presented to:

Bryan Kuhlman

by:

Grandma Janet
& Poppy Bill

on:

October 28, 2007

Confirmation Day

But you, man of God, flee from all this, and pursue righteousness, godliness, faith, love, endurance and gentleness. Fight the good fight of the faith. Take hold of the eternal life to which you were called when you made your good confession in the presence of many witnesses.

—1 Timothy 6:11-12

new international version

revolution

the bible for

teen guys

Youth Specialties

i-vert

ZONDERVAN®

CONTENTS

OLD TESTAMENT

NEW TESTAMENT

FEATURES CONTENTS

BATTLELINES

MATCH-UPS

WeLCOMe TO YOUR NeW BIBLe!

BEFORE YOU GO ANY FARTHER, STOP AND READ THIS.

If you're already familiar with the Bible, then notice that *Revolution* is a little different than other Bibles. It still has all the books of the Bible and all of God's words for you to read and meditate on. But it also has some notes that accompany the Bible text. To get an idea of what those notes are all about, read "You Say You Want a Revolution . . ." starting on page ix. That will help you get the most out of *Revolution*.

What if you're not familiar with the Bible? What if you're not even sure you know God? First things first. Run, don't walk, to page 1640. There you'll find the "Plan of Salvation." It's a short page of info on how you can know God personally. Imagine that—God as your friend, Father and Savior!

Where do you go next? Great question. Here are a few ways you can get into the Word and make sense of it all:

❶ Start on page 6 and read the Match-Up between Cain and Abel. Then read the Bible passage about Cain and Abel. You'll find page numbers for the Bible passage at the end of each Match-Up. There are 50 Match-Ups, nearly one for each week of the year. Try reading one each week.

❷ Check out the reading plans on page 1641. Each reading plan was custom-made for this Bible. Pick one that looks interesting to you and dive in.

❸ What if you want to find out something about a particular topic? There is a subject index that starts on page 1628. Find the topic you're interested in, and do a study of that topic.

Remember, there are many ways to read God's Word. The more you read the Bible, the more comfortable you'll become with it. Talk to other Christians about how they study the Bible. Chances are, they'll have some great ideas for you. Now get started—there's so much waiting for you in the pages ahead!

Be sure to log on to **www.RevolutionBible.com,** a site created especially for readers of this Bible. There you can send us your feedback, as well as your story of how you're trying to live the revolutionary life.

YOU SAY YOU WANT A REVOLUTION . . .

The book you've just opened was written *thousands* of years ago. The guys who put the actual words on paper (or scrolls or parchment or whatever they used back then) knew nothing about the Internet. They never went to a movie, rented a video or watched TV. None of them ever drove a car or made a phone call or tried out for a sports team.

The Bible writers lived in ancient times. Most of them dressed in robes and sandals, wore long beards and spoke languages that few people use today. What could they possibly have in common with a teenage guy living in the twenty-first century?

Well, for one thing, they struggled with lust. When they saw a hot female, their hormones kicked in and they imagined . . . well, the kind of things *you* imagine. What's more, they had to deal with friends who got them into trouble . . . parents who didn't understand them . . . enemies who made life miserable for them . . . rules that seemed to spoil their fun. They wrestled with feelings of anger, fear, excitement, depression, competitiveness, cockiness and insecurity.

Any of these things sound familiar to you?

THE MORE THINGS CHANGE, THE MORE THEY STAY THE SAME

How can a book thousands of years old be so current, so fresh and so timely when most other books are outdated or forgotten months after they're written? Answer: The one who inspired and directed these guys to write the Bible is the definition of current, fresh and timely. He's God himself. Paul, Moses, John and the others who wrote Scripture jotted down the things God wanted them to write—and nothing else.

We don't call the Bible "God's Word" for nothing. The wisdom, instructions and lessons in it come straight from the Almighty. *Everything* that God wants us to know about him, his plan for the world, his will for our lives, and the things he expects from us can be found between the covers of this book.

ONE BOOK CAN DO ALL THAT?

Of course, calling the Bible a book is like calling Tiger Woods a guy who swings a golf club. The description doesn't do justice to what it really is. The Bible is much more than a book; it's a *catalyst*, something that causes change. The truth is, any guy who comes to God's Word with an open mind and an open heart . . . who makes it a priority in his schedule . . . who takes the time to understand what it says . . . will be changed.

We're not just talking about a minor change either. This isn't about simply becoming a "nicer" person. We're talking about an inside-out *revolution*. If you're willing, the Bible will open your eyes to things you've never seen before. It will introduce you to ways of thinking you've never considered before. It will give you answers to questions you didn't even know how to ask. It will give you a confidence in yourself—and your future—that you didn't know was possible.

We're talking about the kind of transformation that makes your friends, family members and even casual acquaintances say, "Whoa, what got into *him*?" Yes, the revolution starts inside you—but it doesn't stay there. The Bible can change you in ways so powerful that it will have an impact on the people around you. Have you ever thought of yourself as a "go-to guy"—someone who knows what's up and who can make a huge contribution in clutch situations? A healthy relationship with God's Word can equip you to become that kind of person.

LOOKING AT GOD'S WORD FROM A GUY'S PERSPECTIVE

Maybe you're still not convinced that the Bible is all that. Maybe you can't shake the opinion that only adults or "religious" people or bookworms read Scripture. If so, this Bible is for you. We've designed this edition of the Bible especially for guys like you. We've highlighted passages that will be especially interesting to you. We've zeroed in on topics and issues that you deal with every day. We've worded spiritual truths in language that's familiar and comfortable to you.

You will find five elements in this Bible designed to emphasize the power and relevance of God's Word for guys:

NOW OR NEVER

These short comments and questions will help you better understand difficult verses—and help you look at familiar verses in a new way.

LIVE THE ADVENTURE

These focused segments are gutsy calls to action and words of encouragement to help you put God's truth to work in your life.

CHALLENGE NOTES

These key passages bring God's Word home in a personal way, as nuggets of advice, comfort and assurance from the Creator himself.

BATTLELINES

These true-to-life interviews feature guys like you who are struggling with tough choices and situations—many of which will seem familiar to you—and are learning to apply God's Word to their daily lives.

MATCH-UPS

These features square off the good guys with the bad guys of the Bible. Learn about the key players in Scripture and pick up some valuable pointers about how to deal with conflict and stand up for what's right.

ONE MORE THING

Making God's Word a major part of your life won't be easy. You're not going to figure out the whole thing overnight. Understanding and being changed by Scripture takes time, work, patience and perseverance.

But here's a promise you can bank on: If you're willing to make the effort . . . if you stick with the Bible through the exciting parts *and* the not-so-exciting ones . . . if you continuously look for ways to apply the things you read to the way you live . . . then you can expect a revolution—one that will not only shake your life to its core, but also change the world around you.

So what are you waiting for? Let the revolution begin.

CONTRIBUTORS

DEVELOPED FOR ZONDERVAN
BY THE LIVINGSTONE CORPORATION

GENERAL EDITOR
Christopher D. Hudson

DEVELOPMENT TEAM
Bruce Barton
Paige Drygas
Pete Gregory
Christopher D. Hudson
Dave Veerman

ZONDERVAN EDITOR
Benjamin D. Irwin

GRAPHIC DESIGN
Kirk Luttrell
Mark Wainwright

SENIOR EDITOR
Randy Southern

ASSOCIATE EDITOR
Pete Gregory

CONTRIBUTING EDITORS
Brian Shipman
Len Woods
Chip Huber

PROJECT CONSULTANTS
Ken Jones, Ph.D.
Jeffrey Gorter, M.S.W., CAC-1
Mark Zurowski

PREFACE TO THE
NEW INTERNATIONAL VERSION

THE NEW INTERNATIONAL VERSION is a completely new translation of the Holy Bible made by over a hundred scholars working directly from the best available Hebrew, Aramaic and Greek texts. It had its beginning in 1965 when, after several years of exploratory study by committees from the Christian Reformed Church and the National Association of Evangelicals, a group of scholars met at Palos Heights, Illinois, and concurred in the need for a new translation of the Bible in contemporary English. This group, though not made up of official church representatives, was transdenominational. Its conclusion was endorsed by a large number of leaders from many denominations who met in Chicago in 1966.

Responsibility for the new version was delegated by the Palos Heights group to a self-governing body of fifteen, the Committee on Bible Translation, composed for the most part of biblical scholars from colleges, universities and seminaries. In 1967 the New York Bible Society (now the International Bible Society) generously undertook the financial sponsorship of the project—a sponsorship that made it possible to enlist the help of many distinguished scholars. The fact that participants from the United States, Great Britain, Canada, Australia and New Zealand worked together gave the project its international scope. That they were from many denominations—including Anglican, Assemblies of God, Baptist, Brethren, Christian Reformed, Church of Christ, Evangelical Free, Lutheran, Mennonite, Methodist, Nazarene, Presbyterian, Wesleyan and other churches—helped to safeguard the translation from sectarian bias.

How it was made helps to give the New International Version its distinctiveness. The translation of each book was assigned to a team of scholars. Next, one of the Intermediate Editorial Committees revised the initial translation, with constant reference to the Hebrew, Aramaic or Greek. Their work then went to one of the General Editorial Committees, which checked it in detail and made another thorough revision. This revision in turn was carefully reviewed by the Committee on Bible Translation, which made further changes and then released the final version for publication. In this way the entire Bible underwent three revisions, during each of which the translation was examined for its faithfulness to the original languages and for its English style.

All this involved many thousands of hours of research and discussion regarding the meaning of the texts and the precise way of putting them into English. It may well be that no other translation has been made by a more thorough process of review and revision from committee to committee than this one.

From the beginning of the project, the Committee on Bible Translation held to certain goals for the New International Version: that it would be an accurate translation and one that would have clarity and literary quality and so prove suitable for public and private reading, teaching, preaching, memorizing and liturgical use. The Committee also sought to preserve some measure of continuity with the long tradition of translating the Scriptures into English.

In working toward these goals, the translators were united in their commitment to the authority and infallibility of the Bible as God's Word in written form. They believe that it contains the divine answer to the deepest needs of humanity, that it sheds unique light on our path in a dark world, and that it sets forth the way to our eternal well-being.

The first concern of the translators has been the accuracy of the translation and its fidelity to the thought of the biblical writers. They have weighed the significance of the lexical and grammatical details of the Hebrew, Aramaic and Greek texts. At the same time, they have striven for more than a word-for-word translation. Because thought patterns and syntax differ from language to language, faithful communication of the meaning of the writers of the Bible demands frequent modifications in sentence structure and constant regard for the contextual meanings of words.

A sensitive feeling for style does not always accompany scholarship. Accordingly the Committee on Bible Translation submitted the developing version to a number of stylistic consultants. Two of them read every book of both Old and New Testaments twice—once before and once after the last major revision—and made invaluable suggestions. Samples of the translation were tested for clarity and ease of reading by various kinds of people—young and old, highly educated and less well educated, ministers and laymen.

Concern for clear and natural English—that the New International Version should be idiomatic but not idiosyncratic, contemporary but not dated—motivated the translators and consultants. At the same time, they tried to reflect the differing styles of the biblical writers. In view of the international use of English, the translators sought to avoid obvious Americanisms on the one hand and obvious Anglicisms on the other. A British edition reflects the comparatively few differences of significant idiom and of spelling.

As for the traditional pronouns "thou," "thee" and "thine" in reference to the Deity, the translators judged that to use these archaisms (along with the old verb forms such as "doest," "wouldest" and "hadst") would violate accuracy in translation. Neither Hebrew, Aramaic nor Greek uses special pronouns for the persons of the Godhead. A present-day translation is not enhanced by forms that in the time of the King James Version were used in everyday speech, whether referring to God or man.

For the Old Testament the standard Hebrew text, the Masoretic Text as published in the latest editions of *Biblia Hebraica,* was used throughout. The Dead Sea Scrolls contain material bearing on an earlier stage of the Hebrew text. They were consulted, as were the Samaritan Pentateuch and the ancient scribal traditions relating to textual changes. Sometimes a variant Hebrew reading in the margin of the Masoretic Text was followed instead of the text itself. Such instances, being variants within the Masoretic tradition, are not specified by footnotes. In rare cases, words in the consonantal text were divided differently from the way they appear in the Masoretic Text. Footnotes indicate this. The translators also consulted the more important early versions—the Septuagint; Aquila, Symmachus and Theodotion; the Vulgate; the Syriac Peshitta; the Targums; and for the Psalms the *Juxta Hebraica* of Jerome. Readings from these versions were occasionally followed where the Masoretic Text seemed doubtful and where accepted principles of textual criticism showed that one or more of these textual witnesses appeared to provide the correct reading. Such instances are footnoted. Sometimes vowel letters and vowel signs did not, in the judgment of the translators, represent the correct vowels for the original consonantal text. Accordingly some words were read with a different set of vowels. These instances are usually not indicated by footnotes.

The Greek text used in translating the New Testament was an eclectic one. No other piece of ancient literature has such an abundance of manuscript witnesses as does the New Testament. Where existing manuscripts differ, the translators made their choice of readings according to accepted principles of New Testament textual criticism. Footnotes call attention to places where there was uncertainty about what the original text was. The best current printed texts of the Greek New Testament were used.

There is a sense in which the work of translation is never wholly finished. This applies to all great literature and uniquely so to the Bible. In 1973 the New Testament in the New International Version was published. Since then, suggestions for corrections and revisions have been received from various sources. The Committee on Bible Translation carefully considered the suggestions and adopted a number of them. These were incorporated in the first printing of the entire Bible in 1978. Additional revisions were made by the Committee on Bible Translation in 1983 and appear in printings after that date.

As in other ancient documents, the precise meaning of the biblical texts is sometimes uncertain. This is more often the case with the Hebrew and Aramaic texts than with the Greek text. Although archaeological and linguistic discoveries in this century aid in understanding difficult passages, some uncertainties remain. The more significant of these have been called to the reader's attention in the footnotes.

In regard to the divine name *YHWH,* commonly referred to as the *Tetragrammaton,* the translators adopted the device used in most English versions of rendering that name as "Lord" in capital letters to distinguish it from *Adonai,* another Hebrew word rendered "Lord," for which small letters are used. Wherever the two names stand together in the Old Testament as a compound name of God, they are rendered "Sovereign Lord."

Because for most readers today the phrases "the Lord of hosts" and "God of hosts" have little meaning, this version renders them "the Lord Almighty" and "God Almighty." These renderings convey the sense of the Hebrew, namely, "he who is sovereign over all the 'hosts' (powers) in heaven and on earth, especially over the 'hosts' (armies) of Israel." For readers unacquainted with Hebrew this does not make clear the distinction between *Sabaoth* ("hosts" or "Almighty") and *Shaddai* (which can also be translated "Almighty"), but the latter occurs infrequently and is always footnoted. When *Adonai* and *YHWH Sabaoth* occur together, they are rendered "the Lord, the Lord Almighty."

As for other proper nouns, the familiar spellings of the King James Version are generally retained. Names traditionally spelled with "ch," except where it is final, are usually spelled in this translation with "k" or "c," since the biblical languages do not have the sound that "ch" frequently indicates in English—for example, in *chant*. For well-known names such as Zechariah, however, the traditional spelling has been retained. Variation in the spelling of names in the original languages has usually not been indicated. Where a person or place has two or more different names in the Hebrew, Aramaic or Greek texts, the more familiar one has generally been used, with footnotes where needed.

To achieve clarity the translators sometimes supplied words not in the original texts but required by the context. If there was uncertainty about such material, it is enclosed in brackets. Also for the sake of clarity or style, nouns, including some proper nouns, are sometimes substituted for pronouns, and vice versa. And though the Hebrew writers often shifted back and forth between first, second and third personal pronouns without change of antecedent, this translation often makes them uniform, in accordance with English style and without the use of footnotes.

Poetical passages are printed as poetry, that is, with indentation of lines and with separate stanzas. These are generally designed to reflect the structure of Hebrew poetry. This poetry is normally characterized by parallelism in balanced lines. Most of the poetry in the Bible is in the Old Testament, and scholars differ regarding the scansion of Hebrew lines. The translators determined the stanza divisions for the most part by analysis of the subject matter. The stanzas therefore serve as poetic paragraphs.

As an aid to the reader, italicized sectional headings are inserted in most of the books. They are not to be regarded as part of the NIV text, are not for oral reading, and are not intended to dictate the interpretation of the sections they head.

The footnotes in this version are of several kinds, most of which need no explanation. Those giving alternative translations begin with "Or" and generally introduce the alternative with the last word preceding it in the text, except when it is a single-word alternative; in poetry quoted in a footnote a slant mark indicates a line division. Footnotes introduced by "Or" do not have uniform significance. In some cases two possible translations were considered to have equal validity. In other cases, though the translators were convinced that the translation in the text was correct, they judged that another interpretation was possible and of sufficient importance to be represented in a footnote.

In the New Testament, footnotes that refer to uncertainty regarding the original text are introduced by "Some manuscripts" or similar expressions. In the Old Testament, evidence for the reading chosen is given first and evidence for the alternative is added after a semicolon (for example: Septuagint; Hebrew *father*). In such notes the term "Hebrew" refers to the Masoretic Text.

It should be noted that minerals, flora and fauna, architectural details, articles of clothing and jewelry, musical instruments and other articles cannot always be identified with precision. Also measures of capacity in the biblical period are particularly uncertain (see the table of weights and measures following the text).

Like all translations of the Bible, made as they are by imperfect man, this one undoubtedly falls short of its goals. Yet we are grateful to God for the extent to which he has enabled us to realize these goals and for the strength he has given us and our colleagues to complete our task. We offer this version of the Bible to him in whose name and for whose glory it has been made. We pray that it will lead many into a better understanding of the Holy Scriptures and a fuller knowledge of Jesus Christ the incarnate Word, of whom the Scriptures so faithfully testify.

The Committee on Bible Translation

June 1978
(Revised August 1983)

Names of the translators and editors may be secured from the International Bible Society, translation sponsors of the New International Version, 1820 Jet Stream Drive, Colorado Springs, Colorado 80921-3696 U.S.A.

THE OLD TESTAMENT

THE OLD
TESTAMENT

« AT A GLANCE

Author
Moses

Audience
People of Israel

Date
1450–1410 B.C. Moses may have completed Genesis before his death on Mount Nebo. The Israelites were camped on the east side of the Jordan River, awaiting their entrance into the promised land.

Setting
The events take place in Mesopotamia, the region known today as the Middle East.

Verse to Remember
I will make you into a great nation and I will bless you; I will make your name great, and you will be a blessing. I will bless those who bless you, and whoever curses you I will curse; and all peoples on earth will be blessed through you (12:2–3).

Theme to Consider
From the beginning, God has desired a relationship with his creation—you!

UNCHANGING TRUTH » When we fell, we fell hard. That's what the book of Genesis shows us again and again. When God created us (the human race), he gave us everything we could possibly want, including the opportunity to choose for ourselves whether to obey or disobey him.

We looked around at paradise, saw how perfect everything would be if we would just follow God's plan . . . and then took off on a sin spree that ruined everything. Creation hasn't been the same since. And once we got a taste of sin, we were hooked. Lying, cheating, sex with strangers, incest, kidnapping, rape, murder, human sacrifice—nothing was too disgusting or too nasty for us.

The thing is, though, no matter how far we fell, no matter how sick and twisted things got, no matter how badly we messed things up, God never stopped loving us. Sure, he called down some scary judgments to remind us how seriously he takes sin, but he never completely wiped us off the face of the earth or abandoned us. He never gave us what we deserved. Why? Because God had a plan to make things right again, a way for us to enjoy the kind of relationship with him that he had in mind all along.

If you've done some things that have seemingly ruined your relationship with God, don't let that be the end of your story. Do something about it. Admit what you've done. Ask God to forgive you, and start again. Remember, God allows "restarts."

LIFE LESSONS »

1. God is the reason the world is a remarkably beautiful place. Every time we notice the amazing wonders of creation, we should praise God for his creative work (1:31).

2. God does not take our sin lightly. Neither should we (6:5–7).

3. God promises to bless people who are faithful to him. If we obey him, he will use us to accomplish his will (6:8—8:19).

4. The fact that we are able to claim Jesus as Savior and Lord today is due to the personal relationship God began with Abraham and his descendants (12:1–3).

THE BEGINNING

1 In the beginning God created the heavens and the earth. [2]Now the earth was[a] formless and empty, darkness was over the surface of the deep, and the Spirit of God was hovering over the waters.

[3]And God said, "Let there be light," and there was light. [4]God saw that the light was good, and he separated the light from the darkness. [5]God called the light "day," and the darkness he called "night." And there was evening, and there was morning—the first day.

[6]And God said, "Let there be an expanse between the waters to separate water from water." [7]So God made the expanse and separated the water under the expanse from the water above it. And it was so. [8]God called the expanse "sky." And there was evening, and there was morning—the second day.

[9]And God said, "Let the water under the sky be gathered to one place, and let dry ground appear." And it was so. [10]God called the dry ground "land," and the gathered waters he called "seas." And God saw that it was good.

[11]Then God said, "Let the land produce vegetation: seed-bearing plants and trees on the land that bear fruit with seed in it, according to their various kinds." And it was so. [12]The land produced vegetation: plants bearing seed according to their kinds and trees bearing fruit with seed in it according to their kinds. And God saw that it was good. [13]And there was evening, and there was morning—the third day.

[14]And God said, "Let there be lights in the expanse of the sky to separate the day from the night, and let them serve as signs to mark seasons and days and years, [15]and let them be lights in the expanse of the sky to give light on the earth." And it was so. [16]God made two great lights—the greater light to govern the day and the lesser light to govern the night. He also made the stars. [17]God set them in the expanse of the sky to give light on the earth, [18]to govern the day and the night, and to separate light from darkness. And God saw that it was good. [19]And there was evening, and there was morning—the fourth day.

[20]And God said, "Let the water teem with living creatures, and let birds fly above the earth across the expanse of the sky." [21]So God created the great creatures of the sea and every living and moving thing with which the water teems, according to their kinds, and every winged bird according to its kind. And God saw that it was good. [22]God blessed them and said, "Be fruitful and increase in number and fill the water in the seas, and let the birds increase on the earth." [23]And there was evening, and there was morning—the fifth day.

[24]And God said, "Let the land produce living creatures according to their kinds: livestock, creatures that move along the ground, and wild animals, each according to its kind." And it was so. [25]God made the wild animals according to their kinds, the livestock according to their kinds, and all the creatures that move along the ground according to their kinds. And God saw that it was good.

[26]Then God said, "Let us make man in our image, in our likeness, and let them rule over the fish of the sea and the birds of the air, over the livestock, over all the earth,[b] and over all the creatures that move along the ground."

[27]So God created man in his own image,
in the image of God he created him;
male and female he created them.

[28]God blessed them and said to them, "Be fruitful and increase in number; fill the earth and

NOW OR NEVER

GE 1:25

When was the last time you noticed something really incredible about God's creation? When was the last time you told God how amazed you are with the world he has made?

---

[a] 2 Or possibly became   [b] 26 Hebrew; Syriac all the wild animals

subdue it. Rule over the fish of the sea and the birds of the air and over every living creature that moves on the ground."

²⁹Then God said, "I give you every seed-bearing plant on the face of the whole earth and every tree that has fruit with seed in it. They will be yours for food. ³⁰And to all the beasts of the earth and all the birds of the air and all the creatures that move on the ground—everything that has the breath of life in it—I give every green plant for food." And it was so.

³¹God saw all that he had made, and it was very good. And there was evening, and there was morning—the sixth day.

To: my_son

heavenly_father: don't give in to your feelings of worthlessness. you weren't made on some assembly line. you're not the product of random chance. I designed you individually and made you in my image. that makes you priceless, not to mention worthy of respect.

GE 1:27

2 Thus the heavens and the earth were completed in all their vast array.

²By the seventh day God had finished the work he had been doing; so on the seventh day he rested[a] from all his work. ³And God blessed the seventh day and made it holy, because on it he rested from all the work of creating that he had done.

ADAM AND EVE

⁴This is the account of the heavens and the earth when they were created.

When the LORD God made the earth and the heavens— ⁵and no shrub of the field had yet appeared on the earth[b] and no plant of the field had yet sprung up, for the LORD God had not sent rain on the earth[b] and there was no man to work the ground, ⁶but streams[c] came up from the earth and watered the whole surface of the ground— ⁷the LORD God formed the man[d] from the dust of the ground and breathed into his nostrils the breath of life, and the man became a living being.

NOW OR NEVER

GE 2:3

God set the pattern for us—six parts work to one part rest. When you work, make sure you give it everything you've got. But don't forget to give yourself time to rest— to recharge your batteries and reconnect with God.

⁸Now the LORD God had planted a garden in the east, in Eden; and there he put the man he had formed. ⁹And the LORD God made all kinds of trees grow out of the ground—trees that were pleasing to the eye and good for food. In the middle of the garden were the tree of life and the tree of the knowledge of good and evil.

¹⁰A river watering the garden flowed from Eden; from there it was separated into four headwaters. ¹¹The name of the first is the Pishon; it winds through the entire land of Havilah, where there is gold. ¹²(The gold of that land is good; aromatic resin[e] and onyx are also there.) ¹³The name of the second river is the Gihon; it winds through the entire land of Cush.[f] ¹⁴The name of the third river is the Tigris; it runs along the east side of Asshur. And the fourth river is the Euphrates.

¹⁵The LORD God took the man and put him in the Garden of Eden to work it and take care of it. ¹⁶And the LORD God commanded the man, "You are free to eat from any tree in the garden; ¹⁷but you must not eat from the tree of the knowledge of good and evil, for when you eat of it you will surely die."

¹⁸The LORD God said, "It is not good for the man to be alone. I will make a helper suitable for him."

¹⁹Now the LORD God had formed out of the ground all the beasts of the field and all the birds of the air. He brought them to the man to see what he would name them; and whatever the man called each living creature, that was its name. ²⁰So the man gave names to all the livestock, the birds of the air and all the beasts of the field.

ª 2 Or ceased; also in verse 3   ᵇ 5 Or land; also in verse 6   ᶜ 6 Or mist   ᵈ 7 The Hebrew for man (adam) sounds like and may be related to the Hebrew for ground (adamah); it is also the name Adam (see Gen. 2:20).   ᵉ 12 Or good; pearls   ᶠ 13 Possibly southeast Mesopotamia

But for Adam[a] no suitable helper was found. [21]So the LORD God caused the man to fall into a deep sleep; and while he was sleeping, he took one of the man's ribs[b] and closed up the place with flesh. [22]Then the LORD God made a woman from the rib[c] he had taken out of the man, and he brought her to the man.

[23]The man said,

> "This is now bone of my bones
> and flesh of my flesh;
> she shall be called 'woman,[d]'
> for she was taken out of man."

[24]For this reason a man will leave his father and mother and be united to his wife, and they will become one flesh. [25]The man and his wife were both naked, and they felt no shame.

THE FALL OF MAN

3 Now the serpent was more crafty than any of the wild animals the LORD God had made. He said to the woman, "Did God really say, 'You must not eat from any tree in the garden'?"

[2]The woman said to the serpent, "We may eat fruit from the trees in the garden, [3]but God did say, 'You must not eat fruit from the tree that is in the middle of the garden, and you must not touch it, or you will die.'"

[4]"You will not surely die," the serpent said to the woman. [5]"For God knows that when you eat of it your eyes will be opened, and you will be like God, knowing good and evil."

[6]When the woman saw that the fruit of the tree was good for food and pleasing to the eye, and also desirable for gaining wisdom, she took some and ate it. She also gave some to her husband, who was with her, and he ate it. [7]Then the eyes of both of them were opened, and they realized they were naked; so they sewed fig leaves together and made coverings for themselves.

[8]Then the man and his wife heard the sound of the LORD God as he was walking in the garden in the cool of the day, and they hid from the LORD God among the trees of the garden. [9]But the LORD God called to the man, "Where are you?"

[10]He answered, "I heard you in the garden, and I was afraid because I was naked; so I hid."

[11]And he said, "Who told you that you were naked? Have you eaten from the tree that I commanded you not to eat from?"

[12]The man said, "The woman you put here with me—she gave me some fruit from the tree, and I ate it."

[13]Then the LORD God said to the woman, "What is this you have done?"

The woman said, "The serpent deceived me, and I ate."

[14]So the LORD God said to the serpent, "Because you have done this,

> "Cursed are you above all the livestock
> and all the wild animals!
> You will crawl on your belly
> and you will eat dust
> all the days of your life.
> [15]And I will put enmity
> between you and the woman,
> and between your offspring[e] and hers;
> he will crush[f] your head,
> and you will strike his heel."

NOW OR NEVER

GE 2:24

Temporary physical hookups always leave at least one of the people involved feeling unsatisfied, insecure, hurt and vulnerable. That's not the case with God's design for a real relationship with someone of the opposite sex.

---

[a] *20* Or *the man* [b] *21* Or *took part of the man's side* [c] *22* Or *part* [d] *23* The Hebrew for *woman* sounds like the Hebrew for *man.*
[e] *15* Or *seed* [f] *15* Or *strike*

16To the woman he said,

"I will greatly increase
your pains in
childbearing;
with pain you will give
birth to
children.
Your desire will be for
your husband,
and he will rule over
you."

17To Adam he said, "Because you listened to your wife and ate from the tree about which I commanded you, 'You must not eat of it,'

> "Cursed is the ground because of you;
> through painful toil you will eat of it
> all the days of your life.
> 18It will produce thorns and thistles for you,
> and you will eat the plants of the field.
> 19By the sweat of your brow
> you will eat your food
> until you return to the ground,
> since from it you were taken;
> for dust you are
> and to dust you will return."

20Adam[a] named his wife Eve,[b] because she would become the mother of all the living.

21The LORD God made garments of skin for Adam and his wife and clothed them. 22And the LORD God said, "The man has now become like one of us, knowing good and evil. He must not be allowed to reach out his hand and take also from the tree of life and eat, and live forever." 23So the LORD God banished him from the Garden of Eden to work the ground from which he had been taken. 24After he drove the man out, he placed on the east side[c] of the Garden of Eden cherubim and a flaming sword flashing back and forth to guard the way to the tree of life.

NOW OR NEVER
GE 3:15

The serpent is Satan and the woman's offspring is Jesus. That means no matter how powerful Satan may seem now, he's already been branded a loser for eternity, because Jesus is going to crush him once and for all. You can bet your life on it.

CAIN AND ABEL

4 Adam[a] lay with his wife Eve, and she became pregnant and gave birth to Cain.[d] She said, "With the help of the LORD I have brought forth[e] a man." 2Later she gave birth to his brother Abel.

Now Abel kept flocks, and Cain worked the soil. 3In the course of time Cain brought some of the fruits of the soil as an offering to the LORD. 4But Abel brought fat portions from some of the firstborn of his flock. The LORD looked with favor on Abel and his offering, 5but on Cain and his offering he did not look with favor. So Cain was very angry, and his face was downcast.

NOW OR NEVER
GE 4:1

How great is sex—that is, sex within marriage? Not only is it part of God's plan for experiencing true love, but it also keeps the human race going! And yes, God made it enjoyable too!

6Then the LORD said to Cain, "Why are you angry? Why is your face downcast? 7If you do what is right, will you not be accepted? But if you do not do what is right, sin is crouching at your door; it desires to have you, but you must master it."

5

---

a 20,1 Or The man   b 20 Eve probably means living.   c 24 Or placed in front   d 1 Cain sounds like the Hebrew for brought forth or acquired.   e 1 Or have acquired

cain

» Adam and Eve's first son
» Worked as a farmer
» Earned a reputation for being indifferent and self-pitying

abel

» Adam and Eve's second son
» Worked as a shepherd
» Earned a reputation for being faithful and conscientious

The Main Event

In Old Testament times, God's people were required to make regular offerings to the Lord. This usually involved sacrificing an animal or a certain portion of produce as a gift to God. Offerings were serious business. Not only were they a way for people to show their thankfulness for what God had done for them, but they were also a means of demonstrating repentance and receiving God's forgiveness for sin. (Remember, this was way before Jesus died as a once-and-for-all sacrifice for our sins.)

When the time came for Cain and Abel to make their offerings, they had two radically different strategies. Cain haphazardly rounded up some of the crops he had been growing, threw them together as a rather pathetic offering, and said, "Here you go, God. Hope you like it. Too bad if you don't." (Maybe he didn't say those exact words, but there's no doubt that was his attitude.)

Abel, on the other hand, went to a lot of trouble to make sure his offering was just right. He carefully examined his flocks and selected the meatiest, least blemished firstborn animals to offer as a sacrifice. Abel worked hard to make sure that his offering was as perfect as it could possibly be.

You know the old saying, "It's the thought that counts"? That was certainly the case here. God knew the thought (or lack of it) that went into Cain and Abel's sacrifices, and he gave each one the response it deserved. God rejected Cain and his offering but welcomed Abel and his offering with open arms.

When Cain saw how God responded, he went ballistic. But instead of dealing with the real issue—his heart—he unleashed his anger and envy on his younger brother. Cain tricked Abel into following him to an isolated field, where he attacked and killed him. When God asked Cain where his brother was, Cain gave the now famous reply, "Am I my brother's keeper?"

Of course, God knew what had really happened. He pronounced a curse on Cain and sentenced him to a lifetime of wandering, with no land to farm and no place to call home.

The Outcome

Cain is remembered today as the first murderer in human history. His name is forever associated with the most violent, heinous crime possible. Abel, on the other hand, is remembered much differently. Hebrews 11 lists the names of Old Testament people whose faith so impressed God that he singled them out as examples for us to follow. That passage is sometimes called "the faith hall of fame," and Abel is the first one on the list.

What's interesting is that the legacies of Cain and Abel were built almost exclusively on this one ill-fated incident. The Bible tells us practically nothing else about either man. All we know is that Abel approached his offering—his responsibility to God—with a positive spirit, and Cain approached his with a negative spirit. And that's really all we need to know.

There are many areas in our lives in which maybe we can get by with less than our best effort—guitar lessons, math homework, basketball practice. But our relationship with the Lord should not be one of them. God demands—and *deserves*—our best efforts, fueled by a genuine desire to please him.

Read more about Cain and Abel in Genesis 4:1–16 (pages 5–7).

⁸Now Cain said to his brother Abel, "Let's go out to the field."ᵃ And while they were in the field, Cain attacked his brother Abel and killed him.

⁹Then the LORD said to Cain, "Where is your brother Abel?"

"I don't know," he replied. "Am I my brother's keeper?"

¹⁰The LORD said, "What have you done? Listen! Your brother's blood cries out to me from the ground. ¹¹Now you are under a curse and driven from the ground, which opened its mouth to receive your brother's blood from your hand. ¹²When you work the ground, it will no longer yield its crops for you. You will be a restless wanderer on the earth."

¹³Cain said to the LORD, "My punishment is more than I can bear. ¹⁴Today you are driving me from the land, and I will be hidden from your presence; I will be a restless wanderer on the earth, and whoever finds me will kill me."

¹⁵But the LORD said to him, "Not soᵇ; if anyone kills Cain, he will suffer vengeance seven times over." Then the LORD put a mark on Cain so that no one who found him would kill him. ¹⁶So Cain went out from the LORD's presence and lived in the land of Nod,ᶜ east of Eden.

¹⁷Cain lay with his wife, and she became pregnant and gave birth to Enoch. Cain was then building a city, and he named it after his son Enoch. ¹⁸To Enoch was born Irad, and Irad was the father of Mehujael, and Mehujael was the father of Methushael, and Methushael was the father of Lamech.

¹⁹Lamech married two women, one named Adah and the other Zillah. ²⁰Adah gave birth to Jabal; he was the father of those who live in tents and raise livestock. ²¹His brother's name was Jubal; he was the father of all who play the harp and flute. ²²Zillah also had a son, Tubal-Cain, who forged all kinds of tools out ofᵈ bronze and iron. Tubal-Cain's sister was Naamah.

²³Lamech said to his wives,

"Adah and Zillah, listen to me;
    wives of Lamech, hear my words.
I have killedᵉ a man for wounding me,
    a young man for injuring me.
²⁴If Cain is avenged seven times,
    then Lamech seventy-seven times."

²⁵Adam lay with his wife again, and she gave birth to a son and named him Seth,ᶠ saying, "God has granted me another child in place of Abel, since Cain killed him." ²⁶Seth also had a son, and he named him Enosh.

At that time men began to call onᵍ the name of the LORD.

FROM ADAM TO NOAH

5 This is the written account of Adam's line.

When God created man, he made him in the likeness of God. ²He created them male and female and blessed them. And when they were created, he called them "man."ʰ

³When Adam had lived 130 years, he had a son in his own likeness, in his own image; and he named him Seth. ⁴After Seth was born, Adam lived 800 years and had other sons and daughters. ⁵Altogether, Adam lived 930 years, and then he died.

⁶When Seth had lived 105 years, he became the fatherⁱ of Enosh. ⁷And after he became the father of Enosh, Seth lived 807 years and had other sons and daughters. ⁸Altogether, Seth lived 912 years, and then he died.

⁹When Enosh had lived 90 years, he became the father of Kenan. ¹⁰And after he became the father of Kenan, Enosh lived 815 years and had other sons and daughters. ¹¹Altogether, Enosh lived 905 years, and then he died.

¹²When Kenan had lived 70 years, he became the father of Mahalalel. ¹³And after he became the father of Mahalalel, Kenan lived 840 years and had other sons and daughters. ¹⁴Altogether, Kenan lived 910 years, and then he died.

¹⁵When Mahalalel had lived 65 years, he became the father of Jared. ¹⁶And after he became the fa-

---

ᵃ 8 Samaritan Pentateuch, Septuagint, Vulgate and Syriac; Masoretic Text does not have *"Let's go out to the field."*   ᵇ 15 Septuagint, Vulgate and Syriac; Hebrew *Very well*   ᶜ 16 *Nod* means *wandering* (see verses 12 and 14).   ᵈ 22 Or *who instructed all who work in*   ᵉ 23 Or *I will kill*   ᶠ 25 *Seth* probably means *granted*.   ᵍ 26 Or *to proclaim*   ʰ 2 Hebrew *adam*   ⁱ 6 *Father* may mean *ancestor*; also in verses 7-26.

ther of Jared, Mahalalel lived 830 years and had other sons and daughters. ¹⁷Altogether, Mahalalel lived 895 years, and then he died.

¹⁸When Jared had lived 162 years, he became the father of Enoch. ¹⁹And after he became the father of Enoch, Jared lived 800 years and had other sons and daughters. ²⁰Altogether, Jared lived 962 years, and then he died.

²¹When Enoch had lived 65 years, he became the father of Methuselah. ²²And after he became the father of Methuselah, Enoch walked with God 300 years and had other sons and daughters. ²³Altogether, Enoch lived 365 years. ²⁴Enoch walked with God; then he was no more, because God took him away.

²⁵When Methuselah had lived 187 years, he became the father of Lamech. ²⁶And after he became the father of Lamech, Methuselah lived 782 years and had other sons and daughters. ²⁷Altogether, Methuselah lived 969 years, and then he died.

²⁸When Lamech had lived 182 years, he had a son. ²⁹He named him Noah[a] and said, "He will comfort us in the labor and painful toil of our hands caused by the ground the LORD has cursed." ³⁰After Noah was born, Lamech lived 595 years and had other sons and daughters. ³¹Altogether, Lamech lived 777 years, and then he died.

³²After Noah was 500 years old, he became the father of Shem, Ham and Japheth.

Making Yourself Known

God's work isn't a job for cowards or chameleons. The kind of people God uses to accomplish his will are those who are willing to step away from the crowd—away from doing what everyone else is doing—in order to take a bold stand for him. If you want to truly follow God, your place will be out in the open, where others can see you and everyone knows whom you serve.

THE FLOOD

6 When men began to increase in number on the earth and daughters were born to them, ²the sons of God saw that the daughters of men were beautiful, and they married any of them they chose. ³Then the LORD said, "My Spirit will not contend with[b] man forever, for he is mortal[c]; his days will be a hundred and twenty years."

⁴The Nephilim were on the earth in those days—and also afterward—when the sons of God went to the daughters of men and had children by them. They were the heroes of old, men of renown.

⁵The LORD saw how great man's wickedness on the earth had become, and that every inclination of the thoughts of his heart was only evil all the time. ⁶The LORD was grieved that he had made man on the earth, and his heart was filled with pain. ⁷So the LORD said, "I will wipe mankind, whom I have created, from the face of the earth—men and animals, and creatures that move along the ground, and birds of the air—for I am grieved that I have made them." ⁸But Noah found favor in the eyes of the LORD.

⁹This is the account of Noah.

Noah was a righteous man, blameless among the people of his time, and he walked with God. ¹⁰Noah had three sons: Shem, Ham and Japheth.

¹¹Now the earth was corrupt in God's sight and was full of violence. ¹²God saw how corrupt the earth had become, for all the people on earth had corrupted their ways. ¹³So God said to Noah, "I am going to put an end to all people, for the earth is filled with violence because of them. I am surely going to destroy both them and the earth. ¹⁴So make yourself an ark of cypress[d] wood; make rooms in it and coat it with pitch inside and out. ¹⁵This is how you are to build it: The ark is to be 450 feet long, 75 feet wide and 45 feet high.[e] ¹⁶Make a roof for it and finish[f] the ark to within 18 inches[g] of the top. Put a door in the side of the ark and make lower, middle and upper decks. ¹⁷I am going to bring floodwaters on the earth to destroy all life under the heavens, every creature that

---

a 29 *Noah* sounds like the Hebrew for *comfort.*   b 3 Or *My spirit will not remain in*   c 3 Or *corrupt*   d 14 The meaning of the Hebrew for this word is uncertain.   e 15 Hebrew *300 cubits long, 50 cubits wide and 30 cubits high* (about 140 meters long, 23 meters wide and 13.5 meters high)   f 16 Or *Make an opening for light by finishing*   g 16 Hebrew *a cubit* (about 0.5 meter) has the breath of life in it. Everything on earth will perish. [18]But I will establish my covenant with you, and you will enter the ark—you and your sons and your wife and your sons' wives with you. [19]You are to bring into the ark two of all living creatures, male and female, to keep them alive with you. [20]Two of every kind of bird, of every kind of animal and of every kind of creature that moves along the ground will come to you to be kept alive. [21]You are to take every kind of food that is to be eaten and store it away as food for you and for them."

[22]Noah did everything just as God commanded him.

7

The LORD then said to Noah, "Go into the ark, you and your whole family, because I have found you righteous in this generation. [2]Take with you seven[a] of every kind of clean animal, a male and its mate, and two of every kind of unclean animal, a male and its mate, [3]and also seven of every kind of bird, male and female, to keep their various kinds alive throughout the earth. [4]Seven days from now I will send rain on the earth for forty days and forty nights, and I will wipe from the face of the earth every living creature I have made."

ПОW ОR ПЕVЕR

GE 6:22

God has a valid reason and a specific purpose for every instruction he gives us. If Noah had ignored God's instructions back in the day, he would have been just another drowning victim when the flood hit. Then who would have been left? Nobody.

[5]And Noah did all that the LORD commanded him.

[6]Noah was six hundred years old when the floodwaters came on the earth. [7]And Noah and his sons and his wife and his sons' wives entered the ark to escape the waters of the flood. [8]Pairs of clean and unclean animals, of birds and of all creatures that move along the ground, [9]male and female, came to Noah and entered the ark, as God had commanded Noah. [10]And after the seven days the floodwaters came on the earth.

[11]In the six hundredth year of Noah's life, on the seventeenth day of the second month—on that day all the springs of the great deep burst forth, and the floodgates of the heavens were opened. [12]And rain fell on the earth forty days and forty nights.

[13]On that very day Noah and his sons, Shem, Ham and Japheth, together with his wife and the wives of his three sons, entered the ark. [14]They had with them every wild animal according to its kind, all livestock according to their kinds, every creature that moves along the ground according to its kind and every bird according to its kind, everything with wings. [15]Pairs of all creatures that have the breath of life in them came to Noah and entered the ark. [16]The animals going in were male and female of every living thing, as God had commanded Noah. Then the LORD shut him in.

[17]For forty days the flood kept coming on the earth, and as the waters increased they lifted the ark high above the earth. [18]The waters rose and increased greatly on the earth, and the ark floated on the surface of the water. [19]They rose greatly on the earth, and all the high mountains under the entire heavens were covered. [20]The waters rose and covered the mountains to a depth of more than twenty feet.[b,c] [21]Every living thing that moved on the earth perished—birds, livestock, wild animals, all the creatures that swarm over the earth, and all mankind. [22]Everything on dry land that had the breath of life in its nostrils died. [23]Every living thing on the face of the earth was wiped out; men and animals and the creatures that move along the ground and the birds of the air were wiped from the earth. Only Noah was left, and those with him in the ark.

[24]The waters flooded the earth for a hundred and fifty days.

8

But God remembered Noah and all the wild animals and the livestock that were with him in the ark, and he sent a wind over the earth, and the waters receded. [2]Now the springs of the deep and the floodgates of the heavens had been closed, and the rain had stopped falling from the sky. [3]The water receded steadily from the earth. At the end of the hundred and fifty days the water had gone down, [4]and on the seventeenth day of the seventh month the ark came to rest on the mountains of Ararat. [5]The waters continued to recede until the tenth month, and on the first day of the tenth month the tops of the mountains became visible.

[6]After forty days Noah opened the window he had made in the ark [7]and sent out a raven, and it kept

---

[a] 2 Or seven pairs; also in verse 3   [b] 20 Hebrew fifteen cubits (about 6.9 meters)   [c] 20 Or rose more than twenty feet, and the mountains were covered

flying back and forth until the water had dried up from the earth. ⁸Then he sent out a dove to see if the water had receded from the surface of the ground. ⁹But the dove could find no place to set its feet because there was water over all the surface of the earth; so it returned to Noah in the ark. He reached out his hand and took the dove and brought it back to himself in the ark. ¹⁰He waited seven more days and again sent out the dove from the ark. ¹¹When the dove returned to him in the evening, there in its beak was a freshly plucked olive leaf! Then Noah knew that the water had receded from the earth. ¹²He waited seven more days and sent the dove out again, but this time it did not return to him.

¹³By the first day of the first month of Noah's six hundred and first year, the water had dried up from the earth. Noah then removed the covering from the ark and saw that the surface of the ground was dry. ¹⁴By the twenty-seventh day of the second month the earth was completely dry.

¹⁵Then God said to Noah, ¹⁶"Come out of the ark, you and your wife and your sons and their wives. ¹⁷Bring out every kind of living creature that is with you—the birds, the animals, and all the creatures that move along the ground—so they can multiply on the earth and be fruitful and increase in number upon it."

¹⁸So Noah came out, together with his sons and his wife and his sons' wives. ¹⁹All the animals and all the creatures that move along the ground and all the birds—everything that moves on the earth—came out of the ark, one kind after another.

²⁰Then Noah built an altar to the LORD and, taking some of all the clean animals and clean birds, he sacrificed burnt offerings on it. ²¹The LORD smelled the pleasing aroma and said in his heart: "Never again will I curse the ground because of man, even though[a] every inclination of his heart is evil from childhood. And never again will I destroy all living creatures, as I have done.

²²"As long as the earth endures,
seedtime and harvest,
cold and heat,
summer and winter,
day and night
will never cease."

GOD'S COVENANT WITH NOAH

9 Then God blessed Noah and his sons, saying to them, "Be fruitful and increase in number and fill the earth. ²The fear and dread of you will fall upon all the beasts of the earth and all the birds of the air, upon every creature that moves along the ground, and upon all the fish of the sea; they are given into your hands. ³Everything that lives and moves will be food for you. Just as I gave you the green plants, I now give you everything.

⁴"But you must not eat meat that has its lifeblood still in it. ⁵And for your lifeblood I will surely demand an accounting. I will demand an accounting from every animal. And from each man, too, I will demand an accounting for the life of his fellow man.

⁶"Whoever sheds the blood of man,
by man shall his blood be shed;
for in the image of God
has God made man.

⁷As for you, be fruitful and increase in number; multiply on the earth and increase upon it."

⁸Then God said to Noah and to his sons with him: ⁹"I now establish my covenant with you and with your descendants after you ¹⁰and with every living creature that was with you—the birds, the livestock and all the wild animals, all those that came out of the ark with you—every living creature on earth. ¹¹I establish my covenant with you: Never again will all life be cut off by the waters of a flood; never again will there be a flood to destroy the earth."

¹²And God said, "This is the sign of the covenant I am making between me and you and every living creature with you, a covenant for all generations to come: ¹³I have set my rainbow in the clouds, and it will be the sign of the covenant between me and the earth. ¹⁴Whenever I bring clouds over the earth and the rainbow appears in the clouds, ¹⁵I will remember my covenant between me and you and all living creatures of every kind. Never again will the waters become a flood to destroy all life. ¹⁶Whenever

---

ª 21 Or man, for

the rainbow appears in the clouds, I will see it and remember the everlasting covenant between God and all living creatures of every kind on the earth."

¹⁷So God said to Noah, "This is the sign of the covenant I have established between me and all life on the earth."

THE SONS OF NOAH

¹⁸The sons of Noah who came out of the ark were Shem, Ham and Japheth. (Ham was the father of Canaan.) ¹⁹These were the three sons of Noah, and from them came the people who were scattered over the earth.

²⁰Noah, a man of the soil, proceeded^a to plant a vineyard. ²¹When he drank some of its wine, he became drunk and lay uncovered inside his tent. ²²Ham, the father of Canaan, saw his father's nakedness and told his two brothers outside. ²³But Shem and Japheth took a garment and laid it across their shoulders; then they walked in backward and covered their father's nakedness. Their faces were turned the other way so that they would not see their father's nakedness.

²⁴When Noah awoke from his wine and found out what his youngest son had done to him, ²⁵he said,

"Cursed be Canaan!
The lowest of slaves
will he be to his brothers."

²⁶He also said,

"Blessed be the LORD, the God of Shem!
May Canaan be the slave of Shem.^b
²⁷ May God extend the territory of Japheth^c;
may Japheth live in the tents of Shem,
and may Canaan be his^d slave."

²⁸After the flood Noah lived 350 years. ²⁹Altogether, Noah lived 950 years, and then he died.

THE TABLE OF NATIONS

10

This is the account of Shem, Ham and Japheth, Noah's sons, who themselves had sons after the flood.

THE JAPHETHITES

²The sons^e of Japheth:
Gomer, Magog, Madai, Javan, Tubal, Meshech and Tiras.
³The sons of Gomer:
Ashkenaz, Riphath and Togarmah.
⁴The sons of Javan:
Elishah, Tarshish, the Kittim and the Rodanim.^f ⁵(From these the maritime peoples spread out into their territories by their clans within their nations, each with its own language.)

THE HAMITES

⁶The sons of Ham:
Cush, Mizraim,^g Put and Canaan.
⁷The sons of Cush:
Seba, Havilah, Sabtah, Raamah and Sabteca.

---

^a 20 Or soil, was the first   ^b 26 Or be his slave   ^c 27 Japheth sounds like the Hebrew for extend.   ^d 27 Or their   ^e 2 Sons may mean descendants or successors or nations; also in verses 3, 4, 6, 7, 20-23, 29 and 31.   ^f 4 Some manuscripts of the Masoretic Text and Samaritan Pentateuch (see also Septuagint and 1 Chron. 1:7); most manuscripts of the Masoretic Text Dodanim   ^g 6 That is, Egypt; also in verse 13

The sons of Raamah:
Sheba and Dedan.

[8]Cush was the father[a] of Nimrod, who grew to be a mighty warrior on the earth. [9]He was a mighty hunter before the LORD; that is why it is said, "Like Nimrod, a mighty hunter before the LORD." [10]The first centers of his kingdom were Babylon, Erech, Akkad and Calneh, in[b] Shinar.[c] [11]From that land he went to Assyria, where he built Nineveh, Rehoboth Ir,[d] Calah [12]and Resen, which is between Nineveh and Calah; that is the great city.

[13]Mizraim was the father of
   the Ludites, Anamites, Lehabites, Naphtuhites, [14]Pathrusites, Casluhites (from whom the Philistines came) and Caphtorites.
[15]Canaan was the father of
   Sidon his firstborn,[e] and of the Hittites, [16]Jebusites, Amorites, Girgashites, [17]Hivites, Arkites, Sinites, [18]Arvadites, Zemarites and Hamathites.

Later the Canaanite clans scattered [19]and the borders of Canaan reached from Sidon toward Gerar as far as Gaza, and then toward Sodom, Gomorrah, Admah and Zeboiim, as far as Lasha.
[20]These are the sons of Ham by their clans and languages, in their territories and nations.

THE SEMITES

[21]Sons were also born to Shem, whose older brother was[f] Japheth; Shem was the ancestor of all the sons of Eber.

[22]The sons of Shem:
   Elam, Asshur, Arphaxad, Lud and Aram.
[23]The sons of Aram:
   Uz, Hul, Gether and Meshech.[g]
[24]Arphaxad was the father of[h] Shelah,
   and Shelah the father of Eber.
[25]Two sons were born to Eber:
   One was named Peleg,[i] because in his time the earth was divided; his brother was named Joktan.
[26]Joktan was the father of
   Almodad, Sheleph, Hazarmaveth, Jerah, [27]Hadoram, Uzal, Diklah, [28]Obal, Abimael, Sheba, [29]Ophir, Havilah and Jobab. All these were sons of Joktan.

[30]The region where they lived stretched from Mesha toward Sephar, in the eastern hill country.
[31]These are the sons of Shem by their clans and languages, in their territories and nations.

[32]These are the clans of Noah's sons, according to their lines of descent, within their nations. From these the nations spread out over the earth after the flood.

THE TOWER OF BABEL

11
Now the whole world had one language and a common speech. [2]As men moved eastward,[j] they found a plain in Shinar[k] and settled there.

[3]They said to each other, "Come, let's make bricks and bake them thoroughly." They used brick instead of stone, and tar for mortar. [4]Then they said, "Come, let us build ourselves

---

NOW OR NEVER

GE 11:4

God does not share his glory with anyone. And why should he? He's the one who created and sustains everything. No one could do anything without the skills and abilities that only God can give us.

---

[a] 8 *Father* may mean *ancestor* or *predecessor* or *founder*; also in verses 13, 15, 24 and 26.   [b] 10 Or *Erech and Akkad—all of them in*   [c] 10 That is, Babylonia   [d] 11 Or *Nineveh with its city squares*   [e] 15 Or *of the Sidonians, the foremost*   [f] 21 Or *Shem, the older brother of*   [g] 23 See Septuagint and 1 Chron. 1:17; Hebrew *Mash*   [h] 24 Hebrew; Septuagint *father of Cainan, and Cainan was the father of*   [i] 25 *Peleg* means *division*.   [j] 2 Or *from the east*; or *in the east*   [k] 2 That is, Babylonia

a city, with a tower that reaches to the heavens, so that we may make a name for ourselves and not be scattered over the face of the whole earth."

⁵But the LORD came down to see the city and the tower that the men were building. ⁶The LORD said, "If as one people speaking the same language they have begun to do this, then nothing they plan to do will be impossible for them. ⁷Come, let us go down and confuse their language so they will not understand each other."

⁸So the LORD scattered them from there over all the earth, and they stopped building the city. ⁹That is why it was called Babelª—because there the LORD confused the language of the whole world. From there the LORD scattered them over the face of the whole earth.

FROM SHEM TO ABRAM

¹⁰This is the account of Shem.

Two years after the flood, when Shem was 100 years old, he became the fatherᵇ of Arphaxad. ¹¹And after he became the father of Arphaxad, Shem lived 500 years and had other sons and daughters.

¹²When Arphaxad had lived 35 years, he became the father of Shelah. ¹³And after he became the father of Shelah, Arphaxad lived 403 years and had other sons and daughters.ᶜ

¹⁴When Shelah had lived 30 years, he became the father of Eber. ¹⁵And after he became the father of Eber, Shelah lived 403 years and had other sons and daughters.

¹⁶When Eber had lived 34 years, he became the father of Peleg. ¹⁷And after he became the father of Peleg, Eber lived 430 years and had other sons and daughters.

¹⁸When Peleg had lived 30 years, he became the father of Reu. ¹⁹And after he became the father of Reu, Peleg lived 209 years and had other sons and daughters.

²⁰When Reu had lived 32 years, he became the father of Serug. ²¹And after he became the father of Serug, Reu lived 207 years and had other sons and daughters.

²²When Serug had lived 30 years, he became the father of Nahor. ²³And after he became the father of Nahor, Serug lived 200 years and had other sons and daughters.

²⁴When Nahor had lived 29 years, he became the father of Terah. ²⁵And after he became the father of Terah, Nahor lived 119 years and had other sons and daughters.

²⁶After Terah had lived 70 years, he became the father of Abram, Nahor and Haran.

²⁷This is the account of Terah.

Terah became the father of Abram, Nahor and Haran. And Haran became the father of Lot. ²⁸While his father Terah was still alive, Haran died in Ur of the Chaldeans, in the land of his birth. ²⁹Abram and Nahor both married. The name of Abram's wife was Sarai, and the name of Nahor's wife was Milcah; she was the daughter of Haran, the father of both Milcah and Iscah. ³⁰Now Sarai was barren; she had no children.

³¹Terah took his son Abram, his grandson Lot son of Haran, and his daughter-in-law Sarai, the wife of his son Abram, and together they set out from Ur of the Chaldeans to go to Canaan. But when they came to Haran, they settled there.

³²Terah lived 205 years, and he died in Haran.

THE CALL OF ABRAM

12 The LORD had said to Abram, "Leave your country, your people and your father's household and go to the land I will show you.

²"I will make you into a great nation
    and I will bless you;
I will make your name great,
    and you will be a blessing.
³I will bless those who bless you,
    and whoever curses you I will curse;

ª 9 That is, Babylon; *Babel* sounds like the Hebrew for *confused*. ᵇ 10 *Father* may mean *ancestor*; also in verses 11-25.
ᶜ 12,13 Hebrew; Septuagint (see also Luke 3:35, 36 and note at Gen. 10:24) *35 years, he became the father of Cainan.* ¹³*And after he became the father of Cainan, Arphaxad lived 430 years and had other sons and daughters, and then he died. When Cainan had lived 130 years, he became the father of Shelah. And after he became the father of Shelah, Cainan lived 330 years and had other sons and daughters*

and all peoples on earth
will be blessed through you."

[4]So Abram left, as the LORD had told him; and Lot went with him. Abram was seventy-five years old when he set out from Haran. [5]He took his wife Sarai, his nephew Lot, all the possessions they had accumulated and the people they had acquired in Haran, and they set out for the land of Canaan, and they arrived there.

[6]Abram traveled through the land as far as the site of the great tree of Moreh at Shechem. At that time the Canaanites were in the land. [7]The LORD appeared to Abram and said, "To your offspring[a] I will give this land." So he built an altar there to the LORD, who had appeared to him.

[8]From there he went on toward the hills east of Bethel and pitched his tent, with Bethel on the west and Ai on the east. There he built an altar to the LORD and called on the name of the LORD. [9]Then Abram set out and continued toward the Negev.

ABRAM IN EGYPT

[10]Now there was a famine in the land, and Abram went down to Egypt to live there for a while because the famine was severe. [11]As he was about to enter Egypt, he said to his wife Sarai, "I know what a beautiful woman you are. [12]When the Egyptians see you, they will say, 'This is his wife.' Then they will kill me but will let you live. [13]Say you are my sister, so that I will be treated well for your sake and my life will be spared because of you."

[14]When Abram came to Egypt, the Egyptians saw that she was a very beautiful woman. [15]And when Pharaoh's officials saw her, they praised her to Pharaoh, and she was taken into his palace. [16]He treated Abram well for her sake, and Abram acquired sheep and cattle, male and female donkeys, menservants and maidservants, and camels.

[17]But the LORD inflicted serious diseases on Pharaoh and his household because of Abram's wife Sarai. [18]So Pharaoh summoned Abram. "What have you done to me?" he said. "Why didn't you tell me she was your wife? [19]Why did you say, 'She is my sister,' so that I took her to be my wife? Now then, here is your wife. Take her and go!" [20]Then Pharaoh gave orders about Abram to his men, and they sent him on his way, with his wife and everything he had.

ABRAM AND LOT SEPARATE

13 So Abram went up from Egypt to the Negev, with his wife and everything he had, and Lot went with him. [2]Abram had become very wealthy in livestock and in silver and gold.

[3]From the Negev he went from place to place until he came to Bethel, to the place between Bethel and Ai where his tent had been earlier [4]and where he had first built an altar. There Abram called on the name of the LORD.

[5]Now Lot, who was moving about with Abram, also had flocks and herds and tents. [6]But the land could not support them while they stayed together, for their possessions were so great that they were not able to stay together. [7]And quarreling arose between Abram's herdsmen and the herdsmen of Lot. The Canaanites and Perizzites were also living in the land at that time.

[8]So Abram said to Lot, "Let's not have any quarreling between you and me, or between your herdsmen and mine, for we are brothers. [9]Is not the whole land before you? Let's part company. If you go to the left, I'll go to the right; if you go to the right, I'll go to the left."

---

[a] 7 Or *seed*

¹⁰Lot looked up and saw that the whole plain of the Jordan was well watered, like the garden of the LORD, like the land of Egypt, toward Zoar. (This was before the LORD destroyed Sodom and Gomorrah.) ¹¹So Lot chose for himself the whole plain of the Jordan and set out toward the east. The two men parted company: ¹²Abram lived in the land of Canaan, while Lot lived among the cities of the plain and pitched his tents near Sodom. ¹³Now the men of Sodom were wicked and were sinning greatly against the LORD.

¹⁴The LORD said to Abram after Lot had parted from him, "Lift up your eyes from where you are and look north and south, east and west. ¹⁵All the land that you see I will give to you and your offspringᵃ forever. ¹⁶I will make your offspring like the dust of the earth, so that if anyone could count the dust, then your offspring could be counted. ¹⁷Go, walk through the length and breadth of the land, for I am giving it to you."

¹⁸So Abram moved his tents and went to live near the great trees of Mamre at Hebron, where he built an altar to the LORD.

NOW OR NEVER
GE 13:7-9

Conflict can develop between even the closest of friends. The key to keeping a friendship solid is to make sure that you always try to do what's best for the other person—even if it means that you have to put aside what you want to do.

ABRAM RESCUES LOT

14 At this time Amraphel king of Shinar,ᵇ Arioch king of Ellasar, Kedorlaomer king of Elam and Tidal king of Goiim ²went to war against Bera king of Sodom, Birsha king of Gomorrah, Shinab king of Admah, Shemeber king of Zeboiim, and the king of Bela (that is, Zoar). ³All these latter kings joined forces in the Valley of Siddim (the Salt Seaᶜ). ⁴For twelve years they had been subject to Kedorlaomer, but in the thirteenth year they rebelled.

⁵In the fourteenth year, Kedorlaomer and the kings allied with him went out and defeated the Rephaites in Ashteroth Karnaim, the Zuzites in Ham, the Emites in Shaveh Kiriathaim ⁶and the Horites in the hill country of Seir, as far as El Paran near the desert. ⁷Then they turned back and went to En Mishpat (that is, Kadesh), and they conquered the whole territory of the Amalekites, as well as the Amorites who were living in Hazazon Tamar.

⁸Then the king of Sodom, the king of Gomorrah, the king of Admah, the king of Zeboiim and the king of Bela (that is, Zoar) marched out and drew up their battle lines in the Valley of Siddim ⁹against Kedorlaomer king of Elam, Tidal king of Goiim, Amraphel king of Shinar and Arioch king of Ellasar—four kings against five. ¹⁰Now the Valley of Siddim was full of tar pits, and when the kings of Sodom and Gomorrah fled, some of the men fell into them and the rest fled to the hills. ¹¹The four kings seized all the goods of Sodom and Gomorrah and all their food; then they went away. ¹²They also carried off Abram's nephew Lot and his possessions, since he was living in Sodom.

¹³One who had escaped came and reported this to Abram the Hebrew. Now Abram was living near the great trees of Mamre the Amorite, a brotherᵈ of Eshcol and Aner, all of whom were allied with Abram. ¹⁴When Abram heard that his relative had been taken captive, he called out the 318 trained men born in his household and went in pursuit as far as Dan. ¹⁵During the night Abram divided his men to attack them and he routed them, pursuing them as far as Hobah, north of Damascus. ¹⁶He

Personal Involvement

When the chips were down, Abram put himself on the line for Lot. He didn't send someone else to do the job. He saddled up with his men and went to rescue his nephew. That's the kind of hands-on commitment God wants from us. Though it's tempting to let someone else do the dirty work when it comes to helping others, you'll find that the response God blesses most is the one with a personal connection—even when it involves personal risk or sacrifice.

»» live the adventure »» Ge 14:14-16

ᵃ *15* Or *seed*; also in verse 16   ᵇ *1* That is, Babylonia; also in verse 9   ᶜ *3* That is, the Dead Sea   ᵈ *13* Or *a relative*; or *an ally* recovered all the goods and brought back his relative Lot and his possessions, together with the women and the other people.

¹⁷After Abram returned from defeating Kedorlaomer and the kings allied with him, the king of Sodom came out to meet him in the Valley of Shaveh (that is, the King's Valley).

¹⁸Then Melchizedek king of Salem[a] brought out bread and wine. He was priest of God Most High, ¹⁹and he blessed Abram, saying,

> "Blessed be Abram by God Most High,
>   Creator[b] of heaven and earth.
> ²⁰And blessed be[c] God Most High,
>   who delivered your enemies into your hand."

Then Abram gave him a tenth of everything.

²¹The king of Sodom said to Abram, "Give me the people and keep the goods for yourself."

²²But Abram said to the king of Sodom, "I have raised my hand to the LORD, God Most High, Creator of heaven and earth, and have taken an oath ²³that I will accept nothing belonging to you, not even a thread or the thong of a sandal, so that you will never be able to say, 'I made Abram rich.' ²⁴I will accept nothing but what my men have eaten and the share that belongs to the men who went with me—to Aner, Eshcol and Mamre. Let them have their share."

GOD'S COVENANT WITH ABRAM

15 After this, the word of the LORD came to Abram in a vision:

> "Do not be afraid, Abram.
>   I am your shield,[d]
>   your very great reward.[e]"

²But Abram said, "O Sovereign LORD, what can you give me since I remain childless and the one who will inherit[f] my estate is Eliezer of Damascus?" ³And Abram said, "You have given me no children; so a servant in my household will be my heir."

⁴Then the word of the LORD came to him: "This man will not be your heir, but a son coming from your own body will be your heir." ⁵He took him outside and said, "Look up at the heavens and count the stars—if indeed you can count them." Then he said to him, "So shall your offspring be."

⁶Abram believed the LORD, and he credited it to him as righteousness.

⁷He also said to him, "I am the LORD, who brought you out of Ur of the Chaldeans to give you this land to take possession of it."

⁸But Abram said, "O Sovereign LORD, how can I know that I will gain possession of it?"

⁹So the LORD said to him, "Bring me a heifer, a goat and a ram, each three years old, along with a dove and a young pigeon."

¹⁰Abram brought all these to him, cut them in two and arranged the halves opposite each other; the birds, however, he did not cut in half. ¹¹Then birds of prey came down on the carcasses, but Abram drove them away.

¹²As the sun was setting, Abram fell into a deep sleep, and a thick and dreadful darkness came over him. ¹³Then the LORD said to him, "Know for certain that your descendants will be strangers in a country not their own, and they will be enslaved and mistreated four hundred years. ¹⁴But I will punish the nation they serve as slaves, and afterward they will come out with great possessions. ¹⁵You, however, will go to your fathers in peace and be buried at a good old age. ¹⁶In the fourth generation your descendants will come back here, for the sin of the Amorites has not yet reached its full measure."

NOW OR NEVER
GE 15:6

God doesn't take our faith lightly. He knows it requires courage to put our trust in him, sight unseen. That's why he always proves himself to be trustworthy when we step out and follow him. What might he be asking you to do?

---

[a] *18* That is, Jerusalem   [b] *19* Or *Possessor*; also in verse 22   [c] *20* Or *And praise be to*   [d] *1* Or *sovereign*   [e] *1* Or *shield; / your reward will be very great*   [f] *2* The meaning of the Hebrew for this phrase is uncertain.

[17]When the sun had set and darkness had fallen, a smoking firepot with a blazing torch appeared and passed between the pieces. [18]On that day the LORD made a covenant with Abram and said, "To your descendants I give this land, from the river[a] of Egypt to the great river, the Euphrates— [19]the land of the Kenites, Kenizzites, Kadmonites, [20]Hittites, Perizzites, Rephaites, [21]Amorites, Canaanites, Girgashites and Jebusites."

NOW OR NEVER
GE 16:1–3

Nothing is impossible for God. He's not restricted by timetables or even biological clocks. He knows exactly what we need and exactly when we need it—even if we don't.

HAGAR AND ISHMAEL

16

Now Sarai, Abram's wife, had borne him no children. But she had an Egyptian maidservant named Hagar; [2]so she said to Abram, "The LORD has kept me from having children. Go, sleep with my maidservant; perhaps I can build a family through her."

Abram agreed to what Sarai said. [3]So after Abram had been living in Canaan ten years, Sarai his wife took her Egyptian maidservant Hagar and gave her to her husband to be his wife. [4]He slept with Hagar, and she conceived.

When she knew she was pregnant, she began to despise her mistress. [5]Then Sarai said to Abram, "You are responsible for the wrong I am suffering. I put my servant in your arms, and now that she knows she is pregnant, she despises me. May the LORD judge between you and me."

[6]"Your servant is in your hands," Abram said. "Do with her whatever you think best." Then Sarai mistreated Hagar; so she fled from her.

[7]The angel of the LORD found Hagar near a spring in the desert; it was the spring that is beside the road to Shur. [8]And he said, "Hagar, servant of Sarai, where have you come from, and where are you going?"

"I'm running away from my mistress Sarai," she answered.

[9]Then the angel of the LORD told her, "Go back to your mistress and submit to her." [10]The angel added, "I will so increase your descendants that they will be too numerous to count."

[11]The angel of the LORD also said to her:

challenge notes

To: my_son

heavenly_father: you are never out of my sight. I know all of your joys and sorrows, your strengths and weaknesses, your triumphs and failures. as long as I'm around, you will never be alone and will never have to rely on your own strength. and I'll be involved in your life forever.

GE 16:7–13

"You are now with child
    and you will have a son.
You shall name him Ishmael,[b]
    for the LORD has heard of your misery.
[12]He will be a wild donkey of a man;
    his hand will be against everyone
    and everyone's hand against him,
and he will live in hostility
    toward[c] all his brothers."

[13]She gave this name to the LORD who spoke to her: "You are the God who sees me," for she said, "I have now seen[d] the One who sees me." [14]That is why the well was called Beer Lahai Roi[e]; it is still there, between Kadesh and Bered.

[15]So Hagar bore Abram a son, and Abram gave the name Ishmael to the son she had borne. [16]Abram was eighty-six years old when Hagar bore him Ishmael.

---

[a] 18 Or Wadi   [b] 11 Ishmael means God hears.   [c] 12 Or live to the east / of   [d] 13 Or seen the back of   [e] 14 Beer Lahai Roi means well of the Living One who sees me.

hagar

VERSUS

sarah

» Sarah's Egyptian maid
» Mother of Abraham's son Ishmael
» Tried to run away from her problems

» Wife of Abraham and mother of the Israelite nation
» Unable to have a child of her own until God miraculously intervened
» Had difficulty waiting on God

The Main Event

God had promised to make Abraham the father of a great nation. The only problem was that Abraham's wife Sarah was infertile. She couldn't have kids. For years, the aging couple prayed and waited. Yet their nursery remained empty.

As she got older, Sarah became more and more panicky about not having kids. (In those days, infertility was thought to be the ultimate curse.) One day she decided to take matters into her own hands. Imitating the cultural practices of the nations around her, Sarah gave her maid Hagar to her husband as a kind of substitute wife and surrogate mother. Abraham must have known Sarah's plan was questionable at best, yet instead of trusting God to do things his way, Abraham wimped out and agreed to sleep with Hagar. And sure enough, Hagar became pregnant.

You can imagine the tension in the household at that point. Not surprisingly, Sarah grew jealous of Hagar, despite the fact that the whole thing was Sarah's idea in the first place. Sarah began to make Hagar's life miserable, and she accused Hagar of gloating about her pregnancy. Hagar responded by taking off. Only an angelic messenger was able to convince her to return.

A few months later, Hagar gave birth to Ishmael. Understandably, he became the "little prince," the darling of the household. Unfortunately for him, his "reign" lasted only a few years. That's when Sarah herself finally became pregnant—just as God had promised. When Sarah gave birth to Isaac, the tension between her and Hagar increased. Each woman wanted her son to be the focus of Abraham's attention and affection.

Rather than taking steps to ease the tension, Sarah pressured Abraham to kick Hagar out of their home. Only after God promised to take care of Ishmael did Abraham send Hagar packing. As Hagar wandered in the desert, God sent an angel to assure her that he would protect and help both her and her son.

The Outcome

What can you learn from the domestic war between Sarah and Hagar? Plenty, actually. First of all, don't be a polygamist—a guy who marries more than one woman. (OK, that was an obvious one.) Second, don't be a passive wuss! Imagine how different this story would be if old Abe had nixed Sarah's shortcut plan instead of letting the ladies talk him into it. Third, don't try to "help" God out (as if he needs it). Wait for him to carry out *his* plan in *his* way, according to *his* timetable. Fourth, deal with conflict. This family feud has festered for thousands of years and is still brewing: Hagar vs. Sarah, Ishmael vs. Isaac, the Arabs vs. the Israelites. What if Abe had said NO or had dealt directly with the conflict? What might be different today?

Read more about Hagar and Sarah in Genesis 16:1–16 (page 17); 21:8–20 (page 24).

THE COVENANT OF CIRCUMCISION

17 When Abram was ninety-nine years old, the Lord appeared to him and said, "I am God Almighty[a]; walk before me and be blameless. ²I will confirm my covenant between me and you and will greatly increase your numbers."

³Abram fell facedown, and God said to him, ⁴"As for me, this is my covenant with you: You will be the father of many nations. ⁵No longer will you be called Abram[b]; your name will be Abraham,[c] for I have made you a father of many nations. ⁶I will make you very fruitful; I will make nations of you, and kings will come from you. ⁷I will establish my covenant as an everlasting covenant between me and you and your descendants after you for the generations to come, to be your God and the God of your descendants after you. ⁸The whole land of Canaan, where you are now an alien, I will give as an everlasting possession to you and your descendants after you; and I will be their God."

⁹Then God said to Abraham, "As for you, you must keep my covenant, you and your descendants after you for the generations to come. ¹⁰This is my covenant with you and your descendants after you, the covenant you are to keep: Every male among you shall be circumcised. ¹¹You are to undergo circumcision, and it will be the sign of the covenant between me and you. ¹²For the generations to come every male among you who is eight days old must be circumcised, including those born in your household or bought with money from a foreigner—those who are not your offspring. ¹³Whether born in your household or bought with your money, they must be circumcised. My covenant in your flesh is to be an everlasting covenant. ¹⁴Any uncircumcised male, who has not been circumcised in the flesh, will be cut off from his people; he has broken my covenant."

¹⁵God also said to Abraham, "As for Sarai your wife, you are no longer to call her Sarai; her name will be Sarah. ¹⁶I will bless her and will surely give you a son by her. I will bless her so that she will be the mother of nations; kings of peoples will come from her."

¹⁷Abraham fell facedown; he laughed and said to himself, "Will a son be born to a man a hundred years old? Will Sarah bear a child at the age of ninety?" ¹⁸And Abraham said to God, "If only Ishmael might live under your blessing!"

¹⁹Then God said, "Yes, but your wife Sarah will bear you a son, and you will call him Isaac.[d] I will establish my covenant with him as an everlasting covenant for his descendants after him. ²⁰And as for Ishmael, I have heard you: I will surely bless him; I will make him fruitful and will greatly increase his numbers. He will be the father of twelve rulers, and I will make him into a great nation. ²¹But my covenant I will establish with Isaac, whom Sarah will bear to you by this time next year." ²²When he had finished speaking with Abraham, God went up from him.

²³On that very day Abraham took his son Ishmael and all those born in his household or bought with his money, every male in his household, and circumcised them, as God told him. ²⁴Abraham was ninety-nine years old when he was circumcised, ²⁵and his son Ishmael was thirteen; ²⁶Abraham and his son Ishmael were both circumcised on that same day. ²⁷And every male in Abraham's household, including those born in his household or bought from a foreigner, was circumcised with him.

THE THREE VISITORS

18 The Lord appeared to Abraham near the great trees of Mamre while he was sitting at the entrance to his tent in the heat of the day. ²Abraham looked up and saw three men standing nearby. When he saw them, he hurried from the entrance of his tent to meet them and bowed low to the ground.

³He said, "If I have found favor in your eyes, my lord,[e] do not pass your servant by. ⁴Let a little water be brought, and then you may all wash your feet and rest under this tree. ⁵Let me get you some-

---

NOW OR NEVER

GE 17:1

You don't have to understand all of the reasons for God's instructions in order to obey them. The fact that God is the infinite, all-powerful, all-knowing, loving Creator of the universe—and you're not—should be reason enough to trust and obey him.

ᵃ 1 Hebrew *El-Shaddai*   ᵇ 5 *Abram* means *exalted father.*   ᶜ 5 *Abraham* means *father of many.*   ᵈ 19 *Isaac* means *he laughs.*
ᵉ 3 Or *O Lord*

thing to eat, so you can be refreshed and then go on your way—now that you have come to your servant."

"Very well," they answered, "do as you say."

[6]So Abraham hurried into the tent to Sarah. "Quick," he said, "get three seahs[a] of fine flour and knead it and bake some bread."

[7]Then he ran to the herd and selected a choice, tender calf and gave it to a servant, who hurried to prepare it. [8]He then brought some curds and milk and the calf that had been prepared, and set these before them. While they ate, he stood near them under a tree.

[9]"Where is your wife Sarah?" they asked him.

"There, in the tent," he said.

[10]Then the Lord[b] said, "I will surely return to you about this time next year, and Sarah your wife will have a son."

Now Sarah was listening at the entrance to the tent, which was behind him. [11]Abraham and Sarah were already old and well advanced in years, and Sarah was past the age of childbearing. [12]So Sarah laughed to herself as she thought, "After I am worn out and my master[c] is old, will I now have this pleasure?"

[13]Then the Lord said to Abraham, "Why did Sarah laugh and say, 'Will I really have a child, now that I am old?' [14]Is anything too hard for the Lord? I will return to you at the appointed time next year and Sarah will have a son."

[15]Sarah was afraid, so she lied and said, "I did not laugh."

But he said, "Yes, you did laugh."

ABRAHAM PLEADS FOR SODOM

[16]When the men got up to leave, they looked down toward Sodom, and Abraham walked along with them to see them on their way. [17]Then the Lord said, "Shall I hide from Abraham what I am about to do? [18]Abraham will surely become a great and powerful nation, and all nations on earth will be blessed through him. [19]For I have chosen him, so that he will direct his children and his household after him to keep the way of the Lord by doing what is right and just, so that the Lord will bring about for Abraham what he has promised him."

[20]Then the Lord said, "The outcry against Sodom and Gomorrah is so great and their sin so grievous [21]that I will go down and see if what they have done is as bad as the outcry that has reached me. If not, I will know."

[22]The men turned away and went toward Sodom, but Abraham remained standing before the Lord.[d] [23]Then Abraham approached him and said: "Will you sweep away the righteous with the wicked? [24]What if there are fifty righteous people in the city? Will you really sweep it away and not spare[e] the place for the sake of the fifty righteous people in it? [25]Far be it from you to do such a thing—to kill the righteous with the wicked, treating the righteous and the wicked alike. Far be it from you! Will not the Judge[f] of all the earth do right?"

[26]The Lord said, "If I find fifty righteous people in the city of Sodom, I will spare the whole place for their sake."

[27]Then Abraham spoke up again: "Now that I have been so bold as to speak to the Lord, though I am nothing but dust and ashes, [28]what if the number of the righteous is five less than fifty? Will you destroy the whole city because of five people?"

"If I find forty-five there," he said, "I will not destroy it."

[29]Once again he spoke to him, "What if only forty are found there?"

He said, "For the sake of forty, I will not do it."

[30]Then he said, "May the Lord not be angry, but let me speak. What if only thirty can be found there?"

He answered, "I will not do it if I find thirty there."

[31]Abraham said, "Now that I have been so bold as to speak to the Lord, what if only twenty can be found there?"

He said, "For the sake of twenty, I will not destroy it."

[a] 6 That is, probably about 20 quarts (about 22 liters)   [b] 10 Hebrew *Then he*   [c] 12 Or *husband*   [d] 22 Masoretic Text; an ancient Hebrew scribal tradition *but the Lord remained standing before Abraham*   [e] 24 Or *forgive*; also in verse 26   [f] 25 Or *Ruler*

³²Then he said, "May the Lord not be angry, but let me speak just once more. What if only ten can be found there?"

He answered, "For the sake of ten, I will not destroy it."

³³When the LORD had finished speaking with Abraham, he left, and Abraham returned home.

SODOM AND GOMORRAH DESTROYED

19 The two angels arrived at Sodom in the evening, and Lot was sitting in the gateway of the city. When he saw them, he got up to meet them and bowed down with his face to the ground. ²"My lords," he said, "please turn aside to your servant's house. You can wash your feet and spend the night and then go on your way early in the morning."

"No," they answered, "we will spend the night in the square."

³But he insisted so strongly that they did go with him and entered his house. He prepared a meal for them, baking bread without yeast, and they ate. ⁴Before they had gone to bed, all the men from every part of the city of Sodom—both young and old—surrounded the house. ⁵They called to Lot, "Where are the men who came to you tonight? Bring them out to us so that we can have sex with them."

⁶Lot went outside to meet them and shut the door behind him ⁷and said, "No, my friends. Don't do this wicked thing. ⁸Look, I have two daughters who have never slept with a man. Let me bring them out to you, and you can do what you like with them. But don't do anything to these men, for they have come under the protection of my roof."

⁹"Get out of our way," they replied. And they said, "This fellow came here as an alien, and now he wants to play the judge! We'll treat you worse than them." They kept bringing pressure on Lot and moved forward to break down the door.

¹⁰But the men inside reached out and pulled Lot back into the house and shut the door. ¹¹Then they struck the men who were at the door of the house, young and old, with blindness so that they could not find the door.

¹²The two men said to Lot, "Do you have anyone else here—sons-in-law, sons or daughters, or anyone else in the city who belongs to you? Get them out of here, ¹³because we are going to destroy this place. The outcry to the LORD against its people is so great that he has sent us to destroy it."

¹⁴So Lot went out and spoke to his sons-in-law, who were pledged to marry*ᵃ* his daughters. He said, "Hurry and get out of this place, because the LORD is about to destroy the city!" But his sons-in-law thought he was joking.

¹⁵With the coming of dawn, the angels urged Lot, saying, "Hurry! Take your wife and your two daughters who are here, or you will be swept away when the city is punished."

¹⁶When he hesitated, the men grasped his hand and the hands of his wife and of his two daughters and led them safely out of the city, for the LORD was merciful to them. ¹⁷As soon as they had brought them out, one of them said, "Flee for your lives! Don't look back, and don't stop anywhere in the plain! Flee to the mountains or you will be swept away!"

¹⁸But Lot said to them, "No, my lords,ᵇ please! ¹⁹Yourᶜ servant has found favor in yourᶜ eyes, and youᶜ have shown great kindness to me in sparing my life. But I can't flee to the mountains; this disaster will overtake me, and I'll die. ²⁰Look, here is a town near enough to run to, and it is small. Let me flee to it—it is very small, isn't it? Then my life will be spared."

²¹He said to him, "Very well, I will grant this request too; I will not overthrow the town you speak of. ²²But flee there quickly, because I cannot do anything until you reach it." (That is why the town was called Zoar.ᵈ)

²³By the time Lot reached Zoar, the sun had risen over the land. ²⁴Then the LORD rained down burning sulfur on Sodom and Gomorrah—from the LORD out of the heavens. ²⁵Thus he overthrew those cities and the entire plain, including all those living in the cities—and also the vegetation in the land. ²⁶But Lot's wife looked back, and she became a pillar of salt.

²⁷Early the next morning Abraham got up and returned to the place where he had stood before the LORD. ²⁸He looked down toward Sodom and Gomorrah, toward all the land of the plain, and he saw dense smoke rising from the land, like smoke from a furnace.

²⁹So when God destroyed the cities of the plain, he remembered Abraham, and he brought Lot out of the catastrophe that overthrew the cities where Lot had lived.

ᵃ *14* Or *were married to*   ᵇ *18* Or *No, Lord*; or *No, my lord*   ᶜ *19* The Hebrew is singular.   ᵈ *22 Zoar* means *small.*

LOT AND HIS DAUGHTERS

³⁰Lot and his two daughters left Zoar and settled in the mountains, for he was afraid to stay in Zoar. He and his two daughters lived in a cave. ³¹One day the older daughter said to the younger, "Our father is old, and there is no man around here to lie with us, as is the custom all over the earth. ³²Let's get our father to drink wine and then lie with him and preserve our family line through our father."

³³That night they got their father to drink wine, and the older daughter went in and lay with him. He was not aware of it when she lay down or when she got up.

³⁴The next day the older daughter said to the younger, "Last night I lay with my father. Let's get him to drink wine again tonight, and you go in and lie with him so we can preserve our family line through our father." ³⁵So they got their father to drink wine that night also, and the younger daughter went and lay with him. Again he was not aware of it when she lay down or when she got up.

NOW OR NEVER

GE 19:30-34

Compromise is never an option when it comes to sin. Doing something wrong— even for reasons that you think are right— will always create more problems than it solves. Where are you feeling the pressure to compromise?

³⁶So both of Lot's daughters became pregnant by their father. ³⁷The older daughter had a son, and she named him Moab ᵃ; he is the father of the Moabites of today. ³⁸The younger daughter also had a son, and she named him Ben-Ammi ᵇ; he is the father of the Ammonites of today.

ABRAHAM AND ABIMELECH

20

Now Abraham moved on from there into the region of the Negev and lived between Kadesh and Shur. For a while he stayed in Gerar, ²and there Abraham said of his wife Sarah, "She is my sister." Then Abimelech king of Gerar sent for Sarah and took her.

³But God came to Abimelech in a dream one night and said to him, "You are as good as dead because of the woman you have taken; she is a married woman."

⁴Now Abimelech had not gone near her, so he said, "Lord, will you destroy an innocent nation? ⁵Did he not say to me, 'She is my sister,' and didn't she also say, 'He is my brother'? I have done this with a clear conscience and clean hands."

⁶Then God said to him in the dream, "Yes, I know you did this with a clear conscience, and so I have kept you from sinning against me. That is why I did not let you touch her. ⁷Now return the man's wife, for he is a prophet, and he will pray for you and you will live. But if you do not return her, you may be sure that you and all yours will die."

⁸Early the next morning Abimelech summoned all his officials, and when he told them all that had happened, they were very much afraid. ⁹Then Abimelech called Abraham in and said, "What have you done to us? How have I wronged you that you have brought such great guilt upon me and my kingdom? You have done things to me that should not be done." ¹⁰And Abimelech asked Abraham, "What was your reason for doing this?"

¹¹Abraham replied, "I said to myself, 'There is surely no fear of God in this place, and they will kill me because of my wife.' ¹²Besides, she really is my sister, the daughter of my father though not of my mother; and she became my wife. ¹³And when God had me wander from my father's household, I said to her, 'This is how you can show your love to me: Everywhere we go, say of me, "He is my brother." ' "

¹⁴Then Abimelech brought sheep and cattle and male and female slaves and gave them to Abraham, and he returned Sarah his wife to him. ¹⁵And Abimelech said, "My land is before you; live wherever you like."

¹⁶To Sarah he said, "I am giving your brother a thousand shekels ᶜ of silver. This is to cover the offense against you before all who are with you; you are completely vindicated."

¹⁷Then Abraham prayed to God, and God healed Abimelech, his wife and his slave girls so they could have children again, ¹⁸for the LORD had closed up every womb in Abimelech's household because of Abraham's wife Sarah.

ᵃ 37 Moab sounds like the Hebrew for from father.   ᵇ 38 Ben-Ammi means son of my people.   ᶜ 16 That is, about 25 pounds (about 11.5 kilograms)

lot

VERSUS

» Abraham's nephew
» Materialistic "friend of the world"
» Always in trouble

abraham

» Lot's uncle
» Spiritual "friend of God"
» Always coming to the aid of those in trouble

The Main Event

Lot is the poster child for weak character and wasted opportunities. He lived his life thinking only of material possessions. His priorities were so twisted, in fact, that he was willing to move his family to Sodom, the most sinful city around.

Lot seemed to be all about acquiring money and stuff. And while he did all right financially speaking, in life he lost much more than he ever gained. For one thing, he lost contact with God. Remember, the Bible says it is impossible to love God *and* money (or the world) at the same time (see Matthew 6:24 and James 4:4). Lot also lost his reputation and credibility. When Lot tried to warn people that God was about to judge Sodom, not even his own sons-in-law took him seriously. They thought it was all a big joke. Finally, Lot lost his family to the evil values of the culture in which he had gotten caught up. His wife died in God's judgment because she couldn't keep from looking back longingly on the life they were leaving behind as they fled Sodom. She couldn't bear to remove herself from her godless lifestyle. Later, Lot's daughters got him drunk to have sex with him and become pregnant. A fitting end to a sad tale.

Abraham, Lot's uncle, was a totally different kind of man. He wasn't perfect, not by any means . . . but he was a man who pursued God above all else. Who wouldn't want Abraham's résumé or legacy? When God prompted him to do things, Abraham obeyed. Period. In a conflict with Lot over pastureland, Abraham basically said, "Hey, take what you want. I'll let you choose. Let's not allow a territorial dispute mess up our relationship." The funny thing is, Abraham always did really well financially—but he did so by focusing on God, not by obsessing over "stuff" (see Matthew 6:33).

The Outcome

Like it or not, we *are* the sum of our choices. Someone has said, "Sow a thought, reap an act. Sow an act, reap a habit. Sow a habit, reap a character. Sow a character, reap a destiny."

The point of this saying is that every decision we make ends up bending us in a certain direction—either toward God or away from him. With every single choice, something huge and eternal is at stake. That's why, like Lot, we can't just drift through life.

Fast forward to your own funeral. What do you want people to say about you? What do you want to be remembered for? A life like Lot's or Abraham's? It's your choice—and today will move you a bit closer to one destination or another.

Read more about Lot and Abraham in Genesis 11–14 (pages 12–16); 18:16–19:38 (pages 20–22.

THE BIRTH OF ISAAC

21

Now the LORD was gracious to Sarah as he had said, and the LORD did for Sarah what he had promised. ²Sarah became pregnant and bore a son to Abraham in his old age, at the very time God had promised him. ³Abraham gave the name Isaac[a] to the son Sarah bore him. ⁴When his son Isaac was eight days old, Abraham circumcised him, as God commanded him. ⁵Abraham was a hundred years old when his son Isaac was born to him.

NOW OR NEVER
GE 21:1-7

God is not bound by the laws of physics or nature. What seems impossible for us is a breeze to him.

⁶Sarah said, "God has brought me laughter, and everyone who hears about this will laugh with me." ⁷And she added, "Who would have said to Abraham that Sarah would nurse children? Yet I have borne him a son in his old age."

HAGAR AND ISHMAEL SENT AWAY

⁸The child grew and was weaned, and on the day Isaac was weaned Abraham held a great feast. ⁹But Sarah saw that the son whom Hagar the Egyptian had borne to Abraham was mocking, ¹⁰and she said to Abraham, "Get rid of that slave woman and her son, for that slave woman's son will never share in the inheritance with my son Isaac."

¹¹The matter distressed Abraham greatly because it concerned his son. ¹²But God said to him, "Do not be so distressed about the boy and your maidservant. Listen to whatever Sarah tells you, because it is through Isaac that your offspring[b] will be reckoned. ¹³I will make the son of the maidservant into a nation also, because he is your offspring."

¹⁴Early the next morning Abraham took some food and a skin of water and gave them to Hagar. He set them on her shoulders and then sent her off with the boy. She went on her way and wandered in the desert of Beersheba.

¹⁵When the water in the skin was gone, she put the boy under one of the bushes. ¹⁶Then she went off and sat down nearby, about a bowshot away, for she thought, "I cannot watch the boy die." And as she sat there nearby, she[c] began to sob.

¹⁷God heard the boy crying, and the angel of God called to Hagar from heaven and said to her, "What is the matter, Hagar? Do not be afraid; God has heard the boy crying as he lies there. ¹⁸Lift the boy up and take him by the hand, for I will make him into a great nation."

¹⁹Then God opened her eyes and she saw a well of water. So she went and filled the skin with water and gave the boy a drink.

²⁰God was with the boy as he grew up. He lived in the desert and became an archer. ²¹While he was living in the Desert of Paran, his mother got a wife for him from Egypt.

THE TREATY AT BEERSHEBA

²²At that time Abimelech and Phicol the commander? of his forces said to Abraham, "God is with you in everything you do. ²³Now swear to me here before God that you will not deal falsely with me or my children or my descendants. Show to me and the country where you are living as an alien the same kindness I have shown to you."

²⁴Abraham said, "I swear it."

²⁵Then Abraham complained to Abimelech about a well of water that Abimelech's servants had seized. ²⁶But Abimelech said, "I don't know who has done this. You did not tell me, and I heard about it only today."

²⁷So Abraham brought sheep and cattle and gave them to Abimelech, and the two men made a treaty. ²⁸Abraham set apart seven ewe lambs from the flock, ²⁹and Abimelech asked Abraham, "What is the meaning of these seven ewe lambs you have set apart by themselves?"

³⁰He replied, "Accept these seven lambs from my hand as a witness that I dug this well."

ᵃ *3 Isaac means he laughs.*   ᵇ *12 Or seed*   ᶜ *16 Hebrew; Septuagint the child*

³¹So that place was called Beersheba,ᵃ because the two men swore an oath there.

³²After the treaty had been made at Beersheba, Abimelech and Phicol the commander of his forces returned to the land of the Philistines. ³³Abraham planted a tamarisk tree in Beersheba, and there he called upon the name of the Lord, the Eternal God. ³⁴And Abraham stayed in the land of the Philistines for a long time.

Facing Faith Challenges

Anyone can *say* they have faith. What counts, though, is what happens when your faith is put to the test. And, sooner or later, your faith *will* be put to the test. If you're serious about living for God, you can expect to face challenge after challenge to your commitment. Are you ready to deal with those challenges when they come?

ABRAHAM TESTED

22

Some time later God tested Abraham. He said to him, "Abraham!"

"Here I am," he replied.

²Then God said, "Take your son, your only son, Isaac, whom you love, and go to the region of Moriah. Sacrifice him there as a burnt offering on one of the mountains I will tell you about."

³Early the next morning Abraham got up and saddled his donkey. He took with him two of his servants and his son Isaac. When he had cut enough wood for the burnt offering, he set out for the place God had told him about. ⁴On the third day Abraham looked up and saw the place in the distance. ⁵He said to his servants, "Stay here with the donkey while I and the boy go over there. We will worship and then we will come back to you."

⁶Abraham took the wood for the burnt offering and placed it on his son Isaac, and he himself carried the fire and the knife. As the two of them went on together, ⁷Isaac spoke up and said to his father Abraham, "Father?"

"Yes, my son?" Abraham replied.

"The fire and wood are here," Isaac said, "but where is the lamb for the burnt offering?"

⁸Abraham answered, "God himself will provide the lamb for the burnt offering, my son." And the two of them went on together.

⁹When they reached the place God had told him about, Abraham built an altar there and arranged the wood on it. He bound his son Isaac and laid him on the altar, on top of the wood. ¹⁰Then he reached out his hand and took the knife to slay his son. ¹¹But the angel of the Lord called out to him from heaven, "Abraham! Abraham!"

"Here I am," he replied.

¹²"Do not lay a hand on the boy," he said. "Do not do anything to him. Now I know that you fear God, because you have not withheld from me your son, your only son."

¹³Abraham looked up and there in a thicket he saw a ramᵇ caught by its horns. He went over and took the ram and sacrificed it as a burnt offering instead of his son. ¹⁴So Abraham called that place The Lord Will Provide. And to this day it is said, "On the mountain of the Lord it will be provided."

¹⁵The angel of the Lord called to Abraham from heaven a second time ¹⁶and said, "I swear by myself, declares the Lord, that because you have done this and have not withheld your son, your only son, ¹⁷I will surely bless you and make your descendants as numerous as the

NOW OR NEVER

GE 22:12

What parts of your life are you holding back from God? More importantly, *why* are you holding them back? And what might happen if you gave everything you have to God?

ᵃ *31 Beersheba* can mean *well of seven* or *well of the oath.* ᵇ *13* Many manuscripts of the Masoretic Text, Samaritan Pentateuch, Septuagint and Syriac; most manuscripts of the Masoretic Text *a ram behind ⸤him⸥*

stars in the sky and as the sand on the seashore. Your descendants will take possession of the cities of their enemies, ¹⁸and through your offspring[a] all nations on earth will be blessed, because you have obeyed me."

¹⁹Then Abraham returned to his servants, and they set off together for Beersheba. And Abraham stayed in Beersheba.

NAHOR'S SONS

²⁰Some time later Abraham was told, "Milcah is also a mother; she has borne sons to your brother Nahor: ²¹Uz the firstborn, Buz his brother, Kemuel (the father of Aram), ²²Kesed, Hazo, Pildash, Jidlaph and Bethuel." ²³Bethuel became the father of Rebekah. Milcah bore these eight sons to Abraham's brother Nahor. ²⁴His concubine, whose name was Reumah, also had sons: Tebah, Gaham, Tahash and Maacah.

challengenotes

To: my_son

heavenly_father: you cannot imagine the incredible blessings that are yours because you're my child. if you will obey me and live according to my word, I'll show you blessing and fulfillment beyond your wildest dreams. and the best thing about these blessings? they last forever!

GE 22:15-18

THE DEATH OF SARAH

23 Sarah lived to be a hundred and twenty-seven years old. ²She died at Kiriath Arba (that is, Hebron) in the land of Canaan, and Abraham went to mourn for Sarah and to weep over her.

³Then Abraham rose from beside his dead wife and spoke to the Hittites.[b] He said, ⁴"I am an alien and a stranger among you. Sell me some property for a burial site here so I can bury my dead."

⁵The Hittites replied to Abraham, ⁶"Sir, listen to us. You are a mighty prince among us. Bury your dead in the choicest of our tombs. None of us will refuse you his tomb for burying your dead."

⁷Then Abraham rose and bowed down before the people of the land, the Hittites. ⁸He said to them, "If you are willing to let me bury my dead, then listen to me and intercede with Ephron son of Zohar on my behalf ⁹so he will sell me the cave of Machpelah, which belongs to him and is at the end of his field. Ask him to sell it to me for the full price as a burial site among you."

¹⁰Ephron the Hittite was sitting among his people and he replied to Abraham in the hearing of all the Hittites who had come to the gate of his city. ¹¹"No, my lord," he said. "Listen to me; I give[c] you the field, and I give[c] you the cave that is in it. I give[c] it to you in the presence of my people. Bury your dead."

¹²Again Abraham bowed down before the people of the land ¹³and he said to Ephron in their hearing, "Listen to me, if you will. I will pay the price of the field. Accept it from me so I can bury my dead there."

¹⁴Ephron answered Abraham, ¹⁵"Listen to me, my lord; the land is worth four hundred shekels[d] of silver, but what is that between me and you? Bury your dead."

¹⁶Abraham agreed to Ephron's terms and weighed out for him the price he had named in the hearing of the Hittites: four hundred shekels of silver, according to the weight current among the merchants.

¹⁷So Ephron's field in Machpelah near Mamre—both the field and the cave in it, and all the trees within the borders of the field—was deeded ¹⁸to Abraham as his property in the presence of all the Hittites who had come to the gate of the city. ¹⁹Afterward Abraham buried his wife Sarah in the cave in the field of Machpelah near Mamre (which is at Hebron) in the land of Canaan. ²⁰So the field and the cave in it were deeded to Abraham by the Hittites as a burial site.

ISAAC AND REBEKAH

24 Abraham was now old and well advanced in years, and the LORD had blessed him in every way. ²He said to the chief[e] servant in his household, the one in charge of all that he had, "Put your hand under my thigh. ³I want you to swear by the LORD, the God of heaven and the God of earth, that you will not get a wife for my son from the daughters of the Canaanites, among whom I am living, ⁴but will go to my country and my own relatives and get a wife for my son Isaac."

---

[a] 18 Or seed   [b] 3 Or the sons of Heth; also in verses 5, 7, 10, 16, 18 and 20   [c] 11 Or sell   [d] 15 That is, about 10 pounds (about 4.5 kilograms)   [e] 2 Or oldest

⁵The servant asked him, "What if the woman is unwilling to come back with me to this land? Shall I then take your son back to the country you came from?"

⁶"Make sure that you do not take my son back there," Abraham said. ⁷"The LORD, the God of heaven, who brought me out of my father's household and my native land and who spoke to me and promised me on oath, saying, 'To your offspring ᵃ I will give this land'—he will send his angel before you so that you can get a wife for my son from there. ⁸If the woman is unwilling to come back with you, then you will be released from this oath of mine. Only do not take my son back there." ⁹So the servant put his hand under the thigh of his master Abraham and swore an oath to him concerning this matter.

¹⁰Then the servant took ten of his master's camels and left, taking with him all kinds of good things from his master. He set out for Aram Naharaim ᵇ and made his way to the town of Nahor. ¹¹He had the camels kneel down near the well outside the town; it was toward evening, the time the women go out to draw water.

¹²Then he prayed, "O LORD, God of my master Abraham, give me success today, and show kindness to my master Abraham. ¹³See, I am standing beside this spring, and the daughters of the townspeople are coming out to draw water. ¹⁴May it be that when I say to a girl, 'Please let down your jar that I may have a drink,' and she says, 'Drink, and I'll water your camels too'—let her be the one you have chosen for your servant Isaac. By this I will know that you have shown kindness to my master."

¹⁵Before he had finished praying, Rebekah came out with her jar on her shoulder. She was the daughter of Bethuel son of Milcah, who was the wife of Abraham's brother Nahor. ¹⁶The girl was very beautiful, a virgin; no man had ever lain with her. She went down to the spring, filled her jar and came up again.

¹⁷The servant hurried to meet her and said, "Please give me a little water from your jar."

¹⁸"Drink, my lord," she said, and quickly lowered the jar to her hands and gave him a drink.

¹⁹After she had given him a drink, she said, "I'll draw water for your camels too, until they have finished drinking." ²⁰So she quickly emptied her jar into the trough, ran back to the well to draw more water, and drew enough for all his camels. ²¹Without saying a word, the man watched her closely to learn whether or not the LORD had made his journey successful.

²²When the camels had finished drinking, the man took out a gold nose ring weighing a beka ᶜ and two gold bracelets weighing ten shekels. ᵈ ²³Then he asked, "Whose daughter are you? Please tell me, is there room in your father's house for us to spend the night?"

²⁴She answered him, "I am the daughter of Bethuel, the son that Milcah bore to Nahor." ²⁵And she added, "We have plenty of straw and fodder, as well as room for you to spend the night."

²⁶Then the man bowed down and worshiped the LORD, ²⁷saying, "Praise be to the LORD, the God of my master Abraham, who has not abandoned his kindness and faithfulness to my master. As for me, the LORD has led me on the journey to the house of my master's relatives."

²⁸The girl ran and told her mother's household about these things. ²⁹Now Rebekah had a brother named Laban, and he hurried out to the man at the spring. ³⁰As soon as he had seen the nose ring, and the bracelets on his sister's arms, and had heard Rebekah tell what the man said to her, he went out to the man and found him standing by the camels near the spring. ³¹"Come, you who are blessed by the LORD," he said. "Why are you standing out here? I have prepared the house and a place for the camels."

³²So the man went to the house, and the camels were unloaded. Straw and fodder were brought for the camels, and water for him and his men to wash their feet. ³³Then food was set before him, but he said, "I will not eat until I have told you what I have to say."

"Then tell us," ⌊Laban⌋ said.

³⁴So he said, "I am Abraham's servant. ³⁵The LORD has blessed my master abundantly, and he has become wealthy. He has given him sheep and cattle, silver and gold, menservants and maidservants, and camels and donkeys. ³⁶My master's wife Sarah has borne him a son in her ᵉ old age, and he has given him everything he owns. ³⁷And my master made me swear an oath, and said, 'You must not get a wife for my son from the daughters of the Canaanites, in whose land I live, ³⁸but go to my father's family and to my own clan, and get a wife for my son.'

³⁹"Then I asked my master, 'What if the woman will not come back with me?'

⁴⁰"He replied, 'The LORD, before whom I have walked, will send his angel with you and make your journey a success, so that you can get a wife for my son from my own clan and from my father's fami-

---

ᵃ 7 Or seed   ᵇ 10 That is, Northwest Mesopotamia   ᶜ 22 That is, about 1/5 ounce (about 5.5 grams)   ᵈ 22 That is, about 4 ounces (about 110 grams)   ᵉ 36 Or his

battlelines

» Surface-level Friends (Friendship)

Q: Hey, can I ask you a question?
A: I don't know. I'm not supposed to talk to strangers. (Smiling) Okay, I guess so.

Q: What is friendship?
A: Friendship? Hmmm, let's see . . . I'd say friendship is, well . . . a relationship between two people, one where they hang out together and . . . I guess, look out for each other.

Q: Anything else?
A: Well, to be friends with someone you gotta have something in common. Similar interests. And you have to keep up with each other, on what's going on in each other's life.

Q: So what about you?
A: What *about* me?

Q: Do you have friends?
A: Well, yeah. Of course.

Q: *Close* friends?
A: What do you mean by "close"?

Q: Well, you said friends look out for each other and stuff. Do you have people who do that for you? People who *really* know the deep stuff going on inside you—your dreams, your disappointments, your hopes, your goals?
A: No, I don't think they know all that stuff. I don't think they'd *want* to know.

Q: So, then, they're really more like acquaintances?
A: No, we're friends. But it's not like we sit around and *talk* all the time, like girls do. We mostly *do* stuff together.

» Beneath the Surface

Because guys are action-oriented, our friendships, as Desmond points out, tend to revolve around doing stuff together. There's nothing wrong with that. However, if our relationships never get beyond seeing movies, shooting hoops or playing video games, we'll find ourselves feeling frustrated and lonely.

Pop culture will try to tell you that real men stand alone, that being open about your struggles and emotions is a sign of weakness. But we're not created in the image of pop culture; we're created in the image of God (see Genesis 1:27). That means, among other things, that we are relational beings. We need other people. We were created to love them and to be loved by them, to work with them, to serve them, to know them and to be known by them.

Don't settle for superficial relationships. Find a band of brothers and open up your lives to one another. Friendship is one of God's most amazing blessings, one of life's greatest joys. It's a big step, but you'll be surprised at how many other people are looking for the same thing.

Read more about friendship at www.RevolutionBible.com.

ly. ⁴¹Then, when you go to my clan, you will be released from my oath even if they refuse to give her to you—you will be released from my oath.'

⁴²"When I came to the spring today, I said, 'O LORD, God of my master Abraham, if you will, please grant success to the journey on which I have come. ⁴³See, I am standing beside this spring; if a maiden comes out to draw water and I say to her, "Please let me drink a little water from your jar," ⁴⁴and if she says to me, "Drink, and I'll draw water for your camels too," let her be the one the LORD has chosen for my master's son.'

⁴⁵"Before I finished praying in my heart, Rebekah came out, with her jar on her shoulder. She went down to the spring and drew water, and I said to her, 'Please give me a drink.'

⁴⁶"She quickly lowered her jar from her shoulder and said, 'Drink, and I'll water your camels too.' So I drank, and she watered the camels also.

⁴⁷"I asked her, 'Whose daughter are you?'

"She said, 'The daughter of Bethuel son of Nahor, whom Milcah bore to him.'

"Then I put the ring in her nose and the bracelets on her arms, ⁴⁸and I bowed down and worshiped the LORD. I praised the LORD, the God of my master Abraham, who had led me on the right road to get the granddaughter of my master's brother for his son. ⁴⁹Now if you will show kindness and faithfulness to my master, tell me; and if not, tell me, so I may know which way to turn."

⁵⁰Laban and Bethuel answered, "This is from the LORD; we can say nothing to you one way or the other. ⁵¹Here is Rebekah; take her and go, and let her become the wife of your master's son, as the LORD has directed."

⁵²When Abraham's servant heard what they said, he bowed down to the ground before the LORD. ⁵³Then the servant brought out gold and silver jewelry and articles of clothing and gave them to Rebekah; he also gave costly gifts to her brother and to her mother. ⁵⁴Then he and the men who were with him ate and drank and spent the night there.

When they got up the next morning, he said, "Send me on my way to my master."

⁵⁵But her brother and her mother replied, "Let the girl remain with us ten days or so; then you[a] may go."

⁵⁶But he said to them, "Do not detain me, now that the LORD has granted success to my journey. Send me on my way so I may go to my master."

⁵⁷Then they said, "Let's call the girl and ask her about it." ⁵⁸So they called Rebekah and asked her, "Will you go with this man?"

"I will go," she said.

⁵⁹So they sent their sister Rebekah on her way, along with her nurse and Abraham's servant and his men. ⁶⁰And they blessed Rebekah and said to her,

"Our sister, may you increase
    to thousands upon thousands;
may your offspring possess
    the gates of their enemies."

⁶¹Then Rebekah and her maids got ready and mounted their camels and went back with the man. So the servant took Rebekah and left.

⁶²Now Isaac had come from Beer Lahai Roi, for he was living in the Negev. ⁶³He went out to the field one evening to meditate,[b] and as he looked up, he saw camels approaching. ⁶⁴Rebekah also looked up and saw Isaac. She got down from her camel ⁶⁵and asked the servant, "Who is that man in the field coming to meet us?"

"He is my master," the servant answered. So she took her veil and covered herself.

⁶⁶Then the servant told Isaac all he had done. ⁶⁷Isaac brought her into the tent of his mother Sarah, and he married Rebekah. So she became his wife, and he loved her; and Isaac was comforted after his mother's death.

THE DEATH OF ABRAHAM

25

Abraham took[c] another wife, whose name was Keturah. ²She bore him Zimran, Jokshan, Medan, Midian, Ishbak and Shuah. ³Jokshan was the father of Sheba and

---

ᵃ 55 Or she   ᵇ 63 The meaning of the Hebrew for this word is uncertain.   ᶜ 1 Or had taken

Dedan; the descendants of Dedan were the Asshurites, the Letushites and the Leummites. [4]The sons of Midian were Ephah, Epher, Hanoch, Abida and Eldaah. All these were descendants of Keturah.

[5]Abraham left everything he owned to Isaac. [6]But while he was still living, he gave gifts to the sons of his concubines and sent them away from his son Isaac to the land of the east.

[7]Altogether, Abraham lived a hundred and seventy-five years. [8]Then Abraham breathed his last and died at a good old age, an old man and full of years; and he was gathered to his people. [9]His sons Isaac and Ishmael buried him in the cave of Machpelah near Mamre, in the field of Ephron son of Zohar the Hittite, [10]the field Abraham had bought from the Hittites.[a] There Abraham was buried with his wife Sarah. [11]After Abraham's death, God blessed his son Isaac, who then lived near Beer Lahai Roi.

ISHMAEL'S SONS

[12]This is the account of Abraham's son Ishmael, whom Sarah's maidservant, Hagar the Egyptian, bore to Abraham.

[13]These are the names of the sons of Ishmael, listed in the order of their birth: Nebaioth the firstborn of Ishmael, Kedar, Adbeel, Mibsam, [14]Mishma, Dumah, Massa, [15]Hadad, Tema, Jetur, Naphish and Kedemah. [16]These were the sons of Ishmael, and these are the names of the twelve tribal rulers according to their settlements and camps. [17]Altogether, Ishmael lived a hundred and thirty-seven years. He breathed his last and died, and he was gathered to his people. [18]His descendants settled in the area from Havilah to Shur, near the border of Egypt, as you go toward Asshur. And they lived in hostility toward[b] all their brothers.

JACOB AND ESAU

[19]This is the account of Abraham's son Isaac.

Abraham became the father of Isaac, [20]and Isaac was forty years old when he married Rebekah daughter of Bethuel the Aramean from Paddan Aram[c] and sister of Laban the Aramean.

[21]Isaac prayed to the LORD on behalf of his wife, because she was barren. The LORD answered his prayer, and his wife Rebekah became pregnant. [22]The babies jostled each other within her, and she said, "Why is this happening to me?" So she went to inquire of the LORD.

[23]The LORD said to her,

"Two nations are in your womb,
 and two peoples from within you will be separated;
 one people will be stronger than the other,
 and the older will serve the younger."

[24]When the time came for her to give birth, there were twin boys in her womb. [25]The first to come out was red, and his whole body was like a hairy garment; so they named him Esau.[d] [26]After this, his brother came out, with his hand grasping Esau's heel; so he was named Jacob.[e] Isaac was sixty years old when Rebekah gave birth to them.

[27]The boys grew up, and Esau became a skillful hunter, a man of the open country, while Jacob was a quiet man, staying among the tents. [28]Isaac, who had a taste for wild game, loved Esau, but Rebekah loved Jacob.

[29]Once when Jacob was cooking some stew, Esau came in from the open country, famished. [30]He said to Jacob, "Quick, let me have some of that red stew! I'm famished!" (That is why he was also called Edom.[f])

[31]Jacob replied, "First sell me your birthright."

[32]"Look, I am about to die," Esau said. "What good is the birthright to me?"

NOW OR NEVER

GE 25:32-33

Always consider the long-term effects of your decisions. Don't let a quick thrill or temporary pleasure ruin the rest of your life. In other words, *think* before you act.

---

[a] 10 Or *the sons of Heth*   [b] 18 Or *lived to the east of*   [c] 20 That is, Northwest Mesopotamia   [d] 25 *Esau* may mean *hairy*; he was also called Edom, which means *red*.   [e] 26 *Jacob* means *he grasps the heel* (figuratively, *he deceives*).   [f] 30 *Edom* means *red*.

³³But Jacob said, "Swear to me first." So he swore an oath to him, selling his birthright to Jacob. ³⁴Then Jacob gave Esau some bread and some lentil stew. He ate and drank, and then got up and left. So Esau despised his birthright.

ISAAC AND ABIMELECH

26 Now there was a famine in the land—besides the earlier famine of Abraham's time—and Isaac went to Abimelech king of the Philistines in Gerar. ²The LORD appeared to Isaac and said, "Do not go down to Egypt; live in the land where I tell you to live. ³Stay in this land for a while, and I will be with you and will bless you. For to you and your descendants I will give all these lands and will confirm the oath I swore to your father Abraham. ⁴I will make your descendants as numerous as the stars in the sky and will give them all these lands, and through your offspring[a] all nations on earth will be blessed, ⁵because Abraham obeyed me and kept my requirements, my commands, my decrees and my laws." ⁶So Isaac stayed in Gerar.

⁷When the men of that place asked him about his wife, he said, "She is my sister," because he was afraid to say, "She is my wife." He thought, "The men of this place might kill me on account of Rebekah, because she is beautiful."

⁸When Isaac had been there a long time, Abimelech king of the Philistines looked down from a window and saw Isaac caressing his wife Rebekah. ⁹So Abimelech summoned Isaac and said, "She is really your wife! Why did you say, 'She is my sister'?"

Isaac answered him, "Because I thought I might lose my life on account of her."

¹⁰Then Abimelech said, "What is this you have done to us? One of the men might well have slept with your wife, and you would have brought guilt upon us."

¹¹So Abimelech gave orders to all the people: "Anyone who molests this man or his wife shall surely be put to death."

¹²Isaac planted crops in that land and the same year reaped a hundredfold, because the LORD blessed him. ¹³The man became rich, and his wealth continued to grow until he became very wealthy. ¹⁴He had so many flocks and herds and servants that the Philistines envied him. ¹⁵So all the wells that his father's servants had dug in the time of his father Abraham, the Philistines stopped up, filling them with earth.

¹⁶Then Abimelech said to Isaac, "Move away from us; you have become too powerful for us."

¹⁷So Isaac moved away from there and encamped in the Valley of Gerar and settled there. ¹⁸Isaac reopened the wells that had been dug in the time of his father Abraham, which the Philistines had stopped up after Abraham died, and he gave them the same names his father had given them.

¹⁹Isaac's servants dug in the valley and discovered a well of fresh water there. ²⁰But the herdsmen of Gerar quarreled with Isaac's herdsmen and said, "The water is ours!" So he named the well Esek,[b] because they disputed with him. ²¹Then they dug another well, but they quarreled over that one also; so he named it Sitnah.[c] ²²He moved on from there and dug another well, and no one quarreled over it. He named it Rehoboth,[d] saying, "Now the LORD has given us room and we will flourish in the land."

NOW OR NEVER
GE 26:16–22

When someone challenges your rights, what is your first reaction? Will you fight to the death (like Isaac could have), or will you defer to your challenger and trust God to provide for you (like Isaac did)?

²³From there he went up to Beersheba. ²⁴That night the LORD appeared to him and said, "I am the God of your father Abraham. Do not be afraid, for I am with you; I will bless you and will increase the number of your descendants for the sake of my servant Abraham."

²⁵Isaac built an altar there and called on the name of the LORD. There he pitched his tent, and there his servants dug a well.

²⁶Meanwhile, Abimelech had come to him from Gerar, with Ahuzzath his personal adviser and Phicol the commander of his forces. ²⁷Isaac asked them, "Why have you come to me, since you were hostile to me and sent me away?"

ᵃ *4 Or* seed   ᵇ *20* Esek *means* dispute.   ᶜ *21* Sitnah *means* opposition.   ᵈ *22* Rehoboth *means* room.

28They answered, "We saw clearly that the LORD was with you; so we said, 'There ought to be a sworn agreement between us'—between us and you. Let us make a treaty with you 29that you will do us no harm, just as we did not molest you but always treated you well and sent you away in peace. And now you are blessed by the LORD."

30Isaac then made a feast for them, and they ate and drank. 31Early the next morning the men swore an oath to each other. Then Isaac sent them on their way, and they left him in peace.

32That day Isaac's servants came and told him about the well they had dug. They said, "We've found water!" 33He called it Shibah,a and to this day the name of the town has been Beersheba.b

34When Esau was forty years old, he married Judith daughter of Beeri the Hittite, and also Basemath daughter of Elon the Hittite. 35They were a source of grief to Isaac and Rebekah.

JACOB GETS ISAAC'S BLESSING

27 When Isaac was old and his eyes were so weak that he could no longer see, he called for Esau his older son and said to him, "My son."

"Here I am," he answered.

2Isaac said, "I am now an old man and don't know the day of my death. 3Now then, get your weapons—your quiver and bow—and go out to the open country to hunt some wild game for me. 4Prepare me the kind of tasty food I like and bring it to me to eat, so that I may give you my blessing before I die."

5Now Rebekah was listening as Isaac spoke to his son Esau. When Esau left for the open country to hunt game and bring it back, 6Rebekah said to her son Jacob, "Look, I overheard your father say to your brother Esau, 7'Bring me some game and prepare me some tasty food to eat, so that I may give you my blessing in the presence of the LORD before I die.' 8Now, my son, listen carefully and do what I tell you: 9Go out to the flock and bring me two choice young goats, so I can prepare some tasty food for your father, just the way he likes it. 10Then take it to your father to eat, so that he may give you his blessing before he dies."

11Jacob said to Rebekah his mother, "But my brother Esau is a hairy man, and I'm a man with smooth skin. 12What if my father touches me? I would appear to be tricking him and would bring down a curse on myself rather than a blessing."

13His mother said to him, "My son, let the curse fall on me. Just do what I say; go and get them for me."

14So he went and got them and brought them to his mother, and she prepared some tasty food, just the way his father liked it. 15Then Rebekah took the best clothes of Esau her older son, which she had in the house, and put them on her younger son Jacob. 16She also covered his hands and the smooth part of his neck with the goatskins. 17Then she handed to her son Jacob the tasty food and the bread she had made.

18He went to his father and said, "My father."

"Yes, my son," he answered. "Who is it?"

19Jacob said to his father, "I am Esau your firstborn. I have done as you told me. Please sit up and eat some of my game so that you may give me your blessing."

20Isaac asked his son, "How did you find it so quickly, my son?"

"The LORD your God gave me success," he replied.

21Then Isaac said to Jacob, "Come near so I can touch you, my son, to know whether you really are my son Esau or not."

22Jacob went close to his father Isaac, who touched him and said, "The voice is the voice of Jacob, but the hands are the hands of Esau." 23He did not recognize him, for his hands were hairy like those of his brother Esau; so he blessed him. 24"Are you really my son Esau?" he asked.

"I am," he replied.

25Then he said, "My son, bring me some of your game to eat, so that I may give you my blessing."

Jacob brought it to him and he ate; and he brought some wine and he drank. 26Then his father Isaac said to him, "Come here, my son, and kiss me."

27So he went to him and kissed him. When Isaac caught the smell of his clothes, he blessed him and said,

---

a 33 *Shibah* can mean *oath* or *seven.* b 33 *Beersheba* can mean *well of the oath* or *well of seven.*

> "Ah, the smell of my son
>   is like the smell of a field
>   that the LORD has blessed.
> 28 May God give you of heaven's dew
>   and of earth's richness—
>   an abundance of grain and new wine.
> 29 May nations serve you
>   and peoples bow down to you.
> Be lord over your brothers,
>   and may the sons of your mother bow down to you.
> May those who curse you be cursed
>   and those who bless you be blessed."

30After Isaac finished blessing him and Jacob had scarcely left his father's presence, his brother Esau came in from hunting. 31He too prepared some tasty food and brought it to his father. Then he said to him, "My father, sit up and eat some of my game, so that you may give me your blessing."

32His father Isaac asked him, "Who are you?"

"I am your son," he answered, "your firstborn, Esau."

33Isaac trembled violently and said, "Who was it, then, that hunted game and brought it to me? I ate it just before you came and I blessed him—and indeed he will be blessed!"

34When Esau heard his father's words, he burst out with a loud and bitter cry and said to his father, "Bless me—me too, my father!"

35But he said, "Your brother came deceitfully and took your blessing."

36Esau said, "Isn't he rightly named Jacob[a]? He has deceived me these two times: He took my birthright, and now he's taken my blessing!" Then he asked, "Haven't you reserved any blessing for me?"

37Isaac answered Esau, "I have made him lord over you and have made all his relatives his servants, and I have sustained him with grain and new wine. So what can I possibly do for you, my son?"

38Esau said to his father, "Do you have only one blessing, my father? Bless me too, my father!" Then Esau wept aloud.

39His father Isaac answered him,

>   "Your dwelling will be
>   away from the earth's richness,
>   away from the dew of heaven above.
> 40 You will live by the sword
>   and you will serve your brother.
> But when you grow restless,
>   you will throw his yoke
>   from off your neck."

JACOB FLEES TO LABAN

41Esau held a grudge against Jacob because of the blessing his father had given him. He said to himself, "The days of mourning for my father are near; then I will kill my brother Jacob."

42When Rebekah was told what her older son Esau had said, she sent for her younger son Jacob and said to him, "Your brother Esau is consoling himself with the thought of killing you. 43Now then, my son, do what I say: Flee at once to my brother Laban in Haran. 44Stay with him for a while until your brother's fury subsides. 45When your brother is no longer angry with you and forgets what you did to him, I'll send word for you to come back from there. Why should I lose both of you in one day?"

46Then Rebekah said to Isaac, "I'm disgusted with living because of these Hittite women. If Jacob takes a wife from among the women of this land, from Hittite women like these, my life will not be worth living."

28 So Isaac called for Jacob and blessed[b] him and commanded him: "Do not marry a Canaanite woman. 2Go at once to Paddan Aram,[c] to the house of your mother's father Bethuel. Take a wife for yourself there, from among the daughters of Laban, your mother's brother.

---

[a] 36 Jacob means he grasps the heel (figuratively, he deceives).   [b] 1 Or greeted   [c] 2 That is, Northwest Mesopotamia; also in verses 5, 6 and 7

[3]May God Almighty[a] bless you and make you fruitful and increase your numbers until you become a community of peoples. [4]May he give you and your descendants the blessing given to Abraham, so that you may take possession of the land where you now live as an alien, the land God gave to Abraham." [5]Then Isaac sent Jacob on his way, and he went to Paddan Aram, to Laban son of Bethuel the Aramean, the brother of Rebekah, who was the mother of Jacob and Esau.

[6]Now Esau learned that Isaac had blessed Jacob and had sent him to Paddan Aram to take a wife from there, and that when he blessed him he commanded him, "Do not marry a Canaanite woman," [7]and that Jacob had obeyed his father and mother and had gone to Paddan Aram. [8]Esau then realized how displeasing the Canaanite women were to his father Isaac; [9]so he went to Ishmael and married Mahalath, the sister of Nebaioth and daughter of Ishmael son of Abraham, in addition to the wives he already had.

JACOB'S DREAM AT BETHEL

[10]Jacob left Beersheba and set out for Haran. [11]When he reached a certain place, he stopped for the night because the sun had set. Taking one of the stones there, he put it under his head and lay down to sleep. [12]He had a dream in which he saw a stairway[b] resting on the earth, with its top reaching to heaven, and the angels of God were ascending and descending on it. [13]There above it[c] stood the LORD, and he said: "I am the LORD, the God of your father Abraham and the God of Isaac. I will give you and your descendants the land on which you are lying. [14]Your descendants will be like the dust of the earth, and you will spread out to the west and to the east, to the north and to the south. All peoples on earth will be blessed through you and your offspring. [15]I am with you and will watch over you wherever you go, and I will bring you back to this land. I will not leave you until I have done what I have promised you."

NOW OR NEVER
GE 28:10–19

You can't rely on someone else's relationship with the Lord—whether it's your parents' or your sibling's or your friend's—to be good enough for you. You've got to establish your own personal relationship with God.

[16]When Jacob awoke from his sleep, he thought, "Surely the LORD is in this place, and I was not aware of it." [17]He was afraid and said, "How awesome is this place! This is none other than the house of God; this is the gate of heaven."

[18]Early the next morning Jacob took the stone he had placed under his head and set it up as a pillar and poured oil on top of it. [19]He called that place Bethel,[d] though the city used to be called Luz. [20]Then Jacob made a vow, saying, "If God will be with me and will watch over me on this journey I am taking and will give me food to eat and clothes to wear [21]so that I return safely to my father's house, then the LORD[e] will be my God [22]and[f] this stone that I have set up as a pillar will be God's house, and of all that you give me I will give you a tenth."

JACOB ARRIVES IN PADDAN ARAM

29

Then Jacob continued on his journey and came to the land of the eastern peoples. [2]There he saw a well in the field, with three flocks of sheep lying near it because the flocks were watered from that well. The stone over the mouth of the well was large. [3]When all the flocks were gathered there, the shepherds would roll the stone away from the well's mouth and water the sheep. Then they would return the stone to its place over the mouth of the well.

[4]Jacob asked the shepherds, "My brothers, where are you from?"

"We're from Haran," they replied.

[5]He said to them, "Do you know Laban, Nahor's grandson?"

"Yes, we know him," they answered.

[6]Then Jacob asked them, "Is he well?"

"Yes, he is," they said, "and here comes his daughter Rachel with the sheep."

---

[a] 3 Hebrew El-Shaddai   [b] 12 Or ladder   [c] 13 Or There beside him   [d] 19 Bethel means house of God.   [e] 20,21 Or Since God . . . father's house, the LORD   [f] 21,22 Or house, and the LORD will be my God, [22]then

⁷"Look," he said, "the sun is still high; it is not time for the flocks to be gathered. Water the sheep and take them back to pasture."

⁸"We can't," they replied, "until all the flocks are gathered and the stone has been rolled away from the mouth of the well. Then we will water the sheep."

⁹While he was still talking with them, Rachel came with her father's sheep, for she was a shepherdess. ¹⁰When Jacob saw Rachel daughter of Laban, his mother's brother, and Laban's sheep, he went over and rolled the stone away from the mouth of the well and watered his uncle's sheep. ¹¹Then Jacob kissed Rachel and began to weep aloud. ¹²He had told Rachel that he was a relative of her father and a son of Rebekah. So she ran and told her father.

¹³As soon as Laban heard the news about Jacob, his sister's son, he hurried to meet him. He embraced him and kissed him and brought him to his home, and there Jacob told him all these things. ¹⁴Then Laban said to him, "You are my own flesh and blood."

JACOB MARRIES LEAH AND RACHEL

After Jacob had stayed with him for a whole month, ¹⁵Laban said to him, "Just because you are a relative of mine, should you work for me for nothing? Tell me what your wages should be."

¹⁶Now Laban had two daughters; the name of the older was Leah, and the name of the younger was Rachel. ¹⁷Leah had weakª eyes, but Rachel was lovely in form, and beautiful. ¹⁸Jacob was in love with Rachel and said, "I'll work for you seven years in return for your younger daughter Rachel."

¹⁹Laban said, "It's better that I give her to you than to some other man. Stay here with me." ²⁰So Jacob served seven years to get Rachel, but they seemed like only a few days to him because of his love for her.

²¹Then Jacob said to Laban, "Give me my wife. My time is completed, and I want to lie with her."

²²So Laban brought together all the people of the place and gave a feast. ²³But when evening came, he took his daughter Leah and gave her to Jacob, and Jacob lay with her. ²⁴And Laban gave his servant girl Zilpah to his daughter as her maidservant.

²⁵When morning came, there was Leah! So Jacob said to Laban, "What is this you have done to me? I served you for Rachel, didn't I? Why have you deceived me?"

²⁶Laban replied, "It is not our custom here to give the younger daughter in marriage before the older one. ²⁷Finish this daughter's bridal week; then we will give you the younger one also, in return for another seven years of work."

²⁸And Jacob did so. He finished the week with Leah, and then Laban gave him his daughter Rachel to be his wife. ²⁹Laban gave his servant girl Bilhah to his daughter Rachel as her maidservant. ³⁰Jacob lay with Rachel also, and he loved Rachel more than Leah. And he worked for Laban another seven years.

JACOB'S CHILDREN

³¹When the LORD saw that Leah was not loved, he opened her womb, but Rachel was barren. ³²Leah became pregnant and gave birth to a son. She named him Reuben,ᵇ for she said, "It is because the LORD has seen my misery. Surely my husband will love me now."

³³She conceived again, and when she gave birth to a son she said, "Because the LORD heard that I am not loved, he gave me this one too." So she named him Simeon.ᶜ

Work Ethic

God doesn't call us to simply sit back and enjoy his blessings; he calls us to a life of active service. Between serving others and maintaining a close relationship with our heavenly Father, we've got a pretty full workload. The good news is that God sees and rewards all service done for him. Those who are faithful to him won't get cheated out of their reward.

»» live the adventure »» Ge 29:20-28

ª 17 Or delicate   ᵇ 32 Reuben sounds like the Hebrew for he has seen my misery; the name means see, a son.   ᶜ 33 Simeon probably means one who hears.

³⁴Again she conceived, and when she gave birth to a son she said, "Now at last my husband will become attached to me, because I have borne him three sons." So he was named Levi.ᵃ

³⁵She conceived again, and when she gave birth to a son she said, "This time I will praise the LORD." So she named him Judah.ᵇ Then she stopped having children.

30 When Rachel saw that she was not bearing Jacob any children, she became jealous of her sister. So she said to Jacob, "Give me children, or I'll die!"

²Jacob became angry with her and said, "Am I in the place of God, who has kept you from having children?"

³Then she said, "Here is Bilhah, my maidservant. Sleep with her so that she can bear children for me and that through her I too can build a family."

⁴So she gave him her servant Bilhah as a wife. Jacob slept with her, ⁵and she became pregnant and bore him a son. ⁶Then Rachel said, "God has vindicated me; he has listened to my plea and given me a son." Because of this she named him Dan.ᶜ

⁷Rachel's servant Bilhah conceived again and bore Jacob a second son. ⁸Then Rachel said, "I have had a great struggle with my sister, and I have won." So she named him Naphtali.ᵈ

⁹When Leah saw that she had stopped having children, she took her maidservant Zilpah and gave her to Jacob as a wife. ¹⁰Leah's servant Zilpah bore Jacob a son. ¹¹Then Leah said, "What good fortune!"ᵉ So she named him Gad.ᶠ

¹²Leah's servant Zilpah bore Jacob a second son. ¹³Then Leah said, "How happy I am! The women will call me happy." So she named him Asher.ᵍ

¹⁴During wheat harvest, Reuben went out into the fields and found some mandrake plants, which he brought to his mother Leah. Rachel said to Leah, "Please give me some of your son's mandrakes."

¹⁵But she said to her, "Wasn't it enough that you took away my husband? Will you take my son's mandrakes too?"

"Very well," Rachel said, "he can sleep with you tonight in return for your son's mandrakes."

¹⁶So when Jacob came in from the fields that evening, Leah went out to meet him. "You must sleep with me," she said. "I have hired you with my son's mandrakes." So he slept with her that night.

¹⁷God listened to Leah, and she became pregnant and bore Jacob a fifth son. ¹⁸Then Leah said, "God has rewarded me for giving my maidservant to my husband." So she named him Issachar.ʰ

¹⁹Leah conceived again and bore Jacob a sixth son. ²⁰Then Leah said, "God has presented me with a precious gift. This time my husband will treat me with honor, because I have borne him six sons." So she named him Zebulun.ⁱ

²¹Some time later she gave birth to a daughter and named her Dinah.

²²Then God remembered Rachel; he listened to her and opened her womb. ²³She became pregnant and gave birth to a son and said, "God has taken away my disgrace." ²⁴She named him Joseph,ʲ and said, "May the LORD add to me another son."

JACOB'S FLOCKS INCREASE

²⁵After Rachel gave birth to Joseph, Jacob said to Laban, "Send me on my way so I can go back to my own homeland. ²⁶Give me my wives and children, for whom I have served you, and I will be on my way. You know how much work I've done for you."

²⁷But Laban said to him, "If I have found favor in your eyes, please stay. I have learned by divination thatᵏ the LORD has blessed me because of you." ²⁸He added, "Name your wages, and I will pay them."

²⁹Jacob said to him, "You know how I have worked for you and how your livestock has fared under my care. ³⁰The little you had before I came has increased greatly, and the LORD has blessed you wherever I have been. But now, when may I do something for my own household?"

³¹"What shall I give you?" he asked.

"Don't give me anything," Jacob replied. "But if you will do this one thing for me, I will go on tending your flocks and watching over them: ³²Let me go through all your flocks today and remove from them every speckled or spotted sheep, every dark-colored lamb and every spotted or speckled goat.

ᵃ *34 Levi* sounds like and may be derived from the Hebrew for *attached.*   ᵇ *35 Judah* sounds like and may be derived from the Hebrew for *praise.*   ᶜ *6 Dan* here means *he has vindicated.*   ᵈ *8 Naphtali* means *my struggle.*   ᵉ *11* Or *"A troop is coming!"*   ᶠ *11 Gad* can mean *good fortune* or *a troop.*   ᵍ *13 Asher* means *happy.*   ʰ *18 Issachar* sounds like the Hebrew for *reward.*   ⁱ *20 Zebulun* probably means *honor.*   ʲ *24 Joseph* means *may he add.*   ᵏ *27* Or possibly *have become rich and*

They will be my wages. 33And my honesty will testify for me in the future, whenever you check on the wages you have paid me. Any goat in my possession that is not speckled or spotted, or any lamb that is not dark-colored, will be considered stolen."

34"Agreed," said Laban. "Let it be as you have said." 35That same day he removed all the male goats that were streaked or spotted, and all the speckled or spotted female goats (all that had white on them) and all the dark-colored lambs, and he placed them in the care of his sons. 36Then he put a three-day journey between himself and Jacob, while Jacob continued to tend the rest of Laban's flocks.

37Jacob, however, took fresh-cut branches from poplar, almond and plane trees and made white stripes on them by peeling the bark and exposing the white inner wood of the branches. 38Then he placed the peeled branches in all the watering troughs, so that they would be directly in front of the flocks when they came to drink. When the flocks were in heat and came to drink, 39they mated in front of the branches. And they bore young that were streaked or speckled or spotted. 40Jacob set apart the young of the flock by themselves, but made the rest face the streaked and dark-colored animals that belonged to Laban. Thus he made separate flocks for himself and did not put them with Laban's animals. 41Whenever the stronger females were in heat, Jacob would place the branches in the troughs in front of the animals so they would mate near the branches, 42but if the animals were weak, he would not place them there. So the weak animals went to Laban and the strong ones to Jacob. 43In this way the man grew exceedingly prosperous and came to own large flocks, and maidservants and menservants, and camels and donkeys.

JACOB FLEES FROM LABAN

31 Jacob heard that Laban's sons were saying, "Jacob has taken everything our father owned and has gained all this wealth from what belonged to our father." 2And Jacob noticed that Laban's attitude toward him was not what it had been.

3Then the LORD said to Jacob, "Go back to the land of your fathers and to your relatives, and I will be with you."

4So Jacob sent word to Rachel and Leah to come out to the fields where his flocks were. 5He said to them, "I see that your father's attitude toward me is not what it was before, but the God of my father has been with me. 6You know that I've worked for your father with all my strength, 7yet your father has cheated me by changing my wages ten times. However, God has not allowed him to harm me. 8If he said, 'The speckled ones will be your wages,' then all the flocks gave birth to speckled young; and if he said, 'The streaked ones will be your wages,' then all the flocks bore streaked young. 9So God has taken away your father's livestock and has given them to me.

10"In breeding season I once had a dream in which I looked up and saw that the male goats mating with the flock were streaked, speckled or spotted. 11The angel of God said to me in the dream, 'Jacob.' I answered, 'Here I am.' 12And he said, 'Look up and see that all the male goats mating with the flock are streaked, speckled or spotted, for I have seen all that Laban has been doing to you. 13I am the God of Bethel, where you anointed a pillar and where you made a vow to me. Now leave this land at once and go back to your native land.' "

14Then Rachel and Leah replied, "Do we still have any share in the inheritance of our father's estate? 15Does he not regard us as foreigners? Not only has he sold us, but he has used up what was paid for us. 16Surely all the wealth that God took away from our father belongs to us and our children. So do whatever God has told you."

17Then Jacob put his children and his wives on camels, 18and he drove all his livestock ahead of him, along with all the goods he had accumulated in Paddan Aram,a to go to his father Isaac in the land of Canaan.

19When Laban had gone to shear his sheep, Rachel stole her father's household gods. 20Moreover, Jacob deceived Laban the Aramean by not telling him he was running away. 21So he fled with all he had, and crossing the River,b he headed for the hill country of Gilead.

LABAN PURSUES JACOB

22On the third day Laban was told that Jacob had fled. 23Taking his relatives with him, he pursued Jacob for seven days and caught up with him in the hill country of Gilead. 24Then God came to Laban the Aramean in a dream at night and said to him, "Be careful not to say anything to Jacob, either good or bad."

---

a 18 That is, Northwest Mesopotamia   b 21 That is, the Euphrates

25Jacob had pitched his tent in the hill country of Gilead when Laban overtook him, and Laban and his relatives camped there too. 26Then Laban said to Jacob, "What have you done? You've deceived me, and you've carried off my daughters like captives in war. 27Why did you run off secretly and deceive me? Why didn't you tell me, so I could send you away with joy and singing to the music of tambourines and harps? 28You didn't even let me kiss my grandchildren and my daughters good-by. You have done a foolish thing. 29I have the power to harm you; but last night the God of your father said to me, 'Be careful not to say anything to Jacob, either good or bad.' 30Now you have gone off because you longed to return to your father's house. But why did you steal my gods?"

31Jacob answered Laban, "I was afraid, because I thought you would take your daughters away from me by force. 32But if you find anyone who has your gods, he shall not live. In the presence of our relatives, see for yourself whether there is anything of yours here with me; and if so, take it." Now Jacob did not know that Rachel had stolen the gods.

33So Laban went into Jacob's tent and into Leah's tent and into the tent of the two maidservants, but he found nothing. After he came out of Leah's tent, he entered Rachel's tent. 34Now Rachel had taken the household gods and put them inside her camel's saddle and was sitting on them. Laban searched through everything in the tent but found nothing.

35Rachel said to her father, "Don't be angry, my lord, that I cannot stand up in your presence; I'm having my period." So he searched but could not find the household gods.

36Jacob was angry and took Laban to task. "What is my crime?" he asked Laban. "What sin have I committed that you hunt me down? 37Now that you have searched through all my goods, what have you found that belongs to your household? Put it here in front of your relatives and mine, and let them judge between the two of us.

38"I have been with you for twenty years now. Your sheep and goats have not miscarried, nor have I eaten rams from your flocks. 39I did not bring you animals torn by wild beasts; I bore the loss myself. And you demanded payment from me for whatever was stolen by day or night. 40This was my situation: The heat consumed me in the daytime and the cold at night, and sleep fled from my eyes. 41It was like this for the twenty years I was in your household. I worked for you fourteen years for your two daughters and six years for your flocks, and you changed my wages ten times. 42If the God of my father, the God of Abraham and the Fear of Isaac, had not been with me, you would surely have sent me away empty-handed. But God has seen my hardship and the toil of my hands, and last night he rebuked you."

43Laban answered Jacob, "The women are my daughters, the children are my children, and the flocks are my flocks. All you see is mine. Yet what can I do today about these daughters of mine, or about the children they have borne? 44Come now, let's make a covenant, you and I, and let it serve as a witness between us."

45So Jacob took a stone and set it up as a pillar. 46He said to his relatives, "Gather some stones." So they took stones and piled them in a heap, and they ate there by the heap. 47Laban called it Jegar Sahadutha,ᵃ and Jacob called it Galeed.ᵇ

48Laban said, "This heap is a witness between you and me today." That is why it was called Galeed. 49It was also called Mizpah,ᶜ because he said, "May the LORD keep watch between you and me when we are away from each other. 50If you mistreat my daughters or if you take any wives besides my daughters, even though no one is with us, remember that God is a witness between you and me."

Surpassing Expectations

»» live the adventure »» Ge 31:38–42

It's one thing to *meet* people's expectations—to do only what's required of you. It's another thing completely to *surpass* people's expectations—to go above and beyond the call of duty in everything you do. When you go the extra mile for people, you not only earn their respect, but you also earn the right to be heard. Remember, people look at what you do before they listen to what you say.

ᵃ 47 The Aramaic *Jegar Sahadutha* means *witness heap*.   ᵇ 47 The Hebrew *Galeed* means *witness heap*.   ᶜ 49 *Mizpah* means *watchtower*.

⁵¹Laban also said to Jacob, "Here is this heap, and here is this pillar I have set up between you and me. ⁵²This heap is a witness, and this pillar is a witness, that I will not go past this heap to your side to harm you and that you will not go past this heap and pillar to my side to harm me. ⁵³May the God of Abraham and the God of Nahor, the God of their father, judge between us."

So Jacob took an oath in the name of the Fear of his father Isaac. ⁵⁴He offered a sacrifice there in the hill country and invited his relatives to a meal. After they had eaten, they spent the night there.

⁵⁵Early the next morning Laban kissed his grandchildren and his daughters and blessed them. Then he left and returned home.

JACOB PREPARES TO MEET ESAU

32 Jacob also went on his way, and the angels of God met him. ²When Jacob saw them, he said, "This is the camp of God!" So he named that place Mahanaim.ᵃ

³Jacob sent messengers ahead of him to his brother Esau in the land of Seir, the country of Edom. ⁴He instructed them: "This is what you are to say to my master Esau: 'Your servant Jacob says, I have been staying with Laban and have remained there till now. ⁵I have cattle and donkeys, sheep and goats, menservants and maidservants. Now I am sending this message to my lord, that I may find favor in your eyes.' "

⁶When the messengers returned to Jacob, they said, "We went to your brother Esau, and now he is coming to meet you, and four hundred men are with him."

⁷In great fear and distress Jacob divided the people who were with him into two groups,ᵇ and the flocks and herds and camels as well. ⁸He thought, "If Esau comes and attacks one group,ᶜ the groupᶜ that is left may escape."

⁹Then Jacob prayed, "O God of my father Abraham, God of my father Isaac, O LORD, who said to me, 'Go back to your country and your relatives, and I will make you prosper,' ¹⁰I am unworthy of all the kindness and faithfulness you have shown your servant. I had only my staff when I crossed this Jordan, but now I have become two groups. ¹¹Save me, I pray, from the hand of my brother Esau, for I am afraid he will come and attack me, and also the mothers with their children. ¹²But you have said, 'I will surely make you prosper and will make your descendants like the sand of the sea, which cannot be counted.' "

¹³He spent the night there, and from what he had with him he selected a gift for his brother Esau: ¹⁴two hundred female goats and twenty male goats, two hundred ewes and twenty rams, ¹⁵thirty female camels with their young, forty cows and ten bulls, and twenty female donkeys and ten male donkeys. ¹⁶He put them in the care of his servants, each herd by itself, and said to his servants, "Go ahead of me, and keep some space between the herds."

¹⁷He instructed the one in the lead: "When my brother Esau meets you and asks, 'To whom do you belong, and where are you going, and who owns all these animals in front of you?' ¹⁸then you are to say, 'They belong to your servant Jacob. They are a gift sent to my lord Esau, and he is coming behind us.' "

¹⁹He also instructed the second, the third and all the others who followed the herds: "You are to say the same thing to Esau when you meet him. ²⁰And be sure to say, 'Your servant Jacob is coming behind us.' " For he thought, "I will pacify him with these gifts I am sending on ahead; later, when I see him, perhaps he will receive me." ²¹So Jacob's gifts went on ahead of him, but he himself spent the night in the camp.

JACOB WRESTLES WITH GOD

²²That night Jacob got up and took his two wives, his two maidservants and his eleven sons and crossed the ford of the Jabbok. ²³After he had sent them across the stream, he sent over all his possessions. ²⁴So Jacob was left alone, and a man wrestled with him till daybreak. ²⁵When the man saw that he could not overpower him, he touched the socket of Jacob's hip so that his hip was wrenched as he wrestled with the man. ²⁶Then the man said, "Let me go, for it is daybreak."

But Jacob replied, "I will not let you go unless you bless me."

²⁷The man asked him, "What is your name?"

"Jacob," he answered.

ᵃ *2 Mahanaim* means *two camps.*   ᵇ *7* Or *camps*; also in verse 10   ᶜ *8* Or *camp*

[28]Then the man said, "Your name will no longer be Jacob, but Israel,[a] because you have struggled with God and with men and have overcome."

[29]Jacob said, "Please tell me your name."

But he replied, "Why do you ask my name?" Then he blessed him there.

[30]So Jacob called the place Peniel,[b] saying, "It is because I saw God face to face, and yet my life was spared."

[31]The sun rose above him as he passed Peniel,[c] and he was limping because of his hip. [32]Therefore to this day the Israelites do not eat the tendon attached to the socket of the hip, because the socket of Jacob's hip was touched near the tendon.

JACOB MEETS ESAU

33 Jacob looked up and there was Esau, coming with his four hundred men; so he divided the children among Leah, Rachel and the two maidservants. [2]He put the maidservants and their children in front, Leah and her children next, and Rachel and Joseph in the rear. [3]He himself went on ahead and bowed down to the ground seven times as he approached his brother.

[4]But Esau ran to meet Jacob and embraced him; he threw his arms around his neck and kissed him. And they wept. [5]Then Esau looked up and saw the women and children. "Who are these with you?" he asked.

Jacob answered, "They are the children God has graciously given your servant."

[6]Then the maidservants and their children approached and bowed down. [7]Next, Leah and her children came and bowed down. Last of all came Joseph and Rachel, and they too bowed down.

[8]Esau asked, "What do you mean by all these droves I met?"

"To find favor in your eyes, my lord," he said.

[9]But Esau said, "I already have plenty, my brother. Keep what you have for yourself."

[10]"No, please!" said Jacob. "If I have found favor in your eyes, accept this gift from me. For to see your face is like seeing the face of God, now that you have received me favorably. [11]Please accept the present that was brought to you, for God has been gracious to me and I have all I need." And because Jacob insisted, Esau accepted it.

[12]Then Esau said, "Let us be on our way; I'll accompany you."

[13]But Jacob said to him, "My lord knows that the children are tender and that I must care for the ewes and cows that are nursing their young. If they are driven hard just one day, all the animals will die. [14]So let my lord go on ahead of his servant, while I move along slowly at the pace of the droves before me and that of the children, until I come to my lord in Seir."

[15]Esau said, "Then let me leave some of my men with you."

"But why do that?" Jacob asked. "Just let me find favor in the eyes of my lord."

[16]So that day Esau started on his way back to Seir. [17]Jacob, however, went to Succoth, where he built a place for himself and made shelters for his livestock. That is why the place is called Succoth.[d]

[18]After Jacob came from Paddan Aram,[e] he arrived safely at the[f] city of Shechem in Canaan and camped within sight of the city. [19]For a hundred pieces of silver,[g] he bought from the sons of Hamor, the father of Shechem, the plot of ground where he pitched his tent. [20]There he set up an altar and called it El Elohe Israel.[h]

Persistence

News flash: God *wants* you to bug him. If you have a request that you believe is in line with God's will, take it to him. If you don't get a response, take it to him again—and again and again. Remind him of the promises in his Word. Ask him for his blessings, and continue to ask until you receive them. As Jacob discovered, the more you wrestle with God, the stronger your faith muscles become.

---

[a] 28 Israel means he struggles with God.   [b] 30 Peniel means face of God.   [c] 31 Hebrew Penuel, a variant of Peniel   [d] 17 Succoth means shelters.   [e] 18 That is, Northwest Mesopotamia   [f] 18 Or arrived at Shalem, a   [g] 19 Hebrew hundred kesitahs; a kesitah was a unit of money of unknown weight and value.   [h] 20 El Elohe Israel can mean God, the God of Israel or mighty is the God of Israel.

DINAH AND THE SHECHEMITES

34

Now Dinah, the daughter Leah had borne to Jacob, went out to visit the women of the land. ²When Shechem son of Hamor the Hivite, the ruler of that area, saw her, he took her and violated her. ³His heart was drawn to Dinah daughter of Jacob, and he loved the girl and spoke tenderly to her. ⁴And Shechem said to his father Hamor, "Get me this girl as my wife."

⁵When Jacob heard that his daughter Dinah had been defiled, his sons were in the fields with his livestock; so he kept quiet about it until they came home.

⁶Then Shechem's father Hamor went out to talk with Jacob. ⁷Now Jacob's sons had come in from the fields as soon as they heard what had happened. They were filled with grief and fury, because Shechem had done a disgraceful thing in ᵃ Israel by lying with Jacob's daughter—a thing that should not be done.

NOW OR NEVER

GE 34:1–4

The best way to avoid trouble is to avoid the people, places and situations you already know could cause problems for you. Why set yourself up to fail?

⁸But Hamor said to them, "My son Shechem has his heart set on your daughter. Please give her to him as his wife. ⁹Intermarry with us; give us your daughters and take our daughters for yourselves. ¹⁰You can settle among us; the land is open to you. Live in it, trade ᵇ in it, and acquire property in it."

¹¹Then Shechem said to Dinah's father and brothers, "Let me find favor in your eyes, and I will give you whatever you ask. ¹²Make the price for the bride and the gift I am to bring as great as you like, and I'll pay whatever you ask me. Only give me the girl as my wife."

¹³Because their sister Dinah had been defiled, Jacob's sons replied deceitfully as they spoke to Shechem and his father Hamor. ¹⁴They said to them, "We can't do such a thing; we can't give our sister to a man who is not circumcised. That would be a disgrace to us. ¹⁵We will give our consent to you on one condition only: that you become like us by circumcising all your males. ¹⁶Then we will give you our daughters and take your daughters for ourselves. We'll settle among you and become one people with you. ¹⁷But if you will not agree to be circumcised, we'll take our sister ᶜ and go."

¹⁸Their proposal seemed good to Hamor and his son Shechem. ¹⁹The young man, who was the most honored of all his father's household, lost no time in doing what they said, because he was delighted with Jacob's daughter. ²⁰So Hamor and his son Shechem went to the gate of their city to speak to their fellow townsmen. ²¹"These men are friendly toward us," they said. "Let them live in our land and trade in it; the land has plenty of room for them. We can marry their daughters and they can marry ours. ²²But the men will consent to live with us as one people only on the condition that our males be circumcised, as they themselves are. ²³Won't their livestock, their property and all their other animals become ours? So let us give our consent to them, and they will settle among us."

²⁴All the men who went out of the city gate agreed with Hamor and his son Shechem, and every male in the city was circumcised.

²⁵Three days later, while all of them were still in pain, two of Jacob's sons, Simeon and Levi, Dinah's brothers, took their swords and attacked the unsuspecting city, killing every male. ²⁶They put Hamor and his son Shechem to the sword and took Dinah from Shechem's house and left. ²⁷The sons of Jacob came upon the dead bodies and looted the city where ᵈ their sister had been defiled. ²⁸They seized their flocks and herds and donkeys and everything else of theirs in the city and out in the fields. ²⁹They carried off all their wealth and all their women and children, taking as plunder everything in the houses.

³⁰Then Jacob said to Simeon and Levi, "You have brought trouble on me by making me a stench to the Canaanites and Perizzites, the people living in this land. We are few in number, and if they join forces against me and attack me, I and my household will be destroyed."

³¹But they replied, "Should he have treated our sister like a prostitute?"

JACOB RETURNS TO BETHEL

35

Then God said to Jacob, "Go up to Bethel and settle there, and build an altar there to God, who appeared to you when you were fleeing from your brother Esau."

ᵃ 7 Or against   ᵇ 10 Or move about freely; also in verse 21   ᶜ 17 Hebrew daughter   ᵈ 27 Or because

[2]So Jacob said to his household and to all who were with him, "Get rid of the foreign gods you have with you, and purify yourselves and change your clothes. [3]Then come, let us go up to Bethel, where I will build an altar to God, who answered me in the day of my distress and who has been with me wherever I have gone." [4]So they gave Jacob all the foreign gods they had and the rings in their ears, and Jacob buried them under the oak at Shechem. [5]Then they set out, and the terror of God fell upon the towns all around them so that no one pursued them.

[6]Jacob and all the people with him came to Luz (that is, Bethel) in the land of Canaan. [7]There he built an altar, and he called the place El Bethel,[a] because it was there that God revealed himself to him when he was fleeing from his brother.

[8]Now Deborah, Rebekah's nurse, died and was buried under the oak below Bethel. So it was named Allon Bacuth.[b]

[9]After Jacob returned from Paddan Aram,[c] God appeared to him again and blessed him. [10]God said to him, "Your name is Jacob,[d] but you will no longer be called Jacob; your name will be Israel.[e]" So he named him Israel.

[11]And God said to him, "I am God Almighty[f]; be fruitful and increase in number. A nation and a community of nations will come from you, and kings will come from your body. [12]The land I gave to Abraham and Isaac I also give to you, and I will give this land to your descendants after you." [13]Then God went up from him at the place where he had talked with him.

[14]Jacob set up a stone pillar at the place where God had talked with him, and he poured out a drink offering on it; he also poured oil on it. [15]Jacob called the place where God had talked with him Bethel.[g]

Genuine Justice

Every human has some sense of justice—even the worst of us. That's not a coincidence. Being created in his image, each of us has a God-given sense of justice. So it's natural to experience feelings of hurt or even anger when you or someone you care about is falsely accused, mistreated or unfairly excluded. But what do you do to make things right? Do you take justice into your own hands? Or do you lay it down before God and ask him for the wisdom, strength and humility to do his will?

THE DEATHS OF RACHEL AND ISAAC

[16]Then they moved on from Bethel. While they were still some distance from Ephrath, Rachel began to give birth and had great difficulty. [17]And as she was having great difficulty in childbirth, the midwife said to her, "Don't be afraid, for you have another son." [18]As she breathed her last—for she was dying—she named her son Ben-Oni.[h] But his father named him Benjamin.[i]

[19]So Rachel died and was buried on the way to Ephrath (that is, Bethlehem). [20]Over her tomb Jacob set up a pillar, and to this day that pillar marks Rachel's tomb.

[21]Israel moved on again and pitched his tent beyond Migdal Eder. [22]While Israel was living in that region, Reuben went in and slept with his father's concubine Bilhah, and Israel heard of it.

Jacob had twelve sons:

[23]The sons of Leah:
Reuben the firstborn of Jacob,
Simeon, Levi, Judah, Issachar and Zebulun.
[24]The sons of Rachel:
Joseph and Benjamin.
[25]The sons of Rachel's maidservant Bilhah:
Dan and Naphtali.
[26]The sons of Leah's maidservant Zilpah:
Gad and Asher.
These were the sons of Jacob, who were born to him in Paddan Aram.

---

[a] 7 El Bethel means God of Bethel.   [b] 8 Allon Bacuth means oak of weeping.   [c] 9 That is, Northwest Mesopotamia; also in verse 26
[d] 10 Jacob means he grasps the heel (figuratively, he deceives).   [e] 10 Israel means he struggles with God.   [f] 11 Hebrew El-Shaddai
[g] 15 Bethel means house of God.   [h] 18 Ben-Oni means son of my trouble.   [i] 18 Benjamin means son of my right hand.

isaac

VERSUS

ishmael

» Son of Abraham and Sarah; his name means "laughter"
» A wealthy owner of sheep and cattle, he was a quiet, reflective man
» Patriarch of the Jewish nation

» Son of Abraham and Hagar; his name means "God hears"
» An expert archer and hunter, he was a "wild donkey of a man"
» Ancestor of the Arab peoples

The Main Event

Unless you're an only child, you know all about sibling rivalry. Being compared to your genius big sister. Feeling as though your parents like your little brother more than they like you. Throw a couple of stepbrothers or half sisters into the mix, and things on the home front can get *really* interesting. For exhibit A, we give you Ishmael and Isaac.

Here's their story in a nutshell: When it seemed as though God wasn't going to come through on his promise of children, Sarah, who was 75 at the time, decided to give him a little "help." She encouraged her husband, Abraham, (who was 85) to sleep with her maid Hagar. As a result of Sarah's plan, Hagar became pregnant and gave birth to Ishmael.

Throughout his entire childhood, Ishmael had his old, doting parents wrapped around his finger. About the time he hit his teenage years, though, God performed a miracle in Abraham and Sarah's lives. At the whopping age of 90, Sarah became pregnant and gave birth to Ishmael's half brother Isaac.

As you can probably guess, the friction level in the family skyrocketed as the boys grew. On the one side, there was Sarah and her precious son Isaac. On the other side, there was Hagar and her strapping teenager Ishmael. And caught right in the middle of all of them was Abraham. Because of the age difference between the boys, it's doubtful they ever fought physically, but that didn't stop Sarah from regarding Ishmael as a threat to Isaac (see Genesis 21:9). So Sarah demanded that Abraham banish Hagar and Ishma-el from their home once and for all. With great sorrow, Abraham did as Sarah asked.

To make a long story short, Ishmael left home and became the father of a nomadic tribe of people. He also became an expert archer and hunter. Isaac, on the other hand, grew up to be a quiet, patient and thoughtful man who made a fortune in the livestock business.

The Outcome

This isn't necessarily a "good guy versus bad guy" story; it's much bigger than that. This is a story about how a little seed of sibling rivalry can sprout into a harvest of animosity.

The suicide bombings you see on the news and the ongoing tension between the Arabs and Jews—according to tradition, they can all be traced back to *this* family squabble, to *this* sibling rivalry. Isaac's descendants are the Jewish people. Ishmael is believed to be the ancestor of the Arab people. Just think about the legacy those two half brothers left.

Ask God to search your heart. What bitter or envious feelings do you have toward a brother or sister, half brother or half sister, stepbrother or stepsister? Favoritism on the part of parents isn't right, but, hey, neither is the jealousy that's stirring in your heart.

Read more about Isaac and Ishmael in Genesis 16–25 (pages 17–31).

27Jacob came home to his father Isaac in Mamre, near Kiriath Arba (that is, Hebron), where Abraham and Isaac had stayed. 28Isaac lived a hundred and eighty years. 29Then he breathed his last and died and was gathered to his people, old and full of years. And his sons Esau and Jacob buried him.

ESAU'S DESCENDANTS

36

This is the account of Esau (that is, Edom).

2Esau took his wives from the women of Canaan: Adah daughter of Elon the Hittite, and Oholibamah daughter of Anah and granddaughter of Zibeon the Hivite— 3also Basemath daughter of Ishmael and sister of Nebaioth.

4Adah bore Eliphaz to Esau, Basemath bore Reuel, 5and Oholibamah bore Jeush, Jalam and Korah. These were the sons of Esau, who were born to him in Canaan.

6Esau took his wives and sons and daughters and all the members of his household, as well as his livestock and all his other animals and all the goods he had acquired in Canaan, and moved to a land some distance from his brother Jacob. 7Their possessions were too great for them to remain together; the land where they were staying could not support them both because of their livestock. 8So Esau (that is, Edom) settled in the hill country of Seir.

9This is the account of Esau the father of the Edomites in the hill country of Seir.

10These are the names of Esau's sons:
Eliphaz, the son of Esau's wife Adah, and Reuel, the son of Esau's wife Basemath.
11The sons of Eliphaz:
Teman, Omar, Zepho, Gatam and Kenaz.
12Esau's son Eliphaz also had a concubine named Timna, who bore him Amalek. These were grandsons of Esau's wife Adah.
13The sons of Reuel:
Nahath, Zerah, Shammah and Mizzah. These were grandsons of Esau's wife Basemath.
14The sons of Esau's wife Oholibamah daughter of Anah and granddaughter of Zibeon, whom she bore to Esau:
Jeush, Jalam and Korah.

15These were the chiefs among Esau's descendants:
The sons of Eliphaz the firstborn of Esau:
Chiefs Teman, Omar, Zepho, Kenaz, 16Korah,ª Gatam and Amalek. These were the chiefs descended from Eliphaz in Edom; they were grandsons of Adah.
17The sons of Esau's son Reuel:
Chiefs Nahath, Zerah, Shammah and Mizzah. These were the chiefs descended from Reuel in Edom; they were grandsons of Esau's wife Basemath.
18The sons of Esau's wife Oholibamah:
Chiefs Jeush, Jalam and Korah. These were the chiefs descended from Esau's wife Oholibamah daughter of Anah.
19These were the sons of Esau (that is, Edom), and these were their chiefs.

20These were the sons of Seir the Horite, who were living in the region:
Lotan, Shobal, Zibeon, Anah, 21Dishon, Ezer and Dishan. These sons of Seir in Edom were Horite chiefs.
22The sons of Lotan:
Hori and Homam.ᵇ Timna was Lotan's sister.
23The sons of Shobal:
Alvan, Manahath, Ebal, Shepho and Onam.
24The sons of Zibeon:
Aiah and Anah. This is the Anah who discovered the hot springsᶜ in the desert while he was grazing the donkeys of his father Zibeon.
25The children of Anah:

ª 16 Masoretic Text; Samaritan Pentateuch (see also Gen. 36:11 and 1 Chron. 1:36) does not have *Korah*.   ᵇ 22 Hebrew *Hemam*, a variant of *Homam* (see 1 Chron. 1:39)   ᶜ 24 Vulgate; Syriac *discovered water*; the meaning of the Hebrew for this word is uncertain.

Dishon and Oholibamah daughter of Anah.

26 The sons of Dishon[a]:
Hemdan, Eshban, Ithran and Keran.

27 The sons of Ezer:
Bilhan, Zaavan and Akan.

28 The sons of Dishan:
Uz and Aran.

29 These were the Horite chiefs:
Lotan, Shobal, Zibeon, Anah, 30Dishon, Ezer and Dishan. These were the Horite chiefs, according to their divisions, in the land of Seir.

THE RULERS OF EDOM

31 These were the kings who reigned in Edom before any Israelite king reigned[b]:
32 Bela son of Beor became king of Edom. His city was named Dinhabah.
33 When Bela died, Jobab son of Zerah from Bozrah succeeded him as king.
34 When Jobab died, Husham from the land of the Temanites succeeded him as king.
35 When Husham died, Hadad son of Bedad, who defeated Midian in the country of Moab, succeeded him as king. His city was named Avith.
36 When Hadad died, Samlah from Masrekah succeeded him as king.
37 When Samlah died, Shaul from Rehoboth on the river[c] succeeded him as king.
38 When Shaul died, Baal-Hanan son of Acbor succeeded him as king.
39 When Baal-Hanan son of Acbor died, Hadad[d] succeeded him as king. His city was named Pau, and his wife's name was Mehetabel daughter of Matred, the daughter of Me-Zahab.

40 These were the chiefs descended from Esau, by name, according to their clans and regions:
Timna, Alvah, Jetheth, 41Oholibamah, Elah, Pinon, 42Kenaz, Teman, Mibzar, 43Magdiel and Iram. These were the chiefs of Edom, according to their settlements in the land they occupied.

This was Esau the father of the Edomites.

JOSEPH'S DREAMS

37

Jacob lived in the land where his father had stayed, the land of Canaan.

2 This is the account of Jacob.

Joseph, a young man of seventeen, was tending the flocks with his brothers, the sons of Bilhah and the sons of Zilpah, his father's wives, and he brought their father a bad report about them.

3 Now Israel loved Joseph more than any of his other sons, because he had been born to him in his old age; and he made a richly ornamented[e] robe for him. 4When his brothers saw that their father loved him more than any of them, they hated him and could not speak a kind word to him.

5 Joseph had a dream, and when he told it to his brothers, they hated him all the more. 6He said to them, "Listen to this dream I had: 7We were binding sheaves of grain out in the field when suddenly my sheaf rose and stood upright, while your sheaves gathered around mine and bowed down to it."

8 His brothers said to him, "Do you intend to reign over us? Will you actually rule us?" And they hated him all the more because of his dream and what he had said.

9 Then he had another dream, and he told it to his brothers. "Listen," he said, "I had another dream, and this time the sun and moon and eleven stars were bowing down to me."

10 When he told his father as well as his brothers, his father rebuked him and said, "What is this dream you had? Will your mother and I and your brothers actually come and bow down to the ground before you?" 11His brothers were jealous of him, but his father kept the matter in mind.

JOSEPH SOLD BY HIS BROTHERS

12 Now his brothers had gone to graze their father's flocks near Shechem, 13and Israel said to Joseph,

45

---

a 26 Hebrew Dishan, a variant of Dishon   b 31 Or before an Israelite king reigned over them   c 37 Possibly the Euphrates
d 39 Many manuscripts of the Masoretic Text, Samaritan Pentateuch and Syriac (see also 1 Chron. 1:50); most manuscripts of the Masoretic Text Hadar   e 3 The meaning of the Hebrew for richly ornamented is uncertain; also in verses 23 and 32.

"As you know, your brothers are grazing the flocks near Shechem. Come, I am going to send you to them."

"Very well," he replied.

¹⁴So he said to him, "Go and see if all is well with your brothers and with the flocks, and bring word back to me." Then he sent him off from the Valley of Hebron.

When Joseph arrived at Shechem, ¹⁵a man found him wandering around in the fields and asked him, "What are you looking for?"

¹⁶He replied, "I'm looking for my brothers. Can you tell me where they are grazing their flocks?"

¹⁷"They have moved on from here," the man answered. "I heard them say, 'Let's go to Dothan.'"

So Joseph went after his brothers and found them near Dothan. ¹⁸But they saw him in the distance, and before he reached them, they plotted to kill him.

¹⁹"Here comes that dreamer!" they said to each other. ²⁰"Come now, let's kill him and throw him into one of these cisterns and say that a ferocious animal devoured him. Then we'll see what comes of his dreams."

²¹When Reuben heard this, he tried to rescue him from their hands. "Let's not take his life," he said. ²²"Don't shed any blood. Throw him into this cistern here in the desert, but don't lay a hand on him." Reuben said this to rescue him from them and take him back to his father.

²³So when Joseph came to his brothers, they stripped him of his robe—the richly ornamented robe he was wearing— ²⁴and they took him and threw him into the cistern. Now the cistern was empty; there was no water in it.

²⁵As they sat down to eat their meal, they looked up and saw a caravan of Ishmaelites coming from Gilead. Their camels were loaded with spices, balm and myrrh, and they were on their way to take them down to Egypt.

²⁶Judah said to his brothers, "What will we gain if we kill our brother and cover up his blood? ²⁷Come, let's sell him to the Ishmaelites and not lay our hands on him; after all, he is our brother, our own flesh and blood." His brothers agreed.

²⁸So when the Midianite merchants came by, his brothers pulled Joseph up out of the cistern and sold him for twenty shekels[a] of silver to the Ishmaelites, who took him to Egypt.

²⁹When Reuben returned to the cistern and saw that Joseph was not there, he tore his clothes. ³⁰He went back to his brothers and said, "The boy isn't there! Where can I turn now?"

³¹Then they got Joseph's robe, slaughtered a goat and dipped the robe in the blood. ³²They took the ornamented robe back to their father and said, "We found this. Examine it to see whether it is your son's robe."

³³He recognized it and said, "It is my son's robe! Some ferocious animal has devoured him. Joseph has surely been torn to pieces."

³⁴Then Jacob tore his clothes, put on sackcloth and mourned for his son many days. ³⁵All his sons and daughters came to comfort him, but he refused to be comforted. "No," he said, "in mourning will I go down to the grave[b] to my son." So his father wept for him.

³⁶Meanwhile, the Midianites[c] sold Joseph in Egypt to Potiphar, one of Pharaoh's officials, the captain of the guard.

JUDAH AND TAMAR

38 At that time, Judah left his brothers and went down to stay with a man of Adullam named Hirah. ²There Judah met the daughter of a Canaanite man named Shua. He married her and lay with her; ³she became pregnant and gave birth to a son, who was named Er. ⁴She conceived again and gave birth to a son and named him Onan. ⁵She gave birth to still another son and named him Shelah. It was at Kezib that she gave birth to him.

NOW OR NEVER
GE 37:18–19

Jealousy is an emotional poison that will work its way out of your system one way or another. If you don't ask for God's help in getting rid of your jealousy, it will eventually damage even your closest relationships.

---

[a] *28* That is, about 8 ounces (about 0.2 kilogram)   [b] *35* Hebrew *Sheol*   [c] *36* Samaritan Pentateuch, Septuagint, Vulgate and Syriac (see also verse 28); Masoretic Text *Medanites*

⁶Judah got a wife for Er, his firstborn, and her name was Tamar. ⁷But Er, Judah's firstborn, was wicked in the LORD's sight; so the LORD put him to death.

⁸Then Judah said to Onan, "Lie with your brother's wife and fulfill your duty to her as a brother-in-law to produce offspring for your brother." ⁹But Onan knew that the offspring would not be his; so whenever he lay with his brother's wife, he spilled his semen on the ground to keep from producing offspring for his brother. ¹⁰What he did was wicked in the LORD's sight; so he put him to death also.

¹¹Judah then said to his daughter-in-law Tamar, "Live as a widow in your father's house until my son Shelah grows up." For he thought, "He may die too, just like his brothers." So Tamar went to live in her father's house.

¹²After a long time Judah's wife, the daughter of Shua, died. When Judah had recovered from his grief, he went up to Timnah, to the men who were shearing his sheep, and his friend Hirah the Adullamite went with him.

¹³When Tamar was told, "Your father-in-law is on his way to Timnah to shear his sheep," ¹⁴she took off her widow's clothes, covered herself with a veil to disguise herself, and then sat down at the entrance to Enaim, which is on the road to Timnah. For she saw that, though Shelah had now grown up, she had not been given to him as his wife.

¹⁵When Judah saw her, he thought she was a prostitute, for she had covered her face. ¹⁶Not realizing that she was his daughter-in-law, he went over to her by the roadside and said, "Come now, let me sleep with you."

"And what will you give me to sleep with you?" she asked.

¹⁷"I'll send you a young goat from my flock," he said.

"Will you give me something as a pledge until you send it?" she asked.

¹⁸He said, "What pledge should I give you?"

"Your seal and its cord, and the staff in your hand," she answered. So he gave them to her and slept with her, and she became pregnant by him. ¹⁹After she left, she took off her veil and put on her widow's clothes again.

²⁰Meanwhile Judah sent the young goat by his friend the Adullamite in order to get his pledge back from the woman, but he did not find her. ²¹He asked the men who lived there, "Where is the shrine prostitute who was beside the road at Enaim?"

"There hasn't been any shrine prostitute here," they said.

²²So he went back to Judah and said, "I didn't find her. Besides, the men who lived there said, 'There hasn't been any shrine prostitute here.'"

²³Then Judah said, "Let her keep what she has, or we will become a laughingstock. After all, I did send her this young goat, but you didn't find her."

²⁴About three months later Judah was told, "Your daughter-in-law Tamar is guilty of prostitution, and as a result she is now pregnant."

Judah said, "Bring her out and have her burned to death!"

²⁵As she was being brought out, she sent a message to her father-in-law. "I am pregnant by the man who owns these," she said. And she added, "See if you recognize whose seal and cord and staff these are."

²⁶Judah recognized them and said, "She is more righteous than I, since I wouldn't give her to my son Shelah." And he did not sleep with her again.

²⁷When the time came for her to give birth, there were twin boys in her womb. ²⁸As she was giving birth, one of them put out his hand; so the midwife took a scarlet thread and tied it on his wrist and said, "This one came out first." ²⁹But when he drew back his hand, his brother came out, and she said, "So this is how you have broken out!" And he was named Perez.ᵃ ³⁰Then his brother, who had the scarlet thread on his wrist, came out and he was given the name Zerah.ᵇ

NOW OR NEVER

GE 38:24–26

There's a word for people who are quick to point out the spiritual flaws and shortcomings in others, while choosing to ignore their own: *hypocrite*. Could that word be used to describe you?

ᵃ 29 Perez means breaking out.   ᵇ 30 Zerah can mean scarlet or brightness.

JOSEPH AND POTIPHAR'S WIFE

39

Now Joseph had been taken down to Egypt. Potiphar, an Egyptian who was one of Pharaoh's officials, the captain of the guard, bought him from the Ishmaelites who had taken him there.

²The LORD was with Joseph and he prospered, and he lived in the house of his Egyptian master. ³When his master saw that the LORD was with him and that the LORD gave him success in everything he did, ⁴Joseph found favor in his eyes and became his attendant. Potiphar put him in charge of his household, and he entrusted to his care everything he owned. ⁵From the time he put him in charge of his household and of all that he owned, the LORD blessed the household of the Egyptian because of Joseph. The blessing of the LORD was on everything Potiphar had, both in the house and in the field. ⁶So he left in Joseph's care everything he had; with Joseph in charge, he did not concern himself with anything except the food he ate.

Now Joseph was well-built and handsome, ⁷and after a while his master's wife took notice of Joseph and said, "Come to bed with me!"

NOW OR NEVER
GE 39:9

No matter what anyone tells you, your body is *not* yours to do whatever you want with; it's God's. He created it. And when you do things to mess up your body, you're damaging God's property.

Purity

» live the adventure » Ge 39:10

Committing yourself to remaining sexually pure isn't simply a matter of signing a pledge or making a commitment to "save yourself" for marriage; it's a matter of making tough decisions every day to take yourself out of lust's way. This involves not only resisting sexual temptation when it comes, but taking proactive steps to avoid tempting thoughts or situations (like certain websites, music or TV channels) in the first place.

---

⁸But he refused. "With me in charge," he told her, "my master does not concern himself with anything in the house; everything he owns he has entrusted to my care. ⁹No one is greater in this house than I am. My master has withheld nothing from me except you, because you are his wife. How then could I do such a wicked thing and sin against God?" ¹⁰And though she spoke to Joseph day after day, he refused to go to bed with her or even be with her.

¹¹One day he went into the house to attend to his duties, and none of the household servants was inside. ¹²She caught him by his cloak and said, "Come to bed with me!" But he left his cloak in her hand and ran out of the house.

¹³When she saw that he had left his cloak in her hand and had run out of the house, ¹⁴she called her household servants. "Look," she said to them, "this Hebrew has been brought to us to make sport of us! He came in here to sleep with me, but I screamed. ¹⁵When he heard me scream for help, he left his cloak beside me and ran out of the house."

¹⁶She kept his cloak beside her until his master came home. ¹⁷Then she told him this story: "That Hebrew slave you brought us came to me to make sport of me. ¹⁸But as soon as I screamed for help, he left his cloak beside me and ran out of the house."

¹⁹When his master heard the story his wife told him, saying, "This is how your slave treated me," he burned with anger. ²⁰Joseph's master took him and put him in prison, the place where the king's prisoners were confined.

But while Joseph was there in the prison, ²¹the LORD was with him; he showed him kindness and granted him favor in the eyes of the prison warden. ²²So the warden put Joseph in charge of all those held in the prison, and he was made responsible for all that was done there. ²³The warden paid no attention to anything under Joseph's care, because the LORD was with Joseph and gave him success in whatever he did.

THE CUPBEARER AND THE BAKER

40

Some time later, the cupbearer and the baker of the king of Egypt offended their master, the king of Egypt. ²Pharaoh was angry with his two officials, the chief cupbearer and the chief baker, ³and put them in custody in the house of the captain of the guard, in the same prison where Joseph was confined. ⁴The captain of the guard assigned them to Joseph, and he attended them.

After they had been in custody for some time, ⁵each of the two men—the cupbearer and the baker of the king of Egypt, who were being held in prison—had a dream the same night, and each dream had a meaning of its own.

⁶When Joseph came to them the next morning, he saw that they were dejected. ⁷So he asked Pharaoh's officials who were in custody with him in his master's house, "Why are your faces so sad today?"

⁸"We both had dreams," they answered, "but there is no one to interpret them."

Then Joseph said to them, "Do not interpretations belong to God? Tell me your dreams."

NOW OR NEVER
GE 40:8

What would you say are the three best things about you? How many of those things can you honestly take sole credit for?

Constancy

We live in a constantly changing world. Interests, successes, hobbies, jobs, houses—even relationships—come and go. The people closest to you right now may be no more than distant memories ten years from now. Through all of your seasons of life, though, one thing will remain constant: God will not forget you. No matter how many other people pass through your life, God will remain. He will pursue you . . . forever.

⁹So the chief cupbearer told Joseph his dream. He said to him, "In my dream I saw a vine in front of me, ¹⁰and on the vine were three branches. As soon as it budded, it blossomed, and its clusters ripened into grapes. ¹¹Pharaoh's cup was in my hand, and I took the grapes, squeezed them into Pharaoh's cup and put the cup in his hand."

¹²"This is what it means," Joseph said to him. "The three branches are three days. ¹³Within three days Pharaoh will lift up your head and restore you to your position, and you will put Pharaoh's cup in his hand, just as you used to do when you were his cupbearer. ¹⁴But when all goes well with you, remember me and show me kindness; mention me to Pharaoh and get me out of this prison. ¹⁵For I was forcibly carried off from the land of the Hebrews, and even here I have done nothing to deserve being put in a dungeon."

¹⁶When the chief baker saw that Joseph had given a favorable interpretation, he said to Joseph, "I too had a dream: On my head were three baskets of bread.ᵃ ¹⁷In the top basket were all kinds of baked goods for Pharaoh, but the birds were eating them out of the basket on my head."

¹⁸"This is what it means," Joseph said. "The three baskets are three days. ¹⁹Within three days Pharaoh will lift off your head and hang you on a tree.ᵇ And the birds will eat away your flesh."

²⁰Now the third day was Pharaoh's birthday, and he gave a feast for all his officials. He lifted up the heads of the chief cupbearer and the chief baker in the presence of his officials: ²¹He restored the chief cupbearer to his position, so that he once again put the cup into Pharaoh's hand, ²²but he hangedᶜ the chief baker, just as Joseph had said to them in his interpretation.

²³The chief cupbearer, however, did not remember Joseph; he forgot him.

ᵃ 16 Or *three wicker baskets*   ᵇ 19 Or *and impale you on a pole*   ᶜ 22 Or *impaled*

PHARAOH'S DREAMS

41

When two full years had passed, Pharaoh had a dream: He was standing by the Nile, ²when out of the river there came up seven cows, sleek and fat, and they grazed among the reeds. ³After them, seven other cows, ugly and gaunt, came up out of the Nile and stood beside those on the riverbank. ⁴And the cows that were ugly and gaunt ate up the seven sleek, fat cows. Then Pharaoh woke up.

⁵He fell asleep again and had a second dream: Seven heads of grain, healthy and good, were growing on a single stalk. ⁶After them, seven other heads of grain sprouted—thin and scorched by the east wind. ⁷The thin heads of grain swallowed up the seven healthy, full heads. Then Pharaoh woke up; it had been a dream.

⁸In the morning his mind was troubled, so he sent for all the magicians and wise men of Egypt. Pharaoh told them his dreams, but no one could interpret them for him.

⁹Then the chief cupbearer said to Pharaoh, "Today I am reminded of my shortcomings. ¹⁰Pharaoh was once angry with his servants, and he imprisoned me and the chief baker in the house of the captain of the guard. ¹¹Each of us had a dream the same night, and each dream had a meaning of its own. ¹²Now a young Hebrew was there with us, a servant of the captain of the guard. We told him our dreams, and he interpreted them for us, giving each man the interpretation of his dream. ¹³And things turned out exactly as he interpreted them to us: I was restored to my position, and the other man was hanged.ᵃ"

¹⁴So Pharaoh sent for Joseph, and he was quickly brought from the dungeon. When he had shaved and changed his clothes, he came before Pharaoh.

¹⁵Pharaoh said to Joseph, "I had a dream, and no one can interpret it. But I have heard it said of you that when you hear a dream you can interpret it."

¹⁶"I cannot do it," Joseph replied to Pharaoh, "but God will give Pharaoh the answer he desires."

¹⁷Then Pharaoh said to Joseph, "In my dream I was standing on the bank of the Nile, ¹⁸when out of the river there came up seven cows, fat and sleek, and they grazed among the reeds. ¹⁹After them, seven other cows came up—scrawny and very ugly and lean. I had never seen such ugly cows in all the land of Egypt. ²⁰The lean, ugly cows ate up the seven fat cows that came up first. ²¹But even after they ate them, no one could tell that they had done so; they looked just as ugly as before. Then I woke up.

²²"In my dreams I also saw seven heads of grain, full and good, growing on a single stalk. ²³After them, seven other heads sprouted—withered and thin and scorched by the east wind. ²⁴The thin heads of grain swallowed up the seven good heads. I told this to the magicians, but none could explain it to me."

²⁵Then Joseph said to Pharaoh, "The dreams of Pharaoh are one and the same. God has revealed to Pharaoh what he is about to do. ²⁶The seven good cows are seven years, and the seven good heads of grain are seven years; it is one and the same dream. ²⁷The seven lean, ugly cows that came up afterward are seven years, and so are the seven worthless heads of grain scorched by the east wind: They are seven years of famine.

²⁸"It is just as I said to Pharaoh: God has shown Pharaoh what he is about to do. ²⁹Seven years of great abundance are coming throughout the land of Egypt, ³⁰but seven years of famine will follow them. Then all the abundance in Egypt will be forgotten, and the famine will ravage the land. ³¹The abundance in the land will not be remembered, because the famine that follows it will be so severe. ³²The reason the dream was given to Pharaoh in two forms is that the matter has been firmly decided by God, and God will do it soon.

³³"And now let Pharaoh look for a discerning and wise man and put him in charge of the land of Egypt. ³⁴Let Pharaoh appoint commissioners over the land to take a fifth of the harvest of Egypt during the seven years of abundance. ³⁵They should collect all the food of these good years that are coming

---

NOW OR NEVER

GE 41:13-14

Only God knows the future. The best way to prepare for whatever lies ahead is to stick close to him.

ᵃ 13 Or *impaled*

and store up the grain under the authority of Pharaoh, to be kept in the cities for food. ³⁶This food should be held in reserve for the country, to be used during the seven years of famine that will come upon Egypt, so that the country may not be ruined by the famine."

³⁷The plan seemed good to Pharaoh and to all his officials. ³⁸So Pharaoh asked them, "Can we find anyone like this man, one in whom is the spirit of God^a?"

³⁹Then Pharaoh said to Joseph, "Since God has made all this known to you, there is no one so discerning and wise as you. ⁴⁰You shall be in charge of my palace, and all my people are to submit to your orders. Only with respect to the throne will I be greater than you."

JOSEPH IN CHARGE OF EGYPT

⁴¹So Pharaoh said to Joseph, "I hereby put you in charge of the whole land of Egypt." ⁴²Then Pharaoh took his signet ring from his finger and put it on Joseph's finger. He dressed him in robes of fine linen and put a gold chain around his neck. ⁴³He had him ride in a chariot as his second-in-command,^b and men shouted before him, "Make way^c!" Thus he put him in charge of the whole land of Egypt.

⁴⁴Then Pharaoh said to Joseph, "I am Pharaoh, but without your word no one will lift hand or foot in all Egypt." ⁴⁵Pharaoh gave Joseph the name Zaphenath-Paneah and gave him Asenath daughter of Potiphera, priest of On,^d to be his wife. And Joseph went throughout the land of Egypt.

⁴⁶Joseph was thirty years old when he entered the service of Pharaoh king of Egypt. And Joseph went out from Pharaoh's presence and traveled throughout Egypt. ⁴⁷During the seven years of abundance the land produced plentifully. ⁴⁸Joseph collected all the food produced in those seven years of abundance in Egypt and stored it in the cities. In each city he put the food grown in the fields surrounding it. ⁴⁹Joseph stored up huge quantities of grain, like the sand of the sea; it was so much that he stopped keeping records because it was beyond measure.

⁵⁰Before the years of famine came, two sons were born to Joseph by Asenath daughter of Potiphera, priest of On. ⁵¹Joseph named his firstborn Manasseh^e and said, "It is because God has made me forget all my trouble and all my father's household." ⁵²The second son he named Ephraim^f and said, "It is because God has made me fruitful in the land of my suffering."

⁵³The seven years of abundance in Egypt came to an end, ⁵⁴and the seven years of famine began, just as Joseph had said. There was famine in all the other lands, but in the whole land of Egypt there was food. ⁵⁵When all Egypt began to feel the famine, the people cried to Pharaoh for food. Then Pharaoh told all the Egyptians, "Go to Joseph and do what he tells you."

⁵⁶When the famine had spread over the whole country, Joseph opened the storehouses and sold grain to the Egyptians, for the famine was severe throughout Egypt. ⁵⁷And all the countries came to Egypt to buy grain from Joseph, because the famine was severe in all the world.

JOSEPH'S BROTHERS GO TO EGYPT

42 When Jacob learned that there was grain in Egypt, he said to his sons, "Why do you just keep looking at each other?" ²He continued, "I have heard that there is grain in Egypt. Go down there and buy some for us, so that we may live and not die."

³Then ten of Joseph's brothers went down to buy grain from Egypt. ⁴But Jacob did not send Benja-

»» live the adventure »» Ge 41:40

Preparation

Treat every experience, good or bad, as a learning opportunity—because it just may be one! You may have no idea what God has in store for you in the future, but you can be sure that he is preparing you for it. Sometimes that preparation will be obvious. Other times, though, you may not even know you're being prepared until you look back on your life and see where God has led you. Then you may begin to understand why.

^a 38 Or of the gods   ^b 43 Or in the chariot of his second-in-command; or in his second chariot   ^c 43 Or Bow down   ^d 45 That is, Heliopolis; also in verse 50   ^e 51 Manasseh sounds like and may be derived from the Hebrew for forget.   ^f 52 Ephraim sounds like the Hebrew for twice fruitful.

min, Joseph's brother, with the others, because he was afraid that harm might come to him. ⁵So Israel's sons were among those who went to buy grain, for the famine was in the land of Canaan also.

⁶Now Joseph was the governor of the land, the one who sold grain to all its people. So when Joseph's brothers arrived, they bowed down to him with their faces to the ground. ⁷As soon as Joseph saw his brothers, he recognized them, but he pretended to be a stranger and spoke harshly to them. "Where do you come from?" he asked.

"From the land of Canaan," they replied, "to buy food."

⁸Although Joseph recognized his brothers, they did not recognize him. ⁹Then he remembered his dreams about them and said to them, "You are spies! You have come to see where our land is unprotected."

¹⁰"No, my lord," they answered. "Your servants have come to buy food. ¹¹We are all the sons of one man. Your servants are honest men, not spies."

¹²"No!" he said to them. "You have come to see where our land is unprotected."

¹³But they replied, "Your servants were twelve brothers, the sons of one man, who lives in the land of Canaan. The youngest is now with our father, and one is no more."

NOW OR NEVER

GE 42:8–9

If God can make a happy ending out of the mess of Joseph's family, what can he do in your life?

¹⁴Joseph said to them, "It is just as I told you: You are spies! ¹⁵And this is how you will be tested: As surely as Pharaoh lives, you will not leave this place unless your youngest brother comes here. ¹⁶Send one of your number to get your brother; the rest of you will be kept in prison, so that your words may be tested to see if you are telling the truth. If you are not, then as surely as Pharaoh lives, you are spies!" ¹⁷And he put them all in custody for three days.

¹⁸On the third day, Joseph said to them, "Do this and you will live, for I fear God: ¹⁹If you are honest men, let one of your brothers stay here in prison, while the rest of you go and take grain back for your starving households. ²⁰But you must bring your youngest brother to me, so that your words may be verified and that you may not die." This they proceeded to do.

²¹They said to one another, "Surely we are being punished because of our brother. We saw how distressed he was when he pleaded with us for his life, but we would not listen; that's why this distress has come upon us."

²²Reuben replied, "Didn't I tell you not to sin against the boy? But you wouldn't listen! Now we must give an accounting for his blood." ²³They did not realize that Joseph could understand them, since he was using an interpreter.

²⁴He turned away from them and began to weep, but then turned back and spoke to them again. He had Simeon taken from them and bound before their eyes.

²⁵Joseph gave orders to fill their bags with grain, to put each man's silver back in his sack, and to give them provisions for their journey. After this was done for them, ²⁶they loaded their grain on their donkeys and left.

²⁷At the place where they stopped for the night one of them opened his sack to get feed for his donkey, and he saw his silver in the mouth of his sack. ²⁸"My silver has been returned," he said to his brothers. "Here it is in my sack."

Their hearts sank and they turned to each other trembling and said, "What is this that God has done to us?"

²⁹When they came to their father Jacob in the land of Canaan, they told him all that had happened to them. They said, ³⁰"The man who is lord over the land spoke harshly to us and treated us as though we were spying on the land. ³¹But we said to him, 'We are honest men; we are not spies. ³²We were twelve brothers, sons of one father. One is no more, and the youngest is now with our father in Canaan.'

³³"Then the man who is lord over the land said to us, 'This is how I will know whether you are honest men: Leave one of your brothers here with me, and take food for your starving households and go. ³⁴But bring your youngest brother to me so I will know that you are not spies but honest men. Then I will give your brother back to you, and you can trade[a] in the land.' "

ᵃ 34 Or move about freely

35As they were emptying their sacks, there in each man's sack was his pouch of silver! When they and their father saw the money pouches, they were frightened. 36Their father Jacob said to them, "You have deprived me of my children. Joseph is no more and Simeon is no more, and now you want to take Benjamin. Everything is against me!"

37Then Reuben said to his father, "You may put both of my sons to death if I do not bring him back to you. Entrust him to my care, and I will bring him back."

38But Jacob said, "My son will not go down there with you; his brother is dead and he is the only one left. If harm comes to him on the journey you are taking, you will bring my gray head down to the grave^a in sorrow."

THE SECOND JOURNEY TO EGYPT

43

Now the famine was still severe in the land. 2So when they had eaten all the grain they had brought from Egypt, their father said to them, "Go back and buy us a little more food."

3But Judah said to him, "The man warned us solemnly, 'You will not see my face again unless your brother is with you.' 4If you will send our brother along with us, we will go down and buy food for you. 5But if you will not send him, we will not go down, because the man said to us, 'You will not see my face again unless your brother is with you.'"

6Israel asked, "Why did you bring this trouble on me by telling the man you had another brother?"

7They replied, "The man questioned us closely about ourselves and our family. 'Is your father still living?' he asked us. 'Do you have another brother?' We simply answered his questions. How were we to know he would say, 'Bring your brother down here'?"

8Then Judah said to Israel his father, "Send the boy along with me and we will go at once, so that we and you and our children may live and not die. 9I myself will guarantee his safety; you can hold me personally responsible for him. If I do not bring him back to you and set him here before you, I will bear the blame before you all my life. 10As it is, if we had not delayed, we could have gone and returned twice."

11Then their father Israel said to them, "If it must be, then do this: Put some of the best products of the land in your bags and take them down to the man as a gift—a little balm and a little honey, some spices and myrrh, some pistachio nuts and almonds. 12Take double the amount of silver with you, for you must return the silver that was put back into the mouths of your sacks. Perhaps it was a mistake. 13Take your brother also and go back to the man at once. 14And may God Almighty^b grant you mercy before the man so that he will let your other brother and Benjamin come back with you. As for me, if I am bereaved, I am bereaved."

15So the men took the gifts and double the amount of silver, and Benjamin also. They hurried down to Egypt and presented themselves to Joseph. 16When Joseph saw Benjamin with them, he said to the steward of his house, "Take these men to my house, slaughter an animal and prepare dinner; they are to eat with me at noon."

17The man did as Joseph told him and took the men to Joseph's house. 18Now the men were frightened when they were taken to his house. They thought, "We were brought here because of the silver that was put back into our sacks the first time. He wants to attack us and overpower us and seize us as slaves and take our donkeys."

» live the adventure » Ge 43:12

Integrity

Reputations aren't just given; they're earned. If you want to be known as someone who is trustworthy and honest, you've got to make tough decisions every day to resist the many opportunities to be dishonest—even when those opportunities may benefit you personally or seemingly make your life easier in the short run. Unfortunately, one little slip—one small lapse in judgment—may be enough to damage your reputation permanently, as far as some people are concerned.

---

[19]So they went up to Joseph's steward and spoke to him at the entrance to the house. [20]"Please, sir," they said, "we came down here the first time to buy food. [21]But at the place where we stopped for the night we opened our sacks and each of us found his silver—the exact weight—in the mouth of his sack. So we have brought it back with us. [22]We have also brought additional silver with us to buy food. We don't know who put our silver in our sacks."

[23]"It's all right," he said. "Don't be afraid. Your God, the God of your father, has given you treasure in your sacks; I received your silver." Then he brought Simeon out to them.

[24]The steward took the men into Joseph's house, gave them water to wash their feet and provided fodder for their donkeys. [25]They prepared their gifts for Joseph's arrival at noon, because they had heard that they were to eat there.

[26]When Joseph came home, they presented to him the gifts they had brought into the house, and they bowed down before him to the ground. [27]He asked them how they were, and then he said, "How is your aged father you told me about? Is he still living?"

[28]They replied, "Your servant our father is still alive and well." And they bowed low to pay him honor.

[29]As he looked about and saw his brother Benjamin, his own mother's son, he asked, "Is this your youngest brother, the one you told me about?" And he said, "God be gracious to you, my son." [30]Deeply moved at the sight of his brother, Joseph hurried out and looked for a place to weep. He went into his private room and wept there.

[31]After he had washed his face, he came out and, controlling himself, said, "Serve the food."

[32]They served him by himself, the brothers by themselves, and the Egyptians who ate with him by themselves, because Egyptians could not eat with Hebrews, for that is detestable to Egyptians. [33]The men had been seated before him in the order of their ages, from the firstborn to the youngest; and they looked at each other in astonishment. [34]When portions were served to them from Joseph's table, Benjamin's portion was five times as much as anyone else's. So they feasted and drank freely with him.

A SILVER CUP IN A SACK

44 Now Joseph gave these instructions to the steward of his house: "Fill the men's sacks with as much food as they can carry, and put each man's silver in the mouth of his sack. [2]Then put my cup, the silver one, in the mouth of the youngest one's sack, along with the silver for his grain." And he did as Joseph said.

[3]As morning dawned, the men were sent on their way with their donkeys. [4]They had not gone far from the city when Joseph said to his steward, "Go after those men at once, and when you catch up with them, say to them, 'Why have you repaid good with evil? [5]Isn't this the cup my master drinks from and also uses for divination? This is a wicked thing you have done.' "

[6]When he caught up with them, he repeated these words to them. [7]But they said to him, "Why does my lord say such things? Far be it from your servants to do anything like that! [8]We even brought back to you from the land of Canaan the silver we found inside the mouths of our sacks. So why would we steal silver or gold from your master's house? [9]If any of your servants is found to have it, he will die; and the rest of us will become my lord's slaves."

[10]"Very well, then," he said, "let it be as you say. Whoever is found to have it will become my slave; the rest of you will be free from blame."

[11]Each of them quickly lowered his sack to the ground and opened it. [12]Then the steward proceeded to search, beginning with the oldest and ending with the youngest. And the cup was found in Benjamin's sack. [13]At this, they tore their clothes. Then they all loaded their donkeys and returned to the city.

[14]Joseph was still in the house when Judah and his brothers came in, and they threw themselves to the ground before him. [15]Joseph said to them, "What is this you have done? Don't you know that a man like me can find things out by divination?"

[16]"What can we say to my lord?" Judah replied. "What can we say? How can we prove our innocence? God has uncovered your servants' guilt. We are now my lord's slaves—we ourselves and the one who was found to have the cup."

[17]But Joseph said, "Far be it from me to do such a thing! Only the man who was found to have the cup will become my slave. The rest of you, go back to your father in peace."

Speaking Up

Do you know anyone who's defenseless—an easy target for torment and ridicule? Maybe you feel like *you're* that person. Whatever the case, there are two important things to remember. First, God is in control. The God who protected Benjamin is the same God who's looking out for you now. Second, you can be a part of God's work in protecting the defenseless, even if you feel weak yourself. Imagine how Judah must have felt, knowing that begging Joseph on Benjamin's behalf could have earned him a death sentence. He wasn't exactly in a great bargaining position. But he courageously stepped in to protect his brother and, indirectly, the interests of his elderly father. Speak up. God is with you.

[18] Then Judah went up to him and said: "Please, my lord, let your servant speak a word to my lord. Do not be angry with your servant, though you are equal to Pharaoh himself. [19] My lord asked his servants, 'Do you have a father or a brother?' [20] And we answered, 'We have an aged father, and there is a young son born to him in his old age. His brother is dead, and he is the only one of his mother's sons left, and his father loves him.'

[21] "Then you said to your servants, 'Bring him down to me so I can see him for myself.' [22] And we said to my lord, 'The boy cannot leave his father; if he leaves him, his father will die.' [23] But you told your servants, 'Unless your youngest brother comes down with you, you will not see my face again.' [24] When we went back to your servant my father, we told him what my lord had said.

[25] "Then our father said, 'Go back and buy a little more food.' [26] But we said, 'We cannot go down. Only if our youngest brother is with us will we go. We cannot see the man's face unless our youngest brother is with us.'

[27] "Your servant my father said to us, 'You know that my wife bore me two sons. [28] One of them went away from me, and I said, "He has surely been torn to pieces." And I have not seen him since. [29] If you take this one from me too and harm comes to him, you will bring my gray head down to the grave[a] in misery.'

[30] "So now, if the boy is not with us when I go back to your servant my father and if my father, whose life is closely bound up with the boy's life, [31] sees that the boy isn't there, he will die. Your servants will bring the gray head of our father down to the grave in sorrow. [32] Your servant guaranteed the boy's safety to my father. I said, 'If I do not bring him back to you, I will bear the blame before you, my father, all my life!'

[33] "Now then, please let your servant remain here as my lord's slave in place of the boy, and let the boy return with his brothers. [34] How can I go back to my father if the boy is not with me? No! Do not let me see the misery that would come upon my father."

JOSEPH MAKES HIMSELF KNOWN

45

Then Joseph could no longer control himself before all his attendants, and he cried out, "Have everyone leave my presence!" So there was no one with Joseph when he made himself known to his brothers. [2] And he wept so loudly that the Egyptians heard him, and Pharaoh's household heard about it.

[3] Joseph said to his brothers, "I am Joseph! Is my father still living?" But his brothers were not able to answer him, because they were terrified at his presence.

[4] Then Joseph said to his brothers, "Come close to me." When they had done so, he said, "I am your brother Joseph, the one you sold into Egypt! [5] And now, do not be distressed and do not be angry with yourselves for selling me here, because it was to save lives that God sent me ahead of you. [6] For two years now there has been famine in the land, and for the next five years there will not be plowing and reaping. [7] But God sent me ahead of you to preserve for you a remnant on earth and to save your lives by a great deliverance.[b]

[8] "So then, it was not you who sent me here, but God. He made me father to Pharaoh, lord of his entire household and ruler of all Egypt. [9] Now hurry back to my father and say to him, 'This is what your son Joseph says: God has made me lord of all Egypt. Come down to me; don't delay. [10] You shall live in the region of Goshen and be near me—you, your children and grandchildren, your flocks and herds,

---

[a] 29 Hebrew *Sheol*; also in verse 31   [b] 7 Or *save you as a great band of survivors*

and all you have. ¹¹I will provide for you there, because five years of famine are still to come. Otherwise you and your household and all who belong to you will become destitute.'

¹²"You can see for yourselves, and so can my brother Benjamin, that it is really I who am speaking to you. ¹³Tell my father about all the honor accorded me in Egypt and about everything you have seen. And bring my father down here quickly."

¹⁴Then he threw his arms around his brother Benjamin and wept, and Benjamin embraced him, weeping. ¹⁵And he kissed all his brothers and wept over them. Afterward his brothers talked with him.

¹⁶When the news reached Pharaoh's palace that Joseph's brothers had come, Pharaoh and all his officials were pleased. ¹⁷Pharaoh said to Joseph, "Tell your brothers, 'Do this: Load your animals and return to the land of Canaan, ¹⁸and bring your father and your families back to me. I will give you the best of the land of Egypt and you can enjoy the fat of the land.'

¹⁹"You are also directed to tell them, 'Do this: Take some carts from Egypt for your children and your wives, and get your father and come. ²⁰Never mind about your belongings, because the best of all Egypt will be yours.' "

²¹So the sons of Israel did this. Joseph gave them carts, as Pharaoh had commanded, and he also gave them provisions for their journey. ²²To each of them he gave new clothing, but to Benjamin he gave three hundred shekels ᵃ of silver and five sets of clothes. ²³And this is what he sent to his father: ten donkeys loaded with the best things of Egypt, and ten female donkeys loaded with grain and bread and other provisions for his journey. ²⁴Then he sent his brothers away, and as they were leaving he said to them, "Don't quarrel on the way!"

²⁵So they went up out of Egypt and came to their father Jacob in the land of Canaan. ²⁶They told him, "Joseph is still alive! In fact, he is ruler of all Egypt." Jacob was stunned; he did not believe them. ²⁷But when they told him everything Joseph had said to them, and when he saw the carts Joseph had sent to carry him back, the spirit of their father Jacob revived. ²⁸And Israel said, "I'm convinced! My son Joseph is still alive. I will go and see him before I die."

JACOB GOES TO EGYPT

46 So Israel set out with all that was his, and when he reached Beersheba, he offered sacrifices to the God of his father Isaac.

²And God spoke to Israel in a vision at night and said, "Jacob! Jacob!"

"Here I am," he replied.

³"I am God, the God of your father," he said. "Do not be afraid to go down to Egypt, for I will make you into a great nation there. ⁴I will go down to Egypt with you, and I will surely bring you back again. And Joseph's own hand will close your eyes."

⁵Then Jacob left Beersheba, and Israel's sons took their father Jacob and their children and their wives in the carts that Pharaoh had sent to transport him. ⁶They also took with them their livestock and the possessions they had acquired in Canaan, and Jacob and all his offspring went to Egypt. ⁷He took with him to Egypt his sons and grandsons and his daughters and granddaughters—all his offspring.

⁸These are the names of the sons of Israel (Jacob and his descendants) who went to Egypt:

Reuben the firstborn of Jacob.
⁹The sons of Reuben:
Hanoch, Pallu, Hezron and Carmi.
¹⁰The sons of Simeon:
Jemuel, Jamin, Ohad, Jakin, Zohar and Shaul the son of a Canaanite woman.
¹¹The sons of Levi:
Gershon, Kohath and Merari.
¹²The sons of Judah:
Er, Onan, Shelah, Perez and Zerah (but Er and Onan had died in the land of Canaan).
The sons of Perez:
Hezron and Hamul.
¹³The sons of Issachar:
Tola, Puah, ᵇ Jashub ᶜ and Shimron.

ᵃ 22 That is, about 7 1/2 pounds (about 3.5 kilograms)   ᵇ 13 Samaritan Pentateuch and Syriac (see also 1 Chron. 7:1); Masoretic Text Puvah   ᶜ 13 Samaritan Pentateuch and some Septuagint manuscripts (see also Num. 26:24 and 1 Chron. 7:1); Masoretic Text Iob

¹⁴ The sons of Zebulun:

Sered, Elon and Jahleel.

¹⁵ These were the sons Leah bore to Jacob in Paddan Aram,ᵃ besides his daughter Dinah. These sons and daughters of his were thirty-three in all.

¹⁶ The sons of Gad:

Zephon,ᵇ Haggi, Shuni, Ezbon, Eri, Arodi and Areli.

¹⁷ The sons of Asher:

Imnah, Ishvah, Ishvi and Beriah.

Their sister was Serah.

The sons of Beriah:

Heber and Malkiel.

¹⁸ These were the children born to Jacob by Zilpah, whom Laban had given to his daughter Leah— sixteen in all.

¹⁹ The sons of Jacob's wife Rachel:

Joseph and Benjamin. ²⁰ In Egypt, Manasseh and Ephraim were born to Joseph by Asenath daughter of Potiphera, priest of On.ᶜ

²¹ The sons of Benjamin:

Bela, Beker, Ashbel, Gera, Naaman, Ehi, Rosh, Muppim, Huppim and Ard.

²² These were the sons of Rachel who were born to Jacob—fourteen in all.

²³ The son of Dan:

Hushim.

²⁴ The sons of Naphtali:

Jahziel, Guni, Jezer and Shillem.

²⁵ These were the sons born to Jacob by Bilhah, whom Laban had given to his daughter Rachel— seven in all.

²⁶ All those who went to Egypt with Jacob—those who were his direct descendants, not counting his sons' wives—numbered sixty-six persons. ²⁷ With the two sonsᵈ who had been born to Joseph in Egypt, the members of Jacob's family, which went to Egypt, were seventyᵉ in all.

²⁸ Now Jacob sent Judah ahead of him to Joseph to get directions to Goshen. When they arrived in the region of Goshen, ²⁹ Joseph had his chariot made ready and went to Goshen to meet his father Israel. As soon as Joseph appeared before him, he threw his arms around his fatherᶠ and wept for a long time.

³⁰ Israel said to Joseph, "Now I am ready to die, since I have seen for myself that you are still alive."

³¹ Then Joseph said to his brothers and to his father's household, "I will go up and speak to Pharaoh and will say to him, 'My brothers and my father's household, who were living in the land of Canaan, have come to me. ³² The men are shepherds; they tend livestock, and they have brought along their flocks and herds and everything they own.' ³³ When Pharaoh calls you in and asks, 'What is your occupation?' ³⁴ you should answer, 'Your servants have tended livestock from our boyhood on, just as our fathers did.' Then you will be allowed to settle in the region of Goshen, for all shepherds are detestable to the Egyptians."

47

Joseph went and told Pharaoh, "My father and brothers, with their flocks and herds and everything they own, have come from the land of Canaan and are now in Goshen." ² He chose five of his brothers and presented them before Pharaoh.

³ Pharaoh asked the brothers, "What is your occupation?"

"Your servants are shepherds," they replied to Pharaoh, "just as our fathers were." ⁴ They also said to him, "We have come to live here awhile, because the famine is severe in Canaan and your servants' flocks have no pasture. So now, please let your servants settle in Goshen."

⁵ Pharaoh said to Joseph, "Your father and your brothers have come to you, ⁶ and the land of Egypt is before you; settle your father and your brothers in the best part of the land. Let them live in Goshen. And if you know of any among them with special ability, put them in charge of my own livestock."

ᵃ *15* That is, Northwest Mesopotamia   ᵇ *16* Samaritan Pentateuch and Septuagint (see also Num. 26:15); Masoretic Text *Ziphion*
ᶜ *20* That is, Heliopolis   ᵈ *27* Hebrew; Septuagint *the nine children*   ᵉ *27* Hebrew (see also Exodus 1:5 and footnote); Septuagint (see also Acts 7:14) *seventy-five*   ᶠ *29* Hebrew *around him*

⁷Then Joseph brought his father Jacob in and presented him before Pharaoh. After Jacob blessed[a] Pharaoh, ⁸Pharaoh asked him, "How old are you?"

⁹And Jacob said to Pharaoh, "The years of my pilgrimage are a hundred and thirty. My years have been few and difficult, and they do not equal the years of the pilgrimage of my fathers." ¹⁰Then Jacob blessed[b] Pharaoh and went out from his presence.

¹¹So Joseph settled his father and his brothers in Egypt and gave them property in the best part of the land, the district of Rameses, as Pharaoh directed. ¹²Joseph also provided his father and his brothers and all his father's household with food, according to the number of their children.

JOSEPH AND THE FAMINE

¹³There was no food, however, in the whole region because the famine was severe; both Egypt and Canaan wasted away because of the famine. ¹⁴Joseph collected all the money that was to be found in Egypt and Canaan in payment for the grain they were buying, and he brought it to Pharaoh's palace. ¹⁵When the money of the people of Egypt and Canaan was gone, all Egypt came to Joseph and said, "Give us food. Why should we die before your eyes? Our money is used up."

¹⁶"Then bring your livestock," said Joseph. "I will sell you food in exchange for your livestock, since your money is gone." ¹⁷So they brought their livestock to Joseph, and he gave them food in exchange for their horses, their sheep and goats, their cattle and donkeys. And he brought them through that year with food in exchange for all their livestock.

¹⁸When that year was over, they came to him the following year and said, "We cannot hide from our lord the fact that since our money is gone and our livestock belongs to you, there is nothing left for our lord except our bodies and our land. ¹⁹Why should we perish before your eyes—we and our land as well? Buy us and our land in exchange for food, and we with our land will be in bondage to Pharaoh. Give us seed so that we may live and not die, and that the land may not become desolate."

²⁰So Joseph bought all the land in Egypt for Pharaoh. The Egyptians, one and all, sold their fields, because the famine was too severe for them. The land became Pharaoh's, ²¹and Joseph reduced the people to servitude,[c] from one end of Egypt to the other. ²²However, he did not buy the land of the priests, because they received a regular allotment from Pharaoh and had food enough from the allotment Pharaoh gave them. That is why they did not sell their land.

²³Joseph said to the people, "Now that I have bought you and your land today for Pharaoh, here is seed for you so you can plant the ground. ²⁴But when the crop comes in, give a fifth of it to Pharaoh. The other four-fifths you may keep as seed for the fields and as food for yourselves and your households and your children."

²⁵"You have saved our lives," they said. "May we find favor in the eyes of our lord; we will be in bondage to Pharaoh."

²⁶So Joseph established it as a law concerning land in Egypt—still in force today—that a fifth of the produce belongs to Pharaoh. It was only the land of the priests that did not become Pharaoh's.

²⁷Now the Israelites settled in Egypt in the region of Goshen. They acquired property there and were fruitful and increased greatly in number.

²⁸Jacob lived in Egypt seventeen years, and the years of his life were a hundred and forty-seven. ²⁹When the time drew near for Israel to die, he called for his son Joseph and said to him, "If I have found favor in your eyes, put your hand under my thigh and promise that you will show me kindness and faithfulness. Do not bury me in Egypt, ³⁰but when I rest with my fathers, carry me out of Egypt and bury me where they are buried."

"I will do as you say," he said.

³¹"Swear to me," he said. Then Joseph swore to him, and Israel worshiped as he leaned on the top of his staff.[d]

MANASSEH AND EPHRAIM

48

Some time later Joseph was told, "Your father is ill." So he took his two sons Manasseh and Ephraim along with him. ²When Jacob was told, "Your son Joseph has come to you," Israel rallied his strength and sat up on the bed.

³Jacob said to Joseph, "God Almighty[e] appeared to me at Luz in the land of Canaan, and there he

---

[a] 7 Or greeted   [b] 10 Or said farewell to   [c] 21 Samaritan Pentateuch and Septuagint (see also Vulgate); Masoretic Text and he moved the people into the cities   [d] 31 Or Israel bowed down at the head of his bed   [e] 3 Hebrew El-Shaddai

blessed me [4]and said to me, 'I am going to make you fruitful and will increase your numbers. I will make you a community of peoples, and I will give this land as an everlasting possession to your descendants after you.'

[5]"Now then, your two sons born to you in Egypt before I came to you here will be reckoned as mine; Ephraim and Manasseh will be mine, just as Reuben and Simeon are mine. [6]Any children born to you after them will be yours; in the territory they inherit they will be reckoned under the names of their brothers. [7]As I was returning from Paddan,[a] to my sorrow Rachel died in the land of Canaan while we were still on the way, a little distance from Ephrath. So I buried her there beside the road to Ephrath" (that is, Bethlehem).

[8]When Israel saw the sons of Joseph, he asked, "Who are these?"

[9]"They are the sons God has given me here," Joseph said to his father.

Then Israel said, "Bring them to me so I may bless them."

[10]Now Israel's eyes were failing because of old age, and he could hardly see. So Joseph brought his sons close to him, and his father kissed them and embraced them.

[11]Israel said to Joseph, "I never expected to see your face again, and now God has allowed me to see your children too."

[12]Then Joseph removed them from Israel's knees and bowed down with his face to the ground. [13]And Joseph took both of them, Ephraim on his right toward Israel's left hand and Manasseh on his left toward Israel's right hand, and brought them close to him. [14]But Israel reached out his right hand and put it on Ephraim's head, though he was the younger, and crossing his arms, he put his left hand on Manasseh's head, even though Manasseh was the firstborn.

[15]Then he blessed Joseph and said,

NOW OR NEVER

GE 48:15

The thing about sheep is they're totally dependent on their shepherd and completely vulnerable apart from him. We'll find ourselves bleating helplessly like sheep if we try living apart from God.

"May the God before whom my fathers
  Abraham and Isaac walked,
the God who has been my shepherd
  all my life to this day,
[16]the Angel who has delivered me from all harm
  —may he bless these boys.
May they be called by my name
  and the names of my fathers Abraham and Isaac,
and may they increase greatly
  upon the earth."

[17]When Joseph saw his father placing his right hand on Ephraim's head he was displeased; so he took hold of his father's hand to move it from Ephraim's head to Manasseh's head. [18]Joseph said to him, "No, my father, this one is the firstborn; put your right hand on his head."

[19]But his father refused and said, "I know, my son, I know. He too will become a people, and he too will become great. Nevertheless, his younger brother will be greater than he, and his descendants will become a group of nations." [20]He blessed them that day and said,

"In your[b] name will Israel pronounce this blessing:
  'May God make you like Ephraim and Manasseh.' "

So he put Ephraim ahead of Manasseh.

[21]Then Israel said to Joseph, "I am about to die, but God will be with you[c] and take you[c] back to the land of your[c] fathers. [22]And to you, as one who is over your brothers, I give the ridge of land[d] I took from the Amorites with my sword and my bow."

---

[a] *7* That is, Northwest Mesopotamia   [b] *20* The Hebrew is singular.   [c] *21* The Hebrew is plural.   [d] *22* Or *And to you I give one portion more than to your brothers—the portion*

JACOB BLESSES HIS SONS

49

Then Jacob called for his sons and said: "Gather around so I can tell you what will happen to you in days to come.

2 "Assemble and listen, sons of Jacob;
    listen to your father Israel.

3 "Reuben, you are my firstborn,
    my might, the first sign of my strength,
    excelling in honor, excelling in power.
4 Turbulent as the waters, you will no longer excel,
    for you went up onto your father's bed,
    onto my couch and defiled it.

5 "Simeon and Levi are brothers—
    their swords[a] are weapons of violence.
6 Let me not enter their council,
    let me not join their assembly,
for they have killed men in their anger
    and hamstrung oxen as they pleased.
7 Cursed be their anger, so fierce,
    and their fury, so cruel!
I will scatter them in Jacob
    and disperse them in Israel.

8 "Judah,[b] your brothers will praise you;
    your hand will be on the neck of your enemies;
    your father's sons will bow down to you.
9 You are a lion's cub, O Judah;
    you return from the prey, my son.
Like a lion he crouches and lies down,
    like a lioness—who dares to rouse him?
10 The scepter will not depart from Judah,
    nor the ruler's staff from between his feet,
until he comes to whom it belongs[c]
    and the obedience of the nations is his.
11 He will tether his donkey to a vine,
    his colt to the choicest branch;

∩OW OR ∩EVER

GE 49:9-10

Despite Judah's personal mistakes and failures, God blessed him. That's good news for all the rest of us who have ever made mistakes or experienced failure.

he will wash his garments in wine,
    his robes in the blood of grapes.
12 His eyes will be darker than wine,
    his teeth whiter than milk.[d]

13 "Zebulun will live by the seashore
    and become a haven for ships;
    his border will extend toward Sidon.

14 "Issachar is a rawboned[e] donkey
    lying down between two saddlebags.[f]
15 When he sees how good is his resting place
    and how pleasant is his land,

---

[a] 5 The meaning of the Hebrew for this word is uncertain.   [b] 8 Judah sounds like and may be derived from the Hebrew for *praise*.
[c] 10 Or *until Shiloh comes; or until he comes to whom tribute belongs*   [d] 12 Or *will be dull from wine, / his teeth white from milk*
[e] 14 Or *strong*   [f] 14 Or *campfires*

joseph

» The eleventh and favorite son of Jacob

» Sold into slavery by his brothers

» Became the second most powerful man in Egypt

his ten older brothers

» The sons of Jacob from his first wife (Leah) and his two mistresses

» Bitter, scheming and jealous

» Ended up owing their lives to Joseph

The Main Event

Maybe Joseph had never heard the old saying, "Some things are better left unsaid." Whether he was naive or cocky, Joseph made the mistake of telling his brothers about an odd dream he had in which he ruled over them.

That was the final straw as far as Joseph's brothers were concerned. They already had to deal with the fact that Joseph was their father's favorite son—something their father, Jacob, made no effort to hide.

Their payback turned out to be brutal. The first chance the brothers got, they beat the stuffing out of their kid brother and threw him into an underground water tank. A little while later, they yanked him out and sold him to some traders who were passing by. Then when they returned to their father, they pretended Joseph was dead.

Things seemed to go from bad to worse for Joseph. He ended up a common slave in faraway Egypt. Over the next few years, he was falsely accused and convicted of attempted rape and thrown into prison.

Yet through it all, Joseph didn't give up his faith or compromise his character. Years passed, and through a remarkable series of God-ordained events, Joseph became like the "vice president" of Egypt.

When a terrible famine hit the region, everyone was forced to travel to Egypt to buy grain, including Joseph's long-lost family. When God orchestrated a reunion between Joseph and his brothers, it was literally a dream come true. There was Joseph, ruling over his brothers!

The Outcome

You'll have to read the whole story of Joseph to appreciate the intrigue and savor the rich details. But what sticks out more than anything else is God's sovereignty and Joseph's amazing response. Joseph wasn't bitter or angry or vengeful. Though his brothers fully expected retaliation for their evil actions years earlier, Joseph chose instead to forgive and bless them. In fact, he showered them with gifts and moved the entire family to Egypt, where they could enjoy ample food and the protection of Pharaoh.

This "Joseph vs. his brothers" match-up is a helpful reminder for us that God is always in control, and he can bring good out of any situation. How can you follow Joseph's example today in the relationships you have and the decisions you make?

Read more about Joseph and his ten brothers in Genesis 37–50 (page 45–64).

he will bend his shoulder to the burden
and submit to forced labor.

16 "Dan[a] will provide justice for his people
as one of the tribes of Israel.
17 Dan will be a serpent by the roadside,
a viper along the path,
that bites the horse's heels
so that its rider tumbles backward.

18 "I look for your deliverance, O Lord.

19 "Gad[b] will be attacked by a band of raiders,
but he will attack them at their heels.

20 "Asher's food will be rich;
he will provide delicacies fit for a king.

21 "Naphtali is a doe set free
that bears beautiful fawns.[c]

22 "Joseph is a fruitful vine,
a fruitful vine near a spring,
whose branches climb over a wall.[d]
23 With bitterness archers attacked him;
they shot at him with hostility.
24 But his bow remained steady,
his strong arms stayed[e] limber,
because of the hand of the Mighty One of Jacob,
because of the Shepherd, the Rock of Israel,
25 because of your father's God, who helps you,
because of the Almighty,[f] who blesses you
with blessings of the heavens above,
blessings of the deep that lies below,
blessings of the breast and womb.
26 Your father's blessings are greater
than the blessings of the ancient mountains,
than[g] the bounty of the age-old hills.
Let all these rest on the head of Joseph,
on the brow of the prince among[h] his brothers.

27 "Benjamin is a ravenous wolf;
in the morning he devours the prey,
in the evening he divides the plunder."

28 All these are the twelve tribes of Israel, and this is what their father said to them when he blessed them, giving each the blessing appropriate to him.

THE DEATH OF JACOB

29 Then he gave them these instructions: "I am about to be gathered to my people. Bury me with my fathers in the cave in the field of Ephron the Hittite, 30 the cave in the field of Machpelah, near Mamre in Canaan, which Abraham bought as a burial place from Ephron the Hittite, along with the field. 31 There Abraham and his wife Sarah were buried, there Isaac and his wife Rebekah were buried, and there I buried Leah. 32 The field and the cave in it were bought from the Hittites.[i]"

---

a 16 *Dan* here means *he provides justice.*   b 19 *Gad* can mean *attack* and *band of raiders.*   c 21 Or *free; / he utters beautiful words*
d 22 Or *Joseph is a wild colt, / a wild colt near a spring, / a wild donkey on a terraced hill*   e 23,24 Or *archers will attack . . . will shoot . . . will remain . . . will stay*   f 25 Hebrew *Shaddai*   g 26 Or *of my progenitors, / as great as*   h 26 Or *the one separated from*
i 32 Or *the sons of Heth*

³³When Jacob had finished giving instructions to his sons, he drew his feet up into the bed, breathed his last and was gathered to his people.

50

Joseph threw himself upon his father and wept over him and kissed him. ²Then Joseph directed the physicians in his service to embalm his father Israel. So the physicians embalmed him, ³taking a full forty days, for that was the time required for embalming. And the Egyptians mourned for him seventy days.

⁴When the days of mourning had passed, Joseph said to Pharaoh's court, "If I have found favor in your eyes, speak to Pharaoh for me. Tell him, ⁵'My father made me swear an oath and said, "I am about to die; bury me in the tomb I dug for myself in the land of Canaan." Now let me go up and bury my father; then I will return.'"

⁶Pharaoh said, "Go up and bury your father, as he made you swear to do."

⁷So Joseph went up to bury his father. All Pharaoh's officials accompanied him—the dignitaries of his court and all the dignitaries of Egypt— ⁸besides all the members of Joseph's household and his brothers and those belonging to his father's household. Only their children and their flocks and herds were left in Goshen. ⁹Chariots and horsemen[a] also went up with him. It was a very large company.

¹⁰When they reached the threshing floor of Atad, near the Jordan, they lamented loudly and bitterly; and there Joseph observed a seven-day period of mourning for his father. ¹¹When the Canaanites who lived there saw the mourning at the threshing floor of Atad, they said, "The Egyptians are holding a solemn ceremony of mourning." That is why that place near the Jordan is called Abel Mizraim.[b]

¹²So Jacob's sons did as he had commanded them: ¹³They carried him to the land of Canaan and buried him in the cave in the field of Machpelah, near Mamre, which Abraham had bought as a burial place from Ephron the Hittite, along with the field. ¹⁴After burying his father, Joseph returned to Egypt, together with his brothers and all the others who had gone with him to bury his father.

JOSEPH REASSURES HIS BROTHERS

¹⁵When Joseph's brothers saw that their father was dead, they said, "What if Joseph holds a grudge against us and pays us back for all the wrongs we did to him?" ¹⁶So they sent word to Joseph, saying, "Your father left these instructions before he died: ¹⁷'This is what you are to say to Joseph: I ask you to forgive your brothers the sins and the wrongs they committed in treating you so badly.' Now please forgive the sins of the servants of the God of your father." When their message came to him, Joseph wept.

¹⁸His brothers then came and threw themselves down before him. "We are your slaves," they said.

¹⁹But Joseph said to them, "Don't be afraid. Am I in the place of God? ²⁰You intended to harm me, but God intended it for good to accomplish what is now being done, the saving of many lives. ²¹So then, don't be afraid. I will provide for you and your children." And he reassured them and spoke kindly to them.

THE DEATH OF JOSEPH

²²Joseph stayed in Egypt, along with all his father's family. He lived a hundred and ten years ²³and saw the third generation of Ephraim's children. Also the children of Makir son of Manasseh were placed at birth on Joseph's knees.[c]

²⁴Then Joseph said to his brothers, "I am about to die. But God will surely come to your aid and

---

» live the adventure » Ge 50:15-21

Leaving Revenge to God

Do you believe God hates sin? Do you believe he sees everything that happens and knows every thought that people have? Do you believe he's powerful enough to carry out judgment on wrongdoers? If so, then leave revenge to him. No matter how justifiable your anger may seem to you, you have no authority to seek vengeance. Only God has that right. Share your feelings with him and allow him to take care of the situation in his own way.

ᵃ 9 Or charioteers   ᵇ 11 Abel Mizraim means mourning of the Egyptians.   ᶜ 23 That is, were counted as his take you up out of this land to the land he promised on oath to Abraham, Isaac and Jacob." 25And Joseph made the sons of Israel swear an oath and said, "God will surely come to your aid, and then you must carry my bones up from this place."

26So Joseph died at the age of a hundred and ten. And after they embalmed him, he was placed in a coffin in Egypt.

challenge notes

To: my_son

GE 50:20

heavenly_father: no problem is too hard for me to solve. no situation is too hopeless for me to change. I can bring good from even the worst of circumstances. in fact, it's my specialty. when you can't see any way out, look to me. trust me to lead you and take care of you.

EXODUS

EXODUS EXODUS

« AT A GLANCE

Author
Moses

Audience
People of Israel

Date
1450–1410 B.C.

Setting
The Israelites went from one bad situation to the next—from being slaves in Egypt to wanderers in the desert.

Verse to Remember
God heard their groaning and he remembered his covenant with Abraham, with Isaac and with Jacob. So God looked on the Israelites and was concerned about them (2:24–25).

Theme to Consider
Exodus is a wonderful word picture of the extraordinary lengths God will go to reach out and rescue those he loves, including you.

UNCHANGING TRUTH » Freedom. That's what it's all about, isn't it?

How many times have you dreamed of being free from your teachers' demands or your parents' rules? How many times have you told yourself, "When I get older, *no one* is going to tell me what to do"?

That's what a lot of guys think of when they hear the word *freedom*. They picture themselves living free and easy, not having to rely on anyone for anything, being able to come and go as they please without anything holding them back.

Here's a news flash for you: Being able to do whatever you want whenever you want is *not* freedom. Why? Because each of us was born with something called a "sin nature." That means we have a natural tendency to do wrong. In fact, it's impossible for us *not* to sin. So what feels like freedom to us is actually something much closer to slavery—slavery to sin.

The only way to be freed from the bondage of sin is to turn our lives over to the Lord and allow him to change us from the inside. So if it's freedom you're looking for, pay attention to the lesson the Israelites learned in the book of Exodus. True freedom comes from obeying God and letting him show you the countless possibilities that are available to you.

LIFE LESSONS »

1. God can work though our weaknesses and shortcomings to help us accomplish things that seem beyond our abilities (4:10–11).

2. God will use any means necessary to make good on his promises (7:14—11:10).

3. The best way to respond to God's awesome work is with heartfelt worship and praise (15:1–21).

4. No situation is hopeless when God is on your side (17:1–7).

THE ISRAELITES OPPRESSED

1 These are the names of the sons of Israel who went to Egypt with Jacob, each with his family: ²Reuben, Simeon, Levi and Judah; ³Issachar, Zebulun and Benjamin; ⁴Dan and Naphtali; Gad and Asher. ⁵The descendants of Jacob numbered seventy[a] in all; Joseph was already in Egypt.

⁶Now Joseph and all his brothers and all that generation died, ⁷but the Israelites were fruitful and multiplied greatly and became exceedingly numerous, so that the land was filled with them.

⁸Then a new king, who did not know about Joseph, came to power in Egypt. ⁹"Look," he said to his people, "the Israelites have become much too numerous for us. ¹⁰Come, we must deal shrewdly with them or they will become even more numerous and, if war breaks out, will join our enemies, fight against us and leave the country."

¹¹So they put slave masters over them to oppress them with forced labor, and they built Pithom and Rameses as store cities for Pharaoh. ¹²But the more they were oppressed, the more they multiplied and spread; so the Egyptians came to dread the Israelites ¹³and worked them ruthlessly. ¹⁴They made their lives bitter with hard labor in brick and mortar and with all kinds of work in the fields; in all their hard labor the Egyptians used them ruthlessly.

¹⁵The king of Egypt said to the Hebrew midwives, whose names were Shiphrah and Puah, ¹⁶"When you help the Hebrew women in childbirth and observe them on the delivery stool, if it is a boy, kill him; but if it is a girl, let her live." ¹⁷The midwives, however, feared God and did not do what the king of Egypt had told them to do; they let the boys live. ¹⁸Then the king of Egypt summoned the midwives and asked them, "Why have you done this? Why have you let the boys live?"

¹⁹The midwives answered Pharaoh, "Hebrew women are not like Egyptian women; they are vigorous and give birth before the midwives arrive."

²⁰So God was kind to the midwives and the people increased and became even more numerous. ²¹And because the midwives feared God, he gave them families of their own.

²²Then Pharaoh gave this order to all his people: "Every boy that is born[b] you must throw into the Nile, but let every girl live."

THE BIRTH OF MOSES

2 Now a man of the house of Levi married a Levite woman, ²and she became pregnant and gave birth to a son. When she saw that he was a fine child, she hid him for three months. ³But when she could hide him no longer, she got a papyrus basket for him and coated it with tar and pitch. Then she placed the child in it and put it among the reeds along the bank of the Nile. ⁴His sister stood at a distance to see what would happen to him.

⁵Then Pharaoh's daughter went down to the Nile to bathe, and her attendants were walking along the river bank. She saw the basket among the reeds and sent her slave girl to get it. ⁶She opened it and saw the baby. He was crying, and she felt sorry for him. "This is one of the Hebrew babies," she said.

⁷Then his sister asked Pharaoh's daughter, "Shall I go and get one of the Hebrew women to nurse the baby for you?"

⁸"Yes, go," she answered. And the girl went and got the baby's mother. ⁹Pharaoh's daughter said to her, "Take this baby and nurse him for me, and I will pay you." So the woman took the baby and nursed him. ¹⁰When the child grew older, she took him to Pharaoh's daughter and he became her son. She named him Moses,[c] saying, "I drew him out of the water."

» live the adventure »» Ex 1:15-17

Doing the Right Thing

Think of the last time you had such a clear-cut choice between doing what's right and doing what's wrong. Maybe it was a good-night kiss that started to go too far. Maybe it was a fool-proof cheating plan that could have saved your grade. Maybe it was a perfect opportunity to stick it to someone you can't stand. Whatever the circumstances, you probably discovered that doing the right thing usually comes with a price, whether it's postponing sexual pleasure, getting a low test grade or being labeled a wimp. Keep in mind, though, that doing what's right also comes with a benefit. God sees—and rewards—every good decision you make.

ᵃ 5 Masoretic Text (see also Gen. 46:27); Dead Sea Scrolls and Septuagint (see also Acts 7:14 and note at Gen. 46:27) *seventy-five*
ᵇ 22 Masoretic Text; Samaritan Pentateuch, Septuagint and Targums *born to the Hebrews*   ᶜ 10 *Moses* sounds like the Hebrew for *draw out.*

MOSES FLEES TO MIDIAN

[11] One day, after Moses had grown up, he went out to where his own people were and watched them at their hard labor. He saw an Egyptian beating a Hebrew, one of his own people. [12] Glancing this way and that and seeing no one, he killed the Egyptian and hid him in the sand. [13] The next day he went out and saw two Hebrews fighting. He asked the one in the wrong, "Why are you hitting your fellow Hebrew?"

[14] The man said, "Who made you ruler and judge over us? Are you thinking of killing me as you killed the Egyptian?" Then Moses was afraid and thought, "What I did must have become known."

[15] When Pharaoh heard of this, he tried to kill Moses, but Moses fled from Pharaoh and went to live in Midian, where he sat down by a well. [16] Now a priest of Midian had seven daughters, and they came to draw water and fill the troughs to water their father's flock. [17] Some shepherds came along and drove them away, but Moses got up and came to their rescue and watered their flock.

[18] When the girls returned to Reuel their father, he asked them, "Why have you returned so early today?"

[19] They answered, "An Egyptian rescued us from the shepherds. He even drew water for us and watered the flock."

[20] "And where is he?" he asked his daughters. "Why did you leave him? Invite him to have something to eat."

[21] Moses agreed to stay with the man, who gave his daughter Zipporah to Moses in marriage. [22] Zipporah gave birth to a son, and Moses named him Gershom,[b] saying, "I have become an alien in a foreign land."

[23] During that long period, the king of Egypt died. The Israelites groaned in their slavery and cried out, and their cry for help because of their slavery went up to God. [24] God heard their groaning and he remembered his covenant with Abraham, with Isaac and with Jacob. [25] So God looked on the Israelites and was concerned about them.

» live the adventure » Ex 2:7-8

Taking the Initiative

You can't always sit back and wait for life to come to you. Sometimes you've got to figure out what needs to be done, roll up your sleeves and do it (or at least get started). Taking the initiative can be a scary thing, because it makes you the point man. You become the person responsible for whatever it is you're doing. That means if things don't go right, you're the one who gets tagged with most of the blame. The funny thing about taking initiative, though, is that the more excitement and confidence you show in tackling a project, the more people you'll find coming out of the woodwork to help you.

MOSES AND THE BURNING BUSH

3 Now Moses was tending the flock of Jethro his father-in-law, the priest of Midian, and he led the flock to the far side of the desert and came to Horeb, the mountain of God. [2] There the angel of the LORD appeared to him in flames of fire from within a bush. Moses saw that though the bush was on fire it did not burn. [3] So Moses thought, "I will go over and see this strange sight—why the bush does not burn up."

[4] When the LORD saw that he had gone over to look, God called to him from within the bush, "Moses! Moses!"

And Moses said, "Here I am."

[5] "Do not come any closer," God said. "Take off your sandals, for the place where you are standing is holy ground." [6] Then he said, "I am the God of your father, the God of Abraham, the God of Isaac and the God of Jacob." At this, Moses hid his face, because he was afraid to look at God.

[7] The LORD said, "I have indeed seen the misery of my people in Egypt. I have heard them crying out

EX 2:23-25

---

challenge notes

To: my_son

heavenly_father: just as I heard the israelites groaning in egypt, I hear your "groaning" today. I know the things you're struggling with at school. I know the doubts you have about your faith. I know the worries that run through your head when you lie in bed at night. I didn't forget about the israelites! I won't forget about you either.

---

a 22 *Gershom* sounds like the Hebrew for *an alien there.*

because of their slave drivers, and I am concerned about their suffering. 8So I have come down to rescue them from the hand of the Egyptians and to bring them up out of that land into a good and spacious land, a land flowing with milk and honey—the home of the Canaanites, Hittites, Amorites, Perizzites, Hivites and Jebusites. 9And now the cry of the Israelites has reached me, and I have seen the way the Egyptians are oppressing them. 10So now, go. I am sending you to Pharaoh to bring my people the Israelites out of Egypt."

11But Moses said to God, "Who am I, that I should go to Pharaoh and bring the Israelites out of Egypt?"

12And God said, "I will be with you. And this will be the sign to you that it is I who have sent you: When you have brought the people out of Egypt, you[a] will worship God on this mountain."

13Moses said to God, "Suppose I go to the Israelites and say to them, 'The God of your fathers has sent me to you,' and they ask me, 'What is his name?' Then what shall I tell them?"

14God said to Moses, "I AM WHO I AM.[b] This is what you are to say to the Israelites: 'I AM has sent me to you.' "

15God also said to Moses, "Say to the Israelites, 'The LORD,[c] the God of your fathers—the God of Abraham, the God of Isaac and the God of Jacob—has sent me to you.' This is my name forever, the name by which I am to be remembered from generation to generation.

16"Go, assemble the elders of Israel and say to them, 'The LORD, the God of your fathers—the God of Abraham, Isaac and Jacob—appeared to me and said: I have watched over you and have seen what has been done to you in Egypt. 17And I have promised to bring you up out of your misery in Egypt into the land of the Canaanites, Hittites, Amorites, Perizzites, Hivites and Jebusites—a land flowing with milk and honey.'

18"The elders of Israel will listen to you. Then you and the elders are to go to the king of Egypt and say to him, 'The LORD, the God of the Hebrews, has met with us. Let us take a three-day journey into the desert to offer sacrifices to the LORD our God.' 19But I know that the king of Egypt will not let you go unless a mighty hand compels him. 20So I will stretch out my hand and strike the Egyptians with all the wonders that I will perform among them. After that, he will let you go.

21"And I will make the Egyptians favorably disposed toward this people, so that when you leave you will not go empty-handed. 22Every woman is to ask her neighbor and any woman living in her house for articles of silver and gold and for clothing, which you will put on your sons and daughters. And so you will plunder the Egyptians."

SIGNS FOR MOSES

4 Moses answered, "What if they do not believe me or listen to me and say, 'The LORD did not appear to you'?"

2Then the LORD said to him, "What is that in your hand?"

"A staff," he replied.

3The LORD said, "Throw it on the ground."

Moses threw it on the ground and it became a snake, and he ran from it. 4Then the LORD said to him, "Reach out your hand and take it by the tail." So Moses reached out and took hold of the snake and it turned back into a staff in his hand. 5"This," said the LORD, "is so that they may believe that the LORD, the God of their fathers—the God of Abraham, the God of Isaac and the God of Jacob—has appeared to you."

6Then the LORD said, "Put your hand inside your cloak." So Moses put his hand into his cloak, and when he took it out, it was leprous,[d] like snow.

7"Now put it back into your cloak," he said. So Moses put his hand back into his cloak, and when he took it out, it was restored, like the rest of his flesh.

NOW OR NEVER
EX 3:5

When you pray or worship God, what kind of an attitude do you bring to the table? Do you give God the respect he deserves? If so, how?

---

a 12 The Hebrew is plural.   b 14 Or I WILL BE WHAT I WILL BE   c 15 The Hebrew for LORD sounds like and may be derived from the Hebrew for I AM in verse 14.   d 6 The Hebrew word was used for various diseases affecting the skin—not necessarily leprosy.

[8]Then the LORD said, "If they do not believe you or pay attention to the first miraculous sign, they may believe the second. [9]But if they do not believe these two signs or listen to you, take some water from the Nile and pour it on the dry ground. The water you take from the river will become blood on the ground."

[10]Moses said to the LORD, "O Lord, I have never been eloquent, neither in the past nor since you have spoken to your servant. I am slow of speech and tongue."

[11]The LORD said to him, "Who gave man his mouth? Who makes him deaf or mute? Who gives him sight or makes him blind? Is it not I, the LORD? [12]Now go; I will help you speak and will teach you what to say."

[13]But Moses said, "O Lord, please send someone else to do it."

[14]Then the LORD's anger burned against Moses and he said, "What about your brother, Aaron the Levite? I know he can speak well. He is already on his way to meet you, and his heart will be glad when he sees you. [15]You shall speak to him and put words in his mouth; I will help both of you speak and will teach you what to do. [16]He will speak to the people for you, and it will be as if he were your mouth and as if you were God to him. [17]But take this staff in your hand so you can perform miraculous signs with it."

MOSES RETURNS TO EGYPT

[18]Then Moses went back to Jethro his father-in-law and said to him, "Let me go back to my own people in Egypt to see if any of them are still alive."

Jethro said, "Go, and I wish you well."

[19]Now the LORD had said to Moses in Midian, "Go back to Egypt, for all the men who wanted to kill you are dead." [20]So Moses took his wife and sons, put them on a donkey and started back to Egypt. And he took the staff of God in his hand.

[21]The LORD said to Moses, "When you return to Egypt, see that you perform before Pharaoh all the wonders I have given you the power to do. But I will harden his heart so that he will not let the people go. [22]Then say to Pharaoh, 'This is what the LORD says: Israel is my firstborn son, [23]and I told you, "Let my son go, so he may worship me." But you refused to let him go; so I will kill your firstborn son.'"

[24]At a lodging place on the way, the LORD met ⌊Moses⌋[a] and was about to kill him. [25]But Zipporah took a flint knife, cut off her son's foreskin and touched ⌊Moses'⌋ feet with it.[b] "Surely you are a bridegroom of blood to me," she said. [26]So the LORD let him alone. (At that time she said "bridegroom of blood," referring to circumcision.)

[27]The LORD said to Aaron, "Go into the desert to meet Moses." So he met Moses at the mountain of God and kissed him. [28]Then Moses told Aaron everything the LORD had sent him to say, and also about all the miraculous signs he had commanded him to perform.

[29]Moses and Aaron brought together all the elders of the Israelites, [30]and Aaron told them everything the LORD had said to Moses. He also performed the signs before the people, [31]and they believed. And when they heard that the LORD was concerned about them and had seen their misery, they bowed down and worshiped.

BRICKS WITHOUT STRAW

5 Afterward Moses and Aaron went to Pharaoh and said, "This is what the LORD, the God of Israel, says: 'Let my people go, so that they may hold a festival to me in the desert.'"

Overcoming Feelings of Incompetence

» live the adventure » Ex 4:10-13

What are the limits of your abilities? Actually, that's a trick question. You can't answer it with any kind of accuracy because you don't have enough information. The fact is, you don't know your limits; only God does. For example, God looked down at Moses, a man herding sheep for his father-in-law, and said, "There's the guy I'm going to use to challenge one of the most powerful leaders in the world, rescue millions of people from slavery and lead them across the desert to their new home." Moses didn't believe it, but God knew better. What do you think the Lord sees when he looks at you?

---

[a] 24 Or ⌊Moses' son⌋; Hebrew him [b] 25 Or and drew near ⌊Moses'⌋ feet

2Pharaoh said, "Who is the LORD, that I should obey him and let Israel go? I do not know the LORD and I will not let Israel go."

3Then they said, "The God of the Hebrews has met with us. Now let us take a three-day journey into the desert to offer sacrifices to the LORD our God, or he may strike us with plagues or with the sword."

4But the king of Egypt said, "Moses and Aaron, why are you taking the people away from their labor? Get back to your work!" 5Then Pharaoh said, "Look, the people of the land are now numerous, and you are stopping them from working."

6That same day Pharaoh gave this order to the slave drivers and foremen in charge of the people: 7"You are no longer to supply the people with straw for making bricks; let them go and gather their own straw. 8But require them to make the same number of bricks as before; don't reduce the quota. They are lazy; that is why they are crying out, 'Let us go and sacrifice to our God.' 9Make the work harder for the men so that they keep working and pay no attention to lies."

10Then the slave drivers and the foremen went out and said to the people, "This is what Pharaoh says: 'I will not give you any more straw. 11Go and get your own straw wherever you can find it, but your work will not be reduced at all.' " 12So the people scattered all over Egypt to gather stubble to use for straw. 13The slave drivers kept pressing them, saying, "Complete the work required of you for each day, just as when you had straw." 14The Israelite foremen appointed by Pharaoh's slave drivers were beaten and were asked, "Why didn't you meet your quota of bricks yesterday or today, as before?"

15Then the Israelite foremen went and appealed to Pharaoh: "Why have you treated your servants this way? 16Your servants are given no straw, yet we are told, 'Make bricks!' Your servants are being beaten, but the fault is with your own people."

17Pharaoh said, "Lazy, that's what you are—lazy! That is why you keep saying, 'Let us go and sacrifice to the LORD.' 18Now get to work. You will not be given any straw, yet you must produce your full quota of bricks."

19The Israelite foremen realized they were in trouble when they were told, "You are not to reduce the number of bricks required of you for each day." 20When they left Pharaoh, they found Moses and Aaron waiting to meet them, 21and they said, "May the LORD look upon you and judge you! You have made us a stench to Pharaoh and his officials and have put a sword in their hand to kill us."

NOW OR NEVER
EX 5:22—6:1

God doesn't work on deadlines. There's no such thing as "too late" when he's involved in a situation. If you want to save yourself some stress, let God do what he wants to do when he wants to do it.

GOD PROMISES DELIVERANCE

22Moses returned to the LORD and said, "O Lord, why have you brought trouble upon this people? Is this why you sent me? 23Ever since I went to Pharaoh to speak in your name, he has brought trouble upon this people, and you have not rescued your people at all."

6 Then the LORD said to Moses, "Now you will see what I will do to Pharaoh: Because of my mighty hand he will let them go; because of my mighty hand he will drive them out of his country."

2God also said to Moses, "I am the LORD. 3I appeared to Abraham, to Isaac and to Jacob as God Almighty,[a] but by my name the LORD[b] I did not make myself known to them.[c] 4I also established my covenant with them to give them the land of Canaan, where they lived as aliens. 5Moreover, I have heard the groaning of the Israelites, whom the Egyptians are enslaving, and I have remembered my covenant.

6"Therefore, say to the Israelites: 'I am the LORD, and I will bring you out from under the yoke of the Egyptians. I will free you from being slaves to them, and I will redeem you with an outstretched arm and with mighty acts of judgment. 7I will take you as my own people, and I will be your God. Then you will know that I am the LORD your God, who brought you out from under the yoke of the Egyptians. 8And I will bring you to the land I swore with uplifted hand to give to Abraham, to Isaac and to Jacob. I will give it to you as a possession. I am the LORD.' "

---

a 3 Hebrew *El-Shaddai*   b 3 See note at Exodus 3:15.   c 3 Or *Almighty, and by my name the LORD did I not let myself be known to them?*

⁹Moses reported this to the Israelites, but they did not listen to him because of their discouragement and cruel bondage.

¹⁰Then the LORD said to Moses, ¹¹"Go, tell Pharaoh king of Egypt to let the Israelites go out of his country."

¹²But Moses said to the LORD, "If the Israelites will not listen to me, why would Pharaoh listen to me, since I speak with faltering lips[a]?"

FAMILY RECORD OF MOSES AND AARON

¹³Now the LORD spoke to Moses and Aaron about the Israelites and Pharaoh king of Egypt, and he commanded them to bring the Israelites out of Egypt.

¹⁴These were the heads of their families[b]:

The sons of Reuben the firstborn son of Israel were Hanoch and Pallu, Hezron and Carmi. These were the clans of Reuben.

¹⁵The sons of Simeon were Jemuel, Jamin, Ohad, Jakin, Zohar and Shaul the son of a Canaanite woman. These were the clans of Simeon.

¹⁶These were the names of the sons of Levi according to their records: Gershon, Kohath and Merari. Levi lived 137 years.

¹⁷The sons of Gershon, by clans, were Libni and Shimei.

¹⁸The sons of Kohath were Amram, Izhar, Hebron and Uzziel. Kohath lived 133 years.

¹⁹The sons of Merari were Mahli and Mushi.

These were the clans of Levi according to their records.

²⁰Amram married his father's sister Jochebed, who bore him Aaron and Moses. Amram lived 137 years.

²¹The sons of Izhar were Korah, Nepheg and Zicri.

²²The sons of Uzziel were Mishael, Elzaphan and Sithri.

²³Aaron married Elisheba, daughter of Amminadab and sister of Nahshon, and she bore him Nadab and Abihu, Eleazar and Ithamar.

²⁴The sons of Korah were Assir, Elkanah and Abiasaph. These were the Korahite clans.

²⁵Eleazar son of Aaron married one of the daughters of Putiel, and she bore him Phinehas.

These were the heads of the Levite families, clan by clan.

²⁶It was this same Aaron and Moses to whom the LORD said, "Bring the Israelites out of Egypt by their divisions." ²⁷They were the ones who spoke to Pharaoh king of Egypt about bringing the Israelites out of Egypt. It was the same Moses and Aaron.

AARON TO SPEAK FOR MOSES

²⁸Now when the LORD spoke to Moses in Egypt, ²⁹he said to him, "I am the LORD. Tell Pharaoh king of Egypt everything I tell you."

³⁰But Moses said to the LORD, "Since I speak with faltering lips, why would Pharaoh listen to me?"

7 Then the LORD said to Moses, "See, I have made you like God to Pharaoh, and your brother Aaron will be your prophet. ²You are to say everything I command you, and your brother Aaron is to tell Pharaoh to let the Israelites go out of his country. ³But I will harden Pharaoh's heart, and though I multiply my miraculous signs and wonders in Egypt, ⁴he will not listen to you. Then I will lay my hand on Egypt and with mighty acts of judgment I will bring out my divisions, my people the Israelites. ⁵And the Egyptians will know that I am the LORD when I stretch out my hand against Egypt and bring the Israelites out of it."

EX 6:6-8

challenge notes

To: my_son

heavenly_father: no matter how often you work out or how much you can bench press, the fact is, you're not that strong. but don't get discouraged; I'm strong enough for both of us—strong enough to deliver you from any obstacle you might ever face.

---

[a] 12 Hebrew *I am uncircumcised of lips*; also in verse 30   [b] 14 The Hebrew for *families* here and in verse 25 refers to units larger than clans.

battlelines

» The Player (Girls)

Q: Word on the street is that you're the ultimate player.
A: (Laughing) Aw, man, that's so wrong. I just like the ladies, that's all. And I know how to treat 'em good.

Q: But you do get around?
A: Hey, I like my freedom, you know what I'm saying? I've got to explore my options. People act all mad, like I'm doing something wrong hanging out with different girls all the time. But do you see a wedding ring on this finger? I'll stop playing the field when I'm ready to settle down and get married—and not a second sooner.

Q: Do you lead girls on?
A: What do you mean?

Q: You know, do you make them think you like them more than you really do?
A: No, man, it's not like that. I just act like a gentleman, you know? I can't help it if they fall for me. Is that *my* fault? And have you seen my MySpace page? It's filled with messages! Every day I get tons of posts from a lot of different girls.

Q: So I guess you really like all the female attention.
A: Who wouldn't? Look, I'm serious. I'm not doing anything wrong. I don't go around whispering, "I love you," to a bunch of girls. And I don't make any promises, all right? This is just what happens when you treat girls right.

» Playing With Emotions

Maybe Matthew's right. Maybe he does possess some kind of rare, inexplicable animal magnetism. Or maybe he's perfected the art of teasing and flirting with the opposite sex. He and God will have to sort that one out.

In the meantime, consider this an opportunity to evaluate your own relational habits. It's never all right to play with people's emotions. It hurts them and, in the end, leaves you feeling empty. Instead, make it your goal to be totally others-centered—concerned more with the feelings and needs of other people than with your own desire for relational conquest. Will you be known as someone who leaves a wake of brokenhearted girls, or as somebody who respects the opposite sex?

As the apostle Paul put it, "Do nothing out of selfish ambition or vain conceit, but in humility consider others better than yourselves. Each of you should look not only to your own interests, but also to the interests of others" (Philippians 2:3–4).

Read more about getting along with girls at www.RevolutionBible.com.

⁶Moses and Aaron did just as the Lord commanded them. ⁷Moses was eighty years old and Aaron eighty-three when they spoke to Pharaoh.

AARON'S STAFF BECOMES A SNAKE

⁸The Lord said to Moses and Aaron, ⁹"When Pharaoh says to you, 'Perform a miracle,' then say to Aaron, 'Take your staff and throw it down before Pharaoh,' and it will become a snake."

¹⁰So Moses and Aaron went to Pharaoh and did just as the Lord commanded. Aaron threw his staff down in front of Pharaoh and his officials, and it became a snake. ¹¹Pharaoh then summoned wise men and sorcerers, and the Egyptian magicians also did the same things by their secret arts: ¹²Each one threw down his staff and it became a snake. But Aaron's staff swallowed up their staffs. ¹³Yet Pharaoh's heart became hard and he would not listen to them, just as the Lord had said.

THE PLAGUE OF BLOOD

¹⁴Then the Lord said to Moses, "Pharaoh's heart is unyielding; he refuses to let the people go. ¹⁵Go to Pharaoh in the morning as he goes out to the water. Wait on the bank of the Nile to meet him, and take in your hand the staff that was changed into a snake. ¹⁶Then say to him, 'The Lord, the God of the Hebrews, has sent me to say to you: Let my people go, so that they may worship me in the desert. But until now you have not listened. ¹⁷This is what the Lord says: By this you will know that I am the Lord: With the staff that is in my hand I will strike the water of the Nile, and it will be changed into blood. ¹⁸The fish in the Nile will die, and the river will stink; the Egyptians will not be able to drink its water.'"

¹⁹The Lord said to Moses, "Tell Aaron, 'Take your staff and stretch out your hand over the waters of Egypt—over the streams and canals, over the ponds and all the reservoirs'—and they will turn to blood. Blood will be everywhere in Egypt, even in the wooden buckets and stone jars."

²⁰Moses and Aaron did just as the Lord had commanded. He raised his staff in the presence of Pharaoh and his officials and struck the water of the Nile, and all the water was changed into blood. ²¹The fish in the Nile died, and the river smelled so bad that the Egyptians could not drink its water. Blood was everywhere in Egypt.

²²But the Egyptian magicians did the same things by their secret arts, and Pharaoh's heart became hard; he would not listen to Moses and Aaron, just as the Lord had said. ²³Instead, he turned and went into his palace, and did not take even this to heart. ²⁴And all the Egyptians dug along the Nile to get drinking water, because they could not drink the water of the river.

THE PLAGUE OF FROGS

²⁵Seven days passed after the Lord struck the Nile. ¹Then the Lord said to Moses, "Go to Pharaoh and say to him, 'This is what the Lord says: Let my people go, so that they may worship me. ²If you refuse to let them go, I will plague your whole country with frogs. ³The Nile will teem with frogs. They will come up into your palace and your bedroom and onto your bed, into the houses of your officials and on your people, and into your ovens and kneading troughs. ⁴The frogs will go up on you and your people and all your officials.'"

⁵Then the Lord said to Moses, "Tell Aaron, 'Stretch out your hand with your staff over the streams and canals and ponds, and make frogs come up on the land of Egypt.'"

⁶So Aaron stretched out his hand over the waters of Egypt, and the frogs came up and covered the land. ⁷But the magicians did the same things by their secret arts; they also made frogs come up on the land of Egypt.

⁸Pharaoh summoned Moses and Aaron and said, "Pray to the Lord to take the frogs away from me and my people, and I will let your people go to offer sacrifices to the Lord."

⁹Moses said to Pharaoh, "I leave to you the honor of setting the time for me to pray for you and your officials and your people that you and your houses may be rid of the frogs, except for those that remain in the Nile."

¹⁰"Tomorrow," Pharaoh said.

Moses replied, "It will be as you say, so that you may know there is no one like the Lord our God. ¹¹The frogs will leave you and your houses, your officials and your people; they will remain only in the Nile."

¹²After Moses and Aaron left Pharaoh, Moses cried out to the Lord about the frogs he had brought

on Pharaoh. ¹³And the LORD did what Moses asked. The frogs died in the houses, in the courtyards and in the fields. ¹⁴They were piled into heaps, and the land reeked of them. ¹⁵But when Pharaoh saw that there was relief, he hardened his heart and would not listen to Moses and Aaron, just as the LORD had said.

THE PLAGUE OF GNATS

¹⁶Then the LORD said to Moses, "Tell Aaron, 'Stretch out your staff and strike the dust of the ground,' and throughout the land of Egypt the dust will become gnats." ¹⁷They did this, and when Aaron stretched out his hand with the staff and struck the dust of the ground, gnats came upon men and animals. All the dust throughout the land of Egypt became gnats. ¹⁸But when the magicians tried to produce gnats by their secret arts, they could not. And the gnats were on men and animals.

¹⁹The magicians said to Pharaoh, "This is the finger of God." But Pharaoh's heart was hard and he would not listen, just as the LORD had said.

NOW OR NEVER

EX 8:15

When you're in a bind and you've run out of options, where do you turn? If you're like a lot of people, you turn to God. So when you humble yourself before God and ask for his intervention, how long does your humility last once he's answered your prayer?

THE PLAGUE OF FLIES

²⁰Then the LORD said to Moses, "Get up early in the morning and confront Pharaoh as he goes to the water and say to him, 'This is what the LORD says: Let my people go, so that they may worship me. ²¹If you do not let my people go, I will send swarms of flies on you and your officials, on your people and into your houses. The houses of the Egyptians will be full of flies, and even the ground where they are.

²²" 'But on that day I will deal differently with the land of Goshen, where my people live; no swarms of flies will be there, so that you will know that I, the LORD, am in this land. ²³I will make a distinctionᵃ between my people and your people. This miraculous sign will occur tomorrow.' "

²⁴And the LORD did this. Dense swarms of flies poured into Pharaoh's palace and into the houses of his officials, and throughout Egypt the land was ruined by the flies.

²⁵Then Pharaoh summoned Moses and Aaron and said, "Go, sacrifice to your God here in the land."

²⁶But Moses said, "That would not be right. The sacrifices we offer the LORD our God would be detestable to the Egyptians. And if we offer sacrifices that are detestable in their eyes, will they not stone us? ²⁷We must take a three-day journey into the desert to offer sacrifices to the LORD our God, as he commands us."

²⁸Pharaoh said, "I will let you go to offer sacrifices to the LORD your God in the desert, but you must not go very far. Now pray for me."

²⁹Moses answered, "As soon as I leave you, I will pray to the LORD, and tomorrow the flies will leave Pharaoh and his officials and his people. Only be sure that Pharaoh does not act deceitfully again by not letting the people go to offer sacrifices to the LORD."

³⁰Then Moses left Pharaoh and prayed to the LORD, ³¹and the LORD did what Moses asked: The flies left Pharaoh and his officials and his people; not a fly remained. ³²But this time also Pharaoh hardened his heart and would not let the people go.

THE PLAGUE ON LIVESTOCK

9 Then the LORD said to Moses, "Go to Pharaoh and say to him, 'This is what the LORD, the God of the Hebrews, says: "Let my people go, so that they may worship me." ²If you refuse to let them go and continue to hold them back, ³the hand of the LORD will bring a terrible plague on your livestock in the field—on your horses and donkeys and camels and on your cattle and sheep and goats. ⁴But the LORD will make a distinction between the livestock of Israel and that of Egypt, so that no animal belonging to the Israelites will die.' "

⁵The LORD set a time and said, "Tomorrow the LORD will do this in the land." ⁶And the next day the

ᵃ 23 Septuagint and Vulgate; Hebrew will put a deliverance

Lord did it: All the livestock of the Egyptians died, but not one animal belonging to the Israelites died. [7]Pharaoh sent men to investigate and found that not even one of the animals of the Israelites had died. Yet his heart was unyielding and he would not let the people go.

Refusing to Quit

How long did it take you to learn to ride a bike without training wheels? Or learn to water-ski? Or complete the last level of your favorite video game? What if you'd given up on bike riding the first time you fell down? What if you'd quit water-skiing the first time you got a mouthful of lake water? What if you'd put away your game cartridge for good the first time you lost? You would have missed the thrill of success and that feeling that comes when your hard work finally pays off. Think about that the next time you get discouraged because a friend or family member refuses to listen to anything you say about God. Remember—persistence pays off.

THE PLAGUE OF BOILS

[8]Then the Lord said to Moses and Aaron, "Take handfuls of soot from a furnace and have Moses toss it into the air in the presence of Pharaoh. [9]It will become fine dust over the whole land of Egypt, and festering boils will break out on men and animals throughout the land."

[10]So they took soot from a furnace and stood before Pharaoh. Moses tossed it into the air, and festering boils broke out on men and animals. [11]The magicians could not stand before Moses because of the boils that were on them and on all the Egyptians. [12]But the Lord hardened Pharaoh's heart and he would not listen to Moses and Aaron, just as the Lord had said to Moses.

THE PLAGUE OF HAIL

[13]Then the Lord said to Moses, "Get up early in the morning, confront Pharaoh and say to him, 'This is what the Lord, the God of the Hebrews, says: Let my people go, so that they may worship me, [14]or this time I will send the full force of my plagues against you and against your officials and your people, so you may know that there is no one like me in all the earth. [15]For by now I could have stretched out my hand and struck you and your people with a plague that would have wiped you off the earth. [16]But I have raised you up[a] for this very purpose, that I might show you my power and that my name might be proclaimed in all the earth. [17]You still set yourself against my people and will not let them go. [18]Therefore, at this time tomorrow I will send the worst hailstorm that has ever fallen on Egypt, from the day it was founded till now. [19]Give an order now to bring your livestock and everything you have in the field to a place of shelter, because the hail will fall on every man and animal that has not been brought in and is still out in the field, and they will die.' "

[20]Those officials of Pharaoh who feared the word of the Lord hurried to bring their slaves and their livestock inside. [21]But those who ignored the word of the Lord left their slaves and livestock in the field.

[22]Then the Lord said to Moses, "Stretch out your hand toward the sky so that hail will fall all over Egypt—on men and animals and on everything growing in the fields of Egypt." [23]When Moses stretched out his staff toward the sky, the Lord sent thunder and hail, and lightning flashed down to the ground. So the Lord rained hail on the land of Egypt; [24]hail fell and lightning flashed back and forth. It was the worst storm in all the land of Egypt since it had become a nation. [25]Throughout Egypt hail struck everything in the fields—both men and animals; it beat down everything growing in the fields and stripped every tree. [26]The only place it did not hail was the land of Goshen, where the Israelites were.

[27]Then Pharaoh summoned Moses and Aaron. "This time I have sinned," he said to them. "The Lord is in the right, and I and my people are in the wrong. [28]Pray to the Lord, for we have had enough thunder and hail. I will let you go; you don't have to stay any longer."

[29]Moses replied, "When I have gone out of the city, I will spread out my hands in prayer to the Lord. The thunder will stop and there will be no more hail, so you may know that the earth is the Lord's. [30]But I know that you and your officials still do not fear the Lord God." [31](The flax and barley were destroyed, since the barley had headed and the flax was in bloom. [32]The wheat and spelt, however, were not destroyed, because they ripen later.)

---

[a] 16 Or have spared you

³³Then Moses left Pharaoh and went out of the city. He spread out his hands toward the LORD; the thunder and hail stopped, and the rain no longer poured down on the land. ³⁴When Pharaoh saw that the rain and hail and thunder had stopped, he sinned again: He and his officials hardened their hearts. ³⁵So Pharaoh's heart was hard and he would not let the Israelites go, just as the LORD had said through Moses.

THE PLAGUE OF LOCUSTS

10 Then the LORD said to Moses, "Go to Pharaoh, for I have hardened his heart and the hearts of his officials so that I may perform these miraculous signs of mine among them ²that you may tell your children and grandchildren how I dealt harshly with the Egyptians and how I performed my signs among them, and that you may know that I am the LORD."

NOW OR NEVER
EX 10:2

Name ten things God has done for you in the past year. Can you do it? If so, how hard did you have to think about it? If you can't name any, why not?

³So Moses and Aaron went to Pharaoh and said to him, "This is what the LORD, the God of the Hebrews, says: 'How long will you refuse to humble yourself before me? Let my people go, so that they may worship me. ⁴If you refuse to let them go, I will bring locusts into your country tomorrow. ⁵They will cover the face of the ground so that it cannot be seen. They will devour what little you have left after the hail, including every tree that is growing in your fields. ⁶They will fill your houses and those of all your officials and all the Egyptians—something neither your fathers nor your forefathers have ever seen from the day they settled in this land till now.'" Then Moses turned and left Pharaoh.

⁷Pharaoh's officials said to him, "How long will this man be a snare to us? Let the people go, so that they may worship the LORD their God. Do you not yet realize that Egypt is ruined?"

⁸Then Moses and Aaron were brought back to Pharaoh. "Go, worship the LORD your God," he said. "But just who will be going?"

⁹Moses answered, "We will go with our young and old, with our sons and daughters, and with our flocks and herds, because we are to celebrate a festival to the LORD."

¹⁰Pharaoh said, "The LORD be with you—if I let you go, along with your women and children! Clearly you are bent on evil.ᵃ ¹¹No! Have only the men go; and worship the LORD, since that's what you have been asking for." Then Moses and Aaron were driven out of Pharaoh's presence.

¹²And the LORD said to Moses, "Stretch out your hand over Egypt so that locusts will swarm over the land and devour everything growing in the fields, everything left by the hail."

¹³So Moses stretched out his staff over Egypt, and the LORD made an east wind blow across the land all that day and all that night. By morning the wind had brought the locusts; ¹⁴they invaded all Egypt and settled down in every area of the country in great numbers. Never before had there been such a plague of locusts, nor will there ever be again. ¹⁵They covered all the ground until it was black. They devoured all that was left after the hail—everything growing in the fields and the fruit on the trees. Nothing green remained on tree or plant in all the land of Egypt.

¹⁶Pharaoh quickly summoned Moses and Aaron and said, "I have sinned against the LORD your God and against you. ¹⁷Now forgive my sin once more and pray to the LORD your God to take this deadly plague away from me."

¹⁸Moses then left Pharaoh and prayed to the LORD. ¹⁹And the LORD changed the wind to a very strong west wind, which caught up the locusts and carried them into the Red Sea.ᵇ Not a locust was left anywhere in Egypt. ²⁰But the LORD hardened Pharaoh's heart, and he would not let the Israelites go.

THE PLAGUE OF DARKNESS

²¹Then the LORD said to Moses, "Stretch out your hand toward the sky so that darkness will spread over Egypt—darkness that can be felt." ²²So Moses stretched out his hand toward the sky, and total darkness covered all Egypt for three days. ²³No one could see anyone else or leave his place for three days. Yet all the Israelites had light in the places where they lived.

ᵃ *10* Or *Be careful, trouble is in store for you!*   ᵇ *19* Hebrew *Yam Suph*; that is, Sea of Reeds

²⁴Then Pharaoh summoned Moses and said, "Go, worship the LORD. Even your women and children may go with you; only leave your flocks and herds behind." ²⁵But Moses said, "You must allow us to have sacrifices and burnt offerings to present to the LORD our God. ²⁶Our livestock too must go with us; not a hoof is to be left behind. We have to use some of them in worshiping the LORD our God, and until we get there we will not know what we are to use to worship the LORD."

²⁷But the LORD hardened Pharaoh's heart, and he was not willing to let them go. ²⁸Pharaoh said to Moses, "Get out of my sight! Make sure you do not appear before me again! The day you see my face you will die."

²⁹"Just as you say," Moses replied, "I will never appear before you again."

THE PLAGUE ON THE FIRSTBORN

11 Now the LORD had said to Moses, "I will bring one more plague on Pharaoh and on Egypt. After that, he will let you go from here, and when he does, he will drive you out completely. ²Tell the people that men and women alike are to ask their neighbors for articles of silver and gold." ³(The LORD made the Egyptians favorably disposed toward the people, and Moses himself was highly regarded in Egypt by Pharaoh's officials and by the people.)

⁴So Moses said, "This is what the LORD says: 'About midnight I will go throughout Egypt. ⁵Every firstborn son in Egypt will die, from the firstborn son of Pharaoh, who sits on the throne, to the first-born son of the slave girl, who is at her hand mill, and all the firstborn of the cattle as well. ⁶There will be loud wailing throughout Egypt—worse than there has ever been or ever will be again. ⁷But among the Israelites not a dog will bark at any man or animal.' Then you will know that the LORD makes a distinction between Egypt and Israel. ⁸All these officials of yours will come to me, bowing down before me and saying, 'Go, you and all the people who follow you!' After that I will leave." Then Moses, hot with anger, left Pharaoh.

⁹The LORD had said to Moses, "Pharaoh will refuse to listen to you—so that my wonders may be multiplied in Egypt." ¹⁰Moses and Aaron performed all these wonders before Pharaoh, but the LORD hardened Pharaoh's heart, and he would not let the Israelites go out of his country.

THE PASSOVER

12 The LORD said to Moses and Aaron in Egypt, ²"This month is to be for you the first month, the first month of your year. ³Tell the whole community of Israel that on the tenth day of this month each man is to take a lamb^a for his family, one for each household. ⁴If any household is too small for a whole lamb, they must share one with their nearest neighbor, having taken into account the number of people there are. You are to determine the amount of lamb needed in accordance with what each person will eat. ⁵The animals you choose must be year-old males without defect, and you may take them from the sheep or the goats. ⁶Take care of them until the fourteenth day of the month, when all the people of the community of Israel must slaughter them at twilight. ⁷Then they are to take some of the blood and put it on the sides and tops of the doorframes of the houses where they eat the lambs. ⁸That same night they are to eat the meat roasted over the fire, along with bitter herbs, and bread made without yeast. ⁹Do not eat the meat raw or cooked in water, but roast it over the fire—head, legs and inner parts. ¹⁰Do not leave any of it till morning; if some is left till morning, you must burn it. ¹¹This is how you are to eat it: with your cloak tucked into your belt, your sandals on your feet and your staff in your hand. Eat it in haste; it is the LORD's Passover.

¹²"On that same night I will pass through Egypt and strike down every firstborn—both men and animals—and I will bring judgment on all the gods of Egypt. I am the LORD. ¹³The blood will be a sign for you on the houses where you are; and when I see the blood, I will pass over you. No destructive plague will touch you when I strike Egypt.

¹⁴"This is a day you are to commemorate; for the generations to come you shall celebrate it as a festival to the LORD—a lasting ordinance. ¹⁵For seven days you are to eat bread made without yeast. On the first day remove the yeast from your houses, for whoever eats anything with yeast in it from the first day through the seventh must be cut off from Israel. ¹⁶On the first day hold a sacred assembly, and another one on the seventh day. Do no work at all on these days, except to prepare food for everyone to eat—that is all you may do.

---

^a *3* The Hebrew word can mean *lamb* or *kid*; also in verse 4.

¹⁷"Celebrate the Feast of Unleavened Bread, because it was on this very day that I brought your divisions out of Egypt. Celebrate this day as a lasting ordinance for the generations to come. ¹⁸In the first month you are to eat bread made without yeast, from the evening of the fourteenth day until the evening of the twenty-first day. ¹⁹For seven days no yeast is to be found in your houses. And whoever eats anything with yeast in it must be cut off from the community of Israel, whether he is an alien or native-born. ²⁰Eat nothing made with yeast. Wherever you live, you must eat unleavened bread."

²¹Then Moses summoned all the elders of Israel and said to them, "Go at once and select the animals for your families and slaughter the Passover lamb. ²²Take a bunch of hyssop, dip it into the blood in the basin and put some of the blood on the top and on both sides of the doorframe. Not one of you shall go out the door of his house until morning. ²³When the LORD goes through the land to strike down the Egyptians, he will see the blood on the top and sides of the doorframe and will pass over that doorway, and he will not permit the destroyer to enter your houses and strike you down.

²⁴"Obey these instructions as a lasting ordinance for you and your descendants. ²⁵When you enter the land that the LORD will give you as he promised, observe this ceremony. ²⁶And when your children ask you, 'What does this ceremony mean to you?' ²⁷then tell them, 'It is the Passover sacrifice to the LORD, who passed over the houses of the Israelites in Egypt and spared our homes when he struck down the Egyptians.'" Then the people bowed down and worshiped. ²⁸The Israelites did just what the LORD commanded Moses and Aaron.

²⁹At midnight the LORD struck down all the firstborn in Egypt, from the firstborn of Pharaoh, who sat on the throne, to the firstborn of the prisoner, who was in the dungeon, and the firstborn of all the livestock as well. ³⁰Pharaoh and all his officials and all the Egyptians got up during the night, and there was loud wailing in Egypt, for there was not a house without someone dead.

THE EXODUS

³¹During the night Pharaoh summoned Moses and Aaron and said, "Up! Leave my people, you and the Israelites! Go, worship the LORD as you have requested. ³²Take your flocks and herds, as you have said, and go. And also bless me."

³³The Egyptians urged the people to hurry and leave the country. "For otherwise," they said, "we will all die!" ³⁴So the people took their dough before the yeast was added, and carried it on their shoulders in kneading troughs wrapped in clothing. ³⁵The Israelites did as Moses instructed and asked the Egyptians for articles of silver and gold and for clothing. ³⁶The LORD had made the Egyptians favorably disposed toward the people, and they gave them what they asked for; so they plundered the Egyptians.

³⁷The Israelites journeyed from Rameses to Succoth. There were about six hundred thousand men on foot, besides women and children. ³⁸Many other people went up with them, as well as large droves of livestock, both flocks and herds. ³⁹With the dough they had brought from Egypt, they baked cakes of unleavened bread. The dough was without yeast because they had been driven out of Egypt and did not have time to prepare food for themselves.

⁴⁰Now the length of time the Israelite people lived in Egypt[a] was 430 years. ⁴¹At the end of the 430 years, to the very day, all the LORD's divisions left Egypt. ⁴²Because the LORD kept vigil that night to bring them out of Egypt, on this night all the Israelites are to keep vigil to honor the LORD for the generations to come.

PASSOVER RESTRICTIONS

⁴³The LORD said to Moses and Aaron, "These are the regulations for the Passover:

"No foreigner is to eat of it. ⁴⁴Any slave you have bought may eat of it after you have circumcised him, ⁴⁵but a temporary resident and a hired worker may not eat of it.

⁴⁶"It must be eaten inside one house; take none of the meat outside the house. Do not break any of the bones. ⁴⁷The whole community of Israel must celebrate it.

⁴⁸"An alien living among you who wants to celebrate the LORD's Passover must have all the males in his household circumcised; then he may take part like one born in the land. No uncircumcised male may eat of it. ⁴⁹The same law applies to the native-born and to the alien living among you."

⁵⁰All the Israelites did just what the LORD had commanded Moses and Aaron. ⁵¹And on that very day the LORD brought the Israelites out of Egypt by their divisions.

ᵃ *40* Masoretic Text; Samaritan Pentateuch and Septuagint *Egypt and Canaan*

battlelines

» Performance Pressure (Sports)

Q: Now that the season's half over, how would you rate things?
A: Pretty good, I guess. We're doing better than a lot of people expected.

Q: What about your role? How do you like being the "go-to guy," the one everyone looks to when the game's on the line?
A: I guess it's kinda cool. I try not to think about it too much. If I did, it would probably mess with my head. Anyway, there's really not that much to say about it. If you make a big play or come through in the clutch, everybody's happy.

Q: And you've done that a few times.
A: Yeah, but I've also let the team down a couple times.

Q: What's that like?
A: Terrible. You replay everything in your head over and over again. Nobody on the team usually says anything, but you know they were counting on you, and you know they're disappointed. It's hard to block all that out. But if you don't forget about it and move on, it'll paralyze you the next time you're in a similar situation.

Q: So would you say the pressure to perform week in and week out is extreme?
A: Oh yeah. People don't really care what you've done during the season or even what you did last week. If you don't come through *today,* in their eyes, you're a loser.

Q: How do you deal with that?
A: I try to get ready physically, mentally and emotionally. I ask God to help me do my best. Then I just go out there and give it all I've got. If we come out on top, great. If we don't, well, at least I can say that I did all I could do. If that's not good enough for other people, so be it. I'm not going to make myself crazy over it. My life is about a whole lot more than what I do in a game that nobody's even going to remember five years from now.

» Measuring Your Worth

What makes us valuable? Winning? Money? Talent? Strength?

Consider the words of an ancient prophet: "This is what the LORD says: 'Let not the wise man boast of his wisdom or the strong man boast of his strength or the rich man boast of his riches, but let him who boasts boast about this: that he understands and knows me, that I am the LORD, who exercises kindness, justice and righteousness on earth, for in these I delight,' declares the LORD" (Jeremiah 9:23–24).

Don't skim over that lightly! Being loved eternally by God and developing a solid relationship with him is where we discover our true worth.

Remember—at the end of the game, God looks at your heart rather than the scoreboard.

Read more about competition at www.RevolutionBible.com.

CONSECRATION OF THE FIRSTBORN

13 The LORD said to Moses, 2"Consecrate to me every firstborn male. The first offspring of every womb among the Israelites belongs to me, whether man or animal."

3Then Moses said to the people, "Commemorate this day, the day you came out of Egypt, out of the land of slavery, because the LORD brought you out of it with a mighty hand. Eat nothing containing yeast. 4Today, in the month of Abib, you are leaving. 5When the LORD brings you into the land of the Canaanites, Hittites, Amorites, Hivites and Jebusites—the land he swore to your forefathers to give you, a land flowing with milk and honey—you are to observe this ceremony in this month: 6For seven days eat bread made without yeast and on the seventh day hold a festival to the LORD. 7Eat unleavened bread during those seven days; nothing with yeast in it is to be seen among you, nor shall any yeast be seen anywhere within your borders. 8On that day tell your son, 'I do this because of what the LORD did for me when I came out of Egypt.' 9This observance will be for you like a sign on your hand and a reminder on your forehead that the law of the LORD is to be on your lips. For the LORD brought you out of Egypt with his mighty hand. 10You must keep this ordinance at the appointed time year after year.

11"After the LORD brings you into the land of the Canaanites and gives it to you, as he promised on oath to you and your forefathers, 12you are to give over to the LORD the first offspring of every womb. All the firstborn males of your livestock belong to the LORD. 13Redeem with a lamb every firstborn donkey, but if you do not redeem it, break its neck. Redeem every firstborn among your sons.

14"In days to come, when your son asks you, 'What does this mean?' say to him, 'With a mighty hand the LORD brought us out of Egypt, out of the land of slavery. 15When Pharaoh stubbornly refused to let us go, the LORD killed every firstborn in Egypt, both man and animal. This is why I sacrifice to the LORD the first male offspring of every womb and redeem each of my firstborn sons.' 16And it will be like a sign on your hand and a symbol on your forehead that the LORD brought us out of Egypt with his mighty hand."

NOW OR NEVER
EX 13:6–9

Think your calendar has enough room for a few more Thanksgiving Day celebrations? Try setting aside a day every month or so to think about the things God has done for you and to give him some special show of appreciation.

CROSSING THE SEA

17When Pharaoh let the people go, God did not lead them on the road through the Philistine country, though that was shorter. For God said, "If they face war, they might change their minds and return to Egypt." 18So God led the people around by the desert road toward the Red Sea.[a] The Israelites went up out of Egypt armed for battle.

19Moses took the bones of Joseph with him because Joseph had made the sons of Israel swear an oath. He had said, "God will surely come to your aid, and then you must carry my bones up with you from this place."[b]

20After leaving Succoth they camped at Etham on the edge of the desert. 21By day the LORD went ahead of them in a pillar of cloud to guide them on their way and by night in a pillar of fire to give them light, so that they could travel by day or night. 22Neither the pillar of cloud by day nor the pillar of fire by night left its place in front of the people.

NOW OR NEVER
EX 13:17–18

God may not always take you on the quickest route, but he'll always get you to where you need to be, when you need to be there.

14 Then the LORD said to Moses, 2"Tell the Israelites to turn back and encamp near Pi Hahiroth, between Migdol and the sea. They are to encamp by the sea, directly opposite Baal Zephon. 3Pharaoh will think, 'The Israelites are wandering around the land in confusion,

---

[a] 18 Hebrew *Yam Suph*; that is, Sea of Reeds   [b] 19 See Gen. 50:25.

hemmed in by the desert.' [4]And I will harden Pharaoh's heart, and he will pursue them. But I will gain glory for myself through Pharaoh and all his army, and the Egyptians will know that I am the LORD." So the Israelites did this.

[5]When the king of Egypt was told that the people had fled, Pharaoh and his officials changed their minds about them and said, "What have we done? We have let the Israelites go and have lost their services!" [6]So he had his chariot made ready and took his army with him. [7]He took six hundred of the best chariots, along with all the other chariots of Egypt, with officers over all of them. [8]The LORD hardened the heart of Pharaoh king of Egypt, so that he pursued the Israelites, who were marching out boldly. [9]The Egyptians—all Pharaoh's horses and chariots, horsemen[a] and troops—pursued the Israelites and overtook them as they camped by the sea near Pi Hahiroth, opposite Baal Zephon.

[10]As Pharaoh approached, the Israelites looked up, and there were the Egyptians, marching after them. They were terrified and cried out to the LORD. [11]They said to Moses, "Was it because there were no graves in Egypt that you brought us to the desert to die? What have you done to us by bringing us out of Egypt? [12]Didn't we say to you in Egypt, 'Leave us alone; let us serve the Egyptians'? It would have been better for us to serve the Egyptians than to die in the desert!"

[13]Moses answered the people, "Do not be afraid. Stand firm and you will see the deliverance the LORD will bring you today. The Egyptians you see today you will never see again. [14]The LORD will fight for you; you need only to be still."

[15]Then the LORD said to Moses, "Why are you crying out to me? Tell the Israelites to move on. [16]Raise your staff and stretch out your hand over the sea to divide the water so that the Israelites can go through the sea on dry ground. [17]I will harden the hearts of the Egyptians so that they will go in after them. And I will gain glory through Pharaoh and all his army, through his chariots and his horsemen. [18]The Egyptians will know that I am the LORD when I gain glory through Pharaoh, his chariots and his horsemen."

NOW OR NEVER

EX 14:13–14

There's nothing remarkable about trusting God and praising him when everything's going your way. But if you can keep that attitude of trust and praise when things go seriously wrong, you're going to open a lot of people's eyes to what a relationship with God is really like.

[19]Then the angel of God, who had been traveling in front of Israel's army, withdrew and went behind them. The pillar of cloud also moved from in front and stood behind them, [20]coming between the armies of Egypt and Israel. Throughout the night the cloud brought darkness to the one side and light to the other side; so neither went near the other all night long.

[21]Then Moses stretched out his hand over the sea, and all that night the LORD drove the sea back with a strong east wind and turned it into dry land. The waters were divided, [22]and the Israelites went through the sea on dry ground, with a wall of water on their right and on their left.

[23]The Egyptians pursued them, and all Pharaoh's horses and chariots and horsemen followed them into the sea. [24]During the last watch of the night the LORD looked down from the pillar of fire and cloud at the Egyptian army and threw it into confusion. [25]He made the wheels of their chariots come off[b] so that they had difficulty driving. And the Egyptians said, "Let's get away from the Israelites! The LORD is fighting for them against Egypt."

[26]Then the LORD said to Moses, "Stretch out your hand over the sea so that the waters may flow back over the Egyptians and their chariots and horsemen." [27]Moses stretched out his hand over the sea, and at daybreak the sea went back to its place. The Egyptians were fleeing toward[c] it, and the LORD swept them into the sea. [28]The water flowed back and covered the chariots and horsemen—the entire army of Pharaoh that had followed the Israelites into the sea. Not one of them survived.

[29]But the Israelites went through the sea on dry ground, with a wall of water on their right and on their left. [30]That day the LORD saved Israel from the hands of the Egyptians, and Israel saw the Egyptians lying dead on the shore. [31]And when the Israelites saw the great power the LORD displayed against the Egyptians, the people feared the LORD and put their trust in him and in Moses his servant.

THE SONG OF MOSES AND MIRIAM

15 Then Moses and the Israelites sang this song to the LORD:

"I will sing to the LORD,
    for he is highly exalted.
The horse and its rider
    he has hurled into the sea.
² The LORD is my strength and my song;
    he has become my salvation.
He is my God, and I will praise him,
    my father's God, and I will exalt him.
³ The LORD is a warrior;
    the LORD is his name.
⁴ Pharaoh's chariots and his army
    he has hurled into the sea.
The best of Pharaoh's officers
    are drowned in the Red Sea. ª
⁵ The deep waters have covered them;
    they sank to the depths like a stone.

⁶ "Your right hand, O LORD,
    was majestic in power.
Your right hand, O LORD,
    shattered the enemy.
⁷ In the greatness of your majesty
    you threw down those who opposed you.
You unleashed your burning anger;
    it consumed them like stubble.
⁸ By the blast of your nostrils
    the waters piled up.
The surging waters stood firm like a wall;
    the deep waters congealed in the heart of the sea.

⁹ "The enemy boasted,
    'I will pursue, I will overtake them.
I will divide the spoils;
    I will gorge myself on them.
I will draw my sword
    and my hand will destroy them.'
¹⁰ But you blew with your breath,
    and the sea covered them.
They sank like lead
    in the mighty waters.

¹¹ "Who among the gods is like you, O LORD?
    Who is like you—
        majestic in holiness,
        awesome in glory,
        working wonders?
¹² You stretched out your right hand
    and the earth swallowed them.

¹³ "In your unfailing love you will lead
    the people you have redeemed.
In your strength you will guide them
    to your holy dwelling.

ª *4* Hebrew *Yam Suph*; that is, Sea of Reeds; also in verse 22

¹⁴The nations will hear and tremble;
    anguish will grip the people of Philistia.
¹⁵The chiefs of Edom will be terrified,
    the leaders of Moab will be seized with trembling,
the people[a] of Canaan will melt away;
¹⁶   terror and dread will fall upon them.
By the power of your arm
    they will be as still as a stone—
until your people pass by, O LORD,
    until the people you bought[b] pass by.
¹⁷You will bring them in and plant them
    on the mountain of your inheritance—
the place, O LORD, you made for your dwelling,
    the sanctuary, O Lord, your hands established.
¹⁸The LORD will reign
    for ever and ever."

¹⁹When Pharaoh's horses, chariots and horsemen[c] went into the sea, the LORD brought the waters of the sea back over them, but the Israelites walked through the sea on dry ground. ²⁰Then Miriam the prophetess, Aaron's sister, took a tambourine in her hand, and all the women followed her, with tambourines and dancing. ²¹Miriam sang to them:

"Sing to the LORD,
    for he is highly exalted.
The horse and its rider
    he has hurled into the sea."

THE WATERS OF MARAH AND ELIM

²²Then Moses led Israel from the Red Sea and they went into the Desert of Shur. For three days they traveled in the desert without finding water. ²³When they came to Marah, they could not drink its water because it was bitter. (That is why the place is called Marah.[d]) ²⁴So the people grumbled against Moses, saying, "What are we to drink?"

²⁵Then Moses cried out to the LORD, and the LORD showed him a piece of wood. He threw it into the water, and the water became sweet.

There the LORD made a decree and a law for them, and there he tested them. ²⁶He said, "If you listen carefully to the voice of the LORD your God and do what is right in his eyes, if you pay attention to his commands and keep all his decrees, I will not bring on you any of the diseases I brought on the Egyptians, for I am the LORD, who heals you."

²⁷Then they came to Elim, where there were twelve springs and seventy palm trees, and they camped there near the water.

MANNA AND QUAIL

16

The whole Israelite community set out from Elim and came to the Desert of Sin, which is between Elim and Sinai, on the fifteenth day of the second month after they had come out of Egypt. ²In the desert the whole community grumbled against Moses and Aaron. ³The Israelites said to them, "If only we had died by the LORD's hand in Egypt! There we sat around pots of meat and ate all the food we wanted, but you have brought us out into this desert to starve this entire assembly to death."

⁴Then the LORD said to Moses, "I will rain down bread from heaven for you. The people are to go out each day and gather enough for that day. In this way I will test them and see whether they will follow my instructions. ⁵On the sixth day they are to prepare what they bring in, and that is to be twice as much as they gather on the other days."

⁶So Moses and Aaron said to all the Israelites, "In the evening you will know that it was the LORD who brought you out of Egypt, ⁷and in the morning you will see the glory of the LORD, because he has heard your grumbling against him. Who are we, that you should grumble against us?" ⁸Moses also

---

^a 15 Or rulers   ^b 16 Or created   ^c 19 Or charioteers   ^d 23 Marah means bitter.

said, "You will know that it was the LORD when he gives you meat to eat in the evening and all the bread you want in the morning, because he has heard your grumbling against him. Who are we? You are not grumbling against us, but against the LORD."

⁹Then Moses told Aaron, "Say to the entire Israelite community, 'Come before the LORD, for he has heard your grumbling.' "

¹⁰While Aaron was speaking to the whole Israelite community, they looked toward the desert, and there was the glory of the LORD appearing in the cloud.

¹¹The LORD said to Moses, ¹²"I have heard the grumbling of the Israelites. Tell them, 'At twilight you will eat meat, and in the morning you will be filled with bread. Then you will know that I am the LORD your God.' "

¹³That evening quail came and covered the camp, and in the morning there was a layer of dew around the camp. ¹⁴When the dew was gone, thin flakes like frost on the ground appeared on the desert floor. ¹⁵When the Israelites saw it, they said to each other, "What is it?" For they did not know what it was.

Moses said to them, "It is the bread the LORD has given you to eat. ¹⁶This is what the LORD has commanded: 'Each one is to gather as much as he needs. Take an omerᵃ for each person you have in your tent.' "

¹⁷The Israelites did as they were told; some gathered much, some little. ¹⁸And when they measured it by the omer, he who gathered much did not have too much, and he who gathered little did not have too little. Each one gathered as much as he needed.

¹⁹Then Moses said to them, "No one is to keep any of it until morning."

²⁰However, some of them paid no attention to Moses; they kept part of it until morning, but it was full of maggots and began to smell. So Moses was angry with them.

²¹Each morning everyone gathered as much as he needed, and when the sun grew hot, it melted away. ²²On the sixth day, they gathered twice as much—two omersᵇ for each person—and the leaders of the community came and reported this to Moses. ²³He said to them, "This is what the LORD commanded: 'Tomorrow is to be a day of rest, a holy Sabbath to the LORD. So bake what you want to bake and boil what you want to boil. Save whatever is left and keep it until morning.' "

²⁴So they saved it until morning, as Moses commanded, and it did not stink or get maggots in it. ²⁵"Eat it today," Moses said, "because today is a Sabbath to the LORD. You will not find any of it on the ground today. ²⁶Six days you are to gather it, but on the seventh day, the Sabbath, there will not be any."

²⁷Nevertheless, some of the people went out on the seventh day to gather it, but they found none. ²⁸Then the LORD said to Moses, "How long will youᶜ refuse to keep my commands and my instructions? ²⁹Bear in mind that the LORD has given you the Sabbath; that is why on the sixth day he gives you bread for two days. Everyone is to stay where he is on the seventh day; no one is to go out." ³⁰So the people rested on the seventh day.

³¹The people of Israel called the bread manna.ᵈ It was white like coriander seed and tasted like wafers made with honey. ³²Moses said, "This is what the LORD has commanded: 'Take an omer of manna and keep it for the generations to come, so they can see the bread I gave you to eat in the desert when I brought you out of Egypt.' "

³³So Moses said to Aaron, "Take a jar and put an omer of manna in it. Then place it before the LORD to be kept for the generations to come."

³⁴As the LORD commanded Moses, Aaron put the manna in front of the Testimony, that it might be kept. ³⁵The Israelites ate manna forty years, until they came to a land that was settled; they ate manna until they reached the border of Canaan.

³⁶(An omer is one tenth of an ephah.)

NOW OR NEVER
EX 16:14–16

Do you ever worry about where your next meal will come from or if you'll have a place to live tomorrow? Ever stop to think that, ultimately, it's God who provides these things? Don't forget to praise God for his everyday blessings.

ᵃ 16 That is, probably about 2 quarts (about 2 liters); also in verses 18, 32, 33 and 36   ᵇ 22 That is, probably about 4 quarts (about 4.5 liters)   ᶜ 28 The Hebrew is plural.   ᵈ 31 Manna means What is it? (see verse 15).

WATER FROM THE ROCK

17 The whole Israelite community set out from the Desert of Sin, traveling from place to place as the LORD commanded. They camped at Rephidim, but there was no water for the people to drink. ²So they quarreled with Moses and said, "Give us water to drink."

Moses replied, "Why do you quarrel with me? Why do you put the LORD to the test?"

³But the people were thirsty for water there, and they grumbled against Moses. They said, "Why did you bring us up out of Egypt to make us and our children and livestock die of thirst?"

⁴Then Moses cried out to the LORD, "What am I to do with these people? They are almost ready to stone me."

⁵The LORD answered Moses, "Walk on ahead of the people. Take with you some of the elders of Israel and take in your hand the staff with which you struck the Nile, and go. ⁶I will stand there before you by the rock at Horeb. Strike the rock, and water will come out of it for the people to drink." So Moses did this in the sight of the elders of Israel. ⁷And he called the place Massah ª and Meribah ᵇ because the Israelites quarreled and because they tested the LORD saying, "Is the LORD among us or not?"

THE AMALEKITES DEFEATED

⁸The Amalekites came and attacked the Israelites at Rephidim. ⁹Moses said to Joshua, "Choose some of our men and go out to fight the Amalekites. Tomorrow I will stand on top of the hill with the staff of God in my hands."

¹⁰So Joshua fought the Amalekites as Moses had ordered, and Moses, Aaron and Hur went to the top of the hill. ¹¹As long as Moses held up his hands, the Israelites were winning, but whenever he lowered his hands, the Amalekites were winning. ¹²When Moses' hands grew tired, they took a stone and put it under him and he sat on it. Aaron and Hur held his hands up—one on one side, one on the other—so that his hands remained steady till sunset. ¹³So Joshua overcame the Amalekite army with the sword.

¹⁴Then the LORD said to Moses, "Write this on a scroll as something to be remembered and make sure that Joshua hears it, because I will completely blot out the memory of Amalek from under heaven."

NOW OR NEVER
EX 17:10–13

Are there people around you who are worn out and need someone to hold up their arms? Maybe your arms are getting tired and you need someone. Ask God. His strength will save you.

¹⁵Moses built an altar and called it The LORD is my Banner. ¹⁶He said, "For hands were lifted up to the throne of the LORD. The ᶜ LORD will be at war against the Amalekites from generation to generation."

JETHRO VISITS MOSES

18 Now Jethro, the priest of Midian and father-in-law of Moses, heard of everything God had done for Moses and for his people Israel, and how the LORD had brought Israel out of Egypt.

²After Moses had sent away his wife Zipporah, his father-in-law Jethro received her ³and her two sons. One son was named Gershom, ᵈ for Moses said, "I have become an alien in a foreign land"; ⁴and the other was named Eliezer, ᵉ for he said, "My father's God was my helper; he saved me from the sword of Pharaoh."

⁵Jethro, Moses' father-in-law, together with Moses' sons and wife, came to him in the desert, where he was camped near the mountain of God. ⁶Jethro had sent word to him, "I, your father-in-law Jethro, am coming to you with your wife and her two sons."

⁷So Moses went out to meet his father-in-law and bowed down and kissed him. They greeted each other and then went into the tent. ⁸Moses told his father-in-law about everything the LORD had done to Pharaoh and the Egyptians for Israel's sake and about all the hardships they had met along the way and how the LORD had saved them.

⁹Jethro was delighted to hear about all the good things the LORD had done for Israel in rescuing

---

ª 7 *Massah* means *testing.*   ᵇ 7 *Meribah* means *quarreling.*   ᶜ 16 Or *"Because a hand was against the throne of the LORD, the*
ᵈ 3 *Gershom* sounds like the Hebrew for *an alien there.*   ᵉ 4 *Eliezer* means *my God is helper.*

them from the hand of the Egyptians. ¹⁰He said, "Praise be to the LORD, who rescued you from the hand of the Egyptians and of Pharaoh, and who rescued the people from the hand of the Egyptians. ¹¹Now I know that the LORD is greater than all other gods, for he did this to those who had treated Israel arrogantly." ¹²Then Jethro, Moses' father-in-law, brought a burnt offering and other sacrifices to God, and Aaron came with all the elders of Israel to eat bread with Moses' father-in-law in the presence of God.

¹³The next day Moses took his seat to serve as judge for the people, and they stood around him from morning till evening. ¹⁴When his father-in-law saw all that Moses was doing for the people, he said, "What is this you are doing for the people? Why do you alone sit as judge, while all these people stand around you from morning till evening?"

¹⁵Moses answered him, "Because the people come to me to seek God's will. ¹⁶Whenever they have a dispute, it is brought to me, and I decide between the parties and inform them of God's decrees and laws."

¹⁷Moses' father-in-law replied, "What you are doing is not good. ¹⁸You and these people who come to you will only wear yourselves out. The work is too heavy for you; you cannot handle it alone. ¹⁹Listen now to me and I will give you some advice, and may God be with you. You must be the people's representative before God and bring their disputes to him. ²⁰Teach them the decrees and laws, and show them the way to live and the duties they are to perform. ²¹But select capable men from all the people—men who fear God, trustworthy men who hate dishonest gain—and appoint them as officials over thousands, hundreds, fifties and tens. ²²Have them serve as judges for the people at all times, but have them bring every difficult case to you; the simple cases they can decide themselves. That will make your load lighter, because they will share it with you. ²³If you do this and God so commands, you will be able to stand the strain, and all these people will go home satisfied."

²⁴Moses listened to his father-in-law and did everything he said. ²⁵He chose capable men from all Israel and made them leaders of the people, officials over thousands, hundreds, fifties and tens. ²⁶They served as judges for the people at all times. The difficult cases they brought to Moses, but the simple ones they decided themselves.

²⁷Then Moses sent his father-in-law on his way, and Jethro returned to his own country.

AT MOUNT SINAI

19 In the third month after the Israelites left Egypt—on the very day—they came to the Desert of Sinai. ²After they set out from Rephidim, they entered the Desert of Sinai, and Israel camped there in the desert in front of the mountain.

³Then Moses went up to God, and the LORD called to him from the mountain and said, "This is what you are to say to the house of Jacob and what you are to tell the people of Israel: ⁴'You yourselves have seen what I did to Egypt, and how I carried you on eagles' wings and brought you to myself. ⁵Now if you obey me fully and keep my covenant, then out of all nations you will be my treasured possession.

Learning From Others

Everyone in your life is a teacher . . . if you're willing to learn. Every person you know has a different set of life experiences, a unique body of knowledge and a distinctive perspective on the world. No one else in the world brings exactly what someone else brings to the table. That means you can come away from every conversation you have with a little more knowledge and wisdom than you had before. The key is to listen and ask questions. Instead of always thinking about what you're going to say next, think of what you can learn.

> live the adventure » Ex 18:13-26

challenge notes

To: my_son

heavenly_father: the privilege of being my son carries the responsibility to live like a child of mine should live. it's your job not only to tell others about me, but also to *show* them what a difference being my child can make in their lives.

EX 19:5-6

Although the whole earth is mine, [6]you[a] will be for me a kingdom of priests and a holy nation.' These are the words you are to speak to the Israelites."

[7]So Moses went back and summoned the elders of the people and set before them all the words the LORD had commanded him to speak. [8]The people all responded together, "We will do everything the LORD has said." So Moses brought their answer back to the LORD.

[9]The LORD said to Moses, "I am going to come to you in a dense cloud, so that the people will hear me speaking with you and will always put their trust in you." Then Moses told the LORD what the people had said.

[10]And the LORD said to Moses, "Go to the people and consecrate them today and tomorrow. Have them wash their clothes [11]and be ready by the third day, because on that day the LORD will come down on Mount Sinai in the sight of all the people. [12]Put limits for the people around the mountain and tell them, 'Be careful that you do not go up the mountain or touch the foot of it. Whoever touches the mountain shall surely be put to death. [13]He shall surely be stoned or shot with arrows; not a hand is to be laid on him. Whether man or animal, he shall not be permitted to live.' Only when the ram's horn sounds a long blast may they go up to the mountain."

[14]After Moses had gone down the mountain to the people, he consecrated them, and they washed their clothes. [15]Then he said to the people, "Prepare yourselves for the third day. Abstain from sexual relations."

[16]On the morning of the third day there was thunder and lightning, with a thick cloud over the mountain, and a very loud trumpet blast. Everyone in the camp trembled. [17]Then Moses led the people out of the camp to meet with God, and they stood at the foot of the mountain. [18]Mount Sinai was covered with smoke, because the LORD descended on it in fire. The smoke billowed up from it like smoke from a furnace, the whole mountain[b] trembled violently, [19]and the sound of the trumpet grew louder and louder. Then Moses spoke and the voice of God answered him.[c]

[20]The LORD descended to the top of Mount Sinai and called Moses to the top of the mountain. So Moses went up [21]and the LORD said to him, "Go down and warn the people so they do not force their way through to see the LORD and many of them perish. [22]Even the priests, who approach the LORD, must consecrate themselves, or the LORD will break out against them."

[23]Moses said to the LORD, "The people cannot come up Mount Sinai, because you yourself warned us, 'Put limits around the mountain and set it apart as holy.' "

[24]The LORD replied, "Go down and bring Aaron up with you. But the priests and the people must not force their way through to come up to the LORD, or he will break out against them."

[25]So Moses went down to the people and told them.

THE TEN COMMANDMENTS

20

And God spoke all these words:

[2]"I am the LORD your God, who brought you out of Egypt, out of the land of slavery.

[3]"You shall have no other gods before[d] me.

[4]"You shall not make for yourself an idol in the form of anything in heaven above or on the earth beneath or in the waters below. [5]You shall not bow down to them or worship them; for I, the LORD your God, am a jealous God, punishing the children for the sin of the fathers to the third and fourth generation of those who hate me, [6]but showing love to a thousand ⌊generations⌋ of those who love me and keep my commandments.

[7]"You shall not misuse the name of the LORD your God, for the LORD will not hold anyone guiltless who misuses his name.

[8]"Remember the Sabbath day by keeping it holy. [9]Six days you shall labor and do all your work,

now or never

EX 20:8-11

The day may have changed, but our need for a "sabbath" rest hasn't. What do you do to make Sunday more than just another day? What are some specific ways you can use your Sundays to honor God?

---

[a] 5,6 Or possession, for the whole earth is mine. [6]You   [b] 18 Most Hebrew manuscripts; a few Hebrew manuscripts and Septuagint all the people   [c] 19 Or and God answered him with thunder   [d] 3 Or besides

battlelines

» Rules of Engagement (Adultery)

Q: How's everything at home?
A: Not good. My dad's been cheating on my mom. He doesn't know that I know, but I found out. At least I *figured* it out.

Q: How do you know?
A: I've known for a while that my mom and dad have been having trouble with their marriage. I also know that my dad's assistant is totally hot. I went to his office a few weeks back, and he didn't know I was coming. When I showed up I saw her massaging his neck. And if that's not enough to convince you, last week I was looking in my dad's car for a missing notebook, and I found a receipt for a hotel room that's not far from his office. So you do the math.

Q: What are you going to do now?
A: I wish I knew. I keep going back and forth in my head. Do I tell my mom? Do I confront my dad? Or do I just shut up and get on with my life? I told a couple of friends about the situation. Tony was like, "That's just how it is. Men cheat; it's in our genes." Chan didn't say much. He mostly just listened. Although he did finally say, "What about your dad's brother? Your dad really looks up to him. Maybe he could help."

Q: Do you think that would work?
A: Maybe. My uncle *is* a solid Christian. Everybody respects him. If anyone could help, he could. I just know that if I sit back and do nothing, I'm gonna hate myself down the road.

» Sticking Your Neck Out

Galatians 6:1 says, "Brothers , if someone is caught in a sin, you who are spiritual should restore him gently. But watch yourself, or you also may be tempted." When people we love are messing up, we don't have the luxury of looking the other way. Real men don't run. Real men deal with trouble head-on, while keeping three things in mind.

❶ Be bold.
Confrontation goes totally against our "live and let live" culture. But if somebody you love is doing something that might ruin his or her life (and others' lives), can you really afford to be silent?

❷ Be gentle.
Your goal is to help bring people back to spiritual, emotional and relational health by "speaking the truth in love" (Ephesians 4:15). If you're too upset to keep your cool, get someone you trust and respect to help.

❸ Be careful.
Ryan's friend Tony was almost right. It is within our genetic make-up to mess up. That should keep us humble, but it doesn't mean we have to sin. It's up to us to decide whether we actually give in to it (see 1 Corinthians 10:13). We do have a choice.

For more on dealing with adultery, go to www.RevolutionBible.com.

[10]but the seventh day is a Sabbath to the LORD your God. On it you shall not do any work, neither you, nor your son or daughter, nor your manservant or maidservant, nor your animals, nor the alien within your gates. [11]For in six days the LORD made the heavens and the earth, the sea, and all that is in them, but he rested on the seventh day. Therefore the LORD blessed the Sabbath day and made it holy.

[12] "Honor your father and your mother, so that you may live long in the land the LORD your God is giving you.

[13] "You shall not murder.

[14] "You shall not commit adultery.

[15] "You shall not steal.

[16] "You shall not give false testimony against your neighbor.

[17] "You shall not covet your neighbor's house. You shall not covet your neighbor's wife, or his manservant or maidservant, his ox or donkey, or anything that belongs to your neighbor."

[18]When the people saw the thunder and lightning and heard the trumpet and saw the mountain in smoke, they trembled with fear. They stayed at a distance [19]and said to Moses, "Speak to us yourself and we will listen. But do not have God speak to us or we will die."

[20]Moses said to the people, "Do not be afraid. God has come to test you, so that the fear of God will be with you to keep you from sinning."

[21]The people remained at a distance, while Moses approached the thick darkness where God was.

IDOLS AND ALTARS

[22]Then the LORD said to Moses, "Tell the Israelites this: 'You have seen for yourselves that I have spoken to you from heaven: [23]Do not make any gods to be alongside me; do not make for yourselves gods of silver or gods of gold.

[24]" 'Make an altar of earth for me and sacrifice on it your burnt offerings and fellowship offerings,[a] your sheep and goats and your cattle. Wherever I cause my name to be honored, I will come to you and bless you. [25]If you make an altar of stones for me, do not build it with dressed stones, for you will defile it if you use a tool on it. [26]And do not go up to my altar on steps, lest your nakedness be exposed on it.'

21

"These are the laws you are to set before them:

HEBREW SERVANTS

[2]"If you buy a Hebrew servant, he is to serve you for six years. But in the seventh year, he shall go free, without paying anything. [3]If he comes alone, he is to go free alone; but if he has a wife when he comes, she is to go with him. [4]If his master gives him a wife and she bears him sons or daughters, the woman and her children shall belong to her master, and only the man shall go free.

[5]"But if the servant declares, 'I love my master and my wife and children and do not want to go free,' [6]then his master must take him before the judges.[b] He shall take him to the door or the doorpost and pierce his ear with an awl. Then he will be his servant for life.

[7]"If a man sells his daughter as a servant, she is not to go free as menservants do. [8]If she does not please the master who has selected her for himself,[c] he must let her be redeemed. He has no right to sell her to foreigners, because he has broken faith with her. [9]If he selects her for his son, he must grant her the rights of a daughter. [10]If he marries another woman, he must not deprive the first one of her food,

---

Respecting Parents

Have you ever thought about how hard it is to be a parent? Think about it. Your folks were once kids like you, with nothing more to worry about than passing an English test or finding something to do on Saturday night. Now they've got people depending on them for food, shelter and clothing—not to mention discipline and life skills. Talk about pressure! And it's not like they went to parenting school or majored in fatherhood and motherhood in college. They've had to learn how to be parents the hard way, through trial and error. Of course they're going to make mistakes—sometimes big ones. But you've got to respect them for who they are and what they're trying to do for you, whether you like it (or agree with it) or not.

---

[a] 24 Traditionally *peace offerings* [b] 6 Or *before God* [c] 8 Or *master so that he does not choose her*

clothing and marital rights. ¹¹If he does not provide her with these three things, she is to go free, without any payment of money.

PERSONAL INJURIES

¹²"Anyone who strikes a man and kills him shall surely be put to death. ¹³However, if he does not do it intentionally, but God lets it happen, he is to flee to a place I will designate. ¹⁴But if a man schemes and kills another man deliberately, take him away from my altar and put him to death.

¹⁵"Anyone who attacks[a] his father or his mother must be put to death.

¹⁶"Anyone who kidnaps another and either sells him or still has him when he is caught must be put to death.

¹⁷"Anyone who curses his father or mother must be put to death.

¹⁸"If men quarrel and one hits the other with a stone or with his fist[b] and he does not die but is confined to bed, ¹⁹the one who struck the blow will not be held responsible if the other gets up and walks around outside with his staff; however, he must pay the injured man for the loss of his time and see that he is completely healed.

²⁰"If a man beats his male or female slave with a rod and the slave dies as a direct result, he must be punished, ²¹but he is not to be punished if the slave gets up after a day or two, since the slave is his property.

²²"If men who are fighting hit a pregnant woman and she gives birth prematurely[c] but there is no serious injury, the offender must be fined whatever the woman's husband demands and the court allows. ²³But if there is serious injury, you are to take life for life, ²⁴eye for eye, tooth for tooth, hand for hand, foot for foot, ²⁵burn for burn, wound for wound, bruise for bruise.

NOW OR NEVER

EX 21:24–25

The next time you're tempted to give someone what you think they deserve, think about what would happen if God gave you what you deserve.

²⁶"If a man hits a manservant or maidservant in the eye and destroys it, he must let the servant go free to compensate for the eye. ²⁷And if he knocks out the tooth of a manservant or maidservant, he must let the servant go free to compensate for the tooth.

²⁸"If a bull gores a man or a woman to death, the bull must be stoned to death, and its meat must not be eaten. But the owner of the bull will not be held responsible. ²⁹If, however, the bull has had the habit of goring and the owner has been warned but has not kept it penned up and it kills a man or woman, the bull must be stoned and the owner also must be put to death. ³⁰However, if payment is demanded of him, he may redeem his life by paying whatever is demanded. ³¹This law also applies if the bull gores a son or daughter. ³²If the bull gores a male or female slave, the owner must pay thirty shekels[d] of silver to the master of the slave, and the bull must be stoned.

³³"If a man uncovers a pit or digs one and fails to cover it and an ox or a donkey falls into it, ³⁴the owner of the pit must pay for the loss; he must pay its owner, and the dead animal will be his.

³⁵"If a man's bull injures the bull of another and it dies, they are to sell the live one and divide both the money and the dead animal equally. ³⁶However, if it was known that the bull had the habit of goring, yet the owner did not keep it penned up, the owner must pay, animal for animal, and the dead animal will be his.

PROTECTION OF PROPERTY

22 "If a man steals an ox or a sheep and slaughters it or sells it, he must pay back five head of cattle for the ox and four sheep for the sheep.

²"If a thief is caught breaking in and is struck so that he dies, the defender is not guilty of bloodshed; ³but if it happens[e] after sunrise, he is guilty of bloodshed.

"A thief must certainly make restitution, but if he has nothing, he must be sold to pay for his theft.

⁴"If the stolen animal is found alive in his possession—whether ox or donkey or sheep—he must pay back double.

ᵃ 15 Or kills   ᵇ 18 Or with a tool   ᶜ 22 Or she has a miscarriage   ᵈ 32 That is, about 12 ounces (about 0.3 kilogram)   ᵉ 3 Or if he strikes him

5 "If a man grazes his livestock in a field or vineyard and lets them stray and they graze in another man's field, he must make restitution from the best of his own field or vineyard.

6 "If a fire breaks out and spreads into thornbushes so that it burns shocks of grain or standing grain or the whole field, the one who started the fire must make restitution.

7 "If a man gives his neighbor silver or goods for safekeeping and they are stolen from the neighbor's house, the thief, if he is caught, must pay back double. 8 But if the thief is not found, the owner of the house must appear before the judges[a] to determine whether he has laid his hands on the other man's property. 9 In all cases of illegal possession of an ox, a donkey, a sheep, a garment, or any other lost property about which somebody says, 'This is mine,' both parties are to bring their cases before the judges. The one whom the judges declare[b] guilty must pay back double to his neighbor.

10 "If a man gives a donkey, an ox, a sheep or any other animal to his neighbor for safekeeping and it dies or is injured or is taken away while no one is looking, 11 the issue between them will be settled by the taking of an oath before the LORD that the neighbor did not lay hands on the other person's property. The owner is to accept this, and no restitution is required. 12 But if the animal was stolen from the neighbor, he must make restitution to the owner. 13 If it was torn to pieces by a wild animal, he shall bring in the remains as evidence and he will not be required to pay for the torn animal.

14 "If a man borrows an animal from his neighbor and it is injured or dies while the owner is not present, he must make restitution. 15 But if the owner is with the animal, the borrower will not have to pay. If the animal was hired, the money paid for the hire covers the loss.

SOCIAL RESPONSIBILITY

16 "If a man seduces a virgin who is not pledged to be married and sleeps with her, he must pay the bride-price, and she shall be his wife. 17 If her father absolutely refuses to give her to him, he must still pay the bride-price for virgins.

18 "Do not allow a sorceress to live.

19 "Anyone who has sexual relations with an animal must be put to death.

20 "Whoever sacrifices to any god other than the LORD must be destroyed.[c]

21 "Do not mistreat an alien or oppress him, for you were aliens in Egypt.

22 "Do not take advantage of a widow or an orphan. 23 If you do and they cry out to me, I will certainly hear their cry. 24 My anger will be aroused, and I will kill you with the sword; your wives will become widows and your children fatherless.

25 "If you lend money to one of my people among you who is needy, do not be like a moneylender; charge him no interest.[d] 26 If you take your neighbor's cloak as a pledge, return it to him by sunset, 27 because his cloak is the only covering he has for his body. What else will he sleep in? When he cries out to me, I will hear, for I am compassionate.

28 "Do not blaspheme God[e] or curse the ruler of your people.

29 "Do not hold back offerings from your granaries or your vats.[f]

"You must give me the firstborn of your sons. 30 Do the same with your cattle and your sheep. Let them stay with their mothers for seven days, but give them to me on the eighth day.

31 "You are to be my holy people. So do not eat the meat of an animal torn by wild beasts; throw it to the dogs.

Supporting the Needy

Never pick on someone weaker than you. See, God's got this thing for underdogs. When you've got a choice between standing up for someone being bullied or piling on the abuse, do the courageous thing—the *right* thing. Give the person a helping hand or a good word, even if it causes problems for you. God has a special place in his heart for people who are rejected by others. So if you line up with anyone, make it the underdog.

---

a 8 Or before God; also in verse 9   b 9 Or whom God declares   c 20 The Hebrew term refers to the irrevocable giving over of things or persons to the LORD, often by totally destroying them.   d 25 Or excessive interest   e 28 Or Do not revile the judges   f 29 The meaning of the Hebrew for this phrase is uncertain.

LAWS OF JUSTICE AND MERCY

23

"Do not spread false reports. Do not help a wicked man by being a malicious witness.

2 "Do not follow the crowd in doing wrong. When you give testimony in a lawsuit, do not pervert justice by siding with the crowd, 3 and do not show favoritism to a poor man in his lawsuit.

4 "If you come across your enemy's ox or donkey wandering off, be sure to take it back to him. 5 If you see the donkey of someone who hates you fallen down under its load, do not leave it there; be sure you help him with it.

6 "Do not deny justice to your poor people in their lawsuits. 7 Have nothing to do with a false charge and do not put an innocent or honest person to death, for I will not acquit the guilty.

8 "Do not accept a bribe, for a bribe blinds those who see and twists the words of the righteous.

9 "Do not oppress an alien; you yourselves know how it feels to be aliens, because you were aliens in Egypt.

NOW OR NEVER
EX 23:4-5

What good does it do you to have an enemy? What do you think would happen if you decided to end all of your grudges for good right now and start treating everyone like a friend?

SABBATH LAWS

10 "For six years you are to sow your fields and harvest the crops, 11 but during the seventh year let the land lie unplowed and unused. Then the poor among your people may get food from it, and the wild animals may eat what they leave. Do the same with your vineyard and your olive grove.

12 "Six days do your work, but on the seventh day do not work, so that your ox and your donkey may rest and the slave born in your household, and the alien as well, may be refreshed.

13 "Be careful to do everything I have said to you. Do not invoke the names of other gods; do not let them be heard on your lips.

THE THREE ANNUAL FESTIVALS

14 "Three times a year you are to celebrate a festival to me.

15 "Celebrate the Feast of Unleavened Bread; for seven days eat bread made without yeast, as I commanded you. Do this at the appointed time in the month of Abib, for in that month you came out of Egypt.

"No one is to appear before me empty-handed.

16 "Celebrate the Feast of Harvest with the firstfruits of the crops you sow in your field.

"Celebrate the Feast of Ingathering at the end of the year, when you gather in your crops from the field.

17 "Three times a year all the men are to appear before the Sovereign LORD.

18 "Do not offer the blood of a sacrifice to me along with anything containing yeast.

"The fat of my festival offerings must not be kept until morning.

19 "Bring the best of the firstfruits of your soil to the house of the LORD your God.

"Do not cook a young goat in its mother's milk.

GOD'S ANGEL TO PREPARE THE WAY

20 "See, I am sending an angel ahead of you to guard you along the way and to bring you to the place I have prepared. 21 Pay attention to him and listen to what he says. Do not rebel against him; he will not forgive your rebellion, since my Name is in him. 22 If you listen carefully to what he says and do all that I say, I will be an enemy to your enemies and will oppose those who oppose you. 23 My angel will go ahead of you and bring you into the land of the Amorites, Hittites, Perizzites, Canaanites, Hivites and Jebusites, and I will wipe them out. 24 Do not bow down before their gods or worship them or follow their practices. You must demolish them and break their sacred stones to pieces. 25 Worship the LORD your God, and his blessing will be on your food and water. I will take away sickness from among you, 26 and none will miscarry or be barren in your land. I will give you a full life span.

²⁷"I will send my terror ahead of you and throw into confusion every nation you encounter. I will make all your enemies turn their backs and run. ²⁸I will send the hornet ahead of you to drive the Hivites, Canaanites and Hittites out of your way. ²⁹But I will not drive them out in a single year, because the land would become desolate and the wild animals too numerous for you. ³⁰Little by little I will drive them out before you, until you have increased enough to take possession of the land.

³¹"I will establish your borders from the Red Sea[a] to the Sea of the Philistines,[b] and from the desert to the River.[c] I will hand over to you the people who live in the land and you will drive them out before you. ³²Do not make a covenant with them or with their gods. ³³Do not let them live in your land, or they will cause you to sin against me, because the worship of their gods will certainly be a snare to you."

» live the adventure » Ex 23:24-25

Letting Your Light Shine

The Israelites weren't supposed to worship other gods when they got to the promised land. They were commanded to be *different*. So what about you? How long would it take someone to figure out that you're different? What clues would that person have to work with? Is there anything about the way you talk that

might give it away? How about the way you treat others—is there anything "Christian" about it? How about your priorities or the way you spend your time? What kind of vibes are you sending off?

THE COVENANT CONFIRMED

24

Then he said to Moses, "Come up to the LORD, you and Aaron, Nadab and Abihu, and seventy of the elders of Israel. You are to worship at a distance, ²but Moses alone is to approach the LORD; the others must not come near. And the people may not come up with him."

³When Moses went and told the people all the LORD's words and laws, they responded with one voice, "Everything the LORD has said we will do." ⁴Moses then wrote down everything the LORD had said.

He got up early the next morning and built an altar at the foot of the mountain and set up twelve stone pillars representing the twelve tribes of Israel. ⁵Then he sent young Israelite men, and they offered burnt offerings and sacrificed young bulls as fellowship offerings[d] to the LORD. ⁶Moses took half of the blood and put it in bowls, and the other half he sprinkled on the altar. ⁷Then he took the Book of the Covenant and read it to the people. They responded, "We will do everything the LORD has said; we will obey."

⁸Moses then took the blood, sprinkled it on the people and said, "This is the blood of the covenant that the LORD has made with you in accordance with all these words."

⁹Moses and Aaron, Nadab and Abihu, and the seventy elders of Israel went up ¹⁰and saw the God of Israel. Under his feet was something like a pavement made of sapphire,[e] clear as the sky itself. ¹¹But God did not raise his hand against these leaders of the Israelites; they saw God, and they ate and drank.

¹²The LORD said to Moses, "Come up to me on the mountain and stay here, and I will give you the tablets of stone, with the law and commands I have written for their instruction."

¹³Then Moses set out with Joshua his aide, and Moses went up on the mountain of God. ¹⁴He said to the elders, "Wait here for us until we come back to you. Aaron and Hur are with you, and anyone involved in a dispute can go to them."

¹⁵When Moses went up on the mountain, the cloud covered it, ¹⁶and the glory of the LORD settled on Mount Sinai. For six days the cloud covered the mountain, and on the seventh day the LORD called to Moses from within the cloud. ¹⁷To the Israelites the glory of the LORD looked like a consuming fire on top of the mountain. ¹⁸Then Moses entered the cloud as he went on up the mountain. And he stayed on the mountain forty days and forty nights.

OFFERINGS FOR THE TABERNACLE

25

The LORD said to Moses, ²"Tell the Israelites to bring me an offering. You are to receive the offering for me from each man whose heart prompts him to give. ³These are the offerings you are to receive from them: gold, silver and bronze; ⁴blue, purple and scarlet yarn

---

a *31* Hebrew *Yam Suph*; that is, Sea of Reeds   b *31* That is, the Mediterranean   c *31* That is, the Euphrates   d *5* Traditionally *peace offerings*   e *10* Or *lapis lazuli* and fine linen; goat hair; ⁵ram skins dyed red and hides of sea cowsᵃ; acacia wood; ⁶olive oil for the light; spices for the anointing oil and for the fragrant incense; ⁷and onyx stones and other gems to be mounted on the ephod and breastpiece.

⁸"Then have them make a sanctuary for me, and I will dwell among them. ⁹Make this tabernacle and all its furnishings exactly like the pattern I will show you.

THE ARK

¹⁰"Have them make a chest of acacia wood—two and a half cubits long, a cubit and a half wide, and a cubit and a half high.ᵇ ¹¹Overlay it with pure gold, both inside and out, and make a gold molding around it. ¹²Cast four gold rings for it and fasten them to its four feet, with two rings on one side and two rings on the other. ¹³Then make poles of acacia wood and overlay them with gold. ¹⁴Insert the poles into the rings on the sides of the chest to carry it. ¹⁵The poles are to remain in the rings of this ark; they are not to be removed. ¹⁶Then put in the ark the Testimony, which I will give you.

¹⁷"Make an atonement coverᶜ of pure gold—two and a half cubits long and a cubit and a half wide.ᵈ ¹⁸And make two cherubim out of hammered gold at the ends of the cover. ¹⁹Make one cherub on one end and the second cherub on the other; make the cherubim of one piece with the cover, at the two ends. ²⁰The cherubim are to have their wings spread upward, overshadowing the cover with them. The cherubim are to face each other, looking toward the cover. ²¹Place the cover on top of the ark and put in the ark the Testimony, which I will give you. ²²There, above the cover between the two cherubim that are over the ark of the Testimony, I will meet with you and give you all my commands for the Israelites.

THE TABLE

²³"Make a table of acacia wood—two cubits long, a cubit wide and a cubit and a half high.ᵉ ²⁴Overlay it with pure gold and make a gold molding around it. ²⁵Also make around it a rim a handbreadthᶠ wide and put a gold molding on the rim. ²⁶Make four gold rings for the table and fasten them to the four corners, where the four legs are. ²⁷The rings are to be close to the rim to hold the poles used in carrying the table. ²⁸Make the poles of acacia wood, overlay them with gold and carry the table with them. ²⁹And make its plates and dishes of pure gold, as well as its pitchers and bowls for the pouring out of offerings. ³⁰Put the bread of the Presence on this table to be before me at all times.

THE LAMPSTAND

³¹"Make a lampstand of pure gold and hammer it out, base and shaft; its flowerlike cups, buds and blossoms shall be of one piece with it. ³²Six branches are to extend from the sides of the lampstand—three on one side and three on the other. ³³Three cups shaped like almond flowers with buds and blossoms are to be on one branch, three on the next branch, and the same for all six branches extending from the lampstand. ³⁴And on the lampstand there are to be four cups shaped like almond flowers with buds and blossoms. ³⁵One bud shall be under the first pair of branches extending from the lampstand, a second bud under the second pair, and a third bud under the third pair—six branches in all. ³⁶The buds and branches shall all be of one piece with the lampstand, hammered out of pure gold.

³⁷"Then make its seven lamps and set them up on it so that they light the space in front of it. ³⁸Its wick trimmers and trays are to be of pure gold. ³⁹A talentᵍ of pure gold is to be used for the lampstand and all these accessories. ⁴⁰See that you make them according to the pattern shown you on the mountain.

THE TABERNACLE

26 "Make the tabernacle with ten curtains of finely twisted linen and blue, purple and scarlet yarn, with cherubim worked into them by a skilled craftsman. ²All the curtains are to be the same size—twenty-eight cubits long and four cubits wide.ʰ ³Join five of the curtains together, and do the same with the other five. ⁴Make loops of blue material along the edge of the end curtain in one set, and do the same with the end curtain in the other set. ⁵Make fifty loops on one cur-

---

ᵃ *5* That is, dugongs   ᵇ *10* That is, about 3 3/4 feet (about 1.1 meters) long and 2 1/4 feet (about 0.7 meter) wide and high
ᶜ *17* Traditionally *a mercy seat*   ᵈ *17* That is, about 3 3/4 feet (about 1.1 meters) long and 2 1/4 feet (about 0.7 meter) wide   ᵉ *23* That is, about 3 feet (about 0.9 meter) long and 1 1/2 feet (about 0.5 meter) wide and 2 1/4 feet (about 0.7 meter) high   ᶠ *25* That is, about 3 inches (about 8 centimeters)   ᵍ *39* That is, about 75 pounds (about 34 kilograms)   ʰ *2* That is, about 42 feet (about 12.5 meters) long and 6 feet (about 1.8 meters) wide

tain and fifty loops on the end curtain of the other set, with the loops opposite each other. ⁶Then make fifty gold clasps and use them to fasten the curtains together so that the tabernacle is a unit.

⁷"Make curtains of goat hair for the tent over the tabernacle—eleven altogether. ⁸All eleven curtains are to be the same size—thirty cubits long and four cubits wide.ᵃ ⁹Join five of the curtains together into one set and the other six into another set. Fold the sixth curtain double at the front of the tent. ¹⁰Make fifty loops along the edge of the end curtain in one set and also along the edge of the end curtain in the other set. ¹¹Then make fifty bronze clasps and put them in the loops to fasten the tent together as a unit. ¹²As for the additional length of the tent curtains, the half curtain that is left over is to hang down at the rear of the tabernacle. ¹³The tent curtains will be a cubitᵇ longer on both sides; what is left will hang over the sides of the tabernacle so as to cover it. ¹⁴Make for the tent a covering of ram skins dyed red, and over that a covering of hides of sea cows.ᶜ

¹⁵"Make upright frames of acacia wood for the tabernacle. ¹⁶Each frame is to be ten cubits long and a cubit and a half wide,ᵈ ¹⁷with two projections set parallel to each other. Make all the frames of the tabernacle in this way. ¹⁸Make twenty frames for the south side of the tabernacle ¹⁹and make forty silver bases to go under them—two bases for each frame, one under each projection. ²⁰For the other side, the north side of the tabernacle, make twenty frames ²¹and forty silver bases—two under each frame. ²²Make six frames for the far end, that is, the west end of the tabernacle, ²³and make two frames for the corners at the far end. ²⁴At these two corners they must be double from the bottom all the way to the top, and fitted into a single ring; both shall be like that. ²⁵So there will be eight frames and sixteen silver bases—two under each frame.

²⁶"Also make crossbars of acacia wood: five for the frames on one side of the tabernacle, ²⁷five for those on the other side, and five for the frames on the west, at the far end of the tabernacle. ²⁸The center crossbar is to extend from end to end at the middle of the frames. ²⁹Overlay the frames with gold and make gold rings to hold the crossbars. Also overlay the crossbars with gold.

³⁰"Set up the tabernacle according to the plan shown you on the mountain.

³¹"Make a curtain of blue, purple and scarlet yarn and finely twisted linen, with cherubim worked into it by a skilled craftsman. ³²Hang it with gold hooks on four posts of acacia wood overlaid with gold and standing on four silver bases. ³³Hang the curtain from the clasps and place the ark of the Testimony behind the curtain. The curtain will separate the Holy Place from the Most Holy Place. ³⁴Put the atonement cover on the ark of the Testimony in the Most Holy Place. ³⁵Place the table outside the curtain on the north side of the tabernacle and put the lampstand opposite it on the south side.

³⁶"For the entrance to the tent make a curtain of blue, purple and scarlet yarn and finely twisted linen—the work of an embroiderer. ³⁷Make gold hooks for this curtain and five posts of acacia wood overlaid with gold. And cast five bronze bases for them.

THE ALTAR OF BURNT OFFERING

27 "Build an altar of acacia wood, three cubitsᵉ high; it is to be square, five cubits long and five cubits wide.ᶠ ²Make a horn at each of the four corners, so that the horns and the altar are of one piece, and overlay the altar with bronze. ³Make all its utensils of bronze—its pots to remove the ashes, and its shovels, sprinkling bowls, meat forks and firepans. ⁴Make a grating for it, a bronze network, and make a bronze ring at each of the four corners of the network. ⁵Put it under the ledge of the altar so that it is halfway up the altar. ⁶Make poles of acacia wood for the altar and overlay them with bronze. ⁷The poles are to be inserted into the rings so they will be on two sides of the altar when it is carried. ⁸Make the altar hollow, out of boards. It is to be made just as you were shown on the mountain.

THE COURTYARD

⁹"Make a courtyard for the tabernacle. The south side shall be a hundred cubitsᵍ long and is to have curtains of finely twisted linen, ¹⁰with twenty posts and twenty bronze bases and with silver hooks and bands on the posts. ¹¹The north side shall also be a hundred cubits long and is to have curtains, with twenty posts and twenty bronze bases and with silver hooks and bands on the posts.

ᵃ 8 That is, about 45 feet (about 13.5 meters) long and 6 feet (about 1.8 meters) wide   ᵇ 13 That is, about 1 1/2 feet (about 0.5 meter)   ᶜ 14 That is, dugongs   ᵈ 16 That is, about 15 feet (about 4.5 meters) long and 2 1/4 feet (about 0.7 meter) wide   ᵉ 1 That is, about 4 1/2 feet (about 1.3 meters)   ᶠ 1 That is, about 7 1/2 feet (about 2.3 meters) long and wide   ᵍ 9 That is, about 150 feet (about 46 meters); also in verse 11

¹² "The west end of the courtyard shall be fifty cubits[a] wide and have curtains, with ten posts and ten bases. ¹³On the east end, toward the sunrise, the courtyard shall also be fifty cubits wide. ¹⁴Curtains fifteen cubits[b] long are to be on one side of the entrance, with three posts and three bases, ¹⁵and curtains fifteen cubits long are to be on the other side, with three posts and three bases.

¹⁶ "For the entrance to the courtyard, provide a curtain twenty cubits[c] long, of blue, purple and scarlet yarn and finely twisted linen—the work of an embroiderer—with four posts and four bases. ¹⁷All the posts around the courtyard are to have silver bands and hooks, and bronze bases. ¹⁸The courtyard shall be a hundred cubits long and fifty cubits wide,[d] with curtains of finely twisted linen five cubits[e] high, and with bronze bases. ¹⁹All the other articles used in the service of the tabernacle, whatever their function, including all the tent pegs for it and those for the courtyard, are to be of bronze.

OIL FOR THE LAMPSTAND

²⁰ "Command the Israelites to bring you clear oil of pressed olives for the light so that the lamps may be kept burning. ²¹In the Tent of Meeting, outside the curtain that is in front of the Testimony, Aaron and his sons are to keep the lamps burning before the LORD from evening till morning. This is to be a lasting ordinance among the Israelites for the generations to come.

THE PRIESTLY GARMENTS

28

"Have Aaron your brother brought to you from among the Israelites, along with his sons Nadab and Abihu, Eleazar and Ithamar, so they may serve me as priests. ²Make sacred garments for your brother Aaron, to give him dignity and honor. ³Tell all the skilled men to whom I have given wisdom in such matters that they are to make garments for Aaron, for his consecration, so he may serve me as priest. ⁴These are the garments they are to make: a breastpiece, an ephod, a robe, a woven tunic, a turban and a sash. They are to make these sacred garments for your brother Aaron and his sons, so they may serve me as priests. ⁵Have them use gold, and blue, purple and scarlet yarn, and fine linen.

THE EPHOD

⁶ "Make the ephod of gold, and of blue, purple and scarlet yarn, and of finely twisted linen—the work of a skilled craftsman. ⁷It is to have two shoulder pieces attached to two of its corners, so it can be fastened. ⁸Its skillfully woven waistband is to be like it—of one piece with the ephod and made with gold, and with blue, purple and scarlet yarn, and with finely twisted linen.

⁹ "Take two onyx stones and engrave on them the names of the sons of Israel ¹⁰in the order of their birth—six names on one stone and the remaining six on the other. ¹¹Engrave the names of the sons of Israel on the two stones the way a gem cutter engraves a seal. Then mount the stones in gold filigree settings ¹²and fasten them on the shoulder pieces of the ephod as memorial stones for the sons of Israel. Aaron is to bear the names on his shoulders as a memorial before the LORD. ¹³Make gold filigree settings ¹⁴and two braided chains of pure gold, like a rope, and attach the chains to the settings.

THE BREASTPIECE

¹⁵ "Fashion a breastpiece for making decisions—the work of a skilled craftsman. Make it like the ephod: of gold, and of blue, purple and scarlet yarn, and of finely twisted linen. ¹⁶It is to be square—a span[f] long and a span wide—and folded double. ¹⁷Then mount four rows of precious stones on it. In the first row there shall be a ruby, a topaz and a beryl; ¹⁸in the second row a turquoise, a sapphire[g] and an emerald; ¹⁹in the third row a jacinth, an agate and an amethyst; ²⁰in the fourth row a chrysolite, an onyx and a jasper.[h] Mount them in gold filigree settings. ²¹There are to be twelve stones, one for each of the names of the sons of Israel, each engraved like a seal with the name of one of the twelve tribes.

²² "For the breastpiece make braided chains of pure gold, like a rope. ²³Make two gold rings for it and fasten them to two corners of the breastpiece. ²⁴Fasten the two gold chains to the rings at the corners of the breastpiece, ²⁵and the other ends of the chains to the two settings, attaching them to the shoulder pieces of the ephod at the front. ²⁶Make two gold rings and attach them to the other two cor-

---

ᵃ 12 That is, about 75 feet (about 23 meters); also in verse 13   ᵇ 14 That is, about 22 1/2 feet (about 6.9 meters); also in verse 15
ᶜ 16 That is, about 30 feet (about 9 meters)   ᵈ 18 That is, about 150 feet (about 46 meters) long and 75 feet (about 23 meters)
wide   ᵉ 18 That is, about 7 1/2 feet (about 2.3 meters)   ᶠ 16 That is, about 9 inches (about 22 centimeters)   ᵍ 18 Or lapis lazuli
ʰ 20 The precise identification of some of these precious stones is uncertain.

ners of the breastpiece on the inside edge next to the ephod. ²⁷Make two more gold rings and attach them to the bottom of the shoulder pieces on the front of the ephod, close to the seam just above the waistband of the ephod. ²⁸The rings of the breastpiece are to be tied to the rings of the ephod with blue cord, connecting it to the waistband, so that the breastpiece will not swing out from the ephod.

²⁹"Whenever Aaron enters the Holy Place, he will bear the names of the sons of Israel over his heart on the breastpiece of decision as a continuing memorial before the LORD. ³⁰Also put the Urim and the Thummim in the breastpiece, so they may be over Aaron's heart whenever he enters the presence of the LORD. Thus Aaron will always bear the means of making decisions for the Israelites over his heart before the LORD.

OTHER PRIESTLY GARMENTS

³¹"Make the robe of the ephod entirely of blue cloth, ³²with an opening for the head in its center. There shall be a woven edge like a collarᵃ around this opening, so that it will not tear. ³³Make pomegranates of blue, purple and scarlet yarn around the hem of the robe, with gold bells between them. ³⁴The gold bells and the pomegranates are to alternate around the hem of the robe. ³⁵Aaron must wear it when he ministers. The sound of the bells will be heard when he enters the Holy Place before the LORD and when he comes out, so that he will not die.

³⁶"Make a plate of pure gold and engrave on it as on a seal: HOLY TO THE LORD. ³⁷Fasten a blue cord to it to attach it to the turban; it is to be on the front of the turban. ³⁸It will be on Aaron's forehead, and he will bear the guilt involved in the sacred gifts the Israelites consecrate, whatever their gifts may be. It will be on Aaron's forehead continually so that they will be acceptable to the LORD.

³⁹"Weave the tunic of fine linen and make the turban of fine linen. The sash is to be the work of an embroiderer. ⁴⁰Make tunics, sashes and headbands for Aaron's sons, to give them dignity and honor. ⁴¹After you put these clothes on your brother Aaron and his sons, anoint and ordain them. Consecrate them so they may serve me as priests.

⁴²"Make linen undergarments as a covering for the body, reaching from the waist to the thigh. ⁴³Aaron and his sons must wear them whenever they enter the Tent of Meeting or approach the altar to minister in the Holy Place, so that they will not incur guilt and die.

"This is to be a lasting ordinance for Aaron and his descendants.

CONSECRATION OF THE PRIESTS

29 "This is what you are to do to consecrate them, so they may serve me as priests: Take a young bull and two rams without defect. ²And from fine wheat flour, without yeast, make bread, and cakes mixed with oil, and wafers spread with oil. ³Put them in a basket and present them in it—along with the bull and the two rams. ⁴Then bring Aaron and his sons to the entrance to the Tent of Meeting and wash them with water. ⁵Take the garments and dress Aaron with the tunic, the robe of the ephod, the ephod itself and the breastpiece. Fasten the ephod on him by its skillfully woven waistband. ⁶Put the turban on his head and attach the sacred diadem to the turban. ⁷Take the anointing oil and anoint him by pouring it on his head. ⁸Bring his sons and dress them in tunics ⁹and put headbands on them. Then tie sashes on Aaron and his sons.ᵇ The priesthood is theirs by a lasting ordinance. In this way you shall ordain Aaron and his sons.

¹⁰"Bring the bull to the front of the Tent of Meeting, and Aaron and his sons shall lay their hands on its head. ¹¹Slaughter it in the LORD's presence at the entrance to the Tent of Meeting. ¹²Take some of the bull's blood and put it on the horns of the altar with your finger, and pour out the rest of it at the base of the altar. ¹³Then take all the fat around the inner parts, the covering of the liver, and both kidneys with the fat on them, and burn them on the altar. ¹⁴But burn the bull's flesh and its hide and its offal outside the camp. It is a sin offering.

¹⁵"Take one of the rams, and Aaron and his sons shall lay their hands on its head. ¹⁶Slaughter it and take the blood and sprinkle it against the altar on all sides. ¹⁷Cut the ram into pieces and wash the inner parts and the legs, putting them with the head and the other pieces. ¹⁸Then burn the entire ram on the altar. It is a burnt offering to the LORD, a pleasing aroma, an offering made to the LORD by fire.

¹⁹"Take the other ram, and Aaron and his sons shall lay their hands on its head. ²⁰Slaughter it, take some of its blood and put it on the lobes of the right ears of Aaron and his sons, on the thumbs of their right hands, and on the big toes of their right feet. Then sprinkle blood against the altar on all sides.

ᵃ *32* The meaning of the Hebrew for this word is uncertain.   ᵇ *9* Hebrew; Septuagint *on them*

²¹And take some of the blood on the altar and some of the anointing oil and sprinkle it on Aaron and his garments and on his sons and their garments. Then he and his sons and their garments will be consecrated.

²²"Take from this ram the fat, the fat tail, the fat around the inner parts, the covering of the liver, both kidneys with the fat on them, and the right thigh. (This is the ram for the ordination.) ²³From the basket of bread made without yeast, which is before the LORD, take a loaf, and a cake made with oil, and a wafer. ²⁴Put all these in the hands of Aaron and his sons and wave them before the LORD as a wave offering. ²⁵Then take them from their hands and burn them on the altar along with the burnt offering for a pleasing aroma to the LORD, an offering made to the LORD by fire. ²⁶After you take the breast of the ram for Aaron's ordination, wave it before the LORD as a wave offering, and it will be your share.

²⁷"Consecrate those parts of the ordination ram that belong to Aaron and his sons: the breast that was waved and the thigh that was presented. ²⁸This is always to be the regular share from the Israelites for Aaron and his sons. It is the contribution the Israelites are to make to the LORD from their fellowship offerings.ᵃ

²⁹"Aaron's sacred garments will belong to his descendants so that they can be anointed and ordained in them. ³⁰The son who succeeds him as priest and comes to the Tent of Meeting to minister in the Holy Place is to wear them seven days.

³¹"Take the ram for the ordination and cook the meat in a sacred place. ³²At the entrance to the Tent of Meeting, Aaron and his sons are to eat the meat of the ram and the bread that is in the basket. ³³They are to eat these offerings by which atonement was made for their ordination and consecration. But no one else may eat them, because they are sacred. ³⁴And if any of the meat of the ordination ram or any bread is left over till morning, burn it up. It must not be eaten, because it is sacred.

³⁵"Do for Aaron and his sons everything I have commanded you, taking seven days to ordain them. ³⁶Sacrifice a bull each day as a sin offering to make atonement. Purify the altar by making atonement for it, and anoint it to consecrate it. ³⁷For seven days make atonement for the altar and consecrate it. Then the altar will be most holy, and whatever touches it will be holy.

³⁸"This is what you are to offer on the altar regularly each day: two lambs a year old. ³⁹Offer one in the morning and the other at twilight. ⁴⁰With the first lamb offer a tenth of an ephahᵇ of fine flour mixed with a quarter of a hinᶜ of oil from pressed olives, and a quarter of a hin of wine as a drink offering. ⁴¹Sacrifice the other lamb at twilight with the same grain offering and its drink offering as in the morning—a pleasing aroma, an offering made to the LORD by fire.

⁴²"For the generations to come this burnt offering is to be made regularly at the entrance to the Tent of Meeting before the LORD. There I will meet you and speak to you; ⁴³there also I will meet with the Israelites, and the place will be consecrated by my glory.

⁴⁴"So I will consecrate the Tent of Meeting and the altar and will consecrate Aaron and his sons to serve me as priests. ⁴⁵Then I will dwell among the Israelites and be their God. ⁴⁶They will know that I am the LORD their God, who brought them out of Egypt so that I might dwell among them. I am the LORD their God.

NOW OR NEVER
EX 29:45-46

How close to God do you think you are right now? What can you do to get closer to him—or to make your life a place where he is welcome?

THE ALTAR OF INCENSE

30

"Make an altar of acacia wood for burning incense. ²It is to be square, a cubit long and a cubit wide, and two cubits highᵈ—its horns of one piece with it. ³Overlay the top and all the sides and the horns with pure gold, and make a gold molding around it. ⁴Make two gold rings for the altar below the molding—two on opposite sides—to hold the poles used to carry it. ⁵Make the poles of acacia wood and overlay them with gold. ⁶Put the altar in front of the curtain that is before the ark of the Testimony—before the atonement cover that is over the Testimony—where I will meet with you.

ᵃ 28 Traditionally *peace offerings* ᵇ 40 That is, probably about 2 quarts (about 2 liters) ᶜ 40 That is, probably about 1 quart (about 1 liter) ᵈ 2 That is, about 1 1/2 feet (about 0.5 meter) long and wide and about 3 feet (about 0.9 meter) high

⁷"Aaron must burn fragrant incense on the altar every morning when he tends the lamps. ⁸He must burn incense again when he lights the lamps at twilight so incense will burn regularly before the Lord for the generations to come. ⁹Do not offer on this altar any other incense or any burnt offering or grain offering, and do not pour a drink offering on it. ¹⁰Once a year Aaron shall make atonement on its horns. This annual atonement must be made with the blood of the atoning sin offering for the generations to come. It is most holy to the Lord."

ATONEMENT MONEY

¹¹Then the Lord said to Moses, ¹²"When you take a census of the Israelites to count them, each one must pay the Lord a ransom for his life at the time he is counted. Then no plague will come on them when you number them. ¹³Each one who crosses over to those already counted is to give a half shekel,ª according to the sanctuary shekel, which weighs twenty gerahs. This half shekel is an offering to the Lord. ¹⁴All who cross over, those twenty years old or more, are to give an offering to the Lord. ¹⁵The rich are not to give more than a half shekel and the poor are not to give less when you make the offering to the Lord to atone for your lives. ¹⁶Receive the atonement money from the Israelites and use it for the service of the Tent of Meeting. It will be a memorial for the Israelites before the Lord, making atonement for your lives."

BASIN FOR WASHING

¹⁷Then the Lord said to Moses, ¹⁸"Make a bronze basin, with its bronze stand, for washing. Place it between the Tent of Meeting and the altar, and put water in it. ¹⁹Aaron and his sons are to wash their hands and feet with water from it. ²⁰Whenever they enter the Tent of Meeting, they shall wash with water so that they will not die. Also, when they approach the altar to minister by presenting an offering made to the Lord by fire, ²¹they shall wash their hands and feet so that they will not die. This is to be a lasting ordinance for Aaron and his descendants for the generations to come."

ANOINTING OIL

²²Then the Lord said to Moses, ²³"Take the following fine spices: 500 shekelsᵇ of liquid myrrh, half as much (that is, 250 shekels) of fragrant cinnamon, 250 shekels of fragrant cane, ²⁴500 shekels of cassia—all according to the sanctuary shekel—and a hinᶜ of olive oil. ²⁵Make these into a sacred anointing oil, a fragrant blend, the work of a perfumer. It will be the sacred anointing oil. ²⁶Then use it to anoint the Tent of Meeting, the ark of the Testimony, ²⁷the table and all its articles, the lampstand and its accessories, the altar of incense, ²⁸the altar of burnt offering and all its utensils, and the basin with its stand. ²⁹You shall consecrate them so they will be most holy, and whatever touches them will be holy.

³⁰"Anoint Aaron and his sons and consecrate them so they may serve me as priests. ³¹Say to the Israelites, 'This is to be my sacred anointing oil for the generations to come. ³²Do not pour it on men's bodies and do not make any oil with the same formula. It is sacred, and you are to consider it sacred. ³³Whoever makes perfume like it and whoever puts it on anyone other than a priest must be cut off from his people.' "

INCENSE

³⁴Then the Lord said to Moses, "Take fragrant spices—gum resin, onycha and galbanum—and pure frankincense, all in equal amounts, ³⁵and make a fragrant blend of incense, the work of a perfumer. It is to be salted and pure and sacred. ³⁶Grind some of it to powder and place it in front of the Testimony in the Tent of Meeting, where I will meet with you. It shall be most holy to you. ³⁷Do not make any incense with this formula for yourselves; consider it holy to the Lord. ³⁸Whoever makes any like it to enjoy its fragrance must be cut off from his people."

BEZALEL AND OHOLIAB

31 Then the Lord said to Moses, ²"See, I have chosen Bezalel son of Uri, the son of Hur, of the tribe of Judah, ³and I have filled him with the Spirit of God, with skill, ability and knowledge in all kinds of crafts— ⁴to make artistic designs for work in gold, silver and bronze, ⁵to cut and set stones, to work in wood, and to engage in all kinds of craftsmanship. ⁶Moreover, I have ap-

---

ª 13 That is, about 1/5 ounce (about 6 grams); also in verse 15   ᵇ 23 That is, about 12 1/2 pounds (about 6 kilograms)   ᶜ 24 That is, probably about 4 quarts (about 4 liters) pointed Oholiab son of Ahisamach, of the tribe of Dan, to help him. Also I have given skill to all the craftsmen to make everything I have commanded you: [7]the Tent of Meeting, the ark of the Testimony with the atonement cover on it, and all the other furnishings of the tent— [8]the table and its articles, the pure gold lampstand and all its accessories, the altar of incense, [9]the altar of burnt offering and all its utensils, the basin with its stand— [10]and also the woven garments, both the sacred garments for Aaron the priest and the garments for his sons when they serve as priests, [11]and the anointing oil and fragrant incense for the Holy Place. They are to make them just as I commanded you."

NOW OR NEVER
EX 31:1–11

What are you good at? How can you use your skills to honor God or draw people's attention to him?

THE SABBATH

[12]Then the Lord said to Moses, [13]"Say to the Israelites, 'You must observe my Sabbaths. This will be a sign between me and you for the generations to come, so you may know that I am the Lord, who makes you holy.[a]

[14]" 'Observe the Sabbath, because it is holy to you. Anyone who desecrates it must be put to death; whoever does any work on that day must be cut off from his people. [15]For six days, work is to be done, but the seventh day is a Sabbath of rest, holy to the Lord. Whoever does any work on the Sabbath day must be put to death. [16]The Israelites are to observe the Sabbath, celebrating it for the generations to come as a lasting covenant. [17]It will be a sign between me and the Israelites forever, for in six days the Lord made the heavens and the earth, and on the seventh day he abstained from work and rested.' "

[18]When the Lord finished speaking to Moses on Mount Sinai, he gave him the two tablets of the Testimony, the tablets of stone inscribed by the finger of God.

THE GOLDEN CALF

32

When the people saw that Moses was so long in coming down from the mountain, they gathered around Aaron and said, "Come, make us gods[b] who will go before us. As for this fellow Moses who brought us up out of Egypt, we don't know what has happened to him."

challengenotes

To: **my_son**

heavenly_father: if you're too busy to give me one day out of each week, then you need to change your schedule. not for my sake, but for yours. I gave you this day to rest—to reset your focus on me. if you ignore that, there's always going to be something missing in your life.

[2]Aaron answered them, "Take off the gold earrings that your wives, your sons and your daughters are wearing, and bring them to me." [3]So all the people took off their earrings and brought them to Aaron. [4]He took what they handed him and made it into an idol cast in the shape of a calf, fashioning it with a tool. Then they said, "These are your gods,[c] O Israel, who brought you up out of Egypt."

[5]When Aaron saw this, he built an altar in front of the calf and announced, "Tomorrow there will be a festival to the Lord." [6]So the next day the people rose early and sacrificed burnt offerings and presented fellowship offerings.[d] Afterward they sat down to eat and drink and got up to indulge in revelry.

[7]Then the Lord said to Moses, "Go down, because your people, whom you brought up out of Egypt, have become corrupt. [8]They have been quick to turn away from what I commanded them and have made themselves an idol cast in the shape of a calf. They have bowed down to it and sacrificed to it and have said, 'These are your gods, O Israel, who brought you up out of Egypt.'

[9]"I have seen these people," the Lord said to Moses, "and they are a stiff-necked people. [10]Now

---

[a] 13 Or who sanctifies you; or who sets you apart as holy   [b] 1 Or a god; also in verses 23 and 31   [c] 4 Or This is your god; also in verse 8   [d] 6 Traditionally peace offerings

leave me alone so that my anger may burn against them and that I may destroy them. Then I will make you into a great nation."

¹¹But Moses sought the favor of the LORD his God. "O LORD," he said, "why should your anger burn against your people, whom you brought out of Egypt with great power and a mighty hand? ¹²Why should the Egyptians say, 'It was with evil intent that he brought them out, to kill them in the mountains and to wipe them off the face of the earth'? Turn from your fierce anger; relent and do not bring disaster on your people. ¹³Remember your servants Abraham, Isaac and Israel, to whom you swore by your own self: 'I will make your descendants as numerous as the stars in the sky and I will give your descendants all this land I promised them, and it will be their inheritance forever.'" ¹⁴Then the LORD relented and did not bring on his people the disaster he had threatened.

¹⁵Moses turned and went down the mountain with the two tablets of the Testimony in his hands. They were inscribed on both sides, front and back. ¹⁶The tablets were the work of God; the writing was the writing of God, engraved on the tablets.

¹⁷When Joshua heard the noise of the people shouting, he said to Moses, "There is the sound of war in the camp."

¹⁸Moses replied:

> "It is not the sound of victory,
> it is not the sound of defeat;
> it is the sound of singing that I hear."

¹⁹When Moses approached the camp and saw the calf and the dancing, his anger burned and he threw the tablets out of his hands, breaking them to pieces at the foot of the mountain. ²⁰And he took the calf they had made and burned it in the fire; then he ground it to powder, scattered it on the water and made the Israelites drink it.

²¹He said to Aaron, "What did these people do to you, that you led them into such great sin?"

²²"Do not be angry, my lord," Aaron answered. "You know how prone these people are to evil. ²³They said to me, 'Make us gods who will go before us. As for this fellow Moses who brought us up out of Egypt, we don't know what has happened to him.' ²⁴So I told them, 'Whoever has any gold jewelry, take it off.' Then they gave me the gold, and I threw it into the fire, and out came this calf!"

²⁵Moses saw that the people were running wild and that Aaron had let them get out of control and so become a laughingstock to their enemies. ²⁶So he stood at the entrance to the camp and said, "Whoever is for the LORD, come to me." And all the Levites rallied to him.

²⁷Then he said to them, "This is what the LORD, the God of Israel, says: 'Each man strap a sword to his side. Go back and forth through the camp from one end to the other, each killing his brother and friend and neighbor.'" ²⁸The Levites did as Moses commanded, and that day about three thousand of the people died. ²⁹Then Moses said, "You have been set apart to the LORD today, for you were against your own sons and brothers, and he has blessed you this day."

³⁰The next day Moses said to the people, "You have committed a great sin. But now I will go up to the LORD; perhaps I can make atonement for your sin."

³¹So Moses went back to the LORD and said, "Oh, what a great sin these people have committed! They have made themselves gods of gold. ³²But now, please forgive their sin—but if not, then blot me out of the book you have written."

³³The LORD replied to Moses, "Whoever has sinned against me I will blot out of my book. ³⁴Now go, lead the people to the place I spoke of, and my angel will go before you. However, when the time comes for me to punish, I will punish them for their sin."

³⁵And the LORD struck the people with a plague because of what they did with the calf Aaron had made.

NOW OR NEVER

EX 32:1–10

When was the last time you worshiped an idol? What if someone told you that an idol is anything that has a higher priority in your life than your relationship with God? How would that change your answer?

aaron

moses

» Older brother of Moses
» Israel's first high priest and Moses' mouthpiece
» Weak in pressure situations

» Younger brother of Aaron
» Israel's deliverer and lawgiver
» Strong in pressure situations

The Main Event

If you've seen the movies *The Ten Commandments* or *The Prince of Egypt*, you know the story. God's people were slaves in Egypt, and God picked a guy named Moses (see Exodus 2–4) to lead them to freedom. Moses had the credentials to do the job, but after 40 years of chasing a bunch of sheep around the desert, he didn't have a whole lot of confidence in himself. To give Moses the help he needed, God appointed his brother, Aaron, to serve as Moses' right-hand man—or "press secretary."

For the most part, the brothers made a pretty good team. With some miraculous help from God, they led the Israelites out of Egypt, through the Red Sea and down to Mount Sinai, the so-called mountain of God. That's where God gave his people their charter as a nation—his laws for living.

While Moses was on the mountain receiving God's instructions, the Israelites in the valley below started getting impatient. "Maybe Moses is dead," they grumbled to Aaron. "Make us a new god," they demanded. Amazingly, Aaron caved to the pressure. In a stunning display of wimpiness, Aaron created an idol for the people and then stood by while they fell all over themselves *worshiping* it!

Moses was so furious when he came down the mountain and saw what was going on that he literally broke all ten commandments at once . . . shattering the stone tablets the commandments were written on (which sent a painfully clear message that the Israelites had just broken their covenant with God). Before confronting his spineless brother (whose lame excuse was, "I threw the gold into the fire and the funniest thing happened . . . out came this golden calf, like magic!"), Moses pulverized the idol into dust, mixed it with water and made the people drink it! Later he went back to God and begged him not to wipe out the Israelites.

What a contrast—one brother gave in to the wishes of the crowd while the other stood alone against them. One man was a *thermometer*, a guy who just reflected the spiritual temperature of the people around him. The other man was a *thermostat*, a guy who regulated the spiritual temperature of those around him.

The Outcome

When God made his famous list of the most courageous believers in the Bible (see Hebrews 11), he gave Moses a prominent mention. Aaron's name, however, is nowhere to be found.

Think about what might have been. What if Aaron had displayed a little more faith, a little more courage? What if he had relied upon the limitless strength that God makes available to each of his followers?

You may never be in a situation like the one Moses and Aaron faced, but you will have moments when you can either choose to be strong in the Lord or weak in the face of peer pressure. What do you want your legacy to be?

Read more about Moses and Aaron in Exodus 32 (pages 100–101) and Numbers 12:1–15 (pages 161–162).

33

Then the Lord said to Moses, "Leave this place, you and the people you brought up out of Egypt, and go up to the land I promised on oath to Abraham, Isaac and Jacob, saying, 'I will give it to your descendants.' ²I will send an angel before you and drive out the Canaanites, Amorites, Hittites, Perizzites, Hivites and Jebusites. ³Go up to the land flowing with milk and honey. But I will not go with you, because you are a stiff-necked people and I might destroy you on the way."

⁴When the people heard these distressing words, they began to mourn and no one put on any ornaments. ⁵For the Lord had said to Moses, "Tell the Israelites, 'You are a stiff-necked people. If I were to go with you even for a moment, I might destroy you. Now take off your ornaments and I will decide what to do with you.' " ⁶So the Israelites stripped off their ornaments at Mount Horeb.

THE TENT OF MEETING

⁷Now Moses used to take a tent and pitch it outside the camp some distance away, calling it the "tent of meeting." Anyone inquiring of the Lord would go to the tent of meeting outside the camp. ⁸And whenever Moses went out to the tent, all the people rose and stood at the entrances to their tents, watching Moses until he entered the tent. ⁹As Moses went into the tent, the pillar of cloud would come down and stay at the entrance, while the Lord spoke with Moses. ¹⁰Whenever the people saw the pillar of cloud standing at the entrance to the tent, they all stood and worshiped, each at the entrance to his tent. ¹¹The Lord would speak to Moses face to face, as a man speaks with his friend. Then Moses would return to the camp, but his young aide Joshua son of Nun did not leave the tent.

NOW OR NEVER

EX 33:11

Ever thought about how cool it would be to cross paths with a movie star or pro athlete? But when you come right down to it, they're just people like you or me. So how much cooler is it that God, the Creator of the universe, talked to Moses like a friend—and later died on a cross for *your* sins? Now that's amazing.

MOSES AND THE GLORY OF THE LORD

¹²Moses said to the Lord, "You have been telling me, 'Lead these people,' but you have not let me know whom you will send with me. You have said, 'I know you by name and you have found favor with me.' ¹³If you are pleased with me, teach me your ways so I may know you and continue to find favor with you. Remember that this nation is your people."

¹⁴The Lord replied, "My Presence will go with you, and I will give you rest."

¹⁵Then Moses said to him, "If your Presence does not go with us, do not send us up from here. ¹⁶How will anyone know that you are pleased with me and with your people unless you go with us? What else will distinguish me and your people from all the other people on the face of the earth?"

¹⁷And the Lord said to Moses, "I will do the very thing you have asked, because I am pleased with you and I know you by name."

¹⁸Then Moses said, "Now show me your glory."

¹⁹And the Lord said, "I will cause all my goodness to pass in front of you, and I will proclaim my name, the Lord, in your presence. I will have mercy on whom I will have mercy, and I will have compassion on whom I will have compassion. ²⁰But," he said, "you cannot see my face, for no one may see me and live."

²¹Then the Lord said, "There is a place near me where you may stand on a rock. ²²When my glory passes by, I will put you in a cleft in the rock and cover you with my hand until I have passed by. ²³Then I will remove my hand and you will see my back; but my face must not be seen."

THE NEW STONE TABLETS

34

The Lord said to Moses, "Chisel out two stone tablets like the first ones, and I will write on them the words that were on the first tablets, which you broke. ²Be ready in the morning, and then come up on Mount Sinai. Present yourself to me there on top of the mountain. ³No one is to come with you or be seen anywhere on the mountain; not even the flocks and herds may graze in front of the mountain."

⁴So Moses chiseled out two stone tablets like the first ones and went up Mount Sinai early in the morning, as the LORD had commanded him; and he carried the two stone tablets in his hands. ⁵Then the LORD came down in the cloud and stood there with him and proclaimed his name, the LORD. ⁶And he passed in front of Moses, proclaiming, "The LORD, the LORD, the compassionate and gracious God, slow to anger, abounding in love and faithfulness, ⁷maintaining love to thousands, and forgiving wickedness, rebellion and sin. Yet he does not leave the guilty unpunished; he punishes the children and their children for the sin of the fathers to the third and fourth generation."

⁸Moses bowed to the ground at once and worshiped. ⁹"O Lord, if I have found favor in your eyes," he said, "then let the Lord go with us. Although this is a stiff-necked people, forgive our wickedness and our sin, and take us as your inheritance."

¹⁰Then the LORD said: "I am making a covenant with you. Before all your people I will do wonders never before done in any nation in all the world. The people you live among will see how awesome is the work that I, the LORD, will do for you. ¹¹Obey what I command you today. I will drive out before you the Amorites, Canaanites, Hittites, Perizzites, Hivites and Jebusites. ¹²Be careful not to make a treaty with those who live in the land where you are going, or they will be a snare among you. ¹³Break down their altars, smash their sacred stones and cut down their Asherah poles.ᵃ ¹⁴Do not worship any other god, for the LORD, whose name is Jealous, is a jealous God.

¹⁵"Be careful not to make a treaty with those who live in the land; for when they prostitute themselves to their gods and sacrifice to them, they will invite you and you will eat their sacrifices. ¹⁶And when you choose some of their daughters as wives for your sons and those daughters prostitute themselves to their gods, they will lead your sons to do the same.

¹⁷"Do not make cast idols.

¹⁸"Celebrate the Feast of Unleavened Bread. For seven days eat bread made without yeast, as I commanded you. Do this at the appointed time in the month of Abib, for in that month you came out of Egypt.

¹⁹"The first offspring of every womb belongs to me, including all the firstborn males of your livestock, whether from herd or flock. ²⁰Redeem the firstborn donkey with a lamb, but if you do not redeem it, break its neck. Redeem all your firstborn sons.

"No one is to appear before me empty-handed.

²¹"Six days you shall labor, but on the seventh day you shall rest; even during the plowing season and harvest you must rest.

²²"Celebrate the Feast of Weeks with the firstfruits of the wheat harvest, and the Feast of Ingathering at the turn of the year.ᵇ ²³Three times a year all your men are to appear before the Sovereign LORD, the God of Israel. ²⁴I will drive out nations before you and enlarge your territory, and no one will covet your land when you go up three times each year to appear before the LORD your God.

²⁵"Do not offer the blood of a sacrifice to me along with anything containing yeast, and do not let any of the sacrifice from the Passover Feast remain until morning.

Taking Sin Seriously

Some people will try to tell you that "sin" is an outdated concept or that it's simply the result of poor judgment or a bad upbringing. They'll try to tell you that feeling shame for the things you do wrong is bad for your self-image. Don't listen to them. Sin not only damages your relationship with God, but it can also ruin lives—not just yours, but the lives of people who love you. So it has to be taken seriously. If you don't feel guilt and shame when you've done something wrong, ask God to work on your heart and make you more sensitive to the things that hurt him.

NOW OR NEVER

EX 34:6-7

Reason #2,546,089,611 why God is supremely cool: He doesn't make us guess what he's like or what he wants from us. He doesn't make us rely on the opinions of "experts." He spells out everything we need to know about him in his Word.

ᵃ 13 That is, symbols of the goddess Asherah   ᵇ 22 That is, in the fall

²⁶ "Bring the best of the firstfruits of your soil to the house of the Lord your God.

"Do not cook a young goat in its mother's milk."

²⁷ Then the Lord said to Moses, "Write down these words, for in accordance with these words I have made a covenant with you and with Israel." ²⁸ Moses was there with the Lord forty days and forty nights without eating bread or drinking water. And he wrote on the tablets the words of the covenant—the Ten Commandments.

THE RADIANT FACE OF MOSES

²⁹ When Moses came down from Mount Sinai with the two tablets of the Testimony in his hands, he was not aware that his face was radiant because he had spoken with the Lord. ³⁰ When Aaron and all the Israelites saw Moses, his face was radiant, and they were afraid to come near him. ³¹ But Moses called to them; so Aaron and all the leaders of the community came back to him, and he spoke to them. ³² Afterward all the Israelites came near him, and he gave them all the commands the Lord had given him on Mount Sinai.

³³ When Moses finished speaking to them, he put a veil over his face. ³⁴ But whenever he entered the Lord's presence to speak with him, he removed the veil until he came out. And when he came out and told the Israelites what he had been commanded, ³⁵ they saw that his face was radiant. Then Moses would put the veil back over his face until he went in to speak with the Lord.

SABBATH REGULATIONS

35 Moses assembled the whole Israelite community and said to them, "These are the things the Lord has commanded you to do: ² For six days, work is to be done, but the seventh day shall be your holy day, a Sabbath of rest to the Lord. Whoever does any work on it must be put to death. ³ Do not light a fire in any of your dwellings on the Sabbath day."

MATERIALS FOR THE TABERNACLE

⁴ Moses said to the whole Israelite community, "This is what the Lord has commanded: ⁵ From what you have, take an offering for the Lord. Everyone who is willing is to bring to the Lord an offering of gold, silver and bronze; ⁶ blue, purple and scarlet yarn and fine linen; goat hair; ⁷ ram skins dyed red and hides of sea cows^a; acacia wood; ⁸ olive oil for the light; spices for the anointing oil and for the fragrant incense; ⁹ and onyx stones and other gems to be mounted on the ephod and breastpiece.

¹⁰ "All who are skilled among you are to come and make everything the Lord has commanded: ¹¹ the tabernacle with its tent and its covering, clasps, frames, crossbars, posts and bases; ¹² the ark with its poles and the atonement cover and the curtain that shields it; ¹³ the table with its poles and all its articles and the bread of the Presence; ¹⁴ the lampstand that is for light with its accessories, lamps and oil for the light; ¹⁵ the altar of incense with its poles, the anointing oil and the fragrant incense; the curtain for the doorway at the entrance to the tabernacle; ¹⁶ the altar of burnt offering with its bronze grating, its poles and all its utensils; the bronze basin with its stand; ¹⁷ the curtains of the courtyard with its posts and bases, and the curtain for the entrance to the courtyard; ¹⁸ the tent pegs for the tabernacle and for the courtyard, and their ropes; ¹⁹ the woven garments worn for ministering in the sanctuary—both the sacred garments for Aaron the priest and the garments for his sons when they serve as priests."

²⁰ Then the whole Israelite community withdrew from Moses' presence, ²¹ and everyone who was willing and whose heart moved him came and brought an offering to the Lord for the work on the Tent of Meeting, for all its service, and for the sacred garments. ²² All who were willing, men and women alike, came and brought gold jewelry of all kinds: brooches, earrings, rings and ornaments. They all presented their gold as a wave offering to the Lord. ²³ Everyone who had blue, purple or scarlet yarn or fine linen, or goat hair, ram skins dyed red or hides of sea cows brought them. ²⁴ Those presenting an offering of silver or bronze brought it as an offering to the Lord, and everyone who had acacia wood for any part of the work brought it. ²⁵ Every skilled woman spun with her hands and brought what she had spun—blue, purple or scarlet yarn or fine linen. ²⁶ And all the women who were willing and had the skill spun the goat hair. ²⁷ The leaders brought onyx stones and other gems to be mounted on the ephod and breastpiece. ²⁸ They also brought spices and olive oil for the light and for the anointing oil and for the fragrant incense. ²⁹ All the Israelite men and women who were willing brought to the Lord freewill offerings for all the work the Lord through Moses had commanded them to do.

---

^a 7 That is, dugongs; also in verse 23

BEZALEL AND OHOLIAB

30 Then Moses said to the Israelites, "See, the LORD has chosen Bezalel son of Uri, the son of Hur, of the tribe of Judah, 31 and he has filled him with the Spirit of God, with skill, ability and knowledge in all kinds of crafts— 32 to make artistic designs for work in gold, silver and bronze, 33 to cut and set stones, to work in wood and to engage in all kinds of artistic craftsmanship. 34 And he has given both him and Oholiab son of Ahisamach, of the tribe of Dan, the ability to teach others. 35 He has filled them with skill to do all kinds of work as craftsmen, designers, embroiderers in blue, purple and scarlet yarn, and fine linen, and weavers—all of them master craftsmen and designers.

36

1 So Bezalel, Oholiab and every skilled person to whom the LORD has given skill and ability to know how to carry out all the work of constructing the sanctuary are to do the work just as the LORD has commanded."

2 Then Moses summoned Bezalel and Oholiab and every skilled person to whom the LORD had given ability and who was willing to come and do the work. 3 They received from Moses all the offerings the Israelites had brought to carry out the work of constructing the sanctuary. And the people continued to bring freewill offerings morning after morning. 4 So all the skilled craftsmen who were doing all the work on the sanctuary left their work 5 and said to Moses, "The people are bringing more than enough for doing the work the LORD commanded to be done."

6 Then Moses gave an order and they sent this word throughout the camp: "No man or woman is to make anything else as an offering for the sanctuary." And so the people were restrained from bringing more, 7 because what they already had was more than enough to do all the work.

THE TABERNACLE

8 All the skilled men among the workmen made the tabernacle with ten curtains of finely twisted linen and blue, purple and scarlet yarn, with cherubim worked into them by a skilled craftsman. 9 All the curtains were the same size—twenty-eight cubits long and four cubits wide. a 10 They joined five of the curtains together and did the same with the other five. 11 Then they made loops of blue material along the edge of the end curtain in one set, and the same was done with the end curtain in the other set. 12 They also made fifty loops on one curtain and fifty loops on the end curtain of the other set, with the loops opposite each other. 13 Then they made fifty gold clasps and used them to fasten the two sets of curtains together so that the tabernacle was a unit.

14 They made curtains of goat hair for the tent over the tabernacle—eleven altogether. 15 All eleven curtains were the same size—thirty cubits long and four cubits wide. b 16 They joined five of the curtains into one set and the other six into another set. 17 Then they made fifty loops along the edge of the end curtain in one set and also along the edge of the end curtain in the other set. 18 They made fifty bronze clasps to fasten the tent together as a unit. 19 Then they made for the tent a covering of ram skins dyed red, and over that a covering of hides of sea cows. c

20 They made upright frames of acacia wood for the tabernacle. 21 Each frame was ten cubits long and a cubit and a half wide, d 22 with two projections set parallel to each other. They made all the frames of the tabernacle in this way. 23 They made twenty frames for the south side of the tabernacle 24 and made forty silver bases to go under them—two bases for each frame, one under each projection. 25 For the

» live the adventure » Ex 35:21-22

Learning to Give

God doesn't *need* anything from us. He doesn't depend on us for anything. That's not why he wants us to give. Giving is actually a way of keeping our own priorities straight. If there's any material possession so important to us that we aren't willing to give it up in a second, we've got a big problem in our lives.

---

a 9 That is, about 42 feet (about 12.5 meters) long and 6 feet (about 1.8 meters) wide   b 15 That is, about 45 feet (about 13.5 meters) long and 6 feet (about 1.8 meters) wide   c 19 That is, dugongs   d 21 That is, about 15 feet (about 4.5 meters) long and 2 1/4 feet (about 0.7 meter) wide other side, the north side of the tabernacle, they made twenty frames ²⁶and forty silver bases—two under each frame. ²⁷They made six frames for the far end, that is, the west end of the tabernacle, ²⁸and two frames were made for the corners of the tabernacle at the far end. ²⁹At these two corners the frames were double from the bottom all the way to the top and fitted into a single ring; both were made alike. ³⁰So there were eight frames and sixteen silver bases—two under each frame.

³¹They also made crossbars of acacia wood: five for the frames on one side of the tabernacle, ³²five for those on the other side, and five for the frames on the west, at the far end of the tabernacle. ³³They made the center crossbar so that it extended from end to end at the middle of the frames. ³⁴They overlaid the frames with gold and made gold rings to hold the crossbars. They also overlaid the crossbars with gold.

³⁵They made the curtain of blue, purple and scarlet yarn and finely twisted linen, with cherubim worked into it by a skilled craftsman. ³⁶They made four posts of acacia wood for it and overlaid them with gold. They made gold hooks for them and cast their four silver bases. ³⁷For the entrance to the tent they made a curtain of blue, purple and scarlet yarn and finely twisted linen—the work of an embroiderer; ³⁸and they made five posts with hooks for them. They overlaid the tops of the posts and their bands with gold and made their five bases of bronze.

THE ARK

37 Bezalel made the ark of acacia wood—two and a half cubits long, a cubit and a half wide, and a cubit and a half high.ᵃ ²He overlaid it with pure gold, both inside and out, and made a gold molding around it. ³He cast four gold rings for it and fastened them to its four feet, with two rings on one side and two rings on the other. ⁴Then he made poles of acacia wood and overlaid them with gold. ⁵And he inserted the poles into the rings on the sides of the ark to carry it.

⁶He made the atonement cover of pure gold—two and a half cubits long and a cubit and a half wide.ᵇ ⁷Then he made two cherubim out of hammered gold at the ends of the cover. ⁸He made one cherub on one end and the second cherub on the other; at the two ends he made them of one piece with the cover. ⁹The cherubim had their wings spread upward, overshadowing the cover with them. The cherubim faced each other, looking toward the cover.

THE TABLE

¹⁰Theyᶜ made the table of acacia wood—two cubits long, a cubit wide, and a cubit and a half high.ᵈ ¹¹Then they overlaid it with pure gold and made a gold molding around it. ¹²They also made around it a rim a handbreadthᵉ wide and put a gold molding on the rim. ¹³They cast four gold rings for the table and fastened them to the four corners, where the four legs were. ¹⁴The rings were put close to the rim to hold the poles used in carrying the table. ¹⁵The poles for carrying the table were made of acacia wood and were overlaid with gold. ¹⁶And they made from pure gold the articles for the table—its plates and dishes and bowls and its pitchers for the pouring out of drink offerings.

THE LAMPSTAND

¹⁷They made the lampstand of pure gold and hammered it out, base and shaft; its flowerlike cups, buds and blossoms were of one piece with it. ¹⁸Six branches extended from the sides of the lampstand—three on one side and three on the other. ¹⁹Three cups shaped like almond flowers with buds and blossoms were on one branch, three on the next branch and the same for all six branches extending from the lampstand. ²⁰And on the lampstand were four cups shaped like almond flowers with buds and blossoms. ²¹One bud was under the first pair of branches extending from the lampstand, a second bud under the second pair, and a third bud under the third pair—six branches in all. ²²The buds and the branches were all of one piece with the lampstand, hammered out of pure gold.

²³They made its seven lamps, as well as its wick trimmers and trays, of pure gold. ²⁴They made the lampstand and all its accessories from one talentᶠ of pure gold.

ᵃ *1* That is, about 3 3/4 feet (about 1.1 meters) long and 2 1/4 feet (about 0.7 meter) wide and high   ᵇ *6* That is, about 3 3/4 feet (about 1.1 meters) long and 2 1/4 feet (about 0.7 meter) wide   ᶜ *10* Or *He*; also in verses 11-29   ᵈ *10* That is, about 3 feet (about 0.9 meter) long, 1 1/2 feet (about 0.5 meter) wide, and 2 1/4 feet (about 0.7 meter) high   ᵉ *12* That is, about 3 inches (about 8 centimeters)   ᶠ *24* That is, about 75 pounds (about 34 kilograms)

THE ALTAR OF INCENSE

25 They made the altar of incense out of acacia wood. It was square, a cubit long and a cubit wide, and two cubits high[a]—its horns of one piece with it. 26 They overlaid the top and all the sides and the horns with pure gold, and made a gold molding around it. 27 They made two gold rings below the molding—two on opposite sides—to hold the poles used to carry it. 28 They made the poles of acacia wood and overlaid them with gold.

29 They also made the sacred anointing oil and the pure, fragrant incense—the work of a perfumer.

THE ALTAR OF BURNT OFFERING

38

They[b] built the altar of burnt offering of acacia wood, three cubits[c] high; it was square, five cubits long and five cubits wide.[d] 2 They made a horn at each of the four corners, so that the horns and the altar were of one piece, and they overlaid the altar with bronze. 3 They made all its utensils of bronze—its pots, shovels, sprinkling bowls, meat forks and firepans. 4 They made a grating for the altar, a bronze network, to be under its ledge, halfway up the altar. 5 They cast bronze rings to hold the poles for the four corners of the bronze grating. 6 They made the poles of acacia wood and overlaid them with bronze. 7 They inserted the poles into the rings so they would be on the sides of the altar for carrying it. They made it hollow, out of boards.

BASIN FOR WASHING

8 They made the bronze basin and its bronze stand from the mirrors of the women who served at the entrance to the Tent of Meeting.

THE COURTYARD

9 Next they made the courtyard. The south side was a hundred cubits[e] long and had curtains of finely twisted linen, 10 with twenty posts and twenty bronze bases, and with silver hooks and bands on the posts. 11 The north side was also a hundred cubits long and had twenty posts and twenty bronze bases, with silver hooks and bands on the posts.

12 The west end was fifty cubits[f] wide and had curtains, with ten posts and ten bases, with silver hooks and bands on the posts. 13 The east end, toward the sunrise, was also fifty cubits wide. 14 Curtains fifteen cubits[g] long were on one side of the entrance, with three posts and three bases, 15 and curtains fifteen cubits long were on the other side of the entrance to the courtyard, with three posts and three bases. 16 All the curtains around the courtyard were of finely twisted linen. 17 The bases for the posts were bronze. The hooks and bands on the posts were silver, and their tops were overlaid with silver; so all the posts of the courtyard had silver bands.

18 The curtain for the entrance to the courtyard was of blue, purple and scarlet yarn and finely twisted linen—the work of an embroiderer. It was twenty cubits[h] long and, like the curtains of the courtyard, five cubits[i] high, 19 with four posts and four bronze bases. Their hooks and bands were silver, and their tops were overlaid with silver. 20 All the tent pegs of the tabernacle and of the surrounding courtyard were bronze.

THE MATERIALS USED

21 These are the amounts of the materials used for the tabernacle, the tabernacle of the Testimony, which were recorded at Moses' command by the Levites under the direction of Ithamar son of Aaron, the priest. 22 (Bezalel son of Uri, the son of Hur, of the tribe of Judah, made everything the LORD commanded Moses; 23 with him was Oholiab son of Ahisamach, of the tribe of Dan—a craftsman and designer, and an embroiderer in blue, purple and scarlet yarn and fine linen.) 24 The total amount of the gold from the wave offering used for all the work on the sanctuary was 29 talents and 730 shekels,[j] according to the sanctuary shekel.

25 The silver obtained from those of the community who were counted in the census was 100 talents and 1,775 shekels,[k] according to the sanctuary shekel— 26 one beka per person, that is, half a shekel,[l]

a 25 That is, about 1 1/2 feet (about 0.5 meter) long and wide, and about 3 feet (about 0.9 meter) high   b 1 Or He; also in verses 2-9   c 1 That is, about 4 1/2 feet (about 1.3 meters)   d 1 That is, about 7 1/2 feet (about 2.3 meters) long and wide   e 9 That is, about 150 feet (about 46 meters)   f 12 That is, about 75 feet (about 23 meters)   g 14 That is, about 22 1/2 feet (about 6.9 meters)   h 18 That is, about 30 feet (about 9 meters)   i 18 That is, about 7 1/2 feet (about 2.3 meters)   j 24 The weight of the gold was a little over one ton (about 1 metric ton).   k 25 The weight of the silver was a little over 3 3/4 tons (about 3.4 metric tons).   l 26 That is, about 1/5 ounce (about 5.5 grams)

battlelines

» Dark Comedy (Humor)

Q: What are you watching?
A: Comedy Central. They've got a bunch of stand-up comics on tonight. A few of them have been lame, but there have been these two or three guys who were *hilarious*.

Q: Pretty raw?
A: Yeah, I guess. Most of their material is about sex and stuff. My older sister would *definitely* fail to see the humor here.

Q: See, that's interesting. If a comedy routine would bother *her*, shouldn't it also bother *you*?
A: No, because, um, she's . . . a girl.

Q: So?
A: It's like she's from another planet—she's out of touch.

Q: And your point is?
A: Well, plus she's like a big-time Christian.

Q: And you're not?
A: Well, yeah, I'm a Christian, but—

Q: But what?
A: Don't do this to me, all right? Look—it doesn't *mean* anything. They're just jokes, stupid observations about life. OK, yeah, so it's crude in parts. But it's not like I'm gonna stand up at the dinner table or at church and start repeating these routines or anything. It's just funny, you know? You laugh, and then you forget about it.

Q: You know, I heard a guy once ask, "What does it say about us that so many of the things we *enjoy* watching on TV and in movies are the very same things that God hated so much, that he sent his Son to die for?"
A: You're killing me, man. Give it a rest already!

» Good Clean Fun

Laughter is great. It's good for you. Or, as King Solomon put it, "A cheerful heart is good medicine" (Proverbs 17:22). But what's so funny about humor that uses raw language or puts other people down? What's so great about a stand-up routine loaded with comments that would make a sex therapist blush? Come on! Where's the creativity? Where's the subtlety?

Try this experiment: Make a commitment with your buddies to clean up your jokes and keep track of how much you guys laugh. Are you still laughing? Does your humor change?

One last question for you: Why do you think the definition of "funny" has changed so radically in such a short time?

If you think crude or degrading humor is OK for a Christian, think again. Try remembering this word of warning from the apostle Paul: "But among you there must not be even a hint of sexual immorality, or of any kind of impurity, or of greed, because these are improper for God's holy people. Nor should there be obscenity, foolish talk or coarse joking, which are out of place, but rather thanksgiving" (Ephesians 5:3–4).

Read more about choosing great entertainment at www.RevolutionBible.com.

according to the sanctuary shekel, from everyone who had crossed over to those counted, twenty years old or more, a total of 603,550 men. [27]The 100 talents[a] of silver were used to cast the bases for the sanctuary and for the curtain—100 bases from the 100 talents, one talent for each base. [28]They used the 1,775 shekels[b] to make the hooks for the posts, to overlay the tops of the posts, and to make their bands.

[29]The bronze from the wave offering was 70 talents and 2,400 shekels.[c] [30]They used it to make the bases for the entrance to the Tent of Meeting, the bronze altar with its bronze grating and all its utensils, [31]the bases for the surrounding courtyard and those for its entrance and all the tent pegs for the tabernacle and those for the surrounding courtyard.

THE PRIESTLY GARMENTS

39

From the blue, purple and scarlet yarn they made woven garments for ministering in the sanctuary. They also made sacred garments for Aaron, as the Lord commanded Moses.

THE EPHOD

[2]They[d] made the ephod of gold, and of blue, purple and scarlet yarn, and of finely twisted linen. [3]They hammered out thin sheets of gold and cut strands to be worked into the blue, purple and scarlet yarn and fine linen—the work of a skilled craftsman. [4]They made shoulder pieces for the ephod, which were attached to two of its corners, so it could be fastened. [5]Its skillfully woven waistband was like it—of one piece with the ephod and made with gold, and with blue, purple and scarlet yarn, and with finely twisted linen, as the Lord commanded Moses.

[6]They mounted the onyx stones in gold filigree settings and engraved them like a seal with the names of the sons of Israel. [7]Then they fastened them on the shoulder pieces of the ephod as memorial stones for the sons of Israel, as the Lord commanded Moses.

THE BREASTPIECE

[8]They fashioned the breastpiece—the work of a skilled craftsman. They made it like the ephod: of gold, and of blue, purple and scarlet yarn, and of finely twisted linen. [9]It was square—a span[e] long and a span wide—and folded double. [10]Then they mounted four rows of precious stones on it. In the first row there was a ruby, a topaz and a beryl; [11]in the second row a turquoise, a sapphire[f] and an emerald; [12]in the third row a jacinth, an agate and an amethyst; [13]in the fourth row a chrysolite, an onyx and a jasper.[g] They were mounted in gold filigree settings. [14]There were twelve stones, one for each of the names of the sons of Israel, each engraved like a seal with the name of one of the twelve tribes.

[15]For the breastpiece they made braided chains of pure gold, like a rope. [16]They made two gold filigree settings and two gold rings, and fastened the rings to two of the corners of the breastpiece. [17]They fastened the two gold chains to the rings at the corners of the breastpiece, [18]and the other ends of the chains to the two settings, attaching them to the shoulder pieces of the ephod at the front. [19]They made two gold rings and attached them to the other two corners of the breastpiece on the inside edge next to the ephod. [20]Then they made two more gold rings and attached them to the bottom of the shoulder pieces on the front of the ephod, close to the seam just above the waistband of the ephod. [21]They tied the rings of the breastpiece to the rings of the ephod with blue cord, connecting it to the waistband so that the breastpiece would not swing out from the ephod—as the Lord commanded Moses.

OTHER PRIESTLY GARMENTS

[22]They made the robe of the ephod entirely of blue cloth—the work of a weaver— [23]with an opening in the center of the robe like the opening of a collar,[h] and a band around this opening, so that it would not tear. [24]They made pomegranates of blue, purple and scarlet yarn and finely twisted linen around the hem of the robe. [25]And they made bells of pure gold and attached them around the hem between the pomegranates. [26]The bells and pomegranates alternated around the hem of the robe to be worn for ministering, as the Lord commanded Moses.

---

[a] *27* That is, about 3 3/4 tons (about 3.4 metric tons)   [b] *28* That is, about 45 pounds (about 20 kilograms)   [c] *29* The weight of the bronze was about 2 1/2 tons (about 2.4 metric tons).   [d] *2* Or *He*; also in verses 7, 8 and 22   [e] *9* That is, about 9 inches (about 22 centimeters)   [f] *11* Or *lapis lazuli*   [g] *13* The precise identification of some of these precious stones is uncertain.   [h] *23* The meaning of the Hebrew for this word is uncertain.

27For Aaron and his sons, they made tunics of fine linen—the work of a weaver— 28and the turban of fine linen, the linen headbands and the undergarments of finely twisted linen. 29The sash was of finely twisted linen and blue, purple and scarlet yarn—the work of an embroiderer—as the LORD commanded Moses.

30They made the plate, the sacred diadem, out of pure gold and engraved on it, like an inscription on a seal: HOLY TO THE LORD. 31Then they fastened a blue cord to it to attach it to the turban, as the LORD commanded Moses.

MOSES INSPECTS THE TABERNACLE

32So all the work on the tabernacle, the Tent of Meeting, was completed. The Israelites did everything just as the LORD commanded Moses. 33Then they brought the tabernacle to Moses: the tent and all its furnishings, its clasps, frames, crossbars, posts and bases; 34the covering of ram skins dyed red, the covering of hides of sea cows[a] and the shielding curtain; 35the ark of the Testimony with its poles and the atonement cover; 36the table with all its articles and the bread of the Presence; 37the pure gold lampstand with its row of lamps and all its accessories, and the oil for the light; 38the gold altar, the anointing oil, the fragrant incense, and the curtain for the entrance to the tent; 39the bronze altar with its bronze grating, its poles and all its utensils; the basin with its stand; 40the curtains of the courtyard with its posts and bases, and the curtain for the entrance to the courtyard; the ropes and tent pegs for the courtyard; all the furnishings for the tabernacle, the Tent of Meeting; 41and the woven garments worn for ministering in the sanctuary, both the sacred garments for Aaron the priest and the garments for his sons when serving as priests.

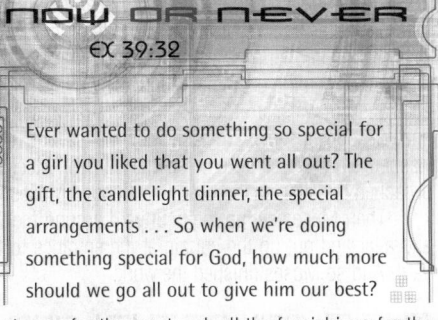

NOW OR NEVER

EX 39:32

Ever wanted to do something so special for a girl you liked that you went all out? The gift, the candlelight dinner, the special arrangements . . . So when we're doing something special for God, how much more should we go all out to give him our best?

42The Israelites had done all the work just as the LORD had commanded Moses. 43Moses inspected the work and saw that they had done it just as the LORD had commanded. So Moses blessed them.

SETTING UP THE TABERNACLE

40 Then the LORD said to Moses: 2"Set up the tabernacle, the Tent of Meeting, on the first day of the first month. 3Place the ark of the Testimony in it and shield the ark with the curtain. 4Bring in the table and set out what belongs on it. Then bring in the lampstand and set up its lamps. 5Place the gold altar of incense in front of the ark of the Testimony and put the curtain at the entrance to the tabernacle.

6"Place the altar of burnt offering in front of the entrance to the tabernacle, the Tent of Meeting; 7place the basin between the Tent of Meeting and the altar and put water in it. 8Set up the courtyard around it and put the curtain at the entrance to the courtyard.

9"Take the anointing oil and anoint the tabernacle and everything in it; consecrate it and all its furnishings, and it will be holy. 10Then anoint the altar of burnt offering and all its utensils; consecrate the altar, and it will be most holy. 11Anoint the basin and its stand and consecrate them.

12"Bring Aaron and his sons to the entrance to the Tent of Meeting and wash them with water. 13Then dress Aaron in the sacred garments, anoint him and consecrate him so he may serve me as priest. 14Bring his sons and dress them in tunics. 15Anoint them just as you anointed their father, so they may serve me as priests. Their anointing will be to a priesthood that will continue for all generations to come." 16Moses did everything just as the LORD commanded him.

17So the tabernacle was set up on the first day of the first month in the second year. 18When Moses set up the tabernacle, he put the bases in place, erected the frames, inserted the crossbars and set up the posts. 19Then he spread the tent over the tabernacle and put the covering over the tent, as the LORD commanded him.

20He took the Testimony and placed it in the ark, attached the poles to the ark and put the atonement

---

a 34 That is, dugongs

cover over it. 21Then he brought the ark into the tabernacle and hung the shielding curtain and shielded the ark of the Testimony, as the LORD commanded him.

22Moses placed the table in the Tent of Meeting on the north side of the tabernacle outside the curtain 23and set out the bread on it before the LORD, as the LORD commanded him. 24He placed the lampstand in the Tent of Meeting opposite the table on the south side of the tabernacle 25and set up the lamps before the LORD, as the LORD commanded him.

26Moses placed the gold altar in the Tent of Meeting in front of the curtain 27and burned fragrant incense on it, as the LORD commanded him. 28Then he put up the curtain at the entrance to the tabernacle.

29He set the altar of burnt offering near the entrance to the tabernacle, the Tent of Meeting, and offered on it burnt offerings and grain offerings, as the LORD commanded him.

30He placed the basin between the Tent of Meeting and the altar and put water in it for washing, 31and Moses and Aaron and his sons used it to wash their hands and feet. 32They washed whenever they entered the Tent of Meeting or approached the altar, as the LORD commanded Moses.

33Then Moses set up the courtyard around the tabernacle and altar and put up the curtain at the entrance to the courtyard. And so Moses finished the work.

THE GLORY OF THE LORD

34Then the cloud covered the Tent of Meeting, and the glory of the LORD filled the tabernacle. 35Moses could not enter the Tent of Meeting because the cloud had settled upon it, and the glory of the LORD filled the tabernacle.

36In all the travels of the Israelites, whenever the cloud lifted from above the tabernacle, they would set out; 37but if the cloud did not lift, they did not set out—until the day it lifted. 38So the cloud of the LORD was over the tabernacle by day, and fire was in the cloud by night, in the sight of all the house of Israel during all their travels.

Working Hard for God

Nothing impresses people like hard work. When your teacher sees you doing a little extra to get your assignments done right, when your boss spots you going above and beyond your assigned duties, when your parents catch a glimpse of you doing something without having to be told—they're all going to come to the conclusion that there's something different about you, something special. That kind of approval means a lot, but God's approval is what matters most. So how hard do you work to please him?

LEVITICUS

« AT A GLANCE

Author
Moses

Audience
People of Israel

Date
1445–1444 B.C.

Setting
The Israelites hear instructions from God at the base of Mount Sinai.

Verse to Remember
I am the LORD who brought you up out of Egypt to be your God; therefore be holy, because I am holy (11:45).

Theme to Consider
Holiness, holiness, holiness! The book of Leviticus establishes the ground rules for how God's people should live. God desires that his people become "set apart" for him.

UNCHANGING TRUTH » Think you're someone special? Well, you are. If you've committed yourself to Christ, you *are* someone very special.

Before your ego blows up too much, though, please realize that *special* doesn't mean "superior." The fact that you're a Christian doesn't mean you're any better or more valuable than your non-Christian friends. It does mean you're different, though. Way different.

For one thing, the fact that you're a Christian means God has a special mission for your life. Maybe you've already discovered some clues about what that mission is—or maybe you're still figuring it out. Either way, the fact remains that you have a remarkable calling and purpose to discover. And that makes you rather unique.

As a Christian, you also have a special set of standards to live by—for example, standards that require you to . . .

- turn the other cheek in situations where others might be looking to dish out some payback,
- show genuine love for people who don't give a rip about you,
- put other people's needs ahead of your own, even when it seems like everyone around you is looking out only for themselves.

Hey, no one said being special (and different from your non-Christian friends) was going to be easy!

In the book of Leviticus, the Israelites begin to discover their own "differentness" through the rules and regulations God set up to make them "separate" from all other people on the planet.

LIFE LESSONS »

1   God doesn't make people guess about what he wants from them; he makes his expectations very clear (1:1–17).

2   Sex is one of God's most awesome gifts to the human race; in fact, it's so incredible that God designed boundaries to keep us from ruining it (18:1–23).

3   God takes sin much more seriously than we do (20:1–27).

THE BURNT OFFERING

1 The Lord called to Moses and spoke to him from the Tent of Meeting. He said, [2]"Speak to the Israelites and say to them: 'When any of you brings an offering to the Lord, bring as your offering an animal from either the herd or the flock.

[3]"'If the offering is a burnt offering from the herd, he is to offer a male without defect. He must present it at the entrance to the Tent of Meeting so that it[a] will be acceptable to the Lord. [4]He is to lay his hand on the head of the burnt offering, and it will be accepted on his behalf to make atonement for him. [5]He is to slaughter the young bull before the Lord, and then Aaron's sons the priests shall bring the blood and sprinkle it against the altar on all sides at the entrance to the Tent of Meeting. [6]He is to skin the burnt offering and cut it into pieces. [7]The sons of Aaron the priest are to put fire on the altar and arrange wood on the fire.

NOW OR NEVER

LEV 1:1–17

God's system of sacrifice was designed (at least in part) to help the Israelites understand just how serious every sin is. How seriously does our world take sin these days? How seriously do you take your own sin?

[8]Then Aaron's sons the priests shall arrange the pieces, including the head and the fat, on the burning wood that is on the altar. [9]He is to wash the inner parts and the legs with water, and the priest is to burn all of it on the altar. It is a burnt offering, an offering made by fire, an aroma pleasing to the Lord.

[10]"'If the offering is a burnt offering from the flock, from either the sheep or the goats, he is to offer a male without defect. [11]He is to slaughter it at the north side of the altar before the Lord, and Aaron's sons the priests shall sprinkle its blood against the altar on all sides. [12]He is to cut it into pieces, and the priest shall arrange them, including the head and the fat, on the burning wood that is on the altar. [13]He is to wash the inner parts and the legs with water, and the priest is to bring all of it and burn it on the altar. It is a burnt offering, an offering made by fire, an aroma pleasing to the Lord.

[14]"'If the offering to the Lord is a burnt offering of birds, he is to offer a dove or a young pigeon. [15]The priest shall bring it to the altar, wring off the head and burn it on the altar; its blood shall be drained out on the side of the altar. [16]He is to remove the crop with its contents[b] and throw it to the east side of the altar, where the ashes are. [17]He shall tear it open by the wings, not severing it completely, and then the priest shall burn it on the wood that is on the fire on the altar. It is a burnt offering, an offering made by fire, an aroma pleasing to the Lord.

THE GRAIN OFFERING

2 "'When someone brings a grain offering to the Lord, his offering is to be of fine flour. He is to pour oil on it, put incense on it [2]and take it to Aaron's sons the priests. The priest shall take a handful of the fine flour and oil, together with all the incense, and burn this as a memorial portion on the altar, an offering made by fire, an aroma pleasing to the Lord. [3]The rest of the grain offering belongs to Aaron and his sons; it is a most holy part of the offerings made to the Lord by fire.

[4]"'If you bring a grain offering baked in an oven, it is to consist of fine flour: cakes made without yeast and mixed with oil, or[c] wafers made without yeast and spread with oil. [5]If your grain offering is prepared on a griddle, it is to be made of fine flour mixed with oil, and without yeast. [6]Crumble it and pour oil on it; it is a grain offering. [7]If your grain offering is cooked in a pan, it is to be made of fine flour and oil. [8]Bring the grain offering made of these things to the Lord; present it to the priest, who shall take it to the altar. [9]He shall take out the memorial portion from the grain offering and burn it on the altar as an offering made by fire, an aroma pleasing to the Lord. [10]The rest of the grain offering belongs to Aaron and his sons; it is a most holy part of the offerings made to the Lord by fire.

[11]"'Every grain offering you bring to the Lord must be made without yeast, for you are not to burn any yeast or honey in an offering made to the Lord by fire. [12]You may bring them to the Lord as an offering of the firstfruits, but they are not to be offered on the altar as a pleasing aroma. [13]Season all your grain offerings with salt. Do not leave the salt of the covenant of your God out of your grain offerings; add salt to all your offerings.

[14]"'If you bring a grain offering of firstfruits to the Lord, offer crushed heads of new grain roasted

---

[a] 3 Or he [b] 16 Or crop and the feathers; the meaning of the Hebrew for this word is uncertain. [c] 4 Or and

in the fire. ¹⁵Put oil and incense on it; it is a grain offering. ¹⁶The priest shall burn the memorial portion of the crushed grain and the oil, together with all the incense, as an offering made to the LORD by fire.

THE FELLOWSHIP OFFERING

3 " 'If someone's offering is a fellowship offering,ᵃ and he offers an animal from the herd, whether male or female, he is to present before the LORD an animal without defect. ²He is to lay his hand on the head of his offering and slaughter it at the entrance to the Tent of Meeting. Then Aaron's sons the priests shall sprinkle the blood against the altar on all sides. ³From the fellowship offering he is to bring a sacrifice made to the LORD by fire: all the fat that covers the inner parts or is connected to them, ⁴both kidneys with the fat on them near the loins, and the covering of the liver, which he will remove with the kidneys. ⁵Then Aaron's sons are to burn it on the altar on top of the burnt offering that is on the burning wood, as an offering made by fire, an aroma pleasing to the LORD.

⁶" 'If he offers an animal from the flock as a fellowship offering to the LORD, he is to offer a male or female without defect. ⁷If he offers a lamb, he is to present it before the LORD. ⁸He is to lay his hand on the head of his offering and slaughter it in front of the Tent of Meeting. Then Aaron's sons shall sprinkle its blood against the altar on all sides. ⁹From the fellowship offering he is to bring a sacrifice made to the LORD by fire: its fat, the entire fat tail cut off close to the backbone, all the fat that covers the inner parts or is connected to them, ¹⁰both kidneys with the fat on them near the loins, and the covering of the liver, which he will remove with the kidneys. ¹¹The priest shall burn them on the altar as food, an offering made to the LORD by fire.

¹²" 'If his offering is a goat, he is to present it before the LORD. ¹³He is to lay his hand on its head and slaughter it in front of the Tent of Meeting. Then Aaron's sons shall sprinkle its blood against the altar on all sides. ¹⁴From what he offers he is to make this offering to the LORD by fire: all the fat that covers the inner parts or is connected to them, ¹⁵both kidneys with the fat on them near the loins, and the covering of the liver, which he will remove with the kidneys. ¹⁶The priest shall burn them on the altar as food, an offering made by fire, a pleasing aroma. All the fat is the LORD's.

¹⁷" 'This is a lasting ordinance for the generations to come, wherever you live: You must not eat any fat or any blood.' "

THE SIN OFFERING

4 The LORD said to Moses, ²"Say to the Israelites: 'When anyone sins unintentionally and does what is forbidden in any of the LORD's commands—

³" 'If the anointed priest sins, bringing guilt on the people, he must bring to the LORD a young bull without defect as a sin offering for the sin he has committed. ⁴He is to present the bull at the entrance to the Tent of Meeting before the LORD. He is to lay his hand on its head and slaughter it before the LORD. ⁵Then the anointed priest shall take some of the bull's blood and carry it into the Tent of Meeting. ⁶He is to dip his finger into the blood and sprinkle some of it seven times before the LORD, in front of the curtain of the sanctuary. ⁷The priest shall then put some of the blood on the horns of the altar of fragrant incense that is before the LORD in the Tent of Meeting. The rest of the bull's blood he shall pour out at the base of the altar of burnt offering at the entrance to the Tent of Meeting. ⁸He shall remove all the fat from the bull of the sin offering—the fat that covers the inner parts or is connected to them, ⁹both kidneys with the fat on them near the loins, and the covering of the liver, which he will remove with the kidneys— ¹⁰just as the fat is removed from the oxᵇ sacrificed as a fellowship offering.ᶜ Then the priest shall burn them on the altar of burnt offering. ¹¹But the hide of the bull and all its flesh, as well as the

NOW OR NEVER

LEV 2:13

Salt was extremely valuable back in the days before refrigerators. Because of its value, the Israelites added it to their sacrifices to symbolize the permanence of their covenant with God. It signified that when it came to their relationship with God, they were in it for the long haul.

ᵃ 1 Traditionally *peace offering*; also in verses 3, 6 and 9   ᵇ 10 The Hebrew word can include both male and female.
ᶜ 10 Traditionally *peace offering*; also in verses 26, 31 and 35

head and legs, the inner parts and offal— ¹²that is, all the rest of the bull—he must take outside the camp to a place ceremonially clean, where the ashes are thrown, and burn it in a wood fire on the ash heap.

¹³" 'If the whole Israelite community sins unintentionally and does what is forbidden in any of the Lord's commands, even though the community is unaware of the matter, they are guilty. ¹⁴When they become aware of the sin they committed, the assembly must bring a young bull as a sin offering and present it before the Tent of Meeting. ¹⁵The elders of the community are to lay their hands on the bull's head before the Lord, and the bull shall be slaughtered before the Lord. ¹⁶Then the anointed priest is to take some of the bull's blood into the Tent of Meeting. ¹⁷He shall dip his finger into the blood and sprinkle it before the Lord seven times in front of the curtain. ¹⁸He is to put some of the blood on the horns of the altar that is before the Lord in the Tent of Meeting. The rest of the blood he shall pour out at the base of the altar of burnt offering at the entrance to the Tent of Meeting. ¹⁹He shall remove all the fat from it and burn it on the altar, ²⁰and do with this bull just as he did with the bull for the sin offering. In this way the priest will make atonement for them, and they will be forgiven. ²¹Then he shall take the bull outside the camp and burn it as he burned the first bull. This is the sin offering for the community.

²²" 'When a leader sins unintentionally and does what is forbidden in any of the commands of the Lord his God, he is guilty. ²³When he is made aware of the sin he committed, he must bring as his offering a male goat without defect. ²⁴He is to lay his hand on the goat's head and slaughter it at the place where the burnt offering is slaughtered before the Lord. It is a sin offering. ²⁵Then the priest shall take some of the blood of the sin offering with his finger and put it on the horns of the altar of burnt offering and pour out the rest of the blood at the base of the altar. ²⁶He shall burn all the fat on the altar as he burned the fat of the fellowship offering. In this way the priest will make atonement for the man's sin, and he will be forgiven.

²⁷" 'If a member of the community sins unintentionally and does what is forbidden in any of the Lord's commands, he is guilty. ²⁸When he is made aware of the sin he committed, he must bring as his offering for the sin he committed a female goat without defect. ²⁹He is to lay his hand on the head of the sin offering and slaughter it at the place of the burnt offering. ³⁰Then the priest is to take some of the blood with his finger and put it on the horns of the altar of burnt offering and pour out the rest of the blood at the base of the altar. ³¹He shall remove all the fat, just as the fat is removed from the fellowship offering, and the priest shall burn it on the altar as an aroma pleasing to the Lord. In this way the priest will make atonement for him, and he will be forgiven.

³²" 'If he brings a lamb as his sin offering, he is to bring a female without defect. ³³He is to lay his hand on its head and slaughter it for a sin offering at the place where the burnt offering is slaughtered. ³⁴Then the priest shall take some of the blood of the sin offering with his finger and put it on the horns of the altar of burnt offering and pour out the rest of the blood at the base of the altar. ³⁵He shall remove all the fat, just as the fat is removed from the lamb of the fellowship offering, and the priest shall burn it on the altar on top of the offerings made to the Lord by fire. In this way the priest will make atonement for him for the sin he has committed, and he will be forgiven.

5 " 'If a person sins because he does not speak up when he hears a public charge to testify regarding something he has seen or learned about, he will be held responsible.

²" 'Or if a person touches anything ceremonially unclean—whether the carcasses of unclean wild animals or of unclean livestock or of unclean creatures that move along the ground—even though he is unaware of it, he has become unclean and is guilty.

³" 'Or if he touches human uncleanness—anything that would make him unclean—even though he is unaware of it, when he learns of it he will be guilty.

⁴" 'Or if a person thoughtlessly takes an oath to do anything, whether good or evil—in any matter one might carelessly swear about—even though he is unaware of it, in any case when he learns of it he will be guilty.

⁵" 'When anyone is guilty in any of these ways, he must confess in what way he has sinned ⁶and, as a penalty for the sin he has committed, he must bring to the Lord a female lamb or goat from the flock as a sin offering; and the priest shall make atonement for him for his sin.

⁷" 'If he cannot afford a lamb, he is to bring two doves or two young pigeons to the Lord as a penalty for his sin—one for a sin offering and the other for a burnt offering. ⁸He is to bring them to the

priest, who shall first offer the one for the sin offering. He is to wring its head from its neck, not sever-ing it completely, ⁹and is to sprinkle some of the blood of the sin offering against the side of the altar; the rest of the blood must be drained out at the base of the altar. It is a sin offering. ¹⁰The priest shall then offer the other as a burnt offering in the prescribed way and make atonement for him for the sin he has committed, and he will be for-given.

¹¹ " 'If, however, he cannot afford two doves or two young pigeons, he is to bring as an of-fering for his sin a tenth of an ephah ᵃ of fine flour for a sin offering. He must not put oil or incense on it, because it is a sin offering. ¹²He is to bring it to the priest, who shall take a handful of it as a memorial portion and burn it on the altar on top of the offerings made to the

ПΩШ OR ПΞVΞR
LEV 5:5

Unconfessed sin is like a virus crashing your Internet connection. You can't expect to get far in your relationship with God if you don't take time to deal with the sin in your life.

LORD by fire. It is a sin offering. ¹³In this way the priest will make atonement for him for any of these sins he has committed, and he will be forgiven. The rest of the offering will belong to the priest, as in the case of the grain offering.' "

THE GUILT OFFERING

¹⁴The LORD said to Moses: ¹⁵"When a person commits a violation and sins unintentionally in regard to any of the LORD's holy things, he is to bring to the LORD as a penalty a ram from the flock, one with-out defect and of the proper value in silver, according to the sanctuary shekel.ᵇ It is a guilt offering. ¹⁶He must make restitution for what he has failed to do in regard to the holy things, add a fifth of the value to that and give it all to the priest, who will make atonement for him with the ram as a guilt offering, and he will be forgiven.

¹⁷"If a person sins and does what is forbidden in any of the LORD's commands, even though he does not know it, he is guilty and will be held responsible. ¹⁸He is to bring to the priest as a guilt offering a ram from the flock, one without defect and of the proper value. In this way the priest will make atone-ment for him for the wrong he has committed unintentionally, and he will be forgiven. ¹⁹It is a guilt of-fering; he has been guilty ofᶜ wrongdoing against the LORD."

6 The LORD said to Moses: ²"If anyone sins and is unfaithful to the LORD by deceiving his neighbor about something entrusted to him or left in his care or stolen, or if he cheats him, ³or if he finds lost property and lies about it, or if he swears falsely, or if he commits any such sin that people may do— ⁴when he thus sins and becomes guilty, he must return what he has stolen or taken by extortion, or what was entrusted to him, or the lost property he found, ⁵or whatever it was he swore falsely about. He must make restitution in full, add a fifth of the value to it and give it all to the owner on the day he presents his guilt offering. ⁶And as a penalty he must bring to the priest, that is, to the LORD, his guilt offering, a ram from the flock, one without defect and of the proper value. ⁷In this way the priest will make atonement for him before the LORD, and he will be forgiven for any of these things he did that made him guilty."

THE BURNT OFFERING

⁸The LORD said to Moses: ⁹"Give Aaron and his sons this command: 'These are the regulations for the burnt offering: The burnt offering is to remain on the altar hearth throughout the night, till morning, and the fire must be kept burning on the altar. ¹⁰The priest shall then put on his linen clothes, with lin-en undergarments next to his body, and shall remove the ashes of the burnt offering that the fire has consumed on the altar and place them beside the altar. ¹¹Then he is to take off these clothes and put on others, and carry the ashes outside the camp to a place that is ceremonially clean. ¹²The fire on the al-tar must be kept burning; it must not go out. Every morning the priest is to add firewood and arrange the burnt offering on the fire and burn the fat of the fellowship offeringsᵈ on it. ¹³The fire must be kept burning on the altar continuously; it must not go out.

ᵃ 11 That is, probably about 2 quarts (about 2 liters) ᵇ 15 That is, about 2/5 ounce (about 11.5 grams) ᶜ 19 Or has made full expiation for his ᵈ 12 Traditionally peace offerings

THE GRAIN OFFERING

14 " 'These are the regulations for the grain offering: Aaron's sons are to bring it before the LORD, in front of the altar. 15 The priest is to take a handful of fine flour and oil, together with all the incense on the grain offering, and burn the memorial portion on the altar as an aroma pleasing to the LORD. 16 Aaron and his sons shall eat the rest of it, but it is to be eaten without yeast in a holy place; they are to eat it in the courtyard of the Tent of Meeting. 17 It must not be baked with yeast; I have given it as their share of the offerings made to me by fire. Like the sin offering and the guilt offering, it is most holy. 18 Any male descendant of Aaron may eat it. It is his regular share of the offerings made to the LORD by fire for the generations to come. Whatever touches them will become holy.ª' "

19 The LORD also said to Moses, 20 "This is the offering Aaron and his sons are to bring to the LORD on the day heᵇ is anointed: a tenth of an ephahᶜ of fine flour as a regular grain offering, half of it in the morning and half in the evening. 21 Prepare it with oil on a griddle; bring it well-mixed and present the grain offering brokenᵈ in pieces as an aroma pleasing to the LORD. 22 The son who is to succeed him as anointed priest shall prepare it. It is the LORD's regular share and is to be burned completely. 23 Every grain offering of a priest shall be burned completely; it must not be eaten."

THE SIN OFFERING

24 The LORD said to Moses, 25 "Say to Aaron and his sons: 'These are the regulations for the sin offering: The sin offering is to be slaughtered before the LORD in the place the burnt offering is slaughtered; it is most holy. 26 The priest who offers it shall eat it; it is to be eaten in a holy place, in the courtyard of the Tent of Meeting. 27 Whatever touches any of the flesh will become holy, and if any of the blood is spattered on a garment, you must wash it in a holy place. 28 The clay pot the meat is cooked in must be broken; but if it is cooked in a bronze pot, the pot is to be scoured and rinsed with water. 29 Any male in a priest's family may eat it; it is most holy. 30 But any sin offering whose blood is brought into the Tent of Meeting to make atonement in the Holy Place must not be eaten; it must be burned.

THE GUILT OFFERING

7 " 'These are the regulations for the guilt offering, which is most holy: 2 The guilt offering is to be slaughtered in the place where the burnt offering is slaughtered, and its blood is to be sprinkled against the altar on all sides. 3 All its fat shall be offered: the fat tail and the fat that covers the inner parts, 4 both kidneys with the fat on them near the loins, and the covering of the liver, which is to be removed with the kidneys. 5 The priest shall burn them on the altar as an offering made to the LORD by fire. It is a guilt offering. 6 Any male in a priest's family may eat it, but it must be eaten in a holy place; it is most holy.

7 " 'The same law applies to both the sin offering and the guilt offering: They belong to the priest who makes atonement with them. 8 The priest who offers a burnt offering for anyone may keep its hide for himself. 9 Every grain offering baked in an oven or cooked in a pan or on a griddle belongs to the priest who offers it, 10 and every grain offering, whether mixed with oil or dry, belongs equally to all the sons of Aaron.

THE FELLOWSHIP OFFERING

11 " 'These are the regulations for the fellowship offeringᵉ a person may present to the LORD:

12 " 'If he offers it as an expression of thankfulness, then along with this thank offering he is to offer

Showing Gratitude

What is your blessing-to-thanking ratio? To figure it out, compare the number of things God does for you every day to the number of things you *specifically* thank him for on a daily basis. Obviously, we're not talking exact figures here, but you should be able to come up with a ballpark estimate. What do you think your ratio is—100 to one? Perhaps 1000 to one? If you want to improve your relationship with God, make an effort to lower that ratio by simply noticing and thanking him for the many things he already does for you every single day.

» live the adventure » Lev 7:12

ª 18 Or Whoever touches them must be holy; similarly in verse 27   ᵇ 20 Or each   ᶜ 20 That is, probably about 2 quarts (about 2 liters)   ᵈ 21 The meaning of the Hebrew for this word is uncertain.   ᵉ 11 Traditionally peace offering; also in verses 13-37 cakes of bread made without yeast and mixed with oil, wafers made without yeast and spread with oil, and cakes of fine flour well-kneaded and mixed with oil. ¹³Along with his fellowship offering of thanksgiving he is to present an offering with cakes of bread made with yeast. ¹⁴He is to bring one of each kind as an offering, a contribution to the Lᴏʀᴅ; it belongs to the priest who sprinkles the blood of the fellowship offerings. ¹⁵The meat of his fellowship offering of thanksgiving must be eaten on the day it is offered; he must leave none of it till morning.

¹⁶" 'If, however, his offering is the result of a vow or is a freewill offering, the sacrifice shall be eaten on the day he offers it, but anything left over may be eaten on the next day. ¹⁷Any meat of the sacrifice left over till the third day must be burned up. ¹⁸If any meat of the fellowship offering is eaten on the third day, it will not be accepted. It will not be credited to the one who offered it, for it is impure; the person who eats any of it will be held responsible.

¹⁹" 'Meat that touches anything ceremonially unclean must not be eaten; it must be burned up. As for other meat, anyone ceremonially clean may eat it. ²⁰But if anyone who is unclean eats any meat of the fellowship offering belonging to the Lᴏʀᴅ, that person must be cut off from his people. ²¹If anyone touches something unclean—whether human uncleanness or an unclean animal or any unclean, detestable thing—and then eats any of the meat of the fellowship offering belonging to the Lᴏʀᴅ, that person must be cut off from his people.' "

EATING FAT AND BLOOD FORBIDDEN

²²The Lᴏʀᴅ said to Moses, ²³"Say to the Israelites: 'Do not eat any of the fat of cattle, sheep or goats. ²⁴The fat of an animal found dead or torn by wild animals may be used for any other purpose, but you must not eat it. ²⁵Anyone who eats the fat of an animal from which an offering by fire may be[a] made to the Lᴏʀᴅ must be cut off from his people. ²⁶And wherever you live, you must not eat the blood of any bird or animal. ²⁷If anyone eats blood, that person must be cut off from his people.' "

THE PRIESTS' SHARE

²⁸The Lᴏʀᴅ said to Moses, ²⁹"Say to the Israelites: 'Anyone who brings a fellowship offering to the Lᴏʀᴅ is to bring part of it as his sacrifice to the Lᴏʀᴅ. ³⁰With his own hands he is to bring the offering made to the Lᴏʀᴅ by fire; he is to bring the fat, together with the breast, and wave the breast before the Lᴏʀᴅ as a wave offering. ³¹The priest shall burn the fat on the altar, but the breast belongs to Aaron and his sons. ³²You are to give the right thigh of your fellowship offerings to the priest as a contribution. ³³The son of Aaron who offers the blood and the fat of the fellowship offering shall have the right thigh as his share. ³⁴From the fellowship offerings of the Israelites, I have taken the breast that is waved and the thigh that is presented and have given them to Aaron the priest and his sons as their regular share from the Israelites.' "

³⁵This is the portion of the offerings made to the Lᴏʀᴅ by fire that were allotted to Aaron and his sons on the day they were presented to serve the Lᴏʀᴅ as priests. ³⁶On the day they were anointed, the Lᴏʀᴅ commanded that the Israelites give this to them as their regular share for the generations to come.

³⁷These, then, are the regulations for the burnt offering, the grain offering, the sin offering, the guilt offering, the ordination offering and the fellowship offering, ³⁸which the Lᴏʀᴅ gave Moses on Mount Sinai on the day he commanded the Israelites to bring their offerings to the Lᴏʀᴅ, in the Desert of Sinai.

THE ORDINATION OF AARON AND HIS SONS

8 The Lᴏʀᴅ said to Moses, ²"Bring Aaron and his sons, their garments, the anointing oil, the bull for the sin offering, the two rams and the basket containing bread made without yeast, ³and gather the entire assembly at the entrance to the Tent of Meeting." ⁴Moses did as the Lᴏʀᴅ commanded him, and the assembly gathered at the entrance to the Tent of Meeting.

⁵Moses said to the assembly, "This is what the Lᴏʀᴅ has commanded to be done." ⁶Then Moses brought Aaron and his sons forward and washed them with water. ⁷He put the tunic on Aaron, tied the sash around him, clothed him with the robe and put the ephod on him. He also tied the ephod to him by its skillfully woven waistband; so it was fastened on him. ⁸He placed the breastpiece on him and put the Urim and Thummim in the breastpiece. ⁹Then he placed the turban on Aaron's head and set the gold plate, the sacred diadem, on the front of it, as the Lᴏʀᴅ commanded Moses.

ᵃ 25 Or fire is

¹⁰Then Moses took the anointing oil and anointed the tabernacle and everything in it, and so consecrated them. ¹¹He sprinkled some of the oil on the altar seven times, anointing the altar and all its utensils and the basin with its stand, to consecrate them. ¹²He poured some of the anointing oil on Aaron's head and anointed him to consecrate him. ¹³Then he brought Aaron's sons forward, put tunics on them, tied sashes around them and put headbands on them, as the LORD commanded Moses.

¹⁴He then presented the bull for the sin offering, and Aaron and his sons laid their hands on its head. ¹⁵Moses slaughtered the bull and took some of the blood, and with his finger he put it on all the horns of the altar to purify the altar. He poured out the rest of the blood at the base of the altar. So he consecrated it to make atonement for it. ¹⁶Moses also took all the fat around the inner parts, the covering of the liver, and both kidneys and their fat, and burned it on the altar. ¹⁷But the bull with its hide and its flesh and its offal he burned up outside the camp, as the LORD commanded Moses.

¹⁸He then presented the ram for the burnt offering, and Aaron and his sons laid their hands on its head. ¹⁹Then Moses slaughtered the ram and sprinkled the blood against the altar on all sides. ²⁰He cut the ram into pieces and burned the head, the pieces and the fat. ²¹He washed the inner parts and the legs with water and burned the whole ram on the altar as a burnt offering, a pleasing aroma, an offering made to the LORD by fire, as the LORD commanded Moses.

²²He then presented the other ram, the ram for the ordination, and Aaron and his sons laid their hands on its head. ²³Moses slaughtered the ram and took some of its blood and put it on the lobe of Aaron's right ear, on the thumb of his right hand and on the big toe of his right foot. ²⁴Moses also brought Aaron's sons forward and put some of the blood on the lobes of their right ears, on the thumbs of their right hands and on the big toes of their right feet. Then he sprinkled blood against the altar on all sides. ²⁵He took the fat, the fat tail, all the fat around the inner parts, the covering of the liver, both kidneys and their fat and the right thigh. ²⁶Then from the basket of bread made without yeast, which was before the LORD, he took a cake of bread, and one made with oil, and a wafer; he put these on the fat portions and on the right thigh. ²⁷He put all these in the hands of Aaron and his sons and waved them before the LORD as a wave offering. ²⁸Then Moses took them from their hands and burned them on the altar on top of the burnt offering as an ordination offering, a pleasing aroma, an offering made to the LORD by fire. ²⁹He also took the breast—Moses' share of the ordination ram—and waved it before the LORD as a wave offering, as the LORD commanded Moses.

³⁰Then Moses took some of the anointing oil and some of the blood from the altar and sprinkled them on Aaron and his garments and on his sons and their garments. So he consecrated Aaron and his garments and his sons and their garments.

³¹Moses then said to Aaron and his sons, "Cook the meat at the entrance to the Tent of Meeting and eat it there with the bread from the basket of ordination offerings, as I commanded, saying,ᵃ 'Aaron and his sons are to eat it.' ³²Then burn up the rest of the meat and the bread. ³³Do not leave the entrance to the Tent of Meeting for seven days, until the days of your ordination are completed, for your ordination will last seven days. ³⁴What has been done today was commanded by the LORD to make atonement for you. ³⁵You must stay at the entrance to the Tent of Meeting day and night for seven days and do what the LORD requires, so you will not die; for that is what I have been commanded." ³⁶So Aaron and his sons did everything the LORD commanded through Moses.

THE PRIESTS BEGIN THEIR MINISTRY

9 On the eighth day Moses summoned Aaron and his sons and the elders of Israel. ²He said to Aaron, "Take a bull calf for your sin offering and a ram for your burnt offering, both without defect, and present them before the LORD. ³Then say to the Israelites: 'Take a male goat for a sin offering, a calf and a lamb—both a year old and without defect—for a burnt offering, ⁴and an oxᵇ and a ram for a fellowship offeringᶜ to sacrifice before the LORD, together with a grain offering mixed with oil. For today the LORD will appear to you.' "

⁵They took the things Moses commanded to the front of the Tent of Meeting, and the entire assembly came near and stood before the LORD. ⁶Then Moses said, "This is what the LORD has commanded you to do, so that the glory of the LORD may appear to you."

⁷Moses said to Aaron, "Come to the altar and sacrifice your sin offering and your burnt offering and

---

ᵃ *31* Or *I was commanded;* ᵇ *4* The Hebrew word can include both male and female; also in verses 18 and 19. ᶜ *4* Traditionally *peace offering;* also in verses 18 and 22

battlelines

» Wake-up Call (Doubt)

Q: Hey, I haven't seen you since you got back from your mission trip to Mexico. How was it?
A: It was okay, I guess. It had its good and bad moments.

Q: What was the *best* moment?
A: I'd have to say it was the look in the kids' eyes at the orphanage when we brought out the bag of toys. I mean, these were second-rate toys—some of them were even used. But these kids had never seen anything like them before. Man, they thought those toys were the coolest.

Q: Cool. So what was the *worst* thing about the trip?
A: Well, the food took some getting used to. Actually, I never *did* get used to it. But that was nothing compared to the poverty.

Q: Pretty bad, huh?
A: It was unbelievable. People living in garbage dumps, wearing rags. Little kids with flies all over them. When I was observing all this, I just started feeling guilty. And then I began getting angry because, when you think about it, some of the worst slums in our whole country are like paradise compared to what those people live in.

Q: Sounds like it hit you pretty hard.
A: (Nodding slowly) Yeah. No doubt. We went there to tell people how much Jesus loves them. And you know, I just couldn't do it! What was I supposed to say? "Hey, little kid, God loves you so much, he lets you live like this!" Why did God choose me to have my life? I mean, it makes you wonder: Does God play favorites?

» Grim Realities

God is all-powerful (see Jeremiah 32:27). God is totally wise (see Daniel 2:20). God is perfectly good (see Psalm 34:8). As a result of sin, however, there is *immense* suffering and injustice in the world (see Genesis 3).

How do we make these truths fit together in a logical way? That, my friend, is the classic dilemma of the ages. Here is where our faith faces its greatest test. But whatever the answer, there's one other truth for you to hold on to: God cares. And because God cares, there will come a day when he will dwell with his people, when he will live right among us (see Revelation 21:3). According to the author of Revelation, when that day comes, "There will be no more death or mourning or crying or pain, for the old order of things has passed away" (v. 4).

Until then, perhaps the honest prayer of a confused and conflicted father in the Gospels is your best bet in times of doubt: "I do believe; help me overcome my unbelief!" (Mark 9:24).

Read more about dealing with doubts at www.RevolutionBible.com.

make atonement for yourself and the people; sacrifice the offering that is for the people and make atonement for them, as the LORD has commanded."

⁸So Aaron came to the altar and slaughtered the calf as a sin offering for himself. ⁹His sons brought the blood to him, and he dipped his finger into the blood and put it on the horns of the altar; the rest of the blood he poured out at the base of the altar. ¹⁰On the altar he burned the fat, the kidneys and the covering of the liver from the sin offering, as the LORD commanded Moses; ¹¹the flesh and the hide he burned up outside the camp.

¹²Then he slaughtered the burnt offering. His sons handed him the blood, and he sprinkled it against the altar on all sides. ¹³They handed him the burnt offering piece by piece, including the head, and he burned them on the altar. ¹⁴He washed the inner parts and the legs and burned them on top of the burnt offering on the altar.

¹⁵Aaron then brought the offering that was for the people. He took the goat for the people's sin offering and slaughtered it and offered it for a sin offering as he did with the first one.

¹⁶He brought the burnt offering and offered it in the prescribed way. ¹⁷He also brought the grain offering, took a handful of it and burned it on the altar in addition to the morning's burnt offering.

¹⁸He slaughtered the ox and the ram as the fellowship offering for the people. His sons handed him the blood, and he sprinkled it against the altar on all sides. ¹⁹But the fat portions of the ox and the ram—the fat tail, the layer of fat, the kidneys and the covering of the liver— ²⁰these they laid on the breasts, and then Aaron burned the fat on the altar. ²¹Aaron waved the breasts and the right thigh before the LORD as a wave offering, as Moses commanded.

²²Then Aaron lifted his hands toward the people and blessed them. And having sacrificed the sin offering, the burnt offering and the fellowship offering, he stepped down.

²³Moses and Aaron then went into the Tent of Meeting. When they came out, they blessed the people; and the glory of the LORD appeared to all the people. ²⁴Fire came out from the presence of the LORD and consumed the burnt offering and the fat portions on the altar. And when all the people saw it, they shouted for joy and fell facedown.

Respect for God

Don't let the fact that you have a personal relationship with God make you lose sight of who he really is. Sometimes it's tempting to treat him just like we would treat another friend or family member—with affection, but not much respect. That's a big mistake. No matter how intimate our relationship with God may be, we must always respond to him with the reverence and awe he deserves. He is the holy Creator of the universe, after all.

»» live the adventure »» Lev 10:1-3

THE DEATH OF NADAB AND ABIHU

10 Aaron's sons Nadab and Abihu took their censers, put fire in them and added incense; and they offered unauthorized fire before the LORD, contrary to his command. ²So fire came out from the presence of the LORD and consumed them, and they died before the LORD. ³Moses then said to Aaron, "This is what the LORD spoke of when he said:

" 'Among those who approach me
    I will show myself holy;
in the sight of all the people
    I will be honored.' "

Aaron remained silent.

⁴Moses summoned Mishael and Elzaphan, sons of Aaron's uncle Uzziel, and said to them, "Come here; carry your cousins outside the camp, away from the front of the sanctuary." ⁵So they came and carried them, still in their tunics, outside the camp, as Moses ordered.

⁶Then Moses said to Aaron and his sons Eleazar and Ithamar, "Do not let your hair become unkempt,ᵃ and do not tear your clothes, or you will die and the LORD will be angry with the whole commu-

---

ᵃ 6 Or Do not uncover your heads

nity. But your relatives, all the house of Israel, may mourn for those the LORD has destroyed by fire. 7Do not leave the entrance to the Tent of Meeting or you will die, because the LORD's anointing oil is on you." So they did as Moses said.

8Then the LORD said to Aaron, 9"You and your sons are not to drink wine or other fermented drink whenever you go into the Tent of Meeting, or you will die. This is a lasting ordinance for the generations to come. 10You must distinguish between the holy and the common, between the unclean and the clean, 11and you must teach the Israelites all the decrees the LORD has given them through Moses."

NOW OR NEVER
LEV 10:10–11

Nothing in your life is "off limits" to God. He wants to be involved in everything—in every decision, every activity, every pursuit. In discerning between "clean" and "unclean," make it your goal to please him.

12Moses said to Aaron and his remaining sons, Eleazar and Ithamar, "Take the grain offering left over from the offerings made to the LORD by fire and eat it prepared without yeast beside the altar, for it is most holy. 13Eat it in a holy place, because it is your share and your sons' share of the offerings made to the LORD by fire; for so I have been commanded. 14But you and your sons and your daughters may eat the breast that was waved and the thigh that was presented. Eat them in a ceremonially clean place; they have been given to you and your children as your share of the Israelites' fellowship offerings.[a] 15The thigh that was presented and the breast that was waved must be brought with the fat portions of the offerings made by fire, to be waved before the LORD as a wave offering. This will be the regular share for you and your children, as the LORD has commanded."

16When Moses inquired about the goat of the sin offering and found that it had been burned up, he was angry with Eleazar and Ithamar, Aaron's remaining sons, and asked, 17"Why didn't you eat the sin offering in the sanctuary area? It is most holy; it was given to you to take away the guilt of the community by making atonement for them before the LORD. 18Since its blood was not taken into the Holy Place, you should have eaten the goat in the sanctuary area, as I commanded."

19Aaron replied to Moses, "Today they sacrificed their sin offering and their burnt offering before the LORD, but such things as this have happened to me. Would the LORD have been pleased if I had eaten the sin offering today?" 20When Moses heard this, he was satisfied.

CLEAN AND UNCLEAN FOOD

11 The LORD said to Moses and Aaron, 2"Say to the Israelites: 'Of all the animals that live on land, these are the ones you may eat: 3You may eat any animal that has a split hoof completely divided and that chews the cud.

4" 'There are some that only chew the cud or only have a split hoof, but you must not eat them. The camel, though it chews the cud, does not have a split hoof; it is ceremonially unclean for you. 5The coney,[b] though it chews the cud, does not have a split hoof; it is unclean for you. 6The rabbit, though it chews the cud, does not have a split hoof; it is unclean for you. 7And the pig, though it has a split hoof completely divided, does not chew the cud; it is unclean for you. 8You must not eat their meat or touch their carcasses; they are unclean for you.

9" 'Of all the creatures living in the water of the seas and the streams, you may eat any that have fins and scales. 10But all creatures in the seas or streams that do not have fins and scales—whether among all the swarming things or among all the other living creatures in the water—you are to detest. 11And since you are to detest them, you must not eat their meat and you must detest their carcasses. 12Anything living in the water that does not have fins and scales is to be detestable to you.

13" 'These are the birds you are to detest and not eat because they are detestable: the eagle, the vulture, the black vulture, 14the red kite, any kind of black kite, 15any kind of raven, 16the horned owl, the screech owl, the gull, any kind of hawk, 17the little owl, the cormorant, the great owl, 18the white owl, the desert owl, the osprey, 19the stork, any kind of heron, the hoopoe and the bat.[c]

20" 'All flying insects that walk on all fours are to be detestable to you. 21There are, however, some winged creatures that walk on all fours that you may eat: those that have jointed legs for hopping on

---

[a] 14 Traditionally *peace offerings*   [b] 5 That is, the hyrax or rock badger   [c] 19 The precise identification of some of the birds, insects and animals in this chapter is uncertain.

the ground. ²²Of these you may eat any kind of locust, katydid, cricket or grasshopper. ²³But all other winged creatures that have four legs you are to detest.

²⁴ 'You will make yourselves unclean by these; whoever touches their carcasses will be unclean till evening. ²⁵Whoever picks up any of their carcasses must wash his clothes, and he will be unclean till evening.

²⁶ 'Every animal that has a split hoof not completely divided or that does not chew the cud is unclean for you; whoever touches ⌊the carcass of⌋ any of them will be unclean. ²⁷Of all the animals that walk on all fours, those that walk on their paws are unclean for you; whoever touches their carcasses will be unclean till evening. ²⁸Anyone who picks up their carcasses must wash his clothes, and he will be unclean till evening. They are unclean for you.

²⁹ 'Of the animals that move about on the ground, these are unclean for you: the weasel, the rat, any kind of great lizard, ³⁰the gecko, the monitor lizard, the wall lizard, the skink and the chameleon. ³¹Of all those that move along the ground, these are unclean for you. Whoever touches them when they are dead will be unclean till evening. ³²When one of them dies and falls on something, that article, whatever its use, will be unclean, whether it is made of wood, cloth, hide or sackcloth. Put it in water; it will be unclean till evening, and then it will be clean. ³³If one of them falls into a clay pot, everything in it will be unclean, and you must break the pot. ³⁴Any food that could be eaten but has water on it from such a pot is unclean, and any liquid that could be drunk from it is unclean. ³⁵Anything that one of their carcasses falls on becomes unclean; an oven or cooking pot must be broken up. They are unclean, and you are to regard them as unclean. ³⁶A spring, however, or a cistern for collecting water remains clean, but anyone who touches one of these carcasses is unclean. ³⁷If a carcass falls on any seeds that are to be planted, they remain clean. ³⁸But if water has been put on the seed and a carcass falls on it, it is unclean for you.

³⁹ 'If an animal that you are allowed to eat dies, anyone who touches the carcass will be unclean till evening. ⁴⁰Anyone who eats some of the carcass must wash his clothes, and he will be unclean till evening. Anyone who picks up the carcass must wash his clothes, and he will be unclean till evening.

⁴¹ 'Every creature that moves about on the ground is detestable; it is not to be eaten. ⁴²You are not to eat any creature that moves about on the ground, whether it moves on its belly or walks on all fours or on many feet; it is detestable. ⁴³Do not defile yourselves by any of these creatures. Do not make yourselves unclean by means of them or be made unclean by them. ⁴⁴I am the LORD your God; consecrate yourselves and be holy, because I am holy. Do not make yourselves unclean by any creature that moves about on the ground. ⁴⁵I am the LORD who brought you up out of Egypt to be your God; therefore be holy, because I am holy.

⁴⁶ 'These are the regulations concerning animals, birds, every living thing that moves in the water and every creature that moves about on the ground. ⁴⁷You must distinguish between the unclean and the clean, between living creatures that may be eaten and those that may not be eaten.' "

challenge notes

To: **my_son**

heavenly_father: you know that I am holy. what you might not know is that if you want to enjoy life in me, you must strive to be holy too—set apart and totally devoted to me. sure, it's impossible for you to be perfect like I am, but I'll give you the strength you need to pursue holiness. and when you fail, get up. start again. I'll be there to help you.

LEV 11:44-45

PURIFICATION AFTER CHILDBIRTH

12 The LORD said to Moses, ²"Say to the Israelites: 'A woman who becomes pregnant and gives birth to a son will be ceremonially unclean for seven days, just as she is unclean during her monthly period. ³On the eighth day the boy is to be circumcised. ⁴Then the woman must wait thirty-three days to be purified from her bleeding. She must not touch anything sacred or go to the sanctuary until the days of her purification are over. ⁵If she gives birth to a daughter, for two weeks the woman will be unclean, as during her period. Then she must wait sixty-six days to be purified from her bleeding.

⁶ 'When the days of her purification for a son or daughter are over, she is to bring to the priest at the entrance to the Tent of Meeting a year-old lamb for a burnt offering and a young pigeon or a dove

for a sin offering. [7]He shall offer them before the LORD to make atonement for her, and then she will be ceremonially clean from her flow of blood.

" 'These are the regulations for the woman who gives birth to a boy or a girl. [8]If she cannot afford a lamb, she is to bring two doves or two young pigeons, one for a burnt offering and the other for a sin offering. In this way the priest will make atonement for her, and she will be clean.' "

REGULATIONS ABOUT INFECTIOUS SKIN DISEASES

13 The LORD said to Moses and Aaron, [2]"When anyone has a swelling or a rash or a bright spot on his skin that may become an infectious skin disease,[a] he must be brought to Aaron the priest or to one of his sons[b] who is a priest. [3]The priest is to examine the sore on his skin, and if the hair in the sore has turned white and the sore appears to be more than skin deep,[c] it is an infectious skin disease. When the priest examines him, he shall pronounce him ceremonially unclean. [4]If the spot on his skin is white but does not appear to be more than skin deep and the hair in it has not turned white, the priest is to put the infected person in isolation for seven days. [5]On the seventh day the priest is to examine him, and if he sees that the sore is unchanged and has not spread in the skin, he is to keep him in isolation another seven days. [6]On the seventh day the priest is to examine him again, and if the sore has faded and has not spread in the skin, the priest shall pronounce him clean; it is only a rash. The man must wash his clothes, and he will be clean. [7]But if the rash does spread in his skin after he has shown himself to the priest to be pronounced clean, he must appear before the priest again. [8]The priest is to examine him, and if the rash has spread in the skin, he shall pronounce him unclean; it is an infectious disease.

[9]"When anyone has an infectious skin disease, he must be brought to the priest. [10]The priest is to examine him, and if there is a white swelling in the skin that has turned the hair white and if there is raw flesh in the swelling, [11]it is a chronic skin disease and the priest shall pronounce him unclean. He is not to put him in isolation, because he is already unclean.

[12]"If the disease breaks out all over his skin and, so far as the priest can see, it covers all the skin of the infected person from head to foot, [13]the priest is to examine him, and if the disease has covered his whole body, he shall pronounce that person clean. Since it has all turned white, he is clean. [14]But whenever raw flesh appears on him, he will be unclean. [15]When the priest sees the raw flesh, he shall pronounce him unclean. The raw flesh is unclean; he has an infectious disease. [16]Should the raw flesh change and turn white, he must go to the priest. [17]The priest is to examine him, and if the sores have turned white, the priest shall pronounce the infected person clean; then he will be clean.

[18]"When someone has a boil on his skin and it heals, [19]and in the place where the boil was, a white swelling or reddish-white spot appears, he must present himself to the priest. [20]The priest is to examine it, and if it appears to be more than skin deep and the hair in it has turned white, the priest shall pronounce him unclean. It is an infectious skin disease that has broken out where the boil was. [21]But if, when the priest examines it, there is no white hair in it and it is not more than skin deep and has faded, then the priest is to put him in isolation for seven days. [22]If it is spreading in the skin, the priest shall pronounce him unclean; it is infectious. [23]But if the spot is unchanged and has not spread, it is only a scar from the boil, and the priest shall pronounce him clean.

[24]"When someone has a burn on his skin and a reddish-white or white spot appears in the raw flesh of the burn, [25]the priest is to examine the spot, and if the hair in it has turned white, and it appears to be more than skin deep, it is an infectious disease that has broken out in the burn. The priest shall pronounce him unclean; it is an infectious skin disease. [26]But if the priest examines it and there is no white hair in the spot and if it is not more than skin deep and has faded, then the priest is to put him in isolation for seven days. [27]On the seventh day the priest is to examine him, and if it is spreading in the skin, the priest shall pronounce him unclean; it is an infectious skin disease. [28]If, however, the spot is unchanged and has not spread in the skin but has faded, it is a swelling from the burn, and the priest shall pronounce him clean; it is only a scar from the burn.

[29]"If a man or woman has a sore on the head or on the chin, [30]the priest is to examine the sore, and if it appears to be more than skin deep and the hair in it is yellow and thin, the priest shall pronounce that person unclean; it is an itch, an infectious disease of the head or chin. [31]But if, when the priest examines this kind of sore, it does not seem to be more than skin deep and there is no black hair in it,

---

[a] 2 Traditionally *leprosy*; the Hebrew word was used for various diseases affecting the skin—not necessarily leprosy; also elsewhere in this chapter.   [b] 2 Or *descendants*   [c] 3 Or *be lower than the rest of the skin*; also elsewhere in this chapter

then the priest is to put the infected person in isolation for seven days. ³²On the seventh day the priest is to examine the sore, and if the itch has not spread and there is no yellow hair in it and it does not appear to be more than skin deep, ³³he must be shaved except for the diseased area, and the priest is to keep him in isolation another seven days. ³⁴On the seventh day the priest is to examine the itch, and if it has not spread in the skin and appears to be no more than skin deep, the priest shall pronounce him clean. He must wash his clothes, and he will be clean. ³⁵But if the itch does spread in the skin after he is pronounced clean, ³⁶the priest is to examine him, and if the itch has spread in the skin, the priest does not need to look for yellow hair; the person is unclean. ³⁷If, however, in his judgment it is unchanged and black hair has grown in it, the itch is healed. He is clean, and the priest shall pronounce him clean.

³⁸"When a man or woman has white spots on the skin, ³⁹the priest is to examine them, and if the spots are dull white, it is a harmless rash that has broken out on the skin; that person is clean.

⁴⁰"When a man has lost his hair and is bald, he is clean. ⁴¹If he has lost his hair from the front of his scalp and has a bald forehead, he is clean. ⁴²But if he has a reddish-white sore on his bald head or forehead, it is an infectious disease breaking out on his head or forehead. ⁴³The priest is to examine him, and if the swollen sore on his head or forehead is reddish-white like an infectious skin disease, ⁴⁴the man is diseased and is unclean. The priest shall pronounce him unclean because of the sore on his head.

⁴⁵"The person with such an infectious disease must wear torn clothes, let his hair be unkempt,ª cover the lower part of his face and cry out, 'Unclean! Unclean!' ⁴⁶As long as he has the infection he remains unclean. He must live alone; he must live outside the camp.

REGULATIONS ABOUT MILDEW

⁴⁷"If any clothing is contaminated with mildew—any woolen or linen clothing, ⁴⁸any woven or knitted material of linen or wool, any leather or anything made of leather— ⁴⁹and if the contamination in the clothing, or leather, or woven or knitted material, or any leather article, is greenish or reddish, it is a spreading mildew and must be shown to the priest. ⁵⁰The priest is to examine the mildew and isolate the affected article for seven days. ⁵¹On the seventh day he is to examine it, and if the mildew has spread in the clothing, or the woven or knitted material, or the leather, whatever its use, it is a destructive mildew; the article is unclean. ⁵²He must burn up the clothing, or the woven or knitted material of wool or linen, or any leather article that has the contamination in it, because the mildew is destructive; the article must be burned up.

⁵³"But if, when the priest examines it, the mildew has not spread in the clothing, or the woven or knitted material, or the leather article, ⁵⁴he shall order that the contaminated article be washed. Then he is to isolate it for another seven days. ⁵⁵After the affected article has been washed, the priest is to examine it, and if the mildew has not changed its appearance, even though it has not spread, it is unclean. Burn it with fire, whether the mildew has affected one side or the other. ⁵⁶If, when the priest examines it, the mildew has faded after the article has been washed, he is to tear the contaminated part out of the clothing, or the leather, or the woven or knitted material. ⁵⁷But if it reappears in the clothing, or in the woven or knitted material, or in the leather article, it is spreading, and whatever has the mildew must be burned with fire. ⁵⁸The clothing, or the woven or knitted material, or any leather article that has been washed and is rid of the mildew, must be washed again, and it will be clean."

⁵⁹These are the regulations concerning contamination by mildew in woolen or linen clothing, woven or knitted material, or any leather article, for pronouncing them clean or unclean.

CLEANSING FROM INFECTIOUS SKIN DISEASES

14 The Lᴏʀᴅ said to Moses, ²"These are the regulations for the diseased person at the time of his ceremonial cleansing, when he is brought to the priest: ³The priest is to go outside the camp and examine him. If the person has been healed of his infectious skin disease,ᵇ ⁴the priest shall order that two live clean birds and some cedar wood, scarlet yarn and hyssop be brought for the one to be cleansed. ⁵Then the priest shall order that one of the birds be killed over fresh water in a clay pot. ⁶He is then to take the live bird and dip it, together with the cedar wood, the scarlet yarn and the hyssop, into the blood of the bird that was killed over the fresh water. ⁷Seven times he shall

---

ª *45* Or *clothes, uncover his head*   ᵇ *3* Traditionally *leprosy*; the Hebrew word was used for various diseases affecting the skin—not necessarily leprosy; also elsewhere in this chapter.

sprinkle the one to be cleansed of the infectious disease and pronounce him clean. Then he is to release the live bird in the open fields.

8 "The person to be cleansed must wash his clothes, shave off all his hair and bathe with water; then he will be ceremonially clean. After this he may come into the camp, but he must stay outside his tent for seven days. 9 On the seventh day he must shave off all his hair; he must shave his head, his beard, his eyebrows and the rest of his hair. He must wash his clothes and bathe himself with water, and he will be clean.

10 "On the eighth day he must bring two male lambs and one ewe lamb a year old, each without defect, along with three-tenths of an ephah[a] of fine flour mixed with oil for a grain offering, and one log[b] of oil. 11 The priest who pronounces him clean shall present both the one to be cleansed and his offerings before the LORD at the entrance to the Tent of Meeting.

12 "Then the priest is to take one of the male lambs and offer it as a guilt offering, along with the log of oil; he shall wave them before the LORD as a wave offering. 13 He is to slaughter the lamb in the holy place where the sin offering and the burnt offering are slaughtered. Like the sin offering, the guilt offering belongs to the priest; it is most holy. 14 The priest is to take some of the blood of the guilt offering and put it on the lobe of the right ear of the one to be cleansed, on the thumb of his right hand and on the big toe of his right foot. 15 The priest shall then take some of the log of oil, pour it in the palm of his own left hand, 16 dip his right forefinger into the oil in his palm, and with his finger sprinkle some of it before the LORD seven times. 17 The priest is to put some of the oil remaining in his palm on the lobe of the right ear of the one to be cleansed, on the thumb of his right hand and on the big toe of his right foot, on top of the blood of the guilt offering. 18 The rest of the oil in his palm the priest shall put on the head of the one to be cleansed and make atonement for him before the LORD.

19 "Then the priest is to sacrifice the sin offering and make atonement for the one to be cleansed from his uncleanness. After that, the priest shall slaughter the burnt offering 20 and offer it on the altar, together with the grain offering, and make atonement for him, and he will be clean.

21 "If, however, he is poor and cannot afford these, he must take one male lamb as a guilt offering to be waved to make atonement for him, together with a tenth of an ephah[c] of fine flour mixed with oil for a grain offering, a log of oil, 22 and two doves or two young pigeons, which he can afford, one for a sin offering and the other for a burnt offering.

23 "On the eighth day he must bring them for his cleansing to the priest at the entrance to the Tent of Meeting, before the LORD. 24 The priest is to take the lamb for the guilt offering, together with the log of oil, and wave them before the LORD as a wave offering. 25 He shall slaughter the lamb for the guilt offering and take some of its blood and put it on the lobe of the right ear of the one to be cleansed, on the thumb of his right hand and on the big toe of his right foot. 26 The priest is to pour some of the oil into the palm of his own left hand, 27 and with his right forefinger sprinkle some of the oil from his palm seven times before the LORD. 28 Some of the oil in his palm he is to put on the same places he put the blood of the guilt offering—on the lobe of the right ear of the one to be cleansed, on the thumb of his right hand and on the big toe of his right foot. 29 The rest of the oil in his palm the priest shall put on the head of the one to be cleansed, to make atonement for him before the LORD. 30 Then he shall sacrifice the doves or the young pigeons, which the person can afford, 31 one[d] as a sin offering and the other as a burnt offering, together with the grain offering. In this way the priest will make atonement before the LORD on behalf of the one to be cleansed."

32 These are the regulations for anyone who has an infectious skin disease and who cannot afford the regular offerings for his cleansing.

CLEANSING FROM MILDEW

33 The LORD said to Moses and Aaron, 34 "When you enter the land of Canaan, which I am giving you as your possession, and I put a spreading mildew in a house in that land, 35 the owner of the house must go and tell the priest, 'I have seen something that looks like mildew in my house.' 36 The priest is to order the house to be emptied before he goes in to examine the mildew, so that nothing in the house will be pronounced unclean. After this the priest is to go in and inspect the house. 37 He is to examine the mildew on the walls, and if it has greenish or reddish depressions that appear to be deeper than the surface of the wall, 38 the priest shall go out the doorway of the house and close it up for seven days.

---

a 10 That is, probably about 6 quarts (about 6.5 liters)   b 10 That is, probably about 2/3 pint (about 0.3 liter); also in verses 12, 15, 21 and 24   c 21 That is, probably about 2 quarts (about 2 liters)   d 31 Septuagint and Syriac; Hebrew 31such as the person can afford, one

39On the seventh day the priest shall return to inspect the house. If the mildew has spread on the walls, 40he is to order that the contaminated stones be torn out and thrown into an unclean place outside the town. 41He must have all the inside walls of the house scraped and the material that is scraped off dumped into an unclean place outside the town. 42Then they are to take other stones to replace these and take new clay and plaster the house.

43"If the mildew reappears in the house after the stones have been torn out and the house scraped and plastered, 44the priest is to go and examine it and, if the mildew has spread in the house, it is a destructive mildew; the house is unclean. 45It must be torn down—its stones, timbers and all the plaster—and taken out of the town to an unclean place.

46"Anyone who goes into the house while it is closed up will be unclean till evening. 47Anyone who sleeps or eats in the house must wash his clothes.

48"But if the priest comes to examine it and the mildew has not spread after the house has been plastered, he shall pronounce the house clean, because the mildew is gone. 49To purify the house he is to take two birds and some cedar wood, scarlet yarn and hyssop. 50He shall kill one of the birds over fresh water in a clay pot. 51Then he is to take the cedar wood, the hyssop, the scarlet yarn and the live bird, dip them into the blood of the dead bird and the fresh water, and sprinkle the house seven times. 52He shall purify the house with the bird's blood, the fresh water, the live bird, the cedar wood, the hyssop and the scarlet yarn. 53Then he is to release the live bird in the open fields outside the town. In this way he will make atonement for the house, and it will be clean."

54These are the regulations for any infectious skin disease, for an itch, 55for mildew in clothing or in a house, 56and for a swelling, a rash or a bright spot, 57to determine when something is clean or unclean.

These are the regulations for infectious skin diseases and mildew.

Preparing for God

What if you knew the girl of your dreams was going to drop by your house for a visit? You'd want the place to look nice, wouldn't you? How far would you go to impress her? Would you pick up your room (or at least shovel everything into your closet)? Would you vacuum and dust the family room? Would you clean the kitchen? That's the situation the Israelites were facing, only with much bigger stakes. God told them that he would be *living* among them. Their responsibility was to make his dwelling place as acceptable as possible.

DISCHARGES CAUSING UNCLEANNESS

15 The Lord said to Moses and Aaron, 2"Speak to the Israelites and say to them: 'When any man has a bodily discharge, the discharge is unclean. 3Whether it continues flowing from his body or is blocked, it will make him unclean. This is how his discharge will bring about uncleanness:

4" 'Any bed the man with a discharge lies on will be unclean, and anything he sits on will be unclean. 5Anyone who touches his bed must wash his clothes and bathe with water, and he will be unclean till evening. 6Whoever sits on anything that the man with a discharge sat on must wash his clothes and bathe with water, and he will be unclean till evening.

7" 'Whoever touches the man who has a discharge must wash his clothes and bathe with water, and he will be unclean till evening.

8" 'If the man with the discharge spits on someone who is clean, that person must wash his clothes and bathe with water, and he will be unclean till evening.

9" 'Everything the man sits on when riding will be unclean, 10and whoever touches any of the things that were under him will be unclean till evening; whoever picks up those things must wash his clothes and bathe with water, and he will be unclean till evening.

11" 'Anyone the man with a discharge touches without rinsing his hands with water must wash his clothes and bathe with water, and he will be unclean till evening.

12" 'A clay pot that the man touches must be broken, and any wooden article is to be rinsed with water.

13 " 'When a man is cleansed from his discharge, he is to count off seven days for his ceremonial cleansing; he must wash his clothes and bathe himself with fresh water, and he will be clean. 14On the eighth day he must take two doves or two young pigeons and come before the LORD to the entrance to the Tent of Meeting and give them to the priest. 15The priest is to sacrifice them, the one for a sin offering and the other for a burnt offering. In this way he will make atonement before the LORD for the man because of his discharge.

16 " 'When a man has an emission of semen, he must bathe his whole body with water, and he will be unclean till evening. 17Any clothing or leather that has semen on it must be washed with water, and it will be unclean till evening. 18When a man lies with a woman and there is an emission of semen, both must bathe with water, and they will be unclean till evening.

19 " 'When a woman has her regular flow of blood, the impurity of her monthly period will last seven days, and anyone who touches her will be unclean till evening.

20 " 'Anything she lies on during her period will be unclean, and anything she sits on will be unclean. 21Whoever touches her bed must wash his clothes and bathe with water, and he will be unclean till evening. 22Whoever touches anything she sits on must wash his clothes and bathe with water, and he will be unclean till evening. 23Whether it is the bed or anything she was sitting on, when anyone touches it, he will be unclean till evening.

24 " 'If a man lies with her and her monthly flow touches him, he will be unclean for seven days; any bed he lies on will be unclean.

25 " 'When a woman has a discharge of blood for many days at a time other than her monthly period or has a discharge that continues beyond her period, she will be unclean as long as she has the discharge, just as in the days of her period. 26Any bed she lies on while her discharge continues will be unclean, as is her bed during her monthly period, and anything she sits on will be unclean, as during her period. 27Whoever touches them will be unclean; he must wash his clothes and bathe with water, and he will be unclean till evening.

28 " 'When she is cleansed from her discharge, she must count off seven days, and after that she will be ceremonially clean. 29On the eighth day she must take two doves or two young pigeons and bring them to the priest at the entrance to the Tent of Meeting. 30The priest is to sacrifice one for a sin offering and the other for a burnt offering. In this way he will make atonement for her before the LORD for the uncleanness of her discharge.

31 " 'You must keep the Israelites separate from things that make them unclean, so they will not die in their uncleanness for defiling my dwelling place,ᵃ which is among them.' "

32These are the regulations for a man with a discharge, for anyone made unclean by an emission of semen, 33for a woman in her monthly period, for a man or a woman with a discharge, and for a man who lies with a woman who is ceremonially unclean.

THE DAY OF ATONEMENT

16 The LORD spoke to Moses after the death of the two sons of Aaron who died when they approached the LORD. 2The LORD said to Moses: "Tell your brother Aaron not to come whenever he chooses into the Most Holy Place behind the curtain in front of the atonement cover on the ark, or else he will die, because I appear in the cloud over the atonement cover.

3"This is how Aaron is to enter the sanctuary area: with a young bull for a sin offering and a ram for a burnt offering. 4He is to put on the sacred linen tunic, with linen undergarments next to his body; he is to tie the linen sash around him and put on the linen turban. These are sacred garments; so he must bathe himself with water before he puts them on. 5From the Israelite community he is to take two male goats for a sin offering and a ram for a burnt offering.

6"Aaron is to offer the bull for his own sin offering to make atonement for himself and his household. 7Then he is to take the two goats and present them before the LORD at the entrance to the Tent of

NOW OR NEVER

LEV 16:1–4

Do you prepare yourself before you worship or spend time alone with God? The high priest had to take care of his own sin before entering the Most Holy Place of the tabernacle. What could you do to better prepare yourself for meaningful worship?

ᵃ 31 Or *my tabernacle*

Meeting. [8]He is to cast lots for the two goats—one lot for the LORD and the other for the scapegoat.[a] [9]Aaron shall bring the goat whose lot falls to the LORD and sacrifice it for a sin offering. [10]But the goat chosen by lot as the scapegoat shall be presented alive before the LORD to be used for making atonement by sending it into the desert as a scapegoat.

[11]"Aaron shall bring the bull for his own sin offering to make atonement for himself and his household, and he is to slaughter the bull for his own sin offering. [12]He is to take a censer full of burning coals from the altar before the LORD and two handfuls of finely ground fragrant incense and take them behind the curtain. [13]He is to put the incense on the fire before the LORD, and the smoke of the incense will conceal the atonement cover above the Testimony, so that he will not die. [14]He is to take some of the bull's blood and with his finger sprinkle it on the front of the atonement cover; then he shall sprinkle some of it with his finger seven times before the atonement cover.

[15]"He shall then slaughter the goat for the sin offering for the people and take its blood behind the curtain and do with it as he did with the bull's blood: He shall sprinkle it on the atonement cover and in front of it. [16]In this way he will make atonement for the Most Holy Place because of the uncleanness and rebellion of the Israelites, whatever their sins have been. He is to do the same for the Tent of Meeting, which is among them in the midst of their uncleanness. [17]No one is to be in the Tent of Meeting from the time Aaron goes in to make atonement in the Most Holy Place until he comes out, having made atonement for himself, his household and the whole community of Israel.

[18]"Then he shall come out to the altar that is before the LORD and make atonement for it. He shall take some of the bull's blood and some of the goat's blood and put it on all the horns of the altar. [19]He shall sprinkle some of the blood on it with his finger seven times to cleanse it and to consecrate it from the uncleanness of the Israelites.

[20]"When Aaron has finished making atonement for the Most Holy Place, the Tent of Meeting and the altar, he shall bring forward the live goat. [21]He is to lay both hands on the head of the live goat and confess over it all the wickedness and rebellion of the Israelites—all their sins—and put them on the goat's head. He shall send the goat away into the desert in the care of a man appointed for the task. [22]The goat will carry on itself all their sins to a solitary place; and the man shall release it in the desert.

[23]"Then Aaron is to go into the Tent of Meeting and take off the linen garments he put on before he entered the Most Holy Place, and he is to leave them there. [24]He shall bathe himself with water in a holy place and put on his regular garments. Then he shall come out and sacrifice the burnt offering for himself and the burnt offering for the people, to make atonement for himself and for the people. [25]He shall also burn the fat of the sin offering on the altar.

[26]"The man who releases the goat as a scapegoat must wash his clothes and bathe himself with water; afterward he may come into the camp. [27]The bull and the goat for the sin offerings, whose blood was brought into the Most Holy Place to make atonement, must be taken outside the camp; their hides, flesh and offal are to be burned up. [28]The man who burns them must wash his clothes and bathe himself with water; afterward he may come into the camp.

[29]"This is to be a lasting ordinance for you: On the tenth day of the seventh month you must deny yourselves[b] and not do any work—whether native-born or an alien living among you— [30]because on this day atonement will be made for you, to cleanse you. Then, before the LORD, you will be clean from all your sins. [31]It is a sabbath of rest, and you must deny yourselves; it is a lasting ordinance. [32]The priest who is anointed and ordained to succeed his father as high priest is to make atonement. He is to put on the sacred linen garments [33]and make atonement for the Most Holy Place, for the Tent of Meeting and the altar, and for the priests and all the people of the community.

[34]"This is to be a lasting ordinance for you: Atonement is to be made once a year for all the sins of the Israelites."

And it was done, as the LORD commanded Moses.

EATING BLOOD FORBIDDEN

17 The LORD said to Moses, [2]"Speak to Aaron and his sons and to all the Israelites and say to them: 'This is what the LORD has commanded: [3]Any Israelite who sacrifices an ox,[c] a lamb or a goat in the camp or outside of it [4]instead of bringing it to the entrance to the Tent of Meeting to present it as an offering to the LORD in front of the tabernacle of the LORD—that man shall

---

[a] 8 That is, the goat of removal; Hebrew azazel; also in verses 10 and 26   [b] 29 Or must fast; also in verse 31   [c] 3 The Hebrew word can include both male and female.

be considered guilty of bloodshed; he has shed blood and must be cut off from his people. ⁵This is so the Israelites will bring to the Lord the sacrifices they are now making in the open fields. They must bring them to the priest, that is, to the Lord, at the entrance to the Tent of Meeting and sacrifice them as fellowship offerings.ᵃ ⁶The priest is to sprinkle the blood against the altar of the Lord at the entrance to the Tent of Meeting and burn the fat as an aroma pleasing to the Lord. ⁷They must no longer offer any of their sacrifices to the goat idolsᵇ to whom they prostitute themselves. This is to be a lasting ordinance for them and for the generations to come.'

⁸"Say to them: 'Any Israelite or any alien living among them who offers a burnt offering or sacrifice ⁹and does not bring it to the entrance to the Tent of Meeting to sacrifice it to the Lord— that man must be cut off from his people.

¹⁰" 'Any Israelite or any alien living among them who eats any blood—I will set my face against that person who eats blood and will cut him off from his people. ¹¹For the life of a creature is in the blood, and I have given it to you to make atonement for yourselves on the altar; it is the blood that makes atonement for one's life. ¹²Therefore I say to the Israelites, "None of you may eat blood, nor may an alien living among you eat blood."

¹³" 'Any Israelite or any alien living among you who hunts any animal or bird that may be eaten must drain out the blood and cover it with earth, ¹⁴because the life of every creature is its blood. That is why I have said to the Israelites, "You must not eat the blood of any creature, because the life of every creature is its blood; anyone who eats it must be cut off."

¹⁵" 'Anyone, whether native-born or alien, who eats anything found dead or torn by wild animals must wash his clothes and bathe with water, and he will be ceremonially unclean till evening; then he will be clean. ¹⁶But if he does not wash his clothes and bathe himself, he will be held responsible.' "

UNLAWFUL SEXUAL RELATIONS

18 The Lord said to Moses, ²"Speak to the Israelites and say to them: 'I am the Lord your God. ³You must not do as they do in Egypt, where you used to live, and you must not do as they do in the land of Canaan, where I am bringing you. Do not follow their practices. ⁴You must obey my laws and be careful to follow my decrees. I am the Lord your God. ⁵Keep my decrees and laws, for the man who obeys them will live by them. I am the Lord.

⁶" 'No one is to approach any close relative to have sexual relations. I am the Lord.

⁷" 'Do not dishonor your father by having sexual relations with your mother. She is your mother; do not have relations with her.

⁸" 'Do not have sexual relations with your father's wife; that would dishonor your father.

⁹" 'Do not have sexual relations with your sister, either your father's daughter or your mother's daughter, whether she was born in the same home or elsewhere.

NOW OR NEVER

LEV 17:11–14

Think God doesn't take sin seriously? In order to gain his forgiveness and make things right with him, something (and, ultimately, some*one*) had to shed blood and die.

Taking a Stand

Let's talk animals. The lemming is a creature so devoted to following the crowd that it will swim into the ocean and drown if it sees other lemmings doing it. The salmon, on the other hand, is a creature designed to go against the flow—literally. During its spawning season, the salmon swims upstream, often against powerful currents, to . . . well, find a lady salmon. Think about that the next time you're faced with a pressure-packed situation. Don't be a lemming. Be a salmon. Swim against the stream. Be the individual God intended you to be.

» live the adventure » Lev 18:3

ᵃ 5 Traditionally *peace offerings*   ᵇ 7 Or *demons*

¹⁰" 'Do not have sexual relations with your son's daughter or your daughter's daughter; that would dishonor you.

¹¹" 'Do not have sexual relations with the daughter of your father's wife, born to your father; she is your sister.

¹²" 'Do not have sexual relations with your father's sister; she is your father's close relative.

¹³" 'Do not have sexual relations with your mother's sister, because she is your mother's close relative.

¹⁴" 'Do not dishonor your father's brother by approaching his wife to have sexual relations; she is your aunt.

¹⁵" 'Do not have sexual relations with your daughter-in-law. She is your son's wife; do not have relations with her.

¹⁶" 'Do not have sexual relations with your brother's wife; that would dishonor your brother.

¹⁷" 'Do not have sexual relations with both a woman and her daughter. Do not have sexual relations with either her son's daughter or her daughter's daughter; they are her close relatives. That is wickedness.

¹⁸" 'Do not take your wife's sister as a rival wife and have sexual relations with her while your wife is living.

¹⁹" 'Do not approach a woman to have sexual relations during the uncleanness of her monthly period.

²⁰" 'Do not have sexual relations with your neighbor's wife and defile yourself with her.

²¹" 'Do not give any of your children to be sacrificed[a] to Molech, for you must not profane the name of your God. I am the LORD.

²²" 'Do not lie with a man as one lies with a woman; that is detestable.

²³" 'Do not have sexual relations with an animal and defile yourself with it. A woman must not present herself to an animal to have sexual relations with it; that is a perversion.

²⁴" 'Do not defile yourselves in any of these ways, because this is how the nations that I am going to drive out before you became defiled. ²⁵Even the land was defiled; so I punished it for its sin, and the land vomited out its inhabitants. ²⁶But you must keep my decrees and my laws. The native-born and the aliens living among you must not do any of these detestable things, ²⁷for all these things were done by the people who lived in the land before you, and the land became defiled. ²⁸And if you defile the land, it will vomit you out as it vomited out the nations that were before you.

²⁹" 'Everyone who does any of these detestable things—such persons must be cut off from their people. ³⁰Keep my requirements and do not follow any of the detestable customs that were practiced before you came and do not defile yourselves with them. I am the LORD your God.' "

VARIOUS LAWS

19 The LORD said to Moses, ²"Speak to the entire assembly of Israel and say to them: 'Be holy because I, the LORD your God, am holy.

³" 'Each of you must respect his mother and father, and you must observe my Sabbaths. I am the LORD your God.

⁴" 'Do not turn to idols or make gods of cast metal for yourselves. I am the LORD your God.

⁵" 'When you sacrifice a fellowship offering[b] to the LORD, sacrifice it in such a way that it will be accepted on your behalf. ⁶It shall be eaten on the day you sacrifice it or on the next day; anything left over until the third day must be burned up. ⁷If any of it is eaten on the third day, it is impure and will not be accepted. ⁸Whoever eats it will be held responsible because he has desecrated what is holy to the LORD; that person must be cut off from his people.

⁹" 'When you reap the harvest of your land, do not reap to the very edges of your field or gather the

---

challenge notes

To: my_son

LEV 18:1-23

heavenly_father: don't believe anyone who says my plan for sex is old-fashioned or out of style. remember, I'm the one who created sex in the first place. I know best how you can fully enjoy it. follow my instructions and you won't have to worry about guilt, shame, STDs or anything else that might damage your experience. you'll be free to discover just how good sex can be.

---

[a] 21 Or *to be passed through the fire*   [b] 5 Traditionally *peace offering*

gleanings of your harvest. [10]Do not go over your vineyard a second time or pick up the grapes that have fallen. Leave them for the poor and the alien. I am the LORD your God.

Respecting the Elderly

What could your grandparents possibly have to say that could ever make a difference in your life? What valuable lesson could your retired neighbor teach you that would even remotely relate to anything going on in your world? Why would you ever need to hear the wisdom of some elderly person in your church? Depends on how serious you are about being successful in your life. If you dismiss older people because they look frail, or because everything they say seems out of date, you'll miss out on a valuable resource. If, however, you take the time and effort to show them respect—listening to them and getting to know them—you'll find that they've seen, done and learned things you can only dream about.

[11]" 'Do not steal.

" 'Do not lie.

" 'Do not deceive one another.

[12]" 'Do not swear falsely by my name and so profane the name of your God. I am the LORD.

[13]" 'Do not defraud your neighbor or rob him.

" 'Do not hold back the wages of a hired man overnight.

[14]" 'Do not curse the deaf or put a stumbling block in front of the blind, but fear your God. I am the LORD.

[15]" 'Do not pervert justice; do not show partiality to the poor or favoritism to the great, but judge your neighbor fairly.

[16]" 'Do not go about spreading slander among your people.

" 'Do not do anything that endangers your neighbor's life. I am the LORD.

[17]" 'Do not hate your brother in your heart. Rebuke your neighbor frankly so you will not share in his guilt.

[18]" 'Do not seek revenge or bear a grudge against one of your people, but love your neighbor as yourself. I am the LORD.

[19]" 'Keep my decrees.

" 'Do not mate different kinds of animals.

" 'Do not plant your field with two kinds of seed.

" 'Do not wear clothing woven of two kinds of material.

[20]" 'If a man sleeps with a woman who is a slave girl promised to another man but who has not been ransomed or given her freedom, there must be due punishment. Yet they are not to be put to death, because she had not been freed. [21]The man, however, must bring a ram to the entrance to the Tent of Meeting for a guilt offering to the LORD. [22]With the ram of the guilt offering the priest is to make atonement for him before the LORD for the sin he has committed, and his sin will be forgiven.

[23]" 'When you enter the land and plant any kind of fruit tree, regard its fruit as forbidden.[a] For three years you are to consider it forbidden[a]; it must not be eaten. [24]In the fourth year all its fruit will be holy, an offering of praise to the LORD. [25]But in the fifth year you may eat its fruit. In this way your harvest will be increased. I am the LORD your God.

[26]" 'Do not eat any meat with the blood still in it.

" 'Do not practice divination or sorcery.

[27]" 'Do not cut the hair at the sides of your head or clip off the edges of your beard.

[28]" 'Do not cut your bodies for the dead or put tattoo marks on yourselves. I am the LORD.

[29]" 'Do not degrade your daughter by making her a prostitute, or the land will turn to prostitution and be filled with wickedness.

[30]" 'Observe my Sabbaths and have reverence for my sanctuary. I am the LORD.

[31]" 'Do not turn to mediums or seek out spiritists, for you will be defiled by them. I am the LORD your God.

[32]" 'Rise in the presence of the aged, show respect for the elderly and revere your God. I am the LORD.

[33]" 'When an alien lives with you in your land, do not mistreat him. [34]The alien living with you must

NOW OR NEVER

LEV 19:33–34

Have you ever felt like an "alien"—an outsider who just doesn't seem to fit in? What about the "aliens"—or new kids—at your school or in your church or neighborhood? How quick are you to make them feel welcome?

---

[a] 23 Hebrew *uncircumcised*

battlelines

» Golden Oldies (Respecting the Elderly)

Q: Are you going to the concert Saturday night?
A: I wish.

Q: You're not going? What's up?
A: It's my grandparents' fiftieth anniversary. So my parents are dragging me 350 miles from home so that I can spend the weekend hugging a bunch of old people and strangers that I don't even know—and that I don't *want* to know.

Q: Where is this all going to happen? Any place fun?
A: Of course not. My grandparents live in some hick town in the middle of nowhere.

Q: Oooh, buddy. Sounds like it could be a very long weekend for you.
A: Count on it. A house that smells like a nursing home. Hours and hours of sitting and talking. Listening to the same stories over and over. Having aunts and uncles say stuff like, "I remember when you were just knee-high to a grasshopper." Being served mounds of ham, coleslaw, baked beans and Jell-O salad. Roosters that wake you up while it's still dark outside . . . Shall I continue? Or do you get the picture?

Q: No, no, I get it. Of course . . . it *could* be a good weekend too.
A: Good for who?

Q: Good for everyone. You never know, this might be the last time you'll ever see some of those people.

» Honoring the Aged

Yes, elderly people can be slow. And sometimes they're a little . . . quirky. Many of them have medical or mental conditions that can make them cranky or unpredictable. But they're also wise. And they are the only link to our past. Their lives give us clues to who we are and where we've come from. Besides, sometimes it can be pretty interesting when you get them to share their stories.

Leviticus 19:32 says, " 'Rise in the presence of the aged, show respect for the elderly and revere your God. I am the LORD.' "

First Peter 5:5 challenges us this way: "Young men, in the same way be submissive to those who are older. All of you, clothe yourselves with humility toward one another, because, 'God opposes the proud but gives grace to the humble.' "

Find an elderly person in your family or church and give him or her the simple gift of your time. You'll be amazed how much joy you can bring to another person's life when you're not too busy asking yourself, "What's in it for me?"

For more ideas on how to relate to your grandparents, check out www.RevolutionBible.com.

be treated as one of your native-born. Love him as yourself, for you were aliens in Egypt. I am the LORD your God.

35 " 'Do not use dishonest standards when measuring length, weight or quantity. 36Use honest scales and honest weights, an honest ephah[a] and an honest hin.[b] I am the LORD your God, who brought you out of Egypt.

37 " 'Keep all my decrees and all my laws and follow them. I am the LORD.' "

PUNISHMENTS FOR SIN

20 The LORD said to Moses, 2"Say to the Israelites: 'Any Israelite or any alien living in Israel who gives[c] any of his children to Molech must be put to death. The people of the community are to stone him. 3I will set my face against that man and I will cut him off from his people; for by giving his children to Molech, he has defiled my sanctuary and profaned my holy name. 4If the people of the community close their eyes when that man gives one of his children to Molech and they fail to put him to death, 5I will set my face against that man and his family and will cut off from their people both him and all who follow him in prostituting themselves to Molech.

6 " 'I will set my face against the person who turns to mediums and spiritists to prostitute himself by following them, and I will cut him off from his people.

7 " 'Consecrate yourselves and be holy, because I am the LORD your God. 8Keep my decrees and follow them. I am the LORD, who makes you holy.[d]

9 " 'If anyone curses his father or mother, he must be put to death. He has cursed his father or his mother, and his blood will be on his own head.

10 " 'If a man commits adultery with another man's wife—with the wife of his neighbor—both the adulterer and the adulteress must be put to death.

11 " 'If a man sleeps with his father's wife, he has dishonored his father. Both the man and the woman must be put to death; their blood will be on their own heads.

12 " 'If a man sleeps with his daughter-in-law, both of them must be put to death. What they have done is a perversion; their blood will be on their own heads.

13 " 'If a man lies with a man as one lies with a woman, both of them have done what is detestable. They must be put to death; their blood will be on their own heads.

14 " 'If a man marries both a woman and her mother, it is wicked. Both he and they must be burned in the fire, so that no wickedness will be among you.

15 " 'If a man has sexual relations with an animal, he must be put to death, and you must kill the animal.

16 " 'If a woman approaches an animal to have sexual relations with it, kill both the woman and the animal. They must be put to death; their blood will be on their own heads.

17 " 'If a man marries his sister, the daughter of either his father or his mother, and they have sexual relations, it is a disgrace. They must be cut off before the eyes of their people. He has dishonored his sister and will be held responsible.

18 " 'If a man lies with a woman during her monthly period and has sexual relations with her, he has exposed the source of her flow, and she has also uncovered it. Both of them must be cut off from their people.

19 " 'Do not have sexual relations with the sister of either your mother or your father, for that would dishonor a close relative; both of you would be held responsible.

20 " 'If a man sleeps with his aunt, he has dishonored his uncle. They will be held responsible; they will die childless.

21 " 'If a man marries his brother's wife, it is an act of impurity; he has dishonored his brother. They will be childless.

NOW OR NEVER
LEV 20:10–21

God's strict laws regulating sex aren't about taking away people's fun; they're about making sure that sex doesn't become just a cheap physical sensation. Sex should be enjoyed within the boundaries God set for us.

---

[a] 36 An ephah was a dry measure.   [b] 36 A hin was a liquid measure.   [c] 2 Or sacrifices; also in verses 3 and 4   [d] 8 Or who sanctifies you; or who sets you apart as holy

22 " 'Keep all my decrees and laws and follow them, so that the land where I am bringing you to live may not vomit you out. 23You must not live according to the customs of the nations I am going to drive out before you. Because they did all these things, I abhorred them. 24But I said to you, "You will possess their land; I will give it to you as an inheritance, a land flowing with milk and honey." I am the LORD your God, who has set you apart from the nations.

25 " 'You must therefore make a distinction between clean and unclean animals and between unclean and clean birds. Do not defile yourselves by any animal or bird or anything that moves along the ground—those which I have set apart as unclean for you. 26You are to be holy to me[a] because I, the LORD, am holy, and I have set you apart from the nations to be my own.

27 " 'A man or woman who is a medium or spiritist among you must be put to death. You are to stone them; their blood will be on their own heads.' "

RULES FOR PRIESTS

21 The LORD said to Moses, "Speak to the priests, the sons of Aaron, and say to them: 'A priest must not make himself ceremonially unclean for any of his people who die, 2except for a close relative, such as his mother or father, his son or daughter, his brother, 3or an unmarried sister who is dependent on him since she has no husband—for her he may make himself unclean. 4He must not make himself unclean for people related to him by marriage,[b] and so defile himself.

5 " 'Priests must not shave their heads or shave off the edges of their beards or cut their bodies. 6They must be holy to their God and must not profane the name of their God. Because they present the offerings made to the LORD by fire, the food of their God, they are to be holy.

7 " 'They must not marry women defiled by prostitution or divorced from their husbands, because priests are holy to their God. 8Regard them as holy, because they offer up the food of your God. Consider them holy, because I the LORD am holy—I who make you holy.[c]

9 " 'If a priest's daughter defiles herself by becoming a prostitute, she disgraces her father; she must be burned in the fire.

10 " 'The high priest, the one among his brothers who has had the anointing oil poured on his head and who has been ordained to wear the priestly garments, must not let his hair become unkempt[d] or tear his clothes. 11He must not enter a place where there is a dead body. He must not make himself unclean, even for his father or mother, 12nor leave the sanctuary of his God or desecrate it, because he has been dedicated by the anointing oil of his God. I am the LORD.

13 " 'The woman he marries must be a virgin. 14He must not marry a widow, a divorced woman, or a woman defiled by prostitution, but only a virgin from his own people, 15so he will not defile his offspring among his people. I am the LORD, who makes him holy.[e]' "

16The LORD said to Moses, 17"Say to Aaron: 'For the generations to come none of your descendants who has a defect may come near to offer the food of his God. 18No man who has any defect may come near: no man who is blind or lame, disfigured or deformed; 19no man with a crippled foot or hand, 20or who is hunchbacked or dwarfed, or who has any eye defect, or who has festering or running sores or damaged testicles. 21No descendant of Aaron the priest who has any defect is to come near to present the offerings made to the LORD by fire. He has a defect; he must not come near to offer the food of his God. 22He may eat the most holy food of his God, as well as the holy food; 23yet because of his defect, he must not go near the curtain or approach the altar, and so desecrate my sanctuary. I am the LORD, who makes them holy.' "

24So Moses told this to Aaron and his sons and to all the Israelites.

22 The LORD said to Moses, 2"Tell Aaron and his sons to treat with respect the sacred offerings the Israelites consecrate to me, so they will not profane my holy name. I am the LORD.

3"Say to them: 'For the generations to come, if any of your descendants is ceremonially unclean and yet comes near the sacred offerings that the Israelites consecrate to the LORD, that person must be cut off from my presence. I am the LORD.

4" 'If a descendant of Aaron has an infectious skin disease[g] or a bodily discharge, he may not eat

---

[a] 26 Or be my holy ones   [b] 4 Or unclean as a leader among his people   [c] 8 Or who sanctify you; or who set you apart as holy   [d] 10 Or not uncover his head   [e] 15 Or who sanctifies him; or who sets him apart as holy   [f] 23 Or who sanctifies them; or who sets them apart as holy   [g] 4 Traditionally leprosy; the Hebrew word was used for various diseases affecting the skin—not necessarily leprosy.

the sacred offerings until he is cleansed. He will also be unclean if he touches something defiled by a corpse or by anyone who has an emission of semen, ⁵or if he touches any crawling thing that makes him unclean, or any person who makes him unclean, whatever the uncleanness may be. ⁶The one who touches any such thing will be unclean till evening. He must not eat any of the sacred offerings unless he has bathed himself with water. ⁷When the sun goes down, he will be clean, and after that he may eat the sacred offerings, for they are his food. ⁸He must not eat anything found dead or torn by wild animals, and so become unclean through it. I am the LORD.

⁹" 'The priests are to keep my requirements so that they do not become guilty and die for treating them with contempt. I am the LORD, who makes them holy.ᵃ

¹⁰" 'No one outside a priest's family may eat the sacred offering, nor may the guest of a priest or his hired worker eat it. ¹¹But if a priest buys a slave with money, or if a slave is born in his household, that slave may eat his food. ¹²If a priest's daughter marries anyone other than a priest, she may not eat any of the sacred contributions. ¹³But if a priest's daughter becomes a widow or is divorced, yet has no children, and she returns to live in her father's house as in her youth, she may eat of her father's food. No unauthorized person, however, may eat any of it.

¹⁴" 'If anyone eats a sacred offering by mistake, he must make restitution to the priest for the offering and add a fifth of the value to it. ¹⁵The priests must not desecrate the sacred offerings the Israelites present to the LORD ¹⁶by allowing them to eat the sacred offerings and so bring upon them guilt requiring payment. I am the LORD, who makes them holy.' "

UNACCEPTABLE SACRIFICES

¹⁷The LORD said to Moses, ¹⁸"Speak to Aaron and his sons and to all the Israelites and say to them: 'If any of you—either an Israelite or an alien living in Israel—presents a gift for a burnt offering to the LORD, either to fulfill a vow or as a freewill offering, ¹⁹you must present a male without defect from the cattle, sheep or goats in order that it may be accepted on your behalf. ²⁰Do not bring anything with a defect, because it will not be accepted on your behalf. ²¹When anyone brings from the herd or flock a fellowship offeringᵇ to the LORD to fulfill a special vow or as a freewill offering, it must be without defect or blemish to be acceptable. ²²Do not offer to the LORD the blind, the injured or the maimed, or anything with warts or festering or running sores. Do not place any of these on the altar as an offering made to the LORD by fire. ²³You may, however, present as a freewill offering an oxᶜ or a sheep that is deformed or stunted, but it will not be accepted in fulfillment of a vow. ²⁴You must not offer to the LORD an animal whose testicles are bruised, crushed, torn or cut. You must not do this in your own land, ²⁵and you must not accept such animals from the hand of a foreigner and offer them as the food of your God. They will not be accepted on your behalf, because they are deformed and have defects.' "

now or never
LEV 22:17–20

If you're just halfheartedly going through the motions in your relationship with God, don't expect that to be good enough. Worship that's meaningless to you is worthless to God.

²⁶The LORD said to Moses, ²⁷"When a calf, a lamb or a goat is born, it is to remain with its mother for seven days. From the eighth day on, it will be acceptable as an offering made to the LORD by fire. ²⁸Do not slaughter a cow or a sheep and its young on the same day.

²⁹"When you sacrifice a thank offering to the LORD, sacrifice it in such a way that it will be accepted on your behalf. ³⁰It must be eaten that same day; leave none of it till morning. I am the LORD.

³¹"Keep my commands and follow them. I am the LORD. ³²Do not profane my holy name. I must be acknowledged as holy by the Israelites. I am the LORD, who makesᵈ you holyᵉ ³³and who brought you out of Egypt to be your God. I am the LORD."

23

The LORD said to Moses, ²"Speak to the Israelites and say to them: 'These are my appointed feasts, the appointed feasts of the LORD, which you are to proclaim as sacred assemblies.

ᵃ 9 Or who sanctifies them; or who sets them apart as holy; also in verse 16   ᵇ 21 Traditionally peace offering   ᶜ 23 The Hebrew word can include both male and female.   ᵈ 32 Or made   ᵉ 32 Or who sanctifies you; or who sets you apart as holy

THE SABBATH

3 " 'There are six days when you may work, but the seventh day is a Sabbath of rest, a day of sacred assembly. You are not to do any work; wherever you live, it is a Sabbath to the LORD.

THE PASSOVER AND UNLEAVENED BREAD

4 " 'These are the LORD's appointed feasts, the sacred assemblies you are to proclaim at their appointed times: 5 The LORD's Passover begins at twilight on the fourteenth day of the first month. 6 On the fifteenth day of that month the LORD's Feast of Unleavened Bread begins; for seven days you must eat bread made without yeast. 7 On the first day hold a sacred assembly and do no regular work. 8 For seven days present an offering made to the LORD by fire. And on the seventh day hold a sacred assembly and do no regular work.' "

FIRSTFRUITS

9 The LORD said to Moses, 10 "Speak to the Israelites and say to them: 'When you enter the land I am going to give you and you reap its harvest, bring to the priest a sheaf of the first grain you harvest. 11 He is to wave the sheaf before the LORD so it will be accepted on your behalf; the priest is to wave it on the day after the Sabbath. 12 On the day you wave the sheaf, you must sacrifice as a burnt offering to the LORD a lamb a year old without defect, 13 together with its grain offering of two-tenths of an ephah[a] of fine flour mixed with oil—an offering made to the LORD by fire, a pleasing

NOW OR NEVER
LEV 23:1-4

Obviously, God thought it was important for his people to worship *together*. How much time do you spend with other Christians? What can you do to make your experiences together a more enjoyable and significant part of your life?

aroma—and its drink offering of a quarter of a hin[b] of wine. 14 You must not eat any bread, or roasted or new grain, until the very day you bring this offering to your God. This is to be a lasting ordinance for the generations to come, wherever you live.

FEAST OF WEEKS

15 " 'From the day after the Sabbath, the day you brought the sheaf of the wave offering, count off seven full weeks. 16 Count off fifty days up to the day after the seventh Sabbath, and then present an offering of new grain to the LORD. 17 From wherever you live, bring two loaves made of two-tenths of an ephah of fine flour, baked with yeast, as a wave offering of firstfruits to the LORD. 18 Present with this bread seven male lambs, each a year old and without defect, one young bull and two rams. They will be a burnt offering to the LORD, together with their grain offerings and drink offerings—an offering made by fire, an aroma pleasing to the LORD. 19 Then sacrifice one male goat for a sin offering and two lambs, each a year old, for a fellowship offering.[c] 20 The priest is to wave the two lambs before the LORD as a wave offering, together with the bread of the firstfruits. They are a sacred offering to the LORD for the priest. 21 On that same day you are to proclaim a sacred assembly and do no regular work. This is to be a lasting ordinance for the generations to come, wherever you live.

22 " 'When you reap the harvest of your land, do not reap to the very edges of your field or gather the gleanings of your harvest. Leave them for the poor and the alien. I am the LORD your God.' "

FEAST OF TRUMPETS

23 The LORD said to Moses, 24 "Say to the Israelites: 'On the first day of the seventh month you are to have a day of rest, a sacred assembly commemorated with trumpet blasts. 25 Do no regular work, but present an offering made to the LORD by fire.' "

DAY OF ATONEMENT

26 The LORD said to Moses, 27 "The tenth day of this seventh month is the Day of Atonement. Hold a sacred assembly and deny yourselves,[d] and present an offering made to the LORD by fire. 28 Do no work

---

[a] *13* That is, probably about 4 quarts (about 4.5 liters); also in verse 17   [b] *13* That is, probably about 1 quart (about 1 liter)
[c] *19* Traditionally *peace offering*   [d] *27* Or *and fast*; also in verses 29 and 32

on that day, because it is the Day of Atonement, when atonement is made for you before the LORD your God. ²⁹Anyone who does not deny himself on that day must be cut off from his people. ³⁰I will destroy from among his people anyone who does any work on that day. ³¹You shall do no work at all. This is to be a lasting ordinance for the generations to come, wherever you live. ³²It is a sabbath of rest for you, and you must deny yourselves. From the evening of the ninth day of the month until the following evening you are to observe your sabbath."

FEAST OF TABERNACLES

³³The LORD said to Moses, ³⁴"Say to the Israelites: 'On the fifteenth day of the seventh month the LORD's Feast of Tabernacles begins, and it lasts for seven days. ³⁵The first day is a sacred assembly; do no regular work. ³⁶For seven days present offerings made to the LORD by fire, and on the eighth day hold a sacred assembly and present an offering made to the LORD by fire. It is the closing assembly; do no regular work.

³⁷(" 'These are the LORD's appointed feasts, which you are to proclaim as sacred assemblies for bringing offerings made to the LORD by fire—the burnt offerings and grain offerings, sacrifices and drink offerings required for each day. ³⁸These offerings are in addition to those for the LORD's Sabbaths andᵃ in addition to your gifts and whatever you have vowed and all the freewill offerings you give to the LORD.)

³⁹" 'So beginning with the fifteenth day of the seventh month, after you have gathered the crops of the land, celebrate the festival to the LORD for seven days; the first day is a day of rest, and the eighth day also is a day of rest. ⁴⁰On the first day you are to take choice fruit from the trees, and palm fronds, leafy branches and poplars, and rejoice before the LORD your God for seven days. ⁴¹Celebrate this as a festival to the LORD for seven days each year. This is to be a lasting ordinance for the generations to come; celebrate it in the seventh month. ⁴²Live in booths for seven days: All native-born Israelites are to live in booths ⁴³so your descendants will know that I had the Israelites live in booths when I brought them out of Egypt. I am the LORD your God.' "

⁴⁴So Moses announced to the Israelites the appointed feasts of the LORD.

OIL AND BREAD SET BEFORE THE LORD

24 The LORD said to Moses, ²"Command the Israelites to bring you clear oil of pressed olives for the light so that the lamps may be kept burning continually. ³Outside the curtain of the Testimony in the Tent of Meeting, Aaron is to tend the lamps before the LORD from evening till morning, continually. This is to be a lasting ordinance for the generations to come. ⁴The lamps on the pure gold lampstand before the LORD must be tended continually.

⁵"Take fine flour and bake twelve loaves of bread, using two-tenths of an ephahᵇ for each loaf. ⁶Set them in two rows, six in each row, on the table of pure gold before the LORD. ⁷Along each row put some pure incense as a memorial portion to represent the bread and to be an offering made to the LORD by fire. ⁸This bread is to be set out before the LORD regularly, Sabbath after Sabbath, on behalf of the Israelites, as a lasting covenant. ⁹It belongs to Aaron and his sons, who are to eat it in a holy place, because it is a most holy part of their regular share of the offerings made to the LORD by fire."

A BLASPHEMER STONED

¹⁰Now the son of an Israelite mother and an Egyptian father went out among the Israelites, and a fight broke out in the camp between him and an Israelite. ¹¹The son of the Israelite woman blasphemed the Name with a curse; so they brought him to Moses. (His mother's name was Shelomith, the daughter of Dibri the Danite.) ¹²They put him in custody until the will of the LORD should be made clear to them.

¹³Then the LORD said to Moses: ¹⁴"Take the blasphemer outside the camp. All those who heard him are to lay their hands on his head, and the entire assembly is to stone him. ¹⁵Say to the Israelites: 'If anyone curses his God, he will be held responsible; ¹⁶anyone who blasphemes the name of the LORD must be put to death. The entire assembly must stone him. Whether an alien or native-born, when he blasphemes the Name, he must be put to death.

¹⁷" 'If anyone takes the life of a human being, he must be put to death. ¹⁸Anyone who takes the life

---

ᵃ *38* Or *These feasts are in addition to the LORD's Sabbaths, and these offerings are*   ᵇ *5* That is, probably about 4 quarts (about 4.5 liters) of someone's animal must make restitution—life for life. ¹⁹If anyone injures his neighbor, whatever he has done must be done to him: ²⁰fracture for fracture, eye for eye, tooth for tooth. As he has injured the other, so he is to be injured. ²¹Whoever kills an animal must make restitution, but whoever kills a man must be put to death. ²²You are to have the same law for the alien and the native-born. I am the LORD your God.' "

²³Then Moses spoke to the Israelites, and they took the blasphemer outside the camp and stoned him. The Israelites did as the LORD commanded Moses.

THE SABBATH YEAR

25 The LORD said to Moses on Mount Sinai, ²"Speak to the Israelites and say to them: 'When you enter the land I am going to give you, the land itself must observe a sabbath to the LORD. ³For six years sow your fields, and for six years prune your vineyards and gather their crops. ⁴But in the seventh year the land is to have a sabbath of rest, a sabbath to the LORD. Do not sow your fields or prune your vineyards. ⁵Do not reap what grows of itself or harvest the grapes of your untended vines. The land is to have a year of rest. ⁶Whatever the land yields during the sabbath year will be food for you—for yourself, your manservant and maidservant, and the hired worker and temporary resident who live among you, ⁷as well as for your livestock and the wild animals in your land. Whatever the land produces may be eaten.

THE YEAR OF JUBILEE

⁸" 'Count off seven sabbaths of years—seven times seven years—so that the seven sabbaths of years amount to a period of forty-nine years. ⁹Then have the trumpet sounded everywhere on the tenth day of the seventh month; on the Day of Atonement sound the trumpet throughout your land. ¹⁰Consecrate the fiftieth year and proclaim liberty throughout the land to all its inhabitants. It shall be a jubilee for you; each one of you is to return to his family property and each to his own clan. ¹¹The fiftieth year shall be a jubilee for you; do not sow and do not reap what grows of itself or harvest the untended vines. ¹²For it is a jubilee and is to be holy for you; eat only what is taken directly from the fields.

¹³" 'In this Year of Jubilee everyone is to return to his own property.

¹⁴" 'If you sell land to one of your countrymen or buy any from him, do not take advantage of each other. ¹⁵You are to buy from your countryman on the basis of the number of years since the Jubilee. And he is to sell to you on the basis of the number of years left for harvesting crops. ¹⁶When the years are many, you are to increase the price, and when the years are few, you are to decrease the price, because what he is really selling you is the number of crops. ¹⁷Do not take advantage of each other, but fear your God. I am the LORD your God.

NOW OR NEVER

LEV 25:23

If you stopped thinking of the things you own as yours and started thinking of them as God's, how would it change the way you live?

¹⁸" 'Follow my decrees and be careful to obey my laws, and you will live safely in the land. ¹⁹Then the land will yield its fruit, and you will eat your fill and live there in safety. ²⁰You may ask, "What will we eat in the seventh year if we do not plant or harvest our crops?" ²¹I will send you such a blessing in the sixth year that the land will yield enough for three years. ²²While you plant during the eighth year, you will eat from the old crop and will continue to eat from it until the harvest of the ninth year comes in.

²³" 'The land must not be sold permanently, because the land is mine and you are but aliens and my tenants. ²⁴Throughout the country that you hold as a possession, you must provide for the redemption of the land.

²⁵" 'If one of your countrymen becomes poor and sells some of his property, his nearest relative is to come and redeem what his countryman has sold. ²⁶If, however, a man has no one to redeem it for him but he himself prospers and acquires sufficient means to redeem it, ²⁷he is to determine the value for the years since he sold it and refund the balance to the man to whom he sold it; he can then go back to his own property. ²⁸But if he does not acquire the means to repay him, what he sold will remain in the possession of the buyer until the Year of Jubilee. It will be returned in the Jubilee, and he can then go back to his property.

²⁹" 'If a man sells a house in a walled city, he retains the right of redemption a full year after its sale. During that time he may redeem it. ³⁰If it is not redeemed before a full year has passed, the house in the walled city shall belong permanently to the buyer and his descendants. It is not to be returned in the Jubilee. ³¹But houses in villages without walls around them are to be considered as open country. They can be redeemed, and they are to be returned in the Jubilee.

³²" 'The Levites always have the right to redeem their houses in the Levitical towns, which they possess. ³³So the property of the Levites is redeemable—that is, a house sold in any town they hold—and is to be returned in the Jubilee, because the houses in the towns of the Levites are their property among the Israelites. ³⁴But the pastureland belonging to their towns must not be sold; it is their permanent possession.

³⁵" 'If one of your countrymen becomes poor and is unable to support himself among you, help him as you would an alien or a temporary resident, so he can continue to live among you. ³⁶Do not take interest of any kind[a] from him, but fear your God, so that your countryman may continue to live among you. ³⁷You must not lend him money at interest or sell him food at a profit. ³⁸I am the LORD your God, who brought you out of Egypt to give you the land of Canaan and to be your God.

³⁹" 'If one of your countrymen becomes poor among you and sells himself to you, do not make him work as a slave. ⁴⁰He is to be treated as a hired worker or a temporary resident among you; he is to work for you until the Year of Jubilee. ⁴¹Then he and his children are to be released, and he will go back to his own clan and to the property of his forefathers. ⁴²Because the Israelites are my servants, whom I brought out of Egypt, they must not be sold as slaves. ⁴³Do not rule over them ruthlessly, but fear your God.

⁴⁴" 'Your male and female slaves are to come from the nations around you; from them you may buy slaves. ⁴⁵You may also buy some of the temporary residents living among you and members of their clans born in your country, and they will become your property. ⁴⁶You can will them to your children as inherited property and can make them slaves for life, but you must not rule over your fellow Israelites ruthlessly.

⁴⁷" 'If an alien or a temporary resident among you becomes rich and one of your countrymen becomes poor and sells himself to the alien living among you or to a member of the alien's clan, ⁴⁸he retains the right of redemption after he has sold himself. One of his relatives may redeem him: ⁴⁹An uncle or a cousin or any blood relative in his clan may redeem him. Or if he prospers, he may redeem himself. ⁵⁰He and his buyer are to count the time from the year he sold himself up to the Year of Jubilee. The price for his release is to be based on the rate paid to a hired man for that number of years. ⁵¹If many years remain, he must pay for his redemption a larger share of the price paid for him. ⁵²If only a few years remain until the Year of Jubilee, he is to compute that and pay for his redemption accordingly. ⁵³He is to be treated as a man hired from year to year; you must see to it that his owner does not rule over him ruthlessly.

⁵⁴" 'Even if he is not redeemed in any of these ways, he and his children are to be released in the Year of Jubilee, ⁵⁵for the Israelites belong to me as servants. They are my servants, whom I brought out of Egypt. I am the LORD your God.

NOW OR NEVER

LEV 26:1

What contemporary idols do you worship? Before you answer, let's rephrase the question: What things in your everyday life rate higher than your relationship with God? Be honest.

REWARD FOR OBEDIENCE

26

" 'Do not make idols or set up an image or a sacred stone for yourselves, and do not place a carved stone in your land to bow down before it. I am the LORD your God. ²" 'Observe my Sabbaths and have reverence for my sanctuary. I am the LORD.

³" 'If you follow my decrees and are careful to obey my commands, ⁴I will send you rain in its season, and the ground will yield its crops and the trees of the field their fruit. ⁵Your threshing will continue until grape harvest and the grape harvest will continue until planting, and you will eat all the food you want and live in safety in your land.

---

^a *36* Or *take excessive interest*; similarly in verse 37

6 " 'I will grant peace in the land, and you will lie down and no one will make you afraid. I will remove savage beasts from the land, and the sword will not pass through your country. 7You will pursue your enemies, and they will fall by the sword before you. 8Five of you will chase a hundred, and a hundred of you will chase ten thousand, and your enemies will fall by the sword before you.

9 " 'I will look on you with favor and make you fruitful and increase your numbers, and I will keep my covenant with you. 10You will still be eating last year's harvest when you will have to move it out to make room for the new. 11I will put my dwelling place^a among you, and I will not abhor you. 12I will walk among you and be your God, and you will be my people. 13I am the LORD your God, who brought you out of Egypt so that you would no longer be slaves to the Egyptians; I broke the bars of your yoke and enabled you to walk with heads held high.

PUNISHMENT FOR DISOBEDIENCE

14 " 'But if you will not listen to me and carry out all these commands, 15and if you reject my decrees and abhor my laws and fail to carry out all my commands and so violate my covenant, 16then I will do this to you: I will bring upon you sudden terror, wasting diseases and fever that will destroy your sight and drain away your life. You will plant seed in vain, because your enemies will eat it. 17I will set my face against you so that you will be defeated by your enemies; those who hate you will rule over you, and you will flee even when no one is pursuing you.

18 " 'If after all this you will not listen to me, I will punish you for your sins seven times over. 19I will break down your stubborn pride and make the sky above you like iron and the ground beneath you like bronze. 20Your strength will be spent in vain, because your soil will not yield its crops, nor will the trees of the land yield their fruit.

21 " 'If you remain hostile toward me and refuse to listen to me, I will multiply your afflictions seven times over, as your sins deserve. 22I will send wild animals against you, and they will rob you of your children, destroy your cattle and make you so few in number that your roads will be deserted.

23 " 'If in spite of these things you do not accept my correction but continue to be hostile toward me, 24I myself will be hostile toward you and will afflict you for your sins seven times over. 25And I will bring the sword upon you to avenge the breaking of the covenant. When you withdraw into your cities, I will send a plague among you, and you will be given into enemy hands. 26When I cut off your supply of bread, ten women will be able to bake your bread in one oven, and they will dole out the bread by weight. You will eat, but you will not be satisfied.

27 " 'If in spite of this you still do not listen to me but continue to be hostile toward me, 28then in my anger I will be hostile toward you, and I myself will punish you for your sins seven times over. 29You will eat the flesh of your sons and the flesh of your daughters. 30I will destroy your high places, cut down your incense altars and pile your dead bodies on the lifeless forms of your idols, and I will abhor you. 31I will turn your cities into ruins and lay waste your sanctuaries, and I will take no delight in the pleasing aroma of your offerings. 32I will lay waste the land, so that your enemies who live there will be appalled. 33I will scatter you among the nations and will draw out my sword and pursue you. Your land will be laid waste, and your cities will lie in ruins. 34Then the land will enjoy its sabbath years all the time that it lies desolate and you are in the country of your enemies; then the land will rest and enjoy its sabbaths. 35All the time that it lies desolate, the land will have the rest it did not have during the sabbaths you lived in it.

36 " 'As for those of you who are left, I will make their hearts so fearful in the lands of their enemies that the sound of a windblown leaf will put them to flight. They will run as though fleeing from the sword, and they will fall, even though no one is pursuing them. 37They will stumble over one another as though fleeing from the sword, even though no one is pursuing them. So you will not be able to stand before your enemies. 38You will perish among the nations; the land of your enemies will devour you. 39Those of you who are left will waste away in the lands of their enemies because of their sins; also because of their fathers' sins they will waste away.

40 " 'But if they will confess their sins and the sins of their fathers—their treachery against me and their hostility toward me, 41which made me hostile toward them so that I sent them into the land of their enemies—then when their uncircumcised hearts are humbled and they pay for their sin, 42I will remember my covenant with Jacob and my covenant with Isaac and my covenant with Abraham, and I will remember the land. 43For the land will be deserted by them and will enjoy its sabbaths while it lies

---

^a 11 Or *my tabernacle*

∩OW OR ∩EVER

LEV 26:40-45

Sometimes God will allow you to suffer the consequences of your sin. If he didn't, you might miss out on some valuable learning experiences. But he will *never* desert you or give up on you, no matter what. Any discipline you experience is meant to bring you closer to God.

desolate without them. They will pay for their sins because they rejected my laws and abhorred my decrees. ⁴⁴Yet in spite of this, when they are in the land of their enemies, I will not reject them or abhor them so as to destroy them completely, breaking my covenant with them. I am the LORD their God. ⁴⁵But for their sake I will remember the covenant with their ancestors whom I brought out of Egypt in the sight of the nations to be their God. I am the LORD.' "

⁴⁶These are the decrees, the laws and the regulations that the LORD established on Mount Sinai between himself and the Israelites through Moses.

REDEEMING WHAT IS THE LORD'S

27

The LORD said to Moses, ²"Speak to the Israelites and say to them: 'If anyone makes a special vow to dedicate persons to the LORD by giving equivalent values, ³set the value of a male between the ages of twenty and sixty at fifty shekels[a] of silver, according to the sanctuary shekel[b]; ⁴and if it is a female, set her value at thirty shekels.[c] ⁵If it is a person between the ages of five and twenty, set the value of a male at twenty shekels[d] and of a female at ten shekels.[e] ⁶If it is a person between one month and five years, set the value of a male at five shekels[f] of silver and that of a female at three shekels[g] of silver. ⁷If it is a person sixty years old or more, set the value of a male at fifteen shekels[h] and of a female at ten shekels. ⁸If anyone making the vow is too poor to pay the specified amount, he is to present the person to the priest, who will set the value for him according to what the man making the vow can afford.

⁹" 'If what he vowed is an animal that is acceptable as an offering to the LORD, such an animal given to the LORD becomes holy. ¹⁰He must not exchange it or substitute a good one for a bad one, or a bad one for a good one; if he should substitute one animal for another, both it and the substitute become holy. ¹¹If what he vowed is a ceremonially unclean animal—one that is not acceptable as an offering to the LORD—the animal must be presented to the priest, ¹²who will judge its quality as good or bad. Whatever value the priest then sets, that is what it will be. ¹³If the owner wishes to redeem the animal, he must add a fifth to its value.

¹⁴" 'If a man dedicates his house as something holy to the LORD, the priest will judge its quality as good or bad. Whatever value the priest then sets, so it will remain. ¹⁵If the man who dedicates his house redeems it, he must add a fifth to its value, and the house will again become his.

¹⁶" 'If a man dedicates to the LORD part of his family land, its value is to be set according to the amount of seed required for it—fifty shekels of silver to a homer[i] of barley seed. ¹⁷If he dedicates his field during the Year of Jubilee, the value that has been set remains. ¹⁸But if he dedicates his field after the Jubilee, the priest will determine the value according to the number of years that remain until the next Year of Jubilee, and its set value will be reduced. ¹⁹If the man who dedicates the field wishes to redeem it, he must add a fifth to its value, and the field will again become his. ²⁰If, however, he does not redeem the field, or if he has sold it to someone else, it can never be redeemed. ²¹When the field is released in the Jubilee, it will become holy, like a field devoted to the LORD; it will become the property of the priests.[j]

²²" 'If a man dedicates to the LORD a field he has bought, which is not part of his family land, ²³the priest will determine its value up to the Year of Jubilee, and the man must pay its value on that day as something holy to the LORD. ²⁴In the Year of Jubilee the field will revert to the person from whom he bought it, the one whose land it was. ²⁵Every value is to be set according to the sanctuary shekel, twenty gerahs to the shekel.

²⁶" 'No one, however, may dedicate the firstborn of an animal, since the firstborn already belongs to the LORD; whether an ox[k] or a sheep, it is the LORD's. ²⁷If it is one of the unclean animals, he may buy it

---

ᵃ *3* That is, about 1 1/4 pounds (about 0.6 kilogram); also in verse 16   ᵇ *3* That is, about 2/5 ounce (about 11.5 grams); also in verse 25   ᶜ *4* That is, about 12 ounces (about 0.3 kilogram)   ᵈ *5* That is, about 8 ounces (about 0.2 kilogram)   ᵉ *5* That is, about 4 ounces (about 110 grams); also in verse 7   ᶠ *6* That is, about 2 ounces (about 55 grams)   ᵍ *6* That is, about 1 1/4 ounces (about 35 grams)   ʰ *7* That is, about 6 ounces (about 170 grams)   ⁱ *16* That is, probably about 6 bushels (about 220 liters)   ʲ *21* Or *priest*   ᵏ *26* The Hebrew word can include both male and female.

back at its set value, adding a fifth of the value to it. If he does not redeem it, it is to be sold at its set value.

28 " 'But nothing that a man owns and devotes[a] to the Lord—whether man or animal or family land—may be sold or redeemed; everything so devoted is most holy to the Lord.

29 " 'No person devoted to destruction[b] may be ransomed; he must be put to death.

30 " 'A tithe of everything from the land, whether grain from the soil or fruit from the trees, belongs to the Lord; it is holy to the Lord. 31 If a man redeems any of his tithe, he must add a fifth of the value to it. 32 The entire tithe of the herd and flock—every tenth animal that passes under the shepherd's rod—will be holy to the Lord. 33 He must not pick out the good from the bad or make any substitution. If he does make a substitution, both the animal and its substitute become holy and cannot be redeemed.' "

34 These are the commands the Lord gave Moses on Mount Sinai for the Israelites.

---

a 28 The Hebrew term refers to the irrevocable giving over of things or persons to the Lord.   b 29 The Hebrew term refers to the irrevocable giving over of things or persons to the Lord, often by totally destroying them.

NUMBERS

NUMBERS

Author
Moses

Audience
People of Israel, wandering in the desert

Date
1444–1405 B.C.

Setting
The people of Israel travel from Mount Sinai through the desert to the borders of the land of Canaan.

Verse to Remember
The LORD replied, "I have forgiven them, as you asked. Nevertheless, as surely as I live and as surely as the glory of the LORD fills the whole earth, not one of the men who saw my glory and the miraculous signs I performed in Egypt and in the desert but who disobeyed me and tested me ten times— not one of them will ever see the land I promised on oath to their forefathers. No one who has treated me with contempt will ever see it" (14:20–23).

Theme to Consider
There are often severe consequences for our rebellion against God. But even though God disciplines us, he remains faithful to his promises, showing great patience and mercy.

UNCHANGING TRUTH » The moment you decide to follow God, you begin a remarkable journey that will last the rest of your days. Your journey is unique; no one else will ever experience exactly what you experience or accomplish what you accomplish. Your journey will take you places you never thought you'd go. Sometimes it will also take you places you'd rather not be.

The scary and exciting—and cool—thing about your journey is that you have no map. You can't say with any certainty what God has in store for you tomorrow, let alone where he will lead you next year. That's where the adventure of faith comes in. God knows exactly where you should be and what you should do every day of your life. If you can learn to trust him—and look for ways to make the most of every day (including every rest stop or detour) along the journey—you're in for the ride of your life.

The Israelites were slow learners when it came to following God's path for their lives. They could have saved themselves a lot of trouble and suffering if they had only learned to let God do the driving and lead them to the right destination—without constantly complaining and questioning from the backseat.

LIFE LESSONS »

1   God wants us to celebrate his blessings regularly and faithfully, with joy and gratitude. (9:1–14).

2   God doesn't mind when we bring our heartfelt questions and doubts to him in a respectful way, but he won't put up with disrespectful grumbling and complaining (11:1–2).

3   We have a responsibility to do whatever it takes to make sure that God's Word stays fresh in our hearts and minds (15:37–41).

4   If you regularly hang out with people who don't make God the top priority in their lives, your relationship with God will definitely suffer (25:1–3).

THE CENSUS

1 The LORD spoke to Moses in the Tent of Meeting in the Desert of Sinai on the first day of the second month of the second year after the Israelites came out of Egypt. He said: 2"Take a census of the whole Israelite community by their clans and families, listing every man by name, one by one. 3You and Aaron are to number by their divisions all the men in Israel twenty years old or more who are able to serve in the army. 4One man from each tribe, each the head of his family, is to help you. 5These are the names of the men who are to assist you:

from Reuben, Elizur son of Shedeur;
6from Simeon, Shelumiel son of Zurishaddai;
7from Judah, Nahshon son of Amminadab;
8from Issachar, Nethanel son of Zuar;
9from Zebulun, Eliab son of Helon;
10from the sons of Joseph:
     from Ephraim, Elishama son of Ammihud;
     from Manasseh, Gamaliel son of Pedahzur;
11from Benjamin, Abidan son of Gideoni;
12from Dan, Ahiezer son of Ammishaddai;
13from Asher, Pagiel son of Ocran;
14from Gad, Eliasaph son of Deuel;
15from Naphtali, Ahira son of Enan."

16These were the men appointed from the community, the leaders of their ancestral tribes. They were the heads of the clans of Israel.

17Moses and Aaron took these men whose names had been given, 18and they called the whole community together on the first day of the second month. The people indicated their ancestry by their clans and families, and the men twenty years old or more were listed by name, one by one, 19as the LORD commanded Moses. And so he counted them in the Desert of Sinai:

20From the descendants of Reuben the firstborn son of Israel:
     All the men twenty years old or more who were able to serve in the army were listed by name, one by one, according to the records of their clans and families. 21The number from the tribe of Reuben was 46,500.

22From the descendants of Simeon:
     All the men twenty years old or more who were able to serve in the army were counted and listed by name, one by one, according to the records of their clans and families. 23The number from the tribe of Simeon was 59,300.

24From the descendants of Gad:
     All the men twenty years old or more who were able to serve in the army were listed by name, according to the records of their clans and families. 25The number from the tribe of Gad was 45,650.

26From the descendants of Judah:
     All the men twenty years old or more who were able to serve in the army were listed by name, according to the records of their clans and families. 27The number from the tribe of Judah was 74,600.

28From the descendants of Issachar:
     All the men twenty years old or more who were able to serve in the army were listed by name, according to the records of their clans and families. 29The number from the tribe of Issachar was 54,400.

30From the descendants of Zebulun:
     All the men twenty years old or more who were able to serve in the army were listed by name, according to the records of their clans and families. 31The number from the tribe of Zebulun was 57,400.

³²From the sons of Joseph:

From the descendants of Ephraim:

All the men twenty years old or more who were able to serve in the army were listed by name, according to the records of their clans and families. ³³The number from the tribe of Ephraim was 40,500.

³⁴From the descendants of Manasseh:

All the men twenty years old or more who were able to serve in the army were listed by name, according to the records of their clans and families. ³⁵The number from the tribe of Manasseh was 32,200.

³⁶From the descendants of Benjamin:

All the men twenty years old or more who were able to serve in the army were listed by name, according to the records of their clans and families. ³⁷The number from the tribe of Benjamin was 35,400.

³⁸From the descendants of Dan:

All the men twenty years old or more who were able to serve in the army were listed by name, according to the records of their clans and families. ³⁹The number from the tribe of Dan was 62,700.

⁴⁰From the descendants of Asher:

All the men twenty years old or more who were able to serve in the army were listed by name, according to the records of their clans and families. ⁴¹The number from the tribe of Asher was 41,500.

⁴²From the descendants of Naphtali:

All the men twenty years old or more who were able to serve in the army were listed by name, according to the records of their clans and families. ⁴³The number from the tribe of Naphtali was 53,400.

⁴⁴These were the men counted by Moses and Aaron and the twelve leaders of Israel, each one representing his family. ⁴⁵All the Israelites twenty years old or more who were able to serve in Israel's army were counted according to their families. ⁴⁶The total number was 603,550.

⁴⁷The families of the tribe of Levi, however, were not counted along with the others. ⁴⁸The LORD had said to Moses: ⁴⁹"You must not count the tribe of Levi or include them in the census of the other Israelites. ⁵⁰Instead, appoint the Levites to be in charge of the tabernacle of the Testimony—over all its furnishings and everything belonging to it. They are to carry the tabernacle and all its furnishings; they are to take care of it and encamp around it. ⁵¹Whenever the tabernacle is to move, the Levites are to take it down, and whenever the tabernacle is to be set up, the Levites shall do it. Anyone else who goes near it shall be put to death. ⁵²The Israelites are to set up their tents by divisions, each man in his own camp under his own standard. ⁵³The Levites, however, are to set up their tents around the tabernacle of the Testimony so that wrath will not fall on the Israelite community. The Levites are to be responsible for the care of the tabernacle of the Testimony."

⁵⁴The Israelites did all this just as the LORD commanded Moses.

NOW OR NEVER
NU 2:1-2

Organizing the people according to families and tribes averted a logistical nightmare. Identifying the people by family and tribe also gave them a sense of belonging and unity. What "tribe" will you choose to belong to?

THE ARRANGEMENT OF THE TRIBAL CAMPS

2 The LORD said to Moses and Aaron: ²"The Israelites are to camp around the Tent of Meeting some distance from it, each man under his standard with the banners of his family."

³On the east, toward the sunrise, the divisions of the camp of Judah are to encamp under their standard. The leader of the people of Judah is Nahshon son of Amminadab. ⁴His division numbers 74,600.

⁵The tribe of Issachar will camp next to them. The leader of the people of Issachar is Nethanel son of Zuar. ⁶His division numbers 54,400.

⁷The tribe of Zebulun will be next. The leader of the people of Zebulun is Eliab son of Helon. ⁸His division numbers 57,400.

⁹All the men assigned to the camp of Judah, according to their divisions, number 186,400. They will set out first.

¹⁰On the south will be the divisions of the camp of Reuben under their standard. The leader of the people of Reuben is Elizur son of Shedeur. ¹¹His division numbers 46,500.

¹²The tribe of Simeon will camp next to them. The leader of the people of Simeon is Shelumiel son of Zurishaddai. ¹³His division numbers 59,300.

¹⁴The tribe of Gad will be next. The leader of the people of Gad is Eliasaph son of Deuel.ᵃ ¹⁵His division numbers 45,650.

¹⁶All the men assigned to the camp of Reuben, according to their divisions, number 151,450. They will set out second.

¹⁷Then the Tent of Meeting and the camp of the Levites will set out in the middle of the camps. They will set out in the same order as they encamp, each in his own place under his standard.

¹⁸On the west will be the divisions of the camp of Ephraim under their standard. The leader of the people of Ephraim is Elishama son of Ammihud. ¹⁹His division numbers 40,500.

²⁰The tribe of Manasseh will be next to them. The leader of the people of Manasseh is Gamaliel son of Pedahzur. ²¹His division numbers 32,200.

²²The tribe of Benjamin will be next. The leader of the people of Benjamin is Abidan son of Gideoni. ²³His division numbers 35,400.

²⁴All the men assigned to the camp of Ephraim, according to their divisions, number 108,100. They will set out third.

²⁵On the north will be the divisions of the camp of Dan, under their standard. The leader of the people of Dan is Ahiezer son of Ammishaddai. ²⁶His division numbers 62,700.

²⁷The tribe of Asher will camp next to them. The leader of the people of Asher is Pagiel son of Ocran. ²⁸His division numbers 41,500.

²⁹The tribe of Naphtali will be next. The leader of the people of Naphtali is Ahira son of Enan. ³⁰His division numbers 53,400.

³¹All the men assigned to the camp of Dan number 157,600. They will set out last, under their standards.

³²These are the Israelites, counted according to their families. All those in the camps, by their divisions, number 603,550. ³³The Levites, however, were not counted along with the other Israelites, as the LORD commanded Moses.

³⁴So the Israelites did everything the LORD commanded Moses; that is the way they encamped under their standards, and that is the way they set out, each with his clan and family.

THE LEVITES

3 This is the account of the family of Aaron and Moses at the time the LORD talked with Moses on Mount Sinai.

²The names of the sons of Aaron were Nadab the firstborn and Abihu, Eleazar and Ithamar. ³Those were the names of Aaron's sons, the anointed priests, who were ordained to serve as priests. ⁴Nadab and Abihu, however, fell dead before the LORD when they made an offering with unauthorized fire before him in the Desert of Sinai. They had no sons; so only Eleazar and Ithamar served as priests during the lifetime of their father Aaron.

⁵The LORD said to Moses, ⁶"Bring the tribe of Levi and present them to Aaron the priest to assist him. ⁷They are to perform duties for him and for the whole community at the Tent of Meeting by doing the work of the tabernacle. ⁸They are to take care of all the furnishings of the Tent of Meeting, fulfilling

---

ᵃ *14* Many manuscripts of the Masoretic Text, Samaritan Pentateuch and Vulgate (see also Num. 1:14); most manuscripts of the Masoretic Text *Reuel* the obligations of the Israelites by doing the work of the tabernacle. ⁹Give the Levites to Aaron and his sons; they are the Israelites who are to be given wholly to him.ᵃ ¹⁰Appoint Aaron and his sons to serve as priests; anyone else who approaches the sanctuary must be put to death."

¹¹The Lord also said to Moses, ¹²"I have taken the Levites from among the Israelites in place of the first male offspring of every Israelite woman. The Levites are mine, ¹³for all the firstborn are mine. When I struck down all the firstborn in Egypt, I set apart for myself every firstborn in Israel, whether man or animal. They are to be mine. I am the Lord."

¹⁴The Lord said to Moses in the Desert of Sinai, ¹⁵"Count the Levites by their families and clans. Count every male a month old or more." ¹⁶So Moses counted them, as he was commanded by the word of the Lord.

¹⁷These were the names of the sons of Levi:

Gershon, Kohath and Merari.

¹⁸These were the names of the Gershonite clans:

Libni and Shimei.

¹⁹The Kohathite clans:

Amram, Izhar, Hebron and Uzziel.

²⁰The Merarite clans:

Mahli and Mushi.

These were the Levite clans, according to their families.

²¹To Gershon belonged the clans of the Libnites and Shimeites; these were the Gershonite clans. ²²The number of all the males a month old or more who were counted was 7,500. ²³The Gershonite clans were to camp on the west, behind the tabernacle. ²⁴The leader of the families of the Gershonites was Eliasaph son of Lael. ²⁵At the Tent of Meeting the Gershonites were responsible for the care of the tabernacle and tent, its coverings, the curtain at the entrance to the Tent of Meeting, ²⁶the curtains of the courtyard, the curtain at the entrance to the courtyard surrounding the tabernacle and altar, and the ropes—and everything related to their use.

²⁷To Kohath belonged the clans of the Amramites, Izharites, Hebronites and Uzzielites; these were the Kohathite clans. ²⁸The number of all the males a month old or more was 8,600.ᵇ The Kohathites were responsible for the care of the sanctuary. ²⁹The Kohathite clans were to camp on the south side of the tabernacle. ³⁰The leader of the families of the Kohathite clans was Elizaphan son of Uzziel. ³¹They were responsible for the care of the ark, the table, the lampstand, the altars, the articles of the sanctuary used in ministering, the curtain, and everything related to their use. ³²The chief leader of the Levites was Eleazar son of Aaron, the priest. He was appointed over those who were responsible for the care of the sanctuary.

³³To Merari belonged the clans of the Mahlites and the Mushites; these were the Merarite clans. ³⁴The number of all the males a month old or more who were counted was 6,200. ³⁵The leader of the families of the Merarite clans was Zuriel son of Abihail; they were to camp on the north side of the tabernacle. ³⁶The Merarites were appointed to take care of the frames of the tabernacle, its crossbars, posts, bases, all its equipment, and everything related to their use, ³⁷as well as the posts of the surrounding courtyard with their bases, tent pegs and ropes.

³⁸Moses and Aaron and his sons were to camp to the east of the tabernacle, toward the sunrise, in front of the Tent of Meeting. They were responsible for the care of the sanctuary on behalf of the Israelites. Anyone else who approached the sanctuary was to be put to death.

³⁹The total number of Levites counted at the Lord's command by Moses and Aaron according to their clans, including every male a month old or more, was 22,000.

⁴⁰The Lord said to Moses, "Count all the firstborn Israelite males who are a month old or more and

ᵃ 9 Most manuscripts of the Masoretic Text; some manuscripts of the Masoretic Text, Samaritan Pentateuch and Septuagint (see also Num. 8:16) *to me*   ᵇ 28 Hebrew; some Septuagint manuscripts *8,300* make a list of their names. ⁴¹Take the Levites for me in place of all the firstborn of the Israelites, and the livestock of the Levites in place of all the firstborn of the livestock of the Israelites. I am the LORD."

⁴²So Moses counted all the firstborn of the Israelites, as the LORD commanded him. ⁴³The total number of firstborn males a month old or more, listed by name, was 22,273.

⁴⁴The LORD also said to Moses, ⁴⁵"Take the Levites in place of all the firstborn of Israel, and the livestock of the Levites in place of their livestock. The Levites are to be mine. I am the LORD. ⁴⁶To redeem the 273 firstborn Israelites who exceed the number of the Levites, ⁴⁷collect five shekelsᵃ for each one, according to the sanctuary shekel, which weighs twenty gerahs. ⁴⁸Give the money for the redemption of the additional Israelites to Aaron and his sons."

⁴⁹So Moses collected the redemption money from those who exceeded the number redeemed by the Levites. ⁵⁰From the firstborn of the Israelites he collected silver weighing 1,365 shekels,ᵇ according to the sanctuary shekel. ⁵¹Moses gave the redemption money to Aaron and his sons, as he was commanded by the word of the LORD.

THE KOHATHITES

4 The LORD said to Moses and Aaron: ²"Take a census of the Kohathite branch of the Levites by their clans and families. ³Count all the men from thirty to fifty years of age who come to serve in the work in the Tent of Meeting.

⁴"This is the work of the Kohathites in the Tent of Meeting: the care of the most holy things. ⁵When the camp is to move, Aaron and his sons are to go in and take down the shielding curtain and cover the ark of the Testimony with it. ⁶Then they are to cover this with hides of sea cows,ᶜ spread a cloth of solid blue over that and put the poles in place.

⁷"Over the table of the Presence they are to spread a blue cloth and put on it the plates, dishes and bowls, and the jars for drink offerings; the bread that is continually there is to remain on it. ⁸Over these they are to spread a scarlet cloth, cover that with hides of sea cows and put its poles in place.

⁹"They are to take a blue cloth and cover the lampstand that is for light, together with its lamps, its wick trimmers and trays, and all its jars for the oil used to supply it. ¹⁰Then they are to wrap it and all its accessories in a covering of hides of sea cows and put it on a carrying frame.

¹¹"Over the gold altar they are to spread a blue cloth and cover that with hides of sea cows and put its poles in place.

¹²"They are to take all the articles used for ministering in the sanctuary, wrap them in a blue cloth, cover that with hides of sea cows and put them on a carrying frame.

¹³"They are to remove the ashes from the bronze altar and spread a purple cloth over it. ¹⁴Then they are to place on it all the utensils used for ministering at the altar, including the firepans, meat forks, shovels and sprinkling bowls. Over it they are to spread a covering of hides of sea cows and put its poles in place.

¹⁵"After Aaron and his sons have finished covering the holy furnishings and all the holy articles, and when the camp is ready to move, the Kohathites are to come to do the carrying. But they must not touch the holy things or they will die. The Kohathites are to carry those things that are in the Tent of Meeting.

¹⁶"Eleazar son of Aaron, the priest, is to have charge of the oil for the light, the fragrant incense, the regular grain offering and the anointing oil. He is to be in charge of the entire tabernacle and everything in it, including its holy furnishings and articles."

¹⁷The LORD said to Moses and Aaron, ¹⁸"See that the Kohathite tribal clans are not cut off from the Levites. ¹⁹So that they may live and not die when they come near the most holy things, do this for them: Aaron and his sons are to go into the sanctuary and assign to each man his work and what he is to carry. ²⁰But the Kohathites must not go in to look at the holy things, even for a moment, or they will die."

THE GERSHONITES

²¹The LORD said to Moses, ²²"Take a census also of the Gershonites by their families and clans. ²³Count all the men from thirty to fifty years of age who come to serve in the work at the Tent of Meeting.

²⁴"This is the service of the Gershonite clans as they work and carry burdens: ²⁵They are to carry the curtains of the tabernacle, the Tent of Meeting, its covering and the outer covering of hides of sea

---

ᵃ 47 That is, about 2 ounces (about 55 grams)   ᵇ 50 That is, about 35 pounds (about 15.5 kilograms)   ᶜ 6 That is, dugongs; also in verses 8, 10, 11, 12, 14 and 25

battlelines

» Fair Share (Materialism)

Q: Why do you keep looking out the window?
A: I'm watching Gavin drive past—again—in his new Honda Ridgeline. This is like his fifteenth trip around the block.

Q: Did you say his *new* Ridgeline?
A: Brand-spanking new.

Q: What's the occasion?
A: He just turned 16 and got his license.

Q: Whoa.
A: Tell me about it. When I turned 16, I got a video game and some new clothes. *He* gets a Ridgeline—brand-new, loaded.

Q: Lucky guy. That's really . . . something.
A: I think the word you're looking for is *un-fair*.

Q: Oh, I don't know. What's it to you if his parents want to get him a car? I mean, if they have the money to do that . . .
A: That's what I'm talking about! Why do his parents have the money and mine don't? It's just one more example of the "haves" and the "have-nots."

Q: Well, remember, it's all relative.
A: You got that right. His relatives can do that kind of stuff and mine can't. His dad's a surgeon. My parents are schoolteachers.

Q: No, that's not what I mean. I mean it's relative in the sense that, yeah, compared to you, Gavin is "rich." But, compared to lots of other people, *you're* rich.
A: Yeah, right.

Q: No, seriously. Your family owns two cars and a house, and probably brings in at least $70K a year. Do you realize that means you're richer than probably 95 percent of the families in the world?

» True Riches

First Timothy 6:6–11 reminds us:

"But godliness with contentment is great gain. For we brought nothing into the world, and we can take nothing out of it. But if we have food and clothing, we will be content with that. People who want to get rich fall into temptation and a trap and into many foolish and harmful desires that plunge men into ruin and destruction. For the love of money is a root of all kinds of evil. Some people, eager for money, have wandered from the faith and pierced themselves with many griefs.

"But you, man of God, flee from all this, and pursue righteousness, godliness, faith, love, endurance and gentleness."

What are you jealous for? In what ways are you not content?

For more on money and contentment, go to www.RevolutionBible.com.

cows, the curtains for the entrance to the Tent of Meeting, ²⁶the curtains of the courtyard surrounding the tabernacle and altar, the curtain for the entrance, the ropes and all the equipment used in its service. The Gershonites are to do all that needs to be done with these things. ²⁷All their service, whether carrying or doing other work, is to be done under the direction of Aaron and his sons. You shall assign to them as their responsibility all they are to carry. ²⁸This is the service of the Gershonite clans at the Tent of Meeting. Their duties are to be under the direction of Ithamar son of Aaron, the priest.

THE MERARITES

²⁹"Count the Merarites by their clans and families. ³⁰Count all the men from thirty to fifty years of age who come to serve in the work at the Tent of Meeting. ³¹This is their duty as they perform service at the Tent of Meeting: to carry the frames of the tabernacle, its crossbars, posts and bases, ³²as well as the posts of the surrounding courtyard with their bases, tent pegs, ropes, all their equipment and everything related to their use. Assign to each man the specific things he is to carry. ³³This is the service of the Merarite clans as they work at the Tent of Meeting under the direction of Ithamar son of Aaron, the priest."

THE NUMBERING OF THE LEVITE CLANS

³⁴Moses, Aaron and the leaders of the community counted the Kohathites by their clans and families. ³⁵All the men from thirty to fifty years of age who came to serve in the work in the Tent of Meeting, ³⁶counted by clans, were 2,750. ³⁷This was the total of all those in the Kohathite clans who served in the Tent of Meeting. Moses and Aaron counted them according to the LORD's command through Moses.

³⁸The Gershonites were counted by their clans and families. ³⁹All the men from thirty to fifty years of age who came to serve in the work at the Tent of Meeting, ⁴⁰counted by their clans and families, were 2,630. ⁴¹This was the total of those in the Gershonite clans who served at the Tent of Meeting. Moses and Aaron counted them according to the LORD's command.

⁴²The Merarites were counted by their clans and families. ⁴³All the men from thirty to fifty years of age who came to serve in the work at the Tent of Meeting, ⁴⁴counted by their clans, were 3,200. ⁴⁵This was the total of those in the Merarite clans. Moses and Aaron counted them according to the LORD's command through Moses.

⁴⁶So Moses, Aaron and the leaders of Israel counted all the Levites by their clans and families. ⁴⁷All the men from thirty to fifty years of age who came to do the work of serving and carrying the Tent of Meeting ⁴⁸numbered 8,580. ⁴⁹At the LORD's command through Moses, each was assigned his work and told what to carry.

Thus they were counted, as the LORD commanded Moses.

THE PURITY OF THE CAMP

5 The LORD said to Moses, ²"Command the Israelites to send away from the camp anyone who has an infectious skin disease^a or a discharge of any kind, or who is ceremonially unclean because of a dead body. ³Send away male and female alike; send them outside the camp so they will not defile their camp, where I dwell among them." ⁴The Israelites did this; they sent them outside the camp. They did just as the LORD had instructed Moses.

RESTITUTION FOR WRONGS

⁵The LORD said to Moses, ⁶"Say to the Israelites: 'When a man or woman wrongs another in any way^b and so is unfaithful to the LORD, that person is guilty ⁷and must confess the sin he has committed. He must make full restitution for his wrong, add one fifth to it and give it all to the person he has wronged. ⁸But if that person has no close relative to whom restitution can be made for the wrong, the restitution belongs to the LORD and must be given to the priest, along with the ram with which atonement is made for him. ⁹All the sacred contributions the Israelites bring to a priest will belong to him. ¹⁰Each man's sacred gifts are his own, but what he gives to the priest will belong to the priest.' "

THE TEST FOR AN UNFAITHFUL WIFE

¹¹Then the LORD said to Moses, ¹²"Speak to the Israelites and say to them: 'If a man's wife goes astray and is unfaithful to him ¹³by sleeping with another man, and this is hidden from her husband

^a 2 Traditionally *leprosy*; the Hebrew word was used for various diseases affecting the skin—not necessarily leprosy.   ^b 6 Or *woman commits any wrong common to mankind*

and her impurity is undetected (since there is no witness against her and she has not been caught in the act), [14]and if feelings of jealousy come over her husband and he suspects his wife and she is impure—or if he is jealous and suspects her even though she is not impure— [15]then he is to take his wife to the priest. He must also take an offering of a tenth of an ephah[a] of barley flour on her behalf. He must not pour oil on it or put incense on it, because it is a grain offering for jealousy, a reminder offering to draw attention to guilt.

[16]" 'The priest shall bring her and have her stand before the LORD. [17]Then he shall take some holy water in a clay jar and put some dust from the tabernacle floor into the water. [18]After the priest has had the woman stand before the LORD, he shall loosen her hair and place in her hands the reminder offering, the grain offering for jealousy, while he himself holds the bitter water that brings a curse. [19]Then the priest shall put the woman under oath and say to her, "If no other man has slept with you and you have not gone astray and become impure while married to your husband, may this bitter water that brings a curse not harm you. [20]But if you have gone astray while married to your husband and you have defiled yourself by sleeping with a man other than your husband"— [21]here the priest is to put the woman under this curse of the oath—"may the LORD cause your people to curse and denounce you when he causes your thigh to waste away and your abdomen to swell.[b] [22]May this water that brings a curse enter your body so that your abdomen swells and your thigh wastes away.[c]"

" 'Then the woman is to say, "Amen. So be it."

[23]" 'The priest is to write these curses on a scroll and then wash them off into the bitter water. [24]He shall have the woman drink the bitter water that brings a curse, and this water will enter her and cause bitter suffering. [25]The priest is to take from her hands the grain offering for jealousy, wave it before the LORD and bring it to the altar. [26]The priest is then to take a handful of the grain offering as a memorial offering and burn it on the altar; after that, he is to have the woman drink the water. [27]If she has defiled herself and been unfaithful to her husband, then when she is made to drink the water that brings a curse, it will go into her and cause bitter suffering; her abdomen will swell and her thigh waste away,[d] and she will become accursed among her people. [28]If, however, the woman has not defiled herself and is free from impurity, she will be cleared of guilt and will be able to have children.

[29]" 'This, then, is the law of jealousy when a woman goes astray and defiles herself while married to her husband, [30]or when feelings of jealousy come over a man because he suspects his wife. The priest is to have her stand before the LORD and is to apply this entire law to her. [31]The husband will be innocent of any wrongdoing, but the woman will bear the consequences of her sin.' "

THE NAZIRITE

6 The LORD said to Moses, [2]"Speak to the Israelites and say to them: 'If a man or woman wants to make a special vow, a vow of separation to the LORD as a Nazirite, [3]he must abstain from wine and other fermented drink and must not drink vinegar made from wine or from other fermented drink. He must not drink grape juice or eat grapes or raisins. [4]As long as he is a Nazirite, he must not eat anything that comes from the grapevine, not even the seeds or skins.

[5]" 'During the entire period of his vow of separation no razor may be used on his head. He must be holy until the period of his separation to the LORD is over; he must let the hair of his head grow long. [6]Throughout the period of his separation to the LORD he must not go near a dead body. [7]Even if his own

---

» live the adventure » Nu 5:5–8

Making Things Right

An apology is a good first step when you do something wrong, but it's just the first step. You also have a responsibility to correct the situation and make things right as much as you possibly can. For instance, if you trash talk or tell a lie about someone, make things right by tracking down everyone who heard or was affected by your comments and telling them the truth. If you steal or destroy something, make things right by returning the items or repaying the amount you owe in damages and stolen goods.

---

[a] 15 That is, probably about 2 quarts (about 2 liters)   [b] 21 Or causes you to have a miscarrying womb and barrenness   [c] 22 Or body and cause you to be barren and have a miscarrying womb   [d] 27 Or suffering; she will have barrenness and a miscarrying womb

father or mother or brother or sister dies, he must not make himself ceremonially unclean on account of them, because the symbol of his separation to God is on his head. 8 Throughout the period of his separation he is consecrated to the LORD.

9 " 'If someone dies suddenly in his presence, thus defiling the hair he has dedicated, he must shave his head on the day of his cleansing—the seventh day. 10 Then on the eighth day he must bring two doves or two young pigeons to the priest at the entrance to the Tent of Meeting. 11 The priest is to offer one as a sin offering and the other as a burnt offering to make atonement for him because he sinned by being in the presence of the dead body. That same day he is to consecrate his head. 12 He must dedicate himself to the LORD for the period of his separation and must bring a year-old male lamb as a guilt offering. The previous days do not count, because he became defiled during his separation.

13 " 'Now this is the law for the Nazirite when the period of his separation is over. He is to be brought to the entrance to the Tent of Meeting. 14 There he is to present his offerings to the LORD: a year-old male lamb without defect for a burnt offering, a year-old ewe lamb without defect for a sin offering, a ram without defect for a fellowship offering,[a] 15 together with their grain offerings and drink offerings, and a basket of bread made without yeast—cakes made of fine flour mixed with oil, and wafers spread with oil.

16 " 'The priest is to present them before the LORD and make the sin offering and the burnt offering. 17 He is to present the basket of unleavened bread and is to sacrifice the ram as a fellowship offering to the LORD, together with its grain offering and drink offering.

18 " 'Then at the entrance to the Tent of Meeting, the Nazirite must shave off the hair that he dedicated. He is to take the hair and put it in the fire that is under the sacrifice of the fellowship offering.

19 " 'After the Nazirite has shaved off the hair of his dedication, the priest is to place in his hands a boiled shoulder of the ram, and a cake and a wafer from the basket, both made without yeast. 20 The priest shall then wave them before the LORD as a wave offering; they are holy and belong to the priest, together with the breast that was waved and the thigh that was presented. After that, the Nazirite may drink wine.

21 " 'This is the law of the Nazirite who vows his offering to the LORD in accordance with his separation, in addition to whatever else he can afford. He must fulfill the vow he has made, according to the law of the Nazirite.' "

NU 6:24-26

challenge notes

To: my_son

heavenly_father: I never ignore faithfulness or take obedience for granted. when you honor me, I will honor you! sometimes I do that by granting one of your prayer requests or by giving you an unshakable sense of peace. bottom line: I love to bless genuine commitment.

THE PRIESTLY BLESSING

22 The LORD said to Moses, 23 "Tell Aaron and his sons, 'This is how you are to bless the Israelites. Say to them:

24 " ' "The LORD bless you
  and keep you;
25 the LORD make his face shine upon you
  and be gracious to you;
26 the LORD turn his face toward you
  and give you peace." '

27 "So they will put my name on the Israelites, and I will bless them."

OFFERINGS AT THE DEDICATION OF THE TABERNACLE

7 When Moses finished setting up the tabernacle, he anointed it and consecrated it and all its furnishings. He also anointed and consecrated the altar and all its utensils. 2 Then the leaders of Israel, the heads of families who were the tribal leaders in charge of those who were counted,

---

[a] 14 Traditionally peace offering; also in verses 17 and 18

made offerings. ³They brought as their gifts before the Lᴏʀᴅ six covered carts and twelve oxen—an ox from each leader and a cart from every two. These they presented before the tabernacle.

⁴The Lᴏʀᴅ said to Moses, ⁵"Accept these from them, that they may be used in the work at the Tent of Meeting. Give them to the Levites as each man's work requires."

⁶So Moses took the carts and oxen and gave them to the Levites. ⁷He gave two carts and four oxen to the Gershonites, as their work required, ⁸and he gave four carts and eight oxen to the Merarites, as their work required. They were all under the direction of Ithamar son of Aaron, the priest. ⁹But Moses did not give any to the Kohathites, because they were to carry on their shoulders the holy things, for which they were responsible.

¹⁰When the altar was anointed, the leaders brought their offerings for its dedication and presented them before the altar. ¹¹For the Lᴏʀᴅ had said to Moses, "Each day one leader is to bring his offering for the dedication of the altar."

¹²The one who brought his offering on the first day was Nahshon son of Amminadab of the tribe of Judah.

¹³His offering was one silver plate weighing a hundred and thirty shekels,ᵃ and one silver sprinkling bowl weighing seventy shekels,ᵇ both according to the sanctuary shekel, each filled with fine flour mixed with oil as a grain offering; ¹⁴one gold dish weighing ten shekels,ᶜ filled with incense; ¹⁵one young bull, one ram and one male lamb a year old, for a burnt offering; ¹⁶one male goat for a sin offering; ¹⁷and two oxen, five rams, five male goats and five male lambs a year old, to be sacrificed as a fellowship offering.ᵈ This was the offering of Nahshon son of Amminadab.

¹⁸On the second day Nethanel son of Zuar, the leader of Issachar, brought his offering.

¹⁹The offering he brought was one silver plate weighing a hundred and thirty shekels, and one silver sprinkling bowl weighing seventy shekels, both according to the sanctuary shekel, each filled with fine flour mixed with oil as a grain offering; ²⁰one gold dish weighing ten shekels, filled with incense; ²¹one young bull, one ram and one male lamb a year old, for a burnt offering; ²²one male goat for a sin offering; ²³and two oxen, five rams, five male goats and five male lambs a year old, to be sacrificed as a fellowship offering. This was the offering of Nethanel son of Zuar.

²⁴On the third day, Eliab son of Helon, the leader of the people of Zebulun, brought his offering.

²⁵His offering was one silver plate weighing a hundred and thirty shekels, and one silver sprinkling bowl weighing seventy shekels, both according to the sanctuary shekel, each filled with fine flour mixed with oil as a grain offering; ²⁶one gold dish weighing ten shekels, filled with incense; ²⁷one young bull, one ram and one male lamb a year old, for a burnt offering; ²⁸one male goat for a sin offering; ²⁹and two oxen, five rams, five male goats and five male lambs a year old, to be sacrificed as a fellowship offering. This was the offering of Eliab son of Helon.

³⁰On the fourth day Elizur son of Shedeur, the leader of the people of Reuben, brought his offering.

³¹His offering was one silver plate weighing a hundred and thirty shekels, and one silver sprinkling bowl weighing seventy shekels, both according to the sanctuary shekel, each filled with fine flour mixed with oil as a grain offering; ³²one gold dish weighing ten shekels, filled with incense; ³³one young bull, one ram and one male lamb a year old, for a burnt offering; ³⁴one male goat for a sin offering; ³⁵and two oxen, five rams, five male goats and five male lambs a year old, to be sacrificed as a fellowship offering. This was the offering of Elizur son of Shedeur.

³⁶On the fifth day Shelumiel son of Zurishaddai, the leader of the people of Simeon, brought his offering.

nᴏᴡ ᴏʀ nᴇᴠᴇʀ

NU 7:4–9

Do you ever wonder what it would be like to have God talk to you personally? Actually, it would be a lot like hearing the Bible read out loud.

ᵃ *13* That is, about 3 1/4 pounds (about 1.5 kilograms); also elsewhere in this chapter   ᵇ *13* That is, about 1 3/4 pounds (about 0.8 kilogram); also elsewhere in this chapter   ᶜ *14* That is, about 4 ounces (about 110 grams); also elsewhere in this chapter   ᵈ *17* Traditionally *peace offering*; also elsewhere in this chapter

³⁷His offering was one silver plate weighing a hundred and thirty shekels, and one silver sprinkling bowl weighing seventy shekels, both according to the sanctuary shekel, each filled with fine flour mixed with oil as a grain offering; ³⁸one gold dish weighing ten shekels, filled with incense; ³⁹one young bull, one ram and one male lamb a year old, for a burnt offering; ⁴⁰one male goat for a sin offering; ⁴¹and two oxen, five rams, five male goats and five male lambs a year old, to be sacrificed as a fellowship offering. This was the offering of Shelumiel son of Zurishaddai.

⁴²On the sixth day Eliasaph son of Deuel, the leader of the people of Gad, brought his offering.
⁴³His offering was one silver plate weighing a hundred and thirty shekels, and one silver sprinkling bowl weighing seventy shekels, both according to the sanctuary shekel, each filled with fine flour mixed with oil as a grain offering; ⁴⁴one gold dish weighing ten shekels, filled with incense; ⁴⁵one young bull, one ram and one male lamb a year old, for a burnt offering; ⁴⁶one male goat for a sin offering; ⁴⁷and two oxen, five rams, five male goats and five male lambs a year old, to be sacrificed as a fellowship offering. This was the offering of Eliasaph son of Deuel.

⁴⁸On the seventh day Elishama son of Ammihud, the leader of the people of Ephraim, brought his offering.
⁴⁹His offering was one silver plate weighing a hundred and thirty shekels, and one silver sprinkling bowl weighing seventy shekels, both according to the sanctuary shekel, each filled with fine flour mixed with oil as a grain offering; ⁵⁰one gold dish weighing ten shekels, filled with incense; ⁵¹one young bull, one ram and one male lamb a year old, for a burnt offering; ⁵²one male goat for a sin offering; ⁵³and two oxen, five rams, five male goats and five male lambs a year old, to be sacrificed as a fellowship offering. This was the offering of Elishama son of Ammihud.

⁵⁴On the eighth day Gamaliel son of Pedahzur, the leader of the people of Manasseh, brought his offering.
⁵⁵His offering was one silver plate weighing a hundred and thirty shekels, and one silver sprinkling bowl weighing seventy shekels, both according to the sanctuary shekel, each filled with fine flour mixed with oil as a grain offering; ⁵⁶one gold dish weighing ten shekels, filled with incense; ⁵⁷one young bull, one ram and one male lamb a year old, for a burnt offering; ⁵⁸one male goat for a sin offering; ⁵⁹and two oxen, five rams, five male goats and five male lambs a year old, to be sacrificed as a fellowship offering. This was the offering of Gamaliel son of Pedahzur.

⁶⁰On the ninth day Abidan son of Gideoni, the leader of the people of Benjamin, brought his offering.
⁶¹His offering was one silver plate weighing a hundred and thirty shekels, and one silver sprinkling bowl weighing seventy shekels, both according to the sanctuary shekel, each filled with fine flour mixed with oil as a grain offering; ⁶²one gold dish weighing ten shekels, filled with incense; ⁶³one young bull, one ram and one male lamb a year old, for a burnt offering; ⁶⁴one male goat for a sin offering; ⁶⁵and two oxen, five rams, five male goats and five male lambs a year old, to be sacrificed as a fellowship offering. This was the offering of Abidan son of Gideoni.

⁶⁶On the tenth day Ahiezer son of Ammishaddai, the leader of the people of Dan, brought his offering.
⁶⁷His offering was one silver plate weighing a hundred and thirty shekels, and one silver sprinkling bowl weighing seventy shekels, both according to the sanctuary shekel, each filled with fine flour mixed with oil as a grain offering; ⁶⁸one gold dish weighing ten shekels, filled with incense; ⁶⁹one young bull, one ram and one male lamb a year old, for a burnt offering; ⁷⁰one male goat for a sin offering; ⁷¹and two oxen, five rams, five male goats and five male lambs a year old, to be sacrificed as a fellowship offering. This was the offering of Ahiezer son of Ammishaddai.

⁷²On the eleventh day Pagiel son of Ocran, the leader of the people of Asher, brought his offering.
⁷³His offering was one silver plate weighing a hundred and thirty shekels, and one silver sprinkling bowl weighing seventy shekels, both according to the sanctuary shekel, each filled with fine flour mixed with oil as a grain offering; ⁷⁴one gold dish weighing ten shekels, filled with incense; ⁷⁵one young bull, one ram and one male lamb a year old, for a burnt offering; ⁷⁶one male

goat for a sin offering; 77and two oxen, five rams, five male goats and five male lambs a year old, to be sacrificed as a fellowship offering. This was the offering of Pagiel son of Ocran.

78On the twelfth day Ahira son of Enan, the leader of the people of Naphtali, brought his offering. 79His offering was one silver plate weighing a hundred and thirty shekels, and one silver sprinkling bowl weighing seventy shekels, both according to the sanctuary shekel, each filled with fine flour mixed with oil as a grain offering; 80one gold dish weighing ten shekels, filled with incense; 81one young bull, one ram and one male lamb a year old, for a burnt offering; 82one male goat for a sin offering; 83and two oxen, five rams, five male goats and five male lambs a year old, to be sacrificed as a fellowship offering. This was the offering of Ahira son of Enan.

84These were the offerings of the Israelite leaders for the dedication of the altar when it was anointed: twelve silver plates, twelve silver sprinkling bowls and twelve gold dishes. 85Each silver plate weighed a hundred and thirty shekels, and each sprinkling bowl seventy shekels. Altogether, the silver dishes weighed two thousand four hundred shekels,a according to the sanctuary shekel. 86The twelve gold dishes filled with incense weighed ten shekels each, according to the sanctuary shekel. Altogether, the gold dishes weighed a hundred and twenty shekels.b 87The total number of animals for the burnt offering came to twelve young bulls, twelve rams and twelve male lambs a year old, together with their grain offering. Twelve male goats were used for the sin offering. 88The total number of animals for the sacrifice of the fellowship offering came to twenty-four oxen, sixty rams, sixty male goats and sixty male lambs a year old. These were the offerings for the dedication of the altar after it was anointed.

89When Moses entered the Tent of Meeting to speak with the LORD, he heard the voice speaking to him from between the two cherubim above the atonement cover on the ark of the Testimony. And he spoke with him.

SETTING UP THE LAMPS

8 The LORD said to Moses, 2"Speak to Aaron and say to him, 'When you set up the seven lamps, they are to light the area in front of the lampstand.'"

3Aaron did so; he set up the lamps so that they faced forward on the lampstand, just as the LORD commanded Moses. 4This is how the lampstand was made: It was made of hammered gold—from its base to its blossoms. The lampstand was made exactly like the pattern the LORD had shown Moses.

THE SETTING APART OF THE LEVITES

5The LORD said to Moses: 6"Take the Levites from among the other Israelites and make them ceremonially clean. 7To purify them, do this: Sprinkle the water of cleansing on them; then have them shave their whole bodies and wash their clothes, and so purify themselves. 8Have them take a young bull with its grain offering of fine flour mixed with oil; then you are to take a second young bull for a sin offering. 9Bring the Levites to the front of the Tent of Meeting and assemble the whole Israelite community. 10You are to bring the Levites before the LORD, and the Israelites are to lay their hands on them. 11Aaron is to present the Levites before the LORD as a wave offering from the Israelites, so that they may be ready to do the work of the LORD.

12"After the Levites lay their hands on the heads of the bulls, use the one for a sin offering to the LORD and the other for a burnt offering, to make atonement for the Levites. 13Have the Levites stand in front of Aaron and his sons and then present them as a wave offering to the LORD. 14In this way you are to set the Levites apart from the other Israelites, and the Levites will be mine.

15"After you have purified the Levites and presented them as a wave offering, they are to come to do their work at the Tent of Meeting. 16They are the Israelites who are to be given wholly to me. I have taken them as my own in place of the firstborn, the first male offspring from every Israelite woman. 17Every firstborn male in Israel, whether man or animal, is mine. When I struck down all the firstborn in Egypt, I set them apart for myself. 18And I have taken the Levites in place of all the firstborn sons in Israel. 19Of all the Israelites, I have given the Levites as gifts to Aaron and his sons to do the work at the Tent of Meeting on behalf of the Israelites and to make atonement for them so that no plague will strike the Israelites when they go near the sanctuary."

20Moses, Aaron and the whole Israelite community did with the Levites just as the LORD commanded Moses. 21The Levites purified themselves and washed their clothes. Then Aaron presented them as

---

a 85 That is, about 60 pounds (about 28 kilograms)   b 86 That is, about 3 pounds (about 1.4 kilograms) a wave offering before the LORD and made atonement for them to purify them. ²²After that, the Levites came to do their work at the Tent of Meeting under the supervision of Aaron and his sons. They did with the Levites just as the LORD commanded Moses.

²³The LORD said to Moses, ²⁴"This applies to the Levites: Men twenty-five years old or more shall come to take part in the work at the Tent of Meeting, ²⁵but at the age of fifty, they must retire from their regular service and work no longer. ²⁶They may assist their brothers in performing their duties at the Tent of Meeting, but they themselves must not do the work. This, then, is how you are to assign the responsibilities of the Levites."

THE PASSOVER

9 The LORD spoke to Moses in the Desert of Sinai in the first month of the second year after they came out of Egypt. He said, ²"Have the Israelites celebrate the Passover at the appointed time. ³Celebrate it at the appointed time, at twilight on the fourteenth day of this month, in accordance with all its rules and regulations."

⁴So Moses told the Israelites to celebrate the Passover, ⁵and they did so in the Desert of Sinai at twilight on the fourteenth day of the first month. The Israelites did everything just as the LORD commanded Moses.

⁶But some of them could not celebrate the Passover on that day because they were ceremonially unclean on account of a dead body. So they came to Moses and Aaron that same day ⁷and said to Moses, "We have become unclean because of a dead body, but why should we be kept from presenting the LORD's offering with the other Israelites at the appointed time?"

⁸Moses answered them, "Wait until I find out what the LORD commands concerning you."

⁹Then the LORD said to Moses, ¹⁰"Tell the Israelites: 'When any of you or your descendants are unclean because of a dead body or are away on a journey, they may still celebrate the LORD's Passover. ¹¹They are to celebrate it on the fourteenth day of the second month at twilight. They are to eat the lamb, together with unleavened bread and bitter herbs. ¹²They must not leave any of it till morning or break any of its bones. When they celebrate the Passover, they must follow all the regulations. ¹³But if a man who is ceremonially clean and not on a journey fails to celebrate the Passover, that person must be cut off from his people because he did not present the LORD's offering at the appointed time. That man will bear the consequences of his sin.

¹⁴"'An alien living among you who wants to celebrate the LORD's Passover must do so in accordance with its rules and regulations. You must have the same regulations for the alien and the native-born.'"

THE CLOUD ABOVE THE TABERNACLE

¹⁵On the day the tabernacle, the Tent of the Testimony, was set up, the cloud covered it. From evening till morning the cloud above the tabernacle looked like fire. ¹⁶That is how it continued to be; the cloud covered it, and at night it looked like fire. ¹⁷Whenever the cloud lifted from above the Tent, the Israelites set out; wherever the cloud settled, the Israelites encamped. ¹⁸At the LORD's command the Israelites set out, and at his command they encamped. As long as the cloud stayed over the tabernacle, they remained in camp. ¹⁹When the cloud remained over the tabernacle a long time, the Israelites obeyed the LORD's order and did not set out. ²⁰Sometimes the cloud was over the tabernacle only a few days; at the LORD's command they would encamp, and then at his command they would set out. ²¹Sometimes the cloud stayed only from evening till morning, and when it lifted in the morning, they set out. Wheth-

Following God

No one can say the Israelites had it easy. After all, they were stuck in the desert for 40 years. But the one thing they had going for them is that they never had to wonder what God wanted them to do. All they had to do was follow the cloud. Unfortunately, following clouds won't work for us today. If you want to know where God wants you to go and what he wants you to do, you have to study his Word, ask for wisdom in making the decisions you face every day, and keep your eyes and heart open for opportunities to serve him.

» live the adventure » Nu 9:15-23

er by day or by night, whenever the cloud lifted, they set out. ²²Whether the cloud stayed over the tabernacle for two days or a month or a year, the Israelites would remain in camp and not set out; but when it lifted, they would set out. ²³At the LORD's command they encamped, and at the LORD's command they set out. They obeyed the LORD's order, in accordance with his command through Moses.

THE SILVER TRUMPETS

10

The LORD said to Moses: ²"Make two trumpets of hammered silver, and use them for calling the community together and for having the camps set out. ³When both are sounded, the whole community is to assemble before you at the entrance to the Tent of Meeting. ⁴If only one is sounded, the leaders—the heads of the clans of Israel—are to assemble before you. ⁵When a trumpet blast is sounded, the tribes camping on the east are to set out. ⁶At the sounding of a second blast, the camps on the south are to set out. The blast will be the signal for setting out. ⁷To gather the assembly, blow the trumpets, but not with the same signal.

⁸"The sons of Aaron, the priests, are to blow the trumpets. This is to be a lasting ordinance for you and the generations to come. ⁹When you go into battle in your own land against an enemy who is oppressing you, sound a blast on the trumpets. Then you will be remembered by the LORD your God and rescued from your enemies. ¹⁰Also at your times of rejoicing—your appointed feasts and New Moon festivals—you are to sound the trumpets over your burnt offerings and fellowship offerings,ᵃ and they will be a memorial for you before your God. I am the LORD your God."

THE ISRAELITES LEAVE SINAI

¹¹On the twentieth day of the second month of the second year, the cloud lifted from above the tabernacle of the Testimony. ¹²Then the Israelites set out from the Desert of Sinai and traveled from place to place until the cloud came to rest in the Desert of Paran. ¹³They set out, this first time, at the LORD's command through Moses.

¹⁴The divisions of the camp of Judah went first, under their standard. Nahshon son of Amminadab was in command. ¹⁵Nethanel son of Zuar was over the division of the tribe of Issachar, ¹⁶and Eliab son of Helon was over the division of the tribe of Zebulun. ¹⁷Then the tabernacle was taken down, and the Gershonites and Merarites, who carried it, set out.

¹⁸The divisions of the camp of Reuben went next, under their standard. Elizur son of Shedeur was in command. ¹⁹Shelumiel son of Zurishaddai was over the division of the tribe of Simeon, ²⁰and Eliasaph son of Deuel was over the division of the tribe of Gad. ²¹Then the Kohathites set out, carrying the holy things. The tabernacle was to be set up before they arrived.

²²The divisions of the camp of Ephraim went next, under their standard. Elishama son of Ammihud was in command. ²³Gamaliel son of Pedahzur was over the division of the tribe of Manasseh, ²⁴and Abidan son of Gideoni was over the division of the tribe of Benjamin.

²⁵Finally, as the rear guard for all the units, the divisions of the camp of Dan set out, under their standard. Ahiezer son of Ammishaddai was in command. ²⁶Pagiel son of Ocran was over the division of the tribe of Asher, ²⁷and Ahira son of Enan was over the division of the tribe of Naphtali. ²⁸This was the order of march for the Israelite divisions as they set out.

²⁹Now Moses said to Hobab son of Reuel the Midianite, Moses' father-in-law, "We are setting out for the place about which the LORD said, 'I will give it to you.' Come with us and we will treat you well, for the LORD has promised good things to Israel."

³⁰He answered, "No, I will not go; I am going back to my own land and my own people."

³¹But Moses said, "Please do not leave us. You know where we should camp in the desert, and you can be our eyes. ³²If you come with us, we will share with you whatever good things the LORD gives us."

³³So they set out from the mountain of the LORD and traveled for three days. The ark of the covenant of the LORD went before them during those three days to find them a place to rest. ³⁴The cloud of the LORD was over them by day when they set out from the camp.

³⁵Whenever the ark set out, Moses said,

> "Rise up, O LORD!
> May your enemies be scattered;
> may your foes flee before you."

ᵃ *10* Traditionally *peace offerings*

36Whenever it came to rest, he said,

> "Return, O LORD,
> to the countless thousands of Israel."

FIRE FROM THE LORD

11 Now the people complained about their hardships in the hearing of the LORD, and when he heard them his anger was aroused. Then fire from the LORD burned among them and consumed some of the outskirts of the camp. 2When the people cried out to Moses, he prayed to the LORD and the fire died down. 3So that place was called Taberah,ᵃ because fire from the LORD had burned among them.

NOW OR NEVER

NU 11:4–6

If you're going to compare the way things are for you with the way things are for someone else, make sure you do it with the right attitude. For every person whose life seems better than yours, there are hundreds of people who would trade places with you in a heartbeat.

QUAIL FROM THE LORD

4The rabble with them began to crave other food, and again the Israelites started wailing and said, "If only we had meat to eat! 5We remember the fish we ate in Egypt at no cost—also the cucumbers, melons, leeks, onions and garlic. 6But now we have lost our appetite; we never see anything but this manna!"

7The manna was like coriander seed and looked like resin. 8The people went around gathering it, and then ground it in a handmill or crushed it in a mortar. They cooked it in a pot or made it into cakes. And it tasted like something made with olive oil. 9When the dew settled on the camp at night, the manna also came down.

10Moses heard the people of every family wailing, each at the entrance to his tent. The LORD became exceedingly angry, and Moses was troubled. 11He asked the LORD, "Why have you brought this trouble on your servant? What have I done to displease you that you put the burden of all these people on me? 12Did I conceive all these people? Did I give them birth? Why do you tell me to carry them in my arms, as a nurse carries an infant, to the land you promised on oath to their forefathers? 13Where can I get meat for all these people? They keep wailing to me, 'Give us meat to eat!' 14I cannot carry all these people by myself; the burden is too heavy for me. 15If this is how you are going to treat me, put me to death right now—if I have found favor in your eyes—and do not let me face my own ruin."

16The LORD said to Moses: "Bring me seventy of Israel's elders who are known to you as leaders and officials among the people. Have them come to the Tent of Meeting, that they may stand there with you. 17I will come down and speak with you there, and I will take of the Spirit that is on you and put the Spirit on them. They will help you carry the burden of the people so that you will not have to carry it alone.

18"Tell the people: 'Consecrate yourselves in preparation for tomorrow, when you will eat meat. The LORD heard you when you wailed, "If only we had meat to eat! We were better off in Egypt!" Now the LORD will give you meat, and you will eat it. 19You will not eat it for just one day, or two days, or five, ten or twenty days, 20but for a whole month—until it comes out of your

Reaching Out for Help

»» live the adventure »» Nu 11:11–17

How do you deal with pressure? Do you keep your feelings, problems and tensions to yourself? If so, there's a better way. Whether you know it or not, God has built a support team around you, people who can step in and help you with your problems. Your team may include your parents, grandparents, Christian friends, youth leaders and other caring people in your church. It might even include people you've never considered close friends or thought were the type who could be much help. Pay attention to the people God brings into your life. If you're willing to watch and listen, you'll see how valuable they are.

ᵃ 3 Taberah means burning.

nostrils and you loathe it—because you have rejected the LORD, who is among you, and have wailed before him, saying, "Why did we ever leave Egypt?" ' "

21But Moses said, "Here I am among six hundred thousand men on foot, and you say, 'I will give them meat to eat for a whole month!' 22Would they have enough if flocks and herds were slaughtered for them? Would they have enough if all the fish in the sea were caught for them?"

23The LORD answered Moses, "Is the LORD's arm too short? You will now see whether or not what I say will come true for you."

24So Moses went out and told the people what the LORD had said. He brought together seventy of their elders and had them stand around the Tent. 25Then the LORD came down in the cloud and spoke with him, and he took of the Spirit that was on him and put the Spirit on the seventy elders. When the Spirit rested on them, they prophesied, but they did not do so again.[a]

26However, two men, whose names were Eldad and Medad, had remained in the camp. They were listed among the elders, but did not go out to the Tent. Yet the Spirit also rested on them, and they prophesied in the camp. 27A young man ran and told Moses, "Eldad and Medad are prophesying in the camp."

28Joshua son of Nun, who had been Moses' aide since youth, spoke up and said, "Moses, my lord, stop them!"

29But Moses replied, "Are you jealous for my sake? I wish that all the LORD's people were prophets and that the LORD would put his Spirit on them!" 30Then Moses and the elders of Israel returned to the camp.

31Now a wind went out from the LORD and drove quail in from the sea. It brought them[b] down all around the camp to about three feet[c] above the ground, as far as a day's walk in any direction. 32All that day and night and all the next day the people went out and gathered quail. No one gathered less than ten homers.[d] Then they spread them out all around the camp. 33But while the meat was still between their teeth and before it could be consumed, the anger of the LORD burned against the people, and he struck them with a severe plague. 34Therefore the place was named Kibroth Hattaavah,[e] because there they buried the people who had craved other food.

35From Kibroth Hattaavah the people traveled to Hazeroth and stayed there.

MIRIAM AND AARON OPPOSE MOSES

12 Miriam and Aaron began to talk against Moses because of his Cushite wife, for he had married a Cushite. 2"Has the LORD spoken only through Moses?" they asked. "Hasn't he also spoken through us?" And the LORD heard this.

3(Now Moses was a very humble man, more humble than anyone else on the face of the earth.)

4At once the LORD said to Moses, Aaron and Miriam, "Come out to the Tent of Meeting, all three of you." So the three of them came out. 5Then the LORD came down in a pillar of cloud; he stood at the entrance to the Tent and summoned Aaron and Miriam. When both of them stepped forward, 6he said, "Listen to my words:

"When a prophet of the LORD is among you,
 I reveal myself to him in visions,
 I speak to him in dreams.
 7But this is not true of my servant Moses;

Humility

»» live the adventure »» Nu 12:1-3

Moses wasn't the type of guy to strike a pose after doing something good. So it might be tempting to assume he had a weak self-image. The truth is, Moses' humility demonstrated great confidence in God. Moses knew exactly who and what he was—a faithful guy being used by God to do some incredible stuff. He also knew exactly who deserved the praise and attention for the things he did—God. Maybe that's why God used him in such remarkable ways. And if you learn to be humble about your talents and abilities, giving all the credit to the One who made you, God will use you to do incredible things too, much like he did with an unassuming guy named Moses.

---

[a] 25 Or prophesied and continued to do so   [b] 31 Or They flew   [c] 31 Hebrew two cubits (about 1 meter)   [d] 32 That is, probably about 60 bushels (about 2.2 kiloliters)   [e] 34 Kibroth Hattaavah means graves of craving.

he is faithful in all my house.
⁸With him I speak face to face,
  clearly and not in riddles;
  he sees the form of the LORD.
Why then were you not afraid
  to speak against my servant Moses?"

⁹The anger of the LORD burned against them, and he left them.

¹⁰When the cloud lifted from above the Tent, there stood Miriam—leprous,ᵃ like snow. Aaron turned toward her and saw that she had leprosy; ¹¹and he said to Moses, "Please, my lord, do not hold against us the sin we have so foolishly committed. ¹²Do not let her be like a stillborn infant coming from its mother's womb with its flesh half eaten away."

¹³So Moses cried out to the LORD, "O God, please heal her!"

¹⁴The LORD replied to Moses, "If her father had spit in her face, would she not have been in disgrace for seven days? Confine her outside the camp for seven days; after that she can be brought back." ¹⁵So Miriam was confined outside the camp for seven days, and the people did not move on till she was brought back.

¹⁶After that, the people left Hazeroth and encamped in the Desert of Paran.

EXPLORING CANAAN

13

The LORD said to Moses, ²"Send some men to explore the land of Canaan, which I am giving to the Israelites. From each ancestral tribe send one of its leaders."

³So at the LORD's command Moses sent them out from the Desert of Paran. All of them were leaders of the Israelites. ⁴These are their names:

from the tribe of Reuben, Shammua son of Zaccur;
⁵from the tribe of Simeon, Shaphat son of Hori;
⁶from the tribe of Judah, Caleb son of Jephunneh;
⁷from the tribe of Issachar, Igal son of Joseph;
⁸from the tribe of Ephraim, Hoshea son of Nun;
⁹from the tribe of Benjamin, Palti son of Raphu;
¹⁰from the tribe of Zebulun, Gaddiel son of Sodi;
¹¹from the tribe of Manasseh (a tribe of Joseph), Gaddi son of Susi;
¹²from the tribe of Dan, Ammiel son of Gemalli;
¹³from the tribe of Asher, Sethur son of Michael;
¹⁴from the tribe of Naphtali, Nahbi son of Vophsi;
¹⁵from the tribe of Gad, Geuel son of Maki.

¹⁶These are the names of the men Moses sent to explore the land. (Moses gave Hoshea son of Nun the name Joshua.)

¹⁷When Moses sent them to explore Canaan, he said, "Go up through the Negev and on into the hill country. ¹⁸See what the land is like and whether the people who live there are strong or weak, few or many. ¹⁹What kind of land do they live in? Is it good or bad? What kind of towns do they live in? Are they unwalled or fortified? ²⁰How is the soil? Is it fertile or poor? Are there trees on it or not? Do your best to bring back some of the fruit of the land." (It was the season for the first ripe grapes.)

challengenotes

To: my_son

heavenly_father: I have promised you my strength and have delivered you countless times—often when you didn't even know I was there. so the next time you encounter enormous obstacles that seem impossible to overcome, remember my faithfulness and trust in me. I'll be right beside you.

NU 13:26-33

²¹So they went up and explored the land from the Desert of Zin as far as Rehob, toward Leboᵇ Hamath. ²²They went up through the Negev and came to Hebron, where Ahiman, Sheshai and Talmai, the

---

ᵃ 10 The Hebrew word was used for various diseases affecting the skin—not necessarily leprosy.   ᵇ 21 Or *toward the entrance to* descendants of Anak, lived. (Hebron had been built seven years before Zoan in Egypt.) 23When they reached the Valley of Eshcol,ᶜ they cut off a branch bearing a single cluster of grapes. Two of them carried it on a pole between them, along with some pomegranates and figs. 24That place was called the Valley of Eshcol because of the cluster of grapes the Israelites cut off there. 25At the end of forty days they returned from exploring the land.

Speaking the Truth

If you've got something truthful to say, say it. Don't worry about how it will affect your popularity. Don't worry about whether people will make fun of you for it. Don't worry about whether they'll argue with you about it. Use your voice to let people know what is true and right. If you're not sure what to say or how to say it, ask God to give you the right words. It's always good to think carefully before you speak, but when you are ready, step out and let your voice be heard.

REPORT ON THE EXPLORATION

26They came back to Moses and Aaron and the whole Israelite community at Kadesh in the Desert of Paran. There they reported to them and to the whole assembly and showed them the fruit of the land. 27They gave Moses this account: "We went into the land to which you sent us, and it does flow with milk and honey! Here is its fruit. 28But the people who live there are powerful, and the cities are fortified and very large. We even saw descendants of Anak there. 29The Amalekites live in the Negev; the Hittites, Jebusites and Amorites live in the hill country; and the Canaanites live near the sea and along the Jordan."

30Then Caleb silenced the people before Moses and said, "We should go up and take possession of the land, for we can certainly do it."

31But the men who had gone up with him said, "We can't attack those people; they are stronger than we are." 32And they spread among the Israelites a bad report about the land they had explored. They said, "The land we explored devours those living in it. All the people we saw there are of great size. 33We saw the Nephilim there (the descendants of Anak come from the Nephilim). We seemed like grasshoppers in our own eyes, and we looked the same to them."

THE PEOPLE REBEL

14 That night all the people of the community raised their voices and wept aloud. 2All the Israelites grumbled against Moses and Aaron, and the whole assembly said to them, "If only we had died in Egypt! Or in this desert! 3Why is the LORD bringing us to this land only to let us fall by the sword? Our wives and children will be taken as plunder. Wouldn't it be better for us to go back to Egypt?" 4And they said to each other, "We should choose a leader and go back to Egypt."

5Then Moses and Aaron fell facedown in front of the whole Israelite assembly gathered there. 6Joshua son of Nun and Caleb son of Jephunneh, who were among those who had explored the land, tore their clothes 7and said to the entire Israelite assembly, "The land we passed through and explored is exceedingly good. 8If the LORD is pleased with us, he will lead us into that land, a land flowing with milk and honey, and will give it to us. 9Only do not rebel against the LORD. And do not be afraid of the people of the land, because we will swallow them up. Their protection is gone, but the LORD is with us. Do not be afraid of them."

NOW OR NEVER

NU 14:5–9

What could you and your Christian buddies accomplish if you had the boldness of Joshua and Caleb? What can you do to develop that kind of confidence in God's ability to work that way in your life?

ᶜ 23 *Eshcol* means *cluster*; also in verse 24.

¹⁰But the whole assembly talked about stoning them. Then the glory of the LORD appeared at the Tent of Meeting to all the Israelites. ¹¹The LORD said to Moses, "How long will these people treat me with contempt? How long will they refuse to believe in me, in spite of all the miraculous signs I have performed among them? ¹²I will strike them down with a plague and destroy them, but I will make you into a nation greater and stronger than they."

¹³Moses said to the LORD, "Then the Egyptians will hear about it! By your power you brought these people up from among them. ¹⁴And they will tell the inhabitants of this land about it. They have already heard that you, O LORD, are with these people and that you, O LORD, have been seen face to face, that your cloud stays over them, and that you go before them in a pillar of cloud by day and a pillar of fire by night. ¹⁵If you put these people to death all at one time, the nations who have heard this report about you will say, ¹⁶'The LORD was not able to bring these people into the land he promised them on oath; so he slaughtered them in the desert.'

¹⁷"Now may the Lord's strength be displayed, just as you have declared: ¹⁸'The LORD is slow to anger, abounding in love and forgiving sin and rebellion. Yet he does not leave the guilty unpunished; he punishes the children for the sin of the fathers to the third and fourth generation.' ¹⁹In accordance with your great love, forgive the sin of these people, just as you have pardoned them from the time they left Egypt until now."

²⁰The LORD replied, "I have forgiven them, as you asked. ²¹Nevertheless, as surely as I live and as surely as the glory of the LORD fills the whole earth, ²²not one of the men who saw my glory and the miraculous signs I performed in Egypt and in the desert but who disobeyed me and tested me ten times— ²³not one of them will ever see the land I promised on oath to their forefathers. No one who has treated me with contempt will ever see it. ²⁴But because my servant Caleb has a different spirit and follows me wholeheartedly, I will bring him into the land he went to, and his descendants will inherit it. ²⁵Since the Amalekites and Canaanites are living in the valleys, turn back tomorrow and set out toward the desert along the route to the Red Sea.ᵃ"

²⁶The LORD said to Moses and Aaron: ²⁷"How long will this wicked community grumble against me? I have heard the complaints of these grumbling Israelites. ²⁸So tell them, 'As surely as I live, declares the LORD, I will do to you the very things I heard you say: ²⁹In this desert your bodies will fall—every one of you twenty years old or more who was counted in the census and who has grumbled against me. ³⁰Not one of you will enter the land I swore with uplifted hand to make your home, except Caleb son of Jephunneh and Joshua son of Nun. ³¹As for your children that you said would be taken as plunder, I will bring them in to enjoy the land you have rejected. ³²But you—your bodies will fall in this desert. ³³Your children will be shepherds here for forty years, suffering for your unfaithfulness, until the last of your bodies lies in the desert. ³⁴For forty years—one year for each of the forty days you explored the land—you will suffer for your sins and know what it is like to have me against me.' ³⁵I, the LORD, have spoken, and I will surely do these

---

challenge notes

To: my_son

NU 14:17-20

heavenly_father: never underestimate my willingness to forgive. even if you fall back into sin, I won't abandon you. if you turn from your sin and ask me to forgive you, I will. I'll make things right between us. but don't underestimate my hatred of sin. the fact that I forgive you doesn't mean there won't be some difficult lessons to be learned as a result of your sin.

»» live the adventure »» Nu 14:24

Being Different

What would a guy with a "different spirit" do today? Would he refuse to join in when his friends started ripping on someone? Would he stand up for someone getting picked on at school? Would he blow off parties where he knew people were going to get wasted? Would he speak up in science class about why he believes God created the universe? Would he invite his non-Christian friends to a youth group activity? What do *you* think he would do to show that he is really set apart?

ᵃ *25* Hebrew *Yam Suph*; that is, Sea of Reeds

battlelines

» Showing Respect (Authority)

Q: Something tells me you're not exactly in a great mood.
A: Oh, it's just my mom. She drives me nuts. The grass has to be mowed today. Now. End of discussion.

Q: The old "while you're under my roof, you'll do as I say" routine, huh?
A: You got it. Man, she's so picky. Everything has to be done exactly the way she wants it, exactly *when* she wants it. Does she ever stop to think that maybe I have a life too? Or plans? Not likely.

Q: Why do you think she gets under your skin so bad?
A: You got me. And, hey, it's not just her. I've got a couple of teachers like that. And my boss can be a total jerk too.

Q: Do you think maybe this is an authority thing—you know, resenting people for telling you what to do?
A: Oh, so now it's *my* fault that people treat me like a kid? The worst is when people just bark out commands—when you can tell they really like having power over you, and when it's obvious they could care less about you as a person. That drives me crazy.

Q: So what options do you have?
A: Well, I could quit my job, but I would probably run into the same thing anywhere else I work. Teachers? I could talk back to them, and feel pretty good . . . for about three seconds. Then they'd make my life miserable. My mom? I don't know what to do about her. Yeah, I know the Bible says I'm supposed to do what she says. You know, show respect. It'd just be a lot easier to do if my mom would go easy on me for once.

» The "S" Word

Submit is the word the Bible uses to describe the way we're supposed to respond to others, especially to those who are have authority over us (see Romans 13:1; Ephesians 5:21; Hebrews 13:17; 1 Peter 2:13). Swallowing our pride and doing what we're told—with the right attitude, no less—is one of the hardest things for a person to do, especially when the people we answer to treat us badly. But according to the Bible, submitting to those in authority is really a way of submitting to God. Check out Paul's instructions to some first-century believers in Ephesians 6:7–8: "Serve wholeheartedly, as if you were serving the Lord, not men, because you know that the Lord will reward everyone for whatever good he does, whether he is slave or free."

Like it or not, authority is a fact of life, whether you're 16 or 60. The better we learn to deal with it now, the better our lives will be later.

Read more about respecting authority at www.RevolutionBible.com.

caleb

VERSUS

» A spy from the tribe of Judah
» Trusted in God's power
» Still eager to fight when Israel entered Canaan

ten spies

» Spies from the other tribes
» Saw only potential problems and pitfalls
» Sentenced by God to die in the wilderness

The Main Event

As the Israelites prepared to enter the land God had promised to give them, Moses sent out a team of 12 spies to gather vital intelligence. The spies slipped into Canaan, took notes of what they saw, and came back 40 days later to brief the rest of the people. It was a *huge* moment in Israel's history.

Ten of the spies offered their report first. "The land is every bit as awesome as God told us," they said. "But the people who live there are *way* scarier than we imagined. They're giants! They're armed to the teeth. We don't stand a chance! We say forget this crazy idea of conquering Canaan."

You can imagine the effect their report had on the Israelites. The people began to murmur and gasp. That's when Caleb jumped up to offer his professional opinion. "Don't panic!" he urged. "The people of Canaan *are* big. But God is bigger! He's promised us victory. We can do this!"

"Impossible!" the other ten spies insisted. To make sure the Israelites got the point, the spies circulated among the crowd, telling anyone who would listen about the terrible things that were certain to happen if they invaded.

The twelfth spy, a guy named Joshua, agreed with Caleb (see Joshua 14:6–9), but by then the damage had already been done. Thanks to the majority report, the people of Israel were freaked out. In fact, they got so worked up that they were ready to put Caleb and Joshua to death for their encouraging remarks.

God protected Joshua and Caleb, but the rest of the Israelites weren't so fortunate. Because the people chose to listen to the ten faithless spies, the entire nation was forced to wander in the desert wilderness south of Canaan for almost 40 years, wondering what might have been.

The Outcome

The match-up between Caleb and the ten spies is a timeless story. Change the names and faces, alter the setting, and it could easily describe a situation at your school or youth group.

There will always be people who see only problems—people who can find a million and one reasons to avoid "going for it." They are content to wander in the wilderness and call it life. The world is full of guys like that.

But God is looking for guys like Caleb, who see possibilities—guys who remember and believe his promises. Guys like this with the boldness and courage to take God at his word will always be in the minority. Ultimately, though, they are the ones who make a real difference in the world.

What about you? Are you willing to stand up against the crowd? Could you stare down a big group of your friends and say, "You're wrong"?

Read more about Caleb and the ten spies in Numbers 13–14 (pages 162–167); Joshua 14:6–15 (pages 256–257).

things to this whole wicked community, which has banded together against me. They will meet their end in this desert; here they will die."

³⁶So the men Moses had sent to explore the land, who returned and made the whole community grumble against him by spreading a bad report about it— ³⁷these men responsible for spreading the bad report about the land were struck down and died of a plague before the LORD. ³⁸Of the men who went to explore the land, only Joshua son of Nun and Caleb son of Jephunneh survived.

³⁹When Moses reported this to all the Israelites, they mourned bitterly. ⁴⁰Early the next morning they went up toward the high hill country. "We have sinned," they said. "We will go up to the place the LORD promised."

⁴¹But Moses said, "Why are you disobeying the LORD's command? This will not succeed! ⁴²Do not go up, because the LORD is not with you. You will be defeated by your enemies, ⁴³for the Amalekites and Canaanites will face you there. Because you have turned away from the LORD, he will not be with you and you will fall by the sword."

⁴⁴Nevertheless, in their presumption they went up toward the high hill country, though neither Moses nor the ark of the LORD's covenant moved from the camp. ⁴⁵Then the Amalekites and Canaanites who lived in that hill country came down and attacked them and beat them down all the way to Hormah.

SUPPLEMENTARY OFFERINGS

1 5 The LORD said to Moses, ²"Speak to the Israelites and say to them: 'After you enter the land I am giving you as a home ³and you present to the LORD offerings made by fire, from the herd or the flock, as an aroma pleasing to the LORD—whether burnt offerings or sacrifices, for special vows or freewill offerings or festival offerings— ⁴then the one who brings his offering shall present to the LORD a grain offering of a tenth of an ephah ᵃ of fine flour mixed with a quarter of a hin ᵇ of oil. ⁵With each lamb for the burnt offering or the sacrifice, prepare a quarter of a hin of wine as a drink offering.

⁶" 'With a ram prepare a grain offering of two-tenths of an ephah ᶜ of fine flour mixed with a third of a hin ᵈ of oil, ⁷and a third of a hin of wine as a drink offering. Offer it as an aroma pleasing to the LORD.

⁸" 'When you prepare a young bull as a burnt offering or sacrifice, for a special vow or a fellowship offering ᵉ to the LORD, ⁹bring with the bull a grain offering of three-tenths of an ephah ᶠ of fine flour mixed with half a hin ᵍ of oil. ¹⁰Also bring half a hin of wine as a drink offering. It will be an offering made by fire, an aroma pleasing to the LORD. ¹¹Each bull or ram, each lamb or young goat, is to be prepared in this manner. ¹²Do this for each one, for as many as you prepare.

¹³" 'Everyone who is native-born must do these things in this way when he brings an offering made by fire as an aroma pleasing to the LORD. ¹⁴For the generations to come, whenever an alien or anyone else living among you presents an offering made by fire as an aroma pleasing to the LORD, he must do exactly as you do. ¹⁵The community is to have the same rules for you and for the alien living among you; this is a lasting ordinance for the generations to come. You and the alien shall be the same before the LORD: ¹⁶The same laws and regulations will apply both to you and to the alien living among you.' "

¹⁷The LORD said to Moses, ¹⁸"Speak to the Israelites and say to them: 'When you enter the land to which I am taking you ¹⁹and you eat the food of the land, present a portion as an offering to the LORD. ²⁰Present a cake from the first of your ground meal and present it as an offering from the threshing floor. ²¹Throughout the generations to come you are to give this offering to the LORD from the first of your ground meal.

OFFERINGS FOR UNINTENTIONAL SINS

²²" 'Now if you unintentionally fail to keep any of these commands the LORD gave Moses— ²³any of the LORD's commands to you through him, from the day the LORD gave them and continuing through the generations to come— ²⁴and if this is done unintentionally without the community being aware of it, then the whole community is to offer a young bull for a burnt offering as an aroma pleasing to the LORD, along with its prescribed grain offering and drink offering, and a male goat for a sin offering. ²⁵The priest is to make atonement for the whole Israelite community, and they will be forgiven, for it was not inten-

---

ᵃ *4* That is, probably about 2 quarts (about 2 liters)   ᵇ *4* That is, probably about 1 quart (about 1 liter); also in verse 5   ᶜ *6* That is, probably about 4 quarts (about 4.5 liters)   ᵈ *6* That is, probably about 1 1/4 quarts (about 1.2 liters); also in verse 7   ᵉ *8* Traditionally *peace offering*   ᶠ *9* That is, probably about 6 quarts (about 6.5 liters)   ᵍ *9* That is, probably about 2 quarts (about 2 liters); also in verse 10 tional and they have brought to the Lord for their wrong an offering made by fire and a sin offering. ²⁶The whole Israelite community and the aliens living among them will be forgiven, because all the people were involved in the unintentional wrong.

²⁷" 'But if just one person sins unintentionally, he must bring a year-old female goat for a sin offering. ²⁸The priest is to make atonement before the Lord for the one who erred by sinning unintentionally, and when atonement has been made for him, he will be forgiven. ²⁹One and the same law applies to everyone who sins unintentionally, whether he is a native-born Israelite or an alien.

³⁰" 'But anyone who sins defiantly, whether native-born or alien, blasphemes the Lord, and that person must be cut off from his people. ³¹Because he has despised the Lord's word and broken his commands, that person must surely be cut off; his guilt remains on him.' "

THE SABBATH-BREAKER PUT TO DEATH

³²While the Israelites were in the desert, a man was found gathering wood on the Sabbath day. ³³Those who found him gathering wood brought him to Moses and Aaron and the whole assembly, ³⁴and they kept him in custody, because it was not clear what should be done to him. ³⁵Then the Lord said to Moses, "The man must die. The whole assembly must stone him outside the camp." ³⁶So the assembly took him outside the camp and stoned him to death, as the Lord commanded Moses.

TASSELS ON GARMENTS

³⁷The Lord said to Moses, ³⁸"Speak to the Israelites and say to them: 'Throughout the generations to come you are to make tassels on the corners of your garments, with a blue cord on each tassel. ³⁹You will have these tassels to look at and so you will remember all the commands of the Lord, that you may obey them and not prostitute yourselves by going after the lusts of your own hearts and eyes. ⁴⁰Then you will remember to obey all my commands and will be consecrated to your God. ⁴¹I am the Lord your God, who brought you out of Egypt to be your God. I am the Lord your God.' "

KORAH, DATHAN AND ABIRAM

16 Korah son of Izhar, the son of Kohath, the son of Levi, and certain Reubenites— Dathan and Abiram, sons of Eliab, and On son of Peleth—became insolent^a ²and rose up against Moses. With them were 250 Israelite men, well-known community leaders who had been appointed members of the council. ³They came as a group to oppose Moses and Aaron and said to them, "You have gone too far! The whole community is holy, every one of them, and the Lord is with them. Why then do you set yourselves above the Lord's assembly?"

⁴When Moses heard this, he fell facedown. ⁵Then he said to Korah and all his followers: "In the morning the Lord will show who belongs to him and who is holy, and he will have that person come near him. The man he chooses he will cause to come near him. ⁶You, Korah, and all your followers are to do this: Take censers ⁷and tomorrow put fire and incense in them before the Lord. The man the Lord chooses will be the one who is holy. You Levites have gone too far!"

⁸Moses also said to Korah, "Now listen, you Levites! ⁹Isn't it enough for you that the God of Israel has separated you from the rest of the Israelite community and brought you near himself to do the work at the Lord's tabernacle and to stand before the community and minister to them? ¹⁰He has brought you and all your fellow Levites near himself, but now you are trying to get the priesthood too. ¹¹It is against

---

^a 1 Or Peleth—took ⌊men⌋

the Lord that you and all your followers have banded together. Who is Aaron that you should grumble against him?"

¹²Then Moses summoned Dathan and Abiram, the sons of Eliab. But they said, "We will not come! ¹³Isn't it enough that you have brought us up out of a land flowing with milk and honey to kill us in the desert? And now you also want to lord it over us? ¹⁴Moreover, you haven't brought us into a land flowing with milk and honey or given us an inheritance of fields and vineyards. Will you gouge out the eyes ofª these men? No, we will not come!"

¹⁵Then Moses became very angry and said to the Lord, "Do not accept their offering. I have not taken so much as a donkey from them, nor have I wronged any of them."

¹⁶Moses said to Korah, "You and all your followers are to appear before the Lord tomorrow—you and they and Aaron. ¹⁷Each man is to take his censer and put incense in it—250 censers in all—and present it before the Lord. You and Aaron are to present your censers also." ¹⁸So each man took his censer, put fire and incense in it, and stood with Moses and Aaron at the entrance to the Tent of Meeting. ¹⁹When Korah had gathered all his followers in opposition to them at the entrance to the Tent of Meeting, the glory of the Lord appeared to the entire assembly. ²⁰The Lord said to Moses and Aaron, ²¹"Separate yourselves from this assembly so I can put an end to them at once."

Controlling the Tongue

Hundreds of men, women and children died because Korah and his buddies couldn't keep their big mouths shut. They were ticked off at Moses and wanted everyone to know it. Unfortunately, they didn't think about the consequences first. There's a lesson to be learned from their example. Once words are spoken, they can't be taken back. We can apologize for the things we say, but we can't erase the damage our words have done. That's why it's always best to think before you speak, especially when you're angry or frustrated.

²²But Moses and Aaron fell facedown and cried out, "O God, God of the spirits of all mankind, will you be angry with the entire assembly when only one man sins?"

²³Then the Lord said to Moses, ²⁴"Say to the assembly, 'Move away from the tents of Korah, Dathan and Abiram.'"

²⁵Moses got up and went to Dathan and Abiram, and the elders of Israel followed him. ²⁶He warned the assembly, "Move back from the tents of these wicked men! Do not touch anything belonging to them, or you will be swept away because of all their sins." ²⁷So they moved away from the tents of Korah, Dathan and Abiram. Dathan and Abiram had come out and were standing with their wives, children and little ones at the entrances to their tents.

²⁸Then Moses said, "This is how you will know that the Lord has sent me to do all these things and that it was not my idea: ²⁹If these men die a natural death and experience only what usually happens to men, then the Lord has not sent me. ³⁰But if the Lord brings about something totally new, and the earth opens its mouth and swallows them, with everything that belongs to them, and they go down alive into the grave,ᵇ then you will know that these men have treated the Lord with contempt."

³¹As soon as he finished saying all this, the ground under them split apart ³²and the earth opened its mouth and swallowed them, with their households and all Korah's men and all their possessions. ³³They went down alive into the grave, with everything they owned; the earth closed over them, and they perished and were gone from the community. ³⁴At their cries, all the Israelites around them fled, shouting, "The earth is going to swallow us too!"

³⁵And fire came out from the Lord and consumed the 250 men who were offering the incense.

³⁶The Lord said to Moses, ³⁷"Tell Eleazar son of Aaron, the priest, to take the censers out of the smoldering remains and scatter the coals some distance away, for the censers are holy— ³⁸the censers of the men who sinned at the cost of their lives. Hammer the censers into sheets to overlay the altar, for they were presented before the Lord and have become holy. Let them be a sign to the Israelites."

³⁹So Eleazar the priest collected the bronze censers brought by those who had been burned up, and he had them hammered out to overlay the altar, ⁴⁰as the Lord directed him through Moses. This was to

---

ª 14 Or you make slaves of; or you deceive   ᵇ 30 Hebrew Sheol; also in verse 33 remind the Israelites that no one except a descendant of Aaron should come to burn incense before the LORD, or he would become like Korah and his followers.

⁴¹The next day the whole Israelite community grumbled against Moses and Aaron. "You have killed the LORD's people," they said.

⁴²But when the assembly gathered in opposition to Moses and Aaron and turned toward the Tent of Meeting, suddenly the cloud covered it and the glory of the LORD appeared. ⁴³Then Moses and Aaron went to the front of the Tent of Meeting, ⁴⁴and the LORD said to Moses, ⁴⁵"Get away from this assembly so I can put an end to them at once." And they fell facedown.

⁴⁶Then Moses said to Aaron, "Take your censer and put incense in it, along with fire from the altar, and hurry to the assembly to make atonement for them. Wrath has come out

now or never

NU 16:41

When you don't like something, don't grumble or complain. Go to the person you have a problem with and spell out what's bothering you. If the two of you can't resolve the issue, bring in a third person to mediate—someone who is older, wiser and whom you both trust (see Matthew 18).

from the LORD; the plague has started." ⁴⁷So Aaron did as Moses said, and ran into the midst of the assembly. The plague had already started among the people, but Aaron offered the incense and made atonement for them. ⁴⁸He stood between the living and the dead, and the plague stopped. ⁴⁹But 14,700 people died from the plague, in addition to those who had died because of Korah. ⁵⁰Then Aaron returned to Moses at the entrance to the Tent of Meeting, for the plague had stopped.

THE BUDDING OF AARON'S STAFF

17 The LORD said to Moses, ²"Speak to the Israelites and get twelve staffs from them, one from the leader of each of their ancestral tribes. Write the name of each man on his staff. ³On the staff of Levi write Aaron's name, for there must be one staff for the head of each ancestral tribe. ⁴Place them in the Tent of Meeting in front of the Testimony, where I meet with you. ⁵The staff belonging to the man I choose will sprout, and I will rid myself of this constant grumbling against you by the Israelites."

⁶So Moses spoke to the Israelites, and their leaders gave him twelve staffs, one for the leader of each of their ancestral tribes, and Aaron's staff was among them. ⁷Moses placed the staffs before the LORD in the Tent of the Testimony.

⁸The next day Moses entered the Tent of the Testimony and saw that Aaron's staff, which represented the house of Levi, had not only sprouted but had budded, blossomed and produced almonds. ⁹Then Moses brought out all the staffs from the LORD's presence to all the Israelites. They looked at them, and each man took his own staff.

¹⁰The LORD said to Moses, "Put back Aaron's staff in front of the Testimony, to be kept

now or never

NU 17:12-13

You don't truly fear the Lord if you fail to do something about the problematic sins that you're aware of in your life. Choosing to commit the same sin over and over again is like spitting in God's face.

as a sign to the rebellious. This will put an end to their grumbling against me, so that they will not die." ¹¹Moses did just as the LORD commanded him.

¹²The Israelites said to Moses, "We will die! We are lost, we are all lost! ¹³Anyone who even comes near the tabernacle of the LORD will die. Are we all going to die?"

DUTIES OF PRIESTS AND LEVITES

18 The LORD said to Aaron, "You, your sons and your father's family are to bear the responsibility for offenses against the sanctuary, and you and your sons alone are to bear the responsibility for offenses against the priesthood. ²Bring your fellow Levites from your ancestral tribe to join you and assist you when you and your sons minister before the Tent of the Testimony. ³They are to be responsible to you and are to perform all the duties of the Tent, but they must not go near the furnishings of the sanctuary or the altar, or both they and you will die. ⁴They are to join you and be responsible for the care of the Tent of Meeting—all the work at the Tent—and no one else may come near where you are.

⁵"You are to be responsible for the care of the sanctuary and the altar, so that wrath will not fall on the Israelites again. ⁶I myself have selected your fellow Levites from among the Israelites as a gift to you, dedicated to the Lord to do the work at the Tent of Meeting. ⁷But only you and your sons may serve as priests in connection with everything at the altar and inside the curtain. I am giving you the service of the priesthood as a gift. Anyone else who comes near the sanctuary must be put to death."

OFFERINGS FOR PRIESTS AND LEVITES

⁸Then the Lord said to Aaron, "I myself have put you in charge of the offerings presented to me; all the holy offerings the Israelites give me I give to you and your sons as your portion and regular share. ⁹You are to have the part of the most holy offerings that is kept from the fire. From all the gifts they bring me as most holy offerings, whether grain or sin or guilt offerings, that part belongs to you and your sons. ¹⁰Eat it as something most holy; every male shall eat it. You must regard it as holy.

¹¹"This also is yours: whatever is set aside from the gifts of all the wave offerings of the Israelites. I give this to you and your sons and daughters as your regular share. Everyone in your household who is ceremonially clean may eat it.

¹²"I give you all the finest olive oil and all the finest new wine and grain they give the Lord as the firstfruits of their harvest. ¹³All the land's firstfruits that they bring to the Lord will be yours. Everyone in your household who is ceremonially clean may eat it.

¹⁴"Everything in Israel that is devotedᵃ to the Lord is yours. ¹⁵The first offspring of every womb, both man and animal, that is offered to the Lord is yours. But you must redeem every firstborn son and every firstborn male of unclean animals. ¹⁶When they are a month old, you must redeem them at the redemption price set at five shekelsᵇ of silver, according to the sanctuary shekel, which weighs twenty gerahs.

¹⁷"But you must not redeem the firstborn of an ox, a sheep or a goat; they are holy. Sprinkle their blood on the altar and burn their fat as an offering made by fire, an aroma pleasing to the Lord. ¹⁸Their meat is to be yours, just as the breast of the wave offering and the right thigh are yours. ¹⁹Whatever is set aside from the holy offerings the Israelites present to the Lord I give to you and your sons and daughters as your regular share. It is an everlasting covenant of salt before the Lord for both you and your offspring."

²⁰The Lord said to Aaron, "You will have no inheritance in their land, nor will you have any share among them; I am your share and your inheritance among the Israelites.

²¹"I give to the Levites all the tithes in Israel as their inheritance in return for the work they do while serving at the Tent of Meeting. ²²From now on the Israelites must not go near the Tent of Meeting, or they will bear the consequences of their sin and will die. ²³It is the Levites who are to do the work at the Tent of Meeting and bear the responsibility for offenses against it. This is a lasting ordinance for the generations to come. They will receive no inheritance among the Israelites. ²⁴Instead, I give to the Levites as their inheritance the tithes that the Israelites present as an offering to the Lord. That is why I said concerning them: 'They will have no inheritance among the Israelites.' "

²⁵The Lord said to Moses, ²⁶"Speak to the Levites and say to them: 'When you receive from the Israelites the tithe I give you as your inheritance, you must present a tenth of that tithe as the Lord's offering. ²⁷Your offering will be reckoned to you as grain from the threshing floor or juice from the winepress. ²⁸In this way you also will present an offering to the Lord from all the tithes you receive from the Israelites. From these tithes you must give the Lord's portion to Aaron the priest. ²⁹You must present as the Lord's portion the best and holiest part of everything given to you.'

³⁰"Say to the Levites: 'When you present the best part, it will be reckoned to you as the product of the threshing floor or the winepress. ³¹You and your households may eat the rest of it anywhere, for it is your wages for your work at the Tent of Meeting. ³²By presenting the best part of it you will not be guilty in this matter; then you will not defile the holy offerings of the Israelites, and you will not die.' "

ᵃ *14* The Hebrew term refers to the irrevocable giving over of things or persons to the Lord. ᵇ *16* That is, about 2 ounces (about 55 grams)

THE WATER OF CLEANSING

19 The Lord said to Moses and Aaron: ²"This is a requirement of the law that the Lord has commanded: Tell the Israelites to bring you a red heifer without defect or blemish and that has never been under a yoke. ³Give it to Eleazar the priest; it is to be taken outside the camp and slaughtered in his presence. ⁴Then Eleazar the priest is to take some of its blood on his finger and sprinkle it seven times toward the front of the Tent of Meeting. ⁵While he watches, the heifer is to be burned—its hide, flesh, blood and offal. ⁶The priest is to take some cedar wood, hyssop and scarlet wool and throw them onto the burning heifer. ⁷After that, the priest must wash his clothes and bathe himself with water. He may then come into the camp, but he will be ceremonially unclean till evening. ⁸The man who burns it must also wash his clothes and bathe with water, and he too will be unclean till evening.

⁹"A man who is clean shall gather up the ashes of the heifer and put them in a ceremonially clean place outside the camp. They shall be kept by the Israelite community for use in the water of cleansing; it is for purification from sin. ¹⁰The man who gathers up the ashes of the heifer must also wash his clothes, and he too will be unclean till evening. This will be a lasting ordinance both for the Israelites and for the aliens living among them.

¹¹"Whoever touches the dead body of anyone will be unclean for seven days. ¹²He must purify himself with the water on the third day and on the seventh day; then he will be clean. But if he does not purify himself on the third and seventh days, he will not be clean. ¹³Whoever touches the dead body of anyone and fails to purify himself defiles the Lord's tabernacle. That person must be cut off from Israel. Because the water of cleansing has not been sprinkled on him, he is unclean; his uncleanness remains on him.

¹⁴"This is the law that applies when a person dies in a tent: Anyone who enters the tent and anyone who is in it will be unclean for seven days, ¹⁵and every open container without a lid fastened on it will be unclean.

¹⁶"Anyone out in the open who touches someone who has been killed with a sword or someone who has died a natural death, or anyone who touches a human bone or a grave, will be unclean for seven days.

¹⁷"For the unclean person, put some ashes from the burned purification offering into a jar and pour fresh water over them. ¹⁸Then a man who is ceremonially clean is to take some hyssop, dip it in the water and sprinkle the tent and all the furnishings and the people who were there. He must also sprinkle anyone who has touched a human bone or a grave or someone who has been killed or someone who has died a natural death. ¹⁹The man who is clean is to sprinkle the unclean person on the third and seventh days, and on the seventh day he is to purify him. The person being cleansed must wash his clothes and bathe with water, and that evening he will be clean. ²⁰But if a person who is unclean does not purify himself, he must be cut off from the community, because he has defiled the sanctuary of the Lord. The water of cleansing has not been sprinkled on him, and he is unclean. ²¹This is a lasting ordinance for them.

"The man who sprinkles the water of cleansing must also wash his clothes, and anyone who touches the water of cleansing will be unclean till evening. ²²Anything that an unclean person touches becomes unclean, and anyone who touches it becomes unclean till evening."

WATER FROM THE ROCK

20 In the first month the whole Israelite community arrived at the Desert of Zin, and they stayed at Kadesh. There Miriam died and was buried.

²Now there was no water for the community, and the people gathered in opposition to Moses and Aaron. ³They quarreled with Moses and said, "If only we had died when our brothers fell dead before the Lord! ⁴Why did you bring the Lord's community into this desert, that we and our livestock should die here? ⁵Why did you bring us up out of Egypt to this terrible place? It has no grain or figs, grapevines or pomegranates. And there is no water to drink!"

⁶Moses and Aaron went from the assembly to the entrance to the Tent of Meeting and fell facedown, and the glory of the Lord appeared to them. ⁷The Lord said to Moses, ⁸"Take the staff, and you and your brother Aaron gather the assembly together. Speak to that rock before their eyes and it will pour out its water. You will bring water out of the rock for the community so they and their livestock can drink."

⁹So Moses took the staff from the Lord's presence, just as he commanded him. ¹⁰He and Aaron

One act of disobedience cost Moses his chance to enter the promised land. If you think that seems unfair, you may be underestimating just how much God cares about the choices we make in life.

gathered the assembly together in front of the rock and Moses said to them, "Listen, you rebels, must we bring you water out of this rock?" ¹¹Then Moses raised his arm and struck the rock twice with his staff. Water gushed out, and the community and their livestock drank.

¹²But the LORD said to Moses and Aaron, "Because you did not trust in me enough to honor me as holy in the sight of the Israelites, you will not bring this community into the land I give them."

¹³These were the waters of Meribah,ª where the Israelites quarreled with the LORD and where he showed himself holy among them.

EDOM DENIES ISRAEL PASSAGE

¹⁴Moses sent messengers from Kadesh to the king of Edom, saying:

"This is what your brother Israel says: You know about all the hardships that have come upon us. ¹⁵Our forefathers went down into Egypt, and we lived there many years. The Egyptians mistreated us and our fathers, ¹⁶but when we cried out to the LORD, he heard our cry and sent an angel and brought us out of Egypt.

"Now we are here at Kadesh, a town on the edge of your territory. ¹⁷Please let us pass through your country. We will not go through any field or vineyard, or drink water from any well. We will travel along the king's highway and not turn to the right or to the left until we have passed through your territory."

¹⁸But Edom answered:

"You may not pass through here; if you try, we will march out and attack you with the sword."

¹⁹The Israelites replied:

"We will go along the main road, and if we or our livestock drink any of your water, we will pay for it. We only want to pass through on foot—nothing else."

²⁰Again they answered:

"You may not pass through."

Then Edom came out against them with a large and powerful army. ²¹Since Edom refused to let them go through their territory, Israel turned away from them.

THE DEATH OF AARON

²²The whole Israelite community set out from Kadesh and came to Mount Hor. ²³At Mount Hor, near the border of Edom, the LORD said to Moses and Aaron, ²⁴"Aaron will be gathered to his people. He will not enter the land I give the Israelites, because both of you rebelled against my command at the waters of Meribah. ²⁵Get Aaron and his son Eleazar and take them up Mount Hor. ²⁶Remove Aaron's garments and put them on his son Eleazar, for Aaron will be gathered to his people; he will die there."

²⁷Moses did as the LORD commanded: They went up Mount Hor in the sight of the whole commu-

Real Obedience

How many of the following statements sound familiar? "One beer won't hurt you." "Smoking one joint isn't going to ruin your life." "Looking at one naked picture on your computer isn't going to mess you up." "One spring break fling isn't going to spoil your sex life when you get married." If Moses were here, he'd laugh bitterly at every one of those lies. He could tell you better than anyone just how one mistake, one moment of carelessness, one act of disobedience can change everything in your life forever.

ª 13 Meribah means quarreling.

nity. [28]Moses removed Aaron's garments and put them on his son Eleazar. And Aaron died there on top of the mountain. Then Moses and Eleazar came down from the mountain, [29]and when the whole community learned that Aaron had died, the entire house of Israel mourned for him thirty days.

ARAD DESTROYED

21 When the Canaanite king of Arad, who lived in the Negev, heard that Israel was coming along the road to Atharim, he attacked the Israelites and captured some of them. [2]Then Israel made this vow to the LORD: "If you will deliver these people into our hands, we will totally destroy[a] their cities." [3]The LORD listened to Israel's plea and gave the Canaanites over to them. They completely destroyed them and their towns; so the place was named Hormah.[b]

THE BRONZE SNAKE

[4]They traveled from Mount Hor along the route to the Red Sea,[c] to go around Edom. But the people grew impatient on the way; [5]they spoke against God and against Moses, and said, "Why have you brought us up out of Egypt to die in the desert? There is no bread! There is no water! And we detest this miserable food!"

[6]Then the LORD sent venomous snakes among them; they bit the people and many Israelites died. [7]The people came to Moses and said, "We sinned when we spoke against the LORD and against you. Pray that the LORD will take the snakes away from us." So Moses prayed for the people.

[8]The LORD said to Moses, "Make a snake and put it up on a pole; anyone who is bitten can look at it and live." [9]So Moses made a bronze snake and put it up on a pole. Then when anyone was bitten by a snake and looked at the bronze snake, he lived.

NOW OR NEVER

NU 21:6–9

Different people need different kinds of healing. Some need physical healing; some need emotional healing; some need spiritual healing. And some need all of the above. How can you point people in need to the only One who can truly heal them?

THE JOURNEY TO MOAB

[10]The Israelites moved on and camped at Oboth. [11]Then they set out from Oboth and camped in Iye Abarim, in the desert that faces Moab toward the sunrise. [12]From there they moved on and camped in the Zered Valley. [13]They set out from there and camped alongside the Arnon, which is in the desert extending into Amorite territory. The Arnon is the border of Moab, between Moab and the Amorites. [14]That is why the Book of the Wars of the LORD says:

> ". . . Waheb in Suphah[d] and the ravines,
>> the Arnon [15]and[e] the slopes of the ravines
> that lead to the site of Ar
>> and lie along the border of Moab."

[16]From there they continued on to Beer, the well where the LORD said to Moses, "Gather the people together and I will give them water."

[17]Then Israel sang this song:

> "Spring up, O well!
>> Sing about it,
> [18]about the well that the princes dug,
>> that the nobles of the people sank—
>> the nobles with scepters and staffs."

Then they went from the desert to Mattanah, [19]from Mattanah to Nahaliel, from Nahaliel to Bamoth, [20]and from Bamoth to the valley in Moab where the top of Pisgah overlooks the wasteland.

---

[a] *2* The Hebrew term refers to the irrevocable giving over of things or persons to the LORD, often by totally destroying them; also in verse 3.   [b] *3 Hormah* means *destruction*.   [c] *4* Hebrew *Yam Suph*; that is, Sea of Reeds   [d] *14* The meaning of the Hebrew for this phrase is uncertain.   [e] *14,15* Or *"I have been given from Suphah and the ravines / of the Arnon* [15]*to*

DEFEAT OF SIHON AND OG

²¹Israel sent messengers to say to Sihon king of the Amorites:

²²"Let us pass through your country. We will not turn aside into any field or vineyard, or drink water from any well. We will travel along the king's highway until we have passed through your territory."

²³But Sihon would not let Israel pass through his territory. He mustered his entire army and marched out into the desert against Israel. When he reached Jahaz, he fought with Israel. ²⁴Israel, however, put him to the sword and took over his land from the Arnon to the Jabbok, but only as far as the Ammonites, because their border was fortified. ²⁵Israel captured all the cities of the Amorites and occupied them, including Heshbon and all its surrounding settlements. ²⁶Heshbon was the city of Sihon king of the Amorites, who had fought against the former king of Moab and had taken from him all his land as far as the Arnon.

²⁷That is why the poets say:

> "Come to Heshbon and let it be rebuilt;
> let Sihon's city be restored.

> ²⁸"Fire went out from Heshbon,
> a blaze from the city of Sihon.
> It consumed Ar of Moab,
> the citizens of Arnon's heights.
> ²⁹Woe to you, O Moab!
> You are destroyed, O people of Chemosh!
> He has given up his sons as fugitives
> and his daughters as captives
> to Sihon king of the Amorites.

> ³⁰"But we have overthrown them;
> Heshbon is destroyed all the way to Dibon.
> We have demolished them as far as Nophah,
> which extends to Medeba."

³¹So Israel settled in the land of the Amorites.

³²After Moses had sent spies to Jazer, the Israelites captured its surrounding settlements and drove out the Amorites who were there. ³³Then they turned and went up along the road toward Bashan, and Og king of Bashan and his whole army marched out to meet them in battle at Edrei.

³⁴The LORD said to Moses, "Do not be afraid of him, for I have handed him over to you, with his whole army and his land. Do to him what you did to Sihon king of the Amorites, who reigned in Heshbon."

³⁵So they struck him down, together with his sons and his whole army, leaving them no survivors. And they took possession of his land.

now or never

NU 21:31–35

No matter what the battle is or who you're going up against, if you're on God's side, you will always beat the odds. Remember this the next time you feel like an underdog fighting a losing battle.

BALAK SUMMONS BALAAM

22 Then the Israelites traveled to the plains of Moab and camped along the Jordan across from Jericho.ᵃ

²Now Balak son of Zippor saw all that Israel had done to the Amorites, ³and Moab was terrified because there were so many people. Indeed, Moab was filled with dread because of the Israelites.

ᵃ 1 Hebrew *Jordan of Jericho*; possibly an ancient name for the Jordan River

⁴The Moabites said to the elders of Midian, "This horde is going to lick up everything around us, as an ox licks up the grass of the field."

So Balak son of Zippor, who was king of Moab at that time, ⁵sent messengers to summon Balaam son of Beor, who was at Pethor, near the River,ª in his native land. Balak said:

"A people has come out of Egypt; they cover the face of the land and have settled next to me. ⁶Now come and put a curse on these people, because they are too powerful for me. Perhaps then I will be able to defeat them and drive them out of the country. For I know that those you bless are blessed, and those you curse are cursed."

⁷The elders of Moab and Midian left, taking with them the fee for divination. When they came to Balaam, they told him what Balak had said.

⁸"Spend the night here," Balaam said to them, "and I will bring you back the answer the LORD gives me." So the Moabite princes stayed with him.

⁹God came to Balaam and asked, "Who are these men with you?"

¹⁰Balaam said to God, "Balak son of Zippor, king of Moab, sent me this message: ¹¹'A people that has come out of Egypt covers the face of the land. Now come and put a curse on them for me. Perhaps then I will be able to fight them and drive them away.' "

¹²But God said to Balaam, "Do not go with them. You must not put a curse on those people, because they are blessed."

¹³The next morning Balaam got up and said to Balak's princes, "Go back to your own country, for the LORD has refused to let me go with you."

¹⁴So the Moabite princes returned to Balak and said, "Balaam refused to come with us."

¹⁵Then Balak sent other princes, more numerous and more distinguished than the first. ¹⁶They came to Balaam and said:

"This is what Balak son of Zippor says: Do not let anything keep you from coming to me, ¹⁷because I will reward you handsomely and do whatever you say. Come and put a curse on these people for me."

¹⁸But Balaam answered them, "Even if Balak gave me his palace filled with silver and gold, I could not do anything great or small to go beyond the command of the LORD my God. ¹⁹Now stay here tonight as the others did, and I will find out what else the LORD will tell me."

²⁰That night God came to Balaam and said, "Since these men have come to summon you, go with them, but do only what I tell you."

BALAAM'S DONKEY

²¹Balaam got up in the morning, saddled his donkey and went with the princes of Moab. ²²But God was very angry when he went, and the angel of the LORD stood in the road to oppose him. Balaam was riding on his donkey, and his two servants were with him. ²³When the donkey saw the angel of the LORD standing in the road with a drawn sword in his hand, she turned off the road into a field. Balaam beat her to get her back on the road.

²⁴Then the angel of the LORD stood in a narrow path between two vineyards, with walls on both sides. ²⁵When the donkey saw the angel of the LORD, she pressed close to the wall, crushing Balaam's foot against it. So he beat her again.

²⁶Then the angel of the LORD moved on ahead and stood in a narrow place where there was no room to turn, either to the right or to the left. ²⁷When the donkey saw the angel of the LORD, she lay down under Balaam, and he was angry and beat her with his staff. ²⁸Then the LORD opened the donkey's mouth, and she said to Balaam, "What have I done to you to make you beat me these three times?"

²⁹Balaam answered the donkey, "You have made a fool of me! If I had a sword in my hand, I would kill you right now."

NOW OR NEVER
NU 22:29

When you start lashing out at other people (or donkeys, in Balaam's case), it's a pretty clear sign that something's wrong inside you. The quicker you figure out what the problem is, the more likely you are to save yourself the embarrassment of having to apologize later.

ª 5 That is, the Euphrates

50 PASSAGES THAT SHOW GOD IS A REVOLUTION GOD

What is God like? Most guys think of him in pretty shallow terms: "the man upstairs," a cosmic grandfather, a heavenly drill sergeant. Umm, yeah . . . not quite. The fact is that God is so much more amazing, adventurous, wild and powerful than any human can ever imagine. Comparing him to earthly images of what we consider cool is useless. How could the most extreme rock climber be more extreme than the One who created him? How could the strongest inside linebacker be stronger than the One who gives him strength? How could the best guitar player understand his instrument more than the One who created music? If you want to find out more about this God, here are some good places to look:

01 » He created the whole world out of nothing . . . nada . . . zilch — GE 1–2
02 » He gave humanity the adventure and responsibility of caring for the earth — GE 1:27–31
03 » He has freedom to choose—and has given that same freedom to humans — GE 2:15–17; 3:1–24
04 » He created women and invented sex — GE 2:20–25
05 » He is fiercely protective of his people and rescues them when they're in trouble — EX 13:17—14:31

06 » He is a "warrior" — EX 15:3
07 » He's creative when it comes to getting our attention—even if it means making donkeys talk — NU 22:28
08 » He has none of the limitations of a human—not even one — NU 23:19; ISA 40:28
09 » He can make the sun stand still — JOS 10:13
10 » He has exercised brutal judgment against those who oppose him — JDG 3:20–22

11 » He uses unlikely people to achieve unlikely victories — 1 SA 17
12 » He's so big that he can't even fit in the heavens — 1 KI 8:27
13 » He surrounds his servants with chariots of fire and angelic warriors — 2 KI 6:17
14 » He "takes out" people who treat him irreverently — 1 CH 13:7–10
15 » He is fiercely competitive with the forces of evil—and wins every time — JOB 1:6–12

16 » He moves mountains and makes the earth shake — JOB 9:5–6
17 » He's real . . . but invisible — JOB 23:8
18 » He stands alone and unchallenged — JOB 23:13–14
19 » His voice is like thunder and his breath like ice — JOB 37:5,10
20 » He laughs at his enemies (and they shake in terror) — PS 2:4–5

21 » He smashes sea monsters and leviathans (whatever those are) — PS 74:13-14

22 » Time really isn't an issue for him—1000 years are like a day — PS 90:4; 93:2

23 » He strikes down mighty kings — PS 136:17-18

24 » He designed the incredibly complex and wonderful human body — PS 139:13

25 » He knocks down wicked people — PS 147:6

26 » He has placed eternity in the heart of every person — ECC 3:11

27 » As a human being, he survived a wilderness trip with no food—for 40 days! — MT 4:1-2

28 » He gives us the command (and the power) to love our enemies — MT 5:44; RO 12:20

29 » He partners with non-spectacular people to accomplish his spectacular plans — MT 10:1-4

30 » He calls his followers to do dangerous, tough, heroic things — MT 10:16-42

31 » He walks on water — MT 14:23-33

32 » He is commander in chief of a vast army of angels ready to do his will — MT 26:53; JOEL 2:11

33 » He can tell a wild thunderstorm to knock it off—and it has to obey — MK 4:37-41

34 » He endured torture and humiliation even though he could have called down the hosts of heaven on his oppressors — MK 15:16-32

35 » He stepped out of eternity into time, the immortal Creator taking the form of a mortal man — JN 1:14

36 » He gave life to the world by laying down his life for us — JN 3:16

37 » He fed a crowd of more than 5,000 people with one little kid's lunch — JN 6:1-14

38 » He raises the dead — JN 11

39 » He weeps — JN 11:35

40 » He can turn weaklings and wusses into lion-hearted men — JN 18:25-27; AC 4:5-14

41 » He can walk through walls — JN 20:26

42 » He can turn murderers into missionaries — AC 8-9

43 » He can use any part of creation—even worms—to deal out justice — AC 12:23

44 » He will get revenge — RO 12:19

45 » He can at any time (and soon will) crush Satan under our feet — RO 16:20

46 » He can enable us to overcome HUGE sins and terrible lifestyle habits — 1 CO 6:9-11

47 » He is completely above superficial judgments — GAL 2:6

48 » He can make a spiritually dead person come to life — EPH 2:1-5

49 » He designed unique individuals for specialized purposes — EPH 2:10

50 » He has decreed that he will hurl Satan and all his followers into the lake of fire — REV 20:10

balaam

donkey

» A well-known sorcerer from Pethor
» Used by God to speak to the Moabites
» Failed to live God's truth

» Generally considered to be one of the dumbest and most stubborn beasts in all of creation
» Used by God to speak to Balaam
» Saved Balaam's life

The Main Event

When the Israelites arrived in Moabite territory, they had to deal with some pretty rotten neighbors. Among other things, Balak (the Moabite king) tried to hire a popular sorcerer named Balaam to put a hex on God's people.

Balaam was a money-hungry guy (see 2 Peter 2:13–15), so he was eager to take the job. God, however, had other plans. He warned Balaam, "Don't do it! Those are my people, and I have blessed them." Even though he was a pagan, Balaam knew that ignoring God's warning would be hazardous to his health, so he told the Moabite king, "Thanks, but no thanks."

The Moabites persisted though. They sent dignitaries to make Balaam feel important. They jacked up the promised price. They practically begged him to take the job. Balaam continued to resist, but he really wanted the big payday. So God let him go with Balak's men. And that's what led to Balaam's face-off with . . . a donkey.

On the way to meet the king of Moab, Balaam's donkey suddenly found itself face-to-face with a well-armed angel sent by God. The donkey wisely veered off the road into a field. Balaam couldn't see the angel, so he beat the donkey until it returned to the road. Later, when the road passed between two vineyard walls, the animal balked again, eventually flopping to the ground. What choice did it have? The angel wasn't about to step aside.

Balaam went ballistic. He began to beat the stuffing out of the poor beast, until finally the donkey spoke. That's right, the donkey spoke—

with a human voice. It turned to Balaam and said (more or less), "Lighten up, dude! What'd I ever do to you?"

At that moment, God opened Balaam's eyes so he could see the angel. More than that, Balaam was able to see the power of Israel's God and the foolishness of trying to curse God's people.

The Outcome

It'd be nice to report that being rebuked by a donkey and encountering a supernatural warrior were enough to change Balaam forever. Unfortunately, the evidence doesn't support that. It seems that Balaam, despite being willing to bless Israel, never quite got over his love of money. Unable to curse the Israelites, Balaam convinced the king of Moab to seduce them with pagan women (see Numbers 25:1; 31:16). When the Israelites later fought against Midian, they killed Balaam in battle. For all we know, Balaam died without ever giving his heart to God. He stumbled upon the light of God's truth, but his heart remained dark.

Balaam's legacy wasn't exactly impressive. You've got to admit, it's pretty embarrassing when you're one-upped spiritually by a donkey.

Read more about Balaam and the donkey in Numbers 22:1–24:25 (pages 175–181); 31:7–16 (page 189); 2 Peter 2:15–16 (page 1585).

³⁰The donkey said to Balaam, "Am I not your own donkey, which you have always ridden, to this day? Have I been in the habit of doing this to you?"

"No," he said.

³¹Then the LORD opened Balaam's eyes, and he saw the angel of the LORD standing in the road with his sword drawn. So he bowed low and fell facedown.

³²The angel of the LORD asked him, "Why have you beaten your donkey these three times? I have come here to oppose you because your path is a reckless one before me.[a] ³³The donkey saw me and turned away from me these three times. If she had not turned away, I would certainly have killed you by now, but I would have spared her."

³⁴Balaam said to the angel of the LORD, "I have sinned. I did not realize you were standing in the road to oppose me. Now if you are displeased, I will go back."

³⁵The angel of the LORD said to Balaam, "Go with the men, but speak only what I tell you." So Balaam went with the princes of Balak.

³⁶When Balak heard that Balaam was coming, he went out to meet him at the Moabite town on the Arnon border, at the edge of his territory. ³⁷Balak said to Balaam, "Did I not send you an urgent summons? Why didn't you come to me? Am I really not able to reward you?"

³⁸"Well, I have come to you now," Balaam replied. "But can I say just anything? I must speak only what God puts in my mouth."

³⁹Then Balaam went with Balak to Kiriath Huzoth. ⁴⁰Balak sacrificed cattle and sheep, and gave some to Balaam and the princes who were with him. ⁴¹The next morning Balak took Balaam up to Bamoth Baal, and from there he saw part of the people.

BALAAM'S FIRST ORACLE

23

Balaam said, "Build me seven altars here, and prepare seven bulls and seven rams for me." ²Balak did as Balaam said, and the two of them offered a bull and a ram on each altar.

³Then Balaam said to Balak, "Stay here beside your offering while I go aside. Perhaps the LORD will come to meet with me. Whatever he reveals to me I will tell you." Then he went off to a barren height.

⁴God met with him, and Balaam said, "I have prepared seven altars, and on each altar I have offered a bull and a ram."

⁵The LORD put a message in Balaam's mouth and said, "Go back to Balak and give him this message."

⁶So he went back to him and found him standing beside his offering, with all the princes of Moab. ⁷Then Balaam uttered his oracle:

> "Balak brought me from Aram,
>   the king of Moab from the eastern mountains.
> 'Come,' he said, 'curse Jacob for me;
>   come, denounce Israel.'
> ⁸How can I curse
>   those whom God has not cursed?
> How can I denounce
>   those whom the LORD has not denounced?
> ⁹From the rocky peaks I see them,
>   from the heights I view them.
> I see a people who live apart
>   and do not consider themselves one of the nations.
> ¹⁰Who can count the dust of Jacob
>   or number the fourth part of Israel?
> Let me die the death of the righteous,
>   and may my end be like theirs!"

¹¹Balak said to Balaam, "What have you done to me? I brought you to curse my enemies, but you have done nothing but bless them!"

¹²He answered, "Must I not speak what the LORD puts in my mouth?"

ª *32* The meaning of the Hebrew for this clause is uncertain.

BALAAM'S SECOND ORACLE

[13]Then Balak said to him, "Come with me to another place where you can see them; you will see only a part but not all of them. And from there, curse them for me." [14]So he took him to the field of Zophim on the top of Pisgah, and there he built seven altars and offered a bull and a ram on each altar.

[15]Balaam said to Balak, "Stay here beside your offering while I meet with him over there."

[16]The LORD met with Balaam and put a message in his mouth and said, "Go back to Balak and give him this message."

[17]So he went to him and found him standing beside his offering, with the princes of Moab. Balak asked him, "What did the LORD say?"

[18]Then he uttered his oracle:

> "Arise, Balak, and listen;
>> hear me, son of Zippor.
> [19]God is not a man, that he should lie,
>> nor a son of man, that he should change his mind.
> Does he speak and then not act?
>> Does he promise and not fulfill?
> [20]I have received a command to bless;
>> he has blessed, and I cannot change it.
>
> [21]"No misfortune is seen in Jacob,
>> no misery observed in Israel.[a]
> The LORD their God is with them;
>> the shout of the King is among them.
> [22]God brought them out of Egypt;
>> they have the strength of a wild ox.
> [23]There is no sorcery against Jacob,
>> no divination against Israel.
> It will now be said of Jacob
>> and of Israel, 'See what God has done!'
> [24]The people rise like a lioness;
>> they rouse themselves like a lion
> that does not rest till he devours his prey
>> and drinks the blood of his victims."

[25]Then Balak said to Balaam, "Neither curse them at all nor bless them at all!"

[26]Balaam answered, "Did I not tell you I must do whatever the LORD says?"

BALAAM'S THIRD ORACLE

[27]Then Balak said to Balaam, "Come, let me take you to another place. Perhaps it will please God to let you curse them for me from there." [28]And Balak took Balaam to the top of Peor, overlooking the wasteland.

[29]Balaam said, "Build me seven altars here, and prepare seven bulls and seven rams for me." [30]Balak did as Balaam had said, and offered a bull and a ram on each altar.

24 Now when Balaam saw that it pleased the LORD to bless Israel, he did not resort to sorcery as at other times, but turned his face toward the desert. [2]When Balaam looked out and saw Israel encamped tribe by tribe, the Spirit of God came upon him [3]and he uttered his oracle:

> "The oracle of Balaam son of Beor,
>> the oracle of one whose eye sees clearly,

challenge notes

To: **my_son**

NU 23:19

heavenly_father: because I'm God, I'm not limited by human needs, impulses and weaknesses. I won't feed you lies just to make you feel good. I'll never fail to keep my word when I promise to do something for you. let me show you what a perfect friendship can be like.

---

[a] 21 Or *He has not looked on Jacob's offenses / or on the wrongs found in Israel.*

4 the oracle of one who hears the words of God,
  who sees a vision from the Almighty,ᵃ
  who falls prostrate, and whose eyes are opened:

5 "How beautiful are your tents, O Jacob,
  your dwelling places, O Israel!

6 "Like valleys they spread out,
  like gardens beside a river,
 like aloes planted by the LORD,
  like cedars beside the waters.
7 Water will flow from their buckets;
  their seed will have abundant water.

"Their king will be greater than Agag;
  their kingdom will be exalted.

8 "God brought them out of Egypt;
  they have the strength of a wild ox.
They devour hostile nations
  and break their bones in pieces;
  with their arrows they pierce them.
9 Like a lion they crouch and lie down,
  like a lioness—who dares to rouse them?

"May those who bless you be blessed
  and those who curse you be cursed!"

10 Then Balak's anger burned against Balaam. He struck his hands together and said to him, "I summoned you to curse my enemies, but you have blessed them these three times. 11 Now leave at once and go home! I said I would reward you handsomely, but the LORD has kept you from being rewarded."

12 Balaam answered Balak, "Did I not tell the messengers you sent me, 13 'Even if Balak gave me his palace filled with silver and gold, I could not do anything of my own accord, good or bad, to go beyond the command of the LORD—and I must say only what the LORD says'? 14 Now I am going back to my people, but come, let me warn you of what this people will do to your people in days to come."

BALAAM'S FOURTH ORACLE

15 Then he uttered his oracle:

"The oracle of Balaam son of Beor,
  the oracle of one whose eye sees clearly,
16 the oracle of one who hears the words of God,
  who has knowledge from the Most High,
who sees a vision from the Almighty,
  who falls prostrate, and whose eyes are opened:

17 "I see him, but not now;
  I behold him, but not near.
A star will come out of Jacob;
  a scepter will rise out of Israel.
He will crush the foreheads of Moab,
  the skullsᵇ ofᶜ all the sons of Sheth.ᵈ
18 Edom will be conquered;
  Seir, his enemy, will be conquered,
  but Israel will grow strong.
19 A ruler will come out of Jacob
  and destroy the survivors of the city."

ᵃ 4 Hebrew *Shaddai*; also in verse 16 ᵇ 17 Samaritan Pentateuch (see also Jer. 48:45); the meaning of the word in the Masoretic Text is uncertain. ᶜ 17 Or possibly *Moab, / batter* ᵈ 17 Or *all the noisy boasters*

BALAAM'S FINAL ORACLES

20 Then Balaam saw Amalek and uttered his oracle:

"Amalek was first among the nations,
but he will come to ruin at last."

21 Then he saw the Kenites and uttered his oracle:

"Your dwelling place is secure,
your nest is set in a rock;
22 yet you Kenites will be destroyed
when Asshur takes you captive."

23 Then he uttered his oracle:

"Ah, who can live when God does this?[a]
24   Ships will come from the shores of Kittim;
they will subdue Asshur and Eber,
but they too will come to ruin."

25 Then Balaam got up and returned home and Balak went his own way.

MOAB SEDUCES ISRAEL

25 While Israel was staying in Shittim, the men began to indulge in sexual immorality with Moabite women, 2who invited them to the sacrifices to their gods. The people ate and bowed down before these gods. 3So Israel joined in worshiping the Baal of Peor. And the LORD's anger burned against them.

4 The LORD said to Moses, "Take all the leaders of these people, kill them and expose them in broad daylight before the LORD, so that the LORD's fierce anger may turn away from Israel."

5 So Moses said to Israel's judges, "Each of you must put to death those of your men who have joined in worshiping the Baal of Peor."

6 Then an Israelite man brought to his family a Midianite woman right before the eyes of Moses and the whole assembly of Israel while they were weeping at the entrance to the Tent of Meeting. 7When Phinehas son of Eleazar, the son of Aaron, the priest, saw this, he left the assembly, took a spear in his hand 8and followed the Israelite into the tent. He drove the spear through both of them—through the Israelite and into the woman's body. Then the plague against the Israelites was stopped; 9but those who died in the plague numbered 24,000.

10 The LORD said to Moses, 11 "Phinehas son of Eleazar, the son of Aaron, the priest, has turned my anger away from the Israelites; for he was as zealous as I am for my honor among them, so that in my zeal I did not put an end to them. 12Therefore tell him I am making my covenant of peace with him. 13He and his descendants will have a covenant of a lasting priesthood, because he was zealous for the honor of his God and made atonement for the Israelites."

14 The name of the Israelite who was killed with the Midianite woman was Zimri son of Salu, the leader of a Simeonite family. 15And the name of the Midianite woman who was put to death was Cozbi daughter of Zur, a tribal chief of a Midianite family.

16 The LORD said to Moses, 17 "Treat the Midianites as enemies and kill them, 18because they treated you as enemies when they deceived you in the affair of Peor and their sister Cozbi, the daughter of a Midianite leader, the woman who was killed when the plague came as a result of Peor."

THE SECOND CENSUS

26 After the plague the LORD said to Moses and Eleazar son of Aaron, the priest, 2 "Take a census of the whole Israelite community by families—all those twenty years old or more who are able to serve in the army of Israel." 3So on the plains of Moab by the Jordan across from Jericho,[b] Moses and Eleazar the priest spoke with them and said, 4 "Take a census of the men twenty years old or more, as the LORD commanded Moses."

[a] 23 Masoretic Text; with a different word division of the Hebrew A people will gather from the north.   [b] 3 Hebrew Jordan of Jericho; possibly an ancient name for the Jordan River; also in verse 63

These were the Israelites who came out of Egypt:

⁵The descendants of Reuben, the firstborn son of Israel, were:

through Hanoch, the Hanochite clan;

through Pallu, the Palluite clan;

⁶through Hezron, the Hezronite clan;

through Carmi, the Carmite clan.

⁷These were the clans of Reuben; those numbered were 43,730.

⁸The son of Pallu was Eliab, ⁹and the sons of Eliab were Nemuel, Dathan and Abiram. The same Dathan and Abiram were the community officials who rebelled against Moses and Aaron and were among Korah's followers when they rebelled against the LORD. ¹⁰The earth opened its mouth and swallowed them along with Korah, whose followers died when the fire devoured the 250 men. And they served as a warning sign. ¹¹The line of Korah, however, did not die out.

¹²The descendants of Simeon by their clans were:

through Nemuel, the Nemuelite clan;

through Jamin, the Jaminite clan;

through Jakin, the Jakinite clan;

¹³through Zerah, the Zerahite clan;

through Shaul, the Shaulite clan.

¹⁴These were the clans of Simeon; there were 22,200 men.

¹⁵The descendants of Gad by their clans were:

through Zephon, the Zephonite clan;

through Haggi, the Haggite clan;

through Shuni, the Shunite clan;

¹⁶through Ozni, the Oznite clan;

through Eri, the Erite clan;

¹⁷through Arodi,ᵃ the Arodite clan;

through Areli, the Arelite clan.

¹⁸These were the clans of Gad; those numbered were 40,500.

¹⁹Er and Onan were sons of Judah, but they died in Canaan.

²⁰The descendants of Judah by their clans were:

through Shelah, the Shelanite clan;

through Perez, the Perezite clan;

through Zerah, the Zerahite clan.

²¹The descendants of Perez were:

through Hezron, the Hezronite clan;

through Hamul, the Hamulite clan.

²²These were the clans of Judah; those numbered were 76,500.

²³The descendants of Issachar by their clans were:

through Tola, the Tolaite clan;

through Puah, the Puiteᵇ clan;

²⁴through Jashub, the Jashubite clan;

through Shimron, the Shimronite clan.

²⁵These were the clans of Issachar; those numbered were 64,300.

²⁶The descendants of Zebulun by their clans were:

through Sered, the Seredite clan;

through Elon, the Elonite clan;

through Jahleel, the Jahleelite clan.

²⁷These were the clans of Zebulun; those numbered were 60,500.

²⁸The descendants of Joseph by their clans through Manasseh and Ephraim were:

ᵃ 17 Samaritan Pentateuch and Syriac (see also Gen. 46:16); Masoretic Text *Arod*   ᵇ 23 Samaritan Pentateuch, Septuagint, Vulgate and Syriac (see also 1 Chron. 7:1); Masoretic Text *through Puvah, the Punite*

29 The descendants of Manasseh:
  through Makir, the Makirite clan (Makir was the father of Gilead);
  through Gilead, the Gileadite clan.
  30 These were the descendants of Gilead:
  through Iezer, the Iezerite clan;
  through Helek, the Helekite clan;
    31 through Asriel, the Asrielite clan;
  through Shechem, the Shechemite clan;
    32 through Shemida, the Shemidaite clan;
  through Hepher, the Hepherite clan.
    33 (Zelophehad son of Hepher had no sons; he had only daughters, whose names were Mahlah, Noah, Hoglah, Milcah and Tirzah.)
34 These were the clans of Manasseh; those numbered were 52,700.

35 These were the descendants of Ephraim by their clans:
  through Shuthelah, the Shuthelahite clan;
  through Beker, the Bekerite clan;
  through Tahan, the Tahanite clan.
  36 These were the descendants of Shuthelah:
  through Eran, the Eranite clan.
37 These were the clans of Ephraim; those numbered were 32,500.

These were the descendants of Joseph by their clans.

38 The descendants of Benjamin by their clans were:
  through Bela, the Belaite clan;
  through Ashbel, the Ashbelite clan;
  through Ahiram, the Ahiramite clan;
    39 through Shupham,[a] the Shuphamite clan;
  through Hupham, the Huphamite clan.
  40 The descendants of Bela through Ard and Naaman were:
  through Ard,[b] the Ardite clan;
  through Naaman, the Naamite clan.
41 These were the clans of Benjamin; those numbered were 45,600.

42 These were the descendants of Dan by their clans:
  through Shuham, the Shuhamite clan.
These were the clans of Dan: 43 All of them were Shuhamite clans; and those numbered were 64,400.

44 The descendants of Asher by their clans were:
  through Imnah, the Imnite clan;
  through Ishvi, the Ishvite clan;
  through Beriah, the Beriite clan;
  45 and through the descendants of Beriah:
  through Heber, the Heberite clan;
  through Malkiel, the Malkielite clan.
  46 (Asher had a daughter named Serah.)
47 These were the clans of Asher; those numbered were 53,400.

48 The descendants of Naphtali by their clans were:
  through Jahzeel, the Jahzeelite clan;
  through Guni, the Gunite clan;
  49 through Jezer, the Jezerite clan;
  through Shillem, the Shillemite clan.
50 These were the clans of Naphtali; those numbered were 45,400.

---

a 39 A few manuscripts of the Masoretic Text, Samaritan Pentateuch, Vulgate and Syriac (see also Septuagint); most manuscripts of the Masoretic Text *Shephupham*   b 40 Samaritan Pentateuch and Vulgate (see also Septuagint); Masoretic Text does not have *through Ard*.

51 The total number of the men of Israel was 601,730.

52 The LORD said to Moses, 53 "The land is to be allotted to them as an inheritance based on the number of names. 54 To a larger group give a larger inheritance, and to a smaller group a smaller one; each is to receive its inheritance according to the number of those listed. 55 Be sure that the land is distributed by lot. What each group inherits will be according to the names for its ancestral tribe. 56 Each inheritance is to be distributed by lot among the larger and smaller groups."

57 These were the Levites who were counted by their clans:
through Gershon, the Gershonite clan;
through Kohath, the Kohathite clan;
through Merari, the Merarite clan.
58 These also were Levite clans:
the Libnite clan,
the Hebronite clan,
the Mahlite clan,
the Mushite clan,
the Korahite clan.
(Kohath was the forefather of Amram; 59 the name of Amram's wife was Jochebed, a descendant of Levi, who was born to the Levites[a] in Egypt. To Amram she bore Aaron, Moses and their sister Miriam. 60 Aaron was the father of Nadab and Abihu, Eleazar and Ithamar. 61 But Nadab and Abihu died when they made an offering before the LORD with unauthorized fire.)

62 All the male Levites a month old or more numbered 23,000. They were not counted along with the other Israelites because they received no inheritance among them.

63 These are the ones counted by Moses and Eleazar the priest when they counted the Israelites on the plains of Moab by the Jordan across from Jericho. 64 Not one of them was among those counted by Moses and Aaron the priest when they counted the Israelites in the Desert of Sinai. 65 For the LORD had told those Israelites they would surely die in the desert, and not one of them was left except Caleb son of Jephunneh and Joshua son of Nun.

ZELOPHEHAD'S DAUGHTERS

27 The daughters of Zelophehad son of Hepher, the son of Gilead, the son of Makir, the son of Manasseh, belonged to the clans of Manasseh son of Joseph. The names of the daughters were Mahlah, Noah, Hoglah, Milcah and Tirzah. They approached 2 the entrance to the Tent of Meeting and stood before Moses, Eleazar the priest, the leaders and the whole assembly, and said, 3 "Our father died in the desert. He was not among Korah's followers, who banded together against the LORD, but he died for his own sin and left no sons. 4 Why should our father's name disappear from his clan because he had no son? Give us property among our father's relatives."

5 So Moses brought their case before the LORD 6 and the LORD said to him, 7 "What Zelophehad's daughters are saying is right. You must certainly give them property as an inheritance among their father's relatives and turn their father's inheritance over to them.

8 "Say to the Israelites, 'If a man dies and leaves no son, turn his inheritance over to his daughter. 9 If he has no daughter, give his inheritance to his brothers. 10 If he has no brothers, give his inheritance to his father's brothers. 11 If his father had no brothers, give his inheritance to the nearest relative in his clan, that he may possess it. This is to be a legal requirement for the Israelites, as the LORD commanded Moses.'"

JOSHUA TO SUCCEED MOSES

12 Then the LORD said to Moses, "Go up this mountain in the Abarim range and see the land I have given the Israelites. 13 After you have seen it, you too will be gathered to your people, as your brother Aaron was, 14 for when the community rebelled at the waters in the Desert of Zin, both of you disobeyed my command to honor me as holy before their eyes." (These were the waters of Meribah Kadesh, in the Desert of Zin.)

---

a 59 Or Jochebed, a daughter of Levi, who was born to Levi

[15]Moses said to the LORD, [16]"May the LORD, the God of the spirits of all mankind, appoint a man over this community [17]to go out and come in before them, one who will lead them out and bring them in, so the LORD's people will not be like sheep without a shepherd."

[18]So the LORD said to Moses, "Take Joshua son of Nun, a man in whom is the spirit,[a] and lay your hand on him. [19]Have him stand before Eleazar the priest and the entire assembly and commission him in their presence. [20]Give him some of your authority so the whole Israelite community will obey him. [21]He is to stand before Eleazar the priest, who will obtain decisions for him by inquiring of the Urim before the LORD. At his command he and the entire community of the Israelites will go out, and at his command they will come in."

[22]Moses did as the LORD commanded him. He took Joshua and had him stand before Eleazar the priest and the whole assembly. [23]Then he laid his hands on him and commissioned him, as the LORD instructed through Moses.

now or never

NU 27:16

Are you a potential leader? Think carefully before you answer no. Chances are, there are at least a few people in your life— maybe a younger sibling, cousin or teammate—who already look up to you whether you realize it or not.

DAILY OFFERINGS

28 The LORD said to Moses, [2]"Give this command to the Israelites and say to them: 'See that you present to me at the appointed time the food for my offerings made by fire, as an aroma pleasing to me.' [3]Say to them: 'This is the offering made by fire that you are to present to the LORD: two lambs a year old without defect, as a regular burnt offering each day. [4]Prepare one lamb in the morning and the other at twilight, [5]together with a grain offering of a tenth of an ephah[b] of fine flour mixed with a quarter of a hin[c] of oil from pressed olives. [6]This is the regular burnt offering instituted at Mount Sinai as a pleasing aroma, an offering made to the LORD by fire. [7]The accompanying drink offering is to be a quarter of a hin of fermented drink with each lamb. Pour out the drink offering to the LORD at the sanctuary. [8]Prepare the second lamb at twilight, along with the same kind of grain offering and drink offering that you prepare in the morning. This is an offering made by fire, an aroma pleasing to the LORD.

SABBATH OFFERINGS

[9]"'On the Sabbath day, make an offering of two lambs a year old without defect, together with its drink offering and a grain offering of two-tenths of an ephah[d] of fine flour mixed with oil. [10]This is the burnt offering for every Sabbath, in addition to the regular burnt offering and its drink offering.

MONTHLY OFFERINGS

[11]"'On the first of every month, present to the LORD a burnt offering of two young bulls, one ram and seven male lambs a year old, all without defect. [12]With each bull there is to be a grain offering of three-tenths of an ephah[e] of fine flour mixed with oil; with the ram, a grain offering of two-tenths of an ephah of fine flour mixed with oil; [13]and with each lamb, a grain offering of a tenth of an ephah of fine flour mixed with oil. This is for a burnt offering, a pleasing aroma, an offering made to the LORD by fire. [14]With each bull there is to be a drink offering of half a hin[f] of wine; with the ram, a third of a hin[g]; and with each lamb, a quarter of a hin. This is the monthly burnt offering to be made at each new moon during the year. [15]Besides the regular burnt offering with its drink offering, one male goat is to be presented to the LORD as a sin offering.

THE PASSOVER

[16]"'On the fourteenth day of the first month the LORD's Passover is to be held. [17]On the fifteenth day of this month there is to be a festival; for seven days eat bread made without yeast. [18]On the first day

[a] 18 Or Spirit   [b] 5 That is, probably about 2 quarts (about 2 liters); also in verses 13, 21 and 29   [c] 5 That is, probably about 1 quart (about 1 liter); also in verses 7 and 14   [d] 9 That is, probably about 4 quarts (about 4.5 liters); also in verses 12, 20 and 28   [e] 12 That is, probably about 6 quarts (about 6.5 liters); also in verses 20 and 28   [f] 14 That is, probably about 2 quarts (about 2 liters)   [g] 14 That is, probably about 1 1/4 quarts (about 1.2 liters)

hold a sacred assembly and do no regular work. ¹⁹Present to the LORD an offering made by fire, a burnt offering of two young bulls, one ram and seven male lambs a year old, all without defect. ²⁰With each bull prepare a grain offering of three-tenths of an ephah of fine flour mixed with oil; with the ram, two-tenths; ²¹and with each of the seven lambs, one-tenth. ²²Include one male goat as a sin offering to make atonement for you. ²³Prepare these in addition to the regular morning burnt offering. ²⁴In this way prepare the food for the offering made by fire every day for seven days as an aroma pleasing to the LORD; it is to be prepared in addition to the regular burnt offering and its drink offering. ²⁵On the seventh day hold a sacred assembly and do no regular work.

FEAST OF WEEKS

²⁶" 'On the day of firstfruits, when you present to the LORD an offering of new grain during the Feast of Weeks, hold a sacred assembly and do no regular work. ²⁷Present a burnt offering of two young bulls, one ram and seven male lambs a year old as an aroma pleasing to the LORD. ²⁸With each bull there is to be a grain offering of three-tenths of an ephah of fine flour mixed with oil; with the ram, two-tenths; ²⁹and with each of the seven lambs, one-tenth. ³⁰Include one male goat to make atonement for you. ³¹Prepare these together with their drink offerings, in addition to the regular burnt offering and its grain offering. Be sure the animals are without defect.

FEAST OF TRUMPETS

29 " 'On the first day of the seventh month hold a sacred assembly and do no regular work. It is a day for you to sound the trumpets. ²As an aroma pleasing to the LORD, prepare a burnt offering of one young bull, one ram and seven male lambs a year old, all without defect. ³With the bull prepare a grain offering of three-tenths of an ephah ᵃ of fine flour mixed with oil; with the ram, two-tenths ᵇ; ⁴and with each of the seven lambs, one-tenth. ᶜ ⁵Include one male goat as a sin offering to make atonement for you. ⁶These are in addition to the monthly and daily burnt offerings with their grain offerings and drink offerings as specified. They are offerings made to the LORD by fire—a pleasing aroma.

DAY OF ATONEMENT

⁷" 'On the tenth day of this seventh month hold a sacred assembly. You must deny yourselves ᵈ and do no work. ⁸Present as an aroma pleasing to the LORD a burnt offering of one young bull, one ram and seven male lambs a year old, all without defect. ⁹With the bull prepare a grain offering of three-tenths of an ephah of fine flour mixed with oil; with the ram, two-tenths; ¹⁰and with each of the seven lambs, one-tenth. ¹¹Include one male goat as a sin offering, in addition to the sin offering for atonement and the regular burnt offering with its grain offering, and their drink offerings.

FEAST OF TABERNACLES

¹²" 'On the fifteenth day of the seventh month, hold a sacred assembly and do no regular work. Celebrate a festival to the LORD for seven days. ¹³Present an offering made by fire as an aroma pleasing to the LORD, a burnt offering of thirteen young bulls, two rams and fourteen male lambs a year old, all without defect. ¹⁴With each of the thirteen bulls prepare a grain offering of three-tenths of an ephah of fine flour mixed with oil; with each of the two rams, two-tenths; ¹⁵and with each of the fourteen lambs, one-tenth. ¹⁶Include one male goat as a sin offering, in addition to the regular burnt offering with its grain offering and drink offering.

¹⁷" 'On the second day prepare twelve young bulls, two rams and fourteen male lambs a year old, all without defect. ¹⁸With the bulls, rams and lambs, prepare their grain offerings and drink offerings according to the number specified. ¹⁹Include one male goat as a sin offering, in addition to the regular burnt offering with its grain offering, and their drink offerings.

²⁰" 'On the third day prepare eleven bulls, two rams and fourteen male lambs a year old, all without defect. ²¹With the bulls, rams and lambs, prepare their grain offerings and drink offerings according to the number specified. ²²Include one male goat as a sin offering, in addition to the regular burnt offering with its grain offering and drink offering.

²³" 'On the fourth day prepare ten bulls, two rams and fourteen male lambs a year old, all without

---

ᵃ 3 That is, probably about 6 quarts (about 6.5 liters); also in verses 9 and 14   ᵇ 3 That is, probably about 4 quarts (about 4.5 liters); also in verses 9 and 14   ᶜ 4 That is, probably about 2 quarts (about 2 liters); also in verses 10 and 15   ᵈ 7 Or *must fast*

battlelines

» Taking Responsibility (Abortion)

Q: Did you ever think you'd be in this situation?
A: No way! We were serious about waiting—to have sex, I mean. But we messed up. I pushed us over the edge—it's my fault. Ever since it happened, I've felt terrible; but I kept telling myself, *I made a mistake, but it was just the one time. It won't happen again.*

Q: And now she's pregnant?
A: Yeah. Man, I can't believe this happened. We did it one time. *Once!* And now our whole lives are changed forever.

Q: Who knows about it?
A: She told her best friend, and now you know too. That's it. Nobody else knows. Her mom would be destroyed. My parents would go through the roof.

Q: So what are you thinking about?
A: I have no idea. It feels like a dream. I'm not ready to get married! And she's not ready to be a mom. I don't know what to do. I don't even know what our options are . . . except that for a few hundred dollars we could make this whole nightmare go away.

Q: You guys aren't really thinking about an abortion, are you?
A: I don't know. To be honest, the thought has crossed my mind. I don't care how much you believe abortion is wrong; when it's *you* in the situation, you start saying things like, "Yeah, but what about *this* and what about *that?*" Your beliefs start getting a little shaky, you know?

Q: So what do you think you'll do?
A: Honestly, I have no clue. Right now the hardest part is figuring out how to tell her mom and my parents. I'm just so used to having options—you know, ways to cover up my mistakes. But I can't cover up this one. It's like there's nowhere to hide. And deep down, I know that it's a human life growing inside of her . . .

» A Real Man's Response

Alex's problem isn't unique. Sadly, there are lots of guys—Christian guys even—who have made the same mistake . . . including one of the most famous heroes in the Bible. His name was King David, and you can read about his story in 2 Samuel 11–12. There's a lot to learn from David's affair with Bathsheba. Here are just a few lessons:

1. Covering up sin #1 (adultery) with sin #2 (murder) only made David's life, his guilt and his punishment worse. Come clean now, and don't compound your sins (see 2 Samuel 11:1–3)

2. Sin always has devastating consequences—even after we confess and are forgiven. If you've messed up, be man enough to accept responsibility and face the consequences, instead of looking for an easy way out (see 2 Samuel 11:14; 12:11–14).

3. It's important to seek out and listen to godly counsel. You don't have to be alone in a situation like this (see 2 Samuel 12:1–14).

4. Last, but not least, the best news a guy could hope for: When you confess your wrongdoing, God *will* forgive you and take your sin away (see 2 Samuel 12:13).

Read more about dealing with a pregnancy at www.RevolutionBible.com.

defect. 24With the bulls, rams and lambs, prepare their grain offerings and drink offerings according to the number specified. 25Include one male goat as a sin offering, in addition to the regular burnt offering with its grain offering and drink offering.

26" 'On the fifth day prepare nine bulls, two rams and fourteen male lambs a year old, all without defect. 27With the bulls, rams and lambs, prepare their grain offerings and drink offerings according to the number specified. 28Include one male goat as a sin offering, in addition to the regular burnt offering with its grain offering and drink offering.

29" 'On the sixth day prepare eight bulls, two rams and fourteen male lambs a year old, all without defect. 30With the bulls, rams and lambs, prepare their grain offerings and drink offerings according to the number specified. 31Include one male goat as a sin offering, in addition to the regular burnt offering with its grain offering and drink offering.

32" 'On the seventh day prepare seven bulls, two rams and fourteen male lambs a year old, all without defect. 33With the bulls, rams and lambs, prepare their grain offerings and drink offerings according to the number specified. 34Include one male goat as a sin offering, in addition to the regular burnt offering with its grain offering and drink offering.

35" 'On the eighth day hold an assembly and do no regular work. 36Present an offering made by fire as an aroma pleasing to the LORD, a burnt offering of one bull, one ram and seven male lambs a year old, all without defect. 37With the bull, the ram and the lambs, prepare their grain offerings and drink offerings according to the number specified. 38Include one male goat as a sin offering, in addition to the regular burnt offering with its grain offering and drink offering.

39" 'In addition to what you vow and your freewill offerings, prepare these for the LORD at your appointed feasts: your burnt offerings, grain offerings, drink offerings and fellowship offerings.^{a} ' "

40Moses told the Israelites all that the LORD commanded him.

VOWS

30

Moses said to the heads of the tribes of Israel: "This is what the LORD commands: 2When a man makes a vow to the LORD or takes an oath to obligate himself by a pledge, he must not break his word but must do everything he said.

3"When a young woman still living in her father's house makes a vow to the LORD or obligates herself by a pledge 4and her father hears about her vow or pledge but says nothing to her, then all her vows and every pledge by which she obligated herself will stand. 5But if her father forbids her when he hears about it, none of her vows or the pledges by which she obligated herself will stand; the LORD will release her because her father has forbidden her.

6"If she marries after she makes a vow or after her lips utter a rash promise by which she obligates herself 7and her husband hears about it but says nothing to her, then her vows or the pledges by which she obligated herself will stand. 8But if her husband forbids her when he hears about it, he nullifies the vow that obligates her or the rash promise by which she obligates herself, and the LORD will release her.

9"Any vow or obligation taken by a widow or divorced woman will be binding on her.

10"If a woman living with her husband makes a vow or obligates herself by a pledge under oath 11and her husband hears about it but says nothing to her and does not forbid her, then all her vows or the pledges by which she obligated herself will stand. 12But if her husband nullifies them when he hears about them, then none of the vows or pledges that came from her lips will stand. Her husband has nullified them, and the LORD will release her. 13Her husband may confirm or nullify any vow she makes or any sworn pledge to deny herself. 14But if her husband says nothing to her about it from day to day, then he confirms all her vows or the pledges binding on her. He confirms them by saying nothing to her when he hears about them. 15If, however, he nullifies them some time after he hears about them, then he is responsible for her guilt."

16These are the regulations the LORD gave Moses concerning relationships between a man and his wife, and between a father and his young daughter still living in his house.

VENGEANCE ON THE MIDIANITES

31

The LORD said to Moses, 2"Take vengeance on the Midianites for the Israelites. After that, you will be gathered to your people."

3So Moses said to the people, "Arm some of your men to go to war against the Midianites and to

---

^{a} 39 Traditionally *peace offerings*

carry out the LORD's vengeance on them. [4]Send into battle a thousand men from each of the tribes of Israel." [5]So twelve thousand men armed for battle, a thousand from each tribe, were supplied from the clans of Israel. [6]Moses sent them into battle, a thousand from each tribe, along with Phinehas son of Eleazar, the priest, who took with him articles from the sanctuary and the trumpets for signaling.

[7]They fought against Midian, as the LORD commanded Moses, and killed every man. [8]Among their victims were Evi, Rekem, Zur, Hur and Reba—the five kings of Midian. They also killed Balaam son of Beor with the sword. [9]The Israelites captured the Midianite women and children and took all the Midianite herds, flocks and goods as plunder. [10]They burned all the towns where the Midianites had settled, as well as all their camps. [11]They took all the plunder and spoils, including the people and animals, [12]and brought the captives, spoils and plunder to Moses and Eleazar the priest and the Israelite assembly at their camp on the plains of Moab, by the Jordan across from Jericho.[a]

�∩OW OR ∩EVER
NU 31:1–3

Sometimes God used the Israelites to carry out his vengeance, but that doesn't mean he's going to ask you to strap on Kevlar and grenade launchers to enforce his justice. Carrying out God's vengeance might seem cool, but imagine just how gruesome and difficult it really was.

[13]Moses, Eleazar the priest and all the leaders of the community went to meet them outside the camp. [14]Moses was angry with the officers of the army—the commanders of thousands and commanders of hundreds—who returned from the battle.

[15]"Have you allowed all the women to live?" he asked them. [16]"They were the ones who followed Balaam's advice and were the means of turning the Israelites away from the LORD in what happened at Peor, so that a plague struck the LORD's people. [17]Now kill all the boys. And kill every woman who has slept with a man, [18]but save for yourselves every girl who has never slept with a man.

[19]"All of you who have killed anyone or touched anyone who was killed must stay outside the camp seven days. On the third and seventh days you must purify yourselves and your captives. [20]Purify every garment as well as everything made of leather, goat hair or wood."

[21]Then Eleazar the priest said to the soldiers who had gone into battle, "This is the requirement of the law that the LORD gave Moses: [22]Gold, silver, bronze, iron, tin, lead [23]and anything else that can withstand fire must be put through the fire, and then it will be clean. But it must also be purified with the water of cleansing. And whatever cannot withstand fire must be put through that water. [24]On the seventh day wash your clothes and you will be clean. Then you may come into the camp."

DIVIDING THE SPOILS

[25]The LORD said to Moses, [26]"You and Eleazar the priest and the family heads of the community are to count all the people and animals that were captured. [27]Divide the spoils between the soldiers who took part in the battle and the rest of the community. [28]From the soldiers who fought in the battle, set apart as tribute for the LORD one out of every five hundred, whether persons, cattle, donkeys, sheep or goats. [29]Take this tribute from their half share and give it to Eleazar the priest as the LORD's part. [30]From the Israelites' half, select one out of every fifty, whether persons, cattle, donkeys, sheep, goats or other animals. Give them to the Levites, who are responsible for the care of the LORD's tabernacle." [31]So Moses and Eleazar the priest did as the LORD commanded Moses.

[32]The plunder remaining from the spoils that the soldiers took was 675,000 sheep, [33]72,000 cattle, [34]61,000 donkeys [35]and 32,000 women who had never slept with a man. [36]The half share of those who fought in the battle was:

337,500 sheep, [37]of which the tribute for the LORD was 675;
[38]36,000 cattle, of which the tribute for the LORD was 72;
[39]30,500 donkeys, of which the tribute for the LORD was 61;
[40]16,000 people, of which the tribute for the LORD was 32.

[41]Moses gave the tribute to Eleazar the priest as the LORD's part, as the LORD commanded Moses. [42]The half belonging to the Israelites, which Moses set apart from that of the fighting men— [43]the

---

[a] 12 Hebrew *Jordan of Jericho*; possibly an ancient name for the Jordan River

community's half—was 337,500 sheep, ⁴⁴36,000 cattle, ⁴⁵30,500 donkeys ⁴⁶and 16,000 people. ⁴⁷From the Israelites' half, Moses selected one out of every fifty persons and animals, as the LORD command- ed him, and gave them to the Levites, who were responsible for the care of the LORD's tabernacle.

⁴⁸Then the officers who were over the units of the army—the commanders of thousands and com- manders of hundreds—went to Moses ⁴⁹and said to him, "Your servants have counted the soldiers un- der our command, and not one is missing. ⁵⁰So we have brought as an offering to the LORD the gold articles each of us acquired—armlets, bracelets, signet rings, earrings and necklaces—to make atone- ment for ourselves before the LORD."

⁵¹Moses and Eleazar the priest accepted from them the gold—all the crafted articles. ⁵²All the gold from the commanders of thousands and commanders of hundreds that Moses and Eleazar presented as a gift to the LORD weighed 16,750 shekels.ᵃ ⁵³Each soldier had taken plunder for himself. ⁵⁴Moses and Eleazar the priest accepted the gold from the commanders of thousands and commanders of hundreds and brought it into the Tent of Meeting as a memorial for the Israelites before the LORD.

THE TRANSJORDAN TRIBES

32

The Reubenites and Gadites, who had very large herds and flocks, saw that the lands of Jazer and Gilead were suitable for livestock. ²So they came to Moses and Eleazar the priest and to the leaders of the community, and said, ³"Ataroth, Dibon, Jazer, Nimrah, Hesh- bon, Elealeh, Sebam, Nebo and Beon— ⁴the land the LORD subdued before the people of Israel—are suitable for livestock, and your servants have livestock. ⁵If we have found favor in your eyes," they said, "let this land be given to your servants as our possession. Do not make us cross the Jordan."

⁶Moses said to the Gadites and Reubenites, "Shall your countrymen go to war while you sit here? ⁷Why do you discourage the Israelites from going over into the land the LORD has given them? ⁸This is what your fathers did when I sent them from Kadesh Barnea to look over the land. ⁹After they went up to the Valley of Eshcol and viewed the land, they discouraged the Israelites from entering the land the LORD had given them. ¹⁰The LORD's anger was aroused that day and he swore this oath: ¹¹'Because they have not followed me wholeheartedly, not one of the men twenty years old or more who came up out of Egypt will see the land I promised on oath to Abraham, Isaac and Jacob— ¹²not one except Caleb son of Jephunneh the Kenizzite and Joshua son of Nun, for they followed the LORD wholeheartedly.' ¹³The LORD's anger burned against Israel and he made them wander in the desert forty years, until the whole generation of those who had done evil in his sight was gone.

¹⁴"And here you are, a brood of sinners, standing in the place of your fathers and making the LORD even more angry with Israel. ¹⁵If you turn away from following him, he will again leave all this people in the desert, and you will be the cause of their destruction."

¹⁶Then they came up to him and said, "We would like to build pens here for our livestock and cit- ies for our women and children. ¹⁷But we are ready to arm ourselves and go ahead of the Israelites un- til we have brought them to their place. Meanwhile our women and children will live in fortified cities, for protection from the inhabitants of the land. ¹⁸We will not return to our homes until every Israelite has received his inheritance. ¹⁹We will not receive any inheritance with them on the other side of the Jor- dan, because our inheritance has come to us on the east side of the Jordan."

²⁰Then Moses said to them, "If you will do this—if you will arm yourselves before the LORD for bat- tle, ²¹and if all of you will go armed over the Jordan before the LORD until he has driven his enemies out before him— ²²then when the land is subdued before the LORD, you may return and be free from your obligation to the LORD and to Israel. And this land will be your possession before the LORD.

²³"But if you fail to do this, you will be sinning against the LORD; and you may be sure that your sin will find you out. ²⁴Build cities for your women and children, and pens for your flocks, but do what you have promised."

²⁵The Gadites and Reubenites said to Moses, "We your servants will do as our lord commands. ²⁶Our children and wives, our flocks and herds will remain here in the cities of Gilead. ²⁷But your ser- vants, every man armed for battle, will cross over to fight before the LORD, just as our lord says."

²⁸Then Moses gave orders about them to Eleazar the priest and Joshua son of Nun and to the fam- ily heads of the Israelite tribes. ²⁹He said to them, "If the Gadites and Reubenites, every man armed for battle, cross over the Jordan with you before the LORD, then when the land is subdued before you, give

---

ᵃ 52 That is, about 420 pounds (about 190 kilograms)

them the land of Gilead as their possession. ³⁰But if they do not cross over with you armed, they must accept their possession with you in Canaan."

³¹The Gadites and Reubenites answered, "Your servants will do what the LORD has said. ³²We will cross over before the LORD into Canaan armed, but the property we inherit will be on this side of the Jordan."

³³Then Moses gave to the Gadites, the Reubenites and the half-tribe of Manasseh son of Joseph the kingdom of Sihon king of the Amorites and the kingdom of Og king of Bashan—the whole land with its cities and the territory around them.

³⁴The Gadites built up Dibon, Ataroth, Aroer, ³⁵Atroth Shophan, Jazer, Jogbehah, ³⁶Beth Nimrah and Beth Haran as fortified cities, and built pens for their flocks. ³⁷And the Reubenites rebuilt Heshbon, Elealeh and Kiriathaim, ³⁸as well as Nebo and Baal Meon (these names were changed) and Sibmah. They gave names to the cities they rebuilt.

³⁹The descendants of Makir son of Manasseh went to Gilead, captured it and drove out the Amorites who were there. ⁴⁰So Moses gave Gilead to the Makirites, the descendants of Manasseh, and they settled there. ⁴¹Jair, a descendant of Manasseh, captured their settlements and called them Havvoth Jair.ᵃ ⁴²And Nobah captured Kenath and its surrounding settlements and called it Nobah after himself.

STAGES IN ISRAEL'S JOURNEY

33

Here are the stages in the journey of the Israelites when they came out of Egypt by divisions under the leadership of Moses and Aaron. ²At the LORD's command Moses recorded the stages in their journey. This is their journey by stages:

³The Israelites set out from Rameses on the fifteenth day of the first month, the day after the Passover. They marched out boldly in full view of all the Egyptians, ⁴who were burying all their firstborn, whom the LORD had struck down among them; for the LORD had brought judgment on their gods.

⁵The Israelites left Rameses and camped at Succoth.

⁶They left Succoth and camped at Etham, on the edge of the desert.

⁷They left Etham, turned back to Pi Hahiroth, to the east of Baal Zephon, and camped near Migdol.

⁸They left Pi Hahirothᵇ and passed through the sea into the desert, and when they had traveled for three days in the Desert of Etham, they camped at Marah.

⁹They left Marah and went to Elim, where there were twelve springs and seventy palm trees, and they camped there.

¹⁰They left Elim and camped by the Red Sea.ᶜ

¹¹They left the Red Sea and camped in the Desert of Sin.

¹²They left the Desert of Sin and camped at Dophkah.

¹³They left Dophkah and camped at Alush.

¹⁴They left Alush and camped at Rephidim, where there was no water for the people to drink.

¹⁵They left Rephidim and camped in the Desert of Sinai.

¹⁶They left the Desert of Sinai and camped at Kibroth Hattaavah.

¹⁷They left Kibroth Hattaavah and camped at Hazeroth.

¹⁸They left Hazeroth and camped at Rithmah.

¹⁹They left Rithmah and camped at Rimmon Perez.

²⁰They left Rimmon Perez and camped at Libnah.

²¹They left Libnah and camped at Rissah.

²²They left Rissah and camped at Kehelathah.

²³They left Kehelathah and camped at Mount Shepher.

²⁴They left Mount Shepher and camped at Haradah.

²⁵They left Haradah and camped at Makheloth.

²⁶They left Makheloth and camped at Tahath.

²⁷They left Tahath and camped at Terah.

²⁸They left Terah and camped at Mithcah.

ᵃ 41 Or them the settlements of Jair   ᵇ 8 Many manuscripts of the Masoretic Text, Samaritan Pentateuch and Vulgate; most manuscripts of the Masoretic Text left from before Hahiroth   ᶜ 10 Hebrew Yam Suph; that is, Sea of Reeds; also in verse 11

²⁹They left Mithcah and camped at Hashmonah.

³⁰They left Hashmonah and camped at Moseroth.

³¹They left Moseroth and camped at Bene Jaakan.

³²They left Bene Jaakan and camped at Hor Haggidgad.

³³They left Hor Haggidgad and camped at Jotbathah.

³⁴They left Jotbathah and camped at Abronah.

³⁵They left Abronah and camped at Ezion Geber.

³⁶They left Ezion Geber and camped at Kadesh, in the Desert of Zin.

³⁷They left Kadesh and camped at Mount Hor, on the border of Edom. ³⁸At the LORD's command Aaron the priest went up Mount Hor, where he died on the first day of the fifth month of the fortieth year after the Israelites came out of Egypt. ³⁹Aaron was a hundred and twenty-three years old when he died on Mount Hor.

⁴⁰The Canaanite king of Arad, who lived in the Negev of Canaan, heard that the Israelites were coming.

⁴¹They left Mount Hor and camped at Zalmonah.

⁴²They left Zalmonah and camped at Punon.

⁴³They left Punon and camped at Oboth.

⁴⁴They left Oboth and camped at Iye Abarim, on the border of Moab.

⁴⁵They left Iyimᵃ and camped at Dibon Gad.

⁴⁶They left Dibon Gad and camped at Almon Diblathaim.

⁴⁷They left Almon Diblathaim and camped in the mountains of Abarim, near Nebo.

⁴⁸They left the mountains of Abarim and camped on the plains of Moab by the Jordan across from Jericho.ᵇ ⁴⁹There on the plains of Moab they camped along the Jordan from Beth Jeshimoth to Abel Shittim.

⁵⁰On the plains of Moab by the Jordan across from Jericho the LORD said to Moses, ⁵¹"Speak to the Israelites and say to them: 'When you cross the Jordan into Canaan, ⁵²drive out all the inhabitants of the land before you. Destroy all their carved images and their cast idols, and demolish all their high places. ⁵³Take possession of the land and settle in it, for I have given you the land to possess. ⁵⁴Distribute the land by lot, according to your clans. To a larger group give a larger inheritance, and to a smaller group a smaller one. Whatever falls to them by lot will be theirs. Distribute it according to your ancestral tribes.

⁵⁵" 'But if you do not drive out the inhabitants of the land, those you allow to remain will become barbs in your eyes and thorns in your sides. They will give you trouble in the land where you will live. ⁵⁶And then I will do to you what I plan to do to them.' "

now or never

NU 33:55

A "problem sin" is like a monster in a horror movie. If you don't take care of it once and for all, it will come back to haunt you . . . again and again and again.

BOUNDARIES OF CANAAN

34

The LORD said to Moses, ²"Command the Israelites and say to them: 'When you enter Canaan, the land that will be allotted to you as an inheritance will have these boundaries:

³" 'Your southern side will include some of the Desert of Zin along the border of Edom. On the east, your southern boundary will start from the end of the Salt Sea,ᶜ ⁴cross south of Scorpionᵈ Pass, continue on to Zin and go south of Kadesh Barnea. Then it will go to Hazar Addar and over to Azmon, ⁵where it will turn, join the Wadi of Egypt and end at the Sea.ᵉ

⁶" 'Your western boundary will be the coast of the Great Sea. This will be your boundary on the west.

⁷" 'For your northern boundary, run a line from the Great Sea to Mount Hor ⁸and from Mount Hor

---

ᵃ *45* That is, Iye Abarim   ᵇ *48* Hebrew *Jordan of Jericho*; possibly an ancient name for the Jordan River; also in verse 50   ᶜ *3* That is, the Dead Sea; also in verse 12   ᵈ *4* Hebrew *Akrabbim*   ᵉ *5* That is, the Mediterranean; also in verses 6 and 7 to Lebo[a] Hamath. Then the boundary will go to Zedad, [9]continue to Ziphron and end at Hazar Enan. This will be your boundary on the north.

[10]" 'For your eastern boundary, run a line from Hazar Enan to Shepham. [11]The boundary will go down from Shepham to Riblah on the east side of Ain and continue along the slopes east of the Sea of Kinnereth.[b] [12]Then the boundary will go down along the Jordan and end at the Salt Sea.

" 'This will be your land, with its boundaries on every side.' "

[13]Moses commanded the Israelites: "Assign this land by lot as an inheritance. The LORD has ordered that it be given to the nine and a half tribes, [14]because the families of the tribe of Reuben, the tribe of Gad and the half-tribe of Manasseh have received their inheritance. [15]These two and a half tribes have received their inheritance on the east side of the Jordan of Jericho,[c] toward the sunrise."

[16]The LORD said to Moses, [17]"These are the names of the men who are to assign the land for you as an inheritance: Eleazar the priest and Joshua son of Nun. [18]And appoint one leader from each tribe to help assign the land. [19]These are their names:

Caleb son of Jephunneh,
    from the tribe of Judah;
[20]Shemuel son of Ammihud,
    from the tribe of Simeon;
[21]Elidad son of Kislon,
    from the tribe of Benjamin;
[22]Bukki son of Jogli,
    the leader from the tribe of Dan;
[23]Hanniel son of Ephod,
    the leader from the tribe of Manasseh son of Joseph;
[24]Kemuel son of Shiphtan,
    the leader from the tribe of Ephraim son of Joseph;
[25]Elizaphan son of Parnach,
    the leader from the tribe of Zebulun;
[26]Paltiel son of Azzan,
    the leader from the tribe of Issachar;
[27]Ahihud son of Shelomi,
    the leader from the tribe of Asher;
[28]Pedahel son of Ammihud,
    the leader from the tribe of Naphtali."

[29]These are the men the LORD commanded to assign the inheritance to the Israelites in the land of Canaan.

TOWNS FOR THE LEVITES

35 On the plains of Moab by the Jordan across from Jericho,[d] the LORD said to Moses, [2]"Command the Israelites to give the Levites towns to live in from the inheritance the Israelites will possess. And give them pasturelands around the towns. [3]Then they will have towns to live in and pasturelands for their cattle, flocks and all their other livestock.

[4]"The pasturelands around the towns that you give the Levites will extend out fifteen hundred feet[e] from the town wall. [5]Outside the town, measure three thousand feet[f] on the east side, three thousand on the south side, three thousand on the west and three thousand on the north, with the town in the center. They will have this area as pastureland for the towns.

CITIES OF REFUGE

[6]"Six of the towns you give the Levites will be cities of refuge, to which a person who has killed someone may flee. In addition, give them forty-two other towns. [7]In all you must give the Levites forty-eight towns, together with their pasturelands. [8]The towns you give the Levites from the land the Israelites possess are to be given in proportion to the inheritance of each tribe: Take many towns from a tribe that has many, but few from one that has few."

---

[a] 8 Or *to the entrance to*   [b] 11 That is, Galilee   [c] 15 *Jordan of Jericho* was possibly an ancient name for the Jordan River.
[d] 1 Hebrew *Jordan of Jericho*; possibly an ancient name for the Jordan River   [e] 4 Hebrew *a thousand cubits* (about 450 meters)
[f] 5 Hebrew *two thousand cubits* (about 900 meters)

⁹Then the LORD said to Moses: ¹⁰"Speak to the Israelites and say to them: 'When you cross the Jordan into Canaan, ¹¹select some towns to be your cities of refuge, to which a person who has killed someone accidentally may flee. ¹²They will be places of refuge from the avenger, so that a person accused of murder may not die before he stands trial before the assembly. ¹³These six towns you give will be your cities of refuge. ¹⁴Give three on this side of the Jordan and three in Canaan as cities of refuge. ¹⁵These six towns will be a place of refuge for Israelites, aliens and any other people living among them, so that anyone who has killed another accidentally can flee there.

¹⁶" 'If a man strikes someone with an iron object so that he dies, he is a murderer; the murderer shall be put to death. ¹⁷Or if anyone has a stone in his hand that could kill, and he strikes someone so that he dies, he is a murderer; the murderer shall be put to death. ¹⁸Or if anyone has a wooden object in his hand that could kill, and he hits someone so that he dies, he is a murderer; the murderer shall be put to death. ¹⁹The avenger of blood shall put the murderer to death; when he meets him, he shall put him to death. ²⁰If anyone with malice aforethought shoves another or throws something at him intentionally so that he dies ²¹or if in hostility he hits him with his fist so that he dies, that person shall be put to death; he is a murderer. The avenger of blood shall put the murderer to death when he meets him.

²²" 'But if without hostility someone suddenly shoves another or throws something at him unintentionally ²³or, without seeing him, drops a stone on him that could kill him, and he dies, then since he was not his enemy and he did not intend to harm him, ²⁴the assembly must judge between him and the avenger of blood according to these regulations. ²⁵The assembly must protect the one accused of murder from the avenger of blood and send him back to the city of refuge to which he fled. He must stay there until the death of the high priest, who was anointed with the holy oil.

²⁶" 'But if the accused ever goes outside the limits of the city of refuge to which he has fled ²⁷and the avenger of blood finds him outside the city, the avenger of blood may kill the accused without being guilty of murder. ²⁸The accused must stay in his city of refuge until the death of the high priest; only after the death of the high priest may he return to his own property.

²⁹" 'These are to be legal requirements for you throughout the generations to come, wherever you live.

³⁰" 'Anyone who kills a person is to be put to death as a murderer only on the testimony of witnesses. But no one is to be put to death on the testimony of only one witness.

³¹" 'Do not accept a ransom for the life of a murderer, who deserves to die. He must surely be put to death.

³²" 'Do not accept a ransom for anyone who has fled to a city of refuge and so allow him to go back and live on his own land before the death of the high priest.

³³" 'Do not pollute the land where you are. Bloodshed pollutes the land, and atonement cannot be made for the land on which blood has been shed, except by the blood of the one who shed it. ³⁴Do not defile the land where you live and where I dwell, for I, the LORD, dwell among the Israelites.' "

NOW OR NEVER
NU 35:20-25

God's interested not only in what we do, but also, perhaps even more, in our reasons for doing what we do. Motivation is huge. If you're doing the right things for the wrong reasons, it's not going to deepen your relationship with God.

INHERITANCE OF ZELOPHEHAD'S DAUGHTERS

36 The family heads of the clan of Gilead son of Makir, the son of Manasseh, who were from the clans of the descendants of Joseph, came and spoke before Moses and the leaders, the heads of the Israelite families. ²They said, "When the LORD commanded my lord to give the land as an inheritance to the Israelites by lot, he ordered you to give the inheritance of our brother Zelophehad to his daughters. ³Now suppose they marry men from other Israelite tribes; then their inheritance will be taken from our ancestral inheritance and added to that of the tribe they marry into. And so part of the inheritance allotted to us will be taken away. ⁴When the Year of Jubilee for the Israelites comes, their inheritance will be added to that of the tribe into which they marry, and their property will be taken from the tribal inheritance of our forefathers."

⁵Then at the Lord's command Moses gave this order to the Israelites: "What the tribe of the descendants of Joseph is saying is right. ⁶This is what the Lord commands for Zelophehad's daughters: They may marry anyone they please as long as they marry within the tribal clan of their father. ⁷No inheritance in Israel is to pass from tribe to tribe, for every Israelite shall keep the tribal land inherited from his forefathers. ⁸Every daughter who inherits land in any Israelite tribe must marry someone in her father's tribal clan, so that every Israelite will possess the inheritance of his fathers. ⁹No inheritance may pass from tribe to tribe, for each Israelite tribe is to keep the land it inherits."

¹⁰So Zelophehad's daughters did as the Lord commanded Moses. ¹¹Zelophehad's daughters—Mahlah, Tirzah, Hoglah, Milcah and Noah—married their cousins on their father's side. ¹²They married within the clans of the descendants of Manasseh son of Joseph, and their inheritance remained in their father's clan and tribe.

¹³These are the commands and regulations the Lord gave through Moses to the Israelites on the plains of Moab by the Jordan across from Jericho.ᵃ

ᵃ *13* Hebrew *Jordan of Jericho*; possibly an ancient name for the Jordan River

DEUTERONOMY

Author
Moses

Audience
The next generation of the people of Israel, just before they enter the promised land

Date
1407–1406 B.C.

Setting
Moses delivers his farewell speech to the Israelites on the plains of Moab, east of the Jordan River.

Verse to Remember
And now, O Israel, what does the LORD your God ask of you but to fear the LORD your God, to walk in all his ways, to love him, to serve the LORD your God with all your heart and with all your soul, and to observe the LORD's commands and decrees that I am giving you today for your own good? (10:12–13).

Theme to Consider
The book of Deuteronomy is a call to *remember* what God has done for you and then to *respond* with a renewed commitment to love, trust and obey him completely.

UNCHANGING TRUTH » If the Bible were a TV series, the book of Deuteronomy would be a flashback episode. With his time on earth running out and the Israelites ready to enter the promised land, Moses took one last opportunity to remind the people of Israel—in great detail—who they were, where they came from and how they got where they were.

What if someone asked you those same three things about your spiritual life—who you are, where you came from and how you got where you are now? Could you answer?

We live in a busy world. Depending on your interests, you probably have a million different things competing for your attention: sports, homework, youth group and an after-school job—not to mention time with your friends and family. If you're like most people, you barely have time to think about what's going to happen a day or two from now, let alone to think about what happened several months or even several years ago.

That's a problem, because one of the things God wants from us is a spirit of gratitude for the things he's done for us. And we can't develop that spirit without taking a backward glance now and then to discover how we got from point A to point B. That's why it's a good idea to make a habit of reminding yourself of how God . . .

- got you out of certain jams,
- protected you when you were in danger,
- gave you peace and comfort when you really needed it,
- answered some of your most intense prayers.

Instead of taking a been-there, done-that attitude toward the past, learn to make it a part of your present. Always be prepared to talk about the things God has done for you, and don't be shy about offering words of thanks as often as possible.

LIFE LESSONS »

1 Never underestimate what God can do (1:26–36).

2 Sin always has consequences, even for God's people (3:21–29).

3 Anyone who doesn't commit to follow and serve God in each area of their life can't legitimately claim to fully love God (6:5).

THE COMMAND TO LEAVE HOREB

1 These are the words Moses spoke to all Israel in the desert east of the Jordan—that is, in the Arabah—opposite Suph, between Paran and Tophel, Laban, Hazeroth and Dizahab. ²(It takes eleven days to go from Horeb to Kadesh Barnea by the Mount Seir road.)

³In the fortieth year, on the first day of the eleventh month, Moses proclaimed to the Israelites all that the LORD had commanded him concerning them. ⁴This was after he had defeated Sihon king of the Amorites, who reigned in Heshbon, and at Edrei had defeated Og king of Bashan, who reigned in Ashtaroth.

⁵East of the Jordan in the territory of Moab, Moses began to expound this law, saying:

⁶The LORD our God said to us at Horeb, "You have stayed long enough at this mountain. ⁷Break camp and advance into the hill country of the Amorites; go to all the neighboring peoples in the Arabah, in the mountains, in the western foothills, in the Negev and along the coast, to the land of the Canaanites and to Lebanon, as far as the great river, the Euphrates. ⁸See, I have given you this land. Go in and take possession of the land that the LORD swore he would give to your fathers—to Abraham, Isaac and Jacob—and to their descendants after them."

THE APPOINTMENT OF LEADERS

⁹At that time I said to you, "You are too heavy a burden for me to carry alone. ¹⁰The LORD your God has increased your numbers so that today you are as many as the stars in the sky. ¹¹May the LORD, the God of your fathers, increase you a thousand times and bless you as he has promised! ¹²But how can I bear your problems and your burdens and your disputes all by myself? ¹³Choose some wise, understanding and respected men from each of your tribes, and I will set them over you."

¹⁴You answered me, "What you propose to do is good."

¹⁵So I took the leading men of your tribes, wise and respected men, and appointed them to have authority over you—as commanders of thousands, of hundreds, of fifties and of tens and as tribal officials. ¹⁶And I charged your judges at that time: Hear the disputes between your brothers and judge fairly, whether the case is between brother Israelites or between one of them and an alien. ¹⁷Do not show partiality in judging; hear both small and great alike. Do not be afraid of any man, for judgment belongs to God. Bring me any case too hard for you, and I will hear it. ¹⁸And at that time I told you everything you were to do.

SPIES SENT OUT

¹⁹Then, as the LORD our God commanded us, we set out from Horeb and went toward the hill country of the Amorites through all that vast and dreadful desert that you have seen, and so we reached Kadesh Barnea. ²⁰Then I said to you, "You have reached the hill country of the Amorites, which the LORD our God is giving us. ²¹See, the LORD your God has given you the land. Go up and take possession of it as the LORD, the God of your fathers, told you. Do not be afraid; do not be discouraged."

²²Then all of you came to me and said, "Let us send men ahead to spy out the land for us and bring back a report about the route we are to take and the towns we will come to."

²³The idea seemed good to me; so I selected twelve of you, one man from each tribe. ²⁴They left and went up into the hill country, and came to the Valley of Eshcol and explored it. ²⁵Taking with them some of the fruit of the land, they brought it down to us and reported, "It is a good land that the LORD our God is giving us."

Showing Equality

It's one thing to *say* that God created all human beings to be equal; it's another thing to live like you believe it. For example, are you comfortable around people of different races or ethnic backgrounds? Are you comfortable around people who might not fit in with your usual crowd of friends? Do you tell racist jokes or laugh when other people tell them? Do you treat people differently just because they may not have as much money or education as you do? Do you think God would like to see you make any changes in the way you think about and treat people who are different from you?

» live the adventure » Dt 1:16-17

esau

VERSUS

jacob

» Isaac's oldest and favorite son, the twin brother of Jacob

» A hairy outdoorsman

» Willing to give up long-term blessing for immediate pleasure

» Rebekah's darling baby boy

» A crafty, conniving guy who was touched and changed by God

» Renamed Israel by God, he became the father of the 12 tribes

The Main Event

It's tough to have a brother. It's even harder to have a *twin* brother. You constantly get compared to each other. You constantly feel the need to compete. You love each other . . . but sometimes you hate each other.

That, in a nutshell, is the story of Esau and Jacob. They were twins all right, but about the only thing they had in common was their date of birth.

From the womb, Esau (who came out first) was covered in red hair. He was a classic "good ol' boy" who loved hunting and roaming the fields. Smooth-skinned Jacob, on the other hand, liked to hang around the house. He was a "mama's boy." But what Jacob may have lacked in brawn, he more than made up for in brains.

Like a world-class con man, Jacob took advantage of his big brother's foolishness and grabbed the lion's share of the family fortune. With his mom's help, he even tricked his dad into giving him the all-important paternal blessing. In other words, Jacob took practically everything that Esau had coming to him as the firstborn son.

Needless to say, Esau wasn't too happy with his younger brother. In fact, he intended to kill Jacob. That's when Jacob decided to hit the road. Out on his own, Jacob worked hard, married well and built up a nice fortune. But more important, Jacob finally responded to God's grace and, in time, became a different man. God even renamed him Israel.

The brothers remained apart for years . . . until Jacob decided it was time to make things right. He arranged a meeting with Esau, but became terrified as the reunion drew near. Jacob was certain that Esau still carried a murderous grudge against him. He tried to soften Esau's heart by sending ahead a caravan of expensive gifts. But Esau didn't want Jacob's stuff; he just wanted his long-lost brother back. When they finally met face-to-face, Esau shocked Jacob by grabbing him, putting a man-sized bear hug on him, and refusing to let go. He bawled like a baby, and the estranged brothers were reunited.

The Outcome

In the big scheme of things, the match-up between Jacob and Esau isn't a story about one man winning and another man losing. It's a story of the miraculous grace of God. If God can transform a con man like Jacob and help a guy like Esau swap bitterness for love, imagine what he can do for you!

You don't need to have a twin or even a brother to learn something valuable from the story of Esau and Jacob. Are you at times the con man who works other people over for your own interests? Do you have a murderous temper? Do you have a strained relationship that needs fixin'? If you answered yes to any of these questions, then you qualify for an Esau-and-Jacob-style transformation. Let God get to work on you now.

Read more about Esau and Jacob in Genesis 25–36 (pages 29–45).

26But you were unwilling to go up; you rebelled against the command of the LORD your God. 27You grumbled in your tents and said, "The LORD hates us; so he brought us out of Egypt to deliver us into the hands of the Amorites to destroy us. 28Where can we go? Our brothers have made us lose heart. They say, 'The people are stronger and taller than we are; the cities are large, with walls up to the sky. We even saw the Anakites there.'"

29Then I said to you, "Do not be terrified; do not be afraid of them. 30The LORD your God, who is going before you, will fight for you, as he did for you in Egypt, before your very eyes, 31and in the desert. There you saw how the LORD your God carried you, as a father carries his son, all the way you went until you reached this place."

32In spite of this, you did not trust in the LORD your God, 33who went ahead of you on your journey, in fire by night and in a cloud by day, to search out places for you to camp and to show you the way you should go.

34When the LORD heard what you said, he was angry and solemnly swore: 35"Not a man of this evil generation shall see the good land I swore to give your forefathers, 36except Caleb son of Jephunneh. He will see it, and I will give him and his descendants the land he set his feet on, because he followed the LORD wholeheartedly."

37Because of you the LORD became angry with me also and said, "You shall not enter it, either. 38But your assistant, Joshua son of Nun, will enter it. Encourage him, because he will lead Israel to inherit it. 39And the little ones that you said would be taken captive, your children who do not yet know good from bad—they will enter the land. I will give it to them and they will take possession of it. 40But as for you, turn around and set out toward the desert along the route to the Red Sea.a"

41Then you replied, "We have sinned against the LORD. We will go up and fight, as the LORD our God commanded us." So every one of you put on his weapons, thinking it easy to go up into the hill country.

42But the LORD said to me, "Tell them, 'Do not go up and fight, because I will not be with you. You will be defeated by your enemies.'"

43So I told you, but you would not listen. You rebelled against the LORD's command and in your arrogance you marched up into the hill country. 44The Amorites who lived in those hills came out against you; they chased you like a swarm of bees and beat you down from Seir all the way to Hormah. 45You came back and wept before the LORD, but he paid no attention to your weeping and turned a deaf ear to you. 46And so you stayed in Kadesh many days—all the time you spent there.

WANDERINGS IN THE DESERT

2 Then we turned back and set out toward the desert along the route to the Red Sea,a as the LORD had directed me. For a long time we made our way around the hill country of Seir.

2Then the LORD said to me, 3"You have made your way around this hill country long enough; now turn north. 4Give the people these orders: 'You are about to pass through the territory of your brothers the descendants of Esau, who live in Seir. They will be afraid of you, but be very careful. 5Do not provoke them to war, for I will not give you any of their land, not even enough to put your foot on. I have given Esau the hill country of Seir as his own. 6You are to pay them in silver for the food you eat and the water you drink.'"

7The LORD your God has blessed you in all the work of your hands. He has watched over your journey through this vast desert. These forty years the LORD your God has been with you, and you have not lacked anything.

DT 2:7

challenge notes

To: **my_son**

heavenly_father: your skills, abilities and power may be limited, but mine aren't. if you give me your best effort, I can turn it into something incredible. whatever the "work of your hands" may be—studying, soccer, cutting the grass, talking to a friend about me—I am your source of strength and blessing. at the end of your journey, look back on all of your years and count whether you have ever lacked anything you have needed.

a 40,1 Hebrew Yam Suph; that is, Sea of Reeds

⁸So we went on past our brothers the descendants of Esau, who live in Seir. We turned from the Arabah road, which comes up from Elath and Ezion Geber, and traveled along the desert road of Moab. ⁹Then the LORD said to me, "Do not harass the Moabites or provoke them to war, for I will not give you any part of their land. I have given Ar to the descendants of Lot as a possession."

¹⁰(The Emites used to live there—a people strong and numerous, and as tall as the Anakites. ¹¹Like the Anakites, they too were considered Rephaites, but the Moabites called them Emites. ¹²Horites used to live in Seir, but the descendants of Esau drove them out. They destroyed the Horites from before them and settled in their place, just as Israel did in the land the LORD gave them as their possession.)

¹³And the LORD said, "Now get up and cross the Zered Valley." So we crossed the valley. ¹⁴Thirty-eight years passed from the time we left Kadesh Barnea until we crossed the Zered Valley. By then, that entire generation of fighting men had perished from the camp, as the LORD had sworn to them. ¹⁵The LORD's hand was against them until he had completely eliminated them from the camp.

¹⁶Now when the last of these fighting men among the people had died, ¹⁷the LORD said to me, ¹⁸"Today you are to pass by the region of Moab at Ar. ¹⁹When you come to the Ammonites, do not harass them or provoke them to war, for I will not give you possession of any land belonging to the Ammonites. I have given it as a possession to the descendants of Lot."

²⁰(That too was considered a land of the Rephaites, who used to live there; but the Ammonites called them Zamzummites. ²¹They were a people strong and numerous, and as tall as the Anakites. The LORD destroyed them from before the Ammonites, who drove them out and settled in their place. ²²The LORD had done the same for the descendants of Esau, who lived in Seir, when he destroyed the Horites from before them. They drove them out and have lived in their place to this day. ²³And as for the Avvites who lived in villages as far as Gaza, the Caphtorites coming out from Caphtor[a] destroyed them and settled in their place.)

DEFEAT OF SIHON KING OF HESHBON

²⁴"Set out now and cross the Arnon Gorge. See, I have given into your hand Sihon the Amorite, king of Heshbon, and his country. Begin to take possession of it and engage him in battle. ²⁵This very day I will begin to put the terror and fear of you on all the nations under heaven. They will hear reports of you and will tremble and be in anguish because of you."

²⁶From the desert of Kedemoth I sent messengers to Sihon king of Heshbon offering peace and saying, ²⁷"Let us pass through your country. We will stay on the main road; we will not turn aside to the right or to the left. ²⁸Sell us food to eat and water to drink for their price in silver. Only let us pass through on foot— ²⁹as the descendants of Esau, who live in Seir, and the Moabites, who live in Ar, did for us—until we cross the Jordan into the land the LORD our God is giving us." ³⁰But Sihon king of Heshbon refused to let us pass through. For the LORD your God had made his spirit stubborn and his heart obstinate in order to give him into your hands, as he has now done.

³¹The LORD said to me, "See, I have begun to deliver Sihon and his country over to you. Now begin to conquer and possess his land."

³²When Sihon and all his army came out to meet us in battle at Jahaz, ³³the LORD our God delivered him over to us and we struck him down, together with his sons and his whole army. ³⁴At that time we took all his towns and completely destroyed[b] them—men, women and children. We left no survivors. ³⁵But the livestock and the plunder from the towns we had captured we carried off for ourselves. ³⁶From Aroer on the rim of the Arnon Gorge, and from the town in the gorge, even as far as Gilead, not one town was too strong for us. The LORD our God gave us all of them. ³⁷But in accordance with the command of the LORD our God, you did not encroach on any of the land of the Ammonites, neither the land along the course of the Jabbok nor that around the towns in the hills.

DEFEAT OF OG KING OF BASHAN

3 Next we turned and went up along the road toward Bashan, and Og king of Bashan with his whole army marched out to meet us in battle at Edrei. ²The LORD said to me, "Do not be afraid of him, for I have handed him over to you with his whole army and his land. Do to him what you did to Sihon king of the Amorites, who reigned in Heshbon."

³So the LORD our God also gave into our hands Og king of Bashan and all his army. We struck them

---

[a] *23* That is, Crete   [b] *34* The Hebrew term refers to the irrevocable giving over of things or persons to the LORD, often by totally destroying them.

down, leaving no survivors. [4]At that time we took all his cities. There was not one of the sixty cities that we did not take from them—the whole region of Argob, Og's kingdom in Bashan. [5]All these cities were fortified with high walls and with gates and bars, and there were also a great many unwalled villages. [6]We completely destroyed[a] them, as we had done with Sihon king of Heshbon, destroying[a] every city—men, women and children. [7]But all the livestock and the plunder from their cities we carried off for ourselves.

[8]So at that time we took from these two kings of the Amorites the territory east of the Jordan, from the Arnon Gorge as far as Mount Hermon. [9](Hermon is called Sirion by the Sidonians; the Amorites call it Senir.) [10]We took all the towns on the plateau, and all Gilead, and all Bashan as far as Salecah and Edrei, towns of Og's kingdom in Bashan. [11](Only Og king of Bashan was left of the remnant of the Rephaites. His bed[b] was made of iron and was more than thirteen feet long and six feet wide.[c] It is still in Rabbah of the Ammonites.)

DIVISION OF THE LAND

[12]Of the land that we took over at that time, I gave the Reubenites and the Gadites the territory north of Aroer by the Arnon Gorge, including half the hill country of Gilead, together with its towns. [13]The rest of Gilead and also all of Bashan, the kingdom of Og, I gave to the half-tribe of Manasseh. (The whole region of Argob in Bashan used to be known as a land of the Rephaites. [14]Jair, a descendant of Manasseh, took the whole region of Argob as far as the border of the Geshurites and the Maacathites; it was named after him, so that to this day Bashan is called Havvoth Jair.[d]) [15]And I gave Gilead to Makir. [16]But to the Reubenites and the Gadites I gave the territory extending from Gilead down to the Arnon Gorge (the middle of the gorge being the border) and out to the Jabbok River, which is the border of the Ammonites. [17]Its western border was the Jordan in the Arabah, from Kinnereth to the Sea of the Arabah (the Salt Sea[e]), below the slopes of Pisgah.

[18]I commanded you at that time: "The LORD your God has given you this land to take possession of it. But all your able-bodied men, armed for battle, must cross over ahead of your brother Israelites. [19]However, your wives, your children and your livestock (I know you have much livestock) may stay in the towns I have given you, [20]until the LORD gives rest to your brothers as he has to you, and they too have taken over the land that the LORD your God is giving them, across the Jordan. After that, each of you may go back to the possession I have given you."

MOSES FORBIDDEN TO CROSS THE JORDAN

[21]At that time I commanded Joshua: "You have seen with your own eyes all that the LORD your God has done to these two kings. The LORD will do the same to all the kingdoms over there where you are going. [22]Do not be afraid of them; the LORD your God himself will fight for you."

[23]At that time I pleaded with the LORD: [24]"O Sovereign LORD, you have begun to show to your servant your greatness and your strong hand. For what god is there in heaven or on earth who can do the deeds and mighty works you do? [25]Let me go over and see the good land beyond the Jordan—that fine hill country and Lebanon."

[26]But because of you the LORD was angry with me and would not listen to me. "That is enough," the LORD said. "Do not speak to me anymore about this matter. [27]Go up to the top of Pisgah and look west and north and south and east. Look at the land with your own eyes, since you are not going to cross this Jordan. [28]But commission Joshua, and encourage and strengthen him, for he will lead this people across and will cause them to inherit the land that you will see." [29]So we stayed in the valley near Beth Peor.

OBEDIENCE COMMANDED

4 Hear now, O Israel, the decrees and laws I am about to teach you. Follow them so that you may live and may go in and take possession of the land that the LORD, the God of your fathers, is giving you. [2]Do not add to what I command you and do not subtract from it, but keep the commands of the LORD your God that I give you.

[3]You saw with your own eyes what the LORD did at Baal Peor. The LORD your God destroyed from

---

[a] *6* The Hebrew term refers to the irrevocable giving over of things or persons to the LORD, often by totally destroying them.
[b] *11* Or *sarcophagus*   [c] *11* Hebrew *nine cubits long and four cubits wide* (about 4 meters long and 1.8 meters wide)   [d] *14* Or *called the settlements of Jair*   [e] *17* That is, the Dead Sea

among you everyone who followed the Baal of Peor, 4but all of you who held fast to the LORD your God are still alive today.

5See, I have taught you decrees and laws as the LORD my God commanded me, so that you may follow them in the land you are entering to take possession of it. 6Observe them carefully, for this will show your wisdom and understanding to the nations, who will hear about all these decrees and say, "Surely this great nation is a wise and understanding people." 7What other nation is so great as to have their gods near them the way the LORD our God is near us whenever we pray to him? 8And what other nation is so great as to have such righteous decrees and laws as this body of laws I am setting before you today?

9Only be careful, and watch yourselves closely so that you do not forget the things your eyes have seen or let them slip from your heart as long as you live. Teach them to your children and to their children after them. 10Remember the day you stood before the LORD your God at Horeb, when he said to me, "Assemble the people before me to hear my words so that they may learn to revere me as long as they live in the land and may teach them to their children." 11You came near and stood at the foot of the mountain while it blazed with fire to the very heavens, with black clouds and deep darkness. 12Then the LORD spoke to you out of the fire. You heard the sound of words but saw no form; there was only a voice. 13He declared to you his covenant, the Ten Commandments, which he commanded you to follow and then wrote them on two stone tablets. 14And the LORD directed me at that time to teach you the decrees and laws you are to follow in the land that you are crossing the Jordan to possess.

IDOLATRY FORBIDDEN

15You saw no form of any kind the day the LORD spoke to you at Horeb out of the fire. Therefore watch yourselves very carefully, 16so that you do not become corrupt and make for yourselves an idol, an image of any shape, whether formed like a man or a woman, 17or like any animal on earth or any bird that flies in the air, 18or like any creature that moves along the ground or any fish in the waters below. 19And when you look up to the sky and see the sun, the moon and the stars—all the heavenly array—do not be enticed into bowing down to them and worshiping things the LORD your God has apportioned to all the nations under heaven. 20But as for you, the LORD took you and brought you out of the iron-smelting furnace, out of Egypt, to be the people of his inheritance, as you now are.

21The LORD was angry with me because of you, and he solemnly swore that I would not cross the Jordan and enter the good land the LORD your God is giving you as your inheritance. 22I will die in this land; I will not cross the Jordan; but you are about to cross over and take possession of that good land. 23Be careful not to forget the covenant of the LORD your God that he made with you; do not make for yourselves an idol in the form of anything the LORD your God has forbidden. 24For the LORD your God is a consuming fire, a jealous God.

25After you have had children and grandchildren and have lived in the land a long time—if you then become corrupt and make any kind of idol, doing evil in the eyes of the LORD your God and provoking him to anger, 26I call heaven and earth as witnesses against you this day that you will quickly perish from the land that you are crossing the Jordan to possess. You will not live there long but will certainly be destroyed. 27The LORD will scatter you among the peoples, and only a few of you will survive among the nations to which the LORD will drive you. 28There you will worship man-made gods of wood and stone, which cannot see or hear or eat or smell. 29But if from there you seek the LORD your God, you will find him if you look for him with all your heart and with all your soul. 30When you are in distress and all these things have happened to you, then in later days you will return to the LORD your God and obey him. 31For the LORD your God is a merciful God; he will not abandon or destroy you or forget the covenant with your forefathers, which he confirmed to them by oath.

Getting Close to God

Remember the tractor beam in *Star Wars*—you know, the whole "locked in" idea? That's a good illustration of what happens to us when we pray. No matter where we are or what we're doing, the moment we begin talking to God, we are immediately locked in to his presence. That doesn't mean we actually *see* him, but it does mean we can have a private, one-on-one conversation with him.

THE LORD IS GOD

32Ask now about the former days, long before your time, from the day God created man on the earth; ask from one end of the heavens to the other. Has anything so great as this ever happened, or has anything like it ever been heard of? 33Has any other people heard the voice of God[a] speaking out of fire, as you have, and lived? 34Has any god ever tried to take for himself one nation out of another nation, by testings, by miraculous signs and wonders, by war, by a mighty hand and an outstretched arm, or by great and awesome deeds, like all the things the LORD your God did for you in Egypt before your very eyes?

35You were shown these things so that you might know that the LORD is God; besides him there is no other. 36From heaven he made you hear his voice to discipline you. On earth he showed you his great fire, and you heard his words from out of the fire. 37Because he loved your forefathers and chose their descendants after them, he brought you out of Egypt by his Presence and his great strength, 38to drive out before you nations greater and stronger than you and to bring you into their land to give it to you for your inheritance, as it is today.

39Acknowledge and take to heart this day that the LORD is God in heaven above and on the earth below. There is no other. 40Keep his decrees and commands, which I am giving you today, so that it may go well with you and your children after you and that you may live long in the land the LORD your God gives you for all time.

challenge notes

To: my_son

heavenly_father: no matter what you're guilty of, no matter how many people you've hurt or how long you've neglected our relationship, I will always be right here—ready to reconnect and make things right in our relationship.

DT 4:29-30

now or never

DT 4:32–35

Look at the challenge God throws down here: "Is there any other god with the power to create the universe and the love to personally take care of you? No? Then your best bet is to listen to me!"

CITIES OF REFUGE

41Then Moses set aside three cities east of the Jordan, 42to which anyone who had killed a person could flee if he had unintentionally killed his neighbor without malice aforethought. He could flee into one of these cities and save his life. 43The cities were these: Bezer in the desert plateau, for the Reubenites; Ramoth in Gilead, for the Gadites; and Golan in Bashan, for the Manassites.

INTRODUCTION TO THE LAW

44This is the law Moses set before the Israelites. 45These are the stipulations, decrees and laws Moses gave them when they came out of Egypt 46and were in the valley near Beth Peor east of the Jordan, in the land of Sihon king of the Amorites, who reigned in Heshbon and was defeated by Moses and the Israelites as they came out of Egypt. 47They took possession of his land and the land of Og king of Bashan, the two Amorite kings east of the Jordan. 48This land extended from Aroer on the rim of the Arnon Gorge to Mount Siyon[b] (that is, Hermon), 49and included all the Arabah east of the Jordan, as far as the Sea of the Arabah,[c] below the slopes of Pisgah.

THE TEN COMMANDMENTS

5 Moses summoned all Israel and said:

Hear, O Israel, the decrees and laws I declare in your hearing today. Learn them and be sure to follow them. 2The LORD our God made a covenant with us at Horeb. 3It was not with our fathers that the LORD made this covenant, but with us, with all of us who are alive here today. 4The LORD spoke to you face to face out of the fire on the mountain. 5(At that time I stood between the LORD and you to declare to you the word of the LORD, because you were afraid of the fire and did not go up the mountain.) And he said:

---

a 33 Or of a god   b 48 Hebrew; Syriac (see also Deut. 3:9) Sirion   c 49 That is, the Dead Sea

⁶ "I am the LORD your God, who brought you out of Egypt, out of the land of slavery.

⁷ "You shall have no other gods before[a] me.

⁸ "You shall not make for yourself an idol in the form of anything in heaven above or on the earth beneath or in the waters below. ⁹You shall not bow down to them or worship them; for I, the LORD your God, am a jealous God, punishing the children for the sin of the fathers to the third and fourth generation of those who hate me, ¹⁰but showing love to a thousand ⌐generations⌐ of those who love me and keep my commandments.

NOW OR NEVER

DT 5:1

Reading God's Word isn't enough. Memorizing it isn't enough. If you want to make a difference in the world, you've got to do what God's Word says.

¹¹ "You shall not misuse the name of the LORD your God, for the LORD will not hold anyone guiltless who misuses his name.

¹² "Observe the Sabbath day by keeping it holy, as the LORD your God has commanded you. ¹³Six days you shall labor and do all your work, ¹⁴but the seventh day is a Sabbath to the LORD your God. On it you shall not do any work, neither you, nor your son or daughter, nor your manservant or maidservant, nor your ox, your donkey or any of your animals, nor the alien within your gates, so that your manservant and maidservant may rest, as you do. ¹⁵Remember that you were slaves in Egypt and that the LORD your God brought you out of there with a mighty hand and an outstretched arm. Therefore the LORD your God has commanded you to observe the Sabbath day.

¹⁶ "Honor your father and your mother, as the LORD your God has commanded you, so that you may live long and that it may go well with you in the land the LORD your God is giving you.

¹⁷ "You shall not murder.

¹⁸ "You shall not commit adultery.

¹⁹ "You shall not steal.

²⁰ "You shall not give false testimony against your neighbor.

²¹ "You shall not covet your neighbor's wife. You shall not set your desire on your neighbor's house or land, his manservant or maidservant, his ox or donkey, or anything that belongs to your neighbor."

²²These are the commandments the LORD proclaimed in a loud voice to your whole assembly there on the mountain from out of the fire, the cloud and the deep darkness; and he added nothing more. Then he wrote them on two stone tablets and gave them to me.

²³When you heard the voice out of the darkness, while the mountain was ablaze with fire, all the leading men of your tribes and your elders came to me. ²⁴And you said, "The LORD our God has shown us his glory and his majesty, and we have heard his voice from the fire. Today we have seen that a man can live even if God speaks with him. ²⁵But now, why should we die? This great fire will consume us, and we will die if we hear the voice of the LORD our God any longer. ²⁶For what mortal man has ever heard the voice of the living God speaking out of fire, as we have, and survived? ²⁷Go near and listen to all that the LORD our God says. Then tell us whatever the LORD our God tells you. We will listen and obey."

²⁸The LORD heard you when you spoke to me and the LORD said to me, "I have heard what this people said to you. Everything they said was good. ²⁹Oh, that their hearts would be inclined to fear me and keep all my commands always, so that it might go well with them and their children forever!

³⁰ "Go, tell them to return to their tents. ³¹But you stay here with me so that I may give you all the commands, decrees and laws you are to teach them to follow in the land I am giving them to possess."

³²So be careful to do what the LORD your God has commanded you; do not turn aside to the right or

---

ᵃ 7 Or besides

to the left. ³³Walk in all the way that the Lord your God has commanded you, so that you may live and prosper and prolong your days in the land that you will possess.

LOVE THE LORD YOUR GOD

6 These are the commands, decrees and laws the Lord your God directed me to teach you to observe in the land that you are crossing the Jordan to possess, ²so that you, your children and their children after them may fear the Lord your God as long as you live by keeping all his decrees and commands that I give you, and so that you may enjoy long life. ³Hear, O Israel, and be careful to obey so that it may go well with you and that you may increase greatly in a land flowing with milk and honey, just as the Lord, the God of your fathers, promised you.

⁴Hear, O Israel: The Lord our God, the Lord is one.^a ⁵Love the Lord your God with all your heart and with all your soul and with all your strength. ⁶These commandments that I give you today are to be upon your hearts. ⁷Impress them on your children. Talk about them when you sit at home and when you walk along the road, when you lie down and when you get up. ⁸Tie them as symbols on your hands and bind them on your foreheads. ⁹Write them on the doorframes of your houses and on your gates.

¹⁰When the Lord your God brings you into the land he swore to your fathers, to Abraham, Isaac and Jacob, to give you—a land with large, flourishing cities you did not build, ¹¹houses filled with all kinds of good things you did not provide, wells you did not dig, and vineyards and olive groves you did not plant—then when you eat and are satisfied, ¹²be careful that you do not forget the Lord, who brought you out of Egypt, out of the land of slavery.

¹³Fear the Lord your God, serve him only and take your oaths in his name. ¹⁴Do not follow other gods, the gods of the peoples around you; ¹⁵for the Lord your God, who is among you, is a jealous God and his anger will burn against you, and he will destroy you from the face of the land. ¹⁶Do not test the Lord your God as you did at Massah. ¹⁷Be sure to keep the commands of the Lord your God and the stipulations and decrees he has given you. ¹⁸Do what is right and good in the Lord's sight, so that it may go well with you and you may go in and take over the good land that the Lord promised on oath to your forefathers, ¹⁹thrusting out all your enemies before you, as the Lord said.

²⁰In the future, when your son asks you, "What is the meaning of the stipulations, decrees and laws the Lord our God has commanded you?" ²¹tell him: "We were slaves of Pharaoh in Egypt, but the Lord brought us out of Egypt with a mighty hand. ²²Before our eyes the Lord sent miraculous signs and wonders—great and terrible—upon Egypt and Pharaoh and his whole household. ²³But he brought us out from there to bring us in and give us the land that he promised on oath to our forefathers. ²⁴The Lord commanded us to obey all these decrees and to fear the Lord our God, so that we might always prosper and be kept alive, as is the case today. ²⁵And if we are careful to obey all this law before the Lord our God, as he has commanded us, that will be our righteousness."

DRIVING OUT THE NATIONS

7 When the Lord your God brings you into the land you are entering to possess and drives out before you many nations—the Hittites, Girgashites, Amorites, Canaanites, Perizzites, Hivites and Jebusites, seven nations larger and stronger than you— ²and when the Lord your God has delivered them over to you and you have defeated them, then you must destroy them totally.^b Make no

---

> ## Pleasing God
>
> Think about the way you act when you fall in love—or at least into serious "like"—with a girl. You know, when you can't seem to get her off your mind, and when you want to do everything you can to make her happy. It's not that different from what an ideal relationship with God is like. It just so happens that what makes God happy is obedience. The question is, are you so into God that you'll do anything to please him?
>
> »» live the adventure »» Dt 6:4-6

^a 4 Or *The Lord our God is one Lord*; or *The Lord is our God, the Lord is one*; or *The Lord is our God, the Lord alone*   ^b 2 The Hebrew term refers to the irrevocable giving over of things or persons to the Lord, often by totally destroying them; also in verse 26.

treaty with them, and show them no mercy. ³Do not intermarry with them. Do not give your daughters to their sons or take their daughters for your sons, ⁴for they will turn your sons away from following me to serve other gods, and the LORD's anger will burn against you and will quickly destroy you. ⁵This is what you are to do to them: Break down their altars, smash their sacred stones, cut down their Asherah poles³ and burn their idols in the fire. ⁶For you are a people holy to the LORD your God. The LORD your God has chosen you out of all the peoples on the face of the earth to be his people, his treasured possession.

⁷The LORD did not set his affection on you and choose you because you were more numerous than other peoples, for you were the fewest of all peoples. ⁸But it was because the LORD loved you and kept the oath he swore to your forefathers that he brought you out with a mighty hand and redeemed you from the land of slavery, from the power of Pharaoh king of Egypt. ⁹Know therefore that the LORD your God is God; he is the faithful God, keeping his covenant of love to a thousand generations of those who love him and keep his commands. ¹⁰But

> those who hate him he will repay to their face by destruction;
> he will not be slow to repay to their face those who hate him.

¹¹Therefore, take care to follow the commands, decrees and laws I give you today.

¹²If you pay attention to these laws and are careful to follow them, then the LORD your God will keep his covenant of love with you, as he swore to your forefathers. ¹³He will love you and bless you and increase your numbers. He will bless the fruit of your womb, the crops of your land—your grain, new wine and oil—the calves of your herds and the lambs of your flocks in the land that he swore to your forefathers to give you. ¹⁴You will be blessed more than any other people; none of your men or women will be childless, nor any of your livestock without young. ¹⁵The LORD will keep you free from every disease. He will not inflict on you the horrible diseases you knew in Egypt, but he will inflict them on all who hate you. ¹⁶You must destroy all the peoples the LORD your God gives over to you. Do not look on them with pity and do not serve their gods, for that will be a snare to you.

¹⁷You may say to yourselves, "These nations are stronger than we are. How can we drive them out?" ¹⁸But do not be afraid of them; remember well what the LORD your God did to Pharaoh and to all Egypt. ¹⁹You saw with your own eyes the great trials, the miraculous signs and wonders, the mighty hand and outstretched arm, with which the LORD your God brought you out. The LORD your God will do the same to all the peoples you now fear. ²⁰Moreover, the LORD your God will send the hornet among them until even the survivors who hide from you have perished. ²¹Do not be terrified by them, for the LORD your God, who is among you, is a great and awesome God. ²²The LORD your God will drive out those nations before you, little by little. You will not be allowed to eliminate them all at once, or the wild animals will multiply around you. ²³But the LORD your God will deliver them over to you, throwing them into great confusion until they are destroyed. ²⁴He will give their kings into your hand, and you will wipe out their names from under heaven. No one will be able to stand up against you; you will destroy them. ²⁵The images of their gods you are to burn in the fire. Do not covet the silver and gold on them, and do not take it for yourselves, or you will be ensnared by it, for it is detestable to the LORD your God. ²⁶Do not bring a detestable thing into your house or you, like it, will be set apart for destruction. Utterly abhor and detest it, for it is set apart for destruction.

>> live the adventure >> Dt 7:12

Keeping Your Word

Are you a man of your word? When you tell someone you'll meet him at a certain place and time, do you always show up—even if you get a better offer in the meantime? When you promise someone you won't tell anyone her secret, do you always keep that promise—even when the secret seems too good to keep to yourself? If a man is only as good as his word, how good would people say you are? Are you better than most? How about compared to God?

ª 5 That is, symbols of the goddess Asherah; here and elsewhere in Deuteronomy

DO NOT FORGET THE LORD

8 Be careful to follow every command I am giving you today, so that you may live and increase and may enter and possess the land that the LORD promised on oath to your forefathers. ²Remember how the LORD your God led you all the way in the desert these forty years, to humble you and to test you in order to know what was in your heart, whether or not you would keep his commands. ³He humbled you, causing you to hunger and then feeding you with manna, which neither you nor your fathers had known, to teach you that man does not live on bread alone but on every word that comes from the mouth of the LORD. ⁴Your clothes did not wear out and your feet did not swell during these forty years. ⁵Know then in your heart that as a man disciplines his son, so the LORD your God disciplines you.

⁶Observe the commands of the LORD your God, walking in his ways and revering him. ⁷For the LORD your God is bringing you into a good land—a land with streams and pools of water, with springs flowing in the valleys and hills; ⁸a land with wheat and barley, vines and fig trees, pomegranates, olive oil and honey; ⁹a land where bread will not be scarce and you will lack nothing; a land where the rocks are iron and you can dig copper out of the hills.

¹⁰When you have eaten and are satisfied, praise the LORD your God for the good land he has given you. ¹¹Be careful that you do not forget the LORD your God, failing to observe his commands, his laws and his decrees that I am giving you this day. ¹²Otherwise, when you eat and are satisfied, when you build fine houses and settle down, ¹³and when your herds and flocks grow large and your silver and gold increase and all you have is multiplied, ¹⁴then your heart will become proud and you will forget the LORD your God, who brought you out of Egypt, out of the land of slavery. ¹⁵He led you through the vast and dreadful desert, that thirsty and waterless land, with its venomous snakes and scorpions. He brought you water out of hard rock. ¹⁶He gave you manna to eat in the desert, something your fathers had never known, to humble and to test you so that in the end it might go well with you. ¹⁷You may say to yourself, "My power and the strength of my hands have produced this wealth for me." ¹⁸But remember the LORD your God, for it is he who gives you the ability to produce wealth, and so confirms his covenant, which he swore to your forefathers, as it is today.

¹⁹If you ever forget the LORD your God and follow other gods and worship and bow down to them, I testify against you today that you will surely be destroyed. ²⁰Like the nations the LORD destroyed before you, so you will be destroyed for not obeying the LORD your God.

NOT BECAUSE OF ISRAEL'S RIGHTEOUSNESS

9 Hear, O Israel. You are now about to cross the Jordan to go in and dispossess nations greater and stronger than you, with large cities that have walls up to the sky. ²The people are strong and tall—Anakites! You know about them and have heard it said: "Who can stand up against the Anakites?" ³But be assured today that the LORD your God is the one who goes across ahead of you like

NOW OR NEVER
DT 8:3

What would happen to you physically if you went days, weeks or even months without food? The same thing happens to you spiritually when you go days, weeks or months without studying God's Word—you starve spiritually and lose your strength.

Distributing Credit

How do you feel when someone compliments you for something you didn't do? How do you respond? Do you take the credit yourself? Or do you pass it along to the people who really deserve it? Do you ever give God credit for your talents and abilities? Do you believe he *deserves* credit for them? Do yourself a favor—never fall into the trap of believing your own hype.

»» live the adventure »» Dt 8:11–18

a devouring fire. He will destroy them; he will subdue them before you. And you will drive them out and annihilate them quickly, as the LORD has promised you.

4After the LORD your God has driven them out before you, do not say to yourself, "The LORD has brought me here to take possession of this land because of my righteousness." No, it is on account of the wickedness of these nations that the LORD is going to drive them out before you. 5It is not because of your righteousness or your integrity that you are going in to take possession of their land; but on account of the wickedness of these nations, the LORD your God will drive them out before you, to accomplish what he swore to your fathers, to Abraham, Isaac and Jacob. 6Understand, then, that it is not because of your righteousness that the LORD your God is giving you this good land to possess, for you are a stiff-necked people.

THE GOLDEN CALF

7Remember this and never forget how you provoked the LORD your God to anger in the desert. From the day you left Egypt until you arrived here, you have been rebellious against the LORD. 8At Horeb you aroused the LORD's wrath so that he was angry enough to destroy you. 9When I went up on the mountain to receive the tablets of stone, the tablets of the covenant that the LORD had made with you, I stayed on the mountain forty days and forty nights; I ate no bread and drank no water. 10The LORD gave me two stone tablets inscribed by the finger of God. On them were all the commandments the LORD proclaimed to you on the mountain out of the fire, on the day of the assembly.

11At the end of the forty days and forty nights, the LORD gave me the two stone tablets, the tablets of the covenant. 12Then the LORD told me, "Go down from here at once, because your people whom you brought out of Egypt have become corrupt. They have turned away quickly from what I commanded them and have made a cast idol for themselves."

13And the LORD said to me, "I have seen this people, and they are a stiff-necked people indeed! 14Let me alone, so that I may destroy them and blot out their name from under heaven. And I will make you into a nation stronger and more numerous than they."

15So I turned and went down from the mountain while it was ablaze with fire. And the two tablets of the covenant were in my hands.a 16When I looked, I saw that you had sinned against the LORD your God; you had made for yourselves an idol cast in the shape of a calf. You had turned aside quickly from the way that the LORD had commanded you. 17So I took the two tablets and threw them out of my hands, breaking them to pieces before your eyes.

18Then once again I fell prostrate before the LORD for forty days and forty nights; I ate no bread and drank no water, because of all the sin you had committed, doing what was evil in the LORD's sight and so provoking him to anger. 19I feared the anger and wrath of the LORD, for he was angry enough with you to destroy you. But again the LORD listened to me. 20And the LORD was angry enough with Aaron to destroy him, but at that time I prayed for Aaron too. 21Also I took that sinful thing of yours, the calf you had made, and burned it in the fire. Then I crushed it and ground it to powder as fine as dust and threw the dust into a stream that flowed down the mountain.

22You also made the LORD angry at Taberah, at Massah and at Kibroth Hattaavah.

23And when the LORD sent you out from Kadesh Barnea, he said, "Go up and take possession of the land I have given you." But you rebelled against the command of the LORD your God. You did not trust him or obey him. 24You have been rebellious against the LORD ever since I have known you.

25I lay prostrate before the LORD those forty days and forty nights because the LORD had said he would destroy you. 26I prayed to the LORD and said, "O Sovereign LORD, do not destroy your people, your own inheritance that you redeemed by your great power and brought out of Egypt with a mighty hand. 27Remember your servants Abraham, Isaac and Jacob. Overlook the stubbornness of this people, their wickedness and their sin. 28Otherwise, the country from which you brought us will say, 'Because the LORD was not able to take them into the land he had promised them, and because he hated them, he brought them out to put them to death in the desert.' 29But they are your people, your inheritance that you brought out by your great power and your outstretched arm."

TABLETS LIKE THE FIRST ONES

10 At that time the LORD said to me, "Chisel out two stone tablets like the first ones and come up to me on the mountain. Also make a wooden chest.b 2I will write on

---

a 15 Or And I had the two tablets of the covenant with me, one in each hand   b 1 That is, an ark the tablets the words that were on the first tablets, which you broke. Then you are to put them in the chest."

³So I made the ark out of acacia wood and chiseled out two stone tablets like the first ones, and I went up on the mountain with the two tablets in my hands. ⁴The LORD wrote on these tablets what he had written before, the Ten Commandments he had proclaimed to you on the mountain, out of the fire, on the day of the assembly. And the LORD gave them to me. ⁵Then I came back down the mountain and put the tablets in the ark I had made, as the LORD commanded me, and they are there now.

⁶(The Israelites traveled from the wells of the Jaakanites to Moserah. There Aaron died and was buried, and Eleazar his son succeeded him as priest. ⁷From there they traveled to Gudgodah and on to Jotbathah, a land with streams of water. ⁸At that time the LORD set apart the tribe of Levi to carry the ark of the covenant of the LORD, to stand before the LORD to minister and to pronounce blessings in his name, as they still do today. ⁹That is why the Levites have no share or inheritance among their brothers; the LORD is their inheritance, as the LORD your God told them.)

¹⁰Now I had stayed on the mountain forty days and nights, as I did the first time, and the LORD listened to me at this time also. It was not his will to destroy you. ¹¹"Go," the LORD said to me, "and lead the people on their way, so that they may enter and possess the land that I swore to their fathers to give them."

NOW OR NEVER
DT 10:12–13

When was the last time you showed real respect for God? When was the last time you made a conscious choice to obey him even though you clearly had another choice? When was the last time you told him how much he means to you?

FEAR THE LORD

¹²And now, O Israel, what does the LORD your God ask of you but to fear the LORD your God, to walk in all his ways, to love him, to serve the LORD your God with all your heart and with all your soul, ¹³and to observe the LORD's commands and decrees that I am giving you today for your own good?

¹⁴To the LORD your God belong the heavens, even the highest heavens, the earth and everything in it. ¹⁵Yet the LORD set his affection on your forefathers and loved them, and he chose you, their descendants, above all the nations, as it is today. ¹⁶Circumcise your hearts, therefore, and do not be stiffnecked any longer. ¹⁷For the LORD your God is God of gods and Lord of lords, the great God, mighty and awesome, who shows no partiality and accepts no bribes. ¹⁸He defends the cause of the fatherless and the widow, and loves the alien, giving him food and clothing. ¹⁹And you are to love those who are aliens, for you yourselves were aliens in Egypt. ²⁰Fear the LORD your God and serve him. Hold fast to him and take your oaths in his name. ²¹He is your praise; he is your God, who performed for you those great and awesome wonders you saw with your own eyes. ²²Your forefathers who went down into Egypt were seventy in all, and now the LORD your God has made you as numerous as the stars in the sky.

challenge notes

To: **my_son**

heavenly_father: think about times when you've been rejected, ignored or made fun of—when you've felt like a loser or an outsider. let the embarrassment and hurt you felt be your motivation to never let that happen to someone else. always be quick to stand up for people and make them feel welcome so they never have to go through what you experienced.

DT 10:19

LOVE AND OBEY THE LORD

11 Love the LORD your God and keep his requirements, his decrees, his laws and his commands always. ²Remember today that your children were not the ones who saw and experienced the discipline of the LORD your God: his majesty, his mighty hand, his outstretched arm; ³the signs he performed and the things he did in the heart of Egypt, both to Pharaoh king of Egypt and to his whole country; ⁴what he did to the Egyptian army, to its horses and chariots, how he overwhelmed them with the waters of the Red Seaᵃ as they were pursuing you, and how the LORD brought lasting ruin

---

ᵃ 4 Hebrew *Yam Suph*; that is, Sea of Reeds

battlelines

» True Lies (Sex)

Q: Hey, Brad . . . Brad . . . oh, Bradley . . .
A: Huh? What? Oh, hey. What's up? Sorry, I wasn't listening.

Q: Yeah, I noticed. You were zoning out there. You ok?
A: Me? Yeah, I'm fine. I was just . . . well, thinking about a conversation I just had with a friend.

Q: Who was it?
A: Oh, you probably don't know him. His name is Keith.

Q: Keith? Oh, as in Mr. Big-time Chick Magnet, Keith?
A: Yeah, that's the guy. Anyway, we were playing ball during lunch today, and he started telling me about how he hooked up with not one, but two different girls this past weekend.

Q: Uh-oh. That sounds like trouble.
A: Yeah, it was. And you didn't even hear the details. Even if you had, you wouldn't believe the stuff he said. Either he's the world's greatest liar, or he's seen way too many porn videos.

Q: So how did you respond when he was telling you all this stuff?
A: Well, not too well. I mean, I didn't exactly stop him from telling me about it. I know what you're going to say: "You shouldn't fill your head with those kinds of thoughts." That's just what my dad would say too. But I don't get why I should miss out on that kind of action just because I'm a Christian. I bet if I wanted to, I could hook up with some of the girls I know pretty easily.

» A Few Reminders

Whether he knows it or not, Brad is falling for the same lie that tripped up Adam and Eve in Eden (see Genesis 3:1–7): God isn't good. He's withholding something wonderful from us. So forget his rules! Let's do what we want!

Just remember what that kind of thinking caused humanity's first couple—a lifetime of fear, guilt, shame, alienation and trouble. The question we have to ask ourselves is, Is such a miserable reality worth a few fleeting moments of exhilaration?

Here's something else to think about. If God cares about our desires—and the fact that he created sex should be proof enough that he does—then maybe his rules are in place for good reason. Maybe his rules exist to protect us and to help us enjoy God's creation as he intended. And perhaps the courageous, trusting souls who stay within God's boundaries will find something a million times better than what Keith is getting (see Deuteronomy 11:27; 28:2).

Read more about sex and abstinence at www.RevolutionBible.com.

on them. ⁵It was not your children who saw what he did for you in the desert until you arrived at this place, ⁶and what he did to Dathan and Abiram, sons of Eliab the Reubenite, when the earth opened its mouth right in the middle of all Israel and swallowed them up with their households, their tents and every living thing that belonged to them. ⁷But it was your own eyes that saw all these great things the LORD has done.

⁸Observe therefore all the commands I am giving you today, so that you may have the strength to go in and take over the land that you are crossing the Jordan to possess, ⁹and so that you may live long in the land that the LORD swore to your forefathers to give to them and their descendants, a land flowing with milk and honey. ¹⁰The land you are entering to take over is not like the land of Egypt, from which you have come, where you planted your seed and irrigated it by foot as in a vegetable garden. ¹¹But the land you are crossing the Jordan to take possession of is a land of mountains and valleys that drinks rain from heaven. ¹²It is a land the LORD your God cares for; the eyes of the LORD your God are continually on it from the beginning of the year to its end.

¹³So if you faithfully obey the commands I am giving you today—to love the LORD your God and to serve him with all your heart and with all your soul— ¹⁴then I will send rain on your land in its season, both autumn and spring rains, so that you may gather in your grain, new wine and oil. ¹⁵I will provide grass in the fields for your cattle, and you will eat and be satisfied.

¹⁶Be careful, or you will be enticed to turn away and worship other gods and bow down to them. ¹⁷Then the LORD's anger will burn against you, and he will shut the heavens so that it will not rain and the ground will yield no produce, and you will soon perish from the good land the LORD is giving you. ¹⁸Fix these words of mine in your hearts and minds; tie them as symbols on your hands and bind them on your foreheads. ¹⁹Teach them to your children, talking about them when you sit at home and when you walk along the road, when you lie down and when you get up. ²⁰Write them on the doorframes of your houses and on your gates, ²¹so that your days and the days of your children may be many in the land that the LORD swore to give your forefathers, as many as the days that the heavens are above the earth.

²²If you carefully observe all these commands I am giving you to follow—to love the LORD your God, to walk in all his ways and to hold fast to him— ²³then the LORD will drive out all these nations before you, and you will dispossess nations larger and stronger than you. ²⁴Every place where you set your foot will be yours: Your territory will extend from the desert to Lebanon, and from the Euphrates River to the western sea.ᵃ ²⁵No man will be able to stand against you. The LORD your God, as he promised you, will put the terror and fear of you on the whole land, wherever you go.

²⁶See, I am setting before you today a blessing and a curse— ²⁷the blessing if you obey the commands of the LORD your God that I am giving you today; ²⁸the curse if you disobey the commands of the LORD your God and turn from the way that I command you today by following other gods, which you have not known. ²⁹When the LORD your God has brought you into the land you are entering to possess, you are to proclaim on Mount Gerizim the blessings, and on Mount Ebal the curses. ³⁰As you know, these mountains are across the Jordan, west of the road,ᵇ toward the setting sun, near the great trees of Moreh, in the territory of those Canaanites living in the Arabah in the vicinity of Gilgal. ³¹You are about to cross the Jordan to enter and take possession of the land the LORD your God is giving you. When you have taken it over and are living there, ³²be sure that you obey all the decrees and laws I am setting before you today.

NOW OR NEVER

DT 11:18

How many Bible passages can you recite from memory? How many songs on the radio can you sing along with from memory? Why is the second number higher than the first?

THE ONE PLACE OF WORSHIP

12

These are the decrees and laws you must be careful to follow in the land that the LORD, the God of your fathers, has given you to possess—as long as you live in the land. ²Destroy completely all the places on the high mountains and on the hills and under every spread-

---

ᵃ 24 That is, the Mediterranean   ᵇ 30 Or Jordan, westward

ing tree where the nations you are dispossessing worship their gods. ³Break down their altars, smash their sacred stones and burn their Asherah poles in the fire; cut down the idols of their gods and wipe out their names from those places.

⁴You must not worship the LORD your God in their way. ⁵But you are to seek the place the LORD your God will choose from among all your tribes to put his Name there for his dwelling. To that place you must go; ⁶there bring your burnt offerings and sacrifices, your tithes and special gifts, what you have vowed to give and your freewill offerings, and the firstborn of your herds and flocks. ⁷There, in the presence of the LORD your God, you and your families shall eat and shall rejoice in everything you have put your hand to, because the LORD your God has blessed you.

⁸You are not to do as we do here today, everyone as he sees fit, ⁹since you have not yet reached the resting place and the inheritance the LORD your God is giving you. ¹⁰But you will cross the Jordan and settle in the land the LORD your God is giving you as an inheritance, and he will give you rest from all your enemies around you so that you will live in safety. ¹¹Then to the place the LORD your God will choose as a dwelling for his Name—there you are to bring everything I command you: your burnt offerings and sacrifices, your tithes and special gifts, and all the choice possessions you have vowed to the LORD. ¹²And there rejoice before the LORD your God, you, your sons and daughters, your menservants and maidservants, and the Levites from your towns, who have no allotment or inheritance of their own. ¹³Be careful not to sacrifice your burnt offerings anywhere you please. ¹⁴Offer them only at the place the LORD will choose in one of your tribes, and there observe everything I command you.

¹⁵Nevertheless, you may slaughter your animals in any of your towns and eat as much of the meat as you want, as if it were gazelle or deer, according to the blessing the LORD your God gives you. Both the ceremonially unclean and the clean may eat it. ¹⁶But you must not eat the blood; pour it out on the ground like water. ¹⁷You must not eat in your own towns the tithe of your grain and new wine and oil, or the firstborn of your herds and flocks, or whatever you have vowed to give, or your freewill offerings or special gifts. ¹⁸Instead, you are to eat them in the presence of the LORD your God at the place the LORD your God will choose—you, your sons and daughters, your menservants and maidservants, and the Levites from your towns—and you are to rejoice before the LORD your God in everything you put your hand to. ¹⁹Be careful not to neglect the Levites as long as you live in your land.

²⁰When the LORD your God has enlarged your territory as he promised you, and you crave meat and say, "I would like some meat," then you may eat as much of it as you want. ²¹If the place where the LORD your God chooses to put his Name is too far away from you, you may slaughter animals from the herds and flocks the LORD has given you, as I have commanded you, and in your own towns you may eat as much of them as you want. ²²Eat them as you would gazelle or deer. Both the ceremonially unclean and the clean may eat. ²³But be sure you do not eat the blood, because the blood is the life, and you must not eat the life with the meat. ²⁴You must not eat the blood; pour it out on the ground like water. ²⁵Do not eat it, so that it may go well with you and your children after you, because you will be doing what is right in the eyes of the LORD.

²⁶But take your consecrated things and whatever you have vowed to give, and go to the place the LORD will choose. ²⁷Present your burnt offerings on the altar of the LORD your God, both the meat and the blood. The blood of your sacrifices must be poured beside the altar of the LORD your God, but you may eat the meat. ²⁸Be careful to obey all these regulations I am giving you, so that it may always go well with you and your children after you, because you will be doing what is good and right in the eyes of the LORD your God.

Worshiping God

What do you look for in your ideal place of worship? What makes your church meaningful to you? What changes would you like to see happen in your church? These are all important questions, but none of them is as important as this one: What do *you* bring to the table, as far as your church is concerned? Remember, worship isn't a spectator sport; it's a participation event. If you're not using your talents and abilities in your church and youth ministry, you're robbing people in your church of something pretty good.

²⁹The LORD your God will cut off before you the nations you are about to invade and dispossess. But when you have driven them out and settled in their land, ³⁰and after they have been destroyed before you, be careful not to be ensnared by inquiring about their gods, saying, "How do these nations serve their gods? We will do the same." ³¹You must not worship the LORD your God in their way, because in worshiping their gods, they do all kinds of detestable things the LORD hates. They even burn their sons and daughters in the fire as sacrifices to their gods.

³²See that you do all I command you; do not add to it or take away from it.

NOW OR NEVER
DT 12:32

God doesn't give us the freedom to choose which Biblical commandments we'll follow or which of his moral instructions we'll apply to our lives. It's all or nothing.

WORSHIPING OTHER GODS

13 If a prophet, or one who foretells by dreams, appears among you and announces to you a miraculous sign or wonder, ²and if the sign or wonder of which he has spoken takes place, and he says, "Let us follow other gods" (gods you have not known) "and let us worship them," ³you must not listen to the words of that prophet or dreamer. The LORD your God is testing you to find out whether you love him with all your heart and with all your soul. ⁴It is the LORD your God you must follow, and him you must revere. Keep his commands and obey him; serve him and hold fast to him. ⁵That prophet or dreamer must be put to death, because he preached rebellion against the LORD your God, who brought you out of Egypt and redeemed you from the land of slavery; he has tried to turn you from the way the LORD your God commanded you to follow. You must purge the evil from among you.

⁶If your very own brother, or your son or daughter, or the wife you love, or your closest friend secretly entices you, saying, "Let us go and worship other gods" (gods that neither you nor your fathers have known, ⁷gods of the peoples around you, whether near or far, from one end of the land to the other), ⁸do not yield to him or listen to him. Show him no pity. Do not spare him or shield him. ⁹You must certainly put him to death. Your hand must be the first in putting him to death, and then the hands of all the people. ¹⁰Stone him to death, because he tried to turn you away from the LORD your God, who brought you out of Egypt, out of the land of slavery. ¹¹Then all Israel will hear and be afraid, and no one among you will do such an evil thing again.

¹²If you hear it said about one of the towns the LORD your God is giving you to live in ¹³that wicked men have arisen among you and have led the people of their town astray, saying, "Let us go and worship other gods" (gods you have not known), ¹⁴then you must inquire, probe and investigate it thoroughly. And if it is true and it has been proved that this detestable thing has been done among you, ¹⁵you must certainly put to the sword all who live in that town. Destroy it

NOW OR NEVER
DT 13:6-8

If your friends get in the way of your relationship with God, it's time to find new friends who will instead encourage you in your faith!

completely,ᵃ both its people and its livestock. ¹⁶Gather all the plunder of the town into the middle of the public square and completely burn the town and all its plunder as a whole burnt offering to the LORD your God. It is to remain a ruin forever, never to be rebuilt. ¹⁷None of those condemned thingsᵃ shall be found in your hands, so that the LORD will turn from his fierce anger; he will show you mercy, have compassion on you, and increase your numbers, as he promised on oath to your forefathers, ¹⁸because you obey the LORD your God, keeping all his commands that I am giving you today and doing what is right in his eyes.

ᵃ *15,17* The Hebrew term refers to the irrevocable giving over of things or persons to the LORD, often by totally destroying them.

CLEAN AND UNCLEAN FOOD

14 You are the children of the LORD your God. Do not cut yourselves or shave the front of your heads for the dead, ²for you are a people holy to the LORD your God. Out of all the peoples on the face of the earth, the LORD has chosen you to be his treasured possession.

³Do not eat any detestable thing. ⁴These are the animals you may eat: the ox, the sheep, the goat, ⁵the deer, the gazelle, the roe deer, the wild goat, the ibex, the antelope and the mountain sheep.[a] ⁶You may eat any animal that has a split hoof divided in two and that chews the cud. ⁷However, of those that chew the cud or that have a split hoof completely divided you may not eat the camel, the rabbit or the coney.[b] Although they chew the cud, they do not have a split hoof; they are ceremonially unclean for you. ⁸The pig is also unclean; although it has a split hoof, it does not chew the cud. You are not to eat their meat or touch their carcasses.

⁹Of all the creatures living in the water, you may eat any that has fins and scales. ¹⁰But anything that does not have fins and scales you may not eat; for you it is unclean.

¹¹You may eat any clean bird. ¹²But these you may not eat: the eagle, the vulture, the black vulture, ¹³the red kite, the black kite, any kind of falcon, ¹⁴any kind of raven, ¹⁵the horned owl, the screech owl, the gull, any kind of hawk, ¹⁶the little owl, the great owl, the white owl, ¹⁷the desert owl, the osprey, the cormorant, ¹⁸the stork, any kind of heron, the hoopoe and the bat.

¹⁹All flying insects that swarm are unclean to you; do not eat them. ²⁰But any winged creature that is clean you may eat.

²¹Do not eat anything you find already dead. You may give it to an alien living in any of your towns, and he may eat it, or you may sell it to a foreigner. But you are a people holy to the LORD your God.

Do not cook a young goat in its mother's milk.

TITHES

²²Be sure to set aside a tenth of all that your fields produce each year. ²³Eat the tithe of your grain, new wine and oil, and the firstborn of your herds and flocks in the presence of the LORD your God at the place he will choose as a dwelling for his Name, so that you may learn to revere the LORD your God always. ²⁴But if that place is too distant and you have been blessed by the LORD your God and cannot carry your tithe (because the place where the LORD will choose to put his Name is so far away), ²⁵then exchange your tithe for silver, and take the silver with you and go to the place the LORD your God will choose. ²⁶Use the silver to buy whatever you like: cattle, sheep, wine or other fermented drink, or anything you wish. Then you and your household shall eat there in the presence of the LORD your God and rejoice. ²⁷And do not neglect the Levites living in your towns, for they have no allotment or inheritance of their own.

²⁸At the end of every three years, bring all the tithes of that year's produce and store it in your towns, ²⁹so that the Levites (who have no allotment or inheritance of their own) and the aliens, the fatherless and the widows who live in your towns may come and eat and be satisfied, and so that the LORD your God may bless you in all the work of your hands.

NOW OR NEVER
DT 14:22

If you believe that everything you have is a gift from God, how lame—not to mention selfish—is it not to give at least part of what you have back to him by giving your money to the church and to God's work around the world?

THE YEAR FOR CANCELING DEBTS

15 At the end of every seven years you must cancel debts. ²This is how it is to be done: Every creditor shall cancel the loan he has made to his fellow Israelite. He shall not require payment from his fellow Israelite or brother, because the LORD's time for canceling debts has been proclaimed. ³You may require payment from a foreigner, but you must cancel any debt your brother owes you. ⁴However, there should be no poor among you, for in the land the LORD your God is giving you to possess as your inheritance, he will richly bless you, ⁵if only you fully obey the LORD your God and are careful to follow all these commands I am giving you today. ⁶For the LORD your God will

---

[a] 5 The precise identification of some of the birds and animals in this chapter is uncertain.   [b] 7 That is, the hyrax or rock badger

bless you as he has promised, and you will lend to many nations but will borrow from none. You will rule over many nations but none will rule over you.

» live the adventure » Dt 15:7-11

Helping the Needy

What difference could you make in the life of a needy person? If you made up your mind to get involved in the life of someone who needed you, what could you do? Could you change the life of a younger kid (maybe even a sibling) in need of a mentor? Could you be an answer to prayer for a mentally challenged or wheelchair-bound kid in your school? Could you supply enough money to buy a month's worth of food and medicine for an AIDS orphan in East Africa? The possibilities are endless, and there are people all over who need what you can offer.

[7]If there is a poor man among your brothers in any of the towns of the land that the LORD your God is giving you, do not be hardhearted or tightfisted toward your poor brother. [8]Rather be openhanded and freely lend him whatever he needs. [9]Be careful not to harbor this wicked thought: "The seventh year, the year for canceling debts, is near," so that you do not show ill will toward your needy brother and give him nothing. He may then appeal to the LORD against you, and you will be found guilty of sin. [10]Give generously to him and do so without a grudging heart; then because of this the LORD your God will bless you in all your work and in everything you put your hand to. [11]There will always be poor people in the land. Therefore I command you to be openhanded toward your brothers and toward the poor and needy in your land.

FREEING SERVANTS

[12]If a fellow Hebrew, a man or a woman, sells himself to you and serves you six years, in the seventh year you must let him go free. [13]And when you release him, do not send him away empty-handed. [14]Supply him liberally from your flock, your threshing floor and your winepress. Give to him as the LORD your God has blessed you. [15]Remember that you were slaves in Egypt and the LORD your God redeemed you. That is why I give you this command today.

[16]But if your servant says to you, "I do not want to leave you," because he loves you and your family and is well off with you, [17]then take an awl and push it through his ear lobe into the door, and he will become your servant for life. Do the same for your maidservant.

[18]Do not consider it a hardship to set your servant free, because his service to you these six years has been worth twice as much as that of a hired hand. And the LORD your God will bless you in everything you do.

THE FIRSTBORN ANIMALS

[19]Set apart for the LORD your God every firstborn male of your herds and flocks. Do not put the firstborn of your oxen to work, and do not shear the firstborn of your sheep. [20]Each year you and your family are to eat them in the presence of the LORD your God at the place he will choose. [21]If an animal has a defect, is lame or blind, or has any serious flaw, you must not sacrifice it to the LORD your God. [22]You are to eat it in your own towns. Both the ceremonially unclean and the clean may eat it, as if it were gazelle or deer. [23]But you must not eat the blood; pour it out on the ground like water.

PASSOVER

16 Observe the month of Abib and celebrate the Passover of the LORD your God, because in the month of Abib he brought you out of Egypt by night. [2]Sacrifice as the Passover to the LORD your God an animal from your flock or herd at the place the LORD will choose as a dwelling for his Name. [3]Do not eat it with bread made with yeast, but for seven days eat unleavened bread, the bread of affliction, because you left Egypt in haste—so that all the days of your life you may remember the time of your departure from Egypt. [4]Let no yeast be found in your possession in all your land for seven days. Do not let any of the meat you sacrifice on the evening of the first day remain until morning.

[5]You must not sacrifice the Passover in any town the LORD your God gives you [6]except in the place he will choose as a dwelling for his Name. There you must sacrifice the Passover in the evening, when

battlelines

» Fitting In (Friendship)

Q: It's been almost two months now. What do you think of your new school?
A: I think it's hard.

Q: What, the classes?
A: Well, yeah, a little bit. But mainly I think it's hard *socially*.

Q: Having trouble fitting in?
A: Sort of.

Q: What's the problem?
A: Part of it is where I live. We're renting a house east of town. It's not really in a neighborhood, so there's no one next door or down the street to hang out with.

Q: What about kids from church?
A: I see some of them in the halls at school, but I don't have any classes with them. Besides, I haven't really clicked with any of them yet, if you know what I mean.

Q: Extracurricular activities?
A: I'm no good at sports, and I don't play any band instruments.

Q: What do you do at lunch?
A: I bring my lunch, so I just kind of sit in the courtyard.

Q: By yourself?
A: Usually. A couple of times I've gone up to a group of guys and sat near them, but they just kind of ignore me. They're not like, "Get out of here!" or anything. They just don't really include me in the conversation. It's like they already have their little group, and I'm just crashing the party.

Q: That's gotta be tough.
A: I guess it could be worse. They could be dragging me into the bathroom to give me a swirlie or something. But, yeah, it's hard.

Q: No clubs or anything else you could participate in?
A: I don't think so. At least, none that I'm aware of. But my youth group is going on a retreat this weekend and some of the kids from school will be there. Maybe something good will come out of that.

» Finding Friends

Aden's situation is a good reminder for us to be sensitive to the plight of new people. Keep your eyes open for those on the fringes who need to be included. Make it your goal to welcome newcomers and make them a part of your group (see Galatians 6:10). If you have any pull with your group of friends, use that influence to encourage them to make new people feel included.

And if you're in Aden's situation right now, read Psalm 25, noting especially David's heartfelt plea in verse 16: "Turn to me and be gracious to me, for I am lonely and afflicted." Even mighty kings like David have experienced loneliness. Above all, remember that God cares. Ask him to meet your need in a unique way and to bring the right people into your life.

Read more about friendship at www.RevolutionBible.com.

the sun goes down, on the anniversary[a] of your departure from Egypt. [7]Roast it and eat it at the place the LORD your God will choose. Then in the morning return to your tents. [8]For six days eat unleavened bread and on the seventh day hold an assembly to the LORD your God and do no work.

FEAST OF WEEKS

[9]Count off seven weeks from the time you begin to put the sickle to the standing grain. [10]Then celebrate the Feast of Weeks to the LORD your God by giving a freewill offering in proportion to the blessings the LORD your God has given you. [11]And rejoice before the LORD your God at the place he will choose as a dwelling for his Name—you, your sons and daughters, your menservants and maidservants, the Levites in your towns, and the aliens, the fatherless and the widows living among you. [12]Remember that you were slaves in Egypt, and follow carefully these decrees.

FEAST OF TABERNACLES

[13]Celebrate the Feast of Tabernacles for seven days after you have gathered the produce of your threshing floor and your winepress. [14]Be joyful at your Feast—you, your sons and daughters, your menservants and maidservants, and the Levites, the aliens, the fatherless and the widows who live in your towns. [15]For seven days celebrate the Feast to the LORD your God at the place the LORD will choose. For the LORD your God will bless you in all your harvest and in all the work of your hands, and your joy will be complete.

[16]Three times a year all your men must appear before the LORD your God at the place he will choose: at the Feast of Unleavened Bread, the Feast of Weeks and the Feast of Tabernacles. No man should appear before the LORD empty-handed: [17]Each of you must bring a gift in proportion to the way the LORD your God has blessed you.

JUDGES

[18]Appoint judges and officials for each of your tribes in every town the LORD your God is giving you, and they shall judge the people fairly. [19]Do not pervert justice or show partiality. Do not accept a bribe, for a bribe blinds the eyes of the wise and twists the words of the righteous. [20]Follow justice and justice alone, so that you may live and possess the land the LORD your God is giving you.

WORSHIPING OTHER GODS

[21]Do not set up any wooden Asherah pole[b] beside the altar you build to the LORD your God, [22]and do not erect a sacred stone, for these the LORD your God hates.

17 Do not sacrifice to the LORD your God an ox or a sheep that has any defect or flaw in it, for that would be detestable to him.

[2]If a man or woman living among you in one of the towns the LORD gives you is found doing evil in the eyes of the LORD your God in violation of his covenant, [3]and contrary to my command has worshiped other gods, bowing down to them or to the sun or the moon or the stars of the sky, [4]and this has been brought to your attention, then you must investigate it thoroughly. If it is true and it has been proved that this detestable thing has been done in Israel, [5]take the man or woman who has done this evil deed to your city gate and stone that person to death. [6]On the testimony of two or three witnesses a man shall be put to death, but no one shall be put to death on the testimony of only one witness. [7]The hands of the witnesses must be the first in putting him to death, and then the hands of all the people. You must purge the evil from among you.

LAW COURTS

[8]If cases come before your courts that are too difficult for you to judge—whether bloodshed, lawsuits

NOW OR NEVER
DT 17:1

God doesn't want our leftovers. Our personal time with him, which would include prayer and Bible study, should be the number one priority on our daily schedule. Everything else should have to be worked around God, not the other way around.

[a] 6 Or *down, at the time of day*   [b] 21 Or *Do not plant any tree dedicated to Asherah*

or assaults—take them to the place the LORD your God will choose. ⁹Go to the priests, who are Levites, and to the judge who is in office at that time. Inquire of them and they will give you the verdict. ¹⁰You must act according to the decisions they give you at the place the LORD will choose. Be careful to do everything they direct you to do. ¹¹Act according to the law they teach you and the decisions they give you. Do not turn aside from what they tell you, to the right or to the left. ¹²The man who shows contempt for the judge or for the priest who stands ministering there to the LORD your God must be put to death. You must purge the evil from Israel. ¹³All the people will hear and be afraid, and will not be contemptuous again.

THE KING

¹⁴When you enter the land the LORD your God is giving you and have taken possession of it and settled in it, and you say, "Let us set a king over us like all the nations around us," ¹⁵be sure to appoint over you the king the LORD your God chooses. He must be from among your own brothers. Do not place a foreigner over you, one who is not a brother Israelite. ¹⁶The king, moreover, must not acquire great numbers of horses for himself or make the people return to Egypt to get more of them, for the LORD has told you, "You are not to go back that way again." ¹⁷He must not take many wives, or his heart will be led astray. He must not accumulate large amounts of silver and gold.

¹⁸When he takes the throne of his kingdom, he is to write for himself on a scroll a copy of this law, taken from that of the priests, who are Levites. ¹⁹It is to be with him, and he is to read it all the days of his life so that he may learn to revere the LORD his God and follow carefully all the words of this law and these decrees ²⁰and not consider himself better than his brothers and turn from the law to the right or to the left. Then he and his descendants will reign a long time over his kingdom in Israel.

OFFERINGS FOR PRIESTS AND LEVITES

18 The priests, who are Levites—indeed the whole tribe of Levi—are to have no allotment or inheritance with Israel. They shall live on the offerings made to the LORD by fire, for that is their inheritance. ²They shall have no inheritance among their brothers; the LORD is their inheritance, as he promised them.

³This is the share due the priests from the people who sacrifice a bull or a sheep: the shoulder, the jowls and the inner parts. ⁴You are to give them the firstfruits of your grain, new wine and oil, and the first wool from the shearing of your sheep, ⁵for the LORD your God has chosen them and their descendants out of all your tribes to stand and minister in the LORD's name always.

⁶If a Levite moves from one of your towns anywhere in Israel where he is living, and comes in all earnestness to the place the LORD will choose, ⁷he may minister in the name of the LORD his God like all his fellow Levites who serve there in the presence of the LORD. ⁸He is to share equally in their benefits, even though he has received money from the sale of family possessions.

DETESTABLE PRACTICES

⁹When you enter the land the LORD your God is giving you, do not learn to imitate the detestable ways of the nations there. ¹⁰Let no one be found among you who sacrifices his son or daughter in ª the fire, who practices divination or sorcery, interprets omens, engages in witchcraft, ¹¹or casts spells, or who is a medium or spiritist or who consults the dead. ¹²Anyone who does these things is detestable to the LORD, and because of these detestable practices the LORD your God will drive out those nations before you. ¹³You must be blameless before the LORD your God.

NOW OR NEVER
DT 18:9–12

Everyone gets tempted to walk on the wild side every once in a while, because it always seems like that's where the real fun is. But no one ever tells you what the cost of that fun might be and just how fast the high wears off.

THE PROPHET

¹⁴The nations you will dispossess listen to those who practice sorcery or divination. But as for you, the LORD your God has not permitted you to do so. ¹⁵The LORD your God will raise up for you a proph-

---

ª 10 Or who makes his son or daughter pass through

et like me from among your own brothers. You must listen to him. ¹⁶For this is what you asked of the LORD your God at Horeb on the day of the assembly when you said, "Let us not hear the voice of the LORD our God nor see this great fire anymore, or we will die."

¹⁷The LORD said to me: "What they say is good. ¹⁸I will raise up for them a prophet like you from among their brothers; I will put my words in his mouth, and he will tell them everything I command him. ¹⁹If anyone does not listen to my words that the prophet speaks in my name, I myself will call him to account. ²⁰But a prophet who presumes to speak in my name anything I have not commanded him to say, or a prophet who speaks in the name of other gods, must be put to death."

²¹You may say to yourselves, "How can we know when a message has not been spoken by the LORD?" ²²If what a prophet proclaims in the name of the LORD does not take place or come true, that is a message the LORD has not spoken. That prophet has spoken presumptuously. Do not be afraid of him.

CITIES OF REFUGE

19 When the LORD your God has destroyed the nations whose land he is giving you, and when you have driven them out and settled in their towns and houses, ²then set aside for yourselves three cities centrally located in the land the LORD your God is giving you to possess. ³Build roads to them and divide into three parts the land the LORD your God is giving you as an inheritance, so that anyone who kills a man may flee there.

⁴This is the rule concerning the man who kills another and flees there to save his life—one who kills his neighbor unintentionally, without malice aforethought. ⁵For instance, a man may go into the forest with his neighbor to cut wood, and as he swings his ax to fell a tree, the head may fly off and hit his neighbor and kill him. That man may flee to one of these cities and save his life. ⁶Otherwise, the avenger of blood might pursue him in a rage, overtake him if the distance is too great, and kill him even though he is not deserving of death, since he did it to his neighbor without malice aforethought. ⁷This is why I command you to set aside for yourselves three cities.

⁸If the LORD your God enlarges your territory, as he promised on oath to your forefathers, and gives you the whole land he promised them, ⁹because you carefully follow all these laws I command you today—to love the LORD your God and to walk always in his ways—then you are to set aside three more cities. ¹⁰Do this so that innocent blood will not be shed in your land, which the LORD your God is giving you as your inheritance, and so that you will not be guilty of bloodshed.

¹¹But if a man hates his neighbor and lies in wait for him, assaults and kills him, and then flees to one of these cities, ¹²the elders of his town shall send for him, bring him back from the city, and hand him over to the avenger of blood to die. ¹³Show him no pity. You must purge from Israel the guilt of shedding innocent blood, so that it may go well with you.

¹⁴Do not move your neighbor's boundary stone set up by your predecessors in the inheritance you receive in the land the LORD your God is giving you to possess.

WITNESSES

¹⁵One witness is not enough to convict a man accused of any crime or offense he may have committed. A matter must be established by the testimony of two or three witnesses.

¹⁶If a malicious witness takes the stand to accuse a man of a crime, ¹⁷the two men involved in the dispute must stand in the presence of the LORD before the priests and the judges who are in office at the time. ¹⁸The judges must make a thorough investigation, and if the witness proves to be a liar, giving false testimony against his brother, ¹⁹then do to him as he intended to do to his brother. You must purge the evil from among you. ²⁰The rest of the people will hear of this and be afraid, and never again will such an evil thing be done among you. ²¹Show no pity: life for life, eye for eye, tooth for tooth, hand for hand, foot for foot.

GOING TO WAR

20 When you go to war against your enemies and see horses and chariots and an army greater than yours, do not be afraid of them, because the LORD your God, who brought you up out of Egypt, will be with you. ²When you are about to go into battle, the priest shall come forward and address the army. ³He shall say: "Hear, O Israel, today you are going into battle against your enemies. Do not be fainthearted or afraid; do not be terrified or give way to panic before them. ⁴For the Lᴏʀᴅ your God is the one who goes with you to fight for you against your enemies to give you victory."

⁵The officers shall say to the army: "Has anyone built a new house and not dedicated it? Let him go home, or he may die in battle and someone else may dedicate it. ⁶Has anyone planted a vineyard and not begun to enjoy it? Let him go home, or he may die in battle and someone else enjoy it. ⁷Has anyone become pledged to a woman and not married her? Let him go home, or he may die in battle and someone else marry her." ⁸Then the officers shall add, "Is any man afraid or fainthearted? Let him go home so that his brothers will not become disheartened too." ⁹When the officers have finished speaking to the army, they shall appoint commanders over it.

¹⁰When you march up to attack a city, make its people an offer of peace. ¹¹If they accept and open their gates, all the people in it shall be subject to forced labor and shall work for you. ¹²If they refuse to make peace and they engage you in battle, lay siege to that city. ¹³When the Lᴏʀᴅ your God delivers it into your hand, put to the sword all the men in it. ¹⁴As for the women, the children, the livestock and everything else in the city, you may take these as plunder for yourselves. And you may use the plunder the Lᴏʀᴅ your God gives you from your enemies. ¹⁵This is how you are to treat all the cities that are at a distance from you and do not belong to the nations nearby.

¹⁶However, in the cities of the nations the Lᴏʀᴅ your God is giving you as an inheritance, do not leave alive anything that breathes. ¹⁷Completely destroy[a] them—the Hittites, Amorites, Canaanites, Perizzites, Hivites and Jebusites—as the Lᴏʀᴅ your God has commanded you. ¹⁸Otherwise, they will teach you to follow all the detestable things they do in worshiping their gods, and you will sin against the Lᴏʀᴅ your God.

¹⁹When you lay siege to a city for a long time, fighting against it to capture it, do not destroy its trees by putting an ax to them, because you can eat their fruit. Do not cut them down. Are the trees of the field people, that you should besiege them?[b] ²⁰However, you may cut down trees that you know are not fruit trees and use them to build siege works until the city at war with you falls.

ATONEMENT FOR AN UNSOLVED MURDER

21 If a man is found slain, lying in a field in the land the Lᴏʀᴅ your God is giving you to possess, and it is not known who killed him, ²your elders and judges shall go out and measure the distance from the body to the neighboring towns. ³Then the elders of the town nearest the body shall take a heifer that has never been worked and has never worn a yoke ⁴and lead her down to a valley that has not been plowed or planted and where there is a flowing stream. There in the valley they are to break the heifer's neck. ⁵The priests, the sons of Levi, shall step forward, for the Lᴏʀᴅ your God has chosen them to minister and to pronounce blessings in the name of the Lᴏʀᴅ and to decide all cases of dispute and assault. ⁶Then all the elders of the town nearest the body shall wash their hands over the heifer whose neck was broken in the valley, ⁷and they shall declare: "Our hands did not shed this blood, nor did our eyes see it done. ⁸Accept this atonement for your people Israel, whom you have redeemed, O Lᴏʀᴅ, and do not hold your people guilty of the blood of an innocent man." And the bloodshed will be atoned for. ⁹So you will purge from yourselves the guilt of shedding innocent blood, since you have done what is right in the eyes of the Lᴏʀᴅ.

MARRYING A CAPTIVE WOMAN

¹⁰When you go to war against your enemies and the Lᴏʀᴅ your God delivers them into your hands and you take captives, ¹¹if you notice among the captives a beautiful woman and are attracted to her, you may take her as your wife. ¹²Bring her into your home and have her shave her head, trim her nails ¹³and put aside the clothes she was wearing when captured. After she has lived in your house and mourned her father and mother for a full month, then you may go to her and be her husband and she shall be your wife. ¹⁴If you are not pleased with her, let her go wherever she wishes. You must not sell her or treat her as a slave, since you have dishonored her.

THE RIGHT OF THE FIRSTBORN

¹⁵If a man has two wives, and he loves one but not the other, and both bear him sons but the firstborn is the son of the wife he does not love, ¹⁶when he wills his property to his sons, he must not give

---

[a] 17 The Hebrew term refers to the irrevocable giving over of things or persons to the Lᴏʀᴅ, often by totally destroying them.
[b] 19 Or down to use in the siege, for the fruit trees are for the benefit of man.

the rights of the firstborn to the son of the wife he loves in preference to his actual firstborn, the son of the wife he does not love. [17]He must acknowledge the son of his unloved wife as the firstborn by giving him a double share of all he has. That son is the first sign of his father's strength. The right of the firstborn belongs to him.

A REBELLIOUS SON

[18]If a man has a stubborn and rebellious son who does not obey his father and mother and will not listen to them when they discipline him, [19]his father and mother shall take hold of him and bring him to the elders at the gate of his town. [20]They shall say to the elders, "This son of ours is stubborn and rebellious. He will not obey us. He is a profligate and a drunkard." [21]Then all the men of his town shall stone him to death. You must purge the evil from among you. All Israel will hear of it and be afraid.

VARIOUS LAWS

[22]If a man guilty of a capital offense is put to death and his body is hung on a tree, [23]you must not leave his body on the tree overnight. Be sure to bury him that same day, because anyone who is hung on a tree is under God's curse. You must not desecrate the land the LORD your God is giving you as an inheritance.

22

If you see your brother's ox or sheep straying, do not ignore it but be sure to take it back to him. [2]If the brother does not live near you or if you do not know who he is, take it home with you and keep it until he comes looking for it. Then give it back to him. [3]Do the same if you find your brother's donkey or his cloak or anything he loses. Do not ignore it.

[4]If you see your brother's donkey or his ox fallen on the road, do not ignore it. Help him get it to its feet.

[5]A woman must not wear men's clothing, nor a man wear women's clothing, for the LORD your God detests anyone who does this.

[6]If you come across a bird's nest beside the road, either in a tree or on the ground, and the mother is sitting on the young or on the eggs, do not take the mother with the young. [7]You may take the young, but be sure to let the mother go, so that it may go well with you and you may have a long life.

NOW OR NEVER
DT 22:1–4

Do your neighbors trust you? Have you ever done anything to earn or lose their trust? What can you do to become the kind of neighbor people would like to have in their lives?

[8]When you build a new house, make a parapet around your roof so that you may not bring the guilt of bloodshed on your house if someone falls from the roof.

[9]Do not plant two kinds of seed in your vineyard; if you do, not only the crops you plant but also the fruit of the vineyard will be defiled. [a]

[10]Do not plow with an ox and a donkey yoked together.

[11]Do not wear clothes of wool and linen woven together.

[12]Make tassels on the four corners of the cloak you wear.

MARRIAGE VIOLATIONS

[13]If a man takes a wife and, after lying with her, dislikes her [14]and slanders her and gives her a bad name, saying, "I married this woman, but when I approached her, I did not find proof of her virginity," [15]then the girl's father and mother shall bring proof that she was a virgin to the town elders at the gate. [16]The girl's father will say to the elders, "I gave my daughter in marriage to this man, but he dislikes her. [17]Now he has slandered her and said, 'I did not find your daughter to be a virgin.' But here is the proof of my daughter's virginity." Then her parents shall display the cloth before the elders of the town, [18]and the elders shall take the man and punish him. [19]They shall fine him a hundred shekels of silver [b] and give them to the girl's father, because this man has given an Israelite virgin a bad name. She shall continue to be his wife; he must not divorce her as long as he lives.

[20]If, however, the charge is true and no proof of the girl's virginity can be found, [21]she shall be

---

[a] 9 Or be forfeited to the sanctuary   [b] 19 That is, about 2 1/2 pounds (about 1 kilogram)

brought to the door of her father's house and there the men of her town shall stone her to death. She has done a disgraceful thing in Israel by being promiscuous while still in her father's house. You must purge the evil from among you.

²²If a man is found sleeping with another man's wife, both the man who slept with her and the woman must die. You must purge the evil from Israel.

²³If a man happens to meet in a town a virgin pledged to be married and he sleeps with her, ²⁴you shall take both of them to the gate of that town and stone them to death—the girl because she was in a town and did not scream for help, and the man because he violated another man's wife. You must purge the evil from among you.

²⁵But if out in the country a man happens to meet a girl pledged to be married and rapes her, only the man who has done this shall die. ²⁶Do nothing to the girl; she has committed no sin deserving death. This case is like that of someone who attacks and murders his neighbor, ²⁷for the man found the girl out in the country, and though the betrothed girl screamed, there was no one to rescue her.

²⁸If a man happens to meet a virgin who is not pledged to be married and rapes her and they are discovered, ²⁹he shall pay the girl's father fifty shekels of silver.[a] He must marry the girl, for he has violated her. He can never divorce her as long as he lives.

³⁰A man is not to marry his father's wife; he must not dishonor his father's bed.

EXCLUSION FROM THE ASSEMBLY

23 No one who has been emasculated by crushing or cutting may enter the assembly of the LORD.

²No one born of a forbidden marriage[b] nor any of his descendants may enter the assembly of the LORD, even down to the tenth generation.

³No Ammonite or Moabite or any of his descendants may enter the assembly of the LORD, even down to the tenth generation. ⁴For they did not come to meet you with bread and water on your way when you came out of Egypt, and they hired Balaam son of Beor from Pethor in Aram Naharaim[c] to pronounce a curse on you. ⁵However, the LORD your God would not listen to Balaam but turned the curse into a blessing for you, because the LORD your God loves you. ⁶Do not seek a treaty of friendship with them as long as you live.

⁷Do not abhor an Edomite, for he is your brother. Do not abhor an Egyptian, because you lived as an alien in his country. ⁸The third generation of children born to them may enter the assembly of the LORD.

UNCLEANNESS IN THE CAMP

⁹When you are encamped against your enemies, keep away from everything impure. ¹⁰If one of your men is unclean because of a nocturnal emission, he is to go outside the camp and stay there. ¹¹But as evening approaches he is to wash himself, and at sunset he may return to the camp.

¹²Designate a place outside the camp where you can go to relieve yourself. ¹³As part of your equipment have something to dig with, and when you relieve yourself, dig a hole and cover up your excrement. ¹⁴For the LORD your God moves about in your camp to protect you and to deliver your enemies to you. Your camp must be holy, so that he will not see among you anything indecent and turn away from you.

MISCELLANEOUS LAWS

¹⁵If a slave has taken refuge with you, do not hand him over to his master. ¹⁶Let him live among you wherever he likes and in whatever town he chooses. Do not oppress him.

¹⁷No Israelite man or woman is to become a shrine prostitute. ¹⁸You must not bring the earnings of a female prostitute or of a male prostitute[d] into the house of the LORD your God to pay any vow, because the LORD your God detests them both.

¹⁹Do not charge your brother interest, whether on money or food or anything else that may earn interest. ²⁰You may charge a foreigner interest, but not a brother Israelite, so that the LORD your God may bless you in everything you put your hand to in the land you are entering to possess.

²¹If you make a vow to the LORD your God, do not be slow to pay it, for the LORD your God will

---

[a] *29 That is, about 1 1/4 pounds (about 0.6 kilogram)*   [b] *2 Or one of illegitimate birth*   [c] *4 That is, Northwest Mesopotamia*
[d] *18 Hebrew of a dog*

battlelines

» Fast and Loose (Internet)

Q: Do you have a computer in your room?
A: No. My dad won't let me have a TV or a computer in there.

Q: Why not?
A: He says he's concerned about all the junk on cable and all the bad stuff online.

Q: Cool dad.
A: Yeah, sometimes. But he's also kind of clueless.

Q: Why do you say that?
A: Well, the computer in the family room has a cable modem.

Q: And?
A: Well, you know, it's pretty fast. I mean, it loads real quickly.

Q: So if a guy wanted to sit in your family room and check out some pretty raunchy stuff, he could do it with your parents right in the next room? And they'd never know?
A: You get the picture. It's all pretty easy, actually. I mean, it *would* be pretty easy—so I'm told—to cover up where you've been surfing. If you just know a few things about computers . . . how to hide your tracks.

Q: What about you, Eric? Do you ever get tempted?
A: What do *you* think?

» A Deadly Trap

First Peter 2:11 gives us this sober challenge: "Dear friends, I urge you, as aliens and strangers in the world, to abstain from sinful desires, which war against your soul."

Weird, isn't it? The girls of Internet porn seem so alluring, so delightful, so available, so . . . harmless. *What's the big deal?* we tell ourselves. Better this than doing the real thing, right? Nobody gets hurt. Nobody finds out.

But the truth is, the girls get hurt. The porn industry treats them like cheap objects. (And so do you, if you're surfing porn sites.) Pornography blasts a hole in your soul, giving you a perverted picture of the wonder of sex and an insatiable desire for more. Viewing porn teaches you to treat the girls around you like mere objects—and that has a negative affect on a lot of your relationships. In God's eyes, surfing porn is every bit as serious as doing the real thing. Check out Matthew 5:27–30.

If you're struggling with the temptation of porn, find some friends who will hold you accountable. If you're already in over your head, get help and get it soon from somebody who cares.

Read more about the effects of porn at www.RevolutionBible.com.

certainly demand it of you and you will be guilty of sin. ²²But if you refrain from making a vow, you will not be guilty. ²³Whatever your lips utter you must be sure to do, because you made your vow freely to the LORD your God with your own mouth.

²⁴If you enter your neighbor's vineyard, you may eat all the grapes you want, but do not put any in your basket. ²⁵If you enter your neighbor's grainfield, you may pick kernels with your hands, but you must not put a sickle to his standing grain.

24

If a man marries a woman who becomes displeasing to him because he finds something indecent about her, and he writes her a certificate of divorce, gives it to her and sends her from his house, ²and if after she leaves his house she becomes the wife of another man, ³and her second husband dislikes her and writes her a certificate of divorce, gives it to her and sends her from his house, or if he dies, ⁴then her first husband, who divorced her, is not allowed to marry her again after she has been defiled. That would be detestable in the eyes of the LORD. Do not bring sin upon the land the LORD your God is giving you as an inheritance.

⁵If a man has recently married, he must not be sent to war or have any other duty laid on him. For one year he is to be free to stay at home and bring happiness to the wife he has married.

⁶Do not take a pair of millstones—not even the upper one—as security for a debt, because that would be taking a man's livelihood as security.

⁷If a man is caught kidnapping one of his brother Israelites and treats him as a slave or sells him, the kidnapper must die. You must purge the evil from among you.

⁸In cases of leprous[a] diseases be very careful to do exactly as the priests, who are Levites, instruct you. You must follow carefully what I have commanded them. ⁹Remember what the LORD your God did to Miriam along the way after you came out of Egypt.

¹⁰When you make a loan of any kind to your neighbor, do not go into his house to get what he is offering as a pledge. ¹¹Stay outside and let the man to whom you are making the loan bring the pledge out to you. ¹²If the man is poor, do not go to sleep with his pledge in your possession. ¹³Return his cloak to him by sunset so that he may sleep in it. Then he will thank you, and it will be regarded as a righteous act in the sight of the LORD your God.

¹⁴Do not take advantage of a hired man who is poor and needy, whether he is a brother Israelite or an alien living in one of your towns. ¹⁵Pay him his wages each day before sunset, because he is poor and is counting on it. Otherwise he may cry to the LORD against you, and you will be guilty of sin.

¹⁶Fathers shall not be put to death for their children, nor children put to death for their fathers; each is to die for his own sin.

¹⁷Do not deprive the alien or the fatherless of justice, or take the cloak of the widow as a pledge. ¹⁸Remember that you were slaves in Egypt and the LORD your God redeemed you from there. That is why I command you to do this.

¹⁹When you are harvesting in your field and you overlook a sheaf, do not go back to get it. Leave it for the alien, the fatherless and the widow, so that the LORD your God may bless you in all the work of your hands. ²⁰When you beat the olives from your trees, do not go over the branches a second time. Leave what remains for the alien, the fatherless and the widow. ²¹When you harvest the grapes in your vineyard, do not go over the vines again. Leave what remains for the alien, the fatherless and the widow. ²²Remember that you were slaves in Egypt. That is why I command you to do this.

25

When men have a dispute, they are to take it to court and the judges will decide the case, acquitting the innocent and condemning the guilty. ²If the guilty man deserves to be beaten, the judge shall make him lie down and have him flogged in his presence with the number of lashes his crime deserves, ³but he must not give him more than forty lashes. If he is flogged more than that, your brother will be degraded in your eyes.

⁴Do not muzzle an ox while it is treading out the grain.

⁵If brothers are living together and one of them dies without a son, his widow must not marry outside the family. Her husband's brother shall take her and marry her and fulfill the duty of a brother-in-law to her. ⁶The first son she bears shall carry on the name of the dead brother so that his name will not be blotted out from Israel.

⁷However, if a man does not want to marry his brother's wife, she shall go to the elders at the town gate and say, "My husband's brother refuses to carry on his brother's name in Israel. He will not fulfill the duty of a brother-in-law to me." ⁸Then the elders of his town shall summon him and talk to him. If

---

ᵃ 8 The Hebrew word was used for various diseases affecting the skin—not necessarily leprosy.

he persists in saying, "I do not want to marry her," ⁹his brother's widow shall go up to him in the presence of the elders, take off one of his sandals, spit in his face and say, "This is what is done to the man who will not build up his brother's family line." ¹⁰That man's line shall be known in Israel as The Family of the Unsandaled.

¹¹If two men are fighting and the wife of one of them comes to rescue her husband from his assailant, and she reaches out and seizes him by his private parts, ¹²you shall cut off her hand. Show her no pity.

¹³Do not have two differing weights in your bag—one heavy, one light. ¹⁴Do not have two differing measures in your house—one large, one small. ¹⁵You must have accurate and honest weights and measures, so that you may live long in the land the LORD your God is giving you. ¹⁶For the LORD your God detests anyone who does these things, anyone who deals dishonestly.

¹⁷Remember what the Amalekites did to you along the way when you came out of Egypt. ¹⁸When you were weary and worn out, they met you on your journey and cut off all who were lagging behind; they had no fear of God. ¹⁹When the LORD your God gives you rest from all the enemies around you in the land he is giving you to possess as an inheritance, you shall blot out the memory of Amalek from under heaven. Do not forget!

now or never

DT 25:13–16

What are some other examples of cheating? What does cheating say about the character of the person doing it? What does it say if the person doing it is a Christian?

FIRSTFRUITS AND TITHES

26

When you have entered the land the LORD your God is giving you as an inheritance and have taken possession of it and settled in it, ²take some of the firstfruits of all that you produce from the soil of the land the LORD your God is giving you and put them in a basket. Then go to the place the LORD your God will choose as a dwelling for his Name ³and say to the priest in office at the time, "I declare today to the LORD your God that I have come to the land the LORD swore to our forefathers to give us." ⁴The priest shall take the basket from your hands and set it down in front of the altar of the LORD your God. ⁵Then you shall declare before the LORD your God: "My father was a wandering Aramean, and he went down into Egypt with a few people and lived there and became a great nation, powerful and numerous. ⁶But the Egyptians mistreated us and made us suffer, putting us to hard labor. ⁷Then we cried out to the LORD, the God of our fathers, and the LORD heard our voice and saw our misery, toil and oppression. ⁸So the LORD brought us out of Egypt with a mighty hand and an outstretched arm, with great terror and with miraculous signs and wonders. ⁹He brought us to this place and gave us this land, a land flowing with milk and honey; ¹⁰and now I bring the firstfruits of the soil that you, O LORD, have given me." Place the basket before the LORD your God and bow down before him. ¹¹And you and the Levites and the aliens among you shall rejoice in all the good things the LORD your God has given to you and your household.

¹²When you have finished setting aside a tenth of all your produce in the third year, the year of the tithe, you shall give it to the Levite, the alien, the fatherless and the widow, so that they may eat in your towns and be satisfied. ¹³Then say to the LORD your God: "I have removed from my house the sacred portion and have given it to the Levite, the alien, the fatherless and the widow, according to all you commanded. I have not turned aside from your commands nor have I forgotten any of them. ¹⁴I have not eaten any of the sacred portion while I was in mourning, nor have I removed any of it while I was unclean, nor have I offered any of it to the dead. I have obeyed the LORD my God; I have done everything you commanded me. ¹⁵Look down from heaven, your holy dwelling place, and bless your people Israel and the land you have given us as you promised on oath to our forefathers, a land flowing with milk and honey."

FOLLOW THE LORD'S COMMANDS

¹⁶The LORD your God commands you this day to follow these decrees and laws; carefully observe them with all your heart and with all your soul. ¹⁷You have declared this day that the LORD is your God and that

you will walk in his ways, that you will keep his decrees, commands and laws, and that you will obey him. [18]And the LORD has declared this day that you are his people, his treasured possession as he promised, and that you are to keep all his commands. [19]He has declared that he will set you in praise, fame and honor high above all the nations he has made and that you will be a people holy to the LORD your God, as he promised.

THE ALTAR ON MOUNT EBAL

27 Moses and the elders of Israel commanded the people: "Keep all these commands that I give you today. [2]When you have crossed the Jordan into the land the LORD your God is giving you, set up some large stones and coat them with plaster. [3]Write on them all the words of this law when you have crossed over to enter the land the LORD your God is giving you, a land flowing with milk and honey, just as the LORD, the God of your fathers, promised you. [4]And when you have crossed the Jordan, set up these stones on Mount Ebal, as I command you today, and coat them with plaster. [5]Build there an altar to the LORD your God, an altar of stones. Do not use any iron tool upon them. [6]Build the altar of the LORD your God with fieldstones and offer burnt offerings on it to the LORD your God. [7]Sacrifice fellowship offerings[a] there, eating them and rejoicing in the presence of the LORD your God. [8]And you shall write very clearly all the words of this law on these stones you have set up."

CURSES FROM MOUNT EBAL

[9]Then Moses and the priests, who are Levites, said to all Israel, "Be silent, O Israel, and listen! You have now become the people of the LORD your God. [10]Obey the LORD your God and follow his commands and decrees that I give you today."

[11]On the same day Moses commanded the people:

[12]When you have crossed the Jordan, these tribes shall stand on Mount Gerizim to bless the people: Simeon, Levi, Judah, Issachar, Joseph and Benjamin. [13]And these tribes shall stand on Mount Ebal to pronounce curses: Reuben, Gad, Asher, Zebulun, Dan and Naphtali.

[14]The Levites shall recite to all the people of Israel in a loud voice:

[15]"Cursed is the man who carves an image or casts an idol—a thing detestable to the LORD, the work of the craftsman's hands—and sets it up in secret."

Then all the people shall say, "Amen!"

[16]"Cursed is the man who dishonors his father or his mother."

Then all the people shall say, "Amen!"

[17]"Cursed is the man who moves his neighbor's boundary stone."

Then all the people shall say, "Amen!"

[18]"Cursed is the man who leads the blind astray on the road."

Then all the people shall say, "Amen!"

[19]"Cursed is the man who withholds justice from the alien, the fatherless or the widow."

Then all the people shall say, "Amen!"

[20]"Cursed is the man who sleeps with his father's wife, for he dishonors his father's bed."

Then all the people shall say, "Amen!"

[21]"Cursed is the man who has sexual relations with any animal."

Then all the people shall say, "Amen!"

[22]"Cursed is the man who sleeps with his sister, the daughter of his father or the daughter of his mother."

Then all the people shall say, "Amen!"

[23]"Cursed is the man who sleeps with his mother-in-law."

Then all the people shall say, "Amen!"

---

[a] 7 Traditionally *peace offerings*

24 "Cursed is the man who kills his neighbor secretly."

Then all the people shall say, "Amen!"

25 "Cursed is the man who accepts a bribe to kill an innocent person."

Then all the people shall say, "Amen!"

26 "Cursed is the man who does not uphold the words of this law by carrying them out."

Then all the people shall say, "Amen!"

BLESSINGS FOR OBEDIENCE

28 If you fully obey the LORD your God and carefully follow all his commands I give you today, the LORD your God will set you high above all the nations on earth. 2All these blessings will come upon you and accompany you if you obey the LORD your God:

3 You will be blessed in the city and blessed in the country.

4 The fruit of your womb will be blessed, and the crops of your land and the young of your livestock—the calves of your herds and the lambs of your flocks.

5 Your basket and your kneading trough will be blessed.

6 You will be blessed when you come in and blessed when you go out.

7 The LORD will grant that the enemies who rise up against you will be defeated before you. They will come at you from one direction but flee from you in seven.

8 The LORD will send a blessing on your barns and on everything you put your hand to. The LORD your God will bless you in the land he is giving you.

9 The LORD will establish you as his holy people, as he promised you on oath, if you keep the commands of the LORD your God and walk in his ways. 10 Then all the peoples on earth will see that you are called by the name of the LORD, and they will fear you. 11 The LORD will grant you abundant prosperity—in the fruit of your womb, the young of your livestock and the crops of your ground—in the land he swore to your forefathers to give you.

12 The LORD will open the heavens, the storehouse of his bounty, to send rain on your land in season and to bless all the work of your hands. You will lend to many nations but will borrow from none. 13 The LORD will make you the head, not the tail. If you pay attention to the commands of the LORD your God that I give you this day and carefully follow them, you will always be at the top, never at the bottom. 14 Do not turn aside from any of the commands I give you today, to the right or to the left, following other gods and serving them.

CURSES FOR DISOBEDIENCE

15 However, if you do not obey the LORD your God and do not carefully follow all his commands and decrees I am giving you today, all these curses will come upon you and overtake you:

16 You will be cursed in the city and cursed in the country.

17 Your basket and your kneading trough will be cursed.

18 The fruit of your womb will be cursed, and the crops of your land, and the calves of your herds and the lambs of your flocks.

19 You will be cursed when you come in and cursed when you go out.

20 The LORD will send on you curses, confusion and rebuke in everything you put your hand to, until you are destroyed and come to sudden ruin because of the evil you have done in forsaking him.[a] 21 The LORD will plague you with diseases until he has destroyed you from the land you are entering to possess. 22 The LORD will strike you with wasting disease, with fever and inflammation, with scorching heat and drought, with blight and mildew, which will plague you until you perish. 23 The sky over your head will be bronze, the ground beneath you iron. 24 The LORD will turn the rain of your country into dust and powder; it will come down from the skies until you are destroyed.

25 The LORD will cause you to be defeated before your enemies. You will come at them from one direction but flee from them in seven, and you will become a thing of horror to all the kingdoms on earth. 26 Your carcasses will be food for all the birds of the air and the beasts of the earth, and there will be no one to frighten them away. 27 The LORD will afflict you with the boils of Egypt and with tumors, festering sores and the itch, from which you cannot be cured. 28 The LORD will afflict you with madness, blindness

a 20 Hebrew me

and confusion of mind. ²⁹At midday you will grope about like a blind man in the dark. You will be unsuccessful in everything you do; day after day you will be oppressed and robbed, with no one to rescue you.

³⁰You will be pledged to be married to a woman, but another will take her and ravish her. You will build a house, but you will not live in it. You will plant a vineyard, but you will not even begin to enjoy its fruit. ³¹Your ox will be slaughtered before your eyes, but you will eat none of it. Your donkey will be forcibly taken from you and will not be returned. Your sheep will be given to your enemies, and no one will rescue them. ³²Your sons and daughters will be given to another nation, and you will wear out your eyes watching for them day after day, powerless to lift a hand. ³³A people that you do not know will eat what your land and labor produce, and you will have nothing but cruel oppression all your days. ³⁴The sights you see will drive you mad. ³⁵The LORD will afflict your knees and legs with painful boils that cannot be cured, spreading from the soles of your feet to the top of your head.

³⁶The LORD will drive you and the king you set over you to a nation unknown to you or your fathers. There you will worship other gods, gods of wood and stone. ³⁷You will become a thing of horror and an object of scorn and ridicule to all the nations where the LORD will drive you.

³⁸You will sow much seed in the field but you will harvest little, because locusts will devour it. ³⁹You will plant vineyards and cultivate them but you will not drink the wine or gather the grapes, because worms will eat them. ⁴⁰You will have olive trees throughout your country but you will not use the oil, because the olives will drop off. ⁴¹You will have sons and daughters but you will not keep them, because they will go into captivity. ⁴²Swarms of locusts will take over all your trees and the crops of your land.

⁴³The alien who lives among you will rise above you higher and higher, but you will sink lower and lower. ⁴⁴He will lend to you, but you will not lend to him. He will be the head, but you will be the tail.

⁴⁵All these curses will come upon you. They will pursue you and overtake you until you are destroyed, because you did not obey the LORD your God and observe the commands and decrees he gave you. ⁴⁶They will be a sign and a wonder to you and your descendants forever. ⁴⁷Because you did not serve the LORD your God joyfully and gladly in the time of prosperity, ⁴⁸therefore in hunger and thirst, in nakedness and dire poverty, you will serve the enemies the LORD sends against you. He will put an iron yoke on your neck until he has destroyed you.

⁴⁹The LORD will bring a nation against you from far away, from the ends of the earth, like an eagle swooping down, a nation whose language you will not understand, ⁵⁰a fierce-looking nation without respect for the old or pity for the young. ⁵¹They will devour the young of your livestock and the crops of your land until you are destroyed. They will leave you no grain, new wine or oil, nor any calves of your herds or lambs of your flocks until you are ruined. ⁵²They will lay siege to all the cities throughout your land until the high fortified walls in which you trust fall down. They will besiege all the cities throughout the land the LORD your God is giving you.

⁵³Because of the suffering that your enemy will inflict on you during the siege, you will eat the fruit of the womb, the flesh of the sons and daughters the LORD your God has given you. ⁵⁴Even the most gentle and sensitive man among you will have no compassion on his own brother or the wife he loves or his surviving children, ⁵⁵and he will not give to one of them any of the flesh of his children that he is eating. It will be all he has left because of the suffering your enemy will inflict on you during the siege of all your cities. ⁵⁶The most gentle and sensitive woman among you—so sensitive and gentle that she would not venture to touch the ground with the sole of her foot—will begrudge the husband she loves and her own son or daughter ⁵⁷the afterbirth from her womb and the children she bears. For she intends to eat them secretly during the siege and in the distress that your enemy will inflict on you in your cities.

⁵⁸If you do not carefully follow all the words of this law, which are written in this book, and do not

NOW OR NEVER
DT 28:47

Want to know how to spot someone who's serious about serving God? Look for the Christian with a consistent, positive outlook. God doesn't want to spoil our fun; he wants us to bring the same joy and enthusiasm to serving him that we bring to all the other things we love to do.

revere this glorious and awesome name—the LORD your God— ⁵⁹the LORD will send fearful plagues on you and your descendants, harsh and prolonged disasters, and severe and lingering illnesses. ⁶⁰He will bring upon you all the diseases of Egypt that you dreaded, and they will cling to you. ⁶¹The LORD will also bring on you every kind of sickness and disaster not recorded in this Book of the Law, until you are destroyed. ⁶²You who were as numerous as the stars in the sky will be left but few in number, because you did not obey the LORD your God. ⁶³Just as it pleased the LORD to make you prosper and increase in number, so it will please him to ruin and destroy you. You will be uprooted from the land you are entering to possess.

⁶⁴Then the LORD will scatter you among all nations, from one end of the earth to the other. There you will worship other gods—gods of wood and stone, which neither you nor your fathers have known. ⁶⁵Among those nations you will find no repose, no resting place for the sole of your foot. There the LORD will give you an anxious mind, eyes weary with longing, and a despairing heart. ⁶⁶You will live in constant suspense, filled with dread both night and day, never sure of your life. ⁶⁷In the morning you will say, "If only it were evening!" and in the evening, "If only it were morning!"—because of the terror that will fill your hearts and the sights that your eyes will see. ⁶⁸The LORD will send you back in ships to Egypt on a journey I said you should never make again. There you will offer yourselves for sale to your enemies as male and female slaves, but no one will buy you.

RENEWAL OF THE COVENANT

29 These are the terms of the covenant the LORD commanded Moses to make with the Israelites in Moab, in addition to the covenant he had made with them at Horeb. ²Moses summoned all the Israelites and said to them:

Your eyes have seen all that the LORD did in Egypt to Pharaoh, to all his officials and to all his land. ³With your own eyes you saw those great trials, those miraculous signs and great wonders. ⁴But to this day the LORD has not given you a mind that understands or eyes that see or ears that hear. ⁵During the forty years that I led you through the desert, your clothes did not wear out, nor did the sandals on your feet. ⁶You ate no bread and drank no wine or other fermented drink. I did this so that you might know that I am the LORD your God.

⁷When you reached this place, Sihon king of Heshbon and Og king of Bashan came out to fight against us, but we defeated them. ⁸We took their land and gave it as an inheritance to the Reubenites, the Gadites and the half-tribe of Manasseh.

⁹Carefully follow the terms of this covenant, so that you may prosper in everything you do. ¹⁰All of you are standing today in the presence of the LORD your God—your leaders and chief men, your elders and officials, and all the other men of Israel, ¹¹together with your children and your wives, and the aliens living in your camps who chop your wood and carry your water. ¹²You are standing here in order to enter into a covenant with the LORD your God, a covenant the LORD is making with you this day and sealing with an oath, ¹³to confirm you this day as his people, that he may be your God as he promised you and as he swore to your fathers, Abraham, Isaac and Jacob. ¹⁴I am making this covenant, with its oath, not only with you ¹⁵who are standing here with us today in the presence of the LORD our God but also with those who are not here today.

¹⁶You yourselves know how we lived in Egypt and how we passed through the countries on the way here. ¹⁷You saw among them their detestable images and idols of wood and stone, of silver and gold. ¹⁸Make sure there is no man or woman, clan or tribe among you today whose heart turns away from the LORD our God to go and worship the gods of those nations; make sure there is no root among you that produces such bitter poison.

¹⁹When such a person hears the words of this oath, he invokes a blessing on himself and therefore thinks, "I will be safe, even though I persist in going my own way." This will bring disaster on the watered land as well as the dry.ᵃ ²⁰The LORD will never be willing to forgive him; his wrath and zeal will burn against that man. All the curses written in this book will fall upon him, and the LORD will blot out his name from under heaven. ²¹The LORD will single him out from all the tribes of Israel for disaster, according to all the curses of the covenant written in this Book of the Law.

²²Your children who follow you in later generations and foreigners who come from distant lands will see the calamities that have fallen on the land and the diseases with which the LORD has afflicted it. ²³The

---

ᵃ *19* Or *way, in order to add drunkenness to thirst."*

whole land will be a burning waste of salt and sulfur—nothing planted, nothing sprouting, no vegetation growing on it. It will be like the destruction of Sodom and Gomorrah, Admah and Zeboiim, which the LORD overthrew in fierce anger. 24All the nations will ask: "Why has the LORD done this to this land? Why this fierce, burning anger?"

25And the answer will be: "It is because this people abandoned the covenant of the LORD, the God of their fathers, the covenant he made with them when he brought them out of Egypt. 26They went off and worshiped other gods and bowed down to them, gods they did not know, gods he had not given them. 27Therefore the LORD's anger burned against this land, so that he brought on it all the curses written in this book. 28In furious anger and in great wrath the LORD uprooted them from their land and thrust them into another land, as it is now."

29The secret things belong to the LORD our God, but the things revealed belong to us and to our children forever, that we may follow all the words of this law.

NOW OR NEVER
DT 29:29

You'll never know everything God has done for you, but you'll always know what you need to know in order to worship, serve and love him.

PROSPERITY AFTER TURNING TO THE LORD

30 When all these blessings and curses I have set before you come upon you and you take them to heart wherever the LORD your God disperses you among the nations, 2and when you and your children return to the LORD your God and obey him with all your heart and with all your soul according to everything I command you today, 3then the LORD your God will restore your fortunes[a] and have compassion on you and gather you again from all the nations where he scattered you. 4Even if you have been banished to the most distant land under the heavens, from there the LORD your God will gather you and bring you back. 5He will bring you to the land that belonged to your fathers, and you will take possession of it. He will make you more prosperous and numerous than your fathers. 6The LORD your God will circumcise your hearts and the hearts of your descendants, so that you may love him with all your heart and with all your soul, and live. 7The LORD your God will put all these curses on your enemies who hate and persecute you. 8You will again obey the LORD and follow all his commands I am giving you today. 9Then the LORD your God will make you most prosperous in all the work of your hands and in the fruit of your womb, the young of your livestock and the crops of your land. The LORD will again delight in you and make you prosperous, just as he delighted in your fathers, 10if you obey the LORD your God and keep his commands and decrees that are written in this Book of the Law and turn to the LORD your God with all your heart and with all your soul.

NOW OR NEVER
DT 30:11–14

Don't fall for the lie that the Bible is too hard for you to understand. It's not. If you pray before you read and give the Bible your full attention, God can help you plow through the tough stuff to get to the meaning, purpose and application of a passage.

THE OFFER OF LIFE OR DEATH

11Now what I am commanding you today is not too difficult for you or beyond your reach. 12It is not up in heaven, so that you have to ask, "Who will ascend into heaven to get it and proclaim it to us so we may obey it?" 13Nor is it beyond the sea, so that you have to ask, "Who will cross the sea to get it and proclaim it to us so we may obey it?" 14No, the word is very near you; it is in your mouth and in your heart so you may obey it.

15See, I set before you today life and prosperity, death and destruction. 16For I command you today to love the LORD your God, to walk in his ways, and to keep his commands, decrees and laws; then you will live and increase, and the LORD your God will bless you in the land you are entering to possess.

17But if your heart turns away and you are not obedient, and if you are drawn away to bow down to other gods and worship them, 18I declare to you this day that you will certainly be destroyed. You will

---
a 3 Or *will bring you back from captivity*

not live long in the land you are crossing the Jordan to enter and possess.

¹⁹This day I call heaven and earth as witnesses against you that I have set before you life and death, blessings and curses. Now choose life, so that you and your children may live ²⁰and that you may love the LORD your God, listen to his voice, and hold fast to him. For the LORD is your life, and he will give you many years in the land he swore to give to your fathers, Abraham, Isaac and Jacob.

---

challenge notes

To: my_son

DT 30:15-20

heavenly_father: don't let other people tell you what "fun" is. don't fall for their lies about what it takes to get the most out of life. most important, don't confuse short-term thrills with long-term satisfaction. the only way for you to be truly happy and fulfilled is to follow me and the principles found in my Word.

JOSHUA TO SUCCEED MOSES

31 Then Moses went out and spoke these words to all Israel: ²"I am now a hundred and twenty years old and I am no longer able to lead you. The LORD has said to me, 'You shall not cross the Jordan.' ³The LORD your God himself will cross over ahead of you. He will destroy these nations before you, and you will take possession of their land. Joshua also will cross over ahead of you, as the LORD said. ⁴And the LORD will do to them what he did to Sihon and Og, the kings of the Amorites, whom he destroyed along with their land. ⁵The LORD will deliver them to you, and you must do to them all that I have commanded you. ⁶Be strong and courageous. Do not be afraid or terrified because of them, for the LORD your God goes with you; he will never leave you nor forsake you."

⁷Then Moses summoned Joshua and said to him in the presence of all Israel, "Be strong and courageous, for you must go with this people into the land that the LORD swore to their forefathers to give them, and you must divide it among them as their inheritance. ⁸The LORD himself goes before you and will be with you; he will never leave you nor forsake you. Do not be afraid; do not be discouraged."

THE READING OF THE LAW

⁹So Moses wrote down this law and gave it to the priests, the sons of Levi, who carried the ark of the covenant of the LORD, and to all the elders of Israel. ¹⁰Then Moses commanded them: "At the end of every seven years, in the year for canceling debts, during the Feast of Tabernacles, ¹¹when all Israel comes to appear before the LORD your God at the place he will choose, you shall read this law before them in their hearing. ¹²Assemble the people—men, women and children, and the aliens living in your towns—so they can listen and learn to fear the LORD your God and follow carefully all the words of this law. ¹³Their children, who do not know this law, must hear it and learn to fear the LORD your God as long as you live in the land you are crossing the Jordan to possess."

ISRAEL'S REBELLION PREDICTED

¹⁴The LORD said to Moses, "Now the day of your death is near. Call Joshua and present yourselves at the Tent of Meeting, where I will commission him." So Moses and Joshua came and presented themselves at the Tent of Meeting.

¹⁵Then the LORD appeared at the Tent in a pillar of cloud, and the cloud stood over the entrance to the Tent. ¹⁶And the LORD said to Moses: "You are going to rest with your fathers, and these people will soon prostitute themselves to the foreign gods of the land they are entering. They will forsake me and break the covenant I made with them. ¹⁷On that day I will become angry with them and forsake them; I will hide my face from them, and they will be destroyed. Many disasters and difficulties will come upon them, and on that day they will ask, 'Have not these disasters come upon us because our God is not with us?' ¹⁸And I will certainly hide my face on that day because of all their wickedness in turning to other gods.

¹⁹"Now write down for yourselves this song and teach it to the Israelites and have them sing it, so that it may be a witness for me against them. ²⁰When I have brought them into the land flowing with milk and honey, the land I promised on oath to their forefathers, and when they eat their fill and thrive, they will turn to other gods and worship them, rejecting me and breaking my covenant. ²¹And when many disasters and difficulties come upon them, this song will testify against them, because it will not be

battlelines

» Have to or Get to? (Loving God)

Q: Are you going on the retreat next weekend?
A: I don't have a choice. I'm on the leadership team. I have to be there.

Q: You *have* to go or you *get* to go?
A: What's the difference?

Q: You make it sound like an unpleasant obligation, like taking out the garbage or getting your teeth cleaned.
A: Well, it's not that bad, but to be honest . . . ah, well, never mind. I should probably just shut up.

Q: No, you should probably say what you think. Come on, be honest. Stop pretending.
A: You want me to be honest?

Q: Absolutely. God already knows what you're thinking anyway.
A: Yeah, that's true. I never thought about it like that. Okay, here's the truth: I feel spiritually empty. Just blah. And I don't even care. I mean, I *care*. But I just don't feel *motivated* or even all that concerned. I'm just tired . . . drained inside. I know I'm supposed to feel excited about God and eager to go to church and on retreats and stuff like that. But that's not how I feel. And I don't know how to change it.

Q: So everything just feels like a big obligation, like a chore?
A: Yeah, pretty much. I do stuff because I just know I'm supposed to—because it's the right thing to do.

» Back on Track

There's hardly a person in the Bible who didn't go through dry times and periods of struggle in their spiritual lives. It's a very common thing for people to reach the point Kobe has reached.

It would be nice to be able to give you a tidy little formula of three easy steps: "Just do these things and presto! You'll recover your excitement and passion for God in no time flat or your money back!" Unfortunately, God doesn't work that way. He deals with each of his children differently. He took Elijah into a cave for some major shut-eye, followed by a feast served by ravens. David worshiped his way to recovery. Jeremiah wept. Peter repented.

Your path to a renewed love for Christ and to a deeper faith will be unique. Perhaps God will rekindle your spiritual fire through fellowship (since you *can't* successfully live the Christian life in isolation) or through service (which tends to be a sure fire way to resuscitate faith). Whatever his method, be patient; let God work.

Learn more about God at www.RevolutionBible.com.

forgotten by their descendants. I know what they are disposed to do, even before I bring them into the land I promised them on oath." 22So Moses wrote down this song that day and taught it to the Israelites.

23The Lord gave this command to Joshua son of Nun: "Be strong and courageous, for you will bring the Israelites into the land I promised them on oath, and I myself will be with you."

24After Moses finished writing in a book the words of this law from beginning to end, 25he gave this command to the Levites who carried the ark of the covenant of the Lord: 26"Take this Book of the Law and place it beside the ark of the covenant of the Lord your God. There it will remain as a witness against you. 27For I know how rebellious and stiff-necked you are. If you have been rebellious against the Lord while I am still alive and with you, how much more will you rebel after I die! 28Assemble before me all the elders of your tribes and all your officials, so that I can speak these words in their hearing and call heaven and earth to testify against them. 29For I know that after my death you are sure to become utterly corrupt and to turn from the way I have commanded you. In days to come, disaster will fall upon you because you will do evil in the sight of the Lord and provoke him to anger by what your hands have made."

THE SONG OF MOSES

30And Moses recited the words of this song from beginning to end in the hearing of the whole assembly of Israel:

32

Listen, O heavens, and I will speak;
    hear, O earth, the words of my mouth.
2Let my teaching fall like rain
    and my words descend like dew,
like showers on new grass,
    like abundant rain on tender plants.

3I will proclaim the name of the Lord.
    Oh, praise the greatness of our God!

4He is the Rock, his works are perfect,
    and all his ways are just.
A faithful God who does no wrong,
    upright and just is he.

5They have acted corruptly toward him;
    to their shame they are no longer his children,
but a warped and crooked generation.[a]
6Is this the way you repay the Lord,
    O foolish and unwise people?
Is he not your Father, your Creator,[b]
    who made you and formed you?

now or never
DT 32:4

When facing a fear or when something happens that really shakes you up, what's the first thing you do? Who's the first person you turn to? Why?

7Remember the days of old;
    consider the generations long past.
Ask your father and he will tell you,
    your elders, and they will explain to you.
8When the Most High gave the nations their inheritance,
    when he divided all mankind,
he set up boundaries for the peoples
    according to the number of the sons of Israel.[c]
9For the Lord's portion is his people,
    Jacob his allotted inheritance.

10In a desert land he found him,
    in a barren and howling waste.

---

a 5 Or *Corrupt are they and not his children, / a generation warped and twisted to their shame*   b 6 Or *Father, who bought you*
c 8 Masoretic Text; Dead Sea Scrolls (see also Septuagint) *sons of God*

He shielded him and cared for him;
he guarded him as the apple of his eye,
11 like an eagle that stirs up its nest
and hovers over its young,
that spreads its wings to catch them
and carries them on its pinions.
12 The LORD alone led him;
no foreign god was with him.

13 He made him ride on the heights of the land
and fed him with the fruit of the fields.
He nourished him with honey from the rock,
and with oil from the flinty crag,
14 with curds and milk from herd and flock
and with fattened lambs and goats,
with choice rams of Bashan
and the finest kernels of wheat.
You drank the foaming blood of the grape.

15 Jeshurun[a] grew fat and kicked;
filled with food, he became heavy and sleek.
He abandoned the God who made him
and rejected the Rock his Savior.
16 They made him jealous with their foreign gods
and angered him with their detestable idols.
17 They sacrificed to demons, which are not God—
gods they had not known,
gods that recently appeared,
gods your fathers did not fear.
18 You deserted the Rock, who fathered you;
you forgot the God who gave you birth.

19 The LORD saw this and rejected them
because he was angered by his sons and daughters.
20 "I will hide my face from them," he said,
"and see what their end will be;
for they are a perverse generation,
children who are unfaithful.
21 They made me jealous by what is no god
and angered me with their worthless idols.
I will make them envious by those who are not a people;
I will make them angry by a nation that has no understanding.
22 For a fire has been kindled by my wrath,
one that burns to the realm of death[b] below.
It will devour the earth and its harvests
and set afire the foundations of the mountains.

23 "I will heap calamities upon them
and spend my arrows against them.
24 I will send wasting famine against them,
consuming pestilence and deadly plague;
I will send against them the fangs of wild beasts,
the venom of vipers that glide in the dust.
25 In the street the sword will make them childless;
in their homes terror will reign.
Young men and young women will perish,

---

a 15 Jeshurun means the upright one, that is, Israel.   b 22 Hebrew to Sheol

infants and gray-haired men.
²⁶ I said I would scatter them
and blot out their memory from mankind,
²⁷ but I dreaded the taunt of the enemy,
lest the adversary misunderstand
and say, 'Our hand has triumphed;
the LORD has not done all this.' "

²⁸ They are a nation without sense,
there is no discernment in them.
²⁹ If only they were wise and would understand this
and discern what their end will be!
³⁰ How could one man chase a thousand,
or two put ten thousand to flight,
unless their Rock had sold them,
unless the LORD had given them up?
³¹ For their rock is not like our Rock,
as even our enemies concede.
³² Their vine comes from the vine of Sodom
and from the fields of Gomorrah.
Their grapes are filled with poison,
and their clusters with bitterness.
³³ Their wine is the venom of serpents,
the deadly poison of cobras.

³⁴ "Have I not kept this in reserve
and sealed it in my vaults?
³⁵ It is mine to avenge; I will repay.
In due time their foot will slip;
their day of disaster is near
and their doom rushes upon them."

³⁶ The LORD will judge his people
and have compassion on his servants
when he sees their strength is gone
and no one is left, slave or free.

---

challengenotes

To: my_son

DT 32:37

heavenly_father: I am the Rock—the one and only. nothing is secure and trustworthy like me. if you put your faith in anything but me, you will be disappointed. you can either take my word for it now or discover it for yourself later . . . when you will wish you had believed it earlier.

---

³⁷ He will say: "Now where are
their gods,
the rock they took refuge in,
³⁸ the gods who ate the fat of
their sacrifices
and drank the wine of their
drink offerings?
Let them rise up to help you!
Let them give you shelter!

³⁹ "See now that I myself am He!
There is no god besides me.
I put to death and I bring to life,

I have wounded and I will heal,
and no one can deliver out of my hand.
⁴⁰ I lift my hand to heaven and declare:
As surely as I live forever,
⁴¹ when I sharpen my flashing sword
and my hand grasps it in judgment,
I will take vengeance on my adversaries
and repay those who hate me.

⁴²I will make my arrows drunk with blood,
        while my sword devours flesh:
    the blood of the slain and the captives,
        the heads of the enemy leaders."

⁴³Rejoice, O nations, with his people,ᵃ,ᵇ
        for he will avenge the blood of his servants;
    he will take vengeance on his enemies
        and make atonement for his land and people.

⁴⁴Moses came with Joshuaᶜ son of Nun and spoke all the words of this song in the hearing of the people. ⁴⁵When Moses finished reciting all these words to all Israel, ⁴⁶he said to them, "Take to heart all the words I have solemnly declared to you this day, so that you may command your children to obey carefully all the words of this law. ⁴⁷They are not just idle words for you—they are your life. By them you will live long in the land you are crossing the Jordan to possess."

MOSES TO DIE ON MOUNT NEBO

⁴⁸On that same day the LORD told Moses, ⁴⁹"Go up into the Abarim Range to Mount Nebo in Moab, across from Jericho, and view Canaan, the land I am giving the Israelites as their own possession. ⁵⁰There on the mountain that you have climbed you will die and be gathered to your people, just as your brother Aaron died on Mount Hor and was gathered to his people. ⁵¹This is because both of you broke faith with me in the presence of the Israelites at the waters of Meribah Kadesh in the Desert of Zin and because you did not uphold my holiness among the Israelites. ⁵²Therefore, you will see the land only from a distance; you will not enter the land I am giving to the people of Israel."

NOW OR NEVER
DT 32:46–47

Have you ever heard someone say something like, "Basketball is my life," or "I live to play video games"? What would it take for you to be able to truthfully say something like that about your relationship with the Lord?

MOSES BLESSES THE TRIBES

33 This is the blessing that Moses the man of God pronounced on the Israelites before his death. ²He said:

    "The LORD came from Sinai
        and dawned over them from Seir;
        he shone forth from Mount Paran.
    He came withᵈ myriads of holy ones
        from the south, from his mountain slopes.ᵉ
    ³Surely it is you who love the people;
        all the holy ones are in your hand.
    At your feet they all bow down,
        and from you receive instruction,
    ⁴the law that Moses gave us,
        the possession of the assembly of Jacob.
    ⁵He was king over Jeshurunᶠ
        when the leaders of the people assembled,
        along with the tribes of Israel.

    ⁶"Let Reuben live and not die,
        norᵍ his men be few."

ᵃ 43 Or *Make his people rejoice, O nations*   ᵇ 43 Masoretic Text; Dead Sea Scrolls (see also Septuagint) *people, / and let all the angels worship him /*   ᶜ 44 Hebrew *Hoshea,* a variant of *Joshua*   ᵈ 2 Or *from*   ᵉ 2 The meaning of the Hebrew for this phrase is uncertain.
ᶠ 5 *Jeshurun* means *the upright one,* that is, Israel; also in verse 26.   ᵍ 6 Or *but let*

[7]And this he said about Judah:

> "Hear, O Lord, the cry of Judah;
>   bring him to his people.
> With his own hands he defends his cause.
>   Oh, be his help against his foes!"

[8]About Levi he said:

> "Your Thummim and Urim belong
>   to the man you favored.
> You tested him at Massah;
>   you contended with him at the waters of Meribah.
> [9]He said of his father and mother,
>   'I have no regard for them.'
> He did not recognize his brothers
>   or acknowledge his own children,
> but he watched over your word
>   and guarded your covenant.
> [10]He teaches your precepts to Jacob
>   and your law to Israel.
> He offers incense before you
>   and whole burnt offerings on your altar.
> [11]Bless all his skills, O Lord,
>   and be pleased with the work of his hands.
> Smite the loins of those who rise up against him;
>   strike his foes till they rise no more."

[12]About Benjamin he said:

> "Let the beloved of the Lord rest secure in him,
>   for he shields him all day long,
>   and the one the Lord loves rests between his shoulders."

[13]About Joseph he said:

> "May the Lord bless his land
>   with the precious dew from heaven above
>   and with the deep waters that lie below;
> [14]with the best the sun brings forth
>   and the finest the moon can yield;
> [15]with the choicest gifts of the ancient mountains
>   and the fruitfulness of the everlasting hills;
> [16]with the best gifts of the earth and its fullness
>   and the favor of him who dwelt in the burning bush.
> Let all these rest on the head of Joseph,
>   on the brow of the prince among[a] his brothers.
> [17]In majesty he is like a firstborn bull;
>   his horns are the horns of a wild ox.
> With them he will gore the nations,
>   even those at the ends of the earth.
> Such are the ten thousands of Ephraim;
>   such are the thousands of Manasseh."

[18]About Zebulun he said:

> "Rejoice, Zebulun, in your going out,
>   and you, Issachar, in your tents.

---

[a] 16 Or *of the one separated from*

¹⁹ They will summon peoples to the mountain
and there offer sacrifices of righteousness;
they will feast on the abundance of the seas,
on the treasures hidden in the sand."

²⁰ About Gad he said:

"Blessed is he who enlarges Gad's domain!
Gad lives there like a lion,
tearing at arm or head.
²¹ He chose the best land for himself;
the leader's portion was kept for him.
When the heads of the people assembled,
he carried out the Lord's righteous will,
and his judgments concerning Israel."

²² About Dan he said:

"Dan is a lion's cub,
springing out of Bashan."

²³ About Naphtali he said:

"Naphtali is abounding with the favor of the Lord
and is full of his blessing;
he will inherit southward to the lake."

²⁴ About Asher he said:

"Most blessed of sons is Asher;
let him be favored by his brothers,
and let him bathe his feet in oil.
²⁵ The bolts of your gates will be iron and bronze,
and your strength will equal your days.

²⁶ "There is no one like the God of Jeshurun,
who rides on the heavens to help you
and on the clouds in his majesty.
²⁷ The eternal God is your refuge,
and underneath are the everlasting arms.
He will drive out your enemy before you,
saying, 'Destroy him!'
²⁸ So Israel will live in safety alone;
Jacob's spring is secure
in a land of grain and new wine,
where the heavens drop dew.
²⁹ Blessed are you, O Israel!
Who is like you,
a people saved by the Lord?
He is your shield and helper
and your glorious sword.
Your enemies will cower before you,
and you will trample down their high places.^a"

THE DEATH OF MOSES

34

Then Moses climbed Mount Nebo from the plains of Moab to the top of Pisgah, across from Jericho. There the Lord showed him the whole land—from Gilead to Dan, ² all of Naphtali, the territory of Ephraim and Manasseh, all the land of Judah as far as the western

^a 29 Or *will tread upon their bodies*

sea,[a] ³the Negev and the whole region from the Valley of Jericho, the City of Palms, as far as Zoar. ⁴Then the LORD said to him, "This is the land I promised on oath to Abraham, Isaac and Jacob when I said, 'I will give it to your descendants.' I have let you see it with your eyes, but you will not cross over into it."

DT 33:27

challengenotes

To: my_son

heavenly_father: do you ever think of me as your refuge, a place to go when you feel like the whole world is against you? try me. I can shield you from the messed-up things going on in your life and give you the strength you need to face them and overcome them.

⁵And Moses the servant of the LORD died there in Moab, as the LORD had said. ⁶He buried him[b] in Moab, in the valley opposite Beth Peor, but to this day no one knows where his grave is. ⁷Moses was a hundred and twenty years old when he died, yet his eyes were not weak nor his strength gone. ⁸The Israelites grieved for Moses in the plains of Moab thirty days, until the time of weeping and mourning was over.

⁹Now Joshua son of Nun was filled with the spirit[c] of wisdom because Moses had laid his hands on him. So the Israelites listened to him and did what the LORD had commanded Moses.

¹⁰Since then, no prophet has risen in Israel like Moses, whom the LORD knew face to face, ¹¹who did all those miraculous signs and wonders the LORD sent him to do in Egypt—to Pharaoh and to all his officials and to his whole land. ¹²For no one has ever shown the mighty power or performed the awesome deeds that Moses did in the sight of all Israel.

---

[a] 2 That is, the Mediterranean   [b] 6 Or He was buried   [c] 9 Or Spirit

JOSHUA

Author
Joshua, except for the ending, which may have been written by the high priest Phinehas

Audience
People of Israel

Date
Probably about 1390 B.C.

Setting
Canaan (the promised land), which today is the modern nation of Israel.

Verse to Remember
So the LORD gave Israel all the land he had sworn to give their forefathers, and they took possession of it and settled there (21:43).

Theme to Consider
God gives us second chances! Though the people failed to enter the promised land the first time, God fulfilled his promise to Abraham by giving his people another chance.

UNCHANGING TRUTH » Sooner or later every guy faces a situation that requires him to step up to the plate, call on skills and courage he's not entirely sure he has, and do something greater than he ever thought possible. For Joshua, that situation came when Moses died in the wilderness—just before the Israelites made it to the promised land.

God basically said, "Joshua, here's the story. I'm putting you in charge of all the Israelites. I want you to lead them into battle against the people who are living in the promised land and claim that land for your own."

Assignments don't come much bigger than that. Imagine the expectations, doubts and pressure that Joshua must have faced! But Joshua was more than ready when his big chance came. God handed him the ball, and Joshua ran with it, not stopping till he got to the end zone.

How did Joshua do it? He recognized that the success of his mission didn't depend on his own skills, but on God's power. So he committed himself to following God's instructions down to the smallest detail. When Joshua had a decision to make, he prayed about it. When he faced a situation that seemed overwhelming, he prayed about it. And when he experienced success, the first thing he did was thank God for it.

You're going to face a situation like Joshua's at some point in your life. Actually, you're going to face quite a few challenging situations like his. Though none of them may involve leading millions of people in a military campaign, they will involve risk on your part. God may urge you to take a public—and unpopular—stand on a controversial issue. He may nudge you to share your faith with someone you want acceptance from. He may use you to confront a friend or family member who's about to make a really bad choice.

When he does, remember Joshua's secret to success: Pray, ask God for strength, follow his instructions and give him all of the praise and credit when he comes through.

LIFE LESSONS »

1   Human leaders come and go, but God's power and his work last forever (1:1–6).

2   We don't always have to understand exactly *what* God is going to do in order to obey him (6:1–21).

3   God never forgets those who are faithful to him (6:22–25).

4   The best eulogy we can hope to have spoken at our funeral is the one Joshua got: "servant of the LORD" (24:29).

Meditating on Scripture

Reading the Bible is a great way to become familiar with who God is and what his will is for you. Memorizing Scripture is an effective way to make sure that God's principles are never far from your mind. *Meditating* on God's Word—thinking about it constantly, praying for God to help you understand it more clearly, searching for ways to use its truth in your everyday life—is a sure way to change your heart and life forever.

THE LORD COMMANDS JOSHUA

1 After the death of Moses the servant of the Lord, the Lord said to Joshua son of Nun, Moses' aide: 2 "Moses my servant is dead. Now then, you and all these people, get ready to cross the Jordan River into the land I am about to give to them—to the Israelites. 3 I will give you every place where you set your foot, as I promised Moses. 4 Your territory will extend from the desert to Lebanon, and from the great river, the Euphrates—all the Hittite country—to the Great Sea[a] on the west. 5 No one will be able to stand up against you all the days of your life. As I was with Moses, so I will be with you; I will never leave you nor forsake you.

6 "Be strong and courageous, because you will lead these people to inherit the land I swore to their forefathers to give them. 7 Be strong and very courageous. Be careful to obey all the law my servant Moses gave you; do not turn from it to the right or to the left, that you may be successful wherever you go. 8 Do not let this Book of the Law depart from your mouth; meditate on it day and night, so that you may be careful to do everything written in it. Then you will be prosperous and successful. 9 Have I not commanded you? Be strong and courageous. Do not be terrified; do not be discouraged, for the Lord your God will be with you wherever you go."

10 So Joshua ordered the officers of the people: 11 "Go through the camp and tell the people, 'Get your supplies ready. Three days from now you will cross the Jordan here to go in and take possession of the land the Lord your God is giving you for your own.' "

12 But to the Reubenites, the Gadites and the half-tribe of Manasseh, Joshua said, 13 "Remember the command that Moses the servant of the Lord gave you: 'The Lord your God is giving you rest and has granted you this land.' 14 Your wives, your children and your livestock may stay in the land that Moses gave you east of the Jordan, but all your fighting men, fully armed, must cross over ahead of your brothers. You are to help your brothers 15 until the Lord gives them rest, as he has done for you, and until they too have taken possession of the land that the Lord your God is giving them. After that, you may go back and occupy your own land, which Moses the servant of the Lord gave you east of the Jordan toward the sunrise."

16 Then they answered Joshua, "Whatever you have commanded us we will do, and wherever you send us we will go. 17 Just as we fully obeyed Moses, so we will obey you. Only may the Lord your God be with you as he was with Moses. 18 Whoever rebels against your word and does not obey your words, whatever you may command them, will be put to death. Only be strong and courageous!"

NOW OR NEVER

JOS 1:9

The fact that God is the most powerful being in the universe means that we have the freedom to obey him without worrying about the earthly consequences.

RAHAB AND THE SPIES

2 Then Joshua son of Nun secretly sent two spies from Shittim. "Go, look over the land," he said, "especially Jericho." So they went and entered the house of a prostitute[b] named Rahab and stayed there.

2 The king of Jericho was told, "Look! Some of the Israelites have come here tonight to spy out the

---

[a] *4* That is, the Mediterranean [b] *1* Or possibly *an innkeeper*

land." ³So the king of Jericho sent this message to Rahab: "Bring out the men who came to you and entered your house, because they have come to spy out the whole land."

⁴But the woman had taken the two men and hidden them. She said, "Yes, the men came to me, but I did not know where they had come from. ⁵At dusk, when it was time to close the city gate, the men left. I don't know which way they went. Go after them quickly. You may catch up with them." ⁶(But she had taken them up to the roof and hidden them under the stalks of flax she had laid out on the roof.) ⁷So the men set out in pursuit of the spies on the road that leads to the fords of the Jordan, and as soon as the pursuers had gone out, the gate was shut.

⁸Before the spies lay down for the night, she went up on the roof ⁹and said to them, "I know that the LORD has given this land to you and that a great fear of you has fallen on us, so

NOW OR NEVER

JOS 1:16

What types of authority do you have problems obeying? Generally speaking, do you try to make the lives of authority figures easier or more difficult when you are under their leadership?

that all who live in this country are melting in fear because of you. ¹⁰We have heard how the LORD dried up the water of the Red Sea[a] for you when you came out of Egypt, and what you did to Sihon and Og, the two kings of the Amorites east of the Jordan, whom you completely destroyed.[b] ¹¹When we heard of it, our hearts melted and everyone's courage failed because of you, for the LORD your God is God in heaven above and on the earth below. ¹²Now then, please swear to me by the LORD that you will show kindness to my family, because I have shown kindness to you. Give me a sure sign ¹³that you will spare the lives of my father and mother, my brothers and sisters, and all who belong to them, and that you will save us from death."

¹⁴"Our lives for your lives!" the men assured her. "If you don't tell what we are doing, we will treat you kindly and faithfully when the LORD gives us the land."

¹⁵So she let them down by a rope through the window, for the house she lived in was part of the city wall. ¹⁶Now she had said to them, "Go to the hills so the pursuers will not find you. Hide yourselves there three days until they return, and then go on your way."

¹⁷The men said to her, "This oath you made us swear will not be binding on us ¹⁸unless, when we enter the land, you have tied this scarlet cord in the window through which you let us down, and unless you have brought your father and mother, your brothers and all your family into your house. ¹⁹If anyone goes outside your house into the street, his blood will be on his own head; we will not be responsible. As for anyone who is in the house with you, his blood will be on our head if a hand is laid on him. ²⁰But if you tell what we are doing, we will be released from the oath you made us swear."

²¹"Agreed," she replied. "Let it be as you say." So she sent them away and they departed. And she tied the scarlet cord in the window.

²²When they left, they went into the hills and stayed there three days, until the pursuers had searched all along the road and returned without finding them. ²³Then the two men started back. They went down out of the hills, forded the river and came to Joshua son of Nun and told him everything that had happened to them. ²⁴They said to Joshua, "The LORD has surely given the whole land into our hands; all the people are melting in fear because of us."

CROSSING THE JORDAN

3 Early in the morning Joshua and all the Israelites set out from Shittim and went to the Jordan, where they camped before crossing over. ²After three days the officers went throughout the camp, ³giving orders to the people: "When you see the ark of the covenant of the LORD your God, and the priests, who are Levites, carrying it, you are to move out from your positions and follow it. ⁴Then you will know which way to go, since you have never been this way before. But keep a distance of about a thousand yards[c] between you and the ark; do not go near it."

⁵Joshua told the people, "Consecrate yourselves, for tomorrow the LORD will do amazing things among you."

---

[a] 10 Hebrew *Yam Suph*; that is, Sea of Reeds [b] 10 The Hebrew term refers to the irrevocable giving over of things or persons to the LORD, often by totally destroying them. [c] 4 Hebrew *about two thousand cubits* (about 900 meters)

battlelines

» What They Don't Know . . . (Honesty)

Q: Where were you last night?
A: I went to that new horror movie—*Psycho on Sorority Row*. It was *intense*!

Q: Your parents let you see *that*?
A: Well, not exactly. I told them I was going to see another movie with a couple friends from band. I didn't want to get into an argument about it. I figured what they didn't know wouldn't hurt them.

Q: So you just looked them in the eyes and *lied*? Wow. I never thought of you as a cold-blooded liar.
A: Whoa, man. That's a little harsh. I mean, yeah, I tell little white lies here and there. But not when something big is on the line. I bet I tell the truth 99 percent of the time. That's like an A+ average. I think that's pretty good.

Q: So if I only killed one out of every 100 people, I wouldn't be a murderer?
A: Come on, that's totally different. Murder hurts other people; harmless lies don't.

Q: If murder and lying are so different, why are they both listed in the Ten Commandments?
A: Wrong, Bible Boy! The Ten Commandments don't say "Don't lie." They say not to give false testimony against other people. And last night I never said anything false about other people.

Q: Sure you did.
A: How?

Q: You told your parents your friends went to see that other movie with you.

» . . . Can't Hurt Them?

Is it ever right to tell a lie? Many Christians point to Biblical examples such as Exodus 1:15–22 (the midwives lying to Pharaoh to protect the Hebrew children) and Joshua 2:1–24 (Rahab lying to the king of Jericho to protect the Israelite spies) and say there are extreme occasions when lying is justifiable—for example, when someone's life is on the line.

You may or may not agree with this view, but what's beyond dispute is that Zach's movie shenanigans certainly don't qualify as an "extreme" situation. And chances are slim that any of us will ever find ourselves in a "life or death" situation where lying is our only option.

What's also beyond dispute is that lying simply to get what we want or to cover our tracks is *never* acceptable. (Check out Ephesians 4:25 and Colossians 3:9.) All lying does is establish an unhealthy pattern or a bad habit that can get out of control way too easily. Lying is also hard to reconcile with our commitment to Christ, who describes himself as "the truth" (John 14:6). Since we can't lie to God about anything (see Hebrews 4:13), why should we be dishonest with anyone else?

Go to www.RevolutionBible.com for more.

6Joshua said to the priests, "Take up the ark of the covenant and pass on ahead of the people." So they took it up and went ahead of them.

7And the LORD said to Joshua, "Today I will begin to exalt you in the eyes of all Israel, so they may know that I am with you as I was with Moses. 8Tell the priests who carry the ark of the covenant: 'When you reach the edge of the Jordan's waters, go and stand in the river.' "

9Joshua said to the Israelites, "Come here and listen to the words of the LORD your God. 10This is how you will know that the living God is among you and that he will certainly drive out before you the Canaanites, Hittites, Hivites, Perizzites, Girgashites, Amorites and Jebusites. 11See, the ark of the covenant of the Lord of all the earth will go into the Jordan ahead of you. 12Now then, choose twelve men from the tribes of Israel, one from each tribe. 13And as soon as the priests who carry the ark of the LORD—the Lord of all the earth—set foot in the Jordan, its waters flowing downstream will be cut off and stand up in a heap."

NOW OR NEVER
JOS 3:8–13

God's instructions—his will for you—won't always make complete sense to you. Sometimes it's only after you do what he says that you'll be able to see just how incredible and right he was.

14So when the people broke camp to cross the Jordan, the priests carrying the ark of the covenant went ahead of them. 15Now the Jordan is at flood stage all during harvest. Yet as soon as the priests who carried the ark reached the Jordan and their feet touched the water's edge, 16the water from upstream stopped flowing. It piled up in a heap a great distance away, at a town called Adam in the vicinity of Zarethan, while the water flowing down to the Sea of the Arabah (the Salt Sea[a]) was completely cut off. So the people crossed over opposite Jericho. 17The priests who carried the ark of the covenant of the LORD stood firm on dry ground in the middle of the Jordan, while all Israel passed by until the whole nation had completed the crossing on dry ground.

4 When the whole nation had finished crossing the Jordan, the LORD said to Joshua, 2"Choose twelve men from among the people, one from each tribe, 3and tell them to take up twelve stones from the middle of the Jordan from right where the priests stood and to carry them over with you and put them down at the place where you stay tonight."

4So Joshua called together the twelve men he had appointed from the Israelites, one from each tribe, 5and said to them, "Go over before the ark of the LORD your God into the middle of the Jordan. Each of you is to take up a stone on his shoulder, according to the number of the tribes of the Israelites, 6to serve as a sign among you. In the future, when your children ask you, 'What do these stones mean?' 7tell them that the flow of the Jordan was cut off before the ark of the covenant of the LORD. When it crossed the Jordan, the waters of the Jordan were cut off. These stones are to be a memorial to the people of Israel forever."

NOW OR NEVER
JOS 4:1–3

Want to start an interesting conversation with your parents (or grandparents)? Ask them to tell you about some of the coolest things God has ever done for them over the course of their lives.

8So the Israelites did as Joshua commanded them. They took twelve stones from the middle of the Jordan, according to the number of the tribes of the Israelites, as the LORD had told Joshua; and they carried them over with them to their camp, where they put them down. 9Joshua set up the twelve stones that had been[b] in the middle of the Jordan at the spot where the priests who carried the ark of the covenant had stood. And they are there to this day.

10Now the priests who carried the ark remained standing in the middle of the Jordan until everything the LORD had commanded Joshua was done by the people, just as Moses had directed Joshua. The people hurried over, 11and as soon as all of them had crossed, the ark of the LORD and the priests came to the other side while the people watched. 12The men of Reuben, Gad and the half-tribe of Manasseh crossed over, armed, in front of the Israelites, as Moses had directed them. 13About forty thousand armed for battle crossed over before the LORD to the plains of Jericho for war.

a 16 That is, the Dead Sea   b 9 Or Joshua also set up twelve stones

Journaling

One of the best ways to keep track of the things God does in your life is to write them in a journal. Get into a routine of jotting down things (both big and small) that relate to important people and events in your life and faith journey. Journaling not only helps you stay focused on God's work in your life, it also gives you a record of blessings that you can look back on whenever you start to doubt God.

¹⁴That day the LORD exalted Joshua in the sight of all Israel; and they revered him all the days of his life, just as they had revered Moses.

¹⁵Then the LORD said to Joshua, ¹⁶"Command the priests carrying the ark of the Testimony to come up out of the Jordan."

¹⁷So Joshua commanded the priests, "Come up out of the Jordan."

¹⁸And the priests came up out of the river carrying the ark of the covenant of the LORD. No sooner had they set their feet on the dry ground than the waters of the Jordan returned to their place and ran at flood stage as before.

¹⁹On the tenth day of the first month the people went up from the Jordan and camped at Gilgal on the eastern border of Jericho. ²⁰And Joshua set up at Gilgal the twelve stones they had taken out of the Jordan. ²¹He said to the Israelites, "In the future when your descendants ask their fathers, 'What do these stones mean?' ²²tell them, 'Israel crossed the Jordan on dry ground.' ²³For the LORD your God dried up the Jordan before you until you had crossed over. The LORD your God did to the Jordan just what he had done to the Red Sea ͣ when he dried it up before us until we had crossed over. ²⁴He did this so that all the peoples of the earth might know that the hand of the LORD is powerful and so that you might always fear the LORD your God."

CIRCUMCISION AT GILGAL

5 Now when all the Amorite kings west of the Jordan and all the Canaanite kings along the coast heard how the LORD had dried up the Jordan before the Israelites until we had crossed over, their hearts melted and they no longer had the courage to face the Israelites.

²At that time the LORD said to Joshua, "Make flint knives and circumcise the Israelites again." ³So Joshua made flint knives and circumcised the Israelites at Gibeath Haaraloth. ͣ

⁴Now this is why he did so: All those who came out of Egypt—all the men of military age—died in the desert on the way after leaving Egypt. ⁵All the people that came out had been circumcised, but all the people born in the desert during the journey from Egypt had not. ⁶The Israelites had moved about in the desert forty years until all the men who were of military age when they left Egypt had died, since they had not obeyed the LORD. For the LORD had sworn to them that they would not see the land that he had solemnly promised their fathers to give us, a land flowing with milk and honey. ⁷So he raised up their sons in their place, and these were the ones Joshua circumcised. They were still uncircumcised because they had not been circum-

Persecution

If obeying God seems painless, you're probably not doing it just right. Lots of pieces of God's will go against the way our society says we should live. If you're serious about following the Lord, you're going to stand out—often in ways that aren't exactly comfortable for you. You're going to bother some people. You're going to make them think about things they'd rather not think about. You're going to set yourself up as a target for jokes and abuse. But at least you'll have an easier time than the Israelite men did at Gibeath Haaraloth. Yowsa!

ͣ 23 Hebrew *Yam Suph*; that is, Sea of Reeds   ᵇ 3 *Gibeath Haaraloth* means *hill of foreskins.*

cised on the way. ⁸And after the whole nation had been circumcised, they remained where they were in camp until they were healed.

⁹Then the LORD said to Joshua, "Today I have rolled away the reproach of Egypt from you." So the place has been called Gilgal[a] to this day.

¹⁰On the evening of the fourteenth day of the month, while camped at Gilgal on the plains of Jericho, the Israelites celebrated the Passover. ¹¹The day after the Passover, that very day, they ate some of the produce of the land: unleavened bread and roasted grain. ¹²The manna stopped the day after[b] they ate this food from the land; there was no longer any manna for the Israelites, but that year they ate of the produce of Canaan.

THE FALL OF JERICHO

¹³Now when Joshua was near Jericho, he looked up and saw a man standing in front of him with a drawn sword in his hand. Joshua went up to him and asked, "Are you for us or for our enemies?"

¹⁴"Neither," he replied, "but as commander of the army of the LORD I have now come." Then Joshua fell facedown to the ground in reverence, and asked him, "What message does my Lord[c] have for his servant?"

¹⁵The commander of the LORD's army replied, "Take off your sandals, for the place where you are standing is holy." And Joshua did so.

6 Now Jericho was tightly shut up because of the Israelites. No one went out and no one came in.

²Then the LORD said to Joshua, "See, I have delivered Jericho into your hands, along with its king and its fighting men. ³March around the city once with all the armed men. Do this for six days. ⁴Have seven priests carry trumpets of rams' horns in front of the ark. On the seventh day, march around the city seven times, with the priests blowing the trumpets. ⁵When you hear them sound a long blast on the trumpets, have all the people give a loud shout; then the wall of the city will collapse and the people will go up, every man straight in."

⁶So Joshua son of Nun called the priests and said to them, "Take up the ark of the covenant of the LORD and have seven priests carry trumpets in front of it." ⁷And he ordered the people, "Advance! March around the city, with the armed guard going ahead of the ark of the LORD."

⁸When Joshua had spoken to the people, the seven priests carrying the seven trumpets

now or never

JOS 6:3–5

Ever wonder why God works in such unique ways? Maybe it's because he doesn't want to leave any doubt about who should get the credit for his work.

before the LORD went forward, blowing their trumpets, and the ark of the LORD's covenant followed them. ⁹The armed guard marched ahead of the priests who blew the trumpets, and the rear guard followed the ark. All this time the trumpets were sounding. ¹⁰But Joshua had commanded the people, "Do not give a war cry, do not raise your voices, do not say a word until the day I tell you to shout. Then shout!" ¹¹So he had the ark of the LORD carried around the city, circling it once. Then the people returned to camp and spent the night there.

¹²Joshua got up early the next morning and the priests took up the ark of the LORD. ¹³The seven priests carrying the seven trumpets went forward, marching before the ark of the LORD and blowing the trumpets. The armed men went ahead of them and the rear guard followed the ark of the LORD, while the trumpets kept sounding. ¹⁴So on the second day they marched around the city once and returned to the camp. They did this for six days.

¹⁵On the seventh day, they got up at daybreak and marched around the city seven times in the same manner, except that on that day they circled the city seven times. ¹⁶The seventh time around, when the priests sounded the trumpet blast, Joshua commanded the people, "Shout! For the LORD has given you the city! ¹⁷The city and all that is in it are to be devoted[d] to the LORD. Only Rahab the prostitute[e] and all

---

[a] 9 *Gilgal* sounds like the Hebrew for *roll.*   [b] 12 Or *the day*   [c] 14 Or *lord*   [d] 17 The Hebrew term refers to the irrevocable giving over of things or persons to the LORD, often by totally destroying them; also in verses 18 and 21.   [e] 17 Or possibly *innkeeper*; also in verses 22 and 25

who are with her in her house shall be spared, because she hid the spies we sent. ¹⁸But keep away from the devoted things, so that you will not bring about your own destruction by taking any of them. Otherwise you will make the camp of Israel liable to destruction and bring trouble on it. ¹⁹All the silver and gold and the articles of bronze and iron are sacred to the Lᴏʀᴅ and must go into his treasury."

²⁰When the trumpets sounded, the people shouted, and at the sound of the trumpet, when the people gave a loud shout, the wall collapsed; so every man charged straight in, and they took the city. ²¹They devoted the city to the Lᴏʀᴅ and destroyed with the sword every living thing in it—men and women, young and old, cattle, sheep and donkeys.

²²Joshua said to the two men who had spied out the land, "Go into the prostitute's house and bring her out and all who belong to her, in accordance with your oath to her." ²³So the young men who had done the spying went in and brought out Rahab, her father and mother and brothers and all who belonged to her. They brought out her entire family and put them in a place outside the camp of Israel.

²⁴Then they burned the whole city and everything in it, but they put the silver and gold and the articles of bronze and iron into the treasury of the Lᴏʀᴅ's house. ²⁵But Joshua spared Rahab the prostitute, with her family and all who belonged to her, because she hid the men Joshua had sent as spies to Jericho—and she lives among the Israelites to this day.

²⁶At that time Joshua pronounced this solemn oath: "Cursed before the Lᴏʀᴅ is the man who undertakes to rebuild this city, Jericho:

> "At the cost of his firstborn son
>   will he lay its foundations;
> at the cost of his youngest
>   will he set up its gates."

²⁷So the Lᴏʀᴅ was with Joshua, and his fame spread throughout the land.

ACHAN'S SIN

7 But the Israelites acted unfaithfully in regard to the devoted things ᵃ; Achan son of Carmi, the son of Zimri, ᵇ the son of Zerah, of the tribe of Judah, took some of them. So the Lᴏʀᴅ's anger burned against Israel.

²Now Joshua sent men from Jericho to Ai, which is near Beth Aven to the east of Bethel, and told them, "Go up and spy out the region." So the men went up and spied out Ai.

³When they returned to Joshua, they said, "Not all the people will have to go up against Ai. Send two or three thousand men to take it and do not weary all the people, for only a few men are there." ⁴So about three thousand men went up; but they were routed by the men of Ai, ⁵who killed about thirty-six of them. They chased the Israelites from the city gate as far as the stone quarries ᶜ and struck them down on the slopes. At this the hearts of the people melted and became like water.

⁶Then Joshua tore his clothes and fell facedown to the ground before the ark of the Lᴏʀᴅ, remaining there till evening. The elders of Israel did the same, and sprinkled dust on their heads. ⁷And Joshua said, "Ah, Sovereign Lᴏʀᴅ, why did you ever bring this people across the Jordan to deliver us into the hands of the Amorites to destroy us? If only we had been content to stay on the other side of the Jordan! ⁸O Lord, what can I say, now that Israel has been routed by its enemies? ⁹The Canaanites and the other people of the country will hear about this and they will surround us and wipe out our name from the earth. What then will you do for your own great name?"

¹⁰The Lᴏʀᴅ said to Joshua, "Stand up! What are you doing down on your face? ¹¹Israel has sinned; they have violated my covenant, which I commanded them to keep. They have taken some of the devoted things; they have stolen, they have lied, they have put them with their own possessions. ¹²That is why the Israelites cannot stand against their enemies; they turn their backs and run because they have been made liable to destruction. I will not be with you anymore unless you destroy whatever among you is devoted to destruction.

¹³"Go, consecrate the people. Tell them, 'Consecrate yourselves in preparation for tomorrow; for this is what the Lᴏʀᴅ, the God of Israel, says: That which is devoted is among you, O Israel. You cannot stand against your enemies until you remove it.

¹⁴" 'In the morning, present yourselves tribe by tribe. The tribe that the Lᴏʀᴅ takes shall come for-

---

ᵃ 1 The Hebrew term refers to the irrevocable giving over of things or persons to the Lᴏʀᴅ, often by totally destroying them; also in verses 11, 12, 13 and 15.   ᵇ 1 See Septuagint and 1 Chron. 2:6; Hebrew *Zabdi*; also in verses 17 and 18.   ᶜ 5 Or *as far as Shebarim* ward clan by clan; the clan that the Lord takes shall come forward family by family; and the family that the Lord takes shall come forward man by man. ¹⁵He who is caught with the devoted things shall be destroyed by fire, along with all that belongs to him. He has violated the covenant of the Lord and has done a disgraceful thing in Israel!' "

¹⁶Early the next morning Joshua had Israel come forward by tribes, and Judah was taken. ¹⁷The clans of Judah came forward, and he took the Zerahites. He had the clan of the Zerahites come forward by families, and Zimri was taken. ¹⁸Joshua had his family come forward man by man, and Achan son of Carmi, the son of Zimri, the son of Zerah, of the tribe of Judah, was taken.

¹⁹Then Joshua said to Achan, "My son, give glory to the Lord,ᵃ the God of Israel, and give him the praise.ᵇ Tell me what you have done; do not hide it from me."

²⁰Achan replied, "It is true! I have sinned against the Lord, the God of Israel. This is what I have done: ²¹When I saw in the plunder a beautiful robe from Babylonia,ᶜ two hundred shekelsᵈ of silver and a wedge of gold weighing fifty shekels,ᵉ I coveted them and took them. They are hidden in the ground inside my tent, with the silver underneath."

²²So Joshua sent messengers, and they ran to the tent, and there it was, hidden in his tent, with the silver underneath. ²³They took the things from the tent, brought them to Joshua and all the Israelites and spread them out before the Lord.

²⁴Then Joshua, together with all Israel, took Achan son of Zerah, the silver, the robe, the gold wedge, his sons and daughters, his cattle, donkeys and sheep, his tent and all that he had, to the Valley of Achor. ²⁵Joshua said, "Why have you brought this trouble on us? The Lord will bring trouble on you today."

Then all Israel stoned him, and after they had stoned the rest, they burned them. ²⁶Over Achan they heaped up a large pile of rocks, which remains to this day. Then the Lord turned from his fierce anger. Therefore that place has been called the Valley of Achorᶠ ever since.

AI DESTROYED

8 Then the Lord said to Joshua, "Do not be afraid; do not be discouraged. Take the whole army with you, and go up and attack Ai. For I have delivered into your hands the king of Ai, his people, his city and his land. ²You shall do to Ai and its king as you did to Jericho and its king, except that you may carry off their plunder and livestock for yourselves. Set an ambush behind the city."

³So Joshua and the whole army moved out to attack Ai. He chose thirty thousand of his best fighting men and sent them out at night ⁴with these orders: "Listen carefully. You are to set an ambush behind the city. Don't go very far from it. All of you be on the alert. ⁵I and all those with me will advance on the city, and when the men come out against us, as they did before, we will flee from them. ⁶They will pursue us until we have lured them away from the city, for they will say, 'They are running away from us as they did before.' So when we flee from them, ⁷you are to rise up from ambush and take the city. The Lord your God will give it into your hand. ⁸When you have taken the city, set it on fire. Do what the Lord has commanded. See to it; you have my orders."

⁹Then Joshua sent them off, and they went to the place of ambush and lay in wait between Bethel and Ai, to the west of Ai—but Joshua spent that night with the people.

¹⁰Early the next morning Joshua mustered his men, and he and the leaders of Israel marched before them to Ai. ¹¹The entire force that was with him marched up and approached the city and arrived in front of it. They set up camp north of Ai, with the valley between them and the city. ¹²Joshua had taken about five thousand men and set them in ambush between Bethel and Ai, to the west of the city. ¹³They had the soldiers take up their positions—all those in the camp to the north of the city and the ambush to the west of it. That night Joshua went into the valley.

¹⁴When the king of Ai saw this, he and all the men of the city hurried out early in the morning to meet Israel in battle at a certain place overlooking the Arabah. But he did not know that an ambush had

now or never

JOS 7:24–25

Think sin is a personal matter? Think it's no one else's business but the one doing the sinning? Think again.

ᵃ 19 A solemn charge to tell the truth   ᵇ 19 Or and confess to him   ᶜ 21 Hebrew Shinar   ᵈ 21 That is, about 5 pounds (about 2.3 kilograms)   ᵉ 21 That is, about 1 1/4 pounds (about 0.6 kilogram)   ᶠ 26 Achor means trouble.

been set against him behind the city. 15Joshua and all Israel let themselves be driven back before them, and they fled toward the desert. 16All the men of Ai were called to pursue them, and they pursued Joshua and were lured away from the city. 17Not a man remained in Ai or Bethel who did not go after Israel. They left the city open and went in pursuit of Israel.

18Then the LORD said to Joshua, "Hold out toward Ai the javelin that is in your hand, for into your hand I will deliver the city." So Joshua held out his javelin toward Ai. 19As soon as he did this, the men in the ambush rose quickly from their position and rushed forward. They entered the city and captured it and quickly set it on fire.

20The men of Ai looked back and saw the smoke of the city rising against the sky, but they had no chance to escape in any direction, for the Israelites who had been fleeing toward the desert had turned back against their pursuers. 21For when Joshua and all Israel saw that the ambush had taken the city and that smoke was going up from the city, they turned around and attacked the men of Ai. 22The men of the ambush also came out of the city against them, so that they were caught in the middle, with Israelites on both sides. Israel cut them down, leaving them neither survivors nor fugitives. 23But they took the king of Ai alive and brought him to Joshua.

24When Israel had finished killing all the men of Ai in the fields and in the desert where they had chased them, and when every one of them had been put to the sword, all the Israelites returned to Ai and killed those who were in it. 25Twelve thousand men and women fell that day—all the people of Ai. 26For Joshua did not draw back the hand that held out his javelin until he had destroyed[a] all who lived in Ai. 27But Israel did carry off for themselves the livestock and plunder of this city, as the LORD had instructed Joshua.

28So Joshua burned Ai and made it a permanent heap of ruins, a desolate place to this day. 29He hung the king of Ai on a tree and left him there until evening. At sunset, Joshua ordered them to take his body from the tree and throw it down at the entrance of the city gate. And they raised a large pile of rocks over it, which remains to this day.

THE COVENANT RENEWED AT MOUNT EBAL

30Then Joshua built on Mount Ebal an altar to the LORD, the God of Israel, 31as Moses the servant of the LORD had commanded the Israelites. He built it according to what is written in the Book of the Law of Moses—an altar of uncut stones, on which no iron tool had been used. On it they offered to the LORD burnt offerings and sacrificed fellowship offerings.[b] 32There, in the presence of the Israelites, Joshua copied on stones the law of Moses, which he had written. 33All Israel, aliens and citizens alike, with their elders, officials and judges, were standing on both sides of the ark of the covenant of the LORD, facing those who carried it—the priests, who were Levites. Half of the people stood in front of Mount Gerizim and half of them in front of Mount Ebal, as Moses the servant of the LORD had formerly commanded when he gave instructions to bless the people of Israel.

34Afterward, Joshua read all the words of the law—the blessings and the curses—just as it is written in the Book of the Law. 35There was not a word of all that Moses had commanded that Joshua did not read to the whole assembly of Israel, including the women and children, and the aliens who lived among them.

THE GIBEONITE DECEPTION

9 Now when all the kings west of the Jordan heard about these things—those in the hill country, in the western foothills, and along the entire coast of the Great Sea[c] as far as Lebanon (the kings of the Hittites, Amorites, Canaanites, Perizzites, Hivites and Jebusites)— 2they came together to make war against Joshua and Israel.

3However, when the people of Gibeon heard what Joshua had done to Jericho and Ai, 4they resorted to a ruse: They went as a delegation whose donkeys were loaded[d] with worn-out sacks and old wineskins, cracked and mended. 5The men put worn and patched sandals on their feet and wore old clothes. All the bread of their food supply was dry and moldy. 6Then they went to Joshua in the camp at Gilgal and said to him and the men of Israel, "We have come from a distant country; make a treaty with us."

7The men of Israel said to the Hivites, "But perhaps you live near us. How then can we make a treaty with you?"

---

a 26 The Hebrew term refers to the irrevocable giving over of things or persons to the LORD, often by totally destroying them. b 31 Traditionally peace offerings c 1 That is, the Mediterranean d 4 Most Hebrew manuscripts; some Hebrew manuscripts, Vulgate and Syriac (see also Septuagint) They prepared provisions and loaded their donkeys

⁸"We are your servants," they said to Joshua.

But Joshua asked, "Who are you and where do you come from?"

⁹They answered: "Your servants have come from a very distant country because of the fame of the LORD your God. For we have heard reports of him: all that he did in Egypt, ¹⁰and all that he did to the two kings of the Amorites east of the Jordan—Sihon king of Heshbon, and Og king of Bashan, who reigned in Ashtaroth. ¹¹And our elders and all those living in our country said to us, 'Take provisions for your journey; go and meet them and say to them, "We are your servants; make a treaty with us." ' ¹²This bread of ours was warm when we packed it at home on the day we left to come to you. But now see how dry and moldy it is. ¹³And these wineskins that we filled were new, but see how cracked they are. And our clothes and sandals are worn out by the very long journey."

¹⁴The men of Israel sampled their provisions but did not inquire of the LORD. ¹⁵Then Joshua made a treaty of peace with them to let them live, and the leaders of the assembly ratified it by oath.

¹⁶Three days after they made the treaty with the Gibeonites, the Israelites heard that they were neighbors, living near them. ¹⁷So the Israelites set out and on the third day came to their cities: Gibeon, Kephirah, Beeroth and Kiriath Jearim. ¹⁸But the Israelites did not attack them, because the leaders of the assembly had sworn an oath to them by the LORD, the God of Israel.

The whole assembly grumbled against the leaders, ¹⁹but all the leaders answered, "We have given them our oath by the LORD, the God of Israel, and we cannot touch them now. ²⁰This is what we will do to them: We will let them live, so that wrath will not fall on us for breaking the oath we swore to them." ²¹They continued, "Let them live, but let them be woodcutters and water carriers for the entire community." So the leaders' promise to them was kept.

²²Then Joshua summoned the Gibeonites and said, "Why did you deceive us by saying, 'We live a long way from you,' while actually you live near us? ²³You are now under a curse: You will never cease to serve as woodcutters and water carriers for the house of my God."

²⁴They answered Joshua, "Your servants were clearly told how the LORD your God had commanded his servant Moses to give you the whole land and to wipe out all its inhabitants from before you. So we feared for our lives because of you, and that is why we did this. ²⁵We are now in your hands. Do to us whatever seems good and right to you."

²⁶So Joshua saved them from the Israelites, and they did not kill them. ²⁷That day he made the Gibeonites woodcutters and water carriers for the community and for the altar of the LORD at the place the LORD would choose. And that is what they are to this day.

THE SUN STANDS STILL

10 Now Adoni-Zedek king of Jerusalem heard that Joshua had taken Ai and totally destroyed^a it, doing to Ai and its king as he had done to Jericho and its king, and that the people of Gibeon had made a treaty of peace with Israel and were living near them. ²He and his people were very much alarmed at this, because Gibeon was an important city, like one of the royal cities; it was larger than Ai, and all its men were good fighters. ³So Adoni-Zedek king of Jerusalem appealed to Hoham king of Hebron, Piram king of Jarmuth, Japhia king of Lachish and Debir king of Eglon. ⁴"Come up and help me attack Gibeon," he said, "because it has made peace with Joshua and the Israelites."

⁵Then the five kings of the Amorites—the kings of Jerusalem, Hebron, Jarmuth, Lachish and Eglon—joined forces. They moved up with all their troops and took up positions against Gibeon and attacked it.

⁶The Gibeonites then sent word to Joshua in the camp at Gilgal: "Do not abandon your servants. Come up to us quickly and save us! Help us, because all the Amorite kings from the hill country have joined forces against us."

⁷So Joshua marched up from Gilgal with his entire army, including all the best fighting men. ⁸The LORD said to Joshua, "Do not be afraid of them; I have given them into your hand. Not one of them will be able to withstand you."

⁹After an all-night march from Gilgal, Joshua took them by surprise. ¹⁰The LORD threw them into confusion before Israel, who defeated them in a great victory at Gibeon. Israel pursued them along the road going up to Beth Horon and cut them down all the way to Azekah and Makkedah. ¹¹As they fled before

^a 1 The Hebrew term refers to the irrevocable giving over of things or persons to the LORD, often by totally destroying them; also in verses 28, 35, 37, 39 and 40.

Israel on the road down from Beth Horon to Azekah, the Lord hurled large hailstones down on them from the sky, and more of them died from the hailstones than were killed by the swords of the Israelites.

¹²On the day the Lord gave the Amorites over to Israel, Joshua said to the Lord in the presence of Israel:

> "O sun, stand still over Gibeon,
> O moon, over the Valley of Aijalon."
> ¹³So the sun stood still,
> and the moon stopped,
> till the nation avenged itself onᵇ its enemies,

as it is written in the Book of Jashar.

The sun stopped in the middle of the sky and delayed going down about a full day. ¹⁴There has never been a day like it before or since, a day when the Lord listened to a man. Surely the Lord was fighting for Israel!

¹⁵Then Joshua returned with all Israel to the camp at Gilgal.

FIVE AMORITE KINGS KILLED

¹⁶Now the five kings had fled and hidden in the cave at Makkedah. ¹⁷When Joshua was told that the five kings had been found hiding in the cave at Makkedah, ¹⁸he said, "Roll large rocks up to the mouth of the cave, and post some men there to guard it. ¹⁹But don't stop! Pursue your enemies, attack them from the rear and don't let them reach their cities, for the Lord your God has given them into your hand."

NOW OR NEVER
JOS 10:12–14

Imagine you're on a battlefield fighting for your life and some battle-ax or broadsword could take your head off at any second. Now imagine that the Lord steps in and fights your battle for you. Pretty cool, huh?

---

²⁰So Joshua and the Israelites destroyed them completely—almost to a man—but the few who were left reached their fortified cities. ²¹The whole army then returned safely to Joshua in the camp at Makkedah, and no one uttered a word against the Israelites.

²²Joshua said, "Open the mouth of the cave and bring those five kings out to me." ²³So they brought the five kings out of the cave—the kings of Jerusalem, Hebron, Jarmuth, Lachish and Eglon. ²⁴When they had brought these kings to Joshua, he summoned all the men of Israel and said to the army commanders who had come with him, "Come here and put your feet on the necks of these kings." So they came forward and placed their feet on their necks.

²⁵Joshua said to them, "Do not be afraid; do not be discouraged. Be strong and courageous. This is what the Lord will do to all the enemies you are going to fight." ²⁶Then Joshua struck and killed the kings and hung them on five trees, and they were left hanging on the trees until evening.

²⁷At sunset Joshua gave the order and they took them down from the trees and threw them into the cave where they had been hiding. At the mouth of the cave they placed large rocks, which are there to this day.

²⁸That day Joshua took Makkedah. He put the city and its king to the sword and totally destroyed everyone in it. He left no survivors. And he did to the king of Makkedah as he had done to the king of Jericho.

SOUTHERN CITIES CONQUERED

²⁹Then Joshua and all Israel with him moved on from Makkedah to Libnah and attacked it. ³⁰The Lord also gave that city and its king into Israel's hand. The city and everyone in it Joshua put to the sword. He left no survivors there. And he did to its king as he had done to the king of Jericho.

³¹Then Joshua and all Israel with him moved on from Libnah to Lachish; he took up positions against it and attacked it. ³²The Lord handed Lachish over to Israel, and Joshua took it on the second day. The city and everyone in it he put to the sword, just as he had done to Libnah. ³³Meanwhile, Ho-

---

ᵇ 13 Or *nation triumphed over*

ram king of Gezer had come up to help Lachish, but Joshua defeated him and his army—until no survivors were left.

³⁴Then Joshua and all Israel with him moved on from Lachish to Eglon; they took up positions against it and attacked it. ³⁵They captured it that same day and put it to the sword and totally destroyed everyone in it, just as they had done to Lachish.

³⁶Then Joshua and all Israel with him went up from Eglon to Hebron and attacked it. ³⁷They took the city and put it to the sword, together with its king, its villages and everyone in it. They left no survivors. Just as at Eglon, they totally destroyed it and everyone in it.

³⁸Then Joshua and all Israel with him turned around and attacked Debir. ³⁹They took the city, its king and its villages, and put them to the sword. Everyone in it they totally destroyed. They left no survivors. They did to Debir and its king as they had done to Libnah and its king and to Hebron.

⁴⁰So Joshua subdued the whole region, including the hill country, the Negev, the western foothills and the mountain slopes, together with all their kings. He left no survivors. He totally destroyed all who breathed, just as the LORD, the God of Israel, had commanded. ⁴¹Joshua subdued them from Kadesh Barnea to Gaza and from the whole region of Goshen to Gibeon. ⁴²All these kings and their lands Joshua conquered in one campaign, because the LORD, the God of Israel, fought for Israel.

⁴³Then Joshua returned with all Israel to the camp at Gilgal.

NORTHERN KINGS DEFEATED

11 When Jabin king of Hazor heard of this, he sent word to Jobab king of Madon, to the kings of Shimron and Acshaph, ²and to the northern kings who were in the mountains, in the Arabah south of Kinnereth, in the western foothills and in Naphoth Dor[a] on the west; ³to the Canaanites in the east and west; to the Amorites, Hittites, Perizzites and Jebusites in the hill country; and to the Hivites below Hermon in the region of Mizpah. ⁴They came out with all their troops and a large number of horses and chariots—a huge army, as numerous as the sand on the seashore. ⁵All these kings joined forces and made camp together at the Waters of Merom, to fight against Israel.

⁶The LORD said to Joshua, "Do not be afraid of them, because by this time tomorrow I will hand all of them over to Israel, slain. You are to hamstring their horses and burn their chariots."

⁷So Joshua and his whole army came against them suddenly at the Waters of Merom and attacked them, ⁸and the LORD gave them into the hand of Israel. They defeated them and pursued them all the way to Greater Sidon, to Misrephoth Maim, and to the Valley of Mizpah on the east, until no survivors were left. ⁹Joshua did to them as the LORD had directed: He hamstrung their horses and burned their chariots.

¹⁰At that time Joshua turned back and captured Hazor and put its king to the sword. (Hazor had been the head of all these kingdoms.) ¹¹Everyone in it they put to the sword. They totally destroyed[b] them, not sparing anything that breathed, and he burned up Hazor itself.

¹²Joshua took all these royal cities and their kings and put them to the sword. He totally destroyed them, as Moses the servant of the LORD had commanded. ¹³Yet Israel did not burn any of the cities built on their mounds—except Hazor, which Joshua burned. ¹⁴The Israelites carried off for themselves all the plunder and livestock of these cities, but all the people they put to the sword until they completely destroyed them, not sparing anyone that breathed. ¹⁵As the LORD commanded his servant Moses, so Moses commanded Joshua, and Joshua did it; he left nothing undone of all that the LORD commanded Moses.

¹⁶So Joshua took this entire land: the hill country, all the Negev, the whole region of Goshen, the western foothills, the Arabah and the mountains of Israel with their foothills, ¹⁷from Mount Halak, which rises toward Seir, to Baal Gad in the Valley of Lebanon below Mount Hermon. He captured all their kings and struck them down, putting them to death. ¹⁸Joshua waged war against all these kings for a long

NOW OR NEVER

JOS 11:15

One solid strategy for growing as a man of God is to link up with an older, more mature man who has years of rich experience in following God. Joshua found that person in Moses. Who can you turn to?

ᵃ 2 Or *in the heights of Dor*   ᵇ 11 The Hebrew term refers to the irrevocable giving over of things or persons to the LORD, often by totally destroying them; also in verses 12, 20 and 21.

joshua

VERSUS

canaanites

» Moses' longtime assistant and eventual successor

» Brilliant military commander

» Led the Israelites in conquering Canaan

» Descendants of Ham, Noah's son

» Inhabitants of the promised land before the Israelites arrived

» Notorious idol worshipers

The Main Event

Try to picture this scene:

It's dusk. General Joshua stands on a rocky hill with a small group of his best military commanders. They look down on a blood-soaked valley littered with Canaanite bodies. After seven years and a battle record of 31-1 against the cities of Canaan (the only loss being the humbling setback at Ai; see Joshua 7–8), the Israelites have won the brutal war for the promised land. God has carried out his word, and the children of Israel have a wonderful new homeland.

The steely-eyed Joshua showed no mercy to his enemies. In keeping with what God had commanded Moses, Joshua made sure his troops "completely destroyed them, not sparing anyone that breathed" (Joshua 11:14). The guys from *Braveheart* and *Gladiator* were teddy bears compared to the Israelite commander.

Why such annihilation? The mangled and headless Canaanite body lying near Joshua gives us the answer. This man, whether soldier or king, was part of a pagan society that embraced immorality and rejected the one true God. In fact, the people of Canaan worshiped just about everything *but* God. Imagine living in a society that viewed sleeping with a prostitute as an authorized act of *worship*, and you've got a pretty good idea of what the religious climate was like in Canaan.

What's more, Joshua lived in a day when each country had its own set of gods. And most people measured the might of their gods by the might of their country. So a war between two nations was more than just a human skirmish; it was an all-out battle between the gods of each country. Whichever nation came out on top was thought to have the more powerful gods on its side.

Given this, God was putting his reputation on the line by promising the land of Canaan to the Israelites. And by using Joshua to annihilate the opposition, God showed the world that he is strong enough to deliver on his promises.

The sad part is, despite overwhelming evidence of the power and grace of the one true God, the people of Canaan were unwilling to bow to him. The result was complete devastation.

The Outcome

The great British author C. S. Lewis once wrote that there are only two kinds of people in the world: those, like Joshua, who say to God, "Thy will be done." And those, like the Canaanites, to whom God says, "*Thy* will be done."*

In other words, when you look beyond the surface, the Canaanites weren't fighting Joshua and his army. Ultimately they were fighting God. Refusing to recognize his reality and authority, they steeled their souls against the truth. Despite seven years of war, they continued to defy God. God's response to such defiance is, "All right, have it your way. You don't have to acknowledge me, but you *do* have to pay the price for refusing to do so." Joshua and the people of Israel were simply the instruments of divine judgment that God used to destroy the Canaanites.

What category do you fit in? Are you like the obedient Joshua? Or are you following the example of the doomed Canaanites?

Read more about Joshua and the Canaanites in Joshua 11:16–23 (pages 252–254).

*C. S. Lewis, *The Great Divorce.* Harper San Francisco, 2001.

time. ¹⁹Except for the Hivites living in Gibeon, not one city made a treaty of peace with the Israelites, who took them all in battle. ²⁰For it was the LORD himself who hardened their hearts to wage war against Israel, so that he might destroy them totally, exterminating them without mercy, as the LORD had commanded Moses.

²¹At that time Joshua went and destroyed the Anakites from the hill country: from Hebron, Debir and Anab, from all the hill country of Judah, and from all the hill country of Israel. Joshua totally destroyed them and their towns. ²²No Anakites were left in Israelite territory; only in Gaza, Gath and Ashdod did any survive. ²³So Joshua took the entire land, just as the LORD had directed Moses, and he gave it as an inheritance to Israel according to their tribal divisions.

Then the land had rest from war.

LIST OF DEFEATED KINGS

12 These are the kings of the land whom the Israelites had defeated and whose territory they took over east of the Jordan, from the Arnon Gorge to Mount Hermon, including all the eastern side of the Arabah:

²Sihon king of the Amorites,
who reigned in Heshbon. He ruled from Aroer on the rim of the Arnon Gorge—from the middle of the gorge—to the Jabbok River, which is the border of the Ammonites. This included half of Gilead. ³He also ruled over the eastern Arabah from the Sea of Kinnereth[a] to the Sea of the Arabah (the Salt Sea[b]), to Beth Jeshimoth, and then southward below the slopes of Pisgah.

⁴And the territory of Og king of Bashan,
one of the last of the Rephaites, who reigned in Ashtaroth and Edrei. ⁵He ruled over Mount Hermon, Salecah, all of Bashan to the border of the people of Geshur and Maacah, and half of Gilead to the border of Sihon king of Heshbon.

⁶Moses, the servant of the LORD, and the Israelites conquered them. And Moses the servant of the LORD gave their land to the Reubenites, the Gadites and the half-tribe of Manasseh to be their possession.

⁷These are the kings of the land that Joshua and the Israelites conquered on the west side of the Jordan, from Baal Gad in the Valley of Lebanon to Mount Halak, which rises toward Seir (their lands Joshua gave as an inheritance to the tribes of Israel according to their tribal divisions— ⁸the hill country, the western foothills, the Arabah, the mountain slopes, the desert and the Negev—the lands of the Hittites, Amorites, Canaanites, Perizzites, Hivites and Jebusites):

⁹the king of Jericho	one
the king of Ai (near Bethel)	one
¹⁰the king of Jerusalem	one
the king of Hebron	one
¹¹the king of Jarmuth	one
the king of Lachish	one
¹²the king of Eglon	one
the king of Gezer	one
¹³the king of Debir	one
the king of Geder	one
¹⁴the king of Hormah	one
the king of Arad	one
¹⁵the king of Libnah	one
the king of Adullam	one
¹⁶the king of Makkedah	one
the king of Bethel	one
¹⁷the king of Tappuah	one
the king of Hepher	one
¹⁸the king of Aphek	one
the king of Lasharon	one

---

^a 3 That is, Galilee   ^b 3 That is, the Dead Sea

¹⁹the king of Madon	one
the king of Hazor	one
²⁰the king of Shimron Meron	one
the king of Acshaph	one
²¹the king of Taanach	one
the king of Megiddo	one
²²the king of Kedesh	one
the king of Jokneam in Carmel	one
²³the king of Dor (in Naphoth Dorᵃ)	one
the king of Goyim in Gilgal	one
²⁴the king of Tirzah	one

thirty-one kings in all.

LAND STILL TO BE TAKEN

13 When Joshua was old and well advanced in years, the Lᴏʀᴅ said to him, "You are very old, and there are still very large areas of land to be taken over.

²"This is the land that remains: all the regions of the Philistines and Geshurites: ³from the Shihor River on the east of Egypt to the territory of Ekron on the north, all of it counted as Canaanite (the territory of the five Philistine rulers in Gaza, Ashdod, Ashkelon, Gath and Ekron—that of the Avvites); ⁴from the south, all the land of the Canaanites, from Arah of the Sidonians as far as Aphek, the region of the Amorites, ⁵the area of the Gebalitesᵇ; and all Lebanon to the east, from Baal Gad below Mount Hermon to Leboᶜ Hamath.

⁶"As for all the inhabitants of the mountain regions from Lebanon to Misrephoth Maim, that is, all the Sidonians, I myself will drive them out before the Israelites. Be sure to allocate this land to Israel for an inheritance, as I have instructed you, ⁷and divide it as an inheritance among the nine tribes and half of the tribe of Manasseh."

NOW OR NEVER
JOS 13:1

God doesn't offer a retirement plan to his people. He has important work to keep us busy until the day we die. That's why it's never a good idea to dismiss or underestimate the older members of God's team.

DIVISION OF THE LAND EAST OF THE JORDAN

⁸The other half of Manasseh,ᵈ the Reubenites and the Gadites had received the inheritance that Moses had given them east of the Jordan, as he, the servant of the Lᴏʀᴅ, had assigned it to them.

⁹It extended from Aroer on the rim of the Arnon Gorge, and from the town in the middle of the gorge, and included the whole plateau of Medeba as far as Dibon, ¹⁰and all the towns of Sihon king of the Amorites, who ruled in Heshbon, out to the border of the Ammonites. ¹¹It also included Gilead, the territory of the people of Geshur and Maacah, all of Mount Hermon and all Bashan as far as Salecah— ¹²that is, the whole kingdom of Og in Bashan, who had reigned in Ashtaroth and Edrei and had survived as one of the last of the Rephaites. Moses had defeated them and taken over their land. ¹³But the Israelites did not drive out the people of Geshur and Maacah, so they continue to live among the Israelites to this day.

¹⁴But to the tribe of Levi he gave no inheritance, since the offerings made by fire to the Lᴏʀᴅ, the God of Israel, are their inheritance, as he promised them.

¹⁵This is what Moses had given to the tribe of Reuben, clan by clan:

¹⁶The territory from Aroer on the rim of the Arnon Gorge, and from the town in the middle of the gorge, and the whole plateau past Medeba ¹⁷to Heshbon and all its towns on the plateau, including Dibon, Bamoth Baal, Beth Baal Meon, ¹⁸Jahaz, Kedemoth, Mephaath, ¹⁹Kiriathaim, Sibmah,

---

ᵃ *23* Or *in the heights of Dor* ᵇ *5* That is, the area of Byblos ᶜ *5* Or *to the entrance to* ᵈ *8* Hebrew *With it* (that is, with the other half of Manasseh)

Zereth Shahar on the hill in the valley, ²⁰Beth Peor, the slopes of Pisgah, and Beth Jeshimoth ²¹—all the towns on the plateau and the entire realm of Sihon king of the Amorites, who ruled at Heshbon. Moses had defeated him and the Midianite chiefs, Evi, Rekem, Zur, Hur and Reba—princes allied with Sihon—who lived in that country. ²²In addition to those slain in battle, the Israelites had put to the sword Balaam son of Beor, who practiced divination. ²³The boundary of the Reubenites was the bank of the Jordan. These towns and their villages were the inheritance of the Reubenites, clan by clan.

²⁴This is what Moses had given to the tribe of Gad, clan by clan:

²⁵The territory of Jazer, all the towns of Gilead and half the Ammonite country as far as Aroer, near Rabbah; ²⁶and from Heshbon to Ramath Mizpah and Betonim, and from Mahanaim to the territory of Debir; ²⁷and in the valley, Beth Haram, Beth Nimrah, Succoth and Zaphon with the rest of the realm of Sihon king of Heshbon (the east side of the Jordan, the territory up to the end of the Sea of Kinnereth ª). ²⁸These towns and their villages were the inheritance of the Gadites, clan by clan.

²⁹This is what Moses had given to the half-tribe of Manasseh, that is, to half the family of the descendants of Manasseh, clan by clan:

³⁰The territory extending from Mahanaim and including all of Bashan, the entire realm of Og king of Bashan—all the settlements of Jair in Bashan, sixty towns, ³¹half of Gilead, and Ashtaroth and Edrei (the royal cities of Og in Bashan). This was for the descendants of Makir son of Manasseh—for half of the sons of Makir, clan by clan.

³²This is the inheritance Moses had given when he was in the plains of Moab across the Jordan east of Jericho. ³³But to the tribe of Levi, Moses had given no inheritance; the LORD, the God of Israel, is their inheritance, as he promised them.

DIVISION OF THE LAND WEST OF THE JORDAN

14 Now these are the areas the Israelites received as an inheritance in the land of Canaan, which Eleazar the priest, Joshua son of Nun and the heads of the tribal clans of Israel allotted to them. ²Their inheritances were assigned by lot to the nine-and-a-half tribes, as the LORD had commanded through Moses. ³Moses had granted the two-and-a-half tribes their inheritance east of the Jordan but had not granted the Levites an inheritance among the rest, ⁴for the sons of Joseph had become two tribes—Manasseh and Ephraim. The Levites received no share of the land but only towns to live in, with pasturelands for their flocks and herds. ⁵So the Israelites divided the land, just as the LORD had commanded Moses.

HEBRON GIVEN TO CALEB

⁶Now the men of Judah approached Joshua at Gilgal, and Caleb son of Jephunneh the Kenizzite said to him, "You know what the LORD said to Moses the man of God at Kadesh Barnea about you and me. ⁷I was forty years old when Moses the servant of the LORD sent me from Kadesh Barnea to explore the land. And I brought him back a report according to my convictions, ⁸but my brothers who went up

---

Fighting Sin

If you really struggle with a particular sin, now is the time to make the necessary tough choices and lifestyle changes to drive it from your life. If that means changing your daily routine, do it. If it means finding new friends, do it. If it means getting rid of your Internet hookup or the premium channels on your cable or satellite TV package, do it. If it means seeking professional help, do it. The sins in our life are like the pagan nations that the Israelites let stay in the promised land: The longer they stick around, the more problems they'll cause and the more severe their impact will be.

ª 27 That is, Galilee

with me made the hearts of the people melt with fear. I, however, followed the LORD my God wholeheartedly. 9So on that day Moses swore to me, 'The land on which your feet have walked will be your inheritance and that of your children forever, because you have followed the LORD my God wholeheartedly.'[a]

10"Now then, just as the LORD promised, he has kept me alive for forty-five years since the time he said this to Moses, while Israel moved about in the desert. So here I am today, eighty-five years old! 11I am still as strong today as the day Moses sent me out; I'm just as vigorous to go out to battle now as I was then. 12Now give me this hill country that the LORD promised me that day. You yourself heard then that the Anakites were there and their cities were large and fortified, but, the LORD helping me, I will drive them out just as he said."

13Then Joshua blessed Caleb son of Jephunneh and gave him Hebron as his inheritance. 14So Hebron has belonged to Caleb son of Jephunneh the Kenizzite ever since, because he followed the LORD, the God of Israel, wholeheartedly. 15(Hebron used to be called Kiriath Arba after Arba, who was the greatest man among the Anakites.)

Then the land had rest from war.

ALLOTMENT FOR JUDAH

15 The allotment for the tribe of Judah, clan by clan, extended down to the territory of Edom, to the Desert of Zin in the extreme south.

2Their southern boundary started from the bay at the southern end of the Salt Sea,[b] 3crossed south of Scorpion[c] Pass, continued on to Zin and went over to the south of Kadesh Barnea. Then it ran past Hezron up to Addar and curved around to Karka. 4It then passed along to Azmon and joined the Wadi of Egypt, ending at the sea. This is their[d] southern boundary.

5The eastern boundary is the Salt Sea as far as the mouth of the Jordan.

The northern boundary started from the bay of the sea at the mouth of the Jordan, 6went up to Beth Hoglah and continued north of Beth Arabah to the Stone of Bohan son of Reuben. 7The boundary then went up to Debir from the Valley of Achor and turned north to Gilgal, which faces the Pass of Adummim south of the gorge. It continued along to the waters of En Shemesh and came out at En Rogel. 8Then it ran up the Valley of Ben Hinnom along the southern slope of the Jebusite city (that is, Jerusalem). From there it climbed to the top of the hill west of the Hinnom Valley at the northern end of the Valley of Rephaim. 9From the hilltop the boundary headed toward the spring of the waters of Nephtoah, came out at the towns of Mount Ephron and went down toward Baalah (that is, Kiriath Jearim). 10Then it curved westward from Baalah to Mount Seir, ran along the northern slope of Mount Jearim (that is, Kesalon), continued down to Beth Shemesh and crossed to Timnah. 11It went to the northern slope of Ekron, turned toward Shikkeron, passed along to Mount Baalah and reached Jabneel. The boundary ended at the sea.

12The western boundary is the coastline of the Great Sea.[e] These are the boundaries around the people of Judah by their clans.

13In accordance with the LORD's command to him, Joshua gave to Caleb son of Jephunneh a portion in Judah—Kiriath Arba, that is, Hebron. (Arba was the forefather of Anak.) 14From Hebron Caleb drove out the three Anakites—Sheshai, Ahiman and Talmai—descendants of Anak. 15From there he marched against the people living in Debir (formerly called Kiriath Sepher). 16And Caleb said, "I will give my daughter Acsah in marriage to the man who attacks and captures Kiriath Sepher."

17Othniel son of Kenaz, Caleb's brother, took it; so Caleb gave his daughter Acsah to him in marriage.

18One day when she came to Othniel, she urged him[f] to ask her father for a field. When she got off her donkey, Caleb asked her, "What can I do for you?"

NOW OR NEVER
JOS 15:13

Everyone who remains faithful to God can look forward to an eternal reward. On top of that, God sometimes offers great earthly rewards to those who follow his plan. Both involve reaping what we sow.

---

[a] 9 Deut. 1:36   [b] 2 That is, the Dead Sea; also in verse 5   [c] 3 Hebrew *Akrabbim*   [d] 4 Hebrew *your*   [e] 12 That is, the Mediterranean; also in verse 47   [f] 18 Hebrew and some Septuagint manuscripts; other Septuagint manuscripts (see also note at Judges 1:14) *Othniel, he urged her*

[19]She replied, "Do me a special favor. Since you have given me land in the Negev, give me also springs of water." So Caleb gave her the upper and lower springs.

[20]This is the inheritance of the tribe of Judah, clan by clan:

[21]The southernmost towns of the tribe of Judah in the Negev toward the boundary of Edom were:

Kabzeel, Eder, Jagur, [22]Kinah, Dimonah, Adadah, [23]Kedesh, Hazor, Ithnan, [24]Ziph, Telem, Bealoth, [25]Hazor Hadattah, Kerioth Hezron (that is, Hazor), [26]Amam, Shema, Moladah, [27]Hazar Gaddah, Heshmon, Beth Pelet, [28]Hazar Shual, Beersheba, Biziothiah, [29]Baalah, Iim, Ezem, [30]Eltolad, Kesil, Hormah, [31]Ziklag, Madmannah, Sansannah, [32]Lebaoth, Shilhim, Ain and Rimmon—a total of twenty-nine towns and their villages.

[33]In the western foothills:

Eshtaol, Zorah, Ashnah, [34]Zanoah, En Gannim, Tappuah, Enam, [35]Jarmuth, Adullam, Socoh, Azekah, [36]Shaaraim, Adithaim and Gederah (or Gederothaim)[a]—fourteen towns and their villages.

[37]Zenan, Hadashah, Migdal Gad, [38]Dilean, Mizpah, Joktheel, [39]Lachish, Bozkath, Eglon, [40]Cabbon, Lahmas, Kitlish, [41]Gederoth, Beth Dagon, Naamah and Makkedah—sixteen towns and their villages.

[42]Libnah, Ether, Ashan, [43]Iphtah, Ashnah, Nezib, [44]Keilah, Aczib and Mareshah—nine towns and their villages.

[45]Ekron, with its surrounding settlements and villages; [46]west of Ekron, all that were in the vicinity of Ashdod, together with their villages; [47]Ashdod, its surrounding settlements and villages; and Gaza, its settlements and villages, as far as the Wadi of Egypt and the coastline of the Great Sea.

[48]In the hill country:

Shamir, Jattir, Socoh, [49]Dannah, Kiriath Sannah (that is, Debir), [50]Anab, Eshtemoh, Anim, [51]Goshen, Holon and Giloh—eleven towns and their villages.

[52]Arab, Dumah, Eshan, [53]Janim, Beth Tappuah, Aphekah, [54]Humtah, Kiriath Arba (that is, Hebron) and Zior—nine towns and their villages.

[55]Maon, Carmel, Ziph, Juttah, [56]Jezreel, Jokdeam, Zanoah, [57]Kain, Gibeah and Timnah—ten towns and their villages.

[58]Halhul, Beth Zur, Gedor, [59]Maarath, Beth Anoth and Eltekon—six towns and their villages. [60]Kiriath Baal (that is, Kiriath Jearim) and Rabbah—two towns and their villages.

[61]In the desert:

Beth Arabah, Middin, Secacah, [62]Nibshan, the City of Salt and En Gedi—six towns and their villages.

[63]Judah could not dislodge the Jebusites, who were living in Jerusalem; to this day the Jebusites live there with the people of Judah.

ALLOTMENT FOR EPHRAIM AND MANASSEH

16 The allotment for Joseph began at the Jordan of Jericho,[b] east of the waters of Jericho, and went up from there through the desert into the hill country of Bethel. [2]It went on from Bethel (that is, Luz),[c] crossed over to the territory of the Arkites in Ataroth, [3]descended westward to the territory of the Japhletites as far as the region of Lower Beth Horon and on to Gezer, ending at the sea.

[4]So Manasseh and Ephraim, the descendants of Joseph, received their inheritance.

[5]This was the territory of Ephraim, clan by clan:

The boundary of their inheritance went from Ataroth Addar in the east to Upper Beth Horon [6]and continued to the sea. From Micmethath on the north it curved eastward to Taanath Shiloh, passing by it to Janoah on the east. [7]Then it went down from Janoah to Ataroth and Naarah, touched Jericho and came out at the Jordan. [8]From Tappuah the border went west to the Kanah Ravine and ended at the sea. This was the inheritance of the tribe of the Ephraimites, clan by

---

[a] *36* Or *Gederah and Gederothaim*   [b] *1 Jordan of Jericho* was possibly an ancient name for the Jordan River.   [c] *2* Septuagint; Hebrew *Bethel to Luz*

battlelines

» No Experience Necessary (Virginity)

Q: I can tell something's bugging you.
A: So?

Q: Well, if you need to get anything off your chest, I'll be glad to listen.
A: You'll just think it's stupid.

Q: Try me.
A: OK, here's the deal. I'm the only guy I know of in my class who's still a virgin.

Q: You make virginity sound like a dreaded disease.
A: I didn't mean it like that. I know it's not a bad thing, but it *does* make me feel kinda like a freak. I hear guys talking all the time about how many girls they've been with. And when they find out that my score total is zero, they give me all kinds of grief and start asking me if I'm gay or something.

Q: OK, first of all, choosing not to have sex *doesn't* make you gay. And second, I seriously doubt that the guys you're talking to have done all the things they brag about. In fact, I'll bet most of them are just lying to impress each other.
A: You're probably right. But they're still making my life miserable. And I don't think that's going to change until I actually have sex.

» Good Things Come to Those Who Wait

Anyone who tries to tell you that you're not a man unless you've had sex deserves to be ignored. That kind of talk is just plain stupid.

If you want some *useful* advice about physical love, check out what God says in 1 Thessalonians 4:1,3–5:

"As for other matters, brothers and sisters, we instructed you how to live in order to please God, as in fact you are living. Now we ask you and urge you in the Lord Jesus to do this more and more . . . It is God's will that you should be sanctified: that you should avoid sexual immorality; that each of you should learn to control your own body in a way that is holy and honorable, not in passionate lust like the pagans, who do not know God."

If you want to please God with your body, learn to go against the flow. Resist the urge to hop in the backseat with a girl just to prove your manhood or to get a quick thrill. Save yourself for your future wife . . . and save yourself from all kinds of headaches and heartaches in the process. Give yourself a chance to experience what God wants you to enjoy to the fullest in marriage someday.

Read more about sex and abstinence at www.RevolutionBible.com.

clan. 9It also included all the towns and their villages that were set aside for the Ephraimites within the inheritance of the Manassites.

10They did not dislodge the Canaanites living in Gezer; to this day the Canaanites live among the people of Ephraim but are required to do forced labor.

17 This was the allotment for the tribe of Manasseh as Joseph's firstborn, that is, for Makir, Manasseh's firstborn. Makir was the ancestor of the Gileadites, who had received Gilead and Bashan because the Makirites were great soldiers. 2So this allotment was for the rest of the people of Manasseh—the clans of Abiezer, Helek, Asriel, Shechem, Hepher and Shemida. These are the other male descendants of Manasseh son of Joseph by their clans.

3Now Zelophehad son of Hepher, the son of Gilead, the son of Makir, the son of Manasseh, had no sons but only daughters, whose names were Mahlah, Noah, Hoglah, Milcah and Tirzah. 4They went to Eleazar the priest, Joshua son of Nun, and the leaders and said, "The LORD commanded Moses to give us an inheritance among our brothers." So Joshua gave them an inheritance along with the brothers of their father, according to the LORD's command. 5Manasseh's share consisted of ten tracts of land besides Gilead and Bashan east of the Jordan, 6because the daughters of the tribe of Manasseh received an inheritance among the sons. The land of Gilead belonged to the rest of the descendants of Manasseh.

7The territory of Manasseh extended from Asher to Micmethath east of Shechem. The boundary ran southward from there to include the people living at En Tappuah. 8(Manasseh had the land of Tappuah, but Tappuah itself, on the boundary of Manasseh, belonged to the Ephraimites.) 9Then the boundary continued south to the Kanah Ravine. There were towns belonging to Ephraim lying among the towns of Manasseh, but the boundary of Manasseh was the northern side of the ravine and ended at the sea. 10On the south the land belonged to Ephraim, on the north to Manasseh. The territory of Manasseh reached the sea and bordered Asher on the north and Issachar on the east.

11Within Issachar and Asher, Manasseh also had Beth Shan, Ibleam and the people of Dor, Endor, Taanach and Megiddo, together with their surrounding settlements (the third in the list is Naphoth[a]).

12Yet the Manassites were not able to occupy these towns, for the Canaanites were determined to live in that region. 13However, when the Israelites grew stronger, they subjected the Canaanites to forced labor but did not drive them out completely.

14The people of Joseph said to Joshua, "Why have you given us only one allotment and one portion for an inheritance? We are a numerous people and the LORD has blessed us abundantly."

15"If you are so numerous," Joshua answered, "and if the hill country of Ephraim is too small for you, go up into the forest and clear land for yourselves there in the land of the Perizzites and Rephaites."

16The people of Joseph replied, "The hill country is not enough for us, and all the Canaanites who live in the plain have iron chariots, both those in Beth Shan and its settlements and those in the Valley of Jezreel."

17But Joshua said to the house of Joseph—to Ephraim and Manasseh—"You are numerous and very powerful. You will have not only one allotment 18but the forested hill country as well. Clear it, and its farthest limits will be yours; though the Canaanites have iron chariots and though they are strong, you can drive them out."

DIVISION OF THE REST OF THE LAND

18 The whole assembly of the Israelites gathered at Shiloh and set up the Tent of Meeting there. The country was brought under their control, 2but there were still seven Israelite tribes who had not yet received their inheritance.

3So Joshua said to the Israelites: "How long will you wait before you begin to take possession of the land that the LORD, the God of your fathers, has given you? 4Appoint three men from each tribe. I will send them out to make a survey of the land and to write a description of it, according to the inheritance of each. Then they will return to me. 5You are to divide the land into seven parts. Judah is to remain in its territory on the south and the house of Joseph in its territory on the north. 6After you have written descriptions of the seven parts of the land, bring them here to me and I will cast lots for you in the presence of the LORD our God. 7The Levites, however, do not get a portion among you, because the

---

a 11 That is, Naphoth Dor

priestly service of the LORD is their inheritance. And Gad, Reuben and the half-tribe of Manasseh have already received their inheritance on the east side of the Jordan. Moses the servant of the LORD gave it to them."

⁸As the men started on their way to map out the land, Joshua instructed them, "Go and make a survey of the land and write a description of it. Then return to me, and I will cast lots for you here at Shiloh in the presence of the LORD." ⁹So the men left and went through the land. They wrote its description on a scroll, town by town, in seven parts, and returned to Joshua in the camp at Shiloh. ¹⁰Joshua then cast lots for them in Shiloh in the presence of the LORD, and there he distributed the land to the Israelites according to their tribal divisions.

ALLOTMENT FOR BENJAMIN

¹¹The lot came up for the tribe of Benjamin, clan by clan. Their allotted territory lay between the tribes of Judah and Joseph:

¹²On the north side their boundary began at the Jordan, passed the northern slope of Jericho and headed west into the hill country, coming out at the desert of Beth Aven. ¹³From there it crossed to the south slope of Luz (that is, Bethel) and went down to Ataroth Addar on the hill south of Lower Beth Horon.

¹⁴From the hill facing Beth Horon on the south the boundary turned south along the western side and came out at Kiriath Baal (that is, Kiriath Jearim), a town of the people of Judah. This was the western side.

¹⁵The southern side began at the outskirts of Kiriath Jearim on the west, and the boundary came out at the spring of the waters of Nephtoah. ¹⁶The boundary went down to the foot of the hill facing the Valley of Ben Hinnom, north of the Valley of Rephaim. It continued down the Hinnom Valley along the southern slope of the Jebusite city and so to En Rogel. ¹⁷It then curved north, went to En Shemesh, continued to Geliloth, which faces the Pass of Adummim, and ran down to the Stone of Bohan son of Reuben. ¹⁸It continued to the northern slope of Beth Arabah[a] and on down into the Arabah. ¹⁹It then went to the northern slope of Beth Hoglah and came out at the northern bay of the Salt Sea,[b] at the mouth of the Jordan in the south. This was the southern boundary.

²⁰The Jordan formed the boundary on the eastern side.

These were the boundaries that marked out the inheritance of the clans of Benjamin on all sides.

²¹The tribe of Benjamin, clan by clan, had the following cities:

Jericho, Beth Hoglah, Emek Keziz, ²²Beth Arabah, Zemaraim, Bethel, ²³Avvim, Parah, Ophrah, ²⁴Kephar Ammoni, Ophni and Geba—twelve towns and their villages.

²⁵Gibeon, Ramah, Beeroth, ²⁶Mizpah, Kephirah, Mozah, ²⁷Rekem, Irpeel, Taralah, ²⁸Zelah, Haeleph, the Jebusite city (that is, Jerusalem), Gibeah and Kiriath—fourteen towns and their villages.

This was the inheritance of Benjamin for its clans.

ALLOTMENT FOR SIMEON

19 The second lot came out for the tribe of Simeon, clan by clan. Their inheritance lay within the territory of Judah. ²It included:

Beersheba (or Sheba),[c] Moladah, ³Hazar Shual, Balah, Ezem, ⁴Eltolad, Bethul, Hormah, ⁵Ziklag, Beth Marcaboth, Hazar Susah, ⁶Beth Lebaoth and Sharuhen—thirteen towns and their villages;

⁷Ain, Rimmon, Ether and Ashan—four towns and their villages— ⁸and all the villages around these towns as far as Baalath Beer (Ramah in the Negev).

This was the inheritance of the tribe of the Simeonites, clan by clan. ⁹The inheritance of the Simeonites was taken from the share of Judah, because Judah's portion was more than they needed. So the Simeonites received their inheritance within the territory of Judah.

---

[a] 18 Septuagint; Hebrew *slope facing the Arabah*   [b] 19 That is, the Dead Sea   [c] 2 Or *Beersheba, Sheba*; 1 Chron. 4:28 does not have Sheba.

ALLOTMENT FOR ZEBULUN

[10] The third lot came up for Zebulun, clan by clan:

The boundary of their inheritance went as far as Sarid. [11] Going west it ran to Maralah, touched Dabbesheth, and extended to the ravine near Jokneam. [12] It turned east from Sarid toward the sunrise to the territory of Kisloth Tabor and went on to Daberath and up to Japhia. [13] Then it continued eastward to Gath Hepher and Eth Kazin; it came out at Rimmon and turned toward Neah. [14] There the boundary went around on the north to Hannathon and ended at the Valley of Iphtah El. [15] Included were Kattath, Nahalal, Shimron, Idalah and Bethlehem. There were twelve towns and their villages.

[16] These towns and their villages were the inheritance of Zebulun, clan by clan.

ALLOTMENT FOR ISSACHAR

[17] The fourth lot came out for Issachar, clan by clan. [18] Their territory included:

Jezreel, Kesulloth, Shunem, [19] Hapharaim, Shion, Anaharath, [20] Rabbith, Kishion, Ebez, [21] Remeth, En Gannim, En Haddah and Beth Pazzez. [22] The boundary touched Tabor, Shahazumah and Beth Shemesh, and ended at the Jordan. There were sixteen towns and their villages.

[23] These towns and their villages were the inheritance of the tribe of Issachar, clan by clan.

ALLOTMENT FOR ASHER

[24] The fifth lot came out for the tribe of Asher, clan by clan. [25] Their territory included:

Helkath, Hali, Beten, Acshaph, [26] Allammelech, Amad and Mishal. On the west the boundary touched Carmel and Shihor Libnath. [27] It then turned east toward Beth Dagon, touched Zebulun and the Valley of Iphtah El, and went north to Beth Emek and Neiel, passing Cabul on the left. [28] It went to Abdon,[a] Rehob, Hammon and Kanah, as far as Greater Sidon. [29] The boundary then turned back toward Ramah and went to the fortified city of Tyre, turned toward Hosah and came out at the sea in the region of Aczib, [30] Ummah, Aphek and Rehob. There were twenty-two towns and their villages.

[31] These towns and their villages were the inheritance of the tribe of Asher, clan by clan.

ALLOTMENT FOR NAPHTALI

[32] The sixth lot came out for Naphtali, clan by clan:

[33] Their boundary went from Heleph and the large tree in Zaanannim, passing Adami Nekeb and Jabneel to Lakkum and ending at the Jordan. [34] The boundary ran west through Aznoth Tabor and came out at Hukkok. It touched Zebulun on the south, Asher on the west and the Jordan[b] on the east. [35] The fortified cities were Ziddim, Zer, Hammath, Rakkath, Kinnereth, [36] Adamah, Ramah, Hazor, [37] Kedesh, Edrei, En Hazor, [38] Iron, Migdal El, Horem, Beth Anath and Beth Shemesh. There were nineteen towns and their villages.

[39] These towns and their villages were the inheritance of the tribe of Naphtali, clan by clan.

ALLOTMENT FOR DAN

[40] The seventh lot came out for the tribe of Dan, clan by clan. [41] The territory of their inheritance included:

Zorah, Eshtaol, Ir Shemesh, [42] Shaalabbin, Aijalon, Ithlah, [43] Elon, Timnah, Ekron, [44] Eltekeh, Gibbethon, Baalath, [45] Jehud, Bene Berak, Gath Rimmon, [46] Me Jarkon and Rakkon, with the area facing Joppa.

[47] (But the Danites had difficulty taking possession of their territory, so they went up and attacked Leshem, took it, put it to the sword and occupied it. They settled in Leshem and named it Dan after their forefather.)

[48] These towns and their villages were the inheritance of the tribe of Dan, clan by clan.

ALLOTMENT FOR JOSHUA

[49] When they had finished dividing the land into its allotted portions, the Israelites gave Joshua son of Nun an inheritance among them, [50] as the LORD had commanded. They gave him the town he asked for—Timnath Serah[c] in the hill country of Ephraim. And he built up the town and settled there.

---

[a] 28 Some Hebrew manuscripts (see also Joshua 21:30); most Hebrew manuscripts *Ebron*   [b] 34 Septuagint; Hebrew *west, and Judah, the Jordan,*   [c] 50 Also known as *Timnath Heres* (see Judges 2:9)

battlelines

» Death Watch (Suicide)

Q: What's up? You look like you just lost your best friend.
A: I might be on the verge of that. About six months ago, Collin changed. He fell into some sort of depression. And he's been spiraling down ever since.

Q: Have you talked to him about it?
A: I've tried, but he says he doesn't know why he feels the way he does, so I don't know how to help him.

Q: Summer's coming up. Maybe with the pressures of school out of the picture, things will get better.
A: Yeah, well, I'm not so sure. Sometimes Collin gets so down he jokes about killing himself.

Q: That's not exactly a laughing matter.
A: Most of the time I think he says that stuff just to break the tension. Then again, he might be trying to send out a cry for help. I'm afraid he's in over his head.

Q: You've got to tell his parents—or convince him to.
A: I can't do it. He's sworn me to secrecy.

Q: But what if he *does* try to kill himself? You'll never forgive yourself for not helping him—secret or no secret.
A: But if I *do* spill the beans he might go into an even deeper depression.

Q: I understand your hesitation, but you've got to do *something*.
A: OK, but what?

Q: You need to tell him that you're really concerned. Encourage him to find someone he can talk to.
A: Like who?

Q: I don't know. How about his youth pastor or a counselor at school?
A: Good idea. I'll try to get him to talk to an adult.

» Save a Friend

Proverbs 17:17 says, "A friend loves at all times, and a brother is born for a time of adversity." We're not just talking about a sentimental feeling here. Biblical love is *active*. It involves going the extra mile and doing whatever needs to be done to assist.

Keep in mind that depression is a very real, very powerful condition; it's *not* "just a phase." While many people get better with support and encouragement from loved ones, others need the benefit of professional counseling. If you have a friend who's in a deep funk—maybe even talking about suicide—don't blow it off. Get involved. Be bold and direct. Ask questions. Use your influence to encourage him or her to get help. Don't be afraid to recommend professional counseling, and support your friend in seeking it.

If your friend resists, you need to be willing to break his or her trust. Having a friend angry at you in the short term is a much better option than losing your friend for good. On the other hand, keeping things a secret could mean loving your friend into a grave. Remember—your friend's life is more important than anything else (see John 15:12–13).

For more on helping someone who's considering suicide, go to www.RevolutionBible.com.

51 These are the territories that Eleazar the priest, Joshua son of Nun and the heads of the tribal clans of Israel assigned by lot at Shiloh in the presence of the LORD at the entrance to the Tent of Meeting. And so they finished dividing the land.

CITIES OF REFUGE

20

Then the LORD said to Joshua: 2 "Tell the Israelites to designate the cities of refuge, as I instructed you through Moses, 3 so that anyone who kills a person accidentally and unintentionally may flee there and find protection from the avenger of blood.

4 "When he flees to one of these cities, he is to stand in the entrance of the city gate and state his case before the elders of that city. Then they are to admit him into their city and give him a place to live with them. 5 If the avenger of blood pursues him, they must not surrender the one accused, because he killed his neighbor unintentionally and without malice aforethought. 6 He is to stay in that city until he has stood trial before the assembly and until the death of the high priest who is serving at that time. Then he may go back to his own home in the town from which he fled."

7 So they set apart Kedesh in Galilee in the hill country of Naphtali, Shechem in the hill country of Ephraim, and Kiriath Arba (that is, Hebron) in the hill country of Judah. 8 On the east side of the Jordan of Jericho ᵃ they designated Bezer in the desert on the plateau in the tribe of Reuben, Ramoth in Gilead in the tribe of Gad, and Golan in Bashan in the tribe of Manasseh. 9 Any of the Israelites or any alien living among them who killed someone accidentally could flee to these designated cities and not be killed by the avenger of blood prior to standing trial before the assembly.

TOWNS FOR THE LEVITES

21

Now the family heads of the Levites approached Eleazar the priest, Joshua son of Nun, and the heads of the other tribal families of Israel 2 at Shiloh in Canaan and said to them, "The LORD commanded through Moses that you give us towns to live in, with pasturelands for our livestock." 3 So, as the LORD had commanded, the Israelites gave the Levites the following towns and pasturelands out of their own inheritance:

4 The first lot came out for the Kohathites, clan by clan. The Levites who were descendants of Aaron the priest were allotted thirteen towns from the tribes of Judah, Simeon and Benjamin. 5 The rest of Kohath's descendants were allotted ten towns from the clans of the tribes of Ephraim, Dan and half of Manasseh.

6 The descendants of Gershon were allotted thirteen towns from the clans of the tribes of Issachar, Asher, Naphtali and the half-tribe of Manasseh in Bashan.

7 The descendants of Merari, clan by clan, received twelve towns from the tribes of Reuben, Gad and Zebulun.

8 So the Israelites allotted to the Levites these towns and their pasturelands, as the LORD had commanded through Moses.

9 From the tribes of Judah and Simeon they allotted the following towns by name 10 (these towns were assigned to the descendants of Aaron who were from the Kohathite clans of the Levites, because the first lot fell to them):

11 They gave them Kiriath Arba (that is, Hebron), with its surrounding pastureland, in the hill country of Judah. (Arba was the forefather of Anak.) 12 But the fields and villages around the city they had given to Caleb son of Jephunneh as his possession.

13 So to the descendants of Aaron the priest they gave Hebron (a city of refuge for one accused of murder), Libnah, 14 Jattir, Eshtemoa, 15 Holon, Debir, 16 Ain, Juttah and Beth Shemesh, together with their pasturelands—nine towns from these two tribes.

17 And from the tribe of Benjamin they gave them Gibeon, Geba, 18 Anathoth and Almon, together with their pasturelands—four towns.

19 All the towns for the priests, the descendants of Aaron, were thirteen, together with their pasturelands.

20 The rest of the Kohathite clans of the Levites were allotted towns from the tribe of Ephraim:

21 In the hill country of Ephraim they were given Shechem (a city of refuge for one accused of murder) and Gezer, 22 Kibzaim and Beth Horon, together with their pasturelands—four towns.

ᵃ 8 Jordan of Jericho was possibly an ancient name for the Jordan River.

23Also from the tribe of Dan they received Eltekeh, Gibbethon, 24Aijalon and Gath Rimmon, together with their pasturelands—four towns.

25From half the tribe of Manasseh they received Taanach and Gath Rimmon, together with their pasturelands—two towns.

26All these ten towns and their pasturelands were given to the rest of the Kohathite clans.

27The Levite clans of the Gershonites were given:
from the half-tribe of Manasseh,
Golan in Bashan (a city of refuge for one accused of murder) and Be Eshtarah, together with their pasturelands—two towns;
28from the tribe of Issachar,
Kishion, Daberath, 29Jarmuth and En Gannim, together with their pasturelands—four towns;
30from the tribe of Asher,
Mishal, Abdon, 31Helkath and Rehob, together with their pasturelands—four towns;
32from the tribe of Naphtali,
Kedesh in Galilee (a city of refuge for one accused of murder), Hammoth Dor and Kartan, together with their pasturelands—three towns.
33All the towns of the Gershonite clans were thirteen, together with their pasturelands.

34The Merarite clans (the rest of the Levites) were given:
from the tribe of Zebulun,
Jokneam, Kartah, 35Dimnah and Nahalal, together with their pasturelands—four towns;
36from the tribe of Reuben,
Bezer, Jahaz, 37Kedemoth and Mephaath, together with their pasturelands—four towns;
38from the tribe of Gad,
Ramoth in Gilead (a city of refuge for one accused of murder), Mahanaim, 39Heshbon and Jazer, together with their pasturelands—four towns in all.
40All the towns allotted to the Merarite clans, who were the rest of the Levites, were twelve.

41The towns of the Levites in the territory held by the Israelites were forty-eight in all, together with their pasturelands. 42Each of these towns had pasturelands surrounding it; this was true for all these towns.

43So the LORD gave Israel all the land he had sworn to give their forefathers, and they took possession of it and settled there. 44The LORD gave them rest on every side, just as he had sworn to their forefathers. Not one of their enemies withstood them; the LORD handed all their enemies over to them. 45Not one of all the LORD's good promises to the house of Israel failed; every one was fulfilled.

JOS 21:43-45

challengenotes

To: my_son

heavenly_father: instant gratification is not my plan for your life. I have many wonderful things planned for you, but they will happen on *my* timetable, not yours. don't get impatient. remember, I can see the future. just wait until you see what I have in store for you!

EASTERN TRIBES RETURN HOME

22 Then Joshua summoned the Reubenites, the Gadites and the half-tribe of Manasseh 2and said to them, "You have done all that Moses the servant of the LORD commanded, and you have obeyed me in everything I commanded. 3For a long time now—to this very day—you have not deserted your brothers but have carried out the mission the LORD your God gave you. 4Now that the LORD your God has given your brothers rest as he promised, return to your homes in the land that Moses the servant of the LORD gave you on the other side of the Jordan. 5But be very careful to keep the commandment and the law that Moses the servant of the LORD gave you: to love the LORD your God, to walk in all his ways, to obey his commands, to hold fast to him and to serve him with all your heart and all your soul."

6Then Joshua blessed them and sent them away, and they went to their homes. 7(To the half-tribe of Manasseh Moses had given land in Bashan, and to the other half of the tribe Joshua gave land on the west side of the Jordan with their brothers.) When Joshua sent them home, he blessed them, 8saying, "Return to your homes with your great wealth—with large herds of livestock, with silver, gold, bronze and iron, and a great quantity of clothing—and divide with your brothers the plunder from your enemies."

⁹So the Reubenites, the Gadites and the half-tribe of Manasseh left the Israelites at Shiloh in Canaan to return to Gilead, their own land, which they had acquired in accordance with the command of the LORD through Moses.

¹⁰When they came to Geliloth near the Jordan in the land of Canaan, the Reubenites, the Gadites and the half-tribe of Manasseh built an imposing altar there by the Jordan. ¹¹And when the Israelites heard that they had built the altar on the border of Canaan at Geliloth near the Jordan on the Israelite side, ¹²the whole assembly of Israel gathered at Shiloh to go to war against them.

NOW OR NEVER
JOS 22:5

Talk is cheap, as far as God and most people are concerned. We can yap all we want about how much we love God, but unless we back up our talk with action—by obeying *his* words—all our jawing is worthless.

¹³So the Israelites sent Phinehas son of Eleazar, the priest, to the land of Gilead—to Reuben, Gad and the half-tribe of Manasseh. ¹⁴With him they sent ten of the chief men, one for each of the tribes of Israel, each the head of a family division among the Israelite clans.

¹⁵When they went to Gilead—to Reuben, Gad and the half-tribe of Manasseh—they said to them: ¹⁶"The whole assembly of the LORD says: 'How could you break faith with the God of Israel like this? How could you turn away from the LORD and build yourselves an altar in rebellion against him now? ¹⁷Was not the sin of Peor enough for us? Up to this very day we have not cleansed ourselves from that sin, even though a plague fell on the community of the LORD! ¹⁸And are you now turning away from the LORD?

" 'If you rebel against the LORD today, tomorrow he will be angry with the whole community of Israel. ¹⁹If the land you possess is defiled, come over to the LORD's land, where the LORD's tabernacle stands, and share the land with us. But do not rebel against the LORD or against us by building an altar for yourselves, other than the altar of the LORD our God. ²⁰When Achan son of Zerah acted unfaithfully regarding the devoted things,ª did not wrath come upon the whole community of Israel? He was not the only one who died for his sin.' "

²¹Then Reuben, Gad and the half-tribe of Manasseh replied to the heads of the clans of Israel: ²²"The Mighty One, God, the LORD! The Mighty One, God, the LORD! He knows! And let Israel know! If this has been in rebellion or disobedience to the LORD, do not spare us this day. ²³If we have built our own altar to turn away from the LORD and to offer burnt offerings and grain offerings, or to sacrifice fellowship offeringsᵇ on it, may the LORD himself call us to account.

²⁴"No! We did it for fear that some day your descendants might say to ours, 'What do you have to do with the LORD, the God of Israel? ²⁵The LORD has made the Jordan a boundary between us and you—you Reubenites and Gadites! You have no share in the LORD.' So your descendants might cause ours to stop fearing the LORD.

²⁶"That is why we said, 'Let us get ready and build an altar—but not for burnt offerings or sacrifices.' ²⁷On the contrary, it is to be a witness between us and you and the generations that follow, that we will worship the LORD at his sanctuary with our burnt offerings, sacrifices and fellowship offerings. Then in the future your descendants will not be able to say to ours, 'You have no share in the LORD.'

²⁸"And we said, 'If they ever say this to us, or to our descendants, we will answer: Look at the replica of the LORD's altar, which our fathers built, not for burnt offerings and sacrifices, but as a witness between us and you.'

²⁹"Far be it from us to rebel against the LORD and turn away from him today by building an altar for burnt offerings, grain offerings and sacrifices, other than the altar of the LORD our God that stands before his tabernacle."

³⁰When Phinehas the priest and the leaders of the community—the heads of the clans of the Israelites—heard what Reuben, Gad and Manasseh had to say, they were pleased. ³¹And Phinehas son of Eleazar, the priest, said to Reuben, Gad and Manasseh, "Today we know that the LORD is with us, be-

ª *20* The Hebrew term refers to the irrevocable giving over of things or persons to the LORD, often by totally destroying them.
ᵇ *23* Traditionally *peace offerings*; also in verse 27

cause you have not acted unfaithfully toward the LORD in this matter. Now you have rescued the Israelites from the LORD's hand."

³²Then Phinehas son of Eleazar, the priest, and the leaders returned to Canaan from their meeting with the Reubenites and Gadites in Gilead and reported to the Israelites. ³³They were glad to hear the report and praised God. And they talked no more about going to war against them to devastate the country where the Reubenites and the Gadites lived.

³⁴And the Reubenites and the Gadites gave the altar this name: A Witness Between Us that the LORD is God.

JOSHUA'S FAREWELL TO THE LEADERS

23 After a long time had passed and the LORD had given Israel rest from all their enemies around them, Joshua, by then old and well advanced in years, ²summoned all Israel—their elders, leaders, judges and officials—and said to them: "I am old and well advanced in years. ³You yourselves have seen everything the LORD your God has done to all these nations for your sake; it was the LORD your God who fought for you. ⁴Remember how I have allotted as an inheritance for your tribes all the land of the nations that remain—the nations I conquered—between the Jordan and the Great Sea[a] in the west. ⁵The LORD your God himself will drive them out of your way. He will push them out before you, and you will take possession of their land, as the LORD your God promised you.

⁶"Be very strong; be careful to obey all that is written in the Book of the Law of Moses, without turning aside to the right or to the left. ⁷Do not associate with these nations that remain among you; do not invoke the names of their gods or swear by them. You must not serve them or bow down to them. ⁸But you are to hold fast to the LORD your God, as you have until now.

⁹"The LORD has driven out before you great and powerful nations; to this day no one has been able to withstand you. ¹⁰One of you routs a thousand, because the LORD your God fights for you, just as he promised. ¹¹So be very careful to love the LORD your God.

¹²"But if you turn away and ally yourselves with the survivors of these nations that remain among you and if you intermarry with them and associate with them, ¹³then you may be sure that the LORD your God will no longer drive out these nations before you. Instead, they will become snares and traps for you, whips on your backs and thorns in your eyes, until you perish from this good land, which the LORD your God has given you.

¹⁴"Now I am about to go the way of all the earth. You know with all your heart and soul that not one of all the good promises the LORD your God gave you has failed. Every promise has been fulfilled; not one has failed. ¹⁵But just as every good promise of the LORD your God has come true, so the LORD will bring on you all the evil he has threatened, until he has destroyed you from this good land he has given you. ¹⁶If you violate the covenant of the LORD your God, which he commanded you, and go and serve other gods and bow down to them, the LORD's anger will burn against you, and you will quickly perish from the good land he has given you."

God's Perfect Record

Talk about an impressive streak! In all of recorded history, God has never blown a promise. He's never reneged on a deal. He's done *everything* he's ever agreed to do, and more—much, *much* more. His record is spotless. His faithfulness is perfect. So why not claim, say, God's promise to be with you always? Then take a bold step of faith, and talk about Christ with someone who may not seem interested. Or why not write a paper articulating a Biblical worldview in a class in which the teacher opposes Christianity? Don't fear—God's record speaks for itself.

» live the adventure » Jos. 23:14

THE COVENANT RENEWED AT SHECHEM

24 Then Joshua assembled all the tribes of Israel at Shechem. He summoned the elders, leaders, judges and officials of Israel, and they presented themselves before God.

²Joshua said to all the people, "This is what the LORD, the God of Israel, says: 'Long ago your fore-

---

ᵃ 4 That is, the Mediterranean

fathers, including Terah the father of Abraham and Nahor, lived beyond the River[a] and worshiped other gods. 3But I took your father Abraham from the land beyond the River and led him throughout Canaan and gave him many descendants. I gave him Isaac, 4and to Isaac I gave Jacob and Esau. I assigned the hill country of Seir to Esau, but Jacob and his sons went down to Egypt.

5" 'Then I sent Moses and Aaron, and I afflicted the Egyptians by what I did there, and I brought you out. 6When I brought your fathers out of Egypt, you came to the sea, and the Egyptians pursued them with chariots and horsemen[b] as far as the Red Sea.[c] 7But they cried to the LORD for help, and he put darkness between you and the Egyptians; he brought the sea over them and covered them. You saw with your own eyes what I did to the Egyptians. Then you lived in the desert for a long time.

8" 'I brought you to the land of the Amorites who lived east of the Jordan. They fought against you, but I gave them into your hands. I destroyed them from before you, and you took possession of their land. 9When Balak son of Zippor, the king of Moab, prepared to fight against Israel, he sent for Balaam son of Beor to put a curse on you. 10But I would not listen to Balaam, so he blessed you again and again, and I delivered you out of his hand.

11" 'Then you crossed the Jordan and came to Jericho. The citizens of Jericho fought against you, as did also the Amorites, Perizzites, Canaanites, Hittites, Girgashites, Hivites and Jebusites, but I gave them into your hands. 12I sent the hornet ahead of you, which drove them out before you—also the two Amorite kings. You did not do it with your own sword and bow. 13So I gave you a land on which you did not toil and cities you did not build; and you live in them and eat from vineyards and olive groves that you did not plant.'

14"Now fear the LORD and serve him with all faithfulness. Throw away the gods your forefathers worshiped beyond the River and in Egypt, and serve the LORD. 15But if serving the LORD seems undesirable to you, then choose for yourselves this day whom you will serve, whether the gods your forefathers served beyond the River, or the gods of the Amorites, in whose land you are living. But as for me and my household, we will serve the LORD."

16Then the people answered, "Far be it from us to forsake the LORD to serve other gods! 17It was the LORD our God himself who brought us and our fathers up out of Egypt, from that land of slavery, and performed those great signs before our eyes. He protected us on our entire journey and among all the nations through which we traveled. 18And the LORD drove out before us all the nations, including the Amorites, who lived in the land. We too will serve the LORD, because he is our God."

19Joshua said to the people, "You are not able to serve the LORD. He is a holy God; he is a jealous God. He will not forgive your rebellion and your sins. 20If you forsake the LORD and serve foreign gods, he will turn and bring disaster on you and make an end of you, after he has been good to you."

21But the people said to Joshua, "No! We will serve the LORD."

22Then Joshua said, "You are witnesses against yourselves that you have chosen to serve the LORD."

"Yes, we are witnesses," they replied.

23"Now then," said Joshua, "throw away the foreign gods that are among you and yield your hearts to the LORD, the God of Israel."

24And the people said to Joshua, "We will serve the LORD our God and obey him."

25On that day Joshua made a covenant for the people, and there at Shechem he drew up for them decrees and laws. 26And Joshua recorded these things in the Book of the Law of God. Then he took a large stone and set it up there under the oak near the holy place of the LORD.

Slaves to Righteousness

If you're serious about serving God and living for him, you can't dabble in sin on the side. God isn't interested in recruiting part-time followers or having a "Sunday relationship" with you. He wants to transform everything about your life—the way you act, the way you talk, the way you spend your money, the way you treat others, the way you prioritize what's important to you, even the way you think.

»» live the adventure »» Jos 24:14-15

---

a 2 That is, the Euphrates; also in verses 3, 14 and 15   b 6 Or charioteers   c 6 Hebrew Yam Suph; that is, Sea of Reeds

27"See!" he said to all the people. "This stone will be a witness against us. It has heard all the words the LORD has said to us. It will be a witness against you if you are untrue to your God."

BURIED IN THE PROMISED LAND

28Then Joshua sent the people away, each to his own inheritance.

29After these things, Joshua son of Nun, the servant of the LORD, died at the age of a hundred and ten. 30And they buried him in the land of his inheritance, at Timnath Serah[a] in the hill country of Ephraim, north of Mount Gaash.

31Israel served the LORD throughout the lifetime of Joshua and of the elders who outlived him and who had experienced everything the LORD had done for Israel.

32And Joseph's bones, which the Israelites had brought up from Egypt, were buried at Shechem in the tract of land that Jacob bought for a hundred pieces of silver[b] from the sons of Hamor, the father of Shechem. This became the inheritance of Joseph's descendants.

33And Eleazar son of Aaron died and was buried at Gibeah, which had been allotted to his son Phinehas in the hill country of Ephraim.

---

[a] 30 Also known as Timnath Heres (see Judges 2:9)   [b] 32 Hebrew hundred kesitahs; a kesitah was a unit of money of unknown weight and value.

JUDGES

JUDGES JUDGES

« AT A GLANCE

Author
Unknown (possibly Samuel)

Audience
People of Israel

Date
Between 1043 and 1004 B.C.

Setting
The events take place in the land of Canaan, which today is Israel. In danger of losing the promised land, the Israelites were rescued by many judges during this period.

Verse to Remember
In those days Israel had no king; everyone did as he saw fit (17:6).

Theme to Consider
Judges is a book of bad news/good news. The bad news is that, left to ourselves, we tend to forget God and turn to sin. The good news is that even though God knows what we're like, he still loves us and forgives us when we turn back to him.

UNCHANGING TRUTH » Everything you do has consequences. Some consequences seem relatively minor. For instance, a guy who goes out with his girlfriend's best friend is probably going to lose his girlfriend. Some consequences, though, can do serious—and permanent—damage to your life. For instance, a guy who decides to drive home after drinking at a party stands a good chance of injuring (or killing) himself or someone else.

God forgives us for our sins—the Bible's extremely clear about that. But that doesn't mean he takes away the earthly consequences of our choices. So while God will forgive someone for cheating on his girlfriend, he won't make his girlfriend take him back. And while God will forgive someone for driving drunk, he won't make the criminal charges for it go away. In other words, if you do the crime, chances are you're going to do the time. You'll just do it as a person forgiven by God.

The book of Judges shows us that the Israelites knew all about consequences. When they made God their number-one priority and obeyed his commands, life was great for them. God blessed everything they did, from growing crops to fighting military battles. On the other hand, when they gave in to their urge to worship idols and live like their pagan neighbors, life became miserable for them. God allowed their enemies to invade, pound on them for a while and even capture them as slaves.

LIFE LESSONS »

1   You're never outnumbered if God is on your side (3:31).

2   Never underestimate the smarts and strength of a woman (4:1–24).

3   God doesn't get angry when we have doubts; he's willing to work with us to help us overcome them (6:1–40).

4   Physical strength is a lot less important than spiritual strength (16:1–30).

1 After the death of Joshua, the Israelites asked the LORD, "Who will be the first to go up and fight for us against the Canaanites?"

²The LORD answered, "Judah is to go; I have given the land into their hands."

³Then the men of Judah said to the Simeonites their brothers, "Come up with us into the territory allotted to us, to fight against the Canaanites. We in turn will go with you into yours." So the Simeonites went with them.

⁴When Judah attacked, the LORD gave the Canaanites and Perizzites into their hands and they struck down ten thousand men at Bezek. ⁵It was there that they found Adoni-Bezek and fought against him, putting to rout the Canaanites and Perizzites. ⁶Adoni-Bezek fled, but they chased him and caught him, and cut off his thumbs and big toes.

⁷Then Adoni-Bezek said, "Seventy kings with their thumbs and big toes cut off have picked up scraps under my table. Now God has paid me back for what I did to them." They brought him to Jerusalem, and he died there.

⁸The men of Judah attacked Jerusalem also and took it. They put the city to the sword and set it on fire.

⁹After that, the men of Judah went down to fight against the Canaanites living in the hill country, the Negev and the western foothills. ¹⁰They advanced against the Canaanites living in Hebron (formerly called Kiriath Arba) and defeated Sheshai, Ahiman and Talmai.

¹¹From there they advanced against the people living in Debir (formerly called Kiriath Sepher). ¹²And Caleb said, "I will give my daughter Acsah in marriage to the man who attacks and captures Kiriath Sepher." ¹³Othniel son of Kenaz, Caleb's younger brother, took it; so Caleb gave his daughter Acsah to him in marriage.

¹⁴One day when she came to Othniel, she urged him[a] to ask her father for a field. When she got off her donkey, Caleb asked her, "What can I do for you?"

¹⁵She replied, "Do me a special favor. Since you have given me land in the Negev, give me also springs of water." Then Caleb gave her the upper and lower springs.

¹⁶The descendants of Moses' father-in-law, the Kenite, went up from the City of Palms[b] with the men of Judah to live among the people of the Desert of Judah in the Negev near Arad.

¹⁷Then the men of Judah went with the Simeonites their brothers and attacked the Canaanites living in Zephath, and they totally destroyed[c] the city. Therefore it was called Hormah.[d] ¹⁸The men of Judah also took[e] Gaza, Ashkelon and Ekron—each city with its territory.

¹⁹The LORD was with the men of Judah. They took possession of the hill country, but they were unable to drive the people from the plains, because they had iron chariots. ²⁰As Moses had promised, Hebron was given to Caleb, who drove from it the three sons of Anak. ²¹The Benjamites, however, failed to dislodge the Jebusites, who were living in Jerusalem; to this day the Jebusites live there with the Benjamites.

²²Now the house of Joseph attacked Bethel, and the LORD was with them. ²³When they sent men to spy out Bethel (formerly called Luz), ²⁴the spies saw a man coming out of the city and they said to him, "Show us how to get into the city and we will see that you are treated well." ²⁵So he showed them, and they put the city to the sword but spared the man and his whole family. ²⁶He then went to the land of the Hittites, where he built a city and called it Luz, which is its name to this day.

²⁷But Manasseh did not drive out the people of Beth Shan or Taanach or Dor or Ibleam or Megiddo and their surrounding settlements, for the Canaanites were determined to live in that land. ²⁸When Israel became strong, they pressed the Canaanites into forced labor but never drove them out completely. ²⁹Nor did Ephraim drive out the Canaanites living in Gezer, but the Canaanites continued to live there among them. ³⁰Neither did Zebulun drive out the Canaanites living in Kitron or Nahalol, who remained among them; but they did subject them to forced labor. ³¹Nor did Asher drive out those living in Acco or Sidon or Ahlab or Aczib or Helbah or Aphek or Rehob, ³²and because of this the people of Asher lived among the Canaanite inhabitants of the land. ³³Neither did Naphtali drive out those living in Beth Shemesh or Beth Anath; but the Naphtalites too lived among the Canaanite inhabitants of the land, and those living in Beth Shemesh and Beth Anath became forced laborers for them. ³⁴The Amorites confined

---

ᵃ *14* Hebrew; Septuagint and Vulgate *Othniel, he urged her*   ᵇ *16* That is, Jericho   ᶜ *17* The Hebrew term refers to the irrevocable giving over of things or persons to the LORD, often by totally destroying them.   ᵈ *17 Hormah* means *destruction.*   ᵉ *18* Hebrew; Septuagint *Judah did not take* the Danites to the hill country, not allowing them to come down into the plain. ³⁵And the Amorites were determined also to hold out in Mount Heres, Aijalon and Shaalbim, but when the power of the house of Joseph increased, they too were pressed into forced labor. ³⁶The boundary of the Amorites was from Scorpionª Pass to Sela and beyond.

THE ANGEL OF THE LORD AT BOKIM

2 The angel of the LORD went up from Gilgal to Bokim and said, "I brought you up out of Egypt and led you into the land that I swore to give to your forefathers. I said, 'I will never break my covenant with you, ²and you shall not make a covenant with the people of this land, but you shall break down their altars.' Yet you have disobeyed me. Why have you done this? ³Now therefore I tell you that I will not drive them out before you; they will be ⌐thorns⌐ in your sides and their gods will be a snare to you."

⁴When the angel of the LORD had spoken these things to all the Israelites, the people wept aloud, ⁵and they called that place Bokim.ᵇ There they offered sacrifices to the LORD.

DISOBEDIENCE AND DEFEAT

NOW OR NEVER
JDG 2:16–19

How does God speak to *you*? Does he use your conscience to remind you about things you need forgiveness for? Bring helpful Bible passages to mind when facing tough decisions? Use the words of others to guide you? More important, do you listen?

⁶After Joshua had dismissed the Israelites, they went to take possession of the land, each to his own inheritance. ⁷The people served the LORD throughout the lifetime of Joshua and of the elders who outlived him and who had seen all the great things the LORD had done for Israel.

⁸Joshua son of Nun, the servant of the LORD, died at the age of a hundred and ten. ⁹And they buried him in the land of his inheritance, at Timnath Heresᶜ in the hill country of Ephraim, north of Mount Gaash.

¹⁰After that whole generation had been gathered to their fathers, another generation grew up, who knew neither the LORD nor what he had done for Israel. ¹¹Then the Israelites did evil in the eyes of the LORD and served the Baals. ¹²They forsook the LORD, the God of their fathers, who had brought them out of Egypt. They followed and worshiped various gods of the peoples around them. They provoked the LORD to anger ¹³because they forsook him and served Baal and the Ashtoreths. ¹⁴In his anger against Israel the LORD handed them over to raiders who plundered them. He sold them to their enemies all around, whom they were no longer able to resist. ¹⁵Whenever Israel went out to fight, the hand of the LORD was against them to defeat them, just as he had sworn to them. They were in great distress.

¹⁶Then the LORD raised up judges,ᵈ who saved them out of the hands of these raiders. ¹⁷Yet they would not listen to their judges but prostituted themselves to other gods and worshiped them. Unlike their fathers, they quickly turned from the way in which their fathers had walked, the way of obedience to the LORD's commands. ¹⁸Whenever the LORD raised up a judge for them, he was with the judge and saved them out of the hands of their enemies as long as the judge lived; for the LORD had compassion on them as they groaned under those who oppressed and afflicted them. ¹⁹But when the judge died, the people returned to ways even more corrupt than those of their fathers, following other gods and serving and worshiping them. They refused to give up their evil practices and stubborn ways.

²⁰Therefore the LORD was very angry with Israel and said, "Because this nation has violated the covenant that I

JDG 3:1

challenge notes

To: **my_son**

heavenly_father: the next time you face a challenge in your spiritual life, don't ask me to remove it; ask me for the strength to overcome it. every time you smack down a threat to your relationship with me, every time you turn your back on temptation, you grow a little more as a follower of Jesus.

ª *36* Hebrew *Akrabbim*   ᵇ *5 Bokim* means *weepers.*   ᶜ *9* Also known as *Timnath Serah* (see Joshua 19:50 and 24:30)
ᵈ *16* Or *leaders*; similarly in verses 17–19

laid down for their forefathers and has not listened to me, ²¹I will no longer drive out before them any of the nations Joshua left when he died. ²²I will use them to test Israel and see whether they will keep the way of the Lord and walk in it as their forefathers did." ²³The Lord had allowed those nations to remain; he did not drive them out at once by giving them into the hands of Joshua.

3 These are the nations the Lord left to test all those Israelites who had not experienced any of the wars in Canaan ²(he did this only to teach warfare to the descendants of the Israelites who had not had previous battle experience): ³the five rulers of the Philistines, all the Canaanites, the Sidonians, and the Hivites living in the Lebanon mountains from Mount Baal Hermon to Leboᵃ Hamath. ⁴They were left to test the Israelites to see whether they would obey the Lord's commands, which he had given their forefathers through Moses.

⁵The Israelites lived among the Canaanites, Hittites, Amorites, Perizzites, Hivites and Jebusites. ⁶They took their daughters in marriage and gave their own daughters to their sons, and served their gods.

»» live the adventure »» Jdg 3:15

NOW OR NEVER
JDG 3:1

When God tests us, he isn't trying to tempt us into doing something wrong; he's making sure we're ready for combat. We have an enemy who will do anything to damage our faith and our relationship with God. If we're not ready for a real battle against him, he has a good chance of succeeding.

Accepting Yourself

If you had to make a list of your weaknesses and shortcomings, what would you include? Even if you're left-handed, that probably wouldn't make the list. But it would have for Ehud. In his day, being left-handed was considered something of a handicap. But it was Ehud's left hand that God used to deliver brutal justice—in a very forceful way. Think it was just a coincidence? The writer of Judges didn't think so; he mentioned the fact that Ehud was left-handed not once, but twice. So what do you think about your weaknesses now?

OTHNIEL

⁷The Israelites did evil in the eyes of the Lord; they forgot the Lord their God and served the Baals and the Asherahs. ⁸The anger of the Lord burned against Israel so that he sold them into the hands of Cushan-Rishathaim king of Aram Naharaim,ᵇ to whom the Israelites were subject for eight years. ⁹But when they cried out to the Lord, he raised up for them a deliverer, Othniel son of Kenaz, Caleb's younger brother, who saved them. ¹⁰The Spirit of the Lord came upon him, so that he became Israel's judgeᶜ and went to war. The Lord gave Cushan-Rishathaim king of Aram into the hands of Othniel, who overpowered him. ¹¹So the land had peace for forty years, until Othniel son of Kenaz died.

EHUD

¹²Once again the Israelites did evil in the eyes of the Lord, and because they did this evil the Lord gave Eglon king of Moab power over Israel. ¹³Getting the Ammonites and Amalekites to join him, Eglon came and attacked Israel, and they took possession of the City of Palms.ᵈ ¹⁴The Israelites were subject to Eglon king of Moab for eighteen years.

¹⁵Again the Israelites cried out to the Lord, and he gave them a deliverer—Ehud, a left-handed man, the son of Gera the Benjamite. The Israelites sent him with tribute to Eglon king of Moab. ¹⁶Now Ehud had made a double-edged sword about a foot and a halfᵉ long, which he strapped to his right thigh under his clothing. ¹⁷He presented the tribute to Eglon king of Moab, who was a very fat man. ¹⁸After Ehud had presented the tribute, he sent on their way the men who had carried it. ¹⁹At the idolsᶠ near Gilgal he himself turned back and said, "I have a secret message for you, O king."

The king said, "Quiet!" And all his attendants left him.

ᵃ *3* Or *to the entrance to*   ᵇ *8* That is, Northwest Mesopotamia   ᶜ *10* Or *leader*   ᵈ *13* That is, Jericho   ᵉ *16* Hebrew *a cubit* (about 0.5 meter)   ᶠ *19* Or *the stone quarries*; also in verse 26

ehud

VERSUS

eglon

» **The son of Gera, an Israelite from the tribe of Benjamin**
» **A lefty**
» **Used by God to deliver Israel from the Moabites**

» **The king of Moab, who oppressed Israel for 18 miserable years**
» **A big, fat slob**
» **Assassinated by Ehud in his summer palace**

The Main Event

How is it that, time and time again, the Israelites just didn't get it? God had been crystal clear: "Obey me and find blessing; turn away from me and find trouble."

Whatever the reason, the Israelites clearly did *not* listen. Once again in Judges 3 they found themselves in a mess of their own making. In response to their evil actions, the Lord allowed the Moabites to ride into town and take control for 18 years. The result was nearly two decades of domination at the hands of King Eglon, a Biblical version of Jabba the Hutt from the movie *Star Wars*.

After considerable suffering, the Israelites finally came to their senses and turned back to God. His gracious response was to send a lefty named Ehud. This guy was all business. With the cunning of a secret agent and the steely nerves of a Navy SEAL, Ehud concocted and executed a daring plan.

Ehud was selected to deliver Israel's annual payment (called a "tribute") to the Moabites. After making the payment, he requested a meeting with Eglon, claiming to have a secret message for him. Little did the king know, Ehud was armed and dangerous. Being left-handed, Ehud had managed to conceal a dagger on the side where no one would have expected one to be. When the two men were alone in the king's private quarters, Ehud said, "I have a message from God for you." With that, he whipped out the dagger and jammed it so hard and so far into Eglon's fat belly that the knife completely disappeared—handle and all!

Quickly and quietly, Ehud took off. Gathering some fighters, he led the Israelites in a lightning strike against the occupation army. When the dust settled, the battlefield was littered with more than 10,000 bloody Moabite bodies. Israel was free again, and the people enjoyed peace for 80 years.

The Outcome

This strange, bloody story reminds us that God can use us just the way we are. Being left-handed in Ehud's day was considered an oddity, if not an outright handicap. Supposedly lefties were at a huge disadvantage in military situations.

Ehud could have bought into the conventional wisdom of his day and declared himself unable, unfit and unusable. Instead, when God called, Ehud answered. He made himself available to the Lord, and God used his so-called weakness to give Israel a great victory.

What about you? What weaknesses or quirks do you have? How might God use those for his glory? Are you willing to present yourself, just as you are, to God in order to accomplish his work?

Read more about Ehud and Eglon in Judges 3:12–30 (pages 273–275).

²⁰Ehud then approached him while he was sitting alone in the upper room of his summer palace[a] and said, "I have a message from God for you." As the king rose from his seat, ²¹Ehud reached with his left hand, drew the sword from his right thigh and plunged it into the king's belly. ²²Even the handle sank in after the blade, which came out his back. Ehud did not pull the sword out, and the fat closed in over it. ²³Then Ehud went out to the porch[b]; he shut the doors of the upper room behind him and locked them.

²⁴After he had gone, the servants came and found the doors of the upper room locked. They said, "He must be relieving himself in the inner room of the house." ²⁵They waited to the point of embarrassment, but when he did not open the doors of the room, they took a key and unlocked them. There they saw their lord fallen to the floor, dead.

²⁶While they waited, Ehud got away. He passed by the idols and escaped to Seirah. ²⁷When he arrived there, he blew a trumpet in the hill country of Ephraim, and the Israelites went down with him from the hills, with him leading them.

²⁸"Follow me," he ordered, "for the LORD has given Moab, your enemy, into your hands." So they followed him down and, taking possession of the fords of the Jordan that led to Moab, they allowed no one to cross over. ²⁹At that time they struck down about ten thousand Moabites, all vigorous and strong; not a man escaped. ³⁰That day Moab was made subject to Israel, and the land had peace for eighty years.

SHAMGAR

³¹After Ehud came Shamgar son of Anath, who struck down six hundred Philistines with an oxgoad. He too saved Israel.

DEBORAH

4 After Ehud died, the Israelites once again did evil in the eyes of the LORD. ²So the LORD sold them into the hands of Jabin, a king of Canaan, who reigned in Hazor. The commander of his army was Sisera, who lived in Harosheth Haggoyim. ³Because he had nine hundred iron chariots and had cruelly oppressed the Israelites for twenty years, they cried to the LORD for help.

⁴Deborah, a prophetess, the wife of Lappidoth, was leading[c] Israel at that time. ⁵She held court under the Palm of Deborah between Ramah and Bethel in the hill country of Ephraim, and the Israelites came to her to have their disputes decided. ⁶She sent for Barak son of Abinoam from Kedesh in Naphtali and said to him, "The LORD, the God of Israel, commands you: 'Go, take with you ten thousand men of Naphtali and Zebulun and lead the way to Mount Tabor. ⁷I will lure Sisera, the commander of Jabin's army, with his chariots and his troops to the Kishon River and give him into your hands.'"

⁸Barak said to her, "If you go with me, I will go; but if you don't go with me, I won't go."

⁹"Very well," Deborah said, "I will go with you. But because of the way you are going about this,[d] the honor will not be yours, for the LORD will hand Sisera over to a woman." So Deborah went with Barak to Kedesh, ¹⁰where he summoned Zebulun and Naphtali. Ten thousand men followed him, and Deborah also went with him.

NOW OR NEVER
JDG 4:9

How many chances did you have yesterday to do something "honorable"—maybe protecting someone's dignity or defending the truth about Jesus to a skeptical unbeliever? How many of those opportunities did you make good on? What can you do to increase your percentage tomorrow?

¹¹Now Heber the Kenite had left the other Kenites, the descendants of Hobab, Moses' brother-in-law,[e] and pitched his tent by the great tree in Zaanannim near Kedesh.

¹²When they told Sisera that Barak son of Abinoam had gone up to Mount Tabor, ¹³Sisera gathered together his nine hundred iron chariots and all the men with him, from Harosheth Haggoyim to the Kishon River.

¹⁴Then Deborah said to Barak, "Go! This is the day the LORD has given Sisera into your hands. Has

---

[a] 20 The meaning of the Hebrew for this phrase is uncertain.   [b] 23 The meaning of the Hebrew for this word is uncertain.   [c] 4 Traditionally *judging*   [d] 9 Or *But on the expedition you are undertaking*   [e] 11 Or *father-in-law*

not the LORD gone ahead of you?" So Barak went down Mount Tabor, followed by ten thousand men. ¹⁵At Barak's advance, the LORD routed Sisera and all his chariots and army by the sword, and Sisera abandoned his chariot and fled on foot. ¹⁶But Barak pursued the chariots and army as far as Harosheth Haggoyim. All the troops of Sisera fell by the sword; not a man was left.

¹⁷Sisera, however, fled on foot to the tent of Jael, the wife of Heber the Kenite, because there were friendly relations between Jabin king of Hazor and the clan of Heber the Kenite.

¹⁸Jael went out to meet Sisera and said to him, "Come, my lord, come right in. Don't be afraid." So he entered her tent, and she put a covering over him.

¹⁹"I'm thirsty," he said. "Please give me some water." She opened a skin of milk, gave him a drink, and covered him up.

²⁰"Stand in the doorway of the tent," he told her. "If someone comes by and asks you, 'Is anyone here?' say 'No.'"

²¹But Jael, Heber's wife, picked up a tent peg and a hammer and went quietly to him while he lay fast asleep, exhausted. She drove the peg through his temple into the ground, and he died.

²²Barak came by in pursuit of Sisera, and Jael went out to meet him. "Come," she said, "I will show you the man you're looking for." So he went in with her, and there lay Sisera with the tent peg through his temple—dead.

²³On that day God subdued Jabin, the Canaanite king, before the Israelites. ²⁴And the hand of the Israelites grew stronger and stronger against Jabin, the Canaanite king, until they destroyed him.

Recognizing Your Usefulness

Jacob cheated his twin brother out of everything he had. David arranged to have one of his best soldiers killed after he hooked up with the guy's wife. Moses murdered a man in broad daylight. Paul helped execute Christians for the Jewish leaders of his day. In this passage, God used a woman to overpower a mighty warrior. God makes unusual personnel choices, to say the least. So what makes you think you're any less useful to God than these unlikely people?

THE SONG OF DEBORAH

5 On that day Deborah and Barak son of Abinoam sang this song:

² "When the princes in Israel take the lead,
    when the people willingly offer themselves—
      praise the LORD!

NOW OR NEVER
JDG 5:3

Do you believe all good things come from God? If so, how quick are you to give credit and thanks to him when something good happens to you?

³ "Hear this, you kings! Listen, you rulers!
    I will sing toª the LORD, I will sing;
I will make music toᵇ the LORD, the God of Israel.

⁴ "O LORD, when you went out from Seir,
    when you marched from the land of Edom,
the earth shook, the heavens poured,
    the clouds poured down water.
⁵ The mountains quaked before the LORD,
    the One of Sinai,
before the LORD, the God of Israel.

⁶ "In the days of Shamgar son of Anath,
    in the days of Jael, the roads were abandoned;
    travelers took to winding paths.

ª *3 Or of*   ᵇ *3 Or / with song I will praise*

battlelines

» Mount St. Jacob (Emotions)

Q: What'd you do this weekend?
A: Didn't I already tell you?

Q: No.
A: Oh . . . maybe that's because it's *none of your stinking business!*

Q: Dude, lighten up! I'm just making conversation. What's the matter with you?
A: Look, I'm sorry. I just . . . I don't know. I'm in a bad mood, and I don't know why, OK?

Q: What's the deal?
A: I just feel mad at the whole world. It's not anyone or anything specific. At least it's nothing I can put my finger on. It just seems like every little thing pushes my buttons.

Q: When did this start?
A: Who knows? A month ago. Two. It's just been building up. Look, don't try to psychoanalyze me. I don't have issues with you, OK? I just feel like—I don't know—a volcano ready to erupt.

Q: So have you erupted yet?
A: Not really. But I have been snapping and yelling at people left and right—my parents, my friends, even this girl I like. A few days ago, I threw a dart at my wall as hard as I could, and it went all the way through the sheet rock.

Q: Really?
A: Yeah. But it's not just anger. Some days I'm depressed, like I can't even pull myself out of bed. And last night I got scared. I was home alone, and I heard something in the back bedroom. I nearly ran out of the house. It turned out to be the dog.

Q: So do you have people you can talk to about all this?
A: (Long pause) Maybe. But it's embarrassing, you know? In the big scheme of things, what do I have to complain about? Maybe I just think too much. I'll work it out.

» Dealing With Feelings

Emotions are those things we feel as life "happens" to us. Whether they're good or bad, it's critical that we express them. If we bury them or deny them, we become human versions of a two-liter of Mountain Dew that's been shaken up and left in a blazing hot vehicle. It's only a matter of time before there will be an explosion—and a huge mess!

Painful emotions aren't wrong, but if they're unexpressed or expressed in an unhealthy way, they can cause major trouble. But if they're dealt with in a healthy fashion, bad feelings can draw us closer to God and other people. Consider these Biblical reminders:

● When you feel sad . . . it's OK to be down—even to cry. Jesus did (see John 11:35).

● When you feel angry . . . let it out without hurting others (see Ephesians 4:26–27).

● When you feel afraid, frustrated, helpless, abandoned, guilty or whatever . . . tell God everything that's going on in your heart. Almost half the psalms in the Bible did just this!

Also keep in mind that intense anger can be a sign of underlying hurt or depression. If you feel like your anger is "eating you up," don't be afraid to talk with your pastor or youth pastor or even a professional Christian counselor.

Read more about handling emotions at www.RevolutionBible.com.

⁷Village life ª in Israel ceased,
  ceased until I, ᵇ Deborah, arose,
  arose a mother in Israel.
⁸When they chose new gods,
  war came to the city gates,
  and not a shield or spear was seen
  among forty thousand in Israel.
⁹My heart is with Israel's princes,
  with the willing volunteers among the people.
  Praise the LORD!

¹⁰"You who ride on white donkeys,
  sitting on your saddle blankets,
  and you who walk along the road,
  consider ¹¹the voice of the singers ᶜ at the watering places.
  They recite the righteous acts of the LORD,
  the righteous acts of his warriors ᵈ in Israel.

"Then the people of the LORD
  went down to the city gates.
¹²'Wake up, wake up, Deborah!
  Wake up, wake up, break out in song!
  Arise, O Barak!
  Take captive your captives, O son of Abinoam.'

¹³"Then the men who were left
  came down to the nobles;
  the people of the LORD
  came to me with the mighty.
¹⁴Some came from Ephraim, whose roots were in Amalek;
  Benjamin was with the people who followed you.
  From Makir captains came down,
  from Zebulun those who bear a commander's staff.
¹⁵The princes of Issachar were with Deborah;
  yes, Issachar was with Barak,
  rushing after him into the valley.
  In the districts of Reuben
  there was much searching of heart.
¹⁶Why did you stay among the campfires ᵉ
  to hear the whistling for the flocks?
  In the districts of Reuben
  there was much searching of heart.
¹⁷Gilead stayed beyond the Jordan.
  And Dan, why did he linger by the ships?
  Asher remained on the coast
  and stayed in his coves.
¹⁸The people of Zebulun risked their very lives;
  so did Naphtali on the heights of the field.

¹⁹"Kings came, they fought;
  the kings of Canaan fought
  at Taanach by the waters of Megiddo,
  but they carried off no silver, no plunder.
²⁰From the heavens the stars fought,
  from their courses they fought against Sisera.

ª 7 Or *Warriors* ᵇ 7 Or *you* ᶜ 11 Or *archers*; the meaning of the Hebrew for this word is uncertain. ᵈ 11 Or *villagers*
ᵉ 16 Or *saddlebags*

²¹ The river Kishon swept them away,
the age-old river, the river Kishon.
March on, my soul; be strong!
²² Then thundered the horses' hoofs—
galloping, galloping go his mighty steeds.
²³ 'Curse Meroz,' said the angel of the LORD.
'Curse its people bitterly,
because they did not come to help the LORD,
to help the LORD against the mighty.'

²⁴ "Most blessed of women be Jael,
the wife of Heber the Kenite,
most blessed of tent-dwelling women.
²⁵ He asked for water, and she gave him milk;
in a bowl fit for nobles she brought him curdled milk.
²⁶ Her hand reached for the tent peg,
her right hand for the workman's hammer.
She struck Sisera, she crushed his head,
she shattered and pierced his temple.
²⁷ At her feet he sank,
he fell; there he lay.
At her feet he sank, he fell;
where he sank, there he fell—dead.

²⁸ "Through the window peered Sisera's mother;
behind the lattice she cried out,
'Why is his chariot so long in coming?
Why is the clatter of his chariots delayed?'
²⁹ The wisest of her ladies answer her;
indeed, she keeps saying to herself,
³⁰ 'Are they not finding and dividing the spoils:
a girl or two for each man,
colorful garments as plunder for Sisera,
colorful garments embroidered,
highly embroidered garments for my neck—
all this as plunder?'

³¹ "So may all your enemies perish,
O LORD!
But may they who love you be like
the sun
when it rises in its strength."

Then the land had peace forty years.

GIDEON

6 Again the Israelites did evil in the eyes of the LORD, and for seven years he gave them into the hands of the Midianites. ²Because the power of Midian was so oppressive, the Israelites prepared shelters for themselves in mountain clefts, caves and strongholds. ³Whenever the Israelites planted their crops, the Midianites, Amalekites and other eastern peoples invaded the country. ⁴They camped on the land and ruined the crops all the way to Gaza and did not spare a living thing for Israel, neither sheep nor cattle nor donkeys. ⁵They came up with their livestock and their tents like swarms of locusts. It was impossible to count the men and their

NOW OR NEVER
JDG 5:31

There's no neutral ground in the war between good and evil. The battle is real and way too important.

camels; they invaded the land to ravage it. [6]Midian so impoverished the Israelites that they cried out to the LORD for help.

[7]When the Israelites cried to the LORD because of Midian, [8]he sent them a prophet, who said, "This is what the LORD, the God of Israel, says: I brought you up out of Egypt, out of the land of slavery. [9]I snatched you from the power of Egypt and from the hand of all your oppressors. I drove them from before you and gave you their land. [10]I said to you, 'I am the LORD your God; do not worship the gods of the Amorites, in whose land you live.' But you have not listened to me."

[11]The angel of the LORD came and sat down under the oak in Ophrah that belonged to Joash the Abiezrite, where his son Gideon was threshing wheat in a winepress to keep it from the Midianites. [12]When the angel of the LORD appeared to Gideon, he said, "The LORD is with you, mighty warrior."

[13]"But sir," Gideon replied, "if the LORD is with us, why has all this happened to us? Where are all his wonders that our fathers told us about when they said, 'Did not the LORD bring us up out of Egypt?' But now the LORD has abandoned us and put us into the hand of Midian."

[14]The LORD turned to him and said, "Go in the strength you have and save Israel out of Midian's hand. Am I not sending you?"

[15]"But Lord,[a]" Gideon asked, "how can I save Israel? My clan is the weakest in Manasseh, and I am the least in my family."

[16]The LORD answered, "I will be with you, and you will strike down all the Midianites together."

[17]Gideon replied, "If now I have found favor in your eyes, give me a sign that it is really you talking to me. [18]Please do not go away until I come back and bring my offering and set it before you."

And the LORD said, "I will wait until you return."

[19]Gideon went in, prepared a young goat, and from an ephah[b] of flour he made bread without yeast. Putting the meat in a basket and its broth in a pot, he brought them out and offered them to him under the oak.

[20]The angel of God said to him, "Take the meat and the unleavened bread, place them on this rock, and pour out the broth." And Gideon did so. [21]With the tip of the staff that was in his hand, the angel of the LORD touched the meat and the unleavened bread. Fire flared from the rock, consuming the meat and the bread. And the angel of the LORD disappeared. [22]When Gideon realized that it was the angel of the LORD, he exclaimed, "Ah, Sovereign LORD! I have seen the angel of the LORD face to face!"

[23]But the LORD said to him, "Peace! Do not be afraid. You are not going to die."

[24]So Gideon built an altar to the LORD there and called it The LORD is Peace. To this day it stands in Ophrah of the Abiezrites.

[25]That same night the LORD said to him, "Take the second bull from your father's herd, the one seven years old.[c] Tear down your father's altar to Baal and cut down the Asherah pole[d] beside it. [26]Then build a proper kind of[e] altar to the LORD your God on the top of this height. Using the wood of the Asherah pole that you cut down, offer the second[f] bull as a burnt offering."

[27]So Gideon took ten of his servants and did as the LORD told him. But because he was afraid of his family and the men of the town, he did it at night rather than in the daytime.

[28]In the morning when the men of the town got up, there was Baal's altar, demolished, with the Asherah pole beside it cut down and the second bull sacrificed on the newly built altar!

[29]They asked each other, "Who did this?"

Dealing With Weaknesses

You're not perfect. In fact, you're not even close. A lot of people are way more talented at a lot of things than you'll ever be. OK? Now get over it and move on, because you've got important work to do. That's right, *you*, with all of your weaknesses and shortcomings. God is going to put you in a position to do some extremely important things for him—because he knows you can accomplish them with him in your life. And if you doubt that, what you're really telling God is that you think he's wrong.

---

[a] *15 Or sir*   [b] *19 That is, probably about 3/5 bushel (about 22 liters)*   [c] *25 Or Take a full-grown, mature bull from your father's herd*   [d] *25 That is, a symbol of the goddess Asherah; here and elsewhere in Judges*   [e] *26 Or build with layers of stone an*   [f] *26 Or full-grown; also in verse 28*

When they carefully investigated, they were told, "Gideon son of Joash did it."

[30]The men of the town demanded of Joash, "Bring out your son. He must die, because he has broken down Baal's altar and cut down the Asherah pole beside it."

[31]But Joash replied to the hostile crowd around him, "Are you going to plead Baal's cause? Are you trying to save him? Whoever fights for him shall be put to death by morning! If Baal really is a god, he can defend himself when someone breaks down his altar." [32]So that day they called Gideon "Jerub-Baal,[a]" saying, "Let Baal contend with him," because he broke down Baal's altar.

[33]Now all the Midianites, Amalekites and other eastern peoples joined forces and crossed over the Jordan and camped in the Valley of Jezreel. [34]Then the Spirit of the LORD came upon Gideon, and he blew a trumpet, summoning the Abiezrites to follow him. [35]He sent messengers throughout Manasseh, calling them to arms, and also into Asher, Zebulun and Naphtali, so that they too went up to meet them.

[36]Gideon said to God, "If you will save Israel by my hand as you have promised— [37]look, I will place a wool fleece on the threshing floor. If there is dew only on the fleece and all the ground is dry, then I will know that you will save Israel by my hand, as you said." [38]And that is what happened. Gideon rose early the next day; he squeezed the fleece and wrung out the dew—a bowlful of water.

[39]Then Gideon said to God, "Do not be angry with me. Let me make just one more request. Allow me one more test with the fleece. This time make the fleece dry and the ground covered with dew." [40]That night God did so. Only the fleece was dry; all the ground was covered with dew.

NOW OR NEVER
JDG 6:39–40

Gideon viewed a dew-proof fleece as proof positive that he was the man for God's plan. What have you seen God do that strengthened your confidence in his plan for your life?

GIDEON DEFEATS THE MIDIANITES

7 Early in the morning, Jerub-Baal (that is, Gideon) and all his men camped at the spring of Harod. The camp of Midian was north of them in the valley near the hill of Moreh. [2]The LORD said to Gideon, "You have too many men for me to deliver Midian into their hands. In order that Israel may not boast against me that her own strength has saved her, [3]announce now to the people, 'Anyone who trembles with fear may turn back and leave Mount Gilead.'" So twenty-two thousand men left, while ten thousand remained.

[4]But the LORD said to Gideon, "There are still too many men. Take them down to the water, and I will sift them for you there. If I say, 'This one shall go with you,' he shall go; but if I say, 'This one shall not go with you,' he shall not go."

[5]So Gideon took the men down to the water. There the LORD told him, "Separate those who lap the water with their tongues like a dog from those who kneel down to drink." [6]Three hundred men lapped with their hands to their mouths. All the rest got down on their knees to drink.

[7]The LORD said to Gideon, "With the three hundred men that lapped I will save you and give the Midianites into your hands. Let all the other men go, each to his own place." [8]So Gideon sent the rest of the Israelites to their tents but kept the three hundred, who took over the provisions and trumpets of the others.

Now the camp of Midian lay below him in the valley. [9]During that night the LORD said to Gideon, "Get up, go down against the camp, because I am going to give it into your hands. [10]If you are afraid to attack, go down to the camp with your servant Purah [11]and listen to what they are saying. Afterward, you will be encouraged to attack the camp." So he and Purah his servant went down to the outposts of

NOW OR NEVER
JDG 7:2

You know what would really make Satan happy? To see you try to resist temptation or go into battle against him relying on your own strength and strategies, instead of on the power and presence of God's Holy Spirit within you.

---

[a] 32 Jerub-Baal means *let Baal contend.*

the camp. 12The Midianites, the Amalekites and all the other eastern peoples had settled in the valley, thick as locusts. Their camels could no more be counted than the sand on the seashore.

13Gideon arrived just as a man was telling a friend his dream. "I had a dream," he was saying. "A round loaf of barley bread came tumbling into the Midianite camp. It struck the tent with such force that the tent overturned and collapsed."

14His friend responded, "This can be nothing other than the sword of Gideon son of Joash, the Israelite. God has given the Midianites and the whole camp into his hands."

15When Gideon heard the dream and its interpretation, he worshiped God. He returned to the camp of Israel and called out, "Get up! The LORD has given the Midianite camp into your hands." 16Dividing the three hundred men into three companies, he placed trumpets and empty jars in the hands of all of them, with torches inside.

17"Watch me," he told them. "Follow my lead. When I get to the edge of the camp, do exactly as I do. 18When I and all who are with me blow our trumpets, then from all around the camp blow yours and shout, 'For the LORD and for Gideon.'"

19Gideon and the hundred men with him reached the edge of the camp at the beginning of the middle watch, just after they had changed the guard. They blew their trumpets and broke the jars that were in their hands. 20The three companies blew the trumpets and smashed the jars. Grasping the torches in their left hands and holding in their right hands the trumpets they were to blow, they shouted, "A sword for the LORD and for Gideon!" 21While each man held his position around the camp, all the Midianites ran, crying out as they fled.

22When the three hundred trumpets sounded, the LORD caused the men throughout the camp to turn on each other with their swords. The army fled to Beth Shittah toward Zererah as far as the border of Abel Meholah near Tabbath. 23Israelites from Naphtali, Asher and all Manasseh were called out, and they pursued the Midianites. 24Gideon sent messengers throughout the hill country of Ephraim, saying, "Come down against the Midianites and seize the waters of the Jordan ahead of them as far as Beth Barah."

So all the men of Ephraim were called out and they took the waters of the Jordan as far as Beth Barah. 25They also captured two of the Midianite leaders, Oreb and Zeeb. They killed Oreb at the rock of Oreb, and Zeeb at the winepress of Zeeb. They pursued the Midianites and brought the heads of Oreb and Zeeb to Gideon, who was by the Jordan.

ZEBAH AND ZALMUNNA

8 Now the Ephraimites asked Gideon, "Why have you treated us like this? Why didn't you call us when you went to fight Midian?" And they criticized him sharply.

2But he answered them, "What have I accomplished compared to you? Aren't the gleanings of Ephraim's grapes better than the full grape harvest of Abiezer? 3God gave Oreb and Zeeb, the Midianite leaders, into your hands. What was I able to do compared to you?" At this, their resentment against him subsided.

4Gideon and his three hundred men, exhausted yet keeping up the pursuit, came to the Jordan and crossed it. 5He said to the men of Succoth, "Give my troops some bread; they are worn out, and I am still pursuing Zebah and Zalmunna, the kings of Midian."

6But the officials of Succoth said, "Do you already have the hands of Zebah and Zalmunna in your possession? Why should we give bread to your troops?"

7Then Gideon replied, "Just for that, when the LORD has given Zebah and Zalmunna into my hand, I will tear your flesh with desert thorns and briers."

8From there he went up to Peniel [a] and made the same request of them, but they answered as the men of Succoth had. 9So he said to the men of Peniel, "When I return in triumph, I will tear down this tower."

10Now Zebah and Zalmunna were in Karkor with a force of about fifteen thousand men, all that were left of the armies of the eastern peoples; a hundred and twenty thousand swordsmen had fallen. 11Gideon went up by the route of the nomads east of Nobah and Jogbehah and fell upon the unsuspecting army. 12Zebah and Zalmunna, the two kings of Midian, fled, but he pursued them and captured them, routing their entire army.

13Gideon son of Joash then returned from the battle by the Pass of Heres. 14He caught a young man

---

a 8 Hebrew *Penuel*, a variant of *Peniel*; also in verses 9 and 17 of Succoth and questioned him, and the young man wrote down for him the names of the seventy-seven officials of Succoth, the elders of the town. ¹⁵Then Gideon came and said to the men of Succoth, "Here are Zebah and Zalmunna, about whom you taunted me by saying, 'Do you already have the hands of Zebah and Zalmunna in your possession? Why should we give bread to your exhausted men?' " ¹⁶He took the elders of the town and taught the men of Succoth a lesson by punishing them with desert thorns and briers. ¹⁷He also pulled down the tower of Peniel and killed the men of the town.

¹⁸Then he asked Zebah and Zalmunna, "What kind of men did you kill at Tabor?"

"Men like you," they answered, "each one with the bearing of a prince."

¹⁹Gideon replied, "Those were my brothers, the sons of my own mother. As surely as the Lord lives, if you had spared their lives, I would not kill you." ²⁰Turning to Jether, his oldest son, he said, "Kill them!" But Jether did not draw his sword, because he was only a boy and was afraid.

²¹Zebah and Zalmunna said, "Come, do it yourself. 'As is the man, so is his strength.' " So Gideon stepped forward and killed them, and took the ornaments off their camels' necks.

GIDEON'S EPHOD

²²The Israelites said to Gideon, "Rule over us—you, your son and your grandson—because you have saved us out of the hand of Midian."

²³But Gideon told them, "I will not rule over you, nor will my son rule over you. The Lord will rule over you." ²⁴And he said, "I do have one request, that each of you give me an earring from your share of the plunder." (It was the custom of the Ishmaelites to wear gold earrings.)

²⁵They answered, "We'll be glad to give them." So they spread out a garment, and each man threw a ring from his plunder onto it. ²⁶The weight of the gold rings he asked for came to seventeen hundred shekels,ᵃ not counting the ornaments, the pendants and the purple garments worn by the kings of Midian or the chains that were on their camels' necks. ²⁷Gideon made the gold into an ephod, which he placed in Ophrah, his town. All Israel prostituted themselves by worshiping it there, and it became a snare to Gideon and his family.

NOW OR NEVER
JDG 8:22-23

Gideon didn't want anyone to think that he was responsible for the things God had accomplished through him. How can you make sure that people see God's "fingerprints" on your success?

GIDEON'S DEATH

²⁸Thus Midian was subdued before the Israelites and did not raise its head again. During Gideon's lifetime, the land enjoyed peace forty years.

²⁹Jerub-Baal son of Joash went back home to live. ³⁰He had seventy sons of his own, for he had many wives. ³¹His concubine, who lived in Shechem, also bore him a son, whom he named Abimelech. ³²Gideon son of Joash died at a good old age and was buried in the tomb of his father Joash in Ophrah of the Abiezrites.

³³No sooner had Gideon died than the Israelites again prostituted themselves to the Baals. They set up Baal-Berith as their god and ³⁴did not remember the Lord their God, who had rescued them from the hands of all their enemies on every side. ³⁵They also failed to show kindness to the family of Jerub-Baal (that is, Gideon) for all the good things he had done for them.

ABIMELECH

9 Abimelech son of Jerub-Baal went to his mother's brothers in Shechem and said to them and to all his mother's clan, ²"Ask all the citizens of Shechem, 'Which is better for you: to have all seventy of Jerub-Baal's sons rule over you, or just one man?' Remember, I am your flesh and blood."

³When the brothers repeated all this to the citizens of Shechem, they were inclined to follow Abimelech, for they said, "He is our brother." ⁴They gave him seventy shekelsᵇ of silver from the temple of Baal-Berith, and Abimelech used it to hire reckless adventurers, who became his followers. ⁵He went to his father's home in Ophrah and on one stone murdered his seventy brothers, the sons of Jerub-Baal.

ᵃ *26* That is, about 43 pounds (about 19.5 kilograms)   ᵇ *4* That is, about 1 3/4 pounds (about 0.8 kilogram)

abimelech

VERSUS

jotham

» The son of Gideon by a mistress
» Put to death all of his brothers except Jotham
» Died a humiliating death at the hands of a woman

» The youngest of Gideon's 70 sons
» The only one who escaped death at the hands of Abimelech
» Spoke out boldly against Abimelech and cursed him

The Main Event

Are you ready to rumble?! In this corner, weighing in at an impressive 250 pounds, it's the sheik from Shechem, the Ogre from Ophrah . . . Abimelech the Assassin!

And in this corner, weighing in at a trim 155 pounds, it's the Mouth from the South, the Gerazim Screamer . . . Jotham the Jet!

Round 1: When Gideon dies, his illegitimate son Abimelech immediately tries to grab power.

Round 2: In one of the most shocking and brutal displays in all of Scripture, Abimelech rounds up his 70 half brothers and slaughters them like a flock of sacrificial animals. But the youngest, Jotham, manages to survive the massacre by hiding.

Round 3: When the people gather at Shechem to make Abimelech their king (who's going to resist this guy after round 2?), Jotham, Gideon's only surviving son, pops up on a nearby mountain and yells out a fable, warning everyone of Abimelech's worthless character. Then, before scramming to a place called Beer, he puts a curse on Abimelech and the people of Shechem for their cruelty toward Gideon's family. Jotham's curse predicts that a bloody cycle of mutual destruction will overtake Abimelech and his subjects.

Round 4: Abimelech and the people of Shechem finally get what they deserve. Abimelech summons all the brutality he can muster to put down a rebellion in Shechem, killing women, children and anyone else who gets in his way. But in a battle at the walled city of Thebez, the curse of Jotham lands on Abimelech in the form of a millstone on his skull—dropped off the wall by an unnamed woman.

Winner and new champion? Jotham!

The Outcome

Jotham's willingness to stand up and speak out is commendable. Would you dare do that—plainly in the presence of the guy who had just wiped out your whole family tree? Sure, Jotham spoke out from a distance and then hightailed it to safety after he was done. Still, it was a pretty gutsy move. His actions are a good reminder that our best weapon is always the truth. In many cases, speaking tough words is the boldest thing we can do.

For the record, a millstone was a stone weighing as much as 200 pounds used to crush and grind grain. Basically, the brutal, power-obsessed Abimelech was killed by a woman with a very large, ancient food processor.

Do you back down in the face of trouble? Don't! Be a man of truth. As the writer John Eldredge has counseled, "Let people feel the weight of who you are, and let them deal with it."*

Read more about Jotham and Abimelech in Judges 8–9 (pages 282–286).

*Quoted from *Wild at Heart* by John Eldredge. Copyright 2001. Published by Thomas Nelson, Nashville, TN 37214. Used by permission.

But Jotham, the youngest son of Jerub-Baal, escaped by hiding. ⁶Then all the citizens of Shechem and Beth Millo gathered beside the great tree at the pillar in Shechem to crown Abimelech king.

⁷When Jotham was told about this, he climbed up on the top of Mount Gerizim and shouted to them, "Listen to me, citizens of Shechem, so that God may listen to you. ⁸One day the trees went out to anoint a king for themselves. They said to the olive tree, 'Be our king.'

⁹"But the olive tree answered, 'Should I give up my oil, by which both gods and men are honored, to hold sway over the trees?'

¹⁰"Next, the trees said to the fig tree, 'Come and be our king.'

¹¹"But the fig tree replied, 'Should I give up my fruit, so good and sweet, to hold sway over the trees?'

¹²"Then the trees said to the vine, 'Come and be our king.'

¹³"But the vine answered, 'Should I give up my wine, which cheers both gods and men, to hold sway over the trees?'

¹⁴"Finally all the trees said to the thornbush, 'Come and be our king.'

¹⁵"The thornbush said to the trees, 'If you really want to anoint me king over you, come and take refuge in my shade; but if not, then let fire come out of the thornbush and consume the cedars of Lebanon!'

¹⁶"Now if you have acted honorably and in good faith when you made Abimelech king, and if you have been fair to Jerub-Baal and his family, and if you have treated him as he deserves— ¹⁷and to think that my father fought for you, risked his life to rescue you from the hand of Midian ¹⁸(but today you have revolted against my father's family, murdered his seventy sons on a single stone, and made Abimelech, the son of his slave girl, king over the citizens of Shechem because he is your brother)— ¹⁹if then you have acted honorably and in good faith toward Jerub-Baal and his family today, may Abimelech be your joy, and may you be his, too! ²⁰But if you have not, let fire come out from Abimelech and consume you, citizens of Shechem and Beth Millo, and let fire come out from you, citizens of Shechem and Beth Millo, and consume Abimelech!"

²¹Then Jotham fled, escaping to Beer, and he lived there because he was afraid of his brother Abimelech.

²²After Abimelech had governed Israel three years, ²³God sent an evil spirit between Abimelech and the citizens of Shechem, who acted treacherously against Abimelech. ²⁴God did this in order that the crime against Jerub-Baal's seventy sons, the shedding of their blood, might be avenged on their brother Abimelech and on the citizens of Shechem, who had helped him murder his brothers. ²⁵In opposition to him these citizens of Shechem set men on the hilltops to ambush and rob everyone who passed by, and this was reported to Abimelech.

²⁶Now Gaal son of Ebed moved with his brothers into Shechem, and its citizens put their confidence in him. ²⁷After they had gone out into the fields and gathered the grapes and trodden them, they held a festival in the temple of their god. While they were eating and drinking, they cursed Abimelech. ²⁸Then Gaal son of Ebed said, "Who is Abimelech, and who is Shechem, that we should be subject to him? Isn't he Jerub-Baal's son, and isn't Zebul his deputy? Serve the men of Hamor, Shechem's father! Why should we serve Abimelech? ²⁹If only this people were under my command! Then I would get rid of him. I would say to Abimelech, 'Call out your whole army!' "ᵃ

³⁰When Zebul the governor of the city heard what Gaal son of Ebed said, he was very angry. ³¹Under cover he sent messengers to Abimelech, saying, "Gaal son of Ebed and his brothers have come to Shechem and are stirring up the city against you. ³²Now then, during the night you and your men should come and lie in wait in the fields. ³³In the morning at sunrise, advance against the city. When Gaal and his men come out against you, do whatever your hand finds to do."

³⁴So Abimelech and all his troops set out by night and took up concealed positions near Shechem in four companies. ³⁵Now Gaal son of Ebed had gone out and was standing at the entrance to the city gate just as Abimelech and his soldiers came out from their hiding place.

³⁶When Gaal saw them, he said to Zebul, "Look, people are coming down from the tops of the mountains!"

Zebul replied, "You mistake the shadows of the mountains for men."

³⁷But Gaal spoke up again: "Look, people are coming down from the center of the land, and a company is coming from the direction of the soothsayers' tree."

ᵃ 29 Septuagint; Hebrew *him." Then he said to Abimelech, "Call out your whole army!"*

38 Then Zebul said to him, "Where is your big talk now, you who said, 'Who is Abimelech that we should be subject to him?' Aren't these the men you ridiculed? Go out and fight them!"

39 So Gaal led out[a] the citizens of Shechem and fought Abimelech. 40 Abimelech chased him, and many fell wounded in the flight—all the way to the entrance to the gate. 41 Abimelech stayed in Arumah, and Zebul drove Gaal and his brothers out of Shechem.

42 The next day the people of Shechem went out to the fields, and this was reported to Abimelech. 43 So he took his men, divided them into three companies and set an ambush in the fields. When he saw the people coming out of the city, he rose to attack them. 44 Abimelech and the companies with him rushed forward to a position at the entrance to the city gate. Then two companies rushed upon those in the fields and struck them down. 45 All that day Abimelech pressed his attack against the city until he had captured it and killed its people. Then he destroyed the city and scattered salt over it.

46 On hearing this, the citizens in the tower of Shechem went into the stronghold of the temple of El-Berith. 47 When Abimelech heard that they had assembled there, 48 he and all his men went up Mount Zalmon. He took an ax and cut off some branches, which he lifted to his shoulders. He ordered the men with him, "Quick! Do what you have seen me do!" 49 So all the men cut branches and followed Abimelech. They piled them against the stronghold and set it on fire over the people inside. So all the people in the tower of Shechem, about a thousand men and women, also died.

50 Next Abimelech went to Thebez and besieged it and captured it. 51 Inside the city, however, was a strong tower, to which all the men and women—all the people of the city—fled. They locked themselves in and climbed up on the tower roof. 52 Abimelech went to the tower and stormed it. But as he approached the entrance to the tower to set it on fire, 53 a woman dropped an upper millstone on his head and cracked his skull.

54 Hurriedly he called to his armor-bearer, "Draw your sword and kill me, so that they can't say, 'A woman killed him.' " So his servant ran him through, and he died. 55 When the Israelites saw that Abimelech was dead, they went home.

56 Thus God repaid the wickedness that Abimelech had done to his father by murdering his seventy brothers. 57 God also made the men of Shechem pay for all their wickedness. The curse of Jotham son of Jerub-Baal came on them.

TOLA

10

After the time of Abimelech a man of Issachar, Tola son of Puah, the son of Dodo, rose to save Israel. He lived in Shamir, in the hill country of Ephraim. 2 He led[b] Israel twenty-three years; then he died, and was buried in Shamir.

JAIR

3 He was followed by Jair of Gilead, who led Israel twenty-two years. 4 He had thirty sons, who rode thirty donkeys. They controlled thirty towns in Gilead, which to this day are called Havvoth Jair.[c] 5 When Jair died, he was buried in Kamon.

JEPHTHAH

6 Again the Israelites did evil in the eyes of the LORD. They served the Baals and the Ashtoreths, and the gods of Aram, the gods of Sidon, the gods of Moab, the gods of the Ammonites and the gods of the Philistines. And because the Israelites forsook the LORD and no longer served him, 7 he became angry with them. He sold them into the hands of the Philistines and the Ammonites, 8 who that year shattered and crushed them. For eighteen years they oppressed all the Israelites on the east side of the Jordan in Gilead, the land of the Amorites. 9 The Ammonites also crossed the Jordan to fight against Judah, Benjamin and the house of Ephraim; and Israel was in great distress. 10 Then the Israelites cried out to the LORD, "We have sinned against you, forsaking our God and serving the Baals."

11 The LORD replied, "When the Egyptians, the Amorites, the Ammonites, the Philistines, 12 the Sidonians, the Amalekites and the Maonites[d] oppressed you and you cried to me for help, did I not save you from their hands? 13 But you have forsaken me and served other gods, so I will no longer save you. 14 Go and cry out to the gods you have chosen. Let them save you when you are in trouble!"

15 But the Israelites said to the LORD, "We have sinned. Do with us whatever you think best, but please

---

[a] 39 Or *Gaal went out in the sight of*   [b] 2 Traditionally *judged*; also in verse 3   [c] 4 Or *called the settlements of Jair*   [d] 12 Hebrew; some Septuagint manuscripts *Midianites*

rescue us now." ¹⁶Then they got rid of the foreign gods among them and served the Lord. And he could bear Israel's misery no longer.

¹⁷When the Ammonites were called to arms and camped in Gilead, the Israelites assembled and camped at Mizpah. ¹⁸The leaders of the people of Gilead said to each other, "Whoever will launch the attack against the Ammonites will be the head of all those living in Gilead."

11

Jephthah the Gileadite was a mighty warrior. His father was Gilead; his mother was a prostitute. ²Gilead's wife also bore him sons, and when they were grown up, they drove Jephthah away. "You are not going to get any inheritance in our family," they said, "because you are the son of another woman." ³So Jephthah fled from his brothers and settled in the land of Tob, where a group of adventurers gathered around him and followed him.

⁴Some time later, when the Ammonites made war on Israel, ⁵the elders of Gilead went to get Jephthah from the land of Tob. ⁶"Come," they said, "be our commander, so we can fight the Ammonites."

⁷Jephthah said to them, "Didn't you hate me and drive me from my father's house? Why do you come to me now, when you're in trouble?"

⁸The elders of Gilead said to him, "Nevertheless, we are turning to you now; come with us to fight the Ammonites, and you will be our head over all who live in Gilead."

⁹Jephthah answered, "Suppose you take me back to fight the Ammonites and the Lord gives them to me—will I really be your head?"

¹⁰The elders of Gilead replied, "The Lord is our witness; we will certainly do as you say." ¹¹So Jephthah went with the elders of Gilead, and the people made him head and commander over them. And he repeated all his words before the Lord in Mizpah.

¹²Then Jephthah sent messengers to the Ammonite king with the question: "What do you have against us that you have attacked our country?"

¹³The king of the Ammonites answered Jephthah's messengers, "When Israel came up out of Egypt, they took away my land from the Arnon to the Jabbok, all the way to the Jordan. Now give it back peaceably."

¹⁴Jephthah sent back messengers to the Ammonite king, ¹⁵saying:

"This is what Jephthah says: Israel did not take the land of Moab or the land of the Ammonites. ¹⁶But when they came up out of Egypt, Israel went through the desert to the Red Sea[a] and on to Kadesh. ¹⁷Then Israel sent messengers to the king of Edom, saying, 'Give us permission to go through your country,' but the king of Edom would not listen. They sent also to the king of Moab, and he refused. So Israel stayed at Kadesh.

¹⁸"Next they traveled through the desert, skirted the lands of Edom and Moab, passed along the eastern side of the country of Moab, and camped on the other side of the Arnon. They did not enter the territory of Moab, for the Arnon was its border.

¹⁹"Then Israel sent messengers to Sihon king of the Amorites, who ruled in Heshbon, and said to him, 'Let us pass through your country to our own place.' ²⁰Sihon, however, did not trust Israel[b] to pass through his territory. He mustered all his men and encamped at Jahaz and fought with Israel.

²¹"Then the Lord, the God of Israel, gave Sihon and all his men into Israel's hands, and they defeated them. Israel took over all the land of the Amorites who lived in that country, ²²capturing all of it from the Arnon to the Jabbok and from the desert to the Jordan.

²³"Now since the Lord, the God of Israel, has driven the Amorites out before his people Israel, what right have you to take it over? ²⁴Will you not take what your god Chemosh gives you? Likewise, whatever the Lord our God has given us, we will possess. ²⁵Are you better than Balak son of Zippor, king of Moab? Did he ever quarrel with Israel or fight with them? ²⁶For three hundred years Israel occupied Heshbon, Aroer, the surrounding settlements and all the towns along the Arnon. Why didn't you retake them during that time? ²⁷I have not wronged you, but you are doing me wrong by waging war against me. Let the Lord, the Judge,[c] decide the dispute this day between the Israelites and the Ammonites."

²⁸The king of Ammon, however, paid no attention to the message Jephthah sent him.

²⁹Then the Spirit of the Lord came upon Jephthah. He crossed Gilead and Manasseh, passed through Mizpah of Gilead, and from there he advanced against the Ammonites. ³⁰And Jephthah made a

---

ᵃ *16* Hebrew *Yam Suph*; that is, Sea of Reeds   ᵇ *20 Or however, would not make an agreement for Israel*   ᶜ *27 Or Ruler* vow to the Lord: "If you give the Ammonites into my hands, ³¹whatever comes out of the door of my house to meet me when I return in triumph from the Ammonites will be the Lord's, and I will sacrifice it as a burnt offering."

³²Then Jephthah went over to fight the Ammonites, and the Lord gave them into his hands. ³³He devastated twenty towns from Aroer to the vicinity of Minnith, as far as Abel Keramim. Thus Israel subdued Ammon.

³⁴When Jephthah returned to his home in Mizpah, who should come out to meet him but his daughter, dancing to the sound of tambourines! She was an only child. Except for her he had neither son nor daughter. ³⁵When he saw her, he tore his clothes and cried, "Oh! My daughter! You have made me miserable and wretched, because I have made a vow to the Lord that I cannot break."

now or never

JDG 11:27

If you have a beef that you can't resolve, pray about it. Ask God, the ultimate Judge, to help you see what you need to do to make it right.

³⁶"My father," she replied, "you have given your word to the Lord. Do to me just as you promised, now that the Lord has avenged you of your enemies, the Ammonites. ³⁷But grant me this one request," she said. "Give me two months to roam the hills and weep with my friends, because I will never marry."

³⁸"You may go," he said. And he let her go for two months. She and the girls went into the hills and wept because she would never marry. ³⁹After the two months, she returned to her father and he did to her as he had vowed. And she was a virgin.

now or never

JDG 11:30-35

Always think carefully before you make a promise to someone. Remember, your word is intrinsically tied to your reputation. You can't break it without doing serious damage to the way people view and respect you.

From this comes the Israelite custom ⁴⁰that each year the young women of Israel go out for four days to commemorate the daughter of Jephthah the Gileadite.

JEPHTHAH AND EPHRAIM

12 The men of Ephraim called out their forces, crossed over to Zaphon and said to Jephthah, "Why did you go to fight the Ammonites without calling us to go with you? We're going to burn down your house over your head."

²Jephthah answered, "I and my people were engaged in a great struggle with the Ammonites, and although I called, you didn't save me out of their hands. ³When I saw that you wouldn't help, I took my life in my hands and crossed over to fight the Ammonites, and the Lord gave me the victory over them. Now why have you come up today to fight me?"

⁴Jephthah then called together the men of Gilead and fought against Ephraim. The Gileadites struck them down because the Ephraimites had said, "You Gileadites are renegades from Ephraim and Manasseh." ⁵The Gileadites captured the fords of the Jordan leading to Ephraim, and whenever a survivor of Ephraim said, "Let me cross over," the men of Gilead asked him, "Are you an Ephraimite?" If he replied, "No," ⁶they said, "All right, say 'Shibboleth.' " If he said, "Sibboleth," because he could not pronounce the word correctly, they seized him and killed him at the fords of the Jordan. Forty-two thousand Ephraimites were killed at that time.

⁷Jephthah led* Israel six years. Then Jephthah the Gileadite died, and was buried in a town in Gilead.

IBZAN, ELON AND ABDON

⁸After him, Ibzan of Bethlehem led Israel. ⁹He had thirty sons and thirty daughters. He gave his daughters away in marriage to those outside his clan, and for his sons he brought in thirty young wom-

---

ᵃ 7 Traditionally *judged*; also in verses 8–14

en as wives from outside his clan. Ibzan led Israel seven years. ¹⁰Then Ibzan died, and was buried in Bethlehem.

¹¹After him, Elon the Zebulunite led Israel ten years. ¹²Then Elon died, and was buried in Aijalon in the land of Zebulun.

¹³After him, Abdon son of Hillel, from Pirathon, led Israel. ¹⁴He had forty sons and thirty grandsons, who rode on seventy donkeys. He led Israel eight years. ¹⁵Then Abdon son of Hillel died, and was buried at Pirathon in Ephraim, in the hill country of the Amalekites.

THE BIRTH OF SAMSON

13

Again the Israelites did evil in the eyes of the LORD, so the LORD delivered them into the hands of the Philistines for forty years.

²A certain man of Zorah, named Manoah, from the clan of the Danites, had a wife who was sterile and remained childless. ³The angel of the LORD appeared to her and said, "You are sterile and childless, but you are going to conceive and have a son. ⁴Now see to it that you drink no wine or other fermented drink and that you do not eat anything unclean, ⁵because you will conceive and give birth to a son. No razor may be used on his head, because the boy is to be a Nazirite, set apart to God from birth, and he will begin the deliverance of Israel from the hands of the Philistines."

⁶Then the woman went to her husband and told him, "A man of God came to me. He looked like an angel of God, very awesome. I didn't ask him where he came from, and he didn't tell me his name. ⁷But he said to me, 'You will conceive and give birth to a son. Now then, drink no wine or other fermented drink and do not eat anything unclean, because the boy will be a Nazirite of God from birth until the day of his death.'"

⁸Then Manoah prayed to the LORD: "O Lord, I beg you, let the man of God you sent to us come again to teach us how to bring up the boy who is to be born."

⁹God heard Manoah, and the angel of God came again to the woman while she was out in the field; but her husband Manoah was not with her. ¹⁰The woman hurried to tell her husband, "He's here! The man who appeared to me the other day!"

¹¹Manoah got up and followed his wife. When he came to the man, he said, "Are you the one who talked to my wife?"

"I am," he said.

¹²So Manoah asked him, "When your words are fulfilled, what is to be the rule for the boy's life and work?"

¹³The angel of the LORD answered, "Your wife must do all that I have told her. ¹⁴She must not eat anything that comes from the grapevine, nor drink any wine or other fermented drink nor eat anything unclean. She must do everything I have commanded her."

¹⁵Manoah said to the angel of the LORD, "We would like you to stay until we prepare a young goat for you."

¹⁶The angel of the LORD replied, "Even though you detain me, I will not eat any of your food. But if you prepare a burnt offering, offer it to the LORD." (Manoah did not realize that it was the angel of the LORD.)

¹⁷Then Manoah inquired of the angel of the LORD, "What is your name, so that we may honor you when your word comes true?"

¹⁸He replied, "Why do you ask my name? It is beyond understanding.ᵃ" ¹⁹Then Manoah took a young goat, together with the grain offering, and sacrificed it on a rock to the LORD. And the LORD did an amazing thing while Manoah and his wife watched: ²⁰As the flame blazed up from the altar toward heaven, the angel of the LORD ascended in the flame. Seeing this, Manoah and his wife fell with their faces to the ground. ²¹When the angel of the LORD did not show himself again to Manoah and his wife, Manoah realized that it was the angel of the LORD.

²²"We are doomed to die!" he said to his wife. "We have seen God!"

²³But his wife answered, "If the LORD had meant to kill us, he would not have accepted a burnt offering and grain offering from our hands, nor shown us all these things or now told us this."

²⁴The woman gave birth to a boy and named him Samson. He grew and the LORD blessed him, ²⁵and the Spirit of the LORD began to stir him while he was in Mahaneh Dan, between Zorah and Eshtaol.

ᵃ 18 Or is wonderful

SAMSON'S MARRIAGE

14 Samson went down to Timnah and saw there a young Philistine woman. [2]When he returned, he said to his father and mother, "I have seen a Philistine woman in Timnah; now get her for me as my wife."

[3]His father and mother replied, "Isn't there an acceptable woman among your relatives or among all our people? Must you go to the uncircumcised Philistines to get a wife?"

But Samson said to his father, "Get her for me. She's the right one for me." [4](His parents did not know that this was from the LORD, who was seeking an occasion to confront the Philistines; for at that time they were ruling over Israel.) [5]Samson went down to Timnah together with his father and mother. As they approached the vineyards of Timnah, suddenly a young lion came roaring toward him. [6]The Spirit of the LORD came upon him in power so that he tore the lion apart with his bare hands as he might have torn a young goat. But he told neither his father nor his mother what he had done. [7]Then he went down and talked with the woman, and he liked her.

[8]Some time later, when he went back to marry her, he turned aside to look at the lion's carcass. In it was a swarm of bees and some honey, [9]which he scooped out with his hands and ate as he went along. When he rejoined his parents, he gave them some, and they too ate it. But he did not tell them that he had taken the honey from the lion's carcass.

[10]Now his father went down to see the woman. And Samson made a feast there, as was customary for bridegrooms. [11]When he appeared, he was given thirty companions.

[12]"Let me tell you a riddle," Samson said to them. "If you can give me the answer within the seven days of the feast, I will give you thirty linen garments and thirty sets of clothes. [13]If you can't tell me the answer, you must give me thirty linen garments and thirty sets of clothes."

"Tell us your riddle," they said. "Let's hear it."

[14]He replied,

> "Out of the eater, something to eat;
> out of the strong, something sweet."

For three days they could not give the answer.

[15]On the fourth[a] day, they said to Samson's wife, "Coax your husband into explaining the riddle for us, or we will burn you and your father's household to death. Did you invite us here to rob us?"

[16]Then Samson's wife threw herself on him, sobbing, "You hate me! You don't really love me. You've given my people a riddle, but you haven't told me the answer."

"I haven't even explained it to my father or mother," he replied, "so why should I explain it to you?" [17]She cried the whole seven days of the feast. So on the seventh day he finally told her, because she continued to press him. She in turn explained the riddle to her people.

[18]Before sunset on the seventh day the men of the town said to him,

> "What is sweeter than honey?
> What is stronger than a lion?"

Samson said to them,

> "If you had not plowed with my heifer,
> you would not have solved my riddle."

[19]Then the Spirit of the LORD came upon him in power. He went down to Ashkelon, struck down thirty of their men, stripped them of their belongings and gave their clothes to those who had explained the riddle. Burning with anger, he went up to his father's house. [20]And Samson's wife was given to the friend who had attended him at his wedding.

SAMSON'S VENGEANCE ON THE PHILISTINES

15 Later on, at the time of wheat harvest, Samson took a young goat and went to visit his wife. He said, "I'm going to my wife's room." But her father would not let him go in.

[2]"I was so sure you thoroughly hated her," he said, "that I gave her to your friend. Isn't her younger sister more attractive? Take her instead."

[3]Samson said to them, "This time I have a right to get even with the Philistines; I will really harm

---

[a] 15 Some Septuagint manuscripts and Syriac; Hebrew *seventh*

battlelines

» I'll Show You (Violence)

Q: So that's your plan?
A: What other choice do I have? You heard what he said about me in front of the whole class.

Q: So you're going over to Clint's house to do what?
A: I'm sure I'll think of something.

Q: Just tell me this: What are you hoping to prove?
A: That I'm not going to take abuse from him.

Q: He's a lot bigger than you. What if he decks you?
A: Then at least I'll go down swinging.

Q: I can't blame you for being angry. I'd be upset too. But how is going down to his level gonna fix anything?
A: Do you have a better suggestion?

Q: Yeah. Forget about payback. Think about it. If you cuss him out or take a swing at him or go after him with a three iron, what happens? You make people think you're just as big a jerk as he is.
A: Yeah, but nobody else thinks he's a jerk. Everybody laughs at him.

Q: I think you're wrong. I'll bet deep down a lot of people think he's a jerk. But even if everybody in the whole school thinks he's the coolest guy in the world, that doesn't make it true. God says that Clint's actions are wrong. Period.
A: Yeah, but—

Q: But nothing. What Clint did was wrong. And one day he'll have to explain that to God. All you have to ask yourself right now is, "Am I going to do wrong too?" If you choose that path, you're no better than he is.
A: But—

Q: Don't go there, Jared. Do the right thing. Just ignore Clint. Or, if you really want to be radical, forgive him.
A: I don't know, man.

» Waiting It Out

Jared's friend is right. Revenge (or payback) never really satisfies, and it sure doesn't honor God. And even staying mad is foolish. While you're sitting around obsessing over the behavior of some jerk in your life (and feeling miserable), chances are the jerk is out having a great time! You're not hurting anyone but yourself. A wise person once said, "I will never allow another person to ruin my life by causing me to hate him."

Everyone feels like getting even when they're wronged. It's a natural reaction. However, Christians are called to give a *supernatural* response. God understands when you get hurt. He knows how you feel, so he's given you an example to follow. Instead of fighting back, forgive. Instead of cursing, bless. Instead of repaying evil with evil, repay it with good. That's what Jesus did when his enemies assaulted him physically, verbally and emotionally (see 1 Peter 2:19–23). What's more, he will give you the grace to do the same (see Romans 12:14–21).

Go to www.RevolutionBible.com for more.

them." ⁴So he went out and caught three hundred foxes and tied them tail to tail in pairs. He then fastened a torch to every pair of tails, ⁵lit the torches and let the foxes loose in the standing grain of the Philistines. He burned up the shocks and standing grain, together with the vineyards and olive groves.

⁶When the Philistines asked, "Who did this?" they were told, "Samson, the Timnite's son-in-law, because his wife was given to his friend."

So the Philistines went up and burned her and her father to death. ⁷Samson said to them, "Since you've acted like this, I won't stop until I get my revenge on you." ⁸He attacked them viciously and slaughtered many of them. Then he went down and stayed in a cave in the rock of Etam.

⁹The Philistines went up and camped in Judah, spreading out near Lehi. ¹⁰The men of Judah asked, "Why have you come to fight us?"

NOW OR NEVER

JDG 15:6–11

When someone does something to tick you off, pray about it—immediately. Don't give petty thoughts of revenge a chance to start taking over your brain. Ask God to take care of the situation in his own way, and then let him deal with it.

"We have come to take Samson prisoner," they answered, "to do to him as he did to us."

¹¹Then three thousand men from Judah went down to the cave in the rock of Etam and said to Samson, "Don't you realize that the Philistines are rulers over us? What have you done to us?"

He answered, "I merely did to them what they did to me."

¹²They said to him, "We've come to tie you up and hand you over to the Philistines."

Samson said, "Swear to me that you won't kill me yourselves."

¹³"Agreed," they answered. "We will only tie you up and hand you over to them. We will not kill you." So they bound him with two new ropes and led him up from the rock. ¹⁴As he approached Lehi, the Philistines came toward him shouting. The Spirit of the Lord came upon him in power. The ropes on his arms became like charred flax, and the bindings dropped from his hands. ¹⁵Finding a fresh jawbone of a donkey, he grabbed it and struck down a thousand men.

¹⁶Then Samson said,

"With a donkey's jawbone
 I have made donkeys of them.ᵃ
With a donkey's jawbone
 I have killed a thousand men."

¹⁷When he finished speaking, he threw away the jawbone; and the place was called Ramath Lehi.ᵇ

¹⁸Because he was very thirsty, he cried out to the Lord, "You have given your servant this great victory. Must I now die of thirst and fall into the hands of the uncircumcised?" ¹⁹Then God opened up the hollow place in Lehi, and water came out of it. When Samson drank, his strength returned and he revived. So the spring was called En Hakkore,ᶜ and it is still there in Lehi.

²⁰Samson ledᵈ Israel for twenty years in the days of the Philistines.

SAMSON AND DELILAH

16 One day Samson went to Gaza, where he saw a prostitute. He went in to spend the night with her. ²The people of Gaza were told, "Samson is here!" So they surrounded the place and lay in wait for him all night at the city gate. They made no move during the night, saying, "At dawn we'll kill him."

³But Samson lay there only until the middle of the night. Then he got up and took hold of the doors of the city gate, together with the two posts, and tore them loose, bar and all. He lifted them to his shoulders and carried them to the top of the hill that faces Hebron.

⁴Some time later, he fell in love with a woman in the Valley of Sorek whose name was Delilah. ⁵The rulers of the Philistines went to her and said, "See if you can lure him into showing you the secret of

---

ᵃ *16 Or made a heap or two;* the Hebrew for *donkey* sounds like the Hebrew for *heap.*   ᵇ *17 Ramath Lehi means jawbone hill.*
ᶜ *19 En Hakkore means caller's spring.*   ᵈ *20 Traditionally judged*

his great strength and how we can overpower him so we may tie him up and subdue him. Each one of us will give you eleven hundred shekels[a] of silver."

NOW OR NEVER
JDG 16:16–17

When you get close to your temptation breaking point, don't just stand there. Call for help—first to God and then to your Christian friends and family. Be honest about how you're being tempted, and ask for help in taking the necessary steps to avoid the tempting circumstances.

[6]So Delilah said to Samson, "Tell me the secret of your great strength and how you can be tied up and subdued."

[7]Samson answered her, "If anyone ties me with seven fresh thongs[b] that have not been dried, I'll become as weak as any other man."

[8]Then the rulers of the Philistines brought her seven fresh thongs that had not been dried, and she tied him with them. [9]With men hidden in the room, she called to him, "Samson, the Philistines are upon you!" But he snapped the thongs as easily as a piece of string snaps when it comes close to a flame. So the secret of his strength was not discovered.

[10]Then Delilah said to Samson, "You have made a fool of me; you lied to me. Come now, tell me how you can be tied."

[11]He said, "If anyone ties me securely with new ropes that have never been used, I'll become as weak as any other man."

[12]So Delilah took new ropes and tied him with them. Then, with men hidden in the room, she called to him, "Samson, the Philistines are upon you!" But he snapped the ropes off his arms as if they were threads.

[13]Delilah then said to Samson, "Until now, you have been making a fool of me and lying to me. Tell me how you can be tied."

He replied, "If you weave the seven braids of my head into the fabric ⌐on the loom⌐ and tighten it with the pin, I'll become as weak as any other man." So while he was sleeping, Delilah took the seven braids of his head, wove them into the fabric [14]and[c] tightened it with the pin.

Again she called to him, "Samson, the Philistines are upon you!" He awoke from his sleep and pulled up the pin and the loom, with the fabric.

[15]Then she said to him, "How can you say, 'I love you,' when you won't confide in me? This is the third time you have made a fool of me and haven't told me the secret of your great strength." [16]With such nagging she prodded him day after day until he was tired to death.

[17]So he told her everything. "No razor has ever been used on my head," he said, "because I have been a Nazirite set apart to God since birth. If my head were shaved, my strength would leave me, and I would become as weak as any other man."

[18]When Delilah saw that he had told her everything, she sent word to the rulers of the Philistines, "Come back once more; he has told me everything." So the rulers of the Philistines returned with the silver in their hands. [19]Having put him to sleep on her lap, she called a man to shave off the seven braids of his hair, and so began to subdue him.[d] And his strength left him.

[20]Then she called, "Samson, the Philistines are upon you!"

Dealing With Lust

Because Samson couldn't control his lust, he risked his life to sleep with a prostitute . . . hooked up with a woman who wanted him dead . . . walked into several traps laid by his enemies . . . revealed his most precious secret . . . lost his incredible strength . . . had his eyes gouged out . . . and ended up dying with the people he hated most. The funny thing is, though, most guys can identify with Samson. We know too well how lust can mess up our thinking until we're willing to sacrifice anything for some temporary gratification—if we fall prey to it. With God's help, though, we can win the battle against lust—and end up stronger than Samson.

---

[a] 5 That is, about 28 pounds (about 13 kilograms)   [b] 7 Or *bowstrings*; also in verses 8 and 9 Hebrew "⌐I can, if you weave the seven braids of my head into the fabric ⌐on the loom⌐." "⌐So she   [c] 13,14 Some Septuagint manuscripts; manuscripts *and he began to weaken*   [d] 19 Hebrew; some Septuagint

He awoke from his sleep and thought, "I'll go out as before and shake myself free." But he did not know that the Lord had left him.

²¹Then the Philistines seized him, gouged out his eyes and took him down to Gaza. Binding him with bronze shackles, they set him to grinding in the prison. ²²But the hair on his head began to grow again after it had been shaved.

THE DEATH OF SAMSON

²³Now the rulers of the Philistines assembled to offer a great sacrifice to Dagon their god and to celebrate, saying, "Our god has delivered Samson, our enemy, into our hands."

²⁴When the people saw him, they praised their god, saying,

> "Our god has delivered our enemy
>   into our hands,
>   the one who laid waste our land
>   and multiplied our slain."

²⁵While they were in high spirits, they shouted, "Bring out Samson to entertain us." So they called Samson out of the prison, and he performed for them.

When they stood him among the pillars, ²⁶Samson said to the servant who held his hand, "Put me where I can feel the pillars that support the temple, so that I may lean against them." ²⁷Now the temple was crowded with men and women; all the rulers of the Philistines were there, and on the roof were about three thousand men and women watching Samson perform. ²⁸Then Samson prayed to the Lord, "O Sovereign Lord, remember me. O God, please strengthen me just once more, and let me with one blow get revenge on the Philistines for my two eyes." ²⁹Then Samson reached toward the two central pillars on which the temple stood. Bracing himself against them, his right hand on the one and his left hand on the other, ³⁰Samson said, "Let me die with the Philistines!" Then he pushed with all his might, and down came the temple on the rulers and all the people in it. Thus he killed many more when he died than while he lived.

³¹Then his brothers and his father's whole family went down to get him. They brought him back and buried him between Zorah and Eshtaol in the tomb of Manoah his father. He had led[a] Israel twenty years.

MICAH'S IDOLS

17 Now a man named Micah from the hill country of Ephraim ²said to his mother, "The eleven hundred shekels[b] of silver that were taken from you and about which I heard you utter a curse—I have that silver with me; I took it."

Then his mother said, "The Lord bless you, my son!"

³When he returned the eleven hundred shekels of silver to his mother, she said, "I solemnly consecrate my silver to the Lord for my son to make a carved image and a cast idol. I will give it back to you."

⁴So he returned the silver to his mother, and she took two hundred shekels[c] of silver and gave them to a silversmith, who made them into the image and the idol. And they were put in Micah's house.

⁵Now this man Micah had a shrine, and he made an ephod and some idols and installed one of his sons as his priest. ⁶In those days Israel had no king; everyone did as he saw fit.

⁷A young Levite from Bethlehem in Judah, who had been living within the clan of Judah, ⁸left that town in search of some other place to stay. On his way[d] he came to Micah's house in the hill country of Ephraim.

⁹Micah asked him, "Where are you from?"

"I'm a Levite from Bethlehem in Judah," he said, "and I'm looking for a place to stay."

¹⁰Then Micah said to him, "Live with me and be my father and priest, and I'll give you ten shekels[e] of silver a year, your clothes and your food." ¹¹So the Levite agreed to live with him, and the young man was to him like one of his sons. ¹²Then Micah installed the Levite, and the young man became his priest and lived in his house. ¹³And Micah said, "Now I know that the Lord will be good to me, since this Levite has become my priest."

18

In those days Israel had no king.

And in those days the tribe of the Danites was seeking a place of their own where they might settle, because they had not yet come into an inheritance among the tribes of Israel. 2So the Danites sent five warriors from Zorah and Eshtaol to spy out the land and explore it. These men represented all their clans. They told them, "Go, explore the land."

The men entered the hill country of Ephraim and came to the house of Micah, where they spent the night. 3When they were near Micah's house, they recognized the voice of the young Levite; so they turned in there and asked him, "Who brought you here? What are you doing in this place? Why are you here?"

4He told them what Micah had done for him, and said, "He has hired me and I am his priest."

5Then they said to him, "Please inquire of God to learn whether our journey will be successful."

6The priest answered them, "Go in peace. Your journey has the LORD's approval."

7So the five men left and came to Laish, where they saw that the people were living in safety, like the Sidonians, unsuspecting and secure. And since their land lacked nothing, they were prosperous.ᵃ Also, they lived a long way from the Sidonians and had no relationship with anyone else.ᵇ

8When they returned to Zorah and Eshtaol, their brothers asked them, "How did you find things?"

9They answered, "Come on, let's attack them! We have seen that the land is very good. Aren't you going to do something? Don't hesitate to go there and take it over. 10When you get there, you will find an unsuspecting people and a spacious land that God has put into your hands, a land that lacks nothing whatever."

11Then six hundred men from the clan of the Danites, armed for battle, set out from Zorah and Eshtaol. 12On their way they set up camp near Kiriath Jearim in Judah. This is why the place west of Kiriath Jearim is called Mahaneh Danᶜ to this day. 13From there they went on to the hill country of Ephraim and came to Micah's house.

14Then the five men who had spied out the land of Laish said to their brothers, "Do you know that one of these houses has an ephod, other household gods, a carved image and a cast idol? Now you know what to do." 15So they turned in there and went to the house of the young Levite at Micah's place and greeted him. 16The six hundred Danites, armed for battle, stood at the entrance to the gate. 17The five men who had spied out the land went inside and took the carved image, the ephod, the other household gods and the cast idol while the priest and the six hundred armed men stood at the entrance to the gate.

18When these men went into Micah's house and took the carved image, the ephod, the other household gods and the cast idol, the priest said to them, "What are you doing?"

19They answered him, "Be quiet! Don't say a word. Come with us, and be our father and priest. Isn't it better that you serve a tribe and clan in Israel as priest rather than just one man's household?" 20Then the priest was glad. He took the ephod, the other household gods and the carved image and went along with the people. 21Putting their little children, their livestock and their possessions in front of them, they turned away and left.

22When they had gone some distance from Micah's house, the men who lived near Micah were called together and overtook the Danites. 23As they shouted after them, the Danites turned and said to Micah, "What's the matter with you that you called out your men to fight?"

24He replied, "You took the gods I made, and my priest, and went away. What else do I have? How can you ask, 'What's the matter with you?' "

25The Danites answered, "Don't argue with us, or some hot-tempered men will attack you, and you and your family will lose your lives." 26So the Danites went their way, and Micah, seeing that they were too strong for him, turned around and went back home.

NOW OR NEVER
JDG 18:24

It doesn't matter how strong your belief is, if you put your faith in an empty god, you're going to regret it sooner or later.

ᵃ 7 The meaning of the Hebrew for this clause is uncertain. ᵇ 7 Hebrew; some Septuagint manuscripts with the Arameans ᶜ 12 Mahaneh Dan means Dan's camp.

27Then they took what Micah had made, and his priest, and went on to Laish, against a peaceful and unsuspecting people. They attacked them with the sword and burned down their city. 28There was no one to rescue them because they lived a long way from Sidon and had no relationship with anyone else. The city was in a valley near Beth Rehob.

The Danites rebuilt the city and settled there. 29They named it Dan after their forefather Dan, who was born to Israel—though the city used to be called Laish. 30There the Danites set up for themselves the idols, and Jonathan son of Gershom, the son of Moses,ᵃ and his sons were priests for the tribe of Dan until the time of the captivity of the land. 31They continued to use the idols Micah had made, all the time the house of God was in Shiloh.

A LEVITE AND HIS CONCUBINE

19

In those days Israel had no king.

Now a Levite who lived in a remote area in the hill country of Ephraim took a concubine from Bethlehem in Judah. 2But she was unfaithful to him. She left him and went back to her father's house in Bethlehem, Judah. After she had been there four months, 3her husband went to her to persuade her to return. He had with him his servant and two donkeys. She took him into her father's house, and when her father saw him, he gladly welcomed him. 4His father-in-law, the girl's father, prevailed upon him to stay; so he remained with him three days, eating and drinking, and sleeping there.

5On the fourth day they got up early and he prepared to leave, but the girl's father said to his son-in-law, "Refresh yourself with something to eat; then you can go." 6So the two of them sat down to eat and drink together. Afterward the girl's father said, "Please stay tonight and enjoy yourself." 7And when the man got up to go, his father-in-law persuaded him, so he stayed there that night. 8On the morning of the fifth day, when he rose to go, the girl's father said, "Refresh yourself. Wait till afternoon!" So the two of them ate together.

9Then when the man, with his concubine and his servant, got up to leave, his father-in-law, the girl's father, said, "Now look, it's almost evening. Spend the night here; the day is nearly over. Stay and enjoy yourself. Early tomorrow morning you can get up and be on your way home." 10But, unwilling to stay another night, the man left and went toward Jebus (that is, Jerusalem), with his two saddled donkeys and his concubine.

11When they were near Jebus and the day was almost gone, the servant said to his master, "Come, let's stop at this city of the Jebusites and spend the night."

12His master replied, "No. We won't go into an alien city, whose people are not Israelites. We will go on to Gibeah." 13He added, "Come, let's try to reach Gibeah or Ramah and spend the night in one of those places." 14So they went on, and the sun set as they neared Gibeah in Benjamin. 15There they stopped to spend the night. They went and sat in the city square, but no one took them into his home for the night.

16That evening an old man from the hill country of Ephraim, who was living in Gibeah (the men of the place were Benjamites), came in from his work in the fields. 17When he looked and saw the traveler in the city square, the old man asked, "Where are you going? Where did you come from?"

18He answered, "We are on our way from Bethlehem in Judah to a remote area in the hill country of Ephraim where I live. I have been to Bethlehem in Judah and now I am going to the house of the LORD. No one has taken me into his house. 19We have both straw and fodder for our donkeys and bread and wine for ourselves your servants—me, your maidservant, and the young man with us. We don't need anything."

20"You are welcome at my house," the old man said. "Let me supply whatever you need. Only don't spend the night in the square." 21So he took him into his house and fed his donkeys. After they had washed their feet, they had something to eat and drink.

22While they were enjoying themselves, some of the wicked men of the city surrounded the house. Pounding on the door, they shouted to the old man who owned the house, "Bring out the man who came to your house so we can have sex with him."

23The owner of the house went outside and said to them, "No, my friends, don't be so vile. Since this man is my guest, don't do this disgraceful thing. 24Look, here is my virgin daughter, and his concubine. I will bring them out to you now, and you can use them and do to them whatever you wish. But to this man, don't do such a disgraceful thing."

ᵃ 30 An ancient Hebrew scribal tradition, some Septuagint manuscripts and Vulgate; Masoretic Text *Manasseh*

battlelines

» Out of the Closet (Homosexuality)

Q: What are you going to do?
A: I don't know. I can't get my brain to accept it. I mean, I've hung out with the guy forever. Oh, man . . . we even took showers in the same locker room after track practice! And now I find out that all this time, he's been a—

Q: A what?
A: He's a homosexual. I can't believe it! It gives me the creeps just thinking about it. I don't know what to do. The guy's always been a good friend. And he's never made a move on me or anything. Part of me wants to downplay the whole thing. But another part of me wants to throw up just thinking about it.

Q: What about your other friends?
A: What about them? They're all normal guys . . . at least, I think they are. I have no problem with them.

Q: Are they perfect?
A: Perfect? No. But they're not . . . well, you know—

Q: Gay?
A: Yeah.

Q: So why's homosexuality worse than anything your other friends do wrong?
A: I don't know. It's just twisted.

Q: Yeah, well, so is hate.
A: Hey, I never said I *hated* the guy. I just don't know if we can be close friends anymore. It's different now. If I stay his friend, wouldn't that be like condoning his lifestyle?

Q: You also have to ask: Is it right for you to cut a friend loose? What ever happened to hating the sin, but loving the sinner?
A: Um . . . good point, I guess.

» Guilty by Association?

Homosexual behavior is wrong. No question. Despite some "creative" attempts by certain gay activists to reinterpret the Bible, arguing that it's neutral on the subject or even supportive of the gay lifestyle, Scripture is clear that the God-ordained norm for human sexuality is one man plus one woman for life (see Matthew 19:4–6). Period. No exceptions. Both Testaments declare homosexual behavior to be sinful (see Leviticus 18:22; 20:13; Romans 1:18–32; 1 Corinthians 6:9). But notice this about 1 Corinthians 6 in particular: The same passage that condemns homosexual behavior equally condemns theft, greed and trash talk! Most Christians don't seem to get as worked up over these behaviors. Why not?

Remember that the Bible is clear about God's response to those who are guilty of any sin. He loves them. He cares for them. He wants to change them, and he wants to be deeply involved in their lives. God never condones sin; he calls it what it is (see John 8:1–11). But he also offers every person—gay or straight—forgiveness and freedom from sin.

So before you walk away from a friend who's struggling with his sexuality, spend some time thinking about how Jesus dealt with sinners. If you need some help, try reading Matthew 9:9–13 and Luke 19:1–9.

Go to www.RevolutionBible.com for more.

²⁵But the men would not listen to him. So the man took his concubine and sent her outside to them, and they raped her and abused her throughout the night, and at dawn they let her go. ²⁶At daybreak the woman went back to the house where her master was staying, fell down at the door and lay there until daylight.

²⁷When her master got up in the morning and opened the door of the house and stepped out to continue on his way, there lay his concubine, fallen in the doorway of the house, with her hands on the threshold. ²⁸He said to her, "Get up; let's go." But there was no answer. Then the man put her on his donkey and set out for home.

²⁹When he reached home, he took a knife and cut up his concubine, limb by limb, into twelve parts and sent them into all the areas of Israel. ³⁰Everyone who saw it said, "Such a thing has never been seen or done, not since the day the Israelites came up out of Egypt. Think about it! Consider it! Tell us what to do!"

ISRAELITES FIGHT THE BENJAMITES

20 Then all the Israelites from Dan to Beersheba and from the land of Gilead came out as one man and assembled before the Lord in Mizpah. ²The leaders of all the people of the tribes of Israel took their places in the assembly of the people of God, four hundred thousand soldiers armed with swords. ³(The Benjamites heard that the Israelites had gone up to Mizpah.) Then the Israelites said, "Tell us how this awful thing happened."

⁴So the Levite, the husband of the murdered woman, said, "I and my concubine came to Gibeah in Benjamin to spend the night. ⁵During the night the men of Gibeah came after me and surrounded the house, intending to kill me. They raped my concubine, and she died. ⁶I took my concubine, cut her into pieces and sent one piece to each region of Israel's inheritance, because they committed this lewd and disgraceful act in Israel. ⁷Now, all you Israelites, speak up and give your verdict."

⁸All the people rose as one man, saying, "None of us will go home. No, not one of us will return to his house. ⁹But now this is what we'll do to Gibeah: We'll go up against it as the lot directs. ¹⁰We'll take ten men out of every hundred from all the tribes of Israel, and a hundred from a thousand, and a thousand from ten thousand, to get provisions for the army. Then, when the army arrives at Gibeah[a] in Benjamin, it can give them what they deserve for all this vileness done in Israel." ¹¹So all the men of Israel got together and united as one man against the city.

¹²The tribes of Israel sent men throughout the tribe of Benjamin, saying, "What about this awful crime that was committed among you? ¹³Now surrender those wicked men of Gibeah so that we may put them to death and purge the evil from Israel."

But the Benjamites would not listen to their fellow Israelites. ¹⁴From their towns they came together at Gibeah to fight against the Israelites. ¹⁵At once the Benjamites mobilized twenty-six thousand swordsmen from their towns, in addition to seven hundred chosen men from those living in Gibeah. ¹⁶Among all these soldiers there were seven hundred chosen men who were left-handed, each of whom could sling a stone at a hair and not miss.

¹⁷Israel, apart from Benjamin, mustered four hundred thousand swordsmen, all of them fighting men.

¹⁸The Israelites went up to Bethel[b] and inquired of God. They said, "Who of us shall go first to fight against the Benjamites?"

The Lord replied, "Judah shall go first."

¹⁹The next morning the Israelites got up and pitched camp near Gibeah. ²⁰The men of Israel went out to fight the Benjamites and took up battle positions against them at Gibeah. ²¹The Benjamites came out of Gibeah and cut down twenty-two thousand Israelites on the battlefield that day. ²²But the men of Israel encouraged one another and again took up their positions where they had stationed themselves the first day. ²³The Israelites went up and wept before the Lord until evening, and they inquired of the Lord. They said, "Shall we go up again to battle against the Benjamites, our brothers?"

The Lord answered, "Go up against them."

²⁴Then the Israelites drew near to Benjamin the second day. ²⁵This time, when the Benjamites came out from Gibeah to oppose them, they cut down another eighteen thousand Israelites, all of them armed with swords.

²⁶Then the Israelites, all the people, went up to Bethel, and there they sat weeping before the Lord.

ᵃ *10* One Hebrew manuscript; most Hebrew manuscripts *Geba,* a variant of *Gibeah*   ᵇ *18* Or *to the house of God*; also in verse 26

They fasted that day until evening and presented burnt offerings and fellowship offerings[a] to the LORD. [27]And the Israelites inquired of the LORD. (In those days the ark of the covenant of God was there, [28]with Phinehas son of Eleazar, the son of Aaron, ministering before it.) They asked, "Shall we go up again to battle with Benjamin our brother, or not?"

The LORD responded, "Go, for tomorrow I will give them into your hands."

[29]Then Israel set an ambush around Gibeah. [30]They went up against the Benjamites on the third day and took up positions against Gibeah as they had done before. [31]The Benjamites came out to meet them and were drawn away from the city. They began to inflict casualties on the Israelites as before, so that about thirty men fell in the open field and on the roads—the one leading to Bethel and the other to Gibeah.

[32]While the Benjamites were saying, "We are defeating them as before," the Israelites were saying, "Let's retreat and draw them away from the city to the roads."

[33]All the men of Israel moved from their places and took up positions at Baal Tamar, and the Israelite ambush charged out of its place on the west[b] of Gibeah.[c] [34]Then ten thousand of Israel's finest men made a frontal attack on Gibeah. The fighting was so heavy that the Benjamites did not realize how near disaster was. [35]The LORD defeated Benjamin before Israel, and on that day the Israelites struck down 25,100 Benjamites, all armed with swords. [36]Then the Benjamites saw that they were beaten.

Now the men of Israel had given way before Benjamin, because they relied on the ambush they had set near Gibeah. [37]The men who had been in ambush made a sudden dash into Gibeah, spread out and put the whole city to the sword. [38]The men of Israel had arranged with the ambush that they should send up a great cloud of smoke from the city, [39]and then the men of Israel would turn in the battle.

The Benjamites had begun to inflict casualties on the men of Israel (about thirty), and they said, "We are defeating them as in the first battle." [40]But when the column of smoke began to rise from the city, the Benjamites turned and saw the smoke of the whole city going up into the sky. [41]Then the men of Israel turned on them, and the men of Benjamin were terrified, because they realized that disaster had come upon them. [42]So they fled before the Israelites in the direction of the desert, but they could not escape the battle. And the men of Israel who came out of the towns cut them down there. [43]They surrounded the Benjamites, chased them and easily[d] overran them in the vicinity of Gibeah on the east. [44]Eighteen thousand Benjamites fell, all of them valiant fighters. [45]As they turned and fled toward the desert to the rock of Rimmon, the Israelites cut down five thousand men along the roads. They kept pressing after the Benjamites as far as Gidom and struck down two thousand more.

[46]On that day twenty-five thousand Benjamite swordsmen fell, all of them valiant fighters. [47]But six hundred men turned and fled into the desert to the rock of Rimmon, where they stayed four months. [48]The men of Israel went back to Benjamin and put all the towns to the sword, including the animals and everything else they found. All the towns they came across they set on fire.

WIVES FOR THE BENJAMITES

21

The men of Israel had taken an oath at Mizpah: "Not one of us will give his daughter in marriage to a Benjamite."

[2]The people went to Bethel,[e] where they sat before God until evening, raising their voices and weeping bitterly. [3]"O LORD, the God of Israel," they cried, "why has this happened to Israel? Why should one tribe be missing from Israel today?"

[4]Early the next day the people built an altar and presented burnt offerings and fellowship offerings.[a]

[5]Then the Israelites asked, "Who from all the tribes of Israel has failed to assemble before the LORD?" For they had taken a solemn oath that anyone who failed to assemble before the LORD at Mizpah should certainly be put to death.

[6]Now the Israelites grieved for their brothers, the Benjamites. "Today one tribe is cut off from Israel," they said. [7]"How can we provide wives for those who are left, since we have taken an oath by the LORD not to give them any of our daughters in marriage?" [8]Then they asked, "Which one of the tribes of Israel failed to assemble before the LORD at Mizpah?" They discovered that no one from Jabesh Gilead had come to the camp for the assembly. [9]For when they counted the people, they found that none of the people of Jabesh Gilead were there.

---

[a] 26,4 Traditionally *peace offerings*   [b] 33 Some Septuagint manuscripts and Vulgate; the meaning of the Hebrew for this word is uncertain.   [c] 33 Hebrew *Geba*, a variant of *Gibeah*   [d] 43 The meaning of the Hebrew for this word is uncertain.   [e] 2 Or *to the house of God*

¹⁰So the assembly sent twelve thousand fighting men with instructions to go to Jabesh Gilead and put to the sword those living there, including the women and children. ¹¹"This is what you are to do," they said. "Kill every male and every woman who is not a virgin." ¹²They found among the people living in Jabesh Gilead four hundred young women who had never slept with a man, and they took them to the camp at Shiloh in Canaan.

¹³Then the whole assembly sent an offer of peace to the Benjamites at the rock of Rimmon. ¹⁴So the Benjamites returned at that time and were given the women of Jabesh Gilead who had been spared. But there were not enough for all of them.

¹⁵The people grieved for Benjamin, because the LORD had made a gap in the tribes of Israel. ¹⁶And the elders of the assembly said, "With the women of Benjamin destroyed, how shall we provide wives for the men who are left? ¹⁷The Benjamite survivors must have heirs," they said, "so that a tribe of Israel will not be wiped out. ¹⁸We can't give them our daughters as wives, since we Israelites have taken this oath: 'Cursed be anyone who gives a wife to a Benjamite.' ¹⁹But look, there is the annual festival of the LORD in Shiloh, to the north of Bethel, and east of the road that goes from Bethel to Shechem, and to the south of Lebonah."

²⁰So they instructed the Benjamites, saying, "Go and hide in the vineyards ²¹and watch. When the girls of Shiloh come out to join in the dancing, then rush from the vineyards and each of you seize a wife from the girls of Shiloh and go to the land of Benjamin. ²²When their fathers or brothers complain to us, we will say to them, 'Do us a kindness by helping them, because we did not get wives for them during the war, and you are innocent, since you did not give your daughters to them.' "

²³So that is what the Benjamites did. While the girls were dancing, each man caught one and carried her off to be his wife. Then they returned to their inheritance and rebuilt the towns and settled in them.

²⁴At that time the Israelites left that place and went home to their tribes and clans, each to his own inheritance.

²⁵In those days Israel had no king; everyone did as he saw fit.

Looking Out for Others

Have you ever seen someone fall spiritually? It's not an easy thing to watch, especially if you can remember when that person had a growing relationship with the Lord. The thing you need to keep in mind is that spiritual falls can be prevented—and you can help prevent them. If you know people who are struggling with doubt or going through tough times, talk to them about it. Help them search for and find the answers to their questions. Lend them a listening ear. Pray with them. Instead of leaving them to do as they see fit, let them know that there's someone else in this world who wants to see them stay tight with the Lord.

RUTH

RUTH RUTH

« AT A GLANCE

Author
Unknown

Audience
People of Israel

Date
Sometime around the period of the judges
(1375–1050 B.C.)

Setting
The story is set during the time of the judges, during a temporary period of peace between the nations of Moab and Israel.

Verse to Remember
But Ruth replied, "Don't urge me to leave you or to turn back from you. Where you go I will go, and where you stay I will stay. Your people will be my people and your God my God" (1:16).

Theme to Consider
Ruth and Naomi are wonderful role models of friendship, loyalty and commitment—to God and to each other.

UNCHANGING TRUTH » What makes someone a good friend? A sense of humor? A fun attitude? How about a generous spirit (especially when you're short on cash)?

What about loyalty—knowing that no matter how badly you screw up or how many arguments you start or how many stupid things you say, your friends will never bail on you? How important is that?

Obviously, loyalty is a two-way street. You can't expect it from others without being willing to give it yourself. And that's not an easy thing for most of us to do. Genuine friendships, the kind that last a lifetime, require a lot of hard work. It's easy to give up on someone who ticks us off or does something we disagree with. Often loyalty—the determination to stick with someone *no matter what*—is the only thing that keeps two friends together during the inevitable rough patches and conflicts in the friendship.

If you want to see authentic friendship in action, check out the story of Ruth and her mother-in-law, Naomi; also take note of the kindness and goodness shown by the main man in this story. This is the kind of loyalty God expects from his people—and the kind of loyalty he loves to reward.

LIFE LESSONS »

I God is not bothered and does not get angry when we express our hurt and disappointment to him (1:20–21).

2 Always look for God's fingerprints on the good things that happen to you (2:20).

3 People who are older and wiser than you are can be great sources of advice when you're not sure what to do (3:1–4).

4 A happy ending is possible for anyone's life, no matter how much the person has struggled and suffered in the past (4:13).

NAOMI AND RUTH

1 In the days when the judges ruled,[a] there was a famine in the land, and a man from Bethlehem in Judah, together with his wife and two sons, went to live for a while in the country of Moab. [2]The man's name was Elimelech, his wife's name Naomi, and the names of his two sons were Mahlon and Kilion. They were Ephrathites from Bethlehem, Judah. And they went to Moab and lived there.

[3]Now Elimelech, Naomi's husband, died, and she was left with her two sons. [4]They married Moabite women, one named Orpah and the other Ruth. After they had lived there about ten years, [5]both Mahlon and Kilion also died, and Naomi was left without her two sons and her husband.

[6]When she heard in Moab that the LORD had come to the aid of his people by providing food for them, Naomi and her daughters-in-law prepared to return home from there. [7]With her two daughters-in-law she left the place where she had been living and set out on the road that would take them back to the land of Judah.

[8]Then Naomi said to her two daughters-in-law, "Go back, each of you, to your mother's home. May the LORD show kindness to you, as you have shown to your dead and to me. [9]May the LORD grant that each of you will find rest in the home of another husband."

Then she kissed them and they wept aloud [10]and said to her, "We will go back with you to your people."

[11]But Naomi said, "Return home, my daughters. Why would you come with me? Am I going to have any more sons, who could become your husbands? [12]Return home, my daughters; I am too old to have another husband. Even if I thought there was still hope for me—even if I had a husband tonight and then gave birth to sons— [13]would you wait until they grew up? Would you remain unmarried for them? No, my daughters. It is more bitter for me than for you, because the LORD's hand has gone out against me!"

[14]At this they wept again. Then Orpah kissed her mother-in-law good-by, but Ruth clung to her.

[15]"Look," said Naomi, "your sister-in-law is going back to her people and her gods. Go back with her."

[16]But Ruth replied, "Don't urge me to leave you or to turn back from you. Where you go I will go, and where you stay I will stay. Your people will be my people and your God my God. [17]Where you die I will die, and there I will be buried. May the LORD deal with me, be it ever so severely, if anything but death separates you and me." [18]When Naomi realized that Ruth was determined to go with her, she stopped urging her.

[19]So the two women went on until they came to Bethlehem. When they arrived in Bethlehem, the whole town was stirred because of them, and the women exclaimed, "Can this be Naomi?"

[20]"Don't call me Naomi,[b]" she told them. "Call me Mara,[c] because the Almighty[d] has made my life very bitter. [21]I went away full, but the LORD has brought me back empty. Why call me Naomi? The LORD has afflicted[e] me; the Almighty has brought misfortune upon me."

[22]So Naomi returned from Moab accompanied by Ruth the Moabitess, her daughter-in-law, arriving in Bethlehem as the barley harvest was beginning.

NOW OR NEVER
RU 1:20–21

Have you ever felt abandoned by God? How did your feelings affect your relationship with him?

RUTH MEETS BOAZ

2 Now Naomi had a relative on her husband's side, from the clan of Elimelech, a man of standing, whose name was Boaz.

[2]And Ruth the Moabitess said to Naomi, "Let me go to the fields and pick up the leftover grain behind anyone in whose eyes I find favor."

Naomi said to her, "Go ahead, my daughter." [3]So she went out and began to glean in the fields behind the harvesters. As it turned out, she found herself working in a field belonging to Boaz, who was from the clan of Elimelech.

---

[a] 1 Traditionally judged   [b] 20 Naomi means pleasant; also in verse 21.   [c] 20 Mara means bitter.   [d] 20 Hebrew Shaddai; also in verse 21   [e] 21 Or has testified against

[4]Just then Boaz arrived from Bethlehem and greeted the harvesters, "The LORD be with you!" "The LORD bless you!" they called back.

[5]Boaz asked the foreman of his harvesters, "Whose young woman is that?"

[6]The foreman replied, "She is the Moabitess who came back from Moab with Naomi. [7]She said, 'Please let me glean and gather among the sheaves behind the harvesters.' She went into the field and has worked steadily from morning till now, except for a short rest in the shelter."

[8]So Boaz said to Ruth, "My daughter, listen to me. Don't go and glean in another field and don't go away from here. Stay here with my servant girls. [9]Watch the field where the men are harvesting, and follow along after the girls. I have told the men not to touch you. And whenever you are thirsty, go and get a drink from the water jars the men have filled."

[10]At this, she bowed down with her face to the ground. She exclaimed, "Why have I found such favor in your eyes that you notice me—a foreigner?"

[11]Boaz replied, "I've been told all about what you have done for your mother-in-law since the death of your husband—how you left your father and mother and your homeland and came to live with a people you did not know before. [12]May the LORD repay you for what you have done. May you be richly rewarded by the LORD, the God of Israel, under whose wings you have come to take refuge."

[13]"May I continue to find favor in your eyes, my lord," she said. "You have given me comfort and have spoken kindly to your servant—though I do not have the standing of one of your servant girls."

[14]At mealtime Boaz said to her, "Come over here. Have some bread and dip it in the wine vinegar."

When she sat down with the harvesters, he offered her some roasted grain. She ate all she wanted and had some left over. [15]As she got up to glean, Boaz gave orders to his men, "Even if she gathers among the sheaves, don't embarrass her. [16]Rather, pull out some stalks for her from the bundles and leave them for her to pick up, and don't rebuke her."

[17]So Ruth gleaned in the field until evening. Then she threshed the barley she had gathered, and it amounted to about an ephah.[a] [18]She carried it back to town, and her mother-in-law saw how much she had gathered. Ruth also brought out and gave her what she had left over after she had eaten enough.

[19]Her mother-in-law asked her, "Where did you glean today? Where did you work? Blessed be the man who took notice of you!"

Then Ruth told her mother-in-law about the one at whose place she had been working. "The name of the man I worked with today is Boaz," she said.

[20]"The LORD bless him!" Naomi said to her daughter-in-law. "He has not stopped showing his kindness to the living and the dead." She added, "That man is our close relative; he is one of our kinsman-redeemers."

Being Generous

live the adventure »» Ru 2:14-16

You know what made Boaz such a stand-up guy? He didn't assume somebody else would take care of it when he saw someone in trouble. Instead, he did what he could to help. In Ruth's case, it didn't cost him much up front, just some leftover grain from his field and a little water and bread. But that was enough to keep Ruth and her mother-in-law from going hungry. Not only did Boaz help Ruth, he showed class while doing it. Instead of embarrassing her, Boaz treated her with respect and dignity. Try following his example in the way you treat women.

now or never

RU 2:20-23

The fact that God is all-powerful, all-knowing and concerned with every detail of our lives pretty much rules out the possibility of coincidence or random chance as an explanation of why things happen the way they do.

MOM

---

[a] 17 That is, probably about 3/5 bushel (about 22 liters)

battlelines

» Big Brother Is Watching (Mentors)

Q: Hey, what was the big announcement at church yesterday?
A: Oh, it was no big deal. They're just starting some new "big brother" program.

Q: Big brother?
A: Yeah, where college guys agree to hang out with guys my age and . . . I don't know . . . help us in some way.

Q: Help you how?
A: I'm not exactly sure. It sounds like if I signed up, I'd meet once a week with a college "mentor" to talk about my "spiritual growth."

Q: Cool!
A: You think so? Sounds like meeting with a religious parole officer or something, so he can tell me what to do.

Q: You're missing the point. Mentoring isn't about telling you what to do.
A: Then what is it? Is he like a psychiatrist? Is he going to psychoanalyze me?

Q: No. Here's the deal. If you want to grow in your faith, it helps to have an older, wiser Christian around for support, counsel, encouragement—stuff like that. Look, let's say you set some spiritual goals for yourself. A mentor is a guy who can hold you accountable to those goals— you know, keep you on track.
A: Why can't my friends do that?

Q: They can. But because a mentor is older, he's got a little more life experience. He has a better sense of what works and what doesn't.
A: Well, that clears things up a little.

Q: So do you think you'd be interested in having a mentor?
A: Maybe. I'll have to think about it.

» Disciple Now

When Jesus walked the earth, he selected 12 guys to mentor—to disciple. He could have chosen a thousand people, but he had a better plan. What happened is that his original, small band of disciples went on to find and make other disciples (see Matthew 28:18–20). And then those disciples found others to disciple . . . and so on and so on. The New Testament tells us to follow the same pattern (see 2 Timothy 2:2).

Look around. Scan your life for some older, wiser Christian guys whom you respect. Ask God to provide a mentor, someone who can help you make progress in your Christian faith. Once you've hooked up with a mentor, humble yourself and learn from him. Then turn around and do the same thing for someone else. It may be hard to believe, but there are a lot of people in this world who know less about following God than you do. That means you can make a difference in someone else's spiritual life!

Jesus said to go and make disciples. That command is known as the Great Commission, not the Nice Suggestion.

Read more about the value of a mentor at www.RevolutionBible.com.

40 ADVENTURES YOU CAN LIVE

A lot of non-Christians think that the Christian life is boring. Even more disappointing is that for a lot of Christians, life is boring. Is that because Jesus called us to a life of drudgery or because God is uninteresting and has no sense of adventure? Hardly. This huge misconception is really part of a global deception—Satan's massive marketing campaign against a life of devotion to God. There's a life of adventure to be lived by each man, and you have to live your own. But in case you're feeling unmotivated right now, here are a few ideas to jumpstart your enthusiasm:

» 10 TO REMEMBER

» 01 Hang out with older people—grandparents or an elderly person from church—and ask them to tell you about their life. You'll find that they have a lot of interesting and wise things to say. » *Lev 19:32*

» 02 Fill a box with anything that is an idol in your life—pornography, raunchy movies, video games, ungodly music—and have a bonfire. Ask God to help you resist the temptation to fall victim to those idols again. » *Dt 7:5*

» 03 There are a bunch of Bible reading plans in the back of this Bible and at www.RevolutionBible.com. Find one and do it. » *Ezr 7:10*

» 04 Fast (go without food) for a day; spend the time you'd normally use to eat talking with God. You might be physically hungry, but spiritually you'll never feel more satisfied. » *Ezr 8:23*

» 05 Take a long camping or hiking trip during which you can spend some quiet time with nature and marvel at God's creation. Notice all the life he's created—the birds, the bugs, the trees. Everything you see is from his hands. » *Job 38–39*

» 06 Make a list of things—big and small—you're thankful for. Read the list back to God and remember that everything you have is from him. » *Ps 95:2*

» 07 Save up your money and plan to go on an overseas missions trip with your friends. There are people all over the world who haven't heard the Good News—yet. » *Mt 28:18–20*

» 08 Every person—including you—has his or her own unique gifts, which are of great importance to the church. Get involved with your congregation—play music in the worship band, run the sound board, start a small group, help with kids . . . » *Ro 12:4–8*

» 09 Follow Paul's urging and celebrate your freedom by serving someone who didn't ask for it. This could mean mowing a neighbor's grass or helping a classmate with his homework—find an opportunity and seize it. » *Gal 5:13*

» 10 Get on the Internet and find out what's going on in a country you don't know much about; pray about what you read and find ways that you can help. » *1Ti 2:1–6*

In case some of these aren't your style, or you simply need more to do, here are a few more suggestions:

» 11 Choose a place (either a physical place or a time in your schedule or both) where you can regularly give God your heart » *Ge 13:4*

» 12 Go watch a high school wrestling meet and think about Jacob wrestling with God. » *Ge 32:22–32*

» 13 Watch the movie *The Ten Commandments* and then memorize the actual Ten Commandments. » *Ex 20*

» 14 Start carrying your "spear"—your Bible—with you wherever you go. » *Ne 4:21–23*

» 15 Make a covenant with some close buddies to stay away from porn. » *Job 31:1*

» 16 Find someplace where you can be silent and alone; still your soul and listen for God. » *Ps 46:10*

» 17 The next time you're doing something repetitive (stacking firewood, mowing the lawn, working on your car) talk to God and worship him while you're doing it. » *Ps 71:8*

» 18 Volunteer to help teach the little kids at church. » *Ps 78:6*

» 19 If you haven't already done so, start researching which college you might want to go to » *Pr 1:5*

» 20 Make a list of your biggest goals for the next three years of your life. Pray about each one and ask God to show you his timing. » *Pr 13:12*

» 21 Take your parents out to dinner. » *Pr 17:6*

» 22 Get a bunch of buddies together, collect canned food and take it to a food bank. » *Pr 22:9*

» 23 Write a letter to the local newspaper editor and address a moral issue in your school or town. » *Mt 5:13*

» 24 Clean out your closet and start giving stuff away. » *Mk 10:21*

» 25 Instead of pranks, plan out "secret service"—silently helping people in need. » *Mk 10:45*

» 26 Tell your closest non-Christian friend how you met Christ and how he's changed your life. » *Ac 26*

» 27 Ask a couple of Christian friends what they think your spiritual gift is. » *Ro 12; 1Co 12; 1Pe 4:10*

» 28 Set a goal to run a marathon and start training. » *1Co 9:24–27*

» 29 Think about the glory of God the next time you're making a decision about what movie to see, video game to play or music to listen to. » *1Co 10:31*

» 30 Pray about giving a big chunk of your time or money to your church. » *2Co 9:6–8*

» 31 Choose a relationship in your life that's a struggle—a friend, an enemy, a teacher, family member—and ask God to do miracles through you! » *Eph 3:20*

» 32 Dedicate something to your parents—a sports season, a semester of school, a performance. » *Eph 6:2*

» 33 Make something with your own hands. » *Col 3:23*

» 34 Make it your goal to be an expert in something (sports, music, computers) and use that as a platform to be a witness. » *Col 4:5*

» 35 Keep a list of prayer requests in your pocket; pray throughout the day. » *1Th 5:17*

» 36 Pick a short Bible passage and make it your "training" verse for the next couple of years—memorize it and live by it. » *2Ti 3:16*

» 37 Buy a book about the life of a great missionary and read it. » *Heb 6:12*

» 38 Call your pastor and get a bunch of guys to go camping or paintballing. » *Heb 13:16–17*

» 39 Send a letter or an email of encouragement to a friend you haven't seen in a while. » *3 Jn*

» 40 Daydream about eternity in heaven and the adventures you'll have there. » *Rev 21–22*

[21] Then Ruth the Moabitess said, "He even said to me, 'Stay with my workers until they finish harvesting all my grain.'"

[22] Naomi said to Ruth her daughter-in-law, "It will be good for you, my daughter, to go with his girls, because in someone else's field you might be harmed."

[23] So Ruth stayed close to the servant girls of Boaz to glean until the barley and wheat harvests were finished. And she lived with her mother-in-law.

RUTH AND BOAZ AT THE THRESHING FLOOR

3 One day Naomi her mother-in-law said to her, "My daughter, should I not try to find a home[a] for you, where you will be well provided for? [2] Is not Boaz, with whose servant girls you have been, a kinsman of ours? Tonight he will be winnowing barley on the threshing floor. [3] Wash and perfume yourself, and put on your best clothes. Then go down to the threshing floor, but don't let him know you are there until he has finished eating and drinking. [4] When he lies down, note the place where he is lying. Then go and uncover his feet and lie down. He will tell you what to do."

[5] "I will do whatever you say," Ruth answered. [6] So she went down to the threshing floor and did everything her mother-in-law told her to do.

[7] When Boaz had finished eating and drinking and was in good spirits, he went over to lie down at the far end of the grain pile. Ruth approached quietly, uncovered his feet and lay down. [8] In the middle of the night something startled the man, and he turned and discovered a woman lying at his feet.

[9] "Who are you?" he asked.

"I am your servant Ruth," she said. "Spread the corner of your garment over me, since you are a kinsman-redeemer."

[10] "The LORD bless you, my daughter," he replied. "This kindness is greater than that which you showed earlier: You have not run after the younger men, whether rich or poor. [11] And now, my daughter, don't be afraid. I will do for you all you ask. All my fellow townsmen know that you are a woman of noble character. [12] Although it is true that I am near of kin, there is a kinsman-redeemer nearer than I. [13] Stay here for the night, and in the morning if he wants to redeem, good; let him redeem. But if he is not willing, as surely as the LORD lives I will do it. Lie here until morning."

[14] So she lay at his feet until morning, but got up before anyone could be recognized; and he said, "Don't let it be known that a woman came to the threshing floor."

[15] He also said, "Bring me the shawl you are wearing and hold it out." When she did so, he poured into it six measures of barley and put it on her. Then he[b] went back to town.

[16] When Ruth came to her mother-in-law, Naomi asked, "How did it go, my daughter?"

Then she told her everything Boaz had done for her [17] and added, "He gave me these six measures of barley, saying, 'Don't go back to your mother-in-law empty-handed.'"

[18] Then Naomi said, "Wait, my daughter, until you find out what happens. For the man will not rest until the matter is settled today."

BOAZ MARRIES RUTH

4 Meanwhile Boaz went up to the town gate and sat there. When the kinsman-redeemer he had mentioned came along, Boaz said, "Come over here, my friend, and sit down." So he went over and sat down.

[2] Boaz took ten of the elders of the town and said, "Sit here," and they did so. [3] Then he said to the kinsman-redeemer, "Naomi, who has come back from Moab, is selling the piece of land that belonged to our brother Elimelech. [4] I thought I should bring the matter to your attention and suggest that you buy it in the presence of these seated here and in the presence of the elders of my people. If you will redeem it, do so. But if you[c] will not, tell me, so I will know. For no one has the right to do it except you, and I am next in line."

"I will redeem it," he said.

[5] Then Boaz said, "On the day you buy the land from Naomi and from Ruth the Moabitess, you acquire[d] the dead man's widow, in order to maintain the name of the dead with his property."

---

[a] *1* Hebrew *find rest* (see Ruth 1:9) [b] *15* Most Hebrew manuscripts; many Hebrew manuscripts, Vulgate and Syriac *she* [c] *4* Many Hebrew manuscripts, Septuagint, Vulgate and Syriac; most Hebrew manuscripts *he* [d] *5* Hebrew; Vulgate and Syriac *Naomi, you acquire Ruth the Moabitess,*

⁶At this, the kinsman-redeemer said, "Then I cannot redeem it because I might endanger my own estate. You redeem it yourself. I cannot do it."

⁷(Now in earlier times in Israel, for the redemption and transfer of property to become final, one party took off his sandal and gave it to the other. This was the method of legalizing transactions in Israel.)

⁸So the kinsman-redeemer said to Boaz, "Buy it yourself." And he removed his sandal.

⁹Then Boaz announced to the elders and all the people, "Today you are witnesses that I have bought from Naomi all the property of Elimelech, Kilion and Mahlon. ¹⁰I have also acquired Ruth the Moabitess, Mahlon's widow, as my wife, in order to maintain the name of the dead with his property, so that his name will not disappear from among his family or from the town records. Today you are witnesses!"

¹¹Then the elders and all those at the gate said, "We are witnesses. May the LORD make the woman who is coming into your home like Rachel and Leah, who together built up the house of Israel. May you have standing in Ephrathah and be famous in Bethlehem. ¹²Through the offspring the LORD gives you by this young woman, may your family be like that of Perez, whom Tamar bore to Judah."

NOW OR NEVER
RU 4:8–10

What's the most extreme thing you've ever done to help a friend? How far would you be willing to go in order to help someone you didn't know very well?

THE GENEALOGY OF DAVID

¹³So Boaz took Ruth and she became his wife. Then he went to her, and the LORD enabled her to conceive, and she gave birth to a son. ¹⁴The women said to Naomi: "Praise be to the LORD, who this day has not left you without a kinsman-redeemer. May he become famous throughout Israel! ¹⁵He will renew your life and sustain you in your old age. For your daughter-in-law, who loves you and who is better to you than seven sons, has given him birth."

challengenotes

To: my_son

heavenly_father: don't let tragedy defeat you. I know the emotions you're experiencing, so I can supply you with exactly what you need—whether it's comfort, advice or the helping hand of a good friend—just keep looking to me. there is hope for what lies ahead in my plan for you.

RU 4:15

¹⁶Then Naomi took the child, laid him in her lap and cared for him. ¹⁷The women living there said, "Naomi has a son." And they named him Obed. He was the father of Jesse, the father of David.

¹⁸This, then, is the family line of Perez:

Perez was the father of Hezron,
¹⁹Hezron the father of Ram,
Ram the father of Amminadab,
²⁰Amminadab the father of Nahshon,
Nahshon the father of Salmon,ᵃ
²¹Salmon the father of Boaz,
Boaz the father of Obed,
²²Obed the father of Jesse,
and Jesse the father of David.

ᵃ *20* A few Hebrew manuscripts, some Septuagint manuscripts and Vulgate (see also verse 21 and Septuagint of 1 Chron. 2:11); most Hebrew manuscripts *Salma*

1 SAMUEL

« AT A GLANCE

Author
Unknown (Samuel may have written some of it)

Audience
People of Israel

Date
Sometime after Solomon's death in 931 B.C.

Setting
The nation of Israel went from being led by God to being led by a human king. The book of 1 Samuel begins with the birth of Samuel and ends with the death of King Saul.

Verse to Remember
But Samuel replied: "Does the LORD delight in burnt offerings and sacrifices as much as in obeying the voice of the LORD? To obey is better than sacrifice, and to heed is better than the fat of rams" (15:22).

Theme to Consider
God desires that we worship, obey, serve and follow him with all our heart and not just with superficial words.

UNCHANGING TRUTH » How can God use you? What can he accomplish through you? Be careful how you answer—especially if you don't have a lot of confidence in your spiritual potential at the moment. After all, we're not talking about what you can do; we're talking about what God can do through you. Underestimating your spiritual potential is the same as underestimating God. And underestimating God is just about the biggest mistake a guy can make.

Keeping your faith in God—believing that he has a plan for you—isn't easy. You're always going to have people telling you what you can't do. That's just the way a lot of people see the world. The thing is, though, unless those people are the voice of God himself, they don't know what they're talking about. In other words, no one but God knows your full potential.

David would certainly shout out an "amen" to that. When he announced that he was going to fight the giant Goliath, he didn't get bombarded with encouragement, to say the least. Instead, he heard things like, "You can't do this; you're just a boy." "You can't win this; you're not a warrior." "You can't survive this; you're not wearing any armor." "You can't overcome this; your only weapon is a slingshot and some rocks."

But David knew something the soldiers didn't know. He knew it was God, and not him, who would be doing the fighting. He knew that even a nine-foot-tall, heavily armed warrior was no match for the Creator of the universe. That's why David had the courage to challenge Goliath face-to-face. He didn't underestimate God's power. If you want to be victorious like David, follow his lead and put your faith in God's strength.

LIFE LESSONS »

1   If there's something you really want from the Lord, keep praying for it until you get an answer—one way or the other—no matter how long it takes (1:1–20).

2   God treats our disobedience a lot more seriously than we do (2:22–25).

3   No job is too big for you if God is on your side (17:1–58).

THE BIRTH OF SAMUEL

1 There was a certain man from Ramathaim, a Zuphite[a] from the hill country of Ephraim, whose name was Elkanah son of Jeroham, the son of Elihu, the son of Tohu, the son of Zuph, an Ephraimite. [2]He had two wives; one was called Hannah and the other Peninnah. Peninnah had children, but Hannah had none.

[3]Year after year this man went up from his town to worship and sacrifice to the LORD Almighty at Shiloh, where Hophni and Phinehas, the two sons of Eli, were priests of the LORD. [4]Whenever the day came for Elkanah to sacrifice, he would give portions of the meat to his wife Peninnah and to all her sons and daughters. [5]But to Hannah he gave a double portion because he loved her, and the LORD had closed her womb. [6]And because the LORD had closed her womb, her rival kept provoking her in order to irritate her. [7]This went on year after year. Whenever Hannah went up to the house of the LORD, her rival provoked her till she wept and would not eat. [8]Elkanah her husband would say to her, "Hannah, why are you weeping? Why don't you eat? Why are you downhearted? Don't I mean more to you than ten sons?"

[9]Once when they had finished eating and drinking in Shiloh, Hannah stood up. Now Eli the priest was sitting on a chair by the doorpost of the LORD's temple.[b] [10]In bitterness of soul Hannah wept much and prayed to the LORD. [11]And she made a vow, saying, "O LORD Almighty, if you will only look upon your servant's misery and remember me, and not forget your servant but give her a son, then I will give him to the LORD for all the days of his life, and no razor will ever be used on his head."

[12]As she kept on praying to the LORD, Eli observed her mouth. [13]Hannah was praying in her heart, and her lips were moving but her voice was not heard. Eli thought she was drunk [14]and said to her, "How long will you keep on getting drunk? Get rid of your wine."

[15]"Not so, my lord," Hannah replied, "I am a woman who is deeply troubled. I have not been drinking wine or beer; I was pouring out my soul to the LORD. [16]Do not take your servant for a wicked woman; I have been praying here out of my great anguish and grief."

[17]Eli answered, "Go in peace, and may the God of Israel grant you what you have asked of him."

[18]She said, "May your servant find favor in your eyes." Then she went her way and ate something, and her face was no longer downcast.

[19]Early the next morning they arose and worshiped before the LORD and then went back to their home at Ramah. Elkanah lay with Hannah his wife, and the LORD remembered her. [20]So in the course of time Hannah conceived and gave birth to a son. She named him Samuel,[c] saying, "Because I asked the LORD for him."

» live the adventure » 1Sa 1:18-20

Praying and Worshiping God

Don't treat prayer like a drive-up window at a fast-food restaurant. Don't just place your order and then wait for God to fill it, expecting to get what you want and get it quick. Instead, work on developing a complete prayer and worship time with the Lord. Include more than just your requests in your private conversations with God. Praise him for who he is; confess the things that have damaged your relationship with him; thank him for the things he's done in your life; *then* talk to him about your needs and desires.

HANNAH DEDICATES SAMUEL

[21]When the man Elkanah went up with all his family to offer the annual sacrifice to the LORD and to fulfill his vow, [22]Hannah did not go. She said to her husband, "After the boy is weaned, I will take him and present him before the LORD, and he will live there always."

[23]"Do what seems best to you," Elkanah her husband told her. "Stay here until you have weaned him; only may the LORD make good his[d] word." So the woman stayed at home and nursed her son until she had weaned him.

[24]After he was weaned, she took the boy with her, young as he was, along with a three-year-old bull,[e] an ephah[f] of flour and a skin of wine, and brought him to the house of the LORD at Shiloh. [25]When they

---

[a] *1* Or *from Ramathaim Zuphim*   [b] *9* That is, tabernacle   [c] *20 Samuel* sounds like the Hebrew for *heard of God.*   [d] *23* Masoretic Text; Dead Sea Scrolls, Septuagint and Syriac *your*   [e] *24* Dead Sea Scrolls, Septuagint and Syriac; Masoretic Text *with three bulls*   [f] *24* That is, probably about 3/5 bushel (about 22 liters)

had slaughtered the bull, they brought the boy to Eli, 26and she said to him, "As surely as you live, my lord, I am the woman who stood here beside you praying to the LORD. 27I prayed for this child, and the LORD has granted me what I asked of him. 28So now I give him to the LORD. For his whole life he will be given over to the LORD." And he worshiped the LORD there.

HANNAH'S PRAYER

2 Then Hannah prayed and said:

"My heart rejoices in the LORD;
    in the LORD my horn[a] is lifted high.
My mouth boasts over my enemies,
    for I delight in your deliverance.

2 "There is no one holy[b] like the
        LORD;
    there is no one besides
        you;
    there is no Rock like our
        God.

3 "Do not keep talking so
        proudly
    or let your mouth speak
        such arrogance,
for the LORD is a God who
        knows,
    and by him deeds are weighed.

4 "The bows of the warriors are broken,
    but those who stumbled are armed with strength.
5 Those who were full hire themselves out for food,
    but those who were hungry hunger no more.
She who was barren has borne seven
        children,
    but she who has had many sons
        pines away.

6 "The LORD brings death and makes alive;
    he brings down to the grave[c] and
        raises up.
7 The LORD sends poverty and wealth;
    he humbles and he exalts.
8 He raises the poor from the dust
    and lifts the needy from the ash
        heap;
he seats them with princes
    and has them inherit a throne of honor.

"For the foundations of the earth are the LORD's;
    upon them he has set the world.
9 He will guard the feet of his saints,
    but the wicked will be silenced in darkness.

"It is not by strength that one prevails;
10   those who oppose the LORD will be shattered.
He will thunder against them from heaven;
    the LORD will judge the ends of the earth.

---

a 1 *Horn* here symbolizes strength; also in verse 10.   b 2 Or *no Holy One*   c 6 Hebrew *Sheol*

> "He will give strength to his king
> and exalt the horn of his anointed."

[11]Then Elkanah went home to Ramah, but the boy ministered before the Lord under Eli the priest.

ELI'S WICKED SONS

[12]Eli's sons were wicked men; they had no regard for the Lord. [13]Now it was the practice of the priests with the people that whenever anyone offered a sacrifice and while the meat was being boiled, the servant of the priest would come with a three-pronged fork in his hand. [14]He would plunge it into the pan or kettle or caldron or pot, and the priest would take for himself whatever the fork brought up. This is how they treated all the Israelites who came to Shiloh. [15]But even before the fat was burned, the servant of the priest would come and say to the man who was sacrificing, "Give the priest some meat to roast; he won't accept boiled meat from you, but only raw."

[16]If the man said to him, "Let the fat be burned up first, and then take whatever you want," the servant would then answer, "No, hand it over now; if you don't, I'll take it by force."

[17]This sin of the young men was very great in the Lord's sight, for they[a] were treating the Lord's offering with contempt.

NOW OR NEVER
1SA 2:21

Believe it or not, what God has in store for you is way better than anything on your wish list. If you learn to pray in keeping with God's will and character, he's ready to give you more than you could ask for.

[18]But Samuel was ministering before the Lord—a boy wearing a linen ephod. [19]Each year his mother made him a little robe and took it to him when she went up with her husband to offer the annual sacrifice. [20]Eli would bless Elkanah and his wife, saying, "May the Lord give you children by this woman to take the place of the one she prayed for and gave to the Lord." Then they would go home. [21]And the Lord was gracious to Hannah; she conceived and gave birth to three sons and two daughters. Meanwhile, the boy Samuel grew up in the presence of the Lord.

[22]Now Eli, who was very old, heard about everything his sons were doing to all Israel and how they slept with the women who served at the entrance to the Tent of Meeting. [23]So he said to them, "Why do you do such things? I hear from all the people about these wicked deeds of yours. [24]No, my sons; it is not a good report that I hear spreading among the Lord's people. [25]If a man sins against another man, God[b] may mediate for him; but if a man sins against the Lord, who will intercede for him?" His sons, however, did not listen to their father's rebuke, for it was the Lord's will to put them to death.

[26]And the boy Samuel continued to grow in stature and in favor with the Lord and with men.

PROPHECY AGAINST THE HOUSE OF ELI

[27]Now a man of God came to Eli and said to him, "This is what the Lord says: 'Did I not clearly reveal myself to your father's house when they were in Egypt under Pharaoh? [28]I chose your father out of all the tribes of Israel to be my priest, to go up to my altar, to burn incense, and to wear an ephod in my presence. I also gave your father's house all the offerings made with fire by the Israelites. [29]Why do you[c] scorn my sacrifice and offering that I prescribed for my dwelling? Why do you honor your sons more than me by fattening yourselves on the choice parts of every offering made by my people Israel?'

[30]"Therefore the Lord, the God of Israel, declares: 'I promised that your house and your father's house would minister before me forever.' But now the Lord declares: 'Far be it from me! Those who honor me I will honor, but those who despise me will be disdained. [31]The time is coming when I will cut short your strength and the strength of your father's house, so that there will not be an old man in your family line [32]and you will see distress in my dwelling. Although good will be done to Israel, in your family line there will never be an old man. [33]Every one of you that I do not cut off from my altar will be spared only to blind your eyes with tears and to grieve your heart, and all your descendants will die in the prime of life.

[34]" 'And what happens to your two sons, Hophni and Phinehas, will be a sign to you—they will both

---

[a] 17 Or *men* [b] 25 Or *the judges* [c] 29 The Hebrew is plural.

die on the same day. ³⁵I will raise up for myself a faithful priest, who will do according to what is in my heart and mind. I will firmly establish his house, and he will minister before my anointed one always. ³⁶Then everyone left in your family line will come and bow down before him for a piece of silver and a crust of bread and plead, "Appoint me to some priestly office so I can have food to eat." ' "

THE LORD CALLS SAMUEL

3 The boy Samuel ministered before the LORD under Eli. In those days the word of the LORD was rare; there were not many visions.

²One night Eli, whose eyes were becoming so weak that he could barely see, was lying down in his usual place. ³The lamp of God had not yet gone out, and Samuel was lying down in the temple[a] of the LORD, where the ark of God was. ⁴Then the LORD called Samuel.

Samuel answered, "Here I am." ⁵And he ran to Eli and said, "Here I am; you called me."

But Eli said, "I did not call; go back and lie down." So he went and lay down.

⁶Again the LORD called, "Samuel!" And Samuel got up and went to Eli and said, "Here I am; you called me."

"My son," Eli said, "I did not call; go back and lie down."

⁷Now Samuel did not yet know the LORD: The word of the LORD had not yet been revealed to him.

⁸The LORD called Samuel a third time, and Samuel got up and went to Eli and said, "Here I am; you called me."

Then Eli realized that the LORD was calling the boy. ⁹So Eli told Samuel, "Go and lie down, and if he calls you, say, 'Speak, LORD, for your servant is listening.' " So Samuel went and lay down in his place.

¹⁰The LORD came and stood there, calling as at the other times, "Samuel! Samuel!"

Then Samuel said, "Speak, for your servant is listening."

NOW OR NEVER

1SA 3:9

Sometimes it's difficult to recognize God's calling, even when our hearts are receptive. That's why it's a good thing God is patient with us. His calling may not come in an audible voice, but if you think he's trying to stir up your interest, you'd better be ready to pay attention.

¹¹And the LORD said to Samuel: "See, I am about to do something in Israel that will make the ears of everyone who hears of it tingle. ¹²At that time I will carry out against Eli everything I spoke against his family—from beginning to end. ¹³For I told him that I would judge his family forever because of the sin he knew about; his sons made themselves contemptible,[b] and he failed to restrain them. ¹⁴Therefore, I swore to the house of Eli, 'The guilt of Eli's house will never be atoned for by sacrifice or offering.' "

¹⁵Samuel lay down until morning and then opened the doors of the house of the LORD. He was afraid to tell Eli the vision, ¹⁶but Eli called him and said, "Samuel, my son."

Samuel answered, "Here I am."

¹⁷"What was it he said to you?" Eli asked. "Do not hide it from me. May God deal with you, be it ever so severely, if you hide from me anything he told you." ¹⁸So Samuel told him everything, hiding nothing from him. Then Eli said, "He is the LORD; let him do what is good in his eyes."

¹⁹The LORD was with Samuel as he grew up, and he let none of his words fall to the ground. ²⁰And all Israel from Dan to Beersheba recognized that Samuel was attested as a prophet of the LORD. ²¹The LORD continued to appear at Shiloh, and there he revealed himself to Samuel through his word.

4 And Samuel's word came to all Israel.

THE PHILISTINES CAPTURE THE ARK

Now the Israelites went out to fight against the Philistines. The Israelites camped at Ebenezer, and the Philistines at Aphek. ²The Philistines deployed their forces to meet Israel, and as the battle spread, Israel was defeated by the Philistines, who killed about four thousand of them on the battlefield. ³When the soldiers returned to camp, the elders of Israel asked, "Why did the LORD bring defeat upon us today

---

ª *3* That is, tabernacle   ᵇ *13* Masoretic Text; an ancient Hebrew scribal tradition and Septuagint *sons blasphemed God* before the Philistines? Let us bring the ark of the LORD's covenant from Shiloh, so that it[a] may go with us and save us from the hand of our enemies."

⁴So the people sent men to Shiloh, and they brought back the ark of the covenant of the LORD Almighty, who is enthroned between the cherubim. And Eli's two sons, Hophni and Phinehas, were there with the ark of the covenant of God.

⁵When the ark of the LORD's covenant came into the camp, all Israel raised such a great shout that the ground shook. ⁶Hearing the uproar, the Philistines asked, "What's all this shouting in the Hebrew camp?"

When they learned that the ark of the LORD had come into the camp, ⁷the Philistines were afraid. "A god has come into the camp," they said. "We're in trouble! Nothing like this has happened before. ⁸Woe to us! Who will deliver us from the hand of these mighty gods? They are the gods who struck the Egyptians with all kinds of plagues in the desert. ⁹Be strong, Philistines! Be men, or you will be subject to the Hebrews, as they have been to you. Be men, and fight!"

NOW OR NEVER
1 SA 4:3

If you put your security in worldly things—even things that have value, like the ark had for Israel—you're going to be disappointed. Not even the most reliable person or thing can save us from death. Only God possesses strength over all things.

¹⁰So the Philistines fought, and the Israelites were defeated and every man fled to his tent. The slaughter was very great; Israel lost thirty thousand foot soldiers. ¹¹The ark of God was captured, and Eli's two sons, Hophni and Phinehas, died.

DEATH OF ELI

¹²That same day a Benjamite ran from the battle line and went to Shiloh, his clothes torn and dust on his head. ¹³When he arrived, there was Eli sitting on his chair by the side of the road, watching, because his heart feared for the ark of God. When the man entered the town and told what had happened, the whole town sent up a cry.

¹⁴Eli heard the outcry and asked, "What is the meaning of this uproar?"

The man hurried over to Eli, ¹⁵who was ninety-eight years old and whose eyes were set so that he could not see. ¹⁶He told Eli, "I have just come from the battle line; I fled from it this very day."

Eli asked, "What happened, my son?"

¹⁷The man who brought the news replied, "Israel fled before the Philistines, and the army has suffered heavy losses. Also your two sons, Hophni and Phinehas, are dead, and the ark of God has been captured."

¹⁸When he mentioned the ark of God, Eli fell backward off his chair by the side of the gate. His neck was broken and he died, for he was an old man and heavy. He had led[b] Israel forty years.

¹⁹His daughter-in-law, the wife of Phinehas, was pregnant and near the time of delivery. When she heard the news that the ark of God had been captured and that her father-in-law and her husband were dead, she went into labor and gave birth, but was overcome by her labor pains. ²⁰As she was dying, the women attending her said, "Don't despair; you have given birth to a son." But she did not respond or pay any attention.

²¹She named the boy Ichabod,[c] saying, "The glory has departed from Israel"—because of the capture of the ark of God and the deaths of her father-in-law and her husband. ²²She said, "The glory has departed from Israel, for the ark of God has been captured."

THE ARK IN ASHDOD AND EKRON

5 After the Philistines had captured the ark of God, they took it from Ebenezer to Ashdod. ²Then they carried the ark into Dagon's temple and set it beside Dagon. ³When the people of Ashdod rose early the next day, there was Dagon, fallen on his face on the ground before the ark of the LORD! They took Dagon and put him back in his place. ⁴But the following morning when they rose, there was Dagon, fallen on his face on the ground before the ark of the LORD! His head and hands had been broken off and were lying on the threshold; only his body remained. ⁵That is why to this day neither the priests of Dagon nor any others who enter Dagon's temple at Ashdod step on the threshold.

---

[a] *3 Or he*   [b] *18 Traditionally judged*   [c] *21 Ichabod means no glory.*

⁶The Lord's hand was heavy upon the people of Ashdod and its vicinity; he brought devastation upon them and afflicted them with tumors.ᵃ ⁷When the men of Ashdod saw what was happening, they said, "The ark of the god of Israel must not stay here with us, because his hand is heavy upon us and upon Dagon our god." ⁸So they called together all the rulers of the Philistines and asked them, "What shall we do with the ark of the god of Israel?"

They answered, "Have the ark of the god of Israel moved to Gath." So they moved the ark of the God of Israel.

⁹But after they had moved it, the Lord's hand was against that city, throwing it into a great panic. He afflicted the people of the city, both young and old, with an outbreak of tumors.ᵇ ¹⁰So they sent the ark of God to Ekron.

As the ark of God was entering Ekron, the people of Ekron cried out, "They have brought the ark of the god of Israel around to us to kill us and our people." ¹¹So they called together all the rulers of the Philistines and said, "Send the ark of the god of Israel away; let it go back to its own place, or itᶜ will kill us and our people." For death had filled the city with panic; God's hand was very heavy upon it. ¹²Those who did not die were afflicted with tumors, and the outcry of the city went up to heaven.

THE ARK RETURNED TO ISRAEL

6 When the ark of the Lord had been in Philistine territory seven months, ²the Philistines called for the priests and the diviners and said, "What shall we do with the ark of the Lord? Tell us how we should send it back to its place."

³They answered, "If you return the ark of the god of Israel, do not send it away empty, but by all means send a guilt offering to him. Then you will be healed, and you will know why his hand has not been lifted from you."

⁴The Philistines asked, "What guilt offering should we send to him?"

They replied, "Five gold tumors and five gold rats, according to the number of the Philistine rulers, because the same plague has struck both you and your rulers. ⁵Make models of the tumors and of the rats that are destroying the country, and pay honor to Israel's god. Perhaps he will lift his hand from you and your gods and your land. ⁶Why do you harden your hearts as the Egyptians and Pharaoh did? When heᵈ treated them harshly, did they not send the Israelites out so they could go on their way?

⁷"Now then, get a new cart ready, with two cows that have calved and have never been yoked. Hitch the cows to the cart, but take their calves away and pen them up. ⁸Take the ark of the Lord and put it on the cart, and in a chest beside it put the gold objects you are sending back to him as a guilt offering. Send it on its way, ⁹but keep watching it. If it goes up to its own territory, toward Beth Shemesh, then the Lord has brought this great disaster on us. But if it does not, then we will know that it was not his hand that struck us and that it happened to us by chance."

¹⁰So they did this. They took two such cows and hitched them to the cart and penned up their calves. ¹¹They placed the ark of the Lord on the cart and along with it the chest containing the gold rats and the models of the tumors. ¹²Then the cows went straight up toward Beth Shemesh, keeping on the road and lowing all the way; they did not turn to the right or to the left. The rulers of the Philistines followed them as far as the border of Beth Shemesh.

¹³Now the people of Beth Shemesh were harvesting their wheat in the valley, and when they looked up and saw the ark, they rejoiced at the sight. ¹⁴The cart came to the field of Joshua of Beth Shemesh, and there it stopped beside a large rock. The people chopped up the wood of the cart and sacrificed the cows as a burnt offering to the Lord. ¹⁵The Levites took down the ark of the Lord, together with the chest containing the gold objects, and placed them on the large rock. On that day the people of Beth Shemesh offered burnt offerings and made sacrifices to the Lord. ¹⁶The five rulers of the Philistines saw all this and then returned that same day to Ekron.

¹⁷These are the gold tumors the Philistines sent as a guilt offering to the Lord—one each for Ashdod, Gaza, Ashkelon, Gath and Ekron. ¹⁸And the number of the gold rats was according to the number of Philistine towns belonging to the five rulers—the fortified towns with their country villages. The large rock, on whichᵉ they set the ark of the Lord, is a witness to this day in the field of Joshua of Beth Shemesh.

ᵃ 6 Hebrew; Septuagint and Vulgate *tumors. And rats appeared in their land, and death and destruction were throughout the city*
ᵇ 9 Or *with tumors in the groin* (see Septuagint)   ᶜ 11 Or *he*   ᵈ 6 That is, God   ᵉ 18 A few Hebrew manuscripts (see also Septuagint); most Hebrew manuscripts *villages as far as Greater Abel, where*

¹⁹But God struck down some of the men of Beth Shemesh, putting seventy[a] of them to death because they had looked into the ark of the LORD. The people mourned because of the heavy blow the LORD had dealt them, ²⁰and the men of Beth Shemesh asked, "Who can stand in the presence of the LORD, this holy God? To whom will the ark go up from here?"

²¹Then they sent messengers to the people of Kiriath Jearim, saying, "The Philistines have returned the ark of the LORD. Come down and take it up to your place." **7** ¹So the men of Kiriath Jearim came and took up the ark of the LORD. They took it to Abinadab's house on the hill and consecrated Eleazar his son to guard the ark of the LORD.

SAMUEL SUBDUES THE PHILISTINES AT MIZPAH

²It was a long time, twenty years in all, that the ark remained at Kiriath Jearim, and all the people of Israel mourned and sought after the LORD. ³And Samuel said to the whole house of Israel, "If you are returning to the LORD with all your hearts, then rid yourselves of the foreign gods and the Ashtoreths and commit yourselves to the LORD and serve him only, and he will deliver you out of the hand of the Philistines." ⁴So the Israelites put away their Baals and Ashtoreths, and served the LORD only.

⁵Then Samuel said, "Assemble all Israel at Mizpah and I will intercede with the LORD for you." ⁶When they had assembled at Mizpah, they drew water and poured it out before the LORD. On that day they fasted and there they confessed, "We have sinned against the LORD." And Samuel was leader[b] of Israel at Mizpah.

NOW OR NEVER

1 SA 7:3

If you're still messing around with stuff from your old life of sin, you're not really engaged with God. And if you're not connected to God, then you don't have much of a relationship with him, do you?

⁷When the Philistines heard that Israel had assembled at Mizpah, the rulers of the Philistines came up to attack them. And when the Israelites heard of it, they were afraid because of the Philistines. ⁸They said to Samuel, "Do not stop crying out to the LORD our God for us, that he may rescue us from the hand of the Philistines." ⁹Then Samuel took a suckling lamb and offered it up as a whole burnt offering to the LORD. He cried out to the LORD on Israel's behalf, and the LORD answered him.

¹⁰While Samuel was sacrificing the burnt offering, the Philistines drew near to engage Israel in battle. But that day the LORD thundered with loud thunder against the Philistines and threw them into such a panic that they were routed before the Israelites. ¹¹The men of Israel rushed out of Mizpah and pursued the Philistines, slaughtering them along the way to a point below Beth Car.

¹²Then Samuel took a stone and set it up between Mizpah and Shen. He named it Ebenezer,[c] saying, "Thus far has the LORD helped us." ¹³So the Philistines were subdued and did not invade Israelite territory again.

Throughout Samuel's lifetime, the hand of the LORD was against the Philistines. ¹⁴The towns from Ekron to Gath that the Philistines had captured from Israel were restored to her, and Israel delivered the neighboring territory from the power of the Philistines. And there was peace between Israel and the Amorites.

¹⁵Samuel continued as judge over Israel all the days of his life. ¹⁶From year to year he went on a circuit from Bethel to Gilgal to Mizpah, judging Israel in all those places. ¹⁷But he always went back to Ramah, where his home was, and there he also judged Israel. And he built an altar there to the LORD.

ISRAEL ASKS FOR A KING

8 When Samuel grew old, he appointed his sons as judges for Israel. ²The name of his firstborn was Joel and the name of his second was Abijah, and they served at Beersheba. ³But his sons did not walk in his ways. They turned aside after dishonest gain and accepted bribes and perverted justice.

⁴So all the elders of Israel gathered together and came to Samuel at Ramah. ⁵They said to him, "You are old, and your sons do not walk in your ways; now appoint a king to lead[d] us, such as all the other nations have."

ᵃ 19 A few Hebrew manuscripts; most Hebrew manuscripts and Septuagint *50,070*   ᵇ 6 Traditionally *judge*   ᶜ 12 *Ebenezer* means *stone of help.*   ᵈ 5 Traditionally *judge*; also in verses 6 and 20

battlelines

» One Way or Another (Truth)

Q: You and Malcom hang out a lot.
A: Yeah. He's a great guy. That's what's so confusing.

Q: What do you mean?
A: He's a Muslim. He believes there's no God but Allah. He says Mohammed is his prophet. He thinks Jesus was a great guy and all—even a prophet—but not the Son of God.

Q: It bothers you that he's not a Christian?
A: Yeah, I guess.

Q: Have you ever witnessed to him?
A: Well . . . no . . . but he's witnessed to me.

Q: Really?
A: Yeah, but I'm not going to convert to Islam or anything. I just wonder if maybe Jesus and Mohammed are two roads that end up in the same place. Why does just one have to be right?

Q: Because contradictory ideas can't both be true.
A: What are you talking about?

Q: Jesus' message was, "I am *the* way, *the* truth and *the* life. Follow me." He died and rose from the dead to prove it.
A: And your point is?

Q: My point is that Jesus didn't say, "I am *a* way" or "I am *a* truth." He made an exclusive claim. Jesus' teachings and opposite teachings can't both be true. That's crazy.
A: Crazy, huh?

Q: Yes! Can one plus one equal four?
A: So you're saying Mohammed is wrong?

Q: Who do you think is wrong? Mohammed started a religious movement, and then he died. He's still in his grave today. But Jesus rose from the dead; he's still alive.

» Counterfeit God

When it comes to spirituality, the issue isn't what *seems* good, *feels* right or even what looks like it works. The issue is truth. And if one thing is true, it follows that anything that contradicts it *can't* be true as well.

Some people get bent all out of shape by Christianity's refusal to say that all religions are equally valid. They call followers of Jesus narrow-minded, bigoted, intolerant, arrogant . . . and lots of other words that can't be printed here. But Christians aren't the ones who said, "No one comes to the Father except through me" (John 14:6). That's a statement from the lips of Jesus himself. Those who don't like Jesus' claim to be the only way to God need to take up their beef with him.

It's important to respect other people's right to religious freedom—after all, it's that same right that allows us to worship God freely—but don't buy into the lie that all roads eventually lead to the same destination.

Read more about Christianity at www.RevolutionBible.com.

⁶But when they said, "Give us a king to lead us," this displeased Samuel; so he prayed to the LORD. ⁷And the LORD told him: "Listen to all that the people are saying to you; it is not you they have reject-ed, but they have rejected me as their king. ⁸As they have done from the day I brought them up out of Egypt until this day, forsaking me and serving other gods, so they are doing to you. ⁹Now listen to them; but warn them solemnly and let them know what the king who will reign over them will do."

¹⁰Samuel told all the words of the LORD to the people who were asking him for a king. ¹¹He said, "This is what the king who will reign over you will do: He will take your sons and make them serve with his chariots and horses, and they will run in front of his chariots. ¹²Some he will assign to be commanders of thousands and commanders of fifties, and others to plow his ground and reap his harvest, and still others to make weapons of war and equipment for his chariots. ¹³He will take your daughters to be per-fumers and cooks and bakers. ¹⁴He will take the best of your fields and vineyards and olive groves and give them to his attendants. ¹⁵He will take a tenth of your grain and of your vintage and give it to his of-ficials and attendants. ¹⁶Your menservants and maidservants and the best of your cattleᵃ and donkeys he will take for his own use. ¹⁷He will take a tenth of your flocks, and you yourselves will become his slaves. ¹⁸When that day comes, you will cry out for relief from the king you have chosen, and the LORD will not answer you in that day."

¹⁹But the people refused to listen to Samuel. "No!" they said. "We want a king over us. ²⁰Then we will be like all the other nations, with a king to lead us and to go out before us and fight our battles."

²¹When Samuel heard all that the people said, he repeated it before the LORD. ²²The LORD answered, "Listen to them and give them a king."

Then Samuel said to the men of Israel, "Everyone go back to his town."

SAMUEL ANOINTS SAUL

9 There was a Benjamite, a man of standing, whose name was Kish son of Abiel, the son of Zeror, the son of Becorath, the son of Aphiah of Benjamin. ²He had a son named Saul, an impressive young man without equal among the Israelites—a head taller than any of the others.

³Now the donkeys belonging to Saul's father Kish were lost, and Kish said to his son Saul, "Take one of the servants with you and go and look for the donkeys." ⁴So he passed through the hill country of Ephraim and through the area around Shalisha, but they did not find them. They went on into the dis-trict of Shaalim, but the donkeys were not there. Then he passed through the territory of Benjamin, but they did not find them.

⁵When they reached the district of Zuph, Saul said to the servant who was with him, "Come, let's go back, or my father will stop thinking about the donkeys and start worrying about us."

⁶But the servant replied, "Look, in this town there is a man of God; he is highly respected, and ev-erything he says comes true. Let's go there now. Perhaps he will tell us what way to take."

⁷Saul said to his servant, "If we go, what can we give the man? The food in our sacks is gone. We have no gift to take to the man of God. What do we have?"

⁸The servant answered him again. "Look," he said, "I have a quarter of a shekelᵇ of silver. I will give it to the man of God so that he will tell us what way to take." ⁹(Formerly in Israel, if a man went to in-quire of God, he would say, "Come, let us go to the seer," because the prophet of today used to be called a seer.)

¹⁰"Good," Saul said to his servant. "Come, let's go." So they set out for the town where the man of God was.

¹¹As they were going up the hill to the town, they met some girls coming out to draw water, and they asked them, "Is the seer here?"

¹²"He is," they answered. "He's ahead of you. Hurry now; he has just come to our town today, for the people have a sacrifice at the high place. ¹³As soon as you enter the town, you will find him be-fore he goes up to the high place to eat. The people will not begin eating until he comes, because he must bless the sacrifice; afterward, those who are invited will eat. Go up now; you should find him about this time."

¹⁴They went up to the town, and as they were entering it, there was Samuel, coming toward them on his way up to the high place.

¹⁵Now the day before Saul came, the LORD had revealed this to Samuel: ¹⁶"About this time tomor-row I will send you a man from the land of Benjamin. Anoint him leader over my people Israel; he will

---

ᵃ 16 Septuagint; Hebrew young men   ᵇ 8 That is, about 1/10 ounce (about 3 grams) deliver my people from the hand of the Philistines. I have looked upon my people, for their cry has reached me."

[17]When Samuel caught sight of Saul, the Lord said to him, "This is the man I spoke to you about; he will govern my people."

[18]Saul approached Samuel in the gateway and asked, "Would you please tell me where the seer's house is?"

[19]"I am the seer," Samuel replied. "Go up ahead of me to the high place, for today you are to eat with me, and in the morning I will let you go and will tell you all that is in your heart. [20]As for the donkeys you lost three days ago, do not worry about them; they have been found. And to whom is all the desire of Israel turned, if not to you and all your father's family?"

[21]Saul answered, "But am I not a Benjamite, from the smallest tribe of Israel, and is not my clan the least of all the clans of the tribe of Benjamin? Why do you say such a thing to me?"

[22]Then Samuel brought Saul and his servant into the hall and seated them at the head of those who were invited—about thirty in number. [23]Samuel said to the cook, "Bring the piece of meat I gave you, the one I told you to lay aside."

[24]So the cook took up the leg with what was on it and set it in front of Saul. Samuel said, "Here is what has been kept for you. Eat, because it was set aside for you for this occasion, from the time I said, 'I have invited guests.'" And Saul dined with Samuel that day.

[25]After they came down from the high place to the town, Samuel talked with Saul on the roof of his house. [26]They rose about daybreak and Samuel called to Saul on the roof, "Get ready, and I will send you on your way." When Saul got ready, he and Samuel went outside together. [27]As they were going down to the edge of the town, Samuel said to Saul, "Tell the servant to go on ahead of us"—and the servant did so—"but you stay here awhile, so that I may give you a message from God."

10 Then Samuel took a flask of oil and poured it on Saul's head and kissed him, saying, "Has not the Lord anointed you leader over his inheritance?[a] [2]When you leave today, you will meet two men near Rachel's tomb, at Zelzah on the border of Benjamin. They will say to you, 'The donkeys you set out to look for have been found. And now your father has stopped thinking about them and is worried about you. He is asking, "What shall I do about my son?"'

[3]"Then you will go on from there until you reach the great tree of Tabor. Three men going up to God at Bethel will meet you there. One will be carrying three young goats, another three loaves of bread, and another a skin of wine. [4]They will greet you and offer you two loaves of bread, which you will accept from them.

[5]"After that you will go to Gibeah of God, where there is a Philistine outpost. As you approach the town, you will meet a procession of prophets coming down from the high place with lyres, tambourines, flutes and harps being played before them, and they will be prophesying. [6]The Spirit of the Lord will come upon you in power, and you will prophesy with them; and you will be changed into a different person. [7]Once these signs are fulfilled, do whatever your hand finds to do, for God is with you.

[8]"Go down ahead of me to Gilgal. I will surely come down to you to sacrifice burnt offerings and fellowship offerings,[b] but you must wait seven days until I come to you and tell you what you are to do."

Knowing Your Strengths

Imagine you're the sixth man on your school's basketball team. During a time out, the coach tells you he's putting you in. What do you think would happen if you said, "Me? No way. I'm the slowest guy on the team. Plus, I'm too short to grab rebounds, and my jump shot stinks." That's kind of like what Saul did when he found out God had chosen him to be the first king of Israel. He gave every excuse he could think of as to why he was the wrong person for the job. A much better strategy for Saul and anyone chosen to do God's work is to humbly ask, "What gifts has God given me to do the job right?"

---

[a] 1 Hebrew; Septuagint and Vulgate over his people Israel? You will reign over the Lord's people and save them from the power of their enemies round about. And this will be a sign to you that the Lord has anointed you leader over his inheritance: [b] 8 Traditionally peace offerings

SAUL MADE KING

⁹As Saul turned to leave Samuel, God changed Saul's heart, and all these signs were fulfilled that day. ¹⁰When they arrived at Gibeah, a procession of prophets met him; the Spirit of God came upon him in power, and he joined in their prophesying. ¹¹When all those who had formerly known him saw him prophesying with the prophets, they asked each other, "What is this that has happened to the son of Kish? Is Saul also among the prophets?"

¹²A man who lived there answered, "And who is their father?" So it became a saying: "Is Saul also among the prophets?" ¹³After Saul stopped prophesying, he went to the high place.

¹⁴Now Saul's uncle asked him and his servant, "Where have you been?"

"Looking for the donkeys," he said. "But when we saw they were not to be found, we went to Samuel."

¹⁵Saul's uncle said, "Tell me what Samuel said to you."

¹⁶Saul replied, "He assured us that the donkeys had been found." But he did not tell his uncle what Samuel had said about the kingship.

¹⁷Samuel summoned the people of Israel to the LORD at Mizpah ¹⁸and said to them, "This is what the LORD, the God of Israel, says: 'I brought Israel up out of Egypt, and I delivered you from the power of Egypt and all the kingdoms that oppressed you.' ¹⁹But you have now rejected your God, who saves you out of all your calamities and distresses. And you have said, 'No, set a king over us.' So now present yourselves before the LORD by your tribes and clans."

²⁰When Samuel brought all the tribes of Israel near, the tribe of Benjamin was chosen. ²¹Then he brought forward the tribe of Benjamin, clan by clan, and Matri's clan was chosen. Finally Saul son of Kish was chosen. But when they looked for him, he was not to be found. ²²So they inquired further of the LORD, "Has the man come here yet?"

And the LORD said, "Yes, he has hidden himself among the baggage."

²³They ran and brought him out, and as he stood among the people he was a head taller than any of the others. ²⁴Samuel said to all the people, "Do you see the man the LORD has chosen? There is no one like him among all the people."

Then the people shouted, "Long live the king!"

²⁵Samuel explained to the people the reg-ulations of the kingship. He wrote them down on a scroll and deposited it before the LORD. Then Samuel dismissed the people, each to his own home.

NOW OR NEVER
1SA 10:21–22

God will never pile more on your plate than you can handle. So when you start to feel overwhelmed by everything going on in your life, don't try to run away or hide from it all. Instead, ask God to help you recognize just how much you're capable of.

²⁶Saul also went to his home in Gibeah, accompanied by valiant men whose hearts God had touched. ²⁷But some troublemakers said, "How can this fellow save us?" They despised him and brought him no gifts. But Saul kept silent.

SAUL RESCUES THE CITY OF JABESH

11 Nahash the Ammonite went up and besieged Jabesh Gilead. And all the men of Jabesh said to him, "Make a treaty with us, and we will be subject to you."

²But Nahash the Ammonite replied, "I will make a treaty with you only on the condition that I gouge out the right eye of every one of you and so bring disgrace on all Israel."

³The elders of Jabesh said to him, "Give us seven days so we can send messengers throughout Israel; if no one comes to rescue us, we will surrender to you."

⁴When the messengers came to Gibeah of Saul and reported these terms to the people, they all wept aloud. ⁵Just then Saul was returning from the fields, behind his oxen, and he asked, "What is wrong with the people? Why are they weeping?" Then they repeated to him what the men of Jabesh had said.

⁶When Saul heard their words, the Spirit of God came upon him in power, and he burned with anger. ⁷He took a pair of oxen, cut them into pieces, and sent the pieces by messengers throughout Israel, proclaiming, "This is what will be done to the oxen of anyone who does not follow Saul and Samuel." Then the terror of the LORD fell on the people, and they turned out as one man. ⁸When Saul mus-

tered them at Bezek, the men of Israel numbered three hundred thousand and the men of Judah thirty thousand.

⁹They told the messengers who had come, "Say to the men of Jabesh Gilead, 'By the time the sun is hot tomorrow, you will be delivered.' " When the messengers went and reported this to the men of Jabesh, they were elated. ¹⁰They said to the Ammonites, "Tomorrow we will surrender to you, and you can do to us whatever seems good to you."

¹¹The next day Saul separated his men into three divisions; during the last watch of the night they broke into the camp of the Ammonites and slaughtered them until the heat of the day. Those who survived were scattered, so that no two of them were left together.

SAUL CONFIRMED AS KING

¹²The people then said to Samuel, "Who was it that asked, 'Shall Saul reign over us?' Bring these men to us and we will put them to death."

¹³But Saul said, "No one shall be put to death today, for this day the LORD has rescued Israel."

¹⁴Then Samuel said to the people, "Come, let us go to Gilgal and there reaffirm the kingship." ¹⁵So all the people went to Gilgal and confirmed Saul as king in the presence of the LORD. There they sacrificed fellowship offerings ᵃ before the LORD, and Saul and all the Israelites held a great celebration.

SAMUEL'S FAREWELL SPEECH

12 Samuel said to all Israel, "I have listened to everything you said to me and have set a king over you. ²Now you have a king as your leader. As for me, I am old and gray, and my sons are here with you. I have been your leader from my youth until this day. ³Here I stand. Testify against me in the presence of the LORD and his anointed. Whose ox have I taken? Whose donkey have I taken? Whom have I cheated? Whom have I oppressed? From whose hand have I accepted a bribe to make me shut my eyes? If I have done any of these, I will make it right."

⁴"You have not cheated or oppressed us," they replied. "You have not taken anything from anyone's hand."

⁵Samuel said to them, "The LORD is witness against you, and also his anointed is witness this day, that you have not found anything in my hand."

"He is witness," they said.

⁶Then Samuel said to the people, "It is the LORD who appointed Moses and Aaron and brought your forefathers up out of Egypt. ⁷Now then, stand here, because I am going to confront you with evidence before the LORD as to all the righteous acts performed by the LORD for you and your fathers.

⁸"After Jacob entered Egypt, they cried to the LORD for help, and the LORD sent Moses and Aaron, who brought your forefathers out of Egypt and settled them in this place.

⁹"But they forgot the LORD their God; so he sold them into the hand of Sisera, the commander of the army of Hazor, and into the hands of the Philistines and the king of Moab, who fought against them. ¹⁰They cried out to the LORD and said, 'We have sinned; we have forsaken the LORD and served the Baals and the Ashtoreths. But now deliver us from the hands of our enemies, and we will serve you.' ¹¹Then the LORD sent Jerub-Baal, ᵇ Barak, ᶜ Jephthah and Samuel, ᵈ and he delivered you from the hands of your enemies on every side, so that you lived securely.

¹²"But when you saw that Nahash king of the Ammonites was moving against you, you said to me, 'No, we want a king to rule over us'—even though the LORD your God was your king. ¹³Now here is the king you have chosen, the one you asked for; see, the LORD has set a king over you. ¹⁴If you fear the LORD and serve and obey him and do not rebel against his commands, and if both you and the king who reigns over you follow the LORD your God—good! ¹⁵But if you do not obey the LORD, and if you rebel against his commands, his hand will be against you, as it was against your fathers.

¹⁶"Now then, stand still and see this great thing the LORD is about to do before your eyes! ¹⁷Is it not wheat harvest now? I will call upon the LORD to send thunder and rain. And you will realize what an evil thing you did in the eyes of the LORD when you asked for a king."

¹⁸Then Samuel called upon the LORD, and that same day the LORD sent thunder and rain. So all the people stood in awe of the LORD and of Samuel.

¹⁹The people all said to Samuel, "Pray to the LORD your God for your servants so that we will not

---

ᵃ 15 Traditionally *peace offerings*   ᵇ 11 Also called *Gideon*   ᶜ 11 Some Septuagint manuscripts and Syriac; Hebrew *Bedan*
ᵈ 11 Hebrew; some Septuagint manuscripts and Syriac *Samson*

die, for we have added to all our other sins the evil of asking for a king."

²⁰"Do not be afraid," Samuel replied. "You have done all this evil; yet do not turn away from the LORD, but serve the LORD with all your heart. ²¹Do not turn away after useless idols. They can do you no good, nor can they rescue you, because they are useless. ²²For the sake of his great name the LORD will not reject his people, because the LORD was pleased to make you his own. ²³As for me, far be it from me that I should sin against the LORD by failing to pray for you. And I will teach you the way that is good and right. ²⁴But be sure to fear the LORD and serve him faithfully with all your heart; consider what great things he has done for you. ²⁵Yet if you persist in doing evil, both you and your king will be swept away."

NOW OR NEVER
1SA 12:16–17

Be careful of the things you wish for and ask for in your life. You may find out too late just how dangerous they are when you actually get them.

SAMUEL REBUKES SAUL

13

Saul was ⌊thirty⌋ᵃ years old when he became king, and he reigned over Israel ⌊forty-⌋ᵇ two years.

²Saulᶜ chose three thousand men from Israel; two thousand were with him at Micmash and in the hill country of Bethel, and a thousand were with Jonathan at Gibeah in Benjamin. The rest of the men he sent back to their homes.

³Jonathan attacked the Philistine outpost at Geba, and the Philistines heard about it. Then Saul had the trumpet blown throughout the land and said, "Let the Hebrews hear!" ⁴So all Israel heard the news: "Saul has attacked the Philistine outpost, and now Israel has become a stench to the Philistines." And the people were summoned to join Saul at Gilgal.

⁵The Philistines assembled to fight Israel, with three thousandᵈ chariots, six thousand charioteers, and soldiers as numerous as the sand on the seashore. They went up and camped at Micmash, east of Beth Aven. ⁶When the men of Israel saw that their situation was critical and that their army was hard pressed, they hid in caves and thickets, among the rocks, and in pits and cisterns. ⁷Some Hebrews even crossed the Jordan to the land of Gad and Gilead.

NOW OR NEVER
1SA 12:23

Prayer is certainly better than cash on the list of great gift ideas. Nothing shows how deeply you care about someone more than taking his or her name to the Creator of the universe and asking him to pour out his blessings and grace on that person's life.

Saul remained at Gilgal, and all the troops with him were quaking with fear. ⁸He waited seven days, the time set by Samuel; but Samuel did not come to Gilgal, and Saul's men began to scatter. ⁹So he said, "Bring me the burnt offering and the fellowship offerings.ᵉ" And Saul offered up the burnt offering. ¹⁰Just as he finished making the offering, Samuel arrived, and Saul went out to greet him.

¹¹"What have you done?" asked Samuel.

Saul replied, "When I saw that the men were scattering, and that you did not come at the set time, and that the Philistines were assembling at Micmash, ¹²I thought, 'Now the Philistines will come down against me at Gilgal, and I have not sought the LORD's favor.' So I felt compelled to offer the burnt offering."

¹³"You acted foolishly," Samuel said. "You have not kept the command the LORD your God gave you; if you had, he would have established your kingdom over Israel for all time. ¹⁴But now your kingdom will not endure; the LORD has sought out a man after his own heart and appointed him leader of his people, because you have not kept the LORD's command."

ᵃ *1* A few late manuscripts of the Septuagint; Hebrew does not have *thirty*.   ᵇ *1* See the round number in Acts 13:21; Hebrew does not have *forty-*.   ᶜ *1,2* Or *and when he had reigned over Israel two years,* ²*he*   ᵈ *5* Some Septuagint manuscripts and Syriac; Hebrew *thirty thousand*   ᵉ *9* Traditionally *peace offerings*

Obeying God's Commands

What promises have you received from the Lord? What has he required of you? What areas of your life have you handed over to him and what areas are you holding back for yourself? God doesn't bargain with his people, guaranteeing money, power and fame if we would only do his will. He does, however, reward his people and bless them out of his infinite goodness. On the other hand, if we reject him and his offer of new life, we forfeit the greatest of all of his blessings: eternal life with him.

15 Then Samuel left Gilgal[a] and went up to Gibeah in Benjamin, and Saul counted the men who were with him. They numbered about six hundred.

ISRAEL WITHOUT WEAPONS

16 Saul and his son Jonathan and the men with them were staying in Gibeah[b] in Benjamin, while the Philistines camped at Micmash. 17 Raiding parties went out from the Philistine camp in three detachments. One turned toward Ophrah in the vicinity of Shual, 18 another toward Beth Horon, and the third toward the borderland overlooking the Valley of Zeboim facing the desert.

19 Not a blacksmith could be found in the whole land of Israel, because the Philistines had said, "Otherwise the Hebrews will make swords or spears!" 20 So all Israel went down to the Philistines to have their plowshares, mattocks, axes and sickles[c] sharpened. 21 The price was two thirds of a shekel[d] for sharpening plowshares and mattocks, and a third of a shekel[e] for sharpening forks and axes and for repointing goads.

22 So on the day of the battle not a soldier with Saul and Jonathan had a sword or spear in his hand; only Saul and his son Jonathan had them.

JONATHAN ATTACKS THE PHILISTINES

23 Now a detachment of Philistines had gone out to the pass at Micmash. **14** 1 One day Jonathan son of Saul said to the young man bearing his armor, "Come, let's go over to the Philistine outpost on the other side." But he did not tell his father.

2 Saul was staying on the outskirts of Gibeah under a pomegranate tree in Migron. With him were about six hundred men, 3 among whom was Ahijah, who was wearing an ephod. He was a son of Ichabod's brother Ahitub son of Phinehas, the son of Eli, the LORD's priest in Shiloh. No one was aware that Jonathan had left.

4 On each side of the pass that Jonathan intended to cross to reach the Philistine outpost was a cliff; one was called Bozez, and the other Seneh. 5 One cliff stood to the north toward Micmash, the other to the south toward Geba.

6 Jonathan said to his young armor-bearer, "Come, let's go over to the outpost of those uncircumcised fellows. Perhaps the LORD will act in our behalf. Nothing can hinder the LORD from saving, whether by many or by few."

7 "Do all that you have in mind," his armor-bearer said. "Go ahead; I am with you heart and soul."

8 Jonathan said, "Come, then; we will cross over toward the men and let them see us. 9 If they say to us, 'Wait there until we come to you,' we will stay where we are and not go up to them. 10 But if they say, 'Come up to us,' we will climb up, because that will be our sign that the LORD has given them into our hands."

11 So both of them showed themselves to the Philistine outpost. "Look!" said the Philistines. "The Hebrews are crawling out of the holes they were hiding in." 12 The men of the outpost shouted to Jona-

NOW OR NEVER
1SA 13:11-13

Why is it easier to trust God when things are going well than it is when things are falling apart? The worse matters get in your life, the tighter you need to hold on to your faith in our rock-solid God.

---

[a] 15 Hebrew; Septuagint *Gilgal and went his way; the rest of the people went after Saul to meet the army, and they went out of Gilgal*
[b] 16 Two Hebrew manuscripts; most Hebrew manuscripts *Geba*, a variant of *Gibeah*   [c] 20 Septuagint; Hebrew *plowshares*
[d] 21 Hebrew *pim*; that is, about 1/4 ounce (about 8 grams)   [e] 21 That is, about 1/8 ounce (about 4 grams)

than and his armor-bearer, "Come up to us and we'll teach you a lesson."

So Jonathan said to his armor-bearer, "Climb up after me; the LORD has given them into the hand of Israel."

[13]Jonathan climbed up, using his hands and feet, with his armor-bearer right behind him. The Philistines fell before Jonathan, and his armor-bearer followed and killed behind him. [14]In that first attack Jonathan and his armor-bearer killed some twenty men in an area of about half an acre.[a]

ISRAEL ROUTS THE PHILISTINES

[15]Then panic struck the whole army—those in the camp and field, and those in the outposts and raiding parties—and the ground shook. It was a panic sent by God.[b]

[16]Saul's lookouts at Gibeah in Benjamin saw the army melting away in all directions. [17]Then Saul said to the men who were with him, "Muster the forces and see who has left us." When they did, it was Jonathan and his armor-bearer who were not there.

[18]Saul said to Ahijah, "Bring the ark of God." (At that time it was with the Israelites.)[c] [19]While Saul was talking to the priest, the tumult in the Philistine camp increased more and more. So Saul said to the priest, "Withdraw your hand."

[20]Then Saul and all his men assembled and went to the battle. They found the Philistines in total confusion, striking each other with their swords. [21]Those Hebrews who had previously been with the Philistines and had gone up with them to their camp went over to the Israelites who were with Saul and Jonathan. [22]When all the Israelites who had hidden in the hill country of Ephraim heard that the Philistines were on the run, they joined the battle in hot pursuit. [23]So the LORD rescued Israel that day, and the battle moved on beyond Beth Aven.

JONATHAN EATS HONEY

[24]Now the men of Israel were in distress that day, because Saul had bound the people under an oath, saying, "Cursed be any man who eats food before evening comes, before I have avenged myself on my enemies!" So none of the troops tasted food.

[25]The entire army[d] entered the woods, and there was honey on the ground. [26]When they went into the woods, they saw the honey oozing out, yet no one put his hand to his mouth, because they feared the oath. [27]But Jonathan had not heard that his father had bound the people with the oath, so he reached out the end of the staff that was in his hand and dipped it into the honeycomb. He raised his hand to his mouth, and his eyes brightened.[e] [28]Then one of the soldiers told him, "Your father bound the army under a strict oath, saying, 'Cursed be any man who eats food today!' That is why the men are faint."

[29]Jonathan said, "My father has made trouble for the country. See how my eyes brightened[f] when I tasted a little of this honey. [30]How much better it would have been if the men had eaten today some of the plunder they took from their enemies. Would not the slaughter of the Philistines have been even greater?"

[31]That day, after the Israelites had struck down the Philistines from Micmash to Aijalon, they were exhausted. [32]They pounced on the plunder and, taking sheep, cattle and calves, they butchered them on the ground and ate them, together with the blood. [33]Then someone said to Saul, "Look, the men are sinning against the LORD by eating meat that has blood in it."

"You have broken faith," he said. "Roll a large stone over here at once." [34]Then he said, "Go out among the men and tell them, 'Each of you bring me your cattle and sheep, and slaughter them here and eat them. Do not sin against the LORD by eating meat with blood still in it.'"

NOW OR NEVER
1SA 14:6

There's no such thing as a "fair fight" when God is involved. He has no competition. Nothing can seriously challenge him. That's why whenever you face trouble, your first call should be to the undisputed champion of the universe.

---

[a] 14 Hebrew half a yoke; a "yoke" was the land plowed by a yoke of oxen in one day.   [b] 15 Or a terrible panic   [c] 18 Hebrew; Septuagint "Bring the ephod." (At that time he wore the ephod before the Israelites.)   [d] 25 Or Now all the people of the land   [e] 27 Or his strength was renewed   [f] 29 Or my strength was renewed

So everyone brought his ox that night and slaughtered it there. ³⁵Then Saul built an altar to the LORD; it was the first time he had done this.

³⁶Saul said, "Let us go down after the Philistines by night and plunder them till dawn, and let us not leave one of them alive."

"Do whatever seems best to you," they replied.

But the priest said, "Let us inquire of God here."

³⁷So Saul asked God, "Shall I go down after the Philistines? Will you give them into Israel's hand?" But God did not answer him that day.

³⁸Saul therefore said, "Come here, all you who are leaders of the army, and let us find out what sin has been committed today. ³⁹As surely as the LORD who rescues Israel lives, even if it lies with my son Jonathan, he must die." But not one of the men said a word.

⁴⁰Saul then said to all the Israelites, "You stand over there; I and Jonathan my son will stand over here."

"Do what seems best to you," the men replied.

⁴¹Then Saul prayed to the LORD, the God of Israel, "Give me the right answer."ᵃ And Jonathan and Saul were taken by lot, and the men were cleared. ⁴²Saul said, "Cast the lot between me and Jonathan my son." And Jonathan was taken.

⁴³Then Saul said to Jonathan, "Tell me what you have done."

So Jonathan told him, "I merely tasted a little honey with the end of my staff. And now must I die?"

⁴⁴Saul said, "May God deal with me, be it ever so severely, if you do not die, Jonathan."

⁴⁵But the men said to Saul, "Should Jonathan die—he who has brought about this great deliverance in Israel? Never! As surely as the LORD lives, not a hair of his head will fall to the ground, for he did this today with God's help." So the men rescued Jonathan, and he was not put to death.

⁴⁶Then Saul stopped pursuing the Philistines, and they withdrew to their own land.

⁴⁷After Saul had assumed rule over Israel, he fought against their enemies on every side: Moab, the Ammonites, Edom, the kingsᵇ of Zobah, and the Philistines. Wherever he turned, he inflicted punishment on them.ᶜ ⁴⁸He fought valiantly and defeated the Amalekites, delivering Israel from the hands of those who had plundered them.

SAUL'S FAMILY

⁴⁹Saul's sons were Jonathan, Ishvi and Malki-Shua. The name of his older daughter was Merab, and that of the younger was Michal. ⁵⁰His wife's name was Ahinoam daughter of Ahimaaz. The name of the commander of Saul's army was Abner son of Ner, and Ner was Saul's uncle. ⁵¹Saul's father Kish and Abner's father Ner were sons of Abiel.

⁵²All the days of Saul there was bitter war with the Philistines, and whenever Saul saw a mighty or brave man, he took him into his service.

THE LORD REJECTS SAUL AS KING

15 Samuel said to Saul, "I am the one the LORD sent to anoint you king over his people Israel; so listen now to the message from the LORD. ²This is what the LORD Almighty says: 'I will punish the Amalekites for what they did to Israel when they waylaid them as they came up from Egypt. ³Now go, attack the Amalekites and totally destroyᵈ everything that belongs to them. Do not spare them; put to death men and women, children and infants, cattle and sheep, camels and donkeys.' "

⁴So Saul summoned the men and mustered them at Telaim—two hundred thousand foot soldiers and ten thousand men from Judah. ⁵Saul went to the city of Amalek and set an ambush in the ravine. ⁶Then he said to the Kenites, "Go away, leave the Amalekites so that I do not destroy you along with

---

NOW OR NEVER
1SA 14:35-36

You've got a choice: You can either go to God after everything else has failed, or you can save yourself some frustration and embarrassment by going to him first.

ᵃ *41* Hebrew; Septuagint *"Why have you not answered your servant today? If the fault is in me or my son Jonathan, respond with Urim, but if the men of Israel are at fault, respond with Thummim."*   ᵇ *47* Masoretic Text; Dead Sea Scrolls and Septuagint *king*
ᶜ *47* Hebrew; Septuagint *he was victorious*   ᵈ *3* The Hebrew term refers to the irrevocable giving over of things or persons to the LORD, often by totally destroying them; also in verses 8, 9, 15, 18, 20 and 21.

them; for you showed kindness to all the Israelites when they came up out of Egypt." So the Kenites moved away from the Amalekites.

⁷Then Saul attacked the Amalekites all the way from Havilah to Shur, to the east of Egypt. ⁸He took Agag king of the Amalekites alive, and all his people he totally destroyed with the sword. ⁹But Saul and the army spared Agag and the best of the sheep and cattle, the fat calvesᵃ and lambs—everything that was good. These they were unwilling to destroy completely, but everything that was despised and weak they totally destroyed.

¹⁰Then the word of the LORD came to Samuel: ¹¹"I am grieved that I have made Saul king, because he has turned away from me and has not carried out my instructions." Samuel was troubled, and he cried out to the LORD all that night.

¹²Early in the morning Samuel got up and went to meet Saul, but he was told, "Saul has gone to Carmel. There he has set up a monument in his own honor and has turned and gone on down to Gilgal."

¹³When Samuel reached him, Saul said, "The LORD bless you! I have carried out the LORD's instructions."

¹⁴But Samuel said, "What then is this bleating of sheep in my ears? What is this lowing of cattle that I hear?"

¹⁵Saul answered, "The soldiers brought them from the Amalekites; they spared the best of the sheep and cattle to sacrifice to the LORD your God, but we totally destroyed the rest."

¹⁶"Stop!" Samuel said to Saul. "Let me tell you what the LORD said to me last night."

"Tell me," Saul replied.

¹⁷Samuel said, "Although you were once small in your own eyes, did you not become the head of the tribes of Israel? The LORD anointed you king over Israel. ¹⁸And he sent you on a mission, saying, 'Go and completely destroy those wicked people, the Amalekites; make war on them until you have wiped them out.' ¹⁹Why did you not obey the LORD? Why did you pounce on the plunder and do evil in the eyes of the LORD?"

²⁰"But I did obey the LORD," Saul said. "I went on the mission the LORD assigned me. I completely destroyed the Amalekites and brought back Agag their king. ²¹The soldiers took sheep and cattle from the plunder, the best of what was devoted to God, in order to sacrifice them to the LORD your God at Gilgal."

²²But Samuel replied:

"Does the LORD delight in burnt
offerings and sacrifices
as much as in obeying the voice of
the LORD?
To obey is better than sacrifice,
and to heed is better than the fat of rams.
²³For rebellion is like the sin of divination,
and arrogance like the evil of idolatry.
Because you have rejected the word of the LORD,
he has rejected you as king."

²⁴Then Saul said to Samuel, "I have sinned. I violated the LORD's command and your instructions. I was afraid of the people and so I gave in to them. ²⁵Now I beg you, forgive my sin and come back with me, so that I may worship the LORD."

²⁶But Samuel said to him, "I will not go back with you. You have rejected the word of the LORD, and the LORD has rejected you as king over Israel!"

Showing True Obedience

Obeying God is different than obeying human authority figures such as parents, teachers, coaches and bosses. As far as most people are concerned, the end result is what matters. As long as you do what you're supposed to do, they're satisfied. If on your own time you want to complain, they're probably not going to find out, much less care. That's not the way it works with God. He cares just as much about your attitude as he does about the end result. You can't fake true obedience to God; he knows what you're thinking and feeling 24/7. If that thought scares you, ask God to change your attitude and teach you how to become obedient from the inside out.

ᵃ 9 Or the grown bulls; the meaning of the Hebrew for this phrase is uncertain.

27As Samuel turned to leave, Saul caught hold of the hem of his robe, and it tore. 28Samuel said to him, "The LORD has torn the kingdom of Israel from you today and has given it to one of your neighbors—to one better than you. 29He who is the Glory of Israel does not lie or change his mind; for he is not a man, that he should change his mind."

30Saul replied, "I have sinned. But please honor me before the elders of my people and before Israel; come back with me, so that I may worship the LORD your God." 31So Samuel went back with Saul, and Saul worshiped the LORD.

32Then Samuel said, "Bring me Agag king of the Amalekites."

Agag came to him confidently,a thinking, "Surely the bitterness of death is past."

33But Samuel said,

> "As your sword has made women childless,
> so will your mother be childless among women."

And Samuel put Agag to death before the LORD at Gilgal.

34Then Samuel left for Ramah, but Saul went up to his home in Gibeah of Saul. 35Until the day Samuel died, he did not go to see Saul again, though Samuel mourned for him. And the LORD was grieved that he had made Saul king over Israel.

SAMUEL ANOINTS DAVID

16 The LORD said to Samuel, "How long will you mourn for Saul, since I have rejected him as king over Israel? Fill your horn with oil and be on your way; I am sending you to Jesse of Bethlehem. I have chosen one of his sons to be king."

2But Samuel said, "How can I go? Saul will hear about it and kill me."

The LORD said, "Take a heifer with you and say, 'I have come to sacrifice to the LORD.' 3Invite Jesse to the sacrifice, and I will show you what to do. You are to anoint for me the one I indicate."

4Samuel did what the LORD said. When he arrived at Bethlehem, the elders of the town trembled when they met him. They asked, "Do you come in peace?"

5Samuel replied, "Yes, in peace; I have come to sacrifice to the LORD. Consecrate yourselves and come to the sacrifice with me." Then he consecrated Jesse and his sons and invited them to the sacrifice.

6When they arrived, Samuel saw Eliab and thought, "Surely the LORD's anointed stands here before the LORD."

7But the LORD said to Samuel, "Do not consider his appearance or his height, for I have rejected him. The LORD does not look at the things man looks at. Man looks at the outward appearance, but the LORD looks at the heart."

8Then Jesse called Abinadab and had him pass in front of Samuel. But Samuel said, "The LORD has not chosen this one either." 9Jesse then had Shammah pass by, but Samuel said, "Nor has the LORD chosen this one." 10Jesse had seven of his sons pass before Samuel, but Samuel said to him, "The LORD has not chosen these." 11So he asked Jesse, "Are these all the sons you have?"

"There is still the youngest," Jesse answered, "but he is tending the sheep."

Samuel said, "Send for him; we will not sit downb until he arrives."

12So he sent and had him brought in. He was ruddy, with a fine appearance and handsome features. Then the LORD said, "Rise and anoint him; he is the one."

Building Spiritual Strength

How much time do you spend honing your body, building your muscle mass and increasing your physical strength? How does that compare with the time you spend honing your relationship with God, increasing your Bible knowledge and building your spiritual strength? God isn't interested primarily in how much you can squat or bench-press; he cares about how well you resist temptation, how strong your faith remains during tough times and how many people you can introduce to him.

---

a 32 Or him trembling, yet   b 11 Some Septuagint manuscripts; Hebrew not gather around

¹³So Samuel took the horn of oil and anointed him in the presence of his brothers, and from that day on the Spirit of the LORD came upon David in power. Samuel then went to Ramah.

DAVID IN SAUL'S SERVICE

¹⁴Now the Spirit of the LORD had departed from Saul, and an evilª spirit from the LORD tormented him.

¹⁵Saul's attendants said to him, "See, an evil spirit from God is tormenting you. ¹⁶Let our lord command his servants here to search for someone who can play the harp. He will play when the evil spirit from God comes upon you, and you will feel better."

¹⁷So Saul said to his attendants, "Find someone who plays well and bring him to me."

¹⁸One of the servants answered, "I have seen a son of Jesse of Bethlehem who knows how to play the harp. He is a brave man and a warrior. He speaks well and is a fine-looking man. And the LORD is with him."

¹⁹Then Saul sent messengers to Jesse and said, "Send me your son David, who is with the sheep." ²⁰So Jesse took a donkey loaded with bread, a skin of wine and a young goat and sent them with his son David to Saul.

²¹David came to Saul and entered his service. Saul liked him very much, and David became one of his armor-bearers. ²²Then Saul sent word to Jesse, saying, "Allow David to remain in my service, for I am pleased with him."

²³Whenever the spirit from God came upon Saul, David would take his harp and play. Then relief would come to Saul; he would feel better, and the evil spirit would leave him.

DAVID AND GOLIATH

17 Now the Philistines gathered their forces for war and assembled at Socoh in Judah. They pitched camp at Ephes Dammim, between Socoh and Azekah. ²Saul and the Israelites assembled and camped in the Valley of Elah and drew up their battle line to meet the Philistines. ³The Philistines occupied one hill and the Israelites another, with the valley between them.

⁴A champion named Goliath, who was from Gath, came out of the Philistine camp. He was over nine feetᵇ tall. ⁵He had a bronze helmet on his head and wore a coat of scale armor of bronze weighing five thousand shekelsᶜ; ⁶on his legs he wore bronze greaves, and a bronze javelin was slung on his back. ⁷His spear shaft was like a weaver's rod, and its iron point weighed six hundred shekels.ᵈ His shield bearer went ahead of him.

⁸Goliath stood and shouted to the ranks of Israel, "Why do you come out and line up for battle? Am I not a Philistine, and are you not the servants of Saul? Choose a man and have him come down to me. ⁹If he is able to fight and kill me, we will become your subjects; but if I overcome him and kill him, you will become our subjects and serve us." ¹⁰Then the Philistine said, "This day I defy the ranks of Israel! Give me a man and let us fight each other." ¹¹On hearing the Philistine's words, Saul and all the Israelites were dismayed and terrified.

¹²Now David was the son of an Ephrathite named Jesse, who was from Bethlehem in Judah. Jesse had eight sons, and in Saul's time he was old and well advanced in years. ¹³Jesse's three oldest sons had followed Saul to the war: The firstborn was Eliab; the second, Abinadab; and the third, Shammah. ¹⁴David was the youngest. The three oldest followed Saul, ¹⁵but David went back and forth from Saul to tend his father's sheep at Bethlehem.

¹⁶For forty days the Philistine came forward every morning and evening and took his stand.

¹⁷Now Jesse said to his son David, "Take this ephahᵉ of roasted grain and these ten loaves of bread

---

1SA 16:7

challenge notes

To: my_son

heavenly_father: the next time someone tries to plant doubts in your mind about your importance to me, just remember what I did for david. I took a boy who knew little more than how to take care of sheep and helped him become one of the greatest kings in all of history. imagine what I can do for you!

ª *14* Or *injurious*; also in verses 15, 16 and 23   ᵇ *4* Hebrew *was six cubits and a span* (about 3 meters)   ᶜ *5* That is, about 125 pounds (about 57 kilograms)   ᵈ *7* That is, about 15 pounds (about 7 kilograms)   ᵉ *17* That is, probably about 3/5 bushel (about 22 liters)

Ignoring Criticism

If you can find someone who knows more than God knows, has better credentials than God's, has done more for you than God has done, cares for you more than God cares or has a better plan for your life than God does, then sure—you should pay attention when that person criticizes you for living a godly life or for trying to do God's will. Otherwise, forget about the criticism and focus on pleasing the one whose ideas and opinions matter the most.

for your brothers and hurry to their camp. [18] Take along these ten cheeses to the commander of their unit.[a] See how your brothers are and bring back some assurance[b] from them. [19] They are with Saul and all the men of Israel in the Valley of Elah, fighting against the Philistines."

[20] Early in the morning David left the flock with a shepherd, loaded up and set out, as Jesse had directed. He reached the camp as the army was going out to its battle positions, shouting the war cry. [21] Israel and the Philistines were drawing up their lines facing each other. [22] David left his things with the keeper of supplies, ran to the battle lines and greeted his brothers. [23] As he was talking with them, Goliath, the Philistine champion from Gath, stepped out from his lines and shouted his usual defiance, and David heard it. [24] When the Israelites saw the man, they all ran from him in great fear.

[25] Now the Israelites had been saying, "Do you see how this man keeps coming out? He comes out to defy Israel. The king will give great wealth to the man who kills him. He will also give him his daughter in marriage and will exempt his father's family from taxes in Israel."

[26] David asked the men standing near him, "What will be done for the man who kills this Philistine and removes this disgrace from Israel? Who is this uncircumcised Philistine that he should defy the armies of the living God?"

[27] They repeated to him what they had been saying and told him, "This is what will be done for the man who kills him."

[28] When Eliab, David's oldest brother, heard him speaking with the men, he burned with anger at him and asked, "Why have you come down here? And with whom did you leave those few sheep in the desert? I know how conceited you are and how wicked your heart is; you came down only to watch the battle."

[29] "Now what have I done?" said David. "Can't I even speak?" [30] He then turned away to someone else and brought up the same matter, and the men answered him as before. [31] What David said was overheard and reported to Saul, and Saul sent for him.

[32] David said to Saul, "Let no one lose heart on account of this Philistine; your servant will go and fight him."

[33] Saul replied, "You are not able to go out against this Philistine and fight him; you are only a boy, and he has been a fighting man from his youth."

[34] But David said to Saul, "Your servant has been keeping his father's sheep. When a lion or a bear came and carried off a sheep from the flock, [35] I went after it, struck it and rescued the sheep from its mouth. When it turned on me, I seized it by its hair, struck it and killed it. [36] Your servant has killed both the lion and the bear; this uncircumcised Philistine will be like one of them, because he has defied the armies of the living God. [37] The LORD who delivered me from the paw of the lion and the paw of the bear will deliver me from the hand of this Philistine."

Saul said to David, "Go, and the LORD be with you."

[38] Then Saul dressed David in his own tunic. He put a coat of armor on him and a bronze helmet on

NOW OR NEVER
1SA 17:26

What would you do if you heard someone mocking God? Would you be willing to stick your neck out for his name and reputation?

---

[a] 18 Hebrew *thousand*   [b] 18 Or *some token*; or *some pledge of spoils*

his head. 39David fastened on his sword over the tunic and tried walking around, because he was not used to them.

"I cannot go in these," he said to Saul, "because I am not used to them." So he took them off. 40Then he took his staff in his hand, chose five smooth stones from the stream, put them in the pouch of his shepherd's bag and, with his sling in his hand, approached the Philistine.

41Meanwhile, the Philistine, with his shield bearer in front of him, kept coming closer to David. 42He looked David over and saw that he was only a boy, ruddy and handsome, and he despised him. 43He said to David, "Am I a dog, that you come at me with sticks?" And the Philistine cursed David by his gods. 44"Come here," he said, "and I'll give your flesh to the birds of the air and the beasts of the field!"

1SA 17:28-32

challengenotes

To: my_son

heavenly_father: if you receive criticism for living by my word and doing what I tell you to do, you'll know you're on the right track. the more criticism you get, the more it should motivate you to do the right thing.

45David said to the Philistine, "You come against me with sword and spear and javelin, but I come against you in the name of the LORD Almighty, the God of the armies of Israel, whom you have defied. 46This day the LORD will hand you over to me, and I'll strike you down and cut off your head. Today I will give the carcasses of the Philistine army to the birds of the air and the beasts of the earth, and the whole world will know that there is a God in Israel. 47All those gathered here will know that it is not by sword or spear that the LORD saves; for the battle is the LORD's, and he will give all of you into our hands."

48As the Philistine moved closer to attack him, David ran quickly toward the battle line to meet him. 49Reaching into his bag and taking out a stone, he slung it and struck the Philistine on the forehead. The stone sank into his forehead, and he fell facedown on the ground.

50So David triumphed over the Philistine with a sling and a stone; without a sword in his hand he struck down the Philistine and killed him.

51David ran and stood over him. He took hold of the Philistine's sword and drew it from the scabbard. After he killed him, he cut off his head with the sword.

When the Philistines saw that their hero was dead, they turned and ran. 52Then the men of Israel and Judah surged forward with a shout and pursued the Philistines to the entrance of Gath[a] and to the gates of Ekron. Their dead were strewn along the Shaaraim road to Gath and Ekron. 53When the Israelites returned from chasing the Philistines, they plundered their camp. 54David took the Philistine's head and brought it to Jerusalem, and he put the Philistine's weapons in his own tent.

55As Saul watched David going out to meet the Philistine, he said to Abner, commander of the army, "Abner, whose son is that young man?"

Abner replied, "As surely as you live, O king, I don't know."

56The king said, "Find out whose son this young man is."

57As soon as David returned from killing the Philistine, Abner took him and brought him before Saul, with David still holding the Philistine's head.

58"Whose son are you, young man?" Saul asked him.

David said, "I am the son of your servant Jesse of Bethlehem."

SAUL'S JEALOUSY OF DAVID

18 After David had finished talking with Saul, Jonathan became one in spirit with David, and he loved him as himself. 2From that day Saul kept David with him and did not let him return to his father's house. 3And Jonathan made a covenant with David because he loved him as himself. 4Jonathan took off the robe he was wearing and gave it to David, along with his tunic, and even his sword, his bow and his belt.

5Whatever Saul sent him to do, David did it so successfully[b] that Saul gave him a high rank in the army. This pleased all the people, and Saul's officers as well.

6When the men were returning home after David had killed the Philistine, the women came out from all the towns of Israel to meet King Saul with singing and dancing, with joyful songs and with tambourines and lutes. 7As they danced, they sang:

---

[a] 52 Some Septuagint manuscripts; Hebrew *a valley*   [b] 5 Or *wisely*

"Saul has slain his thousands,
and David his tens of thousands."

»» live the adventure »» 1Sa 18:1-3

Committing to Your Friendships

A true friendship isn't something that happens by accident. It's something that has to be nurtured continuously. The fact that you get along with or like hanging out with someone doesn't automatically make him or her a true friend. In order for a real friendship to develop, you've got to have *commitment*, the willingness to stick with that person no matter what. That means you don't walk away from a trusted friend to make another buddy of yours happy, because your friend said something that irritated you, or because the two of you don't have all the same interests.

[8] Saul was very angry; this refrain galled him. "They have credited David with tens of thousands," he thought, "but me with only thousands. What more can he get but the kingdom?" [9] And from that time on Saul kept a jealous eye on David.

[10] The next day an evil[a] spirit from God came forcefully upon Saul. He was prophesying in his house, while David was playing the harp, as he usually did. Saul had a spear in his hand [11] and he hurled it, saying to himself, "I'll pin David to the wall." But David eluded him twice.

[12] Saul was afraid of David, because the LORD was with David but had left Saul. [13] So he sent David away from him and gave him command over a thousand men, and David led the troops in their campaigns. [14] In everything he did he had great success,[b] because the LORD was with him. [15] When Saul saw how successful[c] he was, he was afraid of him. [16] But all Israel and Judah loved David, because he led them in their campaigns.

[17] Saul said to David, "Here is my older daughter Merab. I will give her to you in marriage; only serve me bravely and fight the battles of the LORD." For Saul said to himself, "I will not raise a hand against him. Let the Philistines do that!"

[18] But David said to Saul, "Who am I, and what is my family or my father's clan in Israel, that I should become the king's son-in-law?" [19] So[d] when the time came for Merab, Saul's daughter, to be given to David, she was given in marriage to Adriel of Meholah.

[20] Now Saul's daughter Michal was in love with David, and when they told Saul about it, he was pleased. [21] "I will give her to him," he thought, "so that she may be a snare to him and so that the hand of the Philistines may be against him." So Saul said to David, "Now you have a second opportunity to become my son-in-law."

[22] Then Saul ordered his attendants: "Speak to David privately and say, 'Look, the king is pleased with you, and his attendants all like you; now become his son-in-law.'"

[23] They repeated these words to David. But David said, "Do you think it is a small matter to become the king's son-in-law? I'm only a poor man and little known."

[24] When Saul's servants told him what David had said, [25] Saul replied, "Say to David, 'The king wants no other price for the bride than a hundred Philistine foreskins, to take revenge on his enemies.'" Saul's plan was to have David fall by the hands of the Philistines.

[26] When the attendants told David these things, he was pleased to become the king's son-in-law. So before the allotted time elapsed, [27] David and his men went out and killed two hundred Philistines. He brought their foreskins and presented the full number to the king so that he might become the king's son-in-law. Then Saul gave him his daughter Michal in marriage.

[28] When Saul realized that the LORD was with David and that his daughter Michal loved David, [29] Saul became still more afraid of him, and he remained his enemy the rest of his days.

NOW OR NEVER
1SA 18:8

Jealousy is like a warning light on the dashboard of a car. It tells us that something is wrong in our spiritual system. Jealousy tells us that we're more concerned about our own wants and priorities than with God's desires and plans.

---

[a] 10 Or *injurious*   [b] 14 Or *he was very wise*   [c] 15 Or *wise*   [d] 19 Or *However,*

[30]The Philistine commanders continued to go out to battle, and as often as they did, David met with more success[a] than the rest of Saul's officers, and his name became well known.

SAUL TRIES TO KILL DAVID

19

Saul told his son Jonathan and all the attendants to kill David. But Jonathan was very fond of David [2]and warned him, "My father Saul is looking for a chance to kill you. Be on your guard tomorrow morning; go into hiding and stay there. [3]I will go out and stand with my father in the field where you are. I'll speak to him about you and will tell you what I find out."

now or never

1 SA 18:14

Jealousy is a double-edged sword. On the one hand, you can expect resentment from some when God blesses you. Jesus got that kind of treatment all the time here on earth. On the other hand, if you let those who are jealous get the best of you, then the enemy has won.

[4]Jonathan spoke well of David to Saul his father and said to him, "Let not the king do wrong to his servant David; he has not wronged you, and what he has done has benefited you greatly. [5]He took his life in his hands when he killed the Philistine. The Lord won a great victory for all Israel, and you saw it and were glad. Why then would you do wrong to an innocent man like David by killing him for no reason?"

[6]Saul listened to Jonathan and took this oath: "As surely as the Lord lives, David will not be put to death."

[7]So Jonathan called David and told him the whole conversation. He brought him to Saul, and David was with Saul as before.

[8]Once more war broke out, and David went out and fought the Philistines. He struck them with such force that they fled before him.

[9]But an evil[b] spirit from the Lord came upon Saul as he was sitting in his house with his spear in his hand. While David was playing the harp, [10]Saul tried to pin him to the wall with his spear, but David eluded him as Saul drove the spear into the wall. That night David made good his escape.

[11]Saul sent men to David's house to watch it and to kill him in the morning. But Michal, David's wife, warned him, "If you don't run for your life tonight, tomorrow you'll be killed." [12]So Michal let David down through a window, and he fled and escaped. [13]Then Michal took an idol[c] and laid it on the bed, covering it with a garment and putting some goats' hair at the head.

[14]When Saul sent the men to capture David, Michal said, "He is ill."

[15]Then Saul sent the men back to see David and told them, "Bring him up to me in his bed so that I may kill him." [16]But when the men entered, there was the idol in the bed, and at the head was some goats' hair.

[17]Saul said to Michal, "Why did you deceive me like this and send my enemy away so that he escaped?"

Michal told him, "He said to me, 'Let me get away. Why should I kill you?' "

[18]When David had fled and made his escape, he went to Samuel at Ramah and told him all that Saul had done to him. Then he and Samuel went to Naioth and stayed there. [19]Word came to Saul: "David is in Naioth at Ramah"; [20]so he sent men to capture him. But when they saw a group of prophets prophesying, with Samuel standing there as their leader, the Spirit of God came upon Saul's men and they also prophesied. [21]Saul was told about it, and he sent more men, and they prophesied too. Saul sent men a third time, and they also prophesied. [22]Finally, he himself left for Ramah and went to the great cistern at Secu. And he asked, "Where are Samuel and David?"

"Over in Naioth at Ramah," they said.

[23]So Saul went to Naioth at Ramah. But the Spirit of God came even upon him, and he walked along prophesying until he came to Naioth. [24]He stripped off his robes and also prophesied in Samuel's presence. He lay that way all that day and night. This is why people say, "Is Saul also among the prophets?"

DAVID AND JONATHAN

20

Then David fled from Naioth at Ramah and went to Jonathan and asked, "What have I done? What is my crime? How have I wronged your father, that he is trying to take my life?"

---

[a] 30 Or *David acted more wisely*   [b] 9 Or *injurious*   [c] 13 Hebrew *teraphim*; also in verse 16

²"Never!" Jonathan replied. "You are not going to die! Look, my father doesn't do anything, great or small, without confiding in me. Why would he hide this from me? It's not so!"

³But David took an oath and said, "Your father knows very well that I have found favor in your eyes, and he has said to himself, 'Jonathan must not know this or he will be grieved.' Yet as surely as the Lord lives and as you live, there is only a step between me and death."

⁴Jonathan said to David, "Whatever you want me to do, I'll do for you."

⁵So David said, "Look, tomorrow is the New Moon festival, and I am supposed to dine with the king; but let me go and hide in the field until the evening of the day after tomorrow. ⁶If your father misses me at all, tell him, 'David earnestly asked my permission to hurry to Bethlehem, his hometown, because an annual sacrifice is being made there for his whole clan.' ⁷If he says, 'Very well,' then your servant is safe. But if he loses his temper, you can be sure that he is determined to harm me. ⁸As for you, show kindness to your servant, for you have brought him into a covenant with you before the Lord. If I am guilty, then kill me yourself! Why hand me over to your father?"

⁹"Never!" Jonathan said. "If I had the least inkling that my father was determined to harm you, wouldn't I tell you?"

¹⁰David asked, "Who will tell me if your father answers you harshly?"

¹¹"Come," Jonathan said, "let's go out into the field." So they went there together.

¹²Then Jonathan said to David: "By the Lord, the God of Israel, I will surely sound out my father by this time the day after tomorrow! If he is favorably disposed toward you, will I not send you word and let you know? ¹³But if my father is inclined to harm you, may the Lord deal with me, be it ever so severely, if I do not let you know and send you away safely. May the Lord be with you as he has been with my father. ¹⁴But show me unfailing kindness like that of the Lord as long as I live, so that I may not be killed, ¹⁵and do not ever cut off your kindness from my family—not even when the Lord has cut off every one of David's enemies from the face of the earth."

¹⁶So Jonathan made a covenant with the house of David, saying, "May the Lord call David's enemies to account." ¹⁷And Jonathan had David reaffirm his oath out of love for him, because he loved him as he loved himself.

¹⁸Then Jonathan said to David: "Tomorrow is the New Moon festival. You will be missed, because your seat will be empty. ¹⁹The day after tomorrow, toward evening, go to the place where you hid when this trouble began, and wait by the stone Ezel. ²⁰I will shoot three arrows to the side of it, as though I were shooting at a target. ²¹Then I will send a boy and say, 'Go, find the arrows.' If I say to him, 'Look, the arrows are on this side of you; bring them here,' then come, because, as surely as the Lord lives, you are safe; there is no danger. ²²But if I say to the boy, 'Look, the arrows are beyond you,' then you must go, because the Lord has sent you away. ²³And about the matter you and I discussed—remember, the Lord is witness between you and me forever."

²⁴So David hid in the field, and when the New Moon festival came, the king sat down to eat. ²⁵He sat in his customary place by the wall, opposite Jonathan,ᵃ and Abner sat next to Saul, but David's place was empty. ²⁶Saul said nothing that day, for he thought, "Something must have happened to David to make him ceremonially unclean—surely he is unclean." ²⁷But the next day, the second day of the month, David's place was empty again. Then Saul said to his son Jonathan, "Why hasn't the son of Jesse come to the meal, either yesterday or today?"

²⁸Jonathan answered, "David earnestly asked me for permission to go to Bethlehem. ²⁹He said, 'Let me go, because our family is observing a sacrifice in the town and my brother has ordered me to be there. If I have found favor in your eyes, let me get away to see my brothers.' That is why he has not come to the king's table."

³⁰Saul's anger flared up at Jonathan and he said to him, "You son of a perverse and rebellious woman! Don't I know that you have sided with the son of Jesse to your own shame and to the shame of the

NOW OR NEVER
1SA 20:17

What's the riskiest, most radical thing you've ever done for a friend? How far would you be willing to go to help a buddy of yours?

ᵃ 25 Septuagint; Hebrew *wall. Jonathan arose*

mother who bore you? ³¹As long as the son of Jesse lives on this earth, neither you nor your kingdom will be established. Now send and bring him to me, for he must die!"

³²"Why should he be put to death? What has he done?" Jonathan asked his father. ³³But Saul hurled his spear at him to kill him. Then Jonathan knew that his father intended to kill David.

³⁴Jonathan got up from the table in fierce anger; on that second day of the month he did not eat, because he was grieved at his father's shameful treatment of David.

³⁵In the morning Jonathan went out to the field for his meeting with David. He had a small boy with him, ³⁶and he said to the boy, "Run and find the arrows I shoot." As the boy ran, he shot an arrow beyond him. ³⁷When the boy came to the place where Jonathan's arrow had fallen, Jonathan called out after him, "Isn't the arrow beyond you?" ³⁸Then he shouted, "Hurry! Go quickly! Don't stop!" The boy picked up the arrow and returned to his master. ³⁹(The boy knew nothing of all this; only Jonathan and David knew.) ⁴⁰Then Jonathan gave his weapons to the boy and said, "Go, carry them back to town."

⁴¹After the boy had gone, David got up from the south side ⌊of the stone⌋ and bowed down before Jonathan three times, with his face to the ground. Then they kissed each other and wept together—but David wept the most.

⁴²Jonathan said to David, "Go in peace, for we have sworn friendship with each other in the name of the LORD, saying, 'The LORD is witness between you and me, and between your descendants and my descendants forever.' " Then David left, and Jonathan went back to the town.

DAVID AT NOB

21 David went to Nob, to Ahimelech the priest. Ahimelech trembled when he met him, and asked, "Why are you alone? Why is no one with you?"

²David answered Ahimelech the priest, "The king charged me with a certain matter and said to me, 'No one is to know anything about your mission and your instructions.' As for my men, I have told them to meet me at a certain place. ³Now then, what do you have on hand? Give me five loaves of bread, or whatever you can find."

⁴But the priest answered David, "I don't have any ordinary bread on hand; however, there is some consecrated bread here—provided the men have kept themselves from women."

⁵David replied, "Indeed women have been kept from us, as usual whenever[a] I set out. The men's things[b] are holy even on missions that are not holy. How much more so today!" ⁶So the priest gave him the consecrated bread, since there was no bread there except the bread of the Presence that had been removed from before the LORD and replaced by hot bread on the day it was taken away.

⁷Now one of Saul's servants was there that day, detained before the LORD; he was Doeg the Edomite, Saul's head shepherd.

⁸David asked Ahimelech, "Don't you have a spear or a sword here? I haven't brought my sword or any other weapon, because the king's business was urgent."

⁹The priest replied, "The sword of Goliath the Philistine, whom you killed in the Valley of Elah, is here; it is wrapped in a cloth behind the ephod. If you want it, take it; there is no sword here but that one."

David said, "There is none like it; give it to me."

DAVID AT GATH

¹⁰That day David fled from Saul and went to Achish king of Gath. ¹¹But the servants of Achish said to him, "Isn't this David, the king of the land? Isn't he the one they sing about in their dances:

> " 'Saul has slain his thousands,
> and David his tens of thousands'?"

¹²David took these words to heart and was very much afraid of Achish king of Gath. ¹³So he pretended to be insane in their presence; and while he was in their hands he acted like a madman, making marks on the doors of the gate and letting saliva run down his beard.

¹⁴Achish said to his servants, "Look at the man! He is insane! Why bring him to me? ¹⁵Am I so short of madmen that you have to bring this fellow here to carry on like this in front of me? Must this man come into my house?"

ᵃ 5 Or *from us in the past few days since*   ᵇ 5 Or *bodies*

battlelines

» It Shouldn't Be This Hard (Learning Disorder)

Q: Hey, Cory. I haven't seen you much around school this week. What's up? Have you been sick?

A: Ha, I wish. I'm not sick, just "special."

Q: Huh?

A: (Sarcastically) Oh, you haven't heard? I thought the whole world knew. Yeah, a bunch of experts got together and figured out that I can't cut it in the normal classes. So now my teachers have to give me all these embarrassing accommodations. I have to work with a specialist every week and take my tests in a separate, quiet room! I feel so stupid.

Q: Wow. I didn't know. I'm sorry.

A: Yeah, me too.

Q: Look, I know this has to be a blow and everything, but *everybody* has weaknesses.

A: Yeah, well they don't have my problem. I get As in worthless classes like art and music . . . and Ds in everything else. I watch my friends breeze through honors classes while I'm barely getting by in the easy classes. So my parents take me to some "professional" for a million tests. And now here we are.

Q: Well, at least now you know what the problem is, so you can start working on the solution, right?

A: Yeah, well, I didn't ask for this. The *solution* is for God to fix what he broke.

Q: You think this is God's fault—that he made a mistake?

A: Sometimes. I mean either God made a mistake, or else he made me an idiot on purpose. Personally, I'm not real happy with either option.

» Why Me?

If you have a learning disability, you probably wonder, "Why me?" The hard truth is, you may never get a good answer to that question—not in this life, anyway. However, there are several facts that are worth remembering:

- We live in a broken world that isn't at all what God originally planned it to be. Adam and Eve's sin negatively affected every part of our lives (see Genesis 3).

- In spite of all this, God loves us, delights in us and is constantly working for our good.

- Each of us has been given valuable skills and important tasks to accomplish.

- We have a fierce enemy who will do anything to knock us out of the fight.

If struggling with a learning disability makes you feel like a loser, remember this: Most learning disabilities have *nothing* to do with intelligence. They just reflect different styles of learning and different ways of focusing and of processing information. It's important to have real and accurate information about learning disabilities so you can develop an effective plan to succeed in school.

For more on dealing with a learning disability, go to www.RevolutionBible.com.

DAVID AT ADULLAM AND MIZPAH

22 David left Gath and escaped to the cave of Adullam. When his brothers and his father's household heard about it, they went down to him there. ²All those who were in distress or in debt or discontented gathered around him, and he became their leader. About four hundred men were with him.

³From there David went to Mizpah in Moab and said to the king of Moab, "Would you let my father and mother come and stay with you until I learn what God will do for me?" ⁴So he left them with the king of Moab, and they stayed with him as long as David was in the stronghold.

⁵But the prophet Gad said to David, "Do not stay in the stronghold. Go into the land of Judah." So David left and went to the forest of Hereth.

SAUL KILLS THE PRIESTS OF NOB

⁶Now Saul heard that David and his men had been discovered. And Saul, spear in hand, was seated under the tamarisk tree on the hill at Gibeah, with all his officials standing around him. ⁷Saul said to them, "Listen, men of Benjamin! Will the son of Jesse give all of you fields and vineyards? Will he make all of you commanders of thousands and commanders of hundreds? ⁸Is that why you have all conspired against me? No one tells me when my son makes a covenant with the son of Jesse. None of you is concerned about me or tells me that my son has incited my servant to lie in wait for me, as he does today."

⁹But Doeg the Edomite, who was standing with Saul's officials, said, "I saw the son of Jesse come to Ahimelech son of Ahitub at Nob. ¹⁰Ahimelech inquired of the LORD for him; he also gave him provisions and the sword of Goliath the Philistine."

¹¹Then the king sent for the priest Ahimelech son of Ahitub and his father's whole family, who were the priests at Nob, and they all came to the king. ¹²Saul said, "Listen now, son of Ahitub."

"Yes, my lord," he answered.

¹³Saul said to him, "Why have you conspired against me, you and the son of Jesse, giving him bread and a sword and inquiring of God for him, so that he has rebelled against me and lies in wait for me, as he does today?"

¹⁴Ahimelech answered the king, "Who of all your servants is as loyal as David, the king's son-in-law, captain of your bodyguard and highly respected in your household? ¹⁵Was that day the first time I inquired of God for him? Of course not! Let not the king accuse your servant or any of his father's family, for your servant knows nothing at all about this whole affair."

¹⁶But the king said, "You will surely die, Ahimelech, you and your father's whole family."

¹⁷Then the king ordered the guards at his side: "Turn and kill the priests of the LORD, because they too have sided with David. They knew he was fleeing, yet they did not tell me."

But the king's officials were not willing to raise a hand to strike the priests of the LORD.

¹⁸The king then ordered Doeg, "You turn and strike down the priests." So Doeg the Edomite turned and struck them down. That day he killed eighty-five men who wore the linen ephod. ¹⁹He also put to the sword Nob, the town of the priests, with its men and women, its children and infants, and its cattle, donkeys and sheep.

²⁰But Abiathar, a son of Ahimelech son of Ahitub, escaped and fled to join David. ²¹He told David that Saul had killed the priests of the LORD. ²²Then David said to Abiathar: "That day, when Doeg the Edomite was there, I knew he would be sure to tell Saul. I am responsible for the death of your father's whole family. ²³Stay with me; don't be afraid; the man who is seeking your life is seeking mine also. You will be safe with me."

DAVID SAVES KEILAH

23 When David was told, "Look, the Philistines are fighting against Keilah and are looting the threshing floors," ²he inquired of the LORD, saying, "Shall I go and attack these Philistines?"

The LORD answered him, "Go, attack the Philistines and save Keilah."

³But David's men said to him, "Here in Judah we are afraid. How much more, then, if we go to Keilah against the Philistine forces!"

⁴Once again David inquired of the LORD, and the LORD answered him, "Go down to Keilah, for I am going to give the Philistines into your hand." ⁵So David and his men went to Keilah, fought the Philis-

tines and carried off their livestock. He inflicted heavy losses on the Philistines and saved the people of Keilah. 6(Now Abiathar son of Ahimelech had brought the ephod down with him when he fled to David at Keilah.)

SAUL PURSUES DAVID

7Saul was told that David had gone to Keilah, and he said, "God has handed him over to me, for David has imprisoned himself by entering a town with gates and bars." 8And Saul called up all his forces for battle, to go down to Keilah to besiege David and his men.

9When David learned that Saul was plotting against him, he said to Abiathar the priest, "Bring the ephod." 10David said, "O LORD, God of Israel, your servant has heard definitely that Saul plans to come to Keilah and destroy the town on account of me. 11Will the citizens of Keilah surrender me to him? Will Saul come down, as your servant has heard? O LORD, God of Israel, tell your servant."

And the LORD said, "He will."

12Again David asked, "Will the citizens of Keilah surrender me and my men to Saul?"

And the LORD said, "They will."

13So David and his men, about six hundred in number, left Keilah and kept moving from place to place. When Saul was told that David had escaped from Keilah, he did not go there.

14David stayed in the desert strongholds and in the hills of the Desert of Ziph. Day after day Saul searched for him, but God did not give David into his hands.

15While David was at Horesh in the Desert of Ziph, he learned that Saul had come out to take his life. 16And Saul's son Jonathan went to David at Horesh and helped him find strength in God. 17"Don't be afraid," he said. "My father Saul will not lay a hand on you. You will be king over Israel, and I will be second to you. Even my father Saul knows this." 18The two of them made a covenant before the LORD. Then Jonathan went home, but David remained at Horesh.

19The Ziphites went up to Saul at Gibeah and said, "Is not David hiding among us in the strongholds at Horesh, on the hill of Hakilah, south of Jeshimon? 20Now, O king, come down whenever it pleases you to do so, and we will be responsible for handing him over to the king."

21Saul replied, "The LORD bless you for your concern for me. 22Go and make further preparation. Find out where David usually goes and who has seen him there. They tell me he is very crafty. 23Find out about all the hiding places he uses and come back to me with definite information.ᵃ Then I will go with you; if he is in the area, I will track him down among all the clans of Judah."

24So they set out and went to Ziph ahead of Saul. Now David and his men were in the Desert of Maon, in the Arabah south of Jeshimon. 25Saul and his men began the search, and when David was told about it, he went down to the rock and stayed in the Desert of Maon. When Saul heard this, he went into the Desert of Maon in pursuit of David.

26Saul was going along one side of the mountain, and David and his men were on the other side, hurrying to get away from Saul. As Saul and his forces were closing in on David and his men to capture them, 27a messenger came to Saul, saying, "Come quickly! The Philistines are raiding the land." 28Then Saul broke off his pursuit of David and went to meet the Philistines. That is why they call this place Sela Hammahlekoth.ᵇ 29And David went up from there and lived in the strongholds of En Gedi.

NOW OR NEVER
1SA 23:7

The fact that you have a golden opportunity staring you in the face doesn't mean it came from God. Satan can make wrong paths look inviting. The only way to know for sure whether an opportunity is right for you is to pray and seek God's guidance.

NOW OR NEVER
1SA 23:16

The best thing you can do for your friends is to help them draw closer to God. You do that not only by praying for them, but also by talking to them about the awesome things God has done—and can do—in their lives.

ᵃ 23 Or me at Nacon   ᵇ 28 Sela Hammahlekoth means rock of parting.

DAVID SPARES SAUL'S LIFE

24

After Saul returned from pursuing the Philistines, he was told, "David is in the Desert of En Gedi." [2]So Saul took three thousand chosen men from all Israel and set out to look for David and his men near the Crags of the Wild Goats.

[3]He came to the sheep pens along the way; a cave was there, and Saul went in to relieve himself. David and his men were far back in the cave. [4]The men said, "This is the day the LORD spoke of when he said[a] to you, 'I will give your enemy into your hands for you to deal with as you wish.' " Then David crept up unnoticed and cut off a corner of Saul's robe.

[5]Afterward, David was conscience-stricken for having cut off a corner of his robe. [6]He said to his men, "The LORD forbid that I should do such a thing to my master, the LORD's anointed, or lift my hand against him; for he is the anointed of the LORD." [7]With these words David rebuked his men and did not allow them to attack Saul. And Saul left the cave and went his way.

[8]Then David went out of the cave and called out to Saul, "My lord the king!" When Saul looked behind him, David bowed down and prostrated himself with his face to the ground. [9]He said to Saul, "Why do you listen when men say, 'David is bent on harming you'? [10]This day you have seen with your own eyes how the LORD delivered you into my hands in the cave. Some urged me to kill you, but I spared you; I said, 'I will not lift my hand against my master, because he is the LORD's anointed.' [11]See, my father, look at this piece of your robe in my hand! I cut off the corner of your robe but did not kill you. Now understand and recognize that I am not guilty of wrongdoing or rebellion. I have not wronged you, but you are hunting me down to take my life. [12]May the LORD judge between you and me. And may the LORD avenge the wrongs you have done to me, but my hand will not touch you. [13]As the old saying goes, 'From evildoers come evil deeds,' so my hand will not touch you.

[14]"Against whom has the king of Israel come out? Whom are you pursuing? A dead dog? A flea? [15]May the LORD be our judge and decide between us. May he consider my cause and uphold it; may he vindicate me by delivering me from your hand."

[16]When David finished saying this, Saul asked, "Is that your voice, David my son?" And he wept aloud. [17]"You are more righteous than I," he said. "You have treated me well, but I have treated you badly. [18]You have just now told me of the good you did to me; the LORD delivered me into your hands, but you did not kill me. [19]When a man finds his enemy, does he let him get away unharmed? May the LORD reward you well for the way you treated me today. [20]I know that you will surely be king and that the kingdom of Israel will be established in your hands. [21]Now swear to me by the LORD that you will not cut off my descendants or wipe out my name from my father's family."

[22]So David gave his oath to Saul. Then Saul returned home, but David and his men went up to the stronghold.

DAVID, NABAL AND ABIGAIL

25

Now Samuel died, and all Israel assembled and mourned for him; and they buried him at his home in Ramah.

Then David moved down into the Desert of Maon.[b] [2]A certain man in Maon, who had property there at Carmel, was very wealthy. He had a thousand goats and three thousand sheep, which he was shearing in Carmel. [3]His name was Nabal and his wife's name was Abigail. She was an intelligent and beautiful woman, but her husband, a Calebite, was surly and mean in his dealings.

[4]While David was in the desert, he heard that Nabal was shearing sheep. [5]So he sent ten young men and said to them, "Go up to Nabal at Carmel and greet him in my name. [6]Say to him: 'Long life to you! Good health to you and your household! And good health to all that is yours!

[7]" 'Now I hear that it is sheep-shearing time. When your shepherds were with us, we did not mistreat them, and the whole time they were at Carmel nothing of theirs was missing. [8]Ask your own servants and they will tell you. Therefore be favorable toward my young men, since we come at a festive time. Please give your servants and your son David whatever you can find for them.' "

[9]When David's men arrived, they gave Nabal this message in David's name. Then they waited.

[10]Nabal answered David's servants, "Who is this David? Who is this son of Jesse? Many servants are breaking away from their masters these days. [11]Why should I take my bread and water, and the meat I have slaughtered for my shearers, and give it to men coming from who knows where?"

[12]David's men turned around and went back. When they arrived, they reported every word. [13]David

---

[a] 4 Or *Today the LORD is saying*   [b] 1 Some Septuagint manuscripts; Hebrew *Paran*

said to his men, "Put on your swords!" So they put on their swords, and David put on his. About four hundred men went up with David, while two hundred stayed with the supplies.

Avoiding Selfishness

If your goal is to please yourself and satisfy your own desires as often as possible, you're going to miss out on a large chunk of God's will for your life. Personal sacrifice is a must for guys who are serious about being used by God to do great things. If you have the courage to step down off the throne of your life, God will show just how much of a difference you can make in the lives of other people.

14One of the servants told Nabal's wife Abigail: "David sent messengers from the desert to give our master his greetings, but he hurled insults at them. 15Yet these men were very good to us. They did not mistreat us, and the whole time we were out in the fields near them nothing was missing. 16Night and day they were a wall around us all the time we were herding our sheep near them. 17Now think it over and see what you can do, because disaster is hanging over our master and his whole household. He is such a wicked man that no one can talk to him."

18Abigail lost no time. She took two hundred loaves of bread, two skins of wine, five dressed sheep, five seahs a of roasted grain, a hundred cakes of raisins and two hundred cakes of pressed figs, and loaded them on donkeys. 19Then she told her servants, "Go on ahead; I'll follow you." But she did not tell her husband Nabal.

20As she came riding her donkey into a mountain ravine, there were David and his men descending toward her, and she met them. 21David had just said, "It's been useless—all my watching over this fellow's property in the desert so that nothing of his was missing. He has paid me back evil for good. 22May God deal with David, b be it ever so severely, if by morning I leave alive one male of all who belong to him!"

23When Abigail saw David, she quickly got off her donkey and bowed down before David with her face to the ground. 24She fell at his feet and said: "My lord, let the blame be on me alone. Please let your servant speak to you; hear what your servant has to say. 25May my lord pay no attention to that wicked man Nabal. He is just like his name—his name is Fool, and folly goes with him. But as for me, your servant, I did not see the men my master sent.

26"Now since the LORD has kept you, my master, from bloodshed and from avenging yourself with your own hands, as surely as the LORD lives and as you live, may your enemies and all who intend to harm my master be like Nabal. 27And let this gift, which your servant has brought to my master, be given to the men who follow you. 28Please forgive your servant's offense, for the LORD will certainly make a lasting dynasty for my master, because he fights the LORD's battles. Let no wrongdoing be found in you as long as you live. 29Even though someone is pursuing you to take your life, the life of my master will be bound securely in the bundle of the living by the LORD your God. But the lives of your enemies he will hurl away as from the pocket of a sling. 30When the LORD has done for my master every good thing he promised concerning him and has appointed him leader over Israel, 31my master will not have on his conscience the staggering burden of needless bloodshed or of having avenged himself. And when the LORD has brought my master success, remember your servant."

32David said to Abigail, "Praise be to the LORD, the God of Israel, who has sent you today to meet me. 33May you be blessed for your good judgment and for keeping me from bloodshed this day and from avenging myself with my own hands. 34Otherwise, as surely as the LORD, the God of Israel, lives, who has kept me from harming you, if you had not come quickly to meet me, not one male belonging to Nabal would have been left alive by daybreak."

35Then David accepted from her hand what she had brought him and said, "Go home in peace. I have heard your words and granted your request."

36When Abigail went to Nabal, he was in the house holding a banquet like that of a king. He was in high spirits and very drunk. So she told him nothing until daybreak. 37Then in the morning, when Nabal was sober, his wife told him all these things, and his heart failed him and he became like a stone. 38About ten days later, the LORD struck Nabal and he died.

---

a 18 That is, probably about a bushel (about 37 liters)   b 22 Some Septuagint manuscripts; Hebrew with David's enemies

³⁹When David heard that Nabal was dead, he said, "Praise be to the Lᴏʀᴅ, who has upheld my cause against Nabal for treating me with contempt. He has kept his servant from doing wrong and has brought Nabal's wrongdoing down on his own head."

Then David sent word to Abigail, asking her to become his wife. ⁴⁰His servants went to Carmel and said to Abigail, "David has sent us to you to take you to become his wife."

⁴¹She bowed down with her face to the ground and said, "Here is your maidservant, ready to serve you and wash the feet of my master's servants." ⁴²Abigail quickly got on a donkey and, attended by her five maids, went with David's messengers and became his wife. ⁴³David had also married Ahinoam of Jezreel, and they both were his wives. ⁴⁴But Saul had given his daughter Michal, David's wife, to Paltiel[a] son of Laish, who was from Gallim.

DAVID AGAIN SPARES SAUL'S LIFE

26 The Ziphites went to Saul at Gibeah and said, "Is not David hiding on the hill of Hakilah, which faces Jeshimon?"

²So Saul went down to the Desert of Ziph, with his three thousand chosen men of Israel, to search there for David. ³Saul made his camp beside the road on the hill of Hakilah facing Jeshimon, but David stayed in the desert. When he saw that Saul had followed him there, ⁴he sent out scouts and learned that Saul had definitely arrived.[b]

⁵Then David set out and went to the place where Saul had camped. He saw where Saul and Abner son of Ner, the commander of the army, had lain down. Saul was lying inside the camp, with the army encamped around him.

⁶David then asked Ahimelech the Hittite and Abishai son of Zeruiah, Joab's brother, "Who will go down into the camp with me to Saul?"

"I'll go with you," said Abishai.

⁷So David and Abishai went to the army by night, and there was Saul, lying asleep inside the camp with his spear stuck in the ground near his head. Abner and the soldiers were lying around him.

⁸Abishai said to David, "Today God has delivered your enemy into your hands. Now let me pin him to the ground with one thrust of my spear; I won't strike him twice."

⁹But David said to Abishai, "Don't destroy him! Who can lay a hand on the Lᴏʀᴅ's anointed and be guiltless? ¹⁰As surely as the Lᴏʀᴅ lives," he said, "the Lᴏʀᴅ himself will strike him; either his time will come and he will die, or he will go into battle and perish. ¹¹But the Lᴏʀᴅ forbid that I should lay a hand on the Lᴏʀᴅ's anointed. Now get the spear and water jug that are near his head, and let's go."

¹²So David took the spear and water jug near Saul's head, and they left. No one saw or knew about it, nor did anyone wake up. They were all sleeping, because the Lᴏʀᴅ had put them into a deep sleep.

¹³Then David crossed over to the other side and stood on top of the hill some distance away; there was a wide space between them. ¹⁴He called out to the army and to Abner son of Ner, "Aren't you going to answer me, Abner?"

Abner replied, "Who are you who calls to the king?"

¹⁵David said, "You're a man, aren't you? And who is like you in Israel? Why didn't you guard your lord the king? Someone came to destroy your lord the king. ¹⁶What you have done is not good. As surely as the Lᴏʀᴅ lives, you and your men deserve to die, because you did not guard your master, the Lᴏʀᴅ's anointed. Look around you. Where are the king's spear and water jug that were near his head?"

¹⁷Saul recognized David's voice and said, "Is that your voice, David my son?"

David replied, "Yes it is, my lord the king." ¹⁸And he added, "Why is my lord pursuing his servant? What have I done, and what wrong am I guilty of? ¹⁹Now let my lord the king listen to his servant's words. If the Lᴏʀᴅ has incited you against me, then may he accept an offering. If, however, men have done it, may they be cursed before the Lᴏʀᴅ! They have now driven me from my share in the Lᴏʀᴅ's inheritance and have said, 'Go, serve other gods.' ²⁰Now do not let my blood fall to the ground far from the presence of the Lᴏʀᴅ. The king of Israel has come out to look for a flea—as one hunts a partridge in the mountains."

²¹Then Saul said, "I have sinned. Come back, David my son. Because you considered my life precious today, I will not try to harm you again. Surely I have acted like a fool and have erred greatly."

²²"Here is the king's spear," David answered. "Let one of your young men come over and get it. ²³The Lᴏʀᴅ rewards every man for his righteousness and faithfulness. The Lᴏʀᴅ delivered you into my

---

ᵃ 44 Hebrew *Palti*, a variant of *Paltiel*   ᵇ 4 Or *had come to Nacon* hands today, but I would not lay a hand on the LORD's anointed. ²⁴As surely as I valued your life today, so may the LORD value my life and deliver me from all trouble."

²⁵Then Saul said to David, "May you be blessed, my son David; you will do great things and surely triumph."

So David went on his way, and Saul returned home.

DAVID AMONG THE PHILISTINES

27 But David thought to himself, "One of these days I will be destroyed by the hand of Saul. The best thing I can do is to escape to the land of the Philistines. Then Saul will give up searching for me anywhere in Israel, and I will slip out of his hand."

²So David and the six hundred men with him left and went over to Achish son of Maoch king of Gath. ³David and his men settled in Gath with Achish. Each man had his family with him, and David had his two wives: Ahinoam of Jezreel and Abigail of Carmel, the widow of Nabal. ⁴When Saul was told that David had fled to Gath, he no longer searched for him.

⁵Then David said to Achish, "If I have found favor in your eyes, let a place be assigned to me in one of the country towns, that I may live there. Why should your servant live in the royal city with you?"

⁶So on that day Achish gave him Ziklag, and it has belonged to the kings of Judah ever since. ⁷David lived in Philistine territory a year and four months.

⁸Now David and his men went up and raided the Geshurites, the Girzites and the Amalekites. (From ancient times these peoples had lived in the land extending to Shur and Egypt.) ⁹Whenever David attacked an area, he did not leave a man or woman alive, but took sheep and cattle, donkeys and camels, and clothes. Then he returned to Achish.

¹⁰When Achish asked, "Where did you go raiding today?" David would say, "Against the Negev of Judah" or "Against the Negev of Jerahmeel" or "Against the Negev of the Kenites." ¹¹He did not leave a man or woman alive to be brought to Gath, for he thought, "They might inform on us and say, 'This is what David did.'" And such was his practice as long as he lived in Philistine territory. ¹²Achish trusted David and said to himself, "He has become so odious to his people, the Israelites, that he will be my servant forever."

SAUL AND THE WITCH OF ENDOR

28 In those days the Philistines gathered their forces to fight against Israel. Achish said to David, "You must understand that you and your men will accompany me in the army."

²David said, "Then you will see for yourself what your servant can do."

Achish replied, "Very well, I will make you my bodyguard for life."

³Now Samuel was dead, and all Israel had mourned for him and buried him in his own town of Ramah. Saul had expelled the mediums and spiritists from the land.

⁴The Philistines assembled and came and set up camp at Shunem, while Saul gathered all the Israelites and set up camp at Gilboa. ⁵When Saul saw the Philistine army, he was afraid; terror filled his heart. ⁶He inquired of the LORD, but the LORD did not answer him by dreams or Urim or prophets. ⁷Saul then said to his attendants, "Find me a woman who is a medium, so I may go and inquire of her."

"There is one in Endor," they said.

⁸So Saul disguised himself, putting on other clothes, and at night he and two men went to the woman. "Consult a spirit for me," he said, "and bring up for me the one I name."

⁹But the woman said to him, "Surely you know what Saul has done. He has cut off the mediums and spiritists from the land. Why have you set a trap for my life to bring about my death?"

¹⁰Saul swore to her by the LORD, "As surely as the LORD lives, you will not be punished for this."

¹¹Then the woman asked, "Whom shall I bring up for you?"

"Bring up Samuel," he said.

¹²When the woman saw Samuel, she cried out at the top of her voice and said to Saul, "Why have you deceived me? You are Saul!"

¹³The king said to her, "Don't be afraid. What do you see?"

The woman said, "I see a spirit[a] coming up out of the ground."

¹⁴"What does he look like?" he asked.

ᵃ 13 Or see spirits; or see gods

"An old man wearing a robe is coming up," she said.

Then Saul knew it was Samuel, and he bowed down and prostrated himself with his face to the ground.

¹⁵Samuel said to Saul, "Why have you disturbed me by bringing me up?"

"I am in great distress," Saul said. "The Philistines are fighting against me, and God has turned away from me. He no longer answers me, either by prophets or by dreams. So I have called on you to tell me what to do."

¹⁶Samuel said, "Why do you consult me, now that the LORD has turned away from you and become your enemy? ¹⁷The LORD has done what he predicted through me. The LORD has torn the kingdom out of your hands and given it to one of your neighbors—to David. ¹⁸Because you did not obey the LORD or carry out his fierce wrath against the Amalekites, the LORD has done this to you today. ¹⁹The LORD will hand over both Israel and you to the Philistines, and tomorrow you and your sons will be with me. The LORD will also hand over the army of Israel to the Philistines."

²⁰Immediately Saul fell full length on the ground, filled with fear because of Samuel's words. His strength was gone, for he had eaten nothing all that day and night.

²¹When the woman came to Saul and saw that he was greatly shaken, she said, "Look, your maidservant has obeyed you. I took my life in my hands and did what you told me to do. ²²Now please listen to your servant and let me give you some food so you may eat and have the strength to go on your way."

²³He refused and said, "I will not eat."

But his men joined the woman in urging him, and he listened to them. He got up from the ground and sat on the couch.

²⁴The woman had a fattened calf at the house, which she butchered at once. She took some flour, kneaded it and baked bread without yeast. ²⁵Then she set it before Saul and his men, and they ate. That same night they got up and left.

ACHISH SENDS DAVID BACK TO ZIKLAG

29

The Philistines gathered all their forces at Aphek, and Israel camped by the spring in Jezreel. ²As the Philistine rulers marched with their units of hundreds and thousands, David and his men were marching at the rear with Achish. ³The commanders of the Philistines asked, "What about these Hebrews?"

Achish replied, "Is this not David, who was an officer of Saul king of Israel? He has already been with me for over a year, and from the day he left Saul until now, I have found no fault in him."

⁴But the Philistine commanders were angry with him and said, "Send the man back, that he may return to the place you assigned him. He must not go with us into battle, or he will turn against us during the fighting. How better could he regain his master's favor than by taking the heads of our own men? ⁵Isn't this the David they sang about in their dances:

> " 'Saul has slain his thousands,
> and David his tens of thousands'?"

⁶So Achish called David and said to him, "As surely as the LORD lives, you have been reliable, and I would be pleased to have you serve with me in the army. From the day you came to me until now, I have found no fault in you, but the rulers don't approve of you. ⁷Turn back and go in peace; do nothing to displease the Philistine rulers."

⁸"But what have I done?" asked David. "What have you found against your servant from the day I came to you until now? Why can't I go and fight against the enemies of my lord the king?"

⁹Achish answered, "I know that you have been as pleasing in my eyes as an angel of God; nevertheless, the Philistine commanders have said, 'He must not go up with us into battle.' ¹⁰Now get up early, along with your master's servants who have come with you, and leave in the morning as soon as it is light."

¹¹So David and his men got up early in the morning to go back to the land of the Philistines, and the Philistines went up to Jezreel.

DAVID DESTROYS THE AMALEKITES

30

David and his men reached Ziklag on the third day. Now the Amalekites had raided the Negev and Ziklag. They had attacked Ziklag and burned it, ²and had taken captive the women and all who were in it, both young and old. They killed none of them, but carried them off as they went on their way.

³When David and his men came to Ziklag, they found it destroyed by fire and their wives and sons and daughters taken captive. ⁴So David and his men wept aloud until they had no strength left to weep. ⁵David's two wives had been captured—Ahinoam of Jezreel and Abigail, the widow of Nabal of Carmel.

⁶David was greatly distressed because the men were talking of stoning him; each one was bitter in spirit because of his sons and daughters. But David found strength in the LORD his God.

⁷Then David said to Abiathar the priest, the son of Ahimelech, "Bring me the ephod." Abiathar brought it to him, ⁸and David inquired of the LORD, "Shall I pursue this raiding party? Will I overtake them?"

"Pursue them," he answered. "You will certainly overtake them and succeed in the rescue."

⁹David and the six hundred men with him came to the Besor Ravine, where some stayed behind, ¹⁰for two hundred men were too exhausted to cross the ravine. But David and four hundred men continued the pursuit.

NOW OR NEVER

1SA 30:6

You can't please everyone. No matter how hard you try, someone will always find a reason to be dissatisfied—and even blame you for it. Your best bet, then, is to try to please God and let him deal with how others respond. After all, his opinion is the only one that really matters.

¹¹They found an Egyptian in a field and brought him to David. They gave him water to drink and food to eat— ¹²part of a cake of pressed figs and two cakes of raisins. He ate and was revived, for he had not eaten any food or drunk any water for three days and three nights.

¹³David asked him, "To whom do you belong, and where do you come from?"

He said, "I am an Egyptian, the slave of an Amalekite. My master abandoned me when I became ill three days ago. ¹⁴We raided the Negev of the Kerethites and the territory belonging to Judah and the Negev of Caleb. And we burned Ziklag."

¹⁵David asked him, "Can you lead me down to this raiding party?"

He answered, "Swear to me before God that you will not kill me or hand me over to my master, and I will take you down to them."

¹⁶He led David down, and there they were, scattered over the countryside, eating, drinking and reveling because of the great amount of plunder they had taken from the land of the Philistines and from Judah. ¹⁷David fought them from dusk until the evening of the next day, and none of them got away, except four hundred young men who rode off on camels and fled. ¹⁸David recovered everything the Amalekites had taken, including his two wives. ¹⁹Nothing was missing: young or old, boy or girl, plunder or anything else they had taken. David brought everything back. ²⁰He took all the flocks and herds, and his men drove them ahead of the other livestock, saying, "This is David's plunder."

²¹Then David came to the two hundred men

NOW OR NEVER

1SA 30:21–25

As far as God is concerned, the people who work behind the scenes as assistants and supporters in his kingdom are just as important as the preachers, teachers and spiritual "superstars" who get all of the attention.

who had been too exhausted to follow him and who were left behind at the Besor Ravine. They came out to meet David and the people with him. As David and his men approached, he greeted them. ²²But all the evil men and troublemakers among David's followers said, "Because they did not go out with us, we will not share with them the plunder we recovered. However, each man may take his wife and children and go."

²³David replied, "No, my brothers, you must not do that with what the LORD has given us. He has protected us and handed over to us the forces that came against us. ²⁴Who will listen to what you say?

The share of the man who stayed with the supplies is to be the same as that of him who went down to the battle. All will share alike." ²⁵David made this a statute and ordinance for Israel from that day to this.

²⁶When David arrived in Ziklag, he sent some of the plunder to the elders of Judah, who were his friends, saying, "Here is a present for you from the plunder of the LORD's enemies."

²⁷He sent it to those who were in Bethel, Ramoth Negev and Jattir; ²⁸to those in Aroer, Siphmoth, Eshtemoa ²⁹and Racal; to those in the towns of the Jerahmeelites and the Kenites; ³⁰to those in Hormah, Bor Ashan, Athach ³¹and Hebron; and to those in all the other places where David and his men had roamed.

SAUL TAKES HIS LIFE

31

Now the Philistines fought against Israel; the Israelites fled before them, and many fell slain on Mount Gilboa. ²The Philistines pressed hard after Saul and his sons, and they killed his sons Jonathan, Abinadab and Malki-Shua. ³The fighting grew fierce around Saul, and when the archers overtook him, they wounded him critically.

⁴Saul said to his armor-bearer, "Draw your sword and run me through, or these uncircumcised fellows will come and run me through and abuse me."

But his armor-bearer was terrified and would not do it; so Saul took his own sword and fell on it. ⁵When the armor-bearer saw that Saul was dead, he too fell on his sword and died with him. ⁶So Saul and his three sons and his armor-bearer and all his men died together that same day.

⁷When the Israelites along the valley and those across the Jordan saw that the Israelite army had fled and that Saul and his sons had died, they abandoned their towns and fled. And the Philistines came and occupied them.

⁸The next day, when the Philistines came to strip the dead, they found Saul and his three sons fallen on Mount Gilboa. ⁹They cut off his head and stripped off his armor, and they sent messengers throughout the land of the Philistines to proclaim the news in the temple of their idols and among their people. ¹⁰They put his armor in the temple of the Ashtoreths and fastened his body to the wall of Beth Shan.

¹¹When the people of Jabesh Gilead heard of what the Philistines had done to Saul, ¹²all their valiant men journeyed through the night to Beth Shan. They took down the bodies of Saul and his sons from the wall of Beth Shan and went to Jabesh, where they burned them. ¹³Then they took their bones and buried them under a tamarisk tree at Jabesh, and they fasted seven days.

2 SAMUEL

Author
Unknown

Audience
People of Israel

Date
930 B.C., written soon after David's reign
(1050–970 B.C.)

Setting
The land of Israel when David ruled as their king.

Verse to Remember
Then David said to Nathan, "I have sinned against the LORD." Nathan replied, "The LORD has taken away your sin. You are not going to die" (12:13).

Theme to Consider
What great news! No matter how terribly we mess up, we can share our pain and sadness with God and ask for forgiveness like David did.

UNCHANGING TRUTH »

Never let your guard down, because temptation can be lurking around any corner. That's what King David would tell you if he were here today. And he would know. Of all the people God used during Bible times, no one fell harder because of temptation's power than David.

The story goes like this: One night David was walking around the roof of his palace when he spotted a beautiful woman named Bathsheba taking a bath on a nearby rooftop. Instead of averting his eyes and walking away like he should have done, David decided to watch for a while. *After all, what's the harm in admiring God's creation? No one gets hurt, right?*

Wrong. David knew better. Every lustful thought is sinful. And if that's not bad enough, once temptation gets rolling, it starts a snowball effect. It never stops with one "harmless" sin. It keeps getting bigger and bigger until . . . well, until lives are ruined. If that seems like an overstatement, consider this: David's little midnight peep show eventually led him to command the murder of Bathsheba's husband, who happened to be one of David's most loyal and talented soldiers. (You can read the whole story in 2 Samuel 11–12.)

Remember, this is *David* we're talking about—the guy who God handpicked and blessed when he was a kid. He was the shepherd who became king of Israel, the man appointed by God himself to be the ancestor of the Messiah. He was the one God called a "man after his own heart." This guy was a spiritual giant.

If temptation could slam him like that, think of what it can do to us. That's why it's important for us to learn to remove ourselves from tempting situations as soon as we recognize them for what they are. The moment you start to think you can play with fire and not get hurt (whether it's viewing porn, smoking pot, gambling or fooling around with your girlfriend), you're setting yourself up to get burned.

LIFE LESSONS »

I   You cannot predict what the Lord ultimately has in store for your life; his plans may be quite different and much greater than you expect (2:4).

2   If God's in your corner, no challenge is too great for you (8:1–14).

3   If you deal with lust before it gets started, you'll save yourself a lot of trouble in the long run (11:1–5).

4   Trying to hide your sin will always get you in more trouble than just admitting it and dealing with it (11:6–27).

DAVID HEARS OF SAUL'S DEATH

1 After the death of Saul, David returned from defeating the Amalekites and stayed in Ziklag two days. ²On the third day a man arrived from Saul's camp, with his clothes torn and with dust on his head. When he came to David, he fell to the ground to pay him honor.

³"Where have you come from?" David asked him.

He answered, "I have escaped from the Israelite camp."

⁴"What happened?" David asked. "Tell me."

He said, "The men fled from the battle. Many of them fell and died. And Saul and his son Jonathan are dead."

⁵Then David said to the young man who brought him the report, "How do you know that Saul and his son Jonathan are dead?"

⁶"I happened to be on Mount Gilboa," the young man said, "and there was Saul, leaning on his spear, with the chariots and riders almost upon him. ⁷When he turned around and saw me, he called out to me, and I said, 'What can I do?'

⁸"He asked me, 'Who are you?'

" 'An Amalekite,' I answered.

⁹"Then he said to me, 'Stand over me and kill me! I am in the throes of death, but I'm still alive.'

¹⁰"So I stood over him and killed him, because I knew that after he had fallen he could not survive. And I took the crown that was on his head and the band on his arm and have brought them here to my lord."

¹¹Then David and all the men with him took hold of their clothes and tore them. ¹²They mourned and wept and fasted till evening for Saul and his son Jonathan, and for the army of the LORD and the house of Israel, because they had fallen by the sword.

¹³David said to the young man who brought him the report, "Where are you from?"

"I am the son of an alien, an Amalekite," he answered.

¹⁴David asked him, "Why were you not afraid to lift your hand to destroy the LORD's anointed?"

¹⁵Then David called one of his men and said, "Go, strike him down!" So he struck him down, and he died. ¹⁶For David had said to him, "Your blood be on your own head. Your own mouth testified against you when you said, 'I killed the LORD's anointed.' "

DAVID'S LAMENT FOR SAUL AND JONATHAN

¹⁷David took up this lament concerning Saul and his son Jonathan, ¹⁸and ordered that the men of Judah be taught this lament of the bow (it is written in the Book of Jashar):

¹⁹ "Your glory, O Israel, lies slain on your heights.
    How the mighty have fallen!

²⁰ "Tell it not in Gath,
       proclaim it not in the streets of Ashkelon,
    lest the daughters of the Philistines be glad,
       lest the daughters of the uncircumcised rejoice.

²¹ "O mountains of Gilboa,
       may you have neither dew nor rain,
       nor fields that yield offerings ⌐of grain⌐.
    For there the shield of the mighty was defiled,
       the shield of Saul—no longer rubbed with oil.
²² From the blood of the slain,
       from the flesh of the mighty,
    the bow of Jonathan did not turn back,
       the sword of Saul did not return unsatisfied.

²³ "Saul and Jonathan—
       in life they were loved and gracious,
       and in death they were not parted.
    They were swifter than eagles,
       they were stronger than lions.

battlelines

» Running Short of Time (Grief)

Q: What's the latest news on your mom?
A: The latest? Let's see. She still has cancer. She's still dying. And the doctors still say there's nothing else they can do.

Q: What about radiation or chemotherapy?
A: They've tried all that. And if they try any more, it won't be the cancer that kills her.

Q: So how are you holding up?
A: I'm not sure right now. When we first got the news, I just lost it. I mean, I got all emotional. Then I went through a time where I was like, "OK, God, I know you *can* heal her. Will you? Please? I have faith." I even wrote letters to a couple of TV preachers who say they have the power of healing, asking them to pray for my mom. They put me on their mailing list, and now I get all these requests for donations.

Q: And your mom's only gotten worse?
A: Yeah.

Q: So have you totally given up hope?
A: It's not like I don't believe God could heal her. He could say the word, and just like that she'd be in perfect health again. But do I believe he *will* do that? Not really. Let's just say things don't look very promising right now.

Q: And that makes you feel . . . what?
A: (Long pause) Mad. Angry. Confused. I mean, you've got all these murderers in prison, drug dealers, child molesters—you name it. Why do some of them get to live long lives? How is that fair? My mom just turned forty. Forty! You're not supposed to die when you're barely out of your thirties. I just can't imagine life without her.

» Losing a Loved One

Need a world-class lesson in how to grieve? Check out 2 Samuel 1. There we find King David burying Saul (his worst enemy) and Jonathan (his best friend). Imagine that experience. David mourned deeply. He didn't keep it bottled up, pretending that everything was OK.

Next, check out John 11:33–36 to see how Jesus reacted when his friend Lazarus died. Jesus definitely wasn't too cool to show his grief. The experience of losing a friend made him *weep*. (Think real men don't cry?) Yet by raising Lazarus, Jesus reminded us who gets the last word over death.

When someone you love dies, it's OK to grieve. It's normal to wrestle with feelings of loss, anger and confusion. But, like David, you can determine not to let the end of another person's life stop you from living your life in a way that pleases God. Remember, God cares about all the pain and death that his people experience. And Jesus' resurrection means that death doesn't get the final say (see 1 Corinthians 15:54–55).

Learn more about grieving at www.RevolutionBible.com.

²⁴"O daughters of Israel,
  weep for Saul,
who clothed you in scarlet and finery,
  who adorned your garments with ornaments of gold.

²⁵"How the mighty have fallen in battle!
  Jonathan lies slain on your heights.
²⁶I grieve for you, Jonathan my brother;
  you were very dear to me.
Your love for me was wonderful,
  more wonderful than that of women.

²⁷"How the mighty have fallen!
  The weapons of war have perished!"

DAVID ANOINTED KING OVER JUDAH

2 In the course of time, David inquired of the LORD. "Shall I go up to one of the towns of Judah?" he asked.

The LORD said, "Go up."

David asked, "Where shall I go?"

"To Hebron," the LORD answered.

²So David went up there with his two wives, Ahinoam of Jezreel and Abigail, the widow of Nabal of Carmel. ³David also took the men who were with him, each with his family, and they settled in Hebron and its towns. ⁴Then the men of Judah came to Hebron and there they anointed David king over the house of Judah.

When David was told that it was the men of Jabesh Gilead who had buried Saul, ⁵he sent messengers to the men of Jabesh Gilead to say to them, "The LORD bless you for showing this kindness to Saul your master by burying him. ⁶May the LORD now show you kindness and faithfulness, and I too will show you the same favor because you have done this. ⁷Now then, be strong and brave, for Saul your master is dead, and the house of Judah has anointed me king over them."

WAR BETWEEN THE HOUSES OF DAVID AND SAUL

⁸Meanwhile, Abner son of Ner, the commander of Saul's army, had taken Ish-Bosheth son of Saul and brought him over to Mahanaim. ⁹He made him king over Gilead, Ashuri[a] and Jezreel, and also over Ephraim, Benjamin and all Israel.

¹⁰Ish-Bosheth son of Saul was forty years old when he became king over Israel, and he reigned two years. The house of Judah, however, followed David. ¹¹The length of time David was king in Hebron over the house of Judah was seven years and six months.

¹²Abner son of Ner, together with the men of Ish-Bosheth son of Saul, left Mahanaim and went to Gibeon. ¹³Joab son of Zeruiah and David's men went out and met them at the pool of Gibeon. One group sat down on one side of the pool and one group on the other side.

¹⁴Then Abner said to Joab, "Let's have some of the young men get up and fight hand to hand in front of us."

"All right, let them do it," Joab said.

¹⁵So they stood up and were counted off—twelve men for Benjamin and Ish-Bosheth son of Saul, and twelve for David. ¹⁶Then each man grabbed his opponent by the head and thrust his dagger into his opponent's side, and they fell down together. So that place in Gibeon was called Helkath Hazzurim.[b]

¹⁷The battle that day was very fierce, and Abner and the men of Israel were defeated by David's men.

¹⁸The three sons of Zeruiah were there: Joab, Abishai and Asahel. Now Asahel was as fleet-footed as a wild gazelle. ¹⁹He chased Abner, turning neither to the right nor to the left as he pursued him. ²⁰Abner looked behind him and asked, "Is that you, Asahel?"

"It is," he answered.

²¹Then Abner said to him, "Turn aside to the right or to the left; take on one of the young men and strip him of his weapons." But Asahel would not stop chasing him.

---

^a 9 Or Asher   ^b 16 Helkath Hazzurim means *field of daggers* or *field of hostilities.*

²²Again Abner warned Asahel, "Stop chasing me! Why should I strike you down? How could I look your brother Joab in the face?"

²³But Asahel refused to give up the pursuit; so Abner thrust the butt of his spear into Asahel's stomach, and the spear came out through his back. He fell there and died on the spot. And every man stopped when he came to the place where Asahel had fallen and died.

²⁴But Joab and Abishai pursued Abner, and as the sun was setting, they came to the hill of Ammah, near Giah on the way to the wasteland of Gibeon. ²⁵Then the men of Benjamin rallied behind Abner. They formed themselves into a group and took their stand on top of a hill.

²⁶Abner called out to Joab, "Must the sword devour forever? Don't you realize that this will end in bitterness? How long before you order your men to stop pursuing their brothers?"

²⁷Joab answered, "As surely as God lives, if you had not spoken, the men would have continued the pursuit of their brothers until morning.ᵃ"

²⁸So Joab blew the trumpet, and all the men came to a halt; they no longer pursued Israel, nor did they fight anymore.

²⁹All that night Abner and his men marched through the Arabah. They crossed the Jordan, continued through the whole Bithronᵇ and came to Mahanaim.

³⁰Then Joab returned from pursuing Abner and assembled all his men. Besides Asahel, nineteen of David's men were found missing. ³¹But David's men had killed three hundred and sixty Benjamites who were with Abner. ³²They took Asahel and buried him in his father's tomb at Bethlehem. Then Joab and his men marched all night and arrived at Hebron by daybreak.

3 The war between the house of Saul and the house of David lasted a long time. David grew stronger and stronger, while the house of Saul grew weaker and weaker.

²Sons were born to David in Hebron:

His firstborn was Amnon the son of Ahinoam of Jezreel;

³his second, Kileab the son of Abigail the widow of Nabal of Carmel;

the third, Absalom the son of Maacah daughter of Talmai king of Geshur;

⁴the fourth, Adonijah the son of Haggith;

the fifth, Shephatiah the son of Abital;

⁵and the sixth, Ithream the son of David's wife Eglah.

These were born to David in Hebron.

ABNER GOES OVER TO DAVID

⁶During the war between the house of Saul and the house of David, Abner had been strengthening his own position in the house of Saul. ⁷Now Saul had had a concubine named Rizpah daughter of Aiah. And Ish-Bosheth said to Abner, "Why did you sleep with my father's concubine?"

⁸Abner was very angry because of what Ish-Bosheth said and he answered, "Am I a dog's head—on Judah's side? This very day I am loyal to the house of your father Saul and to his family and friends. I haven't handed you over to David. Yet now you accuse me of an offense involving this woman! ⁹May God deal with Abner, be it ever so severely, if I do not do for David what the Lord promised him on oath ¹⁰and transfer the kingdom from the house of Saul and establish David's throne over Israel and Judah from Dan to Beersheba." ¹¹Ish-Bosheth did not dare to say another word to Abner, because he was afraid of him.

¹²Then Abner sent messengers on his behalf to say to David, "Whose land is it? Make an agreement with me, and I will help you bring all Israel over to you."

¹³"Good," said David. "I will make an agreement with you. But I demand one thing of you: Do not come into my presence unless you bring Michal daughter of Saul when you come to see me." ¹⁴Then David sent messengers to Ish-Bosheth son of Saul, demanding, "Give me my wife Michal, whom I betrothed to myself for the price of a hundred Philistine foreskins."

¹⁵So Ish-Bosheth gave orders and had her taken away from her husband Paltiel son of Laish. ¹⁶Her husband, however, went with her, weeping behind her all the way to Bahurim. Then Abner said to him, "Go back home!" So he went back.

¹⁷Abner conferred with the elders of Israel and said, "For some time you have wanted to make Da-

vid your king. ¹⁸Now do it! For the LORD promised David, 'By my servant David I will rescue my people Israel from the hand of the Philistines and from the hand of all their enemies.' "

¹⁹Abner also spoke to the Benjamites in person. Then he went to Hebron to tell David everything that Israel and the whole house of Benjamin wanted to do. ²⁰When Abner, who had twenty men with him, came to David at Hebron, David prepared a feast for him and his men. ²¹Then Abner said to David, "Let me go at once and assemble all Israel for my lord the king, so that they may make a compact with you, and that you may rule over all that your heart desires." So David sent Abner away, and he went in peace.

JOAB MURDERS ABNER

²²Just then David's men and Joab returned from a raid and brought with them a great deal of plunder. But Abner was no longer with David in Hebron, because David had sent him away, and he had gone in peace. ²³When Joab and all the soldiers with him arrived, he was told that Abner son of Ner had come to the king and that the king had sent him away and that he had gone in peace.

²⁴So Joab went to the king and said, "What have you done? Look, Abner came to you. Why did you let him go? Now he is gone! ²⁵You know Abner son of Ner; he came to deceive you and observe your movements and find out everything you are doing."

²⁶Joab then left David and sent messengers after Abner, and they brought him back from the well of Sirah. But David did not know it. ²⁷Now when Abner returned to Hebron, Joab took him aside into the gateway, as though to speak with him privately. And there, to avenge the blood of his brother Asahel, Joab stabbed him in the stomach, and he died.

²⁸Later, when David heard about this, he said, "I and my kingdom are forever innocent before the LORD concerning the blood of Abner son of Ner. ²⁹May his blood fall upon the head of Joab and upon all his father's house! May Joab's house never be without someone who has a running sore or leprosy[a] or who leans on a crutch or who falls by the sword or who lacks food."

³⁰(Joab and his brother Abishai murdered Abner because he had killed their brother Asahel in the battle at Gibeon.)

³¹Then David said to Joab and all the people with him, "Tear your clothes and put on sackcloth and walk in mourning in front of Abner." King David himself walked behind the bier. ³²They buried Abner in Hebron, and the king wept aloud at Abner's tomb. All the people wept also.

³³The king sang this lament for Abner:

> "Should Abner have died as the lawless die?
> ³⁴   Your hands were not bound,
>   your feet were not fettered.
>   You fell as one falls before wicked men."

And all the people wept over him again.

³⁵Then they all came and urged David to eat something while it was still day; but David took an oath, saying, "May God deal with me, be it ever so severely, if I taste bread or anything else before the sun sets!"

³⁶All the people took note and were pleased; indeed, everything the king did pleased them. ³⁷So on that day all the people and all Israel knew that the king had no part in the murder of Abner son of Ner.

³⁸Then the king said to his men, "Do you not realize that a prince and a great man has fallen in Israel this day? ³⁹And today, though I am the anointed king, I am weak, and these sons of Zeruiah are too strong for me. May the LORD repay the evildoer according to his evil deeds!"

ISH-BOSHETH MURDERED

4 When Ish-Bosheth son of Saul heard that Abner had died in Hebron, he lost courage, and all Israel became alarmed. ²Now Saul's son had two men who were leaders of raiding bands. One was named Baanah and the other Recab; they were sons of Rimmon the Beerothite from the tribe of Benjamin—Beeroth is considered part of Benjamin, ³because the people of Beeroth fled to Gittaim and have lived there as aliens to this day.

⁴(Jonathan son of Saul had a son who was lame in both feet. He was five years old when the news about Saul and Jonathan came from Jezreel. His nurse picked him up and fled, but as she hurried to leave, he fell and became crippled. His name was Mephibosheth.)

ᵃ 29 The Hebrew word was used for various diseases affecting the skin—not necessarily leprosy.

⁵Now Recab and Baanah, the sons of Rimmon the Beerothite, set out for the house of Ish-Bosheth, and they arrived there in the heat of the day while he was taking his noonday rest. ⁶They went into the inner part of the house as if to get some wheat, and they stabbed him in the stomach. Then Recab and his brother Baanah slipped away.

⁷They had gone into the house while he was lying on the bed in his bedroom. After they stabbed and killed him, they cut off his head. Taking it with them, they traveled all night by way of the Arabah. ⁸They brought the head of Ish-Bosheth to David at Hebron and said to the king, "Here is the head of Ish-Bosheth son of Saul, your enemy, who tried to take your life. This day the LORD has avenged my lord the king against Saul and his offspring."

⁹David answered Recab and his brother Baanah, the sons of Rimmon the Beerothite, "As surely as the LORD lives, who has delivered me out of all trouble, ¹⁰when a man told me, 'Saul is dead,' and thought he was bringing good news, I seized him and put him to death in Ziklag. That was the reward I gave him for his news! ¹¹How much more—when wicked men have killed an innocent man in his own house and on his own bed—should I not now demand his blood from your hand and rid the earth of you!"

¹²So David gave an order to his men, and they killed them. They cut off their hands and feet and hung the bodies by the pool in Hebron. But they took the head of Ish-Bosheth and buried it in Abner's tomb at Hebron.

DAVID BECOMES KING OVER ISRAEL

5 All the tribes of Israel came to David at Hebron and said, "We are your own flesh and blood. ²In the past, while Saul was king over us, you were the one who led Israel on their military campaigns. And the LORD said to you, 'You will shepherd my people Israel, and you will become their ruler.' "

³When all the elders of Israel had come to King David at Hebron, the king made a compact with them at Hebron before the LORD, and they anointed David king over Israel.

⁴David was thirty years old when he became king, and he reigned forty years. ⁵In Hebron he reigned over Judah seven years and six months, and in Jerusalem he reigned over all Israel and Judah thirty-three years.

DAVID CONQUERS JERUSALEM

⁶The king and his men marched to Jerusalem to attack the Jebusites, who lived there. The Jebusites said to David, "You will not get in here; even the blind and the lame can ward you off." They thought, "David cannot get in here." ⁷Nevertheless, David captured the fortress of Zion, the City of David.

⁸On that day, David said, "Anyone who conquers the Jebusites will have to use the water shaftᵃ to reach those 'lame and blind' who are David's enemies.ᵇ" That is why they say, "The 'blind and lame' will not enter the palace."

⁹David then took up residence in the fortress and called it the City of David. He built up the area around it, from the supporting terracesᶜ inward. ¹⁰And he became more and more powerful, because the LORD God Almighty was with him.

¹¹Now Hiram king of Tyre sent messengers to David, along with cedar logs and carpenters and stonemasons, and they built a palace for David. ¹²And David knew that the LORD had established him as king over Israel and had exalted his kingdom for the sake of his people Israel.

¹³After he left Hebron, David took more concubines and wives in Jerusalem, and more sons and daughters were born to him. ¹⁴These are the names of the children born to him there: Shammua, Shobab, Nathan, Solomon, ¹⁵Ibhar, Elishua, Nepheg, Japhia, ¹⁶Elishama, Eliada and Eliphelet.

NOW OR NEVER
2SA 5:12

Which person do you think the Lord will honor and bless—the guy who gives him credit for all of the good things in his life or the guy who promotes himself as being something to brag about?

ᵃ 8 Or *use scaling hooks*   ᵇ 8 Or *are hated by David*   ᶜ 9 Or *the Millo*

DAVID DEFEATS THE PHILISTINES

[17]When the Philistines heard that David had been anointed king over Israel, they went up in full force to search for him, but David heard about it and went down to the stronghold. [18]Now the Philistines had come and spread out in the Valley of Rephaim; [19]so David inquired of the LORD, "Shall I go and attack the Philistines? Will you hand them over to me?"

The LORD answered him, "Go, for I will surely hand the Philistines over to you."

[20]So David went to Baal Perazim, and there he defeated them. He said, "As waters break out, the LORD has broken out against my enemies before me." So that place was called Baal Perazim.[a] [21]The Philistines abandoned their idols there, and David and his men carried them off.

[22]Once more the Philistines came up and spread out in the Valley of Rephaim; [23]so David inquired of the LORD, and he answered, "Do not go straight up, but circle around behind them and attack them in front of the balsam trees. [24]As soon as you hear the sound of marching in the tops of the balsam trees, move quickly, because that will mean the LORD has gone out in front of you to strike the Philistine army." [25]So David did as the LORD commanded him, and he struck down the Philistines all the way from Gibeon[b] to Gezer.

THE ARK BROUGHT TO JERUSALEM

6 David again brought together out of Israel chosen men, thirty thousand in all. [2]He and all his men set out from Baalah of Judah[c] to bring up from there the ark of God, which is called by the Name,[d] the name of the LORD Almighty, who is enthroned between the cherubim that are on the ark. [3]They set the ark of God on a new cart and brought it from the house of Abinadab, which was on the hill. Uzzah and Ahio, sons of Abinadab, were guiding the new cart [4]with the ark of God on it,[e] and Ahio was walking in front of it. [5]David and the whole house of Israel were celebrating with all their might before the LORD, with songs[f] and with harps, lyres, tambourines, sistrums and cymbals.

[6]When they came to the threshing floor of Nacon, Uzzah reached out and took hold of the ark of God, because the oxen stumbled. [7]The LORD's anger burned against Uzzah because of his irreverent act; therefore God struck him down and he died there beside the ark of God.

[8]Then David was angry because the LORD's wrath had broken out against Uzzah, and to this day that place is called Perez Uzzah.[g]

[9]David was afraid of the LORD that day and said, "How can the ark of the LORD ever come to me?" [10]He was not willing to take the ark of the LORD to be with him in the City of David. Instead, he took it aside to the house of Obed-Edom the Gittite. [11]The ark of the LORD remained in the house of Obed-Edom the Gittite for three months, and the LORD blessed him and his entire household.

[12]Now King David was told, "The LORD has blessed the household of Obed-Edom and everything he has, because of the ark of God." So David went down and brought up the ark of God from the house of Obed-Edom to the City of David with rejoicing. [13]When those who were carrying the ark of the LORD had taken six steps, he sacrificed a bull and a fattened calf. [14]David, wearing a linen ephod, danced before the LORD with all his might, [15]while he and the entire house of Israel brought up the ark of the LORD with shouts and the sound of trumpets.

[16]As the ark of the LORD was entering the City of David, Michal daughter of Saul watched from a window. And when she saw King David leaping and dancing before the LORD, she despised him in her heart.

[17]They brought the ark of the LORD and set it in its place inside the tent that David had pitched for it, and David sacrificed burnt offerings and fellowship offerings[h] before the LORD. [18]After he

NOW OR NEVER
2SA 6:21–22

Have you ever let pride or fear about what people will think keep you from doing something you know you should do?

---

[a] 20 Baal Perazim means the lord who breaks out.   [b] 25 Septuagint (see also 1 Chron. 14:16); Hebrew Geba   [c] 2 That is, Kiriath Jearim; Hebrew Baale Judah, a variant of Baalah of Judah   [d] 2 Hebrew; Septuagint and Vulgate do not have the Name.   [e] 3,4 Dead Sea Scrolls and some Septuagint manuscripts; Masoretic Text cart 'and they brought it with the ark of God from the house of Abinadab, which was on the hill   [f] 5 See Dead Sea Scrolls, Septuagint and 1 Chronicles 13:8; Masoretic Text celebrating before the LORD with all kinds of instruments made of pine.   [g] 8 Perez Uzzah means outbreak against Uzzah.   [h] 17 Traditionally peace offerings; also in verse 18

had finished sacrificing the burnt offerings and fellowship offerings, he blessed the people in the name of the LORD Almighty. [19]Then he gave a loaf of bread, a cake of dates and a cake of raisins to each person in the whole crowd of Israelites, both men and women. And all the people went to their homes.

[20]When David returned home to bless his household, Michal daughter of Saul came out to meet him and said, "How the king of Israel has distinguished himself today, disrobing in the sight of the slave girls of his servants as any vulgar fellow would!"

[21]David said to Michal, "It was before the LORD, who chose me rather than your father or anyone from his house when he appointed me ruler over the LORD's people Israel—I will celebrate before the LORD. [22]I will become even more undignified than this, and I will be humiliated in my own eyes. But by these slave girls you spoke of, I will be held in honor."

[23]And Michal daughter of Saul had no children to the day of her death.

now or never

2SA 7:1–16

When it comes to answered prayers, sometimes what seems like a "no" is really just a "not yet." God may have something much better in mind for you if you're willing to wait for his timing.

GOD'S PROMISE TO DAVID

7 After the king was settled in his palace and the LORD had given him rest from all his enemies around him, [2]he said to Nathan the prophet, "Here I am, living in a palace of cedar, while the ark of God remains in a tent."

[3]Nathan replied to the king, "Whatever you have in mind, go ahead and do it, for the LORD is with you."

[4]That night the word of the LORD came to Nathan, saying:

[5]"Go and tell my servant David, 'This is what the LORD says: Are you the one to build me a house to dwell in? [6]I have not dwelt in a house from the day I brought the Israelites up out of Egypt to this day. I have been moving from place to place with a tent as my dwelling. [7]Wherever I have moved with all the Israelites, did I ever say to any of their rulers whom I commanded to shepherd my people Israel, "Why have you not built me a house of cedar?" '

[8]"Now then, tell my servant David, 'This is what the LORD Almighty says: I took you from the pasture and from following the flock to be ruler over my people Israel. [9]I have been with you wherever you have gone, and I have cut off all your enemies from before you. Now I will make your name great, like the names of the greatest men of the earth. [10]And I will provide a place for my people Israel and will plant them so that they can have a home of their own and no longer be disturbed. Wicked people will not oppress them anymore, as they did at the beginning [11]and have done ever since the time I appointed leaders[a] over my people Israel. I will also give you rest from all your enemies.

" 'The LORD declares to you that the LORD himself will establish a house for you: [12]When your days are over and you rest with your fathers, I will raise up your offspring to succeed you, who will come from your own body, and I will establish his kingdom. [13]He is the one who will build a house for my Name, and I will establish the throne of his kingdom forever. [14]I will be his father, and he will be my son. When he does wrong, I will punish him with the rod of men, with floggings inflicted by men. [15]But my love will never be taken away from him, as I took it away from Saul, whom I removed from before you. [16]Your house and your kingdom will endure forever before me[b]; your throne will be established forever.' "

[17]Nathan reported to David all the words of this entire revelation.

challenge notes

To: my_son

heavenly_father: the world is a dangerous place. one day I'll get rid of evil once and for all. until then, I'll be your refuge. when you're tempted to do something wrong, when you don't know who you can trust, come talk to me about it. I can give you the wisdom to choose wisely and the strength to endure the hardships of this world.

2SA 7:10–11

---

[a] 11 Traditionally *judges*   [b] 16 Some Hebrew manuscripts and Septuagint; most Hebrew manuscripts *you*

DAVID'S PRAYER

[18] Then King David went in and sat before the LORD, and he said:

"Who am I, O Sovereign LORD, and what is my family, that you have brought me this far? [19] And as if this were not enough in your sight, O Sovereign LORD, you have also spoken about the future of the house of your servant. Is this your usual way of dealing with man, O Sovereign LORD?

[20] "What more can David say to you? For you know your servant, O Sovereign LORD. [21] For the sake of your word and according to your will, you have done this great thing and made it known to your servant.

[22] "How great you are, O Sovereign LORD! There is no one like you, and there is no God but you, as we have heard with our own ears. [23] And who is like your people Israel—the one nation on earth that God went out to redeem as a people for himself, and to make a name for himself, and to perform great and awesome wonders by driving out nations and their gods from before your people, whom you redeemed from Egypt?[a] [24] You have established your people Israel as your very own forever, and you, O LORD, have become their God.

[25] "And now, LORD God, keep forever the promise you have made concerning your servant and his house. Do as you promised, [26] so that your name will be great forever. Then men will say, 'The LORD Almighty is God over Israel!' And the house of your servant David will be established before you.

[27] "O LORD Almighty, God of Israel, you have revealed this to your servant, saying, 'I will build a house for you.' So your servant has found courage to offer you this prayer. [28] O Sovereign LORD, you are God! Your words are trustworthy, and you have promised these good things to your servant. [29] Now be pleased to bless the house of your servant, that it may continue forever in your sight; for you, O Sovereign LORD, have spoken, and with your blessing the house of your servant will be blessed forever."

Staying Humble

>> live the adventure >> 2Sa 7:18-29

One day you're going to do something that gets you noticed (in a good way), something that makes people say, "Hey, there's something really cool about that guy." When that happens, you're going to face a choice. You can either let people think that there's something special about you, or you can help people understand that there's something special about the One who made you. The choice is yours.

DAVID'S VICTORIES

8 In the course of time, David defeated the Philistines and subdued them, and he took Metheg Ammah from the control of the Philistines.

[2] David also defeated the Moabites. He made them lie down on the ground and measured them off with a length of cord. Every two lengths of them were put to death, and the third length was allowed to live. So the Moabites became subject to David and brought tribute.

[3] Moreover, David fought Hadadezer son of Rehob, king of Zobah, when he went to restore his control along the Euphrates River. [4] David captured a thousand of his chariots, seven thousand charioteers[b] and twenty thousand foot soldiers. He hamstrung all but a hundred of the chariot horses.

[5] When the Arameans of Damascus came to help Hadadezer king of Zobah, David struck down twenty-two thousand of them. [6] He put garrisons in the Aramean kingdom of Damascus, and the Arameans became subject to him and brought tribute. The LORD gave David victory wherever he went.

[7] David took the gold shields that belonged to the officers of Hadadezer and brought them to Jerusalem. [8] From Tebah[c] and Berothai, towns that belonged to Hadadezer, King David took a great quantity of bronze.

[9] When Tou[d] king of Hamath heard that David had defeated the entire army of Hadadezer, [10] he sent

---

[a] 23 See Septuagint and 1 Chron. 17:21; Hebrew *wonders for your land and before your people, whom you redeemed from Egypt, from the nations and their gods.* [b] 4 Septuagint (see also Dead Sea Scrolls and 1 Chron. 18:4); Masoretic Text *captured seventeen hundred of his charioteers* [c] 8 See some Septuagint manuscripts (see also 1 Chron. 18:8); Hebrew *Betah.* [d] 9 Hebrew *Toi,* a variant of *Tou;* also in verse 10

his son Joram[a] to King David to greet him and congratulate him on his victory in battle over Hadadezer, who had been at war with Tou. Joram brought with him articles of silver and gold and bronze.

[11]King David dedicated these articles to the Lord, as he had done with the silver and gold from all the nations he had subdued: [12]Edom[b] and Moab, the Ammonites and the Philistines, and Amalek. He also dedicated the plunder taken from Hadadezer son of Rehob, king of Zobah.

[13]And David became famous after he returned from striking down eighteen thousand Edomites[c] in the Valley of Salt.

[14]He put garrisons throughout Edom, and all the Edomites became subject to David. The Lord gave David victory wherever he went.

DAVID'S OFFICIALS

[15]David reigned over all Israel, doing what was just and right for all his people. [16]Joab son of Zeruiah was over the army; Jehoshaphat son of Ahilud was recorder; [17]Zadok son of Ahitub and Ahimelech son of Abiathar were priests; Seraiah was secretary; [18]Benaiah son of Jehoiada was over the Kerethites and Pelethites; and David's sons were royal advisers.[d]

NOW OR NEVER
2SA 8:15

Don't worry about becoming popular; just concentrate on doing what you know is right—and treating all people with the kind of respect you'd like to receive from them.

DAVID AND MEPHIBOSHETH

9 David asked, "Is there anyone still left of the house of Saul to whom I can show kindness for Jonathan's sake?"

[2]Now there was a servant of Saul's household named Ziba. They called him to appear before David, and the king said to him, "Are you Ziba?"

"Your servant," he replied.

[3]The king asked, "Is there no one still left of the house of Saul to whom I can show God's kindness?"

Ziba answered the king, "There is still a son of Jonathan; he is crippled in both feet."

[4]"Where is he?" the king asked.

Ziba answered, "He is at the house of Makir son of Ammiel in Lo Debar."

[5]So King David had him brought from Lo Debar, from the house of Makir son of Ammiel.

[6]When Mephibosheth son of Jonathan, the son of Saul, came to David, he bowed down to pay him honor.

David said, "Mephibosheth!"

"Your servant," he replied.

[7]"Don't be afraid," David said to him, "for I will surely show you kindness for the sake of your father Jonathan. I will restore to you all the land that belonged to your grandfather Saul, and you will always eat at my table."

[8]Mephibosheth bowed down and said, "What is your servant, that you should notice a dead dog like me?"

[9]Then the king summoned Ziba, Saul's servant, and said to him, "I have given your master's grandson everything that belonged to Saul and his family. [10]You and your sons and your servants are to farm the land for him and bring in the crops, so

Showing Kindness

There's nothing special about being kind to people you like. There's nothing extraordinary about doing favors for people you want to impress or people who can do something for you in return. That's what many politicians do every day. But being kind to people who have no reason to expect kindness from you and have nothing to give you in return? Now that's another thing altogether! In fact, that's the kind of thing that makes people ask, "What's up with that guy? What makes him different from the people who ignore me or make my life miserable?"

» » live the adventure » » 2Sa 9:1–8

---

[a] *10* A variant of *Hadoram*   [b] *12* Some Hebrew manuscripts, Septuagint and Syriac (see also 1 Chron. 18:11); most Hebrew manuscripts *Aram*   [c] *13* A few Hebrew manuscripts, Septuagint and Syriac (see also 1 Chron. 18:12); most Hebrew manuscripts *Aram* (that is, Arameans)   [d] *18* Or *were priests*

that your master's grandson may be provided for. And Mephibosheth, grandson of your master, will always eat at my table." (Now Ziba had fifteen sons and twenty servants.)

¹¹Then Ziba said to the king, "Your servant will do whatever my lord the king commands his servant to do." So Mephibosheth ate at David's[a] table like one of the king's sons.

¹²Mephibosheth had a young son named Mica, and all the members of Ziba's household were servants of Mephibosheth. ¹³And Mephibosheth lived in Jerusalem, because he always ate at the king's table, and he was crippled in both feet.

DAVID DEFEATS THE AMMONITES

10 In the course of time, the king of the Ammonites died, and his son Hanun succeeded him as king. ²David thought, "I will show kindness to Hanun son of Nahash, just as his father showed kindness to me." So David sent a delegation to express his sympathy to Hanun concerning his father.

When David's men came to the land of the Ammonites, ³the Ammonite nobles said to Hanun their lord, "Do you think David is honoring your father by sending men to you to express sympathy? Hasn't David sent them to you to explore the city and spy it out and overthrow it?" ⁴So Hanun seized David's men, shaved off half of each man's beard, cut off their garments in the middle at the buttocks, and sent them away.

⁵When David was told about this, he sent messengers to meet the men, for they were greatly humiliated. The king said, "Stay at Jericho till your beards have grown, and then come back."

⁶When the Ammonites realized that they had become a stench in David's nostrils, they hired twenty thousand Aramean foot soldiers from Beth Rehob and Zobah, as well as the king of Maacah with a thousand men, and also twelve thousand men from Tob.

⁷On hearing this, David sent Joab out with the entire army of fighting men. ⁸The Ammonites came out and drew up in battle formation at the entrance to their city gate, while the Arameans of Zobah and Rehob and the men of Tob and Maacah were by themselves in the open country.

⁹Joab saw that there were battle lines in front of him and behind him; so he selected some of the best troops in Israel and deployed them against the Arameans. ¹⁰He put the rest of the men under the command of Abishai his brother and deployed them against the Ammonites. ¹¹Joab said, "If the Arameans are too strong for me, then you are to come to my rescue; but if the Ammonites are too strong for you, then I will come to rescue you. ¹²Be strong and let us fight bravely for our people and the cities of our God. The LORD will do what is good in his sight."

¹³Then Joab and the troops with him advanced to fight the Arameans, and they fled before him. ¹⁴When the Ammonites saw that the Arameans were fleeing, they fled before Abishai and went inside the city. So Joab returned from fighting the Ammonites and came to Jerusalem.

¹⁵After the Arameans saw that they had been routed by Israel, they regrouped. ¹⁶Hadadezer had Arameans brought from beyond the River[b]; they went to Helam, with Shobach the commander of Hadadezer's army leading them.

¹⁷When David was told of this, he gathered all Israel, crossed the Jordan and went to Helam. The Arameans formed their battle lines to meet David and fought against him. ¹⁸But they fled before Israel, and David killed seven hundred of their charioteers and forty thousand of their foot soldiers.[c] He also

Resisting the Urge to Humiliate

If you've ever been tagged with an embarrassing nickname or been made fun of because of the way you look or what you wear or something you said or did, then you know all too well how intensely humiliating that kind of experience can be. Remember those feelings the next time you're tempted to go off on someone else and have a little fun at their expense. Don't be the kind of guy that people dread seeing because they're afraid of what you'll say. Treat people the way you want others to treat you.

»» live the adventure »» 2Sa 10:4-5

---

[a] 11 Septuagint; Hebrew *my*   [b] 16 That is, the Euphrates   [c] 18 Some Septuagint manuscripts (see also 1 Chron. 19:18); Hebrew *horsemen*

struck down Shobach the commander of their army, and he died there. ¹⁹When all the kings who were vassals of Hadadezer saw that they had been defeated by Israel, they made peace with the Israelites and became subject to them.

So the Arameans were afraid to help the Ammonites anymore.

DAVID AND BATHSHEBA

11 In the spring, at the time when kings go off to war, David sent Joab out with the king's men and the whole Israelite army. They destroyed the Ammonites and besieged Rabbah. But David remained in Jerusalem.

²One evening David got up from his bed and walked around on the roof of the palace. From the roof he saw a woman bathing. The woman was very beautiful, ³and David sent someone to find out about her. The man said, "Isn't this Bathsheba, the daughter of Eliam and the wife of Uriah the Hittite?" ⁴Then David sent messengers to get her. She came to him, and he slept with her. (She had purified herself from her uncleanness.) Then ᵃ she went back home. ⁵The woman conceived and sent word to David, saying, "I am pregnant."

⁶So David sent this word to Joab: "Send me Uriah the Hittite." And Joab sent him to David. ⁷When Uriah came to him, David asked him how Joab was, how the soldiers were and how the war was going. ⁸Then David said to Uriah, "Go down to your house and wash your feet." So Uriah left the palace, and a gift from the king was sent after him. ⁹But Uriah slept at the entrance to the palace with all his master's servants and did not go down to his house.

¹⁰When David was told, "Uriah did not go home," he asked him, "Haven't you just come from a distance? Why didn't you go home?"

¹¹Uriah said to David, "The ark and Israel and Judah are staying in tents, and my master Joab and my lord's men are camped in the open fields. How could I go to my house to eat and drink and lie with my wife? As surely as you live, I will not do such a thing!"

¹²Then David said to him, "Stay here one more day, and tomorrow I will send you back." So Uriah remained in Jerusalem that day and the next. ¹³At David's invitation, he ate and drank with him, and David made him drunk. But in the evening Uriah went out to sleep on his mat among his master's servants; he did not go home.

¹⁴In the morning David wrote a letter to Joab and sent it with Uriah. ¹⁵In it he wrote, "Put Uriah in the front line where the fighting is fiercest. Then withdraw from him so he will be struck down and die."

¹⁶So while Joab had the city under siege, he put Uriah at a place where he knew the strongest defenders were. ¹⁷When the men of the city came out and fought against Joab, some of the men in David's army fell; moreover, Uriah the Hittite died.

¹⁸Joab sent David a full account of the battle. ¹⁹He instructed the messenger: "When you have finished giving the king this account of the battle, ²⁰the king's anger may flare up, and he may ask you, 'Why did you get so close to the city to fight? Didn't you know they would shoot arrows from the wall? ²¹Who killed Abimelech son of Jerub-Besheth ᵇ? Didn't a woman throw an upper millstone on him from the wall, so that he died in Thebez? Why did you get so close to the wall?' If he asks you this, then say to him, 'Also, your servant Uriah the Hittite is dead.' "

²²The messenger set out, and when he arrived he told David everything Joab had sent him to say. ²³The messenger said to David, "The men overpowered us and came out against us in the open, but we drove them back to the entrance to the city gate. ²⁴Then the archers shot arrows at your servants from the wall, and some of the king's men died. Moreover, your servant Uriah the Hittite is dead."

²⁵David told the messenger, "Say this to Joab: 'Don't let this upset you; the sword devours one as well as another. Press the attack against the city and destroy it.' Say this to encourage Joab."

²⁶When Uriah's wife heard that her husband was dead, she mourned for him. ²⁷After the time of mourning was over, David had her brought to his house, and she became his wife and bore him a son. But the thing David had done displeased the LORD.

NATHAN REBUKES DAVID

12 The LORD sent Nathan to David. When he came to him, he said, "There were two men in a certain town, one rich and the other poor. ²The rich man had a very large number of sheep and cattle, ³but the poor man had nothing except one little ewe lamb he had bought.

ᵃ 4 Or *with her. When she purified herself from her uncleanness,*   ᵇ 21 Also known as *Jerub-Baal* (that is, Gideon)

battlelines

» Point of No Return (God's Forgiveness)

Q: You have to tell me more about what you did or I can't help you. Are we talking about something criminal?
A: I don't *think* so. (Burying his face in his hands) I don't know.

Q: Well, then what is it? Porn? Stealing? What? Let me help you here.
A: (Shaking, beginning to cry) It's too bad to go into. Too embarrassing. All I can tell you is I did something I never should have done. And I can't *undo* it. God will never forgive me.

Q: What makes you think that?
A: I really thought becoming a Christian would make me a better person. But I think I'm getting worse . . . if that's possible.

Q: But the Bible says—
A: I *know* what the Bible says. But I don't think it mentions the kind of things I've done.

Q: But it talks about God's grace and forgiveness.
A: Yeah, well, I don't think they apply in my case. My head wants to believe that God would forgive me, but a louder voice inside me keeps screaming, *No way!*

Q: But you're still alive.
A: So? What does that mean?

Q: Well, if God were through with you, why wouldn't he just end your life?
A: Maybe he's getting ready to. Or maybe he's going to torture me with a long life of guilt.

Q: Or maybe he wants to give you a chance to understand that he still loves you.
A: I wish I could believe that.

» Place of Grace

Think you're such a world-class sinner that not even Almighty God can rescue you? Don't flatter yourself! Nothing you could ever do is bigger than what Jesus has already done for you on the cross. It's like the guy who went to his doctor in terrible agony. The doctor's reply? "Don't sweat it. I've got way more medicine than you've got sickness."

God's grace is kind of like that. In the words of an old hymn, it's "greater than all our sin." Look at Jesus. He asked the Father to forgive the very guys who nailed him to the cross. If he was willing to forgive them, he's willing to forgive you too. If you doubt that, it might help to remember that God forgave . . .

● Peter, who denied he ever knew Jesus (see John 18:15–27; 21:15–22)

● David, who slept with another man's wife and then had the guy killed (see 2 Samuel 11–12)

● Paul, whose first career was persecuting Christians (see Acts 7:54—8:3; 9:1–16).

God loves you. Period. No strings attached, no matter what. He'll forgive you, if you just ask him to (see 1 John 1:9–10). And once you've confessed to him, those accusations you keep hearing—they're not from him!

When you're feeling overrun by guilt, visit www.RevolutionBible.com.

He raised it, and it grew up with him and his children. It shared his food, drank from his cup and even slept in his arms. It was like a daughter to him.

⁴"Now a traveler came to the rich man, but the rich man refrained from taking one of his own sheep or cattle to prepare a meal for the traveler who had come to him. Instead, he took the ewe lamb that belonged to the poor man and prepared it for the one who had come to him."

⁵David burned with anger against the man and said to Nathan, "As surely as the LORD lives, the man who did this deserves to die! ⁶He must pay for that lamb four times over, because he did such a thing and had no pity."

⁷Then Nathan said to David, "You are the man! This is what the LORD, the God of Israel, says: 'I anointed you king over Israel, and I delivered you from the hand of Saul. ⁸I gave your master's house to you, and your master's wives into your arms. I gave you the house of Israel and Judah. And if all this had been too little, I would have given you even more. ⁹Why did you despise the word of the LORD by doing what is evil in his eyes? You struck down Uriah the Hittite with the sword and took his wife to be your own. You killed him with the sword of the Ammonites. ¹⁰Now, therefore, the sword will never depart from your house, because you despised me and took the wife of Uriah the Hittite to be your own.'

¹¹"This is what the LORD says: 'Out of your own household I am going to bring calamity upon you. Before your very eyes I will take your wives and give them to one who is close to you, and he will lie with your wives in broad daylight. ¹²You did it in secret, but I will do this thing in broad daylight before all Israel.' "

¹³Then David said to Nathan, "I have sinned against the LORD."

Nathan replied, "The LORD has taken away your sin. You are not going to die. ¹⁴But because by doing this you have made the enemies of the LORD show utter contempt,ᵃ the son born to you will die."

¹⁵After Nathan had gone home, the LORD struck the child that Uriah's wife had borne to David, and he became ill. ¹⁶David pleaded with God for the child. He fasted and went into his house and spent the nights lying on the ground. ¹⁷The elders of his household stood beside him to get him up from the ground, but he refused, and he would not eat any food with them.

¹⁸On the seventh day the child died. David's servants were afraid to tell him that the child was dead, for they thought, "While the child was still living, we spoke to David but he would not listen to us. How can we tell him the child is dead? He may do something desperate."

¹⁹David noticed that his servants were whispering among themselves and he realized the child was dead. "Is the child dead?" he asked.

"Yes," they replied, "he is dead."

²⁰Then David got up from the ground. After he had washed, put on lotions and changed his clothes, he went into the house of the LORD and worshiped. Then he went to his own house, and at his request they served him food, and he ate.

²¹His servants asked him, "Why are you acting this way? While the child was alive, you fasted and wept, but now that the child is dead, you get up and eat!"

²²He answered, "While the child was still alive, I fasted and wept. I thought, 'Who knows? The LORD may be gracious to me and let the child live.' ²³But now that he is dead, why should I fast? Can I bring him back again? I will go to him, but he will not return to me."

²⁴Then David comforted his wife Bathsheba, and he went to her and lay with her. She gave birth to a son, and they named him Solomon. The LORD loved him; ²⁵and because the LORD loved him, he sent word through Nathan the prophet to name him Jedidiah.ᵇ

Waiting for God

Have you ever stared at your phone, waiting for a friend to reply to a text message? You wait and stare ... and wait some more. Finally you get annoyed and give up. Sometimes we treat God that way. We send off a prayer to him and want an instant reply. When the answer doesn't come, we get frustrated. But because of his perfect knowledge, God knows exactly what to do and when to do it, so he's never late in answering our prayers. Consequently, since we don't always know when his answer will come, our best bet is to keep on praying and get on with living our faith journey while we wait.

ᵃ 14 Masoretic Text; an ancient Hebrew scribal tradition *this you have shown utter contempt for the LORD*   ᵇ 25 Jedidiah means *loved by the LORD*.

26Meanwhile Joab fought against Rabbah of the Ammonites and captured the royal citadel. 27Joab then sent messengers to David, saying, "I have fought against Rabbah and taken its water supply. 28Now muster the rest of the troops and besiege the city and capture it. Otherwise I will take the city, and it will be named after me."

29So David mustered the entire army and went to Rabbah, and attacked and captured it. 30He took the crown from the head of their king^a—its weight was a talent^b of gold, and it was set with precious stones—and it was placed on David's head. He took a great quantity of plunder from the city 31and brought out the people who were there, consigning them to labor with saws and with iron picks and axes, and he made them work at brickmaking.^c He did this to all the Ammonite towns. Then David and his entire army returned to Jerusalem.

AMNON AND TAMAR

13

In the course of time, Amnon son of David fell in love with Tamar, the beautiful sister of Absalom son of David.

2Amnon became frustrated to the point of illness on account of his sister Tamar, for she was a virgin, and it seemed impossible for him to do anything to her.

3Now Amnon had a friend named Jonadab son of Shimeah, David's brother. Jonadab was a very shrewd man. 4He asked Amnon, "Why do you, the king's son, look so haggard morning after morning? Won't you tell me?"

Amnon said to him, "I'm in love with Tamar, my brother Absalom's sister."

5"Go to bed and pretend to be ill," Jonadab said. "When your father comes to see you, say to him, 'I would like my sister Tamar to come and give me something to eat. Let her prepare the food in my sight so I may watch her and then eat it from her hand.'"

6So Amnon lay down and pretended to be ill. When the king came to see him, Amnon said to him, "I would like my sister Tamar to come and make some special bread in my sight, so I may eat from her hand."

7David sent word to Tamar at the palace: "Go to the house of your brother Amnon and prepare some food for him." 8So Tamar went to the house of her brother Amnon, who was lying down. She took some dough, kneaded it, made the bread in his sight and baked it. 9Then she took the pan and served him the bread, but he refused to eat.

"Send everyone out of here," Amnon said. So everyone left him. 10Then Amnon said to Tamar, "Bring the food here into my bedroom so I may eat from your hand." And Tamar took the bread she had prepared and brought it to her brother Amnon in his bedroom. 11But when she took it to him to eat, he grabbed her and said, "Come to bed with me, my sister."

12"Don't, my brother!" she said to him. "Don't force me. Such a thing should not be done in Israel! Don't do this wicked thing. 13What about me? Where could I get rid of my disgrace? And what about you? You would be like one of the wicked fools in Israel. Please speak to the king; he will not keep me from being married to you." 14But he refused to listen to her, and since he was stronger than she, he raped her.

15Then Amnon hated her with intense hatred. In fact, he hated her more than he had loved her. Amnon said to her, "Get up and get out!"

16"No!" she said to him. "Sending me away would be a greater wrong than what you have already done to me."

---

^a 30 Or of Milcom (that is, Molech)   ^b 30 That is, about 75 pounds (about 34 kilograms)   ^c 31 The meaning of the Hebrew for this clause is uncertain.

But he refused to listen to her. ¹⁷He called his personal servant and said, "Get this woman out of here and bolt the door after her." ¹⁸So his servant put her out and bolted the door after her. She was wearing a richly ornamented^a robe, for this was the kind of garment the virgin daughters of the king wore. ¹⁹Tamar put ashes on her head and tore the ornamented^b robe she was wearing. She put her hand on her head and went away, weeping aloud as she went.

⌐OW OR ⌐EVER

2SA 13:11–15

The more you give in to lust's snare, the more power it gains over your life. Give in long enough, and you'll find yourself completely controlled by its desires.

²⁰Her brother Absalom said to her, "Has that Amnon, your brother, been with you? Be quiet now, my sister; he is your brother. Don't take this thing to heart." And Tamar lived in her brother Absalom's house, a desolate woman.

²¹When King David heard all this, he was furious. ²²Absalom never said a word to Amnon, either good or bad; he hated Amnon because he had disgraced his sister Tamar.

ABSALOM KILLS AMNON

²³Two years later, when Absalom's sheepshearers were at Baal Hazor near the border of Ephraim, he invited all the king's sons to come there. ²⁴Absalom went to the king and said, "Your servant has had shearers come. Will the king and his officials please join me?"

²⁵"No, my son," the king replied. "All of us should not go; we would only be a burden to you." Although Absalom urged him, he still refused to go, but gave him his blessing.

²⁶Then Absalom said, "If not, please let my brother Amnon come with us."

The king asked him, "Why should he go with you?" ²⁷But Absalom urged him, so he sent with him Amnon and the rest of the king's sons.

²⁸Absalom ordered his men, "Listen! When Amnon is in high spirits from drinking wine and I say to you, 'Strike Amnon down,' then kill him. Don't be afraid. Have not I given you this order? Be strong and brave." ²⁹So Absalom's men did to Amnon what Absalom had ordered. Then all the king's sons got up, mounted their mules and fled.

³⁰While they were on their way, the report came to David: "Absalom has struck down all the king's sons; not one of them is left." ³¹The king stood up, tore his clothes and lay down on the ground; and all his servants stood by with their clothes torn.

³²But Jonadab son of Shimeah, David's brother, said, "My lord should not think that they killed all the princes; only Amnon is dead. This has been Absalom's expressed intention ever since the day Amnon raped his sister Tamar. ³³My lord the king should not be concerned about the report that all the king's sons are dead. Only Amnon is dead."

³⁴Meanwhile, Absalom had fled.

Now the man standing watch looked up and saw many people on the road west of him, coming down the side of the hill. The watchman went and told the king, "I see men in the direction of Horonaim, on the side of the hill."^c

³⁵Jonadab said to the king, "See, the king's sons are here; it has happened just as your servant said."

³⁶As he finished speaking, the king's sons came in, wailing loudly. The king, too, and all his servants wept very bitterly.

³⁷Absalom fled and went to Talmai son of Ammihud, the king of Geshur. But King David mourned for his son every day.

³⁸After Absalom fled and went to Geshur, he stayed there three years. ³⁹And the spirit of the king^d longed to go to Absalom, for he was consoled concerning Amnon's death.

ABSALOM RETURNS TO JERUSALEM

14 Joab son of Zeruiah knew that the king's heart longed for Absalom. ²So Joab sent someone to Tekoa and had a wise woman brought from there. He said to her, "Pre-

---

^a *18* The meaning of the Hebrew for this phrase is uncertain.   ^b *19* The meaning of the Hebrew for this word is uncertain.
^c *34* Septuagint; Hebrew does not have this sentence.   ^d *39* Dead Sea Scrolls and some Septuagint manuscripts; Masoretic Text *But the spirit of David the king*

tend you are in mourning. Dress in mourning clothes, and don't use any cosmetic lotions. Act like a woman who has spent many days grieving for the dead. ³Then go to the king and speak these words to him." And Joab put the words in her mouth.

⁴When the woman from Tekoa went[a] to the king, she fell with her face to the ground to pay him honor, and she said, "Help me, O king!"

⁵The king asked her, "What is troubling you?"

She said, "I am indeed a widow; my husband is dead. ⁶I your servant had two sons. They got into a fight with each other in the field, and no one was there to separate them. One struck the other and killed him. ⁷Now the whole clan has risen up against your servant; they say, 'Hand over the one who struck his brother down, so that we may put him to death for the life of his brother whom he killed; then we will get rid of the heir as well.' They would put out the only burning coal I have left, leaving my husband neither name nor descendant on the face of the earth."

⁸The king said to the woman, "Go home, and I will issue an order in your behalf."

⁹But the woman from Tekoa said to him, "My lord the king, let the blame rest on me and on my father's family, and let the king and his throne be without guilt."

¹⁰The king replied, "If anyone says anything to you, bring him to me, and he will not bother you again."

¹¹She said, "Then let the king invoke the LORD his God to prevent the avenger of blood from adding to the destruction, so that my son will not be destroyed."

"As surely as the LORD lives," he said, "not one hair of your son's head will fall to the ground."

¹²Then the woman said, "Let your servant speak a word to my lord the king."

"Speak," he replied.

¹³The woman said, "Why then have you devised a thing like this against the people of God? When the king says this, does he not convict himself, for the king has not brought back his banished son? ¹⁴Like water spilled on the ground, which cannot be recovered, so we must die. But God does not take away life; instead, he devises ways so that a banished person may not remain estranged from him.

¹⁵"And now I have come to say this to my lord the king because the people have made me afraid. Your servant thought, 'I will speak to the king; perhaps he will do what his servant asks. ¹⁶Perhaps the king will agree to deliver his servant from the hand of the man who is trying to cut off both me and my son from the inheritance God gave us.'

¹⁷"And now your servant says, 'May the word of my lord the king bring me rest, for my lord the king is like an angel of God in discerning good and evil. May the LORD your God be with you.'"

¹⁸Then the king said to the woman, "Do not keep from me the answer to what I am going to ask you."

"Let my lord the king speak," the woman said.

¹⁹The king asked, "Isn't the hand of Joab with you in all this?"

The woman answered, "As surely as you live, my lord the king, no one can turn to the right or to the left from anything my lord the king says. Yes, it was your servant Joab who instructed me to do this and who put all these words into the mouth of your servant. ²⁰Your servant Joab did this to change the present situation. My lord has wisdom like that of an angel of God—he knows everything that happens in the land."

²¹The king said to Joab, "Very well, I will do it. Go, bring back the young man Absalom."

²²Joab fell with his face to the ground to pay him honor, and he blessed the king. Joab said, "Today your servant knows that he has found favor in your eyes, my lord the king, because the king has granted his servant's request."

²³Then Joab went to Geshur and brought Absalom back to Jerusalem. ²⁴But the king said, "He must go to his own house; he must not see my face." So Absalom went to his own house and did not see the face of the king.

²⁵In all Israel there was not a man so highly praised for his handsome appearance as Absalom. From the top of his head to the sole of his foot there was no blemish in him. ²⁶Whenever he cut the hair of his head—he used to cut his hair from time to time when it became too heavy for him—he would weigh it, and its weight was two hundred shekels[b] by the royal standard.

²⁷Three sons and a daughter were born to Absalom. The daughter's name was Tamar, and she became a beautiful woman.

---

[a] 4 Many Hebrew manuscripts, Septuagint, Vulgate and Syriac; most Hebrew manuscripts *spoke*   [b] 26 That is, about 5 pounds (about 2.3 kilograms)

²⁸Absalom lived two years in Jerusalem without seeing the king's face. ²⁹Then Absalom sent for Joab in order to send him to the king, but Joab refused to come to him. So he sent a second time, but he refused to come. ³⁰Then he said to his servants, "Look, Joab's field is next to mine, and he has barley there. Go and set it on fire." So Absalom's servants set the field on fire.

³¹Then Joab did go to Absalom's house and he said to him, "Why have your servants set my field on fire?"

³²Absalom said to Joab, "Look, I sent word to you and said, 'Come here so I can send you to the king to ask, "Why have I come from Geshur? It would be better for me if I were still there!" ' Now then, I want to see the king's face, and if I am guilty of anything, let him put me to death."

³³So Joab went to the king and told him this. Then the king summoned Absalom, and he came in and bowed down with his face to the ground before the king. And the king kissed Absalom.

ABSALOM'S CONSPIRACY

15 In the course of time, Absalom provided himself with a chariot and horses and with fifty men to run ahead of him. ²He would get up early and stand by the side of the road leading to the city gate. Whenever anyone came with a complaint to be placed before the king for a decision, Absalom would call out to him, "What town are you from?" He would answer, "Your servant is from one of the tribes of Israel." ³Then Absalom would say to him, "Look, your claims are valid and proper, but there is no representative of the king to hear you." ⁴And Absalom would add, "If only I were appointed judge in the land! Then everyone who has a complaint or case could come to me and I would see that he gets justice."

⁵Also, whenever anyone approached him to bow down before him, Absalom would reach out his hand, take hold of him and kiss him. ⁶Absalom behaved in this way toward all the Israelites who came to the king asking for justice, and so he stole the hearts of the men of Israel.

⁷At the end of four[a] years, Absalom said to the king, "Let me go to Hebron and fulfill a vow I made to the LORD. ⁸While your servant was living at Geshur in Aram, I made this vow: 'If the LORD takes me back to Jerusalem, I will worship the LORD in Hebron.[b] ' "

⁹The king said to him, "Go in peace." So he went to Hebron.

¹⁰Then Absalom sent secret messengers throughout the tribes of Israel to say, "As soon as you hear the sound of the trumpets, then say, 'Absalom is king in Hebron.' " ¹¹Two hundred men from Jerusalem had accompanied Absalom. They had been invited as guests and went quite innocently, knowing nothing about the matter. ¹²While Absalom was offering sacrifices, he also sent for Ahithophel the Gilonite, David's counselor, to come from Giloh, his hometown. And so the conspiracy gained strength, and Absalom's following kept on increasing.

DAVID FLEES

¹³A messenger came and told David, "The hearts of the men of Israel are with Absalom."

¹⁴Then David said to all his officials who were with him in Jerusalem, "Come! We must flee, or none of us will escape from Absalom. We must leave immediately, or he will move quickly to overtake us and bring ruin upon us and put the city to the sword."

¹⁵The king's officials answered him, "Your servants are ready to do whatever our lord the king chooses."

¹⁶The king set out, with his entire household following him; but he left ten concubines to take care of the palace. ¹⁷So the king set out, with all the people following him, and they halted at a place some distance away. ¹⁸All his men marched past him, along with all the Kerethites and Pelethites; and all the six hundred Gittites who had accompanied him from Gath marched before the king.

¹⁹The king said to Ittai the Gittite, "Why should you come along with us? Go back and stay with King Absalom. You are a foreigner, an exile from your homeland. ²⁰You came only yesterday. And today shall I make you wander about with us, when I do not know where I am going? Go back, and take your countrymen. May kindness and faithfulness be with you."

²¹But Ittai replied to the king, "As surely as the LORD lives, and as my lord the king lives, wherever my lord the king may be, whether it means life or death, there will your servant be."

ᵃ 7 Some Septuagint manuscripts, Syriac and Josephus; Hebrew *forty*   ᵇ 8 Some Septuagint manuscripts; Hebrew does not have *in Hebron*.

361

²²David said to Ittai, "Go ahead, march on." So Ittai the Gittite marched on with all his men and the families that were with him.

²³The whole countryside wept aloud as all the people passed by. The king also crossed the Kidron Valley, and all the people moved on toward the desert.

²⁴Zadok was there, too, and all the Levites who were with him were carrying the ark of the covenant of God. They set down the ark of God, and Abiathar offered sacrifices[a] until all the people had finished leaving the city.

²⁵Then the king said to Zadok, "Take the ark of God back into the city. If I find favor in the LORD's eyes, he will bring me back and let me see it and his dwelling place again. ²⁶But if he says, 'I am not pleased with you,' then I am ready; let him do to me whatever seems good to him."

²⁷The king also said to Zadok the priest, "Aren't you a seer? Go back to the city in peace, with your son Ahimaaz and Jonathan son of Abiathar. You and Abiathar take your two sons with you. ²⁸I will wait at the fords in the desert until word comes from you to inform me." ²⁹So Zadok and Abiathar took the ark of God back to Jerusalem and stayed there.

³⁰But David continued up the Mount of Olives, weeping as he went; his head was covered and he was barefoot. All the people with him covered their heads too and were weeping as they went up. ³¹Now David had been told, "Ahithophel is among the conspirators with Absalom." So David prayed, "O LORD, turn Ahithophel's counsel into foolishness."

³²When David arrived at the summit, where people used to worship God, Hushai the Arkite was there to meet him, his robe torn and dust on his head. ³³David said to him, "If you go with me, you will be a burden to me. ³⁴But if you return to the city and say to Absalom, 'I will be your servant, O king; I was your father's servant in the past, but now I will be your servant,' then you can help me by frustrating Ahithophel's advice. ³⁵Won't the priests Zadok and Abiathar be there with you? Tell them anything you hear in the king's palace. ³⁶Their two sons, Ahimaaz son of Zadok and Jonathan son of Abiathar, are there with them. Send them to me with anything you hear."

³⁷So David's friend Hushai arrived at Jerusalem as Absalom was entering the city.

DAVID AND ZIBA

16 When David had gone a short distance beyond the summit, there was Ziba, the steward of Mephibosheth, waiting to meet him. He had a string of donkeys saddled and loaded with two hundred loaves of bread, a hundred cakes of raisins, a hundred cakes of figs and a skin of wine.

²The king asked Ziba, "Why have you brought these?"

Ziba answered, "The donkeys are for the king's household to ride on, the bread and fruit are for the men to eat, and the wine is to refresh those who become exhausted in the desert."

³The king then asked, "Where is your master's grandson?"

Ziba said to him, "He is staying in Jerusalem, because he thinks, 'Today the house of Israel will give me back my grandfather's kingdom.' "

⁴Then the king said to Ziba, "All that belonged to Mephibosheth is now yours."

"I humbly bow," Ziba said. "May I find favor in your eyes, my lord the king."

SHIMEI CURSES DAVID

⁵As King David approached Bahurim, a man from the same clan as Saul's family came out from there. His name was Shimei son of Gera, and he cursed as he came out. ⁶He pelted David and all the king's officials with stones, though all the troops and the special guard were on David's right and left. ⁷As he cursed, Shimei said, "Get out, get out, you man of blood, you scoundrel! ⁸The LORD has repaid you for all the blood you shed in the household of Saul, in whose place you have reigned. The LORD has handed the kingdom over to your son Absalom. You have come to ruin because you are a man of blood!"

⁹Then Abishai son of Zeruiah said to the king, "Why should this dead dog curse my lord the king? Let me go over and cut off his head."

¹⁰But the king said, "What do you and I have in common, you sons of Zeruiah? If he is cursing because the LORD said to him, 'Curse David,' who can ask, 'Why do you do this?' "

¹¹David then said to Abishai and all his officials, "My son, who is of my own flesh, is trying to take

---

ᵃ *24 Or Abiathar went up*

my life. How much more, then, this Benjamite! Leave him alone; let him curse, for the Lord has told him to. [12]It may be that the Lord will see my distress and repay me with good for the cursing I am receiving today."

[13]So David and his men continued along the road while Shimei was going along the hillside opposite him, cursing as he went and throwing stones at him and showering him with dirt. [14]The king and all the people with him arrived at their destination exhausted. And there he refreshed himself.

THE ADVICE OF AHITHOPHEL AND HUSHAI

[15]Meanwhile, Absalom and all the men of Israel came to Jerusalem, and Ahithophel was with him. [16]Then Hushai the Arkite, David's friend, went to Absalom and said to him, "Long live the king! Long live the king!"

[17]Absalom asked Hushai, "Is this the love you show your friend? Why didn't you go with your friend?"

[18]Hushai said to Absalom, "No, the one chosen by the Lord, by these people, and by all the men of Israel—his I will be, and I will remain with him. [19]Furthermore, whom should I serve? Should I not serve the son? Just as I served your father, so I will serve you."

[20]Absalom said to Ahithophel, "Give us your advice. What should we do?"

[21]Ahithophel answered, "Lie with your father's concubines whom he left to take care of the palace. Then all Israel will hear that you have made yourself a stench in your father's nostrils, and the hands of everyone with you will be strengthened." [22]So they pitched a tent for Absalom on the roof, and he lay with his father's concubines in the sight of all Israel.

[23]Now in those days the advice Ahithophel gave was like that of one who inquires of God. That was how both David and Absalom regarded all of Ahithophel's advice.

17 Ahithophel said to Absalom, "I would[a] choose twelve thousand men and set out tonight in pursuit of David. [2]I would[b] attack him while he is weary and weak. I would[b] strike him with terror, and then all the people with him will flee. I would[b] strike down only the king [3]and bring all the people back to you. The death of the man you seek will mean the return of all; all the people will be unharmed." [4]This plan seemed good to Absalom and to all the elders of Israel.

[5]But Absalom said, "Summon also Hushai the Arkite, so we can hear what he has to say." [6]When Hushai came to him, Absalom said, "Ahithophel has given this advice. Should we do what he says? If not, give us your opinion."

[7]Hushai replied to Absalom, "The advice Ahithophel has given is not good this time. [8]You know your father and his men; they are fighters, and as fierce as a wild bear robbed of her cubs. Besides, your father is an experienced fighter; he will not spend the night with the troops. [9]Even now, he is hidden in a cave or some other place. If he should attack your troops first,[c] whoever hears about it will say, 'There has been a slaughter among the troops who follow Absalom.' [10]Then even the bravest soldier, whose heart is like the heart of a lion, will melt with fear, for all Israel knows that your father is a fighter and that those with him are brave.

[11]"So I advise you: Let all Israel, from Dan to Beersheba—as numerous as the sand on the seashore—be gathered to you, with you yourself leading them into battle. [12]Then we will attack him wherever he may be found, and we will fall on him as dew settles on the ground. Neither he nor any of his men will be left alive. [13]If he withdraws into a city, then all Israel will bring ropes to that city, and we will drag it down to the valley until not even a piece of it can be found."

[14]Absalom and all the men of Israel said, "The advice of Hushai the Arkite is better than that of Ahithophel." For the Lord had determined to frustrate the good advice of Ahithophel in order to bring disaster on Absalom.

[15]Hushai told Zadok and Abiathar, the priests, "Ahithophel has advised Absalom and the elders of Israel to do such and such, but I have advised them to do so and so. [16]Now send a message immedi-

---

NOW OR NEVER

2SA 16:5–14

There's a right way and a wrong way to let people know when you're angry. If you let your rage overtake you, then you're virtually guaranteed to do something you'll have to apologize for (and often face consequences of) later.

---

[a] 1 Or *Let me*   [b] 2 Or *will*   [c] 9 Or *When some of the men fall at the first attack*

battlelines

» *Spiraling Down (Depression)*

Q: What's the latest with Jason?
A: If you ask me, I think he's getting worse. He won't return anyone's phone calls. He never wants to hang out anymore. He sleeps all the time. It's like nobody can get him to talk.

Q: What about seeing a counselor or something? Would he be up for that?
A: I think he went to counseling a few times right after his brother died. But then he quit. He just said it was a lot of money down the drain.

Q: But you were one of his best friends. You guys did everything together.
A: I know. And now he acts like he barely knows me. It's not like I haven't tried to reach out to the guy. I have—in major ways. But he just blows me off. So now I just pray for him. What else can I do, you know?

Q: So, bottom-line, what do you think?
A: I think it's serious. I think Jason needs to be on some kind of major medication, maybe even hospitalized for a while. I don't understand what his parents are thinking. Where are they in all of this? Why don't they wake up and *do* something? It's the saddest thing in the world. Here's this awesome guy completely going under, and nobody's doing anything. If something doesn't happen soon, I'm afraid this is going to end in a real bad way.

» *Getting Help*

Tim's right. Depression is serious business. If you know someone who's depressed, the best thing you can do for that person is to engage yourself in his or her life. At times, you'll probably feel helpless, and you might want to give up and walk away. Don't! Instead, remember some "P"s:

● Pray (like crazy).

● Put together a team of friends committed to helping. (Don't try to do it all yourself.)

● Push and prod (gently but firmly) your depressed friend to seek the necessary medical, psychological and spiritual help. If your friend's already getting treatment, encourage him to stick with it. Don't let him fall for the all-too-common lie, "Nothing is going to help, so why bother trying?" (And yes, there may be a time when it's right to consider talking to your friend's parents. Share your concerns, not your advice. Statements about suicide are the kind of secret you can't afford to keep.)

● Provide ongoing support. Remember, "A friend loves at all times, and a brother is born for adversity" (Proverbs 17:17).

Read more about overcoming depression at www.RevolutionBible.com.

ately and tell David, 'Do not spend the night at the fords in the desert; cross over without fail, or the king and all the people with him will be swallowed up.'"

[17]Jonathan and Ahimaaz were staying at En Rogel. A servant girl was to go and inform them, and they were to go and tell King David, for they could not risk being seen entering the city. [18]But a young man saw them and told Absalom. So the two of them left quickly and went to the house of a man in Bahurim. He had a well in his courtyard, and they climbed down into it. [19]His wife took a covering and spread it out over the opening of the well and scattered grain over it. No one knew anything about it.

[20]When Absalom's men came to the woman at the house, they asked, "Where are Ahimaaz and Jonathan?"

The woman answered them, "They crossed over the brook."[a] The men searched but found no one, so they returned to Jerusalem.

[21]After the men had gone, the two climbed out of the well and went to inform King David. They said to him, "Set out and cross the river at once; Ahithophel has advised such and such against you." [22]So David and all the people with him set out and crossed the Jordan. By daybreak, no one was left who had not crossed the Jordan.

[23]When Ahithophel saw that his advice had not been followed, he saddled his donkey and set out for his house in his hometown. He put his house in order and then hanged himself. So he died and was buried in his father's tomb.

[24]David went to Mahanaim, and Absalom crossed the Jordan with all the men of Israel. [25]Absalom had appointed Amasa over the army in place of Joab. Amasa was the son of a man named Jether,[b] an Israelite[c] who had married Abigail,[d] the daughter of Nahash and sister of Zeruiah the mother of Joab. [26]The Israelites and Absalom camped in the land of Gilead.

[27]When David came to Mahanaim, Shobi son of Nahash from Rabbah of the Ammonites, and Makir son of Ammiel from Lo Debar, and Barzillai the Gileadite from Rogelim [28]brought bedding and bowls and articles of pottery. They also brought wheat and barley, flour and roasted grain, beans and lentils,[e] [29]honey and curds, sheep, and cheese from cows' milk for David and his people to eat. For they said, "The people have become hungry and tired and thirsty in the desert."

NOW OR NEVER
2SA 17:27–29

How can you make people feel more comfortable around you? What can you do to be more sensitive to the needs of others? In particular, when you see others serving God, what can you do to help them accomplish their objective?

ABSALOM'S DEATH

18 David mustered the men who were with him and appointed over them commanders of thousands and commanders of hundreds. [2]David sent the troops out—a third under the command of Joab, a third under Joab's brother Abishai son of Zeruiah, and a third under Ittai the Gittite. The king told the troops, "I myself will surely march out with you."

[3]But the men said, "You must not go out; if we are forced to flee, they won't care about us. Even if half of us die, they won't care; but you are worth ten thousand of us.[f] It would be better now for you to give us support from the city."

[4]The king answered, "I will do whatever seems best to you."

So the king stood beside the gate while all the men marched out in units of hundreds and of thousands. [5]The king commanded Joab, Abishai and Ittai, "Be gentle with the young man Absalom for my sake." And all the troops heard the king giving orders concerning Absalom to each of the commanders.

[6]The army marched into the field to fight Israel, and the battle took place in the forest of Ephraim. [7]There the army of Israel was defeated by David's men, and the casualties that day were great—twenty thousand men. [8]The battle spread out over the whole countryside, and the forest claimed more lives that day than the sword.

[a] 20 Or "They passed by the sheep pen toward the water."   [b] 25 Hebrew *Ithra*, a variant of *Jether*   [c] 25 Hebrew and some Septuagint manuscripts; other Septuagint manuscripts (see also 1 Chron. 2:17) *Ishmaelite* or *Jezreelite*   [d] 25 Hebrew *Abigal*, a variant of *Abigail*   [e] 28 Most Septuagint manuscripts and Syriac; Hebrew *lentils, and roasted grain*   [f] 3 Two Hebrew manuscripts, some Septuagint manuscripts and Vulgate; most Hebrew manuscripts *care; for now there are ten thousand like us*

⁹Now Absalom happened to meet David's men. He was riding his mule, and as the mule went under the thick branches of a large oak, Absalom's head got caught in the tree. He was left hanging in midair, while the mule he was riding kept on going.

¹⁰When one of the men saw this, he told Joab, "I just saw Absalom hanging in an oak tree."

¹¹Joab said to the man who had told him this, "What! You saw him? Why didn't you strike him to the ground right there? Then I would have had to give you ten shekels[a] of silver and a warrior's belt."

¹²But the man replied, "Even if a thousand shekels[b] were weighed out into my hands, I would not lift my hand against the king's son. In our hearing the king commanded you and Abishai and Ittai, 'Protect the young man Absalom for my sake.'[c] ¹³And if I had put my life in jeopardy[d]—and nothing is hidden from the king—you would have kept your distance from me."

¹⁴Joab said, "I'm not going to wait like this for you." So he took three javelins in his hand and plunged them into Absalom's heart while Absalom was still alive in the oak tree. ¹⁵And ten of Joab's armor-bearers surrounded Absalom, struck him and killed him.

¹⁶Then Joab sounded the trumpet, and the troops stopped pursuing Israel, for Joab halted them. ¹⁷They took Absalom, threw him into a big pit in the forest and piled up a large heap of rocks over him. Meanwhile, all the Israelites fled to their homes.

¹⁸During his lifetime Absalom had taken a pillar and erected it in the King's Valley as a monument to himself, for he thought, "I have no son to carry on the memory of my name." He named the pillar after himself, and it is called Absalom's Monument to this day.

DAVID MOURNS

¹⁹Now Ahimaaz son of Zadok said, "Let me run and take the news to the king that the Lord has delivered him from the hand of his enemies."

²⁰"You are not the one to take the news today," Joab told him. "You may take the news another time, but you must not do so today, because the king's son is dead."

²¹Then Joab said to a Cushite, "Go, tell the king what you have seen." The Cushite bowed down before Joab and ran off.

²²Ahimaaz son of Zadok again said to Joab, "Come what may, please let me run behind the Cushite."

But Joab replied, "My son, why do you want to go? You don't have any news that will bring you a reward."

²³He said, "Come what may, I want to run."

So Joab said, "Run!" Then Ahimaaz ran by way of the plain[e] and outran the Cushite.

²⁴While David was sitting between the inner and outer gates, the watchman went up to the roof of the gateway by the wall. As he looked out, he saw a man running alone. ²⁵The watchman called out to the king and reported it.

The king said, "If he is alone, he must have good news." And the man came closer and closer.

²⁶Then the watchman saw another man running, and he called down to the gatekeeper, "Look, another man running alone!"

The king said, "He must be bringing good news, too."

²⁷The watchman said, "It seems to me that the first one runs like Ahimaaz son of Zadok."

"He's a good man," the king said. "He comes with good news."

²⁸Then Ahimaaz called out to the king, "All is well!" He bowed down before the king with his face to the ground and said, "Praise be to the Lord your God! He has delivered up the men who lifted their hands against my lord the king."

²⁹The king asked, "Is the young man Absalom safe?"

Ahimaaz answered, "I saw great confusion just as Joab was about to send the king's servant and me, your servant, but I don't know what it was."

³⁰The king said, "Stand aside and wait here." So he stepped aside and stood there.

³¹Then the Cushite arrived and said, "My lord the king, hear the good news! The Lord has delivered you today from all who rose up against you."

³²The king asked the Cushite, "Is the young man Absalom safe?"

ᵃ 11 That is, about 4 ounces (about 115 grams)   ᵇ 12 That is, about 25 pounds (about 11 kilograms)   ᶜ 12 A few Hebrew manuscripts, Septuagint, Vulgate and Syriac; most Hebrew manuscripts may be translated Absalom, whoever you may be.
ᵈ 13 Or Otherwise, if I had acted treacherously toward him   ᵉ 23 That is, the plain of the Jordan

The Cushite replied, "May the enemies of my lord the king and all who rise up to harm you be like that young man."

³³The king was shaken. He went up to the room over the gateway and wept. As he went, he said: "O my son Absalom! My son, my son Absalom! If only I had died instead of you—O Absalom, my son, my son!"

19

Joab was told, "The king is weeping and mourning for Absalom." ²And for the whole army the victory that day was turned into mourning, because on that day the troops heard it said, "The king is grieving for his son." ³The men stole into the city that day as men steal in who are ashamed when they flee from battle. ⁴The king covered his face and cried aloud, "O my son Absalom! O Absalom, my son, my son!"

⁵Then Joab went into the house to the king and said, "Today you have humiliated all your men, who have just saved your life and the lives of your sons and daughters and the lives of your wives and concubines. ⁶You love those who hate you and hate those who love you. You have made it clear today that the commanders and their men mean nothing to you. I see that you would be pleased if Absalom were alive today and all of us were dead. ⁷Now go out and encourage your men. I swear by the LORD that if you don't go out, not a man will be left with you by nightfall. This will be worse for you than all the calamities that have come upon you from your youth till now."

⁸So the king got up and took his seat in the gateway. When the men were told, "The king is sitting in the gateway," they all came before him.

DAVID RETURNS TO JERUSALEM

Meanwhile, the Israelites had fled to their homes. ⁹Throughout the tribes of Israel, the people were all arguing with each other, saying, "The king delivered us from the hand of our enemies; he is the one who rescued us from the hand of the Philistines. But now he has fled the country because of Absalom; ¹⁰and Absalom, whom we anointed to rule over us, has died in battle. So why do you say nothing about bringing the king back?"

¹¹King David sent this message to Zadok and Abiathar, the priests: "Ask the elders of Judah, 'Why should you be the last to bring the king back to his palace, since what is being said throughout Israel has reached the king at his quarters? ¹²You are my brothers, my own flesh and blood. So why should you be the last to bring back the king?' ¹³And say to Amasa, 'Are you not my own flesh and blood? May God deal with me, be it ever so severely, if from now on you are not the commander of my army in place of Joab.' "

¹⁴He won over the hearts of all the men of Judah as though they were one man. They sent word to the king, "Return, you and all your men." ¹⁵Then the king returned and went as far as the Jordan.

Now the men of Judah had come to Gilgal to go out and meet the king and bring him across the Jordan. ¹⁶Shimei son of Gera, the Benjamite from Bahurim, hurried down with the men of Judah to meet King David. ¹⁷With him were a thousand Benjamites, along with Ziba, the steward of Saul's household, and his fifteen sons and twenty servants. They rushed to the Jordan, where the king was. ¹⁸They crossed at the ford to take the king's household over and to do whatever he wished.

When Shimei son of Gera crossed the Jordan, he fell prostrate before the king ¹⁹and said to him, "May my lord not hold me guilty. Do not remember how your servant did wrong on the day my lord the king left Jerusalem. May the king put it out of his mind. ²⁰For I your servant know that I have sinned, but today I have come here as the first of the whole house of Joseph to come down and meet my lord the king."

»» live the adventure »» 2Sa 19:16–23

Resisting Vengeance

What's your first reaction when someone meddles with your relationships, tarnishes your image or creates havoc in the lives of you and your friends? You want revenge, right? You want to do to that person what he or she did to you—and maybe a little more. It's an understandable reaction . . . but it's a mistake. Revenge belongs to God. Besides, any revenge you get is going to make that person want to get you back. Instead of solving the situation, taking revenge only escalates the conflict.

²¹Then Abishai son of Zeruiah said, "Shouldn't Shimei be put to death for this? He cursed the Lord's anointed."

²²David replied, "What do you and I have in common, you sons of Zeruiah? This day you have become my adversaries! Should anyone be put to death in Israel today? Do I not know that today I am king over Israel?" ²³So the king said to Shimei, "You shall not die." And the king promised him on oath.

²⁴Mephibosheth, Saul's grandson, also went down to meet the king. He had not taken care of his feet or trimmed his mustache or washed his clothes from the day the king left until the day he returned safely. ²⁵When he came from Jerusalem to meet the king, the king asked him, "Why didn't you go with me, Mephibosheth?"

²⁶He said, "My lord the king, since I your servant am lame, I said, 'I will have my donkey saddled and will ride on it, so I can go with the king.' But Ziba my servant betrayed me. ²⁷And he has slandered your servant to my lord the king. My lord the king is like an angel of God; so do whatever pleases you. ²⁸All my grandfather's descendants deserved nothing but death from my lord the king, but you gave your servant a place among those who eat at your table. So what right do I have to make any more appeals to the king?"

²⁹The king said to him, "Why say more? I order you and Ziba to divide the fields."

³⁰Mephibosheth said to the king, "Let him take everything, now that my lord the king has arrived home safely."

³¹Barzillai the Gileadite also came down from Rogelim to cross the Jordan with the king and to send him on his way from there. ³²Now Barzillai was a very old man, eighty years of age. He had provided for the king during his stay in Mahanaim, for he was a very wealthy man. ³³The king said to Barzillai, "Cross over with me and stay with me in Jerusalem, and I will provide for you."

³⁴But Barzillai answered the king, "How many more years will I live, that I should go up to Jerusalem with the king? ³⁵I am now eighty years old. Can I tell the difference between what is good and what is not? Can your servant taste what he eats and drinks? Can I still hear the voices of men and women singers? Why should your servant be an added burden to my lord the king? ³⁶Your servant will cross over the Jordan with the king for a short distance, but why should the king reward me in this way? ³⁷Let your servant return, that I may die in my own town near the tomb of my father and mother. But here is your servant Kimham. Let him cross over with my lord the king. Do for him whatever pleases you."

³⁸The king said, "Kimham shall cross over with me, and I will do for him whatever pleases you. And anything you desire from me I will do for you."

³⁹So all the people crossed the Jordan, and then the king crossed over. The king kissed Barzillai and gave him his blessing, and Barzillai returned to his home.

⁴⁰When the king crossed over to Gilgal, Kimham crossed with him. All the troops of Judah and half the troops of Israel had taken the king over.

⁴¹Soon all the men of Israel were coming to the king and saying to him, "Why did our brothers, the men of Judah, steal the king away and bring him and his household across the Jordan, together with all his men?"

⁴²All the men of Judah answered the men of Israel, "We did this because the king is closely related to us. Why are you angry about it? Have we eaten any of the king's provisions? Have we taken anything for ourselves?"

⁴³Then the men of Israel answered the men of Judah, "We have ten shares in the king; and besides, we have a greater claim on David than you have. So why do you treat us with contempt? Were we not the first to speak of bringing back our king?"

But the men of Judah responded even more harshly than the men of Israel.

SHEBA REBELS AGAINST DAVID

20

Now a troublemaker named Sheba son of Bicri, a Benjamite, happened to be there. He sounded the trumpet and shouted,

> "We have no share in David,
>   no part in Jesse's son!
> Every man to his tent, O Israel!"

²So all the men of Israel deserted David to follow Sheba son of Bicri. But the men of Judah stayed by their king all the way from the Jordan to Jerusalem.

³When David returned to his palace in Jerusalem, he took the ten concubines he had left to take care of the palace and put them in a house under guard. He provided for them, but did not lie with them. They were kept in confinement till the day of their death, living as widows.

⁴Then the king said to Amasa, "Summon the men of Judah to come to me within three days, and be here yourself." ⁵But when Amasa went to summon Judah, he took longer than the time the king had set for him.

⁶David said to Abishai, "Now Sheba son of Bicri will do us more harm than Absalom did. Take your master's men and pursue him, or he will find fortified cities and escape from us." ⁷So Joab's men and the Kerethites and Pelethites and all the mighty warriors went out under the command of Abishai. They marched out from Jerusalem to pursue Sheba son of Bicri.

⁸While they were at the great rock in Gibeon, Amasa came to meet them. Joab was wearing his military tunic, and strapped over it at his waist was a belt with a dagger in its sheath. As he stepped forward, it dropped out of its sheath.

⁹Joab said to Amasa, "How are you, my brother?" Then Joab took Amasa by the beard with his right hand to kiss him. ¹⁰Amasa was not on his guard against the dagger in Joab's hand, and Joab plunged it into his belly, and his intestines spilled out on the ground. Without being stabbed again, Amasa died. Then Joab and his brother Abishai pursued Sheba son of Bicri.

¹¹One of Joab's men stood beside Amasa and said, "Whoever favors Joab, and whoever is for David, let him follow Joab!" ¹²Amasa lay wallowing in his blood in the middle of the road, and the man saw that all the troops came to a halt there. When he realized that everyone who came up to Amasa stopped, he dragged him from the road into a field and threw a garment over him. ¹³After Amasa had been removed from the road, all the men went on with Joab to pursue Sheba son of Bicri.

¹⁴Sheba passed through all the tribes of Israel to Abel Beth Maacah[a] and through the entire region of the Berites, who gathered together and followed him. ¹⁵All the troops with Joab came and besieged Sheba in Abel Beth Maacah. They built a siege ramp up to the city, and it stood against the outer fortifications. While they were battering the wall to bring it down, ¹⁶a wise woman called from the city, "Listen! Listen! Tell Joab to come here so I can speak to him." ¹⁷He went toward her, and she asked, "Are you Joab?"

"I am," he answered.

She said, "Listen to what your servant has to say."

"I'm listening," he said.

¹⁸She continued, "Long ago they used to say, 'Get your answer at Abel,' and that settled it. ¹⁹We are the peaceful and faithful in Israel. You are trying to destroy a city that is a mother in Israel. Why do you want to swallow up the Lᴏʀᴅ's inheritance?"

²⁰"Far be it from me!" Joab replied, "Far be it from me to swallow up or destroy! ²¹That is not the case. A man named Sheba son of Bicri, from the hill country of Ephraim, has lifted up his hand against the king, against David. Hand over this one man, and I'll withdraw from the city."

The woman said to Joab, "His head will be thrown to you from the wall."

²²Then the woman went to all the people with her wise advice, and they cut off the head of Sheba son of Bicri and threw it to Joab. So he sounded the trumpet, and his men dispersed from the city, each returning to his home. And Joab went back to the king in Jerusalem.

²³Joab was over Israel's entire army; Benaiah son of Jehoiada was over the Kerethites and Pelethites; ²⁴Adoniram[b] was in charge of forced labor; Jehoshaphat son of Ahilud was recorder; ²⁵Sheva was secretary; Zadok and Abiathar were priests; ²⁶and Ira the Jairite was David's priest.

THE GIBEONITES AVENGED

21

During the reign of David, there was a famine for three successive years; so David sought the face of the Lᴏʀᴅ. The Lᴏʀᴅ said, "It is on account of Saul and his blood-stained house; it is because he put the Gibeonites to death."

²The king summoned the Gibeonites and spoke to them. (Now the Gibeonites were not a part of Israel but were survivors of the Amorites; the Israelites had sworn to ˪spare˼ them, but Saul in his zeal for Israel and Judah had tried to annihilate them.) ³David asked the Gibeonites, "What shall I do for you? How shall I make amends so that you will bless the Lᴏʀᴅ's inheritance?"

---

[a] *14* Or *Abel, even Beth Maacah*; also in verse 15   [b] *24* Some Septuagint manuscripts (see also 1 Kings 4:6 and 5:14); Hebrew *Adoram*

[4]The Gibeonites answered him, "We have no right to demand silver or gold from Saul or his family, nor do we have the right to put anyone in Israel to death."

"What do you want me to do for you?" David asked.

[5]They answered the king, "As for the man who destroyed us and plotted against us so that we have been decimated and have no place anywhere in Israel, [6]let seven of his male descendants be given to us to be killed and exposed before the LORD at Gibeah of Saul— the LORD's chosen one."

So the king said, "I will give them to you."

[7]The king spared Mephibosheth son of Jonathan, the son of Saul, because of the oath before the LORD between David and Jonathan son of Saul. [8]But the king took Armoni and Mephibosheth, the two sons of Aiah's daughter Rizpah, whom she had borne to Saul, together with the five sons of Saul's daughter Merab,[a] whom she had borne to Adriel son of Barzillai the Meholathite. [9]He handed them over to the Gibeonites, who killed and exposed them on a hill before the LORD. All seven of them fell together; they were put to death during the first days of the harvest, just as the barley harvest was beginning.

[10]Rizpah daughter of Aiah took sackcloth and spread it out for herself on a rock. From the beginning of the harvest till the rain poured down from the heavens on the bodies, she did not let the birds of the air touch them by day or the wild animals by night. [11]When David was told what Aiah's daughter Rizpah, Saul's concubine, had done, [12]he went and took the bones of Saul and his son Jonathan from the citizens of Jabesh Gilead. (They had taken them secretly from the public square at Beth Shan, where the Philistines had hung them after they struck Saul down on Gilboa.) [13]David brought the bones of Saul and his son Jonathan from there, and the bones of those who had been killed and exposed were gathered up.

[14]They buried the bones of Saul and his son Jonathan in the tomb of Saul's father Kish, at Zela in Benjamin, and did everything the king commanded. After that, God answered prayer in behalf of the land.

WARS AGAINST THE PHILISTINES

[15]Once again there was a battle between the Philistines and Israel. David went down with his men to fight against the Philistines, and he became exhausted. [16]And Ishbi-Benob, one of the descendants of Rapha, whose bronze spearhead weighed three hundred shekels[b] and who was armed with a new ˪sword˩, said he would kill David. [17]But Abishai son of Zeruiah came to David's rescue; he struck the Philistine down and killed him. Then David's men swore to him, saying, "Never again will you go out with us to battle, so that the lamp of Israel will not be extinguished."

[18]In the course of time, there was another battle with the Philistines, at Gob. At that time Sibbecai the Hushathite killed Saph, one of the descendants of Rapha.

[19]In another battle with the Philistines at Gob, Elhanan son of Jaare-Oregim[c] the Bethlehemite killed Goliath[d] the Gittite, who had a spear with a shaft like a weaver's rod.

[20]In still another battle, which took place at Gath, there was a huge man with six fingers on each hand and six toes on each foot—twenty-four in all. He also was descended from Rapha. [21]When he taunted Israel, Jonathan son of Shimeah, David's brother, killed him.

[22]These four were descendants of Rapha in Gath, and they fell at the hands of David and his men.

DAVID'S SONG OF PRAISE

22 David sang to the LORD the words of this song when the LORD delivered him from the hand of all his enemies and from the hand of Saul. [2]He said:

"The LORD is my rock, my fortress and my deliverer;
3   my God is my rock, in whom I take refuge,

NOW OR NEVER
2SA 21:1–3

God cannot stand injustice, even when—scratch that—*especially* when the injustice is committed by his people. Are there old sins in your life that you have not reconciled? Have you dealt justly with your friends and enemies alike?

---

[a] *8* Two Hebrew manuscripts, some Septuagint manuscripts and Syriac (see also 1 Samuel 18:19); most Hebrew and Septuagint manuscripts *Michal*   [b] *16* That is, about 7 1/2 pounds (about 3.5 kilograms)   [c] *19* Or *son of Jair the weaver*   [d] *19* Hebrew and Septuagint; 1 Chron. 20:5 *son of Jair killed Lahmi the brother of Goliath*

my shield and the horn[a] of my salvation.
He is my stronghold, my refuge and my savior—
   from violent men you save me.
4 I call to the LORD, who is worthy of praise,
   and I am saved from my enemies.

5 "The waves of death swirled about me;
   the torrents of destruction overwhelmed me.
6 The cords of the grave[b] coiled around me;
   the snares of death confronted me.
7 In my distress I called to the LORD;
   I called out to my God.
From his temple he heard my voice;
   my cry came to his ears.

8 "The earth trembled and quaked,
   the foundations of the heavens[c]
    shook;
   they trembled because he was angry.
9 Smoke rose from his nostrils;
   consuming fire came from his
    mouth,
   burning coals blazed out of it.
10 He parted the heavens and came down;
   dark clouds were under his feet.
11 He mounted the cherubim and flew;
   he soared[d] on the wings of the wind.
12 He made darkness his canopy around
    him—
   the dark[e] rain clouds of the sky.

NOW OR NEVER
2SA 22:7

What would you do if you fell while rock climbing and injured yourself so badly that you couldn't move? You'd yell as loud as you could until help arrived. That same strategy works for spiritual injuries. When you've made a mess of your relationship with God, call out to him. He can repair the damage.

13 Out of the brightness of his presence
   bolts of lightning blazed forth.
14 The LORD thundered from heaven;
   the voice of the Most High resounded.
15 He shot arrows and scattered ⌊the enemies⌋,
   bolts of lightning and routed them.
16 The valleys of the sea were exposed
   and the foundations of the earth laid bare
at the rebuke of the LORD,
   at the blast of breath from his nostrils.

17 "He reached down from on high and took hold of me;
   he drew me out of deep waters.
18 He rescued me from my powerful enemy,
   from my foes, who were too strong for me.
19 They confronted me in the day of my disaster,
   but the LORD was my support.
20 He brought me out into a spacious place;
   he rescued me because he delighted in me.

21 "The LORD has dealt with me according to my righteousness;
   according to the cleanness of my hands he has rewarded me.
22 For I have kept the ways of the LORD;
   I have not done evil by turning from my God.
23 All his laws are before me;

a 3 Horn here symbolizes strength. b 6 Hebrew Sheol c 8 Hebrew; Vulgate and Syriac (see also Psalm 18:7) mountains d 11 Many Hebrew manuscripts (see also Psalm 18:10); most Hebrew manuscripts appeared e 12 Septuagint and Vulgate (see also Psalm 18:11); Hebrew massed

I have not turned away from his decrees.
24 I have been blameless before him
and have kept myself from sin.
25 The LORD has rewarded me according to my righteousness,
according to my cleanness[a] in his sight.

26 "To the faithful you show yourself faithful,
to the blameless you show yourself blameless,
27 to the pure you show yourself pure,
but to the crooked you show yourself shrewd.
28 You save the humble,
but your eyes are on the haughty to bring them low.
29 You are my lamp, O LORD;
the LORD turns my darkness into light.

30 With your help I can advance against a troop[b];
with my God I can scale a wall.

31 "As for God, his way is perfect;
the word of the LORD is flawless.
He is a shield
for all who take refuge in him.
32 For who is God besides the LORD?
And who is the Rock except our God?
33 It is God who arms me with strength[c]
and makes my way perfect.
34 He makes my feet like the feet of a deer;
he enables me to stand on the heights.

NOW OR NEVER
2SA 22:25–27

God can't be fooled. He knows exactly what you're thinking at all times and why you do the things you do. That's why it's always best to approach him with complete openness, no matter how embarrassing the truth may be.

35 He trains my hands for battle;
my arms can bend a bow of bronze.
36 You give me your shield of victory;
you stoop down to make me great.
37 You broaden the path beneath me,
so that my ankles do not turn.

38 "I pursued my enemies and crushed them;
I did not turn back till they were destroyed.
39 I crushed them completely, and they could not rise;
they fell beneath my feet.
40 You armed me with strength for battle;
you made my adversaries bow at my feet.
41 You made my enemies turn their backs in flight,
and I destroyed my foes.
42 They cried for help, but there was no one to save them—
to the LORD, but he did not answer.
43 I beat them as fine as the dust of the earth;
I pounded and trampled them like mud in the streets.

44 "You have delivered me from the attacks of my people;
you have preserved me as the head of nations.
People I did not know are subject to me,
45 and foreigners come cringing to me;
as soon as they hear me, they obey me.

---

[a] 25 Hebrew; Septuagint and Vulgate (see also Psalm 18:24) *to the cleanness of my hands*   [b] 30 Or *can run through a barricade*
[c] 33 Dead Sea Scrolls, some Septuagint manuscripts, Vulgate and Syriac (see also Psalm 18:32); Masoretic Text *who is my strong refuge*

⁴⁶They all lose heart;
    they come trembling ᵃ from their strongholds.

⁴⁷"The LORD lives! Praise be to my Rock!
    Exalted be God, the Rock, my Savior!
⁴⁸He is the God who avenges me,
    who puts the nations under me,
⁴⁹who sets me free from my enemies.

    You exalted me above my
        foes;
    from violent men you
        rescued me.
⁵⁰Therefore I will praise you,
    O LORD, among the
        nations;
    I will sing praises to your
        name.
⁵¹He gives his king great
        victories;
    he shows unfailing
        kindness to his
        anointed,
    to David and his
        descendants forever."

challenge notes

To: **my_son**

heavenly_father: do you know that I am sovereign? do you understand just what that means? can you explain why I must judge sin? I've given you all kinds of clues about what I'm like in my word. the more you read, the more you will come to understand just how incredible I am.

2SA 22:2-51

THE LAST WORDS OF DAVID

23

These are the last words of David:

"The oracle of David son of Jesse,
    the oracle of the man exalted by the Most High,
the man anointed by the God of Jacob,
    Israel's singer of songs ᵇ:

²"The Spirit of the LORD spoke through me;
    his word was on my tongue.
³The God of Israel spoke,
    the Rock of Israel said to me:
'When one rules over men in righteousness,
    when he rules in the fear of God,
⁴he is like the light of morning at sunrise
    on a cloudless morning,
like the brightness after rain
    that brings the grass from the earth.'

⁵"Is not my house right with God?
    Has he not made with me an everlasting covenant,
    arranged and secured in every part?
Will he not bring to fruition my salvation
    and grant me my every desire?
⁶But evil men are all to be cast aside like thorns,
    which are not gathered with the hand.
⁷Whoever touches thorns
    uses a tool of iron or the shaft of a spear;
    they are burned up where they lie."

ᵃ *46* Some Septuagint manuscripts and Vulgate (see also Psalm 18:45); Masoretic Text *they arm themselves.* ᵇ *1* Or *Israel's beloved singer*

DAVID'S MIGHTY MEN

8These are the names of David's mighty men:

Josheb-Basshebeth,ᵃ a Tahkemonite,ᵇ was chief of the Three; he raised his spear against eight hundred men, whom he killedᶜ in one encounter.

9Next to him was Eleazar son of Dodai the Ahohite. As one of the three mighty men, he was with David when they taunted the Philistines gathered ∟at Pas Dammim,ᵈ for battle. Then the men of Israel retreated, 10but he stood his ground and struck down the Philistines till his hand grew tired and froze to the sword. The Lord brought about a great victory that day. The troops returned to Eleazar, but only to strip the dead.

11Next to him was Shammah son of Agee the Hararite. When the Philistines banded together at a place where there was a field full of lentils, Israel's troops fled from them. 12But Shammah took his stand in the middle of the field. He defended it and struck the Philistines down, and the Lord brought about a great victory.

13During harvest time, three of the thirty chief men came down to David at the cave of Adullam, while a band of Philistines was encamped in the Valley of Rephaim. 14At that time David was in the stronghold, and the Philistine garrison was at Bethlehem. 15David longed for water and said, "Oh, that someone would get me a drink of water from the well near the gate of Bethlehem!" 16So the three mighty men broke through the Philistine lines, drew water from the well near the gate of Bethlehem and carried it back to David. But he refused to drink it; instead, he poured it out before the Lord. 17"Far be it from me, O Lord, to do this!" he said. "Is it not the blood of men who went at the risk of their lives?" And David would not drink it.

Such were the exploits of the three mighty men.

18Abishai the brother of Joab son of Zeruiah was chief of the Three.ᵉ He raised his spear against three hundred men, whom he killed, and so he became as famous as the Three. 19Was he not held in greater honor than the Three? He became their commander, even though he was not included among them.

20Benaiah son of Jehoiada was a valiant fighter from Kabzeel, who performed great exploits. He struck down two of Moab's best men. He also went down into a pit on a snowy day and killed a lion. 21And he struck down a huge Egyptian. Although the Egyptian had a spear in his hand, Benaiah went against him with a club. He snatched the spear from the Egyptian's hand and killed him with his own spear. 22Such were the exploits of Benaiah son of Jehoiada; he too was as famous as the three mighty men. 23He was held in greater honor than any of the Thirty, but he was not included among the Three. And David put him in charge of his bodyguard.

24Among the Thirty were:

Asahel the brother of Joab,
Elhanan son of Dodo from Bethlehem,
25Shammah the Harodite,
Elika the Harodite,
26Helez the Paltite,
Ira son of Ikkesh from Tekoa,
27Abiezer from Anathoth,
Mebunnaiᶠ the Hushathite,
28Zalmon the Ahohite,
Maharai the Netophathite,
29Heledᵍ son of Baanah the Netophathite,
Ithai son of Ribai from Gibeah in Benjamin,
30Benaiah the Pirathonite,
Hiddaiʰ from the ravines of Gaash,
31Abi-Albon the Arbathite,
Azmaveth the Barhumite,

ᵃ *8* Hebrew; some Septuagint manuscripts suggest *Ish-Bosheth*, that is, *Esh-Baal* (see also 1 Chron. 11:11 *Jashobeam*).   ᵇ *8* Probably a variant of *Hacmonite* (see 1 Chron. 11:11)   ᶜ *8* Some Septuagint manuscripts (see also 1 Chron. 11:11); Hebrew and other Septuagint manuscripts *Three; it was Adino the Eznite who killed eight hundred men*   ᵈ *9* See 1 Chron. 11:13; Hebrew *gathered there.*   ᵉ *18* Most Hebrew manuscripts (see also 1 Chron. 11:20); two Hebrew manuscripts and Syriac *Thirty*   ᶠ *27* Hebrew; some Septuagint manuscripts (see also 1 Chron. 11:29) *Sibbecai*   ᵍ *29* Some Hebrew manuscripts and Vulgate (see also 1 Chron. 11:30); most Hebrew manuscripts *Heleb*   ʰ *30* Hebrew; some Septuagint manuscripts (see also 1 Chron. 11:32) *Hurai*

32 Eliahba the Shaalbonite,
  the sons of Jashen,
  Jonathan 33 son of[a] Shammah the Hararite,
  Ahiam son of Sharar[b] the Hararite,
34 Eliphelet son of Ahasbai the Maacathite,
  Eliam son of Ahithophel the Gilonite,
35 Hezro the Carmelite,
  Paarai the Arbite,
36 Igal son of Nathan from Zobah,
  the son of Hagri,[c]
37 Zelek the Ammonite,
  Naharai the Beerothite, the armor-bearer of Joab son of Zeruiah,
38 Ira the Ithrite,
  Gareb the Ithrite
39 and Uriah the Hittite.
  There were thirty-seven in all.

DAVID COUNTS THE FIGHTING MEN

24 Again the anger of the LORD burned against Israel, and he incited David against them, saying, "Go and take a census of Israel and Judah."

2 So the king said to Joab and the army commanders[d] with him, "Go throughout the tribes of Israel from Dan to Beersheba and enroll the fighting men, so that I may know how many there are."

3 But Joab replied to the king, "May the LORD your God multiply the troops a hundred times over, and may the eyes of my lord the king see it. But why does my lord the king want to do such a thing?"

4 The king's word, however, overruled Joab and the army commanders; so they left the presence of the king to enroll the fighting men of Israel.

5 After crossing the Jordan, they camped near Aroer, south of the town in the gorge, and then went through Gad and on to Jazer. 6 They went to Gilead and the region of Tahtim Hodshi, and on to Dan Jaan and around toward Sidon. 7 Then they went toward the fortress of Tyre and all the towns of the Hivites and Canaanites. Finally, they went on to Beersheba in the Negev of Judah.

8 After they had gone through the entire land, they came back to Jerusalem at the end of nine months and twenty days.

9 Joab reported the number of the fighting men to the king: In Israel there were eight hundred thousand able-bodied men who could handle a sword, and in Judah five hundred thousand.

10 David was conscience-stricken after he had counted the fighting men, and he said to the LORD, "I have sinned greatly in what I have done. Now, O LORD, I beg you, take away the guilt of your servant. I have done a very foolish thing."

11 Before David got up the next morning, the word of the LORD had come to Gad the prophet, David's seer: 12 "Go and tell David, 'This is what the LORD says: I am giving you three options. Choose one of them for me to carry out against you.'"

13 So Gad went to David and said to him, "Shall there come upon you three[e] years of famine in your land? Or three months of fleeing from your enemies while they pursue you? Or three days of plague in your land? Now then, think it over and decide how I should answer the one who sent me."

14 David said to Gad, "I am in deep distress. Let us fall into the hands of the LORD, for his mercy is great; but do not let me fall into the hands of men."

15 So the LORD sent a plague on Israel from that morning until the end of the time designated, and seventy thousand of the people from Dan to Beersheba died. 16 When the angel stretched out his hand to destroy Jerusalem, the LORD was grieved because of the calamity and said to the angel who was afflicting the people, "Enough! Withdraw your hand." The angel of the LORD was then at the threshing floor of Araunah the Jebusite.

17 When David saw the angel who was striking down the people, he said to the LORD, "I am the one

---

[a] 33 Some Septuagint manuscripts (see also 1 Chron. 11:34); Hebrew does not have son of.   [b] 33 Hebrew; some Septuagint manuscripts (see also 1 Chron. 11:35) Sacar   [c] 36 Some Septuagint manuscripts (see also 1 Chron. 11:38); Hebrew Haggadi   [d] 2 Septuagint (see also verse 4 and 1 Chron. 21:2); Hebrew Joab the army commander   [e] 13 Septuagint (see also 1 Chron. 21:12); Hebrew seven

who has sinned and done wrong. These are but sheep. What have they done? Let your hand fall upon me and my family."

DAVID BUILDS AN ALTAR

¹⁸On that day Gad went to David and said to him, "Go up and build an altar to the Lᴏʀᴅ on the threshing floor of Araunah the Jebusite." ¹⁹So David went up, as the Lᴏʀᴅ had commanded through Gad. ²⁰When Araunah looked and saw the king and his men coming toward him, he went out and bowed down before the king with his face to the ground.

²¹Araunah said, "Why has my lord the king come to his servant?"

"To buy your threshing floor," David answered, "so I can build an altar to the Lᴏʀᴅ, that the plague on the people may be stopped."

²²Araunah said to David, "Let my lord the king take whatever pleases him and offer it up. Here are oxen for the burnt offering, and here are threshing sledges and ox yokes for the wood. ²³O king, Araunah gives all this to the king." Araunah also said to him, "May the Lᴏʀᴅ your God accept you."

²⁴But the king replied to Araunah, "No, I insist on paying you for it. I will not sacrifice to the Lᴏʀᴅ my God burnt offerings that cost me nothing."

So David bought the threshing floor and the oxen and paid fifty shekels[a] of silver for them. ²⁵David built an altar to the Lᴏʀᴅ there and sacrificed burnt offerings and fellowship offerings.[b] Then the Lᴏʀᴅ answered prayer in behalf of the land, and the plague on Israel was stopped.

NOW OR NEVER
2SA 24:22–24

Want to give God a sacrificial gift, something he really desires from you? Start with your time. Carve out a chunk of time from your schedule each week to focus only on serving God and strengthening your relationship with him.

---

a 24 That is, about 1 1/4 pounds (about 0.6 kilogram)   b 25 Traditionally peace offerings

Author
Unknown

Audience
People of Israel

Date
Most likely this book was written during the Babylonian exile of the Israelites, sometime between 560 and 550 B.C.

Setting
Israel is divided into the northern kingdom of Israel and the southern kingdom of Judah (931 B.C.).

Verse to Remember
"As for you, if you walk before me in integrity of heart and uprightness, as David your father did, and do all I command and observe my decrees and laws, I will establish your royal throne over Israel forever, as I promised David your father when I said, 'You shall never fail to have a man on the throne of Israel' " (9:4–5).

Theme to Consider
God couldn't make it much clearer: When we obey him and keep his laws, he will honor us. When we don't, we *will* suffer the consequences, as did the people of Israel.

UNCHANGING TRUTH » The pursuit of money is a waste of time. So are pursuits of adrenaline, popularity, success and pleasure. These are all temporary rewards, guaranteed to lose their value. If you want to go after something with everything you've got, something that will keep its value forever and is really worth your pursuit, make it wisdom.

That's what Solomon did. When the Lord asked the new king of Israel what he wanted—and stood ready to grant him just about any request—Solomon chose wisdom. That's what he wanted more than money, fame or power. He wanted to be able to do his job as king in a way that pleased God and made him an effective leader. In order to do that, he needed wisdom.

When the Lord heard Solomon's request, he was so pleased that he gave the king money, fame and power to go along with his wisdom. Solomon made the right choice and hit the jackpot—big time.

How important is wisdom to you? Keep in mind that wisdom is not the same thing as intelligence. Intelligence is the ability to learn well. Wisdom is the ability to effectively apply truth to everyday situations. Many intelligent people are not wise.

Where does wisdom come from? Different places. Number one is God. He gave Solomon wisdom, and he'll do the same for you. The next time you face a situation you can't figure out or a problem you can't solve, ask God to help you think it through clearly and then apply what you receive from him and his Word.

Mature Christians whose opinions you trust can be another valuable source of wisdom. Get their input on situations that are giving you trouble. Watch what they do. Learn from their example and the way that they deal with difficult people and situations.

Who knows? You, like Solomon, may find that as your wisdom increases, so does your happiness and fulfillment in other areas of life.

LIFE LESSONS »

1   God rewards faithfulness, not performance (3:14).

2   A little wisdom goes a long, long way (3:28).

3   It's your responsibility to make the most of your God-given talents and abilities (4:32–34).

4   Giving in to lust is always a mistake that will complicate your life (11:1–7).

ADONIJAH SETS HIMSELF UP AS KING

1 When King David was old and well advanced in years, he could not keep warm even when they put covers over him. ²So his servants said to him, "Let us look for a young virgin to attend the king and take care of him. She can lie beside him so that our lord the king may keep warm."

³Then they searched throughout Israel for a beautiful girl and found Abishag, a Shunammite, and brought her to the king. ⁴The girl was very beautiful; she took care of the king and waited on him, but the king had no intimate relations with her.

⁵Now Adonijah, whose mother was Haggith, put himself forward and said, "I will be king." So he got chariots and horses[a] ready, with fifty men to run ahead of him. ⁶(His father had never interfered with him by asking, "Why do you behave as you do?" He was also very handsome and was born next after Absalom.)

⁷Adonijah conferred with Joab son of Zeruiah and with Abiathar the priest, and they gave him their support. ⁸But Zadok the priest, Benaiah son of Jehoiada, Nathan the prophet, Shimei and Rei[b] and David's special guard did not join Adonijah.

⁹Adonijah then sacrificed sheep, cattle and fattened calves at the Stone of Zoheleth near En Rogel. He invited all his brothers, the king's sons, and all the men of Judah who were royal officials, ¹⁰but he did not invite Nathan the prophet or Benaiah or the special guard or his brother Solomon.

¹¹Then Nathan asked Bathsheba, Solomon's mother, "Have you not heard that Adonijah, the son of Haggith, has become king without our lord David's knowing it? ¹²Now then, let me advise you how you can save your own life and the life of your son Solomon. ¹³Go in to King David and say to him, 'My lord the king, did you not swear to me your servant: "Surely Solomon your son shall be king after me, and he will sit on my throne"? Why then has Adonijah become king?' ¹⁴While you are still there talking to the king, I will come in and confirm what you have said."

¹⁵So Bathsheba went to see the aged king in his room, where Abishag the Shunammite was attending him. ¹⁶Bathsheba bowed low and knelt before the king.

"What is it you want?" the king asked.

¹⁷She said to him, "My lord, you yourself swore to me your servant by the Lord your God: 'Solomon your son shall be king after me, and he will sit on my throne.' ¹⁸But now Adonijah has become king, and you, my lord the king, do not know about it. ¹⁹He has sacrificed great numbers of cattle, fattened calves, and sheep, and has invited all the king's sons, Abiathar the priest and Joab the commander of the army, but he has not invited Solomon your servant. ²⁰My lord the king, the eyes of all Israel are on you, to learn from you who will sit on the throne of my lord the king after him. ²¹Otherwise, as soon as my lord the king is laid to rest with his fathers, I and my son Solomon will be treated as criminals."

²²While she was still speaking with the king, Nathan the prophet arrived. ²³And they told the king, "Nathan the prophet is here." So he went before the king and bowed with his face to the ground.

²⁴Nathan said, "Have you, my lord the king, declared that Adonijah shall be king after you, and that he will sit on your throne? ²⁵Today he has gone down and sacrificed great numbers of cattle, fattened calves, and sheep. He has invited all the king's sons, the commanders of the army and Abiathar the priest. Right now they are eating and drinking with him and saying, 'Long live King Adonijah!' ²⁶But me your servant, and Zadok the priest, and Benaiah son of Jehoiada, and your servant Solomon he did not invite. ²⁷Is this something my lord the king has done without letting his servants know who should sit on the throne of my lord the king after him?"

DAVID MAKES SOLOMON KING

²⁸Then King David said, "Call in Bathsheba." So she came into the king's presence and stood before him.

²⁹The king then took an oath: "As surely as the Lord lives, who has delivered me out of every trouble, ³⁰I will surely carry out today what I swore to you by the Lord, the God of Israel: Solomon your son shall be king after me, and he will sit on my throne in my place."

³¹Then Bathsheba bowed low with her face to the ground and, kneeling before the king, said, "May my lord King David live forever!"

³²King David said, "Call in Zadok the priest, Nathan the prophet and Benaiah son of Jehoiada." When they came before the king, ³³he said to them: "Take your lord's servants with you and set Solo-

---

[a] 5 Or charioteers   [b] 8 Or and his friends

mon my son on my own mule and take him down to Gihon. ³⁴There have Zadok the priest and Nathan the prophet anoint him king over Israel. Blow the trumpet and shout, 'Long live King Solomon!' ³⁵Then you are to go up with him, and he is to come and sit on my throne and reign in my place. I have appointed him ruler over Israel and Judah."

³⁶Benaiah son of Jehoiada answered the king, "Amen! May the LORD, the God of my lord the king, so declare it. ³⁷As the LORD was with my lord the king, so may he be with Solomon to make his throne even greater than the throne of my lord King David!"

³⁸So Zadok the priest, Nathan the prophet, Benaiah son of Jehoiada, the Kerethites and the Pelethites went down and put Solomon on King David's mule and escorted him to Gihon. ³⁹Zadok the priest took the horn of oil from the sacred tent and anointed Solomon. Then they sounded the trumpet and all the people shouted, "Long live King Solomon!" ⁴⁰And all the people went up after him, playing flutes and rejoicing greatly, so that the ground shook with the sound.

⁴¹Adonijah and all the guests who were with him heard it as they were finishing their feast. On hearing the sound of the trumpet, Joab asked, "What's the meaning of all the noise in the city?"

⁴²Even as he was speaking, Jonathan son of Abiathar the priest arrived. Adonijah said, "Come in. A worthy man like you must be bringing good news."

⁴³"Not at all!" Jonathan answered. "Our lord King David has made Solomon king. ⁴⁴The king has sent with him Zadok the priest, Nathan the prophet, Benaiah son of Jehoiada, the Kerethites and the Pelethites, and they have put him on the king's mule, ⁴⁵and Zadok the priest and Nathan the prophet have anointed him king at Gihon. From there they have gone up cheering, and the city resounds with it. That's the noise you hear. ⁴⁶Moreover, Solomon has taken his seat on the royal throne. ⁴⁷Also, the royal officials have come to congratulate our lord King David, saying, 'May your God make Solomon's name more famous than yours and his throne greater than yours!' And the king bowed in worship on his bed ⁴⁸and said, 'Praise be to the LORD, the God of Israel, who has allowed my eyes to see a successor on my throne today.' "

⁴⁹At this, all Adonijah's guests rose in alarm and dispersed. ⁵⁰But Adonijah, in fear of Solomon, went and took hold of the horns of the altar. ⁵¹Then Solomon was told, "Adonijah is afraid of King Solomon and is clinging to the horns of the altar. He says, 'Let King Solomon swear to me today that he will not put his servant to death with the sword.' "

⁵²Solomon replied, "If he shows himself to be a worthy man, not a hair of his head will fall to the ground; but if evil is found in him, he will die." ⁵³Then King Solomon sent men, and they brought him down from the altar. And Adonijah came and bowed down to King Solomon, and Solomon said, "Go to your home."

now or never

1 KI 1:52

Want to leave an impression people will never forget? When someone tries to take advantage or make a fool of you, fire back with every bit of kindness you have in you.

DAVID'S CHARGE TO SOLOMON

2 When the time drew near for David to die, he gave a charge to Solomon his son.

²"I am about to go the way of all the earth," he said. "So be strong, show yourself a man, ³and observe what the LORD your God requires: Walk in his ways, and keep his decrees and commands, his laws and requirements, as written in the Law of Moses, so that you may prosper in all you do and wherever you go, ⁴and that the LORD may keep his promise to me: 'If your descendants watch how they live, and if they walk faithfully before me with all their heart and soul, you will never fail to have a man on the throne of Israel.'

⁵"Now you yourself know what Joab son of Zeruiah did to me—what he did to the two commanders of Israel's armies, Abner son of Ner and Amasa son of Jether. He killed them, shedding their blood in peacetime as if in battle, and with that blood stained the belt around his waist and the sandals on his feet. ⁶Deal with him according to your wisdom, but do not let his gray head go down to the grave ᵃ in peace.

ᵃ 6 Hebrew *Sheol*; also in verse 9

abner

VERSUS

joab

» King Saul's top general, a scheming man
» Switched loyalties in hopes of becoming David's commander-in-chief
» Killed by Joab

» King David's top military leader, a ruthless man
» Was disloyal to Solomon
» Murdered Abner to avenge the death of his brother

The Main Event

To many of their contemporaries, Abner and Joab surely must have been seen as successful men. Abner commanded King Saul's armies in Israel; Joab was David's "secretary of defense" in Judah. Both men wielded great power. Both were shrewd, brilliant strategists and fierce fighters.

These were two guys whose philosophy of life could be summarized as, "Look out for number one!" and, "Get the other guy before he gets you!" Neither man seemed to care about God's standards for living. On the contrary, both did whatever they thought would get them ahead and keep them on top. For them, the ends justified the means—even if the means included betrayal and murder. These were two guys you definitely would not want to cross.

It was only a matter of time until these two power-hungry, self-centered lives collided. When Abner killed Joab's brother Asahel in an act of self-defense, Joab burned with fierce determination to avenge his brother's death. Later, when Abner transferred his loyalties from Ishbosheth, the son of Saul and the new king of Israel, to David, the up-and-coming king of Judah, Joab felt threatened. He suspected (perhaps rightly so) that Abner intended to replace him.

The Outcome

In the final showdown between the two men, Joab stabbed Abner to death—payback for having killed Joab's brother Asahel. Years later, Solomon had Joab killed to fulfill his father David's dying wish.

If you write off this bloody rivalry as merely a historical footnote, you may miss some powerful lessons. The fact is, millions of men today live by the same principles that Joab and Abner lived (and died) by. They exclude God from their lives. They care only for themselves. They view everyone else as a potential threat. They are willing to scratch, claw, cheat, steal, slander, cut corners, step on others—in short, do just about anything—to get ahead.

Operate like that and you may succeed for a while, but the story of Abner and Joab reminds us that in the end there is a terrible payday. Perhaps not murder, but certainly shame, retribution and regret. Galatians 6:7–8 puts it like this: "Do not be deceived: God cannot be mocked. A man reaps what he sows. The one who sows to please his sinful nature, from that nature will reap destruction; the one who sows to please the Spirit, from the Spirit will reap eternal life."

Read more about Abner and Joab in 2 Samuel 2:8–4:1 (pages 346–348) and 1 Kings 2:1–35 (pages 379–382).

7"But show kindness to the sons of Barzillai of Gilead and let them be among those who eat at your table. They stood by me when I fled from your brother Absalom.

8"And remember, you have with you Shimei son of Gera, the Benjamite from Bahurim, who called down bitter curses on me the day I went to Mahanaim. When he came down to meet me at the Jordan, I swore to him by the LORD: 'I will not put you to death by the sword.' 9But now, do not consider him innocent. You are a man of wisdom; you will know what to do to him. Bring his gray head down to the grave in blood."

10Then David rested with his fathers and was buried in the City of David. 11He had reigned forty years over Israel—seven years in Hebron and thirty-three in Jerusalem. 12So Solomon sat on the throne of his father David, and his rule was firmly established.

SOLOMON'S THRONE ESTABLISHED

13Now Adonijah, the son of Haggith, went to Bathsheba, Solomon's mother. Bathsheba asked him, "Do you come peacefully?"

He answered, "Yes, peacefully." 14Then he added, "I have something to say to you."

"You may say it," she replied.

15"As you know," he said, "the kingdom was mine. All Israel looked to me as their king. But things changed, and the kingdom has gone to my brother; for it has come to him from the LORD. 16Now I have one request to make of you. Do not refuse me."

"You may make it," she said.

17So he continued, "Please ask King Solomon—he will not refuse you—to give me Abishag the Shunammite as my wife."

18"Very well," Bathsheba replied, "I will speak to the king for you."

19When Bathsheba went to King Solomon to speak to him for Adonijah, the king stood up to meet her, bowed down to her and sat down on his throne. He had a throne brought for the king's mother, and she sat down at his right hand.

20"I have one small request to make of you," she said. "Do not refuse me."

The king replied, "Make it, my mother; I will not refuse you."

21So she said, "Let Abishag the Shunammite be given in marriage to your brother Adonijah."

22King Solomon answered his mother, "Why do you request Abishag the Shunammite for Adonijah? You might as well request the kingdom for him—after all, he is my older brother—yes, for him and for Abiathar the priest and Joab son of Zeruiah!"

NOW OR NEVER
1KI 2:19–20

Does your mother know you respect and love her? If so, what evidence does she have? What have you done (or said) to show (or tell) your mom what she means to you?

23Then King Solomon swore by the LORD: "May God deal with me, be it ever so severely, if Adonijah does not pay with his life for this request! 24And now, as surely as the LORD lives—he who has established me securely on the throne of my father David and has founded a dynasty for me as he promised—Adonijah shall be put to death today!" 25So King Solomon gave orders to Benaiah son of Jehoiada, and he struck down Adonijah and he died.

26To Abiathar the priest the king said, "Go back to your fields in Anathoth. You deserve to die, but I will not put you to death now, because you carried the ark of the Sovereign LORD before my father David and shared all my father's hardships." 27So Solomon removed Abiathar from the priesthood of the LORD, fulfilling the word the LORD had spoken at Shiloh about the house of Eli.

28When the news reached Joab, who had conspired with Adonijah though not with Absalom, he fled to the tent of the LORD and took hold of the horns of the altar. 29King Solomon was told that Joab had fled to the tent of the LORD and was beside the altar. Then Solomon ordered Benaiah son of Jehoiada, "Go, strike him down!"

30So Benaiah entered the tent of the LORD and said to Joab, "The king says, 'Come out!'"

But he answered, "No, I will die here."

Benaiah reported to the king, "This is how Joab answered me."

³¹Then the king commanded Benaiah, "Do as he says. Strike him down and bury him, and so clear me and my father's house of the guilt of the innocent blood that Joab shed. ³²The LORD will repay him for the blood he shed, because without the knowledge of my father David he attacked two men and killed them with the sword. Both of them—Abner son of Ner, commander of Israel's army, and Amasa son of Jether, commander of Judah's army—were better men and more upright than he. ³³May the guilt of their blood rest on the head of Joab and his descendants forever. But on David and his descendants, his house and his throne, may there be the LORD's peace forever."

³⁴So Benaiah son of Jehoiada went up and struck down Joab and killed him, and he was buried on his own landᵃ in the desert. ³⁵The king put Benaiah son of Jehoiada over the army in Joab's position and replaced Abiathar with Zadok the priest.

³⁶Then the king sent for Shimei and said to him, "Build yourself a house in Jerusalem and live there, but do not go anywhere else. ³⁷The day you leave and cross the Kidron Valley, you can be sure you will die; your blood will be on your own head."

³⁸Shimei answered the king, "What you say is good. Your servant will do as my lord the king has said." And Shimei stayed in Jerusalem for a long time.

³⁹But three years later, two of Shimei's slaves ran off to Achish son of Maacah, king of Gath, and Shimei was told, "Your slaves are in Gath." ⁴⁰At this, he saddled his donkey and went to Achish at Gath in search of his slaves. So Shimei went away and brought the slaves back from Gath.

⁴¹When Solomon was told that Shimei had gone from Jerusalem to Gath and had returned, ⁴²the king summoned Shimei and said to him, "Did I not make you swear by the LORD and warn you, 'On the day you leave to go anywhere else, you can be sure you will die'? At that time you said to me, 'What you say is good. I will obey.' ⁴³Why then did you not keep your oath to the LORD and obey the command I gave you?"

⁴⁴The king also said to Shimei, "You know in your heart all the wrong you did to my father David. Now the LORD will repay you for your wrongdoing. ⁴⁵But King Solomon will be blessed, and David's throne will remain secure before the LORD forever."

⁴⁶Then the king gave the order to Benaiah son of Jehoiada, and he went out and struck Shimei down and killed him.

The kingdom was now firmly established in Solomon's hands.

SOLOMON ASKS FOR WISDOM

3 Solomon made an alliance with Pharaoh king of Egypt and married his daughter. He brought her to the City of David until he finished building his palace and the temple of the LORD, and the wall around Jerusalem. ²The people, however, were still sacrificing at the high places, because a temple had not yet been built for the Name of the LORD. ³Solomon showed his love for the LORD by walking according to the statutes of his father David, except that he offered sacrifices and burned incense on the high places.

⁴The king went to Gibeon to offer sacrifices, for that was the most important high place, and Solomon offered a thousand burnt offerings on that altar. ⁵At Gibeon the LORD appeared to Solomon during the night in a dream, and God said, "Ask for whatever you want me to give you."

⁶Solomon answered, "You have shown great kindness to your servant, my father David, because he was faithful to you and righteous and upright in heart. You have continued this great kindness to him and have given him a son to sit on his throne this very day.

⁷"Now, O LORD my God, you have made your servant king in place of my father David. But I am only a little child and do not know how to carry out my duties. ⁸Your servant is here among the people you have chosen, a great people, too numerous to count or number. ⁹So give your servant a discerning heart to govern your people and to distinguish between right and wrong. For who is able to govern this great people of yours?"

now or never
1KI 3:2-9

Never try to drag God into your selfish schemes and desires. Make sure when you ask him for something that you're asking for the right reasons.

ᵃ 34 Or buried in his tomb

[10] The Lord was pleased that Solomon had asked for this. [11] So God said to him, "Since you have asked for this and not for long life or wealth for yourself, nor have asked for the death of your enemies but for discernment in administering justice, [12] I will do what you have asked. I will give you a wise and discerning heart, so that there will never have been anyone like you, nor will there ever be. [13] Moreover, I will give you what you have not asked for—both riches and honor—so that in your lifetime you will have no equal among kings. [14] And if you walk in my ways and obey my statutes and commands as David your father did, I will give you a long life." [15] Then Solomon awoke—and he realized it had been a dream.

He returned to Jerusalem, stood before the ark of the Lord's covenant and sacrificed burnt offerings and fellowship offerings.[a] Then he gave a feast for all his court.

1KI 3:7-8

challenge notes

To: my_son

heavenly_father: in case you haven't noticed, I don't usually call big, heroic people to accomplish big, heroic tasks. I call average people and then give them what they need to accomplish the big, heroic tasks. remember this the next time I call you to do something big.

2863   EG C FE

A WISE RULING

[16] Now two prostitutes came to the king and stood before him. [17] One of them said, "My lord, this woman and I live in the same house. I had a baby while she was there with me. [18] The third day after my child was born, this woman also had a baby. We were alone; there was no one in the house but the two of us.

[19] "During the night this woman's son died because she lay on him. [20] So she got up in the middle of the night and took my son from my side while I your servant was asleep. She put him by her breast and put her dead son by my breast. [21] The next morning, I got up to nurse my son—and he was dead! But when I looked at him closely in the morning light, I saw that it wasn't the son I had borne."

[22] The other woman said, "No! The living one is my son; the dead one is yours."

But the first one insisted, "No! The dead one is yours; the living one is mine." And so they argued before the king.

[23] The king said, "This one says, 'My son is alive and your son is dead,' while that one says, 'No! Your son is dead and mine is alive.' "

[24] Then the king said, "Bring me a sword." So they brought a sword for the king. [25] He then gave an order: "Cut the living child in two and give half to one and half to the other."

[26] The woman whose son was alive was filled with compassion for her son and said to the king, "Please, my lord, give her the living baby! Don't kill him!"

But the other said, "Neither I nor you shall have him. Cut him in two!"

[27] Then the king gave his ruling: "Give the living baby to the first woman. Do not kill him; she is his mother."

[28] When all Israel heard the verdict the king had given, they held the king in awe, because they saw that he had wisdom from God to administer justice.

SOLOMON'S OFFICIALS AND GOVERNORS

4 So King Solomon ruled over all Israel. [2] And these were his chief officials:

Azariah son of Zadok—the priest;
[3] Elihoreph and Ahijah, sons of Shisha—secretaries;
Jehoshaphat son of Ahilud—recorder;
[4] Benaiah son of Jehoiada—commander in chief;
Zadok and Abiathar—priests;
[5] Azariah son of Nathan—in charge of the district officers;
Zabud son of Nathan—a priest and personal adviser to the king;

808

---

[a] 15 Traditionally *peace offerings*

battlelines

» Silent Approval (Bullying)

Q: What was all that laughing about?
A: Oh, some friends of mine were just messing with Tuggle again.

Q: Who's Tuggle?
A: Alvin Tuggle—I think that's his name. Anyway, he's just this weird dude who moved here a few weeks ago. Wears ugly suspenders to school. Who wears suspenders? He talks to himself in the cafeteria. Walks around making mental notes into his little tape recorder. Something's not screwed on right, if you know what I mean. I think his cheese has slid off his cracker.

Q: Oh, I get it. You're picking on the different kid.
A: No, man. It's not like that! *I* don't pick on him. It's my friends, and they're just having a little fun. You have to admit, it *is* pretty hilarious.

Q: Whatever happened to standing up for people who are weak?
A: What do you mean?

Q: You know, defending those who can't defend themselves?
A: Man, it's no big deal—it's just a little fun, that's all. Hey, if they didn't joke around with Tuggle, he wouldn't get any attention at all. Besides, if he doesn't like being singled out, then why does he call so much attention to himself by acting so weird?

Q: Yeah, I'm sure Tuggle just *loves* being abused by you guys. Man, I thought you were stronger than that.
A: Hey, I'd say something if my friends really got out of hand.

Q: Yeah, right.

» Defending the Weak

Deep down, Aaron knows the truth. We all do. A real man doesn't pick on the helpless. It's cowardly, cruel, and it's a cheap way to make ourselves feel good at the expense of others. The prophet Micah put it this way: "He has showed you, O man, what is good. And what does the Lord require of you? To act justly and to love mercy and to walk humbly with your God" (Micah 6:8).

Jesus said that his *real* followers show compassion to those who need it most (see Matthew 25:31–46). And that's just what real men do. They show up in tough situations and respond with mercy and compassion. Aaron could use his influence to steer his friends in a different direction. As long as he sits by and says nothing, he's guilty. And, worse, he's a coward.

Read more about bullying at www.RevolutionBible.com.

⁶Ahishar—in charge of the palace;
Adoniram son of Abda—in charge of forced labor.

⁷Solomon also had twelve district governors over all Israel, who supplied provisions for the king and the royal household. Each one had to provide supplies for one month in the year. ⁸These are their names:

Ben-Hur—in the hill country of Ephraim;
⁹Ben-Deker—in Makaz, Shaalbim, Beth Shemesh and Elon Bethhanan;
¹⁰Ben-Hesed—in Arubboth (Socoh and all the land of Hepher were his);
¹¹Ben-Abinadab—in Naphoth Dorᵃ (he was married to Taphath daughter of Solomon);
¹²Baana son of Ahilud—in Taanach and Megiddo, and in all of Beth Shan next to Zarethan below Jezreel, from Beth Shan to Abel Meholah across to Jokmeam;
¹³Ben-Geber—in Ramoth Gilead (the settlements of Jair son of Manasseh in Gilead were his, as well as the district of Argob in Bashan and its sixty large walled cities with bronze gate bars);
¹⁴Ahinadab son of Iddo—in Mahanaim;
¹⁵Ahimaaz—in Naphtali (he had married Basemath daughter of Solomon);
¹⁶Baana son of Hushai—in Asher and in Aloth;
¹⁷Jehoshaphat son of Paruah—in Issachar;
¹⁸Shimei son of Ela—in Benjamin;
¹⁹Geber son of Uri—in Gilead (the country of Sihon king of the Amorites and the country of Og king of Bashan). He was the only governor over the district.

SOLOMON'S DAILY PROVISIONS

²⁰The people of Judah and Israel were as numerous as the sand on the seashore; they ate, they drank and they were happy. ²¹And Solomon ruled over all the kingdoms from the Riverᵇ to the land of the Philistines, as far as the border of Egypt. These countries brought tribute and were Solomon's subjects all his life.

²²Solomon's daily provisions were thirty corsᶜ of fine flour and sixty corsᵈ of meal, ²³ten head of stall-fed cattle, twenty of pasture-fed cattle and a hundred sheep and goats, as well as deer, gazelles, roebucks and choice fowl. ²⁴For he ruled over all the kingdoms west of the River, from Tiphsah to Gaza, and had peace on all sides. ²⁵During Solomon's lifetime Judah and Israel, from Dan to Beersheba, lived in safety, each man under his own vine and fig tree.

²⁶Solomon had fourᵉ thousand stalls for chariot horses, and twelve thousand horses.ᶠ

²⁷The district officers, each in his month, supplied provisions for King Solomon and all who came to the king's table. They saw to it that nothing was lacking. ²⁸They also brought to the proper place their quotas of barley and straw for the chariot horses and the other horses.

SOLOMON'S WISDOM

²⁹God gave Solomon wisdom and very great insight, and a breadth of understanding as measureless as the sand on the seashore. ³⁰Solomon's wisdom was greater than the wisdom of all the men of the East, and greater than all the wisdom of Egypt. ³¹He was wiser than any other man, including Ethan the Ezrahite—wiser than Heman, Calcol and Darda, the sons of Mahol. And his fame spread to all the surrounding nations. ³²He spoke three thousand proverbs and his songs numbered a thousand and five. ³³He described plant life, from the cedar of Lebanon to the hyssop that grows out of walls. He also taught about animals and birds, reptiles and fish. ³⁴Men of all nations came to listen to Solomon's wisdom, sent by all the kings of the world, who had heard of his wisdom.

PREPARATIONS FOR BUILDING THE TEMPLE

5 When Hiram king of Tyre heard that Solomon had been anointed king to succeed his father David, he sent his envoys to Solomon, because he had always been on friendly terms with David. ²Solomon sent back this message to Hiram:

³"You know that because of the wars waged against my father David from all sides, he could not build a temple for the Name of the LORD his God until the LORD put his enemies under his

---

ᵃ 11 Or *in the heights of Dor*   ᵇ 21 That is, the Euphrates; also in verse 24   ᶜ 22 That is, probably about 185 bushels (about 6.6 kiloliters)   ᵈ 22 That is, probably about 375 bushels (about 13.2 kiloliters)   ᵉ 26 Some Septuagint manuscripts (see also 2 Chron. 9:25); Hebrew *forty*   ᶠ 26 Or *charioteers* feet. ⁴But now the LORD my God has given me rest on every side, and there is no adversary or disaster. ⁵I intend, therefore, to build a temple for the Name of the LORD my God, as the LORD told my father David, when he said, 'Your son whom I will put on the throne in your place will build the temple for my Name.'

⁶"So give orders that cedars of Lebanon be cut for me. My men will work with yours, and I will pay you for your men whatever wages you set. You know that we have no one so skilled in felling timber as the Sidonians."

⁷When Hiram heard Solomon's message, he was greatly pleased and said, "Praise be to the LORD today, for he has given David a wise son to rule over this great nation."

⁸So Hiram sent word to Solomon:

"I have received the message you sent me and will do all you want in providing the cedar and pine logs. ⁹My men will haul them down from Lebanon to the sea, and I will float them in rafts by sea to the place you specify. There I will separate them and you can take them away. And you are to grant my wish by providing food for my royal household."

¹⁰In this way Hiram kept Solomon supplied with all the cedar and pine logs he wanted, ¹¹and Solomon gave Hiram twenty thousand cors ᵃ of wheat as food for his household, in addition to twenty thousand baths ᵇ,ᶜ of pressed olive oil. Solomon continued to do this for Hiram year after year. ¹²The LORD gave Solomon wisdom, just as he had promised him. There were peaceful relations between Hiram and Solomon, and the two of them made a treaty.

¹³King Solomon conscripted laborers from all Israel—thirty thousand men. ¹⁴He sent them off to Lebanon in shifts of ten thousand a month, so that they spent one month in Lebanon and two months at home. Adoniram was in charge of the forced labor. ¹⁵Solomon had seventy thousand carriers and eighty thousand stonecutters in the hills, ¹⁶as well as thirty-three hundred ᵈ foremen who supervised the project and directed the workmen. ¹⁷At the king's command they removed from the quarry large blocks of quality stone to provide a foundation of dressed stone for the temple. ¹⁸The craftsmen of Solomon and Hiram and the men of Gebal ᵉ cut and prepared the timber and stone for the building of the temple.

SOLOMON BUILDS THE TEMPLE

6 In the four hundred and eightieth ᶠ year after the Israelites had come out of Egypt, in the fourth year of Solomon's reign over Israel, in the month of Ziv, the second month, he began to build the temple of the LORD.

²The temple that King Solomon built for the LORD was sixty cubits long, twenty wide and thirty high. ᵍ ³The portico at the front of the main hall of the temple extended the width of the temple, that is twenty cubits, ʰ and projected ten cubits ⁱ from the front of the temple. ⁴He made narrow clerestory windows in the temple. ⁵Against the walls of the main hall and inner sanctuary he built a structure around the building, in which there were side rooms. ⁶The lowest floor was five cubits ⁱ wide, the middle floor six cubits ᵏ and the third floor seven. ˡ He made offset ledges around the outside of the temple so that nothing would be inserted into the temple walls.

Cultivating Passion for God

Solomon was a man of vision. Like an all-pro running back weaving through defenders, when he saw an opening, he hit it hard. When he became king, he looked back on all that his father, David, had wanted to do and realized that many of those things could be accomplished. So he laid out his objectives, did a little networking and set his plan in motion. Are you a man of vision? You don't have to build temples to accomplish something for God. Maybe the opportunity in front of you is a job, a leadership role in your church or a change in your personal devotion to God. Whatever it is, see the opening and go for it.

ᵃ *11* That is, probably about 125,000 bushels (about 4,400 kiloliters) ᵇ *11* Septuagint (see also 2 Chron. 2:10); Hebrew *twenty cors*
ᶜ *11* That is, about 115,000 gallons (about 440 kiloliters) ᵈ *16* Hebrew; some Septuagint manuscripts (see also 2 Chron. 2:2,18)
thirty-six hundred ᵉ *18* That is, Byblos ᶠ *1* Hebrew; Septuagint *four hundred and fortieth* ᵍ *2* That is, about 90 feet (about 27
meters) long and 30 feet (about 9 meters) wide and 45 feet (about 13.5 meters) high ʰ *3* That is, about 30 feet (about 9 meters)
ⁱ *3* That is, about 15 feet (about 4.5 meters) ⁱ *6* That is, about 7 1/2 feet (about 2.3 meters); also in verses 10 and 24 ᵏ *6* That is,
about 9 feet (about 2.7 meters) ˡ *6* That is, about 10 1/2 feet (about 3.1 meters)

⁷In building the temple, only blocks dressed at the quarry were used, and no hammer, chisel or any other iron tool was heard at the temple site while it was being built.

⁸The entrance to the lowestᵃ floor was on the south side of the temple; a stairway led up to the middle level and from there to the third. ⁹So he built the temple and completed it, roofing it with beams and cedar planks. ¹⁰And he built the side rooms all along the temple. The height of each was five cubits, and they were attached to the temple by beams of cedar.

¹¹The word of the LORD came to Solomon: ¹²"As for this temple you are building, if you follow my decrees, carry out my regulations and keep all my commands and obey them, I will fulfill through you the promise I gave to David your father. ¹³And I will live among the Israelites and will not abandon my people Israel."

¹⁴So Solomon built the temple and completed it. ¹⁵He lined its interior walls with cedar boards, paneling them from the floor of the temple to the ceiling, and covered the floor of the temple with planks of pine. ¹⁶He partitioned off twenty cubitsᵇ at the rear of the temple with cedar boards from floor to ceiling to form within the temple an inner sanctuary, the Most Holy Place. ¹⁷The main hall in front of this room was forty cubitsᶜ long. ¹⁸The inside of the temple was cedar, carved with gourds and open flowers. Everything was cedar; no stone was to be seen.

¹⁹He prepared the inner sanctuary within the temple to set the ark of the covenant of the LORD there. ²⁰The inner sanctuary was twenty cubits long, twenty wide and twenty high.ᵈ He overlaid the inside with pure gold, and he also overlaid the altar of cedar. ²¹Solomon covered the inside of the temple with pure gold, and he extended gold chains across the front of the inner sanctuary, which was overlaid with gold. ²²So he overlaid the whole interior with gold. He also overlaid with gold the altar that belonged to the inner sanctuary.

²³In the inner sanctuary he made a pair of cherubim of olive wood, each ten cubitsᵉ high. ²⁴One wing of the first cherub was five cubits long, and the other wing five cubits—ten cubits from wing tip to wing tip. ²⁵The second cherub also measured ten cubits, for the two cherubim were identical in size and shape. ²⁶The height of each cherub was ten cubits. ²⁷He placed the cherubim inside the innermost room of the temple, with their wings spread out. The wing of one cherub touched one wall, while the wing of the other touched the other wall, and their wings touched each other in the middle of the room. ²⁸He overlaid the cherubim with gold.

²⁹On the walls all around the temple, in both the inner and outer rooms, he carved cherubim, palm trees and open flowers. ³⁰He also covered the floors of both the inner and outer rooms of the temple with gold.

³¹For the entrance of the inner sanctuary he made doors of olive wood with five-sided jambs. ³²And on the two olive wood doors he carved cherubim, palm trees and open flowers, and overlaid the cherubim and palm trees with beaten gold. ³³In the same way he made four-sided jambs of olive wood for the entrance to the main hall. ³⁴He also made two pine doors, each having two leaves that turned in sockets. ³⁵He carved cherubim, palm trees and open flowers on them and overlaid them with gold hammered evenly over the carvings.

³⁶And he built the inner courtyard of three courses of dressed stone and one course of trimmed cedar beams.

³⁷The foundation of the temple of the LORD was laid in the fourth year, in the month of Ziv. ³⁸In the eleventh year in the month of Bul, the eighth month, the temple was finished in all its details according to its specifications. He had spent seven years building it.

SOLOMON BUILDS HIS PALACE

7 It took Solomon thirteen years, however, to complete the construction of his palace. ²He built the Palace of the Forest of Lebanon a hundred cubits long, fifty wide and thirty high,ᶠ with four rows of cedar columns supporting trimmed cedar beams. ³It was roofed with cedar above the

NOW OR NEVER
1KI 6:11–13

What would God have to do in order to convince you that committing your life to him is a smart move on your part? Hasn't he already given some pretty strong evidence of this fact?

ᵃ 8 Septuagint; Hebrew *middle*   ᵇ 16 That is, about 30 feet (about 9 meters)   ᶜ 17 That is, about 60 feet (about 18 meters)
ᵈ 20 That is, about 30 feet (about 9 meters) long, wide and high   ᵉ 23 That is, about 15 feet (about 4.5 meters)   ᶠ 2 That is, about 150 feet (about 46 meters) long, 75 feet (about 23 meters) wide and 45 feet (about 13.5 meters) high

beams that rested on the columns—forty-five beams, fifteen to a row. ⁴Its windows were placed high in sets of three, facing each other. ⁵All the doorways had rectangular frames; they were in the front part in sets of three, facing each other.^a

⁶He made a colonnade fifty cubits long and thirty wide.^b In front of it was a portico, and in front of that were pillars and an overhanging roof.

⁷He built the throne hall, the Hall of Justice, where he was to judge, and he covered it with cedar from floor to ceiling.^c ⁸And the palace in which he was to live, set farther back, was similar in design. Solomon also made a palace like this hall for Pharaoh's daughter, whom he had married.

⁹All these structures, from the outside to the great courtyard and from foundation to eaves, were made of blocks of high-grade stone cut to size and trimmed with a saw on their inner and outer faces. ¹⁰The foundations were laid with large stones of good quality, some measuring ten cubits^d and some eight.^e ¹¹Above were high-grade stones, cut to size, and cedar beams. ¹²The great courtyard was surrounded by a wall of three courses of dressed stone and one course of trimmed cedar beams, as was the inner courtyard of the temple of the LORD with its portico.

THE TEMPLE'S FURNISHINGS

¹³King Solomon sent to Tyre and brought Huram,^f ¹⁴whose mother was a widow from the tribe of Naphtali and whose father was a man of Tyre and a craftsman in bronze. Huram was highly skilled and experienced in all kinds of bronze work. He came to King Solomon and did all the work assigned to him.

¹⁵He cast two bronze pillars, each eighteen cubits high and twelve cubits around,^g by line. ¹⁶He also made two capitals of cast bronze to set on the tops of the pillars; each capital was five cubits^h high. ¹⁷A network of interwoven chains festooned the capitals on top of the pillars, seven for each capital. ¹⁸He made pomegranates in two rowsⁱ encircling each network to decorate the capitals on top of the pillars.^j He did the same for each capital. ¹⁹The capitals on top of the pillars in the portico were in the shape of lilies, four cubits^k high. ²⁰On the capitals of both pillars, above the bowl-shaped part next to the network, were the two hundred pomegranates in rows all around. ²¹He erected the pillars at the portico of the temple. The pillar to the south he named Jakin^l and the one to the north Boaz.^m ²²The capitals on top were in the shape of lilies. And so the work on the pillars was completed.

²³He made the Sea of cast metal, circular in shape, measuring ten cubits^d from rim to rim and five cubits high. It took a line of thirty cubitsⁿ to measure around it. ²⁴Below the rim, gourds encircled it—ten to a cubit. The gourds were cast in two rows in one piece with the Sea.

²⁵The Sea stood on twelve bulls, three facing north, three facing west, three facing south and three facing east. The Sea rested on top of them, and their hindquarters were toward the center. ²⁶It was a handbreadth^o in thickness, and its rim was like the rim of a cup, like a lily blossom. It held two thousand baths.^p

Using Your Talents

Huram's skill was working with bronze. That's not necessarily the kind of talent that comes to mind when you think about people doing God's work. Yet God found a way to use Huram's abilities for a very significant project. That's important to remember. No matter what your gifts and abilities are— no matter how minor or insignificant they may seem—God will find a way to use them for his glory. He gave them to you for a reason, after all.

>> live the adventure >> 1Ki 7:13-14

^a 5 The meaning of the Hebrew for this verse is uncertain. ^b 6 That is, about 75 feet (about 23 meters) long and 45 feet (about 13.5 meters) wide ^c 7 Vulgate and Syriac; Hebrew floor ^d 10,23 That is, about 15 feet (about 4.5 meters) ^e 10 That is, about 12 feet (about 3.6 meters) ^f 13 Hebrew Hiram, a variant of Huram; also in verses 40 and 45 ^g 15 That is, about 27 feet (about 8.1 meters) high and 18 feet (about 5.4 meters) around ^h 16 That is, about 7 1/2 feet (about 2.3 meters); also in verse 23 ⁱ 18 Two Hebrew manuscripts and Septuagint; most Hebrew manuscripts made the pillars, and there were two rows ^j 18 Many Hebrew manuscripts and Syriac; most Hebrew manuscripts pomegranates ^k 19 That is, about 6 feet (about 1.8 meters); also in verse 38 ^l 21 Jakin probably means he establishes. ^m 21 Boaz probably means in him is strength. ⁿ 23 That is, about 45 feet (about 13.5 meters) ^o 26 That is, about 3 inches (about 8 centimeters) ^p 26 That is, probably about 11,500 gallons (about 44 kiloliters); the Septuagint does not have this sentence.

²⁷He also made ten movable stands of bronze; each was four cubits long, four wide and three high.^a ²⁸This is how the stands were made: They had side panels attached to uprights. ²⁹On the panels between the uprights were lions, bulls and cherubim—and on the uprights as well. Above and below the lions and bulls were wreaths of hammered work. ³⁰Each stand had four bronze wheels with bronze axles, and each had a basin resting on four supports, cast with wreaths on each side. ³¹On the inside of the stand there was an opening that had a circular frame one cubit^b deep. This opening was round, and with its basework it measured a cubit and a half.^c Around its opening there was engraving. The panels of the stands were square, not round. ³²The four wheels were under the panels, and the axles of the wheels were attached to the stand. The diameter of each wheel was a cubit and a half. ³³The wheels were made like chariot wheels; the axles, rims, spokes and hubs were all of cast metal.

³⁴Each stand had four handles, one on each corner, projecting from the stand. ³⁵At the top of the stand there was a circular band half a cubit^d deep. The supports and panels were attached to the top of the stand. ³⁶He engraved cherubim, lions and palm trees on the surfaces of the supports and on the panels, in every available space, with wreaths all around. ³⁷This is the way he made the ten stands. They were all cast in the same molds and were identical in size and shape.

³⁸He then made ten bronze basins, each holding forty baths^e and measuring four cubits across, one basin to go on each of the ten stands. ³⁹He placed five of the stands on the south side of the temple and five on the north. He placed the Sea on the south side, at the southeast corner of the temple. ⁴⁰He also made the basins and shovels and sprinkling bowls.

So Huram finished all the work he had undertaken for King Solomon in the temple of the LORD:

⁴¹the two pillars;
    the two bowl-shaped capitals on top of the pillars;
    the two sets of network decorating the two bowl-shaped capitals on top of the pillars;
⁴²the four hundred pomegranates for the two sets of network (two rows of pomegranates for each
    network, decorating the bowl-shaped capitals on top of the pillars);
⁴³the ten stands with their ten basins;
⁴⁴the Sea and the twelve bulls under it;
⁴⁵the pots, shovels and sprinkling bowls.

All these objects that Huram made for King Solomon for the temple of the LORD were of burnished bronze. ⁴⁶The king had them cast in clay molds in the plain of the Jordan between Succoth and Zarethan. ⁴⁷Solomon left all these things unweighed, because there were so many; the weight of the bronze was not determined.

⁴⁸Solomon also made all the furnishings that were in the LORD's temple:

    the golden altar;
    the golden table on which was the bread of the Presence;
⁴⁹the lampstands of pure gold (five on the right and five on the left, in front of the inner sanctuary);
    the gold floral work and lamps and tongs;
⁵⁰the pure gold basins, wick trimmers, sprinkling bowls, dishes and censers;
    and the gold sockets for the doors of the innermost room, the Most Holy Place, and also for the
    doors of the main hall of the temple.

⁵¹When all the work King Solomon had done for the temple of the LORD was finished, he brought in the things his father David had dedicated—the silver and gold and the furnishings—and he placed them in the treasuries of the LORD's temple.

THE ARK BROUGHT TO THE TEMPLE

8 Then King Solomon summoned into his presence at Jerusalem the elders of Israel, all the heads of the tribes and the chiefs of the Israelite families, to bring up the ark of the LORD's covenant from Zion, the City of David. ²All the men of Israel came together to King Solomon at the time of the festival in the month of Ethanim, the seventh month.

^a *27* That is, about 6 feet (about 1.8 meters) long and wide and about 4 1/2 feet (about 1.3 meters) high   ^b *31* That is, about 1 1/2 feet (about 0.5 meter)   ^c *31* That is, about 2 1/4 feet (about 0.7 meter); also in verse 32   ^d *35* That is, about 3/4 foot (about 0.2 meter)   ^e *38* That is, about 230 gallons (about 880 liters)

³When all the elders of Israel had arrived, the priests took up the ark, ⁴and they brought up the ark of the LORD and the Tent of Meeting and all the sacred furnishings in it. The priests and Levites carried them up, ⁵and King Solomon and the entire assembly of Israel that had gathered about him were before the ark, sacrificing so many sheep and cattle that they could not be recorded or counted.

⁶The priests then brought the ark of the LORD's covenant to its place in the inner sanctuary of the temple, the Most Holy Place, and put it beneath the wings of the cherubim. ⁷The cherubim spread their wings over the place of the ark and overshadowed the ark and its carrying poles. ⁸These poles were so long that their ends could be seen from the Holy Place in front of the inner sanctuary, but not from outside the Holy Place; and they are still there today. ⁹There was nothing in the ark except the two stone tablets that Moses had placed in it at Horeb, where the LORD made a covenant with the Israelites after they came out of Egypt.

¹⁰When the priests withdrew from the Holy Place, the cloud filled the temple of the LORD. ¹¹And the priests could not perform their service because of the cloud, for the glory of the LORD filled his temple.

¹²Then Solomon said, "The LORD has said that he would dwell in a dark cloud; ¹³I have indeed built a magnificent temple for you, a place for you to dwell forever."

¹⁴While the whole assembly of Israel was standing there, the king turned around and blessed them. ¹⁵Then he said:

"Praise be to the LORD, the God of Israel, who with his own hand has fulfilled what he promised with his own mouth to my father David. For he said, ¹⁶'Since the day I brought my people Israel out of Egypt, I have not chosen a city in any tribe of Israel to have a temple built for my Name to be there, but I have chosen David to rule my people Israel.'

¹⁷"My father David had it in his heart to build a temple for the Name of the LORD, the God of Israel. ¹⁸But the LORD said to my father David, 'Because it was in your heart to build a temple for my Name, you did well to have this in your heart. ¹⁹Nevertheless, you are not the one to build the temple, but your son, who is your own flesh and blood—he is the one who will build the temple for my Name.'

²⁰"The LORD has kept the promise he made: I have succeeded David my father and now I sit on the throne of Israel, just as the LORD promised, and I have built the temple for the Name of the LORD, the God of Israel. ²¹I have provided a place there for the ark, in which is the covenant of the LORD that he made with our fathers when he brought them out of Egypt."

SOLOMON'S PRAYER OF DEDICATION

²²Then Solomon stood before the altar of the LORD in front of the whole assembly of Israel, spread out his hands toward heaven ²³and said:

"O LORD, God of Israel, there is no God like you in heaven above or on earth below—you who keep your covenant of love with your servants who continue wholeheartedly in your way. ²⁴You have kept your promise to your servant David my father; with your mouth you have promised and with your hand you have fulfilled it—as it is today.

²⁵"Now LORD, God of Israel, keep for your servant David my father the promises you made to him when you said, 'You shall never fail to have a man to sit before me on the throne of Israel, if only your sons are careful in all they do to walk before me as you have done.' ²⁶And now, O God of Israel, let your word that you promised your servant David my father come true.

²⁷"But will God really dwell on earth? The heavens, even the highest heaven, cannot contain you. How much less this temple I have built! ²⁸Yet give attention to your servant's prayer and his plea for mercy, O LORD my God. Hear the cry and the prayer that your servant is praying in your presence this day. ²⁹May your eyes be open toward this temple night and day, this place of which you said, 'My Name shall be

challenge notes

To: my_son

1 KI 8:27

heavenly_father: I want to be close to you. I want you to actually sense my presence in your life. I want you to be amazed that the One who created the entire universe chose to have an intimate relationship with you.

there,' so that you will hear the prayer your servant prays toward this place. 30Hear the supplication of your servant and of your people Israel when they pray toward this place. Hear from heaven, your dwelling place, and when you hear, forgive.

31"When a man wrongs his neighbor and is required to take an oath and he comes and swears the oath before your altar in this temple, 32then hear from heaven and act. Judge between your servants, condemning the guilty and bringing down on his own head what he has done. Declare the innocent not guilty, and so establish his innocence.

33"When your people Israel have been defeated by an enemy because they have sinned against you, and when they turn back to you and confess your name, praying and making supplication to you in this temple, 34then hear from heaven and forgive the sin of your people Israel and bring them back to the land you gave to their fathers.

35"When the heavens are shut up and there is no rain because your people have sinned against you, and when they pray toward this place and confess your name and turn from their sin because you have afflicted them, 36then hear from heaven and forgive the sin of your servants, your people Israel. Teach them the right way to live, and send rain on the land you gave your people for an inheritance.

37"When famine or plague comes to the land, or blight or mildew, locusts or grasshoppers, or when an enemy besieges them in any of their cities, whatever disaster or disease may come, 38and when a prayer or plea is made by any of your people Israel—each one aware of the afflictions of his own heart, and spreading out his hands toward this temple— 39then hear from heaven, your dwelling place. Forgive and act; deal with each man according to all he does, since you know his heart (for you alone know the hearts of all men), 40so that they will fear you all the time they live in the land you gave our fathers.

41"As for the foreigner who does not belong to your people Israel but has come from a distant land because of your name— 42for men will hear of your great name and your mighty hand and your outstretched arm—when he comes and prays toward this temple, 43then hear from heaven, your dwelling place, and do whatever the foreigner asks of you, so that all the peoples of the earth may know your name and fear you, as do your own people Israel, and may know that this house I have built bears your Name.

44"When your people go to war against their enemies, wherever you send them, and when they pray to the LORD toward the city you have chosen and the temple I have built for your Name, 45then hear from heaven their prayer and their plea, and uphold their cause.

46"When they sin against you—for there is no one who does not sin—and you become angry with them and give them over to the enemy, who takes them captive to his own land, far away or near; 47and if they have a change of heart in the land where they are held captive, and repent and plead with you in the land of their conquerors and say, 'We have sinned, we have done wrong, we have acted wickedly'; 48and if they turn back to you with all their heart and soul in the land of their enemies who took them captive, and pray to you toward the land you gave their fathers, toward the city you have chosen and the temple I have built for your Name; 49then from heaven, your dwelling place, hear their prayer and their plea, and uphold their cause. 50And forgive your people, who have sinned against you; forgive all the offenses they have committed against you, and cause their conquerors to show them mercy; 51for they are your people and your inheritance, whom you brought out of Egypt, out of that iron-smelting furnace.

52"May your eyes be open to your servant's plea and to the plea of your people Israel, and may you listen to them whenever they cry out to you. 53For you singled them out from all the nations of the world to be your own inheritance, just as you declared through your servant Moses when you, O Sovereign LORD, brought our fathers out of Egypt."

54When Solomon had finished all these prayers and supplications to the LORD, he rose from before the altar of the LORD, where he had been kneeling with his hands spread out toward heaven. 55He stood and blessed the whole assembly of Israel in a loud voice, saying:

56"Praise be to the LORD, who has given rest to his people Israel just as he promised. Not one word has failed of all the good promises he gave through his servant Moses. 57May the LORD our God be with us as he was with our fathers; may he never leave us nor forsake us. 58May he turn our hearts to him, to walk in all his ways and to keep the commands, decrees and regulations he gave our fathers. ⁵⁹And may these words of mine, which I have prayed before the LORD, be near to the LORD our God day and night, that he may uphold the cause of his servant and the cause of his people Israel according to each day's need, ⁶⁰so that all the peoples of the earth may know that the LORD is God and that there is no other. ⁶¹But your hearts must be fully committed to the LORD our God, to live by his decrees and obey his commands, as at this time."

THE DEDICATION OF THE TEMPLE

⁶²Then the king and all Israel with him offered sacrifices before the LORD. ⁶³Solomon offered a sacrifice of fellowship offeringsᵃ to the LORD: twenty-two thousand cattle and a hundred and twenty thousand sheep and goats. So the king and all the Israelites dedicated the temple of the LORD.

⁶⁴On that same day the king consecrated the middle part of the courtyard in front of the temple of the LORD, and there he offered burnt offerings, grain offerings and the fat of the fellowship offerings, because the bronze altar before the LORD was too small to hold the burnt offerings, the grain offerings and the fat of the fellowship offerings.

⁶⁵So Solomon observed the festival at that time, and all Israel with him—a vast assembly, people from Leboᵇ Hamath to the Wadi of Egypt. They celebrated it before the LORD our God for seven days and seven days more, fourteen days in all. ⁶⁶On the following day he sent the people away. They blessed the king and then went home, joyful and glad in heart for all the good things the LORD had done for his servant David and his people Israel.

THE LORD APPEARS TO SOLOMON

9 When Solomon had finished building the temple of the LORD and the royal palace, and had achieved all he had desired to do, ²the LORD appeared to him a second time, as he had appeared to him at Gibeon. ³The LORD said to him:

"I have heard the prayer and plea you have made before me; I have consecrated this temple, which you have built, by putting my Name there forever. My eyes and my heart will always be there.

⁴"As for you, if you walk before me in integrity of heart and uprightness, as David your father did, and do all I command and observe my decrees and laws, ⁵I will establish your royal throne over Israel forever, as I promised David your father when I said, 'You shall never fail to have a man on the throne of Israel.'

⁶"But if youᶜ or your sons turn away from me and do not observe the commands and decrees I have given youᶜ and go off to serve other gods and worship them, ⁷then I will cut off Israel from the land I have given them and will reject this temple I have consecrated for my Name. Israel will then become a byword and an object of ridicule among all peoples. ⁸And though this temple is now imposing, all who pass by will be appalled and will scoff and say, 'Why has the LORD done such a thing to this land and to this temple?' ⁹People will answer, 'Because they have forsaken the LORD their God, who brought their fathers out of Egypt, and have embraced other gods, worshiping and serving them—that is why the LORD brought all this disaster on them.' "

now or never
1KI 9:6–9

One of the worst mistakes you can make is to underestimate how strongly God hates sin. Even offenses that seem minor to us can be enough to draw the full force of God's wrath.

SOLOMON'S OTHER ACTIVITIES

¹⁰At the end of twenty years, during which Solomon built these two buildings—the temple of the LORD and the royal palace— ¹¹King Solomon gave twenty towns in Galilee to Hiram king of Tyre, because Hiram had supplied him with all the cedar and pine and gold he wanted. ¹²But when Hiram went

---

ᵃ *63* Traditionally *peace offerings*; also in verse 64   ᵇ *65* Or *from the entrance to*   ᶜ *6* The Hebrew is plural.

from Tyre to see the towns that Solomon had given him, he was not pleased with them. [13]"What kind of towns are these you have given me, my brother?" he asked. And he called them the Land of Cabul,[a] a name they have to this day. [14]Now Hiram had sent to the king 120 talents[b] of gold.

[15]Here is the account of the forced labor King Solomon conscripted to build the LORD's temple, his own palace, the supporting terraces,[c] the wall of Jerusalem, and Hazor, Megiddo and Gezer. [16](Pharaoh king of Egypt had attacked and captured Gezer. He had set it on fire. He killed its Canaanite inhabitants and then gave it as a wedding gift to his daughter, Solomon's wife. [17]And Solomon rebuilt Gezer.) He built up Lower Beth Horon, [18]Baalath, and Tadmor[d] in the desert, within his land, [19]as well as all his store cities and the towns for his chariots and for his horses[e]—whatever he desired to build in Jerusalem, in Lebanon and throughout all the territory he ruled.

[20]All the people left from the Amorites, Hittites, Perizzites, Hivites and Jebusites (these peoples were not Israelites), [21]that is, their descendants remaining in the land, whom the Israelites could not exterminate[f]—these Solomon conscripted for his slave labor force, as it is to this day. [22]But Solomon did not make slaves of any of the Israelites; they were his fighting men, his government officials, his officers, his captains, and the commanders of his chariots and charioteers. [23]They were also the chief officials in charge of Solomon's projects—550 officials supervising the men who did the work.

[24]After Pharaoh's daughter had come up from the City of David to the palace Solomon had built for her, he constructed the supporting terraces.

[25]Three times a year Solomon sacrificed burnt offerings and fellowship offerings[g] on the altar he had built for the LORD, burning incense before the LORD along with them, and so fulfilled the temple obligations.

[26]King Solomon also built ships at Ezion Geber, which is near Elath in Edom, on the shore of the Red Sea.[h] [27]And Hiram sent his men—sailors who knew the sea—to serve in the fleet with Solomon's men. [28]They sailed to Ophir and brought back 420 talents[i] of gold, which they delivered to King Solomon.

THE QUEEN OF SHEBA VISITS SOLOMON

10 When the queen of Sheba heard about the fame of Solomon and his relation to the name of the LORD, she came to test him with hard questions. [2]Arriving at Jerusalem with a very great caravan—with camels carrying spices, large quantities of gold, and precious stones—she came to Solomon and talked with him about all that she had on her mind. [3]Solomon answered all her questions; nothing was too hard for the king to explain to her. [4]When the queen of Sheba saw all the wisdom of Solomon and the palace he had built, [5]the food on his table, the seating of his officials, the attending servants in their robes, his cupbearers, and the burnt offerings he made at[j] the temple of the LORD, she was overwhelmed.

[6]She said to the king, "The report I heard in my own country about your achievements and your wisdom is true. [7]But I did not believe these things until I came and saw with my own eyes. Indeed, not even half was told me; in wisdom and wealth you have far exceeded the report I heard. [8]How happy your men must be! How happy your officials, who continually stand before you and hear your wisdom! [9]Praise be to the LORD your God, who has delighted in you and placed you on the throne of Israel. Because of the LORD's eternal love for Israel, he has made you king, to maintain justice and righteousness."

now or never

1KI 10:6-9

Do you ever thank God for the good things he is doing in the lives of people close to you? That would make a great addition to your personal prayer time.

[10]And she gave the king 120 talents[b] of gold, large quantities of spices, and precious stones. Never again were so many spices brought in as those the queen of Sheba gave to King Solomon.

[11](Hiram's ships brought gold from Ophir; and from there they brought great cargoes of almug-

---

[a] 13 Cabul sounds like the Hebrew for good-for-nothing.   [b] 14,10 That is, about 4 1/2 tons (about 4 metric tons)   [c] 15 Or the Millo; also in verse 24   [d] 18 The Hebrew may also be read Tamar.   [e] 19 Or charioteers   [f] 21 The Hebrew term refers to the irrevocable giving over of things or persons to the LORD, often by totally destroying them.   [g] 25 Traditionally peace offerings   [h] 26 Hebrew Yam Suph; that is, Sea of Reeds   [i] 28 That is, about 16 tons (about 14.5 metric tons)   [j] 5 Or the ascent by which he went up to

wood[a] and precious stones. [12]The king used the almugwood to make supports for the temple of the Lord and for the royal palace, and to make harps and lyres for the musicians. So much almugwood has never been imported or seen since that day.)

[13]King Solomon gave the queen of Sheba all she desired and asked for, besides what he had given her out of his royal bounty. Then she left and returned with her retinue to her own country.

SOLOMON'S SPLENDOR

[14]The weight of the gold that Solomon received yearly was 666 talents,[b] [15]not including the revenues from merchants and traders and from all the Arabian kings and the governors of the land.

[16]King Solomon made two hundred large shields of hammered gold; six hundred bekas[c] of gold went into each shield. [17]He also made three hundred small shields of hammered gold, with three minas[d] of gold in each shield. The king put them in the Palace of the Forest of Lebanon.

[18]Then the king made a great throne inlaid with ivory and overlaid with fine gold. [19]The throne had six steps, and its back had a rounded top. On both sides of the seat were armrests, with a lion standing beside each of them. [20]Twelve lions stood on the six steps, one at either end of each step. Nothing like it had ever been made for any other kingdom. [21]All King Solomon's goblets were gold, and all the household articles in the Palace of the Forest of Lebanon were pure gold. Nothing was made of silver, because silver was considered of little value in Solomon's days. [22]The king had a fleet of trading ships[e] at sea along with the ships of Hiram. Once every three years it returned, carrying gold, silver and ivory, and apes and baboons.

[23]King Solomon was greater in riches and wisdom than all the other kings of the earth. [24]The whole world sought audience with Solomon to hear the wisdom God had put in his heart. [25]Year after year, everyone who came brought a gift—articles of silver and gold, robes, weapons and spices, and horses and mules.

[26]Solomon accumulated chariots and horses; he had fourteen hundred chariots and twelve thousand horses,[f] which he kept in the chariot cities and also with him in Jerusalem. [27]The king made silver as common in Jerusalem as stones, and cedar as plentiful as sycamore-fig trees in the foothills. [28]Solomon's horses were imported from Egypt[g] and from Kue[h]—the royal merchants purchased them from Kue. [29]They imported a chariot from Egypt for six hundred shekels[i] of silver, and a horse for a hundred and fifty.[j] They also exported them to all the kings of the Hittites and of the Arameans.

SOLOMON'S WIVES

11 King Solomon, however, loved many foreign women besides Pharaoh's daughter—Moabites, Ammonites, Edomites, Sidonians and Hittites. [2]They were from nations about which the Lord had told the Israelites, "You must not intermarry with them, because they will surely turn your hearts after their gods." Nevertheless, Solomon held fast to them in love. [3]He had seven hundred wives of royal birth and three hundred concubines, and his wives led him astray. [4]As Solomon grew old, his wives turned his heart after other gods, and his heart was not fully devoted to the Lord his God, as the heart of David his father had been. [5]He followed Ashtoreth the goddess of the Sidonians, and Molech[k] the detestable god of the Ammonites. [6]So Solomon did evil in the eyes of the Lord; he did not follow the Lord completely, as David his father had done.

[7]On a hill east of Jerusalem, Solomon built a high place for Chemosh the detestable god of Moab, and for Molech the detestable god of the Ammonites. [8]He did the same for all his foreign wives, who burned incense and offered sacrifices to their gods.

NOW OR NEVER
1 KI 11:1–8

If someone wanted to divert your attention from your relationship with God, what would be the most effective way to do it? Watch out; the enemy may try to distract you in that very way.

---

[a] 11 Probably a variant of *algumwood*; also in verse 12   [b] 14 That is, about 25 tons (about 23 metric tons)   [c] 16 That is, about 7 1/2 pounds (about 3.5 kilograms)   [d] 17 That is, about 3 3/4 pounds (about 1.7 kilograms)   [e] 22 Hebrew *of ships of Tarshish*   [f] 26 Or *charioteers*   [g] 28 Or possibly *Muzur*, a region in Cilicia; also in verse 29   [h] 28 Probably *Cilicia*   [i] 29 That is, about 15 pounds (about 7 kilograms)   [j] 29 That is, about 3 3/4 pounds (about 1.7 kilograms)   [k] 5 Hebrew *Milcom*; also in verse 33

⁹The Lord became angry with Solomon because his heart had turned away from the Lord, the God of Israel, who had appeared to him twice. ¹⁰Although he had forbidden Solomon to follow other gods, Solomon did not keep the Lord's command. ¹¹So the Lord said to Solomon, "Since this is your attitude and you have not kept my covenant and my decrees, which I commanded you, I will most certainly tear the kingdom away from you and give it to one of your subordinates. ¹²Nevertheless, for the sake of David your father, I will not do it during your lifetime. I will tear it out of the hand of your son. ¹³Yet I will not tear the whole kingdom from him, but will give him one tribe for the sake of David my servant and for the sake of Jerusalem, which I have chosen."

SOLOMON'S ADVERSARIES

¹⁴Then the Lord raised up against Solomon an adversary, Hadad the Edomite, from the royal line of Edom. ¹⁵Earlier when David was fighting with Edom, Joab the commander of the army, who had gone up to bury the dead, had struck down all the men in Edom. ¹⁶Joab and all the Israelites stayed there for six months, until they had destroyed all the men in Edom. ¹⁷But Hadad, still only a boy, fled to Egypt with some Edomite officials who had served his father. ¹⁸They set out from Midian and went to Paran. Then taking men from Paran with them, they went to Egypt, to Pharaoh king of Egypt, who gave Hadad a house and land and provided him with food.

¹⁹Pharaoh was so pleased with Hadad that he gave him a sister of his own wife, Queen Tahpenes, in marriage. ²⁰The sister of Tahpenes bore him a son named Genubath, whom Tahpenes brought up in the royal palace. There Genubath lived with Pharaoh's own children.

²¹While he was in Egypt, Hadad heard that David rested with his fathers and that Joab the commander of the army was also dead. Then Hadad said to Pharaoh, "Let me go, that I may return to my own country."

²²"What have you lacked here that you want to go back to your own country?" Pharaoh asked.

"Nothing," Hadad replied, "but do let me go!"

²³And God raised up against Solomon another adversary, Rezon son of Eliada, who had fled from his master, Hadadezer king of Zobah. ²⁴He gathered men around him and became the leader of a band of rebels when David destroyed the forcesᵃ ᴸof Zobahᴶ; the rebels went to Damascus, where they settled and took control. ²⁵Rezon was Israel's adversary as long as Solomon lived, adding to the trouble caused by Hadad. So Rezon ruled in Aram and was hostile toward Israel.

JEROBOAM REBELS AGAINST SOLOMON

²⁶Also, Jeroboam son of Nebat rebelled against the king. He was one of Solomon's officials, an Ephraimite from Zeredah, and his mother was a widow named Zeruah.

²⁷Here is the account of how he rebelled against the king: Solomon had built the supporting terracesᵇ and had filled in the gap in the wall of the city of David his father. ²⁸Now Jeroboam was a man of standing, and when Solomon saw how well the young man did his work, he put him in charge of the whole labor force of the house of Joseph.

²⁹About that time Jeroboam was going out of Jerusalem, and Ahijah the prophet of Shiloh met him on the way, wearing a new cloak. The two of them were alone out in the country, ³⁰and Ahijah took hold of the new cloak he was wearing and tore it into twelve pieces. ³¹Then he said to Jeroboam, "Take ten pieces for yourself, for this is what the Lord, the God of Israel, says: 'See, I am going to tear the kingdom out of Solomon's hand and give you ten tribes. ³²But for the sake of my servant David and the city of Jerusalem, which I have chosen out of all the tribes of Israel, he will have one tribe. ³³I will do this because they haveᶜ forsaken me and worshiped Ashtoreth the goddess of the Sidonians, Chemosh the god of the Moabites, and Molech the god of the Ammonites, and have not walked in my ways, nor done what is right in my eyes, nor kept my statutes and laws as David, Solomon's father, did.

³⁴" 'But I will not take the whole kingdom out of Solomon's hand; I have made him ruler all the days of his life for the sake of David my servant, whom I chose and who observed my commands and statutes. ³⁵I will take the kingdom from his son's hands and give you ten tribes. ³⁶I will give one tribe to his son so that David my servant may always have a lamp before me in Jerusalem, the city where I chose to put my Name. ³⁷However, as for you, I will take you, and you will rule over all that your heart desires; you will be king over Israel. ³⁸If you do whatever I command you and walk in my ways and do what is right in my eyes by keeping my statutes and commands, as David my servant did, I will be with you. I

ᵃ *24* Hebrew *destroyed them*   ᵇ *27* Or *the Millo*   ᶜ *33* Hebrew; Septuagint, Vulgate and Syriac *because he has* will build you a dynasty as enduring as the one I built for David and will give Israel to you. ³⁹I will humble David's descendants because of this, but not forever.' "

⁴⁰Solomon tried to kill Jeroboam, but Jeroboam fled to Egypt, to Shishak the king, and stayed there until Solomon's death.

SOLOMON'S DEATH

⁴¹As for the other events of Solomon's reign—all he did and the wisdom he displayed—are they not written in the book of the annals of Solomon? ⁴²Solomon reigned in Jerusalem over all Israel forty years. ⁴³Then he rested with his fathers and was buried in the city of David his father. And Rehoboam his son succeeded him as king.

ISRAEL REBELS AGAINST REHOBOAM

12 Rehoboam went to Shechem, for all the Israelites had gone there to make him king. ²When Jeroboam son of Nebat heard this (he was still in Egypt, where he had fled from King Solomon), he returned from ᵃ Egypt. ³So they sent for Jeroboam, and he and the whole assembly of Israel went to Rehoboam and said to him: ⁴"Your father put a heavy yoke on us, but now lighten the harsh labor and the heavy yoke he put on us, and we will serve you."

⁵Rehoboam answered, "Go away for three days and then come back to me." So the people went away.

⁶Then King Rehoboam consulted the elders who had served his father Solomon during his lifetime. "How would you advise me to answer these people?" he asked.

⁷They replied, "If today you will be a servant to these people and serve them and give them a favorable answer, they will always be your servants."

⁸But Rehoboam rejected the advice the elders gave him and consulted the young men who had grown up with him and were serving him. ⁹He asked them, "What is your advice? How should we answer these people who say to me, 'Lighten the yoke your father put on us'?"

¹⁰The young men who had grown up with him replied, "Tell these people who have said to you, 'Your father put a heavy yoke on us, but make our yoke lighter'—tell them, 'My little finger is thicker than my father's waist. ¹¹My father laid on you a heavy yoke; I will make it even heavier. My father scourged you with whips; I will scourge you with scorpions.' "

¹²Three days later Jeroboam and all the people returned to Rehoboam, as the king had said, "Come back to me in three days." ¹³The king answered the people harshly. Rejecting the advice given him by the elders, ¹⁴he followed the advice of the young men and said, "My father made your yoke heavy; I will make it even heavier. My father scourged you with whips; I will scourge you with scorpions." ¹⁵So the king did not listen to the people, for this turn of events was from the LORD, to fulfill the word the LORD had spoken to Jeroboam son of Nebat through Ahijah the Shilonite.

¹⁶When all Israel saw that the king refused to listen to them, they answered the king:

> "What share do we have in David,
>   what part in Jesse's son?
> To your tents, O Israel!
>   Look after your own house, O David!"

Asking for Advice

Asking someone for advice can be tough. For one thing, it means admitting that someone else may know more than you do about certain things. Admitting that requires you to swallow your pride and let others see that you're not quite as together as you'd like them to believe. But those are small sacrifices compared to the value of wise counsel. There are lots of things in this world that you'll have to learn from experience, but that doesn't mean you can't get some help to make the learning process a little easier and to avoid some mistakes along the way. Learn to recognize good advice, and, unlike Rehoboam, follow it.

ᵃ 2 Or *he remained in*

So the Israelites went home. [17]But as for the Israelites who were living in the towns of Judah, Rehoboam still ruled over them.

[18]King Rehoboam sent out Adoniram,[a] who was in charge of forced labor, but all Israel stoned him to death. King Rehoboam, however, managed to get into his chariot and escape to Jerusalem. [19]So Israel has been in rebellion against the house of David to this day.

[20]When all the Israelites heard that Jeroboam had returned, they sent and called him to the assembly and made him king over all Israel. Only the tribe of Judah remained loyal to the house of David.

[21]When Rehoboam arrived in Jerusalem, he mustered the whole house of Judah and the tribe of Benjamin—a hundred and eighty thousand fighting men—to make war against the house of Israel and to regain the kingdom for Rehoboam son of Solomon.

[22]But this word of God came to Shemaiah the man of God: [23]"Say to Rehoboam son of Solomon king of Judah, to the whole house of Judah and Benjamin, and to the rest of the people, [24]'This is what the LORD says: Do not go up to fight against your brothers, the Israelites. Go home, every one of you, for this is my doing.' " So they obeyed the word of the LORD and went home again, as the LORD had ordered.

GOLDEN CALVES AT BETHEL AND DAN

[25]Then Jeroboam fortified Shechem in the hill country of Ephraim and lived there. From there he went out and built up Peniel.[b]

[26]Jeroboam thought to himself, "The kingdom will now likely revert to the house of David. [27]If these people go up to offer sacrifices at the temple of the LORD in Jerusalem, they will again give their allegiance to their lord, Rehoboam king of Judah. They will kill me and return to King Rehoboam."

[28]After seeking advice, the king made two golden calves. He said to the people, "It is too much for you to go up to Jerusalem. Here are your gods, O Israel, who brought you up out of Egypt." [29]One he set up in Bethel, and the other in Dan. [30]And this thing became a sin; the people went even as far as Dan to worship the one there.

[31]Jeroboam built shrines on high places and appointed priests from all sorts of people, even though they were not Levites. [32]He instituted a festival on the fifteenth day of the eighth month, like the festival held in Judah, and offered sacrifices on the altar. This he did in Bethel, sacrificing to the calves he had made. And at Bethel he also installed priests at the high places he had made. [33]On the fifteenth day of the eighth month, a month of his own choosing, he offered sacrifices on the altar he had built at Bethel. So he instituted the festival for the Israelites and went up to the altar to make offerings.

THE MAN OF GOD FROM JUDAH

13

By the word of the LORD a man of God came from Judah to Bethel, as Jeroboam was standing by the altar to make an offering. [2]He cried out against the altar by the word of the LORD: "O altar, altar! This is what the LORD says: 'A son named Josiah will be born to the house of David. On you he will sacrifice the priests of the high places who now make offerings here, and human bones will be burned on you.' " [3]That same day the man of God gave a sign: "This is the sign the LORD has declared: The altar will be split apart and the ashes on it will be poured out."

[4]When King Jeroboam heard what the man of God cried out against the altar at Bethel, he stretched out his hand from the altar and said, "Seize him!" But the hand he stretched out toward the man shriveled up, so that he could not pull it back. [5]Also, the altar was split apart and its ashes poured out according to the sign given by the man of God by the word of the LORD.

[6]Then the king said to the man of God, "Intercede with the LORD your God and pray for me that my hand may be restored." So the man of God interceded with the LORD, and the king's hand was restored and became as it was before.

[7]The king said to the man of God, "Come home with me and have something to eat, and I will give you a gift."

[8]But the man of God answered the king, "Even if you were to give me half your possessions, I would not go with you, nor would I eat bread or drink water here. [9]For I was commanded by the word of the LORD: 'You must not eat bread or drink water or return by the way you came.' " [10]So he took another road and did not return by the way he had come to Bethel.

---

[a] 18 Some Septuagint manuscripts and Syriac (see also 1 Kings 4:6 and 5:14); Hebrew Adoram   [b] 25 Hebrew Penuel, a variant of Peniel

¹¹Now there was a certain old prophet living in Bethel, whose sons came and told him all that the man of God had done there that day. They also told their father what he had said to the king. ¹²Their father asked them, "Which way did he go?" And his sons showed him which road the man of God from Judah had taken. ¹³So he said to his sons, "Saddle the donkey for me." And when they had saddled the donkey for him, he mounted it ¹⁴and rode after the man of God. He found him sitting under an oak tree and asked, "Are you the man of God who came from Judah?"

"I am," he replied.

¹⁵So the prophet said to him, "Come home with me and eat."

¹⁶The man of God said, "I cannot turn back and go with you, nor can I eat bread or drink water with you in this place. ¹⁷I have been told by the word of the LORD: 'You must not eat bread or drink water there or return by the way you came.' "

¹⁸The old prophet answered, "I too am a prophet, as you are. And an angel said to me by the word of the LORD: 'Bring him back with you to your house so that he may eat bread and drink water.' " (But he was lying to him.) ¹⁹So the man of God returned with him and ate and drank in his house.

²⁰While they were sitting at the table, the word of the LORD came to the old prophet who had brought him back. ²¹He cried out to the man of God who had come from Judah, "This is what the LORD says: 'You have defied the word of the LORD and have not kept the command the LORD your God gave you. ²²You came back and ate bread and drank water in the place where he told you not to eat or drink. Therefore your body will not be buried in the tomb of your fathers.' "

²³When the man of God had finished eating and drinking, the prophet who had brought him back saddled his donkey for him. ²⁴As he went on his way, a lion met him on the road and killed him, and his body was thrown down on the road, with both the donkey and the lion standing beside it. ²⁵Some people who passed by saw the body thrown down there, with the lion standing beside the body, and they went and reported it in the city where the old prophet lived.

²⁶When the prophet who had brought him back from his journey heard of it, he said, "It is the man of God who defied the word of the LORD. The LORD has given him over to the lion, which has mauled him and killed him, as the word of the LORD had warned him."

²⁷The prophet said to his sons, "Saddle the donkey for me," and they did so. ²⁸Then he went out and found the body thrown down on the road, with the donkey and the lion standing beside it. The lion had neither eaten the body nor mauled the donkey. ²⁹So the prophet picked up the body of the man of God, laid it on the donkey, and brought it back to his own city to mourn for him and bury him. ³⁰Then he laid the body in his own tomb, and they mourned over him and said, "Oh, my brother!"

³¹After burying him, he said to his sons, "When I die, bury me in the grave where the man of God is buried; lay my bones beside his bones. ³²For the message he declared by the word of the LORD against the altar in Bethel and against all the shrines on the high places in the towns of Samaria will certainly come true."

³³Even after this, Jeroboam did not change his evil ways, but once more appointed priests for the high places from all sorts of people. Anyone who wanted to become a priest he consecrated for the high places. ³⁴This was the sin of the house of Jeroboam that led to its downfall and to its destruction from the face of the earth.

NOW OR NEVER

1KI 14:1-4

When have you felt like hiding from God? How can you deal with shame, get rid of your guilt and repair your most important relationship?

AHIJAH'S PROPHECY AGAINST JEROBOAM

14

At that time Abijah son of Jeroboam became ill, ²and Jeroboam said to his wife, "Go, disguise yourself, so you won't be recognized as the wife of Jeroboam. Then go to Shiloh. Ahijah the prophet is there—the one who told me I would be king over this people. ³Take ten loaves of bread with you, some cakes and a jar of honey, and go to him. He will tell you what will happen to the boy." ⁴So Jeroboam's wife did what he said and went to Ahijah's house in Shiloh. Now Ahijah could not see; his sight was gone because of his age. ⁵But the LORD had told Ahijah,

"Jeroboam's wife is coming to ask you about her son, for he is ill, and you are to give her such and such an answer. When she arrives, she will pretend to be someone else."

⁶So when Ahijah heard the sound of her footsteps at the door, he said, "Come in, wife of Jeroboam. Why this pretense? I have been sent to you with bad news. ⁷Go, tell Jeroboam that this is what the Lord, the God of Israel, says: 'I raised you up from among the people and made you a leader over my people Israel. ⁸I tore the kingdom away from the house of David and gave it to you, but you have not been like my servant David, who kept my commands and followed me with all his heart, doing only what was right in my eyes. ⁹You have done more evil than all who lived before you. You have made for yourself other gods, idols made of metal; you have provoked me to anger and thrust me behind your back.

¹⁰" 'Because of this, I am going to bring disaster on the house of Jeroboam. I will cut off from Jeroboam every last male in Israel—slave or free. I will burn up the house of Jeroboam as one burns dung, until it is all gone. ¹¹Dogs will eat those belonging to Jeroboam who die in the city, and the birds of the air will feed on those who die in the country. The Lord has spoken!'

¹²"As for you, go back home. When you set foot in your city, the boy will die. ¹³All Israel will mourn for him and bury him. He is the only one belonging to Jeroboam who will be buried, because he is the only one in the house of Jeroboam in whom the Lord, the God of Israel, has found anything good.

¹⁴"The Lord will raise up for himself a king over Israel who will cut off the family of Jeroboam. This is the day! What? Yes, even now.ᵃ ¹⁵And the Lord will strike Israel, so that it will be like a reed swaying in the water. He will uproot Israel from this good land that he gave to their forefathers and scatter them beyond the River,ᵇ because they provoked the Lord to anger by making Asherah poles.ᶜ ¹⁶And he will give Israel up because of the sins Jeroboam has committed and has caused Israel to commit."

¹⁷Then Jeroboam's wife got up and left and went to Tirzah. As soon as she stepped over the threshold of the house, the boy died. ¹⁸They buried him, and all Israel mourned for him, as the Lord had said through his servant the prophet Ahijah.

¹⁹The other events of Jeroboam's reign, his wars and how he ruled, are written in the book of the annals of the kings of Israel. ²⁰He reigned for twenty-two years and then rested with his fathers. And Nadab his son succeeded him as king.

REHOBOAM KING OF JUDAH

²¹Rehoboam son of Solomon was king in Judah. He was forty-one years old when he became king, and he reigned seventeen years in Jerusalem, the city the Lord had chosen out of all the tribes of Israel in which to put his Name. His mother's name was Naamah; she was an Ammonite.

²²Judah did evil in the eyes of the Lord. By the sins they committed they stirred up his jealous anger more than their fathers had done. ²³They also set up for themselves high places, sacred stones and Asherah poles on every high hill and under every spreading tree. ²⁴There were even male shrine prostitutes in the land; the people engaged in all the detestable practices of the nations the Lord had driven out before the Israelites.

²⁵In the fifth year of King Rehoboam, Shishak king of Egypt attacked Jerusalem. ²⁶He carried off the treasures of the temple of the Lord and the treasures of the royal palace. He took everything, including all the gold shields Solomon had made. ²⁷So King Rehoboam made bronze shields to replace them and assigned these to the commanders of the guard on duty at the entrance to the royal palace. ²⁸Whenever the king went to the Lord's temple, the guards bore the shields, and afterward they returned them to the guardroom.

²⁹As for the other events of Rehoboam's reign, and all he did, are they not written in the book of the annals of the kings of Judah? ³⁰There was continual warfare between Rehoboam and Jeroboam. ³¹And Rehoboam rested with his fathers and was buried with them in the City of David. His mother's name was Naamah; she was an Ammonite. And Abijahᵈ his son succeeded him as king.

ABIJAH KING OF JUDAH

15 In the eighteenth year of the reign of Jeroboam son of Nebat, Abijahᵉ became king of Judah, ²and he reigned in Jerusalem three years. His mother's name was Maacah daughter of Abishalom.ᶠ

ᵃ 14 The meaning of the Hebrew for this sentence is uncertain. ᵇ 15 That is, the Euphrates ᶜ 15 That is, symbols of the goddess Asherah; here and elsewhere in 1 Kings ᵈ 31 Some Hebrew manuscripts and Septuagint (see also 2 Chron. 12:16); most Hebrew manuscripts *Abijam* ᵉ 1 Some Hebrew manuscripts and Septuagint (see also 2 Chron. 12:16); most Hebrew manuscripts *Abijam*; also in verses 7 and 8 ᶠ 2 A variant of *Absalom*; also in verse 10

³He committed all the sins his father had done before him; his heart was not fully devoted to the Lord his God, as the heart of David his forefather had been. ⁴Nevertheless, for David's sake the Lord his God gave him a lamp in Jerusalem by raising up a son to succeed him and by making Jerusalem strong. ⁵For David had done what was right in the eyes of the Lord and had not failed to keep any of the Lord's commands all the days of his life—except in the case of Uriah the Hittite.

⁶There was war between Rehoboam[a] and Jeroboam throughout ⌊Abijah's⌋ lifetime. ⁷As for the other events of Abijah's reign, and all he did, are they not written in the book of the annals of the kings of Judah? There was war between Abijah and Jeroboam. ⁸And Abijah rested with his fathers and was buried in the City of David. And Asa his son succeeded him as king.

ASA KING OF JUDAH

⁹In the twentieth year of Jeroboam king of Israel, Asa became king of Judah, ¹⁰and he reigned in Jerusalem forty-one years. His grandmother's name was Maacah daughter of Abishalom.

¹¹Asa did what was right in the eyes of the Lord, as his father David had done. ¹²He expelled the male shrine prostitutes from the land and got rid of all the idols his fathers had made. ¹³He even deposed his grandmother Maacah from her position as queen mother, because she had made a repulsive Asherah pole. Asa cut the pole down and burned it in the Kidron Valley. ¹⁴Although he did not remove the high places, Asa's heart was fully committed to the Lord all his life. ¹⁵He brought into the temple of the Lord the silver and gold and the articles that he and his father had dedicated.

NOW OR NEVER
1KI 15:11–14

Do you always need to be told specifically what God wants you to do? Or is knowing the right thing to do a matter of instinct? Remember, the Bible is our ultimate authority on right and wrong.

¹⁶There was war between Asa and Baasha king of Israel throughout their reigns. ¹⁷Baasha king of Israel went up against Judah and fortified Ramah to prevent anyone from leaving or entering the territory of Asa king of Judah.

¹⁸Asa then took all the silver and gold that was left in the treasuries of the Lord's temple and of his own palace. He entrusted it to his officials and sent them to Ben-Hadad son of Tabrimmon, the son of Hezion, the king of Aram, who was ruling in Damascus. ¹⁹"Let there be a treaty between me and you," he said, "as there was between my father and your father. See, I am sending you a gift of silver and gold. Now break your treaty with Baasha king of Israel so he will withdraw from me."

²⁰Ben-Hadad agreed with King Asa and sent the commanders of his forces against the towns of Israel. He conquered Ijon, Dan, Abel Beth Maacah and all Kinnereth in addition to Naphtali. ²¹When Baasha heard this, he stopped building Ramah and withdrew to Tirzah. ²²Then King Asa issued an order to all Judah—no one was exempt—and they carried away from Ramah the stones and timber Baasha had been using there. With them King Asa built up Geba in Benjamin, and also Mizpah.

²³As for all the other events of Asa's reign, all his achievements, all he did and the cities he built, are they not written in the book of the annals of the kings of Judah? In his old age, however, his feet became diseased. ²⁴Then Asa rested with his fathers and was buried with them in the city of his father David. And Jehoshaphat his son succeeded him as king.

NADAB KING OF ISRAEL

²⁵Nadab son of Jeroboam became king of Israel in the second year of Asa king of Judah, and he reigned over Israel two years. ²⁶He did evil in the eyes of the Lord, walking in the ways of his father and in his sin, which he had caused Israel to commit.

²⁷Baasha son of Ahijah of the house of Issachar plotted against him, and he struck him down at Gibbethon, a Philistine town, while Nadab and all Israel were besieging it. ²⁸Baasha killed Nadab in the third year of Asa king of Judah and succeeded him as king.

²⁹As soon as he began to reign, he killed Jeroboam's whole family. He did not leave Jeroboam anyone that breathed, but destroyed them all, according to the word of the Lord given through his servant

---

ᵃ 6 Most Hebrew manuscripts; some Hebrew manuscripts and Syriac *Abijam* (that is, Abijah)

Ahijah the Shilonite— ³⁰because of the sins Jeroboam had committed and had caused Israel to commit, and because he provoked the LORD, the God of Israel, to anger.

³¹As for the other events of Nadab's reign, and all he did, are they not written in the book of the annals of the kings of Israel? ³²There was war between Asa and Baasha king of Israel throughout their reigns.

BAASHA KING OF ISRAEL

³³In the third year of Asa king of Judah, Baasha son of Ahijah became king of all Israel in Tirzah, and he reigned twenty-four years. ³⁴He did evil in the eyes of the LORD, walking in the ways of Jeroboam and in his sin, which he had caused Israel to commit.

16 Then the word of the LORD came to Jehu son of Hanani against Baasha: ²"I lifted you up from the dust and made you leader of my people Israel, but you walked in the ways of Jeroboam and caused my people Israel to sin and to provoke me to anger by their sins. ³So I am about to consume Baasha and his house, and I will make your house like that of Jeroboam son of Nebat. ⁴Dogs will eat those belonging to Baasha who die in the city, and the birds of the air will feed on those who die in the country."

⁵As for the other events of Baasha's reign, what he did and his achievements, are they not written in the book of the annals of the kings of Israel? ⁶Baasha rested with his fathers and was buried in Tirzah. And Elah his son succeeded him as king.

⁷Moreover, the word of the LORD came through the prophet Jehu son of Hanani to Baasha and his house, because of all the evil he had done in the eyes of the LORD, provoking him to anger by the things he did, and becoming like the house of Jeroboam—and also because he destroyed it.

ELAH KING OF ISRAEL

⁸In the twenty-sixth year of Asa king of Judah, Elah son of Baasha became king of Israel, and he reigned in Tirzah two years.

⁹Zimri, one of his officials, who had command of half his chariots, plotted against him. Elah was in Tirzah at the time, getting drunk in the home of Arza, the man in charge of the palace at Tirzah. ¹⁰Zimri came in, struck him down and killed him in the twenty-seventh year of Asa king of Judah. Then he succeeded him as king.

¹¹As soon as he began to reign and was seated on the throne, he killed off Baasha's whole family. He did not spare a single male, whether relative or friend. ¹²So Zimri destroyed the whole family of Baasha, in accordance with the word of the LORD spoken against Baasha through the prophet Jehu— ¹³because of all the sins Baasha and his son Elah had committed and had caused Israel to commit, so that they provoked the LORD, the God of Israel, to anger by their worthless idols.

¹⁴As for the other events of Elah's reign, and all he did, are they not written in the book of the annals of the kings of Israel?

ZIMRI KING OF ISRAEL

¹⁵In the twenty-seventh year of Asa king of Judah, Zimri reigned in Tirzah seven days. The army was encamped near Gibbethon, a Philistine town. ¹⁶When the Israelites in the camp heard that Zimri had plotted against the king and murdered him, they proclaimed Omri, the commander of the army, king over Israel that very day there in the camp. ¹⁷Then Omri and all the Israelites with him withdrew from Gibbethon and laid siege to Tirzah. ¹⁸When Zimri saw that the city was taken, he went into the citadel of the royal palace and set the palace on fire around him. So he died, ¹⁹because of the sins he had committed, doing evil in the eyes of the LORD and walking in the ways of Jeroboam and in the sin he had committed and had caused Israel to commit.

²⁰As for the other events of Zimri's reign, and the rebellion he carried out, are they not written in the book of the annals of the kings of Israel?

OMRI KING OF ISRAEL

²¹Then the people of Israel were split into two factions; half supported Tibni son of Ginath for king, and the other half supported Omri. ²²But Omri's followers proved stronger than those of Tibni son of Ginath. So Tibni died and Omri became king.

²³In the thirty-first year of Asa king of Judah, Omri became king of Israel, and he reigned twelve

years, six of them in Tirzah. 24He bought the hill of Samaria from Shemer for two talents[a] of silver and built a city on the hill, calling it Samaria, after Shemer, the name of the former owner of the hill.

25But Omri did evil in the eyes of the LORD and sinned more than all those before him. 26He walked in all the ways of Jeroboam son of Nebat and in his sin, which he had caused Israel to commit, so that they provoked the LORD, the God of Israel, to anger by their worthless idols.

27As for the other events of Omri's reign, what he did and the things he achieved, are they not written in the book of the annals of the kings of Israel? 28Omri rested with his fathers and was buried in Samaria. And Ahab his son succeeded him as king.

AHAB BECOMES KING OF ISRAEL

29In the thirty-eighth year of Asa king of Judah, Ahab son of Omri became king of Israel, and he reigned in Samaria over Israel twenty-two years. 30Ahab son of Omri did more evil in the eyes of the LORD than any of those before him. 31He not only considered it trivial to commit the sins of Jeroboam son of Nebat, but he also married Jezebel daughter of Ethbaal king of the Sidonians, and began to serve Baal and worship him. 32He set up an altar for Baal in the temple of Baal that he built in Samaria. 33Ahab also made an Asherah pole and did more to provoke the LORD, the God of Israel, to anger than did all the kings of Israel before him.

34In Ahab's time, Hiel of Bethel rebuilt Jericho. He laid its foundations at the cost of his firstborn son Abiram, and he set up its gates at the cost of his youngest son Segub, in accordance with the word of the LORD spoken by Joshua son of Nun.

ELIJAH FED BY RAVENS

17 Now Elijah the Tishbite, from Tishbe[b] in Gilead, said to Ahab, "As the LORD, the God of Israel, lives, whom I serve, there will be neither dew nor rain in the next few years except at my word."

2Then the word of the LORD came to Elijah: 3"Leave here, turn eastward and hide in the Kerith Ravine, east of the Jordan. 4You will drink from the brook, and I have ordered the ravens to feed you there."

5So he did what the LORD had told him. He went to the Kerith Ravine, east of the Jordan, and stayed there. 6The ravens brought him bread and meat in the morning and bread and meat in the evening, and he drank from the brook.

THE WIDOW AT ZAREPHATH

7Some time later the brook dried up because there had been no rain in the land. 8Then the word of the LORD came to him: 9"Go at once to Zarephath of Sidon and stay there. I have commanded a widow in that place to supply you with food." 10So he went to Zarephath. When he came to the town gate, a widow was there gathering sticks. He called to her and asked, "Would you bring me a little water in a jar so I may have a drink?" 11As she was going to get it, he called, "And bring me, please, a piece of bread."

12"As surely as the LORD your God lives," she replied, "I don't have any bread—only a handful of flour in a jar and a little oil in a jug. I am gathering a few sticks to take home and make a meal for myself and my son, that we may eat it—and die."

13Elijah said to her, "Don't be afraid. Go home and do as you have said. But first make a small cake of bread for me from what you have and bring it to me, and then make something for yourself and your son. 14For this is what the LORD, the God of Israel, says: 'The jar of flour will not be used up and the jug of oil will not run dry until the day the LORD gives rain on the land.' "

Responding to Tragedy

When tragedy strikes, what's your response? Maybe you've never encountered the loss of a loved one, or perhaps you know the experience all too well. Do you worry? Get depressed? Angry? All of these are natural responses to tragedy. God understands our emotions—after all, he gave them to us. But he's also given us something else—a perspective on life that's totally different from the world's. God has given us power over death. Every person dies. Even the boy healed through Elijah's prayer eventually died. But Jesus conquered death, sorrow and tragedy once and for all, making eternal life possible for anyone who believes in him.

---

[a] 24 That is, about 150 pounds (about 70 kilograms)   [b] 1 Or Tishbite, of the settlers

¹⁵She went away and did as Elijah had told her. So there was food every day for Elijah and for the woman and her family. ¹⁶For the jar of flour was not used up and the jug of oil did not run dry, in keeping with the word of the LORD spoken by Elijah.

¹⁷Some time later the son of the woman who owned the house became ill. He grew worse and worse, and finally stopped breathing. ¹⁸She said to Elijah, "What do you have against me, man of God? Did you come to remind me of my sin and kill my son?"

¹⁹"Give me your son," Elijah replied. He took him from her arms, carried him to the upper room where he was staying, and laid him on his bed. ²⁰Then he cried out to the LORD, "O LORD my God, have you brought tragedy also upon this widow I am staying with, by causing her son to die?" ²¹Then he stretched himself out on the boy three times and cried to the LORD, "O LORD my God, let this boy's life return to him!"

²²The LORD heard Elijah's cry, and the boy's life returned to him, and he lived. ²³Elijah picked up the child and carried him down from the room into the house. He gave him to his mother and said, "Look, your son is alive!"

²⁴Then the woman said to Elijah, "Now I know that you are a man of God and that the word of the LORD from your mouth is the truth."

ELIJAH AND OBADIAH

18

After a long time, in the third year, the word of the LORD came to Elijah: "Go and present yourself to Ahab, and I will send rain on the land." ²So Elijah went to present himself to Ahab.

Now the famine was severe in Samaria, ³and Ahab had summoned Obadiah, who was in charge of his palace. (Obadiah was a devout believer in the LORD. ⁴While Jezebel was killing off the LORD's prophets, Obadiah had taken a hundred prophets and hidden them in two caves, fifty in each, and had supplied them with food and water.) ⁵Ahab had said to Obadiah, "Go through the land to all the springs and valleys. Maybe we can find some grass to keep the horses and mules alive so we will not have to kill any of our animals." ⁶So they divided the land they were to cover, Ahab going in one direction and Obadiah in another.

⁷As Obadiah was walking along, Elijah met him. Obadiah recognized him, bowed down to the ground, and said, "Is it really you, my lord Elijah?"

⁸"Yes," he replied. "Go tell your master, 'Elijah is here.' "

⁹"What have I done wrong," asked Obadiah, "that you are handing your servant over to Ahab to be put to death? ¹⁰As surely as the LORD your God lives, there is not a nation or kingdom where my master has not sent someone to look for you. And whenever a nation or kingdom claimed you were not there, he made them swear they could not find you. ¹¹But now you tell me to go to my master and say, 'Elijah is here.' ¹²I don't know where the Spirit of the LORD may carry you when I leave you. If I go and tell Ahab and he doesn't find you, he will kill me. Yet I your servant have worshiped the LORD since my youth. ¹³Haven't you heard, my lord, what I did while Jezebel was killing the prophets of the LORD? I hid a hundred of the LORD's prophets in two caves, fifty in each, and supplied them with food and water. ¹⁴And now you tell me to go to my master and say, 'Elijah is here.' He will kill me!"

¹⁵Elijah said, "As the LORD Almighty lives, whom I serve, I will surely present myself to Ahab today."

Counting the Cost

» live the adventure » 1Ki 18:14

If you stay faithful to God long enough, you can expect to face your share of intense situations. Sooner or later, God is going to let you face circumstances like the one Obadiah found himself in, where the stakes are high and so is the stress level. For Obadiah, obeying the Lord meant risking death. Obadiah knew this, but he didn't dismiss the possibility like some reckless hero. He thought about it and even talked it out with Elijah. Then he made the decision to obey the Lord's command and ignore the potential cost to himself, trusting in God to protect him.

¹⁶So Obadiah went to meet Ahab and told him, and Ahab went to meet Elijah. ¹⁷When he saw Elijah, he said to him, "Is that you, you troubler of Israel?"

¹⁸"I have not made trouble for Israel," Elijah replied. "But you and your father's family have. You have abandoned the LORD's commands and have followed the Baals. ¹⁹Now summon the people from all over Israel to meet me on Mount Carmel. And bring the four hundred and fifty prophets of Baal and the four hundred prophets of Asherah, who eat at Jezebel's table."

²⁰So Ahab sent word throughout all Israel and assembled the prophets on Mount Carmel. ²¹Elijah went before the people and said, "How long will you waver between two opinions? If the LORD is God, follow him; but if Baal is God, follow him."

But the people said nothing.

²²Then Elijah said to them, "I am the only one of the LORD's prophets left, but Baal has four hundred and fifty prophets. ²³Get two bulls for us. Let them choose one for themselves, and let them cut it into pieces and put it on the wood but not set fire to it. I will prepare the other bull and put it on the wood but not set fire to it. ²⁴Then you call on the name of your god, and I will call on the name of the LORD. The god who answers by fire—he is God."

Then all the people said, "What you say is good."

NOW OR NEVER

1KI 18:20–21

Do you know people who try to follow God and live according to the world's standards at the same time? How do you show them the dangers of living a double life and the joy of wholeheartedly following God?

²⁵Elijah said to the prophets of Baal, "Choose one of the bulls and prepare it first, since there are so many of you. Call on the name of your god, but do not light the fire." ²⁶So they took the bull given them and prepared it.

Then they called on the name of Baal from morning till noon. "O Baal, answer us!" they shouted. But there was no response; no one answered. And they danced around the altar they had made.

²⁷At noon Elijah began to taunt them. "Shout louder!" he said. "Surely he is a god! Perhaps he is deep in thought, or busy, or traveling. Maybe he is sleeping and must be awakened." ²⁸So they shouted louder and slashed themselves with swords and spears, as was their custom, until their blood flowed. ²⁹Midday passed, and they continued their frantic prophesying until the time for the evening sacrifice. But there was no response, no one answered, no one paid attention.

³⁰Then Elijah said to all the people, "Come here to me." They came to him, and he repaired the altar of the LORD, which was in ruins. ³¹Elijah took twelve stones, one for each of the tribes descended from Jacob, to whom the word of the LORD had come, saying, "Your name shall be Israel." ³²With the stones he built an altar in the name of the LORD, and he dug a trench around it large enough to hold two seahs[a] of seed. ³³He arranged the wood, cut the bull into pieces and laid it on the wood. Then he said to them, "Fill four large jars with water and pour it on the offering and on the wood."

³⁴"Do it again," he said, and they did it again.

"Do it a third time," he ordered, and they did it the third time. ³⁵The water ran down around the altar and even filled the trench.

³⁶At the time of sacrifice, the prophet Elijah stepped forward and prayed: "O LORD, God of Abraham, Isaac and Israel, let it be known today that you are God in Israel and that I am your servant and have done all these things at your command. ³⁷Answer me, O LORD, answer me, so these people will know that you, O LORD, are God, and that you are turning their hearts back again."

³⁸Then the fire of the LORD fell and burned up the sacrifice, the wood, the stones and the soil, and also licked up the water in the trench.

³⁹When all the people saw this, they fell prostrate and cried, "The LORD—he is God! The LORD—he is God!"

⁴⁰Then Elijah commanded them, "Seize the prophets of Baal. Don't let anyone get away!" They seized them, and Elijah had them brought down to the Kishon Valley and slaughtered there.

⁴¹And Elijah said to Ahab, "Go, eat and drink, for there is the sound of a heavy rain." ⁴²So Ahab went

---

ᵃ 32 That is, probably about 13 quarts (about 15 liters)

off to eat and drink, but Elijah climbed to the top of Carmel, bent down to the ground and put his face between his knees.

⁴³"Go and look toward the sea," he told his servant. And he went up and looked.

"There is nothing there," he said.

Seven times Elijah said, "Go back."

⁴⁴The seventh time the servant reported, "A cloud as small as a man's hand is rising from the sea."

So Elijah said, "Go and tell Ahab, 'Hitch up your chariot and go down before the rain stops you.' "

⁴⁵Meanwhile, the sky grew black with clouds, the wind rose, a heavy rain came on and Ahab rode off to Jezreel. ⁴⁶The power of the LORD came upon Elijah and, tucking his cloak into his belt, he ran ahead of Ahab all the way to Jezreel.

ELIJAH FLEES TO HOREB

19 Now Ahab told Jezebel everything Elijah had done and how he had killed all the prophets with the sword. ²So Jezebel sent a messenger to Elijah to say, "May the gods deal with me, be it ever so severely, if by this time tomorrow I do not make your life like that of one of them."

³Elijah was afraid[a] and ran for his life. When he came to Beersheba in Judah, he left his servant there, ⁴while he himself went a day's journey into the desert. He came to a broom tree, sat down under it and prayed that he might die. "I have had enough, LORD," he said. "Take my life; I am no better than my ancestors." ⁵Then he lay down under the tree and fell asleep.

All at once an angel touched him and said, "Get up and eat." ⁶He looked around, and there by his head was a cake of bread baked over hot coals, and a jar of water. He ate and drank and then lay down again.

⁷The angel of the LORD came back a second time and touched him and said, "Get up and eat, for the journey is too much for you." ⁸So he got up and ate and drank. Strengthened by that food, he traveled forty days and forty nights until he reached Horeb, the mountain of God. ⁹There he went into a cave and spent the night.

THE LORD APPEARS TO ELIJAH

And the word of the LORD came to him: "What are you doing here, Elijah?"

¹⁰He replied, "I have been very zealous for the LORD God Almighty. The Israelites have rejected your covenant, broken down your altars, and put your prophets to death with the sword. I am the only one left, and now they are trying to kill me too."

¹¹The LORD said, "Go out and stand on the mountain in the presence of the LORD, for the LORD is about to pass by."

Then a great and powerful wind tore the mountains apart and shattered the rocks before the LORD, but the LORD was not in the wind. After the wind there was an earthquake, but the LORD was not in the earthquake. ¹²After the earthquake came a fire, but the LORD was not in the fire. And after the fire came a gentle whisper. ¹³When Elijah heard it, he pulled his cloak over his face and went out and stood at the mouth of the cave.

Then a voice said to him, "What are you doing here, Elijah?"

¹⁴He replied, "I have been very zealous for the LORD God Almighty. The Israelites have rejected your covenant, broken down your altars, and put your prophets to death with the sword. I am the only one left, and now they are trying to kill me too."

NOW OR NEVER

1KI 19:14

Whether you realize it or not, you're never far from other believers. You just have to seek them out. One of God's most important gifts to us is the support and encouragement of fellow Christians.

¹⁵The LORD said to him, "Go back the way you came, and go to the Desert of Damascus. When you get there, anoint Hazael king over Aram. ¹⁶Also, anoint Jehu son of Nimshi king over Israel, and anoint Elisha son of Shaphat from Abel Meholah to succeed you as prophet. ¹⁷Jehu will put to death any who escape the sword of Hazael, and Elisha will put to death any who escape the sword of Jehu. ¹⁸Yet I

^a 3 Or *Elijah saw*

battlelines

» The Wages of Busyness

Q: I heard you've got mono. Is that true?
A: Unfortunately, yes.

Q: How did you get it? Have you been lip-locking with the ladies?
A: I wish! The doctor says I'm just run down.

Q: From what?
A: Oh, you know—school, church stuff, baseball, piano lessons . . . plus I've been working about 10-15 hours a week.

Q: Man, I'm getting tired just listening to your list!
A: Yeah, well, I do feel pretty wiped out. Like my aunt from Mississippi says, "I feel like I've been chewed up and spit out."

Q: Thanks for that mental image. So what's the treatment? Antibiotics? Vitamins?
A: There is no treatment. Just rest.

Q: You mean, like, sitting around and doing nothing?
A: You got it.

Q: Dude, that would make me crazy!
A: Tell me about it. On the other hand, maybe it's exactly what I need.

» Recapturing Your Sanity

The Bible makes it clear that it's not a sin to rest. In fact, God *wants* us to rest; he set aside an entire day for us to do just that. When the prophet Elijah was super-stressed and on the verge of a total breakdown, God prescribed a regimen of doing nothing but sleeping and eating (see 1 Kings 19:1–18).

Mark 6:31 reports a similar incident in regard to the lives of Jesus and his disciples: "Then, because so many people were coming and going that they did not even have a chance to eat, he [Jesus] said to them, 'Come with me by yourselves to a quiet place and get some rest.' "

The point is, if we try to do too much—if we don't learn to say no and take a little time out every once in a while—we'll eventually wear ourselves out.

Learn more about time management at www.RevolutionBible.com.

reserve seven thousand in Israel—all whose knees have not bowed down to Baal and all whose mouths have not kissed him."

THE CALL OF ELISHA

¹⁹So Elijah went from there and found Elisha son of Shaphat. He was plowing with twelve yoke of oxen, and he himself was driving the twelfth pair. Elijah went up to him and threw his cloak around him. ²⁰Elisha then left his oxen and ran after Elijah. "Let me kiss my father and mother good-by," he said, "and then I will come with you."

"Go back," Elijah replied. "What have I done to you?"

²¹So Elisha left him and went back. He took his yoke of oxen and slaughtered them. He burned the plowing equipment to cook the meat and gave it to the people, and they ate. Then he set out to follow Elijah and became his attendant.

BEN-HADAD ATTACKS SAMARIA

20 Now Ben-Hadad king of Aram mustered his entire army. Accompanied by thirty-two kings with their horses and chariots, he went up and besieged Samaria and attacked it. ²He sent messengers into the city to Ahab king of Israel, saying, "This is what Ben-Hadad says: ³'Your silver and gold are mine, and the best of your wives and children are mine.' "

⁴The king of Israel answered, "Just as you say, my lord the king. I and all I have are yours."

⁵The messengers came again and said, "This is what Ben-Hadad says: 'I sent to demand your silver and gold, your wives and your children. ⁶But about this time tomorrow I am going to send my officials to search your palace and the houses of your officials. They will seize everything you value and carry it away.' "

⁷The king of Israel summoned all the elders of the land and said to them, "See how this man is looking for trouble! When he sent for my wives and my children, my silver and my gold, I did not refuse him."

⁸The elders and the people all answered, "Don't listen to him or agree to his demands."

⁹So he replied to Ben-Hadad's messengers, "Tell my lord the king, 'Your servant will do all you demanded the first time, but this demand I cannot meet.' " They left and took the answer back to Ben-Hadad.

¹⁰Then Ben-Hadad sent another message to Ahab: "May the gods deal with me, be it ever so severely, if enough dust remains in Samaria to give each of my men a handful."

¹¹The king of Israel answered, "Tell him: 'One who puts on his armor should not boast like one who takes it off.' "

¹²Ben-Hadad heard this message while he and the kings were drinking in their tents,^a and he ordered his men: "Prepare to attack." So they prepared to attack the city.

AHAB DEFEATS BEN-HADAD

¹³Meanwhile a prophet came to Ahab king of Israel and announced, "This is what the LORD says: 'Do you see this vast army? I will give it into your hand today, and then you will know that I am the LORD.' "

¹⁴"But who will do this?" asked Ahab.

The prophet replied, "This is what the LORD says: 'The young officers of the provincial commanders will do it.' "

"And who will start the battle?" he asked.

The prophet answered, "You will."

¹⁵So Ahab summoned the young officers of the provincial commanders, 232 men. Then he assembled the rest of the Israelites, 7,000 in all. ¹⁶They set out at noon while Ben-Hadad and the 32 kings allied with him were in their tents getting drunk. ¹⁷The young officers of the provincial commanders went out first.

Now Ben-Hadad had dispatched scouts, who reported, "Men are advancing from Samaria."

¹⁸He said, "If they have come out for peace, take them alive; if they have come out for war, take them alive."

¹⁹The young officers of the provincial commanders marched out of the city with the army behind them ²⁰and each one struck down his opponent. At that, the Arameans fled, with the Israelites in pur-

---

^a 12 Or in Succoth; also in verse 16

suit. But Ben-Hadad king of Aram escaped on horseback with some of his horsemen. ²¹The king of Israel advanced and overpowered the horses and chariots and inflicted heavy losses on the Arameans.

²²Afterward, the prophet came to the king of Israel and said, "Strengthen your position and see what must be done, because next spring the king of Aram will attack you again."

²³Meanwhile, the officials of the king of Aram advised him, "Their gods are gods of the hills. That is why they were too strong for us. But if we fight them on the plains, surely we will be stronger than they. ²⁴Do this: Remove all the kings from their commands and replace them with other officers. ²⁵You must also raise an army like the one you lost—horse for horse and chariot for chariot—so we can fight Israel on the plains. Then surely we will be stronger than they." He agreed with them and acted accordingly.

²⁶The next spring Ben-Hadad mustered the Arameans and went up to Aphek to fight against Israel. ²⁷When the Israelites were also mustered and given provisions, they marched out to meet them. The Israelites camped opposite them like two small flocks of goats, while the Arameans covered the countryside.

²⁸The man of God came up and told the king of Israel, "This is what the Lᴏʀᴅ says: 'Because the Arameans think the Lᴏʀᴅ is a god of the hills and not a god of the valleys, I will deliver this vast army into your hands, and you will know that I am the Lᴏʀᴅ.' "

²⁹For seven days they camped opposite each other, and on the seventh day the battle was joined. The Israelites inflicted a hundred thousand casualties on the Aramean foot soldiers in one day. ³⁰The rest of them escaped to the city of Aphek, where the wall collapsed on twenty-seven thousand of them. And Ben-Hadad fled to the city and hid in an inner room.

³¹His officials said to him, "Look, we have heard that the kings of the house of Israel are merciful. Let us go to the king of Israel with sackcloth around our waists and ropes around our heads. Perhaps he will spare your life."

³²Wearing sackcloth around their waists and ropes around their heads, they went to the king of Israel and said, "Your servant Ben-Hadad says: 'Please let me live.' "

The king answered, "Is he still alive? He is my brother."

³³The men took this as a good sign and were quick to pick up his word. "Yes, your brother Ben-Hadad!" they said.

"Go and get him," the king said. When Ben-Hadad came out, Ahab had him come up into his chariot.

³⁴"I will return the cities my father took from your father," Ben-Hadad offered. "You may set up your own market areas in Damascus, as my father did in Samaria."

⌊Ahab said,⌋ "On the basis of a treaty I will set you free." So he made a treaty with him, and let him go.

A PROPHET CONDEMNS AHAB

³⁵By the word of the Lᴏʀᴅ one of the sons of the prophets said to his companion, "Strike me with your weapon," but the man refused.

³⁶So the prophet said, "Because you have not obeyed the Lᴏʀᴅ, as soon as you leave me a lion will kill you." And after the man went away, a lion found him and killed him.

³⁷The prophet found another man and said, "Strike me, please." So the man struck him and wounded him. ³⁸Then the prophet went and stood by the road waiting for the king. He disguised himself with his headband down over his eyes. ³⁹As the king passed by, the prophet called out to him, "Your servant went into the thick of the battle, and someone came to me with a captive and said, 'Guard this man. If he is missing, it will be your life for his life, or you must pay a talent[a] of silver.' ⁴⁰While your servant was busy here and there, the man disappeared."

"That is your sentence," the king of Israel said. "You have pronounced it yourself."

⁴¹Then the prophet quickly removed the headband from his eyes, and the king of Israel recognized him as one of the prophets. ⁴²He said to the king, "This is what the Lᴏʀᴅ says: 'You have set free a man I had determined should die.[b] Therefore it is your life for his life, your people for his people.' " ⁴³Sullen and angry, the king of Israel went to his palace in Samaria.

ᵃ 39 That is, about 75 pounds (about 34 kilograms)   ᵇ 42 The Hebrew term refers to the irrevocable giving over of things or persons to the Lᴏʀᴅ, often by totally destroying them.

battlelines

» Up in Smoke (Drugs)

Q: I heard a report that marijuana use is way up among teens and young adults. Is that true with the people you know?
A: Yeah, I'd say so. I don't know many hard-core users, but I know a lot of people who experiment and just mess around with it.

Q: Why do you think they do it?
A: Who knows? Probably because they're curious about what it's like. Or maybe just because they're bored. That's what my grandma has been trying to pound into my head my whole life: "Idle hands are the devil's workshop."

Q: Way to go, Grandma!
A: Uh, yeah. Whatever.

Q: So does it tempt *you* at all?
A: Yeah, maybe a little. Sometimes. But do *not* tell my grandma I said that!

Q: What's tempting about it?
A: I don't know—I just want to know what it's like, you know? Why so many people do it. I mean, if it's really such a terrible experience, it wouldn't be so popular, right? Now don't freak out on me or start calling the cops. I'm not saying I'm *going* to do it. I'm just saying it *looks* fun and it *seems* harmless.

Q: But it *is* illegal.
A: Yeah, but so is driving 50 in a 30 miles-per-hour zone.

» Fun or Dangerous?

Is smoking pot fun? A lot of people think it is. But "fun" shouldn't be what determines what we do. The bigger question is this: Does marijuana use glorify God (see 1 Corinthians 10:31)?

And once you get past that question, here are some more things to consider:

● Marijuana use is illegal.

● Marijuana is considered a "gateway" drug. Once you smoke pot, it's that much easier to move on to the next "fun" drug.

● The myth that pot isn't addictive is just that—an urban legend. Pot may not be as *physically* addictive as some drugs, but it is every bit as *psychologically* addictive. That means once you start using, you will *want* to keep using; and then you'll be hooked.

● Pot can do serious damage to your body—especially your brain cells.

Remember, just because it feels good—because it *seems* right—doesn't mean it's good for you (see Proverbs 14:12).

For more on dealing with drugs, go to www.RevolutionBible.com.

NABOTH'S VINEYARD

21 Some time later there was an incident involving a vineyard belonging to Naboth the Jezreelite. The vineyard was in Jezreel, close to the palace of Ahab king of Samaria. ²Ahab said to Naboth, "Let me have your vineyard to use for a vegetable garden, since it is close to my palace. In exchange I will give you a better vineyard or, if you prefer, I will pay you whatever it is worth."

³But Naboth replied, "The LORD forbid that I should give you the inheritance of my fathers."

⁴So Ahab went home, sullen and angry because Naboth the Jezreelite had said, "I will not give you the inheritance of my fathers." He lay on his bed sulking and refused to eat.

⁵His wife Jezebel came in and asked him, "Why are you so sullen? Why won't you eat?"

⁶He answered her, "Because I said to Naboth the Jezreelite, 'Sell me your vineyard; or if you prefer, I will give you another vineyard in its place.' But he said, 'I will not give you my vineyard.' "

⁷Jezebel his wife said, "Is this how you act as king over Israel? Get up and eat! Cheer up. I'll get you the vineyard of Naboth the Jezreelite."

⁸So she wrote letters in Ahab's name, placed his seal on them, and sent them to the elders and nobles who lived in Naboth's city with him. ⁹In those letters she wrote:

NOW OR NEVER
1KI 21:5–10

Coveting—wanting something someone else has—is a "gateway" sin. If you give in to it and dwell on it long enough, it can easily lead to other sin—lying, stealing and even murder.

"Proclaim a day of fasting and seat Naboth in a prominent place among the people. ¹⁰But seat two scoundrels opposite him and have them testify that he has cursed both God and the king. Then take him out and stone him to death."

¹¹So the elders and nobles who lived in Naboth's city did as Jezebel directed in the letters she had written to them. ¹²They proclaimed a fast and seated Naboth in a prominent place among the people. ¹³Then two scoundrels came and sat opposite him and brought charges against Naboth before the people, saying, "Naboth has cursed both God and the king." So they took him outside the city and stoned him to death. ¹⁴Then they sent word to Jezebel: "Naboth has been stoned and is dead."

¹⁵As soon as Jezebel heard that Naboth had been stoned to death, she said to Ahab, "Get up and take possession of the vineyard of Naboth the Jezreelite that he refused to sell you. He is no longer alive, but dead." ¹⁶When Ahab heard that Naboth was dead, he got up and went down to take possession of Naboth's vineyard.

¹⁷Then the word of the LORD came to Elijah the Tishbite: ¹⁸"Go down to meet Ahab king of Israel, who rules in Samaria. He is now in Naboth's vineyard, where he has gone to take possession of it. ¹⁹Say to him, 'This is what the LORD says: Have you not murdered a man and seized his property?' Then say to him, 'This is what the LORD says: In the place where dogs licked up Naboth's blood, dogs will lick up your blood—yes, yours!' "

²⁰Ahab said to Elijah, "So you have found me, my enemy!"

"I have found you," he answered, "because you have sold yourself to do evil in the eyes of the LORD. ²¹'I am going to bring disaster on you. I will consume your descendants and cut off from Ahab every last male in Israel—slave or free. ²²I will make your house like that of Jeroboam son of Nebat and that of Baasha son of Ahijah, because you have provoked me to anger and have caused Israel to sin.'

²³"And also concerning Jezebel the LORD says: 'Dogs will devour Jezebel by the wall of^a Jezreel.'

²⁴"Dogs will eat those belonging to Ahab who die in the city, and the birds of the air will feed on those who die in the country."

²⁵(There was never a man like Ahab, who sold himself to do evil in the eyes of the LORD, urged on by Jezebel his wife. ²⁶He behaved in the vilest manner by going after idols, like the Amorites the LORD drove out before Israel.)

²⁷When Ahab heard these words, he tore his clothes, put on sackcloth and fasted. He lay in sackcloth and went around meekly.

²⁸Then the word of the LORD came to Elijah the Tishbite: ²⁹"Have you noticed how Ahab has hum-

---

^a 23 Most Hebrew manuscripts; a few Hebrew manuscripts, Vulgate and Syriac (see also 2 Kings 9:26) *the plot of ground at*

bled himself before me? Because he has humbled himself, I will not bring this disaster in his day, but I will bring it on his house in the days of his son."

MICAIAH PROPHESIES AGAINST AHAB

22 For three years there was no war between Aram and Israel. ²But in the third year Jehoshaphat king of Judah went down to see the king of Israel. ³The king of Israel had said to his officials, "Don't you know that Ramoth Gilead belongs to us and yet we are doing nothing to retake it from the king of Aram?"

⁴So he asked Jehoshaphat, "Will you go with me to fight against Ramoth Gilead?"

Jehoshaphat replied to the king of Israel, "I am as you are, my people as your people, my horses as your horses." ⁵But Jehoshaphat also said to the king of Israel, "First seek the counsel of the LORD."

⁶So the king of Israel brought together the prophets—about four hundred men—and asked them, "Shall I go to war against Ramoth Gilead, or shall I refrain?"

"Go," they answered, "for the Lord will give it into the king's hand."

⁷But Jehoshaphat asked, "Is there not a prophet of the LORD here whom we can inquire of?"

⁸The king of Israel answered Jehoshaphat, "There is still one man through whom we can inquire of the LORD, but I hate him because he never prophesies anything good about me, but always bad. He is Micaiah son of Imlah."

"The king should not say that," Jehoshaphat replied.

⁹So the king of Israel called one of his officials and said, "Bring Micaiah son of Imlah at once."

¹⁰Dressed in their royal robes, the king of Israel and Jehoshaphat king of Judah were sitting on their thrones at the threshing floor by the entrance of the gate of Samaria, with all the prophets prophesying before them. ¹¹Now Zedekiah son of Kenaanah had made iron horns and he declared, "This is what the LORD says: 'With these you will gore the Arameans until they are destroyed.'"

¹²All the other prophets were prophesying the same thing. "Attack Ramoth Gilead and be victorious," they said, "for the LORD will give it into the king's hand."

¹³The messenger who had gone to summon Micaiah said to him, "Look, as one man the other prophets are predicting success for the king. Let your word agree with theirs, and speak favorably."

¹⁴But Micaiah said, "As surely as the LORD lives, I can tell him only what the LORD tells me."

¹⁵When he arrived, the king asked him, "Micaiah, shall we go to war against Ramoth Gilead, or shall I refrain?"

"Attack and be victorious," he answered, "for the LORD will give it into the king's hand."

¹⁶The king said to him, "How many times must I make you swear to tell me nothing but the truth in the name of the LORD?"

¹⁷Then Micaiah answered, "I saw all Israel scattered on the hills like sheep without a shepherd, and the LORD said, 'These people have no master. Let each one go home in peace.'"

¹⁸The king of Israel said to Jehoshaphat, "Didn't I tell you that he never prophesies anything good about me, but only bad?"

¹⁹Micaiah continued, "Therefore hear the word of the LORD: I saw the LORD sitting on his throne with all the host of heaven standing around him on his right and on his left. ²⁰And the LORD said, 'Who will entice Ahab into attacking Ramoth Gilead and going to his death there?'

"One suggested this, and another that. ²¹Finally, a spirit came forward, stood before the LORD and said, 'I will entice him.'

²²"'By what means?' the LORD asked.

"'I will go out and be a lying spirit in the mouths of all his prophets,' he said.

» live the adventure » 1Ki 22:1–28

Meeting God's Expectations

Few things in life are more difficult than trying to meet other people's expectations. For one thing, rarely will you have just one set of expectations to think about. Your parents expect one thing from you, your coaches and teachers expect another, your friends expect something different, and your girlfriend expects yet something else. Pleasing everyone is virtually impossible. Trying to do so only makes you miserable. Your best bet, then, is to focus on meeting God's expectations for your life, allowing him to help you properly deal with everyone else's.

" 'You will succeed in enticing him,' said the LORD. 'Go and do it.'

²³"So now the LORD has put a lying spirit in the mouths of all these prophets of yours. The LORD has decreed disaster for you."

²⁴Then Zedekiah son of Kenaanah went up and slapped Micaiah in the face. "Which way did the spirit from[a] the LORD go when he went from me to speak to you?" he asked.

²⁵Micaiah replied, "You will find out on the day you go to hide in an inner room."

²⁶The king of Israel then ordered, "Take Micaiah and send him back to Amon the ruler of the city and to Joash the king's son ²⁷and say, 'This is what the king says: Put this fellow in prison and give him nothing but bread and water until I return safely.' "

²⁸Micaiah declared, "If you ever return safely, the LORD has not spoken through me." Then he added, "Mark my words, all you people!"

AHAB KILLED AT RAMOTH GILEAD

²⁹So the king of Israel and Jehoshaphat king of Judah went up to Ramoth Gilead. ³⁰The king of Israel said to Jehoshaphat, "I will enter the battle in disguise, but you wear your royal robes." So the king of Israel disguised himself and went into battle.

³¹Now the king of Aram had ordered his thirty-two chariot commanders, "Do not fight with anyone, small or great, except the king of Israel." ³²When the chariot commanders saw Jehoshaphat, they thought, "Surely this is the king of Israel." So they turned to attack him, but when Jehoshaphat cried out, ³³the chariot commanders saw that he was not the king of Israel and stopped pursuing him.

³⁴But someone drew his bow at random and hit the king of Israel between the sections of his armor. The king told his chariot driver, "Wheel around and get me out of the fighting. I've been wounded." ³⁵All day long the battle raged, and the king was propped up in his chariot facing the Arameans. The blood from his wound ran onto the floor of the chariot, and that evening he died. ³⁶As the sun was setting, a cry spread through the army: "Every man to his town; everyone to his land!"

³⁷So the king died and was brought to Samaria, and they buried him there. ³⁸They washed the chariot at a pool in Samaria (where the prostitutes bathed),[b] and the dogs licked up his blood, as the word of the LORD had declared.

³⁹As for the other events of Ahab's reign, including all he did, the palace he built and inlaid with ivory, and the cities he fortified, are they not written in the book of the annals of the kings of Israel? ⁴⁰Ahab rested with his fathers. And Ahaziah his son succeeded him as king.

JEHOSHAPHAT KING OF JUDAH

⁴¹Jehoshaphat son of Asa became king of Judah in the fourth year of Ahab king of Israel. ⁴²Jehoshaphat was thirty-five years old when he became king, and he reigned in Jerusalem twenty-five years. His mother's name was Azubah daughter of Shilhi. ⁴³In everything he walked in the ways of his father Asa and did not stray from them; he did what was right in the eyes of the LORD. The high places, however, were not removed, and the people continued to offer sacrifices and burn incense there. ⁴⁴Jehoshaphat was also at peace with the king of Israel.

⁴⁵As for the other events of Jehoshaphat's reign, the things he achieved and his military exploits, are they not written in the book of the annals of the kings of Judah? ⁴⁶He rid the land of the rest of the male shrine prostitutes who remained there even after the reign of his father Asa. ⁴⁷There was then no king in Edom; a deputy ruled.

⁴⁸Now Jehoshaphat built a fleet of trading ships[c] to go to Ophir for gold, but they never set sail—they were wrecked at Ezion Geber. ⁴⁹At that time Ahaziah son of Ahab said to Jehoshaphat, "Let my men sail with your men," but Jehoshaphat refused.

⁵⁰Then Jehoshaphat rested with his fathers and was buried with them in the city of David his father. And Jehoram his son succeeded him.

AHAZIAH KING OF ISRAEL

⁵¹Ahaziah son of Ahab became king of Israel in Samaria in the seventeenth year of Jehoshaphat king of Judah, and he reigned over Israel two years. ⁵²He did evil in the eyes of the LORD, because he walked in the ways of his father and mother and in the ways of Jeroboam son of Nebat, who caused Israel to sin. ⁵³He served and worshiped Baal and provoked the LORD, the God of Israel, to anger, just as his father had done.

ᵃ 24 Or Spirit of   ᵇ 38 Or Samaria and cleaned the weapons   ᶜ 48 Hebrew of ships of Tarshish

2 KINGS 2 KINGS 2 KINGS

« AT A GLANCE

Author
Unknown

Audience
People of Israel

Date
Originally, the book was part of 1 Kings and probably was written after the fall of Jerusalem in 586 B.C., but before 550 B.C.

Setting
Israel and Judah have been divided into two separate kingdoms for more than a century.

Verse to Remember
So the LORD said, "I will remove Judah also from my presence as I removed Israel, and I will reject Jerusalem, the city I chose, and this temple, about which I said, 'There shall my Name be' " (23:27).

Theme to Consider
You can't escape God's judgment. Just as God punished Israel and Judah because they rejected him and chose to worship other gods, so too will he judge all who reject him.

UNCHANGING TRUTH » Do you have a mentor? Have you ever thought about finding one? A mentor is someone who pushes you to become the man God has intended you to be. A mentor is someone you can turn to when your Christian life doesn't seem to be working the way it should . . . or when you're facing a situation that seems overwhelming or hopeless . . . or when you just need someone to talk to about life's mysteries. A mentor is like a friend, role model, teacher and cool older brother all rolled into one.

The book of 2 Kings gives us a good illustration of how a mentoring relationship works. Elijah was a veteran prophet. He'd been around the block several times. Elisha, however, was a rookie—eager to serve God, but not entirely sure how to do it. He learned by watching what Elijah did and listening to what he said. Elisha's training was so successful that when the time came for Elijah to head for his heavenly reward, Elisha was able to step in and take his place as a prophet to Israel. The mentoring relationship had worked wonderfully.

If you think this is the part where we recommend finding a mentor for yourself, you're only half right. Having a mentor will certainly make a difference in your life. Anyone who's had a mentor will tell you that it can be a key stimulus in growing your relationship with God. However, *having* a mentor is not nearly as important as *becoming* a mentor to someone else.

Believe it or not, there are younger guys in this world who actually look up to you—or who *would* look up to you if they got the chance to know you. Depending on your situation, those guys might include a younger brother, cousin, neighbor or a kid in the Sunday school class you help out with.

Think about what you can bring to someone else's spiritual life—what advice you can offer, what mistakes you can help that person avoid, what Bible passages you can share, what books you can recommend, what encouragement you can give and what accountability you can provide. Then talk to your youth leader or pastor to find out where and how you could make a difference in someone else's life.

LIFE LESSONS »

1 Being unfaithful to the one true God can land you in big trouble (1:3–4).

2 God has a special place in his heart for those in great need; so should we (4:1–7).

3 Pride often prevents us from doing God's work and accepting what he has done for us (5:11–12)!

4 The fact that we are God's people does not make us immune to his discipline and to the consequences of our sin (17:7).

THE LORD'S JUDGMENT ON AHAZIAH

1 After Ahab's death, Moab rebelled against Israel. ²Now Ahaziah had fallen through the lattice of his upper room in Samaria and injured himself. So he sent messengers, saying to them, "Go and consult Baal-Zebub, the god of Ekron, to see if I will recover from this injury."

³But the angel of the Lord said to Elijah the Tishbite, "Go up and meet the messengers of the king of Samaria and ask them, 'Is it because there is no God in Israel that you are going off to consult Baal-Zebub, the god of Ekron?' ⁴Therefore this is what the Lord says: 'You will not leave the bed you are lying on. You will certainly die!' " So Elijah went.

⁵When the messengers returned to the king, he asked them, "Why have you come back?"

⁶"A man came to meet us," they replied. "And he said to us, 'Go back to the king who sent you and tell him, "This is what the Lord says: Is it because there is no God in Israel that you are sending men to consult Baal-Zebub, the god of Ekron? Therefore you will not leave the bed you are lying on. You will certainly die!" ' "

⁷The king asked them, "What kind of man was it who came to meet you and told you this?"

⁸They replied, "He was a man with a garment of hair and with a leather belt around his waist."
The king said, "That was Elijah the Tishbite."

⁹Then he sent to Elijah a captain with his company of fifty men. The captain went up to Elijah, who was sitting on the top of a hill, and said to him, "Man of God, the king says, 'Come down!' "

¹⁰Elijah answered the captain, "If I am a man of God, may fire come down from heaven and consume you and your fifty men!" Then fire fell from heaven and consumed the captain and his men.

¹¹At this the king sent to Elijah another captain with his fifty men. The captain said to him, "Man of God, this is what the king says, 'Come down at once!' "

¹²"If I am a man of God," Elijah replied, "may fire come down from heaven and consume you and your fifty men!" Then the fire of God fell from heaven and consumed him and his fifty men.

¹³So the king sent a third captain with his fifty men. This third captain went up and fell on his knees before Elijah. "Man of God," he begged, "please have respect for my life and the lives of these fifty men, your servants! ¹⁴See, fire has fallen from heaven and consumed the first two captains and all their men. But now have respect for my life!"

¹⁵The angel of the Lord said to Elijah, "Go down with him; do not be afraid of him." So Elijah got up and went down with him to the king.

¹⁶He told the king, "This is what the Lord says: Is it because there is no God in Israel for you to consult that you have sent messengers to consult Baal-Zebub, the god of Ekron? Because you have done this, you will never leave the bed you are lying on. You will certainly die!" ¹⁷So he died, according to the word of the Lord that Elijah had spoken.

Because Ahaziah had no son, Joram[a] succeeded him as king in the second year of Jehoram son of Jehoshaphat king of Judah. ¹⁸As for all the other events of Ahaziah's reign, and what he did, are they not written in the book of the annals of the kings of Israel?

ELIJAH TAKEN UP TO HEAVEN

2 When the Lord was about to take Elijah up to heaven in a whirlwind, Elijah and Elisha were on their way from Gilgal. ²Elijah said to Elisha, "Stay here; the Lord has sent me to Bethel."
But Elisha said, "As surely as the Lord lives and as you live, I will not leave you." So they went down to Bethel.

³The company of the prophets at Bethel came out to Elisha and asked, "Do you know that the Lord is going to take your master from you today?"

"Yes, I know," Elisha replied, "but do not speak of it."

⁴Then Elijah said to him, "Stay here, Elisha; the Lord has sent me to Jericho."
And he replied, "As surely as the Lord lives and as you live, I will not leave you." So they went to Jericho.

⁵The company of the prophets at Jericho went up to Elisha and asked him, "Do you know that the Lord is going to take your master from you today?"

"Yes, I know," he replied, "but do not speak of it."

⁶Then Elijah said to him, "Stay here; the Lord has sent me to the Jordan."

---

[a] *17* Hebrew *Jehoram,* a variant of *Joram*

And he replied, "As surely as the LORD lives and as you live, I will not leave you." So the two of them walked on.

⊓OW OR ⊓EVER
2KI 2:9–10

Do you know what you want from God? Is it something that would honor and please him? If the answer to both of these questions is yes, start boldly praying about your request today and don't stop until God answers you.

7Fifty men of the company of the prophets went and stood at a distance, facing the place where Elijah and Elisha had stopped at the Jordan. 8Elijah took his cloak, rolled it up and struck the water with it. The water divided to the right and to the left, and the two of them crossed over on dry ground.

9When they had crossed, Elijah said to Elisha, "Tell me, what can I do for you before I am taken from you?"

"Let me inherit a double portion of your spirit," Elisha replied.

10"You have asked a difficult thing," Elijah said, "yet if you see me when I am taken from you, it will be yours—otherwise not."

11As they were walking along and talking together, suddenly a chariot of fire and horses of fire appeared and separated the two of them, and Elijah went up to heaven in a whirlwind. 12Elisha saw this and cried out, "My father! My father! The chariots and horsemen of Israel!" And Elisha saw him no more. Then he took hold of his own clothes and tore them apart.

13He picked up the cloak that had fallen from Elijah and went back and stood on the bank of the Jordan. 14Then he took the cloak that had fallen from him and struck the water with it. "Where now is the LORD, the God of Elijah?" he asked. When he struck the water, it divided to the right and to the left, and he crossed over.

15The company of the prophets from Jericho, who were watching, said, "The spirit of Elijah is resting on Elisha." And they went to meet him and bowed to the ground before him. 16"Look," they said, "we your servants have fifty able men. Let them go and look for your master. Perhaps the Spirit of the LORD has picked him up and set him down on some mountain or in some valley."

"No," Elisha replied, "do not send them."

17But they persisted until he was too ashamed to refuse. So he said, "Send them." And they sent fifty men, who searched for three days but did not find him. 18When they returned to Elisha, who was staying in Jericho, he said to them, "Didn't I tell you not to go?"

HEALING OF THE WATER

19The men of the city said to Elisha, "Look, our lord, this town is well situated, as you can see, but the water is bad and the land is unproductive."

20"Bring me a new bowl," he said, "and put salt in it." So they brought it to him.

21Then he went out to the spring and threw the salt into it, saying, "This is what the LORD says: 'I have healed this water. Never again will it cause death or make the land unproductive.'" 22And the water has remained wholesome to this day, according to the word Elisha had spoken.

ELISHA IS JEERED

23From there Elisha went up to Bethel. As he was walking along the road, some youths came out of the town and jeered at him. "Go on up, you baldhead!" they said. "Go on up, you baldhead!" 24He turned around, looked at them and called down a curse on them in the name of the LORD. Then two bears came

Being Sensitive to Others

Elisha's baldness made him a target for ridicule and abuse. What are some physical shortcomings that make people targets in your school or neighborhood? What do you usually do when the mocking starts? Do you join in, try to stop it or just ignore it? Don't forget that people's physical characteristics are part of God's creative work. And if you make fun of them, you're mocking the work of your Creator.

out of the woods and mauled forty-two of the youths. ²⁵And he went on to Mount Carmel and from there returned to Samaria.

MOAB REVOLTS

3 Joram^a son of Ahab became king of Israel in Samaria in the eighteenth year of Jehoshaphat king of Judah, and he reigned twelve years. ²He did evil in the eyes of the LORD, but not as his father and mother had done. He got rid of the sacred stone of Baal that his father had made. ³Nevertheless he clung to the sins of Jeroboam son of Nebat, which he had caused Israel to commit; he did not turn away from them.

⁴Now Mesha king of Moab raised sheep, and he had to supply the king of Israel with a hundred thousand lambs and with the wool of a hundred thousand rams. ⁵But after Ahab died, the king of Moab rebelled against the king of Israel. ⁶So at that time King Joram set out from Samaria and mobilized all Israel. ⁷He also sent this message to Jehoshaphat king of Judah: "The king of Moab has rebelled against me. Will you go with me to fight against Moab?"

"I will go with you," he replied. "I am as you are, my people as your people, my horses as your horses."

⁸"By what route shall we attack?" he asked.

"Through the Desert of Edom," he answered.

⁹So the king of Israel set out with the king of Judah and the king of Edom. After a roundabout march of seven days, the army had no more water for themselves or for the animals with them.

¹⁰"What!" exclaimed the king of Israel. "Has the LORD called us three kings together only to hand us over to Moab?"

¹¹But Jehoshaphat asked, "Is there no prophet of the LORD here, that we may inquire of the LORD through him?"

An officer of the king of Israel answered, "Elisha son of Shaphat is here. He used to pour water on the hands of Elijah.^b"

¹²Jehoshaphat said, "The word of the LORD is with him." So the king of Israel and Jehoshaphat and the king of Edom went down to him.

¹³Elisha said to the king of Israel, "What do we have to do with each other? Go to the prophets of your father and the prophets of your mother."

"No," the king of Israel answered, "because it was the LORD who called us three kings together to hand us over to Moab."

¹⁴Elisha said, "As surely as the LORD Almighty lives, whom I serve, if I did not have respect for the presence of Jehoshaphat king of Judah, I would not look at you or even notice you. ¹⁵But now bring me a harpist."

While the harpist was playing, the hand of the LORD came upon Elisha ¹⁶and he said, "This is what the LORD says: Make this valley full of ditches. ¹⁷For this is what the LORD says: You will see neither wind nor rain, yet this valley will be filled with water, and you, your cattle and your other animals will drink. ¹⁸This is an easy thing in the eyes of the LORD; he will also hand Moab over to you. ¹⁹You will overthrow every fortified city and every major town. You will cut down every good tree, stop up all the springs, and ruin every good field with stones."

²⁰The next morning, about the time for offering the sacrifice, there it was—water flowing from the direction of Edom! And the land was filled with water.

²¹Now all the Moabites had heard that the kings had come to fight against them; so every man, young and old, who could bear arms was called up and stationed on the border. ²²When they got up early in the morning, the sun was shining on the water. To the Moabites across the way, the water looked red—like blood. ²³"That's blood!" they said. "Those kings must have fought and slaughtered each other. Now to the plunder, Moab!"

²⁴But when the Moabites came to the camp of Israel, the Israelites rose up and fought them until they fled. And the Israelites invaded the land and slaughtered the Moabites. ²⁵They destroyed the towns, and each man threw a stone on every good field until it was covered. They stopped up all the springs and cut down every good tree. Only Kir Hareseth was left with its stones in place, but men armed with slings surrounded it and attacked it as well.

²⁶When the king of Moab saw that the battle had gone against him, he took with him seven hundred

---

^a *1* Hebrew *Jehoram,* a variant of *Joram;* also in verse 6   ^b *11* That is, he was Elijah's personal servant.

swordsmen to break through to the king of Edom, but they failed. ²⁷Then he took his firstborn son, who was to succeed him as king, and offered him as a sacrifice on the city wall. The fury against Israel was great; they withdrew and returned to their own land.

THE WIDOW'S OIL

4 The wife of a man from the company of the prophets cried out to Elisha, "Your servant my husband is dead, and you know that he revered the LORD. But now his creditor is coming to take my two boys as his slaves."

²Elisha replied to her, "How can I help you? Tell me, what do you have in your house?"

"Your servant has nothing there at all," she said, "except a little oil."

³Elisha said, "Go around and ask all your neighbors for empty jars. Don't ask for just a few. ⁴Then go inside and shut the door behind you and your sons. Pour oil into all the jars, and as each is filled, put it to one side."

⁵She left him and afterward shut the door behind her and her sons. They brought the jars to her and she kept pouring. ⁶When all the jars were full, she said to her son, "Bring me another one."

But he replied, "There is not a jar left." Then the oil stopped flowing.

⁷She went and told the man of God, and he said, "Go, sell the oil and pay your debts. You and your sons can live on what is left."

NOW OR NEVER

2KI 4:1–7

God is better than any bank or broker. He can provide unbelievable abundance from practically nothing. Give all that you have to God, however small it may seem, and let him invest it where and how he wants. He guarantees maximum dividends.

THE SHUNAMMITE'S SON RESTORED TO LIFE

⁸One day Elisha went to Shunem. And a well-to-do woman was there, who urged him to stay for a meal. So whenever he came by, he stopped there to eat. ⁹She said to her husband, "I know that this man who often comes our way is a holy man of God. ¹⁰Let's make a small room on the roof and put in it a bed and a table, a chair and a lamp for him. Then he can stay there whenever he comes to us."

¹¹One day when Elisha came, he went up to his room and lay down there. ¹²He said to his servant Gehazi, "Call the Shunammite." So he called her, and she stood before him. ¹³Elisha said to him, "Tell her, 'You have gone to all this trouble for us. Now what can be done for you? Can we speak on your behalf to the king or the commander of the army?'"

She replied, "I have a home among my own people."

¹⁴"What can be done for her?" Elisha asked.

Gehazi said, "Well, she has no son and her husband is old."

¹⁵Then Elisha said, "Call her." So he called her, and she stood in the doorway. ¹⁶"About this time next year," Elisha said, "you will hold a son in your arms."

"No, my lord," she objected. "Don't mislead your servant, O man of God!"

¹⁷But the woman became pregnant, and the next year about that same time she gave birth to a son, just as Elisha had told her.

¹⁸The child grew, and one day he went out to his father, who was with the reapers. ¹⁹"My head! My head!" he said to his father.

His father told a servant, "Carry him to his mother." ²⁰After the servant had lifted him up and carried him to his mother, the boy sat on her lap until noon, and then he died. ²¹She went up and laid him on the bed of the man of God, then shut the door and went out.

²²She called her husband and said, "Please send me one of the servants and a donkey so I can go to the man of God quickly and return."

²³"Why go to him today?" he asked. "It's not the New Moon or the Sabbath."

"It's all right," she said.

²⁴She saddled the donkey and said to her servant, "Lead on; don't slow down for me unless I tell you." ²⁵So she set out and came to the man of God at Mount Carmel.

When he saw her in the distance, the man of God said to his servant Gehazi, "Look! There's the Shunammite! ²⁶Run to meet her and ask her, 'Are you all right? Is your husband all right? Is your child all right?'"

"Everything is all right," she said.

27When she reached the man of God at the mountain, she took hold of his feet. Gehazi came over to push her away, but the man of God said, "Leave her alone! She is in bitter distress, but the LORD has hidden it from me and has not told me why."

28"Did I ask you for a son, my lord?" she said. "Didn't I tell you, 'Don't raise my hopes'?"

29Elisha said to Gehazi, "Tuck your cloak into your belt, take my staff in your hand and run. If you meet anyone, do not greet him, and if anyone greets you, do not answer. Lay my staff on the boy's face."

30But the child's mother said, "As surely as the LORD lives and as you live, I will not leave you." So he got up and followed her.

31Gehazi went on ahead and laid the staff on the boy's face, but there was no sound or response. So Gehazi went back to meet Elisha and told him, "The boy has not awakened."

32When Elisha reached the house, there was the boy lying dead on his couch. 33He went in, shut the door on the two of them and prayed to the LORD. 34Then he got on the bed and lay upon the boy, mouth to mouth, eyes to eyes, hands to hands. As he stretched himself out upon him, the boy's body grew warm. 35Elisha turned away and walked back and forth in the room and then got on the bed and stretched out upon him once more. The boy sneezed seven times and opened his eyes.

36Elisha summoned Gehazi and said, "Call the Shunammite." And he did. When she came, he said, "Take your son." 37She came in, fell at his feet and bowed to the ground. Then she took her son and went out.

DEATH IN THE POT

38Elisha returned to Gilgal and there was a famine in that region. While the company of the prophets was meeting with him, he said to his servant, "Put on the large pot and cook some stew for these men."

39One of them went out into the fields to gather herbs and found a wild vine. He gathered some of its gourds and filled the fold of his cloak. When he returned, he cut them up into the pot of stew, though no one knew what they were. 40The stew was poured out for the men, but as they began to eat it, they cried out, "O man of God, there is death in the pot!" And they could not eat it.

41Elisha said, "Get some flour." He put it into the pot and said, "Serve it to the people to eat." And there was nothing harmful in the pot.

FEEDING OF A HUNDRED

42A man came from Baal Shalishah, bringing the man of God twenty loaves of barley bread baked from the first ripe grain, along with some heads of new grain. "Give it to the people to eat," Elisha said.

43"How can I set this before a hundred men?" his servant asked.

But Elisha answered, "Give it to the people to eat. For this is what the LORD says: 'They will eat and have some left over.'" 44Then he set it before them, and they ate and had some left over, according to the word of the LORD.

NAAMAN HEALED OF LEPROSY

5 Now Naaman was commander of the army of the king of Aram. He was a great man in the sight of his master and highly regarded, because through him the LORD had given victory to Aram. He was a valiant soldier, but he had leprosy.[a]

2Now bands from Aram had gone out and had taken captive a young girl from Israel, and she served Naaman's wife. 3She said to her mistress, "If only my master would see the prophet who is in Samaria! He would cure him of his leprosy."

4Naaman went to his master and told him what the girl from Israel had said. 5"By all means, go," the king of Aram replied. "I will send a letter to the king of Israel." So Naaman left, taking with him ten talents[b]

NOW OR NEVER
2KI 5:3–4

Can you picture yourself giving out some advice or offering some encouragement to someone in your church? The fact that you're young doesn't prevent you from having helpful insights on important matters.

---

[a] 1 The Hebrew word was used for various diseases affecting the skin—not necessarily leprosy; also in verses 3, 6, 7, 11 and 27.
[b] 5 That is, about 750 pounds (about 340 kilograms)

of silver, six thousand shekels[a] of gold and ten sets of clothing. 6The letter that he took to the king of Israel read: "With this letter I am sending my servant Naaman to you so that you may cure him of his leprosy."

7As soon as the king of Israel read the letter, he tore his robes and said, "Am I God? Can I kill and bring back to life? Why does this fellow send someone to me to be cured of his leprosy? See how he is trying to pick a quarrel with me!"

8When Elisha the man of God heard that the king of Israel had torn his robes, he sent him this message: "Why have you torn your robes? Have the man come to me and he will know that there is a prophet in Israel." 9So Naaman went with his horses and chariots and stopped at the door of Elisha's house. 10Elisha sent a messenger to say to him, "Go, wash yourself seven times in the Jordan, and your flesh will be restored and you will be cleansed."

11But Naaman went away angry and said, "I thought that he would surely come out to me and stand and call on the name of the LORD his God, wave his hand over the spot and cure me of my leprosy. 12Are not Abana and Pharpar, the rivers of Damascus, better than any of the waters of Israel? Couldn't I wash in them and be cleansed?" So he turned and went off in a rage.

13Naaman's servants went to him and said, "My father, if the prophet had told you to do some great thing, would you not have done it? How much more, then, when he tells you, 'Wash and be cleansed'!" 14So he went down and dipped himself in the Jordan seven times, as the man of God had told him, and his flesh was restored and became clean like that of a young boy.

15Then Naaman and all his attendants went back to the man of God. He stood before him and said, "Now I know that there is no God in all the world except in Israel. Please accept now a gift from your servant."

16The prophet answered, "As surely as the LORD lives, whom I serve, I will not accept a thing." And even though Naaman urged him, he refused.

17"If you will not," said Naaman, "please let me, your servant, be given as much earth as a pair of mules can carry, for your servant will never again make burnt offerings and sacrifices to any other god but the LORD. 18But may the LORD forgive your servant for this one thing: When my master enters the temple of Rimmon to bow down and he is leaning on my arm and I bow there also—when I bow down in the temple of Rimmon, may the LORD forgive your servant for this."

19"Go in peace," Elisha said.

After Naaman had traveled some distance, 20Gehazi, the servant of Elisha the man of God, said to himself, "My master was too easy on Naaman, this Aramean, by not accepting from him what he brought. As surely as the LORD lives, I will run after him and get something from him."

21So Gehazi hurried after Naaman. When Naaman saw him running toward him, he got down from the chariot to meet him. "Is everything all right?" he asked.

22"Everything is all right," Gehazi answered. "My master sent me to say, 'Two young men from the company of the prophets have just come to me from the hill country of Ephraim. Please give them a talent[b] of silver and two sets of clothing.'"

23"By all means, take two talents," said Naaman. He urged Gehazi to accept them, and then tied up the two talents of silver in two bags, with two sets of clothing. He gave them to two of his servants, and they carried them ahead of Gehazi. 24When Gehazi came to the hill, he took the things from the servants and put them away in the house. He sent the men away and they left. 25Then he went in and stood before his master Elisha.

"Where have you been, Gehazi?" Elisha asked.

Avoiding Arrogance

» live the adventure » 2Ki 5:11–14

How arrogant do people have to be to believe that their plans for their lives are better than God's plans? Pretty arrogant, right? Except that's the way a lot of us live our lives. We get so caught up with satisfying our own desires—hanging out with whomever we want, going wherever we want to go, doing whatever we think is fun—that we forget to humbly invite God to direct our steps.

---

[a] 5 That is, about 150 pounds (about 70 kilograms)　　[b] 22 That is, about 75 pounds (about 34 kilograms)

"Your servant didn't go anywhere," Gehazi answered.

²⁶But Elisha said to him, "Was not my spirit with you when the man got down from his chariot to meet you? Is this the time to take money, or to accept clothes, olive groves, vineyards, flocks, herds, or menservants and maidservants? ²⁷Naaman's leprosy will cling to you and to your descendants forever." Then Gehazi went from Elisha's presence and he was leprous, as white as snow.

AN AXHEAD FLOATS

6 The company of the prophets said to Elisha, "Look, the place where we meet with you is too small for us. ²Let us go to the Jordan, where each of us can get a pole; and let us build a place there for us to live."

And he said, "Go."

³Then one of them said, "Won't you please come with your servants?"

"I will," Elisha replied. ⁴And he went with them.

They went to the Jordan and began to cut down trees. ⁵As one of them was cutting down a tree, the iron axhead fell into the water. "Oh, my lord," he cried out, "it was borrowed!"

⁶The man of God asked, "Where did it fall?" When he showed him the place, Elisha cut a stick and threw it there, and made the iron float. ⁷"Lift it out," he said. Then the man reached out his hand and took it.

ELISHA TRAPS BLINDED ARAMEANS

⁸Now the king of Aram was at war with Israel. After conferring with his officers, he said, "I will set up my camp in such and such a place."

⁹The man of God sent word to the king of Israel: "Beware of passing that place, because the Arameans are going down there." ¹⁰So the king of Israel checked on the place indicated by the man of God. Time and again Elisha warned the king, so that he was on his guard in such places.

¹¹This enraged the king of Aram. He summoned his officers and demanded of them, "Will you not tell me which of us is on the side of the king of Israel?"

¹²"None of us, my lord the king," said one of his officers, "but Elisha, the prophet who is in Israel, tells the king of Israel the very words you speak in your bedroom."

¹³"Go, find out where he is," the king ordered, "so I can send men and capture him." The report came back: "He is in Dothan." ¹⁴Then he sent horses and chariots and a strong force there. They went by night and surrounded the city.

¹⁵When the servant of the man of God got up and went out early the next morning, an army with horses and chariots had surrounded the city. "Oh, my lord, what shall we do?" the servant asked.

¹⁶"Don't be afraid," the prophet answered. "Those who are with us are more than those who are with them."

¹⁷And Elisha prayed, "O LORD, open his eyes so he may see." Then the LORD opened the servant's eyes, and he looked and saw the hills full of horses and chariots of fire all around Elisha.

¹⁸As the enemy came down toward him, Elisha prayed to the LORD, "Strike these people with blindness." So he struck them with blindness, as Elisha had asked.

¹⁹Elisha told them, "This is not the road and this is not the city. Follow me, and I will lead you to the man you are looking for." And he led them to Samaria.

²⁰After they entered the city, Elisha said, "LORD, open the eyes of these men so they can see." Then the LORD opened their eyes and they looked, and there they were, inside Samaria.

²¹When the king of Israel saw them, he asked Elisha, "Shall I kill them, my father? Shall I kill them?"

²²"Do not kill them," he answered. "Would you kill men you have captured with your own sword or bow? Set food and water before them so that they may eat and drink and then go back to their master."

elisha

» Succeeded Elijah as Israel's chief prophet
» Performed numerous miracles
» Tipped off the king of Israel about Aramean troop movements

king of aram

» Probably Ben-Hadad II
» Bitter enemy of Israel
» Tried to kill Elisha for revealing his army's whereabouts to Israel's king

The Main Event

The element of surprise is one of the most effective weapons in successful warfare. The king of Aram, a guy named Ben-Hadad II, understood this well, and he tried to implement surprise in his war against Israel.

Unfortunately for him, the Israelites had an amazing prophet named Elisha on their side. Each time Ben-Hadad devised a new battle strategy, God revealed it to Elisha. Each time Elisha caught wind of a sneak attack, he sent word to Israel's king. The result: The Israelites were constantly able to move their troops into position and hold off the Arameans. As far as the Israelites were concerned, having Elisha around was better than having a sophisticated reconnaissance satellite or a Predator spy plane!

Forced to watch the Israelites thwart one surprise attack after another, King Ben-Hadad was spitting mad. He gathered his top advisors and demanded to know who was responsible for leaking his military secrets. One officer told him that the prophet Elisha was the culprit. "He knows everything," the officer insisted. "Even the words you speak in your bedroom."

"Then capture him!" Ben-Hadad fumed.

Aramean spies scoured the land until they located Elisha in Dothan. When they reported their discovery, the king ordered his army to surround the city. Early the next morning Elisha's servant almost died of fright when he stumbled outside and saw enemy troops in every direction. "What are we going to do?" he asked.

Elisha was unfazed. "Those who are with us are more than those who are with them," he said with some serious cool. Then he prayed for the Lord to open his servant's eyes.

God did just that. The servant looked around in amazement at a vast angelic army that had been invisible to him only seconds before—heavenly warriors charged with keeping God's servants safe. While opening the eyes of Elisha's servant, God closed the eyes of the Aramean army. He struck every single soldier blind. Helpless, they had no choice but to follow Elisha. And he led them straight to the king of Israel.

The Outcome

Is that one of the coolest Bible chapters ever, or what? It reminds us that God's will cannot be thwarted. When you have God's man following God's plan, you've got an unbeatable combination.

The king of Aram was frustrated because he opposed God and his people. Elisha managed to remain calm because he knew the power of God, and he had faith that God would protect his people.

But that's not all there is to the story. Blinded and captured, the enemy's fate was in Elisha's hands. Swift execution would have sent a powerful message to Ben-Hadad not to mess with Israel any longer. But instead, Elisha had the men fed and sent home. Allowing enemy troops to return to Israel's nemesis unharmed must have taken an incredible amount of faith in God's ability to protect. But Elisha's mercy sent an even more powerful message than vengeance would have, and the Aramean thugs gave up their raids on Israel.

Serving God can be a scary proposition sometimes, but God is absolutely dependable. If Elisha could sit down and eat lunch with you, that's exactly what he would tell you.

Read more about Elisha and the King of Aram in 2 Kings 6 (pages 420–422).

²³So he prepared a great feast for them, and after they had finished eating and drinking, he sent them away, and they returned to their master. So the bands from Aram stopped raiding Israel's territory.

FAMINE IN BESIEGED SAMARIA

²⁴Some time later, Ben-Hadad king of Aram mobilized his entire army and marched up and laid siege to Samaria. ²⁵There was a great famine in the city; the siege lasted so long that a donkey's head sold for eighty shekels ᵃ of silver, and a quarter of a cab ᵇ of seed pods ᶜ for five shekels. ᵈ

²⁶As the king of Israel was passing by on the wall, a woman cried to him, "Help me, my lord the king!"

²⁷The king replied, "If the LORD does not help you, where can I get help for you? From the threshing floor? From the winepress?" ²⁸Then he asked her, "What's the matter?"

She answered, "This woman said to me, 'Give up your son so we may eat him today, and tomorrow we'll eat my son.' ²⁹So we cooked my son and ate him. The next day I said to her, 'Give up your son so we may eat him,' but she had hidden him."

³⁰When the king heard the woman's words, he tore his robes. As he went along the wall, the people looked, and there, underneath, he had sackcloth on his body. ³¹He said, "May God deal with me, be it ever so severely, if the head of Elisha son of Shaphat remains on his shoulders today!"

³²Now Elisha was sitting in his house, and the elders were sitting with him. The king sent a messenger ahead, but before he arrived, Elisha said to the elders, "Don't you see how this murderer is sending someone to cut off my head? Look, when the messenger comes, shut the door and hold it shut against him. Is not the sound of his master's footsteps behind him?"

³³While he was still talking to them, the messenger came down to him. And ˪the king˩ said, "This disaster is from the LORD. Why should I wait for the LORD any longer?"

7 Elisha said, "Hear the word of the LORD. This is what the LORD says: About this time tomorrow, a seah ᵉ of flour will sell for a shekel ᶠ and two seahs ᵍ of barley for a shekel at the gate of Samaria."

²The officer on whose arm the king was leaning said to the man of God, "Look, even if the LORD should open the floodgates of the heavens, could this happen?"

"You will see it with your own eyes," answered Elisha, "but you will not eat any of it!"

THE SIEGE LIFTED

³Now there were four men with leprosy ʰ at the entrance of the city gate. They said to each other, "Why stay here until we die? ⁴If we say, 'We'll go into the city'—the famine is there, and we will die. And if we stay here, we will die. So let's go over to the camp of the Arameans and surrender. If they spare us, we live; if they kill us, then we die."

⁵At dusk they got up and went to the camp of the Arameans. When they reached the edge of the camp, not a man was there, ⁶for the Lord had caused the Arameans to hear the sound of chariots and horses and a great army, so that they said to one another, "Look, the king of Israel has hired the Hittite and Egyptian kings to attack us!" ⁷So they got up and fled in the dusk and abandoned their tents and their horses and donkeys. They left the camp as it was and ran for their lives.

⁸The men who had leprosy reached the edge of the camp and entered one of the tents. They ate and drank, and carried away silver, gold and clothes, and went off and hid them. They returned and entered another tent and took some things from it and hid them also.

⁹Then they said to each other, "We're not doing right. This is a day of good news and we are keeping it to ourselves. If we wait until daylight, punishment will overtake us. Let's go at once and report this to the royal palace."

¹⁰So they went and called out to the city gatekeepers and told them, "We went into the Aramean camp and not a man was there—not a sound of anyone—only tethered horses and donkeys, and the tents left just as they were." ¹¹The gatekeepers shouted the news, and it was reported within the palace.

¹²The king got up in the night and said to his officers, "I will tell you what the Arameans have done

---

ᵃ 25 That is, about 2 pounds (about 1 kilogram)   ᵇ 25 That is, probably about 1/2 pint (about 0.3 liter)   ᶜ 25 Or of doves' dung
ᵈ 25 That is, about 2 ounces (about 55 grams)   ᵉ 1 That is, probably about 7 quarts (about 7.3 liters); also in verses 16 and 18
ᶠ 1 That is, about 2/5 ounce (about 11 grams); also in verses 16 and 18   ᵍ 1 That is, probably about 13 quarts (about 15 liters); also in verses 16 and 18   ʰ 3 The Hebrew word is used for various diseases affecting the skin—not necessarily leprosy; also in verse 8.

to us. They know we are starving; so they have left the camp to hide in the countryside, thinking, 'They will surely come out, and then we will take them alive and get into the city.' "

¹³One of his officers answered, "Have some men take five of the horses that are left in the city. Their plight will be like that of all the Israelites left here—yes, they will only be like all these Israelites who are doomed. So let us send them to find out what happened."

¹⁴So they selected two chariots with their horses, and the king sent them after the Aramean army. He commanded the drivers, "Go and find out what has happened." ¹⁵They followed them as far as the Jordan, and they found the whole road strewn with the clothing and equipment the Arameans had thrown away in their headlong flight. So the messengers returned and reported to the king. ¹⁶Then the people went out and plundered the camp of the Arameans. So a seah of flour sold for a shekel, and two seahs of barley sold for a shekel, as the Lord had said.

¹⁷Now the king had put the officer on whose arm he leaned in charge of the gate, and the people trampled him in the gateway, and he died, just as the man of God had foretold when the king came down to his house. ¹⁸It happened as the man of God had said to the king: "About this time tomorrow, a seah of flour will sell for a shekel and two seahs of barley for a shekel at the gate of Samaria."

¹⁹The officer had said to the man of God, "Look, even if the Lord should open the floodgates of the heavens, could this happen?" The man of God had replied, "You will see it with your own eyes, but you will not eat any of it!" ²⁰And that is exactly what happened to him, for the people trampled him in the gateway, and he died.

THE SHUNAMMITE'S LAND RESTORED

8 Now Elisha had said to the woman whose son he had restored to life, "Go away with your family and stay for a while wherever you can, because the Lord has decreed a famine in the land that will last seven years." ²The woman proceeded to do as the man of God said. She and her family went away and stayed in the land of the Philistines seven years.

³At the end of the seven years she came back from the land of the Philistines and went to the king to beg for her house and land. ⁴The king was talking to Gehazi, the servant of the man of God, and had said, "Tell me about all the great things Elisha has done." ⁵Just as Gehazi was telling the king how Elisha had restored the dead to life, the woman whose son Elisha had brought back to life came to beg the king for her house and land.

Gehazi said, "This is the woman, my lord the king, and this is her son whom Elisha restored to life." ⁶The king asked the woman about it, and she told him.

Then he assigned an official to her case and said to him, "Give back everything that belonged to her, including all the income from her land from the day she left the country until now."

HAZAEL MURDERS BEN-HADAD

⁷Elisha went to Damascus, and Ben-Hadad king of Aram was ill. When the king was told, "The man of God has come all the way up here," ⁸he said to Hazael, "Take a gift with you and go to meet the man of God. Consult the Lord through him; ask him, 'Will I recover from this illness?' "

⁹Hazael went to meet Elisha, taking with him as a gift forty camel-loads of all the finest wares of Damascus. He went in and stood before him, and said, "Your son Ben-Hadad king of Aram has sent me to ask, 'Will I recover from this illness?' "

¹⁰Elisha answered, "Go and say to him, 'You will certainly recover'; butᵃ the Lord has revealed to me that he will in fact die." ¹¹He stared at him with a fixed gaze until Hazael felt ashamed. Then the man of God began to weep.

¹²"Why is my lord weeping?" asked Hazael.

"Because I know the harm you will do to the Israelites," he answered. "You will set fire to their fortified places, kill their young men with the sword, dash their little children to the ground, and rip open their pregnant women."

¹³Hazael said, "How could your servant, a mere dog, accomplish such a feat?"

"The Lord has shown me that you will become king of Aram," answered Elisha.

¹⁴Then Hazael left Elisha and returned to his master. When Ben-Hadad asked, "What did Elisha say to you?" Hazael replied, "He told me that you would certainly recover." ¹⁵But the next day he took a thick cloth, soaked it in water and spread it over the king's face, so that he died. Then Hazael succeeded him as king.

ᵃ 10 The Hebrew may also be read *Go and say, 'You will certainly not recover,' for.*

battlelines

» Loose Lips (Sarcasm)

Q: You really had those guys laughing.
A: We were just messing around.

Q: What was so stinking funny? I mean, Henry was almost in tears.
A: Well, last week Brian had to give a presentation in history class. And you've never seen anybody so nervous! He was shaking like a leaf in a hurricane—and stuttering. It was hilarious. I was just imitating him.

Q: But he was standing right there!
A: So?

Q: Don't you think he might have been embarrassed?
A: He knows we were just kidding with him.

Q: Yeah, but what if you made him feel stupid? What if you totally humiliated him?
A: Hey, look, first of all, we were just joking. If he's feeling weird, he shouldn't take himself so seriously. Second, that's the way things are. If you do something crazy or stupid, you'd better be prepared for people to give you some grief over it.

Q: So you wouldn't care if, say, in front of a bunch of girls, Brian started making fun of your love handles?
A: What?! Dude, why do you have to go there? You don't say stuff like that in front of other people!

» Bite Your Tongue!

King Solomon is widely regarded as the wisest person who ever lived—next to Jesus, of course. If that's true, maybe we ought to pay attention to what he had to say about our tongues. Check out these statements:

● "The tongue has the power of life and death" (Proverbs 18:21a).

● "The tongue that brings healing is a tree of life, but a deceitful tongue crushes the spirit" (Proverbs 15:4).

● "Reckless words pierce like a sword, but the tongue of the wise brings healing" (Proverbs 12:18).

● "A man who lacks judgment derides his neighbor, but a man of understanding holds his tongue" (Proverbs 11:12).

● "When words are many, sin is not absent, but he who holds his tongue is wise" (Proverbs 10:19).

Solomon's message is simple: Be careful. Be considerate. Be wise. Watch what you say. Use your mouth to encourage others, not to shred them.

For more, got to www.RevolutionBible.com.

JEHORAM KING OF JUDAH

¹⁶In the fifth year of Joram son of Ahab king of Israel, when Jehoshaphat was king of Judah, Jehoram son of Jehoshaphat began his reign as king of Judah. ¹⁷He was thirty-two years old when he became king, and he reigned in Jerusalem eight years. ¹⁸He walked in the ways of the kings of Israel, as the house of Ahab had done, for he married a daughter of Ahab. He did evil in the eyes of the LORD. ¹⁹Nevertheless, for the sake of his servant David, the LORD was not willing to destroy Judah. He had promised to maintain a lamp for David and his descendants forever.

²⁰In the time of Jehoram, Edom rebelled against Judah and set up its own king. ²¹So Jehoram[a] went to Zair with all his chariots. The Edomites surrounded him and his chariot commanders, but he rose up and broke through by night; his army, however, fled back home. ²²To this day Edom has been in rebellion against Judah. Libnah revolted at the same time.

²³As for the other events of Jehoram's reign, and all he did, are they not written in the book of the annals of the kings of Judah? ²⁴Jehoram rested with his fathers and was buried with them in the City of David. And Ahaziah his son succeeded him as king.

AHAZIAH KING OF JUDAH

²⁵In the twelfth year of Joram son of Ahab king of Israel, Ahaziah son of Jehoram king of Judah began to reign. ²⁶Ahaziah was twenty-two years old when he became king, and he reigned in Jerusalem one year. His mother's name was Athaliah, a granddaughter of Omri king of Israel. ²⁷He walked in the ways of the house of Ahab and did evil in the eyes of the LORD, as the house of Ahab had done, for he was related by marriage to Ahab's family.

²⁸Ahaziah went with Joram son of Ahab to war against Hazael king of Aram at Ramoth Gilead. The Arameans wounded Joram; ²⁹so King Joram returned to Jezreel to recover from the wounds the Arameans had inflicted on him at Ramoth[b] in his battle with Hazael king of Aram.

Then Ahaziah son of Jehoram king of Judah went down to Jezreel to see Joram son of Ahab, because he had been wounded.

JEHU ANOINTED KING OF ISRAEL

9 The prophet Elisha summoned a man from the company of the prophets and said to him, "Tuck your cloak into your belt, take this flask of oil with you and go to Ramoth Gilead. ²When you get there, look for Jehu son of Jehoshaphat, the son of Nimshi. Go to him, get him away from his companions and take him into an inner room. ³Then take the flask and pour the oil on his head and declare, 'This is what the LORD says: I anoint you king over Israel.' Then open the door and run; don't delay!"

⁴So the young man, the prophet, went to Ramoth Gilead. ⁵When he arrived, he found the army officers sitting together. "I have a message for you, commander," he said.

"For which of us?" asked Jehu.

"For you, commander," he replied.

⁶Jehu got up and went into the house. Then the prophet poured the oil on Jehu's head and declared, "This is what the LORD, the God of Israel, says: 'I anoint you king over the LORD's people Israel. ⁷You are to destroy the house of Ahab your master, and I will avenge the blood of my servants the prophets and the blood of all the LORD's servants shed by Jezebel. ⁸The whole house of Ahab will perish. I will cut off from Ahab every last male in Israel—slave or free. ⁹I will make the house of Ahab like the house of Jeroboam son of Nebat and like the house of Baasha son of Ahijah. ¹⁰As for Jezebel, dogs will devour her on the plot of ground at Jezreel, and no one will bury her.' " Then he opened the door and ran.

¹¹When Jehu went out to his fellow officers, one of them asked him, "Is everything all right? Why did this madman come to you?"

"You know the man and the sort of things he says," Jehu replied.

¹²"That's not true!" they said. "Tell us."

Jehu said, "Here is what he told me: 'This is what the LORD says: I anoint you king over Israel.' "

¹³They hurried and took their cloaks and spread them under him on the bare steps. Then they blew the trumpet and shouted, "Jehu is king!"

ᵃ *21* Hebrew *Joram*, a variant of *Jehoram*; also in verses 23 and 24   ᵇ *29* Hebrew *Ramah*, a variant of *Ramoth*

JEHU KILLS JORAM AND AHAZIAH

¹⁴So Jehu son of Jehoshaphat, the son of Nimshi, conspired against Joram. (Now Joram and all Israel had been defending Ramoth Gilead against Hazael king of Aram, ¹⁵but King Joram[a] had returned to Jezreel to recover from the wounds the Arameans had inflicted on him in the battle with Hazael king of Aram.) Jehu said, "If this is the way you feel, don't let anyone slip out of the city to go and tell the news in Jezreel." ¹⁶Then he got into his chariot and rode to Jezreel, because Joram was resting there and Ahaziah king of Judah had gone down to see him.

¹⁷When the lookout standing on the tower in Jezreel saw Jehu's troops approaching, he called out, "I see some troops coming."

"Get a horseman," Joram ordered. "Send him to meet them and ask, 'Do you come in peace?' "

¹⁸The horseman rode off to meet Jehu and said, "This is what the king says: 'Do you come in peace?' "

"What do you have to do with peace?" Jehu replied. "Fall in behind me."

The lookout reported, "The messenger has reached them, but he isn't coming back."

¹⁹So the king sent out a second horseman. When he came to them he said, "This is what the king says: 'Do you come in peace?' "

Jehu replied, "What do you have to do with peace? Fall in behind me."

²⁰The lookout reported, "He has reached them, but he isn't coming back either. The driving is like that of Jehu son of Nimshi—he drives like a madman."

²¹"Hitch up my chariot," Joram ordered. And when it was hitched up, Joram king of Israel and Ahaziah king of Judah rode out, each in his own chariot, to meet Jehu. They met him at the plot of ground that had belonged to Naboth the Jezreelite. ²²When Joram saw Jehu he asked, "Have you come in peace, Jehu?"

"How can there be peace," Jehu replied, "as long as all the idolatry and witchcraft of your mother Jezebel abound?"

²³Joram turned about and fled, calling out to Ahaziah, "Treachery, Ahaziah!"

²⁴Then Jehu drew his bow and shot Joram between the shoulders. The arrow pierced his heart and he slumped down in his chariot. ²⁵Jehu said to Bidkar, his chariot officer, "Pick him up and throw him on the field that belonged to Naboth the Jezreelite. Remember how you and I were riding together in chariots behind Ahab his father when the LORD made this prophecy about him: ²⁶'Yesterday I saw the blood of Naboth and the blood of his sons, declares the LORD, and I will surely make you pay for it on this plot of ground, declares the LORD.'[b] Now then, pick him up and throw him on that plot, in accordance with the word of the LORD."

²⁷When Ahaziah king of Judah saw what had happened, he fled up the road to Beth Haggan.[c] Jehu chased him, shouting, "Kill him too!" They wounded him in his chariot on the way up to Gur near Ibleam, but he escaped to Megiddo and died there. ²⁸His servants took him by chariot to Jerusalem and buried him with his fathers in his tomb in the City of David. ²⁹(In the eleventh year of Joram son of Ahab, Ahaziah had become king of Judah.)

JEZEBEL KILLED

³⁰Then Jehu went to Jezreel. When Jezebel heard about it, she painted her eyes, arranged her hair and looked out of a window. ³¹As Jehu entered the gate, she asked, "Have you come in peace, Zimri, you murderer of your master?"[d]

³²He looked up at the window and called out, "Who is on my side? Who?" Two or three eunuchs looked down at him. ³³"Throw her down!" Jehu said. So they threw her down, and some of her blood spattered the wall and the horses as they trampled her underfoot.

³⁴Jehu went in and ate and drank. "Take care of that cursed woman," he said, "and bury her, for she was a king's daughter." ³⁵But when they went out to bury her, they found nothing except her skull, her feet and her hands. ³⁶They went back and told Jehu, who said, "This is the word of the LORD that he spoke through his servant Elijah the Tishbite: On the plot of ground at Jezreel dogs will devour Jezebel's flesh.[e] ³⁷Jezebel's body will be like refuse on the ground in the plot at Jezreel, so that no one will be able to say, 'This is Jezebel.' "

---

a 15 Hebrew *Jehoram,* a variant of *Joram;* also in verses 17 and 21-24   *b 26* See 1 Kings 21:19.   *c 27* Or *fled by way of the garden house*   *d 31* Or *"Did Zimri have peace, who murdered his master?"*   *e 36* See 1 Kings 21:23.

AHAB'S FAMILY KILLED

10 Now there were in Samaria seventy sons of the house of Ahab. So Jehu wrote letters and sent them to Samaria: to the officials of Jezreel,[a] to the elders and to the guardians of Ahab's children. He said, 2"As soon as this letter reaches you, since your master's sons are with you and you have chariots and horses, a fortified city and weapons, 3choose the best and most worthy of your master's sons and set him on his father's throne. Then fight for your master's house."

4But they were terrified and said, "If two kings could not resist him, how can we?"

5So the palace administrator, the city governor, the elders and the guardians sent this message to Jehu: "We are your servants and we will do anything you say. We will not appoint anyone as king; you do whatever you think best."

6Then Jehu wrote them a second letter, saying, "If you are on my side and will obey me, take the heads of your master's sons and come to me in Jezreel by this time tomorrow."

Now the royal princes, seventy of them, were with the leading men of the city, who were rearing them. 7When the letter arrived, these men took the princes and slaughtered all seventy of them. They put their heads in baskets and sent them to Jehu in Jezreel. 8When the messenger arrived, he told Jehu, "They have brought the heads of the princes."

Then Jehu ordered, "Put them in two piles at the entrance of the city gate until morning."

9The next morning Jehu went out. He stood before all the people and said, "You are innocent. It was I who conspired against my master and killed him, but who killed all these? 10Know then, that not a word the LORD has spoken against the house of Ahab will fail. The LORD has done what he promised through his servant Elijah." 11So Jehu killed everyone in Jezreel who remained of the house of Ahab, as well as all his chief men, his close friends and his priests, leaving him no survivor.

12Jehu then set out and went toward Samaria. At Beth Eked of the Shepherds, 13he met some relatives of Ahaziah king of Judah and asked, "Who are you?"

They said, "We are relatives of Ahaziah, and we have come down to greet the families of the king and of the queen mother."

14"Take them alive!" he ordered. So they took them alive and slaughtered them by the well of Beth Eked—forty-two men. He left no survivor.

15After he left there, he came upon Jehonadab son of Recab, who was on his way to meet him. Jehu greeted him and said, "Are you in accord with me, as I am with you?"

"I am," Jehonadab answered.

"If so," said Jehu, "give me your hand." So he did, and Jehu helped him up into the chariot. 16Jehu said, "Come with me and see my zeal for the LORD." Then he had him ride along in his chariot.

17When Jehu came to Samaria, he killed all who were left there of Ahab's family; he destroyed them, according to the word of the LORD spoken to Elijah.

MINISTERS OF BAAL KILLED

18Then Jehu brought all the people together and said to them, "Ahab served Baal a little; Jehu will serve him much. 19Now summon all the prophets of Baal, all his ministers and all his priests. See that no one is missing, because I am going to hold a great sacrifice for Baal. Anyone who fails to come will no longer live." But Jehu was acting deceptively in order to destroy the ministers of Baal.

20Jehu said, "Call an assembly in honor of Baal." So they proclaimed it. 21Then he sent word

---

a 1 Hebrew; some Septuagint manuscripts and Vulgate *of the city* throughout Israel, and all the ministers of Baal came; not one stayed away. They crowded into the temple of Baal until it was full from one end to the other. ²²And Jehu said to the keeper of the wardrobe, "Bring robes for all the ministers of Baal." So he brought out robes for them.

²³Then Jehu and Jehonadab son of Recab went into the temple of Baal. Jehu said to the ministers of Baal, "Look around and see that no servants of the Lord are here with you—only ministers of Baal." ²⁴So they went in to make sacrifices and burnt offerings. Now Jehu had posted eighty men outside with this warning: "If one of you lets any of the men I am placing in your hands escape, it will be your life for his life."

²⁵As soon as Jehu had finished making the burnt offering, he ordered the guards and officers: "Go in and kill them; let no one escape." So they cut them down with the sword. The guards and officers threw the bodies out and then entered the inner shrine of the temple of Baal. ²⁶They brought the sacred stone out of the temple of Baal and burned it. ²⁷They demolished the sacred stone of Baal and tore down the temple of Baal, and people have used it for a latrine to this day.

²⁸So Jehu destroyed Baal worship in Israel. ²⁹However, he did not turn away from the sins of Jeroboam son of Nebat, which he had caused Israel to commit—the worship of the golden calves at Bethel and Dan.

³⁰The Lord said to Jehu, "Because you have done well in accomplishing what is right in my eyes and have done to the house of Ahab all I had in mind to do, your descendants will sit on the throne of Israel to the fourth generation." ³¹Yet Jehu was not careful to keep the law of the Lord, the God of Israel, with all his heart. He did not turn away from the sins of Jeroboam, which he had caused Israel to commit.

³²In those days the Lord began to reduce the size of Israel. Hazael overpowered the Israelites throughout their territory ³³east of the Jordan in all the land of Gilead (the region of Gad, Reuben and Manasseh), from Aroer by the Arnon Gorge through Gilead to Bashan.

³⁴As for the other events of Jehu's reign, all he did, and all his achievements, are they not written in the book of the annals of the kings of Israel?

³⁵Jehu rested with his fathers and was buried in Samaria. And Jehoahaz his son succeeded him as king. ³⁶The time that Jehu reigned over Israel in Samaria was twenty-eight years.

ATHALIAH AND JOASH

11 When Athaliah the mother of Ahaziah saw that her son was dead, she proceeded to destroy the whole royal family. ²But Jehosheba, the daughter of King Jehoram[a] and sister of Ahaziah, took Joash son of Ahaziah and stole him away from among the royal princes, who were about to be murdered. She put him and his nurse in a bedroom to hide him from Athaliah; so he was not killed. ³He remained hidden with his nurse at the temple of the Lord for six years while Athaliah ruled the land.

⁴In the seventh year Jehoiada sent for the commanders of units of a hundred, the Carites and the guards and had them brought to him at the temple of the Lord. He made a covenant with them and put them under oath at the temple of the Lord. Then he showed them the king's son. ⁵He commanded them, saying, "This is what you are to do: You who are in the three companies that are going on duty on the Sabbath—a third of you guarding the royal palace, ⁶a third at the Sur Gate, and a third at the gate behind the guard, who take turns guarding the temple— ⁷and you who are in the other two companies that normally go off Sabbath duty are all to guard the temple for the king. ⁸Station yourselves around the king, each man with his weapon in his hand. Anyone who approaches your ranks[b] must be put to death. Stay close to the king wherever he goes."

⁹The commanders of units of a hundred did just as Jehoiada the priest ordered. Each one took his

> **now or never**
> 2KI 11:7–8
>
> Is anything important enough to you that you feel as though you need to guard it? If so, why is it so important to you? What are you guarding it from?

---

[a] *2 Hebrew* Joram, *a variant of* Jehoram   [b] *8 Or* approaches the precincts

men—those who were going on duty on the Sabbath and those who were going off duty—and came to Jehoiada the priest. ¹⁰Then he gave the commanders the spears and shields that had belonged to King David and that were in the temple of the LORD. ¹¹The guards, each with his weapon in his hand, stationed themselves around the king—near the altar and the temple, from the south side to the north side of the temple.

¹²Jehoiada brought out the king's son and put the crown on him; he presented him with a copy of the covenant and proclaimed him king. They anointed him, and the people clapped their hands and shouted, "Long live the king!"

¹³When Athaliah heard the noise made by the guards and the people, she went to the people at the temple of the LORD. ¹⁴She looked and there was the king, standing by the pillar, as the custom was. The officers and the trumpeters were beside the king, and all the people of the land were rejoicing and blowing trumpets. Then Athaliah tore her robes and called out, "Treason! Treason!"

¹⁵Jehoiada the priest ordered the commanders of units of a hundred, who were in charge of the troops: "Bring her out between the ranks[a] and put to the sword anyone who follows her." For the priest had said, "She must not be put to death in the temple of the LORD." ¹⁶So they seized her as she reached the place where the horses enter the palace grounds, and there she was put to death.

¹⁷Jehoiada then made a covenant between the LORD and the king and people that they would be the LORD's people. He also made a covenant between the king and the people. ¹⁸All the people of the land went to the temple of Baal and tore it down. They smashed the altars and idols to pieces and killed Mattan the priest of Baal in front of the altars.

Then Jehoiada the priest posted guards at the temple of the LORD. ¹⁹He took with him the commanders of hundreds, the Carites, the guards and all the people of the land, and together they brought the king down from the temple of the LORD and went into the palace, entering by way of the gate of the guards. The king then took his place on the royal throne, ²⁰and all the people of the land rejoiced. And the city was quiet, because Athaliah had been slain with the sword at the palace.

²¹Joash[b] was seven years old when he began to reign.

JOASH REPAIRS THE TEMPLE

12 In the seventh year of Jehu, Joash[c] became king, and he reigned in Jerusalem forty years. His mother's name was Zibiah; she was from Beersheba. ²Joash did what was right in the eyes of the LORD all the years Jehoiada the priest instructed him. ³The high places, however, were not removed; the people continued to offer sacrifices and burn incense there.

⁴Joash said to the priests, "Collect all the money that is brought as sacred offerings to the temple of the LORD—the money collected in the census, the money received from personal vows and the money brought voluntarily to the temple. ⁵Let every priest receive the money from one of the treasurers, and let it be used to repair whatever damage is found in the temple."

⁶But by the twenty-third year of King Joash the priests still had not repaired the temple. ⁷Therefore King Joash summoned Jehoiada the priest and the other priests and asked them, "Why aren't you repairing the damage done to the temple? Take no more money from your treasurers, but hand it over for repairing the temple." ⁸The priests agreed that they would not collect any more money from the people and that they would not repair the temple themselves.

⁹Jehoiada the priest took a chest and bored a hole in its lid. He placed it beside the altar, on the right side as one enters the temple of the LORD. The priests who guarded the entrance put into the chest all the money that was brought to the temple of the LORD. ¹⁰Whenever they saw that there was a large amount of money in the chest, the royal secretary and the high priest came, counted the money that had been brought into the temple of the LORD and put it

NOW OR NEVER
2KI 12:4–10

What present need in your church can you meet (using your God-given skills, resources and abilities)? What's stopping you from meeting that need?

---

[a] 15 Or *out from the precincts*   [b] 21 Hebrew *Jehoash*, a variant of *Joash*   [c] 1 Hebrew *Jehoash*, a variant of *Joash*; also in verses 2, 4, 6, 7 and 18

into bags. ¹¹When the amount had been determined, they gave the money to the men appointed to supervise the work on the temple. With it they paid those who worked on the temple of the LORD—the carpenters and builders, ¹²the masons and stonecutters. They purchased timber and dressed stone for the repair of the temple of the LORD, and met all the other expenses of restoring the temple.

¹³The money brought into the temple was not spent for making silver basins, wick trimmers, sprinkling bowls, trumpets or any other articles of gold or silver for the temple of the LORD; ¹⁴it was paid to the workmen, who used it to repair the temple. ¹⁵They did not require an accounting from those to whom they gave the money to pay the workers, because they acted with complete honesty. ¹⁶The money from the guilt offerings and sin offerings was not brought into the temple of the LORD; it belonged to the priests.

¹⁷About this time Hazael king of Aram went up and attacked Gath and captured it. Then he turned to attack Jerusalem. ¹⁸But Joash king of Judah took all the sacred objects dedicated by his fathers—Jehoshaphat, Jehoram and Ahaziah, the kings of Judah—and the gifts he himself had dedicated and all the gold found in the treasuries of the temple of the LORD and of the royal palace, and he sent them to Hazael king of Aram, who then withdrew from Jerusalem.

¹⁹As for the other events of the reign of Joash, and all he did, are they not written in the book of the annals of the kings of Judah? ²⁰His officials conspired against him and assassinated him at Beth Millo, on the road down to Silla. ²¹The officials who murdered him were Jozabad son of Shimeath and Jehozabad son of Shomer. He died and was buried with his fathers in the City of David. And Amaziah his son succeeded him as king.

JEHOAHAZ KING OF ISRAEL

13 In the twenty-third year of Joash son of Ahaziah king of Judah, Jehoahaz son of Jehu became king of Israel in Samaria, and he reigned seventeen years. ²He did evil in the eyes of the LORD by following the sins of Jeroboam son of Nebat, which he had caused Israel to commit, and he did not turn away from them. ³So the LORD's anger burned against Israel, and for a long time he kept them under the power of Hazael king of Aram and Ben-Hadad his son.

⁴Then Jehoahaz sought the LORD's favor, and the LORD listened to him, for he saw how severely the king of Aram was oppressing Israel. ⁵The LORD provided a deliverer for Israel, and they escaped from the power of Aram. So the Israelites lived in their own homes as they had before. ⁶But they did not turn away from the sins of the house of Jeroboam, which he had caused Israel to commit; they continued in them. Also, the Asherah pole[a] remained standing in Samaria.

⁷Nothing had been left of the army of Jehoahaz except fifty horsemen, ten chariots and ten thousand foot soldiers, for the king of Aram had destroyed the rest and made them like the dust at threshing time.

⁸As for the other events of the reign of Jehoahaz, all he did and his achievements, are they not written in the book of the annals of the kings of Israel? ⁹Jehoahaz rested with his fathers and was buried in Samaria. And Jehoash[b] his son succeeded him as king.

JEHOASH KING OF ISRAEL

¹⁰In the thirty-seventh year of Joash king of Judah, Jehoash son of Jehoahaz became king of Israel in Samaria, and he reigned sixteen years. ¹¹He did evil in the eyes of the LORD and did not turn away from any of the sins of Jeroboam son of Nebat, which he had caused Israel to commit; he continued in them.

Being Honest

A reputation for being honest and trustworthy comes from doing things like following through on your word when you say you're going to do something, resisting the temptation to cheat or act dishonestly and refusing to spread gossip or rumors. Do you have a reputation for being so honest that people don't have to think twice about trusting you?

»» live the adventure »» 2Ki 12:15

ᵃ *6* That is, a symbol of the goddess Asherah; here and elsewhere in 2 Kings   ᵇ *9* Hebrew *Joash*, a variant of *Jehoash*; also in verses 12-14 and 25

¹²As for the other events of the reign of Jehoash, all he did and his achievements, including his war against Amaziah king of Judah, are they not written in the book of the annals of the kings of Israel? ¹³Jehoash rested with his fathers, and Jeroboam succeeded him on the throne. Jehoash was buried in Samaria with the kings of Israel.

¹⁴Now Elisha was suffering from the illness from which he died. Jehoash king of Israel went down to see him and wept over him. "My father! My father!" he cried. "The chariots and horsemen of Israel!"

¹⁵Elisha said, "Get a bow and some arrows," and he did so. ¹⁶"Take the bow in your hands," he said to the king of Israel. When he had taken it, Elisha put his hands on the king's hands.

¹⁷"Open the east window," he said, and he opened it. "Shoot!" Elisha said, and he shot. "The LORD's arrow of victory, the arrow of victory over Aram!" Elisha declared. "You will completely destroy the Arameans at Aphek."

¹⁸Then he said, "Take the arrows," and the king took them. Elisha told him, "Strike the ground." He struck it three times and stopped. ¹⁹The man of God was angry with him and said, "You should have struck the ground five or six times; then you would have defeated Aram and completely destroyed it. But now you will defeat it only three times."

²⁰Elisha died and was buried.

Now Moabite raiders used to enter the country every spring. ²¹Once while some Israelites were burying a man, suddenly they saw a band of raiders; so they threw the man's body into Elisha's tomb. When the body touched Elisha's bones, the man came to life and stood up on his feet.

²²Hazael king of Aram oppressed Israel throughout the reign of Jehoahaz. ²³But the LORD was gracious to them and had compassion and showed concern for them because of his covenant with Abraham, Isaac and Jacob. To this day he has been unwilling to destroy them or banish them from his presence.

²⁴Hazael king of Aram died, and Ben-Hadad his son succeeded him as king. ²⁵Then Jehoash son of Jehoahaz recaptured from Ben-Hadad son of Hazael the towns he had taken in battle from his father Jehoahaz. Three times Jehoash defeated him, and so he recovered the Israelite towns.

challenge notes

To: **my_son**

2KI 13:23

heavenly_father: no sin is bigger than my ability to forgive. no matter how far you fall or how spectacularly you blow it, I'll never leave you. in fact, I'll be there to catch you and restore you when you fall.

AMAZIAH KING OF JUDAH

14 In the second year of Jehoash[a] son of Jehoahaz king of Israel, Amaziah son of Joash king of Judah began to reign. ²He was twenty-five years old when he became king, and he reigned in Jerusalem twenty-nine years. His mother's name was Jehoaddin; she was from Jerusalem. ³He did what was right in the eyes of the LORD, but not as his father David had done. In everything he followed the example of his father Joash. ⁴The high places, however, were not removed; the people continued to offer sacrifices and burn incense there.

⁵After the kingdom was firmly in his grasp, he executed the officials who had murdered his father the king. ⁶Yet he did not put the sons of the assassins to death, in accordance with what is written in the Book of the Law of Moses where the LORD commanded: "Fathers shall not be put to death for their children, nor children put to death for their fathers; each is to die for his own sins."[b]

⁷He was the one who defeated ten thousand Edomites in the Valley of Salt and captured Sela in battle, calling it Joktheel, the name it has to this day.

⁸Then Amaziah sent messengers to Jehoash son of Jehoahaz, the son of Jehu, king of Israel, with the challenge: "Come, meet me face to face."

⁹But Jehoash king of Israel replied to Amaziah king of Judah: "A thistle in Lebanon sent a message to a cedar in Lebanon, 'Give your daughter to my son in marriage.' Then a wild beast in Lebanon came along and trampled the thistle underfoot. ¹⁰You have indeed defeated Edom and now you are arrogant. Glory in your victory, but stay at home! Why ask for trouble and cause your own downfall and that of Judah also?"

¹¹Amaziah, however, would not listen, so Jehoash king of Israel attacked. He and Amaziah king of Judah faced each other at Beth Shemesh in Judah. ¹²Judah was routed by Israel, and every man fled to

---

^a *1* Hebrew *Joash,* a variant of *Jehoash;* also in verses 13, 23 and 27   ^b *6* Deut. 24:16

his home. ¹³Jehoash king of Israel captured Amaziah king of Judah, the son of Joash, the son of Ahaziah, at Beth Shemesh. Then Jehoash went to Jerusalem and broke down the wall of Jerusalem from the Ephraim Gate to the Corner Gate—a section about six hundred feet long.ᵃ ¹⁴He took all the gold and silver and all the articles found in the temple of the LORD and in the treasuries of the royal palace. He also took hostages and returned to Samaria.

¹⁵As for the other events of the reign of Jehoash, what he did and his achievements, including his war against Amaziah king of Judah, are they not written in the book of the annals of the kings of Israel? ¹⁶Jehoash rested with his fathers and was buried in Samaria with the kings of Israel. And Jeroboam his son succeeded him as king.

¹⁷Amaziah son of Joash king of Judah lived for fifteen years after the death of Jehoash son of Jehoahaz king of Israel. ¹⁸As for the other events of Amaziah's reign, are they not written in the book of the annals of the kings of Judah?

¹⁹They conspired against him in Jerusalem, and he fled to Lachish, but they sent men after him to Lachish and killed him there. ²⁰He was brought back by horse and was buried in Jerusalem with his fathers, in the City of David.

²¹Then all the people of Judah took Azariah,ᵇ who was sixteen years old, and made him king in place of his father Amaziah. ²²He was the one who rebuilt Elath and restored it to Judah after Amaziah rested with his fathers.

JEROBOAM II KING OF ISRAEL

²³In the fifteenth year of Amaziah son of Joash king of Judah, Jeroboam son of Jehoash king of Israel became king in Samaria, and he reigned forty-one years. ²⁴He did evil in the eyes of the LORD and did not turn away from any of the sins of Jeroboam son of Nebat, which he had caused Israel to commit. ²⁵He was the one who restored the boundaries of Israel from Leboᶜ Hamath to the Sea of the Arabah,ᵈ in accordance with the word of the LORD, the God of Israel, spoken through his servant Jonah son of Amittai, the prophet from Gath Hepher.

²⁶The LORD had seen how bitterly everyone in Israel, whether slave or free, was suffering; there was no one to help them. ²⁷And since the LORD had not said he would blot out the name of Israel from under heaven, he saved them by the hand of Jeroboam son of Jehoash.

²⁸As for the other events of Jeroboam's reign, all he did, and his military achievements, including how he recovered for Israel both Damascus and Hamath, which had belonged to Yaudi,ᵉ are they not written in the book of the annals of the kings of Israel? ²⁹Jeroboam rested with his fathers, the kings of Israel. And Zechariah his son succeeded him as king.

AZARIAH KING OF JUDAH

15 In the twenty-seventh year of Jeroboam king of Israel, Azariah son of Amaziah king of Judah began to reign. ²He was sixteen years old when he became king, and he reigned in Jerusalem fifty-two years. His mother's name was Jecoliah; she was from Jerusalem. ³He did what was right in the eyes of the LORD, just as his father Amaziah had done. ⁴The high places, however, were not removed; the people continued to offer sacrifices and burn incense there.

⁵The LORD afflicted the king with leprosyᶠ until the day he died, and he lived in a separate house.ᵍ Jotham the king's son had charge of the palace and governed the people of the land.

» live the adventure » 2Ki 15:4

Obeying God Completely

Selective obedience is the same as disobedience, as far as God is concerned. If you're not prepared to be obedient in every situation, you're just asking for trouble. For example, let's say you have a problem with lust. Do you think God would be satisfied if you decided to delete, say, *half* of the objectionable files on your computer? Of course not! As long as you had access to even one X-rated picture, you'd still be vulnerable to lust. That's one of the reasons God demands total obedience from us. He doesn't want sin to get even the smallest foothold in our lives.

ᵃ 13 Hebrew *four hundred cubits* (about 180 meters)   ᵇ 21 Also called *Uzziah*   ᶜ 25 Or *from the entrance to*   ᵈ 25 That is, the Dead Sea   ᵉ 28 Or *Judah*   ᶠ 5 The Hebrew word was used for various diseases affecting the skin—not necessarily leprosy.   ᵍ 5 Or *in a house where he was relieved of responsibility*

» **50 Dumb Things Not to Do**

50

It isn't hard to ruin your life. Millions of guys do it every day. But let's be honest: It's not as cut and dried as that, either. Sometimes in the heat of the moment, guys do dumb stuff. That story is as old as humanity itself . . . literally. In fact, some of the most famous bone-headed blunders in history are retold in the very book you're holding. No doubt about it, these guys did some pretty stupid and ridiculous stuff. So we've listed some of their mistakes and other Biblical warnings against stupidity here . . . not for laughs, but because these are mistakes you just don't want to make.

DISOBEDIENCE

01» Doing exactly what God says not to do »Ge 3:6 :: **02»** Thinking you can hide your sin from God »Ge 3:8; Isa 29:15–16 :: **03»** Blaming others for your own choices and actions »Ge 3:12 :: **04»** Drinking yourself into oblivion »Ge 9:20–25 :: **05»** Letting a sin-sick culture twist your values and pull you away from God »Ge 19 :: **06»** Making impulsive decisions without considering the long-term consequences »Ge 25:29–34 :: **07»** Marrying a girl your parents don't approve of just to tick them off »Ge 28:6–9 :: **08»** Cheating someone for personal gain »Ge 29:15–30; 30:25–43 :: **09»** Trying to take God's will into your own hands »Ex 2:11–15 :: **10»** Letting the crowd talk you into doing stuff you know is wrong »Ex 32 :: **11»** Taking :: 1 SA 2:12–4:1 God's name in vain and using it as a curse »Lev 24:10 :: **12»** Failing to trust a clear promise from God »Nu 14 :: **13»** Lashing out in anger and disrespecting God »Nu 20 :: **14»** Chasing after immoral sexual pleasure

CORRUPTION

19

and all the sin it brings with it »Nu 25 :: **15»** Stubbornly rebelling against your parents and rejecting their counsel »Dt 21:18 :: **16»** Making a big decision without seeking God's guidance »Jos 9 :: **17»** Allowing your desire for women to consume you and rob you of your God-given strength »Jdg 14–16 :: **18»** Living by the philosophy of doing whatever you feel like »Jdg 21:25 :: **19»** Living a corrupt life while pretending to be a spiritual leader »1Sa 2:12—4:1 :: **20»** Thinking you know better than God about how things should be done »1Sa 15 :: **21»** Trying to be some-

DISRESPECT

26

thing you're not »1Sa 17:38–40 :: **22»** Dabbling in the occult—or anything spiritual that doesn't come from God »1Sa 28 :: **23»** Staring at sexual temptation rather than averting your eyes and leaving »2Sa 11:1–5 :: **24»** Clinging to earthly wealth or power rather than giving thanks for God's blessings »2Sa 24 :: **25»** Getting involved with women who do not share your beliefs and convictions »1Ki 11:1–6 :: **26»** Disrespecting elders or others who deserve your appreciation »2Ki 2:23 :: **27»** Living like there is no God »Ps 53 :: **28»** Getting involved with an adulterous woman and being unfaithful to your wife »Pr 5 :: **29»** Being lazy » Pr 10:4; 12:24; 21:25 :: **30»** Having a loose tongue or an undisciplined

BACKSLIDING 41

:: LK 3:7

mouth »Pr 10:31; 13:3; 17:20; 18:21 :: **31»** Thinking you can find lasting happiness in the pleasures of this world »Ecc 2:1–11 :: **32»** Becoming intimately involved with a girl—physically or emotionally—before you're ready for lifelong commitment »SS 3:5 :: **33»** Taking advantage of poor, oppressed or marginalized people »Isa 10:1–4 :: **34»** Trying to run from God's calling in your life »Jnh :: **35»** Doing "religious" things to improve your reputation »Mt 6:5–14 :: **36»** Building your life on anything other than the person and teachings of Jesus »Mt 7:24–27 :: **37»** Talking the talk but not walking the walk »Mt 15:1–9 :: **38»** Living according to religious rules and rituals rather than the spirit of God's Word »Mk 2:23–28 :: **39»** Influencing young or impressionable people in a negative way »Mk 9:42–49 :: **40»** "Hanging around" Jesus without ever really giving him your heart »Mk 14:43–46 :: **41»** "Repenting" of sin but returning to a life of evil and failing to bear fruit »Lk 3:7 :: **42»** Caring about the temporal concerns of life when you could be involved in changing people's lives for eternity »Lk 8:26–37 :: **43»** Thinking you can follow Jesus on our own terms »Lk 9:57–62 :: **44»** Believing that Jesus wants us to do "stuff" for him more than he wants our hearts »Lk 10:38–42 :: **45»** Thinking that this life lasts forever and that Jesus' return isn't really going to happen »Lk

FEARFUL 47

12:35–48 :: **46»** Walking away from faith in Jesus because you don't understand his teaching »Jn 6:50–71 :: **47»** Being fearful or doubting God's love because of earthly things »Ro 8:31–39 :: **48»** Tolerating sexual immorality and other sin in the family of God »1Co 5 :: **49»** Taking God's grace as a license for immoral living—sex before marriage, drunkenness, stealing, etc. »1Co 6:9–11 :: **50»** Giving to God reluctantly or halfheartedly »2Co 9:6–15

6As for the other events of Azariah's reign, and all he did, are they not written in the book of the annals of the kings of Judah? 7Azariah rested with his fathers and was buried near them in the City of David. And Jotham his son succeeded him as king.

ZECHARIAH KING OF ISRAEL

8In the thirty-eighth year of Azariah king of Judah, Zechariah son of Jeroboam became king of Israel in Samaria, and he reigned six months. 9He did evil in the eyes of the LORD, as his fathers had done. He did not turn away from the sins of Jeroboam son of Nebat, which he had caused Israel to commit.

10Shallum son of Jabesh conspired against Zechariah. He attacked him in front of the people,[a] assassinated him and succeeded him as king. 11The other events of Zechariah's reign are written in the book of the annals of the kings of Israel. 12So the word of the LORD spoken to Jehu was fulfilled: "Your descendants will sit on the throne of Israel to the fourth generation."[b]

SHALLUM KING OF ISRAEL

13Shallum son of Jabesh became king in the thirty-ninth year of Uzziah king of Judah, and he reigned in Samaria one month. 14Then Menahem son of Gadi went from Tirzah up to Samaria. He attacked Shallum son of Jabesh in Samaria, assassinated him and succeeded him as king.

15The other events of Shallum's reign, and the conspiracy he led, are written in the book of the annals of the kings of Israel.

16At that time Menahem, starting out from Tirzah, attacked Tiphsah and everyone in the city and its vicinity, because they refused to open their gates. He sacked Tiphsah and ripped open all the pregnant women.

MENAHEM KING OF ISRAEL

17In the thirty-ninth year of Azariah king of Judah, Menahem son of Gadi became king of Israel, and he reigned in Samaria ten years. 18He did evil in the eyes of the LORD. During his entire reign he did not turn away from the sins of Jeroboam son of Nebat, which he had caused Israel to commit.

19Then Pul[c] king of Assyria invaded the land, and Menahem gave him a thousand talents[d] of silver to gain his support and strengthen his own hold on the kingdom. 20Menahem exacted this money from Israel. Every wealthy man had to contribute fifty shekels[e] of silver to be given to the king of Assyria. So the king of Assyria withdrew and stayed in the land no longer.

21As for the other events of Menahem's reign, and all he did, are they not written in the book of the annals of the kings of Israel? 22Menahem rested with his fathers. And Pekahiah his son succeeded him as king.

PEKAHIAH KING OF ISRAEL

23In the fiftieth year of Azariah king of Judah, Pekahiah son of Menahem became king of Israel in Samaria, and he reigned two years. 24Pekahiah did evil in the eyes of the LORD. He did not turn away from the sins of Jeroboam son of Nebat, which he had caused Israel to commit. 25One of his chief officers, Pekah son of Remaliah, conspired against him. Taking fifty men of Gilead with him, he assassinated Pekahiah, along with Argob and Arieh, in the citadel of the royal palace at Samaria. So Pekah killed Pekahiah and succeeded him as king.

26The other events of Pekahiah's reign, and all he did, are written in the book of the annals of the kings of Israel.

PEKAH KING OF ISRAEL

27In the fifty-second year of Azariah king of Judah, Pekah son of Remaliah became king of Israel in Samaria, and he reigned twenty years. 28He did evil in the eyes of the LORD. He did not turn away from the sins of Jeroboam son of Nebat, which he had caused Israel to commit.

29In the time of Pekah king of Israel, Tiglath-Pileser king of Assyria came and took Ijon, Abel Beth Maacah, Janoah, Kedesh and Hazor. He took Gilead and Galilee, including all the land of Naphtali, and deported the people to Assyria. 30Then Hoshea son of Elah conspired against Pekah son of Remaliah.

---

a 10 Hebrew; some Septuagint manuscripts in Ibleam   b 12 2 Kings 10:30   c 19 Also called Tiglath-Pileser   d 19 That is, about 37 tons (about 34 metric tons)   e 20 That is, about 1 1/4 pounds (about 0.6 kilogram)

He attacked and assassinated him, and then succeeded him as king in the twentieth year of Jotham son of Uzziah. ³¹As for the other events of Pekah's reign, and all he did, are they not written in the book of the annals of the kings of Israel?

JOTHAM KING OF JUDAH

³²In the second year of Pekah son of Remaliah king of Israel, Jotham son of Uzziah king of Judah began to reign. ³³He was twenty-five years old when he became king, and he reigned in Jerusalem sixteen years. His mother's name was Jerusha daughter of Zadok. ³⁴He did what was right in the eyes of the LORD, just as his father Uzziah had done. ³⁵The high places, however, were not removed; the people continued to offer sacrifices and burn incense there. Jotham rebuilt the Upper Gate of the temple of the LORD.

³⁶As for the other events of Jotham's reign, and what he did, are they not written in the book of the annals of the kings of Judah? ³⁷(In those days the LORD began to send Rezin king of Aram and Pekah son of Remaliah against Judah.) ³⁸Jotham rested with his fathers and was buried with them in the City of David, the city of his father. And Ahaz his son succeeded him as king.

AHAZ KING OF JUDAH

16 In the seventeenth year of Pekah son of Remaliah, Ahaz son of Jotham king of Judah began to reign. ²Ahaz was twenty years old when he became king, and he reigned in Jerusalem sixteen years. Unlike David his father, he did not do what was right in the eyes of the LORD his God. ³He walked in the ways of the kings of Israel and even sacrificed his son in ª the fire, following the detestable ways of the nations the LORD had driven out before the Israelites. ⁴He offered sacrifices and burned incense at the high places, on the hilltops and under every spreading tree.

⁵Then Rezin king of Aram and Pekah son of Remaliah king of Israel marched up to fight against Jerusalem and besieged Ahaz, but they could not overpower him. ⁶At that time, Rezin king of Aram recovered Elath for Aram by driving out the men of Judah. Edomites then moved into Elath and have lived there to this day.

⁷Ahaz sent messengers to say to Tiglath-Pileser king of Assyria, "I am your servant and vassal. Come up and save me out of the hand of the king of Aram and of the king of Israel, who are attacking me." ⁸And Ahaz took the silver and gold found in the temple of the LORD and in the treasuries of the royal palace and sent it as a gift to the king of Assyria. ⁹The king of Assyria complied by attacking Damascus and capturing it. He deported its inhabitants to Kir and put Rezin to death.

¹⁰Then King Ahaz went to Damascus to meet Tiglath-Pileser king of Assyria. He saw an altar in Damascus and sent to Uriah the priest a sketch of the altar, with detailed plans for its construction. ¹¹So Uriah the priest built an altar in accordance with all the plans that King Ahaz had sent from Damascus and finished it before King Ahaz returned. ¹²When the king came back from Damascus and saw the altar, he approached it and presented offeringsᵇ on it. ¹³He offered up his burnt offering and grain offering, poured out his drink offering, and sprinkled the blood of his fellowship offeringsᶜ on the altar. ¹⁴The bronze altar that stood before the LORD he brought from the front of the temple—from between the new altar and the temple of the LORD—and put it on the north side of the new altar.

¹⁵King Ahaz then gave these orders to Uriah the priest: "On the large new altar, offer the morning burnt offering and the evening grain offering, the king's burnt offering and his grain offering, and the burnt offering of all the people of the land, and their grain offering and their drink offering. Sprinkle on the altar all the blood of the burnt offerings and sacrifices. But I will use the bronze altar for seeking guidance." ¹⁶And Uriah the priest did just as King Ahaz had ordered.

¹⁷King Ahaz took away the side panels and removed the basins from the movable stands. He removed the Sea from the bronze bulls that supported it and set it on a stone base. ¹⁸He took away the Sabbath canopyᵈ that had been built at the temple and removed the royal entryway outside the temple of the LORD, in deference to the king of Assyria.

¹⁹As for the other events of the reign of Ahaz, and what he did, are they not written in the book of the annals of the kings of Judah? ²⁰Ahaz rested with his fathers and was buried with them in the City of David. And Hezekiah his son succeeded him as king.

ª 3 Or even made his son pass through   ᵇ 12 Or and went up   ᶜ 13 Traditionally peace offerings   ᵈ 18 Or the dais of his throne (see Septuagint)

HOSHEA LAST KING OF ISRAEL

17 In the twelfth year of Ahaz king of Judah, Hoshea son of Elah became king of Israel in Samaria, and he reigned nine years. ²He did evil in the eyes of the Lord, but not like the kings of Israel who preceded him.

³Shalmaneser king of Assyria came up to attack Hoshea, who had been Shalmaneser's vassal and had paid him tribute. ⁴But the king of Assyria discovered that Hoshea was a traitor, for he had sent envoys to So[a] king of Egypt, and he no longer paid tribute to the king of Assyria, as he had done year by year. Therefore Shalmaneser seized him and put him in prison. ⁵The king of Assyria invaded the entire land, marched against Samaria and laid siege to it for three years. ⁶In the ninth year of Hoshea, the king of Assyria captured Samaria and deported the Israelites to Assyria. He settled them in Halah, in Gozan on the Habor River and in the towns of the Medes.

ISRAEL EXILED BECAUSE OF SIN

⁷All this took place because the Israelites had sinned against the Lord their God, who had brought them up out of Egypt from under the power of Pharaoh king of Egypt. They worshiped other gods ⁸and followed the practices of the nations the Lord had driven out before them, as well as the practices that the kings of Israel had introduced. ⁹The Israelites secretly did things against the Lord their God that were not right. From watchtower to fortified city they built themselves high places in all their towns. ¹⁰They set up sacred stones and Asherah poles on every high hill and under every spreading tree. ¹¹At every high place they burned incense, as the nations whom the Lord had driven out before them had done. They did wicked things that provoked the Lord to anger. ¹²They worshiped idols, though the Lord had said, "You shall not do this."[b] ¹³The Lord warned Israel and Judah through all his prophets and seers: "Turn from your evil ways. Observe my commands and decrees, in accordance with the entire Law that I commanded your fathers to obey and that I delivered to you through my servants the prophets."

¹⁴But they would not listen and were as stiff-necked as their fathers, who did not trust in the Lord their God. ¹⁵They rejected his decrees and the covenant he had made with their fathers and the warnings he had given them. They followed worthless idols and themselves became worthless. They imitated the nations around them although the Lord had ordered them, "Do not do as they do," and they did the things the Lord had forbidden them to do.

¹⁶They forsook all the commands of the Lord their God and made for themselves two idols cast in the shape of calves, and an Asherah pole. They bowed down to all the starry hosts, and they worshiped Baal. ¹⁷They sacrificed their sons and daughters in[c] the fire. They practiced divination and sorcery and sold themselves to do evil in the eyes of the Lord, provoking him to anger.

¹⁸So the Lord was very angry with Israel and removed them from his presence. Only the tribe of Judah was left, ¹⁹and even Judah did

---

» live the adventure » 2Ki 17:14-15

Playing by the Rules

When you get serious about a sport, one of the first things you have to do is learn the rules. The better you understand the boundaries set by the rules of the game, the more effective you'll be competing within those boundaries. The same holds true for God's work. The better you know the boundaries set by God's determination of right and wrong, the more effective you'll be in living a life that pleases him. (Hint, hint: You're holding the "boundary map" in your hands right now. All you have to do now is read it and learn it.)

NOW OR NEVER
2KI 17:1-14

Everything about God—including his Word, his will and his commands—is perfect. That means any argument or "logical reasoning" against God is flawed and misguided.

---

[a] *4 Or to Sais, to the; So is possibly an abbreviation for Osorkon.*   [b] *12 Exodus 20:4,5*   [c] *17 Or They made their sons and daughters pass through*

not keep the commands of the LORD their God. They followed the practices Israel had introduced. ²⁰Therefore the LORD rejected all the people of Israel; he afflicted them and gave them into the hands of plunderers, until he thrust them from his presence.

²¹When he tore Israel away from the house of David, they made Jeroboam son of Nebat their king. Jeroboam enticed Israel away from following the LORD and caused them to commit a great sin. ²²The Israelites persisted in all the sins of Jeroboam and did not turn away from them ²³until the LORD removed them from his presence, as he had warned through all his servants the prophets. So the people of Israel were taken from their homeland into exile in Assyria, and they are still there.

SAMARIA RESETTLED

²⁴The king of Assyria brought people from Babylon, Cuthah, Avva, Hamath and Sepharvaim and settled them in the towns of Samaria to replace the Israelites. They took over Samaria and lived in its towns. ²⁵When they first lived there, they did not worship the LORD; so he sent lions among them and they killed some of the people. ²⁶It was reported to the king of Assyria: "The people you deported and resettled in the towns of Samaria do not know what the god of that country requires. He has sent lions among them, which are killing them off, because the people do not know what he requires."

²⁷Then the king of Assyria gave this order: "Have one of the priests you took captive from Samaria go back to live there and teach the people what the god of the land requires." ²⁸So one of the priests who had been exiled from Samaria came to live in Bethel and taught them how to worship the LORD.

²⁹Nevertheless, each national group made its own gods in the several towns where they settled, and set them up in the shrines the people of Samaria had made at the high places. ³⁰The men from Babylon made Succoth Benoth, the men from Cuthah made Nergal, and the men from Hamath made Ashima; ³¹the Avvites made Nibhaz and Tartak, and the Sepharvites burned their children in the fire as sacrifices to Adrammelech and Anammelech, the gods of Sepharvaim. ³²They worshiped the LORD, but they also appointed all sorts of their own people to officiate for them as priests in the shrines at the high places. ³³They worshiped the LORD, but they also served their own gods in accordance with the customs of the nations from which they had been brought.

³⁴To this day they persist in their former practices. They neither worship the LORD nor adhere to the decrees and ordinances, the laws and commands that the LORD gave the descendants of Jacob, whom he named Israel. ³⁵When the LORD made a covenant with the Israelites, he commanded them: "Do not worship any other gods or bow down to them, serve them or sacrifice to them. ³⁶But the LORD, who brought you up out of Egypt with mighty power and outstretched arm, is the one you must worship. To him you shall bow down and to him offer sacrifices. ³⁷You must always be careful to keep the decrees and ordinances, the laws and commands he wrote for you. Do not worship other gods. ³⁸Do not forget the covenant I have made with you, and do not worship other gods. ³⁹Rather, worship the LORD your God; it is he who will deliver you from the hand of all your enemies."

⁴⁰They would not listen, however, but persisted in their former practices. ⁴¹Even while these people were worshiping the LORD, they were serving their idols. To this day their children and grandchildren continue to do as their fathers did.

HEZEKIAH KING OF JUDAH

18

In the third year of Hoshea son of Elah king of Israel, Hezekiah son of Ahaz king of Judah began to reign. ²He was twenty-five years old when he became king, and he reigned in Jerusalem twenty-nine years. His mother's name was Abijah ᵃ daughter of Zechariah. ³He did what was right in the eyes of the LORD, just as his father David had done. ⁴He removed the high places, smashed the sacred stones and cut down the Asherah poles. He broke into pieces the bronze snake Moses had made, for up to that time the Israelites had been burning incense to it. (It was called ᵇ Nehushtan. ᶜ)

⁵Hezekiah trusted in the LORD, the God of Israel. There was no one like him among all the kings of Judah, either before him or after him. ⁶He held fast to the LORD and did not cease to follow him; he kept the commands the LORD had given Moses. ⁷And the LORD was with him; he was successful in whatever he undertook. He rebelled against the king of Assyria and did not serve him. ⁸From watchtower to fortified city, he defeated the Philistines, as far as Gaza and its territory.

ᵃ 2 Hebrew *Abi*, a variant of *Abijah*   ᵇ 4 Or *He called it*   ᶜ 4 *Nehushtan* sounds like the Hebrew for *bronze* and *snake* and *unclean thing*.

hezekiah

VERSUS

sennacherib

» Fifteenth king of the tiny Jewish nation of Judah

» Depended on the Lord and led the nation in turning back to God

» Had an effective prayer life

» Ruler of Assyria, the most powerful empire on earth

» Laid siege to Jerusalem

» A cocky, godless man

The Main Event

When Hezekiah became the king of Judah (Israel's southern kingdom) at age 25, everything was a mess. Specifically, his nation was no longer obeying God. Hezekiah saw what happened when the northern kingdom of Israel rejected God and ignored the prophets: They were conquered by invading armies from Assyria.

To avoid the same fate for his kingdom, Hezekiah made it his first priority as king to rid the land of pagan idols and shrines. He reopened the temple of God and reinstituted the Passover celebration. It was a terrific beginning. The young ruler had chops.

Almost immediately, though, the Assyrians began making noise about invading Judah. They threatened to treat the capital city, Jerusalem, the way they had treated the northern kingdom of Israel. In short, they put the squeeze on Hezekiah, big time. The nervous king responded by dipping into the temple treasury and giving the Assyrians large amounts of gold and silver, hoping they'd take the payoff and go away. They didn't.

Instead, Sennacherib, the Assyrian king, sent a letter to Hezekiah. The note brimmed with arrogance. In a nutshell, it said, "You might as well give up. You can't fight me. And don't think for a moment that the Lord is going to protect you. Why, he's the one who told me to come throw you down."

The note demoralized King Hezekiah. But Hezekiah wasn't the only one Sennacherib was trying to intimidate. He wanted to strike fear in the heart of every man, woman and child in Jerusalem. So the Assyrian official who delivered Sennacherib's message stood within earshot of those sitting on the city wall and read the letter out loud . . . in Hebrew, no less, to make sure that all who heard would understand every single word.

Hezekiah's response to the note was to go straight to the source himself. The king marched to the temple and summoned Isaiah, the great prophet of God. He laid the letter out before God and prayed a simple, honest and desperate prayer: "Deliver us from this thug, so that everyone will know you're the one and only God."

Later that same night, the angel of the LORD paid a little visit to the Assyrian camp. By the time he left, 185,000 enemy soldiers lay dead. Sennacherib, who once boasted that not even God could protect Jerusalem from the coming onslaught, was forced to retreat.

The Outcome

The story of Sennacherib and Hezekiah is one of striking contrasts. The leader of a world empire versus the leader of a tiny nation. A godless, cocky ruler versus a godly, humble one. A preying king versus a praying king. A massive army versus a single angel from heaven.

It just goes to show that the battle doesn't necessarily go to the biggest, the strongest or the most confident. Rather, victory belongs to the man who leans fully on God. There's no shame at all in admitting your weakness and calling out to God for help. In fact, there's wisdom and reward in such a strategy!

Take it from Hezekiah: Looking to heaven and crying, "Help!" is often the wisest course of action and your best response to trouble.

Read more about Hezekiah and Sennacherib in 2 Kings 18:17—19:37 (pages 438–441).

⁹In King Hezekiah's fourth year, which was the seventh year of Hoshea son of Elah king of Israel, Shalmaneser king of Assyria marched against Samaria and laid siege to it. ¹⁰At the end of three years the Assyrians took it. So Samaria was captured in Hezekiah's sixth year, which was the ninth year of Hoshea king of Israel. ¹¹The king of Assyria deported Israel to Assyria and settled them in Halah, in Gozan on the Habor River and in towns of the Medes. ¹²This happened because they had not obeyed the LORD their God, but had violated his covenant—all that Moses the servant of the LORD commanded. They neither listened to the commands nor carried them out.

¹³In the fourteenth year of King Hezekiah's reign, Sennacherib king of Assyria attacked all the fortified cities of Judah and captured them. ¹⁴So Hezekiah king of Judah sent this message to the king of Assyria at Lachish: "I have done wrong. Withdraw from me, and I will pay whatever you demand of me." The king of Assyria exacted from Hezekiah king of Judah three hundred talentsᵃ of silver and thirty talentsᵇ of gold. ¹⁵So Hezekiah gave him all the silver that was found in the temple of the LORD and in the treasuries of the royal palace.

¹⁶At this time Hezekiah king of Judah stripped off the gold with which he had covered the doors and doorposts of the temple of the LORD, and gave it to the king of Assyria.

SENNACHERIB THREATENS JERUSALEM

¹⁷The king of Assyria sent his supreme commander, his chief officer and his field commander with a large army, from Lachish to King Hezekiah at Jerusalem. They came up to Jerusalem and stopped at the aqueduct of the Upper Pool, on the road to the Washerman's Field. ¹⁸They called for the king; and Eliakim son of Hilkiah the palace administrator, Shebna the secretary, and Joah son of Asaph the recorder went out to them.

¹⁹The field commander said to them, "Tell Hezekiah:

" 'This is what the great king, the king of Assyria, says: On what are you basing this confidence of yours? ²⁰You say you have strategy and military strength—but you speak only empty words. On whom are you depending, that you rebel against me? ²¹Look now, you are depending on Egypt, that splintered reed of a staff, which pierces a man's hand and wounds him if he leans on it! Such is Pharaoh king of Egypt to all who depend on him. ²²And if you say to me, "We are depending on the LORD our God"—isn't he the one whose high places and altars Hezekiah removed, saying to Judah and Jerusalem, "You must worship before this altar in Jerusalem"?

²³" 'Come now, make a bargain with my master, the king of Assyria: I will give you two thousand horses—if you can put riders on them! ²⁴How can you repulse one officer of the least of my master's officials, even though you are depending on Egypt for chariots and horsemenᶜ? ²⁵Furthermore, have I come to attack and destroy this place without word from the LORD? The LORD himself told me to march against this country and destroy it.' "

²⁶Then Eliakim son of Hilkiah, and Shebna and Joah said to the field commander, "Please speak to your servants in Aramaic, since we understand it. Don't speak to us in Hebrew in the hearing of the people on the wall."

²⁷But the commander replied, "Was it only to your master and you that my master sent me to say these things, and not to the men sitting on the wall—who, like you, will have to eat their own filth and drink their own urine?"

²⁸Then the commander stood and called out in Hebrew: "Hear the word of the great king, the king of Assyria! ²⁹This is what the king says: Do not let Hezekiah deceive you. He cannot deliver you from my hand. ³⁰Do not let Hezekiah persuade you to trust in the LORD when he says, 'The LORD will surely deliver us; this city will not be given into the hand of the king of Assyria.'

³¹"Do not listen to Hezekiah. This is what the king of Assyria says: Make peace with me and come out to me. Then every one of you will eat from his own vine and fig tree and drink water from his own cistern, ³²until I come and take you to a land like your own, a land of grain and new wine, a land of bread and vineyards, a land of olive trees and honey. Choose life and not death!

"Do not listen to Hezekiah, for he is misleading you when he says, 'The LORD will deliver us.' ³³Has the god of any nation ever delivered his land from the hand of the king of Assyria? ³⁴Where are the gods of Hamath and Arpad? Where are the gods of Sepharvaim, Hena and Ivvah? Have they rescued Samar-

---

ᵃ *14* That is, about 11 tons (about 10 metric tons)   ᵇ *14* That is, about 1 ton (about 1 metric ton)   ᶜ *24* Or *charioteers* ia from my hand? ³⁵Who of all the gods of these countries has been able to save his land from me? How then can the LORD deliver Jerusalem from my hand?"

³⁶But the people remained silent and said nothing in reply, because the king had commanded, "Do not answer him."

Dealing With Opposition

How many people do you know who would freak out if you told them that you were going to give up *everything* in your life that didn't honor God? How many of them would try to talk you out of your decision? How many of them would try to test you to see how serious you were? If you're going to build a relationship with God, you can expect opposition—some of it friendly in nature, some of it definitely not. You can also expect the Lord to help you face down that opposition when you ask him to.

³⁷Then Eliakim son of Hilkiah the palace administrator, Shebna the secretary and Joah son of Asaph the recorder went to Hezekiah, with their clothes torn, and told him what the field commander had said.

JERUSALEM'S DELIVERANCE FORETOLD

19 When King Hezekiah heard this, he tore his clothes and put on sackcloth and went into the temple of the LORD. ²He sent Eliakim the palace administrator, Shebna the secretary and the leading priests, all wearing sackcloth, to the prophet Isaiah son of Amoz. ³They told him, "This is what Hezekiah says: This day is a day of distress and rebuke and disgrace, as when children come to the point of birth and there is no strength to deliver them. ⁴It may be that the LORD your God will hear all the words of the field commander, whom his master, the king of Assyria, has sent to ridicule the living God, and that he will rebuke him for the words the LORD your God has heard. Therefore pray for the remnant that still survives."

⁵When King Hezekiah's officials came to Isaiah, ⁶Isaiah said to them, "Tell your master, 'This is what the LORD says: Do not be afraid of what you have heard—those words with which the underlings of the king of Assyria have blasphemed me. ⁷Listen! I am going to put such a spirit in him that when he hears a certain report, he will return to his own country, and there I will have him cut down with the sword.' "

⁸When the field commander heard that the king of Assyria had left Lachish, he withdrew and found the king fighting against Libnah.

⁹Now Sennacherib received a report that Tirhakah, the Cushite[a] king of Egypt, was marching out to fight against him. So he again sent messengers to Hezekiah with this word: ¹⁰"Say to Hezekiah king of Judah: Do not let the god you depend on deceive you when he says, 'Jerusalem will not be handed over to the king of Assyria.' ¹¹Surely you have heard what the kings of Assyria have done to all the countries, destroying them completely. And will you be delivered? ¹²Did the gods of the nations that were destroyed by my forefathers deliver them: the gods of Gozan, Haran, Rezeph and the people of Eden who were in Tel Assar? ¹³Where is the king of Hamath, the king of Arpad, the king of the city of Sepharvaim, or of Hena or Ivvah?"

HEZEKIAH'S PRAYER

¹⁴Hezekiah received the letter from the messengers and read it. Then he went up to the temple of the LORD and spread it out before the LORD. ¹⁵And Hezekiah prayed to the LORD: "O LORD, God of Israel, enthroned between the cherubim, you alone are God over all the kingdoms of the earth. You have made heaven and earth. ¹⁶Give ear, O LORD, and hear; open your eyes, O LORD, and see; listen to the words Sennacherib has sent to insult the living God.

¹⁷"It is true, O LORD, that the Assyrian kings have laid waste these nations and their lands. ¹⁸They have thrown their gods into the fire and destroyed them, for they were not gods but only wood and stone, fashioned by men's hands. ¹⁹Now, O LORD our God, deliver us from his hand, so that all kingdoms on earth may know that you alone, O LORD, are God."

^a *9* That is, from the upper Nile region

²⁰Then Isaiah son of Amoz sent a message to Hezekiah: "This is what the LORD, the God of Israel, says: I have heard your prayer concerning Sennacherib king of Assyria. ²¹This is the word that the LORD has spoken against him:

" 'The Virgin Daughter of Zion
    despises you and mocks you.
The Daughter of Jerusalem
    tosses her head as you flee.
²²Who is it you have insulted and blasphemed?
    Against whom have you raised your voice
and lifted your eyes in pride?
    Against the Holy One of
      Israel!
²³By your messengers
    you have heaped insults on
      the Lord.
And you have said,
    "With my many chariots
I have ascended the heights of
      the mountains,
    the utmost heights of
      Lebanon.

challenge notes

To: **my_son**

heavenly_father: when trouble comes knocking on your door, who will you turn to? bring it before my throne and let me fight your battles for you. I will hear your cries for help, and I won't abandon you.

I have cut down its tallest cedars,
    the choicest of its pines.
I have reached its remotest parts,
    the finest of its forests.
²⁴I have dug wells in foreign lands
    and drunk the water there.
With the soles of my feet
    I have dried up all the streams of Egypt."

²⁵ " 'Have you not heard?
    Long ago I ordained it.
In days of old I planned it;
    now I have brought it to pass,
that you have turned fortified cities
    into piles of stone.
²⁶Their people, drained of power,
    are dismayed and put to shame.
They are like plants in the field,
    like tender green shoots,
like grass sprouting on the roof,
    scorched before it grows up.

²⁷ " 'But I know where you stay
    and when you come and go
    and how you rage against me.
²⁸Because you rage against me
    and your insolence has reached my ears,
I will put my hook in your nose
    and my bit in your mouth,
and I will make you return
    by the way you came.'

²⁹"This will be the sign for you, O Hezekiah:

"This year you will eat what grows by itself,

and the second year what springs from that.
But in the third year sow and reap,
plant vineyards and eat their fruit.
³⁰ Once more a remnant of the house of Judah
will take root below and bear fruit above.
³¹ For out of Jerusalem will come a remnant,
and out of Mount Zion a band of survivors.

The zeal of the LORD Almighty will accomplish this.

³² "Therefore this is what the LORD says concerning the king of Assyria:

"He will not enter this city
or shoot an arrow here.
He will not come before it with shield
or build a siege ramp against it.
³³ By the way that he came he will return;
he will not enter this city,

declares the LORD.

³⁴ I will defend this city and save it,
for my sake and for the sake of David my servant."

³⁵ That night the angel of the LORD went out and put to death a hundred and eighty-five thousand men in the Assyrian camp. When the people got up the next morning—there were all the dead bodies! ³⁶ So Sennacherib king of Assyria broke camp and withdrew. He returned to Nineveh and stayed there. ³⁷ One day, while he was worshiping in the temple of his god Nisroch, his sons Adrammelech and Sharezer cut him down with the sword, and they escaped to the land of Ararat. And Esarhaddon his son succeeded him as king.

HEZEKIAH'S ILLNESS

20 In those days Hezekiah became ill and was at the point of death. The prophet Isaiah son of Amoz went to him and said, "This is what the LORD says: Put your house in order, because you are going to die; you will not recover."

²Hezekiah turned his face to the wall and prayed to the LORD, ³"Remember, O LORD, how I have walked before you faithfully and with wholehearted devotion and have done what is good in your eyes." And Hezekiah wept bitterly.

⁴Before Isaiah had left the middle court, the word of the LORD came to him: ⁵"Go back and tell Hezekiah, the leader of my people, 'This is what the LORD, the God of your father David, says: I have heard your prayer and seen your tears; I will heal you. On the third day from now you will go up to the temple of the LORD. ⁶I will add fifteen years to your life. And I will deliver you and this city from the hand of the king of Assyria. I will defend this city for my sake and for the sake of my servant David.' "

⁷Then Isaiah said, "Prepare a poultice of figs." They did so and applied it to the boil, and he recovered.

⁸Hezekiah had asked Isaiah, "What will be the sign that the LORD will heal me and that I will go up to the temple of the LORD on the third day from now?"

⁹Isaiah answered, "This is the LORD's sign to you that the LORD will do what he has promised: Shall the shadow go forward ten steps, or shall it go back ten steps?"

¹⁰"It is a simple matter for the shadow to go forward ten steps," said Hezekiah. "Rather, have it go back ten steps."

¹¹Then the prophet Isaiah called upon the LORD, and the LORD made the shadow go back the ten steps it had gone down on the stairway of Ahaz.

ENVOYS FROM BABYLON

¹²At that time Merodach-Baladan son of Baladan king of Babylon sent Hezekiah letters and a gift, because he had heard of Hezekiah's illness. ¹³Hezekiah received the messengers and showed them all that was in his storehouses—the silver, the gold, the spices and the fine oil—his armory and every-

thing found among his treasures. There was nothing in his palace or in all his kingdom that Hezekiah did not show them.

¹⁴Then Isaiah the prophet went to King Hezekiah and asked, "What did those men say, and where did they come from?"

"From a distant land," Hezekiah replied. "They came from Babylon."

¹⁵The prophet asked, "What did they see in your palace?"

"They saw everything in my palace," Hezekiah said. "There is nothing among my treasures that I did not show them."

¹⁶Then Isaiah said to Hezekiah, "Hear the word of the LORD: ¹⁷The time will surely come when everything in your palace, and all that your fathers have stored up until this day, will be carried off to Babylon. Nothing will be left, says the LORD. ¹⁸And some of your descendants, your own flesh and blood, that will be born to you, will be taken away, and they will become eunuchs in the palace of the king of Babylon."

¹⁹"The word of the LORD you have spoken is good," Hezekiah replied. For he thought, "Will there not be peace and security in my lifetime?"

²⁰As for the other events of Hezekiah's reign, all his achievements and how he made the pool and the tunnel by which he brought water into the city, are they not written in the book of the annals of the kings of Judah? ²¹Hezekiah rested with his fathers. And Manasseh his son succeeded him as king.

MANASSEH KING OF JUDAH

21 Manasseh was twelve years old when he became king, and he reigned in Jerusalem fifty-five years. His mother's name was Hephzibah. ²He did evil in the eyes of the LORD, following the detestable practices of the nations the LORD had driven out before the Israelites. ³He rebuilt the high places his father Hezekiah had destroyed; he also erected altars to Baal and made an Asherah pole, as Ahab king of Israel had done. He bowed down to all the starry hosts and worshiped them. ⁴He built altars in the temple of the LORD, of which the LORD had said, "In Jerusalem I will put my Name." ⁵In both courts of the temple of the LORD, he built altars to all the starry hosts. ⁶He sacrificed his own son in^a the fire, practiced sorcery and divination, and consulted mediums and spiritists. He did much evil in the eyes of the LORD, provoking him to anger.

⁷He took the carved Asherah pole he had made and put it in the temple, of which the LORD had said to David and to his son Solomon, "In this temple and in Jerusalem, which I have chosen out of all the tribes of Israel, I will put my Name forever. ⁸I will not again make the feet of the Israelites wander from the land I gave their forefathers, if only they will be careful to do everything I commanded them and will keep the whole Law that my servant Moses gave them." ⁹But the people did not listen. Manasseh led them astray, so that they did more evil than the nations the LORD had destroyed before the Israelites.

¹⁰The LORD said through his servants the prophets: ¹¹"Manasseh king of Judah has committed these detestable sins. He has done more evil than the Amorites who preceded him and has led Judah into sin with his idols. ¹²Therefore this is what the LORD, the God of Israel, says: I am going to bring such disaster on Jerusalem and Judah that the ears of everyone who hears of it will tingle. ¹³I will stretch out over Jerusalem the measuring line used against Samaria and the plumb line used against the house of Ahab. I will wipe out Jerusalem as one wipes a dish, wiping it and turning it upside down. ¹⁴I will forsake the remnant of my inheritance and hand them over to their enemies. They will be looted and plundered by all their foes, ¹⁵because they have done evil in my eyes and have provoked me to anger from the day their forefathers came out of Egypt until this day."

¹⁶Moreover, Manasseh also shed so much innocent blood that he filled Jerusalem from end to end—besides the sin that he had caused Judah to commit, so that they did evil in the eyes of the LORD.

¹⁷As for the other events of Manasseh's reign, and all he did, including the sin he committed, are they not written in the book of the annals of the kings of Judah? ¹⁸Manasseh rested with his fathers and was buried in his palace garden, the garden of Uzza. And Amon his son succeeded him as king.

AMON KING OF JUDAH

¹⁹Amon was twenty-two years old when he became king, and he reigned in Jerusalem two years. His mother's name was Meshullemeth daughter of Haruz; she was from Jotbah. ²⁰He did evil in the eyes of the LORD, as his father Manasseh had done. ²¹He walked in all the ways of his father; he worshiped

---

^a 6 Or He made his own son pass through

battlelines

» What's Wrong With That? (Partying)

Q: You were at Kevan's party Saturday night? What were you *thinking*?
A: Oh, come on. You're not going to bash me too, are you? There was nothing wrong with me being at that party.

Q: Chris, it was a total booze-fest.
A: OK, there was a lot of alcohol there. But so what? I didn't have any of it. I think that's a positive witness.

Q: Yeah, except for the fact that everybody else got so drunk they won't even remember that you were sober.
A: Look, you're always talking about being more like Jesus. Didn't Jesus hang out with a rough crowd so he could win them over?

Q: So *that* was your goal? You were actually thinking, "I'm going to try to witness to someone tonight"? Give me a break!
A: OK, I went to have fun and to be with everybody. But in my mind, I'm always aware that I'm a Christian and that many other people aren't. I know I have to be on my toes.

Q: OK, tell me this, and be honest. After Saturday night, did you come away a stronger or weaker Christian—in your own eyes and in the eyes of others?
A: I don't think I came away any worse. I didn't get "polluted by sin," if that's what you mean.

Q: But did you come away stronger? I've heard a few Christians at school express concern that you went to that party.
A: Aw, they're just being self-righteous, judgmental morons. Look, I don't see what's so wrong about going to a stupid party. You want me to have a boring life?

Q: That's your problem. You keep asking, "What's wrong with it?" instead of, "What's right with it?"

» What's Right With That?

There's nothing wrong with parties, per se. And Christian are called to reach out to those who don't know Christ. So how do we decide what to do in situations like the one Chris faced? Ask yourself these questions as you look at the following verses:

- Am I strong enough spiritually to withstand possible temptation in this setting (see Mark 14:38)?

- Do I have a Christian partner or friend who will watch my back (see Mark 6:7; Luke 10:1)?

- Will my presence at this event send the wrong message to less mature believers (see 1 Corinthians 8:7–13)?

- Is my conscience crystal clear regarding the "OK-ness" of this situation (see Romans 14:23)?

- What do my most trusted, godly advisers think about my plans (see Proverbs 11:14; 24:6)?

- Is my bottom-line goal truly to honor God (see 1 Corinthians 10:31)?

For more on Christians and partying, go to www.RevolutionBible.com.

the idols his father had worshiped, and bowed down to them. ²²He forsook the LORD, the God of his fathers, and did not walk in the way of the LORD.

²³Amon's officials conspired against him and assassinated the king in his palace. ²⁴Then the people of the land killed all who had plotted against King Amon, and they made Josiah his son king in his place.

²⁵As for the other events of Amon's reign, and what he did, are they not written in the book of the annals of the kings of Judah? ²⁶He was buried in his grave in the garden of Uzza. And Josiah his son succeeded him as king.

THE BOOK OF THE LAW FOUND

22 Josiah was eight years old when he became king, and he reigned in Jerusalem thirty-one years. His mother's name was Jedidah daughter of Adaiah; she was from Bozkath. ²He did what was right in the eyes of the LORD and walked in all the ways of his father David, not turning aside to the right or to the left.

³In the eighteenth year of his reign, King Josiah sent the secretary, Shaphan son of Azaliah, the son of Meshullam, to the temple of the LORD. He said: ⁴"Go up to Hilkiah the high priest and have him get ready the money that has been brought into the temple of the LORD, which the doorkeepers have collected from the people. ⁵Have them entrust it to the men appointed to supervise the work on the temple. And have these men pay the workers who repair the temple of the LORD— ⁶the carpenters, the builders and the masons. Also have them purchase timber and dressed stone to repair the temple. ⁷But they need not account for the money entrusted to them, because they are acting faithfully."

⁸Hilkiah the high priest said to Shaphan the secretary, "I have found the Book of the Law in the temple of the LORD." He gave it to Shaphan, who read it. ⁹Then Shaphan the secretary went to the king and reported to him: "Your officials have paid out the money that was in the temple of the LORD and have entrusted it to the workers and supervisors at the temple." ¹⁰Then Shaphan the secretary informed the king, "Hilkiah the priest has given me a book." And Shaphan read from it in the presence of the king.

¹¹When the king heard the words of the Book of the Law, he tore his robes. ¹²He gave these orders to Hilkiah the priest, Ahikam son of Shaphan, Acbor son of Micaiah, Shaphan the secretary and Asaiah the king's attendant: ¹³"Go and inquire of the LORD for me and for the people and for all Judah about what is written in this book that has been found. Great is the LORD's anger that burns against us because our fathers have not obeyed the words of this book; they have not acted in accordance with all that is written there concerning us."

¹⁴Hilkiah the priest, Ahikam, Acbor, Shaphan and Asaiah went to speak to the prophetess Huldah, who was the wife of Shallum son of Tikvah, the son of Harhas, keeper of the wardrobe. She lived in Jerusalem, in the Second District.

¹⁵She said to them, "This is what the LORD, the God of Israel, says: Tell the man who sent you to me, ¹⁶'This is what the LORD says: I am going to bring disaster on this place and its people, according to everything written in the book the king of Judah has read. ¹⁷Because they have forsaken me and burned incense to other gods and provoked me to anger by all the idols their hands have made,^a my anger will burn against this place and will not be quenched.' ¹⁸Tell the king of Judah, who sent you to inquire of the LORD, 'This is what the LORD, the God of Israel, says concerning the words you heard: ¹⁹Because your heart was responsive and you humbled yourself before the LORD when you heard what I have spoken against this place and its people, that they would become accursed and laid waste, and because you tore your robes and wept in my presence, I have heard you, declares the LORD. ²⁰Therefore I will gather you to your fathers, and you will be buried in peace. Your eyes will not see all the disaster I am going to bring on this place.' "

So they took her answer back to the king.

NOW OR NEVER

2KI 22:8–13

Leaving your Bible on the shelf when you're trying to deal with the junk in your life is like benching your starting quarterback for the Super Bowl.

---

^a 17 Or *by everything they have done*

23

Then the king called together all the elders of Judah and Jerusalem. ²He went up to the temple of the LORD with the men of Judah, the people of Jerusalem, the priests and the prophets—all the people from the least to the greatest. He read in their hearing all the words of the Book of the Covenant, which had been found in the temple of the LORD. ³The king stood by the pillar and renewed the covenant in the presence of the LORD—to follow the LORD and keep his commands, regulations and decrees with all his heart and all his soul, thus confirming the words of the covenant written in this book. Then all the people pledged themselves to the covenant.

NOW OR NEVER

2KI 23:3

When was the last time you renewed your commitment to follow God? If it's been a while, what are you waiting for?

⁴The king ordered Hilkiah the high priest, the priests next in rank and the doorkeepers to remove from the temple of the LORD all the articles made for Baal and Asherah and all the starry hosts. He burned them outside Jerusalem in the fields of the Kidron Valley and took the ashes to Bethel. ⁵He did away with the pagan priests appointed by the kings of Judah to burn incense on the high places of the towns of Judah and on those around Jerusalem—those who burned incense to Baal, to the sun and moon, to the constellations and to all the starry hosts. ⁶He took the Asherah pole from the temple of the LORD to the Kidron Valley outside Jerusalem and burned it there. He ground it to powder and scattered the dust over the graves of the common people. ⁷He also tore down the quarters of the male shrine prostitutes, which were in the temple of the LORD and where women did weaving for Asherah.

⁸Josiah brought all the priests from the towns of Judah and desecrated the high places, from Geba to Beersheba, where the priests had burned incense. He broke down the shrines*ᵃ* at the gates—at the entrance to the Gate of Joshua, the city governor, which is on the left of the city gate. ⁹Although the priests of the high places did not serve at the altar of the LORD in Jerusalem, they ate unleavened bread with their fellow priests.

¹⁰He desecrated Topheth, which was in the Valley of Ben Hinnom, so no one could use it to sacrifice his son or daughter in*ᵇ* the fire to Molech. ¹¹He removed from the entrance to the temple of the LORD the horses that the kings of Judah had dedicated to the sun. They were in the court near the room of an official named Nathan-Melech. Josiah then burned the chariots dedicated to the sun.

¹²He pulled down the altars the kings of Judah had erected on the roof near the upper room of Ahaz, and the altars Manasseh had built in the two courts of the temple of the LORD. He removed them from there, smashed them to pieces and threw the rubble into the Kidron Valley. ¹³The king also desecrated the high places that were east of Jerusalem on the south of the Hill of Corruption—the ones Solomon king of Israel had built for Ashtoreth the vile goddess of the Sidonians, for Chemosh the vile god of Moab, and for Molech*ᶜ* the detestable god of the people of Ammon. ¹⁴Josiah smashed the sacred stones and cut down the Asherah poles and covered the sites with human bones.

¹⁵Even the altar at Bethel, the high place made by Jeroboam son of Nebat, who had caused Israel to sin—even that altar and high place he demolished. He burned the high place and ground it to powder, and burned the Asherah pole also. ¹⁶Then Josiah looked around, and when he saw the tombs that were there on the hillside, he had the bones removed from them and burned on the altar to defile it, in accordance with the word of the LORD proclaimed by the man of God who foretold these things.

¹⁷The king asked, "What is that tombstone I see?"

The men of the city said, "It marks the tomb of the man of God who came from Judah and pronounced against the altar of Bethel the very things you have done to it."

¹⁸"Leave it alone," he said. "Don't let anyone disturb his bones." So they spared his bones and those of the prophet who had come from Samaria.

¹⁹Just as he had done at Bethel, Josiah removed and defiled all the shrines at the high places that the kings of Israel had built in the towns of Samaria that had provoked the LORD to anger. ²⁰Josiah

---

ᵃ 8 Or high places   ᵇ 10 Or to make his son or daughter pass through   ᶜ 13 Hebrew Milcom slaughtered all the priests of those high places on the altars and burned human bones on them. Then he went back to Jerusalem.

²¹The king gave this order to all the people: "Celebrate the Passover to the LORD your God, as it is written in this Book of the Covenant." ²²Not since the days of the judges who led Israel, nor throughout the days of the kings of Israel and the kings of Judah, had any such Passover been observed. ²³But in the eighteenth year of King Josiah, this Passover was celebrated to the LORD in Jerusalem.

²⁴Furthermore, Josiah got rid of the mediums and spiritists, the household gods, the idols and all the other detestable things seen in Judah and Jerusalem. This he did to fulfill the requirements of the law written in the book that Hilkiah the priest had discovered in the temple of the LORD. ²⁵Neither before nor after Josiah was there a king like him who turned to the LORD as he did—with all his heart and with all his soul and with all his strength, in accordance with all the Law of Moses.

²⁶Nevertheless, the LORD did not turn away from the heat of his fierce anger, which burned against Judah because of all that Manasseh had done to provoke him to anger. ²⁷So the LORD said, "I will remove Judah also from my presence as I removed Israel, and I will reject Jerusalem, the city I chose, and this temple, about which I said, 'There shall my Name be.'ᵃ"

²⁸As for the other events of Josiah's reign, and all he did, are they not written in the book of the annals of the kings of Judah?

²⁹While Josiah was king, Pharaoh Neco king of Egypt went up to the Euphrates River to help the king of Assyria. King Josiah marched out to meet him in battle, but Neco faced him and killed him at Megiddo. ³⁰Josiah's servants brought his body in a chariot from Megiddo to Jerusalem and buried him in his own tomb. And the people of the land took Jehoahaz son of Josiah and anointed him and made him king in place of his father.

Enjoying God

Somewhere along the line, the idea of living a God-honoring life got a bad rap. Christians have gotten pegged as uptight prudes who aren't allowed to do anything more exciting than sing hymns. It's time to change that stereotype. God doesn't want his people to look and act like we just came from a funeral; he wants us to *enjoy* him, to *celebrate* the fact that we have a relationship with him and to be able to laugh and have fun as we live for him.

JEHOAHAZ KING OF JUDAH

³¹Jehoahaz was twenty-three years old when he became king, and he reigned in Jerusalem three months. His mother's name was Hamutal daughter of Jeremiah; she was from Libnah. ³²He did evil in the eyes of the LORD, just as his fathers had done. ³³Pharaoh Neco put him in chains at Riblah in the land of Hamathᵇ so that he might not reign in Jerusalem, and he imposed on Judah a levy of a hundred talentsᶜ of silver and a talentᵈ of gold. ³⁴Pharaoh Neco made Eliakim son of Josiah king in place of his father Josiah and changed Eliakim's name to Jehoiakim. But he took Jehoahaz and carried him off to Egypt, and there he died. ³⁵Jehoiakim paid Pharaoh Neco the silver and gold he demanded. In order to do so, he taxed the land and exacted the silver and gold from the people of the land according to their assessments.

JEHOIAKIM KING OF JUDAH

³⁶Jehoiakim was twenty-five years old when he became king, and he reigned in Jerusalem eleven years. His mother's name was Zebidah daughter of Pedaiah; she was from Rumah. ³⁷And he did evil in the eyes of the LORD, just as his fathers had done.

24 During Jehoiakim's reign, Nebuchadnezzar king of Babylon invaded the land, and Jehoiakim became his vassal for three years. But then he changed his mind and rebelled against Nebuchadnezzar. ²The LORD sent Babylonian,ᵉ Aramean, Moabite and Ammonite raiders against him. He sent them to destroy Judah, in accordance with the word of the LORD proclaimed by

---

ᵃ *27* 1 Kings 8:29   ᵇ *33* Hebrew; Septuagint (see also 2 Chron. 36:3) *Neco at Riblah in Hamath removed him*   ᶜ *33* That is, about 3 3/4 tons (about 3.4 metric tons)   ᵈ *33* That is, about 75 pounds (about 34 kilograms)   ᵉ *2* Or *Chaldean* his servants the prophets. ³Surely these things happened to Judah according to the LORD's command, in order to remove them from his presence because of the sins of Manasseh and all he had done, ⁴including the shedding of innocent blood. For he had filled Jerusalem with innocent blood, and the LORD was not willing to forgive.

⁵As for the other events of Jehoiakim's reign, and all he did, are they not written in the book of the annals of the kings of Judah? ⁶Jehoiakim rested with his fathers. And Jehoiachin his son succeeded him as king.

⁷The king of Egypt did not march out from his own country again, because the king of Babylon had taken all his territory, from the Wadi of Egypt to the Euphrates River.

JEHOIACHIN KING OF JUDAH

⁸Jehoiachin was eighteen years old when he became king, and he reigned in Jerusalem three months. His mother's name was Nehushta daughter of Elnathan; she was from Jerusalem. ⁹He did evil in the eyes of the LORD, just as his father had done.

¹⁰At that time the officers of Nebuchadnezzar king of Babylon advanced on Jerusalem and laid siege to it, ¹¹and Nebuchadnezzar himself came up to the city while his officers were besieging it. ¹²Jehoiachin king of Judah, his mother, his attendants, his nobles and his officials all surrendered to him.

In the eighth year of the reign of the king of Babylon, he took Jehoiachin prisoner. ¹³As the LORD had declared, Nebuchadnezzar removed all the treasures from the temple of the LORD and from the royal palace, and took away all the gold articles that Solomon king of Israel had made for the temple of the LORD. ¹⁴He carried into exile all Jerusalem: all the officers and fighting men, and all the craftsmen and artisans—a total of ten thousand. Only the poorest people of the land were left.

¹⁵Nebuchadnezzar took Jehoiachin captive to Babylon. He also took from Jerusalem to Babylon the king's mother, his wives, his officials and the leading men of the land. ¹⁶The king of Babylon also deported to Babylon the entire force of seven thousand fighting men, strong and fit for war, and a thousand craftsmen and artisans. ¹⁷He made Mattaniah, Jehoiachin's uncle, king in his place and changed his name to Zedekiah.

ZEDEKIAH KING OF JUDAH

¹⁸Zedekiah was twenty-one years old when he became king, and he reigned in Jerusalem eleven years. His mother's name was Hamutal daughter of Jeremiah; she was from Libnah. ¹⁹He did evil in the eyes of the LORD, just as Jehoiakim had done. ²⁰It was because of the LORD's anger that all this happened to Jerusalem and Judah, and in the end he thrust them from his presence.

THE FALL OF JERUSALEM

Now Zedekiah rebelled against the king of Babylon.

25 So in the ninth year of Zedekiah's reign, on the tenth day of the tenth month, Nebuchadnezzar king of Babylon marched against Jerusalem with his whole army. He encamped outside the city and built siege works all around it. ²The city was kept under siege until the eleventh year of King Zedekiah. ³By the ninth day of the ⌐fourth⌐ᵃ month the famine in the city had become so severe that there was no food for the people to eat. ⁴Then the city wall was broken through, and the whole army fled at night through the gate between the two walls near the king's garden, though the Babyloniansᵇ were surrounding the city. They fled toward the Arabah,ᶜ ⁵but the Babylonianᵈ army pursued the king and overtook him in the plains of Jericho. All his soldiers were separated from him and scattered, ⁶and he was captured. He was taken to the king of Babylon at Riblah, where sentence was pronounced on him. ⁷They killed the sons of Zedekiah before his eyes. Then they put out his eyes, bound him with bronze shackles and took him to Babylon.

⁸On the seventh day of the fifth month, in the nineteenth year of Nebuchadnezzar king of Babylon, Nebuzaradan commander of the imperial guard, an official of the king of Babylon, came to Jerusalem. ⁹He set fire to the temple of the LORD, the royal palace and all the houses of Jerusalem. Every important building he burned down. ¹⁰The whole Babylonian army, under the commander of the imperial guard, broke down the walls around Jerusalem. ¹¹Nebuzaradan the commander of the guard carried into exile the people who remained in the city, along with the rest of the populace and those who had gone over

---

ᵃ 3 See Jer. 52:6.   ᵇ 4 Or Chaldeans; also in verses 13, 25 and 26   ᶜ 4 Or the Jordan Valley   ᵈ 5 Or Chaldean; also in verses 10 and 24 to the king of Babylon. [12]But the commander left behind some of the poorest people of the land to work the vineyards and fields.

[13]The Babylonians broke up the bronze pillars, the movable stands and the bronze Sea that were at the temple of the LORD and they carried the bronze to Babylon. [14]They also took away the pots, shovels, wick trimmers, dishes and all the bronze articles used in the temple service. [15]The commander of the imperial guard took away the censers and sprinkling bowls—all that were made of pure gold or silver.

[16]The bronze from the two pillars, the Sea and the movable stands, which Solomon had made for the temple of the LORD, was more than could be weighed. [17]Each pillar was twenty-seven feet[a] high. The bronze capital on top of one pillar was four and a half feet[b] high and was decorated with a network and pomegranates of bronze all around. The other pillar, with its network, was similar.

[18]The commander of the guard took as prisoners Seraiah the chief priest, Zephaniah the priest next in rank and the three doorkeepers. [19]Of those still in the city, he took the officer in charge of the fighting men and five royal advisers. He also took the secretary who was chief officer in charge of conscripting the people of the land and sixty of his men who were found in the city. [20]Nebuzaradan the commander took them all and brought them to the king of Babylon at Riblah. [21]There at Riblah, in the land of Hamath, the king had them executed.

So Judah went into captivity, away from her land.

[22]Nebuchadnezzar king of Babylon appointed Gedaliah son of Ahikam, the son of Shaphan, to be over the people he had left behind in Judah. [23]When all the army officers and their men heard that the king of Babylon had appointed Gedaliah as governor, they came to Gedaliah at Mizpah—Ishmael son of Nethaniah, Johanan son of Kareah, Seraiah son of Tanhumeth the Netophathite, Jaazaniah the son of the Maacathite, and their men. [24]Gedaliah took an oath to reassure them and their men. "Do not be afraid of the Babylonian officials," he said. "Settle down in the land and serve the king of Babylon, and it will go well with you."

[25]In the seventh month, however, Ishmael son of Nethaniah, the son of Elishama, who was of royal blood, came with ten men and assassinated Gedaliah and also the men of Judah and the Babylonians who were with him at Mizpah. [26]At this, all the people from the least to the greatest, together with the army officers, fled to Egypt for fear of the Babylonians.

JEHOIACHIN RELEASED

[27]In the thirty-seventh year of the exile of Jehoiachin king of Judah, in the year Evil-Merodach[c] became king of Babylon, he released Jehoiachin from prison on the twenty-seventh day of the twelfth month. [28]He spoke kindly to him and gave him a seat of honor higher than those of the other kings who were with him in Babylon. [29]So Jehoiachin put aside his prison clothes and for the rest of his life ate regularly at the king's table. [30]Day by day the king gave Jehoiachin a regular allowance as long as he lived.

---

[a] 17 Hebrew *eighteen cubits* (about 8.1 meters)   [b] 17 Hebrew *three cubits* (about 1.3 meters)   [c] 27 Also called *Amel-Marduk*

1 CHRONICLES

Author
Ezra the priest

Audience
The people of Israel, specifically those who survived the exile to Babylon

Date
About 430 B.C.

Setting
Parallels the events of 2 Samuel and tells the religious history of Judah and Israel to show the people how they fit into God's plan.

Verse to Remember
And David knew that the LORD had established him as king over Israel and that his kingdom had been highly exalted for the sake of his people Israel (14:2).

Theme to Consider
The book of 1 Chronicles is a family history—including *your* history and spiritual roots—and an account of God's work throughout history to bring people to him.

UNCHANGING TRUTH » Have you ever heard the expression "Pride goes before a fall"? It's another way of saying that arrogance and ego will always bring you down. It's a lesson David learned the hard way. The book of 1 Chronicles tells us that at the height of David's reign over Israel, he decided (apart from God) to take a census of his army (see chapter 21). It seems that David was feeling pretty good about himself and wanted to find out just how many men were under his command. In other words, his ego blew up.

The Lord's judgment came down hard and fast on David. He sent a plague on the people of Israel that lasted for three days and killed more than 70,000 people—all because David let his pride get out of control. God made it clear that all good things come from him and that he will not allow people to capture his glory for themselves.

Don't let pride take you down too. The next time you start to feel a little too good about who you are, how you look or what you've done, do a quick reality check. Think about who's really responsible for the good things in your life. Then, instead of drumming up praise for yourself, give it to God, the giver of all good things.

LIFE LESSONS »

1   If you can't be trusted to remain faithful to God, he will replace you in his plan with someone whose character can be trusted (10:13–14).

2   When God does something for you, thank him in a way that expresses genuine feelings of gratitude (17:16–27).

3   The fact that God disciplines you does not mean he doesn't love you anymore or that he no longer has any use for you (21:27–29).

TO NOAH'S SONS

1 Adam, Seth, Enosh, [2]Kenan, Mahalalel, Jared, [3]Enoch, Methuselah, Lamech, Noah.

[4]The sons of Noah:[a]
Shem, Ham and Japheth.

THE JAPHETHITES

[5]The sons[b] of Japheth:
Gomer, Magog, Madai, Javan, Tubal, Meshech and Tiras.
[6]The sons of Gomer:
Ashkenaz, Riphath[c] and Togarmah.
[7]The sons of Javan:
Elishah, Tarshish, the Kittim and the Rodanim.

---

challenge notes

To: my_son

heavenly_father: you are not just a face in the crowd. I have called you by name, just like the people you see listed in this genealogy. I know exactly who you are, what you're capable of and what I have in store for you.

1CH 1:1

THE HAMITES

[8]The sons of Ham:
Cush, Mizraim,[d] Put and Canaan.
[9]The sons of Cush:
Seba, Havilah, Sabta, Raamah and Sabteca.
The sons of Raamah:
Sheba and Dedan.
[10]Cush was the father[e] of
Nimrod, who grew to be a mighty warrior on earth.
[11]Mizraim was the father of
the Ludites, Anamites, Lehabites, Naphtuhites, [12]Pathrusites, Casluhites (from whom the Philistines came) and Caphtorites.
[13]Canaan was the father of
Sidon his firstborn,[f] and of the Hittites, [14]Jebusites, Amorites, Girgashites, [15]Hivites, Arkites, Sinites, [16]Arvadites, Zemarites and Hamathites.

THE SEMITES

[17]The sons of Shem:
Elam, Asshur, Arphaxad, Lud and Aram.
The sons of Aram:[g]
Uz, Hul, Gether and Meshech.
[18]Arphaxad was the father of Shelah,
and Shelah the father of Eber.
[19]Two sons were born to Eber:
One was named Peleg,[h] because in his time the earth was divided; his brother was named Joktan.
[20]Joktan was the father of
Almodad, Sheleph, Hazarmaveth, Jerah, [21]Hadoram, Uzal, Diklah, [22]Obal,[i] Abimael, Sheba, [23]Ophir, Havilah and Jobab. All these were sons of Joktan.

[24]Shem, Arphaxad,[j] Shelah,
[25]Eber, Peleg, Reu,

---

[a] 4 Septuagint; Hebrew does not have this line   [b] 5 Sons may mean descendants or successors or nations; also in verses 6–10, 17 and 20.   [c] 6 Many Hebrew manuscripts and Vulgate (see also Septuagint and Gen. 10:3); most Hebrew manuscripts Diphath   [d] 8 That is, Egypt; also in verse 11   [e] 10 Father may mean ancestor or predecessor or founder; also in verses 11, 13, 18 and 20.   [f] 13 Or of the Sidonians, the foremost   [g] 17 One Hebrew manuscript and some Septuagint manuscripts (see also Gen. 10:23); most Hebrew manuscripts do not have this line.   [h] 19 Peleg means division.   [i] 22 Some Hebrew manuscripts and Syriac (see also Gen. 10:28); most Hebrew manuscripts Ebal   [j] 24 Hebrew; some Septuagint manuscripts Arphaxad, Cainan (see also note at Gen. 11:10)

battlelines

» The Pied Piper (Leadership)

Q: Where are your followers today?
A: My what?

Q: Your followers. I've noticed that guys seem drawn to you.
A: What are you talking about?

Q: You just seem to have a definite knack for being able to gather people and get them to do . . . whatever.
A: I never thought of myself like that, but maybe you're right.

Q: So why do you think that is?
A: My unbelievable brilliance?

Q: Um . . . no. I think it's because you're a natural leader.
A: Oh yeah, right. If that's true, how come I've never been president of a club or anything?

Q: Well, some people have titles, and others just have a lot of influence. Sometimes the two overlap, but they don't have to. You're also a Christian, right?
A: Yeah. Definitely.

Q: Do you think you could use your natural leadership ability to influence people for Christ?
A: You mean, like, preaching to them or being a minister?

Q: No, not necessarily. I'm talking about encouraging the people you know—the ones who like you and look up to you—to consider what the Bible says about Christ.
A: You really think they'd listen to me?

Q: There's only one way to find out.

» Leadership Redefined

Forget positions and formal titles. The measure of godly leadership is the ability to influence others and point them in the right direction.

You may not have hundreds of friends who consult you on a regular basis. You may not have even a dozen who are willing to listen to what you think. But you probably know at least a handful of folks who respect you and your opinion. When Solomon became king of Israel he humbly prayed, "Give me wisdom and knowledge, that I may lead this people" (2 Chronicles 1:10). That's not a bad prayer for you.

What are you doing with your daily leadership opportunities? Are you influencing your friends for better or for worse?

Learn more about leadership at www.RevolutionBible.com.

²⁶Serug, Nahor, Terah ²⁷and Abram (that is, Abraham).

THE FAMILY OF ABRAHAM

²⁸The sons of Abraham:
Isaac and Ishmael.

DESCENDANTS OF HAGAR

²⁹These were their descendants:
Nebaioth the firstborn of Ishmael, Kedar, Adbeel, Mibsam, ³⁰Mishma, Dumah, Massa, Hadad, Tema, ³¹Jetur, Naphish and Kedemah. These were the sons of Ishmael.

DESCENDANTS OF KETURAH

³²The sons born to Keturah, Abraham's concubine:
Zimran, Jokshan, Medan, Midian, Ishbak and Shuah.
The sons of Jokshan:
Sheba and Dedan.
³³The sons of Midian:
Ephah, Epher, Hanoch, Abida and Eldaah.
All these were descendants of Keturah.

DESCENDANTS OF SARAH

³⁴Abraham was the father of Isaac.
The sons of Isaac:
Esau and Israel.

ESAU'S SONS

³⁵The sons of Esau:
Eliphaz, Reuel, Jeush, Jalam and Korah.
³⁶The sons of Eliphaz:
Teman, Omar, Zepho,[a] Gatam and Kenaz;
by Timna: Amalek.[b]
³⁷The sons of Reuel:
Nahath, Zerah, Shammah and Mizzah.

THE PEOPLE OF SEIR IN EDOM

³⁸The sons of Seir:
Lotan, Shobal, Zibeon, Anah, Dishon, Ezer and Dishan.
³⁹The sons of Lotan:
Hori and Homam. Timna was Lotan's sister.
⁴⁰The sons of Shobal:
Alvan,[c] Manahath, Ebal, Shepho and Onam.
The sons of Zibeon:
Aiah and Anah.
⁴¹The son of Anah:
Dishon.
The sons of Dishon:
Hemdan,[d] Eshban, Ithran and Keran.
⁴²The sons of Ezer:
Bilhan, Zaavan and Akan.[e]
The sons of Dishan[f]:
Uz and Aran.

---

[a] *36* Many Hebrew manuscripts, some Septuagint manuscripts and Syriac (see also Gen. 36:11); most Hebrew manuscripts *Zephi*
[b] *36* Some Septuagint manuscripts (see also Gen. 36:12); Hebrew *Gatam, Kenaz, Timna and Amalek*   [c] *40* Many Hebrew manuscripts and some Septuagint manuscripts (see also Gen. 36:23); most Hebrew manuscripts *Alian*   [d] *41* Many Hebrew manuscripts and some Septuagint manuscripts (see also Gen. 36:26); most Hebrew manuscripts *Hamran*   [e] *42* Many Hebrew and Septuagint manuscripts (see also Gen. 36:27); most Hebrew manuscripts *Zaavan, Jaakan*   [f] *42* Hebrew *Dishon*, a variant of *Dishan*

THE RULERS OF EDOM

⁴³ These were the kings who reigned in Edom before any Israelite king reigned ᵃ:
Bela son of Beor, whose city was named Dinhabah.

⁴⁴ When Bela died, Jobab son of Zerah from Bozrah succeeded him as king.

⁴⁵ When Jobab died, Husham from the land of the Temanites succeeded him as king.

⁴⁶ When Husham died, Hadad son of Bedad, who defeated Midian in the country of Moab, succeeded him as king. His city was named Avith.

⁴⁷ When Hadad died, Samlah from Masrekah succeeded him as king.

⁴⁸ When Samlah died, Shaul from Rehoboth on the river ᵇ succeeded him as king.

⁴⁹ When Shaul died, Baal-Hanan son of Acbor succeeded him as king.

⁵⁰ When Baal-Hanan died, Hadad succeeded him as king. His city was named Pau, ᶜ and his wife's name was Mehetabel daughter of Matred, the daughter of Me-Zahab. ⁵¹ Hadad also died.

The chiefs of Edom were:
Timna, Alvah, Jetheth, ⁵²Oholibamah, Elah, Pinon, ⁵³Kenaz, Teman, Mibzar, ⁵⁴Magdiel and Iram. These were the chiefs of Edom.

ISRAEL'S SONS

2 These were the sons of Israel:
Reuben, Simeon, Levi, Judah, Issachar, Zebulun, ²Dan, Joseph, Benjamin, Naphtali, Gad and Asher.

JUDAH

TO HEZRON'S SONS

³ The sons of Judah:
Er, Onan and Shelah. These three were born to him by a Canaanite woman, the daughter of Shua. Er, Judah's firstborn, was wicked in the LORD's sight; so the LORD put him to death. ⁴Tamar, Judah's daughter-in-law, bore him Perez and Zerah. Judah had five sons in all.

⁵ The sons of Perez:
Hezron and Hamul.

⁶ The sons of Zerah:
Zimri, Ethan, Heman, Calcol and Darda ᵈ—five in all.

⁷ The son of Carmi:
Achar, ᵉ who brought trouble on Israel by violating the ban on taking devoted things. ᶠ

⁸ The son of Ethan:
Azariah.

⁹ The sons born to Hezron were:
Jerahmeel, Ram and Caleb. ᵍ

FROM RAM SON OF HEZRON

¹⁰ Ram was the father of
Amminadab, and Amminadab the father of Nahshon, the leader of the people of Judah. ¹¹Nahshon was the father of Salmon, ʰ Salmon the father of Boaz, ¹²Boaz the father of Obed and Obed the father of Jesse.

¹³ Jesse was the father of

NOW OR NEVER
1 CH 2:3

These aren't just a bunch of names on a list. Every one of these guys has a story to tell about his relationship with God—or his lack of one. Their life experiences can help us grow and avoid mistakes in our own relationships with God, if we pay attention to how they chose to live.

ᵃ *43* Or *before an Israelite king reigned over them* ᵇ *48* Possibly the Euphrates ᶜ *50* Many Hebrew manuscripts, some Septuagint manuscripts, Vulgate and Syriac (see also Gen. 36:39); most Hebrew manuscripts *Pai* ᵈ *6* Many Hebrew manuscripts, some Septuagint manuscripts and Syriac (see also 1 Kings 4:31); most Hebrew manuscripts *Dara* ᵉ *7 Achar* means *trouble*; *Achar* is called *Achan* in Joshua. ᶠ *7* The Hebrew term refers to the irrevocable giving over of things or persons to the LORD, often by totally destroying them. ᵍ *9* Hebrew *Kelubai*, a variant of *Caleb* ʰ *11* Septuagint (see also Ruth 4:21); Hebrew *Salma*

Eliab his firstborn; the second son was Abinadab, the third Shimea, [14]the fourth Nethanel, the fifth Raddai, [15]the sixth Ozem and the seventh David. [16]Their sisters were Zeruiah and Abigail. Zeruiah's three sons were Abishai, Joab and Asahel. [17]Abigail was the mother of Amasa, whose father was Jether the Ishmaelite.

CALEB SON OF HEZRON

[18]Caleb son of Hezron had children by his wife Azubah (and by Jerioth). These were her sons: Jesher, Shobab and Ardon. [19]When Azubah died, Caleb married Ephrath, who bore him Hur. [20]Hur was the father of Uri, and Uri the father of Bezalel.

[21]Later, Hezron lay with the daughter of Makir the father of Gilead (he had married her when he was sixty years old), and she bore him Segub. [22]Segub was the father of Jair, who controlled twenty-three towns in Gilead. [23](But Geshur and Aram captured Havvoth Jair,[a] as well as Kenath with its surrounding settlements—sixty towns.) All these were descendants of Makir the father of Gilead.

[24]After Hezron died in Caleb Ephrathah, Abijah the wife of Hezron bore him Ashhur the father[b] of Tekoa.

JERAHMEEL SON OF HEZRON

[25]The sons of Jerahmeel the firstborn of Hezron:
Ram his firstborn, Bunah, Oren, Ozem and[c] Ahijah. [26]Jerahmeel had another wife, whose name was Atarah; she was the mother of Onam.
[27]The sons of Ram the firstborn of Jerahmeel:
Maaz, Jamin and Eker.
[28]The sons of Onam:
Shammai and Jada.
The sons of Shammai:
Nadab and Abishur.
[29]Abishur's wife was named Abihail, who bore him Ahban and Molid.
[30]The sons of Nadab:
Seled and Appaim. Seled died without children.
[31]The son of Appaim:
Ishi, who was the father of Sheshan.
Sheshan was the father of Ahlai.
[32]The sons of Jada, Shammai's brother:
Jether and Jonathan. Jether died without children.
[33]The sons of Jonathan:
Peleth and Zaza.
These were the descendants of Jerahmeel.
[34]Sheshan had no sons—only daughters.
He had an Egyptian servant named Jarha. [35]Sheshan gave his daughter in marriage to his servant Jarha, and she bore him Attai.
[36]Attai was the father of Nathan,
Nathan the father of Zabad,
[37]Zabad the father of Ephlal,
Ephlal the father of Obed,
[38]Obed the father of Jehu,
Jehu the father of Azariah,
[39]Azariah the father of Helez,
Helez the father of Eleasah,
[40]Eleasah the father of Sismai,
Sismai the father of Shallum,
[41]Shallum the father of Jekamiah,
and Jekamiah the father of Elishama.

---

[a] *23* Or *captured the settlements of Jair*   [b] *24 Father* may mean *civic leader* or *military leader*; also in verses 42, 45, 49–52 and possibly elsewhere.   [c] *25* Or *Oren and Ozem, by*

THE CLANS OF CALEB

⁴²The sons of Caleb the brother of Jerahmeel:

Mesha his firstborn, who was the father of Ziph, and his son Mareshah,ᵃ who was the father of Hebron.

⁴³The sons of Hebron:

Korah, Tappuah, Rekem and Shema. ⁴⁴Shema was the father of Raham, and Raham the father of Jorkeam. Rekem was the father of Shammai. ⁴⁵The son of Shammai was Maon, and Maon was the father of Beth Zur.

⁴⁶Caleb's concubine Ephah was the mother of Haran, Moza and Gazez. Haran was the father of Gazez.

⁴⁷The sons of Jahdai:

Regem, Jotham, Geshan, Pelet, Ephah and Shaaph.

⁴⁸Caleb's concubine Maacah was the mother of Sheber and Tirhanah. ⁴⁹She also gave birth to Shaaph the father of Madmannah and to Sheva the father of Macbenah and Gibea. Caleb's daughter was Acsah. ⁵⁰These were the descendants of Caleb.

The sons of Hur the firstborn of Ephrathah:

Shobal the father of Kiriath Jearim, ⁵¹Salma the father of Bethlehem, and Hareph the father of Beth Gader.

⁵²The descendants of Shobal the father of Kiriath Jearim were:

Haroeh, half the Manahathites, ⁵³and the clans of Kiriath Jearim: the Ithrites, Puthites, Shumathites and Mishraites. From these descended the Zorathites and Eshtaolites.

⁵⁴The descendants of Salma:

Bethlehem, the Netophathites, Atroth Beth Joab, half the Manahathites, the Zorites, ⁵⁵and the clans of scribesᵇ who lived at Jabez: the Tirathites, Shimeathites and Sucathites. These are the Kenites who came from Hammath, the father of the house of Recab.ᶜ

THE SONS OF DAVID

3 These were the sons of David born to him in Hebron:

The firstborn was Amnon the son of Ahinoam of Jezreel;

the second, Daniel the son of Abigail of Carmel;

²the third, Absalom the son of Maacah daughter of Talmai king of Geshur;

the fourth, Adonijah the son of Haggith;

³the fifth, Shephatiah the son of Abital;

and the sixth, Ithream, by his wife Eglah.

⁴These six were born to David in Hebron, where he reigned seven years and six months. David reigned in Jerusalem thirty-three years, ⁵and these were the children born to him there:

Shammua,ᵈ Shobab, Nathan and Solomon. These four were by Bathshebaᵉ daughter of Ammiel. ⁶There were also Ibhar, Elishua,ᶠ Eliphelet, ⁷Nogah, Nepheg, Japhia, ⁸Elishama, Eliada and Eliphelet—nine in all. ⁹All these were the sons of David, besides his sons by his concubines. And Tamar was their sister.

THE KINGS OF JUDAH

¹⁰Solomon's son was Rehoboam,

Abijah his son,

Asa his son,

Jehoshaphat his son,

¹¹Jehoramᵍ his son,

Ahaziah his son,

Joash his son,

¹²Amaziah his son,

Azariah his son,

ᵃ *42* The meaning of the Hebrew for this phrase is uncertain.   ᵇ *55* Or *of the Sopherites*   ᶜ *55* Or *father of Beth Recab*   ᵈ *5* Hebrew *Shimea,* a variant of *Shammua*   ᵉ *5* One Hebrew manuscript and Vulgate (see also Septuagint and 2 Samuel 11:3); most Hebrew manuscripts *Bathshua*   ᶠ *6* Two Hebrew manuscripts (see also 2 Samuel 5:15 and 1 Chron. 14:5); most Hebrew manuscripts *Elishama*   ᵍ *11* Hebrew *Joram,* a variant of *Jehoram*

Jotham his son,
¹³ Ahaz his son,
Hezekiah his son,
Manasseh his son,
¹⁴ Amon his son,
Josiah his son.
¹⁵ The sons of Josiah:
Johanan the firstborn,
Jehoiakim the second son,
Zedekiah the third,
Shallum the fourth.
¹⁶ The successors of Jehoiakim:
Jehoiachin[a] his son,
and Zedekiah.

THE ROYAL LINE AFTER THE EXILE

¹⁷ The descendants of Jehoiachin the captive:
Shealtiel his son, ¹⁸Malkiram, Pedaiah, Shenazzar, Jekamiah, Hoshama and Nedabiah.
¹⁹ The sons of Pedaiah:
Zerubbabel and Shimei.
The sons of Zerubbabel:
Meshullam and Hananiah.
Shelomith was their sister.
²⁰ There were also five others:
Hashubah, Ohel, Berekiah, Hasadiah and Jushab-Hesed.
²¹ The descendants of Hananiah:
Pelatiah and Jeshaiah, and the sons of Rephaiah, of Arnan, of Obadiah and of Shecaniah.
²² The descendants of Shecaniah:
Shemaiah and his sons:
Hattush, Igal, Bariah, Neariah and Shaphat—six in all.
²³ The sons of Neariah:
Elioenai, Hizkiah and Azrikam—three in all.
²⁴ The sons of Elioenai:
Hodaviah, Eliashib, Pelaiah, Akkub, Johanan, Delaiah and Anani—seven in all.

OTHER CLANS OF JUDAH

4 The descendants of Judah:
Perez, Hezron, Carmi, Hur and Shobal.
² Reaiah son of Shobal was the father of Jahath, and Jahath the father of Ahumai and Lahad. These were the clans of the Zorathites.
³ These were the sons[b] of Etam:
Jezreel, Ishma and Idbash. Their sister was named Hazzelelponi. ⁴Penuel was the father of Gedor, and Ezer the father of Hushah.
These were the descendants of Hur, the firstborn of Ephrathah and father[c] of Bethlehem.
⁵ Ashhur the father of Tekoa had two wives, Helah and Naarah.
⁶ Naarah bore him Ahuzzam, Hepher, Temeni and Haahashtari. These were the descendants of Naarah.
⁷ The sons of Helah:
Zereth, Zohar, Ethnan, ⁸and Koz, who was the father of Anub and Hazzobebah and of the clans of Aharhel son of Harum.

⁹Jabez was more honorable than his brothers. His mother had named him Jabez,[d] saying, "I gave birth to him in pain." ¹⁰Jabez cried out to the God of Israel, "Oh, that you would bless me and enlarge

^a 16 Hebrew Jeconiah, a variant of Jehoiachin; also in verse 17   ^b 3 Some Septuagint manuscripts (see also Vulgate); Hebrew father
^c 4 Father may mean civic leader or military leader; also in verses 12, 14, 17, 18 and possibly elsewhere.   ^d 9 Jabez sounds like the Hebrew for pain.

my territory! Let your hand be with me, and keep me from harm so that I will be free from pain." And God granted his request.

¹¹Kelub, Shuhah's brother, was the father of Mehir, who was the father of Eshton. ¹²Eshton was the father of Beth Rapha, Paseah and Tehinnah the father of Ir Nahash.ᵃ These were the men of Recah.

¹³The sons of Kenaz:
Othniel and Seraiah.
The sons of Othniel:
Hathath and Meonothai.ᵇ ¹⁴Meonothai was the father of Ophrah.
Seraiah was the father of Joab,
the father of Ge Harashim.ᶜ It was called this because its people were craftsmen.
¹⁵The sons of Caleb son of Jephunneh:
Iru, Elah and Naam.
The son of Elah:
Kenaz.
¹⁶The sons of Jehallelel:
Ziph, Ziphah, Tiria and Asarel.
¹⁷The sons of Ezrah:
Jether, Mered, Epher and Jalon. One of Mered's wives gave birth to Miriam, Shammai and Ishbah the father of Eshtemoa. ¹⁸(His Judean wife gave birth to Jered the father of Gedor, Heber the father of Soco, and Jekuthiel the father of Zanoah.) These were the children of Pharaoh's daughter Bithiah, whom Mered had married.
¹⁹The sons of Hodiah's wife, the sister of Naham:
the father of Keilah the Garmite, and Eshtemoa the Maacathite.
²⁰The sons of Shimon:
Amnon, Rinnah, Ben-Hanan and Tilon.
The descendants of Ishi:
Zoheth and Ben-Zoheth.
²¹The sons of Shelah son of Judah:
Er the father of Lecah, Laadah the father of Mareshah and the clans of the linen workers at Beth Ashbea, ²²Jokim, the men of Cozeba, and Joash and Saraph, who ruled in Moab and Jashubi Lehem. (These records are from ancient times.) ²³They were the potters who lived at Netaim and Gederah; they stayed there and worked for the king.

SIMEON

²⁴The descendants of Simeon:
Nemuel, Jamin, Jarib, Zerah and Shaul;
²⁵Shallum was Shaul's son, Mibsam his son and Mishma his son.
²⁶The descendants of Mishma:
Hammuel his son, Zaccur his son and Shimei his son.
²⁷Shimei had sixteen sons and six daughters, but his brothers did not have many children; so their entire clan did not become as numerous as the people of Judah. ²⁸They lived in Beersheba, Moladah, Hazar Shual, ²⁹Bilhah, Ezem, Tolad, ³⁰Bethuel, Hormah, Ziklag, ³¹Beth Marcaboth, Hazar Susim, Beth Biri and Shaaraim. These were their towns until the reign of David. ³²Their surrounding villages were

Understanding the Importance of Prayer

Here's some Bible trivia for you: First Chronicles 4:9–10 is the only passage in the Bible that mentions Jabez. All we know about the guy is that he was "more honorable than his brothers" and that he asked God to meet his needs. Obviously, as far as God is concerned, that's all we *need* to know about Jabez . . . that and the fact that his prayer was answered. The lesson seems pretty obvious: No matter what our needs are, God is concerned about them. And not only is he interested in our needs, he's ready to take care of them.

ᵃ *12* Or *of the city of Nahash* ᵇ *13* Some Septuagint manuscripts and Vulgate; Hebrew does not have *and Meonothai.*
ᶜ *14* Ge Harashim means *valley of craftsmen.*

Etam, Ain, Rimmon, Token and Ashan—five towns— ³³and all the villages around these towns as far as Baalath.ᵃ These were their settlements. And they kept a genealogical record.

³⁴Meshobab, Jamlech, Joshah son of Amaziah, ³⁵Joel, Jehu son of Joshibiah, the son of Seraiah, the son of Asiel, ³⁶also Elioenai, Jaakobah, Jeshohaiah, Asaiah, Adiel, Jesimiel, Benaiah, ³⁷and Ziza son of Shiphi, the son of Allon, the son of Jedaiah, the son of Shimri, the son of Shemaiah.

³⁸The men listed above by name were leaders of their clans. Their families increased greatly, ³⁹and they went to the outskirts of Gedor to the east of the valley in search of pasture for their flocks. ⁴⁰They found rich, good pasture, and the land was spacious, peaceful and quiet. Some Hamites had lived there formerly.

⁴¹The men whose names were listed came in the days of Hezekiah king of Judah. They attacked the Hamites in their dwellings and also the Meunites who were there and completely destroyedᵇ them, as is evident to this day. Then they settled in their place, because there was pasture for their flocks. ⁴²And five hundred of these Simeonites, led by Pelatiah, Neariah, Rephaiah and Uzziel, the sons of Ishi, invaded the hill country of Seir. ⁴³They killed the remaining Amalekites who had escaped, and they have lived there to this day.

REUBEN

5 The sons of Reuben the firstborn of Israel (he was the firstborn, but when he defiled his father's marriage bed, his rights as firstborn were given to the sons of Joseph son of Israel; so he could not be listed in the genealogical record in accordance with his birthright, ²and though Judah was the strongest of his brothers and a ruler came from him, the rights of the firstborn belonged to Joseph)— ³the sons of Reuben the firstborn of Israel:

Hanoch, Pallu, Hezron and Carmi.
⁴The descendants of Joel:
Shemaiah his son, Gog his son,
Shimei his son, ⁵Micah his son,
Reaiah his son, Baal his son,
⁶and Beerah his son, whom Tiglath-Pileserᶜ king of Assyria took into exile. Beerah was a leader of the Reubenites.
⁷Their relatives by clans, listed according to their genealogical records:
Jeiel the chief, Zechariah, ⁸and Bela son of Azaz, the son of Shema, the son of Joel. They settled in the area from Aroer to Nebo and Baal Meon. ⁹To the east they occupied the land up to the edge of the desert that extends to the Euphrates River, because their livestock had increased in Gilead.
¹⁰During Saul's reign they waged war against the Hagrites, who were defeated at their hands; they occupied the dwellings of the Hagrites throughout the entire region east of Gilead.

GAD

¹¹The Gadites lived next to them in Bashan, as far as Salecah:
¹²Joel was the chief, Shapham the second, then Janai and Shaphat, in Bashan.
¹³Their relatives, by families, were:
Michael, Meshullam, Sheba, Jorai, Jacan, Zia and Eber—seven in all.
¹⁴These were the sons of Abihail son of Huri, the son of Jaroah, the son of Gilead, the son of Michael, the son of Jeshishai, the son of Jahdo, the son of Buz.
¹⁵Ahi son of Abdiel, the son of Guni, was head of their family.
¹⁶The Gadites lived in Gilead, in Bashan and its outlying villages, and on all the pasturelands of Sharon as far as they extended.
¹⁷All these were entered in the genealogical records during the reigns of Jotham king of Judah and Jeroboam king of Israel.

¹⁸The Reubenites, the Gadites and the half-tribe of Manasseh had 44,760 men ready for military ser-

---

ᵃ *33* Some Septuagint manuscripts (see also Joshua 19:8); Hebrew *Baal*   ᵇ *41* The Hebrew term refers to the irrevocable giving over of things or persons to the LORD, often by totally destroying them.   ᶜ *6* Hebrew *Tilgath-Pilneser,* a variant of *Tiglath-Pileser*; also in verse 26 vice—able-bodied men who could handle shield and sword, who could use a bow, and who were trained for battle. ¹⁹They waged war against the Hagrites, Jetur, Naphish and Nodab. ²⁰They were helped in fighting them, and God handed the Hagrites and all their allies over to them, because they cried out to him during the battle. He answered their prayers, because they trusted in him. ²¹They seized the livestock of the Hagrites—fifty thousand camels, two hundred fifty thousand sheep and two thousand donkeys. They also took one hundred thousand people captive, ²²and many others fell slain, because the battle was God's. And they occupied the land until the exile.

THE HALF-TRIBE OF MANASSEH

²³The people of the half-tribe of Manasseh were numerous; they settled in the land from Bashan to Baal Hermon, that is, to Senir (Mount Hermon).

²⁴These were the heads of their families: Epher, Ishi, Eliel, Azriel, Jeremiah, Hodaviah and Jahdiel. They were brave warriors, famous men, and heads of their families. ²⁵But they were unfaithful to the God of their fathers and prostituted themselves to the gods of the peoples of the land, whom God had destroyed before them. ²⁶So the God of Israel stirred up the spirit of Pul king of Assyria (that is, Tiglath-Pileser king of Assyria), who took the Reubenites, the Gadites and the half-tribe of Manasseh into exile. He took them to Halah, Habor, Hara and the river of Gozan, where they are to this day.

LEVI

6 The sons of Levi:
Gershon, Kohath and Merari.

²The sons of Kohath:
Amram, Izhar, Hebron and Uzziel.

³The children of Amram:
Aaron, Moses and Miriam.

The sons of Aaron:
Nadab, Abihu, Eleazar and Ithamar.

⁴Eleazar was the father of Phinehas,
Phinehas the father of Abishua,

⁵Abishua the father of Bukki,
Bukki the father of Uzzi,

⁶Uzzi the father of Zerahiah,
Zerahiah the father of Meraioth,

⁷Meraioth the father of Amariah,
Amariah the father of Ahitub,

⁸Ahitub the father of Zadok,
Zadok the father of Ahimaaz,

⁹Ahimaaz the father of Azariah,
Azariah the father of Johanan,

¹⁰Johanan the father of Azariah (it was he who served as priest in the temple Solomon built in Jerusalem),

¹¹Azariah the father of Amariah,
Amariah the father of Ahitub,

¹²Ahitub the father of Zadok,
Zadok the father of Shallum,

¹³Shallum the father of Hilkiah,
Hilkiah the father of Azariah,

¹⁴Azariah the father of Seraiah,
and Seraiah the father of Jehozadak.

¹⁵Jehozadak was deported when the LORD sent Judah and Jerusalem into exile by the hand of Nebuchadnezzar.

¹⁶The sons of Levi:
Gershon,ᵃ Kohath and Merari.

Understanding the Importance of Faith

The world is a dangerous place. Since sin was first introduced to the world, there have always been predators, those who take advantage of weaker people. This was true for the Israelites, who struggled against the conquests of the Assyrians, and it's true for us today in a variety of settings. God extends to us the same offer for help that he gave to the Israelites: "If you will be faithful as my people, I will be your God and protect you." But Israel refused, so they suffered the abuse of many enemy nations. Will you choose to be faithful to God or will you face the enemy alone?

ᵃ *16* Hebrew *Gershom*, a variant of *Gershon*; also in verses 17, 20, 43, 62 and 71

17 These are the names of the sons of Gershon:
    Libni and Shimei.
18 The sons of Kohath:
    Amram, Izhar, Hebron and Uzziel.
19 The sons of Merari:
    Mahli and Mushi.
These are the clans of the Levites listed according to their fathers:
20 Of Gershon:
    Libni his son, Jehath his son,
    Zimmah his son, 21 Joah his son,
    Iddo his son, Zerah his son
    and Jeatherai his son.
22 The descendants of Kohath:
    Amminadab his son, Korah his son,
    Assir his son, 23 Elkanah his son,
    Ebiasaph his son, Assir his son,
    24 Tahath his son, Uriel his son,
    Uzziah his son and Shaul his son.
25 The descendants of Elkanah:
    Amasai, Ahimoth,
    26 Elkanah his son,ᵃ Zophai his son,
    Nahath his son, 27 Eliab his son,
    Jeroham his son, Elkanah his son
    and Samuel his son.ᵇ
28 The sons of Samuel:
    Joelᶜ the firstborn
    and Abijah the second son.
29 The descendants of Merari:
    Mahli, Libni his son,
    Shimei his son, Uzzah his son,
    30 Shimea his son, Haggiah his son
    and Asaiah his son.

THE TEMPLE MUSICIANS

31 These are the men David put in charge of the music in the house of the LORD after the ark came to rest there. 32 They ministered with music before the tabernacle, the Tent of Meeting, until Solomon built the temple of the LORD in Jerusalem. They performed their duties according to the regulations laid down for them.

33 Here are the men who served, together with their sons:
From the Kohathites:
    Heman, the musician,
    the son of Joel, the son of Samuel,
    34 the son of Elkanah, the son of Jeroham,
    the son of Eliel, the son of Toah,
    35 the son of Zuph, the son of Elkanah,
    the son of Mahath, the son of Amasai,
    36 the son of Elkanah, the son of Joel,
    the son of Azariah, the son of Zephaniah,
    37 the son of Tahath, the son of Assir,
    the son of Ebiasaph, the son of Korah,
    38 the son of Izhar, the son of Kohath,
    the son of Levi, the son of Israel;

ᵃ 26 Some Hebrew manuscripts, Septuagint and Syriac; most Hebrew manuscripts Ahimoth ²⁶and Elkanah. The sons of Elkanah:
ᵇ 27 Some Septuagint manuscripts (see also 1 Samuel 1:19,20 and 1 Chron. 6:33,34); Hebrew does not have and Samuel his son.
ᶜ 28 Some Septuagint manuscripts and Syriac (see also 1 Samuel 8:2 and 1 Chron. 6:33); Hebrew does not have Joel.

³⁹and Heman's associate Asaph, who served at his right hand:
Asaph son of Berekiah, the son of Shimea,
⁴⁰the son of Michael, the son of Baaseiah,^a
the son of Malkijah, ⁴¹the son of Ethni,
the son of Zerah, the son of Adaiah,
⁴²the son of Ethan, the son of Zimmah,
the son of Shimei, ⁴³the son of Jahath,
the son of Gershon, the son of Levi;
⁴⁴and from their associates, the Merarites, at his left hand:
Ethan son of Kishi, the son of Abdi,
the son of Malluch, ⁴⁵the son of Hashabiah,
the son of Amaziah, the son of Hilkiah,
⁴⁶the son of Amzi, the son of Bani,
the son of Shemer, ⁴⁷the son of Mahli,
the son of Mushi, the son of Merari,
the son of Levi.

⁴⁸Their fellow Levites were assigned to all the other duties of the tabernacle, the house of God. ⁴⁹But Aaron and his descendants were the ones who presented offerings on the altar of burnt offering and on the altar of incense in connection with all that was done in the Most Holy Place, making atonement for Israel, in accordance with all that Moses the servant of God had commanded.

⁵⁰These were the descendants of Aaron:
Eleazar his son, Phinehas his son,
Abishua his son, ⁵¹Bukki his son,
Uzzi his son, Zerahiah his son,
⁵²Meraioth his son, Amariah his son,
Ahitub his son, ⁵³Zadok his son
and Ahimaaz his son.

⁵⁴These were the locations of their settlements allotted as their territory (they were assigned to the descendants of Aaron who were from the Kohathite clan, because the first lot was for them):

⁵⁵They were given Hebron in Judah with its surrounding pasturelands. ⁵⁶But the fields and villages around the city were given to Caleb son of Jephunneh.

⁵⁷So the descendants of Aaron were given Hebron (a city of refuge), and Libnah,^b Jattir, Eshtemoa, ⁵⁸Hilen, Debir, ⁵⁹Ashan, Juttah^c and Beth Shemesh, together with their pasturelands. ⁶⁰And from the tribe of Benjamin they were given Gibeon,^d Geba, Alemeth and Anathoth, together with their pasturelands.

These towns, which were distributed among the Kohathite clans, were thirteen in all.

⁶¹The rest of Kohath's descendants were allotted ten towns from the clans of half the tribe of Manasseh.

⁶²The descendants of Gershon, clan by clan, were allotted thirteen towns from the tribes of Issachar, Asher and Naphtali, and from the part of the tribe of Manasseh that is in Bashan.

⁶³The descendants of Merari, clan by clan, were allotted twelve towns from the tribes of Reuben, Gad and Zebulun.

⁶⁴So the Israelites gave the Levites these towns and their pasturelands. ⁶⁵From the tribes of Judah, Simeon and Benjamin they allotted the previously named towns.

⁶⁶Some of the Kohathite clans were given as their territory towns from the tribe of Ephraim.

⁶⁷In the hill country of Ephraim they were given Shechem (a city of refuge), and Gezer,^e ⁶⁸Jokmeam, Beth Horon, ⁶⁹Aijalon and Gath Rimmon, together with their pasturelands.

now or never
1CH 6:48-49

Do you feel as though you have a "duty" in your church—some area of service? If so, what is it? If not, do you think you should find one?

---

^a 40 Most Hebrew manuscripts; some Hebrew manuscripts, one Septuagint manuscript and Syriac *Maaseiah*   ^b 57 See Joshua 21:13; Hebrew *given the cities of refuge: Hebron, Libnah.*   ^c 59 Syriac (see also Septuagint and Joshua 21:16); Hebrew does not have *Juttah.*   ^d 60 See Joshua 21:17; Hebrew does not have *Gibeon.*   ^e 67 See Joshua 21:21; Hebrew *given the cities of refuge: Shechem, Gezer.*

[70]And from half the tribe of Manasseh the Israelites gave Aner and Bileam, together with their pasturelands, to the rest of the Kohathite clans.

[71]The Gershonites received the following:

From the clan of the half-tribe of Manasseh

they received Golan in Bashan and also Ashtaroth, together with their pasturelands;

[72]from the tribe of Issachar

they received Kedesh, Daberath, [73]Ramoth and Anem, together with their pasturelands;

[74]from the tribe of Asher

they received Mashal, Abdon, [75]Hukok and Rehob, together with their pasturelands;

[76]and from the tribe of Naphtali

they received Kedesh in Galilee, Hammon and Kiriathaim, together with their pasturelands.

[77]The Merarites (the rest of the Levites) received the following:

From the tribe of Zebulun

they received Jokneam, Kartah,[a] Rimmono and Tabor, together with their pasturelands;

[78]from the tribe of Reuben across the Jordan east of Jericho

they received Bezer in the desert, Jahzah, [79]Kedemoth and Mephaath, together with their pasturelands;

[80]and from the tribe of Gad

they received Ramoth in Gilead, Mahanaim, [81]Heshbon and Jazer, together with their pasturelands.

ISSACHAR

7 The sons of Issachar:

Tola, Puah, Jashub and Shimron—four in all.

[2]The sons of Tola:

Uzzi, Rephaiah, Jeriel, Jahmai, Ibsam and Samuel—heads of their families. During the reign of David, the descendants of Tola listed as fighting men in their genealogy numbered 22,600.

[3]The son of Uzzi:

Izrahiah.

The sons of Izrahiah:

Michael, Obadiah, Joel and Isshiah. All five of them were chiefs. [4]According to their family genealogy, they had 36,000 men ready for battle, for they had many wives and children.

[5]The relatives who were fighting men belonging to all the clans of Issachar, as listed in their genealogy, were 87,000 in all.

BENJAMIN

[6]Three sons of Benjamin:

Bela, Beker and Jediael.

[7]The sons of Bela:

Ezbon, Uzzi, Uzziel, Jerimoth and Iri, heads of families—five in all. Their genealogical record listed 22,034 fighting men.

[8]The sons of Beker:

Zemirah, Joash, Eliezer, Elioenai, Omri, Jeremoth, Abijah, Anathoth and Alemeth. All these were the sons of Beker. [9]Their genealogical record listed the heads of families and 20,200 fighting men.

[10]The son of Jediael:

Bilhan.

The sons of Bilhan:

Jeush, Benjamin, Ehud, Kenaanah, Zethan, Tarshish and Ahishahar. [11]All these sons of Jediael were heads of families. There were 17,200 fighting men ready to go out to war.

[12]The Shuppites and Huppites were the descendants of Ir, and the Hushites the descendants of Aher.

---

[a] 77 See Septuagint and Joshua 21:34; Hebrew does not have *Jokneam, Kartah.*

NAPHTALI

[13] The sons of Naphtali:

Jahziel, Guni, Jezer and Shillem[a]—the descendants of Bilhah.

MANASSEH

[14] The descendants of Manasseh:

Asriel was his descendant through his Aramean concubine. She gave birth to Makir the father of Gilead. [15] Makir took a wife from among the Huppites and Shuppites. His sister's name was Maacah. Another descendant was named Zelophehad, who had only daughters.

[16] Makir's wife Maacah gave birth to a son and named him Peresh. His brother was named Sheresh, and his sons were Ulam and Rakem.

[17] The son of Ulam:

Bedan.

These were the sons of Gilead son of Makir, the son of Manasseh. [18] His sister Hammoleketh gave birth to Ishhod, Abiezer and Mahlah.

[19] The sons of Shemida were:

Ahian, Shechem, Likhi and Aniam.

EPHRAIM

[20] The descendants of Ephraim:

Shuthelah, Bered his son,

Tahath his son, Eleadah his son,

Tahath his son, [21] Zabad his son

and Shuthelah his son.

Ezer and Elead were killed by the native-born men of Gath, when they went down to seize their livestock. [22] Their father Ephraim mourned for them many days, and his relatives came to comfort him. [23] Then he lay with his wife again, and she became pregnant and gave birth to a son. He named him Beriah,[b] because there had been misfortune in his family. [24] His daughter was Sheerah, who built Lower and Upper Beth Horon as well as Uzzen Sheerah.

[25] Rephah was his son, Resheph his son,[c]

Telah his son, Tahan his son,

[26] Ladan his son, Ammihud his son,

Elishama his son, [27] Nun his son

and Joshua his son.

[28] Their lands and settlements included Bethel and its surrounding villages, Naaran to the east, Gezer and its villages to the west, and Shechem and its villages all the way to Ayyah and its villages. [29] Along the borders of Manasseh were Beth Shan, Taanach, Megiddo and Dor, together with their villages. The descendants of Joseph son of Israel lived in these towns.

ASHER

[30] The sons of Asher:

Imnah, Ishvah, Ishvi and Beriah. Their sister was Serah.

[31] The sons of Beriah:

Heber and Malkiel, who was the father of Birzaith.

[32] Heber was the father of Japhlet, Shomer and Hotham and of their sister Shua.

[33] The sons of Japhlet:

Pasach, Bimhal and Ashvath.

These were Japhlet's sons.

[34] The sons of Shomer:

Ahi, Rohgah,[d] Hubbah and Aram.

[35] The sons of his brother Helem:

Zophah, Imna, Shelesh and Amal.

[36] The sons of Zophah:

[a] 13 Some Hebrew and Septuagint manuscripts (see also Gen. 46:24 and Num. 26:49); most Hebrew manuscripts *Shallum*   [b] 23 *Beriah* sounds like the Hebrew for *misfortune*.   [c] 25 Some Septuagint manuscripts; Hebrew does not have *his son*.   [d] 34 Or *of his brother Shomer: Rohgah*

Suah, Harnepher, Shual, Beri, Imrah, ³⁷Bezer, Hod, Shamma, Shilshah, Ithran ᵃ and Beera.

³⁸The sons of Jether:

Jephunneh, Pispah and Ara.

³⁹The sons of Ulla:

Arah, Hanniel and Rizia.

⁴⁰All these were descendants of Asher—heads of families, choice men, brave warriors and outstanding leaders. The number of men ready for battle, as listed in their genealogy, was 26,000.

THE GENEALOGY OF SAUL THE BENJAMITE

8 Benjamin was the father of Bela his firstborn,
Ashbel the second son, Aharah the third,
²Nohah the fourth and Rapha the fifth.

³The sons of Bela were:

Addar, Gera, Abihud, ᵇ ⁴Abishua, Naaman, Ahoah, ⁵Gera, Shephuphan and Huram.

⁶These were the descendants of Ehud, who were heads of families of those living in Geba and were deported to Manahath:

⁷Naaman, Ahijah, and Gera, who deported them and who was the father of Uzza and Ahihud.

⁸Sons were born to Shaharaim in Moab after he had divorced his wives Hushim and Baara. ⁹By his wife Hodesh he had Jobab, Zibia, Mesha, Malcam, ¹⁰Jeuz, Sakia and Mirmah. These were his sons, heads of families. ¹¹By Hushim he had Abitub and Elpaal.

¹²The sons of Elpaal:

Eber, Misham, Shemed (who built Ono and Lod with its surrounding villages), ¹³and Beriah and Shema, who were heads of families of those living in Aijalon and who drove out the inhabitants of Gath.

¹⁴Ahio, Shashak, Jeremoth, ¹⁵Zebadiah, Arad, Eder, ¹⁶Michael, Ishpah and Joha were the sons of Beriah.

¹⁷Zebadiah, Meshullam, Hizki, Heber, ¹⁸Ishmerai, Izliah and Jobab were the sons of Elpaal.

¹⁹Jakim, Zicri, Zabdi, ²⁰Elienai, Zillethai, Eliel, ²¹Adaiah, Beraiah and Shimrath were the sons of Shimei.

²²Ishpan, Eber, Eliel, ²³Abdon, Zicri, Hanan, ²⁴Hananiah, Elam, Anthothijah, ²⁵Iphdeiah and Penuel were the sons of Shashak.

²⁶Shamsherai, Shehariah, Athaliah, ²⁷Jaareshiah, Elijah and Zicri were the sons of Jeroham.

²⁸All these were heads of families, chiefs as listed in their genealogy, and they lived in Jerusalem.

²⁹Jeiel ᶜ the father ᵈ of Gibeon lived in Gibeon.

His wife's name was Maacah, ³⁰and his firstborn son was Abdon, followed by Zur, Kish, Baal, Ner, ᵉ Nadab, ³¹Gedor, Ahio, Zeker ³²and Mikloth, who was the father of Shimeah. They too lived near their relatives in Jerusalem.

³³Ner was the father of Kish, Kish the father of Saul, and Saul the father of Jonathan, Malki-Shua, Abinadab and Esh-Baal. ᶠ

³⁴The son of Jonathan:

Merib-Baal, ᵍ who was the father of Micah.

³⁵The sons of Micah:

Pithon, Melech, Tarea and Ahaz.

³⁶Ahaz was the father of Jehoaddah, Jehoaddah was the father of Alemeth, Azmaveth and Zimri, and Zimri was the father of Moza. ³⁷Moza was the father of Binea; Raphah was his son, Eleasah his son and Azel his son.

³⁸Azel had six sons, and these were their names:

Azrikam, Bokeru, Ishmael, Sheariah, Obadiah and Hanan. All these were the sons of Azel.

³⁹The sons of his brother Eshek:

Ulam his firstborn, Jeush the second son and Eliphelet the third. ⁴⁰The sons of Ulam were brave warriors who could handle the bow. They had many sons and grandsons—150 in all.

All these were the descendants of Benjamin.

ᵃ 37 Possibly a variant of *Jether*   ᵇ 3 Or *Gera the father of Ehud*   ᶜ 29 Some Septuagint manuscripts (see also 1 Chron. 9:35); Hebrew does not have *Jeiel*.   ᵈ 29 *Father* may mean *civic leader* or *military leader.*   ᵉ 30 Some Septuagint manuscripts (see also 1 Chron. 9:36); Hebrew does not have *Ner.*   ᶠ 33 Also known as *Ish-Bosheth*   ᵍ 34 Also known as *Mephibosheth*

battlelines

» Check Me Out (Flirting)

Q: Did I just see you talking to Ashley?
A: You sure did. And I'm telling you, I think I'm in love!

Q: In love?
A: You heard it here first.

Q: After one conversation, you've decided this girl is "the one"?
A: Maybe.

Q: Didn't you say the exact same thing last month about Sarah?
A: Well—

Q: And before that it was Kari. And before that—
A: OK, OK. So I get a little carried away. I'm just having fun.

Q: Is that how all your "discards" see it?
A: What do you mean?

Q: I mean, you lead these girls on for a week or so and make them think you really like them. Then all of a sudden you're gone, interested in someone else.
A: So?

Q: Do you think that's right?
A: Hey, I'm not out to hurt anybody. I'm just looking for the right person for me.

Q: Yeah, well, we all want that eventually. But do you want everybody talking about you? Do you want a reputation for being a player? I'm telling you—you *don't* want girls getting together and comparing notes about you.
A: What's wrong with a little flirting? Everybody does it.

Q: Yeah, that's probably true. But you're going way overboard. You can't go through girls like they're Kleenex!
A: It's working so far.

» The One

Many guys view girls as fish in the sea. They think all you have to do is bait the hook, throw out the line and reel them in when they bite. They believe that if you don't like what you catch, you can always throw it back and keep fishing.

The problem with that kind of thinking is that hooks leave scars. Just like you, girls want to be loved for who they are. They don't want to get jerked around or treated like they're nothing more than the latest catch.

The next time you find yourself tempted to flirt with a girl, and you know deep down you're not really interested in her, think about this passage of Scripture: "Do nothing out of selfish ambition or vain conceit, but in humility consider others better than yourselves. Each of you should look not only to your own interests, but also to the interests of others" (Philippians 2:3–4). Do these verses sum up the way you treat girls?

Read more about getting along with girls at www.RevolutionBible.com.

9 All Israel was listed in the genealogies recorded in the book of the kings of Israel.

THE PEOPLE IN JERUSALEM

The people of Judah were taken captive to Babylon because of their unfaithfulness. ²Now the first to resettle on their own property in their own towns were some Israelites, priests, Levites and temple servants.

³Those from Judah, from Benjamin, and from Ephraim and Manasseh who lived in Jerusalem were:

⁴Uthai son of Ammihud, the son of Omri, the son of Imri, the son of Bani, a descendant of Perez son of Judah.

⁵Of the Shilonites:

Asaiah the firstborn and his sons.

⁶Of the Zerahites:

Jeuel.

The people from Judah numbered 690.

⁷Of the Benjamites:

Sallu son of Meshullam, the son of Hodaviah, the son of Hassenuah;

⁸Ibneiah son of Jeroham; Elah son of Uzzi, the son of Micri; and Meshullam son of Shephatiah, the son of Reuel, the son of Ibnijah.

⁹The people from Benjamin, as listed in their genealogy, numbered 956. All these men were heads of their families.

¹⁰Of the priests:

Jedaiah; Jehoiarib; Jakin;

¹¹Azariah son of Hilkiah, the son of Meshullam, the son of Zadok, the son of Meraioth, the son of Ahitub, the official in charge of the house of God;

¹²Adaiah son of Jeroham, the son of Pashhur, the son of Malkijah; and Maasai son of Adiel, the son of Jahzerah, the son of Meshullam, the son of Meshillemith, the son of Immer.

¹³The priests, who were heads of families, numbered 1,760. They were able men, responsible for ministering in the house of God.

¹⁴Of the Levites:

Shemaiah son of Hasshub, the son of Azrikam, the son of Hashabiah, a Merarite; ¹⁵Bakbakkar, Heresh, Galal and Mattaniah son of Mica, the son of Zicri, the son of Asaph; ¹⁶Obadiah son of Shemaiah, the son of Galal, the son of Jeduthun; and Berekiah son of Asa, the son of Elkanah, who lived in the villages of the Netophathites.

¹⁷The gatekeepers:

Shallum, Akkub, Talmon, Ahiman and their brothers, Shallum their chief ¹⁸being stationed at the King's Gate on the east, up to the present time. These were the gatekeepers belonging to the camp of the Levites. ¹⁹Shallum son of Kore, the son of Ebiasaph, the son of Korah, and his fellow gatekeepers from his family (the Korahites) were responsible for guarding the thresholds of the Tent ᵃ just as their fathers had been responsible for guarding the entrance to the dwelling of the LORD. ²⁰In earlier times Phinehas son of Eleazar was in charge of the gatekeepers, and the LORD was with him. ²¹Zechariah son of Meshelemiah was the gatekeeper at the entrance to the Tent of Meeting.

²²Altogether, those chosen to be gatekeepers at the thresholds numbered 212. They were registered by genealogy in their villages. The gatekeepers had been assigned to their positions of trust by David and Samuel the seer. ²³They and their descendants were in charge of guarding the gates of the house of the LORD—the house called the Tent. ²⁴The gatekeepers were on the four sides: east, west, north and south. ²⁵Their brothers in their villages had to come from time to time and share their duties for seven-day periods. ²⁶But the four principal gatekeepers, who were Levites, were entrusted with the responsibility for the rooms and treasuries in the house of God. ²⁷They would spend the night stationed around the house of God, because they had to guard it; and they had charge of the key for opening it each morning.

²⁸Some of them were in charge of the articles used in the temple service; they counted them when they were brought in and when they were taken out. ²⁹Others were assigned to take care of the furnish-

---

ᵃ *19 That is, the temple; also in verses 21 and 23*

ings and all the other articles of the sanctuary, as well as the flour and wine, and the oil, incense and spices. ³⁰But some of the priests took care of mixing the spices. ³¹A Levite named Mattithiah, the first-born son of Shallum the Korahite, was entrusted with the responsibility for baking the offering bread. ³²Some of their Kohathite brothers were in charge of preparing for every Sabbath the bread set out on the table.

³³Those who were musicians, heads of Levite families, stayed in the rooms of the temple and were exempt from other duties because they were responsible for the work day and night.

³⁴All these were heads of Levite families, chiefs as listed in their genealogy, and they lived in Jerusalem.

THE GENEALOGY OF SAUL

³⁵Jeiel the father[a] of Gibeon lived in Gibeon.

His wife's name was Maacah, ³⁶and his firstborn son was Abdon, followed by Zur, Kish, Baal, Ner, Nadab, ³⁷Gedor, Ahio, Zechariah and Mikloth. ³⁸Mikloth was the father of Shimeam. They too lived near their relatives in Jerusalem.

³⁹Ner was the father of Kish, Kish the father of Saul, and Saul the father of Jonathan, Malki-Shua, Abinadab and Esh-Baal.[b]

⁴⁰The son of Jonathan:

Merib-Baal,[c] who was the father of Micah.

⁴¹The sons of Micah:

Pithon, Melech, Tahrea and Ahaz.[d]

⁴²Ahaz was the father of Jadah, Jadah[e] was the father of Alemeth, Azmaveth and Zimri, and Zimri was the father of Moza. ⁴³Moza was the father of Binea; Rephaiah was his son, Eleasah his son and Azel his son.

⁴⁴Azel had six sons, and these were their names:

Azrikam, Bokeru, Ishmael, Sheariah, Obadiah and Hanan. These were the sons of Azel.

SAUL TAKES HIS LIFE

10 Now the Philistines fought against Israel; the Israelites fled before them, and many fell slain on Mount Gilboa. ²The Philistines pressed hard after Saul and his sons, and they killed his sons Jonathan, Abinadab and Malki-Shua. ³The fighting grew fierce around Saul, and when the archers overtook him, they wounded him.

⁴Saul said to his armor-bearer, "Draw your sword and run me through, or these uncircumcised fellows will come and abuse me."

But his armor-bearer was terrified and would not do it; so Saul took his own sword and fell on it. ⁵When the armor-bearer saw that Saul was dead, he too fell on his sword and died. ⁶So Saul and his three sons died, and all his house died together.

⁷When all the Israelites in the valley saw that the army had fled and that Saul and his sons had died, they abandoned their towns and fled. And the Philistines came and occupied them.

⁸The next day, when the Philistines came to strip the dead, they found Saul and his sons fallen on Mount Gilboa. ⁹They stripped him and took his head and his armor, and sent messengers throughout the land of the Philistines to proclaim the news among their idols and their people. ¹⁰They put his armor in the temple of their gods and hung up his head in the temple of Dagon.

¹¹When all the inhabitants of Jabesh Gilead heard of everything the Philistines had done to Saul, ¹²all their valiant men went and took the bodies of Saul and his sons and brought them to Jabesh. Then they buried their bones under the great tree in Jabesh, and they fasted seven days.

¹³Saul died because he was unfaithful to the LORD; he did not keep the word of the LORD and even consulted a medium for guidance, ¹⁴and did not inquire of the LORD. So the LORD put him to death and turned the kingdom over to David son of Jesse.

DAVID BECOMES KING OVER ISRAEL

11 All Israel came together to David at Hebron and said, "We are your own flesh and blood. ²In the past, even while Saul was king, you were the one who led Israel on their military campaigns. And the LORD your God said to you, 'You will shepherd my people Israel, and you will become their ruler.'"

³When all the elders of Israel had come to King David at Hebron, he made a compact with them at Hebron before the LORD, and they anointed David king over Israel, as the LORD had promised through Samuel.

DAVID CONQUERS JERUSALEM

⁴David and all the Israelites marched to Jerusalem (that is, Jebus). The Jebusites who lived there ⁵said to David, "You will not get in here." Nevertheless, David captured the fortress of Zion, the City of David.

⁶David had said, "Whoever leads the attack on the Jebusites will become commander-in-chief." Joab son of Zeruiah went up first, and so he received the command.

⁷David then took up residence in the fortress, and so it was called the City of David. ⁸He built up the city around it, from the supporting terraces^a to the surrounding wall, while Joab restored the rest of the city. ⁹And David became more and more powerful, because the LORD Almighty was with him.

DAVID'S MIGHTY MEN

¹⁰These were the chiefs of David's mighty men—they, together with all Israel, gave his kingship strong support to extend it over the whole land, as the LORD had promised— ¹¹this is the list of David's mighty men:

Jashobeam,^b a Hacmonite, was chief of the officers^c; he raised his spear against three hundred men, whom he killed in one encounter.

¹²Next to him was Eleazar son of Dodai the Ahohite, one of the three mighty men. ¹³He was with David at Pas Dammim when the Philistines gathered there for battle. At a place where there was a field full of barley, the troops fled from the Philistines. ¹⁴But they took their stand in the middle of the field. They defended it and struck the Philistines down, and the LORD brought about a great victory.

¹⁵Three of the thirty chiefs came down to David to the rock at the cave of Adullam, while a band of Philistines was encamped in the Valley of Rephaim. ¹⁶At that time David was in the stronghold, and the Philistine garrison was at Bethlehem. ¹⁷David longed for water and said, "Oh, that someone would get me a drink of water from the well near the gate of Bethlehem!" ¹⁸So the Three broke through the Philistine lines, drew water from the well near the gate of Bethlehem and carried it back to David. But he refused to drink it; instead, he poured it out before the LORD. ¹⁹"God forbid that I should do this!" he said. "Should I drink the blood of these men who went at the risk of their lives?" Because they risked their lives to bring it back, David would not drink it.

Being Faithful

How faithful are you to your best friend? If you heard some people making fun of him behind his back, would you stand up for him or would you keep your mouth shut? If he did something that made him seriously unpopular at school, would you stick with him or would you try to separate yourself from him? More important, how faithful are you to God? If you heard a science teacher claim that God doesn't exist, would you stand up for him or would you remain quiet? If identifying yourself as a Christian could make you seriously unpopular with your school crowd, would you stick with God or would you try to hide your relationship with him?

NOW OR NEVER
1CH 10:13–14

God is patient with us and his mercy has no end. Because of sin, however, our lives on earth are not infinite. Someday, we *will* die. There will come a day when we will be held accountable for our actions; so if we refuse to be faithful in this life, we'll pay the price in the next.

---

^a 8 Or *the Millo*   ^b 11 Possibly a variant of *Jashob-Baal*   ^c 11 Or *Thirty*; some Septuagint manuscripts *Three* (see also 2 Samuel 23:8)

Such were the exploits of the three mighty men.

²⁰Abishai the brother of Joab was chief of the Three. He raised his spear against three hundred men, whom he killed, and so he became as famous as the Three. ²¹He was doubly honored above the Three and became their commander, even though he was not included among them.

²²Benaiah son of Jehoiada was a valiant fighter from Kabzeel, who performed great exploits. He struck down two of Moab's best men. He also went down into a pit on a snowy day and killed a lion. ²³And he struck down an Egyptian who was seven and a half feet[a] tall. Although the Egyptian had a spear like a weaver's rod in his hand, Benaiah went against him with a club. He snatched the spear from the Egyptian's hand and killed him with his own spear. ²⁴Such were the exploits of Benaiah son of Jehoiada; he too was as famous as the three mighty men. ²⁵He was held in greater honor than any of the Thirty, but he was not included among the Three. And David put him in charge of his bodyguard.

²⁶The mighty men were:
Asahel the brother of Joab,
Elhanan son of Dodo from Bethlehem,
²⁷Shammoth the Harorite,
Helez the Pelonite,
²⁸Ira son of Ikkesh from Tekoa,
Abiezer from Anathoth,
²⁹Sibbecai the Hushathite,
Ilai the Ahohite,
³⁰Maharai the Netophathite,
Heled son of Baanah the Netophathite,
³¹Ithai son of Ribai from Gibeah in Benjamin,
Benaiah the Pirathonite,
³²Hurai from the ravines of Gaash,
Abiel the Arbathite,
³³Azmaveth the Baharumite,
Eliahba the Shaalbonite,
³⁴the sons of Hashem the Gizonite,
Jonathan son of Shagee the Hararite,
³⁵Ahiam son of Sacar the Hararite,
Eliphal son of Ur,
³⁶Hepher the Mekerathite,
Ahijah the Pelonite,
³⁷Hezro the Carmelite,
Naarai son of Ezbai,
³⁸Joel the brother of Nathan,
Mibhar son of Hagri,
³⁹Zelek the Ammonite,
Naharai the Berothite, the armor-bearer of Joab son of Zeruiah,
⁴⁰Ira the Ithrite,
Gareb the Ithrite,
⁴¹Uriah the Hittite,
Zabad son of Ahlai,

NOW OR NEVER
1CH 11:9

What signs do you see in your life that God has been at work? How noticeable do you think those signs are to other people?

Expecting Victory

What's the biggest battle in your life right now? Accepting who you are? Getting along with your parents? Overcoming a sin that keeps dragging you down? Dealing with a jerk at school? Finding loyal friends? Whatever the battle is, it's time to take your stand, just like David did against the Philistines. Go to God in prayer, tell him all about your battle, and ask—no, wait—make that *beg* him to fight for you and give you the kind of victory that David experienced.

» live the adventure » 1Ch 11:14

---

[a] *23 Hebrew five cubits (about 2.3 meters)*

42 Adina son of Shiza the Reubenite, who was chief of the Reubenites, and the thirty with him,
43 Hanan son of Maacah,
   Joshaphat the Mithnite,
44 Uzzia the Ashterathite,
   Shama and Jeiel the sons of Hotham the Aroerite,
45 Jediael son of Shimri,
   his brother Joha the Tizite,
46 Eliel the Mahavite,
   Jeribai and Joshaviah the sons of Elnaam,
   Ithmah the Moabite,
47 Eliel, Obed and Jaasiel the Mezobaite.

WARRIORS JOIN DAVID

12 These were the men who came to David at Ziklag, while he was banished from the presence of Saul son of Kish (they were among the warriors who helped him in battle; 2 they were armed with bows and were able to shoot arrows or to sling stones right-handed or left-handed; they were kinsmen of Saul from the tribe of Benjamin):

3 Ahiezer their chief and Joash the sons of Shemaah the Gibeathite; Jeziel and Pelet the sons of Azmaveth; Beracah, Jehu the Anathothite, 4 and Ishmaiah the Gibeonite, a mighty man among the Thirty, who was a leader of the Thirty; Jeremiah, Jahaziel, Johanan, Jozabad the Gederathite, 5 Eluzai, Jerimoth, Bealiah, Shemariah and Shephatiah the Haruphite; 6 Elkanah, Isshiah, Azarel, Joezer and Jashobeam the Korahites; 7 and Joelah and Zebadiah the sons of Jeroham from Gedor.

8 Some Gadites defected to David at his stronghold in the desert. They were brave warriors, ready for battle and able to handle the shield and spear. Their faces were the faces of lions, and they were as swift as gazelles in the mountains.

9 Ezer was the chief,
   Obadiah the second in command, Eliab the third,
10 Mishmannah the fourth, Jeremiah the fifth,
11 Attai the sixth, Eliel the seventh,
12 Johanan the eighth, Elzabad the ninth,
13 Jeremiah the tenth and Macbannai the eleventh.

14 These Gadites were army commanders; the least was a match for a hundred, and the greatest for a thousand. 15 It was they who crossed the Jordan in the first month when it was overflowing all its banks, and they put to flight everyone living in the valleys, to the east and to the west.

16 Other Benjamites and some men from Judah also came to David in his stronghold. 17 David went out to meet them and said to them, "If you have come to me in peace, to help me, I am ready to have you unite with me. But if you have come to betray me to my enemies when my hands are free from violence, may the God of our fathers see it and judge you."

18 Then the Spirit came upon Amasai, chief of the Thirty, and he said:

"We are yours, O David!
   We are with you, O son of Jesse!
Success, success to you,
   and success to those who help you,
      for your God will help you."

So David received them and made them leaders of his raiding bands.

19 Some of the men of Manasseh defected to David when he went with the Philistines to fight against Saul. (He and his men did not help the Philistines because, after consultation, their rulers sent him away. They said, "It will cost us our heads if he deserts to his master Saul.") 20 When David went to Ziklag, these were the men of Manasseh who defected to him: Adnah, Jozabad, Jediael, Michael, Jozabad, Elihu and Zillethai, leaders of units of a thousand in Manasseh. 21 They helped David against raiding bands, for all of them were brave warriors, and they were command-

ers in his army. ²²Day after day men came to help David, until he had a great army, like the army of God. ᵃ

OTHERS JOIN DAVID AT HEBRON

²³These are the numbers of the men armed for battle who came to David at Hebron to turn Saul's kingdom over to him, as the LORD had said:

²⁴men of Judah, carrying shield and spear—6,800 armed for battle;

²⁵men of Simeon, warriors ready for battle—7,100;

²⁶men of Levi—4,600, ²⁷including Jehoiada, leader of the family of Aaron, with 3,700 men, ²⁸and Zadok, a brave young warrior, with 22 officers from his family;

²⁹men of Benjamin, Saul's kinsmen—3,000, most of whom had remained loyal to Saul's house until then;

³⁰men of Ephraim, brave warriors, famous in their own clans—20,800;

³¹men of half the tribe of Manasseh, designated by name to come and make David king—18,000;

³²men of Issachar, who understood the times and knew what Israel should do—200 chiefs, with all their relatives under their command;

³³men of Zebulun, experienced soldiers prepared for battle with every type of weapon, to help David with undivided loyalty—50,000;

³⁴men of Naphtali—1,000 officers, together with 37,000 men carrying shields and spears;

³⁵men of Dan, ready for battle—28,600;

³⁶men of Asher, experienced soldiers prepared for battle—40,000;

³⁷and from east of the Jordan, men of Reuben, Gad and the half-tribe of Manasseh, armed with every type of weapon—120,000.

³⁸All these were fighting men who volunteered to serve in the ranks. They came to Hebron fully determined to make David king over all Israel. All the rest of the Israelites were also of one mind to make David king. ³⁹The men spent three days there with David, eating and drinking, for their families had supplied provisions for them. ⁴⁰Also, their neighbors from as far away as Issachar, Zebulun and Naphtali came bringing food on donkeys, camels, mules and oxen. There were plentiful supplies of flour, fig cakes, raisin cakes, wine, oil, cattle and sheep, for there was joy in Israel.

BRINGING BACK THE ARK

13 David conferred with each of his officers, the commanders of thousands and commanders of hundreds. ²He then said to the whole assembly of Israel, "If it seems good to you and if it is the will of the LORD our God, let us send word far and wide to the rest of our brothers throughout the territories of Israel, and also to the priests and Levites who are with them in their towns and pasturelands, to come and join us. ³Let us bring the ark of our God back to us, for we did not inquire ofᵇ itᶜ during the reign of Saul." ⁴The whole assembly agreed to do this, because it seemed right to all the people.

⁵So David assembled all the Israelites, from the Shihor River in Egypt to Leboᵈ Hamath, to bring the ark of God from Kiriath Jearim. ⁶David and all the Israelites with him went to Baalah of Judah (Kiriath Jearim) to bring up from there the ark of God the LORD, who is enthroned between the cherubim—the ark that is called by the Name.

⁷They moved the ark of God from Abinadab's house on a new cart, with Uzzah and Ahio guiding it.

Leading by Example

Do you consider yourself a leader? Many guys would probably answer no to that question. They prefer to remain safely anonymous as followers rather than stick their necks out and draw attention to themselves by taking charge. What David discovered, though, is that you can become a leader without really trying to take charge and make change happen. If you commit yourself to following God full-time, people are going to notice and are going to want to join you—maybe even follow your example.

»» live the adventure »» 1Ch 12:22

ᵃ 22 Or *a great and mighty army*   ᵇ 3 Or *we neglected*   ᶜ 3 Or *him*   ᵈ 5 Or *to the entrance to*

[8]David and all the Israelites were celebrating with all their might before God, with songs and with harps, lyres, tambourines, cymbals and trumpets.

[9]When they came to the threshing floor of Kidon, Uzzah reached out his hand to steady the ark, because the oxen stumbled. [10]The Lord's anger burned against Uzzah, and he struck him down because he had put his hand on the ark. So he died there before God.

[11]Then David was angry because the Lord's wrath had broken out against Uzzah, and to this day that place is called Perez Uzzah.[a]

[12]David was afraid of God that day and asked, "How can I ever bring the ark of God to me?" [13]He did not take the ark to be with him in the City of David. Instead, he took it aside to the house of Obed-Edom the Gittite. [14]The ark of God remained with the family of Obed-Edom in his house for three months, and the Lord blessed his household and everything he had.

NOW OR NEVER

1CH 14:1–2

God doesn't help us succeed because he wants us to gain popularity and status with others. First and foremost, God helps us succeed in order to accomplish *his* work.

DAVID'S HOUSE AND FAMILY

14 Now Hiram king of Tyre sent messengers to David, along with cedar logs, stonemasons and carpenters to build a palace for him. [2]And David knew that the Lord had established him as king over Israel and that his kingdom had been highly exalted for the sake of his people Israel.

[3]In Jerusalem David took more wives and became the father of more sons and daughters. [4]These are the names of the children born to him there: Shammua, Shobab, Nathan, Solomon, [5]Ibhar, Elishua, Elpelet, [6]Nogah, Nepheg, Japhia, [7]Elishama, Beeliada[b] and Eliphelet.

DAVID DEFEATS THE PHILISTINES

[8]When the Philistines heard that David had been anointed king over all Israel, they went up in full force to search for him, but David heard about it and went out to meet them. [9]Now the Philistines had come and raided the Valley of Rephaim; [10]so David inquired of God: "Shall I go and attack the Philistines? Will you hand them over to me?"

The Lord answered him, "Go, I will hand them over to you."

[11]So David and his men went up to Baal Perazim, and there he defeated them. He said, "As waters break out, God has broken out against my enemies by my hand." So that place was called Baal Perazim.[c] [12]The Philistines had abandoned their gods there, and David gave orders to burn them in the fire.

[13]Once more the Philistines raided the valley; [14]so David inquired of God again, and God answered him, "Do not go straight up, but circle around them and attack them in front of the balsam trees. [15]As soon as you hear the sound of marching in the tops of the balsam trees, move out to battle, because that will mean God has gone out in front of you to strike the Philistine army." [16]So David did as God commanded him, and they struck down the Philistine army, all the way from Gibeon to Gezer.

[17]So David's fame spread throughout every land, and the Lord made all the nations fear him.

THE ARK BROUGHT TO JERUSALEM

15 After David had constructed buildings for himself in the City of David, he prepared a place for the ark of God and pitched a tent for it. [2]Then David said, "No one but the Levites may carry the ark of God, because the Lord chose them to carry the ark of the Lord and to minister before him forever."

[3]David assembled all Israel in Jerusalem to bring up the ark of the Lord to the place he had prepared for it. [4]He called together the descendants of Aaron and the Levites:

[5]From the descendants of Kohath,

Uriel the leader and 120 relatives;

[6]from the descendants of Merari,

---

[a] 11 *Perez Uzzah* means *outbreak against Uzzah.*   [b] 7 A variant of *Eliada*   [c] 11 *Baal Perazim* means *the lord who breaks out.*

Asaiah the leader and 220 relatives;
⁷from the descendants of Gershon,[a]
Joel the leader and 130 relatives;
⁸from the descendants of Elizaphan,
Shemaiah the leader and 200 relatives;
⁹from the descendants of Hebron,
Eliel the leader and 80 relatives;
¹⁰from the descendants of Uzziel,
Amminadab the leader and 112 relatives.

¹¹Then David summoned Zadok and Abiathar the priests, and Uriel, Asaiah, Joel, Shemaiah, Eliel and Amminadab the Levites. ¹²He said to them, "You are the heads of the Levitical families; you and your fellow Levites are to consecrate yourselves and bring up the ark of the LORD, the God of Israel, to the place I have prepared for it. ¹³It was because you, the Levites, did not bring it up the first time that the LORD our God broke out in anger against us. We did not inquire of him about how to do it in the prescribed way." ¹⁴So the priests and Levites consecrated themselves in order to bring up the ark of the LORD, the God of Israel. ¹⁵And the Levites carried the ark of God with the poles on their shoulders, as Moses had commanded in accordance with the word of the LORD.

¹⁶David told the leaders of the Levites to appoint their brothers as singers to sing joyful songs, accompanied by musical instruments: lyres, harps and cymbals.

¹⁷So the Levites appointed Heman son of Joel; from his brothers, Asaph son of Berekiah; and from their brothers the Merarites, Ethan son of Kushaiah; ¹⁸and with them their brothers next in rank: Zechariah,[b] Jaaziel, Shemiramoth, Jehiel, Unni, Eliab, Benaiah, Maaseiah, Mattithiah, Eliphelehu, Mikneiah, Obed-Edom and Jeiel,[c] the gatekeepers.

¹⁹The musicians Heman, Asaph and Ethan were to sound the bronze cymbals; ²⁰Zechariah, Aziel, Shemiramoth, Jehiel, Unni, Eliab, Maaseiah and Benaiah were to play the lyres according to *alamoth*,[d] ²¹and Mattithiah, Eliphelehu, Mikneiah, Obed-Edom, Jeiel and Azaziah were to play the harps, directing according to *sheminith*.[d] ²²Kenaniah the head Levite was in charge of the singing; that was his responsibility because he was skillful at it.

²³Berekiah and Elkanah were to be doorkeepers for the ark. ²⁴Shebaniah, Joshaphat, Nethanel, Amasai, Zechariah, Benaiah and Eliezer the priests were to blow trumpets before the ark of God. Obed-Edom and Jehiah were also to be doorkeepers for the ark.

²⁵So David and the elders of Israel and the commanders of units of a thousand went to bring up the ark of the covenant of the LORD from the house of Obed-Edom, with rejoicing. ²⁶Because God had helped the Levites who were carrying the ark of the covenant of the LORD, seven bulls and seven rams were sacrificed. ²⁷Now David was clothed in a robe of fine linen, as were all the Levites who were carrying the ark, and as were the singers, and Kenaniah, who was in charge of the singing of the choirs. David also wore a linen ephod. ²⁸So all Israel brought up the ark of the covenant of the LORD with shouts, with the sounding of rams' horns and trumpets, and of cymbals, and the playing of lyres and harps.

²⁹As the ark of the covenant of the LORD was entering the City of David, Michal daughter of Saul watched from a window. And when she saw King David dancing and celebrating, she despised him in her heart.

Learning to Obey

»» live the adventure »» 1Ch 14:10-16

We've got it all backwards. We admire guys who rebel against authority, break rules and do whatever they want. To us, these guys are role models. But that's not how it should be. Real heroes sacrifice their own plans and desires for the good of the team. Genuine role models recognize that there are people who know better than they do, and they choose to obey authority because it's the right thing to do. Let's face it—breaking rules here and there to get ahead in today's world is pretty much par for the course. At least, it *seems* like everyone does it. That's why a guy who plays by the rules and does what God wants can make a big impression.

---

[a] 7 Hebrew *Gershom*, a variant of *Gershon*   [b] 18 Three Hebrew manuscripts and most Septuagint manuscripts (see also verse 20 and 1 Chron. 16:5); most Hebrew manuscripts *Zechariah son and* or *Zechariah, Ben and*   [c] 18 Hebrew; Septuagint (see also verse 21) *Jeiel and Azaziah*   [d] 20,21 Probably a musical term

saul

VERSUS

» Israel's first king
» Stripped of the throne by God for his repeated disobedience
» Became envious and paranoid because of David's popularity

abiathar

» Priest at Nob who survived the massacre of his family
» Became one of David's counselors
» Guarded David's interests when David fled from Absalom

The Main Event

All over the world, even as you read this paragraph, godly people are suffering and dying at the hands of evil men. Why is there such cruelty and barbarism in the world? Where is God in all of this? Why does he stand by and let his followers experience brutality, torture and death?

Perhaps Abiathar asked those same questions. Do you remember his story? He was a priest during the reign of King Saul, which is significant because Saul was one sick dude—spiritually, emotionally and relationally. When he and Abiathar crossed paths, Saul was in the process of a public melt down. He had already lost God's blessing, not to mention the respect and favor of his people. He was also losing touch with reality—in other words, he was losing his mind.

In his semideranged state, Saul made it his life mission—his obsession—to kill David. When he got word from his chief shepherd Doeg that David had paid a visit to Ahimelech and the priests at Nob, Saul had those priests standing in front of him in a flash.

Ahimelech admitted helping David—feeding him and his men, giving David the sword of Goliath and praying for him. Saul was livid. Ahimelech tried to reason with the king, reminding Saul of David's loyalty and pleading ignorance of David's supposed treachery. Unfortunately for Ahimelech, he discovered that there's no way to talk sense to a mad man.

Saul ordered the execution of Ahimelech and 84 other innocent priests. The only one to escape was Abiathar, the son of Ahimelech. He found David and became part of his entourage.

When David later became king, Abiathar became Israel's high priest.

The Outcome

Imagine living through an experience like that—getting an up-close-and-personal view of the murderous face of evil. Could your faith survive? Apparently, Abiathar's did. He had a long career as Israel's high priest.

Abiathar's horrifying encounter with Saul serves as a helpful reminder of several key truths:

Truth #1: Evil and suffering are grim realities in our present fallen world. Don't be shocked by them. When men and women reject God, anything—including the most unimaginable evil—is possible.

Truth #2: The people of God are *not* exempt from pain and heartache. Our faith doesn't offer us a guarantee of worldly security, but it does give the promise of eternal security.

Truth #3: The experiences of your past—no matter how horrific—don't have to keep you from living your life and serving God. Like Abiathar, don't let your past dictate your future.

Truth #4: One day evil and suffering *will* cease forever (see Revelation 21–22).

Read more about Saul and Abiathar in 1 Samuel 22–23 (pages 334–335) and 1 Kings 1–2 (pages 378–382).

16

They brought the ark of God and set it inside the tent that David had pitched for it, and they presented burnt offerings and fellowship offerings[a] before God. ²After David had finished sacrificing the burnt offerings and fellowship offerings, he blessed the people in the name of the LORD. ³Then he gave a loaf of bread, a cake of dates and a cake of raisins to each Israelite man and woman.

⁴He appointed some of the Levites to minister before the ark of the LORD, to make petition, to give thanks, and to praise the LORD, the God of Israel: ⁵Asaph was the chief, Zechariah second, then Jeiel, Shemiramoth, Jehiel, Mattithiah, Eliab, Benaiah, Obed-Edom and Jeiel. They were to play the lyres and harps, Asaph was to sound the cymbals, ⁶and Benaiah and Jahaziel the priests were to blow the trumpets regularly before the ark of the covenant of God.

NOW OR NEVER

1CH 16:1-3

Offer your own sacrifice to God this week. Do something meaningful for him, such as giving up TV for a day and spending that time deepening your personal relationship with him through prayer or reading the Bible.

DAVID'S PSALM OF THANKS

⁷That day David first committed to Asaph and his associates this psalm of thanks to the LORD:

⁸Give thanks to the LORD, call on his name;
 make known among the nations what he has done.
⁹Sing to him, sing praise to him;
 tell of all his wonderful acts.
¹⁰Glory in his holy name;
 let the hearts of those who seek the LORD rejoice.

¹¹Look to the LORD and his strength;
 seek his face always.
¹²Remember the wonders he has done,
 his miracles, and the judgments he pronounced,
¹³O descendants of Israel his servant,
 O sons of Jacob, his chosen ones.

¹⁴He is the LORD our God;
 his judgments are in all the earth.
¹⁵He remembers[b] his covenant forever,
 the word he commanded, for a thousand generations,
¹⁶the covenant he made with Abraham,
 the oath he swore to Isaac.
¹⁷He confirmed it to Jacob as a decree,
 to Israel as an everlasting covenant:
¹⁸"To you I will give the land of Canaan
 as the portion you will inherit."

¹⁹When they were but few in number,
 few indeed, and strangers in it,
²⁰they[c] wandered from nation to nation,
 from one kingdom to another.
²¹He allowed no man to oppress them;
 for their sake he rebuked kings:
²²"Do not touch my anointed ones;
 do my prophets no harm."

²³Sing to the LORD, all the earth;
 proclaim his salvation day after day.

---

[a] 1 Traditionally *peace offerings*; also in verse 2   [b] 15 Some Septuagint manuscripts (see also Psalm 105:8); Hebrew *Remember*
[c] 18-20 One Hebrew manuscript, Septuagint and Vulgate (see also Psalm 105:12); most Hebrew manuscripts *inherit,* / ¹⁹*though you are but few in number,* / *few indeed, and strangers in it."* / ²⁰*They*

²⁴Declare his glory among the nations,
his marvelous deeds among all peoples.
²⁵For great is the Lᴏʀᴅ and most worthy of praise;
he is to be feared above all gods.
²⁶For all the gods of the nations are idols,
but the Lᴏʀᴅ made the heavens.
²⁷Splendor and majesty are before him;
strength and joy in his dwelling
place.
²⁸Ascribe to the Lᴏʀᴅ, O families of
nations,
ascribe to the Lᴏʀᴅ glory and
strength,
²⁹ ascribe to the Lᴏʀᴅ the glory due his
name.
Bring an offering and come before him;
worship the Lᴏʀᴅ in the splendor of
hisᵃ holiness.
³⁰Tremble before him, all the earth!
The world is firmly established; it
cannot be moved.
³¹Let the heavens rejoice, let the earth be
glad;
let them say among the nations, "The
Lᴏʀᴅ reigns!"
³²Let the sea resound, and all that is in it;
let the fields be jubilant, and
everything in them!
³³Then the trees of the forest will sing,
they will sing for joy before the Lᴏʀᴅ,
for he comes to judge the earth.

³⁴Give thanks to the Lᴏʀᴅ, for he is good;
his love endures forever.
³⁵Cry out, "Save us, O God our Savior;
gather us and deliver us from the
nations,
that we may give thanks to your holy name,
that we may glory in your praise."
³⁶Praise be to the Lᴏʀᴅ, the God of Israel,
from everlasting to everlasting.

Then all the people said "Amen" and "Praise the Lᴏʀᴅ."

»» live the adventure »» 1Ch 16:34

Publicizing Your Thankfulness

Have you ever done something nice for someone and not received so much as a thank you in return? How did it feel? Some guys have a hard time thanking someone because expressing gratitude shows humility. It shows that we need other people—and that's not something that every guy wants to admit, even though it's true for all of us. But refusing to be thankful is wrong. It's a version of a sin called pride. And knowing what it feels like not to receive a well-deserved thanks, how can we neglect to give thanks to the Creator of the world, the giver of all good gifts?

³⁷David left Asaph and his associates before the ark of the covenant of the Lᴏʀᴅ to minister there regularly, according to each day's requirements. ³⁸He also left Obed-Edom and his sixty-eight associates to minister with them. Obed-Edom son of Jeduthun, and also Hosah, were gatekeepers.

³⁹David left Zadok the priest and his fellow priests before the tabernacle of the Lᴏʀᴅ at the high place in Gibeon ⁴⁰to present burnt offerings to the Lᴏʀᴅ on the altar of burnt offering regularly, morning and evening, in accordance with everything written in the Law of the Lᴏʀᴅ, which he had given Israel. ⁴¹With them were Heman and Jeduthun and the rest of those chosen and designated by name to give thanks to the Lᴏʀᴅ, "for his love endures forever." ⁴²Heman and Jeduthun were responsible for the sounding of the trumpets and cymbals and for the playing of the other instruments for sacred song. The sons of Jeduthun were stationed at the gate.

⁴³Then all the people left, each for his own home, and David returned home to bless his family.

ᵃ 29 Or Lᴏʀᴅ with the splendor of

GOD'S PROMISE TO DAVID

17

After David was settled in his palace, he said to Nathan the prophet, "Here I am, living in a palace of cedar, while the ark of the covenant of the LORD is under a tent." ²Nathan replied to David, "Whatever you have in mind, do it, for God is with you." ³That night the word of God came to Nathan, saying:

⁴"Go and tell my servant David, 'This is what the LORD says: You are not the one to build me a house to dwell in. ⁵I have not dwelt in a house from the day I brought Israel up out of Egypt to this day. I have moved from one tent site to another, from one dwelling place to another. ⁶Wherever I have moved with all the Israelites, did I ever say to any of their leadersᵃ whom I commanded to shepherd my people, "Why have you not built me a house of cedar?" '

⁷"Now then, tell my servant David, 'This is what the LORD Almighty says: I took you from the pasture and from following the flock, to be ruler over my people Israel. ⁸I have been with you wherever you have gone, and I have cut off all your enemies from before you. Now I will make your name like the names of the greatest men of the earth. ⁹And I will provide a place for my people Israel and will plant them so that they can have a home of their own and no longer be disturbed. Wicked people will not oppress them anymore, as they did at the beginning ¹⁰and have done ever since the time I appointed leaders over my people Israel. I will also subdue all your enemies.

" 'I declare to you that the LORD will build a house for you: ¹¹When your days are over and you go to be with your fathers, I will raise up your offspring to succeed you, one of your own sons, and I will establish his kingdom. ¹²He is the one who will build a house for me, and I will establish his throne forever. ¹³I will be his father, and he will be my son. I will never take my love away from him, as I took it away from your predecessor. ¹⁴I will set him over my house and my kingdom forever; his throne will be established forever.' "

¹⁵Nathan reported to David all the words of this entire revelation.

challenge notes

To: my_son

1CH 17:13

heavenly_father: I promised eternal love to my servant david thousands of years ago, and I have kept that promise by sending my son, Jesus, to die for the sins of the world. if you believe in him, you have a part in that promise of eternal love.

DAVID'S PRAYER

¹⁶Then King David went in and sat before the LORD, and he said:

"Who am I, O LORD God, and what is my family, that you have brought me this far? ¹⁷And as if this were not enough in your sight, O God, you have spoken about the future of the house of your servant. You have looked on me as though I were the most exalted of men, O LORD God.

¹⁸"What more can David say to you for honoring your servant? For you know your servant, ¹⁹O LORD. For the sake of your servant and according to your will, you have done this great thing and made known all these great promises.

²⁰"There is no one like you, O LORD, and there is no God but you, as we have heard with our own ears. ²¹And who is like your people Israel—the one nation on earth whose God went out to redeem a people for himself, and to make

now or never

1CH 17:20

Think about all the things that compete with God for your attention—friends, sports, TV, MySpace, school and anything else you can come up with. It's one thing to say that God deserves priority in your life; it's another thing to make it a reality.

ᵃ 6 Traditionally judges; also in verse 10

a name for yourself, and to perform great and awesome wonders by driving out nations from before your people, whom you redeemed from Egypt? ²²You made your people Israel your very own forever, and you, O LORD, have become their God.

²³"And now, LORD, let the promise you have made concerning your servant and his house be established forever. Do as you promised, ²⁴so that it will be established and that your name will be great forever. Then men will say, 'The LORD Almighty, the God over Israel, is Israel's God!' And the house of your servant David will be established before you.

²⁵"You, my God, have revealed to your servant that you will build a house for him. So your servant has found courage to pray to you. ²⁶O LORD, you are God! You have promised these good things to your servant. ²⁷Now you have been pleased to bless the house of your servant, that it may continue forever in your sight; for you, O LORD, have blessed it, and it will be blessed forever."

DAVID'S VICTORIES

18 In the course of time, David defeated the Philistines and subdued them, and he took Gath and its surrounding villages from the control of the Philistines. ²David also defeated the Moabites, and they became subject to him and brought tribute.

³Moreover, David fought Hadadezer king of Zobah, as far as Hamath, when he went to establish his control along the Euphrates River. ⁴David captured a thousand of his chariots, seven thousand charioteers and twenty thousand foot soldiers. He hamstrung all but a hundred of the chariot horses.

⁵When the Arameans of Damascus came to help Hadadezer king of Zobah, David struck down twenty-two thousand of them. ⁶He put garrisons in the Aramean kingdom of Damascus, and the Arameans became subject to him and brought tribute. The LORD gave David victory everywhere he went.

⁷David took the gold shields carried by the officers of Hadadezer and brought them to Jerusalem. ⁸From Tebah[a] and Cun, towns that belonged to Hadadezer, David took a great quantity of bronze, which Solomon used to make the bronze Sea, the pillars and various bronze articles.

⁹When Tou king of Hamath heard that David had defeated the entire army of Hadadezer king of Zobah, ¹⁰he sent his son Hadoram to King David to greet him and congratulate him on his victory in battle over Hadadezer, who had been at war with Tou. Hadoram brought all kinds of articles of gold and silver and bronze.

¹¹King David dedicated these articles to the LORD, as he had done with the silver and gold he had taken from all these nations: Edom and Moab, the Ammonites and the Philistines, and Amalek.

¹²Abishai son of Zeruiah struck down eighteen thousand Edomites in the Valley of Salt. ¹³He put garrisons in Edom, and all the Edomites became subject to David. The LORD gave David victory everywhere he went.

DAVID'S OFFICIALS

¹⁴David reigned over all Israel, doing what was just and right for all his people. ¹⁵Joab son of Zeruiah was over the army; Jehoshaphat son of Ahilud was recorder; ¹⁶Zadok son of Ahitub and Ahimelech[b] son of Abiathar were priests; Shavsha was secretary; ¹⁷Benaiah son of Jehoiada was over the Kerethites and Pelethites; and David's sons were chief officials at the king's side.

THE BATTLE AGAINST THE AMMONITES

19 In the course of time, Nahash king of the Ammonites died, and his son succeeded him as king. ²David thought, "I will show kindness to Hanun son of Nahash, because his father showed kindness to me." So David sent a delegation to express his sympathy to Hanun concerning his father.

When David's men came to Hanun in the land of the Ammonites to express sympathy to him, ³the Ammonite nobles said to Hanun, "Do you think David is honoring your father by sending men to you to express sympathy? Haven't his men come to you to explore and spy out the country and overthrow it?" ⁴So Hanun seized David's men, shaved them, cut off their garments in the middle at the buttocks, and sent them away.

ᵃ 8 Hebrew *Tibhath*, a variant of *Tebah*   ᵇ 16 Some Hebrew manuscripts, Vulgate and Syriac (see also 2 Samuel 8:17); most Hebrew manuscripts *Abimelech*

battlelines

» Why Wait? (Sexual Purity)

Q: Dude, was that a condom I saw in your wallet?
A: Yes, but it's not what you think.

Q: What else could it be? You actually took one of the condoms they were passing out during "Safe Sex Day"?
A: Just because I took one doesn't mean I'm going to use it. Hey, I'm not even dating anyone. Besides, the only reason I took it is because I didn't feel like announcing to the world that I'm a virgin. I'll probably just end up throwing it away.

Q: Anthony, your friends already know you're a virgin. Why would you feel embarrassed?
A: You know what my friends are like. They're always checking out girls. They surf porn on the Internet. Some of them have even had sex for real.

Q: You sound jealous.
A: Well, yeah, I guess I am . . . a little. Look, I'm not going to deny that I wanna have sex. Why do I have to wait? Nobody else is waiting!

Q: That's not true.
A: You know what I mean. Most people don't wait.

Q: Granted. But in this case, most people happen to be making a wrong decision.
A: See, you're so rational. You're able to think about this stuff clearly. I'm not like that. I get swayed.

Q: Oh, so you think sex isn't a temptation for me? Hey, I've got hormones too!
A: Yeah, but you've got yours under control.

Q: Barely. This is why we need God—and each other. Otherwise, we'll never make it.

» True Love Waits

Remember what happened in Eden in Genesis 2–3? God put up a boundary of sorts—a fence, if you will. He gave Adam and Eve tons of freedom . . . and one restriction. Yet because of that one "don't," Satan was able to convince the first couple that God wasn't to be trusted—that he was keeping something really good from them. Adam and Eve listened to the serpent, and the result, as we all know, was sin and disaster.

Not much has changed since then. God offers us the amazing gift of sex within marriage and says, "Wait!" Satan takes that one restriction (which is actually a protective provision) and hisses, "No, don't wait. Think about all you're missing now."

That's the choice you're facing.

Look at human history. Look at the character of God, and then look at the character of Satan. Look at the statistics on sexually transmitted diseases. Listen to the tearful testimonies of those who didn't wait and paid the price.

Who are you going to listen to?

Read more about sex and abstinence at www.RevolutionBible.com.

⁵When someone came and told David about the men, he sent messengers to meet them, for they were greatly humiliated. The king said, "Stay at Jericho till your beards have grown, and then come back."

⁶When the Ammonites realized that they had become a stench in David's nostrils, Hanun and the Ammonites sent a thousand talents[a] of silver to hire chariots and charioteers from Aram Naharaim,[b] Aram Maacah and Zobah. ⁷They hired thirty-two thousand chariots and charioteers, as well as the king of Maacah with his troops, who came and camped near Medeba, while the Ammonites were mustered from their towns and moved out for battle.

⁸On hearing this, David sent Joab out with the entire army of fighting men. ⁹The Ammonites came out and drew up in battle formation at the entrance to their city, while the kings who had come were by themselves in the open country.

¹⁰Joab saw that there were battle lines in front of him and behind him; so he selected some of the best troops in Israel and deployed them against the Arameans. ¹¹He put the rest of the men under the command of Abishai his brother, and they were deployed against the Ammonites. ¹²Joab said, "If the Arameans are too strong for me, then you are to rescue me; but if the Ammonites are too strong for you, then I will rescue you. ¹³Be strong and let us fight bravely for our people and the cities of our God. The LORD will do what is good in his sight."

¹⁴Then Joab and the troops with him advanced to fight the Arameans, and they fled before him. ¹⁵When the Ammonites saw that the Arameans were fleeing, they too fled before his brother Abishai and went inside the city. So Joab went back to Jerusalem.

¹⁶After the Arameans saw that they had been routed by Israel, they sent messengers and had Arameans brought from beyond the River,[c] with Shophach the commander of Hadadezer's army leading them.

¹⁷When David was told of this, he gathered all Israel and crossed the Jordan; he advanced against them and formed his battle lines opposite them. David formed his lines to meet the Arameans in battle, and they fought against him. ¹⁸But they fled before Israel, and David killed seven thousand of their charioteers and forty thousand of their foot soldiers. He also killed Shophach the commander of their army.

¹⁹When the vassals of Hadadezer saw that they had been defeated by Israel, they made peace with David and became subject to him.

So the Arameans were not willing to help the Ammonites anymore.

NOW OR NEVER
1CH 19:13

What are some things that can rob you of courage? Being outnumbered? Being put on the spot? Being unpopular? If you're facing a challenge and you know that your cause is a godly one, then you can trust that God will bless you and give you the strength you need to fight bravely.

THE CAPTURE OF RABBAH

20 In the spring, at the time when kings go off to war, Joab led out the armed forces. He laid waste the land of the Ammonites and went to Rabbah and besieged it, but David remained in Jerusalem. Joab attacked Rabbah and left it in ruins. ²David took the crown from the head of their king[d]—its weight was found to be a talent[e] of gold, and it was set with precious stones—and it was placed on David's head. He took a great quantity of plunder from the city ³and brought out the people who were there, consigning them to labor with saws and with iron picks and axes. David did this to all the Ammonite towns. Then David and his entire army returned to Jerusalem.

NOW OR NEVER
1CH 20:1-2

David's army wasted its enemies, even though David stayed behind and committed adultery with Bathsheba (see 2 Samuel 11:1–5). When you mess up but don't suffer immediate consequences, do you repent or do you "crown" yourself for your achievements?

ª 6 That is, about 37 tons (about 34 metric tons)   ᵇ 6 That is, Northwest Mesopotamia   ᶜ 16 That is, the Euphrates   ᵈ 2 Or of Milcom, that is, Molech   ᵉ 2 That is, about 75 pounds (about 34 kilograms)

WAR WITH THE PHILISTINES

⁴In the course of time, war broke out with the Philistines, at Gezer. At that time Sibbecai the Hushathite killed Sippai, one of the descendants of the Rephaites, and the Philistines were subjugated.

⁵In another battle with the Philistines, Elhanan son of Jair killed Lahmi the brother of Goliath the Gittite, who had a spear with a shaft like a weaver's rod.

⁶In still another battle, which took place at Gath, there was a huge man with six fingers on each hand and six toes on each foot—twenty-four in all. He also was descended from Rapha. ⁷When he taunted Israel, Jonathan son of Shimea, David's brother, killed him.

⁸These were descendants of Rapha in Gath, and they fell at the hands of David and his men.

DAVID NUMBERS THE FIGHTING MEN

21 Satan rose up against Israel and incited David to take a census of Israel. ²So David said to Joab and the commanders of the troops, "Go and count the Israelites from Beersheba to Dan. Then report back to me so that I may know how many there are."

³But Joab replied, "May the LORD multiply his troops a hundred times over. My lord the king, are they not all my lord's subjects? Why does my lord want to do this? Why should he bring guilt on Israel?"

⁴The king's word, however, overruled Joab; so Joab left and went throughout Israel and then came back to Jerusalem. ⁵Joab reported the number of the fighting men to David: In all Israel there were one million one hundred thousand men who could handle a sword, including four hundred and seventy thousand in Judah.

⁶But Joab did not include Levi and Benjamin in the numbering, because the king's command was repulsive to him. ⁷This command was also evil in the sight of God; so he punished Israel.

⁸Then David said to God, "I have sinned greatly by doing this. Now, I beg you, take away the guilt of your servant. I have done a very foolish thing."

⁹The LORD said to Gad, David's seer, ¹⁰"Go and tell David, 'This is what the LORD says: I am giving you three options. Choose one of them for me to carry out against you.'"

NOW OR NEVER
1CH 21:1-4

The moment you start to think you've got it made, you're at your most vulnerable point spiritually. Satan can use pride—the tendency to trust in your own strength—to bring you down just as easily (and effectively) as he can use lowlier forms of temptation.

¹¹So Gad went to David and said to him, "This is what the LORD says: 'Take your choice: ¹²three years of famine, three months of being swept away[a] before your enemies, with their swords overtaking you, or three days of the sword of the LORD—days of plague in the land, with the angel of the LORD ravaging every part of Israel.' Now then, decide how I should answer the one who sent me."

¹³David said to Gad, "I am in deep distress. Let me fall into the hands of the LORD, for his mercy is very great; but do not let me fall into the hands of men."

¹⁴So the LORD sent a plague on Israel, and seventy thousand men of Israel fell dead. ¹⁵And God sent an angel to destroy Jerusalem. But as the angel was doing so, the LORD saw it and was grieved because of the calamity and said to the angel who was destroying the people, "Enough! Withdraw your hand." The angel of the LORD was then standing at the threshing floor of Araunah[b] the Jebusite.

¹⁶David looked up and saw the angel of the LORD standing between heaven and earth, with a drawn sword in his hand extended over Jerusalem. Then David and the elders, clothed in sackcloth, fell facedown.

¹⁷David said to God, "Was it not I who ordered the fighting men to be counted? I am the one who has sinned and done wrong. These are but sheep. What have they done? O LORD my God, let your hand fall upon me and my family, but do not let this plague remain on your people."

¹⁸Then the angel of the LORD ordered Gad to tell David to go up and build an altar to the LORD on the threshing floor of Araunah the Jebusite. ¹⁹So David went up in obedience to the word that Gad had spoken in the name of the LORD.

ᵃ 12 Hebrew; Septuagint and Vulgate (see also 2 Samuel 24:13) of fleeing   ᵇ 15 Hebrew Ornan, a variant of Araunah; also in verses 18-28

²⁰While Araunah was threshing wheat, he turned and saw the angel; his four sons who were with him hid themselves. ²¹Then David approached, and when Araunah looked and saw him, he left the threshing floor and bowed down before David with his face to the ground.

²²David said to him, "Let me have the site of your threshing floor so I can build an altar to the Lord, that the plague on the people may be stopped. Sell it to me at the full price."

²³Araunah said to David, "Take it! Let my lord the king do whatever pleases him. Look, I will give the oxen for the burnt offerings, the threshing sledges for the wood, and the wheat for the grain offering. I will give all this."

²⁴But King David replied to Araunah, "No, I insist on paying the full price. I will not take for the Lord what is yours, or sacrifice a burnt offering that costs me nothing."

²⁵So David paid Araunah six hundred shekels[a] of gold for the site. ²⁶David built an altar to the Lord there and sacrificed burnt offerings and fellowship offerings.[b] He called on the Lord, and the Lord answered him with fire from heaven on the altar of burnt offering.

²⁷Then the Lord spoke to the angel, and he put his sword back into its sheath. ²⁸At that time, when David saw that the Lord had answered him on the threshing floor of Araunah the Jebusite, he offered sacrifices there. ²⁹The tabernacle of the Lord, which Moses had made in the desert, and the altar of burnt offering were at that time on the high place at Gibeon. ³⁰But David could not go before it to inquire of God, because he was afraid of the sword of the angel of the Lord.

22

Then David said, "The house of the Lord God is to be here, and also the altar of burnt offering for Israel."

PREPARATIONS FOR THE TEMPLE

²So David gave orders to assemble the aliens living in Israel, and from among them he appointed stonecutters to prepare dressed stone for building the house of God. ³He provided a large amount of iron to make nails for the doors of the gateways and for the fittings, and more bronze than could be weighed. ⁴He also provided more cedar logs than could be counted, for the Sidonians and Tyrians had brought large numbers of them to David.

⁵David said, "My son Solomon is young and inexperienced, and the house to be built for the Lord should be of great magnificence and fame and splendor in the sight of all the nations. Therefore I will make preparations for it." So David made extensive preparations before his death.

⁶Then he called for his son Solomon and charged him to build a house for the Lord, the God of Israel. ⁷David said to Solomon: "My son, I had it in my heart to build a house for the Name of the Lord my God. ⁸But this word of the Lord came to me: 'You have shed much blood and have fought many wars. You are not to build a house for my Name, because you have shed much blood on the earth in my sight. ⁹But you will have a son who will be a man of peace and rest, and I will give him rest from all his enemies on every side. His name will be Solomon,[c] and I will grant Israel peace and quiet during his reign. ¹⁰He is the one who will build a house for my Name. He will be my son, and I will be his father. And I will establish the throne of his kingdom over Israel forever.'

¹¹"Now, my son, the Lord be with you, and may you have success and build the house of the Lord your God, as he said you would. ¹²May the Lord give you discretion and understanding when he puts you in command over Israel, so that you may keep the law of the Lord your God. ¹³Then you will have success if you are careful to observe the decrees and laws that the Lord gave Moses for Israel. Be strong and courageous. Do not be afraid or discouraged.

¹⁴"I have taken great pains to provide for the temple of the Lord a hundred thousand talents[d] of gold, a million talents[e] of silver, quantities of bronze and iron too great to be weighed, and wood and stone. And you may add to them. ¹⁵You have many workmen: stonecutters, masons and carpenters, as well as men skilled in every kind of work ¹⁶in gold and silver, bronze and iron—craftsmen beyond number. Now begin the work, and the Lord be with you."

¹⁷Then David ordered all the leaders of Israel to help his son Solomon. ¹⁸He said to them, "Is not the Lord your God with you? And has he not granted you rest on every side? For he has handed the inhabitants of the land over to me, and the land is subject to the Lord and to his people. ¹⁹Now devote your heart and soul to seeking the Lord your God. Begin to build the sanctuary of the Lord God, so that

---

ᵃ 25 That is, about 15 pounds (about 7 kilograms)   ᵇ 26 Traditionally *peace offerings*   ᶜ 9 *Solomon* sounds like and may be derived from the Hebrew for *peace*.   ᵈ 14 That is, about 3,750 tons (about 3,450 metric tons)   ᵉ 14 That is, about 37,500 tons (about 34,500 metric tons) you may bring the ark of the covenant of the Lord and the sacred articles belonging to God into the temple that will be built for the Name of the Lord."

THE LEVITES

23 When David was old and full of years, he made his son Solomon king over Israel. [2]He also gathered together all the leaders of Israel, as well as the priests and Levites. [3]The Levites thirty years old or more were counted, and the total number of men was thirty-eight thousand. [4]David said, "Of these, twenty-four thousand are to supervise the work of the temple of the Lord and six thousand are to be officials and judges. [5]Four thousand are to be gatekeepers and four thousand are to praise the Lord with the musical instruments I have provided for that purpose."

[6]David divided the Levites into groups corresponding to the sons of Levi: Gershon, Kohath and Merari.

GERSHONITES

[7]Belonging to the Gershonites:
   Ladan and Shimei.
   [8]The sons of Ladan:
   Jehiel the first, Zetham and Joel—three in all.
   [9]The sons of Shimei:
   Shelomoth, Haziel and Haran—three in all.
   These were the heads of the families of Ladan.
   [10]And the sons of Shimei:
   Jahath, Ziza,[a] Jeush and Beriah.
   These were the sons of Shimei—four in all.
      [11]Jahath was the first and Ziza the second, but Jeush and Beriah did not have many sons; so they were counted as one family with one assignment.

KOHATHITES

[12]The sons of Kohath:
   Amram, Izhar, Hebron and Uzziel—four in all.
   [13]The sons of Amram:
   Aaron and Moses.
   Aaron was set apart, he and his descendants forever, to consecrate the most holy things, to offer sacrifices before the Lord, to minister before him and to pronounce blessings in his name forever. [14]The sons of Moses the man of God were counted as part of the tribe of Levi.
   [15]The sons of Moses:
   Gershom and Eliezer.
   [16]The descendants of Gershom:
   Shubael was the first.
   [17]The descendants of Eliezer:
   Rehabiah was the first.
   Eliezer had no other sons, but the sons of Rehabiah were very numerous.
   [18]The sons of Izhar:
   Shelomith was the first.
   [19]The sons of Hebron:
   Jeriah the first, Amariah the second, Jahaziel the third and Jekameam the fourth.
   [20]The sons of Uzziel:
   Micah the first and Isshiah the second.

MERARITES

[21]The sons of Merari:
   Mahli and Mushi.
   The sons of Mahli:
   Eleazar and Kish.

---

[a] *10* One Hebrew manuscript, Septuagint and Vulgate (see also verse 11); most Hebrew manuscripts *Zina*

²²Eleazar died without having sons: he had only daughters. Their cousins, the sons of Kish, married them.
²³The sons of Mushi:
Mahli, Eder and Jerimoth—three in all.

²⁴These were the descendants of Levi by their families—the heads of families as they were registered under their names and counted individually, that is, the workers twenty years old or more who served in the temple of the LORD. ²⁵For David had said, "Since the LORD, the God of Israel, has granted rest to his people and has come to dwell in Jerusalem forever, ²⁶the Levites no longer need to carry the tabernacle or any of the articles used in its service." ²⁷According to the last instructions of David, the Levites were counted from those twenty years old or more.

²⁸The duty of the Levites was to help Aaron's descendants in the service of the temple of the LORD: to be in charge of the courtyards, the side rooms, the purification of all sacred things and the performance of other duties at the house of God. ²⁹They were in charge of the bread set out on the table, the flour for the grain offerings, the unleavened wafers, the baking and the mixing, and all measurements of quantity and size. ³⁰They were also to stand every morning to thank and praise the LORD. They were to do the same in the evening ³¹and whenever burnt offerings were presented to the LORD on Sabbaths and at New Moon festivals and at appointed feasts. They were to serve before the LORD regularly in the proper number and in the way prescribed for them.

³²And so the Levites carried out their responsibilities for the Tent of Meeting, for the Holy Place and, under their brothers the descendants of Aaron, for the service of the temple of the LORD.

NOW OR NEVER
1CH 23:30-31

What does your church attendance record look like? Is worship an absolute priority in your life, or is it something you only do when you feel like it?

THE DIVISIONS OF PRIESTS

24

These were the divisions of the sons of Aaron:
The sons of Aaron were Nadab, Abihu, Eleazar and Ithamar. ²But Nadab and Abihu died before their father did, and they had no sons; so Eleazar and Ithamar served as the priests. ³With the help of Zadok a descendant of Eleazar and Ahimelech a descendant of Ithamar, David separated them into divisions for their appointed order of ministering. ⁴A larger number of leaders were found among Eleazar's descendants than among Ithamar's, and they were divided accordingly: sixteen heads of families from Eleazar's descendants and eight heads of families from Ithamar's descendants. ⁵They divided them impartially by drawing lots, for there were officials of the sanctuary and officials of God among the descendants of both Eleazar and Ithamar.

⁶The scribe Shemaiah son of Nethanel, a Levite, recorded their names in the presence of the king and of the officials: Zadok the priest, Ahimelech son of Abiathar and the heads of families of the priests and of the Levites—one family being taken from Eleazar and then one from Ithamar.

⁷The first lot fell to Jehoiarib,
the second to Jedaiah,
⁸the third to Harim,
the fourth to Seorim,
⁹the fifth to Malkijah,
the sixth to Mijamin,
¹⁰the seventh to Hakkoz,
the eighth to Abijah,
¹¹the ninth to Jeshua,
the tenth to Shecaniah,
¹²the eleventh to Eliashib,
the twelfth to Jakim,

13 the thirteenth to Huppah,
   the fourteenth to Jeshebeab,
14 the fifteenth to Bilgah,
   the sixteenth to Immer,
15 the seventeenth to Hezir,
   the eighteenth to Happizzez,
16 the nineteenth to Pethahiah,
   the twentieth to Jehezkel,
17 the twenty-first to Jakin,
   the twenty-second to Gamul,
18 the twenty-third to Delaiah
   and the twenty-fourth to Maaziah.

19 This was their appointed order of ministering when they entered the temple of the LORD, according to the regulations prescribed for them by their forefather Aaron, as the LORD, the God of Israel, had commanded him.

THE REST OF THE LEVITES

20 As for the rest of the descendants of Levi:
   from the sons of Amram: Shubael;
      from the sons of Shubael: Jehdeiah.
   21 As for Rehabiah, from his sons:
      Isshiah was the first.
22 From the Izharites: Shelomoth;
   from the sons of Shelomoth: Jahath.
23 The sons of Hebron: Jeriah the first,[a] Amariah the second, Jahaziel the third and Jekameam the fourth.
24 The son of Uzziel: Micah;
   from the sons of Micah: Shamir.
   25 The brother of Micah: Isshiah;
      from the sons of Isshiah: Zechariah.
26 The sons of Merari: Mahli and Mushi.
   The son of Jaaziah: Beno.
27 The sons of Merari:
   from Jaaziah: Beno, Shoham, Zaccur and Ibri.
28 From Mahli: Eleazar, who had no sons.
29 From Kish: the son of Kish:
   Jerahmeel.
30 And the sons of Mushi: Mahli, Eder and Jerimoth.

These were the Levites, according to their families. 31 They also cast lots, just as their brothers the descendants of Aaron did, in the presence of King David and of Zadok, Ahimelech, and the heads of families of the priests and of the Levites. The families of the oldest brother were treated the same as those of the youngest.

THE SINGERS

25 David, together with the commanders of the army, set apart some of the sons of Asaph, Heman and Jeduthun for the ministry of prophesying, accompanied by harps, lyres and cymbals. Here is the list of the men who performed this service:

2 From the sons of Asaph:
   Zaccur, Joseph, Nethaniah and Asarelah. The sons of Asaph were under the supervision of Asaph, who prophesied under the king's supervision.
3 As for Jeduthun, from his sons:

---

a 23 Two Hebrew manuscripts and some Septuagint manuscripts (see also 1 Chron. 23:19); most Hebrew manuscripts *The sons of Jeriah:*

Gedaliah, Zeri, Jeshaiah, Shimei,[a] Hashabiah and Mattithiah, six in all, under the supervision of their father Jeduthun, who prophesied, using the harp in thanking and praising the LORD. [4]As for Heman, from his sons:

Bukkiah, Mattaniah, Uzziel, Shubael and Jerimoth; Hananiah, Hanani, Eliathah, Giddalti and Romamti-Ezer; Joshbekashah, Mallothi, Hothir and Mahazioth. [5]All these were sons of Heman the king's seer. They were given him through the promises of God to exalt him.[b] God gave Heman fourteen sons and three daughters.

[6]All these men were under the supervision of their fathers for the music of the temple of the LORD, with cymbals, lyres and harps, for the ministry at the house of God. Asaph, Jeduthun and Heman were under the supervision of the king. [7]Along with their relatives—all of them trained and skilled in music for the LORD—they numbered 288. [8]Young and old alike, teacher as well as student, cast lots for their duties.

[9]The first lot, which was for Asaph, fell to Joseph,
    his sons and relatives,[c]   12[d]
  the second to Gedaliah,
    he and his relatives and sons,   12
[10]the third to Zaccur,
    his sons and relatives,   12
[11]the fourth to Izri,[e]
    his sons and relatives,   12
[12]the fifth to Nethaniah,
    his sons and relatives,   12
[13]the sixth to Bukkiah,
    his sons and relatives,   12
[14]the seventh to Jesarelah,[f]
    his sons and relatives,   12
[15]the eighth to Jeshaiah,
    his sons and relatives,   12
[16]the ninth to Mattaniah,
    his sons and relatives,   12
[17]the tenth to Shimei,
    his sons and relatives,   12
[18]the eleventh to Azarel,[g]
    his sons and relatives,   12
[19]the twelfth to Hashabiah,
    his sons and relatives,   12
[20]the thirteenth to Shubael,
    his sons and relatives,   12
[21]the fourteenth to Mattithiah,
    his sons and relatives,   12
[22]the fifteenth to Jerimoth,
    his sons and relatives,   12
[23]the sixteenth to Hananiah,
    his sons and relatives,   12
[24]the seventeenth to Joshbekashah,
    his sons and relatives,   12
[25]the eighteenth to Hanani,
    his sons and relatives,   12
[26]the nineteenth to Mallothi,
    his sons and relatives,   12
[27]the twentieth to Eliathah,
    his sons and relatives,   12

---

[a] 3 One Hebrew manuscript and some Septuagint manuscripts (see also verse 17); most Hebrew manuscripts do not have *Shimei*.
[b] 5 Hebrew *exalt the horn*   [c] 9 See Septuagint; Hebrew does not have *his sons and relatives.*   [d] 9 See the total in verse 7; Hebrew does not have *twelve.*   [e] 11 A variant of *Zeri*   [f] 14 A variant of *Asarelah*   [g] 18 A variant of *Uzziel*

²⁸the twenty-first to Hothir,
his sons and relatives,   12
²⁹the twenty-second to Giddalti,
his sons and relatives,   12
³⁰the twenty-third to Mahazioth,
his sons and relatives,   12
³¹the twenty-fourth to Romamti-Ezer,
his sons and relatives,   12

THE GATEKEEPERS

 The divisions of the gatekeepers:

From the Korahites: Meshelemiah son of Kore, one of the sons of Asaph.
²Meshelemiah had sons:
Zechariah the firstborn,
Jediael the second,
Zebadiah the third,
Jathniel the fourth,
³Elam the fifth,
Jehohanan the sixth
and Eliehoenai the seventh.
⁴Obed-Edom also had sons:
Shemaiah the firstborn,
Jehozabad the second,
Joah the third,
Sacar the fourth,
Nethanel the fifth,
⁵Ammiel the sixth,
Issachar the seventh
and Peullethai the eighth.
(For God had blessed Obed-Edom.)

⁶His son Shemaiah also had sons, who were leaders in their father's family because they were very capable men. ⁷The sons of Shemaiah: Othni, Rephael, Obed and Elzabad; his relatives Elihu and Semakiah were also able men. ⁸All these were descendants of Obed-Edom; they and their sons and their relatives were capable men with the strength to do the work—descendants of Obed-Edom, 62 in all.

⁹Meshelemiah had sons and relatives, who were able men—18 in all.

¹⁰Hosah the Merarite had sons: Shimri the first (although he was not the firstborn, his father had appointed him the first), ¹¹Hilkiah the second, Tabaliah the third and Zechariah the fourth. The sons and relatives of Hosah were 13 in all.

¹²These divisions of the gatekeepers, through their chief men, had duties for ministering in the temple of the LORD, just as their relatives had. ¹³Lots were cast for each gate, according to their families, young and old alike.

¹⁴The lot for the East Gate fell to Shelemiah.ᵃ Then lots were cast for his son Zechariah, a wise counselor, and the lot for the North Gate fell to him. ¹⁵The lot for the South Gate fell to Obed-Edom, and the lot for the storehouse fell to his sons. ¹⁶The lots for the West Gate and the Shalleketh Gate on the upper road fell to Shuppim and Hosah.

Guard was alongside of guard: ¹⁷There were six Levites a day on the east, four a day on the north, four a day on the south and two at a time at the storehouse. ¹⁸As for the court to the west, there were four at the road and two at the court itself.

¹⁹These were the divisions of the gatekeepers who were descendants of Korah and Merari.

ᵃ 14 A variant of *Meshelemiah*

THE TREASURERS AND OTHER OFFICIALS

[20] Their fellow Levites were[a] in charge of the treasuries of the house of God and the treasuries for the dedicated things.

[21] The descendants of Ladan, who were Gershonites through Ladan and who were heads of families belonging to Ladan the Gershonite, were Jehieli, [22] the sons of Jehieli, Zetham and his brother Joel. They were in charge of the treasuries of the temple of the LORD.

[23] From the Amramites, the Izharites, the Hebronites and the Uzzielites:

[24] Shubael, a descendant of Gershom son of Moses, was the officer in charge of the treasuries. [25] His relatives through Eliezer: Rehabiah his son, Jeshaiah his son, Joram his son, Zicri his son and Shelomith his son. [26] Shelomith and his relatives were in charge of all the treasuries for the things dedicated by King David, by the heads of families who were the commanders of thousands and commanders of hundreds, and by the other army commanders. [27] Some of the plunder taken in battle they dedicated for the repair of the temple of the LORD. [28] And everything dedicated by Samuel the seer and by Saul son of Kish, Abner son of Ner and Joab son of Zeruiah, and all the other dedicated things were in the care of Shelomith and his relatives.

[29] From the Izharites: Kenaniah and his sons were assigned duties away from the temple, as officials and judges over Israel.

[30] From the Hebronites: Hashabiah and his relatives—seventeen hundred able men—were responsible in Israel west of the Jordan for all the work of the LORD and for the king's service. [31] As for the Hebronites, Jeriah was their chief according to the genealogical records of their families. In the fortieth year of David's reign a search was made in the records, and capable men among the Hebronites were found at Jazer in Gilead. [32] Jeriah had twenty-seven hundred relatives, who were able men and heads of families, and King David put them in charge of the Reubenites, the Gadites and the half-tribe of Manasseh for every matter pertaining to God and for the affairs of the king.

ARMY DIVISIONS

27 This is the list of the Israelites—heads of families, commanders of thousands and commanders of hundreds, and their officers, who served the king in all that concerned the army divisions that were on duty month by month throughout the year. Each division consisted of 24,000 men.

[2] In charge of the first division, for the first month, was Jashobeam son of Zabdiel. There were 24,000 men in his division. [3] He was a descendant of Perez and chief of all the army officers for the first month.

[4] In charge of the division for the second month was Dodai the Ahohite; Mikloth was the leader of his division. There were 24,000 men in his division.

[5] The third army commander, for the third month, was Benaiah son of Jehoiada the priest. He was chief and there were 24,000 men in his division. [6] This was the Benaiah who was a mighty man among the Thirty and was over the Thirty. His son Ammizabad was in charge of his division.

[7] The fourth, for the fourth month, was Asahel the brother of Joab; his son Zebadiah was his successor. There were 24,000 men in his division.

[8] The fifth, for the fifth month, was the commander Shamhuth the Izrahite. There were 24,000 men in his division.

[9] The sixth, for the sixth month, was Ira the son of Ikkesh the Tekoite. There were 24,000 men in his division.

[10] The seventh, for the seventh month, was Helez the Pelonite, an Ephraimite. There were 24,000 men in his division.

[11] The eighth, for the eighth month, was Sibbecai the Hushathite, a Zerahite. There were 24,000 men in his division.

[12] The ninth, for the ninth month, was Abiezer the Anathothite, a Benjamite. There were 24,000 men in his division.

---

[a] 20 Septuagint; Hebrew *As for the Levites, Ahijah was*

¹³ The tenth, for the tenth month, was Maharai the Netophathite, a Zerahite. There were 24,000 men in his division.

¹⁴ The eleventh, for the eleventh month, was Benaiah the Pirathonite, an Ephraimite. There were 24,000 men in his division.

¹⁵ The twelfth, for the twelfth month, was Heldai the Netophathite, from the family of Othniel. There were 24,000 men in his division.

OFFICERS OF THE TRIBES

¹⁶ The officers over the tribes of Israel:

over the Reubenites: Eliezer son of Zicri;
over the Simeonites: Shephatiah son of Maacah;
¹⁷ over Levi: Hashabiah son of Kemuel;
over Aaron: Zadok;
¹⁸ over Judah: Elihu, a brother of David;
over Issachar: Omri son of Michael;
¹⁹ over Zebulun: Ishmaiah son of Obadiah;
over Naphtali: Jerimoth son of Azriel;
²⁰ over the Ephraimites: Hoshea son of Azaziah;
over half the tribe of Manasseh: Joel son of Pedaiah;
²¹ over the half-tribe of Manasseh in Gilead: Iddo son of Zechariah;
over Benjamin: Jaasiel son of Abner;
²² over Dan: Azarel son of Jeroham.
These were the officers over the tribes of Israel.

²³ David did not take the number of the men twenty years old or less, because the Lord had promised to make Israel as numerous as the stars in the sky. ²⁴ Joab son of Zeruiah began to count the men but did not finish. Wrath came on Israel on account of this numbering, and the number was not entered in the book^a of the annals of King David.

THE KING'S OVERSEERS

²⁵ Azmaveth son of Adiel was in charge of the royal storehouses.

Jonathan son of Uzziah was in charge of the storehouses in the outlying districts, in the towns, the villages and the watchtowers.

²⁶ Ezri son of Kelub was in charge of the field workers who farmed the land.

²⁷ Shimei the Ramathite was in charge of the vineyards.

Zabdi the Shiphmite was in charge of the produce of the vineyards for the wine vats.

²⁸ Baal-Hanan the Gederite was in charge of the olive and sycamore-fig trees in the western foothills.

Joash was in charge of the supplies of olive oil.

²⁹ Shitrai the Sharonite was in charge of the herds grazing in Sharon.

Shaphat son of Adlai was in charge of the herds in the valleys.

³⁰ Obil the Ishmaelite was in charge of the camels.

Jehdeiah the Meronothite was in charge of the donkeys.

³¹ Jaziz the Hagrite was in charge of the flocks.

All these were the officials in charge of King David's property.

³² Jonathan, David's uncle, was a counselor, a man of insight and a scribe. Jehiel son of Hacmoni took care of the king's sons.

³³ Ahithophel was the king's counselor.

Hushai the Arkite was the king's friend. ³⁴ Ahithophel was succeeded by Jehoiada son of Benaiah and by Abiathar.

Joab was the commander of the royal army.

---

^a 24 Septuagint; Hebrew *number*

DAVID'S PLANS FOR THE TEMPLE

28

David summoned all the officials of Israel to assemble at Jerusalem: the officers over the tribes, the commanders of the divisions in the service of the king, the commanders of thousands and commanders of hundreds, and the officials in charge of all the property and livestock belonging to the king and his sons, together with the palace officials, the mighty men and all the brave warriors.

²King David rose to his feet and said: "Listen to me, my brothers and my people. I had it in my heart to build a house as a place of rest for the ark of the covenant of the Lord, for the footstool of our God, and I made plans to build it. ³But God said to me, 'You are not to build a house for my Name, because you are a warrior and have shed blood.'

⁴"Yet the Lord, the God of Israel, chose me from my whole family to be king over Israel forever. He chose Judah as leader, and from the house of Judah he chose my family, and from my father's sons he was pleased to make me king over all Israel. ⁵Of all my sons—and the Lord has given me many—he has chosen my son Solomon to sit on the throne of the kingdom of the Lord over Israel. ⁶He said to me: 'Solomon your son is the one who will build my house and my courts, for I have chosen him to be my son, and I will be his father. ⁷I will establish his kingdom forever if he is unswerving in carrying out my commands and laws, as is being done at this time.'

NOW OR NEVER

1CH 28:8

Name at least three specific commands that you know God has given you to follow. How well have you kept these commands? What changes can you make in your life in order to obey them more consistently?

⁸"So now I charge you in the sight of all Israel and of the assembly of the Lord, and in the hearing of our God: Be careful to follow all the commands of the Lord your God, that you may possess this good land and pass it on as an inheritance to your descendants forever.

⁹"And you, my son Solomon, acknowledge the God of your father, and serve him with wholehearted devotion and with a willing mind, for the Lord searches every heart and understands every motive behind the thoughts. If you seek him, he will be found by you; but if you forsake him, he will reject you forever. ¹⁰Consider now, for the Lord has chosen you to build a temple as a sanctuary. Be strong and do the work."

¹¹Then David gave his son Solomon the plans for the portico of the temple, its buildings, its storerooms, its upper parts, its inner rooms and the place of atonement. ¹²He gave him the plans of all that the Spirit had put in his mind for the courts of the temple of the Lord and all the surrounding rooms, for the treasuries of the temple of God and for the treasuries for the dedicated things. ¹³He gave him instructions for the divisions of the priests and Levites, and for all the work of serving in the temple of the Lord, as well as for all the articles to be used in its service. ¹⁴He designated the weight of gold for all the gold articles to be used in various kinds of service, and the weight of silver for all the silver articles to be used in various kinds of service: ¹⁵the weight of gold for the gold lampstands and their lamps, with the weight for each lampstand and its lamps; and the weight of silver for each silver lampstand and its lamps, according to the use of each lampstand; ¹⁶the weight of gold for each table for consecrated bread; the weight of silver for the silver tables; ¹⁷the weight of pure gold for the forks, sprinkling bowls and pitchers; the weight of gold for each gold dish; the weight of silver for each silver dish; ¹⁸and the weight of the refined gold for the altar of incense. He also gave him the plan for the chariot, that is, the cherubim of gold that spread their wings and shelter the ark of the covenant of the Lord.

¹⁹"All this," David said, "I have in writing from the hand of the Lord upon me, and he gave me understanding in all the details of the plan."

²⁰David also said to Solomon his son, "Be strong and courageous, and do the work. Do not be afraid or discouraged, for the Lord God, my God, is with you. He will not fail you or forsake you until all the work for the service of the temple of the Lord is finished. ²¹The divisions of the priests and Levites are ready for all the work on the temple of God, and every willing man skilled in any craft will help you in all the work. The officials and all the people will obey your every command."

GIFTS FOR BUILDING THE TEMPLE

29

Then King David said to the whole assembly: "My son Solomon, the one whom God has chosen, is young and inexperienced. The task is great, because this palatial structure is not for man but for the LORD God. ²With all my resources I have provided for the temple of my God—gold for the gold work, silver for the silver, bronze for the bronze, iron for the iron and wood for the wood, as well as onyx for the settings, turquoise,ᵃ stones of various colors, and all kinds of fine stone and marble—all of these in large quantities. ³Besides, in my devotion to the temple of my God I now give my personal treasures of gold and silver for the temple of my God, over and above everything I have provided for this holy temple: ⁴three thousand talentsᵇ of gold (gold of Ophir) and seven thousand talentsᶜ of refined silver, for the overlaying of the walls of the buildings, ⁵for the gold work and the silver work, and for all the work to be done by the craftsmen. Now, who is willing to consecrate himself today to the LORD?"

⁶Then the leaders of families, the officers of the tribes of Israel, the commanders of thousands and commanders of hundreds, and the officials in charge of the king's work gave willingly. ⁷They gave toward the work on the temple of God five thousand talentsᵈ and ten thousand daricsᵉ of gold, ten thousand talentsᶠ of silver, eighteen thousand talentsᵍ of bronze and a hundred thousand talentsʰ of iron. ⁸Any who had precious stones gave them to the treasury of the temple of the LORD in the custody of Jehiel the Gershonite. ⁹The people rejoiced at the willing response of their leaders, for they had given freely and wholeheartedly to the LORD. David the king also rejoiced greatly.

DAVID'S PRAYER

¹⁰David praised the LORD in the presence of the whole assembly, saying,

"Praise be to you, O LORD,
God of our father Israel,
from everlasting to everlasting.

¹¹ Yours, O LORD, is the greatness and the power
and the glory and the majesty and the splendor,
for everything in heaven and earth is yours.
Yours, O LORD, is the kingdom;
you are exalted as head over all.
¹² Wealth and honor come from you;
you are the ruler of all things.
In your hands are strength and power
to exalt and give strength to all.
¹³ Now, our God, we give you thanks,
and praise your glorious name.

¹⁴"But who am I, and who are my people, that we should be able to give as generously as this? Everything comes from you, and we have given you only what comes from your hand. ¹⁵We are aliens and strangers in your sight, as were all our forefathers. Our days on earth are like a shadow, without hope. ¹⁶O LORD our God, as for all this abundance that we have provided for building you a temple for your

---

challenge notes

To: my_son

heavenly_father: when you do my work, people will try to tell you that you're wasting your time. don't listen to them. keep your focus on your kingdom assignment and let me handle the other stuff.

1CH 28:20

NOW OR NEVER

1CH 29:1–9

Are you more likely to spend your money on yourself or give a special offering to God and his work?

ᵃ 2 The meaning of the Hebrew for this word is uncertain.   ᵇ 4 That is, about 110 tons (about 100 metric tons)   ᶜ 4 That is, about 260 tons (about 240 metric tons)   ᵈ 7 That is, about 190 tons (about 170 metric tons)   ᵉ 7 That is, about 185 pounds (about 84 kilograms)   ᶠ 7 That is, about 375 tons (about 345 metric tons)   ᵍ 7 That is, about 675 tons (about 610 metric tons)   ʰ 7 That is, about 3,750 tons (about 3,450 metric tons)

Holy Name, it comes from your hand, and all of it belongs to you. [17]I know, my God, that you test the heart and are pleased with integrity. All these things have I given willingly and with honest intent. And now I have seen with joy how willingly your people who are here have given to you. [18]O LORD, God of our fathers Abraham, Isaac and Israel, keep this desire in the hearts of your people forever, and keep their hearts loyal to you. [19]And give my son Solomon the wholehearted devotion to keep your commands, requirements and decrees and to do everything to build the palatial structure for which I have provided."

[20]Then David said to the whole assembly, "Praise the LORD your God." So they all praised the LORD, the God of their fathers; they bowed low and fell prostrate before the LORD and the king.

SOLOMON ACKNOWLEDGED AS KING

[21]The next day they made sacrifices to the LORD and presented burnt offerings to him: a thousand bulls, a thousand rams and a thousand male lambs, together with their drink offerings, and other sacrifices in abundance for all Israel. [22]They ate and drank with great joy in the presence of the LORD that day.

Then they acknowledged Solomon son of David as king a second time, anointing him before the LORD to be ruler and Zadok to be priest. [23]So Solomon sat on the throne of the LORD as king in place of his father David. He prospered and all Israel obeyed him. [24]All the officers and mighty men, as well as all of King David's sons, pledged their submission to King Solomon.

[25]The LORD highly exalted Solomon in the sight of all Israel and bestowed on him royal splendor such as no king over Israel ever had before.

THE DEATH OF DAVID

[26]David son of Jesse was king over all Israel. [27]He ruled over Israel forty years—seven in Hebron and thirty-three in Jerusalem. [28]He died at a good old age, having enjoyed long life, wealth and honor. His son Solomon succeeded him as king.

[29]As for the events of King David's reign, from beginning to end, they are written in the records of Samuel the seer, the records of Nathan the prophet and the records of Gad the seer, [30]together with the details of his reign and power, and the circumstances that surrounded him and Israel and the kingdoms of all the other lands.

Maintaining Your Integrity

Your reputation hinges on the things you do when people are watching. But your *integrity* is built—and destroyed—by the things you do when no one's around. While a good reputation is valuable, integrity is priceless. David knew how important integrity is to God. He also knew that a person's integrity is tested every day. What kinds of things have tested yours? The websites you visit when you're alone at the computer? The music you listen to? The TV shows you watch? The way you spend your money? What choices do you need to make in order to honor God with integrity?

2 CHRONICLES

« AT A GLANCE

Author
Ezra

Audience
People of Israel

Date
About 430 B.C.

Setting
During Solomon's reign in Jerusalem, paralleling
1 and 2 Kings

Verse to Remember
"If my people, who are called by my name, will
humble themselves and pray and seek my face and
turn from their wicked ways, then will I hear from
heaven and will forgive their sin and will heal their
land" (7:14).

Theme to Consider
Hear God's call that echoes through the ages—
come to him, confess to him and receive his healing and forgiveness.

UNCHANGING TRUTH » Have you ever thought about what kind of legacy you'd like to leave? What do you want people to remember about you after you're gone? Will it be something positive, something significant or something you wouldn't want mentioned in front of your family?

It may seem a little early to be thinking about such things—after all, you're still pretty young. Keep in mind, though, that legacies aren't created in a year or two; they're created over a whole lifetime. That means the things you do now will be part of your legacy, whether you like it or not. What's more, many of the people in your life now may not know you when you're 30 or 40 years old. So you will leave a legacy in their eyes that will include only what they see now.

Solomon's legacy is found in the book of 2 Chronicles (among other places in the Bible). Like most legacies, it's a mixed bag, with highlights (choosing wisdom instead of riches and fame, building God's temple) and blunders (marrying pagan women, worshiping idols). What if Solomon had thought more about his legacy—the example he was leaving for others—while he was still alive? Do you think he might have thought twice about messing around with pagan women if he knew that one day that's what people would read about him and remember about his life?

What steps can you take to start building a positive legacy of your own?

LIFE LESSONS »

I   God rewards faithfulness not only in heaven, but here on earth too (9:13–28).

2   No matter how strong your relationship with the Lord is, pride can ruin everything in a heart-beat (32:24–26).

3   God has used young people to accomplish great things in the past—and he still does (34:1–2).

4   Ignoring God and his Word will eventually result in tragedy (36:15–19).

SOLOMON ASKS FOR WISDOM

1 Solomon son of David established himself firmly over his kingdom, for the LORD his God was with him and made him exceedingly great.

²Then Solomon spoke to all Israel—to the commanders of thousands and commanders of hundreds, to the judges and to all the leaders in Israel, the heads of families— ³and Solomon and the whole assembly went to the high place at Gibeon, for God's Tent of Meeting was there, which Moses the LORD's servant had made in the desert. ⁴Now David had brought up the ark of God from Kiriath Jearim to the place he had prepared for it, because he had pitched a tent for it in Jerusalem. ⁵But the bronze altar that Bezalel son of Uri, the son of Hur, had made was in Gibeon in front of the tabernacle of the LORD; so Solomon and the assembly inquired of him there. ⁶Solomon went up to the bronze altar before the LORD in the Tent of Meeting and offered a thousand burnt offerings on it.

⁷That night God appeared to Solomon and said to him, "Ask for whatever you want me to give you."

⁸Solomon answered God, "You have shown great kindness to David my father and have made me king in his place. ⁹Now, LORD God, let your promise to my father David be confirmed, for you have made me king over a people who are as numerous as the dust of the earth. ¹⁰Give me wisdom and knowledge, that I may lead this people, for who is able to govern this great people of yours?"

¹¹God said to Solomon, "Since this is your heart's desire and you have not asked for wealth, riches or honor, nor for the death of your enemies, and since you have not asked for a long life but for wisdom and knowledge to govern my people over whom I have made you king, ¹²therefore wisdom and knowledge will be given you. And I will also give you wealth, riches and honor, such as no king who was before you ever had and none after you will have."

¹³Then Solomon went to Jerusalem from the high place at Gibeon, from before the Tent of Meeting. And he reigned over Israel.

¹⁴Solomon accumulated chariots and horses; he had fourteen hundred chariots and twelve thousand horses,ª which he kept in the chariot cities and also with him in Jerusalem. ¹⁵The king made silver and gold as common in Jerusalem as stones, and cedar as plentiful as sycamore-fig trees in the foothills. ¹⁶Solomon's horses were imported from Egyptᵇ and from Kueᶜ—the royal merchants purchased them from Kue. ¹⁷They imported a chariot from Egypt for six hundred shekelsᵈ of silver, and a horse for a hundred and fifty.ᵉ They also exported them to all the kings of the Hittites and of the Arameans.

challenge notes

To: my_son

heavenly_father: the kind of offer I made to solomon is also available to you. I can meet your needs in my own special way. solomon asked for wisdom, and look how that changed his life! what will you ask for that will change your life for the better?

2CH 1:7

PREPARATIONS FOR BUILDING THE TEMPLE

2 Solomon gave orders to build a temple for the Name of the LORD and a royal palace for himself. ²He conscripted seventy thousand men as carriers and eighty thousand as stonecutters in the hills and thirty-six hundred as foremen over them.

³Solomon sent this message to Hiramᶠ king of Tyre:

"Send me cedar logs as you did for my father David when you sent him cedar to build a palace to live in. ⁴Now I am about to build a temple for the Name of the LORD my God and to dedicate it to him for burning fragrant incense before him, for setting out the consecrated bread regularly, and for making burnt offerings every morning and evening and on Sabbaths and New Moons and at the appointed feasts of the LORD our God. This is a lasting ordinance for Israel.

⁵"The temple I am going to build will be great, because our God is greater than all other gods. ⁶But who is able to build a temple for him, since the heavens, even the highest heavens, cannot contain him? Who then am I to build a temple for him, except as a place to burn sacrifices before him?

ª *14* Or *charioteers*   ᵇ *16* Or possibly *Muzur,* a region in Cilicia; also in verse 17   ᶜ *16* Probably Cilicia   ᵈ *17* That is, about 15 pounds (about 7 kilograms)   ᵉ *17* That is, about 3 3/4 pounds (about 1.7 kilograms)   ᶠ *3* Hebrew *Huram,* a variant of *Hiram;* also in verses 11 and 12

[7] "Send me, therefore, a man skilled to work in gold and silver, bronze and iron, and in purple, crimson and blue yarn, and experienced in the art of engraving, to work in Judah and Jerusalem with my skilled craftsmen, whom my father David provided.

[8] "Send me also cedar, pine and algum[a] logs from Lebanon, for I know that your men are skilled in cutting timber there. My men will work with yours [9] to provide me with plenty of lumber, because the temple I build must be large and magnificent. [10] I will give your servants, the woodsmen who cut the timber, twenty thousand cors[b] of ground wheat, twenty thousand cors of barley, twenty thousand baths[c] of wine and twenty thousand baths of olive oil."

[11] Hiram king of Tyre replied by letter to Solomon:

"Because the LORD loves his people, he has made you their king."

[12] And Hiram added:

"Praise be to the LORD, the God of Israel, who made heaven and earth! He has given King David a wise son, endowed with intelligence and discernment, who will build a temple for the LORD and a palace for himself.

[13] "I am sending you Huram-Abi, a man of great skill, [14] whose mother was from Dan and whose father was from Tyre. He is trained to work in gold and silver, bronze and iron, stone and wood, and with purple and blue and crimson yarn and fine linen. He is experienced in all kinds of engraving and can execute any design given to him. He will work with your craftsmen and with those of my lord, David your father.

[15] "Now let my lord send his servants the wheat and barley and the olive oil and wine he promised, [16] and we will cut all the logs from Lebanon that you need and will float them in rafts by sea down to Joppa. You can then take them up to Jerusalem."

[17] Solomon took a census of all the aliens who were in Israel, after the census his father David had taken; and they were found to be 153,600. [18] He assigned 70,000 of them to be carriers and 80,000 to be stonecutters in the hills, with 3,600 foremen over them to keep the people working.

SOLOMON BUILDS THE TEMPLE

3 Then Solomon began to build the temple of the LORD in Jerusalem on Mount Moriah, where the LORD had appeared to his father David. It was on the threshing floor of Araunah[d] the Jebusite, the place provided by David. [2] He began building on the second day of the second month in the fourth year of his reign.

[3] The foundation Solomon laid for building the temple of God was sixty cubits long and twenty cubits wide[e] (using the cubit of the old standard). [4] The portico at the front of the temple was twenty cubits[f] long across the width of the building and twenty cubits[g] high.

He overlaid the inside with pure gold. [5] He paneled the main hall with pine and covered it with fine gold and decorated it with palm tree and chain designs. [6] He adorned the temple with precious stones. And the gold he used was gold of Parvaim. [7] He overlaid the ceiling beams, doorframes, walls and doors of the temple with gold, and he carved cherubim on the walls.

[8] He built the Most Holy Place, its length corresponding to the width of the temple—twenty cubits long and twenty cubits wide. He overlaid the inside with six hundred talents[h] of fine gold. [9] The gold nails weighed fifty shekels.[i] He also overlaid the upper parts with gold.

[10] In the Most Holy Place he made a pair of sculptured cherubim and overlaid them with gold. [11] The

---

חםש םר חΞΛΞר

2CH 2:5–7

How do you honor a God who is infinitely perfect? Thankfully, whatever skills we have, however small, can be used to glorify God. No matter the situation, if you give God your best and devote your work to him, it will be pleasing and honoring to him.

---

[a] 8 Probably a variant of *almug*; possibly juniper   [b] 10 That is, probably about 125,000 bushels (about 4,400 kiloliters)   [c] 10 That is, probably about 115,000 gallons (about 440 kiloliters)   [d] 1 Hebrew *Ornan*, a variant of *Araunah*   [e] 3 That is, about 90 feet (about 27 meters) long and 30 feet (about 9 meters) wide   [f] 4 That is, about 30 feet (about 9 meters); also in verses 8, 11 and 13   [g] 4 Some Septuagint and Syriac manuscripts; Hebrew *and a hundred and twenty*   [h] 8 That is, about 23 tons (about 21 metric tons)   [i] 9 That is, about 1 1/4 pounds (about 0.6 kilogram)

total wingspan of the cherubim was twenty cubits. One wing of the first cherub was five cubits[a] long and touched the temple wall, while its other wing, also five cubits long, touched the wing of the other cherub. [12]Similarly one wing of the second cherub was five cubits long and touched the other temple wall, and its other wing, also five cubits long, touched the wing of the first cherub. [13]The wings of these cherubim extended twenty cubits. They stood on their feet, facing the main hall.[b]

[14]He made the curtain of blue, purple and crimson yarn and fine linen, with cherubim worked into it.

[15]In the front of the temple he made two pillars, which ⌐together⌐ were thirty-five cubits[c] long, each with a capital on top measuring five cubits. [16]He made interwoven chains[d] and put them on top of the pillars. He also made a hundred pomegranates and attached them to the chains. [17]He erected the pillars in the front of the temple, one to the south and one to the north. The one to the south he named Jakin[e] and the one to the north Boaz.[f]

THE TEMPLE'S FURNISHINGS

4 He made a bronze altar twenty cubits long, twenty cubits wide and ten cubits high.[g] [2]He made the Sea of cast metal, circular in shape, measuring ten cubits from rim to rim and five cubits[h] high. It took a line of thirty cubits[i] to measure around it. [3]Below the rim, figures of bulls encircled it—ten to a cubit.[j] The bulls were cast in two rows in one piece with the Sea.

[4]The Sea stood on twelve bulls, three facing north, three facing west, three facing south and three facing east. The Sea rested on top of them, and their hindquarters were toward the center. [5]It was a handbreadth[k] in thickness, and its rim was like the rim of a cup, like a lily blossom. It held three thousand baths.[l]

[6]He then made ten basins for washing and placed five on the south side and five on the north. In them the things to be used for the burnt offerings were rinsed, but the Sea was to be used by the priests for washing.

[7]He made ten gold lampstands according to the specifications for them and placed them in the temple, five on the south side and five on the north.

[8]He made ten tables and placed them in the temple, five on the south side and five on the north. He also made a hundred gold sprinkling bowls.

[9]He made the courtyard of the priests, and the large court and the doors for the court, and overlaid the doors with bronze. [10]He placed the Sea on the south side, at the southeast corner.

[11]He also made the pots and shovels and sprinkling bowls.

So Huram finished the work he had undertaken for King Solomon in the temple of God:

[12]the two pillars;
the two bowl-shaped capitals on top of the pillars;
the two sets of network decorating the two bowl-shaped capitals on top of the pillars;
[13]the four hundred pomegranates for the two sets of network (two rows of pomegranates for each network, decorating the bowl-shaped capitals on top of the pillars);
[14]the stands with their basins;
[15]the Sea and the twelve bulls under it;

Striving for Excellence

"Good enough" wasn't good enough for Solomon. He could have lowered his sights a little, cut a few corners to save time and money and still have created an impressive temple for the Lord. But Solomon viewed his work on the temple as a gift to God, wasn't about to offer anything less than his best. That's why Solomon sweated every detail and spared no expense to create something truly spectacular. What do you have to offer the Lord? A talent for art or music? An ability to build or fix things? A knack for organizing or managing? Think about how you can present your gifts to God in a way that goes beyond "good enough" and becomes spectacular.

---

[a] 11 That is, about 7 1/2 feet (about 2.3 meters); also in verse 15   [b] 13 Or facing inward   [c] 15 That is, about 52 feet (about 16 meters)   [d] 16 Or possibly made chains in the inner sanctuary; the meaning of the Hebrew for this phrase is uncertain.   [e] 17 Jakin probably means he establishes.   [f] 17 Boaz probably means in him is strength.   [g] 1 That is, about 30 feet (about 9 meters) long and wide, and about 15 feet (about 4.5 meters) high   [h] 2 That is, about 7 1/2 feet (about 2.3 meters)   [i] 2 That is, about 45 feet (about 13.5 meters)   [j] 3 That is, about 1 1/2 feet (about 0.5 meter)   [k] 5 That is, about 3 inches (about 8 centimeters)   [l] 5 That is, about 17,500 gallons (about 66 kiloliters)

battlelines

» *Flying Off the Handle (Short Fuse)*

Q: In trouble?
A: Yep.

Q: What happened?
A: I mouthed off to my teacher. She was nagging me again about something stupid, and I just went off on her. Boom! Before I even realized what I was doing, I was standing at the front of the room, yelling back at her—right in her face.

Q: Yikes.
A: Yeah. Even my friends were all wide-eyed and stuff. I don't even want to think of what the punishment might be.

Q: Why do you think you got so angry?
A: I couldn't tell you.

Q: Did this just happen out of the blue or something?
A: No, not exactly. Lately I've just been on edge. I've been ripping into everybody. Everything that happens just ticks me off. For example, the other day I was digging through this drawer trying to find something, and I couldn't find it. All of sudden I just yanked the whole drawer out and threw it across the room. It put a big gash in the wall behind my bed. I was like, "What in the world just happened?"

Q: Sounds like something's going on inside you, something you need to check out.
A: Yeah, something. I don't know what.

» *Reeling It In*

The phrases we use to describe *anger* might sound funny—"flipping your lid," "blowing your stack," "going ballistic"—but the results of angry outbursts are anything but humorous. When we give in to angry impulses, we create hurt feelings, shattered souls and damaged relationships, not to mention a wounded reputation—for us and for Christ!

Cain, the son of Adam and Eve, was warned by God about his simmering rage toward his younger brother Abel:

"Then the Lord said to Cain, 'Why are you angry? Why is your face downcast?... Sin is crouching at your door; it desires to have you, but you must master it' " (Genesis 4:6–7).

Cain ignored God's warning and failed to master his emotion. His anger had him for lunch, resulting in Abel's murder.

God's warning to Cain is absolutely valid for us today. Be *very* careful how you respond whenever anger is in your heart. You might regret it.

Read more about handling anger at www.RevolutionBible.com.

[16] the pots, shovels, meat forks and all related articles.

All the objects that Huram-Abi made for King Solomon for the temple of the LORD were of polished bronze. [17] The king had them cast in clay molds in the plain of the Jordan between Succoth and Zarethan.[a] [18] All these things that Solomon made amounted to so much that the weight of the bronze was not determined.

[19] Solomon also made all the furnishings that were in God's temple:

the golden altar;

the tables on which was the bread of the Presence;

[20] the lampstands of pure gold with their lamps, to burn in front of the inner sanctuary as prescribed;

[21] the gold floral work and lamps and tongs (they were solid gold);

[22] the pure gold wick trimmers, sprinkling bowls, dishes and censers; and the gold doors of the temple: the inner doors to the Most Holy Place and the doors of the main hall.

5 When all the work Solomon had done for the temple of the LORD was finished, he brought in the things his father David had dedicated—the silver and gold and all the furnishings—and he placed them in the treasuries of God's temple.

THE ARK BROUGHT TO THE TEMPLE

[2] Then Solomon summoned to Jerusalem the elders of Israel, all the heads of the tribes and the chiefs of the Israelite families, to bring up the ark of the LORD's covenant from Zion, the City of David. [3] And all the men of Israel came together to the king at the time of the festival in the seventh month.

[4] When all the elders of Israel had arrived, the Levites took up the ark, [5] and they brought up the ark and the Tent of Meeting and all the sacred furnishings in it. The priests, who were Levites, carried them up; [6] and King Solomon and the entire assembly of Israel that had gathered about him were before the ark, sacrificing so many sheep and cattle that they could not be recorded or counted.

[7] The priests then brought the ark of the LORD's covenant to its place in the inner sanctuary of the temple, the Most Holy Place, and put it beneath the wings of the cherubim. [8] The cherubim spread their wings over the place of the ark and covered the ark and its carrying poles. [9] These poles were so long that their ends, extending from the ark, could be seen from in front of the inner sanctuary, but not from outside the Holy Place; and they are still there today. [10] There was nothing in the ark except the two tablets that Moses had placed in it at Horeb, where the LORD made a covenant with the Israelites after they came out of Egypt.

[11] The priests then withdrew from the Holy Place. All the priests who were there had consecrated themselves, regardless of their divisions. [12] All the Levites who were musicians—Asaph, Heman, Jeduthun and their sons and relatives—stood on the east side of the altar, dressed in fine linen and playing cymbals, harps and lyres. They were accompanied by 120 priests sounding trumpets. [13] The trumpeters and singers joined in unison, as with one voice, to give praise and thanks to the LORD. Accompanied by trumpets, cymbals and other instruments, they raised their voices in praise to the LORD and sang:

"He is good;
his love endures forever."

Then the temple of the LORD was filled with a cloud, [14] and the priests could not perform their service because of the cloud, for the glory of the LORD filled the temple of God.

6 Then Solomon said, "The LORD has said that he would dwell in a dark cloud; [2] I have built a magnificent temple for you, a place for you to dwell forever."

[3] While the whole assembly of Israel was standing there, the king turned around and blessed them. [4] Then he said:

"Praise be to the LORD, the God of Israel, who with his hands has fulfilled what he promised with his mouth to my father David. For he said, [5] 'Since the day I brought my people out of Egypt, I have not chosen a city in any tribe of Israel to have a temple built for my Name to be there, nor have I chosen anyone to be the leader over my people Israel. [6] But now I have chosen Jerusalem for my Name to be there, and I have chosen David to rule my people Israel.'

---

[a] 17 Hebrew *Zeredatha*, a variant of *Zarethan*

⁷"My father David had it in his heart to build a temple for the Name of the LORD, the God of Israel. ⁸But the LORD said to my father David, 'Because it was in your heart to build a temple for my Name, you did well to have this in your heart. ⁹Nevertheless, you are not the one to build the temple, but your son, who is your own flesh and blood—he is the one who will build the temple for my Name.'

2Ch 6:6
»» live the adventure »»

Honoring God's Name

What does the name of God mean to you? Do you call yourself a Christian? If so, what impact does being identified with Christ have on the way you live your life? God takes his name seriously, and so should we. The third commandment forbids misuse of his name in any way (see Exodus 20:7). That means if we claim to be God's followers and if we take the name *Christian* seriously, then we'd better make sure that our words and actions accurately reflect the name we've taken.

¹⁰"The LORD has kept the promise he made. I have succeeded David my father and now I sit on the throne of Israel, just as the LORD promised, and I have built the temple for the Name of the LORD, the God of Israel. ¹¹There I have placed the ark, in which is the covenant of the LORD that he made with the people of Israel."

SOLOMON'S PRAYER OF DEDICATION

¹²Then Solomon stood before the altar of the LORD in front of the whole assembly of Israel and spread out his hands. ¹³Now he had made a bronze platform, five cubits[a] long, five cubits wide and three cubits[b] high, and had placed it in the center of the outer court. He stood on the platform and then knelt down before the whole assembly of Israel and spread out his hands toward heaven. ¹⁴He said:

"O LORD, God of Israel, there is no God like you in heaven or on earth—you who keep your covenant of love with your servants who continue wholeheartedly in your way. ¹⁵You have kept your promise to your servant David my father; with your mouth you have promised and with your hand you have fulfilled it—as it is today.

¹⁶"Now LORD, God of Israel, keep for your servant David my father the promises you made to him when you said, 'You shall never fail to have a man to sit before me on the throne of Israel, if only your sons are careful in all they do to walk before me according to my law, as you have done.' ¹⁷And now, O LORD, God of Israel, let your word that you promised your servant David come true.

¹⁸"But will God really dwell on earth with men? The heavens, even the highest heavens, cannot contain you. How much less this temple I have built! ¹⁹Yet give attention to your servant's prayer and his plea for mercy, O LORD my God. Hear the cry and the prayer that your servant is praying in your presence. ²⁰May your eyes be open toward this temple day and night, this place of which you said you would put your Name there. May you hear the prayer your servant prays toward this place. ²¹Hear the supplications of your servant and of your people Israel when they pray toward this place. Hear from heaven, your dwelling place; and when you hear, forgive.

²²"When a man wrongs his neighbor and is required to take an oath and he comes and swears the oath before your altar in this temple, ²³then hear from heaven and act. Judge between your servants, repaying the guilty by bringing down on his own head what he has done. Declare the innocent not guilty and so establish his innocence.

²⁴"When your people Israel have been defeated by an enemy because they have sinned against you and when they turn back and confess your name, praying and making supplication before you in this temple, ²⁵then hear from heaven and forgive the sin of your people Israel and bring them back to the land you gave to them and their fathers.

²⁶"When the heavens are shut up and there is no rain because your people have sinned against you, and when they pray toward this place and confess your name and turn from their sin because you have afflicted them, ²⁷then hear from heaven and forgive the sin of your ser-

---

[a] 13 That is, about 7 1/2 feet (about 2.3 meters)   [b] 13 That is, about 4 1/2 feet (about 1.3 meters)

vants, your people Israel. Teach them the right way to live, and send rain on the land you gave your people for an inheritance.

28 "When famine or plague comes to the land, or blight or mildew, locusts or grasshoppers, or when enemies besiege them in any of their cities, whatever disaster or disease may come, 29 and when a prayer or plea is made by any of your people Israel—each one aware of his afflictions and pains, and spreading out his hands toward this temple— 30 then hear from heaven, your dwelling place. Forgive, and deal with each man according to all he does, since you know his heart (for you alone know the hearts of men), 31 so that they will fear you and walk in your ways all the time they live in the land you gave our fathers.

32 "As for the foreigner who does not belong to your people Israel but has come from a distant land because of your great name and your mighty hand and your outstretched arm—when he comes and prays toward this temple, 33 then hear from heaven, your dwelling place, and do whatever the foreigner asks of you, so that all the peoples of the earth may know your name and fear you, as do your own people Israel, and may know that this house I have built bears your Name.

34 "When your people go to war against their enemies, wherever you send them, and when they pray to you toward this city you have chosen and the temple I have built for your Name, 35 then hear from heaven their prayer and their plea, and uphold their cause.

36 "When they sin against you—for there is no one who does not sin—and you become angry with them and give them over to the enemy, who takes them captive to a land far away or near; 37 and if they have a change of heart in the land where they are held captive, and repent and plead with you in the land of their captivity and say, 'We have sinned, we have done wrong and acted wickedly'; 38 and if they turn back to you with all their heart and soul in the land of their captivity where they were taken, and pray toward the land you gave their fathers, toward the city you have chosen and toward the temple I have built for your Name; 39 then from heaven, your dwelling place, hear their prayer and their pleas, and uphold their cause. And forgive your people, who have sinned against you.

40 "Now, my God, may your eyes be open and your ears attentive to the prayers offered in this place.

41 "Now arise, O LORD God, and come to your resting place,
    you and the ark of your might.
May your priests, O LORD God, be clothed with salvation,
    may your saints rejoice in your goodness.
42 O LORD God, do not reject your anointed one.
    Remember the great love promised to David your servant."

THE DEDICATION OF THE TEMPLE

7 When Solomon finished praying, fire came down from heaven and consumed the burnt offering and the sacrifices, and the glory of the LORD filled the temple. 2 The priests could not enter the temple of the LORD because the glory of the LORD filled it. 3 When all the Israelites saw the fire coming down and the glory of the LORD above the temple, they knelt on the pavement with their faces to the ground, and they worshiped and gave thanks to the LORD, saying,

"He is good;
    his love endures forever."

4 Then the king and all the people offered sacrifices before the LORD. 5 And King Solomon offered a sacrifice of twenty-two thousand head of cattle and a hundred and twenty thousand sheep and goats. So the king and all the people dedicated the temple of God. 6 The priests took their positions, as did the Levites with the LORD's musical instruments, which King David had made for praising the LORD and which were used when he gave thanks, saying, "His love endures forever." Opposite the Levites, the priests blew their trumpets, and all the Israelites were standing.

7 Solomon consecrated the middle part of the courtyard in front of the temple of the LORD, and there he offered burnt offerings and the fat of the fellowship offerings,[a] because the bronze altar he had made could not hold the burnt offerings, the grain offerings and the fat portions.

---

a 7 Traditionally *peace offerings*

[8]So Solomon observed the festival at that time for seven days, and all Israel with him—a vast assembly, people from Lebo[a] Hamath to the Wadi of Egypt. [9]On the eighth day they held an assembly, for they had celebrated the dedication of the altar for seven days and the festival for seven days more. [10]On the twenty-third day of the seventh month he sent the people to their homes, joyful and glad in heart for the good things the LORD had done for David and Solomon and for his people Israel.

THE LORD APPEARS TO SOLOMON

[11]When Solomon had finished the temple of the LORD and the royal palace, and had succeeded in carrying out all he had in mind to do in the temple of the LORD and in his own palace, [12]the LORD appeared to him at night and said:

"I have heard your prayer and have chosen this place for myself as a temple for sacrifices.

[13]"When I shut up the heavens so that there is no rain, or command locusts to devour the land or send a plague among my people, [14]if my people, who are called by my name, will humble themselves and pray and seek my face and turn from their wicked ways, then will I hear from heaven and will forgive their sin and will heal their land. [15]Now my eyes will be open and my ears attentive to the prayers offered in this place. [16]I have chosen and consecrated this temple so that my Name may be there forever. My eyes and my heart will always be there.

[17]"As for you, if you walk before me as David your father did, and do all I command, and observe my decrees and laws, [18]I will establish your royal throne, as I covenanted with David your father when I said, 'You shall never fail to have a man to rule over Israel.'

[19]"But if you[b] turn away and forsake the decrees and commands I have given you[b] and go off to serve other gods and worship them, [20]then I will uproot Israel from my land, which I have given them, and will reject this temple I have consecrated for my Name. I will make it a byword and an object of ridicule among all peoples. [21]And though this temple is now so imposing, all who pass by will be appalled and say, 'Why has the LORD done such a thing to this land and to this temple?' [22]People will answer, 'Because they have forsaken the LORD, the God of their fathers, who brought them out of Egypt, and have embraced other gods, worshiping and serving them—that is why he brought all this disaster on them.' "

2CH 7:14

challenge notes

To: my_son

heavenly_father: attitude is extremely important to me. if you want my help, the first thing you need to do is come to me with the right spirit. don't be afraid to seek me out, but always make sure you do it with a humble attitude rather than demanding my help because you think you deserve it.

SOLOMON'S OTHER ACTIVITIES

8 At the end of twenty years, during which Solomon built the temple of the LORD and his own palace, [2]Solomon rebuilt the villages that Hiram[c] had given him, and settled Israelites in them. [3]Solomon then went to Hamath Zobah and captured it. [4]He also built up Tadmor in the desert and all the store cities he had built in Hamath. [5]He rebuilt Upper Beth Horon and Lower Beth Horon as fortified cities, with walls and with gates and bars, [6]as well as Baalath and all his store cities, and all the cities for his chariots and for his horses[d]—whatever he desired to build in Jerusalem, in Lebanon and throughout all the territory he ruled.

[7]All the people left from the Hittites, Amorites, Perizzites, Hivites and Jebusites (these peoples were not Israelites), [8]that is, their descendants remaining in the land, whom the Israelites had not destroyed—these Solomon conscripted for his slave labor force, as it is to this day. [9]But Solomon did not make slaves of the Israelites for his work; they were his fighting men, commanders of his captains, and commanders of his chariots and charioteers. [10]They were also King Solomon's chief officials—two hundred and fifty officials supervising the men.

[11]Solomon brought Pharaoh's daughter up from the City of David to the palace he had built for her,

---

[a] 8 Or *from the entrance to*   [b] 19 The Hebrew is plural.   [c] 2 Hebrew *Huram,* a variant of *Hiram;* also in verse 18
[d] 6 Or *charioteers*

for he said, "My wife must not live in the palace of David king of Israel, because the places the ark of the LORD has entered are holy."

¹²On the altar of the LORD that he had built in front of the portico, Solomon sacrificed burnt offerings to the LORD, ¹³according to the daily requirement for offerings commanded by Moses for Sabbaths, New Moons and the three annual feasts—the Feast of Unleavened Bread, the Feast of Weeks and the Feast of Tabernacles. ¹⁴In keeping with the ordinance of his father David, he appointed the divisions of the priests for their duties, and the Levites to lead the praise and to assist the priests according to each day's requirement. He also appointed the gatekeepers by divisions for the various gates, because this was what David the man of God had ordered. ¹⁵They did not deviate from the king's commands to the priests or to the Levites in any matter, including that of the treasuries.

¹⁶All Solomon's work was carried out, from the day the foundation of the temple of the LORD was laid until its completion. So the temple of the LORD was finished.

¹⁷Then Solomon went to Ezion Geber and Elath on the coast of Edom. ¹⁸And Hiram sent him ships commanded by his own officers, men who knew the sea. These, with Solomon's men, sailed to Ophir and brought back four hundred and fifty talents[a] of gold, which they delivered to King Solomon.

THE QUEEN OF SHEBA VISITS SOLOMON

9 When the queen of Sheba heard of Solomon's fame, she came to Jerusalem to test him with hard questions. Arriving with a very great caravan—with camels carrying spices, large quantities of gold, and precious stones—she came to Solomon and talked with him about all she had on her mind. ²Solomon answered all her questions; nothing was too hard for him to explain to her. ³When the queen of Sheba saw the wisdom of Solomon, as well as the palace he had built, ⁴the food on his table, the seating of his officials, the attending servants in their robes, the cupbearers in their robes and the burnt offerings he made at[b] the temple of the LORD, she was overwhelmed.

⁵She said to the king, "The report I heard in my own country about your achievements and your wisdom is true. ⁶But I did not believe what they said until I came and saw with my own eyes. Indeed, not even half the greatness of your wisdom was told me; you have far exceeded the report I heard. ⁷How happy your men must be! How happy your officials, who continually stand before you and hear your wisdom! ⁸Praise be to the LORD your God, who has delighted in you and placed you on his throne as king to rule for the LORD your God. Because of the love of your God for Israel and his desire to uphold them forever, he has made you king over them, to maintain justice and righteousness."

⁹Then she gave the king 120 talents[c] of gold, large quantities of spices, and precious stones. There had never been such spices as those the queen of Sheba gave to King Solomon.

¹⁰(The men of Hiram and the men of Solomon brought gold from Ophir; they also brought algum-

---

Learning True Obedience

Sometimes honoring God requires effort. This was true for the people who followed God during Solomon's time, and it's true for us today. Is it possible to obey every one of God's instructions exactly as he intends? Not on this side of eternity. Should that keep us from trying? No. God is just as interested in the attitude of your heart as he is in your actions. Which attitude do you think pleases him more—the one that says, "I can't possibly do everything God expects of me, so I'll just do what I can and let the rest slide," or the one that says, "I messed up the last time I tried to obey God, but I learned from my mistake and now I'm ready to try again"?

live the adventure >> 2Ch 8:14-15

NOW OR NEVER
2CH 9:5-8

When you spot God's blessings in other people's lives—things like a healthy dose of wisdom, a good sense of humor, a loving family, good friends—point them out. You may help them see things in a way they never have before.

---

a 18 That is, about 17 tons (about 16 metric tons)   b 4 Or the ascent by which he went up to   c 9 That is, about 4 1/2 tons (about 4 metric tons) wood^a and precious stones. ¹¹The king used the algumwood to make steps for the temple of the Lord and for the royal palace, and to make harps and lyres for the musicians. Nothing like them had ever been seen in Judah.)

¹²King Solomon gave the queen of Sheba all she desired and asked for; he gave her more than she had brought to him. Then she left and returned with her retinue to her own country.

SOLOMON'S SPLENDOR

¹³The weight of the gold that Solomon received yearly was 666 talents,^b ¹⁴not including the revenues brought in by merchants and traders. Also all the kings of Arabia and the governors of the land brought gold and silver to Solomon.

¹⁵King Solomon made two hundred large shields of hammered gold; six hundred bekas^c of hammered gold went into each shield. ¹⁶He also made three hundred small shields of hammered gold, with three hundred bekas^d of gold in each shield. The king put them in the Palace of the Forest of Lebanon.

¹⁷Then the king made a great throne inlaid with ivory and overlaid with pure gold. ¹⁸The throne had six steps, and a footstool of gold was attached to it. On both sides of the seat were armrests, with a lion standing beside each of them. ¹⁹Twelve lions stood on the six steps, one at either end of each step. Nothing like it had ever been made for any other kingdom. ²⁰All King Solomon's goblets were gold, and all the household articles in the Palace of the Forest of Lebanon were pure gold. Nothing was made of silver, because silver was considered of little value in Solomon's day. ²¹The king had a fleet of trading ships^e manned by Hiram's^f men. Once every three years it returned, carrying gold, silver and ivory, and apes and baboons.

²²King Solomon was greater in riches and wisdom than all the other kings of the earth. ²³All the kings of the earth sought audience with Solomon to hear the wisdom God had put in his heart. ²⁴Year after year, everyone who came brought a gift—articles of silver and gold, and robes, weapons and spices, and horses and mules.

²⁵Solomon had four thousand stalls for horses and chariots, and twelve thousand horses,^g which he kept in the chariot cities and also with him in Jerusalem. ²⁶He ruled over all the kings from the River^h to the land of the Philistines, as far as the border of Egypt. ²⁷The king made silver as common in Jerusalem as stones, and cedar as plentiful as sycamore-fig trees in the foothills. ²⁸Solomon's horses were imported from Egyptⁱ and from all other countries.

SOLOMON'S DEATH

²⁹As for the other events of Solomon's reign, from beginning to end, are they not written in the records of Nathan the prophet, in the prophecy of Ahijah the Shilonite and in the visions of Iddo the seer concerning Jeroboam son of Nebat? ³⁰Solomon reigned in Jerusalem over all Israel forty years. ³¹Then he rested with his fathers and was buried in the city of David his father. And Rehoboam his son succeeded him as king.

ISRAEL REBELS AGAINST REHOBOAM

10

Rehoboam went to Shechem, for all the Israelites had gone there to make him king. ²When Jeroboam son of Nebat heard this (he was in Egypt, where he had fled from King Solomon), he returned from Egypt. ³So they sent for Jeroboam, and he and all Israel went to Rehoboam and said to him: ⁴"Your father put a heavy yoke on us, but now lighten the harsh labor and the heavy yoke he put on us, and we will serve you."

⁵Rehoboam answered, "Come back to me in three days." So the people went away.

⁶Then King Rehoboam consulted the elders who had served his father Solomon during his lifetime. "How would you advise me to answer these people?" he asked.

⁷They replied, "If you will be kind to these people and please them and give them a favorable answer, they will always be your servants."

⁸But Rehoboam rejected the advice the elders gave him and consulted the young men who had

---

^a *10* Probably a variant of *almugwood*   ^b *13* That is, about 25 tons (about 23 metric tons)   ^c *15* That is, about 7 1/2 pounds (about 3.5 kilograms)   ^d *16* That is, about 3 3/4 pounds (about 1.7 kilograms)   ^e *21* Hebrew *of ships that could go to Tarshish*   ^f *21* Hebrew *Huram,* a variant of *Hiram*   ^g *25* Or *charioteers*   ^h *26* That is, the Euphrates   ⁱ *28* Or possibly *Muzur,* a region in Cilicia

grown up with him and were serving him. ⁹He asked them, "What is your advice? How should we answer these people who say to me, 'Lighten the yoke your father put on us'?"

¹⁰The young men who had grown up with him replied, "Tell the people who have said to you, 'Your father put a heavy yoke on us, but make our yoke lighter'—tell them, 'My little finger is thicker than my father's waist. ¹¹My father laid on you a heavy yoke; I will make it even heavier. My father scourged you with whips; I will scourge you with scorpions.'"

¹²Three days later Jeroboam and all the people returned to Rehoboam, as the king had said, "Come back to me in three days." ¹³The king answered them harshly. Rejecting the advice of the elders, ¹⁴he followed the advice of the young men and said, "My father made your yoke heavy; I will make it even heavier. My father scourged you with whips; I will scourge you with scorpions." ¹⁵So the king did not listen to the people, for this turn of events was from God, to fulfill the word the LORD had spoken to Jeroboam son of Nebat through Ahijah the Shilonite.

NOW OR NEVER

2CH 10:8

What kind of attitude do you demonstrate when someone tries to offer you advice? Do you roll your eyes, cross your arms and wait impatiently for the person to finish? Or do you make a real effort to understand what he or she is saying and see what you might learn from it?

¹⁶When all Israel saw that the king refused to listen to them, they answered the king:

"What share do we have in David,
    what part in Jesse's son?
To your tents, O Israel!
    Look after your own house, O David!"

So all the Israelites went home. ¹⁷But as for the Israelites who were living in the towns of Judah, Rehoboam still ruled over them.

¹⁸King Rehoboam sent out Adoniram,ᵃ who was in charge of forced labor, but the Israelites stoned him to death. King Rehoboam, however, managed to get into his chariot and escape to Jerusalem. ¹⁹So Israel has been in rebellion against the house of David to this day.

11 When Rehoboam arrived in Jerusalem, he mustered the house of Judah and Benjamin—a hundred and eighty thousand fighting men—to make war against Israel and to regain the kingdom for Rehoboam.

²But this word of the LORD came to Shemaiah the man of God: ³"Say to Rehoboam son of Solomon king of Judah and to all the Israelites in Judah and Benjamin, ⁴'This is what the LORD says: Do not go up to fight against your brothers. Go home, every one of you, for this is my doing.'" So they obeyed the words of the LORD and turned back from marching against Jeroboam.

REHOBOAM FORTIFIES JUDAH

⁵Rehoboam lived in Jerusalem and built up towns for defense in Judah: ⁶Bethlehem, Etam, Tekoa, ⁷Beth Zur, Soco, Adullam, ⁸Gath, Mareshah, Ziph, ⁹Adoraim, Lachish, Azekah, ¹⁰Zorah, Aijalon and Hebron. These were fortified cities in Judah and Benjamin. ¹¹He strengthened their defenses and put commanders in them, with supplies of food, olive oil and wine. ¹²He put shields and spears in all the cities, and made them very strong. So Judah and Benjamin were his.

¹³The priests and Levites from all their districts throughout Israel sided with him. ¹⁴The Levites even abandoned their pasturelands and property, and came to Judah and Jerusalem because Jeroboam and his sons had rejected them as priests of the LORD. ¹⁵And he appointed his own priests for the high places and for the goat and calf idols he had made. ¹⁶Those from every tribe of Israel who set their hearts on seeking the LORD, the God of Israel, followed the Levites to Jerusalem to offer sacrifices to the LORD, the God of their fathers. ¹⁷They strengthened the kingdom of Judah and supported Rehoboam son of Solomon three years, walking in the ways of David and Solomon during this time.

REHOBOAM'S FAMILY

¹⁸Rehoboam married Mahalath, who was the daughter of David's son Jerimoth and of Abihail, the

---

ᵃ 18 Hebrew *Hadoram,* a variant of *Adoniram*

daughter of Jesse's son Eliab. ¹⁹She bore him sons: Jeush, Shemariah and Zaham. ²⁰Then he married Maacah daughter of Absalom, who bore him Abijah, Attai, Ziza and Shelomith. ²¹Rehoboam loved Maacah daughter of Absalom more than any of his other wives and concubines. In all, he had eighteen wives and sixty concubines, twenty-eight sons and sixty daughters.

²²Rehoboam appointed Abijah son of Maacah to be the chief prince among his brothers, in order to make him king. ²³He acted wisely, dispersing some of his sons throughout the districts of Judah and Benjamin, and to all the fortified cities. He gave them abundant provisions and took many wives for them.

SHISHAK ATTACKS JERUSALEM

12 After Rehoboam's position as king was established and he had become strong, he and all Israel[a] with him abandoned the law of the LORD. ²Because they had been unfaithful to the LORD, Shishak king of Egypt attacked Jerusalem in the fifth year of King Rehoboam. ³With twelve hundred chariots and sixty thousand horsemen and the innumerable troops of Libyans, Sukkites and Cushites[b] that came with him from Egypt, ⁴he captured the fortified cities of Judah and came as far as Jerusalem.

⁵Then the prophet Shemaiah came to Rehoboam and to the leaders of Judah who had assembled in Jerusalem for fear of Shishak, and he said to them, "This is what the LORD says, 'You have abandoned me; therefore, I now abandon you to Shishak.' "

⁶The leaders of Israel and the king humbled themselves and said, "The LORD is just."

⁷When the LORD saw that they humbled themselves, this word of the LORD came to Shemaiah: "Since they have humbled themselves, I will not destroy them but will soon give them deliverance. My wrath will not be poured out on Jerusalem through Shishak. ⁸They will, however, become subject to him, so that they may learn the difference between serving me and serving the kings of other lands."

⁹When Shishak king of Egypt attacked Jerusalem, he carried off the treasures of the temple of the LORD and the treasures of the royal palace. He took everything, including the gold shields Solomon had made. ¹⁰So King Rehoboam made bronze shields to replace them and assigned these to the commanders of the guard on duty at the entrance to the royal palace. ¹¹Whenever the king went to the LORD's temple, the guards went with him, bearing the shields, and afterward they returned them to the guardroom.

¹²Because Rehoboam humbled himself, the LORD's anger turned from him, and he was not totally destroyed. Indeed, there was some good in Judah.

¹³King Rehoboam established himself firmly in Jerusalem and continued as king. He was forty-one years old when he became king, and he reigned seventeen years in Jerusalem, the city the LORD had chosen out of all the tribes of Israel in which to put his Name. His mother's name was Naamah; she was an Ammonite. ¹⁴He did evil because he had not set his heart on seeking the LORD.

¹⁵As for the events of Rehoboam's reign, from beginning to end, are they not written in the records of Shemaiah the prophet and of Iddo the seer that deal with genealogies? There was continual warfare between Rehoboam and Jeroboam. ¹⁶Rehoboam rested with his fathers and was buried in the City of David. And Abijah his son succeeded him as king.

ABIJAH KING OF JUDAH

13 In the eighteenth year of the reign of Jeroboam, Abijah became king of Judah, ²and he reigned in Jerusalem three years. His mother's name was Maacah,[c] a daughter[d] of Uriel of Gibeah.

There was war between Abijah and Jeroboam. ³Abijah went into battle with a force of four hundred thousand able fighting men, and Jeroboam drew up a battle line against him with eight hundred thousand able troops.

⁴Abijah stood on Mount Zemaraim, in the hill country of Ephraim, and said, "Jeroboam and all Israel, listen to me! ⁵Don't you know that the LORD, the God of Israel, has given the kingship of Israel to David and his descendants forever by a covenant of salt? ⁶Yet Jeroboam son of Nebat, an official of Solomon son of David, rebelled against his master. ⁷Some worthless scoundrels gathered around him and opposed Rehoboam son of Solomon when he was young and indecisive and not strong enough to resist them.

---

[a] *1* That is, Judah, as frequently in 2 Chronicles   [b] *3* That is, people from the upper Nile region   [c] *2* Most Septuagint manuscripts and Syriac (see also 2 Chron. 11:20 and 1 Kings 15:2); Hebrew *Micaiah*   [d] *2* Or *granddaughter*

8"And now you plan to resist the kingdom of the LORD, which is in the hands of David's descendants. You are indeed a vast army and have with you the golden calves that Jeroboam made to be your gods. 9But didn't you drive out the priests of the LORD, the sons of Aaron, and the Levites, and make priests of your own as the peoples of other lands do? Whoever comes to consecrate himself with a young bull and seven rams may become a priest of what are not gods.

10"As for us, the LORD is our God, and we have not forsaken him. The priests who serve the LORD are sons of Aaron, and the Levites assist them. 11Every morning and evening they present burnt offerings and fragrant incense to the LORD. They set out the bread on the ceremonially clean table and light the lamps on the gold lampstand every evening. We are observing the requirements of the LORD our God. But you have forsaken him. 12God is with us; he is our leader. His priests with their trumpets will sound the battle cry against you. Men of Israel, do not fight against the LORD, the God of your fathers, for you will not succeed."

13Now Jeroboam had sent troops around to the rear, so that while he was in front of Judah the ambush was behind them. 14Judah turned and saw that they were being attacked at both front and rear. Then they cried out to the LORD. The priests blew their trumpets 15and the men of Judah raised the battle cry. At the sound of their battle cry, God routed Jeroboam and all Israel before Abijah and Judah. 16The Israelites fled before Judah, and God delivered them into their hands. 17Abijah and his men inflicted heavy losses on them, so that there were five hundred thousand casualties among Israel's able men. 18The men of Israel were subdued on that occasion, and the men of Judah were victorious because they relied on the LORD, the God of their fathers.

19Abijah pursued Jeroboam and took from him the towns of Bethel, Jeshanah and Ephron, with their surrounding villages. 20Jeroboam did not regain power during the time of Abijah. And the LORD struck him down and he died.

21But Abijah grew in strength. He married fourteen wives and had twenty-two sons and sixteen daughters.

22The other events of Abijah's reign, what he did and what he said, are written in the annotations of the prophet Iddo.

14

And Abijah rested with his fathers and was buried in the City of David. Asa his son succeeded him as king, and in his days the country was at peace for ten years.

ASA KING OF JUDAH

2Asa did what was good and right in the eyes of the LORD his God. 3He removed the foreign altars and the high places, smashed the sacred stones and cut down the Asherah poles.ᵃ 4He commanded Judah to seek the LORD, the God of their fathers, and to obey his laws and commands. 5He removed the high places and incense altars in every town in Judah, and the kingdom was at peace under him. 6He built up the fortified cities of Judah, since the land was at peace. No one was at war with him during those years, for the LORD gave him rest.

7"Let us build up these towns," he said to Judah, "and put walls around them, with towers, gates and bars. The land is still ours, because we have sought the LORD our God; we sought him and he has given us rest on every side." So they built and prospered.

8Asa had an army of three hundred thousand men from Judah, equipped with large shields and with spears, and two hundred and eighty thousand from Benjamin, armed with small shields and with bows. All these were brave fighting men.

9Zerah the Cushite marched out against them with a vast armyᵇ and three hundred chariots, and

---

Relying on God

Do you think you could ever have the kind of confident faith Abijah had? His opponent was twice as big as he was; his army was outnumbered 800,000 to 400,000 (see 13:3). But Abijah never even hesitated when the time for battle came. Why? Because he relied on the Lord. He did what he believed was right and trusted God to help him deal with the outcome. Do you ever feel outnumbered or overpowered at home, school or work? Try asking the Lord to get involved. Let him reverse the odds for you.

ᵃ 3 That is, symbols of the goddess Asherah; here and elsewhere in 2 Chronicles   ᵇ 9 Hebrew *with an army of a thousand thousands* or *with an army of thousands upon thousands* came as far as Mareshah. ¹⁰Asa went out to meet him, and they took up battle positions in the Valley of Zephathah near Mareshah.

¹¹Then Asa called to the Lord his God and said, "Lord, there is no one like you to help the powerless against the mighty. Help us, O Lord our God, for we rely on you, and in your name we have come against this vast army. O Lord, you are our God; do not let man prevail against you."

¹²The Lord struck down the Cushites before Asa and Judah. The Cushites fled, ¹³and Asa and his army pursued them as far as Gerar. Such a great number of Cushites fell that they could not recover; they were crushed before the Lord and his forces. The men of Judah carried off a large amount of plunder. ¹⁴They destroyed all the villages around Gerar, for the terror of the Lord had fallen upon them. They plundered all these villages, since there was much booty there. ¹⁵They also attacked the camps of the herdsmen and carried off droves of sheep and goats and camels. Then they returned to Jerusalem.

NOW OR NEVER

2CH 14:11

This is the flip side of foolish pride. Recognizing and admitting that you are powerless without God is the best strategy for getting his help.

ASA'S REFORM

15 The Spirit of God came upon Azariah son of Oded. ²He went out to meet Asa and said to him, "Listen to me, Asa and all Judah and Benjamin. The Lord is with you when you are with him. If you seek him, he will be found by you, but if you forsake him, he will forsake you. ³For a long time Israel was without the true God, without a priest to teach and without the law. ⁴But in their distress they turned to the Lord, the God of Israel, and sought him, and he was found by them. ⁵In those days it was not safe to travel about, for all the inhabitants of the lands were in great turmoil. ⁶One nation was being crushed by another and one city by another, because God was troubling them with every kind of distress. ⁷But as for you, be strong and do not give up, for your work will be rewarded."

⁸When Asa heard these words and the prophecy of Azariah son of[a] Oded the prophet, he took courage. He removed the detestable idols from the whole land of Judah and Benjamin and from the towns he had captured in the hills of Ephraim. He repaired the altar of the Lord that was in front of the portico of the Lord's temple.

⁹Then he assembled all Judah and Benjamin and the people from Ephraim, Manasseh and Simeon who had settled among them, for large numbers had come over to him from Israel when they saw that the Lord his God was with him.

¹⁰They assembled at Jerusalem in the third month of the fifteenth year of Asa's reign. ¹¹At that time they sacrificed to the Lord seven hundred head of cattle and seven thousand sheep and goats from the plunder they had brought back. ¹²They entered into a covenant to seek the Lord, the God of their fathers, with all their heart and soul. ¹³All who would not seek the Lord, the God of Israel, were to be put to death, whether small or great, man or woman. ¹⁴They took an oath to the Lord with loud acclamation, with shouting and with trumpets and horns. ¹⁵All Judah rejoiced about the oath because they had sworn it wholeheartedly. They sought God eagerly, and he was found by them. So the Lord gave them rest on every side.

¹⁶King Asa also deposed his grandmother Maacah from her position as queen mother, because she had made a repulsive Asherah pole. Asa cut the pole down, broke it up and burned it in the Kidron Valley. ¹⁷Although he did not remove the high places from Israel, Asa's heart was fully committed ⌐to the

NOW OR NEVER

2CH 15:1-4

What are you seeking in your life? Happiness? Security? Companionship? A clear sense of direction? All of these things can be found in the one thing that matters more than all of them put together: a life dedicated to pursuing God. That's where your search should begin—and end.

---

[a] 8 Vulgate and Syriac (see also Septuagint and verse 1); Hebrew does not have *Azariah son of*.

battlelines

» Ready to Explode (Anger)

Q: I heard you got suspended.
A: Yeah, three days. For fighting.

Q: What happened?
A: This guy was mouthing off at me, and I told him to shut up. He wouldn't, so I shoved him pretty hard against the lockers. He took a swing at me, and the next thing I know, a couple coaches are pulling me off him. I think I busted his lip open.

Q: Just like that, huh?
A: Yeah, it all happened so fast. I don't know . . . I just kind of lost it.

Q: Does that happen a lot?
A: Fighting? No, that's the first time I've ever actually gotten in a fight. But it's not the first time I've *wanted* to take a swing at somebody—that's for sure.

Q: So you have a pretty bad temper?
A: I guess—I don't always show it. Lately it seems like *everything* irritates me. People just tick me off. And before I know it, I'm seriously considering doing some damage to somebody's face.

Q: And this time you finally turned your thoughts into action, huh?
A: Yeah, and look where it got me. I'm going to get zeroes on three different tests. Not to mention the fact that I'm grounded for two weeks.

Q: Learn any lessons?
A: I just wish I could figure out why I get so mad about little stuff. My dad says God made our emotions to be like lights on a dashboard. When one of them starts flashing, means it's time to check under the hood.

Q: How do you do that—how do you look under the hood of your life?
A: I'm not sure, but I've gotta find out.

» Checking Under the Hood

Shane's dad is right. Emotions aren't wrong. They just . . . *are.* They reflect what's going on in our hearts and lives. That's why, when we find ourselves feeling extreme anger or deep sadness, when we're nervous or grouchy or depressed, it's wise to check under the hood before our emotions cause us to lash out at someone in a physically or verbally violent fashion.

God will help us do this. The psalmist prayed, "Search me, O God, and know my heart; test me and know my anxious thoughts. See if there is any offensive way in me, and lead me in the way everlasting" (Psalm 139:23–24).

Friends can be a big help too. Solomon wrote, "The purposes of a man's heart are deep waters, but a man of understanding draws them out" (Proverbs 20:5). In other words, a wise parent, friend, youth pastor, teacher or counselor can help you figure out what's going on inside. Don't be afraid to talk about your emotions before you find them exploding out of you.

Read more about handling your emotions at www.RevolutionBible.com.

LORDᵈ all his life. ¹⁸He brought into the temple of God the silver and gold and the articles that he and his father had dedicated.

¹⁹There was no more war until the thirty-fifth year of Asa's reign.

ASA'S LAST YEARS

16 In the thirty-sixth year of Asa's reign Baasha king of Israel went up against Judah and fortified Ramah to prevent anyone from leaving or entering the territory of Asa king of Judah.

²Asa then took the silver and gold out of the treasuries of the LORD's temple and of his own palace and sent it to Ben-Hadad king of Aram, who was ruling in Damascus. ³"Let there be a treaty between me and you," he said, "as there was between my father and your father. See, I am sending you silver and gold. Now break your treaty with Baasha king of Israel so he will withdraw from me."

⁴Ben-Hadad agreed with King Asa and sent the commanders of his forces against the towns of Israel. They conquered Ijon, Dan, Abel Maimᵃ and all the store cities of Naphtali. ⁵When Baasha heard this, he stopped building Ramah and abandoned his work. ⁶Then King Asa brought all the men of Judah, and they carried away from Ramah the stones and timber Baasha had been using. With them he built up Geba and Mizpah.

⁷At that time Hanani the seer came to Asa king of Judah and said to him: "Because you relied on the king of Aram and not on the LORD your God, the army of the king of Aram has escaped from your hand. ⁸Were not the Cushitesᵇ and Libyans a mighty army with great numbers of chariots and horsemenᶜ? Yet when you relied on the LORD, he delivered them into your hand. ⁹For the eyes of the LORD range throughout the earth to strengthen those whose hearts are fully committed to him. You have done a foolish thing, and from now on you will be at war."

¹⁰Asa was angry with the seer because of this; he was so enraged that he put him in prison. At the same time Asa brutally oppressed some of the people.

¹¹The events of Asa's reign, from beginning to end, are written in the book of the kings of Judah and Israel. ¹²In the thirty-ninth year of his reign Asa was afflicted with a disease in his feet. Though his disease was severe, even in his illness he did not seek help from the LORD, but only from the physicians. ¹³Then in the forty-first year of his reign Asa died and rested with his fathers. ¹⁴They buried him in the tomb that he had cut out for himself in the City of David. They laid him on a bier covered with spices and various blended perfumes, and they made a huge fire in his honor.

NOW OR NEVER

2CH 16:7–10

If you're going to trust God, do it boldly and completely. Don't just give him certain areas of your life and keep others for yourself because you're not sure what he'll do with them. Take a risk and give him everything.

JEHOSHAPHAT KING OF JUDAH

17 Jehoshaphat his son succeeded him as king and strengthened himself against Israel. ²He stationed troops in all the fortified cities of Judah and put garrisons in Judah and in the towns of Ephraim that his father Asa had captured.

³The LORD was with Jehoshaphat because in his early years he walked in the ways his father David had followed. He did not consult the Baals ⁴but sought the God of his father and followed his commands rather than the practices of Israel. ⁵The LORD established the kingdom under his control; and all Judah brought gifts to Jehoshaphat, so that he had great wealth and honor. ⁶His heart was devoted to the ways of the LORD; furthermore, he removed the high places and the Asherah poles from Judah.

⁷In the third year of his reign he sent his officials Ben-Hail, Obadiah, Zechariah, Nethanel and Micaiah to teach in the towns of Judah. ⁸With them were certain Levites—Shemaiah, Nethaniah, Zebadiah, Asahel, Shemiramoth, Jehonathan, Adonijah, Tobijah and Tob-Adonijah—and the priests Elishama and Jehoram. ⁹They taught throughout Judah, taking with them the Book of the Law of the LORD; they went around to all the towns of Judah and taught the people.

¹⁰The fear of the LORD fell on all the kingdoms of the lands surrounding Judah, so that they did not

---

ᵃ 4 Also known as *Abel Beth Maacah*   ᵇ 8 That is, people from the upper Nile region   ᶜ 8 Or *charioteers* make war with Jehoshaphat. ¹¹Some Philistines brought Jehoshaphat gifts and silver as tribute, and the Arabs brought him flocks: seven thousand seven hundred rams and seven thousand seven hundred goats.

¹²Jehoshaphat became more and more powerful; he built forts and store cities in Judah ¹³and had large supplies in the towns of Judah. He also kept experienced fighting men in Jerusalem. ¹⁴Their enrollment by families was as follows:

From Judah, commanders of units of 1,000:
Adnah the commander, with 300,000 fighting men;
¹⁵next, Jehohanan the commander, with 280,000;
¹⁶next, Amasiah son of Zicri, who volunteered himself for the service of the LORD, with 200,000.
¹⁷From Benjamin:
Eliada, a valiant soldier, with 200,000 men armed with bows and shields;
¹⁸next, Jehozabad, with 180,000 men armed for battle.

¹⁹These were the men who served the king, besides those he stationed in the fortified cities throughout Judah.

MICAIAH PROPHESIES AGAINST AHAB

18 Now Jehoshaphat had great wealth and honor, and he allied himself with Ahab by marriage. ²Some years later he went down to visit Ahab in Samaria. Ahab slaughtered many sheep and cattle for him and the people with him and urged him to attack Ramoth Gilead. ³Ahab king of Israel asked Jehoshaphat king of Judah, "Will you go with me against Ramoth Gilead?"

Jehoshaphat replied, "I am as you are, and my people as your people; we will join you in the war." ⁴But Jehoshaphat also said to the king of Israel, "First seek the counsel of the LORD."

⁵So the king of Israel brought together the prophets—four hundred men—and asked them, "Shall we go to war against Ramoth Gilead, or shall I refrain?"

"Go," they answered, "for God will give it into the king's hand."

⁶But Jehoshaphat asked, "Is there not a prophet of the LORD here whom we can inquire of?"

⁷The king of Israel answered Jehoshaphat, "There is still one man through whom we can inquire of the LORD, but I hate him because he never prophesies anything good about me, but always bad. He is Micaiah son of Imlah."

"The king should not say that," Jehoshaphat replied.

⁸So the king of Israel called one of his officials and said, "Bring Micaiah son of Imlah at once."

⁹Dressed in their royal robes, the king of Israel and Jehoshaphat king of Judah were sitting on their thrones at the threshing floor by the entrance to the gate of Samaria, with all the prophets prophesying before them. ¹⁰Now Zedekiah son of Kenaanah had made iron horns, and he declared, "This is what the LORD says: 'With these you will gore the Arameans until they are destroyed.'"

¹¹All the other prophets were prophesying the same thing. "Attack Ramoth Gilead and be victorious," they said, "for the LORD will give it into the king's hand."

¹²The messenger who had gone to summon Micaiah said to him, "Look, as one man the other prophets are predicting success for the king. Let your word agree with theirs, and speak favorably."

¹³But Micaiah said, "As surely as the LORD lives, I can tell him only what my God says."

¹⁴When he arrived, the king asked him, "Micaiah, shall we go to war against Ramoth Gilead, or shall I refrain?"

"Attack and be victorious," he answered, "for they will be given into your hand."

¹⁵The king said to him, "How many times must I make you swear to tell me nothing but the truth in the name of the LORD?"

¹⁶Then Micaiah answered, "I saw all Israel scattered on the hills like sheep without a shepherd, and the LORD said, 'These people have no master. Let each one go home in peace.' "

NOW OR NEVER

2CH 18:12–13

When was the last time you were tempted to lie? Why would it have been an easier way out than telling the truth? What's the problem with trying to take the easy way out? If you've never experienced the consequences of a lie that seemed like a good idea at the time, someday you probably will.

¹⁷The king of Israel said to Jehoshaphat, "Didn't I tell you that he never prophesies anything good about me, but only bad?"

¹⁸Micaiah continued, "Therefore hear the word of the LORD: I saw the LORD sitting on his throne with all the host of heaven standing on his right and on his left. ¹⁹And the LORD said, 'Who will entice Ahab king of Israel into attacking Ramoth Gilead and going to his death there?'

"One suggested this, and another that. ²⁰Finally, a spirit came forward, stood before the LORD and said, 'I will entice him.'

" 'By what means?' the LORD asked.

²¹" 'I will go and be a lying spirit in the mouths of all his prophets,' he said.

" 'You will succeed in enticing him,' said the LORD. 'Go and do it.'

²²"So now the LORD has put a lying spirit in the mouths of these prophets of yours. The LORD has decreed disaster for you."

²³Then Zedekiah son of Kenaanah went up and slapped Micaiah in the face. "Which way did the spirit from[a] the LORD go when he went from me to speak to you?" he asked.

²⁴Micaiah replied, "You will find out on the day you go to hide in an inner room."

²⁵The king of Israel then ordered, "Take Micaiah and send him back to Amon the ruler of the city and to Joash the king's son, ²⁶and say, 'This is what the king says: Put this fellow in prison and give him nothing but bread and water until I return safely.' "

²⁷Micaiah declared, "If you ever return safely, the LORD has not spoken through me." Then he added, "Mark my words, all you people!"

AHAB KILLED AT RAMOTH GILEAD

²⁸So the king of Israel and Jehoshaphat king of Judah went up to Ramoth Gilead. ²⁹The king of Israel said to Jehoshaphat, "I will enter the battle in disguise, but you wear your royal robes." So the king of Israel disguised himself and went into battle.

³⁰Now the king of Aram had ordered his chariot commanders, "Do not fight with anyone, small or great, except the king of Israel." ³¹When the chariot commanders saw Jehoshaphat, they thought, "This is the king of Israel." So they turned to attack him, but Jehoshaphat cried out, and the LORD helped him. God drew them away from him, ³²for when the chariot commanders saw that he was not the king of Israel, they stopped pursuing him.

³³But someone drew his bow at random and hit the king of Israel between the sections of his armor. The king told the chariot driver, "Wheel around and get me out of the fighting. I've been wounded." ³⁴All day long the battle raged, and the king of Israel propped himself up in his chariot facing the Arameans until evening. Then at sunset he died.

19 When Jehoshaphat king of Judah returned safely to his palace in Jerusalem, ²Jehu the seer, the son of Hanani, went out to meet him and said to the king, "Should you help the wicked and love[b] those who hate the LORD? Because of this, the wrath of the LORD is upon you. ³There is, however, some good in you, for you have rid the land of the Asherah poles and have set your heart on seeking God."

JEHOSHAPHAT APPOINTS JUDGES

⁴Jehoshaphat lived in Jerusalem, and he went out again among the people from Beersheba to the hill country of Ephraim and turned them back to the LORD, the God of their fathers. ⁵He appointed judges in the land, in each of the fortified cities of Judah. ⁶He told them, "Consider carefully what you do,

---

ᵃ 23 Or *Spirit of*   ᵇ 2 Or *and make alliances with*

because you are not judging for man but for the LORD, who is with you whenever you give a verdict. ⁷Now let the fear of the LORD be upon you. Judge carefully, for with the LORD our God there is no injustice or partiality or bribery."

⁸In Jerusalem also, Jehoshaphat appointed some of the Levites, priests and heads of Israelite families to administer the law of the LORD and to settle disputes. And they lived in Jerusalem. ⁹He gave them these orders: "You must serve faithfully and wholeheartedly in the fear of the LORD. ¹⁰In every case that comes before you from your fellow countrymen who live in the cities—whether bloodshed or other concerns of the law, commands, decrees or ordinances—you are to warn them not to sin against the LORD; otherwise his wrath will come on you and your brothers. Do this, and you will not sin.

¹¹"Amariah the chief priest will be over you in any matter concerning the LORD, and Zebadiah son of Ishmael, the leader of the tribe of Judah, will be over you in any matter concerning the king, and the Levites will serve as officials before you. Act with courage, and may the LORD be with those who do well."

JEHOSHAPHAT DEFEATS MOAB AND AMMON

20 After this, the Moabites and Ammonites with some of the Meunites ᵃ came to make war on Jehoshaphat.

²Some men came and told Jehoshaphat, "A vast army is coming against you from Edom,ᵇ from the other side of the Sea.ᶜ It is already in Hazazon Tamar" (that is, En Gedi). ³Alarmed, Jehoshaphat resolved to inquire of the LORD, and he proclaimed a fast for all Judah. ⁴The people of Judah came together to seek help from the LORD; indeed, they came from every town in Judah to seek him.

⁵Then Jehoshaphat stood up in the assembly of Judah and Jerusalem at the temple of the LORD in the front of the new courtyard ⁶and said:

"O LORD, God of our fathers, are you not the God who is in heaven? You rule over all the kingdoms of the nations. Power and might are in your hand, and no one can withstand you. ⁷O our God, did you not drive out the inhabitants of this land before your people Israel and give it forever to the descendants of Abraham your friend? ⁸They have lived in it and have built in it a sanctuary for your Name, saying, ⁹'If calamity comes upon us, whether the sword of judgment, or plague or famine, we will stand in your presence before this temple that bears your Name and will cry out to you in our distress, and you will hear us and save us.'

¹⁰"But now here are men from Ammon, Moab and Mount Seir, whose territory you would not allow Israel to invade when they came from Egypt; so they turned away from them and did not destroy them. ¹¹See how they are repaying us by coming to drive us out of the possession you gave us as an inheritance. ¹²O our God, will you not judge them? For we have no power to face this vast army that is attacking us. We do not know what to do, but our eyes are upon you."

¹³All the men of Judah, with their wives and children and little ones, stood there before the LORD. ¹⁴Then the Spirit of the LORD came upon Jahaziel son of Zechariah, the son of Benaiah, the son of Jeiel, the son of Mattaniah, a Levite and descendant of Asaph, as he stood in the assembly.

¹⁵He said: "Listen, King Jehoshaphat and all who live in Judah and Jerusalem! This is what the LORD says to you: 'Do not be afraid or discouraged because of this vast army. For the battle is not yours, but God's. ¹⁶Tomorrow march down against them. They will be climbing up by the Pass of Ziz, and you will

Showing Courage

Courage isn't a lack of fear—it's a determination not to let fear stop you from doing what needs to be done. Everyone gets a little freaked out; there's nothing cowardly about admitting that. When you face a situation that makes you fearful, your first reaction probably will be to run, hide and do anything you can to protect yourself. Courage is overcoming that impulse, asking God for help and continuing on.

ᵃ 1 Some Septuagint manuscripts; Hebrew *Ammonites*   ᵇ 2 One Hebrew manuscript; most Hebrew manuscripts, Septuagint and Vulgate *Aram*   ᶜ 2 That is, the Dead Sea find them at the end of the gorge in the Desert of Jeruel. [17]You will not have to fight this battle. Take up your positions; stand firm and see the deliverance the LORD will give you, O Judah and Jerusalem. Do not be afraid; do not be discouraged. Go out to face them tomorrow, and the LORD will be with you.' "

[18]Jehoshaphat bowed with his face to the ground, and all the people of Judah and Jerusalem fell down in worship before the LORD. [19]Then some Levites from the Kohathites and Korahites stood up and praised the LORD, the God of Israel, with a very loud voice.

[20]Early in the morning they left for the Desert of Tekoa. As they set out, Jehoshaphat stood and said, "Listen to me, Judah and people of Jerusalem! Have faith in the LORD your God and you will be upheld; have faith in his prophets and you will be successful." [21]After consulting the people, Jehoshaphat appointed men to sing to the LORD and to praise him for the splendor of his[a] holiness as they went out at the head of the army, saying:

> "Give thanks to the LORD,
> for his love endures forever."

[22]As they began to sing and praise, the LORD set ambushes against the men of Ammon and Moab and Mount Seir who were invading Judah, and they were defeated. [23]The men of Ammon and Moab rose up against the men from Mount Seir to destroy and annihilate them. After they finished slaughtering the men from Seir, they helped to destroy one another.

[24]When the men of Judah came to the place that overlooks the desert and looked toward the vast army, they saw only dead bodies lying on the ground; no one had escaped. [25]So Jehoshaphat and his men went to carry off their plunder, and they found among them a great amount of equipment and clothing[b] and also articles of value—more than they could take away. There was so much plunder that it took three days to collect it. [26]On the fourth day they assembled in the Valley of Beracah, where they praised the LORD. This is why it is called the Valley of Beracah[c] to this day.

[27]Then, led by Jehoshaphat, all the men of Judah and Jerusalem returned joyfully to Jerusalem, for the LORD had given them cause to rejoice over their enemies. [28]They entered Jerusalem and went to the temple of the LORD with harps and lutes and trumpets.

[29]The fear of God came upon all the kingdoms of the countries when they heard how the LORD had fought against the enemies of Israel. [30]And the kingdom of Jehoshaphat was at peace, for his God had given him rest on every side.

THE END OF JEHOSHAPHAT'S REIGN

[31]So Jehoshaphat reigned over Judah. He was thirty-five years old when he became king of Judah, and he reigned in Jerusalem twenty-five years. His mother's name was Azubah daughter of Shilhi. [32]He walked in the ways of his father Asa and did not stray from them; he did what was right in the eyes of the LORD. [33]The high places, however, were not removed, and the people still had not set their hearts on the God of their fathers.

[34]The other events of Jehoshaphat's reign, from beginning to end, are written in the annals of Jehu son of Hanani, which are recorded in the book of the kings of Israel.

NOW OR NEVER
2CH 20:15

Being the underdog may be scary, but it's also pretty cool. Nothing earns people's respect like someone who overcomes big odds or stares down a seemingly unbeatable enemy. That's the kind of opportunity for victory that God likes to give to his people.

NOW OR NEVER
2CH 20:20

The world defines success by external appearances and temporary success. Hollywood and Wall Street are evidence of that. But true success—not defined by time or money or human achievement—depends on the power of God and your faith in him.

---

[a] 21 Or him with the splendor of   [b] 25 Some Hebrew manuscripts and Vulgate; most Hebrew manuscripts corpses   [c] 26 Beracah means praise.

³⁵Later, Jehoshaphat king of Judah made an alliance with Ahaziah king of Israel, who was guilty of wickedness. ³⁶He agreed with him to construct a fleet of trading ships.ᵃ After these were built at Ezion Geber, ³⁷Eliezer son of Dodavahu of Mareshah prophesied against Jehoshaphat, saying, "Because you have made an alliance with Ahaziah, the Lᴏʀᴅ will destroy what you have made." The ships were wrecked and were not able to set sail to trade.ᵇ

21 Then Jehoshaphat rested with his fathers and was buried with them in the City of David. And Jehoram his son succeeded him as king. ²Jehoram's brothers, the sons of Jehoshaphat, were Azariah, Jehiel, Zechariah, Azariahu, Michael and Shephatiah. All these were sons of Jehoshaphat king of Israel.ᶜ ³Their father had given them many gifts of silver and gold and articles of value, as well as fortified cities in Judah, but he had given the kingdom to Jehoram because he was his firstborn son.

JEHORAM KING OF JUDAH

⁴When Jehoram established himself firmly over his father's kingdom, he put all his brothers to the sword along with some of the princes of Israel. ⁵Jehoram was thirty-two years old when he became king, and he reigned in Jerusalem eight years. ⁶He walked in the ways of the kings of Israel, as the house of Ahab had done, for he married a daughter of Ahab. He did evil in the eyes of the Lᴏʀᴅ. ⁷Nevertheless, because of the covenant the Lᴏʀᴅ had made with David, the Lᴏʀᴅ was not willing to destroy the house of David. He had promised to maintain a lamp for him and his descendants forever.

⁸In the time of Jehoram, Edom rebelled against Judah and set up its own king. ⁹So Jehoram went there with his officers and all his chariots. The Edomites surrounded him and his chariot commanders, but he rose up and broke through by night. ¹⁰To this day Edom has been in rebellion against Judah.

Libnah revolted at the same time, because Jehoram had forsaken the Lᴏʀᴅ, the God of his fathers. ¹¹He had also built high places on the hills of Judah and had caused the people of Jerusalem to prostitute themselves and had led Judah astray.

¹²Jehoram received a letter from Elijah the prophet, which said:

"This is what the Lᴏʀᴅ, the God of your father David, says: 'You have not walked in the ways of your father Jehoshaphat or of Asa king of Judah. ¹³But you have walked in the ways of the kings of Israel, and you have led Judah and the people of Jerusalem to prostitute themselves, just as the house of Ahab did. You have also murdered your own brothers, members of your father's house, men who were better than you. ¹⁴So now the Lᴏʀᴅ is about to strike your people, your sons, your wives and everything that is yours, with a heavy blow. ¹⁵You yourself will be very ill with a lingering disease of the bowels, until the disease causes your bowels to come out.' "

¹⁶The Lᴏʀᴅ aroused against Jehoram the hostility of the Philistines and of the Arabs who lived near the Cushites. ¹⁷They attacked Judah, invaded it and carried off all the goods found in the king's palace, together with his sons and wives. Not a son was left to him except Ahaziah,ᵈ the youngest.

¹⁸After all this, the Lᴏʀᴅ afflicted Jehoram with an incurable disease of the bowels. ¹⁹In the course of time, at the end of the second year, his bowels came out because of the disease, and he died in great pain. His people made no fire in his honor, as they had for his fathers.

²⁰Jehoram was thirty-two years old when he became king, and he reigned in Jerusalem eight years. He passed away, to no one's regret, and was buried in the City of David, but not in the tombs of the kings.

AHAZIAH KING OF JUDAH

22 The people of Jerusalem made Ahaziah, Jehoram's youngest son, king in his place, since the raiders, who came with the Arabs into the camp, had killed all the older sons. So Ahaziah son of Jehoram king of Judah began to reign.

²Ahaziah was twenty-twoᵉ years old when he became king, and he reigned in Jerusalem one year. His mother's name was Athaliah, a granddaughter of Omri.

³He too walked in the ways of the house of Ahab, for his mother encouraged him in doing wrong. ⁴He did evil in the eyes of the Lᴏʀᴅ, as the house of Ahab had done, for after his father's death they became his advisers, to his undoing. ⁵He also followed their counsel when he went with Joramᶠ son of

---

ᵃ *36* Hebrew *of ships that could go to Tarshish*   ᵇ *37* Hebrew *sail for Tarshish*   ᶜ *2* That is, Judah, as frequently in 2 Chronicles
ᵈ *17* Hebrew *Jehoahaz*, a variant of *Ahaziah*   ᵉ *2* Some Septuagint manuscripts and Syriac (see also 2 Kings 8:26); Hebrew *forty-two*
ᶠ *5* Hebrew *Jehoram*, a variant of *Joram*; also in verses 6 and 7

Ahab king of Israel to war against Hazael king of Aram at Ramoth Gilead. The Arameans wounded Joram; ⁶so he returned to Jezreel to recover from the wounds they had inflicted on him at Ramoth ᵃ in his battle with Hazael king of Aram.

Then Ahaziah ᵇ son of Jehoram king of Judah went down to Jezreel to see Joram son of Ahab because he had been wounded.

⁷Through Ahaziah's visit to Joram, God brought about Ahaziah's downfall. When Ahaziah arrived, he went out with Joram to meet Jehu son of Nimshi, whom the Lord had anointed to destroy the house of Ahab. ⁸While Jehu was executing judgment on the house of Ahab, he found the princes of Judah and the sons of Ahaziah's relatives, who had been attending Ahaziah, and he killed them. ⁹He then went in search of Ahaziah, and his men captured him while he was hiding in Samaria. He was brought to Jehu and put to death. They buried him, for they said, "He was a son of Jehoshaphat, who sought the Lord with all his heart." So there was no one in the house of Ahaziah powerful enough to retain the kingdom.

ATHALIAH AND JOASH

¹⁰When Athaliah the mother of Ahaziah saw that her son was dead, she proceeded to destroy the whole royal family of the house of Judah. ¹¹But Jehosheba, ᶜ the daughter of King Jehoram, took Joash son of Ahaziah and stole him away from among the royal princes who were about to be murdered and put him and his nurse in a bedroom. Because Jehosheba, ᶜ the daughter of King Jehoram and wife of the priest Jehoiada, was Ahaziah's sister, she hid the child from Athaliah so she could not kill him. ¹²He remained hidden with them at the temple of God for six years while Athaliah ruled the land.

23 In the seventh year Jehoiada showed his strength. He made a covenant with the commanders of units of a hundred: Azariah son of Jeroham, Ishmael son of Jehohanan, Azariah son of Obed, Maaseiah son of Adaiah, and Elishaphat son of Zicri. ²They went throughout Judah and gathered the Levites and the heads of Israelite families from all the towns. When they came to Jerusalem, ³the whole assembly made a covenant with the king at the temple of God.

Jehoiada said to them, "The king's son shall reign, as the Lord promised concerning the descendants of David. ⁴Now this is what you are to do: A third of you priests and Levites who are going on duty on the Sabbath are to keep watch at the doors, ⁵a third of you at the royal palace and a third at the Foundation Gate, and all the other men are to be in the courtyards of the temple of the Lord. ⁶No one is to enter the temple of the Lord except the priests and Levites on duty; they may enter because they are consecrated, but all the other men are to guard what the Lord has assigned to them. ᵈ ⁷The Levites are to station themselves around the king, each man with his weapons in his hand. Anyone who enters the temple must be put to death. Stay close to the king wherever he goes."

⁸The Levites and all the men of Judah did just as Jehoiada the priest ordered. Each one took his men—those who were going on duty on the Sabbath and those who were going off duty—for Jehoiada the priest had not released any of the divisions. ⁹Then he gave the commanders of units of a hundred the spears and the large and small shields that had belonged to King David and that were in the temple of God. ¹⁰He stationed all the men, each with his weapon in his hand, around the king—near the altar and the temple, from the south side to the north side of the temple.

¹¹Jehoiada and his sons brought out the king's son and put the crown on him; they presented him with a copy of the covenant and proclaimed him king. They anointed him and shouted, "Long live the king!"

¹²When Athaliah heard the noise of the people running and cheering the king, she went to them at the temple of the Lord. ¹³She looked, and there was the king, standing by his pillar at the entrance. The officers and the trumpeters were beside the king, and all the people of the land were rejoicing and blowing trumpets, and singers with musical instruments were leading the praises. Then Athaliah tore her robes and shouted, "Treason! Treason!"

¹⁴Jehoiada the priest sent out the commanders of units of a hundred, who were in charge of the troops, and said to them: "Bring her out between the ranks ᵉ and put to the sword anyone who follows her." For the priest had said, "Do not put her to death at the temple of the Lord." ¹⁵So they seized her as she reached the entrance of the Horse Gate on the palace grounds, and there they put her to death.

¹⁶Jehoiada then made a covenant that he and the people and the king ᶠ would be the Lord's people.

ᵃ 6 Hebrew *Ramah*, a variant of *Ramoth*   ᵇ 6 Some Hebrew manuscripts, Septuagint, Vulgate and Syriac (see also 2 Kings 8:29); most Hebrew manuscripts *Azariah*   ᶜ 11 Hebrew *Jehoshabeath*, a variant of *Jehosheba*   ᵈ 6 Or *to observe the Lord's command ⌐ not to enter⌐*   ᵉ 14 Or *out from the precincts*   ᶠ 16 Or *covenant between ⌐the Lord⌐ and the people and the king that they* (see 2 Kings 11:17)

battlelines

» The Chameleon (Identity)

Q: What would you say is your best quality?
A: Well, let's see, I'm pretty easygoing. I don't get rattled very easily.

Q: That's good. What about your *worst* quality?
A: That's easy. I'm too much of a people pleaser.

Q: What do you mean?
A: I don't stick my neck out. I never take a stand. I just try to fit in and make everybody feel happy and comfortable.

Q: Why?
A: *Why?* What do I look like, a psychiatrist? How should I know? Maybe because I'm . . . "Chameleon Man." I change to fit my surroundings, you know. I act one way around my Christian friends and then another way with my friends who aren't into God. I guess that makes me a total fake, huh?

Q: Well . . .
A: No, it's OK. You can say it. It's true. I see it. To be honest, that's what I *hate* about myself. I'm weak.

Q: What are you going to do about it?
A: Try to grow a backbone. Try to get comfortable with the fact that it's OK if some people don't like me. In fact, when I think about it, I should *expect* some people not to like me, right?

Q: Yeah, that's probably true. So you know that if you *do* try to change, you're going to catch some heat for it?
A: (Sighs) I know. I think Jesus told us that—expect persecution. Yeah, well, it's about time. Guess we'll see what I'm really made of, huh?

» Making the Change

One of the best Biblical examples of taking a bold stand is found in the life of a woman named Queen Esther. She was, by all accounts, a flawless beauty; but she found herself in an unenviable situation. She could either keep her mouth shut, allowing many innocent people to be executed, or she could speak up and risk losing her own life in the process.

Esther chose to risk it all and speak up. You'll find her story in Esther 4. Think about her courageous words in verse 16: "I will go to the king, even though it is against the law. And if I perish, I perish."

Wow. We need more *men* like that—guys who will lay it all on the line. Strong guys who will do what's right and let the chips fall where they may.

Be honest—isn't that the kind of guy you really want to be?

Go to www.RevolutionBible.com for more.

17All the people went to the temple of Baal and tore it down. They smashed the altars and idols and killed Mattan the priest of Baal in front of the altars.

18Then Jehoiada placed the oversight of the temple of the LORD in the hands of the priests, who were Levites, to whom David had made assignments in the temple, to present the burnt offerings of the LORD as written in the Law of Moses, with rejoicing and singing, as David had ordered. 19He also stationed doorkeepers at the gates of the LORD's temple so that no one who was in any way unclean might enter.

20He took with him the commanders of hundreds, the nobles, the rulers of the people and all the people of the land and brought the king down from the temple of the LORD. They went into the palace through the Upper Gate and seated the king on the royal throne, 21and all the people of the land rejoiced. And the city was quiet, because Athaliah had been slain with the sword.

JOASH REPAIRS THE TEMPLE

24 Joash was seven years old when he became king, and he reigned in Jerusalem forty years. His mother's name was Zibiah; she was from Beersheba. 2Joash did what was right in the eyes of the LORD all the years of Jehoiada the priest. 3Jehoiada chose two wives for him, and he had sons and daughters.

4Some time later Joash decided to restore the temple of the LORD. 5He called together the priests and Levites and said to them, "Go to the towns of Judah and collect the money due annually from all Israel, to repair the temple of your God. Do it now." But the Levites did not act at once.

6Therefore the king summoned Jehoiada the chief priest and said to him, "Why haven't you required the Levites to bring in from Judah and Jerusalem the tax imposed by Moses the servant of the LORD and by the assembly of Israel for the Tent of the Testimony?"

7Now the sons of that wicked woman Athaliah had broken into the temple of God and had used even its sacred objects for the Baals.

8At the king's command, a chest was made and placed outside, at the gate of the temple of the LORD. 9A proclamation was then issued in Judah and Jerusalem that they should bring to the LORD the tax that Moses the servant of God had required of Israel in the desert. 10All the officials and all the people brought their contributions gladly, dropping them into the chest until it was full. 11Whenever the chest was brought in by the Levites to the king's officials and they saw that there was a large amount of money, the royal secretary and the officer of the chief priest would come and empty the chest and carry it back to its place. They did this regularly and collected a great amount of money. 12The king and Jehoiada gave it to the men who carried out the work required for the temple of the LORD. They hired masons and carpenters to restore the LORD's temple, and also workers in iron and bronze to repair the temple.

13The men in charge of the work were diligent, and the repairs progressed under them. They rebuilt the temple of God according to its original design and reinforced it. 14When they had finished, they brought the rest of the money to the king and Jehoiada, and with it were made articles for the LORD's temple: articles for the service and for the burnt offerings, and also dishes and other objects of gold and silver. As long as Jehoiada lived, burnt offerings were presented continually in the temple of the LORD.

15Now Jehoiada was old and full of years, and he died at the age of a hundred and thirty. 16He was buried with the kings in the City of David, because of the good he had done in Israel for God and his temple.

Being Diligent

live the adventure >> 2Ch 24:13

Rebuilding the temple must have been a frustrating job at times. The workers had to follow precise plans. If their measurements were off even slightly, they had to start over. At one time or another, most of the workers probably got so frustrated that they wanted to quit. But they didn't give in to their frustration, their fatigue or their restlessness. They just kept working. They ignored the distractions around them and focused on getting the job done right. That's the kind of work ethic God appreciates and blesses.

¹⁷After the death of Jehoiada, the officials of Judah came and paid homage to the king, and he listened to them. ¹⁸They abandoned the temple of the Lord, the God of their fathers, and worshiped Asherah poles and idols. Because of their guilt, God's anger came upon Judah and Jerusalem. ¹⁹Although the Lord sent prophets to the people to bring them back to him, and though they testified against them, they would not listen.

²⁰Then the Spirit of God came upon Zechariah son of Jehoiada the priest. He stood before the people and said, "This is what God says: 'Why do you disobey the Lord's commands? You will not prosper. Because you have forsaken the Lord, he has forsaken you.'"

²¹But they plotted against him, and by order of the king they stoned him to death in the courtyard of the Lord's temple. ²²King Joash did not remember the kindness Zechariah's father Jehoiada had shown him but killed his son, who said as he lay dying, "May the Lord see this and call you to account."

²³At the turn of the year,^a the army of Aram marched against Joash; it invaded Judah and Jerusalem and killed all the leaders of the people. They sent all the plunder to their king in Damascus. ²⁴Although the Aramean army had come with only a few men, the Lord delivered into their hands a much larger army. Because Judah had forsaken the Lord, the God of their fathers, judgment was executed on Joash. ²⁵When the Arameans withdrew, they left Joash severely wounded. His officials conspired against him for murdering the son of Jehoiada the priest, and they killed him in his bed. So he died and was buried in the City of David, but not in the tombs of the kings.

²⁶Those who conspired against him were Zabad,^b son of Shimeath an Ammonite woman, and Jehozabad, son of Shimrith^c a Moabite woman. ²⁷The account of his sons, the many prophecies about him, and the record of the restoration of the temple of God are written in the annotations on the book of the kings. And Amaziah his son succeeded him as king.

AMAZIAH KING OF JUDAH

25 Amaziah was twenty-five years old when he became king, and he reigned in Jerusalem twenty-nine years. His mother's name was Jehoaddin^d; she was from Jerusalem. ²He did what was right in the eyes of the Lord, but not wholeheartedly. ³After the kingdom was firmly in his control, he executed the officials who had murdered his father the king. ⁴Yet he did not put their sons to death, but acted in accordance with what is written in the Law, in the Book of Moses, where the Lord commanded: "Fathers shall not be put to death for their children, nor children put to death for their fathers; each is to die for his own sins."^e

⁵Amaziah called the people of Judah together and assigned them according to their families to commanders of thousands and commanders of hundreds for all Judah and Benjamin. He then mustered those twenty years old or more and found that there were three hundred thousand men ready for military service, able to handle the spear and shield. ⁶He also hired a hundred thousand fighting men from Israel for a hundred talents^f of silver.

⁷But a man of God came to him and said, "O king, these troops from Israel must not march with you, for the Lord is not with Israel—not with any of the people of Ephraim. ⁸Even if you go and fight courageously in battle, God will overthrow you before the enemy, for God has the power to help or to overthrow." ⁹Amaziah asked the man of God, "But what about the hundred talents I paid for these Israelite troops?"

NOW OR NEVER
2CH 25:8

God is in control over not only the lives of his people, but those of his enemies as well. No one is ever so rich or so powerful that he or she can't be humbled in an instant by God.

The man of God replied, "The Lord can give you much more than that."

¹⁰So Amaziah dismissed the troops who had come to him from Ephraim and sent them home. They were furious with Judah and left for home in a great rage.

---

^a *23* Probably in the spring   ^b *26* A variant of *Jozabad*   ^c *26* A variant of *Shomer*   ^d *1* Hebrew *Jehoaddan*, a variant of *Jehoaddin*
^e *4* Deut. 24:16   ^f *6* That is, about 3 3/4 tons (about 3.4 metric tons); also in verse 9

¹¹Amaziah then marshaled his strength and led his army to the Valley of Salt, where he killed ten thousand men of Seir. ¹²The army of Judah also captured ten thousand men alive, took them to the top of a cliff and threw them down so that all were dashed to pieces.

¹³Meanwhile the troops that Amaziah had sent back and had not allowed to take part in the war raided Judean towns from Samaria to Beth Horon. They killed three thousand people and carried off great quantities of plunder.

¹⁴When Amaziah returned from slaughtering the Edomites, he brought back the gods of the people of Seir. He set them up as his own gods, bowed down to them and burned sacrifices to them. ¹⁵The anger of the LORD burned against Amaziah, and he sent a prophet to him, who said, "Why do you consult this people's gods, which could not save their own people from your hand?"

¹⁶While he was still speaking, the king said to him, "Have we appointed you an adviser to the king? Stop! Why be struck down?"

So the prophet stopped but said, "I know that God has determined to destroy you, because you have done this and have not listened to my counsel."

¹⁷After Amaziah king of Judah consulted his advisers, he sent this challenge to Jehoash^a son of Jehoahaz, the son of Jehu, king of Israel: "Come, meet me face to face."

¹⁸But Jehoash king of Israel replied to Amaziah king of Judah: "A thistle in Lebanon sent a message to a cedar in Lebanon, 'Give your daughter to my son in marriage.' Then a wild beast in Lebanon came along and trampled the thistle underfoot. ¹⁹You say to yourself that you have defeated Edom, and now you are arrogant and proud. But stay at home! Why ask for trouble and cause your own downfall and that of Judah also?"

²⁰Amaziah, however, would not listen, for God so worked that he might hand them over to ⌊Jehoash⌋, because they sought the gods of Edom. ²¹So Jehoash king of Israel attacked. He and Amaziah king of Judah faced each other at Beth Shemesh in Judah. ²²Judah was routed by Israel, and every man fled to his home. ²³Jehoash king of Israel captured Amaziah king of Judah, the son of Joash, the son of Ahaziah,^b at Beth Shemesh. Then Jehoash brought him to Jerusalem and broke down the wall of Jerusalem from the Ephraim Gate to the Corner Gate—a section about six hundred feet^c long. ²⁴He took all the gold and silver and all the articles found in the temple of God that had been in the care of Obed-Edom, together with the palace treasures and the hostages, and returned to Samaria.

²⁵Amaziah son of Joash king of Judah lived for fifteen years after the death of Jehoash son of Jehoahaz king of Israel. ²⁶As for the other events of Amaziah's reign, from beginning to end, are they not written in the book of the kings of Judah and Israel? ²⁷From the time that Amaziah turned away from following the LORD, they conspired against him in Jerusalem and he fled to Lachish, but they sent men after him to Lachish and killed him there. ²⁸He was brought back by horse and was buried with his fathers in the City of Judah.

UZZIAH KING OF JUDAH

26

Then all the people of Judah took Uzziah,^d who was sixteen years old, and made him king in place of his father Amaziah. ²He was the one who rebuilt Elath and restored it to Judah after Amaziah rested with his fathers.

³Uzziah was sixteen years old when he became king, and he reigned in Jerusalem fifty-two years. His mother's name was Jecoliah; she was from Jerusalem. ⁴He did what was right in the eyes of the LORD, just as his father Amaziah had done. ⁵He sought God during the days of Zechariah, who instructed him in the fear^e of God. As long as he sought the LORD, God gave him success.

⁶He went to war against the Philistines and broke down the walls of Gath, Jabneh and Ashdod. He then

NOW OR NEVER

2CH 26:5

If your quest is only for success, you'll never achieve it—at least not in God's eyes. If your quest is to please God in everything you do, then you'll find real success.

---

^a 17 Hebrew Joash, a variant of Jehoash; also in verses 18, 21, 23 and 25   ^b 23 Hebrew Jehoahaz, a variant of Ahaziah   ^c 23 Hebrew four hundred cubits (about 180 meters)   ^d 1 Also called Azariah   ^e 5 Many Hebrew manuscripts, Septuagint and Syriac; other Hebrew manuscripts vision

rebuilt towns near Ashdod and elsewhere among the Philistines. [7]God helped him against the Philistines and against the Arabs who lived in Gur Baal and against the Meunites. [8]The Ammonites brought tribute to Uzziah, and his fame spread as far as the border of Egypt, because he had become very powerful.

[9]Uzziah built towers in Jerusalem at the Corner Gate, at the Valley Gate and at the angle of the wall, and he fortified them. [10]He also built towers in the desert and dug many cisterns, because he had much livestock in the foothills and in the plain. He had people working his fields and vineyards in the hills and in the fertile lands, for he loved the soil.

[11]Uzziah had a well-trained army, ready to go out by divisions according to their numbers as mustered by Jeiel the secretary and Maaseiah the officer under the direction of Hananiah, one of the royal officials. [12]The total number of family leaders over the fighting men was 2,600. [13]Under their command was an army of 307,500 men trained for war, a powerful force to support the king against his enemies. [14]Uzziah provided shields, spears, helmets, coats of armor, bows and slingstones for the entire army. [15]In Jerusalem he made machines designed by skillful men for use on the towers and on the corner defenses to shoot arrows and hurl large stones. His fame spread far and wide, for he was greatly helped until he became powerful.

NOW OR NEVER
2CH 26:16

Uzziah was a pretty good king at first. But somewhere along the way, he got tired of giving God all the credit for Judah's success. His pride got out of control. Eventually God cut him down to size, and Uzziah became a leper for the rest of his life. Any question how God feels about human pride?

[16]But after Uzziah became powerful, his pride led to his downfall. He was unfaithful to the LORD his God, and entered the temple of the LORD to burn incense on the altar of incense. [17]Azariah the priest with eighty other courageous priests of the LORD followed him in. [18]They confronted him and said, "It is not right for you, Uzziah, to burn incense to the LORD. That is for the priests, the descendants of Aaron, who have been consecrated to burn incense. Leave the sanctuary, for you have been unfaithful; and you will not be honored by the LORD God."

[19]Uzziah, who had a censer in his hand ready to burn incense, became angry. While he was raging at the priests in their presence before the incense altar in the LORD's temple, leprosy[a] broke out on his forehead. [20]When Azariah the chief priest and all the other priests looked at him, they saw that he had leprosy on his forehead, so they hurried him out. Indeed, he himself was eager to leave, because the LORD had afflicted him.

[21]King Uzziah had leprosy until the day he died. He lived in a separate house[b]—leprous, and excluded from the temple of the LORD. Jotham his son had charge of the palace and governed the people of the land.

[22]The other events of Uzziah's reign, from beginning to end, are recorded by the prophet Isaiah son of Amoz. [23]Uzziah rested with his fathers and was buried near them in a field for burial that belonged to the kings, for people said, "He had leprosy." And Jotham his son succeeded him as king.

JOTHAM KING OF JUDAH

27 Jotham was twenty-five years old when he became king, and he reigned in Jerusalem sixteen years. His mother's name was Jerusha daughter of Zadok. [2]He did what was right in the eyes of the LORD, just as his father Uzziah had done, but unlike him he did not enter the temple of the LORD. The people, however, continued their corrupt practices. [3]Jotham rebuilt the Upper Gate of the temple of the LORD and did extensive work on the wall at the hill of Ophel. [4]He built towns in the Judean hills and forts and towers in the wooded areas.

[5]Jotham made war on the king of the Ammonites and conquered them. That year the Ammonites paid him a hundred talents[c] of silver, ten thousand cors[d] of wheat and ten thousand cors of barley. The Ammonites brought him the same amount also in the second and third years.

[6]Jotham grew powerful because he walked steadfastly before the LORD his God.

[7]The other events in Jotham's reign, including all his wars and the other things he did, are written

---

[a] 19 The Hebrew word was used for various diseases affecting the skin—not necessarily leprosy; also in verses 20, 21 and 23.   [b] 21 Or *in a house where he was relieved of responsibilities*   [c] 5 That is, about 3 3/4 tons (about 3.4 metric tons)   [d] 5 That is, probably about 62,000 bushels (about 2,200 kiloliters)

in the book of the kings of Israel and Judah. ⁸He was twenty-five years old when he became king, and he reigned in Jerusalem sixteen years. ⁹Jotham rested with his fathers and was buried in the City of David. And Ahaz his son succeeded him as king.

AHAZ KING OF JUDAH

28 Ahaz was twenty years old when he became king, and he reigned in Jerusalem sixteen years. Unlike David his father, he did not do what was right in the eyes of the LORD. ²He walked in the ways of the kings of Israel and also made cast idols for worshiping the Baals. ³He burned sacrifices in the Valley of Ben Hinnom and sacrificed his sons in the fire, following the detestable ways of the nations the LORD had driven out before the Israelites. ⁴He offered sacrifices and burned incense at the high places, on the hilltops and under every spreading tree.

⁵Therefore the LORD his God handed him over to the king of Aram. The Arameans defeated him and took many of his people as prisoners and brought them to Damascus.

He was also given into the hands of the king of Israel, who inflicted heavy casualties on him. ⁶In one day Pekah son of Remaliah killed a hundred and twenty thousand soldiers in Judah—because Judah had forsaken the LORD, the God of their fathers. ⁷Zicri, an Ephraimite warrior, killed Maaseiah the king's son, Azrikam the officer in charge of the palace, and Elkanah, second to the king. ⁸The Israelites took captive from their kinsmen two hundred thousand wives, sons and daughters. They also took a great deal of plunder, which they carried back to Samaria.

⁹But a prophet of the LORD named Oded was there, and he went out to meet the army when it returned to Samaria. He said to them, "Because the LORD, the God of your fathers, was angry with Judah, he gave them into your hand. But you have slaughtered them in a rage that reaches to heaven. ¹⁰And now you intend to make the men and women of Judah and Jerusalem your slaves. But aren't you also guilty of sins against the LORD your God? ¹¹Now listen to me! Send back your fellow countrymen you have taken as prisoners, for the LORD's fierce anger rests on you."

¹²Then some of the leaders in Ephraim—Azariah son of Jehohanan, Berekiah son of Meshillemoth, Jehizkiah son of Shallum, and Amasa son of Hadlai—confronted those who were arriving from the war. ¹³"You must not bring those prisoners here," they said, "or we will be guilty before the LORD. Do you intend to add to our sin and guilt? For our guilt is already great, and his fierce anger rests on Israel."

¹⁴So the soldiers gave up the prisoners and plunder in the presence of the officials and all the assembly. ¹⁵The men designated by name took the prisoners, and from the plunder they clothed all who were naked. They provided them with clothes and sandals, food and drink, and healing balm. All those who were weak they put on donkeys. So they took them back to their fellow countrymen at Jericho, the City of Palms, and returned to Samaria.

NOW OR NEVER
2CH 28:22

Blaming God for the consequences of sinful choices in your life is like blaming a lifeguard for allowing you to get caught in a riptide after he had warned you about dangerous water conditions.

¹⁶At that time King Ahaz sent to the king[a] of Assyria for help. ¹⁷The Edomites had again come and attacked Judah and carried away prisoners, ¹⁸while the Philistines had raided towns in the foothills and in the Negev of Judah. They captured and occupied Beth Shemesh, Aijalon and Gederoth, as well as Soco, Timnah and Gimzo, with their surrounding villages. ¹⁹The LORD had humbled Judah because of Ahaz king of Israel,[b] for he had promoted wickedness in Judah and had been most unfaithful to the LORD. ²⁰Tiglath-Pileser[c] king of Assyria came to him, but he gave him trouble instead of help. ²¹Ahaz took some of the things from the temple of the LORD and from the royal palace and from the princes and presented them to the king of Assyria, but that did not help him.

²²In his time of trouble King Ahaz became even more unfaithful to the LORD. ²³He offered sacrifices to the gods of Damascus, who had defeated him; for he thought, "Since the gods of the kings of Aram have helped them, I will sacrifice to them so they will help me." But they were his downfall and the downfall of all Israel.

---

[a] *16* One Hebrew manuscript, Septuagint and Vulgate (see also 2 Kings 16:7); most Hebrew manuscripts *kings*   [b] *19* That is, Judah, as frequently in 2 Chronicles   [c] *20* Hebrew *Tilgath-Pilneser,* a variant of *Tiglath-Pileser*

24Ahaz gathered together the furnishings from the temple of God and took them away.[a] He shut the doors of the LORD's temple and set up altars at every street corner in Jerusalem. 25In every town in Judah he built high places to burn sacrifices to other gods and provoked the LORD, the God of his fathers, to anger.

26The other events of his reign and all his ways, from beginning to end, are written in the book of the kings of Judah and Israel. 27Ahaz rested with his fathers and was buried in the city of Jerusalem, but he was not placed in the tombs of the kings of Israel. And Hezekiah his son succeeded him as king.

HEZEKIAH PURIFIES THE TEMPLE

29

Hezekiah was twenty-five years old when he became king, and he reigned in Jerusalem twenty-nine years. His mother's name was Abijah daughter of Zechariah. 2He did what was right in the eyes of the LORD, just as his father David had done.

3In the first month of the first year of his reign, he opened the doors of the temple of the LORD and repaired them. 4He brought in the priests and the Levites, assembled them in the square on the east side 5and said: "Listen to me, Levites! Consecrate yourselves now and consecrate the temple of the LORD, the God of your fathers. Remove all defilement from the sanctuary. 6Our fathers were unfaithful; they did evil in the eyes of the LORD our God and forsook him. They turned their faces away from the LORD's dwelling place and turned their backs on him. 7They also shut the doors of the portico and put out the lamps. They did not burn incense or present any burnt offerings at the sanctuary to the God of Israel. 8Therefore, the anger of the LORD has fallen on Judah and Jerusalem; he has made them an object of dread and horror and scorn, as you can see with your own eyes. 9This is why our fathers have fallen by the sword and why our sons and daughters and our wives are in captivity. 10Now I intend to make a covenant with the LORD, the God of Israel, so that his fierce anger will turn away from us. 11My sons, do not be negligent now, for the LORD has chosen you to stand before him and serve him, to minister before him and to burn incense."

12Then these Levites set to work:
from the Kohathites,
Mahath son of Amasai and Joel son of Azariah;
from the Merarites,
Kish son of Abdi and Azariah son of Jehallelel;
from the Gershonites,
Joah son of Zimmah and Eden son of Joah;
13from the descendants of Elizaphan,
Shimri and Jeiel;
from the descendants of Asaph,
Zechariah and Mattaniah;
14from the descendants of Heman,
Jehiel and Shimei;
from the descendants of Jeduthun,
Shemaiah and Uzziel.

15When they had assembled their brothers and consecrated themselves, they went in to purify the temple of the LORD, as the king had ordered, following the word of the LORD. 16The priests went into the sanctuary of the LORD to purify it. They brought out to the courtyard of the LORD's temple everything unclean that they found in the temple of the LORD. The Levites took it and carried it out to the Kidron Valley. 17They began the consecration on the first day of the first month, and by the eighth day of the month they reached the portico of the LORD. For eight more days they consecrated the temple of the LORD itself, finishing on the sixteenth day of the first month.

18Then they went in to King Hezekiah and reported: "We have purified the entire temple of the LORD, the altar of burnt offering with all its utensils, and the table for setting out the consecrated bread, with all its articles. 19We have prepared and consecrated all the articles that King Ahaz removed in his unfaithfulness while he was king. They are now in front of the LORD's altar."

20Early the next morning King Hezekiah gathered the city officials together and went up to the temple of the LORD. 21They brought seven bulls, seven rams, seven male lambs and seven male goats as a sin offering for the kingdom, for the sanctuary and for Judah. The king commanded the priests, the de-

---

[a] 24 Or *and cut them up*

scendants of Aaron, to offer these on the altar of the Lord. ²²So they slaughtered the bulls, and the priests took the blood and sprinkled it on the altar; next they slaughtered the rams and sprinkled their blood on the altar; then they slaughtered the lambs and sprinkled their blood on the altar. ²³The goats for the sin offering were brought before the king and the assembly, and they laid their hands on them. ²⁴The priests then slaughtered the goats and presented their blood on the altar for a sin offering to atone for all Israel, because the king had ordered the burnt offering and the sin offering for all Israel.

²⁵He stationed the Levites in the temple of the Lord with cymbals, harps and lyres in the way prescribed by David and Gad the king's seer and Nathan the prophet; this was commanded by the Lord through his prophets. ²⁶So the Levites stood ready with David's instruments, and the priests with their trumpets.

²⁷Hezekiah gave the order to sacrifice the burnt offering on the altar. As the offering began, singing to the Lord began also, accompanied by trumpets and the instruments of David king of Israel. ²⁸The whole assembly bowed in worship, while the singers sang and the trumpeters played. All this continued until the sacrifice of the burnt offering was completed.

²⁹When the offerings were finished, the king and everyone present with him knelt down and worshiped. ³⁰King Hezekiah and his officials ordered the Levites to praise the Lord with the words of David and of Asaph the seer. So they sang praises with gladness and bowed their heads and worshiped.

³¹Then Hezekiah said, "You have now dedicated yourselves to the Lord. Come and bring sacrifices and thank offerings to the temple of the Lord." So the assembly brought sacrifices and thank offerings, and all whose hearts were willing brought burnt offerings.

³²The number of burnt offerings the assembly brought was seventy bulls, a hundred rams and two hundred male lambs—all of them for burnt offerings to the Lord. ³³The animals consecrated as sacrifices amounted to six hundred bulls and three thousand sheep and goats. ³⁴The priests, however, were too few to skin all the burnt offerings; so their kinsmen the Levites helped them until the task was finished and until other priests had been consecrated, for the Levites had been more conscientious in consecrating themselves than the priests had been. ³⁵There were burnt offerings in abundance, together with the fat of the fellowship offerings[a] and the drink offerings that accompanied the burnt offerings.

So the service of the temple of the Lord was reestablished. ³⁶Hezekiah and all the people rejoiced at what God had brought about for his people, because it was done so quickly.

HEZEKIAH CELEBRATES THE PASSOVER

30 Hezekiah sent word to all Israel and Judah and also wrote letters to Ephraim and Manasseh, inviting them to come to the temple of the Lord in Jerusalem and celebrate the Passover to the Lord, the God of Israel. ²The king and his officials and the whole assembly in Jerusalem decided to celebrate the Passover in the second month. ³They had not been able to celebrate it at the regular time because not enough priests had consecrated themselves and the people had not assembled in Jerusalem. ⁴The plan seemed right both to the king and to the whole assembly. ⁵They decided to send a proclamation throughout Israel, from Beersheba to Dan, calling the people to come to Jerusalem and celebrate the Passover to the Lord, the God of Israel. It had not been celebrated in large numbers according to what was written.

⁶At the king's command, couriers went throughout Israel and Judah with letters from the king and from his officials, which read:

"People of Israel, return to the Lord, the God of Abraham, Isaac and Israel, that he may return to you who are left, who have escaped from the hand of the kings of Assyria. ⁷Do not be like your fathers and brothers, who were unfaithful to the Lord, the God of their fathers, so that he made them an object of horror, as you see. ⁸Do not be stiff-necked, as your fathers were; submit to the Lord. Come to the sanctuary, which he has consecrated forever. Serve the Lord your God, so that his fierce anger will turn away from you. ⁹If you return to the Lord, then your brothers and your children will be shown compassion by their captors and will come back to this land, for the Lord your God is gracious and compassionate. He will not turn his face from you if you return to him."

¹⁰The couriers went from town to town in Ephraim and Manasseh, as far as Zebulun, but the people scorned and ridiculed them. ¹¹Nevertheless, some men of Asher, Manasseh and Zebulun humbled

---

a 35 Traditionally *peace offerings*

themselves and went to Jerusalem. [12]Also in Judah the hand of God was on the people to give them unity of mind to carry out what the king and his officials had ordered, following the word of the LORD.

[13]A very large crowd of people assembled in Jerusalem to celebrate the Feast of Unleavened Bread in the second month. [14]They removed the altars in Jerusalem and cleared away the incense altars and threw them into the Kidron Valley.

[15]They slaughtered the Passover lamb on the fourteenth day of the second month. The priests and the Levites were ashamed and consecrated themselves and brought burnt offerings to the temple of the LORD. [16]Then they took up their regular positions as prescribed in the Law of Moses the man of God. The priests sprinkled the blood handed to them by the Levites. [17]Since many in the crowd had not consecrated themselves, the Levites had to kill the Passover lambs for all those who were not ceremonially clean and could not consecrate ⌊their lambs⌋ to the LORD. [18]Although most of the many people who came from Ephraim, Manasseh, Issachar and Zebulun had not purified themselves, yet they ate the Passover, contrary to what was written. But Hezekiah prayed for them, saying, "May the LORD, who is good, pardon everyone [19]who sets his heart on seeking God—the LORD, the God of his fathers—even if he is not clean according to the rules of the sanctuary." [20]And the LORD heard Hezekiah and healed the people.

[21]The Israelites who were present in Jerusalem celebrated the Feast of Unleavened Bread for seven days with great rejoicing, while the Levites and priests sang to the LORD every day, accompanied by the LORD's instruments of praise.[a]

[22]Hezekiah spoke encouragingly to all the Levites, who showed good understanding of the service of the LORD. For the seven days they ate their assigned portion and offered fellowship offerings[b] and praised the LORD, the God of their fathers.

[23]The whole assembly then agreed to celebrate the festival seven more days; so for another seven days they celebrated joyfully. [24]Hezekiah king of Judah provided a thousand bulls and seven thousand sheep and goats for the assembly, and the officials provided them with a thousand bulls and ten thousand sheep and goats. A great number of priests consecrated themselves. [25]The entire assembly of Judah rejoiced, along with the priests and Levites and all who had assembled from Israel, including the aliens who had come from Israel and those who lived in Judah. [26]There was great joy in Jerusalem, for since the days of Solomon son of David king of Israel there had been nothing like this in Jerusalem. [27]The priests and the Levites stood to bless the people, and God heard them, for their prayer reached heaven, his holy dwelling place.

31 When all this had ended, the Israelites who were there went out to the towns of Judah, smashed the sacred stones and cut down the Asherah poles. They destroyed the high places and the altars throughout Judah and Benjamin and in Ephraim and Manasseh. After they had destroyed all of them, the Israelites returned to their own towns and to their own property.

Learning to Be Repentant

Have you ever done something so wrong or made a mistake so serious that you changed the way you live so that you wouldn't repeat it? In other words, have you ever done something that made you say, "I will never do *that* again"? That's what repentance is. And that's the kind of attitude God wants us to have *every* time we sin. Instead of tossing off a halfhearted "Sorry about that," we need to allow God to change us—not only externally but also in our hearts, to prevent that sin from happening again.

nOW OR n-EVER
2CH 30:22

How do you respond when you see one of your buddies living in obedience to God? Does it matter to you? Look for ways to encourage and be encouraged by your Christian friends.

---

[a] 21 Or *priests praised the LORD every day with resounding instruments belonging to the LORD*   [b] 22 Traditionally *peace offerings*

CONTRIBUTIONS FOR WORSHIP

[2]Hezekiah assigned the priests and Levites to divisions—each of them according to their duties as priests or Levites—to offer burnt offerings and fellowship offerings,[a] to minister, to give thanks and to sing praises at the gates of the Lord's dwelling. [3]The king contributed from his own possessions for the morning and evening burnt offerings and for the burnt offerings on the Sabbaths, New Moons and appointed feasts as written in the Law of the Lord. [4]He ordered the people living in Jerusalem to give the portion due the priests and Levites so they could devote themselves to the Law of the Lord. [5]As soon as the order went out, the Israelites generously gave the firstfruits of their grain, new wine, oil and honey and all that the fields produced. They brought a great amount, a tithe of everything. [6]The men of Israel and Judah who lived in the towns of Judah also brought a tithe of their herds and flocks and a tithe of the holy things dedicated to the Lord their God, and they piled them in heaps. [7]They began doing this in the third month and finished in the seventh month. [8]When Hezekiah and his officials came and saw the heaps, they praised the Lord and blessed his people Israel.

[9]Hezekiah asked the priests and Levites about the heaps; [10]and Azariah the chief priest, from the family of Zadok, answered, "Since the people began to bring their contributions to the temple of the Lord, we have had enough to eat and plenty to spare, because the Lord has blessed his people, and this great amount is left over."

[11]Hezekiah gave orders to prepare storerooms in the temple of the Lord, and this was done. [12]Then they faithfully brought in the contributions, tithes and dedicated gifts. Conaniah, a Levite, was in charge of these things, and his brother Shimei was next in rank. [13]Jehiel, Azaziah, Nahath, Asahel, Jerimoth, Jozabad, Eliel, Ismakiah, Mahath and Benaiah were supervisors under Conaniah and Shimei his brother, by appointment of King Hezekiah and Azariah the official in charge of the temple of God.

[14]Kore son of Imnah the Levite, keeper of the East Gate, was in charge of the freewill offerings given to God, distributing the contributions made to the Lord and also the consecrated gifts. [15]Eden, Miniamin, Jeshua, Shemaiah, Amariah and Shecaniah assisted him faithfully in the towns of the priests, distributing to their fellow priests according to their divisions, old and young alike.

[16]In addition, they distributed to the males three years old or more whose names were in the genealogical records—all who would enter the temple of the Lord to perform the daily duties of their various tasks, according to their responsibilities and their divisions. [17]And they distributed to the priests enrolled by their families in the genealogical records and likewise to the Levites twenty years old or more, according to their responsibilities and their divisions. [18]They included all the little ones, the wives, and the sons and daughters of the whole community listed in these genealogical records. For they were faithful in consecrating themselves.

[19]As for the priests, the descendants of Aaron, who lived on the farm lands around their towns or in any other towns, men were designated by name to distribute portions to every male among them and to all who were recorded in the genealogies of the Levites.

[20]This is what Hezekiah did throughout Judah, doing what was good and right and faithful before the Lord his God. [21]In everything that he undertook in the service of God's temple and in obedience to the law and the commands, he sought his God and worked wholeheartedly. And so he prospered.

SENNACHERIB THREATENS JERUSALEM

32 After all that Hezekiah had so faithfully done, Sennacherib king of Assyria came and invaded Judah. He laid siege to the fortified cities, thinking to conquer them for himself. [2]When Hezekiah saw that Sennacherib had come and that he intended to make war on Jerusalem, [3]he consulted with his officials and military staff about blocking off the water from the springs outside the city, and they helped him. [4]A large force of men assembled, and they blocked all the springs and the stream that flowed through the land. "Why should the kings[b] of Assyria come and find plenty of water?" they said. [5]Then he worked hard repairing all the broken sections of the wall and building towers on it. He built another wall outside that one and reinforced the supporting terraces[c] of the City of David. He also made large numbers of weapons and shields.

[6]He appointed military officers over the people and assembled them before him in the square at the city gate and encouraged them with these words: [7]"Be strong and courageous. Do not be afraid or discouraged because of the king of Assyria and the vast army with him, for there is a greater power with

---

[a] 2 Traditionally *peace offerings*   [b] 4 Hebrew; Septuagint and Syriac *king*   [c] 5 Or *the Millo*

us than with him. [8]With him is only the arm of flesh, but with us is the LORD our God to help us and to fight our battles." And the people gained confidence from what Hezekiah the king of Judah said.

[9]Later, when Sennacherib king of Assyria and all his forces were laying siege to Lachish, he sent his officers to Jerusalem with this message for Hezekiah king of Judah and for all the people of Judah who were there:

[10]"This is what Sennacherib king of Assyria says: On what are you basing your confidence, that you remain in Jerusalem under siege? [11]When Hezekiah says, 'The LORD our God will save us from the hand of the king of Assyria,' he is misleading you, to let you die of hunger and thirst. [12]Did not Hezekiah himself remove this god's high places and altars, saying to Judah and Jerusalem, 'You must worship before one altar and burn sacrifices on it'?

[13]"Do you not know what I and my fathers have done to all the peoples of the other lands? Were the gods of those nations ever able to deliver their land from my hand? [14]Who of all the gods of these nations that my fathers destroyed has been able to save his people from me? How then can your god deliver you from my hand? [15]Now do not let Hezekiah deceive you and mislead you like this. Do not believe him, for no god of any nation or kingdom has been able to deliver his people from my hand or the hand of my fathers. How much less will your god deliver you from my hand!"

[16]Sennacherib's officers spoke further against the LORD God and against his servant Hezekiah. [17]The king also wrote letters insulting the LORD, the God of Israel, and saying this against him: "Just as the gods of the peoples of the other lands did not rescue their people from my hand, so the god of Hezekiah will not rescue his people from my hand." [18]Then they called out in Hebrew to the people of Jerusalem who were on the wall, to terrify them and make them afraid in order to capture the city. [19]They spoke about the God of Jerusalem as they did about the gods of the other peoples of the world—the work of men's hands.

[20]King Hezekiah and the prophet Isaiah son of Amoz cried out in prayer to heaven about this. [21]And the LORD sent an angel, who annihilated all the fighting men and the leaders and officers in the camp of the Assyrian king. So he withdrew to his own land in disgrace. And when he went into the temple of his god, some of his sons cut him down with the sword.

[22]So the LORD saved Hezekiah and the people of Jerusalem from the hand of Sennacherib king of Assyria and from the hand of all others. He took care of them[a] on every side. [23]Many brought offerings to Jerusalem for the LORD and valuable gifts for Hezekiah king of Judah. From then on he was highly regarded by all the nations.

HEZEKIAH'S PRIDE, SUCCESS AND DEATH

[24]In those days Hezekiah became ill and was at the point of death. He prayed to the LORD, who answered him and gave him a miraculous sign. [25]But Hezekiah's heart was proud and he did not respond to the kindness shown him; therefore the LORD's wrath was on him and on Judah and Jerusalem. [26]Then Hezekiah repented of the pride of his heart, as did the people of Jerusalem; therefore the LORD's wrath did not come upon them during the days of Hezekiah.

[27]Hezekiah had very great riches and honor, and he made treasuries for his silver and gold and for his precious stones, spices, shields and all kinds of valuables. [28]He also made buildings to store the harvest of grain, new wine and oil; and he made stalls for various kinds of cattle, and pens for the flocks. [29]He built villages and acquired great numbers of flocks and herds, for God had given him very great riches.

[30]It was Hezekiah who blocked the upper outlet of the Gihon spring and channeled the water down to the west side of the City of David. He succeeded in everything he undertook. [31]But when envoys were sent by the rulers of Babylon to ask him about the miraculous sign that had occurred in the land, God left him to test him and to know everything that was in his heart.

[32]The other events of Hezekiah's reign and his acts of devotion are written in the vision of the prophet Isaiah son of Amoz in the book of the kings of Judah and Israel. [33]Hezekiah rested with his fathers and was buried on the hill where the tombs of David's descendants are. All Judah and the people of Jerusalem honored him when he died. And Manasseh his son succeeded him as king.

[a] 22 Hebrew; Septuagint and Vulgate *He gave them rest*

33

Manasseh was twelve years old when he became king, and he reigned in Jerusalem fifty-five years. ²He did evil in the eyes of the LORD, following the detestable practices of the nations the LORD had driven out before the Israelites. ³He rebuilt the high places his father Hezekiah had demolished; he also erected altars to the Baals and made Asherah poles. He bowed down to all the starry hosts and worshiped them. ⁴He built altars in the temple of the LORD, of which the LORD had said, "My Name will remain in Jerusalem forever." ⁵In both courts of the temple of the LORD, he built altars to all the starry hosts. ⁶He sacrificed his sons in[a] the fire in the Valley of Ben Hinnom, practiced sorcery, divination and witchcraft, and consulted mediums and spiritists. He did much evil in the eyes of the LORD, provoking him to anger.

⁷He took the carved image he had made and put it in God's temple, of which God had said to David and to his son Solomon, "In this temple and in Jerusalem, which I have chosen out of all the tribes of Israel, I will put my Name forever. ⁸I will not again make the feet of the Israelites leave the land I assigned to your forefathers, if only they will be careful to do everything I commanded them concerning all the laws, decrees and ordinances given through Moses." ⁹But Manasseh led Judah and the people of Jerusalem astray, so that they did more evil than the nations the LORD had destroyed before the Israelites.

¹⁰The LORD spoke to Manasseh and his people, but they paid no attention. ¹¹So the LORD brought against them the army commanders of the king of Assyria, who took Manasseh prisoner, put a hook in his nose, bound him with bronze shackles and took him to Babylon. ¹²In his distress he sought the favor of the LORD his God and humbled himself greatly before the God of his fathers. ¹³And when he prayed to him, the LORD was moved by his entreaty and listened to his plea; so he brought him back to Jerusalem and to his kingdom. Then Manasseh knew that the LORD is God.

NOW OR NEVER
2CH 33:11–13

God has proven that he will do whatever it takes to get our attention and to make us recognize him for who he really is. Do yourself a big favor. Don't wait until someone brings out nose hooks and bronze shackles to humble yourself before God.

¹⁴Afterward he rebuilt the outer wall of the City of David, west of the Gihon spring in the valley, as far as the entrance of the Fish Gate and encircling the hill of Ophel; he also made it much higher. He stationed military commanders in all the fortified cities in Judah.

¹⁵He got rid of the foreign gods and removed the image from the temple of the LORD, as well as all the altars he had built on the temple hill and in Jerusalem; and he threw them out of the city. ¹⁶Then he restored the altar of the LORD and sacrificed fellowship offerings[b] and thank offerings on it, and told Judah to serve the LORD, the God of Israel. ¹⁷The people, however, continued to sacrifice at the high places, but only to the LORD their God.

¹⁸The other events of Manasseh's reign, including his prayer to his God and the words the seers spoke to him in the name of the LORD, the God of Israel, are written in the annals of the kings of Israel.[c] ¹⁹His prayer and how God was moved by his entreaty, as well as all his sins and unfaithfulness, and the sites where he built high places and set up Asherah poles and idols before he humbled himself— all are written in the records of the seers.[d] ²⁰Manasseh rested with his fathers and was buried in his palace. And Amon his son succeeded him as king.

AMON KING OF JUDAH

²¹Amon was twenty-two years old when he became king, and he reigned in Jerusalem two years. ²²He did evil in the eyes of the LORD, as his father Manasseh had done. Amon worshiped and offered sacrifices to all the idols Manasseh had made. ²³But unlike his father Manasseh, he did not humble himself before the LORD; Amon increased his guilt.

²⁴Amon's officials conspired against him and assassinated him in his palace. ²⁵Then the people of the land killed all who had plotted against King Amon, and they made Josiah his son king in his place.

---

[a] 6 Or He made his sons pass through   [b] 16 Traditionally peace offerings   [c] 18 That is, Judah, as frequently in 2 Chronicles
[d] 19 One Hebrew manuscript and Septuagint; most Hebrew manuscripts of Hozai

JOSIAH'S REFORMS

34

Josiah was eight years old when he became king, and he reigned in Jerusalem thirty-one years. [2]He did what was right in the eyes of the LORD and walked in the ways of his father David, not turning aside to the right or to the left.

[3]In the eighth year of his reign, while he was still young, he began to seek the God of his father David. In his twelfth year he began to purge Judah and Jerusalem of high places, Asherah poles, carved idols and cast images. [4]Under his direction the altars of the Baals were torn down; he cut to pieces the incense altars that were above them, and smashed the Asherah poles, the idols and the images. These he broke to pieces and scattered over the graves of those who had sacrificed to them. [5]He burned the bones of the priests on their altars, and so he purged Judah and Jerusalem. [6]In the towns of Manasseh, Ephraim and Simeon, as far as Naphtali, and in the ruins around them, [7]he tore down the altars and the Asherah poles and crushed the idols to powder and cut to pieces all the incense altars throughout Israel. Then he went back to Jerusalem.

[8]In the eighteenth year of Josiah's reign, to purify the land and the temple, he sent Shaphan son of Azaliah and Maaseiah the ruler of the city, with Joah son of Joahaz, the recorder, to repair the temple of the LORD his God.

[9]They went to Hilkiah the high priest and gave him the money that had been brought into the temple of God, which the Levites who were the doorkeepers had collected from the people of Manasseh, Ephraim and the entire remnant of Israel and from all the people of Judah and Benjamin and the inhabitants of Jerusalem. [10]Then they entrusted it to the men appointed to supervise the work on the LORD's temple. These men paid the workers who repaired and restored the temple. [11]They also gave money to the carpenters and builders to purchase dressed stone, and timber for joists and beams for the buildings that the kings of Judah had allowed to fall into ruin.

[12]The men did the work faithfully. Over them to direct them were Jahath and Obadiah, Levites descended from Merari, and Zechariah and Meshullam, descended from Kohath. The Levites—all who were skilled in playing musical instruments— [13]had charge of the laborers and supervised all the workers from job to job. Some of the Levites were secretaries, scribes and doorkeepers.

THE BOOK OF THE LAW FOUND

[14]While they were bringing out the money that had been taken into the temple of the LORD, Hilkiah the priest found the Book of the Law of the LORD that had been given through Moses. [15]Hilkiah said to Shaphan the secretary, "I have found the Book of the Law in the temple of the LORD." He gave it to Shaphan.

[16]Then Shaphan took the book to the king and reported to him: "Your officials are doing everything that has been committed to them. [17]They have paid out the money that was in the temple of the LORD and have entrusted it to the supervisors and workers." [18]Then Shaphan the secretary informed the king, "Hilkiah the priest has given me a book." And Shaphan read from it in the presence of the king.

[19]When the king heard the words of the Law, he tore his robes. [20]He gave these orders to Hilkiah, Ahikam son of Shaphan, Abdon son of Micah,[a] Shaphan the secretary and Asaiah the king's attendant: [21]"Go and inquire of the LORD for me and for the remnant in Israel and Judah about what is written in this book that has been found. Great is the LORD's anger that is poured out on us because our fathers

Enjoying Your Youth

Some people will tell you that your youth is a liability when it comes to your faith. They'll to tell you that you're too young to appreciate what Christ has done for you or too immature to be trusted with anything important. Don't listen to them. Your youth is an asset. By starting a relationship with God when you're young, you have a chance to grow in him, mature and be used by him in ways that some adults may never experience.

»» live the adventure »» 2Ch 34:1-2

---

[a] 20 Also called *Acbor son of Micaiah*

have not kept the word of the LORD; they have not acted in accordance with all that is written in this book."

²²Hilkiah and those the king had sent with him[a] went to speak to the prophetess Huldah, who was the wife of Shallum son of Tokhath,[b] the son of Hasrah,[c] keeper of the wardrobe. She lived in Jerusalem, in the Second District.

²³She said to them, "This is what the LORD, the God of Israel, says: Tell the man who sent you to me, ²⁴'This is what the LORD says: I am going to bring disaster on this place and its people—all the curses written in the book that has been read in the presence of the king of Judah. ²⁵Because they have forsaken me and burned incense to other gods and provoked me to anger by all that their hands have made,[d] my anger will be poured out on this place and will not be quenched.' ²⁶Tell the king of Judah, who sent you to inquire of the LORD, 'This is what the LORD, the God of Israel, says concerning the words you heard: ²⁷Because your heart was responsive and you humbled yourself before God when you heard what he spoke against this place and its people, and because you humbled yourself before me and tore your robes and wept in my presence, I have heard you, declares the LORD. ²⁸Now I will gather you to your fathers, and you will be buried in peace. Your eyes will not see all the disaster I am going to bring on this place and on those who live here.' "

So they took her answer back to the king.

²⁹Then the king called together all the elders of Judah and Jerusalem. ³⁰He went up to the temple of the LORD with the men of Judah, the people of Jerusalem, the priests and the Levites—all the people from the least to the greatest. He read in their hearing all the words of the Book of the Covenant, which had been found in the temple of the LORD. ³¹The king stood by his pillar and renewed the covenant in the presence of the LORD—to follow the LORD and keep his commands, regulations and decrees with all his heart and all his soul, and to obey the words of the covenant written in this book.

³²Then he had everyone in Jerusalem and Benjamin pledge themselves to it; the people of Jerusalem did this in accordance with the covenant of God, the God of their fathers.

³³Josiah removed all the detestable idols from all the territory belonging to the Israelites, and he had all who were present in Israel serve the LORD their God. As long as he lived, they did not fail to follow the LORD, the God of their fathers.

challenge notes

To: my_son

2CH 34:27

heavenly_father: never use my willingness to forgive as an excuse to do whatever you want. don't fall into the trap of believing that all you have to do is say "oops" to make everything instantly better. I offer forgiveness to people who are *truly* sorry for what they've done and who are committed to turning from their sin.

JOSIAH CELEBRATES THE PASSOVER

35

Josiah celebrated the Passover to the LORD in Jerusalem, and the Passover lamb was slaughtered on the fourteenth day of the first month. ²He appointed the priests to their duties and encouraged them in the service of the LORD's temple. ³He said to the Levites, who instructed all Israel and who had been consecrated to the LORD: "Put the sacred ark in the temple that Solomon son of David king of Israel built. It is not to be carried about on your shoulders. Now serve the LORD your God and his people Israel. ⁴Prepare yourselves by families in your divisions, according to the directions written by David king of Israel and by his son Solomon.

⁵"Stand in the holy place with a group of Levites for each subdivision of the families of your fellow countrymen, the lay people. ⁶Slaughter the Passover lambs, consecrate yourselves and prepare ⌊the lambs⌋ for your fellow countrymen, doing what the LORD commanded through Moses."

⁷Josiah provided for all the lay people who were there a total of thirty thousand sheep and goats for the Passover offerings, and also three thousand cattle—all from the king's own possessions.

⁸His officials also contributed voluntarily to the people and the priests and Levites. Hilkiah, Zechariah and Jehiel, the administrators of God's temple, gave the priests twenty-six hundred Passover offerings and three hundred cattle. ⁹Also Conaniah along with Shemaiah and Nethanel, his brothers, and

[a] *22* One Hebrew manuscript, Vulgate and Syriac; most Hebrew manuscripts do not have *had sent with him.* [b] *22* Also called *Tikvah*
[c] *22* Also called *Harhas* [d] *25* Or *by everything they have done*

Hashabiah, Jeiel and Jozabad, the leaders of the Levites, provided five thousand Passover offerings and five hundred head of cattle for the Levites.

¹⁰The service was arranged and the priests stood in their places with the Levites in their divisions as the king had ordered. ¹¹The Passover lambs were slaughtered, and the priests sprinkled the blood handed to them, while the Levites skinned the animals. ¹²They set aside the burnt offerings to give them to the subdivisions of the families of the people to offer to the LORD, as is written in the Book of Moses. They did the same with the cattle. ¹³They roasted the Passover animals over the fire as prescribed, and boiled the holy offerings in pots, caldrons and pans and served them quickly to all the people. ¹⁴After this, they made preparations for themselves and for the priests, because the priests, the descendants of Aaron, were sacrificing the burnt offerings and the fat portions until nightfall. So the Levites made preparations for themselves and for the Aaronic priests.

¹⁵The musicians, the descendants of Asaph, were in the places prescribed by David, Asaph, Heman and Jeduthun the king's seer. The gatekeepers at each gate did not need to leave their posts, because their fellow Levites made the preparations for them.

¹⁶So at that time the entire service of the LORD was carried out for the celebration of the Passover and the offering of burnt offerings on the altar of the LORD, as King Josiah had ordered. ¹⁷The Israelites who were present celebrated the Passover at that time and observed the Feast of Unleavened Bread for seven days. ¹⁸The Passover had not been observed like this in Israel since the days of the prophet Samuel; and none of the kings of Israel had ever celebrated such a Passover as did Josiah, with the priests, the Levites and all Judah and Israel who were there with the people of Jerusalem. ¹⁹This Passover was celebrated in the eighteenth year of Josiah's reign.

THE DEATH OF JOSIAH

²⁰After all this, when Josiah had set the temple in order, Neco king of Egypt went up to fight at Carchemish on the Euphrates, and Josiah marched out to meet him in battle. ²¹But Neco sent messengers to him, saying, "What quarrel is there between you and me, O king of Judah? It is not you I am attacking at this time, but the house with which I am at war. God has told me to hurry; so stop opposing God, who is with me, or he will destroy you."

²²Josiah, however, would not turn away from him, but disguised himself to engage him in battle. He would not listen to what Neco had said at God's command but went to fight him on the plain of Megiddo.

²³Archers shot King Josiah, and he told his officers, "Take me away; I am badly wounded." ²⁴So they took him out of his chariot, put him in the other chariot he had and brought him to Jerusalem, where he died. He was buried in the tombs of his fathers, and all Judah and Jerusalem mourned for him.

²⁵Jeremiah composed laments for Josiah, and to this day all the men and women singers commemorate Josiah in the laments. These became a tradition in Israel and are written in the Laments.

²⁶The other events of Josiah's reign and his acts of devotion, according to what is written in the Law of the LORD— ²⁷all the events, from beginning to end, are written in the book of the kings of Israel and

36

Judah. ¹And the people of the land took Jehoahaz son of Josiah and made him king in Jerusalem in place of his father.

JEHOAHAZ KING OF JUDAH

²Jehoahaz[a] was twenty-three years old when he became king, and he reigned in Jerusalem three months. ³The king of Egypt dethroned him in Jerusalem and imposed on Judah a levy of a hundred talents[b] of silver and a talent[c] of gold. ⁴The king of Egypt made Eliakim, a brother of Jehoahaz, king over Judah and Jerusalem and changed Eliakim's name to Jehoiakim. But Neco took Eliakim's brother Jehoahaz and carried him off to Egypt.

JEHOIAKIM KING OF JUDAH

⁵Jehoiakim was twenty-five years old when he became king, and he reigned in Jerusalem eleven years. He did evil in the eyes of the LORD his God. ⁶Nebuchadnezzar king of Babylon attacked him and bound him with bronze shackles to take him to Babylon. ⁷Nebuchadnezzar also took to Babylon articles from the temple of the LORD and put them in his temple[d] there.

---

[a] *2* Hebrew *Joahaz*, a variant of *Jehoahaz*; also in verse 4   [b] *3* That is, about 3 3/4 tons (about 3.4 metric tons)   [c] *3* That is, about 75 pounds (about 34 kilograms)   [d] *7* Or *palace*

[8]The other events of Jehoiakim's reign, the detestable things he did and all that was found against him, are written in the book of the kings of Israel and Judah. And Jehoiachin his son succeeded him as king.

JEHOIACHIN KING OF JUDAH

[9]Jehoiachin was eighteen[a] years old when he became king, and he reigned in Jerusalem three months and ten days. He did evil in the eyes of the LORD. [10]In the spring, King Nebuchadnezzar sent for him and brought him to Babylon, together with articles of value from the temple of the LORD, and he made Jehoiachin's uncle,[b] Zedekiah, king over Judah and Jerusalem.

ZEDEKIAH KING OF JUDAH

[11]Zedekiah was twenty-one years old when he became king, and he reigned in Jerusalem eleven years. [12]He did evil in the eyes of the LORD his God and did not humble himself before Jeremiah the prophet, who spoke the word of the LORD. [13]He also rebelled against King Nebuchadnezzar, who had made him take an oath in God's name. He became stiff-necked and hardened his heart and would not turn to the LORD, the God of Israel. [14]Furthermore, all the leaders of the priests and the people became more and more unfaithful, following all the detestable practices of the nations and defiling the temple of the LORD, which he had consecrated in Jerusalem.

THE FALL OF JERUSALEM

[15]The LORD, the God of their fathers, sent word to them through his messengers again and again, because he had pity on his people and on his dwelling place. [16]But they mocked God's messengers, despised his words and scoffed at his prophets until the wrath of the LORD was aroused against his people and there was no remedy. [17]He brought up against them the king of the Babylonians,[c] who killed their young men with the sword in the sanctuary, and spared neither young man nor young woman, old man or aged. God handed all of them over to Nebuchadnezzar. [18]He carried to Babylon all the articles from the temple of God, both large and small, and the treasures of the LORD's temple and the treasures of the king and his officials. [19]They set fire to God's temple and broke down the wall of Jerusalem; they burned all the palaces and destroyed everything of value there.

[20]He carried into exile to Babylon the remnant, who escaped from the sword, and they became servants to him and his sons until the kingdom of Persia came to power. [21]The land enjoyed its sabbath rests; all the time of its desolation it rested, until the seventy years were completed in fulfillment of the word of the LORD spoken by Jeremiah.

[22]In the first year of Cyrus king of Persia, in order to fulfill the word of the LORD spoken by Jeremiah, the LORD moved the heart of Cyrus king of Persia to make a proclamation throughout his realm and to put it in writing:

[23]"This is what Cyrus king of Persia says:

" 'The LORD, the God of heaven, has given me all the kingdoms of the earth and he has appointed me to build a temple for him at Jerusalem in Judah. Anyone of his people among you—may the LORD his God be with him, and let him go up.' "

---

[a] 9 One Hebrew manuscript, some Septuagint manuscripts and Syriac (see also 2 Kings 24:8); most Hebrew manuscripts *eight*
[b] 10 Hebrew *brother,* that is, relative (see 2 Kings 24:17)   [c] 17 Or *Chaldeans*

EZRA

« AT A GLANCE

Author
Ezra (probably)

Audience
People of Israel

Date
Written probably around 450 B.C.

Setting
The Israelites who had been exiled to Babylon had returned to the promised land.

Verse to Remember
For seven days they celebrated with joy the Feast of Unleavened Bread, because the Lord had filled them with joy by changing the attitude of the king of Assyria, so that he assisted them in the work on the house of God, the God of Israel (6:22).

Theme to Consider
God is always faithful to keeping his word and working out his plan and purpose.

UNCHANGING TRUTH » God gives second chances. The Israelites understood that better than anyone. When they turned their backs on the Lord and started worshiping other gods, God allowed their enemies (in this case, the Babylonians) to defeat them and carry them away from the promised land as prisoners.

But that wasn't the end of the story. After the Israelites had spent decades in Babylonian captivity, God gave them a chance for a fresh start. He allowed them to return to their homeland to begin rebuilding the city of Jerusalem, starting with the most important building—the temple.

God punished the Israelites for their sin, but he never forgot about them, gave up on them or stopped loving them. After their punishment was over, God wiped their record clean and let them start fresh again.

God still gives second chances today. No matter what you've done in the past (or what you do in the future), no matter how many people you've hurt by your actions, no matter how guilty or undeserving you feel, God will never forget you, give up on you or stop loving you. If you ask him for mercy, he will wipe your record clean—as in, completely clean—and give you the chance to start fresh and rebuild your life into something incredible.

LIFE LESSONS »

I. God can use anyone, even people you wouldn't expect, to get his work done (1:1–4).

2. One of the most important steps in fixing a damaged relationship with God is worship (3:10–11).

3. Asking God to forgive you isn't something you should do casually or thoughtlessly (10:1).

CYRUS HELPS THE EXILES TO RETURN

1 In the first year of Cyrus king of Persia, in order to fulfill the word of the LORD spoken by Jeremiah, the LORD moved the heart of Cyrus king of Persia to make a proclamation throughout his realm and to put it in writing:

2 "This is what Cyrus king of Persia says:

" 'The LORD, the God of heaven, has given me all the kingdoms of the earth and he has appointed me to build a temple for him at Jerusalem in Judah. 3 Anyone of his people among you—may his God be with him, and let him go up to Jerusalem in Judah and build the temple of the LORD, the God of Israel, the God who is in Jerusalem. 4 And the people of any place where survivors may now be living are to provide him with silver and gold, with goods and livestock, and with freewill offerings for the temple of God in Jerusalem.' "

5 Then the family heads of Judah and Benjamin, and the priests and Levites—everyone whose heart God had moved—prepared to go up and build the house of the LORD in Jerusalem. 6 All their neighbors assisted them with articles of silver and gold, with goods and livestock, and with valuable gifts, in addition to all the freewill offerings. 7 Moreover, King Cyrus brought out the articles belonging to the temple of the LORD, which Nebuchadnezzar had carried away from Jerusalem and had placed in the temple of his god.[a] 8 Cyrus king of Persia had them brought by Mithredath the treasurer, who counted them out to Sheshbazzar the prince of Judah.

9 This was the inventory:

gold dishes	30
silver dishes	1,000
silver pans[b]	29
10 gold bowls	30
matching silver bowls	410
other articles	1,000

11 In all, there were 5,400 articles of gold and of silver. Sheshbazzar brought all these along when the exiles came up from Babylon to Jerusalem.

NOW OR NEVER

EZR 1:1-4

No one is beyond God's reach, not even the pagan king of an enemy country. Think about that the next time you decide it's hopeless to talk to someone about Jesus.

THE LIST OF THE EXILES WHO RETURNED

2 Now these are the people of the province who came up from the captivity of the exiles, whom Nebuchadnezzar king of Babylon had taken captive to Babylon (they returned to Jerusalem and Judah, each to his own town, 2 in company with Zerubbabel, Jeshua, Nehemiah, Seraiah, Reelaiah, Mordecai, Bilshan, Mispar, Bigvai, Rehum and Baanah):

The list of the men of the people of Israel:

3 the descendants of Parosh	2,172
4 of Shephatiah	372
5 of Arah	775
6 of Pahath-Moab (through the line of Jeshua and Joab)	2,812
7 of Elam	1,254
8 of Zattu	945
9 of Zaccai	760
10 of Bani	642
11 of Bebai	623

---

a 7 Or *gods*   b 9 The meaning of the Hebrew for this word is uncertain.

¹² of Azgad	1,222
¹³ of Adonikam	666
¹⁴ of Bigvai	2,056
¹⁵ of Adin	454
¹⁶ of Ater (through Hezekiah)	98
¹⁷ of Bezai	323
¹⁸ of Jorah	112
¹⁹ of Hashum	223
²⁰ of Gibbar	95
²¹ the men of Bethlehem	123
²² of Netophah	56
²³ of Anathoth	128
²⁴ of Azmaveth	42
²⁵ of Kiriath Jearim,ᵃ Kephirah and Beeroth	743
²⁶ of Ramah and Geba	621
²⁷ of Micmash	122
²⁸ of Bethel and Ai	223
²⁹ of Nebo	52
³⁰ of Magbish	156
³¹ of the other Elam	1,254
³² of Harim	320
³³ of Lod, Hadid and Ono	725
³⁴ of Jericho	345
³⁵ of Senaah	3,630

³⁶ The priests:

the descendants of Jedaiah (through the family of Jeshua)	973
³⁷ of Immer	1,052
³⁸ of Pashhur	1,247
³⁹ of Harim	1,017

⁴⁰ The Levites:

the descendants of Jeshua and Kadmiel (through the line of Hodaviah)	74

⁴¹ The singers:

the descendants of Asaph	128

⁴² The gatekeepers of the temple:

the descendants of Shallum, Ater, Talmon, Akkub, Hatita and Shobai	139

⁴³ The temple servants:

the descendants of
Ziha, Hasupha, Tabbaoth,
⁴⁴ Keros, Siaha, Padon,
⁴⁵ Lebanah, Hagabah, Akkub,
⁴⁶ Hagab, Shalmai, Hanan,
⁴⁷ Giddel, Gahar, Reaiah,
⁴⁸ Rezin, Nekoda, Gazzam,
⁴⁹ Uzza, Paseah, Besai,

ᵃ 25 See Septuagint (see also Neh. 7:29); Hebrew Kiriath Arim.

⁵⁰Asnah, Meunim, Nephusim,
⁵¹Bakbuk, Hakupha, Harhur,
⁵²Bazluth, Mehida, Harsha,
⁵³Barkos, Sisera, Temah,
⁵⁴Neziah and Hatipha

⁵⁵The descendants of the servants of Solomon:

the descendants of
Sotai, Hassophereth, Peruda,
⁵⁶Jaala, Darkon, Giddel,
⁵⁷Shephatiah, Hattil,
Pokereth-Hazzebaim and Ami

⁵⁸The temple servants and the descendants
of the servants of Solomon   392

⁵⁹The following came up from the towns of Tel Melah, Tel Harsha, Kerub, Addon and Immer, but they could not show that their families were descended from Israel:

⁶⁰The descendants of
Delaiah, Tobiah and Nekoda   652

⁶¹And from among the priests:

The descendants of
Hobaiah, Hakkoz and Barzillai (a man who had married a daughter of Barzillai the Gileadite and was called by that name).
⁶²These searched for their family records, but they could not find them and so were excluded from the priesthood as unclean. ⁶³The governor ordered them not to eat any of the most sacred food until there was a priest ministering with the Urim and Thummim.

⁶⁴The whole company numbered 42,360, ⁶⁵besides their 7,337 menservants and maidservants; and they also had 200 men and women singers. ⁶⁶They had 736 horses, 245 mules, ⁶⁷435 camels and 6,720 donkeys.

⁶⁸When they arrived at the house of the LORD in Jerusalem, some of the heads of the families gave freewill offerings toward the rebuilding of the house of God on its site. ⁶⁹According to their ability they gave to the treasury for this work 61,000 drachmas ᵃ of gold, 5,000 minas ᵇ of silver and 100 priestly garments.
⁷⁰The priests, the Levites, the singers, the gatekeepers and the temple servants settled in their own towns, along with some of the other people, and the rest of the Israelites settled in their towns.

REBUILDING THE ALTAR

3 When the seventh month came and the Israelites had settled in their towns, the people assembled as one man in Jerusalem. ²Then Jeshua son of Jozadak and his fellow priests and Zerubbabel son of Shealtiel and his associates began to build the altar of the God of Israel to sacrifice burnt offerings on it, in accordance with what is written in the Law of Moses the man of God. ³Despite their fear of the peoples around them, they built the altar on its foundation and sacrificed burnt offerings on it to the LORD, both the morning and evening sacrifices.

Being Generous

If you decided to set aside, say, 10 percent of the money you earn every month to help a needy person or for a special project, how would that affect you? What would you be forced to give up, cut back on or do without? Think about it. Would it be a minor inconvenience or would it feel like the end of the world? One more thing: What if you knew that giving away, say, 25 percent of your monthly earnings (no matter how little that might be) could literally change someone else's life forever?

»» live the adventure »» Ezr 2:68-69

ᵃ 69 That is, about 1,100 pounds (about 500 kilograms)   ᵇ 69 That is, about 3 tons (about 2.9 metric tons)

⁴Then in accordance with what is written, they celebrated the Feast of Tabernacles with the required number of burnt offerings prescribed for each day. ⁵After that, they presented the regular burnt offerings, the New Moon sacrifices and the sacrifices for all the appointed sacred feasts of the LORD, as well as those brought as freewill offerings to the LORD. ⁶On the first day of the seventh month they began to offer burnt offerings to the LORD, though the foundation of the LORD's temple had not yet been laid.

REBUILDING THE TEMPLE

⁷Then they gave money to the masons and carpenters, and gave food and drink and oil to the people of Sidon and Tyre, so that they would bring cedar logs by sea from Lebanon to Joppa, as authorized by Cyrus king of Persia.

⁸In the second month of the second year after their arrival at the house of God in Jerusalem, Zerubbabel son of Shealtiel, Jeshua son of Jozadak and the rest of their brothers (the priests and the Levites and all who had returned from the captivity to Jerusalem) began the work, appointing Levites twenty years of age and older to supervise the building of the house of the LORD. ⁹Jeshua and his sons and brothers and Kadmiel and his sons (descendants of Hodaviah[a]) and the sons of Henadad and their sons and brothers—all Levites—joined together in supervising those working on the house of God.

¹⁰When the builders laid the foundation of the temple of the LORD, the priests in their vestments and with trumpets, and the Levites (the sons of Asaph) with cymbals, took their places to praise the LORD, as prescribed by David king of Israel. ¹¹With praise and thanksgiving they sang to the LORD:

> "He is good;
> his love to Israel endures forever."

And all the people gave a great shout of praise to the LORD, because the foundation of the house of the LORD was laid. ¹²But many of the older priests and Levites and family heads, who had seen the former temple, wept aloud when they saw the foundation of this temple being laid, while many others shouted for joy. ¹³No one could distinguish the sound of the shouts of joy from the sound of weeping, because the people made so much noise. And the sound was heard far away.

OPPOSITION TO THE REBUILDING

4 When the enemies of Judah and Benjamin heard that the exiles were building a temple for the LORD, the God of Israel, ²they came to Zerubbabel and to the heads of the families and said, "Let us help you build because, like you, we seek your God and have been sacrificing to him since the time of Esarhaddon king of Assyria, who brought us here."

³But Zerubbabel, Jeshua and the rest of the heads of the families of Israel answered, "You have no part with us in building a temple to our God. We alone will build it for the LORD, the God of Israel, as King Cyrus, the king of Persia, commanded us."

⁴Then the peoples around them set out to discourage the people of Judah and make them afraid to go on building.[b] ⁵They hired counselors to work against them and frustrate their plans during the entire reign of Cyrus king of Persia and down to the reign of Darius king of Persia.

LATER OPPOSITION UNDER XERXES AND ARTAXERXES

⁶At the beginning of the reign of Xerxes,[c] they lodged an accusation against the people of Judah and Jerusalem.

---

[a] 9 Hebrew Yehudah, probably a variant of Hodaviah   [b] 4 Or and troubled them as they built   [c] 6 Hebrew Ahasuerus, a variant of Xerxes' Persian name

zerubbabel

VERSUS

» Descendant of the royal family of Judah
» Returned with the Jewish exiles from Babylon in 537 B.C.
» Laid the foundation for the temple

rehum

» A commanding officer in Jerusalem
» Returned from exile in Babylon with Zerubbabel
» Succeeded in temporarily halting the work on God's temple

The Main Event

Some people are impossible to please. They're called naysayers. They're against everything you try to do. Propose an idea, start a project, and they'll shoot a million holes in it. They'll give you countless reasons why you shouldn't even bother trying. They complain and criticize, oppose and pick apart. They're expert fault-finders. They're like human versions of those small dogs that keep yipping and yapping until you feel like you're going to lose your mind.

That's the kind of guy Rehum was. The Bible doesn't tell us what his problem was or why he was so down on the idea of Zerubbabel leading the Jewish people in rebuilding God's temple. Maybe he didn't like the fact that it wasn't his idea. Maybe he was a control freak. Whatever the reason, the guy had real issues, so he and his cohort Shimshai picked up their prissy little pen and fired off a prissy little letter to the king of Persia.

On the other side of the conflict, there were folks like Zerubbabel. They were the dreamers, the risk takers, the energetic visionaries. They saw noble things that could be done and said, "Come on, let's do it together!" They loved a challenge. Problem solving was their gift.

Obviously when an irresistible force like Zerubbabel meets an immovable obstacle like Rehum, something has to give. In this case, Rehum prevailed. His negative (not to mention deceptive) letter worked. Artaxerxes issued a restraining order and the project stopped for 16 years. But that's not the end of the story.

The Outcome

God sent the prophets Haggai and Zechariah to encourage the faithful Israelites to complete their work on the temple. The people, discouraged and disheartened, were stirred by the divine reminder that the Messiah would one day walk in the temple they were building. With a second wind and a fresh vision, Zerubbabel and his coworkers returned to their building project with renewed commitment. Meanwhile, back in Babylon, the original decree authorizing the Israelites to rebuild the temple was rediscovered. The king gave the order that no one should interfere with the temple construction, on penalty of death. Four years later, the temple was a done deal.

The face-off between Zerubbabel and Rehum serves as a helpful reminder for us. While it's true that you can't always silence your critics, it's also true that you can't always keep a good man down. Not permanently anyway.

Do you tend to be more like Zerubbabel, taking risks and staying faithful, or more like Rehum, always critical and negative? Why do you suppose that's the case? If you're naturally critical, try asking God to help you become more of an encourager and less of a discourager.

Read more about Zerubbabel and Rehum in Ezra 4:1–23 (pages 536–538).

7And in the days of Artaxerxes king of Persia, Bishlam, Mithredath, Tabeel and the rest of his associates wrote a letter to Artaxerxes. The letter was written in Aramaic script and in the Aramaic language.[a, b]

8Rehum the commanding officer and Shimshai the secretary wrote a letter against Jerusalem to Artaxerxes the king as follows:

9Rehum the commanding officer and Shimshai the secretary, together with the rest of their associates—the judges and officials over the men from Tripolis, Persia,[c] Erech and Babylon, the Elamites of Susa, 10and the other people whom the great and honorable Ashurbanipal[d] deported and settled in the city of Samaria and elsewhere in Trans-Euphrates.

11(This is a copy of the letter they sent him.)

To King Artaxerxes,

From your servants, the men of Trans-Euphrates:

12The king should know that the Jews who came up to us from you have gone to Jerusalem and are rebuilding that rebellious and wicked city. They are restoring the walls and repairing the foundations.

13Furthermore, the king should know that if this city is built and its walls are restored, no more taxes, tribute or duty will be paid, and the royal revenues will suffer. 14Now since we are under obligation to the palace and it is not proper for us to see the king dishonored, we are sending this message to inform the king, 15so that a search may be made in the archives of your predecessors. In these records you will find that this city is a rebellious city, troublesome to kings and provinces, a place of rebellion from ancient times. That is why this city was destroyed. 16We inform the king that if this city is built and its walls are restored, you will be left with nothing in Trans-Euphrates.

17The king sent this reply:

To Rehum the commanding officer, Shimshai the secretary and the rest of their associates living in Samaria and elsewhere in Trans-Euphrates:

Greetings.

18The letter you sent us has been read and translated in my presence. 19I issued an order and a search was made, and it was found that this city has a long history of revolt against kings and has been a place of rebellion and sedition. 20Jerusalem has had powerful kings ruling over the whole of Trans-Euphrates, and taxes, tribute and duty were paid to them. 21Now issue an order to these men to stop work, so that this city will not be rebuilt until I so order. 22Be careful not to neglect this matter. Why let this threat grow, to the detriment of the royal interests?

23As soon as the copy of the letter of King Artaxerxes was read to Rehum and Shimshai the secretary and their associates, they went immediately to the Jews in Jerusalem and compelled them by force to stop.

24Thus the work on the house of God in Jerusalem came to a standstill until the second year of the reign of Darius king of Persia.

TATTENAI'S LETTER TO DARIUS

5 Now Haggai the prophet and Zechariah the prophet, a descendant of Iddo, prophesied to the Jews in Judah and Jerusalem in the name of the God of Israel, who was over them. 2Then Zerubbabel son of Shealtiel and Jeshua son of Jozadak set to work to rebuild the house of God in Jerusalem. And the prophets of God were with them, helping them.

3At that time Tattenai, governor of Trans-Euphrates, and Shethar-Bozenai and their associates went to them and asked, "Who authorized you to rebuild this temple and restore this structure?" 4They also

---

[a] 7 Or *written in Aramaic and translated*   [b] 7 The text of Ezra 4:8—6:18 is in Aramaic.   [c] 9 Or *officials, magistrates and governors over the men from*   [d] 10 Aramaic *Osnappar*, a variant of *Ashurbanipal*

battlelines

» Locked Up (Homosexuality)

Q: Derek, man, you have got to clue me in. What's wrong?

A: Why does everyone want to talk about my problems? They're *my* problems aren't they? Look, I really don't want to talk about this.

Q: C'mon man! I know something's going on. You never hang out with the guys anymore, you look depressed all the time, and I can tell something is going on between you and the other guys. Did you get into some kind of argument or something?

A: No, I didn't get into an argument with anyone . . . yet. Look, if you're so observant, why don't you go ask one of them what's wrong with me? They seem to know better than I do.

Q: What are you talking about?

A: Just ask them—they'll tell you everything you want to know. They'll tell you that I never date girls, even though all my close friends are girls. They'll tell you that I'm real sensitive. They'll tell you that I'm not interested in "guy stuff." In other words, they'll tell you that I'm gay.

Q: Derek, you can't know for sure what they . . .

A: Give me a break! You know what they think about me. And don't tell me you haven't thought the same things yourself. Hey, maybe it's all true. Maybe I am gay.

» The Straight Scoop

In a letter to the Christians in Rome (see Romans 1:18–32), written more than 19 centuries ago, the apostle Paul made it clear that our human sexuality is a God-given identity. And God intended for it to be expressed between one man and one woman within the covenant of lifelong marriage.

Paul also made it clear that what we *do* with our sexuality—that is, our sexual behavior—is something that we *can* control (see 1 Corinthians 6:9–11), with God's help. Doing things with our bodies and minds that are contrary to God's design is sin. But like all other sin in our lives, God extends his forgiveness and gives us the strength to resist temptation—if we accept his offer.

If you're struggling with your sexuality, know this: God loves you. He's not indifferent to your struggle. Ask him to help you control your mind and your body. His Holy Spirit can work to shape and strengthen you in those areas of your life that you still need to surrender to him. If necessary, seek out the support of a trusted Christian counselor.

For more on struggling with homosexual feelings, go to www.RevolutionBible.com.

asked, "What are the names of the men constructing this building?"[a] 5But the eye of their God was watching over the elders of the Jews, and they were not stopped until a report could go to Darius and his written reply be received.

6This is a copy of the letter that Tattenai, governor of Trans-Euphrates, and Shethar-Bozenai and their associates, the officials of Trans-Euphrates, sent to King Darius. 7The report they sent him read as follows:

To King Darius:

Cordial greetings.

8The king should know that we went to the district of Judah, to the temple of the great God. The people are building it with large stones and placing the timbers in the walls. The work is being carried on with diligence and is making rapid progress under their direction.

9We questioned the elders and asked them, "Who authorized you to rebuild this temple and restore this structure?" 10We also asked them their names, so that we could write down the names of their leaders for your information.

11This is the answer they gave us:

"We are the servants of the God of heaven and earth, and we are rebuilding the temple that was built many years ago, one that a great king of Israel built and finished. 12But because our fathers angered the God of heaven, he handed them over to Nebuchadnezzar the Chaldean, king of Babylon, who destroyed this temple and deported the people to Babylon.

13"However, in the first year of Cyrus king of Babylon, King Cyrus issued a decree to rebuild this house of God. 14He even removed from the temple[b] of Babylon the gold and silver articles of the house of God, which Nebuchadnezzar had taken from the temple in Jerusalem and brought to the temple[b] in Babylon.

"Then King Cyrus gave them to a man named Sheshbazzar, whom he had appointed governor, 15and he told him, 'Take these articles and go and deposit them in the temple in Jerusalem. And rebuild the house of God on its site.' 16So this Sheshbazzar came and laid the foundations of the house of God in Jerusalem. From that day to the present it has been under construction but is not yet finished."

17Now if it pleases the king, let a search be made in the royal archives of Babylon to see if King Cyrus did in fact issue a decree to rebuild this house of God in Jerusalem. Then let the king send us his decision in this matter.

THE DECREE OF DARIUS

6 King Darius then issued an order, and they searched in the archives stored in the treasury at Babylon. 2A scroll was found in the citadel of Ecbatana in the province of Media, and this was written on it:

Memorandum:

3In the first year of King Cyrus, the king issued a decree concerning the temple of God in Jerusalem:

Let the temple be rebuilt as a place to present sacrifices, and let its foundations be laid. It is to be ninety feet[c] high and ninety feet wide, 4with three courses of large stones and one of timbers. The costs are to be paid by the royal treasury. 5Also, the gold and silver articles of the house of God, which Nebuchadnezzar took from the temple in Jerusalem and brought to Babylon, are to be returned to their places in the temple in Jerusalem; they are to be deposited in the house of God.

6Now then, Tattenai, governor of Trans-Euphrates, and Shethar-Bozenai and you, their fellow officials of that province, stay away from there. 7Do not interfere with the work on this temple of God. Let the governor of the Jews and the Jewish elders rebuild this house of God on its site.

---

[a] 4 See Septuagint; Aramaic *We told them the names of the men constructing this building.*   [b] 14 Or *palace*   [c] 3 Aramaic *sixty cubits* (about 27 meters)

[8]Moreover, I hereby decree what you are to do for these elders of the Jews in the construction of this house of God:

The expenses of these men are to be fully paid out of the royal treasury, from the revenues of Trans-Euphrates, so that the work will not stop. [9]Whatever is needed— young bulls, rams, male lambs for burnt offerings to the God of heaven, and wheat, salt, wine and oil, as requested by the priests in Jerusalem—must be given them daily without fail, [10]so that they may offer sacrifices pleasing to the God of heaven and pray for the well-being of the king and his sons.

[11]Furthermore, I decree that if anyone changes this edict, a beam is to be pulled from his house and he is to be lifted up and impaled on it. And for this crime his house is to be made a pile of rubble. [12]May God, who has caused his Name to dwell there, overthrow any king or people who lifts a hand to change this decree or to destroy this temple in Jerusalem.

I Darius have decreed it. Let it be carried out with diligence.

now or never
EZR 6:16–22

If you're familiar with the Bible, you've probably noticed that sacrifice is a big deal throughout Scripture. It's an easy term to throw around—but a difficult thing to do. To make a sacrifice means giving up something important. What do you think God is asking *you* to sacrifice?

» live the adventure » Ezr 6:20

Being Pure

God is completely holy. That means that he is pure and without any blemishes. In order for us to be his people, we too have to be pure. Otherwise coming to God's throne is like trying to mix oil and water. In the Bible there's a tight relationship between purity and obedience. But we're wrong if we think it's just about doing the right thing. Obedience involves a heart that is right before God. And if what you're doing on the outside doesn't match what's going on inside, you might as well drop the act, because God knows it's not real. But he can and will change your heart and remake you if you ask him to. And he'll do it from the inside out.

COMPLETION AND DEDICATION OF THE TEMPLE

[13]Then, because of the decree King Darius had sent, Tattenai, governor of Trans-Euphrates, and Shethar-Bozenai and their associates carried it out with diligence. [14]So the elders of the Jews continued to build and prosper under the preaching of Haggai the prophet and Zechariah, a descendant of Iddo. They finished building the temple according to the command of the God of Israel and the decrees of Cyrus, Darius and Artaxerxes, kings of Persia. [15]The temple was completed on the third day of the month Adar, in the sixth year of the reign of King Darius.

[16]Then the people of Israel—the priests, the Levites and the rest of the exiles—celebrated the dedication of the house of God with joy. [17]For the dedication of this house of God they offered a hundred bulls, two hundred rams, four hundred male lambs and, as a sin offering for all Israel, twelve male goats, one for each of the tribes of Israel. [18]And they installed the priests in their divisions and the Levites in their groups for the service of God at Jerusalem, according to what is written in the Book of Moses.

THE PASSOVER

[19]On the fourteenth day of the first month, the exiles celebrated the Passover. [20]The priests and Levites had purified themselves and were all ceremonially clean. The Levites slaughtered the Passover lamb for all the exiles, for their brothers the priests and for themselves. [21]So the Israelites who had returned from the exile ate it, together with all who had separated themselves from the unclean practices of their Gentile neighbors in order to seek the LORD, the God of Israel. [22]For seven days they celebrated with joy the Feast of Unleavened Bread, because the LORD had filled them with joy by changing the attitude of the king of Assyria, so that he assisted them in the work on the house of God, the God of Israel.

EZRA COMES TO JERUSALEM

7 After these things, during the reign of Artaxerxes king of Persia, Ezra son of Seraiah, the son of Azariah, the son of Hilkiah, ²the son of Shallum, the son of Zadok, the son of Ahitub, ³the son of Amariah, the son of Azariah, the son of Meraioth, ⁴the son of Zerahiah, the son of Uzzi, the son of Bukki, ⁵the son of Abishua, the son of Phinehas, the son of Eleazar, the son of Aaron the chief priest— ⁶this Ezra came up from Babylon. He was a teacher well versed in the Law of Moses, which the LORD, the God of Israel, had given. The king had granted him everything he asked, for the hand of the LORD his God was on him. ⁷Some of the Israelites, including priests, Levites, singers, gatekeepers and temple servants, also came up to Jerusalem in the seventh year of King Artaxerxes.

⁸Ezra arrived in Jerusalem in the fifth month of the seventh year of the king. ⁹He had begun his journey from Babylon on the first day of the first month, and he arrived in Jerusalem on the first day of the fifth month, for the gracious hand of his God was on him. ¹⁰For Ezra had devoted himself to the study and observance of the Law of the LORD, and to teaching its decrees and laws in Israel.

KING ARTAXERXES' LETTER TO EZRA

¹¹This is a copy of the letter King Artaxerxes had given to Ezra the priest and teacher, a man learned in matters concerning the commands and decrees of the LORD for Israel:

¹² ᵃ Artaxerxes, king of kings,

To Ezra the priest, a teacher of the Law of the God of heaven:

Greetings.

¹³Now I decree that any of the Israelites in my kingdom, including priests and Levites, who wish to go to Jerusalem with you, may go. ¹⁴You are sent by the king and his seven advisers to inquire about Judah and Jerusalem with regard to the Law of your God, which is in your hand. ¹⁵Moreover, you are to take with you the silver and gold that the king and his advisers have freely given to the God of Israel, whose dwelling is in Jerusalem, ¹⁶together with all the silver and gold you may obtain from the province of Babylon, as well as the freewill offerings of the people and priests for the temple of their God in Jerusalem. ¹⁷With this money be sure to buy bulls, rams and male lambs, together with their grain offerings and drink offerings, and sacrifice them on the altar of the temple of your God in Jerusalem.

¹⁸You and your brother Jews may then do whatever seems best with the rest of the silver and gold, in accordance with the will of your God. ¹⁹Deliver to the God of Jerusalem all the articles entrusted to you for worship in the temple of your God. ²⁰And anything else needed for the temple of your God that you may have occasion to supply, you may provide from the royal treasury.

²¹Now I, King Artaxerxes, order all the treasurers of Trans-Euphrates to provide with diligence whatever Ezra the priest, a teacher of the Law of the God of heaven, may ask of you— ²²up to a hundred talents ᵇ of silver, a hundred cors ᶜ of wheat, a hundred baths ᵈ of wine, a hundred baths ᵈ of olive oil, and salt without limit. ²³Whatever the God of heaven has prescribed, let it be done with diligence for the temple of the God of heaven. Why should there be wrath against the realm of the king and of his sons? ²⁴You are also to know that you have no authority to impose taxes, tribute or duty on any of the priests, Levites, singers, gatekeepers, temple servants or other workers at this house of God.

²⁵And you, Ezra, in accordance with the wisdom of your God, which you possess, appoint magistrates and judges to administer justice to all the people of Trans-Euphrates—all who know the laws of your God. And you are to teach any who do not know them. ²⁶Whoever does not obey the law of your God and the law of the king must surely be punished by death, banishment, confiscation of property, or imprisonment.

²⁷Praise be to the LORD, the God of our fathers, who has put it into the king's heart to bring honor to the house of the LORD in Jerusalem in this way ²⁸and who has extended his good favor to me before the king and his advisers and all the king's powerful officials. Because the hand of the LORD my God was on me, I took courage and gathered leading men from Israel to go up with me.

ᵃ 12 The text of Ezra 7:12-26 is in Aramaic.   ᵇ 22 That is, about 3 3/4 tons (about 3.4 metric tons)   ᶜ 22 That is, probably about 600 bushels (about 22 kiloliters)   ᵈ 22 That is, probably about 600 gallons (about 2.2 kiloliters)

8

These are the family heads and those registered with them who came up with me from Babylon during the reign of King Artaxerxes:

²of the descendants of Phinehas, Gershom;
  of the descendants of Ithamar, Daniel;
  of the descendants of David, Hattush ³of the descendants of Shecaniah;

  of the descendants of Parosh, Zechariah, and with him were registered 150 men;
⁴of the descendants of Pahath-Moab, Eliehoenai son of Zerahiah, and with him 200 men;
⁵of the descendants of Zattu,ᵃ Shecaniah son of Jahaziel, and with him 300 men;
⁶of the descendants of Adin, Ebed son of Jonathan, and with him 50 men;
⁷of the descendants of Elam, Jeshaiah son of Athaliah, and with him 70 men;
⁸of the descendants of Shephatiah, Zebadiah son of Michael, and with him 80 men;
⁹of the descendants of Joab, Obadiah son of Jehiel, and with him 218 men;
¹⁰of the descendants of Bani,ᵇ Shelomith son of Josiphiah, and with him 160 men;
¹¹of the descendants of Bebai, Zechariah son of Bebai, and with him 28 men;
¹²of the descendants of Azgad, Johanan son of Hakkatan, and with him 110 men;
¹³of the descendants of Adonikam, the last ones, whose names were Eliphelet, Jeuel and Shemaiah, and with them 60 men;
¹⁴of the descendants of Bigvai, Uthai and Zaccur, and with them 70 men.

THE RETURN TO JERUSALEM

¹⁵I assembled them at the canal that flows toward Ahava, and we camped there three days. When I checked among the people and the priests, I found no Levites there. ¹⁶So I summoned Eliezer, Ariel, Shemaiah, Elnathan, Jarib, Elnathan, Nathan, Zechariah and Meshullam, who were leaders, and Joiarib and Elnathan, who were men of learning, ¹⁷and I sent them to Iddo, the leader in Casiphia. I told them what to say to Iddo and his kinsmen, the temple servants in Casiphia, so that they might bring attendants to us for the house of our God. ¹⁸Because the gracious hand of our God was on us, they brought us Sherebiah, a capable man, from the descendants of Mahli son of Levi, the son of Israel, and Sherebiah's sons and brothers, 18 men; ¹⁹and Hashabiah, together with Jeshaiah from the descendants of Merari, and his brothers and nephews, 20 men. ²⁰They also brought 220 of the temple servants—a body that David and the officials had established to assist the Levites. All were registered by name.

²¹There, by the Ahava Canal, I proclaimed a fast, so that we might humble ourselves before our God and ask him for a safe journey for us and our children, with all our possessions. ²²I was ashamed to ask the king for soldiers and horsemen to protect us from enemies on the road, because we had told the king, "The gracious hand of our God is on everyone who looks to him, but his great anger is against all who forsake him." ²³So we fasted and petitioned our God about this, and he answered our prayer.

²⁴Then I set apart twelve of the leading priests, together with Sherebiah, Hashabiah and ten of their brothers, ²⁵and I weighed out to them the offering of silver and gold and the articles that the king, his advisers, his officials and all Israel present there had donated for the house of our God. ²⁶I weighed out to them 650 talentsᶜ of silver, silver articles weighing 100 talents,ᵈ 100 talentsᵈ of gold, ²⁷20 bowls of gold valued at 1,000 darics,ᵉ and two fine articles of polished bronze, as precious as gold.

²⁸I said to them, "You as well as these articles are consecrated to the LORD. The silver and gold are a freewill offering to the LORD, the God of your fathers. ²⁹Guard them carefully until you weigh them out

NOW OR NEVER
EZR 8:21-23

If you knew you were going to face physical danger, you'd take steps to protect yourself. Keep in mind that spiritual danger is just as real as, and even more harmful than, physical danger. That's why you need to keep yourself spiritually safe by avoiding dangerous (and tempting) situations.

ᵃ *5* Some Septuagint manuscripts (also 1 Esdras 8:32); Hebrew does not have *Zattu*.   ᵇ *10* Some Septuagint manuscripts (also 1 Esdras 8:36); Hebrew does not have *Bani*.   ᶜ *26* That is, about 25 tons (about 22 metric tons)   ᵈ *26* That is, about 3 3/4 tons (about 3.4 metric tons)   ᵉ *27* That is, about 19 pounds (about 8.5 kilograms)

ezra

VERSUS

roaming bandits

» Jewish priest with a deep knowledge of God's Word
» Led exiles back to Jerusalem
» Concerned with the spiritual well-being of his people

» Nationality and number unknown
» Lurked along the road between Mesopotamia and Palestine
» Notorious for robbing and harassing travelers

The Main Event

When we travel, we worry mostly about flat tires, catching our connecting flights or finding cheap gas and a clean restroom.

When Ezra took a caravan of several thousand Israelites on a 700-plus-mile trek from exile in Babylon back to their Jewish homeland, he had far more sinister problems to worry about. The "highway" they traveled, which was a major trade route at the time, was a magnet for no-good thugs and vicious gangs. These "land pirates" would hide along the road and attack unsuspecting travelers. Victims who managed to escape with their lives and the clothes on their backs counted themselves very fortunate.

Because Ezra had the king's blessing to leave Babylon for Jerusalem, he could have asked for a military escort. However, he had been telling anyone who would listen about God's sure faithfulness, great power and constant protection of his people. Somehow, in light of all these grandiose claims, it seemed a bit hypocritical to request armed guards. It was time for Ezra to put up or shut up, to practice what he preached. So he decided to trust solely in God. Just before departing, he called for a time of prayer and fasting to ask God for a safe journey. Then he and his fellow travelers loaded up their precious cargo of gold and silver (materials intended for use in the rebuilt temple in Jerusalem) and headed straight into dangerous territory.

In his "journal" Ezra described the trip this way: "The hand of our God was on us, and he protected us from enemies and bandits along the way" (Ezra 8:31). That's it. A ho-hum, matter-of-fact statement about the faithfulness of God.

The Outcome

Ezra was both a man's man and a man of God. He not only told others about the faithfulness of God, but when push came to shove, he lived that truth. Boldly stepping out in faith, he relied on the Lord, not human might, for protection. And God did not let him down.

We all have "roaming bandits" in our lives—maybe not literal robbers waiting to grab our wallets, but other dangers and obstacles, other tests and challenges to our faith. Will we back away in fear? Or will we press ahead in faith? That's the big question. That's the decision that separates those who just talk the talk from those who are willing to walk the walk.

Read more about Ezra and the roaming bandits in Ezra 8:15–32 (pages 543–545).

in the chambers of the house of the LORD in Jerusalem before the leading priests and the Levites and the family heads of Israel." ³⁰Then the priests and Levites received the silver and gold and sacred articles that had been weighed out to be taken to the house of our God in Jerusalem.

³¹On the twelfth day of the first month we set out from the Ahava Canal to go to Jerusalem. The hand of our God was on us, and he protected us from enemies and bandits along the way. ³²So we arrived in Jerusalem, where we rested three days.

³³On the fourth day, in the house of our God, we weighed out the silver and gold and the sacred articles into the hands of Meremoth son of Uriah, the priest. Eleazar son of Phinehas was with him, and so were the Levites Jozabad son of Jeshua and Noadiah son of Binnui. ³⁴Everything was accounted for by number and weight, and the entire weight was recorded at that time.

³⁵Then the exiles who had returned from captivity sacrificed burnt offerings to the God of Israel: twelve bulls for all Israel, ninety-six rams, seventy-seven male lambs and, as a sin offering, twelve male goats. All this was a burnt offering to the LORD. ³⁶They also delivered the king's orders to the royal satraps and to the governors of Trans-Euphrates, who then gave assistance to the people and to the house of God.

EZRA'S PRAYER ABOUT INTERMARRIAGE

9 After these things had been done, the leaders came to me and said, "The people of Israel, including the priests and the Levites, have not kept themselves separate from the neighboring peoples with their detestable practices, like those of the Canaanites, Hittites, Perizzites, Jebusites, Ammonites, Moabites, Egyptians and Amorites. ²They have taken some of their daughters as wives for themselves and their sons, and have mingled the holy race with the peoples around them. And the leaders and officials have led the way in this unfaithfulness."

³When I heard this, I tore my tunic and cloak, pulled hair from my head and beard and sat down appalled. ⁴Then everyone who trembled at the words of the God of Israel gathered around me because of this unfaithfulness of the exiles. And I sat there appalled until the evening sacrifice.

⁵Then, at the evening sacrifice, I rose from my self-abasement, with my tunic and cloak torn, and fell on my knees with my hands spread out to the LORD my God ⁶and prayed:

"O my God, I am too ashamed and disgraced to lift up my face to you, my God, because our sins are higher than our heads and our guilt has reached to the heavens. ⁷From the days of our forefathers until now, our guilt has been great. Because of our sins, we and our kings and our priests have been subjected to the sword and captivity, to pillage and humiliation at the hand of foreign kings, as it is today.

EZR 9:6

challengenotes

To: my_son

heavenly_father: never be too ashamed to confess your sin, no matter what you've done. I know about your sin already, and I still love you. in fact, I'm just waiting for you to ask me to make things right between us again! get serious about seeking my forgiveness. I'm serious about being ready to forgive.

⁸"But now, for a brief moment, the LORD our God has been gracious in leaving us a remnant and giving us a firm place in his sanctuary, and so our God gives light to our eyes and a little relief in our bondage. ⁹Though we are slaves, our God has not deserted us in our bondage. He has shown us kindness in the sight of the kings of Persia: He has granted us new life to rebuild the house of our God and repair its ruins, and he has given us a wall of protection in Judah and Jerusalem.

¹⁰"But now, O our God, what can we say after this? For we have disregarded the commands ¹¹you gave through your servants the prophets when you said: 'The land you are entering to possess is a land polluted by the corruption of its peoples. By their detestable practices they have filled it with their impurity from one end to the other. ¹²Therefore, do not give your daughters in marriage to their sons or take their daughters for your sons. Do not seek a treaty of friendship with them at any time, that you may be strong and eat the good things of the land and leave it to your children as an everlasting inheritance.'

¹³"What has happened to us is a result of our evil deeds and our great guilt, and yet, our God, you have punished us less than our sins have deserved and have given us a remnant like

this. ¹⁴Shall we again break your commands and intermarry with the peoples who commit such detestable practices? Would you not be angry enough with us to destroy us, leaving us no remnant or survivor? ¹⁵O LORD, God of Israel, you are righteous! We are left this day as a remnant. Here we are before you in our guilt, though because of it not one of us can stand in your presence."

THE PEOPLE'S CONFESSION OF SIN

10 While Ezra was praying and confessing, weeping and throwing himself down before the house of God, a large crowd of Israelites—men, women and children—gathered around him. They too wept bitterly. ²Then Shecaniah son of Jehiel, one of the descendants of Elam, said to Ezra, "We have been unfaithful to our God by marrying foreign women from the peoples around us. But in spite of this, there is still hope for Israel. ³Now let us make a covenant before our God to send away all these women and their children, in accordance with the counsel of my lord and of those who fear the commands of our God. Let it be done according to the Law. ⁴Rise up; this matter is in your hands. We will support you, so take courage and do it."

NOW OR NEVER

EZR 9:1–15

Can you picture yourself as a married man? Ezra knew it was wrong for God's people to marry anyone who didn't worship the Lord. How important is it to you that the person you marry someday is a believer?

⁵So Ezra rose up and put the leading priests and Levites and all Israel under oath to do what had been suggested. And they took the oath. ⁶Then Ezra withdrew from before the house of God and went to the room of Jehohanan son of Eliashib. While he was there, he ate no food and drank no water, because he continued to mourn over the unfaithfulness of the exiles.

⁷A proclamation was then issued throughout Judah and Jerusalem for all the exiles to assemble in Jerusalem. ⁸Anyone who failed to appear within three days would forfeit all his property, in accordance with the decision of the officials and elders, and would himself be expelled from the assembly of the exiles.

⁹Within the three days, all the men of Judah and Benjamin had gathered in Jerusalem. And on the twentieth day of the ninth month, all the people were sitting in the square before the house of God, greatly distressed by the occasion and because of the rain. ¹⁰Then Ezra the priest stood up and said to them, "You have been unfaithful; you have married foreign women, adding to Israel's guilt. ¹¹Now make confession to the LORD, the God of your fathers, and do his will. Separate yourselves from the peoples around you and from your foreign wives."

NOW OR NEVER

EZR 10:6–8

Owning up to your mistakes isn't easy. But failing to take responsibility can have serious consequences. When you identify a sin in your life, confess it, identify what you need to change and then do it.

¹²The whole assembly responded with a loud voice: "You are right! We must do as you say. ¹³But there are many people here and it is the rainy season; so we cannot stand outside. Besides, this matter cannot be taken care of in a day or two, because we have sinned greatly in this thing. ¹⁴Let our officials act for the whole assembly. Then let everyone in our towns who has married a foreign woman come at a set time, along with the elders and judges of each town, until the fierce anger of our God in this matter is turned away from us." ¹⁵Only Jonathan son of Asahel and Jahzeiah son of Tikvah, supported by Meshullam and Shabbethai the Levite, opposed this.

¹⁶So the exiles did as was proposed. Ezra the priest selected men who were family heads, one from each family division, and all of them designated by name. On the first day of the tenth month they sat down to investigate the cases, ¹⁷and by the first day of the first month they finished dealing with all the men who had married foreign women.

18 Among the descendants of the priests, the following had married foreign women:

From the descendants of Jeshua son of Jozadak, and his brothers: Maaseiah, Eliezer, Jarib and Gedaliah. 19(They all gave their hands in pledge to put away their wives, and for their guilt they each presented a ram from the flock as a guilt offering.)

20 From the descendants of Immer:
Hanani and Zebadiah.

21 From the descendants of Harim:
Maaseiah, Elijah, Shemaiah, Jehiel and Uzziah.

22 From the descendants of Pashhur:
Elioenai, Maaseiah, Ishmael, Nethanel, Jozabad and Elasah.

23 Among the Levites:

Jozabad, Shimei, Kelaiah (that is, Kelita), Pethahiah, Judah and Eliezer.

24 From the singers:
Eliashib.
From the gatekeepers:
Shallum, Telem and Uri.

25 And among the other Israelites:

From the descendants of Parosh:
Ramiah, Izziah, Malkijah, Mijamin, Eleazar, Malkijah and Benaiah.

26 From the descendants of Elam:
Mattaniah, Zechariah, Jehiel, Abdi, Jeremoth and Elijah.

27 From the descendants of Zattu:
Elioenai, Eliashib, Mattaniah, Jeremoth, Zabad and Aziza.

28 From the descendants of Bebai:
Jehohanan, Hananiah, Zabbai and Athlai.

29 From the descendants of Bani:
Meshullam, Malluch, Adaiah, Jashub, Sheal and Jeremoth.

30 From the descendants of Pahath-Moab:
Adna, Kelal, Benaiah, Maaseiah, Mattaniah, Bezalel, Binnui and Manasseh.

31 From the descendants of Harim:
Eliezer, Ishijah, Malkijah, Shemaiah, Shimeon, 32Benjamin, Malluch and Shemariah.

33 From the descendants of Hashum:
Mattenai, Mattattah, Zabad, Eliphelet, Jeremai, Manasseh and Shimei.

34 From the descendants of Bani:
Maadai, Amram, Uel, 35Benaiah, Bedeiah, Keluhi, 36Vaniah, Meremoth, Eliashib, 37Mattaniah, Mattenai and Jaasu.

38 From the descendants of Binnui:a
Shimei, 39Shelemiah, Nathan, Adaiah, 40Macnadebai, Shashai, Sharai, 41Azarel, Shelemiah, Shemariah, 42Shallum, Amariah and Joseph.

43 From the descendants of Nebo:
Jeiel, Mattithiah, Zabad, Zebina, Jaddai, Joel and Benaiah.

44All these had married foreign women, and some of them had children by these wives.b

---

a 37,38 See Septuagint (also 1 Esdras 9:34); Hebrew Jaasu 38and Bani and Binnui,   b 44 Or and they sent them away with their children

NEHEMIAH

Author
Unknown (possibly Nehemiah)

Audience
People of Judah

Date
About 445–432 B.C.

Setting
Nehemiah, along with many who were exiled to Babylon, returned to Jerusalem to rebuild the walls (440 B.C.).

Verse to Remember
So the wall was completed on the twenty-fifth of Elul, in fifty-two days. When all our enemies heard about this, all the surrounding nations were afraid and lost their self-confidence, because they realized that this work had been done with the help of our God (6:15–16).

Theme to Consider
When we place our faith in God, he can help us overcome any opposition or obstacle—no matter how great.

UNCHANGING TRUTH » Any goal worth achieving, whether it's making the varsity team or starting a food pantry in your community, has to be worth fighting for. That's important to remember, because with every major goal you attempt and every big job you try to complete, you're going to face doubters, questioners and opponents.

The doubters are the ones who will tell you that you've set your goals too high or that the job you've taken on is too big for someone like you. They'll say that you don't have the experience or skills to do what you want to do. They may claim to have your best interests at heart—and maybe they do—but that doesn't make them right.

The questioners are the ones who will tell you that you're doing things the wrong way. They'll insist that if you don't follow their instructions, or if you don't do things the way everyone else does, you've got no chance of success. They may try to pass themselves off as advisors or experts, but unless they take the time to understand your unique situation, their advice may be more harmful than helpful.

The opponents are the ones who simply want to see you fail. They may be afraid that your success will make them look bad in comparison. They may see you as competition and want to do everything they can to beat you. Or they may not like you, plain and simple. Whatever their motivation, opponents can do serious damage—if you let them get to you.

The key to dealing with doubters, questioners and opponents is to do what Nehemiah did when he was trying to rebuild the wall around Jerusalem: pray. Ask the Lord to bless your efforts, to keep you on track and to give you the wisdom to know which advice to accept and which advice to reject.

LIFE LESSONS »

I   No prayer request is too big for God to answer (2:1–9).

2   Don't let other people's criticism and opposition keep you from doing what you know is right in God's eyes (4:1–23).

3   Don't get so wrapped up in your own goals that you ignore people in need (5:1–19).

NEHEMIAH'S PRAYER

1 The words of Nehemiah son of Hacaliah:

In the month of Kislev in the twentieth year, while I was in the citadel of Susa, ²Hanani, one of my brothers, came from Judah with some other men, and I questioned them about the Jewish remnant that survived the exile, and also about Jerusalem.

³They said to me, "Those who survived the exile and are back in the province are in great trouble and disgrace. The wall of Jerusalem is broken down, and its gates have been burned with fire."

⁴When I heard these things, I sat down and wept. For some days I mourned and fasted and prayed before the God of heaven. ⁵Then I said:

"O Lᴏʀᴅ, God of heaven, the great and awesome God, who keeps his covenant of love with those who love him and obey his commands, ⁶let your ear be attentive and your eyes open to hear the prayer your servant is praying before you day and night for your servants, the people of Israel. I confess the sins we Israelites, including myself and my father's house, have committed against you. ⁷We have acted very wickedly toward you. We have not obeyed the commands, decrees and laws you gave your servant Moses.

⁸"Remember the instruction you gave your servant Moses, saying, 'If you are unfaithful, I will scatter you among the nations, ⁹but if you return to me and obey my commands, then even if your exiled people are at the farthest horizon, I will gather them from there and bring them to the place I have chosen as a dwelling for my Name.'

¹⁰"They are your servants and your people, whom you redeemed by your great strength and your mighty hand. ¹¹O Lord, let your ear be attentive to the prayer of this your servant and to the prayer of your servants who delight in revering your name. Give your servant success today by granting him favor in the presence of this man."

I was cupbearer to the king.

ARTAXERXES SENDS NEHEMIAH TO JERUSALEM

2 In the month of Nisan in the twentieth year of King Artaxerxes, when wine was brought for him, I took the wine and gave it to the king. I had not been sad in his presence before; ²so the king asked me, "Why does your face look so sad when you are not ill? This can be nothing but sadness of heart."

I was very much afraid, ³but I said to the king, "May the king live forever! Why should my face not look sad when the city where my fathers are buried lies in ruins, and its gates have been destroyed by fire?"

⁴The king said to me, "What is it you want?"

Then I prayed to the God of heaven, ⁵and I answered the king, "If it pleases the king and if your servant has found favor in his sight, let him send me to the city in Judah where my fathers are buried so that I can rebuild it."

⁶Then the king, with the queen sitting beside him, asked me, "How long will your journey take, and when will you get back?" It pleased the king to send me; so I set a time.

⁷I also said to him, "If it pleases the king, may I have letters to the governors of Trans-Euphrates, so that they will provide me safe-conduct until I arrive in Judah? ⁸And may I have a letter to Asaph, keeper of the king's forest, so he will give me timber to make beams for the gates of the citadel by the temple and for the city wall and for the residence I will occupy?" And because the gracious hand of my God was upon me, the king granted my requests. ⁹So I went to the governors of Trans-Euphrates and gave them the king's letters. The king had also sent army officers and cavalry with me.

¹⁰When Sanballat the Horonite and Tobiah the Ammonite official heard about this, they were very much disturbed that someone had come to promote the welfare of the Israelites.

NEHEMIAH INSPECTS JERUSALEM'S WALLS

¹¹I went to Jerusalem, and after staying there three days ¹²I set out during the night with a few men. I had not told anyone what my God had put in my heart to do for Jerusalem. There were no mounts with me except the one I was riding on.

¹³By night I went out through the Valley Gate toward the Jackalᵃ Well and the Dung Gate, examin-

---

ᵃ *13* Or *Serpent* or *Fig*

ing the walls of Jerusalem, which had been broken down, and its gates, which had been destroyed by fire. ¹⁴Then I moved on toward the Fountain Gate and the King's Pool, but there was not enough room for my mount to get through; ¹⁵so I went up the valley by night, examining the wall. Finally, I turned back and reentered through the Valley Gate. ¹⁶The officials did not know where I had gone or what I was doing, because as yet I had said nothing to the Jews or the priests or nobles or officials or any others who would be doing the work.

¹⁷Then I said to them, "You see the trouble we are in: Jerusalem lies in ruins, and its gates have been burned with fire. Come, let us rebuild the wall of Jerusalem, and we will no longer be in disgrace." ¹⁸I also told them about the gracious hand of my God upon me and what the king had said to me.

They replied, "Let us start rebuilding." So they began this good work.

¹⁹But when Sanballat the Horonite, Tobiah the Ammonite official and Geshem the Arab heard about it, they mocked and ridiculed us. "What is this you are doing?" they asked. "Are you rebelling against the king?"

²⁰I answered them by saying, "The God of heaven will give us success. We his servants will start rebuilding, but as for you, you have no share in Jerusalem or any claim or historic right to it."

BUILDERS OF THE WALL

3 Eliashib the high priest and his fellow priests went to work and rebuilt the Sheep Gate. They dedicated it and set its doors in place, building as far as the Tower of the Hundred, which they dedicated, and as far as the Tower of Hananel. ²The men of Jericho built the adjoining section, and Zaccur son of Imri built next to them.

³The Fish Gate was rebuilt by the sons of Hassenaah. They laid its beams and put its doors and bolts and bars in place. ⁴Meremoth son of Uriah, the son of Hakkoz, repaired the next section. Next to him Meshullam son of Berekiah, the son of Meshezabel, made repairs, and next to him Zadok son of Baana also made repairs. ⁵The next section was repaired by the men of Tekoa, but their nobles would not put their shoulders to the work under their supervisors.[a]

⁶The Jeshanah[b] Gate was repaired by Joiada son of Paseah and Meshullam son of Besodeiah. They laid its beams and put its doors and bolts and bars in place. ⁷Next to them, repairs were made by men from Gibeon and Mizpah—Melatiah of Gibeon and Jadon of Meronoth—places under the authority of the governor of Trans-Euphrates. ⁸Uzziel son of Harhaiah, one of the goldsmiths, repaired the next section; and Hananiah, one of the perfume-makers, made repairs next to that. They restored[c] Jerusalem as far as the Broad Wall. ⁹Rephaiah son of Hur, ruler of a half-district of Jerusalem, repaired the next section. ¹⁰Adjoining this, Jedaiah son of Harumaph made repairs opposite his house, and Hattush son of Hashabneiah made repairs next to him. ¹¹Malkijah son of Harim and Hasshub son of Pahath-Moab repaired another section and the Tower of the Ovens. ¹²Shallum son of Hallohesh, ruler of a half-district of Jerusalem, repaired the next section with the help of his daughters.

¹³The Valley Gate was repaired by Hanun and the residents of Zanoah. They rebuilt it and put its doors and bolts and bars in place. They also repaired five hundred yards[d] of the wall as far as the Dung Gate.

¹⁴The Dung Gate was repaired by Malkijah son of Recab, ruler of the district of Beth Hakkerem. He rebuilt it and put its doors and bolts and bars in place.

¹⁵The Fountain Gate was repaired by Shallun son of Col-Hozeh, ruler of the district of Mizpah. He rebuilt it, roofing it over and putting its doors and bolts and bars in place. He also repaired the wall of the Pool of Siloam,[e] by the King's Garden, as far as the steps going down from the City of David. ¹⁶Beyond him, Nehemiah son of Azbuk, ruler of a half-district of Beth Zur, made repairs up to a point opposite the tombs[f] of David, as far as the artificial pool and the House of the Heroes.

¹⁷Next to him, the repairs were made by the Levites under Rehum son of Bani. Beside him, Hashabiah, ruler of half the district of Keilah, carried out repairs for his district. ¹⁸Next to him, the repairs were made by their countrymen under Binnui[g] son of Henadad, ruler of the other half-district of Keilah. ¹⁹Next to him, Ezer son of Jeshua, ruler of Mizpah, repaired another section, from a point facing the ascent to

---

[a] 5 Or their Lord or the governor   [b] 6 Or Old   [c] 8 Or They left out part of   [d] 13 Hebrew a thousand cubits (about 450 meters)
[e] 15 Hebrew Shelah, a variant of Shiloah, that is, Siloam   [f] 16 Hebrew; Septuagint, some Vulgate manuscripts and Syriac tomb
[g] 18 Two Hebrew manuscripts and Syriac (see also Septuagint and verse 24); most Hebrew manuscripts Bavvai

battlelines

» Peculiar People (Compassion)

Q: What's your weekend looking like?
A: Probably the usual. Maybe check out a movie Friday night and hang out with some friends. Sleep late on Saturday. Try to get motivated to do a little reading. Actually, I need to do a *lot* of reading. I'm supposed to have some 500-page novel read by the end of next week! Then church on Sunday. You know, the usual.

Q: To be honest, that sounds *incredibly* boring.
A: (Laughing) Yeah, well, thanks a lot. What can I say? My life *is* boring. I live in Dullsville. It is what it is. But get this. I've also been thinking about giving Ken a call. Now *that* would be an adventure.

Q: Why? Who's Ken?
A: He's this new guy around here, and he's definitely on a different wavelength. People pick on him and mess with him all the time. And, I don't know, I just feel bad for him—like I need to try to reach out to him or something.

Q: Really? What makes you feel that way?
A: I've just been thinking about how Jesus interacted with people. He always treated everyone with total respect. And when I think about that, I feel bad about the way certain people get left out.

Q: So you're actually going to give Ken a call?
A: Yeah, who knows . . . maybe we'll dress up like Trekkies and go to a big sci-fi convention or something.

» Gut-Wrenching!

A former tax-collector named Matthew—a guy who knew all too well how it feels to be a total social outcast (tax collectors didn't win many popularity contests in ancient Israel)—had this to say about Jesus: "When he saw the crowds, he had compassion on them, because they were harassed and helpless, like sheep without a shepherd" (Matthew 9:36).

Interestingly, the Greek word for *compassion* in that verse literally means "to be moved in the guts." The point? Real compassion isn't just an emotion; it's emotion that leads to *action*. Jesus got a knot in his stomach when he saw people who were hurting. He just knew he had to do something, so he took action. Is that how you respond when you see hurting people?

Discover ways you can reach out to others at www.RevolutionBible.com.

the armory as far as the angle. 20Next to him, Baruch son of Zabbai zealously repaired another section, from the angle to the entrance of the house of Eliashib the high priest. 21Next to him, Meremoth son of Uriah, the son of Hakkoz, repaired another section, from the entrance of Eliashib's house to the end of it.

22The repairs next to him were made by the priests from the surrounding region. 23Beyond them, Benjamin and Hasshub made repairs in front of their house; and next to them, Azariah son of Maaseiah, the son of Ananiah, made repairs beside his house. 24Next to him, Binnui son of Henadad repaired another section, from Azariah's house to the angle and the corner, 25and Palal son of Uzai worked opposite the angle and the tower projecting from the upper palace near the court of the guard. Next to him, Pedaiah son of Parosh 26and the temple servants living on the hill of Ophel made repairs up to a point opposite the Water Gate toward the east and the projecting tower. 27Next to them, the men of Tekoa repaired another section, from the great projecting tower to the wall of Ophel.

28Above the Horse Gate, the priests made repairs, each in front of his own house. 29Next to them, Zadok son of Immer made repairs opposite his house. Next to him, Shemaiah son of Shecaniah, the guard at the East Gate, made repairs. 30Next to him, Hananiah son of Shelemiah, and Hanun, the sixth son of Zalaph, repaired another section. Next to them, Meshullam son of Berekiah made repairs opposite his living quarters. 31Next to him, Malkijah, one of the goldsmiths, made repairs as far as the house of the temple servants and the merchants, opposite the Inspection Gate, and as far as the room above the corner; 32and between the room above the corner and the Sheep Gate the goldsmiths and merchants made repairs.

OPPOSITION TO THE REBUILDING

4 When Sanballat heard that we were rebuilding the wall, he became angry and was greatly incensed. He ridiculed the Jews, 2and in the presence of his associates and the army of Samaria, he said, "What are those feeble Jews doing? Will they restore their wall? Will they offer sacrifices? Will they finish in a day? Can they bring the stones back to life from those heaps of rubble—burned as they are?"

3Tobiah the Ammonite, who was at his side, said, "What they are building—if even a fox climbed up on it, he would break down their wall of stones!"

4Hear us, O our God, for we are despised. Turn their insults back on their own heads. Give them over as plunder in a land of captivity. 5Do not cover up their guilt or blot out their sins from your sight, for they have thrown insults in the face of[a] the builders.

6So we rebuilt the wall till all of it reached half its height, for the people worked with all their heart.

7But when Sanballat, Tobiah, the Arabs, the Ammonites and the men of Ashdod heard that the repairs to Jerusalem's walls had gone ahead and that the gaps were being closed, they were very angry. 8They all plotted together to come and fight against Jerusalem and stir up trouble against it. 9But we prayed to our God and posted a guard day and night to meet this threat.

10Meanwhile, the people in Judah said, "The strength of the laborers is giving out, and there is so much rubble that we cannot rebuild the wall."

11Also our enemies said, "Before they know it or see us, we will be right there among them and will kill them and put an end to the work."

NOW OR NEVER
NE 4:4–5

When someone insults you, do you fight back, taking matters into your own hands? Instead, try leaving justice in God's hands, even if it's difficult to do. It worked pretty well for Nehemiah.

12Then the Jews who lived near them came and told us ten times over, "Wherever you turn, they will attack us."

13Therefore I stationed some of the people behind the lowest points of the wall at the exposed places, posting them by families, with their swords, spears and bows. 14After I looked things over, I stood up and said to the nobles, the officials and the rest of the people, "Don't be afraid of them. Remember

---

a 5 Or *have provoked you to anger before*

the Lord, who is great and awesome, and fight for your brothers, your sons and your daughters, your wives and your homes."

¹⁵When our enemies heard that we were aware of their plot and that God had frustrated it, we all returned to the wall, each to his own work.

» live the adventure » Ne 4:16-17

Using Your Ingenuity

Do you ever feel like you're overwhelmed by the tasks in front of you? Sometimes the job seems impossibly complicated and nothing is going right until . . . things get worse. Now there are people who are actually trying to make your job harder! That's the point at which most people just throw their hands up in hopelessness and say, "I give up." But some people strap a sword to their belt, pick up their tools and get to work, determined to finish what they've started and ready for whatever opposition they might face. When things get rough, what's your strategy?

¹⁶From that day on, half of my men did the work, while the other half were equipped with spears, shields, bows and armor. The officers posted themselves behind all the people of Judah ¹⁷who were building the wall. Those who carried materials did their work with one hand and held a weapon in the other, ¹⁸and each of the builders wore his sword at his side as he worked. But the man who sounded the trumpet stayed with me.

¹⁹Then I said to the nobles, the officials and the rest of the people, "The work is extensive and spread out, and we are widely separated from each other along the wall. ²⁰Wherever you hear the sound of the trumpet, join us there. Our God will fight for us!"

²¹So we continued the work with half the men holding spears, from the first light of dawn till the stars came out. ²²At that time I also said to the people, "Have every man and his helper stay inside Jerusalem at night, so they can serve us as guards by night and workmen by day." ²³Neither I nor my brothers nor my men nor the guards with me took off our clothes; each had his weapon, even when he went for water.[a]

NEHEMIAH HELPS THE POOR

5 Now the men and their wives raised a great outcry against their Jewish brothers. ²Some were saying, "We and our sons and daughters are numerous; in order for us to eat and stay alive, we must get grain."

³Others were saying, "We are mortgaging our fields, our vineyards and our homes to get grain during the famine."

⁴Still others were saying, "We have had to borrow money to pay the king's tax on our fields and vineyards. ⁵Although we are of the same flesh and blood as our countrymen and though our sons are as good as theirs, yet we have to subject our sons and daughters to slavery. Some of our daughters have already been enslaved, but we are powerless, because our fields and our vineyards belong to others."

⁶When I heard their outcry and these charges, I was very angry. ⁷I pondered them in my mind and then accused the nobles and officials. I told them, "You are exacting usury from your own countrymen!" So I called together a large meeting to deal with them ⁸and said: "As far as possible, we have bought back our Jewish brothers who were sold to the Gentiles. Now you are selling your brothers, only for them to be sold back to us!" They kept quiet, because they could find nothing to say.

⁹So I continued, "What you are doing is not right. Shouldn't you walk in the fear of our God to avoid the reproach of our Gentile enemies? ¹⁰I and my brothers and my men are also lending the people money and grain. But let the exacting of usury stop! ¹¹Give back to them immediately their fields, vineyards, olive groves and houses, and also the usury you are charging them—the hundredth part of the money, grain, new wine and oil."

challenge notes

To: my_son

NE 4:20-21

heavenly_father: here's a promise you can hold on to: no matter where you are or what you're facing, you will never fight a battle alone. you'll never have to rely solely on your own strength.

---

[a] 23 The meaning of the Hebrew for this clause is uncertain.

¹²"We will give it back," they said. "And we will not demand anything more from them. We will do as you say."

Then I summoned the priests and made the nobles and officials take an oath to do what they had promised. ¹³I also shook out the folds of my robe and said, "In this way may God shake out of his house and possessions every man who does not keep this promise. So may such a man be shaken out and emptied!"

At this the whole assembly said, "Amen," and praised the Lord. And the people did as they had promised.

¹⁴Moreover, from the twentieth year of King Artaxerxes, when I was appointed to be their governor in the land of Judah, until his thirty-second year—twelve years—neither I nor my brothers ate the food allotted to the governor. ¹⁵But the earlier governors—those preceding me—placed a heavy burden on the people and took forty shekels[a] of silver from them in addition to food and wine. Their assistants also lorded it over the people. But out of reverence for God I did not act like that. ¹⁶Instead, I devoted myself to the work on this wall. All my men were assembled there for the work; we[b] did not acquire any land.

¹⁷Furthermore, a hundred and fifty Jews and officials ate at my table, as well as those who came to us from the surrounding nations. ¹⁸Each day one ox, six choice sheep and some poultry were prepared for me, and every ten days an abundant supply of wine of all kinds. In spite of all this, I never demanded the food allotted to the governor, because the demands were heavy on these people.

¹⁹Remember me with favor, O my God, for all I have done for these people.

NOW OR NEVER
NE 5:9–10

Taking advantage of people or being dishonest is wrong, regardless of who, when or where. Imagine if you weren't a Christian and someone who claimed to follow God was taking advantage of you. What would you think of that person's religion?

Learning to Endure

How's your physical endurance? Can you run a mile without stopping? Five miles? A marathon? How far can you swim or skate without a break? What about your mental toughness? How long can you put up with people doubting you, questioning the things you do or trying their hardest to make you fail? That's what you're up against when you sign on to do God's work. The better your endurance is, the more successful you'll be in your kingdom work.

»» live the adventure »» Ne 6:1–15

FURTHER OPPOSITION TO THE REBUILDING

6 When word came to Sanballat, Tobiah, Geshem the Arab and the rest of our enemies that I had rebuilt the wall and not a gap was left in it—though up to that time I had not set the doors in the gates— ²Sanballat and Geshem sent me this message: "Come, let us meet together in one of the villages[c] on the plain of Ono."

But they were scheming to harm me; ³so I sent messengers to them with this reply: "I am carrying on a great project and cannot go down. Why should the work stop while I leave it and go down to you?" ⁴Four times they sent me the same message, and each time I gave them the same answer.

⁵Then, the fifth time, Sanballat sent his aide to me with the same message, and in his hand was an unsealed letter ⁶in which was written:

"It is reported among the nations—and Geshem[d] says it is true—that you and the Jews are plotting to revolt, and therefore you are building the wall. Moreover, according to these reports you are about to become their king ⁷and have even appointed prophets to make

---

^a *15* That is, about 1 pound (about 0.5 kilogram)   ^b *16* Most Hebrew manuscripts; some Hebrew manuscripts, Septuagint, Vulgate and Syriac *I*   ^c *2* Or *in Kephirim*   ^d *6* Hebrew *Gashmu,* a variant of *Geshem*

this proclamation about you in Jerusalem: 'There is a king in Judah!' Now this report will get back to the king; so come, let us confer together."

⁸I sent him this reply: "Nothing like what you are saying is happening; you are just making it up out of your head."

⁹They were all trying to frighten us, thinking, "Their hands will get too weak for the work, and it will not be completed."

ᴸBut I prayed,ᴶ "Now strengthen my hands."

¹⁰One day I went to the house of Shemaiah son of Delaiah, the son of Mehetabel, who was shut in at his home. He said, "Let us meet in the house of God, inside the temple, and let us close the temple doors, because men are coming to kill you—by night they are coming to kill you."

¹¹But I said, "Should a man like me run away? Or should one like me go into the temple to save his life? I will not go!" ¹²I realized that God had not sent him, but that he had prophesied against me because Tobiah and Sanballat had hired him. ¹³He had been hired to intimidate me so that I would commit a sin by doing this, and then they would give me a bad name to discredit me.

¹⁴Remember Tobiah and Sanballat, O my God, because of what they have done; remember also the prophetess Noadiah and the rest of the prophets who have been trying to intimidate me.

THE COMPLETION OF THE WALL

¹⁵So the wall was completed on the twenty-fifth of Elul, in fifty-two days. ¹⁶When all our enemies heard about this, all the surrounding nations were afraid and lost their self-confidence, because they realized that this work had been done with the help of our God.

¹⁷Also, in those days the nobles of Judah were sending many letters to Tobiah, and replies from Tobiah kept coming to them. ¹⁸For many in Judah were under oath to him, since he was son-in-law to Shecaniah son of Arah, and his son Jehohanan had married the daughter of Meshullam son of Berekiah. ¹⁹Moreover, they kept reporting to me his good deeds and then telling him what I said. And Tobiah sent letters to intimidate me.

NOW OR NEVER
NE 6:1–14

What intimidates you? After you've answered that question, try this one: If you know that God—who is all-powerful and all-knowing—is behind you, why should anyone or anything intimidate you?

7 After the wall had been rebuilt and I had set the doors in place, the gatekeepers and the singers and the Levites were appointed. ²I put in charge of Jerusalem my brother Hanani, along withᵃ Hananiah the commander of the citadel, because he was a man of integrity and feared God more than most men do. ³I said to them, "The gates of Jerusalem are not to be opened until the sun is hot. While the gatekeepers are still on duty, have them shut the doors and bar them. Also appoint residents of Jerusalem as guards, some at their posts and some near their own houses."

THE LIST OF THE EXILES WHO RETURNED

⁴Now the city was large and spacious, but there were few people in it, and the houses had not yet been rebuilt. ⁵So my God put it into my heart to assemble the nobles, the officials and the common people for registration by families. I found the genealogical record of those who had been the first to return. This is what I found written there:

⁶These are the people of the province who came up from the captivity of the exiles whom Nebuchadnezzar king of Babylon had taken captive (they returned to Jerusalem and Judah, each to his own town, ⁷in company with Zerubbabel, Jeshua, Nehemiah, Azariah, Raamiah, Nahamani, Mordecai, Bilshan, Mispereth, Bigvai, Nehum and Baanah):

The list of the men of Israel:

⁸the descendants of Parosh	2,172
⁹of Shephatiah	372

ᵃ 2 Or Hanani, that is,

nehemiah

sanballat

» An Israelite cupbearer to the Persian king

» Returned to Jerusalem to rebuild the city walls

» A man of prayer and action

» Governor of Samaria, the region just north of Judea

» Opposed Nehemiah

» A petty, angry man who wanted control and power

The Main Event

Have you ever been bullied? If so, you're familiar with that nauseating feeling of intimidation, the soul-shaking threat of harm. Bullies—whether they're common criminals, international terrorists or just some big lug from the wrestling team—thrive on their ability to unnerve people and generate fear.

Sanballat was a world-class bully. When Nehemiah showed up (all the way from Persia) with a God-given desire to rebuild Jerusalem's walls, Sanballat "became angry and was greatly incensed" (Nehemiah 4:1). (That's the Bible's way of saying he was pretty ticked.) It didn't matter that Nehemiah had royal authorization to tackle the project; Sanballat was upset because his agenda was disturbed. Maybe he had his eyes on the governorship of Judah. Maybe he thought Nehemiah posed a threat to his political authority. Whatever the case, Sanballat took it upon himself to put a stop to the construction. So he gathered up some of his goon friends (chiefly Tobiah the Ammonite and Geshem the Arab) and launched a bullying campaign.

Sanballat ridiculed the Jews. He and his cronies fired insults at them. They plotted attacks and tried to stir up trouble. They tried to trick Nehemiah into an ambush. They began spreading lies about his motives. They threatened anyone who would listen. They tried like crazy to stop work on the walls with the twin weapons of fear and intimidation.

But none of their efforts could deter Nehemiah. In a brilliant display of leadership and courage, he kept the vision of rebuilt walls before the people. Sanballat's tactics may have rattled Nehemiah at times, but through prayer and lots of hard work on everyone's part, the monumental task of building the city walls was completed in less than two months.

The Outcome

Bullies use their power (whatever form it may take) to get what they want. And if that means humiliating someone at the same time, even better (as far as bullies are concerned). But real strength isn't pushing people around and blackmailing others to get what you want. Remember, even the most powerful and fearsome dictators in the world are subject to the authority and judgment of God.

Real strength is righteousness under pressure and the will to be obedient to God in the face of intimidation, temptation or even physical threat. When you face a bully, ask God to give you the wisdom to know what to do and the courage to do it.

Where do you get this kind of strength—especially when a bully is as fearsome or powerful as Sanballat? Nehemiah gives us the secret: "But I prayed, 'Now strengthen my hands' " (Nehemiah 6:9).

Ask God right now for the inner power to take on the frightening bullies in your life.

Read more about Nehemiah and Sanballat in Nehemiah 1:1—6:19 (pages 549-555).

¹⁰ of Arah	652
¹¹ of Pahath-Moab (through the line of Jeshua and Joab)	2,818
¹² of Elam	1,254
¹³ of Zattu	845
¹⁴ of Zaccai	760
¹⁵ of Binnui	648
¹⁶ of Bebai	628
¹⁷ of Azgad	2,322
¹⁸ of Adonikam	667
¹⁹ of Bigvai	2,067
²⁰ of Adin	655
²¹ of Ater (through Hezekiah)	98
²² of Hashum	328
²³ of Bezai	324
²⁴ of Hariph	112
²⁵ of Gibeon	95
²⁶ the men of Bethlehem and Netophah	188
²⁷ of Anathoth	128
²⁸ of Beth Azmaveth	42
²⁹ of Kiriath Jearim, Kephirah and Beeroth	743
³⁰ of Ramah and Geba	621
³¹ of Micmash	122
³² of Bethel and Ai	123
³³ of the other Nebo	52
³⁴ of the other Elam	1,254
³⁵ of Harim	320
³⁶ of Jericho	345
³⁷ of Lod, Hadid and Ono	721
³⁸ of Senaah	3,930

³⁹ The priests:

the descendants of Jedaiah (through the family of Jeshua)	973
⁴⁰ of Immer	1,052
⁴¹ of Pashhur	1,247
⁴² of Harim	1,017

⁴³ The Levites:

the descendants of Jeshua (through Kadmiel through the line of Hodaviah)	74

⁴⁴ The singers:

the descendants of Asaph	148

⁴⁵ The gatekeepers:

the descendants of Shallum, Ater, Talmon, Akkub, Hatita and Shobai	138

⁴⁶ The temple servants:

the descendants of
Ziha, Hasupha, Tabbaoth,
⁴⁷ Keros, Sia, Padon,
⁴⁸ Lebana, Hagaba, Shalmai,

49 Hanan, Giddel, Gahar,
50 Reaiah, Rezin, Nekoda,
51 Gazzam, Uzza, Paseah,
52 Besai, Meunim, Nephusim,
53 Bakbuk, Hakupha, Harhur,
54 Bazluth, Mehida, Harsha,
55 Barkos, Sisera, Temah,
56 Neziah and Hatipha

57 The descendants of the servants of Solomon:

the descendants of
Sotai, Sophereth, Perida,
58 Jaala, Darkon, Giddel,
59 Shephatiah, Hattil,
Pokereth-Hazzebaim and Amon

60 The temple servants and the descendants
of the servants of Solomon   392

61 The following came up from the towns of Tel Melah, Tel Harsha, Kerub, Addon and Immer, but they could not show that their families were descended from Israel:

62 the descendants of
Delaiah, Tobiah and Nekoda   642

63 And from among the priests:

the descendants of
Hobaiah, Hakkoz and Barzillai (a man who had married a daughter of Barzillai the Gileadite and was called by that name).

64 These searched for their family records, but they could not find them and so were excluded from the priesthood as unclean. 65 The governor, therefore, ordered them not to eat any of the most sacred food until there should be a priest ministering with the Urim and Thummim.

66 The whole company numbered 42,360, 67 besides their 7,337 menservants and maidservants; and they also had 245 men and women singers. 68 There were 736 horses, 245 mules,[a] 69 435 camels and 6,720 donkeys.

70 Some of the heads of the families contributed to the work. The governor gave to the treasury 1,000 drachmas[b] of gold, 50 bowls and 530 garments for priests. 71 Some of the heads of the families gave to the treasury for the work 20,000 drachmas[c] of gold and 2,200 minas[d] of silver. 72 The total given by the rest of the people was 20,000 drachmas of gold, 2,000 minas[e] of silver and 67 garments for priests.

73 The priests, the Levites, the gatekeepers, the singers and the temple servants, along with certain of the people and the rest of the Israelites, settled in their own towns.

EZRA READS THE LAW

8 When the seventh month came and the Israelites had settled in their towns, 1 all the people assembled as one man in the square before the Water Gate. They told Ezra the scribe to bring out the Book of the Law of Moses, which the LORD had commanded for Israel.

NOW OR NEVER
NE 8:1–3

What's the average amount of time you spend reading God's Word every week? Do you think that number is too low, too high or just right? Why?

---

a 68 Some Hebrew manuscripts (see also Ezra 2:66); most Hebrew manuscripts do not have this verse.   b 70 That is, about 19 pounds (about 8.5 kilograms)   c 71 That is, about 375 pounds (about 170 kilograms); also in verse 72   d 71 That is, about 1 1/3 tons (about 1.2 metric tons)   e 72 That is, about 1 1/4 tons (about 1.1 metric tons)

²So on the first day of the seventh month Ezra the priest brought the Law before the assembly, which was made up of men and women and all who were able to understand. ³He read it aloud from daybreak till noon as he faced the square before the Water Gate in the presence of the men, women and others who could understand. And all the people listened attentively to the Book of the Law.

⁴Ezra the scribe stood on a high wooden platform built for the occasion. Beside him on his right stood Mattithiah, Shema, Anaiah, Uriah, Hilkiah and Maaseiah; and on his left were Pedaiah, Mishael, Malkijah, Hashum, Hashbaddanah, Zechariah and Meshullam.

⁵Ezra opened the book. All the people could see him because he was standing above them; and as he opened it, the people all stood up. ⁶Ezra praised the LORD, the great God; and all the people lifted their hands and responded, "Amen! Amen!" Then they bowed down and worshiped the LORD with their faces to the ground.

⁷The Levites—Jeshua, Bani, Sherebiah, Jamin, Akkub, Shabbethai, Hodiah, Maaseiah, Kelita, Azariah, Jozabad, Hanan and Pelaiah—instructed the people in the Law while the people were standing there. ⁸They read from the Book of the Law of God, making it clear[a] and giving the meaning so that the people could understand what was being read.

⁹Then Nehemiah the governor, Ezra the priest and scribe, and the Levites who were instructing the people said to them all, "This day is sacred to the LORD your God. Do not mourn or weep." For all the people had been weeping as they listened to the words of the Law.

¹⁰Nehemiah said, "Go and enjoy choice food and sweet drinks, and send some to those who have nothing prepared. This day is sacred to our Lord. Do not grieve, for the joy of the LORD is your strength."

¹¹The Levites calmed all the people, saying, "Be still, for this is a sacred day. Do not grieve."

¹²Then all the people went away to eat and drink, to send portions of food and to celebrate with great joy, because they now understood the words that had been made known to them.

¹³On the second day of the month, the heads of all the families, along with the priests and the Levites, gathered around Ezra the scribe

NOW OR NEVER
NE 8:10-11

God knows when we're genuinely sorry for our sin, and he wants us to freely express our remorse. But even in the midst of our sadness, God is still great and worthy of praise. That's why we should never let our sinful past keep us from worshiping him.

to give attention to the words of the Law. ¹⁴They found written in the Law, which the LORD had commanded through Moses, that the Israelites were to live in booths during the feast of the seventh month ¹⁵and that they should proclaim this word and spread it throughout their towns and in Jerusalem: "Go out into the hill country and bring back branches from olive and wild olive trees, and from myrtles, palms and shade trees, to make booths"—as it is written.[b]

¹⁶So the people went out and brought back branches and built themselves booths on their own roofs, in their courtyards, in the courts of the house of God and in the square by the Water Gate and the one by the Gate of Ephraim. ¹⁷The whole company that had returned from exile built booths and lived in them. From the days of Joshua son of Nun until that day, the Israelites had not celebrated it like this. And their joy was very great.

¹⁸Day after day, from the first day to the last, Ezra read from the Book of the Law of God. They celebrated the feast for seven days, and on the eighth day, in accordance with the regulation, there was an assembly.

THE ISRAELITES CONFESS THEIR SINS

9 On the twenty-fourth day of the same month, the Israelites gathered together, fasting and wearing sackcloth and having dust on their heads. ²Those of Israelite descent had separated themselves from all foreigners. They stood in their places and confessed their sins and the wickedness of their fathers. ³They stood where they were and read from the Book of the Law of the LORD their God for a quarter of the day, and spent another quarter in confession and in worshiping the LORD their God. ⁴Standing on the stairs were the Levites—Jeshua, Bani, Kadmiel, Shebaniah, Bunni, Sherebiah, Bani and Kenani—who called with loud voices to the LORD their God. ⁵And the Levites—Jeshua, Kad-

---

a 8 Or God, translating it   b 15 See Lev. 23:37-40.

miel, Bani, Hashabneiah, Sherebiah, Hodiah, Shebaniah and Pethahiah—said: "Stand up and praise the Lord your God, who is from everlasting to everlasting. [a]"

"Blessed be your glorious name, and may it be exalted above all blessing and praise. [6]You alone are the Lord. You made the heavens, even the highest heavens, and all their starry host, the earth and all that is on it, the seas and all that is in them. You give life to everything, and the multitudes of heaven worship you.

[7]"You are the Lord God, who chose Abram and brought him out of Ur of the Chaldeans and named him Abraham. [8]You found his heart faithful to you, and you made a covenant with him to give to his descendants the land of the Canaanites, Hittites, Amorites, Perizzites, Jebusites and Girgashites. You have kept your promise because you are righteous.

[9]"You saw the suffering of our forefathers in Egypt; you heard their cry at the Red Sea. [b] [10]You sent miraculous signs and wonders against Pharaoh, against all his officials and all the people of his land, for you knew how arrogantly the Egyptians treated them. You made a name for yourself, which remains to this day. [11]You divided the sea before them, so that they passed through it on dry ground, but you hurled their pursuers into the depths, like a stone into mighty waters. [12]By day you led them with a pillar of cloud, and by night with a pillar of fire to give them light on the way they were to take.

[13]"You came down on Mount Sinai; you spoke to them from heaven. You gave them regulations and laws that are just and right, and decrees and commands that are good. [14]You made known to them your holy Sabbath and gave them commands, decrees and laws through your servant Moses. [15]In their hunger you gave them bread from heaven and in their thirst you brought them water from the rock; you told them to go in and take possession of the land you had sworn with uplifted hand to give them.

[16]"But they, our forefathers, became arrogant and stiff-necked, and did not obey your commands. [17]They refused to listen and failed to remember the miracles you performed among them. They became stiff-necked and in their rebellion appointed a leader in order to return to their slavery. But you are a forgiving God, gracious and compassionate, slow to anger and abounding in love. Therefore you did not desert them, [18]even when they cast for themselves an image of a calf and said, 'This is your god, who brought you up out of Egypt,' or when they committed awful blasphemies.

[19]"Because of your great compassion you did not abandon them in the desert. By day the pillar of cloud did not cease to guide them on their path, nor the pillar of fire by night to shine on the way they were to take. [20]You gave your good Spirit to instruct them. You did not withhold your manna from their mouths, and you gave them water for their thirst. [21]For forty years you sustained them in the desert; they lacked nothing, their clothes did not wear out nor did their feet become swollen.

[22]"You gave them kingdoms and nations, allotting to them even the remotest frontiers. They took over the country of Sihon [c] king of Heshbon and the country of Og king of Bashan. [23]You made their sons as numerous as the stars in the sky, and you brought them into the land that you told their fathers to enter and possess. [24]Their sons went in and took possession of the land. You subdued before them the Canaanites, who lived in the land; you handed the Canaanites over to them, along with their kings and the peoples of the land, to deal with them as they pleased. [25]They captured fortified cities and fertile land; they took possession of houses filled with all kinds of good things, wells already dug, vineyards, olive groves and fruit trees in abundance. They ate to the full and were well-nourished; they reveled in your great goodness.

challenge notes

To: my_son

NE 9:17

heavenly_father: do yourself a favor. when you realize that you've disobeyed me or given in to temptation, come to me for forgiveness immediately. I will forgive you; that's always a given. the quicker we patch up our relationship, the better off your life will be.

---

[a] 5 Or *God for ever and ever* [b] 9 Hebrew *Yam Suph*, that is, Sea of Reeds [c] 22 One Hebrew manuscript and Septuagint; most Hebrew manuscripts *Sihon, that is, the country of the*

40 IDEAS FOR A FUN DATE

This Bible probably just got a lot more interesting, didn't it? But before you get carried away, let's be honest. Dating is a hot button topic in a lot of homes. And whether your parents are the type who would rather you look for a wife instead of a girlfriend or the type who are happy for you to casually date girls, all Christians should agree on one thing: Love between a male and a female is one of the most important, precious gifts that God has given us, and it shouldn't be taken lightly. That's clear from the very first marriage in Genesis 2. Following are some fun ideas for a date. Whether you try them out this weekend or a couple of years from now, use this list as a reminder of how special God has intended love to be between a man and a woman.

» 10 TO REMEMBER

» 01 Get creative! Have a theme date. For example: England. Eat English muffins with Earl Grey tea and chase it down with fish and chips. If you really want to make her laugh, speak in a British accent. Cheerio!

» 02 Venture out. It seems as though every weekend a community is celebrating something. Visit a nearby small-town festival (e.g., the Bologna Festival, the Catfish Festival, whatever). It will be an adventure and you just might make some new friends.

» 03 Learn. Tackle a new activity together—riding a unicycle, rock climbing, wakeboarding. Since you both will be beginners, it will be a great opportunity to learn together and help each other.

» 04 Take a walk down memory lane. Before your parents can try to embarrass you with snapshots of your "gawky" phase, just get it all out in the open and watch old home videos of each other.

» 05 Shoot some hoops. See who can make the most free throws out of 25.

» 06 Help others. Make a care package for a missionary family supported by your church. You'll be able to spend time together while doing something nice for someone else.

» 07 Go a little wild—at the zoo!

» 08 Get in touch with your inner chef by making homemade waffles or pancakes. Get creative and use different syrups and fruits for toppings. Yummy!

» 09 Head outdoors. Attend a free concert in your local park. Walk there together, if possible.

» 10 Get artistic. Grab a camera and shoot some pictures of your neighborhood, your mom's garden, your dog, whatever. Print them out or download them to share with your friends.

...tes to plan? Don't let these great ideas pass you by:

...

...nic food together.

...et store.

... fishing pole and go fishing.

...ater and go canoeing or kayaking.

...ard game outside.

...h other's picture with finger paint or watercolor.

...ld piece of furniture at a garage sale . . . refinish it and give it to one of your moms.

...t the local museum.

...s.

...staurant and pretend to be from another country.

...little league ball game and cheer for every kid.

...anes and go bowling.

...our bikes for an all-day bike ride.

...ol.

...es shopping at a second-hand store.

...eighbor kid to a park or to get an ice cream cone.

...lea market and see who can buy the most unusual item for less than $2.

...: to the driving range and hit some golf balls.

...nis.

... old silent Charlie Chaplin movie.

...ther a jigsaw puzzle.

...colate chip cookies and give them to someone.

...e nearest airport and watch the planes take off.

...hed or fence or something around your house (be sure to clear it with your

...irst!).

...coffee shop and play chess or checkers.

... and castle.

...t your closet and take the unwanted stuff to Goodwill or to the Salvation Army.

... back riding.

...ocal park and play. Take turns pushing each other on the swings.

26 "But they were disobedient and rebelled against you; they put your law behind their backs. They killed your prophets, who had admonished them in order to turn them back to you; they committed awful blasphemies. 27 So you handed them over to their enemies, who oppressed them. But when they were oppressed they cried out to you. From heaven you heard them, and in your great compassion you gave them deliverers, who rescued them from the hand of their enemies.

28 "But as soon as they were at rest, they again did what was evil in your sight. Then you abandoned them to the hand of their enemies so that they ruled over them. And when they cried out to you again, you heard from heaven, and in your compassion you delivered them time after time.

29 "You warned them to return to your law, but they became arrogant and disobeyed your commands. They sinned against your ordinances, by which a man will live if he obeys them. Stubbornly they turned their backs on you, became stiff-necked and refused to listen. 30 For many years you were patient with them. By your Spirit you admonished them through your prophets. Yet they paid no attention, so you handed them over to the neighboring peoples. 31 But in your great mercy you did not put an end to them or abandon them, for you are a gracious and merciful God.

now or never

NE 9:29

After all of the times we've disobeyed God and ignored his will for us, it's incredible that he still answers us and comes through for us when we cry out to him.

32 "Now therefore, O our God, the great, mighty and awesome God, who keeps his covenant of love, do not let all this hardship seem trifling in your eyes—the hardship that has come upon us, upon our kings and leaders, upon our priests and prophets, upon our fathers and all your people, from the days of the kings of Assyria until today. 33 In all that has happened to us, you have been just; you have acted faithfully, while we did wrong. 34 Our kings, our leaders, our priests and our fathers did not follow your law; they did not pay attention to your commands or the warnings you gave them. 35 Even while they were in their kingdom, enjoying your great goodness to them in the spacious and fertile land you gave them, they did not serve you or turn from their evil ways.

36 "But see, we are slaves today, slaves in the land you gave our forefathers so they could eat its fruit and the other good things it produces. 37 Because of our sins, its abundant harvest goes to the kings you have placed over us. They rule over our bodies and our cattle as they please. We are in great distress.

THE AGREEMENT OF THE PEOPLE

38 "In view of all this, we are making a binding agreement, putting it in writing, and our leaders, our Levites and our priests are affixing their seals to it."

10 Those who sealed it were:

Nehemiah the governor, the son of Hacaliah.

Zedekiah, 2 Seraiah, Azariah, Jeremiah,
3 Pashhur, Amariah, Malkijah,
4 Hattush, Shebaniah, Malluch,
5 Harim, Meremoth, Obadiah,
6 Daniel, Ginnethon, Baruch,
7 Meshullam, Abijah, Mijamin,
8 Maaziah, Bilgai and Shemaiah.
These were the priests.

9 The Levites:

Jeshua son of Azaniah, Binnui of the sons of Henadad, Kadmiel,

¹⁰and their associates: Shebaniah,
Hodiah, Kelita, Pelaiah, Hanan,
¹¹Mica, Rehob, Hashabiah,
¹²Zaccur, Sherebiah, Shebaniah,
¹³Hodiah, Bani and Beninu.

¹⁴The leaders of the people:

Parosh, Pahath-Moab, Elam, Zattu, Bani,
¹⁵Bunni, Azgad, Bebai,
¹⁶Adonijah, Bigvai, Adin,
¹⁷Ater, Hezekiah, Azzur,
¹⁸Hodiah, Hashum, Bezai,
¹⁹Hariph, Anathoth, Nebai,
²⁰Magpiash, Meshullam, Hezir,
²¹Meshezabel, Zadok, Jaddua,
²²Pelatiah, Hanan, Anaiah,
²³Hoshea, Hananiah, Hasshub,
²⁴Hallohesh, Pilha, Shobek,
²⁵Rehum, Hashabnah, Maaseiah,
²⁶Ahiah, Hanan, Anan,
²⁷Malluch, Harim and Baanah.

²⁸"The rest of the people—priests, Levites, gatekeepers, singers, temple servants and all who separated themselves from the neighboring peoples for the sake of the Law of God, together with their wives and all their sons and daughters who are able to understand— ²⁹all these now join their brothers the nobles, and bind themselves with a curse and an oath to follow the Law of God given through Moses the servant of God and to obey carefully all the commands, regulations and decrees of the LORD our Lord.

³⁰"We promise not to give our daughters in marriage to the peoples around us or take their daughters for our sons.

³¹"When the neighboring peoples bring merchandise or grain to sell on the Sabbath, we will not buy from them on the Sabbath or on any holy day. Every seventh year we will forgo working the land and will cancel all debts.

³²"We assume the responsibility for carrying out the commands to give a third of a shekel^a each year for the service of the house of our God: ³³for the bread set out on the table; for the regular grain offerings and burnt offerings; for the offerings on the Sabbaths, New Moon festivals and appointed feasts; for the holy offerings; for sin offerings to make atonement for Israel; and for all the duties of the house of our God.

³⁴"We—the priests, the Levites and the people—have cast lots to determine when each of our families is to bring to the house of our God at set times each year a contribution of wood to burn on the altar of the LORD our God, as it is written in the Law.

³⁵"We also assume responsibility for bringing to the house of the LORD each year the firstfruits of our crops and of every fruit tree.

³⁶"As it is also written in the Law, we will bring the firstborn of our sons and of our cattle, of our herds and of our flocks to the house of our God, to the priests ministering there.

³⁷"Moreover, we will bring to the storerooms of the house of our God, to the priests, the first of our ground meal, of our ⌊grain⌋ offerings, of the fruit of all our trees and of our new wine and oil. And we will bring a tithe of our crops to the Levites, for it is the Levites who collect the tithes in all the towns where we work. ³⁸A priest descended from Aaron is to accompany the Levites when they receive the tithes, and the Levites are to bring a tenth of the tithes up to the house of our God, to the storerooms of the treasury. ³⁹The people of Israel, including the Levites, are to

---

---

^a *32* That is, about 1/8 ounce (about 4 grams)

bring their contributions of grain, new wine and oil to the storerooms where the articles for the sanctuary are kept and where the ministering priests, the gatekeepers and the singers stay.

"We will not neglect the house of our God."

THE NEW RESIDENTS OF JERUSALEM

11 Now the leaders of the people settled in Jerusalem, and the rest of the people cast lots to bring one out of every ten to live in Jerusalem, the holy city, while the remaining nine were to stay in their own towns. ²The people commended all the men who volunteered to live in Jerusalem.

³These are the provincial leaders who settled in Jerusalem (now some Israelites, priests, Levites, temple servants and descendants of Solomon's servants lived in the towns of Judah, each on his own property in the various towns, ⁴while other people from both Judah and Benjamin lived in Jerusalem):

From the descendants of Judah:

Athaiah son of Uzziah, the son of Zechariah, the son of Amariah, the son of Shephatiah, the son of Mahalalel, a descendant of Perez; ⁵and Maaseiah son of Baruch, the son of Col-Hozeh, the son of Hazaiah, the son of Adaiah, the son of Joiarib, the son of Zechariah, a descendant of Shelah. ⁶The descendants of Perez who lived in Jerusalem totaled 468 able men.

⁷From the descendants of Benjamin:

Sallu son of Meshullam, the son of Joed, the son of Pedaiah, the son of Kolaiah, the son of Maaseiah, the son of Ithiel, the son of Jeshaiah, ⁸and his followers, Gabbai and Sallai—928 men. ⁹Joel son of Zicri was their chief officer, and Judah son of Hassenuah was over the Second District of the city.

¹⁰From the priests:

Jedaiah; the son of Joiarib; Jakin; ¹¹Seraiah son of Hilkiah, the son of Meshullam, the son of Zadok, the son of Meraioth, the son of Ahitub, supervisor in the house of God, ¹²and their associates, who carried on work for the temple—822 men; Adaiah son of Jeroham, the son of Pelaliah, the son of Amzi, the son of Zechariah, the son of Pashhur, the son of Malkijah, ¹³and his associates, who were heads of families—242 men; Amashsai son of Azarel, the son of Ahzai, the son of Meshillemoth, the son of Immer, ¹⁴and his[a] associates, who were able men—128. Their chief officer was Zabdiel son of Haggedolim.

¹⁵From the Levites:

Shemaiah son of Hasshub, the son of Azrikam, the son of Hashabiah, the son of Bunni; ¹⁶Shabbethai and Jozabad, two of the heads of the Levites, who had charge of the outside work of the house of God; ¹⁷Mattaniah son of Mica, the son of Zabdi, the son of Asaph, the director who led in thanksgiving and prayer; Bakbukiah, second among his associates; and Abda son of Shammua, the son of Galal, the son of Jeduthun. ¹⁸The Levites in the holy city totaled 284.

¹⁹The gatekeepers:

Akkub, Talmon and their associates, who kept watch at the gates—172 men.

²⁰The rest of the Israelites, with the priests and Levites, were in all the towns of Judah, each on his ancestral property.

²¹The temple servants lived on the hill of Ophel, and Ziha and Gishpa were in charge of them.

²²The chief officer of the Levites in Jerusalem was Uzzi son of Bani, the son of Hashabiah, the son of Mattaniah, the son of Mica. Uzzi was one of Asaph's descendants, who were the singers responsible for the service of the house of God. ²³The singers were under the king's orders, which regulated their daily activity.

²⁴Pethahiah son of Meshezabel, one of the descendants of Zerah son of Judah, was the king's agent in all affairs relating to the people.

²⁵As for the villages with their fields, some of the people of Judah lived in Kiriath Arba and its sur-

---

ᵃ *14* Most Septuagint manuscripts; Hebrew *their*

battlelines

» Professor Pagan (Atheism)

Q: How's school going?
A: So far, so good . . . except for my U.S. History class.

Q: Why? What's the deal?
A: It turns out that my teacher, Mrs. Richardson, is about as anti-Christian as you can get. She thinks religion is a crutch for weaklings. She's even got one of those Darwin fish on her car. I'm telling you, this woman is whacked. No matter what we're talking about, she always finds a way to go off on some rant against the church.

Q: At least you only have her for one semester, right?
A: Yeah, but it could be a long four months. See, she did this exercise the first day of class, where she read off this long list of agree/disagree statements. And now I see why she did it. She basically wanted to find out who her Christian students were . . . so

she could spend the rest of the semester bashing them.

Q: She bashes you?
A: Oh, man, does she ever! Me and two other people . . . every class. Mostly she makes all these snide little remarks. And you should have seen what she did with my first essay. I wrote 500 words, and I'll bet she wrote at least 2,500 words in red in the margins. I got a C- because of "flawed reasoning"—which basically means I disagree with her beliefs.

Q: What are you going to do?
A: I'm just going to stick it out—and try not to let her push my buttons. I've actually started meeting with the other two Christians taking the class. We get together and pray before class once a week—for her and for ourselves. That helps a little. But it's still pretty awful.

» The Real Enemy

When you're dealing with someone who's antagonistic about Christ, it helps to remember that your real struggle is not against that person but against the one the Bible calls Satan, or the devil (see Ephesians 6:12). He is the one who "has blinded the minds of unbelievers, so that they cannot see the light of the gospel" (2 Corinthians 4:4).

It's not always easy, but Jesus calls us to love those who try to make our lives miserable: "Love your enemies and pray for those who persecute you, that you may be children of your Father in heaven" (Matthew 5:44–45). Trent has chosen a wise course of action: prayer, patience and perseverance. Who knows? Maybe down the road in a one-on-one meeting, Trent's attitude will open up a door for him to share his faith. He can be sure that Mrs. Richardson and his classmates are watching closely to see how he'll respond, to see just how real, how genuine, this Jesus thing is.

Learn more about understanding and sharing your faith at www.RevolutionBible.com.

rounding settlements, in Dibon and its settlements, in Jekabzeel and its villages, ²⁶in Jeshua, in Moladah, in Beth Pelet, ²⁷in Hazar Shual, in Beersheba and its settlements, ²⁸in Ziklag, in Meconah and its settlements, ²⁹in En Rimmon, in Zorah, in Jarmuth, ³⁰Zanoah, Adullam and their villages, in Lachish and its fields, and in Azekah and its settlements. So they were living all the way from Beersheba to the Valley of Hinnom.

³¹The descendants of the Benjamites from Geba lived in Micmash, Aija, Bethel and its settlements, ³²in Anathoth, Nob and Ananiah, ³³in Hazor, Ramah and Gittaim, ³⁴in Hadid, Zeboim and Neballat, ³⁵in Lod and Ono, and in the Valley of the Craftsmen.

³⁶Some of the divisions of the Levites of Judah settled in Benjamin.

PRIESTS AND LEVITES

12 These were the priests and Levites who returned with Zerubbabel son of Shealtiel and with Jeshua:

Seraiah, Jeremiah, Ezra,
²Amariah, Malluch, Hattush,
³Shecaniah, Rehum, Meremoth,
⁴Iddo, Ginnethon,ᵃ Abijah,
⁵Mijamin,ᵇ Moadiah, Bilgah,
⁶Shemaiah, Joiarib, Jedaiah,
⁷Sallu, Amok, Hilkiah and Jedaiah.

These were the leaders of the priests and their associates in the days of Jeshua.

⁸The Levites were Jeshua, Binnui, Kadmiel, Sherebiah, Judah, and also Mattaniah, who, together with his associates, was in charge of the songs of thanksgiving. ⁹Bakbukiah and Unni, their associates, stood opposite them in the services.

¹⁰Jeshua was the father of Joiakim, Joiakim the father of Eliashib, Eliashib the father of Joiada, ¹¹Joiada the father of Jonathan, and Jonathan the father of Jaddua.

¹²In the days of Joiakim, these were the heads of the priestly families:

of Seraiah's family, Meraiah;
of Jeremiah's, Hananiah;
¹³of Ezra's, Meshullam;
of Amariah's, Jehohanan;
¹⁴of Malluch's, Jonathan;
of Shecaniah's,ᶜ Joseph;
¹⁵of Harim's, Adna;
of Meremoth's,ᵈ Helkai;
¹⁶of Iddo's, Zechariah;
of Ginnethon's, Meshullam;
¹⁷of Abijah's, Zicri;
of Miniamin's and of Moadiah's, Piltai;
¹⁸of Bilgah's, Shammua;
of Shemaiah's, Jehonathan;
¹⁹of Joiarib's, Mattenai;
of Jedaiah's, Uzzi;
²⁰of Sallu's, Kallai;
of Amok's, Eber;
²¹of Hilkiah's, Hashabiah;
of Jedaiah's, Nethanel.

²²The family heads of the Levites in the days of Eliashib, Joiada, Johanan and Jaddua, as well as those of the priests, were recorded in the reign of Darius the Persian. ²³The family heads among the descendants of Levi up to the time of Johanan son of Eliashib were recorded in the book of the annals. ²⁴And the leaders of the Levites were Hashabiah, Sherebiah, Jeshua son of Kadmiel, and their associ-

---

ᵃ *4* Many Hebrew manuscripts and Vulgate (see also Neh. 12:16); most Hebrew manuscripts *Ginnethoi*   ᵇ *5* A variant of *Miniamin*
ᶜ *14* Very many Hebrew manuscripts, some Septuagint manuscripts and Syriac (see also Neh. 12:3); most Hebrew manuscripts
Shebaniah's   ᵈ *15* Some Septuagint manuscripts (see also Neh. 12:3); Hebrew *Meraioth's*

ates, who stood opposite them to give praise and thanksgiving, one section responding to the other, as prescribed by David the man of God.

²⁵Mattaniah, Bakbukiah, Obadiah, Meshullam, Talmon and Akkub were gatekeepers who guarded the storerooms at the gates. ²⁶They served in the days of Joiakim son of Jeshua, the son of Jozadak, and in the days of Nehemiah the governor and of Ezra the priest and scribe.

DEDICATION OF THE WALL OF JERUSALEM

²⁷At the dedication of the wall of Jerusalem, the Levites were sought out from where they lived and were brought to Jerusalem to celebrate joyfully the dedication with songs of thanksgiving and with the music of cymbals, harps and lyres. ²⁸The singers also were brought together from the region around Jerusalem—from the villages of the Netophathites, ²⁹from Beth Gilgal, and from the area of Geba and Azmaveth, for the singers had built villages for themselves around Jerusalem. ³⁰When the priests and Levites had purified themselves ceremonially, they purified the people, the gates and the wall.

³¹I had the leaders of Judah go up on top ᵃ of the wall. I also assigned two large choirs to give thanks. One was to proceed on top ᵇ of the wall to the right, toward the Dung Gate. ³²Hoshaiah and half the leaders of Judah followed them, ³³along with Azariah, Ezra, Meshullam, ³⁴Judah, Benjamin, Shemaiah, Jeremiah, ³⁵as well as some priests with trumpets, and also Zechariah son of Jonathan, the son of Shemaiah, the son of Mattaniah, the son of Micaiah, the son of Zaccur, the son of Asaph, ³⁶and his associates—Shemaiah, Azarel, Milalai, Gilalai, Maai, Nethanel, Judah and Hanani—with musical instruments ⌞prescribed by⌟ David the man of God. Ezra the scribe led the procession. ³⁷At the Fountain Gate they continued directly up the steps of the City of David on the ascent to the wall and passed above the house of David to the Water Gate on the east.

³⁸The second choir proceeded in the opposite direction. I followed them on top ᶜ of the wall, together with half the people—past the Tower of the Ovens to the Broad Wall, ³⁹over the Gate of Ephraim, the Jeshanah ᵈ Gate, the Fish Gate, the Tower of Hananel and the Tower of the Hundred, as far as the Sheep Gate. At the Gate of the Guard they stopped.

⁴⁰The two choirs that gave thanks then took their places in the house of God; so did I, together with half the officials, ⁴¹as well as the priests—Eliakim, Maaseiah, Miniamin, Micaiah, Elioenai, Zechariah and Hananiah with their trumpets— ⁴²and also Maaseiah, Shemaiah, Eleazar, Uzzi, Jehohanan, Malkijah, Elam and Ezer. The choirs sang under the direction of Jezrahiah. ⁴³And on that day they offered great sacrifices, rejoicing because God had given them great joy. The women and children also rejoiced. The sound of rejoicing in Jerusalem could be heard far away.

⁴⁴At that time men were appointed to be in charge of the storerooms for the contributions, firstfruits and tithes. From the fields around the towns they were to bring into the storerooms the portions required by the Law for the priests and the Levites, for Judah was pleased with the ministering priests and Levites. ⁴⁵They performed the service of their God and the service of purification, as did also the singers and gatekeepers, according to the commands of David and his son Solomon. ⁴⁶For long ago, in the days of David and Asaph, there had been directors for the singers and for the songs of praise and thanksgiving to God. ⁴⁷So in the days of Zerubbabel and of Nehemiah, all Israel contributed the daily portions for the singers and gatekeepers. They also set aside the portion for the other Levites, and the Levites set aside the portion for the descendants of Aaron.

NEHEMIAH'S FINAL REFORMS

13 On that day the Book of Moses was read aloud in the hearing of the people and there it was found written that no Ammonite or Moabite should ever be admitted into the assembly of God, ²because they had not met the Israelites with food and water but had hired Balaam to call a curse down on them. (Our God, however, turned the curse into a blessing.) ³When the people heard this law, they excluded from Israel all who were of foreign descent.

⁴Before this, Eliashib the priest had been put in charge of the storerooms of the house of our God. He was closely associated with Tobiah, ⁵and he had provided him with a large room formerly used to store the grain offerings and incense and temple articles, and also the tithes of grain, new wine and oil prescribed for the Levites, singers and gatekeepers, as well as the contributions for the priests.

⁶But while all this was going on, I was not in Jerusalem, for in the thirty-second year of Artaxerxes king of Babylon I had returned to the king. Some time later I asked his permission ⁷and came back to

ᵃ *31* Or *go alongside*　　ᵇ *31* Or *proceed alongside*　　ᶜ *38* Or *them alongside*　　ᵈ *39* Or *Old*

Jerusalem. Here I learned about the evil thing Eliashib had done in providing Tobiah a room in the courts of the house of God. ⁸I was greatly displeased and threw all Tobiah's household goods out of the room. ⁹I gave orders to purify the rooms, and then I put back into them the equipment of the house of God, with the grain offerings and the incense.

NOW OR NEVER

NE 13:4–22

There's no such thing as a secret sin in God's eyes. He sees everything that happens and, sooner or later, he will expose the things we do in private. That's why it's so much better to deal with sin immediately.

¹⁰I also learned that the portions assigned to the Levites had not been given to them, and that all the Levites and singers responsible for the service had gone back to their own fields. ¹¹So I rebuked the officials and asked them, "Why is the house of God neglected?" Then I called them together and stationed them at their posts.

¹²All Judah brought the tithes of grain, new wine and oil into the storerooms. ¹³I put Shelemiah the priest, Zadok the scribe, and a Levite named Pedaiah in charge of the storerooms and made Hanan son of Zaccur, the son of Mattaniah, their assistant, because these men were considered trustworthy. They were made responsible for distributing the supplies to their brothers.

¹⁴Remember me for this, O my God, and do not blot out what I have so faithfully done for the house of my God and its services.

¹⁵In those days I saw men in Judah treading winepresses on the Sabbath and bringing in grain and loading it on donkeys, together with wine, grapes, figs and all other kinds of loads. And they were bringing all this into Jerusalem on the Sabbath. Therefore I warned them against selling food on that day. ¹⁶Men from Tyre who lived in Jerusalem were bringing in fish and all kinds of merchandise and selling them in Jerusalem on the Sabbath to the people of Judah. ¹⁷I rebuked the nobles of Judah and said to them, "What is this wicked thing you are doing—desecrating the Sabbath day? ¹⁸Didn't your forefathers do the same things, so that our God brought all this calamity upon us and upon this city? Now you are stirring up more wrath against Israel by desecrating the Sabbath."

¹⁹When evening shadows fell on the gates of Jerusalem before the Sabbath, I ordered the doors to be shut and not opened until the Sabbath was over. I stationed some of my own men at the gates so that no load could be brought in on the Sabbath day. ²⁰Once or twice the merchants and sellers of all kinds of goods spent the night outside Jerusalem. ²¹But I warned them and said, "Why do you spend the night by the wall? If you do this again, I will lay hands on you." From that time on they no longer came on the Sabbath. ²²Then I commanded the Levites to purify themselves and go and guard the gates in order to keep the Sabbath day holy.

Remember me for this also, O my God, and show mercy to me according to your great love.

²³Moreover, in those days I saw men of Judah who had married women from Ashdod, Ammon and Moab. ²⁴Half of their children spoke the language of Ashdod or the language of one of the other peoples, and did not know how to speak the language of Judah. ²⁵I rebuked them and called curses down on them. I beat some of the men and pulled out their hair. I made them take an oath in God's name and said: "You are not to give

Developing Trust

If you've ever had a girlfriend who cheated on you, parents who split up or a friend who betrayed you, then you know how painful it feels to have your trust broken. If you lose faith in someone, it makes it very difficult to have any kind of relationship with that person. That's bad news in dating relationships, friendships, even families—but it's absolutely detrimental to Christian fellowship. If you can't trust your Christian friends or if they can't trust you, you're going to have a hard time working together and developing community the way God expects. Can you be trusted?

»» live the adventure »» Ne 13:13

your daughters in marriage to their sons, nor are you to take their daughters in marriage for your sons or for yourselves. 26Was it not because of marriages like these that Solomon king of Israel sinned? Among the many nations there was no king like him. He was loved by his God, and God made him king over all Israel, but even he was led into sin by foreign women. 27Must we hear now that you too are doing all this terrible wickedness and are being unfaithful to our God by marrying foreign women?"

28One of the sons of Joiada son of Eliashib the high priest was son-in-law to Sanballat the Horonite. And I drove him away from me.

29Remember them, O my God, because they defiled the priestly office and the covenant of the priesthood and of the Levites.

30So I purified the priests and the Levites of everything foreign, and assigned them duties, each to his own task. 31I also made provision for contributions of wood at designated times, and for the firstfruits.

Remember me with favor, O my God.

ESTHER

Author
Unknown

Audience
Jews who were not living in Israel

Date
About 470 B.C.

Setting
These Jews were living under the rule of Gentiles in Susa, the capital of the Persian Empire.

Verse to Remember
"For if you remain silent at this time, relief and deliverance for the Jews will arise from another place, but you and your father's family will perish. And who knows but that you have come to royal position for such a time as this?" (4:14).

Theme to Consider
God uses ordinary people (like Esther and us!) to accomplish extraordinary things for his purposes.

UNCHANGING TRUTH » You've heard people talk about being in the right place at the right time. The thing is, though, if you're serious about seeking and fulfilling God's will for your life, you're *always* going to be in the right place at just the right time.

You see, there's no such thing as a coincidence when God is at work. Things don't *just happen*; they happen because God wants them to happen. He puts certain people in certain situations at certain times for a specific reason.

Take Esther's selection as queen, for example (see 2:1–18). King Xerxes may have thought the choice was his, but it wasn't; it was really God's. By making Esther queen, God put her in a key position to stop Haman's plan to destroy the Jews (see 4:14). When you look back at the story now, you can clearly see the perfection of God's timing and his plan for Esther. God put her in the right place at the right time to deliver his people and display his power.

So why has God put you where you are? That's the million-dollar question. Why has he surrounded you with the people in your peer group? Why has he given you the talents and abilities you possess? Why has he opened certain doors in your life?

You probably aren't able to see God's plan for you in its entirety right now, but be assured that he has one. And if you seek his guidance and follow him obediently, you'll be able to look back one day and see the perfection of his plan for your life.

LIFE LESSONS »

1. God often works behind the scenes, putting his people right where he wants them in order to accomplish his purpose (4:14).

2. Always be prepared to use whatever power and influence God gives you to help people in need, no matter what the risk (4:16).

3. Sooner or later, evil people reap what they sow (7:10).

QUEEN VASHTI DEPOSED

1 This is what happened during the time of Xerxes,[a] the Xerxes who ruled over 127 provinces stretching from India to Cush[b]: [2]At that time King Xerxes reigned from his royal throne in the citadel of Susa, [3]and in the third year of his reign he gave a banquet for all his nobles and officials. The military leaders of Persia and Media, the princes, and the nobles of the provinces were present.

[4]For a full 180 days he displayed the vast wealth of his kingdom and the splendor and glory of his majesty. [5]When these days were over, the king gave a banquet, lasting seven days, in the enclosed garden of the king's palace, for all the people from the least to the greatest, who were in the citadel of Susa. [6]The garden had hangings of white and blue linen, fastened with cords of white linen and purple material to silver rings on marble pillars. There were couches of gold and silver on a mosaic pavement of porphyry, marble, mother-of-pearl and other costly stones. [7]Wine was served in goblets of gold, each one different from the other, and the royal wine was abundant, in keeping with the king's liberality. [8]By the king's command each guest was allowed to drink in his own way, for the king instructed all the wine stewards to serve each man what he wished.

[9]Queen Vashti also gave a banquet for the women in the royal palace of King Xerxes.

[10]On the seventh day, when King Xerxes was in high spirits from wine, he commanded the seven eunuchs who served him—Mehuman, Biztha, Harbona, Bigtha, Abagtha, Zethar and Carcas— [11]to bring before him Queen Vashti, wearing her royal crown, in order to display her beauty to the people and nobles, for she was lovely to look at. [12]But when the attendants delivered the king's command, Queen Vashti refused to come. Then the king became furious and burned with anger.

[13]Since it was customary for the king to consult experts in matters of law and justice, he spoke with the wise men who understood the times [14]and were closest to the king—Carshena, Shethar, Admatha, Tarshish, Meres, Marsena and Memucan, the seven nobles of Persia and Media who had special access to the king and were highest in the kingdom.

[15]"According to law, what must be done to Queen Vashti?" he asked. "She has not obeyed the command of King Xerxes that the eunuchs have taken to her."

[16]Then Memucan replied in the presence of the king and the nobles, "Queen Vashti has done wrong, not only against the king but also against all the nobles and the peoples of all the provinces of King Xerxes. [17]For the queen's conduct will become known to all the women, and so they will despise their husbands and say, 'King Xerxes commanded Queen Vashti to be brought before him, but she would not come.' [18]This very day the Persian and Median women of the nobility who have heard about the queen's conduct will respond to all the king's nobles in the same way. There will be no end of disrespect and discord.

[19]"Therefore, if it pleases the king, let him issue a royal decree and let it be written in the laws of Persia and Media, which cannot be repealed, that Vashti is never again to enter the presence of King Xerxes. Also let the king give her royal position to someone else who is better than she. [20]Then when the king's edict is proclaimed throughout all his vast realm, all the women will respect their husbands, from the least to the greatest."

[21]The king and his nobles were pleased with this advice, so the king did as Memucan proposed. [22]He sent dispatches to all parts of the kingdom, to each province in its own script and to each people in its own language, proclaiming in each people's tongue that every man should be ruler over his own household.

ESTHER MADE QUEEN

2 Later when the anger of King Xerxes had subsided, he remembered Vashti and what she had done and what he had decreed about her. [2]Then the king's personal attendants proposed, "Let a search be made for beautiful young virgins for the king. [3]Let the king appoint commissioners in every province of his realm to bring all these beautiful girls into the harem at the citadel of Susa. Let them be placed under the care of Hegai, the king's eunuch, who is in charge of the women; and let beauty treatments be given to them. [4]Then let the girl who pleases the king be queen instead of Vashti." This advice appealed to the king, and he followed it.

[5]Now there was in the citadel of Susa a Jew of the tribe of Benjamin, named Mordecai son of Jair, the son of Shimei, the son of Kish, [6]who had been carried into exile from Jerusalem by Nebuchadnezzar king of Babylon, among those taken captive with Jehoiachin[c] king of Judah. [7]Mordecai had a cous-

---

[a] 1 Hebrew *Ahasuerus*, a variant of Xerxes' Persian name; here and throughout Esther   [b] 1 That is, the upper Nile region   [c] 6 Hebrew *Jeconiah*, a variant of *Jehoiachin*

in named Hadassah, whom he had brought up because she had neither father nor mother. This girl, who was also known as Esther, was lovely in form and features, and Mordecai had taken her as his own daughter when her father and mother died.

8When the king's order and edict had been proclaimed, many girls were brought to the citadel of Susa and put under the care of Hegai. Esther also was taken to the king's palace and entrusted to Hegai, who had charge of the harem. 9The girl pleased him and won his favor. Immediately he provided her with her beauty treatments and special food. He assigned to her seven maids selected from the king's palace and moved her and her maids into the best place in the harem.

10Esther had not revealed her nationality and family background, because Mordecai had forbidden her to do so. 11Every day he walked back and forth near the courtyard of the harem to find out how Esther was and what was happening to her.

12Before a girl's turn came to go in to King Xerxes, she had to complete twelve months of beauty treatments prescribed for the women, six months with oil of myrrh and six with perfumes and cosmetics. 13And this is how she would go to the king: Anything she wanted was given her to take with her from the harem to the king's palace. 14In the evening she would go there and in the morning return to another part of the harem to the care of Shaashgaz, the king's eunuch who was in charge of the concubines. She would not return to the king unless he was pleased with her and summoned her by name.

15When the turn came for Esther (the girl Mordecai had adopted, the daughter of his uncle Abihail) to go to the king, she asked for nothing other than what Hegai, the king's eunuch who was in charge of the harem, suggested. And Esther won the favor of everyone who saw her. 16She was taken to King Xerxes in the royal residence in the tenth month, the month of Tebeth, in the seventh year of his reign.

17Now the king was attracted to Esther more than to any of the other women, and she won his favor and approval more than any of the other virgins. So he set a royal crown on her head and made her queen instead of Vashti. 18And the king gave a great banquet, Esther's banquet, for all his nobles and officials. He proclaimed a holiday throughout the provinces and distributed gifts with royal liberality.

MORDECAI UNCOVERS A CONSPIRACY

19When the virgins were assembled a second time, Mordecai was sitting at the king's gate. 20But Esther had kept secret her family background and nationality just as Mordecai had told her to do, for she continued to follow Mordecai's instructions as she had done when he was bringing her up.

21During the time Mordecai was sitting at the king's gate, Bigthana[a] and Teresh, two of the king's officers who guarded the doorway, became angry and conspired to assassinate King Xerxes. 22But Mordecai found out about the plot and told Queen Esther, who in turn reported it to the king, giving credit to Mordecai. 23And when the report was investigated and found to be true, the two officials were hanged on a gallows.[b] All this was recorded in the book of the annals in the presence of the king.

HAMAN'S PLOT TO DESTROY THE JEWS

3 After these events, King Xerxes honored Haman son of Hammedatha, the Agagite, elevating him and giving him a seat of honor higher than that of all the other nobles. 2All the royal officials at the king's gate knelt down and paid honor to Haman, for the king had commanded this concerning him. But Mordecai would not kneel down or pay him honor.

»» live the adventure »» Est 2:19-23

Speaking Up

If you know of someone being picked on or plotted against and you do nothing about it, you're an accomplice to the crime. Bullies and people who make life miserable for others rarely stop the abuse on their own. They have to be stopped . . . by someone like you. We're not talking about becoming a thug or a vigilante, policing the streets for jerks and bullies; we're talking about exposing the things you know are going on and speaking up about them, instead of averting your eyes and pretending not to notice.

---

a 21 Hebrew *Bigthan*, a variant of *Bigthana*   b 23 Or *were hung* (or *impaled*) *on poles*; similarly elsewhere in Esther

³Then the royal officials at the king's gate asked Mordecai, "Why do you disobey the king's command?" ⁴Day after day they spoke to him but he refused to comply. Therefore they told Haman about it to see whether Mordecai's behavior would be tolerated, for he had told them he was a Jew.

⁵When Haman saw that Mordecai would not kneel down or pay him honor, he was enraged. ⁶Yet having learned who Mordecai's people were, he scorned the idea of killing only Mordecai. Instead Haman looked for a way to destroy all Mordecai's people, the Jews, throughout the whole kingdom of Xerxes.

⁷In the twelfth year of King Xerxes, in the first month, the month of Nisan, they cast the *pur* (that is, the lot) in the presence of Haman to select a day and month. And the lot fell onª the twelfth month, the month of Adar.

⁸Then Haman said to King Xerxes, "There is a certain people dispersed and scattered among the peoples in all the provinces of your kingdom whose customs are different from those of all other peoples and who do not obey the king's laws; it is not in the king's best interest to tolerate them. ⁹If it pleases the king, let a decree be issued to destroy them, and I will put ten thousand talentsᵇ of silver into the royal treasury for the men who carry out this business."

¹⁰So the king took his signet ring from his finger and gave it to Haman son of Hammedatha, the Agagite, the enemy of the Jews. ¹¹"Keep the money," the king said to Haman, "and do with the people as you please."

¹²Then on the thirteenth day of the first month the royal secretaries were summoned. They wrote out in the script of each province and in the language of each people all Haman's orders to the king's satraps, the governors of the various provinces and the nobles of the various peoples. These were written in the name of King Xerxes himself and sealed with his own ring. ¹³Dispatches were sent by couriers to all the king's provinces with the order to destroy, kill and annihilate all the Jews—young and old, women and little children—on a single day, the thirteenth day of the twelfth month, the month of Adar, and to plunder their goods. ¹⁴A copy of the text of the edict was to be issued as law in every province and made known to the people of every nationality so they would be ready for that day.

¹⁵Spurred on by the king's command, the couriers went out, and the edict was issued in the citadel of Susa. The king and Haman sat down to drink, but the city of Susa was bewildered.

NOW OR NEVER

EST 3:14

Don't follow any law, rule, command or instruction that requires you to disobey God's Word. Instead, respectfully explain why you can't go along with it and be prepared for whatever comes as a result of your faithfulness to God.

MORDECAI PERSUADES ESTHER TO HELP

4 When Mordecai learned of all that had been done, he tore his clothes, put on sackcloth and ashes, and went out into the city, wailing loudly and bitterly. ²But he went only as far as the king's gate, because no one clothed in sackcloth was allowed to enter it. ³In every province to which the edict and order of the king came, there was great mourning among the Jews, with fasting, weeping and wailing. Many lay in sackcloth and ashes.

⁴When Esther's maids and eunuchs came and told her about Mordecai, she was in great distress. She sent clothes for him to put on instead of his sackcloth, but he would not accept them. ⁵Then Esther summoned Hathach, one of the king's eunuchs assigned to attend her, and ordered him to find out what was troubling Mordecai and why.

⁶So Hathach went out to Mordecai in the open square of the city in front of the king's gate. ⁷Mordecai told him everything that had happened to him, including the exact amount of money Haman had promised to pay into the royal treasury for the destruction of the Jews. ⁸He also gave him a copy of the text of the edict for their annihilation, which had been published in Susa, to show to Esther and explain it to her, and he told him to urge her to go into the king's presence to beg for mercy and plead with him for her people.

ª *7* Septuagint; Hebrew does not have *And the lot fell on.*   ᵇ *9* That is, about 375 tons (about 345 metric tons)

haman

VERSUS

» Second in command in Persia
» Tried to execute Mordecai and exterminate the rest of the Jews
» Became the victim of his own murderous plan

mordecai

» A Jewish exile living in Persia
» Had a beautiful young cousin named Esther
» Uncovered an assassination plot against King Xerxes

The Main Event

Why hasn't someone in Hollywood made a movie about Haman and Mordecai? It would sure sell some popcorn. It's an awesome story, filled with great characters and all kinds of thrills and surprises.

Get this: Mordecai was living in exile in Persia with his young cousin Esther, who just happened to be drop-dead gorgeous. Through a wild series of events, Esther actually became the queen of Persia. Meanwhile, Mordecai overheard some men plotting to assassinate the king, and he was able to get word to the palace in time to thwart the attack. Thanks to Mordecai's quick work, the king owed him a big favor.

While Mordecai was busy saving the king's life, Haman was basking in his own power and glory. As the second in command in Persia, Haman loved the fact that everyone in the nation bowed to him—everyone except for the king, of course . . . and Mordecai. Mordecai refused to lower himself in Haman's presence. His attitude infuriated Haman so much that the Persian official dreamed up a scheme to get rid of Mordecai. But he didn't stop there. Haman devised a plan to wipe out the entire Jewish population of Persia.

When Mordecai learned of Haman's plan, he met with his cousin, Queen Esther, and convinced her that she was the last, best hope of the Jewish people. The queen swung into action—risking her life to do so—and began appealing to the king for the safety of her people.

About that same time, the king discovered that he had never thanked Mordecai for saving his life. Haman watched in horror as his bitter enemy Mordecai was honored before all the people of the city and eventually given Haman's old job! Not only did King Xerxes (Ahasuerus) come up with a plan to save the Jews from extermination (with a little help from Mordecai), he also sentenced Haman to hang on the very gallows that Haman had built for Mordecai!

Even now, thousands of years later, the Jewish people celebrate the Feast of Purim to commemorate their amazing rescue from genocide at the hands of the evil Haman.

The Outcome

What words could we use to describe Mordecai? Brave . . . bold . . . strong . . . caring . . . unselfish . . . devout . . . honest . . . concerned. Do you think there's a connection between those character qualities and the position of honor he eventually attained?

What words could we use to describe Haman? Bitter . . . proud . . . greedy . . . self-serving . . . ambitious . . . power-hungry . . . vengeful. Do you think there's a connection between those traits and the sad end to his life?

How much Mordecai is in you? How much Haman is in you? What needs to change? What will be your first step?

Read more about Haman and Mordecai in Esther 1:1—10:3 (pages 570–579).

⁹Hathach went back and reported to Esther what Mordecai had said. ¹⁰Then she instructed him to say to Mordecai, ¹¹"All the king's officials and the people of the royal provinces know that for any man or woman who approaches the king in the inner court without being summoned the king has but one law: that he be put to death. The only exception to this is for the king to extend the gold scepter to him and spare his life. But thirty days have passed since I was called to go to the king."

¹²When Esther's words were reported to Mordecai, ¹³he sent back this answer: "Do not think that because you are in the king's house you alone of all the Jews will escape. ¹⁴For if you remain silent at this time, relief and deliverance for the Jews will arise from another place, but you and your father's family will perish. And who knows but that you have come to royal position for such a time as this?"

¹⁵Then Esther sent this reply to Mordecai: ¹⁶"Go, gather together all the Jews who are in Susa, and fast for me. Do not eat or drink for three days, night or day. I and my maids will fast as you do. When this is done, I will go to the king, even though it is against the law. And if I perish, I perish."

¹⁷So Mordecai went away and carried out all of Esther's instructions.

ESTHER'S REQUEST TO THE KING

5 On the third day Esther put on her royal robes and stood in the inner court of the palace, in front of the king's hall. The king was sitting on his royal throne in the hall, facing the entrance. ²When he saw Queen Esther standing in the court, he was pleased with her and held out to her the gold scepter that was in his hand. So Esther approached and touched the tip of the scepter.

³Then the king asked, "What is it, Queen Esther? What is your request? Even up to half the kingdom, it will be given you."

⁴"If it pleases the king," replied Esther, "let the king, together with Haman, come today to a banquet I have prepared for him."

⁵"Bring Haman at once," the king said, "so that we may do what Esther asks."

So the king and Haman went to the banquet Esther had prepared. ⁶As they were drinking wine, the king again asked Esther, "Now what is your petition? It will be given you. And what is your request? Even up to half the kingdom, it will be granted."

⁷Esther replied, "My petition and my request is this: ⁸If the king regards me with favor and if it pleases the king to grant my petition and fulfill my request, let the king and Haman come tomorrow to the banquet I will prepare for them. Then I will answer the king's question."

HAMAN'S RAGE AGAINST MORDECAI

⁹Haman went out that day happy and in high spirits. But when he saw Mordecai at the king's gate and observed that he neither rose nor showed fear in his presence, he was filled with rage against Mordecai. ¹⁰Nevertheless, Haman restrained himself and went home.

Calling together his friends and Zeresh, his wife, ¹¹Haman boasted to them about his vast wealth, his many sons, and all the ways the king had honored him and how he had elevated him above the other nobles and officials. ¹²"And that's not all," Haman added. "I'm the only person Queen Esther invited to accompany the king to the banquet she gave. And she has invited me along with the king tomorrow. ¹³But all this gives me no satisfaction as long as I see that Jew Mordecai sitting at the king's gate."

¹⁴His wife Zeresh and all his friends said to him, "Have a gallows built, seventy-five feet[a] high, and ask the king in the morning to have Mordecai hanged on it. Then go with the king to the dinner and be happy." This suggestion delighted Haman, and he had the gallows built.

NOW OR NEVER
EST 5:9–10

Every person deserves your respect; however, only God deserves your reverence. Never forget that even the most powerful or intimidating person you meet is still just a person, with his or her own set of flaws and weaknesses—whether you see them or not.

ᵃ 14 Hebrew *fifty cubits* (about 23 meters)

battlelines

» Outlook on Life (Attitude)

Q: On a scale of one to ten, with one being "not at all" and ten being "totally," how would you rate yourself when it comes to being negative about life?
A: Hmmm. I guess about a six and a half—maybe a seven.

Q: So you're pretty cynical?
A: Well, my *parents* say I am. They're always asking, "Why do you have to be so sarcastic? You and your friends are always making fun of people! You're always criticizing everything. Why can't you be more positive?"

Q: Do you think they're right?
A: I don't know. Maybe.

Q: Why do you think you do it?
A: It's just a habit, I guess. If I see something, I just go off on it. Like, if a person is *really* into something, then it becomes like a challenge to point out how stupid and lame it really is.

Q: Do you think your negativity ever gets out of hand?
A: Maybe I go too far sometimes—making fun of stuff, acting like everything is stupid, ripping on people for the way they dress or for stuff they like or the things they say. It always seems like the bigger the crowd, the worse it gets. It's like each person has to say or do something to top what somebody else said.

Q: Do you see that kind of message anywhere else?
A: Oh, yeah. The funniest guys on TV are the ones who'll say just about anything. They're the ones who slam everybody and make a joke out of everything. Those are the guys that make me laugh.

» Checking Your Attitude

There's nothing wrong with being funny. Even the occasional dose of sarcasm can help get a good point across. But how much is too much? Try this experiment. The next time you're with your friends, sit back and listen to the conversation. Don't say anything—just observe. Try counting the number of negative, cutting or sarcastic comments you hear in ten minutes.

Rather than going along with our ultra-cynical culture and thinking up new ways to put other people down, the Bible instructs us to figure out ways to encourage others: "And let us consider how we may spur one another on toward love and good deeds" (Hebrews 10:24).

Go to www.RevolutionBible.com for more.

MORDECAI HONORED

6 That night the king could not sleep; so he ordered the book of the chronicles, the record of his reign, to be brought in and read to him. ²It was found recorded there that Mordecai had exposed Bigthana and Teresh, two of the king's officers who guarded the doorway, who had conspired to assassinate King Xerxes.

³"What honor and recognition has Mordecai received for this?" the king asked.

"Nothing has been done for him," his attendants answered.

⁴The king said, "Who is in the court?" Now Haman had just entered the outer court of the palace to speak to the king about hanging Mordecai on the gallows he had erected for him.

⁵His attendants answered, "Haman is standing in the court."

"Bring him in," the king ordered.

⁶When Haman entered, the king asked him, "What should be done for the man the king delights to honor?"

Now Haman thought to himself, "Who is there that the king would rather honor than me?" ⁷So he answered the king, "For the man the king delights to honor, ⁸have them bring a royal robe the king has worn and a horse the king has ridden, one with a royal crest placed on its head. ⁹Then let the robe and horse be entrusted to one of the king's most noble princes. Let them robe the man the king delights to honor, and lead him on the horse through the city streets, proclaiming before him, 'This is what is done for the man the king delights to honor!' "

¹⁰"Go at once," the king commanded Haman. "Get the robe and the horse and do just as you have suggested for Mordecai the Jew, who sits at the king's gate. Do not neglect anything you have recommended."

¹¹So Haman got the robe and the horse. He robed Mordecai, and led him on horseback through the city streets, proclaiming before him, "This is what is done for the man the king delights to honor!"

¹²Afterward Mordecai returned to the king's gate. But Haman rushed home, with his head covered in grief, ¹³and told Zeresh his wife and all his friends everything that had happened to him.

His advisers and his wife Zeresh said to him, "Since Mordecai, before whom your downfall has started, is of Jewish origin, you cannot stand against him—you will surely come to ruin!" ¹⁴While they were still talking with him, the king's eunuchs arrived and hurried Haman away to the banquet Esther had prepared.

HAMAN HANGED

7 So the king and Haman went to dine with Queen Esther, ²and as they were drinking wine on that second day, the king again asked, "Queen Esther, what is your petition? It will be given you. What is your request? Even up to half the kingdom, it will be granted."

³Then Queen Esther answered, "If I have found favor with you, O king, and if it pleases your majesty, grant me my life—this is my petition. And spare my people—this is my request. ⁴For I and my people have been sold for destruction and slaughter and annihilation. If we had merely been sold as male and female slaves, I would have kept quiet, because no such distress would justify disturbing the king.ᵃ"

⁵King Xerxes asked Queen Esther, "Who is he? Where is the man who has dared to do such a thing?"

⁶Esther said, "The adversary and enemy is this vile Haman."

Then Haman was terrified before the king and queen. ⁷The king got up in a rage, left his wine and went out into the palace garden. But Haman, realizing that the king had already decided his fate, stayed behind to beg Queen Esther for his life.

⁸Just as the king returned from the palace garden to the banquet hall, Haman was falling on the couch where Esther was reclining.

The king exclaimed, "Will he even molest the queen while she is with me in the house?"

As soon as the word left the king's mouth, they covered Haman's face. ⁹Then Harbona, one of the eunuchs attending the king, said, "A gallows seventy-five feetᵇ high stands by Haman's house. He had it made for Mordecai, who spoke up to help the king."

ᵃ *4 Or quiet, but the compensation our adversary offers cannot be compared with the loss the king would suffer*   ᵇ *9 Hebrew fifty cubits* (about 23 meters)

The king said, "Hang him on it!" [10]So they hanged Haman on the gallows he had prepared for Mordecai. Then the king's fury subsided.

Dealing With Poisonous Emotions

Pride, jealousy and lust for power are like cancer. Unless you do something about them, they will continue to spread, doing more and more damage until they ultimately destroy you, just as they did Haman. If you're struggling with these feelings, talk to God about them. Ask him to help you calm your emotions and get your head straight so that you don't do anything you'll regret later.

THE KING'S EDICT IN BEHALF OF THE JEWS

8 That same day King Xerxes gave Queen Esther the estate of Haman, the enemy of the Jews. And Mordecai came into the presence of the king, for Esther had told how he was related to her. [2]The king took off his signet ring, which he had reclaimed from Haman, and presented it to Mordecai. And Esther appointed him over Haman's estate.

[3]Esther again pleaded with the king, falling at his feet and weeping. She begged him to put an end to the evil plan of Haman the Agagite, which he had devised against the Jews. [4]Then the king extended the gold scepter to Esther and she arose and stood before him.

[5]"If it pleases the king," she said, "and if he regards me with favor and thinks it the right thing to do, and if he is pleased with me, let an order be written overruling the dispatches that Haman son of Hammedatha, the Agagite, devised and wrote to destroy the Jews in all the king's provinces. [6]For how can I bear to see disaster fall on my people? How can I bear to see the destruction of my family?"

[7]King Xerxes replied to Queen Esther and to Mordecai the Jew, "Because Haman attacked the Jews, I have given his estate to Esther, and they have hanged him on the gallows. [8]Now write another decree in the king's name in behalf of the Jews as seems best to you, and seal it with the king's signet ring—for no document written in the king's name and sealed with his ring can be revoked."

[9]At once the royal secretaries were summoned—on the twenty-third day of the third month, the month of Sivan. They wrote out all Mordecai's orders to the Jews, and to the satraps, governors and nobles of the 127 provinces stretching from India to Cush.[a] These orders were written in the script of each province and the language of each people and also to the Jews in their own script and language. [10]Mordecai wrote in the name of King Xerxes, sealed the dispatches with the king's signet ring, and sent them by mounted couriers, who rode fast horses especially bred for the king.

[11]The king's edict granted the Jews in every city the right to assemble and protect themselves; to destroy, kill and annihilate any armed force of any nationality or province that might attack them and their women and children; and to plunder the property of their enemies. [12]The day appointed for the Jews to do this in all the provinces of King Xerxes was the thirteenth day of the twelfth month, the month of Adar. [13]A copy of the text of the edict was to be issued as law in every province and made known to the people of every nationality so that the Jews would be ready on that day to avenge themselves on their enemies.

[14]The couriers, riding the royal horses, raced out, spurred on by the king's command. And the edict was also issued in the citadel of Susa.

EST 8:7

challenge notes

To: my_son

heavenly_father: it takes courage to speak out against evil, and sometimes doing so can put you in physical danger. remember, though, the greater the risk, the greater the reward. not only will I be with you in everything you face, I will empower you to accomplish incredible things for me.

[a] *9* That is, the upper Nile region

¹⁵Mordecai left the king's presence wearing royal garments of blue and white, a large crown of gold and a purple robe of fine linen. And the city of Susa held a joyous celebration. ¹⁶For the Jews it was a time of happiness and joy, gladness and honor. ¹⁷In every province and in every city, wherever the edict of the king went, there was joy and gladness among the Jews, with feasting and celebrating. And many people of other nationalities became Jews because fear of the Jews had seized them.

TRIUMPH OF THE JEWS

9 On the thirteenth day of the twelfth month, the month of Adar, the edict commanded by the king was to be carried out. On this day the enemies of the Jews had hoped to overpower them, but now the tables were turned and the Jews got the upper hand over those who hated them. ²The Jews assembled in their cities in all the provinces of King Xerxes to attack those seeking their destruction. No one could stand against them, because the people of all the other nationalities were afraid of them. ³And all the nobles of the provinces, the satraps, the governors and the king's administrators helped the Jews, because fear of Mordecai had seized them. ⁴Mordecai was prominent in the palace; his reputation spread throughout the provinces, and he became more and more powerful.

⁵The Jews struck down all their enemies with the sword, killing and destroying them, and they did what they pleased to those who hated them. ⁶In the citadel of Susa, the Jews killed and destroyed five hundred men. ⁷They also killed Parshandatha, Dalphon, Aspatha, ⁸Poratha, Adalia, Aridatha, ⁹Parmashta, Arisai, Aridai and Vaizatha, ¹⁰the ten sons of Haman son of Hammedatha, the enemy of the Jews. But they did not lay their hands on the plunder.

¹¹The number of those slain in the citadel of Susa was reported to the king that same day. ¹²The king said to Queen Esther, "The Jews have killed and destroyed five hundred men and the ten sons of Haman in the citadel of Susa. What have they done in the rest of the king's provinces? Now what is your petition? It will be given you. What is your request? It will also be granted."

¹³"If it pleases the king," Esther answered, "give the Jews in Susa permission to carry out this day's edict tomorrow also, and let Haman's ten sons be hanged on gallows."

¹⁴So the king commanded that this be done. An edict was issued in Susa, and they hanged the ten sons of Haman. ¹⁵The Jews in Susa came together on the fourteenth day of the month of Adar, and they put to death in Susa three hundred men, but they did not lay their hands on the plunder.

¹⁶Meanwhile, the remainder of the Jews who were in the king's provinces also assembled to protect themselves and get relief from their enemies. They killed seventy-five thousand of them but did not lay their hands on the plunder. ¹⁷This happened on the thirteenth day of the month of Adar, and on the fourteenth they rested and made it a day of feasting and joy.

PURIM CELEBRATED

¹⁸The Jews in Susa, however, had assembled on the thirteenth and fourteenth, and then on the fifteenth they rested and made it a day of feasting and joy.

¹⁹That is why rural Jews—those living in villages—observe the fourteenth of the month of Adar as a day of joy and feasting, a day for giving presents to each other.

²⁰Mordecai recorded these events, and he sent letters to all the Jews throughout the provinces of King Xerxes, near and far, ²¹to have them celebrate annually the fourteenth and fifteenth days of the month of Adar ²²as the time when the Jews got relief from their enemies, and as the month when their sorrow was turned into joy and their mourning into a day of celebration. He wrote them to observe the days as days of feasting and joy and giving presents of food to one another and gifts to the poor.

²³So the Jews agreed to continue the celebration they had begun, doing what Mordecai had written to them. ²⁴For Haman son of Hammedatha, the Agagite, the enemy of all the Jews, had plotted against the Jews to destroy them and had cast the *pur* (that is, the lot) for their ruin and destruction. ²⁵But when the plot came to the king's atten-

NOW OR NEVER
EST 9:20-22

When you read the Bible, be sure to share with someone your amazement at what you read. God still enjoys being praised for his miraculous works—even works he did long ago.

tion,[a] he issued written orders that the evil scheme Haman had devised against the Jews should come back onto his own head, and that he and his sons should be hanged on the gallows. 26(Therefore these days were called Purim, from the word *pur*.) Because of everything written in this letter and because of what they had seen and what had happened to them, 27the Jews took it upon themselves to establish the custom that they and their descendants and all who join them should without fail observe these two days every year, in the way prescribed and at the time appointed. 28These days should be remembered and observed in every generation by every family, and in every province and in every city. And these days of Purim should never cease to be celebrated by the Jews, nor should the memory of them die out among their descendants.

29So Queen Esther, daughter of Abihail, along with Mordecai the Jew, wrote with full authority to confirm this second letter concerning Purim. 30And Mordecai sent letters to all the Jews in the 127 provinces of the kingdom of Xerxes—words of goodwill and assurance— 31to establish these days of Purim at their designated times, as Mordecai the Jew and Queen Esther had decreed for them, and as they had established for themselves and their descendants in regard to their times of fasting and lamentation. 32Esther's decree confirmed these regulations about Purim, and it was written down in the records.

THE GREATNESS OF MORDECAI

10

King Xerxes imposed tribute throughout the empire, to its distant shores. 2And all his acts of power and might, together with a full account of the greatness of Mordecai to which the king had raised him, are they not written in the book of the annals of the kings of Media and Persia? 3Mordecai the Jew was second in rank to King Xerxes, preeminent among the Jews, and held in high esteem by his many fellow Jews, because he worked for the good of his people and spoke up for the welfare of all the Jews.

NOW OR NEVER
EST 10:3

Living in a way that pleases God shows character, and character commands respect. Even if some people make fun of the way you live, the only affirmation that really matters comes from a powerful and perfect God.

---

a 25 Or *when Esther came before the king*

JOB

Author
Unknown

Audience
People of Israel

Date
Unknown

Setting
Job lived in the land of Uz, an area of Edom, southeast of the Dead Sea.

Verse to Remember
"Though he slay me, yet will I hope in him; I will surely defend my ways to his face" (13:15).

Theme to Consider
We may never understand why there is suffering in our world, but we can learn the lesson Job learned: Even during tough circumstances, we can trust God because he is in complete control.

UNCHANGING TRUTH » Why does God allow good people to suffer? For that matter, why does he allow bad things to happen at all?

How many times have you asked yourself, your parents, your Sunday school teacher or your youth leader questions like these? Have you ever been given an answer that made sense to you?

Believe it or not, things happen for a reason. That includes the suffering we experience during our lives. Like Job, you may not always know the reason or purpose for your pain. But even if you did know, would it really help? The problem is that when you're in the middle of hard times, knowing the reason probably won't offer as much comfort as you think.

What *can* give you comfort—if you accept it—is God's promise to never abandon you. You may have to endure some pretty rough stuff in your life (if you haven't already), but you'll never have to endure any of it alone. You'll also never have to rely on your own strength to get through it. If you stay in touch with God, he will give you the strength, comfort, support and peace of mind you need to get back on your feet again.

Job was a righteous man, and he suffered. Jesus was perfect, and he suffered. No matter how obedient and faithful you are, you will experience suffering at some point in your life. The question is, who will you turn to when you do?

LIFE LESSONS »

1 Satan attacks us where he thinks we're most vulnerable (1:13–19).

2 Just because you consider a person a friend doesn't mean that he or she will always be supportive or will always give good advice (15:1–6).

3 When you feel as though God is being unfair to you, think about all the incredible things he's done for you in the past (29:1–6).

PROLOGUE

1 In the land of Uz there lived a man whose name was Job. This man was blameless and upright; he feared God and shunned evil. ²He had seven sons and three daughters, ³and he owned seven thousand sheep, three thousand camels, five hundred yoke of oxen and five hundred donkeys, and had a large number of servants. He was the greatest man among all the people of the East.

⁴His sons used to take turns holding feasts in their homes, and they would invite their three sisters to eat and drink with them. ⁵When a period of feasting had run its course, Job would send and have them purified. Early in the morning he would sacrifice a burnt offering for each of them, thinking, "Perhaps my children have sinned and cursed God in their hearts." This was Job's regular custom.

JOB'S FIRST TEST

⁶One day the angels[a] came to present themselves before the LORD, and Satan[b] also came with them. ⁷The LORD said to Satan, "Where have you come from?"

Satan answered the LORD, "From roaming through the earth and going back and forth in it."

⁸Then the LORD said to Satan, "Have you considered my servant Job? There is no one on earth like him; he is blameless and upright, a man who fears God and shuns evil."

⁹"Does Job fear God for nothing?" Satan replied. ¹⁰"Have you not put a hedge around him and his household and everything he has? You have blessed the work of his hands, so that his flocks and herds are spread throughout the land. ¹¹But stretch out your hand and strike everything he has, and he will surely curse you to your face."

¹²The LORD said to Satan, "Very well, then, everything he has is in your hands, but on the man himself do not lay a finger."

Then Satan went out from the presence of the LORD.

¹³One day when Job's sons and daughters were feasting and drinking wine at the oldest brother's house, ¹⁴a messenger came to Job and said, "The oxen were plowing and the donkeys were grazing nearby, ¹⁵and the Sabeans attacked and carried them off. They put the servants to the sword, and I am the only one who has escaped to tell you!"

¹⁶While he was still speaking, another messenger came and said, "The fire of God fell from the sky and burned up the sheep and the servants, and I am the only one who has escaped to tell you!"

¹⁷While he was still speaking, another messenger came and said, "The Chaldeans formed three raiding parties and swept down on your camels and carried them off. They put the servants to the sword, and I am the only one who has escaped to tell you!"

¹⁸While he was still speaking, yet another messenger came and said, "Your sons and daughters were feasting and drinking wine at the oldest brother's house, ¹⁹when suddenly a mighty wind swept in from the desert

---

Considering Your Reputation

How do you think a conversation between God and Satan about *you* might go? If God asked, "Have you considered my servant _____?" how would he describe you? What strengths and positive qualities would he mention? How do you think Satan would reply? What weaknesses or negative qualities would he mention in an attempt to question your devotion to God?

---

challenge notes

To: my_son

heavenly_father: because of his unparalleled integrity and perseverance, job is an inspiration to suffering people everywhere. you can be one too, depending on how you respond to tough times. believe it or not, people are watching you, and they will be impacted—one way or another—by your life.

JOB 1:8

ᵃ 6 Hebrew *the sons of God*   ᵇ 6 *Satan* means *accuser.*

and struck the four corners of the house. It collapsed on them and they are dead, and I am the only one who has escaped to tell you!"

[20]At this, Job got up and tore his robe and shaved his head. Then he fell to the ground in worship [21]and said:

> "Naked I came from my mother's
> womb,
> and naked I will depart. [a]
> The LORD gave and the LORD has taken
> away;
> may the name of the LORD be
> praised."

[22]In all this, Job did not sin by charging God with wrongdoing.

JOB'S SECOND TEST

2 On another day the angels [b] came to present themselves before the LORD, and Satan also came with them to present himself before him. [2]And the LORD said to Satan, "Where have you come from?"

Satan answered the LORD, "From roaming through the earth and going back and forth in it."

[3]Then the LORD said to Satan, "Have you considered my servant Job? There is no one on earth like him; he is blameless and upright, a man who fears God and shuns evil. And he still maintains his integrity, though you incited me against him to ruin him without any reason."

[4]"Skin for skin!" Satan replied. "A man will give all he has for his own life. [5]But stretch out your hand and strike his flesh and bones, and he will surely curse you to your face."

[6]The LORD said to Satan, "Very well, then, he is in your hands; but you must spare his life."

[7]So Satan went out from the presence of the LORD and afflicted Job with painful sores from the soles of his feet to the top of his head. [8]Then Job took a piece of broken pottery and scraped himself with it as he sat among the ashes.

[9]His wife said to him, "Are you still holding on to your integrity? Curse God and die!"

[10]He replied, "You are talking like a foolish [c] woman. Shall we accept good from God, and not trouble?"

In all this, Job did not sin in what he said.

JOB'S THREE FRIENDS

[11]When Job's three friends, Eliphaz the Temanite, Bildad the Shuhite and Zophar the Naamathite, heard about all the troubles that had come upon him, they set out from their homes and met together by agreement to go and sympathize with him and comfort him. [12]When they saw him from a distance, they could hardly recognize him; they began to weep aloud, and they tore their robes and sprinkled dust on their heads. [13]Then they sat on the ground with him for seven days and seven nights. No one said a word to him, because they saw how great his suffering was.

Staying Humble

Notice how Job stayed humble, even when he was suffering. He didn't try to put himself at the center of the tragedy. He didn't turn the whole thing into a pity party for himself. He didn't ask, "How could God do this to *me*?" He said, "I praised God when things were going great in my life, and I'm going to do the same now." That's the kind of attitude that honors and pleases God.

NOW OR NEVER
JOB 2:2-7

What would you think of someone who only wanted to be your friend when things were going well and then dropped you like a bad habit when things got rough?

---

[a] 21 Or *will return there*   [b] 1 Hebrew *the sons of God*   [c] 10 The Hebrew word rendered *foolish* denotes moral deficiency.

3

After this, Job opened his mouth and cursed the day of his birth. [2] He said:

[3] "May the day of my birth perish,
   and the night it was said, 'A boy is born!'
[4] That day—may it turn to darkness;
   may God above not care about it;
   may no light shine upon it.
[5] May darkness and deep shadow[a] claim
      it once more;
   may a cloud settle over it;
   may blackness overwhelm its light.
[6] That night—may thick darkness
      seize it;
   may it not be included among the
      days of the year
   nor be entered in any of the
      months.
[7] May that night be barren;
   may no shout of joy be heard in it.
[8] May those who curse days[b] curse that
      day,
   those who are ready to rouse
      Leviathan.
[9] May its morning stars become dark;
   may it wait for daylight in vain
   and not see the first rays of dawn,
[10] for it did not shut the doors of the womb
      on me
   to hide trouble from my eyes.

[11] "Why did I not perish at birth,
   and die as I came from the womb?
[12] Why were there knees to receive me
   and breasts that I might be nursed?
[13] For now I would be lying down in
      peace;
   I would be asleep and at rest
[14] with kings and counselors of the
      earth,
   who built for themselves places now lying in ruins,
[15] with rulers who had gold,
   who filled their houses with silver.
[16] Or why was I not hidden in the ground like a stillborn child,
   like an infant who never saw the light of day?
[17] There the wicked cease from turmoil,
   and there the weary are at rest.
[18] Captives also enjoy their ease;
   they no longer hear the slave driver's shout.
[19] The small and the great are there,
   and the slave is freed from his master.

[20] "Why is light given to those in misery,
   and life to the bitter of soul,
[21] to those who long for death that does not come,

---

[a] *5* Or *and the shadow of death*   [b] *8* Or *the sea*

who search for it more than for hidden treasure,
22 who are filled with gladness
and rejoice when they reach the grave?
23 Why is life given to a man
whose way is hidden,
whom God has hedged in?
24 For sighing comes to me instead of food;
my groans pour out like water.
25 What I feared has come upon me;
what I dreaded has happened to me.
26 I have no peace, no quietness;
I have no rest, but only turmoil."

ELIPHAZ

4

Then Eliphaz the Temanite replied:

2 "If someone ventures a word with you, will you be impatient?
But who can keep from speaking?
3 Think how you have instructed many,
how you have strengthened feeble hands.
4 Your words have supported those who stumbled;
you have strengthened faltering knees.
5 But now trouble comes to you, and you are discouraged;
it strikes you, and you are dismayed.
6 Should not your piety be your confidence
and your blameless ways your hope?

7 "Consider now: Who, being innocent, has ever perished?
Where were the upright ever destroyed?
8 As I have observed, those who plow evil
and those who sow trouble reap it.
9 At the breath of God they are destroyed;
at the blast of his anger they perish.
10 The lions may roar and growl,
yet the teeth of the great lions are broken.
11 The lion perishes for lack of prey,
and the cubs of the lioness are scattered.

12 "A word was secretly brought to me,
my ears caught a whisper of it.
13 Amid disquieting dreams in the night,
when deep sleep falls on men,
14 fear and trembling seized me
and made all my bones shake.

NOW OR NEVER

JOB 4:6–7

If suffering only happened to "bad" people, it would be a lot easier to understand and accept. But dealing with the fact that good people also suffer requires a lot more faith in God.

15 A spirit glided past my face,
and the hair on my body stood on end.
16 It stopped,
but I could not tell what it was.
A form stood before my eyes,
and I heard a hushed voice:
17 'Can a mortal be more righteous than God?
Can a man be more pure than his Maker?

battlelines

» The Mystery of Unanswered Prayer

Q: I heard the news. I'm so sorry.
A: Yeah . . . I still can't believe she's gone. She was just 14. You know, I prayed and prayed every day that God would heal her. But nothing changed. She died—the same as if I'd never prayed a word. So either God wasn't listening to me for some reason, or prayer just doesn't work.

Q: I don't know. In a way, maybe prayer works no matter what happens.
A: Then how do you explain Becca's death?

Q: I can't. I just know that if I called you on the phone and asked you to do something for me and you refused, I wouldn't say, "The phone doesn't work." Prayer is how we connect with God, but it doesn't mean he always answers our prayers the way we want him to. Believe me, though: He hears what you're asking.
A: Don't try to tell me that God "healed" Becca by taking her to heaven.

Q: It's not what any of us were praying for. And it doesn't make the pain any easier to deal with. But, yeah . . . since Becca was a Christian, she's now healed forever. I understand what you're saying, though. You asked for healing now—here on this earth—and that didn't happen.
A: Exactly. So why didn't God answer *that* prayer? Would that have been too much?

Q: I don't have the answer, Tyrone. I wish things had turned out differently. All I can tell you is that lots of people in the Bible felt ignored or even tricked by God, just like you do now. But instead of turning away from him, they ran *toward* him and told him exactly how they felt.
A: Like who?

Q: Like Job. Like David and the prophets. Ever read the Psalms? Or Jeremiah? Man, talk about honest! Those guys spilled their guts before God. They unloaded their doubts, anger, hurt . . . everything.

» Honest to God

Get this fixed in your head and heart: God *does* answer prayer. Sometimes he gives us what we ask for . . . sometimes he doesn't. The night before being crucified to pay for our sin, Jesus begged the Father for a way out. The Father didn't grant Jesus' request; but he did give his Son the strength he needed to face what was coming (see Luke 22:42–43). So when your cries seem to be falling on deaf ears, don't stop praying.

Also keep in mind that it's always OK to tell God how you're really feeling. (Do you think he doesn't already know what's in your heart?) Consider the shocking prayer that Jeremiah spoke at a particularly low point in his prophetic ministry: "O LORD, you deceived me and I was deceived; you overpowered me and prevailed. I am ridiculed all day long; everyone mocks me" (Jeremiah 20:7). Pretty gutsy, huh?

You can and should tell God *everything* (see Philippians 4:6–7)—not only your concerns, but also your feelings of being "blown off." He will patiently listen to your complaints.

If you're unsure about how to get started, check out these Bible passages for some ideas: Psalm 6:1–10; 13:1–6; Habakkuk 1:2–11; Zechariah 1:11–17; Revelation 6:9–11.

Discover more ways to improve your prayer life at www.RevolutionBible.com.

¹⁸ If God places no trust in his servants,
    if he charges his angels with error,
¹⁹ how much more those who live in houses of clay,
    whose foundations are in the dust,
    who are crushed more readily than a moth!
²⁰ Between dawn and dusk they are broken to pieces;
    unnoticed, they perish forever.
²¹ Are not the cords of their tent pulled up,
    so that they die without wisdom?'ᵃ

5 "Call if you will, but who will answer you?
    To which of the holy ones will you turn?
² Resentment kills a fool,
    and envy slays the simple.
³ I myself have seen a fool taking root,
    but suddenly his house was cursed.
⁴ His children are far from safety,
    crushed in court without a defender.
⁵ The hungry consume his harvest,
    taking it even from among thorns,
    and the thirsty pant after his wealth.
⁶ For hardship does not spring from the soil,
    nor does trouble sprout from the ground.
⁷ Yet man is born to trouble
    as surely as sparks fly upward.

⁸ "But if it were I, I would appeal to God;
    I would lay my cause before him.
⁹ He performs wonders that cannot be fathomed,
    miracles that cannot be counted.
¹⁰ He bestows rain on the earth;
    he sends water upon the countryside.
¹¹ The lowly he sets on high,
    and those who mourn are lifted to safety.
¹² He thwarts the plans of the crafty,
    so that their hands achieve no
        success.
¹³ He catches the wise in their craftiness,
    and the schemes of the wily are
        swept away.
¹⁴ Darkness comes upon them in the
        daytime;
    at noon they grope as in the night.
¹⁵ He saves the needy from the sword in
        their mouth;
    he saves them from the clutches of
        the powerful.
¹⁶ So the poor have hope,
    and injustice shuts its mouth.

NOW OR NEVER

JOB 5:17–18

Always think through the advice you get before you follow it. Sometimes what seems like a good suggestion can end up causing problems rather than solving them.

¹⁷ "Blessed is the man whom God corrects;
    so do not despise the discipline of the Almighty.ᵇ
¹⁸ For he wounds, but he also binds up;
    he injures, but his hands also heal.
¹⁹ From six calamities he will rescue you;

ᵃ *21* Some interpreters end the quotation after verse 17.   ᵇ *17* Hebrew *Shaddai;* here and throughout Job

in seven no harm will befall you.
²⁰ In famine he will ransom you from death,
    and in battle from the stroke of the sword.
²¹ You will be protected from the lash of the tongue,
    and need not fear when destruction comes.
²² You will laugh at destruction and famine,
    and need not fear the beasts of the earth.
²³ For you will have a covenant with the stones of the field,
    and the wild animals will be at peace with you.
²⁴ You will know that your tent is secure;
    you will take stock of your property and find nothing missing.
²⁵ You will know that your children will be many,
    and your descendants like the grass of the earth.
²⁶ You will come to the grave in full vigor,
    like sheaves gathered in season.

²⁷ "We have examined this, and it is true.
    So hear it and apply it to yourself."

JOB 6

Then Job replied:

² "If only my anguish could be weighed
    and all my misery be placed on the scales!
³ It would surely outweigh the sand of the seas—
    no wonder my words have been impetuous.
⁴ The arrows of the Almighty are in me,
    my spirit drinks in their poison;
    God's terrors are marshaled against me.
⁵ Does a wild donkey bray when it has grass,
    or an ox bellow when it has fodder?
⁶ Is tasteless food eaten without salt,
    or is there flavor in the white of an egg[a]?

NOW OR NEVER
JOB 6:1–4

Have you ever wanted to say to God, "That's not fair!"? It's an understandable reaction to suffering, but do you think it's a legitimate complaint to lodge against the Creator of the universe? How do you think he would respond?

⁷ I refuse to touch it;
    such food makes me ill.

⁸ "Oh, that I might have my request,
    that God would grant what I hope for,
⁹ that God would be willing to crush me,
    to let loose his hand and cut me off!
¹⁰ Then I would still have this consolation—
    my joy in unrelenting pain—
    that I had not denied the words of the Holy One.

¹¹ "What strength do I have, that I should still hope?
    What prospects, that I should be patient?
¹² Do I have the strength of stone?
    Is my flesh bronze?
¹³ Do I have any power to help myself,
    now that success has been driven from me?

---

[a] 6 The meaning of the Hebrew for this phrase is uncertain.

¹⁴ "A despairing man should have the devotion of his friends,
   even though he forsakes the fear of the Almighty.
¹⁵ But my brothers are as undependable as intermittent streams,
   as the streams that overflow
¹⁶ when darkened by thawing ice
   and swollen with melting snow,
¹⁷ but that cease to flow in the dry season,
   and in the heat vanish from their channels.
¹⁸ Caravans turn aside from their routes;
   they go up into the wasteland and perish.
¹⁹ The caravans of Tema look for water,
   the traveling merchants of Sheba look in hope.
²⁰ They are distressed, because they had been confident;
   they arrive there, only to be disappointed.
²¹ Now you too have proved to be of no help;
   you see something dreadful and are afraid.
²² Have I ever said, 'Give something on my behalf,
   pay a ransom for me from your wealth,
²³ deliver me from the hand of the enemy,
   ransom me from the clutches of the ruthless'?

²⁴ "Teach me, and I will be quiet;
   show me where I have been wrong.
²⁵ How painful are honest words!
   But what do your arguments prove?
²⁶ Do you mean to correct what I say,
   and treat the words of a despairing man as wind?
²⁷ You would even cast lots for the fatherless
   and barter away your friend.

²⁸ "But now be so kind as to look at me.
   Would I lie to your face?
²⁹ Relent, do not be unjust;
   reconsider, for my integrity is at stake.ᵃ
³⁰ Is there any wickedness on my lips?
   Can my mouth not discern malice?

"Does not man have hard service on earth?
   Are not his days like those of a hired man?
² Like a slave longing for the evening shadows,
   or a hired man waiting eagerly for his wages,
³ so I have been allotted months of futility,
   and nights of misery have been assigned to me.
⁴ When I lie down I think, 'How long before I get up?'
   The night drags on, and I toss till dawn.
⁵ My body is clothed with worms and scabs,
   my skin is broken and festering.

⁶ "My days are swifter than a weaver's shuttle,
   and they come to an end without hope.
⁷ Remember, O God, that my life is but a breath;
   my eyes will never see happiness again.
⁸ The eye that now sees me will see me no longer;
   you will look for me, but I will be no more.
⁹ As a cloud vanishes and is gone,
   so he who goes down to the graveᵇ does not return.

ᵃ *29 Or my righteousness still stands*   ᵇ *9 Hebrew Sheol*

¹⁰ He will never come to his house again;
  his place will know him no more.

¹¹ "Therefore I will not keep silent;
  I will speak out in the anguish of my spirit,
  I will complain in the bitterness of my soul.
¹² Am I the sea, or the monster of the deep,
  that you put me under guard?
¹³ When I think my bed will comfort me
  and my couch will ease my complaint,
¹⁴ even then you frighten me with dreams
  and terrify me with visions,
¹⁵ so that I prefer strangling and death,
  rather than this body of mine.
¹⁶ I despise my life; I would not live forever.
  Let me alone; my days have no meaning.

¹⁷ "What is man that you make so much of him,
  that you give him so much attention,
¹⁸ that you examine him every morning
  and test him every moment?
¹⁹ Will you never look away from me,
  or let me alone even for an instant?
²⁰ If I have sinned, what have I done to you,
  O watcher of men?
  Why have you made me your target?
  Have I become a burden to you?ᵃ
²¹ Why do you not pardon my offenses
  and forgive my sins?
  For I will soon lie down in the dust;
  you will search for me, but I will be no more."

BILDAD

 Then Bildad the Shuhite replied:

² "How long will you say such things?
  Your words are a blustering wind.
³ Does God pervert justice?
  Does the Almighty pervert what is right?
⁴ When your children sinned against him,
  he gave them over to the penalty of their sin.
⁵ But if you will look to God
  and plead with the Almighty,
⁶ if you are pure and upright,
  even now he will rouse himself on your behalf
  and restore you to your rightful place.
⁷ Your beginnings will seem humble,
  so prosperous will your future be.

⁸ "Ask the former generations
  and find out what their fathers learned,
⁹ for we were born only yesterday and know nothing,
  and our days on earth are but a shadow.

ᵃ 20 A few manuscripts of the Masoretic Text, an ancient Hebrew scribal tradition and Septuagint; most manuscripts of the Masoretic Text
I have become a burden to myself.

¹⁰ Will they not instruct you and tell you?
　　Will they not bring forth words from their understanding?
¹¹ Can papyrus grow tall where there is no marsh?
　　Can reeds thrive without water?
¹² While still growing and uncut,
　　they wither more quickly than grass.
¹³ Such is the destiny of all who forget
　　　　God;
　　so perishes the hope of the godless.
¹⁴ What he trusts in is fragile[a];
　　what he relies on is a spider's web.
¹⁵ He leans on his web, but it gives way;
　　he clings to it, but it does not hold.
¹⁶ He is like a well-watered plant in the
　　　　sunshine,
　　spreading its shoots over the
　　　　garden;
¹⁷ it entwines its roots around a pile of
　　　　rocks
　　and looks for a place among the
　　　　stones.
¹⁸ But when it is torn from its spot,
　　that place disowns it and says, 'I
　　　　never saw you.'
¹⁹ Surely its life withers away,
　　and[b] from the soil other plants grow.

²⁰ "Surely God does not reject a blameless
　　　　man
　　or strengthen the hands of evildoers.
²¹ He will yet fill your mouth with laughter
　　and your lips with shouts of joy.
²² Your enemies will be clothed in shame,
　　and the tents of the wicked will be no
　　　　more."

Learning to Look Ahead

When your life is in shambles, it's hard to see anything beyond your immediate circumstances. The idea of time healing all wounds seems like a cruel joke when you're talking about losing a loved one, getting dumped by your girlfriend or being the guy everybody makes fun of at school. That's why the only solution that makes sense is to turn to the only One who has perspective enough to see the big picture. Ask God for the strength to survive your hurt and the ability to catch a glimpse of the bright future he's got planned for you.

JOB 9

Then Job replied:

² "Indeed, I know that this is true.
　　But how can a mortal be righteous before God?
³ Though one wished to dispute with him,
　　he could not answer him one time out of a thousand.
⁴ His wisdom is profound, his power is vast.
　　Who has resisted him and come out unscathed?
⁵ He moves mountains without their knowing it
　　and overturns them in his anger.
⁶ He shakes the earth from its place
　　and makes its pillars tremble.
⁷ He speaks to the sun and it does not shine;
　　he seals off the light of the stars.
⁸ He alone stretches out the heavens
　　and treads on the waves of the sea.
⁹ He is the Maker of the Bear and Orion,

---

[a] 14 The meaning of the Hebrew for this word is uncertain.　　[b] 19 Or Surely all the joy it has / is that

the Pleiades and the constellations of the south.
¹⁰ He performs wonders that cannot be fathomed,
    miracles that cannot be counted.
¹¹ When he passes me, I cannot see him;
    when he goes by, I cannot perceive him.
¹² If he snatches away, who can stop him?
    Who can say to him, 'What are you doing?'
¹³ God does not restrain his anger;
    even the cohorts of Rahab cowered at his feet.

¹⁴ "How then can I dispute with him?
    How can I find words to argue with him?
¹⁵ Though I were innocent, I could not answer him;
    I could only plead with my Judge for mercy.
¹⁶ Even if I summoned him and he responded,
    I do not believe he would give me a hearing.
¹⁷ He would crush me with a storm
    and multiply my wounds for no reason.
¹⁸ He would not let me regain my breath
    but would overwhelm me with misery.
¹⁹ If it is a matter of strength, he is mighty!
    And if it is a matter of justice, who will summon him[a]?
²⁰ Even if I were innocent, my mouth would condemn me;
    if I were blameless, it would pronounce me guilty.

²¹ "Although I am blameless,
    I have no concern for myself;
    I despise my own life.
²² It is all the same; that is why I say,
    'He destroys both the blameless and the wicked.'
²³ When a scourge brings sudden death,
    he mocks the despair of the innocent.
²⁴ When a land falls into the hands of the wicked,
    he blindfolds its judges.
    If it is not he, then who is it?

²⁵ "My days are swifter than a runner;
    they fly away without a glimpse of joy.
²⁶ They skim past like boats of papyrus,
    like eagles swooping down on their prey.
²⁷ If I say, 'I will forget my complaint,
    I will change my expression, and smile,'
²⁸ I still dread all my sufferings,
    for I know you will not hold me innocent.
²⁹ Since I am already found guilty,
    why should I struggle in vain?
³⁰ Even if I washed myself with soap[b]
    and my hands with washing soda,
³¹ you would plunge me into a slime pit
    so that even my clothes would detest me.

³² "He is not a man like me that I might answer him,
    that we might confront each other in court.
³³ If only there were someone to arbitrate between us,
    to lay his hand upon us both,

---

[a] *19* See Septuagint; Hebrew *me.*   [b] *30* Or *snow*

10

³⁴ someone to remove God's rod from me,
so that his terror would frighten me no more.
³⁵ Then I would speak up without fear of him,
but as it now stands with me, I cannot.

"I loathe my very life;
therefore I will give free rein to my complaint
and speak out in the bitterness of my soul.
² I will say to God: Do not condemn me,
but tell me what charges you have against me.
³ Does it please you to oppress me,
to spurn the work of your hands,
while you smile on the schemes of the wicked?
⁴ Do you have eyes of flesh?
Do you see as a mortal sees?
⁵ Are your days like those of a mortal
or your years like those of a man,
⁶ that you must search out my faults
and probe after my sin—
⁷ though you know that I am not guilty
and that no one can rescue me from your hand?

now or never
JOB 10:8–12

God created you for a purpose—and being overcome by tragedy is not part of it. One of the best ways to work through suffering is to ask God to help you keep focused on his purpose for your life.

⁸ "Your hands shaped me and made me.
Will you now turn and destroy me?
⁹ Remember that you molded me like clay.
Will you now turn me to dust again?
¹⁰ Did you not pour me out like milk
and curdle me like cheese,
¹¹ clothe me with skin and flesh
and knit me together with bones and sinews?
¹² You gave me life and showed me kindness,
and in your providence watched over my spirit.

¹³ "But this is what you concealed in your heart,
and I know that this was in your mind:
¹⁴ If I sinned, you would be watching me
and would not let my offense go unpunished.
¹⁵ If I am guilty—woe to me!
Even if I am innocent, I cannot lift my head,
for I am full of shame
and drowned in ᵃ my affliction.
¹⁶ If I hold my head high, you stalk me like a lion
and again display your awesome power against me.
¹⁷ You bring new witnesses against me
and increase your anger toward me;
your forces come against me wave upon wave.

¹⁸ "Why then did you bring me out of the womb?
I wish I had died before any eye saw me.
¹⁹ If only I had never come into being,
or had been carried straight from the womb to the grave!
²⁰ Are not my few days almost over?
Turn away from me so I can have a moment's joy

ᵃ 15 Or and aware of

²¹ before I go to the place of no return,
    to the land of gloom and deep shadow,ᵃ
²² to the land of deepest night,
    of deep shadow and disorder,
    where even the light is like darkness."

ZOPHAR

11

Then Zophar the Naamathite replied:

² "Are all these words to go unanswered?
    Is this talker to be vindicated?
³ Will your idle talk reduce men to silence?
    Will no one rebuke you when you mock?
⁴ You say to God, 'My beliefs are flawless
    and I am pure in your sight.'
⁵ Oh, how I wish that God would speak,
    that he would open his lips against you
⁶ and disclose to you the secrets of wisdom,
    for true wisdom has two sides.
    Know this: God has even forgotten some of your sin.

⁷ "Can you fathom the mysteries of God?
    Can you probe the limits of the Almighty?
⁸ They are higher than the heavens—what can you do?
    They are deeper than the depths of the graveᵇ—what can you know?
⁹ Their measure is longer than the earth
    and wider than the sea.

¹⁰ "If he comes along and confines you in prison
    and convenes a court, who can oppose him?
¹¹ Surely he recognizes deceitful men;
    and when he sees evil, does he not take note?
¹² But a witless man can no more become wise
    than a wild donkey's colt can be born a man.ᶜ

¹³ "Yet if you devote your heart to him
    and stretch out your hands to him,
¹⁴ if you put away the sin that is in your hand
    and allow no evil to dwell in your tent,
¹⁵ then you will lift up your face without shame;
    you will stand firm and without fear.
¹⁶ You will surely forget your trouble,
    recalling it only as waters gone by.
¹⁷ Life will be brighter than noonday,
    and darkness will become like morning.
¹⁸ You will be secure, because there is hope;
    you will look about you and take your rest in safety.
¹⁹ You will lie down, with no one to make you afraid,
    and many will court your favor.
²⁰ But the eyes of the wicked will fail,
    and escape will elude them;
    their hope will become a dying gasp."

ᵃ 21 Or and the shadow of death; also in verse 22   ᵇ 8 Hebrew than Sheol   ᶜ 12 Or wild donkey can be born tame

12

Then Job replied:

2 "Doubtless you are the people,
    and wisdom will die with you!
3 But I have a mind as well as you;
    I am not inferior to you.
    Who does not know all these things?

4 "I have become a laughingstock to my friends,
    though I called upon God and he answered—
    a mere laughingstock, though righteous and blameless!
5 Men at ease have contempt for misfortune
    as the fate of those whose feet are slipping.
6 The tents of marauders are undisturbed,
    and those who provoke God are secure—
    those who carry their god in their hands. [a]

7 "But ask the animals, and they will teach you,
    or the birds of the air, and they will tell you;
8 or speak to the earth, and it will teach you,
    or let the fish of the sea inform you.
9 Which of all these does not know
    that the hand of the Lord has done this?
10 In his hand is the life of every creature
    and the breath of all mankind.
11 Does not the ear test words
    as the tongue tastes food?
12 Is not wisdom found among the aged?
    Does not long life bring understanding?

now or never

JOB 12:13-14

Do you believe God is wise, powerful and
caring enough to bring good out of any
circumstance? If so, what kind of good
can he bring out of a tragedy?

13 "To God belong wisdom and power;
    counsel and understanding are his.
14 What he tears down cannot be rebuilt;
    the man he imprisons cannot be
        released.
15 If he holds back the waters, there is
        drought;
    if he lets them loose, they devastate
        the land.
16 To him belong strength and victory;
    both deceived and deceiver are his.
17 He leads counselors away stripped
    and makes fools of judges.
18 He takes off the shackles put on by kings
    and ties a loincloth [b] around their waist.
19 He leads priests away stripped
    and overthrows men long established.
20 He silences the lips of trusted advisers
    and takes away the discernment of elders.
21 He pours contempt on nobles
    and disarms the mighty.
22 He reveals the deep things of darkness
    and brings deep shadows into the light.
23 He makes nations great, and destroys them;

---

a 6 Or secure / in what God's hand brings them   b 18 Or shackles of kings / and ties a belt

he enlarges nations, and disperses them.
²⁴ He deprives the leaders of the earth of their reason;
he sends them wandering through a trackless waste.
²⁵ They grope in darkness with no light;
he makes them stagger like drunkards.

"My eyes have seen all this,
my ears have heard and understood it.
² What you know, I also know;
I am not inferior to you.
³ But I desire to speak to the Almighty
and to argue my case with God.
⁴ You, however, smear me with lies;
you are worthless physicians, all of you!
⁵ If only you would be altogether silent!
For you, that would be wisdom.
⁶ Hear now my argument;
listen to the plea of my lips.
⁷ Will you speak wickedly on God's behalf?
Will you speak deceitfully for him?
⁸ Will you show him partiality?
Will you argue the case for God?
⁹ Would it turn out well if he examined you?
Could you deceive him as you might deceive men?
¹⁰ He would surely rebuke you
if you secretly showed partiality.
¹¹ Would not his splendor terrify you?
Would not the dread of him fall on you?
¹² Your maxims are proverbs of ashes;
your defenses are defenses of clay.

¹³ "Keep silent and let me speak;
then let come to me what may.
¹⁴ Why do I put myself in jeopardy
and take my life in my hands?
¹⁵ Though he slay me, yet will I hope in him;
I will surely[a] defend my ways to his face.
¹⁶ Indeed, this will turn out for my deliverance,
for no godless man would dare come before him!
¹⁷ Listen carefully to my words;
let your ears take in what I say.
¹⁸ Now that I have prepared my case,
I know I will be vindicated.
¹⁹ Can anyone bring charges against me?
If so, I will be silent and die.

²⁰ "Only grant me these two things, O God,
and then I will not hide from you:
²¹ Withdraw your hand far from me,
and stop frightening me with your terrors.
²² Then summon me and I will answer,
or let me speak, and you reply.
²³ How many wrongs and sins have I committed?
Show me my offense and my sin.
²⁴ Why do you hide your face

ª 15 Or He will surely slay me; I have no hope — / yet I will

and consider me your enemy?
25 Will you torment a windblown leaf?
  Will you chase after dry chaff?
26 For you write down bitter things against me
  and make me inherit the sins of my youth.
27 You fasten my feet in shackles;
  you keep close watch on all my paths
  by putting marks on the soles of my feet.

28 "So man wastes away like something rotten,
  like a garment eaten by moths.

14

"Man born of woman
  is of few days and full of trouble.
2 He springs up like a flower and withers away;
  like a fleeting shadow, he does not endure.
3 Do you fix your eye on such a one?
  Will you bring him[a] before you for judgment?

4 Who can bring what is pure from the
    impure?
  No one!
5 Man's days are determined;
  you have decreed the number of his
    months
  and have set limits he cannot exceed.
6 So look away from him and let him
    alone,
  till he has put in his time like a hired
    man.

NOW OR NEVER
JOB 14:5

What would you do if you found out you had only seven days to live? Would you make any big changes in the way you spend your time? Can anyone but God really know how many days we have left?

7 "At least there is hope for a tree:
  If it is cut down, it will sprout again,
  and its new shoots will not fail.
8 Its roots may grow old in the ground
  and its stump die in the soil,
9 yet at the scent of water it will bud
  and put forth shoots like a plant.
10 But man dies and is laid low;
  he breathes his last and is no more.
11 As water disappears from the sea
  or a riverbed becomes parched and dry,
12 so man lies down and does not rise;
  till the heavens are no more, men will not awake
  or be roused from their sleep.

13 "If only you would hide me in the grave[b]
  and conceal me till your anger has passed!
  If only you would set me a time
  and then remember me!
14 If a man dies, will he live again?
  All the days of my hard service
  I will wait for my renewal[c] to come.
15 You will call and I will answer you;
  you will long for the creature your hands have made.
16 Surely then you will count my steps
  but not keep track of my sin.

---

[a] 3 Septuagint, Vulgate and Syriac; Hebrew *me*   [b] 13 Hebrew *Sheol*   [c] 14 Or *release*

17 My offenses will be sealed up in a bag;
    you will cover over my sin.

18 "But as a mountain erodes and crumbles
    and as a rock is moved from its place,
19 as water wears away stones
    and torrents wash away the soil,
    so you destroy man's hope.
20 You overpower him once for all, and he is gone;
    you change his countenance and send him away.
21 If his sons are honored, he does not know it;
    if they are brought low, he does not see it.
22 He feels but the pain of his own body
    and mourns only for himself."

ELIPHAZ

15

Then Eliphaz the Temanite replied:

2 "Would a wise man answer with empty notions
    or fill his belly with the hot east wind?
3 Would he argue with useless words,
    with speeches that have no value?
4 But you even undermine piety
    and hinder devotion to God.
5 Your sin prompts your mouth;
    you adopt the tongue of the crafty.
6 Your own mouth condemns you, not mine;
    your own lips testify against you.

7 "Are you the first man ever born?
    Were you brought forth before the hills?
8 Do you listen in on God's council?
    Do you limit wisdom to yourself?
9 What do you know that we do not know?
    What insights do you have that we do not have?
10 The gray-haired and the aged are on our side,
    men even older than your father.
11 Are God's consolations not enough for you,
    words spoken gently to you?
12 Why has your heart carried you away,
    and why do your eyes flash,
13 so that you vent your rage against God
    and pour out such words from your mouth?

14 "What is man, that he could be pure,
    or one born of woman, that he could be righteous?
15 If God places no trust in his holy ones,
    if even the heavens are not pure in his eyes,
16 how much less man, who is vile and corrupt,
    who drinks up evil like water!

17 "Listen to me and I will explain to you;
    let me tell you what I have seen,
18 what wise men have declared,
    hiding nothing received from their fathers
19 (to whom alone the land was given
    when no alien passed among them):

job

» A rich, godly man from the land of Uz

» Suffered at the hands of Satan

» Eventually was granted a one-on-one appointment with God

his three "friends"

» Eliphaz, Bildad and Zophar

» Were sympathetic and compassionate to Job . . . at first

» Became Job's accusers

The Main Event

Little did Job know that he was the subject of a cosmic wager between God Almighty and Satan. Poor guy. What would he have done if he'd known that, for at least a little while, he was the focal point of a showdown between God and the devil?

All Job knew for sure was that his entire world had been carpet-bombed right before his eyes. When the smoke finally cleared, Job had lost everything, including his family (except for his nagging wife), his fortune and his health. He was wrecked, wiped out, wasting away . . . and left to wonder why.

When Job's three best buddies—Eliphaz the Temanite, Bildad the Shuhite, and Zophar the Naamathite—heard the news about his suffering, they hustled over. They soon discovered that his situation was even more tragic than they'd heard. The three of them came unglued. For a solid week, they sat with Job, grieving with him, saying nothing.

After that, they did what most guys are prone to do. They began to try to "fix" Job's problem. They offered solutions and explanations. They claimed to know the cause of Job's suffering, insisting that God was angered by some secret sin in his life. Maybe they were trying to help, but before long, Job's "comforters" became his tormentors. Tempers flared, and gentle pats on the back turned into accusing fingers in the face.

Just what Job needed—on top of everything else, his own friends turned on him. Could it get any worse than that?

The Outcome

The names of Job and his three "friends" should not be on the list of the great match-ups in the Bible. Eliphaz, Bildad and Zophar were supposed to be on Job's team, not on his back! They were supposed to be helping him, not hurting him.

File this away in your memory: When a friend is suffering, you want to be an ally, not an enemy. You want to come alongside your friend and offer encouragement; don't add to the problem by piling on discouragement.

Most important, resist the impulse to offer advice and reasons. Simply offer your presence. Just being there will do more good than even the best advice you could hope to give. And even if you think you know the reason for someone else's suffering (and be assured, you do not, at least not as well as you think you do), what good does that do? Head knowledge doesn't take away heart pain!

Be supportive, thoughtful and, above all, loving. Learn to listen. Pray for comfort from above. That's how you can avoid becoming an adversary to friends in trouble.

Read more about Job and his three friends in Job 1:1–42:17 (pages 581–631).

²⁰ All his days the wicked man suffers torment,
   the ruthless through all the years stored up for him.
²¹ Terrifying sounds fill his ears;
   when all seems well, marauders attack him.
²² He despairs of escaping the darkness;
   he is marked for the sword.
²³ He wanders about—food for vultures[a];
   he knows the day of darkness is at hand.
²⁴ Distress and anguish fill him with terror;
   they overwhelm him, like a king poised to attack,
²⁵ because he shakes his fist at God
   and vaunts himself against the Almighty,
²⁶ defiantly charging against him
   with a thick, strong shield.

²⁷ "Though his face is covered with fat
   and his waist bulges with flesh,
²⁸ he will inhabit ruined towns
   and houses where no one lives,
   houses crumbling to rubble.
²⁹ He will no longer be rich and his wealth
   will not endure,
   nor will his possessions spread over
   the land.
³⁰ He will not escape the darkness;
   a flame will wither his shoots,
   and the breath of God's mouth will
   carry him away.
³¹ Let him not deceive himself by trusting
   what is worthless,
   for he will get nothing in return.
³² Before his time he will be paid in full,
   and his branches will not flourish.
³³ He will be like a vine stripped of its
   unripe grapes,
   like an olive tree shedding its
   blossoms.
³⁴ For the company of the godless will be
   barren,
   and fire will consume the tents of
   those who love bribes.
³⁵ They conceive trouble and give birth to
   evil;
   their womb fashions deceit."

Building a Support Group

Do yourself a favor: Find people you can go to for help when you really need it. When the bottom drops out of your world, you don't want to share your feelings with boneheaded friends who are just going to crack jokes or avoid the issue because they can't handle a deep conversation. You don't want friends who will point fingers for no good reason and offer cheap, simplistic answers to your problems. Surround yourself with people who will empathize with you, listen and make a real effort to give comfort.

JOB 16

Then Job replied:

² "I have heard many things like these;
   miserable comforters are you all!
³ Will your long-winded speeches never end?
   What ails you that you keep on arguing?
⁴ I also could speak like you,
   if you were in my place;

---

a 23 Or about, looking for food

I could make fine speeches against you
and shake my head at you.
⁵ But my mouth would encourage you;
comfort from my lips would bring you relief.

⁶ "Yet if I speak, my pain is not relieved;
and if I refrain, it does not go away.
⁷ Surely, O God, you have worn me out;
you have devastated my entire household.
⁸ You have bound me—and it has become a witness;
my gauntness rises up and testifies against me.
⁹ God assails me and tears me in his anger
and gnashes his teeth at me;
my opponent fastens on me his piercing eyes.
¹⁰ Men open their mouths to jeer at me;
they strike my cheek in scorn
and unite together against me.
¹¹ God has turned me over to evil men
and thrown me into the clutches of the wicked.
¹² All was well with me, but he shattered me;
he seized me by the neck and crushed me.
He has made me his target;
¹³   his archers surround me.
Without pity, he pierces my kidneys
and spills my gall on the ground.
¹⁴ Again and again he bursts upon me;
he rushes at me like a warrior.

¹⁵ "I have sewed sackcloth over my skin
and buried my brow in the dust.
¹⁶ My face is red with weeping,
deep shadows ring my eyes;
¹⁷ yet my hands have been free of violence
and my prayer is pure.

¹⁸ "O earth, do not cover my blood;
may my cry never be laid to rest!
¹⁹ Even now my witness is in heaven;
my advocate is on high.
²⁰ My intercessor is my friend[a]
as my eyes pour out tears to God;
²¹ on behalf of a man he pleads with God
as a man pleads for his friend.

²² "Only a few years will pass
before I go on the journey of no return.

17

¹ My spirit is broken,
my days are cut short,
the grave awaits me.
² Surely mockers surround me;
my eyes must dwell on their hostility.

³ "Give me, O God, the pledge you demand.
Who else will put up security for me?
⁴ You have closed their minds to understanding;
therefore you will not let them triumph.

ᵃ 20 Or *My friends treat me with scorn*

⁵ If a man denounces his friends for reward,
   the eyes of his children will fail.

⁶ "God has made me a byword to everyone,
   a man in whose face people spit.
⁷ My eyes have grown dim with grief;
   my whole frame is but a shadow.
⁸ Upright men are appalled at this;
   the innocent are aroused against the ungodly.
⁹ Nevertheless, the righteous will hold to their ways,
   and those with clean hands will grow stronger.

¹⁰ "But come on, all of you, try again!
   I will not find a wise man among you.
¹¹ My days have passed, my plans are shattered,
   and so are the desires of my heart.
¹² These men turn night into day;
   in the face of darkness they say, 'Light is near.'
¹³ If the only home I hope for is the grave,ª
   if I spread out my bed in darkness,
¹⁴ if I say to corruption, 'You are my father,'
   and to the worm, 'My mother' or 'My sister,'
¹⁵ where then is my hope?
   Who can see any hope for me?
¹⁶ Will it go down to the gates of deathª?
   Will we descend together into the dust?"

BILDAD
18

Then Bildad the Shuhite replied:

² "When will you end these speeches?
   Be sensible, and then we can talk.
³ Why are we regarded as cattle
   and considered stupid in your sight?
⁴ You who tear yourself to pieces in your anger,
   is the earth to be abandoned for your sake?
   Or must the rocks be moved from their place?

⁵ "The lamp of the wicked is snuffed out;
   the flame of his fire stops burning.
⁶ The light in his tent becomes dark;
   the lamp beside him goes out.
⁷ The vigor of his step is weakened;
   his own schemes throw him down.
⁸ His feet thrust him into a net
   and he wanders into its mesh.
⁹ A trap seizes him by the heel;
   a snare holds him fast.
¹⁰ A noose is hidden for him on the ground;
   a trap lies in his path.
¹¹ Terrors startle him on every side
   and dog his every step.
¹² Calamity is hungry for him;
   disaster is ready for him when he falls.
¹³ It eats away parts of his skin;

ª *13,16* Hebrew *Sheol*

death's firstborn devours his limbs.
14 He is torn from the security of his tent
and marched off to the king of terrors.
15 Fire resides[a] in his tent;
burning sulfur is scattered over his dwelling.
16 His roots dry up below
and his branches wither above.
17 The memory of him perishes from the earth;
he has no name in the land.
18 He is driven from light into darkness
and is banished from the world.
19 He has no offspring or descendants among his people,
no survivor where once he lived.
20 Men of the west are appalled at his fate;
men of the east are seized with horror.
21 Surely such is the dwelling of an evil man;
such is the place of one who knows not God."

Then Job replied:

2 "How long will you torment me
and crush me with words?
3 Ten times now you have reproached me;
shamelessly you attack me.
4 If it is true that I have gone astray,
my error remains my concern alone.
5 If indeed you would exalt yourselves above me
and use my humiliation against me,
6 then know that God has wronged me
and drawn his net around me.

7 "Though I cry, 'I've been wronged!' I get no response;
though I call for help, there is no justice.
8 He has blocked my way so I cannot pass;
he has shrouded my paths in darkness.
9 He has stripped me of my honor
and removed the crown from my head.
10 He tears me down on every side till I am gone;
he uproots my hope like a tree.
11 His anger burns against me;
he counts me among his enemies.
12 His troops advance in force;
they build a siege ramp against me
and encamp around my tent.

13 "He has alienated my brothers from me;
my acquaintances are completely estranged from me.
14 My kinsmen have gone away;
my friends have forgotten me.
15 My guests and my maidservants count me a stranger;
they look upon me as an alien.
16 I summon my servant, but he does not answer,
though I beg him with my own mouth.
17 My breath is offensive to my wife;

---

a 15 Or *Nothing he had remains*

I am loathsome to my own brothers.
18 Even the little boys scorn me;
  when I appear, they ridicule me.
19 All my intimate friends detest me;
  those I love have turned against me.
20 I am nothing but skin and bones;
  I have escaped with only the skin of my teeth. [a]

21 "Have pity on me, my friends, have pity,
  for the hand of God has struck me.
22 Why do you pursue me as God does?
  Will you never get enough of my
   flesh?

23 "Oh, that my words were recorded,
  that they were written on a scroll,
24 that they were inscribed with an iron
  tool on [b] lead,
  or engraved in rock forever!
25 I know that my Redeemer [c] lives,
  and that in the end he will stand
   upon the earth. [d]

NOW OR NEVER
JOB 19:25

Who is your Redeemer? How do you know he lives? What difference does it make in your daily life?

26 And after my skin has been destroyed,
  yet [e] in [f] my flesh I will see God;
27 I myself will see him
  with my own eyes—I, and not another.
  How my heart yearns within me!

28 "If you say, 'How we will hound him,
  since the root of the trouble lies in him, [g]'
29 you should fear the sword yourselves;
  for wrath will bring punishment by the sword,
  and then you will know that there is judgment. [h]"

ZOPHAR
20

Then Zophar the Naamathite replied:

2 "My troubled thoughts prompt me to answer
  because I am greatly disturbed.
3 I hear a rebuke that dishonors me,
  and my understanding inspires me to reply.

4 "Surely you know how it has been from
  of old,
  ever since man [i] was placed on the
   earth,
5 that the mirth of the wicked is brief,
  the joy of the godless lasts but a
   moment.
6 Though his pride reaches to the heavens
  and his head touches the clouds,
7 he will perish forever, like his own dung;
  those who have seen him will say,
   'Where is he?'

NOW OR NEVER
JOB 20:5

How would you explain this idea to a friend who believes you've got to have all the fun you can while you can?

a 20 Or only my gums   b 24 Or and   c 25 Or defender   d 25 Or upon my grave   e 26 Or And after I awake, / though this body
has been destroyed, / then   f 26 Or / apart from   g 28 Many Hebrew manuscripts, Septuagint and Vulgate; most Hebrew manuscripts
me   h 29 Or / that you may come to know the Almighty   i 4 Or Adam

⁸Like a dream he flies away, no more to be found,
    banished like a vision of the night.
⁹The eye that saw him will not see him again;
    his place will look on him no more.
¹⁰His children must make amends to the poor;
    his own hands must give back his wealth.
¹¹The youthful vigor that fills his bones
    will lie with him in the dust.

¹²"Though evil is sweet in his mouth
    and he hides it under his tongue,
¹³though he cannot bear to let it go
    and keeps it in his mouth,
¹⁴yet his food will turn sour in his stomach;
    it will become the venom of serpents within him.
¹⁵He will spit out the riches he swallowed;
    God will make his stomach vomit them up.
¹⁶He will suck the poison of serpents;
    the fangs of an adder will kill him.
¹⁷He will not enjoy the streams,
    the rivers flowing with honey and cream.
¹⁸What he toiled for he must give back uneaten;
    he will not enjoy the profit from his trading.
¹⁹For he has oppressed the poor and left them destitute;
    he has seized houses he did not build.

²⁰"Surely he will have no respite from his craving;
    he cannot save himself by his treasure.
²¹Nothing is left for him to devour;
    his prosperity will not endure.
²²In the midst of his plenty, distress will overtake him;
    the full force of misery will come upon him.
²³When he has filled his belly,
    God will vent his burning anger against him
    and rain down his blows upon him.
²⁴Though he flees from an iron weapon,
    a bronze-tipped arrow pierces him.
²⁵He pulls it out of his back,
    the gleaming point out of his liver.
    Terrors will come over him;
²⁶   total darkness lies in wait for his treasures.
    A fire unfanned will consume him
    and devour what is left in his tent.
²⁷The heavens will expose his guilt;
    the earth will rise up against him.
²⁸A flood will carry off his house,
    rushing waters[a] on the day of God's wrath.
²⁹Such is the fate God allots the wicked,
    the heritage appointed for them by God."

21

Then Job replied:

²"Listen carefully to my words;
    let this be the consolation you give me.

ᵃ 28 Or *The possessions in his house will be carried off, / washed away*

³Bear with me while I speak,
and after I have spoken, mock on.

⁴"Is my complaint directed to man?
Why should I not be impatient?
⁵Look at me and be astonished;
clap your hand over your mouth.
⁶When I think about this, I am terrified;
trembling seizes my body.
⁷Why do the wicked live on,
growing old and increasing in power?
⁸They see their children established around them,
their offspring before their eyes.
⁹Their homes are safe and free from fear;
the rod of God is not upon them.
¹⁰Their bulls never fail to breed;
their cows calve and do not miscarry.
¹¹They send forth their children as a flock;
their little ones dance about.
¹²They sing to the music of tambourine and harp;
they make merry to the sound of the flute.
¹³They spend their years in prosperity
and go down to the grave[a] in peace.[b]
¹⁴Yet they say to God, 'Leave us alone!
We have no desire to know your ways.
¹⁵Who is the Almighty, that we should serve him?
What would we gain by praying to him?'
¹⁶But their prosperity is not in their own hands,
so I stand aloof from the counsel of the wicked.

¹⁷"Yet how often is the lamp of the wicked snuffed out?
How often does calamity come upon them,
the fate God allots in his anger?
¹⁸How often are they like straw before the wind,
like chaff swept away by a gale?
¹⁹It is said, 'God stores up a man's punishment for his sons.'
Let him repay the man himself, so that he will know it!
²⁰Let his own eyes see his destruction;
let him drink of the wrath of the Almighty.[c]
²¹For what does he care about the family he leaves behind
when his allotted months come to an end?

²²"Can anyone teach knowledge to God,
since he judges even the highest?
²³One man dies in full vigor,
completely secure and at ease,
²⁴his body[d] well nourished,
his bones rich with marrow.
²⁵Another man dies in bitterness of soul,
never having enjoyed anything good.
²⁶Side by side they lie in the dust,
and worms cover them both.

²⁷"I know full well what you are thinking,
the schemes by which you would wrong me.

ᵃ *13* Hebrew *Sheol*   ᵇ *13* Or *in an instant*   ᶜ *17-20* Verses 17 and 18 may be taken as exclamations and 19 and 20 as declarations.
ᵈ *24* The meaning of the Hebrew for this word is uncertain.

²⁸ You say, 'Where now is the great man's house,
    the tents where wicked men lived?'
²⁹ Have you never questioned those who travel?
    Have you paid no regard to their accounts—
³⁰ that the evil man is spared from the day of calamity,
    that he is delivered from^a the day of wrath?
³¹ Who denounces his conduct to his face?
    Who repays him for what he has done?
³² He is carried to the grave,
    and watch is kept over his tomb.
³³ The soil in the valley is sweet to him;
    all men follow after him,
    and a countless throng goes^b before him.

³⁴ "So how can you console me with your nonsense?
    Nothing is left of your answers but falsehood!"

Then Eliphaz the Temanite replied:

² "Can a man be of benefit to God?
    Can even a wise man benefit him?
³ What pleasure would it give the Almighty if you were righteous?
    What would he gain if your ways were blameless?

⁴ "Is it for your piety that he rebukes you
    and brings charges against you?
⁵ Is not your wickedness great?
    Are not your sins endless?
⁶ You demanded security from your brothers for no reason;
    you stripped men of their clothing, leaving them naked.
⁷ You gave no water to the weary
    and you withheld food from the hungry,
⁸ though you were a powerful man, owning land—
    an honored man, living on it.
⁹ And you sent widows away empty-handed
    and broke the strength of the fatherless.
¹⁰ That is why snares are all around you,
    why sudden peril terrifies you,
¹¹ why it is so dark you cannot see,
    and why a flood of water covers you.

¹² "Is not God in the heights of heaven?
    And see how lofty are the highest stars!
¹³ Yet you say, 'What does God know?
    Does he judge through such darkness?
¹⁴ Thick clouds veil him, so he does not see us
    as he goes about in the vaulted heavens.'
¹⁵ Will you keep to the old path
    that evil men have trod?
¹⁶ They were carried off before their time,
    their foundations washed away by a flood.
¹⁷ They said to God, 'Leave us alone!
    What can the Almighty do to us?'
¹⁸ Yet it was he who filled their houses with good things,

---

^a 30 Or man is reserved for the day of calamity, / that he is brought forth to   ^b 33 Or / as a countless throng went

so I stand aloof from the counsel of the wicked.

19 "The righteous see their ruin and rejoice;
   the innocent mock them, saying,
20 'Surely our foes are destroyed,
   and fire devours their wealth.'

21 "Submit to God and be at peace with him;
   in this way prosperity will come to you.
22 Accept instruction from his mouth
   and lay up his words in your heart.
23 If you return to the Almighty, you will be restored:
   If you remove wickedness far from your tent
24 and assign your nuggets to the dust,
   your gold of Ophir to the rocks in the ravines,
25 then the Almighty will be your gold,
   the choicest silver for you.
26 Surely then you will find delight in the Almighty
   and will lift up your face to God.
27 You will pray to him, and he will hear you,
   and you will fulfill your vows.
28 What you decide on will be done,
   and light will shine on your ways.
29 When men are brought low and you say, 'Lift them up!'
   then he will save the downcast.
30 He will deliver even one who is not innocent,
   who will be delivered through the cleanness of your hands."

JOB 23

Then Job replied:

2 "Even today my complaint is bitter;
   his hand[a] is heavy in spite of[b] my groaning.
3 If only I knew where to find him;
   if only I could go to his dwelling!
4 I would state my case before him
   and fill my mouth with arguments.
5 I would find out what he would answer me,
   and consider what he would say.

6 Would he oppose me with
      great power?
   No, he would not press
      charges against me.
7 There an upright man could present
      his case before him,
   and I would be delivered
      forever from my judge.

8 "But if I go to the east, he is
      not there;
   if I go to the west, I do not
      find him.

9 When he is at work in the north, I do not see him;
   when he turns to the south, I catch no glimpse of him.
10 But he knows the way that I take;

---

challenge notes

To: my_son

heavenly_father: I created you, so I know exactly what you're made of. that's important to remember because I've promised to never let you face anything that is too much for you to endure. yes, you will suffer—but stick with me and you'll come out the other side as pure as gold.

JOB 23:10

---

a 2 Septuagint and Syriac; Hebrew / the hand on me   b 2 Or heavy on me in

when he has tested me, I will come forth as gold.
¹¹ My feet have closely followed his steps;
  I have kept to his way without turning aside.
¹² I have not departed from the commands of his lips;
  I have treasured the words of his mouth more than my daily bread.

¹³ "But he stands alone, and who can oppose him?
  He does whatever he pleases.
¹⁴ He carries out his decree against me,
  and many such plans he still has in store.
¹⁵ That is why I am terrified before him;
  when I think of all this, I fear him.
¹⁶ God has made my heart faint;
  the Almighty has terrified me.
¹⁷ Yet I am not silenced by the darkness,
  by the thick darkness that covers my face.

24

"Why does the Almighty not set times for judgment?
  Why must those who know him look in vain for such days?
² Men move boundary stones;
  they pasture flocks they have stolen.
³ They drive away the orphan's donkey
  and take the widow's ox in pledge.
⁴ They thrust the needy from the path
  and force all the poor of the land into hiding.
⁵ Like wild donkeys in the desert,
  the poor go about their labor of foraging food;
  the wasteland provides food for their children.
⁶ They gather fodder in the fields
  and glean in the vineyards of the wicked.
⁷ Lacking clothes, they spend the night naked;
  they have nothing to cover themselves in the cold.
⁸ They are drenched by mountain rains
  and hug the rocks for lack of shelter.
⁹ The fatherless child is snatched from the breast;
  the infant of the poor is seized for a debt.
¹⁰ Lacking clothes, they go about naked;
  they carry the sheaves, but still go hungry.
¹¹ They crush olives among the terraces ᵃ;
  they tread the winepresses, yet suffer thirst.
¹² The groans of the dying rise from the city,
  and the souls of the wounded cry out for help.
  But God charges no one with wrongdoing.

¹³ "There are those who rebel against the light,
  who do not know its ways
  or stay in its paths.
¹⁴ When daylight is gone, the murderer rises up
  and kills the poor and needy;
  in the night he steals forth like a thief.
¹⁵ The eye of the adulterer watches for dusk;
  he thinks, 'No eye will see me,'
  and he keeps his face concealed.
¹⁶ In the dark, men break into houses,
  but by day they shut themselves in;

ᵃ 11 Or *olives between the millstones*; the meaning of the Hebrew for this word is uncertain.

battlelines

» Angry at God

Q: What's the news on your knee?
A: The orthopedic surgeon said it's one of the worst knee injuries he's ever seen. He pretty much told me to forget about playing next season.

Q: I'm sorry to hear that.
A: Yeah, me too.

Q: How are you handling it?
A: Not very well. I keep thinking, *Why now?* I've been playing sports 24/7 for, like, 12 years. Never had an injury. Never missed a game. Then, boom, I just totally blow out my knee—MCL, ACL—everything just shredded.

Q: But I'm sure your faith has been a comfort to you through all of this, right?
A: A comfort? I guess this is where I'm supposed to say something like, "Everything happens for a reason, and I have a sense of peace about it all." Forget it. That's not how I feel. If you want the truth, then, no, my faith hasn't been a comfort at all. If anything, it's made things worse. I mean, isn't God supposed to be in charge of things? Doesn't he control everything in the universe?

Q: Well, yeah.
A: Well, then that means he either *caused* this to happen or he *allowed* it to happen. Either way, it stinks. No senior season. No college recruiters will see me play, so no scholarship. God picked the one thing I love to do more than anything else—the one thing I'm really good at—and took it away. Tell me . . . what's *that* about? And please don't quote the Bible to me. If one more person tells me that "God works all things together for good" or to "trust the Lord with all your heart and blah, blah, blah," I think I'm gonna hurl.

» Arguing With God

Some people are horrified when they hear Christians like Grant express deep pain and confusion with such shocking bluntness. But a careful reading of the Bible shows all sorts of people—even *giants* of the faith like Moses, David, Jeremiah and John the Baptist—wrestling with genuine anguish and real frustration. And if you want to read some *seriously* dark prayers, desperate cries and angry questions, check out Psalms 13, 17, 88 and 142. Or try reading the book of Lamentations. (It's really short.)

There's nothing bad about being honest with God. Sometimes that's just a part of what it means to "fight the good fight" of faith. It's only when we turn our backs on God that our doubt becomes destructive. Just remember: If God is really in control (and he is), then he can handle a few honest questions from his people. Nothing you can say will shock him or cause him to feel differently about you.

Read more about being honest with God at www.RevolutionBible.com.

they want nothing to do with the light.
¹⁷ For all of them, deep darkness is their morning ª;
 they make friends with the terrors of darkness. ᵇ

¹⁸ "Yet they are foam on the surface of the water;
 their portion of the land is cursed,
 so that no one goes to the vineyards.
¹⁹ As heat and drought snatch away the melted snow,
 so the grave ᶜ snatches away those who have sinned.
²⁰ The womb forgets them,
 the worm feasts on them;
evil men are no longer remembered
 but are broken like a tree.
²¹ They prey on the barren and childless woman,
 and to the widow show no kindness.
²² But God drags away the mighty by his power;
 though they become established, they have no assurance of life.
²³ He may let them rest in a feeling of security,
 but his eyes are on their ways.
²⁴ For a little while they are exalted, and then they are gone;
 they are brought low and gathered up like all others;
 they are cut off like heads of grain.

²⁵ "If this is not so, who can prove me false
 and reduce my words to nothing?"

BILDAD 25

Then Bildad the Shuhite replied:

² "Dominion and awe belong to God;
 he establishes order in the heights of heaven.
³ Can his forces be numbered?
 Upon whom does his light not rise?
⁴ How then can a man be righteous before God?
 How can one born of woman be pure?
⁵ If even the moon is not bright
 and the stars are not pure in his eyes,
⁶ how much less man, who is but a maggot—
 a son of man, who is only a worm!"

JOB 26

Then Job replied:

² "How you have helped the powerless!
 How you have saved the arm that is feeble!
³ What advice you have offered to one without wisdom!
 And what great insight you have displayed!
⁴ Who has helped you utter these words?
 And whose spirit spoke from your mouth?

⁵ "The dead are in deep anguish,
 those beneath the waters and all that live in them.
⁶ Death ᶜ is naked before God;
 Destruction ᵈ lies uncovered.
⁷ He spreads out the northern ⌊skies⌋ over empty space;

ª *17 Or them, their morning is like the shadow of death*   ᵇ *17 Or of the shadow of death*   ᶜ *19,6 Hebrew Sheol*   ᵈ *6 Hebrew Abaddon*

he suspends the earth over nothing.
8 He wraps up the waters in his clouds,
yet the clouds do not burst under their weight.
9 He covers the face of the full moon,
spreading his clouds over it.
10 He marks out the horizon on the face of the waters
for a boundary between light and darkness.
11 The pillars of the heavens quake,
aghast at his rebuke.
12 By his power he churned up the sea;
by his wisdom he cut Rahab to pieces.
13 By his breath the skies became fair;
his hand pierced the gliding serpent.
14 And these are but the outer fringe of his works;
how faint the whisper we hear of him!
Who then can understand the thunder of his power?"

27

And Job continued his discourse:

2 "As surely as God lives, who has denied me justice,
the Almighty, who has made me taste bitterness of soul,
3 as long as I have life within me,
the breath of God in my nostrils,
4 my lips will not speak wickedness,
and my tongue will utter no deceit.
5 I will never admit you are in the right;
till I die, I will not deny my integrity.
6 I will maintain my righteousness and never let go of it;
my conscience will not reproach me as long as I live.

7 "May my enemies be like the wicked,
my adversaries like the unjust!
8 For what hope has the godless when he is cut off,
when God takes away his life?
9 Does God listen to his cry
when distress comes upon him?
10 Will he find delight in the Almighty?
Will he call upon God at all times?

11 "I will teach you about the power of God;
the ways of the Almighty I will not conceal.
12 You have all seen this yourselves.
Why then this meaningless talk?

13 "Here is the fate God allots to the wicked,
the heritage a ruthless man receives from the Almighty:
14 However many his children, their fate is the sword;
his offspring will never have enough to eat.
15 The plague will bury those who survive him,
and their widows will not weep for them.
16 Though he heaps up silver like dust
and clothes like piles of clay,
17 what he lays up the righteous will wear,

---

now or never
JOB 27:11

What three things do you think are most important for a new Christian to understand about the way God works? How long did it take you to learn those things? If you'd learned them earlier, how would it have made a difference in your life?

and the innocent will divide his silver.
¹⁸ The house he builds is like a moth's cocoon,
    like a hut made by a watchman.
¹⁹ He lies down wealthy, but will do so no more;
    when he opens his eyes, all is gone.
²⁰ Terrors overtake him like a flood;
    a tempest snatches him away in the night.
²¹ The east wind carries him off, and he is gone;
    it sweeps him out of his place.
²² It hurls itself against him without mercy
    as he flees headlong from its power.
²³ It claps its hands in derision
    and hisses him out of his place.

28

"There is a mine for silver
    and a place where gold is refined.
² Iron is taken from the earth,
    and copper is smelted from ore.
³ Man puts an end to the darkness;
    he searches the farthest recesses
    for ore in the blackest darkness.
⁴ Far from where people dwell he cuts a shaft,
    in places forgotten by the foot of man;
    far from men he dangles and sways.
⁵ The earth, from which food comes,
    is transformed below as by fire;
⁶ sapphires ᵃ come from its rocks,
    and its dust contains nuggets of gold.
⁷ No bird of prey knows that hidden path,
    no falcon's eye has seen it.
⁸ Proud beasts do not set foot on it,
    and no lion prowls there.

⁹ Man's hand assaults the flinty rock
    and lays bare the roots of the
        mountains.
¹⁰ He tunnels through the rock;
    his eyes see all its treasures.
¹¹ He searches ᵇ the sources of the rivers
    and brings hidden things to light.

¹² "But where can wisdom be found?
    Where does understanding dwell?
¹³ Man does not comprehend its worth;
    it cannot be found in the land of the
        living.
¹⁴ The deep says, 'It is not in me';
    the sea says, 'It is not with me.'

NOW OR NEVER
JOB 28:12-23

Don't listen to explanations about why
God allows bad things to happen to good
people if those explanations come from
people who don't know God in the first
place. No one can fully understand all of
God's purposes—least of all those who
have no relationship with him.

¹⁵ It cannot be bought with the finest gold,
    nor can its price be weighed in silver.
¹⁶ It cannot be bought with the gold of Ophir,
    with precious onyx or sapphires.
¹⁷ Neither gold nor crystal can compare with it,
    nor can it be had for jewels of gold.
¹⁸ Coral and jasper are not worthy of mention;
    the price of wisdom is beyond rubies.

ᵃ 6 Or *lapis lazuli*; also in verse 16   ᵇ 11 Septuagint, Aquila and Vulgate; Hebrew *He dams up*

¹⁹ The topaz of Cush cannot compare with it;
   it cannot be bought with pure gold.

²⁰ "Where then does wisdom come from?
   Where does understanding dwell?
²¹ It is hidden from the eyes of every living thing,
   concealed even from the birds of the air.
²² Destruction ᵃ and Death say,
   'Only a rumor of it has reached our ears.'
²³ God understands the way to it
   and he alone knows where it dwells,
²⁴ for he views the ends of the earth
   and sees everything under the heavens.
²⁵ When he established the force of the wind
   and measured out the waters,
²⁶ when he made a decree for the rain
   and a path for the thunderstorm,
²⁷ then he looked at wisdom and appraised it;
   he confirmed it and tested it.
²⁸ And he said to man,
   'The fear of the Lord—that is wisdom,
   and to shun evil is understanding.' "

 Job continued his discourse:

² "How I long for the months gone by,
   for the days when God watched over me,
³ when his lamp shone upon my head
   and by his light I walked through darkness!
⁴ Oh, for the days when I was in my prime,
   when God's intimate friendship blessed my house,
⁵ when the Almighty was still with me
   and my children were around me,
⁶ when my path was drenched with cream
   and the rock poured out for me streams of olive oil.

⁷ "When I went to the gate of the city
   and took my seat in the public square,
⁸ the young men saw me and stepped aside
   and the old men rose to their feet;
⁹ the chief men refrained from speaking
   and covered their mouths with their hands;
¹⁰ the voices of the nobles were hushed,
   and their tongues stuck to the roof of their mouths.
¹¹ Whoever heard me spoke well of me,
   and those who saw me commended me,
¹² because I rescued the poor who cried for help,
   and the fatherless who had none to assist him.
¹³ The man who was dying blessed me;
   I made the widow's heart sing.
¹⁴ I put on righteousness as my clothing;
   justice was my robe and my turban.
¹⁵ I was eyes to the blind
   and feet to the lame.
¹⁶ I was a father to the needy;

ᵃ 22 Hebrew *Abaddon*

I took up the case of the stranger.
¹⁷ I broke the fangs of the wicked
and snatched the victims from their teeth.

¹⁸ "I thought, 'I will die in my own house,
my days as numerous as the grains of sand.
¹⁹ My roots will reach to the water,
and the dew will lie all night on my branches.
²⁰ My glory will remain fresh in me,
the bow ever new in my hand.'

²¹ "Men listened to me expectantly,
waiting in silence for my counsel.
²² After I had spoken, they spoke no more;
my words fell gently on their ears.
²³ They waited for me as for showers
and drank in my words as the spring rain.
²⁴ When I smiled at them, they scarcely believed it;
the light of my face was precious to them.^a
²⁵ I chose the way for them and sat as their chief;
I dwelt as a king among his troops;
I was like one who comforts mourners.

"But now they mock me,
men younger than I,
whose fathers I would have disdained
to put with my sheep dogs.
² Of what use was the strength of their hands to me,
since their vigor had gone from them?
³ Haggard from want and hunger,
they roamed^b the parched land
in desolate wastelands at night.
⁴ In the brush they gathered salt herbs,
and their food^c was the root of the broom tree.
⁵ They were banished from their fellow men,
shouted at as if they were thieves.
⁶ They were forced to live in the dry stream beds,
among the rocks and in holes in the ground.
⁷ They brayed among the bushes
and huddled in the undergrowth.
⁸ A base and nameless brood,
they were driven out of the land.

⁹ "And now their sons mock me in song;
I have become a byword among them.
¹⁰ They detest me and keep their distance;
they do not hesitate to spit in my face.
¹¹ Now that God has unstrung my bow and afflicted me,
they throw off restraint in my presence.
¹² On my right the tribe^d attacks;
they lay snares for my feet,
they build their siege ramps against me.
¹³ They break up my road;
they succeed in destroying me—
without anyone's helping them.^e

---

^a *24* The meaning of the Hebrew for this clause is uncertain.   ^b *3* Or *gnawed*   ^c *4* Or *fuel*   ^d *12* The meaning of the Hebrew for this word is uncertain.   ^e *13* Or *me. / 'No one can help him,' , they say,*.

¹⁴ They advance as through a gaping breach;
　　amid the ruins they come rolling in.
¹⁵ Terrors overwhelm me;
　　my dignity is driven away as by the wind,
　　my safety vanishes like a cloud.

¹⁶ "And now my life ebbs away;
　　days of suffering grip me.
¹⁷ Night pierces my bones;
　　my gnawing pains never rest.
¹⁸ In his great power ⌊God⌋ becomes like clothing to me*ᵉ*;
　　he binds me like the neck of my garment.
¹⁹ He throws me into the mud,
　　and I am reduced to dust and ashes.

²⁰ "I cry out to you, O God, but you do not answer;
　　I stand up, but you merely look at me.
²¹ You turn on me ruthlessly;
　　with the might of your hand you attack me.
²² You snatch me up and drive me before the wind;
　　you toss me about in the storm.
²³ I know you will bring me down to death,
　　to the place appointed for all the living.

²⁴ "Surely no one lays a hand on a broken man
　　when he cries for help in his distress.
²⁵ Have I not wept for those in trouble?
　　Has not my soul grieved for the poor?
²⁶ Yet when I hoped for good, evil came;
　　when I looked for light, then came darkness.
²⁷ The churning inside me never stops;
　　days of suffering confront me.
²⁸ I go about blackened, but not by the sun;
　　I stand up in the assembly and cry for help.
²⁹ I have become a brother of jackals,
　　a companion of owls.
³⁰ My skin grows black and peels;
　　my body burns with fever.
³¹ My harp is tuned to mourning,
　　and my flute to the sound of wailing.

NOW OR NEVER
JOB 31:1

Job made a covenant not to lust after women. Are you willing to make a covenant like that? What changes would you have to make in your daily routine in order to keep it?

31
¹ "I made a covenant with my eyes
　　not to look lustfully at a girl.
² For what is man's lot from God above,
　　his heritage from the Almighty on high?
³ Is it not ruin for the wicked,
　　disaster for those who do wrong?
⁴ Does he not see my ways
　　and count my every step?

⁵ "If I have walked in falsehood
　　or my foot has hurried after deceit—
⁶ let God weigh me in honest scales

ᵃ 18 Hebrew; Septuagint ⌊God⌋ grasps my clothing

battlelines

» Porn Again Christians (Pornography)

Q: What percentage of your friends would you say are involved in porn?
A: Define "involved."

Q: I mean, they look at it on a regular basis.
A: Sheesh, I don't know. I mean, I know some guys who are addicts. They're online everyday. But most of my friends are more into movies. That's probably my biggest weakness too. A still picture is pretty tempting. But moving pictures and real-life action? It's hard to take your eyes off it.

Q: Is that stuff hard to find?
A: Are you kidding? Most video stores stock unrated versions of movies—or director's cuts. You can find some serious skin in those. And I've got tons of friends who get premium cable channels. Have you ever seen the stuff that's on those channels late at night? And I know one guy who fills his mobile device with the stuff. He calls it his "iPorn."

Q: So it's a problem?
A: Yeah . . . big time. Even among my friends who go to church and know it's wrong.

Q: Why do you think that is?
A: Because the people who make those movies know how to hook you so that you can hardly look away.

» The Big Lie

The Bible says that the devil is real. It calls him our enemy and says that he "prowls around like a roaring lion looking for someone to devour" (1 Peter 5:8). Jesus compared Satan to a thief who "comes only to steal and kill and destroy" (John 10:10) and called him the ultimate liar—in fact, "the father of lies" (John 8:44). With this in mind, consider the world of porn. How many guys are being devoured by it? How many men have had their relationships cut short or their marriages destroyed because of their obsession with pornography?

This alluring but deadly business steals its victims' ability to develop and maintain healthy relationships. It lies about women and sex. It substitutes sexual perversion for intimacy. It makes us feel like men without requiring us to *be* men. And in true demonic fashion, it always leaves us feeling empty and guilty the moment the pleasure is over.

God wants you to enjoy the gift of sex the way he meant for it to be enjoyed (in a faithful marriage relationship). Pornography corrodes this gift like an acid, and someday it could cause long-term damage to your marriage. Do yourself a favor: Don't let the porn industry sink its claws into you.

Read more about the effects of porn at www.RevolutionBible.com.

and he will know that I am blameless—
⁷if my steps have turned from the path,
    if my heart has been led by my eyes,
    or if my hands have been defiled,
⁸then may others eat what I have sown,
    and may my crops be uprooted.

⁹"If my heart has been enticed by a woman,
    or if I have lurked at my neighbor's door,
¹⁰then may my wife grind another man's grain,
    and may other men sleep with her.
¹¹For that would have been shameful,
    a sin to be judged.
¹²It is a fire that burns to Destructionᵃ;
    it would have uprooted my harvest.

¹³"If I have denied justice to my menservants and maidservants
    when they had a grievance against me,
¹⁴what will I do when God confronts me?
    What will I answer when called to account?
¹⁵Did not he who made me in the womb make them?
    Did not the same one form us both within our mothers?

¹⁶"If I have denied the desires of the poor
    or let the eyes of the widow grow weary,
¹⁷if I have kept my bread to myself,
    not sharing it with the fatherless—
¹⁸but from my youth I reared him as would a father,
    and from my birth I guided the widow—
¹⁹if I have seen anyone perishing for lack of clothing,
    or a needy man without a garment,
²⁰and his heart did not bless me
    for warming him with the fleece from my sheep,
²¹if I have raised my hand against the fatherless,
    knowing that I had influence in court,
²²then let my arm fall from the shoulder,
    let it be broken off at the joint.
²³For I dreaded destruction from God,
    and for fear of his splendor I could not do such things.

²⁴"If I have put my trust in gold
    or said to pure gold, 'You are my security,'
²⁵if I have rejoiced over my great wealth,
    the fortune my hands had gained,
²⁶if I have regarded the sun in its radiance
    or the moon moving in splendor,
²⁷so that my heart was secretly enticed
    and my hand offered them a kiss of homage,
²⁸then these also would be sins to be judged,
    for I would have been unfaithful to God on high.

²⁹"If I have rejoiced at my enemy's misfortune
    or gloated over the trouble that came to him—
³⁰I have not allowed my mouth to sin
    by invoking a curse against his life—
³¹if the men of my household have never said,

ᵃ 12 Hebrew *Abaddon*

'Who has not had his fill of Job's meat?'—
³²but no stranger had to spend the night in the street,
for my door was always open to the traveler—
³³if I have concealed my sin as men do,ª
by hiding my guilt in my heart
³⁴because I so feared the crowd
and so dreaded the contempt of the clans
that I kept silent and would not go outside—

³⁵("Oh, that I had someone to hear me!
I sign now my defense—let the Almighty answer me;
let my accuser put his indictment in writing.
³⁶Surely I would wear it on my shoulder,
I would put it on like a crown.
³⁷I would give him an account of my
every step;
like a prince I would approach
him.)—

³⁸"if my land cries out against me
and all its furrows are wet with tears,
³⁹if I have devoured its yield without
payment
or broken the spirit of its tenants,
⁴⁰then let briers come up instead of wheat
and weeds instead of barley."

The words of Job are ended.

ELIHU

32

So these three men stopped answering Job, because he was righteous in his own eyes. ²But Elihu son of Barakel the Buzite, of the family of Ram, became very angry with Job for justifying himself rather than God. ³He was also angry with the three friends, because they had found no way to refute Job, and yet had condemned him.ᵇ ⁴Now Elihu had waited before speaking to Job because they were older than he. ⁵But when he saw that the three men had nothing more to say, his anger was aroused.

⁶So Elihu son of Barakel the Buzite said:

"I am young in years,
and you are old;
that is why I was fearful,
not daring to tell you what I know.
⁷I thought, 'Age should speak;
advanced years should teach wisdom.'
⁸But it is the spiritᶜ in a man,
the breath of the Almighty, that gives him understanding.
⁹It is not only the oldᵈ who are wise,
not only the aged who understand what is right.

¹⁰"Therefore I say: Listen to me;
I too will tell you what I know.
¹¹I waited while you spoke,

Knowing When to Share Your Opinions

There's nothing wrong with having an opinion, especially when it concerns people you care about. But the fact that you have one doesn't automatically mean it needs to be shared. The fact is, like everyone else, you're not perfect. And neither are your opinions. Before you tell someone they're doing something wrong or need to change something about themselves, make sure you have thoughtfully and prayerfully considered your counsel. Ask God to give you the words to say; and more important, ask for wisdom about whether you should say anything at all.

»» live the adventure »» Job 32:1

ª 33 Or as Adam did   ᵇ 3 Masoretic Text; an ancient Hebrew scribal tradition Job, and so had condemned God   ᶜ 8 Or Spirit; also in verse 18   ᵈ 9 Or many; or great

I listened to your reasoning;
  while you were searching for words,
¹² I gave you my full attention.
  But not one of you has proved Job wrong;
    none of you has answered his arguments.
¹³ Do not say, 'We have found wisdom;
    let God refute him, not man.'
¹⁴ But Job has not marshaled his words against me,
    and I will not answer him with your arguments.

¹⁵ "They are dismayed and have no more to say;
    words have failed them.
¹⁶ Must I wait, now that they are silent,
    now that they stand there with no reply?
¹⁷ I too will have my say;
    I too will tell what I know.
¹⁸ For I am full of words,
    and the spirit within me compels me;
¹⁹ inside I am like bottled-up wine,
    like new wineskins ready to burst.
²⁰ I must speak and find relief;
    I must open my lips and reply.
²¹ I will show partiality to no one,
    nor will I flatter any man;
²² for if I were skilled in flattery,
    my Maker would soon take me away.

"But now, Job, listen to my words;
    pay attention to everything I say.
² I am about to open my mouth;
    my words are on the tip of my tongue.
³ My words come from an upright heart;
    my lips sincerely speak what I know.
⁴ The Spirit of God has made me;
    the breath of the Almighty gives me life.
⁵ Answer me then, if you can;
    prepare yourself and confront me.
⁶ I am just like you before God;
    I too have been taken from clay.
⁷ No fear of me should alarm you,
    nor should my hand be heavy upon you.

⁸ "But you have said in my hearing—
    I heard the very words—
⁹ 'I am pure and without sin;
    I am clean and free from guilt.
¹⁰ Yet God has found fault with me;
    he considers me his enemy.
¹¹ He fastens my feet in shackles;
    he keeps close watch on all my paths.'

¹² "But I tell you, in this you are not right,
    for God is greater than man.
¹³ Why do you complain to him
    that he answers none of man's words ᵃ?
¹⁴ For God does speak—now one way, now another—

ᵃ *13 Or that he does not answer for any of his actions*

though man may not perceive it.
¹⁵ In a dream, in a vision of the night,
    when deep sleep falls on men
    as they slumber in their beds,
¹⁶ he may speak in their ears
    and terrify them with warnings,
¹⁷ to turn man from wrongdoing
    and keep him from pride,
¹⁸ to preserve his soul from the pit,ᵃ
    his life from perishing by the sword.ᵇ
¹⁹ Or a man may be chastened on a bed of pain
    with constant distress in his bones,
²⁰ so that his very being finds food repulsive
    and his soul loathes the choicest meal.
²¹ His flesh wastes away to nothing,
    and his bones, once hidden, now stick out.
²² His soul draws near to the pit,ᶜ
    and his life to the messengers of death.ᵈ

²³ "Yet if there is an angel on his side
    as a mediator, one out of a thousand,
    to tell a man what is right for him,
²⁴ to be gracious to him and say,
    'Spare him from going down to the pitᵉ;
    I have found a ransom for him'—
²⁵ then his flesh is renewed like a child's;
    it is restored as in the days of his youth.
²⁶ He prays to God and finds favor with him,
    he sees God's face and shouts for joy;
    he is restored by God to his righteous state.
²⁷ Then he comes to men and says,
    'I sinned, and perverted what was right,
    but I did not get what I deserved.
²⁸ He redeemed my soul from going down to the pit,ᶠ
    and I will live to enjoy the light.'

²⁹ "God does all these things to a man—
    twice, even three times—
³⁰ to turn back his soul from the pit,ᵍ
    that the light of life may shine on him.

³¹ "Pay attention, Job, and listen to me;
    be silent, and I will speak.
³² If you have anything to say, answer me;
    speak up, for I want you to be cleared.
³³ But if not, then listen to me;
    be silent, and I will teach you wisdom."

 Then Elihu said:

² "Hear my words, you wise men;
    listen to me, you men of learning.
³ For the ear tests words
    as the tongue tastes food.

ᵃ 18 Or *preserve him from the grave*   ᵇ 18 Or *from crossing the River*   ᶜ 22 Or *He draws near to the grave*   ᵈ 22 Or *to the dead*
ᵉ 24 Or *grave*   ᶠ 28 Or *redeemed me from going down to the grave*   ᵍ 30 Or *turn him back from the grave*

4 Let us discern for ourselves what is right;
  let us learn together what is good.

5 "Job says, 'I am innocent,
  but God denies me justice.
6 Although I am right,
  I am considered a liar;
 although I am guiltless,
  his arrow inflicts an incurable wound.'
7 What man is like Job,
  who drinks scorn like water?
8 He keeps company with evildoers;
  he associates with wicked men.
9 For he says, 'It profits a man nothing
  when he tries to please God.'

10 "So listen to me, you men of understanding.
   Far be it from God to do evil,
   from the Almighty to do wrong.
11 He repays a man for what he has done;
   he brings upon him what his conduct deserves.
12 It is unthinkable that God would do wrong,
   that the Almighty would pervert justice.
13 Who appointed him over the earth?
   Who put him in charge of the whole world?
14 If it were his intention
   and he withdrew his spirit a and breath,
15 all mankind would perish together
   and man would return to the dust.

16 "If you have understanding, hear this;
   listen to what I say.
17 Can he who hates justice govern?
   Will you condemn the just and mighty One?
18 Is he not the One who says to kings, 'You are worthless,'
   and to nobles, 'You are wicked,'
19 who shows no partiality to princes
   and does not favor the rich over the poor,
   for they are all the work of his hands?
20 They die in an instant, in the middle of the night;
   the people are shaken and they pass away;
   the mighty are removed without human hand.

21 "His eyes are on the ways of men;
   he sees their every step.
22 There is no dark place, no deep shadow,
   where evildoers can hide.
23 God has no need to examine men further,
   that they should come before him for judgment.
24 Without inquiry he shatters the mighty
   and sets up others in their place.
25 Because he takes note of their deeds,
   he overthrows them in the night and they are crushed.
26 He punishes them for their wickedness
   where everyone can see them,
27 because they turned from following him

---

a 14 Or Spirit

and had no regard for any of his ways.
28 They caused the cry of the poor to come before him,
so that he heard the cry of the needy.
29 But if he remains silent, who can condemn him?
If he hides his face, who can see him?
Yet he is over man and nation alike,
30   to keep a godless man from ruling,
from laying snares for the people.

31 "Suppose a man says to God,
'I am guilty but will offend no more.
32 Teach me what I cannot see;
if I have done wrong, I will not do so again.'
33 Should God then reward you on your terms,
when you refuse to repent?
You must decide, not I;
so tell me what you know.

34 "Men of understanding declare,
wise men who hear me say to me,
35 'Job speaks without knowledge;
his words lack insight.'
36 Oh, that Job might be tested to the utmost
for answering like a wicked man!
37 To his sin he adds rebellion;
scornfully he claps his hands among us
and multiplies his words against God."

 Then Elihu said:

2 "Do you think this is just?
You say, 'I will be cleared by God.ᵃ'
3 Yet you ask him, 'What profit is it to me,ᵇ
and what do I gain by not sinning?'

4 "I would like to reply to you
and to your friends with you.
5 Look up at the heavens and see;
gaze at the clouds so high above you.
6 If you sin, how does that affect him?
If your sins are many, what does that do to him?
7 If you are righteous, what do you give to him,
or what does he receive from your hand?
8 Your wickedness affects only a man like yourself,
and your righteousness only the sons of men.

9 "Men cry out under a load of oppression;
they plead for relief from the arm of the powerful.
10 But no one says, 'Where is God my Maker,
who gives songs in the night,
11 who teaches more to us than toᶜ the beasts of the earth
and makes us wiser thanᵈ the birds of the air?'
12 He does not answer when men cry out
because of the arrogance of the wicked.
13 Indeed, God does not listen to their empty plea;
the Almighty pays no attention to it.

ᵃ 2 Or *My righteousness is more than God's*   ᵇ 3 Or *you*   ᶜ 11 Or *teaches us by*   ᵈ 11 Or *us wise by*

¹⁴How much less, then, will he listen
    when you say that you do not see him,
that your case is before him
    and you must wait for him,
¹⁵and further, that his anger never punishes
    and he does not take the least notice of wickedness.ᵃ
¹⁶So Job opens his mouth with empty talk;
    without knowledge he multiplies words."

Elihu continued:

²"Bear with me a little longer and I will show you
    that there is more to be said in God's behalf.
³I get my knowledge from afar;
    I will ascribe justice to my Maker.
⁴Be assured that my words are not false;
    one perfect in knowledge is with you.

⁵"God is mighty, but does not despise men;
    he is mighty, and firm in his purpose.
⁶He does not keep the wicked alive
    but gives the afflicted their rights.
⁷He does not take his eyes off the righteous;
    he enthrones them with kings
    and exalts them forever.
⁸But if men are bound in chains,
    held fast by cords of affliction,
⁹he tells them what they have done—
    that they have sinned arrogantly.
¹⁰He makes them listen to correction
    and commands them to repent of their evil.
¹¹If they obey and serve him,
    they will spend the rest of their days in prosperity
    and their years in contentment.
¹²But if they do not listen,
    they will perish by the swordᵇ
    and die without knowledge.

¹³"The godless in heart harbor resentment;
    even when he fetters them, they do not cry for help.
¹⁴They die in their youth,
    among male prostitutes of the shrines.
¹⁵But those who suffer he delivers in their suffering;
    he speaks to them in their affliction.

¹⁶"He is wooing you from the jaws of distress
    to a spacious place free from restriction,
    to the comfort of your table laden with choice food.
¹⁷But now you are laden with the judgment due the wicked;
    judgment and justice have taken hold of you.
¹⁸Be careful that no one entices you by riches;
    do not let a large bribe turn you aside.
¹⁹Would your wealth
    or even all your mighty efforts
    sustain you so you would not be in distress?

ᵃ *15* Symmachus, Theodotion and Vulgate; the meaning of the Hebrew for this word is uncertain.   ᵇ *12* Or *will cross the River*

²⁰Do not long for the night,
  to drag people away from their homes.ᵃ
²¹Beware of turning to evil,
  which you seem to prefer to affliction.

²²"God is exalted in his power.
  Who is a teacher like him?
²³Who has prescribed his ways for him,
  or said to him, 'You have done wrong'?
²⁴Remember to extol his work,
  which men have praised in song.
²⁵All mankind has seen it;
  men gaze on it from afar.

²⁶How great is God—beyond our
  understanding!
  The number of his years is past
  finding out.

²⁷"He draws up the drops of water,
  which distill as rain to the streamsᵇ;
²⁸the clouds pour down their moisture
  and abundant showers fall on
  mankind.
²⁹Who can understand how he spreads
  out the clouds,
  how he thunders from his pavilion?
³⁰See how he scatters his lightning about
  him,
  bathing the depths of the sea.

now or never
JOB 36:26

What would you say to a guy who argues that it's impossible to have a relationship with a God who is beyond our understanding? You might start with the fact that it's possible because God is the One who initiates personal relationships with us.

³¹This is the way he governsᶜ the nations
  and provides food in abundance.
³²He fills his hands with lightning
  and commands it to strike its mark.
³³His thunder announces the coming storm;
  even the cattle make known its approach.ᵈ

37 "At this my heart pounds
  and leaps from its place.
²Listen! Listen to the roar of his voice,
  to the rumbling that comes from his mouth.
³He unleashes his lightning beneath the whole heaven
  and sends it to the ends of the earth.
⁴After that comes the sound of his roar;
  he thunders with his majestic voice.
  When his voice resounds,
  he holds nothing back.
⁵God's voice thunders in marvelous ways;
  he does great things beyond our understanding.
⁶He says to the snow, 'Fall on the earth,'
  and to the rain shower, 'Be a mighty downpour.'
⁷So that all men he has made may know his work,
  he stops every man from his labor.ᵉ
⁸The animals take cover;
  they remain in their dens.

ᵃ *20* The meaning of the Hebrew for verses 18-20 is uncertain.   ᵇ *27* Or *distill from the mist as rain*   ᶜ *31* Or *nourishes*
ᵈ *33* Or *announces his coming— / the One zealous against evil*   ᵉ *7* Or / *he fills all men with fear by his power*

⁹ The tempest comes out from its chamber,
   the cold from the driving winds.
¹⁰ The breath of God produces ice,
   and the broad waters become frozen.
¹¹ He loads the clouds with moisture;
   he scatters his lightning through them.
¹² At his direction they swirl around
   over the face of the whole earth
   to do whatever he commands them.
¹³ He brings the clouds to punish men,
   or to water his earth[a] and show his love.

¹⁴ "Listen to this, Job;
   stop and consider God's wonders.
¹⁵ Do you know how God controls the clouds
   and makes his lightning flash?
¹⁶ Do you know how the clouds hang poised,
   those wonders of him who is perfect in knowledge?
¹⁷ You who swelter in your clothes
   when the land lies hushed under the south wind,
¹⁸ can you join him in spreading out the skies,
   hard as a mirror of cast bronze?

¹⁹ "Tell us what we should say to him;
   we cannot draw up our case because of our darkness.
²⁰ Should he be told that I want to speak?
   Would any man ask to be swallowed up?
²¹ Now no one can look at the sun,
   bright as it is in the skies
   after the wind has swept them clean.
²² Out of the north he comes in golden splendor;
   God comes in awesome majesty.
²³ The Almighty is beyond our reach and exalted in power;
   in his justice and great righteousness, he does not oppress.
²⁴ Therefore, men revere him,
   for does he not have regard for all the wise in heart?[b]"

THE LORD SPEAKS

38

Then the LORD answered Job out of the storm. He said:

² "Who is this that darkens my counsel
   with words without knowledge?
³ Brace yourself like a man;
   I will question you,
   and you shall answer me.

⁴ "Where were you when I laid the earth's foundation?
   Tell me, if you understand.
⁵ Who marked off its dimensions? Surely you know!
   Who stretched a measuring line across it?
⁶ On what were its footings set,
   or who laid its cornerstone—
⁷ while the morning stars sang together
   and all the angels[c] shouted for joy?

⁸ "Who shut up the sea behind doors

ᵃ 13 Or *to favor them*   ᵇ 24 Or *for he does not have regard for any who think they are wise.*   ᶜ 7 Hebrew *the sons of God*

when it burst forth from the womb,
⁹ when I made the clouds its garment
and wrapped it in thick darkness,
¹⁰ when I fixed limits for it
and set its doors and bars in place,
¹¹ when I said, 'This far you may come and
no farther;
here is where your proud waves
halt'?

¹² "Have you ever given orders to the
morning,
or shown the dawn its place,
¹³ that it might take the earth by the edges
and shake the wicked out of it?
¹⁴ The earth takes shape like clay under a
seal;
its features stand out like those of a
garment.
¹⁵ The wicked are denied their light,
and their upraised arm is broken.

¹⁶ "Have you journeyed to the springs of
the sea
or walked in the recesses of the
deep?
¹⁷ Have the gates of death been shown to
you?
Have you seen the gates of the
shadow of death ᵃ?
¹⁸ Have you comprehended the vast
expanses of the earth?
Tell me, if you know all this.

¹⁹ "What is the way to the abode of light?
And where does darkness reside?
²⁰ Can you take them to their places?
Do you know the paths to their dwellings?
²¹ Surely you know, for you were already born!
You have lived so many years!

²² "Have you entered the storehouses of the snow
or seen the storehouses of the hail,
²³ which I reserve for times of trouble,
for days of war and battle?
²⁴ What is the way to the place where the lightning is dispersed,
or the place where the east winds are scattered over the earth?
²⁵ Who cuts a channel for the torrents of rain,
and a path for the thunderstorm,
²⁶ to water a land where no man lives,
a desert with no one in it,
²⁷ to satisfy a desolate wasteland
and make it sprout with grass?
²⁸ Does the rain have a father?
Who fathers the drops of dew?
²⁹ From whose womb comes the ice?

Trusting God's Wisdom

The next time you get the urge to tell God what he should do—or to complain because he hasn't done what you want him to—try answering some of the questions in this passage. Were you involved in creating the foundation of the earth? Are you responsible for the awesome details of nature? Can you make the sun rise simply by telling it to? Remind yourself of who it is you're trying to boss around.

ᵃ 17 Or *gates of deep shadows*

Who gives birth to the frost from the heavens
30 when the waters become hard as stone,
    when the surface of the deep is frozen?

31 "Can you bind the beautiful[a] Pleiades?
    Can you loose the cords of Orion?
32 Can you bring forth the constellations in their seasons[b]
    or lead out the Bear[c] with its cubs?
33 Do you know the laws of the heavens?
    Can you set up ⌊God's⌋[d] dominion over the earth?

34 "Can you raise your voice to the clouds
    and cover yourself with a flood of water?
35 Do you send the lightning bolts on their way?
    Do they report to you, 'Here we are'?
36 Who endowed the heart[e] with wisdom
    or gave understanding to the mind[e]?
37 Who has the wisdom to count the clouds?
    Who can tip over the water jars of the heavens
38 when the dust becomes hard
    and the clods of earth stick together?

39 "Do you hunt the prey for the lioness
    and satisfy the hunger of the lions
40 when they crouch in their dens
    or lie in wait in a thicket?
41 Who provides food for the raven
    when its young cry out to God
    and wander about for lack of food?

"Do you know when the mountain goats give birth?
    Do you watch when the doe bears her fawn?
2 Do you count the months till they bear?
    Do you know the time they give birth?
3 They crouch down and bring forth their young;
    their labor pains are ended.
4 Their young thrive and grow strong in the wilds;
    they leave and do not return.

5 "Who let the wild donkey go free?
    Who untied his ropes?
6 I gave him the wasteland as his home,
    the salt flats as his habitat.
7 He laughs at the commotion in the town;
    he does not hear a driver's shout.
8 He ranges the hills for his pasture
    and searches for any green thing.

9 "Will the wild ox consent to serve you?
    Will he stay by your manger at night?
10 Can you hold him to the furrow with a harness?
    Will he till the valleys behind you?
11 Will you rely on him for his great strength?
    Will you leave your heavy work to him?
12 Can you trust him to bring in your grain
    and gather it to your threshing floor?

---

[a] 31 Or the twinkling; or the chains of the   [b] 32 Or the morning star in its season   [c] 32 Or out Leo   [d] 33 Or his; or their
[e] 36 The meaning of the Hebrew for this word is uncertain.

¹³ "The wings of the ostrich flap joyfully,
  but they cannot compare with the pinions and feathers of the stork.
¹⁴ She lays her eggs on the ground
  and lets them warm in the sand,
¹⁵ unmindful that a foot may crush them,
  that some wild animal may trample them.
¹⁶ She treats her young harshly, as if they were not hers;
  she cares not that her labor was in vain,
¹⁷ for God did not endow her with wisdom
  or give her a share of good sense.
¹⁸ Yet when she spreads her feathers to run,
  she laughs at horse and rider.

¹⁹ "Do you give the horse his strength
  or clothe his neck with a flowing mane?
²⁰ Do you make him leap like a locust,
  striking terror with his proud snorting?
²¹ He paws fiercely, rejoicing in his strength,
  and charges into the fray.
²² He laughs at fear, afraid of nothing;
  he does not shy away from the sword.
²³ The quiver rattles against his side,
  along with the flashing spear and lance.
²⁴ In frenzied excitement he eats up the ground;
  he cannot stand still when the trumpet sounds.
²⁵ At the blast of the trumpet he snorts, 'Aha!'
  He catches the scent of battle from afar,
  the shout of commanders and the battle cry.

²⁶ "Does the hawk take flight by your wisdom
  and spread his wings toward the south?
²⁷ Does the eagle soar at your command
  and build his nest on high?
²⁸ He dwells on a cliff and stays there at night;
  a rocky crag is his stronghold.
²⁹ From there he seeks out his food;
  his eyes detect it from afar.
³⁰ His young ones feast on blood,
  and where the slain are, there is he."

 40 The LORD said to Job:

² "Will the one who contends with the Almighty correct him?
  Let him who accuses God answer him!"

³ Then Job answered the LORD:

⁴ "I am unworthy—how can I reply to you?
  I put my hand over my mouth.
⁵ I spoke once, but I have no answer—
  twice, but I will say no more."

⁶ Then the LORD spoke to Job out of the storm:

⁷ "Brace yourself like a man;
  I will question you,
  and you shall answer me.

⁸ "Would you discredit my justice?

Would you condemn me to justify yourself?
⁹ Do you have an arm like God's,
and can your voice thunder like his?
¹⁰ Then adorn yourself with glory and splendor,
and clothe yourself in honor and majesty.

¹¹ Unleash the fury of your wrath,
look at every proud man and bring
him low,
¹² look at every proud man and humble
him,
crush the wicked where they stand.
¹³ Bury them all in the dust together;
shroud their faces in the grave.
¹⁴ Then I myself will admit to you
that your own right hand can save
you.

¹⁵ "Look at the behemoth,ᵃ
which I made along with you
and which feeds on grass like an ox.

now or never

JOB 40:8–14

The next time you're tempted to question God's fairness, think about how fair it was that his blameless Son died to pay for our sins.

¹⁶ What strength he has in his loins,
what power in the muscles of his belly!
¹⁷ His tailᵇ sways like a cedar;
the sinews of his thighs are close-knit.
¹⁸ His bones are tubes of bronze,
his limbs like rods of iron.
¹⁹ He ranks first among the works of God,
yet his Maker can approach him with his sword.
²⁰ The hills bring him their produce,
and all the wild animals play nearby.
²¹ Under the lotus plants he lies,
hidden among the reeds in the marsh.
²² The lotuses conceal him in their shadow;
the poplars by the stream surround him.
²³ When the river rages, he is not alarmed;
he is secure, though the Jordan should surge against his mouth.
²⁴ Can anyone capture him by the eyes,ᶜ
or trap him and pierce his nose?

41

"Can you pull in the leviathanᵈ with a fishhook
or tie down his tongue with a rope?
² Can you put a cord through his nose
or pierce his jaw with a hook?
³ Will he keep begging you for mercy?
Will he speak to you with gentle words?
⁴ Will he make an agreement with you
for you to take him as your slave for life?
⁵ Can you make a pet of him like a bird
or put him on a leash for your girls?
⁶ Will traders barter for him?
Will they divide him up among the merchants?
⁷ Can you fill his hide with harpoons
or his head with fishing spears?
⁸ If you lay a hand on him,
you will remember the struggle and never do it again!

ᵃ 15 Possibly the hippopotamus or the elephant   ᵇ 17 Possibly trunk   ᶜ 24 Or *by a water hole*   ᵈ 1 Possibly the crocodile

⁹Any hope of subduing him is false;
    the mere sight of him is overpowering.
¹⁰No one is fierce enough to rouse him.
    Who then is able to stand against me?
¹¹Who has a claim against me that I must pay?
    Everything under heaven belongs to me.

¹²"I will not fail to speak of his limbs,
    his strength and his graceful form.
¹³Who can strip off his outer coat?
    Who would approach him with a bridle?
¹⁴Who dares open the doors of his mouth,
    ringed about with his fearsome teeth?
¹⁵His back hasᵃ rows of shields
    tightly sealed together;
¹⁶each is so close to the next
    that no air can pass between.
¹⁷They are joined fast to one another;
    they cling together and cannot be parted.
¹⁸His snorting throws out flashes of light;
    his eyes are like the rays of dawn.
¹⁹Firebrands stream from his mouth;
    sparks of fire shoot out.
²⁰Smoke pours from his nostrils
    as from a boiling pot over a fire of reeds.
²¹His breath sets coals ablaze,
    and flames dart from his mouth.
²²Strength resides in his neck;
    dismay goes before him.
²³The folds of his flesh are tightly joined;
    they are firm and immovable.
²⁴His chest is hard as rock,
    hard as a lower millstone.
²⁵When he rises up, the mighty are terrified;
    they retreat before his thrashing.
²⁶The sword that reaches him has no effect,
    nor does the spear or the dart or the javelin.
²⁷Iron he treats like straw
    and bronze like rotten wood.
²⁸Arrows do not make him flee;
    slingstones are like chaff to him.
²⁹A club seems to him but a piece of straw;
    he laughs at the rattling of the lance.
³⁰His undersides are jagged potsherds,
    leaving a trail in the mud like a threshing sledge.
³¹He makes the depths churn like a boiling caldron
    and stirs up the sea like a pot of ointment.
³²Behind him he leaves a glistening wake;
    one would think the deep had white hair.
³³Nothing on earth is his equal—
    a creature without fear.
³⁴He looks down on all that are haughty;
    he is king over all that are proud."

ᵃ 15 Or His pride is his

JOB

Then Job replied to the Lᴏʀᴅ:

2 "I know that you can do all things;
no plan of yours can be thwarted.

challengenotes

To: my_son

heavenly_father: you've never had a cry for help go unan-swered. I've listened to every one of your emergency calls, and I've responded in ways you may not have expected or recog-nized. I also know what trouble spots lie ahead for you, and I'll be there again when you call.

but now my eyes have seen you.
6 Therefore I despise myself
and repent in dust and ashes."

3 ᴌYou asked,ᴊ 'Who is this that
obscures my counsel
without knowledge?'
Surely I spoke of things I
did not understand,
things too wonderful for me
to know.

4 ᴌ"You said,ᴊ 'Listen now, and I
will speak;
I will question you,
and you shall answer me.'
5 My ears had heard of you

EPILOGUE

7 After the Lᴏʀᴅ had said these things to Job, he said to Eli-phaz the Temanite, "I am angry with you and your two friends, because you have not spoken of me what is right, as my servant Job has. 8 So now take seven bulls and seven rams and go to my servant Job and sacrifice a burnt offering for yourselves. My servant Job will pray for you, and I will accept his prayer and not deal with you according to your folly. You have not spoken of me what is right, as my servant Job has." 9 So Eliphaz the Te-manite, Bildad the Shuhite and Zophar the Naamathite did what the Lᴏʀᴅ told them; and the Lᴏʀᴅ accepted Job's prayer.

10 After Job had prayed for his friends, the Lᴏʀᴅ made him prosperous again and gave him twice as much as he had before. 11 All his brothers and sisters and everyone who had known him before came and ate with him in his house. They comforted and consoled him over all the trouble the Lᴏʀᴅ had brought upon him, and each one gave him a piece of silver[a] and a gold ring. 12 The Lᴏʀᴅ blessed the latter part of Job's life more than the first. He had fourteen thousand sheep, six thousand camels, a thousand yoke of oxen and a thousand donkeys. 13 And he also had seven sons and three daughters. 14 The first daughter he named Jemimah, the second Keziah and the third Keren-Hap-puch. 15 Nowhere in all the land were there found women as beautiful as Job's daughters, and their father granted them an inheritance along with their brothers.

16 After this, Job lived a hundred and forty years; he saw his children and their children to the fourth generation. 17 And so he died, old and full of years.

Holding on to Hope

Few people have ever suffered the way Job did. Yet even when things looked darkest for him, there was a light at the end of the tunnel. If Job had given up, cursed God and killed himself— which is what his wife suggested (see 2:9)—he never would have experienced the incredible bless-ings God had in store for him on the other side of his suffering. No matter how dark things get for you now, hold on to the hope that some-day you'll see God's light at the end of the tunnel.

» live the adventure » Job 42:10-17

---

a 11 Hebrew *him a kesitah*; a kesitah was a unit of money of unknown weight and value.

PSALMS

PSALMS PSALMS

« AT A GLANCE

Authors
David, Asaph, the Sons of Korah, Solomon, Heman, Ethan and Moses

Audience
People of Israel (different psalms were written for specific audiences)

Date
The Psalms were written between the time of Moses (1440 B.C.) and the Babylonian captivity (586 B.C.).

Setting
Many psalms were read or sung in Israelite worship in God's temple.

Verse to Remember
Let everything that has breath praise the LORD. Praise the LORD (150:6).

Theme to Consider
What are you feeling? Sorrow? Regret? Fear? Anger? Joy? You'll find it all expressed here in the writing of the psalmists, who poured out their hearts to God. Tell God whatever you're feeling. He wants to hear from you.

UNCHANGING TRUTH » Real men don't cry. Real men keep their feelings to themselves. Real men never show weakness. Real men suck it up, ignore the pain and keep moving. Real men never let anyone know what's going on inside.

Wrong. Wrong. Wrong. Wrong. Wrong.

Those clichés might sound good on a highlight film or look nice on a T-shirt, but they are nowhere near the truth. When you come right down to it, even the best human effort from the world's strongest man isn't much better than a halfhearted one from a small child. Compared to God, all humans are frail and feeble. We all need God.

The definition of masculinity has been rewritten to include the attributes of an emotionless robot. But men were not created to be that way. God gave us the ability and the need to express ourselves and to share our deepest, most intimate feelings both with other humans and with our Creator.

Take David as an example. No one would accuse this guy of being a wuss. He was a man who killed a bear and a lion with his bare hands—not to mention a giant named Goliath. Yet when you look at the things he wrote in the book of Psalms, it becomes pretty clear that David wasn't afraid to express his emotions.

You shouldn't be either. Maybe you're not the writer type who can craft poems about life and God and stuff. That's cool. But you can still express your deepest feelings to him in prayer. Regardless of what anyone tells you, emotions aren't something to keep inside—even if you're a man's man. God built you with a need to get things off your chest. Besides, sharing your emotions with God is a great way to get close to him.

LIFE LESSONS »

1 Pride and arrogance will always get in the way of a healthy relationship with God (10:2–6).

2 No matter how dark or frightening things get, God is always with us (23:4).

3 Worship is job #1 for all believers (100:1–5).

4 Keeping God's Word fresh in your mind is a good way to avoid the temptation to turn from his will (119:11).

BOOK I

PSALMS 1-41

PSALM 1

¹ Blessed is the man
who does not walk in the counsel of the wicked
or stand in the way of sinners
or sit in the seat of mockers.
² But his delight is in the law of the LORD,
and on his law he meditates day and
night.
³ He is like a tree planted by streams of
water,
which yields its fruit in season
and whose leaf does not wither.
Whatever he does prospers.

⁴ Not so the wicked!
They are like chaff
that the wind blows away.
⁵ Therefore the wicked will not stand in the
judgment,
nor sinners in the assembly of the
righteous.

⁶ For the LORD watches over the way of the
righteous,
but the way of the wicked will perish.

PSALM 2

¹ Why do the nations conspire ᵃ
and the peoples plot in vain?
² The kings of the earth take their stand
and the rulers gather together
against the LORD
and against his Anointed One. ᵇ
³ "Let us break their chains," they say,
"and throw off their fetters."

⁴ The One enthroned in heaven laughs;
the Lord scoffs at them.
⁵ Then he rebukes them in his anger
and terrifies them in his wrath,
saying,
⁶ "I have installed my King ᶜ
on Zion, my holy hill."

⁷ I will proclaim the decree of the LORD:

He said to me, "You are my Son ᵈ;
today I have become your Father. ᵉ
⁸ Ask of me,
and I will make the nations your inheritance,
the ends of the earth your possession.

Choosing Your Friends Wisely

Did you choose the friends you have now, or did they choose you? What led you to start hanging out with them? Would God be excited about your choice of friends? If you have friends who make it hard for you to live the way God wants, be willing to make a difficult sacrifice. Being in this world but not of it means that your influence on unbelievers should be greater than their influence on you.

ᵃ 1 Hebrew; Septuagint *rage*   ᵇ 2 Or *anointed one*   ᶜ 6 Or *king*   ᵈ 7 Or *son*; also in verse 12   ᵉ 7 Or *have begotten you*

hushai

VERSUS

» A friend of King David
» Stuck around to "advise" Absalom
» Used his position as royal advisor to undermine Absalom's rule

absalom

» David's good-looking son
» Carried out a plan to steal the throne from his father
» Killed by Joab, the commander of David's army

The Main Event

What a schmoozer! What a snake! Can you believe Absalom actually stole the kingdom from his own dad?

Using his movie-star good looks and his charming (but totally insincere) personality, Absalom managed to snow all the right people. Like an expert politician, he pressed the flesh, kissed babies and told everyone, "I feel your pain." The next thing anyone knew, David was on the run and Absalom was the new ruler in town.

Enter Hushai, David's long-time trusted adviser. He was prepared to accompany David, wherever he might go. But David had a better idea. "Here's how you can best help me," David told him. "Go back and tell Absalom how you served me and that you're willing to serve him now. Then use your position as an insider to give my boy 'bad counsel' and to keep me posted on his plans."

Hushai obeyed. A short time later, when Absalom was all set to follow the advice of the sniveling Ahithophel ("Take a small number of troops and go after David right away!"), Hushai spoke up. He suggested taking more time to mobilize the entire army in order to squash David like a bug once and for all.

Everything worked like a charm. The vain Absalom dug the idea of a big, grandiose military campaign. And the delay bought enough time to get word to David and enable him to come up with a strategy of his own.

The result was that Absalom's rebellion was quickly crushed—thanks largely to Hushai. As for Absalom, he got his head caught in an oak tree while retreating from his battle with David's army. When David's military commander, Joab, showed up, he used Absalom for a quick round of javelin practice.

The Outcome

Good looks and charm can only get a guy so far. At some point, you also have to have some depth. You have to know something. You have to be something—preferably a man of character.

Absalom was unable to tell the difference between wise and foolish counsel. He seemed incapable of making sound decisions. Time after time, he did really dumb things. Perhaps it was a kind of ironic mercy that Absalom died so young. Think about it. How would he have coped, what would he have had left to fall back on if he reached the age of 60 and . . . lost all of his hair?

The picture we get of Hushai is a guy who may not have been as photogenic as Absalom. He probably didn't get mobbed when he entered a room. A lot of people wouldn't have even noticed him, much less given him the time of day. So what? He was loyal, wise and courageous. (Just think about what might have happened to him if someone had found out he was working undercover for David.) These are the qualities that really matter . . . and really last.

Read more about Hushai and Absalom in 2 Samuel 15:32–37; 16:15—18:15 (pages 362–366).

9 You will rule them with an iron scepter[a];
   you will dash them to pieces like pottery."

10 Therefore, you kings, be wise;
   be warned, you rulers of the earth.
11 Serve the LORD with fear
   and rejoice with trembling.
12 Kiss the Son, lest he be angry
   and you be destroyed in your way,
  for his wrath can flare up in a moment.
   Blessed are all who take refuge in him.

PSALM 3

A psalm of David. When he fled from his son Absalom.

1 O LORD, how many are my foes!
   How many rise up against me!
2 Many are saying of me,
   "God will not deliver him."   *Selah*[b]

3 But you are a shield around me, O LORD;
   you bestow glory on me and lift[c] up my head.
4 To the LORD I cry aloud,
   and he answers me from his holy hill.   *Selah*

5 I lie down and sleep;
   I wake again, because the LORD sustains me.
6 I will not fear the tens of thousands
   drawn up against me on every side.

7 Arise, O LORD!
   Deliver me, O my God!
  Strike all my enemies on the jaw;
   break the teeth of the wicked.

8 From the LORD comes deliverance.
   May your blessing be on your people.   *Selah*

PSALM 4

For the director of music. With stringed instruments. A psalm of David.

1 Answer me when I call to you,
   O my righteous God.
  Give me relief from my distress;
   be merciful to me and hear my prayer.

2 How long, O men, will you turn my glory into shame[d]?
   How long will you love delusions and seek
     false gods[e]?   *Selah*
3 Know that the LORD has set apart the godly for himself;
   the LORD will hear when I call to him.

4 In your anger do not sin;
   when you are on your beds,
   search your hearts and be silent.   *Selah*
5 Offer right sacrifices
   and trust in the LORD.

---

[a] *9 Or will break them with a rod of iron*   [b] *2 A word of uncertain meaning, occurring frequently in the Psalms; possibly a musical term*
[c] *3 Or LORD, / my Glorious One, who lifts*   [d] *2 Or you dishonor my Glorious One*   [e] *2 Or seek lies*

⁶Many are asking, "Who can show us any good?"
    Let the light of your face shine upon us, O LORD.
⁷You have filled my heart with greater joy
    than when their grain and new wine
        abound.
⁸I will lie down and sleep in peace,
    for you alone, O LORD,
    make me dwell in safety.

PSALM 5

For the director of music. For flutes.
    A psalm of David.

¹Give ear to my words, O LORD,
    consider my sighing.
²Listen to my cry for help,
    my King and my God,
    for to you I pray.
³In the morning, O LORD, you hear my
        voice;
    in the morning I lay my requests
        before you
    and wait in expectation.

⁴You are not a God who takes pleasure in
        evil;
    with you the wicked cannot dwell.
⁵The arrogant cannot stand in your
        presence;
    you hate all who do wrong.
⁶You destroy those who tell lies;
    bloodthirsty and deceitful men
    the LORD abhors.

⁷But I, by your great mercy,
    will come into your house;
in reverence will I bow down
    toward your holy temple.
⁸Lead me, O LORD, in your righteousness
    because of my enemies—
    make straight your way before me.

⁹Not a word from their mouth can be trusted;
    their heart is filled with destruction.
Their throat is an open grave;
    with their tongue they speak deceit.
¹⁰Declare them guilty, O God!
    Let their intrigues be their downfall.
Banish them for their many sins,
    for they have rebelled against you.

¹¹But let all who take refuge in you be glad;
    let them ever sing for joy.
Spread your protection over them,
    that those who love your name may rejoice in you.
¹²For surely, O LORD, you bless the righteous;
    you surround them with your favor as with a shield.

Dealing With Anger

Anger is not a sin. If someone does something that ticks you off, you don't have to pretend it doesn't bother you. It's what you do with your anger that matters. The first thing you need to do is cool down—wait for your emotions to settle down; *then* work things out with the person who made you angry. Tell them how you feel and why—without getting in their face. If they apologize, forgive them and let it go. If they don't, turn things over to God. Ask him to help you get rid of your anger. Then leave it to him to deal with the other person.

»» live the adventure »» Ps 4:4

PSALM 6

For the director of music. With stringed instruments. According to *sheminith.*[a] A psalm of David.

1 O LORD, do not rebuke me in your anger
  or discipline me in your wrath.
2 Be merciful to me, LORD, for I am faint;
  O LORD, heal me, for my bones are in agony.
3 My soul is in anguish.
  How long, O LORD, how long?

4 Turn, O LORD, and deliver me;
  save me because of your unfailing
  love.
5 No one remembers you when he is dead.
  Who praises you from the grave[b]?

6 I am worn out from groaning;
  all night long I flood my bed with
  weeping
  and drench my couch with tears.
7 My eyes grow weak with sorrow;
  they fail because of all my foes.

8 Away from me, all you who do evil,
  for the LORD has heard my weeping.
9 The LORD has heard my cry for mercy;
  the LORD accepts my prayer.
10 All my enemies will be ashamed and
  dismayed;
  they will turn back in sudden
  disgrace.

PSALM 7

A *shiggaion*[c] of David, which he sang to the LORD concerning Cush, a Benjamite.

1 O LORD my God, I take refuge in you;
  save and deliver me from all who
  pursue me,
2 or they will tear me like a lion
  and rip me to pieces with no one to
  rescue me.

3 O LORD my God, if I have done this
  and there is guilt on my hands—
4 if I have done evil to him who is at peace with me
  or without cause have robbed my foe—
5 then let my enemy pursue and overtake me;
  let him trample my life to the ground
  and make me sleep in the dust.   *Selah*

6 Arise, O LORD, in your anger;
  rise up against the rage of my enemies.
  Awake, my God; decree justice.
7 Let the assembled peoples gather around you.
  Rule over them from on high;

> *live the adventure* >> Ps 5:3

Setting Aside Time for God

David had a great reason to spend time praying to God in the morning. After starting each new day talking to God about the things going on in his life, David could spend the rest of the day watching and waiting for God to work in his life. There's nothing cooler than seeing something you prayed for happen a few hours later. It's a great way to build your faith in and love for God.

---

[a] Title: Probably a musical term   [b] 5 Hebrew *Sheol*   [c] Title: Probably a literary or musical term

8   let the LORD judge the peoples.
  Judge me, O LORD, according to my
      righteousness,
    according to my integrity, O Most
      High.
9 O righteous God,
    who searches minds and hearts,
  bring to an end the violence of the
      wicked
  and make the righteous secure.

10 My shield[a] is God Most High,
    who saves the upright in heart.
11 God is a righteous judge,
    a God who expresses his wrath every
      day.
12 If he does not relent,
    he[b] will sharpen his sword;
  he will bend and string his bow.
13 He has prepared his deadly weapons;
    he makes ready his flaming arrows.

14 He who is pregnant with evil
    and conceives trouble gives birth to
      disillusionment.
15 He who digs a hole and scoops it out
    falls into the pit he has made.
16 The trouble he causes recoils on
      himself;
    his violence comes down on his own
      head.

17 I will give thanks to the LORD because of his righteousness
    and will sing praise to the name of the LORD Most High.

Letting God Take Care of Enemies

Enemies can make your life a nightmare. Whether they really want to hurt you or just want to make you look stupid every chance they get, enemies add major stress to your life—stress that you don't need or want. More often than not, trying to deal with them yourself only makes matters worse (or, in some cases, gets you a beating). That's why it's great to have a friend like God who can fight your battles for you and be a source of peace and comfort.

PSALM 8

For the director of music. According to *gittith*.[c] A psalm of David.

1 O LORD, our Lord,
    how majestic is your name in all the earth!

  You have set your glory
    above the heavens.
2 From the lips of children and infants
    you have ordained praise[d]
  because of your enemies,
    to silence the foe and the avenger.

3 When I consider your heavens,
    the work of your fingers,
  the moon and the stars,
    which you have set in place,
4 what is man that you are mindful of him,
    the son of man that you care for him?
5 You made him a little lower than the heavenly beings[e]
    and crowned him with glory and honor.

---

[a] 10 Or *sovereign*   [b] 12 Or *If a man does not repent, / God*   [c] Title: Probably a musical term   [d] 2 Or *strength*   [e] 5 Or *than God*

⁶You made him ruler over the works of your hands;
  you put everything under his feet:
⁷all flocks and herds,
  and the beasts of the field,
⁸the birds of the air,
  and the fish of the sea,
  all that swim the paths of the seas.

⁹O LORD, our Lord,
  how majestic is your name in all the earth!

now or never
PS 8:6–8

How good a job do you think humans are doing as rulers (that is, caretakers) of the earth? What are we doing right? What are some things you'd like to change? Remember, you don't have to be a politician or scientist to care about the environment

PSALM 9 ᵃ

For the director of music. To ⌊the tune of⌋ "The Death of the Son." A psalm of David.

¹I will praise you, O LORD, with all my heart;
  I will tell of all your wonders.
²I will be glad and rejoice in you;
  I will sing praise to your name, O Most High.

³My enemies turn back;
  they stumble and perish before you.
⁴For you have upheld my right and my cause;
  you have sat on your throne, judging righteously.
⁵You have rebuked the nations and destroyed the wicked;
  you have blotted out their name for ever and ever.
⁶Endless ruin has overtaken the enemy,
  you have uprooted their cities;
  even the memory of them has perished.

⁷The LORD reigns forever;
  he has established his throne for judgment.
⁸He will judge the world in righteousness;
  he will govern the peoples with justice.
⁹The LORD is a refuge for the oppressed,
  a stronghold in times of trouble.
¹⁰Those who know your name will trust in you,
  for you, LORD, have never forsaken those who seek you.

¹¹Sing praises to the LORD, enthroned in Zion;
  proclaim among the nations what he has done.
¹²For he who avenges blood remembers;
  he does not ignore the cry of the afflicted.

Appreciating God's Concern

It's pretty incredible when you think about it. The God who carved out the Grand Canyon cares about the things going on in your family. The God who raised up Mount Everest is concerned about how you're dealing with pressure at school. The God who filled the Pacific Ocean has a personal interest in the way you spend your weekends. The God who put every star and planet in the universe in its place wants to hear from you and talk to you every day. How should you respond to that kind of attention? The same way David did—with complete awe and wonder.

»» live the adventure »» Ps 8:4–9

ᵃ Psalms 9 and 10 may have been originally a single acrostic poem, the stanzas of which begin with the successive letters of the Hebrew alphabet. In the Septuagint they constitute one psalm.

13 O Lord, see how my enemies persecute me!
　　Have mercy and lift me up from the gates of death,
14 that I may declare your praises
　　in the gates of the Daughter of Zion
　　and there rejoice in your salvation.
15 The nations have fallen into the pit they have dug;
　　their feet are caught in the net they have hidden.
16 The Lord is known by his justice;
　　the wicked are ensnared by the work of their
　　　　hands.　　　　　　　　　　　　　*Higgaion.*[a] *Selah*
17 The wicked return to the grave,[b]
　　all the nations that forget God.
18 But the needy will not always be forgotten,
　　nor the hope of the afflicted ever perish.

19 Arise, O Lord, let not man triumph;
　　let the nations be judged in your presence.
20 Strike them with terror, O Lord;
　　let the nations know they are but men.　　　　*Selah*

PSALM 10[c]

1 Why, O Lord, do you stand far off?
　　Why do you hide yourself in times of
　　　　trouble?

2 In his arrogance the wicked man hunts
　　　　down the weak,
　　who are caught in the schemes he
　　　　devises.
3 He boasts of the cravings of his heart;
　　he blesses the greedy and reviles the
　　　　Lord.
4 In his pride the wicked does not seek
　　　　him;
　　in all his thoughts there is no room
　　　　for God.
5 His ways are always prosperous;
　　he is haughty and your laws are far
　　　　from him;
　　he sneers at all his enemies.
6 He says to himself, "Nothing will shake
　　　　me;
　　I'll always be happy and never have
　　　　trouble."
7 His mouth is full of curses and lies and
　　　　threats;
　　trouble and evil are under his
　　　　tongue.
8 He lies in wait near the villages;
　　from ambush he murders the
　　　　innocent,
　　watching in secret for his victims.
9 He lies in wait like a lion in cover;

Closing the Distance Between You and God

» live the adventure » Ps 10:1

Have you ever been hanging out with your buddies when trouble comes along and—wham!—your friends are gone and you're on your own? At some point in your life, you're going to be disappointed by a close friend or relative. Stuff like this makes it easy to doubt that God is really with us. Even David, a "man after God's own heart," wondered where God was more than a few times. Don't let the imperfection of your earthly relationships define your relationship with your heavenly Father. No matter what the circumstances, God will never abandon you.

---

[a] *16* Or *Meditation*; possibly a musical notation   [b] *17* Hebrew *Sheol*   [c] Psalms 9 and 10 may have been originally a single acrostic poem, the stanzas of which begin with the successive letters of the Hebrew alphabet. In the Septuagint they constitute one psalm.

he lies in wait to catch the helpless;
he catches the helpless and drags them off in his net.
¹⁰His victims are crushed, they collapse;
they fall under his strength.
¹¹He says to himself, "God has forgotten;
he covers his face and never sees."

¹²Arise, LORD! Lift up your hand, O God.
Do not forget the helpless.
¹³Why does the wicked man revile God?
Why does he say to himself,
"He won't call me to account"?
¹⁴But you, O God, do see trouble and grief;
you consider it to take it in hand.
The victim commits himself to you;
you are the helper of the fatherless.
¹⁵Break the arm of the wicked and evil
man;
call him to account for his
wickedness
that would not be found out.

¹⁶The LORD is King for ever and ever;
the nations will perish from his land.
¹⁷You hear, O LORD, the desire of the
afflicted;
you encourage them, and you listen to
their cry,
¹⁸defending the fatherless and the
oppressed,
in order that man, who is of the earth,
may terrify no more.

PSALM 11

For the director of music. Of David.

¹In the LORD I take refuge.
How then can you say to me:
"Flee like a bird to your mountain.
²For look, the wicked bend their bows;
they set their arrows against the
strings
to shoot from the shadows
at the upright in heart.
³When the foundations are being
destroyed,
what can the righteous do^a?"

⁴The LORD is in his holy temple;
the LORD is on his heavenly throne.
He observes the sons of men;
his eyes examine them.
⁵The LORD examines the righteous,
but the wicked^b and those who love violence
his soul hates.

»» live the adventure »» Ps 10:4-6

Keeping a Healthy Perspective on Money

Ever seen one of those TV shows in which celebrities take you on tours of their homes and show off all their stuff? You can see some pretty wild things—some cool, some cheesy. The one thing you won't see, though, is humility. That's because money messes with your head. The more Ferraris, swimming pools, and home theater systems you surround yourself with, the more you start to think you've got it made—that you don't need anyone. No wonder Jesus said it's easier for a camel to make it through a needle's eye than for a rich person to make it to heaven (see Matthew 19:24).

---

^a 3 Or *what is the Righteous One doing*   ^b 5 Or *The LORD, the Righteous One, examines the wicked, /*

⁶On the wicked he will rain
  fiery coals and burning sulfur;
  a scorching wind will be their lot.

⁷For the LORD is righteous,
  he loves justice;
  upright men will see his face.

PSALM 12

For the director of music. According to *sheminith.*ª A psalm of David.

¹Help, LORD, for the godly are no more;
  the faithful have vanished from among men.
²Everyone lies to his neighbor;
  their flattering lips speak with
    deception.

³May the LORD cut off all flattering lips
  and every boastful tongue
⁴that says, "We will triumph with our
    tongues;
  we own our lipsᵇ—who is our
    master?"

⁵"Because of the oppression of the
    weak
  and the groaning of the needy,
I will now arise," says the LORD.
  "I will protect them from those who
    malign them."
⁶And the words of the LORD are
    flawless,
  like silver refined in a
    furnace of clay,
  purified seven times.

⁷O LORD, you will keep us safe
  and protect us from such
    people forever.
⁸The wicked freely strut about
  when what is vile is
    honored among men.

NOW OR NEVER
PS 12:1

Ever feel like the only person in your neighborhood, your school or even your family who cares about doing what's right? Don't let it discourage you. One day your faithfulness will be rewarded by the One who sees everything. God guarantees it.

challenge notes

To: my_son

PS 12:3

heavenly_father: not all flattery is good. anyone who tries to make you think that you are something special apart from me is misleading you. don't invest your hope in human qualities. place your trust in me.

PSALM 13

For the director of music. A psalm of David.

¹How long, O LORD? Will you forget me forever?
  How long will you hide your face from me?
²How long must I wrestle with my thoughts
  and every day have sorrow in my heart?
  How long will my enemy triumph over me?

³Look on me and answer, O LORD my God.
  Give light to my eyes, or I will sleep in death;
⁴my enemy will say, "I have overcome him,"
  and my foes will rejoice when I fall.

ª Title: Probably a musical term   ᵇ 4 Or / *our lips are our plowshares*

battlelines

» Gorilla Warfare (Evolution)

Q: What are you reading?
A: Biology text book.

Q: What's the topic?
A: Origins of life, formation of the species . . . basically it's evolution. We've got a huge test tomorrow.

Q: Sounds like you're not into biology.
A: Actually, I like the labs and stuff. It's just the evolution part that's getting to me.

Q: Why?
A: I've always been taught that the earth was formed in six days and all human beings descended from Adam and Eve. Now I'm taking a test where the "right" answer is that the earth was created over billions of years, and Adam and Eve aren't even mentioned.

Q: So you don't buy into evolution?
A: I don't know. I'm not sure how both evolution and the Bible can be true.

Q: What does your teacher think about the Bible?
A: He doesn't talk about it, but I know he goes to church. It might be easier to know who to believe if the guy was an atheist or something.

Q: So what are you going to do?
A: Well, I have to take the test. And I guess taking a test isn't the same thing as saying that I believe in something, right?

Q: And what will you say if it comes up in class?
A: I guess I'll just say what I believe—that one way or the other, God created everything. I'd kind of like to ask my teacher point blank what he believes about the Bible.

» Origin(al) Thinking

Whatever you may think about the origins of the universe, some things are clear:

Biblical Fact: The first sentence in the Bible declares God to be the Creator of the universe. If we say we believe the Bible, we have to accept this claim.

Philosophical Truth: The elegant design of the universe argues powerfully for the existence of an intelligent Architect. (Would *anyone* honestly conclude that a complex sentence found written in the sand at the beach was the work of random waves and wind?)

Scientific Reality: A small but growing number of respected biologists, physicists and chemists are beginning to embrace the idea that however (and whenever) the universe came into existence, there had to be an intelligent force bringing it all together.

True science is not something we should be afraid of. Good, honest science uncovers truth that's consistent with the Bible. Many of the greatest scientists in history—people like Copernicus, Kepler, Galileo, Kelvin, Isaac Newton, Robert Boyle and Gregor Mendel—were devout believers who found no contradiction between their spiritual beliefs and their academic quests. The science we need to be wary of is biased science, which is based less on real evidence and more on atheistic presuppositions.

Read more about God and creation at www.RevolutionBible.com.

⁵But I trust in your unfailing love;
    my heart rejoices in your salvation.
⁶I will sing to the LORD,
    for he has been good to me.

PSALM 14

For the director of music. Of David.

¹The fool[a] says in his heart,
    "There is no God."
They are corrupt, their deeds are vile;
    there is no one who does good.

²The LORD looks down from heaven
    on the sons of men
to see if there are any who understand,
    any who seek God.
³All have turned aside,
    they have together become corrupt;
there is no one who does good,
    not even one.

⁴Will evildoers never learn—
    those who devour my people as men eat bread
    and who do not call on the LORD?
⁵There they are, overwhelmed with dread,
    for God is present in the company of the righteous.
⁶You evildoers frustrate the plans of the poor,
    but the LORD is their refuge.

⁷Oh, that salvation for Israel would come out of Zion!
    When the LORD restores the fortunes of his people,
    let Jacob rejoice and Israel be glad!

PSALM 15

A psalm of David.

¹LORD, who may dwell in your sanctuary?
    Who may live on your holy hill?

²He whose walk is blameless
    and who does what is righteous,
who speaks the truth from his heart
³   and has no slander on his tongue,
who does his neighbor no wrong
    and casts no slur on his fellowman,
⁴who despises a vile man
    but honors those who fear the LORD,
who keeps his oath
    even when it hurts,
⁵who lends his money without usury
    and does not accept a bribe against the innocent.

He who does these things
    will never be shaken.

ᵃ *1* The Hebrew words rendered *fool* in Psalms denote one who is morally deficient.

battlelines

» Jack the Ripper (Slander)

Q: Somebody said Coach Rogers gave you a hard time today.
A: Yeah, he went off on me big time.

Q: What's the deal?
A: The deal? The deal is he's a total jerk. I think he's bitter at the world because he never made it as an athlete, and he knows he's even worse as a coach.

Q: What are you talking about?
A: Haven't you heard? I thought everybody knew about him. What a loser! After high school, the only scholarship offer he got was from some no-name junior college. So he walked on at the state university and made the team. But he was third string, and sat the bench the whole time. He wasn't even good enough to play in college, let alone make it to the pros. I think he blew out a knee too. After that, he tried to be an assistant coach at the small-college level, but he couldn't cut it, so he got fired. Now he's coaching a high school JV team and taking out all his anger on us. He's such an idiot.

Q: Sounds like you're pretty angry too.
A: It's not just me. Nobody can stand him. And you should see the way he's always checking out the girls. What a sicko!

» Hold Everything . . . Especially That Tongue

Trashing other people has an odd way of making us feel powerful. That's why it's so tempting to point out everybody else's faults and spread juicy rumors. But here's the real truth—what God has to say on the subject:

- "Do not go about spreading slander among your people" (Leviticus 19:16).

- "Lord, who may dwell in your sanctuary? Who may live on your holy hill? He whose walk is blameless . . . and has no slander on his tongue" (Psalm 15:1–3).

- "Whoever spreads slander is a fool" (Proverbs 10:18).

- "And do not grieve the Holy Spirit of God . . . Get rid of all bitterness, rage and anger, brawling and slander, along with every form of malice" (Ephesians 4:30–31).

A vicious mouth says way more about the person who's doing the talking than it does about the person who's being trashed. Hold your tongue and ask God to give you a heart that isn't easily overcome by bitterness.

Learn more about the power of words at www.RevolutionBible.com.

PSALM 16

A *miktam*[a] of David.

1 Keep me safe, O God,
   for in you I take refuge.

2 I said to the LORD, "You are my Lord;
   apart from you I have no good thing."
3 As for the saints who are in the land,
   they are the glorious ones in whom is all my delight.[b]
4 The sorrows of those will increase
   who run after other gods.
 I will not pour out their libations of blood
   or take up their names on my lips.

5 LORD, you have assigned me my portion and my cup;
   you have made my lot secure.
6 The boundary lines have fallen for me in pleasant places;
   surely I have a delightful inheritance.

7 I will praise the LORD, who counsels me;
   even at night my heart instructs me.
8 I have set the LORD always before me.
   Because he is at my right hand,
   I will not be shaken.

9 Therefore my heart is glad and my tongue rejoices;
   my body also will rest secure,
10 because you will not abandon me to the grave,[c]
   nor will you let your Holy One[d] see decay.
11 You have made[e] known to me the path of life;
   you will fill me with joy in your presence,
   with eternal pleasures at your right hand.

PSALM 17

A prayer of David.

1 Hear, O LORD, my righteous plea;
   listen to my cry.
 Give ear to my prayer—
   it does not rise from deceitful lips.
2 May my vindication come from you;
   may your eyes see what is right.

3 Though you probe my heart and examine me at night,
   though you test me, you will find nothing;
   I have resolved that my mouth will not sin.
4 As for the deeds of men—
   by the word of your lips
 I have kept myself
   from the ways of the violent.
5 My steps have held to your paths;
   my feet have not slipped.

6 I call on you, O God, for you will answer me;
   give ear to me and hear my prayer.

---

[a] Title: Probably a literary or musical term   [b] 3 Or *As for the pagan priests who are in the land / and the nobles in whom all delight, I said:*   [c] 10 Hebrew *Sheol*   [d] 10 Or *your faithful one*   [e] 11 Or *You will make*

⁷Show the wonder of your great love,
  you who save by your right hand
    those who take refuge in you from their foes.
⁸Keep me as the apple of your eye;
  hide me in the shadow of your wings
⁹from the wicked who assail me,
  from my mortal enemies who surround me.

¹⁰They close up their callous hearts,
  and their mouths speak with arrogance.
¹¹They have tracked me down, they now surround me,
  with eyes alert, to throw me to the ground.
¹²They are like a lion hungry for prey,
  like a great lion crouching in cover.

¹³Rise up, O Lord, confront them, bring them down;
  rescue me from the wicked by your sword.
¹⁴O Lord, by your hand save me from such men,
  from men of this world whose reward is in this life.

You still the hunger of those you cherish;
  their sons have plenty,
  and they store up wealth for their children.
¹⁵And I—in righteousness I will see your face;
  when I awake, I will be satisfied with seeing your likeness.

PSALM 18

For the director of music. Of David the servant of the Lord. He sang to the Lord the words of this song when the Lord delivered him from the hand of all his enemies and from the hand of Saul. He said:

¹I love you, O Lord, my strength.

²The Lord is my rock, my fortress and my deliverer;
  my God is my rock, in whom I take refuge.

He is my shield and the horn ᵃ of my salvation, my stronghold.
³I call to the Lord, who is worthy of praise,
  and I am saved from my enemies.

⁴The cords of death entangled me;
  the torrents of destruction overwhelmed me.
⁵The cords of the grave ᵇ coiled around me;
  the snares of death confronted me.
⁶In my distress I called to the Lord;
  I cried to my God for help.

NOW OR NEVER
PS 18:1–2

David describes the Lord as a rock and a fortress. What would you compare him to? During one of your quiet times this week, try coming up with an analogy that's helpful to you.

From his temple he heard my voice;
  my cry came before him, into his ears.

⁷The earth trembled and quaked,
  and the foundations of the mountains shook;
    they trembled because he was angry.
⁸Smoke rose from his nostrils;
  consuming fire came from his mouth,

ᵃ 2 Horn here symbolizes strength.   ᵇ 5 Hebrew Sheol

burning coals blazed out of it.
⁹ He parted the heavens and came down;
dark clouds were under his feet.
¹⁰ He mounted the cherubim and flew;
he soared on the wings of the wind.
¹¹ He made darkness his covering, his canopy around him—
the dark rain clouds of the sky.
¹² Out of the brightness of his presence clouds advanced,
with hailstones and bolts of lightning.
¹³ The Lᴏʀᴅ thundered from heaven;
the voice of the Most High resounded. ᵃ
¹⁴ He shot his arrows and scattered ⌊the enemies⌋,
great bolts of lightning and routed them.
¹⁵ The valleys of the sea were exposed
and the foundations of the earth laid bare
at your rebuke, O Lᴏʀᴅ,
at the blast of breath from your nostrils.

¹⁶ He reached down from on high and took hold of me;
he drew me out of deep waters.
¹⁷ He rescued me from my powerful enemy,
from my foes, who were too strong for me.
¹⁸ They confronted me in the day of my disaster,
but the Lᴏʀᴅ was my support.
¹⁹ He brought me out into a spacious place;
he rescued me because he delighted in me.

²⁰ The Lᴏʀᴅ has dealt with me according to my righteousness;
according to the cleanness of my hands he has rewarded me.
²¹ For I have kept the ways of the Lᴏʀᴅ;
I have not done evil by turning from my God.
²² All his laws are before me;
I have not turned away from his decrees.
²³ I have been blameless before him
and have kept myself from sin.
²⁴ The Lᴏʀᴅ has rewarded me according to my righteousness,
according to the cleanness of my hands in his sight.

²⁵ To the faithful you show yourself faithful,
to the blameless you show yourself blameless,
²⁶ to the pure you show yourself pure,
but to the crooked you show yourself shrewd.
²⁷ You save the humble
but bring low those whose eyes are haughty.
²⁸ You, O Lᴏʀᴅ, keep my lamp burning;
my God turns my darkness into light.
²⁹ With your help I can advance against a troop ᵇ;
with my God I can scale a wall.

³⁰ As for God, his way is perfect;
the word of the Lᴏʀᴅ is flawless.
He is a shield
for all who take refuge in him.
³¹ For who is God besides the Lᴏʀᴅ?
And who is the Rock except our God?

ᵃ *13* Some Hebrew manuscripts and Septuagint (see also 2 Samuel 22:14); most Hebrew manuscripts *resounded, / amid hailstones and bolts of lightning*   ᵇ *29* Or *can run through a barricade*

³²It is God who arms me with strength
and makes my way perfect.
³³He makes my feet like the feet of a deer;
he enables me to stand on the heights.
³⁴He trains my hands for battle;
my arms can bend a bow of bronze.
³⁵You give me your shield of victory,
and your right hand sustains me;
you stoop down to make me great.
³⁶You broaden the path beneath me,
so that my ankles do not turn.

³⁷I pursued my enemies and overtook
them;
I did not turn back till they were
destroyed.
³⁸I crushed them so that they could not
rise;
they fell beneath my feet.
³⁹You armed me with strength for battle;
you made my adversaries bow at my
feet.
⁴⁰You made my enemies turn their backs in
flight,
and I destroyed my foes.
⁴¹They cried for help, but there was no one
to save them—
to the Lord, but he did not answer.
⁴²I beat them as fine as dust borne on the
wind;
I poured them out like mud in the
streets.

⁴³You have delivered me from the attacks of
the people;
you have made me the head of
nations;
people I did not know are subject
to me.
⁴⁴As soon as they hear me, they obey me;
foreigners cringe before me.
⁴⁵They all lose heart;
they come trembling from their
strongholds.

⁴⁶The Lord lives! Praise be to my Rock!
Exalted be God my Savior!
⁴⁷He is the God who avenges me,
who subdues nations under me,
⁴⁸   who saves me from my enemies.
You exalted me above my foes;
from violent men you rescued me.
⁴⁹Therefore I will praise you among the nations, O Lord;
I will sing praises to your name.
⁵⁰He gives his king great victories;
he shows unfailing kindness to his anointed,
to David and his descendants forever.

Trusting God's Plan

Do you believe God's way is really perfect? Do you believe his Word is totally flawless? Think carefully before you answer. If you say you believe God's plan is perfect, then you have no reason not to follow it. Otherwise, it's like saying you've met the perfect girl and then looking around for someone else to date.

PSALM 19

For the director of music. A psalm of David.

¹ The heavens declare the glory of God;
  the skies proclaim the work of his hands.
² Day after day they pour forth speech;
  night after night they display knowledge.
³ There is no speech or language
  where their voice is not heard.ᵃ

⁴ Their voiceᵇ goes out into all the earth,
  their words to the ends of the world.

In the heavens he has pitched a tent for
  the sun,
⁵ which is like a bridegroom coming
  forth from his pavilion,
  like a champion rejoicing to run his
  course.
⁶ It rises at one end of the heavens
  and makes its circuit to the other;
  nothing is hidden from its heat.

⁷ The law of the LORD is perfect,
  reviving the soul.

now or never

PS 19:1

Not believing in God after seeing the awesome things in nature is like not believing that a thinking, living being painted the Mona Lisa. You have to explain the work somehow.

The statutes of the LORD are trustworthy,
  making wise the simple.
⁸ The precepts of the LORD are right,
  giving joy to the heart.
The commands of the LORD are radiant,
  giving light to the eyes.
⁹ The fear of the LORD is pure,
  enduring forever.
The ordinances of the LORD are sure
  and altogether righteous.

¹⁰ They are more precious than
  gold,
  than much pure gold;
  they are sweeter than honey,
  than honey from the comb.
¹¹ By them is your servant
  warned;
  in keeping them there is
  great reward.

¹² Who can discern his errors?
  Forgive my hidden faults.
¹³ Keep your servant also from
  willful sins;

challenge notes

To: my_son

heavenly_father: I've filled the world with testimony about my character and work. if you ever doubt me, just observe the vast universe. if I could design a perfect plan for the millions of galaxies in space, then you can trust that I've done the same for you.

72863   6 G C F E

may they not rule over me.
Then will I be blameless,
  innocent of great transgression.

¹⁴ May the words of my mouth and the meditation of my heart
  be pleasing in your sight,
  O LORD, my Rock and my Redeemer.

ᵃ *3 Or They have no speech, there are no words; / no sound is heard from them*   ᵇ *4 Septuagint, Jerome and Syriac; Hebrew line*

PSALM 20

For the director of music. A psalm of David.

¹ May the LORD answer you when you are in distress;
may the name of the God of Jacob protect you.
² May he send you help from the
sanctuary
and grant you support from Zion.
³ May he remember all your sacrifices
and accept your burnt offerings.
Selah
⁴ May he give you the desire of your heart
and make all your plans succeed.
⁵ We will shout for joy when you are
victorious
and will lift up our banners in the
name of our God.
May the LORD grant all your requests.

⁶ Now I know that the LORD saves his
anointed;
he answers him from his holy heaven
with the saving power of his right hand.
⁷ Some trust in chariots and some in horses,
but we trust in the name of the LORD
our God.
⁸ They are brought to their knees and fall,
but we rise up and stand firm.

⁹ O LORD, save the king!
Answer[a] us when we call!

PSALM 21

For the director of music. A psalm of David.

¹ O LORD, the king rejoices in your
strength.
How great is his joy in the victories
you give!
² You have granted him the desire of his
heart
and have not withheld the request of
his lips. *Selah*
³ You welcomed him with rich blessings
and placed a crown of pure gold on
his head.
⁴ He asked you for life, and you gave it to
him—
length of days, for ever and ever.
⁵ Through the victories you gave, his glory
is great;
you have bestowed on him splendor
and majesty.
⁶ Surely you have granted him eternal
blessings

NOW OR NEVER
PS 20:7

Where do your non-Christian friends put
their trust? How can you help them see
that anything besides God is temporary
and that nothing or nobody is as trustworthy he is?

Recognizing God's Work

What does nature tell us about
God? For one thing, it tells us
that he appreciates beauty. He
could have made a sunset look
any way he wanted, but look at
the masterpiece he painted in
the sky. Nature also tells us
that God appreciates diversity.
He didn't stop with one or two
different types of insects;
he made thousands. He
wasn't satisfied with just
land animals; he made
sea creatures and birds
too. Look closely and
you'll see that nature tells
us that God is concerned
with even the tiniest de-
tails of life. He designed
every creature so it's perfectly suited to its environment. Enjoying God's
creation can give us more
than enough reason to
worship him.

»» live the adventure »» Ps 19:1-4

ᵃ *9* Or *save! / O King, answer*

and made him glad with the joy of your presence.
⁷For the king trusts in the LORD;
    through the unfailing love of the Most High
    he will not be shaken.

⁸Your hand will lay hold on all your enemies;
    your right hand will seize your foes.
⁹At the time of your appearing
    you will make them like a fiery furnace.
 In his wrath the LORD will swallow them up,
    and his fire will consume them.
¹⁰You will destroy their descendants from the earth,
    their posterity from mankind.
¹¹Though they plot evil against you
    and devise wicked schemes, they cannot succeed;
¹²for you will make them turn their backs
    when you aim at them with drawn bow.

¹³Be exalted, O LORD, in your strength;
    we will sing and praise your might.

PSALM 22

For the director of music. To ⌊the tune of⌋ "The Doe of the Morning."
A psalm of David.

¹My God, my God, why have you forsaken me?
    Why are you so far from saving me,
    so far from the words of my groaning?

²O my God, I cry out by day, but you do
    not answer,
    by night, and am not silent.

³Yet you are enthroned as the Holy One;
    you are the praise of Israel.[a]
⁴In you our fathers put their trust;
    they trusted and you delivered them.
⁵They cried to you and were saved;
    in you they trusted and were not
    disappointed.

⁶But I am a worm and not a man,
    scorned by men and despised by the
    people.

NOW OR NEVER
PS 22:1

If these words seem familiar, it's because Jesus quoted them when he was hanging from the cross. Jesus (like David) knew firsthand what suffering was like. That's why it makes sense to cry out to him when you're going through hard times.

⁷All who see me mock me;
    they hurl insults, shaking their heads:
⁸"He trusts in the LORD;
    let the LORD rescue him.
 Let him deliver him,
    since he delights in him."

⁹Yet you brought me out of the womb;
    you made me trust in you
    even at my mother's breast.
¹⁰From birth I was cast upon you;
    from my mother's womb you have been my God.
¹¹Do not be far from me,

---

[a] 3 Or *Yet you are holy, / enthroned on the praises of Israel*

for trouble is near
    and there is no one to help.

12 Many bulls surround me;
    strong bulls of Bashan encircle me.
13 Roaring lions tearing their prey
    open their mouths wide against me.
14 I am poured out like water,
    and all my bones are out of joint.
My heart has turned to wax;
    it has melted away within me.
15 My strength is dried up like a potsherd,
    and my tongue sticks to the roof of my mouth;
    you lay me[a] in the dust of death.
16 Dogs have surrounded me;
    a band of evil men has encircled me,
    they have pierced[b] my hands and my feet.
17 I can count all my bones;
    people stare and gloat over me.
18 They divide my garments among them
    and cast lots for my clothing.

19 But you, O LORD, be not far off;
    O my Strength, come quickly to help me.
20 Deliver my life from the sword,
    my precious life from the power of the dogs.
21 Rescue me from the mouth of the lions;
    save[c] me from the horns of the wild oxen.

22 I will declare your name to my brothers;
    in the congregation I will praise you.
23 You who fear the LORD, praise him!
    All you descendants of Jacob, honor him!
    Revere him, all you descendants of Israel!
24 For he has not despised or disdained
    the suffering of the afflicted one;
he has not hidden his face from him
    but has listened to his cry for help.

25 From you comes the theme of my praise in the great assembly;
    before those who fear you[d] will I fulfill my vows.
26 The poor will eat and be satisfied;
    they who seek the LORD will praise him—
    may your hearts live forever!
27 All the ends of the earth
    will remember and turn to the LORD,
and all the families of the nations
    will bow down before him,
28 for dominion belongs to the LORD
    and he rules over the nations.

29 All the rich of the earth will feast and worship;
    all who go down to the dust will kneel before him—
    those who cannot keep themselves alive.
30 Posterity will serve him;

---

[a] 15 Or / I am laid   [b] 16 Some Hebrew manuscripts, Septuagint and Syriac; most Hebrew manuscripts / like the lion,   [c] 21 Or / you have heard   [d] 25 Hebrew him

future generations will be told about the Lord.
³¹ They will proclaim his righteousness
to a people yet unborn—
for he has done it.

PSALM 23

A psalm of David.

¹ The LORD is my shepherd, I shall not be
in want.
² He makes me lie down in green
pastures,
he leads me beside quiet waters,
³ he restores my soul.
He guides me in paths of righteousness
for his name's sake.
⁴ Even though I walk
through the valley of the shadow of
death,ᵃ
I will fear no evil,
for you are with me;
your rod and your staff,
they comfort me.

⁵ You prepare a table before me
in the presence of my enemies.
You anoint my head with oil;
my cup overflows.
⁶ Surely goodness and love will follow
me
all the days of my life,
and I will dwell in the house of the LORD
forever.

PSALM 24

Of David. A psalm.

¹ The earth is the LORD's, and everything in it,
the world, and all who live in it;
² for he founded it upon the seas
and established it upon the waters.

³ Who may ascend the hill of the LORD?
Who may stand in his holy place?
⁴ He who has clean hands and a pure heart,
who does not lift up his soul to an idol
or swear by what is false.ᵇ
⁵ He will receive blessing from the LORD
and vindication from God his Savior.
⁶ Such is the generation of those who seek him,
who seek your face, O God of Jacob.ᶜ   Selah

⁷ Lift up your heads, O you gates;
be lifted up, you ancient doors,
that the King of glory may come in.

Finding Comfort in Dark Times

What's the closest you've ever come to being in the "valley of the shadow of death"? Was it the death of a friend or neighbor? Maybe a life-threatening illness for a close family member? A potentially deadly accident you were in? God is the only One who can offer the kind of comfort and security you need during the worst times of your life. Your best bet is to draw as close to him as you possibly can and let him guard your every step.

ᵃ 4 Or *through the darkest valley*   ᵇ 4 Or *swear falsely*   ᶜ 6 Two Hebrew manuscripts and Syriac (see also Septuagint); most Hebrew manuscripts *face, Jacob*

8 Who is this King of glory?
   The Lord strong and mighty,
   the Lord mighty in battle.
9 Lift up your heads, O you gates;
   lift them up, you ancient doors,
   that the King of glory may come in.
10 Who is he, this King of glory?
   The Lord Almighty—
   he is the King of glory.   *Selah*

PSALM 25 [a]

Of David.

1 To you, O Lord, I lift up my soul;
2   in you I trust, O my God.
   Do not let me be put to shame,
      nor let my enemies triumph over me.

3 No one whose hope is in you
      will ever be put to shame,
   but they will be put to shame
      who are treacherous without excuse.

4 Show me your ways, O Lord,
      teach me your paths;
5 guide me in your truth and teach me,
      for you are God my Savior,
      and my hope is in you all day long.
6 Remember, O Lord, your great mercy
         and love,
      for they are from of old.
7 Remember not the sins of my youth

NOW OR NEVER
PS 25:4–5

Notice that David didn't say, "Make me smart, God." He didn't want an immediate brain transplant. Instead, he used words like "show," "teach" and "guide." David knew that becoming wise required a process of learning and maturing.

   and my rebellious ways;
   according to your love remember me,
      for you are good, O Lord.

8 Good and upright is the Lord;
      therefore he instructs sinners in his ways.
9 He guides the humble in what is right
      and teaches them his way.

10 All the ways of the Lord are loving and
         faithful
      for those who keep the demands of
         his covenant.
11 For the sake of your name, O Lord,
      forgive my iniquity, though it is
         great.
12 Who, then, is the man that fears the
         Lord?
      He will instruct him in the way
         chosen for him.
13 He will spend his days in prosperity,
      and his descendants will inherit the
         land.

NOW OR NEVER
PS 25:7

What sins of your "youth" would you like God to forget? The good news is that if you're serious about wanting to get rid of them forever, God can make it happen.

14 The Lord confides in those who fear him;
      he makes his covenant known to them.

---

a This psalm is an acrostic poem, the verses of which begin with the successive letters of the Hebrew alphabet.

[15] My eyes are ever on the LORD,
for only he will release my feet from the snare.

[16] Turn to me and be gracious to me,
for I am lonely and afflicted.
[17] The troubles of my heart have multiplied;
free me from my anguish.
[18] Look upon my affliction and my distress
and take away all my sins.
[19] See how my enemies have increased
and how fiercely they hate me!
[20] Guard my life and rescue me;
let me not be put to shame,
for I take refuge in you.
[21] May integrity and uprightness protect me,
because my hope is in you.

[22] Redeem Israel, O God,
from all their troubles!

PSALM 26

Of David.

[1] Vindicate me, O LORD,
for I have led a blameless life;
I have trusted in the LORD
without wavering.
[2] Test me, O LORD, and try me,
examine my heart and my mind;
[3] for your love is ever before me,
and I walk continually in your truth.
[4] I do not sit with deceitful men,
nor do I consort with hypocrites;
[5] I abhor the assembly of evildoers
and refuse to sit with the wicked.
[6] I wash my hands in innocence,
and go about your altar, O LORD,
[7] proclaiming aloud your praise
and telling of all your wonderful deeds.
[8] I love the house where you live, O LORD,
the place where your glory dwells.

[9] Do not take away my soul along with sinners,
my life with bloodthirsty men,
[10] in whose hands are wicked schemes,
whose right hands are full of bribes.
[11] But I lead a blameless life;
redeem me and be merciful to me.

[12] My feet stand on level ground;
in the great assembly I will praise the LORD.

PSALM 27

Of David.

[1] The LORD is my light and my salvation—
whom shall I fear?

The LORD is the stronghold of my life—
    of whom shall I be afraid?
2 When evil men advance against me
    to devour my flesh,[a]
when my enemies and my foes attack me,
    they will stumble and fall.
3 Though an army besiege me,
    my heart will not fear;
though war break out against me,
    even then will I be confident.

4 One thing I ask of the LORD,
    this is what I seek:
that I may dwell in the house of the LORD
    all the days of my life,
to gaze upon the beauty of the LORD
    and to seek him in his temple.
5 For in the day of trouble
    he will keep me safe in his dwelling;
he will hide me in the shelter of his tabernacle
    and set me high upon a rock.
6 Then my head will be exalted
    above the enemies who surround me;
at his tabernacle will I sacrifice with shouts of joy;
    I will sing and make music to the LORD.

7 Hear my voice when I call, O LORD;
    be merciful to me and answer me.
8 My heart says of you, "Seek his[b] face!"
    Your face, LORD, I will seek.
9 Do not hide your face from me,
    do not turn your servant away in anger;
    you have been my helper.
Do not reject me or forsake me,
    O God my Savior.
10 Though my father and mother forsake me,
    the LORD will receive me.
11 Teach me your way, O LORD;
    lead me in a straight path
    because of my oppressors.
12 Do not turn me over to the desire of my foes,
    for false witnesses rise up against me,
    breathing out violence.

13 I am still confident of this:
    I will see the goodness of the LORD
    in the land of the living.
14 Wait for the LORD;
    be strong and take heart
    and wait for the LORD.

PSALM 28

Of David.

1 To you I call, O LORD my Rock;
    do not turn a deaf ear to me.

---

a 2 Or *to slander me*   b 8 Or *To you, O my heart, he has said, "Seek my*

For if you remain silent,
    I will be like those who have gone down to the pit.
² Hear my cry for mercy
    as I call to you for help,
    as I lift up my hands
        toward your Most Holy Place.

³ Do not drag me away with the wicked,
    with those who do evil,
who speak cordially with their neighbors
    but harbor malice in their hearts.
⁴ Repay them for their deeds
    and for their evil work;
repay them for what their hands have done
    and bring back upon them what they deserve.
⁵ Since they show no regard for the works of the Lord
    and what his hands have done,
he will tear them down
    and never build them up again.

NOW OR NEVER
PS 28:1–3

Do you ever feel as though God isn't listening? Do you have a prayer that hasn't been answered? Is it possible you've received an answer without knowing it? Remember, God may not respond the way we expect; but he always hears our prayers.

⁶ Praise be to the Lord,
    for he has heard my cry for mercy.
⁷ The Lord is my strength and my shield;
    my heart trusts in him, and I am helped.
My heart leaps for joy
    and I will give thanks to him in song.

⁸ The Lord is the strength of his people,
    a fortress of salvation for his anointed one.
⁹ Save your people and bless your inheritance;
    be their shepherd and carry them forever.

NOW OR NEVER
PS 29:1–2

You can't be in a tight relationship with God unless you're really engaged in worshiping him. Imagine if you were engaged to marry a beautiful girl but never told her how much you loved her or how beautiful she was. What kind of relationship would that be?

PSALM 29

A psalm of David.

¹ Ascribe to the Lord, O mighty ones,
    ascribe to the Lord glory and strength.
² Ascribe to the Lord the glory due his name;
    worship the Lord in the splendor of his[a] holiness.

³ The voice of the Lord is over the waters;
    the God of glory thunders,
    the Lord thunders over the mighty waters.
⁴ The voice of the Lord is powerful;
    the voice of the Lord is majestic.
⁵ The voice of the Lord breaks the cedars;
    the Lord breaks in pieces the cedars of Lebanon.
⁶ He makes Lebanon skip like a calf,

ª 2 Or Lord with the splendor of

Sirion[a] like a young wild ox.
7 The voice of the LORD strikes
with flashes of lightning.
8 The voice of the LORD shakes the desert;
the LORD shakes the Desert of
Kadesh.
9 The voice of the LORD twists the oaks[b]
and strips the forests bare.
And in his temple all cry, "Glory!"

10 The LORD sits[c] enthroned over the flood;
the LORD is enthroned as King
forever.
11 The LORD gives strength to his people;
the LORD blesses his people with
peace.

now or never
PS 29:4–9

If you were going to illustrate God's power using modern examples from your own experiences, what kind of things would you highlight? Try writing them down and sharing them with someone who needs a fresh perspective.

PSALM 30

A psalm. A song. For the dedication of the temple.[d] Of David.

1 I will exalt you, O LORD,
for you lifted me out of the depths
and did not let my enemies gloat over me.
2 O LORD my God, I called to you for help
and you healed me.
3 O LORD, you brought me up from the grave[e];
you spared me from going down into the pit.

4 Sing to the LORD, you saints of his;
praise his holy name.
5 For his anger lasts only a moment,
but his favor lasts a lifetime;
weeping may remain for a night,
but rejoicing comes in the morning.

6 When I felt secure, I said,
"I will never be shaken."
7 O LORD, when you favored me,
you made my mountain[f] stand firm;
but when you hid your face,
I was dismayed.

8 To you, O LORD, I called;
to the Lord I cried for mercy:
9 "What gain is there in my destruction,[g]
in my going down into the pit?
Will the dust praise you?
Will it proclaim your faithfulness?
10 Hear, O LORD, and be merciful to me;
O LORD, be my help."

11 You turned my wailing into dancing;
you removed my sackcloth and clothed me with joy,
12 that my heart may sing to you and not be silent.
O LORD my God, I will give you thanks forever.

---

a 6 That is, Mount Hermon   b 9 Or LORD makes the deer give birth   c 10 Or sat   d Title: Or palace   e 3 Hebrew Sheol   f 7 Or hill country   g 9 Or there if I am silenced

For the director of music. A psalm of David.

¹ In you, O LORD, I have taken refuge;
　let me never be put to shame;
　　deliver me in your righteousness.
² Turn your ear to me,
　come quickly to my rescue;
　be my rock of refuge,
　　a strong fortress to save me.
³ Since you are my rock and my fortress,
　for the sake of your name lead and guide me.
⁴ Free me from the trap that is set for me,
　for you are my refuge.
⁵ Into your hands I commit my spirit;
　redeem me, O LORD, the God of truth.

⁶ I hate those who cling to worthless idols;
　I trust in the LORD.
⁷ I will be glad and rejoice in your love,
　for you saw my affliction
　　and knew the anguish of my soul.
⁸ You have not handed me over to the enemy
　but have set my feet in a spacious place.

⁹ Be merciful to me, O LORD, for I am in distress;
　my eyes grow weak with sorrow,
　　my soul and my body with grief.
¹⁰ My life is consumed by anguish
　and my years by groaning;
　my strength fails because of my affliction,ᵃ
　　and my bones grow weak.
¹¹ Because of all my enemies,
　I am the utter contempt of my neighbors;
　I am a dread to my friends—
　　those who see me on the street flee from me.
¹² I am forgotten by them as though I were dead;
　I have become like broken pottery.
¹³ For I hear the slander of many;
　there is terror on every side;
　they conspire against me
　　and plot to take my life.

¹⁴ But I trust in you, O LORD;
　I say, "You are my God."
¹⁵ My times are in your hands;
　deliver me from my enemies
　　and from those who pursue me.
¹⁶ Let your face shine on your servant;
　save me in your unfailing love.
¹⁷ Let me not be put to shame, O LORD,
　for I have cried out to you;
　but let the wicked be put to shame
　　and lie silent in the grave.ᵇ
¹⁸ Let their lying lips be silenced,

ᵃ 10 Or guilt   ᵇ 17 Hebrew Sheol

for with pride and contempt
   they speak arrogantly against the righteous.

19 How great is your goodness,
      which you have stored up for those who fear you,
   which you bestow in the sight of men
      on those who take refuge in you.
20 In the shelter of your presence you hide them
      from the intrigues of men;
   in your dwelling you keep them safe
      from accusing tongues.

21 Praise be to the LORD,
      for he showed his wonderful love to me
   when I was in a besieged city.
22 In my alarm I said,
      "I am cut off from your sight!"
   Yet you heard my cry for mercy
      when I called to you for help.

23 Love the LORD, all his saints!
      The LORD preserves the faithful,
   but the proud he pays back in full.
24 Be strong and take heart,
      all you who hope in the LORD.

PSALM 32

Of David. A *maskil.*[a]

1 Blessed is he
      whose transgressions are forgiven,
      whose sins are covered.
2 Blessed is the man
      whose sin the LORD does not count against him
      and in whose spirit is no deceit.

3 When I kept silent,
      my bones wasted away
      through my groaning all day long.
4 For day and night
      your hand was heavy upon me;
   my strength was sapped
      as in the heat of summer.   *Selah*
5 Then I acknowledged my sin to you
      and did not cover up my iniquity.
   I said, "I will confess
      my transgressions to the LORD"—
   and you forgave
      the guilt of my sin.   *Selah*

6 Therefore let everyone who is godly pray to you
      while you may be found;
   surely when the mighty waters rise,
      they will not reach him.
7 You are my hiding place;

NOW OR NEVER

PS 32:3

Sin isn't something to mess around with. The longer you try to ignore it, the more it will eat away at your conscience. That's why it's important to confess your sin as soon as possible and ask God to wipe it out of your life for good.

---

a Title: Probably a literary or musical term

you will protect me from trouble
and surround me with songs of deliverance. *Selah*

[8] I will instruct you and teach you in the
way you should go;
I will counsel you and watch over
you.
[9] Do not be like the horse or the mule,
which have no understanding
but must be controlled by bit and bridle
or they will not come to you.
[10] Many are the woes of the wicked,
but the LORD's unfailing love
surrounds the man who trusts in him.

[11] Rejoice in the LORD and be glad, you
righteous;
sing, all you who are upright in
heart!

PSALM 33

[1] Sing joyfully to the LORD, you righteous;
it is fitting for the upright to praise
him.
[2] Praise the LORD with the harp;
make music to him on the
ten-stringed lyre.
[3] Sing to him a new song;
play skillfully, and shout for joy.

[4] For the word of the LORD is right and
true;
he is faithful in all he does.
[5] The LORD loves righteousness and
justice;
the earth is full of his unfailing love.

[6] By the word of the LORD were the heavens made,
their starry host by the breath of his mouth.
[7] He gathers the waters of the sea into jars[a];
he puts the deep into storehouses.
[8] Let all the earth fear the LORD;
let all the people of the world revere
him.
[9] For he spoke, and it came to be;
he commanded, and it stood firm.
[10] The LORD foils the plans of the nations;
he thwarts the purposes of the
peoples.
[11] But the plans of the LORD stand firm
forever,
the purposes of his heart through all
generations.

[12] Blessed is the nation whose God is the LORD,
the people he chose for his inheritance.

Treating Sin Seriously

When you do something that hurts your relationship with God, don't just try to shrug it off. Don't just say, "Oops, my bad," and leave it at that. Treat sin as seriously as David did. Step up to the plate, admit what you did wrong and beg God for his forgiveness. That's the only way to make things right with God again.

» live the adventure » Ps 32:1-5

NOW OR NEVER
PS 33:1

Do you ever sing? When you're by yourself, do you find yourself rocking along with the tunes coming out of your speakers? Did you realize that with the right song, you can wail away and praise God at the same time? Think about it.

---

a 7 Or *sea as into a heap*

battlelines

» Sifting Through the Options (Future)

Q: So what have you decided about college?

A: (Groans) Oh, you had to bring up *that* topic.

Q: What's the problem?

A: I'm stuck. I have no idea what to do. I've gone over it in my mind a million times. All the pros and cons. I've asked every wise person I know. I've been praying for months. And after all that, everything is about as clear as mud to me. You don't have any advice for me, do you?

Q: Me? No. I just ask the questions. I don't do answers.

A: Some help you are.

Q: So what does it all come down to?

A: Three really good schools. Three different majors. All stuff I'm interested in. All potentially good programs that could lead to good careers.

Q: You're unusual.

A: Thanks a lot.

Q: No, seriously, I think it's cool that you're interested in so many things. But it's a little unusual, don't you think? Some guys can't even think of one thing they really care about—except sports or girls.

A: Yeah, well, it's driving me nuts. I feel like a little kid when you ask him what he wants to be when he grows up and he rattles off a bunch of different things. But, honestly, I *do* want variety in my life. If I only get one chance in this world, I want to make the most of it. It's just hard to know where to start.

» A Little Wisdom, Please

Frankly, Evan needs to chill. He's got a lot to feel good about. He has a passion for life, a hunger to learn, a desire to use his abilities to do something worthwhile and, most important, a willingness to follow God. Those are all *huge* assets that point to a bright future. Evan also has this going for him: God's promise to give wisdom to those who follow him (see Psalm 32:8; James 1:5–6).

Put it all together and you've got a solid foundation for success. Now Evan can make prayerful, careful decisions, realizing that college choices are not life and death—not when your heart belongs to God and your deepest desire is to live for him. Pick a school, Evan. If it doesn't end up being what you imagined, what have you lost? One semester? Compared to the wisdom you've gained, it's still a good deal.

Discover tools that will help plan your future at www.RevolutionBible.com.

¹³From heaven the Lord looks down
and sees all mankind;
¹⁴from his dwelling place he watches
all who live on earth—
¹⁵he who forms the hearts of all,
who considers everything they do.
¹⁶No king is saved by the size of his army;
no warrior escapes by his great strength.
¹⁷A horse is a vain hope for deliverance;
despite all its great strength it cannot save.
¹⁸But the eyes of the Lord are on those who fear him,
on those whose hope is in his unfailing love,
¹⁹to deliver them from death
and keep them alive in famine.

²⁰We wait in hope for the Lord;
he is our help and our shield.
²¹In him our hearts rejoice,
for we trust in his holy name.
²²May your unfailing love rest upon us, O Lord,
even as we put our hope in you.

PSALM 34 ª

Of David. When he pretended to be insane before Abimelech, who
drove him away, and he left.

¹I will extol the Lord at all times;
his praise will always be on my lips.
²My soul will boast in the Lord;
let the afflicted hear and rejoice.
³Glorify the Lord with me;
let us exalt his name together.

⁴I sought the Lord, and he answered me;
he delivered me from all my fears.
⁵Those who look to him are radiant;
their faces are never covered with
shame.
⁶This poor man called, and the Lord
heard him;
he saved him out of all his troubles.
⁷The angel of the Lord encamps around
those who fear him,
and he delivers them.

⁸Taste and see that the Lord is good;
blessed is the man who takes refuge
in him.
⁹Fear the Lord, you his saints,
for those who fear him lack nothing.
¹⁰The lions may grow weak and hungry,
but those who seek the Lord lack no good thing.
¹¹Come, my children, listen to me;
I will teach you the fear of the Lord.
¹²Whoever of you loves life

NOW OR NEVER
PS 34:8

You can get a lot of encouragement from
hearing what God has done in other people's lives. Eventually, though, you have to
take the plunge yourself to see what he
can do in your life. That's what it means
to "taste and see that the Lord is good."

ª This psalm is an acrostic poem, the verses of which begin with the successive letters of the Hebrew alphabet.

and desires to see many good days,
¹³ keep your tongue from evil
and your lips from speaking lies.
¹⁴ Turn from evil and do good;
seek peace and pursue it.

¹⁵ The eyes of the LORD are on the righteous
and his ears are attentive to their cry;
¹⁶ the face of the LORD is against those who do evil,
to cut off the memory of them from the earth.

¹⁷ The righteous cry out, and the LORD hears them;
he delivers them from all their troubles.
¹⁸ The LORD is close to the brokenhearted
and saves those who are crushed in spirit.

¹⁹ A righteous man may have many troubles,
but the LORD delivers him from them all;
²⁰ he protects all his bones,
not one of them will be broken.

²¹ Evil will slay the wicked;
the foes of the righteous will be condemned.
²² The LORD redeems his servants;
no one will be condemned who takes refuge in him.

PSALM 35

Of David.

¹ Contend, O LORD, with those who contend with me;
fight against those who fight against me.
² Take up shield and buckler;
arise and come to my aid.
³ Brandish spear and javelin[a]
against those who pursue me.
Say to my soul,
"I am your salvation."

⁴ May those who seek my life
be disgraced and put to shame;
may those who plot my ruin
be turned back in dismay.
⁵ May they be like chaff before the wind,
with the angel of the LORD driving them away;
⁶ may their path be dark and slippery,
with the angel of the LORD pursuing them.
⁷ Since they hid their net for me without cause
and without cause dug a pit for me,
⁸ may ruin overtake them by surprise—
may the net they hid entangle them,
may they fall into the pit, to their ruin.
⁹ Then my soul will rejoice in the LORD
and delight in his salvation.
¹⁰ My whole being will exclaim,
"Who is like you, O LORD?

---

^a 3 Or and block the way

You rescue the poor from those too strong for them,
    the poor and needy from those who rob them."

11 Ruthless witnesses come forward;
    they question me on things I know nothing about.
12 They repay me evil for good
    and leave my soul forlorn.
13 Yet when they were ill, I put on sackcloth
    and humbled myself with fasting.
When my prayers returned to me unanswered,
14   I went about mourning
    as though for my friend or brother.
I bowed my head in grief
    as though weeping for my mother.
15 But when I stumbled, they gathered in glee;
    attackers gathered against me when I was unaware.
    They slandered me without ceasing.
16 Like the ungodly they maliciously mocked[a];
    they gnashed their teeth at me.
17 O Lord, how long will you look on?
    Rescue my life from their ravages,
    my precious life from these lions.
18 I will give you thanks in the great assembly;
    among throngs of people I will praise you.

19 Let not those gloat over me
    who are my enemies without cause;
let not those who hate me without reason
    maliciously wink the eye.
20 They do not speak peaceably,
    but devise false accusations
    against those who live quietly in the land.
21 They gape at me and say, "Aha! Aha!
    With our own eyes we have seen it."

22 O Lord, you have seen this; be not silent.
    Do not be far from me, O Lord.
23 Awake, and rise to my defense!
    Contend for me, my God and Lord.
24 Vindicate me in your righteousness, O Lord my God;
    do not let them gloat over me.
25 Do not let them think, "Aha, just what we wanted!"
    or say, "We have swallowed him up."

26 May all who gloat over my distress
    be put to shame and confusion;
may all who exalt themselves over me
    be clothed with shame and disgrace.
27 May those who delight in my vindication
    shout for joy and gladness;
may they always say, "The Lord be exalted,
    who delights in the well-being of his servant."
28 My tongue will speak of your righteousness
    and of your praises all day long.

---

[a] 16 Septuagint; Hebrew may mean *ungodly circle of mockers*.

PSALM 36

For the director of music. Of David the servant of the Lord.

[1] An oracle is within my heart
   concerning the sinfulness of the wicked:[a]
There is no fear of God
   before his eyes.
[2] For in his own eyes he flatters himself
   too much to detect or hate his sin.
[3] The words of his mouth are wicked and deceitful;
   he has ceased to be wise and to do good.
[4] Even on his bed he plots evil;
   he commits himself to a sinful course
   and does not reject what is wrong.

[5] Your love, O Lord, reaches to the heavens,
   your faithfulness to the skies.
[6] Your righteousness is like the mighty mountains,
   your justice like the great deep.
O Lord, you preserve both man and beast.
[7]   How priceless is your unfailing love!
Both high and low among men
   find[b] refuge in the shadow of your wings.
[8] They feast on the abundance of your house;
   you give them drink from your river of delights.
[9] For with you is the fountain of life;
   in your light we see light.

[10] Continue your love to those who know you,
   your righteousness to the upright in heart.
[11] May the foot of the proud not come against me,
   nor the hand of the wicked drive me away.
[12] See how the evildoers lie fallen—
   thrown down, not able to rise!

PSALM 37 [c]

Of David.

[1] Do not fret because of evil men
   or be envious of those who do wrong;
[2] for like the grass they will soon wither,
   like green plants they will soon die
   away.

[3] Trust in the Lord and do good;
   dwell in the land and enjoy safe
   pasture.
[4] Delight yourself in the Lord
   and he will give you the desires of
   your heart.
[5] Commit your way to the Lord;
   trust in him and he will do this:
[6] He will make your righteousness shine
   like the dawn,

now or never
PS 37:1-2

Do you ever find yourself wishing that you had the freedom to sin without being accountable to God? Guard yourself against such thoughts. Sin never fulfills our deepest longings. Worse than that, it always leads to death.

---

[a] 1 Or heart: / Sin proceeds from the wicked.   [b] 7 Or love, O God! / Men find; or love! / Both heavenly beings and men / find   [c] This psalm is an acrostic poem, the stanzas of which begin with the successive letters of the Hebrew alphabet.

the justice of your cause like the noonday sun.

7 Be still before the LORD and wait patiently for him;
   do not fret when men succeed in their ways,
   when they carry out their wicked schemes.

8 Refrain from anger and turn from wrath;
   do not fret—it leads only to evil.
9 For evil men will be cut off,
   but those who hope in the LORD will inherit the land.

10 A little while, and the wicked will be no more;
    though you look for them, they will not be found.
11 But the meek will inherit the land
    and enjoy great peace.

12 The wicked plot against the righteous
    and gnash their teeth at them;
13 but the Lord laughs at the wicked,
    for he knows their day is coming.

14 The wicked draw the sword
    and bend the bow
   to bring down the poor and needy,
    to slay those whose ways are upright.
15 But their swords will pierce their own hearts,
    and their bows will be broken.

16 Better the little that the righteous have
    than the wealth of many wicked;
17 for the power of the wicked will be broken,
    but the LORD upholds the righteous.

18 The days of the blameless are known to the LORD,
    and their inheritance will endure forever.
19 In times of disaster they will not wither;
    in days of famine they will enjoy plenty.

20 But the wicked will perish:
    The LORD's enemies will be like the beauty of the fields,
    they will vanish—vanish like smoke.

21 The wicked borrow and do not repay,
    but the righteous give generously;
22 those the LORD blesses will inherit the land,
    but those he curses will be cut off.

23 If the LORD delights in a man's way,
    he makes his steps firm;
24 though he stumble, he will not fall,
    for the LORD upholds him with his hand.

25 I was young and now I am old,
    yet I have never seen the righteous forsaken
    or their children begging bread.
26 They are always generous and lend freely;
    their children will be blessed.

27 Turn from evil and do good;
    then you will dwell in the land forever.
28 For the LORD loves the just

and will not forsake his faithful ones.

They will be protected forever,
    but the offspring of the wicked will be cut off;
29 the righteous will inherit the land
    and dwell in it forever.

30 The mouth of the righteous man utters wisdom,
    and his tongue speaks what is just.
31 The law of his God is in his heart;
    his feet do not slip.

32 The wicked lie in wait for the righteous,
    seeking their very lives;
33 but the Lord will not leave them in their power
    or let them be condemned when brought to trial.

34 Wait for the Lord
    and keep his way.
He will exalt you to inherit the land;
    when the wicked are cut off, you will see it.

35 I have seen a wicked and ruthless man
    flourishing like a green tree in its native soil,
36 but he soon passed away and was no more;
    though I looked for him, he could not be found.

37 Consider the blameless, observe the upright;
    there is a future[a] for the man of peace.
38 But all sinners will be destroyed;
    the future[b] of the wicked will be cut off.

39 The salvation of the righteous comes from the Lord;
    he is their stronghold in time of trouble.
40 The Lord helps them and delivers them;
    he delivers them from the wicked and saves them,
    because they take refuge in him.

PSALM 38

A psalm of David. A petition.

1 O Lord, do not rebuke me in your anger
    or discipline me in your wrath.
2 For your arrows have pierced me,
    and your hand has come down upon me.
3 Because of your wrath there is no health in my body;
    my bones have no soundness because of my sin.
4 My guilt has overwhelmed me
    like a burden too heavy to bear.

5 My wounds fester and are loathsome
    because of my sinful folly.
6 I am bowed down and brought very low;
    all day long I go about mourning.
7 My back is filled with searing pain;
    there is no health in my body.
8 I am feeble and utterly crushed;
    I groan in anguish of heart.

a 37 Or there will be posterity   b 38 Or posterity

⁹ All my longings lie open before you, O Lord;
    my sighing is not hidden from you.
¹⁰ My heart pounds, my strength fails me;
    even the light has gone from my eyes.
¹¹ My friends and companions avoid me because of my wounds;
    my neighbors stay far away.
¹² Those who seek my life set their traps,
    those who would harm me talk of my ruin;
    all day long they plot deception.

¹³ I am like a deaf man, who cannot hear,
    like a mute, who cannot open his mouth;
¹⁴ I have become like a man who does not
    hear,
    whose mouth can offer no reply.
¹⁵ I wait for you, O LORD;
    you will answer, O Lord my God.
¹⁶ For I said, "Do not let them gloat
    or exalt themselves over me when
    my foot slips."

¹⁷ For I am about to fall,
    and my pain is ever with me.
¹⁸ I confess my iniquity;
    I am troubled by my sin.
¹⁹ Many are those who are my vigorous
    enemies;
    those who hate me without reason are numerous.
²⁰ Those who repay my good with evil
    slander me when I pursue what is good.

²¹ O LORD, do not forsake me;
    be not far from me, O my God.
²² Come quickly to help me,
    O Lord my Savior.

NOW OR NEVER
PS 38:1–22

Feeling bad? Want to feel better? Follow David's example. Pour out your heart to God. Tell him what's happening, how you're feeling, what you're afraid will happen if something doesn't change . . . and how desperately you need him. Then wait for God to come to your aid.

PSALM 39

For the director of music. For Jeduthun. A psalm of David.

¹ I said, "I will watch my ways
    and keep my tongue from sin;
I will put a muzzle on my mouth
    as long as the wicked are in my presence."
² But when I was silent and still,
    not even saying anything good,
    my anguish increased.
³ My heart grew hot within me,
    and as I meditated, the fire burned;
    then I spoke with my tongue:

⁴ "Show me, O LORD, my life's end
    and the number of my days;
    let me know how fleeting is my life.
⁵ You have made my days a mere handbreadth;
    the span of my years is as nothing before you.
    Each man's life is but a breath.   Selah
⁶ Man is a mere phantom as he goes to and fro:

He bustles about, but only in vain;
he heaps up wealth, not knowing who will get it.

7 "But now, Lord, what do I look for?
My hope is in you.
8 Save me from all my transgressions;
do not make me the scorn of fools.
9 I was silent; I would not open my mouth,
for you are the one who has done this.
10 Remove your scourge from me;
I am overcome by the blow of your hand.
11 You rebuke and discipline men for their sin;
you consume their wealth like a moth—
each man is but a breath.   *Selah*

12 "Hear my prayer, O Lord,
listen to my cry for help;
be not deaf to my weeping.
For I dwell with you as an alien,
a stranger, as all my fathers were.
13 Look away from me, that I may rejoice again
before I depart and am no more."

PSALM 40

For the director of music. Of David. A psalm.

1 I waited patiently for the Lord;
he turned to me and heard my cry.

NOW OR NEVER
PS 40:1

Waiting is hard, isn't it? Especially when you know what you want. The thing is, what seems like a good thing today can turn out to be a big mistake tomorrow. Waiting on God will help you avoid the fallout from those kinds of mistakes.

2 He lifted me out of the slimy pit,
out of the mud and mire;
he set my feet on a rock
and gave me a firm place to stand.
3 He put a new song in my mouth,
a hymn of praise to our God.
Many will see and fear
and put their trust in the Lord.

4 Blessed is the man
who makes the Lord his trust,
who does not look to the proud,
to those who turn aside to false
gods. [a]

5 Many, O Lord my God,
are the wonders you have done.
The things you planned for us
no one can recount to you;
were I to speak and tell of them,
they would be too many to declare.

6 Sacrifice and offering you did not desire,
but my ears you have pierced [b, c];
burnt offerings and sin offerings
you did not require.
7 Then I said, "Here I am, I have come—
it is written about me in the scroll. [d]

[a] 4 Or to falsehood   [b] 6 Hebrew; Septuagint but a body you have prepared for me (see also Symmachus and Theodotion)
[c] 6 Or opened   [d] 7 Or come / with the scroll written for me

⁸ I desire to do your will, O my God;
   your law is within my heart."

⁹ I proclaim righteousness in the great assembly;
   I do not seal my lips,
   as you know, O LORD.
¹⁰ I do not hide your righteousness in my heart;
   I speak of your faithfulness and salvation.
   I do not conceal your love and your truth
   from the great assembly.

¹¹ Do not withhold your mercy from me, O LORD;
   may your love and your truth always protect me.
¹² For troubles without number surround me;
   my sins have overtaken me, and I cannot see.
   They are more than the hairs of my head,
   and my heart fails within me.

¹³ Be pleased, O LORD, to save me;
   O LORD, come quickly to help me.
¹⁴ May all who seek to take my life
   be put to shame and confusion;
   may all who desire my ruin
   be turned back in disgrace.
¹⁵ May those who say to me, "Aha! Aha!"
   be appalled at their own shame.
¹⁶ But may all who seek you
   rejoice and be glad in you;
   may those who love your salvation always say,
   "The LORD be exalted!"

¹⁷ Yet I am poor and needy;
   may the Lord think of me.
   You are my help and my deliverer;
   O my God, do not delay.

NOW OR NEVER
PS 41:1

Human nature tells us to hang out with
the powerful, the popular and the good-
looking. God tells us to hang out with
those who are forgotten, ignored or
ridiculed by the popular crowd. He also
promises to bless those who humble
themselves and obey this call.

PSALM 41

For the director of music. A psalm of David.

¹ Blessed is he who has regard for the
      weak;
   the LORD delivers him in times of
      trouble.
² The LORD will protect him and preserve
      his life;
   he will bless him in the land
   and not surrender him to the desire
      of his foes.
³ The LORD will sustain him on his sickbed
   and restore him from his bed of
      illness.

⁴ I said, "O LORD, have mercy on me;
   heal me, for I have sinned against you."
⁵ My enemies say of me in malice,
   "When will he die and his name perish?"
⁶ Whenever one comes to see me,
   he speaks falsely, while his heart gathers slander;

then he goes out and spreads it abroad.

[7] All my enemies whisper together against me;
    they imagine the worst for me, saying,
[8] "A vile disease has beset him;
    he will never get up from the place where he lies."
[9] Even my close friend, whom I trusted,
    he who shared my bread,
    has lifted up his heel against me.

[10] But you, O LORD, have mercy on me;
    raise me up, that I may repay them.
[11] I know that you are pleased with me,
    for my enemy does not triumph over me.
[12] In my integrity you uphold me
    and set me in your presence forever.

[13] Praise be to the LORD, the God of Israel,
    from everlasting to everlasting.
            Amen and Amen.

BOOK II

PSALMS 42-72

PSALM 42 [a]

For the director of music. A *maskil* [b] of the Sons of Korah.

[1] As the deer pants for streams of water,
    so my soul pants for you, O God.
[2] My soul thirsts for God, for the living God.
    When can I go and meet with God?
[3] My tears have been my food
    day and night,
while men say to me all day long,
    "Where is your God?"
[4] These things I remember
    as I pour out my soul:
how I used to go with the multitude,
    leading the procession to the house
        of God,
with shouts of joy and thanksgiving
    among the festive throng.

[5] Why are you downcast, O my soul?
    Why so disturbed within me?

NOW OR NEVER

PS 42:1-4

Do you know what David is talking about missing in this passage? The time he spent worshiping God at the temple. How do you feel when you miss church? Is worship just a chore to you, or is it something that you crave?

Put your hope in God,
    for I will yet praise him,
    my Savior and [6] my God.

My [c] soul is downcast within me;
    therefore I will remember you
from the land of the Jordan,
    the heights of Hermon—from Mount Mizar.
[7] Deep calls to deep
    in the roar of your waterfalls;

---

[a] In many Hebrew manuscripts Psalms 42 and 43 constitute one psalm.   [b] Title: Probably a literary or musical term   [c] *5,6* A few Hebrew manuscripts, Septuagint and Syriac; most Hebrew manuscripts *praise him for his saving help. / ⁶O my God, my*

all your waves and breakers
    have swept over me.

[8] By day the LORD directs his love,
    at night his song is with me—
    a prayer to the God of my life.

[9] I say to God my Rock,
    "Why have you forgotten me?
Why must I go about mourning,
    oppressed by the enemy?"
[10] My bones suffer mortal agony
    as my foes taunt me,
saying to me all day long,
    "Where is your God?"

[11] Why are you downcast, O my soul?
    Why so disturbed within me?
Put your hope in God,
    for I will yet praise him,
    my Savior and my God.

PSALM 43 [a]

[1] Vindicate me, O God,
    and plead my cause against an ungodly nation;
    rescue me from deceitful and wicked men.
[2] You are God my stronghold.
    Why have you rejected me?
Why must I go about mourning,
    oppressed by the enemy?
[3] Send forth your light and your truth,
    let them guide me;
let them bring me to your holy mountain,
    to the place where you dwell.
[4] Then will I go to the altar of God,
    to God, my joy and my delight.
I will praise you with the harp,
    O God, my God.

[5] Why are you downcast, O my soul?
    Why so disturbed within me?
Put your hope in God,
    for I will yet praise him,
    my Savior and my God.

PSALM 44

For the director of music. Of the Sons of Korah. A *maskil*.[b]

[1] We have heard with our ears, O God;
    our fathers have told us
what you did in their days,
    in days long ago.
[2] With your hand you drove out the nations
    and planted our fathers;
you crushed the peoples

---

[a] In many Hebrew manuscripts Psalms 42 and 43 constitute one psalm.   [b] Title: Probably a literary or musical term

and made our fathers flourish.

3 It was not by their sword that they won the land,
    nor did their arm bring them victory;

it was your right hand, your arm,
    and the light of your face, for you
        loved them.

What did you know about God before you became a Christian? Who told you about him? What could you teach an unbeliever about God? Just as important, who could you teach?

4 You are my King and my God,
    who decrees[a] victories for Jacob.
5 Through you we push back our
        enemies;
    through your name we trample our
        foes.
6 I do not trust in my bow,
    my sword does not bring me victory;
7 but you give us victory over our
        enemies,
    you put our adversaries to shame.
8 In God we make our boast all day long,
    and we will praise your name forever.   *Selah*

9 But now you have rejected and humbled us;
    you no longer go out with our armies.
10 You made us retreat before the enemy,
    and our adversaries have plundered us.
11 You gave us up to be devoured like sheep
    and have scattered us among the nations.
12 You sold your people for a pittance,
    gaining nothing from their sale.

13 You have made us a reproach to our neighbors,
    the scorn and derision of those around us.
14 You have made us a byword among the nations;
    the peoples shake their heads at us.
15 My disgrace is before me all day long,
    and my face is covered with shame
16 at the taunts of those who reproach and revile me,
    because of the enemy, who is bent on revenge.

17 All this happened to us,
    though we had not forgotten you
    or been false to your covenant.
18 Our hearts had not turned back;
    our feet had not strayed from your path.
19 But you crushed us and made us a haunt for jackals
    and covered us over with deep darkness.

20 If we had forgotten the name of our God
    or spread out our hands to a foreign god,
21 would not God have discovered it,
    since he knows the secrets of the heart?
22 Yet for your sake we face death all day long;
    we are considered as sheep to be slaughtered.

23 Awake, O Lord! Why do you sleep?
    Rouse yourself! Do not reject us forever.

a 4 Septuagint, Aquila and Syriac; Hebrew *King, O God; / command*

24 Why do you hide your face
    and forget our misery and oppression?

25 We are brought down to the dust;
    our bodies cling to the ground.
26 Rise up and help us;
    redeem us because of your unfailing love.

PSALM 45

For the director of music. To the tune of "Lilies." Of the Sons of
Korah. A *maskil*.ᵃ A wedding song.

1 My heart is stirred by a noble theme
    as I recite my verses for the king;
    my tongue is the pen of a skillful writer.

2 You are the most excellent of men
    and your lips have been anointed with grace,
    since God has blessed you forever.
3 Gird your sword upon your side, O mighty one;
    clothe yourself with splendor and majesty.
4 In your majesty ride forth victoriously
    in behalf of truth, humility and righteousness;
    let your right hand display awesome deeds.
5 Let your sharp arrows pierce the hearts of the king's enemies;
    let the nations fall beneath your feet.
6 Your throne, O God, will last for ever and ever;
    a scepter of justice will be the scepter of your kingdom.
7 You love righteousness and hate wickedness;
    therefore God, your God, has set you above your companions
    by anointing you with the oil of joy.
8 All your robes are fragrant with myrrh and aloes and cassia;
    from palaces adorned with ivory
    the music of the strings makes you glad.
9 Daughters of kings are among your honored women;
    at your right hand is the royal bride in gold of Ophir.

10 Listen, O daughter, consider and give ear:
    Forget your people and your father's house.
11 The king is enthralled by your beauty;
    honor him, for he is your lord.
12 The Daughter of Tyre will come with a gift,ᵇ
    men of wealth will seek your favor.

13 All glorious is the princess within her chamber;
    her gown is interwoven with gold.
14 In embroidered garments she is led to the king;
    her virgin companions follow her
    and are brought to you.
15 They are led in with joy and gladness;
    they enter the palace of the king.

16 Your sons will take the place of your fathers;
    you will make them princes throughout the land.
17 I will perpetuate your memory through all generations;
    therefore the nations will praise you for ever and ever.

ᵃ Title: Probably a literary or musical term   ᵇ 12 Or *A Tyrian robe is among the gifts*

PSALM 46

For the director of music. Of the Sons of Korah. According to *alamoth.*[a]
A song.

1 God is our refuge and strength,
    an ever-present help in trouble.
2 Therefore we will not fear, though the earth give way
    and the mountains fall into the heart of the sea,
3 though its waters roar and foam
    and the mountains quake with their surging.   *Selah*

4 There is a river whose streams make glad the city of God,
    the holy place where the Most High dwells.
5 God is within her, she will not fall;
    God will help her at break of day.
6 Nations are in uproar, kingdoms fall;
    he lifts his voice, the earth melts.

challengenotes

To: **my_son**

PS 46:10

heavenly_father: in all the noise of today's world, it's easy to lose sight of what's really important—namely, me. that's why silence—a time for solitude and meditating on my word—should be a regular part of your day.

7 The LORD Almighty is with us;
    the God of Jacob is our
        fortress.   *Selah*

8 Come and see the works of the
        LORD,
    the desolations he has
        brought on the earth.
9 He makes wars cease to the
        ends of the earth;
    he breaks the bow and
        shatters the spear,

    he burns the shields[b] with fire.
10 "Be still, and know that I am God;
    I will be exalted among the nations,
    I will be exalted in the earth."

11 The LORD Almighty is with us;
    the God of Jacob is our fortress.   *Selah*

PSALM 47

For the director of music. Of the Sons of Korah. A psalm.

1 Clap your hands, all you nations;
    shout to God with cries of joy.
2 How awesome is the LORD Most High,
    the great King over all the earth!
3 He subdued nations under us,
    peoples under our feet.
4 He chose our inheritance for us,
    the pride of Jacob, whom he loved.   *Selah*

5 God has ascended amid shouts of joy,
    the LORD amid the sounding of trumpets.
6 Sing praises to God, sing praises;
    sing praises to our King, sing praises.

7 For God is the King of all the earth;
    sing to him a psalm[c] of praise.

---

a Title: Probably a musical term   b 9 Or *chariots*   c 7 Or *a maskil* (probably a literary or musical term)

⁸ God reigns over the nations;
    God is seated on his holy throne.
⁹ The nobles of the nations assemble
    as the people of the God of Abraham,
for the kingsᵃ of the earth belong to God;
    he is greatly exalted.

PSALM 48

A song. A psalm of the Sons of Korah.

¹ Great is the LORD, and most worthy of praise,
    in the city of our God, his holy mountain.
² It is beautiful in its loftiness,
    the joy of the whole earth.
Like the utmost heights of Zaphonᵇ is Mount Zion,
    theᶜ city of the Great King.
³ God is in her citadels;
    he has shown himself to be her fortress.

⁴ When the kings joined forces,
    when they advanced together,
⁵ they saw ⌊her⌋ and were astounded;
    they fled in terror.
⁶ Trembling seized them there,
    pain like that of a woman in labor.
⁷ You destroyed them like ships of Tarshish
    shattered by an east wind.

⁸ As we have heard,
    so have we seen
in the city of the LORD Almighty,
    in the city of our God:
    God makes her secure forever.   *Selah*

⁹ Within your temple, O God,
    we meditate on your unfailing love.
¹⁰ Like your name, O God,
    your praise reaches to the ends of the earth;
    your right hand is filled with righteousness.
¹¹ Mount Zion rejoices,
    the villages of Judah are glad
    because of your judgments.

¹² Walk about Zion, go around her,
    count her towers,
¹³ consider well her ramparts,
    view her citadels,
    that you may tell of them to the next generation.
¹⁴ For this God is our God for ever and ever;
    he will be our guide even to the end.

PSALM 49

For the director of music. Of the Sons of Korah. A psalm.

¹ Hear this, all you peoples;
    listen, all who live in this world,

ᵃ *9* Or *shields*   ᵇ *2 Zaphon* can refer to a sacred mountain or the direction north.   ᶜ *2* Or *earth, / Mount Zion, on the northern side / of the*

² both low and high,
   rich and poor alike:
³ My mouth will speak words of wisdom;
   the utterance from my heart will give understanding.
⁴ I will turn my ear to a proverb;
   with the harp I will expound my riddle:

⁵ Why should I fear when evil days come,
   when wicked deceivers surround me—
⁶ those who trust in their wealth
   and boast of their great riches?
⁷ No man can redeem the life of another
   or give to God a ransom for him—
⁸ the ransom for a life is costly,
   no payment is ever enough—
⁹ that he should live on forever
   and not see decay.

¹⁰ For all can see that wise men die;
   the foolish and the senseless alike perish
   and leave their wealth to others.
¹¹ Their tombs will remain their houses^a forever,
   their dwellings for endless generations,
   though they had^b named lands after themselves.

¹² But man, despite his riches, does not endure;
   he is^c like the beasts that perish.

¹³ This is the fate of those who trust in themselves,
   and of their followers, who approve their sayings.   *Selah*

¹⁴ Like sheep they are destined for the
   grave,^d
   and death will feed on them.
The upright will rule over them in the
   morning;
   their forms will decay in the grave,^d
   far from their princely mansions.
¹⁵ But God will redeem my life^e from the
   grave;
   he will surely take me to himself.
                                        Selah

¹⁶ Do not be overawed when a man grows
   rich,
   when the splendor of his house
   increases;

NOW OR NEVER
PS 49:15

The average person's life span is about 77 years; the average Christian's life span is forever. No matter what the excuse is for not becoming a Christian, it pales in comparison to the rewards that come from following Jesus.

¹⁷ for he will take nothing with him when he dies,
   his splendor will not descend with him.
¹⁸ Though while he lived he counted himself blessed—
   and men praise you when you prosper—
¹⁹ he will join the generation of his fathers,
   who will never see the light ⌊of life⌋.

²⁰ A man who has riches without understanding
   is like the beasts that perish.

---

^a *11* Septuagint and Syriac; Hebrew *In their thoughts their houses will remain*   ^b *11* Or */ for they have*   ^c *12* Hebrew; Septuagint and Syriac read verse 12 the same as verse 20.   ^d *14* Hebrew *Sheol*; also in verse 15   ^e *15* Or *soul*

A psalm of Asaph.

¹ The Mighty One, God, the LORD,
    speaks and summons the earth
    from the rising of the sun to the place where it sets.
² From Zion, perfect in beauty,
    God shines forth.
³ Our God comes and will not be silent;
    a fire devours before him,
    and around him a tempest rages.
⁴ He summons the heavens above,
    and the earth, that he may judge his people:
⁵ "Gather to me my consecrated ones,
    who made a covenant with me by sacrifice."
⁶ And the heavens proclaim his righteousness,
    for God himself is judge.   *Selah*

⁷ "Hear, O my people, and I will speak,
    O Israel, and I will testify against you:
    I am God, your God.
⁸ I do not rebuke you for your sacrifices
    or your burnt offerings, which are ever before me.
⁹ I have no need of a bull from your stall
    or of goats from your pens,
¹⁰ for every animal of the forest is mine,
    and the cattle on a thousand hills.
¹¹ I know every bird in the mountains,
    and the creatures of the field are mine.
¹² If I were hungry I would not tell you,
    for the world is mine, and all that is in it.
¹³ Do I eat the flesh of bulls
    or drink the blood of goats?
¹⁴ Sacrifice thank offerings to God,
    fulfill your vows to the Most High,
¹⁵ and call upon me in the day of trouble;
    I will deliver you, and you will honor me."

¹⁶ But to the wicked, God says:

"What right have you to recite my laws
    or take my covenant on your lips?
¹⁷ You hate my instruction
    and cast my words behind you.
¹⁸ When you see a thief, you join with him;
    you throw in your lot with adulterers.
¹⁹ You use your mouth for evil
    and harness your tongue to deceit.
²⁰ You speak continually against your brother
    and slander your own mother's son.
²¹ These things you have done and I kept silent;
    you thought I was altogether[a] like you.
    But I will rebuke you
    and accuse you to your face.

---

[a] *21 Or thought the 'I AM' was*

22 "Consider this, you who forget God,
    or I will tear you to pieces, with none to rescue:
23 He who sacrifices thank offerings honors me,
    and he prepares the way
    so that I may show him[a] the salvation of God."

PSALM 51

For the director of music. A psalm of David. When the prophet Nathan
came to him after David had committed adultery with Bathsheba.

1 Have mercy on me, O God,
    according to your unfailing love;
according to your great compassion
    blot out my transgressions.
2 Wash away all my iniquity
    and cleanse me from my sin.

3 For I know my transgressions,
    and my sin is always before me.
4 Against you, you only, have I sinned
    and done what is evil in your sight,
so that you are proved right when you
    speak
    and justified when you judge.
5 Surely I was sinful at birth,
    sinful from the time my mother
        conceived me.
6 Surely you desire truth in the inner
        parts[b];
    you teach[c] me wisdom in the inmost
        place.

7 Cleanse me with hyssop, and I will be
        clean;
    wash me, and I will be whiter than
        snow.
8 Let me hear joy and gladness;
    let the bones you have crushed
        rejoice.
9 Hide your face from my sins
    and blot out all my iniquity.

10 Create in me a pure heart, O God,
    and renew a steadfast spirit within me.
11 Do not cast me from your presence
    or take your Holy Spirit from me.
12 Restore to me the joy of your salvation
    and grant me a willing spirit, to
        sustain me.

13 Then I will teach transgressors your ways,
    and sinners will turn back to you.
14 Save me from bloodguilt, O God,
    the God who saves me,
    and my tongue will sing of your righteousness.

Fixing Your Relationship With God

Nothing is lonelier than being separated from God by sin. If you don't believe that, check out David's words in this psalm. David, the revered king of Israel, had just screwed up big time. (You can get the whole story in 2 Samuel 11–12.) But he didn't care about how his sin was going to affect *him* or what people were saying about him. He was distraught over how sin had affected his relationship with God. That's why his prayer was so intense. He had to know that everything was made right with his most important relationship before dealing with anything else.

---

a 23 Or and to him who considers his way / I will show   b 6 The meaning of the Hebrew for this phrase is uncertain.   c 6 Or you
desired . . . / you taught

battlelines

» Crossing the Line (God's Forgiveness)

Q: Owen, there *is* no line. The fact is, you can't sin more than God can forgive!
A: Man, my head believes you, but my heart just can't. You wouldn't understand.

Q: Why do you feel that way?
A: Because I knew the right thing to do, and I ignored it. I deliberately chose to do something I knew was wrong.

Q: But isn't that what everybody does when they sin? Remember David, the "man after God's own heart"? You think he didn't know it was wrong to have sex with Bathsheba and then have her husband murdered? Yet God forgave him.
A: I know that. But it just feels too easy. Anyway, when I *do* tell God I'm sorry, I still feel awful. It's like this voice keeps whispering, "You fake. You hypocrite. You loser."

Q: Do you think that voice is coming from God? No way, man. The Bible says he *does* forgive. He even *forgets*. He doesn't condemn his own people. Now the devil—he loves to accuse us of stuff.
A: Oh, OK, the devil. Yeah, right.

Q: I'm serious. God convicts us of sin in order to draw us back to him. He wants to forgive us and help us move on. Satan does the opposite. He tries to overwhelm us with guilt to push us further from God.
A: But if I'm really forgiven, why do I still *feel* guilty?

Q: I'm telling you, man, it's Satan. He's the one who wants to knock you out of the battle and keep you down. He's the one saying, "You're pathetic. You blew it. You're a failure." Meanwhile, God's Spirit is saying, "Yes, you did something you shouldn't have. Let's deal with it and move on." It comes down to this, Owen: Who are you going to listen to?

» Forgiven!

First John 1:9 says it clearly: "If we confess our sins, he is faithful and just and will forgive us our sins and purify us from all unrighteousness."

When we've blown it somehow, our responsibility is to confess. That means to agree with God—to say the same thing about our sin that he says, to have the same attitude toward it that he has. And what does he say? That our sin is wrong, unnecessary and even foolish. But more than that, he says it is *forgiven*. He wants us to leave our sin behind and move on with our lives.

What's God's role in all this? To forgive us and make us pure. How do we know he will? Look at 1 John 1:9 again. He's *faithful*! He always does what he says he will do. If you're still not convinced, check out these other great passages on forgiveness: Psalm 51; Isaiah 38:10–20; Zechariah 3:1–5; John 8:1–11.

Remember, one of Satan's favorite tactics is to use feelings of shame and guilt to isolate us from God and from other believers. It may sound difficult, but talking about your guilt with a trustworthy friend, youth pastor or godly adult can help.

When you're feeling overrun by guilt, visit www.RevolutionBible.com.

¹⁵ O Lord, open my lips,
and my mouth will declare your praise.

¹⁶ You do not delight in sacrifice, or I
would bring it;
you do not take pleasure in burnt
offerings.
¹⁷ The sacrifices of God are[a] a broken
spirit;
a broken and contrite heart,
O God, you will not despise.

¹⁸ In your good pleasure make Zion
prosper;
build up the walls of Jerusalem.
¹⁹ Then there will be righteous sacrifices,
whole burnt offerings to delight you;
then bulls will be offered on your
altar.

NOW OR NEVER
PS 51:1-19

David wrote Psalm 51 as a public confession of his sin with Bathsheba (see 2 Samuel 11–12). Are you man enough to admit your failures to others, or do you try to hide them and pretend they don't exist?

PSALM 52

For the director of music. A *maskil*[b] of David. When Doeg the Edomite had gone to Saul and told him: "David has gone to the house of Ahimelech."

¹ Why do you boast of evil, you mighty man?
Why do you boast all day long,
you who are a disgrace in the eyes of God?
² Your tongue plots destruction;
it is like a sharpened razor,
you who practice deceit.
³ You love evil rather than good,
falsehood rather than speaking the truth. *Selah*

⁴ You love every harmful word,
O you deceitful tongue!

⁵ Surely God will bring you down to
everlasting ruin:
He will snatch you up and tear you
from your tent;
he will uproot you from the land of
the living. *Selah*
⁶ The righteous will see and fear;
they will laugh at him, saying,
⁷ "Here now is the man
who did not make God his
stronghold

NOW OR NEVER
PS 52:1-5

Do you know guys who like to brag about the ungodly things they do? Guys who are proud of their reputation as druggies or players or partyers? David warns that one day God will cause them to regret the things they've done.

but trusted in his great wealth
and grew strong by destroying others!"

⁸ But I am like an olive tree
flourishing in the house of God;
I trust in God's unfailing love
for ever and ever.
⁹ I will praise you forever for what you have done;
in your name I will hope, for your name is good.
I will praise you in the presence of your saints.

---

a 17 Or *My sacrifice, O God, is*   b Title: Probably a literary or musical term

PSALM 53

For the director of music. According to *mahalath*.[a] A *maskil*[b] of David.

¹ The fool says in his heart,
  "There is no God."
 They are corrupt, and their ways are vile;
  there is no one who does good.

² God looks down from heaven
   on the sons of men
 to see if there are any who understand,
  any who seek God.
³ Everyone has turned away,
  they have together become corrupt;
 there is no one who does good,
  not even one.

⁴ Will the evildoers never learn—
  those who devour my people as men
   eat bread
 and who do not call on God?
⁵ There they were, overwhelmed with
   dread,
 where there was nothing to dread.
 God scattered the bones of those who
   attacked you;
 you put them to shame, for God
   despised them.

⁶ Oh, that salvation for Israel would come out of Zion!
  When God restores the fortunes of his people,
   let Jacob rejoice and Israel be glad!

NOW OR NEVER
PS 53:1

This isn't about being an atheist. It's about living your life as though God doesn't exist . . . or as though his instructions don't matter. You can talk about loving and obeying God all you want, but if your actions don't match your words, you're a liar and a fool.

PSALM 54

For the director of music. With stringed instruments. A *maskil*[b] of David. When the Ziphites had gone to Saul and said, "Is not David hiding among us?"

¹ Save me, O God, by your name;
  vindicate me by your might.
² Hear my prayer, O God;
  listen to the words of my mouth.

³ Strangers are attacking me;
  ruthless men seek my life—
   men without regard for God.   *Selah*

⁴ Surely God is my help;
  the Lord is the one who sustains me.

⁵ Let evil recoil on those who slander me;
  in your faithfulness destroy them.

⁶ I will sacrifice a freewill offering to you;
  I will praise your name, O LORD,
   for it is good.
⁷ For he has delivered me from all my troubles,
  and my eyes have looked in triumph on my foes.

ᵃ Title: Probably a musical term   ᵇ Title: Probably a literary or musical term

For the director of music. With stringed instruments. A *maskil*[a]
of David.

¹ Listen to my prayer, O God,
  do not ignore my plea;
² hear me and answer me.
  My thoughts trouble me and I am distraught
³   at the voice of the enemy,
    at the stares of the wicked;
  for they bring down suffering upon me
    and revile me in their anger.

⁴ My heart is in anguish within me;
  the terrors of death assail me.
⁵ Fear and trembling have beset me;
  horror has overwhelmed me.
⁶ I said, "Oh, that I had the wings of a dove!
  I would fly away and be at rest—
⁷ I would flee far away
  and stay in the desert;

                                        Selah
⁸ I would hurry to my place of shelter,
  far from the tempest and storm."

⁹ Confuse the wicked, O Lord, confound
    their speech,
  for I see violence and strife in the
    city.
¹⁰ Day and night they prowl about on its
    walls;
  malice and abuse are within it.
¹¹ Destructive forces are at work in the city;
  threats and lies never leave its
    streets.

¹² If an enemy were insulting me,
    I could endure it;
  if a foe were raising himself against me,
    I could hide from him.
¹³ But it is you, a man like myself,
    my companion, my close friend,
¹⁴ with whom I once enjoyed sweet fellowship
    as we walked with the throng at the house of God.

¹⁵ Let death take my enemies by surprise;
    let them go down alive to the grave,[b]
  for evil finds lodging among them.

¹⁶ But I call to God,
    and the LORD saves me.
¹⁷ Evening, morning and noon
    I cry out in distress,
    and he hears my voice.
¹⁸ He ransoms me unharmed
    from the battle waged against me,
    even though many oppose me.

NOW OR NEVER

PS 55:6–8

Do you have a safe place to go when
things get too intense in the real world?
There's nothing wrong with that. Everyone
needs a little rest now and then; even
Jesus did. In fact, God invites you to rest
in him when you need comfort or peace
of mind.

ᵃ Title: Probably a literary or musical term   ᵇ 15 Hebrew *Sheol*

¹⁹God, who is enthroned forever,
 will hear them and afflict them—   *Selah*
men who never change their ways
 and have no fear of God.

²⁰My companion attacks his friends;
 he violates his covenant.
²¹His speech is smooth as butter,
 yet war is in his heart;
his words are more soothing than oil,
 yet they are drawn swords.

²²Cast your cares on the LORD
 and he will sustain you;
he will never let the righteous fall.
²³But you, O God, will bring down the
  wicked
 into the pit of corruption;
bloodthirsty and deceitful men
 will not live out half their days.

But as for me, I trust in you.

PSALM 56

For the director of music. To ⌊the tune of⌋
"A Dove on Distant Oaks." Of David. A *miktam.*[a]
When the Philistines had seized him in Gath.

¹Be merciful to me, O God, for men hotly
  pursue me;
 all day long they press their attack.
²My slanderers pursue me all day long;
 many are attacking me in their pride.

³When I am afraid,
 I will trust in you.
⁴In God, whose word I praise,
 in God I trust; I will not be afraid.
 What can mortal man do to me?

⁵All day long they twist my words;
 they are always plotting to harm me.
⁶They conspire, they lurk,
 they watch my steps,
 eager to take my life.

⁷On no account let them escape;
 in your anger, O God, bring down the nations.
⁸Record my lament;
 list my tears on your scroll[b]—
 are they not in your record?

⁹Then my enemies will turn back
 when I call for help.
 By this I will know that God is for me.
¹⁰In God, whose word I praise,
 in the LORD, whose word I praise—
¹¹in God I trust; I will not be afraid.

Scheduling Time to Pray

With your busy schedule, how much time do you carve out for prayer? Twenty minutes a day? Ten minutes? The Bible doesn't give us precise figures on how long or how often we should pray. David seemed to like three-a-days ("evening, morning and noon"). Make prayer part of your regular schedule. Give it the same priority you give to working, going to school, studying, exercising or anything else scheduled on your daily calendar.

live the adventure »» Ps 55:16–17

---

[a] Title: Probably a literary or musical term [b] *8* Or / *put my tears in your wineskin*

What can man do to me?

12 I am under vows to you, O God;
    I will present my thank offerings to you.
13 For you have delivered me[a] from death
    and my feet from stumbling,
  that I may walk before God
    in the light of life.[b]

PSALM 57

For the director of music. ⌐To the tune of⌐ "Do Not Destroy." Of David.
A *miktam*.[c] When he had fled from Saul into the cave.

1 Have mercy on me, O God, have mercy on me,
    for in you my soul takes refuge.
  I will take refuge in the shadow of your wings
    until the disaster has passed.

2 I cry out to God Most High,
    to God, who fulfills ⌐his purpose⌐ for me.
3 He sends from heaven and saves me,
    rebuking those who hotly pursue me;   *Selah*
  God sends his love and his faithfulness.

4 I am in the midst of lions;
    I lie among ravenous beasts—
  men whose teeth are spears and arrows,
    whose tongues are sharp swords.

5 Be exalted, O God, above the heavens;
    let your glory be over all the earth.

6 They spread a net for my feet—
    I was bowed down in distress.
  They dug a pit in my path—
    but they have fallen into it themselves.   *Selah*

7 My heart is steadfast, O God,
    my heart is steadfast;
    I will sing and make music.
8 Awake, my soul!
    Awake, harp and lyre!
    I will awaken the dawn.

9 I will praise you, O Lord, among the nations;
    I will sing of you among the peoples.
10 For great is your love, reaching to the heavens;
    your faithfulness reaches to the skies.

11 Be exalted, O God, above the heavens;
    let your glory be over all the earth.

PSALM 58

For the director of music. ⌐To the tune of⌐ "Do Not Destroy." Of David.
A *miktam*.[c]

1 Do you rulers indeed speak justly?
    Do you judge uprightly among men?

---

[a] 13 Or *my soul*   [b] 13 Or *the land of the living*   [c] Title: Probably a literary or musical term

²No, in your heart you devise injustice,
and your hands mete out violence on the earth.
³Even from birth the wicked go astray;
from the womb they are wayward and speak lies.
⁴Their venom is like the venom of a snake,
like that of a cobra that has stopped its ears,
⁵that will not heed the tune of the charmer,
however skillful the enchanter may be.

⁶Break the teeth in their mouths, O God;
tear out, O LORD, the fangs of the lions!

⁷Let them vanish like water that flows
away;
when they draw the bow, let their
arrows be blunted.
⁸Like a slug melting away as it moves
along,
like a stillborn child, may they not
see the sun.

⁹Before your pots can feel ˌthe heat ofˌ
the thorns—
whether they be green or dry—the
wicked will be swept away. ª
¹⁰The righteous will be glad when they are
avenged,
when they bathe their feet in the blood of the wicked.
¹¹Then men will say,
"Surely the righteous still are rewarded;
surely there is a God who judges the earth."

NOW OR NEVER
PS 58:9–11

Someday, the people who boastfully revel
in sin will look to those who follow Jesus
and regret not obeying God and accepting
the truth about his Son.

PSALM 59

For the director of music. ˌTo the tune ofˌ "Do Not Destroy." Of David.
A *miktam.* ᵇ When Saul had sent men to watch David's house in order
to kill him.

¹Deliver me from my enemies, O God;
protect me from those who rise up against me.
²Deliver me from evildoers
and save me from bloodthirsty men.

³See how they lie in wait for me!
Fierce men conspire against me
for no offense or sin of mine, O LORD.
⁴I have done no wrong, yet they are ready to attack me.
Arise to help me; look on my plight!
⁵O LORD God Almighty, the God of Israel,
rouse yourself to punish all the nations;
show no mercy to wicked traitors.   *Selah*

⁶They return at evening,
snarling like dogs,
and prowl about the city.
⁷See what they spew from their mouths—
they spew out swords from their lips,
and they say, "Who can hear us?"

ª *9* The meaning of the Hebrew for this verse is uncertain.   ᵇ Title: Probably a literary or musical term

50 WAYS TO BE A BETTER FRIEND

How often do you find yourself wishing that you had more friends? Maybe you're the kind of person who always has tons of friends. In that case, how often do you wish that you had better relationships with the friends you have? Who wouldn't want more friends or better relationships? There's an old, overused saying that to have friends, you have to be a friend. But overused or not, the Bible seems to agree with this little proverb. Here are some ways that you and your friends can strengthen your relationships. And to make this stuff happen, it's gotta start with you:

TRUE FRIENDSHIP

⁸But you, O LORD, laugh at them;
 you scoff at all those nations.

⁹O my Strength, I watch for you;
 you, O God, are my fortress, ¹⁰my loving God.

God will go before me
 and will let me gloat over those who slander me.
¹¹But do not kill them, O Lord our shield,ᵃ
 or my people will forget.
In your might make them wander about,
 and bring them down.
¹²For the sins of their mouths,
 for the words of their lips,
 let them be caught in their pride.
For the curses and lies they utter,
¹³ consume them in wrath,
 consume them till they are no more.
Then it will be known to the ends of the earth
 that God rules over Jacob.   *Selah*

¹⁴They return at evening,
 snarling like dogs,
 and prowl about the city.
¹⁵They wander about for food
 and howl if not satisfied.
¹⁶But I will sing of your strength,
 in the morning I will sing of your love;
for you are my fortress,
 my refuge in times of trouble.

¹⁷O my Strength, I sing praise to you;
 you, O God, are my fortress, my loving God.

PSALM 60

For the director of music. To ₗthe tune of₎ "The Lily of the Covenant." A
*miktam*ᵇ of David. For teaching. When he fought Aram Naharaimᶜ and
Aram Zobah, ᵈ and when Joab returned and struck down twelve
thousand Edomites in the Valley of Salt.

¹You have rejected us, O God, and burst forth upon us;
 you have been angry—now restore us!
²You have shaken the land and torn it open;
 mend its fractures, for it is quaking.
³You have shown your people desperate times;
 you have given us wine that makes us stagger.

⁴But for those who fear you, you have raised a banner
 to be unfurled against the bow.   *Selah*

⁵Save us and help us with your right hand,
 that those you love may be delivered.
⁶God has spoken from his sanctuary:
 "In triumph I will parcel out Shechem
 and measure off the Valley of Succoth.
⁷Gilead is mine, and Manasseh is mine;

ᵃ *11* Or *sovereign*   ᵇ Title: Probably a literary or musical term   ᶜ Title: That is, Arameans of Northwest Mesopotamia   ᵈ Title: That is, Arameans of central Syria

Ephraim is my helmet,
    Judah my scepter.
8 Moab is my washbasin,
    upon Edom I toss my sandal;
    over Philistia I shout in triumph."

9 Who will bring me to the fortified city?
    Who will lead me to Edom?
10 Is it not you, O God, you who have rejected us
    and no longer go out with our armies?
11 Give us aid against the enemy,
    for the help of man is worthless.
12 With God we will gain the victory,
    and he will trample down our enemies.

PSALM 61

For the director of music. With stringed instruments. Of David.

1 Hear my cry, O God;
    listen to my prayer.

2 From the ends of the earth I call to you,
    I call as my heart grows faint;
    lead me to the rock that is higher than I.
3 For you have been my refuge,
    a strong tower against the foe.

4 I long to dwell in your tent forever
    and take refuge in the shelter of your wings.   *Selah*
5 For you have heard my vows, O God;
    you have given me the heritage of those who fear your name.

6 Increase the days of the king's life,
    his years for many generations.
7 May he be enthroned in God's presence forever;
    appoint your love and faithfulness to protect him.

8 Then will I ever sing praise to your name
    and fulfill my vows day after day.

PSALM 62

For the director of music. For Jeduthun. A psalm of David.

1 My soul finds rest in God alone;
    my salvation comes from him.
2 He alone is my rock and my salvation;
    he is my fortress, I will never be shaken.

3 How long will you assault a man?
    Would all of you throw him down—
    this leaning wall, this tottering fence?
4 They fully intend to topple him
    from his lofty place;
    they take delight in lies.
With their mouths they bless,
    but in their hearts they curse.   *Selah*

5 Find rest, O my soul, in God alone;
    my hope comes from him.

⁶He alone is my rock and my salvation;
    he is my fortress, I will not be shaken.
⁷My salvation and my honor depend on God[a];
    he is my mighty rock, my refuge.
⁸Trust in him at all times, O people;
    pour out your hearts to him,
    for God is our refuge.   *Selah*

⁹Lowborn men are but a breath,
    the highborn are but a lie;
if weighed on a balance, they are nothing;
    together they are only a breath.
¹⁰Do not trust in extortion
    or take pride in stolen goods;
though your riches increase,
    do not set your heart on them.

¹¹One thing God has spoken,
    two things have I heard:
that you, O God, are strong,
¹²   and that you, O Lord, are loving.
Surely you will reward each person
    according to what he has done.

PSALM 63

A psalm of David. When he was in the Desert of Judah.

¹O God, you are my God,
    earnestly I seek you;
my soul thirsts for you,
    my body longs for you,
in a dry and weary land
    where there is no water.

²I have seen you in the sanctuary
    and beheld your power and your glory.
³Because your love is better than life,
    my lips will glorify you.
⁴I will praise you as long as I live,
    and in your name I will lift up my
        hands.
⁵My soul will be satisfied as with the
        richest of foods;
    with singing lips my mouth will
        praise you.

⁶On my bed I remember you;
    I think of you through the watches of
        the night.
⁷Because you are my help,
    I sing in the shadow of your wings.

⁸My soul clings to you;
    your right hand upholds me.

⁹They who seek my life will be destroyed;
    they will go down to the depths of the earth.

NOW OR NEVER

PS 63:6

Before you drift off to sleep each night, take a few minutes to think about the things God did for you during the last 24 hours; then thank him for those things.

ª 7 Or / God Most High is my salvation and my honor

battlelines

» Smoke Signals (Prayer)

Q: Hey, are you going to be at the prayer meeting on Thursday morning?
A: I doubt it.

Q: Join the club. There are a bunch of us who can't make it. We're planning on just praying where we are at the same time.
A: Well, to be honest, I can't promise I'll be doing that either.

Q: Why not?
A: Look, I just don't know about prayer any more, you know? Lately it feels forced and kind of empty. Some people make it sound like when they pray, they have this spiritual jolt or this miraculous experience during which they actually *feel* God or *hear* him.

Q: And?
A: And I never have. Most times it's like I'm talking to a blank ceiling. I'm not saying that's the deal; I'm just saying that's what it feels like to me. Like I'm just spouting words, just talking.

Q: I hear you. I feel like that sometimes and wonder if God is really listening.
A: Exactly! So, um, listen, if people ask where I am, don't make a big deal about it, OK? I mean, let's just keep this between us.

Q: No problem.
A: Oh, and while you're praying, would you mind sending up a smoke signal for me?

» Points on Prayer

A Norwegian pastor by the name of O. Hallesby once said, "Prayer is something deeper than words. It is present in the soul before it has been formulated in words. And it abides in the soul after the last words of prayer have passed over our lips."*

In other words, prayer isn't a grocery list. It isn't just a matter of trying to get things from God. Prayer is a personal conversation with our Creator that expresses the deepest longings of our souls.

Look at what David wrote in Psalm 63:1:

"O God, you are my God, earnestly I seek you; my soul thirsts for you, my body longs for you, in a dry and weary land where there is no water."

No matter how you feel, no matter how things seem, if you are praying from a pure heart (see Psalm 66:18 and Proverbs 15:8), God will hear you and respond. Remember, he *delights* in your attempts to reach out to him in prayer!

Find ways to improve your prayer life at www.RevolutionBible.com.

* O. Hallesby, *Prayer*. Augsburg Fortress Publishers, 1994.

¹⁰ They will be given over to the sword
and become food for jackals.

¹¹ But the king will rejoice in God;
all who swear by God's name will praise him,
while the mouths of liars will be silenced.

PSALM 64

For the director of music. A psalm of David.

¹ Hear me, O God, as I voice my complaint;
protect my life from the threat of the enemy.
² Hide me from the conspiracy of the wicked,
from that noisy crowd of evildoers.

³ They sharpen their tongues like swords
and aim their words like deadly arrows.
⁴ They shoot from ambush at the innocent man;
they shoot at him suddenly, without fear.

⁵ They encourage each other in evil plans,
they talk about hiding their snares;
they say, "Who will see them^a?"
⁶ They plot injustice and say,
"We have devised a perfect plan!"
Surely the mind and heart of man are cunning.

⁷ But God will shoot them with arrows;
suddenly they will be struck down.
⁸ He will turn their own tongues against them
and bring them to ruin;
all who see them will shake their heads in scorn.

⁹ All mankind will fear;
they will proclaim the works of God
and ponder what he has done.
¹⁰ Let the righteous rejoice in the LORD
and take refuge in him;
let all the upright in heart praise him!

PSALM 65

For the director of music. A psalm of David. A song.

¹ Praise awaits^b you, O God, in Zion;
to you our vows will be fulfilled.
² O you who hear prayer,
to you all men will come.
³ When we were overwhelmed by sins,

Enjoying God's Attention

The cool thing about prayer is that God hears everything we say. We're not just tossing requests into space, hoping they get picked up by some distant satellite. God gives us his full attention when we start talking. David was so blown away by the idea of a God who listens that he gave the Lord a special nickname: "you who answer prayer." You've got to admit, that's a whole lot better than "you who could care less about what we have to say."

» live the adventure » Ps 65:2

---

^a 5 Or us   ^b 1 Or befits; the meaning of the Hebrew for this word is uncertain.

you forgave[a] our transgressions.
⁴Blessed are those you choose
    and bring near to live in your courts!
We are filled with the good things of your house,
    of your holy temple.

⁵You answer us with awesome deeds of righteousness,
    O God our Savior,
the hope of all the ends of the earth
    and of the farthest seas,
⁶who formed the mountains by your power,
    having armed yourself with strength,
⁷who stilled the roaring of the seas,
    the roaring of their waves,
    and the turmoil of the nations.
⁸Those living far away fear your wonders;
    where morning dawns and evening fades
    you call forth songs of joy.

⁹You care for the land and water it;
    you enrich it abundantly.
The streams of God are filled with water
    to provide the people with grain,
    for so you have ordained it.[b]
¹⁰You drench its furrows
    and level its ridges;
you soften it with showers
    and bless its crops.
¹¹You crown the year with your bounty,
    and your carts overflow with abundance.
¹²The grasslands of the desert overflow;
    the hills are clothed with gladness.
¹³The meadows are covered with flocks
    and the valleys are mantled with grain;
    they shout for joy and sing.

PSALM 66

For the director of music. A song. A psalm.

¹Shout with joy to God, all the earth!
²   Sing the glory of his name;
    make his praise glorious!
³Say to God, "How awesome are your deeds!
    So great is your power
    that your enemies cringe before you.
⁴All the earth bows down to you;
    they sing praise to you,
    they sing praise to your name."   *Selah*

⁵Come and see what God has done,
    how awesome his works in man's behalf!
⁶He turned the sea into dry land,
    they passed through the waters on foot—
    come, let us rejoice in him.
⁷He rules forever by his power,

---

[a] 3 Or *made atonement for*   [b] 9 Or *for that is how you prepare the land*

his eyes watch the nations—
let not the rebellious rise up against him.   *Selah*

8 Praise our God, O peoples,
let the sound of his praise be heard;
9 he has preserved our lives
and kept our feet from slipping.
10 For you, O God, tested us;
you refined us like silver.
11 You brought us into prison
and laid burdens on our backs.
12 You let men ride over our heads;
we went through fire and water,
but you brought us to a place of
abundance.

13 I will come to your temple with burnt
offerings
and fulfill my vows to you—
14 vows my lips promised and my mouth
spoke
when I was in trouble.
15 I will sacrifice fat animals to you
and an offering of rams;
I will offer bulls and goats.   *Selah*

16 Come and listen, all you who fear God;
let me tell you what he has done
for me.
17 I cried out to him with my mouth;
his praise was on my tongue.
18 If I had cherished sin in my heart,
the Lord would not have listened;
19 but God has surely listened
and heard my voice in prayer.
20 Praise be to God,
who has not rejected my prayer
or withheld his love from me!

PSALM 67

For the director of music. With stringed instruments.
A psalm. A song.

1 May God be gracious to us and bless us
and make his face shine upon us,   *Selah*
2 that your ways may be known on earth,
your salvation among all nations.

3 May the peoples praise you, O God;
may all the peoples praise you.
4 May the nations be glad and sing for joy,
for you rule the peoples justly
and guide the nations of the earth.   *Selah*
5 May the peoples praise you, O God;
may all the peoples praise you.

6 Then the land will yield its harvest,
and God, our God, will bless us.

live the adventure »» Ps 66:10-12

Taking Your Pain to God

The guy who wrote this psalm obviously had personal experience with suffering. But he was determined not to let his pain have the last word. He knew there was something beyond his suffering. He knew that no matter how difficult things got, God would make good out of bad. That's a good thing to keep in mind when things go wrong in your life. Whether it's your parents' crumbling marriage, your dad's job situation, problems with a jerk at school or something you've never told anyone else, God can turn it into something good— if you trust him.

⁷God will bless us,
and all the ends of the earth will fear him.

PSALM 68

For the director of music. Of David. A psalm. A song.

¹May God arise, may his enemies be scattered;
may his foes flee before him.
²As smoke is blown away by the wind,
may you blow them away;
as wax melts before the fire,
may the wicked perish before God.
³But may the righteous be glad
and rejoice before God;
may they be happy and joyful.

⁴Sing to God, sing praise to his name,
extol him who rides on the clouds ᵃ—
his name is the LORD—
and rejoice before him.
⁵A father to the fatherless, a defender of widows,
is God in his holy dwelling.
⁶God sets the lonely in families, ᵇ
he leads forth the prisoners with singing;
but the rebellious live in a sun-scorched land.

⁷When you went out before your people, O God,
when you marched through the wasteland,   *Selah*
⁸the earth shook,
the heavens poured down rain,
before God, the One of Sinai,
before God, the God of Israel.
⁹You gave abundant showers, O God;
you refreshed your weary inheritance.
¹⁰Your people settled in it,
and from your bounty, O God, you provided for the poor.

¹¹The Lord announced the word,
and great was the company of those who proclaimed it:
¹²"Kings and armies flee in haste;
in the camps men divide the plunder.
¹³Even while you sleep among the campfires, ᶜ
the wings of ⌊my⌋ dove are sheathed with silver,
its feathers with shining gold."
¹⁴When the Almighty ᵈ scattered the kings in the land,
it was like snow fallen on Zalmon.

¹⁵The mountains of Bashan are majestic mountains;
rugged are the mountains of Bashan.
¹⁶Why gaze in envy, O rugged mountains,
at the mountain where God chooses to reign,
where the LORD himself will dwell forever?
¹⁷The chariots of God are tens of thousands
and thousands of thousands;
the Lord ⌊has come⌋ from Sinai into his sanctuary.

ᵃ *4* Or *I prepare the way for him who rides through the deserts*   ᵇ *6* Or *the desolate in a homeland*   ᶜ *13* Or *saddlebags*
ᵈ *14* Hebrew *Shaddai*

18 When you ascended on high,
      you led captives in your train;
      you received gifts from men,
   even from[a] the rebellious—
      that you,[b] O LORD God, might dwell there.

19 Praise be to the Lord, to God our Savior,
      who daily bears our burdens.   *Selah*
20 Our God is a God who saves;
      from the Sovereign LORD comes escape from death.

21 Surely God will crush the heads of his enemies,
      the hairy crowns of those who go on in their sins.
22 The Lord says, "I will bring them from Bashan;
      I will bring them from the depths of the sea,
23 that you may plunge your feet in the blood of your foes,
      while the tongues of your dogs have their share."

24 Your procession has come into view, O God,
      the procession of my God and King into the sanctuary.
25 In front are the singers, after them the musicians;
      with them are the maidens playing tambourines.
26 Praise God in the great congregation;
      praise the LORD in the assembly of Israel.
27 There is the little tribe of Benjamin, leading them,
      there the great throng of Judah's princes,
      and there the princes of Zebulun and of Naphtali.

28 Summon your power, O God[c];
      show us your strength, O God, as you have done before.
29 Because of your temple at Jerusalem
      kings will bring you gifts.
30 Rebuke the beast among the reeds,
      the herd of bulls among the calves of the nations.
   Humbled, may it bring bars of silver.
      Scatter the nations who delight in war.
31 Envoys will come from Egypt;
      Cush[d] will submit herself to God.

32 Sing to God, O kingdoms of the earth,
      sing praise to the Lord,   *Selah*
33 to him who rides the ancient skies above,
      who thunders with mighty voice.
34 Proclaim the power of God,
      whose majesty is over Israel,
      whose power is in the skies.
35 You are awesome, O God, in your sanctuary;
      the God of Israel gives power and strength to his people.

   Praise be to God!

PSALM 69

For the director of music. To ⌊the tune of⌋ "Lilies." Of David.

1 Save me, O God,
      for the waters have come up to my neck.

---

[a] *18* Or *gifts for men, / even*   [b] *18* Or *they*   [c] *28* Many Hebrew manuscripts, Septuagint and Syriac; most Hebrew manuscripts *Your God has summoned power for you*   [d] *31* That is, the upper Nile region

²I sink in the miry depths,
　　where there is no foothold.
I have come into the deep waters;
　　the floods engulf me.
³I am worn out calling for help;
　　my throat is parched.
My eyes fail,
　　looking for my God.

now or never

PS 69:1–3

Think of the last time you felt the emotions that David describes in these verses.
What did you do to try to make yourself
feel better? Did it work? What will you do
the next time you feel that way?

⁴Those who hate me without reason
　　outnumber the hairs of my head;
many are my enemies without cause,
　　those who seek to destroy me.
I am forced to restore
　　what I did not steal.

⁵You know my folly, O God;
　　my guilt is not hidden from you.

⁶May those who hope in you
　　not be disgraced because of me,
　　O Lord, the LORD Almighty;
may those who seek you
　　not be put to shame because of me,
　　O God of Israel.

⁷For I endure scorn for your sake,
　　and shame covers my face.
⁸I am a stranger to my brothers,
　　an alien to my own mother's sons;
⁹for zeal for your house consumes me,
　　and the insults of those who insult you fall on me.
¹⁰When I weep and fast,
　　I must endure scorn;
¹¹when I put on sackcloth,
　　people make sport of me.
¹²Those who sit at the gate mock me,
　　and I am the song of the drunkards.

¹³But I pray to you, O LORD,
　　in the time of your favor;
in your great love, O God,
　　answer me with your sure salvation.
¹⁴Rescue me from the mire,
　　do not let me sink;
deliver me from those who hate me,
　　from the deep waters.
¹⁵Do not let the floodwaters engulf me
　　or the depths swallow me up
　　or the pit close its mouth over me.
¹⁶Answer me, O LORD, out of the goodness of your love;
　　in your great mercy turn to me.
¹⁷Do not hide your face from your servant;
　　answer me quickly, for I am in trouble.
¹⁸Come near and rescue me;
　　redeem me because of my foes.

¹⁹You know how I am scorned, disgraced and shamed;
　　all my enemies are before you.

²⁰ Scorn has broken my heart
    and has left me helpless;
  I looked for sympathy, but there was none,
    for comforters, but I found none.
²¹ They put gall in my food
    and gave me vinegar for my thirst.

²² May the table set before them become a snare;
    may it become retribution and^a a trap.
²³ May their eyes be darkened so they cannot see,
    and their backs be bent forever.
²⁴ Pour out your wrath on them;
    let your fierce anger overtake them.
²⁵ May their place be deserted;
    let there be no one to dwell in their tents.
²⁶ For they persecute those you wound
    and talk about the pain of those you hurt.
²⁷ Charge them with crime upon crime;
    do not let them share in your salvation.
²⁸ May they be blotted out of the book of life
    and not be listed with the righteous.

²⁹ I am in pain and distress;
    may your salvation, O God, protect me.

³⁰ I will praise God's name in song
    and glorify him with thanksgiving.
³¹ This will please the LORD more than an ox,
    more than a bull with its horns and hoofs.
³² The poor will see and be glad—
    you who seek God, may your hearts live!
³³ The LORD hears the needy
    and does not despise his captive people.

³⁴ Let heaven and earth praise him,
    the seas and all that move in them,
³⁵ for God will save Zion
    and rebuild the cities of Judah.
  Then people will settle there and possess it;
³⁶   the children of his servants will inherit it,
    and those who love his name will dwell there.

PSALM 70

For the director of music. Of David. A petition.

¹ Hasten, O God, to save me;
    O LORD, come quickly to help me.
² May those who seek my life
    be put to shame and confusion;
  may all who desire my ruin
    be turned back in disgrace.
³ May those who say to me, "Aha! Aha!"
    turn back because of their shame.
⁴ But may all who seek you
    rejoice and be glad in you;
  may those who love your salvation always say,

---

^a 22 Or snare / and their fellowship become

"Let God be exalted!"

5 Yet I am poor and needy;
   come quickly to me, O God.
You are my help and my deliverer;
   O LORD, do not delay.

PSALM 71

1 In you, O LORD, I have taken refuge;
   let me never be put to shame.
2 Rescue me and deliver me in your righteousness;
   turn your ear to me and save me.
3 Be my rock of refuge,
   to which I can always go;
give the command to save me,
   for you are my rock and my fortress.
4 Deliver me, O my God, from the hand of the wicked,
   from the grasp of evil and cruel men.

NOW OR NEVER
PS 71:5-6

Identify five specific examples of how the Lord has taken care of you up to this point in your life. Now set aside a few minutes to thank him for each specific example.

5 For you have been my hope,
      O Sovereign LORD,
   my confidence since my youth.
6 From birth I have relied on you;
   you brought me forth from my
         mother's womb.
   I will ever praise you.
7 I have become like a portent to many,
   but you are my strong refuge.
8 My mouth is filled with your praise,
   declaring your splendor all day long.

9 Do not cast me away when I am old;
   do not forsake me when my strength
         is gone.

10 For my enemies speak against me;
   those who wait to kill me conspire together.
11 They say, "God has forsaken him;
   pursue him and seize him,
   for no one will rescue him."
12 Be not far from me, O God;
   come quickly, O my God, to help me.
13 May my accusers perish in shame;
   may those who want to harm me
   be covered with scorn and disgrace.

14 But as for me, I will always have hope;
   I will praise you more and more.
15 My mouth will tell of your righteousness,
   of your salvation all day long,
   though I know not its measure.
16 I will come and proclaim your mighty acts, O Sovereign LORD;
   I will proclaim your righteousness, yours alone.
17 Since my youth, O God, you have taught me,
   and to this day I declare your marvelous deeds.
18 Even when I am old and gray,
   do not forsake me, O God,
   till I declare your power to the next generation,

your might to all who are to come.

¹⁹ Your righteousness reaches to the skies, O God,
    you who have done great things.
    Who, O God, is like you?
²⁰ Though you have made me see troubles, many and bitter,
    you will restore my life again;
  from the depths of the earth
    you will again bring me up.
²¹ You will increase my honor
    and comfort me once again.

²² I will praise you with the harp
    for your faithfulness, O my God;
  I will sing praise to you with the lyre,
    O Holy One of Israel.
²³ My lips will shout for joy
    when I sing praise to you—
    I, whom you have redeemed.
²⁴ My tongue will tell of your righteous acts
    all day long,
  for those who wanted to harm me
    have been put to shame and confusion.

PSALM 72

Of Solomon.

¹ Endow the king with your justice, O God,
    the royal son with your righteousness.
² He will[a] judge your people in righteousness,
    your afflicted ones with justice.
³ The mountains will bring prosperity to the people,
    the hills the fruit of righteousness.
⁴ He will defend the afflicted among the people
    and save the children of the needy;
    he will crush the oppressor.

⁵ He will endure[b] as long as the sun,
    as long as the moon, through all generations.
⁶ He will be like rain falling on a mown field,
    like showers watering the earth.
⁷ In his days the righteous will flourish;
    prosperity will abound till the moon is no more.

⁸ He will rule from sea to sea
    and from the River[c] to the ends of the earth.[d]
⁹ The desert tribes will bow before him
    and his enemies will lick the dust.
¹⁰ The kings of Tarshish and of distant shores
    will bring tribute to him;
  the kings of Sheba and Seba
    will present him gifts.
¹¹ All kings will bow down to him
    and all nations will serve him.

¹² For he will deliver the needy who cry out,

ᵃ *2* Or *May he*; similarly in verses 3-11 and 17   ᵇ *5* Septuagint; Hebrew *You will be feared*   ᶜ *8* That is, the Euphrates   ᵈ *8* Or *the end of the land*

the afflicted who have no one to help.
¹³ He will take pity on the weak and the needy
and save the needy from death.
¹⁴ He will rescue them from oppression and violence,
for precious is their blood in his sight.

¹⁵ Long may he live!
May gold from Sheba be given him.
May people ever pray for him
and bless him all day long.
¹⁶ Let grain abound throughout the land;
on the tops of the hills may it sway.
Let its fruit flourish like Lebanon;
let it thrive like the grass of the field.
¹⁷ May his name endure forever;
may it continue as long as the sun.

All nations will be blessed through him,
and they will call him blessed.

¹⁸ Praise be to the Lord God, the God of Israel,
who alone does marvelous deeds.
¹⁹ Praise be to his glorious name forever;
may the whole earth be filled with his glory.
Amen and Amen.

²⁰ This concludes the prayers of David son of Jesse.

BOOK III

Psalms 73-89

PSALM 73

A psalm of Asaph.

¹ Surely God is good to Israel,
to those who are pure in heart.

² But as for me, my feet had almost slipped;
I had nearly lost my foothold.
³ For I envied the arrogant
when I saw the prosperity of the wicked.

⁴ They have no struggles;
their bodies are healthy and strong.ᵃ
⁵ They are free from the burdens common to man;
they are not plagued by human ills.
⁶ Therefore pride is their necklace;
they clothe themselves with violence.
⁷ From their callous hearts comes iniquityᵇ;
the evil conceits of their minds know no limits.
⁸ They scoff, and speak with malice;
in their arrogance they threaten oppression.
⁹ Their mouths lay claim to heaven,
and their tongues take possession of the earth.
¹⁰ Therefore their people turn to them

ᵃ 4 With a different word division of the Hebrew; Masoretic Text *struggles at their death; / their bodies are healthy*   ᵇ 7 Syriac (see also
Septuagint); Hebrew *Their eyes bulge with fat*

and drink up waters in abundance.ᵃ
11 They say, "How can God know?
   Does the Most High have knowledge?"

12 This is what the wicked are like—
   always carefree, they increase in wealth.

13 Surely in vain have I kept my heart pure;
   in vain have I washed my hands in innocence.
14 All day long I have been plagued;
   I have been punished every morning.

15 If I had said, "I will speak thus,"
   I would have betrayed your children.
16 When I tried to understand all this,
   it was oppressive to me
17 till I entered the sanctuary of God;
   then I understood their final destiny.

18 Surely you place them on slippery ground;
   you cast them down to ruin.
19 How suddenly are they destroyed,
   completely swept away by terrors!
20 As a dream when one awakes,
   so when you arise, O Lord,
   you will despise them as fantasies.

21 When my heart was grieved
   and my spirit embittered,
22 I was senseless and ignorant;
   I was a brute beast before you.

23 Yet I am always with you;
   you hold me by my right hand.
24 You guide me with your counsel,
   and afterward you will take me into glory.
25 Whom have I in heaven but you?
   And earth has nothing I desire besides you.
26 My flesh and my heart may fail,
   but God is the strength of my heart
   and my portion forever.

27 Those who are far from you will perish;
   you destroy all who are unfaithful to you.
28 But as for me, it is good to be near God.
   I have made the Sovereign LORD my refuge;
   I will tell of all your deeds.

PSALM 74

A *maskil*ᵇ of Asaph.

1 Why have you rejected us forever, O God?
   Why does your anger smolder against the sheep of your pasture?
2 Remember the people you purchased of old,
   the tribe of your inheritance, whom you redeemed—
   Mount Zion, where you dwelt.
3 Turn your steps toward these everlasting ruins,

ᵃ *10* The meaning of the Hebrew for this verse is uncertain.   ᵇ Title: Probably a literary or musical term all this destruction the enemy has brought on the sanctuary.

4 Your foes roared in the place where you met with us;
  they set up their standards as signs.
5 They behaved like men wielding axes
  to cut through a thicket of trees.
6 They smashed all the carved paneling
  with their axes and hatchets.
7 They burned your sanctuary to the ground;
  they defiled the dwelling place of your Name.
8 They said in their hearts, "We will crush them completely!"
  They burned every place where God was worshiped in the land.
9 We are given no miraculous signs;
  no prophets are left,
  and none of us knows how long this will be.

10 How long will the enemy mock you, O God?
  Will the foe revile your name forever?
11 Why do you hold back your hand, your right hand?
  Take it from the folds of your garment and destroy them!

12 But you, O God, are my king from of old;
  you bring salvation upon the earth.
13 It was you who split open the sea by your power;
  you broke the heads of the monster in the waters.
14 It was you who crushed the heads of Leviathan
  and gave him as food to the creatures of the desert.
15 It was you who opened up springs and streams;
  you dried up the ever flowing rivers.
16 The day is yours, and yours also the night;
  you established the sun and moon.
17 It was you who set all the boundaries of the earth;
  you made both summer and winter.

18 Remember how the enemy has mocked you, O Lord,
  how foolish people have reviled your name.
19 Do not hand over the life of your dove to wild beasts;
  do not forget the lives of your afflicted people forever.
20 Have regard for your covenant,
  because haunts of violence fill the dark places of the land.
21 Do not let the oppressed retreat in disgrace;
  may the poor and needy praise your name.

22 Rise up, O God, and defend your cause;
  remember how fools mock you all day long.
23 Do not ignore the clamor of your adversaries,
  the uproar of your enemies, which rises continually.

PSALM 75

For the director of music. ⌊To the tune of⌋ "Do Not Destroy." A psalm of
Asaph. A song.

1 We give thanks to you, O God,
  we give thanks, for your Name is near;
  men tell of your wonderful deeds.

2 You say, "I choose the appointed time;
  it is I who judge uprightly.

³When the earth and all its people quake,
    it is I who hold its pillars firm.   *Selah*
⁴To the arrogant I say, 'Boast no more,'
    and to the wicked, 'Do not lift up your horns.
⁵Do not lift your horns against heaven;
    do not speak with outstretched neck.' "

⁶No one from the east or the west
    or from the desert can exalt a man.
⁷But it is God who judges:
    He brings one down, he exalts another.
⁸In the hand of the LORD is a cup
    full of foaming wine mixed with spices;
he pours it out, and all the wicked of the earth
    drink it down to its very dregs.

⁹As for me, I will declare this forever;
    I will sing praise to the God of Jacob.
¹⁰I will cut off the horns of all the wicked,
    but the horns of the righteous will be lifted up.

PSALM 76

For the director of music. With stringed instruments. A psalm of
Asaph. A song.

¹In Judah God is known;
    his name is great in Israel.
²His tent is in Salem,
    his dwelling place in Zion.
³There he broke the flashing arrows,
    the shields and the swords, the weapons of war.   *Selah*

⁴You are resplendent with light,
    more majestic than mountains rich with game.
⁵Valiant men lie plundered,
    they sleep their last sleep;
not one of the warriors
    can lift his hands.
⁶At your rebuke, O God of Jacob,
    both horse and chariot lie still.
⁷You alone are to be feared.
    Who can stand before you when you are angry?
⁸From heaven you pronounced judgment,
    and the land feared and was quiet—
⁹when you, O God, rose up to judge,
    to save all the afflicted of the land.   *Selah*
¹⁰Surely your wrath against men brings you praise,
    and the survivors of your wrath are restrained.ᵃ

¹¹Make vows to the LORD your God and fulfill them;
    let all the neighboring lands
    bring gifts to the One to be feared.
¹²He breaks the spirit of rulers;
    he is feared by the kings of the earth.

ᵃ *10* Or *Surely the wrath of men brings you praise, / and with the remainder of wrath you arm yourself*

For the director of music. For Jeduthun. Of Asaph. A psalm.

¹ I cried out to God for help;
   I cried out to God to hear me.
² When I was in distress, I sought the Lord;
   at night I stretched out untiring hands
   and my soul refused to be comforted.

³ I remembered you, O God, and I groaned;
   I mused, and my spirit grew faint.
                                    Selah

⁴ You kept my eyes from closing;
   I was too troubled to speak.
⁵ I thought about the former days,
   the years of long ago;
⁶ I remembered my songs in the night.
   My heart mused and my spirit
      inquired:

⁷ "Will the Lord reject forever?
   Will he never show his favor again?
⁸ Has his unfailing love vanished forever?
   Has his promise failed for all time?
⁹ Has God forgotten to be merciful?
   Has he in anger withheld his
      compassion?"   *Selah*

¹⁰ Then I thought, "To this I will appeal:
   the years of the right hand of the
      Most High."
¹¹ I will remember the deeds of the LORD;
   yes, I will remember your miracles of
      long ago.
¹² I will meditate on all your works
   and consider all your mighty deeds.

¹³ Your ways, O God, are holy.
   What god is so great as our God?
¹⁴ You are the God who performs miracles;
   you display your power among the
      peoples.
¹⁵ With your mighty arm you redeemed
      your people,
   the descendants of Jacob and Joseph.
                                    Selah

¹⁶ The waters saw you, O God,
   the waters saw you and writhed;
   the very depths were convulsed.
¹⁷ The clouds poured down water,
   the skies resounded with thunder;
   your arrows flashed back and forth.
¹⁸ Your thunder was heard in the whirlwind,
   your lightning lit up the world;
   the earth trembled and quaked.
¹⁹ Your path led through the sea,
   your way through the mighty waters,
   though your footprints were not seen.

Speaking to God Like a Friend

Asaph (the guy who wrote Psalm 77) knew God so well that he wasn't afraid to ask tough questions when he got depressed. If all you knew of God were stories of his judgment and destruction, you might be afraid to talk to him the way Asaph did in his prayer. You might worry about getting zapped by a lightning bolt. But Asaph wasn't worried. He knew God wouldn't punish him for sharing his deepest feelings. He was comfortable talking to the Lord about anything. How do you feel when you talk to God?

²⁰ You led your people like a flock
    by the hand of Moses and Aaron.

PSALM 78

A *maskil*[a] of Asaph.

¹ O my people, hear my teaching;
    listen to the words of my mouth.
² I will open my mouth in parables,
    I will utter hidden things, things from of old—
³ what we have heard and known,
    what our fathers have told us.
⁴ We will not hide them from their children;
    we will tell the next generation
the praiseworthy deeds of the LORD,
    his power, and the wonders he has done.
⁵ He decreed statutes for Jacob
    and established the law in Israel,
which he commanded our forefathers
    to teach their children,
⁶ so the next generation would know them,
    even the children yet to be born,
    and they in turn would tell their children.
⁷ Then they would put their trust in God
    and would not forget his deeds
    but would keep his commands.
⁸ They would not be like their forefathers—
    a stubborn and rebellious generation,
whose hearts were not loyal to God,
    whose spirits were not faithful to him.

⁹ The men of Ephraim, though armed with bows,
    turned back on the day of battle;
¹⁰ they did not keep God's covenant
    and refused to live by his law.
¹¹ They forgot what he had done,
    the wonders he had shown them.
¹² He did miracles in the sight of their fathers
    in the land of Egypt, in the region of Zoan.
¹³ He divided the sea and led them through;
    he made the water stand firm like a wall.
¹⁴ He guided them with the cloud by day
    and with light from the fire all night.
¹⁵ He split the rocks in the desert
    and gave them water as abundant as the seas;
¹⁶ he brought streams out of a rocky crag
    and made water flow down like rivers.

¹⁷ But they continued to sin against him,
    rebelling in the desert against the Most High.
¹⁸ They willfully put God to the test
    by demanding the food they craved.
¹⁹ They spoke against God, saying,
    "Can God spread a table in the desert?
²⁰ When he struck the rock, water gushed out,

---

a Title: Probably a literary or musical term

and streams flowed abundantly.
But can he also give us food?
Can he supply meat for his people?"
21 When the Lord heard them, he was very angry;
his fire broke out against Jacob,
and his wrath rose against Israel,
22 for they did not believe in God
or trust in his deliverance.
23 Yet he gave a command to the skies above
and opened the doors of the heavens;
24 he rained down manna for the people to eat,
he gave them the grain of heaven.
25 Men ate the bread of angels;
he sent them all the food they could eat.
26 He let loose the east wind from the heavens
and led forth the south wind by his power.
27 He rained meat down on them like dust,
flying birds like sand on the seashore.

28 He made them come down inside their
camp,
all around their tents.
29 They ate till they had more than enough,
for he had given them what they
craved.
30 But before they turned from the food
they craved,
even while it was still in their
mouths,
31 God's anger rose against them;
he put to death the sturdiest among
them,
cutting down the young men of
Israel.

ΠOW OR ΠEVER
PS 78:1–72

There's no expiration date on the things you can praise God for. If you see something about God in the Bible that impresses you or helps you understand him a little better, say a prayer and give him the credit he deserves.

32 In spite of all this, they kept on sinning;
in spite of his wonders, they did not believe.
33 So he ended their days in futility
and their years in terror.
34 Whenever God slew them, they would seek him;
they eagerly turned to him again.
35 They remembered that God was their Rock,
that God Most High was their Redeemer.
36 But then they would flatter him with their mouths,
lying to him with their tongues;
37 their hearts were not loyal to him,
they were not faithful to his covenant.
38 Yet he was merciful;
he forgave their iniquities
and did not destroy them.
Time after time he restrained his anger
and did not stir up his full wrath.
39 He remembered that they were but flesh,
a passing breeze that does not return.

40 How often they rebelled against him in the desert
and grieved him in the wasteland!

⁴¹ Again and again they put God to the test;
     they vexed the Holy One of Israel.
⁴² They did not remember his power—
     the day he redeemed them from the oppressor,
⁴³ the day he displayed his miraculous signs in Egypt,
     his wonders in the region of Zoan.
⁴⁴ He turned their rivers to blood;
     they could not drink from their streams.
⁴⁵ He sent swarms of flies that devoured them,
     and frogs that devastated them.
⁴⁶ He gave their crops to the grasshopper,
     their produce to the locust.
⁴⁷ He destroyed their vines with hail
     and their sycamore-figs with sleet.
⁴⁸ He gave over their cattle to the hail,
     their livestock to bolts of lightning.
⁴⁹ He unleashed against them his hot anger,
     his wrath, indignation and hostility—
     a band of destroying angels.
⁵⁰ He prepared a path for his anger;
     he did not spare them from death
     but gave them over to the plague.
⁵¹ He struck down all the firstborn of Egypt,
     the firstfruits of manhood in the tents of Ham.
⁵² But he brought his people out like a flock;
     he led them like sheep through the desert.
⁵³ He guided them safely, so they were unafraid;
     but the sea engulfed their enemies.
⁵⁴ Thus he brought them to the border of his holy land,
     to the hill country his right hand had taken.
⁵⁵ He drove out nations before them
     and allotted their lands to them as an inheritance;
     he settled the tribes of Israel in their homes.

⁵⁶ But they put God to the test
     and rebelled against the Most High;
     they did not keep his statutes.
⁵⁷ Like their fathers they were disloyal and faithless,
     as unreliable as a faulty bow.
⁵⁸ They angered him with their high places;
     they aroused his jealousy with their idols.
⁵⁹ When God heard them, he was very angry;
     he rejected Israel completely.
⁶⁰ He abandoned the tabernacle of Shiloh,
     the tent he had set up among men.
⁶¹ He sent ⌊the ark of⌋ his might into captivity,
     his splendor into the hands of the enemy.
⁶² He gave his people over to the sword;
     he was very angry with his inheritance.
⁶³ Fire consumed their young men,
     and their maidens had no wedding songs;
⁶⁴ their priests were put to the sword,
     and their widows could not weep.

⁶⁵ Then the Lord awoke as from sleep,
     as a man wakes from the stupor of wine.

⁶⁶ He beat back his enemies;
    he put them to everlasting shame.
⁶⁷ Then he rejected the tents of Joseph,
    he did not choose the tribe of Ephraim;
⁶⁸ but he chose the tribe of Judah,
    Mount Zion, which he loved.
⁶⁹ He built his sanctuary like the heights,
    like the earth that he established forever.
⁷⁰ He chose David his servant
    and took him from the sheep pens;
⁷¹ from tending the sheep he brought him
    to be the shepherd of his people Jacob,
    of Israel his inheritance.
⁷² And David shepherded them with integrity of heart;
    with skillful hands he led them.

PSALM 79

A psalm of Asaph.

¹ O God, the nations have invaded your inheritance;
    they have defiled your holy temple,
    they have reduced Jerusalem to rubble.
² They have given the dead bodies of your servants
    as food to the birds of the air,
    the flesh of your saints to the beasts of the earth.
³ They have poured out blood like water
    all around Jerusalem,
    and there is no one to bury the dead.
⁴ We are objects of reproach to our neighbors,
    of scorn and derision to those around us.

⁵ How long, O LORD? Will you be angry forever?
    How long will your jealousy burn like fire?
⁶ Pour out your wrath on the nations
    that do not acknowledge you,
  on the kingdoms
    that do not call on your name;
⁷ for they have devoured Jacob
    and destroyed his homeland.
⁸ Do not hold against us the sins of the fathers;
    may your mercy come quickly to meet us,
    for we are in desperate need.

⁹ Help us, O God our Savior,
    for the glory of your name;
  deliver us and forgive our sins
    for your name's sake.
¹⁰ Why should the nations say,
    "Where is their God?"
  Before our eyes, make known among the nations
    that you avenge the outpoured blood of your servants.
¹¹ May the groans of the prisoners come before you;
    by the strength of your arm
    preserve those condemned to die.

¹² Pay back into the laps of our neighbors seven times
    the reproach they have hurled at you, O Lord.

¹³ Then we your people, the sheep of your pasture,
    will praise you forever;
from generation to generation
    we will recount your praise.

PSALM 80

For the director of music. To ˌthe tune ofˌ "The Lilies of the Covenant."
Of Asaph. A psalm.

¹ Hear us, O Shepherd of Israel,
    you who lead Joseph like a flock;
you who sit enthroned between the cherubim, shine forth
²   before Ephraim, Benjamin and Manasseh.
Awaken your might;
    come and save us.

³ Restore us, O God;
    make your face shine upon us,
    that we may be saved.

⁴ O LORD God Almighty,
    how long will your anger smolder
    against the prayers of your people?
⁵ You have fed them with the bread of tears;
    you have made them drink tears by the bowlful.
⁶ You have made us a source of contention to our neighbors,
    and our enemies mock us.

⁷ Restore us, O God Almighty;
    make your face shine upon us,
    that we may be saved.

⁸ You brought a vine out of Egypt;
    you drove out the nations and planted it.
⁹ You cleared the ground for it,
    and it took root and filled the land.
¹⁰ The mountains were covered with its shade,
    the mighty cedars with its branches.
¹¹ It sent out its boughs to the Sea,ᵃ
    its shoots as far as the River.ᵇ

¹² Why have you broken down its walls
    so that all who pass by pick its grapes?
¹³ Boars from the forest ravage it
    and the creatures of the field feed on it.
¹⁴ Return to us, O God Almighty!
    Look down from heaven and see!
Watch over this vine,
¹⁵   the root your right hand has planted,
    the sonᶜ you have raised up for yourself.

¹⁶ Your vine is cut down, it is burned with fire;
    at your rebuke your people perish.
¹⁷ Let your hand rest on the man at your right hand,
    the son of man you have raised up for yourself.
¹⁸ Then we will not turn away from you;
    revive us, and we will call on your name.

ᵃ *11* Probably the Mediterranean   ᵇ *11* That is, the Euphrates   ᶜ *15* Or *branch*

jael

VERSUS

sisera

» Wife of Heber the Kenite, a man loyal to the Canaanites
» Killed Sisera
» Praised in the song of Deborah and Barak (see Judges 5)

» Commander of the Canaanite armies under King Jabin
» Defeated by Deborah and Barak in battle
» Killed by Jael while he slept

The Main Event

Classic Bible riddle #29: What was the last thing to go through Sisera's mind? Answer: A big tent peg, compliments of a quick-thinking woman named Jael.

Here's how the bloody Jael vs. Sisera match-up unfolded:

During the dark, depressing period known as the time of the judges, the stubborn people of Israel repeatedly turned away from God. On one of these occasions, the Lord allowed them to be tormented and bullied by Canaanite thugs under the command of General Sisera. With a ferocious fleet of 900 chariots, he made life miserable for the Israelites—for two solid decades. When the people had finally had enough, they humbled themselves and begged God for help.

In response, God graciously raised up Deborah and Barak to lead Israel in an uprising that resulted in a rout of the Canaanite invaders. While the Israelites were making quick work of Sisera's army, Sisera leaped from his chariot and took off on foot. He sought shelter at the homestead of Heber, whose clan was loyal to Jabin, the Canaanite king.

Jael, Heber's wife, met Sisera outside her tent. She invited him inside, where he'd be safe from any Israelite search parties. (In that culture, a man wasn't allowed to go into a woman's tent unless she was his wife.) Jael gave Sisera a tall glass of milk, and soon the exhausted general was fast asleep.

That's when Jael grabbed a big mallet and the longest tent stake she could find. She crept quietly back into the tent, and . . . BAM, BAM, BAM, BAM! She nailed Sisera's head to the ground.

The Outcome

What's the application of a gruesome story like this? The most obvious one is that what goes around comes around. Or as the apostle Paul put it, "Do not be deceived: God cannot be mocked. A man reaps what he sows" (Galatians 6:7). Sisera lived by the sword, and ultimately he died by the sword.

Another truth is the importance of courage. Jael was bold and decisive (a big contrast from Barak, who was afraid to lead the charge into battle by himself). In a day when women were considered mere property, Jael took a huge risk by breaking from her husband and his family to stand with the people of God. She must have been scared to death, but she did what needed to be done.

Read more about Jael and Sisera in Judges 4–5 (pages 275–279).

¹⁹ Restore us, O LORD God Almighty;
  make your face shine upon us,
  that we may be saved.

PSALM 81

For the director of music. According to gittith.^a *Of Asaph.*

¹ Sing for joy to God our strength;
  shout aloud to the God of Jacob!
² Begin the music, strike the tambourine,
  play the melodious harp and lyre.

³ Sound the ram's horn at the New Moon,
  and when the moon is full, on the day of our Feast;
⁴ this is a decree for Israel,
  an ordinance of the God of Jacob.
⁵ He established it as a statute for Joseph
  when he went out against Egypt,
  where we heard a language we did not understand.^b

⁶ He says, "I removed the burden from their shoulders;
  their hands were set free from the basket.
⁷ In your distress you called and I rescued you,
  I answered you out of a thundercloud;
  I tested you at the waters of Meribah.   *Selah*

⁸ "Hear, O my people, and I will warn you—
  if you would but listen to me, O Israel!
⁹ You shall have no foreign god among you;
  you shall not bow down to an alien god.
¹⁰ I am the LORD your God,
  who brought you up out of Egypt.
  Open wide your mouth and I will fill it.

¹¹ "But my people would not listen to me;
  Israel would not submit to me.
¹² So I gave them over to their stubborn hearts
  to follow their own devices.

¹³ "If my people would but listen to me,
  if Israel would follow my ways,
¹⁴ how quickly would I subdue their enemies
  and turn my hand against their foes!
¹⁵ Those who hate the LORD would cringe before him,
  and their punishment would last forever.
¹⁶ But you would be fed with the finest of wheat;
  with honey from the rock I would satisfy you."

PSALM 82

A psalm of Asaph.

¹ God presides in the great assembly;
  he gives judgment among the "gods":

² "How long will you^c defend the unjust
  and show partiality to the wicked?   *Selah*
³ Defend the cause of the weak and fatherless;

---

^a Title: Probably a musical term   ^b 5 Or *I and we heard a voice we had not known*   ^c 2 The Hebrew is plural.

battlelines

» Feeling Helpless (Abuse)

Q: You're saying he's actually *hit* her?
A: Once that I've seen. I'm sure there have been other times. I've seen the bruises.

Q: Dude, what are you going to do?
A: What *can* I do? He outweighs me by 50 pounds. The one time I actually stepped between him and my mom, he put me in a headlock and started screaming in my ear and threatening me. I was just waiting for him to start smacking *me* around too.

Q: Why's he so angry?
A: Who knows?

Q: Does he ever do more than hit?
A: He yells a lot, if that's what you mean. At my mom, at me, at my little brother. He's always telling us how stupid we are. He also likes to throw things and slam doors. One time he even spit in my face.

Q: Man, that's out of control.
A: Tell me about it. I know I have to do something. I can't let it go on. I've thought about calling the police, but then I think, *Even if they arrest him, he'll eventually get out. And then what?* I told my mom that we should just pack up and leave one day while he's at work—and stay away until he gets some counseling or something.

Q: Yeah, that might work.
A: But part of me would really like to take care of this myself.

Q: What do you mean?
A: You know . . . just hit him as hard as I can. Knock him out when he least expects it. I'd like to give him some payback for all the times he's hurt us. Does that shock you?

Q: Man, I'm already *beyond* shocked by everything else you've told me.
A: I know I'm not supposed to say this, but sometimes I *hate* my dad. And on really bad days, I like to think about ways to . . . do serious damage to him. It's kind of scary to talk about, but that's how I feel.

» The Avenger

It's a tough question: Why doesn't God "step up" and fight for people who are weak and mistreated? At the very least, why doesn't he give us the green light to carry out vengeance on behalf of the abused?

There are no easy answers to these questions—just these Biblical principles:

- Be patient. God is the just judge of the universe. Ultimately he will right every wrong and punish all evil. "Do not take revenge, my friends, but leave room for God's wrath, for it is written: 'It is mine to avenge; I will repay,' says the Lord" (Romans 12:19).

- Be prayerful. James 5:16 says that "the prayer of a righteous man is powerful and effective." Prayer moves the heart of the One with the power to change things.

- Be protective. Psalm 82:3 tells us to "defend the cause of the weak . . . maintain the rights of the poor and oppressed." Abuse is a crime and needs to be reported. A lot of people think that reporting abuse will only make things worse, but in reality the opposite is true: If abuse is left unchecked, it will just get worse. Don't go it alone; consider talking to a trusted youth pastor, school counselor or even a professional counselor.

Find help for dealing with abusive situations at www.RevolutionBible.com.

maintain the rights of the poor and oppressed.
4 Rescue the weak and needy;
    deliver them from the hand of the wicked.

5 "They know nothing, they understand nothing.
    They walk about in darkness;
    all the foundations of the earth are shaken.

6 "I said, 'You are "gods";
    you are all sons of the Most High.'
7 But you will die like mere men;
    you will fall like every other ruler."

8 Rise up, O God, judge the earth,
    for all the nations are your inheritance.

PSALM 83

A song. A psalm of Asaph.

1 O God, do not keep silent;
    be not quiet, O God, be not still.
2 See how your enemies are astir,
    how your foes rear their heads.
3 With cunning they conspire against your people;
    they plot against those you cherish.
4 "Come," they say, "let us destroy them as a nation,
    that the name of Israel be remembered no more."

5 With one mind they plot together;
    they form an alliance against you—
6 the tents of Edom and the Ishmaelites,
    of Moab and the Hagrites,
7 Gebal,[a] Ammon and Amalek,
    Philistia, with the people of Tyre.
8 Even Assyria has joined them
    to lend strength to the descendants of Lot.   *Selah*

9 Do to them as you did to Midian,
    as you did to Sisera and Jabin at the river Kishon,
10 who perished at Endor
    and became like refuse on the ground.
11 Make their nobles like Oreb and Zeeb,
    all their princes like Zebah and Zalmunna,
12 who said, "Let us take possession
    of the pasturelands of God."

13 Make them like tumbleweed, O my God,
    like chaff before the wind.
14 As fire consumes the forest
    or a flame sets the mountains ablaze,
15 so pursue them with your tempest
    and terrify them with your storm.
16 Cover their faces with shame
    so that men will seek your name, O LORD.

17 May they ever be ashamed and dismayed;
    may they perish in disgrace.

a 7 That is, Byblos

18 Let them know that you, whose name is the LORD—
    that you alone are the Most High over all the earth.

PSALM 84

For the director of music. According to gittith.[a] *Of the Sons of Korah.*
A psalm.

1 How lovely is your dwelling place,
    O LORD Almighty!
2 My soul yearns, even faints,
    for the courts of the LORD;
my heart and my flesh cry out
    for the living God.

3 Even the sparrow has found a home,
    and the swallow a nest for herself,
    where she may have her young—
a place near your altar,
    O LORD Almighty, my King and my God.
4 Blessed are those who dwell in your house;
    they are ever praising you.   Selah

5 Blessed are those whose strength is in you,
    who have set their hearts on pilgrimage.
6 As they pass through the Valley of Baca,
    they make it a place of springs;
    the autumn rains also cover it with pools.[b]
7 They go from strength to strength,
    till each appears before God in Zion.

8 Hear my prayer, O LORD God Almighty;
    listen to me, O God of Jacob.   Selah
9 Look upon our shield,[c] O God;
    look with favor on your anointed one.

10 Better is one day in your courts
    than a thousand elsewhere;
I would rather be a doorkeeper in the house of my God
    than dwell in the tents of the wicked.
11 For the LORD God is a sun and shield;
    the LORD bestows favor and honor;
no good thing does he withhold
    from those whose walk is blameless.

12 O LORD Almighty,
    blessed is the man who trusts in you.

PSALM 85

For the director of music. Of the Sons of Korah. A psalm.

1 You showed favor to your land, O LORD;
    you restored the fortunes of Jacob.
2 You forgave the iniquity of your people
    and covered all their sins.   Selah
3 You set aside all your wrath
    and turned from your fierce anger.

---

[a] Title: Probably a musical term   [b] 6 Or *blessings*   [c] 9 Or *sovereign*

4 Restore us again, O God our Savior,
    and put away your displeasure toward us.
5 Will you be angry with us forever?
    Will you prolong your anger through all generations?
6 Will you not revive us again,
    that your people may rejoice in you?
7 Show us your unfailing love, O LORD,
    and grant us your salvation.

8 I will listen to what God the LORD will say;
    he promises peace to his people, his saints—
    but let them not return to folly.
9 Surely his salvation is near those who fear him,
    that his glory may dwell in our land.

10 Love and faithfulness meet together;
    righteousness and peace kiss each other.
11 Faithfulness springs forth from the earth,
    and righteousness looks down from heaven.
12 The LORD will indeed give what is good,
    and our land will yield its harvest.
13 Righteousness goes before him
    and prepares the way for his steps.

PSALM 86

A prayer of David.

1 Hear, O LORD, and answer me,
    for I am poor and needy.
2 Guard my life, for I am devoted to you.
    You are my God; save your servant
    who trusts in you.
3 Have mercy on me, O Lord,
    for I call to you all day long.
4 Bring joy to your servant,
    for to you, O Lord,
    I lift up my soul.

5 You are forgiving and good, O Lord,
    abounding in love to all who call to you.
6 Hear my prayer, O LORD;
    listen to my cry for mercy.
7 In the day of my trouble I will call to you,
    for you will answer me.

8 Among the gods there is none like you, O Lord;
    no deeds can compare with yours.
9 All the nations you have made
    will come and worship before you, O Lord;
    they will bring glory to your name.
10 For you are great and do marvelous deeds;
    you alone are God.

11 Teach me your way, O LORD,
    and I will walk in your truth;
give me an undivided heart,
    that I may fear your name.
12 I will praise you, O Lord my God, with all my heart;

I will glorify your name forever.
¹³ For great is your love toward me;
you have delivered me from the depths of the grave.^a

¹⁴ The arrogant are attacking me, O God;
a band of ruthless men seeks my life—
men without regard for you.
¹⁵ But you, O Lord, are a compassionate and gracious God,
slow to anger, abounding in love and faithfulness.
¹⁶ Turn to me and have mercy on me;
grant your strength to your servant
and save the son of your maidservant.^b
¹⁷ Give me a sign of your goodness,
that my enemies may see it and be put to shame,
for you, O Lord, have helped me and comforted me.

PSALM 87

Of the Sons of Korah. A psalm. A song.

¹ He has set his foundation on the holy mountain;
²   the Lord loves the gates of Zion
more than all the dwellings of Jacob.
³ Glorious things are said of you,
O city of God: *Selah*
⁴ "I will record Rahab^c and Babylon
among those who acknowledge me—
Philistia too, and Tyre, along with Cush^d—
and will say, 'This^e one was born in Zion.' "

⁵ Indeed, of Zion it will be said,
"This one and that one were born in her,
and the Most High himself will establish her."
⁶ The Lord will write in the register of the peoples:
"This one was born in Zion."   *Selah*
⁷ As they make music they will sing,
"All my fountains are in you."

PSALM 88

*A song. A psalm of the Sons of Korah. For the director of music.
According to* mahalath leannoth.^f *A* maskil^g *of Heman the Ezrahite.*

¹ O Lord, the God who saves me,
day and night I cry out before you.
² May my prayer come before you;
turn your ear to my cry.

³ For my soul is full of trouble
and my life draws near the grave.^a
⁴ I am counted among those who go down to the pit;
I am like a man without strength.
⁵ I am set apart with the dead,
like the slain who lie in the grave,
whom you remember no more,
who are cut off from your care.

---

^a *13,3* Hebrew Sheol   ^b *16* Or *save your faithful son*   ^c *4* A poetic name for Egypt   ^d *4* That is, the upper Nile region
^e *4* Or *"O Rahab and Babylon, / Philistia, Tyre and Cush, / I will record concerning those who acknowledge me: / 'This*   ^f Title: Possibly
a tune, "The Suffering of Affliction"   ^g Title: Probably a literary or musical term

⁶ You have put me in the lowest pit,
    in the darkest depths.
⁷ Your wrath lies heavily upon me;
    you have overwhelmed me with all your waves. *Selah*
⁸ You have taken from me my closest friends
    and have made me repulsive to them.
  I am confined and cannot escape;
⁹   my eyes are dim with grief.

  I call to you, O Lᴏʀᴅ, every day;
    I spread out my hands to you.
¹⁰ Do you show your wonders to the dead?
    Do those who are dead rise up and praise you? *Selah*
¹¹ Is your love declared in the grave,
    your faithfulness in Destructionᵃ?
¹² Are your wonders known in the place of darkness,
    or your righteous deeds in the land of oblivion?

¹³ But I cry to you for help, O Lᴏʀᴅ;
    in the morning my prayer comes before you.
¹⁴ Why, O Lᴏʀᴅ, do you reject me
    and hide your face from me?

¹⁵ From my youth I have been afflicted and close to death;
    I have suffered your terrors and am in despair.
¹⁶ Your wrath has swept over me;
    your terrors have destroyed me.
¹⁷ All day long they surround me like a flood;
    they have completely engulfed me.
¹⁸ You have taken my companions and loved ones from me;
    the darkness is my closest friend.

PSALM 89

A *maskil*ᵇ of Ethan the Ezrahite.

¹ I will sing of the Lᴏʀᴅ's great love forever;
    with my mouth I will make your faithfulness known through all
        generations.
² I will declare that your love stands firm forever,
    that you established your faithfulness in heaven itself.

³ You said, "I have made a covenant with my chosen one,
    I have sworn to David my servant,
⁴ 'I will establish your line forever
    and make your throne firm through all generations.' " *Selah*

⁵ The heavens praise your wonders, O Lᴏʀᴅ,
    your faithfulness too, in the assembly of the holy ones.
⁶ For who in the skies above can compare with the Lᴏʀᴅ?
    Who is like the Lᴏʀᴅ among the heavenly beings?
⁷ In the council of the holy ones God is greatly feared;
    he is more awesome than all who surround him.
⁸ O Lᴏʀᴅ God Almighty, who is like you?
    You are mighty, O Lᴏʀᴅ, and your faithfulness surrounds you.

⁹ You rule over the surging sea;
    when its waves mount up, you still them.

ᵃ *11* Hebrew *Abaddon*   ᵇ Title: Probably a literary or musical term

¹⁰ You crushed Rahab like one of the slain;
>> with your strong arm you scattered your enemies.
¹¹ The heavens are yours, and yours also the earth;
>> you founded the world and all that is in it.
¹² You created the north and the south;
>> Tabor and Hermon sing for joy at your name.
¹³ Your arm is endued with power;
>> your hand is strong, your right hand exalted.

¹⁴ Righteousness and justice are the foundation of your throne;
>> love and faithfulness go before you.
¹⁵ Blessed are those who have learned to acclaim you,
>> who walk in the light of your presence, O Lord.
¹⁶ They rejoice in your name all day long;
>> they exult in your righteousness.
¹⁷ For you are their glory and strength,
>> and by your favor you exalt our horn.^a
¹⁸ Indeed, our shield^b belongs to the Lord,
>> our king to the Holy One of Israel.

¹⁹ Once you spoke in a vision,
>> to your faithful people you said:
>> "I have bestowed strength on a warrior;
>> I have exalted a young man from among the people.
²⁰ I have found David my servant;
>> with my sacred oil I have anointed him.
²¹ My hand will sustain him;
>> surely my arm will strengthen him.
²² No enemy will subject him to tribute;
>> no wicked man will oppress him.
²³ I will crush his foes before him
>> and strike down his adversaries.
²⁴ My faithful love will be with him,
>> and through my name his horn^a will be exalted.
²⁵ I will set his hand over the sea,
>> his right hand over the rivers.
²⁶ He will call out to me, 'You are my Father,
>> my God, the Rock my Savior.'
²⁷ I will also appoint him my firstborn,
>> the most exalted of the kings of the earth.
²⁸ I will maintain my love to him forever,
>> and my covenant with him will never fail.
²⁹ I will establish his line forever,
>> his throne as long as the heavens endure.

³⁰ "If his sons forsake my law
>> and do not follow my statutes,
³¹ if they violate my decrees
>> and fail to keep my commands,
³² I will punish their sin with the rod,
>> their iniquity with flogging;
³³ but I will not take my love from him,
>> nor will I ever betray my faithfulness.
³⁴ I will not violate my covenant
>> or alter what my lips have uttered.

---

[a] *17,24 Horn* here symbolizes strong one.   [b] *18* Or *sovereign*

35 Once for all, I have sworn by my holiness—
 and I will not lie to David—
36 that his line will continue forever
 and his throne endure before me like the sun;
37 it will be established forever like the moon,
 the faithful witness in the sky."   *Selah*

38 But you have rejected, you have spurned,
 you have been very angry with your anointed one.
39 You have renounced the covenant with your servant
 and have defiled his crown in the dust.
40 You have broken through all his walls
 and reduced his strongholds to ruins.
41 All who pass by have plundered him;
 he has become the scorn of his neighbors.
42 You have exalted the right hand of his foes;
 you have made all his enemies rejoice.
43 You have turned back the edge of his sword
 and have not supported him in battle.
44 You have put an end to his splendor
 and cast his throne to the ground.
45 You have cut short the days of his youth;
 you have covered him with a mantle of shame.   *Selah*

46 How long, O LORD? Will you hide yourself forever?
 How long will your wrath burn like fire?
47 Remember how fleeting is my life.
 For what futility you have created all men!
48 What man can live and not see death,
 or save himself from the power of the grave[a]?   *Selah*
49 O Lord, where is your former great love,
 which in your faithfulness you swore to David?
50 Remember, Lord, how your servant has[b] been mocked,
 how I bear in my heart the taunts of all the nations,
51 the taunts with which your enemies have mocked, O LORD,
 with which they have mocked every step of your anointed one.

52 Praise be to the LORD forever!
 Amen and Amen.

BOOK IV

Psalms 90–106

PSALM 90

A prayer of Moses the man of God.

1 Lord, you have been our dwelling place
 throughout all generations.
2 Before the mountains were born
 or you brought forth the earth and the world,
 from everlasting to everlasting you are God.

3 You turn men back to dust,
 saying, "Return to dust, O sons of men."
4 For a thousand years in your sight

---

a 48 Hebrew *Sheol*   b 50 Or *your servants have*

moses

VERSUS

» Raised in the royal household by one of Pharaoh's daughters

» Handpicked by God to be Israel's deliverer and lawgiver

» The humblest man on earth

pharaoh

» Possibly Ramses II

» Cruel leader who enslaved the Hebrew people

» A proud man who refused to acknowledge the one true God

The Main Event

Name a guy in this world who doesn't want to "be somebody." You can't. We all want to achieve, succeed and be recognized. We all want to feel significant, to do something lasting and important.

Take Moses, for example. A Hebrew by birth, he escaped the poverty and misery of his people and grew up as the adopted grandson of the king of Egypt. With such a privileged upbringing and impressive education, there's no telling where Moses might have ended up and what he might have accomplished.

However, Moses' potential to do great things as a privileged member of the royal household ended when he impulsively killed an Egyptian who was beating a Hebrew slave. After the killing, Moses had to leave the country fast. With nowhere else to go, he took a job herding sheep in the middle of nowhere.

At that point, most people would have said to stick a fork in the guy, because he's done. All hopes of greatness and all chances of doing something important would have seemed out of the question at that point. As far as public opinion was concerned, Moses might as well have tattooed a big "L" for "loser" right in the middle of his forehead.

In contrast to Moses, there was Pharaoh, the leader of the world's first great superpower. Pharaoh was wealthy beyond words. He had the power to do almost anything. He was revered, feared—even worshiped as a god. He built pyramids and drank out of golden goblets. If anyone in this story was primed for everlasting success and fame, it was Pharaoh . . . right?

Before you answer that question, let's fast-forward about 40 years. That's when God suddenly yanked Moses away from his flocks and said, "Forget about sheep; I want you to shepherd my people. In fact, I'm going to use you to deliver them from Egyptian slavery."

Armed with only a walking stick, Moses reluctantly obeyed God's call. And wouldn't you know it, God made good on his promise. He humbled the arrogant Pharaoh and crushed his famed army. Even more amazing is the fact that God used an 80-year-old fugitive and former shepherd named Moses to guide his people to the promised land.

The Outcome

We never know what tomorrow holds, do we? We can't see the future. We don't have a clue what God may do in us and through our lives.

Right now we look around and see other guys with talent, smarts, connections, wealth and worldly ambition. The temptation is to think, *That's what I need in order to be significant. I can be important too if I meet the right people, go to the right places, find the right career and own the right stuff.*

Moses would give us some different advice. He would tell us to spend our lives walking with God and listening for his voice. He would urge us to be faithful, patient and humble . . . to keep obeying, to love and serve the Lord with all of our hearts.

If you're willing to do those things, you (like Moses) will find out—when it really counts—just how important your life can be.

Read more about Moses and Pharaoh in Exodus 4–15 (pages 68–83).

are like a day that has just gone by,
or like a watch in the night.

⁵ You sweep men away in the sleep of
death;
they are like the new grass of the
morning—
⁶ though in the morning it springs up
new,
by evening it is dry and withered.

⁷ We are consumed by your anger
and terrified by your indignation.
⁸ You have set our iniquities before you,
our secret sins in the light of your
presence.
⁹ All our days pass away under your
wrath;

∏OW OR ∏EVER

PS 90:4

God isn't controlled by time like we are.
He doesn't have deadlines, he never has to
rush, and he's never late. He works according to his own perfect timing and
makes things happen exactly when they're
supposed to happen.

we finish our years with a moan.
¹⁰ The length of our days is seventy years—
or eighty, if we have the strength;
yet their span ᵃ is but trouble and sorrow,
for they quickly pass, and we fly away.

¹¹ Who knows the power of your anger?
For your wrath is as great as the fear that is due you.
¹² Teach us to number our days aright,
that we may gain a heart of wisdom.

¹³ Relent, O Lᴏʀᴅ! How long will it be?
Have compassion on your servants.
¹⁴ Satisfy us in the morning with your unfailing love,
that we may sing for joy and be glad all our days.
¹⁵ Make us glad for as many days as you have afflicted us,
for as many years as we have seen trouble.
¹⁶ May your deeds be shown to your servants,
your splendor to their children.

¹⁷ May the favor ᵇ of the Lord our God rest upon us;
establish the work of our hands for us—
yes, establish the work of our hands.

PSALM 91

¹ He who dwells in the shelter of the Most High
will rest in the shadow of the Almighty. ᶜ
² I will say ᵈ of the Lᴏʀᴅ, "He is my refuge and my fortress,
my God, in whom I trust."

³ Surely he will save you from the fowler's snare
and from the deadly pestilence.
⁴ He will cover you with his feathers,
and under his wings you will find refuge;
his faithfulness will be your shield and rampart.
⁵ You will not fear the terror of night,
nor the arrow that flies by day,
⁶ nor the pestilence that stalks in the darkness,
nor the plague that destroys at midday.

ᵃ 10 Or yet the best of them   ᵇ 17 Or beauty   ᶜ 1 Hebrew Shaddai   ᵈ 2 Or He says

7 A thousand may fall at your side,
    ten thousand at your right hand,
    but it will not come near you.
8 You will only observe with your eyes
    and see the punishment of the wicked.

9 If you make the Most High your dwelling—
    even the LORD, who is my refuge—
10 then no harm will befall you,
    no disaster will come near your tent.
11 For he will command his angels concerning you
    to guard you in all your ways;
12 they will lift you up in their hands,
    so that you will not strike your foot against a stone.
13 You will tread upon the lion and the cobra;
    you will trample the great lion and the serpent.

14 "Because he loves me," says the LORD, "I will rescue him;
    I will protect him, for he acknowledges my name.
15 He will call upon me, and I will answer him;
    I will be with him in trouble,
    I will deliver him and honor him.
16 With long life will I satisfy him
    and show him my salvation."

PSALM 92

A psalm. A song. For the Sabbath day.

1 It is good to praise the LORD
    and make music to your name, O Most High,
2 to proclaim your love in the morning
    and your faithfulness at night,
3 to the music of the ten-stringed lyre
    and the melody of the harp.

4 For you make me glad by your deeds, O LORD;
    I sing for joy at the works of your hands.
5 How great are your works, O LORD,
    how profound your thoughts!
6 The senseless man does not know,
    fools do not understand,
7 that though the wicked spring up like grass
    and all evildoers flourish,
they will be forever destroyed.

8 But you, O LORD, are exalted forever.

9 For surely your enemies, O LORD,
    surely your enemies will perish;
    all evildoers will be scattered.
10 You have exalted my horn[a] like that of a wild ox;
    fine oils have been poured upon me.
11 My eyes have seen the defeat of my adversaries;
    my ears have heard the rout of my wicked foes.

12 The righteous will flourish like a palm tree,
    they will grow like a cedar of Lebanon;

---

a 10 *Horn* here symbolizes strength.

¹³ planted in the house of the LORD,
    they will flourish in the courts of our God.
¹⁴ They will still bear fruit in old age,
    they will stay fresh and green,
¹⁵ proclaiming, "The LORD is upright;
    he is my Rock, and there is no wickedness in him."

PSALM 93

¹ The LORD reigns, he is robed in majesty;
    the LORD is robed in majesty
    and is armed with strength.
The world is firmly established;
    it cannot be moved.
² Your throne was established long ago;
    you are from all eternity.

³ The seas have lifted up, O LORD,
    the seas have lifted up their voice;
    the seas have lifted up their pounding waves.
⁴ Mightier than the thunder of the great waters,
    mightier than the breakers of the sea—
    the LORD on high is mighty.

⁵ Your statutes stand firm;
    holiness adorns your house
    for endless days, O LORD.

PSALM 94

¹ O LORD, the God who avenges,
    O God who avenges, shine forth.
² Rise up, O Judge of the earth;
    pay back to the proud what they deserve.
³ How long will the wicked, O LORD,
    how long will the wicked be jubilant?

⁴ They pour out arrogant words;
    all the evildoers are full of boasting.
⁵ They crush your people, O LORD;
    they oppress your inheritance.
⁶ They slay the widow and the alien;
    they murder the fatherless.
⁷ They say, "The LORD does not see;
    the God of Jacob pays no heed."

⁸ Take heed, you senseless ones among
    the people;
    you fools, when will you become
    wise?
⁹ Does he who implanted the ear not
    hear?
    Does he who formed the eye not see?
¹⁰ Does he who disciplines nations not punish?
    Does he who teaches man lack knowledge?
¹¹ The LORD knows the thoughts of man;
    he knows that they are futile.

¹² Blessed is the man you discipline, O LORD,

NOW OR NEVER

PS 94:1–11

Step into the psalmists' shoes for a moment. Using Psalm 94 (and others like it) as a model, write out how you would warn people who ignore God and live the way they want to live.

the man you teach from your law;
¹³ you grant him relief from days of trouble,
till a pit is dug for the wicked.
¹⁴ For the LORD will not reject his people;
he will never forsake his inheritance.
¹⁵ Judgment will again be founded on righteousness,
and all the upright in heart will follow it.

¹⁶ Who will rise up for me against the wicked?
Who will take a stand for me against evildoers?
¹⁷ Unless the LORD had given me help,
I would soon have dwelt in the silence of death.
¹⁸ When I said, "My foot is slipping,"
your love, O LORD, supported me.
¹⁹ When anxiety was great within me,
your consolation brought joy to my soul.

²⁰ Can a corrupt throne be allied with you—
one that brings on misery by its decrees?
²¹ They band together against the righteous
and condemn the innocent to death.
²² But the LORD has become my fortress,
and my God the rock in whom I take refuge.
²³ He will repay them for their sins
and destroy them for their wickedness;
the LORD our God will destroy them.

PSALM 95

¹ Come, let us sing for joy to the LORD;
let us shout aloud to the Rock of our salvation.
² Let us come before him with thanksgiving
and extol him with music and song.

³ For the LORD is the great God,
the great King above all gods.
⁴ In his hand are the depths of the earth,
and the mountain peaks belong to him.
⁵ The sea is his, for he made it,
and his hands formed the dry land.

⁶ Come, let us bow down in worship,
let us kneel before the LORD our Maker;
⁷ for he is our God
and we are the people of his pasture,
the flock under his care.

Today, if you hear his voice,
⁸   do not harden your hearts as you did at Meribah,[a]
as you did that day at Massah[b] in the desert,
⁹ where your fathers tested and tried me,
though they had seen what I did.
¹⁰ For forty years I was angry with that generation;
I said, "They are a people whose hearts go astray,
and they have not known my ways."
¹¹ So I declared on oath in my anger,
"They shall never enter my rest."

[a] 8 Meribah means quarreling.   [b] 8 Massah means testing.

PSALM 96

1 Sing to the LORD a new song;
    sing to the LORD, all the earth.
2 Sing to the LORD, praise his name;
    proclaim his salvation day after day.
3 Declare his glory among the nations,
    his marvelous deeds among all peoples.

4 For great is the LORD and most worthy of praise;
    he is to be feared above all gods.
5 For all the gods of the nations are idols,
    but the LORD made the heavens.
6 Splendor and majesty are before him;
    strength and glory are in his sanctuary.

7 Ascribe to the LORD, O families of nations,
    ascribe to the LORD glory and strength.
8 Ascribe to the LORD the glory due his name;
    bring an offering and come into his courts.
9 Worship the LORD in the splendor of his[a] holiness;
    tremble before him, all the earth.

10 Say among the nations, "The LORD reigns."
    The world is firmly established, it cannot be moved;
    he will judge the peoples with equity.
11 Let the heavens rejoice, let the earth be glad;
    let the sea resound, and all that is in it;
12   let the fields be jubilant, and everything in them.
Then all the trees of the forest will sing for joy;
13   they will sing before the LORD, for he comes,
    he comes to judge the earth.
He will judge the world in righteousness
    and the peoples in his truth.

PSALM 97

1 The LORD reigns, let the earth be glad;
    let the distant shores rejoice.

2 Clouds and thick darkness surround him;
    righteousness and justice are the foundation of his throne.
3 Fire goes before him
    and consumes his foes on every side.
4 His lightning lights up the world;
    the earth sees and trembles.
5 The mountains melt like wax before the LORD,
    before the Lord of all the earth.
6 The heavens proclaim his righteousness,
    and all the peoples see his glory.

7 All who worship images are put to shame,
    those who boast in idols—
    worship him, all you gods!

8 Zion hears and rejoices
    and the villages of Judah are glad
    because of your judgments, O LORD.

---

[a] 9 Or LORD with the splendor of

⁹For you, O Lᴏʀᴅ, are the Most High over all the earth;
  you are exalted far above all gods.

¹⁰Let those who love the Lᴏʀᴅ hate evil,
  for he guards the lives of his faithful ones
  and delivers them from the hand of the wicked.
¹¹Light is shed upon the righteous
  and joy on the upright in heart.
¹²Rejoice in the Lᴏʀᴅ, you who are righteous,
  and praise his holy name.

PSALM 98

A psalm.

¹Sing to the Lᴏʀᴅ a new song,
  for he has done marvelous things;
his right hand and his holy arm
  have worked salvation for him.
²The Lᴏʀᴅ has made his salvation known
  and revealed his righteousness to the nations.
³He has remembered his love
  and his faithfulness to the house of Israel;
all the ends of the earth have seen
  the salvation of our God.

⁴Shout for joy to the Lᴏʀᴅ, all the earth,
  burst into jubilant song with music;
⁵make music to the Lᴏʀᴅ with the harp,
  with the harp and the sound of singing,
⁶with trumpets and the blast of the ram's horn—
  shout for joy before the Lᴏʀᴅ, the King.

⁷Let the sea resound, and everything in it,
  the world, and all who live in it.
⁸Let the rivers clap their hands,
  let the mountains sing together for joy;
⁹let them sing before the Lᴏʀᴅ,
  for he comes to judge the earth.
He will judge the world in righteousness
  and the peoples with equity.

PSALM 99

¹The Lᴏʀᴅ reigns,
  let the nations tremble;
he sits enthroned between the cherubim,
  let the earth shake.
²Great is the Lᴏʀᴅ in Zion;
  he is exalted over all the nations.
³Let them praise your great and awesome name—
  he is holy.

⁴The King is mighty, he loves justice—
  you have established equity;
in Jacob you have done
  what is just and right.
⁵Exalt the Lᴏʀᴅ our God

and worship at his footstool;
    he is holy.

⁶Moses and Aaron were among his priests,
    Samuel was among those who called on his name;
  they called on the LORD
    and he answered them.
⁷He spoke to them from the pillar of cloud;
    they kept his statutes and the decrees he gave them.

⁸O LORD our God,
    you answered them;
  you were to Israel ᵃ a forgiving God,
    though you punished their misdeeds. ᵇ
⁹Exalt the LORD our God
    and worship at his holy mountain,
    for the LORD our God is holy.

PSALM 100

A psalm. For giving thanks.

¹Shout for joy to the LORD, all the earth.
²   Worship the LORD with gladness;
    come before him with joyful songs.
³Know that the LORD is God.
    It is he who made us, and we are his ᶜ;
    we are his people, the sheep of his pasture.

⁴Enter his gates with thanksgiving
    and his courts with praise;
    give thanks to him and praise his name.
⁵For the LORD is good and his love endures forever;
    his faithfulness continues through all generations.

PSALM 101

Of David. A psalm.

¹I will sing of your love and justice;
    to you, O LORD, I will sing praise.
²I will be careful to lead a blameless life—
    when will you come to me?

I will walk in my house
    with blameless heart.
³I will set before my eyes
    no vile thing.

The deeds of faithless men I hate;
    they will not cling to me.
⁴Men of perverse heart shall be far from me;
    I will have nothing to do with evil.

⁵Whoever slanders his neighbor in secret,
    him will I put to silence;
  whoever has haughty eyes and a proud heart,
    him will I not endure.

ᵃ *8* Hebrew *them*   ᵇ *8* Or *| an avenger of the wrongs done to them*   ᶜ *3* Or *and not we ourselves*

⁶My eyes will be on the faithful in the land,
   that they may dwell with me;
he whose walk is blameless
   will minister to me.

⁷No one who practices deceit
   will dwell in my house;
no one who speaks falsely
   will stand in my presence.

⁸Every morning I will put to silence
   all the wicked in the land;
I will cut off every evildoer
   from the city of the LORD.

PSALM 102

A prayer of an afflicted man. When he is faint and pours out his lament
before the LORD.

¹Hear my prayer, O LORD;
   let my cry for help come to you.
²Do not hide your face from me
   when I am in distress.
Turn your ear to me;
   when I call, answer me quickly.

³For my days vanish like smoke;
   my bones burn like glowing embers.
⁴My heart is blighted and withered like
         grass;
   I forget to eat my food.
⁵Because of my loud groaning
   I am reduced to skin and bones.
⁶I am like a desert owl,
   like an owl among the ruins.
⁷I lie awake; I have become
   like a bird alone on a roof.
⁸All day long my enemies taunt me;
   those who rail against me use my
         name as a curse.
⁹For I eat ashes as my food
   and mingle my drink with tears
¹⁰because of your great wrath,
   for you have taken me up and thrown
         me aside.
¹¹My days are like the evening shadow;
   I wither away like grass.

¹²But you, O LORD, sit enthroned forever;
   your renown endures through all
         generations.
¹³You will arise and have compassion on
         Zion,
   for it is time to show favor to her;
   the appointed time has come.
¹⁴For her stones are dear to your servants;
   her very dust moves them to pity.

Getting Creative With Your Prayers

One thing that made the psalmists such great pray-ers is that they worked hard to keep their prayers fresh, interesting and heartfelt. They used their God-given creativity to express their true feelings in original and innovative ways. In this psalm, the writer could have said, *God, I feel lonely*. Instead, he used what he knew about nature to get his point across in a more poetic way. (In case you're wondering, desert owls live in isolated, lonely places.) Does God demand that kind of creativity in every prayer? Of course not. Does he appreciate the effort? What do you think?

15 The nations will fear the name of the LORD,
    all the kings of the earth will revere your glory.
16 For the LORD will rebuild Zion
    and appear in his glory.
17 He will respond to the prayer of the destitute;
    he will not despise their plea.

18 Let this be written for a future generation,
    that a people not yet created may praise the LORD:
19 "The LORD looked down from his sanctuary on high,
    from heaven he viewed the earth,
20 to hear the groans of the prisoners
    and release those condemned to death."
21 So the name of the LORD will be declared in Zion
    and his praise in Jerusalem
22 when the peoples and the kingdoms
    assemble to worship the LORD.

23 In the course of my life[a] he broke my strength;
    he cut short my days.
24 So I said:
    "Do not take me away, O my God, in the midst of my days;
    your years go on through all generations.
25 In the beginning you laid the foundations of the earth,
    and the heavens are the work of your hands.
26 They will perish, but you remain;
    they will all wear out like a garment.
    Like clothing you will change them
    and they will be discarded.
27 But you remain the same,
    and your years will never end.
28 The children of your servants will live in your presence;
    their descendants will be established before you."

PSALM 103

Of David.

1 Praise the LORD, O my soul;
    all my inmost being, praise his holy name.
2 Praise the LORD, O my soul,
    and forget not all his benefits—
3 who forgives all your sins
    and heals all your diseases,
4 who redeems your life from the pit
    and crowns you with love and compassion,
5 who satisfies your desires with good things
    so that your youth is renewed like the eagle's.

6 The LORD works righteousness
    and justice for all the oppressed.

7 He made known his ways to Moses,
    his deeds to the people of Israel:
8 The LORD is compassionate and gracious,
    slow to anger, abounding in love.
9 He will not always accuse,

a 23 Or By his power

nor will he harbor his anger forever;
10 he does not treat us as our sins deserve
   or repay us according to our iniquities.
11 For as high as the heavens are above the earth,
   so great is his love for those who fear him;
12 as far as the east is from the west,
   so far has he removed our transgressions from us.
13 As a father has compassion on his children,
   so the LORD has compassion on those who fear him;
14 for he knows how we are formed,
   he remembers that we are dust.
15 As for man, his days are like grass,
   he flourishes like a flower of the field;
16 the wind blows over it and it is gone,
   and its place remembers it no more.
17 But from everlasting to everlasting
   the LORD's love is with those who fear him,
   and his righteousness with their children's children—
18 with those who keep his covenant
   and remember to obey his precepts.

19 The LORD has established his throne in heaven,
   and his kingdom rules over all.

20 Praise the LORD, you his angels,
   you mighty ones who do his bidding,
   who obey his word.
21 Praise the LORD, all his heavenly hosts,
   you his servants who do his will.
22 Praise the LORD, all his works
   everywhere in his dominion.

Praise the LORD, O my soul.

PSALM 104

1 Praise the LORD, O my soul.

O LORD my God, you are very great;
   you are clothed with splendor and majesty.
2 He wraps himself in light as with a garment;
   he stretches out the heavens like a tent
3   and lays the beams of his upper chambers on their waters.
   He makes the clouds his chariot
   and rides on the wings of the wind.
4 He makes winds his messengers,ª
   flames of fire his servants.

5 He set the earth on its foundations;
   it can never be moved.
6 You covered it with the deep as with a garment;
   the waters stood above the mountains.
7 But at your rebuke the waters fled,
   at the sound of your thunder they took to flight;
8 they flowed over the mountains,
   they went down into the valleys,
   to the place you assigned for them.

ª 4 Or angels

⁹ You set a boundary they cannot cross;
  never again will they cover the earth.

¹⁰ He makes springs pour water into the ravines;
  it flows between the mountains.
¹¹ They give water to all the beasts of the field;
  the wild donkeys quench their thirst.
¹² The birds of the air nest by the waters;
  they sing among the branches.
¹³ He waters the mountains from his upper chambers;
  the earth is satisfied by the fruit of his work.
¹⁴ He makes grass grow for the cattle,
  and plants for man to cultivate—
  bringing forth food from the earth:
¹⁵ wine that gladdens the heart of man,
  oil to make his face shine,
  and bread that sustains his heart.
¹⁶ The trees of the Lord are well watered,
  the cedars of Lebanon that he planted.
¹⁷ There the birds make their nests;
  the stork has its home in the pine trees.
¹⁸ The high mountains belong to the wild goats;
  the crags are a refuge for the coneys. ᵃ

¹⁹ The moon marks off the seasons,
  and the sun knows when to go down.
²⁰ You bring darkness, it becomes night,
  and all the beasts of the forest prowl.
²¹ The lions roar for their prey
  and seek their food from God.
²² The sun rises, and they steal away;
  they return and lie down in their dens.
²³ Then man goes out to his work,
  to his labor until evening.

²⁴ How many are your works, O Lord!
  In wisdom you made them all;
  the earth is full of your creatures.
²⁵ There is the sea, vast and spacious,
  teeming with creatures beyond number—
  living things both large and small.
²⁶ There the ships go to and fro,
  and the leviathan, which you formed to frolic there.

²⁷ These all look to you
  to give them their food at the proper time.
²⁸ When you give it to them,
  they gather it up;
  when you open your hand,
  they are satisfied with good things.
²⁹ When you hide your face,
  they are terrified;
  when you take away their breath,
  they die and return to the dust.
³⁰ When you send your Spirit,
  they are created,

ᵃ 18 That is, the hyrax or rock badger

and you renew the face of the earth.

31 May the glory of the LORD endure forever;
  may the LORD rejoice in his works—
32 he who looks at the earth, and it trembles,
  who touches the mountains, and they smoke.

33 I will sing to the LORD all my life;
  I will sing praise to my God as long as I live.
34 May my meditation be pleasing to him,
  as I rejoice in the LORD.
35 But may sinners vanish from the earth
  and the wicked be no more.

Praise the LORD, O my soul.

Praise the LORD. [a]

PSALM 105

1 Give thanks to the LORD, call on his name;
  make known among the nations what he has done.
2 Sing to him, sing praise to him;
  tell of all his wonderful acts.
3 Glory in his holy name;
  let the hearts of those who seek the LORD rejoice.
4 Look to the LORD and his strength;
  seek his face always.

5 Remember the wonders he has done,
  his miracles, and the judgments he pronounced,
6 O descendants of Abraham his servant,
  O sons of Jacob, his chosen ones.
7 He is the LORD our God;
  his judgments are in all the earth.

8 He remembers his covenant forever,
  the word he commanded, for a thousand generations,
9 the covenant he made with Abraham,
  the oath he swore to Isaac.
10 He confirmed it to Jacob as a decree,
  to Israel as an everlasting covenant:
11 "To you I will give the land of Canaan
  as the portion you will inherit."

12 When they were but few in number,
  few indeed, and strangers in it,
13 they wandered from nation to nation,
  from one kingdom to another.
14 He allowed no one to oppress them;
  for their sake he rebuked kings:
15 "Do not touch my anointed ones;
  do my prophets no harm."

16 He called down famine on the land
  and destroyed all their supplies of food;
17 and he sent a man before them—
  Joseph, sold as a slave.

---

a *35* Hebrew *Hallelu Yah*; in the Septuagint this line stands at the beginning of Psalm 105.

18 They bruised his feet with shackles,
    his neck was put in irons,
19 till what he foretold came to pass,
    till the word of the LORD proved him true.
20 The king sent and released him,
    the ruler of peoples set him free.
21 He made him master of his household,
    ruler over all he possessed,
22 to instruct his princes as he pleased
    and teach his elders wisdom.

23 Then Israel entered Egypt;
    Jacob lived as an alien in the land of Ham.
24 The LORD made his people very fruitful;
    he made them too numerous for their foes,
25 whose hearts he turned to hate his people,
    to conspire against his servants.
26 He sent Moses his servant,
    and Aaron, whom he had chosen.
27 They performed his miraculous signs among them,
    his wonders in the land of Ham.
28 He sent darkness and made the land dark—
    for had they not rebelled against his words?
29 He turned their waters into blood,
    causing their fish to die.
30 Their land teemed with frogs,
    which went up into the bedrooms of their rulers.
31 He spoke, and there came swarms of flies,
    and gnats throughout their country.
32 He turned their rain into hail,
    with lightning throughout their land;
33 he struck down their vines and fig trees
    and shattered the trees of their country.
34 He spoke, and the locusts came,
    grasshoppers without number;
35 they ate up every green thing in their land,
    ate up the produce of their soil.
36 Then he struck down all the firstborn in their land,
    the firstfruits of all their manhood.

37 He brought out Israel, laden with silver and gold,
    and from among their tribes no one faltered.
38 Egypt was glad when they left,
    because dread of Israel had fallen on them.
39 He spread out a cloud as a covering,
    and a fire to give light at night.
40 They asked, and he brought them quail
    and satisfied them with the bread of heaven.
41 He opened the rock, and water gushed out;
    like a river it flowed in the desert.

42 For he remembered his holy promise
    given to his servant Abraham.
43 He brought out his people with rejoicing,
    his chosen ones with shouts of joy;
44 he gave them the lands of the nations,
    and they fell heir to what others had toiled for—

45 that they might keep his precepts
and observe his laws.

Praise the LORD. [a]

PSALM 106

1 Praise the LORD. [b]

Give thanks to the LORD, for he is good;
his love endures forever.
2 Who can proclaim the mighty acts of the LORD
or fully declare his praise?
3 Blessed are they who maintain justice,
who constantly do what is right.
4 Remember me, O LORD, when you show favor to your people,
come to my aid when you save them,
5 that I may enjoy the prosperity of your chosen ones,
that I may share in the joy of your nation
and join your inheritance in giving praise.

6 We have sinned, even as our fathers did;
we have done wrong and acted wickedly.
7 When our fathers were in Egypt,
they gave no thought to your miracles;
they did not remember your many kindnesses,
and they rebelled by the sea, the Red Sea. [c]
8 Yet he saved them for his name's sake,
to make his mighty power known.
9 He rebuked the Red Sea, and it dried up;
he led them through the depths as through a desert.
10 He saved them from the hand of the foe;
from the hand of the enemy he redeemed them.
11 The waters covered their adversaries;
not one of them survived.
12 Then they believed his promises
and sang his praise.

13 But they soon forgot what he had done
and did not wait for his counsel.
14 In the desert they gave in to their craving;
in the wasteland they put God to the test.
15 So he gave them what they asked for,
but sent a wasting disease upon them.

16 In the camp they grew envious of Moses
and of Aaron, who was consecrated to the LORD.
17 The earth opened up and swallowed Dathan;
it buried the company of Abiram.
18 Fire blazed among their followers;
a flame consumed the wicked.

19 At Horeb they made a calf
and worshiped an idol cast from metal.
20 They exchanged their Glory
for an image of a bull, which eats grass.

---

[a] 45 Hebrew *Hallelu Yah*   [b] 1 Hebrew *Hallelu Yah*; also in verse 48   [c] 7 Hebrew *Yam Suph*; that is, Sea of Reeds; also in verses 9 and 22

²¹ They forgot the God who saved them,
who had done great things in Egypt,
²² miracles in the land of Ham
and awesome deeds by the Red Sea.
²³ So he said he would destroy them—
had not Moses, his chosen one,
stood in the breach before him
to keep his wrath from destroying them.

²⁴ Then they despised the pleasant land;
they did not believe his promise.
²⁵ They grumbled in their tents
and did not obey the LORD.
²⁶ So he swore to them with uplifted hand
that he would make them fall in the desert,
²⁷ make their descendants fall among the nations
and scatter them throughout the lands.

²⁸ They yoked themselves to the Baal of Peor
and ate sacrifices offered to lifeless gods;
²⁹ they provoked the LORD to anger by their wicked deeds,
and a plague broke out among them.
³⁰ But Phinehas stood up and intervened,
and the plague was checked.
³¹ This was credited to him as righteousness
for endless generations to come.

³² By the waters of Meribah they angered the LORD,
and trouble came to Moses because of them;
³³ for they rebelled against the Spirit of God,
and rash words came from Moses' lips. [a]

³⁴ They did not destroy the peoples
as the LORD had commanded them,
³⁵ but they mingled with the nations
and adopted their customs.
³⁶ They worshiped their idols,
which became a snare to them.
³⁷ They sacrificed their sons
and their daughters to demons.
³⁸ They shed innocent blood,
the blood of their sons and daughters,
whom they sacrificed to the idols of Canaan,
and the land was desecrated by their blood.
³⁹ They defiled themselves by what they did;
by their deeds they prostituted themselves.

⁴⁰ Therefore the LORD was angry with his people
and abhorred his inheritance.
⁴¹ He handed them over to the nations,
and their foes ruled over them.
⁴² Their enemies oppressed them
and subjected them to their power.
⁴³ Many times he delivered them,
but they were bent on rebellion
and they wasted away in their sin.

---

^a 33 Or against his spirit, / and rash words came from his lips

⁴⁴But he took note of their distress
　　when he heard their cry;
⁴⁵for their sake he remembered his covenant
　　and out of his great love he relented.
⁴⁶He caused them to be pitied
　　by all who held them captive.

⁴⁷Save us, O LORD our God,
　　and gather us from the nations,
　that we may give thanks to your holy name
　　and glory in your praise.

⁴⁸Praise be to the LORD, the God of Israel,
　　from everlasting to everlasting.
　Let all the people say, "Amen!"

　Praise the LORD.

BOOK V

PSALMS 107-150

PSALM 107

¹Give thanks to the LORD, for he is good;
　　his love endures forever.
²Let the redeemed of the LORD say this—
　　those he redeemed from the hand of the foe,
³those he gathered from the lands,
　　from east and west, from north and south.ᵃ

⁴Some wandered in desert wastelands,
　　finding no way to a city where they could settle.
⁵They were hungry and thirsty,
　　and their lives ebbed away.
⁶Then they cried out to the LORD in their trouble,
　　and he delivered them from their distress.
⁷He led them by a straight way
　　to a city where they could settle.
⁸Let them give thanks to the LORD for his unfailing love
　　and his wonderful deeds for men,
⁹for he satisfies the thirsty
　　and fills the hungry with good things.

¹⁰Some sat in darkness and the deepest gloom,
　　prisoners suffering in iron chains,
¹¹for they had rebelled against the words of God
　　and despised the counsel of the Most High.
¹²So he subjected them to bitter labor;
　　they stumbled, and there was no one to help.
¹³Then they cried to the LORD in their trouble,
　　and he saved them from their distress.
¹⁴He brought them out of darkness and the deepest gloom
　　and broke away their chains.
¹⁵Let them give thanks to the LORD for his unfailing love
　　and his wonderful deeds for men,
¹⁶for he breaks down gates of bronze

ᵃ 3 Hebrew *north and the sea*

and cuts through bars of iron.

17 Some became fools through their rebellious ways
and suffered affliction because of their iniquities.
18 They loathed all food
and drew near the gates of death.
19 Then they cried to the LORD in their trouble,
and he saved them from their distress.
20 He sent forth his word and healed them;
he rescued them from the grave.
21 Let them give thanks to the LORD for his unfailing love
and his wonderful deeds for men.
22 Let them sacrifice thank offerings
and tell of his works with songs of joy.

23 Others went out on the sea in ships;
they were merchants on the mighty waters.
24 They saw the works of the LORD,
his wonderful deeds in the deep.
25 For he spoke and stirred up a tempest
that lifted high the waves.
26 They mounted up to the heavens and went down to the depths;
in their peril their courage melted away.
27 They reeled and staggered like drunken men;
they were at their wits' end.
28 Then they cried out to the LORD in their trouble,
and he brought them out of their distress.
29 He stilled the storm to a whisper;
the waves of the sea were hushed.
30 They were glad when it grew calm,
and he guided them to their desired haven.
31 Let them give thanks to the LORD for his unfailing love
and his wonderful deeds for men.
32 Let them exalt him in the assembly of the people
and praise him in the council of the elders.

33 He turned rivers into a desert,
flowing springs into thirsty ground,
34 and fruitful land into a salt waste,
because of the wickedness of those who lived there.
35 He turned the desert into pools of water
and the parched ground into flowing springs;
36 there he brought the hungry to live,
and they founded a city where they could settle.
37 They sowed fields and planted vineyards
that yielded a fruitful harvest;
38 he blessed them, and their numbers greatly increased,
and he did not let their herds diminish.

39 Then their numbers decreased, and they were humbled
by oppression, calamity and sorrow;
40 he who pours contempt on nobles
made them wander in a trackless waste.
41 But he lifted the needy out of their affliction
and increased their families like flocks.
42 The upright see and rejoice,
but all the wicked shut their mouths.

⁴³Whoever is wise, let him heed these things
  and consider the great love of the LORD.

PSALM 108

A song. A psalm of David.

¹My heart is steadfast, O God;
  I will sing and make music with all my soul.
²Awake, harp and lyre!
  I will awaken the dawn.
³I will praise you, O LORD, among the nations;
  I will sing of you among the peoples.
⁴For great is your love, higher than the heavens;
  your faithfulness reaches to the skies.
⁵Be exalted, O God, above the heavens,
  and let your glory be over all the earth.

⁶Save us and help us with your right hand,
  that those you love may be delivered.
⁷God has spoken from his sanctuary:
  "In triumph I will parcel out Shechem
  and measure off the Valley of Succoth.
⁸Gilead is mine, Manasseh is mine;
  Ephraim is my helmet,
  Judah my scepter.
⁹Moab is my washbasin,
  upon Edom I toss my sandal;
  over Philistia I shout in triumph."

¹⁰Who will bring me to the fortified city?
  Who will lead me to Edom?
¹¹Is it not you, O God, you who have rejected us
  and no longer go out with our armies?
¹²Give us aid against the enemy,
  for the help of man is worthless.
¹³With God we will gain the victory,
  and he will trample down our enemies.

PSALM 109

For the director of music. Of David. A psalm.

¹O God, whom I praise,
  do not remain silent,
²for wicked and deceitful men
  have opened their mouths against me;
  they have spoken against me with lying tongues.
³With words of hatred they surround me;
  they attack me without cause.
⁴In return for my friendship they accuse me,
  but I am a man of prayer.
⁵They repay me evil for good,
  and hatred for my friendship.

⁶Appoint[a] an evil man[b] to oppose him;
  let an accuser[c] stand at his right hand.

---

[a] 6 Or They say: "Appoint (with quotation marks at the end of verse 19)   [b] 6 Or the Evil One   [c] 6 Or let Satan

7 When he is tried, let him be found guilty,
 and may his prayers condemn him.
8 May his days be few;
 may another take his place of leadership.
9 May his children be fatherless
 and his wife a widow.
10 May his children be wandering beggars;
 may they be driven[a] from their ruined homes.
11 May a creditor seize all he has;
 may strangers plunder the fruits of his labor.
12 May no one extend kindness to him
 or take pity on his fatherless children.
13 May his descendants be cut off,
 their names blotted out from the next generation.
14 May the iniquity of his fathers be remembered before the LORD;
 may the sin of his mother never be blotted out.
15 May their sins always remain before the LORD,
 that he may cut off the memory of them from the earth.

16 For he never thought of doing a kindness,
 but hounded to death the poor
 and the needy and the brokenhearted.
17 He loved to pronounce a curse—
 may it[b] come on him;
 he found no pleasure in blessing—
 may it be[c] far from him.
18 He wore cursing as his garment;
 it entered into his body like water,
 into his bones like oil.
19 May it be like a cloak wrapped about him,
 like a belt tied forever around him.
20 May this be the LORD's payment to my accusers,
 to those who speak evil of me.

21 But you, O Sovereign LORD,
 deal well with me for your name's sake;
 out of the goodness of your love, deliver me.
22 For I am poor and needy,
 and my heart is wounded within me.
23 I fade away like an evening shadow;
 I am shaken off like a locust.
24 My knees give way from fasting;
 my body is thin and gaunt.
25 I am an object of scorn to my accusers;
 when they see me, they shake their heads.

26 Help me, O LORD my God;
 save me in accordance with your love.
27 Let them know that it is your hand,
 that you, O LORD, have done it.
28 They may curse, but you will bless;
 when they attack they will be put to shame,
 but your servant will rejoice.
29 My accusers will be clothed with disgrace
 and wrapped in shame as in a cloak.

---

a 10 Septuagint; Hebrew sought   b 17 Or curse, / and it has   c 17 Or blessing, / and it is

³⁰ With my mouth I will greatly extol the L<small>ORD</small>;
in the great throng I will praise him.
³¹ For he stands at the right hand of the needy one,
to save his life from those who condemn him.

PSALM 110

Of David. A psalm.

¹ The L<small>ORD</small> says to my Lord:
"Sit at my right hand
until I make your enemies
a footstool for your feet."

² The L<small>ORD</small> will extend your mighty scepter from Zion;
you will rule in the midst of your enemies.
³ Your troops will be willing
on your day of battle.
Arrayed in holy majesty,
from the womb of the dawn
you will receive the dew of your youth.^a

⁴ The L<small>ORD</small> has sworn
and will not change his mind:
"You are a priest forever,
in the order of Melchizedek."

⁵ The Lord is at your right hand;
he will crush kings on the day of his wrath.
⁶ He will judge the nations, heaping up the dead
and crushing the rulers of the whole earth.
⁷ He will drink from a brook beside the way^b;
therefore he will lift up his head.

PSALM 111 ^c

¹ Praise the L<small>ORD</small>.^d

I will extol the L<small>ORD</small> with all my heart
in the council of the upright and in the assembly.

² Great are the works of the L<small>ORD</small>;
they are pondered by all who delight in them.
³ Glorious and majestic are his deeds,
and his righteousness endures forever.
⁴ He has caused his wonders to be remembered;
the L<small>ORD</small> is gracious and compassionate.
⁵ He provides food for those who fear him;
he remembers his covenant forever.
⁶ He has shown his people the power of his works,
giving them the lands of other nations.
⁷ The works of his hands are faithful and just;
all his precepts are trustworthy.
⁸ They are steadfast for ever and ever,
done in faithfulness and uprightness.
⁹ He provided redemption for his people;
he ordained his covenant forever—

---

^a 3 Or / your young men will come to you like the dew   ^b 7 Or / The One who grants succession will set him in authority   ^c This psalm is an acrostic poem, the lines of which begin with the successive letters of the Hebrew alphabet.   ^d 1 Hebrew Hallelu Yah

david

» A Jewish shepherd who loved God
» The youngest son of Jesse
» The future king of Israel

VERSUS

goliath

» A loud, pagan Philistine warrior
» Stood more than nine feet tall
» Killed by David

The Main Event

Long-time enemies, the Israelites and Philistines were ready to duke it out. Rather than resort to all-out war, the Philistines proposed the idea of having each nation put forth its most fearsome warrior for a kind of winner-take-all duel.

The proposal was a no-brainer for the Philistines. After all, they had Goliath, a human mountain, on their side. In his armor, Goliath must have looked like a tank with legs. His spear was the size of a small telephone pole. Take the tallest NBA player, mix him with the meanest NFL linebacker—on steroids, no less—and well, you start to get the picture of what Goliath was like.

Every morning this mutant would walk out into the valley separating the two armies and engage in some serious trash talk. He challenged the manhood of the Jewish soldiers. He mocked their God. Yet none of the Israelites were willing to step forward to take on Goliath.

About that time, David wandered on to the scene, sent by his father to deliver supplies to his older brothers who were in the Israelite army. David was just a teenager, maybe not even all the way through puberty. But when he heard Goliath mouthing off, he was furious. "Who is this jerk who dares to taunt the armies of the living God?" he asked.

When David saw that no one else was going to stand up for the Lord, he volunteered to take on Goliath himself. The result was a pretty comical scene. A massive warrior towering over a skinny little shepherd boy. A trained killing machine with industrial-sized armor squaring off against a kid with a slingshot and, more important, a heart full of faith. It was the greatest mismatch in history.

Poor Goliath never had a chance.

The Outcome

One well-placed stone from David's sling put Goliath facedown on the ground. To make sure that he stayed down, David raced over and hacked off the giant's big, shaggy head. The stunned Israelites spent the rest of the day chasing down the fleeing Philistine soldiers.

We could quote hokey clichés such as, "The bigger they come, the harder they fall" or "It's not the size of the dog in the fight; it's the size of the fight in the dog," but the real lesson here is wild-eyed faith.

Are you willing to put yourself in situations in which, if God doesn't come through, you're going down? Sounds scary, doesn't it? But it's that radical kind of risk-taking that separates the men from the boys.

Read more about David and Goliath in 1 Samuel 17 (pages 326–328).

holy and awesome is his name.

¹⁰ The fear of the LORD is the beginning of wisdom;
all who follow his precepts have good understanding.
To him belongs eternal praise.

PSALM 112 ᵃ

¹ Praise the LORD. ᵇ

Blessed is the man who fears the LORD,
who finds great delight in his commands.

² His children will be mighty in the land;
the generation of the upright will be blessed.
³ Wealth and riches are in his house,
and his righteousness endures forever.
⁴ Even in darkness light dawns for the upright,
for the gracious and compassionate and righteous man. ᶜ
⁵ Good will come to him who is generous and lends freely,
who conducts his affairs with justice.
⁶ Surely he will never be shaken;
a righteous man will be remembered forever.
⁷ He will have no fear of bad news;
his heart is steadfast, trusting in the LORD.
⁸ His heart is secure, he will have no fear;
in the end he will look in triumph on his foes.
⁹ He has scattered abroad his gifts to the poor,
his righteousness endures forever;
his horn ᵈ will be lifted high in honor.

¹⁰ The wicked man will see and be vexed,
he will gnash his teeth and waste away;
the longings of the wicked will come to nothing.

PSALM 113

¹ Praise the LORD. ᵉ

Praise, O servants of the LORD,
praise the name of the LORD.
² Let the name of the LORD be praised,
both now and forevermore.
³ From the rising of the sun to the place where it sets,
the name of the LORD is to be praised.

⁴ The LORD is exalted over all the nations,
his glory above the heavens.
⁵ Who is like the LORD our God,
the One who sits enthroned on high,
⁶ who stoops down to look
on the heavens and the earth?

⁷ He raises the poor from the dust
and lifts the needy from the ash heap;
⁸ he seats them with princes,
with the princes of their people.

ᵃ This psalm is an acrostic poem, the lines of which begin with the successive letters of the Hebrew alphabet.   ᵇ 1 Hebrew *Hallelu Yah*
ᶜ 4 Or / for ⌊the LORD⌋ is gracious and compassionate and righteous   ᵈ 9 *Horn* here symbolizes dignity.   ᵉ 1 Hebrew *Hallelu Yah*; also
in verse 9

⁹He settles the barren woman in her home
  as a happy mother of children.

  Praise the LORD.

PSALM 114

¹When Israel came out of Egypt,
  the house of Jacob from a people of foreign tongue,
²Judah became God's sanctuary,
  Israel his dominion.

³The sea looked and fled,
  the Jordan turned back;
⁴the mountains skipped like rams,
  the hills like lambs.

⁵Why was it, O sea, that you fled,
  O Jordan, that you turned back,
⁶you mountains, that you skipped like rams,
  you hills, like lambs?

⁷Tremble, O earth, at the presence of the Lord,
  at the presence of the God of Jacob,
⁸who turned the rock into a pool,
  the hard rock into springs of water.

PSALM 115

¹Not to us, O LORD, not to us
  but to your name be the glory,
  because of your love and faithfulness.

²Why do the nations say,
  "Where is their God?"
³Our God is in heaven;
  he does whatever pleases him.
⁴But their idols are silver and gold,
  made by the hands of men.
⁵They have mouths, but cannot speak,
  eyes, but they cannot see;
⁶they have ears, but cannot hear,
  noses, but they cannot smell;
⁷they have hands, but cannot feel,
  feet, but they cannot walk;
  nor can they utter a sound with their throats.
⁸Those who make them will be like them,
  and so will all who trust in them.

⁹O house of Israel, trust in the LORD—
  he is their help and shield.
¹⁰O house of Aaron, trust in the LORD—
  he is their help and shield.
¹¹You who fear him, trust in the LORD—
  he is their help and shield.

¹²The LORD remembers us and will bless us:
  He will bless the house of Israel,
  he will bless the house of Aaron,
¹³he will bless those who fear the LORD—

small and great alike.

14 May the LORD make you increase,
    both you and your children.
15 May you be blessed by the LORD,
    the Maker of heaven and earth.

16 The highest heavens belong to the LORD,
    but the earth he has given to man.
17 It is not the dead who praise the LORD,
    those who go down to silence;
18 it is we who extol the LORD,
    both now and forevermore.

Praise the LORD.[a]

PSALM 116

1 I love the LORD, for he heard my voice;
    he heard my cry for mercy.
2 Because he turned his ear to me,
    I will call on him as long as I live.

3 The cords of death entangled me,
    the anguish of the grave[b] came upon me;
    I was overcome by trouble and sorrow.
4 Then I called on the name of the LORD:
    "O LORD, save me!"

5 The LORD is gracious and righteous;
    our God is full of compassion.
6 The LORD protects the simplehearted;
    when I was in great need, he saved me.

7 Be at rest once more, O my soul,
    for the LORD has been good to you.

8 For you, O LORD, have delivered my soul from death,
    my eyes from tears,
    my feet from stumbling,
9 that I may walk before the LORD
    in the land of the living.
10 I believed; therefore[c] I said,
    "I am greatly afflicted."
11 And in my dismay I said,
    "All men are liars."

12 How can I repay the LORD
    for all his goodness to me?
13 I will lift up the cup of salvation
    and call on the name of the LORD.
14 I will fulfill my vows to the LORD
    in the presence of all his people.

15 Precious in the sight of the LORD
    is the death of his saints.
16 O LORD, truly I am your servant;
    I am your servant, the son of your maidservant[d];
    you have freed me from my chains.

---

[a] 18 Hebrew Hallelu Yah   [b] 3 Hebrew Sheol   [c] 10 Or believed even when   [d] 16 Or servant, your faithful son

¹⁷ I will sacrifice a thank offering to you
and call on the name of the LORD.
¹⁸ I will fulfill my vows to the LORD
in the presence of all his people,
¹⁹ in the courts of the house of the LORD—
in your midst, O Jerusalem.

Praise the LORD. ᵃ

ⓝⓞⓦ ⓞⓡ ⓝⓔⓥⓔⓡ
PS 117:1-2

This entire psalm is 29 words long. Sometimes you can say something pretty important about God in just a sentence or two. You don't necessarily need a ton of words to express who God really is.

PSALM 117

¹ Praise the LORD, all you nations;
extol him, all you peoples.
² For great is his love toward us,
and the faithfulness of the LORD
endures forever.

Praise the LORD. ᵃ

PSALM 118

¹ Give thanks to the LORD, for he is good;
his love endures forever.

² Let Israel say:
"His love endures forever."
³ Let the house of Aaron say:
"His love endures forever."
⁴ Let those who fear the LORD say:
"His love endures forever."

⁵ In my anguish I cried to the LORD,
and he answered by setting me free.
⁶ The LORD is with me; I will not be afraid.
What can man do to me?
⁷ The LORD is with me; he is my helper.
I will look in triumph on my enemies.

⁸ It is better to take refuge in the LORD
than to trust in man.
⁹ It is better to take refuge in the LORD
than to trust in princes.

¹⁰ All the nations surrounded me,
but in the name of the LORD I cut them off.
¹¹ They surrounded me on every side,
but in the name of the LORD I cut them off.
¹² They swarmed around me like bees,
but they died out as quickly as burning thorns;
in the name of the LORD I cut them off.

¹³ I was pushed back and about to fall,
but the LORD helped me.
¹⁴ The LORD is my strength and my song;
he has become my salvation.

¹⁵ Shouts of joy and victory
resound in the tents of the righteous:
"The LORD's right hand has done mighty things!

ᵃ 19,2 Hebrew *Hallelu Yah*

16 The Lord's right hand is lifted high;
  the Lord's right hand has done mighty things!"

17 I will not die but live,
  and will proclaim what the Lord has done.
18 The Lord has chastened me severely,
  but he has not given me over to death.

19 Open for me the gates of righteousness;
  I will enter and give thanks to the Lord.
20 This is the gate of the Lord
  through which the righteous may enter.
21 I will give you thanks, for you answered me;
  you have become my salvation.

22 The stone the builders rejected
  has become the capstone;
23 the Lord has done this,
  and it is marvelous in our eyes.
24 This is the day the Lord has made;
  let us rejoice and be glad in it.

25 O Lord, save us;
  O Lord, grant us success.
26 Blessed is he who comes in the name of the Lord.
  From the house of the Lord we bless you. [a]
27 The Lord is God,
  and he has made his light shine upon us.
  With boughs in hand, join in the festal procession
  up [b] to the horns of the altar.

28 You are my God, and I will give you thanks;
  you are my God, and I will exalt you.

29 Give thanks to the Lord, for he is good;
  his love endures forever.

PSALM 119 [c]

א ALEPH

1 Blessed are they whose ways are blameless,
  who walk according to the law of the Lord.
2 Blessed are they who keep his statutes
  and seek him with all their heart.
3 They do nothing wrong;
  they walk in his ways.
4 You have laid down precepts
  that are to be fully obeyed.
5 Oh, that my ways were steadfast
  in obeying your decrees!
6 Then I would not be put to shame
  when I consider all your commands.
7 I will praise you with an upright heart
  as I learn your righteous laws.
8 I will obey your decrees;
  do not utterly forsake me.

---

[a] 26 The Hebrew is plural.   [b] 27 Or *Bind the festal sacrifice with ropes / and take it*   [c] This psalm is an acrostic poem; the verses of each stanza begin with the same letter of the Hebrew alphabet.

battlelines

» Insert One Foot (Think First)

Q: I can't believe you said that.
A: Neither can I. It just slipped out. I was mad, that's all.

Q: I'll bet you'll pay big-time for it.
A: Yeah, you're probably right. I ought to just staple my lips together.

Q: So is this becoming a regular thing?
A: Yeah, lately. I don't know why. It's like my mouth is totally out of control. My parents start asking me 100 questions, and before I know it, I'm lying. Looking them right in the eyes and just flat-out lying. Or if I start losing at a computer game, the next thing I know, I'm cussing my head off. If someone makes me mad, things I don't want to say just come gushing out.

Q: Sounds like you've got a big problem to tackle.
A: (Pause) I don't know what to do. I mean, right after I blurt stuff out, it's like I want to lasso the words back into my mouth. Instant guilt. And then I think, *OK, that's it. No more.* But then, 30 seconds later, I'm back at it—doing it again in a different situation.

Q: So what are you going to do about it?
A: What *can* I do? It's a habit, like smoking. I think I'm addicted.

Q: I don't buy that. I think you can control what you say.
A: How?

Q: I think whatever you put in your head is what will come out of your mouth.
A: So I shouldn't watch movies with lots of bad language, is that what you're saying?

Q: Well, it's probably not *that* simple. All I can tell you is that when I spend time with God daily, reading the Bible and praying—when my heart is focused on him—I find I don't struggle as much with my mouth.

» Taming the Tongue

Controlling your mouth is one of the toughest things you'll ever do. But the secret to success doesn't lie in biting your tongue the moment the words start coming out. That's like trying to deal with nasty tap water coming from your kitchen faucet by tinkering with the hot and cold knobs.

To win the battle of the tongue, you need to focus your efforts on dealing with what's in your *mind* and *heart*. Jesus said, "The good man brings good things out of the good stored up in his heart, and the evil man brings evil things out of the evil stored up in his heart. For out of the overflow of his heart his mouth speaks" (Luke 6:45).

Make God the focus of your life, and godly words will come from your mouth (see Psalm 119:9–11 and James 3:1–12).

Go to www.RevolutionBible.com for more.

ב BETH

9 How can a young man keep his way pure?
    By living according to your word.
10 I seek you with all my heart;
    do not let me stray from your commands.
11 I have hidden your word in my heart
    that I might not sin against you.
12 Praise be to you, O Lord;
    teach me your decrees.
13 With my lips I recount
    all the laws that come from your mouth.
14 I rejoice in following your statutes
    as one rejoices in great riches.
15 I meditate on your precepts
    and consider your ways.
16 I delight in your decrees;
    I will not neglect your word.

ג GIMEL

17 Do good to your servant, and I will live;
    I will obey your word.
18 Open my eyes that I may see
    wonderful things in your law.
19 I am a stranger on earth;
    do not hide your commands
        from me.

now or never
PS 119:9

One of the most difficult tasks for Christian guys is to remain sexually pure. There is temptation at every corner. Whether you're 15 or 50, you will always encounter the pressure to give in. But David's words are a good reminder of how to remain pure.

20 My soul is consumed with longing
    for your laws at all times.
21 You rebuke the arrogant, who are cursed
    and who stray from your commands.
22 Remove from me scorn and contempt,
    for I keep your statutes.
23 Though rulers sit together and slander me,
    your servant will meditate on your decrees.
24 Your statutes are my delight;
    they are my counselors.

ד DALETH

25 I am laid low in the dust;
    preserve my life according to your word.
26 I recounted my ways and you answered me;
    teach me your decrees.
27 Let me understand the teaching of your precepts;
    then I will meditate on your wonders.
28 My soul is weary with sorrow;
    strengthen me according to your word.
29 Keep me from deceitful ways;
    be gracious to me through your law.
30 I have chosen the way of truth;
    I have set my heart on your laws.
31 I hold fast to your statutes, O Lord;
    do not let me be put to shame.
32 I run in the path of your commands,
    for you have set my heart free.

³³ Teach me, O Lord, to follow your decrees;
 then I will keep them to the end.
³⁴ Give me understanding, and I will keep your law
 and obey it with all my heart.
³⁵ Direct me in the path of your commands,
 for there I find delight.
³⁶ Turn my heart toward your statutes
 and not toward selfish gain.
³⁷ Turn my eyes away from worthless things;
 preserve my life according to your word. ᵃ
³⁸ Fulfill your promise to your servant,
 so that you may be feared.
³⁹ Take away the disgrace I dread,
 for your laws are good.
⁴⁰ How I long for your precepts!
 Preserve my life in your
 righteousness.

ו WAW

⁴¹ May your unfailing love come to me,
 O Lord,
 your salvation according to your
 promise;
⁴² then I will answer the one who taunts me,
 for I trust in your word.
⁴³ Do not snatch the word of truth from my
 mouth,
 for I have put my hope in your laws.
⁴⁴ I will always obey your law,
 for ever and ever.
⁴⁵ I will walk about in freedom,
 for I have sought out your precepts.
⁴⁶ I will speak of your statutes before kings
 and will not be put to shame,
⁴⁷ for I delight in your commands
 because I love them.
⁴⁸ I lift up my hands to ᵇ your commands,
 which I love,
 and I meditate on your decrees.

ז ZAYIN

⁴⁹ Remember your word to your servant,
 for you have given me hope.
⁵⁰ My comfort in my suffering is this:
 Your promise preserves my life.
⁵¹ The arrogant mock me without restraint,
 but I do not turn from your law.
⁵² I remember your ancient laws, O Lord,
 and I find comfort in them.
⁵³ Indignation grips me because of the wicked,
 who have forsaken your law.

Focusing on God's Word

Turning your heart toward God's statutes is like tuning in to a radio station. It's like asking God to hit the right preset button on your heart so it picks up his Word clearly. If you're tuned in to the Bible, anything else that tries to come through your frequency—whether it's temptation, doubt or false teaching—is going to sound like static.

»» live the adventure »» Ps 119:36

ᵃ *37* Two manuscripts of the Masoretic Text and Dead Sea Scrolls; most manuscripts of the Masoretic Text *life in your way*   ᵇ *48* Or *for*

⁵⁴ Your decrees are the theme of my song
    wherever I lodge.
⁵⁵ In the night I remember your name, O LORD,
    and I will keep your law.
⁵⁶ This has been my practice:
    I obey your precepts.

ח HETH

⁵⁷ You are my portion, O LORD;
    I have promised to obey your words.
⁵⁸ I have sought your face with all my heart;
    be gracious to me according to your promise.
⁵⁹ I have considered my ways
    and have turned my steps to your statutes.
⁶⁰ I will hasten and not delay
    to obey your commands.
⁶¹ Though the wicked bind me with ropes,
    I will not forget your law.
⁶² At midnight I rise to give you thanks
    for your righteous laws.
⁶³ I am a friend to all who fear you,
    to all who follow your precepts.
⁶⁴ The earth is filled with your love, O LORD;
    teach me your decrees.

ט TETH

⁶⁵ Do good to your servant
    according to your word, O LORD.
⁶⁶ Teach me knowledge and good judgment,
    for I believe in your commands.
⁶⁷ Before I was afflicted I went astray,
    but now I obey your word.
⁶⁸ You are good, and what you do is good;
    teach me your decrees.
⁶⁹ Though the arrogant have smeared me with lies,
    I keep your precepts with all my heart.
⁷⁰ Their hearts are callous and unfeeling,
    but I delight in your law.
⁷¹ It was good for me to be afflicted
    so that I might learn your decrees.
⁷² The law from your mouth is more precious to me
    than thousands of pieces of silver and gold.

י YODH

⁷³ Your hands made me and formed me;
    give me understanding to learn your commands.
⁷⁴ May those who fear you rejoice when they see me,
    for I have put my hope in your word.
⁷⁵ I know, O LORD, that your laws are righteous,
    and in faithfulness you have afflicted me.
⁷⁶ May your unfailing love be my comfort,
    according to your promise to your servant.
⁷⁷ Let your compassion come to me that I may live,
    for your law is my delight.

⁷⁸ May the arrogant be put to shame for wronging me without cause;
    but I will meditate on your precepts.
⁷⁹ May those who fear you turn to me,
    those who understand your statutes.
⁸⁰ May my heart be blameless toward your decrees,
    that I may not be put to shame.

כ KAPH

⁸¹ My soul faints with longing for your salvation,
    but I have put my hope in your word.
⁸² My eyes fail, looking for your promise;
    I say, "When will you comfort me?"
⁸³ Though I am like a wineskin in the smoke,
    I do not forget your decrees.
⁸⁴ How long must your servant wait?
    When will you punish my persecutors?
⁸⁵ The arrogant dig pitfalls for me,
    contrary to your law.
⁸⁶ All your commands are trustworthy;
    help me, for men persecute me without cause.
⁸⁷ They almost wiped me from the earth,
    but I have not forsaken your precepts.
⁸⁸ Preserve my life according to your love,
    and I will obey the statutes of your mouth.

ל LAMEDH

⁸⁹ Your word, O Lord, is eternal;
    it stands firm in the heavens.
⁹⁰ Your faithfulness continues through all generations;
    you established the earth, and it endures.
⁹¹ Your laws endure to this day,
    for all things serve you.
⁹² If your law had not been my delight,
    I would have perished in my affliction.
⁹³ I will never forget your precepts,
    for by them you have preserved my life.
⁹⁴ Save me, for I am yours;
    I have sought out your precepts.
⁹⁵ The wicked are waiting to destroy me,
    but I will ponder your statutes.
⁹⁶ To all perfection I see a limit;
    but your commands are boundless.

מ MEM

⁹⁷ Oh, how I love your law!
    I meditate on it all day long.
⁹⁸ Your commands make me wiser than my enemies,
    for they are ever with me.
⁹⁹ I have more insight than all my teachers,
    for I meditate on your statutes.
¹⁰⁰ I have more understanding than the elders,
    for I obey your precepts.
¹⁰¹ I have kept my feet from every evil path
    so that I might obey your word.

¹⁰² I have not departed from your laws,
for you yourself have taught me.
¹⁰³ How sweet are your words to my taste,
sweeter than honey to my mouth!
¹⁰⁴ I gain understanding from your precepts;
therefore I hate every wrong path.

נ NUN

¹⁰⁵ Your word is a lamp to my feet
and a light for my path.
¹⁰⁶ I have taken an oath and confirmed it,
that I will follow your righteous laws.
¹⁰⁷ I have suffered much;
preserve my life, O LORD, according to your word.
¹⁰⁸ Accept, O LORD, the willing praise of my mouth,
and teach me your laws.

¹⁰⁹ Though I constantly take my
life in my hands,
I will not forget your law.
¹¹⁰ The wicked have set a snare
for me,
but I have not strayed from
your precepts.
¹¹¹ Your statutes are my heritage
forever;
they are the joy of my heart.
¹¹² My heart is set on keeping
your decrees
to the very end.

challengenotes

To: my_son

PS 119:105

heavenly_father: as long as you have my word, you'll never be lost. when you're unsure about a decision, when life's mysteries have you totally confused, when you just need some reassurance—you can always find the guidance you need in scripture.

ס SAMEKH

¹¹³ I hate double-minded men,
but I love your law.
¹¹⁴ You are my refuge and my shield;
I have put my hope in your word.
¹¹⁵ Away from me, you evildoers,
that I may keep the commands of my God!
¹¹⁶ Sustain me according to your promise, and I will live;
do not let my hopes be dashed.
¹¹⁷ Uphold me, and I will be delivered;
I will always have regard for your decrees.
¹¹⁸ You reject all who stray from your decrees,
for their deceitfulness is in vain.
¹¹⁹ All the wicked of the earth you discard like dross;
therefore I love your statutes.
¹²⁰ My flesh trembles in fear of you;
I stand in awe of your laws.

ע AYIN

¹²¹ I have done what is righteous and just;
do not leave me to my oppressors.
¹²² Ensure your servant's well-being;
let not the arrogant oppress me.

123 My eyes fail, looking for your salvation,
   looking for your righteous promise.
124 Deal with your servant according to your love
   and teach me your decrees.
125 I am your servant; give me discernment
   that I may understand your statutes.
126 It is time for you to act, O LORD;
   your law is being broken.
127 Because I love your commands
   more than gold, more than pure gold,
128 and because I consider all your precepts right,
   I hate every wrong path.

ְפ PE

129 Your statutes are wonderful;
   therefore I obey them.
130 The unfolding of your words gives light;
   it gives understanding to the simple.
131 I open my mouth and pant,
   longing for your commands.
132 Turn to me and have mercy on me,
   as you always do to those who love your name.
133 Direct my footsteps according to your word;
   let no sin rule over me.
134 Redeem me from the oppression of men,
   that I may obey your precepts.
135 Make your face shine upon your servant
   and teach me your decrees.
136 Streams of tears flow from my eyes,
   for your law is not obeyed.

צ TSADHE

137 Righteous are you, O LORD,
   and your laws are right.
138 The statutes you have laid down are righteous;
   they are fully trustworthy.
139 My zeal wears me out,
   for my enemies ignore your words.
140 Your promises have been thoroughly tested,
   and your servant loves them.
141 Though I am lowly and despised,
   I do not forget your precepts.
142 Your righteousness is everlasting
   and your law is true.
143 Trouble and distress have come upon me,
   but your commands are my delight.
144 Your statutes are forever right;
   give me understanding that I may live.

ק QOPH

145 I call with all my heart; answer me, O LORD,
   and I will obey your decrees.
146 I call out to you; save me
   and I will keep your statutes.

147 I rise before dawn and cry for help;
    I have put my hope in your word.
148 My eyes stay open through the watches of the night,
    that I may meditate on your promises.
149 Hear my voice in accordance with your love;
    preserve my life, O LORD, according to your laws.
150 Those who devise wicked schemes are near,
    but they are far from your law.
151 Yet you are near, O LORD,
    and all your commands are true.
152 Long ago I learned from your statutes
    that you established them to last forever.

ר RESH

153 Look upon my suffering and deliver me,
    for I have not forgotten your law.
154 Defend my cause and redeem me;
    preserve my life according to your promise.
155 Salvation is far from the wicked,
    for they do not seek out your decrees.
156 Your compassion is great, O LORD;
    preserve my life according to your laws.
157 Many are the foes who persecute me,
    but I have not turned from your statutes.
158 I look on the faithless with loathing,
    for they do not obey your word.
159 See how I love your precepts;
    preserve my life, O LORD, according to your love.
160 All your words are true;
    all your righteous laws are eternal.

ש SIN AND SHIN

161 Rulers persecute me without cause,
    but my heart trembles at your word.
162 I rejoice in your promise
    like one who finds great spoil.
163 I hate and abhor falsehood
    but I love your law.
164 Seven times a day I praise you
    for your righteous laws.
165 Great peace have they who love your law,
    and nothing can make them stumble.
166 I wait for your salvation, O LORD,
    and I follow your commands.
167 I obey your statutes,
    for I love them greatly.
168 I obey your precepts and your statutes,
    for all my ways are known to you.

ת TAW

169 May my cry come before you, O LORD;
    give me understanding according to your word.
170 May my supplication come before you;
    deliver me according to your promise.

171 May my lips overflow with praise,
    for you teach me your decrees.
172 May my tongue sing of your word,
    for all your commands are righteous.
173 May your hand be ready to help me,
    for I have chosen your precepts.
174 I long for your salvation, O LORD,
    and your law is my delight.
175 Let me live that I may praise you,
    and may your laws sustain me.
176 I have strayed like a lost sheep.
    Seek your servant,
    for I have not forgotten your commands.

PSALM 120

A song of ascents.

1 I call on the LORD in my distress,
    and he answers me.
2 Save me, O LORD, from lying lips
    and from deceitful tongues.

3 What will he do to you,
    and what more besides, O deceitful tongue?
4 He will punish you with a warrior's sharp arrows,
    with burning coals of the broom tree.

5 Woe to me that I dwell in Meshech,
    that I live among the tents of Kedar!
6 Too long have I lived
    among those who hate peace.
7 I am a man of peace;
    but when I speak, they are for war.

PSALM 121

A song of ascents.

1 I lift up my eyes to the hills—
    where does my help come from?
2 My help comes from the LORD,
    the Maker of heaven and earth.

3 He will not let your foot slip—
    he who watches over you will not slumber;
4 indeed, he who watches over Israel
    will neither slumber nor sleep.

5 The LORD watches over you—
    the LORD is your shade at your right hand;
6 the sun will not harm you by day,
    nor the moon by night.

7 The LORD will keep you from all harm—
    he will watch over your life;
8 the LORD will watch over your coming and going
    both now and forevermore.

NOW OR NEVER

PS 121:1–8

Where do your eyes look to when you're in trouble? When you need help, where do you turn first? Your parents? Your buddies? Your youth leaders? That's all good, but do you go to God in prayer first?

PSALM 122

A song of ascents. Of David.

1 I rejoiced with those who said to me,
   "Let us go to the house of the LORD."
2 Our feet are standing
   in your gates, O Jerusalem.

3 Jerusalem is built like a city
   that is closely compacted together.
4 That is where the tribes go up,
   the tribes of the LORD,
 to praise the name of the LORD
   according to the statute given to Israel.
5 There the thrones for judgment stand,
   the thrones of the house of David.

6 Pray for the peace of Jerusalem:
   "May those who love you be secure.
7 May there be peace within your walls
   and security within your citadels."
8 For the sake of my brothers and friends,
   I will say, "Peace be within you."
9 For the sake of the house of the LORD our God,
   I will seek your prosperity.

PSALM 123

A song of ascents.

1 I lift up my eyes to you,
   to you whose throne is in heaven.
2 As the eyes of slaves look to the hand of their master,
   as the eyes of a maid look to the hand of her mistress,
      so our eyes look to the LORD
         our God,
      till he shows us his mercy.

3 Have mercy on us, O LORD,
      have mercy on us,
   for we have endured much
      contempt.
4 We have endured much ridicule
      from the proud,
   much contempt from the
      arrogant.

challengenotes

To: my_son

PS 124:1-5

heavenly_father: have you ever stopped to think about what life would be like without me? what if you didn't have my protection from evil or my plan for your life? what if you didn't have my reward to look forward to when you die? think about it.

PSALM 124

A song of ascents. Of David.

1 If the LORD had not been on our side—
   let Israel say—
2 if the LORD had not been on our side
   when men attacked us,
3 when their anger flared against us,
   they would have swallowed us alive;
4 the flood would have engulfed us,
   the torrent would have swept over us,

⁵the raging waters
    would have swept us away.

⁶Praise be to the LORD,
    who has not let us be torn by their teeth.
⁷We have escaped like a bird
    out of the fowler's snare;
  the snare has been broken,
    and we have escaped.
⁸Our help is in the name of the LORD,
    the Maker of heaven and earth.

PSALM 125

A song of ascents.

¹Those who trust in the LORD are like
    Mount Zion,
  which cannot be shaken but endures
    forever.
²As the mountains surround Jerusalem,
    so the LORD surrounds his people
    both now and forevermore.

³The scepter of the wicked will not remain
    over the land allotted to the righteous,
  for then the righteous might use
    their hands to do evil.

⁴Do good, O LORD, to those who are good,
    to those who are upright in heart.
⁵But those who turn to crooked ways
    the LORD will banish with the
        evildoers.

Peace be upon Israel.

PSALM 126

A song of ascents.

¹When the LORD brought back the captives
        to ᵃ Zion,
    we were like men who dreamed.ᵇ
²Our mouths were filled with laughter,
    our tongues with songs of joy.
  Then it was said among the nations,
    "The LORD has done great things for
        them."
³The LORD has done great things for us,
    and we are filled with joy.

⁴Restore our fortunes,ᶜ O LORD,
    like streams in the Negev.
⁵Those who sow in tears
    will reap with songs of joy.
⁶He who goes out weeping,
    carrying seed to sow,

Showing Your Joy

Do you have joy in your heart? If so, does it show on the outside too? One of the best ways to let people know that there's something different about you is to maintain a content, joyful attitude when everyone else is feeling a bit low, despite the temptation to whine and complain with the rest.

»» live the adventure »» Ps 126:1-3

ᵃ *1 Or* LORD *restored the fortunes of*   ᵇ *1 Or men restored to health*   ᶜ *4 Or Bring back our captives*

will return with songs of joy,
    carrying sheaves with him.

PSALM 127

A song of ascents. Of Solomon.

¹Unless the LORD builds the house,
    its builders labor in vain.

To: **my_son**

heavenly_father: my plan for your life is based on everything I
know about you—including what you're capable of doing well
and what will bring you the deepest satisfaction. it doesn't
make sense for you to choose your own path. nothing can satisfy you like following my will.

Unless the LORD watches over
    the city,
    the watchmen stand guard
    in vain.
²In vain you rise early
    and stay up late,
toiling for food to eat—
    for he grants sleep to ᵃ
    those he loves.

³Sons are a heritage from the
    LORD,
    children a reward from him.

⁴Like arrows in the hands of a warrior
    are sons born in one's youth.
⁵Blessed is the man
    whose quiver is full of them.
They will not be put to shame
    when they contend with their enemies in the gate.

PSALM 128

A song of ascents.

¹Blessed are all who fear the LORD,
    who walk in his ways.

now or never

PS 127:3

Do you think your parents consider you a
reward? Are you like an arrow in the
hands of a warrior— strong, sharp and
true?

²You will eat the fruit of your labor;
    blessings and prosperity will be
    yours.
³Your wife will be like a fruitful vine
    within your house;
your sons will be like olive shoots
    around your table.
⁴Thus is the man blessed
    who fears the LORD.

⁵May the LORD bless you from Zion
    all the days of your life;
may you see the prosperity of
    Jerusalem,
⁶   and may you live to see your children's children.

Peace be upon Israel.

PSALM 129

A song of ascents.

¹They have greatly oppressed me from my youth—
    let Israel say—

ᵃ *2 Or eat— / for while they sleep he provides for*

² they have greatly oppressed me from my youth,
  but they have not gained the victory over me.
³ Plowmen have plowed my back
  and made their furrows long.
⁴ But the LORD is righteous;
  he has cut me free from the cords of the wicked.

⁵ May all who hate Zion
  be turned back in shame.
⁶ May they be like grass on the roof,
  which withers before it can grow;
⁷ with it the reaper cannot fill his hands,
  nor the one who gathers fill his arms.
⁸ May those who pass by not say,
  "The blessing of the LORD be upon you;
  we bless you in the name of the LORD."

PSALM 130

A song of ascents.

¹ Out of the depths I cry to you, O LORD;
²   O Lord, hear my voice.
Let your ears be attentive
  to my cry for mercy.

³ If you, O LORD, kept a record of sins,
  O Lord, who could stand?
⁴ But with you there is forgiveness;
  therefore you are feared.

⁵ I wait for the LORD, my soul waits,
  and in his word I put my hope.
⁶ My soul waits for the Lord
  more than watchmen wait for the morning,
  more than watchmen wait for the morning.

⁷ O Israel, put your hope in the LORD,
  for with the LORD is unfailing love
  and with him is full redemption.
⁸ He himself will redeem Israel
  from all their sins.

PSALM 131

A song of ascents. Of David.

¹ My heart is not proud, O LORD,
  my eyes are not haughty;
I do not concern myself with great matters
  or things too wonderful for me.
² But I have stilled and quieted my soul;
  like a weaned child with its mother,
  like a weaned child is my soul within me.

³ O Israel, put your hope in the LORD
  both now and forevermore.

PSALM 132

A song of ascents.

1 O LORD, remember David
     and all the hardships he endured.

2 He swore an oath to the LORD
     and made a vow to the Mighty One of Jacob:
3 "I will not enter my house
     or go to my bed—
4 I will allow no sleep to my eyes,
     no slumber to my eyelids,
5 till I find a place for the LORD,
     a dwelling for the Mighty One of Jacob."

6 We heard it in Ephrathah,
     we came upon it in the fields of Jaar[a][b]
7 "Let us go to his dwelling place;
     let us worship at his footstool—
8 arise, O LORD, and come to your resting place,
     you and the ark of your might.
9 May your priests be clothed with righteousness;
     may your saints sing for joy."

10 For the sake of David your servant,
     do not reject your anointed one.

11 The LORD swore an oath to David,
     a sure oath that he will not revoke:
"One of your own descendants
     I will place on your throne—
12 if your sons keep my covenant
     and the statutes I teach them,
then their sons will sit
     on your throne for ever and ever."

13 For the LORD has chosen Zion,
     he has desired it for his dwelling:
14 "This is my resting place for ever and ever;
     here I will sit enthroned, for I have desired it—
15 I will bless her with abundant provisions;
     her poor will I satisfy with food.
16 I will clothe her priests with salvation,
     and her saints will ever sing for joy.

17 "Here I will make a horn[c] grow for David
     and set up a lamp for my anointed one.
18 I will clothe his enemies with shame,
     but the crown on his head will be resplendent."

PSALM 133

A song of ascents. Of David.

1 How good and pleasant it is
     when brothers live together in unity!
2 It is like precious oil poured on the head,

[a] 6 That is, Kiriath Jearim [b] 6 Or heard of it in Ephrathah, / we found it in the fields of Jaar. (And no quotes around verses 7-9)
[c] 17 Horn here symbolizes strong one, that is, king.

running down on the beard,
running down on Aaron's beard,
down upon the collar of his robes.
³ It is as if the dew of Hermon
were falling on Mount Zion.
For there the LORD bestows his blessing,
even life forevermore.

PSALM 134

A song of ascents.

¹ Praise the LORD, all you servants of the LORD
who minister by night in the house of the LORD.
² Lift up your hands in the sanctuary
and praise the LORD.

³ May the LORD, the Maker of heaven and earth,
bless you from Zion.

PSALM 135

¹ Praise the LORD.ª

Praise the name of the LORD;
praise him, you servants of the LORD,
² you who minister in the house of the LORD,
in the courts of the house of our God.

³ Praise the LORD, for the LORD is good;
sing praise to his name, for that is pleasant.
⁴ For the LORD has chosen Jacob to be his own,
Israel to be his treasured possession.

⁵ I know that the LORD is great,
that our Lord is greater than all gods.
⁶ The LORD does whatever pleases him,
in the heavens and on the earth,
in the seas and all their depths.
⁷ He makes clouds rise from the ends of the earth;
he sends lightning with the rain
and brings out the wind from his storehouses.

⁸ He struck down the firstborn of Egypt,
the firstborn of men and animals.
⁹ He sent his signs and wonders into your midst, O Egypt,
against Pharaoh and all his servants.
¹⁰ He struck down many nations
and killed mighty kings—
¹¹ Sihon king of the Amorites,
Og king of Bashan
and all the kings of Canaan—
¹² and he gave their land as an inheritance,
an inheritance to his people Israel.

¹³ Your name, O LORD, endures forever,
your renown, O LORD, through all generations.

ª *1* Hebrew *Hallelu Yah*; also in verses 3 and 21

14 For the LORD will vindicate his people
    and have compassion on his servants.

15 The idols of the nations are silver and gold,
    made by the hands of men.
16 They have mouths, but cannot speak,
    eyes, but they cannot see;
17 they have ears, but cannot hear,
    nor is there breath in their mouths.
18 Those who make them will be like them,
    and so will all who trust in them.

19 O house of Israel, praise the LORD;
    O house of Aaron, praise the LORD;
20 O house of Levi, praise the LORD;
    you who fear him, praise the LORD.
21 Praise be to the LORD from Zion,
    to him who dwells in Jerusalem.

Praise the LORD.

PSALM 136

1 Give thanks to the LORD, for he is good.
    His love endures forever.
2 Give thanks to the God of gods.
    His love endures forever.
3 Give thanks to the Lord of lords:
    His love endures forever.

4 to him who alone does great wonders,
    His love endures forever.
5 who by his understanding made the
    heavens,
    His love endures forever.
6 who spread out the earth upon the waters,
    His love endures forever.
7 who made the great lights—
    His love endures forever.
8 the sun to govern the day,
    His love endures forever.
9 the moon and stars to govern the night;
    His love endures forever.

10 to him who struck down the firstborn of
    Egypt
    His love endures forever.
11 and brought Israel out from among them
    His love endures forever.
12 with a mighty hand and outstretched arm;
    His love endures forever.

13 to him who divided the Red Sea[a]
    asunder
    His love endures forever.
14 and brought Israel through the midst of it,
    His love endures forever.

Giving Thanks to the Lord

»» live the adventure »» Ps 136:1-26

Looking back on your own life, what things could you thank God for? How about starting with basic life necessities like David did—food to eat, oxygen to breathe, earth to walk on? If you're having trouble finding reasons to thank God, think about a newborn baby: Babies are completely helpless. How quickly would a newborn starve or be injured without the provision and protection of loving parents? On the grand scale of the universe, adult human beings aren't so different. Where would we be without the provision and protection of a loving Father? We have a lot to be thankful for.

---

a 13 Hebrew *Yam Suph*; that is, Sea of Reeds; also in verse 15

15 but swept Pharaoh and his army into the Red Sea;

His love endures forever.

16 to him who led his people through the desert,

His love endures forever.

17 who struck down great kings,

His love endures forever.

18 and killed mighty kings—

His love endures forever.

19 Sihon king of the Amorites

His love endures forever.

20 and Og king of Bashan—

His love endures forever.

21 and gave their land as an inheritance,

His love endures forever.

22 an inheritance to his servant Israel;

His love endures forever.

23 to the One who remembered us in our low estate

His love endures forever.

24 and freed us from our enemies,

His love endures forever.

25 and who gives food to every creature.

His love endures forever.

26 Give thanks to the God of heaven.

His love endures forever.

PSALM 137

1 By the rivers of Babylon we sat and wept
   when we remembered Zion.

2 There on the poplars
   we hung our harps,
3 for there our captors asked us
   for songs,
   our tormentors demanded
   songs of joy;
   they said, "Sing us one of
   the songs of Zion!"

4 How can we sing the songs of
   the LORD
   while in a foreign land?

challengenotes

PS 136:13

To: my_son

heavenly_father: the psalmist was right. my love *does* endure forever. so does my strength. the same power that held back the waters of the red sea can help to hold back the pressures of your everyday life! you just have to ask.

5 If I forget you, O Jerusalem,
   may my right hand forget ⌐its skill⌐.
6 May my tongue cling to the roof of my mouth
   if I do not remember you,
   if I do not consider Jerusalem
   my highest joy.

7 Remember, O LORD, what the Edomites did
   on the day Jerusalem fell.
   "Tear it down," they cried,
      "tear it down to its foundations!"

8 O Daughter of Babylon, doomed to destruction,
   happy is he who repays you
   for what you have done to us—

⁹he who seizes your infants
and dashes them against the rocks.

PSALM 138

Of David.

¹I will praise you, O LORD, with all my heart;
before the "gods" I will sing your praise.
²I will bow down toward your holy temple
and will praise your name
for your love and your faithfulness,
for you have exalted above all things
your name and your word.
³When I called, you answered me;
you made me bold and stouthearted.

⁴May all the kings of the earth praise you, O LORD,
when they hear the words of your mouth.
⁵May they sing of the ways of the LORD,
for the glory of the LORD is great.

⁶Though the LORD is on high, he looks upon the lowly,
but the proud he knows from afar.
⁷Though I walk in the midst of trouble,
you preserve my life;
you stretch out your hand against the anger of my foes,
with your right hand you save me.
⁸The LORD will fulfill ⌊his purpose⌋ for me;
your love, O LORD, endures forever—
do not abandon the works of your hands.

PSALM 139

For the director of music. Of David. A psalm.

¹O LORD, you have searched me
and you know me.
²You know when I sit and when I rise;
you perceive my thoughts from afar.
³You discern my going out and my lying down;
you are familiar with all my ways.

⁴Before a word is on my tongue
you know it completely,
O LORD.

⁵You hem me in—behind and
before;
you have laid your hand
upon me.
⁶Such knowledge is too
wonderful for me,
too lofty for me to attain.

challenge notes

To: my_son

heavenly_father: I know *everything* about you—the things you do in secret, the ugly thoughts you hide from even your closest friends. if that makes you feel a bit ashamed, good. then you can confess, be forgiven and be restored.

PS 139:1-4

⁷Where can I go from your Spirit?
Where can I flee from your presence?
⁸If I go up to the heavens, you are there;
if I make my bed in the depths,ᵃ you are there.

ᵃ *8* Hebrew *Sheol*

battlelines

» Joe Average? (Inferiority)

Q: I can tell you're out of sorts, Andrew. What's up?
A: I'm just frustrated.

Q: How come?
A: Oh, I'm basically just sick of my life. That and I stink at everything I do.

Q: Oh, well if that's all . . . come on! What are you talking about? What makes you say that?
A: The *facts* make me say that!

Q: OK, I'm not following you here.
A: Go down the list. First of all, look at me. I mean, I know I'm not the worst-looking guy around; but let's face it, I'm not going to turn any heads either. You don't have to be a genius to see why I've never had a girlfriend.

Q: Now, wait a minute. Maybe you're not going to be chosen as "Sexiest Man Alive," but don't you think you're being just a *little* harsh on yourself?
A: No, let me finish. I haven't mentioned school yet. I make all Bs and Cs—and I'm not even taking any really hard classes. Socially, I'm doing OK. I have a handful of friends, but most people don't even know who I am. Or they don't care. And then there are sports. Think about this: Our soccer team is *terrible*. We haven't won a game all year. In fact, we've only scored one goal. And I'm *second string*! What does that tell you about my skill level?

Q: It tells me soccer's not your biggest strength.
A: That's just it—*nothing* is my biggest strength! I'm one big . . . nothing. I'm average, or below average, in everything.

» 20/20 Vision

It's a fact: We will always be able to find people who can do something better than we can. Occasionally an extraordinarily rare person like Tiger Woods gets to be the best at something. Even then it's usually just one thing and only for a brief time. There's just too much talent in this world.

Here's another fact: You've got some strengths. You do excel in certain areas, and you certainly have the capacity to be good at specific things (see Psalm 139:13–14). You just have to discover your God-given abilities and develop them.

One final reminder: Don't get so wrapped up in being able to *do* particular things that you forget to *be* what you're meant to be: a radical follower of God. It's something that all who know Christ can excel at!

Go to www.RevolutionBible.com for more.

⁹ If I rise on the wings of the dawn,
  if I settle on the far side of the sea,
¹⁰ even there your hand will guide me,
  your right hand will hold me fast.

¹¹ If I say, "Surely the darkness will hide
    me
  and the light become night around
    me,"
¹² even the darkness will not be dark
    to you;
  the night will shine like the day,
  for darkness is as light to you.

¹³ For you created my inmost being;
  you knit me together in my mother's
    womb.
¹⁴ I praise you because I am fearfully and
    wonderfully made;
  your works are wonderful,
  I know that full well.
¹⁵ My frame was not hidden from you
  when I was made in the secret place.
  When I was woven together in the
    depths of the earth,
¹⁶   your eyes saw my unformed body.
  All the days ordained for me
  were written in your book
  before one of them came to be.

¹⁷ How precious toᵃ me are your thoughts,
    O God!
  How vast is the sum of them!
¹⁸ Were I to count them,
  they would outnumber the grains of sand.
  When I awake,
  I am still with you.

Opening Your Heart to God

What would God find if he searched the contents of your heart right now? Would he discover any grudges against people who've ticked you off this week? Would he observe any lust for girls who are in your classes? The good news is that no matter what evil is lodged in your heart right now, God can blast it out. If you're willing to let him sweep out your heart, he will transform it into the kind of place he'd like to live.

now or never
PS 139:15-16

If you ever start to feel like a nobody, remind yourself that God had an important plan for your life... before you were born! In other words, you have a destiny to fulfill.

¹⁹ If only you would slay the wicked,
    O God!
  Away from me, you bloodthirsty men!
²⁰ They speak of you with evil intent;
  your adversaries misuse your name.
²¹ Do I not hate those who hate you,
    O LORD,
  and abhor those who rise up against
    you?
²² I have nothing but hatred for them;
  I count them my enemies.

²³ Search me, O God, and know my heart;
  test me and know my anxious
    thoughts.
²⁴ See if there is any offensive way in me,
  and lead me in the way everlasting.

ᵃ 17 Or concerning

PSALM 140

For the director of music. A psalm of David.

¹ Rescue me, O Lᴏʀᴅ, from evil men;
  protect me from men of violence,
² who devise evil plans in their hearts
  and stir up war every day.
³ They make their tongues as sharp as a serpent's;
  the poison of vipers is on their lips.   *Selah*

⁴ Keep me, O Lᴏʀᴅ, from the hands of the wicked;
  protect me from men of violence
  who plan to trip my feet.
⁵ Proud men have hidden a snare for me;
  they have spread out the cords of their
    net
  and have set traps for me along my
    path.   *Selah*

⁶ O Lᴏʀᴅ, I say to you, "You are my God."
  Hear, O Lᴏʀᴅ, my cry for mercy.
⁷ O Sovereign Lᴏʀᴅ, my strong deliverer,
  who shields my head in the day of
    battle—
⁸ do not grant the wicked their desires,
    O Lᴏʀᴅ;
  do not let their plans succeed,
  or they will become proud.   *Selah*

⁹ Let the heads of those who surround me
  be covered with the trouble their lips
    have caused.
¹⁰ Let burning coals fall upon them;
  may they be thrown into the fire,
  into miry pits, never to rise.
¹¹ Let slanderers not be established in the
    land;
  may disaster hunt down men of
    violence.

¹² I know that the Lᴏʀᴅ secures justice for
    the poor
  and upholds the cause of the
    needy.
¹³ Surely the righteous will praise your
    name
  and the upright will live before you.

PSALM 141

A psalm of David.

¹ O Lᴏʀᴅ, I call to you; come quickly to me.
  Hear my voice when I call to you.
² May my prayer be set before you like incense;
  may the lifting up of my hands be like the evening sacrifice.

³ Set a guard over my mouth, O Lᴏʀᴅ;
  keep watch over the door of my lips.

» live the adventure » Ps 140:8

Battling the Spiritual Enemy

David lived in a very different time from the one we live in now. His enemies were nine feet tall, carried spears, swords and axes; and they wanted to hack him to pieces. That could explain why David got so emotional when he prayed. Our enemies look a lot different than David's did—but they're no less dangerous. When you're battling against sin and temptation, you're really battling against the evil one: Satan. Don't let your guard down. And don't ever trust in your own strength. Make it a spiritual battle and call on your heavenly Commander.

battlelines

» Get Me Out of Here (Family Conflict)

Q: You ready to roll?
A: You bet. Stomp on that pedal and get me the heck out of here.

Q: Why the big rush?
A: Just drive, all right? The farther I get from that house, the better off I'll be. I can't deal with one more minute of their yelling and screaming.

Q: Are you in trouble or something?
A: Me? No. I haven't done anything. It's my mom and my sister. Put them in the same room for five minutes and they're at each other's throats. Sometimes I let myself get dragged into their little dramas, but not to-day.

Q: What about your dad? What does he do about their fights?
A: Oh, at some point he usually charges into the room, starts making all kinds of threats and telling everybody to shut up. Sounds like a real fun time, huh?

Q: Is that why you never ask me inside?
A: I never really thought about it, but, yeah, I guess. I don't ask *anyone* to come in. Like I want my friends to see *that* mess!

Q: So how do you cope?
A: One word: iPod.

Q: And it's like that *every* day?
A: Just about. I'd say my mom and sister have a big blowout about five days a week. My dad and I tangle too—at least once a week. I can tell he's disappointed in me. He wanted a jock for a son. That's why he's always on my case.

Q: Can you remember ever having a good time with your whole family?
A: Sure. We went on a camping trip together about three years ago. It was really nice. We actually laughed together. Sat there talking around the campfire for a couple hours. Yeah, that was pretty awesome.

» Home Remedy

You don't have to graduate high school or run away from home to experience peace in your family. Though you can't control what other members of your family do, you can play a major role in reducing conflict and bringing peace to your home. Among other things, you can . . .

● Pray. James 5:16 says, "The prayer of a righteous man is powerful and effective." Ask the God of peace to bring calm to your family. Ask him to bless your efforts to promote peace in your home (see Matthew 5:9).

● Guard your tongue. Better yet, bite your tongue whenever you're tempted to make a cutting remark. Use words of kindness and encouragement to build up other members of your family . . . instead of tearing them down with angry words (see Ephesians 4:29).

● Resist the urge to bicker about stupid little things. Many of the domestic battles we fight just aren't worth our effort or energy (see Proverbs 17:14; 20:3).

● Forgive. Let go of your grudges and past hurts, and then move on (see Colossians 3:13).

Your family driving you crazy? Find ways to get along at www.RevolutionBible.com.

⁴Let not my heart be drawn to what is evil,
    to take part in wicked deeds
with men who are evildoers;
    let me not eat of their delicacies.

⁵Let a righteous man[a] strike me—it is a kindness;
    let him rebuke me—it is oil on my head.
    My head will not refuse it.

Yet my prayer is ever against the deeds of evildoers;
⁶   their rulers will be thrown down from the cliffs,
    and the wicked will learn that my words were well spoken.
⁷ᴸThey will say,ᴶ "As one plows and breaks up the earth,
    so our bones have been scattered at the mouth of the grave.[b]"

⁸But my eyes are fixed on you, O Sovereign LORD;
    in you I take refuge—do not give me over to death.
⁹Keep me from the snares they have laid for me,
    from the traps set by evildoers.
¹⁰Let the wicked fall into their own nets,
    while I pass by in safety.

PSALM 142

A *maskil*[c] of David. When he was in the cave. A prayer.

¹I cry aloud to the LORD;
    I lift up my voice to the LORD for mercy.
²I pour out my complaint before him;
    before him I tell my trouble.

³When my spirit grows faint within me,
    it is you who know my way.
In the path where I walk
    men have hidden a snare for me.
⁴Look to my right and see;
    no one is concerned for me.
I have no refuge;
    no one cares for my life.

⁵I cry to you, O LORD;
    I say, "You are my refuge,
    my portion in the land of the living."
⁶Listen to my cry,
    for I am in desperate need;
rescue me from those who pursue me,
    for they are too strong for me.
⁷Set me free from my prison,
    that I may praise your name.

Then the righteous will gather about me
    because of your goodness to me.

PSALM 143

A psalm of David.

¹O LORD, hear my prayer,
    listen to my cry for mercy;

---

[a] *5* Or *Let the Righteous One*   [b] *7* Hebrew *Sheol*   [c] Title: Probably a literary or musical term

in your faithfulness and righteousness
come to my relief.
2 Do not bring your servant into judgment,
for no one living is righteous before you.

3 The enemy pursues me,
he crushes me to the ground;
he makes me dwell in darkness
like those long dead.
4 So my spirit grows faint within me;
my heart within me is dismayed.

5 I remember the days of long ago;
I meditate on all your works
and consider what your hands have
done.
6 I spread out my hands to you;
my soul thirsts for you like a parched
land.   *Selah*

7 Answer me quickly, O LORD;
my spirit fails.
Do not hide your face from me
or I will be like those who go down
to the pit.
8 Let the morning bring me word of your
unfailing love,
for I have put my trust in you.
Show me the way I should go,
for to you I lift up my soul.
9 Rescue me from my enemies, O LORD,
for I hide myself in you.
10 Teach me to do your will,
for you are my God;
may your good Spirit
lead me on level ground.

11 For your name's sake, O LORD, preserve
my life;
in your righteousness, bring me out of trouble.
12 In your unfailing love, silence my enemies;
destroy all my foes,
for I am your servant.

Being Persistent With God

This has got to be the thousandth time David begged God to rescue him from his enemies. You'd think that after a while God would say, "Enough already! Stop asking me to rescue you!" But he didn't do that to David, and he won't do that to you. If you have a strong conviction about a request you've taken to God, be persistent. Don't let the fact that you haven't gotten an answer yet discourage you. Remember, God has his own schedule for doing things. He wants us to pursue him, to seek close fellowship with him.

»» live the adventure »» Ps 143:9

PSALM 144

Of David.

1 Praise be to the LORD my Rock,
who trains my hands for war,
my fingers for battle.
2 He is my loving God and my fortress,
my stronghold and my deliverer,
my shield, in whom I take refuge,
who subdues peoples[a] under me.

3 O LORD, what is man that you care for him,

---

[a] 2 Many manuscripts of the Masoretic Text, Dead Sea Scrolls, Aquila, Jerome and Syriac; most manuscripts of the Masoretic Text *subdues my people*

the son of man that you think of him?
4 Man is like a breath;
his days are like a fleeting shadow.

5 Part your heavens, O Lord, and come down;
touch the mountains, so that they smoke.
6 Send forth lightning and scatter ⌊the enemies⌋;
shoot your arrows and rout them.
7 Reach down your hand from on high;
deliver me and rescue me
from the mighty waters,
from the hands of foreigners
8 whose mouths are full of lies,
whose right hands are deceitful.

9 I will sing a new song to you, O God;
on the ten-stringed lyre I will make music to you,
10 to the One who gives victory to kings,
who delivers his servant David from the deadly sword.

11 Deliver me and rescue me
from the hands of foreigners
whose mouths are full of lies,
whose right hands are deceitful.

12 Then our sons in their youth
will be like well-nurtured plants,
and our daughters will be like pillars
carved to adorn a palace.
13 Our barns will be filled
with every kind of provision.
Our sheep will increase by thousands,
by tens of thousands in our fields;
14   our oxen will draw heavy loads. a
There will be no breaching of walls,
no going into captivity,
no cry of distress in our streets.
15 Blessed are the people of whom this is true;
blessed are the people whose God is the Lord.

PSALM 145 b

A psalm of praise. Of David.

1 I will exalt you, my God the King;
I will praise your name for ever and ever.
2 Every day I will praise you
and extol your name for ever and ever.

3 Great is the Lord and most worthy of praise;
his greatness no one can fathom.
4 One generation will commend your works to another;
they will tell of your mighty acts.
5 They will speak of the glorious splendor of your majesty,
and I will meditate on your wonderful works. c

---

a 14 Or *our chieftains will be firmly established*   b This psalm is an acrostic poem, the verses of which (including verse 13b) begin with the successive letters of the Hebrew alphabet.   c 5 Dead Sea Scrolls and Syriac (see also Septuagint); Masoretic Text *On the glorious splendor of your majesty / and on your wonderful works I will meditate*

⁶ They will tell of the power of your awesome works,
      and I will proclaim your great deeds.
⁷ They will celebrate your abundant goodness
      and joyfully sing of your righteousness.

⁸ The LORD is gracious and compassionate,
      slow to anger and rich in love.
⁹ The LORD is good to all;
      he has compassion on all he has made.
¹⁰ All you have made will praise you, O LORD;
      your saints will extol you.
¹¹ They will tell of the glory of your kingdom
      and speak of your might,
¹² so that all men may know of your mighty acts
      and the glorious splendor of your kingdom.
¹³ Your kingdom is an everlasting kingdom,
      and your dominion endures through all generations.

The LORD is faithful to all his promises
      and loving toward all he has made. ᵃ
¹⁴ The LORD upholds all those who fall
      and lifts up all who are bowed down.
¹⁵ The eyes of all look to you,
      and you give them their food at the proper time.
¹⁶ You open your hand
      and satisfy the desires of every living thing.

¹⁷ The LORD is righteous in all his ways
      and loving toward all he has made.
¹⁸ The LORD is near to all who call on him,
      to all who call on him in truth.
¹⁹ He fulfills the desires of those who fear him;
      he hears their cry and saves them.
²⁰ The LORD watches over all who love him,
      but all the wicked he will destroy.

²¹ My mouth will speak in praise of the LORD.
      Let every creature praise his holy name
      for ever and ever.

PSALM 146

¹ Praise the LORD. ᵇ

Praise the LORD, O my soul.
²   I will praise the LORD all my life;
      I will sing praise to my God as long as I live.

³ Do not put your trust in princes,
      in mortal men, who cannot save.
⁴ When their spirit departs, they return to the ground;
      on that very day their plans come to nothing.

⁵ Blessed is he whose help is the God of Jacob,
      whose hope is in the LORD his God,
⁶ the Maker of heaven and earth,
      the sea, and everything in them—

ᵃ *13* One manuscript of the Masoretic Text, Dead Sea Scrolls and Syriac (see also Septuagint); most manuscripts of the Masoretic Text do not have the last two lines of verse 13.   ᵇ *1* Hebrew *Hallelu Yah*; also in verse 10

the LORD, who remains faithful forever.
⁷He upholds the cause of the oppressed
and gives food to the hungry.
The LORD sets prisoners free,
⁸ the LORD gives sight to the blind,
the LORD lifts up those who are bowed down,
the LORD loves the righteous.
⁹The LORD watches over the alien
and sustains the fatherless and the widow,
but he frustrates the ways of the wicked.

¹⁰The LORD reigns forever,
your God, O Zion, for all generations.

Praise the LORD.

PSALM 147

¹Praise the LORD.ᵃ

How good it is to sing praises to our God,
how pleasant and fitting to praise him!

²The LORD builds up Jerusalem;
he gathers the exiles of Israel.
³He heals the brokenhearted
and binds up their wounds.

⁴He determines the number of the stars
and calls them each by name.
⁵Great is our Lord and mighty in power;
his understanding has no limit.
⁶The LORD sustains the humble
but casts the wicked to the ground.

⁷Sing to the LORD with thanksgiving;
make music to our God on the harp.
⁸He covers the sky with clouds;
he supplies the earth with rain
and makes grass grow on the hills.
⁹He provides food for the cattle
and for the young ravens when they call.

¹⁰His pleasure is not in the strength of the horse,
nor his delight in the legs of a man;
¹¹the LORD delights in those who fear him,
who put their hope in his unfailing love.

¹²Extol the LORD, O Jerusalem;
praise your God, O Zion,
¹³for he strengthens the bars of your gates
and blesses your people within you.
¹⁴He grants peace to your borders
and satisfies you with the finest of wheat.

¹⁵He sends his command to the earth;
his word runs swiftly.
¹⁶He spreads the snow like wool
and scatters the frost like ashes.

ᵃ 1 Hebrew *Hallelu Yah*; also in verse 20

¹⁷ He hurls down his hail like pebbles.
    Who can withstand his icy blast?
¹⁸ He sends his word and melts them;
    he stirs up his breezes, and the waters flow.

¹⁹ He has revealed his word to Jacob,
    his laws and decrees to Israel.
²⁰ He has done this for no other nation;
    they do not know his laws.

Praise the LORD.

PSALM 148

¹ Praise the LORD. ^a

Praise the LORD from the heavens,
    praise him in the heights above.
² Praise him, all his angels,
    praise him, all his heavenly hosts.
³ Praise him, sun and moon,
    praise him, all you shining stars.
⁴ Praise him, you highest heavens
    and you waters above the skies.
⁵ Let them praise the name of the LORD,
    for he commanded and they were created.
⁶ He set them in place for ever and ever;
    he gave a decree that will never pass away.

⁷ Praise the LORD from the earth,
    you great sea creatures and all ocean depths,
⁸ lightning and hail, snow and clouds,
    stormy winds that do his bidding,
⁹ you mountains and all hills,
    fruit trees and all cedars,
¹⁰ wild animals and all cattle,
    small creatures and flying birds,
¹¹ kings of the earth and all nations,
    you princes and all rulers on earth,
¹² young men and maidens,
    old men and children.

¹³ Let them praise the name of the LORD,
    for his name alone is exalted;
    his splendor is above the earth and the heavens.
¹⁴ He has raised up for his people a horn, ^b
    the praise of all his saints,
    of Israel, the people close to his heart.

Praise the LORD.

PSALM 149

¹ Praise the LORD. ^c

Sing to the LORD a new song,
    his praise in the assembly of the saints.

^a *1* Hebrew *Hallelu Yah*; also in verse 14   ^b *14 Horn* here symbolizes strong one, that is, king.   ^c *1* Hebrew *Hallelu Yah*; also in verse 9

2 Let Israel rejoice in their Maker;
    let the people of Zion be glad in their King.
3 Let them praise his name with dancing
    and make music to him with tambourine and harp.
4 For the LORD takes delight in his people;
    he crowns the humble with salvation.
5 Let the saints rejoice in this honor
    and sing for joy on their beds.

6 May the praise of God be in their mouths
    and a double-edged sword in their hands,
7 to inflict vengeance on the nations
    and punishment on the peoples,
8 to bind their kings with fetters,
    their nobles with shackles of iron,
9 to carry out the sentence written against them.
    This is the glory of all his saints.

Praise the LORD.

PSALM 150

1 Praise the LORD.[a]

Praise God in his sanctuary;
    praise him in his mighty heavens.
2 Praise him for his acts of power;
    praise him for his surpassing
        greatness.
3 Praise him with the sounding of the
        trumpet,
    praise him with the harp and lyre,
4 praise him with tambourine and
        dancing,
    praise him with the strings and flute,
5 praise him with the clash of cymbals,
    praise him with resounding cymbals.

6 Let everything that has breath praise the
    LORD.

Praise the LORD.

NOW OR NEVER
PS 150:3–5

What would you add to this list? What are some unique ways you can praise the Lord? God gave you talents and abilities. What better tribute is there than using them to honor him?

---

a 1 Hebrew *Hallelu Yah*; also in verse 6

PROVERBS

Author
King Solomon

Audience
People of Israel

Date
Solomon wrote the majority of these proverbs during his reign, but they weren't compiled and edited until centuries later, around 700 B.C.

Setting
Solomon was Israel's king during a time when the nation was faithful to God. Solomon wrote these wise sayings before he himself became caught up in materialism and idolatry.

Verse to Remember
The fear of the LORD is the beginning of knowledge, but fools despise wisdom and discipline (1:7).

Theme to Consider
Allow these wise sayings to help you develop attitudes and behaviors that are pleasing to God.

UNCHANGING TRUTH » Want some advice? It doesn't really matter whether you answer yes or no to that question. You're going to get it anyway—plenty of it and for the rest of your life, even from people you don't want to listen to. You're always going to have people around you telling you what you should and shouldn't do, what is and isn't right for you.

That's not necessarily a bad thing. Good advice can change your life. People who tell you things like . . .

• "You're letting your God-given talents go to waste"
• "Don't mistake lust for love; love will last, lust won't"
• "Finishing your education will pay big dividends later"

. . . can help you avoid big mistakes and open your eyes to possibilities you've never considered before—if you listen to them. Of course, bad advice can change your life too. People who tell you things like . . .

• "Just take whatever job pays the most money"
• "You'll never get the bulk you need to play at the next level without steroids"
• "You're not going to turn into an addict from smoking one joint"

. . . can wreck your health, your self-esteem and your future—if you listen to them. You're responsible for separating good advice from bad advice. That can be tricky sometimes, but God has given you a head start in recognizing solid advice by filling an entire book with his counsel.

LIFE LESSONS »

1 People will take advantage of you if you let them (1:10–19).

2 God is the ultimate source of all wisdom (3:19).

3 Living foolishly may seem more fun and exciting than living wisely, but the end result of foolishness is tragedy and regret (9:13–18).

4 Greed can make a person do things that he or she would otherwise think are foolish (15:27).

PROLOGUE: PURPOSE AND THEME

1 The proverbs of Solomon son of David, king of Israel:

2 for attaining wisdom and discipline;
   for understanding words of insight;
3 for acquiring a disciplined and prudent life,
   doing what is right and just and fair;
4 for giving prudence to the simple,
   knowledge and discretion to the young—
5 let the wise listen and add to their learning,
   and let the discerning get guidance—
6 for understanding proverbs and parables,
   the sayings and riddles of the wise.

7 The fear of the LORD is the beginning of knowledge,
   but fools[a] despise wisdom and discipline.

EXHORTATIONS TO EMBRACE WISDOM

WARNING AGAINST ENTICEMENT

8 Listen, my son, to your father's instruction
   and do not forsake your mother's teaching.
9 They will be a garland to grace your head
   and a chain to adorn your neck.

10 My son, if sinners entice you,
    do not give in to them.
11 If they say, "Come along with us;
    let's lie in wait for someone's blood,
    let's waylay some harmless soul;
12 let's swallow them alive, like the grave,[b]
    and whole, like those who go down
       to the pit;
13 we will get all sorts of valuable things
    and fill our houses with plunder;
14 throw in your lot with us,
    and we will share a common
       purse"—

15 my son, do not go along with them,
    do not set foot on their paths;
16 for their feet rush into sin,
    they are swift to shed blood.
17 How useless to spread a net
    in full view of all the birds!
18 These men lie in wait for their own blood;
    they waylay only themselves!
19 Such is the end of all who go after ill-gotten gain;
    it takes away the lives of those who get it.

WARNING AGAINST REJECTING WISDOM

20 Wisdom calls aloud in the street,
    she raises her voice in the public squares;
21 at the head of the noisy streets[c] she cries out,
    in the gateways of the city she makes her speech:

NOW OR NEVER
PR 1:7

The "fear of the LORD" is not a horror-movie kind of terror; it's an attitude of total respect and reverence for who God is and what he's capable of doing.

---

[a] 7 The Hebrew words rendered *fool* in Proverbs, and often elsewhere in the Old Testament, denote one who is morally deficient.
[b] 12 Hebrew *Sheol*   [c] 21 Hebrew; Septuagint / *on the tops of the walls*

22 "How long will you simple ones[a] love your simple ways?
   How long will mockers delight in mockery
   and fools hate knowledge?
23 If you had responded to my rebuke,
   I would have poured out my heart to you
   and made my thoughts known to you.
24 But since you rejected me when I called
   and no one gave heed when I stretched out my hand,
25 since you ignored all my advice
   and would not accept my rebuke,
26 I in turn will laugh at your disaster;
   I will mock when calamity overtakes you—
27 when calamity overtakes you like a storm,
   when disaster sweeps over you like a whirlwind,
   when distress and trouble overwhelm you.

28 "Then they will call to me but I will not answer;
   they will look for me but will not find me.
29 Since they hated knowledge
   and did not choose to fear the LORD,
30 since they would not accept my advice
   and spurned my rebuke,
31 they will eat the fruit of their ways
   and be filled with the fruit of their schemes.
32 For the waywardness of the simple will kill them,
   and the complacency of fools will destroy them;
33 but whoever listens to me will live in safety
   and be at ease, without fear of harm."

MORAL BENEFITS OF WISDOM

2

My son, if you accept my words
   and store up my commands within you,
2 turning your ear to wisdom
   and applying your heart to understanding,
3 and if you call out for insight
   and cry aloud for understanding,
4 and if you look for it as for silver
   and search for it as for hidden treasure,
5 then you will understand the fear of the LORD
   and find the knowledge of God.
6 For the LORD gives wisdom,
   and from his mouth come knowledge and understanding.
7 He holds victory in store for the upright,
   he is a shield to those whose walk is blameless,

Claiming God's Promise of Wisdom

As treasure hunts go, the search for wisdom probably seems a lot less exciting than, say, a search for a million dollars. But can money help you when you're struggling with doubts about God or about how to live your life? Can money give you clear direction when you're not sure about your future? Can money help you resist a temptation that could potentially destroy your life? Wisdom can do all those things and more—things that money just can't do.

a 22 The Hebrew word rendered *simple* in Proverbs generally denotes one without moral direction and inclined to evil.

⁸for he guards the course of the just
  and protects the way of his faithful ones.

⁹Then you will understand what is right and just
  and fair—every good path.
¹⁰For wisdom will enter your heart,
  and knowledge will be pleasant to your soul.
¹¹Discretion will protect you,
  and understanding will guard you.

¹²Wisdom will save you from the ways of wicked men,
  from men whose words are perverse,
¹³who leave the straight paths
  to walk in dark ways,
¹⁴who delight in doing wrong
  and rejoice in the perverseness of evil,
¹⁵whose paths are crooked
  and who are devious in their ways.

¹⁶It will save you also from the adulteress,
  from the wayward wife with her seductive words,
¹⁷who has left the partner of her youth
  and ignored the covenant she made before God.ª
¹⁸For her house leads down to death
  and her paths to the spirits of the dead.
¹⁹None who go to her return
  or attain the paths of life.

²⁰Thus you will walk in the ways of good men
  and keep to the paths of the righteous.
²¹For the upright will live in the land,
  and the blameless will remain in it;
²²but the wicked will be cut off from the land,
  and the unfaithful will be torn from it.

FURTHER BENEFITS OF WISDOM

3 My son, do not forget my teaching,
  but keep my commands in your heart,
²for they will prolong your life many years
  and bring you prosperity.

challengenotes

To: my_son

heavenly_father: why are you still holding back certain areas of your life from me? is it because you don't think I can change them? or is it because you're afraid of what I might do with them?

PR 3:5-6

³Let love and faithfulness never leave you;
  bind them around your neck,
  write them on the tablet of your heart.
⁴Then you will win favor and a good name
  in the sight of God and man.

⁵Trust in the LORD with all your heart
⁶and lean not on your own understanding;
  in all your ways acknowledge him,
  and he will make your paths straight.ᵇ

ª 17 Or covenant of her God   ᵇ 6 Or will direct your paths

⁷Do not be wise in your own eyes;
 fear the LORD and shun evil.
⁸This will bring health to your body
 and nourishment to your bones.

⁹Honor the LORD with your wealth,
 with the firstfruits of all your crops;
¹⁰then your barns will be filled to overflowing,
 and your vats will brim over with new wine.

¹¹My son, do not despise the LORD's discipline
 and do not resent his rebuke,
¹²because the LORD disciplines those he loves,
 as a fatherᵃ the son he delights in.

¹³Blessed is the man who finds wisdom,
 the man who gains understanding,
¹⁴for she is more profitable than silver
 and yields better returns than gold.
¹⁵She is more precious than rubies;
 nothing you desire can compare with her.
¹⁶Long life is in her right hand;
 in her left hand are riches and honor.
¹⁷Her ways are pleasant ways,
 and all her paths are peace.
¹⁸She is a tree of life to those who embrace her;
 those who lay hold of her will be blessed.

¹⁹By wisdom the LORD laid the earth's foundations,
 by understanding he set the heavens in place;
²⁰by his knowledge the deeps were divided,
 and the clouds let drop the dew.

²¹My son, preserve sound judgment and discernment,
 do not let them out of your sight;
²²they will be life for you,
 an ornament to grace your neck.
²³Then you will go on your way in safety,
 and your foot will not stumble;
²⁴when you lie down, you will not be afraid;
 when you lie down, your sleep will be sweet.
²⁵Have no fear of sudden disaster
 or of the ruin that overtakes the wicked,
²⁶for the LORD will be your confidence
 and will keep your foot from being snared.

NOW OR NEVER

PR 3:27–28

What's your first instinct when you see someone in trouble, whether it's a stranded motorist or a geek getting ripped on in gym class—to stop and help, or to just keep going and mind your own business?

²⁷Do not withhold good from those who deserve it,
 when it is in your power to act.
²⁸Do not say to your neighbor,
 "Come back later; I'll give it tomorrow"—
 when you now have it with you.

²⁹Do not plot harm against your neighbor,

ᵃ *12* Hebrew; Septuagint / *and he punishes*

who lives trustfully near you.
³⁰ Do not accuse a man for no reason—
    when he has done you no harm.

³¹ Do not envy a violent man
    or choose any of his ways,
³² for the LORD detests a perverse man
    but takes the upright into his confidence.

³³ The LORD'S curse is on the house of the wicked,
    but he blesses the home of the righteous.
³⁴ He mocks proud mockers
    but gives grace to the humble.
³⁵ The wise inherit honor,
    but fools he holds up to shame.

WISDOM IS SUPREME

Listen, my sons, to a father's instruction;
    pay attention and gain understanding.
² I give you sound learning,
    so do not forsake my teaching.
³ When I was a boy in my father's house,
    still tender, and an only child of my mother,
⁴ he taught me and said,
    "Lay hold of my words with all your heart;
    keep my commands and you will live.
⁵ Get wisdom, get understanding;
    do not forget my words or swerve from them.
⁶ Do not forsake wisdom, and she will protect you;
    love her, and she will watch over you.
⁷ Wisdom is supreme; therefore get wisdom.
    Though it cost all you have,ᵃ get understanding.
⁸ Esteem her, and she will exalt you;
    embrace her, and she will honor you.
⁹ She will set a garland of grace on your head
    and present you with a crown of splendor."

¹⁰ Listen, my son, accept what I say,
    and the years of your life will be many.
¹¹ I guide you in the way of wisdom
    and lead you along straight paths.
¹² When you walk, your steps will not be hampered;
    when you run, you will not stumble.
¹³ Hold on to instruction, do not let it go;
    guard it well, for it is your life.
¹⁴ Do not set foot on the path of the wicked
    or walk in the way of evil men.
¹⁵ Avoid it, do not travel on it;
    turn from it and go on your way.
¹⁶ For they cannot sleep till they do evil;
    they are robbed of slumber till they make someone fall.
¹⁷ They eat the bread of wickedness
    and drink the wine of violence.
¹⁸ The path of the righteous is like the first gleam of dawn,
    shining ever brighter till the full light of day.

ᵃ 7 Or *Whatever else you get*

¹⁹But the way of the wicked is like deep darkness;
they do not know what makes them stumble.

²⁰My son, pay attention to what I say;
listen closely to my words.
²¹Do not let them out of your sight,
keep them within your heart;
²²for they are life to those who find them
and health to a man's whole body.
²³Above all else, guard your heart,
for it is the wellspring of life.
²⁴Put away perversity from your mouth;
keep corrupt talk far from your lips.
²⁵Let your eyes look straight ahead,
fix your gaze directly before you.
²⁶Make level ᵃ paths for your feet
and take only ways that are firm.
²⁷Do not swerve to the right or the left;
keep your foot from evil.

WARNING AGAINST ADULTERY

5   My son, pay attention to my wisdom,
listen well to my words of insight,
²that you may maintain discretion
and your lips may preserve knowledge.
³For the lips of an adulteress drip honey,
and her speech is smoother than oil;
⁴but in the end she is bitter as gall,
sharp as a double-edged sword.
⁵Her feet go down to death;
her steps lead straight to the grave. ᵇ
⁶She gives no thought to the way of life;
her paths are crooked, but she knows it not.

⁷Now then, my sons, listen to me;
do not turn aside from what I say.
⁸Keep to a path far from her,
do not go near the door of her house,
⁹lest you give your best strength to others
and your years to one who is cruel,
¹⁰lest strangers feast on your wealth
and your toil enrich another man's house.
¹¹At the end of your life you will groan,
when your flesh and body are spent.
¹²You will say, "How I hated discipline!
How my heart spurned correction!
¹³I would not obey my teachers
or listen to my instructors.
¹⁴I have come to the brink of utter ruin
in the midst of the whole assembly."

¹⁵Drink water from your own cistern,
running water from your own well.
¹⁶Should your springs overflow in the streets,
your streams of water in the public squares?

ᵃ *26* Or *Consider the*   ᵇ *5* Hebrew *Sheol*

battlelines

» Flicker Tape Parade (Pure Thoughts)

Q: Hey, I thought you were spending the night at Taylor's house.
A: If you'd been there, you would have left early too. I'll probably never live this night down.

Q: What happened?
A: Everything started out fine. We ate pizza. Shot some pool. Just goofed off. Then Taylor says, "Hey, guys, get in here. You're going to want to see this!" I thought he had some goofy video or home movie or something. Man, was I wrong.

Q: I can already see where this is going.
A: You got it. Hard-core porn. I guess it was his dad's. Anyway, there I am surrounded by all these guys, and it just gets wilder and wilder. I couldn't believe my eyes.

Q: So you just got up and left?
A: Well, I sat there for probably five minutes, mostly staring at the floor. I didn't want to make a big scene or have everybody

think I was weird or something. I didn't know what to do. So I acted like I was going to get a refill on my drink and I slipped out.

Q: Has anyone called?
A: No. Until that tape's over, I doubt they'll even notice I'm gone. But at some point they will. Dude, what am I going to say on Monday?

Q: I don't know, but you did the right thing. I'm proud of you. And God is too.
A: Yeah, well, I'm not so sure about that.

Q: Why not?
A: Because I did peek at the video a few times. I was curious, I guess. And even though I got up and left, I *wanted* to see that film. And now I can't stop thinking about those images. And the worst part is, if I thought I could watch that video by myself and get away with it, I'd probably do it. *Now* how proud are you?

» Wanting Isn't Doing

Let's get three things straight:

1   It isn't sinful for a guy to be attracted to the visual elements of sex—or even to be curious about sex. God wired you that way. He also set up a great system called marriage, where all your curiosity can be satisfied. One day you'll get all the excitement you need with your wife (see Proverbs 5:15–20).

2   Porn is one of Satan's sad and deceptive counterfeits to God's perfect plan. Like all other sexual perversions, porn will leave you feeling empty and frustrated. You were made for total, amazing intimacy with a real woman for life, not for stimulating yourself while looking at a video, Internet or magazine image of a total stranger.

3   If you are a follower of Jesus, you are a new creature (see 2 Corinthians 5:17). And even though something in you yearns to look at porn, the new creation in you wants more than anything else to follow God and to do what is right.

Read more about the effects of porn at www.RevolutionBible.com.

17 Let them be yours alone,
   never to be shared with strangers.
18 May your fountain be blessed,
   and may you rejoice in the wife of your youth.
19 A loving doe, a graceful deer—
   may her breasts satisfy you always,
   may you ever be captivated by her love.
20 Why be captivated, my son, by an adulteress?
   Why embrace the bosom of another man's wife?

21 For a man's ways are in full view of the LORD,
   and he examines all his paths.
22 The evil deeds of a wicked man ensnare him;
   the cords of his sin hold him fast.
23 He will die for lack of discipline,
   led astray by his own great folly.

WARNINGS AGAINST FOLLY

My son, if you have put up security for your neighbor,
   if you have struck hands in pledge for another,
2 if you have been trapped by what you
         said,
   ensnared by the words of your
         mouth,
3 then do this, my son, to free yourself,
   since you have fallen into your
         neighbor's hands:
   Go and humble yourself;
   press your plea with your neighbor!
4 Allow no sleep to your eyes,
   no slumber to your eyelids.
5 Free yourself, like a gazelle from the
         hand of the hunter,
   like a bird from the snare of the
         fowler.

6 Go to the ant, you sluggard;
   consider its ways and be wise!
7 It has no commander,
   no overseer or ruler,
8 yet it stores its provisions in summer
   and gathers its food at harvest.

9 How long will you lie there, you
         sluggard?
   When will you get up from your
         sleep?
10 A little sleep, a little slumber,
   a little folding of the hands to rest—
11 and poverty will come on you like a
         bandit
   and scarcity like an armed man. [a]

12 A scoundrel and villain,
   who goes about with a corrupt mouth,
13   who winks with his eye,

---

a 11 Or like a vagrant / and scarcity like a beggar

signals with his feet
and motions with his fingers,
¹⁴ who plots evil with deceit in his heart—
he always stirs up dissension.
¹⁵ Therefore disaster will overtake him in an instant;
he will suddenly be destroyed—without remedy.

¹⁶ There are six things the LORD hates,
seven that are detestable to him:
¹⁷ haughty eyes,
a lying tongue,
hands that shed innocent blood,
¹⁸ a heart that devises wicked schemes,
feet that are quick to rush into evil,
¹⁹ a false witness who pours out lies
and a man who stirs up dissension among brothers.

WARNING AGAINST ADULTERY

²⁰ My son, keep your father's commands
and do not forsake your mother's teaching.
²¹ Bind them upon your heart forever;
fasten them around your neck.
²² When you walk, they will guide you;
when you sleep, they will watch over
you;
when you awake, they will speak to
you.
²³ For these commands are a lamp,
this teaching is a light,
and the corrections of discipline
are the way to life,
²⁴ keeping you from the immoral woman,
from the smooth tongue of the
wayward wife.

NOW OR NEVER

PR 6:16–19

Do you see any of the things on God's "hate list" in your own life? If so, what can you do to correct the situation and remove those things from your life?

²⁵ Do not lust in your heart after her beauty
or let her captivate you with her eyes,
²⁶ for the prostitute reduces you to a loaf of bread,
and the adulteress preys upon your very life.
²⁷ Can a man scoop fire into his lap
without his clothes being burned?
²⁸ Can a man walk on hot coals
without his feet being scorched?
²⁹ So is he who sleeps with another man's wife;
no one who touches her will go unpunished.

³⁰ Men do not despise a thief if he steals
to satisfy his hunger when he is starving.
³¹ Yet if he is caught, he must pay sevenfold,
though it costs him all the wealth of his house.
³² But a man who commits adultery lacks judgment;
whoever does so destroys himself.
³³ Blows and disgrace are his lot,
and his shame will never be wiped away;
³⁴ for jealousy arouses a husband's fury,
and he will show no mercy when he takes revenge.
³⁵ He will not accept any compensation;
he will refuse the bribe, however great it is.

7

My son, keep my words
  and store up my commands within you.
[2] Keep my commands and you will live;
  guard my teachings as the apple of your eye.
[3] Bind them on your fingers;
  write them on the tablet of your heart.
[4] Say to wisdom, "You are my sister,"
  and call understanding your kinsman;
[5] they will keep you from the adulteress,
  from the wayward wife with her seductive words.

[6] At the window of my house
  I looked out through the lattice.

---

challengenotes

To: my_son

heavenly_father: a good way to keep my word stored in your
heart is to memorize it word for word so that you don't have
to look it up to remember how it goes. you'll find after a while
that *my* words become *your* words.

PR 7:1-2

72863   B G C FE

---

[7] I saw among the simple,
  I noticed among the young
    men,
  a youth who lacked
    judgment.
[8] He was going down the street
    near her corner,
  walking along in the
    direction of her
    house
[9] at twilight, as the day was
    fading,
  as the dark of night set in.

[10] Then out came a woman to meet him,
  dressed like a prostitute and with crafty intent.
[11] (She is loud and defiant,
  her feet never stay at home;
[12] now in the street, now in the squares,
  at every corner she lurks.)
[13] She took hold of him and kissed him
  and with a brazen face she said:

[14] "I have fellowship offerings[a] at home;
  today I fulfilled my vows.
[15] So I came out to meet you;
  I looked for you and have found you!
[16] I have covered my bed
  with colored linens from Egypt.
[17] I have perfumed my bed
  with myrrh, aloes and cinnamon.
[18] Come, let's drink deep of love till morning;
  let's enjoy ourselves with love!
[19] My husband is not at home;
  he has gone on a long journey.
[20] He took his purse filled with money
  and will not be home till full moon."

[21] With persuasive words she led him astray;
  she seduced him with her smooth talk.
[22] All at once he followed her
  like an ox going to the slaughter,

---

[a] 14 Traditionally *peace offerings*

like a deer[a] stepping into a noose[b]
23   till an arrow pierces his liver,
  like a bird darting into a snare,
    little knowing it will cost him his life.

24 Now then, my sons, listen to me;
    pay attention to what I say.
25 Do not let your heart turn to her ways
    or stray into her paths.
26 Many are the victims she has brought down;
    her slain are a mighty throng.
27 Her house is a highway to the grave,[c]
    leading down to the chambers of death.

WISDOM'S CALL

Does not wisdom call out?
    Does not understanding raise her voice?
2 On the heights along the way,
    where the paths meet, she takes her stand;
3 beside the gates leading into the city,
    at the entrances, she cries aloud:
4 "To you, O men, I call out;
    I raise my voice to all mankind.
5 You who are simple, gain prudence;
    you who are foolish, gain understanding.
6 Listen, for I have worthy things to say;
    I open my lips to speak what is right.
7 My mouth speaks what is true,
    for my lips detest wickedness.
8 All the words of my mouth are just;
    none of them is crooked or perverse.
9 To the discerning all of them are right;
    they are faultless to those who have knowledge.
10 Choose my instruction instead of silver,
    knowledge rather than choice gold,
11 for wisdom is more precious than rubies,
    and nothing you desire can compare with her.

12 "I, wisdom, dwell together with prudence;
    I possess knowledge and discretion.
13 To fear the LORD is to hate evil;
    I hate pride and arrogance,
    evil behavior and perverse speech.
14 Counsel and sound judgment are mine;
    I have understanding and power.
15 By me kings reign
    and rulers make laws that are just;
16 by me princes govern,
    and all nobles who rule on earth.[d]
17 I love those who love me,
    and those who seek me find me.
18 With me are riches and honor,
    enduring wealth and prosperity.
19 My fruit is better than fine gold;

---

a 22 Syriac (see also Septuagint); Hebrew *fool*   b 22 The meaning of the Hebrew for this line is uncertain.   c 27 Hebrew *Sheol*
d 16 Many Hebrew manuscripts and Septuagint; most Hebrew manuscripts *and nobles—all righteous rulers*

what I yield surpasses choice silver.
20 I walk in the way of righteousness,
     along the paths of justice,
21 bestowing wealth on those who love me
     and making their treasuries full.

22 "The LORD brought me forth as the first of his works,[a,b]
     before his deeds of old;
23 I was appointed[c] from eternity,
     from the beginning, before the world began.
24 When there were no oceans, I was given birth,
     when there were no springs abounding with water;
25 before the mountains were settled in place,
     before the hills, I was given birth,
26 before he made the earth or its fields
     or any of the dust of the world.
27 I was there when he set the heavens in place,
     when he marked out the horizon on the face of the deep,
28 when he established the clouds above
     and fixed securely the fountains of the deep,
29 when he gave the sea its boundary
     so the waters would not overstep his command,
   and when he marked out the foundations of the earth.
30   Then I was the craftsman at his side.
   I was filled with delight day after day,
     rejoicing always in his presence,
31 rejoicing in his whole world
     and delighting in mankind.

32 "Now then, my sons, listen to me;
     blessed are those who keep my ways.
33 Listen to my instruction and be wise;
     do not ignore it.
34 Blessed is the man who listens to me,
     watching daily at my doors,
     waiting at my doorway.
35 For whoever finds me finds life
     and receives favor from the LORD.
36 But whoever fails to find me harms himself;
     all who hate me love death."

INVITATIONS OF WISDOM AND OF FOLLY

9 Wisdom has built her house;
     she has hewn out its seven pillars.
2 She has prepared her meat and mixed her wine;
     she has also set her table.
3 She has sent out her maids, and she calls
     from the highest point of the city.
4 "Let all who are simple come in here!"
     she says to those who lack judgment.
5 "Come, eat my food
     and drink the wine I have mixed.
6 Leave your simple ways and you will live;
     walk in the way of understanding.

a 22 Or way; or dominion   b 22 Or The LORD possessed me at the beginning of his work; or The LORD brought me forth at the beginning
of his work   c 23 Or fashioned

⁷ "Whoever corrects a mocker invites insult;
  whoever rebukes a wicked man incurs abuse.
⁸ Do not rebuke a mocker or he will hate you;
  rebuke a wise man and he will love you.
⁹ Instruct a wise man and he will be wiser still;
  teach a righteous man and he will add to his learning.

¹⁰ "The fear of the LORD is the beginning of wisdom,
  and knowledge of the Holy One is understanding.
¹¹ For through me your days will be many,
  and years will be added to your life.
¹² If you are wise, your wisdom will reward you;
  if you are a mocker, you alone will suffer."

¹³ The woman Folly is loud;
  she is undisciplined and without knowledge.
¹⁴ She sits at the door of her house,
  on a seat at the highest point of the city,
¹⁵ calling out to those who pass by,
  who go straight on their way.

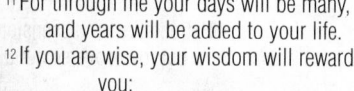

NOW OR NEVER
PR 9:10-12

If you want to be wise, start by showing a little wisdom in your attitude toward God. Once you've figured out what your relationship with him should be like, you can apply the wisdom he gives you to other areas of your life.

¹⁶ "Let all who are simple come in here!"
  she says to those who lack judgment.
¹⁷ "Stolen water is sweet;
  food eaten in secret is delicious!"
¹⁸ But little do they know that the dead are there,
  that her guests are in the depths of the grave.ᵃ

PROVERBS OF SOLOMON

10

The proverbs of Solomon:

A wise son brings joy to his father,
  but a foolish son grief to his mother.

² Ill-gotten treasures are of no value,
  but righteousness delivers from death.

³ The LORD does not let the righteous go hungry
  but he thwarts the craving of the wicked.

⁴ Lazy hands make a man poor,
  but diligent hands bring wealth.

⁵ He who gathers crops in summer is a wise son,
  but he who sleeps during harvest is a disgraceful son.

⁶ Blessings crown the head of the righteous,
  but violence overwhelms the mouth of the wicked.ᵇ

⁷ The memory of the righteous will be a blessing,
  but the name of the wicked will rot.

⁸ The wise in heart accept commands,
  but a chattering fool comes to ruin.

⁹ The man of integrity walks securely,

ᵃ 18 Hebrew Sheol ᵇ 6 Or but the mouth of the wicked conceals violence; also in verse 11 but he who takes crooked paths will be found out.

10 He who winks maliciously causes grief,
and a chattering fool comes to ruin.

11 The mouth of the righteous is a fountain of life,
but violence overwhelms the mouth of the wicked.

12 Hatred stirs up dissension,
but love covers over all wrongs.

13 Wisdom is found on the lips of the discerning,
but a rod is for the back of him who lacks judgment.

14 Wise men store up knowledge,
but the mouth of a fool invites ruin.

15 The wealth of the rich is their fortified city,
but poverty is the ruin of the poor.

16 The wages of the righteous bring them life,
but the income of the wicked brings them punishment.

17 He who heeds discipline shows the way to life,
but whoever ignores correction leads others astray.

18 He who conceals his hatred has lying lips,
and whoever spreads slander is a fool.

19 When words are many, sin is not absent,
but he who holds his tongue is wise.

20 The tongue of the righteous is choice silver,
but the heart of the wicked is of little value.

21 The lips of the righteous nourish many,
but fools die for lack of judgment.

22 The blessing of the LORD brings wealth,
and he adds no trouble to it.

23 A fool finds pleasure in evil conduct,
but a man of understanding delights in wisdom.

24 What the wicked dreads will overtake him;
what the righteous desire will be granted.

25 When the storm has swept by, the wicked are gone,
but the righteous stand firm forever.

26 As vinegar to the teeth and smoke to the eyes,
so is a sluggard to those who send him.

27 The fear of the LORD adds length to life,
but the years of the wicked are cut short.

Living With Integrity

»» live the adventure »» Pr 10:9

Being careless about what you say and do creates a lot of extra work and stress for you. Think about it. If you tell a lie, you always have to remember what you said so you don't slip up. Spread a rumor, and you always have to worry about the wrong person finding out what you said. If you steal, you'll always have to worry about getting caught and having your reputation ruined. Living with integrity, on the other hand, allows you to relax around others and live free from the burden of a guilty conscience.

battlelines

» The Big Lie (Stealing)

Q: Hey, Adam, in your circle of friends, how big a problem is stealing?
A: Stealing?

Q: Yeah, for example, going into a convenience store and helping yourself to the old "five finger discount." Or sneaking money from your dad's wallet when he's not looking?
A: Oh, I'd say it's pretty common. Not everybody does it—at least not the shoplifting thing. But yeah, it happens. And other stuff too.

Q: Like what?
A: Like paying for one movie and then staying to watch a couple more. I know a lot of people who do that. And I know some older guys who go out to eat at different restaurants around town, and then when things get busy, they slip out one by one without paying.

Q: Pretty creative.
A: I guess. Pretty illegal too. My sister preaches to me about ripping songs and games off the Internet and burning CDs. She says that's stealing. I don't know . . . what do you think?

Q: Well, I know if I were an artist trying to make a living, I would rather sell ten copies of my CD than sell one copy and have ten people pass it around and copy it. Wouldn't you?
A: Yeah, I guess if a guy makes his living by writing songs, that's true. I see your point.

» The Bigger Truth

Shoplifting. Cheating in school. "Borrowing" stuff, knowing you'll never return it. Copying music without paying for it. Where in the world did Christians get the idea that it's no big deal to take what isn't ours? The Bible is crystal clear on the issue:

- "You shall not steal" (Exodus 20:15).

- "Ill-gotten treasures are of no value, but righteousness delivers from death" (Proverbs 10:2).

- "He who robs his father or mother and says, 'It's not wrong'—he is partner to him who destroys" (Proverbs 28:24).

- "He who has been stealing must steal no longer, but must work, doing something useful with his own hands, that he may have something to share with those in need" (Ephesians 4:28).

When it comes to taking what's not yours, be different . . . be radical . . . be right.

Find help in making right choices at www.RevolutionBible.com.

28 The prospect of the righteous is joy,
   but the hopes of the wicked come to nothing.

29 The way of the LORD is a refuge for the righteous,
   but it is the ruin of those who do evil.

30 The righteous will never be uprooted,
   but the wicked will not remain in the land.

31 The mouth of the righteous brings forth wisdom,
   but a perverse tongue will be cut out.

32 The lips of the righteous know what is fitting,
   but the mouth of the wicked only what is perverse.

11

The LORD abhors dishonest scales,
   but accurate weights are his delight.

2 When pride comes, then comes disgrace,
   but with humility comes wisdom.

3 The integrity of the upright guides them,
   but the unfaithful are destroyed by their duplicity.

4 Wealth is worthless in the day of wrath,
   but righteousness delivers from death.

5 The righteousness of the blameless makes a straight way for them,
   but the wicked are brought down by their own wickedness.

6 The righteousness of the upright delivers them,
   but the unfaithful are trapped by evil desires.

7 When a wicked man dies, his hope perishes;
   all he expected from his power comes to nothing.

8 The righteous man is rescued from trouble,
   and it comes on the wicked instead.

9 With his mouth the godless destroys his neighbor,
   but through knowledge the righteous escape.

10 When the righteous prosper, the city rejoices;
   when the wicked perish, there are shouts of joy.

11 Through the blessing of the upright a city is exalted,
   but by the mouth of the wicked it is destroyed.

12 A man who lacks judgment derides his neighbor,
   but a man of understanding holds his tongue.

13 A gossip betrays a confidence,
   but a trustworthy man keeps a secret.

14 For lack of guidance a nation falls,
   but many advisers make victory sure.

15 He who puts up security for another will surely suffer,
   but whoever refuses to strike hands in pledge is safe.

16 A kindhearted woman gains respect,
   but ruthless men gain only wealth.

17 A kind man benefits himself,
   but a cruel man brings trouble on himself.

18 The wicked man earns deceptive wages,
  but he who sows righteousness reaps a sure reward.

19 The truly righteous man attains life,
  but he who pursues evil goes to his death.

20 The LORD detests men of perverse heart
  but he delights in those whose ways are blameless.

21 Be sure of this: The wicked will not go unpunished,
  but those who are righteous will go free.

22 Like a gold ring in a pig's snout
  is a beautiful woman who shows no discretion.

23 The desire of the righteous ends only in
    good,
  but the hope of the wicked only in
    wrath.

24 One man gives freely, yet gains even
    more;
  another withholds unduly, but comes
    to poverty.

25 A generous man will prosper;
  he who refreshes others will himself
    be refreshed.

26 People curse the man who hoards grain,
  but blessing crowns him who is
    willing to sell.

27 He who seeks good finds goodwill,
  but evil comes to him who searches
    for it.

28 Whoever trusts in his riches will fall,
  but the righteous will thrive like a
    green leaf.

29 He who brings trouble on his family will
    inherit only wind,
  and the fool will be servant to the
    wise.

30 The fruit of the righteous is a tree of
    life,
  and he who wins souls is wise.

31 If the righteous receive their due on earth,
  how much more the ungodly and the sinner!

12

Whoever loves discipline loves knowledge,
  but he who hates correction is stupid.

2 A good man obtains favor from the LORD,
  but the LORD condemns a crafty man.

3 A man cannot be established through wickedness,
  but the righteous cannot be uprooted.

4 A wife of noble character is her husband's crown,
  but a disgraceful wife is like decay in his bones.

»» live the adventure »» Pr 11.17-21

Demonstrating Character

People notice character, whether you realize it or not. Everything you do says something about your character—the way you react when you find out your best friend made the team and you didn't, the way you listen when someone shares something personal with you, the way you act during worship services . . . even the way you treat your little brother or sister. The first step in developing a good character is to remember that everything you do— even in private—is being watched by an audience of one: God.

⁵ The plans of the righteous are just,
   but the advice of the wicked is deceitful.

⁶ The words of the wicked lie in wait for blood,
   but the speech of the upright rescues them.

⁷ Wicked men are overthrown and are no more,
   but the house of the righteous stands firm.

⁸ A man is praised according to his wisdom,
   but men with warped minds are despised.

⁹ Better to be a nobody and yet have a servant
   than pretend to be somebody and have no food.

¹⁰ A righteous man cares for the needs of his animal,
   but the kindest acts of the wicked are cruel.

¹¹ He who works his land will have abundant food,
   but he who chases fantasies lacks judgment.

¹² The wicked desire the plunder of evil men,
   but the root of the righteous flourishes.

¹³ An evil man is trapped by his sinful talk,
   but a righteous man escapes trouble.

¹⁴ From the fruit of his lips a man is filled with good things
   as surely as the work of his hands rewards him.

¹⁵ The way of a fool seems right to him,
   but a wise man listens to advice.

¹⁶ A fool shows his annoyance at once,
   but a prudent man overlooks an insult.

¹⁷ A truthful witness gives honest testimony,
   but a false witness tells lies.

¹⁸ Reckless words pierce like a sword,
   but the tongue of the wise brings healing.

¹⁹ Truthful lips endure forever,
   but a lying tongue lasts only a moment.

²⁰ There is deceit in the hearts of those who plot evil,
   but joy for those who promote peace.

²¹ No harm befalls the righteous,
   but the wicked have their fill of trouble.

²² The LORD detests lying lips,
   but he delights in men who are truthful.

²³ A prudent man keeps his knowledge to himself,
   but the heart of fools blurts out folly.

²⁴ Diligent hands will rule,
   but laziness ends in slave labor.

²⁵ An anxious heart weighs a man down,
   but a kind word cheers him up.

²⁶ A righteous man is cautious in friendship,[a]

---

[a] 26 Or man is a guide to his neighbor

but the way of the wicked leads them astray.

²⁷ The lazy man does not roast^a his game,
    but the diligent man prizes his possessions.

²⁸ In the way of righteousness there is life;
    along that path is immortality.

A wise son heeds his father's instruction,
    but a mocker does not listen to rebuke.

² From the fruit of his lips a man enjoys good things,
    but the unfaithful have a craving for violence.

³ He who guards his lips guards his life,
    but he who speaks rashly will come to ruin.

⁴ The sluggard craves and gets nothing,
    but the desires of the diligent are fully satisfied.

⁵ The righteous hate what is false,
    but the wicked bring shame and disgrace.

⁶ Righteousness guards the man of integrity,
    but wickedness overthrows the sinner.

⁷ One man pretends to be rich, yet has nothing;
    another pretends to be poor, yet has great wealth.

⁸ A man's riches may ransom his life,
    but a poor man hears no threat.

⁹ The light of the righteous shines brightly,
    but the lamp of the wicked is snuffed out.

¹⁰ Pride only breeds quarrels,
    but wisdom is found in those who take advice.

¹¹ Dishonest money dwindles away,
    but he who gathers money little by little makes it grow.

¹² Hope deferred makes the heart sick,
    but a longing fulfilled is a tree of life.

¹³ He who scorns instruction will pay for it,
    but he who respects a command is rewarded.

¹⁴ The teaching of the wise is a fountain of life,
    turning a man from the snares of death.

¹⁵ Good understanding wins favor,
    but the way of the unfaithful is hard.^b

¹⁶ Every prudent man acts out of knowledge,
    but a fool exposes his folly.

¹⁷ A wicked messenger falls into trouble,
    but a trustworthy envoy brings healing.

¹⁸ He who ignores discipline comes to poverty and shame,
    but whoever heeds correction is honored.

¹⁹ A longing fulfilled is sweet to the soul,
    but fools detest turning from evil.

---

^a *27* The meaning of the Hebrew for this word is uncertain.   ^b *15* Or *unfaithful does not endure*

battlelines

» "Show Me the Money" (Gambling)

Q: Is it true that you've got $1,200 in gambling debts?
A: Actually it's $1,230—but who's counting?

Q: Dude, how did that happen?
A: It's not hard. Ten bucks here, twenty-five there. Then you go double or nothing. It doesn't take long to add up. I know one guy who's lost $2,600 at some offshore gaming sites.

Q: Why didn't you quit when the debt started piling up?
A: Well, you always think you can reverse it. Get on a roll, you know? Or maybe you get a tip or a hunch. Or someone offers another bet and you think, *I can't lose!*

Q: What kind of things do you bet on?
A: Mostly college and pro games—but some stupid stuff too.

Q: Like what?
A: Like test scores, what movie is gonna win the Oscar, pick-up games. I lost $50 a couple weeks ago betting this skinny dude he couldn't eat two extra large pizzas by himself without hurling.

Q: He did it?
A: He did it.

Q: So, are you, like, in trouble? Do you use a bookie? I mean, are you gonna get your thumbs broken by some guy named Tony?
A: (Smiling weakly) No, I don't think I have to worry about that. But I can't just welch on a bet, you know? I have to pay up. I've got some serious work ahead of me.

Q: Do you think you're addicted to gambling? I mean, can you quit?
A: I *have* to quit. It's stupid. It's not a good way to make money. From now on, I'll just settle for friendly bets, with a Coke or a burger on the line, but nothing more than that.

» A Sure Bet

Gambling is a serious problem; it can be just as addictive as alcohol, drugs or sex. It destroys thousands of families each year and is anything but "harmless fun."

Besides, if it's money you're after, there are much surer ways to get it than gambling. The casinos in Vegas, Atlantic City and elsewhere don't stay in business by filling their customers' pockets. Proverbs 13:11 warns, "Dishonest money dwindles away, but he who gathers money little by little makes it grow." Regularly stashing money away in a savings account is a much better way than gambling to build some cash. It may not be flashy, but it works.

If you've become caught in gambling's grip—or if you know someone who has—it's time to act. Check out your local Gamblers Anonymous chapter for support and encouragement. Also, seek professional counseling before the problem gets any worse.

Keep your sanity—and your thumbs—in one piece. Declare all bets off limits.

Learn more about handling money wisely at www.RevolutionBible.com.

²⁰ He who walks with the wise grows wise,
  but a companion of fools suffers harm.

²¹ Misfortune pursues the sinner,
  but prosperity is the reward of the righteous.

²² A good man leaves an inheritance for his children's children,
  but a sinner's wealth is stored up for the righteous.

²³ A poor man's field may produce abundant food,
  but injustice sweeps it away.

²⁴ He who spares the rod hates his son,
  but he who loves him is careful to discipline him.

²⁵ The righteous eat to their hearts' content,
  but the stomach of the wicked goes hungry.

14

The wise woman builds her house,
  but with her own hands the foolish one tears hers down.

² He whose walk is upright fears the LORD,
  but he whose ways are devious despises him.

³ A fool's talk brings a rod to his back,
  but the lips of the wise protect them.

⁴ Where there are no oxen, the manger is empty,
  but from the strength of an ox comes an abundant harvest.

⁵ A truthful witness does not deceive,
  but a false witness pours out lies.

⁶ The mocker seeks wisdom and finds none,
  but knowledge comes easily to the discerning.

⁷ Stay away from a foolish man,
  for you will not find knowledge on
  his lips.

⁸ The wisdom of the prudent is to give
  thought to their ways,
  but the folly of fools is deception.

⁹ Fools mock at making amends for sin,
  but goodwill is found among the
  upright.

¹⁰ Each heart knows its own bitterness,
  and no one else can share its joy.

NOW OR NEVER
PR 14:12

What are some things that seem harmless and fun at first, but eventually lead to serious problems? What advice would you give to a friend who's just started messing around with, say, cigarettes, pot, alcohol or porn?

¹¹ The house of the wicked will be destroyed,
  but the tent of the upright will flourish.

¹² There is a way that seems right to a man,
  but in the end it leads to death.

¹³ Even in laughter the heart may ache,
  and joy may end in grief.

¹⁴ The faithless will be fully repaid for their ways,
  and the good man rewarded for his.

¹⁵ A simple man believes anything,
  but a prudent man gives thought to his steps.

¹⁶ A wise man fears the L<small>ORD</small> and shuns evil,
　　but a fool is hotheaded and reckless.

¹⁷ A quick-tempered man does foolish things,
　　and a crafty man is hated.

¹⁸ The simple inherit folly,
　　but the prudent are crowned with knowledge.

¹⁹ Evil men will bow down in the presence of the good,
　　and the wicked at the gates of the righteous.

²⁰ The poor are shunned even by their neighbors,
　　but the rich have many friends.

²¹ He who despises his neighbor sins,
　　but blessed is he who is kind to the needy.

²² Do not those who plot evil go astray?
　　But those who plan what is good find^a love and faithfulness.

²³ All hard work brings a profit,
　　but mere talk leads only to poverty.

²⁴ The wealth of the wise is their crown,
　　but the folly of fools yields folly.

²⁵ A truthful witness saves lives,
　　but a false witness is deceitful.

²⁶ He who fears the L<small>ORD</small> has a secure fortress,
　　and for his children it will be a refuge.

²⁷ The fear of the L<small>ORD</small> is a fountain of life,
　　turning a man from the snares of death.

²⁸ A large population is a king's glory,
　　but without subjects a prince is ruined.

²⁹ A patient man has great understanding,
　　but a quick-tempered man displays folly.

³⁰ A heart at peace gives life to the body,
　　but envy rots the bones.

³¹ He who oppresses the poor shows contempt for their Maker,
　　but whoever is kind to the needy honors God.

³² When calamity comes, the wicked are brought down,
　　but even in death the righteous have a refuge.

³³ Wisdom reposes in the heart of the discerning
　　and even among fools she lets herself be known.^b

³⁴ Righteousness exalts a nation,
　　but sin is a disgrace to any people.

³⁵ A king delights in a wise servant,
　　but a shameful servant incurs his wrath.

A gentle answer turns away wrath,
　　but a harsh word stirs up anger.

² The tongue of the wise commends knowledge,
　　but the mouth of the fool gushes folly.

---

^a *22* Or *show*　　^b *33* Hebrew; Septuagint and Syriac / *but in the heart of fools she is not known*

³The eyes of the LORD are everywhere,
  keeping watch on the wicked and the good.

⁴The tongue that brings healing is a tree of life,
  but a deceitful tongue crushes the spirit.

⁵A fool spurns his father's discipline,
  but whoever heeds correction shows prudence.

⁶The house of the righteous contains great treasure,
  but the income of the wicked brings them trouble.

⁷The lips of the wise spread knowledge;
  not so the hearts of fools.

⁸The LORD detests the sacrifice of the wicked,
  but the prayer of the upright pleases him.

⁹The LORD detests the way of the wicked
  but he loves those who pursue
    righteousness.

¹⁰Stern discipline awaits him who leaves
    the path;
  he who hates correction will die.

¹¹Death and Destruction[a] lie open before
    the LORD—
  how much more the hearts of men!

¹²A mocker resents correction;
  he will not consult the wise.

¹³A happy heart makes the face cheerful,
  but heartache crushes the spirit.

¹⁴The discerning heart seeks knowledge,
  but the mouth of a fool feeds on
    folly.

¹⁵All the days of the oppressed are
    wretched,
  but the cheerful heart has a continual
    feast.

¹⁶Better a little with the fear of the LORD
  than great wealth with turmoil.

¹⁷Better a meal of vegetables where there is
    love
  than a fattened calf with hatred.

¹⁸A hot-tempered man stirs up
    dissension,
  but a patient man calms a quarrel.

¹⁹The way of the sluggard is blocked with
    thorns,
  but the path of the upright is a highway.

²⁰A wise son brings joy to his father,
  but a foolish man despises his mother.

Learning to Accept Discipline

Did your parents ever give you the line "I'm doing this for your own good" just before they lowered the boom on you with a grounding or some other punishment? Well, surprise, surprise—it turns out they were telling the truth. Discipline prepares you for life in the big, bad world. If you don't get it from your parents, who love you and want the best for you, you're going to get it later on from someone who cares a whole lot less about you and your feelings.

» live the adventure » Pr 15:10

---

a 11 Hebrew *Sheol and Abaddon*

²¹ Folly delights a man who lacks judgment,
  but a man of understanding keeps a straight course.

²² Plans fail for lack of counsel,
  but with many advisers they succeed.

²³ A man finds joy in giving an apt reply—
  and how good is a timely word!

²⁴ The path of life leads upward for the wise
  to keep him from going down to the
  grave.ᵃ

²⁵ The LORD tears down the proud man's
  house
  but he keeps the widow's boundaries
  intact.

²⁶ The LORD detests the thoughts of the
  wicked,
  but those of the pure are pleasing to
  him.

²⁷ A greedy man brings trouble to his family,
  but he who hates bribes will live.

²⁸ The heart of the righteous weighs its
  answers,
  but the mouth of the wicked gushes
  evil.

²⁹ The LORD is far from the wicked
  but he hears the prayer of the
  righteous.

³⁰ A cheerful look brings joy to the heart,
  and good news gives health to the
  bones.

³¹ He who listens to a life-giving rebuke
  will be at home among the wise.

³² He who ignores discipline despises himself,
  but whoever heeds correction gains understanding.

³³ The fear of the LORD teaches a man wisdom,ᵇ
  and humility comes before honor.

16 To man belong the plans of the heart,
  but from the LORD comes the reply of the tongue.

² All a man's ways seem innocent to him,
  but motives are weighed by the LORD.

³ Commit to the LORD whatever you do,
  and your plans will succeed.

⁴ The LORD works out everything for his own ends—
  even the wicked for a day of disaster.

⁵ The LORD detests all the proud of heart.
  Be sure of this: They will not go unpunished.

Seeking Advice

»» live the adventure »» Pr 15:22

The president of the United States has plenty of advisers. So why shouldn't you? You think you're smarter than the president? (Don't answer that.) Here's the deal. Every so often we encounter situations that are completely new to us or that are beyond our comfort level. When that happens, we have a choice. We can either guess at the right thing to do and hope for the best, or we can talk to people who have experienced similar circumstances, find out what they did and how it turned out, and then incorporate their advice into our decision-making process.

ᵃ 24 Hebrew *Sheol*   ᵇ 33 Or *Wisdom teaches the fear of the LORD*

battlelines

» I'm the One (Pride)

Q: Did you see the heavyweight fight on TV this weekend?
A: Yeah, I like that guy who won.

Q: Really? Not me. He's way too cocky—too full of himself.
A: I think he just knows he's the best.

Q: Yeah, well, he'd better enjoy it. Sooner or later somebody will come along and knock him on his back. I hope it's sooner rather than later. I'd like to see that.
A: So you don't like the guy just because he knows he's good?

Q: I just can't stand people who strut around like they're so awesome. Like those football players who sack the quarterback and then show off with a victory dance. They act like they just did something special, when that's what they're *supposed* to do! That's their *job*, for crying out loud!

A: Sounds like you've been thinking about this a lot.

Q: Look, I don't hand somebody their order at work and then pump my fist in the air and do a jig around the cash register. It's dumb. It's arrogant.
A: Man, if I was the best in the world at something, I'd definitely let people know about it.

Q: See, that's what I'm talking about. If you're so great at something, why do you have to advertise it? I think when you show off it just shows how insecure you are.
A: So you must not like Shaun and most of the other guys on the basketball team.

Q: It's not that I don't like them. I just don't see why they have to be so full of themselves. Just because they can put a ball in a hoop, they act like they're better than everybody else. And I don't think they are.

» Who's the One?

Pride is a deadly disease. C. S. Lewis called it the "Great Sin" and once said that as long as we are looking down on everything and everybody, we can't possibly see the One who is above us.*

Not only does pride keep us from God, it also sets us up for trouble. The Bible warns, "When pride comes, then comes disgrace, but with humility comes wisdom" (Proverbs 11:2) and "Pride goes before destruction, a haughty spirit before a fall" (Proverbs 16:18). Eventually those who think they're all that discover that they're nothing without God in their lives.

Watch out for cockiness and arrogance in your own heart. Few things are less attractive to others.

Go to www.RevolutionBible.com for more.

*C. S. Lewis, *Mere Christianity*, Zondervan, 2001.

⁶ Through love and faithfulness sin is atoned for;
    through the fear of the LORD a man avoids evil.

⁷ When a man's ways are pleasing to the LORD,
    he makes even his enemies live at peace with him.

⁸ Better a little with righteousness
    than much gain with injustice.

⁹ In his heart a man plans his course,
    but the LORD determines his steps.

¹⁰ The lips of a king speak as an oracle,
    and his mouth should not betray justice.

¹¹ Honest scales and balances are from the LORD;
    all the weights in the bag are of his making.

¹² Kings detest wrongdoing,
    for a throne is established through righteousness.

¹³ Kings take pleasure in honest lips;
    they value a man who speaks the truth.

¹⁴ A king's wrath is a messenger of death,
    but a wise man will appease it.

¹⁵ When a king's face brightens, it means life;
    his favor is like a rain cloud in spring.

¹⁶ How much better to get wisdom than gold,
    to choose understanding rather than silver!

¹⁷ The highway of the upright avoids evil;
    he who guards his way guards his life.

¹⁸ Pride goes before destruction,
    a haughty spirit before a fall.

¹⁹ Better to be lowly in spirit and among the oppressed
    than to share plunder with the proud.

²⁰ Whoever gives heed to instruction prospers,
    and blessed is he who trusts in the LORD.

²¹ The wise in heart are called discerning,
    and pleasant words promote instruction.ᵃ

²² Understanding is a fountain of life to those who have it,
    but folly brings punishment to fools.

²³ A wise man's heart guides his mouth,
    and his lips promote instruction.ᵇ

²⁴ Pleasant words are a honeycomb,
    sweet to the soul and healing to the bones.

²⁵ There is a way that seems right to a man,
    but in the end it leads to death.

²⁶ The laborer's appetite works for him;
    his hunger drives him on.

²⁷ A scoundrel plots evil,
    and his speech is like a scorching fire.

ᵃ 21 Or words make a man persuasive   ᵇ 23 Or mouth / and makes his lips persuasive

²⁸ A perverse man stirs up dissension,
and a gossip separates close friends.

²⁹ A violent man entices his neighbor
and leads him down a path that is
not good.

³⁰ He who winks with his eye is plotting
perversity;
he who purses his lips is bent on
evil.

³¹ Gray hair is a crown of splendor;
it is attained by a righteous life.

³² Better a patient man than a warrior,
a man who controls his temper than
one who takes a city.

NOW OR NEVER

PR 16:32

What kinds of situations really tick you
off? When was the last time your temper
got you in trouble?

³³ The lot is cast into the lap,
but its every decision is from the Lᴏʀᴅ.

17 Better a dry crust with peace and quiet
than a house full of feasting,ᵃ with strife.

² A wise servant will rule over a disgraceful son,
and will share the inheritance as one of the brothers.

³ The crucible for silver and the furnace for gold,
but the Lᴏʀᴅ tests the heart.

⁴ A wicked man listens to evil lips;
a liar pays attention to a malicious tongue.

⁵ He who mocks the poor shows contempt for their Maker;
whoever gloats over disaster will not go unpunished.

⁶ Children's children are a crown to the aged,
and parents are the pride of their children.

⁷ Arrogantᵇ lips are unsuited to a fool—
how much worse lying lips to a ruler!

⁸ A bribe is a charm to the one who gives it;
wherever he turns, he succeeds.

⁹ He who covers over an offense promotes love,
but whoever repeats the matter separates close friends.

¹⁰ A rebuke impresses a man of discernment
more than a hundred lashes a fool.

¹¹ An evil man is bent only on rebellion;
a merciless official will be sent against him.

¹² Better to meet a bear robbed of her cubs
than a fool in his folly.

¹³ If a man pays back evil for good,
evil will never leave his house.

¹⁴ Starting a quarrel is like breaching a dam;
so drop the matter before a dispute breaks out.

ᵃ 1 Hebrew *sacrifices*   ᵇ 7 Or *Eloquent*

¹⁵ Acquitting the guilty and condemning the innocent—
the LORD detests them both.

¹⁶ Of what use is money in the hand of a fool,
since he has no desire to get wisdom?

¹⁷ A friend loves at all times,
and a brother is born for adversity.

¹⁸ A man lacking in judgment strikes hands in pledge
and puts up security for his neighbor.

¹⁹ He who loves a quarrel loves sin;
he who builds a high gate invites destruction.

²⁰ A man of perverse heart does not prosper;
he whose tongue is deceitful falls into trouble.

²¹ To have a fool for a son brings grief;
there is no joy for the father of a fool.

²² A cheerful heart is good medicine,
but a crushed spirit dries up the bones.

²³ A wicked man accepts a bribe in secret
to pervert the course of justice.

²⁴ A discerning man keeps wisdom in view,
but a fool's eyes wander to the ends of the earth.

²⁵ A foolish son brings grief to his father
and bitterness to the one who bore him.

²⁶ It is not good to punish an innocent man,
or to flog officials for their integrity.

²⁷ A man of knowledge uses words with restraint,
and a man of understanding is even-tempered.

²⁸ Even a fool is thought wise if he keeps silent,
and discerning if he holds his tongue.

 An unfriendly man pursues selfish ends;
he defies all sound judgment.

² A fool finds no pleasure in understanding
but delights in airing his own opinions.

³ When wickedness comes, so does contempt,
and with shame comes disgrace.

⁴ The words of a man's mouth are deep waters,
but the fountain of wisdom is a bubbling brook.

⁵ It is not good to be partial to the wicked
or to deprive the innocent of justice.

⁶ A fool's lips bring him strife,
and his mouth invites a beating.

⁷ A fool's mouth is his undoing,
and his lips are a snare to his soul.

⁸ The words of a gossip are like choice morsels;
they go down to a man's inmost parts.

battlelines

» Tasty Morsels (Gossip)

Q: What are you grinning about?
A: Oh, man, I just heard some hot news. Get this: Last night, a bunch of people saw Chandler get in a car with Kim.

Q: So?
A: So . . . they drove to Kim's. Her parents are out of town. You know what I'm saying?

Q: Yeah, but how do you know it's true?
A: Because everybody says so! Let's just say the rumors are flying! Anyway, things got pretty wild.

Q: And you *know* this to be a fact?
A: Dude, are you deaf? Everybody's talking about it. I know everything that went on.

Q: So you were there?
A: Well, no. But I've heard about it. Everybody's talking.

Q: But you can't say you *really* know what happened, can you?
A: Hey, I've got good sources. I heard from two different people.

Q: Were they there?
A: Well, no.

Q: Look, even if what you heard is true—and you don't know that it is—why do you want to go around talking about it? That's pathetic. Get a life! You're just trashing other people's reputations.
A: Hey, they're the ones who chose to do this. Nobody held a gun to their heads. Now they have to deal with the consequences.

Q: Oh, yeah, you're right. Now I remember. When Jesus caught the woman in adultery, he ran all over Galilee telling everybody, right?
A: Whatever.

» INSIDE SCOOP

Proverbs 18:8 says, "The words of a gossip are like choice morsels; they go down to a man's inmost parts."

In other words, a juicy rumor is like an irresistible delicacy—but it has a fishhook inside. It just sits there in front of you, begging to be sampled and enjoyed. If you bite, you find this "hot, new scoop" tastes delicious—and you find yourself hooked.

What usually happens next is that you compound the sin by sharing the "morsel" with others. Not only that, you allow the factoid—true or not—to sink deep into your heart and mind. The result is that every time you see the people in question, you automatically match them up with the dirt you have on them.

There's a better way. Present yourself—even your ears and your mouth—to God as "instruments of righteousness" (Romans 6:13). Determine now that you will be a dead end for every piece of gossip that comes your way.

Read more about the effects of gossip at www.RevolutionBible.com.

⁹One who is slack in his work
  is brother to one who destroys.

¹⁰The name of the LORD is a strong tower;
  the righteous run to it and are safe.

¹¹The wealth of the rich is their fortified city;
  they imagine it an unscalable wall.

¹²Before his downfall a man's heart is proud,
  but humility comes before honor.

¹³He who answers before listening—
  that is his folly and his shame.

¹⁴A man's spirit sustains him in sickness,
  but a crushed spirit who can bear?

¹⁵The heart of the discerning acquires knowledge;
  the ears of the wise seek it out.

¹⁶A gift opens the way for the giver
  and ushers him into the presence of the great.

¹⁷The first to present his case seems right,
  till another comes forward and questions him.

NOW OR NEVER

PR 18:21

When was the last time someone said something that really hurt you (whether you showed it or not)? When was the last time you said something that really hurt someone else?

¹⁸Casting the lot settles disputes
  and keeps strong opponents apart.

¹⁹An offended brother is more unyielding
  than a fortified city,
  and disputes are like the barred gates
  of a citadel.

²⁰From the fruit of his mouth a man's
  stomach is filled;
  with the harvest from his lips he is
  satisfied.

²¹The tongue has the power of life and
  death,
  and those who love it will eat its
  fruit.

²²He who finds a wife finds what is good
  and receives favor from the LORD.

²³A poor man pleads for mercy,
  but a rich man answers harshly.

²⁴A man of many companions may come to ruin,
  but there is a friend who sticks closer than a brother.

19

Better a poor man whose walk is blameless
  than a fool whose lips are perverse.

²It is not good to have zeal without knowledge,
  nor to be hasty and miss the way.

³A man's own folly ruins his life,
  yet his heart rages against the LORD.

⁴Wealth brings many friends,
  but a poor man's friend deserts him.

⁵A false witness will not go unpunished,
    and he who pours out lies will not go free.

⁶Many curry favor with a ruler,
    and everyone is the friend of a man who gives gifts.

⁷A poor man is shunned by all his relatives—
    how much more do his friends avoid him!
  Though he pursues them with pleading,
    they are nowhere to be found.ᵃ

⁸He who gets wisdom loves his own soul;
    he who cherishes understanding prospers.

⁹A false witness will not go unpunished,
    and he who pours out lies will perish.

¹⁰It is not fitting for a fool to live in luxury—
    how much worse for a slave to rule over princes!

¹¹A man's wisdom gives him patience;
    it is to his glory to overlook an offense.

¹²A king's rage is like the roar of a lion,
    but his favor is like dew on the grass.

¹³A foolish son is his father's ruin,
    and a quarrelsome wife is like a constant dripping.

¹⁴Houses and wealth are inherited from parents,
    but a prudent wife is from the Lord.

¹⁵Laziness brings on deep sleep,
    and the shiftless man goes hungry.

¹⁶He who obeys instructions guards his life,
    but he who is contemptuous of his ways will die.

¹⁷He who is kind to the poor lends to the Lord,
    and he will reward him for what he has done.

¹⁸Discipline your son, for in that there is hope;
    do not be a willing party to his death.

¹⁹A hot-tempered man must pay the penalty;
    if you rescue him, you will have to do it again.

²⁰Listen to advice and accept instruction,
    and in the end you will be wise.

²¹Many are the plans in a man's heart,
    but it is the Lord's purpose that prevails.

²²What a man desires is unfailing loveᵇ;
    better to be poor than a liar.

²³The fear of the Lord leads to life:
    Then one rests content, untouched by trouble.

²⁴The sluggard buries his hand in the dish;
    he will not even bring it back to his mouth!

²⁵Flog a mocker, and the simple will learn prudence;
    rebuke a discerning man, and he will gain knowledge.

ᵃ *7 The meaning of the Hebrew for this sentence is uncertain.*   ᵇ *22 Or A man's greed is his shame*

26 He who robs his father and drives out his mother
   is a son who brings shame and disgrace.

27 Stop listening to instruction, my son,
   and you will stray from the words of knowledge.

28 A corrupt witness mocks at justice,
   and the mouth of the wicked gulps down evil.

29 Penalties are prepared for mockers,
   and beatings for the backs of fools.

20 Wine is a mocker and beer a brawler;
   whoever is led astray by them is not wise.

2 A king's wrath is like the roar of a lion;
   he who angers him forfeits his life.

3 It is to a man's honor to avoid strife,
   but every fool is quick to quarrel.

now or never

PR 20:1

What's the dumbest or scariest thing you've ever seen anyone do when he or she was under the influence of drugs or alcohol? Do you think that person learned a lesson from the incident?

4 A sluggard does not plow in season;
   so at harvest time he looks but finds
      nothing.

5 The purposes of a man's heart are deep
      waters,
   but a man of understanding draws
      them out.

6 Many a man claims to have unfailing
      love,
   but a faithful man who can find?

7 The righteous man leads a blameless
      life;
   blessed are his children after
      him.

8 When a king sits on his throne to judge,
   he winnows out all evil with his eyes.

9 Who can say, "I have kept my heart pure;
   I am clean and without sin"?

10 Differing weights and differing measures—
   the LORD detests them both.

11 Even a child is known by his actions,
   by whether his conduct is pure and right.

12 Ears that hear and eyes that see—
   the LORD has made them both.

13 Do not love sleep or you will grow poor;
   stay awake and you will have food to spare.

14 "It's no good, it's no good!" says the buyer;
   then off he goes and boasts about his purchase.

15 Gold there is, and rubies in abundance,
   but lips that speak knowledge are a rare jewel.

16 Take the garment of one who puts up security for a stranger;
   hold it in pledge if he does it for a wayward woman.

17 Food gained by fraud tastes sweet to a man,
  but he ends up with a mouth full of gravel.

18 Make plans by seeking advice;
  if you wage war, obtain guidance.

19 A gossip betrays a confidence;
  so avoid a man who talks too much.

20 If a man curses his father or mother,
  his lamp will be snuffed out in pitch darkness.

21 An inheritance quickly gained at the beginning
  will not be blessed at the end.

22 Do not say, "I'll pay you back for this wrong!"
  Wait for the LORD, and he will deliver you.

23 The LORD detests differing weights,
  and dishonest scales do not please him.

24 A man's steps are directed by the LORD.
  How then can anyone understand his own way?

25 It is a trap for a man to dedicate something rashly
  and only later to consider his vows.

26 A wise king winnows out the wicked;
  he drives the threshing wheel over them.

27 The lamp of the LORD searches the spirit of a man ª;
  it searches out his inmost being.

28 Love and faithfulness keep a king safe;
  through love his throne is made secure.

29 The glory of young men is their strength,
  gray hair the splendor of the old.

30 Blows and wounds cleanse away evil,
  and beatings purge the inmost being.

The king's heart is in the hand of the LORD;
  he directs it like a watercourse wherever he pleases.

2 All a man's ways seem right to him,
  but the LORD weighs the heart.

3 To do what is right and just
  is more acceptable to the LORD than sacrifice.

4 Haughty eyes and a proud heart,
  the lamp of the wicked, are sin!

5 The plans of the diligent lead to profit
  as surely as haste leads to poverty.

6 A fortune made by a lying tongue
  is a fleeting vapor and a deadly snare. ᵇ

7 The violence of the wicked will drag them away,
  for they refuse to do what is right.

ª 27 Or *The spirit of man is the LORD's lamp*   ᵇ 6 Some Hebrew manuscripts, Septuagint and Vulgate; most Hebrew manuscripts *vapor for those who seek death*

⁸ The way of the guilty is devious,
   but the conduct of the innocent is upright.

⁹ Better to live on a corner of the roof
   than share a house with a quarrelsome wife.

¹⁰ The wicked man craves evil;
   his neighbor gets no mercy from him.

¹¹ When a mocker is punished, the simple gain wisdom;
   when a wise man is instructed, he gets knowledge.

¹² The Righteous One ᵃ takes note of the house of the wicked
   and brings the wicked to ruin.

¹³ If a man shuts his ears to the cry of the poor,
   he too will cry out and not be answered.

¹⁴ A gift given in secret soothes anger,
   and a bribe concealed in the cloak pacifies great wrath.

¹⁵ When justice is done, it brings joy to the righteous
   but terror to evildoers.

¹⁶ A man who strays from the path of understanding
   comes to rest in the company of the dead.

¹⁷ He who loves pleasure will become poor;
   whoever loves wine and oil will never be rich.

¹⁸ The wicked become a ransom for the righteous,
   and the unfaithful for the upright.

¹⁹ Better to live in a desert
   than with a quarrelsome and ill-tempered wife.

²⁰ In the house of the wise are stores of choice food and oil,
   but a foolish man devours all he has.

²¹ He who pursues righteousness and love
   finds life, prosperity ᵇ and honor.

²² A wise man attacks the city of the mighty
   and pulls down the stronghold in which they trust.

²³ He who guards his mouth and his tongue
   keeps himself from calamity.

²⁴ The proud and arrogant man—"Mocker" is his name;
   he behaves with overweening pride.

²⁵ The sluggard's craving will be the death of him,
   because his hands refuse to work.

²⁶ All day long he craves for more,
   but the righteous give without sparing.

²⁷ The sacrifice of the wicked is detestable—
   how much more so when brought with evil intent!

²⁸ A false witness will perish,
   and whoever listens to him will be destroyed forever. ᶜ

²⁹ A wicked man puts up a bold front,
   but an upright man gives thought to his ways.

ᵃ *12 Or The righteous man*   ᵇ *21 Or righteousness*   ᶜ *28 Or / but the words of an obedient man will live on*

30 There is no wisdom, no insight, no plan
   that can succeed against the Lord.

31 The horse is made ready for the day of battle,
   but victory rests with the Lord.

22 A good name is more desirable than great riches;
   to be esteemed is better than silver or gold.

2 Rich and poor have this in common:
   The Lord is the Maker of them all.

3 A prudent man sees danger and takes refuge,
   but the simple keep going and suffer for it.

4 Humility and the fear of the Lord
   bring wealth and honor and life.

5 In the paths of the wicked lie thorns and
      snares,
   but he who guards his soul stays far
      from them.

6 Train[a] a child in the way he should go,
   and when he is old he will not turn
      from it.

7 The rich rule over the poor,
   and the borrower is servant to the
      lender.

8 He who sows wickedness reaps trouble,
   and the rod of his fury will be
      destroyed.

9 A generous man will himself be blessed,
   for he shares his food with the poor.

10 Drive out the mocker, and out goes strife;
   quarrels and insults are ended.

11 He who loves a pure heart and whose
      speech is gracious
   will have the king for his friend.

12 The eyes of the Lord keep watch over
      knowledge,
   but he frustrates the words of the
      unfaithful.

13 The sluggard says, "There is a lion
      outside!"
   or, "I will be murdered in the streets!"

14 The mouth of an adulteress is a deep pit;
   he who is under the Lord's wrath will fall into it.

15 Folly is bound up in the heart of a child,
   but the rod of discipline will drive it far from him.

16 He who oppresses the poor to increase his wealth
   and he who gives gifts to the rich—both come to poverty.

Giving Generously

Have you ever tried an extreme sport—biking or boarding or skating? Here's another activity for you to consider: extreme giving. That's right. Instead of making sure that you have enough money for lunch or your weekend plans or whatever, do the outrageous thing by giving a major chunk of your cash to people in need. Worry about yourself later.

»» live the adventure »» Pr 22:9

a 6 Or Start

SAYINGS OF THE WISE

17 Pay attention and listen to the sayings of the wise;
  apply your heart to what I teach,
18 for it is pleasing when you keep them in your heart
  and have all of them ready on your lips.
19 So that your trust may be in the LORD,
  I teach you today, even you.
20 Have I not written thirty[a] sayings for you,
  sayings of counsel and knowledge,
21 teaching you true and reliable words,
  so that you can give sound answers
  to him who sent you?

22 Do not exploit the poor because they are poor
  and do not crush the needy in court,
23 for the LORD will take up their case
  and will plunder those who plunder them.

24 Do not make friends with a hot-tempered man,
  do not associate with one easily angered,
25 or you may learn his ways
  and get yourself ensnared.

26 Do not be a man who strikes hands in pledge
  or puts up security for debts;
27 if you lack the means to pay,
  your very bed will be snatched from under you.

28 Do not move an ancient boundary stone
  set up by your forefathers.

29 Do you see a man skilled in his work?
  He will serve before kings;
  he will not serve before obscure men.

23

When you sit to dine with a ruler,
  note well what[b] is before you,
2 and put a knife to your throat
  if you are given to gluttony.

3 Do not crave his delicacies,
  for that food is deceptive.

4 Do not wear yourself out to get rich;
  have the wisdom to show restraint.
5 Cast but a glance at riches,
  and they are gone,
  for they will surely sprout wings
  and fly off to the sky like an eagle.

challenge notes

To: my_son

heavenly_father: money is overrated. the things you think will bring you happiness quickly become just "things" once you have them. they'll leave you bored and dissatisfied. so no matter what your financial situation is, remember—the only thing that can bring true satisfaction is me.

PR 23:4-5

6 Do not eat the food of a stingy man,
  do not crave his delicacies;
7 for he is the kind of man
  who is always thinking about the cost.[c]

---

[a] 20 Or not formerly written; or not written excellent   [b] 1 Or who   [c] 7 Or for as he thinks within himself, / so he is; or for as he puts on a feast, / so he is

"Eat and drink," he says to you,
　　but his heart is not with you.
8 You will vomit up the little you have eaten
　　and will have wasted your compliments.

9 Do not speak to a fool,
　　for he will scorn the wisdom of your words.

10 Do not move an ancient boundary stone
　　or encroach on the fields of the fatherless,
11 for their Defender is strong;
　　he will take up their case against you.

12 Apply your heart to instruction
　　and your ears to words of knowledge.

13 Do not withhold discipline from a child;
　　if you punish him with the rod, he will not die.
14 Punish him with the rod
　　and save his soul from death. a

15 My son, if your heart is wise,
　　then my heart will be glad;
16 my inmost being will rejoice
　　when your lips speak what is right.

17 Do not let your heart envy sinners,
　　but always be zealous for the fear of the LORD.
18 There is surely a future hope for you,
　　and your hope will not be cut off.

19 Listen, my son, and be wise,
　　and keep your heart on the right path.

20 Do not join those who drink too much
　　　　wine
　　　　or gorge themselves on meat,
21 for drunkards and gluttons become
　　　　poor,
　　　　and drowsiness clothes them in rags.

22 Listen to your father, who gave you life,
　　　　and do not despise your mother
　　　　　when she is old.
23 Buy the truth and do not sell it;
　　　　get wisdom, discipline and
　　　　　understanding.
24 The father of a righteous man has great
　　　　　joy;

NOW OR NEVER
PR 23:22-25

What three words best describe your father? How about your mother? What three words best describe your relationship with your parents?

he who has a wise son delights in him.
25 May your father and mother be glad;
　　may she who gave you birth rejoice!

26 My son, give me your heart
　　and let your eyes keep to my ways,
27 for a prostitute is a deep pit
　　and a wayward wife is a narrow well.
28 Like a bandit she lies in wait,
　　and multiplies the unfaithful among men.

---

a 14 Hebrew *Sheol*

²⁹ Who has woe? Who has sorrow?
　　Who has strife? Who has complaints?
　　Who has needless bruises? Who has bloodshot eyes?
³⁰ Those who linger over wine,
　　who go to sample bowls of mixed wine.
³¹ Do not gaze at wine when it is red,
　　when it sparkles in the cup,
　　when it goes down smoothly!
³² In the end it bites like a snake
　　and poisons like a viper.
³³ Your eyes will see strange sights
　　and your mind imagine confusing things.
³⁴ You will be like one sleeping on the high seas,
　　lying on top of the rigging.
³⁵ "They hit me," you will say, "but I'm not hurt!
　　They beat me, but I don't feel it!
　　When will I wake up
　　so I can find another drink?"

Do not envy wicked men,
　　do not desire their company;
² for their hearts plot violence,
　　and their lips talk about making trouble.

³ By wisdom a house is built,
　　and through understanding it is established;
⁴ through knowledge its rooms are filled
　　with rare and beautiful treasures.

⁵ A wise man has great power,
　　and a man of knowledge increases strength;
⁶ for waging war you need guidance,
　　and for victory many advisers.

⁷ Wisdom is too high for a fool;
　　in the assembly at the gate he has nothing to say.

⁸ He who plots evil
　　will be known as a schemer.
⁹ The schemes of folly are sin,
　　and men detest a mocker.

¹⁰ If you falter in times of trouble,
　　how small is your strength!

¹¹ Rescue those being led away to death;
　　hold back those staggering toward slaughter.
¹² If you say, "But we knew nothing about this,"
　　does not he who weighs the heart perceive it?
　　Does not he who guards your life know it?
　　Will he not repay each person according to what he has done?

¹³ Eat honey, my son, for it is good;
　　honey from the comb is sweet to your taste.
¹⁴ Know also that wisdom is sweet to your soul;
　　if you find it, there is a future hope for you,
　　and your hope will not be cut off.

¹⁵ Do not lie in wait like an outlaw against a righteous man's house,
　　do not raid his dwelling place;

60 of Satan's Favorite Lies

Jesus sized up the devil by calling him the world's biggest liar. Satan is not only real and powerful, but he's also deceptive. We need to be able to recognize his lies. Here are some of the messages we are bombarded with:

01» The universe is just a fluke—it doesn't prove anything about God »Ge 1–2 **02»** Real men have sex every chance they get »Ge 39:6–12 **03»** Real men fight their own battles »Ex 14:14 **04»** You're your own god »1Ki 8:60 **05»** You're your own man—you don't owe anyone anything »Job 33:4 **06»** Real men don't talk about their feelings »Ps 6 **07»** There are no guarantees in life »Ps 37:23 **08»** You'll never shake that sin from your life »Ps 103:12 **09»** You're stupid »Pr 2:1–5 **10»** Christians are prudes—they think sex is dirty »Pr 5:15–20; SS 1–8 **11»** Only the aggressive survive, so do whatever it takes to get rich quick »Pr 13:11 **12»** A friend is someone who improves your social status »Pr 17:17 **13»** Money will solve all your problems »Pr 30:8 **14»** You don't have what it takes »Isa 41:10 **15»** Smarts, strength and money are what really matter in life »Jer 9:23–24 **16»** God doesn't care about your thoughts—just what you say and do » Jer 17:10 **17»** Your future is hopeless »Jer 29:11–13 **18»** Live it up while you're young . . . you've got plenty of time »Mt 4:17 **19»** God only wants complex, heady thinkers »Mt 18:4 **20»** When things don't work out between you and your wife, just get a divorce »Mt 19:6 **21»** The Christian life is boring and empty »Jn 10:10 **22»** Real men don't cry »Jn 11:35 **23»** Jesus didn't really rise from the dead—it's just a story »Jn 20; 1Co 15:3–8 **24»** God helps those who help themselves »Ac 20:35 **25»** Hoping in something you've never seen will only end in disappointment »Ro 5:5 **26»** Sin is not that big a deal »Ro 6:23 **27»** You can't overcome sinful thoughts—why fight them? »Ro 8:6 **28»** So what if God's promises are true? Who wants to live a boring life anyway? »1Co 2:9 **29»** Hooking up with a girl for a little fun is harmless »1Co 6:18–20 **30»** Some temptations

THERE IS NO CREATOR

1

HOPLESSNESS

17

:: JER 29:11-13

RESURRECTION

23

"REAL MAN: ONE WHO OVERCOMES SINFUL THOUGHTS

are irresistible, so you might as well give in »1Co 10:13 :: **31»** As long as you believe the right things, it doesn't matter how you live »1Co 10:31 :: **32»** Real love is all about sex »1Co 13:4–7 :: **33»** Why give up a life of fun just to follow a bunch of dumb rules? »2Co 4:17–18 :: **34»** You're weak »2Co 12:9 :: **35»** If you're smart about covering up your sin, no one will ever know »Gal 6:7 :: **36»** You've got nothing to contribute »Eph 2:10 :: **37»** It's better to bury your anger than to let it out »Eph 4:26–27 :: **38»** You don't owe forgiveness to anybody »Eph 4:32 :: **39»** Women exist solely to serve and satisfy men »Eph 5:25–33 :: **40»** Your life is small, boring and insignificant »Eph 6:10–12 :: **41»** You'll never become anything worthwhile »Php 1:6 :: **42»** Asking other people for help is a sign of weakness »Php 4:14–18 :: **43»** A little white lie never hurt anybody »Col 3:9 :: **44»** Oral sex isn't wrong—because it isn't sex »1Th 4:3–8; Gal 5:19 :: **45»** Jesus wasn't really human »1Ti 2:5 :: **46»** The guy who dies with the most toys wins »1Ti 6:7 :: **47»** Doing whatever it takes to make a lot of money is fine as long as you share some with people who need it »1Ti 6:10 :: **48»** The Christian life is for weaklings »2Ti 2:3 :: **49»** If you blow it, God is guaranteed to blow you off »2Ti 2:13 :: **50»** Getting to heaven is based on trying hard to be a good person »Titus 3:5–7 :: **51»** Jesus wasn't (and isn't) really God »Heb 1:1–4 :: **52»** You're on your own—and you're going down »Heb 13:6 :: **53»** Hardship is a signal that it's time to give up »Jas 1:2–3 :: **54»** Pornography doesn't hurt anyone. Besides, it's better to look than to actually do the deed »Jas 1:14–15 :: **55»** You don't need to explain your faith to anyone »1Pe 3:15–16 :: **56»** Life is supposed to be easy »1Pe 4:12–13 :: **57»** You will never be loved »1Jn 4:16 :: **58»** Everybody's doing it »Rev 14:4 :: **59»** If God really loves people, he won't send anybody to hell »Rev 20:11–15 :: **60»** Heaven is a stupid dream—this world is all there is »Rev 21–22

:: 1TI 2:5

IDENTITY 45

PORNOGRAPHY

54

battlelines

» Sticking It Out (Commitment)

Q: Isn't it great being on the wrestling team this year?
A: I guess.

Q: I'm not sensing that you're very excited about it.
A: Don't get me wrong. I'm glad I made the team. It's definitely an honor. And my dad's real proud. I'm just wondering now if I made the right choice.

Q: Why?
A: Well, being on the team sort of takes over your life. The fact that we've won state titles six out of the last ten years is a *huge* deal. So you've got all this working out and running and trying to make weight. Plus, you still have tons of homework to do. Every day it's work out, school, practice, study, sleep. And the only thing that changes on the weekend is the school part. So you don't have much of a life when you're on the

wrestling team. And—don't tell anyone I said this—but it gets old after a while.

Q: Didn't you realize what you were getting into?
A: I thought I did. I mean, I like wrestling and all. But most of the guys on the team are hard-core wrestling freaks. They *love* this stuff. It's all they care about or think about . . . well, that and girls. But it's not like I'm ever going to get a college scholarship or go to the Olympics. So what am I doing this for? I miss hanging out with my friends. And I'll bet I haven't picked up my guitar in a month.

Q: You're not thinking of bailing, are you?
A: Honestly? I'd like to. But if I did, I know I'd catch all kinds of grief.

» What About Reneging?

If Hayden quits, he lets the team down. He sets a bad example for others and possibly a dangerous precedent for himself. If he walks away now, it will just make it easier for him to renege on a commitment the next time he doesn't feel like sticking it out.

It's important to prioritize (and limit) your commitments in order to maintain a healthy balance in your life (and to avoid burnout). But it's also important to keep your word once you've made a commitment to do something. It takes great integrity to finish out a commitment when all you want to do is quit. Face it: If it were easy, it wouldn't take character to finish (see Proverbs 24:10).

Learn more about making tough choices at www.RevolutionBible.com.

¹⁶for though a righteous man falls seven times, he rises again,
but the wicked are brought down by calamity.

¹⁷Do not gloat when your enemy falls;
when he stumbles, do not let your heart rejoice,
¹⁸or the LORD will see and disapprove
and turn his wrath away from him.

¹⁹Do not fret because of evil men
or be envious of the wicked,
²⁰for the evil man has no future hope,
and the lamp of the wicked will be snuffed out.

²¹Fear the LORD and the king, my son,
and do not join with the rebellious,
²²for those two will send sudden destruction upon them,
and who knows what calamities they can bring?

FURTHER SAYINGS OF THE WISE

²³These also are sayings of the wise:

To show partiality in judging is not good:
²⁴Whoever says to the guilty, "You are innocent"—
peoples will curse him and nations denounce him.
²⁵But it will go well with those who convict the guilty,
and rich blessing will come upon them.

²⁶An honest answer
is like a kiss on the lips.

²⁷Finish your outdoor work
and get your fields ready;
after that, build your house.

²⁸Do not testify against your neighbor without cause,
or use your lips to deceive.
²⁹Do not say, "I'll do to him as he has done to me;
I'll pay that man back for what he did."

³⁰I went past the field of the sluggard,
past the vineyard of the man who lacks judgment;
³¹thorns had come up everywhere,
the ground was covered with weeds,
and the stone wall was in ruins.
³²I applied my heart to what I observed
and learned a lesson from what I saw:
³³A little sleep, a little slumber,
a little folding of the hands to rest—
³⁴and poverty will come on you like a bandit
and scarcity like an armed man.[a]

MORE PROVERBS OF SOLOMON

These are more proverbs of Solomon, copied by the men of Hezekiah king of Judah:

²It is the glory of God to conceal a matter;
to search out a matter is the glory of kings.

---

[a] 34 Or like a vagrant / and scarcity like a beggar

³As the heavens are high and the earth is deep,
    so the hearts of kings are unsearchable.

⁴Remove the dross from the silver,
    and out comes material for[a] the silversmith;
⁵remove the wicked from the king's presence,
    and his throne will be established through righteousness.

⁶Do not exalt yourself in the king's presence,
    and do not claim a place among great men;
⁷it is better for him to say to you, "Come up here,"
    than for him to humiliate you before a nobleman.

  What you have seen with your eyes
⁸   do not bring[b] hastily to court,
for what will you do in the end
    if your neighbor puts you to shame?

⁹If you argue your case with a neighbor,
    do not betray another man's confidence,
¹⁰or he who hears it may shame you
    and you will never lose your bad reputation.

¹¹A word aptly spoken
    is like apples of gold in settings of silver.

¹²Like an earring of gold or an ornament of fine gold
    is a wise man's rebuke to a listening ear.

¹³Like the coolness of snow at harvest time
    is a trustworthy messenger to those who send him;
    he refreshes the spirit of his masters.

¹⁴Like clouds and wind without rain
    is a man who boasts of gifts he does not give.

¹⁵Through patience a ruler can be persuaded,
    and a gentle tongue can break a bone.

¹⁶If you find honey, eat just enough—
    too much of it, and you will vomit.
¹⁷Seldom set foot in your neighbor's house—
    too much of you, and he will hate you.

¹⁸Like a club or a sword or a sharp arrow
    is the man who gives false testimony
    against his neighbor.

¹⁹Like a bad tooth or a lame foot
    is reliance on the unfaithful in times
    of trouble.

NOW OR N·E·V·ER
PR 25:19

What does a person have to do to earn your trust? Have you ever been burned by someone you trusted and figured out later that you shouldn't have trusted them in the first place? If so, what did you learn from the experience?

²⁰Like one who takes away a garment on a cold day,
    or like vinegar poured on soda,
    is one who sings songs to a heavy heart.

²¹If your enemy is hungry, give him food to eat;
    if he is thirsty, give him water to drink.
²²In doing this, you will heap burning coals on his head,
    and the LORD will reward you.

---

[a] 4 Or comes a vessel from   [b] 7,8 Or nobleman / on whom you had set your eyes. / ⁸Do not go

²³ As a north wind brings rain,
so a sly tongue brings angry looks.

²⁴ Better to live on a corner of the roof
than share a house with a quarrelsome wife.

²⁵ Like cold water to a weary soul
is good news from a distant land.

²⁶ Like a muddied spring or a polluted well
is a righteous man who gives way to the wicked.

²⁷ It is not good to eat too much honey,
nor is it honorable to seek one's own honor.

²⁸ Like a city whose walls are broken down
is a man who lacks self-control.

 Like snow in summer or rain in harvest,
honor is not fitting for a fool.

² Like a fluttering sparrow or a darting swallow,
an undeserved curse does not come to rest.

³ A whip for the horse, a halter for the donkey,
and a rod for the backs of fools!

⁴ Do not answer a fool according to his folly,
or you will be like him yourself.

⁵ Answer a fool according to his folly,
or he will be wise in his own eyes.

⁶ Like cutting off one's feet or drinking violence
is the sending of a message by the hand of a fool.

⁷ Like a lame man's legs that hang limp
is a proverb in the mouth of a fool.

⁸ Like tying a stone in a sling
is the giving of honor to a fool.

⁹ Like a thornbush in a drunkard's hand
is a proverb in the mouth of a fool.

¹⁰ Like an archer who wounds at random
is he who hires a fool or any passer-by.

¹¹ As a dog returns to its vomit,
so a fool repeats his folly.

¹² Do you see a man wise in his own eyes?
There is more hope for a fool than for him.

¹³ The sluggard says, "There is a lion in the road,
a fierce lion roaming the streets!"

¹⁴ As a door turns on its hinges,
so a sluggard turns on his bed.

¹⁵ The sluggard buries his hand in the dish;
he is too lazy to bring it back to his mouth.

¹⁶ The sluggard is wiser in his own eyes
than seven men who answer discreetly.

¹⁷ Like one who seizes a dog by the ears
is a passer-by who meddles in a quarrel not his own.

¹⁸ Like a madman shooting
firebrands or deadly arrows
¹⁹ is a man who deceives his neighbor
and says, "I was only joking!"

²⁰ Without wood a fire goes out;
without gossip a quarrel dies down.

²¹ As charcoal to embers and as wood to fire,
so is a quarrelsome man for kindling strife.

²² The words of a gossip are like choice morsels;
they go down to a man's inmost parts.

²³ Like a coating of glaze^a over earthenware
are fervent lips with an evil heart.

²⁴ A malicious man disguises himself with his lips,
but in his heart he harbors deceit.
²⁵ Though his speech is charming, do not believe him,
for seven abominations fill his heart.
²⁶ His malice may be concealed by deception,
but his wickedness will be exposed in the assembly.

²⁷ If a man digs a pit, he will fall into it;
if a man rolls a stone, it will roll back on him.

²⁸ A lying tongue hates those it hurts,
and a flattering mouth works ruin.

27

Do not boast about tomorrow,
for you do not know what a day may bring forth.

² Let another praise you, and not your own mouth;
someone else, and not your own lips.

nОШ ОR ПEVER

PR 27:2

No matter how proud you are of something you've done or how oblivious other people seem to be in regard to your accomplishments, resist the temptation to praise yourself. You'll only make yourself look desperate for attention.

³ Stone is heavy and sand a burden,
but provocation by a fool is heavier
than both.

⁴ Anger is cruel and fury overwhelming,
but who can stand before
jealousy?

⁵ Better is open rebuke
than hidden love.

⁶ Wounds from a friend can be trusted,
but an enemy multiplies kisses.

⁷ He who is full loathes honey,
but to the hungry even what is bitter
tastes sweet.

⁸ Like a bird that strays from its nest
is a man who strays from his home.

⁹ Perfume and incense bring joy to the heart,
and the pleasantness of one's friend springs from his earnest counsel.

---

^a *23* With a different word division of the Hebrew; Masoretic Text *of silver dross*

battlelines

» Low Life (Friendship)

Q: Well, that *is* a dicey situation. You're in a real tight spot.
A: Thanks for stating the obvious. So what am I supposed to do? I can't just blow off my best friend. I also can't let him keep going down this path. He's starting to hang out with a pretty wild crowd. He's got this edge now. I don't know what happened to him.

Q: Have you talked to him about it?
A: What am I supposed to say? "Hey, Clay, did you notice you're becoming a total jerk? In fact, you're such a loser, I can't hang out with you anymore. Have a nice day!" I know I wouldn't want to hear that.

Q: I'm not saying you should heap a bunch of condemnation on the guy. I'm saying maybe you should dig a little bit to find out why he's going downhill all of the sudden. Something's obviously going on in his life. The truth is, he's probably dying to talk about it. What he needs is a friend.
A: So how do I do that?

Q: Start at the beginning. How has Clay changed the most?
A: He's stopped coming to church.

Q: That's just a symptom. What prompted that? Why did he stop coming? What was going on in his life before that?
A: Nothing, really . . . except that his dad got activated for military service overseas. He shipped out a few weeks ago, and he probably won't be home for at least a year. But Clay never talks about that; he never acts like it's a big deal.

Q: Maybe his dad leaving has something to do with all of this.
A: You think?

» Higher Love

Why are so many guys such risk takers in so many areas of life and such wusses when it comes to friendships? It doesn't take a genius to figure out that when your friend is in trouble, it's time to engage. Move in. Start asking questions. What does the book of Proverbs say?

● "Better is open rebuke than hidden love" (27:5).

● "Wounds from a friend can be trusted, but an enemy multiplies kisses" (27:6).

The point is that true friends don't stand idly by wringing their hands when trouble is obviously brewing. They don't watch silently as their buddies go down in flames.

You may feel like you're butting in, and your friend may be uncomfortable with your efforts to help. So what? Love rides to the rescue. Love means you have to help, ask, listen, pray, encourage . . . and sometimes say hard things.

Read more about friendship at www.RevolutionBible.com.

¹⁰ Do not forsake your friend and the friend of your father,
  and do not go to your brother's house when disaster strikes you—
  better a neighbor nearby than a brother far away.

¹¹ Be wise, my son, and bring joy to my heart;
  then I can answer anyone who treats me with contempt.

¹² The prudent see danger and take refuge,
  but the simple keep going and suffer for it.

¹³ Take the garment of one who puts up security for a stranger;
  hold it in pledge if he does it for a wayward woman.

¹⁴ If a man loudly blesses his neighbor early in the morning,
  it will be taken as a curse.

¹⁵ A quarrelsome wife is like
  a constant dripping on a rainy day;
¹⁶ restraining her is like restraining the wind
  or grasping oil with the hand.

¹⁷ As iron sharpens iron,
  so one man sharpens another.

¹⁸ He who tends a fig tree will eat its fruit,
  and he who looks after his master will
  be honored.

¹⁹ As water reflects a face,
  so a man's heart reflects the man.

²⁰ Death and Destruction[a] are never satisfied,
  and neither are the eyes of man.

²¹ The crucible for silver and the furnace for
  gold,
  but man is tested by the praise he
  receives.

²² Though you grind a fool in a mortar,
  grinding him like grain with a pestle,
  you will not remove his folly from him.

²³ Be sure you know the condition of your
  flocks,
  give careful attention to your herds;
²⁴ for riches do not endure forever,
  and a crown is not secure for all
  generations.
²⁵ When the hay is removed and new
  growth appears
  and the grass from the hills is gathered in,
²⁶ the lambs will provide you with clothing,
  and the goats with the price of a field.
²⁷ You will have plenty of goats' milk
  to feed you and your family
  and to nourish your servant girls.

Sharpening One Another

If you found out that one of your Christian buddies was doing something he shouldn't—something potentially harmful to himself or his relationship with God—would you say anything to him about it? If he told you to back off, would you bring up the subject again (with a compassionate spirit, of course)? That's what "sharpening" one another is all about. It's about saying—and listening to—the tough things that need to be said in order for us to be at our sharpest as followers of God.

»» live the adventure »» Pr 27:17

28

The wicked man flees though no one pursues,
  but the righteous are as bold as a lion.

ᵃ 20 Hebrew *Sheol and Abaddon*

2 When a country is rebellious, it has many rulers,
    but a man of understanding and knowledge maintains order.

3 A ruler[a] who oppresses the poor
    is like a driving rain that leaves no crops.

4 Those who forsake the law praise the wicked,
    but those who keep the law resist them.

5 Evil men do not understand justice,
    but those who seek the LORD understand it fully.

6 Better a poor man whose walk is blameless
    than a rich man whose ways are perverse.

7 He who keeps the law is a discerning son,
    but a companion of gluttons disgraces his father.

now or never

PR 28:6

Do you think rich people are more likely to make better choices in life than poor people are? Which is worth more to you— a life lived faithfully to God or an armload of cash?

8 He who increases his wealth by exorbitant interest
    amasses it for another, who will be kind to the poor.

9 If anyone turns a deaf ear to the law,
    even his prayers are detestable.

10 He who leads the upright along an evil path
    will fall into his own trap,
    but the blameless will receive a good inheritance.

11 A rich man may be wise in his own eyes,
    but a poor man who has discernment sees through him.

12 When the righteous triumph, there is great elation;
    but when the wicked rise to power, men go into hiding.

13 He who conceals his sins does not prosper,
    but whoever confesses and renounces them finds mercy.

14 Blessed is the man who always fears the LORD,
    but he who hardens his heart falls into trouble.

15 Like a roaring lion or a charging bear
    is a wicked man ruling over a helpless people.

16 A tyrannical ruler lacks judgment,
    but he who hates ill-gotten gain will enjoy a long life.

17 A man tormented by the guilt of murder
    will be a fugitive till death;
    let no one support him.

18 He whose walk is blameless is kept safe,
    but he whose ways are perverse will suddenly fall.

19 He who works his land will have abundant food,
    but the one who chases fantasies will have his fill of poverty.

20 A faithful man will be richly blessed,
    but one eager to get rich will not go unpunished.

---

a 3 Or A poor man

²¹ To show partiality is not good—
    yet a man will do wrong for a piece of bread.

²² A stingy man is eager to get rich
    and is unaware that poverty awaits him.

²³ He who rebukes a man will in the end gain more favor
    than he who has a flattering tongue.

²⁴ He who robs his father or mother
    and says, "It's not wrong"—
    he is partner to him who destroys.

²⁵ A greedy man stirs up dissension,
    but he who trusts in the LORD will prosper.

²⁶ He who trusts in himself is a fool,
    but he who walks in wisdom is kept safe.

²⁷ He who gives to the poor will lack nothing,
    but he who closes his eyes to them receives many curses.

²⁸ When the wicked rise to power, people go into hiding;
    but when the wicked perish, the righteous thrive.

 A man who remains stiff-necked after many rebukes
    will suddenly be destroyed—without remedy.

² When the righteous thrive, the people rejoice;
    when the wicked rule, the people groan.

³ A man who loves wisdom brings joy to his father,
    but a companion of prostitutes squanders his wealth.

⁴ By justice a king gives a country stability,
    but one who is greedy for bribes tears it down.

⁵ Whoever flatters his neighbor
    is spreading a net for his feet.

⁶ An evil man is snared by his own sin,
    but a righteous one can sing and be glad.

⁷ The righteous care about justice for the poor,
    but the wicked have no such concern.

⁸ Mockers stir up a city,
    but wise men turn away anger.

⁹ If a wise man goes to court with a fool,
    the fool rages and scoffs, and there is no peace.

¹⁰ Bloodthirsty men hate a man of integrity
    and seek to kill the upright.

¹¹ A fool gives full vent to his anger,
    but a wise man keeps himself under control.

¹² If a ruler listens to lies,
    all his officials become wicked.

¹³ The poor man and the oppressor have this in common:
    The LORD gives sight to the eyes of both.

¹⁴ If a king judges the poor with fairness,
    his throne will always be secure.

¹⁵ The rod of correction imparts wisdom,
but a child left to himself disgraces his mother.

¹⁶ When the wicked thrive, so does sin,
but the righteous will see their downfall.

¹⁷ Discipline your son, and he will give you peace;
he will bring delight to your soul.

¹⁸ Where there is no revelation, the people cast off restraint;
but blessed is he who keeps the law.

¹⁹ A servant cannot be corrected by mere words;
though he understands, he will not respond.

²⁰ Do you see a man who speaks in haste?
There is more hope for a fool than for him.

²¹ If a man pampers his servant from youth,
he will bring grief[a] in the end.

²² An angry man stirs up dissension,
and a hot-tempered one commits many sins.

²³ A man's pride brings him low,
but a man of lowly spirit gains honor.

²⁴ The accomplice of a thief is his own enemy;
he is put under oath and dare not testify.

²⁵ Fear of man will prove to be a snare,
but whoever trusts in the LORD is kept safe.

²⁶ Many seek an audience with a ruler,
but it is from the LORD that man gets justice.

²⁷ The righteous detest the dishonest;
the wicked detest the upright.

SAYINGS OF AGUR

The sayings of Agur son of Jakeh—an oracle[b]:

This man declared to Ithiel,
to Ithiel and to Ucal:[c]

² "I am the most ignorant of men;
I do not have a man's understanding.
³ I have not learned wisdom,
nor have I knowledge of the Holy One.
⁴ Who has gone up to heaven and come down?
Who has gathered up the wind in the hollow of his hands?
Who has wrapped up the waters in his cloak?
Who has established all the ends of the earth?
What is his name, and the name of his son?
Tell me if you know!

⁵ "Every word of God is flawless;
he is a shield to those who take refuge in him.

---

a 21 The meaning of the Hebrew for this word is uncertain.　*b 1* Or *Jakeh of Massa*　*c 1* Masoretic Text; with a different word division of the Hebrew *declared, "I am weary, O God; / I am weary, O God, and faint.*

6 Do not add to his words,
    or he will rebuke you and prove you a liar.

7 "Two things I ask of you, O LORD;
    do not refuse me before I die:
8 Keep falsehood and lies far from me;
    give me neither poverty nor riches,
    but give me only my daily bread.
9 Otherwise, I may have too much and disown you
    and say, 'Who is the LORD?'
  Or I may become poor and steal,
    and so dishonor the name of my God.

10 "Do not slander a servant to his master,
    or he will curse you, and you will pay for it.

11 "There are those who curse their fathers
    and do not bless their mothers;
12 those who are pure in their own eyes
    and yet are not cleansed of their filth;
13 those whose eyes are ever so haughty,
    whose glances are so disdainful;
14 those whose teeth are swords
    and whose jaws are set with knives
  to devour the poor from the earth,
    the needy from among mankind.

15 "The leech has two daughters.
    'Give! Give!' they cry.

  "There are three things that are never satisfied,
    four that never say, 'Enough!':
16 the grave,ᵃ the barren womb,
    land, which is never satisfied with water,
    and fire, which never says, 'Enough!'

17 "The eye that mocks a father,
    that scorns obedience to a mother,
  will be pecked out by the ravens of the valley,
    will be eaten by the vultures.

18 "There are three things that are too amazing for me,
    four that I do not understand:
19 the way of an eagle in the sky,
    the way of a snake on a rock,
  the way of a ship on the high seas,
    and the way of a man with a maiden.

20 "This is the way of an adulteress:
    She eats and wipes her mouth
    and says, 'I've done nothing wrong.'

21 "Under three things the earth trembles,
    under four it cannot bear up:
22 a servant who becomes king,
    a fool who is full of food,
23 an unloved woman who is married,
    and a maidservant who displaces her mistress.

ᵃ 16 Hebrew *Sheol*

²⁴ "Four things on earth are small,
    yet they are extremely wise:
²⁵ Ants are creatures of little strength,
    yet they store up their food in the summer;
²⁶ coneys[a] are creatures of little power,
    yet they make their home in the crags;
²⁷ locusts have no king,
    yet they advance together in ranks;
²⁸ a lizard can be caught with the hand,
    yet it is found in kings' palaces.

²⁹ "There are three things that are stately in their stride,
    four that move with stately bearing:
³⁰ a lion, mighty among beasts,
    who retreats before nothing;
³¹ a strutting rooster, a he-goat,
    and a king with his army around him.[b]

³² "If you have played the fool and exalted
        yourself,
    or if you have planned evil,
    clap your hand over your mouth!
³³ For as churning the milk produces
        butter,
    and as twisting the nose produces
        blood,
    so stirring up anger produces strife."

SAYINGS OF KING LEMUEL

31

The sayings of King Lemuel—an oracle[c] his mother taught him:

² "O my son, O son of my womb,
    O son of my vows,[d]
³ do not spend your strength on women,
    your vigor on those who ruin kings.

⁴ "It is not for kings, O Lemuel—
    not for kings to drink wine,
    not for rulers to crave beer,
⁵ lest they drink and forget what the law
        decrees,
    and deprive all the oppressed of their
        rights.
⁶ Give beer to those who are perishing,
    wine to those who are in
        anguish;
⁷ let them drink and forget their
        poverty
    and remember their misery no more.

⁸ "Speak up for those who cannot speak for themselves,
    for the rights of all who are destitute.
⁹ Speak up and judge fairly;
    defend the rights of the poor and needy."

Getting Involved

Are you willing to do what it takes to speak up for people who can't speak for themselves? To take care of people who can't take care of themselves? To defend those who can't defend themselves? To provide for people who can't provide for themselves? If you don't have what it takes right now, God can give it to you. All you have to do is ask for the courage and the love that comes straight from the heart of God.

»» live the adventure »» Pr 31:8-9

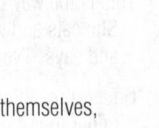

---

[a] *26* That is, the hyrax or rock badger   [b] *31* Or *king secure against revolt*   [c] *1* Or *of Lemuel king of Massa, which*   [d] *2* Or */ the answer to my prayers*

10 [a] A wife of noble character who can find?
　　She is worth far more than rubies.
11 Her husband has full confidence in her
　　and lacks nothing of value.
12 She brings him good, not harm,
　　all the days of her life.
13 She selects wool and flax
　　and works with eager hands.
14 She is like the merchant ships,
　　bringing her food from afar.

15 She gets up while it is still dark;
　　she provides food for her family
　　and portions for her servant girls.
16 She considers a field and buys it;
　　out of her earnings she plants a
　　vineyard.
17 She sets about her work vigorously;
　　her arms are strong for her tasks.
18 She sees that her trading is profitable,
　　and her lamp does not go out at
　　night.
19 In her hand she holds the distaff
　　and grasps the spindle with her
　　fingers.

∏Oꟼ OR ∏EVER
PR 31:10–31

If you were writing your own list to describe the ideal woman for you, what qualities and characteristics would you include? What things from the list in Proverbs 31 are most important to you in a future wife?

20 She opens her arms to the poor
　　and extends her hands to the needy.
21 When it snows, she has no fear for her household;
　　for all of them are clothed in scarlet.
22 She makes coverings for her bed;
　　she is clothed in fine linen and purple.
23 Her husband is respected at the city gate,
　　where he takes his seat among the elders of the land.
24 She makes linen garments and sells them,
　　and supplies the merchants with sashes.
25 She is clothed with strength and dignity;
　　she can laugh at the days to come.
26 She speaks with wisdom,
　　and faithful instruction is on her tongue.
27 She watches over the affairs of her household
　　and does not eat the bread of idleness.
28 Her children arise and call her blessed;
　　her husband also, and he praises her:
29 "Many women do noble things,
　　but you surpass them all."
30 Charm is deceptive, and beauty is fleeting;
　　but a woman who fears the LORD is to be praised.
31 Give her the reward she has earned,
　　and let her works bring her praise at the city gate.

---

[a] *10* Verses 10-31 are an acrostic, each verse beginning with a successive letter of the Hebrew alphabet.

ECCLESIASTES

« AT A GLANCE

Author
King Solomon (probably)

Audience
The people under Solomon's rule

Date
Possibly around 935 B.C.

Setting
Solomon went through a time in his life when he was apart from God, experimenting with sins like idolatry and materialism. In the book of Ecclesiastes he reflects on his experiences.

Verse to Remember
Now all has been heard; here is the conclusion of the matter: Fear God and keep his commandments, for this is the whole duty of man (12:13).

Theme to Consider
Life is meaningless apart from a relationship with the Lord. Solomon found that power, popularity, prestige and pleasure really don't satisfy. Only God can bring joy, satisfaction and fulfillment into our lives.

UNCHANGING TRUTH » Balance is the key to a healthy life. At least, that's what Solomon taught. He said there is a time for everything—laughing, crying, celebrating, mourning and even a time to search for answers (see 3:1–8). The key to experiencing all life has to offer, according to Solomon, is allowing God to guide you and be your source of strength throughout the different seasons of life—without getting stuck in any one of them.

That's easier said than done. Let's face it: Some seasons are a lot more enjoyable than others. Who wants to cry when you can keep laughing? Who wants to work when you can keep partying? Who wants to search for answers when you can just chill out and relax?

If there's such a thing as an expert on this topic, it was Solomon. As if possessing unmatched wisdom wasn't enough, this guy was loaded with cash. And he made the most of it, dedicating his life to buying, building and acquiring whatever he wanted. About the only thing that interrupted Solomon's spending sprees was his relentless pursuit of women.

So what does a guy who has all the money, toys and women he ever wanted say when he looks back on his life? "Everything was meaningless, a chasing after the wind; nothing was gained under the sun" (2:11). In other words, most of Solomon's life turned out to be one big waste of time.

That's what a lack of balance can do to a person. The secret to avoiding a fate such as Solomon faced is keeping everything in its God-ordained place. When it's time to have fun, give it all you've got. But when it's time to work, give that everything you've got too. Enjoy the time you spend with your friends, but never at the expense of time spent with your Creator.

You may not always know when the seasons of life are changing, but God does. And if you stay close to him, he will help you live the life that Solomon wished he would've lived.

LIFE LESSONS »

1. If all you care about are thrills, excitement and fun, you'll eventually discover—probably when you become bored or depressed—that you've wasted your life (2:1–3).

2. A good friend is more valuable than money or possessions (4:9–12).

3. The quicker you are to get angry, the more likely you are to do something you'll later regret (7:9).

4. Honoring and obeying God is the only thing that can fill your deepest need (12:13).

EVERYTHING IS MEANINGLESS

1 The words of the Teacher,[a] son of David, king in Jerusalem:

> 2 "Meaningless! Meaningless!"
>   says the Teacher.
> "Utterly meaningless!
>   Everything is meaningless."

> 3 What does man gain from all his labor
>   at which he toils under the sun?
> 4 Generations come and generations go,
>   but the earth remains forever.
> 5 The sun rises and the sun sets,
>   and hurries back to where it rises.
> 6 The wind blows to the south
>   and turns to the north;
> round and round it goes,
>   ever returning on its course.
> 7 All streams flow into the sea,
>   yet the sea is never full.
> To the place the streams come from,
>   there they return again.
> 8 All things are wearisome,
>   more than one can say.
> The eye never has enough of seeing,
>   nor the ear its fill of hearing.
> 9 What has been will be again,
>   what has been done will be done again;
>   there is nothing new under the sun.
> 10 Is there anything of which one can say,
>   "Look! This is something new"?
> It was here already, long ago;
>   it was here before our time.
> 11 There is no remembrance of men of old,
>   and even those who are yet to come
> will not be remembered
>   by those who follow.

WISDOM IS MEANINGLESS

12 I, the Teacher, was king over Israel in Jerusalem. 13 I devoted myself to study and to explore by wisdom all that is done under heaven. What a heavy burden God has laid on men! 14 I have seen all the things that are done under the sun; all of them are meaningless, a chasing after the wind.

> 15 What is twisted cannot be straightened;
>   what is lacking cannot be counted.

16 I thought to myself, "Look, I have grown and increased in wisdom more than anyone who has ruled over Jerusalem before me; I have experienced much of wisdom and knowledge." 17 Then I applied myself to the understanding of wisdom, and also of madness and folly, but I learned that this, too, is a chasing after the wind.

> 18 For with much wisdom comes much sorrow;
>   the more knowledge, the more grief.

---

a 1 Or *leader of the assembly*; also in verses 2 and 12

PLEASURES ARE MEANINGLESS

2 I thought in my heart, "Come now, I will test you with pleasure to find out what is good." But that also proved to be meaningless. [2]"Laughter," I said, "is foolish. And what does pleasure accomplish?" [3]I tried cheering myself with wine, and embracing folly—my mind still guiding me with wisdom. I wanted to see what was worthwhile for men to do under heaven during the few days of their lives.

[4]I undertook great projects: I built houses for myself and planted vineyards. [5]I made gardens and parks and planted all kinds of fruit trees in them. [6]I made reservoirs to water groves of flourishing trees. [7]I bought male and female slaves and had other slaves who were born in my house. I also owned more herds and flocks than anyone in Jerusalem before me. [8]I amassed silver and gold for myself, and the treasure of kings and provinces. I acquired men and women singers, and a harem[a] as well—the delights of the heart of man. [9]I became greater by far than anyone in Jerusalem before me. In all this my wisdom stayed with me.

> [10]I denied myself nothing my eyes desired;
> I refused my heart no pleasure.
> My heart took delight in all my work,
> and this was the reward for all my labor.
> [11]Yet when I surveyed all that my hands had done
> and what I had toiled to achieve,
> everything was meaningless, a chasing after the wind;
> nothing was gained under the sun.

WISDOM AND FOLLY ARE MEANINGLESS

> [12]Then I turned my thoughts to consider wisdom,
> and also madness and folly.
> What more can the king's successor do
> than what has already been done?
> [13]I saw that wisdom is better than folly,
> just as light is better than darkness.
> [14]The wise man has eyes in his head,
> while the fool walks in the darkness;
> but I came to realize
> that the same fate overtakes them both.

[15]Then I thought in my heart,

> "The fate of the fool will overtake me also.
> What then do I gain by being wise?"
> I said in my heart,
> "This too is meaningless."
> [16]For the wise man, like the fool, will not be long remembered;
> in days to come both will be forgotten.
> Like the fool, the wise man too must die!

TOIL IS MEANINGLESS

[17]So I hated life, because the work that is done under the sun was grievous to me. All of it is meaningless, a chasing after the wind. [18]I hated all the things I had toiled for under the sun, because I must leave them to the one who comes after me. [19]And who knows whether he will be a wise man or a fool? Yet he will have control over all the work into which I have poured my effort and skill under the sun. This too is meaningless. [20]So my heart began to despair over all my toilsome labor under the sun. [21]For a man may do his work with wisdom, knowledge and skill, and then he must leave all he owns to someone who has not worked for it. This too is meaningless and a great misfortune. [22]What does a man get for all the toil and anxious striving with which he labors under the sun? [23]All his days his work is pain and grief; even at night his mind does not rest. This too is meaningless.

---

[a] 8 The meaning of the Hebrew for this phrase is uncertain.

24A man can do nothing better than to eat and drink and find satisfaction in his work. This too, I see, is from the hand of God, 25for without him, who can eat or find enjoyment? 26To the man who pleases him, God gives wisdom, knowledge and happiness, but to the sinner he gives the task of gathering and storing up wealth to hand it over to the one who pleases God. This too is meaningless, a chasing after the wind.

A TIME FOR EVERYTHING

3 There is a time for everything,
and a season for every activity under heaven:

2a time to be born and a time to die,
a time to plant and a time to uproot,
3a time to kill and a time to heal,
a time to tear down and a time to build,
4a time to weep and a time to laugh,
a time to mourn and a time to dance,
5a time to scatter stones and a time to gather them,
a time to embrace and a time to refrain,
6a time to search and a time to give up,

a time to keep and a time to throw away,
7 a time to tear and a time to mend,
a time to be silent and a time to speak,
8 a time to love and a time to hate,
a time for war and a time for peace.

9What does the worker gain from his toil? 10I have seen the burden God has laid on men. 11He has made everything beautiful in its time. He has also set eternity in the hearts of men; yet they cannot fathom what God has done from beginning to end. 12I know that there is nothing better for men than to be happy and do good while they live. 13That everyone may eat and drink, and find satisfaction in all his toil—this is the gift of God. 14I know that everything God does will endure forever; nothing can be added to it and nothing taken from it. God does it so that men will revere him.

15Whatever is has already been,
and what will be has been before;
and God will call the past to account.a

16And I saw something else under the sun:

In the place of judgment—wickedness was there,
in the place of justice—wickedness was there.

17I thought in my heart,

"God will bring to judgment
both the righteous and the wicked,

NOW OR NEVER
ECC 3:1–8

Do you ever feel out of step with the rest of the world—lonely when everyone else seems to be with friends, bored when everyone else seems to be having a good time, struggling when everyone else seems to be breezing through life?

Enjoying Satisfaction

What kinds of things give you satisfaction? Getting an A on a paper you nearly killed yourself to finish? Learning the chords to one of your favorite songs? Increasing the weight on your bench press bar by 20 pounds? Whatever it is that gives you satisfaction or makes you feel good about yourself, give thanks to God for it. He's the one who gives true satisfaction and joy.

»» live the adventure »» Ecc 2:24–26

---

a 15 Or God calls back the past

for there will be a time for every activity,
a time for every deed."

[18]I also thought, "As for men, God tests them so that they may see that they are like the animals. [19]Man's fate is like that of the animals; the same fate awaits them both: As one dies, so dies the other. All have the same breath[a]; man has no advantage over the animal. Everything is meaningless. [20]All go to the same place; all come from dust, and to dust all return. [21]Who knows if the spirit of man rises upward and if the spirit of the animal[b] goes down into the earth?"

[22]So I saw that there is nothing better for a man than to enjoy his work, because that is his lot. For who can bring him to see what will happen after him?

OPPRESSION, TOIL, FRIENDLESSNESS

4 Again I looked and saw all the oppression that was taking place under the sun:

I saw the tears of the oppressed—
and they have no comforter;
power was on the side of their oppressors—
and they have no comforter.
[2]And I declared that the dead,
who had already died,
are happier than the living,
who are still alive.
[3]But better than both
is he who has not yet been,
who has not seen the evil
that is done under the sun.

[4]And I saw that all labor and all achievement spring from man's envy of his neighbor. This too is meaningless, a chasing after the wind.

[5]The fool folds his hands
and ruins himself.
[6]Better one handful with tranquillity
than two handfuls with toil
and chasing after the wind.

[7]Again I saw something meaningless under the sun:

NOW OR NEVER
ECC 4:9–12

Do you have a friend you can count on when you really need help? More important, are you the kind of person that others can count on when they need a godly friend?

[8]There was a man all alone;
he had neither son nor brother.
There was no end to his toil,
yet his eyes were not content with his
wealth.
"For whom am I toiling," he asked,
"and why am I depriving myself of
enjoyment?"
This too is meaningless—
a miserable business!

[9]Two are better than one,
because they have a good return for
their work:
[10]If one falls down,
his friend can help him up.
But pity the man who falls
and has no one to help him up!
[11]Also, if two lie down together, they will keep warm.

---

[a] 19 Or *spirit*   [b] 21 Or *Who knows the spirit of man, which rises upward, or the spirit of the animal, which*

But how can one keep warm alone?
¹²Though one may be overpowered,
two can defend themselves.
A cord of three strands is not quickly broken.

ADVANCEMENT IS MEANINGLESS

¹³Better a poor but wise youth than an old but foolish king who no longer knows how to take warning. ¹⁴The youth may have come from prison to the kingship, or he may have been born in poverty within his kingdom. ¹⁵I saw that all who lived and walked under the sun followed the youth, the king's successor. ¹⁶There was no end to all the people who were before them. But those who came later were not pleased with the successor. This too is meaningless, a chasing after the wind.

STAND IN AWE OF GOD

5 Guard your steps when you go to the house of God. Go near to listen rather than to offer the sacrifice of fools, who do not know that they do wrong.

²Do not be quick with your mouth,
do not be hasty in your heart
to utter anything before God.
God is in heaven
and you are on earth,
so let your words be few.
³As a dream comes when there are many cares,
so the speech of a fool when there are many words.

⁴When you make a vow to God, do not delay in fulfilling it. He has no pleasure in fools; fulfill your vow. ⁵It is better not to vow than to make a vow and not fulfill it. ⁶Do not let your mouth lead you into sin. And do not protest to the ⌊temple⌋ messenger, "My vow was a mistake." Why should God be angry at what you say and destroy the work of your hands? ⁷Much dreaming and many words are meaningless. Therefore stand in awe of God.

RICHES ARE MEANINGLESS

⁸If you see the poor oppressed in a district, and justice and rights denied, do not be surprised at such things; for one official is eyed by a higher one, and over them both are others higher still. ⁹The increase from the land is taken by all; the king himself profits from the fields.

¹⁰Whoever loves money never has money
enough;
whoever loves wealth is never
satisfied with his income.
This too is meaningless.

¹¹As goods increase,
so do those who consume them.
And what benefit are they to the owner
except to feast his eyes on them?

¹²The sleep of a laborer is sweet,
whether he eats little or much,
but the abundance of a rich man
permits him no sleep.

NOW OR NEVER
ECC 5:10

What's your relationship with money and possessions? Would you describe it as a passing interest? Wishful thinking? A serious obsession? Do you think you have a healthy, Biblical attitude about material things?

¹³I have seen a grievous evil under the sun:

wealth hoarded to the harm of its owner,
¹⁴   or wealth lost through some misfortune,
so that when he has a son
there is nothing left for him.
¹⁵Naked a man comes from his mother's womb,

and as he comes, so he departs.
He takes nothing from his labor
that he can carry in his hand.

¹⁶This too is a grievous evil:

As a man comes, so he departs,
and what does he gain,
since he toils for the wind?
¹⁷All his days he eats in darkness,
with great frustration, affliction and anger.

¹⁸Then I realized that it is good and proper for a man to eat and drink, and to find satisfaction in his toilsome labor under the sun during the few days of life God has given him—for this is his lot. ¹⁹Moreover, when God gives any man wealth and possessions, and enables him to enjoy them, to accept his lot and be happy in his work—this is a gift of God. ²⁰He seldom reflects on the days of his life, because God keeps him occupied with gladness of heart.

6 I have seen another evil under the sun, and it weighs heavily on men: ²God gives a man wealth, possessions and honor, so that he lacks nothing his heart desires, but God does not enable him to enjoy them, and a stranger enjoys them instead. This is meaningless, a grievous evil.

³A man may have a hundred children and live many years; yet no matter how long he lives, if he cannot enjoy his prosperity and does not receive proper burial, I say that a stillborn child is better off than he. ⁴It comes without meaning, it departs in darkness, and in darkness its name is shrouded. ⁵Though it never saw the sun or knew anything, it has more rest than does that man— ⁶even if he lives a thousand years twice over but fails to enjoy his prosperity. Do not all go to the same place?

⁷All man's efforts are for his mouth,
yet his appetite is never satisfied.
⁸What advantage has a wise man
over a fool?
What does a poor man gain
by knowing how to conduct himself before others?
⁹Better what the eye sees
than the roving of the appetite.
This too is meaningless,
a chasing after the wind.

¹⁰Whatever exists has already been named,
and what man is has been known;
no man can contend
with one who is stronger than he.
¹¹The more the words,
the less the meaning,
and how does that profit anyone?

¹²For who knows what is good for a man in life, during the few and meaningless days he passes through like a shadow? Who can tell him what will happen under the sun after he is gone?

WISDOM

7 A good name is better than fine perfume,
and the day of death better than the day of birth.
²It is better to go to a house of mourning
than to go to a house of feasting,
for death is the destiny of every man;
the living should take this to heart.
³Sorrow is better than laughter,
because a sad face is good for the heart.
⁴The heart of the wise is in the house of mourning,

but the heart of fools is in the house of pleasure.
⁵ It is better to heed a wise man's rebuke
than to listen to the song of fools.
⁶ Like the crackling of thorns under the pot,
so is the laughter of fools.
This too is meaningless.

⁷ Extortion turns a wise man into a fool,
and a bribe corrupts the heart.

⁸ The end of a matter is better than its beginning,
and patience is better than pride.
⁹ Do not be quickly provoked in your spirit,
for anger resides in the lap of fools.

¹⁰ Do not say, "Why were the old days better than these?"
For it is not wise to ask such questions.

¹¹ Wisdom, like an inheritance, is a good
thing
and benefits those who see the sun.
¹² Wisdom is a shelter
as money is a shelter,
but the advantage of knowledge is this:
that wisdom preserves the life of its
possessor.

¹³ Consider what God has done:

Who can straighten
what he has made crooked?
¹⁴ When times are good, be happy;
but when times are bad, consider:
God has made the one
as well as the other.
Therefore, a man cannot discover
anything about his future.

¹⁵ In this meaningless life of mine I have seen both of these:

a righteous man perishing in his
righteousness,
and a wicked man living long in his
wickedness.
¹⁶ Do not be overrighteous,
neither be overwise—
why destroy yourself?
¹⁷ Do not be overwicked,
and do not be a fool—
why die before your time?
¹⁸ It is good to grasp the one
and not let go of the other.
The man who fears God will avoid all ⌐extremes⌐.ᵃ

¹⁹ Wisdom makes one wise man more powerful
than ten rulers in a city.

²⁰ There is not a righteous man on earth
who does what is right and never sins.

Using Your Wisdom

Wisdom can protect you from people who pretend to be your friends but are really trying to take advantage of you. Wisdom can protect you from losing your head when your life starts to crash down all around you. Wisdom can protect you from making a decision that will haunt you for the rest of your life. These are just a few of the reasons that God puts such a high priority on the pursuit of wisdom.

» live the adventure » Ecc 7:12

ᵃ 18 Or *will follow them both*

²¹ Do not pay attention to every word people say,
    or you may hear your servant cursing you—
²² for you know in your heart
    that many times you yourself have cursed others.

²³ All this I tested by wisdom and I said,

"I am determined to be wise"—
    but this was beyond me.
²⁴ Whatever wisdom may be,
    it is far off and most profound—
    who can discover it?
²⁵ So I turned my mind to understand,
    to investigate and to search out wisdom and the scheme of things
and to understand the stupidity of wickedness
    and the madness of folly.

²⁶ I find more bitter than death
    the woman who is a snare,
whose heart is a trap
    and whose hands are chains.
The man who pleases God will escape her,
    but the sinner she will ensnare.

²⁷ "Look," says the Teacher,ᵃ "this is what I have discovered:

"Adding one thing to another to discover the scheme of things—
²⁸   while I was still searching
    but not finding—
I found one ⌞upright⌟ man among a thousand,
    but not one ⌞upright⌟ woman among them all.
²⁹ This only have I found:
    God made mankind upright,
    but men have gone in search of many schemes."

Who is like the wise man?
    Who knows the explanation of things?
Wisdom brightens a man's face
    and changes its hard appearance.

OBEY THE KING

² Obey the king's command, I say, because you took an oath before God. ³ Do not be in a hurry to leave the king's presence. Do not stand up for a bad cause, for he will do whatever he pleases. ⁴ Since a king's word is supreme, who can say to him, "What are you doing?"

⁵ Whoever obeys his command will come to no harm,
    and the wise heart will know the proper time and procedure.
⁶ For there is a proper time and procedure for every matter,
    though a man's misery weighs heavily upon him.

⁷ Since no man knows the future,
    who can tell him what is to come?
⁸ No man has power over the wind to contain itᵇ;
    so no one has power over the day of his death.
As no one is discharged in time of war,
    so wickedness will not release those who practice it.

⁹ All this I saw, as I applied my mind to everything done under the sun. There is a time when a man

---

ᵃ 27 Or *leader of the assembly*   ᵇ 8 Or *over his spirit to retain it* lords it over others to his own[a] hurt. [10]Then too, I saw the wicked buried—those who used to come and go from the holy place and receive praise[b] in the city where they did this. This too is meaningless.

[11]When the sentence for a crime is not quickly carried out, the hearts of the people are filled with schemes to do wrong. [12]Although a wicked man commits a hundred crimes and still lives a long time, I know that it will go better with God-fearing men, who are reverent before God. [13]Yet because the wicked do not fear God, it will not go well with them, and their days will not lengthen like a shadow.

[14]There is something else meaningless that occurs on earth: righteous men who get what the wicked deserve, and wicked men who get what the righteous deserve. This too, I say, is meaningless. [15]So I commend the enjoyment of life, because nothing is better for a man under the sun than to eat and drink and be glad. Then joy will accompany him in his work all the days of the life God has given him under the sun.

[16]When I applied my mind to know wisdom and to observe man's labor on earth—his eyes not seeing sleep day or night— [17]then I saw all that God has done. No one can comprehend what goes on under the sun. Despite all his efforts to search it out, man cannot discover its meaning. Even if a wise man claims he knows, he cannot really comprehend it.

A COMMON DESTINY FOR ALL

9 So I reflected on all this and concluded that the righteous and the wise and what they do are in God's hands, but no man knows whether love or hate awaits him. [2]All share a common destiny—the righteous and the wicked, the good and the bad,[c] the clean and the unclean, those who offer sacrifices and those who do not.

> As it is with the good man,
>> so with the sinner;
> as it is with those who take oaths,
>> so with those who are afraid to take them.

[3]This is the evil in everything that happens under the sun: The same destiny overtakes all. The hearts of men, moreover, are full of evil and there is madness in their hearts while they live, and afterward they join the dead. [4]Anyone who is among the living has hope[d]—even a live dog is better off than a dead lion!

NOW OR NEVER

ECC 9:4–7

Someone once said, "There's only one guarantee about life—and that's death." No one can be sure about tomorrow, so make the most of today.

[5]For the living know that they will die,
>> but the dead know nothing;
> they have no further reward,
>> and even the memory of them is
>>> forgotten.
[6]Their love, their hate
>> and their jealousy have long since
>>> vanished;
> never again will they have a part
>> in anything that happens under the
>>> sun.

[7]Go, eat your food with gladness, and drink your wine with a joyful heart, for it is now that God favors what you do. [8]Always be clothed in white, and always anoint your head with oil. [9]Enjoy life with your wife, whom you love, all the days of this meaningless life that God has given you under the sun—all your meaningless days. For this is your lot in life and in your toilsome labor under the sun. [10]Whatever your hand finds to do, do it with all your might, for in the grave,[e] where you are going, there is neither working nor planning nor knowledge nor wisdom.

[11]I have seen something else under the sun:

> The race is not to the swift

---

[a] 9 Or *to their*   [b] 10 Some Hebrew manuscripts and Septuagint (Aquila); most Hebrew manuscripts *and are forgotten*   [c] 2 Septuagint (Aquila), Vulgate and Syriac; Hebrew does not have *and the bad*.   [d] 4 Or *What then is to be chosen? With all who live, there is hope*   [e] 10 Hebrew *Sheol*

or the battle to the strong,
nor does food come to the wise
or wealth to the brilliant
or favor to the learned;
but time and chance happen to them all.

¹²Moreover, no man knows when his hour will come:

As fish are caught in a cruel net,
or birds are taken in a snare,
so men are trapped by evil times
that fall unexpectedly upon them.

WISDOM BETTER THAN FOLLY

¹³I also saw under the sun this example of wisdom that greatly impressed me: ¹⁴There was once a small city with only a few people in it. And a powerful king came against it, surrounded it and built huge siegeworks against it. ¹⁵Now there lived in that city a man poor but wise, and he saved the city by his wisdom. But nobody remembered that poor man. ¹⁶So I said, "Wisdom is better than strength." But the poor man's wisdom is despised, and his words are no longer heeded.

¹⁷The quiet words of the wise are more to
be heeded
than the shouts of a ruler of fools.
¹⁸Wisdom is better than weapons of
war,
but one sinner destroys much
good.

As dead flies give perfume a bad smell,
so a little folly outweighs wisdom
and honor.
²The heart of the wise inclines to the right,
but the heart of the fool to the left.
³Even as he walks along the road,
the fool lacks sense
and shows everyone how stupid he is.
⁴If a ruler's anger rises against you,
do not leave your post;
calmness can lay great errors to rest.

⁵There is an evil I have seen under the sun,
the sort of error that arises from a ruler:
⁶Fools are put in many high positions,
while the rich occupy the low ones.
⁷I have seen slaves on horseback,
while princes go on foot like slaves.

⁸Whoever digs a pit may fall into it;
whoever breaks through a wall may be bitten by a snake.
⁹Whoever quarries stones may be injured by them;
whoever splits logs may be endangered by them.

¹⁰If the ax is dull
and its edge unsharpened,
more strength is needed
but skill will bring success.

Expecting the Unexpected

Making plans for the future is a wise thing to do; otherwise, you'll just drift from place to place with no goals and no direction. However, counting on your plans to go exactly as you intend is a setup for disappointment. Life is full of unexpected twists and turns—some of them good, some not so good. The best way to plan for life's ups and downs is to learn to be flexible and creative. If your old plan gets shot down by unexpected circumstances, come up with a new one and keep moving forward.

battlelines

» Thinking About Drinking

Q: You're how old?
A: Fifteen.

Q: How hard would it be for you to get alcohol if you wanted it?
A: About as hard as it would be to get a glass of orange juice.

Q: No way.
A: Oh, please. Most of my friends' parents have wet bars stocked with everything you could possibly want. And everybody knows which liquor stores check IDs and which ones don't. Besides, there's always somebody with an older brother or a college friend who can hook you up.

Q: How many of your friends drink?
A: Depends on what you mean by *drink*. If you're talking about getting wasted every weekend, it's maybe one out of four. But if you're just talking about having a beer or two at a party with some friends, it's probably 90 or 95 percent. Put it this way: I can probably count on both hands the people I know who *don't* drink.

Q: So do *you* drink?
A: Um . . . well, not yet.

Q: Do you think you *will* at some point?
A: It's hard to say. I definitely feel the pressure. But at the same time, I don't think you really *need* alcohol to have fun. And, if you do, how sad is that? I just can't help thinking about all the bad stuff that can happen. It's like, "Woo-hoo, look at me. I got blitzed at a party the other night, knocked up some girl I've never even seen before, wound up on the losing end of a fistfight, crashed my car into a mailbox and puked all over the place. Am I cool, or what!?" You know what I mean? It just seems like a huge gamble—but without the big payoff.

» The Bible and the Bottle

Let's be honest. The Bible never says, "Thou shalt not drink." But it does warn of the many different ways alcohol abuse can mess up our lives (see Proverbs 20:1; 23:29–35). It says that drunkenness is wrong (see Ephesians 5:18). On top of that, Scripture calls us to obey government authority (see Romans 13:1). So the Bible sends a pretty strong message about underage drinking.

Alcohol has a particularly dangerous, addictive potential for teens. The biggest alcohol-related problem among teenagers isn't daily or even compulsive drinking; it's *binge* drinking. Some guys can go days or weeks without touching a brew—and, in the process, convince themselves that they don't have a drinking problem. But when they *do* drink, they can't stop. Sometimes they literally drink themselves to death.

The Bible says, "Whether you eat or drink or whatever you do, do it all for the glory of God" (1 Corinthians 10:31). Perhaps *that's* the biggest issue for a teen guy wanting to follow Christ. If it's against the law for you, if your parents wouldn't approve and if it could lead to all sorts of other problems, how exactly can you *drink* to the glory of God?

Read more about Christians and alcohol at www.RevolutionBible.com.

11 If a snake bites before it is charmed,
    there is no profit for the charmer.

12 Words from a wise man's mouth are gracious,
    but a fool is consumed by his own lips.
13 At the beginning his words are folly;
    at the end they are wicked madness—
14   and the fool multiplies words.

No one knows what is coming—
    who can tell him what will happen after him?

15 A fool's work wearies him;
    he does not know the way to town.

16 Woe to you, O land whose king was a servant[a]
    and whose princes feast in the morning.
17 Blessed are you, O land whose king is of noble birth
    and whose princes eat at a proper time—
    for strength and not for drunkenness.

18 If a man is lazy, the rafters sag;
    if his hands are idle, the house leaks.

19 A feast is made for laughter,
    and wine makes life merry,
    but money is the answer for everything.

20 Do not revile the king even in your thoughts,
    or curse the rich in your bedroom,
because a bird of the air may carry your words,
    and a bird on the wing may report what you say.

BREAD UPON THE WATERS

11 Cast your bread upon the waters,
    for after many days you will find it again.
2 Give portions to seven, yes to eight,
    for you do not know what disaster may come upon the land.

3 If clouds are full of water,
    they pour rain upon the earth.
Whether a tree falls to the south or to
    the north,
    in the place where it falls, there will it
    lie.
4 Whoever watches the wind will not
    plant;
    whoever looks at the clouds will not
    reap.

5 As you do not know the path of the wind,
    or how the body is formed[b] in a
    mother's womb,
so you cannot understand the work of
    God,
    the Maker of all things.

6 Sow your seed in the morning,
    and at evening let not your hands be idle,

∏OⱲ OR ∏EVER
ECC 11:5

It's tempting to complain about why God made us the way that he did. But we can't really know all of his purposes—and what little we do know takes a lifetime to learn. God has a purpose for you. Hang around to find out what it is.

---

a 16 Or *king is a child*   b 5 Or *know how life* (or *the spirit*) / *enters the body being formed*

for you do not know which will succeed,
    whether this or that,
    or whether both will do equally well.

REMEMBER YOUR CREATOR WHILE YOUNG

[7]Light is sweet,
    and it pleases the eyes to see the sun.
[8]However many years a man may live,
    let him enjoy them all.
But let him remember the days of darkness,
    for they will be many.
    Everything to come is meaningless.

[9]Be happy, young man, while you are young,
    and let your heart give you joy in the days of your youth.
Follow the ways of your heart
    and whatever your eyes see,
but know that for all these things
    God will bring you to judgment.
[10]So then, banish anxiety from your heart
    and cast off the troubles of your body,
    for youth and vigor are meaningless.

Remember your Creator
    in the days of your youth,
before the days of trouble come
    and the years approach when you will say,
    "I find no pleasure in them"—
[2]before the sun and the light
    and the moon and the stars grow dark,
    and the clouds return after the rain;
[3]when the keepers of the house tremble,
    and the strong men stoop,
when the grinders cease because they are few,
    and those looking through the windows grow dim;
[4]when the doors to the street are closed
    and the sound of grinding fades;
when men rise up at the sound of birds,
    but all their songs grow faint;
[5]when men are afraid of heights
    and of dangers in the streets;
when the almond tree blossoms
    and the grasshopper drags himself along
    and desire no longer is stirred.
Then man goes to his eternal home
    and mourners go about the streets.

[6]Remember him—before the silver cord is severed,
    or the golden bowl is broken;
before the pitcher is shattered at the spring,
    or the wheel broken at the well,
[7]and the dust returns to the ground it came from,
    and the spirit returns to God who gave it.

[8]"Meaningless! Meaningless!" says the Teacher.[a]
    "Everything is meaningless!"

---

[a] 8 Or *the leader of the assembly*; also in verses 9 and 10

THE CONCLUSION OF THE MATTER

⁹Not only was the Teacher wise, but also he imparted knowledge to the people. He pondered and searched out and set in order many proverbs. ¹⁰The Teacher searched to find just the right words, and what he wrote was upright and true.

¹¹The words of the wise are like goads, their collected sayings like firmly embedded nails—given by one Shepherd. ¹²Be warned, my son, of anything in addition to them.

Of making many books there is no end, and much study wearies the body.

¹³Now all has been heard;
here is the conclusion of the matter:
Fear God and keep his commandments,
for this is the whole ⌊duty⌋ of man.
¹⁴For God will bring every deed into judgment,
including every hidden thing,
whether it is good or evil.

challenge notes

To: my_son

ECC 12:10-13

heavenly_father: things get more complicated as you grow older. the pressures of the world can make you lose sight of what's important. but if you come to me now, we can build a relationship that will be a stronghold for you during the storms of life.

SONG OF SONGS

Author
King Solomon (probably)

Audience
People of Israel

Date
Early in Solomon's reign, around 965 B.C.

Setting
The king's palace and the Shulammite woman's vineyard (in Israel).

Verse to Remember
Many waters cannot quench love; rivers cannot wash it away. If one were to give all the wealth of his house for love, it would be utterly scorned (8:7).

Theme to Consider
Sex is God's amazing gift to a husband and wife. Song of Songs gives us a proper perspective of this human love between a man and a woman.

UNCHANGING TRUTH » Have you ever heard someone complain that God wants to spoil our fun when it comes to sex? Show that person Song of Songs. This short, eight-chapter book features pure passion and genuine sexuality in such a wonderful context that it shows just how pathetic pornography and other distortions of sex really are. And the fact that God made this book part of his written Word illustrates just how much he wants us to enjoy his gift of sex.

Don't get the wrong idea, though. We're not talking about Bible porn here. This isn't some green light for quick thrills or erotic fantasies. We're talking about *complete* sex—the kind of physical, emotional and even spiritual union that God had in mind when he created this pleasure experience for our bodies.

In other words, we're talking about sex between a husband and a wife. We're talking about the freedom two people in such a relationship have to explore each other's bodies and please one another without guilt, shame, embarrassment, damaged reputations or rejection—not to mention extramarital pregnancy and STDs.

In a world of instant gratification, the idea of waiting for sex seems ridiculously prudish, old-fashioned and sometimes even impossible. But it's not. God is available 24/7 to help you when your appetite for sex gets out of control.

Remember, good things do come to those who wait . . . and incredible things happen to those who wait to have sex as God intended it.

LIFE LESSONS »

1   Your real friends will be thrilled for you when you fall in love (1:4b).

2   Passion is an important (and legitimate) part of any intimate relationship (2:8–13).

3   Love can be expressed in any number of ways—the more romantic and personal, the better (4:1–7).

1 Solomon's Song of Songs.

BELOVED[a]

2 Let him kiss me with the kisses of his mouth—
   for your love is more delightful than wine.
3 Pleasing is the fragrance of your perfumes;
   your name is like perfume poured out.
   No wonder the maidens love you!
4 Take me away with you—let us hurry!
   Let the king bring me into his chambers.

FRIENDS

We rejoice and delight in you[b];
   we will praise your love more than
      wine.

BELOVED

How right they are to adore you!

5 Dark am I, yet lovely,
   O daughters of Jerusalem,
   dark like the tents of Kedar,
   like the tent curtains of Solomon.[c]
6 Do not stare at me because I am dark,
   because I am darkened by the sun.
My mother's sons were angry with me
   and made me take care of the
      vineyards;
   my own vineyard I have neglected.
7 Tell me, you whom I love, where you
      graze your flock
   and where you rest your sheep at
      midday.
Why should I be like a veiled woman
   beside the flocks of your friends?

FRIENDS

8 If you do not know, most beautiful of
      women,
   follow the tracks of the sheep
and graze your young goats
   by the tents of the shepherds.

LOVER

9 I liken you, my darling, to a mare
   harnessed to one of the chariots of Pharaoh.
10 Your cheeks are beautiful with earrings,
   your neck with strings of jewels.
11 We will make you earrings of gold,
   studded with silver.

Waiting for Sex

Having sex outside of God's plan (meaning outside of marriage) is like secretly raiding the Christmas tree before Christmas morning. What joy is there for you or anyone else if you open a gift that was intended for someone else? And even if the gift you opened was meant for you, would that make it right? No. When you have sex outside of marriage, you take and give a priceless gift at the wrong time, and maybe to the wrong person. And worst of all, it's certain that you are hurting the ultimate gift-giver, God, whose plan is for you and your future wife to enjoy your sexual union.

---

a Primarily on the basis of the gender of the Hebrew pronouns used, male and female speakers are indicated in the margins by the captions *Lover* and *Beloved* respectively. The words of others are marked *Friends*. In some instances the divisions and their captions are debatable. b 4 The Hebrew is masculine singular. c 5 Or *Salma*

BELOVED

¹²While the king was at his table,
my perfume spread its fragrance.
¹³My lover is to me a sachet of myrrh
resting between my breasts.
¹⁴My lover is to me a cluster of henna blossoms
from the vineyards of En Gedi.

LOVER

¹⁵How beautiful you are, my darling!
Oh, how beautiful!
Your eyes are doves.

BELOVED

¹⁶How handsome you are, my lover!
Oh, how charming!
And our bed is verdant.

LOVER

¹⁷The beams of our house are cedars;
our rafters are firs.

BELOVED[a]

2

I am a rose[b] of Sharon,
a lily of the valleys.

LOVER

²Like a lily among thorns
is my darling among the maidens.

BELOVED

³Like an apple tree among the trees of the forest
is my lover among the young men.
I delight to sit in his shade,
and his fruit is sweet to my taste.
⁴He has taken me to the banquet hall,
and his banner over me is love.
⁵Strengthen me with raisins,
refresh me with apples,
for I am faint with love.
⁶His left arm is under my head,
and his right arm embraces me.
⁷Daughters of Jerusalem, I charge you
by the gazelles and by the does of
the field:
Do not arouse or awaken love
until it so desires.

⁸Listen! My lover!
Look! Here he comes,

NOW OR NEVER

SS 2:4

What kind of lover will you be for your
wife? Will you be selfish, demanding and
irritable? Or will you be a provider, a pro-
tector and a nurturer? What banner will
you fly over your household?

leaping across the mountains,
bounding over the hills.
⁹My lover is like a gazelle or a young stag.
Look! There he stands behind our wall,

---

[a] Or *Lover*   [b] *1* Possibly a member of the crocus family

battlelines

» The New Girl (Cheating)

Q: What are you drooling at?
A: The new girl. See her over there—the one in the jean shorts? Man, oh man. I think I need to give her a call.

Q: Hold it. I thought you and Stacey were a thing.
A: Well . . . yeah, we are. But, I mean, we've been together for what, four months? Things are a little stale, if you know what I mean.

Q: So you're saying you want to dump her?
A: No, man! Not at all. I don't want to *dump* her. I'm just curious. Gotta check out all the possibilities, keep my options open, you know?

Q: What would Stacey say about your plan?
A: Why does she need to know? It's not like we're married. What about that old saying, "All's fair in love and war"? And like *she* doesn't notice other *guys*? . . . Oh, dude,

there goes the new girl. Look at the way she walks!

Q: So you're saying you can cheat all you want before you're married, but not after?
A: Where are you getting this "cheating" stuff? Isn't dating supposed to be about playing the field to make sure you find the right person? How can I do that unless I check out every option?

Q: I just think if that's the way you're going to operate, then you owe it to Stacey to cut her loose. I mean, it's one thing to check out your options. It's another to cheat on your girlfriend. That's just practice for cheating on your wife someday.
A: Stop it! Like I would cheat on my *wife*!

Q: You might if you develop those kinds of habits while you're single. Think about it.

» Girlfriend or Wife?

Faithfulness starts now, not later. The way you treat women today is a very good indicator of how you'll treat your future wife. There's nothing magical about saying the words "I do" in a wedding ceremony that guarantees a guy like Jay will suddenly morph into a man of strong commitment. A man will stay true to his bride only if he's already developed a faithful character over time.

You can do a lot of things now to invest in a great future marriage. If you're going to spend time with one girl in order to get to know her, then rein in your roving eyes. Keep the same rules for your girlfriend now that you plan to have for your wife later:

- Be faithful to her and her alone (see Proverbs 5:15–18).

- Remain sexually pure until marriage (see Hebrews 13:4).

- Treat her like a queen (see Song of Solomon 2:14).

- Remember the Golden Rule (see Matthew 7:12). You'd be furious if your girlfriend cheated on you—so don't do it to her!

Read more about getting along with girls at www.RevolutionBible.com.

gazing through the windows,
peering through the lattice.
¹⁰ My lover spoke and said to me,
"Arise, my darling,
my beautiful one, and come with me.
¹¹ See! The winter is past;
the rains are over and gone.
¹² Flowers appear on the earth;
the season of singing has come,
the cooing of doves
is heard in our land.
¹³ The fig tree forms its early fruit;
the blossoming vines spread their fragrance.
Arise, come, my darling;
my beautiful one, come with me."

LOVER

¹⁴ My dove in the clefts of the rock,
in the hiding places on the mountainside,
show me your face,
let me hear your voice;
for your voice is sweet,
and your face is lovely.
¹⁵ Catch for us the foxes,
the little foxes
that ruin the vineyards,
our vineyards that are in bloom.

BELOVED

¹⁶ My lover is mine and I am his;
he browses among the lilies.
¹⁷ Until the day breaks
and the shadows flee,
turn, my lover,
and be like a gazelle
or like a young stag
on the rugged hills. ª

All night long on my bed
I looked for the one my heart loves;
I looked for him but did not find him.
² I will get up now and go about the city,
through its streets and squares;
I will search for the one my heart loves.
So I looked for him but did not find him.
³ The watchmen found me
as they made their rounds in the city.
"Have you seen the one my heart loves?"
⁴ Scarcely had I passed them
when I found the one my heart loves.
I held him and would not let him go
till I had brought him to my mother's house,
to the room of the one who conceived me.
⁵ Daughters of Jerusalem, I charge you

ª 17 Or *the hills of Bether*

by the gazelles and by the does of the field:
Do not arouse or awaken love
until it so desires.

⁶Who is this coming up from the desert
like a column of smoke,
perfumed with myrrh and incense
made from all the spices of the
merchant?
⁷Look! It is Solomon's carriage,
escorted by sixty warriors,
the noblest of Israel,
⁸all of them wearing the sword,
all experienced in battle,
each with his sword at his side,
prepared for the terrors of the night.
⁹King Solomon made for himself the
carriage;
he made it of wood from Lebanon.
¹⁰Its posts he made of silver,
its base of gold.
Its seat was upholstered with purple,
its interior lovingly inlaid
by ª the daughters of Jerusalem.
¹¹Come out, you daughters of Zion,
and look at King Solomon wearing
the crown,
the crown with which his mother
crowned him
on the day of his wedding,
the day his heart rejoiced.

Guarding Against Lust

Solomon uses a poetic term for it: "Do not arouse or awaken love." But you get the idea of what he's talking about, don't you? Letting your hormones run wild, awaking desires that you just can't control even when you think you can. Whether you call it first base or second base, you know there's a point where innocent romance becomes not-so-innocent lust. That's the point you have to stop from reaching. When lust gets even the tiniest foothold in your life, it sets in motion a pattern of sin that can do life-changing damage.

LOVER
4

How beautiful you are, my darling!
Oh, how beautiful!
Your eyes behind your veil are doves.
Your hair is like a flock of goats
descending from Mount Gilead.
²Your teeth are like a flock of sheep just
shorn,
coming up from the washing.
Each has its twin;
not one of them is alone.
³Your lips are like a scarlet ribbon;
your mouth is lovely.
Your temples behind your veil
are like the halves of a pomegranate.
⁴Your neck is like the tower of David,
built with elegance ª;
on it hang a thousand shields,
all of them shields of warriors.

NOW OR NEVER
SS 4:1–7

Do you feel a little weird reading Solomon's love notes to his fiancée? There's a sense in which the passion between a husband and wife is a private thing. But at the same time, Solomon couldn't keep quiet about his love . . . and rightly so.

⁵Your two breasts are like two fawns,
like twin fawns of a gazelle
that browse among the lilies.

ª 10 Or *its inlaid interior a gift of love / from*   ᵇ 4 The meaning of the Hebrew for this word is uncertain.

⁶Until the day breaks
  and the shadows flee,
I will go to the mountain of myrrh
  and to the hill of incense.
⁷All beautiful you are, my darling;
  there is no flaw in you.

⁸Come with me from Lebanon, my bride,
  come with me from Lebanon.
Descend from the crest of Amana,
  from the top of Senir, the summit of Hermon,
from the lions' dens
  and the mountain haunts of the leopards.
⁹You have stolen my heart, my sister, my bride;
  you have stolen my heart
with one glance of your eyes,
  with one jewel of your necklace.
¹⁰How delightful is your love, my sister, my bride!
  How much more pleasing is your love than wine,
  and the fragrance of your perfume than any spice!
¹¹Your lips drop sweetness as the honeycomb, my bride;
  milk and honey are under your tongue.
  The fragrance of your garments is like that of Lebanon.
¹²You are a garden locked up, my sister, my bride;
  you are a spring enclosed, a sealed fountain.
¹³Your plants are an orchard of pomegranates
  with choice fruits,
  with henna and nard,
¹⁴   nard and saffron,
  calamus and cinnamon,
  with every kind of incense tree,
  with myrrh and aloes
  and all the finest spices.
¹⁵You are^a a garden fountain,
  a well of flowing water
  streaming down from Lebanon.

BELOVED

¹⁶Awake, north wind,
  and come, south wind!
Blow on my garden,
  that its fragrance may spread abroad.
Let my lover come into his garden
  and taste its choice fruits.

LOVER

I have come into my garden, my sister, my bride;
  I have gathered my myrrh with my spice.
I have eaten my honeycomb and my honey;
  I have drunk my wine and my milk.

FRIENDS

Eat, O friends, and drink;
  drink your fill, O lovers.

---

^a *15* Or *I am* (spoken by the *Beloved*)

² I slept but my heart was awake.
Listen! My lover is knocking:
"Open to me, my sister, my darling,
my dove, my flawless one.
My head is drenched with dew,
my hair with the dampness of the night."
³ I have taken off my robe—
must I put it on again?
I have washed my feet—
must I soil them again?
⁴ My lover thrust his hand through the latch-opening;
my heart began to pound for him.
⁵ I arose to open for my lover,
and my hands dripped with myrrh,
my fingers with flowing myrrh,
on the handles of the lock.
⁶ I opened for my lover,
but my lover had left; he was gone.
My heart sank at his departure.[a]
I looked for him but did not find him.
I called him but he did not answer.
⁷ The watchmen found me
as they made their rounds in the city.
They beat me, they bruised me;
they took away my cloak,
those watchmen of the walls!
⁸ O daughters of Jerusalem, I charge you—
if you find my lover,
what will you tell him?
Tell him I am faint with love.

FRIENDS

⁹ How is your beloved better than others,
most beautiful of women?
How is your beloved better than others,
that you charge us so?

BELOVED

¹⁰ My lover is radiant and ruddy,
outstanding among ten thousand.
¹¹ His head is purest gold;
his hair is wavy
and black as a raven.
¹² His eyes are like doves
by the water streams,
washed in milk,
mounted like jewels.
¹³ His cheeks are like beds of spice
yielding perfume.
His lips are like lilies
dripping with myrrh.
¹⁴ His arms are rods of gold
set with chrysolite.

ᵃ *6* Or *heart had gone out to him when he spoke*

battlelines

» *The Great Constant (Sex)*

Q: Wow. What exactly were they trying to sell in that commercial?
A: I know. Why do they have to do that? Like I don't already have enough problems with daydreaming about sex!

Q: Struggling, huh?
A: That's a nice way of putting it. Everywhere I look, sex is shoved in my face—TV, movies, CD covers, ads . . . even some of the girls at school, with the way they dress! No wonder sex is on my mind 24/7.

Q: So do you—
A: And then my friends talking nonstop about what they did or what they'd like to do with this girl or that one. I'm not going to lie; I think I'm becoming obsessed.

Q: So, what is—
A: And I know all about what the Bible says, and I believe in it. I want to do the right thing and wait until I'm married. But, dude, I'm 14! I probably won't get married until I'm at least 23 or 24. That's ten years! And I'm thinking, is that even possible? I mean, give me some kind of pill or something that mellows me out!

» *The Great Challenge*

Here's the bottom line: As a guy, you have been hardwired by God to be attracted to females. There's nothing wrong with sexual desire . . . as long as you play by God's rules.

If you think God is anti-sex, you need to read Song of Songs, an erotic love poem in the Old Testament about amazing marital sex. Why would that be in the Bible if sex is a bad thing?

The issue is self-control. In the same way God doesn't want us giving in to every impulse to eat or lash out or spend money, he wants us to keep a tight rein on our sexual desires. And we're not alone in this struggle—he will help us. Remember that one of the fruits of the Spirit—that is, the Holy Spirit that God gives to his people—is self-control (see Galatians 5:22–23).

Read more about dealing with sexual temptation at www.RevolutionBible.com.

His body is like polished ivory
    decorated with sapphires.[a]
[15] His legs are pillars of marble
    set on bases of pure gold.
His appearance is like Lebanon,
    choice as its cedars.
[16] His mouth is sweetness itself;
    he is altogether lovely.
This is my lover, this my friend,
    O daughters of Jerusalem.

FRIENDS

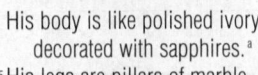

Where has your lover gone,
    most beautiful of women?
Which way did your lover turn,
    that we may look for him with you?

BELOVED

[2] My lover has gone down to his garden,
    to the beds of spices,
to browse in the gardens
    and to gather lilies.
[3] I am my lover's and my lover is mine;
    he browses among the lilies.

LOVER

[4] You are beautiful, my darling, as Tirzah,
    lovely as Jerusalem,
    majestic as troops with banners.
[5] Turn your eyes from me;
    they overwhelm me.
Your hair is like a flock of goats
    descending from Gilead.
[6] Your teeth are like a flock of sheep
    coming up from the washing.
Each has its twin,
    not one of them is alone.
[7] Your temples behind your veil
    are like the halves of a pomegranate.
[8] Sixty queens there may be,
    and eighty concubines,
    and virgins beyond number;
[9] but my dove, my perfect one, is unique,
    the only daughter of her mother,
    the favorite of the one who bore her.
The maidens saw her and called her blessed;
    the queens and concubines praised her.

FRIENDS

[10] Who is this that appears like the dawn,
    fair as the moon, bright as the sun,
    majestic as the stars in procession?

---

[a] *14* Or *lapis lazuli*

LOVER

¹¹ I went down to the grove of nut trees
    to look at the new growth in the valley,
to see if the vines had budded
    or the pomegranates were in bloom.
¹² Before I realized it,
    my desire set me among the royal chariots of my people. ᵃ

FRIENDS

¹³ Come back, come back, O Shulammite;
    come back, come back, that we may gaze on you!

LOVER

Why would you gaze on the Shulammite
    as on the dance of Mahanaim?

7

How beautiful your sandaled feet,
    O prince's daughter!
Your graceful legs are like jewels,
    the work of a craftsman's hands.
² Your navel is a rounded goblet
    that never lacks blended wine.
Your waist is a mound of wheat
    encircled by lilies.
³ Your breasts are like two fawns,
    twins of a gazelle.

⁴ Your neck is like an ivory tower.
    Your eyes are the pools of Heshbon
    by the gate of Bath Rabbim.
Your nose is like the tower of Lebanon
    looking toward Damascus.
⁵ Your head crowns you like Mount
        Carmel.
    Your hair is like royal tapestry;
    the king is held captive by its
        tresses.
⁶ How beautiful you are and how
        pleasing,
    O love, with your delights!
⁷ Your stature is like that of the palm,
    and your breasts like clusters of fruit.

NOW OR NEVER
SS 7:10

How do you feel about someone "belonging" to you? How do you feel about belonging to someone else? What do you think it means to fully give yourself to a partner for life?

⁸ I said, "I will climb the palm tree;
    I will take hold of its fruit."
May your breasts be like the clusters of the vine,
    the fragrance of your breath like apples,
⁹   and your mouth like the best wine.

BELOVED

May the wine go straight to my lover,
    flowing gently over lips and teeth. ᵇ
¹⁰ I belong to my lover,
    and his desire is for me.
¹¹ Come, my lover, let us go to the countryside,

ᵃ *12* Or *among the chariots of Amminadab;* or *among the chariots of the people of the prince*   ᵇ *9* Septuagint, Aquila, Vulgate and Syriac; Hebrew *lips of sleepers*

let us spend the night in the villages.ᵃ
¹²Let us go early to the vineyards
to see if the vines have budded,
if their blossoms have opened,
and if the pomegranates are in bloom—
there I will give you my love.
¹³The mandrakes send out their fragrance,
and at our door is every delicacy,
both new and old,
that I have stored up for you, my lover.

If only you were to me like a brother,
who was nursed at my mother's breasts!
Then, if I found you outside,
I would kiss you,
and no one would despise me.
²I would lead you
and bring you to my mother's house—
she who has taught me.

challenge notes

To: **my_son**

heavenly_father: you won't believe the priceless gift that's waiting for you on your wedding night. it's everything you've heard it is, and more . . . much more. but if you open it before the right time, you will ruin it for yourself.

SS 8:4

I would give you spiced wine
to drink,
the nectar of my pomegranates.
³His left arm is under my head
and his right arm embraces
me.
⁴Daughters of Jerusalem,
I charge you:
Do not arouse or awaken
love
until it so desires.

FRIENDS

⁵Who is this coming up from the desert
leaning on her lover?

BELOVED

Under the apple tree I roused you;
there your mother conceived you,
there she who was in labor gave you birth.
⁶Place me like a seal over your heart,
like a seal on your arm;
for love is as strong as death,
its jealousyᵇ unyielding as the grave.ᶜ
It burns like blazing fire,
like a mighty flame.ᵈ
⁷Many waters cannot quench love;
rivers cannot wash it away.
If one were to give
all the wealth of his house for love,
itᵉ would be utterly scorned.

FRIENDS

⁸We have a young sister,
and her breasts are not yet grown.

ᵃ *11* Or *henna bushes*   ᵇ *6* Or *ardor*   ᶜ *6* Hebrew *Sheol*   ᵈ *6* Or */ like the very flame of the* LORD   ᵉ *7* Or *he*

What shall we do for our sister
   for the day she is spoken for?
⁹ If she is a wall,
   we will build towers of silver on her.
If she is a door,
   we will enclose her with panels of cedar.

BELOVED

¹⁰ I am a wall,
   and my breasts are like towers.
Thus I have become in his eyes
   like one bringing contentment.
¹¹ Solomon had a vineyard in Baal Hamon;
   he let out his vineyard to tenants.
Each was to bring for its fruit
   a thousand shekels ª of silver.
¹² But my own vineyard is mine to give;
   the thousand shekels are for you, O Solomon,
   and two hundred ᵇ are for those who tend its fruit.

LOVER

¹³ You who dwell in the gardens
   with friends in attendance,
   let me hear your voice!

BELOVED

¹⁴ Come away, my lover,
   and be like a gazelle
or like a young stag
   on the spice-laden mountains.

ª *11* That is, about 25 pounds (about 11.5 kilograms); also in verse 12   ᵇ *12* That is, about 5 pounds (about 2.3 kilograms)

ISAIAH

« AT A GLANCE

Author
The prophet Isaiah, son of Amoz

Audience
People of Judah and Jerusalem

Date
Between 701 and 681 B.C.

Setting
Isaiah spoke to the people during a rough time in Judah when the Assyrians were becoming more of a threat to them.

Verse to Remember
We all, like sheep, have gone astray, each of us has turned to his own way; and the LORD has laid on him the iniquity of us all (53:6).

Theme to Consider
God, who is holy, must punish his people for their sin. But God is also compassionate, and he provided a way to save his people from condemnation through Jesus Christ, the Messiah.

UNCHANGING TRUTH » The future's not always hard to predict. Sometimes it's painfully obvious. All you have to do is take a good look at the present. Think about it. If you sit around watching TV and playing video games all summer instead of training, it's a no-brainer that you're not going to impress the coach when practice starts next season. If you cheat on your girlfriend, it shouldn't come as a surprise when your relationship takes an ugly nosedive. If you treat your friends like dirt, it's not unexpected that they will distance themselves from you one by one.

And the easiest prediction of all? If you don't put God at the center of everything you do, you will never be completely happy or satisfied with your life.

The prophet Isaiah was making some different kinds of predictions. His job was to tell the people of Judah that God was fed up with their disobedience and unfaithfulness. He warned the people that God's judgment was coming. He gave them a glimpse of what the future would be like—both the bad and the good.

LIFE LESSONS »

I   If you let your pride go unchecked, it will damage your relationship with the Lord (2:11).

2   When God gives you something to do, give it everything you've got for as long as it takes (6:8–13).

3   The best way to respond to all of the good things God has done for you is with joy and a positive attitude (35:9–10).

4   Jesus fulfilled prophecies that were written hundreds of years before his birth; that's just one of the many reasons we can trust that he is the Savior of the world (53:12).

1

The vision concerning Judah and Jerusalem that Isaiah son of Amoz saw during the reigns of Uzziah, Jotham, Ahaz and Hezekiah, kings of Judah.

A REBELLIOUS NATION

² Hear, O heavens! Listen, O earth!
For the LORD has spoken:

NOW OR NEVER

ISA 1:2

People rebel when they think they know more than the people who are telling them what to do. Since no one knows more than God, it's always a bad idea to rebel against him.

"I reared children and brought them up,
but they have rebelled against me.
³ The ox knows his master,
the donkey his owner's manger,
but Israel does not know,
my people do not understand."

⁴ Ah, sinful nation,
a people loaded with guilt,
a brood of evildoers,
children given to corruption!
They have forsaken the LORD;
they have spurned the Holy One of
Israel
and turned their backs on him.

⁵ Why should you be beaten anymore?
Why do you persist in rebellion?
Your whole head is injured,
your whole heart afflicted.
⁶ From the sole of your foot to the top of your head
there is no soundness—
only wounds and welts
and open sores,
not cleansed or bandaged
or soothed with oil.

⁷ Your country is desolate,
your cities burned with fire;
your fields are being stripped by foreigners
right before you,
laid waste as when overthrown by strangers.
⁸ The Daughter of Zion is left
like a shelter in a vineyard,
like a hut in a field of melons,
like a city under siege.
⁹ Unless the LORD Almighty
had left us some survivors,
we would have become like Sodom,
we would have been like Gomorrah.

¹⁰ Hear the word of the LORD,
you rulers of Sodom;
listen to the law of our God,
you people of Gomorrah!
¹¹ "The multitude of your sacrifices—
what are they to me?" says the LORD.
"I have more than enough of burnt offerings,
of rams and the fat of fattened animals;
I have no pleasure
in the blood of bulls and lambs and goats.

¹² When you come to appear before me,
who has asked this of you,
this trampling of my courts?
¹³ Stop bringing meaningless offerings!
Your incense is detestable to me.
New Moons, Sabbaths and convocations—

challengenotes

To: my_son

heavenly_father: as long as you live, I will never give up on you or turn my back on you. no sin is terrible enough to make me stop loving you. when you come to me looking for a second chance, I'll be there to give you one. just make sure you come with a repentant heart and a humble spirit.

I cannot bear your evil
assemblies.
¹⁴ Your New Moon festivals and
your appointed feasts
my soul hates.
They have become a burden to
me;
I am weary of bearing them.
¹⁵ When you spread out your
hands in prayer,
I will hide my eyes from
you;
even if you offer many prayers,
I will not listen.

Your hands are full of blood;
¹⁶   wash and make yourselves clean.
Take your evil deeds
out of my sight!
Stop doing wrong,
¹⁷   learn to do right!
Seek justice,
encourage the oppressed.ᵃ
Defend the cause of the fatherless,
plead the case of the widow.

¹⁸ "Come now, let us reason together,"
says the LORD.
"Though your sins are like scarlet,
they shall be as white as snow;
though they are red as crimson,
they shall be like wool.
¹⁹ If you are willing and obedient,
you will eat the best from the land;
²⁰ but if you resist and rebel,
you will be devoured by the sword."
For the mouth of the LORD
has spoken.

²¹ See how the faithful city
has become a harlot!
She once was full of justice;
righteousness used to dwell in
her—
but now murderers!
²² Your silver has become dross,
your choice wine is diluted with
water.
²³ Your rulers are rebels,
companions of thieves;

Understanding God's Forgiveness

Certain things can mark you for life. One bad decision . . . one moment of anger . . . one stupid act . . . one ignorant comment. A moment can change the way people look at you forever. No matter how much you apologize or try to make things right, some people will never be able to forget a serious slip up. Fortunately, God is not one of those people. Your reputation in his eyes becomes spotless the moment you repent and seek his forgiveness.

» » live the adventure » » Isa 1:18

ᵃ *17* Or / *rebuke the oppressor*

they all love bribes
and chase after gifts.
They do not defend the cause of the fatherless;
the widow's case does not come before them.
24 Therefore the Lord, the LORD Almighty,
the Mighty One of Israel, declares:
"Ah, I will get relief from my foes
and avenge myself on my enemies.
25 I will turn my hand against you;
I will thoroughly purge away your dross
and remove all your impurities.
26 I will restore your judges as in days of old,
your counselors as at the beginning.
Afterward you will be called
the City of Righteousness,
the Faithful City."

27 Zion will be redeemed with justice,
her penitent ones with righteousness.
28 But rebels and sinners will both be broken,
and those who forsake the LORD will perish.

29 "You will be ashamed because of the sacred oaks
in which you have delighted;
you will be disgraced because of the gardens
that you have chosen.
30 You will be like an oak with fading leaves,
like a garden without water.
31 The mighty man will become tinder
and his work a spark;
both will burn together,
with no one to quench the fire."

THE MOUNTAIN OF THE LORD

 This is what Isaiah son of Amoz saw concerning Judah and Jerusalem:

2 In the last days

the mountain of the LORD's temple will be established
as chief among the mountains;
it will be raised above the hills,
and all nations will stream to it.

3 Many peoples will come and say,

"Come, let us go up to the mountain of the LORD,
to the house of the God of Jacob.
He will teach us his ways,
so that we may walk in his paths."
The law will go out from Zion,
the word of the LORD from Jerusalem.
4 He will judge between the nations
and will settle disputes for many peoples.
They will beat their swords into plowshares
and their spears into pruning hooks.
Nation will not take up sword against nation,
nor will they train for war anymore.

⁵ Come, O house of Jacob,
    let us walk in the light of the LORD.

THE DAY OF THE LORD

⁶ You have abandoned your people,
    the house of Jacob.
They are full of superstitions from the East;
    they practice divination like the Philistines
    and clasp hands with pagans.
⁷ Their land is full of silver and gold;
    there is no end to their treasures.
Their land is full of horses;
    there is no end to their chariots.
⁸ Their land is full of idols;
    they bow down to the work of their hands,
    to what their fingers have made.
⁹ So man will be brought low
    and mankind humbled—
    do not forgive them. ª

¹⁰ Go into the rocks,
    hide in the ground
from dread of the LORD
    and the splendor of his majesty!
¹¹ The eyes of the arrogant man will be humbled
    and the pride of men brought low;
    the LORD alone will be exalted in that day.

¹² The LORD Almighty has a day in store
    for all the proud and lofty,
    for all that is exalted
    (and they will be humbled),
¹³ for all the cedars of Lebanon, tall and lofty,
    and all the oaks of Bashan,
¹⁴ for all the towering mountains
    and all the high hills,
¹⁵ for every lofty tower
    and every fortified wall,
¹⁶ for every trading ship ᵇ
    and every stately vessel.
¹⁷ The arrogance of man will be brought low
    and the pride of men humbled;
    the LORD alone will be exalted in that day,
¹⁸   and the idols will totally disappear.

¹⁹ Men will flee to caves in the rocks
    and to holes in the ground
from dread of the LORD
    and the splendor of his majesty,
    when he rises to shake the earth.
²⁰ In that day men will throw away
    to the rodents and bats
their idols of silver and idols of gold,
    which they made to worship.
²¹ They will flee to caverns in the rocks

ª *9 Or not raise them up*   ᵇ *16 Hebrew every ship of Tarshish*

and to the overhanging crags
from dread of the LORD
and the splendor of his majesty,
when he rises to shake the earth.

22 Stop trusting in man,
who has but a breath in his nostrils.
Of what account is he?

JUDGMENT ON JERUSALEM AND JUDAH

3 See now, the Lord,
the LORD Almighty,
is about to take from Jerusalem and Judah
both supply and support:
all supplies of food and all supplies of water,
2 the hero and warrior,
the judge and prophet,
the soothsayer and elder,
3 the captain of fifty and man of rank,
the counselor, skilled craftsman and clever enchanter.

4 I will make boys their officials;
mere children will govern them.
5 People will oppress each other—
man against man, neighbor against neighbor.
The young will rise up against the old,
the base against the honorable.

6 A man will seize one of his brothers
at his father's home, and say,
"You have a cloak, you be our leader;
take charge of this heap of ruins!"
7 But in that day he will cry out,
"I have no remedy.
I have no food or clothing in my house;
do not make me the leader of the people."

8 Jerusalem staggers,
Judah is falling;
their words and deeds are against the
LORD,
defying his glorious presence.
9 The look on their faces testifies against
them;
they parade their sin like Sodom;
they do not hide it.
Woe to them!
They have brought disaster upon
themselves.

10 Tell the righteous it will be well with them,
for they will enjoy the fruit of their
deeds.

NOW OR NEVER

ISA 3:10–11

Do you ever feel discouraged in your faith,
like you're the only guy trying to do the
right thing? Take Isaiah's words here as an
encouragement and a warning: The righteous will prosper, but the wicked will find
disaster.

11 Woe to the wicked! Disaster is upon them!
They will be paid back for what their hands have done.

12 Youths oppress my people,
women rule over them.

O my people, your guides lead you astray;
they turn you from the path.

¹³ The Lord takes his place in court;
he rises to judge the people.
¹⁴ The Lord enters into judgment
against the elders and leaders of his people:
"It is you who have ruined my vineyard;
the plunder from the poor is in your houses.
¹⁵ What do you mean by crushing my people
and grinding the faces of the poor?"
declares the Lord,
the Lord Almighty.

¹⁶ The Lord says,
"The women of Zion are haughty,
walking along with outstretched necks,
flirting with their eyes,
tripping along with mincing steps,
with ornaments jingling on their
ankles.
¹⁷ Therefore the Lord will bring sores on
the heads of the women of
Zion;
the Lord will make their scalps
bald."

¹⁸In that day the Lord will snatch away their finery: the bangles and headbands and crescent necklaces, ¹⁹the earrings and bracelets and veils, ²⁰the headdresses and ankle chains and sashes, the perfume bottles and charms, ²¹the signet rings and nose rings, ²²the fine robes and the capes and cloaks, the purses ²³and mirrors, and the linen garments and tiaras and shawls.

²⁴Instead of fragrance there will be a
stench;
instead of a sash, a rope;
instead of well-dressed hair, baldness;
instead of fine clothing, sackcloth;
instead of beauty, branding.
²⁵ Your men will fall by the sword,
your warriors in battle.
²⁶ The gates of Zion will lament and
mourn;
destitute, she will sit on the ground.
In that day seven women
will take hold of one man
and say, "We will eat our own food
and provide our own clothes;
only let us be called by your name.
Take away our disgrace!"

4

Concentrating on What's Inside

How much time do you spend getting ready to meet the world? Five minutes? A half hour? More than an hour? How does that compare to the time you spend meeting with the Lord? It's OK to want to look presentable—as long as it doesn't become your number-one priority. Remember, God cares most about what's going on *inside* you.

THE BRANCH OF THE LORD

²In that day the Branch of the Lord will be beautiful and glorious, and the fruit of the land will be the pride and glory of the survivors in Israel. ³Those who are left in Zion, who remain in Jerusalem, will be called holy, all who are recorded among the living in Jerusalem. ⁴The Lord will wash away the filth

of the women of Zion; he will cleanse the bloodstains from Jerusalem by a spirit[a] of judgment and a spirit[a] of fire. 5Then the LORD will create over all of Mount Zion and over those who assemble there a cloud of smoke by day and a glow of flaming fire by night; over all the glory will be a canopy. 6It will be a shelter and shade from the heat of the day, and a refuge and hiding place from the storm and rain.

THE SONG OF THE VINEYARD

I will sing for the one I love
    a song about his vineyard:
My loved one had a vineyard
    on a fertile hillside.
2He dug it up and cleared it of stones
    and planted it with the choicest vines.
He built a watchtower in it
    and cut out a winepress as well.
Then he looked for a crop of good grapes,
    but it yielded only bad fruit.

3"Now you dwellers in Jerusalem and men of Judah,
    judge between me and my vineyard.
4What more could have been done for my vineyard
    than I have done for it?
When I looked for good grapes,
    why did it yield only bad?
5Now I will tell you
    what I am going to do to my vineyard:
I will take away its hedge,
    and it will be destroyed;
I will break down its wall,
    and it will be trampled.
6I will make it a wasteland,
    neither pruned nor cultivated,
    and briers and thorns will grow there.
I will command the clouds
    not to rain on it."

7The vineyard of the LORD Almighty
    is the house of Israel,
and the men of Judah
    are the garden of his delight.
And he looked for justice, but saw bloodshed;
    for righteousness, but heard cries of distress.

WOES AND JUDGMENTS

8Woe to you who add house to house
    and join field to field
till no space is left
    and you live alone in the land.

9The LORD Almighty has declared in my hearing:

"Surely the great houses will become desolate,
    the fine mansions left without occupants.
10A ten-acre[b] vineyard will produce only a bath[c] of wine,
    a homer[d] of seed only an ephah[e] of grain."

---

a 4 Or the Spirit   b 10 Hebrew ten-yoke, that is, the land plowed by 10 yoke of oxen in one day   c 10 That is, probably about 6 gallons (about 22 liters)   d 10 That is, probably about 6 bushels (about 220 liters)   e 10 That is, probably about 3/5 bushel (about 22 liters)

¹¹Woe to those who rise early in the morning
    to run after their drinks,
who stay up late at night
    till they are inflamed with wine.
¹²They have harps and lyres at their banquets,
    tambourines and flutes and wine,
but they have no regard for the deeds of the LORD,
    no respect for the work of his hands.
¹³Therefore my people will go into exile
    for lack of understanding;
their men of rank will die of hunger

and their masses will be parched
    with thirst.
¹⁴Therefore the grave^a enlarges its
    appetite
and opens its mouth without limit;
into it will descend their nobles and
    masses
with all their brawlers and revelers.
¹⁵So man will be brought low
    and mankind humbled,
the eyes of the arrogant humbled.
¹⁶But the LORD Almighty will be exalted by
    his justice,
and the holy God will show himself
    holy by his righteousness.

NOW OR NEVER
ISA 5:11–13

Let this be a warning to partyers everywhere. If all you think about is getting wasted with your buddies or where the next party is, your focus is terribly misplaced. Since when does a passing night of "fun" take priority over an eternity of happiness?

¹⁷Then sheep will graze as in their own pasture;
    lambs will feed^b among the ruins of the rich.

¹⁸Woe to those who draw sin along with cords of deceit,
    and wickedness as with cart ropes,
¹⁹to those who say, "Let God hurry,
    let him hasten his work
    so we may see it.
Let it approach,
    let the plan of the Holy One of Israel come,
    so we may know it."

²⁰Woe to those who call evil good
    and good evil,
who put darkness for light
    and light for darkness,
who put bitter for sweet
    and sweet for bitter.

²¹Woe to those who are wise in their own eyes
    and clever in their own sight.

²²Woe to those who are heroes at drinking wine
    and champions at mixing drinks,
²³who acquit the guilty for a bribe,
    but deny justice to the innocent.
²⁴Therefore, as tongues of fire lick up straw
    and as dry grass sinks down in the flames,
so their roots will decay
    and their flowers blow away like dust;

---

^a *14* Hebrew *Sheol*   ^b *17* Septuagint; Hebrew / *strangers will eat*

for they have rejected the law of the LORD Almighty
 and spurned the word of the Holy One of Israel.
²⁵ Therefore the LORD's anger burns against his people;
 his hand is raised and he strikes them down.
The mountains shake,
 and the dead bodies are like refuse in the streets.

Yet for all this, his anger is not turned away,
 his hand is still upraised.

²⁶ He lifts up a banner for the distant nations,
 he whistles for those at the ends of the earth.
Here they come,
 swiftly and speedily!
²⁷ Not one of them grows tired or stumbles,
 not one slumbers or sleeps;
not a belt is loosened at the waist,
 not a sandal thong is broken.
²⁸ Their arrows are sharp,
 all their bows are strung;
their horses' hoofs seem like flint,
 their chariot wheels like a whirlwind.
²⁹ Their roar is like that of the lion,
 they roar like young lions;
they growl as they seize their prey
 and carry it off with no one to rescue.
³⁰ In that day they will roar over it
 like the roaring of the sea.
And if one looks at the land,
 he will see darkness and distress;
 even the light will be darkened by the
 clouds.

ISAIAH'S COMMISSION

6 In the year that King Uzziah died, I saw the Lord seated on a throne, high and exalted, and the train of his robe filled the temple. ²Above him were seraphs, each with six wings: With two wings they covered their faces, with two they covered their feet, and with two they were flying. ³And they were calling to one another:

 "Holy, holy, holy is the LORD Almighty;
 the whole earth is full of his glory."

⁴At the sound of their voices the doorposts and thresholds shook and the temple was filled with smoke.

⁵"Woe to me!" I cried. "I am ruined! For I am a man of unclean lips, and I live among a people of unclean lips, and my eyes have seen the King, the LORD Almighty."

⁶Then one of the seraphs flew to me with a live coal in his hand, which he had taken with tongs from the altar. ⁷With it he touched my mouth and said, "See, this has touched your lips; your guilt is taken away and your sin atoned for."

⁸Then I heard the voice of the Lord saying, "Whom shall I send? And who will go for us?"
And I said, "Here am I. Send me!"
⁹He said, "Go and tell this people:

 " 'Be ever hearing, but never understanding;
 be ever seeing, but never perceiving.'
¹⁰ Make the heart of this people calloused;

Volunteering for Service

Right now, God may be looking for someone to explain his forgiveness to a student at school who's struggling with guilt . . . or start a winter coat collection for the homeless people in your community . . . or share his love by hanging out with the guy in your church who no one can stand. Will you be that person? Will you step up to the plate like Isaiah did and say, "Here am I: send me"?

       make their ears dull
       and close their eyes.[a]
   Otherwise they might see with their eyes,
       hear with their ears,
       understand with their hearts,
       and turn and be healed."

¹¹Then I said, "For how long, O Lord?"
And he answered:

   "Until the cities lie ruined
       and without inhabitant,
   until the houses are left deserted
       and the fields ruined and ravaged,
   ¹²until the LORD has sent everyone far away
       and the land is utterly forsaken.
   ¹³And though a tenth remains in the land,
       it will again be laid waste.
   But as the terebinth and oak
       leave stumps when they are cut down,
       so the holy seed will be the stump in the land."

THE SIGN OF IMMANUEL

7 When Ahaz son of Jotham, the son of Uzziah, was king of Judah, King Rezin of Aram and Pekah son of Remaliah king of Israel marched up to fight against Jerusalem, but they could not overpower it.

²Now the house of David was told, "Aram has allied itself with[b] Ephraim"; so the hearts of Ahaz and his people were shaken, as the trees of the forest are shaken by the wind.

³Then the LORD said to Isaiah, "Go out, you and your son Shear-Jashub,[c] to meet Ahaz at the end of the aqueduct of the Upper Pool, on the road to the Washerman's Field. ⁴Say to him, 'Be careful, keep calm and don't be afraid. Do not lose heart because of these two smoldering stubs of firewood—because of the fierce anger of Rezin and Aram and of the son of Remaliah. ⁵Aram, Ephraim and Remaliah's son have plotted your ruin, saying, ⁶"Let us invade Judah; let us tear it apart and divide it among ourselves, and make the son of Tabeel king over it." ⁷Yet this is what the Sovereign LORD says:

   " 'It will not take place,
       it will not happen,
   ⁸for the head of Aram is Damascus,
       and the head of Damascus is only Rezin.
   Within sixty-five years
       Ephraim will be too shattered to be a people.
   ⁹The head of Ephraim is Samaria,
       and the head of Samaria is only Remaliah's son.
   If you do not stand firm in your faith,
       you will not stand at all.' "

¹⁰Again the LORD spoke to Ahaz, ¹¹"Ask the LORD your God for a sign, whether in the deepest depths or in the highest heights."

¹²But Ahaz said, "I will not ask; I will not put the LORD to the test."

¹³Then Isaiah said, "Hear now, you house of David! Is it not enough to try the patience of men? Will you try the patience of my God also? ¹⁴Therefore the Lord himself will give you[d] a sign: The virgin will be with child and will give birth to a son, and[e] will call him Immanuel.[f] ¹⁵He will eat curds and honey when he knows enough to reject the wrong and choose the right. ¹⁶But before the boy knows enough

---

[a] *9,10* Hebrew; Septuagint *'You will be ever hearing, but never understanding; / you will be ever seeing, but never perceiving.' / ¹⁰This people's heart has become calloused; / they hardly hear with their ears, / and they have closed their eyes*   [b] *2* Or *has set up camp in*   [c] *3 Shear-Jashub* means *a remnant will return.*   [d] *14* The Hebrew is plural.   [e] *14* Masoretic Text; Dead Sea Scrolls *and he* or *and they*   [f] *14 Immanuel* means *God with us.*

to reject the wrong and choose the right, the land of the two kings you dread will be laid waste. [17]The LORD will bring on you and on your people and on the house of your father a time unlike any since Ephraim broke away from Judah—he will bring the king of Assyria."

[18]In that day the LORD will whistle for flies from the distant streams of Egypt and for bees from the land of Assyria. [19]They will all come and settle in the steep ravines and in the crevices in the rocks, on all the thornbushes and at all the water holes. [20]In that day the Lord will use a razor hired from beyond the River[a]—the king of Assyria—to shave your head and the hair of your legs, and to take off your beards also. [21]In that day, a man will keep alive a young cow and two goats. [22]And because of the abundance of the milk they give, he will have curds to eat. All who remain in the land will eat curds and honey. [23]In that day, in every place where there were a thousand vines worth a thousand silver shekels,[b] there will be only briers and thorns. [24]Men will go there with bow and arrow, for the land will be covered with briers and thorns. [25]As for all the hills once cultivated by the hoe, you will no longer go there for fear of the briers and thorns; they will become places where cattle are turned loose and where sheep run.

ASSYRIA, THE LORD'S INSTRUMENT

8 The LORD said to me, "Take a large scroll and write on it with an ordinary pen: Maher-Shalal-Hash-Baz.[c] [2]And I will call in Uriah the priest and Zechariah son of Jeberekiah as reliable witnesses for me."

[3]Then I went to the prophetess, and she conceived and gave birth to a son. And the LORD said to me, "Name him Maher-Shalal-Hash-Baz. [4]Before the boy knows how to say 'My father' or 'My mother,' the wealth of Damascus and the plunder of Samaria will be carried off by the king of Assyria."

[5]The LORD spoke to me again:

> [6]"Because this people has rejected
>   the gently flowing waters of Shiloah
> and rejoices over Rezin
>   and the son of Remaliah,

> [7]therefore the Lord is about to bring
>   against them
>   the mighty floodwaters of the
>   River[a]—
>   the king of Assyria with all his pomp.
> It will overflow all its channels,
>   run over all its banks
> [8]and sweep on into Judah, swirling over it,
>   passing through it and reaching up
>   to the neck.
> Its outspread wings will cover the
>   breadth of your land,
>   O Immanuel[d]!"

NOW OR NEVER
ISA 8:11–13

Who is it that you fear? A tough guy at school? Your coach? A certain teacher? The only one you should fear is God—not because he is merciless or mean, but because he is powerful and just.

> [9]Raise the war cry,[e] you nations, and be shattered!
>   Listen, all you distant lands.
> Prepare for battle, and be shattered!
> Prepare for battle, and be shattered!
> [10]Devise your strategy, but it will be thwarted;
>   propose your plan, but it will not stand,
>   for God is with us.[f]

FEAR GOD

[11]The LORD spoke to me with his strong hand upon me, warning me not to follow the way of this people. He said:

---

[a] 20,7 That is, the Euphrates   [b] 23 That is, about 25 pounds (about 11.5 kilograms)   [c] 1 Maher-Shalal-Hash-Baz means quick to the plunder, swift to the spoil; also in verse 3.   [d] 8 Immanuel means God with us.   [e] 9 Or Do your worst
[f] 10 Hebrew Immanuel

12 "Do not call conspiracy
  everything that these people call
    conspiracy[a];
do not fear what they fear,
  and do not dread it.
13 The LORD Almighty is the one you are to
    regard as holy,
  he is the one you are to fear,
  he is the one you are to dread,
14 and he will be a sanctuary;
  but for both houses of Israel he will
    be
  a stone that causes men to stumble
    and a rock that makes them fall.
  And for the people of Jerusalem he will
    be
  a trap and a snare.
15 Many of them will stumble;
  they will fall and be broken,
  they will be snared and captured."

16 Bind up the testimony
  and seal up the law among my
    disciples.
17 I will wait for the LORD,
  who is hiding his face from the
    house of Jacob.
I will put my trust in him.

Understanding Whose Opinion Matters

If you weren't sure whether a certain shirt looked good on you or not, who would you listen to? Your grandma, who says it makes you look handsome (but says that about everything you wear)? Or a cheerleader at school who tells you it makes you look like a dork? Whose opinion matters to you more in that situation? Whose opinion matters to you when it comes to the way you live your life? If your first answer is anyone but God, you're trying to please the wrong people.

18 Here am I, and the children the LORD has given me. We are signs and symbols in Israel from the LORD Almighty, who dwells on Mount Zion.

19 When men tell you to consult mediums and spiritists, who whisper and mutter, should not a people inquire of their God? Why consult the dead on behalf of the living? 20 To the law and to the testimony! If they do not speak according to this word, they have no light of dawn. 21 Distressed and hungry, they will roam through the land; when they are famished, they will become enraged and, looking upward, will curse their king and their God. 22 Then they will look toward the earth and see only distress and darkness and fearful gloom, and they will be thrust into utter darkness.

TO US A CHILD IS BORN

9 Nevertheless, there will be no more gloom for those who were in distress. In the past he humbled the land of Zebulun and the land of Naphtali, but in the future he will honor Galilee of the Gentiles, by the way of the sea, along the Jordan—

2 The people walking in darkness
  have seen a great light;
on those living in the land of the shadow of death[b]
  a light has dawned.
3 You have enlarged the nation
  and increased their joy;
they rejoice before you
  as people rejoice at the harvest,
as men rejoice
  when dividing the plunder.
4 For as in the day of Midian's defeat,

---

[a] 12 Or Do not call for a treaty / every time these people call for a treaty   [b] 2 Or land of darkness

you have shattered
the yoke that burdens them,
the bar across their shoulders,
the rod of their oppressor.
⁵ Every warrior's boot used in battle
and every garment rolled in blood
will be destined for burning,
will be fuel for the fire.

⁶ For to us a child is born,
to us a son is given,
and the government will be on his
shoulders.
And he will be called
Wonderful Counselor,ᵃ Mighty God,
Everlasting Father, Prince of Peace.
⁷ Of the increase of his government and
peace
there will be no end.
He will reign on David's throne
and over his kingdom,
establishing and upholding it
with justice and righteousness

nOW OR nEVER
ISA 9:6-7

Does this passage seem familiar? You probably hear it quoted at least once every Christmas season. Jesus is the one who lifted the "gloom" (v. 1) for people everywhere by offering us the only way to escape sin and death.

from that time on and forever.
The zeal of the LORD Almighty
will accomplish this.

THE LORD'S ANGER AGAINST ISRAEL

⁸ The Lord has sent a message against Jacob;
it will fall on Israel.
⁹ All the people will know it—
Ephraim and the inhabitants of Samaria—
who say with pride
and arrogance of heart,
¹⁰ "The bricks have fallen down,
but we will rebuild with dressed stone;
the fig trees have been felled,
but we will replace them with cedars."
¹¹ But the LORD has strengthened Rezin's foes against them
and has spurred their enemies on.
¹² Arameans from the east and Philistines from the west
have devoured Israel with open mouth.

Yet for all this, his anger is not turned away,
his hand is still upraised.

¹³ But the people have not returned to him who struck them,
nor have they sought the LORD Almighty.
¹⁴ So the LORD will cut off from Israel both head and tail,
both palm branch and reed in a single day;
¹⁵ the elders and prominent men are the head,
the prophets who teach lies are the tail.
¹⁶ Those who guide this people mislead them,
and those who are guided are led astray.
¹⁷ Therefore the Lord will take no pleasure in the young men,
nor will he pity the fatherless and widows,

ᵃ 6 Or Wonderful, Counselor

for everyone is ungodly and wicked,
    every mouth speaks vileness.

Yet for all this, his anger is not turned away,
    his hand is still upraised.

18 Surely wickedness burns like a fire;
    it consumes briers and thorns,
it sets the forest thickets ablaze,
    so that it rolls upward in a column of smoke.
19 By the wrath of the LORD Almighty
    the land will be scorched
and the people will be fuel for the fire;
    no one will spare his brother.
20 On the right they will devour,
    but still be hungry;
on the left they will eat,
    but not be satisfied.
Each will feed on the flesh of his own offspring[a]:
21   Manasseh will feed on Ephraim, and Ephraim on Manasseh;
    together they will turn against Judah.

Yet for all this, his anger is not turned away,
    his hand is still upraised.

10 Woe to those who make unjust laws,
    to those who issue oppressive decrees,
2 to deprive the poor of their rights
    and withhold justice from the oppressed of my people,
    making widows their prey
    and robbing the fatherless.
3 What will you do on the day of
    reckoning,
    when disaster comes from
    afar?
To whom will you run for help?
    Where will you leave your
    riches?
4 Nothing will remain but to
    cringe among the
    captives
    or fall among the slain.

Yet for all this, his anger is not turned away,
    his hand is still upraised.

GOD'S JUDGMENT ON ASSYRIA

5 "Woe to the Assyrian, the rod of my anger,
    in whose hand is the club of my wrath!
6 I send him against a godless nation,
    I dispatch him against a people who anger me,
to seize loot and snatch plunder,
    and to trample them down like mud in the streets.
7 But this is not what he intends,
    this is not what he has in mind;
    his purpose is to destroy,

[a] 20 Or arm

to put an end to many nations.
8 'Are not my commanders all kings?' he says.
9 'Has not Calno fared like Carchemish?
  Is not Hamath like Arpad,
    and Samaria like Damascus?
10 As my hand seized the kingdoms of the idols,
    kingdoms whose images excelled those of Jerusalem and Samaria—
11 shall I not deal with Jerusalem and her images
    as I dealt with Samaria and her idols?' "

12 When the Lord has finished all his work against Mount Zion and Jerusalem, he will say, "I will punish the king of Assyria for the willful pride of his heart and the haughty look in his eyes. 13 For he says:

" 'By the strength of my hand I have done this,
    and by my wisdom, because I have understanding.
  I removed the boundaries of nations,
    I plundered their treasures;
    like a mighty one I subdued[a] their kings.
14 As one reaches into a nest,
    so my hand reached for the wealth of the nations;
  as men gather abandoned eggs,
    so I gathered all the countries;
  not one flapped a wing,
    or opened its mouth to chirp.' "

15 Does the ax raise itself above him who swings it,
    or the saw boast against him who uses it?
  As if a rod were to wield him who lifts it up,
    or a club brandish him who is not wood!
16 Therefore, the Lord, the LORD Almighty,
    will send a wasting disease upon his sturdy warriors;
  under his pomp a fire will be kindled
    like a blazing flame.
17 The Light of Israel will become a fire,
    their Holy One a flame;
  in a single day it will burn and consume
    his thorns and his briers.
18 The splendor of his forests and fertile fields
    it will completely destroy,
    as when a sick man wastes away.
19 And the remaining trees of his forests will be so few
    that a child could write them down.

THE REMNANT OF ISRAEL

20 In that day the remnant of Israel,
    the survivors of the house of Jacob,
  will no longer rely on him
    who struck them down
  but will truly rely on the LORD,
    the Holy One of Israel.
21 A remnant will return,[b] a remnant of Jacob
    will return to the Mighty God.
22 Though your people, O Israel, be like the sand by the sea,
    only a remnant will return.

---

a 13 Or / I subdued the mighty;   b 21 Hebrew shear-jashub; also in verse 22

Destruction has been decreed,
> overwhelming and righteous.
23 The Lord, the LORD Almighty, will carry out
> the destruction decreed upon the whole land.

24 Therefore, this is what the Lord, the LORD Almighty, says:

"O my people who live in Zion,
> do not be afraid of the Assyrians,
who beat you with a rod
> and lift up a club against you, as Egypt did.
25 Very soon my anger against you will end
> and my wrath will be directed to their destruction."

26 The LORD Almighty will lash them with a whip,
> as when he struck down Midian at the rock of Oreb;
and he will raise his staff over the waters,
> as he did in Egypt.
27 In that day their burden will be lifted from your shoulders,
> their yoke from your neck;
the yoke will be broken
> because you have grown so fat. [a]

28 They enter Aiath;
> they pass through Migron;
> they store supplies at Micmash.
29 They go over the pass, and say,
> "We will camp overnight at Geba."
Ramah trembles;
> Gibeah of Saul flees.
30 Cry out, O Daughter of Gallim!
> Listen, O Laishah!
> Poor Anathoth!
31 Madmenah is in flight;
> the people of Gebim take cover.
32 This day they will halt at Nob;
> they will shake their fist
at the mount of the Daughter of Zion,
> at the hill of Jerusalem.

33 See, the Lord, the LORD Almighty,
> will lop off the boughs with great power.
The lofty trees will be felled,
> the tall ones will be brought low.
34 He will cut down the forest thickets with an ax;
> Lebanon will fall before the Mighty One.

THE BRANCH FROM JESSE

11 A shoot will come up from the stump of Jesse;
> from his roots a Branch will bear fruit.
2 The Spirit of the LORD will rest on him—
> the Spirit of wisdom and of understanding,
> the Spirit of counsel and of power,
> the Spirit of knowledge and of the fear of the LORD—
3 and he will delight in the fear of the LORD.

He will not judge by what he sees with his eyes,

---
[a] 27 Hebrew; Septuagint *broken / from your shoulders*

or decide by what he hears with his ears;
⁴but with righteousness he will judge the needy,
   with justice he will give decisions for the poor of the earth.
He will strike the earth with the rod of his mouth;
   with the breath of his lips he will slay the wicked.
⁵Righteousness will be his belt
   and faithfulness the sash around his waist.

⁶The wolf will live with the lamb,
   the leopard will lie down with the goat,
the calf and the lion and the yearling ᵃ together;
   and a little child will lead them.
⁷The cow will feed with the bear,
   their young will lie down together,
   and the lion will eat straw like the ox.
⁸The infant will play near the hole of the cobra,
   and the young child put his hand
      into the viper's nest.
⁹They will neither harm nor destroy
   on all my holy mountain,
for the earth will be full of the knowledge of the LORD
   as the waters cover the sea.

NOW OR NEVER
ISA 11:6–9

Everything will change when Jesus re-turns—even the way animals treat each other. Can you imagine being able to pet a lion or a crocodile? The new earth that God has planned is going to be an incredi-ble place to live.

¹⁰In that day the Root of Jesse will stand as a banner for the peoples; the nations will rally to him, and his place of rest will be glorious. ¹¹In that day the Lord will reach out his hand a second time to re-claim the remnant that is left of his people from Assyria, from Lower Egypt, from Upper Egypt,ᵇ from Cush,ᶜ from Elam, from Babylonia,ᵈ from Hamath and from the islands of the sea.

¹²He will raise a banner for the nations
   and gather the exiles of Israel;
he will assemble the scattered people of Judah
   from the four quarters of the earth.
¹³Ephraim's jealousy will vanish,
   and Judah's enemiesᵉ will be cut off;
Ephraim will not be jealous of Judah,
   nor Judah hostile toward Ephraim.
¹⁴They will swoop down on the slopes of Philistia to the west;
   together they will plunder the people to the east.
They will lay hands on Edom and Moab,
   and the Ammonites will be subject to them.
¹⁵The LORD will dry up
   the gulf of the Egyptian sea;
with a scorching wind he will sweep his hand
   over the Euphrates River.ᶠ
He will break it up into seven streams
   so that men can cross over in sandals.
¹⁶There will be a highway for the remnant of his people
   that is left from Assyria,
as there was for Israel
   when they came up from Egypt.

ᵃ 6 Hebrew; Septuagint *lion will feed*   ᵇ 11 Hebrew *from Pathros*   ᶜ 11 That is, the upper Nile region   ᵈ 11 Hebrew *Shinar*   ᵉ 13 Or *hostility*   ᶠ 15 Hebrew *the River*

SONGS OF PRAISE

12 In that day you will say:

"I will praise you, O LORD.
  Although you were angry with me,
your anger has turned away
  and you have comforted me.
2 Surely God is my salvation;
  I will trust and not be afraid.
The LORD, the LORD, is my strength and
    my song;
  he has become my salvation."
3 With joy you will draw water
  from the wells of salvation.

4 In that day you will say:

"Give thanks to the LORD, call on his
    name;
  make known among the nations what
    he has done,
  and proclaim that his name is exalted.
5 Sing to the LORD, for he has done
    glorious things;
  let this be known to all the world.
6 Shout aloud and sing for joy, people of
    Zion,
  for great is the Holy One of Israel
    among you."

A PROPHECY AGAINST BABYLON

13 An oracle concerning Babylon that Isaiah son of Amoz saw:

2 Raise a banner on a bare hilltop,
  shout to them;
beckon to them
  to enter the gates of the nobles.
3 I have commanded my holy ones;
  I have summoned my warriors to carry out my wrath—
  those who rejoice in my triumph.

4 Listen, a noise on the mountains,
  like that of a great multitude!
Listen, an uproar among the kingdoms,
  like nations massing together!
The LORD Almighty is mustering
  an army for war.
5 They come from faraway lands,
  from the ends of the heavens—
the LORD and the weapons of his wrath—
  to destroy the whole country.

6 Wail, for the day of the LORD is near;
  it will come like destruction from the Almighty. a
7 Because of this, all hands will go limp,

Understanding Courage

What are your biggest fears? Embarrassing yourself in public? Getting stuck in a tight space? Being left alone? Getting beaten up by a bully? God can help you deal with them. Notice Isaiah doesn't say God will snap his fingers and make your fears instantly go away. That's not the way God works. He wants you to depend on him in every situation—especially when you're scared. So if you're nervous about, say, speaking in front of a crowd, God won't suddenly make you the world's most confident and gifted public speaker. Instead, he will be the strength you need to get through your speech, sentence by sentence.

---

a 6 Hebrew *Shaddai*

every man's heart will melt.
⁸ Terror will seize them,
pain and anguish will grip them;
they will writhe like a woman in labor.
They will look aghast at each other,
their faces aflame.

⁹ See, the day of the LORD is coming
—a cruel day, with wrath and fierce anger—
to make the land desolate
and destroy the sinners within it.
¹⁰ The stars of heaven and their constellations
will not show their light.
The rising sun will be darkened
and the moon will not give its light.
¹¹ I will punish the world for its evil,
the wicked for their sins.
I will put an end to the arrogance of the haughty
and will humble the pride of the ruthless.
¹² I will make man scarcer than pure gold,
more rare than the gold of Ophir.
¹³ Therefore I will make the heavens tremble;
and the earth will shake from its place
at the wrath of the LORD Almighty,
in the day of his burning anger.

¹⁴ Like a hunted gazelle,
like sheep without a shepherd,
each will return to his own people,
each will flee to his native land.
¹⁵ Whoever is captured will be thrust through;
all who are caught will fall by the sword.
¹⁶ Their infants will be dashed to pieces before their eyes;
their houses will be looted and their wives ravished.

¹⁷ See, I will stir up against them the Medes,
who do not care for silver
and have no delight in gold.
¹⁸ Their bows will strike down the young
men;
they will have no mercy on infants
nor will they look with compassion
on children.
¹⁹ Babylon, the jewel of kingdoms,
the glory of the Babylonians'ᵃ pride,
will be overthrown by God
like Sodom and Gomorrah.
²⁰ She will never be inhabited
or lived in through all generations;
no Arab will pitch his tent there,
no shepherd will rest his flocks
there.

now or never
ISA 13:19–22

Search all you want—you won't find Babylon on any current world map. That's because it doesn't exist. Like every other promise in the Bible, God's vow that Babylon would never again be inhabited holds true today.

²¹ But desert creatures will lie there,
jackals will fill her houses;
there the owls will dwell,

ᵃ 19 Or Chaldeans'

and there the wild goats will leap about.
²²Hyenas will howl in her strongholds,
        jackals in her luxurious palaces.
Her time is at hand,
        and her days will not be prolonged.

14

The LORD will have compassion on Jacob;
        once again he will choose Israel
        and will settle them in their own land.
Aliens will join them
        and unite with the house of Jacob.
²Nations will take them
        and bring them to their own place.
And the house of Israel will possess the nations
        as menservants and maidservants in the LORD's land.
They will make captives of their captors
        and rule over their oppressors.

³On the day the LORD gives you relief from suffering and turmoil and cruel bondage, ⁴you will take up this taunt against the king of Babylon:

now or never
ISA 14:4

Think about this verse the next time you hear about Christians being oppressed because of their faith. No matter how much power oppressors seem to have now, one day the tables will be turned. And God's judgment is fiercer than anything we could dish out.

How the oppressor has come to an end!
        How his fury[a] has ended!
⁵The LORD has broken the rod of the
        wicked,
        the scepter of the rulers,
⁶which in anger struck down peoples
        with unceasing blows,
and in fury subdued nations
        with relentless aggression.
⁷All the lands are at rest and at peace;
        they break into singing.
⁸Even the pine trees and the cedars of
        Lebanon
exult over you and say,
"Now that you have been laid low,
        no woodsman comes to cut us down."

⁹The grave[b] below is all astir
        to meet you at your coming;
it rouses the spirits of the departed to greet you—
        all those who were leaders in the world;
it makes them rise from their thrones—
        all those who were kings over the nations.
¹⁰They will all respond,
        they will say to you,
"You also have become weak, as we are;
        you have become like us."
¹¹All your pomp has been brought down to the grave,
        along with the noise of your harps;
maggots are spread out beneath you
        and worms cover you.

¹²How you have fallen from heaven,
        O morning star, son of the dawn!

---

[a] 4 Dead Sea Scrolls, Septuagint and Syriac; the meaning of the word in the Masoretic Text is uncertain.   [b] 9 Hebrew *Sheol*; also in verses 11 and 15

You have been cast down to the earth,
you who once laid low the nations!
¹³ You said in your heart,
"I will ascend to heaven;
I will raise my throne
above the stars of God;
I will sit enthroned on the mount of
assembly,
on the utmost heights of the sacred
mountain. ᵃ
¹⁴ I will ascend above the tops of the
clouds;
I will make myself like the Most
High."
¹⁵ But you are brought down to the grave,
to the depths of the pit.

NOW OR NEVER
ISA 14:12–15

Ever wonder what made Satan the way he is? This passage may be a veiled reference to him, so here's your answer. It was pride. He wasn't satisfied with being just another one of God's countless creatures. He wanted glory that only God deserves. His ego led to his downfall.

¹⁶ Those who see you stare at you,
they ponder your fate:
"Is this the man who shook the earth
and made kingdoms tremble,
¹⁷ the man who made the world a desert,
who overthrew its cities
and would not let his captives go home?"

¹⁸ All the kings of the nations lie in state,
each in his own tomb.
¹⁹ But you are cast out of your tomb
like a rejected branch;
you are covered with the slain,
with those pierced by the sword,
those who descend to the stones of the pit.
Like a corpse trampled underfoot,
²⁰ you will not join them in burial,
for you have destroyed your land
and killed your people.

The offspring of the wicked
will never be mentioned again.
²¹ Prepare a place to slaughter his sons
for the sins of their forefathers;
they are not to rise to inherit the land
and cover the earth with their cities.

²² "I will rise up against them,"
declares the Lord Almighty.
"I will cut off from Babylon her name and survivors,
her offspring and descendants,"

declares the Lord.

²³ "I will turn her into a place for owls
and into swampland;
I will sweep her with the broom of destruction,"
declares the Lord Almighty.

ᵃ *13* Or *the north*; Hebrew *Zaphon*

A PROPHECY AGAINST ASSYRIA

²⁴The LORD Almighty has sworn,

"Surely, as I have planned, so it will be,
and as I have purposed, so it will stand.
²⁵I will crush the Assyrian in my land;
on my mountains I will trample him down.
His yoke will be taken from my people,
and his burden removed from their shoulders."

²⁶This is the plan determined for the whole world;
this is the hand stretched out over all nations.
²⁷For the LORD Almighty has purposed, and who can thwart him?
His hand is stretched out, and who can turn it back?

A PROPHECY AGAINST THE PHILISTINES

²⁸This oracle came in the year King Ahaz died:

²⁹Do not rejoice, all you Philistines,
that the rod that struck you is broken;
from the root of that snake will spring
up a viper,
its fruit will be a darting, venomous
serpent.
³⁰The poorest of the poor will find
pasture,
and the needy will lie down in safety.
But your root I will destroy by famine;
it will slay your survivors.

³¹Wail, O gate! Howl, O city!
Melt away, all you Philistines!
A cloud of smoke comes from the north,
and there is not a straggler in its
ranks.

NOW OR NEVER
ISA 14:27

No one can stop God's will from being accomplished. His purposes are like a freight train rumbling down the tracks. If you're not on board, you're either going to get left behind or run over.

³²What answer shall be given
to the envoys of that nation?
"The LORD has established Zion,
and in her his afflicted people will find refuge."

A PROPHECY AGAINST MOAB

15

An oracle concerning Moab:

Ar in Moab is ruined,
destroyed in a night!
Kir in Moab is ruined,
destroyed in a night!
²Dibon goes up to its temple,
to its high places to weep;
Moab wails over Nebo and Medeba.
Every head is shaved
and every beard cut off.
³In the streets they wear sackcloth;
on the roofs and in the public squares
they all wail,
prostrate with weeping.
⁴Heshbon and Elealeh cry out,

their voices are heard all the way to Jahaz.
Therefore the armed men of Moab cry out,
and their hearts are faint.

⁵My heart cries out over Moab;
her fugitives flee as far as Zoar,
as far as Eglath Shelishiyah.
They go up the way to Luhith,
weeping as they go;
on the road to Horonaim
they lament their destruction.
⁶The waters of Nimrim are dried up
and the grass is withered;
the vegetation is gone
and nothing green is left.
⁷So the wealth they have acquired and stored up
they carry away over the Ravine of the Poplars.
⁸Their outcry echoes along the border of Moab;
their wailing reaches as far as Eglaim,
their lamentation as far as Beer Elim.
⁹Dimon's ᵃ waters are full of blood,
but I will bring still more upon Dimon ᵃ—
a lion upon the fugitives of Moab
and upon those who remain in the land.

16

Send lambs as tribute
to the ruler of the land,
from Sela, across the desert,
to the mount of the Daughter of Zion.
²Like fluttering birds
pushed from the nest,
so are the women of Moab
at the fords of the Arnon.

³"Give us counsel,
render a decision.
Make your shadow like night—
at high noon.
Hide the fugitives,
do not betray the refugees.
⁴Let the Moabite fugitives stay with you;
be their shelter from the destroyer."

The oppressor will come to an end,
and destruction will cease;
the aggressor will vanish from the land.
⁵In love a throne will be established;
in faithfulness a man will sit on it—
one from the house ᵇ of David—
one who in judging seeks justice
and speeds the cause of righteousness.

⁶We have heard of Moab's pride—
her overweening pride and conceit,
her pride and her insolence—

ᵃ *9* Masoretic Text; Dead Sea Scrolls, some Septuagint manuscripts and Vulgate *Dibon*   ᵇ *5* Hebrew *tent*

but her boasts are empty.
7 Therefore the Moabites wail,
they wail together for Moab.
Lament and grieve
for the men[a] of Kir Hareseth.
8 The fields of Heshbon wither,
the vines of Sibmah also.
The rulers of the nations
have trampled down the choicest vines,
which once reached Jazer
and spread toward the desert.
Their shoots spread out
and went as far as the sea.
9 So I weep, as Jazer weeps,
for the vines of Sibmah.
O Heshbon, O Elealeh,
I drench you with tears!
The shouts of joy over your ripened fruit
and over your harvests have been
stilled.
10 Joy and gladness are taken away from
the orchards;
no one sings or shouts in the
vineyards;
no one treads out wine at the presses,
for I have put an end to the shouting.
11 My heart laments for Moab like a harp,
my inmost being for Kir Hareseth.
12 When Moab appears at her high place,
she only wears herself out;
when she goes to her shrine to pray,
it is to no avail.

13 This is the word the LORD has already spoken concerning Moab. 14 But now the LORD says: "Within three years, as a servant bound by contract would count them, Moab's splendor and all her many people will be despised, and her survivors will be very few and feeble."

AN ORACLE AGAINST DAMASCUS

17

An oracle concerning Damascus:

"See, Damascus will no longer be a city
but will become a heap of ruins.
2 The cities of Aroer will be deserted
and left to flocks, which will lie down,
with no one to make them afraid.
3 The fortified city will disappear from Ephraim,
and royal power from Damascus;
the remnant of Aram will be
like the glory of the Israelites,"

declares the LORD Almighty.

4 "In that day the glory of Jacob will fade;
the fat of his body will waste away.
5 It will be as when a reaper gathers the standing grain
and harvests the grain with his arm—

a 7 Or "raisin cakes," a wordplay

as when a man gleans heads of grain
in the Valley of Rephaim.
⁶ Yet some gleanings will remain,
as when an olive tree is beaten,
leaving two or three olives on the topmost branches,
four or five on the fruitful boughs,"
declares the LORD, the God of Israel.

⁷ In that day men will look to their Maker
and turn their eyes to the Holy One of Israel.
⁸ They will not look to the altars,
the work of their hands,
and they will have no regard for the Asherah poles[a]
and the incense altars their fingers have made.

⁹ In that day their strong cities, which they left because of the Israelites, will be like places abandoned to thickets and undergrowth. And all will be desolation.

¹⁰ You have forgotten God your Savior;
you have not remembered the Rock, your fortress.
Therefore, though you set out the finest plants
and plant imported vines,
¹¹ though on the day you set them out, you
make them grow,
and on the morning when you plant
them, you bring them to bud,
yet the harvest will be as nothing
in the day of disease and incurable
pain.

¹² Oh, the raging of many nations—
they rage like the raging sea!
Oh, the uproar of the peoples—
they roar like the roaring of great
waters!

¹³ Although the peoples roar like the roar of surging waters,
when he rebukes them they flee far away,
driven before the wind like chaff on the hills,
like tumbleweed before a gale.
¹⁴ In the evening, sudden terror!
Before the morning, they are gone!
This is the portion of those who loot us,
the lot of those who plunder us.

NOW OR NEVER
ISA 17:10–11

What does the way you live say about God's role in your life? Is he just an afterthought to you? Ask God to help you make him the centerpiece of your daily life—even when things around you get crazy.

A PROPHECY AGAINST CUSH

18

Woe to the land of whirring wings[b]
along the rivers of Cush,[c]
² which sends envoys by sea
in papyrus boats over the water.

Go, swift messengers,
to a people tall and smooth-skinned,
to a people feared far and wide,
an aggressive nation of strange speech,
whose land is divided by rivers.

³ All you people of the world,

---

[a] 8 That is, symbols of the goddess Asherah   [b] 1 Or of locusts   [c] 1 That is, the upper Nile region

you who live on the earth,
when a banner is raised on the mountains,
you will see it,
and when a trumpet sounds,
you will hear it.

4 This is what the LORD says to me:
"I will remain quiet and will look on from my dwelling place,
like shimmering heat in the sunshine,
like a cloud of dew in the heat of harvest."

5 For, before the harvest, when the blossom is gone
and the flower becomes a ripening grape,
he will cut off the shoots with pruning knives,
and cut down and take away the spreading branches.

6 They will all be left to the mountain birds of prey
and to the wild animals;
the birds will feed on them all summer,
the wild animals all winter.

7 At that time gifts will be brought to the LORD Almighty

from a people tall and smooth-skinned,
from a people feared far and wide,
an aggressive nation of strange speech,
whose land is divided by rivers—

the gifts will be brought to Mount Zion, the place of the Name of the LORD Almighty.

A PROPHECY ABOUT EGYPT

19

An oracle concerning Egypt:

See, the LORD rides on a swift cloud
and is coming to Egypt.
The idols of Egypt tremble before him,
and the hearts of the Egyptians melt within them.

2 "I will stir up Egyptian against Egyptian—
brother will fight against brother,
neighbor against neighbor,
city against city,
kingdom against kingdom.

3 The Egyptians will lose heart,
and I will bring their plans to nothing;
they will consult the idols and the spirits of the dead,
the mediums and the spiritists.

4 I will hand the Egyptians over
to the power of a cruel master,
and a fierce king will rule over them,"
declares the Lord, the LORD Almighty.

5 The waters of the river will dry up,
and the riverbed will be parched and dry.

6 The canals will stink;
the streams of Egypt will dwindle and dry up.
The reeds and rushes will wither,

7 also the plants along the Nile,
at the mouth of the river.
Every sown field along the Nile
will become parched, will blow away and be no more.

⁸The fishermen will groan and lament,
  all who cast hooks into the Nile;
 those who throw nets on the water
  will pine away.
⁹Those who work with combed flax will despair,
  the weavers of fine linen will lose hope.
¹⁰The workers in cloth will be dejected,
  and all the wage earners will be sick at heart.

¹¹The officials of Zoan are nothing but fools;
  the wise counselors of Pharaoh give senseless advice.
 How can you say to Pharaoh,
  "I am one of the wise men,
  a disciple of the ancient kings"?

¹²Where are your wise men now?
  Let them show you and make known
 what the LORD Almighty
  has planned against Egypt.
¹³The officials of Zoan have become fools,
  the leaders of Memphisᵃ are deceived;
 the cornerstones of her peoples
  have led Egypt astray.
¹⁴The LORD has poured into them
  a spirit of dizziness;
 they make Egypt stagger in all that she does,
  as a drunkard staggers around in his vomit.
¹⁵There is nothing Egypt can do—
  head or tail, palm branch or reed.

¹⁶In that day the Egyptians will be like women. They will shudder with fear at the uplifted hand that the LORD Almighty raises against them. ¹⁷And the land of Judah will bring terror to the Egyptians; everyone to whom Judah is mentioned will be terrified, because of what the LORD Almighty is planning against them.

¹⁸In that day five cities in Egypt will speak the language of Canaan and swear allegiance to the LORD Almighty. One of them will be called the City of Destruction.ᵇ

¹⁹In that day there will be an altar to the LORD in the heart of Egypt, and a monument to the LORD at its border. ²⁰It will be a sign and witness to the LORD Almighty in the land of Egypt. When they cry out to the LORD because of their oppressors, he will send them a savior and defender, and he will rescue them. ²¹So the LORD will make himself known to the Egyptians, and in that day they will acknowledge the LORD. They will worship with sacrifices and grain offerings; they will make vows to the LORD and keep them. ²²The LORD will strike Egypt with a plague; he will strike them and heal them. They will turn to the LORD, and he will respond to their pleas and heal them.

²³In that day there will be a highway from Egypt to Assyria. The Assyrians will go to Egypt and the Egyptians to Assyria. The Egyptians and Assyrians will worship together. ²⁴In that day Israel will be the third, along with Egypt and Assyria, a blessing on the earth. ²⁵The LORD Almighty will bless them, saying, "Blessed be Egypt my people, Assyria my handiwork, and Israel my inheritance."

A PROPHECY AGAINST EGYPT AND CUSH

20 In the year that the supreme commander, sent by Sargon king of Assyria, came to Ashdod and attacked and captured it— ²at that time the LORD spoke through Isaiah son of Amoz. He said to him, "Take off the sackcloth from your body and the sandals from your feet." And he did so, going around stripped and barefoot.

³Then the LORD said, "Just as my servant Isaiah has gone stripped and barefoot for three years, as a sign and portent against Egypt and Cush,ᶜ ⁴so the king of Assyria will lead away stripped and bare-

---

ᵃ 13 Hebrew Noph   ᵇ 18 Most manuscripts of the Masoretic Text; some manuscripts of the Masoretic Text, Dead Sea Scrolls and Vulgate City of the Sun (that is, Heliopolis)   ᶜ 3 That is, the upper Nile region; also in verse 5

battlelines

» Joystick . . . Joystuck (Gaming)

Q: Did you say you have a Nintendo system *and* an Xbox?
A: That's right. And my best friend has a PlayStation and a GameCube.

Q: So you've got all the systems covered. What about games?
A: Between the two of us, we've probably got 100 games or so.

Q: That's a lot of software.
A: Yeah, but there are always new ones coming out, so that number will keep going up.

Q: How many hours a week would you say you spend playing all these games?
A: Well, my parents get on my case for playing during the week—you know, on school days. They say I'm too obsessed or whatever. So mostly we play on weekends.

Q: So how many hours on weekends?
A: I don't know. Ten hours. Maybe twelve.

Q: Don't you get tired of it? Just sitting in front of a screen all weekend?
A: No way! Like I said, there are always new games coming out, and each one has a bunch of levels. Plus, if you get the cheat codes, you can go really deep into a game.

Q: With all that practice, you guys must be pretty good.
A: You got that right. Jay and I can beat anybody.

Q: What does that do for your future?
A: What do you mean?

Q: Well, they don't exactly give scholarships for *gaming*, do they?
A: Look, nobody ever said this was a career move. It's just a hobby. It's something we like to do. Some guys play cards. Others play guitar. And 99.9 percent of *them* aren't going to play cards or write music for their career, you know? But, hey, they always need people to come up with new games and to test them. So who knows?

» Redeeming the Time

Hobbies are fine—unless they become all-consuming. When any recreational pursuit, whether it's fishing, skiing, collecting something or whatever, begins to control your life and eat up every free moment, something has to change.

Why? Well, for starters, life is short: "Man is like a breath; his days are like a fleeting shadow" (Psalm 144:4). Second, we are warned to make the most of our brief time here on earth (see Ephesians 5:15–16). Third, at the end of this life, "we must all appear before the judgment seat of Christ, that each one may receive what is due him for the things done while in the body, whether good or bad" (2 Corinthians 5:10).

The point? You want to do something worthwhile with your life, right? You'll need more than a hobby or two to succeed.

Read more at www.RevolutionBible.com.

foot the Egyptian captives and Cushite exiles, young and old, with buttocks bared—to Egypt's shame. ⁵Those who trusted in Cush and boasted in Egypt will be afraid and put to shame. ⁶In that day the people who live on this coast will say, 'See what has happened to those we relied on, those we fled to for help and deliverance from the king of Assyria! How then can we escape?' "

A PROPHECY AGAINST BABYLON

21

An oracle concerning the Desert by the Sea:

> Like whirlwinds sweeping through the southland,
>> an invader comes from the desert,
>> from a land of terror.

> ²A dire vision has been shown to me:
>> The traitor betrays, the looter takes loot.
> Elam, attack! Media, lay siege!
>> I will bring to an end all the groaning she caused.

> ³At this my body is racked with pain,
>> pangs seize me, like those of a woman in labor;
> I am staggered by what I hear,
>> I am bewildered by what I see.
> ⁴My heart falters,
>> fear makes me tremble;
> the twilight I longed for
>> has become a horror to me.

> ⁵They set the tables,
>> they spread the rugs,
>> they eat, they drink!
> Get up, you officers,
>> oil the shields!

⁶This is what the Lord says to me:

> "Go, post a lookout
>> and have him report what he sees.
> ⁷When he sees chariots
>> with teams of horses,
> riders on donkeys
>> or riders on camels,
> let him be alert,
>> fully alert."

⁸And the lookoutᵃ shouted,

> "Day after day, my lord, I stand on the watchtower;
>> every night I stay at my post.
> ⁹Look, here comes a man in a chariot
>> with a team of horses.
> And he gives back the answer:
>> 'Babylon has fallen, has fallen!
> All the images of its gods
>> lie shattered on the ground!' "

> ¹⁰O my people, crushed on the threshing floor,
>> I tell you what I have heard
> from the Lᴏʀᴅ Almighty,
>> from the God of Israel.

ᵃ 8 Dead Sea Scrolls and Syriac; Masoretic Text A lion

A PROPHECY AGAINST EDOM

¹¹An oracle concerning Dumah^a:

> Someone calls to me from Seir,
> "Watchman, what is left of the night?
> Watchman, what is left of the night?"
> ¹²The watchman replies,
> "Morning is coming, but also the night.
> If you would ask, then ask;
> and come back yet again."

A PROPHECY AGAINST ARABIA

¹³An oracle concerning Arabia:

> You caravans of Dedanites,
> who camp in the thickets of Arabia,
> ¹⁴ bring water for the thirsty;
> you who live in Tema,
> bring food for the fugitives.
> ¹⁵They flee from the sword,
> from the drawn sword,
> from the bent bow
> and from the heat of battle.

¹⁶This is what the Lord says to me: "Within one year, as a servant bound by contract would count it, all the pomp of Kedar will come to an end. ¹⁷The survivors of the bowmen, the warriors of Kedar, will be few." The LORD, the God of Israel, has spoken.

A PROPHECY ABOUT JERUSALEM

22 An oracle concerning the Valley of Vision:

> What troubles you now,
> that you have all gone up on the roofs,
> ²O town full of commotion,
> O city of tumult and revelry?
> Your slain were not killed by the sword,
> nor did they die in battle.
> ³All your leaders have fled together;
> they have been captured without using the bow.
> All you who were caught were taken prisoner together,
> having fled while the enemy was still far away.
> ⁴Therefore I said, "Turn away from me;
> let me weep bitterly.
> Do not try to console me
> over the destruction of my people."
>
> ⁵The Lord, the LORD Almighty, has a day
> of tumult and trampling and terror
> in the Valley of Vision,
> a day of battering down walls
> and of crying out to the mountains.
> ⁶Elam takes up the quiver,
> with her charioteers and horses;
> Kir uncovers the shield.
> ⁷Your choicest valleys are full of chariots,

---

^a *11 Dumah* means *silence* or *stillness*, a wordplay on *Edom*.

and horsemen are posted at the city gates;
8   the defenses of Judah are stripped away.

And you looked in that day
    to the weapons in the Palace of the Forest;
9 you saw that the City of David
    had many breaches in its defenses;
you stored up water
    in the Lower Pool.
10 You counted the buildings in Jerusalem
    and tore down houses to strengthen the wall.
11 You built a reservoir between the two walls
    for the water of the Old Pool,
but you did not look to the One who made it,
                    or have regard for the One who
                        planned it long ago.

12 The Lord, the LORD Almighty,
        called you on that day
    to weep and to wail,
        to tear out your hair and put on
            sackcloth.
13 But see, there is joy and revelry,
        slaughtering of cattle and killing of
            sheep,
        eating of meat and drinking of wine!
    "Let us eat and drink," you say,
        "for tomorrow we die!"

NOW OR NEVER

ISA 22:13

There's nothing wrong with having fun—as long as it doesn't become an idol or an all-consuming pursuit. Walking with God is so rich and his purposes are so incredible. Don't miss out on the real meaning of life because you're off chasing good times.

14 The LORD Almighty has revealed this in my hearing: "Till your dying day this sin will not be atoned for," says the Lord, the LORD Almighty.

15 This is what the Lord, the LORD Almighty, says:

"Go, say to this steward,
    to Shebna, who is in charge of the palace:
16 What are you doing here and who gave you permission
    to cut out a grave for yourself here,
hewing your grave on the height
    and chiseling your resting place in the rock?

17 "Beware, the LORD is about to take firm hold of you
    and hurl you away, O you mighty man.
18 He will roll you up tightly like a ball
    and throw you into a large country.
There you will die
    and there your splendid chariots will remain—
    you disgrace to your master's house!
19 I will depose you from your office,
    and you will be ousted from your position.

20 "In that day I will summon my servant, Eliakim son of Hilkiah. 21 I will clothe him with your robe and fasten your sash around him and hand your authority over to him. He will be a father to those who live in Jerusalem and to the house of Judah. 22 I will place on his shoulder the key to the house of David; what he opens no one can shut, and what he shuts no one can open. 23 I will drive him like a peg into a firm place; he will be a seat[a] of honor for the house of his father. 24 All the glory of his family will hang on him: its offspring and offshoots—all its lesser vessels, from the bowls to all the jars.

a 23 Or throne

"In that day," declares the LORD Almighty, "the peg driven into the firm place will give way; it will be sheared off and will fall, and the load hanging on it will be cut down." The LORD has spoken.

A PROPHECY ABOUT TYRE

23

An oracle concerning Tyre:

Wail, O ships of Tarshish!
　　For Tyre is destroyed
　　and left without house or harbor.
From the land of Cyprus[a]
　　word has come to them.

2 Be silent, you people of the island
　　and you merchants of Sidon,
　　whom the seafarers have enriched.
3 On the great waters
　　came the grain of the Shihor;
the harvest of the Nile[b] was the revenue of Tyre,
　　and she became the marketplace of the nations.

4 Be ashamed, O Sidon, and you, O fortress of the sea,
　　for the sea has spoken:
"I have neither been in labor nor given birth;
　　I have neither reared sons nor brought up daughters."
5 When word comes to Egypt,
　　they will be in anguish at the report from Tyre.

6 Cross over to Tarshish;
　　wail, you people of the island.
7 Is this your city of revelry,
　　the old, old city,
whose feet have taken her
　　to settle in far-off lands?
8 Who planned this against Tyre,
　　the bestower of crowns,
whose merchants are princes,
　　whose traders are renowned in the earth?
9 The LORD Almighty planned it,
　　to bring low the pride of all glory
　　and to humble all who are renowned on the earth.

10 Till[c] your land as along the Nile,
　　O Daughter of Tarshish,
　　for you no longer have a harbor.
11 The LORD has stretched out his hand over the sea
　　and made its kingdoms tremble.
He has given an order concerning Phoenicia[d]
　　that her fortresses be destroyed.
12 He said, "No more of your reveling,
　　O Virgin Daughter of Sidon, now crushed!

"Up, cross over to Cyprus[a];
　　even there you will find no rest."
13 Look at the land of the Babylonians,[e]
　　this people that is now of no account!

---

[a] 1,12 Hebrew *Kittim*　　[b] 2,3 Masoretic Text; one Dead Sea Scroll *Sidon, / who cross over the sea; / your envoys* [3]*are on the great waters. / The grain of the Shihor, / the harvest of the Nile,*　　[c] 10 Dead Sea Scrolls and some Septuagint manuscripts; Masoretic Text *Go through*　　[d] 11 Hebrew *Canaan*　　[e] 13 Or *Chaldeans*

The Assyrians have made it
    a place for desert creatures;
they raised up their siege towers,
they stripped its fortresses bare
    and turned it into a ruin.

¹⁴Wail, you ships of Tarshish;
    your fortress is destroyed!

¹⁵At that time Tyre will be forgotten for seventy years, the span of a king's life. But at the end of these seventy years, it will happen to Tyre as in the song of the prostitute:

¹⁶"Take up a harp, walk through the city,
    O prostitute forgotten;
play the harp well, sing many a song,
    so that you will be remembered."

¹⁷At the end of seventy years, the LORD will deal with Tyre. She will return to her hire as a prostitute and will ply her trade with all the kingdoms on the face of the earth. ¹⁸Yet her profit and her earnings will be set apart for the LORD; they will not be stored up or hoarded. Her profits will go to those who live before the LORD, for abundant food and fine clothes.

THE LORD'S DEVASTATION OF THE EARTH

24

See, the LORD is going to lay waste the earth
    and devastate it;
he will ruin its face
    and scatter its inhabitants—

²it will be the same
    for priest as for people,
    for master as for servant,
    for mistress as for maid,
    for seller as for buyer,
    for borrower as for lender,
    for debtor as for creditor.
³The earth will be completely laid waste
    and totally plundered.
            The LORD has spoken
                this word.

⁴The earth dries up and withers,
    the world languishes and withers,
    the exalted of the earth languish.
⁵The earth is defiled by its people;
    they have disobeyed the laws,
violated the statutes
    and broken the everlasting covenant.
⁶Therefore a curse consumes the earth;
    its people must bear their guilt.
Therefore earth's inhabitants are burned up,
    and very few are left.
⁷The new wine dries up and the vine withers;
    all the merrymakers groan.
⁸The gaiety of the tambourines is stilled,
    the noise of the revelers has stopped,
    the joyful harp is silent.
⁹No longer do they drink wine with a song;
    the beer is bitter to its drinkers.
¹⁰The ruined city lies desolate;

NOW OR NEVER

ISA 24:1–3

When you think about the end of the world, what do you imagine it will be like? This chapter gives us some pretty sobering clues. Remember though, no matter how it all goes down, God will be in complete control.

the entrance to every house is barred.
11 In the streets they cry out for wine;
all joy turns to gloom,
all gaiety is banished from the earth.
12 The city is left in ruins,
its gate is battered to pieces.
13 So will it be on the earth
and among the nations,
as when an olive tree is beaten,
or as when gleanings are left after the grape harvest.

14 They raise their voices, they shout for joy;
from the west they acclaim the LORD's majesty.
15 Therefore in the east give glory to the LORD;
exalt the name of the LORD, the God of Israel,
in the islands of the sea.
16 From the ends of the earth we hear singing:
"Glory to the Righteous One."

But I said, "I waste away, I waste away!
Woe to me!
The treacherous betray!
With treachery the treacherous betray!"
17 Terror and pit and snare await you,
O people of the earth.
18 Whoever flees at the sound of terror
will fall into a pit;
whoever climbs out of the pit
will be caught in a snare.

The floodgates of the heavens are opened,
the foundations of the earth shake.
19 The earth is broken up,
the earth is split asunder,
the earth is thoroughly shaken.
20 The earth reels like a drunkard,
it sways like a hut in the wind;
so heavy upon it is the guilt of its rebellion
that it falls—never to rise again.

21 In that day the LORD will punish
the powers in the heavens above
and the kings on the earth below.
22 They will be herded together
like prisoners bound in a dungeon;
they will be shut up in prison
and be punished[a] after many days.
23 The moon will be abashed, the sun ashamed;
for the LORD Almighty will reign
on Mount Zion and in Jerusalem,
and before its elders, gloriously.

PRAISE TO THE LORD

25

O LORD, you are my God;
I will exalt you and praise your name,
for in perfect faithfulness

[a] 22 Or released

you have done marvelous things,
   things planned long ago.
²You have made the city a heap of rubble,
   the fortified town a ruin,
the foreigners' stronghold a city no more;
   it will never be rebuilt.
³Therefore strong peoples will honor you;
   cities of ruthless nations will revere you.
⁴You have been a refuge for the poor,
   a refuge for the needy in his distress,
a shelter from the storm
   and a shade from the heat.
For the breath of the ruthless
   is like a storm driving against a wall
⁵   and like the heat of the desert.
You silence the uproar of foreigners;
   as heat is reduced by the shadow of a cloud,
   so the song of the ruthless is stilled.

now or never

ISA 25:9

Think about what it means for you to be saved . . . what horrible suffering Jesus had to endure for your sins . . . the amazing eternity you have to look forward to. Reflect on these things and let God know that you don't treat his awesome gift lightly.

⁶On this mountain the Lord Almighty will prepare
   a feast of rich food for all peoples,
a banquet of aged wine—
   the best of meats and the finest of wines.
⁷On this mountain he will destroy
   the shroud that enfolds all peoples,
the sheet that covers all nations;
   ⁸he will swallow up death forever.
The Sovereign Lord will wipe away the tears
   from all faces;
he will remove the disgrace of his people
   from all the earth.

         The Lord has spoken.

⁹In that day they will say,

"Surely this is our God;
   we trusted in him, and he saved us.
This is the Lord, we trusted in him;
   let us rejoice and be glad in his salvation."

¹⁰The hand of the Lord will rest on this mountain;
   but Moab will be trampled under him
   as straw is trampled down in the manure.
¹¹They will spread out their hands in it,
   as a swimmer spreads out his hands to swim.
God will bring down their pride
   despite the cleverness^a of their hands.
¹²He will bring down your high fortified walls
   and lay them low;
he will bring them down to the ground,
   to the very dust.

---

^a *11* The meaning of the Hebrew for this word is uncertain.

A SONG OF PRAISE

26

In that day this song will be sung in the land of Judah:

We have a strong city;
God makes salvation
its walls and ramparts.
2 Open the gates
that the righteous nation may enter,
the nation that keeps faith.
3 You will keep in perfect peace
him whose mind is steadfast,
because he trusts in you.

challenge**notes**

To: my_son

ISA 26:3-4

heavenly_father: the more you try to solve your own problems,
the more stress you're going to create for yourself. the only
way to find real peace is to place everything in my hands. trust
me to lead you to where you need to be. I've never steered
anyone wrong.

4 Trust in the LORD forever,
for the LORD, the LORD, is
the Rock eternal.
5 He humbles those who dwell
on high,
he lays the lofty city low;
he levels it to the ground
and casts it down to the dust.
6 Feet trample it down—
the feet of the oppressed,
the footsteps of the poor.

7 The path of the righteous is
level;
O upright One, you make the way of the righteous smooth.
8 Yes, LORD, walking in the way of your laws,[a]
we wait for you;
your name and renown
are the desire of our hearts.
9 My soul yearns for you in the night;
in the morning my spirit longs for you.
When your judgments come upon the earth,
the people of the world learn righteousness.
10 Though grace is shown to the wicked,
they do not learn righteousness;
even in a land of uprightness they go on doing evil
and regard not the majesty of the LORD.
11 O LORD, your hand is lifted high,
but they do not see it.
Let them see your zeal for your people and be put to shame;
let the fire reserved for your enemies consume them.

12 LORD, you establish peace for us;
all that we have accomplished you have done for us.
13 O LORD, our God, other lords besides you have ruled over us,
but your name alone do we honor.
14 They are now dead, they live no more;
those departed spirits do not rise.
You punished them and brought them to ruin;
you wiped out all memory of them.
15 You have enlarged the nation, O LORD;
you have enlarged the nation.

---

a 8 Or judgments

You have gained glory for yourself;
        you have extended all the borders of the land.

¹⁶ LORD, they came to you in their distress;
        when you disciplined them,
        they could barely whisper a prayer.ᵃ
¹⁷ As a woman with child and about to give birth
        writhes and cries out in her pain,
        so were we in your presence, O LORD.
¹⁸ We were with child, we writhed in pain,
        but we gave birth to wind.
    We have not brought salvation to the earth;
        we have not given birth to people of the world.

¹⁹ But your dead will live;
        their bodies will rise.
    You who dwell in the dust,
        wake up and shout for joy.
    Your dew is like the dew of the morning;
        the earth will give birth to her dead.

²⁰ Go, my people, enter your rooms
        and shut the doors behind you;
    hide yourselves for a little while
        until his wrath has passed by.
²¹ See, the LORD is coming out of his dwelling
        to punish the people of the earth for their sins.
    The earth will disclose the blood shed upon her;
        she will conceal her slain no longer.

DELIVERANCE OF ISRAEL

In that day,

    the LORD will punish with his sword,
        his fierce, great and powerful sword,
    Leviathan the gliding serpent,
        Leviathan the coiling serpent;
    he will slay the monster of the sea.

²In that day—

    "Sing about a fruitful vineyard:
³   I, the LORD, watch over it;
        I water it continually.
    I guard it day and night
        so that no one may harm it.
⁴   I am not angry.
    If only there were briers and thorns confronting me!
        I would march against them in battle;
        I would set them all on fire.
⁵ Or else let them come to me for refuge;
        let them make peace with me,
        yes, let them make peace with me."

⁶ In days to come Jacob will take root,
        Israel will bud and blossom
        and fill all the world with fruit.

ᵃ *16* The meaning of the Hebrew for this clause is uncertain.

⁷ Has ⌊the Lord⌋ struck her
    as he struck down those who struck her?
Has she been killed
    as those were killed who killed her?
⁸ By warfare[a] and exile you contend with her—
    with his fierce blast he drives her out,
    as on a day the east wind blows.
⁹ By this, then, will Jacob's guilt be atoned for,
    and this will be the full fruitage of the removal of his sin:
When he makes all the altar stones
    to be like chalk stones crushed to pieces,
no Asherah poles[b] or incense altars
    will be left standing.
¹⁰ The fortified city stands desolate,
    an abandoned settlement, forsaken like the desert;
there the calves graze,
    there they lie down;
    they strip its branches bare.
¹¹ When its twigs are dry, they are broken off
    and women come and make fires with them.
For this is a people without understanding;
    so their Maker has no compassion on them,
    and their Creator shows them no favor.

¹²In that day the Lord will thresh from the flowing Euphrates[c] to the Wadi of Egypt, and you, O Israelites, will be gathered up one by one. ¹³And in that day a great trumpet will sound. Those who were perishing in Assyria and those who were exiled in Egypt will come and worship the Lord on the holy mountain in Jerusalem.

WOE TO EPHRAIM

Woe to that wreath, the pride of Ephraim's drunkards,
    to the fading flower, his glorious beauty,
set on the head of a fertile valley—
    to that city, the pride of those laid low by wine!
² See, the Lord has one who is powerful and strong.
    Like a hailstorm and a destructive wind,
like a driving rain and a flooding downpour,
    he will throw it forcefully to the ground.
³ That wreath, the pride of Ephraim's drunkards,
    will be trampled underfoot.
⁴ That fading flower, his glorious beauty,
    set on the head of a fertile valley,
will be like a fig ripe before harvest—
    as soon as someone sees it and takes it in his hand,
    he swallows it.

⁵ In that day the Lord Almighty
    will be a glorious crown,
a beautiful wreath
    for the remnant of his people.
⁶ He will be a spirit of justice
    to him who sits in judgment,
a source of strength
    to those who turn back the battle at the gate.

---

[a] *8* See Septuagint; the meaning of the Hebrew for this word is uncertain.   [b] *9* That is, symbols of the goddess Asherah   [c] *12* Hebrew *River*

⁷And these also stagger from wine
    and reel from beer:
Priests and prophets stagger from beer
    and are befuddled with wine;
they reel from beer,
    they stagger when seeing visions,
    they stumble when rendering decisions.
⁸All the tables are covered with vomit
    and there is not a spot without filth.

⁹"Who is it he is trying to teach?
    To whom is he explaining his message?
To children weaned from their milk,
    to those just taken from the breast?
¹⁰For it is:
    Do and do, do and do,
    rule on rule, rule on rule ª;
    a little here, a little there."

¹¹Very well then, with foreign lips and strange tongues
    God will speak to this people,
¹²to whom he said,
    "This is the resting place, let the weary rest";
and, "This is the place of repose"—
    but they would not listen.
¹³So then, the word of the Lᴏʀᴅ to them will become:
    Do and do, do and do,
    rule on rule, rule on rule;
    a little here, a little there—
so that they will go and fall backward,
    be injured and snared and captured.

¹⁴Therefore hear the word of the Lᴏʀᴅ, you scoffers
    who rule this people in Jerusalem.
¹⁵You boast, "We have entered into a covenant with death,
    with the grave ᵇ we have made an agreement.
When an overwhelming scourge sweeps by,
    it cannot touch us,
for we have made a lie our refuge
    and falsehood ᶜ our hiding place."

¹⁶So this is what the Sovereign Lᴏʀᴅ says:

    "See, I lay a stone in Zion,
        a tested stone,
    a precious cornerstone for a sure foundation;
        the one who trusts will never be dismayed.
¹⁷I will make justice the measuring line
    and righteousness the plumb line;
hail will sweep away your refuge, the lie,
    and water will overflow your hiding place.
¹⁸Your covenant with death will be annulled;
    your agreement with the grave will not stand.
When the overwhelming scourge sweeps by,
    you will be beaten down by it.

ª *10* Hebrew / *sav lasav sav lasav / kav lakav kav lakav* (possibly meaningless sounds; perhaps a mimicking of the prophet's words); also in verse 13 ᵇ *15* Hebrew *Sheol*; also in verse 18 ᶜ *15* Or *false gods*

¹⁹As often as it comes it will carry you away;
  morning after morning, by day and by night,
  it will sweep through."

The understanding of this message
  will bring sheer terror.
²⁰The bed is too short to stretch out on,
  the blanket too narrow to wrap around you.
²¹The LORD will rise up as he did at Mount Perazim,
  he will rouse himself as in the Valley of Gibeon—
to do his work, his strange work,
  and perform his task, his alien task.
²²Now stop your mocking,
  or your chains will become heavier;
the Lord, the LORD Almighty, has told me
  of the destruction decreed against the whole land.

²³Listen and hear my voice;
  pay attention and hear what I say.
²⁴When a farmer plows for planting, does he plow continually?
  Does he keep on breaking up and harrowing the soil?
²⁵When he has leveled the surface,
  does he not sow caraway and scatter cummin?
Does he not plant wheat in its place,ᵃ
  barley in its plot,ᵃ
  and spelt in its field?
²⁶His God instructs him
  and teaches him the right way.

²⁷Caraway is not threshed with a sledge,
  nor is a cartwheel rolled over cummin;
caraway is beaten out with a rod,
  and cummin with a stick.
²⁸Grain must be ground to make bread;
  so one does not go on threshing it forever.
Though he drives the wheels of his threshing cart over it,
  his horses do not grind it.
²⁹All this also comes from the LORD Almighty,
  wonderful in counsel and magnificent in wisdom.

WOE TO DAVID'S CITY

 Woe to you, Ariel, Ariel,
  the city where David settled!
Add year to year
  and let your cycle of festivals go on.
²Yet I will besiege Ariel;
  she will mourn and lament,
  she will be to me like an altar hearth.ᵇ
³I will encamp against you all around;
  I will encircle you with towers
  and set up my siege works against you.
⁴Brought low, you will speak from the ground;
  your speech will mumble out of the dust.
Your voice will come ghostlike from the earth;
  out of the dust your speech will whisper.

ᵃ 25 The meaning of the Hebrew for this word is uncertain.   ᵇ 2 The Hebrew for *altar hearth* sounds like the Hebrew for *Ariel*.

battlelines

» Face Off (Hypocrisy)

Q: Why do you feel like a hypocrite?
A: It's like this: I have a devotional time every morning. I go to church at least twice a week. I know exactly how I'm supposed to live. But if my parents tell me I can't see a movie I want to see—or something like that—I do it anyway. Or, like the other morning . . . I was in my bedroom doing my daily Bible reading, and I spilled orange juice on myself. The next thing I knew, I was cussing my head off—during my Bible study! Now *that's* a problem.

Q: You're right. It is a problem.
A: So why am I such a hypocrite? I mean, if I'm doing all the right things, why don't I obey God better? Why am I such a Jekyll and Hyde?

Q: Maybe you're *not* doing all the right things.
A: I just told you that I read my Bible and pray and go to church.

Q: Right. You keep talking about how you're doing *stuff*—church, devotions, yada, yada, yada—but you don't talk about God as though you have a strong connection with him personally.
A: I'm not following you.

Q: The Christian life is supposed to be a relationship. You talk about it like it's a performance or a checklist or something. You rattle off all this stuff you're doing *for* God. But isn't the whole point to be *with* him—to get to know him?
A: Yeah, I guess so.

Q: I mean, how would Courtney feel if you described your relationship with her the way you describe your relationship with God? "Well, I call her for about five minutes each morning, and I go see her twice a week for an hour or so."
A: You're right. That would be a pretty shallow relationship. When you put it like that, it does kind of sound more like a business arrangement than a relationship.

» Face It

When Jesus came on the scene, Israel was full of hypocrisy. Religious people everywhere were wearing themselves out with empty religious activity. People were just going through the motions, performing dead rituals. Jesus looked at all their hoop-jumping and remembered the words of Isaiah: "These people honor me with their lips, but their hearts are far from me" (Matthew 15:8).

Not much has changed in 2,000 years. Lots of church people know the truth and use the correct religious lingo, but their lives don't change.

Reading the Bible, praying and going to church are great tools for building a relationship with God. But that's all they are—tools. There's nothing magical about them. Sitting in front of an open Bible doesn't guarantee anything. Reading a chapter of Scripture is not the same thing as seeking God. Mumbling a quick prayer isn't the same as talking to God.

If you find yourself battling hypocrisy, do a "ritual check." Are you doing things *for* God, but not spending time *with* him? Do whatever it takes to throw yourself back into God's presence. Remember, it's hard to walk away from God when you are holding his hand.

Read more about breaking hypocrisy at www.RevolutionBible.com.

⁵But your many enemies will become like fine dust,
   the ruthless hordes like blown chaff.
Suddenly, in an instant,
⁶   the LORD Almighty will come
with thunder and earthquake and great noise,
   with windstorm and tempest and flames of a devouring fire.
⁷Then the hordes of all the nations that fight against Ariel,
   that attack her and her fortress and besiege her,
will be as it is with a dream,
   with a vision in the night—
⁸as when a hungry man dreams that he
      is eating,
   but he awakens, and his hunger
      remains;
as when a thirsty man dreams that he is
      drinking,
   but he awakens faint, with his thirst
      unquenched.
So will it be with the hordes of all the
      nations
   that fight against Mount Zion.

⁹Be stunned and amazed,
   blind yourselves and be sightless;
be drunk, but not from wine,
   stagger, but not from beer.
¹⁰The LORD has brought over you a deep
      sleep:
   He has sealed your eyes (the
      prophets);
   he has covered your heads (the seers).

¹¹For you this whole vision is nothing but words sealed in a scroll. And if you give the scroll to someone who can read, and say to him, "Read this, please," he will answer, "I can't; it is sealed." ¹²Or if you give the scroll to someone who cannot read, and say, "Read this, please," he will answer, "I don't know how to read."

¹³The Lord says:

"These people come near to me with
      their mouth
   and honor me with their lips,
   but their hearts are far from me.
Their worship of me
   is made up only of rules taught by men.ᵃ
¹⁴Therefore once more I will astound these people
   with wonder upon wonder;
the wisdom of the wise will perish,
   the intelligence of the intelligent will vanish."
¹⁵Woe to those who go to great depths
   to hide their plans from the LORD,
who do their work in darkness and think,
   "Who sees us? Who will know?"
¹⁶You turn things upside down,

Understanding Real Worship

Do you ever feel like your worship is empty, like you're just going through the motions? Do you sing the worship choruses at church without thinking about what they mean? Do you constantly look down at your watch during the sermon, counting the minutes until church is over? When you pray, do you find yourself repeating the words and phrases of other people just so you have something to say? Guess what? That stuff doesn't mean any more to God than it does to you. He'd much rather have an honest relationship with you than your artificial worship. Start there and ask God to help you worship him with your whole heart and life.

ᵃ 13 Hebrew; Septuagint *They worship me in vain; / their teachings are but rules taught by men*

as if the potter were thought to be like the clay!
Shall what is formed say to him who formed it,
  "He did not make me"?
  Can the pot say of the potter,
  "He knows nothing"?

¹⁷ In a very short time, will not Lebanon be
  turned into a fertile field
  and the fertile field seem like a
   forest?
¹⁸ In that day the deaf will hear the words
   of the scroll,
  and out of gloom and darkness
   the eyes of the blind will see.
¹⁹ Once more the humble will rejoice in the
   LORD;
  the needy will rejoice in the Holy One of Israel.
²⁰ The ruthless will vanish,
  the mockers will disappear,
  and all who have an eye for evil will be cut down—
²¹ those who with a word make a man out to be guilty,
  who ensnare the defender in court
  and with false testimony deprive the innocent of justice.

²² Therefore this is what the LORD, who redeemed Abraham, says to the house of Jacob:

  "No longer will Jacob be ashamed;
  no longer will their faces grow pale.
²³ When they see among them their children,
  the work of my hands,
  they will keep my name holy;
  they will acknowledge the holiness of the Holy One of Jacob,
  and will stand in awe of the God of Israel.
²⁴ Those who are wayward in spirit will gain understanding;
  those who complain will accept instruction."

NOW OR NEVER
ISA 29:18–19

A day is coming when believers who have been dealt a tough hand in this life will find out just how incredible the Lord can be. No suffering is permanent. That's God's promise to those who trust in him.

WOE TO THE OBSTINATE NATION

30

  "Woe to the obstinate children,"
   declares the LORD,
  "to those who carry out plans that are not mine,
   forming an alliance, but not by my Spirit,
   heaping sin upon sin;
² who go down to Egypt
  without consulting me;
  who look for help to Pharaoh's protection,
  to Egypt's shade for refuge.
³ But Pharaoh's protection will be to your shame,
  Egypt's shade will bring you disgrace.
⁴ Though they have officials in Zoan
  and their envoys have arrived in Hanes,
⁵ everyone will be put to shame
  because of a people useless to them,
  who bring neither help nor advantage,
  but only shame and disgrace."

⁶ An oracle concerning the animals of the Negev:

  Through a land of hardship and distress,

of lions and lionesses,
of adders and darting snakes,
the envoys carry their riches on donkeys' backs,
their treasures on the humps of camels,
to that unprofitable nation,
⁷ to Egypt, whose help is utterly useless.
Therefore I call her
Rahab the Do-Nothing.

⁸ Go now, write it on a tablet for them,
inscribe it on a scroll,
that for the days to come
it may be an everlasting witness.
⁹ These are rebellious people, deceitful children,
children unwilling to listen to the Lord's instruction.
¹⁰ They say to the seers,
"See no more visions!"
and to the prophets,
"Give us no more visions of what is right!
Tell us pleasant things,
prophesy illusions.
¹¹ Leave this way,
get off this path,
and stop confronting us
with the Holy One of Israel!"

¹² Therefore, this is what the Holy One of Israel says:

"Because you have rejected this message,
relied on oppression
and depended on deceit,
¹³ this sin will become for you
like a high wall, cracked and bulging,
that collapses suddenly, in an instant.
¹⁴ It will break in pieces like pottery,
shattered so mercilessly
that among its pieces not a fragment will be found
for taking coals from a hearth
or scooping water out of a cistern."

¹⁵ This is what the Sovereign Lord, the Holy One of Israel, says:

"In repentance and rest is your salvation,
in quietness and trust is your strength,
but you would have none of it.
¹⁶ You said, 'No, we will flee on horses.'
Therefore you will flee!
You said, 'We will ride off on swift horses.'
Therefore your pursuers will be swift!
¹⁷ A thousand will flee
at the threat of one;
at the threat of five
you will all flee away,
till you are left
like a flagstaff on a mountaintop,
like a banner on a hill."

¹⁸ Yet the LORD longs to be gracious to you;
he rises to show you compassion.
For the LORD is a God of justice.
Blessed are all who wait for him!

¹⁹ O people of Zion, who live in Jerusalem, you will weep no more. How gracious he will be when you cry for help! As soon as he hears, he will answer you. ²⁰ Although the Lord gives you the bread of adversity and the water of affliction, your teachers will be hidden no more; with your own eyes you will see them. ²¹ Whether you turn to the right or to the left, your ears will hear a voice behind you, saying, "This is the way; walk in it." ²² Then you will defile your idols overlaid with silver and your images covered with gold; you will throw them away like a menstrual cloth and say to them, "Away with you!"

NOW OR NEVER

ISA 30:18

God isn't some angry, psychotic judge who's just itching to condemn people to hell. His desire is to show mercy and compassion. The only people who don't experience his grace are those who willfully reject it.

²³ He will also send you rain for the seed you sow in the ground, and the food that comes from the land will be rich and plentiful. In that day your cattle will graze in broad meadows. ²⁴ The oxen and donkeys that work the soil will eat fodder and mash, spread out with fork and shovel. ²⁵ In the day of great slaughter, when the towers fall, streams of water will flow on every high mountain and every lofty hill. ²⁶ The moon will shine like the sun, and the sunlight will be seven times brighter, like the light of seven full days, when the LORD binds up the bruises of his people and heals the wounds he inflicted.

²⁷ See, the Name of the LORD comes from afar,
with burning anger and dense clouds of smoke;
his lips are full of wrath,
and his tongue is a consuming fire.
²⁸ His breath is like a rushing torrent,
rising up to the neck.
He shakes the nations in the sieve of destruction;
he places in the jaws of the peoples
a bit that leads them astray.
²⁹ And you will sing
as on the night you celebrate a holy festival;
your hearts will rejoice
as when people go up with flutes
to the mountain of the LORD,
to the Rock of Israel.
³⁰ The LORD will cause men to hear his majestic voice
and will make them see his arm coming down
with raging anger and consuming fire,
with cloudburst, thunderstorm and hail.
³¹ The voice of the LORD will shatter Assyria;
with his scepter he will strike them down.
³² Every stroke the LORD lays on them
with his punishing rod
will be to the music of tambourines and harps,
as he fights them in battle with the blows of his arm.
³³ Topheth has long been prepared;
it has been made ready for the king.
Its fire pit has been made deep and wide,
with an abundance of fire and wood;
the breath of the LORD,

like a stream of burning sulfur,
        sets it ablaze.

WOE TO THOSE WHO RELY ON EGYPT

31

Woe to those who go down to Egypt for help,
        who rely on horses,
    who trust in the multitude of their chariots
        and in the great strength of their horsemen,
    but do not look to the Holy One of Israel,
        or seek help from the LORD.
² Yet he too is wise and can bring disaster;
        he does not take back his words.
    He will rise up against the house of the wicked,
        against those who help evildoers.
³ But the Egyptians are men and not God;
        their horses are flesh and not spirit.
    When the LORD stretches out his hand,
        he who helps will stumble,
        he who is helped will fall;
        both will perish together.

⁴ This is what the LORD says to me:

    "As a lion growls,
        a great lion over his prey—
    and though a whole band of shepherds
        is called together against him,
    he is not frightened by their shouts
        or disturbed by their clamor—
    so the LORD Almighty will come down
        to do battle on Mount Zion and on its heights.
⁵ Like birds hovering overhead,
        the LORD Almighty will shield Jerusalem;
    he will shield it and deliver it,
        he will 'pass over' it and will rescue it."

⁶ Return to him you have so greatly revolted against, O Israelites. ⁷ For in that day every one of you
will reject the idols of silver and gold your sinful hands have made.

⁸ "Assyria will fall by a sword that is not of man;
        a sword, not of mortals, will devour them.
    They will flee before the sword
        and their young men will be put to forced labor.
⁹ Their stronghold will fall because of terror;
        at sight of the battle standard their commanders will panic,"
    declares the LORD,
        whose fire is in Zion,
        whose furnace is in Jerusalem.

THE KINGDOM OF RIGHTEOUSNESS

32

See, a king will reign in righteousness
        and rulers will rule with justice.
² Each man will be like a shelter from the wind
        and a refuge from the storm,
    like streams of water in the desert
        and the shadow of a great rock in a thirsty land.

³ Then the eyes of those who see will no longer be closed,

and the ears of those who hear will listen.
⁴The mind of the rash will know and understand,
and the stammering tongue will be fluent and clear.
⁵No longer will the fool be called noble
nor the scoundrel be highly respected.
⁶For the fool speaks folly,
his mind is busy with evil:
He practices ungodliness
and spreads error concerning the LORD;
the hungry he leaves empty
and from the thirsty he withholds water.
⁷The scoundrel's methods are wicked,
he makes up evil schemes
to destroy the poor with lies,
even when the plea of the needy is
just.
⁸But the noble man makes noble plans,
and by noble deeds he stands.

THE WOMEN OF JERUSALEM

⁹You women who are so complacent,
rise up and listen to me;
you daughters who feel secure,
hear what I have to say!
¹⁰In little more than a year
you who feel secure will tremble;
the grape harvest will fail,
and the harvest of fruit will not come.
¹¹Tremble, you complacent women;
shudder, you daughters who feel
secure!
Strip off your clothes,
put sackcloth around your waists.
¹²Beat your breasts for the pleasant fields,
for the fruitful vines
¹³and for the land of my people,
a land overgrown with thorns and
briers—
yes, mourn for all houses of merriment
and for this city of revelry.
¹⁴The fortress will be abandoned,
the noisy city deserted;
citadel and watchtower will become a
wasteland forever,
the delight of donkeys, a pasture for flocks,
¹⁵till the Spirit is poured upon us from on high,
and the desert becomes a fertile field,
and the fertile field seems like a forest.
¹⁶Justice will dwell in the desert
and righteousness live in the fertile field.
¹⁷The fruit of righteousness will be peace;
the effect of righteousness will be quietness and confidence forever.
¹⁸My people will live in peaceful dwelling places,
in secure homes,
in undisturbed places of rest.

«« live the adventure »» Isa 32:17

Understanding True Confidence

Do you ever put on a fake personality when you're around your friends or teammates? Do you ever try to make people think you're more confident than you really are? Fake confidence may fool people who don't know you very well, but it doesn't do much else for you. The only thing that can help you feel completely confident is living the way God wants you to live. If you know that you have God's power and blessing in your life, you will have nothing to fear or feel insecure about.

¹⁹ Though hail flattens the forest
and the city is leveled completely,
²⁰ how blessed you will be,
sowing your seed by every stream,
and letting your cattle and donkeys range free.

DISTRESS AND HELP

33

Woe to you, O destroyer,
you who have not been destroyed!
Woe to you, O traitor,
you who have not been betrayed!
When you stop destroying,
you will be destroyed;
when you stop betraying,
you will be betrayed.

² O Lord, be gracious to us;
we long for you.
Be our strength every morning,
our salvation in time of distress.
³ At the thunder of your voice, the peoples flee;
when you rise up, the nations scatter.
⁴ Your plunder, O nations, is harvested as by young locusts;
like a swarm of locusts men pounce on it.

⁵ The Lord is exalted, for he dwells on high;
he will fill Zion with justice and righteousness.
⁶ He will be the sure foundation for your times,
a rich store of salvation and wisdom and knowledge;
the fear of the Lord is the key to this treasure.[a]

⁷ Look, their brave men cry aloud in the streets;
the envoys of peace weep bitterly.
⁸ The highways are deserted,
no travelers are on the roads.
The treaty is broken,
its witnesses[b] are despised,
no one is respected.
⁹ The land mourns[c] and wastes away,
Lebanon is ashamed and withers;
Sharon is like the Arabah,
and Bashan and Carmel drop their leaves.

¹⁰ "Now will I arise," says the Lord.
"Now will I be exalted;
now will I be lifted up.
¹¹ You conceive chaff,
you give birth to straw;
your breath is a fire that consumes you.
¹² The peoples will be burned as if to lime;
like cut thornbushes they will be set ablaze."

NOW OR NEVER

ISA 32:18–20

How many wars are going on in the world today? What would it take to stop them all? The answer is Jesus. The only way to remove the hatred, evil and violence that cause war is to change this world from the inside out—which is exactly what Jesus will do when he comes back.

NOW OR NEVER

ISA 33:2

Do you acknowledge your need for God's strength every morning? You'd be surprised what a little heaven-sent strength can do when you're dealing with parents who constantly fight or a teacher who grades you unfairly or a punk at school who wants to rearrange your face.

---

[a] 6 Or *is a treasure from him*　　[b] 8 Dead Sea Scrolls; Masoretic Text / *the cities*　　[c] 9 Or *dries up*

¹³ You who are far away, hear what I have done;
    you who are near, acknowledge my power!
¹⁴ The sinners in Zion are terrified;
    trembling grips the godless:
"Who of us can dwell with the consuming fire?
    Who of us can dwell with everlasting burning?"
¹⁵ He who walks righteously
    and speaks what is right,
who rejects gain from extortion
    and keeps his hand from accepting bribes,
who stops his ears against plots of murder
    and shuts his eyes against contemplating evil—
¹⁶ this is the man who will dwell on the heights,
    whose refuge will be the mountain fortress.
His bread will be supplied,
    and water will not fail him.

¹⁷ Your eyes will see the king in his beauty
    and view a land that stretches afar.
¹⁸ In your thoughts you will ponder the former terror:
    "Where is that chief officer?
Where is the one who took the revenue?
    Where is the officer in charge of the towers?"
¹⁹ You will see those arrogant people no more,
    those people of an obscure speech,
    with their strange, incomprehensible tongue.

²⁰ Look upon Zion, the city of our festivals;
    your eyes will see Jerusalem,
    a peaceful abode, a tent that will not be moved;
its stakes will never be pulled up,
    nor any of its ropes broken.
²¹ There the LORD will be our Mighty One.
    It will be like a place of broad rivers and streams.
No galley with oars will ride them,
    no mighty ship will sail them.
²² For the LORD is our judge,
    the LORD is our lawgiver,
the LORD is our king;
    it is he who will save us.

²³ Your rigging hangs loose:
    The mast is not held secure,
    the sail is not spread.
Then an abundance of spoils will be divided
    and even the lame will carry off plunder.
²⁴ No one living in Zion will say, "I am ill";
    and the sins of those who dwell there will be forgiven.

JUDGMENT AGAINST THE NATIONS

Come near, you nations, and listen;
    pay attention, you peoples!
Let the earth hear, and all that is in it,
    the world, and all that comes out of it!
² The LORD is angry with all nations;
    his wrath is upon all their armies.

He will totally destroy[a] them,
   he will give them over to slaughter.
3 Their slain will be thrown out,
   their dead bodies will send up a stench;
   the mountains will be soaked with their blood.
4 All the stars of the heavens will be dissolved
   and the sky rolled up like a scroll;
all the starry host will fall
   like withered leaves from the vine,
   like shriveled figs from the fig tree.

5 My sword has drunk its fill in the heavens;
   see, it descends in judgment on Edom,
   the people I have totally destroyed.
6 The sword of the LORD is bathed in blood,
   it is covered with fat—
the blood of lambs and goats,
   fat from the kidneys of rams.
For the LORD has a sacrifice in Bozrah
   and a great slaughter in Edom.
7 And the wild oxen will fall with them,
   the bull calves and the great bulls.
Their land will be drenched with blood,
   and the dust will be soaked with fat.

8 For the LORD has a day of vengeance,
   a year of retribution, to uphold Zion's cause.
9 Edom's streams will be turned into pitch,
   her dust into burning sulfur;
   her land will become blazing pitch!
10 It will not be quenched night and day;
   its smoke will rise forever.
From generation to generation it will lie desolate;
   no one will ever pass through it again.
11 The desert owl[b] and screech owl[b] will possess it;
   the great owl[b] and the raven will nest there.
God will stretch out over Edom
   the measuring line of chaos
   and the plumb line of desolation.
12 Her nobles will have nothing there to be called a kingdom,
   all her princes will vanish away.
13 Thorns will overrun her citadels,
   nettles and brambles her strongholds.
She will become a haunt for jackals,
   a home for owls.
14 Desert creatures will meet with hyenas,
   and wild goats will bleat to each other;
there the night creatures will also repose
   and find for themselves places of rest.
15 The owl will nest there and lay eggs,
   she will hatch them, and care for her young under the shadow of her wings;
there also the falcons will gather,
   each with its mate.

---

[a] 2 The Hebrew term refers to the irrevocable giving over of things or persons to the LORD, often by totally destroying them; also in verse 5. [b] 11 The precise identification of these birds is uncertain.

¹⁶Look in the scroll of the Lord and read:

> None of these will be missing,
>> not one will lack her mate.
> For it is his mouth that has given the order,
>> and his Spirit will gather them together.
> ¹⁷He allots their portions;
>> his hand distributes them by measure.
> They will possess it forever
>> and dwell there from generation to generation.

JOY OF THE REDEEMED

35

> The desert and the parched land will be glad;
>> the wilderness will rejoice and blossom.
> Like the crocus, ²it will burst into bloom;
>> it will rejoice greatly and shout for joy.
> The glory of Lebanon will be given to it,
>> the splendor of Carmel and Sharon;
> they will see the glory of the Lord,
>> the splendor of our God.

> ³Strengthen the feeble hands,
>> steady the knees that give way;
> ⁴say to those with fearful hearts,
>> "Be strong, do not fear;
> your God will come,
>> he will come with vengeance;
> with divine retribution
>> he will come to save you."

> ⁵Then will the eyes of the blind be
>> opened
>> and the ears of the deaf unstopped.
> ⁶Then will the lame leap like a deer,
>> and the mute tongue shout for joy.
> Water will gush forth in the wilderness
>> and streams in the desert.
> ⁷The burning sand will become a pool,
>> the thirsty ground bubbling springs.
> In the haunts where jackals once lay,
>> grass and reeds and papyrus will grow.

> ⁸And a highway will be there;
>> it will be called the Way of Holiness.

NOW OR NEVER
ISA 35:5–6

Think of some additional transformations the Lord could guide in the future. Think of things that have special meaning to you, such as the healing of someone close to you or the mending of a broken relationship. Remember that only God has the power to make all things new.

> The unclean will not journey on it;
>> it will be for those who walk in that Way;
>> wicked fools will not go about on it.^a
> ⁹No lion will be there,
>> nor will any ferocious beast get up on it;
>> they will not be found there.
> But only the redeemed will walk there,
> ¹⁰ and the ransomed of the Lord will return.
> They will enter Zion with singing;
>> everlasting joy will crown their heads.
> Gladness and joy will overtake them,
>> and sorrow and sighing will flee away.

^a 8 Or / the simple will not stray from it

SENNACHERIB THREATENS JERUSALEM

36 In the fourteenth year of King Hezekiah's reign, Sennacherib king of Assyria attacked all the fortified cities of Judah and captured them. ²Then the king of Assyria sent his field commander with a large army from Lachish to King Hezekiah at Jerusalem. When the commander stopped at the aqueduct of the Upper Pool, on the road to the Washerman's Field, ³Eliakim son of Hilkiah the palace administrator, Shebna the secretary, and Joah son of Asaph the recorder went out to him.

⁴The field commander said to them, "Tell Hezekiah,

" 'This is what the great king, the king of Assyria, says: On what are you basing this confidence of yours? ⁵You say you have strategy and military strength—but you speak only empty words. On whom are you depending, that you rebel against me? ⁶Look now, you are depending on Egypt, that splintered reed of a staff, which pierces a man's hand and wounds him if he leans on it! Such is Pharaoh king of Egypt to all who depend on him. ⁷And if you say to me, "We are depending on the LORD our God"—isn't he the one whose high places and altars Hezekiah removed, saying to Judah and Jerusalem, "You must worship before this altar"?

⁸" 'Come now, make a bargain with my master, the king of Assyria: I will give you two thousand horses—if you can put riders on them! ⁹How then can you repulse one officer of the least of my master's officials, even though you are depending on Egypt for chariots and horsemen? ¹⁰Furthermore, have I come to attack and destroy this land without the LORD? The LORD himself told me to march against this country and destroy it.' "

¹¹Then Eliakim, Shebna and Joah said to the field commander, "Please speak to your servants in Aramaic, since we understand it. Don't speak to us in Hebrew in the hearing of the people on the wall."

¹²But the commander replied, "Was it only to your master and you that my master sent me to say these things, and not to the men sitting on the wall—who, like you, will have to eat their own filth and drink their own urine?"

¹³Then the commander stood and called out in Hebrew, "Hear the words of the great king, the king of Assyria! ¹⁴This is what the king says: Do not let Hezekiah deceive you. He cannot deliver you! ¹⁵Do not let Hezekiah persuade you to trust in the LORD when he says, 'The LORD will surely deliver us; this city will not be given into the hand of the king of Assyria.'

¹⁶"Do not listen to Hezekiah. This is what the king of Assyria says: Make peace with me and come out to me. Then every one of you will eat from his own vine and fig tree and drink water from his own cistern, ¹⁷until I come and take you to a land like your own—a land of grain and new wine, a land of bread and vineyards.

¹⁸"Do not let Hezekiah mislead you when he says, 'The LORD will deliver us.' Has the god of any nation ever delivered his land from the hand of the king of Assyria? ¹⁹Where are the gods of Hamath and Arpad? Where are the gods of Sepharvaim? Have they rescued Samaria from my hand? ²⁰Who of all the gods of these countries has been able to save his land from me? How then can the LORD deliver Jerusalem from my hand?"

²¹But the people remained silent and said nothing in reply, because the king had commanded, "Do not answer him."

²²Then Eliakim son of Hilkiah the palace administrator, Shebna the secretary, and Joah son of Asaph the recorder went to Hezekiah, with their clothes torn, and told him what the field commander had said.

JERUSALEM'S DELIVERANCE FORETOLD

37 When King Hezekiah heard this, he tore his clothes and put on sackcloth and went into the temple of the LORD. ²He sent Eliakim the palace administrator, Shebna the secretary, and the leading priests, all wearing sackcloth, to the prophet Isaiah son of Amoz. ³They told him, "This is what Hezekiah says: This day is a day of distress and rebuke and disgrace, as when children come to the point of birth and there is no strength to deliver them. ⁴It may be that the LORD your God will hear the words of the field commander, whom his master, the king of Assyria, has sent to ridicule the living God, and that he will rebuke him for the words the LORD your God has heard. Therefore pray for the remnant that still survives."

⁵When King Hezekiah's officials came to Isaiah, ⁶Isaiah said to them, "Tell your master, 'This is what the LORD says: Do not be afraid of what you have heard—those words with which the underlings of the

king of Assyria have blasphemed me. ⁷Listen! I am going to put a spirit in him so that when he hears a certain report, he will return to his own country, and there I will have him cut down with the sword.' "

⁸When the field commander heard that the king of Assyria had left Lachish, he withdrew and found the king fighting against Libnah.

⁹Now Sennacherib received a report that Tirhakah, the Cushite[a] king ⌊of Egypt⌋, was marching out to fight against him. When he heard it, he sent messengers to Hezekiah with this word: ¹⁰"Say to Hezekiah king of Judah: Do not let the god you depend on deceive you when he says, 'Jerusalem will not be handed over to the king of Assyria.' ¹¹Surely you have heard what the kings of Assyria have done to all the countries, destroying them completely. And will you be delivered? ¹²Did the gods of the nations that were destroyed by my forefathers deliver them—the gods of Gozan, Haran, Rezeph and the people of Eden who were in Tel Assar? ¹³Where is the king of Hamath, the king of Arpad, the king of the city of Sepharvaim, or of Hena or Ivvah?"

HEZEKIAH'S PRAYER

¹⁴Hezekiah received the letter from the messengers and read it. Then he went up to the temple of the LORD and spread it out before the LORD. ¹⁵And Hezekiah prayed to the LORD: ¹⁶"O LORD Almighty, God of Israel, enthroned between the cherubim, you alone are God over all the kingdoms of the earth. You have made heaven and earth. ¹⁷Give ear, O LORD, and hear; open your eyes, O LORD, and see; listen to all the words Sennacherib has sent to insult the living God.

¹⁸"It is true, O LORD, that the Assyrian kings have laid waste all these peoples and their lands. ¹⁹They have thrown their gods into the fire and destroyed them, for they were not gods but only wood and stone, fashioned by human hands. ²⁰Now, O LORD our God, deliver us from his hand, so that all kingdoms on earth may know that you alone, O LORD, are God.[b]"

SENNACHERIB'S FALL

²¹Then Isaiah son of Amoz sent a message to Hezekiah: "This is what the LORD, the God of Israel, says: Because you have prayed to me concerning Sennacherib king of Assyria, ²²this is the word the LORD has spoken against him:

"The Virgin Daughter of Zion
　despises and mocks you.
The Daughter of Jerusalem
　tosses her head as you flee.
²³Who is it you have insulted and
　blasphemed?
Against whom have you raised your
　voice
and lifted your eyes in pride?
　Against the Holy One of Israel!
²⁴By your messengers
　you have heaped insults on the Lord.
And you have said,
'With my many chariots
I have ascended the heights of the
　mountains,
　the utmost heights of Lebanon.
I have cut down its tallest cedars,
　the choicest of its pines.
I have reached its remotest heights,
　the finest of its forests.

Understanding How to Pray

When was the last time you *really* prayed? We're not talking about the few quick words you toss out when you're asked to pray at the dinner table or with your small group at church. We're talking about the kind of praying you do when you've got nowhere else to turn. We're talking about the kind of praying Hezekiah did when he knew big trouble was coming his way. Keep in mind that no request is too big or too small to take to God. The more areas of your life you submit to him, the more evidence of his awesome power you'll see.

» live the adventure » Isa 37:14-20

---

[a] *9* That is, from the upper Nile region   [b] *20* Dead Sea Scrolls (see also 2 Kings 19:19); Masoretic Text *alone are the LORD*

²⁵ I have dug wells in foreign lands^a
and drunk the water there.
With the soles of my feet
I have dried up all the streams of Egypt.'

²⁶ "Have you not heard?
Long ago I ordained it.
In days of old I planned it;
now I have brought it to pass,
that you have turned fortified cities
into piles of stone.
²⁷ Their people, drained of power,
are dismayed and put to shame.
They are like plants in the field,
like tender green shoots,
like grass sprouting on the roof,
scorched^b before it grows up.

²⁸ "But I know where you stay
and when you come and go
and how you rage against me.
²⁹ Because you rage against me
and because your insolence has reached my ears,
I will put my hook in your nose
and my bit in your mouth,
and I will make you return
by the way you came.

³⁰ "This will be the sign for you, O Hezekiah:

"This year you will eat what grows by itself,
and the second year what springs from that.
But in the third year sow and reap,
plant vineyards and eat their fruit.
³¹ Once more a remnant of the house of Judah
will take root below and bear fruit above.
³² For out of Jerusalem will come a remnant,
and out of Mount Zion a band of survivors.
The zeal of the LORD Almighty
will accomplish this.

³³ "Therefore this is what the LORD says concerning the king of Assyria:

"He will not enter this city
or shoot an arrow here.
He will not come before it with shield
or build a siege ramp against it.
³⁴ By the way that he came he will return;
he will not enter this city,"

declares the LORD.

³⁵ "I will defend this city and save it,
for my sake and for the sake of David my servant!"

³⁶ Then the angel of the LORD went out and put to death a hundred and eighty-five thousand men in the Assyrian camp. When the people got up the next morning—there were all the dead bodies! ³⁷ So Sennacherib king of Assyria broke camp and withdrew. He returned to Nineveh and stayed there.

---

^a 25 Dead Sea Scrolls (see also 2 Kings 19:24); Masoretic Text does not have *in foreign lands.* ^b 27 Some manuscripts of the Masoretic Text, Dead Sea Scrolls and some Septuagint manuscripts (see also 2 Kings 19:26); most manuscripts of the Masoretic Text *roof / and terraced fields*

³⁸One day, while he was worshiping in the temple of his god Nisroch, his sons Adrammelech and Sharezer cut him down with the sword, and they escaped to the land of Ararat. And Esarhaddon his son succeeded him as king.

NOW OR NEVER
ISA 37:36

This is a perfect example of why no enemy should scare you. God can cut anyone down to size—no matter how unstoppable or intimidating they may seem.

HEZEKIAH'S ILLNESS

38 In those days Hezekiah became ill and was at the point of death. The prophet Isaiah son of Amoz went to him and said, "This is what the LORD says: Put your house in order, because you are going to die; you will not recover."

²Hezekiah turned his face to the wall and prayed to the LORD, ³"Remember, O LORD, how I have walked before you faithfully and with wholehearted devotion and have done what is good in your eyes." And Hezekiah wept bitterly.

⁴Then the word of the LORD came to Isaiah: ⁵"Go and tell Hezekiah, 'This is what the LORD, the God of your father David, says: I have heard your prayer and seen your tears; I will add fifteen years to your life. ⁶And I will deliver you and this city from the hand of the king of Assyria. I will defend this city.

⁷"'This is the LORD's sign to you that the LORD will do what he has promised: ⁸I will make the shadow cast by the sun go back the ten steps it has gone down on the stairway of Ahaz.'" So the sunlight went back the ten steps it had gone down.

⁹A writing of Hezekiah king of Judah after his illness and recovery:

¹⁰I said, "In the prime of my life
must I go through the gates of death ᵃ
and be robbed of the rest of my years?"
¹¹I said, "I will not again see the LORD,
the LORD, in the land of the living;
no longer will I look on mankind,
or be with those who now dwell in this world. ᵇ
¹²Like a shepherd's tent my house
has been pulled down and taken from me.
Like a weaver I have rolled up my life,
and he has cut me off from the loom;
day and night you made an end of me.
¹³I waited patiently till dawn,
but like a lion he broke all my bones;
day and night you made an end of me.
¹⁴I cried like a swift or thrush,
I moaned like a mourning dove.
My eyes grew weak as I looked to the heavens.
I am troubled; O Lord, come to my aid!"

¹⁵But what can I say?
He has spoken to me, and he himself has done this.
I will walk humbly all my years
because of this anguish of my soul.
¹⁶Lord, by such things men live;
and my spirit finds life in them too.
You restored me to health
and let me live.
¹⁷Surely it was for my benefit

ᵃ *10* Hebrew *Sheol*   ᵇ *11* A few Hebrew manuscripts; most Hebrew manuscripts *in the place of cessation*

that I suffered such anguish.
In your love you kept me
from the pit of destruction;
you have put all my sins
behind your back.
18 For the grave[a] cannot praise you,
death cannot sing your praise;
those who go down to the pit
cannot hope for your faithfulness.
19 The living, the living—they praise you,
as I am doing today;
fathers tell their children
about your faithfulness.

20 The LORD will save me,
and we will sing with stringed instruments
all the days of our lives
in the temple of the LORD.

21 Isaiah had said, "Prepare a poultice of figs and apply it to the boil, and he will recover."
22 Hezekiah had asked, "What will be the sign that I will go up to the temple of the LORD?"

ENVOYS FROM BABYLON

39 At that time Merodach-Baladan son of Baladan king of Babylon sent Hezekiah letters and a gift, because he had heard of his illness and recovery. 2 Hezekiah received the envoys gladly and showed them what was in his storehouses—the silver, the gold, the spices, the fine oil, his entire armory and everything found among his treasures. There was nothing in his palace or in all his kingdom that Hezekiah did not show them.

3 Then Isaiah the prophet went to King Hezekiah and asked, "What did those men say, and where did they come from?"

"From a distant land," Hezekiah replied. "They came to me from Babylon."

4 The prophet asked, "What did they see in your palace?"

"They saw everything in my palace," Hezekiah said. "There is nothing among my treasures that I did not show them."

5 Then Isaiah said to Hezekiah, "Hear the word of the LORD Almighty: 6 The time will surely come when everything in your palace, and all that your fathers have stored up until this day, will be carried off to Babylon. Nothing will be left, says the LORD. 7 And some of your descendants, your own flesh and blood who will be born to you, will be taken away, and they will become eunuchs in the palace of the king of Babylon."

8 "The word of the LORD you have spoken is good," Hezekiah replied. For he thought, "There will be peace and security in my lifetime."

COMFORT FOR GOD'S PEOPLE

40 Comfort, comfort my people,
says your God.
2 Speak tenderly to Jerusalem,
and proclaim to her
that her hard service has been completed,
that her sin has been paid for,
that she has received from the LORD's hand
double for all her sins.

3 A voice of one calling:
"In the desert prepare
the way for the LORD[b];

---

a 18 Hebrew *Sheol*   b 3 Or *A voice of one calling in the desert: / "Prepare the way for the LORD*

make straight in the wilderness
   a highway for our God.[a]
⁴Every valley shall be raised up,
   every mountain and hill made low;
the rough ground shall become level,
   the rugged places a plain.
⁵And the glory of the LORD will be revealed,
   and all mankind together will see it.

     For the mouth of the LORD has spoken."

⁶A voice says, "Cry out."
   And I said, "What shall I cry?"

"All men are like grass,
   and all their glory is like the flowers of the field.
⁷The grass withers and the flowers fall,
   because the breath of the LORD blows on them.
Surely the people are grass.
⁸The grass withers and the flowers fall,
   but the word of our God stands forever."

⁹You who bring good tidings to Zion,
   go up on a high mountain.
You who bring good tidings to Jerusalem,[b]
   lift up your voice with a shout,
lift it up, do not be afraid;
   say to the towns of Judah,
   "Here is your God!"
¹⁰See, the Sovereign LORD comes with power,
   and his arm rules for him.
See, his reward is with him,
   and his recompense accompanies him.
¹¹He tends his flock like a shepherd:
   He gathers the lambs in his arms
and carries them close to his heart;
   he gently leads those that have young.

¹²Who has measured the waters in the hollow of his hand,
   or with the breadth of his hand marked off the heavens?
Who has held the dust of the earth in a basket,
   or weighed the mountains on the scales
   and the hills in a balance?
¹³Who has understood the mind[c] of the LORD,
   or instructed him as his counselor?
¹⁴Whom did the LORD consult to enlighten him,
   and who taught him the right way?
Who was it that taught him knowledge
   or showed him the path of understanding?

¹⁵Surely the nations are like a drop in a bucket;
   they are regarded as dust on the scales;
   he weighs the islands as though they were fine dust.
¹⁶Lebanon is not sufficient for altar fires,
   nor its animals enough for burnt offerings.
¹⁷Before him all the nations are as nothing;

---

^a 3 Hebrew; Septuagint *make straight the paths of our God* ^b 9 Or *O Zion, bringer of good tidings, / go up on a high mountain. / O Jerusalem, bringer of good tidings* ^c 13 Or *Spirit*; or *spirit*

they are regarded by him as worthless
and less than nothing.

18 To whom, then, will you compare God?
What image will you compare him to?
19 As for an idol, a craftsman casts it,
and a goldsmith overlays it with gold
and fashions silver chains for it.
20 A man too poor to present such an offering
selects wood that will not rot.
He looks for a skilled craftsman
to set up an idol that will not topple.

21 Do you not know?
Have you not heard?
Has it not been told you from the beginning?
Have you not understood since the earth was founded?
22 He sits enthroned above the circle of the earth,
and its people are like grasshoppers.
He stretches out the heavens like a canopy,
and spreads them out like a tent to live in.
23 He brings princes to naught
and reduces the rulers of this world to nothing.
24 No sooner are they planted,
no sooner are they sown,
no sooner do they take root in the ground,
than he blows on them and they wither,
and a whirlwind sweeps them away like chaff.

25 "To whom will you compare me?
Or who is my equal?" says the Holy One.
26 Lift your eyes and look to the heavens:
Who created all these?

now or never

ISA 40:28–31

Ever get tired of saying no when everyone else seems to be saying yes? Ever get tired of trusting God when everything seems to go wrong? Don't throw your commitment away just because life gets difficult. Ask God to give you the strength you need to stay faithful to him.

He who brings out the starry host one by one,
and calls them each by name.
Because of his great power and mighty strength,
not one of them is missing.

27 Why do you say, O Jacob,
and complain, O Israel,
"My way is hidden from the LORD;
my cause is disregarded by my God"?
28 Do you not know?
Have you not heard?

The LORD is the everlasting God,
the Creator of the ends of the earth.
He will not grow tired or weary,
and his understanding no one can fathom.
29 He gives strength to the weary
and increases the power of the weak.
30 Even youths grow tired and weary,
and young men stumble and fall;
31 but those who hope in the LORD
will renew their strength.

They will soar on wings like eagles;
  they will run and not grow weary,
  they will walk and not be faint.

THE HELPER OF ISRAEL

41

"Be silent before me, you islands!
  Let the nations renew their strength!
Let them come forward and speak;
  let us meet together at the place of judgment.

² "Who has stirred up one from the east,
  calling him in righteousness to his service ᵃ?
He hands nations over to him
  and subdues kings before him.
He turns them to dust with his sword,
  to windblown chaff with his bow.
³ He pursues them and moves on unscathed,
  by a path his feet have not traveled before.
⁴ Who has done this and carried it through,
  calling forth the generations from the beginning?
I, the LORD—with the first of them
  and with the last—I am he."

⁵ The islands have seen it and fear;
  the ends of the earth tremble.
They approach and come forward;
⁶   each helps the other
  and says to his brother, "Be strong!"
⁷ The craftsman encourages the goldsmith,
  and he who smooths with the hammer
  spurs on him who strikes the anvil.
He says of the welding, "It is good."
  He nails down the idol so it will not topple.

⁸ "But you, O Israel, my servant,
  Jacob, whom I have chosen,
  you descendants of Abraham my friend,
⁹ I took you from the ends of the earth,
  from its farthest corners I called you.
I said, 'You are my servant';
  I have chosen you and have not rejected you.
¹⁰ So do not fear, for I am with you;
  do not be dismayed, for I am your God.
I will strengthen you and help you;
  I will uphold you with my righteous right hand.

¹¹ "All who rage against you
  will surely be ashamed and disgraced;
those who oppose you
  will be as nothing and perish.
¹² Though you search for your enemies,
  you will not find them.
Those who wage war against you
  will be as nothing at all.
¹³ For I am the LORD, your God,
  who takes hold of your right hand

ᵃ 2 Or / whom victory meets at every step

battlelines

» Looking Forward (Fear)

Q: Hey, I've noticed you've been kind of quiet lately. You're not your usual self. What's up?
A: I think it's starting to hit me that everything in my life is about to change. After graduation, then what? I have no idea what I'm going to do.

Q: I thought you were going to enlist in the Army.
A: Well, yeah, I was thinking about that, but I'm not so sure anymore. This whole war on terrorism is kind of freaking me out.

Q: So what else would you do?
A: I've been thinking a lot lately about going to school. Maybe doing a year of basic courses at the community college, then transferring to Tech if my grades are good enough. Maybe get some kind of computer degree.

Q: Sounds like a good move. From what I hear, there are always going to be plenty of computer jobs available.
A: Maybe, but I hear the math requirements are pretty tough. I just hope I can pass all the classes. (Laughs) So many things to be worried about, so little time.

Q: Why? What else are you worried about?
A: Let's see . . . World War III. More terrorist attacks. A bad economy. How's that for a start?

Q: Anything more personal?
A: Personal worries? Well, I'm a little afraid I won't be able to get into college. And then there's not being able to finish college. And not being able to support myself or my family. Settling for some mindless job that I hate. Living a totally boring life. That's probably what I'm most afraid of.

Q: I'm sorry I asked. Now you've got me starting to worry.

» Looking Up

Isaiah 41:10 offers a helpful reminder for Spencer—and anyone else who's battling fear and uncertainty about the future: "So do not fear, for I am with you; do not be dismayed, for I am your God. I will strengthen you and help you; I will uphold you with my righteous right hand."

Think about that. No matter what situations or circumstances you face, as a child of God through faith in Christ, you can be assured of God's companionship and strength. What's more, God made the church to be a place where believers can "carry each other's burdens"—including your fears and uncertainties (Galatians 6:2).

Remember, everyone has fears, but dealing with them head-on shows real courage.

Discover tools that will help you feel good about your future at RevolutionBible.com.

and says to you, Do not fear;
  I will help you.
¹⁴ Do not be afraid, O worm Jacob,
  O little Israel,
for I myself will help you," declares the LORD,
  your Redeemer, the Holy One of Israel.
¹⁵ "See, I will make you into a threshing sledge,
  new and sharp, with many teeth.
You will thresh the mountains and crush them,
  and reduce the hills to chaff.
¹⁶ You will winnow them, the wind will pick them up,
  and a gale will blow them away.
But you will rejoice in the LORD
  and glory in the Holy One of Israel.

¹⁷ "The poor and needy search for water,
  but there is none;
  their tongues are parched with thirst.
But I the LORD will answer them;
  I, the God of Israel, will not forsake them.
¹⁸ I will make rivers flow on barren heights,
  and springs within the valleys.
I will turn the desert into pools of water,
  and the parched ground into springs.
¹⁹ I will put in the desert
  the cedar and the acacia, the myrtle and the olive.
I will set pines in the wasteland,
  the fir and the cypress together,
²⁰ so that people may see and know,
  may consider and understand,
that the hand of the LORD has done this,
  that the Holy One of Israel has created it.

²¹ "Present your case," says the LORD.
  "Set forth your arguments," says Jacob's King.
²² "Bring in ⌊your idols⌋ to tell us
  what is going to happen.
Tell us what the former things were,
  so that we may consider them
  and know their final outcome.
Or declare to us the things to come,
²³ tell us what the future holds,
  so we may know that you are gods.
Do something, whether good or bad,
  so that we will be dismayed and filled with fear.
²⁴ But you are less than nothing
  and your works are utterly worthless;
  he who chooses you is detestable.

²⁵ "I have stirred up one from the north, and he comes—
  one from the rising sun who calls on my name.
He treads on rulers as if they were mortar,
  as if he were a potter treading the clay.
²⁶ Who told of this from the beginning, so we could know,
  or beforehand, so we could say, 'He was right'?
No one told of this,
  no one foretold it,

no one heard any words from you.
²⁷I was the first to tell Zion, 'Look, here they are!'
I gave to Jerusalem a messenger of good tidings.
²⁸I look but there is no one—
no one among them to give counsel,
no one to give answer when I ask them.
²⁹See, they are all false!
Their deeds amount to nothing;
their images are but wind and confusion.

THE SERVANT OF THE LORD

42

"Here is my servant, whom I uphold,
my chosen one in whom I delight;
I will put my Spirit on him
and he will bring justice to the nations.
²He will not shout or cry out,
or raise his voice in the streets.

³A bruised reed he will not break,
and a smoldering wick he will not
snuff out.
In faithfulness he will bring forth justice;
⁴he will not falter or be discouraged
till he establishes justice on earth.
In his law the islands will put their
hope."

⁵This is what God the LORD says—
he who created the heavens and
stretched them out,
who spread out the earth and all that
comes out of it,

NOW OR NEVER
ISA 42:3

The "bruised reed" and "smoldering wick" refer to outcasts—those who are considered weak or are overlooked by others. Who does that describe at your school? Do you think you treat those people in a godly way? How can you imitate Christ's example?

who gives breath to its people,
and life to those who walk on it:
⁶"I, the LORD, have called you in righteousness;
I will take hold of your hand.
I will keep you and will make you
to be a covenant for the people
and a light for the Gentiles,
⁷to open eyes that are blind,
to free captives from prison
and to release from the dungeon those who sit in darkness.

⁸"I am the LORD; that is my name!
I will not give my glory to another
or my praise to idols.
⁹See, the former things have taken place,
and new things I declare;
before they spring into being
I announce them to you."

SONG OF PRAISE TO THE LORD

¹⁰Sing to the LORD a new song,
his praise from the ends of the earth,
you who go down to the sea, and all that is in it,
you islands, and all who live in them.
¹¹Let the desert and its towns raise their voices;

let the settlements where Kedar lives rejoice.
Let the people of Sela sing for joy;
 let them shout from the mountaintops.
¹² Let them give glory to the LORD
 and proclaim his praise in the islands.
¹³ The LORD will march out like a mighty man,
 like a warrior he will stir up his zeal;
with a shout he will raise the battle cry
 and will triumph over his enemies.

¹⁴ "For a long time I have kept silent,
 I have been quiet and held myself back.
But now, like a woman in childbirth,
 I cry out, I gasp and pant.
¹⁵ I will lay waste the mountains and hills
 and dry up all their vegetation;
I will turn rivers into islands
 and dry up the pools.
¹⁶ I will lead the blind by ways they have not known,
 along unfamiliar paths I will guide them;
I will turn the darkness into light before them
 and make the rough places smooth.
These are the things I will do;
 I will not forsake them.
¹⁷ But those who trust in idols,
 who say to images, 'You are our gods,'
 will be turned back in utter shame.

ISRAEL BLIND AND DEAF

¹⁸ "Hear, you deaf;
 look, you blind, and see!
¹⁹ Who is blind but my servant,
 and deaf like the messenger I send?
Who is blind like the one committed to me,
 blind like the servant of the LORD?
²⁰ You have seen many things, but have paid no attention;
 your ears are open, but you hear nothing."
²¹ It pleased the LORD
 for the sake of his righteousness
 to make his law great and glorious.
²² But this is a people plundered and looted,
 all of them trapped in pits
 or hidden away in prisons.
They have become plunder,
 with no one to rescue them;
they have been made loot,
 with no one to say, "Send them back."

²³ Which of you will listen to this
 or pay close attention in time to come?
²⁴ Who handed Jacob over to become loot,
 and Israel to the plunderers?
Was it not the LORD,
 against whom we have sinned?
For they would not follow his ways;
 they did not obey his law.

²⁵So he poured out on them his burning anger,
the violence of war.
It enveloped them in flames, yet they did not understand;
it consumed them, but they did not take it to heart.

ISRAEL'S ONLY SAVIOR
43

But now, this is what the LORD says—
he who created you, O Jacob,
he who formed you, O Israel:

---

challengenotes

To: my_son

heavenly_father: in moses' day, I held back the waters of the red sea while the israelites marched across on dry land. I held back the flames of nebuchadnezzar's furnace so that shadrach, meshach and abednego never even got warm. do you have any doubt that I can protect you?

ISA 43:1-3

"Fear not, for I have redeemed you;
I have summoned you by name; you are mine.
²When you pass through the waters,
I will be with you;
and when you pass through the rivers,
they will not sweep over you.
When you walk through the fire,
you will not be burned;
the flames will not set you ablaze.
³For I am the LORD, your God,
the Holy One of Israel, your Savior;
I give Egypt for your ransom,
Cush^a and Seba in your stead.
⁴Since you are precious and honored in my sight,
and because I love you,
I will give men in exchange for you,
and people in exchange for your life.
⁵Do not be afraid, for I am with you;
I will bring your children from the east
and gather you from the west.
⁶I will say to the north, 'Give them up!'
and to the south, 'Do not hold them back.'
Bring my sons from afar
and my daughters from the ends of the earth—
⁷everyone who is called by my name,
whom I created for my glory,
whom I formed and made."

⁸Lead out those who have eyes but are blind,
who have ears but are deaf.
⁹All the nations gather together
and the peoples assemble.
Which of them foretold this
and proclaimed to us the former things?

Understanding God's Purpose

What does God want me to do with my life? Usually when people ask that question, they're debating issues like whether they should attend a local college or an out-of-state university . . . marry a high school sweetheart or date freely in college . . . major in something they're interested in or something they know will get them a good job after they graduate. The answer is much simpler, though. God wants you to give him glory in the way you live. That's it. Whether you're a single investment banker or a married plumber, your number-one priority should be to give glory to God. When you love God with all of your heart, the rest will fall into place.

»» live the adventure »» Isa 43:7

^a *3* That is, the upper Nile region

battlelines

» The Big Break up (Rejection)

Q: Hey, I, uh . . . heard the news.
A: Yeah, you and everybody else in the world. It must have been on CNN this morning.

Q: I'm sorry, man.
A: Yeah, well, what can you do? It happens, I guess.

Q: Did you see it coming? Did you have any warning?
A: Not really. The other night she just said, "Look, I care about you, but not like I used to. This isn't working out. I want to date other people." All of the sudden, out of nowhere.

Q: Ouch! That hurts.
A: Yeah, it was harsh. But even worse was the fact that within two days she was already going out with Richard.

Q: Aw, man, that's wrong. Are you pretty ripped about it?
A: Yeah. And confused. But when you boil it down, it's pretty simple. She dumped me for him. Obviously he's got something I don't.

Q: Dude, don't do that to yourself. You don't know that for sure.
A: How can I not? Christy and I were together for almost a year, and the minute this big jock comes along, boom! It's over. I feel like an idiot! You think I don't know everybody is talking? I'm embarrassed to show my face in school!

» Real Validation

If you've ever been where Seth is, you know what he's feeling. It's devastating to get dumped. Among other things, rejection makes you feel like a total loser.

But that's not what you are. That's just a lie from the enemy. Your value and worth do not depend on the emotions and decisions of some girl. Notice what God said to the people of Israel:

"Fear not, for I have redeemed you; I have summoned you by name; you are mine. When you pass through the waters, I will be with you; and when you pass through the rivers, they will not sweep over you. When you walk through the fire, you will not be burned; the flames will not set you ablaze. For I am the LORD, your God, the Holy One of Israel, your Savior . . . You are precious and honored in my sight, and . . . I love you" (Isaiah 43:1b–4).

No matter what happens in your life, no matter what other people say about you, define yourself by God's measure, not theirs.

When you find yourself feeling rejected, log on to www.RevolutionBible.com.

Let them bring in their witnesses to prove they were right,
    so that others may hear and say, "It is true."
10 "You are my witnesses," declares the LORD,
    "and my servant whom I have chosen,
so that you may know and believe me
    and understand that I am he.
Before me no god was formed,
    nor will there be one after me.
11 I, even I, am the LORD,
    and apart from me there is no savior.
12 I have revealed and saved and proclaimed—
    I, and not some foreign god among you.
You are my witnesses," declares the LORD, "that I am God.
13   Yes, and from ancient days I am he.
No one can deliver out of my hand.
    When I act, who can reverse it?"

GOD'S MERCY AND ISRAEL'S UNFAITHFULNESS

14 This is what the LORD says—
    your Redeemer, the Holy One of Israel:
"For your sake I will send to Babylon
    and bring down as fugitives all the Babylonians,ᵃ
    in the ships in which they took pride.
15 I am the LORD, your Holy One,
    Israel's Creator, your King."

16 This is what the LORD says—
    he who made a way through the sea,
    a path through the mighty waters,
17 who drew out the chariots and horses,
    the army and reinforcements together,
and they lay there, never to rise again,
    extinguished, snuffed out like a wick:

18 "Forget the former things;
    do not dwell on the past.
19 See, I am doing a new thing!
    Now it springs up; do you not
        perceive it?
I am making a way in the desert
    and streams in the wasteland.
20 The wild animals honor me,
    the jackals and the owls,
because I provide water in the desert
    and streams in the wasteland,
to give drink to my people, my chosen,
    21 the people I formed for myself
    that they may proclaim my praise.

NOW OR NEVER
ISA 43:18–19

What "new thing" is God doing in your life?
While his character never changes, God's
methods and means for accomplishing his
purposes are creative and fresh. Make sure
you never say "never." Following God is an
adventure from beginning to end.

22 "Yet you have not called upon me, O Jacob,
    you have not wearied yourselves for me, O Israel.
23 You have not brought me sheep for burnt offerings,
    nor honored me with your sacrifices.
I have not burdened you with grain offerings
    nor wearied you with demands for incense.
24 You have not bought any fragrant calamus for me,

ᵃ 14 Or *Chaldeans*

or lavished on me the fat of your sacrifices.
But you have burdened me with your sins
    and wearied me with your offenses.

25 "I, even I, am he who blots out
    your transgressions, for my own sake,
    and remembers your sins no more.
26 Review the past for me,
    let us argue the matter together;
    state the case for your innocence.
27 Your first father sinned;
    your spokesmen rebelled against me.
28 So I will disgrace the dignitaries of your temple,
    and I will consign Jacob to destruction[a]
    and Israel to scorn.

ISRAEL THE CHOSEN

"But now listen, O Jacob, my servant,
    Israel, whom I have chosen.
2 This is what the LORD says—
    he who made you, who formed you in the womb,
    and who will help you:
Do not be afraid, O Jacob, my servant,
    Jeshurun, whom I have chosen.
3 For I will pour water on the thirsty land,
    and streams on the dry ground;
I will pour out my Spirit on your offspring,
    and my blessing on your descendants.
4 They will spring up like grass in a meadow,
    like poplar trees by flowing streams.
5 One will say, 'I belong to the LORD';
    another will call himself by the name of Jacob;
still another will write on his hand, 'The LORD's,'
    and will take the name Israel.

THE LORD, NOT IDOLS

6 "This is what the LORD says—
    Israel's King and Redeemer, the LORD Almighty:
I am the first and I am the last;
    apart from me there is no God.
7 Who then is like me? Let him proclaim it.
    Let him declare and lay out before me
what has happened since I established my ancient people,
    and what is yet to come—
    yes, let him foretell what will come.
8 Do not tremble, do not be afraid.
    Did I not proclaim this and foretell it long ago?
You are my witnesses. Is there any God besides me?
    No, there is no other Rock; I know not one."

9 All who make idols are nothing,
    and the things they treasure are worthless.
Those who would speak up for them are blind;
    they are ignorant, to their own shame.

---

a 28 The Hebrew term refers to the irrevocable giving over of things or persons to the LORD, often by totally destroying them.

¹⁰ Who shapes a god and casts an idol,
    which can profit him nothing?
¹¹ He and his kind will be put to shame;
    craftsmen are nothing but men.
Let them all come together and take their stand;
    they will be brought down to terror and infamy.

¹² The blacksmith takes a tool
    and works with it in the coals;
he shapes an idol with hammers,
    he forges it with the might of his arm.
He gets hungry and loses his strength;
    he drinks no water and grows faint.
¹³ The carpenter measures with a line
    and makes an outline with a marker;
he roughs it out with chisels
    and marks it with compasses.
He shapes it in the form of man,
    of man in all his glory,
    that it may dwell in a shrine.

¹⁴ He cut down cedars,
    or perhaps took a cypress or oak.
He let it grow among the trees of the forest,
    or planted a pine, and the rain made it grow.
¹⁵ It is man's fuel for burning;
    some of it he takes and warms himself,
    he kindles a fire and bakes bread.
But he also fashions a god and worships it;
    he makes an idol and bows down to it.

---

challengenotes

To: my_son

heavenly_father: you don't have the authority to judge other people, but you do have the responsibility to examine their beliefs. if anyone tries to convince you that there are higher powers in this world besides me, don't believe them. I alone am God.

ISA 44:6-23

---

¹⁶ Half of the wood he burns in the fire;
    over it he prepares his meal,
    he roasts his meat and eats his fill.
He also warms himself and says,
    "Ah! I am warm; I see the fire."
¹⁷ From the rest he makes a god, his idol;
    he bows down to it and worships.
He prays to it and says,
    "Save me; you are my god."
¹⁸ They know nothing, they understand nothing;
    their eyes are plastered over so they cannot see,
    and their minds closed so they cannot understand.
¹⁹ No one stops to think,
    no one has the knowledge or understanding to say,
"Half of it I used for fuel;
    I even baked bread over its coals,
    I roasted meat and I ate.
Shall I make a detestable thing from what is left?
    Shall I bow down to a block of wood?"
²⁰ He feeds on ashes, a deluded heart misleads him;

he cannot save himself, or say,
"Is not this thing in my right hand a lie?"

21 "Remember these things, O Jacob,
    for you are my servant, O Israel.
I have made you, you are my servant;
    O Israel, I will not forget you.
22 I have swept away your offenses like a cloud,
    your sins like the morning mist.
Return to me,
    for I have redeemed you."

23 Sing for joy, O heavens, for the LORD has done this;
    shout aloud, O earth beneath.
Burst into song, you mountains,
    you forests and all your trees,
for the LORD has redeemed Jacob,
    he displays his glory in Israel.

JERUSALEM TO BE INHABITED

24 "This is what the LORD says—
    your Redeemer, who formed you in the womb:

I am the LORD,
who has made all things,
who alone stretched out the heavens,
who spread out the earth by myself,

25 who foils the signs of false prophets
    and makes fools of diviners,
who overthrows the learning of the wise
    and turns it into nonsense,
26 who carries out the words of his servants
    and fulfills the predictions of his messengers,

who says of Jerusalem, 'It shall be inhabited,'
    of the towns of Judah, 'They shall be built,'
    and of their ruins, 'I will restore them,'
27 who says to the watery deep, 'Be dry,
    and I will dry up your streams,'
28 who says of Cyrus, 'He is my shepherd
    and will accomplish all that I please;
    he will say of Jerusalem, "Let it be rebuilt,"
    and of the temple, "Let its foundations be laid." '

"This is what the LORD says to his anointed,
    to Cyrus, whose right hand I take hold of
to subdue nations before him
    and to strip kings of their armor,
to open doors before him
    so that gates will not be shut:
2 I will go before you
    and will level the mountains[a];
I will break down gates of bronze
    and cut through bars of iron.

---

a 2 Dead Sea Scrolls and Septuagint; the meaning of the word in the Masoretic Text is uncertain.

³I will give you the treasures of darkness,
　riches stored in secret places,
so that you may know that I am the LORD,
　the God of Israel, who summons you by name.
⁴For the sake of Jacob my servant,
　of Israel my chosen,
I summon you by name
　and bestow on you a title of honor,
　though you do not acknowledge me.
⁵I am the LORD, and there is no other;
　apart from me there is no God.
I will strengthen you,
　though you have not acknowledged
　me,
⁶so that from the rising of the sun
　to the place of its setting
men may know there is none besides
　me.
　I am the LORD, and there is no other.
⁷I form the light and create darkness,
　I bring prosperity and create
　disaster;
　I, the LORD, do all these things.

⁸"You heavens above, rain down
　righteousness;
　let the clouds shower it down.
Let the earth open wide,
　let salvation spring up,
let righteousness grow with it;
　I, the LORD, have created it.

⁹"Woe to him who quarrels with his Maker,
　to him who is but a potsherd among
　　the potsherds on the ground.
Does the clay say to the potter,
　'What are you making?'
Does your work say,
　'He has no hands'?
¹⁰Woe to him who says to his father,
　'What have you begotten?'
or to his mother,
　'What have you brought to birth?'

¹¹"This is what the LORD says—
　the Holy One of Israel, and its Maker:
Concerning things to come,
　do you question me about my children,
　or give me orders about the work of my hands?
¹²It is I who made the earth
　and created mankind upon it.
My own hands stretched out the heavens;
　I marshaled their starry hosts.
¹³I will raise up Cyrus[a] in my righteousness:
　I will make all his ways straight.

»» live the adventure »» Isa 45:5-9

Accepting God's Authority

Would you ever try to tell a doctor that your diagnosis of an injury is better than hers? Would you ever claim to understand the Bible better than your pastor does? Would you tell an airline pilot that he should turn the controls of the plane over to you? How much worse is it to try to tell God that he should have done something different with you? Never forget that God is the *perfect* Creator. He made you the way you are for a reason. If you don't understand what that reason is, be patient and trust him. He'll show you.

ª 13 Hebrew *him*

He will rebuild my city
    and set my exiles free,
but not for a price or reward,
    says the Lord Almighty."

¹⁴This is what the Lord says:

"The products of Egypt and the merchandise of Cush,ᵃ
    and those tall Sabeans—
they will come over to you
    and will be yours;
they will trudge behind you,
    coming over to you in chains.
They will bow down before you
    and plead with you, saying,
'Surely God is with you, and there is no other;
    there is no other god.' "

¹⁵Truly you are a God who hides himself,
    O God and Savior of Israel.
¹⁶All the makers of idols will be put to shame and disgraced;
    they will go off into disgrace together.
¹⁷But Israel will be saved by the Lord
    with an everlasting salvation;
you will never be put to shame or disgraced,
    to ages everlasting.

¹⁸For this is what the Lord says—
he who created the heavens,
    he is God;
he who fashioned and made the earth,
    he founded it;
he did not create it to be empty,
    but formed it to be inhabited—
he says:
"I am the Lord,
    and there is no other.
¹⁹I have not spoken in secret,
    from somewhere in a land of darkness;
I have not said to Jacob's descendants,
    'Seek me in vain.'
I, the Lord, speak the truth;
    I declare what is right.

²⁰"Gather together and come;
    assemble, you fugitives from the nations.
Ignorant are those who carry about idols of wood,
    who pray to gods that cannot save.
²¹Declare what is to be, present it—
    let them take counsel together.
Who foretold this long ago,
    who declared it from the distant past?
Was it not I, the Lord?
    And there is no God apart from me,
a righteous God and a Savior;
    there is none but me.

ᵃ 14 That is, the upper Nile region

²² "Turn to me and be saved,
    all you ends of the earth;
    for I am God, and there is no other.
²³ By myself I have sworn,
    my mouth has uttered in all integrity
    a word that will not be revoked:
  Before me every knee will bow;
    by me every tongue will swear.
²⁴ They will say of me, 'In the LORD alone
    are righteousness and strength.' "
  All who have raged against him
    will come to him and be put to shame.
²⁵ But in the LORD all the descendants of Israel
    will be found righteous and will exult.

GODS OF BABYLON
46

Bel bows down, Nebo stoops low;
    their idols are borne by beasts of burden.[a]
The images that are carried about are burdensome,
    a burden for the weary.
² They stoop and bow down together;
    unable to rescue the burden,
    they themselves go off into captivity.

³ "Listen to me, O house of Jacob,
    all you who remain of the house of Israel,
  you whom I have upheld since you were conceived,
    and have carried since your birth.
⁴ Even to your old age and gray hairs
    I am he, I am he who will sustain you.
  I have made you and I will carry you;
    I will sustain you and I will rescue you.

⁵ "To whom will you compare me or count me equal?
    To whom will you liken me that we may be compared?
⁶ Some pour out gold from their bags
    and weigh out silver on the scales;
  they hire a goldsmith to make it into a god,
    and they bow down and worship it.
⁷ They lift it to their shoulders and carry it;
    they set it up in its place, and there it stands.
    From that spot it cannot move.
  Though one cries out to it, it does not answer;
    it cannot save him from his troubles.

⁸ "Remember this, fix it in mind,
    take it to heart, you rebels.
⁹ Remember the former things, those of long ago;
    I am God, and there is no other;
    I am God, and there is none like me.
¹⁰ I make known the end from the beginning,
    from ancient times, what is still to come.
  I say: My purpose will stand,
    and I will do all that I please.

ᵃ 1 Or *are but beasts and cattle*

¹¹From the east I summon a bird of prey;
    from a far-off land, a man to fulfill my purpose.
What I have said, that will I bring about;
    what I have planned, that will I do.
¹²Listen to me, you stubborn-hearted,
    you who are far from righteousness.
¹³I am bringing my righteousness near,
    it is not far away;
    and my salvation will not be delayed.
I will grant salvation to Zion,
    my splendor to Israel.

THE FALL OF BABYLON

47

"Go down, sit in the dust,
    Virgin Daughter of Babylon;
sit on the ground without a throne,
    Daughter of the Babylonians.^a
No more will you be called
    tender or delicate.
²Take millstones and grind flour;
    take off your veil.
Lift up your skirts, bare your legs,
    and wade through the streams.
³Your nakedness will be exposed
    and your shame uncovered.
I will take vengeance;
    I will spare no one."

⁴Our Redeemer—the LORD Almighty is his name—
    is the Holy One of Israel.

⁵"Sit in silence, go into darkness,
    Daughter of the Babylonians;
no more will you be called
    queen of kingdoms.
⁶I was angry with my people
    and desecrated my inheritance;
I gave them into your hand,
    and you showed them no mercy.
Even on the aged
    you laid a very heavy yoke.
⁷You said, 'I will continue forever—
    the eternal queen!'
But you did not consider these things
    or reflect on what might happen.

⁸"Now then, listen, you wanton creature,
    lounging in your security
and saying to yourself,
    'I am, and there is none besides me.
I will never be a widow
    or suffer the loss of children.'
⁹Both of these will overtake you
    in a moment, on a single day:
    loss of children and widowhood.

^a *1* Or *Chaldeans*; also in verse 5

They will come upon you in full measure,
in spite of your many sorceries
and all your potent spells.
¹⁰ You have trusted in your wickedness
and have said, 'No one sees me.'
Your wisdom and knowledge mislead you
when you say to yourself,
'I am, and there is none besides me.'
¹¹ Disaster will come upon you,
and you will not know how to conjure it away.
A calamity will fall upon you
that you cannot ward off with a ransom;
a catastrophe you cannot foresee
will suddenly come upon you.

¹² "Keep on, then, with your magic spells
and with your many sorceries,
which you have labored at since childhood.
Perhaps you will succeed,
perhaps you will cause terror.
¹³ All the counsel you have received has only worn you out!
Let your astrologers come forward,
those stargazers who make predictions month by month,
let them save you from what is coming upon you.
¹⁴ Surely they are like stubble;
the fire will burn them up.
They cannot even save themselves
from the power of the flame.
Here are no coals to warm anyone;
here is no fire to sit by.
¹⁵ That is all they can do for you—
these you have labored with
and trafficked with since childhood.
Each of them goes on in his error;
there is not one that can save you.

STUBBORN ISRAEL

"Listen to this, O house of Jacob,
you who are called by the name of Israel
and come from the line of Judah,
you who take oaths in the name of the LORD
and invoke the God of Israel—
but not in truth or righteousness—
² you who call yourselves citizens of the holy city
and rely on the God of Israel—
the LORD Almighty is his name:
³ I foretold the former things long ago,
my mouth announced them and I made them known;
then suddenly I acted, and they came to pass.
⁴ For I knew how stubborn you were;
the sinews of your neck were iron,
your forehead was bronze.
⁵ Therefore I told you these things long ago;
before they happened I announced them to you
so that you could not say,
'My idols did them;

my wooden image and metal god ordained them.'
⁶ You have heard these things; look at them all.
  Will you not admit them?

"From now on I will tell you of new things,
  of hidden things unknown to you.
⁷ They are created now, and not long ago;
  you have not heard of them before today.
So you cannot say,
  'Yes, I knew of them.'
⁸ You have neither heard nor understood;
  from of old your ear has not been open.
Well do I know how treacherous you are;
  you were called a rebel from birth.
⁹ For my own name's sake I delay my wrath;
  for the sake of my praise I hold it back from you,
  so as not to cut you off.
¹⁰ See, I have refined you, though not as silver;
  I have tested you in the furnace of affliction.
¹¹ For my own sake, for my own sake, I do this.
  How can I let myself be defamed?
  I will not yield my glory to another.

ISRAEL FREED

¹² "Listen to me, O Jacob,
  Israel, whom I have called:
I am he;
  I am the first and I am the last.

NOW OR NEVER
ISA 48:17–18

God could force you to obey him if he wanted to. He is God, after all. But he chose a different way. Through his Word he teaches you what you need to do in order to find true success, peace and happiness. But it's up to you to pay attention to his instructions.

¹³ My own hand laid the foundations of the earth,
  and my right hand spread out the heavens;
when I summon them,
  they all stand up together.

¹⁴ "Come together, all of you, and listen:
  Which of ⌊the idols⌋ has foretold these things?
The Lord's chosen ally
  will carry out his purpose against Babylon;
  his arm will be against the Babylonians. ᵃ

¹⁵ I, even I, have spoken;
  yes, I have called him.
I will bring him,
  and he will succeed in his mission.

¹⁶ "Come near me and listen to this:

"From the first announcement I have not spoken in secret;
  at the time it happens, I am there."

And now the Sovereign Lord has sent me,
  with his Spirit.

¹⁷ This is what the Lord says—
  your Redeemer, the Holy One of Israel:

ᵃ *14* Or *Chaldeans*; also in verse 20

"I am the LORD your God,
　　who teaches you what is best for you,
　　who directs you in the way you should go.
18 If only you had paid attention to my commands,
　　your peace would have been like a river,
　　your righteousness like the waves of the sea.
19 Your descendants would have been like the sand,
　　your children like its numberless grains;
　their name would never be cut off
　　nor destroyed from before me."

20 Leave Babylon,
　　flee from the Babylonians!
Announce this with shouts of
　　joy
　and proclaim it.
Send it out to the ends of the
　　earth;
　　say, "The LORD has
　　　redeemed his servant
　　　Jacob."
21 They did not thirst when he led
　　　them through the
　　　deserts;
　he made water flow for
　　them from the rock;

challenge notes

To: my_son

ISA 48:18

heavenly_father: don't give yourself reason to have regrets.
trust in the fact that I know exactly what I'm doing. listen to
me. let me guide your steps. that way, when you look back on
your life, instead of wondering what might have been, you will
be able to celebrate what is.

he split the rock
　and water gushed out.

22 "There is no peace," says the LORD, "for the wicked."

THE SERVANT OF THE LORD

49

Listen to me, you islands;
　hear this, you distant nations:
Before I was born the LORD called me;
　from my birth he has made mention of my name.
2 He made my mouth like a sharpened sword,
　in the shadow of his hand he hid me;
he made me into a polished arrow
　and concealed me in his quiver.
3 He said to me, "You are my servant,
　Israel, in whom I will display my splendor."
4 But I said, "I have labored to no purpose;
　I have spent my strength in vain and for nothing.
Yet what is due me is in the LORD's hand,
　and my reward is with my God."

5 And now the LORD says—
　he who formed me in the womb to be his servant
to bring Jacob back to him
　and gather Israel to himself,
for I am honored in the eyes of the LORD
　and my God has been my strength—
6 he says:
"It is too small a thing for you to be my servant
　to restore the tribes of Jacob
　and bring back those of Israel I have kept.

I will also make you a light for the Gentiles,
   that you may bring my salvation to the ends of the earth."

7 This is what the LORD says—
   the Redeemer and Holy One of
      Israel—
to him who was despised and abhorred
      by the nation,
   to the servant of rulers:
"Kings will see you and rise up,
   princes will see and bow down,
because of the LORD, who is faithful,
   the Holy One of Israel, who has
      chosen you."

NOW OR NEVER
ISA 49:6

God promised to make the Jewish people a "light" for non-Jewish people (Gentiles). He kept that promise by sending Jesus—who was a Jew—to bring salvation. He also used the first Christians—most of whom were Jewish—to share the Good News with their Gentile neighbors. Are you a "light" to the people around you?

RESTORATION OF ISRAEL

8 This is what the LORD says:

"In the time of my favor I will answer you,
   and in the day of salvation I will help you;
I will keep you and will make you
      to be a covenant for the people,
to restore the land
      and to reassign its desolate
         inheritances,
9 to say to the captives, 'Come out,'
      and to those in darkness, 'Be free!'

"They will feed beside the roads
      and find pasture on every barren hill.
10 They will neither hunger nor thirst,
      nor will the desert heat or the sun beat
         upon them.
He who has compassion on them will
         guide them
      and lead them beside springs of water.
11 I will turn all my mountains into roads,
      and my highways will be raised up.
12 See, they will come from afar—
      some from the north, some from the
         west,
      some from the region of Aswan.ᵃ"

13 Shout for joy, O heavens;
      rejoice, O earth;
      burst into song, O mountains!
For the LORD comforts his people
      and will have compassion on his
         afflicted ones.

14 But Zion said, "The LORD has forsaken
      me,
      the Lord has forgotten me."

15 "Can a mother forget the baby at her breast
      and have no compassion on the child she has borne?

Understanding God's Love

Can you imagine anyone loving you more than your mom does? Can you imagine anyone wanting to see you succeed more than she does? Can you imagine anyone who cares more about your safety than she does? Multiply your mom's affection for you by about a billion, and you'll start to get an idea of just how deeply God loves you. The difference between God and your mom is that in addition to his concern for you, God has the power to guide and direct your life in a way that will bring you ultimate meaning.

» live the adventure » Isa 49:15-16

ᵃ 12 Dead Sea Scrolls; Masoretic Text *Sinim*

Though she may forget,
    I will not forget you!
16 See, I have engraved you on the palms of my hands;
    your walls are ever before me.
17 Your sons hasten back,
    and those who laid you waste depart from you.
18 Lift up your eyes and look around;
    all your sons gather and come to you.
As surely as I live," declares the Lord,
    "you will wear them all as ornaments;
    you will put them on, like a bride.

19 "Though you were ruined and made desolate
    and your land laid waste,
now you will be too small for your people,
    and those who devoured you will be far away.
20 The children born during your bereavement
    will yet say in your hearing,
'This place is too small for us;
    give us more space to live in.'
21 Then you will say in your heart,
    'Who bore me these?
I was bereaved and barren;
    I was exiled and rejected.
    Who brought these up?
I was left all alone,
    but these—where have they come from?' "

22 This is what the Sovereign Lord says:

"See, I will beckon to the Gentiles,
    I will lift up my banner to the peoples;
they will bring your sons in their arms
    and carry your daughters on their shoulders.
23 Kings will be your foster fathers,
    and their queens your nursing mothers.
They will bow down before you with their faces to the ground;
    they will lick the dust at your feet.
Then you will know that I am the Lord;
    those who hope in me will not be disappointed."

24 Can plunder be taken from warriors,
    or captives rescued from the fierce a?

25 But this is what the Lord says:

"Yes, captives will be taken from warriors,
    and plunder retrieved from the fierce;
I will contend with those who contend with you,
    and your children I will save.
26 I will make your oppressors eat their own flesh;
    they will be drunk on their own blood, as with wine.
Then all mankind will know
    that I, the Lord, am your Savior,
    your Redeemer, the Mighty One of Jacob."

---

a 24 Dead Sea Scrolls, Vulgate and Syriac (see also Septuagint and verse 25); Masoretic Text *righteous*

battlelines

» Winning Is Everything

Q: You look like a man on a mission. Where are you headed?
A: To see my English teacher. See this paper? She gave me a B.

Q: What's wrong with a B?
A: Losers make Bs.

Q: Ruben, don't be so hard on yourself. It's one test. Just study harder next time.
A: I *did* study. And then she put stuff on the test that wasn't even in the chapter.

Q: So it's your teacher's fault?
A: Well, it isn't *mine*!

Q: You know, yesterday after you guys lost to Central, somebody told me you went off on Gary in the locker room.
A: If he had done what he was supposed to do, we could have won. He cost us the game.

Q: It's all about winning with you, isn't it?
A: Yeah, so what? What's wrong with that? That's the way the world works. There's the guy who's the best, and then there's everybody else. You think losers get respect?

Q: Well, I know that you could have a perfect GPA, become the best basketball player in history and still be a jerk who nobody respects.
A: What?

Q: I'm just saying that trying to do your best is fine, but twenty years from now—heck, *five* years from now—nobody's going to remember that you made a B on a stupid test. And nobody's going to remember who won yesterday's basketball game. In the big scheme of things, it just doesn't matter that much.
A: You're saying winning doesn't matter?

Q: No, not if you're keeping score with grades and awards and points in a game. You can have all that stuff and still be a loser.

» Winning Is One Thing

Our culture seems to believe that winning is everything. If you're not careful, you could get swept up in the foolish notion that being "better" than others is the best way to get respect and honor.

The thing is, if you leave a trail of offended or wounded people in your wake while trying to be the best, you will lose the very thing you're trying to earn—respect. Don't get addicted to winning. Be careful that you don't become arrogant and self-centered. Remember, Jesus had a very different notion of what makes a person great: "If anyone wants to be first, he must be the very last, and the servant of all" (Mark 9:35). Learn to win like Jesus did—by making your twin goals to please God and serve others.

Read more about how to keep winning in perspective at www.RevolutionBible.com.

50

This is what the LORD says:

"Where is your mother's certificate of divorce
    with which I sent her away?
Or to which of my creditors
    did I sell you?
Because of your sins you were sold;
    because of your transgressions your mother was sent away.
2 When I came, why was there no one?
    When I called, why was there no one to answer?
Was my arm too short to ransom you?
    Do I lack the strength to rescue you?
By a mere rebuke I dry up the sea,
    I turn rivers into a desert;
their fish rot for lack of water
    and die of thirst.
3 I clothe the sky with darkness
    and make sackcloth its covering."

4 The Sovereign LORD has given me an
        instructed tongue,
    to know the word that sustains the
        weary.
He wakens me morning by morning,
    wakens my ear to listen like one
        being taught.
5 The Sovereign LORD has opened my ears,
    and I have not been rebellious;
    I have not drawn back.
6 I offered my back to those who beat me,
    my cheeks to those who pulled out
        my beard;
I did not hide my face
    from mocking and spitting.
7 Because the Sovereign LORD helps me,
    I will not be disgraced.
Therefore have I set my face like flint,
    and I know I will not be put to shame.
8 He who vindicates me is near.
    Who then will bring charges against
        me?
    Let us face each other!
Who is my accuser?
    Let him confront me!
9 It is the Sovereign LORD who helps me.
    Who is he that will condemn me?
They will all wear out like a garment;
    the moths will eat them up.

10 Who among you fears the LORD
    and obeys the word of his servant?
Let him who walks in the dark,
    who has no light,
trust in the name of the LORD
    and rely on his God.

Looking for God's Light

In what areas of your life do you feel like you're wandering in the dark? Are you clueless when it comes to controlling your sexual thoughts . . . setting future goals . . . getting along with your parents . . . telling others about Jesus . . . deciding what to do about a relationship with a certain girl? Don't trust your own instincts when you can't see. Don't let faulty counsel from people around you determine what you do. Ask God to shine his light on you—to guide you with his wisdom.

»» live the adventure »» Isa 50:10–11

¹¹ But now, all you who light fires
and provide yourselves with flaming torches,
go, walk in the light of your fires
and of the torches you have set ablaze.
This is what you shall receive from my hand:
You will lie down in torment.

EVERLASTING SALVATION FOR ZION

51

"Listen to me, you who pursue righteousness
and who seek the LORD:
Look to the rock from which you were cut
and to the quarry from which you were hewn;
² look to Abraham, your father,
and to Sarah, who gave you birth.
When I called him he was but one,
and I blessed him and made him
many.
³ The LORD will surely comfort Zion
and will look with compassion on all
her ruins;
he will make her deserts like Eden,
her wastelands like the garden of the
LORD.
Joy and gladness will be found in her,
thanksgiving and the sound of
singing.

⁴ "Listen to me, my people;
hear me, my nation:
The law will go out from me;
my justice will become a light to the
nations.
⁵ My righteousness draws near speedily,
my salvation is on the way,
and my arm will bring justice to the
nations.
The islands will look to me
and wait in hope for my arm.
⁶ Lift up your eyes to the heavens,
look at the earth beneath;
the heavens will vanish like smoke,
the earth will wear out like a garment
and its inhabitants die like flies.
But my salvation will last forever,
my righteousness will never fail.

⁷ "Hear me, you who know what is right,
you people who have my law in your hearts:
Do not fear the reproach of men
or be terrified by their insults.
⁸ For the moth will eat them up like a garment;
the worm will devour them like wool.
But my righteousness will last forever,
my salvation through all generations."

⁹ Awake, awake! Clothe yourself with strength,
O arm of the LORD;

Knowing God's Law

Do you think you could drive to a friend's house across town without breaking any traffic laws—even if you had a police officer watching you the whole way? You could if you knew the rules of the road by heart and really cared about obeying the law. That same principle is true for living a life that pleases God. If you know his Word by heart—if you really care about demonstrating your love for him—you can stay faithful to him no matter how many people you have waiting for you to fall flat on your face.

awake, as in days gone by,
    as in generations of old.
Was it not you who cut Rahab to pieces,
    who pierced that monster through?
[10] Was it not you who dried up the sea,
    the waters of the great deep,
who made a road in the depths of the sea
    so that the redeemed might cross over?
[11] The ransomed of the LORD will return.
    They will enter Zion with singing;
    everlasting joy will crown their heads.
Gladness and joy will overtake them,
    and sorrow and sighing will flee away.

[12] "I, even I, am he who comforts you.
    Who are you that you fear mortal men,
    the sons of men, who are but grass,
[13] that you forget the LORD your Maker,
    who stretched out the heavens
    and laid the foundations of the earth,
that you live in constant terror every day
    because of the wrath of the oppressor,
    who is bent on destruction?
For where is the wrath of the oppressor?
[14]   The cowering prisoners will soon be set free;
they will not die in their dungeon,
    nor will they lack bread.
[15] For I am the LORD your God,
    who churns up the sea so that its waves roar—
    the LORD Almighty is his name.
[16] I have put my words in your mouth
    and covered you with the shadow of my hand—
I who set the heavens in place,
    who laid the foundations of the earth,
    and who say to Zion, 'You are my people.' "

THE CUP OF THE LORD'S WRATH

[17] Awake, awake!
    Rise up, O Jerusalem,
you who have drunk from the hand of the LORD
    the cup of his wrath,
you who have drained to its dregs
    the goblet that makes men stagger.
[18] Of all the sons she bore
    there was none to guide her;
of all the sons she reared
    there was none to take her by the hand.
[19] These double calamities have come upon you—
    who can comfort you?—
ruin and destruction, famine and sword—
    who can[a] console you?
[20] Your sons have fainted;
    they lie at the head of every street,
    like antelope caught in a net.

---

[a] 19 Dead Sea Scrolls, Septuagint, Vulgate and Syriac; Masoretic Text / how can I

They are filled with the wrath of the Lord
and the rebuke of your God.

²¹ Therefore hear this, you afflicted one,
made drunk, but not with wine.
²² This is what your Sovereign Lord says,
your God, who defends his people:
"See, I have taken out of your hand
the cup that made you stagger;
from that cup, the goblet of my wrath,
you will never drink again.
²³ I will put it into the hands of your
tormentors,
who said to you,
'Fall prostrate that we may walk over
you.'
And you made your back like the ground,
like a street to be walked over."

52 Awake, awake, O Zion,
clothe yourself with strength.
Put on your garments of splendor,
O Jerusalem, the holy city.
The uncircumcised and defiled
will not enter you again.
² Shake off your dust;
rise up, sit enthroned, O Jerusalem.
Free yourself from the chains on your
neck,
O captive Daughter of Zion.

³ For this is what the Lord says:

"You were sold for nothing,
and without money you will be
redeemed."

⁴ For this is what the Sovereign Lord says:

"At first my people went down to Egypt to
live;
lately, Assyria has oppressed them.

⁵ "And now what do I have here?" declares the Lord.

"For my people have been taken away for nothing,
and those who rule them mock,ᵃ"

"And all day long
my name is constantly blasphemed.
⁶ Therefore my people will know my name;
therefore in that day they will know
that it is I who foretold it.
Yes, it is I."

⁷ How beautiful on the mountains
are the feet of those who bring good news,
who proclaim peace,

Spreading God's Good News

Where have you taken God's good news of salvation? To the dining room table? To the school hallway after class? To the parking lot after soccer practice? To the inner city on a missions project? God has given you the honor and privilege of spreading his gospel. Don't think of it as a burden. A message as awesome as the one about Christ ought to be the most exciting thing in our lives—so exciting that we can't help but share it.

declares the Lord.

ᵃ 5 Dead Sea Scrolls and Vulgate; Masoretic Text *wail*

who bring good tidings,
who proclaim salvation,
who say to Zion,
"Your God reigns!"
[8] Listen! Your watchmen lift up their voices;
together they shout for joy.
When the LORD returns to Zion,
they will see it with their own eyes.
[9] Burst into songs of joy together,
you ruins of Jerusalem,
for the LORD has comforted his people,
he has redeemed Jerusalem.
[10] The LORD will lay bare his holy arm
in the sight of all the nations,
and all the ends of the earth will see
the salvation of our God.

[11] Depart, depart, go out from there!
Touch no unclean thing!
Come out from it and be pure,
you who carry the vessels of the LORD.
[12] But you will not leave in haste
or go in flight;
for the LORD will go before you,
the God of Israel will be your rear
guard.

THE SUFFERING AND GLORY OF THE SERVANT

[13] See, my servant will act wisely[a];
he will be raised and lifted up and
highly exalted.
[14] Just as there were many who were
appalled at him[b]—
his appearance was so disfigured
beyond that of any man
and his form marred beyond human
likeness—
[15] so will he sprinkle many nations,[c]
and kings will shut their mouths
because of him.
For what they were not told, they will see,
and what they have not heard, they
will understand.

53

Who has believed our message
and to whom has the arm of the LORD been revealed?
[2] He grew up before him like a tender shoot,
and like a root out of dry ground.
He had no beauty or majesty to attract us to him,
nothing in his appearance that we should desire him.
[3] He was despised and rejected by men,
a man of sorrows, and familiar with suffering.
Like one from whom men hide their faces
he was despised, and we esteemed him not.

Looking Beyond the Surface

How do you picture Jesus? Most paintings and movies depict a lean, white guy with a contemplative look—tall and graceful. You might imagine long, brown hair and a neatly trimmed beard. But that's probably not an accurate representation. This verse suggests that Jesus was a pretty average-looking guy and maybe even a little below average. Imagine what a mistake it would have been for the people of Jesus' day to judge him based on his appearance. Don't make the same mistake with people today. Look beyond a person's appearance and try to understand who they really are.

---

[a] 13 Or *will prosper*   [b] 14 Hebrew *you*   [c] 15 Hebrew; Septuagint *so will many nations marvel at him*

⁴Surely he took up our infirmities
and carried our sorrows,
yet we considered him stricken by God,
smitten by him, and afflicted.

⁵But he was pierced for our
transgressions,
he was crushed for our iniquities;
the punishment that brought us peace
was upon him,
and by his wounds we are healed.
⁶We all, like sheep, have gone astray,
each of us has turned to his own way;
and the LORD has laid on him
the iniquity of us all.

⁷He was oppressed and afflicted,
yet he did not open his mouth;
he was led like a lamb to the slaughter,
and as a sheep before her shearers is silent,
so he did not open his mouth.
⁸By oppressionᵃ and judgment he was taken away.
And who can speak of his descendants?
For he was cut off from the land of the living;
for the transgression of my people he was stricken.ᵇ
⁹He was assigned a grave with the wicked,
and with the rich in his death,
though he had done no violence,
nor was any deceit in his mouth.

¹⁰Yet it was the LORD's will to crush him and cause him to suffer,
and though the LORD makesᶜ his life a guilt offering,
he will see his offspring and prolong his days,
and the will of the LORD will prosper in his hand.
¹¹After the suffering of his soul,
he will see the light ⌞of life⌟ᵈ and be satisfiedᵉ;
by his knowledgeᶠ my righteous servant will justify many,
and he will bear their iniquities.
¹²Therefore I will give him a portion among the great,ᵍ
and he will divide the spoils with the strong,ʰ
because he poured out his life unto death,
and was numbered with the transgressors.
For he bore the sin of many,
and made intercession for the transgressors.

NOW OR NEVER
ISA 53:3–9

When people tell you there's nothing special about the Bible, show them Isaiah 53. Isaiah predicted that the Savior would be rejected, despised, pierced (as in, nailed to a cross and stabbed with a spear), executed with criminals and buried in a rich man's tomb. Seven hundred years later, all of it came true!

THE FUTURE GLORY OF ZION

54

"Sing, O barren woman,
you who never bore a child;
burst into song, shout for joy,
you who were never in labor;
because more are the children of the desolate woman
than of her who has a husband,"

says the LORD.

ᵃ 8 Or *From arrest*   ᵇ 8 Or *away. / Yet who of his generation considered / that he was cut off from the land of the living / for the transgression of my people, / to whom the blow was due?*   ᶜ 10 Hebrew *though you make*   ᵈ 11 Dead Sea Scrolls (see also Septuagint); Masoretic Text does not have the *light ⌞of life⌟*.   ᵉ 11 Or (with Masoretic Text) ¹¹*He will see the result of the suffering of his soul / and be satisfied*   ᶠ 11 Or *by knowledge of him*   ᵍ 12 Or *many*   ʰ 12 Or *numerous*

2 "Enlarge the place of your tent,
     stretch your tent curtains wide,
     do not hold back;
   lengthen your cords,
     strengthen your stakes.
3 For you will spread out to the right and to the left;
     your descendants will dispossess nations
     and settle in their desolate cities.

4 "Do not be afraid; you will not suffer shame.
     Do not fear disgrace; you will not be humiliated.
   You will forget the shame of your youth
     and remember no more the reproach of your widowhood.
5 For your Maker is your husband—
     the LORD Almighty is his name—
   the Holy One of Israel is your Redeemer;
     he is called the God of all the earth.
6 The LORD will call you back
     as if you were a wife deserted and distressed in spirit—
   a wife who married young,
     only to be rejected," says your God.
7 "For a brief moment I abandoned you,
     but with deep compassion I will bring you back.
8 In a surge of anger
     I hid my face from you for a moment,
   but with everlasting kindness
     I will have compassion on you,"
   says the LORD your Redeemer.

9 "To me this is like the days of Noah,
     when I swore that the waters of Noah would never again cover the earth.
   So now I have sworn not to be angry with you,
     never to rebuke you again.
10 Though the mountains be shaken
     and the hills be removed,
   yet my unfailing love for you will not be shaken
     nor my covenant of peace be removed,"
   says the LORD, who has compassion on you.

11 "O afflicted city, lashed by storms and not comforted,
     I will build you with stones of turquoise,[a]
     your foundations with sapphires.[b]
12 I will make your battlements of rubies,
     your gates of sparkling jewels,
     and all your walls of precious stones.
13 All your sons will be taught by the LORD,
     and great will be your children's peace.
14 In righteousness you will be established:
   Tyranny will be far from you;
     you will have nothing to fear.
   Terror will be far removed;
     it will not come near you.
15 If anyone does attack you, it will not be my doing;
     whoever attacks you will surrender to you.

---

[a] 11 The meaning of the Hebrew for this word is uncertain.   [b] 11 Or lapis lazuli

50 WAYS TO BE RADICAL FOR GOD

The world doesn't need a bunch of weak, cowardly, half hearted Christian guys who are just playing the church game. The world needs men who are willing to live with passion, strength and fierce conviction. It needs men who are hungry for God and who don't get sucked into the world's foolish traps. Here are 50 ways that you can be radical for God, starting right now:

01 »	Live as though everything you possess actually belongs to God . . . because it does	PS 24:1
02 »	Memorize Scripture as a shield against sin	PS 119:11
03 »	Obey Christ's commands regardless of what others think or say	PS 119:51
04 »	Ask God to search your heart, to show you where you need to change	PS 139:23
05 »	Live life like a beacon of light on a mountain	MT 5:14
06 »	Pray authentic prayers—talk to God, not to anyone else who might be listening	MT 6:5–8
07 »	Commit every ounce of strength in your body, soul and mind to loving God	LK 10:27
08 »	Look out for other people the same way that you look out for yourself	LK 10:27
09 »	Repent: Turn away from sin and from anything that's not pleasing to God	AC 17:30
10 »	Instead of being ashamed, defend the honor of the gospel the same way that you would defend yourself	RO 1:16–17
11 »	Be a trendsetter in living for Jesus—instead of a follower who lives like the world	RO 12:2
12 »	Don't follow the crowd	RO 12:2
13 »	When trouble comes, refuse to lose your temper, use bad language or complain	RO 12:12
14 »	Look for Christians in need and find ways to meet their needs	RO 12:13
15 »	Pray for the people who give you the most grief	RO 12:14
16 »	Be a peacemaker, not a guy who picks fights	RO 12:16
17 »	Look after loners and be a friend to people who are considered uncool	RO 12:16
18 »	Go the extra mile to resolve conflicts	RO 12:18
19 »	Let God get revenge and settle scores, not you	RO 12:19
20 »	Learn to submit to people in authority	RO 13:1

RADICAL FOR GOD

¹⁶ "See, it is I who created the blacksmith
    who fans the coals into flame
    and forges a weapon fit for its work.
And it is I who have created the destroyer to work havoc;
¹⁷   no weapon forged against you will prevail,
    and you will refute every tongue that accuses you.
This is the heritage of the servants of the LORD,
    and this is their vindication from me,"

                            declares the LORD.

INVITATION TO THE THIRSTY

55

"Come, all you who are thirsty,
    come to the waters;
and you who have no money,
    come, buy and eat!
Come, buy wine and milk
    without money and without cost.
² Why spend money on what is not bread,
    and your labor on what does not
       satisfy?
Listen, listen to me, and eat what is
       good,
    and your soul will delight in the
       richest of fare.
³ Give ear and come to me;
    hear me, that your soul may live.
I will make an everlasting covenant with
       you,
    my faithful love promised to David.
⁴ See, I have made him a witness to the
       peoples,
    a leader and commander of the
       peoples.
⁵ Surely you will summon nations you
       know not,
    and nations that do not know you will
       hasten to you,
because of the LORD your God,
    the Holy One of Israel,
    for he has endowed you with
       splendor."

⁶ Seek the LORD while he may be found;
    call on him while he is near.
⁷ Let the wicked forsake his way
    and the evil man his thoughts.
Let him turn to the LORD, and he will have mercy on him,
    and to our God, for he will freely pardon.

⁸ "For my thoughts are not your thoughts,
    neither are your ways my ways,"

                            declares the LORD.

⁹ "As the heavens are higher than the earth,
    so are my ways higher than your ways
    and my thoughts than your thoughts.
¹⁰ As the rain and the snow

Satisfying Your Spiritual Hunger

You know how you can eat certain things such as cotton candy, air-popped popcorn or a salad and still be hungry? That's the way it is when you try to fill your soul with anything but God. Each of us is born with a God-shaped hole in our lives. If you try to satisfy that need with sex or work or material possessions or friends or music or Wicca or anything else, you're going to find yourself spiritually hungry. Only the Lord can truly satisfy you.

»» live the adventure »» Isa 55:1-2

come down from heaven,
and do not return to it
without watering the earth
and making it bud and flourish,
so that it yields seed for the sower and bread for the eater,
11 so is my word that goes out from my mouth:
It will not return to me empty,
but will accomplish what I desire
and achieve the purpose for which I sent it.
12 You will go out in joy
and be led forth in peace;
the mountains and hills
will burst into song before you,
and all the trees of the field
will clap their hands.
13 Instead of the thornbush will grow the pine tree,
and instead of briers the myrtle will grow.
This will be for the LORD's renown,
for an everlasting sign,
which will not be destroyed."

SALVATION FOR OTHERS

This is what the LORD says:

"Maintain justice
and do what is right,
for my salvation is close at hand
and my righteousness will soon be revealed.
2 Blessed is the man who does this,
the man who holds it fast,
who keeps the Sabbath without desecrating it,
and keeps his hand from doing any evil."

3 Let no foreigner who has bound himself to the LORD say,
"The LORD will surely exclude me from his people."
And let not any eunuch complain,
"I am only a dry tree."

4 For this is what the LORD says:

"To the eunuchs who keep my Sabbaths,
who choose what pleases me
and hold fast to my covenant—
5 to them I will give within my temple and its walls
a memorial and a name
better than sons and daughters;
I will give them an everlasting name
that will not be cut off.
6 And foreigners who bind themselves to the LORD
to serve him,
to love the name of the LORD,
and to worship him,
all who keep the Sabbath without desecrating it
and who hold fast to my covenant—
7 these I will bring to my holy mountain
and give them joy in my house of prayer.
Their burnt offerings and sacrifices

will be accepted on my altar;
for my house will be called
a house of prayer for all nations."
⁸ The Sovereign LORD declares—
he who gathers the exiles of Israel:
"I will gather still others to them
besides those already gathered."

GOD'S ACCUSATION AGAINST THE WICKED

⁹ Come, all you beasts of the field,
come and devour, all you beasts of the forest!
¹⁰ Israel's watchmen are blind,
they all lack knowledge;
they are all mute dogs,
they cannot bark;
they lie around and dream,
they love to sleep.
¹¹ They are dogs with mighty appetites;
they never have enough.
They are shepherds who lack understanding;
they all turn to their own way,
each seeks his own gain.
¹² "Come," each one cries, "let me get wine!
Let us drink our fill of beer!
And tomorrow will be like today,
or even far better."

57 The righteous perish,
and no one ponders it in his heart;
devout men are taken away,
and no one understands
that the righteous are taken away
to be spared from evil.

ISA 57:1-2

This is why the funeral of a Christian can be full of both happiness and sadness at the same time. We mourn the fact that loved ones are no longer with us, but we celebrate the fact that they're experiencing incredible peace.

² Those who walk uprightly
enter into peace;
they find rest as they lie in death.

³ "But you—come here, you sons of a sorceress,
you offspring of adulterers and prostitutes!
⁴ Whom are you mocking?
At whom do you sneer
and stick out your tongue?
Are you not a brood of rebels,
the offspring of liars?
⁵ You burn with lust among the oaks
and under every spreading tree;

you sacrifice your children in the ravines
and under the overhanging crags.
⁶ ⌊The idols⌋ among the smooth stones of the ravines are your portion;
they, they are your lot.
Yes, to them you have poured out drink offerings
and offered grain offerings.
In the light of these things, should I relent?

⁷ You have made your bed on a high and lofty hill;
  there you went up to offer your sacrifices.
⁸ Behind your doors and your doorposts
  you have put your pagan symbols.
 Forsaking me, you uncovered your bed,
  you climbed into it and opened it wide;
 you made a pact with those whose beds you love,
  and you looked on their nakedness.
⁹ You went to Molech[a] with olive oil
  and increased your perfumes.
 You sent your ambassadors[b] far away;
  you descended to the grave[c] itself!
¹⁰ You were wearied by all your ways,
  but you would not say, 'It is hopeless.'
 You found renewal of your strength,
  and so you did not faint.

¹¹ "Whom have you so dreaded and feared
  that you have been false to me,
 and have neither remembered me
  nor pondered this in your hearts?
 Is it not because I have long been silent
  that you do not fear me?
¹² I will expose your righteousness and
  your works,
  and they will not benefit you.
¹³ When you cry out for help,
  let your collection ⌊of idols⌋ save you!
 The wind will carry all of them off,
  a mere breath will blow them away.
 But the man who makes me his refuge
  will inherit the land
  and possess my holy mountain."

COMFORT FOR THE CONTRITE

¹⁴ And it will be said:

 "Build up, build up, prepare the road!
  Remove the obstacles out of the way
   of my people."
¹⁵ For this is what the high and lofty One says—
  he who lives forever, whose name is holy:
 "I live in a high and holy place,
  but also with him who is contrite and lowly in spirit,
 to revive the spirit of the lowly
  and to revive the heart of the contrite.
¹⁶ I will not accuse forever,
  nor will I always be angry,
 for then the spirit of man would grow faint before me—
  the breath of man that I have created.
¹⁷ I was enraged by his sinful greed;
  I punished him, and hid my face in anger,
  yet he kept on in his willful ways.
¹⁸ I have seen his ways, but I will heal him;
  I will guide him and restore comfort to him,

Learning to Be Humble

How low can you go? That's the question to ask if you want to be successful in God's eyes. God isn't impressed by what your parents do for a living, what kind of clothes you wear or how many people envy you at school. He cares about how humble you are. He cares about how readily you confess your sin and seek his forgiveness. He cares about how willing you are to get your hands dirty to help others. He cares about how quick you are to deflect praise and give credit to him instead of hogging the spotlight yourself.

---

¹⁹ creating praise on the lips of the mourners in Israel.
Peace, peace, to those far and near,"
  says the Lᴏʀᴅ. "And I will heal them."
²⁰ But the wicked are like the tossing sea,
  which cannot rest,
  whose waves cast up mire and mud.
²¹ "There is no peace," says my God, "for the wicked."

TRUE FASTING

58

"Shout it aloud, do not hold back.
  Raise your voice like a trumpet.
Declare to my people their rebellion
  and to the house of Jacob their sins.
² For day after day they seek me out;
  they seem eager to know my ways,
as if they were a nation that does what is right
  and has not forsaken the commands of its God.
They ask me for just decisions
  and seem eager for God to come near them.
³ 'Why have we fasted,' they say,
  'and you have not seen it?
Why have we humbled ourselves,
  and you have not noticed?'

"Yet on the day of your fasting, you do as you please
  and exploit all your workers.
⁴ Your fasting ends in quarreling and strife,
  and in striking each other with wicked fists.
You cannot fast as you do today
  and expect your voice to be heard on high.
⁵ Is this the kind of fast I have chosen,
  only a day for a man to humble himself?
Is it only for bowing one's head like a reed
  and for lying on sackcloth and ashes?
Is that what you call a fast,
  a day acceptable to the Lᴏʀᴅ?

⁶ "Is not this the kind of fasting I have chosen:
to loose the chains of injustice
  and untie the cords of the yoke,
to set the oppressed free
  and break every yoke?
⁷ Is it not to share your food with the hungry
  and to provide the poor wanderer with shelter—
when you see the naked, to clothe him,
  and not to turn away from your own flesh and blood?
⁸ Then your light will break forth like the dawn,
  and your healing will quickly appear;
then your righteousness ᵃ will go before you,
  and the glory of the Lᴏʀᴅ will be your rear guard.
⁹ Then you will call, and the Lᴏʀᴅ will answer;
  you will cry for help, and he will say: Here am I.

"If you do away with the yoke of oppression,
  with the pointing finger and malicious talk,

ᵃ 8 Or *your righteous One*

¹⁰ and if you spend yourselves in behalf of the hungry
  and satisfy the needs of the oppressed,
then your light will rise in the darkness,
  and your night will become like the noonday.
¹¹ The LORD will guide you always;
  he will satisfy your needs in a sun-scorched land
  and will strengthen your frame.
You will be like a well-watered garden,
  like a spring whose waters never fail.
¹² Your people will rebuild the ancient ruins
  and will raise up the age-old foundations;
you will be called Repairer of Broken Walls,
  Restorer of Streets with Dwellings.

¹³ "If you keep your feet from breaking the Sabbath
  and from doing as you please on my holy day,
if you call the Sabbath a delight
  and the LORD's holy day honorable,
and if you honor it by not going your own way
  and not doing as you please or speaking idle words,
¹⁴ then you will find your joy in the LORD,
  and I will cause you to ride on the heights of the land
  and to feast on the inheritance of your father Jacob."
The mouth of the LORD has spoken.

SIN, CONFESSION AND REDEMPTION

59

Surely the arm of the LORD is not too short to save,
  nor his ear too dull to hear.
² But your iniquities have separated
  you from your God;
your sins have hidden his face from you,
  so that he will not hear.
³ For your hands are stained with blood,
  your fingers with guilt.
Your lips have spoken lies,
  and your tongue mutters wicked things.
⁴ No one calls for justice;
  no one pleads his case with integrity.
They rely on empty arguments and speak lies;
  they conceive trouble and give birth to evil.
⁵ They hatch the eggs of vipers
  and spin a spider's web.
Whoever eats their eggs will die,
  and when one is broken, an adder is hatched.
⁶ Their cobwebs are useless for clothing;
  they cannot cover themselves with what they make.
Their deeds are evil deeds,
  and acts of violence are in their hands.
⁷ Their feet rush into sin;
  they are swift to shed innocent blood.
Their thoughts are evil thoughts;
  ruin and destruction mark their ways.
⁸ The way of peace they do not know;
  there is no justice in their paths.
They have turned them into crooked roads;
  no one who walks in them will know peace.

⁹So justice is far from us,
   and righteousness does not reach us.
We look for light, but all is darkness;
   for brightness, but we walk in deep shadows.
¹⁰Like the blind we grope along the wall,
   feeling our way like men without eyes.
At midday we stumble as if it were twilight;
   among the strong, we are like the dead.
¹¹We all growl like bears;
   we moan mournfully like doves.
We look for justice, but find none;
   for deliverance, but it is far away.

¹²For our offenses are many in your sight,
   and our sins testify against us.
Our offenses are ever with us,
   and we acknowledge our iniquities:
¹³rebellion and treachery against the LORD,
   turning our backs on our God,
fomenting oppression and revolt,
   uttering lies our hearts have conceived.
¹⁴So justice is driven back,
   and righteousness stands at a distance;
truth has stumbled in the streets,
   honesty cannot enter.
¹⁵Truth is nowhere to be found,
   and whoever shuns evil becomes a prey.

The LORD looked and was displeased
   that there was no justice.
¹⁶He saw that there was no one,
   he was appalled that there was no one to intervene;
so his own arm worked salvation for him,
   and his own righteousness sustained him.
¹⁷He put on righteousness as his breastplate,
   and the helmet of salvation on his head;
he put on the garments of vengeance
   and wrapped himself in zeal as in a cloak.
¹⁸According to what they have done,
   so will he repay
wrath to his enemies
   and retribution to his foes;
he will repay the islands their due.
¹⁹From the west, men will fear the name of the LORD,
   and from the rising of the sun, they will revere his glory.
For he will come like a pent-up flood
   that the breath of the LORD drives along.ᵃ

²⁰"The Redeemer will come to Zion,
   to those in Jacob who repent of their sins,"

                                 declares the LORD.

²¹"As for me, this is my covenant with them," says the LORD. "My Spirit, who is on you, and my words that I have put in your mouth will not depart from your mouth, or from the mouths of your children, or from the mouths of their descendants from this time on and forever," says the LORD.

ᵃ 19 Or When the enemy comes in like a flood, / the Spirit of the LORD will put him to flight

THE GLORY OF ZION

60

"Arise, shine, for your light has come,
and the glory of the LORD rises upon you.
² See, darkness covers the earth
and thick darkness is over the peoples,
but the LORD rises upon you
and his glory appears over you.
³ Nations will come to your light,
and kings to the brightness of your dawn.

⁴ "Lift up your eyes and look about you:
All assemble and come to you;
your sons come from afar,
and your daughters are carried on the arm.
⁵ Then you will look and be radiant,
your heart will throb and swell with joy;
the wealth on the seas will be brought to you,
to you the riches of the nations will come.
⁶ Herds of camels will cover your land,
young camels of Midian and Ephah.
And all from Sheba will come,
bearing gold and incense
and proclaiming the praise of the LORD.
⁷ All Kedar's flocks will be gathered to you,
the rams of Nebaioth will serve you;
they will be accepted as offerings on my altar,
and I will adorn my glorious temple.

⁸ "Who are these that fly along like clouds,
like doves to their nests?
⁹ Surely the islands look to me;
in the lead are the ships of Tarshish,ᵃ
bringing your sons from afar,
with their silver and gold,
to the honor of the LORD your God,
the Holy One of Israel,
for he has endowed you with splendor.

¹⁰ "Foreigners will rebuild your walls,
and their kings will serve you.
Though in anger I struck you,
in favor I will show you compassion.
¹¹ Your gates will always stand open,
they will never be shut, day or night,
so that men may bring you the wealth of the nations—
their kings led in triumphal procession.
¹² For the nation or kingdom that will not serve you will perish;
it will be utterly ruined.

¹³ "The glory of Lebanon will come to you,
the pine, the fir and the cypress together,
to adorn the place of my sanctuary;
and I will glorify the place of my feet.
¹⁴ The sons of your oppressors will come bowing before you;
all who despise you will bow down at your feet

ᵃ 9 Or the trading ships

and will call you the City of the Lord,
    Zion of the Holy One of Israel.

15 "Although you have been forsaken and hated,
    with no one traveling through,
I will make you the everlasting pride
    and the joy of all generations.
16 You will drink the milk of nations
    and be nursed at royal breasts.
Then you will know that I, the Lord, am your Savior,
    your Redeemer, the Mighty One of Jacob.
17 Instead of bronze I will bring you gold,
    and silver in place of iron.
Instead of wood I will bring you bronze,
    and iron in place of stones.
I will make peace your governor
    and righteousness your ruler.
18 No longer will violence be heard in your land,
    nor ruin or destruction within your borders,
but you will call your walls Salvation
    and your gates Praise.
19 The sun will no more be your light by day,
    nor will the brightness of the moon shine on you,
for the Lord will be your everlasting light,
    and your God will be your glory.
20 Your sun will never set again,
    and your moon will wane no more;
the Lord will be your everlasting light,
    and your days of sorrow will end.
21 Then will all your people be righteous
    and they will possess the land forever.
They are the shoot I have planted,
    the work of my hands,
for the display of my splendor.
22 The least of you will become a thousand,
    the smallest a mighty nation.
I am the Lord;
    in its time I will do this swiftly."

THE YEAR OF THE LORD'S FAVOR

61

The Spirit of the Sovereign Lord is on me,
    because the Lord has anointed me
    to preach good news to the poor.
He has sent me to bind up the brokenhearted,
    to proclaim freedom for the captives
    and release from darkness for the prisoners, [a]
2 to proclaim the year of the Lord's favor
    and the day of vengeance of our God,
to comfort all who mourn,
3   and provide for those who grieve in Zion—
to bestow on them a crown of beauty
    instead of ashes,
the oil of gladness
    instead of mourning,

---

[a] 1 Hebrew; Septuagint the blind

battlelines

» Outside the Box (Serving Others)

Q: You're soaking wet. What happened? Did you just hit a water buffalo or something?
A: Funny. No, I just came from the youth group car wash.

Q: Are you guys raising money for a trip or something?
A: No, this thing was totally free. We refused to take donations.

Q: You're kidding, right?
A: No, I'm serious. Most of the people who came by had the same expression on their faces that you do. It was kinda funny. They kept asking, "What's the catch?"

Q: So you spent all afternoon working, and you didn't make a dime?
A: Nope. But we had fun. We laughed a lot, and I learned some things.

Q: Like what?
A: Like how selfish I usually am. Like how hard it is for people to let others do something nice for them. Like how I need to spend more time serving other people.

Q: So are you thinking of becoming a pastor or something like that?
A: No, not really. I'm just starting to realize how much time I spend sitting around saying, "There's nothing to do, there's nothing to do." The truth is, there's plenty to do. People everywhere are in need.

Q: So what started all this, anyway?
A: I'm not exactly sure. My youth pastor did a series on what it means to be a Christian. I always thought it meant just believing in Jesus. But he really challenged that idea and encouraged us to *live* what we believe. Some other people in the youth group started *doing* something with their faith, and I guess it was contagious. Hey, maybe I've caught the real disease.

» Think It or Live It?

Most Christians live in nice, comfortable little boxes of self-centeredness. They see their faith as a way to get their own needs and desires met. Few dare to venture outside of their boxes and devote their time to serving other people.

Contrast that approach to life with Jesus' stated mission: "For even the Son of Man did not come to be served, but to serve, and to give his life as a ransom for many" (Mark 10:45).

That's not to say that a lifestyle of serving and giving should feel comfortable or natural to you. Serving others requires you to break out of your comfort zone and do extraordinary, sacrificial things—through the power of the Holy Spirit. It takes a real man to go from just *thinking* about being a Christian to actually *living* his faith.

Discover ways you can reach out to others at www.RevolutionBible.com.

and a garment of praise
    instead of a spirit of despair.
They will be called oaks of righteousness,
    a planting of the Lord
    for the display of his splendor.

4 They will rebuild the ancient ruins
    and restore the places long devastated;
they will renew the ruined cities
    that have been devastated for generations.
5 Aliens will shepherd your flocks;
    foreigners will work your fields and vineyards.
6 And you will be called priests of the Lord,
    you will be named ministers of our
        God.
You will feed on the wealth of nations,
    and in their riches you will boast.

7 Instead of their shame
    my people will receive a double
        portion,
and instead of disgrace
    they will rejoice in their inheritance;
and so they will inherit a double portion
    in their land,
    and everlasting joy will be theirs.

8 "For I, the Lord, love justice;
    I hate robbery and iniquity.
In my faithfulness I will reward them
    and make an everlasting covenant
        with them.
9 Their descendants will be known among
        the nations
    and their offspring among the
        peoples.
All who see them will acknowledge
    that they are a people the Lord has
        blessed."

10 I delight greatly in the Lord;
    my soul rejoices in my God.
For he has clothed me with garments of
        salvation
    and arrayed me in a robe of
        righteousness,
as a bridegroom adorns his head like a
        priest,
    and as a bride adorns herself with her jewels.
11 For as the soil makes the sprout come up
    and a garden causes seeds to grow,
so the Sovereign Lord will make righteousness and praise
    spring up before all nations.

ZION'S NEW NAME

62

For Zion's sake I will not keep silent,
    for Jerusalem's sake I will not remain quiet,

>> live the adventure >> Isa 61:10

Understanding How God Sees You

When your parents look at you, what do they see? What do your friends see? What do your coaches see? What do your teachers see? What do your coworkers see? What do people who don't know you see? Sometimes it's hard to figure out exactly what people think of you. Fortunately, that's not the case when it comes to God. The Bible tells us very clearly what he thinks of us. If you've made Jesus the Savior and Lord of your life, God doesn't see you as a person guilty of a long list of sins and missteps. He sees someone who is *perfectly* righteous!

till her righteousness shines out like the dawn,
    her salvation like a blazing torch.
2 The nations will see your righteousness,
    and all kings your glory;
you will be called by a new name
    that the mouth of the LORD will bestow.
3 You will be a crown of splendor in the LORD's hand,
    a royal diadem in the hand of your God.
4 No longer will they call you Deserted,
    or name your land Desolate.
But you will be called Hephzibah,ᵃ
    and your land Beulahᵇ;
for the LORD will take delight in you,
    and your land will be married.
5 As a young man marries a maiden,
    so will your sonsᶜ marry you;
as a bridegroom rejoices over his bride,
    so will your God rejoice over you.

6 I have posted watchmen on your walls, O Jerusalem;
    they will never be silent day or night.
You who call on the LORD,
    give yourselves no rest,
7 and give him no rest till he establishes Jerusalem
    and makes her the praise of the earth.

8 The LORD has sworn by his right hand
    and by his mighty arm:
"Never again will I give your grain
    as food for your enemies,
and never again will foreigners drink the new wine
    for which you have toiled;
9 but those who harvest it will eat it
    and praise the LORD,
and those who gather the grapes will drink it
    in the courts of my sanctuary."

10 Pass through, pass through the gates!
    Prepare the way for the people.
Build up, build up the highway!
    Remove the stones.
Raise a banner for the nations.

11 The LORD has made proclamation
    to the ends of the earth:
"Say to the Daughter of Zion,
    'See, your Savior comes!
See, his reward is with him,
    and his recompense accompanies him.' "
12 They will be called the Holy People,
    the Redeemed of the LORD;
and you will be called Sought After,
    the City No Longer Deserted.

ᵃ 4 *Hephzibah* means *my delight is in her.*   ᵇ 4 *Beulah* means *married.*   ᶜ 5 Or *Builder*

63

Who is this coming from Edom,
from Bozrah, with his garments stained crimson?
Who is this, robed in splendor,
striding forward in the greatness of his strength?

"It is I, speaking in righteousness,
mighty to save."

2 Why are your garments red,
like those of one treading the winepress?

3 "I have trodden the winepress alone;
from the nations no one was with me.
I trampled them in my anger
and trod them down in my wrath;
their blood spattered my garments,
and I stained all my clothing.
4 For the day of vengeance was in my heart,
and the year of my redemption has come.
5 I looked, but there was no one to help,
I was appalled that no one gave support;
so my own arm worked salvation for me,
and my own wrath sustained me.
6 I trampled the nations in my anger;
in my wrath I made them drunk
and poured their blood on the ground."

PRAISE AND PRAYER

7 I will tell of the kindnesses of the LORD,
the deeds for which he is to be praised,
according to all the LORD has done for us—
yes, the many good things he has done
for the house of Israel,
according to his compassion and many kindnesses.
8 He said, "Surely they are my people,
sons who will not be false to me";
and so he became their Savior.
9 In all their distress he too was distressed,
and the angel of his presence saved them.
In his love and mercy he redeemed them;
he lifted them up and carried them
all the days of old.
10 Yet they rebelled
and grieved his Holy Spirit.
So he turned and became their enemy
and he himself fought against them.

11 Then his people recalled [a] the days of old,
the days of Moses and his people—
where is he who brought them through the sea,
with the shepherd of his flock?
Where is he who set
his Holy Spirit among them,
12 who sent his glorious arm of power
to be at Moses' right hand,

[a] 11 Or But may he recall

who divided the waters before them,
to gain for himself everlasting renown,
¹³who led them through the depths?
Like a horse in open country,
they did not stumble;
¹⁴like cattle that go down to the plain,
they were given rest by the Spirit of the LORD.
This is how you guided your people
to make for yourself a glorious name.

¹⁵Look down from heaven and see
from your lofty throne, holy and glorious.
Where are your zeal and your might?
Your tenderness and compassion are withheld from us.
¹⁶But you are our Father,
though Abraham does not know us
or Israel acknowledge us;
you, O LORD, are our Father,
our Redeemer from of old is your name.
¹⁷Why, O LORD, do you make us wander from your ways
and harden our hearts so we do not revere you?
Return for the sake of your servants,
the tribes that are your inheritance.
¹⁸For a little while your people possessed your holy place,
but now our enemies have trampled down your sanctuary.
¹⁹We are yours from of old;
but you have not ruled over them,
they have not been called by your name.ᵃ

64

Oh, that you would rend the heavens and come down,
that the mountains would tremble before you!
²As when fire sets twigs ablaze
and causes water to boil,
come down to make your name known to your enemies
and cause the nations to quake before you!
³For when you did awesome things that we did not expect,
you came down, and the mountains trembled before you.
⁴Since ancient times no one has heard,
no ear has perceived,
no eye has seen any God besides you,
who acts on behalf of those who wait
for him.
⁵You come to the help of those who
gladly do right,
who remember your ways.
But when we continued to sin against
them,
you were angry.
How then can we be saved?
⁶All of us have become like one who is
unclean,
and all our righteous acts are like
filthy rags;
we all shrivel up like a leaf,

NOW OR NEVER
ISA 64:6

Think you can impress God with how good you are? Think again. The "filthy rags" in this verse refer to the cloths women in ancient times wore during their menstrual bleeding. Gross! Yet that's what God thinks of the good deeds people try to do to "earn" their way into heaven.

ᵃ 19 Or *We are like those you have never ruled, / like those never called by your name*

and like the wind our sins sweep us away.
⁷ No one calls on your name
　　or strives to lay hold of you;
for you have hidden your face from us
　　and made us waste away because of our sins.

⁸ Yet, O LORD, you are our Father.
　　We are the clay, you are the potter;
　　we are all the work of your hand.
⁹ Do not be angry beyond measure, O LORD;
　　do not remember our sins forever.
Oh, look upon us, we pray,
　　for we are all your people.
¹⁰ Your sacred cities have become a desert;
　　even Zion is a desert, Jerusalem a desolation.
¹¹ Our holy and glorious temple, where our fathers praised you,
　　has been burned with fire,
　　and all that we treasured lies in ruins.
¹² After all this, O LORD, will you hold yourself back?
　　Will you keep silent and punish us beyond measure?

JUDGMENT AND SALVATION

"I revealed myself to those who did not ask for me;
　　I was found by those who did not seek me.
To a nation that did not call on my name,
　　I said, 'Here am I, here am I.'
² All day long I have held out my hands
　　to an obstinate people,
who walk in ways not good,
　　pursuing their own imaginations—
³ a people who continually provoke me
　　to my very face,
offering sacrifices in gardens
　　and burning incense on altars of brick;
⁴ who sit among the graves
　　and spend their nights keeping secret vigil;
who eat the flesh of pigs,
　　and whose pots hold broth of unclean meat;
⁵ who say, 'Keep away; don't come near me,
　　for I am too sacred for you!'
Such people are smoke in my nostrils,
　　a fire that keeps burning all day.

⁶ "See, it stands written before me:
　　I will not keep silent but will pay back in full;
　　I will pay it back into their laps—
⁷ both your sins and the sins of your fathers,"
　　says the LORD.
"Because they burned sacrifices on the mountains
　　and defied me on the hills,
I will measure into their laps
　　the full payment for their former deeds."

⁸ This is what the LORD says:

"As when juice is still found in a cluster of grapes
　　and men say, 'Don't destroy it,

there is yet some good in it,'
so will I do in behalf of my servants;
I will not destroy them all.
⁹I will bring forth descendants from Jacob,
and from Judah those who will possess my mountains;
my chosen people will inherit them,
and there will my servants live.
¹⁰Sharon will become a pasture for flocks,
and the Valley of Achor a resting place for herds,
for my people who seek me.

¹¹"But as for you who forsake the LORD
and forget my holy mountain,
who spread a table for Fortune
and fill bowls of mixed wine for Destiny,
¹²I will destine you for the sword,
and you will all bend down for the slaughter;
for I called but you did not answer,
I spoke but you did not listen.
You did evil in my sight
and chose what displeases me."

¹³Therefore this is what the Sovereign LORD says:

"My servants will eat,
but you will go hungry;
my servants will drink,
but you will go thirsty;
my servants will rejoice,
but you will be put to shame.
¹⁴My servants will sing
out of the joy of their hearts,
but you will cry out
from anguish of heart
and wail in brokenness of spirit.
¹⁵You will leave your name
to my chosen ones as a curse;
the Sovereign LORD will put you to death,
but to his servants he will give another name.
¹⁶Whoever invokes a blessing in the land
will do so by the God of truth;
he who takes an oath in the land
will swear by the God of truth.
For the past troubles will be forgotten
and hidden from my eyes.

NEW HEAVENS AND A NEW EARTH

¹⁷"Behold, I will create
new heavens and a new earth.
The former things will not be remembered,
nor will they come to mind.
¹⁸But be glad and rejoice forever
in what I will create,
for I will create Jerusalem to be a delight
and its people a joy.
¹⁹I will rejoice over Jerusalem
and take delight in my people;

the sound of weeping and of crying
    will be heard in it no more.

20 "Never again will there be in it
    an infant who lives but a few days,

or an old man who does not live out
        his years;
he who dies at a hundred
    will be thought a mere youth;
he who fails to reach[a] a hundred
    will be considered accursed.
21 They will build houses and dwell in
        them;
    they will plant vineyards and eat their
        fruit.
22 No longer will they build houses and
        others live in them,
    or plant and others eat.
For as the days of a tree,
    so will be the days of my people;

NOW OR NEVER
ISA 65:17–25

What do you look forward to most in the new world God has planned? Forgetting all the worries of this world? Not having to see anyone suffer? Not having to worry about death?

my chosen ones will long enjoy
        the works of their hands.
23 They will not toil in vain
    or bear children doomed to misfortune;
for they will be a people blessed by the LORD,
    they and their descendants with them.
24 Before they call I will answer;
    while they are still speaking I will hear.
25 The wolf and the lamb will feed together,
    and the lion will eat straw like the ox,
    but dust will be the serpent's food.
They will neither harm nor destroy
    on all my holy mountain,"

says the LORD.

JUDGMENT AND HOPE

66

This is what the LORD says:

"Heaven is my throne,
    and the earth is my footstool.
Where is the house you will build for me?
    Where will my resting place be?
2 Has not my hand made all these things,
    and so they came into being?"

declares the LORD.

"This is the one I esteem:
    he who is humble and contrite in spirit,
    and trembles at my word.
3 But whoever sacrifices a bull
    is like one who kills a man,
and whoever offers a lamb,
    like one who breaks a dog's neck;
whoever makes a grain offering
    is like one who presents pig's blood,

[a] 20 Or / the sinner who reaches

and whoever burns memorial incense,
    like one who worships an idol.
They have chosen their own ways,
    and their souls delight in their abominations;
⁴so I also will choose harsh treatment for them
    and will bring upon them what they dread.
For when I called, no one answered,
    when I spoke, no one listened.
They did evil in my sight
    and chose what displeases me."

⁵Hear the word of the LORD,
    you who tremble at his word:
"Your brothers who hate you,
    and exclude you because of my name, have said,
'Let the LORD be glorified,
    that we may see your joy!'
Yet they will be put to shame.
⁶Hear that uproar from the city,
    hear that noise from the temple!
It is the sound of the LORD
    repaying his enemies all they deserve.

⁷"Before she goes into labor,
    she gives birth;
before the pains come upon her,
    she delivers a son.
⁸Who has ever heard of such a thing?
    Who has ever seen such things?
Can a country be born in a day
    or a nation be brought forth in a moment?
Yet no sooner is Zion in labor
    than she gives birth to her children.
⁹Do I bring to the moment of birth
    and not give delivery?" says the LORD.
"Do I close up the womb
    when I bring to delivery?" says your God.
¹⁰"Rejoice with Jerusalem and be glad for her,
    all you who love her;
rejoice greatly with her,
    all you who mourn over her.
¹¹For you will nurse and be satisfied
    at her comforting breasts;
you will drink deeply
    and delight in her overflowing abundance."

¹²For this is what the LORD says:

"I will extend peace to her like a river,
    and the wealth of nations like a flooding stream;
you will nurse and be carried on her arm
    and dandled on her knees.
¹³As a mother comforts her child,
    so will I comfort you;
and you will be comforted over Jerusalem."

¹⁴When you see this, your heart will rejoice
    and you will flourish like grass;

the hand of the LORD will be made known to his servants,
　　but his fury will be shown to his foes.
[15] See, the LORD is coming with fire,
　　and his chariots are like a whirlwind;
he will bring down his anger with fury,
　　and his rebuke with flames of fire.
[16] For with fire and with his sword
　　the LORD will execute judgment upon all men,
　　and many will be those slain by the LORD.

[17] "Those who consecrate and purify themselves to go into the gardens, following the one in the midst of[a] those who eat the flesh of pigs and rats and other abominable things—they will meet their end together," declares the LORD.

[18] "And I, because of their actions and their imaginations, am about to come[b] and gather all nations and tongues, and they will come and see my glory.

[19] "I will set a sign among them, and I will send some of those who survive to the nations—to Tarshish, to the Libyans[c] and Lydians (famous as archers), to Tubal and Greece, and to the distant islands that have not heard of my fame or seen my glory. They will proclaim my glory among the nations. [20] And they will bring all your brothers, from all the nations, to my holy mountain in Jerusalem as an offering to the LORD—on horses, in chariots and wagons, and on mules and camels," says the LORD. "They will bring them, as the Israelites bring their grain offerings, to the temple of the LORD in ceremonially clean vessels. [21] And I will select some of them also to be priests and Levites," says the LORD.

[22] "As the new heavens and the new earth that I make will endure before me," declares the LORD, "so will your name and descendants endure. [23] From one New Moon to another and from one Sabbath to another, all mankind will come and bow down before me," says the LORD. [24] "And they will go out and look upon the dead bodies of those who rebelled against me; their worm will not die, nor will their fire be quenched, and they will be loathsome to all mankind."

---

[a] 17 Or *gardens behind one of your temples, and*　[b] 18 The meaning of the Hebrew for this clause is uncertain.　[c] 19 Some Septuagint manuscripts *Put* (Libyans); Hebrew *Pul*

JEREMIAH

Author
Jeremiah

Audience
People of Judah and Jerusalem

Date
Jeremiah wrote during his years of ministry, which began in 626 B.C. and ended sometime after the fall of Jerusalem in 586 B.C.

Setting
Jeremiah spoke to the people of Judah during the reigns of Josiah, Jehoahaz, Jehoiakim, Jehoiachin and Zedekiah, the last five kings of Judah.

Verses to Remember
"But I gave them this command: Obey me, and I will be your God and you will be my people. Walk in all the ways I command you, that it may go well with you. But they did not listen or pay attention; instead, they followed the stubborn inclinations of their evil hearts. They went backward and not forward" (7:23–24).

Theme to Consider
Judah was dying spiritually, and Jeremiah was sent to plead with the people to stop sinning and return to God. Because they wouldn't listen, they were sent as captives to Babylon. God, however, remained faithful to his covenant by keeping some of them alive and later bringing them back to Jerusalem.

UNCHANGING TRUTH » How good are you at learning from other people's mistakes? When you hear about . . .

- a guy at school who got his girlfriend pregnant
- a teenager killed while driving recklessly
- a relative diagnosed with lung cancer after smoking two packs a day for most of his life
- a former athlete dealing with mental and physical damage caused by steroids

. . . do you say, "That could never happen to me"? Or do you say, "Lord, please give me the wisdom, self-control and strength I need to make sure that never happens to me"?

Do you have the wisdom to change certain things in your life when you see evidence of the damage they can do? Please answer yes . . . for your sake. The fact that you're a Christian doesn't mean you'll escape the consequences of your sins. The fact that you say you're sorry doesn't solve anything if you don't change the way you live. Remember—part of living in a sinful world is that we still face the temporal consequences and damage caused by sin in our lives.

The people of Judah failed to learn from other people's mistakes. They watched God judge the northern kingdom of Israel because of the Israelites' disobedience. Yet Judah still refused to obey God. That's why he sent the prophet Jeremiah to warn them that their judgment was coming soon.

Don't make the same mistake as the people of Judah. Learn from the experiences of others.

LIFE LESSONS »

1. God has a unique plan for your life—one that he planned for you before you were born (1:5).

2. God is willing to make things rough in your life if that's what it takes to get your attention (9:7).

3. Trusting the Lord and letting him guide your life *always* leads to success (29:11).

4. No matter how bad things get, stay faithful; God will come through in the end (52:27b–34).

1

The words of Jeremiah son of Hilkiah, one of the priests at Anathoth in the territory of Benjamin. ²The word of the Lord came to him in the thirteenth year of the reign of Josiah son of Amon king of Judah, ³and through the reign of Jehoiakim son of Josiah king of Judah, down to the fifth month of the eleventh year of Zedekiah son of Josiah king of Judah, when the people of Jerusalem went into exile.

THE CALL OF JEREMIAH

⁴The word of the Lord came to me, saying,

⁵ "Before I formed you in the womb I knew ͣ you,
before you were born I set you apart;
I appointed you as a prophet to the nations."

challenge notes

To: my_son

heavenly_father: I've had a plan for your life since before you were conceived. I put together every strand of DNA in your body; I made sure that you were perfectly equipped to carry out my plan. that's why you never have to worry about accomplishing the things I call you to do.

JER 1:5

⁶"Ah, Sovereign Lord," I said, "I do not know how to speak; I am only a child."

⁷But the Lord said to me, "Do not say, 'I am only a child.' You must go to everyone I send you to and say whatever I command you. ⁸Do not be afraid of them, for I am with you and will rescue you," declares the Lord.

⁹Then the Lord reached out his hand and touched my mouth and said to me, "Now, I have put my words in your mouth. ¹⁰See, today I appoint you over nations and kingdoms to uproot and tear down, to destroy and overthrow, to build and to plant."

¹¹The word of the Lord came to me: "What do you see, Jeremiah?"

"I see the branch of an almond tree," I replied.

¹²The Lord said to me, "You have seen correctly, for I am watching ᵇ to see that my word is fulfilled."

¹³The word of the Lord came to me again: "What do you see?"

"I see a boiling pot, tilting away from the north," I answered.

¹⁴The Lord said to me, "From the north disaster will be poured out on all who live in the land. ¹⁵I am about to summon all the peoples of the northern kingdoms," declares the Lord.

NOW OR NEVER

JER 1:6

Here's Biblical example #3,822 of God using a humble person to do incredible things. Go ahead—try counting the number of times in the Bible when God used a proud, arrogant, self-sufficient person to do his work. But don't hold your breath.

"Their kings will come and set up their thrones
in the entrance of the gates of Jerusalem;
they will come against all her surrounding walls
and against all the towns of Judah.
¹⁶I will pronounce my judgments on my people
because of their wickedness in forsaking me,
in burning incense to other gods
and in worshiping what their hands have made.

¹⁷"Get yourself ready! Stand up and say to them whatever I command you. Do not be terrified by them, or I will terrify you before them. ¹⁸Today I have made you a fortified city, an iron pillar and a bronze wall to stand against the whole land—against the kings of Judah, its officials, its priests and the people of the land. ¹⁹They will fight against you but will not overcome you, for I am with you and will rescue you," declares the Lord.

ͣ 5 Or chose   ᵇ 12 The Hebrew for watching sounds like the Hebrew for almond tree.

ISRAEL FORSAKES GOD

2 The word of the LORD came to me: ²"Go and proclaim in the hearing of Jerusalem:

" 'I remember the devotion of your
youth,
how as a bride you loved me
and followed me through the desert,
through a land not sown.
³Israel was holy to the LORD,
the firstfruits of his harvest;
all who devoured her were held guilty,
and disaster overtook them,' "
declares the LORD.

⁴Hear the word of the LORD, O house of
Jacob,
all you clans of the house of Israel.

⁵This is what the LORD says:

"What fault did your fathers find in me,
that they strayed so far from me?
They followed worthless idols
and became worthless themselves.
⁶They did not ask, 'Where is the LORD,
who brought us up out of Egypt
and led us through the barren wilderness,
through a land of deserts and rifts,
a land of drought and darkness,ᵃ
a land where no one travels and no
one lives?'
⁷I brought you into a fertile land
to eat its fruit and rich produce.
But you came and defiled my land
and made my inheritance detestable.
⁸The priests did not ask,
'Where is the LORD?'
Those who deal with the law did not know me;
the leaders rebelled against me.

The prophets prophesied by
Baal,
following worthless idols.

⁹"Therefore I bring charges
against you again,"
declares the LORD.
"And I will bring charges
against your
children's children.
¹⁰Cross over to the coasts of
Kittimᵇ and look,
send to Kedarᶜ and observe
closely;
see if there has ever been anything like this:
¹¹Has a nation ever changed its gods?

Breaking Your Silence

Do you have the courageous spirit needed to stand up for what's right? When you hear your friends talk about bulking up with steroids . . . or smoking pot on weekends . . . or treating girls like sex objects, do you ever speak the truth about God's commands for righteous living? At the very least, are you willing to distance yourself from the kind of life your friends have chosen? Are you willing to risk losing friendships and even making some enemies in order to spread God's truth like Jeremiah did?

challenge notes

To: my_son

heavenly_father: in regard to your faith, starting strong is important, but finishing strong is the ultimate goal. you'll face people who will hammer away at your passion and situations that will test your commitment. that's when you must do everything you can to stay true to your faith.

ᵃ 6 Or *and the shadow of death*   ᵇ 10 That is, Cyprus and western coastlands   ᶜ 10 The home of Bedouin tribes in the Syro-Arabian desert

(Yet they are not gods at all.)
But my people have exchanged their[a] Glory
for worthless idols.
12 Be appalled at this, O heavens,
and shudder with great horror,"

declares the LORD.

13 "My people have committed two sins:
They have forsaken me,
the spring of living water,
and have dug their own cisterns,
broken cisterns that cannot hold water.
14 Is Israel a servant, a slave by birth?
Why then has he become plunder?
15 Lions have roared;
they have growled at him.
They have laid waste his land;
his towns are burned and deserted.
16 Also, the men of Memphis[b] and Tahpanhes
have shaved the crown of your head.[c]
17 Have you not brought this on yourselves
by forsaking the LORD your God
when he led you in the way?
18 Now why go to Egypt
to drink water from the Shihor[d]?
And why go to Assyria
to drink water from the River[e]?
19 Your wickedness will punish you;
your backsliding will rebuke you.
Consider then and realize
how evil and bitter it is for you
when you forsake the LORD your God
and have no awe of me,"

declares the Lord,
the LORD Almighty.

NOW OR NEVER
JER 2:19

The problem with turning away from God again and again is that it gets easier to do each time. If you're not careful, you will quickly become more comfortable living apart from God than you are living close to him.

20 "Long ago you broke off your yoke
and tore off your bonds;
you said, 'I will not serve you!'
Indeed, on every high hill
and under every spreading tree
you lay down as a prostitute.
21 I had planted you like a choice vine
of sound and reliable stock.
How then did you turn against me
into a corrupt, wild vine?
22 Although you wash yourself with soda
and use an abundance of soap,
the stain of your guilt is still before me,"

declares the Sovereign LORD.

23 "How can you say, 'I am not defiled;
I have not run after the Baals'?
See how you behaved in the valley;
consider what you have done.

---

a 11 Masoretic Text; an ancient Hebrew scribal tradition *my*   b 16 Hebrew *Noph*   c 16 Or *have cracked your skull*   d 18 That is, a branch of the Nile   e 18 That is, the Euphrates

You are a swift she-camel
running here and there,
24 a wild donkey accustomed to the desert,
sniffing the wind in her craving—
in her heat who can restrain her?
Any males that pursue her need not tire themselves;
at mating time they will find her.
25 Do not run until your feet are bare
and your throat is dry.
But you said, 'It's no use!
I love foreign gods,
and I must go after them.'

26 "As a thief is disgraced when he is
caught,
so the house of Israel is disgraced—
they, their kings and their officials,
their priests and their prophets.
27 They say to wood, 'You are my father,'
and to stone, 'You gave me birth.'
They have turned their backs to me
and not their faces;
yet when they are in trouble, they say,
'Come and save us!'
28 Where then are the gods you made for
yourselves?
Let them come if they can save you
when you are in trouble!
For you have as many gods
as you have towns, O Judah.

29 "Why do you bring charges against me?
You have all rebelled against me,"
declares the LORD.
30 "In vain I punished your people;
they did not respond to correction.
Your sword has devoured your prophets
like a ravening lion.

31 "You of this generation, consider the word of the LORD:

"Have I been a desert to Israel
or a land of great darkness?
Why do my people say, 'We are free to roam;
we will come to you no more'?
32 Does a maiden forget her jewelry,
a bride her wedding ornaments?
Yet my people have forgotten me,
days without number.
33 How skilled you are at pursuing love!
Even the worst of women can learn from your ways.
34 On your clothes men find
the lifeblood of the innocent poor,
though you did not catch them breaking in.
Yet in spite of all this
35 you say, 'I am innocent;
he is not angry with me.'

>> live the adventure >> Jer 2:32

Remembering God

Have you ever forgotten to show up for a big game you were supposed to play in? Have you ever had a final exam completely slip your mind? Have you ever blanked and forgotten to pick up a girl you had a date with? No way, right? Those are things we rarely forget about. But have you ever forgotten about God, acting as if he didn't exist for an entire day or more? If your relationship with the Lord is important to you, treat it that way. Make him a vital part of every day.

But I will pass judgment on you
　　because you say, 'I have not sinned.'
36 Why do you go about so much,
　　changing your ways?
You will be disappointed by Egypt
　　as you were by Assyria.
37 You will also leave that place
　　with your hands on your head,
for the LORD has rejected those you trust;
　　you will not be helped by them.

"If a man divorces his wife
　　and she leaves him and marries another man,
should he return to her again?
　　Would not the land be completely defiled?
But you have lived as a prostitute with many lovers—
　　would you now return to me?"

　　　　　　　　　　　　　　　　　　　　　declares the LORD.

2 "Look up to the barren heights and see.
　　Is there any place where you have not been ravished?
By the roadside you sat waiting for lovers,
　　sat like a nomad[a] in the desert.
You have defiled the land
　　with your prostitution and wickedness.
3 Therefore the showers have been withheld,
　　and no spring rains have fallen.
Yet you have the brazen look of a prostitute;
　　you refuse to blush with shame.
4 Have you not just called to me:
　　'My Father, my friend from my youth,
5 will you always be angry?
　　Will your wrath continue forever?'
This is how you talk,
　　but you do all the evil you can."

UNFAITHFUL ISRAEL

6 During the reign of King Josiah, the LORD said to me, "Have you seen what faithless Israel has done? She has gone up on every high hill and under every spreading tree and has committed adultery there. 7 I thought that after she had done all this she would return to me but she did not, and her unfaithful sister Judah saw it. 8 I gave faithless Israel her certificate of divorce and sent her away because of all her adulteries. Yet I saw that her unfaithful sister Judah had no fear; she also went out and committed adultery. 9 Because Israel's immorality mattered so little to her, she defiled the land and committed adultery with stone and wood. 10 In spite of all this, her unfaithful sister Judah did not return to me with all her heart, but only in pretense," declares the LORD.

11 The LORD said to me, "Faithless Israel is more righteous than unfaithful Judah. 12 Go, proclaim this message toward the north:

　　" 'Return, faithless Israel,' declares the LORD,
　　　　'I will frown on you no longer,
　　for I am merciful,' declares the LORD,
　　　　'I will not be angry forever.
13 Only acknowledge your guilt—
　　　　you have rebelled against the LORD your God,

---

a 2 Or an Arab

battlelines

» Dad? What Dad? (Absent Parents)

Q: You're acting funny.
A: What do you mean?

Q: I don't know. You look bummed.
A: Yeah. I guess I am.

Q: What's up?
A: Look around. All these friends of mine with their dads. I keep thinking, *What would that be like?* I've never experienced it, and I never will. My dad left when I was seven.

Q: Do you have any contact with him?
A: He sends money every now and then, but I haven't seen him in more than a year. We talk about every six months or so.

Q: What's that like?
A: They're usually awkward conversations with long pauses, like neither of us has anything to say. And this year he forgot my birthday. He didn't even bother to send a card.

Q: I'm sorry, David. That's a rotten deal.
A: Yeah. It really stinks.

Q: I guess there's nothing I can say.
A: You could do what other people have done. Give me a little sermon, a little "rah-rah" pep talk. Quote some Bible verse about how God wants to be my father.

Q: Well, as weird as that must sound to you, it is true, you know.
A: Yeah, I guess at some level I *do* believe that. It's just hard. I don't want to insult God or anything, but it would be nice to have a flesh-and-blood father show up at one of my games.

Q: I hear you.
A: Let me ask you this: Why do you think God let my dad run out on us?

Q: Well, I think your dad made a wrong choice—a really, *really* bad decision. And I don't think God's any happier with your dad's decision than you are. But I also think that somehow or another God can fill the big hole in your life.

» Ultimate Dad

Of all the names for God—King, Judge, Creator, Lord, Savior—perhaps the most incredible is Father. It sounds almost too good to be true. The almighty ruler of the universe as our cosmic dad?

According to Jesus, yes. The word he used for the heavenly Father—the one that is found in Romans 8:15—is *Abba,* an intimate term of endearment, a title overflowing with love, affection and tenderness.

If you're one of the millions of guys like David, and you're having a hard time sorting things out, here's a truth to cling to: God your heavenly Father loves you and watches over you at all times. You can bank on it.

Learn more about God your Father at www.RevolutionBible.com.

you have scattered your favors to foreign gods
 under every spreading tree,
 and have not obeyed me,' "

declares the LORD.

¹⁴"Return, faithless people," declares the LORD, "for I am your husband. I will choose you—one from a town and two from a clan—and bring you to Zion. ¹⁵Then I will give you shepherds after my own heart, who will lead you with knowledge and understanding. ¹⁶In those days, when your numbers have increased greatly in the land," declares the LORD, "men will no longer say, 'The ark of the covenant of the LORD.' It will never enter their minds or be remembered; it will not be missed, nor will another one be made.

challenge notes

To: my_son

JER 3:12-14

heavenly_father: when you ignore me to follow your own desires, it's like cheating on me. that's how seriously I take our relationship. the good news is that if you come to me with true sorrow and a desire to repent, I will forgive you and forget about your unfaithfulness.

¹⁷At that time they will call Jerusalem The Throne of the LORD, and all nations will gather in Jerusalem to honor the name of the LORD. No longer will they follow the stubbornness of their evil hearts. ¹⁸In those days the house of Judah will join the house of Israel, and together they will come from a northern land to the land I gave your forefathers as an inheritance.

¹⁹"I myself said,

" 'How gladly would I treat you like sons
 and give you a desirable land,
 the most beautiful inheritance of any nation.'
I thought you would call me 'Father'
 and not turn away from following me.
²⁰But like a woman unfaithful to her husband,
 so you have been unfaithful to me, O house of Israel,"

declares the LORD.

²¹A cry is heard on the barren heights,
 the weeping and pleading of the people of Israel,
because they have perverted their ways
 and have forgotten the LORD their God.

²²"Return, faithless people;
 I will cure you of backsliding."

"Yes, we will come to you,
 for you are the LORD our God.
²³Surely the ⌐idolatrous⌐ commotion on the hills
 and mountains is a deception;
surely in the LORD our God
 is the salvation of Israel.
²⁴From our youth shameful gods have consumed
 the fruits of our fathers' labor—
their flocks and herds,
 their sons and daughters.
²⁵Let us lie down in our shame,
 and let our disgrace cover us.
We have sinned against the LORD our God,
 both we and our fathers;
from our youth till this day
 we have not obeyed the LORD our God."

4

"If you will return, O Israel,
return to me,"

declares the LORD.

"If you put your detestable idols out of my sight
and no longer go astray,
²and if in a truthful, just and righteous way
you swear, 'As surely as the LORD lives,'
then the nations will be blessed by him
and in him they will glory."

³This is what the LORD says to the men of Judah and to Jerusalem:

"Break up your unplowed ground
and do not sow among thorns.
⁴Circumcise yourselves to the LORD,
circumcise your hearts,
you men of Judah and people of Jerusalem,
or my wrath will break out and burn like fire
because of the evil you have done—
burn with no one to quench it.

DISASTER FROM THE NORTH

⁵"Announce in Judah and proclaim in Jerusalem and say:
'Sound the trumpet throughout the land!'
Cry aloud and say:
'Gather together!
Let us flee to the fortified cities!'
⁶Raise the signal to go to Zion!
Flee for safety without delay!
For I am bringing disaster from the
north,
even terrible destruction."

⁷A lion has come out of his lair;
a destroyer of nations has set out.
He has left his place
to lay waste your land.
Your towns will lie in ruins
without inhabitant.

NOW OR NEVER

JER 4:4

You know what circumcision is, right? (It's when the skin around the head of the penis is cut off.) You also know that it's irreversible, right? Once you've been circumcised, there's no turning back. That's the kind of commitment God wants from us—one that can't be changed.

⁸So put on sackcloth,
lament and wail,
for the fierce anger of the LORD
has not turned away from us.

⁹"In that day," declares the LORD,
"the king and the officials will lose heart,
the priests will be horrified,
and the prophets will be appalled."

¹⁰Then I said, "Ah, Sovereign LORD, how completely you have deceived this people and Jerusalem by saying, 'You will have peace,' when the sword is at our throats."

¹¹At that time this people and Jerusalem will be told, "A scorching wind from the barren heights in the desert blows toward my people, but not to winnow or cleanse; ¹²a wind too strong for that comes from me.ᵃ Now I pronounce my judgments against them."

¹³Look! He advances like the clouds,
his chariots come like a whirlwind,

ᵃ 12 Or comes at my command

battlelines

» The Big Rejection (Failure)

Q: I heard the news. Sorry, man.
A: Hey, stuff happens.

Q: So why didn't they give you the lead role?
A: Beats me. Maybe they didn't think I looked the part. Maybe they wanted somebody taller. Or maybe Antwon is just a better actor than I am.

Q: But you *did* make the cast, right?
A: Yeah, I'm in the chorus. I'm one of the "townspeople." Yeehaw. I get to be on stage with 6,000 other extras—probably standing almost in the wings.

Q: No lines?
A: Nope. Not one. My mom keeps telling me, "Remember, Tanner, there are no little parts, just people who choose to be little."

Q: What does that mean?
A: Oh, you know, everyone in the production is important, every role matters, blah, blah, blah.

Q: Well, I guess that *is* true.
A: Yeah, it is. But I'm thinking, *Why can't I get a* real *part—just once?* Last year it was the same thing. I prepared for my audition for, like, a month. And then . . . nothing. What kills me is that I really love the theater. I can't think of anything else I really want to do. Is it asking too much for God to give me just a little success? I'm not even talking about a lead role, just a small part.

Q: I don't know what to tell you. It *is* hard to understand.
A: I mean, why torture me with this desire if I'm just gonna keep failing?

» The Big Reminder

Two failed business ventures. Eight times defeated in political campaigns. One nervous breakdown. Called by many the greatest president of the United States of America. Know who this is? Abe Lincoln. OK, OK, you've probably heard this one a million times in history class by now, right? But ask yourself this question: Do you have the kind of determination that people will talk about long after you're gone?

That's a great challenge for Tanner—and for anyone else who's ever tasted failure (that is, all of us). The Bible is filled with stories of people who failed . . . but persevered. They stubbornly continued to trust God and move forward. As a result, they became men and women of character. And in the process, they accomplished some pretty spectacular things.

Feel like a failure? Tuck this verse away in your head and heart: "Be on your guard; stand firm in the faith; be men of courage; be strong" (1 Corinthians 16:13). In other words, don't quit!

Learn more about overcoming failure at www.RevolutionBible.com.

his horses are swifter than eagles.
Woe to us! We are ruined!
¹⁴ O Jerusalem, wash the evil from your heart and be saved.
How long will you harbor wicked thoughts?
¹⁵ A voice is announcing from Dan,
proclaiming disaster from the hills of Ephraim.
¹⁶ "Tell this to the nations,
proclaim it to Jerusalem:
'A besieging army is coming from a distant land,
raising a war cry against the cities of Judah.
¹⁷ They surround her like men guarding a field,
because she has rebelled against me,' "

declares the Lord.

¹⁸ "Your own conduct and actions
have brought this upon you.
This is your punishment.
How bitter it is!
How it pierces to the heart!"

¹⁹ Oh, my anguish, my anguish!
I writhe in pain.
Oh, the agony of my heart!
My heart pounds within me,
I cannot keep silent.
For I have heard the sound of the trumpet;
I have heard the battle cry.
²⁰ Disaster follows disaster;
the whole land lies in ruins.
In an instant my tents are destroyed,
my shelter in a moment.
²¹ How long must I see the battle standard
and hear the sound of the trumpet?

²² "My people are fools;
they do not know me.
They are senseless children;
they have no understanding.
They are skilled in doing evil;
they know not how to do good."

²³ I looked at the earth,
and it was formless and empty;
and at the heavens,
and their light was gone.
²⁴ I looked at the mountains,
and they were quaking;
all the hills were swaying.
²⁵ I looked, and there were no people;
every bird in the sky had flown away.
²⁶ I looked, and the fruitful land was a desert;
all its towns lay in ruins
before the Lord, before his fierce anger.

²⁷ This is what the Lord says:

"The whole land will be ruined,
though I will not destroy it completely.
²⁸ Therefore the earth will mourn

and the heavens above grow dark,
because I have spoken and will not relent,
I have decided and will not turn back."

29 At the sound of horsemen and archers
every town takes to flight.
Some go into the thickets;
some climb up among the rocks.
All the towns are deserted;
no one lives in them.

30 What are you doing, O devastated one?
Why dress yourself in scarlet
and put on jewels of gold?
Why shade your eyes with paint?
You adorn yourself in vain.
Your lovers despise you;
they seek your life.

31 I hear a cry as of a woman in labor,
a groan as of one bearing her first child—
the cry of the Daughter of Zion gasping for breath,
stretching out her hands and saying,
"Alas! I am fainting;
my life is given over to murderers."

NOT ONE IS UPRIGHT

5

"Go up and down the streets of Jerusalem,
look around and consider,
search through her squares.
If you can find but one person
who deals honestly and seeks the truth,
I will forgive this city.
2 Although they say, 'As surely as the LORD lives,'
still they are swearing falsely."

3 O LORD, do not your eyes look for truth?
You struck them, but they felt no pain;
you crushed them, but they refused correction.
They made their faces harder than stone
and refused to repent.
4 I thought, "These are only the poor;
they are foolish,
for they do not know the way of the LORD,
the requirements of their God.
5 So I will go to the leaders
and speak to them;
surely they know the way of the LORD,
the requirements of their God."
But with one accord they too had broken off the yoke
and torn off the bonds.
6 Therefore a lion from the forest will attack them,
a wolf from the desert will ravage them,
a leopard will lie in wait near their towns
to tear to pieces any who venture out,
for their rebellion is great
and their backslidings many.

⁷ "Why should I forgive you?
  Your children have forsaken me
  and sworn by gods that are not gods.
I supplied all their needs,
  yet they committed adultery
  and thronged to the houses of prostitutes.
⁸ They are well-fed, lusty stallions,
  each neighing for another man's wife.
⁹ Should I not punish them for this?"
  declares the LORD.
  "Should I not avenge myself
  on such a nation as this?

¹⁰ "Go through her vineyards and ravage them,
  but do not destroy them completely.
Strip off her branches,
  for these people do not belong to the LORD.
¹¹ The house of Israel and the house of Judah
  have been utterly unfaithful to me,"

declares the LORD.

¹² They have lied about the LORD;
  they said, "He will do
  nothing!
No harm will come to us;
  we will never see sword or
  famine.
¹³ The prophets are but wind
  and the word is not in
  them;
  so let what they say be
  done to them."

---

challengenotes

To: **my_son**

heavenly_father: don't listen to anyone who says I'm too loving to punish sin or too busy to be interested in your daily activities and decisions. both of these statements are lies. I am capable of much more than you could ever imagine.

JER 5:12

---

¹⁴ Therefore this is what the LORD God Almighty says:

"Because the people have spoken these words,
  I will make my words in your mouth a fire
  and these people the wood it consumes.
¹⁵ O house of Israel," declares the LORD,
  "I am bringing a distant nation against you—
an ancient and enduring nation,
  a people whose language you do not know,
  whose speech you do not understand.
¹⁶ Their quivers are like an open grave;
  all of them are mighty warriors.
¹⁷ They will devour your harvests and food,
  devour your sons and daughters;
they will devour your flocks and herds,
  devour your vines and fig trees.
With the sword they will destroy
  the fortified cities in which you trust.

¹⁸ "Yet even in those days," declares the LORD, "I will not destroy you completely. ¹⁹ And when the people ask, 'Why has the LORD our God done all this to us?' you will tell them, 'As you have forsaken me and served foreign gods in your own land, so now you will serve foreigners in a land not your own.'

²⁰ "Announce this to the house of Jacob
  and proclaim it in Judah:

²¹ Hear this, you foolish and senseless people,
     who have eyes but do not see,
     who have ears but do not hear:
²² Should you not fear me?" declares the LORD.
     "Should you not tremble in my presence?
I made the sand a boundary for the sea,
     an everlasting barrier it cannot cross.
The waves may roll, but they cannot prevail;
     they may roar, but they cannot cross it.
²³ But these people have stubborn and rebellious hearts;
     they have turned aside and gone away.
²⁴ They do not say to themselves,
     'Let us fear the LORD our God,
who gives autumn and spring rains in season,
     who assures us of the regular weeks of harvest.'
²⁵ Your wrongdoings have kept these away;
     your sins have deprived you of good.

²⁶ "Among my people are wicked men
     who lie in wait like men who snare birds
     and like those who set traps to catch men.
²⁷ Like cages full of birds,
     their houses are full of deceit;
they have become rich and powerful
²⁸   and have grown fat and sleek.
Their evil deeds have no limit;
     they do not plead the case of the fatherless to win it,
     they do not defend the rights of the poor.
²⁹ Should I not punish them for this?"
     declares the LORD.
"Should I not avenge myself
     on such a nation as this?

³⁰ "A horrible and shocking thing
     has happened in the land:
³¹ The prophets prophesy lies,
     the priests rule by their own authority,
and my people love it this way.
     But what will you do in the end?

JERUSALEM UNDER SIEGE

6

"Flee for safety, people of Benjamin!
     Flee from Jerusalem!
Sound the trumpet in Tekoa!
     Raise the signal over Beth Hakkerem!
For disaster looms out of the north,
     even terrible destruction.
² I will destroy the Daughter of Zion,
     so beautiful and delicate.
³ Shepherds with their flocks will come against her;
     they will pitch their tents around her,
     each tending his own portion."

⁴ "Prepare for battle against her!
     Arise, let us attack at noon!
But, alas, the daylight is fading,
     and the shadows of evening grow long.

⁵So arise, let us attack at night
      and destroy her fortresses!"

⁶This is what the LORD Almighty says:

      "Cut down the trees
            and build siege ramps against Jerusalem.
      This city must be punished;
            it is filled with oppression.
      ⁷As a well pours out its water,
            so she pours out her wickedness.
      Violence and destruction resound in her;
            her sickness and wounds are ever before me.
      ⁸Take warning, O Jerusalem,
            or I will turn away from you
      and make your land desolate
            so no one can live in it."

⁹This is what the LORD Almighty says:

      "Let them glean the remnant of Israel
            as thoroughly as a vine;
      pass your hand over the branches again,
            like one gathering grapes."

      ¹⁰To whom can I speak and give warning?
            Who will listen to me?
      Their ears are closed[a]
            so they cannot hear.
      The word of the LORD is offensive to them;
            they find no pleasure in it.
      ¹¹But I am full of the wrath of the LORD,
            and I cannot hold it in.

      "Pour it out on the children in the street
            and on the young men gathered together;
      both husband and wife will be caught in it,
            and the old, those weighed down with years.
      ¹²Their houses will be turned over to others,
            together with their fields and their wives,
      when I stretch out my hand
            against those who live in the land,"

                                                    declares the LORD.

      ¹³"From the least to the greatest,
            all are greedy for gain;
      prophets and priests alike,
            all practice deceit.
      ¹⁴They dress the wound of my people
            as though it were not serious.
      'Peace, peace,' they say,
            when there is no peace.
      ¹⁵Are they ashamed of their loathsome conduct?
            No, they have no shame at all;
            they do not even know how to blush.
      So they will fall among the fallen;
            they will be brought down when I punish them,"

                                                    says the LORD.

ᵃ *10* Hebrew *uncircumcised*

¹⁶This is what the LORD says:

> "Stand at the crossroads and look;
> ask for the ancient paths,
> ask where the good way is, and walk in it,
> and you will find rest for your souls.
> But you said, 'We will not walk in it.'
> ¹⁷I appointed watchmen over you and said,
> 'Listen to the sound of the trumpet!'
> But you said, 'We will not listen.'
> ¹⁸Therefore hear, O nations;
> observe, O witnesses,
> what will happen to them.
> ¹⁹Hear, O earth:
> I am bringing disaster on this people,
> the fruit of their schemes,
> because they have not listened to my
> words
> and have rejected my law.
> ²⁰What do I care about incense from Sheba
> or sweet calamus from a distant land?
> Your burnt offerings are not acceptable;
> your sacrifices do not please me."

²¹Therefore this is what the LORD says:

> "I will put obstacles before this people.
> Fathers and sons alike will stumble
> over them;
> neighbors and friends will perish."

²²This is what the LORD says:

> "Look, an army is coming
> from the land of the north;
> a great nation is being stirred up
> from the ends of the earth.
> ²³They are armed with bow and spear;
> they are cruel and show no mercy.
> They sound like the roaring sea
> as they ride on their horses;
> they come like men in battle formation
> to attack you, O Daughter of Zion."

> ²⁴We have heard reports about them,
> and our hands hang limp.
> Anguish has gripped us,
> pain like that of a woman in labor.
> ²⁵Do not go out to the fields
> or walk on the roads,
> for the enemy has a sword,
> and there is terror on every side.
> ²⁶O my people, put on sackcloth
> and roll in ashes;
> mourn with bitter wailing
> as for an only son,
> for suddenly the destroyer
> will come upon us.

Appreciating the Past

People have been trying to improve on God's plan for thousands of years. They're still trying. Turn on the TV any time of the day or night, and you'll find someone trying to sell you a new product, a new lifestyle or a new way of thinking designed to bring you happiness and satisfaction. The truth is, nothing can even come close to matching God's original blueprint. If you want what's best for your life, forget about the cutting-edge; you've got to look back. That's where real fulfillment is found.

27 "I have made you a tester of metals
    and my people the ore,
that you may observe
    and test their ways.
28 They are all hardened rebels,
    going about to slander.
They are bronze and iron;
    they all act corruptly.
29 The bellows blow fiercely
    to burn away the lead with fire,
but the refining goes on in vain;
    the wicked are not purged out.
30 They are called rejected silver,
    because the LORD has rejected them."

FALSE RELIGION WORTHLESS

7 This is the word that came to Jeremiah from the LORD: 2 "Stand at the gate of the LORD's house and there proclaim this message:

" 'Hear the word of the LORD, all you people of Judah who come through these gates to worship the LORD. 3 This is what the LORD Almighty, the God of Israel, says: Reform your ways and your actions, and I will let you live in this place. 4 Do not trust in deceptive words and say, "This is the temple of the LORD, the temple of the LORD, the temple of the LORD!" 5 If you really change your ways and your actions and deal with each other justly, 6 if you do not oppress the alien, the fatherless or the widow and do not shed innocent blood in this place, and if you do not follow other gods to your own harm, 7 then I will let you live in this place, in the land I gave your forefathers for ever and ever. 8 But look, you are trusting in deceptive words that are worthless.

9 " 'Will you steal and murder, commit adultery and perjury,[a] burn incense to Baal and follow other gods you have not known, 10 and then come and stand before me in this house, which bears my Name, and say, "We are safe"—safe to do all these detestable things? 11 Has this house, which bears my Name, become a den of robbers to you? But I have been watching! declares the LORD.

12 " 'Go now to the place in Shiloh where I first made a dwelling for my Name, and see what I did to it because of the wickedness of my people Israel. 13 While you were doing all these things, declares the LORD, I spoke to you again and again, but you did not listen; I called you, but you did not answer. 14 Therefore, what I did to Shiloh I will now do to the house that bears my Name, the temple you trust in, the place I gave to you and your fathers. 15 I will thrust you from my presence, just as I did all your brothers, the people of Ephraim.'

16 "So do not pray for this people nor offer any plea or petition for them; do not plead with me, for I will not listen to you. 17 Do you not see what they are doing in the towns of Judah and in the streets of Jerusalem? 18 The children gather wood, the fathers light the fire, and the women knead the dough and make cakes of bread for the Queen of Heaven. They pour out drink offerings to other gods to provoke me to anger. 19 But am I the one they are provoking? declares the LORD. Are they not rather harming themselves, to their own shame?

20 " 'Therefore this is what the Sovereign LORD says: My anger and my wrath will be poured out on this place, on man and beast, on the trees of the field and on the fruit of the ground, and it will burn and not be quenched.

21 " 'This is what the LORD Almighty, the God of Israel, says: Go ahead, add your burnt offerings to your other sacrifices and eat the meat yourselves! 22 For when I brought your forefathers out of Egypt and spoke to them, I did not just give them commands about burnt offerings and sacrifices, 23 but I gave them this command: Obey me, and I will be your God and you will be my people. Walk in all the ways I command you, that it may go well with you. 24 But they did not listen or pay attention; instead, they followed the stubborn inclinations of their evil hearts. They went backward and not forward. 25 From the time your forefathers left Egypt until now, day after day, again and again I sent you my servants the prophets. 26 But they did not listen to me or pay attention. They were stiff-necked and did more evil than their forefathers.'

---

a 9 Or and swear by false gods

battlelines

» To Each His Own? (Pluralism)

Q: You spent most of your life down in the "Bible Belt"?

A: Yep. Churches on every corner. And just about everybody says they're Christian.

Q: So I guess living up here is kind of like culture shock.

A: Oh, yeah! Probably the guy I've gotten to know best is Sayed. He's a Muslim, and he's one of the nicest guys you'll ever meet. Anyway, we've had some interesting religious discussions, that's for sure.

Q: Not too many Muslims where you're from, huh?

A: Heck, no. I think we had one Jewish family and a handful of Mormons in my hometown. Everybody else was either Baptist or Methodist. Here you have everything under the sun. In fact, there's this one girl in my fifth-hour class who's big into New Age stuff.

Q: Like what?

A: Crystals, meditation . . . stuff like that. I've got to tell you, though, she seems pretty normal. She's nice enough. And man, is she good-looking! You should see her in her yoga tights!

Q: Or maybe not.

A: OK, sorry. Anyway, you get the point. It's just weird. I'm hearing about stuff I've never even thought of. All these different viewpoints. It makes me wonder: Do I believe Christianity because it's true or just because it's the only perspective I've ever been taught?

» True Truth

Many people today speak in terms of "my truth" and "your truth"—as if truth is a matter of personal preference. The Bible takes a radically different view, speaking matter-of-factly against any teaching that departs from faith in Jesus as the only way to God.

Paul warned, "See to it that no one takes you captive through hollow and deceptive philosophy, which depends on human tradition and the basic principles of this world rather than on Christ" (Colossians 2:8).

Later, in the last letter he ever wrote, the apostle said, "But mark this: There will be terrible times in the last days. People will be lovers of themselves, lovers of money, boastful, proud, abusive, disobedient to their parents, ungrateful, unholy, without love, unforgiving, slanderous, without self-control, brutal, not lovers of the good, treacherous, rash, conceited, lovers of pleasure rather than lovers of God—having a form of godliness but denying its power. Have nothing to do with them" (2 Timothy 3:1–5).

Don't let human bias—whether it's your own or someone else's—define truth for you. True truth is found in one place: the life and teachings of Jesus, who is the Son of the one true God.

Read more about Christianity at www.RevolutionBible.com.

27"When you tell them all this, they will not listen to you; when you call to them, they will not answer. 28Therefore say to them, 'This is the nation that has not obeyed the LORD its God or responded to correction. Truth has perished; it has vanished from their lips. 29Cut off your hair and throw it away; take up a lament on the barren heights, for the LORD has rejected and abandoned this generation that is under his wrath.

THE VALLEY OF SLAUGHTER

30" 'The people of Judah have done evil in my eyes, declares the LORD. They have set up their detestable idols in the house that bears my Name and have defiled it. 31They have built the high places of Topheth in the Valley of Ben Hinnom to burn their sons and daughters in the fire—something I did not command, nor did it enter my mind. 32So beware, the days are coming, declares the LORD, when people will no longer call it Topheth or the Valley of Ben Hinnom, but the Valley of Slaughter, for they will bury the dead in Topheth until there is no more room. 33Then the carcasses of this people will become food for the birds of the air and the beasts of the earth, and there will be no one to frighten them away. 34I will bring an end to the sounds of joy and gladness and to the voices of bride and bridegroom in the towns of Judah and the streets of Jerusalem, for the land will become desolate.

8 " 'At that time, declares the LORD, the bones of the kings and officials of Judah, the bones of the priests and prophets, and the bones of the people of Jerusalem will be removed from their graves. 2They will be exposed to the sun and the moon and all the stars of the heavens, which they have loved and served and which they have followed and consulted and worshiped. They will not be gathered up or buried, but will be like refuse lying on the ground. 3Wherever I banish them, all the survivors of this evil nation will prefer death to life, declares the LORD Almighty.'

SIN AND PUNISHMENT

4"Say to them, 'This is what the LORD says:

" 'When men fall down, do they not
  get up?
When a man turns away, does he not
  return?
5Why then have these people turned away?
  Why does Jerusalem always turn away?
They cling to deceit;
  they refuse to return.
6I have listened attentively,
  but they do not say what is right.
No one repents of his wickedness,
  saying, "What have I done?"
Each pursues his own course
  like a horse charging into battle.
7Even the stork in the sky
  knows her appointed seasons,
and the dove, the swift and the thrush
  observe the time of their migration.
But my people do not know
  the requirements of the LORD.

»»» live the adventure »» Jer 7.22-23

Walking With God

Are you ever tempted to view your Christian faith like a job? Do you clock in for an hour or so every Sunday morning to do your "work" of praying, singing and staying awake during the sermon . . . and then clock out for the rest of the week? That's not the kind of commitment God's looking for. He wants a 24/7 relationship with you. He'll make it worth your while too. If you choose to walk with him, he'll walk with you. And when you have the all-powerful Creator of the universe walking beside you, *anything* is possible.

⁸ " 'How can you say, "We are wise,
    for we have the law of the LORD,"
when actually the lying pen of the scribes
    has handled it falsely?
⁹ The wise will be put to shame;
    they will be dismayed and trapped.
Since they have rejected the word of the LORD,
    what kind of wisdom do they have?
¹⁰ Therefore I will give their wives to other
        men
    and their fields to new owners.
From the least to the greatest,
    all are greedy for gain;
prophets and priests alike,
    all practice deceit.
¹¹ They dress the wound of my people
    as though it were not serious.
"Peace, peace," they say,
    when there is no peace.
¹² Are they ashamed of their loathsome
        conduct?
No, they have no shame at all;
    they do not even know how to blush.
So they will fall among the fallen;
    they will be brought down when they are punished,

says the LORD.

¹³ " 'I will take away their harvest,

declares the LORD.

There will be no grapes on the vine.
There will be no figs on the tree,
    and their leaves will wither.
What I have given them
    will be taken from them.^{a'} "

¹⁴ "Why are we sitting here?
    Gather together!
Let us flee to the fortified cities
    and perish there!
For the LORD our God has doomed us to perish
    and given us poisoned water to drink,
    because we have sinned against him.
¹⁵ We hoped for peace
    but no good has come,
for a time of healing
    but there was only terror.
¹⁶ The snorting of the enemy's horses
    is heard from Dan;
at the neighing of their stallions
    the whole land trembles.
They have come to devour
    the land and everything in it,
    the city and all who live there."

¹⁷ "See, I will send venomous snakes among you,

NOW OR NEVER
JER 8:9

Anyone—whether it's a professor, an author or some other "expert"—who denies the truth of God's Word will be exposed as a fool one day. That's why it's important not to let people like that govern your thinking now.

---

^a *13* The meaning of the Hebrew for this sentence is uncertain.

vipers that cannot be charmed,
and they will bite you,"

declares the LORD.

18 O my Comforter[a] in sorrow,
my heart is faint within me.
19 Listen to the cry of my people
from a land far away:
"Is the LORD not in Zion?
Is her King no longer there?"

"Why have they provoked me to anger with their images,
with their worthless foreign idols?"

20 "The harvest is past,
the summer has ended,
and we are not saved."

21 Since my people are crushed, I am crushed;
I mourn, and horror grips me.
22 Is there no balm in Gilead?
Is there no physician there?
Why then is there no healing
for the wound of my people?

9 1 Oh, that my head were a spring of water
and my eyes a fountain of tears!
I would weep day and night
for the slain of my people.
2 Oh, that I had in the desert
a lodging place for travelers,
so that I might leave my people
and go away from them;
for they are all adulterers,
a crowd of unfaithful people.

3 "They make ready their tongue
like a bow, to shoot lies;
it is not by truth
that they triumph[b] in the land.
They go from one sin to another;
they do not acknowledge me,"

declares the LORD.

4 "Beware of your friends;
do not trust your brothers.
For every brother is a deceiver,[c]
and every friend a slanderer.
5 Friend deceives friend,
and no one speaks the truth.
They have taught their tongues to lie;
they weary themselves with sinning.
6 You[d] live in the midst of deception;
in their deceit they refuse to acknowledge me,"

declares the LORD.

---

[a] 18 The meaning of the Hebrew for this word is uncertain.   [b] 3 Or lies; / they are not valiant for truth   [c] 4 Or a deceiving Jacob
[d] 6 That is, Jeremiah (the Hebrew is singular)

[7]Therefore this is what the LORD Almighty says:

> "See, I will refine and test them,
>   for what else can I do
>   because of the sin of my people?
> [8]Their tongue is a deadly arrow;
>   it speaks with deceit.
> With his mouth each speaks cordially to his neighbor,
>   but in his heart he sets a trap for him.
> [9]Should I not punish them for this?"
>   declares the LORD.
> "Should I not avenge myself
>   on such a nation as this?"

> [10]I will weep and wail for the mountains
>   and take up a lament concerning the desert pastures.
> They are desolate and untraveled,
>   and the lowing of cattle is not heard.
> The birds of the air have fled
>   and the animals are gone.

> [11]"I will make Jerusalem a heap of ruins,
>   a haunt of jackals;
> and I will lay waste the towns of Judah
>   so no one can live there."

[12]What man is wise enough to understand this? Who has been instructed by the LORD and can explain it? Why has the land been ruined and laid waste like a desert that no one can cross?

[13]The LORD said, "It is because they have forsaken my law, which I set before them; they have not obeyed me or followed my law. [14]Instead, they have followed the stubbornness of their hearts; they have followed the Baals, as their fathers taught them." [15]Therefore, this is what the LORD Almighty, the God of Israel, says: "See, I will make this people eat bitter food and drink poisoned water. [16]I will scatter them among nations that neither they nor their fathers have known, and I will pursue them with the sword until I have destroyed them."

[17]This is what the LORD Almighty says:

> "Consider now! Call for the wailing
>   women to come;
>   send for the most skillful of them.
> [18]Let them come quickly
>   and wail over us
> till our eyes overflow with tears
>   and water streams from our eyelids.
> [19]The sound of wailing is heard from Zion:
>   'How ruined we are!
>   How great is our shame!
> We must leave our land
>   because our houses are in ruins.'"

> [20]Now, O women, hear the word of the LORD;
>   open your ears to the words of his mouth.
> Teach your daughters how to wail;
>   teach one another a lament.
> [21]Death has climbed in through our windows

Understanding God's Discipline

God can't have an authentic relationship with people who disobey him or treat him like an afterthought. That's a problem, because he really wants a meaningful relationship with us. In fact, he wants it so much that he is willing, at times, to allow suffering and hardship to enter our lives in order to push us closer to him. So remember, when you suffer the consequences of your own sin, God isn't out to destroy you. He simply loves you too much to let you keep ruining your life with sin.

and has entered our fortresses;
it has cut off the children from the streets
and the young men from the public
squares.

22 Say, "This is what the LORD declares:

" 'The dead bodies of men will lie
like refuse on the open field,
like cut grain behind the reaper,
with no one to gather them.' "

23 This is what the LORD says:

"Let not the wise man boast of his
wisdom
or the strong man boast of his
strength
or the rich man boast of his riches,
24 but let him who boasts boast about this:
that he understands and knows me,
that I am the LORD, who exercises
kindness,
justice and righteousness on earth,
for in these I delight,"
declares the LORD.

25 "The days are coming," declares the LORD, "when I will
punish all who are circumcised only in the flesh— 26 Egypt,
Judah, Edom, Ammon, Moab and all who live in the desert in
distant places.[a] For all these nations are really uncircumcised,
and even the whole house of Israel is uncircumcised in heart."

GOD AND IDOLS

10
Hear what the LORD says to you, O house
of Israel. 2 This is what the LORD says:
"Do not learn the ways of the nations
or be terrified by signs in the sky,
though the nations are terrified by them.

Knowing What's Important

What is your greatest source of
confidence? Is it your witty humor, your strength in the weight
room or the loads of money your
parents have? None of these
things are bad in and of themselves. But, like even the best
gifts that God gives us, they can
become idols. In fact, anything
that competes for God's
place in our heart is an
idol. As a man created in
God's image, be confident
and bold for the right reasons: God, who is the
all-powerful Creator of
the universe, made you,
knows you and has
called you to himself.

---

challengenotes

To: my_son

heavenly_father: don't let non-christian friends or family members discourage your relationship with me. don't let their
wrong ideas about how to live and what to believe affect the
way you think. remember, my way is truth. everything else will
lead you astray.

2863   B G C FE

3 For the customs of the peoples
are worthless;
they cut a tree out of the
forest,
and a craftsman shapes it
with his chisel.
4 They adorn it with silver and
gold;
they fasten it with hammer
and nails
so it will not totter.
5 Like a scarecrow in a melon
patch,

their idols cannot speak;
they must be carried
because they cannot walk.
Do not fear them;

---

[a] 26 Or *desert and who clip the hair by their foreheads*

they can do no harm
nor can they do any good."

6 No one is like you, O Lord;
    you are great,
    and your name is mighty in power.
7 Who should not revere you,
    O King of the nations?
    This is your due.
Among all the wise men of the nations
    and in all their kingdoms,
    there is no one like you.
8 They are all senseless and foolish;
    they are taught by worthless wooden idols.
9 Hammered silver is brought from Tarshish
    and gold from Uphaz.
What the craftsman and goldsmith have made
    is then dressed in blue and purple—
    all made by skilled workers.
10 But the Lord is the true God;
    he is the living God, the eternal King.
When he is angry, the earth trembles;
    the nations cannot endure his wrath.

11 "Tell them this: 'These gods, who did not make the heavens and the earth, will perish from the earth and from under the heavens.' " a

12 But God made the earth by his power;
    he founded the world by his wisdom
    and stretched out the heavens by his understanding.
13 When he thunders, the waters in the heavens roar;
    he makes clouds rise from the ends of the earth.
He sends lightning with the rain
    and brings out the wind from his storehouses.

14 Everyone is senseless and without knowledge;
    every goldsmith is shamed by his idols.
His images are a fraud;
    they have no breath in them.
15 They are worthless, the objects of mockery;
    when their judgment comes, they will perish.
16 He who is the Portion of Jacob is not like these,
    for he is the Maker of all things,
    including Israel, the tribe of his inheritance—
    the Lord Almighty is his name.

COMING DESTRUCTION

17 Gather up your belongings to leave the land,
    you who live under siege.
18 For this is what the Lord says:
    "At this time I will hurl out
    those who live in this land;
I will bring distress on them
    so that they may be captured."

19 Woe to me because of my injury!

---

a 11 The text of this verse is in Aramaic.

My wound is incurable!
Yet I said to myself,
"This is my sickness, and I must endure it."
20 My tent is destroyed;
all its ropes are snapped.
My sons are gone from me and are no more;
no one is left now to pitch my tent
or to set up my shelter.
21 The shepherds are senseless
and do not inquire of the LORD;
so they do not prosper
and all their flock is scattered.
22 Listen! The report is coming—
a great commotion from the land of the north!
It will make the towns of Judah desolate,
a haunt of jackals.

JEREMIAH'S PRAYER

23 I know, O LORD, that a man's life is not his own;
it is not for man to direct his steps.
24 Correct me, LORD, but only with justice—
not in your anger,
lest you reduce me to nothing.
25 Pour out your wrath on the nations
that do not acknowledge you,
on the peoples who do not call on your name.
For they have devoured Jacob;
they have devoured him completely
and destroyed his homeland.

THE COVENANT IS BROKEN

11 This is the word that came to Jeremiah from the LORD: 2 "Listen to the terms of this covenant and tell them to the people of Judah and to those who live in Jerusalem. 3 Tell them that this is what the LORD, the God of Israel, says: 'Cursed is the man who does not obey the terms of this covenant— 4 the terms I commanded your forefathers when I brought them out of Egypt, out of the iron-smelting furnace.' I said, 'Obey me and do everything I command you, and you will be my people, and I will be your God. 5 Then I will fulfill the oath I swore to your forefathers, to give them a land flowing with milk and honey'—the land you possess today."

I answered, "Amen, LORD."

6 The LORD said to me, "Proclaim all these words in the towns of Judah and in the streets of Jerusalem: 'Listen to the terms of this covenant and follow them. 7 From the time I brought your forefathers up from Egypt until today, I warned them again and again, saying, "Obey me." 8 But they did not listen or pay attention; instead, they followed the stubbornness of their evil hearts. So I brought on them all the curses of the covenant I had commanded them to follow but that they did not keep.' "

9 Then the LORD said to me, "There is a conspiracy among the people of Judah and those who live in Jerusalem. 10 They have returned to the sins of their forefathers, who refused to listen to my words. They have followed other gods to serve them. Both the house of Israel and the house of Judah have broken the covenant I made with their forefathers. 11 Therefore this is what the LORD says: 'I will bring on them a disaster they cannot escape. Although they cry out to me, I will not listen to them. 12 The towns of Judah and the people of Jerusalem will go and cry out to the gods to whom they burn incense, but they will not help them at all when disaster strikes. 13 You have as many gods as you have towns, O Judah; and the altars you have set up to burn incense to that shameful god Baal are as many as the streets of Jerusalem.'

14 "Do not pray for this people nor offer any plea or petition for them, because I will not listen when they call to me in the time of their distress.

¹⁵ "What is my beloved doing in my temple
　　as she works out her evil schemes with many?
　　Can consecrated meat avert ∟your punishment⌐?
　When you engage in your wickedness,
　　then you rejoice. ^a"

¹⁶ The LORD called you a thriving olive tree
　　with fruit beautiful in form.
　But with the roar of a mighty storm
　　he will set it on fire,
　　and its branches will be broken.

¹⁷The LORD Almighty, who planted you, has decreed disaster for you, because the house of Israel and the house of Judah have done evil and provoked me to anger by burning incense to Baal.

PLOT AGAINST JEREMIAH

¹⁸Because the LORD revealed their plot to me, I knew it, for at that time he showed me what they were doing. ¹⁹I had been like a gentle lamb led to the slaughter; I did not realize that they had plotted against me, saying,

NOW OR NEVER
JER 11:18–20

Many people consider God's teachings a threat to their lifestyle. They don't take kindly to people who believe that Jesus is the only answer and that life without him is meaningless. That's why, if you're serious about your relationship with God, you can expect to take a lot of heat for it.

"Let us destroy the tree and its fruit;
　　let us cut him off from the land of the
　　　living,
　　that his name be remembered no
　　　more."
²⁰ But, O LORD Almighty, you who judge
　　righteously
　　and test the heart and mind,
　let me see your vengeance upon them,
　　for to you I have committed my
　　　cause.

²¹ "Therefore this is what the LORD says about the men of Anathoth who are seeking your life and saying, 'Do not prophesy in the name of the LORD or you will die by our hands'— ²²therefore this is what the LORD Almighty says: 'I will punish them. Their young men will die by the sword, their sons and daughters by famine. ²³Not even a remnant will be left to them, because I will bring disaster on the men of Anathoth in the year of their punishment.' "

JEREMIAH'S COMPLAINT

12

You are always righteous, O LORD,
　　when I bring a case before you.

NOW OR NEVER
JER 12:1

If you've got a beef with God, lay it all out—respectfully, reverently and honestly. Don't worry about hurting his feelings. He already knows what you're thinking anyway. Besides, no one else has the power or the answers that he holds.

Yet I would speak with you about your
　　justice:
　Why does the way of the wicked
　　prosper?
　Why do all the faithless live at ease?
² You have planted them, and they have
　　taken root;
　they grow and bear fruit.
　You are always on their lips
　　but far from their hearts.
³ Yet you know me, O LORD;
　　you see me and test my thoughts
　　　about you.

---

^a 15 Or *Could consecrated meat avert your punishment? / Then you would rejoice*

Drag them off like sheep to be butchered!
    Set them apart for the day of slaughter!
4 How long will the land lie parched[a]
    and the grass in every field be withered?
Because those who live in it are wicked,
    the animals and birds have perished.
Moreover, the people are saying,
    "He will not see what happens to us."

GOD'S ANSWER

5 "If you have raced with men on foot
    and they have worn you out,
    how can you compete with horses?
If you stumble in safe country,[b]
    how will you manage in the thickets by[c] the Jordan?
6 Your brothers, your own family—
    even they have betrayed you;
    they have raised a loud cry against you.
Do not trust them,
    though they speak well of you.

7 "I will forsake my house,
    abandon my inheritance;
I will give the one I love
    into the hands of her enemies.
8 My inheritance has become to me
    like a lion in the forest.
She roars at me;
    therefore I hate her.
9 Has not my inheritance become to me
    like a speckled bird of prey
    that other birds of prey surround and attack?
Go and gather all the wild beasts;
    bring them to devour.
10 Many shepherds will ruin my vineyard
    and trample down my field;
they will turn my pleasant field
    into a desolate wasteland.
11 It will be made a wasteland,
    parched and desolate before me;
the whole land will be laid waste
    because there is no one who cares.
12 Over all the barren heights in the desert
    destroyers will swarm,
for the sword of the LORD will devour
    from one end of the land to the other;
    no one will be safe.
13 They will sow wheat but reap thorns;
    they will wear themselves out but gain nothing.
So bear the shame of your harvest
    because of the LORD's fierce anger."

14 This is what the LORD says: "As for all my wicked neighbors who seize the inheritance I gave my people Israel, I will uproot them from their lands and I will uproot the house of Judah from among them. 15 But after I uproot them, I will again have compassion and will bring each of them back to his own in-

---

a 4 Or *land mourn*   b 5 Or *If you put your trust in a land of safety*   c 5 Or *the flooding of* heritance and his own country. ¹⁶And if they learn well the ways of my people and swear by my name, saying, 'As surely as the LORD lives'—even as they once taught my people to swear by Baal—then they will be established among my people. ¹⁷But if any nation does not listen, I will completely uproot and destroy it," declares the LORD.

A LINEN BELT

13 This is what the LORD said to me: "Go and buy a linen belt and put it around your waist, but do not let it touch water." ²So I bought a belt, as the LORD directed, and put it around my waist.

³Then the word of the LORD came to me a second time: ⁴"Take the belt you bought and are wearing around your waist, and go now to Perath[a] and hide it there in a crevice in the rocks." ⁵So I went and hid it at Perath, as the LORD told me.

⁶Many days later the LORD said to me, "Go now to Perath and get the belt I told you to hide there." ⁷So I went to Perath and dug up the belt and took it from the place where I had hidden it, but now it was ruined and completely useless.

⁸Then the word of the LORD came to me: ⁹"This is what the LORD says: 'In the same way I will ruin the pride of Judah and the great pride of Jerusalem. ¹⁰These wicked people, who refuse to listen to my words, who follow the stubbornness of their hearts and go after other gods to serve and worship them, will be like this belt—completely useless! ¹¹For as a belt is bound around a man's waist, so I bound the whole house of Israel and the whole house of Judah to me,' declares the LORD, 'to be my people for my renown and praise and honor. But they have not listened.'

WINESKINS

¹²"Say to them: 'This is what the LORD, the God of Israel, says: Every wineskin should be filled with wine.' And if they say to you, 'Don't we know that every wineskin should be filled with wine?' ¹³then tell them, 'This is what the LORD says: I am going to fill with drunkenness all who live in this land, including the kings who sit on David's throne, the priests, the prophets and all those living in Jerusalem. ¹⁴I will smash them one against the other, fathers and sons alike, declares the LORD. I will allow no pity or mercy or compassion to keep me from destroying them.' "

THREAT OF CAPTIVITY

¹⁵Hear and pay attention,
    do not be arrogant,
        for the LORD has spoken.

¹⁶Give glory to the LORD your God
        before he brings the darkness,
    before your feet stumble
        on the darkening hills.
You hope for light,
        but he will turn it to thick darkness
        and change it to deep gloom.
¹⁷But if you do not listen,
        I will weep in secret
        because of your pride;
    my eyes will weep bitterly,
        overflowing with tears,
        because the LORD's flock will be taken
                captive.

NOW OR NEVER
JER 13:15

When was the last time you got the feeling that God was trying to tell you something? How long did it take for you to get the message? What did you do? If you plan on hearing what God wants to teach you, then you'd better be prepared to listen with a humble heart.

¹⁸Say to the king and to the queen mother,
    "Come down from your thrones,
    for your glorious crowns
        will fall from your heads."
¹⁹The cities in the Negev will be shut up,

ª *4* Or possibly *the Euphrates*; also in verses 5-7

and there will be no one to open them.
All Judah will be carried into exile,
   carried completely away.

20 Lift up your eyes and see
   those who are coming from the north.
Where is the flock that was entrusted to you,
   the sheep of which you boasted?
21 What will you say when ⌐the LORD⌐ sets over you
   those you cultivated as your special allies?
Will not pain grip you
   like that of a woman in labor?
22 And if you ask yourself,
   "Why has this happened to me?"—
it is because of your many sins
   that your skirts have been torn off
   and your body mistreated.
23 Can the Ethiopianª change his skin
   or the leopard its spots?
Neither can you do good
   who are accustomed to doing evil.

24 "I will scatter you like chaff
   driven by the desert wind.
25 This is your lot,
   the portion I have decreed for you,"

declares the LORD,

"because you have forgotten me
   and trusted in false gods.
26 I will pull up your skirts over your face
   that your shame may be seen—
27 your adulteries and lustful neighings,
   your shameless prostitution!
I have seen your detestable acts
   on the hills and in the fields.
Woe to you, O Jerusalem!
   How long will you be unclean?"

DROUGHT, FAMINE, SWORD

14

This is the word of the LORD to Jeremiah concerning the drought:

2 "Judah mourns,
   her cities languish;
they wail for the land,
   and a cry goes up from Jerusalem.
3 The nobles send their servants for water;
   they go to the cisterns
   but find no water.
They return with their jars unfilled;
   dismayed and despairing,
   they cover their heads.
4 The ground is cracked
   because there is no rain in the land;
the farmers are dismayed
   and cover their heads.

ª 23 Hebrew *Cushite* (probably a person from the upper Nile region)

5 Even the doe in the field
    deserts her newborn fawn
    because there is no grass.
6 Wild donkeys stand on the barren heights
    and pant like jackals;
    their eyesight fails
    for lack of pasture."

7 Although our sins testify against us,
    O Lord, do something for the sake of
        your name.
For our backsliding is great;
    we have sinned against you.
8 O Hope of Israel,
    its Savior in times of distress,
why are you like a stranger in the land,
    like a traveler who stays only a
        night?
9 Why are you like a man taken by
        surprise,
    like a warrior powerless to save?
You are among us, O Lord,

now or never

JER 14:9

Bearing your family name tells the world who you belong to. Likewise, bearing the name of Christ is a way of advertising that you belong to him. The way you live your life says something either good or bad about that name—about the One you claim to follow.

and we bear your name;
    do not forsake us!

10 This is what the Lord says about this people:

"They greatly love to wander;
    they do not restrain their feet.
So the Lord does not accept them;
    he will now remember their wickedness
    and punish them for their sins."

11 Then the Lord said to me, "Do not pray for the well-being of this people. 12 Although they fast, I will not listen to their cry; though they offer burnt offerings and grain offerings, I will not accept them. Instead, I will destroy them with the sword, famine and plague."

13 But I said, "Ah, Sovereign Lord, the prophets keep telling them, 'You will not see the sword or suffer famine. Indeed, I will give you lasting peace in this place.' "

14 Then the Lord said to me, "The prophets are prophesying lies in my name. I have not sent them or appointed them or spoken to them. They are prophesying to you false visions, divinations, idolatries[a] and the delusions of their own minds. 15 Therefore, this is what the Lord says about the prophets who are prophesying in my name: I did not send them, yet they are saying, 'No sword or famine will touch this land.' Those same prophets will perish by sword and famine. 16 And the people they are prophesying to will be thrown out into the streets of Jerusalem because of the famine and sword. There will be no one to bury them or their wives, their sons or their daughters. I will pour out on them the calamity they deserve.

17 "Speak this word to them:

" 'Let my eyes overflow with tears
    night and day without ceasing;
for my virgin daughter—my people—
    has suffered a grievous wound,
    a crushing blow.
18 If I go into the country,
    I see those slain by the sword;
if I go into the city,

---
a 14 Or visions, worthless divinations

I see the ravages of famine.
Both prophet and priest
    have gone to a land they know not.' "

¹⁹ Have you rejected Judah completely?
    Do you despise Zion?
Why have you afflicted us
    so that we cannot be healed?
We hoped for peace
    but no good has come,
for a time of healing
    but there is only terror.
²⁰ O Lord, we acknowledge our wickedness
    and the guilt of our fathers;
    we have indeed sinned against you.
²¹ For the sake of your name do not despise us;
    do not dishonor your glorious throne.
Remember your covenant with us
    and do not break it.
²² Do any of the worthless idols of the nations bring rain?
    Do the skies themselves send down showers?
No, it is you, O Lord our God.
    Therefore our hope is in you,
    for you are the one who does all this.

15 Then the Lord said to me: "Even if Moses and Samuel were to stand before me, my heart would not go out to this people. Send them away from my presence! Let them go! ²And if they ask you, 'Where shall we go?' tell them, 'This is what the Lord says:

" 'Those destined for death, to death;
those for the sword, to the sword;
those for starvation, to starvation;
those for captivity, to captivity.'

³"I will send four kinds of destroyers against them," declares the Lord, "the sword to kill and the dogs to drag away and the birds of the air and the beasts of the earth to devour and destroy. ⁴I will make them abhorrent to all the kingdoms of the earth because of what Manasseh son of Hezekiah king of Judah did in Jerusalem.

⁵ "Who will have pity on you, O Jerusalem?
    Who will mourn for you?
    Who will stop to ask how you are?
⁶ You have rejected me," declares the Lord.
    "You keep on backsliding.
So I will lay hands on you and destroy you;
    I can no longer show compassion.
⁷ I will winnow them with a winnowing fork
    at the city gates of the land.
I will bring bereavement and destruction on my people,
    for they have not changed their ways.
⁸ I will make their widows more numerous
    than the sand of the sea.
At midday I will bring a destroyer
    against the mothers of their young men;
suddenly I will bring down on them
    anguish and terror.
⁹ The mother of seven will grow faint
    and breathe her last.

Her sun will set while it is still day;
  she will be disgraced and humiliated.
I will put the survivors to the sword
  before their enemies,"

declares the LORD.

¹⁰ Alas, my mother, that you gave me birth,
  a man with whom the whole land strives and contends!
I have neither lent nor borrowed,
  yet everyone curses me.

¹¹ The LORD said,

"Surely I will deliver you for a good purpose;
  surely I will make your enemies plead
    with you
  in times of disaster and times of
    distress.

¹² "Can a man break iron—
  iron from the north—or bronze?
¹³ Your wealth and your treasures
  I will give as plunder, without charge,
because of all your sins
  throughout your country.
¹⁴ I will enslave you to your enemies
  in[a] a land you do not know,
for my anger will kindle a fire
  that will burn against you."

¹⁵ You understand, O LORD;
  remember me and care for me.
  Avenge me on my persecutors.
You are long-suffering—do not take me
    away;
  think of how I suffer reproach for your
    sake.
¹⁶ When your words came, I ate them;
  they were my joy and my heart's
    delight,
for I bear your name,
  O LORD God Almighty.
¹⁷ I never sat in the company of revelers,
  never made merry with them;
I sat alone because your hand was on me
  and you had filled me with
    indignation.
¹⁸ Why is my pain unending
  and my wound grievous and incurable?
Will you be to me like a deceptive brook,
  like a spring that fails?

¹⁹ Therefore this is what the LORD says:

"If you repent, I will restore you
  that you may serve me;

» live the adventure » Jer 15:16

Developing a Passion for God's Word

How excited do you get about God's Word? Do you consider it your "joy" and your "heart's delight"? If not, the problem may be in the way you think about it. If you think of God's Word as a bunch of rules and old stories that don't make much sense, you're not going to view it with a lot of excitement or respect. But if you think of it as a personal letter from God to *you*—the story of all he's done to save you, filled with instructions about how to be satisfied in him— you're going to want to get all you can out of it.

ᵃ *14* Some Hebrew manuscripts, Septuagint and Syriac (see also Jer. 17:4); most Hebrew manuscripts *I will cause your enemies to bring you / into*

if you utter worthy, not worthless, words,
   you will be my spokesman.
Let this people turn to you,
   but you must not turn to them.
²⁰ I will make you a wall to this people,
   a fortified wall of bronze;
they will fight against you
   but will not overcome you,
for I am with you
   to rescue and save you,"

declares the Lord.

²¹ "I will save you from the hands of the wicked
   and redeem you from the grasp of the cruel."

DAY OF DISASTER

16 Then the word of the Lord came to me: ²"You must not marry and have sons or daughters in this place." ³For this is what the Lord says about the sons and daughters born in this land and about the women who are their mothers and the men who are their fathers: ⁴"They will die of deadly diseases. They will not be mourned or buried but will be like refuse lying on the ground. They will perish by sword and famine, and their dead bodies will become food for the birds of the air and the beasts of the earth."

⁵For this is what the Lord says: "Do not enter a house where there is a funeral meal; do not go to mourn or show sympathy, because I have withdrawn my blessing, my love and my pity from this people," declares the Lord. ⁶"Both high and low will die in this land. They will not be buried or mourned, and no one will cut himself or shave his head for them. ⁷No one will offer food to comfort those who mourn for the dead—not even for a father or a mother—nor will anyone give them a drink to console them.

⁸"And do not enter a house where there is feasting and sit down to eat and drink. ⁹For this is what the Lord Almighty, the God of Israel, says: Before your eyes and in your days I will bring an end to the sounds of joy and gladness and to the voices of bride and bridegroom in this place.

¹⁰"When you tell these people all this and they ask you, 'Why has the Lord decreed such a great disaster against us? What wrong have we done? What sin have we committed against the Lord our God?' ¹¹then say to them, 'It is because your fathers forsook me,' declares the Lord, 'and followed other gods and served and worshiped them. They forsook me and did not keep my law. ¹²But you have behaved more wickedly than your fathers. See how each of you is following the stubbornness of his evil heart instead of obeying me. ¹³So I will throw you out of this land into a land neither you nor your fathers have known, and there you will serve other gods day and night, for I will show you no favor.'

NOW OR NEVER
JER 16:10–13

Name three reasons why people you know (including yourself) disobey God's rules for living. Then imagine how God would respond to each reason. Do that the next time you're tempted to disobey, and you may save yourself a whole lot of trouble.

¹⁴"However, the days are coming," declares the Lord, "when men will no longer say, 'As surely as the Lord lives, who brought the Israelites up out of Egypt,' ¹⁵but they will say, 'As surely as the Lord lives, who brought the Israelites up out of the land of the north and out of all the countries where he had banished them.' For I will restore them to the land I gave their forefathers.

¹⁶"But now I will send for many fishermen," declares the Lord, "and they will catch them. After that I will send for many hunters, and they will hunt them down on every mountain and hill and from the crevices of the rocks. ¹⁷My eyes are on all their ways; they are not hidden from me, nor is their sin concealed from my eyes. ¹⁸I will repay them double for their wickedness and their sin, because they have defiled my land with the lifeless forms of their vile images and have filled my inheritance with their detestable idols."

¹⁹ O L<small>ORD</small>, my strength and my fortress,
    my refuge in time of distress,
to you the nations will come
    from the ends of the earth and say,
"Our fathers possessed nothing but false gods,
    worthless idols that did them no good.
²⁰ Do men make their own gods?
    Yes, but they are not gods!"

²¹ "Therefore I will teach them—
    this time I will teach them
    my power and might.
Then they will know
    that my name is the L<small>ORD</small>.

"Judah's sin is engraved with an iron tool,
    inscribed with a flint point,
on the tablets of their hearts
    and on the horns of their altars.
² Even their children remember
    their altars and Asherah poles^a
beside the spreading trees
    and on the high hills.
³ My mountain in the land
    and your^b wealth and all your treasures
I will give away as plunder,
    together with your high places,
    because of sin throughout your country.
⁴ Through your own fault you will lose
    the inheritance I gave you.
I will enslave you to your enemies
    in a land you do not know,
for you have kindled my anger,
    and it will burn forever."

⁵ This is what the L<small>ORD</small> says:

"Cursed is the one who trusts in man,
    who depends on flesh for his strength
    and whose heart turns away from the L<small>ORD</small>.
⁶ He will be like a bush in the wastelands;
    he will not see prosperity when it comes.
He will dwell in the parched places of the desert,
    in a salt land where no one lives.

⁷ "But blessed is the man who trusts in the L<small>ORD</small>,
    whose confidence is in him.
⁸ He will be like a tree planted by the water
    that sends out its roots by the stream.
It does not fear when heat comes;
    its leaves are always green.
It has no worries in a year of drought
    and never fails to bear fruit."

⁹ The heart is deceitful above all things
    and beyond cure.
    Who can understand it?

^a *2* That is, symbols of the goddess Asherah   ^b *2,3* Or *hills / ³and the mountains of the land. / Your*

10 "I the LORD search the heart
  and examine the mind,
to reward a man according to his
    conduct,
  according to what his deeds deserve."

11 Like a partridge that hatches eggs it did
    not lay
  is the man who gains riches by
    unjust means.
When his life is half gone, they will
    desert him,
  and in the end he will prove to be a
    fool.

12 A glorious throne, exalted from the
    beginning,
  is the place of our sanctuary.
13 O LORD, the hope of Israel,
  all who forsake you will be put to
    shame.
Those who turn away from you will be
    written in the dust
  because they have forsaken the LORD,
    the spring of living water.

14 Heal me, O LORD, and I will be healed;
  save me and I will be saved,
  for you are the one I praise.
15 They keep saying to me,
  "Where is the word of the LORD?
  Let it now be fulfilled!"
16 I have not run away from being your shepherd;
  you know I have not desired the day of despair.
  What passes my lips is open before you.
17 Do not be a terror to me;
  you are my refuge in the day of disaster.
18 Let my persecutors be put to shame,
  but keep me from shame;
let them be terrified,
  but keep me from terror.
Bring on them the day of disaster;
  destroy them with double destruction.

Keeping Your Heart in Check

Have you ever fallen for a girl you knew would cause real problems in your life? Have you ever *really* wanted something you knew wasn't good for you? If so, you know how easily your heart can be fooled. That's why following your "heart's desire" never guarantees hapiness . . . unless your heart's desire is to please God. Don't let your heart control your actions unless it's in tune with God's plans and desires for you.

KEEPING THE SABBATH HOLY

19 This is what the LORD said to me: "Go and stand at the gate of the people, through which the kings of Judah go in and out; stand also at all the other gates of Jerusalem. 20 Say to them, 'Hear the word of the LORD, O kings of Judah and all people of Judah and everyone living in Jerusalem who come through these gates. 21 This is what the LORD says: Be careful not to carry a load on the Sabbath day or bring it through the gates of Jerusalem. 22 Do not bring a load out of your houses or do any work on the Sabbath, but keep the Sabbath day holy, as I commanded your forefathers. 23 Yet they did not listen or pay attention; they were stiff-necked and would not listen or respond to discipline. 24 But if you are careful to obey me, declares the LORD, and bring no load through the gates of this city on the Sabbath, but keep the Sabbath day holy by not doing any work on it, 25 then kings who sit on David's throne will come through the gates of this city with their officials. They and their officials will come riding in chariots and on horses, accompanied by the men of Judah and those living in Jerusalem, and this city will be inhabited forever. 26 People will come from the towns of Judah and the villages around Jerusalem, from

the territory of Benjamin and the western foothills, from the hill country and the Negev, bringing burnt offerings and sacrifices, grain offerings, incense and thank offerings to the house of the LORD. 27But if you do not obey me to keep the Sabbath day holy by not carrying any load as you come through the gates of Jerusalem on the Sabbath day, then I will kindle an unquenchable fire in the gates of Jerusalem that will consume her fortresses.' "

AT THE POTTER'S HOUSE

18 This is the word that came to Jeremiah from the LORD: 2"Go down to the potter's house, and there I will give you my message." 3So I went down to the potter's house, and I saw him working at the wheel. 4But the pot he was shaping from the clay was marred in his hands; so the potter formed it into another pot, shaping it as seemed best to him.

5Then the word of the LORD came to me: 6"O house of Israel, can I not do with you as this potter does?" declares the LORD. "Like clay in the hand of the potter, so are you in my hand, O house of Israel. 7If at any time I announce that a nation or kingdom is to be uprooted, torn down and destroyed, 8and if that nation I warned repents of its evil, then I will relent and not inflict on it the disaster I had planned. 9And if at another time I announce that a nation or kingdom is to be built up and planted, 10and if it does evil in my sight and does not obey me, then I will reconsider the good I had intended to do for it.

11"Now therefore say to the people of Judah and those living in Jerusalem, 'This is what the LORD says: Look! I am preparing a disaster for you and devising a plan against you. So turn from your evil ways, each one of you, and reform your ways and your actions.' 12But they will reply, 'It's no use. We will continue with our own plans; each of us will follow the stubbornness of his evil heart.' "

NOW OR NEVER
JER 18:1–10

The Bible says that each one of us is a lump of clay in God's hands. What do you think he's shaping you to be? What "rough edges" in your life would you like to see him smooth out?

13Therefore this is what the LORD says:

> "Inquire among the nations:
> Who has ever heard anything like this?
> A most horrible thing has been done
> by Virgin Israel.
> 14Does the snow of Lebanon
> ever vanish from its rocky slopes?
> Do its cool waters from distant sources
> ever cease to flow?[a]
> 15Yet my people have forgotten me;
> they burn incense to worthless idols,
> which made them stumble in their ways
> and in the ancient paths.
> They made them walk in bypaths
> and on roads not built up.
> 16Their land will be laid waste,
> an object of lasting scorn;
> all who pass by will be appalled
> and will shake their heads.
> 17Like a wind from the east,
> I will scatter them before their enemies;
> I will show them my back and not my face
> in the day of their disaster."

---

[a] 14 The meaning of the Hebrew for this sentence is uncertain.

battlelines

» The Fine Line (Partying)

Q: So you're going to have 150 people at your house this weekend!?
A: Yeah, maybe more . . . It's going to be insane. I'm probably not even going to know a lot of them since a bunch of them are college kids.

Q: College kids? How do you know anyone who's in college?
A: I don't. But my buddies do. And they're not just any college kids. They're college *girls* . . . and I've heard they're hot. Man, I can't wait . . .

Q: Oh, man. Just what you and a bunch of your hormone-driven buddies need. Ethan, I have to be honest with you: This doesn't sound like a great idea.
A: Dude, relax. My parents said it was OK. Our house is out in the woods, so the noise won't bother anyone. Besides, most of my buddies are pretty clean-cut guys. What could go wrong?

Q: Ethan, college parties aren't exactly video games and ping-pong. This is a whole different animal. Maybe *your* friends are clean-cut, but you don't know the others. There's no way to control what happens once 150 people show up. Besides, drooling over "hot" college girls probably isn't the best idea for a guy who's trying to keep his mind clean.
A: Hey, I'm a good kid. I do my homework, I go to youth group every week, and I've never once—not even *once*—touched a girl. This is just a party, not a sin fest. Besides, would you want to track down 150 people to tell them the whole thing is off just because it *might* get out of hand?

» Dangerous Opportunity?

Hanging out with friends is a good thing. In fact, it's a Biblical thing (see Acts 2:46; Hebrews 10:25). Fellowship should be about encouraging solid Christian living. And there's plenty of room within Christian living for some crazy fun.

But there are some environments that open up doors for unholy living. And guys who are smart will err on the side of caution and avoid those settings like the plague. Sometimes we are presented with a situation in which there isn't a "right" or a "wrong" choice, but discernment is all about seeing between right and wrong and choosing what's *best*.

Christian living is all about sacrificing yourself and your own desires for the sake of God's will (see Romans 12:1–2). Questionable party scenes with hot college girls may be something you need to sacrifice, but instead of focusing only on your displeasure about what you have to give up, remember that righteous living is pleasing to God.

Read more about Christians and partying at www.RevolutionBible.com.

¹⁸They said, "Come, let's make plans against Jeremiah; for the teaching of the law by the priest will not be lost, nor will counsel from the wise, nor the word from the prophets. So come, let's attack him with our tongues and pay no attention to anything he says."

¹⁹Listen to me, O Lᴏʀᴅ;
    hear what my accusers are saying!
²⁰Should good be repaid with evil?
    Yet they have dug a pit for me.
Remember that I stood before you
    and spoke in their behalf
to turn your wrath away from them.
²¹So give their children over to famine;
    hand them over to the power of the sword.
Let their wives be made childless and widows;
    let their men be put to death,
their young men slain by the sword in battle.
²²Let a cry be heard from their houses
    when you suddenly bring invaders against them,
for they have dug a pit to capture me
    and have hidden snares for my feet.
²³But you know, O Lᴏʀᴅ,
    all their plots to kill me.
Do not forgive their crimes
    or blot out their sins from your sight.
Let them be overthrown before you;
    deal with them in the time of your anger.

19

This is what the Lᴏʀᴅ says: "Go and buy a clay jar from a potter. Take along some of the elders of the people and of the priests ²and go out to the Valley of Ben Hinnom, near the entrance of the Potsherd Gate. There proclaim the words I tell you, ³and say, 'Hear the word of the Lᴏʀᴅ, O kings of Judah and people of Jerusalem. This is what the Lᴏʀᴅ Almighty, the God of Israel, says: Listen! I am going to bring a disaster on this place that will make the ears of everyone who hears of it tingle. ⁴For they have forsaken me and made this a place of foreign gods; they have burned sacrifices in it to gods that neither they nor their fathers nor the kings of Judah ever knew, and they have filled this place with the blood of the innocent. ⁵They have built the high places of Baal to burn their sons in the fire as offerings to Baal—something I did not command or mention, nor did it enter my mind. ⁶So beware, the days are coming, declares the Lᴏʀᴅ, when people will no longer call this place Topheth or the Valley of Ben Hinnom, but the Valley of Slaughter.

⁷" 'In this place I will ruinᵃ the plans of Judah and Jerusalem. I will make them fall by the sword before their enemies, at the hands of those who seek their lives, and I will give their carcasses as food to the birds of the air and the beasts of the earth. ⁸I will devastate this city and make it an object of scorn; all who pass by will be appalled and will scoff because of all its wounds. ⁹I will make them eat the flesh of their sons and daughters, and they will eat one another's flesh during the stress of the siege imposed on them by the enemies who seek their lives.'

¹⁰"Then break the jar while those who go with you are watching, ¹¹and say to them, 'This is what the Lᴏʀᴅ Almighty says: I will smash this nation and this city just as this potter's jar is smashed and cannot be repaired. They will bury the dead in Topheth until there is no more room. ¹²This is what I

ⁿᴏᴡ ᴏʀ ⁿᴇᴠᴇʀ

JER 19:1-6

Do you fear the consequences of your sin? Do your ears "tingle" and does your heart race as you read God's words proclaiming judgment for all of your sins? Remember God's holiness and fear his awesome judgment!

ᵃ *7* The Hebrew for *ruin* sounds like the Hebrew for *jar* (see verses 1 and 10).

will do to this place and to those who live here, declares the LORD. I will make this city like Topheth. ¹³The houses in Jerusalem and those of the kings of Judah will be defiled like this place, Topheth— all the houses where they burned incense on the roofs to all the starry hosts and poured out drink offerings to other gods.' "

¹⁴Jeremiah then returned from Topheth, where the LORD had sent him to prophesy, and stood in the court of the LORD's temple and said to all the people, ¹⁵"This is what the LORD Almighty, the God of Israel, says: 'Listen! I am going to bring on this city and the villages around it every disaster I pronounced against them, because they were stiff-necked and would not listen to my words.' "

JEREMIAH AND PASHHUR

20

When the priest Pashhur son of Immer, the chief officer in the temple of the LORD, heard Jeremiah prophesying these things, ²he had Jeremiah the prophet beaten and put in the stocks at the Upper Gate of Benjamin at the LORD's temple. ³The next day, when Pashhur released him from the stocks, Jeremiah said to him, "The LORD's name for you is not Pashhur, but Magor-Missabib.ᵃ ⁴For this is what the LORD says: 'I will make you a terror to yourself and to all your friends; with your own eyes you will see them fall by the sword of their enemies. I will hand all Judah over to the king of Babylon, who will carry them away to Babylon or put them to the sword. ⁵I will hand over to their enemies all the wealth of this city—all its products, all its valuables and all the treasures of the kings of Judah. They will take it away as plunder and carry it off to Babylon. ⁶And you, Pashhur, and all who live in your house will go into exile to Babylon. There you will die and be buried, you and all your friends to whom you have prophesied lies.' "

JEREMIAH'S COMPLAINT

⁷O LORD, you deceivedᵇ me, and I was
    deceivedᵇ;
  you overpowered me and prevailed.
I am ridiculed all day long;
    everyone mocks me.
⁸Whenever I speak, I cry out
    proclaiming violence and destruction.
So the word of the LORD has brought me
    insult and reproach all day long.
⁹But if I say, "I will not mention him
    or speak any more in his name,"
his word is in my heart like a fire,
    a fire shut up in my bones.
I am weary of holding it in;
    indeed, I cannot.
¹⁰I hear many whispering,
    "Terror on every side!
    Report him! Let's report him!"
All my friends
    are waiting for me to slip, saying,
"Perhaps he will be deceived;
    then we will prevail over him
    and take our revenge on him."

¹¹But the LORD is with me like a mighty
    warrior;
  so my persecutors will stumble and
    not prevail.
They will fail and be thoroughly disgraced;
    their dishonor will never be forgotten.

Doing What's Right—Even When It Hurts

Have you ever been given a task to do and wished that someone else had been picked for the job? Have you ever wanted to shrug off responsibility but realized that you couldn't? Being a follower of God often means going against the crowd and being different, either by speaking the truth when it's unpopular or refusing to be a part of something that just isn't right. Don't expect it to be easy. But if you have a heart devoted to God, his truth will burn "like a fire" inside you, and your desire will be to honor and obey him.

ᵃ 3 *Magor-Missabib* means *terror on every side.*   ᵇ 7 Or *persuaded*

jeremiah

» A man of God who was known as the "weeping prophet"
» Legendary for obeying God's call
» Often persecuted for faithfully delivering God's message

pashhur

» A priest and the son of Immer
» His name could mean "ease" or "tranquility"
» Had Jeremiah beaten and locked up for his discouraging prophecies

The Main Event

Jeremiah's job was to deliver God's messages to the Israelites. And that's what he did, faithfully and obediently. Since the Israelites weren't exactly on God's good side, most of Jeremiah's messages contained bad news.

As you might imagine, Jeremiah's job made him pretty unpopular with the general population. One man in particular, though, took his dislike of Jeremiah to the next level. His name was Pashhur, and he served as a priest (believe it or not).

When Jeremiah delivered a message from God that hit a little too close to home, Pashhur used his considerable religious authority to do something about it. He ordered a goon squad to rough up Jeremiah and then had the prophet locked up—all for the "crime" of speaking the words of God.

After a night in jail, Jeremiah was released. As he left, he looked Pashhur in the eye and said (in so many words), "Everybody around here might call you Pashhur—which means 'ease'—but God's name for you is 'Magor-Missabib'—which means 'terror on every side.' And, by the way, you'd better pack your bags, pal. You're going away into Babylonian captivity, and you're gonna die there."

It was Jeremiah's bold way of saying, "You can lock me in jail all you want, Pashhur. You can beat me up and try to shut me up. But I'm not backing down. God's Word is what it is. What he has said, he will do. Judgment's coming. Deal with it."

The Outcome

From a worldly perspective, Pashhur won his battle against Jeremiah. He clearly had the upper hand. It's not hard to imagine him and his henchmen laughing and mocking Jeremiah as the bloodied and bruised prophet walked out the prison door. But Jeremiah's predictions proved true in the end—not surprisingly, considering the source (God). Everything Jeremiah prophesied eventually happened. In the end, he was vindicated.

This incident serves as a reminder of a disturbing truth of the Christian life. Sometimes we will suffer for doing the things God tells us to do. In fact, the Bible promises it (see 2 Timothy 3:12). That's the way things work in a sinful world that's alienated from God.

Like Jeremiah, we might feel shocked, even betrayed, when our obedience brings trouble. But as Christian men, we have no choice but to do what God says. A bold willingness to follow God no matter what is the place where spirituality and masculinity come together to accomplish eternally significant things.

Read more about Jeremiah and Pashhur in Jeremiah 20:1–18 (pages 1002–1004).

¹²O LORD Almighty, you who examine the righteous
 and probe the heart and mind,
let me see your vengeance upon them,
 for to you I have committed my cause.

¹³Sing to the LORD!
 Give praise to the LORD!
He rescues the life of the needy
 from the hands of the wicked.

¹⁴Cursed be the day I was born!
 May the day my mother bore me not be blessed!
¹⁵Cursed be the man who brought my father the news,
 who made him very glad, saying,
 "A child is born to you—a son!"
¹⁶May that man be like the towns
 the LORD overthrew without pity.
May he hear wailing in the morning,
 a battle cry at noon.
¹⁷For he did not kill me in the womb,
 with my mother as my grave,
 her womb enlarged forever.
¹⁸Why did I ever come out of the womb
 to see trouble and sorrow
 and to end my days in shame?

GOD REJECTS ZEDEKIAH'S REQUEST

21 The word came to Jeremiah from the LORD when King Zedekiah sent to him Pashhur son of Malkijah and the priest Zephaniah son of Maaseiah. They said: ²"Inquire now of the LORD for us because Nebuchadnezzar[a] king of Babylon is attacking us. Perhaps the LORD will perform wonders for us as in times past so that he will withdraw from us."

³But Jeremiah answered them, "Tell Zedekiah, ⁴'This is what the LORD, the God of Israel, says: I am about to turn against you the weapons of war that are in your hands, which you are using to fight the king of Babylon and the Babylonians[b] who are outside the wall besieging you. And I will gather them inside this city. ⁵I myself will fight against you with an outstretched hand and a mighty arm in anger and fury and great wrath. ⁶I will strike down those who live in this city—both men and animals—and they will die of a terrible plague. ⁷After that, declares the LORD, I will hand over Zedekiah king of Judah, his officials and the people in this city who survive the plague, sword and famine, to Nebuchadnezzar king of Babylon and to their enemies who seek their lives. He will put them to the sword; he will show them no mercy or pity or compassion.'

now or never

JER 21:1–7

God answers prayer—though sometimes not how we want him to, as King Zedekiah discovered. If you're not living in obedience to God, why should you expect him to listen to you when you ask for stuff?

⁸"Furthermore, tell the people, 'This is what the LORD says: See, I am setting before you the way of life and the way of death. ⁹Whoever stays in this city will die by the sword, famine or plague. But whoever goes out and surrenders to the Babylonians who are besieging you will live; he will escape with his life. ¹⁰I have determined to do this city harm and not good, declares the LORD. It will be given into the hands of the king of Babylon, and he will destroy it with fire.'

¹¹"Moreover, say to the royal house of Judah, 'Hear the word of the LORD; ¹²O house of David, this is what the LORD says:

---

[a] 2 Hebrew *Nebuchadrezzar*, of which *Nebuchadnezzar* is a variant; here and often in Jeremiah and Ezekiel [b] 4 Or *Chaldeans*; also in verse 9

" 'Administer justice every morning;
    rescue from the hand of his oppressor
    the one who has been robbed,
or my wrath will break out and burn like fire
    because of the evil you have done—
    burn with no one to quench it.
¹³I am against you, ⌊Jerusalem,⌋
    you who live above this valley
    on the rocky plateau,

                      declares the LORD—

you who say, "Who can come against us?
    Who can enter our refuge?"
¹⁴I will punish you as your deeds deserve,

                      declares the LORD.

I will kindle a fire in your forests
    that will consume everything around you.' "

JUDGMENT AGAINST EVIL KINGS

22 This is what the LORD says: "Go down to the palace of the king of Judah and pro-claim this message there: ²'Hear the word of the LORD, O king of Judah, you who sit on David's throne—you, your officials and your people who come through these gates. ³This is what the LORD says: Do what is just and right. Rescue from the hand of his oppressor the one who has been robbed. Do no wrong or violence to the alien, the fatherless or the widow, and do not shed innocent blood in this place. ⁴For if you are careful to carry out these commands, then kings who sit on David's throne will come through the gates of this palace, riding in chariots and on horses, accompanied by their officials and their people. ⁵But if you do not obey these commands, declares the LORD, I swear by myself that this palace will become a ruin.' "

⁶For this is what the LORD says about the palace of the king of Judah:

"Though you are like Gilead to me,
    like the summit of Lebanon,
I will surely make you like a desert,
    like towns not inhabited.
⁷I will send destroyers against you,
    each man with his weapons,
and they will cut up your fine cedar beams
    and throw them into the fire.

⁸"People from many nations will pass by this city and will ask one another, 'Why has the LORD done such a thing to this great city?' ⁹And the answer will be: 'Because they have forsaken the covenant of the LORD their God and have worshiped and served other gods.' "

¹⁰Do not weep for the dead ⌊king⌋ or mourn his loss;
    rather, weep bitterly for him who is exiled,
because he will never return
    nor see his native land again.

¹¹For this is what the LORD says about Shallum[a] son of Josiah, who succeeded his father as king of Judah but has gone from this place: "He will never return. ¹²He will die in the place where they have led him captive; he will not see this land again."

¹³"Woe to him who builds his palace by unrighteousness,
    his upper rooms by injustice,
making his countrymen work for nothing,
    not paying them for their labor.
¹⁴He says, 'I will build myself a great palace

---

[a] 11 Also called Jehoahaz

with spacious upper rooms.'
So he makes large windows in it,
    panels it with cedar
    and decorates it in red.

¹⁵ "Does it make you a king
    to have more and more cedar?
Did not your father have food and drink?
    He did what was right and just,
    so all went well with him.
¹⁶ He defended the cause of the poor and needy,
    and so all went well.
Is that not what it means to know me?"
    declares the LORD.
¹⁷ "But your eyes and your heart
    are set only on dishonest gain,
on shedding innocent blood
    and on oppression and extortion."

¹⁸ Therefore this is what the LORD says about Jehoiakim son of Josiah king of Judah:

"They will not mourn for him:
    'Alas, my brother! Alas, my sister!'
They will not mourn for him:
    'Alas, my master! Alas, his splendor!'
¹⁹ He will have the burial of a donkey—
    dragged away and thrown
    outside the gates of Jerusalem."

²⁰ "Go up to Lebanon and cry out,
    let your voice be heard in Bashan,
cry out from Abarim,
    for all your allies are crushed.
²¹ I warned you when you felt secure,
    but you said, 'I will not listen!'

Avoiding Greed

Shallum wanted an impressive palace and was willing to walk all over anyone to get it. Sound familiar? Do you know someone who cares more about things than about people? Do you know people who would rather buy something they don't need than use their money to help someone in serious need? God makes it pretty clear how he feels about selfishness and greed. In the end it cost Shallum everything—he was taken away as a captive and eventually died in exile. There's a lot we can learn from Shallum's experience.

NOW OR NEVER
JER 22:24–27

You can read where this prophecy came true in 2 Kings 24:8–17. The Lord backs up every one of his prophecies and promises with action. That's why we can believe him.

This has been your way from your youth;
    you have not obeyed me.
²² The wind will drive all your shepherds away,
    and your allies will go into exile.
Then you will be ashamed and disgraced
    because of all your wickedness.
²³ You who live in 'Lebanon,'ᵃ
    who are nestled in cedar buildings,
how you will groan when pangs come upon you,
    pain like that of a woman in labor!

²⁴ "As surely as I live," declares the LORD, "even if you, Jehoiachinᵇ son of Jehoiakim king of Judah, were a signet ring on my right hand, I would still pull you off. ²⁵ I will hand you over to those who seek your life, those you fear—to Nebuchadnezzar king of Babylon and to the Babylonians.ᶜ ²⁶ I will hurl you

ᵃ 23 That is, the palace in Jerusalem (see 1 Kings 7:2)   ᵇ 24 Hebrew Coniah, a variant of Jehoiachin; also in verse 28
ᶜ 25 Or Chaldeans

and the mother who gave you birth into another country, where neither of you was born, and there you both will die. ²⁷You will never come back to the land you long to return to."

²⁸Is this man Jehoiachin a despised, broken pot,
  an object no one wants?
Why will he and his children be hurled out,
  cast into a land they do not know?
²⁹O land, land, land,
  hear the word of the LORD!
³⁰This is what the LORD says:
"Record this man as if childless,
  a man who will not prosper in his lifetime,
for none of his offspring will prosper,
  none will sit on the throne of David
  or rule anymore in Judah."

THE RIGHTEOUS BRANCH

23 "Woe to the shepherds who are destroying and scattering the sheep of my pasture!" declares the LORD. ²Therefore this is what the LORD, the God of Israel, says to the shepherds who tend my people: "Because you have scattered my flock and driven them away and have not bestowed care on them, I will bestow punishment on you for the evil you have done," declares the LORD. ³"I myself will gather the remnant of my flock out of all the countries where I have driven them and will bring them back to their pasture, where they will be fruitful and increase in number. ⁴I will place shepherds over them who will tend them, and they will no longer be afraid or terrified, nor will any be missing," declares the LORD.

⁵"The days are coming," declares the LORD,
  "when I will raise up to David ᵃ a righteous Branch,
a King who will reign wisely
  and do what is just and right in the land.
⁶In his days Judah will be saved
  and Israel will live in safety.
This is the name by which he will be called:
  The LORD Our Righteousness.

⁷"So then, the days are coming," declares the LORD, "when people will no longer say, 'As surely as the LORD lives, who brought the Israelites up out of Egypt,' ⁸but they will say, 'As surely as the LORD lives, who brought the descendants of Israel up out of the land of the north and out of all the countries where he had banished them.' Then they will live in their own land."

LYING PROPHETS

⁹Concerning the prophets:

My heart is broken within me;
  all my bones tremble.
I am like a drunken man,
  like a man overcome by wine,
because of the LORD
  and his holy words.
¹⁰The land is full of adulterers;
  because of the curse ᵇ the land lies parched ᶜ
  and the pastures in the desert are withered.
The ⌐prophets⌐ follow an evil course
  and use their power unjustly.

ᵃ 5 Or *up from David's line*   ᵇ 10 Or *because of these things*   ᶜ 10 Or *land mourns*

¹¹"Both prophet and priest are godless;
even in my temple I find their wickedness,"

declares the LORD.

¹²"Therefore their path will become slippery;
they will be banished to darkness
and there they will fall.
I will bring disaster on them
in the year they are punished,"

declares the LORD.

¹³"Among the prophets of Samaria
I saw this repulsive thing:
They prophesied by Baal
and led my people Israel astray.
¹⁴And among the prophets of Jerusalem
I have seen something horrible:
They commit adultery and live a lie.
They strengthen the hands of evildoers,
so that no one turns from his wickedness.
They are all like Sodom to me;
the people of Jerusalem are like Gomorrah."

¹⁵Therefore, this is what the LORD Almighty says concerning the prophets:

"I will make them eat bitter food
and drink poisoned water,
because from the prophets of Jerusalem
ungodliness has spread throughout the land."

¹⁶This is what the LORD Almighty says:

"Do not listen to what the prophets are prophesying to you;
they fill you with false hopes.
They speak visions from their own minds,
not from the mouth of the LORD.
¹⁷They keep saying to those who despise me,
'The LORD says: You will have peace.'
And to all who follow the stubbornness of their hearts
they say, 'No harm will come to you.'
¹⁸But which of them has stood in the council of the LORD
to see or to hear his word?
Who has listened and heard his word?
¹⁹See, the storm of the LORD
will burst out in wrath,
a whirlwind swirling down
on the heads of the wicked.
²⁰The anger of the LORD will not turn back
until he fully accomplishes
the purposes of his heart.
In days to come
you will understand it clearly.
²¹I did not send these prophets,
yet they have run with their message;
I did not speak to them,
yet they have prophesied.
²²But if they had stood in my council,
they would have proclaimed my words to my people

and would have turned them from their evil ways
and from their evil deeds.

²³ "Am I only a God nearby,"

declares the LORD,

"and not a God far away?
²⁴ Can anyone hide in secret places
so that I cannot see him?"

declares the LORD.

"Do not I fill heaven and earth?"

declares the LORD.

²⁵ "I have heard what the prophets say who prophesy lies in my name. They say, 'I had a dream! I had a dream!' ²⁶How long will this continue in the hearts of these lying prophets, who prophesy the delusions of their own minds? ²⁷They think the dreams they tell one another will make my people forget my name, just as their fathers forgot my name through Baal worship. ²⁸Let the prophet who has a dream tell his dream, but let the one who has my word speak it faithfully. For what has straw to do with grain?" declares the LORD. ²⁹"Is not my word like fire," declares the LORD, "and like a hammer that breaks a rock in pieces?

³⁰"Therefore," declares the LORD, "I am against the prophets who steal from one another words supposedly from me. ³¹Yes," declares the LORD, "I am against the prophets who wag their own tongues and yet declare, 'The LORD declares.' ³²Indeed, I am against those who prophesy false dreams," declares the LORD. "They tell them and lead my people astray with their reckless lies, yet I did not send or appoint them. They do not benefit these people in the least," declares the LORD.

FALSE ORACLES AND FALSE PROPHETS

³³"When these people, or a prophet or a priest, ask you, 'What is the oracle[a] of the LORD?' say to them, 'What oracle?[b] I will forsake you, declares the LORD.' ³⁴If a prophet or a priest or anyone else claims, 'This is the oracle of the LORD,' I will punish that man and his household. ³⁵This is what each of you keeps on saying to his friend or relative: 'What is the LORD's answer?' or 'What has the LORD spoken?' ³⁶But you must not mention 'the oracle of the LORD' again, because every man's own word becomes his oracle and so you distort the words of the living God, the LORD Almighty, our God. ³⁷This is what you keep saying to a prophet: 'What is the LORD's answer to you?' or 'What has the LORD spoken?' ³⁸Although you claim, 'This is the oracle of the LORD,' this is what the LORD says: You used the words, 'This is the oracle of the LORD,' even though I told you that you must not claim, 'This is the oracle of the LORD.' ³⁹Therefore, I will surely forget you and cast you out of my presence along with the city I gave to you and your fathers. ⁴⁰I will bring upon you everlasting disgrace—everlasting shame that will not be forgotten."

NOW OR NEVER
JER 23:30–32

If you tell someone you're speaking for God, you'd better make sure that what you say is consistent with his Word. Similarly, if people tell you they're speaking for God, you'd better make sure their message also lines up with the Word.

TWO BASKETS OF FIGS

24

After Jehoiachin[c] son of Jehoiakim king of Judah and the officials, the craftsmen and the artisans of Judah were carried into exile from Jerusalem to Babylon by Nebuchadnezzar king of Babylon, the LORD showed me two baskets of figs placed in front of the temple of the LORD. ²One basket had very good figs, like those that ripen early; the other basket had very poor figs, so bad they could not be eaten.

³Then the LORD asked me, "What do you see, Jeremiah?"

"Figs," I answered. "The good ones are very good, but the poor ones are so bad they cannot be eaten."

---

[a] 33 Or burden (see Septuagint and Vulgate)   [b] 33 Hebrew; Septuagint and Vulgate 'You are the burden. (The Hebrew for oracle and burden is the same.)   [c] 1 Hebrew Jeconiah, a variant of Jehoiachin

4Then the word of the Lord came to me: 5"This is what the Lord, the God of Israel, says: 'Like these good figs, I regard as good the exiles from Judah, whom I sent away from this place to the land of the Babylonians.[a] 6My eyes will watch over them for their good, and I will bring them back to this land. I will build them up and not tear them down; I will plant them and not uproot them. 7I will give them a heart to know me, that I am the Lord. They will be my people, and I will be their God, for they will return to me with all their heart.

8" 'But like the poor figs, which are so bad they cannot be eaten,' says the Lord, 'so will I deal with Zedekiah king of Judah, his officials and the survivors from Jerusalem, whether they remain in this land or live in Egypt. 9I will make them abhorrent and an offense to all the kingdoms of the earth, a reproach and a byword, an object of ridicule and cursing, wherever I banish them. 10I will send the sword, famine and plague against them until they are destroyed from the land I gave to them and their fathers.' "

now or never

JER 24:7

How would you explain to a non-Christian friend what it means to know God with your heart? What else could you tell your friend about the Lord—from your own personal experience—that he or she might not know?

SEVENTY YEARS OF CAPTIVITY

25 The word came to Jeremiah concerning all the people of Judah in the fourth year of Jehoiakim son of Josiah king of Judah, which was the first year of Nebuchadnezzar king of Babylon. 2So Jeremiah the prophet said to all the people of Judah and to all those living in Jerusalem: 3For twenty-three years—from the thirteenth year of Josiah son of Amon king of Judah until this very day—the word of the Lord has come to me and I have spoken to you again and again, but you have not listened.

4And though the Lord has sent all his servants the prophets to you again and again, you have not listened or paid any attention. 5They said, "Turn now, each of you, from your evil ways and your evil practices, and you can stay in the land the Lord gave to you and your fathers for ever and ever. 6Do not follow other gods to serve and worship them; do not provoke me to anger with what your hands have made. Then I will not harm you."

7"But you did not listen to me," declares the Lord, "and you have provoked me with what your hands have made, and you have brought harm to yourselves."

8Therefore the Lord Almighty says this: "Because you have not listened to my words, 9I will summon all the peoples of the north and my servant Nebuchadnezzar king of Babylon," declares the Lord, "and I will bring them against this land and its inhabitants and against all the surrounding nations. I will completely destroy[b] them and make them an object of horror and scorn, and an everlasting ruin. 10I will banish from them the sounds of joy and gladness, the voices of bride and bridegroom, the sound of millstones and the light of the lamp. 11This whole country will become a desolate wasteland, and these nations will serve the king of Babylon seventy years.

12"But when the seventy years are fulfilled, I will punish the king of Babylon and his nation, the land of the Babylonians,[a] for their guilt," declares the Lord, "and will make it desolate forever. 13I will bring upon that land all the things I have spoken against it, all that are written in this book and prophesied by Jeremiah against all the nations. 14They themselves will be enslaved by many nations and great kings; I will repay them according to their deeds and the work of their hands."

THE CUP OF GOD'S WRATH

15This is what the Lord, the God of Israel, said to me: "Take from my hand this cup filled with the wine of my wrath and make all the nations to whom I send you drink it. 16When they drink it, they will stagger and go mad because of the sword I will send among them."

17So I took the cup from the Lord's hand and made all the nations to whom he sent me drink it: 18Jerusalem and the towns of Judah, its kings and officials, to make them a ruin and an object of horror and

---

a 5,12 Or Chaldeans   b 9 The Hebrew term refers to the irrevocable giving over of things or persons to the Lord, often by totally destroying them.

scorn and cursing, as they are today; ¹⁹Pharaoh king of Egypt, his attendants, his officials and all his people, ²⁰and all the foreign people there; all the kings of Uz; all the kings of the Philistines (those of Ashkelon, Gaza, Ekron, and the people left at Ashdod); ²¹Edom, Moab and Ammon; ²²all the kings of Tyre and Sidon; the kings of the coastlands across the sea; ²³Dedan, Tema, Buz and all who are in distant places ᵃ; ²⁴all the kings of Arabia and all the kings of the foreign people who live in the desert; ²⁵all the kings of Zimri, Elam and Media; ²⁶and all the kings of the north, near and far, one after the other— all the kingdoms on the face of the earth. And after all of them, the king of Sheshach ᵇ will drink it too.

²⁷"Then tell them, 'This is what the Lᴏʀᴅ Almighty, the God of Israel, says: Drink, get drunk and vomit, and fall to rise no more because of the sword I will send among you.' ²⁸But if they refuse to take the cup from your hand and drink, tell them, 'This is what the Lᴏʀᴅ Almighty says: You must drink it! ²⁹See, I am beginning to bring disaster on the city that bears my Name, and will you indeed go unpunished? You will not go unpunished, for I am calling down a sword upon all who live on the earth, declares the Lᴏʀᴅ Almighty.'

³⁰"Now prophesy all these words against them and say to them:

" 'The Lᴏʀᴅ will roar from on high;
    he will thunder from his holy dwelling
    and roar mightily against his land.
He will shout like those who tread the grapes,
    shout against all who live on the earth.
³¹ The tumult will resound to the ends of the earth,
    for the Lᴏʀᴅ will bring charges against the nations;
he will bring judgment on all mankind
    and put the wicked to the sword,' "

                                                                                    declares the Lᴏʀᴅ.

³²This is what the Lᴏʀᴅ Almighty says:

"Look! Disaster is spreading
    from nation to nation;
a mighty storm is rising
    from the ends of the earth."

³³At that time those slain by the Lᴏʀᴅ will be everywhere—from one end of the earth to the other. They will not be mourned or gathered up or buried, but will be like refuse lying on the ground.

³⁴Weep and wail, you shepherds;
    roll in the dust, you leaders of the flock.
For your time to be slaughtered has
    come;
you will fall and be shattered like fine
    pottery.
³⁵ The shepherds will have nowhere to flee,
    the leaders of the flock no place to
    escape.
³⁶Hear the cry of the shepherds,
    the wailing of the leaders of the flock,
for the Lᴏʀᴅ is destroying their
    pasture.
³⁷ The peaceful meadows will be laid waste
    because of the fierce anger of the
    Lᴏʀᴅ.

NOW OR NEVER
JER 25:30–38

This is a sneak preview of things to come. The message is loud and clear: God is not one to mess around with. Do whatever it takes to stay close to him.

³⁸Like a lion he will leave his lair,
    and their land will become desolate
because of the sword ᶜ of the oppressor
    and because of the Lᴏʀᴅ's fierce anger.

JEREMIAH 25:38

1011

ᵃ 23 Or who clip the hair by their foreheads   ᵇ 26 Sheshach is a cryptogram for Babylon.   ᶜ 38 Some Hebrew manuscripts and Septuagint (see also Jer. 46:16 and 50:16); most Hebrew manuscripts anger

JEREMIAH THREATENED WITH DEATH

26 Early in the reign of Jehoiakim son of Josiah king of Judah, this word came from the LORD: ²"This is what the LORD says: Stand in the courtyard of the LORD's house and speak to all the people of the towns of Judah who come to worship in the house of the LORD. Tell them everything I command you; do not omit a word. ³Perhaps they will listen and each will turn from his evil way. Then I will relent and not bring on them the disaster I was planning because of the evil they have done. ⁴Say to them, 'This is what the LORD says: If you do not listen to me and follow my law, which I have set before you, ⁵and if you do not listen to the words of my servants the prophets, whom I have sent to you again and again (though you have not listened), ⁶then I will make this house like Shiloh and this city an object of cursing among all the nations of the earth.' "

⁷The priests, the prophets and all the people heard Jeremiah speak these words in the house of the LORD. ⁸But as soon as Jeremiah finished telling all the people everything the LORD had commanded him to say, the priests, the prophets and all the people seized him and said, "You must die! ⁹Why do you prophesy in the LORD's name that this house will be like Shiloh and this city will be desolate and deserted?" And all the people crowded around Jeremiah in the house of the LORD.

¹⁰When the officials of Judah heard about these things, they went up from the royal palace to the house of the LORD and took their places at the entrance of the New Gate of the LORD's house. ¹¹Then the priests and the prophets said to the officials and all the people, "This man should be sentenced to death because he has prophesied against this city. You have heard it with your own ears!"

¹²Then Jeremiah said to all the officials and all the people: "The LORD sent me to prophesy against this house and this city all the things you have heard. ¹³Now reform your ways and your actions and obey the LORD your God. Then the LORD will relent and not bring the disaster he has pronounced against you. ¹⁴As for me, I am in your hands; do with me whatever you think is good and right. ¹⁵Be assured, however, that if you put me to death, you will bring the guilt of innocent blood on yourselves and on this city and on those who live in it, for in truth the LORD has sent me to you to speak all these words in your hearing."

¹⁶Then the officials and all the people said to the priests and the prophets, "This man should not be sentenced to death! He has spoken to us in the name of the LORD our God."

¹⁷Some of the elders of the land stepped forward and said to the entire assembly of people, ¹⁸"Micah of Moresheth prophesied in the days of Hezekiah king of Judah. He told all the people of Judah, 'This is what the LORD Almighty says:

" 'Zion will be plowed like a field,
    Jerusalem will become a heap of rubble,
    the temple hill a mound overgrown with thickets.'ᵃ

¹⁹"Did Hezekiah king of Judah or anyone else in Judah put him to death? Did not Hezekiah fear the LORD and seek his favor? And did not the LORD relent, so that he did not bring the disaster he pronounced against them? We are about to bring a terrible disaster on ourselves!"

²⁰(Now Uriah son of Shemaiah from Kiriath Jearim was another man who prophesied in the name of the LORD; he prophesied the same things against this city and this land as Jeremiah did. ²¹When King Jehoiakim and all his officers and officials heard his words, the king sought to put him to death. But Uriah heard of it and fled in fear to Egypt. ²²King Jehoiakim, however, sent Elnathan son of Acbor to Egypt, along with some other men. ²³They brought Uriah out of Egypt and took him to King Jehoiakim, who had him struck down with a sword and his body thrown into the burial place of the common people.)

²⁴Furthermore, Ahikam son of Shaphan supported Jeremiah, and so he was not handed over to the people to be put to death.

NOW OR NEVER
JER 26:7-9

What's the worst response you've ever gotten when you tried to talk to someone about Jesus? You can't control how others react, but remember—God still may be using your words (no matter how lame they seem to you) to bring about a change in that person's life.

ᵃ *18* Micah 3:12

JUDAH TO SERVE NEBUCHADNEZZAR

27 Early in the reign of Zedekiah[a] son of Josiah king of Judah, this word came to Jeremiah from the LORD: ²This is what the LORD said to me: "Make a yoke out of straps and crossbars and put it on your neck. ³Then send word to the kings of Edom, Moab, Ammon, Tyre and Sidon through the envoys who have come to Jerusalem to Zedekiah king of Judah. ⁴Give them a message for their masters and say, 'This is what the LORD Almighty, the God of Israel, says: "Tell this to your masters: ⁵With my great power and outstretched arm I made the earth and its people and the animals that are on it, and I give it to anyone I please. ⁶Now I will hand all your countries over to my servant Nebuchadnezzar king of Babylon; I will make even the wild animals subject to him. ⁷All nations will serve him and his son and his grandson until the time for his land comes; then many nations and great kings will subjugate him.

⁸" ' "If, however, any nation or kingdom will not serve Nebuchadnezzar king of Babylon or bow its neck under his yoke, I will punish that nation with the sword, famine and plague, declares the LORD, until I destroy it by his hand. ⁹So do not listen to your prophets, your diviners, your interpreters of dreams, your mediums or your sorcerers who tell you, 'You will not serve the king of Babylon.' ¹⁰They prophesy lies to you that will only serve to remove you far from your lands; I will banish you and you will perish. ¹¹But if any nation will bow its neck under the yoke of the king of Babylon and serve him, I will let that nation remain in its own land to till it and to live there, declares the LORD." ' "

¹²I gave the same message to Zedekiah king of Judah. I said, "Bow your neck under the yoke of the king of Babylon; serve him and his people, and you will live. ¹³Why will you and your people die by the sword, famine and plague with which the LORD has threatened any nation that will not serve the king of Babylon? ¹⁴Do not listen to the words of the prophets who say to you, 'You will not serve the king of Babylon,' for they are prophesying lies to you. ¹⁵'I have not sent them,' declares the LORD. 'They are prophesying lies in my name. Therefore, I will banish you and you will perish, both you and the prophets who prophesy to you.' "

¹⁶Then I said to the priests and all these people, "This is what the LORD says: Do not listen to the prophets who say, 'Very soon now the articles from the LORD's house will be brought back from Babylon.' They are prophesying lies to you. ¹⁷Do not listen to them. Serve the king of Babylon, and you will live. Why should this city become a ruin? ¹⁸If they are prophets and have the word of the LORD, let them plead with the LORD Almighty that the furnishings remaining in the house of the LORD and in the palace of the king of Judah and in Jerusalem not be taken to Babylon. ¹⁹For this is what the LORD Almighty says about the pillars, the Sea, the movable stands and the other furnishings that are left in this city, ²⁰which Nebuchadnezzar king of Babylon did not take away when he carried Jehoiachin[b] son of Jehoiakim king of Judah into exile from Jerusalem to Babylon, along with all the nobles of Judah and Jerusalem— ²¹yes, this is what the LORD Almighty, the God of Israel, says about the things that are left in the house of the LORD and in the palace of the king of Judah and in Jerusalem: ²²'They will be taken to Babylon and there they will remain until the day I come for them,' declares the LORD. 'Then I will bring them back and restore them to this place.' "

NOW OR NEVER
JER 27:14–15

How many lies have you heard about the Christian life? Has anyone ever told you that salvation is a free ticket to heaven, and, therefore, we can live it up and sin all we want? That prayer doesn't really do anything? There are still plenty of "false prophets" around. Beware of their lies.

THE FALSE PROPHET HANANIAH

28 In the fifth month of that same year, the fourth year, early in the reign of Zedekiah king of Judah, the prophet Hananiah son of Azzur, who was from Gibeon, said to me in the house of the LORD in the presence of the priests and all the people: ²"This is what the LORD Almighty, the God of Israel, says: 'I will break the yoke of the king of Babylon. ³Within two years I will bring back to this place all the articles of the LORD's house that Nebuchadnezzar king of Babylon removed from here and took to Babylon. ⁴I will also bring back to this place Jehoiachin[b] son of Jehoia-

---

[a] 1 A few Hebrew manuscripts and Syriac (see also Jer. 27:3, 12 and 28:1); most Hebrew manuscripts *Jehoiakim* (Most Septuagint manuscripts do not have this verse.)   [b] 20,4 Hebrew *Jeconiah*, a variant of *Jehoiachin*

hananiah

VERSUS

jeremiah

» A self-appointed prophet who promised good times
» Confronted by Jeremiah for deceiving the nation
» Died for being a false prophet

» A prophet of God who delivered hard-to-stomach messages
» Wore a yoke on his neck to illustrate the nation's future captivity
» Persevered to the end

The Main Event

Being an Old Testament prophet was a tough gig. God often asked his prophets to do some crazy stuff. For example, he once told Jeremiah to walk around town with a big yoke around his neck—the kind oxen wear when they're plowing. The reason? God wanted to give the Israelites a vivid picture of the political domination that awaited them in Babylon.

Like a good prophet, Jeremiah obeyed. As he acted out this strange prophecy, he warned the people against "feel-good" prophets bearing user-friendly messages. "Don't believe anyone who tells you that we're going to escape judgment," Jeremiah said. "We're not. Anyone who says that is a liar."

The next thing you know, a prophet named Hananiah popped up and directly contradicted the words of Jeremiah. Hananiah's upbeat message and confident assurances were a breath of fresh air to the people of Israel. Even Jeremiah longed for Hananiah's words to come true, but he warned the would-be prophet that his prediction of good times ran against everything Jeremiah and just about every other prophet of God had been saying for years. But when Hananiah grabbed the yoke from Jeremiah's neck and shattered it on the ground for special dramatic effect, he had almost everyone convinced.

Jeremiah walked away from the incident shaking his head. Later, however, he returned with a fresh word from God for Hananiah. He accused him of being a self-appointed, dishonest fake. And then he gave the false prophet this direct quote from the Lord's mouth: "I am about to remove you from the face of the earth. This very year you are going to die."

Two months later, Hananiah was pushing up daisies, leaving no doubt who the real prophet in town was.

The Outcome

Perhaps Hananiah had good intentions. Perhaps he just wanted to make the people feel better. Or maybe his true motives were utterly selfish. Maybe he wanted respect, acclaim and popularity. Whatever the case, he hadn't been called by God, and he sure didn't have a message from God. As a result, he committed the ultimate no-no by claiming to speak for God. He gave the people false hope, and it cost him dearly.

Contrast Hananiah's behavior with Jeremiah's. The authentic, faithful prophet wasn't concerned with being liked or making people feel good. He was concerned only with speaking the truth and living it out. ("You want me to wear *what* on my neck?! OK, God, if you say so . . . You want me to say *that*?! OK, God. The people aren't going to like it, but you're the boss.")

Telling people what they want to hear might pay off in the short term. But in the long run it will always do more damage than good.

Read more about Hananiah and Jeremiah in Jeremiah 28 (pages 1013–1015).

kim king of Judah and all the other exiles from Judah who went to Babylon,' declares the LORD, 'for I will break the yoke of the king of Babylon.' "

⁵Then the prophet Jeremiah replied to the prophet Hananiah before the priests and all the people who were standing in the house of the LORD. ⁶He said, "Amen! May the LORD do so! May the LORD fulfill the words you have prophesied by bringing the articles of the LORD's house and all the exiles back to this place from Babylon. ⁷Nevertheless, listen to what I have to say in your hearing and in the hearing of all the people: ⁸From early times the prophets who preceded you and me have prophesied war, disaster and plague against many countries and great kingdoms. ⁹But the prophet who prophesies peace will be recognized as one truly sent by the LORD only if his prediction comes true."

¹⁰Then the prophet Hananiah took the yoke off the neck of the prophet Jeremiah and broke it, ¹¹and he said before all the people, "This is what the LORD says: 'In the same way will I break the yoke of Nebuchadnezzar king of Babylon off the neck of all the nations within two years.' " At this, the prophet Jeremiah went on his way.

¹²Shortly after the prophet Hananiah had broken the yoke off the neck of the prophet Jeremiah, the word of the LORD came to Jeremiah: ¹³"Go and tell Hananiah, 'This is what the LORD says: You have broken a wooden yoke, but in its place you will get a yoke of iron. ¹⁴This is what the LORD Almighty, the God of Israel, says: I will put an iron yoke on the necks of all these nations to make them serve Nebuchadnezzar king of Babylon, and they will serve him. I will even give him control over the wild animals.' "

¹⁵Then the prophet Jeremiah said to Hananiah the prophet, "Listen, Hananiah! The LORD has not sent you, yet you have persuaded this nation to trust in lies. ¹⁶Therefore, this is what the LORD says: 'I am about to remove you from the face of the earth. This very year you are going to die, because you have preached rebellion against the LORD.' "

¹⁷In the seventh month of that same year, Hananiah the prophet died.

NOW OR NEVER

JER 28:13–14

Let's face it: Certain parts of God's message are unpleasant to hear. No one wants to be told that they're a sinner or that people who reject Jesus go to hell when they die. But God isn't going to sugarcoat his message just to make people happy. Our job is to tell the truth of his Word no matter what.

A LETTER TO THE EXILES

29 This is the text of the letter that the prophet Jeremiah sent from Jerusalem to the surviving elders among the exiles and to the priests, the prophets and all the other people Nebuchadnezzar had carried into exile from Jerusalem to Babylon. ²(This was after King Jehoiachinᵃ and the queen mother, the court officials and the leaders of Judah and Jerusalem, the craftsmen and the artisans had gone into exile from Jerusalem.) ³He entrusted the letter to Elasah son of Shaphan and to Gemariah son of Hilkiah, whom Zedekiah king of Judah sent to King Nebuchadnezzar in Babylon. It said:

⁴This is what the LORD Almighty, the God of Israel, says to all those I carried into exile from Jerusalem to Babylon: ⁵"Build houses and settle down; plant gardens and eat what they produce. ⁶Marry and have sons and daughters; find wives for your sons and give your daughters in marriage, so that they too may have sons and daughters. Increase in number there; do not decrease. ⁷Also, seek the peace and prosperity of the city to which I have carried you into exile. Pray to the LORD for it, because if it prospers, you too will prosper." ⁸Yes, this is what the LORD Almighty, the God of Israel, says: "Do not let the prophets and diviners among you deceive you. Do not listen to the dreams you encourage them to have. ⁹They are prophesying lies to you in my name. I have not sent them," declares the LORD.

¹⁰This is what the LORD says: "When seventy years are completed for Babylon, I will come to you and fulfill my gracious promise to bring you back to this place. ¹¹For I know the plans I have for you," declares the LORD, "plans to prosper you and not to harm you, plans to give you hope and a future. ¹²Then you will call upon me and come and pray to me, and I will listen to you. ¹³You will seek me and find me when you seek me with all your heart. ¹⁴I will be found by

---

ᵃ 2 Hebrew *Jeconiah*, a variant of *Jehoiachin*

battlelines

» Pressure's On (Stress)

Q: How's the big college hunt going?
A: Not so great.

Q: What? I thought you had a lock on OSU. I thought it was a done deal.
A: Yeah, me too. Turns out my test scores were a bit low.

Q: Sorry, dude. So now what?
A: I wish I knew. That's the fourth school that's said, "Not here. Not you. Have a nice life."

Q: Yeah, but be realistic. It's not like you're applying to Homer Simpson Junior College. I mean, these are pretty elite schools. It's tough to get in. Lots of quality people get turned away.
A: At OSU?

Q: Well, it *is* out of state. And they have only so many slots for out-of-state students.
A: Look, I appreciate what you're trying to do—cheer me up and all—but the bottom line is I'm running out of time, and all my big plans are coming unraveled. I have no idea what's ahead, and that's unbelievably stressful, OK? I have certain goals, and if I can't get into the right school, everything I've been working for will go out the window.

» Rest for the Restless

Speaking to the stressed-out Jews who were exiled in Babylon—and wondering what their future held—the prophet Jeremiah conveyed this message from God:

" 'For I know the plans I have for you,' declares the Lord, 'plans to prosper you and not to harm you, plans to give you hope and a future. Then you will call upon me and come and pray to me, and I will listen to you. You will seek me and find me when you seek me with all your heart' " (Jeremiah 29:11–13).

If you read that passage carefully and thoughtfully, what you'll discover is a God who cares, a God who longs to lead you into a place of great promise. Don't despair and don't stress! Trust the Lord.

Discover tools that will help plan your future at www.RevolutionBible.com.

you," declares the LORD, "and will bring you back from captivity.[a] I will gather you from all the nations and places where I have banished you," declares the LORD, "and will bring you back to the place from which I carried you into exile."

» live the adventure » Jer 29:11-14

Understanding God's Plan for You

Do you ever feel like you have a big "X" painted on your back? Like you're a target for people who just want to make your life miserable? The teacher who won't listen to your (very good) reasons for turning in a paper late. The coach who refuses to consider you for anything but a spot on the bench. The punk who goes out of his way to find you between classes just to mock you for leaving last weekend's party when everyone started drinking. No matter how bad things get, don't forget that there is someone who never wants anything but the absolute best for you.

15You may say, "The LORD has raised up prophets for us in Babylon," 16but this is what the LORD says about the king who sits on David's throne and all the people who remain in this city, your countrymen who did not go with you into exile— 17yes, this is what the LORD Almighty says: "I will send the sword, famine and plague against them and I will make them like poor figs that are so bad they cannot be eaten. 18I will pursue them with the sword, famine and plague and will make them abhorrent to all the kingdoms of the earth and an object of cursing and horror, of scorn and reproach, among all the nations where I drive them. 19For they have not listened to my words," declares the LORD, "words that I sent to them again and again by my servants the prophets. And you exiles have not listened either," declares the LORD.

20Therefore, hear the word of the LORD, all you exiles whom I have sent away from Jerusalem to Babylon. 21This is what the LORD Almighty, the God of Israel, says about Ahab son of Kolaiah and Zedekiah son of Maaseiah, who are prophesying lies to you in my name: "I will hand them over to Nebuchadnezzar king of Babylon, and he will put them to death before your very eyes. 22Because of them, all the exiles from Judah who are in Babylon will use this curse: 'The LORD treat you like Zedekiah and Ahab, whom the king of Babylon burned in the fire.' 23For they have done outrageous things in Israel; they have committed adultery with their neighbors' wives and in my name have spoken lies, which I did not tell them to do. I know it and am a witness to it," declares the LORD.

MESSAGE TO SHEMAIAH

24Tell Shemaiah the Nehelamite, 25"This is what the LORD Almighty, the God of Israel, says: You sent letters in your own name to all the people in Jerusalem, to Zephaniah son of Maaseiah the priest, and to all the other priests. You said to Zephaniah, 26'The LORD has appointed you priest in place of Jehoiada to be in charge of the house of the LORD; you should put any madman who acts like a prophet into the stocks and neck-irons. 27So why have you not reprimanded Jeremiah from Anathoth, who poses as a prophet among you? 28He has sent this message to us in Babylon: It will be a long time. Therefore build houses and settle down; plant gardens and eat what they produce.' "

29Zephaniah the priest, however, read the letter to Jeremiah the prophet. 30Then the word of the LORD came to Jeremiah: 31"Send this message to all the exiles: 'This is what the LORD says about Shemaiah the Nehelamite: Because Shemaiah has prophesied to you, even though I did not send him, and has led you to believe a lie, 32this is what the LORD says: I will surely punish Shemaiah the Nehelamite and his descendants. He will have no one left among this people, nor will he see the good things I will do for my people, declares the LORD, because he has preached rebellion against me.' "

RESTORATION OF ISRAEL

30 This is the word that came to Jeremiah from the LORD: 2"This is what the LORD, the God of Israel, says: 'Write in a book all the words I have spoken to you. 3The days are coming,' declares the LORD, 'when I will bring my people Israel and Judah back from captivity[b] and restore them to the land I gave their forefathers to possess,' says the LORD."

[a] 14 Or will restore your fortunes   [b] 3 Or will restore the fortunes of my people Israel and Judah

⁴These are the words the LORD spoke concerning Israel and Judah: ⁵"This is what the LORD says:

" 'Cries of fear are heard—
terror, not peace.
⁶Ask and see:
Can a man bear children?
Then why do I see every strong man
with his hands on his stomach like a woman in labor,
every face turned deathly pale?
⁷How awful that day will be!
None will be like it.
It will be a time of trouble for Jacob,
but he will be saved out of it.

⁸"'In that day,' declares the LORD Almighty,
'I will break the yoke off their necks
and will tear off their bonds;
no longer will foreigners enslave them.
⁹Instead, they will serve the LORD their God
and David their king,
whom I will raise up for them.

NOW OR NEVER

JER 30:10–11

When your friends turn on you . . . when you can't talk to your parents . . . when your whole world seems to collapse around you, God will stay by your side. Lean on him, and he'll help you through your loneliness and pain.

¹⁰"'So do not fear, O Jacob my servant;
do not be dismayed, O Israel,'
declares the LORD.
'I will surely save you out of a distant place,
your descendants from the land of their exile.
Jacob will again have peace and security,
and no one will make him afraid.
¹¹I am with you and will save you,'
declares the LORD.
'Though I completely destroy all the nations
among which I scatter you,
I will not completely destroy you.
I will discipline you but only with justice;
I will not let you go entirely unpunished.'

¹²"This is what the LORD says:

" 'Your wound is incurable,
your injury beyond healing.
¹³There is no one to plead your cause,
no remedy for your sore,
no healing for you.
¹⁴All your allies have forgotten you;
they care nothing for you.
I have struck you as an enemy would
and punished you as would the cruel,
because your guilt is so great
and your sins so many.
¹⁵Why do you cry out over your wound,
your pain that has no cure?
Because of your great guilt and many sins
I have done these things to you.

16 " 'But all who devour you will be devoured;
   all your enemies will go into exile.
Those who plunder you will be plundered;
   all who make spoil of you I will despoil.
17 But I will restore you to health
   and heal your wounds,'

declares the LORD,

'because you are called an outcast,
   Zion for whom no one cares.'

18 "This is what the LORD says:

" 'I will restore the fortunes of Jacob's tents
   and have compassion on his dwellings;
the city will be rebuilt on her ruins,
   and the palace will stand in its proper place.
19 From them will come songs of thanksgiving
   and the sound of rejoicing.
I will add to their numbers,
   and they will not be decreased;
I will bring them honor,
   and they will not be disdained.
20 Their children will be as in days of old,
   and their community will be established before me;
   I will punish all who oppress them.
21 Their leader will be one of their own;
   their ruler will arise from among them.
I will bring him near and he will come close to me,
   for who is he who will devote himself
   to be close to me?'

declares the LORD.

22 " 'So you will be my people,
   and I will be your God.' "

23 See, the storm of the LORD
   will burst out in wrath,
a driving wind swirling down
   on the heads of the wicked.
24 The fierce anger of the LORD will not turn back
   until he fully accomplishes
   the purposes of his heart.
In days to come
   you will understand this.

31

"At that time," declares the LORD, "I will be the God of all the clans of Israel, and they will be my people."
2 This is what the LORD says:

"The people who survive the sword
   will find favor in the desert;
I will come to give rest to Israel."

3 The LORD appeared to us in the past,ª saying:

"I have loved you with an everlasting love;
   I have drawn you with loving-kindness.

ª 3 Or LORD has appeared to us from afar

leah

VERSUS

rachel

» Older daughter of Laban
» Given to Jacob in marriage as a trick
» Mother of Jacob's first four sons

» Younger daughter of Laban—and a real babe (Genesis 29:17)
» The love of Jacob's life
» Mother of Joseph and Benjamin, Jacob's favorite sons

The Main Event

Have you ever watched one of those obscure college football bowl games in mid-December? We're talking about games with names like the Amalgamated Federal Credit Union Holiday Bowl—the kind you find on ESPN at 3:00 in the morning, between podunk colleges like Northeastern Iowa Technical Institute and Brookhaven Junior College at Hazelhurst.

Obviously, they're games only die-hard sports junkies (or school alumni) would watch. Most of us wouldn't even have a clue whom to root for. But sometimes these games end up being just as exciting as the more famous bowl games that feature the big-name schools.

That's kind of like this match-up between Leah and Rachel. Neither one of them is what you'd call a major player in the Bible. Yet their story is just as cool as some of the more famous ones you've heard since you were a kid.

Leah and Rachel were sisters, the daughters of Laban. Leah was the older one; Rachel was the cuter one. When Jacob showed up at their home, he was immediately smitten with the shapely, drop-dead gorgeous Rachel. In fact, Jacob was so head over heels for Rachel that he agreed to work for Laban for seven years just for the right to marry her. Can you imagine that—seven years of hard labor for a girl?

When the time came for the big wedding night, Laban surprised Jacob by switching his daughters at the altar. As a result, Jacob ended up marrying Leah instead of Rachel . . . without knowing it. He didn't find out the truth until the next morning. When Jacob complained to Laban, his father-in-law struck another deal: seven more years of labor for the right to marry Rachel. Jacob agreed and finally got the girl he really wanted.

Before long, Jacob had two wives vying for his affection in a bizarre way. Leah and Rachel competed to see who could give Jacob the most children. When Rachel had trouble getting pregnant, she gave Jacob her servant to sleep with. Not to be outdone, Leah gave Jacob her servant to sleep with. Soon Jacob's house was filled with children from four different women. Even though it was a fairly common practice in that culture, you can imagine the problems this situation caused—jealousy, hurt feelings, bitter rivalry and preferential treatment, just to name a few.

The Outcome

Look up dysfunction in the dictionary, and if you don't see a picture of Jacob's clan . . . well, you should. To be truthful, nobody in this story comes out looking good—except God.

Despite the horrible choices and wrong attitudes of Rachel and Leah (and all the rest), God continued to work out his plan for Jacob's life and held this fractured family together. Jacob's descendants became the 12 tribes of Israel. From one of those tribes came Jesus, the Savior of the world.

On the one hand, you can rejoice that God is so good, so wise and so willing to bring good out of your bad decisions. On the other hand, though, you'd better make a commitment to create fewer messes from which you need God to rescue you!

Read more about Leah and Rachel in Genesis 29–35 (pages 34–44).

⁴"I will build you up again
     and you will be rebuilt, O Virgin Israel.
 Again you will take up your tambourines
     and go out to dance with the joyful.
⁵Again you will plant vineyards
     on the hills of Samaria;
 the farmers will plant them
     and enjoy their fruit.
⁶There will be a day when watchmen cry out
     on the hills of Ephraim,
 'Come, let us go up to Zion,
     to the LORD our God.' "

⁷This is what the LORD says:

"Sing with joy for Jacob;
     shout for the foremost of the nations.
 Make your praises heard, and say,
 'O LORD, save your people,
     the remnant of Israel.'
⁸See, I will bring them from the land of the north
     and gather them from the ends of the earth.
 Among them will be the blind and the lame,
     expectant mothers and women in labor;
     a great throng will return.
⁹They will come with weeping;
     they will pray as I bring them back.
 I will lead them beside streams of water
     on a level path where they will not stumble,
 because I am Israel's father,
     and Ephraim is my firstborn son.

¹⁰"Hear the word of the LORD, O nations;
     proclaim it in distant coastlands:
 'He who scattered Israel will gather them
     and will watch over his flock like a shepherd.'
¹¹For the LORD will ransom Jacob
     and redeem them from the hand of those stronger than they.
¹²They will come and shout for joy on the heights of Zion;
     they will rejoice in the bounty of the LORD—
 the grain, the new wine and the oil,
     the young of the flocks and herds.
 They will be like a well-watered garden,
     and they will sorrow no more.
¹³Then maidens will dance and be glad,
     young men and old as well.
 I will turn their mourning into gladness;
     I will give them comfort and joy instead of sorrow.
¹⁴I will satisfy the priests with abundance,
     and my people will be filled with my bounty,"

declares the LORD.

¹⁵This is what the LORD says:

"A voice is heard in Ramah,
     mourning and great weeping,
 Rachel weeping for her children

and refusing to be comforted,
because her children are no more."

16This is what the LORD says:

"Restrain your voice from weeping
and your eyes from tears,
for your work will be rewarded,"

declares the LORD.

"They will return from the land of the enemy.
17So there is hope for your future,"

declares the LORD.

"Your children will return to their
own land.

18"I have surely heard Ephraim's moaning:
'You disciplined me like an unruly
calf,
and I have been disciplined.
Restore me, and I will return,
because you are the LORD my God.
19After I strayed,
I repented;
after I came to understand,
I beat my breast.
I was ashamed and humiliated
because I bore the disgrace of my
youth.'
20Is not Ephraim my dear son,
the child in whom I delight?
Though I often speak against him,
I still remember him.
Therefore my heart yearns for him;
I have great compassion for him,"
declares the LORD.

21"Set up road signs;
put up guideposts.
Take note of the highway,
the road that you take.
Return, O Virgin Israel,
return to your towns.
22How long will you wander,
O unfaithful daughter?
The LORD will create a new thing on
earth—
a woman will surrounda a man."

Learning to Repent

» » live the adventure » » Jer 31:19

Have you ever *really* disappointed someone? Have you ever done something that made people change their opinion of you—for the worse? Maybe it was getting caught being too physical with your girlfriend, some embarrassing files on your computer hard drive or coming home wasted after a party. If you've ever had an experience like one of these, you know what regret feels like. You know what it's like to want to go back and erase what you did so that people aren't disappointed in you. That's what genuine repentance is like. It's the desire to get rid of your sin and start over so that God will look at you with pride again.

23This is what the LORD Almighty, the God of Israel, says: "When I bring them back from captivity,b the people in the land of Judah and in its towns will once again use these words: 'The LORD bless you, O righteous dwelling, O sacred mountain.' 24People will live together in Judah and all its towns—farmers and those who move about with their flocks. 25I will refresh the weary and satisfy the faint."

26At this I awoke and looked around. My sleep had been pleasant to me.

27"The days are coming," declares the LORD, "when I will plant the house of Israel and the house of Judah with the offspring of men and of animals. 28Just as I watched over them to uproot and tear down,

---

a 22 Or will go about ˌseekingˌ; or will protect   b 23 Or I restore their fortunes and to overthrow, destroy and bring disaster, so I will watch over them to build and to plant," declares the LORD. ²⁹"In those days people will no longer say,

> 'The fathers have eaten sour grapes,
>   and the children's teeth are set on edge.'

³⁰Instead, everyone will die for his own sin; whoever eats sour grapes—his own teeth will be set on edge.

> ³¹"The time is coming," declares the LORD,
>   "when I will make a new covenant
> with the house of Israel
>   and with the house of Judah.
> ³²It will not be like the covenant
>   I made with their forefathers
> when I took them by the hand
>   to lead them out of Egypt,
> because they broke my covenant,
>   though I was a husband to ᵃ them, ᵇ"
>
> declares the LORD.

> ³³"This is the covenant I will make with the house of Israel
>   after that time," declares the LORD.
> "I will put my law in their minds
>   and write it on their hearts.
> I will be their God,
>   and they will be my people.
> ³⁴No longer will a man teach his neighbor,
>   or a man his brother, saying, 'Know the LORD,'
> because they will all know me,
>   from the least of them to the greatest,"
>
> declares the LORD.
>
> "For I will forgive their wickedness
>   and will remember their sins no more."

³⁵This is what the LORD says,

> he who appoints the sun
>   to shine by day,
> who decrees the moon and stars
>   to shine by night,
> who stirs up the sea
>   so that its waves roar—
>   the LORD Almighty is his name:
> ³⁶"Only if these decrees vanish from my sight,"
>   declares the LORD,
> "will the descendants of Israel ever cease
>   to be a nation before me."

³⁷This is what the LORD says:

> "Only if the heavens above can be measured
>   and the foundations of the earth below be searched out
> will I reject all the descendants of Israel
>   because of all they have done,"
>
> declares the LORD.

³⁸"The days are coming," declares the LORD, "when this city will be rebuilt for me from the Tower of Hananel to the Corner Gate. ³⁹The measuring line will stretch from there straight to the hill of Gareb and

---

ᵃ *32* Hebrew; Septuagint and Syriac / *and I turned away from*   ᵇ *32* Or *was their master* then turn to Goah. ⁴⁰The whole valley where dead bodies and ashes are thrown, and all the terraces out to the Kidron Valley on the east as far as the corner of the Horse Gate, will be holy to the LORD. The city will never again be uprooted or demolished."

JEREMIAH BUYS A FIELD

32 This is the word that came to Jeremiah from the LORD in the tenth year of Zedekiah king of Judah, which was the eighteenth year of Nebuchadnezzar. ²The army of the king of Babylon was then besieging Jerusalem, and Jeremiah the prophet was confined in the court-yard of the guard in the royal palace of Judah.

³Now Zedekiah king of Judah had imprisoned him there, saying, "Why do you prophesy as you do? You say, 'This is what the LORD says: I am about to hand this city over to the king of Babylon, and he will capture it. ⁴Zedekiah king of Judah will not escape out of the hands of the Babylonians^a but will certainly be handed over to the king of Babylon, and will speak with him face to face and see him with his own eyes. ⁵He will take Zedekiah to Babylon, where he will remain until I deal with him, declares the LORD. If you fight against the Babylonians, you will not succeed.' "

⁶Jeremiah said, "The word of the LORD came to me: ⁷Hanamel son of Shallum your uncle is going to come to you and say, 'Buy my field at Anathoth, because as nearest relative it is your right and duty to buy it.'

⁸"Then, just as the LORD had said, my cousin Hanamel came to me in the courtyard of the guard and said, 'Buy my field at Anathoth in the territory of Benjamin. Since it is your right to redeem it and possess it, buy it for yourself.'

"I knew that this was the word of the LORD; ⁹so I bought the field at Anathoth from my cousin Hanamel and weighed out for him seventeen shekels^b of silver. ¹⁰I signed and sealed the deed, had it witnessed, and weighed out the silver on the scales. ¹¹I took the deed of purchase—the sealed copy containing the terms and conditions, as well as the unsealed copy— ¹²and I gave this deed to Baruch son of Neriah, the son of Mahseiah, in the presence of my cousin Hanamel and of the witnesses who had signed the deed and of all the Jews sitting in the courtyard of the guard.

¹³"In their presence I gave Baruch these instructions: ¹⁴'This is what the LORD Almighty, the God of Israel, says: Take these documents, both the sealed and unsealed copies of the deed of purchase, and put them in a clay jar so they will last a long time. ¹⁵For this is what the LORD Almighty, the God of Israel, says: Houses, fields and vineyards will again be bought in this land.'

¹⁶"After I had given the deed of purchase to Baruch son of Neriah, I prayed to the LORD:

¹⁷"Ah, Sovereign LORD, you have made the heavens and the earth by your great power and out-stretched arm. Nothing is too hard for you. ¹⁸You show love to thousands but bring the punishment for the fathers' sins into the laps of their children after them. O great and powerful God, whose name is the LORD Almighty, ¹⁹great are your purposes and mighty are your deeds. Your eyes are open to all the ways of men; you reward everyone according to his conduct and as his deeds deserve. ²⁰You performed miraculous signs and wonders in Egypt and have continued them to this day, both in Israel and among all mankind, and have gained the renown that is still yours. ²¹You brought your people Israel out of Egypt with signs and wonders, by a mighty hand and an outstretched arm and with great terror. ²²You gave them this land you had sworn to give

---

Trusting in God's Strength

There are certain questions that even the best teachers can't answer. There are certain problems that even the best counselors can't help you with. There are certain situations that even the best bodyguards can't protect you from. But nothing is beyond God's ability. He created the entire universe from nothing, and he can supply you with anything you need, whether it's the courage to admit to your parents that you screwed up . . . the wisdom and sensitivity to end a dating relationship that you know isn't right . . . or the discipline to avoid a potentially compromising situation at a party.

---

^a 4 Or Chaldeans; also in verses 5, 24, 25, 28, 29 and 43   ^b 9 That is, about 7 ounces (about 200 grams)

their forefathers, a land flowing with milk and honey. ²³They came in and took possession of it, but they did not obey you or follow your law; they did not do what you commanded them to do. So you brought all this disaster upon them.

²⁴"See how the siege ramps are built up to take the city. Because of the sword, famine and plague, the city will be handed over to the Babylonians who are attacking it. What you said has happened, as you now see. ²⁵And though the city will be handed over to the Babylonians, you, O Sovereign LORD, say to me, 'Buy the field with silver and have the transaction witnessed.'"

²⁶Then the word of the LORD came to Jeremiah: ²⁷"I am the LORD, the God of all mankind. Is anything too hard for me? ²⁸Therefore, this is what the LORD says: I am about to hand this city over to the Babylonians and to Nebuchadnezzar king of Babylon, who will capture it. ²⁹The Babylonians who are attacking this city will come in and set it on fire; they will burn it down, along with the houses where the people provoked me to anger by burning incense on the roofs to Baal and by pouring out drink offerings to other gods.

³⁰"The people of Israel and Judah have done nothing but evil in my sight from their youth; indeed, the people of Israel have done nothing but provoke me with what their hands have made, declares the LORD. ³¹From the day it was built until now, this city has so aroused my anger and wrath that I must remove it from my sight. ³²The people of Israel and Judah have provoked me by all the evil they have done—they, their kings and officials, their priests and prophets, the men of Judah and the people of Jerusalem. ³³They turned their backs to me and not their faces; though I taught them again and again, they would not listen or respond to discipline. ³⁴They set up their abominable idols in the house that bears my Name and defiled it. ³⁵They built high places for Baal in the Valley of Ben Hinnom to sacrifice their sons and daughters ᵃ to Molech, though I never commanded, nor did it enter my mind, that they should do such a detestable thing and so make Judah sin.

³⁶"You are saying about this city, 'By the sword, famine and plague it will be handed over to the king of Babylon'; but this is what the LORD, the God of Israel, says: ³⁷I will surely gather them from all the lands where I banish them in my furious anger and great wrath; I will bring them back to this place and let them live in safety. ³⁸They will be my people, and I will be their God. ³⁹I will give them singleness of heart and action, so that they will always fear me for their own good and the good of their children after them. ⁴⁰I will make an everlasting covenant with them: I will never stop doing good to them, and I will inspire them to fear me, so that they will never turn away from me. ⁴¹I will rejoice in doing them good and will assuredly plant them in this land with all my heart and soul.

⁴²"This is what the LORD says: As I have brought all this great calamity on this people, so I will give them all the prosperity I have promised them. ⁴³Once more fields will be bought in this land of which you say, 'It is a desolate waste, without men or animals, for it has been handed over to the Babylonians.' ⁴⁴Fields will be bought for silver, and deeds will be signed, sealed and witnessed in the territory of Benjamin, in the villages around Jerusalem, in the towns of Judah and in the towns of the hill country, of the western foothills and of the Negev, because I will restore their fortunes, ᵇ declares the LORD."

challenge notes

To: my_son

JER 33:3

heavenly_father: when you call to me, I will not abandon you. notice how I have answered the call of the many faithful believers who lived before you. all things are at my disposal—wisdom, power, comfort—whatever you need. all you have to do is call my name.

PROMISE OF RESTORATION

33 While Jeremiah was still confined in the courtyard of the guard, the word of the LORD came to him a second time: ²"This is what the LORD says, he who made the earth, the LORD who formed it and established it—the LORD is his name: ³'Call to me and I will answer you and tell you great and unsearchable things you do not know.' ⁴For this is what the LORD, the God of Israel, says about the houses in this city and the royal palaces of Judah that have been torn down to be used against the siege ramps and the sword ⁵in the fight with the Babyloniansᶜ: 'They will be filled

---

ᵃ 35 Or *to make their sons and daughters pass through the fire.*   ᵇ 44 Or *will bring them back from captivity*   ᶜ 5 Or *Chaldeans* with the dead bodies of the men I will slay in my anger and wrath. I will hide my face from this city because of all its wickedness.

6 " 'Nevertheless, I will bring health and healing to it; I will heal my people and will let them enjoy abundant peace and security. 7I will bring Judah and Israel back from captivity[a] and will rebuild them as they were before. 8I will cleanse them from all the sin they have committed against me and will forgive all their sins of rebellion against me. 9Then this city will bring me renown, joy, praise and honor before all nations on earth that hear of all the good things I do for it; and they will be in awe and will tremble at the abundant prosperity and peace I provide for it.'

10"This is what the LORD says: 'You say about this place, "It is a desolate waste, without men or animals." Yet in the towns of Judah and the streets of Jerusalem that are deserted, inhabited by neither men nor animals, there will be heard once more 11the sounds of joy and gladness, the voices of bride and bridegroom, and the voices of those who bring thank offerings to the house of the LORD, saying,

"Give thanks to the LORD Almighty,
    for the LORD is good;
    his love endures forever."

For I will restore the fortunes of the land as they were before,' says the LORD.

12"This is what the LORD Almighty says: 'In this place, desolate and without men or animals—in all its towns there will again be pastures for shepherds to rest their flocks. 13In the towns of the hill country, of the western foothills and of the Negev, in the territory of Benjamin, in the villages around Jerusalem and in the towns of Judah, flocks will again pass under the hand of the one who counts them,' says the LORD.

14" 'The days are coming,' declares the LORD, 'when I will fulfill the gracious promise I made to the house of Israel and to the house of Judah.

15" 'In those days and at that time
    I will make a righteous Branch sprout from David's line;
    he will do what is just and right in the land.
16In those days Judah will be saved
    and Jerusalem will live in safety.
This is the name by which it[b] will be called:
    The LORD Our Righteousness.'

17For this is what the LORD says: 'David will never fail to have a man to sit on the throne of the house of Israel, 18nor will the priests, who are Levites, ever fail to have a man to stand before me continually to offer burnt offerings, to burn grain offerings and to present sacrifices.' "

19The word of the LORD came to Jeremiah: 20"This is what the LORD says: 'If you can break my covenant with the day and my covenant with the night, so that day and night no longer come at their appointed time, 21then my covenant with David my servant—and my covenant with the Levites who are priests ministering before me—can be broken and David will no longer have a descendant to reign on his throne. 22I will make the descendants of David my servant and the Levites who minister before me as countless as the stars of the sky and as measureless as the sand on the seashore.' "

23The word of the LORD came to Jeremiah: 24"Have you not noticed that these people are saying, 'The LORD has rejected the two kingdoms[c] he chose'? So they despise my people and no longer regard them as a nation. 25This is what the LORD says: 'If I have not established my covenant with day and night and the fixed laws of heaven and earth, 26then I will reject the descendants of Jacob and David my servant and will not choose one of his sons to rule over the descendants of Abraham, Isaac and Jacob. For I will restore their fortunes[d] and have compassion on them.' "

WARNING TO ZEDEKIAH

34 While Nebuchadnezzar king of Babylon and all his army and all the kingdoms and peoples in the empire he ruled were fighting against Jerusalem and all its surrounding towns, this word came to Jeremiah from the LORD: 2"This is what the LORD, the God of Israel, says: Go to Zedekiah king of Judah and tell him, 'This is what the LORD says: I am about to hand this city over to the king of Babylon, and he will burn it down. 3You will not escape from his grasp but will

---

a 7 Or will restore the fortunes of Judah and Israel   b 16 Or he   c 24 Or families   d 26 Or will bring them back from captivity surely be captured and handed over to him. You will see the king of Babylon with your own eyes, and he will speak with you face to face. And you will go to Babylon.

⁴" 'Yet hear the promise of the LORD, O Zedekiah king of Judah. This is what the LORD says concerning you: You will not die by the sword; ⁵you will die peacefully. As people made a funeral fire in honor of your fathers, the former kings who preceded you, so they will make a fire in your honor and lament, "Alas, O master!" I myself make this promise, declares the LORD.' "

⁶Then Jeremiah the prophet told all this to Zedekiah king of Judah, in Jerusalem, ⁷while the army of the king of Babylon was fighting against Jerusalem and the other cities of Judah that were still holding out—Lachish and Azekah. These were the only fortified cities left in Judah.

NOW OR NEVER

JER 34:1–5

Have you ever blown it so badly that you knew there was nothing you could do to fix things? When you face the consequences, accept them honorably. But ask God to forgive you and to restore your relationship with him. The backlash from sin stings, but God's forgiveness heals every time.

FREEDOM FOR SLAVES

⁸The word came to Jeremiah from the LORD after King Zedekiah had made a covenant with all the people in Jerusalem to proclaim freedom for the slaves. ⁹Everyone was to free his Hebrew slaves, both male and female; no one was to hold a fellow Jew in bondage. ¹⁰So all the officials and people who entered into this covenant agreed that they would free their male and female slaves and no longer hold them in bondage. They agreed, and set them free. ¹¹But afterward they changed their minds and took back the slaves they had freed and enslaved them again.

¹²Then the word of the LORD came to Jeremiah: ¹³"This is what the LORD, the God of Israel, says: I made a covenant with your forefathers when I brought them out of Egypt, out of the land of slavery. I said, ¹⁴'Every seventh year each of you must free any fellow Hebrew who has sold himself to you. After he has served you six years, you must let him go free.'ᵃ Your fathers, however, did not listen to me or pay attention to me. ¹⁵Recently you repented and did what is right in my sight: Each of you proclaimed freedom to his countrymen. You even made a covenant before me in the house that bears my Name. ¹⁶But now you have turned around and profaned my name; each of you has taken back the male and female slaves you had set free to go where they wished. You have forced them to become your slaves again.

¹⁷"Therefore, this is what the LORD says: You have not obeyed me; you have not proclaimed freedom for your fellow countrymen. So I now proclaim 'freedom' for you, declares the LORD—'freedom' to fall by the sword, plague and famine. I will make you abhorrent to all the kingdoms of the earth. ¹⁸The men who have violated my covenant and have not fulfilled the terms of the covenant they made before me, I will treat like the calf they cut in two and then walked between its pieces. ¹⁹The leaders of Judah and Jerusalem, the court officials, the priests and all the people of the land who walked between the pieces of the calf, ²⁰I will hand over to their enemies who seek their lives. Their dead bodies will become food for the birds of the air and the beasts of the earth.

²¹"I will hand Zedekiah king of Judah and his officials over to their enemies who seek their lives, to the army of the king of Babylon, which has withdrawn from you. ²²I am going to give the order, declares the LORD, and I will bring them back to this city. They will fight against it, take it and burn it down. And I will lay waste the towns of Judah so no one can live there."

THE RECABITES

35 This is the word that came to Jeremiah from the LORD during the reign of Jehoiakim son of Josiah king of Judah: ²"Go to the Recabite family and invite them to come to one of the side rooms of the house of the LORD and give them wine to drink."

³So I went to get Jaazaniah son of Jeremiah, the son of Habazziniah, and his brothers and all his sons—the whole family of the Recabites. ⁴I brought them into the house of the LORD, into the room of the sons of Hanan son of Igdaliah the man of God. It was next to the room of the officials, which was

ᵃ *14* Deut. 15:12

over that of Maaseiah son of Shallum the doorkeeper. 5Then I set bowls full of wine and some cups before the men of the Recabite family and said to them, "Drink some wine."

6But they replied, "We do not drink wine, because our forefather Jonadab son of Recab gave us this command: 'Neither you nor your descendants must ever drink wine. 7Also you must never build houses, sow seed or plant vineyards; you must never have any of these things, but must always live in tents. Then you will live a long time in the land where you are nomads.' 8We have obeyed everything our forefather Jonadab son of Recab commanded us. Neither we nor our wives nor our sons and daughters have ever drunk wine 9or built houses to live in or had vineyards, fields or crops. 10We have lived in tents and have fully obeyed everything our forefather Jonadab commanded us. 11But when Nebuchadnezzar king of Babylon invaded this land, we said, 'Come, we must go to Jerusalem to escape the Babylonian[a] and Aramean armies.' So we have remained in Jerusalem."

12Then the word of the LORD came to Jeremiah, saying: 13"This is what the LORD Almighty, the God of Israel, says: Go and tell the men of Judah and the people of Jerusalem, 'Will you not learn a lesson and obey my words?' declares the LORD. 14'Jonadab son of Recab ordered his sons not to drink wine and this command has been kept. To this day they do not drink wine, because they obey their forefather's command. But I have spoken to you again and again, yet you have not obeyed me. 15Again and again I sent all my servants the prophets to you. They said, "Each of you must turn from your wicked ways and reform your actions; do not follow other gods to serve them. Then you will live in the land I have given to you and your fathers." But you have not paid attention or listened to me. 16The descendants of Jonadab son of Recab have carried out the command their forefather gave them, but these people have not obeyed me.'

now or never

JER 35:12–16

Picture a man you admire—maybe it's a coach, a close mentor or your dad. If he asked you to commit to running five miles a day or to watching your younger siblings, you'd want to do it, right? What about pleasing God? Would any amount of effort spent trying to please him be too much?

17"Therefore, this is what the LORD God Almighty, the God of Israel, says: 'Listen! I am going to bring on Judah and on everyone living in Jerusalem every disaster I pronounced against them. I spoke to them, but they did not listen; I called to them, but they did not answer.' "

18Then Jeremiah said to the family of the Recabites, "This is what the LORD Almighty, the God of Israel, says: 'You have obeyed the command of your forefather Jonadab and have followed all his instructions and have done everything he ordered.' 19Therefore, this is what the LORD Almighty, the God of Israel, says: 'Jonadab son of Recab will never fail to have a man to serve me.' "

JEHOIAKIM BURNS JEREMIAH'S SCROLL

36 In the fourth year of Jehoiakim son of Josiah king of Judah, this word came to Jeremiah from the LORD: 2"Take a scroll and write on it all the words I have spoken to you concerning Israel, Judah and all the other nations from the time I began speaking to you in the reign of Josiah till now. 3Perhaps when the people of Judah hear about every disaster I plan to inflict on them, each of them will turn from his wicked way; then I will forgive their wickedness and their sin."

4So Jeremiah called Baruch son of Neriah, and while Jeremiah dictated all the words the LORD had spoken to him, Baruch wrote them on the scroll. 5Then Jeremiah told Baruch, "I am restricted; I cannot go to the LORD's temple. 6So you go to the house of the LORD on a day of fasting and read to the people from the scroll the words of the LORD that you wrote as I dictated. Read them to all the people of Judah who come in from their towns. 7Perhaps they will bring their petition before the LORD, and each will turn from his wicked ways, for the anger and wrath pronounced against this people by the LORD are great."

8Baruch son of Neriah did everything Jeremiah the prophet told him to do; at the LORD's temple he read the words of the LORD from the scroll. 9In the ninth month of the fifth year of Jehoiakim son of Josiah king of Judah, a time of fasting before the LORD was proclaimed for all the people in Jerusalem and those who had come from the towns of Judah. 10From the room of Gemariah son of Shaphan the sec-

[a] 11 Or *Chaldean*

battlelines

» Who Am I? (Popularity)

What are you laughing at?

Q: I'm sorry, but those clothes—they're just not "you."
A: Hey, I'm busting out, trying something new. What's wrong with that?

Q: Nothing. It's just so out of character, don't you think? You just usually dress . . .
A: What, boring?

Q: No. Just jeans. Basic stuff. I mean, you don't usually call attention to yourself with clothes like that.
A: Yeah, well, I'm just looking for my own style.

Q: Your *own* style? Come on! Your style looks an awful lot like the style of the guys you've been hanging out with lately.
A: Maybe this happens to be my style too.

Q: OK, if you say so.

A: Look, I hear what you're saying. It's definitely a change. But this is how all my friends dress. I'm just trying not to stick out like a sore thumb. I'll get used to it.

Q: Keyshawn, you used to tell me you would never let people tell you what to do.
A: I won't.

Q: But here you are, letting your friends tell you how to dress. They've got you wearing stuff you don't even like.
A: Lighten up! They're just clothes, all right? At the end of the day, does it really matter what I wear or what anybody else wears?

Q: That's my point! It doesn't matter. At least it shouldn't. The question is, can you be yourself around your friends, or will they only accept you if you dress and talk like they do? Who is the real Keyshawn?
A: The "real Keyshawn"? Most days I don't have a clue.

» I Am Who I Am

One of the saddest things in the world is the guy who is so clueless about who he is, so desperate for approval that he becomes a chameleon. Depending on the situation, he switches vocabulary, attitudes or even behavior in a frantic attempt to fit in and find acceptance. Or, like Keyshawn, he goes out and blows his money on clothes he normally wouldn't wear.

Christian guys are called to a gutsier way of living . . . and to have a different kind of wardrobe: "Therefore, as God's chosen people, holy and dearly loved, clothe yourselves with compassion, kindness, humility, gentleness and patience. Bear with each other and forgive whatever grievances you may have against one another. Forgive as the Lord forgave you" (Colossians 3:12–13).

Notice that before we find the freedom and courage to focus on others, we first must understand how deeply we are loved by God. Once we're secure in his acceptance, we can finally be the people he created us to be. And we no longer have to play roles that others expect us to play.

Read more about popularity at www.RevolutionBible.com.

retary, which was in the upper courtyard at the entrance of the New Gate of the temple, Baruch read to all the people at the LORD's temple the words of Jeremiah from the scroll.

11When Micaiah son of Gemariah, the son of Shaphan, heard all the words of the LORD from the scroll, 12he went down to the secretary's room in the royal palace, where all the officials were sitting: Elishama the secretary, Delaiah son of Shemaiah, Elnathan son of Acbor, Gemariah son of Shaphan, Zedekiah son of Hananiah, and all the other officials. 13After Micaiah told them everything he had heard Baruch read to the people from the scroll, 14all the officials sent Jehudi son of Nethaniah, the son of Shelemiah, the son of Cushi, to say to Baruch, "Bring the scroll from which you have read to the people and come." So Baruch son of Neriah went to them with the scroll in his hand. 15They said to him, "Sit down, please, and read it to us."

now or never

JER 36:4-32

If you find one faithful friend in your life, consider yourself blessed . . . and do everything you can to keep the friendship growing. A true friend is more valuable than a house, a car or anything else you could own. Material possessions will come and go, but a real friend will stand by you.

So Baruch read it to them. 16When they heard all these words, they looked at each other in fear and said to Baruch, "We must report all these words to the king." 17Then they asked Baruch, "Tell us, how did you come to write all this? Did Jeremiah dictate it?"

18"Yes," Baruch replied, "he dictated all these words to me, and I wrote them in ink on the scroll."

19Then the officials said to Baruch, "You and Jeremiah, go and hide. Don't let anyone know where you are."

20After they put the scroll in the room of Elishama the secretary, they went to the king in the courtyard and reported everything to him. 21The king sent Jehudi to get the scroll, and Jehudi brought it from the room of Elishama the secretary and read it to the king and all the officials standing beside him. 22It was the ninth month and the king was sitting in the winter apartment, with a fire burning in the firepot in front of him. 23Whenever Jehudi had read three or four columns of the scroll, the king cut them off with a scribe's knife and threw them into the firepot, until the entire scroll was burned in the fire. 24The king and all his attendants who heard all these words showed no fear, nor did they tear their clothes. 25Even though Elnathan, Delaiah and Gemariah urged the king not to burn the scroll, he would not listen to them. 26Instead, the king commanded Jerahmeel, a son of the king, Seraiah son of Azriel and Shelemiah son of Abdeel to arrest Baruch the scribe and Jeremiah the prophet. But the LORD had hidden them.

27After the king burned the scroll containing the words that Baruch had written at Jeremiah's dictation, the word of the LORD came to Jeremiah: 28"Take another scroll and write on it all the words that were on the first scroll, which Jehoiakim king of Judah burned up. 29Also tell Jehoiakim king of Judah, 'This is what the LORD says: You burned that scroll and said, "Why did you write on it that the king of Babylon would certainly come and destroy this land and cut off both men and animals from it?" 30Therefore, this is what the LORD says about Jehoiakim king of Judah: He will have no one to sit on the throne of David; his body will be thrown out and exposed to the heat by day and the frost by night. 31I will punish him and his children and his attendants for their wickedness; I will bring on them and those living in Jerusalem and the people of Judah every disaster I pronounced against them, because they have not listened.' "

32So Jeremiah took another scroll and gave it to the scribe Baruch son of Neriah, and as Jeremiah dictated, Baruch wrote on it all the words of the scroll that Jehoiakim king of Judah had burned in the fire. And many similar words were added to them.

JEREMIAH IN PRISON

37

Zedekiah son of Josiah was made king of Judah by Nebuchadnezzar king of Babylon; he reigned in place of Jehoiachin[a] son of Jehoiakim. 2Neither he nor his attendants nor the people of the land paid any attention to the words the LORD had spoken through Jeremiah the prophet.

3King Zedekiah, however, sent Jehucal son of Shelemiah with the priest Zephaniah son of Maase-

[a] 1 Hebrew Coniah, a variant of Jehoiachin

iah to Jeremiah the prophet with this message: "Please pray to the Lord our God for us."

4Now Jeremiah was free to come and go among the people, for he had not yet been put in prison. 5Pharaoh's army had marched out of Egypt, and when the Babylonians[a] who were besieging Jerusalem heard the report about them, they withdrew from Jerusalem.

6Then the word of the Lord came to Jeremiah the prophet: 7"This is what the Lord, the God of Israel, says: Tell the king of Judah, who sent you to inquire of me, 'Pharaoh's army, which has marched out to support you, will go back to its own land, to Egypt. 8Then the Babylonians will return and attack this city; they will capture it and burn it down.'

9"This is what the Lord says: Do not deceive yourselves, thinking, 'The Babylonians will surely leave us.' They will not! 10Even if you were to defeat the entire Babylonian[b] army that is attacking you and only wounded men were left in their tents, they would come out and burn this city down."

11After the Babylonian army had withdrawn from Jerusalem because of Pharaoh's army, 12Jeremiah started to leave the city to go to the territory of Benjamin to get his share of the property among the people there. 13But when he reached the Benjamin Gate, the captain of the guard, whose name was Irijah son of Shelemiah, the son of Hananiah, arrested him and said, "You are deserting to the Babylonians!"

14"That's not true!" Jeremiah said. "I am not deserting to the Babylonians." But Irijah would not listen to him; instead, he arrested Jeremiah and brought him to the officials. 15They were angry with Jeremiah and had him beaten and imprisoned in the house of Jonathan the secretary, which they had made into a prison.

16Jeremiah was put into a vaulted cell in a dungeon, where he remained a long time. 17Then King Zedekiah sent for him and had him brought to the palace, where he asked him privately, "Is there any word from the Lord?"

"Yes," Jeremiah replied, "you will be handed over to the king of Babylon."

18Then Jeremiah said to King Zedekiah, "What crime have I committed against you or your officials or this people, that you have put me in prison? 19Where are your prophets who prophesied to you, 'The king of Babylon will not attack you or this land'? 20But now, my lord the king, please listen. Let me bring my petition before you: Do not send me back to the house of Jonathan the secretary, or I will die there."

21King Zedekiah then gave orders for Jeremiah to be placed in the courtyard of the guard and given bread from the street of the bakers each day until all the bread in the city was gone. So Jeremiah remained in the courtyard of the guard.

NOW OR NEVER

JER 37:11–17

Jeremiah didn't deserve imprisonment, but no one listened to him. You'd think that after a while, he might start blaming God for his problems. But he didn't. He kept delivering the messages God told him to deliver and trusted God to take care of him. And, of course, God did—just as he will take care of you when your situation looks bleak.

JEREMIAH THROWN INTO A CISTERN

38 Shephatiah son of Mattan, Gedaliah son of Pashhur, Jehucal[c] son of Shelemiah, and Pashhur son of Malkijah heard what Jeremiah was telling all the people when he said, 2"This is what the Lord says: 'Whoever stays in this city will die by the sword, famine or plague, but whoever goes over to the Babylonians[d] will live. He will escape with his life; he will live.' 3And this is what the Lord says: 'This city will certainly be handed over to the army of the king of Babylon, who will capture it.' "

4Then the officials said to the king, "This man should be put to death. He is discouraging the soldiers who are left in this city, as well as all the people, by the things he is saying to them. This man is not seeking the good of these people but their ruin."

5"He is in your hands," King Zedekiah answered. "The king can do nothing to oppose you."

6So they took Jeremiah and put him into the cistern of Malkijah, the king's son, which was in the courtyard of the guard. They lowered Jeremiah by ropes into the cistern; it had no water in it, only mud, and Jeremiah sank down into the mud.

7But Ebed-Melech, a Cushite,[a] an official[b] in the royal palace, heard that they had put Jeremiah into

---

[a] 5 Or *Chaldeans*; also in verses 8, 9, 13 and 14   [b] 10 Or *Chaldean*; also in verse 11   [c] 1 Hebrew *Jucal*, a variant of *Jehucal*
[d] 2 Or *Chaldeans*; also in verses 18, 19 and 23

the cistern. While the king was sitting in the Benjamin Gate, [8]Ebed-Melech went out of the palace and said to him, [9]"My lord the king, these men have acted wickedly in all they have done to Jeremiah the prophet. They have thrown him into a cistern, where he will starve to death when there is no longer any bread in the city."

[10]Then the king commanded Ebed-Melech the Cushite, "Take thirty men from here with you and lift Jeremiah the prophet out of the cistern before he dies."

[11]So Ebed-Melech took the men with him and went to a room under the treasury in the palace. He took some old rags and worn-out clothes from there and let them down with ropes to Jeremiah in the cistern. [12]Ebed-Melech the Cushite said to Jeremiah, "Put these old rags and worn-out clothes under your arms to pad the ropes." Jeremiah did so, [13]and they pulled him up with the ropes and lifted him out of the cistern. And Jeremiah remained in the courtyard of the guard.

ZEDEKIAH QUESTIONS JEREMIAH AGAIN

[14]Then King Zedekiah sent for Jeremiah the prophet and had him brought to the third entrance to the temple of the LORD. "I am going to ask you something," the king said to Jeremiah. "Do not hide anything from me."

[15]Jeremiah said to Zedekiah, "If I give you an answer, will you not kill me? Even if I did give you counsel, you would not listen to me."

[16]But King Zedekiah swore this oath secretly to Jeremiah: "As surely as the LORD lives, who has given us breath, I will neither kill you nor hand you over to those who are seeking your life."

[17]Then Jeremiah said to Zedekiah, "This is what the LORD God Almighty, the God of Israel, says: 'If you surrender to the officers of the king of Babylon, your life will be spared and this city will not be burned down; you and your family will live. [18]But if you will not surrender to the officers of the king of Babylon, this city will be handed over to the Babylonians and they will burn it down; you yourself will not escape from their hands.'"

[19]King Zedekiah said to Jeremiah, "I am afraid of the Jews who have gone over to the Babylonians, for the Babylonians may hand me over to them and they will mistreat me."

[20]"They will not hand you over," Jeremiah replied. "Obey the LORD by doing what I tell you. Then it will go well with you, and your life will be spared. [21]But if you refuse to surrender, this is what the LORD has revealed to me: [22]All the women left in the palace of the king of Judah will be brought out to the officials of the king of Babylon. Those women will say to you:

> " 'They misled you and overcame you—
>   those trusted friends of yours.
> Your feet are sunk in the mud;
>   your friends have deserted you.'

[23]"All your wives and children will be brought out to the Babylonians. You yourself will not escape from their hands but will be captured by the king of Babylon; and this city will[c] be burned down."

[24]Then Zedekiah said to Jeremiah, "Do not let anyone know about this conversation, or you may die. [25]If the officials hear that I talked with you, and they come to you and say, 'Tell us what you said to the king and what the king said to you; do not hide it from us or we will kill you,' [26]then tell them, 'I was pleading with the king not to send me back to Jonathan's house to die there.'"

Taking Risks for Others

Ebed-Melech risked his own life to save Jeremiah. In the process, he made himself a target for the people who were making Jeremiah's life miserable. If you have the guts to stand up for those who are being pushed around or laughed at, you may become a target too. But if doing the right thing never involved risk, why would God look for courageous, obedient servants? The Lord protected and blessed Ebed-Melech, and he will protect and bless you.

---

[a] 7 Probably from the upper Nile region   [b] 7 Or a eunuch   [c] 23 Or and you will cause this city to

²⁷All the officials did come to Jeremiah and question him, and he told them everything the king had ordered him to say. So they said no more to him, for no one had heard his conversation with the king. ²⁸And Jeremiah remained in the courtyard of the guard until the day Jerusalem was captured.

THE FALL OF JERUSALEM

39 This is how Jerusalem was taken: ¹In the ninth year of Zedekiah king of Judah, in the tenth month, Nebuchadnezzar king of Babylon marched against Jerusalem with his whole army and laid siege to it. ²And on the ninth day of the fourth month of Zedekiah's eleventh year, the city wall was broken through. ³Then all the officials of the king of Babylon came and took seats in the Middle Gate: Nergal-Sharezer of Samgar, Nebo-Sarsekim ᵃ a chief officer, Nergal-Sharezer a high official and all the other officials of the king of Babylon. ⁴When Zedekiah king of Judah and all the soldiers saw them, they fled; they left the city at night by way of the king's garden, through the gate between the two walls, and headed toward the Arabah. ᵇ

⁵But the Babylonian ᶜ army pursued them and overtook Zedekiah in the plains of Jericho. They captured him and took him to Nebuchadnezzar king of Babylon at Riblah in the land of Hamath, where he pronounced sentence on him. ⁶There at Riblah the king of Babylon slaughtered the sons of Zedekiah before his eyes and also killed all the nobles of Judah. ⁷Then he put out Zedekiah's eyes and bound him with bronze shackles to take him to Babylon.

⁸The Babylonians ᵈ set fire to the royal palace and the houses of the people and broke down the walls of Jerusalem. ⁹Nebuzaradan commander of the imperial guard carried into exile to Babylon the people who remained in the city, along with those who had gone over to him, and the rest of the people. ¹⁰But Nebuzaradan the commander of the guard left behind in the land of Judah some of the poor people, who owned nothing; and at that time he gave them vineyards and fields.

¹¹Now Nebuchadnezzar king of Babylon had given these orders about Jeremiah through Nebuzaradan commander of the imperial guard: ¹²"Take him and look after him; don't harm him but do for him whatever he asks." ¹³So Nebuzaradan the commander of the guard, Nebushazban a chief officer, Nergal-Sharezer a high official and all the other officers of the king of Babylon ¹⁴sent and had Jeremiah taken out of the courtyard of the guard. They turned him over to Gedaliah son of Ahikam, the son of Shaphan, to take him back to his home. So he remained among his own people.

¹⁵While Jeremiah had been confined in the courtyard of the guard, the word of the Lᴏʀᴅ came to him: ¹⁶"Go and tell Ebed-Melech the Cushite, 'This is what the Lᴏʀᴅ Almighty, the God of Israel, says: I am about to fulfill my words against this city through disaster, not prosperity. At that time they will be fulfilled before your eyes. ¹⁷But I will rescue you on that day, declares the Lᴏʀᴅ; you will not be handed over to those you fear. ¹⁸I will save you; you will not fall by the sword but will escape with your life, because you trust in me, declares the Lᴏʀᴅ.' "

JEREMIAH FREED

40 The word came to Jeremiah from the Lᴏʀᴅ after Nebuzaradan commander of the imperial guard had released him at Ramah. He had found Jeremiah bound in chains among all the captives from Jerusalem and Judah who were being carried into exile to Babylon. ²When the commander of the guard found Jeremiah, he said to him, "The Lᴏʀᴅ your God decreed this disaster for this place. ³And now the Lᴏʀᴅ has brought it about; he has done just as he said he would. All this happened because you people sinned against the Lᴏʀᴅ and did not obey him. ⁴But today I am freeing you from the chains on your wrists. Come with me to Babylon, if you like, and I will look after you; but if you do not want to, then don't come. Look, the whole country lies before you; go wherever you please." ⁵However, before Jeremiah turned to go, ᵉ Nebuzaradan added, "Go back to Gedaliah son of Ahikam, the son of Shaphan, whom the king of Babylon has appointed over the towns of Judah, and live with him among the people, or go anywhere else you please."

Then the commander gave him provisions and a present and let him go. ⁶So Jeremiah went to Gedaliah son of Ahikam at Mizpah and stayed with him among the people who were left behind in the land.

GEDALIAH ASSASSINATED

⁷When all the army officers and their men who were still in the open country heard that the king of

---

ᵃ *3* Or *Nergal-Sharezer, Samgar-Nebo, Sarsekim*   ᵇ *4* Or *the Jordan Valley*   ᶜ *5* Or *Chaldean*   ᵈ *8* Or *Chaldeans*   ᵉ *5* Or *Jeremiah answered*

Babylon had appointed Gedaliah son of Ahikam as governor over the land and had put him in charge of the men, women and children who were the poorest in the land and who had not been carried into exile to Babylon, 8they came to Gedaliah at Mizpah—Ishmael son of Nethaniah, Johanan and Jonathan the sons of Kareah, Seraiah son of Tanhumeth, the sons of Ephai the Netophathite, and Jaazaniah[a] the son of the Maacathite, and their men. 9Gedaliah son of Ahikam, the son of Shaphan, took an oath to reassure them and their men. "Do not be afraid to serve the Babylonians,[b]" he said. "Settle down in the land and serve the king of Babylon, and it will go well with you. 10I myself will stay at Mizpah to represent you before the Babylonians who come to us, but you are to harvest the wine, summer fruit and oil, and put them in your storage jars, and live in the towns you have taken over."

11When all the Jews in Moab, Ammon, Edom and all the other countries heard that the king of Babylon had left a remnant in Judah and had appointed Gedaliah son of Ahikam, the son of Shaphan, as governor over them, 12they all came back to the land of Judah, to Gedaliah at Mizpah, from all the countries where they had been scattered. And they harvested an abundance of wine and summer fruit.

13Johanan son of Kareah and all the army officers still in the open country came to Gedaliah at Mizpah 14and said to him, "Don't you know that Baalis king of the Ammonites has sent Ishmael son of Nethaniah to take your life?" But Gedaliah son of Ahikam did not believe them.

15Then Johanan son of Kareah said privately to Gedaliah in Mizpah, "Let me go and kill Ishmael son of Nethaniah, and no one will know it. Why should he take your life and cause all the Jews who are gathered around you to be scattered and the remnant of Judah to perish?"

16But Gedaliah son of Ahikam said to Johanan son of Kareah, "Don't do such a thing! What you are saying about Ishmael is not true."

41 In the seventh month Ishmael son of Nethaniah, the son of Elishama, who was of royal blood and had been one of the king's officers, came with ten men to Gedaliah son of Ahikam at Mizpah. While they were eating together there, 2Ishmael son of Nethaniah and the ten men who were with him got up and struck down Gedaliah son of Ahikam, the son of Shaphan, with the sword, killing the one whom the king of Babylon had appointed as governor over the land. 3Ishmael also killed all the Jews who were with Gedaliah at Mizpah, as well as the Babylonian[c] soldiers who were there.

4The day after Gedaliah's assassination, before anyone knew about it, 5eighty men who had shaved off their beards, torn their clothes and cut themselves came from Shechem, Shiloh and Samaria, bringing grain offerings and incense with them to the house of the LORD. 6Ishmael son of Nethaniah went out from Mizpah to meet them, weeping as he went. When he met them, he said, "Come to Gedaliah son of Ahikam." 7When they went into the city, Ishmael son of Nethaniah and the men who were with him slaughtered them and threw them into a cistern. 8But ten of them said to Ishmael, "Don't kill us! We have wheat and barley, oil and honey, hidden in a field." So he let them alone and did not kill them with the others. 9Now the cistern where he threw all the bodies of the men he had killed along with Gedaliah was the one King Asa had made as part of his defense against Baasha king of Israel. Ishmael son of Nethaniah filled it with the dead.

10Ishmael made captives of all the rest of the people who were in Mizpah—the king's daughters along with all the others who were left there, over whom Nebuzaradan commander of the imperial guard had appointed Gedaliah son of Ahikam. Ishmael son of Nethaniah took them captive and set out to cross over to the Ammonites.

11When Johanan son of Kareah and all the army officers who were with him heard about all the crimes Ishmael son of Nethaniah had committed, 12they took all their men and went to fight Ishmael son of Nethaniah. They caught up with him near the great pool in Gibeon. 13When all the people Ishmael had with him saw Johanan son of Kareah and the army officers who were with him, they were glad. 14All the people Ishmael had taken captive at Mizpah turned and went over to Johanan son of Kareah. 15But Ishmael son of Nethaniah and eight of his men escaped from Johanan and fled to the Ammonites.

FLIGHT TO EGYPT

16Then Johanan son of Kareah and all the army officers who were with him led away all the survivors from Mizpah whom he had recovered from Ishmael son of Nethaniah after he had assassinated Gedaliah son of Ahikam: the soldiers, women, children and court officials he had brought from Gibeon. 17And they went on, stopping at Geruth Kimham near Bethlehem on their way to Egypt 18to escape

---

a 8 Hebrew *Jezaniah*, a variant of *Jaazaniah*   b 9 Or *Chaldeans*; also in verse 10   c 3 Or *Chaldean*

asa

» **King of Judah, the southern kingdom**

» **His reign began well but ended poorly**

» **Got Ben-Hadad to attack Baasha**

baasha

» **King of Israel, the northern kingdom**

» **His entire reign was marked by evil**

» **Attacked by Ben-Hadad's army**

The Main Event

As far as kings go, Asa was mostly decent. For the first few years of his reign, he tried hard to please God. He demolished pagan idols throughout the land. He encouraged the people of Judah to return to God—to seek him and to obey his commands.

When the massive Egyptian army set out to attack Judah, Asa practiced what he preached. He humbly called upon God and watched as God gave his troops a miraculous victory. The army of Judah thrashed its enemy and went home with the spoils of war.

Toward the end of his reign, King Asa underwent an unexpected (and unfortunate) turnaround. The evil King Baasha of Israel began threatening Judah, beefing up his military presence right in Asa's backyard. But this time, rather than crying out to God for rescue, Asa decided to go with "plan B." He dipped into the royal treasury and offered a huge payoff to King Ben-Hadad of Aram in exchange for some tag-team help against Israel.

The plan worked, at least on the surface. Ben-Hadad broke his treaty with Baasha and launched an attack on northern Israel. Ben-Hadad's army cut through Baasha's boys like a hot knife going through butter. Baasha was smart enough to throw in the towel; he abandoned his military buildup on Judah's border to go take care of things in the north. End of story, right?

Wrong. Along came the prophet Hanani, who said to King Asa: "I know it looks like you've succeeded, but I'm here to tell you that you just messed up royally." (Pun intended.) Then Hanani lowered the boom: "You forgot the Lord. If you had asked for his help, you wouldn't have needed Ben-Hadad. In fact, God would've handed you Ben-Hadad's army on a silver platter. But since you failed to put your trust in God, from now on your country will be faced with one war after another."

Asa wasn't exactly thrilled with this message. He took out his anger on the messenger. He threw poor Hanani in the slammer and lived the rest of his life in a seriously bad mood.

The Outcome

Which is worse: to live your whole life disregarding God (as Baasha did) or to start out following God and then turn away from him in your final years (as Asa did)?

Obviously neither option is good. The ideal is to follow God all the days of your life. "Love the Lord your God with all your heart and with all your soul and with all your mind," Jesus said in Matthew 22:37. Not just with part of your heart or for just part of your life. God wants all of you, for all of your days.

That means you have to guard your heart. You have to make it your top priority to listen and to talk to God. Otherwise, you'll become spiritually cold. You need to decide once and for all to live your life God's way. You need to have people in your life like Hanani, who will look you in the eye and shoot straight with you. And when you're messing up, you need to be willing to acknowledge your sin. That's the only way to finish well.

Read more about King Asa and King Baasha in 1 Kings 15:1—16:7 (pages 399—401) and 2 Chronicles 14—16 (pages 506—509).

the Babylonians.[a] They were afraid of them because Ishmael son of Nethaniah had killed Gedaliah son of Ahikam, whom the king of Babylon had appointed as governor over the land.

42

Then all the army officers, including Johanan son of Kareah and Jezaniah[b] son of Hoshaiah, and all the people from the least to the greatest approached ²Jeremiah the prophet and said to him, "Please hear our petition and pray to the LORD your God for this entire remnant. For as you now see, though we were once many, now only a few are left. ³Pray that the LORD your God will tell us where we should go and what we should do."

⁴"I have heard you," replied Jeremiah the prophet. "I will certainly pray to the LORD your God as you have requested; I will tell you everything the LORD says and will keep nothing back from you."

⁵Then they said to Jeremiah, "May the LORD be a true and faithful witness against us if we do not act in accordance with everything the LORD your God sends you to tell us. ⁶Whether it is favorable or unfavorable, we will obey the LORD our God, to whom we are sending you, so that it will go well with us, for we will obey the LORD our God."

⁷Ten days later the word of the LORD came to Jeremiah. ⁸So he called together Johanan son of Kareah and all the army officers who were with him and all the people from the least to the greatest. ⁹He said to them, "This is what the LORD, the God of Israel, to whom you sent me to present your petition, says: ¹⁰'If you stay in this land, I will build you up and not tear you down; I will plant you and not uproot you, for I am grieved over the disaster I have inflicted on you. ¹¹Do not be afraid of the king of Babylon, whom you now fear. Do not be afraid of him, declares the LORD, for I am with you and will save you and deliver you from his hands. ¹²I will show you compassion so that he will have compassion on you and restore you to your land.'

¹³"However, if you say, 'We will not stay in this land,' and so disobey the LORD your God, ¹⁴and if you say, 'No, we will go and live in Egypt, where we will not see war or hear the trumpet or be hungry for bread,' ¹⁵then hear the word of the LORD, O remnant of Judah. This is what the LORD Almighty, the God of Israel, says: 'If you are determined to go to Egypt and you do go to settle there, ¹⁶then the sword you fear will overtake you there, and the famine you dread will follow you into Egypt, and there you will die. ¹⁷Indeed, all who are determined to go to Egypt to settle there will die by the sword, famine and plague; not one of them will survive or escape the disaster I will bring on them.' ¹⁸This is what the LORD Almighty, the God of Israel, says: 'As my anger and wrath have been poured out on those who lived in Jerusalem, so will my wrath be poured out on you when you go to Egypt. You will be an object of cursing and horror, of condemnation and reproach; you will never see this place again.'

¹⁹"O remnant of Judah, the LORD has told you, 'Do not go to Egypt.' Be sure of this: I warn you today ²⁰that you made a fatal mistake[c] when you sent me to the LORD your God and said, 'Pray to the LORD our God for us; tell us everything he says and we will do it.' ²¹I have told you today, but you still have not obeyed the LORD your God in all he sent me to tell you. ²²So now, be sure of this: You will die by the sword, famine and plague in the place where you want to go to settle."

43

When Jeremiah finished telling the people all the words of the LORD their God— everything the LORD had sent him to tell them— ²Azariah son of Hoshaiah and Johanan son of Kareah and all the arrogant men said to Jeremiah, "You are lying! The LORD our God has not sent you to say, 'You must not go to Egypt to settle there.' ³But Baruch son of Neriah is inciting you against us to hand us over to the Babylonians,[a] so they may kill us or carry us into exile to Babylon."

⁴So Johanan son of Kareah and all the army officers and all the people disobeyed the LORD's com-

Seeking God's Direction

The Israelites were in a jam and knew they needed help. So they turned to God and asked for it. They did the right thing . . . well, almost. If you read the rest of the story, you'll find that the Israelites already had in mind the answer they wanted from God. When his response wasn't what they wanted to hear, they accused Jeremiah of being a liar. Imagine how the faithful prophet must have felt. When you find yourself under the gun, ask God for help—but be prepared to accept whatever response he may give. Crying out for help takes humility, but obedience requires faith.

ᵃ 18,3 Or *Chaldeans*   ᵇ 1 Hebrew; Septuagint (see also 43:2) *Azariah*   ᶜ 20 Or *you erred in your hearts* mand to stay in the land of Judah. 5Instead, Johanan son of Kareah and all the army officers led away all the remnant of Judah who had come back to live in the land of Judah from all the nations where they had been scattered. 6They also led away all the men, women and children and the king's daughters whom Nebuzaradan commander of the imperial guard had left with Gedaliah son of Ahikam, the son of Shaphan, and Jeremiah the prophet and Baruch son of Neriah. 7So they entered Egypt in disobedience to the LORD and went as far as Tahpanhes.

8In Tahpanhes the word of the LORD came to Jeremiah: 9"While the Jews are watching, take some large stones with you and bury them in clay in the brick pavement at the entrance to Pharaoh's palace in Tahpanhes. 10Then say to them, 'This is what the LORD Almighty, the God of Israel, says: I will send for my servant Nebuchadnezzar king of Babylon, and I will set his throne over these stones I have buried here; he will spread his royal canopy above them. 11He will come and attack Egypt, bringing death to those destined for death, captivity to those destined for captivity, and the sword to those destined for the sword. 12He a will set fire to the temples of the gods of Egypt; he will burn their temples and take their gods captive. As a shepherd wraps his garment around him, so will he wrap Egypt around himself and depart from there unscathed. 13There in the temple of the sun b in Egypt he will demolish the sacred pillars and will burn down the temples of the gods of Egypt.' "

DISASTER BECAUSE OF IDOLATRY

44 This word came to Jeremiah concerning all the Jews living in Lower Egypt—in Migdol, Tahpanhes and Memphis c—and in Upper Egypt d: 2"This is what the LORD Almighty, the God of Israel, says: You saw the great disaster I brought on Jerusalem and on all the towns of Judah. Today they lie deserted and in ruins 3because of the evil they have done. They provoked me to anger by burning incense and by worshiping other gods that neither they nor you nor your fathers ever knew. 4Again and again I sent my servants the prophets, who said, 'Do not do this detestable thing that I hate!' 5But they did not listen or pay attention; they did not turn from their wickedness or stop burning incense to other gods. 6Therefore, my fierce anger was poured out; it raged against the towns of Judah and the streets of Jerusalem and made them the desolate ruins they are today.

7"Now this is what the LORD God Almighty, the God of Israel, says: Why bring such great disaster on yourselves by cutting off from Judah the men and women, the children and infants, and so leave yourselves without a remnant? 8Why provoke me to anger with what your hands have made, burning incense to other gods in Egypt, where you have come to live? You will destroy yourselves and make yourselves an object of cursing and reproach among all the nations on earth. 9Have you forgotten the wickedness committed by your fathers and by the kings and queens of Judah and the wickedness committed by you and your wives in the land of Judah and the streets of Jerusalem? 10To this day they have not humbled themselves or shown reverence, nor have they followed my law and the decrees I set before you and your fathers.

11"Therefore, this is what the LORD Almighty, the God of Israel, says: I am determined to bring disaster on you and to destroy all Judah. 12I will take away the remnant of Judah who were determined to go to Egypt to settle there. They will all perish in Egypt; they will fall by the sword or die from famine. From the least to the greatest, they will die by sword or famine. They will become an object of cursing and horror, of condemnation and reproach. 13I will punish those who live in Egypt with the sword, famine and plague, as I punished Jerusalem. 14None of the remnant of Judah who have gone to live in Egypt will escape or survive to return to the land of Judah, to which they long to return and live; none will return except a few fugitives."

15Then all the men who knew that their wives were burning incense to other gods, along with all the women who were present—a large assembly—and all the people living in Lower and Upper Egypt, e said to Jeremiah, 16"We will not listen to the message you have spoken to us in the name of the LORD!

---

a 12 Or I   b 13 Or in Heliopolis   c 1 Hebrew Noph   d 1 Hebrew in Pathros   e 15 Hebrew in Egypt and Pathros

17We will certainly do everything we said we would: We will burn incense to the Queen of Heaven and will pour out drink offerings to her just as we and our fathers, our kings and our officials did in the towns of Judah and in the streets of Jerusalem. At that time we had plenty of food and were well off and suffered no harm. 18But ever since we stopped burning incense to the Queen of Heaven and pouring out drink offerings to her, we have had nothing and have been perishing by sword and famine."

19The women added, "When we burned incense to the Queen of Heaven and poured out drink offerings to her, did not our husbands know that we were making cakes like her image and pouring out drink offerings to her?"

20Then Jeremiah said to all the people, both men and women, who were answering him, 21"Did not the LORD remember and think about the incense burned in the towns of Judah and the streets of Jerusalem by you and your fathers, your kings and your officials and the people of the land? 22When the LORD could no longer endure your wicked actions and the detestable things you did, your land became an object of cursing and a desolate waste without inhabitants, as it is today. 23Because you have burned incense and have sinned against the LORD and have not obeyed him or followed his law or his decrees or his stipulations, this disaster has come upon you, as you now see."

24Then Jeremiah said to all the people, including the women, "Hear the word of the LORD, all you people of Judah in Egypt. 25This is what the LORD Almighty, the God of Israel, says: You and your wives have shown by your actions what you promised when you said, 'We will certainly carry out the vows we made to burn incense and pour out drink offerings to the Queen of Heaven.'

"Go ahead then, do what you promised! Keep your vows! 26But hear the word of the LORD, all Jews living in Egypt: 'I swear by my great name,' says the LORD, 'that no one from Judah living anywhere in Egypt will ever again invoke my name or swear, "As surely as the Sovereign LORD lives." 27For I am watching over them for harm, not for good; the Jews in Egypt will perish by sword and famine until they are all destroyed. 28Those who escape the sword and return to the land of Judah from Egypt will be very few. Then the whole remnant of Judah who came to live in Egypt will know whose word will stand—mine or theirs.

29" 'This will be the sign to you that I will punish you in this place,' declares the LORD, 'so that you will know that my threats of harm against you will surely stand.' 30This is what the LORD says: 'I am going to hand Pharaoh Hophra king of Egypt over to his enemies who seek his life, just as I handed Zedekiah king of Judah over to Nebuchadnezzar king of Babylon, the enemy who was seeking his life.' "

NOW OR NEVER

JER 45:5

Baruch's brother Seraiah was on his way to becoming a big man in the kingdom. Even though Baruch had been faithful in his duties, God had a lower-profile plan for his life. Don't chase after fame or popularity. God is the only audience we ever need to worry about pleasing.

A MESSAGE TO BARUCH

45 This is what Jeremiah the prophet told Baruch son of Neriah in the fourth year of Jehoiakim son of Josiah king of Judah, after Baruch had written on a scroll the words Jeremiah was then dictating: 2"This is what the LORD, the God of Israel, says to you, Baruch: 3You said, 'Woe to me! The LORD has added sorrow to my pain; I am worn out with groaning and find no rest.' "

4The LORD said, "Say this to him: 'This is what the LORD says: I will overthrow what I have built and uproot what I have planted, throughout the land. 5Should you then seek great things for yourself? Seek them not. For I will bring disaster on all people, declares the LORD, but wherever you go I will let you escape with your life.' "

A MESSAGE ABOUT EGYPT

46 This is the word of the LORD that came to Jeremiah the prophet concerning the nations:

2Concerning Egypt:

This is the message against the army of Pharaoh Neco king of Egypt, which was defeated at Carchemish on the Euphrates River by Nebuchadnezzar king of Babylon in the fourth year of Jehoiakim son of Josiah king of Judah:

³ "Prepare your shields, both large and small,
    and march out for battle!
⁴ Harness the horses,
    mount the steeds!
Take your positions
    with helmets on!
Polish your spears,
    put on your armor!
⁵ What do I see?
    They are terrified,
they are retreating,
    their warriors are defeated.
They flee in haste
    without looking back,
    and there is terror on every side,"

declares the LORD.

⁶ "The swift cannot flee
    nor the strong escape.
In the north by the River Euphrates
    they stumble and fall.

⁷ "Who is this that rises like the Nile,
    like rivers of surging waters?
⁸ Egypt rises like the Nile,
    like rivers of surging waters.
She says, 'I will rise and cover the earth;
    I will destroy cities and their people.'
⁹ Charge, O horses!
    Drive furiously, O charioteers!
March on, O warriors—
    men of Cush^a and Put who carry shields,
    men of Lydia who draw the bow.
¹⁰ But that day belongs to the Lord, the LORD Almighty—
    a day of vengeance, for vengeance on his foes.
The sword will devour till it is satisfied,
    till it has quenched its thirst with blood.
For the Lord, the LORD Almighty, will offer sacrifice
    in the land of the north by the River Euphrates.

¹¹ "Go up to Gilead and get balm,
    O Virgin Daughter of Egypt.
But you multiply remedies in vain;
    there is no healing for you.
¹² The nations will hear of your shame;
    your cries will fill the earth.
One warrior will stumble over another;
    both will fall down together."

¹³ This is the message the LORD spoke to Jeremiah the prophet about the coming of Nebuchadnezzar king of Babylon to attack Egypt:

¹⁴ "Announce this in Egypt, and proclaim it in Migdol;
    proclaim it also in Memphis^b and Tahpanhes:

---

^a 9 That is, the upper Nile region   ^b 14 Hebrew Noph; also in verse 19

'Take your positions and get ready,
    for the sword devours those around you.'
15 Why will your warriors be laid low?
    They cannot stand, for the LORD will push them down.
16 They will stumble repeatedly;
    they will fall over each other.
They will say, 'Get up, let us go back
    to our own people and our native lands,
    away from the sword of the oppressor.'
17 There they will exclaim,
    'Pharaoh king of Egypt is only a loud noise;
    he has missed his opportunity.'

18 "As surely as I live," declares the King,
    whose name is the LORD Almighty,
"one will come who is like Tabor among the mountains,
    like Carmel by the sea.
19 Pack your belongings for exile,
    you who live in Egypt,
for Memphis will be laid waste
    and lie in ruins without inhabitant.

20 "Egypt is a beautiful heifer,
    but a gadfly is coming
    against her from the north.
21 The mercenaries in her ranks
    are like fattened calves.
They too will turn and flee together,
    they will not stand their ground,
for the day of disaster is coming upon them,
    the time for them to be punished.
22 Egypt will hiss like a fleeing serpent
    as the enemy advances in force;
they will come against her with axes,
    like men who cut down trees.
23 They will chop down her forest,"
                                              declares the LORD,
    "dense though it be.
They are more numerous than locusts,
    they cannot be counted.
24 The Daughter of Egypt will be put to shame,
    handed over to the people of the north."

25 The LORD Almighty, the God of Israel, says: "I am about to bring punishment on Amon god of Thebes,[a] on Pharaoh, on Egypt and her gods and her kings, and on those who rely on Pharaoh. 26 I will hand them over to those who seek their lives, to Nebuchadnezzar king of Babylon and his officers. Later, however, Egypt will be inhabited as in times past," declares the LORD.

27 "Do not fear, O Jacob my servant;
    do not be dismayed, O Israel.
I will surely save you out of a distant place,
    your descendants from the land of their exile.
Jacob will again have peace and security,
    and no one will make him afraid.
28 Do not fear, O Jacob my servant,
    for I am with you," declares the LORD.

---

[a] 25 Hebrew No

> "Though I completely destroy all the nations
>   among which I scatter you,
>   I will not completely destroy you.
> I will discipline you but only with justice;
>   I will not let you go entirely unpunished."

A MESSAGE ABOUT THE PHILISTINES

This is the word of the LORD that came to Jeremiah the prophet concerning the Philistines before Pharaoh attacked Gaza:

2 This is what the LORD says:

> "See how the waters are rising in the north;
>   they will become an overflowing torrent.
> They will overflow the land and everything in it,
>   the towns and those who live in them.
> The people will cry out;
>   all who dwell in the land will wail
> 3 at the sound of the hoofs of galloping steeds,
>   at the noise of enemy chariots
>   and the rumble of their wheels.
> Fathers will not turn to help their children;
>   their hands will hang limp.
> 4 For the day has come
>   to destroy all the Philistines
> and to cut off all survivors
>   who could help Tyre and Sidon.
> The LORD is about to destroy the Philistines,
>   the remnant from the coasts of Caphtor.ᵃ
> 5 Gaza will shave her head in mourning;
>   Ashkelon will be silenced.
> O remnant on the plain,
>   how long will you cut yourselves?
>
> 6 " 'Ah, sword of the LORD,' ⌊you cry,⌋
>   'how long till you rest?
> Return to your scabbard;
>   cease and be still.'
> 7 But how can it rest
>   when the LORD has commanded it,
> when he has ordered it
>   to attack Ashkelon and the coast?"

A MESSAGE ABOUT MOAB

Concerning Moab:

This is what the LORD Almighty, the God of Israel, says:

> "Woe to Nebo, for it will be ruined.
>   Kiriathaim will be disgraced and captured;
>   the strongholdᵇ will be disgraced and shattered.
> 2 Moab will be praised no more;
>   in Heshbonᶜ men will plot her downfall:
>   'Come, let us put an end to that nation.'
> You too, O Madmen,ᵈ will be silenced;

ᵃ 4 That is, Crete   ᵇ 1 Or /Misgab   ᶜ 2 The Hebrew for Heshbon sounds like the Hebrew for plot.   ᵈ 2 The name of the Moabite town Madmen sounds like the Hebrew for be silenced.

battlelines

» Surrounded (Alcoholism)

Q: Whoa! It smells like a brewery in here. Don't tell me—
A: Yeah, my dad's drinking again.

Q: I thought he quit.
A: He did—for a while. He just stopped cold turkey. I was so proud of him. But then about six weeks ago, he drank a beer with his supper. "Just one," he said. After that it was three or four a night. Then my older brothers got in on the act. Now . . . well, see for yourself. (Opens a trash can to reveal dozens of empty cans.)

Q: Wow. I'm sorry to hear that. So with your dad and your brothers sitting around drinking all the time, are you ever tempted?
A: Are you kidding? Have you ever seen my dad the morning after a binge? Last week I found him passed out on the bathroom floor, lying in his own puke. Heck, no. I don't ever touch the stuff.

Q: Not even one beer?
A: No way! Alcoholism runs in my family. My grandpa drank himself to death. My dad and both my brothers are on the same path. We're talking about some seriously weak genes. Or weak resistance to temptation. Or both.

Q: And your mom?
A: She doesn't say anything. She always cleans up the mess and covers for my dad. She calls his boss and makes up excuses when he's too hung over to show up for work on time. And then she goes to church and prays. But nothing ever seems to change. I'm telling you, I'm just hanging on until I get out of high school.

» Spirits or Spirit?

Why do people drink? More important, why do some people become "problem drinkers"? For many, there may be a biological or genetic factor. For others, it's simply an escape from reality. They use drinking as a way to forget—for a while, at least—the problems they're facing. The brutal truth is that alcohol doesn't *solve* anything. In fact, when it's abused, it creates a whole new set of problems.

God has a better solution. He wants us to be filled with his Holy Spirit so that we can deal head-on with our problems and live in a way that pleases him (see Ephesians 5:18). He wants us to be filled with the fruit of the Spirit (see Galatians 5:22–23) instead of the "fruit" of alcohol.

If a friend or family member is struggling with alcoholism, it's not up to you to stop his or her drinking. But you don't have to deal with the situation alone either. Seek out the support of a trusted youth pastor or possibly a professional counselor. They'll be able to help.

Read more about Christians and alcohol at www.RevolutionBible.com.

the sword will pursue you.
³ Listen to the cries from Horonaim,
    cries of great havoc and destruction.
⁴ Moab will be broken;
    her little ones will cry out.ª
⁵ They go up the way to Luhith,
    weeping bitterly as they go;
on the road down to Horonaim
    anguished cries over the destruction are heard.
⁶ Flee! Run for your lives;
    become like a bushᵇ in the desert.
⁷ Since you trust in your deeds and riches,
    you too will be taken captive,
and Chemosh will go into exile,
    together with his priests and officials.
⁸ The destroyer will come against every town,
    and not a town will escape.
The valley will be ruined
    and the plateau destroyed,
    because the Lord has spoken.
⁹ Put salt on Moab,
    for she will be laid wasteᶜ;
her towns will become desolate,
    with no one to live in them.

¹⁰ "A curse on him who is lax in doing the Lord's work!
    A curse on him who keeps his sword from bloodshed!

¹¹ "Moab has been at rest from youth,
    like wine left on its dregs,
not poured from one jar to another—
    she has not gone into exile.
So she tastes as she did,
    and her aroma is unchanged.
¹² But days are coming,"
    declares the Lord,
"when I will send men who pour from jars,
    and they will pour her out;
they will empty her jars
    and smash her jugs.
¹³ Then Moab will be ashamed of Chemosh,
    as the house of Israel was ashamed
    when they trusted in Bethel.

¹⁴ "How can you say, 'We are warriors,
    men valiant in battle'?
¹⁵ Moab will be destroyed and her towns invaded;
    her finest young men will go down in the slaughter,"
    declares the King, whose name is the Lord Almighty.
¹⁶ "The fall of Moab is at hand;
    her calamity will come quickly.
¹⁷ Mourn for her, all who live around her,
    all who know her fame;
say, 'How broken is the mighty scepter,
    how broken the glorious staff!'

ª 4 Hebrew; Septuagint / *proclaim it to Zoar*   ᵇ 6 Or *like Aroer*   ᶜ 9 Or *Give wings to Moab, / for she will fly away*

18 "Come down from your glory
and sit on the parched ground,
O inhabitants of the Daughter of Dibon,
for he who destroys Moab
will come up against you
and ruin your fortified cities.
19 Stand by the road and watch,
you who live in Aroer.
Ask the man fleeing and the woman escaping,
ask them, 'What has happened?'
20 Moab is disgraced, for she is shattered.
Wail and cry out!
Announce by the Arnon
that Moab is destroyed.
21 Judgment has come to the plateau—
to Holon, Jahzah and Mephaath,
22   to Dibon, Nebo and Beth Diblathaim,
23   to Kiriathaim, Beth Gamul and Beth Meon,
24   to Kerioth and Bozrah—
to all the towns of Moab, far and near.
25 Moab's horn[a] is cut off;
her arm is broken,"

declares the LORD.

26 "Make her drunk,
for she has defied the LORD.
Let Moab wallow in her vomit;
let her be an object of ridicule.
27 Was not Israel the object of your ridicule?
Was she caught among thieves,
that you shake your head in scorn
whenever you speak of her?
28 Abandon your towns and dwell among the rocks,
you who live in Moab.
Be like a dove that makes its nest
at the mouth of a cave.

29 "We have heard of Moab's pride—
her overweening pride and conceit,
her pride and arrogance
and the haughtiness of her heart.
30 I know her insolence but it is futile,"

declares the LORD,

"and her boasts accomplish nothing.
31 Therefore I wail over Moab,
for all Moab I cry out,
I moan for the men of Kir Hareseth.
32 I weep for you, as Jazer weeps,
O vines of Sibmah.
Your branches spread as far as the sea;
they reached as far as the sea of Jazer.
The destroyer has fallen
on your ripened fruit and grapes.
33 Joy and gladness are gone
from the orchards and fields of Moab.

---

a 25 Horn here symbolizes strength.

I have stopped the flow of wine from the presses;
     no one treads them with shouts of joy.
Although there are shouts,
     they are not shouts of joy.

³⁴ "The sound of their cry rises
     from Heshbon to Elealeh and Jahaz,
from Zoar as far as Horonaim and Eglath Shelishiyah,
     for even the waters of Nimrim are dried up.
³⁵ In Moab I will put an end
     to those who make offerings on the high places
     and burn incense to their gods,"

declares the LORD.

³⁶ "So my heart laments for Moab like a flute;
     it laments like a flute for the men of Kir Hareseth.
     The wealth they acquired is gone.
³⁷ Every head is shaved
     and every beard cut off;
every hand is slashed
     and every waist is covered with sackcloth.
³⁸ On all the roofs in Moab
     and in the public squares
there is nothing but mourning,
     for I have broken Moab
     like a jar that no one wants,"

declares the LORD.

³⁹ "How shattered she is! How they wail!
     How Moab turns her back in shame!
Moab has become an object of ridicule,
     an object of horror to all those around her."

⁴⁰ This is what the LORD says:

"Look! An eagle is swooping down,
     spreading its wings over Moab.
⁴¹ Kerioth[a] will be captured
     and the strongholds taken.
In that day the hearts of Moab's warriors
     will be like the heart of a woman in labor.
⁴² Moab will be destroyed as a nation
     because she defied the LORD.
⁴³ Terror and pit and snare await you,
     O people of Moab,"

declares the LORD.

⁴⁴ "Whoever flees from the terror
     will fall into a pit,
whoever climbs out of the pit
     will be caught in a snare;
for I will bring upon Moab
     the year of her punishment,"

declares the LORD.

⁴⁵ "In the shadow of Heshbon
     the fugitives stand helpless,
for a fire has gone out from Heshbon,
     a blaze from the midst of Sihon;

it burns the foreheads of Moab,
the skulls of the noisy boasters.
46 Woe to you, O Moab!
The people of Chemosh are destroyed;
your sons are taken into exile
and your daughters into captivity.

47 "Yet I will restore the fortunes of Moab
in days to come,"

declares the LORD.

Here ends the judgment on Moab.

A MESSAGE ABOUT AMMON

49
Concerning the Ammonites:

This is what the LORD says:

"Has Israel no sons?
Has she no heirs?
Why then has Molech[a] taken possession of Gad?
Why do his people live in its towns?
2 But the days are coming,"
declares the LORD,
"when I will sound the battle cry
against Rabbah of the Ammonites;
it will become a mound of ruins,
and its surrounding villages will be set on fire.
Then Israel will drive out
those who drove her out,"

says the LORD.

3 "Wail, O Heshbon, for Ai is destroyed!
Cry out, O inhabitants of Rabbah!
Put on sackcloth and mourn;
rush here and there inside the walls,
for Molech will go into exile,
together with his priests and officials.
4 Why do you boast of your valleys,
boast of your valleys so fruitful?
O unfaithful daughter,
you trust in your riches and say,
'Who will attack me?'
5 I will bring terror on you
from all those around you,"

declares the Lord, the LORD Almighty.

"Every one of you will be driven away,
and no one will gather the fugitives.

6 "Yet afterward, I will restore the fortunes of the Ammonites,"

declares the LORD.

A MESSAGE ABOUT EDOM

7 Concerning Edom:

This is what the LORD Almighty says:

"Is there no longer wisdom in Teman?

---

a 1 Or their king; Hebrew malcam; also in verse 3

Has counsel perished from the prudent?
 Has their wisdom decayed?
⁸Turn and flee, hide in deep caves,
 you who live in Dedan,
for I will bring disaster on Esau
 at the time I punish him.
⁹If grape pickers came to you,
 would they not leave a few grapes?
If thieves came during the night,
 would they not steal only as much as they wanted?
¹⁰But I will strip Esau bare;
 I will uncover his hiding places,
 so that he cannot conceal himself.
His children, relatives and neighbors will perish,
 and he will be no more.
¹¹Leave your orphans; I will protect their lives.
 Your widows too can trust in me."

¹²This is what the LORD says: "If those who do not deserve to drink the cup must drink it, why should you go unpunished? You will not go unpunished, but must drink it. ¹³I swear by myself," declares the LORD, "that Bozrah will become a ruin and an object of horror, of reproach and of cursing; and all its towns will be in ruins forever."

¹⁴I have heard a message from the LORD:
 An envoy was sent to the nations to say,
 "Assemble yourselves to attack it!
 Rise up for battle!"

¹⁵"Now I will make you small among the nations,
 despised among men.
¹⁶The terror you inspire
 and the pride of your heart have deceived you,
you who live in the clefts of the rocks,
 who occupy the heights of the hill.
Though you build your nest as high as the eagle's,
 from there I will bring you down,"

declares the LORD.

¹⁷"Edom will become an object of horror;
 all who pass by will be appalled and will scoff
 because of all its wounds.
¹⁸As Sodom and Gomorrah were overthrown,
 along with their neighboring towns,"

says the LORD,

"so no one will live there;
 no man will dwell in it.

¹⁹"Like a lion coming up from Jordan's thickets
 to a rich pastureland,
I will chase Edom from its land in an instant.
 Who is the chosen one I will appoint for this?
Who is like me and who can challenge me?
 And what shepherd can stand against me?"
²⁰Therefore, hear what the LORD has planned against Edom,
 what he has purposed against those who live in Teman:
The young of the flock will be dragged away;
 he will completely destroy their pasture because of them.

21 At the sound of their fall the earth will tremble;
   their cry will resound to the Red Sea.[a]
22 Look! An eagle will soar and swoop down,
   spreading its wings over Bozrah.
   In that day the hearts of Edom's warriors
   will be like the heart of a woman in labor.

A MESSAGE ABOUT DAMASCUS

23 Concerning Damascus:

"Hamath and Arpad are dismayed,
   for they have heard bad news.
They are disheartened,
   troubled like[b] the restless sea.
24 Damascus has become feeble,
   she has turned to flee
   and panic has gripped her;
anguish and pain have seized her,
   pain like that of a woman in labor.
25 Why has the city of renown not been abandoned,
   the town in which I delight?
26 Surely, her young men will fall in the streets;
   all her soldiers will be silenced in that day,"

declares the LORD Almighty.

27 "I will set fire to the walls of Damascus;
   it will consume the fortresses of Ben-Hadad."

A MESSAGE ABOUT KEDAR AND HAZOR

28 Concerning Kedar and the kingdoms of Hazor, which Nebuchadnezzar king of Babylon attacked:

This is what the LORD says:

"Arise, and attack Kedar
   and destroy the people of the East.
29 Their tents and their flocks will be taken;
   their shelters will be carried off
   with all their goods and camels.
Men will shout to them,
   'Terror on every side!'

30 "Flee quickly away!
   Stay in deep caves, you who live in Hazor,"

declares the LORD.

"Nebuchadnezzar king of Babylon has plotted against you;
   he has devised a plan against you.

31 "Arise and attack a nation at ease,
   which lives in confidence,"

declares the LORD,

"a nation that has neither gates nor bars;
   its people live alone.
32 Their camels will become plunder,
   and their large herds will be booty.
I will scatter to the winds those who are in distant places[c]
   and will bring disaster on them from every side,"

declares the LORD.

---

[a] 21 Hebrew Yam Suph; that is, Sea of Reeds   [b] 23 Hebrew on or by   [c] 32 Or who clip the hair by their foreheads

33 "Hazor will become a haunt of jackals,
    a desolate place forever.
No one will live there;
    no man will dwell in it."

A MESSAGE ABOUT ELAM

34 This is the word of the LORD that came to Jeremiah the prophet concerning Elam, early in the reign of Zedekiah king of Judah:

35 This is what the LORD Almighty says:

"See, I will break the bow of Elam,
    the mainstay of their might.
36 I will bring against Elam the four winds
    from the four quarters of the heavens;
I will scatter them to the four winds,
    and there will not be a nation
    where Elam's exiles do not go.
37 I will shatter Elam before their foes,
    before those who seek their lives;
I will bring disaster upon them,
    even my fierce anger,"
                        declares the LORD.
"I will pursue them with the sword
    until I have made an end of them.
38 I will set my throne in Elam
    and destroy her king and officials,"
                        declares the LORD.

39 "Yet I will restore the fortunes of Elam
    in days to come,"
                        declares the LORD.

A MESSAGE ABOUT BABYLON

50 This is the word the LORD spoke through Jeremiah the prophet concerning Babylon and the land of the Babylonians[a]:

2 "Announce and proclaim among the
        nations,
    lift up a banner and proclaim it;
    keep nothing back, but say,
'Babylon will be captured;
    Bel will be put to shame,
    Marduk filled with terror.
Her images will be put to shame
    and her idols filled with terror.'
3 A nation from the north will attack her
    and lay waste her land.
No one will live in it;
    both men and animals will flee away.

4 "In those days, at that time,"
    declares the LORD,
"the people of Israel and the people of Judah together
    will go in tears to seek the LORD their God.

Enjoying God's Protection

Anyone who messes with God's people messes with God. He may not always stop everybody who tries to make your life miserable, but he will protect you in every situation. All you have to do is ask . . . and then cling to him no matter what. God will make sure that justice is done in the end. Someday those who mess with God's people will pay for their evil in a big way.

---

a 1 Or *Chaldeans*; also in verses 8, 25, 35 and 45

⁵They will ask the way to Zion
and turn their faces toward it.
They will come and bind themselves to the LORD
in an everlasting covenant
that will not be forgotten.

⁶"My people have been lost sheep;
their shepherds have led them astray
and caused them to roam on the mountains.
They wandered over mountain and hill
and forgot their own resting place.
⁷Whoever found them devoured them;
their enemies said, 'We are not guilty,
for they sinned against the LORD, their true pasture,
the LORD, the hope of their fathers.'

⁸"Flee out of Babylon;
leave the land of the Babylonians,
and be like the goats that lead the flock.
⁹For I will stir up and bring against Babylon
an alliance of great nations from the land of the north.
They will take up their positions against her,
and from the north she will be captured.
Their arrows will be like skilled warriors
who do not return empty-handed.
¹⁰So Babylonia^a will be plundered;
all who plunder her will have their fill,"

declares the LORD.

¹¹"Because you rejoice and are glad,
you who pillage my inheritance,
because you frolic like a heifer threshing grain
and neigh like stallions,
¹²your mother will be greatly ashamed;
she who gave you birth will be disgraced.
She will be the least of the nations—
a wilderness, a dry land, a desert.
¹³Because of the LORD'S anger she will not be inhabited
but will be completely desolate.
All who pass Babylon will be horrified and scoff
because of all her wounds.

¹⁴"Take up your positions around Babylon,
all you who draw the bow.
Shoot at her! Spare no arrows,
for she has sinned against the LORD.
¹⁵Shout against her on every side!
She surrenders, her towers fall,
her walls are torn down.
Since this is the vengeance of the LORD,
take vengeance on her;
do to her as she has done to others.
¹⁶Cut off from Babylon the sower,
and the reaper with his sickle at harvest.
Because of the sword of the oppressor

---

^a 10 Or *Chaldea*

let everyone return to his own people,
let everyone flee to his own land.

¹⁷ "Israel is a scattered flock
    that lions have chased away.
The first to devour him
    was the king of Assyria;
the last to crush his bones
    was Nebuchadnezzar king of Babylon."

¹⁸ Therefore this is what the LORD Almighty, the God of Israel, says:

"I will punish the king of Babylon and his land
    as I punished the king of Assyria.
¹⁹ But I will bring Israel back to his own pasture
    and he will graze on Carmel and Bashan;
his appetite will be satisfied
    on the hills of Ephraim and Gilead.
²⁰ In those days, at that time,"
    declares the LORD,
"search will be made for Israel's guilt,
    but there will be none,
and for the sins of Judah,
    but none will be found,
    for I will forgive the remnant I spare.

²¹ "Attack the land of Merathaim
    and those who live in Pekod.
Pursue, kill and completely destroy[a] them,"

declares the LORD.

"Do everything I have commanded you.
²² The noise of battle is in the land,
    the noise of great destruction!
²³ How broken and shattered
    is the hammer of the whole earth!
How desolate is Babylon
    among the nations!
²⁴ I set a trap for you, O Babylon,
    and you were caught before you knew it;
you were found and captured
    because you opposed the LORD.
²⁵ The LORD has opened his arsenal
    and brought out the weapons of his wrath,
for the Sovereign LORD Almighty has work to do
    in the land of the Babylonians.
²⁶ Come against her from afar.
    Break open her granaries;
    pile her up like heaps of grain.
Completely destroy her
    and leave her no remnant.
²⁷ Kill all her young bulls;
    let them go down to the slaughter!
Woe to them! For their day has come,
    the time for them to be punished.
²⁸ Listen to the fugitives and refugees from Babylon

---

[a] 21 The Hebrew term refers to the irrevocable giving over of things or persons to the LORD, often by totally destroying them; also in verse 26.

declaring in Zion
how the Lord our God has taken vengeance,
   vengeance for his temple.

29 "Summon archers against Babylon,
   all those who draw the bow.
Encamp all around her;
   let no one escape.
Repay her for her deeds;
   do to her as she has done.
For she has defied the Lord,
   the Holy One of Israel.
30 Therefore, her young men will fall in the streets;
   all her soldiers will be silenced in that day,"

declares the Lord.

31 "See, I am against you, O arrogant one,"
   declares the Lord, the Lord Almighty,
"for your day has come,
   the time for you to be punished.
32 The arrogant one will stumble and fall
   and no one will help her up;
I will kindle a fire in her towns
   that will consume all who are around her."

33 This is what the Lord Almighty says:

"The people of Israel are oppressed,
   and the people of Judah as well.
All their captors hold them fast,
   refusing to let them go.
34 Yet their Redeemer is strong;
   the Lord Almighty is his name.
He will vigorously defend their cause
   so that he may bring rest to their land,
   but unrest to those who live in Babylon.

35 "A sword against the Babylonians!"
   declares the Lord—
"against those who live in Babylon
   and against her officials and wise men!
36 A sword against her false prophets!
   They will become fools.
A sword against her warriors!
   They will be filled with terror.
37 A sword against her horses and chariots
   and all the foreigners in her ranks!
   They will become women.
A sword against her treasures!
   They will be plundered.
38 A drought on[a] her waters!
   They will dry up.
For it is a land of idols,
   idols that will go mad with terror.

39 "So desert creatures and hyenas will live there,
   and there the owl will dwell.

---
[a] 38 Or A sword against

It will never again be inhabited
or lived in from generation to generation.
40 As God overthrew Sodom and Gomorrah
along with their neighboring towns,"

declares the LORD,

"so no one will live there;
no man will dwell in it.

41 "Look! An army is coming from the north;
a great nation and many kings
are being stirred up from the ends of the earth.
42 They are armed with bows and spears;
they are cruel and without mercy.
They sound like the roaring sea
as they ride on their horses;
they come like men in battle formation
to attack you, O Daughter of Babylon.
43 The king of Babylon has heard reports about them,
and his hands hang limp.
Anguish has gripped him,
pain like that of a woman in labor.
44 Like a lion coming up from Jordan's thickets
to a rich pastureland,
I will chase Babylon from its land in an instant.
Who is the chosen one I will appoint for this?
Who is like me and who can challenge me?
And what shepherd can stand against me?"
45 Therefore, hear what the LORD has planned against Babylon,
what he has purposed against the land of the Babylonians:
The young of the flock will be dragged away;
he will completely destroy their pasture because of them.
46 At the sound of Babylon's capture the earth will tremble;
its cry will resound among the nations.

51 This is what the LORD says:

"See, I will stir up the spirit of a destroyer
against Babylon and the people of Leb Kamai.[a]
2 I will send foreigners to Babylon
to winnow her and to devastate her land;
they will oppose her on every side
in the day of her disaster.
3 Let not the archer string his bow,
nor let him put on his armor.
Do not spare her young men;
completely destroy[b] her army.
4 They will fall down slain in Babylon,[c]
fatally wounded in her streets.
5 For Israel and Judah have not been forsaken
by their God, the LORD Almighty,
though their land[d] is full of guilt
before the Holy One of Israel.

6 "Flee from Babylon!

JEREMIAH 51:6

a 1 *Leb Kamai* is a cryptogram for Chaldea, that is, Babylonia.   b 3 The Hebrew term refers to the irrevocable giving over of things or persons to the LORD, often by totally destroying them.   c 4 Or *Chaldea*   d 5 Or *I and the land of the Babylonians*

Run for your lives!
    Do not be destroyed because of her sins.
It is time for the LORD's vengeance;
    he will pay her what she deserves.
⁷Babylon was a gold cup in the LORD's hand;
    she made the whole earth drunk.
The nations drank her wine;
    therefore they have now gone mad.
⁸Babylon will suddenly fall and be broken.
    Wail over her!
Get balm for her pain;
    perhaps she can be healed.

⁹ " 'We would have healed Babylon,
    but she cannot be healed;
let us leave her and each go to his own land,
    for her judgment reaches to the skies,
    it rises as high as the clouds.'

¹⁰ " 'The LORD has vindicated us;
    come, let us tell in Zion
    what the LORD our God has done.'

¹¹ "Sharpen the arrows,
    take up the shields!
The LORD has stirred up the kings of the Medes,
    because his purpose is to destroy Babylon.
The LORD will take vengeance,
    vengeance for his temple.
¹²Lift up a banner against the walls of Babylon!
    Reinforce the guard,
station the watchmen,
    prepare an ambush!
The LORD will carry out his purpose,
    his decree against the people of Babylon.
¹³You who live by many waters
    and are rich in treasures,
your end has come,
    the time for you to be cut off.
¹⁴The LORD Almighty has sworn by himself:
    I will surely fill you with men, as with a swarm of locusts,
    and they will shout in triumph over you.

¹⁵ "He made the earth by his power;
    he founded the world by his wisdom
    and stretched out the heavens by his understanding.
¹⁶When he thunders, the waters in the heavens roar;
    he makes clouds rise from the ends of the earth.
He sends lightning with the rain
    and brings out the wind from his storehouses.

¹⁷ "Every man is senseless and without knowledge;
    every goldsmith is shamed by his idols.
His images are a fraud;
    they have no breath in them.
¹⁸They are worthless, the objects of mockery;
    when their judgment comes, they will perish.
¹⁹He who is the Portion of Jacob is not like these,

for he is the Maker of all things,
including the tribe of his inheritance—
the Lord Almighty is his name.

20 "You are my war club,
my weapon for battle—
with you I shatter nations,
with you I destroy kingdoms,
21 with you I shatter horse and rider,
with you I shatter chariot and driver,
22 with you I shatter man and woman,
with you I shatter old man and youth,
with you I shatter young man and maiden,
23 with you I shatter shepherd and flock,
with you I shatter farmer and oxen,
with you I shatter governors and officials.

24 "Before your eyes I will repay Babylon and all who live in Babylonia[a] for all the wrong they have done in Zion," declares the Lord.

25 "I am against you, O destroying mountain,
you who destroy the whole earth,"

declares the Lord.

"I will stretch out my hand against you,
roll you off the cliffs,
and make you a burned-out mountain.
26 No rock will be taken from you for a cornerstone,
nor any stone for a foundation,
for you will be desolate forever,"

declares the Lord.

27 "Lift up a banner in the land!
Blow the trumpet among the nations!
Prepare the nations for battle against her;
summon against her these kingdoms:
Ararat, Minni and Ashkenaz.
Appoint a commander against her;
send up horses like a swarm of locusts.
28 Prepare the nations for battle against her—
the kings of the Medes,
their governors and all their officials,
and all the countries they rule.
29 The land trembles and writhes,
for the Lord's purposes against Babylon stand—
to lay waste the land of Babylon
so that no one will live there.
30 Babylon's warriors have stopped fighting;
they remain in their strongholds.
Their strength is exhausted;
they have become like women.
Her dwellings are set on fire;
the bars of her gates are broken.
31 One courier follows another
and messenger follows messenger
to announce to the king of Babylon
that his entire city is captured,

---

a 24 Or Chaldea; also in verse 35

³² the river crossings seized,
 the marshes set on fire,
 and the soldiers terrified."

³³ This is what the LORD Almighty, the God of Israel, says:

 "The Daughter of Babylon is like a threshing floor
  at the time it is trampled;
  the time to harvest her will soon come."

³⁴ "Nebuchadnezzar king of Babylon has devoured us,
 he has thrown us into confusion,
 he has made us an empty jar.
Like a serpent he has swallowed us
 and filled his stomach with our delicacies,
 and then has spewed us out.
³⁵ May the violence done to our flesh^a be upon Babylon,"
 say the inhabitants of Zion.
"May our blood be on those who live in Babylonia,"
 says Jerusalem.

³⁶ Therefore, this is what the LORD says:

 "See, I will defend your cause
  and avenge you;
 I will dry up her sea
  and make her springs dry.
³⁷ Babylon will be a heap of ruins,
 a haunt of jackals,
an object of horror and scorn,
 a place where no one lives.
³⁸ Her people all roar like young lions,
 they growl like lion cubs.
³⁹ But while they are aroused,
 I will set out a feast for them
 and make them drunk,
so that they shout with laughter—
 then sleep forever and not awake,"

declares the LORD.

⁴⁰ "I will bring them down
 like lambs to the slaughter,
 like rams and goats.

⁴¹ "How Sheshach^b will be captured,
 the boast of the whole earth seized!
What a horror Babylon will be
 among the nations!
⁴² The sea will rise over Babylon;
 its roaring waves will cover her.
⁴³ Her towns will be desolate,
 a dry and desert land,
a land where no one lives,
 through which no man travels.
⁴⁴ I will punish Bel in Babylon
 and make him spew out what he has swallowed.
The nations will no longer stream to him.
 And the wall of Babylon will fall.

---

^a *35* Or *done to us and to our children* ^b *41 Sheshach* is a cryptogram for Babylon.

45 "Come out of her, my people!
    Run for your lives!
    Run from the fierce anger of the Lord.
46 Do not lose heart or be afraid
    when rumors are heard in the land;
  one rumor comes this year, another the next,
    rumors of violence in the land
    and of ruler against ruler.
47 For the time will surely come
    when I will punish the idols of Babylon;
  her whole land will be disgraced
    and her slain will all lie fallen within her.
48 Then heaven and earth and all that is in them
    will shout for joy over Babylon,
  for out of the north
    destroyers will attack her,"

                                        declares the Lord.

49 "Babylon must fall because of Israel's slain,
    just as the slain in all the earth
    have fallen because of Babylon.
50 You who have escaped the sword,
    leave and do not linger!
  Remember the Lord in a distant land,
    and think on Jerusalem."

51 "We are disgraced,
    for we have been insulted
    and shame covers our faces,
  because foreigners have entered
    the holy places of the Lord's house."

52 "But days are coming," declares the Lord,
    "when I will punish her idols,
  and throughout her land
    the wounded will groan.
53 Even if Babylon reaches the sky
    and fortifies her lofty stronghold,
    I will send destroyers against her,"

                                        declares the Lord.

54 "The sound of a cry comes from Babylon,
    the sound of great destruction
    from the land of the Babylonians.[a]
55 The Lord will destroy Babylon;
    he will silence her noisy din.
  Waves ⌊of enemies⌋ will rage like great waters;
    the roar of their voices will resound.
56 A destroyer will come against Babylon;
    her warriors will be captured,
    and their bows will be broken.
  For the Lord is a God of retribution;
    he will repay in full.
57 I will make her officials and wise men drunk,
    her governors, officers and warriors as well;

[a] 54 Or Chaldeans

they will sleep forever and not awake,"
declares the King, whose name is the LORD Almighty.

⁵⁸This is what the LORD Almighty says:

"Babylon's thick wall will be leveled
and her high gates set on fire;
the peoples exhaust themselves for
nothing,
the nations' labor is only fuel for the
flames."

⁵⁹This is the message Jeremiah gave to the staff officer Seraiah son of Neriah, the son of Mahseiah, when he went to Babylon with Zedekiah king of Judah in the fourth year of his reign. ⁶⁰Jeremiah had written on a scroll about all the disasters that would come upon Babylon—all that had been recorded concerning Babylon. ⁶¹He said to Seraiah, "When you get to Babylon, see that you read all these words aloud. ⁶²Then say, 'O LORD, you have said you will destroy this place, so that neither man nor animal will live in it; it will be desolate forever.' ⁶³When you finish reading this scroll, tie a stone to it and throw it into the Euphrates. ⁶⁴Then say, 'So will Babylon sink to rise no more because of the disaster I will bring upon her. And her people will fall.' "

The words of Jeremiah end here.

THE FALL OF JERUSALEM

52

Zedekiah was twenty-one years old when he became king, and he reigned in Jerusalem eleven years. His mother's name was Hamutal daughter of Jeremiah; she was from Libnah. ²He did evil in the eyes of the LORD, just as Jehoiakim had done. ³It was because of the LORD's anger that all this happened to Jerusalem and Judah, and in the end he thrust them from his presence.

Now Zedekiah rebelled against the king of Babylon.

⁴So in the ninth year of Zedekiah's reign, on the tenth day of the tenth month, Nebuchadnezzar king of Babylon marched against Jerusalem with his whole army. They camped outside the city and built siege works all around it. ⁵The city was kept under siege until the eleventh year of King Zedekiah.

⁶By the ninth day of the fourth month the famine in the city had become so severe that there was no food for the people to eat. ⁷Then the city wall was broken through, and the whole army fled. They left the city at night through the gate between the two walls near the king's garden, though the Babylonians[a] were surrounding the city. They fled toward the Arabah,[b] ⁸but the Babylonian[c] army pursued King Zedekiah and overtook him in the plains of Jericho. All his soldiers were separated from him and scattered, ⁹and he was captured.

He was taken to the king of Babylon at Riblah in the land of Hamath, where he pronounced sentence on him. ¹⁰There at Riblah the king of Babylon slaughtered the sons of Zedekiah before his eyes; he also killed all the officials of Judah. ¹¹Then he put out Zedekiah's eyes, bound him with bronze shackles and took him to Babylon, where he put him in prison till the day of his death.

¹²On the tenth day of the fifth month, in the nineteenth year of Nebuchadnezzar king of Babylon, Nebuzaradan commander of the imperial guard, who served the king of Babylon, came to Jerusalem. ¹³He set fire to the temple of the LORD, the royal palace and all the houses of Jerusalem. Every important building he burned down. ¹⁴The whole Babylonian army under the commander of the imperial guard broke down all the walls around Jerusalem. ¹⁵Nebuzaradan the commander of the guard carried into exile some of the poorest people and those who remained in the city, along with the rest of the

Answering the Tough Call

Let's reset the scene. Judah is about to be destroyed by the Babylonians. The people of Judah are about to be captured and taken back to Babylon where who knows what might happen to them. In the middle of all this violence and bloodshed, Jeremiah wanted Seraiah to stand up and announce that God is going to destroy Babylon.

Talk about gut-check time! Obeying Jeremiah's (and God's) instructions would have meant serious danger—maybe even death—for Seraiah. The thing about obeying God, though, is that the tougher the task he calls you to, the more strength and courage he gives you to do it.

---

[a] 7 Or *Chaldeans*; also in verse 17   [b] 7 Or *the Jordan Valley*   [c] 8 Or *Chaldean*; also in verse 14

craftsmen[a] and those who had gone over to the king of Babylon. [16]But Nebuzaradan left behind the rest of the poorest people of the land to work the vineyards and fields.

[17]The Babylonians broke up the bronze pillars, the movable stands and the bronze Sea that were at the temple of the LORD and they carried all the bronze to Babylon. [18]They also took away the pots, shovels, wick trimmers, sprinkling bowls, dishes and all the bronze articles used in the temple service. [19]The commander of the imperial guard took away the basins, censers, sprinkling bowls, pots, lampstands, dishes and bowls used for drink offerings—all that were made of pure gold or silver.

[20]The bronze from the two pillars, the Sea and the twelve bronze bulls under it, and the movable stands, which King Solomon had made for the temple of the LORD, was more than could be weighed. [21]Each of the pillars was eighteen cubits high and twelve cubits in circumference[b]; each was four fingers thick, and hollow. [22]The bronze capital on top of the one pillar was five cubits[c] high and was decorated with a network and pomegranates of bronze all around. The other pillar, with its pomegranates, was similar. [23]There were ninety-six pomegranates on the sides; the total number of pomegranates above the surrounding network was a hundred.

[24]The commander of the guard took as prisoners Seraiah the chief priest, Zephaniah the priest next in rank and the three doorkeepers. [25]Of those still in the city, he took the officer in charge of the fighting men, and seven royal advisers. He also took the secretary who was chief officer in charge of conscripting the people of the land and sixty of his men who were found in the city. [26]Nebuzaradan the commander took them all and brought them to the king of Babylon at Riblah. [27]There at Riblah, in the land of Hamath, the king had them executed.

So Judah went into captivity, away from her land. [28]This is the number of the people Nebuchadnezzar carried into exile:

in the seventh year, 3,023 Jews;
[29]in Nebuchadnezzar's eighteenth year,
    832 people from Jerusalem;
[30]in his twenty-third year,
    745 Jews taken into exile by Nebuzaradan the commander of the imperial guard.
    There were 4,600 people in all.

NOW OR NEVER
JER 52:31–34

Notice how, despite all the negative stuff that happens in the book of Jeremiah, the story ends on a good note. There's a lesson here. No matter how bad life gets, God delights in showing undeserved mercy to his people.

JEHOIACHIN RELEASED

[31]In the thirty-seventh year of the exile of Jehoiachin king of Judah, in the year Evil-Merodach[d] became king of Babylon, he released Jehoiachin king of Judah and freed him from prison on the twenty-fifth day of the twelfth month. [32]He spoke kindly to him and gave him a seat of honor higher than those of the other kings who were with him in Babylon. [33]So Jehoiachin put aside his prison clothes and for the rest of his life ate regularly at the king's table. [34]Day by day the king of Babylon gave Jehoiachin a regular allowance as long as he lived, till the day of his death.

---

[a] 15 Or *populace*   [b] 21 That is, about 27 feet (about 8.1 meters) high and 18 feet (about 5.4 meters) in circumference   [c] 22 That is, about 7 1/2 feet (about 2.3 meters)   [d] 31 Also called *Amel-Marduk*

LAMENTATIONS

« AT A GLANCE

Author
Jeremiah

Audience
People of Judah and Jerusalem

Date
Shortly after the fall of Jerusalem in 586 B.C.

Setting
Jerusalem had been utterly destroyed by the Babylonians. The people were killed, tortured or taken as prisoners.

Verses to Remember
Because of the LORD's great love we are not consumed, for his compassions never fail. They are new every morning; great is your faithfulness (3:22–23).

Theme to Consider
In the midst of hopelessness, Jeremiah had faith in God's character and in his promise to bring his people back to himself someday.

UNCHANGING TRUTH » Very few people make it out of this world without being blindsided by tragedy at least once in their lives. For some, it's the sudden death of a loved one. For others, it's a serious illness or injury. And for various people, it's a financial disaster that turns their family upside down. Maybe you've already experienced your share of tragedies, maybe not.

The thing is, no one can predict how they will react when tragedy strikes. One thing you need to know, though, is that when the bottom seemingly drops out of your world, you'll face one of the most important decisions of your life: What part God will play in the aftermath. Your first option is to make God your enemy and blame him for the tragedy—to say things like, "How could you let this happen? I put my faith in you because I thought you were supposed to be loving!"

Your second option is to rely on God as your greatest source of strength, depending on him to get you through the tragedy. That doesn't mean you ignore your feelings of anger, fear, hurt, confusion and hopelessness, pretending they aren't there; it means you share them with God. You tell him exactly how you're feeling—a hundred times a day, if you need to—and ask him to give you the strength and faith you need to keep your feelings of rage and pain from dragging you away from the protection of his grip.

Do yourself a lifelong favor—choose the second option. Don't separate yourself from the only One who can bring true peace and joy back into your life, the only One who can help you begin to put your life back together again. Don't try to carry the emotional pain all by yourself; give it to the One whose strength is limitless.

Jeremiah was a man who knew tragedy. When he wrote the book of Lamentations, he was still shell-shocked from watching as his home and his city were destroyed, and his friends and neighbors either killed or carried away as captives by the hated Babylonians. Though you may not find much comfort in Jeremiah's writings, you will find words of grief and suffering that may help express your own feelings in the wake of tragedy.

LIFE LESSONS »

1. Sometimes God uses extreme methods to get his people's undivided attention (1:12–15).

2. God never stops doing good things in the lives of people who maintain a close relationship with him (3:22–23).

3. When you know you've done something wrong, the wisest thing to do is to confess it immediately and seek God's forgiveness (3:40–50).

1

[a]How deserted lies the city,
    once so full of people!
How like a widow is she,
    who once was great among the nations!
She who was queen among the provinces
    has now become a slave.

NOW OR NEVER

LA 1:1

Is your life pretty good right now? How
would you describe your relationship with
God? What can you do to make sure that
you don't get spiritually complacent like
the Israelites did?

[2]Bitterly she weeps at night,
    tears are upon her cheeks.
Among all her lovers
    there is none to comfort her.
All her friends have betrayed her;
    they have become her enemies.

[3]After affliction and harsh labor,
    Judah has gone into exile.
She dwells among the nations;
    she finds no resting place.
All who pursue her have overtaken her
    in the midst of her distress.

[4]The roads to Zion mourn,
    for no one comes to her appointed feasts.
All her gateways are desolate,
    her priests groan,
her maidens grieve,
    and she is in bitter anguish.

[5]Her foes have become her masters;
    her enemies are at ease.
The LORD has brought her grief
    because of her many sins.
Her children have gone into exile,
    captive before the foe.

[6]All the splendor has departed
    from the Daughter of Zion.
Her princes are like deer
    that find no pasture;
in weakness they have fled
    before the pursuer.

[7]In the days of her affliction and wandering
    Jerusalem remembers all the treasures
    that were hers in days of old.
When her people fell into enemy hands,
    there was no one to help her.
Her enemies looked at her
    and laughed at her destruction.

[8]Jerusalem has sinned greatly
    and so has become unclean.
All who honored her despise her,
    for they have seen her nakedness;
she herself groans
    and turns away.

[a] This chapter is an acrostic poem, the verses of which begin with the successive letters of the Hebrew alphabet.

⁹Her filthiness clung to her skirts;
    she did not consider her future.
Her fall was astounding;
    there was none to comfort her.
"Look, O LORD, on my affliction,
    for the enemy has triumphed."

¹⁰The enemy laid hands
    on all her treasures;
she saw pagan nations
    enter her sanctuary—
those you had forbidden
    to enter your assembly.

¹¹All her people groan
    as they search for bread;
they barter their treasures for food
    to keep themselves alive.
"Look, O LORD, and consider,
    for I am despised."

¹²"Is it nothing to you, all you who pass by?
    Look around and see.
Is any suffering like my suffering
    that was inflicted on me,
that the LORD brought on me
    in the day of his fierce anger?

¹³"From on high he sent fire,
    sent it down into my bones.
He spread a net for my feet
    and turned me back.
He made me desolate,
    faint all the day long.

¹⁴"My sins have been bound into a yokeᵃ;
    by his hands they were woven together.
They have come upon my neck
    and the Lord has sapped my strength.
He has handed me over
    to those I cannot withstand.

¹⁵"The Lord has rejected
    all the warriors in my midst;
he has summoned an army against me
    toᵇ crush my young men.
In his winepress the Lord has trampled
    the Virgin Daughter of Judah.

¹⁶"This is why I weep
    and my eyes overflow with tears.
No one is near to comfort me,
    no one to restore my spirit.
My children are destitute
    because the enemy has prevailed."

¹⁷Zion stretches out her hands,
    but there is no one to comfort her.

ᵃ *14* Most Hebrew manuscripts; Septuagint *He kept watch over my sins*   ᵇ *15* Or *has set a time for me / when he will*

The LORD has decreed for Jacob
    that his neighbors become his foes;
Jerusalem has become
    an unclean thing among them.

18 "The LORD is righteous,
    yet I rebelled against his command.
Listen, all you peoples;
    look upon my suffering.
My young men and maidens
    have gone into exile.

19 "I called to my allies
    but they betrayed me.
My priests and my elders
    perished in the city
while they searched for food
    to keep themselves alive.

20 "See, O LORD, how distressed I am!
    I am in torment within,
and in my heart I am disturbed,
    for I have been most rebellious.
Outside, the sword bereaves;
    inside, there is only death.

21 "People have heard my groaning,
    but there is no one to comfort me.
All my enemies have heard of my distress;
    they rejoice at what you have done.
May you bring the day you have announced
    so they may become like me.

22 "Let all their wickedness come before you;
    deal with them
as you have dealt with me
    because of all my sins.
My groans are many
    and my heart is faint."

2

aHow the Lord has covered the Daughter of Zion
    with the cloud of his angerb!
He has hurled down the splendor of Israel
    from heaven to earth;
he has not remembered his footstool
    in the day of his anger.

2 Without pity the Lord has swallowed up
    all the dwellings of Jacob;
in his wrath he has torn down
    the strongholds of the Daughter of Judah.
He has brought her kingdom and its princes
    down to the ground in dishonor.

3 In fierce anger he has cut off
    every hornc of Israel.

---

a This chapter is an acrostic poem, the verses of which begin with the successive letters of the Hebrew alphabet.   b 1 Or *How the Lord in his anger / has treated the Daughter of Zion with contempt*   c 3 Or / *all the strength*; or *every king*; horn here symbolizes strength.

battlelines

» The Bitterness Battle (Bitterness/Blame)

Q: How's it going?
A: Are you just making conversation, or do you *really* want to know?

Q: No, I want to know. What's up?
A: Everything. My mom is—man, don't even get me started. I'll end up saying something I shouldn't.

Q: Like what?
A: Well, you know she moved out about three months ago. According to her, my dad wasn't any good. He wasn't making enough money. He didn't have any ambition. All he cared about was watching sports on TV. So now my mom's in California living the good life, and here we are—my dad, my younger brother and me.

Q: That's harsh.
A: Yeah. My dad is just destroyed. It's like she sucked the life right out of him. He couldn't focus at work and lost his job. And now he's too unstable to do anything else. I don't know what we're going to do. Meanwhile, my mom keeps calling and emailing, saying that my little brother and I should move out to California to live with her.

Q: What are you going to do?
A: I don't know. But tell me this: How am I *not* supposed to resent my mom for what she's done to our family? I know, I know; if I'm a Christian, I'm supposed to forgive. But it's not like she did something once and then acted sorry. She *keeps* causing us pain, every single day. And she's *not* sorry—not even a little bit. Now my dad is like a shell of what he used to be. Tell me, how can I *not* be bitter toward her?

» Letting It Go

This is a tough situation. And Hsin is asking some good questions. It's the most natural thing in the world to be furious at someone who has caused you this kind of pain. If you're facing a situation similar to Hsin's, you need to deal with the pain head-on before it consumes you. Accept support from brothers and sisters in Christ, and consider seeking the assistance of a Christian counselor.

Ephesians 4:30–32 says, "Do not grieve the Holy Spirit of God, with whom you were sealed for the day of redemption. Get rid of all bitterness, rage and anger . . . Be kind and compassionate to one another, forgiving each other, just as in Christ God forgave you."

God's not just looking out for the people who need forgiveness; he's also looking out for those who have been wronged. God warns against hatred and bitterness because in the end, an unforgiving spirit hurts only one person—you. Forgiving someone doesn't make what he or she did to you alright; it makes *you* alright.

Read more about the effects of bitterness at www.RevolutionBible.com.

He has withdrawn his right hand
  at the approach of the enemy.
He has burned in Jacob like a flaming fire
  that consumes everything around it.

⁴Like an enemy he has strung his bow;
  his right hand is ready.
Like a foe he has slain
  all who were pleasing to the eye;
he has poured out his wrath like fire
  on the tent of the Daughter of Zion.

⁵The Lord is like an enemy;
  he has swallowed up Israel.
He has swallowed up all her palaces
  and destroyed her strongholds.
He has multiplied mourning and lamentation
  for the Daughter of Judah.

⁶He has laid waste his dwelling like a garden;
  he has destroyed his place of meeting.
The LORD has made Zion forget
  her appointed feasts and her Sabbaths;
in his fierce anger he has spurned
  both king and priest.

⁷The Lord has rejected his altar
  and abandoned his sanctuary.
He has handed over to the enemy
  the walls of her palaces;
they have raised a shout in the house of the LORD
  as on the day of an appointed feast.

⁸The LORD determined to tear down
  the wall around the Daughter of Zion.
He stretched out a measuring line
  and did not withhold his hand from destroying.
He made ramparts and walls lament;
  together they wasted away.

⁹Her gates have sunk into the ground;
  their bars he has broken and destroyed.
Her king and her princes are exiled among the nations,
  the law is no more,
and her prophets no longer find
  visions from the LORD.

¹⁰The elders of the Daughter of Zion
  sit on the ground in silence;
they have sprinkled dust on their heads
  and put on sackcloth.
The young women of Jerusalem
  have bowed their heads to the ground.

¹¹My eyes fail from weeping,
  I am in torment within,
my heart is poured out on the ground
  because my people are destroyed,
because children and infants faint
  in the streets of the city.

12 They say to their mothers,
    "Where is bread and wine?"
as they faint like wounded men
    in the streets of the city,
as their lives ebb away
    in their mothers' arms.

13 What can I say for you?
    With what can I compare you,
    O Daughter of Jerusalem?
To what can I liken you,
    that I may comfort you,
    O Virgin Daughter of Zion?
Your wound is as deep as the sea.
    Who can heal you?

14 The visions of your prophets
    were false and worthless;
they did not expose your sin
    to ward off your captivity.
The oracles they gave you
    were false and misleading.

15 All who pass your way
    clap their hands at you;
they scoff and shake their heads
    at the Daughter of Jerusalem:
"Is this the city that was called
    the perfection of beauty,
    the joy of the whole earth?"

16 All your enemies open their mouths
    wide against you;
they scoff and gnash their teeth
    and say, "We have swallowed her up.
This is the day we have waited for;
    we have lived to see it."

17 The Lord has done what he planned;
    he has fulfilled his word,
    which he decreed long ago.
He has overthrown you without pity,
    he has let the enemy gloat over you,
    he has exalted the horn[a] of your foes.

18 The hearts of the people
    cry out to the Lord.
O wall of the Daughter of Zion,
    let your tears flow like a river
    day and night;
give yourself no relief,
    your eyes no rest.

19 Arise, cry out in the night,
    as the watches of the night begin;
pour out your heart like water
    in the presence of the Lord.

[a] 17 Horn here symbolizes strength.

Lift up your hands to him
 for the lives of your children,
who faint from hunger
 at the head of every street.

20 "Look, O Lord, and consider:
 Whom have you ever treated like this?
Should women eat their offspring,
 the children they have cared for?
Should priest and prophet be killed
 in the sanctuary of the Lord?

21 "Young and old lie together
 in the dust of the streets;
my young men and maidens
 have fallen by the sword.
You have slain them in the day of your anger;
 you have slaughtered them without pity.

22 "As you summon to a feast day,
 so you summoned against me terrors on every side.
In the day of the Lord's anger
 no one escaped or survived;
those I cared for and reared,
 my enemy has destroyed."

^aI am the man who has seen affliction
 by the rod of his wrath.
2 He has driven me away and made me walk
 in darkness rather than light;
3 indeed, he has turned his hand against me
 again and again, all day long.

4 He has made my skin and my flesh
  grow old
  and has broken my bones.
5 He has besieged me and surrounded me
 with bitterness and hardship.
6 He has made me dwell in darkness
 like those long dead.

7 He has walled me in so I cannot escape;
 he has weighed me down with
  chains.
8 Even when I call out or cry for help,
 he shuts out my prayer.
9 He has barred my way with blocks of
  stone;
 he has made my paths crooked.

10 Like a bear lying in wait,
 like a lion in hiding,
11 he dragged me from the path and mangled me
 and left me without help.
12 He drew his bow
 and made me the target for his arrows.

now or never

LA 3:1

Have you ever endured a time of intense suffering? Did that experience bring you closer to God or drive you away from him? We don't always understand why we suffer, and trusting God through hardship requires a lot of faith and humility. But the price to pay for rejecting God's goodness is too huge to measure.

---

^a This chapter is an acrostic poem; the verses of each stanza begin with the successive letters of the Hebrew alphabet, and the verses within each stanza begin with the same letter.

13 He pierced my heart
with arrows from his quiver.
14 I became the laughingstock of all my
people;
they mock me in song all day long.
15 He has filled me with bitter herbs
and sated me with gall.

16 He has broken my teeth with gravel;
he has trampled me in the dust.
17 I have been deprived of peace;
I have forgotten what prosperity is.
18 So I say, "My splendor is gone
and all that I had hoped from the
LORD."

19 I remember my affliction and my
wandering,
the bitterness and the gall.
20 I well remember them,
and my soul is downcast within me.
21 Yet this I call to mind
and therefore I have hope:

22 Because of the LORD's great love we are
not consumed,
for his compassions never fail.
23 They are new every morning;
great is your faithfulness.
24 I say to myself, "The LORD is my portion;
therefore I will wait for him."

25 The LORD is good to those whose hope
is in him,
to the one who seeks him;
26 it is good to wait quietly
for the salvation of the LORD.
27 It is good for a man to bear the yoke
while he is young.

Depending on God's Faithfulness

If you're like most people, you're going to face times when life seems overwhelming—even pointless—and you can't get excited about the thought of facing another day. That's when God's daily outpouring of grace is essential. The fact that God's blessings are "new every morning" suggests that, if we ask, he will give us the strength, motivation and encouragement to make it through the day ahead— no matter what we encounter.

challenge notes

To: my_son

heavenly_father: I will never leave you hanging. if you put your faith in me, I promise to make it worth your while. you don't know where or when my deliverance will come, but you can absolutely count on it coming.

28 Let him sit alone in silence,
for the LORD has laid it on
him.
29 Let him bury his face in the
dust—
there may yet be hope.
30 Let him offer his cheek to one
who would strike
him,
and let him be filled with
disgrace.

31 For men are not cast off
by the Lord forever.

32 Though he brings grief, he will show compassion,
so great is his unfailing love.
33 For he does not willingly bring affliction
or grief to the children of men.

³⁴ To crush underfoot
    all prisoners in the land,
³⁵ to deny a man his rights
    before the Most High,
³⁶ to deprive a man of justice—
    would not the Lord see such things?

³⁷ Who can speak and have it happen
    if the Lord has not decreed it?
³⁸ Is it not from the mouth of the Most High
    that both calamities and good things come?
³⁹ Why should any living man complain
    when punished for his sins?

⁴⁰ Let us examine our ways and test them,
    and let us return to the Lord.
⁴¹ Let us lift up our hearts and our hands
    to God in heaven, and say:
⁴² "We have sinned and rebelled
    and you have not forgiven.

⁴³ "You have covered yourself with anger and pursued us;
    you have slain without pity.
⁴⁴ You have covered yourself with a cloud
    so that no prayer can get through.
⁴⁵ You have made us scum and refuse
    among the nations.

⁴⁶ "All our enemies have opened their mouths
    wide against us.
⁴⁷ We have suffered terror and pitfalls,
    ruin and destruction."
⁴⁸ Streams of tears flow from my eyes
    because my people are destroyed.

⁴⁹ My eyes will flow unceasingly,
    without relief,
⁵⁰ until the Lord looks down
    from heaven and sees.
⁵¹ What I see brings grief to my soul
    because of all the women of my city.

⁵² Those who were my enemies without cause
    hunted me like a bird.
⁵³ They tried to end my life in a pit
    and threw stones at me;
⁵⁴ the waters closed over my head,
    and I thought I was about to be cut off.

⁵⁵ I called on your name, O Lord,
    from the depths of the pit.
⁵⁶ You heard my plea: "Do not close your ears
    to my cry for relief."
⁵⁷ You came near when I called you,
    and you said, "Do not fear."

⁵⁸ O Lord, you took up my case;
    you redeemed my life.
⁵⁹ You have seen, O Lord, the wrong done to me.

4

Uphold my cause!
60 You have seen the depth of their vengeance,
all their plots against me.

61 O LORD, you have heard their insults,
all their plots against me—
62 what my enemies whisper and mutter
against me all day long.
63 Look at them! Sitting or standing,
they mock me in their songs.

64 Pay them back what they deserve, O LORD,
for what their hands have done.
65 Put a veil over their hearts,
and may your curse be on them!
66 Pursue them in anger and destroy them
from under the heavens of the LORD.

ᵃHow the gold has lost its luster,
the fine gold become dull!
The sacred gems are scattered
at the head of every street.

2 How the precious sons of Zion,
once worth their weight in gold,
are now considered as pots of clay,
the work of a potter's hands!

3 Even jackals offer their breasts
to nurse their young,
but my people have become heartless
like ostriches in the desert.

4 Because of thirst the infant's tongue
sticks to the roof of its mouth;
the children beg for bread,
but no one gives it to them.

5 Those who once ate delicacies
are destitute in the streets.
Those nurtured in purple
now lie on ash heaps.

6 The punishment of my people
is greater than that of Sodom,
which was overthrown in a moment
without a hand turned to help her.

7 Their princes were brighter than snow
and whiter than milk,
their bodies more ruddy than rubies,
their appearance like sapphires.ᵇ

8 But now they are blacker than soot;
they are not recognized in the streets.
Their skin has shriveled on their bones;
it has become as dry as a stick.

9 Those killed by the sword are better off

Appreciating God's Grace

»» live the adventure »» La 4:4-16

The people of Israel had their homes destroyed and were taken as prisoners to a foreign country—all because of their habit of disobeying God. Those of us today who have made a habit of disobedience should look at the Israelites' fate and take a hint. God takes the sin of his people very seriously. The good news is that Jesus took the punishment we deserved when he died for us on the cross. But that doesn't give us the right to live however we want. God expects his children to live out their faith.

ᵃ This chapter is an acrostic poem, the verses of which begin with the successive letters of the Hebrew alphabet.   ᵇ 7 Or *lapis lazuli*

than those who die of famine;
    racked with hunger, they waste away
        for lack of food from the field.

10 With their own hands compassionate women
    have cooked their own children,
who became their food
    when my people were destroyed.

11 The LORD has given full vent to his wrath;
    he has poured out his fierce anger.
He kindled a fire in Zion
    that consumed her foundations.

12 The kings of the earth did not believe,
    nor did any of the world's people,
that enemies and foes could enter
    the gates of Jerusalem.

13 But it happened because of the sins of her prophets
    and the iniquities of her priests,
who shed within her
    the blood of the righteous.

14 Now they grope through the streets
    like men who are blind.
They are so defiled with blood
    that no one dares to touch their garments.

15 "Go away! You are unclean!" men cry to them.
    "Away! Away! Don't touch us!"
When they flee and wander about,
    people among the nations say,
    "They can stay here no longer."

16 The LORD himself has scattered them;
    he no longer watches over them.
The priests are shown no honor,
    the elders no favor.

17 Moreover, our eyes failed,
    looking in vain for help;
from our towers we watched
    for a nation that could not save us.

18 Men stalked us at every step,
    so we could not walk in our streets.
Our end was near, our days were numbered,
    for our end had come.

19 Our pursuers were swifter
    than eagles in the sky;
they chased us over the mountains
    and lay in wait for us in the desert.

20 The LORD's anointed, our very life breath,
    was caught in their traps.
We thought that under his shadow
    we would live among the nations.

21 Rejoice and be glad, O Daughter of Edom,

you who live in the land of Uz.
But to you also the cup will be passed;
  you will be drunk and stripped naked.

²² O Daughter of Zion, your punishment will end;
  he will not prolong your exile.
But, O Daughter of Edom, he will punish your sin
  and expose your wickedness.

5

Remember, O LORD, what has happened to us;
  look, and see our disgrace.
² Our inheritance has been turned over to aliens,
  our homes to foreigners.
³ We have become orphans and fatherless,
  our mothers like widows.
⁴ We must buy the water we drink;
  our wood can be had only at a price.
⁵ Those who pursue us are at our heels;
  we are weary and find no rest.
⁶ We submitted to Egypt and Assyria
  to get enough bread.
⁷ Our fathers sinned and are no more,
  and we bear their punishment.
⁸ Slaves rule over us,
  and there is none to free us from
    their hands.
⁹ We get our bread at the risk of our lives
  because of the sword in the desert.
¹⁰ Our skin is hot as an oven,
  feverish from hunger.
¹¹ Women have been ravished in Zion,
  and virgins in the towns of Judah.

NOW OR NEVER

LA 5:1

Do you ever find yourself embarrassed by your sin? Imagine, for instance, your parents catching you looking at pornography. Do you think God cares that your pride is wounded when it's because of your own mistakes? Take a lesson from Lamentations. Bring your plea for mercy before him.

¹² Princes have been hung up by their hands;
  elders are shown no respect.
¹³ Young men toil at the millstones;
  boys stagger under loads of wood.
¹⁴ The elders are gone from the city gate;
  the young men have stopped their music.
¹⁵ Joy is gone from our hearts;
  our dancing has turned to mourning.
¹⁶ The crown has fallen from our head.
  Woe to us, for we have sinned!
¹⁷ Because of this our hearts are faint,
  because of these things our eyes grow dim
¹⁸ for Mount Zion, which lies desolate,
  with jackals prowling over it.

¹⁹ You, O LORD, reign forever;
  your throne endures from generation to generation.
²⁰ Why do you always forget us?
  Why do you forsake us so long?
²¹ Restore us to yourself, O LORD, that we may return;
  renew our days as of old
²² unless you have utterly rejected us
  and are angry with us beyond measure.

70 PROMISES OF GOD

Have you ever heard the saying, "The only sure things in life are death and taxes"? Hopefully, you won't have to worry about either for a while. Neither one is a party. But there is one other item you can add to that short list, and this one is both encouraging and relevant. It's . . . the promises of God. The Bible is filled with covenant pledges from God about things that he either will do or has already done. You might search the Scriptures for a lifetime and not find them all, but we've given you a fighting chance. Here are a few of God's promises:

» 01 Obedience to God's Word brings eternal prosperity and success » *Jos 1:8*
» 02 Not only is God strong, but he also goes with you wherever you are . . . so be courageous » *Jos 1:9*
» 03 God won't evaluate you by the superficial standards of the world » *1Sa 16:7*
» 04 When you are feeling oppressed, God is your stronghold and refuge » *Ps 9:9*
» 05 God is the shepherd of your soul—the One who meets your true needs » *Ps 23:1*

» 06 Even in the darkest periods of life, God's favor and grace are just around the corner » *Ps 30:4–5*
» 07 Those who look to God need never fear or be ashamed » *Ps 34:4–5*
» 08 God listens to those who are pure in heart » *Ps 34:17; 66:18*
» 09 Pursue God with all your heart, and he will give you your heart's desire » *Ps 37:4*
» 10 God will punish his enemies and those who oppose his people » *Ps 59:9–10*

» 11 God will help you bear your daily burdens » *Ps 68:19*
» 12 God doesn't withhold any good thing from his people » *Ps 84:11*
» 13 Those who seek God and live according to his ways will be blessed » *Ps 119:1–2*
» 14 If you keep God's Word in your heart, you will be able to guard yourself against sin » *Ps 119:9–11*
» 15 God protects his people from evil » *Ps 121:7*

» 16 God understands everything about your life » *Ps 139:3*
» 17 When you trust in God, he takes care of everything » *Pr 3:5–6*
» 18 God displays great gentleness in handling his people » *Isa 40:11*
» 19 When you hope in God, he will renew your strength » *Isa 40:31*
» 20 We have no reason to be afraid or discouraged because we have God's strength » *Isa 41:10*

» 21 God is with his people to the very end of their lives » *Isa 46:4*
» 22 God has a purpose for your life, and he's in complete control » *Isa 46:9–10*
» 23 God is good in times of trouble » *Na 1:7*
» 24 God never changes » *Mal 3:6*
» 25 God shows mercy to those who are merciful » *Mt 5:7*

» 26 God will provide for every need you have » *Mt 6:32–34*
» 27 Those who serve God by serving his people will be exalted » *Mt 20:26–27*
» 28 God is sitting next to you right now and will be with you right to the end » *Mt 28:20*
» 29 If you believe in Jesus, you have the right to be considered a child of God » *Jn 1:12*
» 30 God (and no one/nothing else) satisfies the deep thirsts of your soul » *Jn 7:37–39*

» 31 God gives followers of Jesus an unbelievably rich life » *Jn 10:10*

» 32 God is preparing an eternal home for you in paradise » *Jn 14:2–3*

» 33 If you obey God, you will experience his love and joy » *Jn 15:9–11*

» 34 We can actually be friends with God » *Jn 15:15*

» 35 God has already overcome the trouble we have not yet faced » *Jn 16:33*

» 36 God will use you to spread the truth about his Son » *Ac 1:8*

» 37 God uses trials and difficulties to shape us and strengthen us » *Ro 5:3*

» 38 If Jesus' death on the cross means our death to sin, his resurrection means our eternal life » *Ro 6:3–5*

» 39 Christians have been spared from condemnation » *Ro 8:1*

» 40 Faithfulness now leads to glory later » *Ro 8:18*

» 41 God works in all things—troubles and successes alike—for your good » *Ro 8:28*

» 42 God forgives our sin when we trust Christ—and someday he will glorify us! » *Ro 8:30*

» 43 God will give you the strength you need to resist every kind of temptation » *1Co 10:13*

» 44 God will continue to make you just like Jesus » *2Co 3:18*

» 45 God constantly renews his people every day of their lives » *2Co 4:16*

» 46 Those who believe in Jesus become brand-new people inside » *2Co 5:17*

» 47 God provides encouragement to the discouraged » *2Co 7:5–6*

» 48 When you are weakest, Christ's power will prove strongest in your life » *2Co 12:9*

» 49 When the Holy Spirit fills us, our lives are completely different » *Gal 5:22–23*

» 50 You will reap what you sow » *Gal 6:7*

» 51 God showers us with every spiritual blessing » *Eph 1:3*

» 52 God can do WAY more than you can ask for or imagine » *Eph 3:20*

» 53 God will complete in you what he began when he saved you » *Php 1:6*

» 54 God can give you the desire to obey him and the ability to please him » *Php 2:13*

» 55 We have guaranteed citizenship in heaven » *Php 3:20*

» 56 God can calm any anxiousness in your heart and mind » *Php 4:6–7*

» 57 You can do anything through God who gives you strength » *Php 4:13*

» 58 You have all you need in Christ; you are complete in him » *Col 2:9–10*

» 59 God is patient with even the worst of sinners » *1Ti 1:16*

» 60 God will provide for your every need, and he can make you content with less » *1Ti 6:6–8*

» 61 God expects power, love and self-discipline from us—because he graciously gave us the spirit of those things » *2Ti 1:7*

» 62 God understands your temptations and struggles » *Heb 4:14–15*

» 63 We can approach God anywhere, anytime, no matter what our circumstances are » *Heb 4:16*

» 64 Jesus lives to intercede on behalf of sinners like us » *Heb 7:24–25*

» 65 Those who seek God will be rewarded » *Heb 11:6*

» 66 The perfect wisdom of God is yours for the asking » *Jas 1:5*

» 67 God promises the crown of life to the person who is steadfastly devoted to him » *Jas 1:12*

» 68 The prayer of a righteous person (you, if you've trusted Jesus) is powerful and effective » *Jas 5:16*

» 69 No matter the circumstances or what people say, we are truly free in Christ » *1Pe 2:16*

» 70 If you fail to know God, you won't understand those who follow him » *1Jn 3:1*

EZEKIEL

« AT A GLANCE

Author
Ezekiel

Audience
The Jews in captivity in Babylon

Date
Between 593 and 571 B.C.

Setting
Ezekiel the priest prophesied to his fellow Jews
who were taken as prisoners to Babylon in 597 B.C.

Verses to Remember
"For I will take you out of the nations; I will gather
you from all the countries and bring you back into
your own land. I will sprinkle clean water on you,
and you will be clean; I will cleanse you from all
your impurities and from all your idols. I will give
you a new heart and put a new spirit in you; I will
remove from you your heart of stone and give you
a heart of flesh" (36:24–26).

Theme to Consider
In part 1 of the book, Ezekiel warned that God would
punish the people for their sins. Later in the book (after that first part came true!), Ezekiel comforted the
people by assuring them that God would someday
bring them back to Jerusalem and restore the temple.

UNCHANGING TRUTH » Do you ever have trouble understanding certain parts of the
Bible? You're not alone. All Christians struggle occasionally to make sense of God's Word. And why
wouldn't they? Let's face it, it's not exactly like reading *Sports Illustrated*.

Why is the Bible such a challenge? Because God designed it that way! Don't be confused. God is perfectly willing to give us the wisdom and insight we need to understand his Word, but he's not going to
dumb it down for us.

Matthew 22:37 says, "'Love the Lord your God with all your heart and with all your soul and with all
your mind.'" Look at those last three words again: *all your mind*. When it comes to reading his Word, God
wants our brains to be involved along with our eyes.

Working to figure out what certain difficult Bible passages mean is a way of showing God how much
you want to know him. The more effort you put into it, the more desire you show. That's why it's a mistake
to approach Bible study with a casual, half hearted attitude. If you're going to make sense of God's Word—
if you're going to grasp what he wants you to understand in it—you've got to bring passion and desire to
the time you spend studying it.

The book of Ezekiel might be one of the biggest brain busters in the Bible. It's full of odd visions, ancient prophecies and historical references. But it also contains some of the coolest events and most incredible promises in all of Scripture. In other words, it's a book worth diving into . . . with all of your brain-
power.

LIFE LESSONS »

1   You have a responsibility to make sure that your Christian friends and family members stay
faithful to the Lord (3:20–21).

2   If you're serious about your relationship with God, you can expect him to ask you to do some
things that make you uncomfortable (5:1–4).

3   You can't keep anything secret from God (8:5–16).

THE LIVING CREATURES AND THE GLORY OF THE LORD

1 In the[a] thirtieth year, in the fourth month on the fifth day, while I was among the exiles by the Kebar River, the heavens were opened and I saw visions of God.

[2] On the fifth of the month—it was the fifth year of the exile of King Jehoiachin— [3] the word of the LORD came to Ezekiel the priest, the son of Buzi,[b] by the Kebar River in the land of the Babylonians.[c] There the hand of the LORD was upon him.

[4] I looked, and I saw a windstorm coming out of the north—an immense cloud with flashing lightning and surrounded by brilliant light. The center of the fire looked like glowing metal, [5] and in the fire was what looked like four living creatures. In appearance their form was that of a man, [6] but each of them had four faces and four wings. [7] Their legs were straight; their feet were like those of a calf and gleamed like burnished bronze. [8] Under their wings on their four sides they had the hands of a man. All four of them had faces and wings, [9] and their wings touched one another. Each one went straight ahead; they did not turn as they moved.

[10] Their faces looked like this: Each of the four had the face of a man, and on the right side each had the face of a lion, and on the left the face of an ox; each also had the face of an eagle. [11] Such were their faces. Their wings were spread out upward; each had two wings, one touching the wing of another creature on either side, and two wings covering its body. [12] Each one went straight ahead. Wherever the spirit would go, they would go, without turning as they went. [13] The appearance of the living creatures was like burning coals of fire or like torches. Fire moved back and forth among the creatures; it was bright, and lightning flashed out of it. [14] The creatures sped back and forth like flashes of lightning.

[15] As I looked at the living creatures, I saw a wheel on the ground beside each creature with its four faces. [16] This was the appearance and structure of the wheels: They sparkled like chrysolite, and all four looked alike. Each appeared to be made like a wheel intersecting a wheel. [17] As they moved, they would go in any one of the four directions the creatures faced; the wheels did not turn about[d] as the creatures went. [18] Their rims were high and awesome, and all four rims were full of eyes all around.

[19] When the living creatures moved, the wheels beside them moved; and when the living creatures rose from the ground, the wheels also rose. [20] Wherever the spirit would go, they would go, and the wheels would rise along with them, because the spirit of the living creatures was in the wheels. [21] When the creatures moved, they also moved; when the creatures stood still, they also stood still; and when the creatures rose from the ground, the wheels rose along with them, because the spirit of the living creatures was in the wheels.

[22] Spread out above the heads of the living creatures was what looked like an expanse, sparkling like ice, and awesome. [23] Under the expanse their wings were stretched out one toward the other, and each had two wings covering its body. [24] When the creatures moved, I heard the sound of their wings, like the roar of rushing waters, like the voice of the Almighty,[e] like the tumult of an army. When they stood still, they lowered their wings.

[25] Then there came a voice from above the expanse over their heads as they stood with lowered wings.

Recognizing God's Call

You may never experience a vision from God like Ezekiel did, but you can still know his will for your life. Start by taking a good look at who you are. What strengths and skills do you have? God gave them to you for a reason. Use them to honor him. Next, think about the non-Christians you know. God put them in your life for a purpose. Share with them the good news about God. Then take a look at the needy people around you. God put them in your life for a reason too. Share with them the countless blessings that God has given you. Focus on these things, and you'll *know* what God's will for you is—just like Ezekiel did.

NOW OR NEVER
EZE 1:25-28

Having a personal relationship with God doesn't mean you can treat him like "one of the guys." He deserves the kind of respect and awe that Ezekiel showed him.

---

[a] 1 Or my; [b] 3 Or *Ezekiel son of Buzi the priest* [c] 3 Or *Chaldeans* [d] 17 Or *aside* [e] 24 Hebrew *Shaddai*

26Above the expanse over their heads was what looked like a throne of sapphire,[a] and high above on the throne was a figure like that of a man. 27I saw that from what appeared to be his waist up he looked like glowing metal, as if full of fire, and that from there down he looked like fire; and brilliant light surrounded him. 28Like the appearance of a rainbow in the clouds on a rainy day, so was the radiance around him.

This was the appearance of the likeness of the glory of the LORD. When I saw it, I fell facedown, and I heard the voice of one speaking.

challenge notes

To: my_son

EZE 2:3

heavenly_father: just as I sent ezekiel to the israelites, I have sent you to the people in your home, your neighborhood, your school and your community. it's your job to tell people about me, whether they listen to you or not. don't let them down. let them know how much I have to offer.

EZEKIEL'S CALL

2 He said to me, "Son of man, stand up on your feet and I will speak to you." 2As he spoke, the Spirit came into me and raised me to my feet, and I heard him speaking to me.

3He said: "Son of man, I am sending you to the Israelites, to a rebellious nation that has rebelled against me; they and their fathers have been in revolt against me to this very day. 4The people to whom I am sending you are obstinate and stubborn. Say to them, 'This is what the Sovereign LORD says.' 5And whether they listen or fail to listen—for they are a rebellious house—they will know that a prophet has been among them. 6And you, son of man, do not be afraid of them or their words. Do not be afraid, though briers and thorns are all around you and you live among scorpions. Do not be afraid of what they say or terrified by them, though they are a rebellious house. 7You must speak my words to them, whether they listen or fail to listen, for they are rebellious. 8But you, son of man, listen to what I say to you. Do not rebel like that rebellious house; open your mouth and eat what I give you."

9Then I looked, and I saw a hand stretched out to me. In it was a scroll, 10which he unrolled before me. On both sides of it were written words of lament and mourning and woe.

3 And he said to me, "Son of man, eat what is before you, eat this scroll; then go and speak to the house of Israel." 2So I opened my mouth, and he gave me the scroll to eat.

3Then he said to me, "Son of man, eat this scroll I am giving you and fill your stomach with it." So I ate it, and it tasted as sweet as honey in my mouth.

4He then said to me: "Son of man, go now to the house of Israel and speak my words to them. 5You are not being sent to a people of obscure speech and difficult language, but to the house of Israel— 6not to many peoples of obscure speech and difficult language, whose words you cannot understand. Surely if I had sent you to them, they would have listened to you. 7But the house of Israel is not willing to listen to you because they are not willing to listen to me, for the whole house of Israel is hardened and obstinate. 8But I will make you as unyielding and hardened as they are. 9I will make your forehead like the hardest stone, harder than flint. Do not be afraid of them or terrified by them, though they are a rebellious house."

NOW OR NEVER
EZE 2:5

Who is easier to talk to about spiritual things: a close friend or someone you barely know? How might your friendship with someone make it hard for you to have a serious spiritual conversation? Would you worry too much about what he or she might think?

10And he said to me, "Son of man, listen carefully and take to heart all the words I speak to you. 11Go now to your countrymen in exile and speak to them. Say to them, 'This is what the Sovereign LORD says,' whether they listen or fail to listen."

12Then the Spirit lifted me up, and I heard behind me a loud rumbling sound—May the glory of the LORD be praised in his dwelling place!— 13the sound of the wings of the living creatures brushing against each other and the sound of the wheels beside them, a loud rumbling sound. 14The Spirit then lifted me up and took me away, and I went in bitterness and in the anger of my spirit, with the strong

---

a 26 Or lapis lazuli

hand of the LORD upon me. ¹⁵I came to the exiles who lived at Tel Abib near the Kebar River. And there, where they were living, I sat among them for seven days—overwhelmed.

WARNING TO ISRAEL

¹⁶At the end of seven days the word of the LORD came to me: ¹⁷"Son of man, I have made you a watchman for the house of Israel; so hear the word I speak and give them warning from me. ¹⁸When I say to a wicked man, 'You will surely die,' and you do not warn him or speak out to dissuade him from his evil ways in order to save his life, that wicked man will die forᵃ his sin, and I will hold you accountable for his blood. ¹⁹But if you do warn the wicked man and he does not turn from his wickedness or from his evil ways, he will die for his sin; but you will have saved yourself.

NOW OR NEVER

EZE 3:20-21

Do you have someone close to you who will warn you when he sees dangers in the way you're living? It's important that you have someone living in your life with the guts and the freedom to confront you when you need it.

²⁰"Again, when a righteous man turns from his righteousness and does evil, and I put a stumbling block before him, he will die. Since you did not warn him, he will die for his sin. The righteous things he did will not be remembered, and I will hold you accountable for his blood. ²¹But if you do warn the righteous man not to sin and he does not sin, he will surely live because he took warning, and you will have saved yourself."

²²The hand of the LORD was upon me there, and he said to me, "Get up and go out to the plain, and there I will speak to you." ²³So I got up and went out to the plain. And the glory of the LORD was standing there, like the glory I had seen by the Kebar River, and I fell facedown.

²⁴Then the Spirit came into me and raised me to my feet. He spoke to me and said: "Go, shut yourself inside your house. ²⁵And you, son of man, they will tie with ropes; you will be bound so that you cannot go out among the people. ²⁶I will make your tongue stick to the roof of your mouth so that you will be silent and unable to rebuke them, though they are a rebellious house. ²⁷But when I speak to you, I will open your mouth and you shall say to them, 'This is what the Sovereign LORD says.' Whoever will listen let him listen, and whoever will refuse let him refuse; for they are a rebellious house.

SIEGE OF JERUSALEM SYMBOLIZED

4 "Now, son of man, take a clay tablet, put it in front of you and draw the city of Jerusalem on it. ²Then lay siege to it: Erect siege works against it, build a ramp up to it, set up camps against it and put battering rams around it. ³Then take an iron pan, place it as an iron wall between you and the city and turn your face toward it. It will be under siege, and you shall besiege it. This will be a sign to the house of Israel.

⁴"Then lie on your left side and put the sin of the house of Israel upon yourself.ᵇ You are to bear their sin for the number of days you lie on your side. ⁵I have assigned you the same number of days as the years of their sin. So for 390 days you will bear the sin of the house of Israel.

⁶"After you have finished this, lie down again, this time on your right side, and bear the sin of the house of Judah. I have assigned you 40 days, a day for each year. ⁷Turn your face toward the siege of

Understanding God's Rewards

Ezekiel's life on earth wasn't exactly a summer day at the beach. God's plan for him included a ton of responsibility, but not a lot of reward—at least not the immediate payoff that most of us would want and expect. Ezekiel's reward came after his life on earth ended. That's when God blessed him beyond his wildest dreams. Learn from Ezekiel's experience. Don't always expect earthly rewards for doing God's work. Keep your sights focused on eternity, because that's when the real payoff will happen.

»» live the adventure »» Eze 3:24—4:8

ᵃ 18 Or in; also in verses 19 and 20   ᵇ 4 Or your side

Jerusalem and with bared arm prophesy against her. ⁸I will tie you up with ropes so that you cannot turn from one side to the other until you have finished the days of your siege.

⁹"Take wheat and barley, beans and lentils, millet and spelt; put them in a storage jar and use them to make bread for yourself. You are to eat it during the 390 days you lie on your side. ¹⁰Weigh out twenty shekels ᵃ of food to eat each day and eat it at set times. ¹¹Also measure out a sixth of a hin ᵇ of water and drink it at set times. ¹²Eat the food as you would a barley cake; bake it in the sight of the people, using human excrement for fuel." ¹³The Lord said, "In this way the people of Israel will eat defiled food among the nations where I will drive them."

¹⁴Then I said, "Not so, Sovereign Lord! I have never defiled myself. From my youth until now I have never eaten anything found dead or torn by wild animals. No unclean meat has ever entered my mouth."

¹⁵"Very well," he said, "I will let you bake your bread over cow manure instead of human excrement."

¹⁶He then said to me: "Son of man, I will cut off the supply of food in Jerusalem. The people will eat rationed food in anxiety and drink rationed water in despair, ¹⁷for food and water will be scarce. They will be appalled at the sight of each other and will waste away because of ᶜ their sin.

now or never

EZE 4:1–8

If Ezekiel was confused by God's bizarre instructions, he didn't show it. He followed them to the letter. Some of the things God asks you to do may not make sense right away, but that's OK. God doesn't expect you to understand everything; he just expects you to obey him.

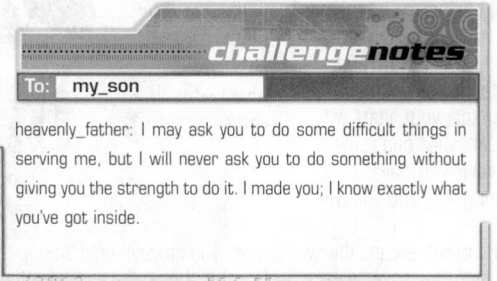

challengenotes

To: my_son

heavenly_father: I may ask you to do some difficult things in serving me, but I will never ask you to do something without giving you the strength to do it. I made you; I know exactly what you've got inside.

EZE 4:4–13

5 "Now, son of man, take a sharp sword and use it as a barber's razor to shave your head and your beard. Then take a set of scales and divide up the hair. ²When the days of your siege come to an end, burn a third of the hair with fire inside the city. Take a third and strike it with the sword all around the city. And scatter a third to the wind. For I will pursue them with drawn sword. ³But take a few strands of hair and tuck them away in the folds of your garment. ⁴Again, take a few of these and throw them into the fire and burn them up. A fire will spread from there to the whole house of Israel.

⁵"This is what the Sovereign Lord says: This is Jerusalem, which I have set in the center of the nations, with countries all around her. ⁶Yet in her wickedness she has rebelled against my laws and decrees more than the nations and countries around her. She has rejected my laws and has not followed my decrees.

⁷"Therefore this is what the Sovereign Lord says: You have been more unruly than the nations around you and have not followed my decrees or kept my laws. You have not even ᵈ conformed to the standards of the nations around you.

⁸"Therefore this is what the Sovereign Lord says: I myself am against you, Jerusalem, and I will inflict punishment on you in the sight of the nations. ⁹Because of all your detestable idols, I will do to you what I have never done before and will never do again. ¹⁰Therefore in your midst fathers will eat their children, and children will eat their fathers. I will inflict punishment on you and will scatter all your survivors to the winds. ¹¹Therefore as surely as I live, declares the Sovereign Lord, because you have defiled my sanctuary with all your vile images and detestable practices, I myself will withdraw my favor; I will not look on you with pity or spare you. ¹²A third of your people will die of the plague or perish by famine inside you; a third will fall by the sword outside your walls; and a third I will scatter to the winds and pursue with drawn sword.

¹³"Then my anger will cease and my wrath against them will subside, and I will be avenged. And when I have spent my wrath upon them, they will know that I the Lord have spoken in my zeal.

ᵃ *10* That is, about 8 ounces (about 0.2 kilogram)   ᵇ *11* That is, about 2/3 quart (about 0.6 liter)   ᶜ *17* Or *away in*   ᵈ *7* Most Hebrew manuscripts; some Hebrew manuscripts and Syriac *You have*

14 "I will make you a ruin and a reproach among the nations around you, in the sight of all who pass by. 15 You will be a reproach and a taunt, a warning and an object of horror to the nations around you when I inflict punishment on you in anger and in wrath and with stinging rebuke. I the LORD have spoken. 16 When I shoot at you with my deadly and destructive arrows of famine, I will shoot to destroy you. I will bring more and more famine upon you and cut off your supply of food. 17 I will send famine and wild beasts against you, and they will leave you childless. Plague and bloodshed will sweep through you, and I will bring the sword against you. I the LORD have spoken."

A PROPHECY AGAINST THE MOUNTAINS OF ISRAEL

6 The word of the LORD came to me: 2 "Son of man, set your face against the mountains of Israel; prophesy against them 3 and say: 'O mountains of Israel, hear the word of the Sovereign LORD. This is what the Sovereign LORD says to the mountains and hills, to the ravines and valleys: I am about to bring a sword against you, and I will destroy your high places. 4 Your altars will be demolished and your incense altars will be smashed; and I will slay your people in front of your idols. 5 I will lay the dead bodies of the Israelites in front of their idols, and I will scatter your bones around your altars. 6 Wherever you live, the towns will be laid waste and the high places demolished, so that your altars will be laid waste and devastated, your idols smashed and ruined, your incense altars broken down, and what you have made wiped out. 7 Your people will fall slain among you, and you will know that I am the LORD.

8 " 'But I will spare some, for some of you will escape the sword when you are scattered among the lands and nations. 9 Then in the nations where they have been carried captive, those who escape will remember me—how I have been grieved by their adulterous hearts, which have turned away from me, and by their eyes, which have lusted after their idols. They will loathe themselves for the evil they have done and for all their detestable practices. 10 And they will know that I am the LORD; I did not threaten in vain to bring this calamity on them.

11 " 'This is what the Sovereign LORD says: Strike your hands together and stamp your feet and cry out "Alas!" because of all the wicked and detestable practices of the house of Israel, for they will fall by the sword, famine and plague. 12 He that is far away will die of the plague, and he that is near will fall by the sword, and he that survives and is spared will die of famine. So will I spend my wrath upon them. 13 And they will know that I am the LORD, when their people lie slain among their idols around their altars, on every high hill and on all the mountaintops, under every spreading tree and every leafy oak—places where they offered fragrant incense to all their idols. 14 And I will stretch out my hand against them and make the land a desolate waste from the desert to Diblah[a]—wherever they live. Then they will know that I am the LORD.' "

Recognizing God for Who He Is

Sooner or later, *everyone* will know exactly who God is. Some people will discover the truth about him in his Word. Some people will discover it through the testimony of Christian friends. And others will discover it when they face his final judgment. Unfortunately, by that time it will be too late for the truth to save them. That's why it's important for you to share the news about God with others whenever you have the opportunity. Let them find out sooner, rather than later, what God is all about.

now or never

EZE 6:8

If God were as cruel as some people think he is, imagine how many more terrible things he might do when his people disobey him. The fact that he puts limits on his judgment shows just how much he loves us.

---

a 14 Most Hebrew manuscripts; a few Hebrew manuscripts *Riblah*

battlelines

» Strangers in the House (Blended Families)

Q: Has it even been a year yet?
A: Nope. Ten months. Can you believe that? In ten months I've watched my parents split up, my mom move away and some woman I don't know—with two kids I can't stand—move into my house.

Q: So what's she like?
A: Dad's new wife? She's OK, I guess. I mean, she'll never be my mom, but she tries hard. She's nice enough. Maybe a little *too* nice. But her little kids are driving me crazy. I used to have the place all to myself, but now the rug rats are in control.

Q: So do your new brother and sister like you?
A: Hey, don't call them that. They are *not* my brother and sister. They never will be.

Q: Sounds a little harsh.
A: Yeah, well, I want my life back.

Q: Hey, I agree that it'd be great to have your old life back. But you and I both know that's not going to happen.
A: Gee, thanks for the encouragement.

Q: No, hear me out. I just want to help. What can *you* do to make your new life better?
A: Nothing. It's out of my hands.

Q: Come on, there has to be *something* you can do to make the situation better. You're a smart guy.
A: Yeah, well, too bad I'm not a rich guy. Then I could get my own place.

Q: True. But until you hit the jackpot, let's try to figure out a more realistic plan.
A: I'm all ears.

» New Kids on the Block

Siblings are a challenge—especially if they're step-siblings. You may wonder, *Who are these strange people invading my space and getting on my nerves?* If you're dealing with a situation like this, you can either grumble, choosing to remain frustrated and ticked off, or you can try to make the best of it. Here's how:

- Determine to be "big" no matter what. Refuse to get petty or hold grudges.

- Be thankful. Instead of obsessing over everything that's wrong with your life, spend time thanking God for all the good things in it (see 1 Thessalonians 5:18). You'll be amazed how such an attitude can alter your perspective.

- Pray consistently for your new family. It's hard to hate people you're praying for.

- Keep the lines of communication open with your parents. Don't keep your feelings bottled up. Make it your goal to understand and to be understood.

- It's OK if it takes some time getting used to family change. Be patient and take heart. God hasn't forgotten you. He's got great plans ahead for you!

Read more about getting along with your family at www.RevolutionBible.com.

THE END HAS COME

7 The word of the LORD came to me: ²"Son of man, this is what the Sovereign LORD says to the land of Israel: The end! The end has come upon the four corners of the land. ³The end is now upon you and I will unleash my anger against you. I will judge you according to your conduct and repay you for all your detestable practices. ⁴I will not look on you with pity or spare you; I will surely repay you for your conduct and the detestable practices among you. Then you will know that I am the LORD.

⁵"This is what the Sovereign LORD says: Disaster! An unheard-of[a] disaster is coming. ⁶The end has come! The end has come! It has roused itself against you. It has come! ⁷Doom has come upon you—you who dwell in the land. The time has come, the day is near; there is panic, not joy, upon the mountains. ⁸I am about to pour out my wrath on you and spend my anger against you; I will judge you according to your conduct and repay you for all your detestable practices. ⁹I will not look on you with pity or spare you; I will repay you in accordance with your conduct and the detestable practices among you. Then you will know that it is I the LORD who strikes the blow.

¹⁰"The day is here! It has come! Doom has burst forth, the rod has budded, arrogance has blossomed! ¹¹Violence has grown into[b] a rod to punish wickedness; none of the people will be left, none of that crowd—no wealth, nothing of value. ¹²The time has come, the day has arrived. Let not the buyer rejoice nor the seller grieve, for wrath is upon the whole crowd. ¹³The seller will not recover the land he has sold as long as both of them live, for the vision concerning the whole crowd will not be reversed. Because of their sins, not one of them will preserve his life. ¹⁴Though they blow the trumpet and get everything ready, no one will go into battle, for my wrath is upon the whole crowd.

¹⁵"Outside is the sword, inside are plague and famine; those in the country will die by the sword, and those in the city will be devoured by famine and plague. ¹⁶All who survive and escape will be in the mountains, moaning like doves of the valleys, each because of his sins. ¹⁷Every hand will go limp, and every knee will become as weak as water. ¹⁸They will put on sackcloth and be clothed with terror. Their faces will be covered with shame and their heads will be shaved. ¹⁹They will throw their silver into the streets, and their gold will be an unclean thing. Their silver and gold will not be able to save them in the day of the LORD's wrath. They will not satisfy their hunger or fill their stomachs with it, for it has made them stumble into sin. ²⁰They were proud of their beautiful jewelry and used it to make their detestable idols and vile images. Therefore I will turn these into an unclean thing for them. ²¹I will hand it all over as plunder to foreigners and as loot to the wicked of the earth, and they will defile it. ²²I will turn my face away from them, and they will desecrate my treasured place; robbers will enter it and desecrate it.

²³"Prepare chains, because the land is full of bloodshed and the city is full of violence. ²⁴I will bring the most wicked of the nations to take possession of their houses; I will put an end to the pride of the mighty, and their sanctuaries will be desecrated. ²⁵When terror comes, they will seek peace, but there

Understanding God's Justice

Some people would look at these verses and ask, "How could a loving God do this?" They don't understand that love is just one of God's many attributes. God is also perfectly just, which means he demands complete payment for sin. So you might ask, "Then how could a just God show love to sinners?" God's justice and love come together magnificently in his plan of salvation. Someone had to be punished for the sins of the world (because God's justice demands it). That someone was Jesus, who was sent by God for that very purpose (because God loves us). The only way to escape God's judgment is to have the payment for your sins covered by the blood of Jesus' sacrifice.

challenge notes

To: my_son

heavenly_father: I've given fair warning about the reality of my judgment. for years my people have proclaimed that a day of judgment is coming. when that day arrives, those who rejected me will have no one but themselves to blame for the suffering that comes as a result.

EZE 7:10

---

[a] 5 Most Hebrew manuscripts; some Hebrew manuscripts and Syriac *Disaster after*   [b] 11 Or *The violent one has become*

will be none. 26Calamity upon calamity will come, and rumor upon rumor. They will try to get a vision from the prophet; the teaching of the law by the priest will be lost, as will the counsel of the elders. 27The king will mourn, the prince will be clothed with despair, and the hands of the people of the land will tremble. I will deal with them according to their conduct, and by their own standards I will judge them. Then they will know that I am the LORD."

IDOLATRY IN THE TEMPLE

8 In the sixth year, in the sixth month on the fifth day, while I was sitting in my house and the elders of Judah were sitting before me, the hand of the Sovereign LORD came upon me there. 2I looked, and I saw a figure like that of a man.ª From what appeared to be his waist down he was like fire, and from there up his appearance was as bright as glowing metal. 3He stretched out what looked like a hand and took me by the hair of my head. The Spirit lifted me up between earth and heaven and in visions of God he took me to Jerusalem, to the entrance to the north gate of the inner court, where the idol that provokes to jealousy stood. 4And there before me was the glory of the God of Israel, as in the vision I had seen in the plain.

5Then he said to me, "Son of man, look toward the north." So I looked, and in the entrance north of the gate of the altar I saw this idol of jealousy.

6And he said to me, "Son of man, do you see what they are doing—the utterly detestable things the house of Israel is doing here, things that will drive me far from my sanctuary? But you will see things that are even more detestable."

7Then he brought me to the entrance to the court. I looked, and I saw a hole in the wall. 8He said to me, "Son of man, now dig into the wall." So I dug into the wall and saw a doorway there.

9And he said to me, "Go in and see the wicked and detestable things they are doing here." 10So I went in and looked, and I saw portrayed all over the walls all kinds of crawling things and detestable animals and all the idols of the house of Israel. 11In front of them stood seventy elders of the house of Israel, and Jaazaniah son of Shaphan was standing among them. Each had a censer in his hand, and a fragrant cloud of incense was rising.

12He said to me, "Son of man, have you seen what the elders of the house of Israel are doing in the darkness, each at the shrine of his own idol? They say, 'The LORD does not see us; the LORD has forsaken the land.'" 13Again, he said, "You will see them doing things that are even more detestable."

14Then he brought me to the entrance to the north gate of the house of the LORD, and

EZE 8:5–16

*challenge*notes

To: my_son

heavenly_father: I see the things you do in secret. if you're ashamed to do something where other people can see you, it's because I created you to discern good from bad by way of this thing called your conscience.

I saw women sitting there, mourning for Tammuz. 15He said to me, "Do you see this, son of man? You will see things that are even more detestable than this."

16He then brought me into the inner court of the house of the LORD, and there at the entrance to the temple, between the portico and the altar, were about twenty-five men. With their backs toward the temple of the LORD and their faces toward the east, they were bowing down to the sun in the east.

17He said to me, "Have you seen this, son of man? Is it a trivial matter for the house of Judah to do the detestable things they are doing here? Must they also fill the land with violence and continually provoke me to anger? Look at them putting the branch to their nose! 18Therefore I will deal with them in anger; I will not look on them with pity or spare them. Although they shout in my ears, I will not listen to them."

IDOLATERS KILLED

9 Then I heard him call out in a loud voice, "Bring the guards of the city here, each with a weapon in his hand." 2And I saw six men coming from the direction of the upper gate, which faces north, each with a deadly weapon in his hand. With them was a man clothed in linen who had a writing kit at his side. They came in and stood beside the bronze altar.

3Now the glory of the God of Israel went up from above the cherubim, where it had been, and moved

ª 2 Or *saw a fiery figure*

to the threshold of the temple. Then the LORD called to the man clothed in linen who had the writing kit at his side ⁴and said to him, "Go throughout the city of Jerusalem and put a mark on the foreheads of those who grieve and lament over all the detestable things that are done in it."

⁵As I listened, he said to the others, "Follow him through the city and kill, without showing pity or compassion. ⁶Slaughter old men, young men and maidens, women and children, but do not touch anyone who has the mark. Begin at my sanctuary." So they began with the elders who were in front of the temple.

⁷Then he said to them, "Defile the temple and fill the courts with the slain. Go!" So they went out and began killing throughout the city. ⁸While they were killing and I was left alone, I fell facedown, crying out, "Ah, Sovereign LORD! Are you going to destroy the entire remnant of Israel in this outpouring of your wrath on Jerusalem?"

⁹He answered me, "The sin of the house of Israel and Judah is exceedingly great; the land is full of bloodshed and the city is full of injustice. They say, 'The LORD has forsaken the land; the LORD does not see.' ¹⁰So I will not look on them with pity or spare them, but I will bring down on their own heads what they have done."

¹¹Then the man in linen with the writing kit at his side brought back word, saying, "I have done as you commanded."

now or never

EZE 9:4

Are you ever disgusted by things you see on TV or hear on the radio? Do you ever experience remorse for something you said to someone? God wants you to be sensitive to his will . . . and disturbed when people (including yourself) reject it.

THE GLORY DEPARTS FROM THE TEMPLE

10

I looked, and I saw the likeness of a throne of sapphire[a] above the expanse that was over the heads of the cherubim. ²The LORD said to the man clothed in linen, "Go in among the wheels beneath the cherubim. Fill your hands with burning coals from among the cherubim and scatter them over the city." And as I watched, he went in.

³Now the cherubim were standing on the south side of the temple when the man went in, and a cloud filled the inner court. ⁴Then the glory of the LORD rose from above the cherubim and moved to the threshold of the temple. The cloud filled the temple, and the court was full of the radiance of the glory of the LORD. ⁵The sound of the wings of the cherubim could be heard as far away as the outer court, like the voice of God Almighty[b] when he speaks.

⁶When the LORD commanded the man in linen, "Take fire from among the wheels, from among the cherubim," the man went in and stood beside a wheel. ⁷Then one of the cherubim reached out his hand to the fire that was among them. He took up some of it and put it into the hands of the man in linen, who took it and went out. ⁸(Under the wings of the cherubim could be seen what looked like the hands of a man.)

⁹I looked, and I saw beside the cherubim four wheels, one beside each of the cherubim; the wheels sparkled like chrysolite. ¹⁰As for their appearance, the four of them looked alike; each was like a wheel intersecting a wheel. ¹¹As they moved, they would go in any one of the four directions the cherubim faced; the wheels did not turn about[c] as the cherubim went. The cherubim went in whatever direction the head faced, without turning as they went. ¹²Their entire bodies, including their backs, their hands and their wings, were completely full of eyes, as were their four wheels. ¹³I heard the wheels being called "the whirling wheels." ¹⁴Each of the cherubim had four faces: One face was that of a cherub, the second the face of a man, the third the face of a lion, and the fourth the face of an eagle.

¹⁵Then the cherubim rose upward. These were the living creatures I had seen by the Kebar River. ¹⁶When the cherubim moved, the wheels beside them moved; and when the cherubim spread their wings to rise from the ground, the wheels did not leave their side. ¹⁷When the cherubim stood still, they also stood still; and when the cherubim rose, they rose with them, because the spirit of the living creatures was in them.

¹⁸Then the glory of the LORD departed from over the threshold of the temple and stopped above the cherubim. ¹⁹While I watched, the cherubim spread their wings and rose from the ground, and as they

---

ª *1* Or *lapis lazuli*   ᵇ *5* Hebrew *El-Shaddai*   ᶜ *11* Or *aside*

battlelines

» The Mouth of the South (Being Judgmental)

Q: Hey.
A: Hey, yourself. What's with the clown shirt?

Q: Huh?
A: That shirt . . . sheesh, it looks like something my crazy Uncle Louie would wear.

Q: Oooo-kay, thanks for the fashion tip there, Travis. So what have I missed?
A: Oh, it's been quite an eventful lunch hour so far. Some tall, ugly chick dropped her lunch tray. That was kinda fun. We gave her a standing "O." Then we were graced with a visit from Brandon Carter, star quarterback of Hampton High, and his jock entourage of total suck-ups. Oh, and that wonderful moment also included a bubble-headed cheerleader who was basically ready to become the mother of Brandon's child right here in the cafeteria.

Q: Wow. All that, huh?
A: Yeah, and Jake was just telling us about a new band geek. Some transfer student. Just what we need . . . another drummer in the old Hampton High marching band.

Q: Man, Travis, why are you so negative?
A: What, do you think everybody should be chipper and peppy like you?

» A Critical Spirit

Maybe you know somebody like Travis. Always quick to stick a negative label on everyone. Always ready to criticize anything.

Or maybe you *are* somebody like Travis.

Whatever the case, being judgmental and harsh isn't cool. It isn't funny. And it certainly isn't the best way to make friends or fit in. If anything, a "take no prisoners" tongue merely reveals an incredibly insecure individual. Over time, people who constantly put others down find themselves very alone.

Try measuring your conversation against this standard: "Do not let any unwholesome talk come out of your mouths, but only what is helpful for building others up according to their needs, that it may benefit those who listen" (Ephesians 4:29).

Learn more about the power of words at www.RevolutionBible.com.

went, the wheels went with them. They stopped at the entrance to the east gate of the LORD's house, and the glory of the God of Israel was above them.

20These were the living creatures I had seen beneath the God of Israel by the Kebar River, and I realized that they were cherubim. 21Each had four faces and four wings, and under their wings was what looked like the hands of a man. 22Their faces had the same appearance as those I had seen by the Kebar River. Each one went straight ahead.

JUDGMENT ON ISRAEL'S LEADERS

11 Then the Spirit lifted me up and brought me to the gate of the house of the LORD that faces east. There at the entrance to the gate were twenty-five men, and I saw among them Jaazaniah son of Azzur and Pelatiah son of Benaiah, leaders of the people.

2The LORD said to me, "Son of man, these are the men who are plotting evil and giving wicked advice in this city. 3They say, 'Will it not soon be time to build houses?ª This city is a cooking pot, and we are the meat.' 4Therefore prophesy against them; prophesy, son of man."

5Then the Spirit of the LORD came upon me, and he told me to say: "This is what the LORD says: That is what you are saying, O house of Israel, but I know what is going through your mind. 6You have killed many people in this city and filled its streets with the dead.

7"Therefore this is what the Sovereign LORD says: The bodies you have thrown there are the meat and this city is the pot, but I will drive you out of it. 8You fear the sword, and the sword is what I will bring against you, declares the Sovereign LORD. 9I will drive you out of the city and hand you over to foreigners and inflict punishment on you. 10You will fall by the sword, and I will execute judgment on you at the borders of Israel. Then you will know that I am the LORD. 11This city will not be a pot for you, nor will you be the meat in it; I will execute judgment on you at the borders of Israel. 12And you will know that I am the LORD, for you have not followed my decrees or kept my laws but have conformed to the standards of the nations around you."

13Now as I was prophesying, Pelatiah son of Benaiah died. Then I fell facedown and cried out in a loud voice, "Ah, Sovereign LORD! Will you completely destroy the remnant of Israel?"

14The word of the LORD came to me: 15"Son of man, your brothers—your brothers who are your blood relativesᵇ and the whole house of Israel—are those of whom the people of Jerusalem have said, 'They areᶜ far away from the LORD; this land was given to us as our possession.'

PROMISED RETURN OF ISRAEL

16"Therefore say: 'This is what the Sovereign LORD says: Although I sent them far away among the nations and scattered them among the countries, yet for a little while I have been a sanctuary for them in the countries where they have gone.'

17"Therefore say: 'This is what the Sovereign LORD says: I will gather you from the nations and bring you back from the countries where you have been scattered, and I will give you back the land of Israel again.'

18"They will return to it and remove all its vile images and detestable idols. 19I will give them an undivided heart and put a new spirit in them; I will remove from them their heart of stone and give them a heart of flesh. 20Then they will follow my decrees and be careful to keep my laws. They will be my people, and I will be their God. 21But as for those whose

---

ª 3 Or *This is not the time to build houses.* ᵇ 15 Or *are in exile with you* (see Septuagint and Syriac) ᶜ 15 Or *those to whom the people of Jerusalem have said, 'Stay* hearts are devoted to their vile images and detestable idols, I will bring down on their own heads what they have done, declares the Sovereign LORD."

²²Then the cherubim, with the wheels beside them, spread their wings, and the glory of the God of Israel was above them. ²³The glory of the LORD went up from within the city and stopped above the mountain east of it. ²⁴The Spirit lifted me up and brought me to the exiles in Babylonia[a] in the vision given by the Spirit of God.

Then the vision I had seen went up from me, ²⁵and I told the exiles everything the LORD had shown me.

THE EXILE SYMBOLIZED

12

The word of the LORD came to me: ²"Son of man, you are living among a rebellious people. They have eyes to see but do not see and ears to hear but do not hear, for they are a rebellious people.

³"Therefore, son of man, pack your belongings for exile and in the daytime, as they watch, set out and go from where you are to another place. Perhaps they will understand, though they are a rebellious house. ⁴During the daytime, while they watch, bring out your belongings packed for exile. Then in the evening, while they are watching, go out like those who go into exile. ⁵While they watch, dig through the wall and take your belongings out through it. ⁶Put them on your shoulder as they are watching and carry them out at dusk. Cover your face so that you cannot see the land, for I have made you a sign to the house of Israel."

⁷So I did as I was commanded. During the day I brought out my things packed for exile. Then in the evening I dug through the wall with my hands. I took my belongings out at dusk, carrying them on my shoulders while they watched.

⁸In the morning the word of the LORD came to me: ⁹"Son of man, did not that rebellious house of Israel ask you, 'What are you doing?'

¹⁰"Say to them, 'This is what the Sovereign LORD says: This oracle concerns the prince in Jerusalem and the whole house of Israel who are there.' ¹¹Say to them, 'I am a sign to you.'

"As I have done, so it will be done to them. They will go into exile as captives.

¹²"The prince among them will put his things on his shoulder at dusk and leave, and a hole will be dug in the wall for him to go through. He will cover his face so that he cannot see the land. ¹³I will spread my net for him, and he will be caught in my snare; I will bring him to Babylonia, the land of the Chaldeans, but he will not see it, and there he will die. ¹⁴I will scatter to the winds all those around him—his staff and all his troops—and I will pursue them with drawn sword.

¹⁵"They will know that I am the LORD, when I disperse them among the nations and scatter them through the countries. ¹⁶But I will spare a few of them from the sword, famine and plague, so that in the nations where they go they may acknowledge all their detestable practices. Then they will know that I am the LORD."

¹⁷The word of the LORD came to me: ¹⁸"Son of man, tremble as you eat your food, and shudder in fear as you drink your water. ¹⁹Say to the people of the land: 'This is what the Sovereign LORD says about those living in Jerusalem and in the land of Israel: They will eat their food in anxiety and drink their water in despair, for their land will be stripped of everything in it because of the violence of all who live there. ²⁰The inhabited towns will be laid waste and the land will be desolate. Then you will know that I am the LORD.' "

²¹The word of the LORD came to me: ²²"Son of man, what is this proverb you have in the land of Israel: 'The days go by and every vision comes to nothing'? ²³Say to them, 'This is what the Sovereign LORD says: I am going to put an end to this proverb, and they will no longer quote it in Israel.' Say to them, 'The days are near when every vision will be fulfilled. ²⁴For there will be no more false visions or flattering divinations among the people of Israel. ²⁵But I the LORD will speak what I will,

NOW OR NEVER
EZE 12:21-23

So when are all of the prophets' predictions about the future going to be fulfilled? Any day now. Literally. That's how you should treat the Bible's prophecies about the future. If you live each day as though it could be your last, you never have to worry about being taken by surprise when the end comes.

and it shall be fulfilled without delay. For in your days, you rebellious house, I will fulfill whatever I say, declares the Sovereign LORD.' "

26The word of the LORD came to me: 27"Son of man, the house of Israel is saying, 'The vision he sees is for many years from now, and he prophesies about the distant future.'

28"Therefore say to them, 'This is what the Sovereign LORD says: None of my words will be delayed any longer; whatever I say will be fulfilled, declares the Sovereign LORD.' "

FALSE PROPHETS CONDEMNED

13 The word of the LORD came to me: 2"Son of man, prophesy against the prophets of Israel who are now prophesying. Say to those who prophesy out of their own imagination: 'Hear the word of the LORD! 3This is what the Sovereign LORD says: Woe to the foolisha prophets who follow their own spirit and have seen nothing! 4Your prophets, O Israel, are like jackals among ruins. 5You have not gone up to the breaks in the wall to repair it for the house of Israel so that it will stand firm in the battle on the day of the LORD. 6Their visions are false and their divinations a lie. They say, "The LORD declares," when the LORD has not sent them; yet they expect their words to be fulfilled. 7Have you not seen false visions and uttered lying divinations when you say, "The LORD declares," though I have not spoken?

8" 'Therefore this is what the Sovereign LORD says: Because of your false words and lying visions, I am against you, declares the Sovereign LORD. 9My hand will be against the prophets who see false visions and utter lying divinations. They will not belong to the council of my people or be listed in the records of the house of Israel, nor will they enter the land of Israel. Then you will know that I am the Sovereign LORD.

10" 'Because they lead my people astray, saying, "Peace," when there is no peace, and because, when a flimsy wall is built, they cover it with whitewash, 11therefore tell those who cover it with whitewash that it is going to fall. Rain will come in torrents, and I will send hailstones hurtling down, and violent winds will burst forth. 12When the wall collapses, will people not ask you, "Where is the whitewash you covered it with?"

13" 'Therefore this is what the Sovereign LORD says: In my wrath I will unleash a violent wind, and in my anger hailstones and torrents of rain will fall with destructive fury. 14I will tear down the wall you have covered with whitewash and will level it to the ground so that its foundation will be laid bare. When itb falls, you will be destroyed in it; and you will know that I am the LORD. 15So I will spend my wrath against the wall and against those who covered it with whitewash. I will say to you, "The wall is gone and so are those who whitewashed it, 16those prophets of Israel who prophesied to Jerusalem and saw visions of peace for her when there was no peace, declares the Sovereign LORD." '

17"Now, son of man, set your face against the daughters of your people who prophesy out of their own imagination. Prophesy against them 18and say, 'This is what the Sovereign LORD says: Woe to the women who sew magic charms on all their wrists and make veils of various lengths for their heads in order to ensnare people. Will you ensnare the lives of my people but preserve your own? 19You have profaned me among my people for a few handfuls of barley and scraps of bread. By lying to my people, who listen to lies, you have killed those who should not have died and have spared those who should not live.

20" 'Therefore this is what the Sovereign LORD says: I am against your magic charms with which you ensnare people like birds and I will tear them from your arms; I will set free the people that you ensnare like birds. 21I will tear off your veils and save my people from your hands, and they will no longer fall

---

Being Honest With Yourself

God despises people who trick others into believing something that is false. But false prophets aren't the only deceivers you have to worry about. You also have to keep an eye on yourself. Under the right circumstances, you can convince yourself of just about anything. Have you ever talked yourself into believing that if no one sees you, you can get away with certain sins? Or that your sins are minor compared to someone else's? Or that confessing your sins in prayer is only something you do for "major" screwups? Be careful what you allow yourself to believe.

>> live the adventure >> Eze 13:10-12

---

a 3 Or wicked   b 14 Or the city

prey to your power. Then you will know that I am the LORD. ²²Because you disheartened the righteous with your lies, when I had brought them no grief, and because you encouraged the wicked not to turn from their evil ways and so save their lives, ²³therefore you will no longer see false visions or practice divination. I will save my people from your hands. And then you will know that I am the LORD.' "

IDOLATERS CONDEMNED

14 Some of the elders of Israel came to me and sat down in front of me. ²Then the word of the LORD came to me: ³"Son of man, these men have set up idols in their hearts and put wicked stumbling blocks before their faces. Should I let them inquire of me at all? ⁴Therefore speak to them and tell them, 'This is what the Sovereign LORD says: When any Israelite sets up idols in his heart and puts a wicked stumbling block before his face and then goes to a prophet, I the LORD will answer him myself in keeping with his great idolatry. ⁵I will do this to recapture the hearts of the people of Israel, who have all deserted me for their idols.'

⁶"Therefore say to the house of Israel, 'This is what the Sovereign LORD says: Repent! Turn from your idols and renounce all your detestable practices!

⁷" 'When any Israelite or any alien living in Israel separates himself from me and sets up idols in his heart and puts a wicked stumbling block before his face and then goes to a prophet to inquire of me, I the LORD will answer him myself. ⁸I will set my face against that man and make him an example and a byword. I will cut him off from my people. Then you will know that I am the LORD.

⁹" 'And if the prophet is enticed to utter a prophecy, I the LORD have enticed that prophet, and I will stretch out my hand against him and destroy him from among my people Israel. ¹⁰They will bear their guilt—the prophet will be as guilty as the one who consults him. ¹¹Then the people of Israel will no longer stray from me, nor will they defile themselves anymore with all their sins. They will be my people, and I will be their God, declares the Sovereign LORD.' "

NOW OR NEVER
EZE 14:7

You don't have to bow down in front of a statue to be an idol worshiper. Anything that has a higher priority in your life than God is an idol. Do you have any "idols of the heart" that you need to destroy?

JUDGMENT INESCAPABLE

¹²The word of the LORD came to me: ¹³"Son of man, if a country sins against me by being unfaithful and I stretch out my hand against it to cut off its food supply and send famine upon it and kill its men and their animals, ¹⁴even if these three men—Noah, Daniel[a] and Job—were in it, they could save only themselves by their righteousness, declares the Sovereign LORD.

¹⁵"Or if I send wild beasts through that country and they leave it childless and it becomes desolate so that no one can pass through it because of the beasts, ¹⁶as surely as I live, declares the Sovereign LORD, even if these three men were in it, they could not save their own sons or daughters. They alone would be saved, but the land would be desolate.

¹⁷"Or if I bring a sword against that country and say, 'Let the sword pass throughout the land,' and I kill its men and their animals, ¹⁸as surely as I live, declares the Sovereign LORD, even if these three men were in it, they could not save their own sons or daughters. They alone would be saved.

¹⁹"Or if I send a plague into that land and pour out my wrath upon it through bloodshed, killing its men and their animals, ²⁰as surely as I live, declares the Sovereign LORD, even if Noah, Daniel and Job were in it, they could save neither son nor daughter. They would save only themselves by their righteousness.

²¹"For this is what the Sovereign LORD says: How much worse will it be when I send against Jerusalem my four dreadful judgments—sword and famine and wild beasts and plague—to kill its men and their animals! ²²Yet there will be some survivors—sons and daughters who will be brought out of it. They will come to you, and when you see their conduct and their actions, you will be consoled regarding the disaster I have brought upon Jerusalem—every disaster I have brought upon it. ²³You will be consoled when you see their conduct and their actions, for you will know that I have done nothing in it without cause, declares the Sovereign LORD."

ᵃ *14* Or *Danel*; the Hebrew spelling may suggest a person other than the prophet Daniel; also in verse 20.

JERUSALEM, A USELESS VINE

15 The word of the LORD came to me: ²"Son of man, how is the wood of a vine better than that of a branch on any of the trees in the forest? ³Is wood ever taken from it to make anything useful? Do they make pegs from it to hang things on? ⁴And after it is thrown on the fire as fuel and the fire burns both ends and chars the middle, is it then useful for anything? ⁵If it was not useful for anything when it was whole, how much less can it be made into something useful when the fire has burned it and it is charred?

⁶"Therefore this is what the Sovereign LORD says: As I have given the wood of the vine among the trees of the forest as fuel for the fire, so will I treat the people living in Jerusalem. ⁷I will set my face against them. Although they have come out of the fire, the fire will yet consume them. And when I set my face against them, you will know that I am the LORD. ⁸I will make the land desolate because they have been unfaithful, declares the Sovereign LORD."

AN ALLEGORY OF UNFAITHFUL JERUSALEM

16 The word of the LORD came to me: ²"Son of man, confront Jerusalem with her detestable practices ³and say, 'This is what the Sovereign LORD says to Jerusalem: Your ancestry and birth were in the land of the Canaanites; your father was an Amorite and your mother a Hittite. ⁴On the day you were born your cord was not cut, nor were you washed with water to make you clean, nor were you rubbed with salt or wrapped in cloths. ⁵No one looked on you with pity or had compassion enough to do any of these things for you. Rather, you were thrown out into the open field, for on the day you were born you were despised.

⁶" 'Then I passed by and saw you kicking about in your blood, and as you lay there in your blood I said to you, "Live!"ᵃ ⁷I made you grow like a plant of the field. You grew up and developed and became the most beautiful of jewels.ᵇ Your breasts were formed and your hair grew, you who were naked and bare.

⁸" 'Later I passed by, and when I looked at you and saw that you were old enough for love, I spread the corner of my garment over you and covered your nakedness. I gave you my solemn oath and entered into a covenant with you, declares the Sovereign LORD, and you became mine.

⁹" 'I bathedᶜ you with water and washed the blood from you and put ointments on you. ¹⁰I clothed you with an embroidered dress and put leather sandals on you. I dressed you in fine linen and covered you with costly garments. ¹¹I adorned you with jewelry: I put bracelets on your arms and a necklace around your neck, ¹²and I put a ring on your nose, earrings on your ears and a beautiful crown on your head. ¹³So you were adorned with gold and silver; your clothes were of fine linen and costly fabric and embroidered cloth. Your food was fine flour, honey and olive oil. You became very beautiful and rose to be a queen. ¹⁴And your fame spread among the nations on account of your beauty, because the splendor I had given you made your beauty perfect, declares the Sovereign LORD.

¹⁵" 'But you trusted in your beauty and used your fame to become a prostitute. You lavished your favors on anyone who passed by and your beauty became his.ᵈ ¹⁶You took some of your garments to make gaudy high places, where you carried on your prostitution. Such things should not happen, nor should they ever occur. ¹⁷You also took the fine jewelry I gave you, the jewelry made of my gold and silver, and you made for yourself male idols and engaged in prostitution with them. ¹⁸And you took your embroidered clothes to put on them, and you offered my oil and incense before them. ¹⁹Also the food I provided for you—the fine flour, olive oil and honey I gave you to eat—you offered as fragrant incense before them. That is what happened, declares the Sovereign LORD.

²⁰" 'And you took your sons and daughters whom you bore to me and sacrificed them as food to the idols. Was your prostitution not enough? ²¹You slaughtered my children and sacrificed themᵉ to the idols. ²²In all your detestable practices and your prostitution you did not remember the days of your youth, when you were naked and bare, kicking about in your blood.

²³" 'Woe! Woe to you, declares the Sovereign LORD. In addition to all your other wickedness, ²⁴you built a mound for yourself and made a lofty shrine in every public square. ²⁵At the head of every street you built your lofty shrines and degraded your beauty, offering your body with increasing promiscuity to anyone who passed by. ²⁶You engaged in prostitution with the Egyptians, your lustful neighbors, and

---

ᵃ *6* A few Hebrew manuscripts, Septuagint and Syriac; most Hebrew manuscripts *"Live!" And as you lay there in your blood I said to you, "Live!"*   ᵇ *7* Or *became mature*   ᶜ *9* Or *I had bathed*   ᵈ *15* Most Hebrew manuscripts; one Hebrew manuscript (see some Septuagint manuscripts) *by. Such a thing should not happen*   ᵉ *21* Or *and made them pass through ⸤the fire⸥*

battlelines

» Making the Grade (Grades)

Q: You look stressed.
A: Yeah, well, I'm pretty wigged out about my grades right now.

Q: What do *you* have to worry about? You've got a 4.0 GPA.
A: Not if I don't ace my next physics test.

Q: So what if you don't? What if you get a B on the test? Your GPA will drop all the way to what? A 3.9? That's still awesome. What are you worried about?
A: Getting into Michigan. I'm out of state, remember? They only take so many applicants. My SAT scores are OK, but not great. So my GPA is a big deal. I *need* a 4.0.

Q: Yeah, but there's other stuff that factors in—recommendations, interviews, essays, extracurricular activities.
A: You just don't get it, do you?

Q: Apparently not. I didn't realize there's only one university in the whole world where you can go to prepare yourself for a successful career. So, yeah, your entire life really hinges on this *one grade*.
A: (Shaking his head) You're not helping me here—you know that?

» Bonus Points

Why do some guys put so much pressure on themselves? It's one thing to set high academic goals for yourself and work hard to reach them, but it's another thing altogether to stress out over grades and come unglued if you don't ace every test.

Remember, God is way more concerned about your heart, your character and the kind of person you are than he is about your transcript. He cares far more about how much wisdom—that is, skill in living his way—you possess than about how much "book learning" you can regurgitate in an exam booklet.

Do your best . . . then give yourself a break (see Philippians 4:6–7).

Feeling pressure from school? Read more about giving yourself a break at www.RevolutionBible.com

provoked me to anger with your increasing promiscuity. ²⁷So I stretched out my hand against you and reduced your territory; I gave you over to the greed of your enemies, the daughters of the Philistines, who were shocked by your lewd conduct. ²⁸You engaged in prostitution with the Assyrians too, because you were insatiable; and even after that, you still were not satisfied. ²⁹Then you increased your promiscuity to include Babylonia,ᵃ a land of merchants, but even with this you were not satisfied.

³⁰" 'How weak-willed you are, declares the Sovereign LORD, when you do all these things, acting like a brazen prostitute! ³¹When you built your mounds at the head of every street and made your lofty shrines in every public square, you were unlike a prostitute, because you scorned payment.

³²" 'You adulterous wife! You prefer strangers to your own husband! ³³Every prostitute receives a fee, but you give gifts to all your lovers, bribing them to come to you from everywhere for your illicit favors. ³⁴So in your prostitution you are the opposite of others; no one runs after you for your favors. You are the very opposite, for you give payment and none is given to you.

³⁵" 'Therefore, you prostitute, hear the word of the LORD! ³⁶This is what the Sovereign LORD says: Because you poured out your wealthᵇ and exposed your nakedness in your promiscuity with your lovers, and because of all your detestable idols, and because you gave them your children's blood, ³⁷therefore I am going to gather all your lovers, with whom you found pleasure, those you loved as well as those you hated. I will gather them against you from all around and will strip you in front of them, and they will see all your nakedness. ³⁸I will sentence you to the punishment of women who commit adultery and who shed blood; I will bring upon you the blood vengeance of my wrath and jealous anger. ³⁹Then I will hand you over to your lovers, and they will tear down your mounds and destroy your lofty shrines. They will strip you of your clothes and take your fine jewelry and leave you naked and bare. ⁴⁰They will bring a mob against you, who will stone you and hack you to pieces with their swords. ⁴¹They will burn down your houses and inflict punishment on you in the sight of many women. I will put a stop to your prostitution, and you will no longer pay your lovers. ⁴²Then my wrath against you will subside and my jealous anger will turn away from you; I will be calm and no longer angry.

⁴³" 'Because you did not remember the days of your youth but enraged me with all these things, I will surely bring down on your head what you have done, declares the Sovereign LORD. Did you not add lewdness to all your other detestable practices?

⁴⁴" 'Everyone who quotes proverbs will quote this proverb about you: "Like mother, like daughter." ⁴⁵You are a true daughter of your mother, who despised her husband and her children; and you are a true sister of your sisters, who despised their husbands and their children. Your mother was a Hittite and your father an Amorite. ⁴⁶Your older sister was Samaria, who lived to the north of you with her daughters; and your younger sister, who lived to the south of you with her daughters, was Sodom. ⁴⁷You not only walked in their ways and copied their detestable practices, but in all your ways you soon became more depraved than they. ⁴⁸As surely as I live, declares the Sovereign LORD, your sister Sodom and her daughters never did what you and your daughters have done.

⁴⁹" 'Now this was the sin of your sister Sodom: She and her daughters were arrogant, overfed and unconcerned; they did not help the poor and needy. ⁵⁰They were haughty and did detestable things before me. Therefore I did away with them as you have seen. ⁵¹Samaria did not commit half the sins you did. You have done more detestable things than they, and have made your sisters seem righteous by all these things you have done. ⁵²Bear your disgrace, for you have furnished some justification for your sisters. Because your sins were more vile than theirs, they appear more righteous than you. So then, be ashamed and bear your disgrace, for you have made your sisters appear righteous.

⁵³" 'However, I will restore the fortunes of Sodom and her daughters and of Samaria and her daughters, and your fortunes along with them, ⁵⁴so that you may bear your disgrace and be ashamed of all you have done in giving them comfort. ⁵⁵And your sisters, Sodom with her daughters and Samaria with her daughters, will return to what they were before; and you and your daughters will return to what you were before. ⁵⁶You would not even mention your sister Sodom in the day of your pride, ⁵⁷before your wickedness was uncovered. Even so, you are now scorned by the daughters of Edomᶜ and all her neighbors and the daughters of the Philistines—all those around you who despise you. ⁵⁸You will bear the consequences of your lewdness and your detestable practices, declares the LORD.

⁵⁹" 'This is what the Sovereign LORD says: I will deal with you as you deserve, because you have despised my oath by breaking the covenant. ⁶⁰Yet I will remember the covenant I made with you in the days of your youth, and I will establish an everlasting covenant with you. ⁶¹Then you will remember your

ᵃ 29 Or Chaldea   ᵇ 36 Or lust   ᶜ 57 Many Hebrew manuscripts and Syriac; most Hebrew manuscripts, Septuagint and Vulgate Aram ways and be ashamed when you receive your sisters, both those who are older than you and those who are younger. I will give them to you as daughters, but not on the basis of my covenant with you. ⁶²So I will establish my covenant with you, and you will know that I am the Lord. ⁶³Then, when I make atonement for you for all you have done, you will remember and be ashamed and never again open your mouth because of your humiliation, declares the Sovereign Lord.' "

TWO EAGLES AND A VINE

17 The word of the Lord came to me: ²"Son of man, set forth an allegory and tell the house of Israel a parable. ³Say to them, 'This is what the Sovereign Lord says: A great eagle with powerful wings, long feathers and full plumage of varied colors came to Lebanon. Taking hold of the top of a cedar, ⁴he broke off its topmost shoot and carried it away to a land of merchants, where he planted it in a city of traders.

⁵" 'He took some of the seed of your land and put it in fertile soil. He planted it like a willow by abundant water, ⁶and it sprouted and became a low, spreading vine. Its branches turned toward him, but its roots remained under it. So it became a vine and produced branches and put out leafy boughs.

⁷" 'But there was another great eagle with powerful wings and full plumage. The vine now sent out its roots toward him from the plot where it was planted and stretched out its branches to him for water. ⁸It had been planted in good soil by abundant water so that it would produce branches, bear fruit and become a splendid vine.'

⁹"Say to them, 'This is what the Sovereign Lord says: Will it thrive? Will it not be uprooted and stripped of its fruit so that it withers? All its new growth will wither. It will not take a strong arm or many people to pull it up by the roots. ¹⁰Even if it is transplanted, will it thrive? Will it not wither completely when the east wind strikes it—wither away in the plot where it grew?' "

¹¹Then the word of the Lord came to me: ¹²"Say to this rebellious house, 'Do you not know what these things mean?' Say to them: 'The king of Babylon went to Jerusalem and carried off her king and her nobles, bringing them back with him to Babylon. ¹³Then he took a member of the royal family and made a treaty with him, putting him under oath. He also carried away the leading men of the land, ¹⁴so that the kingdom would be brought low, unable to rise again, surviving only by keeping his treaty. ¹⁵But the king rebelled against him by sending his envoys to Egypt to get horses and a large army. Will he succeed? Will he who does such things escape? Will he break the treaty and yet escape?

¹⁶" 'As surely as I live, declares the Sovereign Lord, he shall die in Babylon, in the land of the king who put him on the throne, whose oath he despised and whose treaty he broke. ¹⁷Pharaoh with his mighty army and great horde will be of no help to him in war, when ramps are built and siege works erected to destroy many lives. ¹⁸He despised the oath by breaking the covenant. Because he had given his hand in pledge and yet did all these things, he shall not escape.

¹⁹" 'Therefore this is what the Sovereign Lord says: As surely as I live, I will bring down on his head my oath that he despised and my covenant that he broke. ²⁰I will spread my net for him, and he will be caught in my snare. I will bring him to Babylon and execute judgment upon him there because he was unfaithful to me. ²¹All his fleeing troops will fall by the sword, and the survivors will be scattered to the winds. Then you will know that I the Lord have spoken.

²²" 'This is what the Sovereign Lord says: I myself will take a shoot from the very top of a cedar and plant it; I will break off a tender sprig from its topmost shoots and plant it on a high and lofty mountain. ²³On the mountain heights of Israel I will plant it; it will produce branches and bear fruit and become a splendid cedar. Birds of every kind will nest in it; they will find shelter in the shade of its branches. ²⁴All the trees of the field will know that I the Lord bring down the tall tree and make the low tree grow tall. I dry up the green tree and make the dry tree flourish.

" 'I the Lord have spoken, and I will do it.' "

THE SOUL WHO SINS WILL DIE

18 The word of the Lord came to me: ²"What do you people mean by quoting this proverb about the land of Israel:

" 'The fathers eat sour grapes,
   and the children's teeth are set on edge'?

³"As surely as I live, declares the Sovereign Lord, you will no longer quote this proverb in Israel.

4For every living soul belongs to me, the father as well as the son—both alike belong to me. The soul who sins is the one who will die.

5 "Suppose there is a righteous man
who does what is just and right.
6 He does not eat at the mountain shrines
or look to the idols of the house of
Israel.
He does not defile his neighbor's wife
or lie with a woman during her period.
7 He does not oppress anyone,
but returns what he took in pledge
for a loan.
He does not commit robbery
but gives his food to the hungry
and provides clothing for the naked.
8 He does not lend at usury
or take excessive interest.ᵃ
He withholds his hand from doing wrong
and judges fairly between man and
man.
9 He follows my decrees
and faithfully keeps my laws.
That man is righteous;
he will surely live,
declares the Sovereign LORD.

10 "Suppose he has a violent son, who sheds blood or does any of these other thingsᵇ 11(though the father has done none of them):

"He eats at the mountain shrines.
He defiles his neighbor's wife.
12 He oppresses the poor and needy.
He commits robbery.
He does not return what he took in pledge.
He looks to the idols.
He does detestable things.
13 He lends at usury and takes excessive interest.

Will such a man live? He will not! Because he has done all these detestable things, he will surely be put to death and his blood will be on his own head.

14 "But suppose this son has a son who sees all the sins his father commits, and though he sees them, he does not do such things:

15 "He does not eat at the mountain shrines
or look to the idols of the house of Israel.
He does not defile his neighbor's wife.
16 He does not oppress anyone
or require a pledge for a loan.
He does not commit robbery
but gives his food to the hungry
and provides clothing for the naked.
17 He withholds his hand from sinᶜ
and takes no usury or excessive interest.
He keeps my laws and follows my decrees.

Breaking Free of Your Past

Do you ever feel like a victim of your family's mistakes? Do you ever get the feeling that people look at you a certain way because of something your parents or siblings or even grandparents did? Here's good news from the Lord: You don't have to feel guilty for your family's past. For one thing, God never judges you for something someone else did. For another thing, he can give you the strength you need to break any cycle of sin in your family— no matter how terrible or damaging that cycle is.

>> live the adventure >> Eze 18:1-21

ᵃ 8 Or take interest; similarly in verses 13 and 17   ᵇ 10 Or things to a brother   ᶜ 17 Septuagint (see also verse 8); Hebrew from the poor

He will not die for his father's sin; he will surely live. ¹⁸But his father will die for his own sin, because he practiced extortion, robbed his brother and did what was wrong among his people.

¹⁹"Yet you ask, 'Why does the son not share the guilt of his father?' Since the son has done what is just and right and has been careful to keep all my decrees, he will surely live. ²⁰The soul who sins is the one who will die. The son will not share the guilt of the father, nor will the father share the guilt of the son. The righteousness of the righteous man will be credited to him, and the wickedness of the wicked will be charged against him.

²¹"But if a wicked man turns away from all the sins he has committed and keeps all my decrees and does what is just and right, he will surely live; he will not die. ²²None of the offenses he has committed will be remembered against him. Because of the righteous things he has done, he will live. ²³Do I take any pleasure in the death of the wicked? declares the Sovereign LORD. Rather, am I not pleased when they turn from their ways and live?

²⁴"But if a righteous man turns from his righteousness and commits sin and does the same detestable things the wicked man does, will he live? None of the righteous things he has done will be remembered. Because of the unfaithfulness he is guilty of and because of the sins he has committed, he will die.

²⁵"Yet you say, 'The way of the Lord is not just.' Hear, O house of Israel: Is my way unjust? Is it not your ways that are unjust? ²⁶If a righteous man turns from his righteousness and commits sin, he will die for it; because of the sin he has committed he will die. ²⁷But if a wicked man turns away from the wickedness he has committed and does what is just and right, he will save his life. ²⁸Because he considers all the offenses he has committed and turns away from them, he will surely live; he will not die. ²⁹Yet the house of Israel says, 'The way of the Lord is not just.' Are my ways unjust, O house of Israel? Is it not your ways that are unjust?

³⁰"Therefore, O house of Israel, I will judge you, each one according to his ways, declares the Sovereign LORD. Repent! Turn away from all your offenses; then sin will not be your downfall. ³¹Rid yourselves of all the offenses you have committed, and get a new heart and a new spirit. Why will you die, O house of Israel? ³²For I take no pleasure in the death of anyone, declares the Sovereign LORD. Repent and live!

NOW OR NEVER
EZE 18:20

If your parents are divorced, you may have gone through a period of blaming yourself for it. Maybe you still do, but God doesn't see it that way. As far as he's concerned, your parents are responsible for their own decisions and actions. Don't let someone else's past shape your future.

A LAMENT FOR ISRAEL'S PRINCES

19
"Take up a lament concerning the princes of Israel ²and say:

" 'What a lioness was your mother
among the lions!
She lay down among the young lions
and reared her cubs.
³She brought up one of her cubs,
and he became a strong lion.
He learned to tear the prey
and he devoured men.
⁴The nations heard about him,
and he was trapped in their pit.
They led him with hooks
to the land of Egypt.

⁵" 'When she saw her hope unfulfilled,
her expectation gone,
she took another of her cubs
and made him a strong lion.

⁶He prowled among the lions,
　for he was now a strong lion.
He learned to tear the prey
　and he devoured men.
⁷He broke down[a] their strongholds
　and devastated their towns.
The land and all who were in it
　were terrified by his roaring.
⁸Then the nations came against him,
　those from regions round about.
They spread their net for him,
　and he was trapped in their pit.
⁹With hooks they pulled him into a cage
　and brought him to the king of Babylon.
They put him in prison,
　so his roar was heard no longer
　on the mountains of Israel.

10 " 'Your mother was like a vine in your vineyard[b]
　planted by the water;
it was fruitful and full of branches
　because of abundant water.
¹¹Its branches were strong,
　fit for a ruler's scepter.
It towered high
　above the thick foliage,
conspicuous for its height
　and for its many branches.
¹²But it was uprooted in fury
　and thrown to the ground.
The east wind made it shrivel,
　it was stripped of its fruit;
its strong branches withered
　and fire consumed them.
¹³Now it is planted in the desert,
　in a dry and thirsty land.
¹⁴Fire spread from one of its main[c] branches
　and consumed its fruit.
No strong branch is left on it
　fit for a ruler's scepter.'

This is a lament and is to be used as a lament."

REBELLIOUS ISRAEL

20 In the seventh year, in the fifth month on the tenth day, some of the elders of Israel came to inquire of the LORD, and they sat down in front of me.

²Then the word of the LORD came to me: ³"Son of man, speak to the elders of Israel and say to them, 'This is what the Sovereign LORD says: Have you come to inquire of me? As surely as I live, I will not let you inquire of me, declares the Sovereign LORD.'

⁴"Will you judge them? Will you judge them, son of man? Then confront them with the detestable practices of their fathers ⁵and say to them: 'This is what the Sovereign LORD says: On the day I chose Israel, I swore with uplifted hand to the descendants of the house of Jacob and revealed myself to them in Egypt. With uplifted hand I said to them, "I am the LORD your God." ⁶On that day I swore to them that I would bring them out of Egypt into a land I had searched out for them, a land flowing with milk and

---

[a] 7 Targum (see Septuagint); Hebrew *He knew*　[b] 10 Two Hebrew manuscripts; most Hebrew manuscripts *your blood*　[c] 14 Or *from under its*

honey, the most beautiful of all lands. ⁷And I said to them, "Each of you, get rid of the vile images you have set your eyes on, and do not defile yourselves with the idols of Egypt. I am the LORD your God."

Watching What You Watch

Vile images come in all shapes and sizes. For Israel, they were pagan idols worshiped in the place of God. For us today, vile images can be found in music videos, porn magazines, nude celebrity websites, pay cable channels and thousands of other places. Although it's always best to avoid them altogether, sometimes it's hard to block them out entirely. But you can control the way you respond to them. Don't give them space to settle down in your memory. Vile images ruined the lives of many Israelites, and they'll ruin your life too . . . if you give them the chance.

⁸ " 'But they rebelled against me and would not listen to me; they did not get rid of the vile images they had set their eyes on, nor did they forsake the idols of Egypt. So I said I would pour out my wrath on them and spend my anger against them in Egypt. ⁹But for the sake of my name I did what would keep it from being profaned in the eyes of the nations they lived among and in whose sight I had revealed myself to the Israelites by bringing them out of Egypt. ¹⁰Therefore I led them out of Egypt and brought them into the desert. ¹¹I gave them my decrees and made known to them my laws, for the man who obeys them will live by them. ¹²Also I gave them my Sabbaths as a sign between us, so they would know that I the LORD made them holy.

¹³ " 'Yet the people of Israel rebelled against me in the desert. They did not follow my decrees but rejected my laws—although the man who obeys them will live by them—and they utterly desecrated my Sabbaths. So I said I would pour out my wrath on them and destroy them in the desert. ¹⁴But for the sake of my name I did what would keep it from being profaned in the eyes of the nations in whose sight I had brought them out. ¹⁵Also with uplifted hand I swore to them in the desert that I would not bring them into the land I had given them—a land flowing with milk and honey, most beautiful of all lands— ¹⁶because they rejected my laws and did not follow my decrees and desecrated my Sabbaths. For their hearts were devoted to their idols. ¹⁷Yet I looked on them with pity and did not destroy them or put an end to them in the desert. ¹⁸I said to their children in the desert, "Do not follow the statutes of your fathers or keep their laws or defile yourselves with their idols. ¹⁹I am the LORD your God; follow my decrees and be careful to keep my laws. ²⁰Keep my Sabbaths holy, that they may be a sign between us. Then you will know that I am the LORD your God."

²¹ " 'But the children rebelled against me: They did not follow my decrees, they were not careful to keep my laws—although the man who obeys them will live by them—and they desecrated my Sabbaths. So I said I would pour out my wrath on them and spend my anger against them in the desert. ²²But I withheld my hand, and for the sake of my name I did what would keep it from being profaned in the eyes of the nations in whose sight I had brought them out. ²³Also with uplifted hand I swore to them in the desert that I would disperse them among the nations and scatter them through the countries, ²⁴because they had not obeyed my laws but had rejected my decrees and desecrated my Sabbaths, and their eyes ⌐lusted⌐ after their fathers' idols. ²⁵I also gave them over to statutes that were not good and laws they could not live by; ²⁶I let them become defiled through their gifts—the sacrifice of every firstborn[a]—that I might fill them with horror so they would know that I am the LORD.'

²⁷"Therefore, son of man, speak to the people of Israel and say to them, 'This is what the Sovereign LORD says: In this also your fathers blasphemed me by forsaking me: ²⁸When I brought them into the land I had sworn to give them and they saw any high hill or any leafy tree, there they offered their sacrifices, made offerings that provoked me to anger, presented their fragrant incense and poured out their drink offerings. ²⁹Then I said to them: What is this high place you go to?' " (It is called Bamah[b] to this day.)

JUDGMENT AND RESTORATION

³⁰"Therefore say to the house of Israel: 'This is what the Sovereign LORD says: Will you defile yourselves the way your fathers did and lust after their vile images? ³¹When you offer your gifts—the sacrifice of your sons in[c] the fire—you continue to defile yourselves with all your idols to this day. Am I

---

[a] 26 Or —making every firstborn pass through ⌐the fire⌐   [b] 29 Bamah means high place.   [c] 31 Or —making your sons pass through

to let you inquire of me, O house of Israel? As surely as I live, declares the Sovereign LORD, I will not let you inquire of me.

32 " 'You say, "We want to be like the nations, like the peoples of the world, who serve wood and stone." But what you have in mind will never happen. 33 As surely as I live, declares the Sovereign LORD, I will rule over you with a mighty hand and an outstretched arm and with outpoured wrath. 34 I will bring you from the nations and gather you from the countries where you have been scattered—with a mighty hand and an outstretched arm and with outpoured wrath. 35 I will bring you into the desert of the nations and there, face to face, I will execute judgment upon you. 36 As I judged your fathers in the desert of the land of Egypt, so I will judge you, declares the Sovereign LORD. 37 I will take note of you as you pass under my rod, and I will bring you into the bond of the covenant. 38 I will purge you of those who revolt and rebel against me. Although I will bring them out of the land where they are living, yet they will not enter the land of Israel. Then you will know that I am the LORD.

39 " 'As for you, O house of Israel, this is what the Sovereign LORD says: Go and serve your idols, every one of you! But afterward you will surely listen to me and no longer profane my holy name with your gifts and idols. 40 For on my holy mountain, the high mountain of Israel, declares the Sovereign LORD, there in the land the entire house of Israel will serve me, and there I will accept them. There I will require your offerings and your choice gifts,[a] along with all your holy sacrifices. 41 I will accept you as fragrant incense when I bring you out from the nations and gather you from the countries where you have been scattered, and I will show myself holy among you in the sight of the nations. 42 Then you will know that I am the LORD, when I bring you into the land of Israel, the land I had sworn with uplifted hand to give to your fathers. 43 There you will remember your conduct and all the actions by which you have defiled yourselves, and you will loathe yourselves for all the evil you have done. 44 You will know that I am the LORD, when I deal with you for my name's sake and not according to your evil ways and your corrupt practices, O house of Israel, declares the Sovereign LORD.' "

now or never

EZE 20:39

Sometimes God has to get people's attention through tough times or tragedy before they'll listen. Maybe some of your friends or family fit this description. If so, you need to be ready to share God's truth with them when the critical moment arrives.

PROPHECY AGAINST THE SOUTH

45 The word of the LORD came to me: 46 "Son of man, set your face toward the south; preach against the south and prophesy against the forest of the southland. 47 Say to the southern forest: 'Hear the word of the LORD. This is what the Sovereign LORD says: I am about to set fire to you, and it will consume all your trees, both green and dry. The blazing flame will not be quenched, and every face from south to north will be scorched by it. 48 Everyone will see that I the LORD have kindled it; it will not be quenched.' "

49 Then I said, "Ah, Sovereign LORD! They are saying of me, 'Isn't he just telling parables?' "

BABYLON, GOD'S SWORD OF JUDGMENT

21 The word of the LORD came to me: 2 "Son of man, set your face against Jerusalem and preach against the sanctuary. Prophesy against the land of Israel 3 and say to her: 'This is what the LORD says: I am against you. I will draw my sword from its scabbard and cut off from you both the righteous and the wicked. 4 Because I am going to cut off the righteous and the wicked, my sword will be unsheathed against everyone from south to north. 5 Then all people will know that I the LORD have drawn my sword from its scabbard; it will not return again.'

6 "Therefore groan, son of man! Groan before them with broken heart and bitter grief. 7 And when they ask you, 'Why are you groaning?' you shall say, 'Because of the news that is coming. Every heart will melt and every hand go limp; every spirit will become faint and every knee become as weak as water.' It is coming! It will surely take place, declares the Sovereign LORD."

8 The word of the LORD came to me: 9 "Son of man, prophesy and say, 'This is what the Lord says:

---

a 40 Or and the gifts of your firstfruits

" 'A sword, a sword,
  sharpened and polished—
10 sharpened for the slaughter,
   polished to flash like lightning!

" 'Shall we rejoice in the scepter of my son ⌊Judah⌋? The sword despises every such stick.

11 " 'The sword is appointed to be polished,
    to be grasped with the hand;
   it is sharpened and polished,
    made ready for the hand of the slayer.
12 Cry out and wail, son of man,
    for it is against my people;
   it is against all the princes of Israel.
   They are thrown to the sword
    along with my people.
   Therefore beat your breast.

13 " 'Testing will surely come. And what if the scepter ⌊of Judah⌋, which the sword despises, does not continue? declares the Sovereign Lord.'

14 "So then, son of man, prophesy
    and strike your hands together.
   Let the sword strike twice,
    even three times.
   It is a sword for slaughter—
    a sword for great slaughter,
    closing in on them from every side.
15 So that hearts may melt
    and the fallen be many,
   I have stationed the sword for slaughter[a]
    at all their gates.
   Oh! It is made to flash like lightning,
    it is grasped for slaughter.
16 O sword, slash to the right,
    then to the left,
   wherever your blade is turned.
17 I too will strike my hands together,
    and my wrath will subside.
   I the Lord have spoken."

18 The word of the Lord came to me: 19 "Son of man, mark out two roads for the sword of the king of Babylon to take, both starting from the same country. Make a signpost where the road branches off to the city. 20 Mark out one road for the sword to come against Rabbah of the Ammonites and another against Judah and fortified Jerusalem. 21 For the king of Babylon will stop at the fork in the road, at the junction of the two roads, to seek an omen: He will cast lots with arrows, he will consult his idols, he will examine the liver. 22 Into his right hand will come the lot for Jerusalem, where he is to set up battering rams, to give the command to slaughter, to sound the battle cry, to set battering rams against the gates, to build a ramp and to erect siege works. 23 It will seem like a false omen to those who have sworn allegiance to him, but he will remind them of their guilt and take them captive.

24 "Therefore this is what the Sovereign Lord says: 'Because you people have brought to mind your guilt by your open rebellion, revealing your sins in all that you do—because you have done this, you will be taken captive.

25 " 'O profane and wicked prince of Israel, whose day has come, whose time of punishment has reached its climax, 26 this is what the Sovereign Lord says: Take off the turban, remove the crown. It will

---

[a] 15 Septuagint; the meaning of the Hebrew for this word is uncertain.

battlelines

» The Silver Screen (Movies)

Q: Big plans tonight, Dustin?
A: I'm probably gonna eat some pizza and catch a movie with the guys.

Q: Sounds good. What's playing now?
A: Mostly stuff I've already seen. But there's one new flick starting today that everybody's pumped to see. It's called *Death Angel*.

Q: Oh yeah. I've seen the previews for that. Looks pretty intense . . . pretty graphic.
A: Well, it *is* a horror movie. So, yeah, it'll definitely have some blood and guts, but probably no worse than a lot of the stuff that's already out there. It'll have some language, I'm sure, and maybe some skin too . . . but nothing I haven't heard or seen 100 times.

Q: Doesn't all that stuff affect you?
A: Not the language. You hear those words everyday. The violence . . . well, that's just Hollywood special effects. But I guess the sex scenes probably aren't the best images to be putting into my mind.

Q: So why do you go?
A: To be with the guys. To have something to do. Meet girls. Get out of the house. I mean, if I didn't go, I'd just sit at home and go crazy. Plus everybody will be talking about the movie next week, and I don't want to be totally out of it.

» The Discerning Moviegoer

First Hezekiah 3:5 plainly states, "Thou shalt not watch movies."

Just kidding. There's no such verse and no such command in the Bible. However, there *are* numerous verses that tell us to be careful about what we focus our minds on. Philippians 4:8 is one example: "Finally, brothers, whatever is true, whatever is noble, whatever is right, whatever is pure, whatever is lovely, whatever is admirable—if anything is excellent or praiseworthy—think about such things." Gratuitous language, violence and sex scenes—apart from not fitting well with the above list—can have a bigger affect on your heart and mind than you might realize.

In short, we need to practice discernment. Some movies convey truth in a powerful way and are well worth seeing. Others promote wrong or stupid ideas, and they do so very badly. We should avoid them like a rotten piece of fruit.

Read more about making good entertainment choices at www.RevolutionBible.com.

not be as it was: The lowly will be exalted and the exalted will be brought low. ²⁷A ruin! A ruin! I will make it a ruin! It will not be restored until he comes to whom it rightfully belongs; to him I will give it.'

²⁸"And you, son of man, prophesy and say, 'This is what the Sovereign LORD says about the Ammonites and their insults:

> " 'A sword, a sword,
>> drawn for the slaughter,
>> polished to consume
>> and to flash like lightning!
> ²⁹Despite false visions concerning you
>> and lying divinations about you,
> it will be laid on the necks
>> of the wicked who are to be slain,
> whose day has come,
>> whose time of punishment has reached its climax.
> ³⁰Return the sword to its scabbard.
>> In the place where you were created,
> in the land of your ancestry,
>> I will judge you.
> ³¹I will pour out my wrath upon you
>> and breathe out my fiery anger against you;
> I will hand you over to brutal men,
>> men skilled in destruction.
> ³²You will be fuel for the fire,
>> your blood will be shed in your land,
> you will be remembered no more;
>> for I the LORD have spoken.' "

JERUSALEM'S SINS

22 The word of the LORD came to me: ²"Son of man, will you judge her? Will you judge this city of bloodshed? Then confront her with all her detestable practices ³and say: 'This is what the Sovereign LORD says: O city that brings on herself doom by shedding blood in her midst and defiles herself by making idols, ⁴you have become guilty because of the blood you have shed and have become defiled by the idols you have made. You have brought your days to a close, and the end of your years has come. Therefore I will make you an object of scorn to the nations and a laughingstock to all the countries. ⁵Those who are near and those who are far away will mock you, O infamous city, full of turmoil.

⁶" 'See how each of the princes of Israel who are in you uses his power to shed blood. ⁷In you they have treated father and mother with contempt; in you they have oppressed the alien and mistreated the fatherless and the widow. ⁸You have despised my holy things and desecrated my Sabbaths. ⁹In you are slanderous men bent on shedding blood; in you are those who eat at the mountain shrines and commit lewd acts. ¹⁰In you are those who dishonor their fathers' bed; in you are those who violate women during their period, when they are ceremonially unclean. ¹¹In you one man commits a detestable offense with his neighbor's wife, another shamefully defiles his daughter-in-law, and another violates his sister, his own father's daughter. ¹²In you men accept bribes to shed blood; you take usury and excessive interest^a and make unjust gain from your neighbors by extortion. And you have forgotten me, declares the Sovereign LORD.

¹³" 'I will surely strike my hands together at the unjust gain you have made and at the blood you

NOW OR NEVER
EZE 22:6–12

Notice that one of the sins God singles out is treating one's parents badly (alongside murder and adultery, no less). Your parents are God's gift to you. If you don't treat them that way, you show contempt for God's blessing in your life. When you honor your parents, it's a way of showing God your gratitude.

---

^a 12 Or *usury and interest*

have shed in your midst. [14]Will your courage endure or your hands be strong in the day I deal with you? I the LORD have spoken, and I will do it. [15]I will disperse you among the nations and scatter you through the countries; and I will put an end to your uncleanness. [16]When you have been defiled[a] in the eyes of the nations, you will know that I am the LORD.' "

[17]Then the word of the LORD came to me: [18]"Son of man, the house of Israel has become dross to me; all of them are the copper, tin, iron and lead left inside a furnace. They are but the dross of silver. [19]Therefore this is what the Sovereign LORD says: 'Because you have all become dross, I will gather you into Jerusalem. [20]As men gather silver, copper, iron, lead and tin into a furnace to melt it with a fiery blast, so will I gather you in my anger and my wrath and put you inside the city and melt you. [21]I will gather you and I will blow on you with my fiery wrath, and you will be melted inside her. [22]As silver is melted in a furnace, so you will be melted inside her, and you will know that I the LORD have poured out my wrath upon you.' "

[23]Again the word of the LORD came to me: [24]"Son of man, say to the land, 'You are a land that has had no rain or showers[b] in the day of wrath.' [25]There is a conspiracy of her princes[c] within her like a roaring lion tearing its prey; they devour people, take treasures and precious things and make many widows within her. [26]Her priests do violence to my law and profane my holy things; they do not distinguish between the holy and the common; they teach that there is no difference between the unclean and the clean; and they shut their eyes to the keeping of my Sabbaths, so that I am profaned among them. [27]Her officials within her are like wolves tearing their prey; they shed blood and kill people to make unjust gain. [28]Her prophets whitewash these deeds for them by false visions and lying divinations. They say, 'This is what the Sovereign LORD says'—when the LORD has not spoken. [29]The people of the land practice extortion and commit robbery; they oppress the poor and needy and mistreat the alien, denying them justice.

[30]"I looked for a man among them who would build up the wall and stand before me in the gap on behalf of the land so I would not have to destroy it, but I found none. [31]So I will pour out my wrath on them and consume them with my fiery anger, bringing down on their own heads all they have done, declares the Sovereign LORD."

Standing in the Gap

God is looking for young men to "stand . . . in the gap" between him and the many people who don't know him. He's looking for guys who will intercede for others, who will lay themselves on the line to bring people to him. He's looking for guys who will ignore their fears and say the tough things that unsaved people need to hear. Do you have the guts to stand in the gap between God and your non-Christian friends and loved ones?

» live the adventure » Eze 22:30

TWO ADULTEROUS SISTERS

23

The word of the LORD came to me: [2]"Son of man, there were two women, daughters of the same mother. [3]They became prostitutes in Egypt, engaging in prostitution from their youth. In that land their breasts were fondled and their virgin bosoms caressed. [4]The older was named Oholah, and her sister was Oholibah. They were mine and gave birth to sons and daughters. Oholah is Samaria, and Oholibah is Jerusalem.

[5]"Oholah engaged in prostitution while she was still mine; and she lusted after her lovers, the Assyrians—warriors [6]clothed in blue, governors and commanders, all of them handsome young men, and mounted horsemen. [7]She gave herself as a prostitute to all the elite of the Assyrians and defiled herself with all the idols of everyone she lusted after. [8]She did not give up the prostitution she began in Egypt, when during her youth men slept with her, caressed her virgin bosom and poured out their lust upon her.

[9]"Therefore I handed her over to her lovers, the Assyrians, for whom she lusted. [10]They stripped her naked, took away her sons and daughters and killed her with the sword. She became a byword among women, and punishment was inflicted on her.

[11]"Her sister Oholibah saw this, yet in her lust and prostitution she was more depraved than her sis-

---

[a] 16 Or *When I have allotted you your inheritance*   [b] 24 Septuagint; Hebrew *has not been cleansed or rained on*   [c] 25 Septuagint; Hebrew *prophets*

ter. [12]She too lusted after the Assyrians—governors and commanders, warriors in full dress, mounted horsemen, all handsome young men. [13]I saw that she too defiled herself; both of them went the same way.

[14]"But she carried her prostitution still further. She saw men portrayed on a wall, figures of Chaldeans[a] portrayed in red, [15]with belts around their waists and flowing turbans on their heads; all of them looked like Babylonian chariot officers, natives of Chaldea.[b] [16]As soon as she saw them, she lusted after them and sent messengers to them in Chaldea. [17]Then the Babylonians came to her, to the bed of love, and in their lust they defiled her. After she had been defiled by them, she turned away from them in disgust. [18]When she carried on her prostitution openly and exposed her nakedness, I turned away from her in disgust, just as I had turned away from her sister. [19]Yet she became more and more promiscuous as she recalled the days of her youth, when she was a prostitute in Egypt. [20]There she lusted after her lovers, whose genitals were like those of donkeys and whose emission was like that of horses. [21]So you longed for the lewdness of your youth, when in Egypt your bosom was caressed and your young breasts fondled.[c]

[22]"Therefore, Oholibah, this is what the Sovereign LORD says: I will stir up your lovers against you, those you turned away from in disgust, and I will bring them against you from every side— [23]the Babylonians and all the Chaldeans, the men of Pekod and Shoa and Koa, and all the Assyrians with them, handsome young men, all of them governors and commanders, chariot officers and men of high rank, all mounted on horses. [24]They will come against you with weapons,[d] chariots and wagons and with a throng of people; they will take up positions against you on every side with large and small shields and with helmets. I will turn you over to them for punishment, and they will punish you according to their standards. [25]I will direct my jealous anger against you, and they will deal with you in fury. They will cut off your noses and your ears, and those of you who are left will fall by the sword. They will take away your sons and daughters, and those of you who are left will be consumed by fire. [26]They will also strip you of your clothes and take your fine jewelry. [27]So I will put a stop to the lewdness and prostitution you began in Egypt. You will not look on these things with longing or remember Egypt anymore.

[28]"For this is what the Sovereign LORD says: I am about to hand you over to those you hate, to those you turned away from in disgust. [29]They will deal with you in hatred and take away everything you have worked for. They will leave you naked and bare, and the shame of your prostitution will be exposed. Your lewdness and promiscuity [30]have brought this upon you, because you lusted after the nations and defiled yourself with their idols. [31]You have gone the way of your sister; so I will put her cup into your hand.

[32]"This is what the Sovereign LORD says:

> "You will drink your sister's cup,
>   a cup large and deep;
> it will bring scorn and derision,
>   for it holds so much.
> [33]You will be filled with drunkenness and sorrow,
>   the cup of ruin and desolation,
>   the cup of your sister Samaria.
> [34]You will drink it and drain it dry;
>   you will dash it to pieces
>   and tear your breasts.

I have spoken, declares the Sovereign LORD.

[35]"Therefore this is what the Sovereign LORD says: Since you have forgotten me and thrust me behind your back, you must bear the consequences of your lewdness and prostitution."

[36]The LORD said to me: "Son of man, will you judge Oholah and Oholibah? Then confront them with their detestable practices, [37]for they have committed adultery and blood is on their hands. They committed adultery with their idols; they even sacrificed their children, whom they bore to me,[e] as food for them. [38]They have also done this to me: At that same time they defiled my sanctuary and desecrated my Sabbaths. [39]On the very day they sacrificed their children to their idols, they entered my sanctuary and desecrated it. That is what they did in my house.

---

[a] *14* Or *Babylonians*   [b] *15* Or *Babylonia*; also in verse 16   [c] *21* Syriac (see also verse 3); Hebrew *caressed because of your young breasts*   [d] *24* The meaning of the Hebrew for this word is uncertain.   [e] *37* Or *even made the children they bore to me pass through the fire*

40"They even sent messengers for men who came from far away, and when they arrived you bathed yourself for them, painted your eyes and put on your jewelry. 41You sat on an elegant couch, with a table spread before it on which you had placed the incense and oil that belonged to me.

42"The noise of a carefree crowd was around her; Sabeans[a] were brought from the desert along with men from the rabble, and they put bracelets on the arms of the woman and her sister and beautiful crowns on their heads. 43Then I said about the one worn out by adultery, 'Now let them use her as a prostitute, for that is all she is.' 44And they slept with her. As men sleep with a prostitute, so they slept with those lewd women, Oholah and Oholibah. 45But righteous men will sentence them to the punishment of women who commit adultery and shed blood, because they are adulterous and blood is on their hands.

46"This is what the Sovereign Lord says: Bring a mob against them and give them over to terror and plunder. 47The mob will stone them and cut them down with their swords; they will kill their sons and daughters and burn down their houses.

48"So I will put an end to lewdness in the land, that all women may take warning and not imitate you. 49You will suffer the penalty for your lewdness and bear the consequences of your sins of idolatry. Then you will know that I am the Sovereign Lord."

THE COOKING POT

24 In the ninth year, in the tenth month on the tenth day, the word of the Lord came to me: 2"Son of man, record this date, this very date, because the king of Babylon has laid siege to Jerusalem this very day. 3Tell this rebellious house a parable and say to them: 'This is what the Sovereign Lord says:

" 'Put on the cooking pot; put it on
        and pour water into it.
4Put into it the pieces of meat,
        all the choice pieces—the leg and the shoulder.
Fill it with the best of these bones;
5   take the pick of the flock.
Pile wood beneath it for the bones;
        bring it to a boil
        and cook the bones in it.

6" 'For this is what the Sovereign Lord says:

" 'Woe to the city of bloodshed,
        to the pot now encrusted,
        whose deposit will not go away!
Empty it piece by piece
        without casting lots for them.

7" 'For the blood she shed is in her midst:
        She poured it on the bare rock;
she did not pour it on the ground,
        where the dust would cover it.
8To stir up wrath and take revenge
        I put her blood on the bare rock,
        so that it would not be covered.

9" 'Therefore this is what the Sovereign Lord says:

" 'Woe to the city of bloodshed!
        I, too, will pile the wood high.
10So heap on the wood
        and kindle the fire.
Cook the meat well,
        mixing in the spices;

---

and let the bones be charred.
¹¹ Then set the empty pot on the coals
till it becomes hot and its copper glows
so its impurities may be melted
and its deposit burned away.
¹² It has frustrated all efforts;
its heavy deposit has not been removed,
not even by fire.

¹³ " 'Now your impurity is lewdness. Because I tried to cleanse you but you would not be cleansed from your impurity, you will not be clean again until my wrath against you has subsided.

¹⁴ " 'I the LORD have spoken. The time has come for me to act. I will not hold back; I will not have pity, nor will I relent. You will be judged according to your conduct and your actions, declares the Sovereign LORD.' "

EZEKIEL'S WIFE DIES

¹⁵The word of the LORD came to me: ¹⁶"Son of man, with one blow I am about to take away from you the delight of your eyes. Yet do not lament or weep or shed any tears. ¹⁷Groan quietly; do not mourn for the dead. Keep your turban fastened and your sandals on your feet; do not cover the lower part of your face or eat the customary food ∟of mourners⌋."

¹⁸So I spoke to the people in the morning, and in the evening my wife died. The next morning I did as I had been commanded.

¹⁹Then the people asked me, "Won't you tell us what these things have to do with us?"

²⁰So I said to them, "The word of the LORD came to me: ²¹Say to the house of Israel, 'This is what the Sovereign LORD says: I am about to desecrate my sanctuary—the stronghold in which you take pride, the delight of your eyes, the object of your affection. The sons and daughters you left behind will fall by the sword. ²²And you will do as I have done. You will not cover the lower part of your face or eat the customary food ∟of mourners⌋. ²³You will keep your turbans on your heads and your sandals on your feet. You will not mourn or weep but will waste away because of^a your sins and groan among yourselves. ²⁴Ezekiel will be a sign to you; you will do just as he has done. When this happens, you will know that I am the Sovereign LORD.'

²⁵"And you, son of man, on the day I take away their stronghold, their joy and glory, the delight of their eyes, their heart's desire, and their sons and daughters as well— ²⁶on that day a fugitive will come to tell you the news. ²⁷At that time your mouth will be opened; you will speak with him and will no longer be silent. So you will be a sign to them, and they will know that I am the LORD."

Understanding God's Desire for Faithfulness

If you've ever wondered how far God would go to get people's attention in order to bring them to him, here's your answer. Before you accuse God of being unfair, though, keep in mind that he's the one who gave Ezekiel's wife her life in the first place. Yes, the death of his wife must have been a devastating blow to Ezekiel. Yes, not being able to grieve for her must have stretched Ezekiel's faith to the breaking point. Deep down, though, Ezekiel knew that staying obedient to God—the One who controls all life and death—was the only response that made sense.

A PROPHECY AGAINST AMMON

25 The word of the LORD came to me: ²"Son of man, set your face against the Ammonites and prophesy against them. ³Say to them, 'Hear the word of the Sovereign LORD. This is what the Sovereign LORD says: Because you said "Aha!" over my sanctuary when it was desecrated and over the land of Israel when it was laid waste and over the people of Judah when they went into exile, ⁴therefore I am going to give you to the people of the East as a possession. They will set up their camps and pitch their tents among you; they will eat your fruit and drink your milk. ⁵I will turn Rabbah into a pasture for camels and Ammon into a resting place for sheep. Then you will know

^a 23 Or away in

samson

VERSUS

» A Hebrew judge (deliverer) from the tribe of Dan

» A man blessed with supernatural strength

» Had a weakness for pretty women

philistines

» "Sea Peoples" who migrated to Canaan

» Israel's archenemies to the west

» Fierce warriors with superior military "technology"

The Main Event

You know the old saying that history repeats itself? That's a perfect way to describe the time of the judges in Israel. Here's how the cycle worked: The Israelites would sin against God; God would allow an enemy nation to come in and oppress his people; humbled and miserable, the Israelites would cry out for help; God would send a judge or deliverer; the Israelites would enjoy a time of peace . . . until their next bout of unfaithfulness. Then it was déjà vu all over again.

Not surprisingly, the dominant philosophy of that era could be summed up as, "Do whatever you want" (see Judges 21:25). Sound familiar?

Of all Israel's tormentors, the Philistines were probably the worst. They lived along the Mediterranean Sea and were constantly pushing inland. They used their superior military expertise and strength to great advantage. If you saw the movie *Braveheart*, with the ragged Scots fighting on foot with hoes and shovels against the well-armed English on horseback, you get the idea.

When the situation with the Philistines got really awful, God sent help in the form of Samson. Samson was a one-man wrecking crew, a long-haired jokester blessed with superhuman (make that "supernatural") strength. One time, for example, Samson grabbed the jawbone of a donkey and took out more than a thousand Philistines. Another time he picked up the front gate to the Philistine city of Gaza and transplanted it to a hilltop outside of town. We're talking about a scary, freak-of-nature type of power.

Yet for all his strength, Samson had one enormous weakness—women. He was constantly hooking up with shady ladies. One of them, a temptress named Delilah, caused his downfall. After she sweet-talked him into giving away the secret to his strength, Samson was captured and blinded by the Philistines. But even in his humiliation and death, Samson got the last laugh, bringing down a huge temple on the heads of thousands of his enemies.

The Outcome

Perhaps the best response to Samson's life is, "Wow," not only with a sense of awe for what he accomplished, but also with a sense of regret for what he might have done if only he had developed a close relationship with God.

Samson reminds us that we all have strengths and weaknesses. He reminds us that God can accomplish great things through us despite all our shortcomings. But he also reminds us that if we're not careful, our flaws can prevent us from accomplishing even greater things for God. Samson is the poster child for the millions of potentially great men throughout the ages who have thrown it all away for a pretty face.

Don't throw away your opportunities to make a difference. Keep yourself pure. Don't get cocky. Remember that God is your true source of strength.

Read more about Samson and the Philistines in Judges 13–16 (pages 289–294).

that I am the LORD. ⁶For this is what the Sovereign LORD says: Because you have clapped your hands and stamped your feet, rejoicing with all the malice of your heart against the land of Israel, ⁷therefore I will stretch out my hand against you and give you as plunder to the nations. I will cut you off from the nations and exterminate you from the countries. I will destroy you, and you will know that I am the LORD.' "

A PROPHECY AGAINST MOAB

⁸"This is what the Sovereign LORD says: 'Because Moab and Seir said, "Look, the house of Judah has become like all the other nations," ⁹therefore I will expose the flank of Moab, beginning at its frontier towns—Beth Jeshimoth, Baal Meon and Kiriathaim—the glory of that land. ¹⁰I will give Moab along with the Ammonites to the people of the East as a possession, so that the Ammonites will not be remembered among the nations; ¹¹and I will inflict punishment on Moab. Then they will know that I am the LORD.' "

A PROPHECY AGAINST EDOM

¹²"This is what the Sovereign LORD says: 'Because Edom took revenge on the house of Judah and became very guilty by doing so, ¹³therefore this is what the Sovereign LORD says: I will stretch out my hand against Edom and kill its men and their animals. I will lay it waste, and from Teman to Dedan they will fall by the sword. ¹⁴I will take vengeance on Edom by the hand of my people Israel, and they will deal with Edom in accordance with my anger and my wrath; they will know my vengeance, declares the Sovereign LORD.' "

A PROPHECY AGAINST PHILISTIA

¹⁵"This is what the Sovereign LORD says: 'Because the Philistines acted in vengeance and took revenge with malice in their hearts, and with ancient hostility sought to destroy Judah, ¹⁶therefore this is what the Sovereign LORD says: I am about to stretch out my hand against the Philistines, and I will cut off the Kerethites and destroy those remaining along the coast. ¹⁷I will carry out great vengeance on them and punish them in my wrath. Then they will know that I am the LORD, when I take vengeance on them.' "

A PROPHECY AGAINST TYRE

26 In the eleventh year, on the first day of the month, the word of the LORD came to me: ²"Son of man, because Tyre has said of Jerusalem, 'Aha! The gate to the nations is broken, and its doors have swung open to me; now that she lies in ruins I will prosper,' ³therefore this is what the Sovereign LORD says: I am against you, O Tyre, and I will bring many nations against you, like the sea casting up its waves. ⁴They will destroy the walls of Tyre and pull down her towers; I will scrape away her rubble and make her a bare rock. ⁵Out in the sea she will become a place to spread fishnets, for I have spoken, declares the Sovereign LORD. She will become plunder for the nations, ⁶and her settlements on the mainland will be ravaged by the sword. Then they will know that I am the LORD.

⁷"For this is what the Sovereign LORD says: From the north I am going to bring against Tyre Nebuchadnezzar[a] king of Babylon, king of kings, with horses and chariots, with horsemen and a great army. ⁸He will ravage your settlements on the mainland with the sword; he will set up siege works against you, build a ramp up to your walls and raise his shields against you. ⁹He will direct the blows of his battering rams against your walls and demolish your towers with his weapons. ¹⁰His horses will be so many that they will cover you with dust. Your walls will tremble at the noise of the war horses, wagons and chariots when he enters your gates as men enter a city whose walls have been broken through. ¹¹The hoofs of

NOW OR NEVER
EZE 26:1–21

By 332 B.C., Tyre was destroyed as Ezekiel had predicted. Was it a lucky guess on Ezekiel's part? Get real. When the Bible says something is going to happen, bank on it.

---

[a] 7 Hebrew Nebuchadrezzar, of which Nebuchadnezzar is a variant; here and often in Ezekiel and Jeremiah

his horses will trample all your streets; he will kill your people with the sword, and your strong pillars will fall to the ground. 12 They will plunder your wealth and loot your merchandise; they will break down your walls and demolish your fine houses and throw your stones, timber and rubble into the sea. 13 I will put an end to your noisy songs, and the music of your harps will be heard no more. 14 I will make you a bare rock, and you will become a place to spread fishnets. You will never be rebuilt, for I the LORD have spoken, declares the Sovereign LORD.

15 "This is what the Sovereign LORD says to Tyre: Will not the coastlands tremble at the sound of your fall, when the wounded groan and the slaughter takes place in you? 16 Then all the princes of the coast will step down from their thrones and lay aside their robes and take off their embroidered garments. Clothed with terror, they will sit on the ground, trembling every moment, appalled at you. 17 Then they will take up a lament concerning you and say to you:

" 'How you are destroyed, O city of renown,
peopled by men of the sea!
You were a power on the seas,
you and your citizens;
you put your terror
on all who lived there.
18 Now the coastlands tremble
on the day of your fall;
the islands in the sea
are terrified at your collapse.'

19 "This is what the Sovereign LORD says: When I make you a desolate city, like cities no longer inhabited, and when I bring the ocean depths over you and its vast waters cover you, 20 then I will bring you down with those who go down to the pit, to the people of long ago. I will make you dwell in the earth below, as in ancient ruins, with those who go down to the pit, and you will not return or take your place[a] in the land of the living. 21 I will bring you to a horrible end and you will be no more. You will be sought, but you will never again be found, declares the Sovereign LORD."

A LAMENT FOR TYRE

27

The word of the LORD came to me: 2 "Son of man, take up a lament concerning Tyre. 3 Say to Tyre, situated at the gateway to the sea, merchant of peoples on many coasts, 'This is what the Sovereign LORD says:

" 'You say, O Tyre,
"I am perfect in beauty."
4 Your domain was on the high seas;
your builders brought your beauty to perfection.
5 They made all your timbers
of pine trees from Senir[b];
they took a cedar from Lebanon
to make a mast for you.
6 Of oaks from Bashan
they made your oars;
of cypress wood[c] from the coasts of Cyprus[d]
they made your deck, inlaid with ivory.
7 Fine embroidered linen from Egypt was your sail
and served as your banner;
your awnings were of blue and purple
from the coasts of Elishah.
8 Men of Sidon and Arvad were your oarsmen;
your skilled men, O Tyre, were aboard as your seamen.

---

a 20 Septuagint; Hebrew *return, and I will give glory*   b 5 That is, Hermon   c 6 Targum; the Masoretic Text has a different division of the consonants.   d 6 Hebrew *Kittim*

⁹ Veteran craftsmen of Gebal ᵃ were on board
    as shipwrights to caulk your seams.
All the ships of the sea and their sailors
    came alongside to trade for your wares.

¹⁰ " 'Men of Persia, Lydia and Put
    served as soldiers in your army.
They hung their shields and helmets on your walls,
    bringing you splendor.
¹¹ Men of Arvad and Helech
    manned your walls on every side;
men of Gammad
    were in your towers.
They hung their shields around your walls;
    they brought your beauty to perfection.

¹² " 'Tarshish did business with you because of your great wealth of goods; they exchanged silver, iron, tin and lead for your merchandise.

¹³ " 'Greece, Tubal and Meshech traded with you; they exchanged slaves and articles of bronze for your wares.

¹⁴ " 'Men of Beth Togarmah exchanged work horses, war horses and mules for your merchandise.

¹⁵ " 'The men of Rhodes ᵇ traded with you, and many coastlands were your customers; they paid you with ivory tusks and ebony.

¹⁶ " 'Aram ᶜ did business with you because of your many products; they exchanged turquoise, purple fabric, embroidered work, fine linen, coral and rubies for your merchandise.

¹⁷ " 'Judah and Israel traded with you; they exchanged wheat from Minnith and confections, ᵈ honey, oil and balm for your wares.

¹⁸ " 'Damascus, because of your many products and great wealth of goods, did business with you in wine from Helbon and wool from Zahar.

¹⁹ " 'Danites and Greeks from Uzal bought your merchandise; they exchanged wrought iron, cassia and calamus for your wares.

²⁰ " 'Dedan traded in saddle blankets with you.

²¹ " 'Arabia and all the princes of Kedar were your customers; they did business with you in lambs, rams and goats.

²² " 'The merchants of Sheba and Raamah traded with you; for your merchandise they exchanged the finest of all kinds of spices and precious stones, and gold.

²³ " 'Haran, Canneh and Eden and merchants of Sheba, Asshur and Kilmad traded with you. ²⁴ In your marketplace they traded with you beautiful garments, blue fabric, embroidered work and multicolored rugs with cords twisted and tightly knotted.

²⁵ " 'The ships of Tarshish serve
    as carriers for your wares.
You are filled with heavy cargo
    in the heart of the sea.
²⁶ Your oarsmen take you
    out to the high seas.
But the east wind will break you to pieces
    in the heart of the sea.
²⁷ Your wealth, merchandise and wares,
    your mariners, seamen and shipwrights,
your merchants and all your soldiers,
    and everyone else on board
will sink into the heart of the sea
    on the day of your shipwreck.

ᵃ *9* That is, Byblos   ᵇ *15* Septuagint; Hebrew *Dedan*   ᶜ *16* Most Hebrew manuscripts; some Hebrew manuscripts and Syriac *Edom*
ᵈ *17* The meaning of the Hebrew for this word is uncertain.

28 The shorelands will quake
  when your seamen cry out.
29 All who handle the oars
  will abandon their ships;
 the mariners and all the seamen
  will stand on the shore.
30 They will raise their voice
  and cry bitterly over you;
 they will sprinkle dust on their heads
  and roll in ashes.
31 They will shave their heads because of you
  and will put on sackcloth.
 They will weep over you with anguish of soul
  and with bitter mourning.
32 As they wail and mourn over you,
  they will take up a lament concerning you:
 "Who was ever silenced like Tyre,
  surrounded by the sea?"
33 When your merchandise went out on the seas,
  you satisfied many nations;
 with your great wealth and your wares
  you enriched the kings of the earth.
34 Now you are shattered by the sea
  in the depths of the waters;
 your wares and all your company
  have gone down with you.
35 All who live in the coastlands
  are appalled at you;
 their kings shudder with horror
  and their faces are distorted with fear.
36 The merchants among the nations hiss at you;
  you have come to a horrible end
  and will be no more.' "

A PROPHECY AGAINST THE KING OF TYRE

 The word of the LORD came to me: 2 "Son of man, say to the ruler of Tyre, 'This is what the Sovereign LORD says:

 " 'In the pride of your heart
  you say, "I am a god;
 I sit on the throne of a god
  in the heart of the seas."
 But you are a man and not a god,
  though you think you are as wise as a god.
3 Are you wiser than Daniel[a]?
  Is no secret hidden from you?
4 By your wisdom and understanding
  you have gained wealth for yourself
 and amassed gold and silver
  in your treasuries.
5 By your great skill in trading
  you have increased your wealth,
 and because of your wealth
  your heart has grown proud.

---

a 3 Or Danel; the Hebrew spelling may suggest a person other than the prophet Daniel.

6 " 'Therefore this is what the Sovereign LORD says:

" 'Because you think you are wise,
    as wise as a god,
7 I am going to bring foreigners against you,
    the most ruthless of nations;
they will draw their swords against your beauty and wisdom
    and pierce your shining splendor.
8 They will bring you down to the pit,
    and you will die a violent death
    in the heart of the seas.
9 Will you then say, "I am a god,"
    in the presence of those who kill you?
You will be but a man, not a god,
    in the hands of those who slay you.
10 You will die the death of the uncircumcised
    at the hands of foreigners.

I have spoken, declares the Sovereign LORD.' "

11 The word of the LORD came to me: 12 "Son of man, take up a lament concerning the king of Tyre and say to him: 'This is what the Sovereign LORD says:

" 'You were the model of perfection,
    full of wisdom and perfect in beauty.
13 You were in Eden,
    the garden of God;
every precious stone adorned you:
    ruby, topaz and emerald,
    chrysolite, onyx and jasper,
    sapphire,[a] turquoise and beryl.[b]
Your settings and mountings[c] were
    made of gold;
on the day you were created they
    were prepared.
14 You were anointed as a guardian
    cherub,
    for so I ordained you.
You were on the holy mount of God;
    you walked among the fiery stones.
15 You were blameless in your ways
    from the day you were created
    till wickedness was found in you.
16 Through your widespread trade
    you were filled with violence,
    and you sinned.
So I drove you in disgrace from the mount of God,
    and I expelled you, O guardian cherub,
    from among the fiery stones.
17 Your heart became proud
    on account of your beauty,
and you corrupted your wisdom
    because of your splendor.
So I threw you to the earth;
    I made a spectacle of you before kings.

now or never

EZE 28:11–19

Do you ever find yourself confused by God's judgment? Does it seem harsh or unfair? Read this account of how wonderful God made humanity . . . and how far we fell. The most amazing part of the story is not told here—when he sent his Son to redeem us.

---

a 13 Or *lapis lazuli*   b 13 The precise identification of some of these precious stones is uncertain.   c 13 The meaning of the Hebrew for this phrase is uncertain.

¹⁸By your many sins and dishonest trade
>   you have desecrated your sanctuaries.
> So I made a fire come out from you,
>   and it consumed you,
> and I reduced you to ashes on the ground
>   in the sight of all who were watching.
> ¹⁹All the nations who knew you
>   are appalled at you;
> you have come to a horrible end
>   and will be no more.' "

A PROPHECY AGAINST SIDON

²⁰The word of the LORD came to me: ²¹"Son of man, set your face against Sidon; prophesy against her ²²and say: 'This is what the Sovereign LORD says:

> " 'I am against you, O Sidon,
>   and I will gain glory within you.
> They will know that I am the LORD,
>   when I inflict punishment on her
>   and show myself holy within her.
> ²³I will send a plague upon her
>   and make blood flow in her streets.
> The slain will fall within her,
>   with the sword against her on every
>   side.
> Then they will know that I am the
>   LORD.

²⁴" 'No longer will the people of Israel have malicious neighbors who are painful briers and sharp thorns. Then they will know that I am the Sovereign LORD.

²⁵" 'This is what the Sovereign LORD says: When I gather the people of Israel from the nations where they have been scattered, I will show myself holy among them in the sight of the nations. Then they will live in their own land, which I gave to my servant Jacob. ²⁶They will live there in safety and will build houses and plant vineyards; they will live in safety when I inflict punishment on all their neighbors who maligned them. Then they will know that I am the LORD their God.' "

A PROPHECY AGAINST EGYPT

29

In the tenth year, in the tenth month on the twelfth day, the word of the LORD came to me: ²"Son of man, set your face against Pharaoh king of Egypt and prophesy against him and against all Egypt. ³Speak to him and say: 'This is what the Sovereign LORD says:

> " 'I am against you, Pharaoh king of Egypt,
>   you great monster lying among your streams.
> You say, "The Nile is mine;
>   I made it for myself."
> ⁴But I will put hooks in your jaws
>   and make the fish of your streams stick to your scales.
> I will pull you out from among your streams,
>   with all the fish sticking to your scales.
> ⁵I will leave you in the desert,
>   you and all the fish of your streams.

Keeping a Lid on Your Ego

» live the adventure » Eze 29:3

What kind of power trip would you have to be on to actually try to convince people that *you* created the Nile River? When you think about it, though, taking credit for the Nile really isn't much different from taking pride in the fact that you're good-looking . . . or that you have good hand-eye coordination . . . or that you're a wiz with computers. After all, everything good comes from God. If you take credit for your talents and abilities, you're not much different from the egomaniac that ruled over Egypt thousands of years ago.

You will fall on the open field
　　and not be gathered or picked up.
I will give you as food
　　to the beasts of the earth and the birds of the air.

⁶Then all who live in Egypt will know that I am the LORD.

" 'You have been a staff of reed for the house of Israel. ⁷When they grasped you with their hands, you splintered and you tore open their shoulders; when they leaned on you, you broke and their backs were wrenched.ᵃ

⁸" 'Therefore this is what the Sovereign LORD says: I will bring a sword against you and kill your men and their animals. ⁹Egypt will become a desolate wasteland. Then they will know that I am the LORD.

" 'Because you said, "The Nile is mine; I made it," ¹⁰therefore I am against you and against your streams, and I will make the land of Egypt a ruin and a desolate waste from Migdol to Aswan, as far as the border of Cush.ᵇ ¹¹No foot of man or animal will pass through it; no one will live there for forty years. ¹²I will make the land of Egypt desolate among devastated lands, and her cities will lie desolate forty years among ruined cities. And I will disperse the Egyptians among the nations and scatter them through the countries.

¹³" 'Yet this is what the Sovereign LORD says: At the end of forty years I will gather the Egyptians from the nations where they were scattered. ¹⁴I will bring them back from captivity and return them to Upper Egypt,ᶜ the land of their ancestry. There they will be a lowly kingdom. ¹⁵It will be the lowliest of kingdoms and will never again exalt itself above the other nations. I will make it so weak that it will never again rule over the nations. ¹⁶Egypt will no longer be a source of confidence for the people of Israel but will be a reminder of their sin in turning to her for help. Then they will know that I am the Sovereign LORD.' "

¹⁷In the twenty-seventh year, in the first month on the first day, the word of the LORD came to me: ¹⁸"Son of man, Nebuchadnezzar king of Babylon drove his army in a hard campaign against Tyre; every head was rubbed bare and every shoulder made raw. Yet he and his army got no reward from the campaign he led against Tyre. ¹⁹Therefore this is what the Sovereign LORD says: I am going to give Egypt to Nebuchadnezzar king of Babylon, and he will carry off its wealth. He will loot and plunder the land as pay for his army. ²⁰I have given him Egypt as a reward for his efforts because he and his army did it for me, declares the Sovereign LORD.

²¹"On that day I will make a hornᵈ grow for the house of Israel, and I will open your mouth among them. Then they will know that I am the LORD."

A LAMENT FOR EGYPT

30

The word of the LORD came to me: ²"Son of man, prophesy and say: 'This is what the Sovereign LORD says:

" 'Wail and say,
　　"Alas for that day!"
³For the day is near,
　　the day of the LORD is near—
a day of clouds,
　　a time of doom for the nations.
⁴A sword will come against Egypt,
　　and anguish will come upon Cush.ᵉ
When the slain fall in Egypt,
　　her wealth will be carried away
　　and her foundations torn down.

⁵Cush and Put, Lydia and all Arabia, Libyaᶠ and the people of the covenant land will fall by the sword along with Egypt.

⁶" 'This is what the LORD says:

ᵃ 7 Syriac (see also Septuagint and Vulgate); Hebrew *and you caused their backs to stand*　ᵇ 10 That is, the upper Nile region
ᶜ 14 Hebrew *to Pathros*　ᵈ 21 *Horn* here symbolizes strength.　ᵉ 4 That is, the upper Nile region; also in verses 5 and 9
ᶠ 5 Hebrew *Cub*

" 'The allies of Egypt will fall
    and her proud strength will fail.
From Migdol to Aswan
    they will fall by the sword within her,

declares the Sovereign LORD.

7 " 'They will be desolate
    among desolate lands,
and their cities will lie
    among ruined cities.
8 Then they will know that I am the LORD,
    when I set fire to Egypt
    and all her helpers are crushed.

9 " 'On that day messengers will go out from me in ships to frighten Cush out of her complacency. Anguish will take hold of them on the day of Egypt's doom, for it is sure to come.

10 " 'This is what the Sovereign LORD says:

" 'I will put an end to the hordes of Egypt
    by the hand of Nebuchadnezzar king of Babylon.
11 He and his army—the most ruthless of nations—
    will be brought in to destroy the land.
They will draw their swords against Egypt
    and fill the land with the slain.
12 I will dry up the streams of the Nile
    and sell the land to evil men;
by the hand of foreigners
    I will lay waste the land and everything in it.

I the LORD have spoken.

13 " 'This is what the Sovereign LORD says:

" 'I will destroy the idols
    and put an end to the images in Memphis.ᵃ
No longer will there be a prince in Egypt,
    and I will spread fear throughout the land.
14 I will lay waste Upper Egypt,ᵇ
    set fire to Zoan
    and inflict punishment on Thebes.ᶜ
15 I will pour out my wrath on Pelusium,ᵈ
    the stronghold of Egypt,
    and cut off the hordes of Thebes.
16 I will set fire to Egypt;
    Pelusium will writhe in agony.
Thebes will be taken by storm;
    Memphis will be in constant distress.
17 The young men of Heliopolisᵉ and Bubastisᶠ
    will fall by the sword,
    and the cities themselves will go into captivity.
18 Dark will be the day at Tahpanhes
    when I break the yoke of Egypt;
    there her proud strength will come to an end.
She will be covered with clouds,
    and her villages will go into captivity.

ᵃ 13 Hebrew *Noph*; also in verse 16   ᵇ 14 Hebrew *waste Pathros*   ᶜ 14 Hebrew *No*; also in verses 15 and 16   ᵈ 15 Hebrew *Sin*; also in verse 16   ᵉ 17 Hebrew *Awen* (or *On*)   ᶠ 17 Hebrew *Pi Beseth*

battlelines

» Beauty and the Beasts (Sex)

Q: How does your little sister like high school?

A: She thinks it's OK. She's definitely made a splash, that's for sure.

Q: How so?

A: Well, she's on the swim team, you know?

Q: I get it, "making a splash." Very funny.

A: No, no, no. I didn't mean it like that. I meant, well, some guy snapped her picture with his camera phone while she was in the pool. Now they're passing her photo around like she's a swimsuit model or something. The comments they make are really disturbing.

Q: They get pretty crude, huh?

A: Oh, man, you can't even imagine. They're always making comments about her body and saying things like, "Let me come sleep over at your house!" Stuff like that. I'm like, "You guys are sick! She's my little sister! If I catch any of you guys within 100 yards of her, that's it!"

Q: Wow, that must be really awkward.

A: Yeah, but it has been good in one way.

Q: What's that?

A: It's made me realize that I've done the exact same thing. I've looked at girls as just bodies. I didn't think about who they are or what they're like as human beings. All I cared about is what they looked like. A bunch of us used to sit around at lunch and rate girls like cattle. I never stopped to think that each one of them is somebody's sister or daughter.

» True Beauty

We can thank Hugh Hefner (founder of *Playboy* magazine) and the rest of the world's pornographers for selling the sick, selfish notion that women exist solely to serve as sexual playthings.

In the minds of many men, a woman's intellect, heart and inner qualities mean nothing. To them, all that matters is her body. They look at females as nothing more than a means of fulfilling their perverted sexual fantasies.

The Bible paints a different picture of what women should mean to us. Instead of seducing them and trying to use them, we have a responsibility to serve them and consider their needs as more important than our own (see Philippians 2:1–4). Is that how you treat the females in your life?

Read more about dealing with sexual temptation at www.RevolutionBible.com.

¹⁹So I will inflict punishment on Egypt,
and they will know that I am the LORD.' "

²⁰In the eleventh year, in the first month on the seventh day, the word of the LORD came to me: ²¹"Son of man, I have broken the arm of Pharaoh king of Egypt. It has not been bound up for healing or put in a splint so as to become strong enough to hold a sword. ²²Therefore this is what the Sovereign LORD says: I am against Pharaoh king of Egypt. I will break both his arms, the good arm as well as the broken one, and make the sword fall from his hand. ²³I will disperse the Egyptians among the nations and scatter them through the countries. ²⁴I will strengthen the arms of the king of Babylon and put my sword in his hand, but I will break the arms of Pharaoh, and he will groan before him like a mortally wounded man. ²⁵I will strengthen the arms of the king of Babylon, but the arms of Pharaoh will fall limp. Then they will know that I am the LORD, when I put my sword into the hand of the king of Babylon and he brandishes it against Egypt. ²⁶I will disperse the Egyptians among the nations and scatter them through the countries. Then they will know that I am the LORD."

A CEDAR IN LEBANON

31

In the eleventh year, in the third month on the first day, the word of the LORD came to me: ²"Son of man, say to Pharaoh king of Egypt and to his hordes:

" 'Who can be compared with you in majesty?
³ Consider Assyria, once a cedar in Lebanon,
   with beautiful branches overshadowing the forest;
it towered on high,
   its top above the thick foliage.
⁴ The waters nourished it,
   deep springs made it grow tall;
their streams flowed
   all around its base
and sent their channels
   to all the trees of the field.
⁵ So it towered higher
   than all the trees of the field;
its boughs increased
   and its branches grew long,
   spreading because of abundant
      waters.
⁶ All the birds of the air
   nested in its boughs,
all the beasts of the field
   gave birth under its branches;
all the great nations
   lived in its shade.
⁷ It was majestic in beauty,
   with its spreading boughs,

NOW OR NEVER
EZE 31:1–11

Example #23,512 of why it's a bad idea to let your ego run wild. You've got a choice. You can either develop a humble spirit on your own, or you can wait for God to humble you.

for its roots went down
   to abundant waters.
⁸ The cedars in the garden of God
   could not rival it,
nor could the pine trees
   equal its boughs,
nor could the plane trees
   compare with its branches—
no tree in the garden of God
   could match its beauty.
⁹ I made it beautiful
   with abundant branches,

EZEKIEL 32:8

the envy of all the trees of Eden
in the garden of God.

[10] " 'Therefore this is what the Sovereign Lord says: Because it towered on high, lifting its top above the thick foliage, and because it was proud of its height, [11] I handed it over to the ruler of the nations, for him to deal with according to its wickedness. I cast it aside, [12] and the most ruthless of foreign nations cut it down and left it. Its boughs fell on the mountains and in all the valleys; its branches lay broken in all the ravines of the land. All the nations of the earth came out from under its shade and left it. [13] All the birds of the air settled on the fallen tree, and all the beasts of the field were among its branches. [14] Therefore no other trees by the waters are ever to tower proudly on high, lifting their tops above the thick foliage. No other trees so well-watered are ever to reach such a height; they are all destined for death, for the earth below, among mortal men, with those who go down to the pit.

[15] " 'This is what the Sovereign Lord says: On the day it was brought down to the grave[a] I covered the deep springs with mourning for it; I held back its streams, and its abundant waters were restrained. Because of it I clothed Lebanon with gloom, and all the trees of the field withered away. [16] I made the nations tremble at the sound of its fall when I brought it down to the grave with those who go down to the pit. Then all the trees of Eden, the choicest and best of Lebanon, all the trees that were well-watered, were consoled in the earth below. [17] Those who lived in its shade, its allies among the nations, had also gone down to the grave with it, joining those killed by the sword.

[18] " 'Which of the trees of Eden can be compared with you in splendor and majesty? Yet you, too, will be brought down with the trees of Eden to the earth below; you will lie among the uncircumcised, with those killed by the sword.

" 'This is Pharaoh and all his hordes, declares the Sovereign Lord.' "

A LAMENT FOR PHARAOH

 In the twelfth year, in the twelfth month on the first day, the word of the Lord came to me: [2] "Son of man, take up a lament concerning Pharaoh king of Egypt and say to him:

" 'You are like a lion among the nations;
    you are like a monster in the seas
thrashing about in your streams,
    churning the water with your feet
    and muddying the streams.

[3] " 'This is what the Sovereign Lord says:

" 'With a great throng of people
    I will cast my net over you,
    and they will haul you up in my net.
[4] I will throw you on the land
    and hurl you on the open field.
I will let all the birds of the air settle on you
    and all the beasts of the earth gorge themselves on you.
[5] I will spread your flesh on the mountains
    and fill the valleys with your remains.
[6] I will drench the land with your flowing blood
    all the way to the mountains,
    and the ravines will be filled with your flesh.
[7] When I snuff you out, I will cover the heavens
    and darken their stars;
I will cover the sun with a cloud,
    and the moon will not give its light.
[8] All the shining lights in the heavens
    I will darken over you;
I will bring darkness over your land,

                            declares the Sovereign Lord.

---

[a] 15 Hebrew *Sheol*; also in verses 16 and 17

1115

⁹I will trouble the hearts of many peoples
    when I bring about your destruction among the nations,
    among[a] lands you have not known.
¹⁰I will cause many peoples to be appalled at you,
    and their kings will shudder with horror because of you
    when I brandish my sword before them.
On the day of your downfall
    each of them will tremble
    every moment for his life.

¹¹" 'For this is what the Sovereign LORD says:

" 'The sword of the king of Babylon
    will come against you.
¹²I will cause your hordes to fall
    by the swords of mighty men—
    the most ruthless of all nations.
They will shatter the pride of Egypt,
    and all her hordes will be overthrown.
¹³I will destroy all her cattle
    from beside abundant waters
no longer to be stirred by the foot of man
    or muddied by the hoofs of cattle.
¹⁴Then I will let her waters settle
    and make her streams flow like oil,

declares the Sovereign LORD.

¹⁵When I make Egypt desolate
    and strip the land of everything in it,
when I strike down all who live there,
    then they will know that I am the LORD.'

¹⁶"This is the lament they will chant for her. The daughters of the nations will chant it; for Egypt and all her hordes they will chant it, declares the Sovereign LORD."

¹⁷In the twelfth year, on the fifteenth day of the month, the word of the LORD came to me: ¹⁸"Son of man, wail for the hordes of Egypt and consign to the earth below both her and the daughters of mighty nations, with those who go down to the pit. ¹⁹Say to them, 'Are you more favored than others? Go down and be laid among the uncircumcised.' ²⁰They will fall among those killed by the sword. The sword is drawn; let her be dragged off with all her hordes. ²¹From within the grave[b] the mighty leaders will say of Egypt and her allies, 'They have come down and they lie with the uncircumcised, with those killed by the sword.'

²²"Assyria is there with her whole army; she is surrounded by the graves of all her slain, all who have fallen by the sword. ²³Their graves are in the depths of the pit and her army lies around her grave. All who had spread terror in the land of the living are slain, fallen by the sword.

²⁴"Elam is there, with all her hordes around her grave. All of them are slain, fallen by the sword. All who had spread terror in the land of the living went down uncircumcised to the earth below. They bear their shame with those who go down to the pit. ²⁵A bed is made for her among the slain, with all her hordes around her grave. All of them are uncircumcised, killed by the sword. Because their terror had spread in the land of the living, they bear their shame with those who go down to the pit; they are laid among the slain.

²⁶"Meshech and Tubal are there, with all their hordes around their graves. All of them are uncircumcised, killed by the sword because they spread their terror in the land of the living. ²⁷Do they not lie with the other uncircumcised warriors who have fallen, who went down to the grave with their weapons of war, whose swords were placed under their heads? The punishment for their sins rested on their bones, though the terror of these warriors had stalked through the land of the living.

---

[a] 9 Hebrew; Septuagint *bring you into captivity among the nations, / to*   [b] 21 Hebrew *Sheol*; also in verse 27

28 "You too, O Pharaoh, will be broken and will lie among the uncircumcised, with those killed by the sword.

29 "Edom is there, her kings and all her princes; despite their power, they are laid with those killed by the sword. They lie with the uncircumcised, with those who go down to the pit.

30 "All the princes of the north and all the Sidonians are there; they went down with the slain in disgrace despite the terror caused by their power. They lie uncircumcised with those killed by the sword and bear their shame with those who go down to the pit.

31 "Pharaoh—he and all his army—will see them and he will be consoled for all his hordes that were killed by the sword, declares the Sovereign LORD. 32 Although I had him spread terror in the land of the living, Pharaoh and all his hordes will be laid among the uncircumcised, with those killed by the sword, declares the Sovereign LORD."

NOW OR NEVER

EZE 33:1–6

Do you ever feel like a "watchman"? Who do you know that needs to be warned about what happens to people who reject God? Are you up for the job?

EZEKIEL A WATCHMAN

33

The word of the LORD came to me: 2 "Son of man, speak to your countrymen and say to them: 'When I bring the sword against a land, and the people of the land choose one of their men and make him their watchman, 3 and he sees the sword coming against the land and blows the trumpet to warn the people, 4 then if anyone hears the trumpet but does not take warning and the sword comes and takes his life, his blood will be on his own head. 5 Since he heard the sound of the trumpet but did not take warning, his blood will be on his own head. If he had taken warning, he would have saved himself. 6 But if the watchman sees the sword coming and does not blow the trumpet to warn the people and the sword comes and takes the life of one of them, that man will be taken away because of his sin, but I will hold the watchman accountable for his blood.'

7 "Son of man, I have made you a watchman for the house of Israel; so hear the word I speak and give them warning from me. 8 When I say to the wicked, 'O wicked man, you will surely die,' and you do not speak out to dissuade him from his ways, that wicked man will die for a his sin, and I will hold you accountable for his blood. 9 But if you do warn the wicked man to turn from his ways and he does not do so, he will die for his sin, but you will have saved yourself.

10 "Son of man, say to the house of Israel, 'This is what you are saying: "Our offenses and sins weigh us down, and we are wasting away because of b them. How then can we live?" ' 11 Say to them, 'As surely as I live, declares the Sovereign LORD, I take no pleasure in the death of the wicked, but rather that they turn from their ways and live. Turn! Turn from your evil ways! Why will you die, O house of Israel?'

12 "Therefore, son of man, say to your countrymen, 'The righteousness of the righteous man will not save him when he disobeys, and the wickedness of the wicked man will not cause him to fall when he turns from it. The righteous man, if he sins, will not be allowed to live because of his former righteousness.' 13 If I tell the righteous man that he will surely live, but

Dealing With God's Judgment

» live the adventure » Eze 33:10–11

Yes, God judges people who reject him. But that doesn't mean he enjoys it. He gets no pleasure out of seeing sinners fry, no matter how evil they are. We shouldn't either. Sure, it's frustrating to see evil people get ahead in this world. But that doesn't mean we should root for their eternal suffering. A better idea is to do everything we can to help them understand the transformational truth of God's salvation. Instead of condemning them, try introducing them to God's life-changing power.

---

a 8 Or in; also in verse 9   b 10 Or away in

then he trusts in his righteousness and does evil, none of the righteous things he has done will be remembered; he will die for the evil he has done. ¹⁴And if I say to the wicked man, 'You will surely die,' but he then turns away from his sin and does what is just and right— ¹⁵if he gives back what he took in pledge for a loan, returns what he has stolen, follows the decrees that give life, and does no evil, he will surely live; he will not die. ¹⁶None of the sins he has committed will be remembered against him. He has done what is just and right; he will surely live.

¹⁷"Yet your countrymen say, 'The way of the Lord is not just.' But it is their way that is not just. ¹⁸If a righteous man turns from his righteousness and does evil, he will die for it. ¹⁹And if a wicked man turns away from his wickedness and does what is just and right, he will live by doing so. ²⁰Yet, O house of Israel, you say, 'The way of the Lord is not just.' But I will judge each of you according to his own ways."

JERUSALEM'S FALL EXPLAINED

²¹In the twelfth year of our exile, in the tenth month on the fifth day, a man who had escaped from Jerusalem came to me and said, "The city has fallen!" ²²Now the evening before the man arrived, the hand of the LORD was upon me, and he opened my mouth before the man came to me in the morning. So my mouth was opened and I was no longer silent.

²³Then the word of the LORD came to me: ²⁴"Son of man, the people living in those ruins in the land of Israel are saying, 'Abraham was only one man, yet he possessed the land. But we are many; surely the land has been given to us as our possession.' ²⁵Therefore say to them, 'This is what the Sovereign LORD says: Since you eat meat with the blood still in it and look to your idols and shed blood, should you then possess the land? ²⁶You rely on your sword, you do detestable things, and each of you defiles his neighbor's wife. Should you then possess the land?'

²⁷"Say this to them: 'This is what the Sovereign LORD says: As surely as I live, those who are left in the ruins will fall by the sword, those out in the country I will give to the wild animals to be devoured, and those in strongholds and caves will die of a plague. ²⁸I will make the land a desolate waste, and her proud strength will come to an end, and the mountains of Israel will become desolate so that no one will cross them. ²⁹Then they will know that I am the LORD, when I have made the land a desolate waste because of all the detestable things they have done.'

³⁰"As for you, son of man, your countrymen are talking together about you by the walls and at the doors of the houses, saying to each other, 'Come and hear the message that has come from the LORD.' ³¹My people come to you, as they usually do, and sit before you to listen to your words, but they do not put them into practice. With their mouths they express devotion, but their hearts are greedy for unjust gain. ³²Indeed, to them you are nothing more than one who sings love songs with a beautiful voice and plays an instrument well, for they hear your words but do not put them into practice.

³³"When all this comes true—and it surely will—then they will know that a prophet has been among them."

SHEPHERDS AND SHEEP

34 The word of the LORD came to me: ²"Son of man, prophesy against the shepherds of Israel; prophesy and say to them: 'This is what the Sovereign LORD says: Woe to the shepherds of Israel who only take care of themselves! Should not shepherds take care of the flock? ³You eat the curds, clothe yourselves with the wool and slaughter the choice animals, but you do not take care of the flock. ⁴You have not strengthened the weak or healed the sick or bound up the injured. You have not brought back the strays or searched for the lost. You have ruled them harshly and brutally. ⁵So they were scattered because there was no shepherd, and when they were scattered they became food for all the wild animals. ⁶My sheep wandered over all the mountains and on every high hill. They were scattered over the whole earth, and no one searched or looked for them.

⁷" 'Therefore, you shepherds, hear the word of the LORD: ⁸As surely as I live, declares the Sovereign LORD, because my flock lacks a shepherd and so has been plundered and has become food for all the wild animals, and because my shepherds did not search for my flock but cared for themselves rather than for my flock, ⁹therefore, O shepherds, hear the word of the LORD: ¹⁰This is what the Sovereign LORD says: I am against the shepherds and will hold them accountable for my flock. I will remove them from tending the flock so that the shepherds can no longer feed themselves. I will rescue my flock from their mouths, and it will no longer be food for them.

11 " 'For this is what the Sovereign LORD says: I myself will search for my sheep and look after them. 12 As a shepherd looks after his scattered flock when he is with them, so will I look after my sheep. I will rescue them from all the places where they were scattered on a day of clouds and darkness. 13 I will bring them out from the nations and gather them from the countries, and I will bring them into their own land. I will pasture them on the mountains of Israel, in the ravines and in all the settlements in the land. 14 I will tend them in a good pasture, and the mountain heights of Israel will be their grazing land. There they will lie down in good grazing land, and there they will feed in a rich pasture on the mountains of Israel. 15 I myself will tend my sheep and have them lie down, declares the Sovereign LORD. 16 I will search for the lost and bring back the strays. I will bind up the injured and strengthen the weak, but the sleek and the strong I will destroy. I will shepherd the flock with justice.

17 " 'As for you, my flock, this is what the Sovereign LORD says: I will judge between one sheep and another, and between rams and goats. 18 Is it not enough for you to feed on the good pasture? Must you also trample the rest of your pasture with your feet? Is it not enough for you to drink clear water? Must you also muddy the rest with your feet? 19 Must my flock feed on what you have trampled and drink what you have muddied with your feet?

20 " 'Therefore this is what the Sovereign LORD says to them: See, I myself will judge between the fat sheep and the lean sheep. 21 Because you shove with flank and shoulder, butting all the weak sheep with your horns until you have driven them away, 22 I will save my flock, and they will no longer be plundered. I will judge between one sheep and another. 23 I will place over them one shepherd, my servant David, and he will tend them; he will tend them and be their shepherd. 24 I the LORD will be their God, and my servant David will be prince among them. I the LORD have spoken.

25 " 'I will make a covenant of peace with them and rid the land of wild beasts so that they may live in the desert and sleep in the forests in safety. 26 I will bless them and the places surrounding my hill.ᵃ I will send down showers in season; there will be showers of blessing. 27 The trees of the field will yield their fruit and the ground will yield its crops; the people will be secure in their land. They will know that I am the LORD, when I break the bars of their yoke and rescue them from the hands of those who enslaved them. 28 They will no longer be plundered by the nations, nor will wild animals devour them. They will live in safety, and no one will make them afraid. 29 I will provide for them a land renowned for its crops, and they will no longer be victims of famine in the land or bear the scorn of the nations. 30 Then they will know that I, the LORD their God, am with them and that they, the house of Israel, are my people, declares the Sovereign LORD. 31 You my sheep, the sheep of my pasture, are people, and I am your God, declares the Sovereign LORD.' "

now or never
EZE 34:26

"Showers of blessing"? That's a pretty sweet promise. Imagine good things happening in your life at the same rate that rain falls from the sky on a spring day. That's the kind of future that God has in store for those who are faithful to him.

now or never
EZE 35:5–6

Are you turned off by bloodshed and senseless violence? Not just in real life, but in the movies you watch and the video games you play? Do you think God might have a problem with some of your entertainment choices?

A PROPHECY AGAINST EDOM

35

The word of the LORD came to me: 2 "Son of man, set your face against Mount Seir; prophesy against it 3 and say: 'This is what the Sovereign LORD says: I am against you, Mount Seir, and I will stretch out my hand against you and make you a desolate waste. 4 I will turn your towns into ruins and you will be desolate. Then you will know that I am the LORD.

5 " 'Because you harbored an ancient hostility and delivered the Israelites over to the sword at the time of their calamity, the time their punishment reached its climax, 6 therefore as surely as I live, de-

---

ᵃ 26 Or I will make them and the places surrounding my hill a blessing clares the Sovereign LORD, I will give you over to bloodshed and it will pursue you. Since you did not hate bloodshed, bloodshed will pursue you. 7I will make Mount Seir a desolate waste and cut off from it all who come and go. 8I will fill your mountains with the slain; those killed by the sword will fall on your hills and in your valleys and in all your ravines. 9I will make you desolate forever; your towns will not be inhabited. Then you will know that I am the LORD.

10" 'Because you have said, "These two nations and countries will be ours and we will take possession of them," even though I the LORD was there, 11therefore as surely as I live, declares the Sovereign LORD, I will treat you in accordance with the anger and jealousy you showed in your hatred of them and I will make myself known among them when I judge you. 12Then you will know that I the LORD have heard all the contemptible things you have said against the mountains of Israel. You said, "They have been laid waste and have been given over to us to devour." 13You boasted against me and spoke against me without restraint, and I heard it. 14This is what the Sovereign LORD says: While the whole earth rejoices, I will make you desolate. 15Because you rejoiced when the inheritance of the house of Israel became desolate, that is how I will treat you. You will be desolate, O Mount Seir, you and all of Edom. Then they will know that I am the LORD.' "

A PROPHECY TO THE MOUNTAINS OF ISRAEL

36 "Son of man, prophesy to the mountains of Israel and say, 'O mountains of Israel, hear the word of the LORD. 2This is what the Sovereign LORD says: The enemy said of you, "Aha! The ancient heights have become our possession." ' 3Therefore prophesy and say, 'This is what the Sovereign LORD says: Because they ravaged and hounded you from every side so that you became the possession of the rest of the nations and the object of people's malicious talk and slander, 4therefore, O mountains of Israel, hear the word of the Sovereign LORD: This is what the Sovereign LORD says to the mountains and hills, to the ravines and valleys, to the desolate ruins and the deserted towns that have been plundered and ridiculed by the rest of the nations around you— 5this is what the Sovereign LORD says: In my burning zeal I have spoken against the rest of the nations, and against all Edom, for with glee and with malice in their hearts they made my land their own possession so that they might plunder its pastureland.' 6Therefore prophesy concerning the land of Israel and say to the mountains and hills, to the ravines and valleys: 'This is what the Sovereign LORD says: I speak in my jealous wrath because you have suffered the scorn of the nations. 7Therefore this is what the Sovereign LORD says: I swear with uplifted hand that the nations around you will also suffer scorn.

8" 'But you, O mountains of Israel, will produce branches and fruit for my people Israel, for they will soon come home. 9I am concerned for you and will look on you with favor; you will be plowed and sown, 10and I will multiply the number of people upon you, even the whole house of Israel. The towns will be inhabited and the ruins rebuilt. 11I will increase the number of men and animals upon you, and they will be fruitful and become numerous. I will settle people on you as in the past and will make you prosper more than before. Then you will know that I am the LORD. 12I will cause people, my people Israel, to walk upon you. They will possess you, and you will be their inheritance; you will never again deprive them of their children.

13" 'This is what the Sovereign LORD says: Because people say to you, "You devour men and deprive your nation of its children," 14therefore you will no longer devour men or make your nation childless, declares the Sovereign LORD. 15No longer will I make you hear the taunts of the nations, and no longer will you suffer the scorn of the peoples or cause your nation to fall, declares the Sovereign LORD.' "

16Again the word of the LORD came to me: 17"Son of man, when the people of Israel were living in their own land, they defiled it by their conduct and their actions. Their conduct was like a woman's monthly uncleanness in my sight. 18So I poured out my wrath on them because they had shed blood in the land and because they had defiled it with their idols. 19I dispersed them among the nations, and they were scattered through the countries; I judged them according to their conduct and their actions. 20And wherever they went among the nations they profaned my holy name, for it was said of them, 'These are the LORD's people, and yet they had to leave his land.' 21I had concern for my holy name, which the house of Israel profaned among the nations where they had gone.

22"Therefore say to the house of Israel, 'This is what the Sovereign LORD says: It is not for your sake, O house of Israel, that I am going to do these things, but for the sake of my holy name, which you have profaned among the nations where you have gone. 23I will show the holiness of my great name, which has

battlelines

» Pity Party of Four (Siblings)

Q: Nice shirt.
A: Shut up. I had to wear one of my brother's stupid dress shirts because he keeps borrowing all of my clothes. This was the only clean thing in our closet!

Q: That's got to be pretty irritating, huh?
A: You want to talk about irritating? My six-year-old brother always leaves the bathroom floor soaking wet. I consider it a good day when the puddle is just water, if you know what I mean. And my four-year-old sister thinks the funniest game in the world is to hide our stuff while we're at school. I've had it with them. I want my own room. I want to do the "Survivor" thing and vote them all out of the house.

Q: Funny.
A: Yeah, well, I'm half serious. I don't see how I'm going to survive till college.

Q: Ah, but then you'll miss them.
A: Yeah, like I'd miss a bad case of mono.

Q: What if I told you that even Jesus had trouble with his siblings?
A: How do you know? I thought the Bible didn't say much about Jesus' early years.

Q: That's true, but we do know Jesus lived with or near his family until he was about 30. Try doing that. And we know that his own brothers didn't even believe in him at first. They thought he'd lost his mind.
A: So what did he do? Please tell me that he blinked them into the next zip code or something.

Q: Nope. He was too busy doing what God sent him to do.
A: Wow. I think if I had Jesus' power, I'd be tempted to use it for a little payback.

Q: Well, eventually you'd probably miss your family and want to zap them back into your life.
A: I doubt it.

» Party of One

Who *doesn't* dream about being an only child (or at least having thoughtful sisters and easy-to-live-with brothers)? The fact is, though, changing your circumstances doesn't automatically make life easier. In order for that to happen, you must learn to resist the "if only" trap. If you live your life thinking *If only things were different, then I'd be happy,* you'll be miserable until the day you die. Instead, take charge of your situation. Play the hand you've been dealt. Love your siblings. Or, as the apostle Paul put it:

"Bear with each other and forgive whatever grievances you may have against one another. Forgive as the Lord forgave you" (Colossians 3:13).

Your family driving you crazy? Find ways to get along at www.RevolutionBible.com.

been profaned among the nations, the name you have profaned among them. Then the nations will know that I am the LORD, declares the Sovereign LORD, when I show myself holy through you before their eyes.

24 " 'For I will take you out of the nations; I will gather you from all the countries and bring you back into your own land. 25 I will sprinkle clean water on you, and you will be clean; I will cleanse you from all your impurities and from all your idols. 26 I will give you a new heart and put a new spirit in you; I will remove from you your heart of stone and give you a heart of flesh. 27 And I will put my Spirit in you and move you to follow my decrees and be careful to keep my laws. 28 You will live in the land I gave your forefathers; you will be my people, and I will be your God. 29 I will save you from all your uncleanness. I will call for the grain and make it plentiful and will not bring famine upon you. 30 I will increase the fruit of the trees and the crops of the field, so that you will no longer suffer disgrace among the nations because of famine. 31 Then you will remember your evil ways and wicked deeds, and you will loathe yourselves for your sins and detestable practices. 32 I want you to know that I am not doing this for your sake, declares the Sovereign LORD. Be ashamed and disgraced for your conduct, O house of Israel!

33 " 'This is what the Sovereign LORD says: On the day I cleanse you from all your sins, I will resettle your towns, and the ruins will be rebuilt. 34 The desolate land will be cultivated instead of lying desolate in the sight of all who pass through it. 35 They will say, "This land that was laid waste has become like the garden of Eden; the cities that were lying in ruins, desolate and destroyed, are now fortified and inhabited." 36 Then the nations around you that remain will know that I the LORD have rebuilt what was destroyed and have replanted what was desolate. I the LORD have spoken, and I will do it.'

37 "This is what the Sovereign LORD says: Once again I will yield to the plea of the house of Israel and do this for them: I will make their people as numerous as sheep, 38 as numerous as the flocks for offerings at Jerusalem during her appointed feasts. So will the ruined cities be filled with flocks of people. Then they will know that I am the LORD."

THE VALLEY OF DRY BONES

37 The hand of the LORD was upon me, and he brought me out by the Spirit of the LORD and set me in the middle of a valley; it was full of bones. 2 He led me back and forth among them, and I saw a great many bones on the floor of the valley, bones that were very dry. 3 He asked me, "Son of man, can these bones live?"

I said, "O Sovereign LORD, you alone know."

4 Then he said to me, "Prophesy to these bones and say to them, 'Dry bones, hear the word of the LORD! 5 This is what the Sovereign LORD says to these bones: I will make breath[a] enter you, and you will come to life. 6 I will attach tendons to you and make flesh come upon you and cover you with skin; I will put breath in you, and you will come to life. Then you will know that I am the LORD.' "

7 So I prophesied as I was commanded. And as I was prophesying, there was a noise, a rattling sound, and the bones came together, bone to bone. 8 I looked, and tendons and flesh appeared on them and skin covered them, but there was no breath in them.

9 Then he said to me, "Prophesy to the breath; prophesy, son of man, and say to it, 'This is what the Sovereign LORD says: Come from the four winds, O breath, and breathe into these slain, that they may live.' " 10 So I prophesied as he commanded me, and breath entered them; they came to life and stood up on their feet—a vast army.

11 Then he said to me: "Son of man, these bones are the whole house of Israel. They say, 'Our bones are dried up and our hope is gone; we are cut off.' 12 Therefore prophesy and say to them: 'This is what

» live the adventure » Eze 37:1-14

Understanding What God Is Capable Of

Skeletons coming to life? It sounds like something you'd see in a horror movie, not the Bible. But this happens to be one of the coolest demonstrations of God's power in all of the Old Testament. The idea here is that nothing is hopeless where God is concerned. Nothing is beyond his ability to repair and restore. His awesome power can accomplish things that you can't even imagine.

---

a 5 The Hebrew for this word can also mean *wind* or *spirit* (see verses 6-14).

the Sovereign LORD says: O my people, I am going to open your graves and bring you up from them; I will bring you back to the land of Israel. ¹³Then you, my people, will know that I am the LORD, when I open your graves and bring you up from them. ¹⁴I will put my Spirit in you and you will live, and I will settle you in your own land. Then you will know that I the LORD have spoken, and I have done it, declares the LORD.' "

ONE NATION UNDER ONE KING

¹⁵The word of the LORD came to me: ¹⁶"Son of man, take a stick of wood and write on it, 'Belonging to Judah and the Israelites associated with him.' Then take another stick of wood, and write on it, 'Ephraim's stick, belonging to Joseph and all the house of Israel associated with him.' ¹⁷Join them together into one stick so that they will become one in your hand.

¹⁸"When your countrymen ask you, 'Won't you tell us what you mean by this?' ¹⁹say to them, 'This is what the Sovereign LORD says: I am going to take the stick of Joseph—which is in Ephraim's hand—and of the Israelite tribes associated with him, and join it to Judah's stick, making them a single stick of wood, and they will become one in my hand.' ²⁰Hold before their eyes the sticks you have written on ²¹and say to them, 'This is what the Sovereign LORD says: I will take the Israelites out of the nations where they have gone. I will gather them from all around and bring them back into their own land. ²²I will make them one nation in the land, on the mountains of Israel. There will be one king over all of them and they will never again be two nations or be divided into two kingdoms. ²³They will no longer defile themselves with their idols and vile images or with any of their offenses, for I will save them from all their sinful backsliding,ᵃ and I will cleanse them. They will be my people, and I will be their God.

²⁴" 'My servant David will be king over them, and they will all have one shepherd. They will follow my laws and be careful to keep my decrees. ²⁵They will live in the land I gave to my servant Jacob, the land where your fathers lived. They and their children and their children's children will live there forever, and David my servant will be their prince forever. ²⁶I will make a covenant of peace with them; it will be an everlasting covenant. I will establish them and increase their numbers, and I will put my sanctuary among them forever. ²⁷My dwelling place will be with them; I will be their God, and they will be my people. ²⁸Then the nations will know that I the LORD make Israel holy, when my sanctuary is among them forever.' "

A PROPHECY AGAINST GOG

38

The word of the LORD came to me: ²"Son of man, set your face against Gog, of the land of Magog, the chief prince ofᵇ Meshech and Tubal; prophesy against him ³and say: 'This is what the Sovereign LORD says: I am against you, O Gog, chief prince ofᶜ Meshech and Tubal. ⁴I will turn you around, put hooks in your jaws and bring you out with your whole army—your horses, your horsemen fully armed, and a great horde with large and small shields, all of them brandishing their swords. ⁵Persia, Cushᵈ and Put will be with them, all with shields and helmets, ⁶also Gomer with all its troops, and Beth Togarmah from the far north with all its troops—the many nations with you.

⁷" 'Get ready; be prepared, you and all the hordes gathered about you, and take command of them. ⁸After many days you will be called to arms. In future years you will invade a land that has recovered from war, whose people were gathered from many nations to the mountains of Israel, which had long been desolate. They had been brought out from the nations, and now all of them live in safety. ⁹You and all your troops and the many nations with you will go up, advancing like a storm; you will be like a cloud covering the land.

¹⁰" 'This is what the Sovereign LORD says: On that day thoughts will come into your mind and you will devise an evil scheme. ¹¹You will say, "I will invade a land of unwalled villages; I will attack a peaceful and unsuspecting people—all of them living without walls and without gates and bars. ¹²I will plunder and loot and turn my hand against the resettled ruins and the people gathered from the nations, rich in livestock and goods, living at the center of the land." ¹³Sheba and Dedan and the merchants of Tarshish and all her villagesᵉ will say to you, "Have you come to plunder? Have you gathered your hordes to loot, to carry off silver and gold, to take away livestock and goods and to seize much plunder?" '

¹⁴"Therefore, son of man, prophesy and say to Gog: 'This is what the Sovereign LORD says: In that

---

ᵃ 23 Many Hebrew manuscripts (see also Septuagint); most Hebrew manuscripts *all their dwelling places where they sinned*   ᵇ 2 Or *the prince of Rosh,*   ᶜ 3 Or *Gog, prince of Rosh,*   ᵈ 5 That is, the upper Nile region   ᵉ 13 Or *her strong lions* day, when my people Israel are living in safety, will you not take notice of it? 15You will come from your place in the far north, you and many nations with you, all of them riding on horses, a great horde, a mighty army. 16You will advance against my people Israel like a cloud that covers the land. In days to come, O Gog, I will bring you against my land, so that the nations may know me when I show myself holy through you before their eyes.

17" 'This is what the Sovereign LORD says: Are you not the one I spoke of in former days by my servants the prophets of Israel? At that time they prophesied for years that I would bring you against them. 18This is what will happen in that day: When Gog attacks the land of Israel, my hot anger will be aroused, declares the Sovereign LORD. 19In my zeal and fiery wrath I declare that at that time there shall be a great earthquake in the land of Israel. 20The fish of the sea, the birds of the air, the beasts of the field, every creature that moves along the ground, and all the people on the face of the earth will tremble at my presence. The mountains will be overturned, the cliffs will crumble and every wall will fall to the ground. 21I will summon a sword against Gog on all my mountains, declares the Sovereign LORD. Every man's sword will be against his brother. 22I will execute judgment upon him with plague and bloodshed; I will pour down torrents of rain, hailstones and burning sulfur on him and on his troops and on the many nations with him. 23And so I will show my greatness and my holiness, and I will make myself known in the sight of many nations. Then they will know that I am the LORD.'

39 "Son of man, prophesy against Gog and say: 'This is what the Sovereign LORD says: I am against you, O Gog, chief prince of[a] Meshech and Tubal. 2I will turn you around and drag you along. I will bring you from the far north and send you against the mountains of Israel. 3Then I will strike your bow from your left hand and make your arrows drop from your right hand. 4On the mountains of Israel you will fall, you and all your troops and the nations with you. I will give you as food to all kinds of carrion birds and to the wild animals. 5You will fall in the open field, for I have spoken, declares the Sovereign LORD. 6I will send fire on Magog and on those who live in safety in the coastlands, and they will know that I am the LORD.

7" 'I will make known my holy name among my people Israel. I will no longer let my holy name be profaned, and the nations will know that I the LORD am the Holy One in Israel. 8It is coming! It will surely take place, declares the Sovereign LORD. This is the day I have spoken of.

9" 'Then those who live in the towns of Israel will go out and use the weapons for fuel and burn them up—the small and large shields, the bows and arrows, the war clubs and spears. For seven years they will use them for fuel. 10They will not need to gather wood from the fields or cut it from the forests, because they will use the weapons for fuel. And they will plunder those who plundered them and loot those who looted them, declares the Sovereign LORD.

11" 'On that day I will give Gog a burial place in Israel, in the valley of those who travel east toward[b] the Sea.[c] It will block the way of travelers, because Gog and all his hordes will be buried there. So it will be called the Valley of Hamon Gog.[d]

12" 'For seven months the house of Israel will be burying them in order to cleanse the land. 13All the people of the land will bury them, and the day I am glorified will be a memorable day for them, declares the Sovereign LORD.

14" 'Men will be regularly employed to cleanse the land. Some will go throughout the land and, in addition to them, others will bury those that remain on the ground. At the end of the seven months they will begin their search. 15As they go through the land and one of them sees a human bone, he will set up a marker beside it until the gravediggers have buried it in the Valley of Hamon Gog. 16(Also a town called Hamonah[e] will be there.) And so they will cleanse the land.'

17"Son of man, this is what the Sovereign LORD says: Call out to every kind of bird and all the wild animals: 'Assemble and come together from all around to the sacrifice I am preparing for you, the great sacrifice on the mountains of Israel. There you will eat flesh and drink blood. 18You will eat the flesh of mighty men and drink the blood of the princes of the earth as if they were rams and lambs, goats and bulls—all of them fattened animals from Bashan. 19At the sacrifice I am preparing for you, you will eat fat till you are glutted and drink blood till you are drunk. 20At my table you will eat your fill of horses and riders, mighty men and soldiers of every kind,' declares the Sovereign LORD.

21"I will display my glory among the nations, and all the nations will see the punishment I inflict and the hand I lay upon them. 22From that day forward the house of Israel will know that I am the LORD their

God. 23And the nations will know that the people of Israel went into exile for their sin, because they were unfaithful to me. So I hid my face from them and handed them over to their enemies, and they all fell by the sword. 24I dealt with them according to their uncleanness and their offenses, and I hid my face from them.

25"Therefore this is what the Sovereign LORD says: I will now bring Jacob back from captivity[a] and will have compassion on all the people of Israel, and I will be zealous for my holy name. 26They will forget their shame and all the unfaithfulness they showed toward me when they lived in safety in their land with no one to make them afraid. 27When I have brought them back from the nations and have gathered them from the countries of their enemies, I will show myself holy through them in the sight of many nations. 28Then they will know that I am the LORD their God, for though I sent them into exile among the nations, I will gather them to their own land, not leaving any behind. 29I will no longer hide my face from them, for I will pour out my Spirit on the house of Israel, declares the Sovereign LORD."

THE NEW TEMPLE AREA

40 In the twenty-fifth year of our exile, at the beginning of the year, on the tenth of the month, in the fourteenth year after the fall of the city—on that very day the hand of the LORD was upon me and he took me there. 2In visions of God he took me to the land of Israel and set me on a very high mountain, on whose south side were some buildings that looked like a city. 3He took me there, and I saw a man whose appearance was like bronze; he was standing in the gateway with a linen cord and a measuring rod in his hand. 4The man said to me, "Son of man, look with your eyes and hear with your ears and pay attention to everything I am going to show you, for that is why you have been brought here. Tell the house of Israel everything you see."

THE EAST GATE TO THE OUTER COURT

5I saw a wall completely surrounding the temple area. The length of the measuring rod in the man's hand was six long cubits, each of which was a cubit[b] and a handbreadth.[c] He measured the wall; it was one measuring rod thick and one rod high. 6Then he went to the gate facing east. He climbed its steps and measured the threshold of the gate; it was one rod deep.[d] 7The alcoves for the guards were one rod long and one rod wide, and the projecting walls between the alcoves were five cubits thick. And the threshold of the gate next to the portico facing the temple was one rod deep. 8Then he measured the portico of the gateway; 9it[e] was eight cubits deep and its jambs were two cubits thick. The portico of the gateway faced the temple.

Recognizing God's Grace

Alcoves? Porticos? Cubits? A guy can get lost reading all this detail. But don't let all the design specs fool you. The real story here is God's plan for his people. By their sin, the people of Israel had condemned themselves to a life of warfare and turmoil. They thought that God had forgotten them. But nothing could have been further from the truth. All the while God had plans to restore his people to himself, and his instructions here to Ezekiel are symbolic of just how much he was concerned with Israel's welfare. Now that's grace.

>» live the adventure >» Eze 40:5-9

---

a 25 Or now restore the fortunes of Jacob   b 5 The common cubit was about 1 1/2 feet (about 0.5 meter).   c 5 That is, about 3 inches (about 8 centimeters)   d 6 Septuagint; Hebrew deep, the first threshold, one rod deep   e 8,9 Many Hebrew manuscripts, Septuagint, Vulgate and Syriac; most Hebrew manuscripts gateway facing the temple; it was one rod deep. 9Then he measured the portico of the gateway; it

¹⁰Inside the east gate were three alcoves on each side; the three had the same measurements, and the faces of the projecting walls on each side had the same measurements. ¹¹Then he measured the width of the entrance to the gateway; it was ten cubits and its length was thirteen cubits. ¹²In front of each alcove was a wall one cubit high, and the alcoves were six cubits square. ¹³Then he measured the gateway from the top of the rear wall of one alcove to the top of the opposite one; the distance was twenty-five cubits from one parapet opening to the opposite one. ¹⁴He measured along the faces of the projecting walls all around the inside of the gateway—sixty cubits. The measurement was up to the portico[a] facing the courtyard.[b] ¹⁵The distance from the entrance of the gateway to the far end of its portico was fifty cubits. ¹⁶The alcoves and the projecting walls inside the gateway were surmounted by narrow parapet openings all around, as was the portico; the openings all around faced inward. The faces of the projecting walls were decorated with palm trees.

THE OUTER COURT

¹⁷Then he brought me into the outer court. There I saw some rooms and a pavement that had been constructed all around the court; there were thirty rooms along the pavement. ¹⁸It abutted the sides of the gateways and was as wide as they were long; this was the lower pavement. ¹⁹Then he measured the distance from the inside of the lower gateway to the outside of the inner court; it was a hundred cubits on the east side as well as on the north.

THE NORTH GATE

²⁰Then he measured the length and width of the gate facing north, leading into the outer court. ²¹Its alcoves—three on each side—its projecting walls and its portico had the same measurements as those of the first gateway. It was fifty cubits long and twenty-five cubits wide. ²²Its openings, its portico and its palm tree decorations had the same measurements as those of the gate facing east. Seven steps led up to it, with its portico opposite them. ²³There was a gate to the inner court facing the north gate, just as there was on the east. He measured from one gate to the opposite one; it was a hundred cubits.

THE SOUTH GATE

²⁴Then he led me to the south side and I saw a gate facing south. He measured its jambs and its portico, and they had the same measurements as the others. ²⁵The gateway and its portico had narrow openings all around, like the openings of the others. It was fifty cubits long and twenty-five cubits wide. ²⁶Seven steps led up to it, with its portico opposite them; it had palm tree decorations on the faces of the projecting walls on each side. ²⁷The inner court also had a gate facing south, and he measured from this gate to the outer gate on the south side; it was a hundred cubits.

GATES TO THE INNER COURT

²⁸Then he brought me into the inner court through the south gate, and he measured the south gate; it had the same measurements as the others. ²⁹Its alcoves, its projecting walls and its portico had the same measurements as the others. The gateway and its portico had openings all around. It was fifty cubits long and twenty-five cubits wide. ³⁰(The porticoes of the gateways around the inner court were twenty-five cubits wide and five cubits deep.) ³¹Its portico faced the outer court; palm trees decorated its jambs, and eight steps led up to it.

³²Then he brought me to the inner court on the east side, and he measured the gateway; it had the same measurements as the others. ³³Its alcoves, its projecting walls and its portico had the same measurements as the others. The gateway and its portico had openings all around. It was fifty cubits long and twenty-five cubits wide. ³⁴Its portico faced the outer court; palm trees decorated the jambs on either side, and eight steps led up to it.

³⁵Then he brought me to the north gate and measured it. It had the same measurements as the others, ³⁶as did its alcoves, its projecting walls and its portico, and it had openings all around. It was fifty cubits long and twenty-five cubits wide. ³⁷Its portico[c] faced the outer court; palm trees decorated the jambs on either side, and eight steps led up to it.

ᵃ 14 Septuagint; Hebrew *projecting wall*   ᵇ 14 The meaning of the Hebrew for this verse is uncertain.   ᶜ 37 Septuagint (see also verses 31 and 34); Hebrew *jambs*

THE ROOMS FOR PREPARING SACRIFICES

³⁸A room with a doorway was by the portico in each of the inner gateways, where the burnt offerings were washed. ³⁹In the portico of the gateway were two tables on each side, on which the burnt offerings, sin offerings and guilt offerings were slaughtered. ⁴⁰By the outside wall of the portico of the gateway, near the steps at the entrance to the north gateway were two tables, and on the other side of the steps were two tables. ⁴¹So there were four tables on one side of the gateway and four on the other—eight tables in all—on which the sacrifices were slaughtered. ⁴²There were also four tables of dressed stone for the burnt offerings, each a cubit and a half long, a cubit and a half wide and a cubit high. On them were placed the utensils for slaughtering the burnt offerings and the other sacrifices. ⁴³And double-pronged hooks, each a handbreadth long, were attached to the wall all around. The tables were for the flesh of the offerings.

ROOMS FOR THE PRIESTS

⁴⁴Outside the inner gate, within the inner court, were two rooms, one ᵃ at the side of the north gate and facing south, and another at the side of the south ᵇ gate and facing north. ⁴⁵He said to me, "The room facing south is for the priests who have charge of the temple, ⁴⁶and the room facing north is for the priests who have charge of the altar. These are the sons of Zadok, who are the only Levites who may draw near to the LORD to minister before him."

⁴⁷Then he measured the court: It was square—a hundred cubits long and a hundred cubits wide. And the altar was in front of the temple.

THE TEMPLE

⁴⁸He brought me to the portico of the temple and measured the jambs of the portico; they were five cubits wide on either side. The width of the entrance was fourteen cubits and its projecting walls were ᶜ three cubits wide on either side. ⁴⁹The portico was twenty cubits wide, and twelve ᵈ cubits from front to back. It was reached by a flight of stairs, ᵉ and there were pillars on each side of the jambs.

41 Then the man brought me to the outer sanctuary and measured the jambs; the width of the jambs was six cubits ᶠ on each side. ᵍ ²The entrance was ten cubits wide, and the projecting walls on each side of it were five cubits wide. He also measured the outer sanctuary; it was forty cubits long and twenty cubits wide.

³Then he went into the inner sanctuary and measured the jambs of the entrance; each was two cubits wide. The entrance was six cubits wide, and the projecting walls on each side of it were seven cubits wide. ⁴And he measured the length of the inner sanctuary; it was twenty cubits, and its width was twenty cubits across the end of the outer sanctuary. He said to me, "This is the Most Holy Place."

⁵Then he measured the wall of the temple; it was six cubits thick, and each side room around the temple was four cubits wide. ⁶The side rooms were on three levels, one above another, thirty on each level. There were ledges all around the wall of the temple to serve as supports for the side rooms, so that the supports were not inserted into the wall of the temple. ⁷The side rooms all around the temple were wider at each successive level. The structure surrounding the temple was built in ascending stages, so that the rooms widened as one went upward. A stairway went up from the lowest floor to the top floor through the middle floor.

⁸I saw that the temple had a raised base all around it, forming the foundation of the side rooms. It was the length of the rod, six long cubits. ⁹The outer wall of the side rooms was five cubits thick. The open area between the side rooms of the temple ¹⁰and the ⌐priests'⌐ rooms was twenty cubits wide all around the temple. ¹¹There were entrances to the side rooms from the open area, one on the north and another on the south; and the base adjoining the open area was five cubits wide all around.

¹²The building facing the temple courtyard on the west side was seventy cubits wide. The wall of the building was five cubits thick all around, and its length was ninety cubits.

¹³Then he measured the temple; it was a hundred cubits long, and the temple courtyard and the building with its walls were also a hundred cubits long. ¹⁴The width of the temple courtyard on the east, including the front of the temple, was a hundred cubits.

ᵃ 44 Septuagint; Hebrew *were rooms for singers, which were*   ᵇ 44 Septuagint; Hebrew *east*   ᶜ 48 Septuagint; Hebrew *entrance was*
ᵈ 49 Septuagint; Hebrew *eleven*   ᵉ 49 Hebrew; Septuagint *Ten steps led up to it*   ᶠ 1 The common cubit was about 1 1/2 feet (about
0.5 meter).   ᵍ 1 One Hebrew manuscript and Septuagint; most Hebrew manuscripts *side, the width of the tent*

15 Then he measured the length of the building facing the courtyard at the rear of the temple, including its galleries on each side; it was a hundred cubits.

The outer sanctuary, the inner sanctuary and the portico facing the court, 16 as well as the thresholds and the narrow windows and galleries around the three of them—everything beyond and including the threshold was covered with wood. The floor, the wall up to the windows, and the windows were covered. 17 In the space above the outside of the entrance to the inner sanctuary and on the walls at regular intervals all around the inner and outer sanctuary 18 were carved cherubim and palm trees. Palm trees alternated with cherubim. Each cherub had two faces: 19 the face of a man toward the palm tree on one side and the face of a lion toward the palm tree on the other. They were carved all around the whole temple. 20 From the floor to the area above the entrance, cherubim and palm trees were carved on the wall of the outer sanctuary.

21 The outer sanctuary had a rectangular doorframe, and the one at the front of the Most Holy Place was similar. 22 There was a wooden altar three cubits high and two cubits square[a]; its corners, its base[b] and its sides were of wood. The man said to me, "This is the table that is before the LORD." 23 Both the outer sanctuary and the Most Holy Place had double doors. 24 Each door had two leaves—two hinged leaves for each door. 25 And on the doors of the outer sanctuary were carved cherubim and palm trees like those carved on the walls, and there was a wooden overhang on the front of the portico. 26 On the sidewalls of the portico were narrow windows with palm trees carved on each side. The side rooms of the temple also had overhangs.

ROOMS FOR THE PRIESTS

42 Then the man led me northward into the outer court and brought me to the rooms opposite the temple courtyard and opposite the outer wall on the north side. 2 The building whose door faced north was a hundred cubits[c] long and fifty cubits wide. 3 Both in the section twenty cubits from the inner court and in the section opposite the pavement of the outer court, gallery faced gallery at the three levels. 4 In front of the rooms was an inner passageway ten cubits wide and a hundred cubits[d] long. Their doors were on the north. 5 Now the upper rooms were narrower, for the galleries took more space from them than from the rooms on the lower and middle floors of the building. 6 The rooms on the third floor had no pillars, as the courts had; so they were smaller in floor space than those on the lower and middle floors. 7 There was an outer wall parallel to the rooms and the outer court; it extended in front of the rooms for fifty cubits. 8 While the row of rooms on the side next to the outer court was fifty cubits long, the row on the side nearest the sanctuary was a hundred cubits long. 9 The lower rooms had an entrance on the east side as one enters them from the outer court.

10 On the south side[e] along the length of the wall of the outer court, adjoining the temple courtyard and opposite the outer wall, were rooms 11 with a passageway in front of them. These were like the rooms on the north; they had the same length and width, with similar exits and dimensions. Similar to the doorways on the north 12 were the doorways of the rooms on the south. There was a doorway at the beginning of the passageway that was parallel to the corresponding wall extending eastward, by which one enters the rooms.

13 Then he said to me, "The north and south rooms facing the temple courtyard are the priests' rooms, where the priests who approach the LORD will eat the most holy offerings. There they will put the most holy offerings—the grain offerings, the sin offerings and the guilt offerings—for the place is holy. 14 Once the priests enter the holy precincts, they are not to go into the outer court until they leave behind the garments in which they minister, for these are holy. They are to put on other clothes before they go near the places that are for the people."

15 When he had finished measuring what was inside the temple area, he led me out by the east gate and measured the area all around: 16 He measured the east side with the measuring rod; it was five hundred cubits.[f] 17 He measured the north side; it was five hundred cubits[g] by the measuring rod. 18 He measured the south side; it was five hundred cubits by the measuring rod. 19 Then he turned to the west side and measured; it was five hundred cubits by the measuring rod. 20 So he measured the area on all four sides. It had a wall around it, five hundred cubits long and five hundred cubits wide, to separate the holy from the common.

---

a 22 Septuagint; Hebrew *long*   b 22 Septuagint; Hebrew *length*   c 2 The common cubit was about 1 1/2 feet (about 0.5 meter).
d 4 Septuagint and Syriac; Hebrew *and one cubit*   e 10 Septuagint; Hebrew *Eastward*   f 16 See Septuagint of verse 17; Hebrew *rods*; also in verses 18 and 19.   g 17 Septuagint; Hebrew *rods*

battlelines

» The Christian Bubble (Fitting In)

Q: Big plans for the weekend?
A: Not really. Our youth retreat was last weekend. But *this* weekend is pretty bleak. No fun stuff at all.

Q: What about your friends outside the youth group? Do you ever do anything with them?
A: Well, we see each other at school and track practice. But that's about it.

Q: Why?
A: Because we have nothing in common. Some of those guys may be Christians—*maybe*. But most of them don't ever think about God. They're too busy partying. And I'm not going to do that, so I see those guys when I see them. But I don't go out of my way to hang with them.

Q: So this is your way of taking a stand?
A: I've never really thought about taking a stand. I just don't think I should go to those kinds of parties if I'm a Christian.

Q: Have you ever thought about asking your partying friends to do something with you, like maybe even come to your youth group?
A: Are you serious? I don't think so. I'm pretty sure they wouldn't come. They'd think what we do is totally lame.

Q: How do you know? Have you ever asked?
A: Why ask? Why would they want to do church stuff?

Q: OK, forget "church stuff" then. You like paintball, right?
A: Yeah. Definitely.

Q: Why don't you ask a couple of them to do that with you?
A: I guess I could. I just always figured they wouldn't want to.

» Bursting the Bubble

When it comes to relating to non-believers (or "pre-believers" as one optimistic Christian calls them), many followers of Jesus go to one of two extremes. One group's motto is "Run! Avoid! Hide!" They can go months without having a meaningful conversation with a non-Christian.

The other group says, "Sure! Whatever!" and goes along with the crowd. These people often end up doing things that go against their faith and compromise their witness.

Jesus taught and modeled a third approach. He compared believers to salt and light (see Matthew 5:13–16). Those are great analogies, because both salt and light have to touch something in order to make a difference. Neither is made to be hidden away. As salt and light, we are to influence our friends for good. And we can only do that as we rub shoulders with them.

Make sure you have a partner to keep you accountable (see Luke 10:1), commit to staying pure, and then take Jesus to your non-Christian friends. That's the best way to take a stand *and* make a difference.

Learn more about sharing Christ with others at www.RevolutionBible.com.

THE GLORY RETURNS TO THE TEMPLE

43
Then the man brought me to the gate facing east, [2]and I saw the glory of the God of Israel coming from the east. His voice was like the roar of rushing waters, and the land was radiant with his glory. [3]The vision I saw was like the vision I had seen when he[a] came to destroy the city and like the visions I had seen by the Kebar River, and I fell facedown. [4]The glory of the LORD entered the temple through the gate facing east. [5]Then the Spirit lifted me up and brought me into the inner court, and the glory of the LORD filled the temple.

[6]While the man was standing beside me, I heard someone speaking to me from inside the temple. [7]He said: "Son of man, this is the place of my throne and the place for the soles of my feet. This is where I will live among the Israelites forever. The house of Israel will never again defile my holy name—neither they nor their kings—by their prostitution[b] and the lifeless idols[c] of their kings at their high places. [8]When they placed their threshold next to my threshold and their doorposts beside my doorposts, with only a wall between me and them, they defiled my holy name by their detestable practices. So I destroyed them in my anger. [9]Now let them put away from me their prostitution and the lifeless idols of their kings, and I will live among them forever.

[10]"Son of man, describe the temple to the people of Israel, that they may be ashamed of their sins. Let them consider the plan, [11]and if they are ashamed of all they have done, make known to them the design of the temple—its arrangement, its exits and entrances—its whole design and all its regulations[d] and laws. Write these down before them so that they may be faithful to its design and follow all its regulations.

[12]"This is the law of the temple: All the surrounding area on top of the mountain will be most holy. Such is the law of the temple.

THE ALTAR

[13]"These are the measurements of the altar in long cubits, that cubit being a cubit[e] and a handbreadth[f]: Its gutter is a cubit deep and a cubit wide, with a rim of one span[g] around the edge. And this is the height of the altar: [14]From the gutter on the ground up to the lower ledge it is two cubits high and a cubit wide, and from the smaller ledge up to the larger ledge it is four cubits high and a cubit wide. [15]The altar hearth is four cubits high, and four horns project upward from the hearth. [16]The altar hearth is square, twelve cubits long and twelve cubits wide. [17]The upper ledge also is square, fourteen cubits long and fourteen cubits wide, with a rim of half a cubit and a gutter of a cubit all around. The steps of the altar face east."

[18]Then he said to me, "Son of man, this is what the Sovereign LORD says: These will be the regulations for sacrificing burnt offerings and sprinkling blood upon the altar when it is built: [19]You are to give a young bull as a sin offering to the priests, who are Levites, of the family of Zadok, who come near to minister before me, declares the Sovereign LORD. [20]You are to take some of its blood and put it on the four horns of the altar and on the four corners of the upper ledge and all around the rim, and so purify the altar and make atonement for it. [21]You are to take the bull for the sin offering and burn it in the designated part of the temple area outside the sanctuary.

[22]"On the second day you are to offer a male goat without defect for a sin offering, and the altar is to be purified as it was purified with the bull. [23]When you have finished purifying it, you are to offer a young bull and a ram from the flock, both without defect. [24]You are to offer them before the LORD, and the priests are to sprinkle salt on them and sacrifice them as a burnt offering to the LORD.

[25]"For seven days you are to provide a male goat daily for a sin offering; you are also to provide a young bull and a ram from the flock, both without defect. [26]For seven days they are to make atonement for the altar and cleanse it; thus they will dedicate it. [27]At the end of these days, from the eighth day on, the priests are to present your burnt offerings and fellowship offerings[h] on the altar. Then I will accept you, declares the Sovereign LORD."

---

[a] 3 Some Hebrew manuscripts and Vulgate; most Hebrew manuscripts I   [b] 7 Or their spiritual adultery; also in verse 9   [c] 7 Or the corpses; also in verse 9   [d] 11 Some Hebrew manuscripts and Septuagint; most Hebrew manuscripts regulations and its whole design   [e] 13 The common cubit was about 1 1/2 feet (about 0.5 meter).   [f] 13 That is, about 3 inches (about 8 centimeters)   [g] 13 That is, about 9 inches (about 22 centimeters)   [h] 27 Traditionally peace offerings

44

Then the man brought me back to the outer gate of the sanctuary, the one facing east, and it was shut. ²The LORD said to me, "This gate is to remain shut. It must not be opened; no one may enter through it. It is to remain shut because the LORD, the God of Israel, has entered through it. ³The prince himself is the only one who may sit inside the gateway to eat in the presence of the LORD. He is to enter by way of the portico of the gateway and go out the same way."

⁴Then the man brought me by way of the north gate to the front of the temple. I looked and saw the glory of the LORD filling the temple of the LORD, and I fell facedown.

⁵The LORD said to me, "Son of man, look carefully, listen closely and give attention to everything I tell you concerning all the regulations regarding the temple of the LORD. Give attention to the entrance of the temple and all the exits of the sanctuary. ⁶Say to the rebellious house of Israel, 'This is what the Sovereign LORD says: Enough of your detestable practices, O house of Israel! ⁷In addition to all your other detestable practices, you brought foreigners uncircumcised in heart and flesh into my sanctuary, desecrating my temple while you offered me food, fat and blood, and you broke my covenant. ⁸Instead of carrying out your duty in regard to my holy things, you put others in charge of my sanctuary. ⁹This is what the Sovereign LORD says: No foreigner uncircumcised in heart and flesh is to enter my sanctuary, not even the foreigners who live among the Israelites.

¹⁰" 'The Levites who went far from me when Israel went astray and who wandered from me after their idols must bear the consequences of their sin. ¹¹They may serve in my sanctuary, having charge of the gates of the temple and serving in it; they may slaughter the burnt offerings and sacrifices for the people and stand before the people and serve them. ¹²But because they served them in the presence of their idols and made the house of Israel fall into sin, therefore I have sworn with uplifted hand that they must bear the consequences of their sin, declares the Sovereign LORD. ¹³They are not to come near to serve me as priests or come near any of my holy things or my most holy offerings; they must bear the shame of their detestable practices. ¹⁴Yet I will put them in charge of the duties of the temple and all the work that is to be done in it.

¹⁵" 'But the priests, who are Levites and descendants of Zadok and who faithfully carried out the duties of my sanctuary when the Israelites went astray from me, are to come near to minister before me; they are to stand before me to offer sacrifices of fat and blood, declares the Sovereign LORD. ¹⁶They alone are to enter my sanctuary; they alone are to come near my table to minister before me and perform my service.

¹⁷" 'When they enter the gates of the inner court, they are to wear linen clothes; they must not wear any woolen garment while ministering at the gates of the inner court or inside the temple. ¹⁸They are to wear linen turbans on their heads and linen undergarments around their waists. They must not wear anything that makes them perspire. ¹⁹When they go out into the outer court where the people are, they are to take off the clothes they have been ministering in and are to leave them in the sacred rooms, and put on other clothes, so that they do not consecrate the people by means of their garments.

²⁰" 'They must not shave their heads or let their hair grow long, but they are to keep the hair of their heads trimmed. ²¹No priest is to drink wine when he enters the inner court. ²²They must not marry widows or divorced women; they may marry only virgins of Israelite descent or widows of priests. ²³They are to teach my people the difference between the holy and the common and show them how to distinguish between the unclean and the clean.

²⁴" 'In any dispute, the priests are to serve as judges and decide it according to my ordinances. They are to keep my laws and my decrees for all my appointed feasts, and they are to keep my Sabbaths holy.

²⁵" 'A priest must not defile himself by going near a dead person; however, if the dead person was his father or mother, son or daughter, brother or unmarried sister, then he may defile himself. ²⁶After he is cleansed, he must wait seven days. ²⁷On the day he goes into the inner court of the sanctuary to minister in the sanctuary, he is to offer a sin offering for himself, declares the Sovereign LORD.

²⁸" 'I am to be the only inheritance the priests have. You are to give them no possession in Israel; I will be their possession. ²⁹They will eat the grain offerings, the sin offerings and the guilt offerings; and everything in Israel devoted[a] to the LORD will belong to them. ³⁰The best of all the firstfruits and of all your special gifts will belong to the priests. You are to give them the first portion of your ground meal so that a blessing may rest on your household. ³¹The priests must not eat anything, bird or animal, found dead or torn by wild animals.

ᵃ *29* The Hebrew term refers to the irrevocable giving over of things or persons to the LORD.

DIVISION OF THE LAND

45

" 'When you allot the land as an inheritance, you are to present to the LORD a portion of the land as a sacred district, 25,000 cubits long and 20,000[a] cubits wide;
the entire area will be holy. [2]Of this, a section 500 cubits square is to be for the sanctuary, with 50 cubits around it for open land. [3]In the sacred district, measure off a section 25,000 cubits[b] long and
10,000 cubits[c] wide. In it will be the sanctuary, the Most Holy Place. [4]It will be the sacred portion of the
land for the priests, who minister in the sanctuary and who draw near to minister before the LORD. It will
be a place for their houses as well as a holy place for the sanctuary. [5]An area 25,000 cubits long and
10,000 cubits wide will belong to the Levites, who serve in the temple, as their possession for towns
to live in.[d]

[6]" 'You are to give the city as its property an area 5,000 cubits wide and 25,000 cubits long, adjoining the sacred portion; it will belong to the whole house of Israel.

[7]" 'The prince will have the land bordering each side of the area formed by the sacred district and
the property of the city. It will extend westward from the west side and eastward from the east side, running lengthwise from the western to the eastern border parallel to one of the tribal portions. [8]This land
will be his possession in Israel. And my princes will no longer oppress my people but will allow the
house of Israel to possess the land according to their tribes.

[9]" 'This is what the Sovereign LORD says: You have gone far enough, O princes of Israel! Give up
your violence and oppression and do what is just and right. Stop dispossessing my people, declares
the Sovereign LORD. [10]You are to use accurate scales, an accurate ephah[e] and an accurate bath.[f] [11]The
ephah and the bath are to be the same size, the bath containing a tenth of a homer[g] and the ephah a
tenth of a homer; the homer is to be the standard measure for both. [12]The shekel[h] is to consist of twenty gerahs. Twenty shekels plus twenty-five shekels plus fifteen shekels equal one mina.[i]

OFFERINGS AND HOLY DAYS

[13]" 'This is the special gift you are to offer: a sixth of an ephah from each homer of wheat and a sixth
of an ephah from each homer of barley. [14]The prescribed portion of oil, measured by the bath, is a tenth
of a bath from each cor (which consists of ten baths or one homer, for ten baths are equivalent to a homer). [15]Also one sheep is to be taken from every flock of two hundred from the well-watered pastures
of Israel. These will be used for the grain offerings, burnt offerings and fellowship offerings[j] to make
atonement for the people, declares the Sovereign LORD. [16]All the people of the land will participate in
this special gift for the use of the prince in Israel. [17]It will be the duty of the prince to provide the burnt
offerings, grain offerings and drink offerings at the festivals, the New Moons and the Sabbaths—at all
the appointed feasts of the house of Israel. He will provide the sin offerings, grain offerings, burnt offerings and fellowship offerings to make atonement for the house of Israel.

[18]" 'This is what the Sovereign LORD says: In the first month on the first day you are to take a young
bull without defect and purify the sanctuary. [19]The priest is to take some of the blood of the sin offering
and put it on the doorposts of the temple, on the four corners of the upper ledge of the altar and on the
gateposts of the inner court. [20]You are to do the same on the seventh day of the month for anyone who
sins unintentionally or through ignorance; so you are to make atonement for the temple.

[21]" 'In the first month on the fourteenth day you are to observe the Passover, a feast lasting seven
days, during which you shall eat bread made without yeast. [22]On that day the prince is to provide a bull
as a sin offering for himself and for all the people of the land. [23]Every day during the seven days of the
Feast he is to provide seven bulls and seven rams without defect as a burnt offering to the LORD, and a
male goat for a sin offering. [24]He is to provide as a grain offering an ephah for each bull and an ephah
for each ram, along with a hin[k] of oil for each ephah.

[25]" 'During the seven days of the Feast, which begins in the seventh month on the fifteenth day, he
is to make the same provision for sin offerings, burnt offerings, grain offerings and oil.

46

" 'This is what the Sovereign LORD says: The gate of the inner court facing east is
to be shut on the six working days, but on the Sabbath day and on the day of the
New Moon it is to be opened. [2]The prince is to enter from the outside through the portico of the gate-

---

[a] *1* Septuagint (see also verses 3 and 5 and 48:9); Hebrew *10,000*   [b] *3* That is, about 7 miles (about 12 kilometers)   [c] *3* That is,
about 3 miles (about 5 kilometers)   [d] *5* Septuagint; Hebrew *temple; they will have as their possession 20 rooms*   [e] *10* An ephah was
a dry measure.   [f] *10* A bath was a liquid measure.   [g] *11* A homer was a dry measure.   [h] *12* A shekel weighed about 2/5 ounce
(about 11.5 grams).   [i] *12* That is, 60 shekels; the common mina was 50 shekels.   [j] *15* Traditionally *peace offerings*; also in verse 17
[k] *24* That is, probably about 4 quarts (about 4 liters)

way and stand by the gatepost. The priests are to sacrifice his burnt offering and his fellowship offerings.[a] He is to worship at the threshold of the gateway and then go out, but the gate will not be shut until evening. [3]On the Sabbaths and New Moons the people of the land are to worship in the presence of the LORD at the entrance to that gateway. [4]The burnt offering the prince brings to the LORD on the Sabbath day is to be six male lambs and a ram, all without defect. [5]The grain offering given with the ram is to be an ephah,[b] and the grain offering with the lambs is to be as much as he pleases, along with a hin[c] of oil for each ephah. [6]On the day of the New Moon he is to offer a young bull, six lambs and a ram, all without defect. [7]He is to provide as a grain offering one ephah with the bull, one ephah with the ram, and with the lambs as much as he wants to give, along with a hin of oil with each ephah. [8]When the prince enters, he is to go in through the portico of the gateway, and he is to come out the same way.

[9]" 'When the people of the land come before the LORD at the appointed feasts, whoever enters by the north gate to worship is to go out the south gate; and whoever enters by the south gate is to go out the north gate. No one is to return through the gate by which he entered, but each is to go out the opposite gate. [10]The prince is to be among them, going in when they go in and going out when they go out.

[11]" 'At the festivals and the appointed feasts, the grain offering is to be an ephah with a bull, an ephah with a ram, and with the lambs as much as one pleases, along with a hin of oil for each ephah. [12]When the prince provides a freewill offering to the LORD—whether a burnt offering or fellowship offerings—the gate facing east is to be opened for him. He shall offer his burnt offering or his fellowship offerings as he does on the Sabbath day. Then he shall go out, and after he has gone out, the gate will be shut.

[13]" 'Every day you are to provide a year-old lamb without defect for a burnt offering to the LORD; morning by morning you shall provide it. [14]You are also to provide with it morning by morning a grain offering, consisting of a sixth of an ephah with a third of a hin of oil to moisten the flour. The presenting of this grain offering to the LORD is a lasting ordinance. [15]So the lamb and the grain offering and the oil shall be provided morning by morning for a regular burnt offering.

[16]" 'This is what the Sovereign LORD says: If the prince makes a gift from his inheritance to one of his sons, it will also belong to his descendants; it is to be their property by inheritance. [17]If, however, he makes a gift from his inheritance to one of his servants, the servant may keep it until the year of freedom; then it will revert to the prince. His inheritance belongs to his sons only; it is theirs. [18]The prince must not take any of the inheritance of the people, driving them off their property. He is to give his sons their inheritance out of his own property, so that none of my people will be separated from his property.' "

[19]Then the man brought me through the entrance at the side of the gate to the sacred rooms facing north, which belonged to the priests, and showed me a place at the western end. [20]He said to me, "This is the place where the priests will cook the guilt offering and the sin offering and bake the grain offering, to avoid bringing them into the outer court and consecrating the people."

[21]He then brought me to the outer court and led me around to its four corners, and I saw in each corner another court. [22]In the four corners of the outer court were enclosed[d] courts, forty cubits long and thirty cubits wide; each of the courts in the four corners was the same size. [23]Around the inside of each of the four courts was a ledge of stone, with places for fire built all around under the ledge. [24]He said to me, "These are the kitchens where those who minister at the temple will cook the sacrifices of the people."

THE RIVER FROM THE TEMPLE

47

The man brought me back to the entrance of the temple, and I saw water coming out from under the threshold of the temple toward the east (for the temple faced east). The water was coming down from under the south side of the temple, south of the altar. [2]He then brought me out through the north gate and led me around the outside to the outer gate facing east, and the water was flowing from the south side.

[3]As the man went eastward with a measuring line in his hand, he measured off a thousand cubits[e] and then led me through water that was ankle-deep. [4]He measured off another thousand cubits and led me through water that was knee-deep. He measured off another thousand and led me through water that

---

[a] *2* Traditionally *peace offerings*; also in verse 12   [b] *5* That is, probably about 3/5 bushel (about 22 liters)   [c] *5* That is, probably about 4 quarts (about 4 liters)   [d] *22* The meaning of the Hebrew for this word is uncertain.   [e] *3* That is, about 1,500 feet (about 450 meters)

was up to the waist. [5]He measured off another thousand, but now it was a river that I could not cross, because the water had risen and was deep enough to swim in—a river that no one could cross. [6]He asked me, "Son of man, do you see this?"

Then he led me back to the bank of the river. [7]When I arrived there, I saw a great number of trees on each side of the river. [8]He said to me, "This water flows toward the eastern region and goes down into the Arabah,[a] where it enters the Sea.[b] When it empties into the Sea,[b] the water there becomes fresh. [9]Swarms of living creatures will live wherever the river flows. There will be large numbers of fish, because this water flows there and makes the salt water fresh; so where the river flows everything will live. [10]Fishermen will stand along the shore; from En Gedi to En Eglaim there will be places for spreading nets. The fish will be of many kinds—like the fish of the Great Sea.[c] [11]But the swamps and marshes will not become fresh; they will be left for salt. [12]Fruit trees of all kinds will grow on both banks of the river. Their leaves will not wither, nor will their fruit fail. Every month they will bear, because the water from the sanctuary flows to them. Their fruit will serve for food and their leaves for healing."

THE BOUNDARIES OF THE LAND

[13]This is what the Sovereign LORD says: "These are the boundaries by which you are to divide the land for an inheritance among the twelve tribes of Israel, with two portions for Joseph. [14]You are to divide it equally among them. Because I swore with uplifted hand to give it to your forefathers, this land will become your inheritance.

[15]"This is to be the boundary of the land:

"On the north side it will run from the Great Sea by the Hethlon road past Lebo[d] Hamath to Zedad, [16]Berothah[e] and Sibraim (which lies on the border between Damascus and Hamath), as far as Hazer Hatticon, which is on the border of Hauran. [17]The boundary will extend from the sea to Hazar Enan,[f] along the northern border of Damascus, with the border of Hamath to the north. This will be the north boundary.

[18]"On the east side the boundary will run between Hauran and Damascus, along the Jordan between Gilead and the land of Israel, to the eastern sea and as far as Tamar.[g] This will be the east boundary.

[19]"On the south side it will run from Tamar as far as the waters of Meribah Kadesh, then along the Wadi ∟of Egypt⌐ to the Great Sea. This will be the south boundary.

[20]"On the west side, the Great Sea will be the boundary to a point opposite Lebo[h] Hamath. This will be the west boundary.

[21]"You are to distribute this land among yourselves according to the tribes of Israel. [22]You are to allot it as an inheritance for yourselves and for the aliens who have settled among you and who have children. You are to consider them as native-born Israelites; along with you they are to be allotted an inheritance among the tribes of Israel. [23]In whatever tribe the alien settles, there you are to give him his inheritance," declares the Sovereign LORD.

THE DIVISION OF THE LAND

48

"These are the tribes, listed by name: At the northern frontier, Dan will have one portion; it will follow the Hethlon road to Lebo[i] Hamath; Hazar Enan and the northern border of Damascus next to Hamath will be part of its border from the east side to the west side.

[2]"Asher will have one portion; it will border the territory of Dan from east to west.

[3]"Naphtali will have one portion; it will border the territory of Asher from east to west.

[4]"Manasseh will have one portion; it will border the territory of Naphtali from east to west.

[5]"Ephraim will have one portion; it will border the territory of Manasseh from east to west.

[6]"Reuben will have one portion; it will border the territory of Ephraim from east to west.

[7]"Judah will have one portion; it will border the territory of Reuben from east to west.

[8]"Bordering the territory of Judah from east to west will be the portion you are to present as a spe-

---

[a] 8 Or the Jordan Valley   [b] 8 That is, the Dead Sea   [c] 10 That is, the Mediterranean; also in verses 15, 19 and 20   [d] 15 Or past the entrance to   [e] 15,16 See Septuagint and Ezekiel 48:1; Hebrew road to go into Zedad, [16]Hamath, Berothah   [f] 17 Hebrew Enon, a variant of Enan   [g] 18 Septuagint and Syriac; Hebrew Israel. You will measure to the eastern sea   [h] 20 Or opposite the entrance to   [i] 1 Or to the entrance to

cial gift. It will be 25,000 cubits[a] wide, and its length from east to west will equal one of the tribal portions; the sanctuary will be in the center of it.

⁹"The special portion you are to offer to the Lᴏʀᴅ will be 25,000 cubits long and 10,000 cubits[b] wide. ¹⁰This will be the sacred portion for the priests. It will be 25,000 cubits long on the north side, 10,000 cubits wide on the west side, 10,000 cubits wide on the east side and 25,000 cubits long on the south side. In the center of it will be the sanctuary of the Lᴏʀᴅ. ¹¹This will be for the consecrated priests, the Zadokites, who were faithful in serving me and did not go astray as the Levites did when the Israelites went astray. ¹²It will be a special gift to them from the sacred portion of the land, a most holy portion, bordering the territory of the Levites.

¹³"Alongside the territory of the priests, the Levites will have an allotment 25,000 cubits long and 10,000 cubits wide. Its total length will be 25,000 cubits and its width 10,000 cubits. ¹⁴They must not sell or exchange any of it. This is the best of the land and must not pass into other hands, because it is holy to the Lᴏʀᴅ.

¹⁵"The remaining area, 5,000 cubits wide and 25,000 cubits long, will be for the common use of the city, for houses and for pastureland. The city will be in the center of it ¹⁶and will have these measurements: the north side 4,500 cubits, the south side 4,500 cubits, the east side 4,500 cubits, and the west side 4,500 cubits. ¹⁷The pastureland for the city will be 250 cubits on the north, 250 cubits on the south, 250 cubits on the east, and 250 cubits on the west. ¹⁸What remains of the area, bordering on the sacred portion and running the length of it, will be 10,000 cubits on the east side and 10,000 cubits on the west side. Its produce will supply food for the workers of the city. ¹⁹The workers from the city who farm it will come from all the tribes of Israel. ²⁰The entire portion will be a square, 25,000 cubits on each side. As a special gift you will set aside the sacred portion, along with the property of the city.

²¹"What remains on both sides of the area formed by the sacred portion and the city property will belong to the prince. It will extend eastward from the 25,000 cubits of the sacred portion to the eastern border, and westward from the 25,000 cubits to the western border. Both these areas running the length of the tribal portions will belong to the prince, and the sacred portion with the temple sanctuary will be in the center of them. ²²So the property of the Levites and the property of the city will lie in the center of the area that belongs to the prince. The area belonging to the prince will lie between the border of Judah and the border of Benjamin.

²³"As for the rest of the tribes: Benjamin will have one portion; it will extend from the east side to the west side.

²⁴"Simeon will have one portion; it will border the territory of Benjamin from east to west.

²⁵"Issachar will have one portion; it will border the territory of Simeon from east to west.

²⁶"Zebulun will have one portion; it will border the territory of Issachar from east to west.

²⁷"Gad will have one portion; it will border the territory of Zebulun from east to west.

²⁸"The southern boundary of Gad will run south from Tamar to the waters of Meribah Kadesh, then along the Wadi ᴸof Egyptᴸ to the Great Sea.[c]

²⁹"This is the land you are to allot as an inheritance to the tribes of Israel, and these will be their portions," declares the Sovereign Lᴏʀᴅ.

THE GATES OF THE CITY

³⁰"These will be the exits of the city: Beginning on the north side, which is 4,500 cubits long, ³¹the gates of the city will be named after the tribes of Israel. The three gates on the north side will be the gate of Reuben, the gate of Judah and the gate of Levi.

³²"On the east side, which is 4,500 cubits long, will be three gates: the gate of Joseph, the gate of Benjamin and the gate of Dan.

³³"On the south side, which measures 4,500 cubits, will be three gates: the gate of Simeon, the gate of Issachar and the gate of Zebulun.

³⁴"On the west side, which is 4,500 cubits long, will be three gates: the gate of Gad, the gate of Asher and the gate of Naphtali.

³⁵"The distance all around will be 18,000 cubits.

"And the name of the city from that time on will be:

THE Lᴏʀᴅ ɪs ᴛʜᴇʀᴇ."

---

[a] 8 That is, about 7 miles (about 12 kilometers)   [b] 9 That is, about 3 miles (about 5 kilometers)   [c] 28 That is, the Mediterranean

DANIEL

DANIEL DANIEL DANIEL

« AT A GLANCE

Author
Daniel

Audience
The captives in Babylon

Date
About 535 B.C.

Setting
Daniel, a Jew, was taken captive to Babylon by King Nebuchadnezzar in 605 B.C. He served in the government of the kings of Babylon, and then Persia, for nearly 70 years

Verses to Remember
"Praise be to the name of God for ever and ever; wisdom and power are his. He changes times and seasons; he sets up kings and deposes them. He gives wisdom to the wise and knowledge to the discerning. He reveals deep and hidden things; he knows what lies in darkness, and light dwells with him" (2:20–22).

Theme to Consider
God is in control over everything—heaven and earth, nature, nations and his people. Because of this, we can trust him completely. The book of Daniel was written to encourage the exiled Jews to have hope in God.

UNCHANGING TRUTH » If you tried hard enough, you could probably skate through life without too many people knowing you're a Christian. You could hone your skill at "flying under the radar" so you wouldn't stand out in a crowd. To avoid revealing too much about your personal beliefs, you could learn to keep your mouth shut whenever people talk about God or spiritual things. You could roll your eyes and complain about your parents making you go to church whenever someone tries to make Sunday morning plans with you. If you wanted, you could live your entire Christian life anonymously.

And what a hypocritical, frustrating and dishonest life that would be.

God doesn't call us to be anonymous faces in a crowd. He calls us to stand out. He calls us to be lights in the world, to live in a way that draws people's attention to him. God doesn't want secret agents. He wants bold disciples who will jump at every opportunity to demonstrate their faith in public (and sometimes risky) ways.

Throughout your life, you're going to face situations that demand that you either stand up for God or conceal your relationship with him. The Old Testament prophet Daniel faced this choice when the king of Babylon made it illegal—and punishable by death—to pray to anyone but him. Daniel, who was well-known as a hardcore man of prayer and a follower of the Hebrew God, was faced with a choice: He could either submit to the thugs who "suggested" he stop praying, or he could risk his life by continuing to pray faithfully.

Daniel chose to make a bold stand for God by continuing with his daily prayers. As a result, he was arrested and sentenced to death. (You can read the rest of his incredible story in Daniel 6.)

What about you? Do you have the guts to stand up and say, "I will obey God; and if you've got a problem with that, bring it on, because I'm ready to go all the way for my faith"?

LIFE LESSONS »

I   God will reward you for keeping yourself pure (1:8–21).

2   Trusting God means putting your life in his hands—literally (3:16–18).

3   Always keep your God-given gifts sharp, because you never know when you might get the call, and the game-winning play will be in your hands (5:1–29).

1 In the third year of the reign of Jehoiakim king of Judah, Nebuchadnezzar king of Babylon came to Jerusalem and besieged it. ²And the Lord delivered Jehoiakim king of Judah into his hand, along with some of the articles from the temple of God. These he carried off to the temple of his god in Babylonia[a] and put in the treasure house of his god.

³Then the king ordered Ashpenaz, chief of his court officials, to bring in some of the Israelites from the royal family and the nobility— ⁴young men without any physical defect, handsome, showing aptitude for every kind of learning, well informed, quick to understand, and qualified to serve in the king's palace. He was to teach them the language and literature of the Babylonians.[b] ⁵The king assigned them a daily amount of food and wine from the king's table. They were to be trained for three years, and after that they were to enter the king's service.

⁶Among these were some from Judah: Daniel, Hananiah, Mishael and Azariah. ⁷The chief official gave them new names: to Daniel, the name Belteshazzar; to Hananiah, Shadrach; to Mishael, Meshach; and to Azariah, Abednego.

NOW OR NEVER

DA 1:8–16

Daniel took his commitment to keep himself pure seriously. No amount of pressure could make him cave in. Are you committed to anything that strongly? What have you done to honor God with the body he has given you?

Showing Character in Tough Times

» live the adventure » Da 1:18–21

Daniel's story is one big advertisement for the value of character. Think about it: Daniel was living under the worst of conditions. His homeland had been destroyed, and he was living as an exile working for the king who had overrun his homeland. No one would have blamed Daniel if he'd had a bad attitude toward his job. But that wasn't Daniel's style. His *character* wouldn't allow him to give less than his best. As a result, God blessed Daniel's work, and the king promoted him to a place of importance in the government—a place where Daniel could use his influence to accomplish God's work. What do you think God could accomplish through you?

---

⁸But Daniel resolved not to defile himself with the royal food and wine, and he asked the chief official for permission not to defile himself this way. ⁹Now God had caused the official to show favor and sympathy to Daniel, ¹⁰but the official told Daniel, "I am afraid of my lord the king, who has assigned your[c] food and drink. Why should he see you looking worse than the other young men your age? The king would then have my head because of you."

¹¹Daniel then said to the guard whom the chief official had appointed over Daniel, Hananiah, Mishael and Azariah, ¹²"Please test your servants for ten days: Give us nothing but vegetables to eat and water to drink. ¹³Then compare our appearance with that of the young men who eat the royal food, and treat your servants in accordance with what you see." ¹⁴So he agreed to this and tested them for ten days.

¹⁵At the end of the ten days they looked healthier and better nourished than any of the young men who ate the royal food. ¹⁶So the guard took away their choice food and the wine they were to drink and gave them vegetables instead.

¹⁷To these four young men God gave knowledge and understanding of all kinds of literature and learning. And Daniel could understand visions and dreams of all kinds.

¹⁸At the end of the time set by the king to bring them in, the chief official presented them to Nebuchadnezzar. ¹⁹The king talked with them, and he found none equal to Daniel, Hananiah, Mishael and Azariah; so they entered the king's service. ²⁰In every matter of wisdom and understanding about which the king questioned them, he found them ten times better than all the magicians and enchanters in his whole kingdom.

²¹And Daniel remained there until the first year of King Cyrus.

ᵃ 2 Hebrew *Shinar*   ᵇ 4 Or *Chaldeans*   ᶜ 10 The Hebrew for *your* and *you* in this verse is plural.

NEBUCHADNEZZAR'S DREAM

2 In the second year of his reign, Nebuchadnezzar had dreams; his mind was troubled and he could not sleep. ²So the king summoned the magicians, enchanters, sorcerers and astrologers[a] to tell him what he had dreamed. When they came in and stood before the king, ³he said to them, "I have had a dream that troubles me and I want to know what it means.[b]"

⁴Then the astrologers answered the king in Aramaic,[c] "O king, live forever! Tell your servants the dream, and we will interpret it."

⁵The king replied to the astrologers, "This is what I have firmly decided: If you do not tell me what my dream was and interpret it, I will have you cut into pieces and your houses turned into piles of rubble. ⁶But if you tell me the dream and explain it, you will receive from me gifts and rewards and great honor. So tell me the dream and interpret it for me."

⁷Once more they replied, "Let the king tell his servants the dream, and we will interpret it."

⁸Then the king answered, "I am certain that you are trying to gain time, because you realize that this is what I have firmly decided: ⁹If you do not tell me the dream, there is just one penalty for you. You have conspired to tell me misleading and wicked things, hoping the situation will change. So then, tell me the dream, and I will know that you can interpret it for me."

¹⁰The astrologers answered the king, "There is not a man on earth who can do what the king asks! No king, however great and mighty, has ever asked such a thing of any magician or enchanter or astrologer. ¹¹What the king asks is too difficult. No one can reveal it to the king except the gods, and they do not live among men."

¹²This made the king so angry and furious that he ordered the execution of all the wise men of Babylon. ¹³So the decree was issued to put the wise men to death, and men were sent to look for Daniel and his friends to put them to death.

¹⁴When Arioch, the commander of the king's guard, had gone out to put to death the wise men of Babylon, Daniel spoke to him with wisdom and tact. ¹⁵He asked the king's officer, "Why did the king issue such a harsh decree?" Arioch then explained the matter to Daniel. ¹⁶At this, Daniel went in to the king and asked for time, so that he might interpret the dream for him.

¹⁷Then Daniel returned to his house and explained the matter to his friends Hananiah, Mishael and Azariah. ¹⁸He urged them to plead for mercy from the God of heaven concerning this mystery, so that he and his friends might not be executed with the rest of the wise men of Babylon. ¹⁹During the night the mystery was revealed to Daniel in a vision. Then Daniel praised the God of heaven ²⁰and said:

"Praise be to the name of God for ever and ever;
    wisdom and power are his.
²¹ He changes times and seasons;
    he sets up kings and deposes them.
He gives wisdom to the wise
    and knowledge to the discerning.
²² He reveals deep and hidden things;
    he knows what lies in darkness,
    and light dwells with him.
²³ I thank and praise you, O God of my fathers:
    You have given me wisdom and power,
you have made known to me what we asked of you,
    you have made known to us the dream of the king."

DANIEL INTERPRETS THE DREAM

²⁴Then Daniel went to Arioch, whom the king had appointed to execute the wise men of Babylon, and said to him, "Do not execute the wise men of Babylon. Take me to the king, and I will interpret his dream for him."

²⁵Arioch took Daniel to the king at once and said, "I have found a man among the exiles from Judah who can tell the king what his dream means."

---

[a] *2* Or *Chaldeans*; also in verses 4, 5 and 10   [b] *3* Or *was*   [c] *4* The text from here through chapter 7 is in Aramaic.

²⁶The king asked Daniel (also called Belteshazzar), "Are you able to tell me what I saw in my dream and interpret it?"

²⁷Daniel replied, "No wise man, enchanter, magician or diviner can explain to the king the mystery he has asked about, ²⁸but there is a God in heaven who reveals mysteries. He has shown King Nebuchadnezzar what will happen in days to come. Your dream and the visions that passed through your mind as you lay on your bed are these:

²⁹"As you were lying there, O king, your mind turned to things to come, and the revealer of mysteries showed you what is going to happen. ³⁰As for me, this mystery has been revealed to me, not because I have greater wisdom than other living men, but so that you, O king, may know the interpretation and that you may understand what went through your mind.

³¹"You looked, O king, and there before you stood a large statue—an enormous, dazzling statue, awesome in appearance. ³²The head of the statue was made of pure gold, its chest and arms of silver, its belly and thighs of bronze, ³³its legs of iron, its feet partly of iron and partly of baked clay. ³⁴While you were watching, a rock was cut out, but not by human hands. It struck the statue on its feet of iron and clay and smashed them. ³⁵Then the iron, the clay, the bronze, the silver and the gold were broken to pieces at the same time and became like chaff on a threshing floor in the summer. The wind swept them away without leaving a trace. But the rock that struck the statue became a huge mountain and filled the whole earth.

³⁶"This was the dream, and now we will interpret it to the king. ³⁷You, O king, are the king of kings. The God of heaven has given you dominion and power and might and glory; ³⁸in your hands he has placed mankind and the beasts of the field and the birds of the air. Wherever they live, he has made you ruler over them all. You are that head of gold.

³⁹"After you, another kingdom will rise, inferior to yours. Next, a third kingdom, one of bronze, will rule over the whole earth. ⁴⁰Finally, there will be a fourth kingdom, strong as iron—for iron breaks and smashes everything—and as iron breaks things to pieces, so it will crush and break all the others. ⁴¹Just as you saw that the feet and toes were partly of baked clay and partly of iron, so this will be a divided kingdom; yet it will have some of the strength of iron in it, even as you saw iron mixed with clay. ⁴²As the toes were partly iron and partly clay, so this kingdom will be partly strong and partly brittle. ⁴³And just as you saw the iron mixed with baked clay, so the people will be a mixture and will not remain united, any more than iron mixes with clay.

⁴⁴"In the time of those kings, the God of heaven will set up a kingdom that will never be destroyed, nor will it be left to another people. It will crush all those kingdoms and bring them to an end, but it will itself endure forever. ⁴⁵This is the meaning of the vision of the rock cut out of a mountain, but not by human hands—a rock that broke the iron, the bronze, the clay, the silver and the gold to pieces.

"The great God has shown the king what will take place in the future. The dream is true and the interpretation is trustworthy."

⁴⁶Then King Nebuchadnezzar fell prostrate before Daniel and paid him honor and ordered that an offering and incense be presented to him. ⁴⁷The king said to Daniel, "Surely your God is the God of gods and the Lord of kings and a revealer of mysteries, for you were able to reveal this mystery."

⁴⁸Then the king placed Daniel in a high position and lavished many gifts on him. He made him ruler over the entire province of Babylon and placed him in charge of all its wise men. ⁴⁹Moreover, at Daniel's request the king appointed Shadrach, Meshach and Abednego administrators over the province of Babylon, while Daniel himself remained at the royal court.

» live the adventure » Da 2:27–28

Giving Credit to God

Do you think Daniel was tempted even for a moment to take the credit for his amazing ability to interpret dreams? Not likely. Why? Because Daniel probably never fooled himself into thinking he was that powerful. He knew that he, like any other guy, didn't possess some natural human ability to interpret dreams. How many guys do you know who have a knack for that kind of thing? Daniel understood the source of his strength—he was an instrument, a tool that God used to accomplish a certain goal. How careful are you to give God the credit for the talents and abilities other people see in you when your gifts are on display?

3 King Nebuchadnezzar made an image of gold, ninety feet high and nine feet[a] wide, and set it up on the plain of Dura in the province of Babylon. ²He then summoned the satraps, prefects, governors, advisers, treasurers, judges, magistrates and all the other provincial officials to come to the dedication of the image he had set up. ³So the satraps, prefects, governors, advisers, treasurers, judges, magistrates and all the other provincial officials assembled for the dedication of the image that King Nebuchadnezzar had set up, and they stood before it.

⁴Then the herald loudly proclaimed, "This is what you are commanded to do, O peoples, nations and men of every language: ⁵As soon as you hear the sound of the horn, flute, zither, lyre, harp, pipes and all kinds of music, you must fall down and worship the image of gold that King Nebuchadnezzar has set up. ⁶Whoever does not fall down and worship will immediately be thrown into a blazing furnace."

⁷Therefore, as soon as they heard the sound of the horn, flute, zither, lyre, harp and all kinds of music, all the peoples, nations and men of every language fell down and worshiped the image of gold that King Nebuchadnezzar had set up.

⁸At this time some astrologers[b] came forward and denounced the Jews. ⁹They said to King Nebuchadnezzar, "O king, live forever! ¹⁰You have issued a decree, O king, that everyone who hears the sound of the horn, flute, zither, lyre, harp, pipes and all kinds of music must fall down and worship the image of gold, ¹¹and that whoever does not fall down and worship will be thrown into a blazing furnace. ¹²But there are some Jews whom you have set over the affairs of the province of Babylon—Shadrach, Meshach and Abednego—who pay no attention to you, O king. They neither serve your gods nor worship the image of gold you have set up."

¹³Furious with rage, Nebuchadnezzar summoned Shadrach, Meshach and Abednego. So these men were brought before the king, ¹⁴and Nebuchadnezzar said to them, "Is it true, Shadrach, Meshach and Abednego, that you do not serve my gods or worship the image of gold I have set up? ¹⁵Now when you hear the sound of the horn, flute, zither, lyre, harp, pipes and all kinds of music, if you are ready to fall down and worship the image I made, very good. But if you do not worship it, you will be thrown immediately into a blazing furnace. Then what god will be able to rescue you from my hand?"

¹⁶Shadrach, Meshach and Abednego replied to the king, "O Nebuchadnezzar, we do not need to defend ourselves before you in this matter. ¹⁷If we are thrown into the blazing furnace, the God we serve is able to save us from it, and he will rescue us from your hand, O king. ¹⁸But even if he does not, we want you to know, O king, that we will not serve your gods or worship the image of gold you have set up."

¹⁹Then Nebuchadnezzar was furious with Shadrach, Meshach and Abednego, and his attitude toward them changed. He ordered the furnace heated seven times hotter than usual ²⁰and commanded some of the strongest soldiers in his army to tie up Shadrach, Meshach and Abednego and

---

NOW OR NEVER

DA 3:1–12

Be honest: If you'd been on the plain of Dura with Shadrach, Meshach, Abednego and the rest of the people, and you could see the blazing furnace waiting for anyone who refused to bow down, would you have been on your feet or on your face when the horns blew?

» live the adventure » Da 3:16-18

Learning Extreme Faith

This might be the most courageous statement of faith anyone has ever uttered. It's one thing to say, "I will obey God because I know he's going to protect me." It's a whole different ball game to say, "I'm going to obey God even if he allows me to burn to death." That's the kind of extreme faith that leaves a lasting impression on everyone who witnesses it. (Look at the effect it had on the arrogant King Nebuchadnezzar in verses 28–29.) That's the kind of extreme faith that God uses to produce miracles.

ª 1 Aramaic *sixty cubits high and six cubits wide* (about 27 meters high and 2.7 meters wide) ᵇ 8 Or *Chaldeans* throw them into the blazing furnace. ²¹So these men, wearing their robes, trousers, turbans and other clothes, were bound and thrown into the blazing furnace. ²²The king's command was so urgent and the furnace so hot that the flames of the fire killed the soldiers who took up Shadrach, Meshach and Abednego, ²³and these three men, firmly tied, fell into the blazing furnace.

²⁴Then King Nebuchadnezzar leaped to his feet in amazement and asked his advisers, "Weren't there three men that we tied up and threw into the fire?"

They replied, "Certainly, O king."

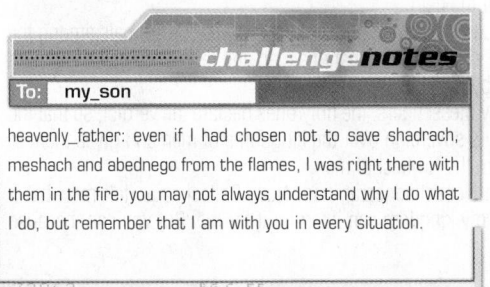

challengenotes

To: my_son

heavenly_father: even if I had chosen not to save shadrach, meshach and abednego from the flames, I was right there with them in the fire. you may not always understand why I do what I do, but remember that I am with you in every situation.

²⁵He said, "Look! I see four men walking around in the fire, unbound and unharmed, and the fourth looks like a son of the gods."

²⁶Nebuchadnezzar then approached the opening of the blazing furnace and shouted, "Shadrach, Meshach and Abednego, servants of the Most High God, come out! Come here!"

So Shadrach, Meshach and Abednego came out of the fire, ²⁷and the satraps, prefects, governors and royal advisers crowded around them. They saw that the fire had not harmed their bodies, nor was a hair of their heads singed; their robes were not scorched, and there was no smell of fire on them.

²⁸Then Nebuchadnezzar said, "Praise be to the God of Shadrach, Meshach and Abednego, who has sent his angel and rescued his servants! They trusted in him and defied the king's command and were willing to give up their lives rather than serve or worship any god except their own God. ²⁹Therefore I decree that the people of any nation or language who say anything against the God of Shadrach, Meshach and Abednego be cut into pieces and their houses be turned into piles of rubble, for no other god can save in this way."

³⁰Then the king promoted Shadrach, Meshach and Abednego in the province of Babylon.

NEBUCHADNEZZAR'S DREAM OF A TREE

4 King Nebuchadnezzar,

To the peoples, nations and men of every language, who live in all the world:

May you prosper greatly!

²It is my pleasure to tell you about the miraculous signs and wonders that the Most High God has performed for me.

³How great are his signs,
　　how mighty his wonders!
His kingdom is an eternal kingdom;
　　his dominion endures from generation to generation.

⁴I, Nebuchadnezzar, was at home in my palace, contented and prosperous. ⁵I had a dream that made me afraid. As I was lying in my bed, the images and visions that passed through my mind terrified me. ⁶So I commanded that all the wise men of Babylon be brought before me to interpret the dream for me. ⁷When the magicians, enchanters, astrologersᵃ and diviners came, I told them the dream, but they could not interpret it for me. ⁸Finally, Daniel came into my presence and I told him the dream. (He is called Belteshazzar, after the name of my god, and the spirit of the holy gods is in him.)

⁹I said, "Belteshazzar, chief of the magicians, I know that the spirit of the holy gods is in you, and no mystery is too difficult for you. Here is my dream; interpret it for me. ¹⁰These are the visions I saw while lying in my bed: I looked, and there before me stood a tree in the middle of the land. Its height was enormous. ¹¹The tree grew large and strong and its top touched the sky; it was visible to the ends of the earth. ¹²Its leaves were beautiful, its fruit abundant, and on it

---

ᵃ 7 Or *Chaldeans*

was food for all. Under it the beasts of the field found shelter, and the birds of the air lived in its branches; from it every creature was fed.

[13]"In the visions I saw while lying in my bed, I looked, and there before me was a messenger,[a] a holy one, coming down from heaven. [14]He called in a loud voice: 'Cut down the tree and trim off its branches; strip off its leaves and scatter its fruit. Let the animals flee from under it and the birds from its branches. [15]But let the stump and its roots, bound with iron and bronze, remain in the ground, in the grass of the field.

" 'Let him be drenched with the dew of heaven, and let him live with the animals among the plants of the earth. [16]Let his mind be changed from that of a man and let him be given the mind of an animal, till seven times[b] pass by for him.

[17]" 'The decision is announced by messengers, the holy ones declare the verdict, so that the living may know that the Most High is sovereign over the kingdoms of men and gives them to anyone he wishes and sets over them the lowliest of men.'

[18]"This is the dream that I, King Nebuchadnezzar, had. Now, Belteshazzar, tell me what it means, for none of the wise men in my kingdom can interpret it for me. But you can, because the spirit of the holy gods is in you."

DANIEL INTERPRETS THE DREAM

[19]Then Daniel (also called Belteshazzar) was greatly perplexed for a time, and his thoughts terrified him. So the king said, "Belteshazzar, do not let the dream or its meaning alarm you."

Belteshazzar answered, "My lord, if only the dream applied to your enemies and its meaning to your adversaries! [20]The tree you saw, which grew large and strong, with its top touching the sky, visible to the whole earth, [21]with beautiful leaves and abundant fruit, providing food for all, giving shelter to the beasts of the field, and having nesting places in its branches for the birds of the air— [22]you, O king, are that tree! You have become great and strong; your greatness has grown until it reaches the sky, and your dominion extends to distant parts of the earth.

[23]"You, O king, saw a messenger, a holy one, coming down from heaven and saying, 'Cut down the tree and destroy it, but leave the stump, bound with iron and bronze, in the grass of the field, while its roots remain in the ground. Let him be drenched with the dew of heaven; let him live like the wild animals, until seven times pass by for him.'

[24]"This is the interpretation, O king, and this is the decree the Most High has issued against my lord the king: [25]You will be driven away from people and will live with the wild animals; you will eat grass like cattle and be drenched with the dew of heaven. Seven times will pass by for you until you acknowledge that the Most High is sovereign over the kingdoms of men and gives them to anyone he wishes. [26]The command to leave the stump of the tree with its roots means that your kingdom will be restored to you when you acknowledge that Heaven rules. [27]Therefore, O king, be pleased to accept my advice: Renounce your sins by doing what is right, and your wickedness by being kind to the oppressed. It may be that then your prosperity will continue."

THE DREAM IS FULFILLED

[28]All this happened to King Nebuchadnezzar. [29]Twelve months later, as the king was walking on the roof of the royal palace of Babylon, [30]he said, "Is not this the great Babylon I have built as the royal residence, by my mighty power and for the glory of my majesty?"

[31]The words were still on his lips when

NOW OR NEVER

DA 4:28–32

If there's one thing God won't put up with, it's pride. He cut King Nebuchadnezzar down to size, and he'll do the same to anyone else who tries to act like they are God.

a voice came from heaven, "This is what is decreed for you, King Nebuchadnezzar: Your royal authority has been taken from you. [32]You will be driven away from people and will live with the wild animals; you will eat grass like cattle. Seven times will pass by for you until you acknowl-

---

[a] 13 Or watchman; also in verses 17 and 23   [b] 16 Or years; also in verses 23, 25 and 32

edge that the Most High is sovereign over the kingdoms of men and gives them to anyone he wishes."

³³Immediately what had been said about Nebuchadnezzar was fulfilled. He was driven away from people and ate grass like cattle. His body was drenched with the dew of heaven until his hair grew like the feathers of an eagle and his nails like the claws of a bird.

³⁴At the end of that time, I, Nebuchadnezzar, raised my eyes toward heaven, and my sanity was restored. Then I praised the Most High; I honored and glorified him who lives forever.

> His dominion is an eternal dominion;
>> his kingdom endures from generation to generation.
> ³⁵All the peoples of the earth
>> are regarded as nothing.
> He does as he pleases
>> with the powers of heaven
>> and the peoples of the earth.
> No one can hold back his hand
>> or say to him: "What have you done?"

³⁶At the same time that my sanity was restored, my honor and splendor were returned to me for the glory of my kingdom. My advisers and nobles sought me out, and I was restored to my throne and became even greater than before. ³⁷Now I, Nebuchadnezzar, praise and exalt and glorify the King of heaven, because everything he does is right and all his ways are just. And those who walk in pride he is able to humble.

THE WRITING ON THE WALL

5 King Belshazzar gave a great banquet for a thousand of his nobles and drank wine with them. ²While Belshazzar was drinking his wine, he gave orders to bring in the gold and silver goblets that Nebuchadnezzar his father ᵃ had taken from the temple in Jerusalem, so that the king and his nobles, his wives and his concubines might drink from them. ³So they brought in the gold goblets that had been taken from the temple of God in Jerusalem, and the king and his nobles, his wives and his concubines drank from them. ⁴As they drank the wine, they praised the gods of gold and silver, of bronze, iron, wood and stone.

⁵Suddenly the fingers of a human hand appeared and wrote on the plaster of the wall, near the lampstand in the royal palace. The king watched the hand as it wrote. ⁶His face turned pale and he was so frightened that his knees knocked together and his legs gave way.

⁷The king called out for the enchanters, astrologers ᵇ and diviners to be brought and said to these wise men of Babylon, "Whoever reads this writing and tells me what it means will be clothed in purple and have a gold chain placed around his neck, and he will be made the third highest ruler in the kingdom."

⁸Then all the king's wise men came in, but they could not read the writing or tell the king what it meant. ⁹So King Belshazzar became even more terrified and his face grew more pale. His nobles were baffled.

¹⁰The queen, ᶜ hearing the voices of the king and his nobles, came into the banquet hall. "O king, live forever!" she said. "Don't be alarmed! Don't look so pale! ¹¹There is a man in your kingdom who has the spirit of the holy gods in him. In the time of your father he was found to have insight and intelligence and wisdom like that of the gods. King Nebuchadnezzar your father—your father the king, I say—appointed him chief of the magicians, enchanters, astrologers and diviners. ¹²This man Daniel, whom the king called Belteshazzar, was found to have a keen mind and knowledge and understanding, and also the ability to interpret dreams, explain riddles and solve difficult problems. Call for Daniel, and he will tell you what the writing means."

¹³So Daniel was brought before the king, and the king said to him, "Are you Daniel, one of the exiles my father the king brought from Judah? ¹⁴I have heard that the spirit of the gods is in you and that you have insight, intelligence and outstanding wisdom. ¹⁵The wise men and enchanters were brought before me to read this writing and tell me what it means, but they could not explain it. ¹⁶Now I have

---

ᵃ 2 Or *ancestor*; or *predecessor*; also in verses 11, 13 and 18   ᵇ 7 Or *Chaldeans*; also in verse 11   ᶜ 10 Or *queen mother* heard that you are able to give interpretations and to solve difficult problems. If you can read this writing and tell me what it means, you will be clothed in purple and have a gold chain placed around your neck, and you will be made the third highest ruler in the kingdom."

[17] Then Daniel answered the king, "You may keep your gifts for yourself and give your rewards to someone else. Nevertheless, I will read the writing for the king and tell him what it means.

[18] "O king, the Most High God gave your father Nebuchadnezzar sovereignty and greatness and glory and splendor. [19] Because of the high position he gave him, all the peoples and nations and men of every language dreaded and feared him. Those the king wanted to put to death, he put to death; those he wanted to spare, he spared; those he wanted to promote, he promoted; and those he wanted to humble, he humbled. [20] But when his heart became arrogant and hardened with pride, he was deposed from his royal throne and stripped of his glory. [21] He was driven away from people and given the mind of an animal; he lived with the wild donkeys and ate grass like cattle; and his body was drenched with the dew of heaven, until he acknowledged that the Most High God is sovereign over the kingdoms of men and sets over them anyone he wishes.

[22] "But you his son,[a] O Belshazzar, have not humbled yourself, though you knew all this. [23] Instead, you have set yourself up against the Lord of heaven. You had the goblets from his temple brought to you, and you and your nobles, your wives and your concubines drank wine from them. You praised the gods of silver and gold, of bronze, iron, wood and stone, which cannot see or hear or understand. But you did not honor the God who holds in his hand your life and all your ways. [24] Therefore he sent the hand that wrote the inscription.

[25] "This is the inscription that was written:

MENE, MENE, TEKEL, PARSIN[b]

[26] "This is what these words mean:

Mene[c]: God has numbered the days of your reign and brought it to an end.
[27] *Tekel*[d]: You have been weighed on the scales and found wanting.
[28] *Peres*[e]: Your kingdom is divided and given to the Medes and Persians."

[29] Then at Belshazzar's command, Daniel was clothed in purple, a gold chain was placed around his neck, and he was proclaimed the third highest ruler in the kingdom.

[30] That very night Belshazzar, king of the Babylonians,[f] was slain, [31] and Darius the Mede took over the kingdom, at the age of sixty-two.

DANIEL IN THE DEN OF LIONS

6 It pleased Darius to appoint 120 satraps to rule throughout the kingdom, [2] with three administrators over them, one of whom was Daniel. The satraps were made accountable to them so that the king might not suffer loss. [3] Now Daniel so distinguished himself among the administrators and the satraps by his exceptional qualities that the king planned to set him over the whole kingdom. [4] At this, the administrators and the satraps tried to find grounds for charges against Daniel in his conduct of government affairs, but they were unable to do so. They could find no corruption in him, because he was trustworthy and neither corrupt nor negligent. [5] Finally these men said, "We will never find any basis for charges against this man Daniel unless it has something to do with the law of his God."

Living a Blameless Life

>> live the adventure >> Da 6:4–5

It's human nature to look for flaws, weaknesses and scandals in other people's lives. And let's be real here—usually you don't have to look very hard to find those things. After all, no one's perfect, right? But what if someone couldn't dig up any dirt on you? What if you were consistently honest and fair in the way you treated people? What if you refused to let your emotions get the best of you under *any* circumstances? What if you learned to say no to the temptations that come your way? If you had a spotless record like Daniel's, what kind of message about God's work in your life would it send to the people who know you?

---

[a] 22 Or *descendant*; or *successor*   [b] 25 Aramaic *UPARSIN* (that is, *AND PARSIN*)   [c] 26 *Mene* can mean *numbered* or *mina* (a unit of money).   [d] 27 *Tekel* can mean *weighed* or *shekel*.   [e] 28 *Peres* (the singular of *Parsin*) can mean *divided* or *Persia* or *a half mina* or *a half shekel*.   [f] 30 Or *Chaldeans*

daniel

VERSUS

government officers

» A young Jewish exile
» A distinguished civil servant and advisor to kings
» Remembered as one of Israel's greatest prophets

» Godless men who sought position, power, prestige and personal gain
» Jealous of Daniel's wisdom and ability
» Largely forgotten by history

The Main Event

Daniel was barely old enough to shave when a horde of foreign invaders yanked him out of his home and shipped him off to Babylon. Talk about a tough break! Except for the company of a few other Jewish captives, there was nothing familiar about Daniel's new life. Immersed in a foreign culture, he faced a monumental choice: learn a whole new language and adjust to life apart from his family and his beloved homeland . . . or be miserable for the rest of his days.

Daniel decided to make the best of a bad situation. He remained faithful, studied hard and excelled at everything he did. He was so impressive that important officials in the Babylonian government took notice of him. Because of Daniel's God-given wisdom and expertise, he was promoted over all the Babylonian officials his age. As you might guess, that caused many of his peers in the government to despise him.

The same story repeated itself when the Persian army rolled into town. Daniel quickly distinguished himself in the eyes of the new king and, as a result, jealous Persian officials sought to discredit him. They looked for some flaw in his character, an unethical practice they could tie to his past. They pored over his life, but the worst accusation they could come up with was that Daniel worshiped the God of Israel.

So these shifty wannabes tricked King Darius into issuing a decree forbidding prayers offered to anyone but the king himself. Needless to say, Daniel ignored this law; and when he did, the Persian officials jumped all over him, demanding a death sentence for his "crime."

King Darius had no choice. Any decree signed into law by the Persian king was irrevocable. Despite all his best efforts to save Daniel, in the end Darius had to carry out his own law. He ordered Daniel to be thrown into a den of starving lions for an entire night. After carrying out the sentence, King Darius couldn't sleep a wink. Ironically, Daniel probably slept just fine. That's because God closed the mouths of the lions and kept him safe. The next morning, when King Darius found Daniel unharmed, he ordered Daniel's accusers to be executed.

The Outcome

Here's a secret to tuck away: If you closely follow God, develop your gifts and use your abilities to serve him with excellence, you will be successful. Like cream, you'll rise to the top. You'll get noticed—maybe even promoted and honored—and you'll be envied.

That's the way the world generally works. But no matter how others treat you—despite how they try to discredit you—if your heart is right, then in God's eyes you'll be a major success.

Read more about Daniel and the government officers in Daniel 1 (pages 1137–1138); 2:10–49 (pages 1138–1139); 6 (pages 1144–1147).

6So the administrators and the satraps went as a group to the king and said: "O King Darius, live forever! 7The royal administrators, prefects, satraps, advisers and governors have all agreed that the king should issue an edict and enforce the decree that anyone who prays to any god or man during the next thirty days, except to you, O king, shall be thrown into the lions' den. 8Now, O king, issue the decree and put it in writing so that it cannot be altered—in accordance with the laws of the Medes and Persians, which cannot be repealed." 9So King Darius put the decree in writing.

10Now when Daniel learned that the decree had been published, he went home to his upstairs room where the windows opened toward Jerusalem. Three times a day he got down on his knees and prayed, giving thanks to his God, just as he had done before. 11Then these men went as a group and found Daniel praying and asking God for help. 12So they went to the king and spoke to him about his royal decree: "Did you not publish a decree that during the next thirty days anyone who prays to any god or man except to you, O king, would be thrown into the lions' den?"

The king answered, "The decree stands—in accordance with the laws of the Medes and Persians, which cannot be repealed."

13Then they said to the king, "Daniel, who is one of the exiles from Judah, pays no attention to you, O king, or to the decree you put in writing. He still prays three times a day." 14When the king heard this, he was greatly distressed; he was determined to rescue Daniel and made every effort until sundown to save him.

15Then the men went as a group to the king and said to him, "Remember, O king, that according to the law of the Medes and Persians no decree or edict that the king issues can be changed."

16So the king gave the order, and they brought Daniel and threw him into the lions' den. The king said to Daniel, "May your God, whom you serve continually, rescue you!"

17A stone was brought and placed over the mouth of the den, and the king sealed it with his own signet ring and with the rings of his nobles, so that Daniel's situation might not be changed. 18Then the king returned to his palace and spent the night without eating and without any entertainment being brought to him. And he could not sleep.

19At the first light of dawn, the king got up and hurried to the lions' den. 20When he came near the den, he called to Daniel in an anguished voice, "Daniel, servant of the living God, has your God, whom you serve continually, been able to rescue you from the lions?"

21Daniel answered, "O king, live forever! 22My God sent his angel, and he shut the mouths of the lions. They have not hurt me, because I was found innocent in his sight. Nor have I ever done any wrong before you, O king."

23The king was overjoyed and gave orders to lift Daniel out of the den. And when Daniel was lifted from the den, no wound was found on him, because he had trusted in his God.

24At the king's command, the men who had falsely accused Daniel were brought in and thrown into the lions' den, along with their wives and children. And before they reached the floor of the den, the lions overpowered them and crushed all their bones.

25Then King Darius wrote to all the peoples, nations and men of every language throughout the land:

"May you prosper greatly!

NOW OR NEVER
DA 6:6–10

What do you think Daniel—a guy who valued his time with God so much that he was willing to die for it—would say to you about your prayer life?

NOW OR NEVER
DA 6:21–22

If God could keep Daniel safe for an entire night in a dark pit with a bunch of starving lions, what dangers do you think he can protect you from? Or rather, what dangers can't he protect you from?

26 "I issue a decree that in every part of my kingdom people must fear and reverence the God of Daniel.

> "For he is the living God
>   and he endures forever;
> his kingdom will not be destroyed,
>   his dominion will never end.
> 27 He rescues and he saves;
>   he performs signs and wonders
>   in the heavens and on the earth.
> He has rescued Daniel
>   from the power of the lions."

28 So Daniel prospered during the reign of Darius and the reign of Cyrus[a] the Persian.

DANIEL'S DREAM OF FOUR BEASTS

7 In the first year of Belshazzar king of Babylon, Daniel had a dream, and visions passed through his mind as he was lying on his bed. He wrote down the substance of his dream. 2 Daniel said: "In my vision at night I looked, and there before me were the four winds of heaven churning up the great sea. 3 Four great beasts, each different from the others, came up out of the sea.

4 "The first was like a lion, and it had the wings of an eagle. I watched until its wings were torn off and it was lifted from the ground so that it stood on two feet like a man, and the heart of a man was given to it.

5 "And there before me was a second beast, which looked like a bear. It was raised up on one of its sides, and it had three ribs in its mouth between its teeth. It was told, 'Get up and eat your fill of flesh!'

6 "After that, I looked, and there before me was another beast, one that looked like a leopard. And on its back it had four wings like those of a bird. This beast had four heads, and it was given authority to rule.

7 "After that, in my vision at night I looked, and there before me was a fourth beast—terrifying and frightening and very powerful. It had large iron teeth; it crushed and devoured its victims and trampled underfoot whatever was left. It was different from all the former beasts, and it had ten horns.

8 "While I was thinking about the horns, there before me was another horn, a little one, which came up among them; and three of the first horns were uprooted before it. This horn had eyes like the eyes of a man and a mouth that spoke boastfully.

9 "As I looked,

> "thrones were set in place,
>   and the Ancient of Days took his seat.
> His clothing was as white as snow;
>   the hair of his head was white like wool.
> His throne was flaming with fire,
>   and its wheels were all ablaze.
> 10 A river of fire was flowing,
>   coming out from before him.
> Thousands upon thousands attended him;
>   ten thousand times ten thousand stood before him.
> The court was seated,
>   and the books were opened.

11 "Then I continued to watch because of the boastful words the horn was speaking. I kept looking until the beast was slain and its body destroyed and thrown into the blazing fire. 12 (The other beasts had been stripped of their authority, but were allowed to live for a period of time.)

13 "In my vision at night I looked, and there before me was one like a son of man, coming with the clouds of heaven. He approached the Ancient of Days and was led into his presence. 14 He was given authority, glory and sovereign power; all peoples, nations and men of every language worshiped him. His dominion is an everlasting dominion that will not pass away, and his kingdom is one that will never be destroyed.

---

a 28 Or Darius, that is, the reign of Cyrus

THE INTERPRETATION OF THE DREAM

¹⁵"I, Daniel, was troubled in spirit, and the visions that passed through my mind disturbed me. ¹⁶I approached one of those standing there and asked him the true meaning of all this.

"So he told me and gave me the interpretation of these things: ¹⁷'The four great beasts are four kingdoms that will rise from the earth. ¹⁸But the saints of the Most High will receive the kingdom and will possess it forever—yes, for ever and ever.'

¹⁹"Then I wanted to know the true meaning of the fourth beast, which was different from all the others and most terrifying, with its iron teeth and bronze claws—the beast that crushed and devoured its victims and trampled underfoot whatever was left. ²⁰I also wanted to know about the ten horns on its head and about the other horn that came up, before which three of them fell—the horn that looked more imposing than the others and that had eyes and a mouth that spoke boastfully. ²¹As I watched, this horn was waging war against the saints and defeating them, ²²until the Ancient of Days came and pronounced judgment in favor of the saints of the Most High, and the time came when they possessed the kingdom.

²³"He gave me this explanation: 'The fourth beast is a fourth kingdom that will appear on earth. It will be different from all the other kingdoms and will devour the whole earth, trampling it down and crushing it. ²⁴The ten horns are ten kings who will come from this kingdom. After them another king will arise, different from the earlier ones; he will subdue three kings. ²⁵He will speak against the Most High and oppress his saints and try to change the set times and the laws. The saints will be handed over to him for a time, times and half a time.ᵃ

²⁶" 'But the court will sit, and his power will be taken away and completely destroyed forever. ²⁷Then the sovereignty, power and greatness of the kingdoms under the whole heaven will be handed over to the saints, the people of the Most High. His kingdom will be an everlasting kingdom, and all rulers will worship and obey him.'

²⁸"This is the end of the matter. I, Daniel, was deeply troubled by my thoughts, and my face turned pale, but I kept the matter to myself."

DANIEL'S VISION OF A RAM AND A GOAT

8 In the third year of King Belshazzar's reign, I, Daniel, had a vision, after the one that had already appeared to me. ²In my vision I saw myself in the citadel of Susa in the province of Elam; in the vision I was beside the Ulai Canal. ³I looked up, and there before me was a ram with two horns, standing beside the canal, and the horns were long. One of the horns was longer than the other but grew up later. ⁴I watched the ram as he charged toward the west and the north and the south. No animal could stand against him, and none could rescue from his power. He did as he pleased and became great.

⁵As I was thinking about this, suddenly a goat with a prominent horn between his eyes came from the west, crossing the whole earth without touching the ground. ⁶He came toward the two-horned ram I had seen standing beside the canal and charged at him in great rage. ⁷I saw him attack the ram furiously, striking the ram and shattering his two horns. The ram was powerless to stand against him; the goat knocked him to the ground and trampled on him, and none could rescue the ram from his power. ⁸The goat became very great, but at the height of his power his large horn was broken off, and in its place four prominent horns grew up toward the four winds of heaven.

⁹Out of one of them came another horn, which started small but grew in power to the south and to the east and toward the Beautiful Land. ¹⁰It grew until it reached the host of the heavens, and it threw some of the starry host down to the earth and trampled on them. ¹¹It set itself up to be as great as the Prince of the host; it took away the daily sacrifice from him, and the place of his sanctuary was brought low. ¹²Because of rebellion, the host ∟of the saints⌐ ᵇ and the daily sacrifice were given over to it. It prospered in everything it did, and truth was thrown to the ground.

¹³Then I heard a holy one speaking, and another holy one said to him, "How long will it take for the vision to be fulfilled—the vision concerning the daily sacrifice, the rebellion that causes desolation, and the surrender of the sanctuary and of the host that will be trampled underfoot?"

¹⁴He said to me, "It will take 2,300 evenings and mornings; then the sanctuary will be reconsecrated."

ᵃ 25 Or for a year, two years and half a year   ᵇ 12 Or rebellion, the armies

the angel

» God's messenger
» Sent in response to Daniel's prayers
» Opposed by a powerful demonic spirit called "the prince of the Persian kingdom"

VERSUS

the prince of persia

» Apparently a demon or evil spirit
» Exercised power or control over the region of Persia
» Overcome with the help of Michael, the archangel of God

The Main Event

Do you believe that one person's prayers are enough to set in motion a battle between the spiritual forces of good and evil? Before you answer, check out the prophet Daniel's experience in Daniel 10.

Daniel had been doing some serious praying for three weeks, focusing his thoughts on God and interceding for his fellow Jews. One day, while he and some other guys were out walking by the Tigris River, Daniel had a heavenly vision. He saw a "man" with a face like lightning and eyes like flaming torches. This guy was a sight to behold, and when he spoke, it sounded like an entire crowd of people was talking all at once.

The Bible never tells us this heavenly messenger's name. But whoever it was, his appearance was enough to make Daniel shake in his boots (or sandals). None of Daniel's companions could see the messenger, but they could certainly feel his presence. It filled them with so much terror that they all ran away and hid.

Daniel discovered that the messenger was an angelic answer to prayer—a prayer Daniel first started praying three weeks earlier. But get this—the angelic messenger had been intercepted by the "prince of the Persian kingdom"! This wasn't a human prince, but a spiritual one—an evil spirit or demonic power who had managed to hold up God's messenger for 21 days. In other words, what we have in this story is an actual report of spiritual warfare—two fantastic, indescribable angelic beings (one good and one evil) duking it out . . . all because of the prayers of a guy named Daniel.

Daniel's visitor reported that this super-heavyweight match was a draw until Michael the archangel of God stepped into the celestial ring and tipped the scales in the unnamed messenger's favor.

The Outcome

Based on this remarkable glimpse into the invisible world of spiritual warfare, we can draw at least three conclusions:

1. The idea of spiritual warfare is a lot more real than many people think.

2. Our prayers matter a whole lot more than most of us imagine.

3. There's a danger in becoming too concerned with silly, worldly stuff and not concerned enough with deeper, bigger spiritual realities.

Remember the story of the Israelites' battle with the Amalekites in Exodus 17? While Joshua was down on the battlefield, Moses was lifting his hands up to God on a nearby hill. According to the Bible, Joshua never would have prevailed without Moses' prayer cover. What does that tell you?

Read more about the angel and the prince of Persia in Daniel 10:1–21 (pages 1151– 1152).

THE INTERPRETATION OF THE VISION

15While I, Daniel, was watching the vision and trying to understand it, there before me stood one who looked like a man. 16And I heard a man's voice from the Ulai calling, "Gabriel, tell this man the meaning of the vision."

17As he came near the place where I was standing, I was terrified and fell prostrate. "Son of man," he said to me, "understand that the vision concerns the time of the end."

18While he was speaking to me, I was in a deep sleep, with my face to the ground. Then he touched me and raised me to my feet.

19He said: "I am going to tell you what will happen later in the time of wrath, because the vision concerns the appointed time of the end.a 20The two-horned ram that you saw represents the kings of Media and Persia. 21The shaggy goat is the king of Greece, and the large horn between his eyes is the first king. 22The four horns that replaced the one that was broken off represent four kingdoms that will emerge from his nation but will not have the same power.

23"In the latter part of their reign, when rebels have become completely wicked, a stern-faced king, a master of intrigue, will arise. 24He will become very strong, but not by his own power. He will cause astounding devastation and will succeed in whatever he does. He will destroy the mighty men and the holy people. 25He will cause deceit to prosper, and he will consider himself superior. When they feel secure, he will destroy many and take his stand against the Prince of princes. Yet he will be destroyed, but not by human power.

26"The vision of the evenings and mornings that has been given you is true, but seal up the vision, for it concerns the distant future."

27I, Daniel, was exhausted and lay ill for several days. Then I got up and went about the king's business. I was appalled by the vision; it was beyond understanding.

DANIEL'S PRAYER

9 In the first year of Darius son of Xerxesb (a Mede by descent), who was made ruler over the Babylonianc kingdom— 2in the first year of his reign, I, Daniel, understood from the Scriptures, according to the word of the LORD given to Jeremiah the prophet, that the desolation of Jerusalem would last seventy years. 3So I turned to the Lord God and pleaded with him in prayer and petition, in fasting, and in sackcloth and ashes.

4I prayed to the LORD my God and confessed:

"O Lord, the great and awesome God, who keeps his covenant of love with all who love him and obey his commands, 5we have sinned and done wrong. We have been wicked and have rebelled; we have turned away from your commands and laws. 6We have not listened to your servants the prophets, who spoke in your name to our kings, our princes and our fathers, and to all the people of the land.

7"Lord, you are righteous, but this day we are covered with shame—the men of Judah and people of Jerusalem and all Israel, both near and far, in all the countries where you have scattered us because of our unfaithfulness to you. 8O LORD, we and our kings, our princes and our fathers are covered with shame because we have sinned against you. 9The Lord our God is merciful and forgiving, even though we have rebelled against him; 10we have not obeyed the LORD our God or kept the laws he gave us through his servants the prophets. 11All Israel has transgressed your law and turned away, refusing to obey you.

NOW OR NEVER

DA 9:4–18

How many people do you generally pray for? Your family? Friends? Your youth leader? Your pastor? Teachers? The president? Christians around the world? Daniel mentioned all the people of Israel in his prayer. How do you decide who to bring before God's throne?

"Therefore the curses and sworn judgments written in the Law of Moses, the servant of God, have been poured out on us, because we have sinned against you. 12You have fulfilled the words spoken against us and against our rulers by bringing upon us great disaster. Under the whole

---

a 19 Or *because the end will be at the appointed time*   b 1 Hebrew *Ahasuerus*   c 1 Or *Chaldean* heaven nothing has ever been done like what has been done to Jerusalem. ¹³Just as it is written in the Law of Moses, all this disaster has come upon us, yet we have not sought the favor of the Lᴏʀᴅ our God by turning from our sins and giving attention to your truth. ¹⁴The Lᴏʀᴅ did not hesitate to bring the disaster upon us, for the Lᴏʀᴅ our God is righteous in everything he does; yet we have not obeyed him.

¹⁵"Now, O Lord our God, who brought your people out of Egypt with a mighty hand and who made for yourself a name that endures to this day, we have sinned, we have done wrong. ¹⁶O Lord, in keeping with all your righteous acts, turn away your anger and your wrath from Jerusalem, your city, your holy hill. Our sins and the iniquities of our fathers have made Jerusalem and your people an object of scorn to all those around us.

¹⁷"Now, our God, hear the prayers and petitions of your servant. For your sake, O Lord, look with favor on your desolate sanctuary. ¹⁸Give ear, O God, and hear; open your eyes and see the desolation of the city that bears your Name. We do not make requests of you because we are righteous, but because of your great mercy. ¹⁹O Lord, listen! O Lord, forgive! O Lord, hear and act! For your sake, O my God, do not delay, because your city and your people bear your Name."

challenge notes

To: **my_son**

heavenly_father: when daniel had something weighing heavily on his mind, he poured out his feelings in prayer to me. he praised me, confessed his sins and told me exactly what his desires were. I answered daniel, and I will answer you when you bring your heartfelt prayers to me.

DA 9:4-19

THE SEVENTY "SEVENS"

²⁰While I was speaking and praying, confessing my sin and the sin of my people Israel and making my request to the Lᴏʀᴅ my God for his holy hill— ²¹while I was still in prayer, Gabriel, the man I had seen in the earlier vision, came to me in swift flight about the time of the evening sacrifice. ²²He instructed me and said to me, "Daniel, I have now come to give you insight and understanding. ²³As soon as you began to pray, an answer was given, which I have come to tell you, for you are highly esteemed. Therefore, consider the message and understand the vision:

²⁴"Seventy 'sevens'[a] are decreed for your people and your holy city to finish[b] transgression, to put an end to sin, to atone for wickedness, to bring in everlasting righteousness, to seal up vision and prophecy and to anoint the most holy.[c]

²⁵"Know and understand this: From the issuing of the decree[d] to restore and rebuild Jerusalem until the Anointed One,[e] the ruler, comes, there will be seven 'sevens,' and sixty-two 'sevens.' It will be rebuilt with streets and a trench, but in times of trouble. ²⁶After the sixty-two 'sevens,' the Anointed One will be cut off and will have nothing.[f] The people of the ruler who will come will destroy the city and the sanctuary. The end will come like a flood: War will continue until the end, and desolations have been decreed. ²⁷He will confirm a covenant with many for one 'seven.'[g] In the middle of the 'seven'[g] he will put an end to sacrifice and offering. And on a wing ⌊of the temple⌋ he will set up an abomination that causes desolation, until the end that is decreed is poured out on him.[h]"[i]

DANIEL'S VISION OF A MAN

10 In the third year of Cyrus king of Persia, a revelation was given to Daniel (who was called Belteshazzar). Its message was true and it concerned a great war.[j] The understanding of the message came to him in a vision.

²At that time I, Daniel, mourned for three weeks. ³I ate no choice food; no meat or wine touched my lips; and I used no lotions at all until the three weeks were over.

⁴On the twenty-fourth day of the first month, as I was standing on the bank of the great river, the Tigris, ⁵I looked up and there before me was a man dressed in linen, with a belt of the finest gold around

---

[a] 24 Or 'weeks'; also in verses 25 and 26   [b] 24 Or restrain   [c] 24 Or Most Holy Place; or most holy One   [d] 25 Or word
[e] 25 Or an anointed one; also in verse 26   [f] 26 Or off and will have no one; or off, but not for himself   [g] 27 Or 'week'   [h] 27 Or it
[i] 27 Or And one who causes desolation will come upon the pinnacle of the abominable ⌊temple⌋, until the end that is decreed is poured out on the desolated ⌊city⌋   [j] 1 Or true and burdensome

his waist. [6]His body was like chrysolite, his face like lightning, his eyes like flaming torches, his arms and legs like the gleam of burnished bronze, and his voice like the sound of a multitude.

[7]I, Daniel, was the only one who saw the vision; the men with me did not see it, but such terror overwhelmed them that they fled and hid themselves. [8]So I was left alone, gazing at this great vision; I had no strength left, my face turned deathly pale and I was helpless. [9]Then I heard him speaking, and as I listened to him, I fell into a deep sleep, my face to the ground.

[10]A hand touched me and set me trembling on my hands and knees. [11]He said, "Daniel, you who are highly esteemed, consider carefully the words I am about to speak to you, and stand up, for I have now been sent to you." And when he said this to me, I stood up trembling.

[12]Then he continued, "Do not be afraid, Daniel. Since the first day that you set your mind to gain understanding and to humble yourself before your God, your words were heard, and I have come in response to them. [13]But the prince of the Persian kingdom resisted me twenty-one days. Then Michael, one of the chief princes, came to help me, because I was detained there with the king of Persia. [14]Now I have come to explain to you what will happen to your people in the future, for the vision concerns a time yet to come."

[15]While he was saying this to me, I bowed with my face toward the ground and was speechless. [16]Then one who looked like a man[a] touched my lips, and I opened my mouth and began to speak. I said to the one standing before me, "I am overcome with anguish because of the vision, my lord, and I am helpless. [17]How can I, your servant, talk with you, my lord? My strength is gone and I can hardly breathe."

[18]Again the one who looked like a man touched me and gave me strength. [19]"Do not be afraid, O man highly esteemed," he said. "Peace! Be strong now; be strong."

When he spoke to me, I was strengthened and said, "Speak, my lord, since you have given me strength."

[20]So he said, "Do you know why I have come to you? Soon I will return to fight against the prince of Persia, and when I go, the prince of Greece will come; [21]but first I will tell you what is written in the Book of Truth. (No one supports me against them except Michael, your prince. [1]And in the first year of Darius the Mede, I took my stand to support and protect him.)

THE KINGS OF THE SOUTH AND THE NORTH

[2]"Now then, I tell you the truth: Three more kings will appear in Persia, and then a fourth, who will be far richer than all the others. When he has gained power by his wealth, he will stir up everyone against the kingdom of Greece. [3]Then a mighty king will appear, who will rule with great power and do as he pleases. [4]After he has appeared, his empire will be broken up and parceled out toward the four winds of heaven. It will not go to his descendants, nor will it have the power he exercised, because his empire will be uprooted and given to others.

[5]"The king of the South will become strong, but one of his commanders will become even stronger than he and will rule his own kingdom with great power. [6]After some years, they will become allies. The daughter of the king of the South will go to the king of the North to make an alliance, but she will not retain her power, and he and his power[b] will not last. In those days she will be handed over, together with her royal escort and her father[c] and the one who supported her.

[7]"One from her family line will arise to take her place. He will attack the forces of the king of the North and enter his fortress; he will fight against them and be victorious. [8]He will also seize their gods, their metal images and their valuable articles of silver and gold and carry them off to Egypt. For some years he will leave the king of the North alone. [9]Then the king of the North will invade the realm of the king of the South but will retreat to his own country. [10]His sons will prepare for war and assemble a great army, which will sweep on like an irresistible flood and carry the battle as far as his fortress.

[11]"Then the king of the South will march out in a rage and fight against the king of the North, who will raise a large army, but it will be defeated. [12]When the army is carried off, the king of the South will be filled with pride and will slaughter many thousands, yet he will not remain triumphant. [13]For the king of the North will muster another army, larger than the first; and after several years, he will advance with a huge army fully equipped.

[14]"In those times many will rise against the king of the South. The violent men among your own

---

[a] 16 Most manuscripts of the Masoretic Text; one manuscript of the Masoretic Text, Dead Sea Scrolls and Septuagint *Then something that looked like a man's hand*   [b] 6 Or *offspring*   [c] 6 Or *child* (see Vulgate and Syriac)

people will rebel in fulfillment of the vision, but without success. ¹⁵Then the king of the North will come and build up siege ramps and will capture a fortified city. The forces of the South will be powerless to resist; even their best troops will not have the strength to stand. ¹⁶The invader will do as he pleases; no one will be able to stand against him. He will establish himself in the Beautiful Land and will have the power to destroy it. ¹⁷He will determine to come with the might of his entire kingdom and will make an alliance with the king of the South. And he will give him a daughter in marriage in order to overthrow the kingdom, but his plansᵃ will not succeed or help him. ¹⁸Then he will turn his attention to the coast-lands and will take many of them, but a commander will put an end to his insolence and will turn his insolence back upon him. ¹⁹After this, he will turn back toward the fortresses of his own country but will stumble and fall, to be seen no more.

²⁰"His successor will send out a tax collector to maintain the royal splendor. In a few years, howev-er, he will be destroyed, yet not in anger or in battle.

²¹"He will be succeeded by a contemptible person who has not been given the honor of royalty. He will invade the kingdom when its people feel secure, and he will seize it through intrigue. ²²Then an overwhelming army will be swept away before him; both it and a prince of the covenant will be de-stroyed. ²³After coming to an agreement with him, he will act deceitfully, and with only a few people he will rise to power. ²⁴When the richest provinces feel secure, he will invade them and will achieve what neither his fathers nor his forefathers did. He will distribute plunder, loot and wealth among his follow-ers. He will plot the overthrow of fortresses—but only for a time.

²⁵"With a large army he will stir up his strength and courage against the king of the South. The king of the South will wage war with a large and very powerful army, but he will not be able to stand because of the plots devised against him. ²⁶Those who eat from the king's provisions will try to destroy him; his army will be swept away, and many will fall in battle. ²⁷The two kings, with their hearts bent on evil, will sit at the same table and lie to each other, but to no avail, because an end will still come at the appoint-ed time. ²⁸The king of the North will return to his own country with great wealth, but his heart will be set against the holy covenant. He will take action against it and then return to his own country.

²⁹"At the appointed time he will invade the South again, but this time the outcome will be different from what it was before. ³⁰Ships of the western coast-landsᵇ will oppose him, and he will lose heart. Then he will turn back and vent his fury against the holy covenant. He will return and show favor to those who forsake the holy covenant.

³¹"His armed forces will rise up to desecrate the temple fortress and will abolish the daily sacrifice. Then they will set up the abomination that causes desolation. ³²With flattery he will corrupt those who have violated the covenant, but the people who know their God will firmly resist him.

³³"Those who are wise will instruct many, though for a time they will fall by the sword or

NOW OR NEVER

DA 11:32

The secret to true success in any situation is knowing God. If you have a clear idea of what pleases God, you can make decisions using that as a benchmark. If you know what God is capable of, you can face even the toughest circumstances with confi-dence and courage.

be burned or captured or plundered. ³⁴When they fall, they will receive a little help, and many who are not sincere will join them. ³⁵Some of the wise will stumble, so that they may be refined, purified and made spotless until the time of the end, for it will still come at the appointed time.

THE KING WHO EXALTS HIMSELF

³⁶"The king will do as he pleases. He will exalt and magnify himself above every god and will say unheard-of things against the God of gods. He will be successful until the time of wrath is completed, for what has been determined must take place. ³⁷He will show no regard for the gods of his fathers or for the one desired by women, nor will he regard any god, but will exalt himself above them all. ³⁸In-stead of them, he will honor a god of fortresses; a god unknown to his fathers he will honor with gold and silver, with precious stones and costly gifts. ³⁹He will attack the mightiest fortresses with the help of a foreign god and will greatly honor those who acknowledge him. He will make them rulers over many people and will distribute the land at a price.ᶜ

ᵃ 17 Or but she   ᵇ 30 Hebrew of Kittim   ᶜ 39 Or land for a reward

40 "At the time of the end the king of the South will engage him in battle, and the king of the North will storm out against him with chariots and cavalry and a great fleet of ships. He will invade many countries and sweep through them like a flood. 41 He will also invade the Beautiful Land. Many countries will fall, but Edom, Moab and the leaders of Ammon will be delivered from his hand. 42 He will extend his power over many countries; Egypt will not escape. 43 He will gain control of the treasures of gold and silver and all the riches of Egypt, with the Libyans and Nubians in submission. 44 But reports from the east and the north will alarm him, and he will set out in a great rage to destroy and annihilate many. 45 He will pitch his royal tents between the seas at[a] the beautiful holy mountain. Yet he will come to his end, and no one will help him.

THE END TIMES

12

"At that time Michael, the great prince who protects your people, will arise. There will be a time of distress such as has not happened from the beginning of nations until then. But at that time your people—everyone whose name is found written in the book—will be delivered. 2 Multitudes who sleep in the dust of the earth will awake: some to everlasting life, others to shame and everlasting contempt. 3 Those who are wise[b] will shine like the brightness of the heavens, and those who lead many to righteousness, like the stars for ever and ever. 4 But you, Daniel, close up and seal the words of the scroll until the time of the end. Many will go here and there to increase knowledge."

5 Then I, Daniel, looked, and there before me stood two others, one on this bank of the river and one on the opposite bank. 6 One of them said to the man clothed in linen, who was above the waters of the river, "How long will it be before these astonishing things are fulfilled?"

7 The man clothed in linen, who was above the waters of the river, lifted his right hand and his left hand toward heaven, and I heard him swear by him who lives forever, saying, "It will be for a time, times and half a time.[c] When the power of the holy people has been finally broken, all these things will be completed."

8 I heard, but I did not understand. So I asked, "My lord, what will the outcome of all this be?"

9 He replied, "Go your way, Daniel, because the words are closed up and sealed until the time of the end. 10 Many will be purified, made spotless and refined, but the wicked will continue to be wicked. None of the wicked will understand, but those who are wise will understand.

11 "From the time that the daily sacrifice is abolished and the abomination that causes desolation is set up, there will be 1,290 days. 12 Blessed is the one who waits for and reaches the end of the 1,335 days.

13 "As for you, go your way till the end. You will rest, and then at the end of the days you will rise to receive your allotted inheritance."

Praying for Wisdom

Every day must have been an adventure (and not always a fun one) for Daniel. Despite his accomplishments, reputation and fame, he was always an outsider—an Israelite in a Babylonian government, a worshiper of God in an ungodly nation. He had enemies constantly trying to take him down and not many friends rushing to his defense. So what does a guy do when he doesn't know who to trust or where to turn? He prays to God for wisdom and strength.

»» live the adventure »» Da 12:3

---

[a] 45 Or the sea and   [b] 3 Or who impart wisdom   [c] 7 Or a year, two years and half a year

HOSEA

Author
Hosea

Audience
Primarily the northern kingdom of Israel

Date
About 715 B.C.

Setting
Hosea lived during the time of the end of the northern kingdom, which fell to the Assyrians in 722 B.C.

Verse to Remember
But you must return to your God; maintain love and justice, and wait for your God always (12:6).

Theme to Consider
Even though Israel committed spiritual adultery by worshiping other gods, God was loyal to his people by loving them and offering them forgiveness.

UNCHANGING TRUTH » Have you ever loved, liked or even just cared about a girl who didn't feel the same way about you? Have you ever been in a relationship that you thought was something special, but turned out to not really mean anything to the other person? Have you ever had your heart broken? Have you ever been cheated on?

If you answered yes to any of these questions, then you've had a small taste of the kind of relationship woes God has experienced since the earliest days of the human race.

For reasons we'll never be able to understand, God loves us. We've certainly done nothing to deserve his love. In fact, we've done just about everything we can to earn his disgust. We've abandoned him, ignored him and even hooked up with other gods (both actual idols and the things we "worship" by giving them a higher priority in our lives than God). In relationship terms, we've been unfaithful. Very unfaithful.

Yet God still loves us. In fact, he loves us so much that he sacrificed his own Son so that we can live with him forever after we die. That's what makes our unfaithfulness so offensive. After all that God has done for us, after the amazing love he's shown us, we still wander away from him whenever something that seems more exciting or more thrilling catches our eye.

How do you think God responds to our unfaithfulness? Actually, you don't have to wonder. God gave us a living, breathing example through the relationship of Hosea and his adulterous wife.

LIFE LESSONS »

1. Sometimes God asks difficult things of his people, but he rewards those who choose to be faithful in those moments (1:2–3).

2. God sees us for exactly who and what we are (2:5–8).

3. God's love for us is so great that he will pursue us even after we've walked away from him (3:1).

1

The word of the Lord that came to Hosea son of Beeri during the reigns of Uzziah, Jotham, Ahaz and Hezekiah, kings of Judah, and during the reign of Jeroboam son of Jehoash[a] king of Israel:

HOSEA'S WIFE AND CHILDREN

²When the Lord began to speak through Hosea, the Lord said to him, "Go, take to yourself an adulterous wife and children of unfaithfulness, because the land is guilty of the vilest adultery in departing from the Lord." ³So he married Gomer daughter of Diblaim, and she conceived and bore him a son.

⁴Then the Lord said to Hosea, "Call him Jezreel, because I will soon punish the house of Jehu for the massacre at Jezreel, and I will put an end to the kingdom of Israel. ⁵In that day I will break Israel's bow in the Valley of Jezreel."

⁶Gomer conceived again and gave birth to a daughter. Then the Lord said to Hosea, "Call her Lo-Ruhamah,[b] for I will no longer show love to the house of Israel, that I should at all forgive them. ⁷Yet I will show love to the house of Judah; and I will save them—not by bow, sword or battle, or by horses and horsemen, but by the Lord their God."

NOW OR NEVER

HOS 1:2

Do you consider yourself faithful to God? Is there anything that draws your attention and affection away from him?

⁸After she had weaned Lo-Ruhamah, Gomer had another son. ⁹Then the Lord said, "Call him Lo-Ammi,[c] for you are not my people, and I am not your God.

¹⁰"Yet the Israelites will be like the sand on the seashore, which cannot be measured or counted. In the place where it was said to them, 'You are not my people,' they will be called 'sons of the living God.' ¹¹The people of Judah and the people of Israel will be reunited, and they will appoint one leader and will come up out of the land, for great will be the day of Jezreel.

2

"Say of your brothers, 'My people,' and of your sisters, 'My loved one.'

ISRAEL PUNISHED AND RESTORED

²"Rebuke your mother, rebuke her,
　　for she is not my wife,
　　and I am not her husband.
Let her remove the adulterous look from her face
　　and the unfaithfulness from between her breasts.
³Otherwise I will strip her naked
　　and make her as bare as on the day she was born;
I will make her like a desert,
　　turn her into a parched land,
　　and slay her with thirst.
⁴I will not show my love to her children,
　　because they are the children of adultery.
⁵Their mother has been unfaithful
　　and has conceived them in disgrace.
She said, 'I will go after my lovers,
　　who give me my food and my water,
　　my wool and my linen, my oil and my drink.'
⁶Therefore I will block her path with thornbushes;
　　I will wall her in so that she cannot find her way.
⁷She will chase after her lovers but not catch them;
　　she will look for them but not find them.
Then she will say,

---

[a] 1 Hebrew *Joash*, a variant of *Jehoash*　　[b] 6 *Lo-Ruhamah* means *not loved*.　　[c] 9 *Lo-Ammi* means *not my people*.

'I will go back to my husband as at first,
    for then I was better off than now.'
⁸ She has not acknowledged that I was the one
    who gave her the grain, the new wine and oil,
  who lavished on her the silver and gold—
    which they used for Baal.

⁹ "Therefore I will take away my grain when it ripens,
    and my new wine when it is ready.
  I will take back my wool and my linen,
    intended to cover her nakedness.
¹⁰ So now I will expose her lewdness
    before the eyes of her lovers;
  no one will take her out of my hands.
¹¹ I will stop all her celebrations:
    her yearly festivals, her New Moons,
    her Sabbath days—all her appointed feasts.
¹² I will ruin her vines and her fig trees,
    which she said were her pay from her lovers;
  I will make them a thicket,
    and wild animals will devour them.
¹³ I will punish her for the days
    she burned incense to the Baals;
  she decked herself with rings and jewelry,
    and went after her lovers,
    but me she forgot,"

declares the LORD.

¹⁴ "Therefore I am now going to allure her;
    I will lead her into the desert
    and speak tenderly to her.
¹⁵ There I will give her back her vineyards,
    and will make the Valley of Achorᵃ a door of hope.
  There she will singᵇ as in the days of her youth,
    as in the day she came up out of Egypt.

¹⁶ "In that day," declares the LORD,
    "you will call me 'my husband';
    you will no longer call me 'my master.ᶜ'
¹⁷ I will remove the names of the Baals from her lips;
    no longer will their names be invoked.
¹⁸ In that day I will make a covenant for them
    with the beasts of the field and the birds of the air
    and the creatures that move along the ground.
  Bow and sword and battle
    I will abolish from the land,
    so that all may lie down in safety.
¹⁹ I will betroth you to me forever;
    I will betroth you inᵈ righteousness and justice,
    inᵉ love and compassion.
²⁰ I will betroth you in faithfulness,
    and you will acknowledge the LORD.

²¹ "In that day I will respond,"
    declares the LORD—
  "I will respond to the skies,

ᵃ 15 Achor means trouble.   ᵇ 15 Or respond   ᶜ 16 Hebrew baal   ᵈ 19 Or with; also in verse 20   ᵉ 19 Or with

and they will respond to the earth;
²² and the earth will respond to the grain,
the new wine and oil,
and they will respond to Jezreel.[a]
²³ I will plant her for myself in the land;
I will show my love to the one I called 'Not my loved one.'[b]
I will say to those called 'Not my people,'[c] 'You are my people';
and they will say, 'You are my God.' "

HOSEA'S RECONCILIATION WITH HIS WIFE

3 The Lord said to me, "Go, show your love to your wife again, though she is loved by another and is an adulteress. Love her as the Lord loves the Israelites, though they turn to other gods and love the sacred raisin cakes."

² So I bought her for fifteen shekels[d] of silver and about a homer and a lethek[e] of barley. ³ Then I told her, "You are to live with[f] me many days; you must not be a prostitute or be intimate with any man, and I will live with[f] you."

⁴ For the Israelites will live many days without king or prince, without sacrifice or sacred stones, without ephod or idol. ⁵ Afterward the Israelites will return and seek the Lord their God and David their king. They will come trembling to the Lord and to his blessings in the last days.

NOW OR NEVER
HOS 3:1

If someone you loved completely rejected you for another guy, how would you react if she came back after six months or so, apologized and said she wanted to start a relationship with you again?

THE CHARGE AGAINST ISRAEL

4 Hear the word of the Lord, you Israelites,
because the Lord has a charge to bring
against you who live in the land:
"There is no faithfulness, no love,
no acknowledgment of God in the land.
² There is only cursing,[g] lying and murder,
stealing and adultery;

they break all bounds,
and bloodshed follows bloodshed.
³ Because of this the land mourns,[h]
and all who live in it waste away;
the beasts of the field and the birds of
the air
and the fish of the sea are dying.

⁴ "But let no man bring a charge,
let no man accuse another,
for your people are like those
who bring charges against a priest.
⁵ You stumble day and night,
and the prophets stumble with you.

NOW OR NEVER
HOS 4:1

Do you ever acknowledge the Lord to your friends and family? Does his name come up often in your conversations? Do you make it clear to the people who know you how important he is to you?

So I will destroy your mother—
⁶ my people are destroyed from lack of knowledge.

"Because you have rejected knowledge,
I also reject you as my priests;
because you have ignored the law of your God,

---

^a 22 *Jezreel* means *God plants.*   ^b 23 Hebrew *Lo-Ruhamah*   ^c 23 Hebrew *Lo-Ammi*   ^d 2 That is, about 6 ounces (about 170 grams)
^e 2 That is, probably about 10 bushels (about 330 liters)   ^f 3 Or *wait for*   ^g 2 That is, to pronounce a curse upon   ^h 3 Or *dries up*

I also will ignore your children.
⁷ The more the priests increased,
    the more they sinned against me;
    they exchanged[a] their[b] Glory for something disgraceful.
⁸ They feed on the sins of my people
    and relish their wickedness.
⁹ And it will be: Like people, like priests.
    I will punish both of them for their ways
    and repay them for their deeds.

¹⁰ "They will eat but not have enough;
    they will engage in prostitution but not increase,
because they have deserted the LORD
    to give themselves ¹¹to prostitution,
to old wine and new,
    which take away the understanding ¹²of my people.
They consult a wooden idol
    and are answered by a stick of wood.
A spirit of prostitution leads them astray;
    they are unfaithful to their God.
¹³ They sacrifice on the mountaintops
    and burn offerings on the hills,
under oak, poplar and terebinth,
    where the shade is pleasant.
Therefore your daughters turn to prostitution
    and your daughters-in-law to adultery.

¹⁴ "I will not punish your daughters
    when they turn to prostitution,
nor your daughters-in-law
    when they commit adultery,
because the men themselves consort with harlots
    and sacrifice with shrine prostitutes—
    a people without understanding will come to ruin!

¹⁵ "Though you commit adultery, O Israel,
    let not Judah become guilty.

"Do not go to Gilgal;
    do not go up to Beth Aven.[c]
    And do not swear, 'As surely as the LORD lives!'
¹⁶ The Israelites are stubborn,
    like a stubborn heifer.
How then can the LORD pasture them
    like lambs in a meadow?
¹⁷ Ephraim is joined to idols;
    leave him alone!
¹⁸ Even when their drinks are gone,
    they continue their prostitution;
    their rulers dearly love shameful ways.
¹⁹ A whirlwind will sweep them away,
    and their sacrifices will bring them shame.

---

[a] 7 Syriac and an ancient Hebrew scribal tradition; Masoretic Text *I will exchange*   [b] 7 Masoretic Text; an ancient Hebrew scribal tradition *my*   [c] 15 *Beth Aven* means *house of wickedness* (a name for Bethel, which means *house of God*).

"Hear this, you priests!
    Pay attention, you Israelites!
Listen, O royal house!
    This judgment is against you:
You have been a snare at Mizpah,
    a net spread out on Tabor.
2 The rebels are deep in slaughter.
    I will discipline all of them.
3 I know all about Ephraim;
    Israel is not hidden from me.
Ephraim, you have now turned to prostitution;
    Israel is corrupt.

4 "Their deeds do not permit them
    to return to their God.
A spirit of prostitution is in their heart;
    they do not acknowledge the LORD.
5 Israel's arrogance testifies against them;
    the Israelites, even Ephraim, stumble in their sin;
    Judah also stumbles with them.
6 When they go with their flocks and herds
        to seek the LORD,
    they will not find him;
    he has withdrawn himself from them.
7 They are unfaithful to the LORD;
    they give birth to illegitimate children.
Now their New Moon festivals
    will devour them and their fields.

8 "Sound the trumpet in Gibeah,
    the horn in Ramah.
Raise the battle cry in Beth Aven[a];
    lead on, O Benjamin.
9 Ephraim will be laid waste
    on the day of reckoning.
Among the tribes of Israel
    I proclaim what is certain.
10 Judah's leaders are like those
    who move boundary stones.
I will pour out my wrath on them
    like a flood of water.
11 Ephraim is oppressed,
        trampled in judgment,
    intent on pursuing idols.[b]
12 I am like a moth to Ephraim,
    like rot to the people of Judah.

13 "When Ephraim saw his sickness,
    and Judah his sores,
then Ephraim turned to Assyria,
    and sent to the great king for help.
But he is not able to cure you,
    not able to heal your sores.

---

[a] 8 Beth Aven means house of wickedness (a name for Bethel, which means house of God).   [b] 11 The meaning of the Hebrew for this word is uncertain.

¹⁴ For I will be like a lion to Ephraim,
　　like a great lion to Judah.
I will tear them to pieces and go away;
I will carry them off, with no one to rescue them.
¹⁵ Then I will go back to my place
　　until they admit their guilt.
And they will seek my face;
　　in their misery they will earnestly seek me."

ISRAEL UNREPENTANT

6 "Come, let us return to the LORD.
He has torn us to pieces
　　but he will heal us;

he has injured us
　　but he will bind up our wounds.
² After two days he will revive us;
　　on the third day he will restore us,
　　that we may live in his presence.
³ Let us acknowledge the LORD;
　　let us press on to acknowledge him.
As surely as the sun rises,
　　he will appear;
he will come to us like the winter rains,
　　like the spring rains that water the earth."

⁴ "What can I do with you, Ephraim?
　　What can I do with you, Judah?

NOW OR NEVER
HOS 6:3

God is more dependable than the sunrise.
You can always count on him being there
when you need him. But how dependable
are you? When he gives you a job to do,
can he count on you to complete it every
time?

Your love is like the morning mist,
　　like the early dew that disappears.
⁵ Therefore I cut you in pieces with my prophets,
I killed you with the words of my mouth;
　　my judgments flashed like lightning upon you.
⁶ For I desire mercy, not sacrifice,
　　and acknowledgment of God rather than burnt offerings.

⁷ Like Adam,ᵃ they have broken
　　the covenant—
　　they were unfaithful to me
　　there.
⁸ Gilead is a city of wicked men,
　　stained with footprints of
　　blood.
⁹ As marauders lie in ambush
　　for a man,
　　so do bands of priests;
they murder on the road to
　　Shechem,
　　committing shameful
　　crimes.

challengenotes

To: my_son

HOS 6:6

heavenly_father: show me your love through your actions. show it by resisting the things that pull you away from me and by displaying a heart that remains loyal to me. show it by acknowledging who I am and by giving me credit for what I've done in your life. show it by telling others about me.

¹⁰ I have seen a horrible thing
　　in the house of Israel.
There Ephraim is given to prostitution
　　and Israel is defiled.

¹¹ "Also for you, Judah,
　　a harvest is appointed.

ᵃ 7 Or *As at Adam*; or *Like men*

7

"Whenever I would restore the fortunes of my people,
¹   whenever I would heal Israel,
the sins of Ephraim are exposed
   and the crimes of Samaria revealed.
They practice deceit,
   thieves break into houses,
   bandits rob in the streets;
² but they do not realize
   that I remember all their evil deeds.
Their sins engulf them;
   they are always before me.

³ "They delight the king with their
      wickedness,
   the princes with their lies.
⁴ They are all adulterers,
   burning like an oven
whose fire the baker need not stir
   from the kneading of the dough till it
      rises.
⁵ On the day of the festival of our king
   the princes become inflamed with
      wine,
   and he joins hands with the
      mockers.
⁶ Their hearts are like an oven;
   they approach him with intrigue.
Their passion smolders all night;
   in the morning it blazes like a
      flaming fire.
⁷ All of them are hot as an oven;
   they devour their rulers.
All their kings fall,
   and none of them calls on me.

⁸ "Ephraim mixes with the nations;
   Ephraim is a flat cake not turned over.
⁹ Foreigners sap his strength,
   but he does not realize it.
His hair is sprinkled with gray,
   but he does not notice.
¹⁰ Israel's arrogance testifies against him,
   but despite all this
he does not return to the LORD his God
   or search for him.

¹¹ "Ephraim is like a dove,
   easily deceived and senseless—
now calling to Egypt,
   now turning to Assyria.
¹² When they go, I will throw my net over them;
   I will pull them down like birds of the air.
When I hear them flocking together,
   I will catch them.
¹³ Woe to them,
   because they have strayed from me!
Destruction to them,

Walking the Walk

How real is your love for God? Do you still believe in him when things are going bad like you do when things are going great? Is he a major part of your daily life or just someone you think about for an hour or two on Sundays (and maybe Wednesdays)? Are you confident that you know him well, or is he really just more of an acquaintance? One more question: If someone treated you the way you treat God, would you know that person really loved you?

» live the adventure » Hos 7:8–10

battlelines

» Stepping Out? (Divorce)

Q: I heard you had an interesting experience this weekend.
A: I'm not sure I'd call it "interesting." "Strange" is more like it.

Q: What happened?
A: My mom actually went on a date.

Q: Really?
A: Yeah, some guy from where she works. He was nice enough, I guess. It was just weird to see my mom going out with some guy I don't even know.

Q: How long have your parents been divorced?
A: About two years, I guess. At the time, even though I definitely wasn't happy about it, I thought, *All they ever do is fight and yell anyway.* I thought divorce was the only way that we'd ever have any peace in the house.

Q: So has it been more peaceful?
A: We don't have the daily yelling anymore, if that's what you mean. But the tension is still there. Whenever we go see my dad on weekends, my mom gets in a bad mood and makes all these little comments about him. And when we get to my dad's place, he makes sure he takes a few shots back at her.

Q: Sounds tough.
A: Well, I've got friends in situations that are a lot worse. But, yeah, it's a mess. It makes it easy to see why God says he hates divorce. Look at the results. In my opinion, divorce creates more problems than it fixes.

» Breaking Up?

The statement Terrance is referring to is found in Malachi 2:16. Ever wonder why God speaks so forcefully against married couples who call it quits? Because marriage is designed to be a living picture of the kind of intimate relationship the Father, Son and Holy Spirit enjoy, as well as the kind of relationship God wants to have with his people. Walking away destroys that picture. It's also because God knows that divorce almost always creates a heartbreaking mess for those involved.

You can't alter what your parents do or what they've done in the past. However, you *can* determine right now to do the marriage thing right, if marriage is a part of what God has in store for you. It's not too early to prepare yourself for a lasting marriage that honors God and results in great fulfillment.

What traits do you think will be most important when choosing your future mate?

Learn more about living with divorced parents at www.RevolutionBible.com.

because they have rebelled against me!
I long to redeem them
but they speak lies against me.
14 They do not cry out to me from their hearts
but wail upon their beds.
They gather together[a] for grain and new wine
but turn away from me.
15 I trained them and strengthened them,
but they plot evil against me.
16 They do not turn to the Most High;
they are like a faulty bow.
Their leaders will fall by the sword
because of their insolent words.
For this they will be ridiculed
in the land of Egypt.

ISRAEL TO REAP THE WHIRLWIND

8 "Put the trumpet to your lips!
An eagle is over the house of the LORD
because the people have broken my covenant
and rebelled against my law.
2 Israel cries out to me,
'O our God, we acknowledge you!'
3 But Israel has rejected what is good;
an enemy will pursue him.
4 They set up kings without my consent;
they choose princes without my approval.
With their silver and gold
they make idols for themselves
to their own destruction.
5 Throw out your calf-idol, O Samaria!
My anger burns against them.
How long will they be incapable of purity?
6   They are from Israel!
This calf—a craftsman has made it;
it is not God.
It will be broken in pieces,
that calf of Samaria.

7 "They sow the wind
and reap the whirlwind.
The stalk has no head;
it will produce no flour.
Were it to yield grain,
foreigners would swallow it up.
8 Israel is swallowed up;
now she is among the nations
like a worthless thing.
9 For they have gone up to Assyria
like a wild donkey wandering alone.
Ephraim has sold herself to lovers.
10 Although they have sold themselves among the nations,
I will now gather them together.

---

[a] 14 Most Hebrew manuscripts; some Hebrew manuscripts and Septuagint *They slash themselves*

They will begin to waste away
    under the oppression of the mighty king.

11 "Though Ephraim built many altars for sin offerings,
    these have become altars for sinning.
12 I wrote for them the many things of my law,
    but they regarded them as something alien.
13 They offer sacrifices given to me
    and they eat the meat,
but the LORD is not pleased with them.
Now he will remember their wickedness
    and punish their sins:
They will return to Egypt.
14 Israel has forgotten his Maker
    and built palaces;
Judah has fortified many towns.
But I will send fire upon their cities
    that will consume their fortresses."

PUNISHMENT FOR ISRAEL

Do not rejoice, O Israel;
    do not be jubilant like the other nations.
For you have been unfaithful to your God;
    you love the wages of a prostitute
    at every threshing floor.
2 Threshing floors and winepresses will not feed the people;
    the new wine will fail them.
3 They will not remain in the LORD's land;
    Ephraim will return to Egypt
    and eat unclean[a] food in Assyria.
4 They will not pour out wine offerings to the LORD,
    nor will their sacrifices please him.
Such sacrifices will be to them like the bread of mourners;
    all who eat them will be unclean.
This food will be for themselves;
    it will not come into the temple of the LORD.

5 What will you do on the day of your appointed feasts,
    on the festival days of the LORD?
6 Even if they escape from destruction,
    Egypt will gather them,
    and Memphis will bury them.
Their treasures of silver will be taken over by briers,
    and thorns will overrun their tents.
7 The days of punishment are coming,
    the days of reckoning are at hand.
    Let Israel know this.
Because your sins are so many
    and your hostility so great,
the prophet is considered a fool,
    the inspired man a maniac.
8 The prophet, along with my God,
    is the watchman over Ephraim,[b]
yet snares await him on all his paths,
    and hostility in the house of his God.

---

[a] 3 That is, ceremonially unclean   [b] 8 Or The prophet is the watchman over Ephraim, / the people of my God

hosea

VERSUS

» A prophet to Israel
» Commanded by God to marry an immoral woman
» Witnessed the fall of Samaria

company of priests

» Were supposed to point the people to God
» Led people into immorality
» Were more interested in financial gain than holiness

The Main Event

In the final days of the northern kingdom of Israel, things got really bad, spiritually speaking. The entire land was littered with idols and shrines to false gods. Almost everyone in the nation had embraced some kind of pagan religion—including the kind that actually encouraged worshipers to have sex with temple prostitutes! The prevailing attitude seemed to be, "Why just worship the God of Abraham, Isaac and Jacob when all these other erotic religions are available?"

What made the situation even worse is that Israel's priests let it all happen. In fact, many of them participated in the pagan rituals! They were quick to forget about the one true God when money, sex and power were available to them.

As you might imagine, God was ticked and saddened—furious and heartbroken all at once. He sent a prophet named Hosea to his rebellious nation. Not only did God instruct Hosea to speak harsh warnings to the people, he also commanded his prophet to provide Israel with a shocking, living picture of their great sin. God actually directed Hosea to marry a promiscuous woman named Gomer.

Gomer cheated on Hosea like crazy. She hopped in and out of beds (and maybe even had sex with some of Israel's religious leaders). She even became a prostitute and was eventually made a slave. Can you imagine the embarrassment, hurt and disgrace Hosea felt? Wherever he went, people must have talked, pointed and laughed at the fool who had married an adulterous woman.

Hosea must've wept. Yet, led by God, he continued to love and care for his wayward wife. When Gomer hit rock bottom, Hosea showed up—but not to judge or sneer. Because of his love for his wife—and in order to illustrate God's undying devotion to Israel—Hosea purchased Gomer's freedom, took her home as his wife and showed his love to her once again. Amazing!

The Outcome

The prophet Hosea and the idolatrous priests of Israel don't deserve to be mentioned in the same breath. Hosea towers over them as a faithful servant of God—obedient to the Lord's commands and willing to suffer greatly, even when that suffering involved unbelievable personal pain and embarrassment.

The religious leaders Hosea was sent to confront were users. Posers. Fakes. Hypocrites. They had no desire to teach the people the ways of God. Nor did they model what it means to walk with God. They were faithless, disobedient men, eager only for personal pleasure and gain.

You don't have to be a genius to figure out which kind of man God prefers. However, you do have to decide which kind of man you will be.

Read more about Hosea and the company of priests in Hosea 1–4 (pages 1156–1159).

⁹ They have sunk deep into corruption,
    as in the days of Gibeah.
God will remember their wickedness
    and punish them for their sins.

¹⁰ "When I found Israel,
    it was like finding grapes in the desert;
when I saw your fathers,
    it was like seeing the early fruit on the fig tree.
But when they came to Baal Peor,
    they consecrated themselves to that shameful idol
    and became as vile as the thing they loved.
¹¹ Ephraim's glory will fly away like a bird—
    no birth, no pregnancy, no conception.
¹² Even if they rear children,
    I will bereave them of every one.
Woe to them
    when I turn away from them!
¹³ I have seen Ephraim, like Tyre,
    planted in a pleasant place.
But Ephraim will bring out
    their children to the slayer."

¹⁴ Give them, O Lᴏʀᴅ—
    what will you give them?
Give them wombs that miscarry
    and breasts that are dry.

¹⁵ "Because of all their wickedness in Gilgal,
    I hated them there.
Because of their sinful deeds,
    I will drive them out of my house.
I will no longer love them;
    all their leaders are rebellious.
¹⁶ Ephraim is blighted,
    their root is withered,
    they yield no fruit.
Even if they bear children,
    I will slay their cherished offspring."

¹⁷ My God will reject them
    because they have not obeyed him;
    they will be wanderers among the nations.

Israel was a spreading vine;
    he brought forth fruit for himself.
As his fruit increased,
    he built more altars;
as his land prospered,
    he adorned his sacred stones.
² Their heart is deceitful,
    and now they must bear their guilt.
The Lᴏʀᴅ will demolish their altars
    and destroy their sacred stones.

³ Then they will say, "We have no king
    because we did not revere the Lᴏʀᴅ.

But even if we had a king,
 what could he do for us?"
⁴ They make many promises,
 take false oaths
 and make agreements;
therefore lawsuits spring up
 like poisonous weeds in a plowed field.
⁵ The people who live in Samaria fear
 for the calf-idol of Beth Aven. ᵃ
Its people will mourn over it,
 and so will its idolatrous priests,
those who had rejoiced over its splendor,
 because it is taken from them into exile.
⁶ It will be carried to Assyria
 as tribute for the great king.
Ephraim will be disgraced;
 Israel will be ashamed of its wooden idols. ᵇ
⁷ Samaria and its king will float away
 like a twig on the surface of the waters.
⁸ The high places of wickednessᶜ will be destroyed—
 it is the sin of Israel.
Thorns and thistles will grow up
 and cover their altars.
Then they will say to the mountains, "Cover us!"
 and to the hills, "Fall on us!"

⁹ "Since the days of Gibeah, you have sinned, O Israel,
 and there you have remained. ᵈ
Did not war overtake
 the evildoers in Gibeah?
¹⁰ When I please, I will punish them;
 nations will be gathered against them
 to put them in bonds for their double sin.
¹¹ Ephraim is a trained heifer
 that loves to thresh;
so I will put a yoke
 on her fair neck.
I will drive Ephraim,
 Judah must plow,
 and Jacob must break up the ground.
¹² Sow for yourselves righteousness,
 reap the fruit of unfailing love,
and break up your unplowed ground;
 for it is time to seek the LORD,
until he comes
 and showers righteousness on you.
¹³ But you have planted wickedness,
 you have reaped evil,
 you have eaten the fruit of deception.
Because you have depended on your own strength
 and on your many warriors,
¹⁴ the roar of battle will rise against your people,
 so that all your fortresses will be devastated—

ᵃ *5 Beth Aven* means *house of wickedness* (a name for Bethel, which means *house of God*).   ᵇ *6 Or its counsel*   ᶜ *8* Hebrew *aven*, a reference to Beth Aven (a derogatory name for Bethel)   ᵈ *9 Or there a stand was taken*

as Shalman devastated Beth Arbel on the day of battle,
when mothers were dashed to the ground with their children.
15 Thus will it happen to you, O Bethel,
because your wickedness is great.
When that day dawns,
the king of Israel will be completely destroyed.

GOD'S LOVE FOR ISRAEL

11 "When Israel was a child, I loved him,
and out of Egypt I called my son.
2 But the more I a called Israel,
the further they went from me. b
They sacrificed to the Baals
and they burned incense to images.
3 It was I who taught Ephraim to walk,
taking them by the arms;
but they did not realize
it was I who healed them.
4 I led them with cords of human kindness,
with ties of love;
I lifted the yoke from their neck
and bent down to feed them.

NOW OR NEVER

HOS 11:1–11

Have you ever thought about what it means when you call God your Father? How is your relationship with him similar to your relationship with your earthly dad? How is it different? Do you ever find yourself seeing God the same way you view your dad?

---

5 "Will they not return to Egypt
and will not Assyria rule over them
because they refuse to repent?
6 Swords will flash in their cities,
will destroy the bars of their gates
and put an end to their plans.
7 My people are determined to turn from
me.
Even if they call to the Most High,
he will by no means exalt them.

8 "How can I give you up, Ephraim?
How can I hand you over, Israel?
How can I treat you like Admah?
How can I make you like Zeboiim?
My heart is changed within me;
all my compassion is aroused.
9 I will not carry out my fierce anger,
nor will I turn and devastate Ephraim.
For I am God, and not man—
the Holy One among you.
I will not come in wrath. c
10 They will follow the LORD;
he will roar like a lion.
When he roars,
his children will come trembling from the west.
11 They will come trembling
like birds from Egypt,
like doves from Assyria.
I will settle them in their homes,"
declares the LORD.

12

¹²Ephraim has surrounded me with lies,
the house of Israel with deceit.
And Judah is unruly against God,
even against the faithful Holy One.
¹Ephraim feeds on the wind;
he pursues the east wind all day
and multiplies lies and violence.
He makes a treaty with Assyria
and sends olive oil to Egypt.
²The Lord has a charge to bring against Judah;
he will punish Jacobᵃ according to his ways
and repay him according to his deeds.
³In the womb he grasped his brother's heel;
as a man he struggled with God.
⁴He struggled with the angel and
overcame him;
he wept and begged for his favor.
He found him at Bethel
and talked with him there—
⁵the Lord God Almighty,
the Lord is his name of renown!
⁶But you must return to your God;
maintain love and justice,
and wait for your God always.

⁷The merchant uses dishonest scales;
he loves to defraud.
⁸Ephraim boasts,
"I am very rich; I have become wealthy.
With all my wealth they will not find
in me
any iniquity or sin."

⁹"I am the Lord your God,
⌊who brought you⌋ out ofᵇ Egypt;
I will make you live in tents again,
as in the days of your appointed feasts.
¹⁰I spoke to the prophets,
gave them many visions
and told parables through them."

¹¹Is Gilead wicked?
Its people are worthless!
Do they sacrifice bulls in Gilgal?
Their altars will be like piles of stones
on a plowed field.
¹²Jacob fled to the country of Aramᶜ;
Israel served to get a wife,
and to pay for her he tended sheep.
¹³The Lord used a prophet to bring Israel up from Egypt,
by a prophet he cared for him.
¹⁴But Ephraim has bitterly provoked him to anger;
his Lord will leave upon him the guilt of his bloodshed
and will repay him for his contempt.

Keeping Money in Its Place

Money can buy you a sweet house and lots of nice stuff to surround yourself with . . . for about 80 years or so, if you live that long. But 80 years doesn't sound that great when you compare it to eternity. If you let money come between you and God, it'll be like trading a million years of incredible happiness for a few moments of quick thrills.

»» live the adventure »» Hos 12:8

ᵃ *2 Jacob* means *he grasps the heel* (figuratively, *he deceives*). ᵇ *9* Or *God / ever since you were in* ᶜ *12* That is, Northwest Mesopotamia

When Ephraim spoke, men trembled;
    he was exalted in Israel.
But he became guilty of Baal worship and died.
² Now they sin more and more;
    they make idols for themselves from their silver,
cleverly fashioned images,
    all of them the work of craftsmen.
It is said of these people,
    "They offer human sacrifice
    and kiss[a] the calf-idols."
³ Therefore they will be like the morning mist,
    like the early dew that disappears,
    like chaff swirling from a threshing floor,
    like smoke escaping through a window.

⁴ "But I am the LORD your God,
    ⌊who brought you⌋ out of[b] Egypt.
You shall acknowledge no God but me,
    no Savior except me.
⁵ I cared for you in the desert,
    in the land of burning heat.
⁶ When I fed them, they were satisfied;
    when they were satisfied, they became proud;
    then they forgot me.
⁷ So I will come upon them like a lion,
    like a leopard I will lurk by the path.
⁸ Like a bear robbed of her cubs,
    I will attack them and rip them open.
Like a lion I will devour them;
    a wild animal will tear them apart.

⁹ "You are destroyed, O Israel,
    because you are against me, against your helper.
¹⁰ Where is your king, that he may save you?
    Where are your rulers in all your towns,
of whom you said,
    'Give me a king and princes'?
¹¹ So in my anger I gave you a king,
    and in my wrath I took him away.
¹² The guilt of Ephraim is stored up,
    his sins are kept on record.
¹³ Pains as of a woman in childbirth come to him,
    but he is a child without wisdom;
when the time arrives,
    he does not come to the opening of the womb.

¹⁴ "I will ransom them from the power of the grave[c];
    I will redeem them from death.
Where, O death, are your plagues?
    Where, O grave,[c] is your destruction?

"I will have no compassion,
¹⁵   even though he thrives among his brothers.
An east wind from the LORD will come,
    blowing in from the desert;

ᵃ 2 Or "Men who sacrifice / kiss   ᵇ 4 Or God / ever since you were in   ᶜ 14 Hebrew Sheol

his spring will fail
and his well dry up.
His storehouse will be plundered
of all its treasures.
¹⁶ The people of Samaria must bear their guilt,
because they have rebelled against their God.
They will fall by the sword;
their little ones will be dashed to the ground,
their pregnant women ripped open."

REPENTANCE TO BRING BLESSING

14 Return, O Israel, to the LORD your God.
Your sins have been your downfall!
² Take words with you
and return to the LORD.
Say to him:
"Forgive all our sins
and receive us graciously,
that we may offer the fruit of our lips.^a
³ Assyria cannot save us;
we will not mount war-horses.
We will never again say 'Our gods'
to what our own hands have made,
for in you the fatherless find
compassion."

⁴ "I will heal their waywardness
and love them freely,
for my anger has turned away from
them.
⁵ I will be like the dew to Israel;
he will blossom like a lily.
Like a cedar of Lebanon
he will send down his roots;
⁶   his young shoots will grow.
His splendor will be like an olive tree,
his fragrance like a cedar of Lebanon.
⁷ Men will dwell again in his shade.
He will flourish like the grain.
He will blossom like a vine,
and his fame will be like the wine from Lebanon.
⁸ O Ephraim, what more have I^b to do with idols?
I will answer him and care for him.
I am like a green pine tree;
your fruitfulness comes from me."

⁹ Who is wise? He will realize these things.
Who is discerning? He will understand them.
The ways of the LORD are right;
the righteous walk in them,
but the rebellious stumble in them.

Walking in the Ways of the Lord

Think of God's plan for your life as a road map that shows you the perfect route to get from point A to point B. How much sense would it make for you to ignore the map and stumble around blindly, trying to find your own way through the highways and byways of life?

>> live the adventure >> Hos 14:9

---

^a 2 Or offer our lips as sacrifices of bulls   ^b 8 Or What more has Ephraim

« AT A GLANCE

Author
Joel

Audience
The people of Judah

Date
Probably about 835 B.C.

Setting
The people of Judah had become wealthy and complacent. They stopped relying on God and instead worshiped idols.

Verse to Remember
"And everyone who calls on the name of the LORD will be saved; for on Mount Zion and in Jerusalem there will be deliverance, as the LORD has said, among the survivors whom the LORD calls" (2:32).

Theme to Consider
Joel warned the people of Judah that God would judge them by sending a locust plague against them. He urged them to turn to God and repent so they would be saved on the day of judgment.

UNCHANGING TRUTH » Jesus is coming.

You've probably heard that since the day you became a Christian, if not before. Some people talk about Jesus' return like it's something to be excited about. They see it as the ultimate blessing—the start of a perfect life with God. Others—specifically, those who don't know Jesus—would rather not think about his return; for them it's something to dread or fear.

The prophet Joel saw it both ways. When God punished his people with a plague of locusts that wreaked havoc throughout Judah, Joel saw it as a small taste of what the "day of the LORD" would be like for anyone who disobeys God. But for those who humble themselves, repent and seek God's forgiveness, the "day of the LORD" will be an incredible time of blessing—a time when God makes everything new and dwells with his people forever (see Joel 3:17; Revelation 21:3–5).

How do you feel when you think about Jesus' return? Is it something you're anxious, even excited for? It should be, if you've put your trust in Jesus for salvation. At the same time, if you have friends and loved ones who haven't yet accepted Jesus as Lord and Savior, you may be a little nervous about it. You may even feel as though you're racing against the hand of time.

The tricky thing about Jesus' return is that we don't have a timetable for it. It could literally happen at any moment. That's why the best way to prepare for it is with action. Do everything in your power—and God's power—to make sure that you and everyone you know will be ready when the big day comes.

LIFE LESSONS »

1. God can use anything in the natural world—even locusts—to accomplish his work (1:4).

2. Genuine repentance involves much more than simply saying, "I'm sorry" (1:13–14).

3. God is ready and willing to save anyone who calls on his name (2:32).

1

The word of the LORD that came to Joel son of Pethuel.

AN INVASION OF LOCUSTS

2 Hear this, you elders;
    listen, all who live in the land.
Has anything like this ever happened in your days
    or in the days of your forefathers?
3 Tell it to your children,
    and let your children tell it to their
        children,
    and their children to the next
        generation.
4 What the locust swarm has left
    the great locusts have eaten;
what the great locusts have left
    the young locusts have eaten;
what the young locusts have left
    other locusts [a] have eaten.

5 Wake up, you drunkards, and weep!
    Wail, all you drinkers of wine;
wail because of the new wine,
    for it has been snatched from your
        lips.
6 A nation has invaded my land,
    powerful and without number;
it has the teeth of a lion,
    the fangs of a lioness.
7 It has laid waste my vines
    and ruined my fig trees.
It has stripped off their bark
    and thrown it away,
    leaving their branches white.

8 Mourn like a virgin [b] in sackcloth
    grieving for the husband [c] of her
        youth.
9 Grain offerings and drink offerings
    are cut off from the house of the
        LORD.
The priests are in mourning,
    those who minister before the LORD.
10 The fields are ruined,
    the ground is dried up [d];
the grain is destroyed,
    the new wine is dried up,
    the oil fails.
11 Despair, you farmers,
    wail, you vine growers;
grieve for the wheat and the barley,
    because the harvest of the field is destroyed.
12 The vine is dried up
    and the fig tree is withered;

Remembering What God Has Done

Do you think you'll have stories to tell your kids and grandkids about the incredible things you've seen God do? Do you have any stories yet? The prophet Joel commanded the people of Judah to pay close attention to his message; he wanted them to share the story of God's judgment with their children so none of them would forget the difficult lesson they were being taught. Do yourself a favor—start keeping a journal. Develop a habit of writing about what you've seen God do and what you've learned.

»» live the adventure »» Joel 1:3

---

[a] 4 The precise meaning of the four Hebrew words used here for locusts is uncertain.   [b] 8 Or young woman   [c] 8 Or betrothed
[d] 10 Or ground mourns

the pomegranate, the palm and the apple tree—
all the trees of the field—are dried up.
Surely the joy of mankind
is withered away.

A CALL TO REPENTANCE

[13] Put on sackcloth, O priests, and mourn;
wail, you who minister before the altar.

Come, spend the night in sackcloth,
you who minister before my God;
for the grain offerings and drink
offerings
are withheld from the house of your
God.

[14] Declare a holy fast;
call a sacred assembly.
Summon the elders
and all who live in the land
to the house of the LORD your God,
and cry out to the LORD.

NOW OR NEVER
JOEL 1:13

"Don't do _____. It's bad for you." You've probably heard that line a thousand times, right? Hard to believe when you see people around you doing _____ and nothing bad happens to them, right? But check out the mourning and the torture that the Israelites endured—all because of sin.

[15] Alas for that day!
For the day of the LORD is near;
it will come like destruction from the Almighty.[a]

[16] Has not the food been cut off
before our very eyes—
joy and gladness
from the house of our God?
[17] The seeds are shriveled
beneath the clods.[b]
The storehouses are in ruins,
the granaries have been broken down,
for the grain has dried up.
[18] How the cattle moan!
The herds mill about
because they have no pasture;
even the flocks of sheep are suffering.

[19] To you, O LORD, I call,
for fire has devoured the open pastures
and flames have burned up all the trees of the field.
[20] Even the wild animals pant for you;
the streams of water have dried up
and fire has devoured the open pastures.

AN ARMY OF LOCUSTS

2 Blow the trumpet in Zion;
sound the alarm on my holy hill.
Let all who live in the land tremble,
for the day of the LORD is coming.
It is close at hand—
[2] a day of darkness and gloom,
a day of clouds and blackness.
Like dawn spreading across the mountains

---

[a] 15 Hebrew *Shaddai* [b] 17 The meaning of the Hebrew for this word is uncertain.

a large and mighty army comes,
such as never was of old
nor ever will be in ages to come.

³ Before them fire devours,
behind them a flame blazes.
Before them the land is like the garden of Eden,
behind them, a desert waste—
nothing escapes them.
⁴ They have the appearance of horses;
they gallop along like cavalry.
⁵ With a noise like that of chariots
they leap over the mountaintops,
like a crackling fire consuming stubble,
like a mighty army drawn up for battle.

⁶ At the sight of them, nations are in
anguish;
every face turns pale.
⁷ They charge like warriors;
they scale walls like soldiers.
They all march in line,
not swerving from their course.
⁸ They do not jostle each other;
each marches straight ahead.
They plunge through defenses
without breaking ranks.
⁹ They rush upon the city;
they run along the wall.
They climb into the houses;
like thieves they enter through the
windows.

¹⁰ Before them the earth shakes,
the sky trembles,
the sun and moon are darkened,
and the stars no longer shine.
¹¹ The LORD thunders
at the head of his army;
his forces are beyond number,
and mighty are those who obey his
command.
The day of the LORD is great;
it is dreadful.
Who can endure it?

REND YOUR HEART

¹² "Even now," declares the LORD,
"return to me with all your heart,
with fasting and weeping and mourning."

¹³ Rend your heart
and not your garments.
Return to the LORD your God,
for he is gracious and compassionate,
slow to anger and abounding in love,
and he relents from sending calamity.

Dealing With Guilt

»» live the adventure »» Joel 2:12-13

When was the last time you felt really guilty about something? How do you handle it? Are you more likely to swallow your pride and apologize, or do you try to forget about the incident and wait for your guilt to fade away? Obviously, the first option is the better one, especially when the person you hurt is God. Not only will he forgive you, but he'll also take away your nagging guilt—if you let him.

¹⁴Who knows? He may turn and have pity
    and leave behind a blessing—
grain offerings and drink offerings
    for the LORD your God.

¹⁵Blow the trumpet in Zion,
    declare a holy fast,
    call a sacred assembly.
¹⁶Gather the people,
    consecrate the assembly;
bring together the elders,
    gather the children,
    those nursing at the breast.
Let the bridegroom leave his room
    and the bride her chamber.
¹⁷Let the priests, who minister before the LORD,
    weep between the temple porch and the altar.
Let them say, "Spare your people, O LORD.
    Do not make your inheritance an object of scorn,
    a byword among the nations.
Why should they say among the peoples,
    'Where is their God?' "

THE LORD'S ANSWER

¹⁸Then the LORD will be jealous for his land
    and take pity on his people.

¹⁹The LORD will reply ᵃ to them:

"I am sending you grain, new wine and oil,
    enough to satisfy you fully;
never again will I make you
    an object of scorn to the nations.

²⁰"I will drive the northern army far from you,
    pushing it into a parched and barren land,
with its front columns going into the eastern sea ᵇ
    and those in the rear into the western sea. ᶜ
And its stench will go up;
    its smell will rise."

Surely he has done great things. ᵈ
²¹   Be not afraid, O land;
    be glad and rejoice.
Surely the LORD has done great things.
²²   Be not afraid, O wild animals,
    for the open pastures are becoming green.
The trees are bearing their fruit;
    the fig tree and the vine yield their riches.
²³Be glad, O people of Zion,
    rejoice in the LORD your God,
for he has given you
    the autumn rains in righteousness. ᵉ
He sends you abundant showers,
    both autumn and spring rains, as before.

ᵃ *18,19* Or *LORD was jealous . . . / and took pity . . . / ¹⁹The LORD replied*   ᵇ *20* That is, the Dead Sea   ᶜ *20* That is, the Mediterranean
ᵈ *20* Or *rise. / Surely it has done great things."*   ᵉ *23* Or *the teacher for righteousness:*

²⁴ The threshing floors will be filled with grain;
　　the vats will overflow with new wine and oil.

²⁵ "I will repay you for the years the locusts have eaten—
　　the great locust and the young locust,
　　the other locusts and the locust swarm ª—
　　my great army that I sent among you.
²⁶ You will have plenty to eat, until you are full,
　　and you will praise the name of the LORD your God,
　　who has worked wonders for you;
　　never again will my people be shamed.
²⁷ Then you will know that I am in Israel,
　　that I am the LORD your God,
　　and that there is no other;
　　never again will my people be shamed.

THE DAY OF THE LORD

²⁸ "And afterward,
　　I will pour out my Spirit on all people.
　Your sons and daughters will prophesy,
　　your old men will dream dreams,
　　your young men will see visions.
²⁹ Even on my servants, both men and women,
　　I will pour out my Spirit in those days.
³⁰ I will show wonders in the heavens
　　and on the earth,
　　blood and fire and billows of smoke.
³¹ The sun will be turned to darkness
　　and the moon to blood

before the coming of the
great and dreadful
day of the LORD.
³² And everyone who calls
on the name of the LORD
will be saved;
for on Mount Zion and in
Jerusalem
there will be deliverance,
as the LORD has said,
among the survivors
whom the LORD calls.

challengenotes

To: **my_son**

heavenly_father: the day is coming when it will be too late to turn to me. before that day arrives, though, anyone who calls on me will be saved. that's news your unbelieving friends and loved ones desperately need to hear. will you be the one to tell them?

THE NATIONS JUDGED

"In those days and at that time,
　　when I restore the fortunes of Judah and Jerusalem,
² I will gather all nations
　　and bring them down to the Valley of Jehoshaphat.ᵇ
There I will enter into judgment against them
　　concerning my inheritance, my people Israel,
for they scattered my people among the nations
　　and divided up my land.
³ They cast lots for my people
　　and traded boys for prostitutes;

ª 25 The precise meaning of the four Hebrew words used here for locusts is uncertain.　　ᵇ 2 Jehoshaphat means the LORD judges; also in verse 12.

battlelines

» Not Normal (Spiritual Growth)

Q: How long have you been a Christian, Philip?
A: Let's see, I'm fifteen now, so . . . about nine years.

Q: Really? Nine years?
A: Yep.

Q: What have been some of the biggest changes Christ has made in your life?
A: Changes?

Q: Yeah, you know. How has Jesus made a difference in your attitudes, actions, values—stuff like that?
A: I don't know. I guess I could say that because of him I don't get drunk or go to wild parties.

Q: What about things like joy and peace?
A: What about them?

Q: Would you say you're a joyful person?
A: Joyful?

Q: Yeah.
A: No, not really.

Q: Do you worry a lot?
A: My friends think I do.

Q: So on a scale of one to ten, how much would you say you've grown in your faith over the last two or three years?
A: I could lie and give myself a seven. But the truth is, it's more like . . . a two.

» Healthy Things Grow

When a new baby doesn't grow, the child's parents and doctor get alarmed. Why? Because healthy things grow. That's the way the world works. No growth equals poor health. The same principle applies to your relationship with God. Consider this passage, which was written to a church full of stagnant believers: "Brothers, I could not address you as spiritual but as worldly—mere infants in Christ. I gave you milk, not solid food, for you were not yet ready for it. Indeed, you are still not ready. You are still worldly" (1 Corinthians 3:1–3).

Would you think it was weird if a guy at your school was still acting like he did in kindergarten? Is it any less strange when followers of Jesus act no differently than they did before putting their trust in God? God wants his children to grow in unity, love, faith and obedience.

Learn more about growing as a Christian at www.RevolutionBible.com.

they sold girls for wine
that they might drink.

4 "Now what have you against me, O Tyre and Sidon and all you regions of Philistia? Are you repaying me for something I have done? If you are paying me back, I will swiftly and speedily return on your own heads what you have done. 5 For you took my silver and my gold and carried off my finest treasures to your temples. 6 You sold the people of Judah and Jerusalem to the Greeks, that you might send them far from their homeland.

7 "See, I am going to rouse them out of the places to which you sold them, and I will return on your own heads what you have done. 8 I will sell your sons and daughters to the people of Judah, and they will sell them to the Sabeans, a nation far away." The Lord has spoken.

now or never

JOEL 3:16

If the pressures of your daily life get to be too much for you, ask God to give you refuge—a quiet place of safety with him. He can see you through all of life's challenges.

9 Proclaim this among the nations:
Prepare for war!
Rouse the warriors!
Let all the fighting men draw near
and attack.
10 Beat your plowshares into swords
and your pruning hooks into spears.
Let the weakling say,
"I am strong!"
11 Come quickly, all you nations from
every side,
and assemble there.

Bring down your warriors, O Lord!

12 "Let the nations be roused;
let them advance into the Valley of Jehoshaphat,
for there I will sit
to judge all the nations on every side.
13 Swing the sickle,
for the harvest is ripe.
Come, trample the grapes,
for the winepress is full
and the vats overflow—
so great is their wickedness!"

14 Multitudes, multitudes
in the valley of decision!
For the day of the Lord is near
in the valley of decision.
15 The sun and moon will be darkened,
and the stars no longer shine.
16 The Lord will roar from Zion
and thunder from Jerusalem;
the earth and the sky will tremble.
But the Lord will be a refuge for his people,
a stronghold for the people of Israel.

BLESSINGS FOR GOD'S PEOPLE

17 "Then you will know that I, the Lord your God,
dwell in Zion, my holy hill.
Jerusalem will be holy;
never again will foreigners invade her.

18 "In that day the mountains will drip new wine,
and the hills will flow with milk;

all the ravines of Judah will run with water.
A fountain will flow out of the Lord's house
    and will water the valley of acacias. [a]
19 But Egypt will be desolate,
    Edom a desert waste,
because of violence done to the people of Judah,
    in whose land they shed innocent blood.
20 Judah will be inhabited forever
    and Jerusalem through all generations.
21 Their bloodguilt, which I have not pardoned,
    I will pardon."

The Lord dwells in Zion!

---

[a] 18 Or *Valley of Shittim*

AMOS

« AT A GLANCE

Author
Amos, a shepherd and fig-grower from Tekoa in Judah

Audience
The northern kingdom of Israel

Date
About 760–750 B.C.

Setting
Some wealthy people in Israel were oppressing the poor. The Assyrians were about to conquer Israel, and the wealthy Israelites would then become their slaves.

Verses to Remember
Hear this word the Lord has spoken against you, O people of Israel—against the whole family I brought up out of Egypt: "You only have I chosen of all the families of the earth; therefore I will punish you for all your sins" (3:1–2).

Theme to Consider
Amos prophesied God's judgment on Israel for their sins of idolatry and oppression of the poor.

UNCHANGING TRUTH » When was the last time you complained about something being unfair? If you're like most of us, it probably had to do with something that happened (or didn't happen) to *you*. Injustices are easy to spot when *you're* the one who's being treated unfairly. They're not nearly as obvious, though, when other people are the ones getting the short end of the stick.

What about the poor and needy people in your community? Do you think it's fair that they have so little when so many others have so much?

What do you think should be done for . . .

- single mothers who have no one to watch their kids while they work?
- inner city kids who can't play outside because of gang violence?
- elderly people who can't afford to buy the medication they need?
- parents in third-world countries who helplessly watch their children starve to death?
- innocent people who have been wrongly convicted of crimes because they couldn't afford a good lawyer?
- homeless people who have no place to go when the weather gets brutal?

If you answered some of these questions with an "I don't know," that's OK. There aren't a lot of easy solutions when it comes to making sure that life is fair for others. Thinking about the problems is a necessary first step though. Many people choose to ignore them altogether, which only makes things worse.

God certainly doesn't ignore these problems. He's very concerned about people who are overlooked and treated unfairly in this world. And he's looking for Christians with the guts to stand up for them, get involved in their lives and give them a hand.

Amos warned the people of Israel that God judges those who overlook the poor and needy. That warning still applies to us today—especially to the few of us that have so much in comparison to the many who have so little.

LIFE LESSONS »

1. God judges people based on the way they treat the poor and needy (5:11–13).

2. Rituals and traditions by themselves mean nothing to God. If your worship isn't sincere, don't bother giving it to the Lord (5:21–23).

3. God has complete control over nature. All of creation is under his power (9:5–6).

1 The words of Amos, one of the shepherds of Tekoa—what he saw concerning Israel two years before the earthquake, when Uzziah was king of Judah and Jeroboam son of Jehoash[a] was king of Israel.

²He said:

> "The LORD roars from Zion
>   and thunders from Jerusalem;
> the pastures of the shepherds dry up,[b]
>   and the top of Carmel withers."

JUDGMENT ON ISRAEL'S NEIGHBORS

³This is what the LORD says:

> "For three sins of Damascus,
>   even for four, I will not turn back ⌐my wrath⌐.
> Because she threshed Gilead
>   with sledges having iron teeth,
> ⁴I will send fire upon the house of Hazael
>   that will consume the fortresses of
>   Ben-Hadad.
> ⁵I will break down the gate of Damascus;
>   I will destroy the king who is in[c] the
>   Valley of Aven[d]
> and the one who holds the scepter in
>   Beth Eden.
> The people of Aram will go into exile
>   to Kir,"
>
> says the LORD.

⁶This is what the LORD says:

> "For three sins of Gaza,
>   even for four, I will not turn back ⌐my
>   wrath⌐.
> Because she took captive whole
>   communities
>   and sold them to Edom,
> ⁷I will send fire upon the walls of Gaza
>   that will consume her fortresses.
> ⁸I will destroy the king[e] of Ashdod
>   and the one who holds the scepter in
>   Ashkelon.
> I will turn my hand against Ekron,
>   till the last of the Philistines is dead,"
>   says the Sovereign LORD.

⁹This is what the LORD says:

> "For three sins of Tyre,
>   even for four, I will not turn back ⌐my wrath⌐.
> Because she sold whole communities of captives to Edom,
>   disregarding a treaty of brotherhood,
> ¹⁰I will send fire upon the walls of Tyre
>   that will consume her fortresses."

¹¹This is what the LORD says:

Showing Loyalty

Do you consider yourself a loyal person? How far does your loyalty stretch? Would you stay loyal to a friend who . . . blew off your birthday party . . . revealed an embarrassing secret about you that he swore he would never tell . . . made a crude joke about your sister . . . went out with your girlfriend behind your back? If you did remain loyal to a friend—even under extreme conditions—what message do you think that would send to him and the people who know you?

"For three sins of Edom,
　　even for four, I will not turn back ⌐my wrath⌐.
Because he pursued his brother with a sword,
　　stifling all compassion, ª
because his anger raged continually
　　and his fury flamed unchecked,
¹²I will send fire upon Teman
　　that will consume the fortresses of Bozrah."

¹³This is what the LORD says:

"For three sins of Ammon,
　　even for four, I will not turn back ⌐my wrath⌐.
Because he ripped open the pregnant women of Gilead
　　in order to extend his borders,
¹⁴I will set fire to the walls of Rabbah
　　that will consume her fortresses
amid war cries on the day of battle,
　　amid violent winds on a stormy day.
¹⁵Her kingᵇ will go into exile,
　　he and his officials together,"

　　　　　　　　　　　　　　　　　　　　　　　says the LORD.

 This is what the LORD says:

"For three sins of Moab,
　　even for four, I will not turn back ⌐my wrath⌐.
Because he burned, as if to lime,
　　the bones of Edom's king,
²I will send fire upon Moab
　　that will consume the fortresses of Kerioth. ᶜ
Moab will go down in great tumult
　　amid war cries and the blast of the trumpet.
³I will destroy her ruler
　　and kill all her officials with him,"

　　　　　　　　　　　　　　　　　　　　　　　says the LORD.

⁴This is what the LORD says:

"For three sins of Judah,
　　even for four, I will not turn back ⌐my wrath⌐.
Because they have rejected the law of the LORD
　　and have not kept his decrees,
because they have been led astray by false gods, ᵈ
　　the godsᵉ their ancestors followed,
⁵I will send fire upon Judah
　　that will consume the fortresses of Jerusalem."

JUDGMENT ON ISRAEL

⁶This is what the LORD says:

"For three sins of Israel,
　　even for four, I will not turn back ⌐my wrath⌐.
They sell the righteous for silver,
　　and the needy for a pair of sandals.
⁷They trample on the heads of the poor
　　as upon the dust of the ground

ª 11 Or sword / and destroyed his allies　　ᵇ 15 Or / Molech; Hebrew malcam　　ᶜ 2 Or of her cities　　ᵈ 4 Or by lies　　ᵉ 4 Or lies

and deny justice to the oppressed.
Father and son use the same girl
and so profane my holy name.
⁸ They lie down beside every altar
on garments taken in pledge.
In the house of their god
they drink wine taken as fines.

⁹ "I destroyed the Amorite before them,
though he was tall as the cedars
and strong as the oaks.
I destroyed his fruit above
and his roots below.

¹⁰ "I brought you up out of Egypt,
and I led you forty years in the desert
to give you the land of the Amorites.

¹¹ I also raised up prophets from among your sons
and Nazirites from among your young men.
Is this not true, people of Israel?"
declares the LORD.
¹² "But you made the Nazirites drink wine
and commanded the prophets not to
prophesy.

¹³ "Now then, I will crush you
as a cart crushes when loaded with
grain.
¹⁴ The swift will not escape,
the strong will not muster their
strength,
and the warrior will not save his life.
¹⁵ The archer will not stand his ground,
the fleet-footed soldier will not get
away,
and the horseman will not save his
life.
¹⁶ Even the bravest warriors
will flee naked on that day,"
declares the LORD.

NOW OR NEVER
AM 2:14–16

The Israelites were God's chosen people,
his favored nation. Yet even they had to
pay for their sins. No one is above God's
judgment.

WITNESSES SUMMONED AGAINST ISRAEL

3 Hear this word the LORD has spoken against you, O
people of Israel—against the whole family I brought
up out of Egypt:

² "You only have I chosen
of all the families of the earth;
therefore I will punish you
for all your sins."

³ Do two walk together
unless they have agreed to do so?
⁴ Does a lion roar in the thicket
when he has no prey?
Does he growl in his den
when he has caught nothing?

Appreciating God's Justice

On the one hand, God's judgment is pretty scary to consider—especially if you have friends and loved ones who aren't Christians. On the other hand, it's comforting to know that God sees and remembers every evil thing that happens. Nothing gets past him. The things that no one else seems to notice—the secret sins, the lies that destroy lives—God notices and despises.

»» live the adventure »» Am 2:15-16

⁵Does a bird fall into a trap on the ground
   where no snare has been set?
Does a trap spring up from the earth
   when there is nothing to catch?
⁶When a trumpet sounds in a city,
   do not the people tremble?
When disaster comes to a city,
   has not the Lᴏʀᴅ caused it?

⁷Surely the Sovereign Lᴏʀᴅ does nothing
   without revealing his plan
   to his servants the prophets.

⁸The lion has roared—
   who will not fear?
The Sovereign Lᴏʀᴅ has spoken—
   who can but prophesy?

⁹Proclaim to the fortresses of Ashdod
   and to the fortresses of Egypt:
"Assemble yourselves on the mountains of Samaria;
   see the great unrest within her
   and the oppression among her people."

¹⁰"They do not know how to do right," declares the Lᴏʀᴅ,
   "who hoard plunder and loot in their fortresses."

¹¹Therefore this is what the Sovereign Lᴏʀᴅ says:

"An enemy will overrun the land;
   he will pull down your strongholds
   and plunder your fortresses."

¹²This is what the Lᴏʀᴅ says:

"As a shepherd saves from the lion's mouth
   only two leg bones or a piece of an ear,
so will the Israelites be saved,
those who sit in Samaria
   on the edge of their beds
   and in Damascus on their couches. ᵃ"

¹³"Hear this and testify against the house of Jacob," declares the Lord, the Lᴏʀᴅ God Almighty.

¹⁴"On the day I punish Israel for her sins,
   I will destroy the altars of Bethel;
the horns of the altar will be cut off
   and fall to the ground.
¹⁵I will tear down the winter house
   along with the summer house;
the houses adorned with ivory will be destroyed
   and the mansions will be demolished,"

                                declares the Lᴏʀᴅ.

ISRAEL HAS NOT RETURNED TO GOD

4 Hear this word, you cows of Bashan on Mount Samaria,
   you women who oppress the poor and crush the needy
   and say to your husbands, "Bring us some drinks!"
²The Sovereign Lᴏʀᴅ has sworn by his holiness:

ᵃ *12* The meaning of the Hebrew for this line is uncertain.

"The time will surely come
when you will be taken away with hooks,
the last of you with fishhooks.
³ You will each go straight out
through breaks in the wall,
and you will be cast out toward
Harmon,ᵃ"

declares the LORD.

⁴ "Go to Bethel and sin;
go to Gilgal and sin yet more.
Bring your sacrifices every morning,
your tithes every three years.ᵇ
⁵ Burn leavened bread as a thank offering
and brag about your freewill
offerings—
boast about them, you Israelites,
for this is what you love to do,"

declares the Sovereign LORD.

NOW OR NEVER

AM 4:1–2

Have you ever been guilty of taking advantage of someone else in order to get something you wanted? Did you apologize for it—not just to God, but to the person you took advantage of?

⁶ "I gave you empty stomachsᶜ in every city
and lack of bread in every town,
yet you have not returned to me,"

declares the LORD.

⁷ "I also withheld rain from you
when the harvest was still three months away.
I sent rain on one town,
but withheld it from another.
One field had rain;
another had none and dried up.
⁸ People staggered from town to town for water
but did not get enough to drink,
yet you have not returned to me,"

declares the LORD.

challengenotes

To: my_son

heavenly_father: your faithfulness and obedience mean so much to me that I will go to great lengths to get them. if that means holding back some of the good things in your life to get your attention, then don't be surprised. besides, in the end, you'll be glad I did.

AM 4:7–9

⁹ "Many times I struck your
gardens and
vineyards,
I struck them with blight
and mildew.
Locusts devoured your fig and
olive trees,
yet you have not returned to
me,"
declares the LORD.

¹⁰ "I sent plagues among you
as I did to Egypt.
I killed your young men with the sword,
along with your captured horses.
I filled your nostrils with the stench of your camps,
yet you have not returned to me,"

declares the LORD.

ᵃ 3 Masoretic Text; with a different word division of the Hebrew (see Septuagint) *out, O mountain of oppression*   ᵇ 4 Or *tithes on the third day*   ᶜ 6 Hebrew *you cleanness of teeth*

[11] "I overthrew some of you
  as I[a] overthrew Sodom and Gomorrah.
You were like a burning stick snatched from the fire,
  yet you have not returned to me,"

declares the LORD.

[12] "Therefore this is what I will do to you, Israel,
  and because I will do this to you,
  prepare to meet your God, O Israel."

[13] He who forms the mountains,
  creates the wind,
  and reveals his thoughts to man,
he who turns dawn to darkness,
  and treads the high places of the earth—
  the LORD God Almighty is his name.

A LAMENT AND CALL TO REPENTANCE

5 Hear this word, O house of Israel, this lament I take up concerning you:

[2] "Fallen is Virgin Israel,
  never to rise again,
  deserted in her own land,
  with no one to lift her up."

[3] This is what the Sovereign LORD says:

"The city that marches out a thousand strong for Israel
  will have only a hundred left;
the town that marches out a hundred strong
  will have only ten left."

[4] This is what the LORD says to the house of Israel:

"Seek me and live;
[5] do not seek Bethel,
  do not go to Gilgal,
  do not journey to Beersheba.
For Gilgal will surely go into exile,
  and Bethel will be reduced to nothing.[b]"
[6] Seek the LORD and live,
  or he will sweep through the house
    of Joseph like a fire;
it will devour,
  and Bethel will have no one to
    quench it.

[7] You who turn justice into bitterness
  and cast righteousness to the ground
[8] (he who made the Pleiades and Orion,
  who turns blackness into dawn
  and darkens day into night,
who calls for the waters of the sea
  and pours them out over the face of the land—
  the LORD is his name—
[9] he flashes destruction on the stronghold
  and brings the fortified city to ruin),

NOW OR NEVER

AM 5:7–13

What's good about the way our nation treats poor and needy people? What areas need serious improvement? How do you fit in the bigger picture? What can you do to help?

---

[a] 11 Hebrew *God*   [b] 5 Or *grief*; or *wickedness*; Hebrew *aven*, a reference to Beth Aven (a derogatory name for Bethel)

¹⁰ you hate the one who reproves in court
and despise him who tells the truth.

¹¹ You trample on the poor
and force him to give you grain.
Therefore, though you have built stone mansions,
you will not live in them;
though you have planted lush vineyards,
you will not drink their wine.
¹² For I know how many are your offenses
and how great your sins.

You oppress the righteous and take bribes
and you deprive the poor of justice in the courts.
¹³ Therefore the prudent man keeps quiet in such times,
for the times are evil.

¹⁴ Seek good, not evil,
that you may live.
Then the Lord God Almighty will be with you,
just as you say he is.
¹⁵ Hate evil, love good;
maintain justice in the courts.
Perhaps the Lord God Almighty will have mercy
on the remnant of Joseph.

¹⁶ Therefore this is what the Lord, the Lord God Almighty, says:

"There will be wailing in all the streets
and cries of anguish in every public square.
The farmers will be summoned to weep
and the mourners to wail.
¹⁷ There will be wailing in all the vineyards,
for I will pass through your midst,"

says the Lord.

THE DAY OF THE LORD

¹⁸ Woe to you who long
for the day of the Lord!
Why do you long for the day of the Lord?
That day will be darkness, not light.
¹⁹ It will be as though a man fled from a lion
only to meet a bear,
as though he entered his house
and rested his hand on the wall
only to have a snake bite him.
²⁰ Will not the day of the Lord be darkness, not light—
pitch-dark, without a ray of brightness?

²¹ "I hate, I despise your religious feasts;
I cannot stand your assemblies.
²² Even though you bring me burnt offerings and grain offerings,
I will not accept them.
Though you bring choice fellowship offerings, ^a
I will have no regard for them.
²³ Away with the noise of your songs!
I will not listen to the music of your harps.

---

^a 22 Traditionally *peace offerings*

²⁴But let justice roll on like a river,
        righteousness like a never-failing stream!

²⁵"Did you bring me sacrifices and offerings
        forty years in the desert, O house of Israel?
²⁶You have lifted up the shrine of your king,
        the pedestal of your idols,
        the star of your god ͣ—
    which you made for yourselves.
²⁷Therefore I will send you into exile beyond Damascus,"
        says the LORD, whose name is God Almighty.

WOE TO THE COMPLACENT

Woe to you who are complacent in Zion,
        and to you who feel secure on Mount Samaria,
    you notable men of the foremost nation,
        to whom the people of Israel come!
²Go to Calneh and look at it;
        go from there to great Hamath,
        and then go down to Gath in Philistia.
    Are they better off than your two kingdoms?
        Is their land larger than yours?
³You put off the evil day
        and bring near a reign of terror.
⁴You lie on beds inlaid with ivory
        and lounge on your couches.
    You dine on choice lambs
        and fattened calves.
⁵You strum away on your harps like David
        and improvise on musical instruments.
⁶You drink wine by the bowlful
        and use the finest lotions,
        but you do not grieve over the ruin of Joseph.
⁷Therefore you will be among the first to go into exile;
        your feasting and lounging will end.

THE LORD ABHORS THE PRIDE OF ISRAEL

⁸The Sovereign LORD has sworn by himself—the LORD God Almighty declares:

    "I abhor the pride of Jacob
        and detest his fortresses;
    I will deliver up the city
        and everything in it."

⁹If ten men are left in one house, they too will die. ¹⁰And if a relative who is to burn the bodies comes to carry them out of the house and asks anyone still hiding there, "Is anyone with you?" and he says, "No," then he will say, "Hush! We must not mention the name of the LORD."

    ¹¹For the LORD has given the command,
        and he will smash the great house into pieces
        and the small house into bits.

    ¹²Do horses run on the rocky crags?
        Does one plow there with oxen?
    But you have turned justice into poison

ͣ 26 Or lifted up Sakkuth your king / and Kaiwan your idols, / your star-gods; Septuagint lifted up the shrine of Molech / and the star of your god Rephan, / their idols

battlelines

» Gutter Mouth (Swearing)

[Wes is telling a story about going to the mall with his friends. Without even knowing it, he swears several times.]

Q: Dude, do you kiss your girlfriend with that mouth?
A: What?

Q: Do you realize that just about every other word out of your mouth is a swear word?
A: Whatever. That's not true.

Q: Dude, I'm telling you. If I had a tape recorder, I could prove it to you.
A: Yeah, well, so what? They're just words. I don't mean anything by them. Besides, everybody talks that way.

Q: Not everybody talks that way.
A: OK, not *everybody*. But you know what I mean.

Q: Do you think talking like that is really necessary?
A: Sometimes it is.

Q: All right, let me ask you this: Do you think that kind of talk honors God? I mean, you claim to be a Christian.
A: Aw, don't go getting all "holy" on me.

Q: I'm not. Look, sometimes I slip too. I'm not perfect. But you have to admit, when some people hear you talk like that, they're going to question whether Jesus really makes a difference in your life.
A: Well, I guess. I've never thought of it like that.

» What's It Gonna Be?

The apostle James thought it was ironic that we use the same mouth to praise God one minute and to curse others the next. His conclusion? "My brothers, this should not be" (James 3:10). James understood that the words that pour out of your mouth are a good indicator of what's inside.

The apostle Paul put it this way: "But among you there must not be even a hint of sexual immorality, or of any kind of impurity, or of greed, because these are improper for God's holy people. Nor should there be obscenity, foolish talk or coarse joking, which are out of place, but rather thanksgiving" (Ephesians 5:3-4).

What's coming out of *your* mouth? Need a little oral cleansing? If so, you'd better start with your heart (see Matthew 15:18).

Does the language you use need a makeover? Read more at www.RevolutionBible.com.

and the fruit of righteousness into bitterness—
¹³you who rejoice in the conquest of Lo Debar ᵃ
and say, "Did we not take Karnaim ᵇ by our own strength?"

¹⁴For the Lord God Almighty declares,
"I will stir up a nation against you, O house of Israel,
that will oppress you all the way
from Lebo ᶜ Hamath to the valley of the Arabah."

LOCUSTS, FIRE AND A PLUMB LINE

7 This is what the Sovereign Lord showed me: He was preparing swarms of locusts after the king's share had been harvested and just as the second crop was coming up. ²When they had stripped the land clean, I cried out, "Sovereign Lord, forgive! How can Jacob survive? He is so small!"

³So the Lord relented.

"This will not happen," the Lord said.

⁴This is what the Sovereign Lord showed me: The Sovereign Lord was calling for judgment by fire; it dried up the great deep and devoured the land. ⁵Then I cried out, "Sovereign Lord, I beg you, stop! How can Jacob survive? He is so small!"

⁶So the Lord relented.

"This will not happen either," the Sovereign Lord said.

⁷This is what he showed me: The Lord was standing by a wall that had been built true to plumb, with a plumb line in his hand. ⁸And the Lord asked me, "What do you see, Amos?"

"A plumb line," I replied.

Then the Lord said, "Look, I am setting a plumb line among my people Israel; I will spare them no longer.

⁹ "The high places of Isaac will be
destroyed
and the sanctuaries of Israel will be
ruined;
with my sword I will rise against the
house of Jeroboam."

AMOS AND AMAZIAH

¹⁰Then Amaziah the priest of Bethel sent a message to Jeroboam king of Israel: "Amos is raising a conspiracy against you in the very heart of Israel. The land cannot bear all his words. ¹¹For this is what Amos is saying:

" 'Jeroboam will die by the sword,
and Israel will surely go into exile,
away from their native land.' "

¹²Then Amaziah said to Amos, "Get out, you seer! Go back to the land of Judah. Earn your bread there and do your prophesying there. ¹³Don't prophesy anymore at Bethel, because this is the king's sanctuary and the temple of the kingdom."

¹⁴Amos answered Amaziah, "I was neither a prophet nor a prophet's son, but I was a shepherd, and I also took care of sycamore-fig trees. ¹⁵But the Lord took me from tending the flock and said to me, 'Go, prophesy to my people Israel.' ¹⁶Now then, hear the word of the Lord. You say,

" 'Do not prophesy against Israel,
and stop preaching against the house of Isaac.'

Recognizing Your Potential

Amos was a quiet farmer and shepherd when God called him to deliver one of the most important messages in Israel's history. You can bet that more than once Amos wondered, *Why me?* But he didn't let his uncertainty or insecurity get in the way of his faithfulness. Amos simply did everything God told him to do. Remember Amos's example the next time you face a God-sized challenge that intimidates you.

»» live the adventure »» Am 7:14-15

ᵃ *13 Lo Debar* means *nothing.* ᵇ *13 Karnaim* means *horns; horn* here symbolizes strength. ᶜ *14* Or *from the entrance to*

¹⁷"Therefore this is what the LORD says:

> " 'Your wife will become a prostitute in the city,
>> and your sons and daughters will fall by the sword.
> Your land will be measured and divided up,
>> and you yourself will die in a pagan^a country.
> And Israel will certainly go into exile,
>> away from their native land.' "

A BASKET OF RIPE FRUIT

8 This is what the Sovereign LORD showed me: a basket of ripe fruit. ²"What do you see, Amos?" he asked.

"A basket of ripe fruit," I answered.

Then the LORD said to me, "The time is ripe for my people Israel; I will spare them no longer.

³"In that day," declares the Sovereign LORD, "the songs in the temple will turn to wailing.^b Many, many bodies—flung everywhere! Silence!"

> ⁴Hear this, you who trample the needy
>> and do away with the poor of the land,

⁵saying,

> "When will the New Moon be over
>> that we may sell grain,
> and the Sabbath be ended
>> that we may market wheat?"—
> skimping the measure,
>> boosting the price
>> and cheating with dishonest scales,
> ⁶buying the poor with silver
>> and the needy for a pair of sandals,
>> selling even the sweepings with the wheat.

⁷The LORD has sworn by the Pride of Jacob: "I will never forget anything they have done.

> ⁸"Will not the land tremble for this,
>> and all who live in it mourn?
> The whole land will rise like the Nile;
>> it will be stirred up and then sink
>> like the river of Egypt.

⁹"In that day," declares the Sovereign LORD,

> "I will make the sun go down at noon
>> and darken the earth in broad daylight.
> ¹⁰I will turn your religious feasts into mourning
>> and all your singing into weeping.
> I will make all of you wear sackcloth
>> and shave your heads.
> I will make that time like mourning for an only son
>> and the end of it like a bitter day.

> ¹¹"The days are coming," declares the Sovereign LORD,
>> "when I will send a famine through the land—
> not a famine of food or a thirst for water,
>> but a famine of hearing the words of the LORD.
> ¹²Men will stagger from sea to sea
>> and wander from north to east,

^a 17 Hebrew an unclean   ^b 3 Or "the temple singers will wail"

searching for the word of the LORD,
    but they will not find it.

13 "In that day

    "the lovely young women and strong young men
        will faint because of thirst.
14 They who swear by the shame[a] of Samaria,
    or say, 'As surely as your god lives, O Dan,'
    or, 'As surely as the god[b] of Beersheba lives'—
they will fall,
    never to rise again."

ISRAEL TO BE DESTROYED

9 I saw the Lord standing by the altar, and he said:

    "Strike the tops of the pillars
        so that the thresholds shake.
Bring them down on the heads of all the people;
    those who are left I will kill with the sword.
Not one will get away,
    none will escape.
2 Though they dig down to the depths of the grave,[c]
    from there my hand will take them.
Though they climb up to the heavens,
    from there I will bring them down.
3 Though they hide themselves on the top of Carmel,
    there I will hunt them down and seize them.
Though they hide from me at the bottom of the sea,
    there I will command the serpent to bite them.
4 Though they are driven into exile by their enemies,
    there I will command the sword to slay them.
I will fix my eyes upon them
    for evil and not for good."

5 The Lord, the LORD Almighty,
    he who touches the earth and it melts,
    and all who live in it mourn—
the whole land rises like the Nile,
    then sinks like the river of Egypt—
6 he who builds his lofty palace[d] in the heavens
    and sets its foundation[e] on the earth,
who calls for the waters of the sea
    and pours them out over the face of the land—
    the LORD is his name.

7 "Are not you Israelites
    the same to me as the Cushites[f]?"

        declares the LORD.

    "Did I not bring Israel up from Egypt,
        the Philistines from Caphtor[g]
        and the Arameans from Kir?

8 "Surely the eyes of the Sovereign LORD
        are on the sinful kingdom.

---

a 14 Or *by Ashima*; or *by the idol*   b 14 Or *power*   c 2 Hebrew *to Sheol*   d 6 The meaning of the Hebrew for this phrase is uncertain.   e 6 The meaning of the Hebrew for this word is uncertain.   f 7 That is, people from the upper Nile region   g 7 That is, Crete

I will destroy it
  from the face of the earth—
yet I will not totally destroy
  the house of Jacob,"

          declares the LORD.

9 "For I will give the command,
  and I will shake the house of Israel
  among all the nations
as grain is shaken in a sieve,
  and not a pebble will reach the ground.
10 All the sinners among my people
  will die by the sword,
all those who say,
  'Disaster will not overtake or meet us.'

ISRAEL'S RESTORATION

11 "In that day I will restore
  David's fallen tent.
I will repair its broken places,
  restore its ruins,
  and build it as it used to be,

12 so that they may possess the remnant of
  Edom
  and all the nations that bear my
  name,[a]"

        declares the LORD,
      who will do these things.

13 "The days are coming," declares the LORD,

"when the reaper will be overtaken by
  the plowman
and the planter by the one treading
  grapes.
New wine will drip from the mountains
  and flow from all the hills.
14 I will bring back my exiled[b] people Israel;
  they will rebuild the ruined cities and live in them.
They will plant vineyards and drink their wine;
  they will make gardens and eat their fruit.
15 I will plant Israel in their own land,
  never again to be uprooted
  from the land I have given them,"

        says the LORD your God.

NOW OR NEVER

AM 9:9–15

God's judgment is like nasty-tasting medicine; it's hard to take sometimes, but it keeps you healthy and vital, protecting you against spiritual illness.

---

[a] 12 Hebrew; Septuagint *so that the remnant of men / and all the nations that bear my name may seek the Lord;*   [b] 14 Or *will restore the fortunes of my*

OBADIAH

Author
Obadiah

Audience
The Edomites and the Jews in Judah

Date
Probably during the Babylonian attacks on Jerusalem (605–586 B.C.)

Setting
The Edomites, who were descendants of Esau and related to the Israelites, had constantly harassed the people of Israel. Centuries earlier they had refused to allow the Israelites to pass through their land as the Israelites journeyed to Canaan. Now the Edomites had taken advantage of Judah's defeat and misfortune.

Verse to Remember
"Because of the violence against your brother Jacob, you will be covered with shame; you will be destroyed forever" (10).

Theme to Consider
God will judge those who oppress his people. Obadiah prophesied the destruction of Edom because of the Edomites' cruelty toward the people of Judah.

UNCHANGING TRUTH » One of the weird side effects of seeing someone else suffer is the temptation to start feeling secure in yourself by entertaining thoughts like, *Better him than me*, or even, *She had it coming*. If you really let temptation run wild, you might even convince yourself that your lack of suffering somehow makes you better than those who are hurting.

Wrong.

The suffering of other people is a call for empathy and action from God's people. At least it should be. We should never sit and gloat over other people's misfortunes. We shouldn't just give a halfhearted, "Oh, that's too bad." Other people's suffering should shake us up. It should make us want to do something—anything—to help.

The book of Obadiah makes that point abundantly clear in just 21 verses. Apparently, the Edomites were getting quite a kick out of the suffering of their Israelite cousins. God sent Obadiah to tell them just what a bad idea that was.

LIFE LESSONS »

1 Selfish pride always leads to a downfall (3).

2 God frowns on people who ignore or laugh at the suffering of others (11).

3 No one will escape God's judgment (18).

¹The vision of Obadiah.

This is what the Sovereign LORD says about Edom—

We have heard a message from the LORD:
  An envoy was sent to the nations to say,
  "Rise, and let us go against her for battle"—

² "See, I will make you small among the nations;
    you will be utterly despised.
³ The pride of your heart has deceived you,
    you who live in the clefts of the rocksª
    and make your home on the heights,
  you who say to yourself,
    'Who can bring me down to the ground?'
⁴ Though you soar like the eagle
    and make your nest among the stars,
    from there I will bring you down,"

                                        declares the LORD.

⁵ "If thieves came to you,
    if robbers in the night—
  Oh, what a disaster awaits you—
    would they not steal only as much as
      they wanted?
  If grape pickers came to you,
    would they not leave a few grapes?
⁶ But how Esau will be ransacked,
    his hidden treasures pillaged!
⁷ All your allies will force you to the
      border;
  your friends will deceive and
      overpower you;
  those who eat your bread will set a trap
      for you,ᵇ
    but you will not detect it.

⁸ "In that day," declares the LORD,
    "will I not destroy the wise men of
      Edom,
  men of understanding in the
      mountains of Esau?
⁹ Your warriors, O Teman, will be terrified,
    and everyone in Esau's mountains
    will be cut down in the slaughter.
¹⁰ Because of the violence against your
      brother Jacob,
  you will be covered with shame;
    you will be destroyed forever.
¹¹ On the day you stood aloof
    while strangers carried off his wealth
  and foreigners entered his gates
    and cast lots for Jerusalem,
    you were like one of them.
¹² You should not look down on your brother
    in the day of his misfortune,

Understanding Discipline

No one is beyond God's discipline. David was the king of Israel when God allowed his newborn son to die because of his sin. Jonah was one of God's chosen prophets, but that didn't stop the Lord from having him spend three days in the stomach of a fish until he changed his attitude. If you don't stay faithful to God, you can expect his discipline too. God loves you too much to let you destroy your life with sin.

ª *3* Or *of Sela*   ᵇ *7* The meaning of the Hebrew for this clause is uncertain.

battlelines

» Getting Prepped (Fitting In)

Q: Well, well, well, lookie here. It's Mr. Prep School himself. How's it going so far?
A: Not so good.

Q: What's not so good about it?
A: Everything. They make you wear dress shoes, khakis and a navy blazer every day. Every class is a killer. Last year I breezed through school without cracking a book. Now my nose is stuck in one all the time! But the worst part is having no girls in my classes. It's *all guys*. Is that insane or what?

Q: Look at it this way: At least you'll be better prepared for college when you finish.
A: That's the theory. But that's *four years* away. Meanwhile, I have absolutely nothing in common with any of the guys at school. I'm telling you, it's like prison—or like I moved to a different country.

Q: Sounds like you're experiencing a case of culture shock.
A: Huh?

Q: You know, just when you start getting used to certain situations and people, everything changes. It's like you said— you're living in a whole different culture: Preppieland. All new customs, a totally different language.
A: But I don't want to learn a new language. I liked my old language.

Q: So how are you going to make it through it if you don't adapt?
A: Adapt, huh? That doesn't sound like much fun.

Q: Aren't there any other new guys there too?
A: Yeah, a couple. They look just as lost as me.

Q: Sounds like a good place to start.

» Preparing for Life

You don't necessarily have to pack up and move to another country to experience culture shock. It can occur when your family moves to a new neighborhood, when you change schools, when you join a new club or when you switch churches. Talk to guys whose parents are in the military—they know all about culture shock, about having to roll with the punches of frequent change.

The fact is that you will experience various types of culture shock many times between now and the time you die. Learning to adapt is a skill we all need to acquire. No matter what your situation is, though, you'll find that the adjusting process goes a lot more smoothly if you can find a friend or two who are in the same boat as you.

The apostle Paul is a great role model in this regard. God led him all over the known world to preach and start new churches. His life was far from easy. He got stretched in ways most of us never will. Yet here's what he concluded: "That is why, for Christ's sake, I delight in weaknesses, in insults, in hardships, in persecutions, in difficulties. For when I am weak, then I am strong" (2 Corinthians 12:10).

Read more about fitting in at www.RevolutionBible.com.

nor rejoice over the people of Judah
in the day of their destruction,
nor boast so much
in the day of their trouble.

∩□ᴡ □ʀ ∩−Ξ−∨−Ξ−ʀ

OB 11

One of the reasons many people don't respond to the suffering of others is that
they're afraid of doing or saying the wrong
thing. Don't let that fear stop you from
helping someone who is hurting. If you refuse to help, you're no different from
those who actively oppress the needy.

¹³ You should not march through the gates
of my people
in the day of their disaster,
nor look down on them in their calamity
in the day of their disaster,
nor seize their wealth
in the day of their disaster.
¹⁴ You should not wait at the crossroads
to cut down their fugitives,
nor hand over their survivors
in the day of their trouble.

¹⁵ "The day of the LORD is near
for all nations.

As you have done, it will be done to you;
your deeds will return upon your own head.
¹⁶ Just as you drank on my holy hill,
so all the nations will drink continually;
they will drink and drink
and be as if they had never been.
¹⁷ But on Mount Zion will be deliverance;
it will be holy,
and the house of Jacob
will possess its inheritance.
¹⁸ The house of Jacob will be a fire
and the house of Joseph a flame;
the house of Esau will be stubble,
and they will set it on fire and consume it.
There will be no survivors
from the house of Esau."

The LORD has spoken.

¹⁹ People from the Negev will occupy
the mountains of Esau,
and people from the foothills will possess
the land of the Philistines.
They will occupy the fields of Ephraim and Samaria,
and Benjamin will possess Gilead.
²⁰ This company of Israelite exiles who are in Canaan
will possess ⌊the land⌋ as far as Zarephath;
the exiles from Jerusalem who are in Sepharad
will possess the towns of the Negev.
²¹ Deliverers will go up on[a] Mount Zion
to govern the mountains of Esau.
And the kingdom will be the LORD'S.

ª 21 Or *from*

JONAH

Author
Jonah

Audience
People of Israel

Date
Probably about 785–750 B.C.

Setting
Jonah is sent to Nineveh, the most important city in Assyria, to tell the people to repent.

Verse to Remember
"O LORD, is this not what I said when I was still at home? That is why I was so quick to flee to Tarshish. I knew that you are a gracious and compassionate God, slow to anger and abounding in love, a God who relents from sending calamity" (4:1–2).

Theme to Consider
Jonah's story brings us the encouraging message that no one is beyond hope. God's grace and mercy extend to all who seek his forgiveness.

UNCHANGING TRUTH » You were created for a purpose. God has made this clear by setting out specific things for you to do in your life. Maybe God's plan for you involves leading certain friends to Christ. Maybe he sees you as a volunteer youth leader, a river guide at a Christian adventure camp or a mentor to a kid with no dad. Only God knows exactly what he has planned for you. Only he can see the entire script of your life from the day you're born to the day you die.

The thing about being created for a special purpose, though, is that if you're not fulfilling that purpose, you'll soon know it. You may not know exactly what's wrong, but you'll know something's missing. And even success, fame and tons of money won't help you fill the void.

The prophet Jonah discovered that God's plan for his life wasn't something to take lightly. He found out that you can't choose to ignore it without suffering serious consequences. He also discovered just how far God is willing to go in order to make sure that his work gets done through his servants.

What about you? Do you fully realize what it means to be created for a purpose? Do you have a passion to serve God with your whole life? If so, are you eager to get started? Uncertain about what to do? Overwhelmed by it all? Don't hesitate to go to God with any questions or doubts you may have. Like any great father, he wants you to succeed. And you won't find anyone else around with more resources at his disposal.

If you're still not sure what God has in store for you, just keep obeying his Word, listening to him in your prayer time and watching for open doors in your life. He'll lead you to the place he wants you to go and show you what to do when you get there. And when he does, make sure you obey . . . because there just might be some big stinky fish swimming around out there with your name on it!

LIFE LESSONS »

1. You can't escape God or his calling in your life, no matter how hard you try (1:1–9).

2. God is willing to go to extreme measures to get your attention and help you understand the benefits of following his instructions (1:17).

3. The Word of God can affect people in totally unexpected ways and produce remarkable changes in their lives (3:3–9).

60 Things Real Men Do

It's one thing to talk about what a Revolution Man is. But how do you know what a Revolution Man does? Does he guzzle beer with pretty girls at poolside parties like in the commercials? Does he carry automatic weapons and kick the snot out of bad guys like in the movies? Does he crack witty jokes and have lots of popular friends like the cool kids at school? And what about the whole sports thing? Authentic masculinity isn't defined by pop culture or fads. It's defined by the One who created men in the first place—God. Looking for some ideas about how to be the Revolution Man that God intended you to be? How about 60? Starting right now, make a commitment to:

01» Study, obey and teach God's Word »Ezr 7:10 :: 02» Keep your promises no matter what »Ps 15:4b :: 03» Trust God's provision »Ps 37:3,5 :: 04» Talk to people boldly and honestly about God's truth »Ps 105:1 :: 05» Use your mouth to heal, not to cut others down »Pr 12:18 :: 06» Choose your friends wisely »Pr 14:7 :: 07» Control your anger »Pr 14:29 :: 08» Accept valid criticism from others »Pr 15:32 :: 09» Listen to advice because it makes you wiser »Pr 19:20 :: 10» Develop a desire for what is right and good »Mt 5:6 ::

:: MT 7:7

11» Make peace with difficult people »Mt 5:9 :: 12» Ask for forgiveness »Mt 6:12 :: 13» Do the right thing for the right reason »Mt 6:16 :: 14» Give up chasing after material possessions »Mt 6:19 :: 15» Focus on spiritual matters rather than earthly and material stuff »Mt 6:33 :: 16» Seek God relentlessly »Mt 7:7 :: 17» Build your life on the solid rock of Christ »Mt 7:24-27 :: 18» Forgive »Lk 17:3 :: 19» Worship »Jn 4:24 :: 20» Cry »Jn 11:35 :: 21» Love people sincerely »Jn 13:34-35; Gal 5:14 :: 22» Refuse to adopt worldly attitudes and actions »Ro 12:2 :: 23» Find out what gift God has given you and use it for his glory »Ro 12:8 :: 24» Hate what is wrong »Ro 12:9 :: 25» Be patient during tough times »Ro

REF: 080

1

16 SEEK GOD

WORK HARD 26

"REAL MAN: ONE WHO IS PATIENT WITH PEOPLE

30

12:12 :: **26»** Work hard to get along with others »Ro 12:16,18 :: **27»** Be satisfied not to seek revenge »Ro 12:17,19 :: **28»** Respect people in authority—even those who aren't great leaders »Ro 13:1 :: **29»** Allow Jesus to control you »Ro 13:14 :: **30»** Look for an escape route when faced with temptation »1Co 10:13 :: **31»** Seek to please God no matter where you are or who you're with »2Co 5:9 :: **32»** Be ready for "the big day" (that is, the day of judgment) »2Co 5:10 :: **33»** Block out jealous thoughts »Gal 5:26 :: **34»** Work on being humble »Eph 4:2 :: **35»** Continue growing in your faith »Eph 4:15 :: **36»** Speak the truth 100 percent of the time »Eph 4:25 :: **37»** Show kindness »Eph 4:32 :: **38»** Imitate Jesus' selfless love »Eph 5:1-2 :: **39»** Make the most of every day; live each one as if it's your last »Eph 5:16 :: **40»** Let the Spirit of God fill you »Eph 5:18 :: **41»** Honor your parents »Eph 6:2 :: **42»** Teach your kids to love and obey God »Eph 6:4 :: **43»** Look to God for strength »Eph 6:10 :: **44»** Pray »Eph 6:18 :: **45»** Live selflessly; always think of others first »Php 2:3 :: **46»** Steer clear of sexual temptation »1Th 4:3 :: **47»** Stay sexually pure before marriage »1Th 4:3 :: **48»** Be patient with weak and difficult people »1Th 5:14 :: **49»** Thank God in every situation »1Th 5:18 :: **50»** Work hard »2Th 3:11-12 :: **51»** Show respect to older people »1Ti 5:1 :: **52»** Respect girls like sisters »1Ti 5:1-2 :: **53»** View money as a gift from God and not as an idol »1Ti 6:6-10 :: **54»** Stay sexually pure during marriage »Heb 13:4 :: **55»** Ask God for wisdom »Jas 1:5 :: **56»** Listen to others »Jas 1:19 :: **57»** Obey God's commands »Jas 1:22 :: **58»** Stay close to God »Jas 4:8 :: **59»** Live so that people see Jesus in you »1Pe 2:12 :: **60»** Confess your sins »1Jn 1:9

HONOR PARENTS

41

:: EPH 6:2

CONFESS YOUR SINS

60

JONAH FLEES FROM THE LORD

1 The word of the LORD came to Jonah son of Amittai: ²"Go to the great city of Nineveh and preach against it, because its wickedness has come up before me."

³But Jonah ran away from the LORD and headed for Tarshish. He went down to Joppa, where he found a ship bound for that port. After paying the fare, he went aboard and sailed for Tarshish to flee from the LORD.

⁴Then the LORD sent a great wind on the sea, and such a violent storm arose that the ship threatened to break up. ⁵All the sailors were afraid and each cried out to his own god. And they threw the cargo into the sea to lighten the ship.

But Jonah had gone below deck, where he lay down and fell into a deep sleep. ⁶The captain went to him and said, "How can you sleep? Get up and call on your god! Maybe he will take notice of us, and we will not perish."

⁷Then the sailors said to each other, "Come, let us cast lots to find out who is responsible for this calamity." They cast lots and the lot fell on Jonah.

⁸So they asked him, "Tell us, who is responsible for making all this trouble for us? What do you do? Where do you come from? What is your country? From what people are you?"

⁹He answered, "I am a Hebrew and I worship the LORD, the God of heaven, who made the sea and the land."

¹⁰This terrified them and they asked, "What have you done?" (They knew he was running away from the LORD, because he had already told them so.)

¹¹The sea was getting rougher and rougher. So they asked him, "What should we do to you to make the sea calm down for us?"

¹²"Pick me up and throw me into the sea," he replied, "and it will become calm. I know that it is my fault that this great storm has come upon you."

¹³Instead, the men did their best to row back to land. But they could not, for the sea grew even wilder than before. ¹⁴Then they cried to the LORD, "O LORD, please do not let us die for taking this man's life. Do not hold us accountable for killing an innocent man, for you, O LORD, have done as you pleased." ¹⁵Then they took Jonah and threw him overboard, and the raging sea grew calm. ¹⁶At this the men greatly feared the LORD, and they offered a sacrifice to the LORD and made vows to him.

¹⁷But the LORD provided a great fish to swallow Jonah, and Jonah was inside the fish three days and three nights.

JONAH'S PRAYER

2 From inside the fish Jonah prayed to the LORD his God. ²He said:

"In my distress I called to the LORD,
    and he answered me.
From the depths of the grave ª I called for help,
    and you listened to my cry.
³ You hurled me into the deep,
    into the very heart of the seas,
    and the currents swirled about me;
all your waves and breakers
    swept over me.
⁴I said, 'I have been banished

Facing Tough Challenges

God gave Jonah a tough job, no question. The idea of bringing God's message to the evil Ninevites probably turned Jonah's stomach. But he didn't even *attempt* to do what he was told. Jonah took off like a coward, hoping to outrun his call. He found out the hard way that he couldn't run (or swim) fast enough. What if Jonah had said, "Lord, I'm not sure I can carry out this assignment, and I don't even know if I understand what you're trying to do; but I'll give it a try"? You can bet God would have helped him. Keep that in mind the next time you face an assignment from God that you're not sure you can handle.

» live the adventure » Jnh 1:3

ª 2 Hebrew *Sheol*

jonah

VERSUS

» A Hebrew prophet
» The first missionary sent to a pagan nation
» Struggled with major attitude and obedience problems

the ninevites

» Citizens of Assyria's capital
» Known for their wickedness, cruelty and worship of false gods
» Turned to God in response to Jonah's preaching

The Main Event

When Jonah heard the voice of God telling him to pack his bags and head to Nineveh, he nearly fell out of his chair. His thoughts probably went something like this: *Warn the Ninevites of judgment? Give one of the most evil nations in the world a chance at God's mercy? Why? Why should I do anything to help the enemies of God? At best, they'll mock me. At worst, they'll kill me. I say, "Let 'em fry!"*

So instead of setting his cruise control on 70 and heading in a northeasterly direction for about 500 miles, Jonah bought a boat ticket and headed due west. Needless to say, it didn't turn out to be the cruise he had hoped for. God wasn't about to let his rebellious servant off the hook that easily.

It took a violent storm at sea, a field trip inside the gastrointestinal tract of an enormous fish and some serious soul-searching . . . but eventually Jonah saw things God's way. He did an about-face and made his way to Nineveh, delivering God's word once he got there. Then, to his utter shock, the Ninevites actually listened and responded. They declared a fast, put on sackcloth (a sign of mourning) and, at the king's urging, cried out to God for forgiveness. In short, the entire city turned to God.

Great story, huh? Nice, happy ending, right? It wasn't the response Jonah had hoped for. He was actually ticked that God would show compassion to the people of Nineveh. He took a seat outside the city, finding shelter beneath a shady plant (lovingly provided by God) and waited for God to rain down his fiery judgment on the Ninevites. But God's judgment never came. This merciful turn of events really put Jonah in a bad mood. "I knew it!" he fumed. "I just knew it! That's so like God—to forgive the same godless bunch I've been warning of judgment. Thanks a lot, God, for making me look like an idiot!"

The Outcome

What an interesting, odd little story! Everybody and everything in it (the storm, the fish, the Ninevites) are obedient to God—everyone except Jonah, that is. At the end of the book, the moody prophet is more concerned about his shady plant (which ended up being chewed on by a worm) than about the fate of an entire city.

Jonah's experience shows us the consequences of disobedience and the ugliness of being judgmental and harsh. The lesson? When God gives us an assignment, even a hard and confusing one, we need to carry it out immediately—and with the right attitude.

The Ninevites' experience shows us the importance of humility and the wonder of God's love and mercy. The lesson there? When God warns you to repent and turn around, don't hesitate! And when people that you don't think deserve God's mercy receive it, celebrate.

Read more about Jonah and the Ninevites in Jonah 1–4 (pages 1201–1204).

from your sight;
yet I will look again
toward your holy temple.'
⁵ The engulfing waters threatened me,ª
the deep surrounded me;
seaweed was wrapped around my head.
⁶ To the roots of the mountains I sank down;
the earth beneath barred me in forever.
But you brought my life up from the pit,
O LORD my God.

⁷ "When my life was ebbing away,
I remembered you, LORD,
and my prayer rose to you,
to your holy temple.

⁸ "Those who cling to worthless idols
forfeit the grace that could be theirs.
⁹ But I, with a song of thanksgiving,
will sacrifice to you.
What I have vowed I will make good.
Salvation comes from the LORD."

¹⁰And the LORD commanded the fish, and it vomited Jonah onto dry land.

JONAH GOES TO NINEVEH

3 Then the word of the LORD came to Jonah a second time: ²"Go to the great city of Nineveh and proclaim to it the message I give you."

³Jonah obeyed the word of the LORD and went to Nineveh. Now Nineveh was a very important city—a visit required three days. ⁴On the first day, Jonah started into the city. He proclaimed: "Forty more days and Nineveh will be overturned." ⁵The Ninevites believed God. They declared a fast, and all of them, from the greatest to the least, put on sackcloth.

⁶When the news reached the king of Nineveh, he rose from his throne, took off his royal robes, covered himself with sackcloth and sat down in the dust. ⁷Then he issued a proclamation in Nineveh:

"By the decree of the king and his nobles:

Do not let any man or beast, herd or flock, taste anything; do not let them eat or drink. ⁸But let man and beast be covered with sackcloth. Let everyone call urgently on God. Let them give up their evil ways and their violence. ⁹Who knows? God may yet relent and with compassion turn from his fierce anger so that we will not perish."

¹⁰When God saw what they did and how they turned from their evil ways, he had compassion and did not bring upon them the destruction he had threatened.

NOW OR NEVER

JNH 3:4

It wasn't Jonah's words that won over the Ninevites. It was the power of God speaking through those words. Remember that the next time you stumble through telling your own faith story or trying to explain to someone who Jesus is and what he's done for you.

JONAH'S ANGER AT THE LORD'S COMPASSION

4 But Jonah was greatly displeased and became angry. ²He prayed to the LORD, "O LORD, is this not what I said when I was still at home? That is why I was so quick to flee to Tarshish. I knew that you are a gracious and compassionate God, slow to anger and abounding in love, a God who relents from sending calamity. ³Now, O LORD, take away my life, for it is better for me to die than to live."

ª 5 Or *waters were at my throat*

⁴But the LORD replied, "Have you any right to be angry?"

⁵Jonah went out and sat down at a place east of the city. There he made himself a shelter, sat in its shade and waited to see what would happen to the city. ⁶Then the LORD God provided a vine and made it grow up over Jonah to give shade for his head to ease his discomfort, and Jonah was very happy about the vine. ⁷But at dawn the next day God provided a worm, which chewed the vine so that it withered. ⁸When the sun rose, God provided a scorching east wind, and the sun blazed on Jonah's head so that he grew faint. He wanted to die, and said, "It would be better for me to die than to live."

challenge notes

To: my_son

heavenly_father: you'll find plenty of things in this world to be angry about, but my work is not one of them. if you have sincere questions about why I do certain things, ask me. I'll find a way to help you understand. but don't allow an honest question to turn into grumbling or bitterness.

JNH 4:1-4

⁹But God said to Jonah, "Do you have a right to be angry about the vine?"

"I do," he said. "I am angry enough to die."

¹⁰But the LORD said, "You have been concerned about this vine, though you did not tend it or make it grow. It sprang up overnight and died overnight. ¹¹But Nineveh has more than a hundred and twenty thousand people who cannot tell their right hand from their left, and many cattle as well. Should I not be concerned about that great city?"

MICAH

MICAH MICAH

« AT A GLANCE

Author
Micah

Audience
People of Israel and Judah

Date
Likely written between 742 and 687 B.C., during the reigns of Jotham, Ahaz and Hezekiah

Setting
Micah lived during the time of Isaiah and Hosea. He predicted the fall of both Israel and Judah because of the people's sin.

Verse to Remember
"Who is a God like you, who pardons sin and forgives the transgression of the remnant of his inheritance? You do not stay angry forever but delight to show mercy" (7:18).

Theme to Consider
Micah makes it clear what God hates: unkindness, idolatry, injustice and empty worship. God still hates these today. But God offers forgiveness and love to all who turn to him.

UNCHANGING TRUTH » Where do you go when things start looking hopeless? Where do you turn when . . .

- your girlfriend gives you the "let's just be friends" speech?
- your parents start talking about divorce?
- school becomes a waking nightmare?
- you can't stand the way you look?
- you've messed up big-time and you can't escape your past?
- you can't shake those feelings of not being good enough?

Look to God when feelings of hopelessness start to set in. No matter what the situation is, God can help you through it. No problem is too big for him to handle, and no problem is too small for him to be concerned about.

As long as God exists, hope exists for us. The prophet Micah understood that, and he wanted the Israelites to understand it, too—during one of the darkest periods in their nation's history.

Fight the temptation to blame God for your situation or to pull away from him in anger. Instead, draw closer to him. Spend more time with him. Pour out your heart to him. Let him know exactly how you feel. And hold on . . . because he'll give you the strength you need.

LIFE LESSONS »

1   Be careful who you listen to. Many people will try to lead you away from God's truth (2:6–11).

2   Even in the midst of judgment, God will not forget his people (2:12–13).

3   Leadership always carries with it responsibility. God holds spiritual leaders accountable for the things they do (and don't do) on behalf of those who rely on them (3:1–3).

4   God allows us to suffer the consequences of our sins, but he also gives us a chance to be made right with him (7:8–10).

1 The word of the LORD that came to Micah of Moresheth during the reigns of Jotham, Ahaz and Hezekiah, kings of Judah—the vision he saw concerning Samaria and Jerusalem.

²Hear, O peoples, all of you,
    listen, O earth and all who are in it,
that the Sovereign LORD may witness against you,
    the Lord from his holy temple.

JUDGMENT AGAINST SAMARIA AND JERUSALEM

³Look! The LORD is coming from his dwelling place;
    he comes down and treads the high places of the earth.
⁴The mountains melt beneath him
    and the valleys split apart,
like wax before the fire,
    like water rushing down a slope.
⁵All this is because of Jacob's transgression,
    because of the sins of the house of Israel.
What is Jacob's transgression?
    Is it not Samaria?
What is Judah's high place?
    Is it not Jerusalem?

⁶"Therefore I will make Samaria a heap of rubble,
    a place for planting vineyards.
I will pour her stones into the valley
    and lay bare her foundations.
⁷All her idols will be broken to pieces;
    all her temple gifts will be burned with fire;
    I will destroy all her images.
Since she gathered her gifts from the wages of prostitutes,
    as the wages of prostitutes they will again be used."

WEEPING AND MOURNING

⁸Because of this I will weep and wail;
    I will go about barefoot and naked.
I will howl like a jackal
    and moan like an owl.
⁹For her wound is incurable;
    it has come to Judah.
Itᵃ has reached the very gate of my people,
    even to Jerusalem itself.
¹⁰Tell it not in Gathᵇ;
    weep not at all.ᶜ
In Beth Ophrahᵈ
    roll in the dust.
¹¹Pass on in nakedness and shame,
    you who live in Shaphir.ᵉ
Those who live in Zaananᶠ
    will not come out.
Beth Ezel is in mourning;
    its protection is taken from you.
¹²Those who live in Marothᵍ writhe in pain,
    waiting for relief,

ᵃ 9 Or He   ᵇ 10 Gath sounds like the Hebrew for tell.   ᶜ 10 Hebrew; Septuagint may suggest not in Acco. The Hebrew for in Acco sounds like the Hebrew for weep.   ᵈ 10 Beth Ophrah means house of dust.   ᵉ 11 Shaphir means pleasant.   ᶠ 11 Zaanan sounds like the Hebrew for come out.   ᵍ 12 Maroth sounds like the Hebrew for bitter.

because disaster has come from the LORD,
    even to the gate of Jerusalem.
¹³ You who live in Lachish,ᵃ
    harness the team to the chariot.
You were the beginning of sin
    to the Daughter of Zion,
for the transgressions of Israel
    were found in you.
¹⁴ Therefore you will give parting gifts
    to Moresheth Gath.
The town of Aczibᵇ will prove deceptive
    to the kings of Israel.
¹⁵ I will bring a conqueror against you
    who live in Mareshah.ᶜ
He who is the glory of Israel
    will come to Adullam.
¹⁶ Shave your heads in mourning
    for the children in whom you delight;
make yourselves as bald as the vulture,
    for they will go from you into exile.

MAN'S PLANS AND GOD'S

Woe to those who plan iniquity,
    to those who plot evil on their beds!
At morning's light they carry it out
    because it is in their power to do it.
² They covet fields and seize them,
    and houses, and take them.
They defraud a man of his home,
    a fellowman of his inheritance.

³ Therefore, the LORD says:

"I am planning disaster against this people,
    from which you cannot save yourselves.
You will no longer walk proudly,
    for it will be a time of calamity.
⁴ In that day men will ridicule you;
    they will taunt you with this mournful song:
'We are utterly ruined;
    my people's possession is divided up.
He takes it from me!
    He assigns our fields to traitors.' "

⁵ Therefore you will have no one in the assembly of the LORD
    to divide the land by lot.

FALSE PROPHETS

⁶ "Do not prophesy," their prophets say.
    "Do not prophesy about these things;
    disgrace will not overtake us."
⁷ Should it be said, O house of Jacob:
    "Is the Spirit of the LORD angry?
    Does he do such things?"

"Do not my words do good

ᵃ *13 Lachish* sounds like the Hebrew for *team.*   ᵇ *14 Aczib* means *deception.*   ᶜ *15 Mareshah* sounds like the Hebrew for *conqueror.*

to him whose ways are upright?
⁸ Lately my people have risen up
　　like an enemy.
You strip off the rich robe
　　from those who pass by without a
　　　care,
　　like men returning from battle.
⁹ You drive the women of my people
　　from their pleasant homes.
You take away my blessing
　　from their children forever.
¹⁰ Get up, go away!
　　For this is not your resting place,
because it is defiled,
　　it is ruined, beyond all remedy.
¹¹ If a liar and deceiver comes and says,
　　'I will prophesy for you plenty of
　　　wine and beer,'
　　he would be just the prophet for this
　　　people!

DELIVERANCE PROMISED

¹² "I will surely gather all of you, O Jacob;
　　I will surely bring together the
　　　remnant of Israel.
I will bring them together like sheep in a
　　pen,
　　like a flock in its pasture;
　　the place will throng with people.
¹³ One who breaks open the way will go
　　up before them;
　　they will break through the gate and
　　　go out.
Their king will pass through before
　　them,
　　the LORD at their head."

LEADERS AND PROPHETS REBUKED

3 Then I said,

"Listen, you leaders of Jacob,
　　you rulers of the house of Israel.
Should you not know justice,
² 　you who hate good and love evil;
who tear the skin from my people
　　and the flesh from their bones;
³ who eat my people's flesh,
　　strip off their skin
　　and break their bones in pieces;
who chop them up like meat for the pan,
　　like flesh for the pot?"

⁴ Then they will cry out to the LORD,
　　but he will not answer them.
At that time he will hide his face from them
　　because of the evil they have done.

Guarding Against False Teachers

Some people may try to tell you that God is too loving to send people to hell, and others will say he is too uncaring to deserve our love. Neither is true. In fact, anytime someone tells you something about God, even if it sounds right, prayerfully check it against the Bible. Unfortunately, many people who think they know what God is like are going to be in for quite a surprise when they actually stand before him.

5 This is what the LORD says:

"As for the prophets
who lead my people astray,

if one feeds them,
they proclaim 'peace';
if he does not,
they prepare to wage war against him.
6 Therefore night will come over you,
without visions,
and darkness, without divination.
The sun will set for the prophets,
and the day will go dark for them.
7 The seers will be ashamed
and the diviners disgraced.
They will all cover their faces
because there is no answer from God."

now or never

MIC 3:5

Who do you trust to tell you what God is like and what he wants from you? How do you know that they are giving you the real truth? When it comes to knowing God, check everything against the only completely reliable source: the Bible.

8 But as for me, I am filled with power,
with the Spirit of the LORD,
and with justice and might,
to declare to Jacob his transgression,
to Israel his sin.
9 Hear this, you leaders of the house of Jacob,
you rulers of the house of Israel,
who despise justice
and distort all that is right;
10 who build Zion with bloodshed,
and Jerusalem with wickedness.
11 Her leaders judge for a bribe,
her priests teach for a price,
and her prophets tell fortunes for money.
Yet they lean upon the LORD and say,
"Is not the LORD among us?
No disaster will come upon us."
12 Therefore because of you,
Zion will be plowed like a field,
Jerusalem will become a heap of rubble,
the temple hill a mound overgrown with thickets.

THE MOUNTAIN OF THE LORD

4

In the last days

the mountain of the LORD's temple will be established
as chief among the mountains;
it will be raised above the hills,
and peoples will stream to it.

2 Many nations will come and say,

"Come, let us go up to the mountain of the LORD,
to the house of the God of Jacob.
He will teach us his ways,
so that we may walk in his paths."
The law will go out from Zion,
the word of the LORD from Jerusalem.
3 He will judge between many peoples

micah

VERSUS

» A farmer turned prophet
» Primarily dealt with the common people, not the elite
» Delivered bold, uncompromising messages of truth and hope

wealthy israelites

» Wealthy class known for oppressing the poor
» False prophets who said whatever the people wanted to hear
» Condemned strongly by Micah

The Main Event

For most folks, God is a nice idea and little else. He's good to turn to when all else fails. As far as they're concerned, it's best to keep the Almighty in a corner, out of the way. The real deal for them is wealth. Cash is king. Most people want money—the more the better.

The problem is, without God in the picture, people can get pretty ruthless in their quest for riches. Hop into a time machine and travel to any era in any culture, and you'll find plenty of evidence of that ruthlessness.

That was certainly the case in ancient Israel between the years 750 and 690 B.C. God's people were going through the motions, spiritually speaking, while the rich scrambled like crazy to get even richer. Wealthy landowners were taking advantage of the poor in their quest to make even more money. If that weren't bad enough, they also had false prophets who were willing to say practically anything—and claimed that it came from God—in exchange for a buck.

And then Micah appeared on the scene. From a worldly perspective, he was nobody special, just a simple farmer. But the Spirit of God came upon him and gave him a message straight from heaven. And nothing was going to stop him from delivering it.

The Outcome

Micah delivered his message hard and strong—with no compromise, no fear and no backing down. "You crooks are going down!" he told the money-grubbing landowners and false prophets. "You think God doesn't see your corruption? Just wait till you get into his courtroom!" It was the verbal equivalent of a running elbow, a corkscrew leg drop and a flying shoulder block all rolled into one.

Yet Micah's words of prophetic truth also contained nuggets of grace. He promised the people that a ruler was coming from Bethlehem—a great shepherd who would be full of compassion. The news was so great, in fact, that the prophet wrapped up his remarks by saying, "Who is a God like you, who pardons sin and forgives the transgression of the remnant of his inheritance? You do not stay angry forever but delight to show mercy" (Micah 7:18). What a great way to end an unpleasant conversation with unpleasant people—declaring the mercy of God.

Ask yourself: Am I more like Micah or more like the thugs and posers he was rebuking? Do I do what God has shown is good? Do I act in a way that's just? Do I love mercy? Do I walk humbly with God?

Read more about Micah's encounter with the landowners and false prophets in Micah 1–7 (pages 1206–1217).

and will settle disputes for strong nations far and wide.
    They will beat their swords into plowshares
        and their spears into pruning hooks.
    Nation will not take up sword against nation,
        nor will they train for war anymore.
4 Every man will sit under his own vine
        and under his own fig tree,
    and no one will make them afraid,
        for the LORD Almighty has spoken.
5 All the nations may walk
        in the name of their gods;
    we will walk in the name of the LORD
        our God for ever and ever.

THE LORD'S PLAN

6 "In that day," declares the LORD,

    "I will gather the lame;
        I will assemble the exiles
        and those I have brought to grief.
7 I will make the lame a remnant,
        those driven away a strong nation.
    The LORD will rule over them in Mount Zion
        from that day and forever.
8 As for you, O watchtower of the flock,
        O stronghold[a] of the Daughter of Zion,
    the former dominion will be restored to you;
        kingship will come to the Daughter of Jerusalem."

9 Why do you now cry aloud—
        have you no king?
    Has your counselor perished,
        that pain seizes you like that of a woman in labor?
10 Writhe in agony, O Daughter of Zion,
        like a woman in labor,
    for now you must leave the city
        to camp in the open field.
    You will go to Babylon;
        there you will be rescued.
    There the LORD will redeem you
        out of the hand of your enemies.

11 But now many nations
        are gathered against you.
    They say, "Let her be defiled,
        let our eyes gloat over Zion!"
12 But they do not know
        the thoughts of the LORD;
    they do not understand his plan,
        he who gathers them like sheaves to the threshing floor.

13 "Rise and thresh, O Daughter of Zion,
        for I will give you horns of iron;
    I will give you hoofs of bronze
        and you will break to pieces many nations."

a 8 Or hill

You will devote their ill-gotten gains to the Lord,
their wealth to the Lord of all the earth.

A PROMISED RULER FROM BETHLEHEM

5

Marshal your troops, O city of troops,[a]
for a siege is laid against us.
They will strike Israel's ruler
on the cheek with a rod.

2 "But you, Bethlehem Ephrathah,
though you are small among the
clans[b] of Judah,
out of you will come for me
one who will be ruler over Israel,
whose origins[c] are from of old,
from ancient times.[d]"

3 Therefore Israel will be abandoned
until the time when she who is in
labor gives birth
and the rest of his brothers return
to join the Israelites.

4 He will stand and shepherd his flock
in the strength of the Lord,
in the majesty of the name of the Lord his God.
And they will live securely, for then his greatness
will reach to the ends of the earth.
5 And he will be their peace.

DELIVERANCE AND DESTRUCTION

When the Assyrian invades our land
and marches through our fortresses,
we will raise against him seven shepherds,
even eight leaders of men.
6 They will rule[e] the land of Assyria with the sword,
the land of Nimrod with drawn sword.[f]
He will deliver us from the Assyrian
when he invades our land
and marches into our borders.

7 The remnant of Jacob will be
in the midst of many peoples
like dew from the Lord,
like showers on the grass,
which do not wait for man
or linger for mankind.
8 The remnant of Jacob will be among the nations,
in the midst of many peoples,
like a lion among the beasts of the forest,
like a young lion among flocks of sheep,
which mauls and mangles as it goes,
and no one can rescue.
9 Your hand will be lifted up in triumph over your enemies,
and all your foes will be destroyed.

[a] 1 Or *Strengthen your walls, O walled city* [b] 2 Or *rulers* [c] 2 Hebrew *goings out* [d] 2 Or *from days of eternity* [e] 6 Or *crush*
[f] 6 Or *Nimrod in its gates*

¹⁰"In that day," declares the Lᴏʀᴅ,

> "I will destroy your horses from among you
>> and demolish your chariots.
> ¹¹ I will destroy the cities of your land
>> and tear down all your strongholds.
> ¹² I will destroy your witchcraft
>> and you will no longer cast spells.
> ¹³ I will destroy your carved images
>> and your sacred stones from among you;
> you will no longer bow down
>> to the work of your hands.
> ¹⁴ I will uproot from among you your Asherah poles ᵃ
>> and demolish your cities.
> ¹⁵ I will take vengeance in anger and wrath
>> upon the nations that have not obeyed me."

THE LORD'S CASE AGAINST ISRAEL

 Listen to what the Lᴏʀᴅ says:

> "Stand up, plead your case before the mountains;
>> let the hills hear what you have to say.
> ² Hear, O mountains, the Lᴏʀᴅ's accusation;
>> listen, you everlasting foundations of the earth.
> For the Lᴏʀᴅ has a case against his people;
>> he is lodging a charge against Israel.
>
> ³ "My people, what have I done to you?
>> How have I burdened you? Answer me.
> ⁴ I brought you up out of Egypt
>> and redeemed you from the land of slavery.
> I sent Moses to lead you,
>> also Aaron and Miriam.
> ⁵ My people, remember
>> what Balak king of Moab counseled
>> and what Balaam son of Beor answered.
> Remember ⌊your journey⌋ from Shittim to Gilgal,
>> that you may know the righteous acts of the Lᴏʀᴅ."
>
> ⁶ With what shall I come before the Lᴏʀᴅ
>> and bow down before the exalted God?
> Shall I come before him with burnt offerings,
>> with calves a year old?
> ⁷ Will the Lᴏʀᴅ be pleased with thousands of rams,
>> with ten thousand rivers of oil?
> Shall I offer my firstborn for my transgression,
>> the fruit of my body for the sin of my soul?
> ⁸ He has showed you, O man, what is good.
>> And what does the Lᴏʀᴅ require of you?
> To act justly and to love mercy
>> and to walk humbly with your God.

ISRAEL'S GUILT AND PUNISHMENT

> ⁹ Listen! The Lᴏʀᴅ is calling to the city—
>> and to fear your name is wisdom—

ᵃ *14* That is, symbols of the goddess Asherah

battlelines

» Funny Man (Ridicule)

Q: You're lying. They actually formed a *circle* around him?
A: I wouldn't have believed it if I hadn't seen it with my own eyes. I mean, the kid has cerebral palsy. He can't help it if he walks and talks differently. But there they were—most of them were guys you and I hang out with—torturing him with their jokes and imitations of him.

Q: OK, wait a minute. If you *saw* this, please tell me you did something about it.
A: Yeah, well, I tried. But I might have just made things worse.

Q: How?
A: I didn't know what to say or do. It happened so fast.

Q: So what did you do?
A: I said something like, "Come on, guys. Leave him alone; he's not bothering you. Lighten up. Back off."

Q: And what happened?
A: They actually did! A couple of guys mouthed off and tried to stare me down. One of them even questioned my sexuality, if you know what I mean. But it was kind of amazing; they just sorta dispersed.

Q: And what about the kid they were picking on?
A: Oh, man, he disappeared. Boom! I'd never seem him move that fast.

Q: He was pretty humiliated, I guess.
A: Well, yeah, wouldn't you be?

Q: Well, that's awesome that you stuck your neck out for someone else. You put yourself on the line.
A: Yeah, well, don't make me out to be a hero or anything. It had to have been God, because my heart was beating about a hundred miles an hour!

» Underdog Is Here

Raj is the man! What he did was so awesome, so courageous and so right. Think about that scene. Put yourself there. What character do you want to be? The bully, picking on a kid with a disability? Or the guy who stands up for the mistreated and abused and says, "Cut it out"? The answer should be a no-brainer. In our hearts we know what a real man is and what one does in such situations.

Micah 6:8 says, "He has showed you, O man, what is good. And what does the Lord require of you? To act justly and to love mercy and to walk humbly with your God." Treating people with justice and mercy and walking humbly with God—that's the recipe for authentic manhood.

Read more about standing up for others at www.RevolutionBible.com.

"Heed the rod and the One who appointed it.ᵃ
¹⁰ Am I still to forget, O wicked house,
your ill-gotten treasures
and the short ephah,ᵇ which is accursed?
¹¹ Shall I acquit a man with dishonest scales,
with a bag of false weights?
¹² Her rich men are violent;
her people are liars
and their tongues speak deceitfully.
¹³ Therefore, I have begun to destroy you,
to ruin you because of your sins.
¹⁴ You will eat but not be satisfied;
your stomach will still be empty.ᶜ
You will store up but save nothing,
because what you save I will give to
the sword.
¹⁵ You will plant but not harvest;
you will press olives but not use the
oil on yourselves,
you will crush grapes but not drink
the wine.
¹⁶ You have observed the statutes of Omri
and all the practices of Ahab's house,
and you have followed their traditions.
Therefore I will give you over to ruin
and your people to derision;
you will bear the scorn of the
nations.ᵈ"

ISRAEL'S MISERY

7 What misery is mine!
I am like one who gathers summer fruit
at the gleaning of the vineyard;
there is no cluster of grapes to eat,
none of the early figs that I crave.
² The godly have been swept from the land;
not one upright man remains.
All men lie in wait to shed blood;
each hunts his brother with a net.
³ Both hands are skilled in doing evil;
the ruler demands gifts,
the judge accepts bribes,
the powerful dictate what they desire—
they all conspire together.
⁴ The best of them is like a brier,
the most upright worse than a thorn hedge.
The day of your watchmen has come,
the day God visits you.
Now is the time of their confusion.
⁵ Do not trust a neighbor;
put no confidence in a friend.
Even with her who lies in your embrace
be careful of your words.

«« live the adventure »» Mic 6:8

Pleasing God

Have you ever asked yourself,
What does God want from me?
This verse gives you a pretty
straightforward answer. First,
"act justly," meaning you ought
to pursue righteousness and obedience to God in every area of
your life. Second, "love mercy."
God wants you to treat people
not as you think they deserve to
be treated, but as God treats
you—with kindness and genuine
love. Third, "walk
humbly with your God."
In other words, recognize
that even the little human
strength you have comes
from God, so you should
follow him with humility
and stand in awe of his
power.

ᵃ *9* The meaning of the Hebrew for this line is uncertain.   ᵇ *10* An ephah was a dry measure.   ᶜ *14* The meaning of the Hebrew for this word is uncertain.   ᵈ *16* Septuagint; Hebrew *scorn due my people*

⁶For a son dishonors his father,
    a daughter rises up against her mother,
    a daughter-in-law against her mother-in-law—
    a man's enemies are the members of his own household.

⁷But as for me, I watch in hope for the LORD,
    I wait for God my Savior;
    my God will hear me.

ISRAEL WILL RISE

⁸Do not gloat over me, my enemy!
    Though I have fallen, I will rise.
Though I sit in darkness,
    the LORD will be my light.
⁹Because I have sinned against him,
    I will bear the LORD's wrath,
until he pleads my case
    and establishes my right.
He will bring me out into the light;
    I will see his righteousness.
¹⁰Then my enemy will see it
    and will be covered with shame,
she who said to me,
    "Where is the LORD your God?"
My eyes will see her downfall;
    even now she will be trampled underfoot
    like mire in the streets.

¹¹The day for building your walls will come,
    the day for extending your boundaries.
¹²In that day people will come to you
    from Assyria and the cities of Egypt,
    even from Egypt to the Euphrates
    and from sea to sea
    and from mountain to mountain.
¹³The earth will become desolate because of its inhabitants,
    as the result of their deeds.

PRAYER AND PRAISE

¹⁴Shepherd your people with your staff,
    the flock of your inheritance,
which lives by itself in a forest,
    in fertile pasturelands.ᵃ
Let them feed in Bashan and Gilead
    as in days long ago.

¹⁵"As in the days when you came out of Egypt,
    I will show them my wonders."

¹⁶Nations will see and be ashamed,
    deprived of all their power.
They will lay their hands on their mouths
    and their ears will become deaf.
¹⁷They will lick dust like a snake,
    like creatures that crawl on the ground.
They will come trembling out of their dens;

ᵃ 14 Or in the middle of Carmel

they will turn in fear to the LORD our God
and will be afraid of you.

challengenotes

To: **my_son**

heavenly_father: you will never find anyone who offers the kind of pardon and complete forgiveness I offer. when you repent, I wipe your slate clean and give you a fresh start. in fact, I can remove the sin from your life as far as the east is from the west.

18 Who is a God like you,
who pardons sin and
forgives the
transgression
of the remnant of his
inheritance?
You do not stay angry forever
but delight to show mercy.
19 You will again have
compassion on us;
you will tread our sins
underfoot
and hurl all our iniquities into
the depths of the sea.
20 You will be true to Jacob,
and show mercy to Abraham,
as you pledged on oath to our fathers
in days long ago.

NAHUM

UNCHANGING TRUTH ›› Think about the people who have made your life miserable at one time or another. The bullies who picked on you. The so-called friends who betrayed you. The people who started false rumors behind your back. The teachers and coaches who purposely embarrassed you in front of others.

Now picture them standing in front of God's throne, trembling in fear as the Almighty Creator of the universe reminds them of the things they did and pronounces his judgment on them.

Does that image bring a smile to your face? Maybe just a little one? It's OK to admit it if it does. It's part of our nature to want to see people punished for the bad things they do. In fact, our sense of justice comes from God himself, the One who will ultimately judge all evildoers.

Knowing that everyone will one day face God's judgment—and have to answer for everything they have done—should do two things for you. First, it should encourage you to let go of your need to exact revenge. Instead of looking for payback when someone messes with you, you can turn the matter over to God and let him even up the score when and how he sees fit. Second, the thought of God's judgment should serve as a warning for you personally not to take sin lightly. The next time you face a situation in which you're tempted to do something wrong, picture yourself standing in front of God's throne having to answer for that sin.

LIFE LESSONS ››

1   Problems, if we view them and deal with them correctly, can draw us closer to God (1:7).

2   Always, always, always remember sin's present and eternal consequences, and always strive to honor God (1:7–8).

3   God's judgment is complete and terrifying—something to be avoided at all costs (3:1–19).

1

An oracle concerning Nineveh. The book of the vision of Nahum the Elkoshite.

THE LORD'S ANGER AGAINST NINEVEH

2 The LORD is a jealous and avenging God;
   the LORD takes vengeance and is filled with wrath.
The LORD takes vengeance on his foes
   and maintains his wrath against his enemies.
3 The LORD is slow to anger and great in power;
   the LORD will not leave the guilty unpunished.
His way is in the whirlwind and the storm,
   and clouds are the dust of his feet.
4 He rebukes the sea and dries it up;
   he makes all the rivers run dry.
Bashan and Carmel wither
   and the blossoms of Lebanon fade.

NOW OR NEVER
NA 1:3

Can you imagine what life would be like if the Lord wasn't slow to anger? What if he didn't give us a chance to repent after we disobeyed him? What if he punished us immediately whenever we committed a sin?

5 The mountains quake before him
   and the hills melt away.
The earth trembles at his presence,
   the world and all who live in it.
6 Who can withstand his indignation?
   Who can endure his fierce anger?
His wrath is poured out like fire;
   the rocks are shattered before him.

7 The LORD is good,
   a refuge in times of trouble.

He cares for those who trust in him,
8 but with an overwhelming flood
   he will make an end of ⌊Nineveh⌋;
   he will pursue his foes into darkness.

challenge notes

To: my_son

heavenly_father: when you come to me, you don't have to act tough or pretend that nothing scares you. let down your guard. I won't make fun of you or think less of you for sharing your fears and feelings of vulnerability. I'm your refuge. you're always safe with me.

NA 1:7

9 Whatever they plot against the LORD
   he[a] will bring to an end;
   trouble will not come a second time.

10 They will be entangled among thorns
    and drunk from their wine;
    they will be consumed like dry stubble.[b]
11 From you, ⌊O Nineveh,⌋ has one come forth
    who plots evil against the LORD
    and counsels wickedness.

12 This is what the LORD says:

"Although they have allies and are numerous,
   they will be cut off and pass away.

---

a 9 Or *What do you foes plot against the LORD? / He*   b 10 The meaning of the Hebrew for this verse is uncertain.

Although I have afflicted you, ⌞O Judah,⌟
I will afflict you no more.
[13] Now I will break their yoke from your
neck
and tear your shackles away."

[14] The LORD has given a command
concerning you, ⌞Nineveh⌟:
"You will have no descendants to
bear your name.
I will destroy the carved images and
cast idols
that are in the temple of your gods.
I will prepare your grave,
for you are vile."

[15] Look, there on the mountains,
the feet of one who brings good
news,
who proclaims peace!
Celebrate your festivals, O Judah,
and fulfill your vows.
No more will the wicked invade you;
they will be completely destroyed.

NINEVEH TO FALL

2

An attacker advances against you,
⌞Nineveh⌟.
Guard the fortress,
watch the road,
brace yourselves,
marshal all your strength!

[2] The LORD will restore the splendor of Jacob
like the splendor of Israel,
though destroyers have laid them waste
and have ruined their vines.

[3] The shields of his soldiers are red;
the warriors are clad in scarlet.
The metal on the chariots flashes
on the day they are made ready;
the spears of pine are brandished.[a]
[4] The chariots storm through the streets,
rushing back and forth through the squares.
They look like flaming torches;
they dart about like lightning.

[5] He summons his picked troops,
yet they stumble on their way.
They dash to the city wall;
the protective shield is put in place.
[6] The river gates are thrown open
and the palace collapses.
[7] It is decreed[b] that ⌞the city⌟
be exiled and carried away.

Separating From the Crowd

Call it peer pressure or whatever, but you've got to admit, disobeying God is much easier when other people are doing it too. Think about it. If your friends are getting smashed at a party, doesn't it increase the chances that you're going to drink too? If you know that most of your coworkers occasionally lift merchandise after hours, doesn't it make you feel more comfortable doing it yourself? It's easy to be tricked into believing that there's safety in numbers. The fact is, though, God doesn't judge people in numbers. He judges us individually. We must each stand alone before him to accept the consequences we deserve.

---

[a] 3 Hebrew; Septuagint and Syriac / *the horsemen rush to and fro*   [b] 7 The meaning of the Hebrew for this word is uncertain.

Its slave girls moan like doves
and beat upon their breasts.
⁸ Nineveh is like a pool,
and its water is draining away.
"Stop! Stop!" they cry,
but no one turns back.
⁹ Plunder the silver!
Plunder the gold!
The supply is endless,
the wealth from all its treasures!
¹⁰ She is pillaged, plundered, stripped!
Hearts melt, knees give way,
bodies tremble, every face grows pale.

¹¹ Where now is the lions' den,
the place where they fed their young,
where the lion and lioness went,
and the cubs, with nothing to fear?
¹² The lion killed enough for his cubs
and strangled the prey for his mate,
filling his lairs with the kill
and his dens with the prey.

¹³ "I am against you,"
declares the LORD Almighty.
"I will burn up your chariots in smoke,
and the sword will devour your young
lions.
I will leave you no prey on the earth.
The voices of your messengers
will no longer be heard."

WOE TO NINEVEH

3

Woe to the city of blood,
full of lies,
full of plunder,
never without victims!
² The crack of whips,
the clatter of wheels,
galloping horses
and jolting chariots!
³ Charging cavalry,
flashing swords
and glittering spears!
Many casualties,
piles of dead,
bodies without number,
people stumbling over the corpses—
⁴ all because of the wanton lust of a harlot,
alluring, the mistress of sorceries,
who enslaved nations by her prostitution
and peoples by her witchcraft.

⁵ "I am against you," declares the LORD Almighty.
"I will lift your skirts over your face.
I will show the nations your nakedness
and the kingdoms your shame.

Understanding God's Attitude Toward Sin

>>> live the adventure >>> Na 2:13

God isn't big on the view that people get to decide what's right for themselves. He doesn't look at various sins as simply a matter of "lifestyle choices." He doesn't excuse people's actions because of their background or family history. He doesn't see a gray area between righteousness and evil. When people choose to go against him, his commands or his people, God brings the full weight of his judgment on them.

battlelines

» Music Maniac (Media)

Q: I heard that the new sound system you installed in your car is already broken.
A: Yeah, I'm gonna have to take it in and let the pros look at it. Meanwhile, I'm riding around in total silence.

Q: That's not so bad, is it? I mean, it's only temporary.
A: I hate it! I've got to have music playing or I'm, like, in withdrawal.

Q: Is it the music you love or the silence you hate?
A: It's both, I guess. But I do love music.

Q: Aren't you big into that new artist whose CD some stores won't carry because of the violent lyrics in his songs?
A: Yeah, it's really no big deal. Anyway, you should check out the wicked home theater system I set up in our living room. My dad told me to get whatever we needed. He said

I was the expert. So I went for it. I got this flat screen, high-def TV with killer digital speakers. I love to sit out there and crank up MTV and watch videos late at night. It's awesome.

Q: I've noticed the music channels seem to be getting pretty raw these days.
A: Yeah, no doubt. They know how to grab your attention . . . and keep it.

» Minding Your Mind

In one of the apostle Paul's letters, we find this fascinating passage:

"For though we live in the world, we do not wage war as the world does. The weapons we fight with are not the weapons of the world. On the contrary, they have divine power to demolish strongholds. We demolish arguments and every pretension that sets itself up against the knowledge of God, and we take captive every thought to make it obedient to Christ" (2 Corinthians 10:3–5).

Paul's reason for using military terminology is to remind us that we are in a spiritual war. Our adversary, the devil, tries to plant thoughts in our heads—sometimes through the stuff we hear in certain music, movies and TV shows. Satan knows that if he can quietly control the way we think and feel internally, he can influence the way we live life externally.

Be alert. Fight the devil. Round up and destroy every idea in your head that does not square with God's truth.

Read more about making good entertainment choices at www.RevolutionBible.com.

⁶ I will pelt you with filth,
    I will treat you with contempt
    and make you a spectacle.

⁷ All who see you will flee from you and
        say,
    'Nineveh is in ruins—who will
        mourn for her?'
    Where can I find anyone to comfort
        you?"

NOW OR NEVER

NA 3:4

Are there certain sins that you keep going back to again and again, like a moth drawn to a flame?

⁸ Are you better than Thebes,ᵃ
        situated on the Nile,
    with water around her?
    The river was her defense,
        the waters her wall.
⁹ Cushᵇ and Egypt were her boundless
        strength;
    Put and Libya were among her allies.

¹⁰ Yet she was taken captive
        and went into exile.
    Her infants were dashed to pieces
        at the head of every street.
    Lots were cast for her nobles,
        and all her great men were put in chains.
¹¹ You too will become drunk;
        you will go into hiding
        and seek refuge from the enemy.

¹² All your fortresses are like fig trees
        with their first ripe fruit;
    when they are shaken,
        the figs fall into the mouth of the eater.
¹³ Look at your troops—
        they are all women!
    The gates of your land
        are wide open to your enemies;
        fire has consumed their bars.

¹⁴ Draw water for the siege,
        strengthen your defenses!
    Work the clay,
        tread the mortar,
        repair the brickwork!
¹⁵ There the fire will devour you;
        the sword will cut you down
        and, like grasshoppers, consume you.
    Multiply like grasshoppers,
        multiply like locusts!
¹⁶ You have increased the number of your merchants
        till they are more than the stars of the sky,
    but like locusts they strip the land
        and then fly away.
¹⁷ Your guards are like locusts,
        your officials like swarms of locusts
        that settle in the walls on a cold day—

ᵃ *8* Hebrew *No Amon*   ᵇ *9* That is, the upper Nile region

but when the sun appears they fly away,
and no one knows where.

18 O king of Assyria, your shepherds[a] slumber;
your nobles lie down to rest.
Your people are scattered on the mountains
with no one to gather them.
19 Nothing can heal your wound;
your injury is fatal.
Everyone who hears the news about you
claps his hands at your fall,
for who has not felt
your endless cruelty?

---

[a] 18 Or *rulers*

HABAKKUK

HABAKKUK HABAKKUK HABAKKUK

« AT A GLANCE

Author
Habakkuk

Audience
People of Judah

Date
Around 605 B.C.

Setting
Babylon was about to destroy Judah.

Verse to Remember
Though the fig tree does not bud and there are no grapes on the vines, though the olive crop fails and the fields produce no food, though there are no sheep in the pen and no cattle in the stalls, yet I will rejoice in the LORD, I will be joyful in God my Savior (3:17–18).

Theme to Consider
Ever wonder why it appears as though God allows evil to win so often? Join Habakkuk. But after questioning God, Habakkuk concluded that God *is* in control and judgment *will* come; so praise God!

UNCHANGING TRUTH » If you could ask God any question, what would it be? Would you go for personal information, like what you're going to be when you get older . . . who you're going to marry . . . how long you're going to live? Or would you ask him some harder questions, like why he created Satan . . . how dinosaurs fit in to the creation story . . . what heaven is like?

How would you ask your question? Would you be nervous, or would you be bold? What kind of answer would you expect to get?

The Old Testament prophet Habakkuk was given an opportunity like that. In fact, he was allowed to ask God *two* questions, and he made the most of the opportunity. Habakkuk chose two tough questions, both of which had to do with the way God deals with evil. Apparently Habakkuk wasn't a guy to settle for easy answers, because he didn't pull any punches with God. In some places, it even seems as though he's accusing God—in a respectful way, of course.

God didn't get angry about Habakkuk's questions; he patiently answered each one. He wanted Habakkuk to understand him and to know him. God wants *you* to understand and know him too. That's why he won't get mad about any sincere questions you have. If you come across something in the Bible that doesn't make sense to you, ask for God's help in finding answers to your questions. If you get put in a situation that seems unfair to you, ask him to help you understand why. If you see things in the world that don't match what you've been taught, ask him to help you clear things up.

There's no reason for you to hide your questions about the Christian life or the God you worship. Remember, the Lord doesn't punish faithful people for wanting to know more about him!

LIFE LESSONS »

1. God can use anyone to accomplish his work (1:5–11).

2. Expect answers from God when you pray. It's a great way to develop valuable listening skills (2:1).

3. Question God all you want; but when you're finished, make sure you praise him (3:2).

1

The oracle that Habakkuk the prophet received.

HABAKKUK'S COMPLAINT

2 How long, O LORD, must I call for help,
but you do not listen?
Or cry out to you, "Violence!"
but you do not save?
3 Why do you make me look at injustice?
Why do you tolerate wrong?
Destruction and violence are before me;
there is strife, and conflict abounds.
4 Therefore the law is paralyzed,
and justice never prevails.
The wicked hem in the righteous,
so that justice is perverted.

THE LORD'S ANSWER

5 "Look at the nations and watch—
and be utterly amazed.

For I am going to do something in your
days
that you would not believe,
even if you were told.
6 I am raising up the Babylonians,[a]
that ruthless and impetuous people,
who sweep across the whole earth
to seize dwelling places not their
own.
7 They are a feared and dreaded people;
they are a law to themselves
and promote their own honor.
8 Their horses are swifter than leopards,
fiercer than wolves at dusk.

NOW OR NEVER

HAB 1:2

If you have questions about the way God
works, you're not alone. And you're not
being ridiculous either. Habakkuk was one
of God's chosen prophets, and look at the
questions he had!

Their cavalry gallops headlong;
their horsemen come from afar.
They fly like a vulture swooping to devour;
9   they all come bent on violence.
Their hordes[b] advance like a desert wind
and gather prisoners like sand.
10 They deride kings
and scoff at rulers.
They laugh at all fortified cities;
they build earthen ramps and capture them.
11 Then they sweep past like the wind and go on—
guilty men, whose own strength is their god."

HABAKKUK'S SECOND COMPLAINT

12 O LORD, are you not from everlasting?
My God, my Holy One, we will not die.
O LORD, you have appointed them to execute judgment;
O Rock, you have ordained them to punish.
13 Your eyes are too pure to look on evil;
you cannot tolerate wrong.

---

a 6 Or *Chaldeans*   b 9 The meaning of the Hebrew for this word is uncertain.

Why then do you tolerate the treacherous?
   Why are you silent while the wicked
   swallow up those more righteous than themselves?
14 You have made men like fish in the sea,
   like sea creatures that have no ruler.
15 The wicked foe pulls all of them up with hooks,
   he catches them in his net,
he gathers them up in his dragnet;
   and so he rejoices and is glad.
16 Therefore he sacrifices to his net
   and burns incense to his dragnet,
for by his net he lives in luxury
   and enjoys the choicest food.
17 Is he to keep on emptying his net,
   destroying nations without mercy?

I will stand at my watch
   and station myself on the ramparts;
I will look to see what he will say to me,
   and what answer I am to give to this complaint.ᵃ

THE LORD'S ANSWER

2 Then the LORD replied:

  "Write down the revelation
    and make it plain on tablets
    so that a heraldᵇ may run with it.
3 For the revelation awaits an appointed time;
    it speaks of the end
    and will not prove false.
Though it linger, wait for it;
    itᶜ will certainly come and will not delay.

4 "See, he is puffed up;
    his desires are not upright—
    but the righteous will live by his faithᵈ—
5 indeed, wine betrays him;
    he is arrogant and never at rest.
Because he is as greedy as the graveᵉ
    and like death is never satisfied,
he gathers to himself all the nations
    and takes captive all the peoples.

6 "Will not all of them taunt him with ridicule and scorn, saying,

  " 'Woe to him who piles up stolen goods
    and makes himself wealthy by extortion!
    How long must this go on?'
7 Will not your debtorsᶠ suddenly arise?
    Will they not wake up and make you tremble?
    Then you will become their victim.
8 Because you have plundered many nations,
    the peoples who are left will plunder you.
For you have shed man's blood;
    you have destroyed lands and cities and everyone in them.

ᵃ 1 Or *and what to answer when I am rebuked*   ᵇ 2 Or *so that whoever reads it*   ᶜ 3 Or *Though he linger, wait for him; / he*
ᵈ 4 Or *faithfulness*   ᵉ 5 Hebrew *Sheol*   ᶠ 7 Or *creditors*

9 "Woe to him who builds his realm by unjust gain
  to set his nest on high,
  to escape the clutches of ruin!
10 You have plotted the ruin of many peoples,
  shaming your own house and forfeiting your life.
11 The stones of the wall will cry out,
  and the beams of the woodwork will echo it.

12 "Woe to him who builds a city with bloodshed
  and establishes a town by crime!
13 Has not the LORD Almighty determined
  that the people's labor is only fuel for the fire,
  that the nations exhaust themselves for nothing?
14 For the earth will be filled with the knowledge of the glory of the LORD,
  as the waters cover the sea.

15 "Woe to him who gives drink to his neighbors,
  pouring it from the wineskin till they are drunk,
  so that he can gaze on their naked bodies.

16 You will be filled with shame instead of glory.
  Now it is your turn! Drink and be exposed[a]!
  The cup from the LORD's right hand is coming around to you,
  and disgrace will cover your glory.
17 The violence you have done to Lebanon will overwhelm you,
  and your destruction of animals will terrify you.
  For you have shed man's blood;
  you have destroyed lands and cities
  and everyone in them.

NOW OR NEVER
HAB 2:18–20

It's tempting to make fun of the ancient Israelites for worshiping things they created themselves. But think about how many people today put their trust in money, which is also a human creation.

18 "Of what value is an idol, since a man has carved it?
  Or an image that teaches lies?
  For he who makes it trusts in his own creation;
  he makes idols that cannot speak.
19 Woe to him who says to wood, 'Come to life!'
  Or to lifeless stone, 'Wake up!'
  Can it give guidance?
  It is covered with gold and silver;
  there is no breath in it.
20 But the LORD is in his holy temple;
  let all the earth be silent before him."

HABAKKUK'S PRAYER

3 A prayer of Habakkuk the prophet. On shigionoth.[b]

2 LORD, I have heard of your fame;
  I stand in awe of your deeds, O LORD.
  Renew them in our day,
  in our time make them known;
  in wrath remember mercy.

---

[a] 16 Masoretic Text; Dead Sea Scrolls, Aquila, Vulgate and Syriac (see also Septuagint) and stagger   [b] 1 Probably a literary or musical term

othniel

» **Nephew of Caleb**
» **Married Caleb's daughter**
» **A distinguished warrior and judge**

cushan

» **King of Aram Naharaim (or Mesopotamia)**
» **Dominated Israel for eight years**
» **Defeated by Othniel**

The Main Event

It's a somewhat obscure story of only five verses with not a lot of detail. Here's what we know: The Israelites foolishly forgot about the Lord. They dumped the one true God and started chasing after the gods of their neighbors, the Canaanites.

This wasn't like changing churches or switching denominational affiliations. All idol worship is despicable in God's eyes. But the gods Israel turned to, Baal and Asherah, were especially heinous. Baal and Asherah worship involved, among other things, disgusting sexual orgies and human sacrifices . . . of helpless children.

It's no wonder "the anger of the Lord burned against Israel" (Judges 3:8). What's kind of surprising, though, is that God used King Cushan of Mesopotamia to carry out his punishment of the Israelites.

Cushan's full name was Cushan-Rishathaim, which scholars think means "doubly wicked Cushan." That should tell you something right there. He was a really nasty guy. After eight years of his savage reign, the people of Israel were humbled. When they finally cried out to God for help, he graciously sent them a deliverer named Othniel.

Perhaps Othniel was a giant of a man, built like an NFL defensive end or a sculpted WWE champion. We don't know for sure. But we do know a couple things about Othniel. For one thing, he'd seen battle before. He once captured the town of Kiriath Sepher to win a girl's hand in marriage (see Joshua 15:16–17). But the most important thing about Othniel is that the "Spirit of the Lord came upon him" (Judges 3:10). What else do we need to know?

The Outcome

Othniel, filled with the strength of God, overpowered Cushan and all of his soldiers. The result was 40 years of peace in the land of Israel.

Their showdown is a good reminder of our need to be filled with the Holy Spirit (see Ephesians 5:18)—not just in times of crisis, but all the time. When we are controlled by the Spirit, our lives are marked by power (see Acts 1:8) and overflow with "love, joy, peace, patience, kindness, goodness, faithfulness, gentleness and self-control" (Galatians 5:22–23).

The only other option is to rely on our own strength. The results of that are what the Bible calls "acts of the sinful nature," which are "sexual immorality, impurity and debauchery; idolatry and witchcraft; hatred, discord, jealousy, fits of rage, selfish ambition, dissensions, factions and envy; drunkenness, orgies, and the like" (Galatians 5:19–21).

When you see a list like that—plus real-life examples like the wayward Israelites and Cushan—it doesn't seem like much of a choice, does it?

Read more about Othniel and Cushan in Judges 3:7–11 (page 273).

³God came from Teman,
the Holy One from Mount Paran.   *Selah*ᵃ
His glory covered the heavens
and his praise filled the earth.
⁴His splendor was like the sunrise;
rays flashed from his hand,
where his power was hidden.
⁵Plague went before him;
pestilence followed his steps.
⁶He stood, and shook the earth;
he looked, and made the nations tremble.
The ancient mountains crumbled
and the age-old hills collapsed.
His ways are eternal.
⁷I saw the tents of Cushan in distress,
the dwellings of Midian in anguish.

⁸Were you angry with the rivers, O LORD?
Was your wrath against the streams?
Did you rage against the sea
when you rode with your horses
and your victorious chariots?
⁹You uncovered your bow,
you called for many arrows.
Selah
You split the earth with rivers;
¹⁰   the mountains saw you and writhed.
Torrents of water swept by;
the deep roared
and lifted its waves on high.

¹¹Sun and moon stood still in the heavens
at the glint of your flying arrows,
at the lightning of your flashing
spear.
¹²In wrath you strode through the earth
and in anger you threshed the
nations.
¹³You came out to deliver your people,
to save your anointed one.
You crushed the leader of the land of
wickedness,
you stripped him from head to foot.
Selah
¹⁴With his own spear you pierced his
head
when his warriors stormed out to
scatter us,
gloating as though about to devour
the wretched who were in hiding.
¹⁵You trampled the sea with your horses,
churning the great waters.

¹⁶I heard and my heart pounded,
my lips quivered at the sound;

ᵃ *3* A word of uncertain meaning; possibly a musical term; also in verses 9 and 13

decay crept into my bones,
and my legs trembled.
Yet I will wait patiently for the day of calamity
to come on the nation invading us.

17 Though the fig tree does not
bud
and there are no grapes on
the vines,
though the olive crop fails
and the fields produce no
food,
though there are no sheep in
the pen
and no cattle in the stalls,
18 yet I will rejoice in the LORD,
I will be joyful in God my
Savior.

challengenotes

To: my_son

heavenly_father: I have all the strength you need to overcome the obstacles in your path. when your footing gets shaky, call out for me. I'll pull you up to heights you've never dreamed possible.

19 The Sovereign LORD is my strength;
he makes my feet like the feet of a deer,
he enables me to go on the heights.

For the director of music. On my stringed instruments.

ZEPHANIAH

ZEPHANIAH

Author
Zephaniah

Audience
People of Judah

Date
As 1:1 states, during the reign of King Josiah (640–609 B.C.), probably near the beginning of Josiah's reign

Setting
King Manasseh and King Amon had been evil kings of Judah. King Josiah, who ruled after them, tried to make changes for the good in Judah—probably in part because of Zephaniah's warnings.

Verse to Remember
Seek the LORD, all you humble of the land, you who do what he commands. Seek righteousness, seek humility; perhaps you will be sheltered on the day of the LORD's anger (2:3).

Theme to Consider
Zephaniah declared the coming of God's stern judgment, but he wasn't all doom and gloom. The flip side of his message was that someday the people would repent and return to God, and that's always worth celebrating—in our lives too.

UNCHANGING TRUTH » Have you ever heard the expression, "When the cat's away, the mice will play"? Have you ever seen that principle at work—say, when a teacher leaves your class alone for a few minutes? What is it that makes people want to get crazy when authority figures are absent? What is it that tempts . . .

- players to goof off during practice when the coach isn't watching?
- drivers to stomp on the accelerator after they get a safe distance past a cop with a radar gun?
- kids to throw keg parties when their parents are out of town?

More than anything else, it's the possibility of getting away with it. That's what makes a lot of sin tempting. If there's no one around to hand out immediate consequences for disobedience, we start to think that maybe no one will ever find out about it . . . or that no one really cares what we do.

That's the attitude the people of Judah had while Zephaniah was a prophet. They had abandoned any type of contact with God years earlier and figured that his apparent silence was a sign that he didn't care what they did. They seemed to believe that they were untouchable, so they lived as though God wasn't there at all.

Talk about a serious error in judgment! The people of Judah soon found out that God had seen every single one of their sins—and was preparing his judgment for the wickedness he had witnessed.

Don't make the same mistake. Don't let anyone convince you that you can get away with doing something wrong. Remember, God sees everything, and he always cares about the thoughts in our minds, the state of our hearts and the things we do.

LIFE LESSONS »

1 Never underestimate the seriousness of God's judgment (1:2–3).

2 The more genuinely humble you are, the better chance you have of developing a close relationship with God (2:3).

3 If you remain faithful to God, you will never have to fear his eternal judgment (3:15).

1 The word of the LORD that came to Zephaniah son of Cushi, the son of Gedaliah, the son of Amariah, the son of Hezekiah, during the reign of Josiah son of Amon king of Judah:

WARNING OF COMING DESTRUCTION

² "I will sweep away everything
from the face of the earth,"

declares the LORD.

³ "I will sweep away both men and animals;
I will sweep away the birds of the air
and the fish of the sea.
The wicked will have only heaps of rubble[a]
when I cut off man from the face of the earth,"

declares the LORD.

AGAINST JUDAH

⁴ "I will stretch out my hand against Judah
and against all who live in Jerusalem.
I will cut off from this place every
remnant of Baal,
the names of the pagan and the
idolatrous priests—
⁵ those who bow down on the roofs
to worship the starry host,
those who bow down and swear by the
LORD
and who also swear by Molech,[b]
⁶ those who turn back from following the
LORD
and neither seek the LORD nor inquire
of him.
⁷ Be silent before the Sovereign LORD,
for the day of the LORD is near.
The LORD has prepared a sacrifice;
he has consecrated those he has invited.
⁸ On the day of the LORD's sacrifice
I will punish the princes
and the king's sons
and all those clad
in foreign clothes.
⁹ On that day I will punish
all who avoid stepping on the threshold,[c]
who fill the temple of their gods
with violence and deceit.

¹⁰ "On that day," declares the LORD,
"a cry will go up from the Fish Gate,
wailing from the New Quarter,
and a loud crash from the hills.
¹¹ Wail, you who live in the market district[d];
all your merchants will be wiped out,
all who trade with[e] silver will be ruined.
¹² At that time I will search Jerusalem with lamps
and punish those who are complacent,

NOW OR NEVER
ZEP 1:4-6

God promised to punish the people of Judah for putting their trust in the stars instead of in him. Remember that the next time you see someone messing around with astrology or signs of the zodiac. It might seem harmless, but if it encourages you to trust anything but God, it's wrong.

---

[a] 3 The meaning of the Hebrew for this line is uncertain.   [b] 5 Hebrew *Malcam*, that is, Milcom   [c] 9 See 1 Samuel 5:5.   [d] 11 Or *the Mortar*   [e] 11 Or *in*

who are like wine left on its dregs,
who think, 'The Lord will do nothing,
    either good or bad.'
¹³ Their wealth will be plundered,
    their houses demolished.
They will build houses
    but not live in them;
they will plant vineyards
    but not drink the wine.

THE GREAT DAY OF THE LORD

¹⁴ "The great day of the Lord is near—
    near and coming quickly.
Listen! The cry on the day of the Lord will be bitter,
    the shouting of the warrior there.
¹⁵ That day will be a day of wrath,
    a day of distress and anguish,
a day of trouble and ruin,
    a day of darkness and gloom,
    a day of clouds and blackness,
¹⁶ a day of trumpet and battle cry
    against the fortified cities
    and against the corner towers.
¹⁷ I will bring distress on the people
    and they will walk like blind men,
    because they have sinned against the Lord.
Their blood will be poured out like dust
    and their entrails like filth.
¹⁸ Neither their silver nor their gold
    will be able to save them
    on the day of the Lord's wrath.
In the fire of his jealousy
    the whole world will be consumed,
for he will make a sudden end
    of all who live in the earth."

Gather together, gather together,
    O shameful nation,
² before the appointed time arrives
    and that day sweeps on like chaff,
before the fierce anger of the Lord comes upon you,
    before the day of the Lord's wrath comes upon you.
³ Seek the Lord, all you humble of the land,
    you who do what he commands.
Seek righteousness, seek humility;
    perhaps you will be sheltered
    on the day of the Lord's anger.

AGAINST PHILISTIA

⁴ Gaza will be abandoned
    and Ashkelon left in ruins.
At midday Ashdod will be emptied
    and Ekron uprooted.
⁵ Woe to you who live by the sea,
    O Kerethite people;

battlelines

» Can't Get Enough (Contentment)

Q: What would you say is your greatest weakness?
A: My what?

Q: You know, the one thing in life you just can't resist.
A: Oh, that's easy. Technology. Anything electronic.

Q: Really?
A: Absolutely. I could spend a whole day in a good electronics store. My friends don't even like to go with me anymore, because I just walk around the place and drool.

Q: Do you have a lot of gadgets?
A: Not as many as I'd *like* to have. Right now I'm saving up for a laptop.

Q: I thought you already had a computer.
A: Well, yeah, a desktop. But it's almost a year old, and it's already outdated! Lately I've been getting into digital moviemaking; I need something really mobile so I can edit as I go. If I could just get something with a massive hard drive, a ton of RAM and the right software, I'd have my own portable movie studio. Unfortunately, my video camera is pretty basic. I can't do much with it. That's why I've got my eye on the newest model.

Q: Sounds like you'll need to rob a bank or something.
A: Yeah, that's the frustrating part. As soon as I buy one thing, they come out with something better, and I have to start all over again.

» True Satisfaction

The countless commercials and ads we see every day are designed to do two things: (1) make us unhappy with what we've got, and (2) get us to buy whatever they're trying to sell us. That's the deal in a nutshell. Many advertisers are masters of manipulation.

No wonder so many guys like Ramon are constantly wanting and wishing, never happy with what they've got. If that's you, ponder these words from the apostle Paul: "I have learned to be content whatever the circumstances. I know what it is to be in need, and I know what it is to have plenty. I have learned the secret of being content in any and every situation, whether well fed or hungry, whether living in plenty or in want" (Philippians 4:11–12). So what is the secret of being content? In this case, the "secret" is less like confidential info you'd get from an expert and more like a lesson you have to learn. No one can just *tell* you the "secret." Have you learned it?

For more on money and contentment go to www.RevolutionBible.com.

the word of the Lord is against you,
  O Canaan, land of the Philistines.

"I will destroy you,
  and none will be left."

[6] The land by the sea, where the Kerethites[a] dwell,
  will be a place for shepherds and sheep pens.
[7] It will belong to the remnant of the house of Judah;
  there they will find pasture.
In the evening they will lie down
  in the houses of Ashkelon.
The Lord their God will care for them;
  he will restore their fortunes.[b]

AGAINST MOAB AND AMMON

[8] "I have heard the insults of Moab
  and the taunts of the Ammonites,
who insulted my people
  and made threats against their land.
[9] Therefore, as surely as I live,"
  declares the Lord Almighty, the God of Israel,
"surely Moab will become like Sodom,
  the Ammonites like Gomorrah—
a place of weeds and salt pits,
  a wasteland forever.
The remnant of my people will plunder them;
  the survivors of my nation will inherit their land."

[10] This is what they will get in return for their pride,
  for insulting and mocking the people of the Lord Almighty.
[11] The Lord will be awesome to them
  when he destroys all the gods of the land.
The nations on every shore will worship him,
  every one in its own land.

AGAINST CUSH

[12] "You too, O Cushites,[c]
  will be slain by my sword."

AGAINST ASSYRIA

[13] He will stretch out his hand against the north
  and destroy Assyria,
leaving Nineveh utterly desolate
  and dry as the desert.
[14] Flocks and herds will lie down there,
  creatures of every kind.
The desert owl and the screech owl
  will roost on her columns.
Their calls will echo through the windows,
  rubble will be in the doorways,
  the beams of cedar will be exposed.
[15] This is the carefree city
  that lived in safety.

---

[a] 6 The meaning of the Hebrew for this word is uncertain.   [b] 7 Or *will bring back their captives*   [c] 12 That is, people from the upper Nile region

She said to herself,
    "I am, and there is none besides me."
What a ruin she has become,
    a lair for wild beasts!
All who pass by her scoff
    and shake their fists.

THE FUTURE OF JERUSALEM

3

Woe to the city of oppressors,
    rebellious and defiled!
2 She obeys no one,
    she accepts no correction.
She does not trust in the LORD,
    she does not draw near to her God.
3 Her officials are roaring lions,
    her rulers are evening wolves,
    who leave nothing for the morning.
4 Her prophets are arrogant;
    they are treacherous men.
Her priests profane the sanctuary
    and do violence to the law.
5 The LORD within her is righteous;
    he does no wrong.
Morning by morning he dispenses his
        justice,
    and every new day he does not fail,
    yet the unrighteous know no shame.

6 "I have cut off nations;
    their strongholds are demolished.
I have left their streets deserted,
    with no one passing through.
Their cities are destroyed;
    no one will be left—no one at all.
7 I said to the city,
    'Surely you will fear me
    and accept correction!'
Then her dwelling would not be cut off,
    nor all my punishments come upon
        her.
But they were still eager
    to act corruptly in all they did.
8 Therefore wait for me," declares the LORD,
    "for the day I will stand up to testify.a
I have decided to assemble the nations,
    to gather the kingdoms
and to pour out my wrath on them—
    all my fierce anger.
The whole world will be consumed
    by the fire of my jealous anger.

9 "Then will I purify the lips of the peoples,
    that all of them may call on the name of the LORD
    and serve him shoulder to shoulder.
10 From beyond the rivers of Cushb

Remaining Humble Before God

When people talk about arrogance, who do you think of? Do you think of the school football star who pushes people around just because he can? A kid in your youth group who thinks he's so cool because he drives a nice car and has a new girlfriend every month? Or do you think of yourself? One day, God is going to reveal to the whole earth just how great he is, and everyone who put their trust in anything or anyone else will pay the price. Read about the people of Nineveh and remember the price they paid for their pride.

»» live the adventure »» Zep 2:15

---

a 8 Septuagint and Syriac; Hebrew *will rise up to plunder*   b 10 That is, the upper Nile region

my worshipers, my scattered people,
will bring me offerings.
¹¹ On that day you will not be put to shame
for all the wrongs you have done to me,
because I will remove from this city
those who rejoice in their pride.
Never again will you be haughty
on my holy hill.
¹² But I will leave within you
the meek and humble,
who trust in the name of the LORD.
¹³ The remnant of Israel will do no wrong;
they will speak no lies,
nor will deceit be found in their mouths.
They will eat and lie down
and no one will make them afraid."

¹⁴ Sing, O Daughter of Zion;
shout aloud, O Israel!
Be glad and rejoice with all your heart,
O Daughter of Jerusalem!
¹⁵ The LORD has taken away your punishment,
he has turned back your enemy.
The LORD, the King of Israel, is with you;
never again will you fear any harm.
¹⁶ On that day they will say to Jerusalem,
"Do not fear, O Zion;
do not let your hands hang limp.

¹⁷ The LORD your God is with you,
he is mighty to save.
He will take great delight in you,
he will quiet you with his love,
he will rejoice over you
with singing."

¹⁸ "The sorrows for the appointed
feasts
I will remove from you;
they are a burden and a
reproach to you.ᵃ

---

¹⁹ At that time I will deal
with all who oppressed you;
I will rescue the lame
and gather those who have been scattered.
I will give them praise and honor
in every land where they were put to shame.
²⁰ At that time I will gather you;
at that time I will bring you home.
I will give you honor and praise
among all the peoples of the earth
when I restore your fortunesᵇ
before your very eyes,"

says the LORD.

ᵃ *18* Or *"I will gather you who mourn for the appointed feasts; / your reproach is a burden to you*   ᵇ *20* Or *I bring back your captives*

HAGGAI

« AT A GLANCE

Author
Haggai

Audience
The Jewish exiles who had returned to Jerusalem from Babylon

Date
520 B.C.

Setting
The Persian king Cyrus had allowed the Jews to return to Jerusalem to rebuild the temple. The people began rebuilding it, but opposition from their neighbors and then their own apathy caused them to abandon the project.

Verse to Remember
Then the word of the LORD came through the prophet Haggai: "Is it a time for you yourselves to be living in your paneled houses, while this house remains a ruin?" Now this is what the LORD Almighty says: "Give careful thought to your ways" (1:3–5).

Theme to Consider
The situation in the book of Haggai is a challenging reminder to take inventory of our lives and reorder our priorities to reflect God's will. What has God called you to do? Are you doing it?

UNCHANGING TRUTH » We live in a noisy world. We're constantly surrounded by voices trying to convince us to buy this, wear that, eat this, watch that and believe this. One of the few things that can cut through the noise and confusion is the voice of reason.

Everyone is looking for something that has meaning—something that's not just about surface appearances or disposable stuff. People want to know that they have a purpose in this world. More specifically, they want to know what that purpose is.

The prophet Haggai was a voice of reason for the Jews who had returned to their homeland to rebuild Jerusalem after it had been destroyed. Haggai told the people to start with the temple of God so that they could reconnect with the Lord in worship as soon as possible. He gave the people a sense of purpose, and—initially, at least—they responded. They began the temple's reconstruction with fresh enthusiasm.

You can be a voice of reason for the people in your life. You may not be able to convince them to build a temple, but you could . . .

- encourage a friend to put her talents to use by playing guitar for your youth group meetings.
- convince someone you know who's struggling with a personal problem to read a book or Bible passage that helped you through a similar situation.
- challenge your mom to stop smoking by telling her how worried you are about her health (or by promising to wash the dishes every day she stays smoke-free).

Obviously, being a voice of reason isn't something you can or even should do by yourself. It's something that requires God's help. Ask him to give you the wisdom to know what to say, when to say it and how to say it so that it is received well.

LIFE LESSONS »

1 If you care more about your own personal comfort and enjoyment than you do about the Lord's work, you need to change your priorities, or you will ultimately be disappointed with your life (1:2–4).

2 If your relationship with God isn't what it should be, the other areas of your life will seem out of whack as well (1:5–6).

3 When you get serious about worshiping God and doing his work, you will be rewarded with a blessed and meaningful life (2:4–5).

A CALL TO BUILD THE HOUSE OF THE LORD

1 In the second year of King Darius, on the first day of the sixth month, the word of the LORD came through the prophet Haggai to Zerubbabel son of Shealtiel, governor of Judah, and to Joshua[a] son of Jehozadak, the high priest:

2 This is what the LORD Almighty says: "These people say, 'The time has not yet come for the LORD's house to be built.' "

3 Then the word of the LORD came through the prophet Haggai: 4 "Is it a time for you yourselves to be living in your paneled houses, while this house remains a ruin?"

5 Now this is what the LORD Almighty says: "Give careful thought to your ways. 6 You have planted much, but have harvested little. You eat, but never have enough. You drink, but never have your fill. You put on clothes, but are not warm. You earn wages, only to put them in a purse with holes in it."

NOW OR NEVER
HAG 1:9

Do you give anything a higher priority in your life than your relationship with God? If so, what do you think God wants you to do about it?

7 This is what the LORD Almighty says: "Give careful thought to your ways. 8 Go up into the mountains and bring down timber and build the house, so that I may take pleasure in it and be honored," says the LORD. 9 "You expected much, but see, it turned out to be little. What you brought home, I blew away. Why?" declares the LORD Almighty. "Because of my house, which remains a ruin, while each of you is busy with his own house. 10 Therefore, because of you the heavens have withheld their dew and the earth its crops. 11 I called for a drought on the fields and the mountains, on the grain, the new wine, the oil and whatever the ground produces, on men and cattle, and on the labor of your hands."

challenge notes

To: my_son

heavenly_father: four words from me—"I am with you"—were enough to inspire the israelites to rebuild my temple. let those same words inspire you too. I *am* with you, and I will bless everything you do for me.

12 Then Zerubbabel son of Shealtiel, Joshua son of Jehozadak, the high priest, and the whole remnant of the people obeyed the voice of the LORD their God and the message of the prophet Haggai, because the LORD their God had sent him. And the people feared the LORD.

13 Then Haggai, the LORD's messenger, gave this message of the LORD to the people: "I am with you," declares the LORD. 14 So the LORD stirred up the spirit of Zerubbabel son of Shealtiel, governor of Judah, and the spirit of Joshua son of Jehozadak, the high priest, and the spirit of the whole remnant of the people. They came and began to work on the house of the LORD Almighty, their God, 15 on the twenty-fourth day of the sixth month in the second year of King Darius.

THE PROMISED GLORY OF THE NEW HOUSE

2 On the twenty-first day of the seventh month, the word of the LORD came through the prophet Haggai: 2 "Speak to Zerubbabel son of Shealtiel, governor of Judah, to Joshua son of Jehozadak, the high priest, and to the remnant of the people. Ask them, 3 'Who of you is left who saw this house in its former glory? How does it look to you now? Does it not seem to you like nothing? 4 But now be strong, O Zerubbabel,' declares the LORD. 'Be strong, O Joshua son of Jehozadak, the high priest. Be strong, all you people of the land,' declares the LORD, 'and work. For I am with you,' declares the LORD Almighty. 5 'This is what I covenanted with you when you came out of Egypt. And my Spirit remains among you. Do not fear.'

6 "This is what the LORD Almighty says: 'In a little while I will once more shake the heavens and the earth, the sea and the dry land. 7 I will shake all nations, and the desired of all nations will come, and I will fill this house with glory,' says the LORD Almighty. 8 'The silver is mine and the gold is mine,' de-

---

[a] *1* A variant of *Jeshua*; here and elsewhere in Haggai

battlelines

» Waking Up . . . (Thankfulness)

Q: Big plans for Thanksgiving?
A: The usual—going to see my grandparents. Stuffing my pie hole with turkey and dressing. Watching football. Catching some z's. Reading.

Q: So what are you most thankful for?
A: Most thankful for? I would say my family. I feel pretty blessed. I have a lot of friends whose families are just a mess. My folks really love each other, and they're decent parents—better than decent, actually.

Q: Anything else?
A: I've got a good group of friends. And I'm doing well in school this year—way better than I ever thought I could do in algebra!

Q: That's not a bad list. You ought to feel really good.
A: Yeah, I guess I should. I've got a lot to feel good about . . . which is kind of strange, now that I think about it.

Q: Why?
A: Because I always hear myself complaining about my life and how lame it is.

Q: Really?
A: Yeah, I guess it's just a bad habit. I should start a new one—like having a little Thanksgiving celebration every day. Why do we set aside only one day a year for that?

Q: You got me.

» . . . And Smelling the Coffee

If complaining is your thing, you can always find plenty to gripe about in a fallen world. But the flip side is also true. In a world that has been graced by God, there is always much to celebrate.

The apostle Paul once told a group of Christians who were being persecuted for their faith: "Be joyful always; pray continually; give thanks in all circumstances, for this is God's will for you in Christ Jesus" (1 Thessalonians 5:16–18). If that kind of thinking applies to suffering people, how much more does it apply to those of us who have it relatively easy?

If you're having problems keeping track of the good things in your life, grab some paper and a pen. Make a list of all the things you've been given. Then thank your Maker from the depths of your heart as you read through your list.

For more on thankfulness go to www.RevolutionBible.com.

clares the LORD Almighty. 9'The glory of this present house will be greater than the glory of the former house,' says the LORD Almighty. 'And in this place I will grant peace,' declares the LORD Almighty."

BLESSINGS FOR A DEFILED PEOPLE

10On the twenty-fourth day of the ninth month, in the second year of Darius, the word of the LORD came to the prophet Haggai: 11"This is what the LORD Almighty says: 'Ask the priests what the law says: 12If a person carries consecrated meat in the fold of his garment, and that fold touches some bread or stew, some wine, oil or other food, does it become consecrated?' "

The priests answered, "No."

13Then Haggai said, "If a person defiled by contact with a dead body touches one of these things, does it become defiled?"

"Yes," the priests replied, "it becomes defiled."

14Then Haggai said, " 'So it is with this people and this nation in my sight,' declares the LORD. 'Whatever they do and whatever they offer there is defiled.

15" 'Now give careful thought to this from this day on[a]— consider how things were before one stone was laid on another in the LORD's temple. 16When anyone came to a heap of twenty measures, there were only ten. When anyone went to a wine vat to draw fifty measures, there were only twenty. 17I struck all the work of your hands with blight, mildew and hail, yet you did not turn to me,' declares the LORD. 18'From this day on, from this twenty-fourth day of the ninth month, give careful thought to the day when the foundation of the LORD's temple was laid. Give careful thought: 19Is there yet any seed left in the barn? Until now, the vine and the fig tree, the pomegranate and the olive tree have not borne fruit.

" 'From this day on I will bless you.' "

ZERUBBABEL THE LORD'S SIGNET RING

20The word of the LORD came to Haggai a second time on the twenty-fourth day of the month: 21"Tell Zerubbabel governor of Judah that I will shake the heavens and the earth. 22I will overturn royal thrones and shatter the power of the foreign kingdoms. I will overthrow chariots and their drivers; horses and their riders will fall, each by the sword of his brother.

23" 'On that day,' declares the LORD Almighty, 'I will take you, my servant Zerubbabel son of Shealtiel,' declares the LORD, 'and I will make you like my signet ring, for I have chosen you,' declares the LORD Almighty."

Overcoming Opposition

The enemies of Israel couldn't stop the Jewish builders from finishing God's temple. That's because God was with them. That same presence is available to you as you do your kingdom work. Nothing can prevent you from doing what God wants you to do. People may try to distract you or put obstacles in your way, but if you're focused on your work, their efforts to steer you off course will fail.

»» live the adventure »» Hag 2:4-5

a 15 Or to the days past

ZECHARIAH

ZECHARIAH ZECHARIAH ZECHARIAH

« AT A GLANCE »

Author
Zechariah

Audience
The Jewish exiles who had returned to Jerusalem from Babylon

Date
Between about 520 and 480 B.C.

Setting
Zechariah, like Haggai, encouraged the exiles who had returned to Jerusalem from Babylon to obey God and complete the rebuilding of the temple.

Verse to Remember
Rejoice greatly, O Daughter of Zion! Shout, Daughter of Jerusalem! See, your king comes to you, righteous and having salvation, gentle and riding on a donkey, on a colt, the foal of a donkey (9:9).

Theme to Consider
Zechariah challenges his fellow Israelites to finish the work of rebuilding the temple. He also offers a glimpse of events that would take place 500 years later—the coming of the Messiah! The promise is there for us as well: Our King is coming again and will reign forever!

UNCHANGING TRUTH » Where do you get your encouragement? Who fires you up? Who inspires you to dig down deep and find that little "something extra" that often means the difference between success and failure? For some guys, it's a coach or a trainer. For others, it's a certain teacher or a mentor. For others, it's a parent or a friend or a famous role model.

What makes someone a good encourager? An enthusiasm for developing other people? A desire to see them succeed? A willingness to get involved in their lives?

You would make a great encourager. That's a safe bet, because God can give you the skills you need. You see, God wants us to show love to one another, and giving someone encouragement is one of the most loving things you can do.

Encouragement is more than saying things like, "Way to go, man," or "Nice job." It's a way of helping people understand what they're capable of. Let's face it—we all have enough people in our lives whose goal seems to be to keep us down or prevent us from succeeding. Be the kind of person who counteracts those influences. Be a person who builds people up, who points out the talents and abilities in others—abilities that they might be shy to use or even unaware of.

Zechariah encouraged the Israelites to complete the enormous task of rebuilding the temple in Jerusalem. What can you encourage people to do?

LIFE LESSONS »

1   Learn from other people's mistakes. Don't make the same poor choices you see others make (1:2–6).

2   All of the religious traditions and spiritual acts in the world don't mean a thing to God if your heart isn't devoted to him (7:4–7).

3   Part of God's will for every believer is to take care of people in need (7:8–10).

4   No one can oppose God or mistreat his people and get away with it in the long run (12:1–5).

A CALL TO RETURN TO THE LORD

1 In the eighth month of the second year of Darius, the word of the LORD came to the prophet Zechariah son of Berekiah, the son of Iddo:

2 "The LORD was very angry with your forefathers. 3 Therefore tell the people: This is what the LORD Almighty says: 'Return to me,' declares the LORD Almighty, 'and I will return to you,' says the LORD Almighty. 4 Do not be like your forefathers, to whom the earlier prophets proclaimed: This is what the LORD Almighty says: 'Turn from your evil ways and your evil practices.' But they would not listen or pay attention to me, declares the LORD. 5 Where are your forefathers now? And the prophets, do they live forever? 6 But did not my words and my decrees, which I commanded my servants the prophets, overtake your forefathers?

"Then they repented and said, 'The LORD Almighty has done to us what our ways and practices deserve, just as he determined to do.' "

THE MAN AMONG THE MYRTLE TREES

7 On the twenty-fourth day of the eleventh month, the month of Shebat, in the second year of Darius, the word of the LORD came to the prophet Zechariah son of Berekiah, the son of Iddo.

8 During the night I had a vision—and there before me was a man riding a red horse! He was standing among the myrtle trees in a ravine. Behind him were red, brown and white horses.

9 I asked, "What are these, my lord?"

The angel who was talking with me answered, "I will show you what they are."

10 Then the man standing among the myrtle trees explained, "They are the ones the LORD has sent to go throughout the earth."

11 And they reported to the angel of the LORD, who was standing among the myrtle trees, "We have gone throughout the earth and found the whole world at rest and in peace."

12 Then the angel of the LORD said, "LORD Almighty, how long will you withhold mercy from Jerusalem and from the towns of Judah, which you have been angry with these seventy years?" 13 So the LORD spoke kind and comforting words to the angel who talked with me.

14 Then the angel who was speaking to me said, "Proclaim this word: This is what the LORD Almighty says: 'I am very jealous for Jerusalem and Zion, 15 but I am very angry with the nations that feel secure. I was only a little angry, but they added to the calamity.'

16 "Therefore, this is what the LORD says: 'I will return to Jerusalem with mercy, and there my house will be rebuilt. And the measuring line will be stretched out over Jerusalem,' declares the LORD Almighty.

17 "Proclaim further: This is what the LORD Almighty says: 'My towns will again overflow with prosperity, and the LORD will again comfort Zion and choose Jerusalem.' "

FOUR HORNS AND FOUR CRAFTSMEN

18 Then I looked up—and there before me were four horns! 19 I asked the angel who was speaking to me, "What are these?"

He answered me, "These are the horns that scattered Judah, Israel and Jerusalem."

20 Then the LORD showed me four craftsmen. 21 I asked, "What are these coming to do?"

He answered, "These are the horns that scattered Judah so that no one could raise his head, but the craftsmen have come to terrify them and throw down these horns of the nations who lifted up their horns against the land of Judah to scatter its people."

A MAN WITH A MEASURING LINE

2 Then I looked up—and there before me was a man with a measuring line in his hand! 2 I asked, "Where are you going?"

He answered me, "To measure Jerusalem, to find out how wide and how long it is."

3 Then the angel who was speaking to me left, and another angel came to meet him 4 and said to him: "Run, tell that young man, 'Jerusalem will be a city without walls because of the great number of men and livestock in it. 5 And I myself will be a wall of fire around it,' declares the LORD, 'and I will be its glory within.'

6 "Come! Come! Flee from the land of the north," declares the LORD, "for I have scattered you to the four winds of heaven," declares the LORD.

7 "Come, O Zion! Escape, you who live in the Daughter of Babylon!" 8 For this is what the LORD Al-

mighty says: "After he has honored me and has sent me against the nations that have plundered you— for whoever touches you touches the apple of his eye— ⁹I will surely raise my hand against them so that their slaves will plunder them.ᵃ Then you will know that the LORD Almighty has sent me.

¹⁰"Shout and be glad, O Daughter of Zion. For I am coming, and I will live among you," declares the LORD. ¹¹"Many nations will be joined with the LORD in that day and will become my people. I will live among you and you will know that the LORD Almighty has sent me to you. ¹²The LORD will inherit Judah as his portion in the holy land and will again choose Jerusalem. ¹³Be still before the LORD, all mankind, because he has roused himself from his holy dwelling."

CLEAN GARMENTS FOR THE HIGH PRIEST

3 Then he showed me Joshuaᵇ the high priest standing before the angel of the LORD, and Satanᶜ standing at his right side to accuse him. ²The LORD said to Satan, "The LORD rebuke you, Satan! The LORD, who has chosen Jerusalem, rebuke you! Is not this man a burning stick snatched from the fire?"

³Now Joshua was dressed in filthy clothes as he stood before the angel. ⁴The angel said to those who were standing before him, "Take off his filthy clothes."

Then he said to Joshua, "See, I have taken away your sin, and I will put rich garments on you."

⁵Then I said, "Put a clean turban on his head." So they put a clean turban on his head and clothed him, while the angel of the LORD stood by.

⁶The angel of the LORD gave this charge to Joshua: ⁷"This is what the LORD Almighty says:

NOW OR NEVER

ZEC 3:6-7

You won't get a standing ovation every time you do something that pleases God. In fact, most of the obedient things you do will never be noticed by another human being. But God notices them, and he'll reward you—sometimes in this life and most definitely in the life to come.

'If you will walk in my ways and keep my requirements, then you will govern my house and have charge of my courts, and I will give you a place among these standing here.

⁸" 'Listen, O high priest Joshua and your associates seated before you, who are men symbolic of things to come: I am going to bring my servant, the Branch. ⁹See, the stone I have set in front of Joshua! There are seven eyesᵈ on that one stone, and I will engrave an inscription on it,' says the LORD Almighty, 'and I will remove the sin of this land in a single day.

¹⁰" 'In that day each of you will invite his neighbor to sit under his vine and fig tree,' declares the LORD Almighty."

THE GOLD LAMPSTAND AND THE TWO OLIVE TREES

4 Then the angel who talked with me returned and wakened me, as a man is wakened from his sleep. ²He asked me, "What do you see?"

I answered, "I see a solid gold lampstand with a bowl at the top and seven lights on it, with seven channels to the lights. ³Also there are two olive trees by it, one on the right of the bowl and the other on its left."

⁴I asked the angel who talked with me, "What are these, my lord?"

⁵He answered, "Do you not know what these are?"

"No, my lord," I replied.

⁶So he said to me, "This is the word of the LORD to Zerubbabel: 'Not by might nor by power, but by my Spirit,' says the LORD Almighty.

NOW OR NEVER

ZEC 4:6

You don't need any special qualifications, skills or abilities to serve God. All you need is a willing heart. The power of God's Spirit will take care of the rest.

ᵃ 8,9 Or says after . . . eye: ⁹"I . . . plunder them."   ᵇ 1 A variant of Jeshua; here and elsewhere in Zechariah   ᶜ 1 Satan means accuser.   ᵈ 9 Or facets

7 "What[a] are you, O mighty mountain? Before Zerubbabel you will become level ground. Then he will bring out the capstone to shouts of 'God bless it! God bless it!' "

8 Then the word of the LORD came to me: 9 "The hands of Zerubbabel have laid the foundation of this temple; his hands will also complete it. Then you will know that the LORD Almighty has sent me to you.

10 "Who despises the day of small things? Men will rejoice when they see the plumb line in the hand of Zerubbabel.

"(These seven are the eyes of the LORD, which range throughout the earth.)"

11 Then I asked the angel, "What are these two olive trees on the right and the left of the lampstand?"

12 Again I asked him, "What are these two olive branches beside the two gold pipes that pour out golden oil?"

13 He replied, "Do you not know what these are?"

"No, my lord," I said.

14 So he said, "These are the two who are anointed to[b] serve the Lord of all the earth."

THE FLYING SCROLL

 I looked again—and there before me was a flying scroll! 2 He asked me, "What do you see?"

I answered, "I see a flying scroll, thirty feet long and fifteen feet wide.[c]"

3 And he said to me, "This is the curse that is going out over the whole land; for according to what it says on one side, every thief will be banished, and according to what it says on the other, everyone who swears falsely will be banished. 4 The LORD Almighty declares, 'I will send it out, and it will enter the house of the thief and the house of him who swears falsely by my name. It will remain in his house and destroy it, both its timbers and its stones.' "

THE WOMAN IN A BASKET

5 Then the angel who was speaking to me came forward and said to me, "Look up and see what this is that is appearing."

6 I asked, "What is it?"

He replied, "It is a measuring basket.[d]" And he added, "This is the iniquity[e] of the people throughout the land."

7 Then the cover of lead was raised, and there in the basket sat a woman! 8 He said, "This is wickedness," and he pushed her back into the basket and pushed the lead cover down over its mouth.

9 Then I looked up—and there before me were two women, with the wind in their wings! They had wings like those of a stork, and they lifted up the basket between heaven and earth.

10 "Where are they taking the basket?" I asked the angel who was speaking to me.

11 He replied, "To the country of Babylonia[f] to build a house for it. When it is ready, the basket will be set there in its place."

FOUR CHARIOTS

I looked up again—and there before me were four chariots coming out from between two mountains—mountains of bronze! 2 The first chariot had red horses, the second black, 3 the third white, and the fourth dappled—all of them powerful. 4 I asked the angel who was speaking to me, "What are these, my lord?"

5 The angel answered me, "These are the four spirits[g] of heaven, going out from standing in the presence of the Lord of the whole world. 6 The one with the black horses is going toward the north country, the one with the white horses toward the west,[h] and the one with the dappled horses toward the south."

7 When the powerful horses went out, they were straining to go throughout the earth. And he said, "Go throughout the earth!" So they went throughout the earth.

8 Then he called to me, "Look, those going toward the north country have given my Spirit[i] rest in the land of the north."

---

[a] 7 Or Who   [b] 14 Or two who bring oil and   [c] 2 Hebrew twenty cubits long and ten cubits wide (about 9 meters long and 4.5 meters wide)   [d] 6 Hebrew an ephah; also in verses 7-11   [e] 6 Or appearance   [f] 11 Hebrew Shinar   [g] 5 Or winds   [h] 6 Or horses after them   [i] 8 Or spirit

battlelines

» The Little Guy (Dominance)

Q: What's the story on the new guy at school?
A: His name's Akil or Hakim or something like that. Not sure where he's from. He seems like a decent guy, but maybe a little *too* nice.

Q: How can you be too nice?
A: I mean, he's . . . well, kind of weak. He doesn't defend himself. A lot of guys have started picking on him because he just smiles and nods and tries to joke it off. And I think that just encourages them.

Q: You're not picking on him, are you?
A: No! I would never do that.

Q: Do you stick up for him?
A: (Sighing) I *knew* you were going to ask me that. I'd *like* to stick up for him—really, I would. But what good would that do? I'm just one guy.

Q: So what do you do when you notice people giving Akil a hard time?
A: Usually I just . . . um, walk away.

Q: You walk away?
A: Hey, it's not like I'm the guy's knight in shining armor. He's got to learn to take care of himself.

Q: Can I be honest with you?
A: I guess so.

Q: I think you're weaker than Akil.
A: What?

Q: Well, come on! Do you think walking away is a sign of *strength*?
A: Hey, not wanting to get involved doesn't make me weak.

Q: Really? Tell me, how do you feel about yourself when you abandon this guy? Do you feel strong or weak? Proud of yourself or—
A: Look, I don't have time for this. There's the bell. I have to get to class.

» Sticking Up

God gives guys strength so they can make a difference. But way too many guys equate power with bullying. They try to make themselves feel more powerful by picking on those they believe are weak. That's cowardly and cruel. A real man doesn't take advantage of others; he helps them. He uses his strength to honor others and defend them. Paul puts it this way: Carry burdens—don't cause them (see Galatians 6:2). Use your mouth to build others up, not to tear them down (see Ephesians 4:29). In addition, Proverbs 3:27 urges us, "Do not withhold good from those who deserve it, when it is in your power to act."

Here's a challenge: stick your neck out today for somebody in trouble. Is it risky? Sure, it can be. But that's what men do. We need to be willing to run straight into dangerous situations, not away from them.

Read more about bullying at www.RevolutionBible.com.

A CROWN FOR JOSHUA

⁹The word of the LORD came to me: ¹⁰"Take ⌐silver and gold⌐ from the exiles Heldai, Tobijah and Jedaiah, who have arrived from Babylon. Go the same day to the house of Josiah son of Zephaniah. ¹¹Take the silver and gold and make a crown, and set it on the head of the high priest, Joshua son of Jehozadak. ¹²Tell him this is what the LORD Almighty says: 'Here is the man whose name is the Branch, and he will branch out from his place and build the temple of the LORD. ¹³It is he who will build the temple of the LORD, and he will be clothed with majesty and will sit and rule on his throne. And he will be a priest on his throne. And there will be harmony between the two.' ¹⁴The crown will be given to Heldai,ᵃ Tobijah, Jedaiah and Henᵇ son of Zephaniah as a memorial in the temple of the LORD. ¹⁵Those who are far away will come and help to build the temple of the LORD, and you will know that the LORD Almighty has sent me to you. This will happen if you diligently obey the LORD your God."

JUSTICE AND MERCY, NOT FASTING

7 In the fourth year of King Darius, the word of the LORD came to Zechariah on the fourth day of the ninth month, the month of Kislev. ²The people of Bethel had sent Sharezer and Regem-Melech, together with their men, to entreat the LORD ³by asking the priests of the house of the LORD Almighty and the prophets, "Should I mourn and fast in the fifth month, as I have done for so many years?"

⁴Then the word of the LORD Almighty came to me: ⁵"Ask all the people of the land and the priests, 'When you fasted and mourned in the fifth and seventh months for the past seventy years, was it really for me that you fasted? ⁶And when you were eating and drinking, were you not just feasting for yourselves? ⁷Are these not the words the LORD proclaimed through the earlier prophets when Jerusalem and its surrounding towns were at rest and prosperous, and the Negev and the western foothills were settled?' "

NOW OR NEVER
ZEC 7:8–10

As far as God is concerned, everyone who follows him is part of one big team. And God is big on team unity. One thing he won't put up with is dissension, fighting or oppression among teammates.

⁸And the word of the LORD came again to Zechariah: ⁹"This is what the LORD Almighty says: 'Administer true justice; show mercy and compassion to one another. ¹⁰Do not oppress the widow or the fatherless, the alien or the poor. In your hearts do not think evil of each other.'

¹¹"But they refused to pay attention; stubbornly they turned their backs and stopped up their ears. ¹²They made their hearts as hard as flint and would not listen to the law or to the words that the LORD Almighty had sent by his Spirit through the earlier prophets. So the LORD Almighty was very angry.

¹³" 'When I called, they did not listen; so when they called, I would not listen,' says the LORD Almighty. ¹⁴'I scattered them with a whirlwind among all the nations, where they were strangers. The land was left so desolate behind them that no one could come or go. This is how they made the pleasant land desolate.' "

challenge notes

ZEC 7:10

To: my_son

heavenly_father: I've given you special opportunities to serve me by taking care of people in need. it takes a strong man to stand up for people that others overlook. be a man who reaches out to those who need your help.

THE LORD PROMISES TO BLESS JERUSALEM

8 Again the word of the LORD Almighty came to me. ²This is what the LORD Almighty says: "I am very jealous for Zion; I am burning with jealousy for her."

³This is what the LORD says: "I will return to Zion and dwell in Jerusalem. Then Jerusalem will be called the City of Truth, and the mountain of the LORD Almighty will be called the Holy Mountain."

⁴This is what the LORD Almighty says: "Once again men and women of ripe old age will sit in the

---

ᵃ 14 Syriac; Hebrew Helem   ᵇ 14 Or and the gracious one, the streets of Jerusalem, each with cane in hand because of his age. ⁵The city streets will be filled with boys and girls playing there."

⁶This is what the LORD Almighty says: "It may seem marvelous to the remnant of this people at that time, but will it seem marvelous to me?" declares the LORD Almighty.

⁷This is what the LORD Almighty says: "I will save my people from the countries of the east and the west. ⁸I will bring them back to live in Jerusalem; they will be my people, and I will be faithful and righteous to them as their God."

⁹This is what the LORD Almighty says: "You who now hear these words spoken by the prophets who were there when the foundation was laid for the house of the LORD Almighty, let your hands be strong so that the temple may be built. ¹⁰Before that time there were no wages for man or beast. No one could go about his business safely because of his enemy, for I had turned every man against his neighbor. ¹¹But now I will not deal with the remnant of this people as I did in the past," declares the LORD Almighty.

¹²"The seed will grow well, the vine will yield its fruit, the ground will produce its crops, and the heavens will drop their dew. I will give all these things as an inheritance to the remnant of this people. ¹³As you have been an object of cursing among the nations, O Judah and Israel, so will I save you, and you will be a blessing. Do not be afraid, but let your hands be strong."

¹⁴This is what the LORD Almighty says: "Just as I had determined to bring disaster upon you and showed no pity when your fathers angered me," says the LORD Almighty, ¹⁵"so now I have determined to do good again to Jerusalem and Judah. Do not be afraid. ¹⁶These are the things you are to do: Speak the truth to each other, and render true and sound judgment in your courts; ¹⁷do not plot evil against your neighbor, and do not love to swear falsely. I hate all this," declares the LORD.

¹⁸Again the word of the LORD Almighty came to me. ¹⁹This is what the LORD Almighty says: "The fasts of the fourth, fifth, seventh and tenth months will become joyful and glad occasions and happy festivals for Judah. Therefore love truth and peace."

²⁰This is what the LORD Almighty says: "Many peoples and the inhabitants of many cities will yet come, ²¹and the inhabitants of one city will go to another and say, 'Let us go at once to entreat the LORD and seek the LORD Almighty. I myself am going.' ²²And many peoples and powerful nations will come to Jerusalem to seek the LORD Almighty and to entreat him."

²³This is what the LORD Almighty says: "In those days ten men from all languages and nations will take firm hold of one Jew by the hem of his robe and say, 'Let us go with you, because we have heard that God is with you.'"

JUDGMENT ON ISRAEL'S ENEMIES

An Oracle

9 The word of the LORD is against the land of Hadrach
    and will rest upon Damascus—
for the eyes of men and all the tribes of Israel
    are on the LORD—ᵃ
²and upon Hamath too, which borders on it,
    and upon Tyre and Sidon, though they are very skillful.
³Tyre has built herself a stronghold;
    she has heaped up silver like dust,

Obeying God in Love

> » live the adventure » Zec 8:14-17

God's kindness to us is completely undeserved. Nothing we have done and nothing we could ever offer to God could possibly earn his blessing. Still, he chooses to love us and to "do good" to us. Zechariah gives some commands to the people about how they are to live in light of God's plan to restore them: Speak the truth. Stand for justice. Love your neighbor. A man who does these things is a godly man.

---

and gold like the dirt of the streets.
⁴But the Lord will take away her possessions
    and destroy her power on the sea,
    and she will be consumed by fire.
⁵Ashkelon will see it and fear;
    Gaza will writhe in agony,
    and Ekron too, for her hope will wither.
Gaza will lose her king
    and Ashkelon will be deserted.
⁶Foreigners will occupy Ashdod,
    and I will cut off the pride of the Philistines.
⁷I will take the blood from their mouths,
    the forbidden food from between their teeth.
Those who are left will belong to our God
    and become leaders in Judah,
    and Ekron will be like the Jebusites.
⁸But I will defend my house
    against marauding forces.
Never again will an oppressor overrun my people,
    for now I am keeping watch.

THE COMING OF ZION'S KING

⁹Rejoice greatly, O Daughter of Zion!
    Shout, Daughter of Jerusalem!

See, your king[a] comes to you,
    righteous and having salvation,
    gentle and riding on a donkey,
    on a colt, the foal of a donkey.
¹⁰I will take away the chariots from
        Ephraim
    and the war-horses from Jerusalem,
    and the battle bow will be broken.
He will proclaim peace to the nations.
    His rule will extend from sea to sea
    and from the River[b] to the ends of the
        earth.[c]
¹¹As for you, because of the blood of my
        covenant with you,

NOW OR NEVER
ZEC 9:9

Five hundred years after Zechariah made
this prediction, Jesus rode into Jerusalem
for the Passover feast on—you guessed it—
a donkey and a colt (see Matthew 21:1–7
and John 12:14–15). Was it a lucky guess
on Zechariah's part or more evidence that
Jesus is indeed who he says he is?

I will free your prisoners from the waterless pit.
¹²Return to your fortress, O prisoners of hope;
    even now I announce that I will restore twice as much to you.
¹³I will bend Judah as I bend my bow
    and fill it with Ephraim.
I will rouse your sons, O Zion,
    against your sons, O Greece,
    and make you like a warrior's sword.

THE LORD WILL APPEAR

¹⁴Then the Lord will appear over them;
    his arrow will flash like lightning.
The Sovereign Lord will sound the trumpet;
    he will march in the storms of the south,
¹⁵   and the Lord Almighty will shield them.
They will destroy

ª 9 Or King   ᵇ 10 That is, the Euphrates   ᶜ 10 Or the end of the land

and overcome with slingstones.
They will drink and roar as with wine;
   they will be full like a bowl
   used for sprinkling[a] the corners of the altar.
¹⁶ The Lord their God will save them on that day
   as the flock of his people.
They will sparkle in his land
   like jewels in a crown.
¹⁷ How attractive and beautiful they will be!
   Grain will make the young men thrive,
   and new wine the young women.

THE LORD WILL CARE FOR JUDAH

10

Ask the Lord for rain in the springtime;
   it is the Lord who makes the storm clouds.
He gives showers of rain to men,
   and plants of the field to everyone.
² The idols speak deceit,
   diviners see visions that lie;
they tell dreams that are false,
   they give comfort in vain.
Therefore the people wander like sheep
   oppressed for lack of a shepherd.

³ "My anger burns against the shepherds,
   and I will punish the leaders;
for the Lord Almighty will care
   for his flock, the house of Judah,
   and make them like a proud horse in battle.
⁴ From Judah will come the cornerstone,
   from him the tent peg,
   from him the battle bow,
   from him every ruler.
⁵ Together they[b] will be like mighty men
   trampling the muddy streets in battle.
Because the Lord is with them,
   they will fight and overthrow the horsemen.

⁶ "I will strengthen the house of Judah
   and save the house of Joseph.
I will restore them
   because I have compassion on them.
They will be as though
   I had not rejected them,
for I am the Lord their God
   and I will answer them.
⁷ The Ephraimites will become like mighty men,
   and their hearts will be glad as with wine.
Their children will see it and be joyful;
   their hearts will rejoice in the Lord.
⁸ I will signal for them
   and gather them in.
Surely I will redeem them;
   they will be as numerous as before.
⁹ Though I scatter them among the peoples,

ª 15 Or bowl, / like   ᵇ 4,5 Or ruler, all of them together. / ⁵They

yet in distant lands they will remember me.
They and their children will survive,
and they will return.
¹⁰I will bring them back from Egypt
and gather them from Assyria.
I will bring them to Gilead and Lebanon,
and there will not be room enough for them.
¹¹They will pass through the sea of trouble;
the surging sea will be subdued
and all the depths of the Nile will dry up.
Assyria's pride will be brought down
and Egypt's scepter will pass away.
¹²I will strengthen them in the LORD
and in his name they will walk,"

declares the LORD.

11

Open your doors, O Lebanon,
so that fire may devour your cedars!
²Wail, O pine tree, for the cedar has fallen;
the stately trees are ruined!
Wail, oaks of Bashan;
the dense forest has been cut down!
³Listen to the wail of the shepherds;
their rich pastures are destroyed!
Listen to the roar of the lions;
the lush thicket of the Jordan is ruined!

TWO SHEPHERDS

⁴This is what the LORD my God says: "Pasture the flock marked for slaughter. ⁵Their buyers slaughter them and go unpunished. Those who sell them say, 'Praise the LORD, I am rich!' Their own shepherds do not spare them. ⁶For I will no longer have pity on the people of the land," declares the LORD. "I will hand everyone over to his neighbor and his king. They will oppress the land, and I will not rescue them from their hands."

⁷So I pastured the flock marked for slaughter, particularly the oppressed of the flock. Then I took two staffs and called one Favor and the other Union, and I pastured the flock. ⁸In one month I got rid of the three shepherds.

The flock detested me, and I grew weary of them ⁹and said, "I will not be your shepherd. Let the dying die, and the perishing perish. Let those who are left eat one another's flesh."

¹⁰Then I took my staff called Favor and broke it, revoking the covenant I had made with all the nations. ¹¹It was revoked on that day, and so the afflicted of the flock who were watching me knew it was the word of the LORD.

¹²I told them, "If you think it best, give me my pay; but if not, keep it." So they paid me thirty pieces of silver.

¹³And the LORD said to me, "Throw it to the potter"—the handsome price at which they priced me! So I took the thirty pieces of silver and threw them into the house of the LORD to the potter.

¹⁴Then I broke my second staff called Union, breaking the brotherhood between Judah and Israel.

¹⁵Then the LORD said to me, "Take again the equipment of a foolish shepherd. ¹⁶For I am going to raise up a shepherd over the land who will not care for the lost, or seek the young, or heal the injured, or feed the healthy, but will eat the meat of the choice sheep, tearing off their hoofs.

¹⁷"Woe to the worthless shepherd,
who deserts the flock!
May the sword strike his arm and his right eye!
May his arm be completely withered,
his right eye totally blinded!"

battlelines

» *Sibling Rivalry (Competition)*

Q: Hey man, what's up?
A: (Unintelligible grunt)

Q: What?
A: (Louder, mumbled response)

Q: Dude, have you got marbles in your mouth?
A: (Angry, practically snarling) I said, "Nothing"!

Q: Whoa, man, what's with the bad mood?
A: (Frowning, gesturing toward a crowd of nice-looking girls watching a guy skateboard) What else?

Q: Oh, of course. Carlton. Sheesh, he's a girl magnet, that's for sure.
A: Yep. Look at him. He's loving every minute of it.

Q: Well, who wouldn't be? Man, Cade, how can you stand having a little brother like that?
A: It's not easy. He's just, I don't know, blessed, you know? School is a breeze for him, and he never even cracks a book. Pick a sport, and he's awesome at it. Everybody likes him. I'm telling you, the guy is just like that King Midas dude. Everything he touches turns to gold.

Q: So, do you hate him—in a very nice, Christian way, of course?
A: Yeah, well, sometimes I try to. But then the next thing I know, he turns around and does something nice for me. Besides, he's my brother!

» *Brotherly Love*

Comparing ourselves to others is a very natural—and dangerous—thing to do. If we come out on top, we tend to feel cocky. And if we come out on the short end of the stick, we feel second-rate.

The wiser solution is to get comfortable with the truth that God, in his hard-to-understand wisdom, made each of us just the way we are for a reason. Sure, there are others—maybe even siblings—who can do certain things better than you can. But don't forget that you also have a unique set of gifts and abilities. And if *you* don't do what only you can do, the world is left with a hole that no one else can fill. First Peter 4:10 says it best: "Each one should use whatever gift he has received to serve others."

Read more about competition at www.RevolutionBible.com.

JERUSALEM'S ENEMIES TO BE DESTROYED

An Oracle

12 This is the word of the LORD concerning Israel. The LORD, who stretches out the heavens, who lays the foundation of the earth, and who forms the spirit of man within him, declares: ²"I am going to make Jerusalem a cup that sends all the surrounding peoples reeling. Judah will be besieged as well as Jerusalem. ³On that day, when all the nations of the earth are gathered against her, I will make Jerusalem an immovable rock for all the nations. All who try to move it will injure themselves. ⁴On that day I will strike every horse with panic and its rider with madness," declares the LORD. "I will keep a watchful eye over the house of Judah, but I will blind all the horses of the nations. ⁵Then the leaders of Judah will say in their hearts, 'The people of Jerusalem are strong, because the LORD Almighty is their God.'

⁶"On that day I will make the leaders of Judah like a firepot in a woodpile, like a flaming torch among sheaves. They will consume right and left all the surrounding peoples, but Jerusalem will remain intact in her place.

⁷"The LORD will save the dwellings of Judah first, so that the honor of the house of David and of Jerusalem's inhabitants may not be greater than that of Judah. ⁸On that day the LORD will shield those who live in Jerusalem, so that the feeblest among them will be like David, and the house of David will be like God, like the Angel of the LORD going before them. ⁹On that day I will set out to destroy all the nations that attack Jerusalem.

MOURNING FOR THE ONE THEY PIERCED

¹⁰"And I will pour out on the house of David and the inhabitants of Jerusalem a spirit[a] of grace and supplication. They will look on[b] me, the one they have pierced, and they will mourn for him as one mourns for an only child, and grieve bitterly for him as one grieves for a firstborn son. ¹¹On that day the weeping in Jerusalem will be great, like the weeping of Hadad Rimmon in the plain of Megiddo. ¹²The land will mourn, each clan by itself, with their wives by themselves: the clan of the house of David and their wives, the clan of the house of Nathan and their wives, ¹³the clan of the house of Levi and their wives, the clan of Shimei and their wives, ¹⁴and all the rest of the clans and their wives.

CLEANSING FROM SIN

13 "On that day a fountain will be opened to the house of David and the inhabitants of Jerusalem, to cleanse them from sin and impurity.

²"On that day, I will banish the names of the idols from the land, and they will be remembered no more," declares the LORD Almighty. "I will remove both the prophets and the spirit of impurity from the land. ³And if anyone still prophesies, his father and mother, to whom he was born, will say to him, 'You must die, because you have told lies in the LORD's name.' When he prophesies, his own parents will stab him.

⁴"On that day every prophet will be ashamed of his prophetic vision. He will not put on a prophet's garment of hair in order to deceive. ⁵He will say, 'I am not a prophet. I am a farmer; the land has been my livelihood since my youth.[c]' ⁶If someone asks him, 'What are these wounds on your body[d]?' he will answer, 'The wounds I was given at the house of my friends.'

Explaining God's Prophecy

If you know people who refuse to believe what the Bible says about Jesus, ask them to explain how prophets who lived hundreds of years before Jesus was born were able to accurately predict specific details of his life. We're not just talking about one or two details either; we're talking about *dozens* of them. Those accurate predictions aren't the result of coincidence. They are the result of God's work.

»» live the adventure »» Zec 12:10

ᵃ 10 Or *the Spirit*   ᵇ 10 Or *to*   ᶜ 5 Or *farmer; a man sold me in my youth*   ᵈ 6 Or *wounds between your hands*

battlelines

» A Change'll Do You Good? (Change)

Q: What would you say are the three best things about your new home?
A: Three things? Why don't you get back to me in a month or so? I might have an answer for you by then.

Q: Oh, come on! There's gotta be *something* you like about this place.
A: All right, let's see . . . I guess it's pretty cool that the beach is only a few miles away. That's good. And the girls—at least the ones I've met so far—are pretty cute, and they seem friendly enough. Oh, and our house is bigger, so I don't have to share a room with my little brother. That's a *huge* bonus.

Q: See there? I knew you'd think of something. Now . . . what about the *downside* of being the new guy in town?
A: That's easy. Feeling like an outsider. Having people size you up and look at you funny. Not knowing where anything is. Feeling like all your stuff is in boxes—and, actually, it still is.

Q: How many times have you moved?
A: Five times in the last nine years.

Q: Dude, that's some serious traveling!
A: Tell me about it.

Q: So what's your strategy? How do you cope?
A: Well, I used to fight it, but that doesn't change anything. I can't divorce my family. So I can either try to adapt and make the best of it, or I can just be in a bad mood all the time. Maybe it sounds stupid, but about three moves ago, I just decided to think of myself as sort of a modern-day explorer—you know, like those Lewis and Clark guys. I'm like, "OK, here I am, in this whole new town. I guess it's time to check it out and see what's here. Who knows, maybe I'll find something really cool here—even if it only lasts a little while."

» The Great Constant

It's true what they say: The only thing that never changes is God himself. Want proof? Check out God's words in Malachi 3:6: "I the Lord do not change." (Check out Hebrews 13:8 too while you're at it.). He's the one fixed point, the one stable thing in the universe that you can always count on. Everything else—*everything*—is subject to change.

Change happens. You can't control it, but you don't have to let it control you either. Catch a clue from Darius. Learn to lean hard on the unchanging God, but be flexible enough to adapt to your changing world. Decide to make the best of each new situation. Keep the lines of communication open with your parents so they know how you feel.

In many ways, life *is* what you make it as you trust in God.

For more on dealing with change, log on to www.RevolutionBible.com.

THE SHEPHERD STRUCK, THE SHEEP SCATTERED

7 "Awake, O sword, against my shepherd,
    against the man who is close to me!"
    declares the LORD Almighty.
  "Strike the shepherd,
    and the sheep will be scattered,
    and I will turn my hand against the little ones.
  8 In the whole land," declares the LORD,
    "two-thirds will be struck down and perish;
    yet one-third will be left in it.
  9 This third I will bring into the fire;
    I will refine them like silver
    and test them like gold.
  They will call on my name
    and I will answer them;
  I will say, 'They are my people,'
    and they will say, 'The LORD is our God.' "

THE LORD COMES AND REIGNS

14 A day of the LORD is coming when your plunder will be divided among you. 2 I will gather all the nations to Jerusalem to fight against it; the city will be captured, the houses ransacked, and the women raped. Half of the city will go into exile, but the rest of the people will not be taken from the city.

3 Then the LORD will go out and fight against those nations, as he fights in the day of battle. 4 On that day his feet will stand on the Mount of Olives, east of Jerusalem, and the Mount of Olives will be split in two from east to west, forming a great valley, with half of the mountain moving north and half moving south. 5 You will flee by my mountain valley, for it will extend to Azel. You will flee as you fled from the earthquake[a] in the days of Uzziah king of Judah. Then the LORD my God will come, and all the holy ones with him.

6 On that day there will be no light, no cold or frost. 7 It will be a unique day, without daytime or nighttime—a day known to the LORD. When evening comes, there will be light.

8 On that day living water will flow out from Jerusalem, half to the eastern sea[b] and half to the western sea,[c] in summer and in winter.

9 The LORD will be king over the whole earth. On that day there will be one LORD, and his name the only name.

10 The whole land, from Geba to Rimmon, south of Jerusalem, will become like the Arabah. But Jerusalem will be raised up and remain in its place, from the Benjamin Gate to the site of the First Gate, to the Corner Gate, and from the Tower of Hananel to the royal winepresses. 11 It will be inhabited; never again will it be destroyed. Jerusalem will be secure.

12 This is the plague with which the LORD will strike all the nations that fought against Jerusalem: Their flesh will rot while they are still standing on their feet, their eyes will rot in their sockets, and their tongues will rot in their mouths. 13 On that day men will be stricken by the LORD with great panic. Each man will seize the hand of another, and they will attack each other. 14 Judah too will fight at Jerusalem. The wealth of all the surrounding nations will be collected—great quantities of gold and silver and clothing. 15 A similar plague will strike the horses and mules, the camels and donkeys, and all the animals in those camps.

NOW OR NEVER
ZEC 14:9

One day everyone will find out that the Lord is the only true God. Unfortunately, for many people that discovery will come too late. What steps can you take this week to make sure that your friends and loved ones believe while they still have a chance?

a 5 Or 5 My mountain valley will be blocked and will extend to Azel. It will be blocked as it was blocked because of the earthquake
b 8 That is, the Dead Sea   c 8 That is, the Mediterranean

¹⁶Then the survivors from all the nations that have attacked Jerusalem will go up year after year to worship the King, the Lord Almighty, and to celebrate the Feast of Tabernacles. ¹⁷If any of the peoples of the earth do not go up to Jerusalem to worship the King, the Lord Almighty, they will have no rain. ¹⁸If the Egyptian people do not go up and take part, they will have no rain. The Lord^a will bring on them the plague he inflicts on the nations that do not go up to celebrate the Feast of Tabernacles. ¹⁹This will be the punishment of Egypt and the punishment of all the nations that do not go up to celebrate the Feast of Tabernacles.

²⁰On that day HOLY TO THE LORD will be inscribed on the bells of the horses, and the cooking pots in the Lord's house will be like the sacred bowls in front of the altar. ²¹Every pot in Jerusalem and Judah will be holy to the Lord Almighty, and all who come to sacrifice will take some of the pots and cook in them. And on that day there will no longer be a Canaanite^b in the house of the Lord Almighty.

---

^a *18 Or part, then the Lord*   ^b *21 Or merchant*

MALACHI

« AT A GLANCE

Author
Malachi

Audience
Jews in Jerusalem and Judah

Date
About 430 B.C.

Setting
The temple in Jerusalem had been rebuilt, and the city walls had been restored. But the Jews were discouraged, so they didn't worship or obey God wholeheartedly.

Verse to Remember
"I the LORD do not change. So you, O descendants of Jacob, are not destroyed. Ever since the time of your forefathers you have turned away from my decrees and have not kept them. Return to me, and I will return to you," says the LORD Almighty (3:6–7).

Theme to Consider
Don't let apathy and indifference prevent you from enjoying the full benefits of God's love for you.

UNCHANGING TRUTH » Confrontation is no fun for anyone. No one likes to tell other people that they're doing something wrong. (For one thing, it can make a person *very* unpopular.) And certainly no guy likes to be told by someone else that he's doing something wrong.

But a "hands off" policy doesn't work either. Like it or not, we *need* other people to tell us when we've done something hurtful or when our lifestyle starts to drift from obedience to disobedience. And when it comes to confrontation, we have to be willing to speak the truth in love.

Yeah, confrontation is a dirty job, but someone's got to do it. And if you're serious about growing in your relationship with God, that someone is you.

Your friends and loved ones need your gentle and honest confrontation. They may not know they need it. And they may not appreciate it when you give it. But the fact is, a few well-chosen, tough words from you may be all that stands between someone you care for and a mistake or decision that could ruin their life.

Malachi was a guy who understood the importance of confrontation. Look at the way he got in the faces of his fellow Israelites about their poor decisions and faithlessness. His words were tough, but his motive was pure. He wanted to save his people from God's judgment, and he was willing to say anything to do it—no matter how unpopular his words made him.

LIFE LESSONS »

1 God is rightly offended when we give him anything less than our best (1:6–14).

2 Everyone who does evil will face God's wrath and judgment (3:5).

3 God will show compassion and mercy to anyone who turns away from sin and follows him (3:16–18).

1

An oracle: The word of the LORD to Israel through Malachi.[a]

JACOB LOVED, ESAU HATED

2 "I have loved you," says the LORD.

"But you ask, 'How have you loved us?'

"Was not Esau Jacob's brother?" the LORD says. "Yet I have loved Jacob, 3but Esau I have hated, and I have turned his mountains into a wasteland and left his inheritance to the desert jackals."

4Edom may say, "Though we have been crushed, we will rebuild the ruins."

But this is what the LORD Almighty says: "They may build, but I will demolish. They will be called the Wicked Land, a people always under the wrath of the LORD. 5You will see it with your own eyes and say, 'Great is the LORD—even beyond the borders of Israel!'

ПОШ ОР ПЕVER

MAL 1:10–11

What happens when we forget that people of all nations and races have the same Creator, Father and Savior? What will you do the next time you see or hear someone who seems to have forgotten that fact?

BLEMISHED SACRIFICES

6 "A son honors his father, and a servant his master. If I am a father, where is the honor due me? If I am a master, where is the respect due me?" says the LORD Almighty. "It is you, O priests, who show contempt for my name.

"But you ask, 'How have we shown contempt for your name?'

7 "You place defiled food on my altar.

"But you ask, 'How have we defiled you?'

"By saying that the LORD's table is contemptible. 8When you bring blind animals for sacrifice, is that not wrong? When you sacrifice crippled or diseased animals, is that not wrong? Try offering them to your governor! Would he be pleased with you? Would he accept you?" says the LORD Almighty.

9 "Now implore God to be gracious to us. With such offerings from your hands, will he accept you?"—says the LORD Almighty.

10 "Oh, that one of you would shut the temple doors, so that you would not light useless fires on my altar! I am not pleased with you," says the LORD Almighty, "and I will accept no offering from your hands. 11My name will be great among the nations, from the rising to the setting of the sun. In every place incense and pure offerings will be brought to my name, because my name will be great among the nations," says the LORD Almighty.

12 "But you profane it by saying of the Lord's table, 'It is defiled,' and of its food, 'It is contemptible.' 13And you say, 'What a burden!' and you sniff at it contemptuously," says the LORD Almighty.

"When you bring injured, crippled or diseased animals and offer them as sacrifices, should I accept them from your hands?" says the LORD. 14 "Cursed is the cheat who has an acceptable male in his flock and vows to give it, but then sacrifices a blemished animal to the Lord. For I am a great king," says the LORD Almighty, "and my name is to be feared among the nations.

Sacrificing to God

God no longer requires us to bring him livestock, but that doesn't mean he still doesn't desire—and reward—sacrifice. What can you sacrificially bring to God to show him how important he is to you? Your time? Would you be willing to carve out a two- or three-hour block of your weekend and devote that time to one of your church's service ministries? Your money? Would you be willing to give up entertainment (including fast food, movies and video games) for a month and use the money you save to help sponsor a child in another country who needs food, medicine and education?

» live the adventure » Mal 1:14

---

[a] 1 Malachi means my messenger.

battlelines

» Anything Goes? (Tolerance)

Q: What's with all these signs and banners?

A: Don't you know? It's National Tolerance Month or something like that. The Year of Tolerance. OK Day. Whatever they call it.

Q: Which means what exactly?

A: (Sarcastically) That *everything* is okay. No one can question *anything*. Everything is acceptable—except, of course, saying that something is *unacceptable*. Don't you dare do that!

Q: Or else?

A: Or else you'll wish you hadn't. People will call you a bigot, a homophobe, a Bible thumper or something like that. Then they'll make you go to a seminar on sensitivity training. I know one guy who made the big mistake of saying he thought homosexual behavior is wrong.

Q: And?

A: And you would have thought he'd said, "Let's all take drugs and worship Hitler!" No kidding, the poor guy got called before some committee and had to go to this Saturday workshop that lasted six hours, and then he had to write an essay and watch some videos.

» One Thing Stands!

If tolerance means we love people and accept *them* regardless of their views, fine. After all, how can we ever hope to share Jesus' love with people if we don't love them? It's when the word *tolerance* gets redefined to mean that we have to endorse and celebrate any and every *idea* that Christians need to say no. Question: Why is it OK for doctors to be intolerant of germs, for police to be intolerant of criminals, for building inspectors to be intolerant of shoddy construction, but not OK for people of conscience to call certain behaviors morally wrong?

The New Testament writer Jude warned, "But, dear friends, remember what the apostles of our Lord Jesus Christ foretold. They said to you, 'In the last times there will be scoffers who will follow their own ungodly desires.' These are the men who divide you, who follow mere natural instincts and do not have the Spirit" (Jude 17–19).

The point? The desires, teachings, ideas and values of some people are simply wrong. As followers of the truth, we have a responsibility to reject any unbiblical ways of thinking—no matter what the cost is to us.

Read more about Christianity at www.RevolutionBible.com.

ADMONITION FOR THE PRIESTS

2 "And now this admonition is for you, O priests. ²If you do not listen, and if you do not set your heart to honor my name," says the LORD Almighty, "I will send a curse upon you, and I will curse your blessings. Yes, I have already cursed them, because you have not set your heart to honor me.

³ "Because of you I will rebuke[a] your descendants[b]; I will spread on your faces the offal from your festival sacrifices, and you will be carried off with it. ⁴And you will know that I have sent you this admonition so that my covenant with Levi may continue," says the LORD Almighty. ⁵"My covenant was with him, a covenant of life and peace, and I gave them to him; this called for reverence and he revered me and stood in awe of my name. ⁶True instruction was in his mouth and nothing false was found on his lips. He walked with me in peace and uprightness, and turned many from sin.

NOW OR NEVER

MAL 2:2

Do you think it's harder to honor God on the outside (in the way you act), or on the inside (in the way you think and feel)? How hard would it be to make your thoughts and your actions consistent with each other?

⁷"For the lips of a priest ought to preserve knowledge, and from his mouth men should seek instruction—because he is the messenger of the LORD Almighty. ⁸But you have turned from the way and by your teaching have caused many to stumble; you have violated the covenant with Levi," says the LORD Almighty. ⁹"So I have caused you to be despised and humiliated before all the people, because you have not followed my ways but have shown partiality in matters of the law."

JUDAH UNFAITHFUL

¹⁰Have we not all one Father[c]? Did not one God create us? Why do we profane the covenant of our fathers by breaking faith with one another?

¹¹Judah has broken faith. A detestable thing has been committed in Israel and in Jerusalem: Judah has desecrated the sanctuary the LORD loves, by marrying the daughter of a foreign god. ¹²As for the man who does this, whoever he may be, may the LORD cut him off from the tents of Jacob[d]—even though he brings offerings to the LORD Almighty.

¹³Another thing you do: You flood the LORD's altar with tears. You weep and wail because he no longer pays attention to your offerings or accepts them with pleasure from your hands. ¹⁴You ask, "Why?" It is because the LORD is acting as the witness between you and the wife of your youth, because you have broken faith with her, though she is your partner, the wife of your marriage covenant.

¹⁵Has not ⌊the LORD⌋ made them one? In flesh and spirit they are his. And why one? Because he was seeking godly offspring.[e] So guard yourself in your spirit, and do not break faith with the wife of your youth.

¹⁶"I hate divorce," says the LORD God of Israel, "and I hate a man's covering himself[f] with violence as well as with his garment," says the LORD Almighty.

So guard yourself in your spirit, and do not break faith.

THE DAY OF JUDGMENT

¹⁷You have wearied the LORD with your words.

"How have we wearied him?" you ask.

By saying, "All who do evil are good in the eyes of the LORD, and he is pleased with them" or "Where is the God of justice?"

3 "See, I will send my messenger, who will prepare the way before me. Then suddenly the Lord you are seeking will come to his temple; the messenger of the covenant, whom you desire, will come," says the LORD Almighty.

²But who can endure the day of his coming? Who can stand when he appears? For he will be like a refiner's fire or a launderer's soap. ³He will sit as a refiner and purifier of silver; he will purify the Le-

---

ᵃ 3 Or cut off (see Septuagint)   ᵇ 3 Or will blight your grain   ᶜ 10 Or father   ᵈ 12 Or ¹²May the LORD cut off from the tents of Jacob anyone who gives testimony in behalf of the man who does this   ᵉ 15 Or ¹⁵But the one ⌊who is our father⌋ did not do this, not as long as life remained in him. And what was he seeking? An offspring from God   ᶠ 16 Or his wife

1261

vites and refine them like gold and silver. Then the LORD will have men who will bring offerings in righteousness, ⁴and the offerings of Judah and Jerusalem will be acceptable to the LORD, as in days gone by, as in former years.

⁵"So I will come near to you for judgment. I will be quick to testify against sorcerers, adulterers and perjurers, against those who defraud laborers of their wages, who oppress the widows and the fatherless, and deprive aliens of justice, but do not fear me," says the LORD Almighty.

ROBBING GOD

⁶"I the LORD do not change. So you, O descendants of Jacob, are not destroyed. ⁷Ever since the time of your forefathers you have turned away from my decrees and have not kept them. Return to me, and I will return to you," says the LORD Almighty.

"But you ask, 'How are we to return?'

⁸"Will a man rob God? Yet you rob me.

"But you ask, 'How do we rob you?'

"In tithes and offerings. ⁹You are under a curse—the whole nation of you—because you are robbing me. ¹⁰Bring the whole tithe into the storehouse, that there may be food in my house. Test me in this," says the LORD Almighty, "and see if I will not throw open the floodgates of heaven and pour out so much blessing that you will not have room enough for it. ¹¹I will prevent pests from devouring your crops, and the vines in your fields will not cast their fruit," says the LORD Almighty. ¹²"Then all the nations will call you blessed, for yours will be a delightful land," says the LORD Almighty.

¹³"You have said harsh things against me," says the LORD.

"Yet you ask, 'What have we said against you?'

¹⁴"You have said, 'It is futile to serve God. What did we gain by carrying out his requirements and going about like mourners before the LORD Almighty? ¹⁵But now we call the arrogant blessed. Certainly the evildoers prosper, and even those who challenge God escape.' "

¹⁶Then those who feared the LORD talked with each other, and the LORD listened and heard. A scroll of remembrance was written in his presence concerning those who feared the LORD and honored his name.

¹⁷"They will be mine," says the LORD Almighty, "in the day when I make up my treasured possession.ᵃ I will spare them, just as in compassion a man spares his son who serves him. ¹⁸And you will again see the distinction between the righteous and the wicked, between those who serve God and those who do not.

»» live the adventure »» Mal 3:8-10

Giving Back to God

When we give tithes—money to finance the Lord's work—we are responding to God's generosity simply by imitating it. Our money, like everything else we have, comes from God. It's his to begin with. So when we present our offerings at church, all we're doing is giving back to God a portion of what's rightfully his. When we *don't* present our offerings, we're actually pocketing God's possessions. Remember the eighth commandment, "You shall not steal" (Exodus 20:15)? Think you've managed to keep it just because you've never shoplifted? According to Malachi, when you refuse to give back to God a portion of what he's given you, you're stealing.

challenge notes

To: my_son

heavenly_father: when my judgment comes, a lot of people will be scared to death; they'll panic and do everything they can to escape me. you don't have to be one of them. stay close to me and follow my commands, and I will show you kindness and compassion when it matters most.

THE DAY OF THE LORD

4

"Surely the day is coming; it will burn like a furnace. All the arrogant and every evildoer will be stubble, and that day that is coming will set them on fire," says the LORD Almighty. "Not a root or a branch will be left to them. ²But for you who revere my name, the sun of righteousness will rise with healing in its wings. And you will go out and leap like calves released from the stall. ³Then

ᵃ 17 Or Almighty, "my treasured possession, in the day when I act

ahab

VERSUS

» One of Israel's most evil kings
» Married to Jezebel, who influenced the whole nation to worship Baal
» Refused to hear God speaking through the prophet Elijah

elijah

» One of Israel's most spectacular prophets
» Confronted the false priests of Baal in the famous "battle of the gods"
» Heard God speak in a whisper

The Main Event

Think it doesn't matter who you date? Think again. Dating leads to liking, which leads to loving, which eventually leads to marrying. And the person you marry will have a huge impact on your life. Case in point? King Ahab of Israel. He married a scheming, aggressive heathen woman named Jezebel. Before long, she had him and the rest of the nation worshiping her pagan gods, particularly Baal.

God did what God usually does in such situations. He sent someone to wake up his people and turn them around. In this particular instance he called a prophet named Elijah to speak some strong words of rebuke to Ahab and his people.

Ahab responded foolishly. (See Proverbs 12:1 for a nice, short description of the kind of loser Ahab was.) He rejected Elijah's message because it made him uncomfortable. Instead, Ahab chose to listen to his false prophets, who told him only what he wanted to hear. All the while, Jezebel was blowing in his ear, leading him closer and closer to destruction.

So God performed an absolute jaw-dropping miracle to get the people's attention. He instructed Elijah to challenge 850 false prophets to a death match on Mount Carmel. "We'll make sacrifices," Elijah suggested. "I'll make them to my God, and you to your gods. The first god to respond will be declared the one true God."

When the contest started, the pagan holy men danced and gyrated all over the mountaintop in an attempt to get Baal to do something. It was almost comical. They hooted and yelled and even cut themselves with knives. But they got no response. Elijah watched his sweaty, bloody rivals with amusement, and he couldn't resist the opportunity to lay a little smack on them. "What's the matter? Can't Baal hear you? Maybe he's on the road. Maybe he fell asleep!"

When Elijah's turn came, he raised the stakes, drenching his own altar with water. Then he stood up and called on God. The result was immediate and dramatic. Fire roared down from heaven and consumed Elijah's altar, along with everything around it. The Lord left no doubt as to who is the one true God. After the contest, Elijah ordered the people of Israel to hack down the 850 false prophets of Baal.

You would think this miraculous display would have turned Ahab's heart—and maybe even Jezebel's. Sadly, it only hardened them.

The Outcome

After the dramatic contest, Elijah experienced a period of fear and depression. Intimidated by Jezebel's murderous threats, the weary prophet hightailed it into the wilderness and became borderline suicidal. God met him there and spoke to Elijah in a whisper. In time, Elijah recovered and came back rested, strong and ready to serve. He maintained that spirit for the rest of his days on earth, until God miraculously transported him to heaven.

Ahab, meanwhile, continued to let Jezebel manipulate him for evil. Ignoring the one true God, their lives spiraled ever downward. They died gruesome deaths and are remembered all these years later only for their shameful acts.

Think it doesn't matter who you marry? Think again.

Read more about Ahab and Elijah in 1 Kings 17–22 (pages 402–412; 2 Kings 1–2 (pages 414–416).

you will trample down the wicked; they will be ashes under the soles of your feet on the day when I do these things," says the LORD Almighty.

4 "Remember the law of my servant Moses, the decrees and laws I gave him at Horeb for all Israel.

5 "See, I will send you the prophet Elijah before that great and dreadful day of the LORD comes. 6 He will turn the hearts of the fathers to their children, and the hearts of the children to their fathers; or else I will come and strike the land with a curse."

NOW OR NEVER
MAL 4:1–6

How do you feel about the Lord coming back someday? How do you think your non-Christian friends would react if you tried to explain to them in detail what his return means?

THE NEW TESTAMENT

MATTHEW

Author
Matthew, also called Levi, the tax collector

Audience
Greek-speaking Jews

Date
Probably between A.D. 60 and 70

Setting
Matthew most likely wrote from Israel, though some believe he wrote from Syrian Antioch.

Verse to Remember
Simon Peter answered, "You are the Christ, the Son of the living God" (16:16).

Theme to Consider
Matthew's message is clear: Jesus is the long-awaited Messiah, the King of kings and Lord of lords. Examine the evidence and accept Jesus as Lord of your life.

UNCHANGING TRUTH » Do you know what a Christian testimony is? It's like your spiritual autobiography—the story of how you first heard about Jesus, what made you decide to believe in him and trust him with your life, and how things have been different for you since you made that life-changing decision.

Some people have testimonies that would make great movies—full of action, suspense and amazing life transformations. The apostle Matthew's testimony—the story of his experiences with Jesus—actually became the first book of the New Testament.

Most of us, though, have testimonies that aren't quite so dramatic. That doesn't make them any less valuable or significant in God's eyes.

The fact is, *your* testimony may be what inspires friends, family members, classmates or visitors to your youth group to start thinking seriously about Jesus. They may hear something in your story that rings a bell in their own lives. They may see the changes that have happened in your life and start wondering if Jesus can do the same thing for them. Or they may just trust what you say because you're a regular guy—someone they can relate to.

Whatever the reason, your story *can* make a difference in other people's lives. Of course, that's assuming that other people actually *hear* your story. In order for that to happen, you have to be willing to share your faith story. That doesn't mean you have to recite your personal spiritual history the moment you meet someone new. But it does mean you should get comfortable talking about the things Jesus has done in your life so they can see what he can do for real people.

LIFE LESSONS »

1   Being insulted, made fun of or excluded from certain groups at school because of your Christian faith is a sure sign that you're doing something right—and that God will honor you (5:11–12).

2   Your Christian faith isn't something to hide; it's something that should be obvious to everyone who knows you (5:14–16).

3   God rewards people who know what they want—as long as it is consistent with his will and they are willing to keep praying with persistence (7:7–8).

THE GENEALOGY OF JESUS

1 A record of the genealogy of Jesus Christ the son of David, the son of Abraham:

² Abraham was the father of Isaac,
Isaac the father of Jacob,
Jacob the father of Judah and his brothers,
³ Judah the father of Perez and Zerah, whose mother was Tamar,
Perez the father of Hezron,
Hezron the father of Ram,
⁴ Ram the father of Amminadab,
Amminadab the father of Nahshon,
Nahshon the father of Salmon,
⁵ Salmon the father of Boaz, whose mother was Rahab,
Boaz the father of Obed, whose mother was Ruth,
Obed the father of Jesse,
⁶ and Jesse the father of King David.

David was the father of Solomon, whose mother had been Uriah's wife,
⁷ Solomon the father of Rehoboam,
Rehoboam the father of Abijah,
Abijah the father of Asa,
⁸ Asa the father of Jehoshaphat,
Jehoshaphat the father of Jehoram,
Jehoram the father of Uzziah,
⁹ Uzziah the father of Jotham,
Jotham the father of Ahaz,
Ahaz the father of Hezekiah,
¹⁰ Hezekiah the father of Manasseh,
Manasseh the father of Amon,
Amon the father of Josiah,
¹¹ and Josiah the father of Jeconiah[a] and his brothers at the time of the exile to Babylon.

¹² After the exile to Babylon:
Jeconiah was the father of Shealtiel,
Shealtiel the father of Zerubbabel,
¹³ Zerubbabel the father of Abiud,
Abiud the father of Eliakim,
Eliakim the father of Azor,
¹⁴ Azor the father of Zadok,
Zadok the father of Akim,
Akim the father of Eliud,
¹⁵ Eliud the father of Eleazar,
Eleazar the father of Matthan,
Matthan the father of Jacob,
¹⁶ and Jacob the father of Joseph, the husband of Mary, of whom was born Jesus, who is called Christ.

¹⁷ Thus there were fourteen generations in all from Abraham to David, fourteen from David to the exile to Babylon, and fourteen from the exile to the Christ.[b]

Reading the Signs of Prophecy

What's up with all the long, seemingly boring genealogies in the Bible? Back in Jesus' day, a person's family tree was considered a lot more important than it is today. The fact that Jesus was a descendant of King David would have raised at least a few eyebrows among those who didn't believe he was who he claimed to be. After all, the Old Testament prophets had predicted that the Messiah would come from David's family line. So a simple genealogy gives us good reason to believe that Jesus is who he says he is.

»» live the adventure »» Mt 1:6

---

[a] *11* That is, Jehoiachin; also in verse 12   [b] *17* Or *Messiah.* "The Christ" (Greek) and "the Messiah" (Hebrew) both mean "the Anointed One."

THE BIRTH OF JESUS CHRIST

18This is how the birth of Jesus Christ came about: His mother Mary was pledged to be married to Joseph, but before they came together, she was found to be with child through the Holy Spirit. 19Because Joseph her husband was a righteous man and did not want to expose her to public disgrace, he had in mind to divorce her quietly.

20But after he had considered this, an angel of the Lord appeared to him in a dream and said, "Joseph son of David, do not be afraid to take Mary home as your wife, because what is conceived in her is from the Holy Spirit. 21She will give birth to a son, and you are to give him the name Jesus,ᵃ because he will save his people from their sins."

22All this took place to fulfill what the Lord had said through the prophet: 23"The virgin will be with child and will give birth to a son, and they will call him Immanuel"ᵇ—which means, "God with us."

24When Joseph woke up, he did what the angel of the Lord had commanded him and took Mary home as his wife. 25But he had no union with her until she gave birth to a son. And he gave him the name Jesus.

THE VISIT OF THE MAGI

2 After Jesus was born in Bethlehem in Judea, during the time of King Herod, Magiᶜ from the east came to Jerusalem 2and asked, "Where is the one who has been born king of the Jews? We saw his star in the eastᵈ and have come to worship him."

3When King Herod heard this he was disturbed, and all Jerusalem with him. 4When he had called together all the people's chief priests and teachers of the law, he asked them where the Christᵉ was to be born. 5"In Bethlehem in Judea," they replied, "for this is what the prophet has written:

6 " 'But you, Bethlehem, in the land of Judah,
    are by no means least among the rulers of Judah;
  for out of you will come a ruler
    who will be the shepherd of my people Israel.'ᶠ"

7Then Herod called the Magi secretly and found out from them the exact time the star had appeared. 8He sent them to Bethlehem and said, "Go and make a careful search for the child. As soon as you find him, report to me, so that I too may go and worship him."

9After they had heard the king, they went on their way, and the star they had seen in the eastᵍ went ahead of them until it stopped over the place where the child was. 10When they saw the star, they were overjoyed. 11On coming to the house, they saw the child with his mother Mary, and they bowed down and worshiped him. Then they opened their treasures and presented him with gifts of gold and of incense and of myrrh. 12And having been warned in a dream not to go back to Herod, they returned to their country by another route.

NOW OR NEVER
MT 2:11

Your Christmas nativity set is all wrong. The wise men (or Magi) did not visit Jesus at the manger on the night he was born. He was almost a toddler when they visited him at his home several months (or years) later.

THE ESCAPE TO EGYPT

13When they had gone, an angel of the Lord appeared to Joseph in a dream. "Get up," he said, "take the child and his mother and escape to Egypt. Stay there until I tell you, for Herod is going to search for the child to kill him."

14So he got up, took the child and his mother during the night and left for Egypt, 15where he stayed until the death of Herod. And so was fulfilled what the Lord had said through the prophet: "Out of Egypt I called my son."ʰ

16When Herod realized that he had been outwitted by the Magi, he was furious, and he gave orders to kill all the boys in Bethlehem and its vicinity who were two years old and under, in accordance with the time he had learned from the Magi. 17Then what was said through the prophet Jeremiah was fulfilled:

ᵃ 21 Jesus is the Greek form of Joshua, which means the Lᴏʀᴅ saves.　ᵇ 23 Isaiah 7:14　ᶜ 1 Traditionally Wise Men　ᵈ 2 Or star when it rose　ᵉ 4 Or Messiah　ᶠ 6 Micah 5:2　ᵍ 9 Or seen when it rose　ʰ 15 Hosea 11:1

18 "A voice is heard in Ramah,
    weeping and great mourning,
Rachel weeping for her children
    and refusing to be comforted,
because they are no more." [a]

THE RETURN TO NAZARETH

19After Herod died, an angel of the Lord appeared in a dream to Joseph in Egypt 20and said, "Get up, take the child and his mother and go to the land of Israel, for those who were trying to take the child's life are dead."

21So he got up, took the child and his mother and went to the land of Israel. 22But when he heard that Archelaus was reigning in Judea in place of his father Herod, he was afraid to go there. Having been warned in a dream, he withdrew to the district of Galilee, 23and he went and lived in a town called Nazareth. So was fulfilled what was said through the prophets: "He will be called a Nazarene."

JOHN THE BAPTIST PREPARES THE WAY

3 In those days John the Baptist came, preaching in the Desert of Judea 2and saying, "Repent, for the kingdom of heaven is near." 3This is he who was spoken of through the prophet Isaiah:

"A voice of one calling in the desert,
    'Prepare the way for the Lord,
    make straight paths for him.' " [b]

4John's clothes were made of camel's hair, and he had a leather belt around his waist. His food was locusts and wild honey. 5People went out to him from Jerusalem and all Judea and the whole region of the Jordan. 6Confessing their sins, they were baptized by him in the Jordan River.

7But when he saw many of the Pharisees and Sadducees coming to where he was baptizing, he said to them: "You brood of vipers! Who warned you to flee from the coming wrath? 8Produce fruit in keeping with repentance. 9And do not think you can say to yourselves, 'We have Abraham as our father.' I tell you that out of these stones God can raise up children for Abraham. 10The ax is already at the root of the trees, and every tree that does not produce good fruit will be cut down and thrown into the fire.

11"I baptize you with[c] water for repentance. But after me will come one who is more powerful than I, whose sandals I am not fit to carry. He will baptize you with the Holy Spirit and with fire. 12His winnowing fork is in his hand, and he will clear his threshing floor, gathering his wheat into the barn and burning up the chaff with unquenchable fire."

NOW OR NEVER

MT 3:4

John's appearance and eating habits probably made him seem like a bit of a freak to some people. But his lifestyle was a visually powerful rejection of self-indulgence and materialism. God doesn't tell us all to start munching on insects, but he does want his people to stand out in a crowd.

THE BAPTISM OF JESUS

13Then Jesus came from Galilee to the Jordan to be baptized by John. 14But John tried to deter him, saying, "I need to be baptized by you, and do you come to me?"

15Jesus replied, "Let it be so now; it is proper for us to do this to fulfill all righteousness." Then John consented.

16As soon as Jesus was baptized, he went up out of the water. At that moment heaven was opened, and he saw the Spirit of God descending like a dove and lighting on him. 17And a voice from heaven said, "This is my Son, whom I love; with him I am well pleased."

---

[a] 18 Jer. 31:15   [b] 3 Isaiah 40:3   [c] 11 Or in

THE TEMPTATION OF JESUS

4 Then Jesus was led by the Spirit into the desert to be tempted by the devil. ²After fasting forty days and forty nights, he was hungry. ³The tempter came to him and said, "If you are the Son of God, tell these stones to become bread."

⁴Jesus answered, "It is written: 'Man does not live on bread alone, but on every word that comes from the mouth of God.'ᵃ"

⁵Then the devil took him to the holy city and had him stand on the highest point of the temple. ⁶"If you are the Son of God," he said, "throw yourself down. For it is written:

" 'He will command his angels
    concerning you,
and they will lift you up in their
    hands,
so that you will not strike your foot
    against a stone.'ᵇ"

now or never
MT 4:18–20

What do you think made Jesus' disciples drop everything they were doing and follow him? What exactly was it that made you want to turn over your life to his care and control?

⁷Jesus answered him, "It is also written: 'Do not put the Lord your God to the test.'ᶜ"

⁸Again, the devil took him to a very high mountain and showed him all the kingdoms of the world and their splendor. ⁹"All this I will give you," he said, "if you will bow down and worship me."

¹⁰Jesus said to him, "Away from me, Satan! For it is written: 'Worship the Lord your God, and serve him only.'ᵈ"

¹¹Then the devil left him, and angels came and attended him.

JESUS BEGINS TO PREACH

¹²When Jesus heard that John had been put in prison, he returned to Galilee. ¹³Leaving Nazareth, he went and lived in Capernaum, which was by the lake in the area of Zebulun and Naphtali— ¹⁴to fulfill what was said through the prophet Isaiah:

¹⁵ "Land of Zebulun and land of Naphtali,
    the way to the sea, along the Jordan,
    Galilee of the Gentiles—
¹⁶ the people living in darkness
    have seen a great light;
on those living in the land of the shadow
    of death
a light has dawned."ᵉ

¹⁷From that time on Jesus began to preach, "Repent, for the kingdom of heaven is near."

THE CALLING OF THE FIRST DISCIPLES

¹⁸As Jesus was walking beside the Sea of Galilee, he saw two brothers, Simon called Peter and his brother Andrew. They were casting a net into the lake, for they were fishermen. ¹⁹"Come, follow me," Jesus said, "and I will make you fishers of men." ²⁰At once they left their nets and followed him.

²¹Going on from there, he saw two other brothers, James son of Zebedee and his brother John. They were in a boat with their father Zebedee, preparing their nets. Jesus called them, ²²and immediately they left the boat and their father and followed him.

Resisting Temptation

Notice how Jesus dealt with Satan's challenges. He didn't abuse his power by doing the things Satan wanted him to do. Instead he steered clear of the temptations completely. He refused to do anything that might cause him to sin. He also used a weapon that Satan has no defense against: the truth of God's Word. Each time Satan tempted Jesus, Jesus fired back with Scripture, exposing Satan's temptation for the sham that it was. When you're facing the enemy, remember what weapons are at your disposal.

» live the adventure » Mt 4:10

ᵃ *4* Deut. 8:3 ᵇ *6* Psalm 91:11,12 ᶜ *7* Deut. 6:16 ᵈ *10* Deut. 6:13 ᵉ *16* Isaiah 9:1,2

JESUS HEALS THE SICK

23Jesus went throughout Galilee, teaching in their synagogues, preaching the good news of the kingdom, and healing every disease and sickness among the people. 24News about him spread all over Syria, and people brought to him all who were ill with various diseases, those suffering severe pain, the demon-possessed, those having seizures, and the paralyzed, and he healed them. 25Large crowds from Galilee, the Decapolis,ª Jerusalem, Judea and the region across the Jordan followed him.

THE BEATITUDES

5 Now when he saw the crowds, he went up on a mountainside and sat down. His disciples came to him, 2and he began to teach them, saying:

3 "Blessed are the poor in spirit,
　　for theirs is the kingdom of heaven.
4 Blessed are those who mourn,
　　for they will be comforted.
5 Blessed are the meek,
　　for they will inherit the earth.
6 Blessed are those who hunger and thirst
　　for righteousness,
　　for they will be filled.
7 Blessed are the merciful,
　　for they will be shown mercy.
8 Blessed are the pure in heart,
　　for they will see God.
9 Blessed are the peacemakers,
　　for they will be called sons of God.
10 Blessed are those who are persecuted because of righteousness,
　　for theirs is the kingdom of heaven.

11"Blessed are you when people insult you, persecute you and falsely say all kinds of evil against you because of me. 12Rejoice and be glad, because great is your reward in heaven, for in the same way they persecuted the prophets who were before you.

»» live the adventure »» Mt 5:5

Learning to Be Meek

What does it mean to be meek? Who are the truly humble types? They're the guys who don't have to be first all the time. They're the guys who don't bask in the spotlight every chance they get. They're the guys who don't have a problem doing thankless jobs. They're the guys who care more about team stats than personal ones. They're the guys who listen instead of always trying to dominate the conversation. They're the guys who realize they wouldn't have anything if it weren't for God—who recognize all that God has done for them and give him all the credit instead of praising themselves.

challengenotes

To: my_son

heavenly_father: people will make fun of you when they find out that you're serious about your beliefs. some will spread rumors about you. you may even lose a friendship over me. but for every bad thing that happens to you on account of me, I will reward you a million times and more in heaven.

MT 5:11-12

SALT AND LIGHT

13"You are the salt of the earth. But if the salt loses its saltiness, how can it be made salty again? It is no longer good for anything, except to be thrown out and trampled by men.

14"You are the light of the world. A city on a hill cannot be hidden. 15Neither do people light a lamp and put it under a bowl. Instead they put it on its stand, and it gives light to everyone in the house. 16In the same way, let your light shine before men, that they may see your good deeds and praise your Father in heaven.

THE FULFILLMENT OF THE LAW

17"Do not think that I have come to abolish the Law or the Prophets; I have not come to abolish them but to fulfill them. 18I tell you the truth, until heaven and earth disappear, not the smallest letter, not the

ª 25 That is, the Ten Cities

least stroke of a pen, will by any means disappear from the Law until everything is accomplished. [19]Anyone who breaks one of the least of these commandments and teaches others to do the same will be called least in the kingdom of heaven, but whoever practices and teaches these commands will be called great in the kingdom of heaven. [20]For I tell you that unless your righteousness surpasses that of the Pharisees and the teachers of the law, you will certainly not enter the kingdom of heaven.

MURDER

[21]"You have heard that it was said to the people long ago, 'Do not murder,[a] and anyone who murders will be subject to judgment.' [22]But I tell you that anyone who is angry with his brother[b] will be subject to judgment. Again, anyone who says to his brother, 'Raca,'[c] is answerable to the Sanhedrin. But anyone who says, 'You fool!' will be in danger of the fire of hell.

[23]"Therefore, if you are offering your gift at the altar and there remember that your brother has something against you, [24]leave your gift there in front of the altar. First go and be reconciled to your brother; then come and offer your gift.

[25]"Settle matters quickly with your adversary who is taking you to court. Do it while you are still with him on the way, or he may hand you over to the judge, and the judge may hand you over to the officer, and you may be thrown into prison. [26]I tell you the truth, you will not get out until you have paid the last penny.[d]

ADULTERY

[27]"You have heard that it was said, 'Do not commit adultery.'[e] [28]But I tell you that anyone who looks at a woman lustfully has already committed adultery with her in his heart. [29]If your right eye causes you to sin, gouge it out and throw it away. It is better for you to lose one part of your body than for your whole body to be thrown into hell. [30]And if your right hand causes you to sin, cut it off and throw it away. It is better for you to lose one part of your body than for your whole body to go into hell.

DIVORCE

[31]"It has been said, 'Anyone who divorces his wife must give her a certificate of divorce.'[f] [32]But I tell you that anyone who divorces his wife, except for marital unfaithfulness, causes her to become an adulteress, and anyone who marries the divorced woman commits adultery.

OATHS

[33]"Again, you have heard that it was said to the people long ago, 'Do not break your oath, but keep the oaths you have made to the Lord.' [34]But I tell you, Do not swear at all: either by heaven, for it is God's throne; [35]or by the earth, for it is his footstool; or by Jerusalem, for it is the city of the Great King. [36]And do not swear by your head, for you cannot make even one hair white or black. [37]Simply let your 'Yes' be 'Yes,' and your 'No,' 'No'; anything beyond this comes from the evil one.

AN EYE FOR AN EYE

[38]"You have heard that it was said, 'Eye for eye, and tooth for tooth.'[g] [39]But I tell you, Do not resist an evil person. If someone strikes you on the right cheek, turn to him the other also. [40]And if someone wants to sue you and take your tunic, let him have your cloak as well. [41]If someone forces you to go one mile, go with him two miles. [42]Give to the one who asks you, and do not turn away from the one who wants to borrow from you.

LOVE FOR ENEMIES

[43]"You have heard that it was said, 'Love your neighbor[h] and hate your enemy.' [44]But I tell you: Love your enemies[i] and pray for those who persecute you, [45]that you may be sons of your Father in heaven. He causes his sun to rise on the evil and the good, and sends rain on the righteous and the unrighteous. [46]If you love those who love you, what reward will you get? Are not even the tax collectors doing that? [47]And if you greet only your brothers, what are you doing more than others? Do not even pagans do that? [48]Be perfect, therefore, as your heavenly Father is perfect.

[a] *21* Exodus 20:13   [b] *22* Some manuscripts *brother without cause*   [c] *22* An Aramaic term of contempt   [d] *26* Greek *kodrantes*
[e] *27* Exodus 20:14   [f] *31* Deut. 24:1   [g] *38* Exodus 21:24; Lev. 24:20; Deut. 19:21   [h] *43* Lev. 19:18   [i] *44* Some late manuscripts *enemies, bless those who curse you, do good to those who hate you*

GIVING TO THE NEEDY

6

"Be careful not to do your 'acts of righteousness' before men, to be seen by them. If you do, you will have no reward from your Father in heaven.

2 "So when you give to the needy, do not announce it with trumpets, as the hypocrites do in the synagogues and on the streets, to be honored by men. I tell you the truth, they have received their reward in full. 3 But when you give to the needy, do not let your left hand know what your right hand is doing, 4 so that your giving may be in secret. Then your Father, who sees what is done in secret, will reward you.

PRAYER

5 "And when you pray, do not be like the hypocrites, for they love to pray standing in the synagogues and on the street corners to be seen by men. I tell you the truth, they have received their reward in full. 6 But when you pray, go into your room, close the door and pray to your Father, who is unseen. Then your Father, who sees what is done in secret, will reward you. 7 And when you pray, do not keep on babbling like pagans, for they think they will be heard because of their many words. 8 Do not be like them, for your Father knows what you need before you ask him.

9 "This, then, is how you should pray:

"'Our Father in heaven,
hallowed be your name,
10 your kingdom come,
your will be done
on earth as it is in heaven.
11 Give us today our daily bread.
12 Forgive us our debts,
as we also have forgiven our debtors.
13 And lead us not into temptation,
but deliver us from the evil one.a'

» live the adventure » Mt 5:43-48

Dealing With Enemies

Do you have an actual enemy, someone you can't stand or someone who can't stand you (or both)? Do you remember what it was that made you enemies? What do you think would happen if you swallowed your pride and apologized to that person for your part in the conflict—even if it's just for having a negative attitude toward him or her? What if you supported that apology with a few sincere words about your desire to get along? Do you think you'd be made fun of, ignored, yelled at or laughed out of the room? You might be. But your gesture of love might also reduce your enemy total by one. And who wants enemies anyway?

14 For if you forgive men when they sin against you, your heavenly Father will also forgive you. 15 But if you do not forgive men their sins, your Father will not forgive your sins.

NOW OR NEVER
MT 6:9–13

Here's an idea for the next time you spend some quiet time alone with God: Try putting the Lord's Prayer in your own words and using that as your prayer.

FASTING

16 "When you fast, do not look somber as the hypocrites do, for they disfigure their faces to show men they are fasting. I tell you the truth, they have received their reward in full. 17 But when you fast, put oil on your head and wash your face, 18 so that it will not be obvious to men that you are fasting, but only to your Father, who is unseen; and your Father, who sees what is done in secret, will reward you.

TREASURES IN HEAVEN

19 "Do not store up for yourselves treasures on earth, where moth and rust destroy, and where thieves break in and steal. 20 But store up for yourselves treasures in heaven, where moth and rust do not destroy, and where thieves do not break in and steal. 21 For where your treasure is, there your heart will be also.

---

a 13 Or from evil; some late manuscripts one, / for yours is the kingdom and the power and the glory forever. Amen.

²²"The eye is the lamp of the body. If your eyes are good, your whole body will be full of light. ²³But if your eyes are bad, your whole body will be full of darkness. If then the light within you is darkness, how great is that darkness!

nOW OR nEVER
MT 6:19

Have you seen the bumper sticker that says, "The one who dies with the most toys wins"? That attitude is not only wrong, but it's also dangerous. As far as God is concerned, those who die with the most toys have wasted their time on earthly things and put their eternity in jeopardy.

²⁴"No one can serve two masters. Either he will hate the one and love the other, or he will be devoted to the one and despise the other. You cannot serve both God and Money.

DO NOT WORRY

²⁵"Therefore I tell you, do not worry about your life, what you will eat or drink; or about your body, what you will wear. Is not life more important than food, and the body more important than clothes? ²⁶Look at the birds of the air; they do not sow or reap or store away in barns, and yet your heavenly Father feeds them. Are you not much more valuable than they? ²⁷Who of you by worrying can add a single hour to his life^a?

²⁸"And why do you worry about clothes? See how the lilies of the field grow. They do not labor or spin. ²⁹Yet I tell you that not even Solomon in all his splendor was dressed like one of these. ³⁰If that is how God clothes the grass of the field, which is here today and tomorrow is thrown into the fire, will he not much more clothe you, O you of little faith? ³¹So do not worry, saying, 'What shall we eat?' or 'What shall we drink?' or 'What shall we wear?' ³²For the pagans run after all these things, and your heavenly Father knows that you need them. ³³But seek first his kingdom and his righteousness, and all these things will be given to you as well. ³⁴Therefore do not worry about tomorrow, for tomorrow will worry about itself. Each day has enough trouble of its own.

challengenotes

To: my_son

MT 6:25-27

heavenly_father: here's a simple strategy for dealing with worry: take care of the things that you can do something about—the things that are within your power to control—and leave the rest to me.

JUDGING OTHERS

7 "Do not judge, or you too will be judged. ²For in the same way you judge others, you will be judged, and with the measure you use, it will be measured to you.

³"Why do you look at the speck of sawdust in your brother's eye and pay no attention to the plank in your own eye? ⁴How can you say to your brother, 'Let me take the speck out of your eye,' when all the time there is a plank in your own eye? ⁵You hypocrite, first take the plank out of your own eye, and then you will see clearly to remove the speck from your brother's eye.

⁶"Do not give dogs what is sacred; do not throw your pearls to pigs. If you do, they may trample them under their feet, and then turn and tear you to pieces.

ASK, SEEK, KNOCK

⁷"Ask and it will be given to you; seek and you will find; knock and the door will be opened to you. ⁸For everyone who asks receives; he who seeks finds; and to him who knocks, the door will be opened.

⁹"Which of you, if his son asks for bread, will give him a stone? ¹⁰Or if he asks for a fish, will give him a snake? ¹¹If you, then, though you are evil, know how to give good gifts to your children, how much more will your Father in heaven give good gifts to those who ask him! ¹²So in everything, do to others what you would have them do to you, for this sums up the Law and the Prophets.

THE NARROW AND WIDE GATES

¹³"Enter through the narrow gate. For wide is the gate and broad is the road that leads to destruction, and many enter through it. ¹⁴But small is the gate and narrow the road that leads to life, and only a few find it.

---

^{a} 27 Or *single cubit to his height*

battlelines

» The Big Dis (Forgiveness)

Q: Hey, I noticed you and Stephen hanging out the other day.
A: Yeah, he just came over, out of the blue.

Q: What's up with that?
A: You tell me. For years, the whole time we were growing up, we were like best friends. All through childhood. Then a couple of years ago, he blew me off and started hanging out with some other guys. So I'm like, "What's the deal, man? Did I do something or what?" He just said he was sorry. No explanation. Nothing. Now, all of sudden, he's coming by all the time: "Hey, man, let's go do this. Let's go do that." I'm telling you, it's weird, man.

Q: Did you ever say anything more to him about it?
A: What do you mean?

Q: You know, like, "Stephen, why do you want to hang out with me now, after two years of not even giving me the time of day?"
A: Nah. I just figured, "OK, whatever."

Q: So you're not bitter? You're not worried that he might do the same thing again?
A: I never said that. Yeah, I'm a little ticked. I don't get the guy. And I'm not sure I trust him. I mean, what's he thinking? That I didn't notice he didn't want to hang around me for two years? But, at the same time, I think, *Turn the other cheek and all that. Forgive and forget.*

Q: Juan, you're a better man than I am. I'd be tempted to tell him to get lost.
A: Yeah, but we *all* do stupid stuff, you know? We all make mistakes. I figure you have to cut people some slack if you want them to do the same for you.

» No Grudges

Here are three simple truths to keep in mind:

❶ **People are guaranteed to fail you.**

Whether inadvertently or on purpose, people *will* do things that hurt your feelings. Count on it.

❷ **When you are wronged, your first impulse will be to get even.**

We all have a natural tendency to want to make people experience the same kind of hurt, disappointment or anger that they make us feel. In other words, we keep score. And when we dwell on that score, we become bitter.

❸ **God tells us to forgive (see Matthew 6:12–15; Luke 17:3; Colossians 3:13).**

By resisting the urge to keep a record of how others have wronged us—by canceling the debts they owe us (which, by the way, is what forgiveness is all about)—we keep bitterness from taking root in our lives and turning us into angry, resentful creatures. Living with bitterness can eat us up and keep us from enjoying the good things God places in our lives.

For more on forgiving others, log on to www.RevolutionBible.com.

A TREE AND ITS FRUIT

15"Watch out for false prophets. They come to you in sheep's clothing, but inwardly they are ferocious wolves. 16By their fruit you will recognize them. Do people pick grapes from thornbushes, or figs from thistles? 17Likewise every good tree bears good fruit, but a bad tree bears bad fruit. 18A good tree cannot bear bad fruit, and a bad tree cannot bear good fruit. 19Every tree that does not bear good fruit is cut down and thrown into the fire. 20Thus, by their fruit you will recognize them.

21"Not everyone who says to me, 'Lord, Lord,' will enter the kingdom of heaven, but only he who does the will of my Father who is in heaven. 22Many will say to me on that day, 'Lord, Lord, did we not prophesy in your name, and in your name drive out demons and perform many miracles?' 23Then I will tell them plainly, 'I never knew you. Away from me, you evildoers!'

THE WISE AND FOOLISH BUILDERS

24"Therefore everyone who hears these words of mine and puts them into practice is like a wise man who built his house on the rock. 25The rain came down, the streams rose, and the winds blew and beat against that house; yet it did not fall, because it had its foundation on the rock. 26But everyone who hears these words of mine and does not put them into practice is like a foolish man who built his house on sand. 27The rain came down, the streams rose, and the winds blew and beat against that house, and it fell with a great crash."

28When Jesus had finished saying these things, the crowds were amazed at his teaching, 29because he taught as one who had authority, and not as their teachers of the law.

NOW OR NEVER

MT 7:3-5

No one likes a hypocrite. If you feel the need to confront someone about something they're doing wrong, you'd better make sure you examine your own heart and habits first.

THE MAN WITH LEPROSY

8 When he came down from the mountainside, large crowds followed him. 2A man with leprosy[a] came and knelt before him and said, "Lord, if you are willing, you can make me clean." 3Jesus reached out his hand and touched the man. "I am willing," he said. "Be clean!" Immediately he was cured[b] of his leprosy. 4Then Jesus said to him, "See that you don't tell anyone. But go, show yourself to the priest and offer the gift Moses commanded, as a testimony to them."

THE FAITH OF THE CENTURION

5When Jesus had entered Capernaum, a centurion came to him, asking for help. 6"Lord," he said, "my servant lies at home paralyzed and in terrible suffering."

7Jesus said to him, "I will go and heal him."

8The centurion replied, "Lord, I do not deserve to have you come under my roof. But just say the word, and my servant will be healed. 9For I myself am a man under authority, with soldiers under me. I tell this one, 'Go,' and he goes; and that one, 'Come,' and he comes. I say to my servant, 'Do this,' and he does it."

10When Jesus heard this, he was astonished and said to those following him, "I tell you the truth, I have not found anyone in Israel with such great faith. 11I say to you that many will come from the east and the west, and will take their places at the feast with Abraham, Isaac and Jacob in the kingdom of heaven. 12But the subjects of the kingdom will be thrown outside, into the darkness, where there will be weeping and gnashing of teeth."

13Then Jesus said to the centurion, "Go! It will be done just as you believed it would." And his servant was healed at that very hour.

JESUS HEALS MANY

14When Jesus came into Peter's house, he saw Peter's mother-in-law lying in bed with a fever. 15He touched her hand and the fever left her, and she got up and began to wait on him.

---

[a] 2 The Greek word was used for various diseases affecting the skin—not necessarily leprosy.   [b] 3 Greek *made clean*

[16]When evening came, many who were demon-possessed were brought to him, and he drove out the spirits with a word and healed all the sick. [17]This was to fulfill what was spoken through the prophet Isaiah:

> "He took up our infirmities
> and carried our diseases." [a]

THE COST OF FOLLOWING JESUS

[18]When Jesus saw the crowd around him, he gave orders to cross to the other side of the lake. [19]Then a teacher of the law came to him and said, "Teacher, I will follow you wherever you go."

[20]Jesus replied, "Foxes have holes and birds of the air have nests, but the Son of Man has no place to lay his head."

[21]Another disciple said to him, "Lord, first let me go and bury my father."

[22]But Jesus told him, "Follow me, and let the dead bury their own dead."

JESUS CALMS THE STORM

[23]Then he got into the boat and his disciples followed him. [24]Without warning, a furious storm came up on the lake, so that the waves swept over the boat. But Jesus was sleeping. [25]The disciples went and woke him, saying, "Lord, save us! We're going to drown!"

[26]He replied, "You of little faith, why are you so afraid?" Then he got up and rebuked the winds and the waves, and it was completely calm.

[27]The men were amazed and asked, "What kind of man is this? Even the winds and the waves obey him!"

THE HEALING OF TWO DEMON-POSSESSED MEN

[28]When he arrived at the other side in the region of the Gadarenes,[b] two demon-possessed men coming from the tombs met him. They were so violent that no one could pass that way. [29]"What do you want with us, Son of God?" they shouted. "Have you come here to torture us before the appointed time?"

[30]Some distance from them a large herd of pigs was feeding. [31]The demons begged Jesus, "If you drive us out, send us into the herd of pigs."

[32]He said to them, "Go!" So they came out and went into the pigs, and the whole herd rushed down the steep bank into the lake and died in the water. [33]Those tending the pigs ran off, went into the town and reported all this, including what had happened to the demon-possessed men. [34]Then the whole town went out to meet Jesus. And when they saw him, they pleaded with him to leave their region.

JESUS HEALS A PARALYTIC

9 Jesus stepped into a boat, crossed over and came to his own town. [2]Some men brought to him a paralytic, lying on a mat. When Jesus saw their faith, he said to the paralytic, "Take heart, son; your sins are forgiven."

[3]At this, some of the teachers of the law said to themselves, "This fellow is blaspheming!"

[4]Knowing their thoughts, Jesus said, "Why do you entertain evil thoughts in your hearts? [5]Which is easier: to say, 'Your sins are forgiven,' or to say, 'Get up and walk'? [6]But so that you may know that the Son of Man has authority on earth to forgive sins . . ." Then he said to the paralytic, "Get up, take your mat and go home." [7]And the man got up and went home. [8]When the crowd saw this, they were filled with awe; and they praised God, who had given such authority to men.

THE CALLING OF MATTHEW

[9]As Jesus went on from there, he saw a man named Matthew sitting at the tax collector's booth. "Follow me," he told him, and Matthew got up and followed him.

[10]While Jesus was having dinner at Matthew's house, many tax collectors and "sinners" came and ate with him and his disciples. [11]When the Pharisees saw this, they asked his disciples, "Why does your teacher eat with tax collectors and 'sinners'?"

[12]On hearing this, Jesus said, "It is not the healthy who need a doctor, but the sick. [13]But go and learn what this means: 'I desire mercy, not sacrifice.'[c] For I have not come to call the righteous, but sinners."

---

[a] *17* Isaiah 53:4   [b] *28* Some manuscripts *Gergesenes*; others *Gerasenes*   [c] *13* Hosea 6:6

JESUS QUESTIONED ABOUT FASTING

[14] Then John's disciples came and asked him, "How is it that we and the Pharisees fast, but your disciples do not fast?"

[15] Jesus answered, "How can the guests of the bridegroom mourn while he is with them? The time will come when the bridegroom will be taken from them; then they will fast.

[16] "No one sews a patch of unshrunk cloth on an old garment, for the patch will pull away from the garment, making the tear worse. [17] Neither do men pour new wine into old wineskins. If they do, the skins will burst, the wine will run out and the wineskins will be ruined. No, they pour new wine into new wineskins, and both are preserved."

A DEAD GIRL AND A SICK WOMAN

[18] While he was saying this, a ruler came and knelt before him and said, "My daughter has just died. But come and put your hand on her, and she will live." [19] Jesus got up and went with him, and so did his disciples.

[20] Just then a woman who had been subject to bleeding for twelve years came up behind him and touched the edge of his cloak. [21] She said to herself, "If I only touch his cloak, I will be healed."

[22] Jesus turned and saw her. "Take heart, daughter," he said, "your faith has healed you." And the woman was healed from that moment.

[23] When Jesus entered the ruler's house and saw the flute players and the noisy crowd, [24] he said, "Go away. The girl is not dead but asleep." But they laughed at him. [25] After the crowd had been put outside, he went in and took the girl by the hand, and she got up. [26] News of this spread through all that region.

JESUS HEALS THE BLIND AND MUTE

[27] As Jesus went on from there, two blind men followed him, calling out, "Have mercy on us, Son of David!"

[28] When he had gone indoors, the blind men came to him, and he asked them, "Do you believe that I am able to do this?"

"Yes, Lord," they replied.

[29] Then he touched their eyes and said, "According to your faith will it be done to you"; [30] and their sight was restored. Jesus warned them sternly, "See that no one knows about this." [31] But they went out and spread the news about him all over that region.

[32] While they were going out, a man who was demon-possessed and could not talk was brought to Jesus. [33] And when the demon was driven out, the man who had been mute spoke. The crowd was amazed and said, "Nothing like this has ever been seen in Israel."

[34] But the Pharisees said, "It is by the prince of demons that he drives out demons."

THE WORKERS ARE FEW

[35] Jesus went through all the towns and villages, teaching in their synagogues, preaching the good news of the kingdom and healing every disease and sickness. [36] When he saw the crowds, he had compassion on them, because they were harassed and helpless, like sheep without a shepherd. [37] Then he said to his disciples, "The harvest is plentiful but the workers are few. [38] Ask the Lord of the harvest, therefore, to send out workers into his harvest field."

JESUS SENDS OUT THE TWELVE

10 He called his twelve disciples to him and gave them authority to drive out evil[a] spirits and to heal every disease and sickness.

[2] These are the names of the twelve apostles: first, Simon (who is called Peter) and his brother Andrew; James son of Zebedee, and his brother John; [3] Philip and Bartholomew; Thomas and Matthew the tax collector; James son of Alphaeus, and Thaddaeus; [4] Simon the Zealot and Judas Iscariot, who betrayed him.

[5] These twelve Jesus sent out with the following instructions: "Do not go among the Gentiles or enter any town of the Samaritans. [6] Go rather to the lost sheep of Israel. [7] As you go, preach this message: 'The kingdom of heaven is near.' [8] Heal the sick, raise the dead, cleanse those who have leprosy,[b] drive

---

[a] 1 Greek *unclean*   [b] 8 The Greek word was used for various diseases affecting the skin—not necessarily leprosy.

out demons. Freely you have received, freely give. ⁹Do not take along any gold or silver or copper in your belts; ¹⁰take no bag for the journey, or extra tunic, or sandals or a staff; for the worker is worth his keep.

¹¹"Whatever town or village you enter, search for some worthy person there and stay at his house until you leave. ¹²As you enter the home, give it your greeting. ¹³If the home is deserving, let your peace rest on it; if it is not, let your peace return to you. ¹⁴If anyone will not welcome you or listen to your words, shake the dust off your feet when you leave that home or town. ¹⁵I tell you the truth, it will be more bearable for Sodom and Gomorrah on the day of judgment than for that town. ¹⁶I am sending you out like sheep among wolves. Therefore be as shrewd as snakes and as innocent as doves.

¹⁷"Be on your guard against men; they will hand you over to the local councils and flog you in their synagogues. ¹⁸On my account you will be brought before governors and kings as witnesses to them and to the Gentiles. ¹⁹But when they arrest you, do not worry about what to say or how to say it. At that time you will be given what to say, ²⁰for it will not be you speaking, but the Spirit of your Father speaking through you.

²¹"Brother will betray brother to death, and a father his child; children will rebel against their parents and have them put to death. ²²All men will hate you because of me, but he who stands firm to the end will be saved. ²³When you are persecuted in one place, flee to another. I tell you the truth, you will not finish going through the cities of Israel before the Son of Man comes.

²⁴"A student is not above his teacher, nor a servant above his master. ²⁵It is enough for the student to be like his teacher, and the servant like his master. If the head of the house has been called Beelzebub,ᵃ how much more the members of his household!

²⁶"So do not be afraid of them. There is nothing concealed that will not be disclosed, or hidden that will not be made known. ²⁷What I tell you in the dark, speak in the daylight; what is whispered in your ear, proclaim from the roofs. ²⁸Do not be afraid of those who kill the body but cannot kill the soul. Rather, be afraid of the One who can destroy both soul and body in hell. ²⁹Are not two sparrows sold for a pennyᵇ? Yet not one of them will fall to the ground apart from the will of your Father. ³⁰And even the very hairs of your head are all numbered. ³¹So don't be afraid; you are worth more than many sparrows.

³²"Whoever acknowledges me before men, I will also acknowledge him before my Father in heaven. ³³But whoever disowns me before men, I will disown him before my Father in heaven.

³⁴"Do not suppose that I have come to bring peace to the earth. I did not come to bring peace, but a sword. ³⁵For I have come to turn

" 'a man against his father,
a daughter against her mother,
a daughter-in-law against her mother-in-law—
³⁶ a man's enemies will be the members of his own household.'ᶜ

³⁷"Anyone who loves his father or mother more than me is not worthy of me; anyone who loves his son or daughter more than me is not worthy of me; ³⁸and anyone who does not take his cross and follow me is not worthy of me. ³⁹Whoever finds his life will lose it, and whoever loses his life for my sake will find it.

⁴⁰"He who receives you receives me, and he who receives me receives the one who sent me. ⁴¹Anyone who receives a prophet because he is a prophet will receive a prophet's reward, and anyone who receives a righteous man because he is a righteous man will receive a righteous man's reward. ⁴²And if anyone gives even a cup of cold water to one of these little ones because he is my disciple, I tell you the truth, he will certainly not lose his reward."

Dealing With Opposition to Your Faith

Unless everyone you care about is a Christian, at some point your faith is going to cause some friction between you and a friend or family member. Then you'll be faced with a choice: You can either sweep your faith under the rug and agree not to talk about it in order to keep the peace, or you can make it clear to the person how much your faith means to you and let God worry about protecting the friendship. Your choice will say a lot about who means more to you—your friends and family or God.

live the adventure » Mt. 10:34-39

ᵃ 25 Greek *Beezeboul* or *Beelzeboul*   ᵇ 29 Greek *an assarion*   ᶜ 36 Micah 7:6

JESUS AND JOHN THE BAPTIST

11 After Jesus had finished instructing his twelve disciples, he went on from there to teach and preach in the towns of Galilee.[a]

²When John heard in prison what Christ was doing, he sent his disciples ³to ask him, "Are you the one who was to come, or should we expect someone else?"

⁴Jesus replied, "Go back and report to John what you hear and see: ⁵The blind receive sight, the lame walk, those who have leprosy[b] are cured, the deaf hear, the dead are raised, and the good news is preached to the poor. ⁶Blessed is the man who does not fall away on account of me."

⁷As John's disciples were leaving, Jesus began to speak to the crowd about John: "What did you go out into the desert to see? A reed swayed by the wind? ⁸If not, what did you go out to see? A man dressed in fine clothes? No, those who wear fine clothes are in kings' palaces. ⁹Then what did you go out to see? A prophet? Yes, I tell you, and more than a prophet. ¹⁰This is the one about whom it is written:

> " 'I will send my messenger ahead of you,
>   who will prepare your way before you.'[c]

¹¹I tell you the truth: Among those born of women there has not risen anyone greater than John the Baptist; yet he who is least in the kingdom of heaven is greater than he. ¹²From the days of John the Baptist until now, the kingdom of heaven has been forcefully advancing, and forceful men lay hold of it. ¹³For all the Prophets and the Law prophesied until John. ¹⁴And if you are willing to accept it, he is the Elijah who was to come. ¹⁵He who has ears, let him hear.

¹⁶"To what can I compare this generation? They are like children sitting in the marketplaces and calling out to others:

> ¹⁷" 'We played the flute for you,
>   and you did not dance;
> we sang a dirge,
>   and you did not mourn.'

¹⁸For John came neither eating nor drinking, and they say, 'He has a demon.' ¹⁹The Son of Man came eating and drinking, and they say, 'Here is a glutton and a drunkard, a friend of tax collectors and "sinners." ' But wisdom is proved right by her actions."

WOE ON UNREPENTANT CITIES

²⁰Then Jesus began to denounce the cities in which most of his miracles had been performed, because they did not repent. ²¹"Woe to you, Korazin! Woe to you, Bethsaida! If the miracles that were performed in you had been performed in Tyre and Sidon, they would have repented long ago in sackcloth and ashes. ²²But I tell you, it will be more bearable for Tyre and Sidon on the day of judgment than for you. ²³And you, Capernaum, will you be lifted up to the skies? No, you will go down to the depths.[d] If the miracles that were performed in you had been performed in Sodom, it would have remained to this day. ²⁴But I tell you that it will be more bearable for Sodom on the day of judgment than for you."

REST FOR THE WEARY

²⁵At that time Jesus said, "I praise you, Father, Lord of heaven and earth, because you have hidden these things from the wise and learned, and revealed them to little children. ²⁶Yes, Father, for this was your good pleasure.

²⁷"All things have been committed to me by my Father. No one knows the Son except the Father, and no one knows the Father except the Son and those to whom the Son chooses to reveal him.

²⁸"Come to me, all you who are weary and burdened, and I will give you rest. ²⁹Take my yoke upon you and learn from me, for I am gentle and humble in heart, and you will find rest for your souls. ³⁰For my yoke is easy and my burden is light."

---

[a] 1 Greek *in their towns*   [b] 5 The Greek word was used for various diseases affecting the skin—not necessarily leprosy.
[c] 10 Mal. 3:1   [d] 23 Greek *Hades*

LORD OF THE SABBATH

12 At that time Jesus went through the grainfields on the Sabbath. His disciples were hungry and began to pick some heads of grain and eat them. ²When the Pharisees saw this, they said to him, "Look! Your disciples are doing what is unlawful on the Sabbath."

³He answered, "Haven't you read what David did when he and his companions were hungry? ⁴He entered the house of God, and he and his companions ate the consecrated bread—which was not lawful for them to do, but only for the priests. ⁵Or haven't you read in the Law that on the Sabbath the priests in the temple desecrate the day and yet are innocent? ⁶I tell you that one[a] greater than the temple is here. ⁷If you had known what these words mean, 'I desire mercy, not sacrifice,'[b] you would not have condemned the innocent. ⁸For the Son of Man is Lord of the Sabbath."

⁹Going on from that place, he went into their synagogue, ¹⁰and a man with a shriveled hand was there. Looking for a reason to accuse Jesus, they asked him, "Is it lawful to heal on the Sabbath?"

¹¹He said to them, "If any of you has a sheep and it falls into a pit on the Sabbath, will you not take hold of it and lift it out? ¹²How much more valuable is a man than a sheep! Therefore it is lawful to do good on the Sabbath."

¹³Then he said to the man, "Stretch out your hand." So he stretched it out and it was completely restored, just as sound as the other. ¹⁴But the Pharisees went out and plotted how they might kill Jesus.

GOD'S CHOSEN SERVANT

¹⁵Aware of this, Jesus withdrew from that place. Many followed him, and he healed all their sick, ¹⁶warning them not to tell who he was. ¹⁷This was to fulfill what was spoken through the prophet Isaiah:

> ¹⁸ "Here is my servant whom I have chosen,
>   the one I love, in whom I delight;
>   I will put my Spirit on him,
>   and he will proclaim justice to the nations.
> ¹⁹ He will not quarrel or cry out;
>   no one will hear his voice in the streets.
> ²⁰ A bruised reed he will not break,
>   and a smoldering wick he will not snuff out,
>   till he leads justice to victory.
> ²¹   In his name the nations will put their hope."[c]

JESUS AND BEELZEBUB

²²Then they brought him a demon-possessed man who was blind and mute, and Jesus healed him, so that he could both talk and see. ²³All the people were astonished and said, "Could this be the Son of David?"

²⁴But when the Pharisees heard this, they said, "It is only by Beelzebub,[d] the prince of demons, that this fellow drives out demons."

²⁵Jesus knew their thoughts and said to them, "Every kingdom divided against itself will be ruined, and every city or household divided against itself will not stand. ²⁶If Satan drives out Satan, he is divided against himself. How then can his kingdom stand? ²⁷And if I drive out demons by Beelzebub, by whom do your people drive them out? So then, they will be your judges. ²⁸But if I drive out demons by the Spirit of God, then the kingdom of God has come upon you.

²⁹"Or again, how can anyone enter a strong man's house and carry off his possessions unless he first ties up the strong man? Then he can rob his house.

³⁰"He who is not with me is against me, and he who does not gather with me scatters. ³¹And so I tell you, every sin and blasphemy will be forgiven men, but the blasphemy against the Spirit will not be forgiven. ³²Anyone who speaks a word against the Son of Man will be forgiven, but anyone who speaks against the Holy Spirit will not be forgiven, either in this age or in the age to come.

³³"Make a tree good and its fruit will be good, or make a tree bad and its fruit will be bad, for a tree is recognized by its fruit. ³⁴You brood of vipers, how can you who are evil say anything good? For out

---

[a] *6* Or *something*; also in verses 41 and 42   [b] *7* Hosea 6:6   [c] *21* Isaiah 42:1-4   [d] *24* Greek *Beezeboul* or *Beelzeboul*; also in verse 27

of the overflow of the heart the mouth speaks. ³⁵The good man brings good things out of the good stored up in him, and the evil man brings evil things out of the evil stored up in him. ³⁶But I tell you that men will have to give account on the day of judgment for every careless word they have spoken. ³⁷For by your words you will be acquitted, and by your words you will be condemned."

NOW OR NEVER

MT 12:33–35

You can tell a lot about people by the way they talk to and treat others, the jokes they make and the language they use. Based on those behaviors, what might someone be able to tell about you?

THE SIGN OF JONAH

³⁸Then some of the Pharisees and teachers of the law said to him, "Teacher, we want to see a miraculous sign from you."

³⁹He answered, "A wicked and adulterous generation asks for a miraculous sign! But none will be given it except the sign of the prophet Jonah. ⁴⁰For as Jonah was three days and three nights in the belly of a huge fish, so the Son of Man will be three days and three nights in the heart of the earth. ⁴¹The men of Nineveh will stand up at the judgment with this generation and condemn it; for they repented at the preaching of Jonah, and now one[a] greater than Jonah is here. ⁴²The Queen of the South will rise at the judgment with this generation and condemn it; for she came from the ends of the earth to listen to Solomon's wisdom, and now one greater than Solomon is here.

⁴³"When an evil[b] spirit comes out of a man, it goes through arid places seeking rest and does not find it. ⁴⁴Then it says, 'I will return to the house I left.' When it arrives, it finds the house unoccupied, swept clean and put in order. ⁴⁵Then it goes and takes with it seven other spirits more wicked than itself, and they go in and live there. And the final condition of that man is worse than the first. That is how it will be with this wicked generation."

JESUS' MOTHER AND BROTHERS

⁴⁶While Jesus was still talking to the crowd, his mother and brothers stood outside, wanting to speak to him. ⁴⁷Someone told him, "Your mother and brothers are standing outside, wanting to speak to you."[c]

⁴⁸He replied to him, "Who is my mother, and who are my brothers?" ⁴⁹Pointing to his disciples, he said, "Here are my mother and my brothers. ⁵⁰For whoever does the will of my Father in heaven is my brother and sister and mother."

THE PARABLE OF THE SOWER

13 That same day Jesus went out of the house and sat by the lake. ²Such large crowds gathered around him that he got into a boat and sat in it, while all the people stood on the shore. ³Then he told them many things in parables, saying: "A farmer went out to sow his seed. ⁴As he was scattering the seed, some fell along the path, and the birds came and ate it up. ⁵Some fell on rocky places, where it did not have much soil. It sprang up quickly, because the soil was shallow. ⁶But when the sun came up, the plants were scorched, and they withered because they had no root. ⁷Other seed fell among thorns, which grew up and choked the plants. ⁸Still other seed fell on good soil, where it produced a crop—a hundred, sixty or thirty times what was sown. ⁹He who has ears, let him hear."

¹⁰The disciples came to him and asked, "Why do you speak to the people in parables?"

¹¹He replied, "The knowledge of the secrets of the kingdom of heaven has been given to you, but not to them. ¹²Whoever has will be given more, and he will have an abundance. Whoever does not have, even what he has will be taken from him. ¹³This is why I speak to them in parables:

"Though seeing, they do not see;
though hearing, they do not hear or understand.

¹⁴In them is fulfilled the prophecy of Isaiah:

" 'You will be ever hearing but never understanding;
you will be ever seeing but never perceiving.

---

[a] 41 Or *something*; also in verse 42   [b] 43 Greek *unclean*   [c] 47 Some manuscripts do not have verse 47.

¹⁵For this people's heart has become calloused;
they hardly hear with their ears,
and they have closed their eyes.
Otherwise they might see with their eyes,
hear with their ears,
understand with their hearts
and turn, and I would heal them.'ᵃ

¹⁶But blessed are your eyes because they see, and your ears because they hear. ¹⁷For I tell you the truth, many prophets and righteous men longed to see what you see but did not see it, and to hear what you hear but did not hear it.

¹⁸"Listen then to what the parable of the sower means: ¹⁹When anyone hears the message about the kingdom and does not understand it, the evil one comes and snatches away what was sown in his heart. This is the seed sown along the path. ²⁰The one who received the seed that fell on rocky places is the man who hears the word and at once receives it with joy. ²¹But since he has no root, he lasts only a short time. When trouble or persecution comes because of the word, he quickly falls away. ²²The one who received the seed that fell among the thorns is the man who hears the word, but the worries of this life and the deceitfulness of wealth choke it, making it unfruitful. ²³But the one who received the seed that fell on good soil is the man who hears the word and understands it. He produces a crop, yielding a hundred, sixty or thirty times what was sown."

THE PARABLE OF THE WEEDS

²⁴Jesus told them another parable: "The kingdom of heaven is like a man who sowed good seed in his field. ²⁵But while everyone was sleeping, his enemy came and sowed weeds among the wheat, and went away. ²⁶When the wheat sprouted and formed heads, then the weeds also appeared.

²⁷"The owner's servants came to him and said, 'Sir, didn't you sow good seed in your field? Where then did the weeds come from?'

²⁸" 'An enemy did this,' he replied.

"The servants asked him, 'Do you want us to go and pull them up?'

²⁹" 'No,' he answered, 'because while you are pulling the weeds, you may root up the wheat with them. ³⁰Let both grow together until the harvest. At that time I will tell the harvesters: First collect the weeds and tie them in bundles to be burned; then gather the wheat and bring it into my barn.' "

THE PARABLES OF THE MUSTARD SEED AND THE YEAST

³¹He told them another parable: "The kingdom of heaven is like a mustard seed, which a man took and planted in his field. ³²Though it is the smallest of all your seeds, yet when it grows, it is the largest of garden plants and becomes a tree, so that the birds of the air come and perch in its branches."

³³He told them still another parable: "The kingdom of heaven is like yeast that a woman took and mixed into a large amountᵇ of flour until it worked all through the dough."

³⁴Jesus spoke all these things to the crowd in parables; he did not say anything to them without using a parable. ³⁵So was fulfilled what was spoken through the prophet:

"I will open my mouth in parables,
I will utter things hidden since the creation of the world."ᶜ

Growing in Your Faith

What are some things that can "choke" God's Word from your life and keep you from growing as a Christian? For instance, do you have any friends who encourage you to blow off church and youth group meetings? Do you have any priorities that make it hard for you to find time to study God's Word? Are you obsessed with earning more money to spend on yourself? Do you have any habits or unconfessed sins that make it difficult for you to talk to God with a clear conscience? What do you think God wants you to do with the "thorns" in your life?

ᵃ *15* Isaiah 6:9,10   ᵇ *33* Greek *three satas* (probably about 1/2 bushel or 22 liters)   ᶜ *35* Psalm 78:2

THE PARABLE OF THE WEEDS EXPLAINED

36 Then he left the crowd and went into the house. His disciples came to him and said, "Explain to us the parable of the weeds in the field."

37 He answered, "The one who sowed the good seed is the Son of Man. 38 The field is the world, and the good seed stands for the sons of the kingdom. The weeds are the sons of the evil one, 39 and the enemy who sows them is the devil. The harvest is the end of the age, and the harvesters are angels.

40 "As the weeds are pulled up and burned in the fire, so it will be at the end of the age. 41 The Son of Man will send out his angels, and they will weed out of his kingdom everything that causes sin and all who do evil. 42 They will throw them into the fiery furnace, where there will be weeping and gnashing of teeth. 43 Then the righteous will shine like the sun in the kingdom of their Father. He who has ears, let him hear.

THE PARABLES OF THE HIDDEN TREASURE AND THE PEARL

44 "The kingdom of heaven is like treasure hidden in a field. When a man found it, he hid it again, and then in his joy went and sold all he had and bought that field.

45 "Again, the kingdom of heaven is like a merchant looking for fine pearls. 46 When he found one of great value, he went away and sold everything he had and bought it.

THE PARABLE OF THE NET

47 "Once again, the kingdom of heaven is like a net that was let down into the lake and caught all kinds of fish. 48 When it was full, the fishermen pulled it up on the shore. Then they sat down and collected the good fish in baskets, but threw the bad away. 49 This is how it will be at the end of the age. The angels will come and separate the wicked from the righteous 50 and throw them into the fiery furnace, where there will be weeping and gnashing of teeth.

51 "Have you understood all these things?" Jesus asked.

"Yes," they replied.

52 He said to them, "Therefore every teacher of the law who has been instructed about the kingdom of heaven is like the owner of a house who brings out of his storeroom new treasures as well as old."

A PROPHET WITHOUT HONOR

53 When Jesus had finished these parables, he moved on from there. 54 Coming to his hometown, he began teaching the people in their synagogue, and they were amazed. "Where did this man get this wisdom and these miraculous powers?" they asked. 55 "Isn't this the carpenter's son? Isn't his mother's name Mary, and aren't his brothers James, Joseph, Simon and Judas? 56 Aren't all his sisters with us? Where then did this man get all these things?" 57 And they took offense at him.

But Jesus said to them, "Only in his hometown and in his own house is a prophet without honor."

58 And he did not do many miracles there because of their lack of faith.

JOHN THE BAPTIST BEHEADED

14 At that time Herod the tetrarch heard the reports about Jesus, 2 and he said to his attendants, "This is John the Baptist; he has risen from the dead! That is why miraculous powers are at work in him."

3 Now Herod had arrested John and bound him and put him in prison because of Herodias, his brother Philip's wife, 4 for John had been saying to him: "It is not lawful for you to have her." 5 Herod wanted to kill John, but he was afraid of the people, because they considered him a prophet.

6 On Herod's birthday the daughter of Herodias danced for them and pleased Herod so much 7 that he promised with an oath to give her whatever she asked. 8 Prompted by her mother, she said, "Give me here on a platter the head of John the Baptist." 9 The king was distressed, but because of his oaths and his dinner guests, he ordered that her request be granted 10 and had John beheaded in the prison. 11 His head was brought in on a platter and given to the girl, who carried it to her mother. 12 John's disciples came and took his body and buried it. Then they went and told Jesus.

JESUS FEEDS THE FIVE THOUSAND

13 When Jesus heard what had happened, he withdrew by boat privately to a solitary place. Hearing

herod antipas

» Appointed by the Romans to rule Galilee
» Married his half brother's wife
» Was publicly confronted by John the Baptist for his immorality

VERSUS

john the baptist

» The man called by God to announce the coming of the Messiah
» A bold preacher with an uncompromising message of repentance
» Beheaded by Herod

The Main Event

Jesus called John the Baptist the greatest man to ever live (see Matthew 11:11). He was also one of the most unusual.

John lived out in the desert and ate honey-covered bugs. He dressed like Tarzan and looked like someone who had been raised by wolves. When he preached, it was like thunder. Crowds came from everywhere to hear this wild holy man, and many, many people were broken (in a good way) by his piercing words of truth. Unfortunately, Herod Antipas was not one of them.

Herod was the tetrarch (ruler) of Galilee, a political position given to him by the Roman emperor. He might have received his job because he was well qualified. But it's more likely that he got it because he was the son of the legendary Herod the Great. Once he achieved power, Herod decided that he was above the law—the Jewish moral law, that is. When he got the hots for his brother's spouse, he divorced his own wife and shamelessly moved his new lover, Herodias, right into the palace with him.

Predictably, John flipped his lid. He started railing against Herod's scandalous behavior. An embarrassed Herod promptly had John locked up. Yet something about the uncompromising, bold-as-a-lion preacher intrigued the ruler . . . and even scared him a little. Herod loved to summon John from prison to hear him speak. Herodias, on the other hand, was not so enthralled. The more John condemned their adulterous relationship, the more Herodias wanted to silence him once and for all.

Eventually Herodias got her wish. One night Herod threw a banquet to celebrate his birthday. His stepdaughter provided the entertainment,

dancing provocatively for Herod and his guests. Herod was so pleased that he vowed to reward her by giving her whatever she wanted. With a little bit of coaching from her scheming mother, Herod's stepdaughter knew just what to ask for: John the Baptist's head on a platter.

The Outcome

Some people might conclude that the moral of this story is "Watch what you say" or "Don't offend the wrong people." John the Baptist would give you a different take.

John would tell you that the moral of the story is "Don't offend *God*." He would say, "If speaking the truth costs you everything—even your very life—so be it. Better to lose your head than your integrity."

The bottom line is truth. Followers of Jesus are supposed to be people of truth. We can't afford to compromise. We can't be weak. Too many people—including far too many Christians—live compromised lives. They see evil and turn their heads the other way. Their motto? Don't rock the boat. Keep the peace. For them the opinions of people matter more than what God thinks about their behavior. Don't buy into their mindset. Instead take a cue from John the Baptist.

Read more about Herod Antipas and John the Baptist in Matthew 14:1–12 (page 1285); Mark 6:14–29 (page 1318); Luke 9:7–9 (page 1352).

of this, the crowds followed him on foot from the towns. [14]When Jesus landed and saw a large crowd, he had compassion on them and healed their sick.

[15]As evening approached, the disciples came to him and said, "This is a remote place, and it's already getting late. Send the crowds away, so they can go to the villages and buy themselves some food."

[16]Jesus replied, "They do not need to go away. You give them something to eat."

[17]"We have here only five loaves of bread and two fish," they answered.

[18]"Bring them here to me," he said. [19]And he directed the people to sit down on the grass. Taking the five loaves and the two fish and looking up to heaven, he gave thanks and broke the loaves. Then he gave them to the disciples, and the disciples gave them to the people. [20]They all ate and were satisfied, and the disciples picked up twelve basketfuls of broken pieces that were left over. [21]The number of those who ate was about five thousand men, besides women and children.

JESUS WALKS ON THE WATER

[22]Immediately Jesus made the disciples get into the boat and go on ahead of him to the other side, while he dismissed the crowd. [23]After he had dismissed them, he went up on a mountainside by himself to pray. When evening came, he was there alone, [24]but the boat was already a considerable distance[a] from land, buffeted by the waves because the wind was against it.

[25]During the fourth watch of the night Jesus went out to them, walking on the lake. [26]When the disciples saw him walking on the lake, they were terrified. "It's a ghost," they said, and cried out in fear.

[27]But Jesus immediately said to them: "Take courage! It is I. Don't be afraid."

[28]"Lord, if it's you," Peter replied, "tell me to come to you on the water."

[29]"Come," he said.

Then Peter got down out of the boat, walked on the water and came toward Jesus. [30]But when he saw the wind, he was afraid and, beginning to sink, cried out, "Lord, save me!"

[31]Immediately Jesus reached out his hand and caught him. "You of little faith," he said, "why did you doubt?"

[32]And when they climbed into the boat, the wind died down. [33]Then those who were in the boat worshiped him, saying, "Truly you are the Son of God."

[34]When they had crossed over, they landed at Gennesaret. [35]And when the men of that place recognized Jesus, they sent word to all the surrounding country. People brought all their sick to him [36]and begged him to let the sick just touch the edge of his cloak, and all who touched him were healed.

NOW OR NEVER
MT 14:31

Doubts can play with your mind . . . if you let them. They can even make you question your faith. You will always encounter doubt in your life, but you can work through it by reminding yourself that your salvation doesn't depend on you, but on God.

CLEAN AND UNCLEAN

15

Then some Pharisees and teachers of the law came to Jesus from Jerusalem and asked, [2]"Why do your disciples break the tradition of the elders? They don't wash their hands before they eat!"

[3]Jesus replied, "And why do you break the command of God for the sake of your tradition? [4]For God said, 'Honor your father and mother'[b] and 'Anyone who curses his father or mother must be put to death.'[c] [5]But you say that if a man says to his father or mother, 'Whatever help you might otherwise have received from me is a gift devoted to God,' [6]he is not to 'honor his father'[d] with it. Thus you nullify the word of God for the sake of your tradition. [7]You hypocrites! Isaiah was right when he prophesied about you:

[8]" 'These people honor me with their lips,
     but their hearts are far from me.
[9]They worship me in vain;
     their teachings are but rules taught by men.'[e]"

---

[a] 24 Greek many stadia   [b] 4 Exodus 20:12; Deut. 5:16   [c] 4 Exodus 21:17; Lev. 20:9   [d] 6 Some manuscripts father or his mother
[e] 9 Isaiah 29:13

[10]Jesus called the crowd to him and said, "Listen and understand. [11]What goes into a man's mouth does not make him 'unclean,' but what comes out of his mouth, that is what makes him 'unclean.' "

[12]Then the disciples came to him and asked, "Do you know that the Pharisees were offended when they heard this?"

[13]He replied, "Every plant that my heavenly Father has not planted will be pulled up by the roots. [14]Leave them; they are blind guides.[a] If a blind man leads a blind man, both will fall into a pit."

[15]Peter said, "Explain the parable to us."

[16]"Are you still so dull?" Jesus asked them. [17]"Don't you see that whatever enters the mouth goes into the stomach and then out of the body? [18]But the things that come out of the mouth come from the heart, and these make a man 'unclean.' [19]For out of the heart come evil thoughts, murder, adultery, sexual immorality, theft, false testimony, slander. [20]These are what make a man 'unclean'; but eating with unwashed hands does not make him 'unclean.' "

THE FAITH OF THE CANAANITE WOMAN

[21]Leaving that place, Jesus withdrew to the region of Tyre and Sidon. [22]A Canaanite woman from that vicinity came to him, crying out, "Lord, Son of David, have mercy on me! My daughter is suffering terribly from demon-possession."

[23]Jesus did not answer a word. So his disciples came to him and urged him, "Send her away, for she keeps crying out after us."

[24]He answered, "I was sent only to the lost sheep of Israel."

[25]The woman came and knelt before him. "Lord, help me!" she said.

[26]He replied, "It is not right to take the children's bread and toss it to their dogs."

[27]"Yes, Lord," she said, "but even the dogs eat the crumbs that fall from their masters' table."

[28]Then Jesus answered, "Woman, you have great faith! Your request is granted." And her daughter was healed from that very hour.

JESUS FEEDS THE FOUR THOUSAND

[29]Jesus left there and went along the Sea of Galilee. Then he went up on a mountainside and sat down. [30]Great crowds came to him, bringing the lame, the blind, the crippled, the mute and many others, and laid them at his feet; and he healed them. [31]The people were amazed when they saw the mute speaking, the crippled made well, the lame walking and the blind seeing. And they praised the God of Israel.

[32]Jesus called his disciples to him and said, "I have compassion for these people; they have already been with me three days and have nothing to eat. I do not want to send them away hungry, or they may collapse on the way."

[33]His disciples answered, "Where could we get enough bread in this remote place to feed such a crowd?"

[34]"How many loaves do you have?" Jesus asked.

"Seven," they replied, "and a few small fish."

[35]He told the crowd to sit down on the ground. [36]Then he took the seven loaves and the fish, and when he had given thanks, he broke them and gave them to the disciples, and they in turn to the people. [37]They all ate and were satisfied. Afterward the disciples picked up seven basketfuls of broken pieces that were left over. [38]The number of those who ate was four thousand, besides women and children. [39]After Jesus had sent the crowd away, he got into the boat and went to the vicinity of Magadan.

THE DEMAND FOR A SIGN

16

The Pharisees and Sadducees came to Jesus and tested him by asking him to show them a sign from heaven.

[2]He replied,[b] "When evening comes, you say, 'It will be fair weather, for the sky is red,' [3]and in the morning, 'Today it will be stormy, for the sky is red and overcast.' You know how to interpret the appearance of the sky, but you cannot interpret the signs of the times. [4]A wicked and adulterous generation looks for a miraculous sign, but none will be given it except the sign of Jonah." Jesus then left them and went away.

---

[a] 14 Some manuscripts *guides of the blind*   [b] 2 Some early manuscripts do not have the rest of verse 2 and all of verse 3.

THE YEAST OF THE PHARISEES AND SADDUCEES

[5]When they went across the lake, the disciples forgot to take bread. [6]"Be careful," Jesus said to them. "Be on your guard against the yeast of the Pharisees and Sadducees."

[7]They discussed this among themselves and said, "It is because we didn't bring any bread."

[8]Aware of their discussion, Jesus asked, "You of little faith, why are you talking among yourselves about having no bread? [9]Do you still not understand? Don't you remember the five loaves for the five thousand, and how many basketfuls you gathered? [10]Or the seven loaves for the four thousand, and how many basketfuls you gathered? [11]How is it you don't understand that I was not talking to you about bread? But be on your guard against the yeast of the Pharisees and Sadducees." [12]Then they understood that he was not telling them to guard against the yeast used in bread, but against the teaching of the Pharisees and Sadducees.

PETER'S CONFESSION OF CHRIST

[13]When Jesus came to the region of Caesarea Philippi, he asked his disciples, "Who do people say the Son of Man is?"

[14]They replied, "Some say John the Baptist; others say Elijah; and still others, Jeremiah or one of the prophets."

[15]"But what about you?" he asked. "Who do you say I am?"

[16]Simon Peter answered, "You are the Christ,[a] the Son of the living God."

[17]Jesus replied, "Blessed are you, Simon son of Jonah, for this was not revealed to you by man, but by my Father in heaven. [18]And I tell you that you are Peter,[b] and on this rock I will build my church, and the gates of Hades[c] will not overcome it.[d] [19]I will give you the keys of the kingdom of heaven; whatever you bind on earth will be[e] bound in heaven, and whatever you loose on earth will be[e] loosed in heaven." [20]Then he warned his disciples not to tell anyone that he was the Christ.

JESUS PREDICTS HIS DEATH

[21]From that time on Jesus began to explain to his disciples that he must go to Jerusalem and suffer many things at the hands of the elders, chief priests and teachers of the law, and that he must be killed and on the third day be raised to life.

[22]Peter took him aside and began to rebuke him. "Never, Lord!" he said. "This shall never happen to you!"

[23]Jesus turned and said to Peter, "Get behind me, Satan! You are a stumbling block to me; you do not have in mind the things of God, but the things of men."

[24]Then Jesus said to his disciples, "If anyone would come after me, he must deny himself and take up his cross and follow me. [25]For whoever wants to save his life[f] will lose it, but whoever loses his life for me will find it. [26]What good will it be for a man if he gains the whole world, yet forfeits his soul? Or what can a man give in exchange for his soul? [27]For the Son of Man is going to come in his Father's glory with his angels, and then he will reward each person according to what he has done. [28]I tell you the truth, some who are standing here will not taste death before they see the Son of Man coming in his kingdom."

THE TRANSFIGURATION

17 After six days Jesus took with him Peter, James and John the brother of James, and led them up a high mountain by themselves. [2]There he was transfigured before them. His face shone like the sun, and his clothes became as white as the light. [3]Just then there appeared before them Moses and Elijah, talking with Jesus.

[4]Peter said to Jesus, "Lord, it is good for us to be here. If you wish, I will put up three shelters—one for you, one for Moses and one for Elijah."

[5]While he was still speaking, a bright cloud enveloped them, and a voice from the cloud said, "This is my Son, whom I love; with him I am well pleased. Listen to him!"

[6]When the disciples heard this, they fell facedown to the ground, terrified. [7]But Jesus came and touched them. "Get up," he said. "Don't be afraid." [8]When they looked up, they saw no one except Jesus.

---

[a] *16* Or *Messiah*; also in verse 20   [b] *18* *Peter* means *rock.*   [c] *18* Or *hell*   [d] *18* Or *not prove stronger than it*   [e] *19* Or *have been*
[f] *25* The Greek word means either *life* or *soul*; also in verse 26.

[9]As they were coming down the mountain, Jesus instructed them, "Don't tell anyone what you have seen, until the Son of Man has been raised from the dead." [10]The disciples asked him, "Why then do the teachers of the law say that Elijah must come first?" [11]Jesus replied, "To be sure, Elijah comes and will restore all things. [12]But I tell you, Elijah has already come, and they did not recognize him, but have done to him everything they wished. In the same way the Son of Man is going to suffer at their hands." [13]Then the disciples understood that he was talking to them about John the Baptist.

THE HEALING OF A BOY WITH A DEMON

[14]When they came to the crowd, a man approached Jesus and knelt before him. [15]"Lord, have mercy on my son," he said. "He has seizures and is suffering greatly. He often falls into the fire or into the water. [16]I brought him to your disciples, but they could not heal him."

[17]"O unbelieving and perverse generation," Jesus replied, "how long shall I stay with you? How long shall I put up with you? Bring the boy here to me." [18]Jesus rebuked the demon, and it came out of the boy, and he was healed from that moment.

[19]Then the disciples came to Jesus in private and asked, "Why couldn't we drive it out?"

[20]He replied, "Because you have so little faith. I tell you the truth, if you have faith as small as a mustard seed, you can say to this mountain, 'Move from here to there' and it will move. Nothing will be impossible for you.[a]"

[22]When they came together in Galilee, he said to them, "The Son of Man is going to be betrayed into the hands of men. [23]They will kill him, and on the third day he will be raised to life." And the disciples were filled with grief.

THE TEMPLE TAX

[24]After Jesus and his disciples arrived in Capernaum, the collectors of the two-drachma tax came to Peter and asked, "Doesn't your teacher pay the temple tax[b]?"

[25]"Yes, he does," he replied.

When Peter came into the house, Jesus was the first to speak. "What do you think, Simon?" he asked. "From whom do the kings of the earth collect duty and taxes—from their own sons or from others?"

[26]"From others," Peter answered.

"Then the sons are exempt," Jesus said to him. [27]"But so that we may not offend them, go to the lake and throw out your line. Take the first fish you catch; open its mouth and you will find a four-drachma coin. Take it and give it to them for my tax and yours."

THE GREATEST IN THE KINGDOM OF HEAVEN

18

At that time the disciples came to Jesus and asked, "Who is the greatest in the kingdom of heaven?"

[2]He called a little child and had him stand among them. [3]And he said: "I tell you the truth, unless you change and become like little children, you will never enter the kingdom of heaven. [4]Therefore, whoever humbles himself like this child is the greatest in the kingdom of heaven.

[5]"And whoever welcomes a little child like this in my name welcomes me. [6]But if anyone causes one of these little ones who believe in me to sin, it would be better for him to have a large millstone hung around his neck and to be drowned in the depths of the sea.

[7]"Woe to the world because of the things that cause people to sin! Such things must come, but woe to the man through whom they come! [8]If your hand or your foot causes you to sin, cut it off and throw it away. It is better for you to enter life maimed or crippled than to have two hands or two feet and be thrown into eternal fire. [9]And if your eye causes you to sin, gouge it out and throw it away. It is better for you to enter life with one eye than to have two eyes and be thrown into the fire of hell.

THE PARABLE OF THE LOST SHEEP

[10]"See that you do not look down on one of these little ones. For I tell you that their angels in heaven always see the face of my Father in heaven.[c]

---

[a] 20 Some manuscripts you. [21]But this kind does not go out except by prayer and fasting.   [b] 24 Greek the two drachmas   [c] 10 Some manuscripts heaven. [11]The Son of Man came to save what was lost.

12"What do you think? If a man owns a hundred sheep, and one of them wanders away, will he not leave the ninety-nine on the hills and go to look for the one that wandered off? 13And if he finds it, I tell you the truth, he is happier about that one sheep than about the ninety-nine that did not wander off. 14In the same way your Father in heaven is not willing that any of these little ones should be lost.

A BROTHER WHO SINS AGAINST YOU

15"If your brother sins against you,ª go and show him his fault, just between the two of you. If he listens to you, you have won your brother over. 16But if he will not listen, take one or two others along, so that 'every matter may be established by the testimony of two or three witnesses.'ᵇ 17If he refuses to listen to them, tell it to the church; and if he refuses to listen even to the church, treat him as you would a pagan or a tax collector.

now or never
MT 18:15–17

If you have an issue with a friend—no matter who or what caused the issue—you (as a Christian) are the one who should make the first move to patch things up.

18"I tell you the truth, whatever you bind on earth will beᶜ bound in heaven, and whatever you loose on earth will beᶜ loosed in heaven. 19"Again, I tell you that if two of you on earth agree about anything you ask for, it will be done for you by my Father in heaven. 20For where two or three come together in my name, there am I with them."

THE PARABLE OF THE UNMERCIFUL SERVANT

21Then Peter came to Jesus and asked, "Lord, how many times shall I forgive my brother when he sins against me? Up to seven times?"

22Jesus answered, "I tell you, not seven times, but seventy-seven times.ᵈ

23"Therefore, the kingdom of heaven is like a king who wanted to settle accounts with his servants. 24As he began the settlement, a man who owed him ten thousand talentsᵉ was brought to him. 25Since he was not able to pay, the master ordered that he and his wife and his children and all that he had be sold to repay the debt.

26"The servant fell on his knees before him. 'Be patient with me,' he begged, 'and I will pay back everything.' 27The servant's master took pity on him, canceled the debt and let him go.

28"But when that servant went out, he found one of his fellow servants who owed him a hundred denarii.ᶠ He grabbed him and began to choke him. 'Pay back what you owe me!' he demanded.

29"His fellow servant fell to his knees and begged him, 'Be patient with me, and I will pay you back.'

30"But he refused. Instead, he went off and had the man thrown into prison until he could pay the debt. 31When the other servants saw what had happened, they were greatly distressed and went and told their master everything that had happened.

32"Then the master called the servant in. 'You wicked servant,' he said, 'I canceled all that debt of yours because you begged me to. 33Shouldn't you have had mercy on your fellow servant just as I had on you?' 34In anger his master turned him over to the jailers to be tortured, until he should pay back all he owed.

35"This is how my heavenly Father will treat each of you unless you forgive your brother from your heart."

DIVORCE

19

When Jesus had finished saying these things, he left Galilee and went into the region of Judea to the other side of the Jordan. 2Large crowds followed him, and he healed them there.

3Some Pharisees came to him to test him. They asked, "Is it lawful for a man to divorce his wife for any and every reason?"

4"Haven't you read," he replied, "that at the beginning the Creator 'made them male and female,'ᵍ 5and said, 'For this reason a man will leave his father and mother and be united to his wife, and the two

ª 15 Some manuscripts do not have *against you.*   ᵇ 16 Deut. 19:15   ᶜ 18 Or *have been*   ᵈ 22 Or *seventy times seven*   ᵉ 24 That is, millions of dollars   ᶠ 28 That is, a few dollars   ᵍ 4 Gen. 1:27

battlelines

» Why Not? (Sex)

Q: Run that by me one more time. You think sex outside marriage is no big deal?
A: It's not the big deal you make it out to be. One person for life? Please!

Q: So you're saying we're just animals—a pack of dogs in heat? You're saying we can't possibly control our hormones, so we should just do whatever we want?
A: Hey, I'm not saying people should sleep around just for the fun of it.

Q: But you're saying it's OK for people to have 10 or 20 partners over the course of a lifetime?
A: Over 50 years or more? Sure, why not?

Q: But doesn't staying true to one person build character?
A: They say cancer builds character too, but that doesn't mean I want the disease.

Q: Don't you think it's important to learn self-control?
A: I don't know. Why?

Q: Because last time I checked, life doesn't always conform to our timetable. We can't always have what we want when we want it. Sometimes we have to curb our desires for the sake of other people.
A: OK, but what's your point?

Q: My point is, I think you have a shallow view of sex. You seem to think it's something people do for recreation. You're talking more about lust—a few minutes of physical pleasure. It's like sex has no deep meaning for you. And I think that's sad.
A: Really?

Q: Yeah, because to me, sex is going to be this amazing bond—not just physical, but emotional and spiritual too. One day my wife and I will join not just our bodies, but our souls. I'm talking about a whole lifetime together versus a bunch of one-night stands, broken hearts and ruined lives.

» Whine Not

Genesis 2:24 describes love, sex and marriage as they were originally intended: "A man will leave his father and mother and be united to his wife, and they will become one flesh." Pretty simple and straightforward, huh?

Centuries later, Jesus quoted this verse and added, "So they are no longer two, but one. Therefore what God has joined together, let man not separate" (Matthew 19:6).

Here are two quick points to consider when thinking about what the Bible has to say on the topic of sex:

❶ Sex is meant to be a symbol of the complete union—physical, spiritual and emotional—of one man and one woman.

❷ According to Jesus, that glorious linking is intended to last a lifetime.

Think sex is no big deal? No way! Multiple partners? Forget it!

Read more about sex and abstinence at www.RevolutionBible.com.

will become one flesh'ª? ⁶So they are no longer two, but one. Therefore what God has joined together, let man not separate."

nou or never

MT 19:4-6

Divorce is so devastating and painful because it goes against God's plan for families. One of the best things you can do for those who have been affected by divorce—including yourself—is to pray for God's healing love to be present, even in the midst of broken families.

⁷"Why then," they asked, "did Moses command that a man give his wife a certificate of divorce and send her away?"

⁸Jesus replied, "Moses permitted you to divorce your wives because your hearts were hard. But it was not this way from the beginning. ⁹I tell you that anyone who divorces his wife, except for marital unfaithfulness, and marries another woman commits adultery."

¹⁰The disciples said to him, "If this is the situation between a husband and wife, it is better not to marry."

¹¹Jesus replied, "Not everyone can accept this word, but only those to whom it has been given. ¹²For some are eunuchs because they were born that way; others were made that way by men; and others have renounced marriageᵇ because of the kingdom of heaven. The one who can accept this should accept it."

THE LITTLE CHILDREN AND JESUS

¹³Then little children were brought to Jesus for him to place his hands on them and pray for them. But the disciples rebuked those who brought them.

¹⁴Jesus said, "Let the little children come to me, and do not hinder them, for the kingdom of heaven belongs to such as these." ¹⁵When he had placed his hands on them, he went on from there.

THE RICH YOUNG MAN

¹⁶Now a man came up to Jesus and asked, "Teacher, what good thing must I do to get eternal life?"

¹⁷"Why do you ask me about what is good?" Jesus replied. "There is only One who is good. If you want to enter life, obey the commandments."

¹⁸"Which ones?" the man inquired.

Jesus replied, " 'Do not murder, do not commit adultery, do not steal, do not give false testimony, ¹⁹honor your father and mother,'ᶜ and 'love your neighbor as yourself.'ᵈ"

²⁰"All these I have kept," the young man said. "What do I still lack?"

²¹Jesus answered, "If you want to be perfect, go, sell your possessions and give to the poor, and you will have treasure in heaven. Then come, follow me."

²²When the young man heard this, he went away sad, because he had great wealth.

²³Then Jesus said to his disciples, "I tell you the truth, it is hard for a rich man to enter the kingdom of heaven. ²⁴Again I tell you, it is easier for a camel to go through the eye of a needle than for a rich man to enter the kingdom of God."

²⁵When the disciples heard this, they were greatly astonished and asked, "Who then can be saved?"

²⁶Jesus looked at them and said, "With man this is impossible, but with God all things are possible."

²⁷Peter answered him, "We have left everything to follow you! What then will there be for us?"

²⁸Jesus said to them, "I tell you the truth, at the renewal of all things, when the Son of Man sits on his glorious throne, you who have followed me will also sit on twelve thrones, judging the twelve tribes of Israel. ²⁹And everyone who has left houses or brothers or sisters or father or motherᵉ or children or fields for my sake will receive a hundred times as much and will inherit eternal life. ³⁰But many who are first will be last, and many who are last will be first.

THE PARABLE OF THE WORKERS IN THE VINEYARD

20

"For the kingdom of heaven is like a landowner who went out early in the morning to hire men to work in his vineyard. ²He agreed to pay them a denarius for the day and sent them into his vineyard.

ª *5* Gen. 2:24   ᵇ *12* Or *have made themselves eunuchs*   ᶜ *19* Exodus 20:12-16; Deut. 5:16-20   ᵈ *19* Lev. 19:18   ᵉ *29* Some manuscripts *mother or wife*

³"About the third hour he went out and saw others standing in the marketplace doing nothing. ⁴He told them, 'You also go and work in my vineyard, and I will pay you whatever is right.' ⁵So they went.

"He went out again about the sixth hour and the ninth hour and did the same thing. ⁶About the eleventh hour he went out and found still others standing around. He asked them, 'Why have you been standing here all day long doing nothing?'

⁷" 'Because no one has hired us,' they answered.

"He said to them, 'You also go and work in my vineyard.'

⁸"When evening came, the owner of the vineyard said to his foreman, 'Call the workers and pay them their wages, beginning with the last ones hired and going on to the first.'

⁹"The workers who were hired about the eleventh hour came and each received a denarius. ¹⁰So when those came who were hired first, they expected to receive more. But each one of them also received a denarius. ¹¹When they received it, they began to grumble against the landowner. ¹²'These men who were hired last worked only one hour,' they said, 'and you have made them equal to us who have borne the burden of the work and the heat of the day.'

¹³"But he answered one of them, 'Friend, I am not being unfair to you. Didn't you agree to work for a denarius? ¹⁴Take your pay and go. I want to give the man who was hired last the same as I gave you. ¹⁵Don't I have the right to do what I want with my own money? Or are you envious because I am generous?'

¹⁶"So the last will be first, and the first will be last."

JESUS AGAIN PREDICTS HIS DEATH

¹⁷Now as Jesus was going up to Jerusalem, he took the twelve disciples aside and said to them, ¹⁸"We are going up to Jerusalem, and the Son of Man will be betrayed to the chief priests and the teachers of the law. They will condemn him to death ¹⁹and will turn him over to the Gentiles to be mocked and flogged and crucified. On the third day he will be raised to life!"

A MOTHER'S REQUEST

²⁰Then the mother of Zebedee's sons came to Jesus with her sons and, kneeling down, asked a favor of him.

²¹"What is it you want?" he asked.

She said, "Grant that one of these two sons of mine may sit at your right and the other at your left in your kingdom."

²²"You don't know what you are asking," Jesus said to them. "Can you drink the cup I am going to drink?"

"We can," they answered.

²³Jesus said to them, "You will indeed drink from my cup, but to sit at my right or left is not for me to grant. These places belong to those for whom they have been prepared by my Father."

²⁴When the ten heard about this, they were indignant with the two brothers. ²⁵Jesus called them together and said, "You know that the rulers of the Gentiles lord it over them, and their high officials exercise authority over them. ²⁶Not so with you. Instead, whoever wants to become great among you must be your servant, ²⁷and whoever wants to be first must be your slave— ²⁸just as the Son of Man did not come to be served, but to serve, and to give his life as a ransom for many."

TWO BLIND MEN RECEIVE SIGHT

²⁹As Jesus and his disciples were leaving Jericho, a large crowd followed him. ³⁰Two blind men were sitting by the roadside, and when they heard that Jesus was going by, they shouted, "Lord, Son of David, have mercy on us!"

³¹The crowd rebuked them and told them to be quiet, but they shouted all the louder, "Lord, Son of David, have mercy on us!"

³²Jesus stopped and called them. "What do you want me to do for you?" he asked.

³³"Lord," they answered, "we want our sight."

³⁴Jesus had compassion on them and touched their eyes. Immediately they received their sight and followed him.

THE TRIUMPHAL ENTRY

21 As they approached Jerusalem and came to Bethphage on the Mount of Olives, Jesus sent two disciples, ²saying to them, "Go to the village ahead of you, and at once you will find a donkey tied there, with her colt by her. Untie them and bring them to me. ³If anyone says anything to you, tell him that the Lord needs them, and he will send them right away."

⁴This took place to fulfill what was spoken through the prophet:

⁵ "Say to the Daughter of Zion,
    'See, your king comes to you,
gentle and riding on a donkey,
    on a colt, the foal of a donkey.' " ª

⁶The disciples went and did as Jesus had instructed them. ⁷They brought the donkey and the colt, placed their cloaks on them, and Jesus sat on them. ⁸A very large crowd spread their cloaks on the road, while others cut branches from the trees and spread them on the road. ⁹The crowds that went ahead of him and those that followed shouted,

"Hosanna ᵇ to the Son of David!"

"Blessed is he who comes in the name of the Lord!" ᶜ

"Hosanna ᵇ in the highest!"

¹⁰When Jesus entered Jerusalem, the whole city was stirred and asked, "Who is this?"

¹¹The crowds answered, "This is Jesus, the prophet from Nazareth in Galilee."

JESUS AT THE TEMPLE

¹²Jesus entered the temple area and drove out all who were buying and selling there. He overturned the tables of the money changers and the benches of those selling doves. ¹³"It is written," he said to them, " 'My house will be called a house of prayer,'ᵈ but you are making it a 'den of robbers.'ᵉ"

¹⁴The blind and the lame came to him at the temple, and he healed them. ¹⁵But when the chief priests and the teachers of the law saw the wonderful things he did and the children shouting in the temple area, "Hosanna to the Son of David," they were indignant.

¹⁶"Do you hear what these children are saying?" they asked him.

"Yes," replied Jesus, "have you never read,

" 'From the lips of children and infants
    you have ordained praise'ᶠ?"

¹⁷And he left them and went out of the city to Bethany, where he spent the night.

THE FIG TREE WITHERS

¹⁸Early in the morning, as he was on his way back to the city, he was hungry. ¹⁹Seeing a fig tree by the road, he went up to it but found nothing on it except leaves. Then he said to it, "May you never bear fruit again!" Immediately the tree withered.

²⁰When the disciples saw this, they were amazed. "How did the fig tree wither so quickly?" they asked.

Believing in Jesus

live the adventure »» Mt 21:12–16

The religious leaders of Jesus' day had a hard time believing that Jesus was the Son of God because he didn't look the way they thought the Messiah should look or do what they thought he should do. Little kids running around the temple area had an easier time seeing (and praising) Jesus for who he really is. So what about you? Before you became a Christian, what did you think Jesus was like? How did you find out the truth? Now here's the big question: How can you help other people discover the truth about Jesus?

ª 5 Zech. 9:9   ᵇ 9 A Hebrew expression meaning "Save!" which became an exclamation of praise; also in verse 15   ᶜ 9 Psalm 118:26
ᵈ 13 Isaiah 56:7   ᵉ 13 Jer. 7:11   ᶠ 16 Psalm 8:2

²¹Jesus replied, "I tell you the truth, if you have faith and do not doubt, not only can you do what was done to the fig tree, but also you can say to this mountain, 'Go, throw yourself into the sea,' and it will be done. ²²If you believe, you will receive whatever you ask for in prayer."

THE AUTHORITY OF JESUS QUESTIONED

²³Jesus entered the temple courts, and, while he was teaching, the chief priests and the elders of the people came to him. "By what authority are you doing these things?" they asked. "And who gave you this authority?"

²⁴Jesus replied, "I will also ask you one question. If you answer me, I will tell you by what authority I am doing these things. ²⁵John's baptism—where did it come from? Was it from heaven, or from men?"

They discussed it among themselves and said, "If we say, 'From heaven,' he will ask, 'Then why didn't you believe him?' ²⁶But if we say, 'From men'—we are afraid of the people, for they all hold that John was a prophet."

²⁷So they answered Jesus, "We don't know."

Then he said, "Neither will I tell you by what authority I am doing these things.

THE PARABLE OF THE TWO SONS

²⁸"What do you think? There was a man who had two sons. He went to the first and said, 'Son, go and work today in the vineyard.'

²⁹" 'I will not,' he answered, but later he changed his mind and went.

³⁰"Then the father went to the other son and said the same thing. He answered, 'I will, sir,' but he did not go.

³¹"Which of the two did what his father wanted?"

"The first," they answered.

Jesus said to them, "I tell you the truth, the tax collectors and the prostitutes are entering the kingdom of God ahead of you. ³²For John came to you to show you the way of righteousness, and you did not believe him, but the tax collectors and the prostitutes did. And even after you saw this, you did not repent and believe him.

THE PARABLE OF THE TENANTS

³³"Listen to another parable: There was a landowner who planted a vineyard. He put a wall around it, dug a winepress in it and built a watchtower. Then he rented the vineyard to some farmers and went away on a journey. ³⁴When the harvest time approached, he sent his servants to the tenants to collect his fruit.

³⁵"The tenants seized his servants; they beat one, killed another, and stoned a third. ³⁶Then he sent other servants to them, more than the first time, and the tenants treated them the same way. ³⁷Last of all, he sent his son to them. 'They will respect my son,' he said.

³⁸"But when the tenants saw the son, they said to each other, 'This is the heir. Come, let's kill him and take his inheritance.' ³⁹So they took him and threw him out of the vineyard and killed him.

⁴⁰"Therefore, when the owner of the vineyard comes, what will he do to those tenants?"

⁴¹"He will bring those wretches to a wretched end," they replied, "and he will rent the vineyard to other tenants, who will give him his share of the crop at harvest time."

⁴²Jesus said to them, "Have you never read in the Scriptures:

Understanding the Power of Faith

What are the limits of God's power? How much is he willing to do for you and through you? Those are things worth checking out, don't you think? Wouldn't it be a shame to get to heaven and have God say, "I was ready to do so much more for you! Why didn't you ask me?" Do you think God could help an accident victim walk again, despite the doctor's prognosis? Do you think he could change the emotional health of a suicidal classmate? Do you think he could help a loved one with an addiction get clean and stay sober? Are you willing to explore the territory of real faith and find out for yourself?

> " 'The stone the builders rejected
> has become the capstone[a];
> the Lord has done this,
> and it is marvelous in our eyes'[b]?

[43] "Therefore I tell you that the kingdom of God will be taken away from you and given to a people who will produce its fruit. [44] He who falls on this stone will be broken to pieces, but he on whom it falls will be crushed."[c]

[45] When the chief priests and the Pharisees heard Jesus' parables, they knew he was talking about them. [46] They looked for a way to arrest him, but they were afraid of the crowd because the people held that he was a prophet.

THE PARABLE OF THE WEDDING BANQUET

22 Jesus spoke to them again in parables, saying: [2] "The kingdom of heaven is like a king who prepared a wedding banquet for his son. [3] He sent his servants to those who had been invited to the banquet to tell them to come, but they refused to come.

[4] "Then he sent some more servants and said, 'Tell those who have been invited that I have prepared my dinner: My oxen and fattened cattle have been butchered, and everything is ready. Come to the wedding banquet.'

[5] "But they paid no attention and went off— one to his field, another to his business. [6] The rest seized his servants, mistreated them and killed them. [7] The king was enraged. He sent his army and destroyed those murderers and burned their city.

[8] "Then he said to his servants, 'The wedding banquet is ready, but those I invited did not deserve to come. [9] Go to the street corners and invite to the banquet anyone you find.' [10] So the servants went out into the streets and gathered all the people they could find, both good and bad, and the wedding hall was filled with guests.

[11] "But when the king came in to see the guests, he noticed a man there who was not wearing wedding clothes. [12] 'Friend,' he asked, 'how did you get in here without wedding clothes?' The man was speechless.

[13] "Then the king told the attendants, 'Tie him hand and foot, and throw him outside, into the darkness, where there will be weeping and gnashing of teeth.'

[14] "For many are invited, but few are chosen."

NOW OR NEVER
MT 22:3

Have you ever been shot down when you invited someone to become a Christian? If so, what reason(s) did the person give? How did you respond? Did you give up or keep looking (and praying) for opportunities to share your faith?

PAYING TAXES TO CAESAR

[15] Then the Pharisees went out and laid plans to trap him in his words. [16] They sent their disciples to him along with the Herodians. "Teacher," they said, "we know you are a man of integrity and that you teach the way of God in accordance with the truth. You aren't swayed by men, because you pay no attention to who they are. [17] Tell us then, what is your opinion? Is it right to pay taxes to Caesar or not?"

[18] But Jesus, knowing their evil intent, said, "You hypocrites, why are you trying to trap me? [19] Show me the coin used for paying the tax." They brought him a denarius, [20] and he asked them, "Whose portrait is this? And whose inscription?"

[21] "Caesar's," they replied.

Then he said to them, "Give to Caesar what is Caesar's, and to God what is God's."

[22] When they heard this, they were amazed. So they left him and went away.

MARRIAGE AT THE RESURRECTION

[23] That same day the Sadducees, who say there is no resurrection, came to him with a question. [24] "Teacher," they said, "Moses told us that if a man dies without having children, his brother must mar-

---

[a] *42* Or *cornerstone*   [b] *42* Psalm 118:22,23   [c] *44* Some manuscripts do not have verse 44.

ry the widow and have children for him. 25Now there were seven brothers among us. The first one married and died, and since he had no children, he left his wife to his brother. 26The same thing happened to the second and third brother, right on down to the seventh. 27Finally, the woman died. 28Now then, at the resurrection, whose wife will she be of the seven, since all of them were married to her?"

29Jesus replied, "You are in error because you do not know the Scriptures or the power of God. 30At the resurrection people will neither marry nor be given in marriage; they will be like the angels in heaven. 31But about the resurrection of the dead—have you not read what God said to you, 32'I am the God of Abraham, the God of Isaac, and the God of Jacob'a? He is not the God of the dead but of the living." 33When the crowds heard this, they were astonished at his teaching.

THE GREATEST COMMANDMENT

34Hearing that Jesus had silenced the Sadducees, the Pharisees got together. 35One of them, an expert in the law, tested him with this question: 36"Teacher, which is the greatest commandment in the Law?"

37Jesus replied: " 'Love the Lord your God with all your heart and with all your soul and with all your mind.'b 38This is the first and greatest commandment. 39And the second is like it: 'Love your neighbor as yourself.'c 40All the Law and the Prophets hang on these two commandments."

WHOSE SON IS THE CHRIST?

41While the Pharisees were gathered together, Jesus asked them, 42"What do you think about the Christd? Whose son is he?"

"The son of David," they replied.

43He said to them, "How is it then that David, speaking by the Spirit, calls him 'Lord'? For he says,

44 " 'The Lord said to my Lord:
"Sit at my right hand
until I put your enemies
under your feet." 'e

45If then David calls him 'Lord,' how can he be his son?" 46No one could say a word in reply, and from that day on no one dared to ask him any more questions.

SEVEN WOES

23 Then Jesus said to the crowds and to his disciples: 2"The teachers of the law and the Pharisees sit in Moses' seat. 3So you must obey them and do everything they tell you. But do not do what they do, for they do not practice what they preach. 4They tie up heavy loads and put them on men's shoulders, but they themselves are not willing to lift a finger to move them.

5"Everything they do is done for men to see: They make their phylacteriesf wide and the tassels on their garments long; 6they love the place of honor at banquets and the most important seats in the synagogues; 7they love to be greeted in the marketplaces and to have men call them 'Rabbi.'

8"But you are not to be called 'Rabbi,' for you have only one Master and you are all brothers. 9And do not call anyone on earth 'father,' for you have one Father, and he is in heaven. 10Nor are you to be called 'teacher,' for you have one Teacher, the Christ.d 11The greatest among you will be your servant. 12For whoever exalts himself will be humbled, and whoever humbles himself will be exalted.

13"Woe to you, teachers of the law and Pharisees, you hypocrites! You shut the kingdom of heaven in men's faces. You yourselves do not enter, nor will you let those enter who are trying to.g

15"Woe to you, teachers of the law and Pharisees, you hypocrites! You travel over land and sea to win a single convert, and when he becomes one, you make him twice as much a son of hell as you are.

16"Woe to you, blind guides! You say, 'If anyone swears by the temple, it means nothing; but if anyone swears by the gold of the temple, he is bound by his oath.' 17You blind fools! Which is greater: the gold, or the temple that makes the gold sacred? 18You also say, 'If anyone swears by the altar, it means nothing; but if anyone swears by the gift on it, he is bound by his oath.' 19You blind men! Which is greater: the gift, or the altar that makes the gift sacred? 20Therefore, he who swears by the altar swears by it

---

a 32 Exodus 3:6   b 37 Deut. 6:5   c 39 Lev. 19:18   d 42,10 Or Messiah   e 44 Psalm 110:1   f 5 That is, boxes containing Scripture verses, worn on forehead and arm   g 13 Some manuscripts to. 14Woe to you, teachers of the law and Pharisees, you hypocrites! You devour widows' houses and for a show make lengthy prayers. Therefore you will be punished more severely.

and by everything on it. 21And he who swears by the temple swears by it and by the one who dwells in it. 22And he who swears by heaven swears by God's throne and by the one who sits on it.

23"Woe to you, teachers of the law and Pharisees, you hypocrites! You give a tenth of your spices— mint, dill and cummin. But you have neglected the more important matters of the law—justice, mercy and faithfulness. You should have practiced the latter, without neglecting the former. 24You blind guides! You strain out a gnat but swallow a camel.

25"Woe to you, teachers of the law and Pharisees, you hypocrites! You clean the outside of the cup and dish, but inside they are full of greed and self-indulgence. 26Blind Pharisee! First clean the inside of the cup and dish, and then the outside also will be clean.

27"Woe to you, teachers of the law and Pharisees, you hypocrites! You are like whitewashed tombs, which look beautiful on the outside but on the inside are full of dead men's bones and everything un- clean. 28In the same way, on the outside you appear to people as righteous but on the inside you are full of hypocrisy and wickedness.

29"Woe to you, teachers of the law and Pharisees, you hypocrites! You build tombs for the proph- ets and decorate the graves of the righteous. 30And you say, 'If we had lived in the days of our forefa- thers, we would not have taken part with them in shedding the blood of the prophets.' 31So you testify against yourselves that you are the descendants of those who murdered the prophets. 32Fill up, then, the measure of the sin of your forefathers!

33"You snakes! You brood of vipers! How will you escape being condemned to hell? 34Therefore I am sending you prophets and wise men and teachers. Some of them you will kill and crucify; others you will flog in your synagogues and pursue from town to town. 35And so upon you will come all the righteous blood that has been shed on earth, from the blood of righteous Abel to the blood of Zechari- ah son of Berekiah, whom you murdered between the temple and the altar. 36I tell you the truth, all this will come upon this generation.

37"O Jerusalem, Jerusalem, you who kill the prophets and stone those sent to you, how often I have longed to gather your children together, as a hen gathers her chicks under her wings, but you were not willing. 38Look, your house is left to you desolate. 39For I tell you, you will not see me again until you say, 'Blessed is he who comes in the name of the Lord.'ᵃ"

SIGNS OF THE END OF THE AGE

24 Jesus left the temple and was walking away when his disciples came up to him to call his attention to its buildings. 2"Do you see all these things?" he asked. "I tell you the truth, not one stone here will be left on another; every one will be thrown down."

3As Jesus was sitting on the Mount of Olives, the disciples came to him privately. "Tell us," they said, "when will this happen, and what will be the sign of your coming and of the end of the age?"

4Jesus answered: "Watch out that no one deceives you. 5For many will come in my name, claim- ing, 'I am the Christ,ᵇ' and will deceive many. 6You will hear of wars and rumors of wars, but see to it that you are not alarmed. Such things must happen, but the end is still to come. 7Nation will rise against nation, and kingdom against king- dom. There will be famines and earthquakes in various places. 8All these are the beginning of birth pains.

9"Then you will be handed over to be perse- cuted and put to death, and you will be hated by all nations because of me. 10At that time many will turn away from the faith and will betray and hate each other, 11and many false prophets will appear and deceive many people. 12Because of the increase of wickedness, the love of most will grow cold, 13but he who stands firm to the end will be saved. 14And this gospel of the kingdom will be preached in the whole world as a testimo- ny to all nations, and then the end will come.

15"So when you see standing in the holy place 'the abomination that causes desolation,'ᶜ spoken of

now or never
MT 24:9-14

In the Christian life, it's not just about how you start. It's how you finish. If you've stumbled a few times and even lost your way, ask God for his forgiveness and get back in the race. The best is yet to come for those who hang in there till the end!

---

through the prophet Daniel—let the reader understand— ¹⁶then let those who are in Judea flee to the mountains. ¹⁷Let no one on the roof of his house go down to take anything out of the house. ¹⁸Let no one in the field go back to get his cloak. ¹⁹How dreadful it will be in those days for pregnant women and nursing mothers! ²⁰Pray that your flight will not take place in winter or on the Sabbath. ²¹For then there will be great distress, unequaled from the beginning of the world until now—and never to be equaled again. ²²If those days had not been cut short, no one would survive, but for the sake of the elect those days will be shortened. ²³At that time if anyone says to you, 'Look, here is the Christ!' or, 'There he is!' do not believe it. ²⁴For false Christs and false prophets will appear and perform great signs and miracles to deceive even the elect—if that were possible. ²⁵See, I have told you ahead of time.

²⁶"So if anyone tells you, 'There he is, out in the desert,' do not go out; or, 'Here he is, in the inner rooms,' do not believe it. ²⁷For as lightning that comes from the east is visible even in the west, so will be the coming of the Son of Man. ²⁸Wherever there is a carcass, there the vultures will gather.

²⁹"Immediately after the distress of those days

> " 'the sun will be darkened,
>   and the moon will not give its light;
> the stars will fall from the sky,
>   and the heavenly bodies will be shaken.'ᵃ

³⁰"At that time the sign of the Son of Man will appear in the sky, and all the nations of the earth will mourn. They will see the Son of Man coming on the clouds of the sky, with power and great glory. ³¹And he will send his angels with a loud trumpet call, and they will gather his elect from the four winds, from one end of the heavens to the other.

³²"Now learn this lesson from the fig tree: As soon as its twigs get tender and its leaves come out, you know that summer is near. ³³Even so, when you see all these things, you know that itᵇ is near, right at the door. ³⁴I tell you the truth, this generationᶜ will certainly not pass away until all these things have happened. ³⁵Heaven and earth will pass away, but my words will never pass away.

THE DAY AND HOUR UNKNOWN

³⁶"No one knows about that day or hour, not even the angels in heaven, nor the Son,ᵈ but only the Father. ³⁷As it was in the days of Noah, so it will be at the coming of the Son of Man. ³⁸For in the days before the flood, people were eating and drinking, marrying and giving in marriage, up to the day Noah entered the ark; ³⁹and they knew nothing about what would happen until the flood came and took them all away. That is how it will be at the coming of the Son of Man. ⁴⁰Two men will be in the field; one will be taken and the other left. ⁴¹Two women will be grinding with a hand mill; one will be taken and the other left.

⁴²"Therefore keep watch, because you do not know on what day your Lord will come. ⁴³But understand this: If the owner of the house had known at what time of night the thief was coming, he would have kept watch and would not have let his house be broken into. ⁴⁴So you also must be ready, because the Son of Man will come at an hour when you do not expect him.

⁴⁵"Who then is the faithful and wise servant, whom the master has put in charge of the servants in his household to give them their food at the proper time? ⁴⁶It will be good for that servant whose master finds him doing so when he returns. ⁴⁷I tell you the truth, he will put him in charge of all his possessions. ⁴⁸But suppose that servant is wicked and says to himself, 'My master is staying away a long time,' ⁴⁹and he then begins to beat his fellow servants and to eat and drink with drunkards. ⁵⁰The master of that servant will come on a day when he does not expect him and at an hour he is not aware of. ⁵¹He will cut him to pieces and assign him a place with the hypocrites, where there will be weeping and gnashing of teeth.

THE PARABLE OF THE TEN VIRGINS

25 "At that time the kingdom of heaven will be like ten virgins who took their lamps and went out to meet the bridegroom. ²Five of them were foolish and five were wise. ³The foolish ones took their lamps but did not take any oil with them. ⁴The wise, however, took oil in jars along with their lamps. ⁵The bridegroom was a long time in coming, and they all became drowsy and fell asleep.

ᵃ 29 Isaiah 13:10; 34:4   ᵇ 33 Or he   ᶜ 34 Or race   ᵈ 36 Some manuscripts do not have *nor the Son.*

[6] "At midnight the cry rang out: 'Here's the bridegroom! Come out to meet him!'

[7] "Then all the virgins woke up and trimmed their lamps. [8] The foolish ones said to the wise, 'Give us some of your oil; our lamps are going out.'

[9] " 'No,' they replied, 'there may not be enough for both us and you. Instead, go to those who sell oil and buy some for yourselves.'

[10] "But while they were on their way to buy the oil, the bridegroom arrived. The virgins who were ready went in with him to the wedding banquet. And the door was shut.

[11] "Later the others also came. 'Sir! Sir!' they said. 'Open the door for us!'

[12] "But he replied, 'I tell you the truth, I don't know you.'

[13] "Therefore keep watch, because you do not know the day or the hour.

THE PARABLE OF THE TALENTS

[14] "Again, it will be like a man going on a journey, who called his servants and entrusted his property to them. [15] To one he gave five talents[a] of money, to another two talents, and to another one talent, each according to his ability. Then he went on his journey. [16] The man who had received the five talents went at once and put his money to work and gained five more. [17] So also, the one with the two talents gained two more. [18] But the man who had received the one talent went off, dug a hole in the ground and hid his master's money.

[19] "After a long time the master of those servants returned and settled accounts with them. [20] The man who had received the five talents brought the other five. 'Master,' he said, 'you entrusted me with five talents. See, I have gained five more.'

[21] "His master replied, 'Well done, good and faithful servant! You have been faithful with a few things; I will put you in charge of many things. Come and share your master's happiness!'

[22] "The man with the two talents also came. 'Master,' he said, 'you entrusted me with two talents; see, I have gained two more.'

[23] "His master replied, 'Well done, good and faithful servant! You have been faithful with a few things; I will put you in charge of many things. Come and share your master's happiness!'

[24] "Then the man who had received the one talent came. 'Master,' he said, 'I knew that you are a hard man, harvesting where you have not sown and gathering where you have not scattered seed. [25] So I was afraid and went out and hid your talent in the ground. See, here is what belongs to you.'

[26] "His master replied, 'You wicked, lazy servant! So you knew that I harvest where I have not sown and gather where I have not scattered seed? [27] Well then, you should have put my money on deposit with the bankers, so that when I returned I would have received it back with interest.

[28] " 'Take the talent from him and give it to the one who has the ten talents. [29] For everyone who has will be given more, and he will have an abundance. Whoever does not have, even what he has will be taken from him. [30] And throw that worthless servant outside, into the darkness, where there will be weeping and gnashing of teeth.'

NOW OR NEVER

MT 25:31-46

What specific thing can you do this week to help someone who's hungry? What can you do to help a stranger? Someone who needs clothes? Someone who's sick? A prisoner? Can you really afford *not* to help "the least of these"?

THE SHEEP AND THE GOATS

[31] "When the Son of Man comes in his glory, and all the angels with him, he will sit on his throne in heavenly glory. [32] All the nations will be gathered before him, and he will separate the people one from another as a shepherd separates the sheep from the goats. [33] He will put the sheep on his right and the goats on his left.

[34] "Then the King will say to those on his right, 'Come, you who are blessed by my Father; take your inheritance, the kingdom prepared for you since the creation of the world. [35] For I was hungry and you gave me something to eat, I was thirsty and you gave me something to drink, I was a stranger and you invited me in, [36] I needed clothes and you clothed me, I was sick and you looked after me, I was in prison and you came to visit me.'

[37] "Then the righteous will answer him, 'Lord, when did we see you hungry and feed you, or thirsty

---

[a] *15* A talent was worth more than a thousand dollars.

and give you something to drink? ³⁸When did we see you a stranger and invite you in, or needing clothes and clothe you? ³⁹When did we see you sick or in prison and go to visit you?'

⁴⁰"The King will reply, 'I tell you the truth, whatever you did for one of the least of these brothers of mine, you did for me.'

⁴¹"Then he will say to those on his left, 'Depart from me, you who are cursed, into the eternal fire prepared for the devil and his angels. ⁴²For I was hungry and you gave me nothing to eat, I was thirsty and you gave me nothing to drink, ⁴³I was a stranger and you did not invite me in, I needed clothes and you did not clothe me, I was sick and in prison and you did not look after me.'

⁴⁴"They also will answer, 'Lord, when did we see you hungry or thirsty or a stranger or needing clothes or sick or in prison, and did not help you?'

⁴⁵"He will reply, 'I tell you the truth, whatever you did not do for one of the least of these, you did not do for me.'

⁴⁶"Then they will go away to eternal punishment, but the righteous to eternal life."

THE PLOT AGAINST JESUS

26 When Jesus had finished saying all these things, he said to his disciples, ²"As you know, the Passover is two days away—and the Son of Man will be handed over to be crucified."

³Then the chief priests and the elders of the people assembled in the palace of the high priest, whose name was Caiaphas, ⁴and they plotted to arrest Jesus in some sly way and kill him. ⁵"But not during the Feast," they said, "or there may be a riot among the people."

JESUS ANOINTED AT BETHANY

⁶While Jesus was in Bethany in the home of a man known as Simon the Leper, ⁷a woman came to him with an alabaster jar of very expensive perfume, which she poured on his head as he was reclining at the table.

⁸When the disciples saw this, they were indignant. "Why this waste?" they asked. ⁹"This perfume could have been sold at a high price and the money given to the poor."

¹⁰Aware of this, Jesus said to them, "Why are you bothering this woman? She has done a beautiful thing to me. ¹¹The poor you will always have with you, but you will not always have me. ¹²When she poured this perfume on my body, she did it to prepare me for burial. ¹³I tell you the truth, wherever this gospel is preached throughout the world, what she has done will also be told, in memory of her."

JUDAS AGREES TO BETRAY JESUS

¹⁴Then one of the Twelve—the one called Judas Iscariot—went to the chief priests ¹⁵and asked, "What are you willing to give me if I hand him over to you?" So they counted out for him thirty silver coins. ¹⁶From then on Judas watched for an opportunity to hand him over.

THE LORD'S SUPPER

¹⁷On the first day of the Feast of Unleavened Bread, the disciples came to Jesus and asked, "Where do you want us to make preparations for you to eat the Passover?"

¹⁸He replied, "Go into the city to a certain man and tell him, 'The Teacher says: My appointed time is near. I am going to celebrate the Passover with my disciples at your house.' " ¹⁹So the disciples did as Jesus had directed them and prepared the Passover.

²⁰When evening came, Jesus was reclining at the table with the Twelve. ²¹And while they were eating, he said, "I tell you the truth, one of you will betray me."

²²They were very sad and began to say to him one after the other, "Surely not I, Lord?"

²³Jesus replied, "The one who has dipped his hand into the bowl with me will betray me. ²⁴The Son of Man will go just as it is written about him. But woe to that man who betrays the Son of Man! It would be better for him if he had not been born."

²⁵Then Judas, the one who would betray him, said, "Surely not I, Rabbi?"
Jesus answered, "Yes, it is you." ͣ

²⁶While they were eating, Jesus took bread, gave thanks and broke it, and gave it to his disciples, saying, "Take and eat; this is my body."

ͣ *25 Or "You yourself have said it"*

battlelines

» Stressed Out

Q: Shane told me about the big discussion in biology today. Why didn't you speak up?
A: Oh, great. Now everyone knows. You're right. I'm a big screw-up! I should have said something, but I didn't, all right? I wasn't in the mood to be called a religious fanatic for expressing my views on creation. Besides, I'm not sure I could have defended my position. I probably would have screwed that up too!

Q: OK, look: It's not the end of the world. I'm not bashing you. I just wondered if you had a reason for keeping quiet.
A: I can't explain it. I know what I'm supposed to do. Sometimes I even get all fired up about doing it. But when I'm faced with a real-life situation, I wilt. I can't handle all the expectations and pressures. "Do this. Don't do that. Speak up! Shut up!" It's driving me nuts!

Q: Relax. It's OK. Nobody expects you to be perfect.
A: *Everybody* expects me to be perfect. My dad is always preaching at me about my shortcomings. My mom just shakes her head in disappointment. My youth pastor sent me an email last night to "encourage" me, but what it really said between the lines was, "Hey, Troy, get your act together." And I know God sees every mistake I make.

Q: I think you might be reading more into people's feelings about you than what's really there.
A: I'm just telling you what I see.

Q: You're telling me what you *think* you see. Troy, trust me on this. Your judgment right now is probably clouded by all the stress in your life. You're under tons of pressure, man. It's obvious. It's not healthy to walk around beating yourself up for all the ways you imagine you're blowing it. Lighten up.
A: I wish I could. But how?

» Stress Doubt

Mix the STrains of life with the pRESSures of the world, and you get STRESS. Stress results from being pulled in at least two directions at the same time. When God calls you to live one way, and your body, mind, feelings and friends pull you in another direction, stress is the result. Jesus understood stress firsthand. He spent his last night on earth in agony, torn between his Father's will and his own desire to escape the torment of the cross (see Matthew 26:36–46).

How are we supposed to deal with stress? Philippians 4:6–7 says, "Do not be anxious about anything, but in everything, by prayer and petition, with thanksgiving, present your requests to God. And the peace of God, which transcends all understanding, will guard your hearts and your minds in Christ Jesus."

Did you get that? Pray . . . about *everything*. And while you're at it, be thankful for all that God has already done. One result of that kind of prayer life is a deep comfort in knowing that God is good—the kind of peace that can only come from acknowledging that he is in control. Stress can't survive under those conditions!

For more ideas on handling stress, go to www.RevolutionBible.com.

27Then he took the cup, gave thanks and offered it to them, saying, "Drink from it, all of you. 28This is my blood of the ᵃ covenant, which is poured out for many for the forgiveness of sins. 29I tell you, I will not drink of this fruit of the vine from now on until that day when I drink it anew with you in my Father's kingdom."

30When they had sung a hymn, they went out to the Mount of Olives.

JESUS PREDICTS PETER'S DENIAL

31Then Jesus told them, "This very night you will all fall away on account of me, for it is written:

> " 'I will strike the shepherd,
>   and the sheep of the flock will be scattered.'ᵇ

32But after I have risen, I will go ahead of you into Galilee."

33Peter replied, "Even if all fall away on account of you, I never will."

34"I tell you the truth," Jesus answered, "this very night, before the rooster crows, you will disown me three times."

35But Peter declared, "Even if I have to die with you, I will never disown you." And all the other disciples said the same.

GETHSEMANE

36Then Jesus went with his disciples to a place called Gethsemane, and he said to them, "Sit here while I go over there and pray." 37He took Peter and the two sons of Zebedee along with him, and he began to be sorrowful and troubled. 38Then he said to them, "My soul is overwhelmed with sorrow to the point of death. Stay here and keep watch with me."

39Going a little farther, he fell with his face to the ground and prayed, "My Father, if it is possible, may this cup be taken from me. Yet not as I will, but as you will."

40Then he returned to his disciples and found them sleeping. "Could you men not keep watch with me for one hour?" he asked Peter. 41"Watch and pray so that you will not fall into temptation. The spirit is willing, but the body is weak."

42He went away a second time and prayed, "My Father, if it is not possible for this cup to be taken away unless I drink it, may your will be done."

43When he came back, he again found them sleeping, because their eyes were heavy.

NOW OR NEVER
MT 26:40

Have you ever failed or betrayed a friend when he or she really needed you? What does it take to be a true friend even in the midst of tough times?

44So he left them and went away once more and prayed the third time, saying the same thing.

45Then he returned to the disciples and said to them, "Are you still sleeping and resting? Look, the hour is near, and the Son of Man is betrayed into the hands of sinners. 46Rise, let us go! Here comes my betrayer!"

JESUS ARRESTED

47While he was still speaking, Judas, one of the Twelve, arrived. With him was a large crowd armed with swords and clubs, sent from the chief priests and the elders of the people. 48Now the betrayer had arranged a signal with them: "The one I kiss is the man; arrest him." 49Going at once to Jesus, Judas said, "Greetings, Rabbi!" and kissed him.

50Jesus replied, "Friend, do what you came for." ᶜ

Then the men stepped forward, seized Jesus and arrested him. 51With that, one of Jesus' companions reached for his sword, drew it out and struck the servant of the high priest, cutting off his ear.

52"Put your sword back in its place," Jesus said to him, "for all who draw the sword will die by the sword. 53Do you think I cannot call on my Father, and he will at once put at my disposal more than twelve legions of angels? 54But how then would the Scriptures be fulfilled that say it must happen in this way?"

ᵃ 28 Some manuscripts the new   ᵇ 31 Zech. 13:7   ᶜ 50 Or "Friend, why have you come?"

[55]At that time Jesus said to the crowd, "Am I leading a rebellion, that you have come out with swords and clubs to capture me? Every day I sat in the temple courts teaching, and you did not arrest me. [56]But this has all taken place that the writings of the prophets might be fulfilled." Then all the disciples deserted him and fled.

BEFORE THE SANHEDRIN

[57]Those who had arrested Jesus took him to Caiaphas, the high priest, where the teachers of the law and the elders had assembled. [58]But Peter followed him at a distance, right up to the courtyard of the high priest. He entered and sat down with the guards to see the outcome.

[59]The chief priests and the whole Sanhedrin were looking for false evidence against Jesus so that they could put him to death. [60]But they did not find any, though many false witnesses came forward.

Finally two came forward [61]and declared, "This fellow said, 'I am able to destroy the temple of God and rebuild it in three days.' "

[62]Then the high priest stood up and said to Jesus, "Are you not going to answer? What is this testimony that these men are bringing against you?" [63]But Jesus remained silent.

The high priest said to him, "I charge you under oath by the living God: Tell us if you are the Christ,[a] the Son of God."

[64]"Yes, it is as you say," Jesus replied. "But I say to all of you: In the future you will see the Son of Man sitting at the right hand of the Mighty One and coming on the clouds of heaven."

[65]Then the high priest tore his clothes and said, "He has spoken blasphemy! Why do we need any more witnesses? Look, now you have heard the blasphemy. [66]What do you think?"

"He is worthy of death," they answered.

[67]Then they spit in his face and struck him with their fists. Others slapped him [68]and said, "Prophesy to us, Christ. Who hit you?"

PETER DISOWNS JESUS

[69]Now Peter was sitting out in the courtyard, and a servant girl came to him. "You also were with Jesus of Galilee," she said.

[70]But he denied it before them all. "I don't know what you're talking about," he said.

[71]Then he went out to the gateway, where another girl saw him and said to the people there, "This fellow was with Jesus of Nazareth."

[72]He denied it again, with an oath: "I don't know the man!"

[73]After a little while, those standing there went up to Peter and said, "Surely you are one of them, for your accent gives you away."

[74]Then he began to call down curses on himself and he swore to them, "I don't know the man!"

Immediately a rooster crowed. [75]Then Peter remembered the word Jesus had spoken: "Before the rooster crows, you will disown me three times." And he went outside and wept bitterly.

JUDAS HANGS HIMSELF

27 Early in the morning, all the chief priests and the elders of the people came to the decision to put Jesus to death. [2]They bound him, led him away and handed him over to Pilate, the governor.

[3]When Judas, who had betrayed him, saw that Jesus was condemned, he was seized with remorse and returned the thirty silver coins to the chief priests and the elders. [4]"I have sinned," he said, "for I have betrayed innocent blood."

"What is that to us?" they replied. "That's your responsibility."

[5]So Judas threw the money into the temple and left. Then he went away and hanged himself.

[6]The chief priests picked up the coins and said, "It is against the law to put this into the treasury, since it is blood money." [7]So they decided to use the money to buy the potter's field as a burial place for foreigners. [8]That is why it has been called the Field of Blood to this day. [9]Then what was spoken by Jeremiah the prophet was fulfilled: "They took the thirty silver coins, the price set on him by the people of Israel, [10]and they used them to buy the potter's field, as the Lord commanded me."[b]

[a] 63 Or Messiah; also in verse 68   [b] 10 See Zech. 11:12,13; Jer. 19:1-13; 32:6-9.

JESUS BEFORE PILATE

¹¹Meanwhile Jesus stood before the governor, and the governor asked him, "Are you the king of the Jews?"

"Yes, it is as you say," Jesus replied.

¹²When he was accused by the chief priests and the elders, he gave no answer. ¹³Then Pilate asked him, "Don't you hear the testimony they are bringing against you?" ¹⁴But Jesus made no reply, not even to a single charge—to the great amazement of the governor.

¹⁵Now it was the governor's custom at the Feast to release a prisoner chosen by the crowd. ¹⁶At that time they had a notorious prisoner, called Barabbas. ¹⁷So when the crowd had gathered, Pilate asked them, "Which one do you want me to release to you: Barabbas, or Jesus who is called Christ?" ¹⁸For he knew it was out of envy that they had handed Jesus over to him.

¹⁹While Pilate was sitting on the judge's seat, his wife sent him this message: "Don't have anything to do with that innocent man, for I have suffered a great deal today in a dream because of him."

²⁰But the chief priests and the elders persuaded the crowd to ask for Barabbas and to have Jesus executed.

²¹"Which of the two do you want me to release to you?" asked the governor.

"Barabbas," they answered.

²²"What shall I do, then, with Jesus who is called Christ?" Pilate asked.

They all answered, "Crucify him!"

²³"Why? What crime has he committed?" asked Pilate.

But they shouted all the louder, "Crucify him!"

²⁴When Pilate saw that he was getting nowhere, but that instead an uproar was starting, he took water and washed his hands in front of the crowd. "I am innocent of this man's blood," he said. "It is your responsibility!"

²⁵All the people answered, "Let his blood be on us and on our children!"

²⁶Then he released Barabbas to them. But he had Jesus flogged, and handed him over to be crucified.

THE SOLDIERS MOCK JESUS

²⁷Then the governor's soldiers took Jesus into the Praetorium and gathered the whole company of soldiers around him. ²⁸They stripped him and put a scarlet robe on him, ²⁹and then twisted together a crown of thorns and set it on his head. They put a staff in his right hand and knelt in front of him and mocked him. "Hail, king of the Jews!" they said. ³⁰They spit on him, and took the staff and struck him on the head again and again. ³¹After they had mocked him, they took off the robe and put his own clothes on him. Then they led him away to crucify him.

THE CRUCIFIXION

³²As they were going out, they met a man from Cyrene, named Simon, and they forced him to carry the cross. ³³They came to a place called Golgotha (which means The Place of the Skull). ³⁴There they offered Jesus wine to drink, mixed with gall; but after tasting it, he refused to drink it. ³⁵When they had crucified him, they divided up his clothes by casting lots.ª ³⁶And sitting down, they kept watch over him there. ³⁷Above his head they placed the written charge against him: THIS IS JESUS, THE KING OF THE JEWS. ³⁸Two robbers were crucified with him, one on his right and one on his left. ³⁹Those who passed by hurled insults at him, shaking their heads ⁴⁰and saying, "You who are going to destroy the temple and build it in three days, save yourself! Come down from the cross, if you are the Son of God!"

⁴¹In the same way the chief priests, the teachers of the law and the elders mocked him. ⁴²"He saved others," they said, "but he can't save himself! He's the King of Israel! Let him come down now from the cross, and we will believe in him. ⁴³He trusts in God. Let God rescue him now if he wants him, for he said, 'I am the Son of God.' " ⁴⁴In the same way the robbers who were crucified with him also heaped insults on him.

THE DEATH OF JESUS

⁴⁵From the sixth hour until the ninth hour darkness came over all the land. ⁴⁶About the ninth hour

---

ª 35 A few late manuscripts *lots that the word spoken by the prophet might be fulfilled: "They divided my garments among themselves and cast lots for my clothing"* (Psalm 22:18)

Jesus cried out in a loud voice, *"Eloi, Eloi,*[a] *lama sabachthani?"*—which means, "My God, my God, why have you forsaken me?"[b]

⁴⁷When some of those standing there heard this, they said, "He's calling Elijah."

⁴⁸Immediately one of them ran and got a sponge. He filled it with wine vinegar, put it on a stick, and offered it to Jesus to drink. ⁴⁹The rest said, "Now leave him alone. Let's see if Elijah comes to save him."

⁵⁰And when Jesus had cried out again in a loud voice, he gave up his spirit.

⁵¹At that moment the curtain of the temple was torn in two from top to bottom. The earth shook and the rocks split. ⁵²The tombs broke open and the bodies of many holy people who had died were raised to life. ⁵³They came out of the tombs, and after Jesus' resurrection they went into the holy city and appeared to many people.

now or never

MT 27:46

Jesus knows exactly what it's like to be deserted by everyone. The next time you feel abandoned by your friends, family or even God, he's the One you should talk to. He's always listening.

⁵⁴When the centurion and those with him who were guarding Jesus saw the earthquake and all that had happened, they were terrified, and exclaimed, "Surely he was the Son[c] of God!"

⁵⁵Many women were there, watching from a distance. They had followed Jesus from Galilee to care for his needs. ⁵⁶Among them were Mary Magdalene, Mary the mother of James and Joses, and the mother of Zebedee's sons.

THE BURIAL OF JESUS

⁵⁷As evening approached, there came a rich man from Arimathea, named Joseph, who had himself become a disciple of Jesus. ⁵⁸Going to Pilate, he asked for Jesus' body, and Pilate ordered that it be given to him. ⁵⁹Joseph took the body, wrapped it in a clean linen cloth, ⁶⁰and placed it in his own new tomb that he had cut out of the rock. He rolled a big stone in front of the entrance to the tomb and went away. ⁶¹Mary Magdalene and the other Mary were sitting there opposite the tomb.

THE GUARD AT THE TOMB

⁶²The next day, the one after Preparation Day, the chief priests and the Pharisees went to Pilate. ⁶³"Sir," they said, "we remember that while he was still alive that deceiver said, 'After three days I will rise again.' ⁶⁴So give the order for the tomb to be made secure until the third day. Otherwise, his disciples may come and steal the body and tell the people that he has been raised from the dead. This last deception will be worse than the first."

⁶⁵"Take a guard," Pilate answered. "Go, make the tomb as secure as you know how." ⁶⁶So they went and made the tomb secure by putting a seal on the stone and posting the guard.

THE RESURRECTION

28 After the Sabbath, at dawn on the first day of the week, Mary Magdalene and the other Mary went to look at the tomb.

²There was a violent earthquake, for an angel of the Lord came down from heaven and, going to the tomb, rolled back the stone and sat on it. ³His appearance was like lightning, and his clothes were white as snow. ⁴The guards were so afraid of him that they shook and became like dead men.

⁵The angel said to the women, "Do not be afraid, for I know that you are looking for Jesus, who was crucified. ⁶He is not here; he has risen, just as he said. Come and see the place where he lay. ⁷Then go quickly and tell his disciples: 'He has risen from the dead and is going ahead of you into Galilee. There you will see him.' Now I have told you."

⁸So the women hurried away from the tomb, afraid yet filled with joy, and ran to tell his disciples. ⁹Suddenly Jesus met them. "Greetings," he said. They came to him, clasped his feet and worshiped him. ¹⁰Then Jesus said to them, "Do not be afraid. Go and tell my brothers to go to Galilee; there they will see me."

ᵃ *46* Some manuscripts *Eli, Eli*   ᵇ *46* Psalm 22:1   ᶜ *54* Or *a son*

THE GUARDS' REPORT

[11]While the women were on their way, some of the guards went into the city and reported to the chief priests everything that had happened. [12]When the chief priests had met with the elders and devised a plan, they gave the soldiers a large sum of money, [13]telling them, "You are to say, 'His disciples came during the night and stole him away while we were asleep.' [14]If this report gets to the governor, we will satisfy him and keep you out of trouble." [15]So the soldiers took the money and did as they were instructed. And this story has been widely circulated among the Jews to this very day.

THE GREAT COMMISSION

[16]Then the eleven disciples went to Galilee, to the mountain where Jesus had told them to go. [17]When they saw him, they worshiped him; but some doubted. [18]Then Jesus came to them and said, "All authority in heaven and on earth has been given to me. [19]Therefore go and make disciples of all nations, baptizing them in[a] the name of the Father and of the Son and of the Holy Spirit, [20]and teaching them to obey everything I have commanded you. And surely I am with you always, to the very end of the age."

challengenotes

To: my_son

heavenly_father: you never have to feel outnumbered, intimidated or outclassed by anything on earth. why? because I am with you. as my follower, you have 24/7 access to me—to my power and my protection.

MT 28:20

Spreading the Good News

How comfortable do you feel talking about Jesus with others? As with most things in life, the more you do it, the more comfortable and confident you'll become— the more confidence you'll have when those opportunities arise. The best way to practice sharing your faith is to start with friends, family members and other people close to you. Once you get the hang of sharing the story of your own relationship with God, explaining key Bible passages and answering tough questions, you can gradually expand your scope, finding ways to talk about Jesus with people you don't know as well. Ask God to give you opportunities, and you'll be amazed at how he uses you.

---

[a] *19 Or into*; see Acts 8:16; 19:5; Romans 6:3; 1 Cor. 1:13; 10:2 and Gal. 3:27.

MARK

MARK MARK MARK MARK

« AT A GLANCE

Author
John Mark

Audience
Christian Gentiles in Rome

Date
Probably between A.D. 55 and 65

Setting
Mark most likely wrote from Rome, where he received—according to early church sources—the information for his Gospel from the apostle Peter.

Verse to Remember
"For even the Son of Man did not come to be served, but to serve, and to give his life as a ransom for many" (10:45).

Theme to Consider
The book of Mark is a quick-paced, rapid-fire picture of Jesus on earth—healing, teaching, serving and saving. Let this story inspire you to step out in faith!

UNCHANGING TRUTH » Jesus was a man of action. The book of Mark makes that clear. Jesus didn't just teach his disciples (and us) with words; he taught with his hands and feet too. He lived his entire life as an example for others to follow.

Jesus told his disciples to show love to others; then he gave them a model to follow by spending his time with people in need, showing genuine concern for them and relieving their pain and suffering. He told his disciples to love their enemies; then he showed them what he meant by going to the cross for the very people who hated him.

Because he was a man of action, Jesus expects action from his followers as well. He's not satisfied with the guy who sits around talking about the importance of loving others; he's satisfied by the guy who helps the single mom next door by playing with her kids when she has to work late. He's not satisfied by the guy who underlines the words "love your enemies" in his Bible; he's satisfied by the guy who secretly shovels snow for the mean, old retired guy down the block.

Reading Jesus' words and not putting them into action is like memorizing a football playbook but never stepping onto the field. It doesn't really benefit anyone.

So . . . how about it? Are you ready to become a man of action?

LIFE LESSONS »

1. No matter how busy your life gets, always make time for prayer (1:35).

2. Jesus' message of love and forgiveness means more to people who recognize their sin than to people who are satisfied with the way they are (2:17).

3. The bond between Jesus and his followers is stronger than even the bond between family members (3:35).

4. A strong faith in Jesus Christ can lead to incredible things (5:25–34).

JOHN THE BAPTIST PREPARES THE WAY

1 The beginning of the gospel about Jesus Christ, the Son of God.[a]

[2]It is written in Isaiah the prophet:

> "I will send my messenger ahead of you,
>   who will prepare your way"[b]—
> [3]"a voice of one calling in the desert,
> 'Prepare the way for the Lord,
>   make straight paths for him.' "[c]

[4]And so John came, baptizing in the desert region and preaching a baptism of repentance for the forgiveness of sins. [5]The whole Judean countryside and all the people of Jerusalem went out to him. Confessing their sins, they were baptized by him in the Jordan River. [6]John wore clothing made of camel's hair, with a leather belt around his waist, and he ate locusts and wild honey. [7]And this was his message: "After me will come one more powerful than I, the thongs of whose sandals I am not worthy to stoop down and untie. [8]I baptize you with[d] water, but he will baptize you with the Holy Spirit."

NOW OR NEVER
MK 1:7

Here's another example of God using a humble person to accomplish something huge. If you want God to use you for something remarkable, the first thing you need to do is keep your ego in check—not an easy thing to do.

THE BAPTISM AND TEMPTATION OF JESUS

[9]At that time Jesus came from Nazareth in Galilee and was baptized by John in the Jordan. [10]As Jesus was coming up out of the water, he saw heaven being torn open and the Spirit descending on him like a dove. [11]And a voice came from heaven: "You are my Son, whom I love; with you I am well pleased."

[12]At once the Spirit sent him out into the desert, [13]and he was in the desert forty days, being tempted by Satan. He was with the wild animals, and angels attended him.

THE CALLING OF THE FIRST DISCIPLES

[14]After John was put in prison, Jesus went into Galilee, proclaiming the good news of God. [15]"The time has come," he said. "The kingdom of God is near. Repent and believe the good news!"

NOW OR NEVER
MK 1:10

Here's some Bible trivia for you: This is one of the few places in Scripture where the three members of the Trinity—the Father, Son and Holy Spirit—are mentioned together. Jesus is standing in the river; the Father is the voice from heaven; the Holy Spirit descends in the form of a dove.

[16]As Jesus walked beside the Sea of Galilee, he saw Simon and his brother Andrew casting a net into the lake, for they were fishermen. [17]"Come, follow me," Jesus said, "and I will make you fishers of men." [18]At once they left their nets and followed him.

[19]When he had gone a little farther, he saw James son of Zebedee and his brother John in a boat, preparing their nets. [20]Without delay he called them, and they left their father Zebedee in the boat with the hired men and followed him.

JESUS DRIVES OUT AN EVIL SPIRIT

[21]They went to Capernaum, and when the Sabbath came, Jesus went into the synagogue and began to teach. [22]The people were amazed at his teaching, because he taught them as one who had authority, not as the teachers of the law. [23]Just then a man in their synagogue who was possessed by an evil[e] spir-

---

[a] *1* Some manuscripts do not have *the Son of God.*   [b] *2* Mal. 3:1   [c] *3* Isaiah 40:3   [d] *8* Or *in*   [e] *23* Greek *unclean;* also in verses 26 and 27

it cried out, [24] "What do you want with us, Jesus of Nazareth? Have you come to destroy us? I know who you are—the Holy One of God!"

»» live the adventure »» Mk 1:35

Improving Your Prayer Life

You can find some helpful tips for your own personal prayer time in this passage. First of all, try praying early in the day. You don't necessarily have to get up before dawn, but if you make prayer the first thing you do after you wake up, you'll be a whole lot better prepared to face the challenges of the day. Second, find a place where you can be alone—away from interruptions and distractions. The good thing about prayer is that you can do it anywhere—a closet, the shower or even in a car. (Just don't close your eyes if you're driving!)

[25] "Be quiet!" said Jesus sternly. "Come out of him!" [26] The evil spirit shook the man violently and came out of him with a shriek.

[27] The people were all so amazed that they asked each other, "What is this? A new teaching—and with authority! He even gives orders to evil spirits and they obey him." [28] News about him spread quickly over the whole region of Galilee.

JESUS HEALS MANY

[29] As soon as they left the synagogue, they went with James and John to the home of Simon and Andrew. [30] Simon's mother-in-law was in bed with a fever, and they told Jesus about her. [31] So he went to her, took her hand and helped her up. The fever left her and she began to wait on them.

[32] That evening after sunset the people brought to Jesus all the sick and demon-possessed. [33] The whole town gathered at the door, [34] and Jesus healed many who had various diseases. He also drove out many demons, but he would not let the demons speak because they knew who he was.

JESUS PRAYS IN A SOLITARY PLACE

[35] Very early in the morning, while it was still dark, Jesus got up, left the house and went off to a solitary place, where he prayed. [36] Simon and his companions went to look for him, [37] and when they found him, they exclaimed: "Everyone is looking for you!"

[38] Jesus replied, "Let us go somewhere else—to the nearby villages—so I can preach there also. That is why I have come." [39] So he traveled throughout Galilee, preaching in their synagogues and driving out demons.

A MAN WITH LEPROSY

[40] A man with leprosy[a] came to him and begged him on his knees, "If you are willing, you can make me clean."

[41] Filled with compassion, Jesus reached out his hand and touched the man. "I am willing," he said. "Be clean!" [42] Immediately the leprosy left him and he was cured.

[43] Jesus sent him away at once with a strong warning: [44] "See that you don't tell this to anyone. But go, show yourself to the priest and offer the sacrifices that Moses commanded for your cleansing, as a testimony to them." [45] Instead he went out and began to talk freely, spreading the news. As a result, Jesus could no longer enter a town openly but stayed outside in lonely places. Yet the people still came to him from everywhere.

challenge notes

MK 1:40-42

To: my_son

heavenly_father: you don't think I've lost my healing touch, do you? when a loved one is suffering, bring that pain and sickness to me. if it's my will, I'll remove it; if not, I will give you my strength and comfort. and someday everyone who believes in me will experience the ultimate healing.

JESUS HEALS A PARALYTIC

2 A few days later, when Jesus again entered Capernaum, the people heard that he had come home. [2] So many gathered that there was no room left, not even outside the door, and he

---

[a] 40 The Greek word was used for various diseases affecting the skin—not necessarily leprosy.

preached the word to them. ³Some men came, bringing to him a paralytic, carried by four of them. ⁴Since they could not get him to Jesus because of the crowd, they made an opening in the roof above Jesus and, after digging through it, lowered the mat the paralyzed man was lying on. ⁵When Jesus saw their faith, he said to the paralytic, "Son, your sins are forgiven."

⁶Now some teachers of the law were sitting there, thinking to themselves, ⁷"Why does this fellow talk like that? He's blaspheming! Who can forgive sins but God alone?"

⁸Immediately Jesus knew in his spirit that this was what they were thinking in their hearts, and he said to them, "Why are you thinking these things? ⁹Which is easier: to say to the paralytic, 'Your sins are forgiven,' or to say, 'Get up, take your mat and walk'? ¹⁰But that you may know that the Son of Man has authority on earth to forgive sins . . ." He said to the paralytic, ¹¹"I tell you, get up, take your mat and go home." ¹²He got up, took his mat and walked out in full view of them all. This amazed everyone and they praised God, saying, "We have never seen anything like this!"

NOW OR NEVER
MK 2:1–5

How far would you be willing to go to help a friend in need? Make sure your friends know they can count on you when they have nowhere else to turn.

THE CALLING OF LEVI

¹³Once again Jesus went out beside the lake. A large crowd came to him, and he began to teach them. ¹⁴As he walked along, he saw Levi son of Alphaeus sitting at the tax collector's booth. "Follow me," Jesus told him, and Levi got up and followed him.

¹⁵While Jesus was having dinner at Levi's house, many tax collectors and "sinners" were eating with him and his disciples, for there were many who followed him. ¹⁶When the teachers of the law who were Pharisees saw him eating with the "sinners" and tax collectors, they asked his disciples: "Why does he eat with tax collectors and 'sinners'?"

¹⁷On hearing this, Jesus said to them, "It is not the healthy who need a doctor, but the sick. I have not come to call the righteous, but sinners."

JESUS QUESTIONED ABOUT FASTING

¹⁸Now John's disciples and the Pharisees were fasting. Some people came and asked Jesus, "How is it that John's disciples and the disciples of the Pharisees are fasting, but yours are not?"

¹⁹Jesus answered, "How can the guests of the bridegroom fast while he is with them? They cannot, so long as they have him with them. ²⁰But the time will come when the bridegroom will be taken from them, and on that day they will fast.

²¹"No one sews a patch of unshrunk cloth on an old garment. If he does, the new piece will pull away from the old, making the tear worse. ²²And no one pours new wine into old wineskins. If he does, the wine will burst the skins, and both the wine and the wineskins will be ruined. No, he pours new wine into new wineskins."

LORD OF THE SABBATH

²³One Sabbath Jesus was going through the grainfields, and as his disciples walked along, they be-

Spreading the News of God's Forgiveness

Which do you think the paralyzed man was more excited about: having his sins forgiven or being able to walk again? What if you were handicapped and lived in a culture in which people thought your disability was a divine punishment for some unknown sin?

Some people struggle their whole lives with feelings of guilt and worthlessness because of things they've done or things that have happened to them. For them, knowing that they're truly forgiven and can escape their guilt once and for all would be a life-changing experience. If you know people who are struggling with guilt, how can you introduce them to God's forgiveness?

gan to pick some heads of grain. 24The Pharisees said to him, "Look, why are they doing what is unlawful on the Sabbath?"

25He answered, "Have you never read what David did when he and his companions were hungry and in need? 26In the days of Abiathar the high priest, he entered the house of God and ate the consecrated bread, which is lawful only for priests to eat. And he also gave some to his companions."

27Then he said to them, "The Sabbath was made for man, not man for the Sabbath. 28So the Son of Man is Lord even of the Sabbath."

3 Another time he went into the synagogue, and a man with a shriveled hand was there. 2Some of them were looking for a reason to accuse Jesus, so they watched him closely to see if he would heal him on the Sabbath. 3Jesus said to the man with the shriveled hand, "Stand up in front of everyone."

4Then Jesus asked them, "Which is lawful on the Sabbath: to do good or to do evil, to save life or to kill?" But they remained silent.

5He looked around at them in anger and, deeply distressed at their stubborn hearts, said to the man, "Stretch out your hand." He stretched it out, and his hand was completely restored. 6Then the Pharisees went out and began to plot with the Herodians how they might kill Jesus.

CROWDS FOLLOW JESUS

7Jesus withdrew with his disciples to the lake, and a large crowd from Galilee followed. 8When they heard all he was doing, many people came to him from Judea, Jerusalem, Idumea, and the regions across the Jordan and around Tyre and Sidon. 9Because of the crowd he told his disciples to have a small boat ready for him, to keep the people from crowding him. 10For he had healed many, so that those with diseases were pushing forward to touch him. 11Whenever the evil[a] spirits saw him, they fell down before him and cried out, "You are the Son of God." 12But he gave them strict orders not to tell who he was.

THE APPOINTING OF THE TWELVE APOSTLES

13Jesus went up on a mountainside and called to him those he wanted, and they came to him. 14He appointed twelve—designating them apostles[b]—that they might be with him and that he might send them out to preach 15and to have authority to drive out demons. 16These are the twelve he appointed: Simon (to whom he gave the name Peter); 17James son of Zebedee and his brother John (to them he gave the name Boanerges, which means Sons of Thunder); 18Andrew, Philip, Bartholomew, Matthew, Thomas, James son of Alphaeus, Thaddaeus, Simon the Zealot 19and Judas Iscariot, who betrayed him.

JESUS AND BEELZEBUB

20Then Jesus entered a house, and again a crowd gathered, so that he and his disciples were not even able to eat. 21When his family heard about this, they went to take charge of him, for they said, "He is out of his mind."

22And the teachers of the law who came down from Jerusalem said, "He is possessed by Beelzebub[c]! By the prince of demons he is driving out demons."

23So Jesus called them and spoke to them in parables: "How can Satan drive out Satan? 24If a kingdom is divided against itself, that kingdom cannot stand. 25If a house is divided against itself, that house cannot stand. 26And if Satan opposes himself and is divided, he cannot stand; his end has come. 27In fact, no one can enter a strong man's house and carry off his possessions unless he first ties up the strong man. Then he can rob his house. 28I tell you the truth, all the sins and blasphemies of men will be forgiven them. 29But whoever blasphemes against the Holy Spirit will never be forgiven; he is guilty of an eternal sin."

30He said this because they were saying, "He has an evil spirit."

JESUS' MOTHER AND BROTHERS

31Then Jesus' mother and brothers arrived. Standing outside, they sent someone in to call him. 32A crowd was sitting around him, and they told him, "Your mother and brothers are outside looking for you."

---

a 11 Greek unclean; also in verse 30   b 14 Some manuscripts do not have designating them apostles.   c 22 Greek Beezeboul or Beelzeboul

33 "Who are my mother and my brothers?" he asked.

34 Then he looked at those seated in a circle around him and said, "Here are my mother and my brothers! 35 Whoever does God's will is my brother and sister and mother."

THE PARABLE OF THE SOWER

NOW OR NEVER

MK 3:35

4 Again Jesus began to teach by the lake. The crowd that gathered around him was so large that he got into a boat and sat in it out on the lake, while all the people were along the shore at the water's edge. 2 He taught them many things by parables, and in his teaching said: 3 "Listen! A farmer went out to sow his seed. 4 As he was scattering the seed, some fell along the path, and the birds came and ate it up. 5 Some fell on rocky places, where it did not have much soil. It sprang up quickly, because the soil was shallow. 6 But when the sun came up, the plants were scorched, and they withered because they had no root. 7 Other seed fell among thorns, which grew up and choked the plants, so that they did not bear grain. 8 Still other seed fell on good soil. It came up, grew and produced a crop, multiplying thirty, sixty, or even a hundred times."

Do you have a couple of close buddies who are like brothers to you? Have you ever thought about what it means to have the kind of relationship with Jesus that you have with your closest friends and family members?

9 Then Jesus said, "He who has ears to hear, let him hear."

10 When he was alone, the Twelve and the others around him asked him about the parables. 11 He told them, "The secret of the kingdom of God has been given to you. But to those on the outside everything is said in parables 12 so that,

> " 'they may be ever seeing but never perceiving,
> and ever hearing but never understanding;
> otherwise they might turn and be forgiven!'[a]"

13 Then Jesus said to them, "Don't you understand this parable? How then will you understand any parable? 14 The farmer sows the word. 15 Some people are like seed along the path, where the word is sown. As soon as they hear it, Satan comes and takes away the word that was sown in them. 16 Others, like seed sown on rocky places, hear the word and at once receive it with joy. 17 But since they have no root, they last only a short time. When trouble or persecution comes because of the word, they quickly fall away. 18 Still others, like seed sown among thorns, hear the word; 19 but the worries of this life, the deceitfulness of wealth and the desires for other things come in and choke the word, making it unfruitful. 20 Others, like seed sown on good soil, hear the word, accept it, and produce a crop—thirty, sixty or even a hundred times what was sown."

A LAMP ON A STAND

21 He said to them, "Do you bring in a lamp to put it under a bowl or a bed? Instead, don't you put it on its stand? 22 For whatever is hidden is meant to be disclosed, and whatever is concealed is meant to be brought out into the open. 23 If anyone has ears to hear, let him hear."

24 "Consider carefully what you hear," he continued. "With the measure you use, it will be measured to you—and even more. 25 Whoever has will be given more; whoever does not have, even what he has will be taken from him."

THE PARABLE OF THE GROWING SEED

26 He also said, "This is what the kingdom of God is like. A man scatters seed on the ground. 27 Night and day, whether he sleeps or gets up, the seed sprouts and grows, though he does not know how. 28 All by itself the soil produces grain—first the stalk, then the head, then the full kernel in the head. 29 As soon as the grain is ripe, he puts the sickle to it, because the harvest has come."

---

a 12 Isaiah 6:9,10

THE PARABLE OF THE MUSTARD SEED

[30] Again he said, "What shall we say the kingdom of God is like, or what parable shall we use to describe it? [31] It is like a mustard seed, which is the smallest seed you plant in the ground. [32] Yet when planted, it grows and becomes the largest of all garden plants, with such big branches that the birds of the air can perch in its shade."

[33] With many similar parables Jesus spoke the word to them, as much as they could understand. [34] He did not say anything to them without using a parable. But when he was alone with his own disciples, he explained everything.

JESUS CALMS THE STORM

[35] That day when evening came, he said to his disciples, "Let us go over to the other side." [36] Leaving the crowd behind, they took him along, just as he was, in the boat. There were also other boats with him. [37] A furious squall came up, and the waves broke over the boat, so that it was nearly swamped. [38] Jesus was in the stern, sleeping on a cushion. The disciples woke him and said to him, "Teacher, don't you care if we drown?"

[39] He got up, rebuked the wind and said to the waves, "Quiet! Be still!" Then the wind died down and it was completely calm.

[40] He said to his disciples, "Why are you so afraid? Do you still have no faith?"

[41] They were terrified and asked each other, "Who is this? Even the wind and the waves obey him!"

THE HEALING OF A DEMON-POSSESSED MAN

5 They went across the lake to the region of the Gerasenes.[a] [2] When Jesus got out of the boat, a man with an evil[b] spirit came from the tombs to meet him. [3] This man lived in the tombs, and no one could bind him any more, not even with a chain. [4] For he had often been chained hand and foot, but he tore the chains apart and broke the irons on his feet. No one was strong enough to subdue him. [5] Night and day among the tombs and in the hills he would cry out and cut himself with stones.

[6] When he saw Jesus from a distance, he ran and fell on his knees in front of him. [7] He shouted at the top of his voice, "What do you want with me, Jesus, Son of the Most High God? Swear to God that you won't torture me!" [8] For Jesus had said to him, "Come out of this man, you evil spirit!"

[9] Then Jesus asked him, "What is your name?"

"My name is Legion," he replied, "for we are many." [10] And he begged Jesus again and again not to send them out of the area.

[11] A large herd of pigs was feeding on the nearby hillside. [12] The demons begged Jesus, "Send us among the pigs; allow us to go into them." [13] He gave them permission, and the evil spirits came out and went into the pigs. The herd, about two thousand in number, rushed down the steep bank into the lake and were drowned.

[14] Those tending the pigs ran off and reported this in the town and countryside, and the people went out to see what had happened. [15] When they came to Jesus, they saw the man who had been possessed by the legion of demons, sitting there, dressed and in his right mind; and they were afraid. [16] Those who had seen it told the people what had happened to the demon-possessed man—and told about the pigs as well. [17] Then the people began to plead with Jesus to leave their region.

[18] As Jesus was getting into the boat, the man who had been demon-possessed begged to go with him. [19] Jesus did not let him, but said, "Go home to your family and tell them how much the Lord has

---

Helping Others Understand God's Word

Let's face it: The Bible isn't always easy to understand. Even the disciples had a tough time comprehending some of Jesus' teachings. For some people, making sense of the Bible is an obstacle that keeps them from exploring a relationship with Jesus. They figure they can't understand it, so why bother trying? Find ways to explain the Good News to others and make the Bible a little less intimidating for them. Often it takes time to fully understand God's truth. Help people along the way—like Jesus did for his disciples—by making the Bible a regular part of your conversations with friends.

---

[a] 1 Some manuscripts *Gadarenes*; other manuscripts *Gergesenes*   [b] 2 Greek *unclean*; also in verses 8 and 13

done for you, and how he has had mercy on you." ²⁰So the man went away and began to tell in the Decapolis[a] how much Jesus had done for him. And all the people were amazed.

A DEAD GIRL AND A SICK WOMAN

²¹When Jesus had again crossed over by boat to the other side of the lake, a large crowd gathered around him while he was by the lake. ²²Then one of the synagogue rulers, named Jairus, came there. Seeing Jesus, he fell at his feet ²³and pleaded earnestly with him, "My little daughter is dying. Please come and put your hands on her so that she will be healed and live." ²⁴So Jesus went with him.

A large crowd followed and pressed around him. ²⁵And a woman was there who had been subject to bleeding for twelve years. ²⁶She had suffered a great deal under the care of many doctors and had spent all she had, yet instead of getting better she grew worse. ²⁷When she heard about Jesus, she came up behind him in the crowd and touched his cloak, ²⁸because she thought, "If I just touch his clothes, I will be healed." ²⁹Immediately her bleeding stopped and she felt in her body that she was freed from her suffering.

³⁰At once Jesus realized that power had gone out from him. He turned around in the crowd and asked, "Who touched my clothes?"

³¹"You see the people crowding against you," his disciples answered, "and yet you can ask, 'Who touched me?' "

³²But Jesus kept looking around to see who had done it. ³³Then the woman, knowing what had happened to her, came and fell at his feet and, trembling with fear, told him the whole truth. ³⁴He said to her, "Daughter, your faith has healed you. Go in peace and be freed from your suffering."

³⁵While Jesus was still speaking, some men came from the house of Jairus, the synagogue ruler. "Your daughter is dead," they said. "Why bother the teacher any more?"

³⁶Ignoring what they said, Jesus told the synagogue ruler, "Don't be afraid; just believe."

³⁷He did not let anyone follow him except Peter, James and John the brother of James. ³⁸When they came to the home of the synagogue ruler, Jesus saw a commotion, with people crying and wailing loudly. ³⁹He went in and said to them, "Why all this commotion and wailing? The child is not dead but asleep." ⁴⁰But they laughed at him.

After he put them all out, he took the child's father and mother and the disciples who were with him, and went in where the child was. ⁴¹He took her by the hand and said to her, *"Talitha koum!"* (which means, "Little girl, I say to you, get up!"). ⁴²Immediately the girl stood up and walked around (she was twelve years old). At this they were completely astonished. ⁴³He gave strict orders not to let anyone know about this, and told them to give her something to eat.

A PROPHET WITHOUT HONOR

6 Jesus left there and went to his hometown, accompanied by his disciples. ²When the Sabbath came, he began to teach in the synagogue, and many who heard him were amazed.

"Where did this man get these things?" they asked. "What's this wisdom that has been given him, that he even does miracles! ³Isn't this the carpenter? Isn't this Mary's son and the brother of James, Joseph,[b] Judas and Simon? Aren't his sisters here with us?" And they took offense at him.

⁴Jesus said to them, "Only in his hometown, among his relatives and in his own house is a prophet without honor." ⁵He could not do any miracles there, except lay his hands on a few sick people and heal them. ⁶And he was amazed at their lack of faith.

NOW OR NEVER
MK 6:6

Isn't it amazing that the people who knew Jesus the longest—the old lady next door, the local shopkeeper—were most skeptical about his claims of being the Son of God? Maybe it's because they thought they understood him completely and had nothing else to learn from him. Do you ever think that?

JESUS SENDS OUT THE TWELVE

Then Jesus went around teaching from village to village. ⁷Calling the Twelve to him, he sent them out two by two and gave them authority over evil[c] spirits.

ᵃ 20 That is, the Ten Cities   ᵇ 3 Greek *Joses*, a variant of *Joseph*   ᶜ 7 Greek *unclean*

battlelines

» *Cardboard Houses (Poverty)*

Q: What's with the old beat-up shoes? Didn't you just buy a new pair of Nikes?
A: I, um . . . don't have them anymore.

Q: What? Those were brand-new Nikes! What happened?
A: Well, you know that mission trip I went on over spring break—the one to Mexico?

Q: Yeah?
A: Well, we went to this poor village near Tijuana.

Q: Don't tell me somebody stole your shoes!
A: No. We went down there to build houses for people. Man, you should see what they live in—it's unbelievable! Cardboard boxes. Old scraps of tin and plywood nailed together. Everywhere you looked there were little kids in ragged, dirty clothes. It was pretty grim.

Q: So what happened to the shoes?
A: One night we're giving away old clothes to people from the village. And there's this one kid—he was about 13—who had been telling one of our interpreters all day that all he wanted was a pair of shoes. So he's at the end of the line, and by the time he gets up to the table, there aren't any shoes left. And he starts getting all teary eyed.

Q: You didn't.
A: Well, what was I supposed to do? I'm looking down at his bare, dirty feet, and then I look at my brand-new shoes. And, I've got—what, probably six pairs of shoes? His feet looked about the same size as mine.

Q: So you gave him your Nikes?
A: I can't explain it. Suddenly I just didn't want them anymore. It made more sense for him to have them.

Q: Dude, you're a living saint!
A: Hey, I'm just glad I went on the trip. Now that I'm back, it almost makes me sick to see how much time I spend thinking about how to get more stuff. Now I can see how blessed I really am.

Q: You'll get over it in a week or so.
A: I sure hope not.

» *Greedy vs. Needy*

When we're surrounded by greed, it's easy to become greedy ourselves. Most of the time we're not even aware of how materialistic we are. But when we're surrounded by need, our greed becomes obvious, and that can make us feel guilty—even a bit ashamed. (Maybe that's why so many of us change the channel when we're confronted with scenes of starving children on TV.)

You'd think that guilt and shame would be enough to spur most people to action. But it's not. For one thing, most people like their materialistic lifestyles. They're comfortable with the pursuit of things. Besides, they argue, what difference can one person's efforts make in the face of so much poverty?

Someone once said, "Don't let what you cannot do interfere with what you can do!" It's true that you can't clothe and feed the whole world. But you *can* help one person. Take a cue from Julian. Step out of your comfort zone. Look into the eyes of those who have little or nothing. Then give whatever you've got. You'll discover that Jesus wasn't just pulling our leg when he said it's more fulfilling to give than to receive (see Acts 20:35).

Discover ways you can reach out to others at www.RevolutionBible.com.

8These were his instructions: "Take nothing for the journey except a staff—no bread, no bag, no money in your belts. 9Wear sandals but not an extra tunic. 10Whenever you enter a house, stay there until you leave that town. 11And if any place will not welcome you or listen to you, shake the dust off your feet when you leave, as a testimony against them."

12They went out and preached that people should repent. 13They drove out many demons and anointed many sick people with oil and healed them.

JOHN THE BAPTIST BEHEADED

14King Herod heard about this, for Jesus' name had become well known. Some were saying,[a] "John the Baptist has been raised from the dead, and that is why miraculous powers are at work in him."

15Others said, "He is Elijah."

And still others claimed, "He is a prophet, like one of the prophets of long ago."

16But when Herod heard this, he said, "John, the man I beheaded, has been raised from the dead!"

17For Herod himself had given orders to have John arrested, and he had him bound and put in prison. He did this because of Herodias, his brother Philip's wife, whom he had married. 18For John had been saying to Herod, "It is not lawful for you to have your brother's wife." 19So Herodias nursed a grudge against John and wanted to kill him. But she was not able to, 20because Herod feared John and protected him, knowing him to be a righteous and holy man. When Herod heard John, he was greatly puzzled[b]; yet he liked to listen to him.

21Finally the opportune time came. On his birthday Herod gave a banquet for his high officials and military commanders and the leading men of Galilee. 22When the daughter of Herodias came in and danced, she pleased Herod and his dinner guests.

The king said to the girl, "Ask me for anything you want, and I'll give it to you." 23And he promised her with an oath, "Whatever you ask I will give you, up to half my kingdom."

24She went out and said to her mother, "What shall I ask for?"

"The head of John the Baptist," she answered.

25At once the girl hurried in to the king with the request: "I want you to give me right now the head of John the Baptist on a platter."

26The king was greatly distressed, but because of his oaths and his dinner guests, he did not want to refuse her. 27So he immediately sent an executioner with orders to bring John's head. The man went, beheaded John in the prison, 28and brought back his head on a platter. He presented it to the girl, and she gave it to her mother. 29On hearing of this, John's disciples came and took his body and laid it in a tomb.

NOW OR NEVER
MK 6:27–28

Thousands of people are killed every year because of their faith in Jesus. Take advantage of—but don't take lightly—the religious freedom you enjoy. Spread the good news about Jesus to as many people as you possibly can. You have an opportunity that others literally die for.

JESUS FEEDS THE FIVE THOUSAND

30The apostles gathered around Jesus and reported to him all they had done and taught. 31Then, because so many people were coming and going that they did not even have a chance to eat, he said to them, "Come with me by yourselves to a quiet place and get some rest."

32So they went away by themselves in a boat to a solitary place. 33But many who saw them leaving recognized them and ran on foot from all the towns and got there ahead of them. 34When Jesus landed and saw a large crowd, he had compassion on them, because they were like sheep without a shepherd. So he began teaching them many things.

35By this time it was late in the day, so his disciples came to him. "This is a remote place," they said, "and it's already very late. 36Send the people away so they can go to the surrounding countryside and villages and buy themselves something to eat."

37But he answered, "You give them something to eat."

They said to him, "That would take eight months of a man's wages[c]! Are we to go and spend that much on bread and give it to them to eat?"

---

[a] 14 Some early manuscripts He was saying   [b] 20 Some early manuscripts he did many things   [c] 37 Greek take two hundred denarii

[38]"How many loaves do you have?" he asked. "Go and see."

When they found out, they said, "Five—and two fish."

[39]Then Jesus directed them to have all the people sit down in groups on the green grass. [40]So they sat down in groups of hundreds and fifties. [41]Taking the five loaves and the two fish and looking up to heaven, he gave thanks and broke the loaves. Then he gave them to his disciples to set before the people. He also divided the two fish among them all. [42]They all ate and were satisfied, [43]and the disciples picked up twelve basketfuls of broken pieces of bread and fish. [44]The number of the men who had eaten was five thousand.

JESUS WALKS ON THE WATER

[45]Immediately Jesus made his disciples get into the boat and go on ahead of him to Bethsaida, while he dismissed the crowd. [46]After leaving them, he went up on a mountainside to pray.

[47]When evening came, the boat was in the middle of the lake, and he was alone on land. [48]He saw the disciples straining at the oars, because the wind was against them. About the fourth watch of the night he went out to them, walking on the lake. He was about to pass by them, [49]but when they saw him walking on the lake, they thought he was a ghost. They cried out, [50]because they all saw him and were terrified.

Immediately he spoke to them and said, "Take courage! It is I. Don't be afraid." [51]Then he climbed into the boat with them, and the wind died down. They were completely amazed, [52]for they had not understood about the loaves; their hearts were hardened.

[53]When they had crossed over, they landed at Gennesaret and anchored there. [54]As soon as they got out of the boat, people recognized Jesus. [55]They ran throughout that whole region and carried the sick on mats to wherever they heard he was. [56]And wherever he went—into villages, towns or countryside—they placed the sick in the marketplaces. They begged him to let them touch even the edge of his cloak, and all who touched him were healed.

CLEAN AND UNCLEAN

7 The Pharisees and some of the teachers of the law who had come from Jerusalem gathered around Jesus and [2]saw some of his disciples eating food with hands that were "unclean," that is, unwashed. [3](The Pharisees and all the Jews do not eat unless they give their hands a ceremonial washing, holding to the tradition of the elders. [4]When they come from the marketplace they do not eat unless they wash. And they observe many other traditions, such as the washing of cups, pitchers and kettles.[a])

[5]So the Pharisees and teachers of the law asked Jesus, "Why don't your disciples live according to the tradition of the elders instead of eating their food with 'unclean' hands?"

[6]He replied, "Isaiah was right when he prophesied about you hypocrites; as it is written:

NOW OR NEVER

MK 7:8

Do you ever argue with your parents about what a Christian shouldn't do . . . or wear . . . or watch . . . or listen to? Where do you draw the line in each of these areas? How do you tell the difference between mere human rules and ultimate principles or standards to live by?

" 'These people honor me with their lips,
  but their hearts are far from me.
[7]They worship me in vain;
  their teachings are but rules taught by men.'[b]

[8]You have let go of the commands of God and are holding on to the traditions of men."

[9]And he said to them: "You have a fine way of setting aside the commands of God in order to observe[c] your own traditions! [10]For Moses said, 'Honor your father and your mother,'[d] and, 'Anyone who curses his father or mother must be put to death.'[e] [11]But you say that if a man says to his father or mother: 'Whatever help you might otherwise have received from me is Corban' (that is, a gift devoted to God),

---

[a] 4 Some early manuscripts *pitchers, kettles and dining couches*   [b] 6,7 Isaiah 29:13   [c] 9 Some manuscripts *set up*
[d] 10 Exodus 20:12; Deut. 5:16   [e] 10 Exodus 21:17; Lev. 20:9

¹²then you no longer let him do anything for his father or mother. ¹³Thus you nullify the word of God by your tradition that you have handed down. And you do many things like that."

¹⁴Again Jesus called the crowd to him and said, "Listen to me, everyone, and understand this. ¹⁵Nothing outside a man can make him 'unclean' by going into him. Rather, it is what comes out of a man that makes him 'unclean.'ᵃ"

¹⁷After he had left the crowd and entered the house, his disciples asked him about this parable. ¹⁸"Are you so dull?" he asked. "Don't you see that nothing that enters a man from the outside can make him 'unclean'? ¹⁹For it doesn't go into his heart but into his stomach, and then out of his body." (In saying this, Jesus declared all foods "clean.")

²⁰He went on: "What comes out of a man is what makes him 'unclean.' ²¹For from within, out of men's hearts, come evil thoughts, sexual immorality, theft, murder, adultery, ²²greed, malice, deceit, lewdness, envy, slander, arrogance and folly. ²³All these evils come from inside and make a man 'unclean.'"

THE FAITH OF A SYROPHOENICIAN WOMAN

²⁴Jesus left that place and went to the vicinity of Tyre.ᵇ He entered a house and did not want anyone to know it; yet he could not keep his presence secret. ²⁵In fact, as soon as she heard about him, a woman whose little daughter was possessed by an evilᶜ spirit came and fell at his feet. ²⁶The woman was a Greek, born in Syrian Phoenicia. She begged Jesus to drive the demon out of her daughter.

²⁷"First let the children eat all they want," he told her, "for it is not right to take the children's bread and toss it to their dogs."

²⁸"Yes, Lord," she replied, "but even the dogs under the table eat the children's crumbs."

²⁹Then he told her, "For such a reply, you may go; the demon has left your daughter."

³⁰She went home and found her child lying on the bed, and the demon gone.

THE HEALING OF A DEAF AND MUTE MAN

³¹Then Jesus left the vicinity of Tyre and went through Sidon, down to the Sea of Galilee and into the region of the Decapolis.ᵈ ³²There some people brought to him a man who was deaf and could hardly talk, and they begged him to place his hand on the man.

³³After he took him aside, away from the crowd, Jesus put his fingers into the man's ears. Then he spit and touched the man's tongue. ³⁴He looked up to heaven and with a deep sigh said to him, *"Ephphatha!"* (which means, "Be opened!"). ³⁵At this, the man's ears were opened, his tongue was loosened and he began to speak plainly.

³⁶Jesus commanded them not to tell anyone. But the more he did so, the more they kept talking about it. ³⁷People were overwhelmed with amazement. "He has done everything well," they said. "He even makes the deaf hear and the mute speak."

JESUS FEEDS THE FOUR THOUSAND

8 During those days another large crowd gathered. Since they had nothing to eat, Jesus called his disciples to him and said, ²"I have compassion for these people; they have already been with me three days and have nothing to eat. ³If I send them home hungry, they will collapse on the way, because some of them have come a long distance."

⁴His disciples answered, "But where in this remote place can anyone get enough bread to feed them?"

⁵"How many loaves do you have?" Jesus asked.

"Seven," they replied.

⁶He told the crowd to sit down on the ground. When he had taken the seven loaves and given thanks, he broke them and gave them to his disciples to set before the people, and they did so. ⁷They had a few small fish as well; he gave thanks for them also and told the disciples to distribute them. ⁸The people ate and were satisfied. Afterward the disciples picked up seven basketfuls of broken pieces that were left over. ⁹About four thousand men were present. And having sent them away, ¹⁰he got into the boat with his disciples and went to the region of Dalmanutha.

¹¹The Pharisees came and began to question Jesus. To test him, they asked him for a sign from

---

ᵃ *15 Some early manuscripts 'unclean.' ¹⁶If anyone has ears to hear, let him hear.*   ᵇ *24 Many early manuscripts Tyre and Sidon*
ᶜ *25 Greek unclean*   ᵈ *31 That is, the Ten Cities*

heaven. [12]He sighed deeply and said, "Why does this generation ask for a miraculous sign? I tell you the truth, no sign will be given to it." [13]Then he left them, got back into the boat and crossed to the other side.

THE YEAST OF THE PHARISEES AND HEROD

[14]The disciples had forgotten to bring bread, except for one loaf they had with them in the boat. [15]"Be careful," Jesus warned them. "Watch out for the yeast of the Pharisees and that of Herod."

[16]They discussed this with one another and said, "It is because we have no bread."

[17]Aware of their discussion, Jesus asked them: "Why are you talking about having no bread? Do you still not see or understand? Are your hearts hardened? [18]Do you have eyes but fail to see, and ears but fail to hear? And don't you remember? [19]When I broke the five loaves for the five thousand, how many basketfuls of pieces did you pick up?"

"Twelve," they replied.

[20]"And when I broke the seven loaves for the four thousand, how many basketfuls of pieces did you pick up?"

They answered, "Seven."

[21]He said to them, "Do you still not understand?"

THE HEALING OF A BLIND MAN AT BETHSAIDA

[22]They came to Bethsaida, and some people brought a blind man and begged Jesus to touch him. [23]He took the blind man by the hand and led him outside the village. When he had spit on the man's eyes and put his hands on him, Jesus asked, "Do you see anything?"

[24]He looked up and said, "I see people; they look like trees walking around."

[25]Once more Jesus put his hands on the man's eyes. Then his eyes were opened, his sight was restored, and he saw everything clearly. [26]Jesus sent him home, saying, "Don't go into the village. [a]"

PETER'S CONFESSION OF CHRIST

[27]Jesus and his disciples went on to the villages around Caesarea Philippi. On the way he asked them, "Who do people say I am?"

[28]They replied, "Some say John the Baptist; others say Elijah; and still others, one of the prophets."

[29]"But what about you?" he asked. "Who do you say I am?" Peter answered, "You are the Christ. [b]"

[30]Jesus warned them not to tell anyone about him.

JESUS PREDICTS HIS DEATH

[31]He then began to teach them that the Son of Man must suffer many things and be rejected by the elders, chief priests and teachers of the law, and that he must be killed and after three days rise again. [32]He spoke plainly about this, and Peter took him aside and began to rebuke him.

[33]But when Jesus turned and looked at his disciples, he rebuked Peter. "Get behind me, Satan!" he said. "You do not have in mind the things of God, but the things of men."

[34]Then he called the crowd to him along with his disciples and said: "If anyone would come after me, he must deny himself and take up his cross and follow me. [35]For whoever wants

---

[a] *26* Some manuscripts *Don't go and tell anyone in the village*   [b] *29* Or *Messiah*. "The Christ" (Greek) and "the Messiah" (Hebrew) both mean "the Anointed One."

to save his life[a] will lose it, but whoever loses his life for me and for the gospel will save it. 36What good is it for a man to gain the whole world, yet forfeit his soul? 37Or what can a man give in exchange for his soul? 38If anyone is ashamed of me and my words in this adulterous and sinful generation, the Son of Man will be ashamed of him when he comes in his Father's glory with the holy angels."

9

And he said to them, "I tell you the truth, some who are standing here will not taste death before they see the kingdom of God come with power."

THE TRANSFIGURATION

2After six days Jesus took Peter, James and John with him and led them up a high mountain, where they were all alone. There he was transfigured before them. 3His clothes became dazzling white, whiter than anyone in the world could bleach them. 4And there appeared before them Elijah and Moses, who were talking with Jesus.

5Peter said to Jesus, "Rabbi, it is good for us to be here. Let us put up three shelters—one for you, one for Moses and one for Elijah." 6(He did not know what to say, they were so frightened.)

7Then a cloud appeared and enveloped them, and a voice came from the cloud: "This is my Son, whom I love. Listen to him!"

8Suddenly, when they looked around, they no longer saw anyone with them except Jesus.

9As they were coming down the mountain, Jesus gave them orders not to tell anyone what they had seen until the Son of Man had risen from the dead. 10They kept the matter to themselves, discussing what "rising from the dead" meant.

11And they asked him, "Why do the teachers of the law say that Elijah must come first?"

12Jesus replied, "To be sure, Elijah does come first, and restores all things. Why then is it written that the Son of Man must suffer much and be rejected? 13But I tell you, Elijah has come, and they have done to him everything they wished, just as it is written about him."

THE HEALING OF A BOY WITH AN EVIL SPIRIT

14When they came to the other disciples, they saw a large crowd around them and the teachers of the law arguing with them. 15As soon as all the people saw Jesus, they were overwhelmed with wonder and ran to greet him.

16"What are you arguing with them about?" he asked.

17A man in the crowd answered, "Teacher, I brought you my son, who is possessed by a spirit that has robbed him of speech. 18Whenever it seizes him, it throws him to the ground. He foams at the mouth, gnashes his teeth and becomes rigid. I asked your disciples to drive out the spirit, but they could not."

19"O unbelieving generation," Jesus replied, "how long shall I stay with you? How long shall I put up with you? Bring the boy to me."

20So they brought him. When the spirit saw Jesus, it immediately threw the boy into a convulsion. He fell to the ground and rolled around, foaming at the mouth.

21Jesus asked the boy's father, "How long has he been like this?"

"From childhood," he answered. 22"It has often thrown him into fire or water to kill him. But if you can do anything, take pity on us and help us."

23" 'If you can'?" said Jesus. "Everything is possible for him who believes."

24Immediately the boy's father exclaimed, "I do believe; help me overcome my unbelief!"

Overcoming Challenges to Your Faith

No matter how strong your faith is, sooner or later you're going to face a situation that rocks you to your core and makes you question everything you believe about God. It may be the sudden death of a family member, an up-close view of extreme poverty or something you can't even imagine right now. Rather than letting yourself become overwhelmed by doubt, anger or bitterness, do what the desperate father in this Bible story did: Cry out to the Lord and ask for an extra dose of faith to help you get through the difficult times.

---

a 35 The Greek word means either *life* or *soul*; also in verse 36.

25When Jesus saw that a crowd was running to the scene, he rebuked the evil[a] spirit. "You deaf and mute spirit," he said, "I command you, come out of him and never enter him again."

26The spirit shrieked, convulsed him violently and came out. The boy looked so much like a corpse that many said, "He's dead." 27But Jesus took him by the hand and lifted him to his feet, and he stood up.

28After Jesus had gone indoors, his disciples asked him privately, "Why couldn't we drive it out?" 29He replied, "This kind can come out only by prayer.[b]"

30They left that place and passed through Galilee. Jesus did not want anyone to know where they were, 31because he was teaching his disciples. He said to them, "The Son of Man is going to be betrayed into the hands of men. They will kill him, and after three days he will rise." 32But they did not understand what he meant and were afraid to ask him about it.

WHO IS THE GREATEST?

33They came to Capernaum. When he was in the house, he asked them, "What were you arguing about on the road?" 34But they kept quiet because on the way they had argued about who was the greatest.

35Sitting down, Jesus called the Twelve and said, "If anyone wants to be first, he must be the very last, and the servant of all."

36He took a little child and had him stand among them. Taking him in his arms, he said to them, 37"Whoever welcomes one of these little children in my name welcomes me; and whoever welcomes me does not welcome me but the one who sent me."

WHOEVER IS NOT AGAINST US IS FOR US

38"Teacher," said John, "we saw a man driving out demons in your name and we told him to stop, because he was not one of us."

39"Do not stop him," Jesus said. "No one who does a miracle in my name can in the next moment say anything bad about me, 40for whoever is not against us is for us. 41I tell you the truth, anyone who gives you a cup of water in my name because you belong to Christ will certainly not lose his reward.

CAUSING TO SIN

42"And if anyone causes one of these little ones who believe in me to sin, it would be better for him to be thrown into the sea with a large millstone tied around his neck. 43If your hand causes you to sin, cut it off. It is better for you to enter life maimed than with two hands to go into hell, where the fire never goes out.[c] 45And if your foot causes you to sin, cut it off. It is better for you to enter life crippled than to have two feet and be thrown into hell.[d] 47And if your eye causes you to sin, pluck it out. It is better for you to enter the kingdom of God with one eye than to have two eyes and be thrown into hell, 48where

NOW OR NEVER
MK 9:42

Do you have a bad influence in your life—someone who can get you to do things you wouldn't otherwise do? If you're serious about your relationship with God, you need to get rid of that influence—even if it means losing a friendship.

" 'their worm does not die,
   and the fire is not quenched.'[e]

49Everyone will be salted with fire.

50"Salt is good, but if it loses its saltiness, how can you make it salty again? Have salt in yourselves, and be at peace with each other."

DIVORCE

Jesus then left that place and went into the region of Judea and across the Jordan. Again crowds of people came to him, and as was his custom, he taught them.

[a] 25 Greek unclean   [b] 29 Some manuscripts prayer and fasting   [c] 43 Some manuscripts out, 44"where / " 'their worm does not die, / and the fire is not quenched.'   [d] 45 Some manuscripts hell, 46where / " 'their worm does not die, / and the fire is not quenched.'   [e] 48 Isaiah 66:24

²Some Pharisees came and tested him by asking, "Is it lawful for a man to divorce his wife?" ³"What did Moses command you?" he replied.

⁴They said, "Moses permitted a man to write a certificate of divorce and send her away."

⁵"It was because your hearts were hard that Moses wrote you this law," Jesus replied. ⁶"But at the beginning of creation God 'made them male and female.'ᵃ ⁷'For this reason a man will leave his father and mother and be united to his wife,ᵇ ⁸and the two will become one flesh.'ᶜ So they are no longer two, but one. ⁹Therefore what God has joined together, let man not separate."

¹⁰When they were in the house again, the disciples asked Jesus about this. ¹¹He answered, "Anyone who divorces his wife and marries another woman commits adultery against her. ¹²And if she divorces her husband and marries another man, she commits adultery."

THE LITTLE CHILDREN AND JESUS

¹³People were bringing little children to Jesus to have him touch them, but the disciples rebuked them. ¹⁴When Jesus saw this, he was indignant. He said to them, "Let the little children come to me, and do not hinder them, for the kingdom of God belongs to such as these. ¹⁵I tell you the truth, anyone who will not receive the kingdom of God like a little child will never enter it." ¹⁶And he took the children in his arms, put his hands on them and blessed them.

challengenotes

To: my_son

heavenly_father: every possession you have is a gift from me. but never let your heart seek after these gifts in place of a relationship with me. trust me. I will satisfy all of your longings. since before you were even born, I have been storing up for you treasure in heaven.

MK 10:21

THE RICH YOUNG MAN

¹⁷As Jesus started on his way, a man ran up to him and fell on his knees before him. "Good teacher," he asked, "what must I do to inherit eternal life?"

¹⁸"Why do you call me good?" Jesus answered. "No one is good—except God alone. ¹⁹You know the commandments: 'Do not murder, do not commit adultery, do not steal, do not give false testimony, do not defraud, honor your father and mother.'ᵈ"

²⁰"Teacher," he declared, "all these I have kept since I was a boy."

²¹Jesus looked at him and loved him. "One thing you lack," he said. "Go, sell everything you have and give to the poor, and you will have treasure in heaven. Then come, follow me."

²²At this the man's face fell. He went away sad, because he had great wealth.

²³Jesus looked around and said to his disciples, "How hard it is for the rich to enter the kingdom of God!"

²⁴The disciples were amazed at his words. But Jesus said again, "Children, how hard it isᵉ to enter the kingdom of God! ²⁵It is easier for a camel to go through the eye of a needle than for a rich man to enter the kingdom of God."

²⁶The disciples were even more amazed, and said to each other, "Who then can be saved?"

²⁷Jesus looked at them and said, "With man this is impossible, but not with God; all things are possible with God."

²⁸Peter said to him, "We have left everything to follow you!"

²⁹"I tell you the truth," Jesus replied, "no one who has left home or brothers or sisters or mother or father or children or fields for me and the gospel ³⁰will fail to receive a hundred times as much in this present age (homes, brothers, sisters, mothers, children and fields—and with them, persecutions) and in the age to come, eternal life. ³¹But many who are first will be last, and the last first."

now or never

MK 10:22

The rich man allowed money to come between him and a relationship with Jesus. What is your biggest obstacle to living the kind of life the Lord has designed for you?

ᵃ 6 Gen. 1:27   ᵇ 7 Some early manuscripts do not have and be united to his wife.   ᶜ 8 Gen. 2:24   ᵈ 19 Exodus 20:12-16; Deut. 5:16-20   ᵉ 24 Some manuscripts is for those who trust in riches

JESUS AGAIN PREDICTS HIS DEATH

³²They were on their way up to Jerusalem, with Jesus leading the way, and the disciples were astonished, while those who followed were afraid. Again he took the Twelve aside and told them what was going to happen to him. ³³"We are going up to Jerusalem," he said, "and the Son of Man will be betrayed to the chief priests and teachers of the law. They will condemn him to death and will hand him over to the Gentiles, ³⁴who will mock him and spit on him, flog him and kill him. Three days later he will rise."

THE REQUEST OF JAMES AND JOHN

³⁵Then James and John, the sons of Zebedee, came to him. "Teacher," they said, "we want you to do for us whatever we ask."

³⁶"What do you want me to do for you?" he asked.

³⁷They replied, "Let one of us sit at your right and the other at your left in your glory."

³⁸"You don't know what you are asking," Jesus said. "Can you drink the cup I drink or be baptized with the baptism I am baptized with?"

³⁹"We can," they answered.

Jesus said to them, "You will drink the cup I drink and be baptized with the baptism I am baptized with, ⁴⁰but to sit at my right or left is not for me to grant. These places belong to those for whom they have been prepared."

⁴¹When the ten heard about this, they became indignant with James and John. ⁴²Jesus called them together and said, "You know that those who are regarded as rulers of the Gentiles lord it over them, and their high officials exercise authority over them. ⁴³Not so with you. Instead, whoever wants to become great among you must be your servant, ⁴⁴and whoever wants to be first must be slave of all. ⁴⁵For even the Son of Man did not come to be served, but to serve, and to give his life as a ransom for many."

BLIND BARTIMAEUS RECEIVES HIS SIGHT

⁴⁶Then they came to Jericho. As Jesus and his disciples, together with a large crowd, were leaving the city, a blind man, Bartimaeus (that is, the Son of Timaeus), was sitting by the roadside begging. ⁴⁷When he heard that it was Jesus of Nazareth, he began to shout, "Jesus, Son of David, have mercy on me!"

⁴⁸Many rebuked him and told him to be quiet, but he shouted all the more, "Son of David, have mercy on me!"

⁴⁹Jesus stopped and said, "Call him."

So they called to the blind man, "Cheer up! On your feet! He's calling you." ⁵⁰Throwing his cloak aside, he jumped to his feet and came to Jesus.

⁵¹"What do you want me to do for you?" Jesus asked him.

The blind man said, "Rabbi, I want to see."

⁵²"Go," said Jesus, "your faith has healed you." Immediately he received his sight and followed Jesus along the road.

THE TRIUMPHAL ENTRY

11 As they approached Jerusalem and came to Bethphage and Bethany at the Mount of Olives, Jesus sent two of his disciples, ²saying to them, "Go to the village ahead of you, and just as you enter it, you will find a colt tied there, which no one has ever ridden. Untie it and bring it here. ³If anyone asks you, 'Why are you doing this?' tell him, 'The Lord needs it and will send it back here shortly.' "

⁴They went and found a colt outside in the street, tied at a doorway. As they untied it, ⁵some people standing there asked, "What are you doing, untying that colt?" ⁶They answered as Jesus had told them to, and the people let them go. ⁷When they brought the colt to Jesus and threw their cloaks over it, he sat on it. ⁸Many people spread their cloaks on the road, while others spread branches they had cut in the fields. ⁹Those who went ahead and those who followed shouted,

"Hosanna!ᵃ"

"Blessed is he who comes in the name of the Lord!"ᵇ

ᵃ 9 A Hebrew expression meaning "Save!" which became an exclamation of praise; also in verse 10   ᵇ 9 Psalm 118:25,26

[10] "Blessed is the coming kingdom of our father David!"

"Hosanna in the highest!"

[11] Jesus entered Jerusalem and went to the temple. He looked around at everything, but since it was already late, he went out to Bethany with the Twelve.

JESUS CLEARS THE TEMPLE

[12] The next day as they were leaving Bethany, Jesus was hungry. [13] Seeing in the distance a fig tree in leaf, he went to find out if it had any fruit. When he reached it, he found nothing but leaves, because it was not the season for figs. [14] Then he said to the tree, "May no one ever eat fruit from you again." And his disciples heard him say it.

[15] On reaching Jerusalem, Jesus entered the temple area and began driving out those who were buying and selling there. He overturned the tables of the money changers and the benches of those selling doves, [16] and would not allow anyone to carry merchandise through the temple courts. [17] And as he taught them, he said, "Is it not written:

" 'My house will be called
    a house of prayer for all nations'[a]?

But you have made it 'a den of robbers.'[b]"

[18] The chief priests and the teachers of the law heard this and began looking for a way to kill him, for they feared him, because the whole crowd was amazed at his teaching.

[19] When evening came, they[c] went out of the city.

THE WITHERED FIG TREE

[20] In the morning, as they went along, they saw the fig tree withered from the roots. [21] Peter remembered and said to Jesus, "Rabbi, look! The fig tree you cursed has withered!"

[22] "Have[d] faith in God," Jesus answered. [23] "I tell you the truth, if anyone says to this mountain, 'Go, throw yourself into the sea,' and does not doubt in his heart but believes that what he says will happen, it will be done for him. [24] Therefore I tell you, whatever you ask for in prayer, believe that you have received it, and it will be yours. [25] And when you stand praying, if you hold anything against anyone, forgive him, so that your Father in heaven may forgive you your sins.[e]"

THE AUTHORITY OF JESUS QUESTIONED

[27] They arrived again in Jerusalem, and while Jesus was walking in the temple courts, the chief priests, the teachers of the law and the elders came to him. [28] "By what authority are you doing these things?" they asked. "And who gave you authority to do this?"

[29] Jesus replied, "I will ask you one question. Answer me, and I will tell you by what authority I am doing these things. [30] John's baptism—was it from heaven, or from men? Tell me!"

[31] They discussed it among themselves and said, "If we say, 'From heaven,' he will ask, 'Then why didn't you believe him?' [32] But if we say, 'From men' . . ." (They feared the people, for everyone held that John really was a prophet.)

[33] So they answered Jesus, "We don't know."

Jesus said, "Neither will I tell you by what authority I am doing these things."

THE PARABLE OF THE TENANTS

12 He then began to speak to them in parables: "A man planted a vineyard. He put a wall around it, dug a pit for the winepress and built a watchtower. Then he rented the vineyard to some farmers and went away on a journey. [2] At harvest time he sent a servant to the tenants to collect from them some of the fruit of the vineyard. [3] But they seized him, beat him and sent him away empty-handed. [4] Then he sent another servant to them; they struck this man on the head and treated him shamefully. [5] He sent still another, and that one they killed. He sent many others; some of them they beat, others they killed.

---

[a] 17 Isaiah 56:7   [b] 17 Jer. 7:11   [c] 19 Some early manuscripts he   [d] 22 Some early manuscripts If you have   [e] 25 Some manuscripts sins. 26But if you do not forgive, neither will your Father who is in heaven forgive your sins.

⁶"He had one left to send, a son, whom he loved. He sent him last of all, saying, 'They will respect my son.'

⁷"But the tenants said to one another, 'This is the heir. Come, let's kill him, and the inheritance will be ours.' ⁸So they took him and killed him, and threw him out of the vineyard.

⁹"What then will the owner of the vineyard do? He will come and kill those tenants and give the vineyard to others. ¹⁰Haven't you read this scripture:

" 'The stone the builders rejected
    has become the capstone[a];
¹¹the Lord has done this,
    and it is marvelous in our eyes'[b]?"

¹²Then they looked for a way to arrest him because they knew he had spoken the parable against them. But they were afraid of the crowd; so they left him and went away.

PAYING TAXES TO CAESAR

¹³Later they sent some of the Pharisees and Herodians to Jesus to catch him in his words. ¹⁴They came to him and said, "Teacher, we know you are a man of integrity. You aren't swayed by men, because you pay no attention to who they are; but you teach the way of God in accordance with the truth. Is it right to pay taxes to Caesar or not? ¹⁵Should we pay or shouldn't we?"

But Jesus knew their hypocrisy. "Why are you trying to trap me?" he asked. "Bring me a denarius and let me look at it." ¹⁶They brought the coin, and he asked them, "Whose portrait is this? And whose inscription?"

"Caesar's," they replied.

¹⁷Then Jesus said to them, "Give to Caesar what is Caesar's and to God what is God's."

And they were amazed at him.

MARRIAGE AT THE RESURRECTION

¹⁸Then the Sadducees, who say there is no resurrection, came to him with a question. ¹⁹"Teacher," they said, "Moses wrote for us that if a man's brother dies and leaves a wife but no children, the man must marry the widow and have children for his brother. ²⁰Now there were seven brothers. The first one married and died without leaving any children. ²¹The second one married the widow, but he also died, leaving no child. It was the same with the third. ²²In fact, none of the seven left any children. Last of all, the woman died too. ²³At the resurrection[c] whose wife will she be, since the seven were married to her?"

²⁴Jesus replied, "Are you not in error because you do not know the Scriptures or the power of God? ²⁵When the dead rise, they will neither marry nor be given in marriage; they will be like the angels in heaven. ²⁶Now about the dead rising—have you not read in the book of Moses, in the account of the bush, how God said to him, 'I am the God of Abraham, the God of Isaac, and the God of Jacob'[d]? ²⁷He is not the God of the dead, but of the living. You are badly mistaken!"

THE GREATEST COMMANDMENT

²⁸One of the teachers of the law came and heard them debating. Noticing that Jesus had given them a good answer, he asked him, "Of all the commandments, which is the most important?"

²⁹"The most important one," answered Jesus, "is this: 'Hear, O Israel, the Lord our God, the Lord is one.[e] ³⁰Love the Lord your God with all your heart and with all your soul and with all your mind and with all your strength.'[f] ³¹The second is this: 'Love your neighbor as yourself.'[g] There is no commandment greater than these."

³²"Well said, teacher," the man replied. "You are right in saying that God is one and there is no other but him. ³³To love him with all your heart, with all your understanding and with all your strength, and to love your neighbor as yourself is more important than all burnt offerings and sacrifices."

³⁴When Jesus saw that he had answered wisely, he said to him, "You are not far from the kingdom of God." And from then on no one dared ask him any more questions.

---

[a] 10 Or cornerstone   [b] 11 Psalm 118:22,23   [c] 23 Some manuscripts resurrection, when men rise from the dead,   [d] 26 Exodus 3:6
[e] 29 Or the Lord our God is one Lord   [f] 30 Deut. 6:4,5   [g] 31 Lev. 19:18

WHOSE SON IS THE CHRIST?

[35]While Jesus was teaching in the temple courts, he asked, "How is it that the teachers of the law say that the Christ[a] is the son of David? [36]David himself, speaking by the Holy Spirit, declared:

" 'The Lord said to my Lord:
"Sit at my right hand
until I put your enemies
under your feet." '[b]

[37]David himself calls him 'Lord.' How then can he be his son?"

The large crowd listened to him with delight.

[38]As he taught, Jesus said, "Watch out for the teachers of the law. They like to walk around in flowing robes and be greeted in the marketplaces, [39]and have the most important seats in the synagogues and the places of honor at banquets. [40]They devour widows' houses and for a show make lengthy prayers. Such men will be punished most severely."

THE WIDOW'S OFFERING

[41]Jesus sat down opposite the place where the offerings were put and watched the crowd putting their money into the temple treasury. Many rich people threw in large amounts. [42]But a poor widow came and put in two very small copper coins,[c] worth only a fraction of a penny.[d]

[43]Calling his disciples to him, Jesus said, "I tell you the truth, this poor widow has put more into the treasury than all the others. [44]They all gave out of their wealth; but she, out of her poverty, put in everything—all she had to live on."

SIGNS OF THE END OF THE AGE

13 As he was leaving the temple, one of his disciples said to him, "Look, Teacher! What massive stones! What magnificent buildings!"

[2]"Do you see all these great buildings?" replied Jesus. "Not one stone here will be left on another; every one will be thrown down."

[3]As Jesus was sitting on the Mount of Olives opposite the temple, Peter, James, John and Andrew asked him privately, [4]"Tell us, when will these things happen? And what will be the sign that they are all about to be fulfilled?"

[5]Jesus said to them: "Watch out that no one deceives you. [6]Many will come in my name, claiming, 'I am he,' and will deceive many. [7]When you hear of wars and rumors of wars, do not be alarmed. Such things must happen, but the end is still to come. [8]Nation will rise against nation, and kingdom against kingdom. There will be earthquakes in various places, and famines. These are the beginning of birth pains.

[9]"You must be on your guard. You will be handed over to the local councils and flogged in the synagogues. On account of me you will stand before governors and kings as witnesses to them. [10]And the gospel must first be preached to all nations. [11]Whenever you are arrested and brought to trial, do not worry beforehand about what to say. Just say whatever is given you at the time, for it is not you speaking, but the Holy Spirit.

[12]"Brother will betray brother to death, and a father his child. Children will rebel against their parents and have them put to death. [13]All men will hate you because of me, but he who stands firm to the end will be saved.

[14]"When you see 'the abomination that causes desolation'[e] standing where it[f] does not belong—let the reader understand—then let those who are in Judea flee to the mountains. [15]Let no one on the roof of his house go down or enter the house to take anything out. [16]Let no one in the field go back to get his cloak. [17]How dreadful it will be in those days for pregnant women and nursing mothers! [18]Pray that this will not take place in winter, [19]because those will be days of distress unequaled from the beginning, when God created the world, until now—and never to be equaled again. [20]If the Lord had not cut short those days, no one would survive. But for the sake of the elect, whom he has chosen, he has shortened them. [21]At that time if anyone says to you, 'Look, here is the Christ[a]!' or, 'Look, there he is!' do not be-

---

[a] *35,21 Or Messiah*   [b] *36 Psalm 110:1*   [c] *42 Greek two lepta*   [d] *42 Greek kodrantes*   [e] *14 Daniel 9:27; 11:31; 12:11*
[f] *14 Or he; also in verse 29*

» 60 Things Real Men Don't Do

Have you ever seen a football player tackle his own teammate or intentionally run the ball into his own end zone? Have you ever heard of a band or a musician who got on TV and told people not to buy their CD? Probably not. Why? Because it would be against their best interest to do so. It's not consistent with their character. And guess what? The same is true of real men. There are some things they just won't do. Here are 60 of them:

01» Hold anything back from God »Ge 22 02» Hang around sexual temptation »Ge 39:6–12 03» Take credit for a gift or talent that God has given them »Ge 41:16; Da 2:27–28 04» Chase sexual perversity »Lev 18 05» Hold grudges »Lev 19:18 06» Forget about God's work in their lives »Dt 4:9 07» Doubt God's love »Dt 7:9 08» Mess around with the occult »Dt 18:10–12 09» Blow off a direct command from God »1Sa 15 10» Come to God as a last resort for wisdom or help »1Ki 22:5 11» Be intimidated by a bully »Ne 4 12» Doubt God in the midst of hardship »Job 1–2; 42:7–16 13» Look at a girl lustfully »Job 31:1 14» Let anger control their action »Ps 4:4 15» Pretend to be holy while living a sinful life »Ps 50:16 16» Become obsessed with money »Ps 62:10 17» Ignore solid parental advice »Pr 1:8

:: PR 6:6–11

18 LAZINESS

18» Get lazy and sleep when there is work to be done »Pr 6:6–11 19» Run their mouths »Pr 10:19 20» Start fights »Pr 15:18 21» Eat up gossip about other people »Pr 20:19 22» Despise their mothers »Pr 23:22 23» Evade responsibility for wrongdoing »Pr 24:12 24» Join with rebels »Pr 24:21 25» Brag and boast »Pr 27:2 26» Make rash promises to God »Ecc 5:2 27» Cover up other people's sin or their own evil »Ecc 8:3 28» Forget about God »Ecc 12:1 29» Become physically intimate with a girl outside of marriage »SS 2:7; 3:5 30» Reject God because of pressure

29 IMMORALITY

or intimidation »Da 3 **31»** Give up being faithful in marriage »Mal 2:16

32» Do a good deed in order to be recognized »Mt 6:1-2 **33»** Pray in order to impress others »Mt 6:7 **34»** Fear physical danger more than spiritual danger »Mt 10:28 **35»** Chase after the approval of people »Jn 12:43 **36»** Imitate the behavior and standards of the world »Ro 12:2 **37»** Pass judgment on weaker Christians »Ro 14:1 **38»** Show approval for a brother or sister in Christ who continues to sin »1Co 5:11 **39»** Trade freedom in Christ for slavery to the world 1Co »7:23 **40»** Place their own welfare above others' »1Co 10:24 **41»** Give up »2Co 4:16 **42»** Allow their sinful nature to rule their lives »Gal 5:16-17 **43»** Use coarse or abusive language »Eph 4:29 **44»** Get drunk »Eph 5:18 **45»** Live to impress others »Php 2:3 **46»** Think only about themselves »Php 2:4 **47»** Worry »Php 4:6 **48»** Accept legalistic judgments from others »Col 2:16 **49»** Lie »Col 3:9 **50»** Patronize or discourage their kids »Col 3:21 **51»** Disrespect older people—even when they're out of line »1Ti 5:1-2 **52»** Become greedy for stuff and things »1Ti 6:9 **53»** Be embarrassed because of their commitment to Christ »2Ti 1:8 **54»** Cause younger guys to stumble by setting a bad example »Tit 2:6-7 **55»** Forget to share with those in need »Heb 13:16 **56»** Treat "cool" people better than "uncool" people »Jas 2:1 **57»** Grumble and complain »Jas 5:9 **58»** Slip back into old, sinful habits »1Pe 1:14 **59»** Repay evil with evil »1Pe 3:9 **60»** Be naïve about the world's hatred of Christians »1Jn 3:13

FEAR

34

:: MT 10:28

DRUNKENNESS

44

:: EPH 5:18

GRUMBLING

57

lieve it. 22For false Christs and false prophets will appear and perform signs and miracles to deceive the elect—if that were possible. 23So be on your guard; I have told you everything ahead of time.

24"But in those days, following that distress,

" 'the sun will be darkened,
and the moon will not give its light;
25the stars will fall from the sky,
and the heavenly bodies will be shaken.'ª

26"At that time men will see the Son of Man coming in clouds with great power and glory. 27And he will send his angels and gather his elect from the four winds, from the ends of the earth to the ends of the heavens.

28"Now learn this lesson from the fig tree: As soon as its twigs get tender and its leaves come out, you know that summer is near. 29Even so, when you see these things happening, you know that it is near, right at the door. 30I tell you the truth, this generationᵇ will certainly not pass away until all these things have happened. 31Heaven and earth will pass away, but my words will never pass away.

THE DAY AND HOUR UNKNOWN

32"No one knows about that day or hour, not even the angels in heaven, nor the Son, but only the Father. 33Be on guard! Be alertᶜ! You do not know when that time will come. 34It's like a man going away: He leaves his house and puts his servants in charge, each with his assigned task, and tells the one at the door to keep watch.

35"Therefore keep watch because you do not know when the owner of the house will come back—whether in the evening, or at midnight, or when the rooster crows, or at dawn. 36If he comes suddenly, do not let him find you sleeping. 37What I say to you, I say to everyone: 'Watch!' "

JESUS ANOINTED AT BETHANY

14 Now the Passover and the Feast of Unleavened Bread were only two days away, and the chief priests and the teachers of the law were looking for some sly way to arrest Jesus and kill him. 2"But not during the Feast," they said, "or the people may riot."

3While he was in Bethany, reclining at the table in the home of a man known as Simon the Leper, a woman came with an alabaster jar of very expensive perfume, made of pure nard. She broke the jar and poured the perfume on his head.

4Some of those present were saying indignantly to one another, "Why this waste of perfume? 5It could have been sold for more than a year's wagesᵈ and the money given to the poor." And they rebuked her harshly.

6"Leave her alone," said Jesus. "Why are you bothering her? She has done a beautiful thing to me. 7The poor you will always have with you, and you can help them any time you want. But you will not always have me. 8She did what she could. She poured perfume on my body beforehand to prepare for my burial. 9I tell you the truth, wherever the gospel is preached throughout the world, what she has done will also be told, in memory of her."

10Then Judas Iscariot, one of the Twelve, went to the chief priests to betray Jesus to them. 11They were delighted to hear this and promised to give him money. So he watched for an opportunity to hand him over.

THE LORD'S SUPPER

12On the first day of the Feast of Unleavened Bread, when it was customary to sacrifice the Passover lamb, Jesus' disciples asked him, "Where do you want us to go and make preparations for you to eat the Passover?"

13So he sent two of his disciples, telling them, "Go into the city, and a man carrying a jar of water will meet you. Follow him. 14Say to the owner of the house he enters, 'The Teacher asks: Where is my guest room, where I may eat the Passover with my disciples?' 15He will show you a large upper room, furnished and ready. Make preparations for us there."

16The disciples left, went into the city and found things just as Jesus had told them. So they prepared the Passover.

ª 25 Isaiah 13:10; 34:4   ᵇ 30 Or race   ᶜ 33 Some manuscripts alert and pray   ᵈ 5 Greek than three hundred denarii

battlelines

» Party of One (Loneliness)

Q: What do you mean you feel alone? You're with friends every time I see you.
A: I'm *with* people all the time. But sometimes I feel like—I don't know—like I'm drowning in a river or something, and there's no one around to help.

Q: OK, that's valid. Let's go with that. Let's say you feel like you're drowning right now. How do you cry out for help?
A: I don't know. I mean, shouldn't it be kind of obvious that I'm drowning?

Q: If it were an actual river, yes! But we're speaking metaphorically. Your "drowning" isn't always easy for others to see. Your friends have their own stuff to deal with. It's a pretty self-centered world out there. Most people are too focused on themselves.
A: Thanks. That's *real* encouraging.

Q: I'm just saying that if you want help, you've got to ask. I know a lot of your friends. They're not bad guys. They'll be there for you if they know what you need.

But guys aren't always the most observant creatures on earth. You almost have to hit some of them in the head with a two-by-four to get their attention.
A: So you're telling me I'm lonely because people don't know how I feel?

Q: Maybe. Do you tell your friends how you feel?
A: Well . . . not really. Most of the time we're playing video games or going to movies or playing basketball—stuff like that.

Q: There's nothing wrong with that. But you're at a point where life is changing rapidly. You're dealing with a lot of emotions. Your friends are feeling weird and confused too. You have to learn to talk about that stuff.
A: I don't know. That sounds kind of . . . girly. Like a real-life chick flick or something. I'm not very good at talking about that kind of stuff.

» Your Table Is Ready

Guys are great at telling each other what we *think*. Saying what we *feel*, however, is a lot harder. Somewhere along the way, we bought into the stupid idea that it's not masculine to talk about our emotions, much less show them.

Apparently Jesus never got that memo. He expressed his feelings openly. He wept (see John 11:35). He asked his Father why he had been abandoned (see Matthew 27:46). He asked his disciples to watch and pray with him when he felt depressed (see Mark 14:32–34).

It takes strength and courage to deal with your feelings. Covering them up or pretending they don't exist—that's letting fear control you. Bottling them up could lead to an angry explosion somewhere down the road.

As a guy, it really is OK to talk about how you feel. Follow Jesus' lead. Share your feelings with the people closest to you—with the people you trust.

For more ideas on how to talk to others, visit www.RevolutionBible.com.

[17]When evening came, Jesus arrived with the Twelve. [18]While they were reclining at the table eating, he said, "I tell you the truth, one of you will betray me—one who is eating with me."

[19]They were saddened, and one by one they said to him, "Surely not I?"

[20]"It is one of the Twelve," he replied, "one who dips bread into the bowl with me. [21]The Son of Man will go just as it is written about him. But woe to that man who betrays the Son of Man! It would be better for him if he had not been born."

[22]While they were eating, Jesus took bread, gave thanks and broke it, and gave it to his disciples, saying, "Take it; this is my body."

[23]Then he took the cup, gave thanks and offered it to them, and they all drank from it.

[24]"This is my blood of the[a] covenant, which is poured out for many," he said to them. [25]"I tell you the truth, I will not drink again of the fruit of the vine until that day when I drink it anew in the kingdom of God."

[26]When they had sung a hymn, they went out to the Mount of Olives.

JESUS PREDICTS PETER'S DENIAL

[27]"You will all fall away," Jesus told them, "for it is written:

" 'I will strike the shepherd,
and the sheep will be scattered.'[b]

[28]But after I have risen, I will go ahead of you into Galilee."

[29]Peter declared, "Even if all fall away, I will not."

[30]"I tell you the truth," Jesus answered, "today—yes, tonight—before the rooster crows twice[c] you yourself will disown me three times."

[31]But Peter insisted emphatically, "Even if I have to die with you, I will never disown you." And all the others said the same.

GETHSEMANE

[32]They went to a place called Gethsemane, and Jesus said to his disciples, "Sit here while I pray." [33]He took Peter, James and John along with him, and he began to be deeply distressed and troubled. [34]"My soul is overwhelmed with sorrow to the point of death," he said to them. "Stay here and keep watch."

[35]Going a little farther, he fell to the ground and prayed that if possible the hour might pass from him. [36]"Abba,[d] Father," he said, "everything is possible for you. Take this cup from me. Yet not what I will, but what you will."

[37]Then he returned to his disciples and found them sleeping. "Simon," he said to Peter, "are you asleep? Could you not keep watch for one hour? [38]Watch and pray so that you will not fall into temptation. The spirit is willing, but the body is weak."

[39]Once more he went away and prayed the same thing. [40]When he came back, he again found them sleeping, because their eyes were heavy. They did not know what to say to him.

[41]Returning the third time, he said to them, "Are you still sleeping and resting? Enough! The hour has come. Look, the Son of Man is betrayed into the hands of sinners. [42]Rise! Let us go! Here comes my betrayer!"

JESUS ARRESTED

[43]Just as he was speaking, Judas, one of the Twelve, appeared. With him was a crowd armed with swords and clubs, sent from the chief priests, the teachers of the law, and the elders. [44]Now the betrayer had arranged a signal with them: "The one I kiss is the man; arrest him and lead him away under guard." [45]Going at once to Jesus, Judas said, "Rabbi!" and kissed him. [46]The men seized Jesus and arrested him. [47]Then one of those standing near drew his sword and struck the servant of the high priest, cutting off his ear.

[48]"Am I leading a rebellion," said Jesus, "that you have come out with swords and clubs to capture me? [49]Every day I was with you, teaching in the temple courts, and you did not arrest me. But the Scriptures must be fulfilled." [50]Then everyone deserted him and fled.

[a] 24 Some manuscripts the new   [b] 27 Zech. 13:7   [c] 30 Some early manuscripts do not have twice.   [d] 36 Aramaic for Father

[51]A young man, wearing nothing but a linen garment, was following Jesus. When they seized him, [52]he fled naked, leaving his garment behind.

BEFORE THE SANHEDRIN

[53]They took Jesus to the high priest, and all the chief priests, elders and teachers of the law came together. [54]Peter followed him at a distance, right into the courtyard of the high priest. There he sat with the guards and warmed himself at the fire.

[55]The chief priests and the whole Sanhedrin were looking for evidence against Jesus so that they could put him to death, but they did not find any. [56]Many testified falsely against him, but their statements did not agree.

NOW OR NEVER

MK 14:50–51

Put yourself in the disciples' position. The leader you trusted with your future—the one you gave up everything to follow—has just been arrested and in a matter of hours will be sentenced to die. How would you feel? What would you do?

[57]Then some stood up and gave this false testimony against him: [58]"We heard him say, 'I will destroy this man-made temple and in three days will build another, not made by man.'" [59]Yet even then their testimony did not agree.

[60]Then the high priest stood up before them and asked Jesus, "Are you not going to answer? What is this testimony that these men are bringing against you?" [61]But Jesus remained silent and gave no answer.

Again the high priest asked him, "Are you the Christ,[a] the Son of the Blessed One?"

[62]"I am," said Jesus. "And you will see the Son of Man sitting at the right hand of the Mighty One and coming on the clouds of heaven."

[63]The high priest tore his clothes. "Why do we need any more witnesses?" he asked. [64]"You have heard the blasphemy. What do you think?"

They all condemned him as worthy of death. [65]Then some began to spit at him; they blindfolded him, struck him with their fists, and said, "Prophesy!" And the guards took him and beat him.

PETER DISOWNS JESUS

[66]While Peter was below in the courtyard, one of the servant girls of the high priest came by. [67]When she saw Peter warming himself, she looked closely at him.

"You also were with that Nazarene, Jesus," she said.

[68]But he denied it. "I don't know or understand what you're talking about," he said, and went out into the entryway.[b]

[69]When the servant girl saw him there, she said again to those standing around, "This fellow is one of them." [70]Again he denied it.

After a little while, those standing near said to Peter, "Surely you are one of them, for you are a Galilean."

[71]He began to call down curses on himself, and he swore to them, "I don't know this man you're talking about."

[72]Immediately the rooster crowed the second time.[c] Then Peter remembered the word Jesus had spoken to him: "Before the rooster crows twice[d] you will disown me three times." And he broke down and wept.

JESUS BEFORE PILATE

15 Very early in the morning, the chief priests, with the elders, the teachers of the law and the whole Sanhedrin, reached a decision. They bound Jesus, led him away and handed him over to Pilate.

[2]"Are you the king of the Jews?" asked Pilate.

"Yes, it is as you say," Jesus replied.

[3]The chief priests accused him of many things. [4]So again Pilate asked him, "Aren't you going to answer? See how many things they are accusing you of."

---

[a] 61 Or Messiah   [b] 68 Some early manuscripts entryway and the rooster crowed   [c] 72 Some early manuscripts do not have the second time.   [d] 72 Some early manuscripts do not have twice.

5But Jesus still made no reply, and Pilate was amazed.

6Now it was the custom at the Feast to release a prisoner whom the people requested. 7A man called Barabbas was in prison with the insurrectionists who had committed murder in the uprising. 8The crowd came up and asked Pilate to do for them what he usually did.

9"Do you want me to release to you the king of the Jews?" asked Pilate, 10knowing it was out of envy that the chief priests had handed Jesus over to him. 11But the chief priests stirred up the crowd to have Pilate release Barabbas instead.

12"What shall I do, then, with the one you call the king of the Jews?" Pilate asked them.

13"Crucify him!" they shouted.

14"Why? What crime has he committed?" asked Pilate.

But they shouted all the louder, "Crucify him!"

15Wanting to satisfy the crowd, Pilate released Barabbas to them. He had Jesus flogged, and handed him over to be crucified.

THE SOLDIERS MOCK JESUS

16The soldiers led Jesus away into the palace (that is, the Praetorium) and called together the whole company of soldiers. 17They put a purple robe on him, then twisted together a crown of thorns and set it on him. 18And they began to call out to him, "Hail, king of the Jews!" 19Again and again they struck him on the head with a staff and spit on him. Falling on their knees, they paid homage to him. 20And when they had mocked him, they took off the purple robe and put his own clothes on him. Then they led him out to crucify him.

THE CRUCIFIXION

21A certain man from Cyrene, Simon, the father of Alexander and Rufus, was passing by on his way in from the country, and they forced him to carry the cross. 22They brought Jesus to the place called Golgotha (which means The Place of the Skull). 23Then they offered him wine mixed with myrrh, but he did not take it. 24And they crucified him. Dividing up his clothes, they cast lots to see what each would get.

25It was the third hour when they crucified him. 26The written notice of the charge against him read: THE KING OF THE JEWS. 27They crucified two robbers with him, one on his right and one on his left.[a] 29Those who passed by hurled insults at him, shaking their heads and saying, "So! You who are going to destroy the temple and build it in three days, 30come down from the cross and save yourself!"

31In the same way the chief priests and the teachers of the law mocked him among themselves. "He saved others," they said, "but he can't save himself! 32Let this Christ,[b] this King of Israel, come down now from the cross, that we may see and believe." Those crucified with him also heaped insults on him.

THE DEATH OF JESUS

33At the sixth hour darkness came over the whole land until the ninth hour. 34And at the ninth hour Jesus cried out in a loud voice, *"Eloi, Eloi, lama sabachthani?"*—which means, "My God, my God, why have you forsaken me?"[c]

35When some of those standing near heard this, they said, "Listen, he's calling Elijah."

36One man ran, filled a sponge with wine vinegar, put it on a stick, and offered it to Jesus to drink. "Now leave him alone. Let's see if Elijah comes to take him down," he said.

37With a loud cry, Jesus breathed his last.

Knowing Who to Please

Are you a people pleaser? Whose opinion do you value most? Pilate found out what can happen when you let other people's opinions influence you. The next time you're faced with a choice of listening to God or listening to the crowd, consider these facts: People are imperfect; God is perfect. People often let their emotions determine what they do; God lets his perfect wisdom determine what he does. People frequently have no idea what the consequences of their decisions will be; God knows every possible result of every possible decision. People are frequently wrong; God is never wrong. Block out the distractions and listen to God.

---

38 The curtain of the temple was torn in two from top to bottom. 39 And when the centurion, who stood there in front of Jesus, heard his cry and[a] saw how he died, he said, "Surely this man was the Son[b] of God!"

40 Some women were watching from a distance. Among them were Mary Magdalene, Mary the mother of James the younger and of Joses, and Salome. 41 In Galilee these women had followed him and cared for his needs. Many other women who had come up with him to Jerusalem were also there.

THE BURIAL OF JESUS

42 It was Preparation Day (that is, the day before the Sabbath). So as evening approached, 43 Joseph of Arimathea, a prominent member of the Council, who was himself waiting for the kingdom of God, went boldly to Pilate and asked for Jesus' body. 44 Pilate was surprised to hear that he was already dead. Summoning the centurion, he asked him if Jesus had already died. 45 When he learned from the centurion that it was so, he gave the body to Joseph. 46 So Joseph bought some linen cloth, took down the body, wrapped it in the linen, and placed it in a tomb cut out of rock. Then he rolled a stone against the entrance of the tomb. 47 Mary Magdalene and Mary the mother of Joses saw where he was laid.

THE RESURRECTION

16 When the Sabbath was over, Mary Magdalene, Mary the mother of James, and Salome bought spices so that they might go to anoint Jesus' body. 2 Very early on the first day of the week, just after sunrise, they were on their way to the tomb 3 and they asked each other, "Who will roll the stone away from the entrance of the tomb?"

4 But when they looked up, they saw that the stone, which was very large, had been rolled away. 5 As they entered the tomb, they saw a young man dressed in a white robe sitting on the right side, and they were alarmed.

6 "Don't be alarmed," he said. "You are looking for Jesus the Nazarene, who was crucified. He has risen! He is not here. See the place where they laid him. 7 But go, tell his disciples and Peter, 'He is going ahead of you into Galilee. There you will see him, just as he told you.' "

8 Trembling and bewildered, the women went out and fled from the tomb. They said nothing to anyone, because they were afraid.

[The earliest manuscripts and some other ancient witnesses do not have Mark 16:9–20.]

9 When Jesus rose early on the first day of the week, he appeared first to Mary Magdalene, out of whom he had driven seven demons. 10 She went and told those who had been with him and who were mourning and weeping. 11 When they heard that Jesus was alive and that she had seen him, they did not believe it.

12 Afterward Jesus appeared in a different form to two of them while they were walking in the country. 13 These returned and reported it to the rest; but they did not believe them either.

14 Later Jesus appeared to the Eleven as they were eating; he rebuked them for their lack of faith and their stubborn refusal to believe those who had seen him after he had risen.

15 He said to them, "Go into all the world and preach the good news to all creation. 16 Whoever believes and is baptized will be saved, but whoever does not believe will be condemned. 17 And these signs will accompany those who believe: In my name they will drive out demons; they will speak in new tongues; 18 they will pick up snakes with their hands; and when they drink deadly poison, it will not hurt them at all; they will place their hands on sick people, and they will get well."

19 After the Lord Jesus had spoken to them, he was taken up into heaven and he sat at the right hand of God. 20 Then the disciples went out and preached everywhere, and the Lord worked with them and confirmed his word by the signs that accompanied it.

---

[a] 39 Some manuscripts do not have *heard his cry and*   [b] 39 Or *a son*

« AT A GLANCE

Author
Luke, a doctor and Gentile Christian

Audience
Theophilus and the Gentiles

Date
Probably about A.D. 60

Setting
Luke probably wrote from Rome, or perhaps from Caesarea. He wanted the Gentiles to hear the true details about the life of Jesus.

Verse to Remember
"For the Son of Man came to seek and to save what was lost" (19:10).

Theme to Consider
Dr. Luke presents a carefully documented biography of Jesus, the perfect Son of Man, who came to save *all* who are lost. Look for the emphasis on Jesus' relationships with others, and in particular, the prominence given to women and the poor.

UNCHANGING TRUTH » When we talk about Jesus' "sacrifice," we usually think of his death on the cross. But the book of Luke reveals that Jesus' sacrifice started much earlier than that. In fact, it started the moment he took human form.

Remember, when we talk about Jesus, we're talking about God. Jesus is the One who created the world and breathed life into each human being. His power and knowledge were—and still are—limitless. Nothing could harm him or threaten his power.

Yet he abandoned all of that so he could come to Earth and live as one of us. He left his perfect existence in heaven to live a life filled with rejection, ridicule and betrayal on our sinful planet. He gave up his supreme power and became a helpless baby, totally dependent on his human mother to take care of him. He made himself vulnerable to hunger, thirst, pain, sickness, exhaustion and ultimately death. He squeezed infinite divinity into finite humanity—into a pile of flesh roughly five-and-a-half-feet tall.

Can you imagine how agonizing the transition must have been? Can you imagine what kind of love would motivate that type of sacrifice?

You know what Jesus did for you. Now the question is, What are you willing to sacrifice in response?

LIFE LESSONS »

1. When Jesus tells you to do something—don't ask why—just do it (5:4–6).

2. If you're concerned about how much honor and glory you're going to receive, your heart is in the wrong place (9:46–48).

3. God cares deeply about the plight of the poor (12:33).

4. God is willing to grant justice to his people if they're willing to plead for it (18:1–8).

INTRODUCTION

1 Many have undertaken to draw up an account of the things that have been fulfilled[a] among us, [2]just as they were handed down to us by those who from the first were eyewitnesses and servants of the word. [3]Therefore, since I myself have carefully investigated everything from the beginning, it seemed good also to me to write an orderly account for you, most excellent Theophilus, [4]so that you may know the certainty of the things you have been taught.

THE BIRTH OF JOHN THE BAPTIST FORETOLD

[5]In the time of Herod king of Judea there was a priest named Zechariah, who belonged to the priestly division of Abijah; his wife Elizabeth was also a descendant of Aaron. [6]Both of them were upright in the sight of God, observing all the Lord's commandments and regulations blamelessly. [7]But they had no children, because Elizabeth was barren; and they were both well along in years.

[8]Once when Zechariah's division was on duty and he was serving as priest before God, [9]he was chosen by lot, according to the custom of the priesthood, to go into the temple of the Lord and burn incense. [10]And when the time for the burning of incense came, all the assembled worshipers were praying outside.

[11]Then an angel of the Lord appeared to him, standing at the right side of the altar of incense. [12]When Zechariah saw him, he was startled and was gripped with fear. [13]But the angel said to him: "Do not be afraid, Zechariah; your prayer has been heard. Your wife Elizabeth will bear you a son, and you are to give him the name John. [14]He will be a joy and delight to you, and many will rejoice because of his birth, [15]for he will be great in the sight of the Lord. He is never to take wine or other fermented drink, and he will be filled with the Holy Spirit even from birth.[b] [16]Many of the people of Israel will he bring back to the Lord their God. [17]And he will go on before the Lord, in the spirit and power of Elijah, to turn the hearts of the fathers to their children and the disobedient to the wisdom of the righteous—to make ready a people prepared for the Lord."

[18]Zechariah asked the angel, "How can I be sure of this? I am an old man and my wife is well along in years."

[19]The angel answered, "I am Gabriel. I stand in the presence of God, and I have been sent to speak to you and to tell you this good news. [20]And now you will be silent and not able to speak until the day this happens, because you did not believe my words, which will come true at their proper time."

[21]Meanwhile, the people were waiting for Zechariah and wondering why he stayed so long in the temple. [22]When he came out, he could not speak to them. They realized he had seen a vision in the temple, for he kept making signs to them but remained unable to speak.

[23]When his time of service was completed, he returned home. [24]After this his wife Elizabeth became pregnant and for five months remained in seclusion. [25]"The Lord has done this for me," she said. "In these days he has shown his favor and taken away my disgrace among the people."

THE BIRTH OF JESUS FORETOLD

[26]In the sixth month, God sent the angel Gabriel to Nazareth, a town in Galilee, [27]to a virgin pledged to be married to a man named Joseph, a descendant of David. The virgin's name was Mary. [28]The angel went to her and said, "Greetings, you who are highly favored! The Lord is with you."

[29]Mary was greatly troubled at his words and wondered what kind of greeting this might be. [30]But the angel said to her, "Do not be afraid, Mary, you have found favor with God. [31]You will be with child

> ## Supporting Your Beliefs
>
> You never know what kind of response you're going to get when you talk to people about your faith. Some people may like what they hear and decide to trust Jesus on the spot. Some people may walk away before you get your first sentence out. And some people may try to argue with you about your beliefs. That's when it's important to be able to back up your words with evidence from the Bible. For instance, what if someone tried to tell you that Jesus never claimed to be the Son of God? Would you know how to respond? Could you support your beliefs?

live the adventure » Lk 1:3

[a] 1 Or *been surely believed*   [b] 15 Or *from his mother's womb*

and give birth to a son, and you are to give him the name Jesus. ³²He will be great and will be called the Son of the Most High. The Lord God will give him the throne of his father David, ³³and he will reign over the house of Jacob forever; his kingdom will never end."

³⁴"How will this be," Mary asked the angel, "since I am a virgin?"

³⁵The angel answered, "The Holy Spirit will come upon you, and the power of the Most High will overshadow you. So the holy one to be born will be called ᵃ the Son of God. ³⁶Even Elizabeth your relative is going to have a child in her old age, and she who was said to be barren is in her sixth month. ³⁷For nothing is impossible with God."

³⁸"I am the Lord's servant," Mary answered. "May it be to me as you have said." Then the angel left her.

now or never

LK 1:37

Do you believe that miracles still happen today? What defines a miracle? Have you ever seen one? Do you know anyone who has witnessed one?

MARY VISITS ELIZABETH

³⁹At that time Mary got ready and hurried to a town in the hill country of Judea, ⁴⁰where she entered Zechariah's home and greeted Elizabeth. ⁴¹When Elizabeth heard Mary's greeting, the baby leaped in her womb, and Elizabeth was filled with the Holy Spirit. ⁴²In a loud voice she exclaimed: "Blessed are you among women, and blessed is the child you will bear! ⁴³But why am I so favored, that the mother of my Lord should come to me? ⁴⁴As soon as the sound of your greeting reached my ears, the baby in my womb leaped for joy. ⁴⁵Blessed is she who has believed that what the Lord has said to her will be accomplished!"

MARY'S SONG

⁴⁶And Mary said:

"My soul glorifies the Lord
⁴⁷   and my spirit rejoices in God my Savior,
⁴⁸for he has been mindful
      of the humble state of his servant.
   From now on all generations will call
      me blessed,
⁴⁹   for the Mighty One has done great
         things for me—
      holy is his name.
⁵⁰His mercy extends to those who fear
         him,
      from generation to generation.
⁵¹He has performed mighty deeds with his
         arm;
      he has scattered those who are proud
         in their inmost thoughts.

now or never

LK 1:46-55

Mary responded to the Lord's blessings in her life by composing a special song for him. Zechariah did the same (see 1:68-79). If you were going to write a song for God, what would the lyrics be?

⁵²He has brought down rulers from their thrones
      but has lifted up the humble.
⁵³He has filled the hungry with good things
      but has sent the rich away empty.
⁵⁴He has helped his servant Israel,
      remembering to be merciful
⁵⁵to Abraham and his descendants forever,
      even as he said to our fathers."

⁵⁶Mary stayed with Elizabeth for about three months and then returned home.

ᵃ 35 Or So the child to be born will be called holy,

THE BIRTH OF JOHN THE BAPTIST

57When it was time for Elizabeth to have her baby, she gave birth to a son. 58Her neighbors and relatives heard that the Lord had shown her great mercy, and they shared her joy.

59On the eighth day they came to circumcise the child, and they were going to name him after his father Zechariah, 60but his mother spoke up and said, "No! He is to be called John."

61They said to her, "There is no one among your relatives who has that name."

62Then they made signs to his father, to find out what he would like to name the child. 63He asked for a writing tablet, and to everyone's astonishment he wrote, "His name is John." 64Immediately his mouth was opened and his tongue was loosed, and he began to speak, praising God. 65The neighbors were all filled with awe, and throughout the hill country of Judea people were talking about all these things. 66Everyone who heard this wondered about it, asking, "What then is this child going to be?" For the Lord's hand was with him.

ZECHARIAH'S SONG

67His father Zechariah was filled with the Holy Spirit and prophesied:

> 68 "Praise be to the Lord, the God of Israel,
>   because he has come and has redeemed his people.
> 69 He has raised up a horn a of salvation for us
>   in the house of his servant David
> 70 (as he said through his holy prophets of long ago),
> 71 salvation from our enemies
>   and from the hand of all who hate us—
> 72 to show mercy to our fathers
>   and to remember his holy covenant,
> 73   the oath he swore to our father Abraham:
> 74 to rescue us from the hand of our enemies,
>   and to enable us to serve him without fear
> 75   in holiness and righteousness before him all our days.
>
> 76 And you, my child, will be called a prophet of the Most High;
>   for you will go on before the Lord to prepare the way for him,
> 77 to give his people the knowledge of salvation
>   through the forgiveness of their sins,
> 78 because of the tender mercy of our God,
>   by which the rising sun will come to us from heaven
> 79 to shine on those living in darkness
>   and in the shadow of death,
>   to guide our feet into the path of peace."

80And the child grew and became strong in spirit; and he lived in the desert until he appeared publicly to Israel.

THE BIRTH OF JESUS

2 In those days Caesar Augustus issued a decree that a census should be taken of the entire Roman world. 2(This was the first census that took place while Quirinius was governor of Syria.) 3And everyone went to his own town to register.

4So Joseph also went up from the town of Nazareth in Galilee to Judea, to Bethlehem the town of David, because he belonged to the house and line of David. 5He went there to register with Mary, who was pledged to be married to him and was expecting a child. 6While they were there, the time came for the baby to be born, 7and she gave birth to her firstborn, a son. She wrapped him in cloths and placed him in a manger, because there was no room for them in the inn.

THE SHEPHERDS AND THE ANGELS

8And there were shepherds living out in the fields nearby, keeping watch over their flocks at night.

---

a 69 Horn here symbolizes strength.

9An angel of the Lord appeared to them, and the glory of the Lord shone around them, and they were terrified. 10But the angel said to them, "Do not be afraid. I bring you good news of great joy that will be for all the people. 11Today in the town of David a Savior has been born to you; he is Christ[a] the Lord. 12This will be a sign to you: You will find a baby wrapped in cloths and lying in a manger."

13Suddenly a great company of the heavenly host appeared with the angel, praising God and saying,

14 "Glory to God in the highest,
    and on earth peace to men on whom
        his favor rests."

15When the angels had left them and gone into heaven, the shepherds said to one another, "Let's go to Bethlehem and see this thing that has happened, which the Lord has told us about."

16So they hurried off and found Mary and Joseph, and the baby, who was lying in the manger. 17When they had seen him, they spread the word concerning what had been told them about this child, 18and all who heard it were amazed at what the shepherds said to them. 19But Mary treasured up all these things and pondered them in her heart. 20The shepherds returned, glorifying and praising God for all the things they had heard and seen, which were just as they had been told.

NOW OR NEVER
LK 2:7

The Creator of the universe spent his first night on earth in an animal's feeding trough. Think about that the next time you're tempted to question the depth of God's love for you.

JESUS PRESENTED IN THE TEMPLE

21On the eighth day, when it was time to circumcise him, he was named Jesus, the name the angel had given him before he had been conceived.

22When the time of their purification according to the Law of Moses had been completed, Joseph and Mary took him to Jerusalem to present him to the Lord 23(as it is written in the Law of the Lord, "Every firstborn male is to be consecrated to the Lord"[b]), 24and to offer a sacrifice in keeping with what is said in the Law of the Lord: "a pair of doves or two young pigeons."[c]

25Now there was a man in Jerusalem called Simeon, who was righteous and devout. He was waiting for the consolation of Israel, and the Holy Spirit was upon him. 26It had been revealed to him by the Holy Spirit that he would not die before he had seen the Lord's Christ. 27Moved by the Spirit, he went into the temple courts. When the parents brought in the child Jesus to do for him what the custom of the Law required, 28Simeon took him in his arms and praised God, saying:

29 "Sovereign Lord, as you have promised,
    you now dismiss[d] your servant in
        peace.
30 For my eyes have seen your salvation,
31   which you have prepared in the sight
        of all people,
32 a light for revelation to the Gentiles
    and for glory to your people Israel."

Recognizing the Lord's Work

Old Testament prophets had predicted that the Messiah would be born in the city of Bethlehem. However, Joseph and Mary both lived in the city of Nazareth. That was no problem for God though. He simply caused the Roman emperor to order a census that would bring Joseph and Mary to Bethlehem at the exact time Jesus was to be born. In other words, God coordinated everything that needed to happen in order for the Old Testament prophecies to be fulfilled. That's just one example of why there's no such thing as coincidence—because God is involved.

» live the adventure » Lk 2:1-3

---

a 11 Or Messiah. "The Christ" (Greek) and "the Messiah" (Hebrew) both mean "the Anointed One"; also in verse 26.
b 23 Exodus 13:2,12   c 24 Lev. 12:8   d 29 Or promised, / now dismiss

33 The child's father and mother marveled at what was said about him. 34 Then Simeon blessed them and said to Mary, his mother: "This child is destined to cause the falling and rising of many in Israel, and to be a sign that will be spoken against, 35 so that the thoughts of many hearts will be revealed. And a sword will pierce your own soul too."

36 There was also a prophetess, Anna, the daughter of Phanuel, of the tribe of Asher. She was very old; she had lived with her husband seven years after her marriage, 37 and then was a widow until she was eighty-four.ᵃ She never left the temple but worshiped night and day, fasting and praying. 38 Coming up to them at that very moment, she gave thanks to God and spoke about the child to all who were looking forward to the redemption of Jerusalem.

39 When Joseph and Mary had done everything required by the Law of the Lord, they returned to Galilee to their own town of Nazareth. 40 And the child grew and became strong; he was filled with wisdom, and the grace of God was upon him.

THE BOY JESUS AT THE TEMPLE

41 Every year his parents went to Jerusalem for the Feast of the Passover. 42 When he was twelve years old, they went up to the Feast, according to the custom. 43 After the Feast was over, while his parents were returning home, the boy Jesus stayed behind in Jerusalem, but they were unaware of it. 44 Thinking he was in their company, they traveled on for a day. Then they began looking for him among their relatives and friends. 45 When they did not find him, they went back to Jerusalem to look for him. 46 After three days they found him in the temple courts, sitting among the teachers, listening to them and asking them questions. 47 Everyone who heard him was amazed at his understanding and his answers. 48 When his parents saw him, they were astonished. His mother said to him, "Son, why have you treated us like this? Your father and I have been anxiously searching for you."

49 "Why were you searching for me?" he asked. "Didn't you know I had to be in my Father's house?" 50 But they did not understand what he was saying to them.

51 Then he went down to Nazareth with them and was obedient to them. But his mother treasured all these things in her heart. 52 And Jesus grew in wisdom and stature, and in favor with God and men.

JOHN THE BAPTIST PREPARES THE WAY

3 In the fifteenth year of the reign of Tiberius Caesar—when Pontius Pilate was governor of Judea, Herod tetrarch of Galilee, his brother Philip tetrarch of Iturea and Traconitis, and Lysanias tetrarch of Abilene— 2 during the high priesthood of Annas and Caiaphas, the word of God came to John son of Zechariah in the desert. 3 He went into all the country around the Jordan, preaching a baptism of repentance for the forgiveness of sins. 4 As is written in the book of the words of Isaiah the prophet:

"A voice of one calling in the desert,
'Prepare the way for the Lord,
make straight paths for him.
5 Every valley shall be filled in,
every mountain and hill made low.
The crooked roads shall become straight,
the rough ways smooth.
6 And all mankind will see God's salvation.' "ᵇ

Learning to Be Patient

Simeon waited years to see the coming of the Messiah, and his patience finally paid off. Not only did he get to *see* the Messiah, but he also got to hold him in his arms. God loyally rewarded Simeon's long-term faithfulness. There's a lesson in Simeon's story for anyone who's struggling with an unanswered prayer request. Waiting on God isn't always a two- or three-day process; sometimes it's a two- or three-*year* process . . . or longer. If that seems too long to wait, change your perspective. Remember, God's not on your clock; you're on his.

»» live the adventure »» Lk 2:25-32

ᵃ *37* Or *widow for eighty-four years*   ᵇ *6* Isaiah 40:3-5

battlelines

» Go for Broke (Identity)

Q: Hey, man, where have you been hiding for the past few weeks?
A: If I'm not doing homework, I'm either lifting weights or at the pool. I don't have time for anything else.

Q: You've always done pretty well in both school and swimming before. Why the sudden change?
A: Because I'm tired of doing "pretty good." I want to be the best.

Q: Wow. What got you so motivated?
A: My older brother. He's a waste. Drinking all the time, working at the video store. He's got no future ahead of him. I don't want to end up like that. I want to do something with my life. I want to be somebody.

Q: "Be somebody"? So what are you now?
A: I'm a nobody. But not for long.

Q: That's a little extreme, don't you think?
A: Well, I haven't *done* anything. Nobody knows who I am, but they *will* . . . before long. I'm going to show everyone what I can do when I really put my mind to it.

Q: You think all that matters is what you *do*?
A: What else is there?

Q: What about who you *are*?
A: What you do *is* who you are. Isn't that the first thing people ask when they meet you? "What do you do?" I want to be able to give a great answer when someone asks me that question. In fact, I want to get to the point where people don't even have to ask. They just recognize me.

» The Performance Trap

Drew is not alone. Many guys think their value as a person is tied solely to what they do. They believe that they'll only be significant if they achieve lofty goals.

The problem is that you can be a great athlete or a hotshot businessman and still be a total loser. At some point our accomplishments fade into the background, and all we're left with is ourselves. What will we have then?

Yes, you should always do your best for God's glory (see 1 Corinthians 10:31). Yes, you should develop your gifts to their full capacity. But don't neglect your heart. Give attention to your character—to the person you are and to the person you're becoming.

Think about this: Jesus preached and healed and did spectacular things for only the final three years of his life. But what about the first thirty? The Bible doesn't talk about what he did—only about the kind of person he was becoming (see Luke 2:52). Are we to believe that God was only pleased with Jesus during the last 36 months of his life? Maybe Jesus was so effective and influential in the end, when it counted, because he spent his youth drawing near to his Father. Remember, character can give birth to terrific accomplishments, but achievements by themselves can never produce character.

Learn more about growing as a Christian at www.RevolutionBible.com.

[7]John said to the crowds coming out to be baptized by him, "You brood of vipers! Who warned you to flee from the coming wrath? [8]Produce fruit in keeping with repentance. And do not begin to say to yourselves, 'We have Abraham as our father.' For I tell you that out of these stones God can raise up children for Abraham. [9]The ax is already at the root of the trees, and every tree that does not produce good fruit will be cut down and thrown into the fire."

[10]"What should we do then?" the crowd asked.

[11]John answered, "The man with two tunics should share with him who has none, and the one who has food should do the same."

[12]Tax collectors also came to be baptized. "Teacher," they asked, "what should we do?"

[13]"Don't collect any more than you are required to," he told them.

[14]Then some soldiers asked him, "And what should we do?"

He replied, "Don't extort money and don't accuse people falsely—be content with your pay."

[15]The people were waiting expectantly and were all wondering in their hearts if John might possibly be the Christ.[a] [16]John answered them all, "I baptize you with[b] water. But one more powerful than I will come, the thongs of whose sandals I am not worthy to untie. He will baptize you with the Holy Spirit and with fire. [17]His winnowing fork is in his hand to clear his threshing floor and to gather the wheat into his barn, but he will burn up the chaff with unquenchable fire." [18]And with many other words John exhorted the people and preached the good news to them.

[19]But when John rebuked Herod the tetrarch because of Herodias, his brother's wife, and all the other evil things he had done, [20]Herod added this to them all: He locked John up in prison.

THE BAPTISM AND GENEALOGY OF JESUS

[21]When all the people were being baptized, Jesus was baptized too. And as he was praying, heaven was opened [22]and the Holy Spirit descended on him in bodily form like a dove. And a voice came from heaven: "You are my Son, whom I love; with you I am well pleased."

[23]Now Jesus himself was about thirty years old when he began his ministry. He was the son, so it was thought, of Joseph,

the son of Heli, [24]the son of Matthat,
the son of Levi, the son of Melki,
the son of Jannai, the son of Joseph,
[25]the son of Mattathias, the son of Amos,
the son of Nahum, the son of Esli,
the son of Naggai, [26]the son of Maath,
the son of Mattathias, the son of Semein,
the son of Josech, the son of Joda,
[27]the son of Joanan, the son of Rhesa,
the son of Zerubbabel, the son of Shealtiel,
the son of Neri, [28]the son of Melki,
the son of Addi, the son of Cosam,
the son of Elmadam, the son of Er,
[29]the son of Joshua, the son of Eliezer,
the son of Jorim, the son of Matthat,
the son of Levi, [30]the son of Simeon,
the son of Judah, the son of Joseph,
the son of Jonam, the son of Eliakim,
[31]the son of Melea, the son of Menna,
the son of Mattatha, the son of Nathan,
the son of David, [32]the son of Jesse,
the son of Obed, the son of Boaz,
the son of Salmon,[c] the son of Nahshon,
[33]the son of Amminadab, the son of Ram,[d]
the son of Hezron, the son of Perez,

---

[a] 15 Or Messiah   [b] 16 Or in   [c] 32 Some early manuscripts Sala   [d] 33 Some manuscripts Amminadab, the son of Admin, the son of Arni; other manuscripts vary widely.

the son of Judah, 34the son of Jacob,
the son of Isaac, the son of Abraham,
the son of Terah, the son of Nahor,
35the son of Serug, the son of Reu,
the son of Peleg, the son of Eber,
the son of Shelah, 36the son of Cainan,
the son of Arphaxad, the son of Shem,
the son of Noah, the son of Lamech,
37the son of Methuselah, the son of Enoch,
the son of Jared, the son of Mahalalel,
the son of Kenan, 38the son of Enosh,
the son of Seth, the son of Adam,
the son of God.

THE TEMPTATION OF JESUS

4 Jesus, full of the Holy Spirit, returned from the Jordan and was led by the Spirit in the desert, 2where for forty days he was tempted by the devil. He ate nothing during those days, and at the end of them he was hungry.

3The devil said to him, "If you are the Son of God, tell this stone to become bread."

4Jesus answered, "It is written: 'Man does not live on bread alone.'a"

5The devil led him up to a high place and showed him in an instant all the kingdoms of the world. 6And he said to him, "I will give you all their authority and splendor, for it has been given to me, and I can give it to anyone I want to. 7So if you worship me, it will all be yours."

8Jesus answered, "It is written: 'Worship the Lord your God and serve him only.'b"

9The devil led him to Jerusalem and had him stand on the highest point of the temple. "If you are the Son of God," he said, "throw yourself down from here. 10For it is written:

" 'He will command his angels
concerning you
to guard you carefully;
11they will lift you up in their hands,
so that you will not strike your foot
against a stone.'c"

12Jesus answered, "It says: 'Do not put the Lord your God to the test.'d"

13When the devil had finished all this tempting, he left him until an opportune time.

JESUS REJECTED AT NAZARETH

14Jesus returned to Galilee in the power of the Spirit, and news about him spread through the whole countryside. 15He taught in their synagogues, and everyone praised him.

16He went to Nazareth, where he had been brought up, and on the Sabbath day he went into the synagogue, as was his custom. And he stood up to read. 17The scroll of the prophet Isaiah was handed to him. Unrolling it, he found the place where it is written:

18 "The Spirit of the Lord is on me,
because he has anointed me

Dealing With Temptation

Notice how Satan targeted Jesus' most pressing needs and desires in his temptations. Changing the stones to bread would have given Jesus something to eat after 40 days without food. Worshiping Satan would have spared Jesus the intense suffering on the cross. Jumping off the temple and being rescued by God would have shown everyone God's power and Jesus' authority, establishing his kingship and sparing him years of insult from hypocrites like the Pharisees. Satan uses a similar strategy on us. He identifies our needs and desires and offers us tantalizing "shortcuts" that give us a temporary fix to a much deeper need that only God can fill.

» live the adventure » Lk 4:1–11

---

a 4 Deut. 8:3   b 8 Deut. 6:13   c 11 Psalm 91:11,12   d 12 Deut. 6:16

to preach good news to the poor.
He has sent me to proclaim freedom for the prisoners
and recovery of sight for the blind,
to release the oppressed,
19 to proclaim the year of the Lord's favor." [a]

20Then he rolled up the scroll, gave it back to the attendant and sat down. The eyes of everyone in the synagogue were fastened on him, 21and he began by saying to them, "Today this scripture is fulfilled in your hearing."

22All spoke well of him and were amazed at the gracious words that came from his lips. "Isn't this Joseph's son?" they asked.

23Jesus said to them, "Surely you will quote this proverb to me: 'Physician, heal yourself! Do here in your hometown what we have heard that you did in Capernaum.'"

24"I tell you the truth," he continued, "no prophet is accepted in his hometown. 25I assure you that there were many widows in Israel in Elijah's time, when the sky was shut for three and a half years and there was a severe famine throughout the land. 26Yet Elijah was not sent to any of them, but to a widow in Zarephath in the region of Sidon. 27And there were many in Israel with leprosy[b] in the time of Elisha the prophet, yet not one of them was cleansed—only Naaman the Syrian."

28All the people in the synagogue were furious when they heard this. 29They got up, drove him out of the town, and took him to the brow of the hill on which the town was built, in order to throw him down the cliff. 30But he walked right through the crowd and went on his way.

NOW OR NEVER

LK 4:22

What's your mental picture of Jesus? Contemplative? Angelic? Glowing? Yes, he is God's Son. But remember that when he walked on Earth, he was also a normal guy like you. That's why the people who knew him best were "amazed" by his teaching and didn't know quite what to think.

JESUS DRIVES OUT AN EVIL SPIRIT

31Then he went down to Capernaum, a town in Galilee, and on the Sabbath began to teach the people. 32They were amazed at his teaching, because his message had authority.

33In the synagogue there was a man possessed by a demon, an evil[c] spirit. He cried out at the top of his voice, 34"Ha! What do you want with us, Jesus of Nazareth? Have you come to destroy us? I know who you are—the Holy One of God!"

35"Be quiet!" Jesus said sternly. "Come out of him!" Then the demon threw the man down before them all and came out without injuring him.

36All the people were amazed and said to each other, "What is this teaching? With authority and power he gives orders to evil spirits and they come out!" 37And the news about him spread throughout the surrounding area.

JESUS HEALS MANY

38Jesus left the synagogue and went to the home of Simon. Now Simon's mother-in-law was suffering from a high fever, and they asked Jesus to help her. 39So he bent over her and rebuked the fever, and it left her. She got up at once and began to wait on them.

40When the sun was setting, the people brought to Jesus all who had various kinds of sickness, and laying his hands on each one, he healed them. 41Moreover, demons came out of many people, shouting, "You are the Son of God!" But he rebuked them and would not allow them to speak, because they knew he was the Christ.[d]

42At daybreak Jesus went out to a solitary place. The people were looking for him and when they came to where he was, they tried to keep him from leaving them. 43But he said, "I must preach the good news of the kingdom of God to the other towns also, because that is why I was sent." 44And he kept on preaching in the synagogues of Judea.[e]

---

[a] 19 Isaiah 61:1,2   [b] 27 The Greek word was used for various diseases affecting the skin—not necessarily leprosy.   [c] 33 Greek unclean; also in verse 36   [d] 41 Or Messiah   [e] 44 Or the land of the Jews; some manuscripts Galilee

THE CALLING OF THE FIRST DISCIPLES

5 One day as Jesus was standing by the Lake of Gennesaret,[a] with the people crowding around him and listening to the word of God, [2]he saw at the water's edge two boats, left there by the fishermen, who were washing their nets. [3]He got into one of the boats, the one belonging to Simon, and asked him to put out a little from shore. Then he sat down and taught the people from the boat.

[4]When he had finished speaking, he said to Simon, "Put out into deep water, and let down[b] the nets for a catch."

[5]Simon answered, "Master, we've worked hard all night and haven't caught anything. But because you say so, I will let down the nets."

[6]When they had done so, they caught such a large number of fish that their nets began to break. [7]So they signaled their partners in the other boat to come and help them, and they came and filled both boats so full that they began to sink.

[8]When Simon Peter saw this, he fell at Jesus' knees and said, "Go away from me, Lord; I am a sinful man!" [9]For he and all his companions were astonished at the catch of fish they had taken, [10]and so were James and John, the sons of Zebedee, Simon's partners.

Then Jesus said to Simon, "Don't be afraid; from now on you will catch men." [11]So they pulled their boats up on shore, left everything and followed him.

THE MAN WITH LEPROSY

[12]While Jesus was in one of the towns, a man came along who was covered with leprosy.[c] When he saw Jesus, he fell with his face to the ground and begged him, "Lord, if you are willing, you can make me clean."

[13]Jesus reached out his hand and touched the man. "I am willing," he said. "Be clean!" And immediately the leprosy left him.

[14]Then Jesus ordered him, "Don't tell anyone, but go, show yourself to the priest and offer the sacrifices that Moses commanded for your cleansing, as a testimony to them."

[15]Yet the news about him spread all the more, so that crowds of people came to hear him and to be healed of their sicknesses. [16]But Jesus often withdrew to lonely places and prayed.

JESUS HEALS A PARALYTIC

[17]One day as he was teaching, Pharisees and teachers of the law, who had come from every village of Galilee and from Judea and Jerusalem, were sitting there. And the power of the Lord was present for him to heal the sick. [18]Some men came carrying a paralytic on a mat and tried to take him into the house to lay him before Jesus. [19]When they could not find a way to do this because of the crowd, they went up on the roof and lowered him on his mat through the tiles into the middle of the crowd, right in front of Jesus.

[20]When Jesus saw their faith, he said, "Friend, your sins are forgiven."

[21]The Pharisees and the teachers of the law began thinking to themselves, "Who is this fellow who speaks blasphemy? Who can forgive sins but God alone?"

[22]Jesus knew what they were thinking and asked, "Why are you thinking these things in your hearts? [23]Which is easier: to say, 'Your sins are forgiven,' or to say, 'Get up and walk'? [24]But that you may know that the Son of Man has authority on earth to forgive sins . . . ." He said to the paralyzed man, "I tell you, get up, take your mat and go home." [25]Immediately he stood up in front of them, took what he had been lying on and went home praising God. [26]Everyone was amazed and gave praise to God. They were filled with awe and said, "We have seen remarkable things today."

THE CALLING OF LEVI

[27]After this, Jesus went out and saw a tax collector by the name of Levi sitting at his tax booth. "Follow me," Jesus said to him, [28]and Levi got up, left everything and followed him.

[29]Then Levi held a great banquet for Jesus at his house, and a large crowd of tax collectors and others were eating with them. [30]But the Pharisees and the teachers of the law who belonged to their sect complained to his disciples, "Why do you eat and drink with tax collectors and 'sinners'?"

---

[a] *1* That is, Sea of Galilee   [b] *4* The Greek verb is plural.   [c] *12* The Greek word was used for various diseases affecting the skin—not necessarily leprosy.

³¹Jesus answered them, "It is not the healthy who need a doctor, but the sick. ³²I have not come to call the righteous, but sinners to repentance."

JESUS QUESTIONED ABOUT FASTING

³³They said to him, "John's disciples often fast and pray, and so do the disciples of the Pharisees, but yours go on eating and drinking."

³⁴Jesus answered, "Can you make the guests of the bridegroom fast while he is with them? ³⁵But the time will come when the bridegroom will be taken from them; in those days they will fast."

NOW OR NEVER
LK 5:33

Don't fall into the trap of judging other Christians according to whether they do things the exact same way you do them. God has a unique path, plan and purpose for each one of us.

³⁶He told them this parable: "No one tears a patch from a new garment and sews it on an old one. If he does, he will have torn the new garment, and the patch from the new will not match the old. ³⁷And no one pours new wine into old wineskins. If he does, the new wine will burst the skins, the wine will run out and the wineskins will be ruined. ³⁸No, new wine must be poured into new wineskins. ³⁹And no one after drinking old wine wants the new, for he says, 'The old is better.' "

LORD OF THE SABBATH

6 One Sabbath Jesus was going through the grainfields, and his disciples began to pick some heads of grain, rub them in their hands and eat the kernels. ²Some of the Pharisees asked, "Why are you doing what is unlawful on the Sabbath?"

³Jesus answered them, "Have you never read what David did when he and his companions were hungry? ⁴He entered the house of God, and taking the consecrated bread, he ate what is lawful only for priests to eat. And he also gave some to his companions." ⁵Then Jesus said to them, "The Son of Man is Lord of the Sabbath."

⁶On another Sabbath he went into the synagogue and was teaching, and a man was there whose right hand was shriveled. ⁷The Pharisees and the teachers of the law were looking for a reason to accuse Jesus, so they watched him closely to see if he would heal on the Sabbath. ⁸But Jesus knew what they were thinking and said to the man with the shriveled hand, "Get up and stand in front of everyone." So he got up and stood there.

⁹Then Jesus said to them, "I ask you, which is lawful on the Sabbath: to do good or to do evil, to save life or to destroy it?"

¹⁰He looked around at them all, and then said to the man, "Stretch out your hand." He did so, and his hand was completely restored. ¹¹But they were furious and began to discuss with one another what they might do to Jesus.

THE TWELVE APOSTLES

¹²One of those days Jesus went out to a mountainside to pray, and spent the night praying to God. ¹³When morning came, he called his disciples to him and chose twelve of them, whom he also designated apostles: ¹⁴Simon (whom he named Peter), his brother Andrew, James, John, Philip, Bartholomew, ¹⁵Matthew, Thomas, James son of Alphaeus, Simon who was called the Zealot, ¹⁶Judas son of James, and Judas Iscariot, who became a traitor.

BLESSINGS AND WOES

¹⁷He went down with them and stood on a level place. A large crowd of his disciples was there and a great number of people from all over Judea, from Jerusalem, and from the coast of Tyre and Sidon, ¹⁸who had come to hear him and to be healed of their diseases. Those troubled by evilᵃ spirits were cured, ¹⁹and the people all tried to touch him, because power was coming from him and healing them all.

ᵃ 18 Greek unclean

²⁰Looking at his disciples, he said:

"Blessed are you who are poor,
    for yours is the kingdom of God.
²¹Blessed are you who hunger now,
    for you will be satisfied.
Blessed are you who weep now,
    for you will laugh.
²²Blessed are you when men hate you,
    when they exclude you and insult you
    and reject your name as evil,
        because of the Son of Man.

²³"Rejoice in that day and leap for joy, because great is your reward in heaven. For that is how their fathers treated the prophets.

²⁴"But woe to you who are rich,
    for you have already received your
    comfort.
²⁵Woe to you who are well fed now,
    for you will go hungry.
Woe to you who laugh now,
    for you will mourn and weep.
²⁶Woe to you when all men speak well of
    you,
    for that is how their fathers treated the
    false prophets.

LOVE FOR ENEMIES

²⁷"But I tell you who hear me: Love your enemies, do good to those who hate you, ²⁸bless those who curse you, pray for those who mistreat you. ²⁹If someone strikes you on one cheek, turn to him the other also. If someone takes your cloak, do not stop him from taking your tunic. ³⁰Give to everyone who asks you, and if anyone takes what belongs to you, do not demand it back. ³¹Do to others as you would have them do to you.

³²"If you love those who love you, what credit is that to you? Even 'sinners' love those who love them. ³³And if you do good to those who are good to you, what credit is that to you? Even 'sinners' do that. ³⁴And if you lend to those from whom you expect repayment, what credit is that to you? Even 'sinners' lend to 'sinners,' expecting to be repaid in full. ³⁵But love your enemies, do good to them, and lend to them without expecting to get anything back. Then your reward will be great, and you will be sons of the Most High, because he is kind to the ungrateful and wicked. ³⁶Be merciful, just as your Father is merciful.

JUDGING OTHERS

³⁷"Do not judge, and you will not be judged. Do not condemn, and you will not be condemned. Forgive, and you will be forgiven. ³⁸Give, and it will be given to you. A good measure, pressed down, shaken together and running over, will be poured into your lap. For with the measure you use, it will be measured to you."

³⁹He also told them this parable: "Can a blind man lead a blind man? Will they not both fall into a pit? ⁴⁰A student is not above his teacher, but everyone who is fully trained will be like his teacher.

⁴¹"Why do you look at the speck of sawdust in your brother's eye and pay no attention to the plank in your own eye? ⁴²How can you say to your brother, 'Brother, let me take the speck out of your eye,' when you yourself fail to see the plank in your own eye? You hypocrite, first take the plank out of your

Treating Others Well

»» live the adventure »» Lk 6:31

This rule would be a whole lot easier to obey if it said, "Do to others as they do to you," wouldn't it? The whole "eye for an eye" thing seems a lot more appropriate when you're dealing with someone who's wronged you or ticked you off. But vengeance isn't part of Jesus' plan for our relationships; mercy is. How hypocritical is it to thank God for his mercy—for not giving us the punishment we deserve for the things we've done wrong—and then exact revenge or demand punishment for something someone else has done to us?

eye, and then you will see clearly to remove the speck from your brother's eye.

A TREE AND ITS FRUIT

43 "No good tree bears bad fruit, nor does a bad tree bear good fruit. 44 Each tree is recognized by its own fruit. People do not pick figs from thornbushes, or grapes from briers. 45 The good man brings good things out of the good stored up in his heart, and the evil man brings evil things out of the evil stored up in his heart. For out of the overflow of his heart his mouth speaks.

THE WISE AND FOOLISH BUILDERS

46 "Why do you call me, 'Lord, Lord,' and do not do what I say? 47 I will show you what he is like who comes to me and hears my words and puts them into practice. 48 He is like a man building a house, who dug down deep and laid the foundation on rock. When a flood came, the torrent struck that house but could not shake it, because it was well built. 49 But the one who hears my words and does not put them into practice is like a man who built a house on the ground without a foundation. The moment the torrent struck that house, it collapsed and its destruction was complete."

THE FAITH OF THE CENTURION

7 When Jesus had finished saying all this in the hearing of the people, he entered Capernaum. 2 There a centurion's servant, whom his master valued highly, was sick and about to die. 3 The centurion heard of Jesus and sent some elders of the Jews to him, asking him to come and heal his servant. 4 When they came to Jesus, they pleaded earnestly with him, "This man deserves to have you do this, 5 because he loves our nation and has built our synagogue." 6 So Jesus went with them.

He was not far from the house when the centurion sent friends to say to him: "Lord, don't trouble yourself, for I do not deserve to have you come under my roof. 7 That is why I did not even consider myself worthy to come to you. But say the word, and my servant will be healed. 8 For I myself am a man under authority, with soldiers under me. I tell this one, 'Go,' and he goes; and that one, 'Come,' and he comes. I say to my servant, 'Do this,' and he does it."

9 When Jesus heard this, he was amazed at him, and turning to the crowd following him, he said, "I tell you, I have not found such great faith even in Israel." 10 Then the men who had been sent returned to the house and found the servant well.

JESUS RAISES A WIDOW'S SON

11 Soon afterward, Jesus went to a town called Nain, and his disciples and a large crowd went along with him. 12 As he approached the town gate, a dead person was being carried out—the only son of his mother, and she was a widow. And a large crowd from the town was with her. 13 When the Lord saw her, his heart went out to her and he said, "Don't cry."

»» live the adventure »» Lk 6:46-49

Building a Spiritual Foundation

You can save yourself a lot of future problems by making sure that your life is built on solid ground right now. The way to do that is to put Jesus at the center of everything you do—to hear what he says and, more important, to *do* what he says. Whether you're buying a new video game or playing basketball, ask yourself, "What would be the best way to honor the Lord right now?" or the ever-popular, "What would Jesus do?" If you learn to make both major and minor decisions based on the answers to those two questions, you'll build a foundation for your life that will be able to withstand anything Satan throws at you.

NOW OR NEVER
LK 7:6-10

Here is example #21,897 of a person being rewarded in an incredible way for demonstrating a humble attitude of faith. If you want to impress God... don't even try. Just humbly acknowledge who he is.

¹⁴Then he went up and touched the coffin, and those carrying it stood still. He said, "Young man, I say to you, get up!" ¹⁵The dead man sat up and began to talk, and Jesus gave him back to his mother.

¹⁶They were all filled with awe and praised God. "A great prophet has appeared among us," they said. "God has come to help his people." ¹⁷This news about Jesus spread throughout Judeaᵃ and the surrounding country.

JESUS AND JOHN THE BAPTIST

¹⁸John's disciples told him about all these things. Calling two of them, ¹⁹he sent them to the Lord to ask, "Are you the one who was to come, or should we expect someone else?"

²⁰When the men came to Jesus, they said, "John the Baptist sent us to you to ask, 'Are you the one who was to come, or should we expect someone else?' "

²¹At that very time Jesus cured many who had diseases, sicknesses and evil spirits, and gave sight to many who were blind. ²²So he replied to the messengers, "Go back and report to John what you have seen and heard: The blind receive sight, the lame walk, those who have leprosyᵇ are cured, the deaf hear, the dead are raised, and the good news is preached to the poor. ²³Blessed is the man who does not fall away on account of me."

NOW OR NEVER

LK 7:19

Even spiritual giants struggle with doubt. Notice that Jesus didn't make John feel like a loser for temporarily questioning his faith. Instead, Jesus gave John the assurance he needed to believe.

²⁴After John's messengers left, Jesus began to speak to the crowd about John: "What did you go out into the desert to see? A reed swayed by the wind? ²⁵If not, what did you go out to see? A man dressed in fine clothes? No, those who wear expensive clothes and indulge in luxury are in palaces. ²⁶But what did you go out to see? A prophet? Yes, I tell you, and more than a prophet. ²⁷This is the one about whom it is written:

> " 'I will send my messenger ahead of you,
>   who will prepare your way before you.'ᶜ

²⁸I tell you, among those born of women there is no one greater than John; yet the one who is least in the kingdom of God is greater than he."

²⁹(All the people, even the tax collectors, when they heard Jesus' words, acknowledged that God's way was right, because they had been baptized by John. ³⁰But the Pharisees and experts in the law rejected God's purpose for themselves, because they had not been baptized by John.)

³¹"To what, then, can I compare the people of this generation? What are they like? ³²They are like children sitting in the marketplace and calling out to each other:

> " 'We played the flute for you,
>   and you did not dance;
> we sang a dirge,
>   and you did not cry.'

³³For John the Baptist came neither eating bread nor drinking wine, and you say, 'He has a demon.' ³⁴The Son of Man came eating and drinking, and you say, 'Here is a glutton and a drunkard, a friend of tax collectors and "sinners." ' ³⁵But wisdom is proved right by all her children."

JESUS ANOINTED BY A SINFUL WOMAN

³⁶Now one of the Pharisees invited Jesus to have dinner with him, so he went to the Pharisee's house and reclined at the table. ³⁷When a woman who had lived a sinful life in that town learned that Jesus was eating at the Pharisee's house, she brought an alabaster jar of perfume, ³⁸and as she stood behind him at his feet weeping, she began to wet his feet with her tears. Then she wiped them with her hair, kissed them and poured perfume on them.

ᵃ *17* Or *the land of the Jews*   ᵇ *22* The Greek word was used for various diseases affecting the skin—not necessarily leprosy.
ᶜ *27* Mal. 3:1

³⁹When the Pharisee who had invited him saw this, he said to himself, "If this man were a prophet, he would know who is touching him and what kind of woman she is—that she is a sinner."

⁴⁰Jesus answered him, "Simon, I have something to tell you."

"Tell me, teacher," he said.

⁴¹"Two men owed money to a certain moneylender. One owed him five hundred denarii,ᵃ and the other fifty. ⁴²Neither of them had the money to pay him back, so he canceled the debts of both. Now which of them will love him more?"

⁴³Simon replied, "I suppose the one who had the bigger debt canceled."

"You have judged correctly," Jesus said.

⁴⁴Then he turned toward the woman and said to Simon, "Do you see this woman? I came into your house. You did not give me any water for my feet, but she wet my feet with her tears and wiped them with her hair. ⁴⁵You did not give me a kiss, but this woman, from the time I entered, has not stopped kissing my feet. ⁴⁶You did not put oil on my head, but she has poured perfume on my feet. ⁴⁷Therefore, I tell you, her many sins have been forgiven—for she loved much. But he who has been forgiven little loves little."

⁴⁸Then Jesus said to her, "Your sins are forgiven."

⁴⁹The other guests began to say among themselves, "Who is this who even forgives sins?"

⁵⁰Jesus said to the woman, "Your faith has saved you; go in peace."

Responding to God's Forgiveness

Have you ever heard stories about people who were told they had a fatal disease but ended up making a full recovery? Usually those stories end with the people talking about how they're going to make the most of every day thanks to their second chance at life. That's the kind of attitude God expects when he forgives our sins. Think about it: Your old life without Jesus was a dead end. You had nothing to look forward to. But with God's forgiveness everything changes. Not only do you have a chance for a brand-new start, you also have an eternal future in heaven to look forward to. That should put a spark in your life!

THE PARABLE OF THE SOWER

8 After this, Jesus traveled about from one town and village to another, proclaiming the good news of the kingdom of God. The Twelve were with him, ²and also some women who had been cured of evil spirits and diseases: Mary (called Magdalene) from whom seven demons had come out; ³Joanna the wife of Cuza, the manager of Herod's household; Susanna; and many others. These women were helping to support them out of their own means.

⁴While a large crowd was gathering and people were coming to Jesus from town after town, he told this parable: ⁵"A farmer went out to sow his seed. As he was scattering the seed, some fell along the path; it was trampled on, and the birds of the air ate it up. ⁶Some fell on rock, and when it came up, the plants withered because they had no moisture. ⁷Other seed fell among thorns, which grew up with it and choked the plants. ⁸Still other seed fell on good soil. It came up and yielded a crop, a hundred times more than was sown."

When he said this, he called out, "He who has ears to hear, let him hear."

⁹His disciples asked him what this parable meant. ¹⁰He said, "The knowledge of the secrets of the kingdom of God has been given to you, but to others I speak in parables, so that,

" 'though seeing, they may not see;
  though hearing, they may not understand.'ᵇ

NOW OR NEVER
LK 8:5–8

When you talk to people about Jesus, what you're really doing is spreading seeds of truth. You may not see immediate results, but God can cause the seeds you plant to "take root" in people's hearts and minds. At some point in the future, those people may decide to trust Jesus—because of a seed that you planted.

ᵃ *41* A denarius was a coin worth about a day's wages.   ᵇ *10* Isaiah 6:9

[11] "This is the meaning of the parable: The seed is the word of God. [12] Those along the path are the ones who hear, and then the devil comes and takes away the word from their hearts, so that they may not believe and be saved. [13] Those on the rock are the ones who receive the word with joy when they hear it, but they have no root. They believe for a while, but in the time of testing they fall away. [14] The seed that fell among thorns stands for those who hear, but as they go on their way they are choked by life's worries, riches and pleasures, and they do not mature. [15] But the seed on good soil stands for those with a noble and good heart, who hear the word, retain it, and by persevering produce a crop.

A LAMP ON A STAND

[16] "No one lights a lamp and hides it in a jar or puts it under a bed. Instead, he puts it on a stand, so that those who come in can see the light. [17] For there is nothing hidden that will not be disclosed, and nothing concealed that will not be known or brought out into the open. [18] Therefore consider carefully how you listen. Whoever has will be given more; whoever does not have, even what he thinks he has will be taken from him."

JESUS' MOTHER AND BROTHERS

[19] Now Jesus' mother and brothers came to see him, but they were not able to get near him because of the crowd. [20] Someone told him, "Your mother and brothers are standing outside, wanting to see you."

[21] He replied, "My mother and brothers are those who hear God's word and put it into practice."

challenge notes

To: my_son

heavenly_father: I've given you two families—the one you were born into and the one you became a part of when you gave your life to me. what does it mean to be part of my family? it's all about hearing and obeying my word.

LK 8:21

JESUS CALMS THE STORM

[22] One day Jesus said to his disciples, "Let's go over to the other side of the lake." So they got into a boat and set out. [23] As they sailed, he fell asleep. A squall came down on the lake, so that the boat was being swamped, and they were in great danger.

[24] The disciples went and woke him, saying, "Master, Master, we're going to drown!"

He got up and rebuked the wind and the raging waters; the storm subsided, and all was calm. [25] "Where is your faith?" he asked his disciples.

In fear and amazement they asked one another, "Who is this? He commands even the winds and the water, and they obey him."

NOW OR NEVER
LK 8:24

If Jesus can stop a wicked storm in its tracks, do you still believe there's anything in your life too big for him to handle?

THE HEALING OF A DEMON-POSSESSED MAN

[26] They sailed to the region of the Gerasenes, [a] which is across the lake from Galilee. [27] When Jesus stepped ashore, he was met by a demon-possessed man from the town. For a long time this man had not worn clothes or lived in a house, but had lived in the tombs. [28] When he saw Jesus, he cried out and fell at his feet, shouting at the top of his voice, "What do you want with me, Jesus, Son of the Most High God? I beg you, don't torture me!" [29] For Jesus had commanded the evil [b] spirit to come out of the man. Many times it had seized him, and though he was chained hand and foot and kept under guard, he had broken his chains and had been driven by the demon into solitary places.

[30] Jesus asked him, "What is your name?"

"Legion," he replied, because many demons had gone into him. [31] And they begged him repeatedly not to order them to go into the Abyss.

[32] A large herd of pigs was feeding there on the hillside. The demons begged Jesus to let them go

---

[a] *26 Some manuscripts Gadarenes; other manuscripts Gergesenes; also in verse 37*   [b] *29 Greek unclean*

into them, and he gave them permission. 33When the demons came out of the man, they went into the pigs, and the herd rushed down the steep bank into the lake and was drowned.

34When those tending the pigs saw what had happened, they ran off and reported this in the town and countryside, 35and the people went out to see what had happened. When they came to Jesus, they found the man from whom the demons had gone out, sitting at Jesus' feet, dressed and in his right mind; and they were afraid. 36Those who had seen it told the people how the demon-possessed man had been cured. 37Then all the people of the region of the Gerasenes asked Jesus to leave them, because they were overcome with fear. So he got into the boat and left.

38The man from whom the demons had gone out begged to go with him, but Jesus sent him away, saying, 39"Return home and tell how much God has done for you." So the man went away and told all over town how much Jesus had done for him.

A DEAD GIRL AND A SICK WOMAN

40Now when Jesus returned, a crowd welcomed him, for they were all expecting him. 41Then a man named Jairus, a ruler of the synagogue, came and fell at Jesus' feet, pleading with him to come to his house 42because his only daughter, a girl of about twelve, was dying.

As Jesus was on his way, the crowds almost crushed him. 43And a woman was there who had been subject to bleeding for twelve years, [a] but no one could heal her. 44She came up behind him and touched the edge of his cloak, and immediately her bleeding stopped.

45"Who touched me?" Jesus asked.

When they all denied it, Peter said, "Master, the people are crowding and pressing against you."

46But Jesus said, "Someone touched me; I know that power has gone out from me."

47Then the woman, seeing that she could not go unnoticed, came trembling and fell at his feet. In the presence of all the people, she told why she had touched him and how she had been instantly healed. 48Then he said to her, "Daughter, your faith has healed you. Go in peace."

49While Jesus was still speaking, someone came from the house of Jairus, the synagogue ruler. "Your daughter is dead," he said. "Don't bother the teacher any more."

50Hearing this, Jesus said to Jairus, "Don't be afraid; just believe, and she will be healed."

51When he arrived at the house of Jairus, he did not let anyone go in with him except Peter, John and James, and the child's father and mother. 52Meanwhile, all the people were wailing and mourning for her. "Stop wailing," Jesus said. "She is not dead but asleep."

53They laughed at him, knowing that she was dead. 54But he took her by the hand and said, "My child, get up!" 55Her spirit returned, and at once she stood up. Then Jesus told them to give her something to eat. 56Her parents were astonished, but he ordered them not to tell anyone what had happened.

JESUS SENDS OUT THE TWELVE

9 When Jesus had called the Twelve together, he gave them power and authority to drive out all demons and to cure diseases, 2and he sent them out to preach the kingdom of God and to heal the sick. 3He told them: "Take nothing for the journey—no staff, no bag, no bread, no money, no extra tunic. 4Whatever house you enter, stay there until you leave that town. 5If people do not welcome you, shake the dust off your feet when you leave their town, as a testimony against them." 6So they set out and went from village to village, preaching the gospel and healing people everywhere.

7Now Herod the tetrarch heard about all that was going on. And he was perplexed, because some were saying that John had been raised from the dead, 8others that Elijah had appeared, and still others that one of the prophets of long ago had come back to life. 9But Herod said, "I beheaded John. Who, then, is this I hear such things about?" And he tried to see him.

JESUS FEEDS THE FIVE THOUSAND

10When the apostles returned, they reported to Jesus what they had done. Then he took them with him and they withdrew by themselves to a town called Bethsaida, 11but the crowds learned about it and followed him. He welcomed them and spoke to them about the kingdom of God, and healed those who needed healing.

12Late in the afternoon the Twelve came to him and said, "Send the crowd away so they can go to the surrounding villages and countryside and find food and lodging, because we are in a remote place here."

[a] 43 Many manuscripts years, and she had spent all she had on doctors

13He replied, "You give them something to eat."

They answered, "We have only five loaves of bread and two fish—unless we go and buy food for all this crowd." 14(About five thousand men were there.)

But he said to his disciples, "Have them sit down in groups of about fifty each." 15The disciples did so, and everybody sat down. 16Taking the five loaves and the two fish and looking up to heaven, he gave thanks and broke them. Then he gave them to the disciples to set before the people. 17They all ate and were satisfied, and the disciples picked up twelve basketfuls of broken pieces that were left over.

PETER'S CONFESSION OF CHRIST

18Once when Jesus was praying in private and his disciples were with him, he asked them, "Who do the crowds say I am?"

19They replied, "Some say John the Baptist; others say Elijah; and still others, that one of the prophets of long ago has come back to life."

20"But what about you?" he asked. "Who do you say I am?"

Peter answered, "The Christa of God."

21Jesus strictly warned them not to tell this to anyone. 22And he said, "The Son of Man must suffer many things and be rejected by the elders, chief priests and teachers of the law, and he must be killed and on the third day be raised to life."

23Then he said to them all: "If anyone would come after me, he must deny himself and take up his cross daily and follow me. 24For whoever wants to save his life will lose it, but whoever loses his life for me will save it. 25What good is it for a man to gain the whole world, and yet lose or forfeit his very self? 26If anyone is ashamed of me and my words, the Son of Man will be ashamed of him when he comes in his glory and in the glory of the Father and of the holy angels. 27I tell you the truth, some who are standing here will not taste death before they see the kingdom of God."

THE TRANSFIGURATION

28About eight days after Jesus said this, he took Peter, John and James with him and went up onto a mountain to pray. 29As he was praying, the appearance of his face changed, and his clothes became as bright as a flash of lightning. 30Two men, Moses and Elijah, 31appeared in glorious splendor, talking with Jesus. They spoke about his departure, which he was about to bring to fulfillment at Jerusalem. 32Peter and his companions were very sleepy, but when they became fully awake, they saw his glory and the two men standing with him. 33As the men were leaving Jesus, Peter said to him, "Master, it is good for us to be here. Let us put up three shelters—one for you, one for Moses and one for Elijah." (He did not know what he was saying.)

34While he was speaking, a cloud appeared and enveloped them, and they were afraid as they entered the cloud. 35A voice came from the cloud, saying, "This is my Son, whom I have chosen; listen to him." 36When the voice had spoken, they found that Jesus was alone. The disciples kept this to themselves, and told no one at that time what they had seen.

NOW OR NEVER
LK 9:42

Demons aren't just movie monsters; they're actual spiritual beings. But as Jesus proved over and over again in the New Testament, their power is no match for his . . . so we have no reason to fear them.

THE HEALING OF A BOY WITH AN EVIL SPIRIT

37The next day, when they came down from the mountain, a large crowd met him. 38A man in the crowd called out, "Teacher, I beg you to look at my son, for he is my only child. 39A spirit seizes him and he suddenly screams; it throws him into convulsions so that he foams at the mouth. It scarcely ever leaves him and is destroying him. 40I begged your disciples to drive it out, but they could not."

41"O unbelieving and perverse generation," Jesus replied, "how long shall I stay with you and put up with you? Bring your son here."

42Even while the boy was coming, the demon threw him to the ground in a convulsion. But Jesus

a 20 Or Messiah

rebuked the evil[a] spirit, healed the boy and gave him back to his father. 43And they were all amazed at the greatness of God.

While everyone was marveling at all that Jesus did, he said to his disciples, 44"Listen carefully to what I am about to tell you: The Son of Man is going to be betrayed into the hands of men." 45But they did not understand what this meant. It was hidden from them, so that they did not grasp it, and they were afraid to ask him about it.

WHO WILL BE THE GREATEST?

46An argument started among the disciples as to which of them would be the greatest. 47Jesus, knowing their thoughts, took a little child and had him stand beside him. 48Then he said to them, "Whoever welcomes this little child in my name welcomes me; and whoever welcomes me welcomes the one who sent me. For he who is least among you all—he is the greatest."

49"Master," said John, "we saw a man driving out demons in your name and we tried to stop him, because he is not one of us."

50"Do not stop him," Jesus said, "for whoever is not against you is for you."

SAMARITAN OPPOSITION

51As the time approached for him to be taken up to heaven, Jesus resolutely set out for Jerusalem. 52And he sent messengers on ahead, who went into a Samaritan village to get things ready for him; 53but the people there did not welcome him, because he was heading for Jerusalem. 54When the disciples James and John saw this, they asked, "Lord, do you want us to call fire down from heaven to destroy them[b]?" 55But Jesus turned and rebuked them, 56and[c] they went to another village.

THE COST OF FOLLOWING JESUS

57As they were walking along the road, a man said to him, "I will follow you wherever you go."

58Jesus replied, "Foxes have holes and birds of the air have nests, but the Son of Man has no place to lay his head."

59He said to another man, "Follow me."

But the man replied, "Lord, first let me go and bury my father."

60Jesus said to him, "Let the dead bury their own dead, but you go and proclaim the kingdom of God."

61Still another said, "I will follow you, Lord; but first let me go back and say good-by to my family."

62Jesus replied, "No one who puts his hand to the plow and looks back is fit for service in the kingdom of God."

JESUS SENDS OUT THE SEVENTY-TWO

10 After this the Lord appointed seventy-two[d] others and sent them two by two ahead of him to every town and place where he was about to go. 2He told them, "The harvest is plentiful, but the workers are few. Ask the Lord of the harvest, therefore, to send out workers into his harvest field. 3Go! I am sending you out like lambs among wolves. 4Do not take a purse or bag or sandals; and do not greet anyone on the road.

5"When you enter a house, first say, 'Peace to this house.' 6If a man of peace is there, your peace will rest on him; if not, it will return to you. 7Stay in that house, eating and drinking whatever they give you, for the worker deserves his wages. Do not move around from house to house.

8"When you enter a town and are welcomed, eat what is set before you. 9Heal the sick who are there and tell them, 'The kingdom of God is near you.' 10But when you enter a town and are not welcomed,

---

NOW OR NEVER
LK 9:60

Your commitment to Jesus isn't something you can put on the back burner when "more pressing" things come up. If you find you don't have enough time in your calendar for quality time with the One who saved your life, it's time to get rid of some of your other commitments.

---

[a] 42 Greek *unclean*   [b] 54 Some manuscripts *them, even as Elijah did*   [c] 55,56 Some manuscripts *them. And he said, "You do not know what kind of spirit you are of, for the Son of Man did not come to destroy men's lives, but to save them."* 56And   [d] 1 Some manuscripts *seventy*; also in verse 17

go into its streets and say, ¹¹'Even the dust of your town that sticks to our feet we wipe off against you. Yet be sure of this: The kingdom of God is near.' ¹²I tell you, it will be more bearable on that day for Sodom than for that town.

¹³"Woe to you, Korazin! Woe to you, Bethsaida! For if the miracles that were performed in you had been performed in Tyre and Sidon, they would have repented long ago, sitting in sackcloth and ashes. ¹⁴But it will be more bearable for Tyre and Sidon at the judgment than for you. ¹⁵And you, Capernaum, will you be lifted up to the skies? No, you will go down to the depths.ᵃ

¹⁶"He who listens to you listens to me; he who rejects you rejects me; but he who rejects me rejects him who sent me."

¹⁷The seventy-two returned with joy and said, "Lord, even the demons submit to us in your name."

¹⁸He replied, "I saw Satan fall like lightning from heaven. ¹⁹I have given you authority to trample on snakes and scorpions and to overcome all the power of the enemy; nothing will harm you. ²⁰However, do not rejoice that the spirits submit to you, but rejoice that your names are written in heaven."

²¹At that time Jesus, full of joy through the Holy Spirit, said, "I praise you, Father, Lord of heaven and earth, because you have hidden these things from the wise and learned, and revealed them to little children. Yes, Father, for this was your good pleasure.

²²"All things have been committed to me by my Father. No one knows who the Son is except the Father, and no one knows who the Father is except the Son and those to whom the Son chooses to reveal him."

²³Then he turned to his disciples and said privately, "Blessed are the eyes that see what you see. ²⁴For I tell you that many prophets and kings wanted to see what you see but did not see it, and to hear what you hear but did not hear it."

THE PARABLE OF THE GOOD SAMARITAN

²⁵On one occasion an expert in the law stood up to test Jesus. "Teacher," he asked, "what must I do to inherit eternal life?"

²⁶"What is written in the Law?" he replied. "How do you read it?"

²⁷He answered: "'Love the Lord your God with all your heart and with all your soul and with all your strength and with all your mind'ᵇ; and, 'Love your neighbor as yourself.'ᶜ"

²⁸"You have answered correctly," Jesus replied. "Do this and you will live."

²⁹But he wanted to justify himself, so he asked Jesus, "And who is my neighbor?"

³⁰In reply Jesus said: "A man was going down from Jerusalem to Jericho, when he fell into the hands of robbers. They stripped him of his clothes, beat him and went away, leaving him half dead. ³¹A priest happened to be going down the same road, and when he saw the man, he passed by on the other side. ³²So too, a Levite, when he came to the place and saw him, passed by on the other side. ³³But a Samaritan, as he traveled, came where the man was; and when he saw him, he took pity on him. ³⁴He went to him and bandaged his wounds, pour-

---

NOW OR NEVER

LK 10:25–37

How cool would it be to become an *unforgettable person* in someone's life? That's what happens when you're willing to go the distance in loving your neighbor the way Jesus calls us to. Do you think the injured man in Jesus' story could ever forget the Samaritan who helped him?

» live the adventure » Lk 10:33

Identifying Your Neighbors

The law expert had it all backward. He wanted to know who his neighbor was so that he could narrow down the list of people he had to show love to. After all, why show love to the whole neighborhood if you're only really responsible for your next-door neighbors—right?

Wrong. It turns out Jesus has a much broader definition of the word *neighbor*. As far as he's concerned, the question is not "Who is my neighbor?" The question is "Who *isn't* my neighbor?" Who deserves your love, attention and generosity? Anyone who needs it. Jesus has called us to show compassion to everyone.

ᵃ *15* Greek *Hades*   ᵇ *27* Deut. 6:5   ᶜ *27* Lev. 19:18

ing on oil and wine. Then he put the man on his own donkey, took him to an inn and took care of him. ³⁵The next day he took out two silver coins ª and gave them to the innkeeper. 'Look after him,' he said, 'and when I return, I will reimburse you for any extra expense you may have.'

³⁶"Which of these three do you think was a neighbor to the man who fell into the hands of robbers?"

³⁷The expert in the law replied, "The one who had mercy on him."

Jesus told him, "Go and do likewise."

AT THE HOME OF MARTHA AND MARY

³⁸As Jesus and his disciples were on their way, he came to a village where a woman named Martha opened her home to him. ³⁹She had a sister called Mary, who sat at the Lord's feet listening to what he said. ⁴⁰But Martha was distracted by all the preparations that had to be made. She came to him and asked, "Lord, don't you care that my sister has left me to do the work by myself? Tell her to help me!"

⁴¹"Martha, Martha," the Lord answered, "you are worried and upset about many things, ⁴²but only one thing is needed. ᵇ Mary has chosen what is better, and it will not be taken away from her."

challenge notes

To: my_son

heavenly_father: you will always find things to keep you busy if you look hard enough. at some point, though, you need to stop and think about what's really important. your time with me is too valuable to ignore. no matter what else you're trying to get done, it can wait.

LK 10:41-42

JESUS' TEACHING ON PRAYER

11 One day Jesus was praying in a certain place. When he finished, one of his disciples said to him, "Lord, teach us to pray, just as John taught his disciples."

²He said to them, "When you pray, say:

" 'Father, ᶜ
hallowed be your name,
your kingdom come. ᵈ
³Give us each day our daily bread.
⁴Forgive us our sins,
for we also forgive everyone who sins against us. ᵉ
And lead us not into temptation.' ᶠ "

⁵Then he said to them, "Suppose one of you has a friend, and he goes to him at midnight and says, 'Friend, lend me three loaves of bread, ⁶because a friend of mine on a journey has come to me, and I have nothing to set before him.'

⁷"Then the one inside answers, 'Don't bother me. The door is already locked, and my children are with me in bed. I can't get up and give you anything.' ⁸I tell you, though he will not get up and give him the bread because he is his friend, yet because of the man's boldness ᵍ he will get up and give him as much as he needs.

⁹"So I say to you: Ask and it will be given to you; seek and you will find; knock and the door will be opened to you. ¹⁰For everyone

now or never

LK 11:11-13

What prevents you from taking *all* of your needs to God in prayer? Are you afraid he'll reject you? Are you unsure if he can answer them? Whatever the reason, it's not good enough to keep you from enjoying the incredible blessings that come from answered prayer.

who asks receives; he who seeks finds; and to him who knocks, the door will be opened.

¹¹"Which of you fathers, if your son asks for ʰ a fish, will give him a snake instead? ¹²Or if he asks

---

ª 35 Greek *two denarii*   ᵇ 42 Some manuscripts *but few things are needed—or only one*   ᶜ 2 Some manuscripts *Our Father in heaven*   ᵈ 2 Some manuscripts *come. May your will be done on earth as it is in heaven.*   ᵉ 4 Greek *everyone who is indebted to us*   ᶠ 4 Some manuscripts *temptation but deliver us from the evil one*   ᵍ 8 Or *persistence*   ʰ 11 Some manuscripts *for bread, will give him a stone; or if he asks for*

for an egg, will give him a scorpion? [13]If you then, though you are evil, know how to give good gifts to your children, how much more will your Father in heaven give the Holy Spirit to those who ask him!"

JESUS AND BEELZEBUB

[14]Jesus was driving out a demon that was mute. When the demon left, the man who had been mute spoke, and the crowd was amazed. [15]But some of them said, "By Beelzebub,[a] the prince of demons, he is driving out demons." [16]Others tested him by asking for a sign from heaven.

[17]Jesus knew their thoughts and said to them: "Any kingdom divided against itself will be ruined, and a house divided against itself will fall. [18]If Satan is divided against himself, how can his kingdom stand? I say this because you claim that I drive out demons by Beelzebub. [19]Now if I drive out demons by Beelzebub, by whom do your followers drive them out? So then, they will be your judges. [20]But if I drive out demons by the finger of God, then the kingdom of God has come to you.

[21]"When a strong man, fully armed, guards his own house, his possessions are safe. [22]But when someone stronger attacks and overpowers him, he takes away the armor in which the man trusted and divides up the spoils.

[23]"He who is not with me is against me, and he who does not gather with me, scatters.

[24]"When an evil[b] spirit comes out of a man, it goes through arid places seeking rest and does not find it. Then it says, 'I will return to the house I left.' [25]When it arrives, it finds the house swept clean and put in order. [26]Then it goes and takes seven other spirits more wicked than itself, and they go in and live there. And the final condition of that man is worse than the first."

[27]As Jesus was saying these things, a woman in the crowd called out, "Blessed is the mother who gave you birth and nursed you."

[28]He replied, "Blessed rather are those who hear the word of God and obey it."

THE SIGN OF JONAH

[29]As the crowds increased, Jesus said, "This is a wicked generation. It asks for a miraculous sign, but none will be given it except the sign of Jonah. [30]For as Jonah was a sign to the Ninevites, so also will the Son of Man be to this generation. [31]The Queen of the South will rise at the judgment with the men of this generation and condemn them; for she came from the ends of the earth to listen to Solomon's wisdom, and now one[c] greater than Solomon is here. [32]The men of Nineveh will stand up at the judgment with this generation and condemn it; for they repented at the preaching of Jonah, and now one greater than Jonah is here.

NOW OR NEVER

LK 11:29

Do you think more people today would believe that Jesus is who he says he is if they saw him perform the kinds of miracles he did in New Testament times? Why or why not?

THE LAMP OF THE BODY

[33]"No one lights a lamp and puts it in a place where it will be hidden, or under a bowl. Instead he puts it on its stand, so that those who come in may see the light. [34]Your eye is the lamp of your body. When your eyes are good, your whole body also is full of light. But when they are bad, your body also is full of darkness. [35]See to it, then, that the light within you is not darkness. [36]Therefore, if your whole body is full of light, and no part of it dark, it will be completely lighted, as when the light of a lamp shines on you."

SIX WOES

[37]When Jesus had finished speaking, a Pharisee invited him to eat with him; so he went in and reclined at the table. [38]But the Pharisee, noticing that Jesus did not first wash before the meal, was surprised.

[39]Then the Lord said to him, "Now then, you Pharisees clean the outside of the cup and dish, but inside you are full of greed and wickedness. [40]You foolish people! Did not the one who made the outside make the inside also? [41]But give what is inside ⌐the dish⌐[d] to the poor, and everything will be clean for you.

---

[a] 15 Greek Beezeboul or Beelzeboul; also in verses 18 and 19   [b] 24 Greek unclean   [c] 31 Or something; also in verse 32
[d] 41 Or what you have

⁴²"Woe to you Pharisees, because you give God a tenth of your mint, rue and all other kinds of garden herbs, but you neglect justice and the love of God. You should have practiced the latter without leaving the former undone.

⁴³"Woe to you Pharisees, because you love the most important seats in the synagogues and greetings in the marketplaces.

⁴⁴"Woe to you, because you are like unmarked graves, which men walk over without knowing it."

⁴⁵One of the experts in the law answered him, "Teacher, when you say these things, you insult us also."

⁴⁶Jesus replied, "And you experts in the law, woe to you, because you load people down with burdens they can hardly carry, and you yourselves will not lift one finger to help them.

⁴⁷"Woe to you, because you build tombs for the prophets, and it was your forefathers who killed them. ⁴⁸So you testify that you approve of what your forefathers did; they killed the prophets, and you build their tombs. ⁴⁹Because of this, God in his wisdom said, 'I will send them prophets and apostles, some of whom they will kill and others they will persecute.' ⁵⁰Therefore this generation will be held responsible for the blood of all the prophets that has been shed since the beginning of the world, ⁵¹from the blood of Abel to the blood of Zechariah, who was killed between the altar and the sanctuary. Yes, I tell you, this generation will be held responsible for it all.

⁵²"Woe to you experts in the law, because you have taken away the key to knowledge. You yourselves have not entered, and you have hindered those who were entering."

⁵³When Jesus left there, the Pharisees and the teachers of the law began to oppose him fiercely and to besiege him with questions, ⁵⁴waiting to catch him in something he might say.

WARNINGS AND ENCOURAGEMENTS

12 Meanwhile, when a crowd of many thousands had gathered, so that they were trampling on one another, Jesus began to speak first to his disciples, saying: "Be on your guard against the yeast of the Pharisees, which is hypocrisy. ²There is nothing concealed that will not be disclosed, or hidden that will not be made known. ³What you have said in the dark will be heard in the daylight, and what you have whispered in the ear in the inner rooms will be proclaimed from the roofs.

⁴"I tell you, my friends, do not be afraid of those who kill the body and after that can do no more. ⁵But I will show you whom you should fear: Fear him who, after the killing of the body, has power to throw you into hell. Yes, I tell you, fear him. ⁶Are not five sparrows sold for two pennies*? Yet not one of them is forgotten by God. ⁷Indeed, the very hairs of your head are all numbered. Don't be afraid; you are worth more than many sparrows.

⁸"I tell you, whoever acknowledges me before men, the Son of Man will also acknowledge him before the angels of God. ⁹But he who disowns me before men will be disowned before the angels of God. ¹⁰And everyone who speaks a word against the Son of Man will be forgiven, but anyone who blasphemes against the Holy Spirit will not be forgiven.

¹¹"When you are brought before synagogues, rulers and authorities, do not worry about how you will defend yourselves or what you will say, ¹²for the Holy Spirit will teach you at that time what you should say."

THE PARABLE OF THE RICH FOOL

¹³Someone in the crowd said to him, "Teacher, tell my brother to divide the inheritance with me."

¹⁴Jesus replied, "Man, who appointed me a judge or an arbiter between you?" ¹⁵Then he said to them, "Watch out! Be on your guard against all kinds of greed; a man's life does not consist in the abundance of his possessions."

¹⁶And he told them this parable: "The ground of a certain rich man produced a good crop. ¹⁷He thought to himself, 'What shall I do? I have no place to store my crops.'

¹⁸"Then he said, 'This is what I'll do. I will tear down my barns and build bigger ones, and there I will store all my grain and my goods. ¹⁹And I'll say to myself, "You have plenty of good things laid up for many years. Take life easy; eat, drink and be merry." '

²⁰"But God said to him, 'You fool! This very night your life will be demanded from you. Then who will get what you have prepared for yourself?'

²¹"This is how it will be with anyone who stores up things for himself but is not rich toward God."

battlelines

» Spilling the Beans? (Confrontation)

Q: You look whipped.
A: I should—I was up most of the night.

Q: Studying for your math test?
A: Worrying about my brother.

Q: What's up with him?
A: He snuck out again last night. I was sure my parents were going to catch him this time. But, as usual, he snuck back in just before they got up. That's not all though. I found out a few weeks ago he's doing drugs. He told me everything.

Q: That's tough.
A: Yep. My parents know he tells me stuff, so they pump me for information every day. And then Brad expects me to keep his dirty little secrets. What am I supposed to do? I'm getting pulled from both sides.

Q: I don't know, man. I couldn't live like that.
A: I don't think I can either. Right now, it looks like I only have two options, and both of them stink. If I tell my parents what's going on, Brad will never trust me again. But if I keep my mouth shut and let him keep going, something *really* bad could happen. That's an even worse deal. Either way, I'm a bad brother.

Q: So there's your answer.
A: What do you mean?

Q: You said it yourself. One option's a bad deal. But the other is even *worse*.
A: Maybe I could just run away.

Q: You mean, like, join a circus or something?
A: Sure. I've already got experience living in a freak show!

» Black-and-White Choices in a Gray World

Different people respond to conflict in different ways. Some people run away from it. Some look the other way. And some deal with it head-on. So what is the *right* way to handle conflict? While every situation is different, here's something to remember: The small conflict you refuse to address today is likely to become an even bigger deal tomorrow. It's like a cavity in your tooth. You can deal with it now with a $100 filling, or you can pay later with an $800 root canal.

Jesus didn't go around butting heads for no good reason (see Luke 9:38–41), but he didn't run from conflict either (see Luke 12:49–53). As for Nicholas, his brother is risking his own life by experimenting with drugs. Maybe it's time for Nicholas to give his brother an ultimatum before going to their parents. (Jesus lays out the model for loving confrontation in Matthew 18:15–17). Better an angry but alive brother than one who's in jail or worse—dead.

For more on confrontation, go to www.RevolutionBible.com.

DO NOT WORRY

22Then Jesus said to his disciples: "Therefore I tell you, do not worry about your life, what you will eat; or about your body, what you will wear. 23Life is more than food, and the body more than clothes. 24Consider the ravens: They do not sow or reap, they have no storeroom or barn; yet God feeds them. And how much more valuable you are than birds! 25Who of you by worrying can add a single hour to his life[a]? 26Since you cannot do this very little thing, why do you worry about the rest?

27"Consider how the lilies grow. They do not labor or spin. Yet I tell you, not even Solomon in all his splendor was dressed like one of these. 28If that is how God clothes the grass of the field, which is here today, and tomorrow is thrown into the fire, how much more will he clothe you, O you of little faith! 29And do not set your heart on what you will eat or drink; do not worry about it. 30For the pagan world runs after all such things, and your Father knows that you need them. 31But seek his kingdom, and these things will be given to you as well.

32"Do not be afraid, little flock, for your Father has been pleased to give you the kingdom. 33Sell your possessions and give to the poor. Provide purses for yourselves that will not wear out, a treasure in heaven that will not be exhausted, where no thief comes near and no moth destroys. 34For where your treasure is, there your heart will be also.

WATCHFULNESS

35"Be dressed ready for service and keep your lamps burning, 36like men waiting for their master to return from a wedding banquet, so that when he comes and knocks they can immediately open the door for him. 37It will be good for those servants whose master finds them watching when he comes. I tell you the truth, he will dress himself to serve, will have them recline at the table and will come and wait on them. 38It will be good for those servants whose master finds them ready, even if he comes in the second or third watch of the night. 39But understand this: If the owner of the house had known at what hour the thief was coming, he would not have let his house be broken into. 40You also must be ready, because the Son of Man will come at an hour when you do not expect him."

41Peter asked, "Lord, are you telling this parable to us, or to everyone?"

42The Lord answered, "Who then is the faithful and wise manager, whom the master puts in charge of his servants to give them their food allowance at the proper time? 43It will be good for that servant whom the master finds doing so when he returns. 44I tell you the truth, he will put him in charge of all his possessions. 45But suppose the servant says to himself, 'My master is taking a long time in coming,' and he then begins to beat the menservants and maidservants and to eat and drink and get drunk. 46The master of that servant will come on a day when he does not expect him and at an hour he is not aware of. He will cut him to pieces and assign him a place with the unbelievers.

47"That servant who knows his master's will and does not get ready or does not do what his master wants will be beaten with many blows. 48But the one who does not know and does things deserving punishment will be beaten with few blows. From everyone who has been given much, much will be demanded; and from the one who has been entrusted with much, much more will be asked.

NOT PEACE BUT DIVISION

49"I have come to bring fire on the earth, and how I wish it were already kindled! 50But I have a baptism to undergo, and how distressed I am until it is completed! 51Do you think I came to bring peace on

Using What You've Been Given

Do you think you've been blessed with a lot? Don't just think in terms of money and possessions; think about the natural skills, physical health, family, friends and remarkable list of opportunities you've been granted. How do you think it all compares to what other people you know have been given? Based on what you've been given, how much do you think God expects of you? What can you do to live up to his expectations for your life?

---

[a] 25 Or single cubit to his height

earth? No, I tell you, but division. [52]From now on there will be five in one family divided against each other, three against two and two against three. [53]They will be divided, father against son and son against father, mother against daughter and daughter against mother, mother-in-law against daughter-in-law and daughter-in-law against mother-in-law."

INTERPRETING THE TIMES

[54]He said to the crowd: "When you see a cloud rising in the west, immediately you say, 'It's going to rain,' and it does. [55]And when the south wind blows, you say, 'It's going to be hot,' and it is. [56]Hypocrites! You know how to interpret the appearance of the earth and the sky. How is it that you don't know how to interpret this present time?

[57]"Why don't you judge for yourselves what is right? [58]As you are going with your adversary to the magistrate, try hard to be reconciled to him on the way, or he may drag you off to the judge, and the judge turn you over to the officer, and the officer throw you into prison. [59]I tell you, you will not get out until you have paid the last penny.[a]"

REPENT OR PERISH

13 Now there were some present at that time who told Jesus about the Galileans whose blood Pilate had mixed with their sacrifices. [2]Jesus answered, "Do you think that these Galileans were worse sinners than all the other Galileans because they suffered this way? [3]I tell you, no! But unless you repent, you too will all perish. [4]Or those eighteen who died when the tower in Siloam fell on them—do you think they were more guilty than all the others living in Jerusalem? [5]I tell you, no! But unless you repent, you too will all perish."

[6]Then he told this parable: "A man had a fig tree, planted in his vineyard, and he went to look for fruit on it, but did not find any. [7]So he said to the man who took care of the vineyard, 'For three years now I've been coming to look for fruit on this fig tree and haven't found any. Cut it down! Why should it use up the soil?'

[8]"'Sir,' the man replied, 'leave it alone for one more year, and I'll dig around it and fertilize it. [9]If it bears fruit next year, fine! If not, then cut it down.'"

A CRIPPLED WOMAN HEALED ON THE SABBATH

[10]On a Sabbath Jesus was teaching in one of the synagogues, [11]and a woman was there who had been crippled by a spirit for eighteen years. She was bent over and could not straighten up at all. [12]When Jesus saw her, he called her forward and said to her, "Woman, you are set free from your infirmity." [13]Then he put his hands on her, and immediately she straightened up and praised God.

[14]Indignant because Jesus had healed on the Sabbath, the synagogue ruler said to the people, "There are six days for work. So come and be healed on those days, not on the Sabbath."

[15]The Lord answered him, "You hypocrites! Doesn't each of you on the Sabbath untie his ox or donkey from the stall and lead it out to give it water? [16]Then should not this woman, a daughter of Abraham, whom Satan has kept bound for eighteen long years, be set free on the Sabbath day from what bound her?"

[17]When he said this, all his opponents were humiliated, but the people were delighted with all the wonderful things he was doing.

THE PARABLES OF THE MUSTARD SEED AND THE YEAST

[18]Then Jesus asked, "What is the kingdom of God like? What shall I compare it to? [19]It is like a mustard seed, which a man took and planted in his garden. It grew and became a tree, and the birds of the air perched in its branches."

[20]Again he asked, "What shall I compare the kingdom of God to? [21]It is like yeast that a woman took and mixed into a large amount[b] of flour until it worked all through the dough."

THE NARROW DOOR

[22]Then Jesus went through the towns and villages, teaching as he made his way to Jerusalem. [23]Someone asked him, "Lord, are only a few people going to be saved?"

---

[a] 59 Greek *lepton*   [b] 21 Greek *three satas* (probably about 1/2 bushel or 22 liters)

He said to them, 24 "Make every effort to enter through the narrow door, because many, I tell you, will try to enter and will not be able to. 25 Once the owner of the house gets up and closes the door, you will stand outside knocking and pleading, 'Sir, open the door for us.'

"But he will answer, 'I don't know you or where you come from.'

26 "Then you will say, 'We ate and drank with you, and you taught in our streets.'

27 "But he will reply, 'I don't know you or where you come from. Away from me, all you evildoers!'

28 "There will be weeping there, and gnashing of teeth, when you see Abraham, Isaac and Jacob and all the prophets in the kingdom of God, but you yourselves thrown out. 29 People will come from east and west and north and south, and will take their places at the feast in the kingdom of God. 30 Indeed there are those who are last who will be first, and first who will be last."

JESUS' SORROW FOR JERUSALEM

31 At that time some Pharisees came to Jesus and said to him, "Leave this place and go somewhere else. Herod wants to kill you."

32 He replied, "Go tell that fox, 'I will drive out demons and heal people today and tomorrow, and on the third day I will reach my goal.' 33 In any case, I must keep going today and tomorrow and the next day—for surely no prophet can die outside Jerusalem!

34 "O Jerusalem, Jerusalem, you who kill the prophets and stone those sent to you, how often I have longed to gather your children together, as a hen gathers her chicks under her wings, but you were not willing! 35 Look, your house is left to you desolate. I tell you, you will not see me again until you say, 'Blessed is he who comes in the name of the Lord.'[a]"

JESUS AT A PHARISEE'S HOUSE

14 One Sabbath, when Jesus went to eat in the house of a prominent Pharisee, he was being carefully watched. 2 There in front of him was a man suffering from dropsy. 3 Jesus asked the Pharisees and experts in the law, "Is it lawful to heal on the Sabbath or not?" 4 But they remained silent. So taking hold of the man, he healed him and sent him away.

5 Then he asked them, "If one of you has a son[b] or an ox that falls into a well on the Sabbath day, will you not immediately pull him out?" 6 And they had nothing to say.

7 When he noticed how the guests picked the places of honor at the table, he told them this parable: 8 "When someone invites you to a wedding feast, do not take the place of honor, for a person more distinguished than you may have been invited. 9 If so, the host who invited both of you will come and say to you, 'Give this man your seat.' Then, humiliated, you will have to take the least important place. 10 But when you are invited, take the lowest place, so that when your host comes, he will say to you, 'Friend, move up to a better place.' Then you will be honored in the presence of all your fellow guests. 11 For everyone who exalts himself will be humbled, and he who humbles himself will be exalted."

12 Then Jesus said to his host, "When you give a luncheon or dinner, do not invite your friends, your brothers or relatives, or your rich neighbors; if you do, they may invite you back and so you will be repaid. 13 But when you give a banquet, invite the poor, the crippled, the lame, the blind, 14 and you will be blessed. Although they cannot repay you, you will be repaid at the resurrection of the righteous."

THE PARABLE OF THE GREAT BANQUET

15 When one of those at the table with him heard this, he said to Jesus, "Blessed is the man who will eat at the feast in the kingdom of God."

16 Jesus replied: "A certain man was preparing a great banquet and invited many guests. 17 At the time of the banquet he sent his servant to tell those who had been invited, 'Come, for everything is now ready.'

18 "But they all alike began to make excuses. The first said, 'I have just bought a field, and I must go and see it. Please excuse me.'

19 "Another said, 'I have just bought five yoke of oxen, and I'm on my way to try them out. Please excuse me.'

20 "Still another said, 'I just got married, so I can't come.'

21 "The servant came back and reported this to his master. Then the owner of the house became angry and ordered his servant, 'Go out quickly into the streets and alleys of the town and bring in the poor, the crippled, the blind and the lame.'

---

a 35 Psalm 118:26   b 5 Some manuscripts donkey

²²" 'Sir,' the servant said, 'what you ordered has been done, but there is still room.'

²³"Then the master told his servant, 'Go out to the roads and country lanes and make them come in, so that my house will be full. ²⁴I tell you, not one of those men who were invited will get a taste of my banquet.' "

THE COST OF BEING A DISCIPLE

²⁵Large crowds were traveling with Jesus, and turning to them he said: ²⁶"If anyone comes to me and does not hate his father and mother, his wife and children, his brothers and sisters—yes, even his own life—he cannot be my disciple. ²⁷And anyone who does not carry his cross and follow me cannot be my disciple.

²⁸"Suppose one of you wants to build a tower. Will he not first sit down and estimate the cost to see if he has enough money to complete it? ²⁹For if he lays the foundation and is not able to finish it, everyone who sees it will ridicule him, ³⁰saying, 'This fellow began to build and was not able to finish.'

³¹"Or suppose a king is about to go to war against another king. Will he not first sit down and consider whether he is able with ten thousand men to oppose the one coming against him with twenty thousand? ³²If he is not able, he will send a delegation while the other is still a long way off and will ask for terms of peace. ³³In the same way, any of you who does not give up everything he has cannot be my disciple.

³⁴"Salt is good, but if it loses its saltiness, how can it be made salty again? ³⁵It is fit neither for the soil nor for the manure pile; it is thrown out.

"He who has ears to hear, let him hear."

THE PARABLE OF THE LOST SHEEP

15

Now the tax collectors and "sinners" were all gathering around to hear him. ²But the Pharisees and the teachers of the law muttered, "This man welcomes sinners and eats with them."

³Then Jesus told them this parable: ⁴"Suppose one of you has a hundred sheep and loses one of them. Does he not leave the ninety-nine in the open country and go after the lost sheep until he finds it? ⁵And when he finds it, he joyfully puts it on his shoulders ⁶and goes home. Then he calls his friends and neighbors together and says, 'Rejoice with me; I have found my lost sheep.' ⁷I tell you that in the same way there will be more rejoicing in heaven over one sinner who repents than over ninety-nine righteous persons who do not need to repent.

NOW OR NEVER

LK 15:2

Jesus wasn't afraid to rub shoulders with the outcasts of society—the ones who "decent" people wanted nothing to do with. Are you willing to sacrifice your image and spend time with the "unlovable" types?

THE PARABLE OF THE LOST COIN

⁸"Or suppose a woman has ten silver coins^a and loses one. Does she not light a lamp, sweep the house and search carefully until she finds it? ⁹And when she finds it, she calls her friends and neighbors together and says, 'Rejoice with me; I have found my lost coin.' ¹⁰In the same way, I tell you, there is rejoicing in the presence of the angels of God over one sinner who repents."

THE PARABLE OF THE LOST SON

¹¹Jesus continued: "There was a man who had two sons. ¹²The younger one said to his father, 'Father, give me my share of the estate.' So he divided his property between them.

¹³"Not long after that, the younger son got together all he had, set off for a distant country and there squandered his wealth in wild living. ¹⁴After he had spent everything, there was a severe famine in that whole country, and he began to be in need. ¹⁵So he went and hired himself out to a citizen of that country, who sent him to his fields to feed pigs. ¹⁶He longed to fill his stomach with the pods that the pigs were eating, but no one gave him anything.

¹⁷"When he came to his senses, he said, 'How many of my father's hired men have food to spare,

^a 8 Greek ten drachmas, each worth about a day's wages

and here I am starving to death! [18]I will set out and go back to my father and say to him: Father, I have sinned against heaven and against you. [19]I am no longer worthy to be called your son; make me like one of your hired men.' [20]So he got up and went to his father.

"But while he was still a long way off, his father saw him and was filled with compassion for him; he ran to his son, threw his arms around him and kissed him.

[21]"The son said to him, 'Father, I have sinned against heaven and against you. I am no longer worthy to be called your son.[a]'

[22]"But the father said to his servants, 'Quick! Bring the best robe and put it on him. Put a ring on his finger and sandals on his feet. [23]Bring the fattened calf and kill it. Let's have a feast and celebrate. [24]For this son of mine was dead and is alive again; he was lost and is found.' So they began to celebrate.

[25]"Meanwhile, the older son was in the field. When he came near the house, he heard music and dancing. [26]So he called one of the servants and asked him what was going on. [27]'Your brother has come,' he replied, 'and your father has killed the fattened calf because he has him back safe and sound.'

[28]"The older brother became angry and refused to go in. So his father went out and pleaded with him. [29]But he answered his father, 'Look! All these years I've been slaving for you and never disobeyed your orders. Yet you never gave me even a young goat so I could celebrate with my friends. [30]But when this son of yours who has squandered your property with prostitutes comes home, you kill the fattened calf for him!'

[31]" 'My son,' the father said, 'you are always with me, and everything I have is yours. [32]But we had to celebrate and be glad, because this brother of yours was dead and is alive again; he was lost and is found.' "

THE PARABLE OF THE SHREWD MANAGER

16

Jesus told his disciples: "There was a rich man whose manager was accused of wasting his possessions. [2]So he called him in and asked him, 'What is this I hear about you? Give an account of your management, because you cannot be manager any longer.'

[3]"The manager said to himself, 'What shall I do now? My master is taking away my job. I'm not strong enough to dig, and I'm ashamed to beg— [4]I know what I'll do so that, when I lose my job here, people will welcome me into their houses.'

[5]"So he called in each one of his master's debtors. He asked the first, 'How much do you owe my master?'

[6]" 'Eight hundred gallons[b] of olive oil,' he replied.

"The manager told him, 'Take your bill, sit down quickly, and make it four hundred.'

[7]"Then he asked the second, 'And how much do you owe?'

" 'A thousand bushels[c] of wheat,' he replied.

"He told him, 'Take your bill and make it eight hundred.'

[8]"The master commended the dishonest manager because he had acted shrewdly. For the people of this world are more shrewd in dealing with their own kind than are the people of the light. [9]I tell you, use worldly wealth to gain friends for yourselves, so that when it is gone, you will be welcomed into eternal dwellings.

[10]"Whoever can be trusted with very little can also be trusted with much, and whoever is dishonest with very little will also be dishonest with much. [11]So if you have not been trustworthy in handling worldly wealth, who will trust you with true riches? [12]And if you have not been trustworthy with someone else's property, who will give you property of your own?

[13]"No servant can serve two masters. Either he will hate the one and love the other, or he will be devoted to the one and despise the other. You cannot serve both God and Money."

---

[a] 21 Some early manuscripts *son. Make me like one of your hired men.*   [b] 6 Greek *one hundred batous* (probably about 3 kiloliters)
[c] 7 Greek *one hundred korous* (probably about 35 kiloliters)

[14]The Pharisees, who loved money, heard all this and were sneering at Jesus. [15]He said to them, "You are the ones who justify yourselves in the eyes of men, but God knows your hearts. What is highly valued among men is detestable in God's sight.

ADDITIONAL TEACHINGS

[16]"The Law and the Prophets were proclaimed until John. Since that time, the good news of the kingdom of God is being preached, and everyone is forcing his way into it. [17]It is easier for heaven and earth to disappear than for the least stroke of a pen to drop out of the Law.

[18]"Anyone who divorces his wife and marries another woman commits adultery, and the man who marries a divorced woman commits adultery.

THE RICH MAN AND LAZARUS

[19]"There was a rich man who was dressed in purple and fine linen and lived in luxury every day. [20]At his gate was laid a beggar named Lazarus, covered with sores [21]and longing to eat what fell from the rich man's table. Even the dogs came and licked his sores.

[22]"The time came when the beggar died and the angels carried him to Abraham's side. The rich man also died and was buried. [23]In hell,[a] where he was in torment, he looked up and saw Abraham far away, with Lazarus by his side. [24]So he called to him, 'Father Abraham, have pity on me and send Lazarus to dip the tip of his finger in water and cool my tongue, because I am in agony in this fire.'

[25]"But Abraham replied, 'Son, remember that in your lifetime you received your good things, while Lazarus received bad things, but now he is comforted here and you are in agony. [26]And besides all this, between us and you a great chasm has been fixed, so that those who want to go from here to you cannot, nor can anyone cross over from there to us.'

[27]"He answered, 'Then I beg you, father, send Lazarus to my father's house, [28]for I have five brothers. Let him warn them, so that they will not also come to this place of torment.'

[29]"Abraham replied, 'They have Moses and the Prophets; let them listen to them.'

[30]" 'No, father Abraham,' he said, 'but if someone from the dead goes to them, they will repent.'

[31]"He said to him, 'If they do not listen to Moses and the Prophets, they will not be convinced even if someone rises from the dead.' "

SIN, FAITH, DUTY

17 Jesus said to his disciples: "Things that cause people to sin are bound to come, but woe to that person through whom they come. [2]It would be better for him to be thrown into the sea with a millstone tied around his neck than for him to cause one of these little ones to sin. [3]So watch yourselves.

"If your brother sins, rebuke him, and if he repents, forgive him. [4]If he sins against you seven times in a day, and seven times comes back to you and says, 'I repent,' forgive him."

[5]The apostles said to the Lord, "Increase our faith!"

[6]He replied, "If you have faith as small as a mustard seed, you can say to this mulberry tree, 'Be uprooted and planted in the sea,' and it will obey you.

[7]"Suppose one of you had a servant plowing or looking after the sheep. Would he say to the servant when he comes in from the field, 'Come along now and sit down to eat'? [8]Would he not rather say, 'Prepare my supper, get yourself ready and wait on me while I eat and drink; after that you may eat and drink'? [9]Would he thank the servant because he did what he was told to do? [10]So you also, when you have done everything you were told to do, should say, 'We are unworthy servants; we have only done our duty.' "

TEN HEALED OF LEPROSY

[11]Now on his way to Jerusalem, Jesus traveled along the border between Samaria and Galilee. [12]As he was going into a village, ten men who had leprosy[b] met him. They stood at a distance [13]and called out in a loud voice, "Jesus, Master, have pity on us!"

[14]When he saw them, he said, "Go, show yourselves to the priests." And as they went, they were cleansed.

---

[a] *23* Greek *Hades* [b] *12* The Greek word was used for various diseases affecting the skin—not necessarily leprosy.

15One of them, when he saw he was healed, came back, praising God in a loud voice. 16He threw himself at Jesus' feet and thanked him—and he was a Samaritan.

17Jesus asked, "Were not all ten cleansed? Where are the other nine? 18Was no one found to return and give praise to God except this foreigner?" 19Then he said to him, "Rise and go; your faith has made you well."

THE COMING OF THE KINGDOM OF GOD

20Once, having been asked by the Pharisees when the kingdom of God would come, Jesus replied, "The kingdom of God does not come with your careful observation, 21nor will people say, 'Here it is,' or 'There it is,' because the kingdom of God is withina you."

22Then he said to his disciples, "The time is coming when you will long to see one of the days of the Son of Man, but you will not see it. 23Men will tell you, 'There he is!' or 'Here he is!' Do not go running off after them. 24For the Son of Man in his dayb will be like the lightning, which flashes and lights up the sky from one end to the other. 25But first he must suffer many things and be rejected by this generation.

26"Just as it was in the days of Noah, so also will it be in the days of the Son of Man. 27People were eating, drinking, marrying and being given in marriage up to the day Noah entered the ark. Then the flood came and destroyed them all.

28"It was the same in the days of Lot. People were eating and drinking, buying and selling, planting and building. 29But the day Lot left Sodom, fire and sulfur rained down from heaven and destroyed them all.

30"It will be just like this on the day the Son of Man is revealed. 31On that day no one who is on the roof of his house, with his goods inside, should go down to get them. Likewise, no one in the field should go back for anything. 32Remember Lot's wife! 33Whoever tries to keep his life will lose it, and whoever loses his life will preserve it. 34I tell you, on that night two people will be in one bed; one will be taken and the other left. 35Two women will be grinding grain together; one will be taken and the other left.c"

37"Where, Lord?" they asked.

He replied, "Where there is a dead body, there the vultures will gather."

THE PARABLE OF THE PERSISTENT WIDOW

18 Then Jesus told his disciples a parable to show them that they should always pray and not give up. 2He said: "In a certain town there was a judge who neither feared God nor cared about men. 3And there was a widow in that town who kept coming to him with the plea, 'Grant me justice against my adversary.'

4"For some time he refused. But finally he said to himself, 'Even though I don't fear God or care about men, 5yet because this widow keeps bothering me, I will see that she gets justice, so that she won't eventually wear me out with her coming!' "

6And the Lord said, "Listen to what the unjust judge says. 7And will not God bring about justice for his chosen ones, who cry out to him day and night? Will he keep putting them off? 8I tell you, he will see that they get justice, and quickly. However, when the Son of Man comes, will he find faith on the earth?"

---

a 21 Or among   b 24 Some manuscripts do not have in his day.   c 35 Some manuscripts left. 36Two men will be in the field; one will be taken and the other left.

Counting Your Blessings

To avoid making the same mistake the nine ungrateful ex-lepers made, here's an exercise to try during your prayer time this week: Every day for the next week, write down at least ten things God has done in your life that you're thankful for. When you pray, thank God specifically for each one. Here's the catch: Each day's list has to be completely different from the others; you can't repeat any items from a previous day's prayer. That means you'll need to think of 70 different things you're thankful for. Does it sound like a challenge? It might be easier than you think.

THE PARABLE OF THE PHARISEE AND THE TAX COLLECTOR

[9] To some who were confident of their own righteousness and looked down on everybody else, Jesus told this parable: [10] "Two men went up to the temple to pray, one a Pharisee and the other a tax collector. [11] The Pharisee stood up and prayed about[a] himself: 'God, I thank you that I am not like other men— robbers, evildoers, adulterers—or even like this tax collector. [12] I fast twice a week and give a tenth of all I get.'

[13] "But the tax collector stood at a distance. He would not even look up to heaven, but beat his breast and said, 'God, have mercy on me, a sinner.'

[14] "I tell you that this man, rather than the other, went home justified before God. For everyone who exalts himself will be humbled, and he who humbles himself will be exalted."

THE LITTLE CHILDREN AND JESUS

[15] People were also bringing babies to Jesus to have him touch them. When the disciples saw this, they rebuked them. [16] But Jesus called the children to him and said, "Let the little children come to me, and do not hinder them, for the kingdom of God belongs to such as these. [17] I tell you the truth, anyone who will not receive the kingdom of God like a little child will never enter it."

THE RICH RULER

[18] A certain ruler asked him, "Good teacher, what must I do to inherit eternal life?"

[19] "Why do you call me good?" Jesus answered. "No one is good—except God alone. [20] You know the commandments: 'Do not commit adultery, do not murder, do not steal, do not give false testimony, honor your father and mother.'[b]"

[21] "All these I have kept since I was a boy," he said.

[22] When Jesus heard this, he said to him, "You still lack one thing. Sell everything you have and give to the poor, and you will have treasure in heaven. Then come, follow me."

[23] When he heard this, he became very sad, because he was a man of great wealth. [24] Jesus looked at him and said, "How hard it is for the rich to enter the kingdom of God! [25] Indeed, it is easier for a camel to go through the eye of a needle than for a rich man to enter the kingdom of God."

[26] Those who heard this asked, "Who then can be saved?"

[27] Jesus replied, "What is impossible with men is possible with God."

[28] Peter said to him, "We have left all we had to follow you!"

[29] "I tell you the truth," Jesus said to them, "no one who has left home or wife or brothers or parents or children for the sake of the kingdom of God [30] will fail to receive many times as much in this age and, in the age to come, eternal life."

JESUS AGAIN PREDICTS HIS DEATH

[31] Jesus took the Twelve aside and told them, "We are going up to Jerusalem, and everything that is written by the prophets about the Son of Man will be fulfilled. [32] He will be handed over to the Gentiles. They will mock him, insult him, spit on him, flog him and kill him. [33] On the third day he will rise again."

[34] The disciples did not understand any of this. Its meaning was hidden from them, and they did not know what he was talking about.

A BLIND BEGGAR RECEIVES HIS SIGHT

[35] As Jesus approached Jericho, a blind man was sitting by the roadside begging. [36] When he heard the crowd going by, he asked what was happening. [37] They told him, "Jesus of Nazareth is passing by."

[38] He called out, "Jesus, Son of David, have mercy on me!"

[39] Those who led the way rebuked him and told him to be quiet, but he shouted all the more, "Son of David, have mercy on me!"

[40] Jesus stopped and ordered the man to be brought to him. When he came near, Jesus asked him, [41] "What do you want me to do for you?"

"Lord, I want to see," he replied.

[42] Jesus said to him, "Receive your sight; your faith has healed you." [43] Immediately he received his sight and followed Jesus, praising God. When all the people saw it, they also praised God.

---

[a] *11* Or *to*   [b] *20* Exodus 20:12-16; Deut. 5:16-20

ZACCHAEUS THE TAX COLLECTOR

19

Jesus entered Jericho and was passing through. ²A man was there by the name of Zacchaeus; he was a chief tax collector and was wealthy. ³He wanted to see who Jesus was, but being a short man he could not, because of the crowd. ⁴So he ran ahead and climbed a sycamore-fig tree to see him, since Jesus was coming that way.

⁵When Jesus reached the spot, he looked up and said to him, "Zacchaeus, come down immediately. I must stay at your house today." ⁶So he came down at once and welcomed him gladly.

⁷All the people saw this and began to mutter, "He has gone to be the guest of a 'sinner.' "

⁸But Zacchaeus stood up and said to the Lord, "Look, Lord! Here and now I give half of my possessions to the poor, and if I have cheated anybody out of anything, I will pay back four times the amount."

⁹Jesus said to him, "Today salvation has come to this house, because this man, too, is a son of Abraham. ¹⁰For the Son of Man came to seek and to save what was lost."

THE PARABLE OF THE TEN MINAS

¹¹While they were listening to this, he went on to tell them a parable, because he was near Jerusalem and the people thought that the kingdom of God was going to appear at once. ¹²He said: "A man of noble birth went to a distant country to have himself appointed king and then to return. ¹³So he called ten of his servants and gave them ten minas.ᵃ 'Put this money to work,' he said, 'until I come back.'

¹⁴"But his subjects hated him and sent a delegation after him to say, 'We don't want this man to be our king.'

¹⁵"He was made king, however, and returned home. Then he sent for the servants to whom he had given the money, in order to find out what they had gained with it.

¹⁶"The first one came and said, 'Sir, your mina has earned ten more.'

¹⁷" 'Well done, my good servant!' his master replied. 'Because you have been trustworthy in a very small matter, take charge of ten cities.'

¹⁸"The second came and said, 'Sir, your mina has earned five more.'

¹⁹"His master answered, 'You take charge of five cities.'

²⁰"Then another servant came and said, 'Sir, here is your mina; I have kept it laid away in a piece of cloth. ²¹I was afraid of you, because you are a hard man. You take out what you did not put in and reap what you did not sow.'

²²"His master replied, 'I will judge you by your own words, you wicked servant! You knew, did you, that I am a hard man, taking out what I did not put in, and reaping what I did not sow? ²³Why then didn't you put my money on deposit, so that when I came back, I could have collected it with interest?'

²⁴"Then he said to those standing by, 'Take his mina away from him and give it to the one who has ten minas.'

²⁵" 'Sir,' they said, 'he already has ten!'

²⁶"He replied, 'I tell you that to everyone who has, more will be given, but as for the one who has nothing, even what he has will be taken away. ²⁷But those enemies of mine who did not want me to be king over them—bring them here and kill them in front of me.' "

THE TRIUMPHAL ENTRY

²⁸After Jesus had said this, he went on ahead, going up to Jerusalem. ²⁹As he approached Bethphage and Bethany at the hill called the Mount of Olives, he sent two of his disciples, saying to them, ³⁰"Go to the village ahead of you, and as you enter it, you will find a colt tied there, which no one has ever ridden. Untie it and bring it here. ³¹If anyone asks you, 'Why are you untying it?' tell him, 'The Lord needs it.' "

challenge notes

To: my_son

heavenly_father: Jesus doesn't have to be a mystery. I left clues throughout my word to help you recognize him. when you need reassurance about the one you've put your faith in, go back and trace the clues I left through my prophets—and see how I made it all a reality in the gospels.

ᵃ 13 A mina was about three months' wages.

³²Those who were sent ahead went and found it just as he had told them. ³³As they were untying the colt, its owners asked them, "Why are you untying the colt?"

³⁴They replied, "The Lord needs it."

³⁵They brought it to Jesus, threw their cloaks on the colt and put Jesus on it. ³⁶As he went along, people spread their cloaks on the road.

³⁷When he came near the place where the road goes down the Mount of Olives, the whole crowd of disciples began joyfully to praise God in loud voices for all the miracles they had seen:

³⁸ "Blessed is the king who comes in the name of the Lord!" ᵃ

"Peace in heaven and glory in the highest!"

³⁹Some of the Pharisees in the crowd said to Jesus, "Teacher, rebuke your disciples!"

⁴⁰"I tell you," he replied, "if they keep quiet, the stones will cry out."

⁴¹As he approached Jerusalem and saw the city, he wept over it ⁴²and said, "If you, even you, had only known on this day what would bring you peace—but now it is hidden from your eyes. ⁴³The days will come upon you when your enemies will build an embankment against you and encircle you and hem you in on every side. ⁴⁴They will dash you to the ground, you and the children within your walls. They will not leave one stone on another, because you did not recognize the time of God's coming to you."

JESUS AT THE TEMPLE

⁴⁵Then he entered the temple area and began driving out those who were selling. ⁴⁶"It is written," he said to them, " 'My house will be a house of prayer'ᵇ; but you have made it 'a den of robbers.'ᶜ"

⁴⁷Every day he was teaching at the temple. But the chief priests, the teachers of the law and the leaders among the people were trying to kill him. ⁴⁸Yet they could not find any way to do it, because all the people hung on his words.

THE AUTHORITY OF JESUS QUESTIONED

20 One day as he was teaching the people in the temple courts and preaching the gospel, the chief priests and the teachers of the law, together with the elders, came up to him. ²"Tell us by what authority you are doing these things," they said. "Who gave you this authority?"

³He replied, "I will also ask you a question. Tell me, ⁴John's baptism—was it from heaven, or from men?"

⁵They discussed it among themselves and said, "If we say, 'From heaven,' he will ask, 'Why didn't you believe him?' ⁶But if we say, 'From men,' all the people will stone us, because they are persuaded that John was a prophet."

⁷So they answered, "We don't know where it was from."

⁸Jesus said, "Neither will I tell you by what authority I am doing these things."

THE PARABLE OF THE TENANTS

⁹He went on to tell the people this parable: "A man planted a vineyard, rented it to some farmers and went away for a long time. ¹⁰At harvest time he sent a servant to the tenants so they would give him some of the fruit of the vineyard. But the tenants beat him and sent him away empty-handed. ¹¹He sent another servant, but that one also they beat and treated shamefully and sent away empty-handed. ¹²He sent still a third, and they wounded him and threw him out.

¹³"Then the owner of the vineyard said, 'What shall I do? I will send my son, whom I love; perhaps they will respect him.'

¹⁴"But when the tenants saw him, they talked the matter over. 'This is the heir,' they said. 'Let's kill him, and the inheritance will be ours.' ¹⁵So they threw him out of the vineyard and killed him.

"What then will the owner of the vineyard do to them? ¹⁶He will come and kill those tenants and give the vineyard to others."

When the people heard this, they said, "May this never be!"

¹⁷Jesus looked directly at them and asked, "Then what is the meaning of that which is written:

ᵃ *38* Psalm 118:26   ᵇ *46* Isaiah 56:7   ᶜ *46* Jer. 7:11

> " 'The stone the builders rejected
> has become the capstone[a][b]?

¹⁸Everyone who falls on that stone will be broken to pieces, but he on whom it falls will be crushed."

¹⁹The teachers of the law and the chief priests looked for a way to arrest him immediately, because they knew he had spoken this parable against them. But they were afraid of the people.

PAYING TAXES TO CAESAR

²⁰Keeping a close watch on him, they sent spies, who pretended to be honest. They hoped to catch Jesus in something he said so that they might hand him over to the power and authority of the governor. ²¹So the spies questioned him: "Teacher, we know that you speak and teach what is right, and that you do not show partiality but teach the way of God in accordance with the truth. ²²Is it right for us to pay taxes to Caesar or not?"

²³He saw through their duplicity and said to them, ²⁴"Show me a denarius. Whose portrait and inscription are on it?"

²⁵"Caesar's," they replied.

He said to them, "Then give to Caesar what is Caesar's, and to God what is God's."

²⁶They were unable to trap him in what he had said there in public. And astonished by his answer, they became silent.

THE RESURRECTION AND MARRIAGE

²⁷Some of the Sadducees, who say there is no resurrection, came to Jesus with a question. ²⁸"Teacher," they said, "Moses wrote for us that if a man's brother dies and leaves a wife but no children, the man must marry the widow and have children for his brother. ²⁹Now there were seven brothers. The first one married a woman and died childless. ³⁰The second ³¹and then the third married her, and in the same way the seven died, leaving no children. ³²Finally, the woman died too. ³³Now then, at the resurrection whose wife will she be, since the seven were married to her?"

³⁴Jesus replied, "The people of this age marry and are given in marriage. ³⁵But those who are considered worthy of taking part in that age and in the resurrection from the dead will neither marry nor be given in marriage, ³⁶and they can no longer die; for they are like the angels. They are God's children, since they are children of the resurrection. ³⁷But in the account of the bush, even Moses showed that the dead rise, for he calls the Lord 'the God of Abraham, and the God of Isaac, and the God of Jacob.'[c] ³⁸He is not the God of the dead, but of the living, for to him all are alive."

³⁹Some of the teachers of the law responded, "Well said, teacher!" ⁴⁰And no one dared to ask him any more questions.

WHOSE SON IS THE CHRIST?

⁴¹Then Jesus said to them, "How is it that they say the Christ[d] is the Son of David? ⁴²David himself declares in the Book of Psalms:

> " 'The Lord said to my Lord:
> "Sit at my right hand
> ⁴³until I make your enemies
> a footstool for your feet." '[e]

⁴⁴David calls him 'Lord.' How then can he be his son?"

⁴⁵While all the people were listening, Jesus said to his disciples, ⁴⁶"Beware of the teachers of the law. They like to walk around in flowing robes and love to be greeted in the marketplaces and have the most important seats in the synagogues and the places of honor at banquets. ⁴⁷They devour widows' houses and for a show make lengthy prayers. Such men will be punished most severely."

THE WIDOW'S OFFERING

 As he looked up, Jesus saw the rich putting their gifts into the temple treasury. ²He also saw a poor widow put in two very small copper coins.[f] ³"I tell you the truth," he

---

ᵃ 17 Or *cornerstone*　ᵇ 17 Psalm 118:22　ᶜ 37 Exodus 3:6　ᵈ 41 Or *Messiah*　ᵉ 43 Psalm 110:1　ᶠ 2 Greek *two lepta*

battlelines

» You Can Count on Me (Accountability)

Q: How are you doing with the life changes we talked about last month?
A: Well . . . that's hard to say.

Q: Give it a shot. I'll list some of the things you mentioned, and you tell me how you're doing in each area.
A: You mean you want me to grade myself?

Q: Exactly. And tell me the *truth*—not what you think I want to hear.
A: All right—if you insist.

Q: OK, number one—staying away from porn websites.
A: You don't beat around the bush. I'd give myself a B. No . . . make that a B–.

Q: How about resisting physical temptation with your girlfriend?
A: (Groan) I hate this game already. I guess I'd say a . . . C+.

Q: What about reading the Bible and praying everyday?
A: Oooh, you're killing me! I'm definitely in

the toilet on that one. Maybe a D. *Maybe.*

Q: Jesse, don't you have anybody who can help you in these areas?
A: Help me? What do you mean?

Q: You know, an accountability partner. A Christian friend who can pray with you. Somebody you can share your struggles with.
A: That would be kind of embarrassing, don't you think?

Q: Not really. You think you're the only one who struggles? I've got a guy I meet with every week. I can't explain it, but somehow talking about our temptations and praying for each other . . . well, it really helps. It makes me stronger.
A: Really?

Q: Yeah, sometimes I feel stupid having to admit I messed up in a certain area, but it helps to talk things through. We support each other. We talk about the Bible and how to apply it to our lives.

» Getting Real

Making yourself *accountable* means getting real with at least one other Christian guy. It means sharing your successes and failures. It involves praying together and encouraging each other to be more like Jesus. If that seems like a good idea to you, here are some guidelines for meaningful accountability sessions:

● Ask tough but honest questions, and answer each other truthfully (see Galatians 2:11–14; James 5:16). Dishonesty has no place in an accountability relationship. Deception is always the work of the evil one (see John 8:44).

● Don't condemn failure; encourage success. Hebrews 10:24 puts it this way: "And let us consider how we may spur one another on toward love and good deeds"

● Pray for each other faithfully (see Luke 22:31–32).

Learn more about accountability at www.RevolutionBible.com.

said, "this poor widow has put in more than all the others. ⁴All these people gave their gifts out of their wealth; but she out of her poverty put in all she had to live on."

SIGNS OF THE END OF THE AGE

⁵Some of his disciples were remarking about how the temple was adorned with beautiful stones and with gifts dedicated to God. But Jesus said, ⁶"As for what you see here, the time will come when not one stone will be left on another; every one of them will be thrown down."

⁷"Teacher," they asked, "when will these things happen? And what will be the sign that they are about to take place?"

⁸He replied: "Watch out that you are not deceived. For many will come in my name, claiming, 'I am he,' and, 'The time is near.' Do not follow them. ⁹When you hear of wars and revolutions, do not be frightened. These things must happen first, but the end will not come right away."

¹⁰Then he said to them: "Nation will rise against nation, and kingdom against kingdom. ¹¹There will be great earthquakes, famines and pestilences in various places, and fearful events and great signs from heaven.

¹²"But before all this, they will lay hands on you and persecute you. They will deliver you to synagogues and prisons, and you will be brought before kings and governors, and all on account of my name. ¹³This will result in your being witnesses to them. ¹⁴But make up your mind not to worry beforehand how you will defend yourselves. ¹⁵For I will give you words and wisdom that none of your adversaries will be able to resist or contradict. ¹⁶You will be betrayed even by parents, brothers, relatives and friends, and they will put some of you to death. ¹⁷All men will hate you because of me. ¹⁸But not a hair of your head will perish. ¹⁹By standing firm you will gain life.

²⁰"When you see Jerusalem being surrounded by armies, you will know that its desolation is near. ²¹Then let those who are in Judea flee to the mountains, let those in the city get out, and let those in the country not enter the city. ²²For this is the time of punishment in fulfillment of all that has been written. ²³How dreadful it will be in those days for pregnant women and nursing mothers! There will be great distress in the land and wrath against this people. ²⁴They will fall by the sword and will be taken as prisoners to all the nations. Jerusalem will be trampled on by the Gentiles until the times of the Gentiles are fulfilled.

²⁵"There will be signs in the sun, moon and stars. On the earth, nations will be in anguish and perplexity at the roaring and tossing of the sea. ²⁶Men will faint from terror, apprehensive of what is coming on the world, for the heavenly bodies will be shaken. ²⁷At that time they will see the Son of Man coming in a cloud with power and great glory. ²⁸When these things begin to take place, stand up and lift up your heads, because your redemption is drawing near."

²⁹He told them this parable: "Look at the fig tree and all the trees. ³⁰When they sprout leaves, you can see for yourselves and know that summer is near. ³¹Even so, when you see these things happening, you know that the kingdom of God is near.

³²"I tell you the truth, this generationª will certainly not pass away until all these things have happened. ³³Heaven and earth will pass away, but my words will never pass away.

³⁴"Be careful, or your hearts will be weighed down with dissipation, drunkenness and the anxieties of life, and that day will close on you unexpectedly like a trap. ³⁵For it will come upon all those who live on the face of the whole earth. ³⁶Be always on the watch, and pray that you may be able to escape all that is about to happen, and that you may be able to stand before the Son of Man."

³⁷Each day Jesus was teaching at the temple, and each evening he went out to spend the night on the hill called the Mount of Olives, ³⁸and all the people came early in the morning to hear him at the temple.

JUDAS AGREES TO BETRAY JESUS

22 Now the Feast of Unleavened Bread, called the Passover, was approaching, ²and the chief priests and the teachers of the law were looking for some way to get rid of Jesus, for they were afraid of the people. ³Then Satan entered Judas, called Iscariot, one of the Twelve. ⁴And Judas went to the chief priests and the officers of the temple guard and discussed with them how he might betray Jesus. ⁵They were delighted and agreed to give him money. ⁶He consented, and watched for an opportunity to hand Jesus over to them when no crowd was present.

ª 32 Or race

⁷Then came the day of Unleavened Bread on which the Passover lamb had to be sacrificed. ⁸Jesus sent Peter and John, saying, "Go and make preparations for us to eat the Passover."

⁹"Where do you want us to prepare for it?" they asked.

¹⁰He replied, "As you enter the city, a man carrying a jar of water will meet you. Follow him to the house that he enters, ¹¹and say to the owner of the house, 'The Teacher asks: Where is the guest room, where I may eat the Passover with my disciples?' ¹²He will show you a large upper room, all furnished. Make preparations there."

¹³They left and found things just as Jesus had told them. So they prepared the Passover.

¹⁴When the hour came, Jesus and his apostles reclined at the table. ¹⁵And he said to them, "I have eagerly desired to eat this Passover with you before I suffer. ¹⁶For I tell you, I will not eat it again until it finds fulfillment in the kingdom of God."

¹⁷After taking the cup, he gave thanks and said, "Take this and divide it among you. ¹⁸For I tell you I will not drink again of the fruit of the vine until the kingdom of God comes."

¹⁹And he took bread, gave thanks and broke it, and gave it to them, saying, "This is my body given for you; do this in remembrance of me."

²⁰In the same way, after the supper he took the cup, saying, "This cup is the new covenant in my blood, which is poured out for you. ²¹But the hand of him who is going to betray me is with mine on the table. ²²The Son of Man will go as it has been decreed, but woe to that man who betrays him." ²³They began to question among themselves which of them it might be who would do this.

²⁴Also a dispute arose among them as to which of them was considered to be greatest. ²⁵Jesus said to them, "The kings of the Gentiles lord it over them; and those who exercise authority over them call themselves Benefactors. ²⁶But you are not to be like that. Instead, the greatest among you should be like the youngest, and the one who rules like the one who serves. ²⁷For who is greater, the one who is at the table or the one who serves? Is it not the one who is at the table? But I am among you as one who serves. ²⁸You are those who have stood by me in my trials. ²⁹And I confer on you a kingdom, just as my Father conferred one on me, ³⁰so that you may eat and drink at my table in my kingdom and sit on thrones, judging the twelve tribes of Israel.

³¹"Simon, Simon, Satan has asked to sift you[a] as wheat. ³²But I have prayed for you, Simon, that your faith may not fail. And when you have turned back, strengthen your brothers."

³³But he replied, "Lord, I am ready to go with you to prison and to death."

³⁴Jesus answered, "I tell you, Peter, before the rooster crows today, you will deny three times that you know me."

³⁵Then Jesus asked them, "When I sent you without purse, bag or sandals, did you lack anything?"

"Nothing," they answered.

³⁶He said to them, "But now if you have a purse, take it, and also a bag; and if you don't have a sword, sell your cloak and buy one. ³⁷It is written: 'And he was numbered with the transgressors'[b]; and I tell you that this must be fulfilled in me. Yes, what is written about me is reaching its fulfillment."

³⁸The disciples said, "See, Lord, here are two swords."

"That is enough," he replied.

JESUS PRAYS ON THE MOUNT OF OLIVES

³⁹Jesus went out as usual to the Mount of Olives, and his disciples followed him. ⁴⁰On reaching the place, he said to them, "Pray that you will not fall into temptation." ⁴¹He withdrew about a stone's throw beyond them, knelt down and prayed, ⁴²"Father, if you are willing, take this cup from me; yet not my will, but yours be done." ⁴³An angel from heaven appeared to him and strengthened him. ⁴⁴And being in anguish, he prayed more earnestly, and his sweat was like drops of blood falling to the ground.[c]

⁴⁵When he rose from prayer and went back to the disciples, he found them asleep, exhausted from sorrow. ⁴⁶"Why are you sleeping?" he asked them. "Get up and pray so that you will not fall into temptation."

JESUS ARRESTED

⁴⁷While he was still speaking a crowd came up, and the man who was called Judas, one of the Twelve, was leading them. He approached Jesus to kiss him, ⁴⁸but Jesus asked him, "Judas, are you betraying the Son of Man with a kiss?"

---

[a] *31* The Greek is plural.   [b] *37* Isaiah 53:12   [c] *44* Some early manuscripts do not have verses 43 and 44.

[49]When Jesus' followers saw what was going to happen, they said, "Lord, should we strike with our swords?" [50]And one of them struck the servant of the high priest, cutting off his right ear.

[51]But Jesus answered, "No more of this!" And he touched the man's ear and healed him.

[52]Then Jesus said to the chief priests, the officers of the temple guard, and the elders, who had come for him, "Am I leading a rebellion, that you have come with swords and clubs? [53]Every day I was with you in the temple courts, and you did not lay a hand on me. But this is your hour—when darkness reigns."

PETER DISOWNS JESUS

[54]Then seizing him, they led him away and took him into the house of the high priest. Peter followed at a distance. [55]But when they had kindled a fire in the middle of the courtyard and had sat down together, Peter sat down with them. [56]A servant girl saw him seated there in the firelight. She looked closely at him and said, "This man was with him."

[57]But he denied it. "Woman, I don't know him," he said.

[58]A little later someone else saw him and said, "You also are one of them."

"Man, I am not!" Peter replied.

[59]About an hour later another asserted, "Certainly this fellow was with him, for he is a Galilean."

[60]Peter replied, "Man, I don't know what you're talking about!" Just as he was speaking, the rooster crowed. [61]The Lord turned and looked straight at Peter. Then Peter remembered the word the Lord had spoken to him: "Before the rooster crows today, you will disown me three times." [62]And he went outside and wept bitterly.

THE GUARDS MOCK JESUS

[63]The men who were guarding Jesus began mocking and beating him. [64]They blindfolded him and demanded, "Prophesy! Who hit you?" [65]And they said many other insulting things to him.

JESUS BEFORE PILATE AND HEROD

[66]At daybreak the council of the elders of the people, both the chief priests and teachers of the law, met together, and Jesus was led before them. [67]"If you are the Christ,[a]" they said, "tell us."

Jesus answered, "If I tell you, you will not believe me, [68]and if I asked you, you would not answer. [69]But from now on, the Son of Man will be seated at the right hand of the mighty God."

[70]They all asked, "Are you then the Son of God?"

He replied, "You are right in saying I am."

[71]Then they said, "Why do we need any more testimony? We have heard it from his own lips."

23 Then the whole assembly rose and led him off to Pilate. [2]And they began to accuse him, saying, "We have found this man subverting our nation. He opposes payment of taxes to Caesar and claims to be Christ,[b] a king."

[3]So Pilate asked Jesus, "Are you the king of the Jews?"

"Yes, it is as you say," Jesus replied.

[4]Then Pilate announced to the chief priests and the crowd, "I find no basis for a charge against this man."

[5]But they insisted, "He stirs up the people all over Judea[c] by his teaching. He started in Galilee and has come all the way here."

[6]On hearing this, Pilate asked if the man was a Galilean. [7]When he learned that Jesus was under Herod's jurisdiction, he sent him to Herod, who was also in Jerusalem at that time.

[8]When Herod saw Jesus, he was greatly pleased, because for a long time he had been wanting to see him. From what he had heard about him, he hoped to see him perform some miracle. [9]He plied him with many questions, but Jesus gave him no answer. [10]The chief priests and the teachers of the law were standing there, vehemently accusing him. [11]Then Herod and his soldiers ridiculed and mocked him. Dressing him in an elegant robe, they sent him back to Pilate. [12]That day Herod and Pilate became friends—before this they had been enemies.

[13]Pilate called together the chief priests, the rulers and the people, [14]and said to them, "You brought me this man as one who was inciting the people to rebellion. I have examined him in your presence and have found no basis for your charges against him. [15]Neither has Herod, for he sent him back to us; as you can see, he has done nothing to deserve death. [16]Therefore, I will punish him and then release him.[d]"

---

[a] 67 Or Messiah   [b] 2 Or Messiah; also in verses 35 and 39   [c] 5 Or over the land of the Jews   [d] 16 Some manuscripts him." [17]Now he was obliged to release one man to them at the Feast.

[18]With one voice they cried out, "Away with this man! Release Barabbas to us!" [19](Barabbas had been thrown into prison for an insurrection in the city, and for murder.)

[20]Wanting to release Jesus, Pilate appealed to them again. [21]But they kept shouting, "Crucify him! Crucify him!"

[22]For the third time he spoke to them: "Why? What crime has this man committed? I have found in him no grounds for the death penalty. Therefore I will have him punished and then release him."

[23]But with loud shouts they insistently demanded that he be crucified, and their shouts prevailed. [24]So Pilate decided to grant their demand. [25]He released the man who had been thrown into prison for insurrection and murder, the one they asked for, and surrendered Jesus to their will.

THE CRUCIFIXION

[26]As they led him away, they seized Simon from Cyrene, who was on his way in from the country, and put the cross on him and made him carry it behind Jesus. [27]A large number of people followed him, including women who mourned and wailed for him. [28]Jesus turned and said to them, "Daughters of Jerusalem, do not weep for me; weep for yourselves and for your children. [29]For the time will come when you will say, 'Blessed are the barren women, the wombs that never bore and the breasts that never nursed!' [30]Then

> " 'they will say to the mountains, "Fall on us!"
> and to the hills, "Cover us!" ' [a]

[31]For if men do these things when the tree is green, what will happen when it is dry?"

[32]Two other men, both criminals, were also led out with him to be executed. [33]When they came to the place called the Skull, there they crucified him, along with the criminals—one on his right, the other on his left. [34]Jesus said, "Father, forgive them, for they do not know what they are doing." [b] And they divided up his clothes by casting lots.

[35]The people stood watching, and the rulers even sneered at him. They said, "He saved others; let him save himself if he is the Christ of God, the Chosen One."

[36]The soldiers also came up and mocked him. They offered him wine vinegar [37]and said, "If you are the king of the Jews, save yourself."

[38]There was a written notice above him, which read: THIS IS THE KING OF THE JEWS.

[39]One of the criminals who hung there hurled insults at him: "Aren't you the Christ? Save yourself and us!"

[40]But the other criminal rebuked him. "Don't you fear God," he said, "since you are under the same sentence? [41]We are punished justly, for we are getting what our deeds deserve. But this man has done nothing wrong."

[42]Then he said, "Jesus, remember me when you come into your kingdom. [c]"

[43]Jesus answered him, "I tell you the truth, today you will be with me in paradise."

JESUS' DEATH

[44]It was now about the sixth hour, and darkness came over the whole land until the ninth hour, [45]for the sun stopped shining. And the curtain of the temple was torn in two. [46]Jesus called out with a loud voice, "Father, into your hands I commit my spirit." When he had said this, he breathed his last.

[47]The centurion, seeing what had happened, praised God and said, "Surely this was a righteous man." [48]When all the people who had gathered to witness this sight saw what took place, they beat their breasts and went away. [49]But all those who knew him, including the women who had followed him from Galilee, stood at a distance, watching these things.

JESUS' BURIAL

[50]Now there was a man named Joseph, a member of the Council, a good and upright man, [51]who had not consented to their decision and action. He came from the Judean town of Arimathea and he was waiting for the kingdom of God. [52]Going to Pilate, he asked for Jesus' body. [53]Then he took it down, wrapped it in linen cloth and placed it in a tomb cut in the rock, one in which no one had yet been laid. [54]It was Preparation Day, and the Sabbath was about to begin.

[55]The women who had come with Jesus from Galilee followed Joseph and saw the tomb and how

---

[a] *30* Hosea 10:8   [b] *34* Some early manuscripts do not have this sentence.   [c] *42* Some manuscripts *come with your kingly power*

his body was laid in it. 56Then they went home and prepared spices and perfumes. But they rested on the Sabbath in obedience to the commandment.

THE RESURRECTION

24 On the first day of the week, very early in the morning, the women took the spices they had prepared and went to the tomb. 2They found the stone rolled away from the tomb, 3but when they entered, they did not find the body of the Lord Jesus. 4While they were wondering about this, suddenly two men in clothes that gleamed like lightning stood beside them. 5In their fright the women bowed down with their faces to the ground, but the men said to them, "Why do you look for the living among the dead? 6He is not here; he has risen! Remember how he told you, while he was still with you in Galilee: 7'The Son of Man must be delivered into the hands of sinful men, be crucified and on the third day be raised again.'"
8Then they remembered his words.

9When they came back from the tomb, they told all these things to the Eleven and to all the others. 10It was Mary Magdalene, Joanna, Mary the mother of James, and the others with them who told this to the apostles. 11But they did not believe the women, because their words seemed to them like nonsense. 12Peter, however, got up and ran to the tomb. Bending over, he saw the strips of linen lying by themselves, and he went away, wondering to himself what had happened.

NOW OR NEVER
LK 24:11

Do you know anyone who considers the idea of Jesus' resurrection "nonsense"? If so, ask God to reveal the truth to that person . . . and trust God to use you and help you speak the right words at the right time.

ON THE ROAD TO EMMAUS

13Now that same day two of them were going to a village called Emmaus, about seven miles[a] from Jerusalem. 14They were talking with each other about everything that had happened. 15As they talked and discussed these things with each other, Jesus himself came up and walked along with them; 16but they were kept from recognizing him.

17He asked them, "What are you discussing together as you walk along?"

They stood still, their faces downcast. 18One of them, named Cleopas, asked him, "Are you only a visitor to Jerusalem and do not know the things that have happened there in these days?"

19"What things?" he asked.

"About Jesus of Nazareth," they replied. "He was a prophet, powerful in word and deed before God and all the people. 20The chief priests and our rulers handed him over to be sentenced to death, and they crucified him; 21but we had hoped that he was the one who was going to redeem Israel. And what is more, it is the third day since all this took place. 22In addition, some of our women amazed us. They went to the tomb early this morning 23but didn't find his body. They came and told us that they had seen a vision of angels, who said he was alive. 24Then some of our companions went to the tomb and found it just as the women had said, but him they did not see."

25He said to them, "How foolish you are, and how slow of heart to believe all that the prophets have spoken! 26Did not the Christ[b] have to suffer these things and then enter his glory?" 27And beginning with Moses and all the Prophets, he explained to them what was said in all the Scriptures concerning himself.

28As they approached the village to which they were going, Jesus acted as if he were going farther. 29But they urged him strongly, "Stay with us, for it is nearly evening; the day is almost over." So he went in to stay with them.

30When he was at the table with them, he took bread, gave thanks, broke it and began to give it to them. 31Then their eyes were opened and they recognized him, and he disappeared from their sight. 32They asked each other, "Were not our hearts burning within us while he talked with us on the road and opened the Scriptures to us?"

33They got up and returned at once to Jerusalem. There they found the Eleven and those with them, assembled together 34and saying, "It is true! The Lord has risen and has appeared to Simon." 35Then

---

a 13 Greek sixty stadia (about 11 kilometers)   b 26 Or Messiah; also in verse 46 the two told what had happened on the way, and how Jesus was recognized by them when he broke the bread.

JESUS APPEARS TO THE DISCIPLES

³⁶While they were still talking about this, Jesus himself stood among them and said to them, "Peace be with you."

³⁷They were startled and frightened, thinking they saw a ghost. ³⁸He said to them, "Why are you troubled, and why do doubts rise in your minds? ³⁹Look at my hands and my feet. It is I myself! Touch me and see; a ghost does not have flesh and bones, as you see I have."

⁴⁰When he had said this, he showed them his hands and feet. ⁴¹And while they still did not believe it because of joy and amazement, he asked them, "Do you have anything here to eat?" ⁴²They gave him a piece of broiled fish, ⁴³and he took it and ate it in their presence.

⁴⁴He said to them, "This is what I told you while I was still with you: Everything must be fulfilled that is written about me in the Law of Moses, the Prophets and the Psalms."

⁴⁵Then he opened their minds so they could understand the Scriptures. ⁴⁶He told them, "This is what is written: The Christ will suffer and rise from the dead on the third day, ⁴⁷and repentance and forgiveness of sins will be preached in his name to all nations, beginning at Jerusalem. ⁴⁸You are witnesses of these things. ⁴⁹I am going to send you what my Father has promised; but stay in the city until you have been clothed with power from on high."

THE ASCENSION

⁵⁰When he had led them out to the vicinity of Bethany, he lifted up his hands and blessed them. ⁵¹While he was blessing them, he left them and was taken up into heaven. ⁵²Then they worshiped him and returned to Jerusalem with great joy. ⁵³And they stayed continually at the temple, praising God.

JOHN

JOHN JOHN JOHN

Author
John, the apostle, the son of Zebedee and the brother of James

Audience
John probably wrote with Gentile readers in mind, particularly those influenced by the Greek philosophies prevalent at the time.

Date
Probably A.D. 85–90

Setting
Traditionally it has been assumed that John's eyewitness account was the last Gospel written, sometime before John was exiled to the island of Patmos.

Verse to Remember
But these are written that you may believe that Jesus is the Christ, the Son of God, and that by believing you may have life in his name (20:31).

Theme to Consider
John's Gospel is not just a record of Jesus' life; it is a powerful argument that Jesus *is* the heaven-sent Son of God and the only source of eternal life. Believe and be saved!

UNCHANGING TRUTH » If you're serious about your relationship with Jesus, you need to develop the instincts of an investigative journalist. You see, there are many myths out there about Jesus and his teachings, about what his followers are supposed to be like. If you don't challenge those myths and demonstrate how they are wrong, they may confuse your non-Christian friends and family members about the nature of life in Christ. These myths may even distort the way you think of yourself.

The apostle John was a great myth-buster. He reported exactly what he witnessed firsthand as one of Jesus' closest friends, and he refused to let any lie about Jesus go unchallenged. That's why his book is a good place to go for the truth about what Jesus and his followers are really all about.

Myth #1: Jesus' teachings are old-fashioned and out of touch.

Truth: Jesus' teachings are so extreme that the world hasn't caught up with them yet. The "old-fashioned" way of life is to do what your natural instincts tell you to do—to put yourself first, to hurt anyone who hurts you and to satisfy your urges however you can. Jesus gives us a radical solution for overcoming our sinful desires and living in real freedom.

Myth #2: Christianity is about religion.

Truth: If Jesus had been into religion, he would have been a lot more popular while he was on Earth. The religious leaders were the ones who wanted him dead. You see, religion is about people trying to impress God, earning their way to him through good deeds. Jesus said, "The only way you can get to God is through me; ritual and religion can't save anybody."

Myth #3: Following Jesus is a boring way of life.

Truth: Following Jesus (the way he intends) is like living on the edge 24/7. The Lord encourages us to push the boundaries when it comes to our faith. He says, "Ask me for anything that will help you change your world, and I will give it to you."

Don't let anyone lie to you about your faith in Jesus. There's much more to the Christian life than the world knows or wants you to believe.

LIFE LESSONS »

1. God sent Jesus to die for us simply because he loves us (3:16).

2. One person's testimony about Jesus and what he has done can affect many other people (4:39–41).

3. Jesus can do incredible things with even what we have (6:8–13).

4. One of the ways people recognize us as Christians is by the way we treat each other (13:35).

THE WORD BECAME FLESH

1 In the beginning was the Word, and the Word was with God, and the Word was God. ²He was with God in the beginning.

³Through him all things were made; without him nothing was made that has been made. ⁴In him was life, and that life was the light of men. ⁵The light shines in the darkness, but the darkness has not understood[a] it.

⁶There came a man who was sent from God; his name was John. ⁷He came as a witness to testify concerning that light, so that through him all men might believe. ⁸He himself was not the light; he came only as a witness to the light. ⁹The true light that gives light to every man was coming into the world.[b]

¹⁰He was in the world, and though the world was made through him, the world did not recognize him. ¹¹He came to that which was his own, but his own did not receive him. ¹²Yet to all who received him, to those who believed in his name, he gave the right to become children of God— ¹³children born not of natural descent,[c] nor of human decision or a husband's will, but born of God. ¹⁴The Word became flesh and made his dwelling among us. We have seen his glory, the glory of the One and Only,[d] who came from the Father, full of grace and truth.

¹⁵John testifies concerning him. He cries out, saying, "This was he of whom I said, 'He who comes after me has surpassed me because he was before me.'" ¹⁶From the fullness of his grace we have all received one blessing after another. ¹⁷For the law was given through Moses; grace and truth came through Jesus Christ. ¹⁸No one has ever seen God, but God the One and Only,[d,e] who is at the Father's side, has made him known.

JOHN THE BAPTIST DENIES BEING THE CHRIST

¹⁹Now this was John's testimony when the Jews of Jerusalem sent priests and Levites to ask him who he was. ²⁰He did not fail to confess, but confessed freely, "I am not the Christ.[f]"

²¹They asked him, "Then who are you? Are you Elijah?"

He said, "I am not."

"Are you the Prophet?"

He answered, "No."

²²Finally they said, "Who are you? Give us an answer to take back to those who sent us. What do you say about yourself?"

²³John replied in the words of Isaiah the prophet, "I am the voice of one calling in the desert, 'Make straight the way for the Lord.'"[g]

²⁴Now some Pharisees who had been sent ²⁵questioned him, "Why then do you baptize if you are not the Christ, nor Elijah, nor the Prophet?"

²⁶"I baptize with[h] water," John replied, "but among you stands one you do not know. ²⁷He is the one who comes after me, the thongs of whose sandals I am not worthy to untie."

²⁸This all happened at Bethany on the other side of the Jordan, where John was baptizing.

JESUS THE LAMB OF GOD

²⁹The next day John saw Jesus coming toward him and said, "Look, the Lamb of God, who takes away the sin of the world! ³⁰This is the one I meant when I said, 'A man who comes after me has surpassed me because he was before me.' ³¹I myself did not know him, but the reason I came baptizing with water was that he might be revealed to Israel."

---

a 5 Or darkness, and the darkness has not overcome   b 9 Or This was the true light that gives light to every man who comes into the world   c 13 Greek of bloods   d 14,18 Or the Only Begotten   e 18 Some manuscripts but the only (or only begotten) Son   f 20 Or Messiah. "The Christ" (Greek) and "the Messiah" (Hebrew) both mean "the Anointed One"; also in verse 25.   g 23 Isaiah 40:3   h 26 Or in; also in verses 31 and 33

[32]Then John gave this testimony: "I saw the Spirit come down from heaven as a dove and remain on him. [33]I would not have known him, except that the one who sent me to baptize with water told me, 'The man on whom you see the Spirit come down and remain is he who will baptize with the Holy Spirit.' [34]I have seen and I testify that this is the Son of God."

JESUS' FIRST DISCIPLES

[35]The next day John was there again with two of his disciples. [36]When he saw Jesus passing by, he said, "Look, the Lamb of God!"

[37]When the two disciples heard him say this, they followed Jesus. [38]Turning around, Jesus saw them following and asked, "What do you want?"

They said, "Rabbi" (which means Teacher), "where are you staying?"

[39]"Come," he replied, "and you will see."

So they went and saw where he was staying, and spent that day with him. It was about the tenth hour.

[40]Andrew, Simon Peter's brother, was one of the two who heard what John had said and who had followed Jesus. [41]The first thing Andrew did was to find his brother Simon and tell him, "We have found the Messiah" (that is, the Christ). [42]And he brought him to Jesus.

Jesus looked at him and said, "You are Simon son of John. You will be called Cephas" (which, when translated, is Peter[a]).

JESUS CALLS PHILIP AND NATHANAEL

[43]The next day Jesus decided to leave for Galilee. Finding Philip, he said to him, "Follow me."

[44]Philip, like Andrew and Peter, was from the town of Bethsaida. [45]Philip found Nathanael and told him, "We have found the one Moses wrote about in the Law, and about whom the prophets also wrote—Jesus of Nazareth, the son of Joseph."

[46]"Nazareth! Can anything good come from there?" Nathanael asked.

"Come and see," said Philip.

[47]When Jesus saw Nathanael approaching, he said of him, "Here is a true Israelite, in whom there is nothing false."

[48]"How do you know me?" Nathanael asked.

Jesus answered, "I saw you while you were still under the fig tree before Philip called you."

[49]Then Nathanael declared, "Rabbi, you are the Son of God; you are the King of Israel."

[50]Jesus said, "You believe[b] because I told you I saw you under the fig tree. You shall see greater things than that." [51]He then added, "I tell you[c] the truth, you[c] shall see heaven open, and the angels of God ascending and descending on the Son of Man."

Introducing Someone to Jesus

John's simple comment, "Look, the Lamb of God!" was enough to make Andrew and an unnamed disciple want to check out this guy Jesus for themselves. What could you say to your friends that would make them want to find out what Jesus is all about? Do you think it would make a difference to them to hear what Jesus has done for you personally? Do you think they'd like to hear about how Jesus can help them with problems in their lives? Do you think they'd like to know that Jesus can help them overcome feelings of guilt about things in their past?

NOW OR NEVER

JN 1:43–51

If someone brought you to meet Jesus in person, what would he be thinking as you approached? Would he say to himself, "Here is a true man of God—there is nothing false in him"?

---

[a] 42 Both *Cephas* (Aramaic) and *Peter* (Greek) mean *rock*.   [b] 50 Or *Do you believe . . . ?*   [c] 51 The Greek is plural.

JESUS CHANGES WATER TO WINE

2 On the third day a wedding took place at Cana in Galilee. Jesus' mother was there, ²and Jesus and his disciples had also been invited to the wedding. ³When the wine was gone, Jesus' mother said to him, "They have no more wine."

⁴"Dear woman, why do you involve me?" Jesus replied. "My time has not yet come."

⁵His mother said to the servants, "Do whatever he tells you."

⁶Nearby stood six stone water jars, the kind used by the Jews for ceremonial washing, each holding from twenty to thirty gallons.ª

⁷Jesus said to the servants, "Fill the jars with water"; so they filled them to the brim.

⁸Then he told them, "Now draw some out and take it to the master of the banquet."

They did so, ⁹and the master of the banquet tasted the water that had been turned into wine. He did not realize where it had come from, though the servants who had drawn the water knew. Then he called the bridegroom aside ¹⁰and said, "Everyone brings out the choice wine first and then the cheaper wine after the guests have had too much to drink; but you have saved the best till now."

¹¹This, the first of his miraculous signs, Jesus performed at Cana in Galilee. He thus revealed his glory, and his disciples put their faith in him.

NOW OR NEVER

JN 2:5–11

There's an important lesson here: Always be ready to do anything for God, however crazy it might seem. You never know when there's going to be a miracle just around the corner.

JESUS CLEARS THE TEMPLE

¹²After this he went down to Capernaum with his mother and brothers and his disciples. There they stayed for a few days.

¹³When it was almost time for the Jewish Passover, Jesus went up to Jerusalem. ¹⁴In the temple courts he found men selling cattle, sheep and doves, and others sitting at tables exchanging money. ¹⁵So he made a whip out of cords, and drove all from the temple area, both sheep and cattle; he scattered the coins of the money changers and overturned their tables. ¹⁶To those who sold doves he said, "Get these out of here! How dare you turn my Father's house into a market!"

¹⁷His disciples remembered that it is written: "Zeal for your house will consume me."ᵇ

¹⁸Then the Jews demanded of him, "What miraculous sign can you show us to prove your authority to do all this?"

¹⁹Jesus answered them, "Destroy this temple, and I will raise it again in three days."

²⁰The Jews replied, "It has taken forty-six years to build this temple, and you are going to raise it in three days?" ²¹But the temple he had spoken of was his body. ²²After he was raised from the dead, his disciples recalled what he had said. Then they believed the Scripture and the words that Jesus had spoken.

²³Now while he was in Jerusalem at the Passover Feast, many people saw the miraculous signs he was doing and believed in his name.ᶜ ²⁴But Jesus would not entrust himself to them, for he knew all men. ²⁵He did not need man's testimony about man, for he knew what was in a man.

JESUS TEACHES NICODEMUS

3 Now there was a man of the Pharisees named Nicodemus, a member of the Jewish ruling council. ²He came to Jesus at night and said, "Rabbi, we know you are a teacher who has come from God. For no one could perform the miraculous signs you are doing if God were not with him."

³In reply Jesus declared, "I tell you the truth, no one can see the kingdom of God unless he is born again.ᵈ"

⁴"How can a man be born when he is old?" Nicodemus asked. "Surely he cannot enter a second time into his mother's womb to be born!"

ª *6* Greek *two to three metretes* (probably about 75 to 115 liters)   ᵇ *17* Psalm 69:9   ᶜ *23* Or *and believed in him*   ᵈ *3* Or *born from above*; also in verse 7

5Jesus answered, "I tell you the truth, no one can enter the kingdom of God unless he is born of water and the Spirit. 6Flesh gives birth to flesh, but the Spirit[a] gives birth to spirit. 7You should not be surprised at my saying, 'You[b] must be born again.' 8The wind blows wherever it pleases. You hear its sound, but you cannot tell where it comes from or where it is going. So it is with everyone born of the Spirit."

9"How can this be?" Nicodemus asked.

10"You are Israel's teacher," said Jesus, "and do you not understand these things? 11I tell you the truth, we speak of what we know, and we testify to what we have seen, but still you people do not accept our testimony. 12I have spoken to you of earthly things and you do not believe; how then will you believe if I speak of heavenly things? 13No one has ever gone into heaven except the one who came from heaven—the Son of Man.[c] 14Just as Moses lifted up the snake in the desert, so the Son of Man must be lifted up, 15that everyone who believes in him may have eternal life.[d]

NOW OR NEVER
JN 3:16

This is probably the most famous verse in the Bible. Can you quote it without looking? How many other Bible verses have you committed to memory? Try setting a personal goal to memorize at least one passage a week.

16"For God so loved the world that he gave his one and only Son,[e] that whoever believes in him shall not perish but have eternal life. 17For God did not send his Son into the world to condemn the world, but to save the world through him. 18Whoever believes in him is not condemned, but whoever does not believe stands condemned already because he has not believed in the name of God's one and only Son.[f] 19This is the verdict: Light has come into the world, but men loved darkness instead of light because their deeds were evil. 20Everyone who does evil hates the light, and will not come into the light for fear that his deeds will be exposed. 21But whoever lives by the truth comes into the light, so that it may be seen plainly that what he has done has been done through God."[g]

Appreciating God's Love

» live the adventure » Jn 3:16

People have no trouble doubting God's love. We often hear questions like, "If God loves us, why didn't he stop AIDS from killing millions of innocent children in Africa?" or "If God loves us, why did he allow the 9/11 attacks?" or "If God loves us, why does he send people to hell?" These are all tough questions, but here's a tougher one: If God *doesn't* love us, why did he send his own Son to be laughed at, tortured and murdered just so we could have a chance at eternal life?

JOHN THE BAPTIST'S TESTIMONY ABOUT JESUS

22After this, Jesus and his disciples went out into the Judean countryside, where he spent some time with them, and baptized. 23Now John also was baptizing at Aenon near Salim, because there was plenty of water, and people were constantly coming to be baptized. 24(This was before John was put in prison.) 25An argument developed between some of John's disciples and a certain Jew[h] over the matter of ceremonial washing. 26They came to John and said to him, "Rabbi, that man who was with you on the other side of the Jordan—the one you testified about—well, he is baptizing, and everyone is going to him."

27To this John replied, "A man can receive only what is given him from heaven. 28You yourselves can testify that I said, 'I am not the Christ[i] but am sent ahead of him.' 29The bride belongs to the bridegroom. The friend who attends the bridegroom waits and listens for him, and is full of joy when he hears the bridegroom's voice. That joy is mine, and it is now complete. 30He must become greater; I must become less.

31"The one who comes from above is above all; the one who is from the earth belongs to the earth,

---

[a] 6 Or *but spirit*   [b] 7 The Greek is plural.   [c] 13 Some manuscripts *Man, who is in heaven*   [d] 15 Or *believes may have eternal life in him*   [e] 16 Or *his only begotten Son*   [f] 18 Or *God's only begotten Son*   [g] 21 Some interpreters end the quotation after verse 15.
[h] 25 Some manuscripts *and certain Jews*   [i] 28 Or *Messiah*

and speaks as one from the earth. The one who comes from heaven is above all. ³²He testifies to what he has seen and heard, but no one accepts his testimony. ³³The man who has accepted it has certified that God is truthful. ³⁴For the one whom God has sent speaks the words of God, for God[a] gives the Spirit without limit. ³⁵The Father loves the Son and has placed everything in his hands. ³⁶Whoever believes in the Son has eternal life, but whoever rejects the Son will not see life, for God's wrath remains on him."[b]

JESUS TALKS WITH A SAMARITAN WOMAN

4 The Pharisees heard that Jesus was gaining and baptizing more disciples than John, ²although in fact it was not Jesus who baptized, but his disciples. ³When the Lord learned of this, he left Judea and went back once more to Galilee.

⁴Now he had to go through Samaria. ⁵So he came to a town in Samaria called Sychar, near the plot of ground Jacob had given to his son Joseph. ⁶Jacob's well was there, and Jesus, tired as he was from the journey, sat down by the well. It was about the sixth hour.

⁷When a Samaritan woman came to draw water, Jesus said to her, "Will you give me a drink?" ⁸(His disciples had gone into the town to buy food.)

⁹The Samaritan woman said to him, "You are a Jew and I am a Samaritan woman. How can you ask me for a drink?" (For Jews do not associate with Samaritans.[c])

¹⁰Jesus answered her, "If you knew the gift of God and who it is that asks you for a drink, you would have asked him and he would have given you living water."

¹¹"Sir," the woman said, "you have nothing to draw with and the well is deep. Where can you get this living water? ¹²Are you greater than our father Jacob, who gave us the well and drank from it himself, as did also his sons and his flocks and herds?"

¹³Jesus answered, "Everyone who drinks this water will be thirsty again, ¹⁴but whoever drinks the water I give him will never thirst. Indeed, the water I give him will become in him a spring of water welling up to eternal life."

¹⁵The woman said to him, "Sir, give me this water so that I won't get thirsty and have to keep coming here to draw water."

¹⁶He told her, "Go, call your husband and come back."

¹⁷"I have no husband," she replied.

Jesus said to her, "You are right when you say you have no husband. ¹⁸The fact is, you have had five husbands, and the man you now have is not your husband. What you have just said is quite true."

¹⁹"Sir," the woman said, "I can see that you are a prophet. ²⁰Our fathers worshiped on this mountain, but you Jews claim that the place where we must worship is in Jerusalem."

²¹Jesus declared, "Believe me, woman, a time is coming when you will worship the Father neither on this mountain nor in Jerusalem. ²²You Samaritans worship what you do not know; we worship what we do know, for salvation is from the Jews. ²³Yet a time is coming and has now come when the true worshipers will worship the Father in spirit and truth, for they are the kind of worshipers the Father seeks. ²⁴God is spirit, and his worshipers must worship in spirit and in truth."

²⁵The woman said, "I know that Messiah" (called Christ) "is coming. When he comes, he will explain everything to us."

²⁶Then Jesus declared, "I who speak to you am he."

NOW OR NEVER

JN 4:17–18

Jesus knew exactly what the woman had done in her past, yet he was still willing to offer her eternal life. That goes to show that no one is too immoral, too messed up or too evil to be changed by Jesus.

THE DISCIPLES REJOIN JESUS

²⁷Just then his disciples returned and were surprised to find him talking with a woman. But no one asked, "What do you want?" or "Why are you talking with her?"

²⁸Then, leaving her water jar, the woman went back to the town and said to the people, ²⁹"Come, see

---

[a] *34* Greek *he*   [b] *36* Some interpreters end the quotation after verse 30.   [c] *9* Or *do not use dishes Samaritans have used*

a man who told me everything I ever did. Could this be the Christ[a]?" ³⁰They came out of the town and made their way toward him.

³¹Meanwhile his disciples urged him, "Rabbi, eat something."

³²But he said to them, "I have food to eat that you know nothing about."

³³Then his disciples said to each other, "Could someone have brought him food?"

³⁴"My food," said Jesus, "is to do the will of him who sent me and to finish his work. ³⁵Do you not say, 'Four months more and then the harvest'? I tell you, open your eyes and look at the fields! They are ripe for harvest. ³⁶Even now the reaper draws his wages, even now he harvests the crop for eternal life, so that the sower and the reaper may be glad together. ³⁷Thus the saying 'One sows and another reaps' is true. ³⁸I sent you to reap what you have not worked for. Others have done the hard work, and you have reaped the benefits of their labor."

MANY SAMARITANS BELIEVE

³⁹Many of the Samaritans from that town believed in him because of the woman's testimony, "He told me everything I ever did." ⁴⁰So when the Samaritans came to him, they urged him to stay with them, and he stayed two days. ⁴¹And because of his words many more became believers.

⁴²They said to the woman, "We no longer believe just because of what you said; now we have heard for ourselves, and we know that this man really is the Savior of the world."

NOW OR NEVER

JN 4:39–41

Notice the woman's first reaction to her experience with Jesus. She wanted to tell everyone she knew about it. Have you ever felt that way about who Christ is and what he's done in *your* life?

JESUS HEALS THE OFFICIAL'S SON

⁴³After the two days he left for Galilee. ⁴⁴(Now Jesus himself had pointed out that a prophet has no honor in his own country.) ⁴⁵When he arrived in Galilee, the Galileans welcomed him. They had seen all that he had done in Jerusalem at the Passover Feast, for they also had been there.

⁴⁶Once more he visited Cana in Galilee, where he had turned the water into wine. And there was a certain royal official whose son lay sick at Capernaum. ⁴⁷When this man heard that Jesus had arrived in Galilee from Judea, he went to him and begged him to come and heal his son, who was close to death.

⁴⁸"Unless you people see miraculous signs and wonders," Jesus told him, "you will never believe."

⁴⁹The royal official said, "Sir, come down before my child dies."

⁵⁰Jesus replied, "You may go. Your son will live."

The man took Jesus at his word and departed. ⁵¹While he was still on the way, his servants met him with the news that his boy was living. ⁵²When he inquired as to the time when his son got better, they said to him, "The fever left him yesterday at the seventh hour."

⁵³Then the father realized that this was the exact time at which Jesus had said to him, "Your son will live." So he and all his household believed.

⁵⁴This was the second miraculous sign that Jesus performed, having come from Judea to Galilee.

THE HEALING AT THE POOL

5 Some time later, Jesus went up to Jerusalem for a feast of the Jews. ²Now there is in Jerusalem near the Sheep Gate a pool, which in Aramaic is called Bethesda[b] and which is surrounded by five covered colonnades. ³Here a great number of disabled people used to lie—the blind, the lame, the paralyzed.[c] ⁵One who was there had been an invalid for thirty-eight years. ⁶When Jesus saw him lying there and learned that he had been in this condition for a long time, he asked him, "Do you want to get well?"

⁷"Sir," the invalid replied, "I have no one to help me into the pool when the water is stirred. While I am trying to get in, someone else goes down ahead of me."

---

[a] *29* Or *Messiah*   [b] *2* Some manuscripts *Bethzatha*; other manuscripts *Bethsaida*   [c] *3* Some less important manuscripts *paralyzed—and they waited for the moving of the waters.* ⁴*From time to time an angel of the Lord would come down and stir up the waters. The first one into the pool after each such disturbance would be cured of whatever disease he had.*

[8]Then Jesus said to him, "Get up! Pick up your mat and walk." [9]At once the man was cured; he picked up his mat and walked.

The day on which this took place was a Sabbath, [10]and so the Jews said to the man who had been healed, "It is the Sabbath; the law forbids you to carry your mat."

[11]But he replied, "The man who made me well said to me, 'Pick up your mat and walk.' "

[12]So they asked him, "Who is this fellow who told you to pick it up and walk?"

[13]The man who was healed had no idea who it was, for Jesus had slipped away into the crowd that was there.

[14]Later Jesus found him at the temple and said to him, "See, you are well again. Stop sinning or something worse may happen to you." [15]The man went away and told the Jews that it was Jesus who had made him well.

Preparing for Responsibility

Why did Jesus ask the man if he wanted to get well? Wasn't the answer obvious? Imagine for a moment that Jesus hadn't said anything to the man and just healed him. Although the man would have needed Jesus' healing touch all the same, he wouldn't have had the opportunity to express how helpless he was without it. When we verbally express how weak and needy we are, we are humbled. And that's when Jesus demonstrates his strength— right in the midst of our weakness. So when you are weak, admit it and ask for God's strength in your life. Don't be surprised when he tells you to "get up and walk."

LIFE THROUGH THE SON

[16]So, because Jesus was doing these things on the Sabbath, the Jews persecuted him. [17]Jesus said to them, "My Father is always at his work to this very day, and I, too, am working." [18]For this reason the Jews tried all the harder to kill him; not only was he breaking the Sabbath, but he was even calling God his own Father, making himself equal with God.

[19]Jesus gave them this answer: "I tell you the truth, the Son can do nothing by himself; he can do only what he sees his Father doing, because whatever the Father does the Son also does. [20]For the Father loves the Son and shows him all he does. Yes, to your amazement he will show him even greater things than these. [21]For just as the Father raises the dead and gives them life, even so the Son gives life to whom he is pleased to give it. [22]Moreover, the Father judges no one, but has entrusted all judgment to the Son, [23]that all may honor the Son just as they honor the Father. He who does not honor the Son does not honor the Father, who sent him.

[24]"I tell you the truth, whoever hears my word and believes him who sent me has eternal life and will not be condemned; he has crossed over from death to life. [25]I tell you the truth, a time is coming and has now come when the dead will hear the voice of the Son of God and those who hear will live. [26]For as the Father has life in himself, so he has granted the Son to have life in himself. [27]And he has given him authority to judge because he is the Son of Man.

[28]"Do not be amazed at this, for a time is coming when all who are in their graves will hear his voice [29]and come out—those who have done good will rise to live, and those who have done evil will rise to be condemned. [30]By myself I can do nothing; I judge only as I hear, and my judgment is just, for I seek not to please myself but him who sent me.

TESTIMONIES ABOUT JESUS

[31]"If I testify about myself, my testimony is not valid. [32]There is another who testifies in my favor, and I know that his testimony about me is valid.

[33]"You have sent to John and he has testified to the truth. [34]Not that I accept human testimony; but I mention it that you may be saved. [35]John was a lamp that burned and gave light, and you chose for a time to enjoy his light.

[36]"I have testimony weightier than that of John. For the very work that the Father has given me to finish, and which I am doing, testifies that the Father has sent me. [37]And the Father who sent me has himself testified concerning me. You have never heard his voice nor seen his form, [38]nor does his word dwell in you, for you do not believe the one he sent. [39]You diligently study[a] the Scriptures because you

---

[a] 39 Or Study diligently (the imperative)

think that by them you possess eternal life. These are the Scriptures that testify about me, ⁴⁰yet you refuse to come to me to have life.

⁴¹"I do not accept praise from men, ⁴²but I know you. I know that you do not have the love of God in your hearts. ⁴³I have come in my Father's name, and you do not accept me; but if someone else comes in his own name, you will accept him. ⁴⁴How can you believe if you accept praise from one another, yet make no effort to obtain the praise that comes from the only God*?

⁴⁵"But do not think I will accuse you before the Father. Your accuser is Moses, on whom your hopes are set. ⁴⁶If you believed Moses, you would believe me, for he wrote about me. ⁴⁷But since you do not believe what he wrote, how are you going to believe what I say?"

JESUS FEEDS THE FIVE THOUSAND

6 Some time after this, Jesus crossed to the far shore of the Sea of Galilee (that is, the Sea of Tiberias), ²and a great crowd of people followed him because they saw the miraculous signs he had performed on the sick. ³Then Jesus went up on a mountainside and sat down with his disciples. ⁴The Jewish Passover Feast was near.

⁵When Jesus looked up and saw a great crowd coming toward him, he said to Philip, "Where shall we buy bread for these people to eat?" ⁶He asked this only to test him, for he already had in mind what he was going to do.

⁷Philip answered him, "Eight months' wagesᵇ would not buy enough bread for each one to have a bite!"

⁸Another of his disciples, Andrew, Simon Peter's brother, spoke up, ⁹"Here is a boy with five small barley loaves and two small fish, but how far will they go among so many?"

¹⁰Jesus said, "Have the people sit down." There was plenty of grass in that place, and the men sat down, about five thousand of them. ¹¹Jesus then took the loaves, gave thanks, and distributed to those who were seated as much as they wanted. He did the same with the fish.

¹²When they had all had enough to eat, he said to his disciples, "Gather the pieces that are left over. Let nothing be wasted." ¹³So they gathered them and filled twelve baskets with the pieces of the five barley loaves left over by those who had eaten.

¹⁴After the people saw the miraculous sign that Jesus did, they began to say, "Surely this is the Prophet who is to come into the world." ¹⁵Jesus, knowing that they intended to come and make him king by force, withdrew again to a mountain by himself.

JESUS WALKS ON THE WATER

¹⁶When evening came, his disciples went down to the lake, ¹⁷where they got into a boat and set off across the lake for Capernaum. By now it was dark, and Jesus had not yet joined them. ¹⁸A strong wind was blowing and the waters grew rough. ¹⁹When they had rowed three or three and a half miles,ᶜ they saw Jesus approaching the boat, walking on the water; and they were terrified. ²⁰But he said to them, "It is I; don't be afraid." ²¹Then they were willing to take him into the boat, and immediately the boat reached the shore where they were heading.

²²The next day the crowd that had stayed on the opposite shore of the lake realized that only one boat had been there, and that Jesus had not entered it with his disciples, but that they had gone away alone. ²³Then some boats from Tiberias landed near the place where the people had eaten the bread after the Lord had given thanks. ²⁴Once the crowd realized that neither Jesus nor his disciples were there, they got into the boats and went to Capernaum in search of Jesus.

Letting Jesus Use Your Talents

»» live the adventure »» Jn 6:8-9

As you read about this miraculous chow-down, remember to never underestimate God's ability to use what you bring to the table. The fact that the kid in this story had only five loaves and two fish didn't bother Jesus. He didn't say, "I've got 5,000 people to take care of, and this is the best you can do?" Instead, Jesus took the boy's meager little meal, blessed it and used it to feed the entire crowd (with food to spare). The same goes for our talents and abilities. It doesn't depend on what you've got but on Jesus' awesome power to use what you've got. So give him everything you have and say, "Here, Jesus. It isn't much, but you can have it all."

ᵃ *44* Some early manuscripts *the Only One*   ᵇ *7* Greek *two hundred denarii*   ᶜ *19* Greek *rowed twenty-five or thirty stadia* (about 5 or 6 kilometers)

²⁵When they found him on the other side of the lake, they asked him, "Rabbi, when did you get here?"

²⁶Jesus answered, "I tell you the truth, you are looking for me, not because you saw miraculous signs but because you ate the loaves and had your fill. ²⁷Do not work for food that spoils, but for food that endures to eternal life, which the Son of Man will give you. On him God the Father has placed his seal of approval."

²⁸Then they asked him, "What must we do to do the works God requires?"

²⁹Jesus answered, "The work of God is this: to believe in the one he has sent."

³⁰So they asked him, "What miraculous sign then will you give that we may see it and believe you? What will you do? ³¹Our forefathers ate the manna in the desert; as it is written: 'He gave them bread from heaven to eat.'ᵃ"

³²Jesus said to them, "I tell you the truth, it is not Moses who has given you the bread from heaven, but it is my Father who gives you the true bread from heaven. ³³For the bread of God is he who comes down from heaven and gives life to the world."

³⁴"Sir," they said, "from now on give us this bread."

³⁵Then Jesus declared, "I am the bread of life. He who comes to me will never go hungry, and he who believes in me will never be thirsty. ³⁶But as I told you, you have seen me and still you do not believe. ³⁷All that the Father gives me will come to me, and whoever comes to me I will never drive away. ³⁸For I have come down from heaven not to do my will but to do the will of him who sent me. ³⁹And this is the will of him who sent me, that I shall lose none of all that he has given me, but raise them up at the last day. ⁴⁰For my Father's will is that everyone who looks to the Son and believes in him shall have eternal life, and I will raise him up at the last day."

⁴¹At this the Jews began to grumble about him because he said, "I am the bread that came down from heaven." ⁴²They said, "Is this not Jesus, the son of Joseph, whose father and mother we know? How can he now say, 'I came down from heaven'?"

⁴³"Stop grumbling among yourselves," Jesus answered. ⁴⁴"No one can come to me unless the Father who sent me draws him, and I will raise him up at the last day. ⁴⁵It is written in the Prophets: 'They will all be taught by God.'ᵇ Everyone who listens to the Father and learns from him comes to me. ⁴⁶No one has seen the Father except the one who is from God; only he has seen the Father. ⁴⁷I tell you the truth, he who believes has everlasting life. ⁴⁸I am the bread of life. ⁴⁹Your forefathers ate the manna in the desert, yet they died. ⁵⁰But here is the bread that comes down from heaven, which a man may eat and not die. ⁵¹I am the living bread that came down from heaven. If anyone eats of this bread, he will live forever. This bread is my flesh, which I will give for the life of the world."

⁵²Then the Jews began to argue sharply among themselves, "How can this man give us his flesh to eat?"

⁵³Jesus said to them, "I tell you the truth, unless you eat the flesh of the Son of Man and drink his blood, you have no life in you. ⁵⁴Whoever eats my flesh and drinks my blood has eternal life, and I will raise him up at the last day. ⁵⁵For my flesh is real food and my blood is real drink. ⁵⁶Whoever eats my flesh and drinks my blood remains in me, and I in him. ⁵⁷Just as the living Father sent me and I live because of the Father, so the one who feeds on me will live because of me. ⁵⁸This is the bread that came down from heaven. Your forefathers ate manna and died, but he who feeds on this bread will live forever." ⁵⁹He said this while teaching in the synagogue in Capernaum.

MANY DISCIPLES DESERT JESUS

⁶⁰On hearing it, many of his disciples said, "This is a hard teaching. Who can accept it?"

⁶¹Aware that his disciples were grumbling about this, Jesus said to them, "Does this offend you? ⁶²What if you see the Son of Man ascend to where he was before! ⁶³The Spirit gives life; the flesh counts for nothing. The words I have spoken to you are spiritᶜ and they are life. ⁶⁴Yet there are some of you who do not believe." For Jesus had known from the beginning which of them did not believe and who would betray him. ⁶⁵He went on to say, "This is why I told you that no one can come to me unless the Father has enabled him."

⁶⁶From this time many of his disciples turned back and no longer followed him.

⁶⁷"You do not want to leave too, do you?" Jesus asked the Twelve.

ᵃ 31 Exodus 16:4; Neh. 9:15; Psalm 78:24,25   ᵇ 45 Isaiah 54:13   ᶜ 63 Or Spirit

68Simon Peter answered him, "Lord, to whom shall we go? You have the words of eternal life. 69We believe and know that you are the Holy One of God."

70Then Jesus replied, "Have I not chosen you, the Twelve? Yet one of you is a devil!" 71(He meant Judas, the son of Simon Iscariot, who, though one of the Twelve, was later to betray him.)

JESUS GOES TO THE FEAST OF TABERNACLES

7 After this, Jesus went around in Galilee, purposely staying away from Judea because the Jews there were waiting to take his life. 2But when the Jewish Feast of Tabernacles was near, 3Jesus' brothers said to him, "You ought to leave here and go to Judea, so that your disciples may see the miracles you do. 4No one who wants to become a public figure acts in secret. Since you are doing these things, show yourself to the world." 5For even his own brothers did not believe in him.

6Therefore Jesus told them, "The right time for me has not yet come; for you any time is right. 7The world cannot hate you, but it hates me because I testify that what it does is evil. 8You go to the Feast. I am not yet[a] going up to this Feast, because for me the right time has not yet come." 9Having said this, he stayed in Galilee.

10However, after his brothers had left for the Feast, he went also, not publicly, but in secret. 11Now at the Feast the Jews were watching for him and asking, "Where is that man?"

12Among the crowds there was widespread whispering about him. Some said, "He is a good man."

Others replied, "No, he deceives the people." 13But no one would say anything publicly about him for fear of the Jews.

JESUS TEACHES AT THE FEAST

14Not until halfway through the Feast did Jesus go up to the temple courts and begin to teach. 15The Jews were amazed and asked, "How did this man get such learning without having studied?"

16Jesus answered, "My teaching is not my own. It comes from him who sent me. 17If anyone chooses to do God's will, he will find out whether my teaching comes from God or whether I speak on my own. 18He who speaks on his own does so to gain honor for himself, but he who works for the honor of the one who sent him is a man of truth; there is nothing false about him. 19Has not Moses given you the law? Yet not one of you keeps the law. Why are you trying to kill me?"

20"You are demon-possessed," the crowd answered. "Who is trying to kill you?"

21Jesus said to them, "I did one miracle, and you are all astonished. 22Yet, because Moses gave you circumcision (though actually it did not come from Moses, but from the patriarchs), you circumcise a child on the Sabbath. 23Now if a child can be circumcised on the Sabbath so that the law of Moses may not be broken, why are you angry with me for healing the whole man on the Sabbath? 24Stop judging by mere appearances, and make a right judgment."

IS JESUS THE CHRIST?

25At that point some of the people of Jerusalem began to ask, "Isn't this the man they are trying to kill? 26Here he is, speaking publicly, and they are not saying a word to him. Have the authorities really concluded that he is the Christ[b]? 27But we know where this man is from; when the Christ comes, no one will know where he is from."

28Then Jesus, still teaching in the temple courts, cried out, "Yes, you know me, and you know where

Staying Faithful

Yes, Jesus' commands can be tough to follow at times. Yes, his teachings can be hard to understand. Yes, the life he asked us to live isn't always pleasant. And no, we can't do any of it without God's enabling power. But if you ever get tempted to abandon the Lord, ask yourself the questions the disciples asked: Where else will you find ultimate truth? Who else can guarantee you eternal life and fulfillment?

---

a 8 Some early manuscripts do not have yet.   b 26 Or Messiah; also in verses 27, 31, 41 and 42

I am from. I am not here on my own, but he who sent me is true. You do not know him, 29but I know him because I am from him and he sent me."

30At this they tried to seize him, but no one laid a hand on him, because his time had not yet come. 31Still, many in the crowd put their faith in him. They said, "When the Christ comes, will he do more miraculous signs than this man?"

32The Pharisees heard the crowd whispering such things about him. Then the chief priests and the Pharisees sent temple guards to arrest him.

33Jesus said, "I am with you for only a short time, and then I go to the one who sent me. 34You will look for me, but you will not find me; and where I am, you cannot come."

35The Jews said to one another, "Where does this man intend to go that we cannot find him? Will he go where our people live scattered among the Greeks, and teach the Greeks? 36What did he mean when he said, 'You will look for me, but you will not find me,' and 'Where I am, you cannot come'?"

37On the last and greatest day of the Feast, Jesus stood and said in a loud voice, "If anyone is thirsty, let him come to me and drink. 38Whoever believes in me, as[a] the Scripture has said, streams of living water will flow from within him." 39By this he meant the Spirit, whom those who believed in him were later to receive. Up to that time the Spirit had not been given, since Jesus had not yet been glorified.

40On hearing his words, some of the people said, "Surely this man is the Prophet."

41Others said, "He is the Christ."

Still others asked, "How can the Christ come from Galilee? 42Does not the Scripture say that the Christ will come from David's family[b] and from Bethlehem, the town where David lived?" 43Thus the people were divided because of Jesus. 44Some wanted to seize him, but no one laid a hand on him.

Making Smart Judgments

Jesus accused his opponents of making shallow, biased judgments of his ministry. That's the problem with judging strictly by appearance; your conclusions about someone else may be superficial and inaccurate. What if the girl who never smiles or talks during social studies isn't really snobby and conceited like you think? What if she's just too shy to open her mouth? What if the new guy with the thick glasses isn't the geek you think he is? What if he's actually a better athlete than you are? Give people the benefit of the doubt, just like you want others to do for you. Let people surprise you . . . in a good way.

UNBELIEF OF THE JEWISH LEADERS

45Finally the temple guards went back to the chief priests and Pharisees, who asked them, "Why didn't you bring him in?"

46"No one ever spoke the way this man does," the guards declared.

47"You mean he has deceived you also?" the Pharisees retorted. 48"Has any of the rulers or of the Pharisees believed in him? 49No! But this mob that knows nothing of the law—there is a curse on them."

50Nicodemus, who had gone to Jesus earlier and who was one of their own number, asked, 51"Does our law condemn anyone without first hearing him to find out what he is doing?"

52They replied, "Are you from Galilee, too? Look into it, and you will find that a prophet[c] does not come out of Galilee."

NOW OR NEVER
JN 7:42

If the people had done a little investigating, they would have discovered that Jesus *was* born in Bethlehem, just as the prophets had predicted years in advance. (Check out Luke 2 for the full story.) The more you know about Jesus, the easier it is to trust him.

---

[a] 37,38 Or / If anyone is thirsty, let him come to me. / And let him drink, 38who believes in me. / As   [b] 42 Greek seed   [c] 52 Two early manuscripts the Prophet

[The earliest manuscripts and many other ancient witnesses do not have John 7:53–8:11.]

53Then each went to his own home.

8 But Jesus went to the Mount of Olives. **2**At dawn he appeared again in the temple courts, where all the people gathered around him, and he sat down to teach them. **3**The teachers of the law and the Pharisees brought in a woman caught in adultery. They made her stand before the group **4**and said to Jesus, "Teacher, this woman was caught in the act of adultery. **5**In the Law Moses commanded us to stone such women. Now what do you say?" **6**They were using this question as a trap, in order to have a basis for accusing him.

But Jesus bent down and started to write on the ground with his finger. **7**When they kept on questioning him, he straightened up and said to them, "If any one of you is without sin, let him be the first to throw a stone at her." **8**Again he stooped down and wrote on the ground.

9At this, those who heard began to go away one at a time, the older ones first, until only Jesus was left, with the woman still standing there. **10**Jesus straightened up and asked her, "Woman, where are they? Has no one condemned you?"

11"No one, sir," she said.

"Then neither do I condemn you," Jesus declared. "Go now and leave your life of sin."

THE VALIDITY OF JESUS' TESTIMONY

12When Jesus spoke again to the people, he said, "I am the light of the world. Whoever follows me will never walk in darkness, but will have the light of life."

13The Pharisees challenged him, "Here you are, appearing as your own witness; your testimony is not valid."

14Jesus answered, "Even if I testify on my own behalf, my testimony is valid, for I know where I came from and where I am going. But you have no idea where I come from or where I am going. **15**You judge by human standards; I pass judgment on no one. **16**But if I do judge, my decisions are right, because I am not alone. I stand with the Father, who sent me. **17**In your own Law it is written that the testimony of two men is valid. **18**I am one who testifies for myself; my other witness is the Father, who sent me."

19Then they asked him, "Where is your father?"

"You do not know me or my Father," Jesus replied. "If you knew me, you would know my Father also." **20**He spoke these words while teaching in the temple area near the place where the offerings were put. Yet no one seized him, because his time had not yet come.

21Once more Jesus said to them, "I am going away, and you will look for me, and you will die in your sin. Where I go, you cannot come."

22This made the Jews ask, "Will he kill himself? Is that why he says, 'Where I go, you cannot come'?"

23But he continued, "You are from below; I am from above. You are of this world; I am not of this world. **24**I told you that you would die in your sins; if you do not believe that I am ⌊the one I claim to be,⌋[a] you will indeed die in your sins."

25"Who are you?" they asked.

"Just what I have been claiming all along," Jesus replied. **26**"I have much to say in judgment of you. But he who sent me is reliable, and what I have heard from him I tell the world."

27They did not understand that he was telling them about his Father. **28**So Jesus said, "When you have lifted up the Son of Man, then you will know that I am ⌊the one I claim to be⌋ and that I do nothing on my own but speak just what the Father has taught me. **29**The one who sent me is with me; he has not left me alone, for I always do what pleases him." **30**Even as he spoke, many put their faith in him.

THE CHILDREN OF ABRAHAM

31To the Jews who had believed him, Jesus said, "If you hold to my teaching, you are really my disciples. **32**Then you will know the truth, and the truth will set you free."

[a] *24* Or *I am he*; also in verse 28

battlelines

» *The God of Second Chances (Forgiveness)*

Q: Hey, are you going to the True Love Waits rally this weekend?

A: Uh . . . no. I don't think that's the kind of thing I can go to anymore.

Q: What are you talking about? It's for everyone.

A: Not me. Not after . . . well, you know—last summer.

Q: Oh, yeah. But that was a year ago. That's ancient history.

A: No, it's not. Don't you get it? I'm not a virgin anymore. And even if I was, I'm constantly thinking about sex. How can I promise that "true love waits" when I *didn't* wait then and my mind certainly doesn't want to wait now? My future wife—if I ever have one—will know I didn't wait for her, so what's the point?

Q: So you're saying God has just given up on you? That you're condemned to live a miserable life?

A: Basically, yeah.

Q: I thought God specializes in miracles.

A: Yeah, well, it's not like he can undo what I've done.

Q: No, but he can forgive you. And with that forgiveness comes cleansing. It's like you become a "recycled virgin." You get to start over with a clean slate.

A: What I really want is to totally erase what happened.

Q: Well, the truth is, you can't. You'll always have that memory. You can't go back in time and change the events of the past. But *God* can do something about it when you repent. The Bible says he not only forgives our sins, but he also forgets them. From his perspective, your sins are erased—as if they never happened.

A: Do you really believe that?

Q: As a matter of fact, I do.

A: Then will you pray for God to forgive me?

Q: He already has.

» *Starting Over*

If you've already given away your virginity, you have a chance to start over. God offers complete forgiveness to anyone who repents, to anyone who confesses their sin. He can erase everything you've done and everything you've thought about doing. He can repair the damage to your relationship with him. All he asks in return is that you accept his forgiveness and look to him for the strength to do the right thing the next time you're tempted.

In the meantime, hold on to this promise from Hebrews 8:11–12: "No longer will a man teach his neighbor, or a man his brother, saying, 'Know the Lord,' because they will all know me, from the least of them to the greatest, for I will forgive their wickedness and will remember their sins no more."

While you're at it, try memorizing 1 John 1:9. It's a short, life-altering verse that some have called "the Christian's bar of soap."

When you're feeling overrun by guilt, visit www.RevolutionBible.com

³³They answered him, "We are Abraham's descendants[a] and have never been slaves of anyone. How can you say that we shall be set free?"

³⁴Jesus replied, "I tell you the truth, everyone who sins is a slave to sin. ³⁵Now a slave has no permanent place in the family, but a son belongs to it forever. ³⁶So if the Son sets you free, you will be free indeed. ³⁷I know you are Abraham's descendants. Yet you are ready to kill me, because you have no room for my word. ³⁸I am telling you what I have seen in the Father's presence, and you do what you have heard from your father.[b]"

³⁹"Abraham is our father," they answered.

"If you were Abraham's children," said Jesus, "then you would[c] do the things Abraham did. ⁴⁰As it is, you are determined to kill me, a man who has told you the truth that I heard from God. Abraham did not do such things. ⁴¹You are doing the things your own father does."

"We are not illegitimate children," they protested. "The only Father we have is God himself."

THE CHILDREN OF THE DEVIL

⁴²Jesus said to them, "If God were your Father, you would love me, for I came from God and now am here. I have not come on my own; but he sent me. ⁴³Why is my language not clear to you? Because you are unable to hear what I say. ⁴⁴You belong to your father, the devil, and you want to carry out your father's desire. He was a murderer from the beginning, not holding to the truth, for there is no truth in him. When he lies, he speaks his native language, for he is a liar and the father of lies. ⁴⁵Yet because I tell the truth, you do not believe me! ⁴⁶Can any of you prove me guilty of sin? If I am telling the truth, why don't you believe me? ⁴⁷He who belongs to God hears what God says. The reason you do not hear is that you do not belong to God."

THE CLAIMS OF JESUS ABOUT HIMSELF

⁴⁸The Jews answered him, "Aren't we right in saying that you are a Samaritan and demon-possessed?"

⁴⁹"I am not possessed by a demon," said Jesus, "but I honor my Father and you dishonor me. ⁵⁰I am not seeking glory for myself; but there is one who seeks it, and he is the judge. ⁵¹I tell you the truth, if anyone keeps my word, he will never see death."

⁵²At this the Jews exclaimed, "Now we know that you are demon-possessed! Abraham died and so did the prophets, yet you say that if anyone keeps your word, he will never taste death. ⁵³Are you greater than our father Abraham? He died, and so did the prophets. Who do you think you are?"

⁵⁴Jesus replied, "If I glorify myself, my glory means nothing. My Father, whom you claim as your God, is the one who glorifies me. ⁵⁵Though you do not know him, I know him. If I said I did not, I would be a liar like you, but I do know him and keep his word. ⁵⁶Your father Abraham rejoiced at the thought of seeing my day; he saw it and was glad."

⁵⁷"You are not yet fifty years old," the Jews said to him, "and you have seen Abraham!"

⁵⁸"I tell you the truth," Jesus answered, "before Abraham was born, I am!" ⁵⁹At this, they picked up stones to stone him, but Jesus hid himself, slipping away from the temple grounds.

JESUS HEALS A MAN BORN BLIND

9 As he went along, he saw a man blind from birth. ²His disciples asked him, "Rabbi, who sinned, this man or his parents, that he was born blind?"

³"Neither this man nor his parents sinned," said Jesus, "but this happened so that the work of God might be displayed in his life. ⁴As long as it is day, we must do the work of him who sent me. Night is coming, when no one can work. ⁵While I am in the world, I am the light of the world."

⁶Having said this, he spit on the ground, made some mud with the saliva, and put it on the man's eyes. ⁷"Go," he told him, "wash in the Pool of Siloam" (this word means Sent). So the man went and washed, and came home seeing.

⁸His neighbors and those who had formerly seen him begging asked, "Isn't this the same man who used to sit and beg?" ⁹Some claimed that he was.

Others said, "No, he only looks like him."

But he himself insisted, "I am the man."

---

[a] 33 Greek seed; also in verse 37   [b] 38 Or presence. Therefore do what you have heard from the Father.   [c] 39 Some early manuscripts "If you are Abraham's children," said Jesus, "then

[10] "How then were your eyes opened?" they demanded.

[11] He replied, "The man they call Jesus made some mud and put it on my eyes. He told me to go to Siloam and wash. So I went and washed, and then I could see."

[12] "Where is this man?" they asked him.

"I don't know," he said.

THE PHARISEES INVESTIGATE THE HEALING

[13] They brought to the Pharisees the man who had been blind. [14] Now the day on which Jesus had made the mud and opened the man's eyes was a Sabbath. [15] Therefore the Pharisees also asked him how he had received his sight. "He put mud on my eyes," the man replied, "and I washed, and now I see."

[16] Some of the Pharisees said, "This man is not from God, for he does not keep the Sabbath."

But others asked, "How can a sinner do such miraculous signs?" So they were divided.

[17] Finally they turned again to the blind man, "What have you to say about him? It was your eyes he opened."

The man replied, "He is a prophet."

[18] The Jews still did not believe that he had been blind and had received his sight until they sent for the man's parents. [19] "Is this your son?" they asked. "Is this the one you say was born blind? How is it that now he can see?"

[20] "We know he is our son," the parents answered, "and we know he was born blind. [21] But how he can see now, or who opened his eyes, we don't know. Ask him. He is of age; he will speak for himself." [22] His parents said this because they were afraid of the Jews, for already the Jews had decided that anyone who acknowledged that Jesus was the Christ[a] would be put out of the synagogue. [23] That was why his parents said, "He is of age; ask him."

[24] A second time they summoned the man who had been blind. "Give glory to God,[b]" they said. "We know this man is a sinner."

[25] He replied, "Whether he is a sinner or not, I don't know. One thing I do know. I was blind but now I see!"

[26] Then they asked him, "What did he do to you? How did he open your eyes?"

[27] He answered, "I have told you already and you did not listen. Why do you want to hear it again? Do you want to become his disciples, too?"

[28] Then they hurled insults at him and said, "You are this fellow's disciple! We are disciples of Moses! [29] We know that God spoke to Moses, but as for this fellow, we don't even know where he comes from."

[30] The man answered, "Now that is remarkable! You don't know where he comes from, yet he opened my eyes. [31] We know that God does not listen to sinners. He listens to the godly man who does his will. [32] Nobody has ever heard of opening the eyes of a man born blind. [33] If this man were not from God, he could do nothing."

[34] To this they replied, "You were steeped in sin at birth; how dare you lecture us!" And they threw him out.

SPIRITUAL BLINDNESS

[35] Jesus heard that they had thrown him out, and when he found him, he said, "Do you believe in the Son of Man?"

[36] "Who is he, sir?" the man asked. "Tell me so that I may believe in him."

[37] Jesus said, "You have now seen him; in fact, he is the one speaking with you."

[38] Then the man said, "Lord, I believe," and he worshiped him.

[39] Jesus said, "For judgment I have come into this world, so that the blind will see and those who see will become blind."

[40] Some Pharisees who were with him heard him say this and asked, "What? Are we blind too?"

[41] Jesus said, "If you were blind, you would not be guilty of sin; but now that you claim you can see, your guilt remains.

---

[a] 22 Or *Messiah*   [b] 24 A solemn charge to tell the truth (see Joshua 7:19)

THE SHEPHERD AND HIS FLOCK

10

"I tell you the truth, the man who does not enter the sheep pen by the gate, but climbs in by some other way, is a thief and a robber. [2]The man who enters by the gate is the shepherd of his sheep. [3]The watchman opens the gate for him, and the sheep listen to his voice. He calls his own sheep by name and leads them out. [4]When he has brought out all his own, he goes on ahead of them, and his sheep follow him because they know his voice. [5]But they will never follow a stranger; in fact, they will run away from him because they do not recognize a stranger's voice." [6]Jesus used this figure of speech, but they did not understand what he was telling them.

[7]Therefore Jesus said again, "I tell you the truth, I am the gate for the sheep. [8]All who ever came before me were thieves and robbers, but the sheep did not listen to them. [9]I am the gate; whoever enters through me will be saved.[a] He will come in and go out, and find pasture. [10]The thief comes only to steal and kill and destroy; I have come that they may have life, and have it to the full.

[11]"I am the good shepherd. The good shepherd lays down his life for the sheep. [12]The hired hand is not the shepherd who owns the sheep. So when he sees the wolf coming, he abandons the sheep and runs away. Then the wolf attacks the flock and scatters it. [13]The man runs away because he is a hired hand and cares nothing for the sheep.

[14]"I am the good shepherd; I know my sheep and my sheep know me— [15]just as the Father knows me and I know the Father—and I lay down my life for the sheep. [16]I have other sheep that are not of this sheep pen. I must bring them also. They too will listen to my voice, and there shall be one flock and one shepherd. [17]The reason my Father loves me is that I lay down my life—only to take it up again. [18]No one takes it from me, but I lay it down of my own accord. I have authority to lay it down and authority to take it up again. This command I received from my Father."

[19]At these words the Jews were again divided. [20]Many of them said, "He is demon-possessed and raving mad. Why listen to him?"

[21]But others said, "These are not the sayings of a man possessed by a demon. Can a demon open the eyes of the blind?"

THE UNBELIEF OF THE JEWS

[22]Then came the Feast of Dedication[b] at Jerusalem. It was winter, [23]and Jesus was in the temple area walking in Solomon's Colonnade. [24]The Jews gathered around him, saying, "How long will you keep us in suspense? If you are the Christ,[c] tell us plainly."

[25]Jesus answered, "I did tell you, but you do not believe. The miracles I do in my Father's name speak for me, [26]but you do not believe because you are not my sheep. [27]My sheep listen to my voice; I know them, and they follow me. [28]I give them eternal life, and they shall never perish; no one can snatch them out of my hand. [29]My Father, who has given them to me, is greater than all[d]; no one can snatch them out of my Father's hand. [30]I and the Father are one."

[31]Again the Jews picked up stones to stone him, [32]but Jesus said to them, "I have shown you many great miracles from the Father. For which of these do you stone me?"

[33]"We are not stoning you for any of these," replied the Jews, "but for blasphemy, because you, a mere man, claim to be God."

[34]Jesus answered them, "Is it not written in your Law, 'I have said you are gods'[e]? [35]If he called them 'gods,' to whom the word of God came—and the Scripture cannot be broken— [36]what about the one

Appreciating Life in Jesus

Jesus didn't just give us a "Get Out of Hell Free" card when he died for us; he also gave us a purpose for living. Imagine what your life would be like if Jesus hadn't come. You would be in constant "me first" mode; there would be no reason to care much about other people. Life would be one never-ending search for the next quick thrill. Without eternity to look forward to, death would be infinitely more terrifying than it is now. Compare that scenario to the hope we have now thanks to Jesus.

---

[a] 9 Or *kept safe*   [b] 22 That is, Hanukkah   [c] 24 Or *Messiah*   [d] 29 Many early manuscripts *What my Father has given me is greater than all*   [e] 34 Psalm 82:6

whom the Father set apart as his very own and sent into the world? Why then do you accuse me of blasphemy because I said, 'I am God's Son'? ³⁷Do not believe me unless I do what my Father does. ³⁸But if I do it, even though you do not believe me, believe the miracles, that you may know and understand that the Father is in me, and I in the Father." ³⁹Again they tried to seize him, but he escaped their grasp.

⁴⁰Then Jesus went back across the Jordan to the place where John had been baptizing in the early days. Here he stayed ⁴¹and many people came to him. They said, "Though John never performed a miraculous sign, all that John said about this man was true." ⁴²And in that place many believed in Jesus.

THE DEATH OF LAZARUS

11 Now a man named Lazarus was sick. He was from Bethany, the village of Mary and her sister Martha. ²This Mary, whose brother Lazarus now lay sick, was the same one who poured perfume on the Lord and wiped his feet with her hair. ³So the sisters sent word to Jesus, "Lord, the one you love is sick."

⁴When he heard this, Jesus said, "This sickness will not end in death. No, it is for God's glory so that God's Son may be glorified through it." ⁵Jesus loved Martha and her sister and Lazarus. ⁶Yet when he heard that Lazarus was sick, he stayed where he was two more days.

⁷Then he said to his disciples, "Let us go back to Judea."

⁸"But Rabbi," they said, "a short while ago the Jews tried to stone you, and yet you are going back there?"

⁹Jesus answered, "Are there not twelve hours of daylight? A man who walks by day will not stumble, for he sees by this world's light. ¹⁰It is when he walks by night that he stumbles, for he has no light."

¹¹After he had said this, he went on to tell them, "Our friend Lazarus has fallen asleep; but I am going there to wake him up."

¹²His disciples replied, "Lord, if he sleeps, he will get better." ¹³Jesus had been speaking of his death, but his disciples thought he meant natural sleep.

¹⁴So then he told them plainly, "Lazarus is dead, ¹⁵and for your sake I am glad I was not there, so that you may believe. But let us go to him."

¹⁶Then Thomas (called Didymus) said to the rest of the disciples, "Let us also go, that we may die with him."

JESUS COMFORTS THE SISTERS

¹⁷On his arrival, Jesus found that Lazarus had already been in the tomb for four days. ¹⁸Bethany was less than two miles[a] from Jerusalem, ¹⁹and many Jews had come to Martha and Mary to comfort them in the loss of their brother. ²⁰When Martha heard that Jesus was coming, she went out to meet him, but Mary stayed at home.

²¹"Lord," Martha said to Jesus, "if you had been here, my brother would not have died. ²²But I know that even now God will give you whatever you ask."

²³Jesus said to her, "Your brother will rise again."

²⁴Martha answered, "I know he will rise again in the resurrection at the last day."

²⁵Jesus said to her, "I am the resurrection and the life. He who believes in me will live, even though he dies; ²⁶and whoever lives and believes in me will never die. Do you believe this?"

²⁷"Yes, Lord," she told him, "I believe that you are the Christ,[b] the Son of God, who was to come into the world."

²⁸And after she had said this, she went back and called her sister Mary aside. "The Teacher is here," she said, "and is asking for you." ²⁹When Mary heard this, she got up quickly and went to him. ³⁰Now Jesus had not yet entered the village, but was still at the place where Martha had met him. ³¹When the Jews who had been with Mary in the house, comforting her, noticed how quickly she got up and went out, they followed her, supposing she was going to the tomb to mourn there.

³²When Mary reached the place where Jesus was and saw him, she fell at his feet and said, "Lord, if you had been here, my brother would not have died."

³³When Jesus saw her weeping, and the Jews who had come along with her also weeping, he was deeply moved in spirit and troubled. ³⁴"Where have you laid him?" he asked.

"Come and see, Lord," they replied.

³⁵Jesus wept.

ᵃ 18 Greek fifteen stadia (about 3 kilometers)   ᵇ 27 Or Messiah

36Then the Jews said, "See how he loved him!"

37But some of them said, "Could not he who opened the eyes of the blind man have kept this man from dying?"

JESUS RAISES LAZARUS FROM THE DEAD

38Jesus, once more deeply moved, came to the tomb. It was a cave with a stone laid across the entrance. 39"Take away the stone," he said.

"But, Lord," said Martha, the sister of the dead man, "by this time there is a bad odor, for he has been there four days."

40Then Jesus said, "Did I not tell you that if you believed, you would see the glory of God?"

41So they took away the stone. Then Jesus looked up and said, "Father, I thank you that you have heard me. 42I knew that you always hear me, but I said this for the benefit of the people standing here, that they may believe that you sent me."

43When he had said this, Jesus called in a loud voice, "Lazarus, come out!" 44The dead man came out, his hands and feet wrapped with strips of linen, and a cloth around his face.

Jesus said to them, "Take off the grave clothes and let him go."

THE PLOT TO KILL JESUS

45Therefore many of the Jews who had come to visit Mary, and had seen what Jesus did, put their faith in him. 46But some of them went to the Pharisees and told them what Jesus had done. 47Then the chief priests and the Pharisees called a meeting of the Sanhedrin.

"What are we accomplishing?" they asked. "Here is this man performing many miraculous signs. 48If we let him go on like this, everyone will believe in him, and then the Romans will come and take away both our place[a] and our nation."

49Then one of them, named Caiaphas, who was high priest that year, spoke up, "You know nothing at all! 50You do not realize that it is better for you that one man die for the people than that the whole nation perish."

51He did not say this on his own, but as high priest that year he prophesied that Jesus would die for the Jewish nation, 52and not only for that nation but also for the scattered children of God, to bring them together and make them one. 53So from that day on they plotted to take his life.

54Therefore Jesus no longer moved about publicly among the Jews. Instead he withdrew to a region near the desert, to a village called Ephraim, where he stayed with his disciples.

55When it was almost time for the Jewish Passover, many went up from the country to Jerusalem for their ceremonial cleansing before the Passover. 56They kept looking for Jesus, and as they stood in the temple area they asked one another, "What do you think? Isn't he coming to the Feast at all?" 57But the chief priests and Pharisees had given orders that if anyone found out where Jesus was, he should report it so that they might arrest him.

JESUS ANOINTED AT BETHANY

12

Six days before the Passover, Jesus arrived at Bethany, where Lazarus lived, whom Jesus had raised from the dead. 2Here a dinner was given in Jesus' honor. Martha served, while Lazarus was among those reclining at the table with him. 3Then Mary took about a pint[b] of pure nard, an expensive perfume; she poured it on Jesus' feet and wiped his feet with her hair. And the house was filled with the fragrance of the perfume.

4But one of his disciples, Judas Iscariot, who was later to betray him, objected, 5"Why wasn't this perfume sold and the money given to the poor? It was worth a year's wages.[c]" 6He did not say this because he cared about the poor but because he was a thief; as keeper of the money bag, he used to help himself to what was put into it.

7"Leave her alone," Jesus replied. "⌊It was intended⌋ that she should save this perfume for the day of my burial. 8You will always have the poor among you, but you will not always have me."

9Meanwhile a large crowd of Jews found out that Jesus was there and came, not only because of him but also to see Lazarus, whom he had raised from the dead. 10So the chief priests made plans to kill Lazarus as well, 11for on account of him many of the Jews were going over to Jesus and putting their faith in him.

---

a 48 Or *temple*   b 3 Greek *a litra* (probably about 0.5 liter)   c 5 Greek *three hundred denarii*

THE TRIUMPHAL ENTRY

[12]The next day the great crowd that had come for the Feast heard that Jesus was on his way to Jerusalem. [13]They took palm branches and went out to meet him, shouting,

"Hosanna![a]"

"Blessed is he who comes in the name of the Lord!" [b]

"Blessed is the King of Israel!"

[14]Jesus found a young donkey and sat upon it, as it is written,

[15]"Do not be afraid, O Daughter of Zion;
see, your king is coming,
seated on a donkey's colt." [c]

[16]At first his disciples did not understand all this. Only after Jesus was glorified did they realize that these things had been written about him and that they had done these things to him.

[17]Now the crowd that was with him when he called Lazarus from the tomb and raised him from the dead continued to spread the word. [18]Many people, because they had heard that he had given this miraculous sign, went out to meet him. [19]So the Pharisees said to one another, "See, this is getting us nowhere. Look how the whole world has gone after him!"

JESUS PREDICTS HIS DEATH

[20]Now there were some Greeks among those who went up to worship at the Feast. [21]They came to Philip, who was from Bethsaida in Galilee, with a request. "Sir," they said, "we would like to see Jesus." [22]Philip went to tell Andrew; Andrew and Philip in turn told Jesus.

[23]Jesus replied, "The hour has come for the Son of Man to be glorified. [24]I tell you the truth, unless a kernel of wheat falls to the ground and dies, it remains only a single seed. But if it dies, it produces many seeds. [25]The man who loves his life will lose it, while the man who hates his life in this world will keep it for eternal life. [26]Whoever serves me must follow me; and where I am, my servant also will be. My Father will honor the one who serves me.

[27]"Now my heart is troubled, and what shall I say? 'Father, save me from this hour'? No, it was for this very reason I came to this hour. [28]Father, glorify your name!"

Then a voice came from heaven, "I have glorified it, and will glorify it again." [29]The crowd that was there and heard it said it had thundered; others said an angel had spoken to him.

[30]Jesus said, "This voice was for your benefit, not mine. [31]Now is the time for judgment on this world; now the prince of this world will be driven out. [32]But I, when I am lifted up from the earth, will draw all men to myself." [33]He said this to show the kind of death he was going to die.

[34]The crowd spoke up, "We have heard from the Law that the Christ[d] will remain forever, so how can you say, 'The Son of Man must be lifted up'? Who is this 'Son of Man'?"

[35]Then Jesus told them, "You are going to have the light just a little while longer. Walk while you have the light, before darkness overtakes you. The man who walks in the dark does not know where he is going. [36]Put your trust in the light while you have it, so that you may become sons of light." When he had finished speaking, Jesus left and hid himself from them.

THE JEWS CONTINUE IN THEIR UNBELIEF

[37]Even after Jesus had done all these miraculous signs in their presence, they still would not believe in him. [38]This was to fulfill the word of Isaiah the prophet:

"Lord, who has believed our message
and to whom has the arm of the Lord been revealed?" [e]

[39]For this reason they could not believe, because, as Isaiah says elsewhere:

[40]"He has blinded their eyes
and deadened their hearts,

---

[a] *13* A Hebrew expression meaning "Save!" which became an exclamation of praise   [b] *13* Psalm 118:25,26   [c] *15* Zech. 9:9
[d] *34* Or *Messiah*   [e] *38* Isaiah 53:1

so they can neither see with their eyes,
nor understand with their hearts,
nor turn—and I would heal them." [a]

⁴¹Isaiah said this because he saw Jesus' glory and spoke about him.

⁴²Yet at the same time many even among the leaders believed in him. But because of the Pharisees they would not confess their faith for fear they would be put out of the synagogue; ⁴³for they loved praise from men more than praise from God.

⁴⁴Then Jesus cried out, "When a man believes in me, he does not believe in me only, but in the one who sent me. ⁴⁵When he looks at me, he sees the one who sent me. ⁴⁶I have come into the world as a light, so that no one who believes in me should stay in darkness.

⁴⁷"As for the person who hears my words but does not keep them, I do not judge him. For I did not come to judge the world, but to save it. ⁴⁸There is a judge for the one who rejects me and does not accept my words; that very word which I spoke will condemn him at the last day. ⁴⁹For I did not speak of my own accord, but the Father who sent me commanded me what to say and how to say it. ⁵⁰I know that his command leads to eternal life. So whatever I say is just what the Father has told me to say."

JESUS WASHES HIS DISCIPLES' FEET

13 It was just before the Passover Feast. Jesus knew that the time had come for him to leave this world and go to the Father. Having loved his own who were in the world, he now showed them the full extent of his love. [b]

²The evening meal was being served, and the devil had already prompted Judas Iscariot, son of Simon, to betray Jesus. ³Jesus knew that the Father had put all things under his power, and that he had come from God and was returning to God; ⁴so he got up from the meal, took off his outer clothing, and wrapped a towel around his waist. ⁵After that, he poured water into a basin and began to wash his disciples' feet, drying them with the towel that was wrapped around him.

⁶He came to Simon Peter, who said to him, "Lord, are you going to wash my feet?"

⁷Jesus replied, "You do not realize now what I am doing, but later you will understand."

⁸"No," said Peter, "you shall never wash my feet."

Jesus answered, "Unless I wash you, you have no part with me."

⁹"Then, Lord," Simon Peter replied, "not just my feet but my hands and my head as well!"

¹⁰Jesus answered, "A person who has had a bath needs only to wash his feet; his whole body is clean. And you are clean, though not every one of you." ¹¹For he knew who was going to betray him, and that was why he said not every one was clean.

¹²When he had finished washing their feet, he put on his clothes and returned to his place. "Do you understand what I have done for you?" he asked them. ¹³"You call me 'Teacher' and 'Lord,' and rightly so, for that is what I am. ¹⁴Now that I, your Lord and Teacher, have washed your feet, you also should wash one another's feet. ¹⁵I have set you an example that you should do as I have done for you. ¹⁶I tell you the truth, no servant is greater than his master, nor is a messenger greater than the one who sent him. ¹⁷Now that you know these things, you will be blessed if you do them.

Learning to Be a Servant

» live the adventure » Jn 13:13–17

Foot washing in Jesus' day was a disgusting job. The roads of that time were mostly dirt. The preferred footwear was sandals. You can imagine how nasty people's feet got after a long day of walking. That's why lowly servants often got stuck with the job of foot washing. Jesus showed his disciples that anyone who follows him has to be willing to do the jobs no one else wants to do. How about you? Are you willing to get your hands dirty and give up a little status to serve other people?

---

[a] 40 Isaiah 6:10   [b] 1 Or he loved them to the last

JESUS PREDICTS HIS BETRAYAL

[18]"I am not referring to all of you; I know those I have chosen. But this is to fulfill the scripture: 'He who shares my bread has lifted up his heel against me.'[a]

[19]"I am telling you now before it happens, so that when it does happen you will believe that I am He. [20]I tell you the truth, whoever accepts anyone I send accepts me; and whoever accepts me accepts the one who sent me."

[21]After he had said this, Jesus was troubled in spirit and testified, "I tell you the truth, one of you is going to betray me."

[22]His disciples stared at one another, at a loss to know which of them he meant. [23]One of them, the disciple whom Jesus loved, was reclining next to him. [24]Simon Peter motioned to this disciple and said, "Ask him which one he means."

[25]Leaning back against Jesus, he asked him, "Lord, who is it?"

[26]Jesus answered, "It is the one to whom I will give this piece of bread when I have dipped it in the dish." Then, dipping the piece of bread, he gave it to Judas Iscariot, son of Simon. [27]As soon as Judas took the bread, Satan entered into him.

"What you are about to do, do quickly," Jesus told him, [28]but no one at the meal understood why Jesus said this to him. [29]Since Judas had charge of the money, some thought Jesus was telling him to buy what was needed for the Feast, or to give something to the poor. [30]As soon as Judas had taken the bread, he went out. And it was night.

JESUS PREDICTS PETER'S DENIAL

[31]When he was gone, Jesus said, "Now is the Son of Man glorified and God is glorified in him. [32]If God is glorified in him,[b] God will glorify the Son in himself, and will glorify him at once.

[33]"My children, I will be with you only a little longer. You will look for me, and just as I told the Jews, so I tell you now: Where I am going, you cannot come.

[34]"A new command I give you: Love one another. As I have loved you, so you must love one another. [35]By this all men will know that you are my disciples, if you love one another."

[36]Simon Peter asked him, "Lord, where are you going?"

Jesus replied, "Where I am going, you cannot follow now, but you will follow later."

[37]Peter asked, "Lord, why can't I follow you now? I will lay down my life for you."

[38]Then Jesus answered, "Will you really lay down your life for me? I tell you the truth, before the rooster crows, you will disown me three times!

JESUS COMFORTS HIS DISCIPLES

14

"Do not let your hearts be troubled. Trust in God[c]; trust also in me. [2]In my Father's house are many rooms; if it were not so, I would have told you. I am going there to prepare a place for you. [3]And if I go and prepare a place for you, I will come back and take you to be with me that you also may be where I am. [4]You know the way to the place where I am going."

challengenotes

To: my_son

heavenly_father: I have a home ready for you here with me— one where you'll never feel unwanted or unwelcome. you will never feel insecure or unsafe. you will never feel unloved or lonely. best of all, you will never have to leave.

JN 14:3

JESUS THE WAY TO THE FATHER

[5]Thomas said to him, "Lord, we don't know where you are going, so how can we know the way?"

[6]Jesus answered, "I am the way and the truth and the life. No one comes to the Father except through me. [7]If you really knew me, you would know[d] my Father as well. From now on, you do know him and have seen him."

[8]Philip said, "Lord, show us the Father and that will be enough for us."

[9]Jesus answered: "Don't you know me, Philip, even after I have been among you such a long time?

---

[a] 18 Psalm 41:9   [b] 32 Many early manuscripts do not have If God is glorified in him.   [c] 1 Or You trust in God   [d] 7 Some early manuscripts If you really have known me, you will know

Anyone who has seen me has seen the Father. How can you say, 'Show us the Father'? ¹⁰Don't you believe that I am in the Father, and that the Father is in me? The words I say to you are not just my own. Rather, it is the Father, living in me, who is doing his work. ¹¹Believe me when I say that I am in the Father and the Father is in me; or at least believe on the evidence of the miracles themselves. ¹²I tell you the truth, anyone who has faith in me will do what I have been doing. He will do even greater things than these, because I am going to the Father. ¹³And I will do whatever you ask in my name, so that the Son may bring glory to the Father. ¹⁴You may ask me for anything in my name, and I will do it.

JESUS PROMISES THE HOLY SPIRIT

¹⁵"If you love me, you will obey what I command. ¹⁶And I will ask the Father, and he will give you another Counselor to be with you forever— ¹⁷the Spirit of truth. The world cannot accept him, because it neither sees him nor knows him. But you know him, for he lives with you and will be[a] in you. ¹⁸I will not leave you as orphans; I will come to you. ¹⁹Before long, the world will not see me anymore, but you will see me. Because I live, you also will live. ²⁰On that day you will realize that I am in my Father, and you are in me, and I am in you. ²¹Whoever has my commands and obeys them, he is the one who loves me. He who loves me will be loved by my Father, and I too will love him and show myself to him."

²²Then Judas (not Judas Iscariot) said, "But, Lord, why do you intend to show yourself to us and not to the world?"

²³Jesus replied, "If anyone loves me, he will obey my teaching. My Father will love him, and we will come to him and make our home with him. ²⁴He who does not love me will not obey my teaching. These words you hear are not my own; they belong to the Father who sent me.

²⁵"All this I have spoken while still with you. ²⁶But the Counselor, the Holy Spirit, whom the Father will send in my name, will teach you all things and will remind you of everything I have said to you.

²⁷Peace I leave with you; my peace I give you. I do not give to you as the world gives. Do not let your hearts be troubled and do not be afraid.

²⁸"You heard me say, 'I am going away and I am coming back to you.' If you loved me, you would be glad that I am going to the Father, for the Father is greater than I. ²⁹I have told you now before it happens, so that when it does happen you will believe. ³⁰I will not speak with you much longer, for the prince of this world is coming. He has no hold on me, ³¹but the world must learn that I love the Father and that I do exactly what my Father has commanded me.

"Come now; let us leave.

Understanding Jesus' Unique Sacrifice

Jesus suffered and died on the cross because his perfect sacrifice was the only thing that could meet God's requirements for providing salvation. If there were *any* other way for people to get to heaven, that would mean Jesus' death wasn't really necessary . . . and that God sacrificed his Son for nothing. That's why Christians can't accept the teachings of religions that say people have to earn their way to heaven.

live the adventure »» Jn 14:6

NOW OR NEVER

JN 14:23-24

Would you believe a girlfriend who told you that she loved you but snuck out behind your back every now and then to date other guys? Your *actions* are what demonstrate your love for God, not your words.

THE VINE AND THE BRANCHES

15

"I am the true vine, and my Father is the gardener. ²He cuts off every branch in me that bears no fruit, while every branch that does bear fruit he prunes[b] so that it will be even more fruitful. ³You are already clean because of the word I have spoken to you. ⁴Remain in me,

---

ª 17 Some early manuscripts *and is*   ᵇ 2 The Greek for *prunes* also means *cleans*.

battlelines

» Where Is Everybody? (Loneliness)

Q: How about that game Friday night? Could you believe our defense?
A: I didn't go.

Q: You didn't *go*? Are you nuts? It was the state play-off! Why did you stay home?
A: Because I don't like sitting by myself.

Q: Why would you have to sit by yourself? The whole school was there.
A: Yeah, but none of them are my friends.

Q: Get out of town! You have *tons* of friends.
A: No. I have lots of people *around* me. Most of them don't have a clue about who I am. Like, how many know what J.C. stands for?

Q: Well, how would anybody know? That's what you go by. OK, OK, let me guess. Jesus Christ? Julius Caesar?
A: Come on, man, I'm being serious.

Q: What about Hunter? I see you with him a lot.

A: Hunter and I hang out because we have the same class schedule. Big deal. He has plenty of friends, and I'm not one of them. Just because you see us together at school doesn't mean we're friends.

Q: What do you mean by "friend"? What are you looking for?
A: Someone who knows me. Someone I can talk to. Someone who *listens* to me. Someone who comes into a room full of people and looks for *me* in the crowd. Someone who thinks to actually call me once in a while—or drop by my house.

Q: Wow. I never knew. I'm sorry, man.
A: Yeah, well, you and me both. I've tried everything—you know, "To have a friend, you have to be a friend." I call people. I make the effort. But nothing works. People have their own little groups. Just like when we were kids: "Tick tock, the game is locked; no one else can play." That's me—on the outside looking in.

» Friends Are Friends Forever

Ouch. What can you say? J.C.'s situation stinks. We can talk all day long about Jesus being our friend (see John 15:13–17)—it's a great truth—but still, life can get lonely. Can you relate?

So where's God in our loneliness? Does he even notice when we feel all alone? Does he care if we have meaningful friendships? Absolutely! Remember, it was God who saw Adam all by himself, said, "That's not good!" and then made Eve to be his companion (see Genesis 2:18).

What's more, the Bible tells us, "Two are better than one, because they have a good return for their work: If one falls down, his friend can help him up. But pity the man who falls and has no one to help him up! Also, if two lie down together, they will keep warm. But how can one keep warm alone? Though one may be overpowered, two can defend themselves. A cord of three strands is not quickly broken" (Ecclesiastes 4:9–12).

Everybody needs friends. God knows that. He made us for relationships. So don't give up; keep sticking your neck out there. You won't become best buds with everyone, and you can't build solid friendships overnight. But you will eventually find a guy or two you really hit it off with. It's like everything else: The more faithfully and regularly you invest, the greater the eventual payoff will be.

Read more about friendship at www.RevolutionBible.com.

and I will remain in you. No branch can bear fruit by itself; it must remain in the vine. Neither can you bear fruit unless you remain in me.

[5]"I am the vine; you are the branches. If a man remains in me and I in him, he will bear much fruit; apart from me you can do nothing. [6]If anyone does not remain in me, he is like a branch that is thrown away and withers; such branches are picked up, thrown into the fire and burned. [7]If you remain in me and my words remain in you, ask whatever you wish, and it will be given you. [8]This is to my Father's glory, that you bear much fruit, showing yourselves to be my disciples.

[9]"As the Father has loved me, so have I loved you. Now remain in my love. [10]If you obey my commands, you will remain in my love, just as I have obeyed my Father's commands and remain in his love. [11]I have told you this so that my joy may be in you and that your joy may be complete. [12]My command is this: Love each other as I have loved you. [13]Greater love has no one than this, that he lay down his life for his friends. [14]You are my friends if you do what I command. [15]I no longer call you servants, because a servant does not know his master's business. Instead, I have called you friends, for everything that I learned from my Father I have made known to you. [16]You did not choose me, but I chose you and appointed you to go and bear fruit—fruit that will last. Then the Father will give you whatever you ask in my name. [17]This is my command: Love each other.

THE WORLD HATES THE DISCIPLES

[18]"If the world hates you, keep in mind that it hated me first. [19]If you belonged to the world, it would love you as its own. As it is, you do not belong to the world, but I have chosen you out of the world. That is why the world hates you. [20]Remember the words I spoke to you: 'No servant is greater than his master.'[a] If they persecuted me, they will persecute you also. If they obeyed my teaching, they will obey yours also. [21]They will treat you this way because of my name, for they do not know the One who sent me. [22]If I had not come and spoken to them, they would not be guilty of sin. Now, however, they have no excuse for their sin. [23]He who hates me hates my Father as well. [24]If I had not done among them what no one else did, they would not be guilty of sin. But now they have seen these miracles, and yet they have hated both me and my Father. [25]But this is to fulfill what is written in their Law: 'They hated me without reason.'[b]

[26]"When the Counselor comes, whom I will send to you from the Father, the Spirit of truth who goes out from the Father, he will testify about me. [27]And you also must testify, for you have been with me from the beginning.

16 "All this I have told you so that you will not go astray. [2]They will put you out of the synagogue; in fact, a time is coming when anyone who kills you will think he is offering a service to God. [3]They will do such things because they have not known the Father or me. [4]I have told you this, so that when the time comes you will remember that I warned you. I did not tell you this at first because I was with you.

THE WORK OF THE HOLY SPIRIT

[5]"Now I am going to him who sent me, yet none of you asks me, 'Where are you going?' [6]Because I have said these things, you are filled with grief. [7]But I tell you the truth: It is for your good that I am going away. Unless I go away, the Counselor will not come to you; but if I go, I will send him to you. [8]When he comes, he will convict the world of guilt[c] in regard to sin and righteousness and judgment: [9]in regard to sin, because men do not believe in me; [10]in regard to righteousness, because I am going to the Father, where you can see me no longer; [11]and in regard to judgment, because the prince of this world now stands condemned.

[12]"I have much more to say to you, more than you can now bear. [13]But when he, the Spirit of truth, comes, he will guide you into all truth. He will not speak on his own; he will speak only what he hears, and he will tell you what is yet to come. [14]He will bring glory to me by taking from what is mine and making it known to you. [15]All that belongs to the Father is mine. That is why I said the Spirit will take from what is mine and make it known to you.

[16]"In a little while you will see me no more, and then after a little while you will see me."

THE DISCIPLES' GRIEF WILL TURN TO JOY

[17]Some of his disciples said to one another, "What does he mean by saying, 'In a little while you will see me no more, and then after a little while you will see me,' and 'Because I am going to the Fa-

---

[a] 20 John 13:16   [b] 25 Psalms 35:19; 69:4   [c] 8 Or will expose the guilt of the world

ther'?" ¹⁸They kept asking, "What does he mean by 'a little while'? We don't understand what he is saying."

¹⁹Jesus saw that they wanted to ask him about this, so he said to them, "Are you asking one another what I meant when I said, 'In a little while you will see me no more, and then after a little while you will see me'? ²⁰I tell you the truth, you will weep and mourn while the world rejoices. You will grieve, but your grief will turn to joy. ²¹A woman giving birth to a child has pain because her time has come; but when her baby is born she forgets the anguish because of her joy that a child is born into the world. ²²So with you: Now is your time of grief, but I will see you again and you will rejoice, and no one will take away your joy. ²³In that day you will no longer ask me anything. I tell you the truth, my Father will give you whatever you ask in my name. ²⁴Until now you have not asked for anything in my name. Ask and you will receive, and your joy will be complete.

²⁵"Though I have been speaking figuratively, a time is coming when I will no longer use this kind of language but will tell you plainly about my Father. ²⁶In that day you will ask in my name. I am not saying that I will ask the Father on your behalf. ²⁷No, the Father himself loves you because you have loved me and have believed that I came from God. ²⁸I came from the Father and entered the world; now I am leaving the world and going back to the Father."

²⁹Then Jesus' disciples said, "Now you are speaking clearly and without figures of speech. ³⁰Now we can see that you know all things and that you do not even need to have anyone ask you questions. This makes us believe that you came from God."

³¹"You believe at last!"ᵃ Jesus answered. ³²"But a time is coming, and has come, when you will be scattered, each to his own home. You will leave me all alone. Yet I am not alone, for my Father is with me.

³³"I have told you these things, so that in me you may have peace. In this world you will have trouble. But take heart! I have overcome the world."

JESUS PRAYS FOR HIMSELF

17 After Jesus said this, he looked toward heaven and prayed:

"Father, the time has come. Glorify your Son, that your Son may glorify you. ²For you granted him authority over all people that he might give eternal life to all those you have given him. ³Now this is eternal life: that they may know you, the only true God, and Jesus Christ, whom you have sent. ⁴I have brought you glory on earth by completing the work you gave me to do. ⁵And now, Father, glorify me in your presence with the glory I had with you before the world began.

JESUS PRAYS FOR HIS DISCIPLES

⁶"I have revealed youᵇ to those whom you gave me out of the world. They were yours; you gave them to me and they have obeyed your word. ⁷Now they know that everything you have given me comes from you. ⁸For I gave them the words you gave me and they accepted them. They knew with certainty that I came from you, and they believed that you sent me. ⁹I pray for them. I am not praying for the world, but for those you have given me, for they are yours. ¹⁰All I have is yours, and all you have is mine. And glory has come to me through them. ¹¹I will remain in the world no longer, but they are still in the world, and I am coming to you. Holy Father, protect them by the power of your name—the name you gave me—so that they may be one as we are one. ¹²While I was with them, I protected them and kept them safe by that name you gave me. None has been lost except the one doomed to destruction so that Scripture would be fulfilled.

¹³"I am coming to you now, but I say these things while I am still in the world, so that they may have the full measure of my joy within them. ¹⁴I have given them your word and the world has hated them, for they are not of the world any more than I am of the world. ¹⁵My prayer is not that you take them out of the world but that you protect them from the evil one. ¹⁶They are not of the world, even as I am not of it. ¹⁷Sanctifyᶜ them by the truth; your word is truth. ¹⁸As

---

ᵃ *31* Or *"Do you now believe?"*   ᵇ *6* Greek *your name*; also in verse 26   ᶜ *17* Greek *hagiazo (set apart for sacred use* or *make holy)*; also in verse 19 you sent me into the world, I have sent them into the world. [19]For them I sanctify myself, that they too may be truly sanctified.

JESUS PRAYS FOR ALL BELIEVERS

[20]"My prayer is not for them alone. I pray also for those who will believe in me through their message, [21]that all of them may be one, Father, just as you are in me and I am in you. May they also be in us so that the world may believe that you have sent me. [22]I have given them the glory that you gave me, that they may be one as we are one: [23]I in them and you in me. May they be brought to complete unity to let the world know that you sent me and have loved them even as you have loved me.

[24]"Father, I want those you have given me to be with me where I am, and to see my glory, the glory you have given me because you loved me before the creation of the world.

[25]"Righteous Father, though the world does not know you, I know you, and they know that you have sent me. [26]I have made you known to them, and will continue to make you known in order that the love you have for me may be in them and that I myself may be in them."

JESUS ARRESTED

18 When he had finished praying, Jesus left with his disciples and crossed the Kidron Valley. On the other side there was an olive grove, and he and his disciples went into it.

[2]Now Judas, who betrayed him, knew the place, because Jesus had often met there with his disciples. [3]So Judas came to the grove, guiding a detachment of soldiers and some officials from the chief priests and Pharisees. They were carrying torches, lanterns and weapons.

[4]Jesus, knowing all that was going to happen to him, went out and asked them, "Who is it you want?"

[5]"Jesus of Nazareth," they replied.

"I am he," Jesus said. (And Judas the traitor was standing there with them.) [6]When Jesus said, "I am he," they drew back and fell to the ground.

[7]Again he asked them, "Who is it you want?"

And they said, "Jesus of Nazareth."

[8]"I told you that I am he," Jesus answered. "If you are looking for me, then let these men go." [9]This happened so that the words he had spoken would be fulfilled: "I have not lost one of those you gave me."[a]

[10]Then Simon Peter, who had a sword, drew it and struck the high priest's servant, cutting off his right ear. (The servant's name was Malchus.)

[11]Jesus commanded Peter, "Put your sword away! Shall I not drink the cup the Father has given me?"

JESUS TAKEN TO ANNAS

[12]Then the detachment of soldiers with its commander and the Jewish officials arrested Jesus. They bound him [13]and brought him first to Annas, who was the father-in-law of Caiaphas, the high priest that year. [14]Caiaphas was the one who had advised the Jews that it would be good if one man died for the people.

PETER'S FIRST DENIAL

[15]Simon Peter and another disciple were following Jesus. Because this disciple was known to the high priest, he went with Jesus into the high priest's courtyard, [16]but Peter had to wait outside at the

Choosing Your Battles

This wasn't the first time the Jewish authorities tried to nail Jesus, but it was the first time they managed to actually arrest him. That's because it was God's will for it to happen at that time. Peter didn't understand that this was not a time to draw swords and fight. Sometimes God's will is hard to comprehend and accept. If you let it run its course, though, you'll see that he has something incredible planned.

»» live the adventure »» Jn 18:10-11

---

[a] 9 John 6:39

door. The other disciple, who was known to the high priest, came back, spoke to the girl on duty there and brought Peter in.

[17]"You are not one of his disciples, are you?" the girl at the door asked Peter.

He replied, "I am not."

[18]It was cold, and the servants and officials stood around a fire they had made to keep warm. Peter also was standing with them, warming himself.

THE HIGH PRIEST QUESTIONS JESUS

[19]Meanwhile, the high priest questioned Jesus about his disciples and his teaching.

[20]"I have spoken openly to the world," Jesus replied. "I always taught in synagogues or at the temple, where all the Jews come together. I said nothing in secret. [21]Why question me? Ask those who heard me. Surely they know what I said."

[22]When Jesus said this, one of the officials nearby struck him in the face. "Is this the way you answer the high priest?" he demanded.

[23]"If I said something wrong," Jesus replied, "testify as to what is wrong. But if I spoke the truth, why did you strike me?" [24]Then Annas sent him, still bound, to Caiaphas the high priest.[a]

PETER'S SECOND AND THIRD DENIALS

[25]As Simon Peter stood warming himself, he was asked, "You are not one of his disciples, are you?" He denied it, saying, "I am not."

[26]One of the high priest's servants, a relative of the man whose ear Peter had cut off, challenged him, "Didn't I see you with him in the olive grove?" [27]Again Peter denied it, and at that moment a rooster began to crow.

JESUS BEFORE PILATE

[28]Then the Jews led Jesus from Caiaphas to the palace of the Roman governor. By now it was early morning, and to avoid ceremonial uncleanness the Jews did not enter the palace; they wanted to be able to eat the Passover. [29]So Pilate came out to them and asked, "What charges are you bringing against this man?"

[30]"If he were not a criminal," they replied, "we would not have handed him over to you."

[31]Pilate said, "Take him yourselves and judge him by your own law."

"But we have no right to execute anyone," the Jews objected. [32]This happened so that the words Jesus had spoken indicating the kind of death he was going to die would be fulfilled.

[33]Pilate then went back inside the palace, summoned Jesus and asked him, "Are you the king of the Jews?"

NOW OR NEVER

JN 18:27

This was a major choke, no question. But happily, it wasn't the end for Peter . . . not by a long shot. He was forgiven by Jesus and ultimately became the man Jesus trusted most when it came to building the church. Remember Peter's story the next time you do something really stupid.

[34]"Is that your own idea," Jesus asked, "or did others talk to you about me?"

[35]"Am I a Jew?" Pilate replied. "It was your people and your chief priests who handed you over to me. What is it you have done?"

[36]Jesus said, "My kingdom is not of this world. If it were, my servants would fight to prevent my arrest by the Jews. But now my kingdom is from another place."

[37]"You are a king, then!" said Pilate.

Jesus answered, "You are right in saying I am a king. In fact, for this reason I was born, and for this I came into the world, to testify to the truth. Everyone on the side of truth listens to me."

[38]"What is truth?" Pilate asked. With this he went out again to the Jews and said, "I find no basis for a charge against him. [39]But it is your custom for me to release to you one prisoner at the time of the Passover. Do you want me to release 'the king of the Jews'?"

[40]They shouted back, "No, not him! Give us Barabbas!" Now Barabbas had taken part in a rebellion.

---

[a] 24 Or *(Now Annas had sent him, still bound, to Caiaphas the high priest.)*

JESUS SENTENCED TO BE CRUCIFIED

19 Then Pilate took Jesus and had him flogged. ²The soldiers twisted together a crown of thorns and put it on his head. They clothed him in a purple robe ³and went up to him again and again, saying, "Hail, king of the Jews!" And they struck him in the face.

⁴Once more Pilate came out and said to the Jews, "Look, I am bringing him out to you to let you know that I find no basis for a charge against him." ⁵When Jesus came out wearing the crown of thorns and the purple robe, Pilate said to them, "Here is the man!"

⁶As soon as the chief priests and their officials saw him, they shouted, "Crucify! Crucify!"

But Pilate answered, "You take him and crucify him. As for me, I find no basis for a charge against him."

⁷The Jews insisted, "We have a law, and according to that law he must die, because he claimed to be the Son of God."

⁸When Pilate heard this, he was even more afraid, ⁹and he went back inside the palace. "Where do you come from?" he asked Jesus, but Jesus gave him no answer. ¹⁰"Do you refuse to speak to me?" Pilate said. "Don't you realize I have power either to free you or to crucify you?"

¹¹Jesus answered, "You would have no power over me if it were not given to you from above. Therefore the one who handed me over to you is guilty of a greater sin."

¹²From then on, Pilate tried to set Jesus free, but the Jews kept shouting, "If you let this man go, you are no friend of Caesar. Anyone who claims to be a king opposes Caesar."

¹³When Pilate heard this, he brought Jesus out and sat down on the judge's seat at a place known as the Stone Pavement (which in Aramaic is Gabbatha). ¹⁴It was the day of Preparation of Passover Week, about the sixth hour.

"Here is your king," Pilate said to the Jews.

¹⁵But they shouted, "Take him away! Take him away! Crucify him!"

"Shall I crucify your king?" Pilate asked.

"We have no king but Caesar," the chief priests answered.

¹⁶Finally Pilate handed him over to them to be crucified.

THE CRUCIFIXION

So the soldiers took charge of Jesus. ¹⁷Carrying his own cross, he went out to the place of the Skull (which in Aramaic is called Golgotha). ¹⁸Here they crucified him, and with him two others—one on each side and Jesus in the middle.

¹⁹Pilate had a notice prepared and fastened to the cross. It read: JESUS OF NAZARETH, THE KING OF THE JEWS. ²⁰Many of the Jews read this sign, for the place where Jesus was crucified was near the city, and the sign was written in Aramaic, Latin and Greek. ²¹The chief priests of the Jews protested to Pilate, "Do not write 'The King of the Jews,' but that this man claimed to be king of the Jews."

²²Pilate answered, "What I have written, I have written."

²³When the soldiers crucified Jesus, they took his clothes, dividing them into four shares, one for each of them, with the undergarment remaining. This garment was seamless, woven in one piece from top to bottom.

²⁴"Let's not tear it," they said to one another. "Let's decide by lot who will get it."

This happened that the scripture might be fulfilled which said,

> "They divided my garments among them
> and cast lots for my clothing." ª

So this is what the soldiers did.

²⁵Near the cross of Jesus stood his mother, his mother's sister, Mary the wife of Clopas, and Mary Magdalene. ²⁶When Jesus saw his mother there, and the disciple whom he loved standing nearby, he said to his mother, "Dear woman, here is your son," ²⁷and to the disciple, "Here is your mother." From that time on, this disciple took her into his home.

THE DEATH OF JESUS

²⁸Later, knowing that all was now completed, and so that the Scripture would be fulfilled, Jesus said, "I am thirsty." ²⁹A jar of wine vinegar was there, so they soaked a sponge in it, put the sponge on a stalk

---

ª *24* Psalm 22:18

of the hyssop plant, and lifted it to Jesus' lips. 30When he had received the drink, Jesus said, "It is finished." With that, he bowed his head and gave up his spirit.

31Now it was the day of Preparation, and the next day was to be a special Sabbath. Because the Jews did not want the bodies left on the crosses during the Sabbath, they asked Pilate to have the legs broken and the bodies taken down. 32The soldiers therefore came and broke the legs of the first man who had been crucified with Jesus, and then those of the other. 33But when they came to Jesus and found that he was already dead, they did not break his legs. 34Instead, one of the soldiers pierced Jesus' side with a spear, bringing a sudden flow of blood and water. 35The man who saw it has given testimony, and his testimony is true. He knows that he tells the truth, and he testifies so that you also may believe. 36These things happened so that the scripture would be fulfilled: "Not one of his bones will be broken,"a 37and, as another scripture says, "They will look on the one they have pierced."b

THE BURIAL OF JESUS

38Later, Joseph of Arimathea asked Pilate for the body of Jesus. Now Joseph was a disciple of Jesus, but secretly because he feared the Jews. With Pilate's permission, he came and took the body away. 39He was accompanied by Nicodemus, the man who earlier had visited Jesus at night. Nicodemus brought a mixture of myrrh and aloes, about seventy-five pounds.c 40Taking Jesus' body, the two of them wrapped it, with the spices, in strips of linen. This was in accordance with Jewish burial customs. 41At the place where Jesus was crucified, there was a garden, and in the garden a new tomb, in which no one had ever been laid. 42Because it was the Jewish day of Preparation and since the tomb was nearby, they laid Jesus there.

THE EMPTY TOMB

20 Early on the first day of the week, while it was still dark, Mary Magdalene went to the tomb and saw that the stone had been removed from the entrance. 2So she came running to Simon Peter and the other disciple, the one Jesus loved, and said, "They have taken the Lord out of the tomb, and we don't know where they have put him!"

3So Peter and the other disciple started for the tomb. 4Both were running, but the other disciple outran Peter and reached the tomb first. 5He bent over and looked in at the strips of linen lying there but did not go in. 6Then Simon Peter, who was behind him, arrived and went into the tomb. He saw the strips of linen lying there, 7as well as the burial cloth that had been around Jesus' head. The cloth was folded up by itself, separate from the linen. 8Finally the other disciple, who had reached the tomb first, also went inside. He saw and believed. 9(They still did not understand from Scripture that Jesus had to rise from the dead.)

JESUS APPEARS TO MARY MAGDALENE

10Then the disciples went back to their homes, 11but Mary stood outside the tomb crying. As she wept, she bent over to look into the tomb 12and saw two angels in white, seated where Jesus' body had been, one at the head and the other at the foot.

13They asked her, "Woman, why are you crying?"

"They have taken my Lord away," she said, "and I don't know where they have put him." 14At this, she turned around and saw Jesus standing there, but she did not realize that it was Jesus.

15"Woman," he said, "why are you crying? Who is it you are looking for?"

Thinking he was the gardener, she said, "Sir, if you have carried him away, tell me where you have put him, and I will get him."

16Jesus said to her, "Mary."

She turned toward him and cried out in Aramaic, "Rabboni!" (which means Teacher).

17Jesus said, "Do not hold on to me, for I have not yet returned to the Father. Go instead to my brothers and tell them, 'I am returning to my Father and your Father, to my God and your God.'"

18Mary Magdalene went to the disciples with the news: "I have seen the Lord!" And she told them that he had said these things to her.

JESUS APPEARS TO HIS DISCIPLES

19On the evening of that first day of the week, when the disciples were together, with the doors locked for fear of the Jews, Jesus came and stood among them and said, "Peace be with you!" 20After

a 36 Exodus 12:46; Num. 9:12; Psalm 34:20   b 37 Zech. 12:10   c 39 Greek a hundred litrai (about 34 kilograms) he said this, he showed them his hands and side. The disciples were overjoyed when they saw the Lord.

²¹Again Jesus said, "Peace be with you! As the Father has sent me, I am sending you." ²²And with that he breathed on them and said, "Receive the Holy Spirit. ²³If you forgive anyone his sins, they are forgiven; if you do not forgive them, they are not forgiven."

JESUS APPEARS TO THOMAS

²⁴Now Thomas (called Didymus), one of the Twelve, was not with the disciples when Jesus came. ²⁵So the other disciples told him, "We have seen the Lord!"

But he said to them, "Unless I see the nail marks in his hands and put my finger where the nails were, and put my hand into his side, I will not believe it."

²⁶A week later his disciples were in the house again, and Thomas was with them. Though the doors were locked, Jesus came and stood among them and said, "Peace be with you!" ²⁷Then he said to Thomas, "Put your finger here; see my hands. Reach out your hand and put it into my side. Stop doubting and believe."

now or never

JN 20:24-29

Look at the way Jesus handled Thomas. He didn't yell at him for doubting. Jesus gave him the opportunity to strengthen his faith by seeing the evidence for himself. Then Jesus told him to get back in the game.

²⁸Thomas said to him, "My Lord and my God!"

²⁹Then Jesus told him, "Because you have seen me, you have believed; blessed are those who have not seen and yet have believed."

³⁰Jesus did many other miraculous signs in the presence of his disciples, which are not recorded in this book. ³¹But these are written that you may[a] believe that Jesus is the Christ, the Son of God, and that by believing you may have life in his name.

challenge notes

JN 20:29

To: my_son

heavenly_father: very few had the privilege of knowing my Son when I sent him to Earth for a short time. but don't be discouraged that you were not among those who saw him in person. have faith; you will be blessed if you believe in him and give your life to him.

JESUS AND THE MIRACULOUS CATCH OF FISH

21 Afterward Jesus appeared again to his disciples, by the Sea of Tiberias.[b] It happened this way: ²Simon Peter, Thomas (called Didymus), Nathanael from Cana in Galilee, the sons of Zebedee, and two other disciples were together. ³"I'm going out to fish," Simon Peter told them, and they said, "We'll go with you." So they went out and got into the boat, but that night they caught nothing.

⁴Early in the morning, Jesus stood on the shore, but the disciples did not realize that it was Jesus.

⁵He called out to them, "Friends, haven't you any fish?"

"No," they answered.

⁶He said, "Throw your net on the right side of the boat and you will find some." When they did, they were unable to haul the net in because of the large number of fish.

⁷Then the disciple whom Jesus loved said to Peter, "It is the Lord!" As soon as Simon Peter heard him say, "It is the Lord," he wrapped his outer garment around him (for he had taken it off) and jumped into the water. ⁸The other disciples followed in the boat, towing the net full of fish, for they were not far from shore, about a hundred yards.[c] ⁹When they landed, they saw a fire of burning coals there with fish on it, and some bread.

¹⁰Jesus said to them, "Bring some of the fish you have just caught."

¹¹Simon Peter climbed aboard and dragged the net ashore. It was full of large fish, 153, but even with so many the net was not torn. ¹²Jesus said to them, "Come and have breakfast." None of the dis-

---

ª *31* Some manuscripts *may continue to*   ᵇ *1* That is, Sea of Galilee   ᶜ *8* Greek *about two hundred cubits* (about 90 meters) ciples dared ask him, "Who are you?" They knew it was the Lord. [13]Jesus came, took the bread and gave it to them, and did the same with the fish. [14]This was now the third time Jesus appeared to his disciples after he was raised from the dead.

JESUS REINSTATES PETER

[15]When they had finished eating, Jesus said to Simon Peter, "Simon son of John, do you truly love me more than these?"

"Yes, Lord," he said, "you know that I love you."

Jesus said, "Feed my lambs."

[16]Again Jesus said, "Simon son of John, do you truly love me?"

He answered, "Yes, Lord, you know that I love you."

Jesus said, "Take care of my sheep."

[17]The third time he said to him, "Simon son of John, do you love me?"

Peter was hurt because Jesus asked him the third time, "Do you love me?" He said, "Lord, you know all things; you know that I love you."

Jesus said, "Feed my sheep. [18]I tell you the truth, when you were younger you dressed yourself and went where you wanted; but when you are old you will stretch out your hands, and someone else will dress you and lead you where you do not want to go." [19]Jesus said this to indicate the kind of death by which Peter would glorify God. Then he said to him, "Follow me!"

[20]Peter turned and saw that the disciple whom Jesus loved was following them. (This was the one who had leaned back against Jesus at the supper and had said, "Lord, who is going to betray you?") [21]When Peter saw him, he asked, "Lord, what about him?"

[22]Jesus answered, "If I want him to remain alive until I return, what is that to you? You must follow me." [23]Because of this, the rumor spread among the brothers that this disciple would not die. But Jesus did not say that he would not die; he only said, "If I want him to remain alive until I return, what is that to you?"

[24]This is the disciple who testifies to these things and who wrote them down. We know that his testimony is true.

[25]Jesus did many other things as well. If every one of them were written down, I suppose that even the whole world would not have room for the books that would be written.

NOW OR NEVER
JN 21:15-18

The Lord is a master recycler. He can make something new and useful out of something that seems broken or used up. Just ask Peter. No matter how badly you've failed, Jesus offers you the promise of forgiveness and a bright future.

ACTS

ACTS ACTS ACTS

« AT A GLANCE

Author
Luke

Audience
Theophilus

Date
Probably about A.D. 63

Setting
The message of Jesus Christ quickly spread from Jerusalem to all parts of the Roman Empire.

Verse to Remember
"But you will receive power when the Holy Spirit comes on you; and you will be my witnesses in Jerusalem, and in all Judea and Samaria, and to the ends of the earth" (1:8).

Theme to Consider
The book of Acts tells the story of men and women who spread the gospel with the help of the Holy Spirit. Read it and allow the Spirit to move you to boldly share your faith with others.

UNCHANGING TRUTH » Think about your "territory," the area where you spend most of your life. Obviously, it includes your house and your school. But what else is in there? The place you work? Your friends' houses? Your girlfriend's house? The skate park? The mall? The gym or baseball field?

It's important to know what your territory is because that's ground zero for your faith-sharing assignment from God. His plan is for you to start locally, talking to the people in your "territory" about who Jesus is, what he did and how he has impacted your life.

Let's start at the center of your territory. How many people in your house know you're a Christian? Dumb question, right? Of course your family knows that you're a Christian. But how many of them know what that *really* means? How many of them see firsthand the impact that Jesus has on your daily life?

What about your buddies at school? How many of them know about your faith? What steps can you take to start getting the word out? If you want to see some guys who really made it happen, check out the way Peter, Paul and the rest of the early missionaries spread the news about Jesus in the book of Acts.

No one is saying it's going to be easy. The stories of Peter, Paul and the other early Christians show that sooner or later you'll pay a price (maybe even among your family and friends) for identifying yourself as a follower of Christ. The good news is that the more you share your faith, the more comfortable you'll be talking about Jesus . . . and the better you'll get at it.

The better you get at sharing your faith in your "territory," the more God will expand that territory to include greater numbers of people and new places. God changed thousands of lives through the personal ministries of Peter and Paul. Who knows how many lives he will change through you as the Holy Spirit empowers you to be a witness for God?

LIFE LESSONS »

1 What looks like a setback may actually be an opportunity (4:1–22).

2 A person's past doesn't matter when it comes to serving God; the Lord can change anyone and make them fit for service (9:1–20).

3 The Good News of Jesus is for everyone, regardless of how "unworthy" they may seem to us (10:34–38).

JESUS TAKEN UP INTO HEAVEN

1 In my former book, Theophilus, I wrote about all that Jesus began to do and to teach ²until the day he was taken up to heaven, after giving instructions through the Holy Spirit to the apostles he had chosen. ³After his suffering, he showed himself to these men and gave many convincing proofs that he was alive. He appeared to them over a period of forty days and spoke about the kingdom of God. ⁴On one occasion, while he was eating with them, he gave them this command: "Do not leave Jerusalem, but wait for the gift my Father promised, which you have heard me speak about. ⁵For John baptized withᵃ water, but in a few days you will be baptized with the Holy Spirit."

⁶So when they met together, they asked him, "Lord, are you at this time going to restore the kingdom to Israel?"

⁷He said to them: "It is not for you to know the times or dates the Father has set by his own authority. ⁸But you will receive power when the Holy Spirit comes on you; and you will be my witnesses in Jerusalem, and in all Judea and Samaria, and to the ends of the earth."

⁹After he said this, he was taken up before their very eyes, and a cloud hid him from their sight.

¹⁰They were looking intently up into the sky as he was going, when suddenly two men dressed in white stood beside them. ¹¹"Men of Galilee," they said, "why do you stand here looking into the sky? This same Jesus, who has been taken from you into heaven, will come back in the same way you have seen him go into heaven."

NOW OR NEVER
AC 1:3

This is one of several appearances by Jesus after his resurrection. More than 500 people saw him in person after his death. God doesn't just expect us to believe some obscure, 2,000-year-old story; he gave us historical evidence to prove the story true.

MATTHIAS CHOSEN TO REPLACE JUDAS

¹²Then they returned to Jerusalem from the hill called the Mount of Olives, a Sabbath day's walkᵇ from the city. ¹³When they arrived, they went upstairs to the room where they were staying. Those present were Peter, John, James and Andrew; Philip and Thomas, Bartholomew and Matthew; James son of Alphaeus and Simon the Zealot, and Judas son of James. ¹⁴They all joined together constantly in prayer, along with the women and Mary the mother of Jesus, and with his brothers.

¹⁵In those days Peter stood up among the believersᶜ (a group numbering about a hundred and twenty) ¹⁶and said, "Brothers, the Scripture had to be fulfilled which the Holy Spirit spoke long ago through the mouth of David concerning Judas, who served as guide for those who arrested Jesus— ¹⁷he was one of our number and shared in this ministry."

NOW OR NEVER
AC 1:7

People have been talking about Jesus' return (and the end of the world) since the day he left for heaven. The fact is, though, no one knows when he's coming back. That's why it's a good idea to make sure that you're always ready for his return.

¹⁸(With the reward he got for his wickedness, Judas bought a field; there he fell headlong, his body burst open and all his intestines spilled out. ¹⁹Everyone in Jerusalem heard about this, so they called that field in their language Akeldama, that is, Field of Blood.)

²⁰"For," said Peter, "it is written in the book of Psalms,

" 'May his place be deserted;
let there be no one to dwell in it,'ᵈ

and,

" 'May another take his place of leadership.'ᵉ

²¹Therefore it is necessary to choose one of the men who have been with us the whole time the Lord

---

ᵃ *5* Or *in*   ᵇ *12* That is, about 3/4 mile (about 1,100 meters)   ᶜ *15* Greek *brothers*   ᵈ *20* Psalm 69:25   ᵉ *20* Psalm 109:8

Jesus went in and out among us, ²²beginning from John's baptism to the time when Jesus was taken up from us. For one of these must become a witness with us of his resurrection."

²³So they proposed two men: Joseph called Barsabbas (also known as Justus) and Matthias. ²⁴Then they prayed, "Lord, you know everyone's heart. Show us which of these two you have chosen ²⁵to take over this apostolic ministry, which Judas left to go where he belongs." ²⁶Then they cast lots, and the lot fell to Matthias; so he was added to the eleven apostles.

THE HOLY SPIRIT COMES AT PENTECOST

2 When the day of Pentecost came, they were all together in one place. ²Suddenly a sound like the blowing of a violent wind came from heaven and filled the whole house where they were sitting. ³They saw what seemed to be tongues of fire that separated and came to rest on each of them. ⁴All of them were filled with the Holy Spirit and began to speak in other tongues[a] as the Spirit enabled them.

⁵Now there were staying in Jerusalem God-fearing Jews from every nation under heaven. ⁶When they heard this sound, a crowd came together in bewilderment, because each one heard them speaking in his own language. ⁷Utterly amazed, they asked: "Are not all these men who are speaking Galileans? ⁸Then how is it that each of us hears them in his own native language? ⁹Parthians, Medes and Elamites; residents of Mesopotamia, Judea and Cappadocia, Pontus and Asia, ¹⁰Phrygia and Pamphylia, Egypt and the parts of Libya near Cyrene; visitors from Rome ¹¹(both Jews and converts to Judaism); Cretans and Arabs—we hear them declaring the wonders of God in our own tongues!" ¹²Amazed and perplexed, they asked one another, "What does this mean?"

¹³Some, however, made fun of them and said, "They have had too much wine.[b]"

PETER ADDRESSES THE CROWD

¹⁴Then Peter stood up with the Eleven, raised his voice and addressed the crowd: "Fellow Jews and all of you who live in Jerusalem, let me explain this to you; listen carefully to what I say. ¹⁵These men are not drunk, as you suppose. It's only nine in the morning! ¹⁶No, this is what was spoken by the prophet Joel:

AC 2:14

challengenotes

To: my_son

heavenly_father: a few weeks earlier, peter had denied even *knowing* my Son. now he's standing in front of a large group, preaching the good news about him! what changed him? my Holy Spirit. that same Spirit can give you the kind of courage I gave peter . . . if you will ask.

¹⁷" 'In the last days, God says,
   I will pour out my Spirit on
      all people.
Your sons and daughters will
      prophesy,
   your young men will see
      visions,
   your old men will dream
      dreams.
¹⁸Even on my servants, both
      men and women,
   I will pour out my Spirit in
      those days,
and they will prophesy.
¹⁹I will show wonders in the heaven above
   and signs on the earth below,
      blood and fire and billows of smoke.
²⁰The sun will be turned to darkness
   and the moon to blood
      before the coming of the great and glorious day of the Lord.
²¹And everyone who calls
   on the name of the Lord will be saved.'[c]

²²"Men of Israel, listen to this: Jesus of Nazareth was a man accredited by God to you by miracles, wonders and signs, which God did among you through him, as you yourselves know. ²³This man was handed over to you by God's set purpose and foreknowledge; and you, with the help of wicked men,[d]

---

[a] *4 Or languages*; also in verse 11   [b] *13 Or sweet wine*   [c] *21 Joel 2:28-32*   [d] *23 Or of those not having the law* (that is, Gentiles)

put him to death by nailing him to the cross. [24]But God raised him from the dead, freeing him from the agony of death, because it was impossible for death to keep its hold on him. [25]David said about him:

> " 'I saw the Lord always before me.
> Because he is at my right hand,
> I will not be shaken.
> [26]Therefore my heart is glad and my tongue rejoices;
> my body also will live in hope,
> [27]because you will not abandon me to the grave,
> nor will you let your Holy One see decay.
> [28]You have made known to me the paths of life;
> you will fill me with joy in your presence.'[a]

[29]"Brothers, I can tell you confidently that the patriarch David died and was buried, and his tomb is here to this day. [30]But he was a prophet and knew that God had promised him on oath that he would place one of his descendants on his throne. [31]Seeing what was ahead, he spoke of the resurrection of the Christ,[b] that he was not abandoned to the grave, nor did his body see decay. [32]God has raised this Jesus to life, and we are all witnesses of the fact. [33]Exalted to the right hand of God, he has received from the Father the promised Holy Spirit and has poured out what you now see and hear. [34]For David did not ascend to heaven, and yet he said,

> " 'The Lord said to my Lord:
> "Sit at my right hand
> [35]until I make your enemies
> a footstool for your feet." '[c]

[36]"Therefore let all Israel be assured of this: God has made this Jesus, whom you crucified, both Lord and Christ."

[37]When the people heard this, they were cut to the heart and said to Peter and the other apostles, "Brothers, what shall we do?"

[38]Peter replied, "Repent and be baptized, every one of you, in the name of Jesus Christ for the forgiveness of your sins. And you will receive the gift of the Holy Spirit. [39]The promise is for you and your children and for all who are far off—for all whom the Lord our God will call."

[40]With many other words he warned them; and he pleaded with them, "Save yourselves from this corrupt generation." [41]Those who accepted his message were baptized, and about three thousand were added to their number that day.

THE FELLOWSHIP OF THE BELIEVERS

[42]They devoted themselves to the apostles' teaching and to the fellowship, to the breaking of bread and to prayer. [43]Everyone was filled with awe, and many wonders and miraculous signs were done by the apostles. [44]All the believers were together and had everything in common. [45]Selling their possessions and goods, they gave to anyone as he had need. [46]Every day they continued to meet together in the temple courts. They broke bread in their homes and ate together with glad and sincere hearts, [47]praising God and enjoying the favor of all the people. And the Lord added to their number daily those who were being saved.

Meeting People's Deepest Need

>> live the adventure >> Ac 2:37

Check out the way people responded to Peter's message. It's like something clicked inside them, and they suddenly realized how much they needed Jesus. Can you imagine anyone you know responding like that? You might be surprised how many people have the same kind of hunger—without even knowing it. They have no idea how much they need to hear about Jesus. Your words just might click with them and turn their hearts toward God.

---

[a] 28 Psalm 16:8-11 [b] 31 Or Messiah. "The Christ" (Greek) and "the Messiah" (Hebrew) both mean "the Anointed One"; also in verse 36. [c] 35 Psalm 110:1

PETER HEALS THE CRIPPLED BEGGAR

3 One day Peter and John were going up to the temple at the time of prayer—at three in the afternoon. [2]Now a man crippled from birth was being carried to the temple gate called Beautiful, where he was put every day to beg from those going into the temple courts. [3]When he saw Peter and John about to enter, he asked them for money. [4]Peter looked straight at him, as did John. Then Peter said, "Look at us!" [5]So the man gave them his attention, expecting to get something from them.

[6]Then Peter said, "Silver or gold I do not have, but what I have I give you. In the name of Jesus Christ of Nazareth, walk." [7]Taking him by the right hand, he helped him up, and instantly the man's feet and ankles became strong. [8]He jumped to his feet and began to walk. Then he went with them into the temple courts, walking and jumping, and praising God. [9]When all the people saw him walking and praising God, [10]they recognized him as the same man who used to sit begging at the temple gate called Beautiful, and they were filled with wonder and amazement at what had happened to him.

NOW OR NEVER

AC 3:6

Do you believe that you have direct access to Jesus' power? Do you live like you believe it? For instance, when you hear that someone is sick, do you pray for that person? Do you expect your prayers to make an actual difference in that person's life?

PETER SPEAKS TO THE ONLOOKERS

[11]While the beggar held on to Peter and John, all the people were astonished and came running to them in the place called Solomon's Colonnade. [12]When Peter saw this, he said to them: "Men of Israel, why does this surprise you? Why do you stare at us as if by our own power or godliness we had made this man walk? [13]The God of Abraham, Isaac and Jacob, the God of our fathers, has glorified his servant Jesus. You handed him over to be killed, and you disowned him before Pilate, though he had decided to let him go. [14]You disowned the Holy and Righteous One and asked that a murderer be released to you. [15]You killed the author of life, but God raised him from the dead. We are witnesses of this. [16]By faith in the name of Jesus, this man whom you see and know was made strong. It is Jesus' name and the faith that comes through him that has given this complete healing to him, as you can all see.

[17]"Now, brothers, I know that you acted in ignorance, as did your leaders. [18]But this is how God fulfilled what he had foretold through all the prophets, saying that his Christ[a] would suffer. [19]Repent, then, and turn to God, so that your sins may be wiped out, that times of refreshing may come from the Lord, [20]and that he may send the Christ, who has been appointed for you—even Jesus. [21]He must remain in heaven until the time comes for God to restore everything, as he promised long ago through his holy prophets. [22]For Moses said, 'The Lord your God will raise up for you a prophet like me from among your own people; you must listen to everything he tells you. [23]Anyone who does not listen to him will be completely cut off from among his people.'[b]

[24]"Indeed, all the prophets from Samuel on, as many as have spoken, have foretold these days. [25]And you are heirs of the prophets and of the covenant God made with your fathers. He said to Abraham, 'Through your offspring all peoples on earth will be blessed.'[c] [26]When God raised up his servant, he sent him first to you to bless you by turning each of you from your wicked ways."

PETER AND JOHN BEFORE THE SANHEDRIN

4 The priests and the captain of the temple guard and the Sadducees came up to Peter and John while they were speaking to the people. [2]They were greatly disturbed because the apostles were teaching the people and proclaiming in Jesus the resurrection of the dead. [3]They seized Peter and John, and because it was evening, they put them in jail until the next day. [4]But many who heard the message believed, and the number of men grew to about five thousand.

[5]The next day the rulers, elders and teachers of the law met in Jerusalem. [6]Annas the high priest was there, and so were Caiaphas, John, Alexander and the other men of the high priest's family. [7]They had Peter and John brought before them and began to question them: "By what power or what name did you do this?"

---

[a] *18* Or *Messiah*; also in verse 20 [b] *23* Deut. 18:15,18,19 [c] *25* Gen. 22:18; 26:4

8Then Peter, filled with the Holy Spirit, said to them: "Rulers and elders of the people! 9If we are being called to account today for an act of kindness shown to a cripple and are asked how he was healed, 10then know this, you and all the people of Israel: It is by the name of Jesus Christ of Nazareth, whom you crucified but whom God raised from the dead, that this man stands before you healed. 11He is

" 'the stone you builders rejected,
   which has become the capstone.'[a][b]

12Salvation is found in no one else, for there is no other name under heaven given to men by which we must be saved."

13When they saw the courage of Peter and John and realized that they were unschooled, ordinary men, they were astonished and they took note that these men had been with Jesus. 14But since they could see the man who had been healed standing there with them, there was nothing they could say. 15So they ordered them to withdraw from the Sanhedrin and then conferred together. 16"What are we going to do with these men?" they asked. "Everybody living in Jerusalem knows they have done an outstanding miracle, and we cannot deny it. 17But to stop this thing from spreading any further among the people, we must warn these men to speak no longer to anyone in this name."

18Then they called them in again and commanded them not to speak or teach at all in the name of Jesus. 19But Peter and John replied, "Judge for yourselves whether it is right in God's sight to obey you rather than God. 20For we cannot help speaking about what we have seen and heard."

21After further threats they let them go. They could not decide how to punish them, because all the people were praising God for what had happened. 22For the man who was miraculously healed was over forty years old.

THE BELIEVERS' PRAYER

23On their release, Peter and John went back to their own people and reported all that the chief priests and elders had said to them. 24When they heard this, they raised their voices together in prayer to God. "Sovereign Lord," they said, "you made the heaven and the earth and the sea, and everything in them. 25You spoke by the Holy Spirit through the mouth of your servant, our father David:

" 'Why do the nations rage
   and the peoples plot in vain?
26 The kings of the earth take their stand
   and the rulers gather together
against the Lord
   and against his Anointed One.'[c][d]

27Indeed Herod and Pontius Pilate met together with the Gentiles and the people[e] of Israel in this city to conspire against your holy servant Jesus, whom you anointed. 28They did what your power and will had decided beforehand should happen. 29Now, Lord, consider their threats and enable your servants to speak your word with great boldness. 30Stretch out your hand to heal and perform miraculous signs and wonders through the name of your holy servant Jesus."

NOW OR NEVER

AC 4:13

One of the most popular excuses for not talking to people about Jesus is, "I'm just a regular guy; I don't know about theological stuff." But Peter and John were "regular guys." That's what made their ministry so incredible—only God could have empowered them to speak, heal and minister the way they did.

Taking Risks for God

»» live the adventure »» Ac 4:1-4

Peter and John knew the Jewish religious leaders were out to nail them. They knew that talking to people about Jesus could get them arrested—or worse. They knew the risks, but they also knew the potential payoff. So they gambled . . . and came up big. Yes, they were arrested—but not before introducing 2,000 more people to Jesus! What are the risks you face in talking to people at school and in your neighborhood about Jesus? What's the potential payoff? Are you willing to put your own life on the line for Jesus?

---

[a] 11 Or *cornerstone*   [b] 11 Psalm 118:22   [c] 26 That is, Christ or Messiah   [d] 26 Psalm 2:1,2   [e] 27 The Greek is plural.

³¹After they prayed, the place where they were meeting was shaken. And they were all filled with the Holy Spirit and spoke the word of God boldly.

THE BELIEVERS SHARE THEIR POSSESSIONS

³²All the believers were one in heart and mind. No one claimed that any of his possessions was his own, but they shared everything they had. ³³With great power the apostles continued to testify to the resurrection of the Lord Jesus, and much grace was upon them all. ³⁴There were no needy persons among them. For from time to time those who owned lands or houses sold them, brought the money from the sales ³⁵and put it at the apostles' feet, and it was distributed to anyone as he had need.

³⁶Joseph, a Levite from Cyprus, whom the apostles called Barnabas (which means Son of Encouragement), ³⁷sold a field he owned and brought the money and put it at the apostles' feet.

ANANIAS AND SAPPHIRA

5 Now a man named Ananias, together with his wife Sapphira, also sold a piece of property. ²With his wife's full knowledge he kept back part of the money for himself, but brought the rest and put it at the apostles' feet.

³Then Peter said, "Ananias, how is it that Satan has so filled your heart that you have lied to the Holy Spirit and have kept for yourself some of the money you received for the land? ⁴Didn't it belong to you before it was sold? And after it was sold, wasn't the money at your disposal? What made you think of doing such a thing? You have not lied to men but to God."

⁵When Ananias heard this, he fell down and died. And great fear seized all who heard what had happened. ⁶Then the young men came forward, wrapped up his body, and carried him out and buried him.

⁷About three hours later his wife came in, not knowing what had happened. ⁸Peter asked her, "Tell me, is this the price you and Ananias got for the land?"

"Yes," she said, "that is the price."

⁹Peter said to her, "How could you agree to test the Spirit of the Lord? Look! The feet of the men who buried your husband are at the door, and they will carry you out also."

¹⁰At that moment she fell down at his feet and died. Then the young men came in and, finding her dead, carried her out and buried her beside her husband. ¹¹Great fear seized the whole church and all who heard about these events.

THE APOSTLES HEAL MANY

¹²The apostles performed many miraculous signs and wonders among the people. And all the believers used to meet together in Solomon's Colonnade. ¹³No one else dared join them, even though they were highly regarded by the people. ¹⁴Nevertheless, more and more men and women believed in the Lord and were added to their number. ¹⁵As a result, people brought the sick into the streets and laid them on beds and mats so that at least Peter's shadow might fall on some of them as he passed by. ¹⁶Crowds gathered also from the towns around Jerusalem, bringing their sick and those tormented by evilᵃ spirits, and all of them were healed.

THE APOSTLES PERSECUTED

¹⁷Then the high priest and all his associates, who were members of the party of the Sadducees, were filled with jealousy. ¹⁸They arrested the apostles and put them in the public jail. ¹⁹But during the night

---

ᵃ 16 Greek unclean

Sharing What You Have

Do you think an arrangement like this could work in your church today? What kind of message do you think it would send to your community if your church made sure everyone's needs were met? What could you do to help make it possible? Many things have changed in the past 2,000 years, but God's heart isn't one of them. The Lord still expects his people—all of them, not just the rich—to take care of the poor and needy.

» live the adventure » Ac 4:32-35

ananias & sapphira

VERSUS

peter

» A married couple in the early church

» Pretended to give more money to the church than they really did

» Struck dead for lying to God

» A leader of the early church

» Confronted Ananias and Sapphira regarding their deception

» Pronounced judgment on Ananias and Sapphira

The Main Event

In the church's early days, followers of Jesus took giving to the extreme. They shared their possessions with one another. When that wasn't enough, they sold their houses and used the money to meet each other's needs. Their acts of generosity kept getting bigger and bigger. It was about this time that a guy named Barnabas caused heads to turn by giving his church 100 percent of the proceeds from a lucrative real estate transaction. As word spread of his faithful generosity, Barnabas (without seeking it) saw his spiritual reputation get a major boost.

A married couple named Ananias and Sapphira were among those watching. The more they heard folks "ooh" and "ahh" over Barnabas, the more they wanted such acclaim for themselves. So they concocted a scheme. "Let's sell some of our property," they said. "Then we'll give *some* of the profit to the church . . . but we'll let everyone think we gave all of it."

The plan backfired in a surprisingly deadly way. The apostle Peter, with the Holy Spirit's help, saw right through Ananias and Sapphira's ruse. The issue wasn't the amount of their gift, but the couple's dishonest motives. They wanted praise, attention and glory, and they were willing to lie to get it.

Peter sternly confronted Ananias and Sapphira one at a time. After their rebukes, they both dropped dead at Peter's feet.

The Outcome

This sobering story raises a couple of questions.

The first is this: What prompts us to do the things we do? Why do we act in certain ways? Why do we *not* act in other ways? The answer is *motives*. We all have them—those deep, secret desires that influence us. We long internally for security or respect or power or popularity. And so we adjust our lives externally. However, we need to be very careful in this area. Motives matter! God takes deception, dishonesty and pride *very* seriously—especially among his own people. The fact is, if our souls hunger for the wrong things, we will engage in wrong acts. We *must* guard our hearts (see Proverbs 4:23).

The second question is this: How should we respond when other Christians willfully engage in wrong acts? As men of God, we must be willing to step forward and confront others. (Unlike the apostle Peter, we don't have the authority or power to pronounce a judgment of death on someone; however, we *do* have the responsibility to hold our friends accountable.) We should never be cocky or self-righteous, but we must humbly look out for others.

Read more about Ananias and Sapphira and Peter in Acts 5:1–11 (page 1416).

an angel of the Lord opened the doors of the jail and brought them out. [20]"Go, stand in the temple courts," he said, "and tell the people the full message of this new life."

[21]At daybreak they entered the temple courts, as they had been told, and began to teach the people.

When the high priest and his associates arrived, they called together the Sanhedrin—the full assembly of the elders of Israel—and sent to the jail for the apostles. [22]But on arriving at the jail, the officers did not find them there. So they went back and reported, [23]"We found the jail securely locked, with the guards standing at the doors; but when we opened them, we found no one inside." [24]On hearing this report, the captain of the temple guard and the chief priests were puzzled, wondering what would come of this.

[25]Then someone came and said, "Look! The men you put in jail are standing in the temple courts teaching the people." [26]At that, the captain went with his officers and brought the apostles. They did not use force, because they feared that the people would stone them.

[27]Having brought the apostles, they made them appear before the Sanhedrin to be questioned by the high priest. [28]"We gave you strict orders not to teach in this name," he said. "Yet you have filled Jerusalem with your teaching and are determined to make us guilty of this man's blood."

[29]Peter and the other apostles replied: "We must obey God rather than men! [30]The God of our fathers raised Jesus from the dead—whom you had killed by hanging him on a tree. [31]God exalted him to his own right hand as Prince and Savior that he might give repentance and forgiveness of sins to Israel. [32]We are witnesses of these things, and so is the Holy Spirit, whom God has given to those who obey him."

[33]When they heard this, they were furious and wanted to put them to death. [34]But a Pharisee named Gamaliel, a teacher of the law, who was honored by all the people, stood up in the Sanhedrin and ordered that the men be put outside for a little while. [35]Then he addressed them: "Men of Israel, consider carefully what you intend to do to these men. [36]Some time ago Theudas appeared, claiming to be somebody, and about four hundred men rallied to him. He was killed, all his followers were dispersed, and it all came to nothing. [37]After him, Judas the Galilean appeared in the days of the census and led a band of people in revolt. He too was killed, and all his followers were scattered. [38]Therefore, in the present case I advise you: Leave these men alone! Let them go! For if their purpose or activity is of human origin, it will fail. [39]But if it is from God, you will not be able to stop these men; you will only find yourselves fighting against God."

[40]His speech persuaded them. They called the apostles in and had them flogged. Then they ordered them not to speak in the name of Jesus, and let them go.

NOW OR NEVER

AC 5:41–42

Peter and John were the original "Jesus freaks." They were *proud* of the fact that their faith cost them something. If they had to take a beating for Jesus, they were happy to do it—anything to show their love for him. If you're wondering what Christian manhood looks like, just remember Peter and John.

[41]The apostles left the Sanhedrin, rejoicing because they had been counted worthy of suffering disgrace for the Name. [42]Day after day, in the temple courts and from house to house, they never stopped teaching and proclaiming the good news that Jesus is the Christ.[a]

THE CHOOSING OF THE SEVEN

6 In those days when the number of disciples was increasing, the Grecian Jews among them complained against the Hebraic Jews because their widows were being overlooked in the daily distribution of food. [2]So the Twelve gathered all the disciples together and said, "It would not be right for us to neglect the ministry of the word of God in order to wait on tables. [3]Brothers, choose seven men from among you who are known to be full of the Spirit and wisdom. We will turn this responsibility over to them [4]and will give our attention to prayer and the ministry of the word."

[5]This proposal pleased the whole group. They chose Stephen, a man full of faith and of the Holy Spirit; also Philip, Procorus, Nicanor, Timon, Parmenas, and Nicolas from Antioch, a convert to Judaism. [6]They presented these men to the apostles, who prayed and laid their hands on them.

---

[a] 42 Or *Messiah*

caiaphas

VERSUS

» Israel's high priest (top religious leader)
» Instrumental in Jesus' execution
» Cared more about religious power than spiritual truth

stephen

» One of the first deacons of the early church
» The first recorded Christian martyr
» A man of high character, filled with the Spirit of God

The Main Event

As the high priest of Israel, Caiaphas should have been the godliest person in the land. In reality he was totally disinterested in spiritual things. Caiaphas didn't care about God; he cared about power and wealth. He was a political schmoozer, a backstabber who would do anything to get to the top and stay there. Caiaphas liked his cushy position and the prestige that came with it. That's why he used all of his connections and every tool at his disposal to arrange Jesus' execution. Caiaphas viewed the carpenter from Nazareth as trouble, as a threat to his personal security. And he viewed Jesus' followers as more of the same.

Enter Stephen. This brilliant young church leader had been causing quite a ruckus in Jerusalem with his preaching about the resurrected Messiah and his stunning miracles. Dragged in front of the intimidating Caiaphas and his colleagues, Stephen was asked to defend himself.

Stephen might have stopped for a moment to consider that this was the same powerful man who had orchestrated Jesus' crucifixion. He might have toned down his message. He might have played it safe. But he didn't. In a long speech, Stephen slowly but surely made his case that Jesus is the promised Messiah... and that

Caiaphas and his cronies were nothing more than religious fakes. He basically called them hardheaded, hard-hearted pagans.

Not surprisingly, Caiaphas and the other priests went nuts. They mobbed Stephen, dragged him outside and hurled rocks at him until he died. Amazingly, Stephen's last words were a prayer for his killers' forgiveness.

The Outcome

This is a classic good guy vs. bad guy match-up. To the casual onlooker, Stephen was the clear loser of the bout, squashed like a bug by the powerful Caiaphas. To those who can see beyond the surface, however, Stephen was the victor. He was received into heaven by Christ himself. The man whose name means "crown" received the ultimate crown—eternal life with Jesus. He was full of faith, grace, power, wisdom, courage and love.

And Caiaphas? He was just full of himself.

Read more about Caiaphas and Stephen in Acts 4:6 (page 1414); 6:8—7:60 (pages 1420–1422).

[7]So the word of God spread. The number of disciples in Jerusalem increased rapidly, and a large number of priests became obedient to the faith.

STEPHEN SEIZED

[8]Now Stephen, a man full of God's grace and power, did great wonders and miraculous signs among the people. [9]Opposition arose, however, from members of the Synagogue of the Freedmen (as it was called)—Jews of Cyrene and Alexandria as well as the provinces of Cilicia and Asia. These men began to argue with Stephen, [10]but they could not stand up against his wisdom or the Spirit by whom he spoke.

[11]Then they secretly persuaded some men to say, "We have heard Stephen speak words of blasphemy against Moses and against God."

[12]So they stirred up the people and the elders and the teachers of the law. They seized Stephen and brought him before the Sanhedrin. [13]They produced false witnesses, who testified, "This fellow never stops speaking against this holy place and against the law. [14]For we have heard him say that this Jesus of Nazareth will destroy this place and change the customs Moses handed down to us."

[15]All who were sitting in the Sanhedrin looked intently at Stephen, and they saw that his face was like the face of an angel.

STEPHEN'S SPEECH TO THE SANHEDRIN

7 Then the high priest asked him, "Are these charges true?"

[2]To this he replied: "Brothers and fathers, listen to me! The God of glory appeared to our father Abraham while he was still in Mesopotamia, before he lived in Haran. [3]'Leave your country and your people,' God said, 'and go to the land I will show you.'[a]

[4]"So he left the land of the Chaldeans and settled in Haran. After the death of his father, God sent him to this land where you are now living. [5]He gave him no inheritance here, not even a foot of ground. But God promised him that he and his descendants after him would possess the land, even though at that time Abraham had no child. [6]God spoke to him in this way: 'Your descendants will be strangers in a country not their own, and they will be enslaved and mistreated four hundred years. [7]But I will punish the nation they serve as slaves,' God said, 'and afterward they will come out of that country and worship me in this place.'[b] [8]Then he gave Abraham the covenant of circumcision. And Abraham became the father of Isaac and circumcised him eight days after his birth. Later Isaac became the father of Jacob, and Jacob became the father of the twelve patriarchs.

[9]"Because the patriarchs were jealous of Joseph, they sold him as a slave into Egypt. But God was with him [10]and rescued him from all his troubles. He gave Joseph wisdom and enabled him to gain the goodwill of Pharaoh king of Egypt; so he made him ruler over Egypt and all his palace.

[11]"Then a famine struck all Egypt and Canaan, bringing great suffering, and our fathers could not find food. [12]When Jacob heard that there was grain in Egypt, he sent our fathers on their first visit. [13]On their second visit, Joseph told his brothers who he was, and Pharaoh learned about Joseph's family. [14]After this, Joseph sent for his father Jacob and his whole family, seventy-five in all. [15]Then Jacob went down to Egypt, where he and our fathers died. [16]Their bodies were brought back to Shechem and placed in the tomb that Abraham had bought from the sons of Hamor at Shechem for a certain sum of money.

[17]"As the time drew near for God to fulfill his promise to Abraham, the number of our people in Egypt greatly increased.

Understanding What People Need to Hear

Stephen knew the secret to getting his point across was to find a way to capture people's attention. That's why he mentioned Abraham, Joseph and Moses—three of the most beloved people in Jewish history. Stephen knew the Jewish religious leaders would listen to any argument based on Jewish history, so he used that in his talk about Jesus. Learn from Stephen's example. Before you share your faith with someone, think about the things the person is really into—whether it's music, sports, video games or something else. Use those interests as a springboard for talking about Jesus.

---

[a] 3 Gen. 12:1   [b] 7 Gen. 15:13,14

¹⁸Then another king, who knew nothing about Joseph, became ruler of Egypt. ¹⁹He dealt treacherously with our people and oppressed our forefathers by forcing them to throw out their newborn babies so that they would die.

²⁰"At that time Moses was born, and he was no ordinary child.ª For three months he was cared for in his father's house. ²¹When he was placed outside, Pharaoh's daughter took him and brought him up as her own son. ²²Moses was educated in all the wisdom of the Egyptians and was powerful in speech and action.

²³"When Moses was forty years old, he decided to visit his fellow Israelites. ²⁴He saw one of them being mistreated by an Egyptian, so he went to his defense and avenged him by killing the Egyptian. ²⁵Moses thought that his own people would realize that God was using him to rescue them, but they did not. ²⁶The next day Moses came upon two Israelites who were fighting. He tried to reconcile them by saying, 'Men, you are brothers; why do you want to hurt each other?'

²⁷"But the man who was mistreating the other pushed Moses aside and said, 'Who made you ruler and judge over us? ²⁸Do you want to kill me as you killed the Egyptian yesterday?'ᵇ ²⁹When Moses heard this, he fled to Midian, where he settled as a foreigner and had two sons.

³⁰"After forty years had passed, an angel appeared to Moses in the flames of a burning bush in the desert near Mount Sinai. ³¹When he saw this, he was amazed at the sight. As he went over to look more closely, he heard the Lord's voice: ³²'I am the God of your fathers, the God of Abraham, Isaac and Jacob.'ᶜ Moses trembled with fear and did not dare to look.

³³"Then the Lord said to him, 'Take off your sandals; the place where you are standing is holy ground. ³⁴I have indeed seen the oppression of my people in Egypt. I have heard their groaning and have come down to set them free. Now come, I will send you back to Egypt.'ᵈ

³⁵"This is the same Moses whom they had rejected with the words, 'Who made you ruler and judge?' He was sent to be their ruler and deliverer by God himself, through the angel who appeared to him in the bush. ³⁶He led them out of Egypt and did wonders and miraculous signs in Egypt, at the Red Seaᵉ and for forty years in the desert.

³⁷"This is that Moses who told the Israelites, 'God will send you a prophet like me from your own people.'ᶠ ³⁸He was in the assembly in the desert, with the angel who spoke to him on Mount Sinai, and with our fathers; and he received living words to pass on to us.

³⁹"But our fathers refused to obey him. Instead, they rejected him and in their hearts turned back to Egypt. ⁴⁰They told Aaron, 'Make us gods who will go before us. As for this fellow Moses who led us out of Egypt—we don't know what has happened to him!'ᵍ ⁴¹That was the time they made an idol in the form of a calf. They brought sacrifices to it and held a celebration in honor of what their hands had made. ⁴²But God turned away and gave them over to the worship of the heavenly bodies. This agrees with what is written in the book of the prophets:

" 'Did you bring me sacrifices and offerings
    forty years in the desert, O house of Israel?
⁴³You have lifted up the shrine of Molech
    and the star of your god Rephan,
    the idols you made to worship.
Therefore I will send you into exile'ʰ beyond Babylon.

⁴⁴"Our forefathers had the tabernacle of the Testimony with them in the desert. It had been made as God directed Moses, according to the pattern he had seen. ⁴⁵Having received the tabernacle, our fathers under Joshua brought it with them when they took the land from the nations God drove out before them. It remained in the land until the time of David, ⁴⁶who enjoyed God's favor and asked that he might provide a dwelling place for the God of Jacob.ⁱ ⁴⁷But it was Solomon who built the house for him.

⁴⁸"However, the Most High does not live in houses made by men. As the prophet says:

⁴⁹" 'Heaven is my throne,
    and the earth is my footstool.
What kind of house will you build for me?
                                    says the Lord.

ª 20 Or was fair in the sight of God   ᵇ 28 Exodus 2:14   ᶜ 32 Exodus 3:6   ᵈ 34 Exodus 3:5,7,8,10   ᵉ 36 That is, Sea of Reeds   ᶠ 37 Deut. 18:15   ᵍ 40 Exodus 32:1   ʰ 43 Amos 5:25-27   ⁱ 46 Some early manuscripts the house of Jacob

Or where will my resting place be?
⁵⁰Has not my hand made all these things?'ᵃ

⁵¹"You stiff-necked people, with uncircumcised hearts and ears! You are just like your fathers: You always resist the Holy Spirit! ⁵²Was there ever a prophet your fathers did not persecute? They even killed those who predicted the coming of the Righteous One. And now you have betrayed and murdered him— ⁵³you who have received the law that was put into effect through angels but have not obeyed it."

THE STONING OF STEPHEN

⁵⁴When they heard this, they were furious and gnashed their teeth at him. ⁵⁵But Stephen, full of the Holy Spirit, looked up to heaven and saw the glory of God, and Jesus standing at the right hand of God. ⁵⁶"Look," he said, "I see heaven open and the Son of Man standing at the right hand of God."

⁵⁷At this they covered their ears and, yelling at the top of their voices, they all rushed at him, ⁵⁸dragged him out of the city and began to stone him. Meanwhile, the witnesses laid their clothes at the feet of a young man named Saul.

⁵⁹While they were stoning him, Stephen prayed, "Lord Jesus, receive my spirit." ⁶⁰Then he fell on his knees and cried out, "Lord, do not hold this sin against them." When he had said this, he fell asleep.

8 And Saul was there, giving approval to his death.

NOW OR NEVER
AC 7:54—8:1

This "Saul" character who helped kill Stephen (and perhaps several other Christians) later changed his name and cleaned up his act, thanks to a run-in with the resurrected Jesus. You probably know him better as Paul, the guy who wrote most of the New Testament.

THE CHURCH PERSECUTED AND SCATTERED

On that day a great persecution broke out against the church at Jerusalem, and all except the apostles were scattered throughout Judea and Samaria. ²Godly men buried Stephen and mourned deeply for him. ³But Saul began to destroy the church. Going from house to house, he dragged off men and women and put them in prison.

PHILIP IN SAMARIA

⁴Those who had been scattered preached the word wherever they went. ⁵Philip went down to a city in Samaria and proclaimed the Christᵇ there. ⁶When the crowds heard Philip and saw the miraculous signs he did, they all paid close attention to what he said. ⁷With shrieks, evilᶜ spirits came out of many, and many paralytics and cripples were healed. ⁸So there was great joy in that city.

SIMON THE SORCERER

⁹Now for some time a man named Simon had practiced sorcery in the city and amazed all the people of Samaria. He boasted that he was someone great, ¹⁰and all the people, both high and low, gave him their attention and exclaimed, "This man is the divine power known as the Great Power." ¹¹They followed him because he had amazed them for a long time with his magic. ¹²But when they believed Philip as he preached the good news of the kingdom of God and the name of Jesus Christ, they were baptized, both men and women. ¹³Simon himself believed and was baptized. And he followed Philip everywhere, astonished by the great signs and miracles he saw.

NOW OR NEVER
AC 8:1—4

Here's an example of how God can make something good from something bad. The "bad" in this case is the persecution that the Christians in Jerusalem endured. It scattered believers everywhere, spreading the Good News and starting new churches all over the ancient world.

¹⁴When the apostles in Jerusalem heard that Samaria had accepted the word of God, they sent Pe-

ᵃ *50* Isaiah 66:1,2   ᵇ *5* Or *Messiah*   ᶜ *7* Greek *unclean*

simon the sorcerer

» A pagan sorcerer
» Claimed to believe in Jesus and was baptized
» Tried to pay money for the divine ability to bestow the Holy Spirit

VERSUS

simon peter

» A fisherman turned follower of Jesus Christ
» The first great leader of the church
» A bold spokesman for the faith and author of 1 and 2 Peter

The Main Event

Palm readers, mediums and spiritualists are nothing new. They've been around for as long as anyone can remember. They're called shamans in some cultures, sorcerers in others. And while some are obvious fakes who make a living off gullible people, others *do* seem to possess convincing supernatural power.

Take Simon the Sorcerer, for example. For a long time he was a hot commodity in Samaria. Some people watched his tricks in amazement and thought he might possibly be divine—God in the flesh . . . or at least some kind of messenger from the Almighty.

But when Philip came along proclaiming the message of Jesus and authenticating his message with spectacular healings and mind-boggling exorcisms, Simon could only gawk in astonishment and awe. Simon's tricks and powers—which no doubt were demonic in origin—were pretty impressive, but nothing compared to what Philip was doing. In fact, when Simon saw evidence of God's power in Philip, he confessed faith in Jesus.

Later, when the apostles came to Samaria to pray that the new Samaritan believers might receive the Holy Spirit (and be seen by all their Jewish cousins as full partners in the Christian faith), Simon's eyes got wide. In his spiritual immaturity, Simon saw the imparting of the Spirit as a cool trick, a bit of magic that he could add to his repertoire. He offered Peter money, right there on the spot, for the ability.

The always-blunt Peter erupted, "May your money perish with you, because you thought you could buy the gift of God with money! You have no part or share in this ministry, because your heart is not right before God. Repent of this wickedness and pray to the Lord. Perhaps he will forgive you for having such a thought in your heart" (Acts 8:20–22).

The Outcome

Simon the Sorcerer learned from the apostle Peter that God's power is not for sale. It can't be bought. It is a *gift*, given to those whose hearts are made right by God.

Simon also learned that Christian ministry is not about being flashy, making a name for oneself or getting rich off the crowds. The purpose of ministry is to glorify God—specifically through the changed lives of people who come to know him. Whenever you see "Christian" ministers who play to the crowd—always talking about money, preaching or singing in showy ways and drawing undue attention to themselves—you can be sure you are watching something that does not honor God.

Read more about Simon the Sorcerer and Simon Peter in Acts 8:4–25 (pages 1422–1424).

ter and John to them. ¹⁵When they arrived, they prayed for them that they might receive the Holy Spir-it, ¹⁶because the Holy Spirit had not yet come upon any of them; they had simply been baptized into[a] the name of the Lord Jesus. ¹⁷Then Peter and John placed their hands on them, and they received the Holy Spirit.

¹⁸When Simon saw that the Spirit was given at the laying on of the apostles' hands, he offered them money ¹⁹and said, "Give me also this ability so that everyone on whom I lay my hands may receive the Holy Spirit."

²⁰Peter answered: "May your money perish with you, because you thought you could buy the gift of God with money! ²¹You have no part or share in this ministry, because your heart is not right before God. ²²Repent of this wickedness and pray to the Lord. Perhaps he will forgive you for having such a thought in your heart. ²³For I see that you are full of bitterness and captive to sin."

²⁴Then Simon answered, "Pray to the Lord for me so that nothing you have said may happen to me."

²⁵When they had testified and pro-claimed the word of the Lord, Peter and John returned to Jerusalem, preaching the gospel in many Samaritan villages.

challenge notes

To: **my_son**

heavenly_father: if you're serious about understanding my word, I can make it come alive for you. the story of philip and the ethiopian shows just how far I'll go to make my word clear to those who truly want to know me.

AC 8:26-39

PHILIP AND THE ETHIOPIAN

²⁶Now an angel of the Lord said to Philip, "Go south to the road—the desert road—that goes down from Jerusalem to Gaza." ²⁷So he started out, and on his way he met an Ethiopian[b] eunuch, an impor-tant official in charge of all the treasury of Candace, queen of the Ethiopians. This man had gone to Je-rusalem to worship, ²⁸and on his way home was sitting in his chariot reading the book of Isaiah the prophet. ²⁹The Spirit told Philip, "Go to that chariot and stay near it."

³⁰Then Philip ran up to the chariot and heard the man reading Isaiah the prophet. "Do you under-stand what you are reading?" Philip asked.

³¹"How can I," he said, "unless someone explains it to me?" So he invited Philip to come up and sit with him.

³²The eunuch was reading this passage of Scripture:

NOW OR NEVER

AC 8:30–35

Do you have someone you can go to with your questions about the Bible? If not, why don't you ask God to provide some-one?

"He was led like a sheep to the slaughter,
and as a lamb before the shearer is silent,
so he did not open his mouth.
³³In his humiliation he was deprived of justice.
Who can speak of his descendants?
For his life was taken from the earth."[c]

³⁴The eunuch asked Philip, "Tell me, please, who is the prophet talking about, himself or someone else?" ³⁵Then Philip began with that very passage of Scripture and told him the good news about Jesus.

³⁶As they traveled along the road, they came to some water and the eunuch said, "Look, here is wa-ter. Why shouldn't I be baptized?"[d] ³⁸And he gave orders to stop the chariot. Then both Philip and the eunuch went down into the water and Philip baptized him. ³⁹When they came up out of the water, the Spirit of the Lord suddenly took Philip away, and the eunuch did not see him again, but went on his way rejoicing. ⁴⁰Philip, however, appeared at Azotus and traveled about, preaching the gospel in all the towns until he reached Caesarea.

---

[a] *16* Or *in* [b] *27* That is, from the upper Nile region [c] *33* Isaiah 53:7,8 [d] *36* Some late manuscripts *baptized?"* ³⁷Philip said, "If you believe with all your heart, you may." The eunuch answered, "I believe that Jesus Christ is the Son of God."

SAUL'S CONVERSION

9 Meanwhile, Saul was still breathing out murderous threats against the Lord's disciples. He went to the high priest ²and asked him for letters to the synagogues in Damascus, so that if he found any there who belonged to the Way, whether men or women, he might take them as prisoners to Jerusalem. ³As he neared Damascus on his journey, suddenly a light from heaven flashed around him. ⁴He fell to the ground and heard a voice say to him, "Saul, Saul, why do you persecute me?"

⁵"Who are you, Lord?" Saul asked.

"I am Jesus, whom you are persecuting," he replied. ⁶"Now get up and go into the city, and you will be told what you must do."

⁷The men traveling with Saul stood there speechless; they heard the sound but did not see anyone. ⁸Saul got up from the ground, but when he opened his eyes he could see nothing. So they led him by the hand into Damascus. ⁹For three days he was blind, and did not eat or drink anything.

¹⁰In Damascus there was a disciple named Ananias. The Lord called to him in a vision, "Ananias!"

"Yes, Lord," he answered.

¹¹The Lord told him, "Go to the house of Judas on Straight Street and ask for a man from Tarsus named Saul, for he is praying. ¹²In a vision he has seen a man named Ananias come and place his hands on him to restore his sight."

¹³"Lord," Ananias answered, "I have heard many reports about this man and all the harm he has done to your saints in Jerusalem. ¹⁴And he has come here with authority from the chief priests to arrest all who call on your name."

¹⁵But the Lord said to Ananias, "Go! This man is my chosen instrument to carry my name before the Gentiles and their kings and before the people of Israel. ¹⁶I will show him how much he must suffer for my name."

¹⁷Then Ananias went to the house and entered it. Placing his hands on Saul, he said, "Brother Saul, the Lord—Jesus, who appeared to you on the road as you were coming here—has sent me so that you may see again and be filled with the Holy Spirit." ¹⁸Immediately, something like scales fell from Saul's eyes, and he could see again. He got up and was baptized, ¹⁹and after taking some food, he regained his strength.

SAUL IN DAMASCUS AND JERUSALEM

Saul spent several days with the disciples in Damascus. ²⁰At once he began to preach in the synagogues that Jesus is the Son of God. ²¹All those who heard him were astonished and asked, "Isn't he the man who raised havoc in Jerusalem among those who call on this name? And hasn't he come here to take them as prisoners to the chief priests?" ²²Yet Saul grew more and more powerful and baffled the Jews living in Damascus by proving that Jesus is the Christ.ᵃ

²³After many days had gone by, the Jews conspired to kill him, ²⁴but Saul learned of their plan. Day and night they kept close watch on the city gates in order to kill him. ²⁵But his followers took him by night and lowered him in a basket through an opening in the wall.

²⁶When he came to Jerusalem, he tried to join the disciples, but they were all afraid of him, not believing that he really was a disciple. ²⁷But Barnabas took him and brought him to the apostles. He told them how Saul on his journey had seen the Lord and that the Lord had spoken to him, and how in Damascus he had preached fearlessly in the name of Jesus. ²⁸So Saul stayed with them and moved about freely in Jerusalem, speaking boldly in the name of the Lord. ²⁹He talked and debated with the Grecian Jews, but they tried to kill him. ³⁰When the brothers learned of this, they took him down to Caesarea and sent him off to Tarsus.

³¹Then the church throughout Judea, Galilee and Samaria enjoyed a time of peace. It was strengthened; and encouraged by the Holy Spirit, it grew in numbers, living in the fear of the Lord.

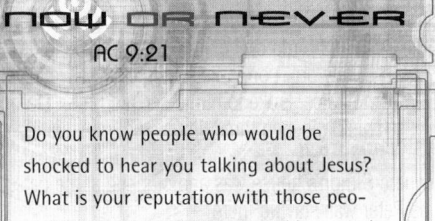

NOW OR NEVER

AC 9:21

Do you know people who would be shocked to hear you talking about Jesus? What is your reputation with those people? Think about what you could say or do to let those people know just how serious you are about your faith.

ᵃ 22 Or *Messiah*

AENEAS AND DORCAS

32As Peter traveled about the country, he went to visit the saints in Lydda. 33There he found a man named Aeneas, a paralytic who had been bedridden for eight years. 34"Aeneas," Peter said to him, "Jesus Christ heals you. Get up and take care of your mat." Immediately Aeneas got up. 35All those who lived in Lydda and Sharon saw him and turned to the Lord.

36In Joppa there was a disciple named Tabitha (which, when translated, is Dorcas[a]), who was always doing good and helping the poor. 37About that time she became sick and died, and her body was washed and placed in an upstairs room. 38Lydda was near Joppa; so when the disciples heard that Peter was in Lydda, they sent two men to him and urged him, "Please come at once!"

39Peter went with them, and when he arrived he was taken upstairs to the room. All the widows stood around him, crying and showing him the robes and other clothing that Dorcas had made while she was still with them.

40Peter sent them all out of the room; then he got down on his knees and prayed. Turning toward the dead woman, he said, "Tabitha, get up." She opened her eyes, and seeing Peter she sat up. 41He took her by the hand and helped her to her feet. Then he called the believers and the widows and presented her to them alive. 42This became known all over Joppa, and many people believed in the Lord. 43Peter stayed in Joppa for some time with a tanner named Simon.

CORNELIUS CALLS FOR PETER

10 At Caesarea there was a man named Cornelius, a centurion in what was known as the Italian Regiment. 2He and all his family were devout and God-fearing; he gave generously to those in need and prayed to God regularly. 3One day at about three in the afternoon he had a vision. He distinctly saw an angel of God, who came to him and said, "Cornelius!"

4Cornelius stared at him in fear. "What is it, Lord?" he asked.

The angel answered, "Your prayers and gifts to the poor have come up as a memorial offering before God. 5Now send men to Joppa to bring back a man named Simon who is called Peter. 6He is staying with Simon the tanner, whose house is by the sea."

7When the angel who spoke to him had gone, Cornelius called two of his servants and a devout soldier who was one of his attendants. 8He told them everything that had happened and sent them to Joppa.

PETER'S VISION

9About noon the following day as they were on their journey and approaching the city, Peter went up on the roof to pray. 10He became hungry and wanted something to eat, and while the meal was being prepared, he fell into a trance. 11He saw heaven opened and something like a large sheet being let down to earth by its four corners. 12It contained all kinds of four-footed animals, as well as reptiles of the earth and birds of the air. 13Then a voice told him, "Get up, Peter. Kill and eat."

14"Surely not, Lord!" Peter replied. "I have never eaten anything impure or unclean."

15The voice spoke to him a second time, "Do not call anything impure that God has made clean."

16This happened three times, and immediately the sheet was taken back to heaven.

17While Peter was wondering about the meaning of the vision, the men sent by Cornelius found out where Simon's house was and stopped at the gate. 18They called out, asking if Simon who was known as Peter was staying there.

19While Peter was still thinking about the vision, the Spirit said to him, "Simon, three[b] men are looking for you. 20So get up and go downstairs. Do not hesitate to go with them, for I have sent them."

21Peter went down and said to the men, "I'm the one you're looking for. Why have you come?"

22The men replied, "We have come from Cornelius the centurion. He is a righteous and God-fearing man, who is respected by all the Jewish people. A holy angel told him to have you come to his house so that he could hear what you have to say." 23Then Peter invited the men into the house to be his guests.

PETER AT CORNELIUS'S HOUSE

The next day Peter started out with them, and some of the brothers from Joppa went along. 24The following day he arrived in Caesarea. Cornelius was expecting them and had called together his rela-

---

[a] 36 Both *Tabitha* (Aramaic) and *Dorcas* (Greek) mean *gazelle*.   [b] 19 One early manuscript *two*; other manuscripts do not have the number.

tives and close friends. 25As Peter entered the house, Cornelius met him and fell at his feet in reverence. 26But Peter made him get up. "Stand up," he said, "I am only a man myself."

27Talking with him, Peter went inside and found a large gathering of people. 28He said to them: "You are well aware that it is against our law for a Jew to associate with a Gentile or visit him. But God has shown me that I should not call any man impure or unclean. 29So when I was sent for, I came without raising any objection. May I ask why you sent for me?"

NOW OR NEVER
AC 10:28

Never let personal feelings or prejudice get in the way of sharing your faith. Everyone ought to hear about the promise of new life in Jesus. Imagine if Peter had never gotten over his prejudice and hadn't obey God's call to take the Good News to the Gentiles (non-Jews).

30Cornelius answered: "Four days ago I was in my house praying at this hour, at three in the afternoon. Suddenly a man in shining clothes stood before me 31and said, 'Cornelius, God has heard your prayer and remembered your gifts to the poor. 32Send to Joppa for Simon who is called Peter. He is a guest in the home of Simon the tanner, who lives by the sea.' 33So I sent for you immediately, and it was good of you to come. Now we are all here in the presence of God to listen to everything the Lord has commanded you to tell us."

34Then Peter began to speak: "I now realize how true it is that God does not show favoritism 35but accepts men from every nation who fear him and do what is right. 36You know the message God sent to the people of Israel, telling the good news of peace through Jesus Christ, who is Lord of all. 37You know what has happened throughout Judea, beginning in Galilee after the baptism that John preached— 38how God anointed Jesus of Nazareth with the Holy Spirit and power, and how he went around doing good and healing all who were under the power of the devil, because God was with him.

39"We are witnesses of everything he did in the country of the Jews and in Jerusalem. They killed him by hanging him on a tree, 40but God raised him from the dead on the third day and caused him to be seen. 41He was not seen by all the people, but by witnesses whom God had already chosen—by us who ate and drank with him after he rose from the dead. 42He commanded us to preach to the people and to testify that he is the one whom God appointed as judge of the living and the dead. 43All the prophets testify about him that everyone who believes in him receives forgiveness of sins through his name."

44While Peter was still speaking these words, the Holy Spirit came on all who heard the message. 45The circumcised believers who had come with Peter were astonished that the gift of the Holy Spirit had been poured out even on the Gentiles. 46For they heard them speaking in tongues[a] and praising God.

Then Peter said, 47"Can anyone keep these people from being baptized with water? They have received the Holy Spirit just as we have." 48So he ordered that they be baptized in the name of Jesus Christ. Then they asked Peter to stay with them for a few days.

PETER EXPLAINS HIS ACTIONS

11 The apostles and the brothers throughout Judea heard that the Gentiles also had received the word of God. 2So when Peter went up to Jerusalem, the circumcised believers criticized him 3and said, "You went into the house of uncircumcised men and ate with them."

4Peter began and explained everything to them precisely as it had happened: 5"I was in the city of Joppa praying, and in a trance I saw a vision. I saw something like a large sheet being let down from heaven by its four corners, and it came down to where I was. 6I looked into it and saw four-footed animals of the earth, wild beasts, reptiles, and birds of the air. 7Then I heard a voice telling me, 'Get up, Peter. Kill and eat.'

8"I replied, 'Surely not, Lord! Nothing impure or unclean has ever entered my mouth.'

9"The voice spoke from heaven a second time, 'Do not call anything impure that God has made clean.' 10This happened three times, and then it was all pulled up to heaven again.

11"Right then three men who had been sent to me from Caesarea stopped at the house where I was staying. 12The Spirit told me to have no hesitation about going with them. These six brothers also went with me, and we entered the man's house. 13He told us how he had seen an angel appear in his house

---
a 46 Or other languages

and say, 'Send to Joppa for Simon who is called Peter. [14]He will bring you a message through which you and all your household will be saved.'

[15]"As I began to speak, the Holy Spirit came on them as he had come on us at the beginning. [16]Then I remembered what the Lord had said: 'John baptized with [a] water, but you will be baptized with the Holy Spirit.' [17]So if God gave them the same gift as he gave us, who believed in the Lord Jesus Christ, who was I to think that I could oppose God?"

[18]When they heard this, they had no further objections and praised God, saying, "So then, God has granted even the Gentiles repentance unto life."

THE CHURCH IN ANTIOCH

[19]Now those who had been scattered by the persecution in connection with Stephen traveled as far as Phoenicia, Cyprus and Antioch, telling the message only to Jews. [20]Some of them, however, men from Cyprus and Cyrene, went to Antioch and began to speak to Greeks also, telling them the good news about the Lord Jesus. [21]The Lord's hand was with them, and a great number of people believed and turned to the Lord.

[22]News of this reached the ears of the church at Jerusalem, and they sent Barnabas to Antioch. [23]When he arrived and saw the evidence of the grace of God, he was glad and encouraged them all to remain true to the Lord with all their hearts. [24]He was a good man, full of the Holy Spirit and faith, and a great number of people were brought to the Lord.

[25]Then Barnabas went to Tarsus to look for Saul, [26]and when he found him, he brought him to Antioch. So for a whole year Barnabas and Saul met with the church and taught great numbers of people. The disciples were called Christians first at Antioch.

[27]During this time some prophets came down from Jerusalem to Antioch. [28]One of them, named Agabus, stood up and through the Spirit predicted that a severe famine would spread over the entire Roman world. (This happened during the reign of Claudius.) [29]The disciples, each according to his ability, decided to provide help for the brothers living in Judea. [30]This they did, sending their gift to the elders by Barnabas and Saul.

PETER'S MIRACULOUS ESCAPE FROM PRISON

12 It was about this time that King Herod arrested some who belonged to the church, intending to persecute them. [2]He had James, the brother of John, put to death with the sword. [3]When he saw that this pleased the Jews, he proceeded to seize Peter also. This happened during the Feast of Unleavened Bread. [4]After arresting him, he put him in prison, handing him over to be guarded by four squads of four soldiers each. Herod intended to bring him out for public trial after the Passover.

[5]So Peter was kept in prison, but the church was earnestly praying to God for him.

challenge notes

To: my_son

AC 12:5-10

heavenly_father: never doubt the power of prayer—especially the power of a prayer offered by a group of faithful believers. I have unimaginable power at my disposal (including an army of angels like the one who freed peter) to respond to your requests.

[6]The night before Herod was to bring him to trial, Peter was sleeping between two soldiers, bound with two chains, and sentries stood guard at the entrance. [7]Suddenly an angel of the Lord appeared and a light shone in the cell. He struck Peter on the side and woke him up. "Quick, get up!" he said, and the chains fell off Peter's wrists.

[8]Then the angel said to him, "Put on your clothes and sandals." And Peter did so. "Wrap your cloak around you and follow me," the angel told him. [9]Peter followed him out of the prison, but he had no idea that what the angel was doing was really happening; he thought he was seeing a vision. [10]They passed the first and second guards and came to the iron gate leading to the city. It opened for them by itself, and they went through it. When they had walked the length of one street, suddenly the angel left him.

---

[a] 16 Or *in*

[11]Then Peter came to himself and said, "Now I know without a doubt that the Lord sent his angel and rescued me from Herod's clutches and from everything the Jewish people were anticipating."

[12]When this had dawned on him, he went to the house of Mary the mother of John, also called Mark, where many people had gathered and were praying. [13]Peter knocked at the outer entrance, and a servant girl named Rhoda came to answer the door. [14]When she recognized Peter's voice, she was so overjoyed she ran back without opening it and exclaimed, "Peter is at the door!"

[15]"You're out of your mind," they told her. When she kept insisting that it was so, they said, "It must be his angel."

[16]But Peter kept on knocking, and when they opened the door and saw him, they were astonished. [17]Peter motioned with his hand for them to be quiet and described how the Lord had brought him out of prison. "Tell James and the brothers about this," he said, and then he left for another place.

[18]In the morning, there was no small commotion among the soldiers as to what had become of Peter. [19]After Herod had a thorough search made for him and did not find him, he cross-examined the guards and ordered that they be executed.

HEROD'S DEATH

Then Herod went from Judea to Caesarea and stayed there a while. [20]He had been quarreling with the people of Tyre and Sidon; they now joined together and sought an audience with him. Having secured the support of Blastus, a trusted personal servant of the king, they asked for peace, because they depended on the king's country for their food supply.

[21]On the appointed day Herod, wearing his royal robes, sat on his throne and delivered a public address to the people. [22]They shouted, "This is the voice of a god, not of a man." [23]Immediately, because Herod did not give praise to God, an angel of the Lord struck him down, and he was eaten by worms and died.

[24]But the word of God continued to increase and spread.

[25]When Barnabas and Saul had finished their mission, they returned from[a] Jerusalem, taking with them John, also called Mark.

BARNABAS AND SAUL SENT OFF

13 In the church at Antioch there were prophets and teachers: Barnabas, Simeon called Niger, Lucius of Cyrene, Manaen (who had been brought up with Herod the tetrarch) and Saul. [2]While they were worshiping the Lord and fasting, the Holy Spirit said, "Set apart for me Barnabas and Saul for the work to which I have called them." [3]So after they had fasted and prayed, they placed their hands on them and sent them off.

ON CYPRUS

[4]The two of them, sent on their way by the Holy Spirit, went down to Seleucia and sailed from there to Cyprus. [5]When they arrived at Salamis, they proclaimed the word of God in the Jewish synagogues. John was with them as their helper.

[6]They traveled through the whole island until they came to Paphos. There they met a Jewish sorcerer and false prophet named Bar-Jesus, [7]who was an attendant of the proconsul, Sergius Paulus. The proconsul, an intelligent man, sent for Barnabas and Saul because he wanted to hear the word of God. [8]But Elymas the sorcerer (for that is what his name means) opposed them and tried to turn the proconsul from the faith. [9]Then Saul, who was also called Paul, filled with the Holy Spirit, looked straight at Elymas and said, [10]"You are a child of the devil and an enemy of everything that is right! You are full of all kinds of deceit and trickery. Will you never stop perverting the right ways of the Lord? [11]Now the hand of the Lord is against you. You are going to be blind, and for a time you will be unable to see the light of the sun."

Immediately mist and darkness came over him, and he groped about, seeking someone to lead him by the hand. [12]When the proconsul saw what had happened, he believed, for he was amazed at the teaching about the Lord.

IN PISIDIAN ANTIOCH

[13]From Paphos, Paul and his companions sailed to Perga in Pamphylia, where John left them to return to Jerusalem. [14]From Perga they went on to Pisidian Antioch. On the Sabbath they entered the syn-

---

[a] 25 Some manuscripts *to*

agogue and sat down. [15]After the reading from the Law and the Prophets, the synagogue rulers sent word to them, saying, "Brothers, if you have a message of encouragement for the people, please speak."

[16]Standing up, Paul motioned with his hand and said: "Men of Israel and you Gentiles who worship God, listen to me! [17]The God of the people of Israel chose our fathers; he made the people prosper during their stay in Egypt, with mighty power he led them out of that country, [18]he endured their conduct[a] for about forty years in the desert, [19]he overthrew seven nations in Canaan and gave their land to his people as their inheritance. [20]All this took about 450 years.

"After this, God gave them judges until the time of Samuel the prophet. [21]Then the people asked for a king, and he gave them Saul son of Kish, of the tribe of Benjamin, who ruled forty years. [22]After removing Saul, he made David their king. He testified concerning him: 'I have found David son of Jesse a man after my own heart; he will do everything I want him to do.'

[23]"From this man's descendants God has brought to Israel the Savior Jesus, as he promised. [24]Before the coming of Jesus, John preached repentance and baptism to all the people of Israel. [25]As John was completing his work, he said: 'Who do you think I am? I am not that one. No, but he is coming after me, whose sandals I am not worthy to untie.'

[26]"Brothers, children of Abraham, and you God-fearing Gentiles, it is to us that this message of salvation has been sent. [27]The people of Jerusalem and their rulers did not recognize Jesus, yet in condemning him they fulfilled the words of the prophets that are read every Sabbath. [28]Though they found no proper ground for a death sentence, they asked Pilate to have him executed. [29]When they had carried out all that was written about him, they took him down from the tree and laid him in a tomb. [30]But God raised him from the dead, [31]and for many days he was seen by those who had traveled with him from Galilee to Jerusalem. They are now his witnesses to our people.

[32]"We tell you the good news: What God promised our fathers [33]he has fulfilled for us, their children, by raising up Jesus. As it is written in the second Psalm:

"'You are my Son;
today I have become your Father.'[b][c]

[34]The fact that God raised him from the dead, never to decay, is stated in these words:

"'I will give you the holy and sure blessings promised to David.'[d]

[35]So it is stated elsewhere:

"'You will not let your Holy One see decay.'[e]

[36]"For when David had served God's purpose in his own generation, he fell asleep; he was buried with his fathers and his body decayed. [37]But the one whom God raised from the dead did not see decay.

[38]"Therefore, my brothers, I want you to know that through Jesus the forgiveness of sins is proclaimed to you. [39]Through him everyone who believes is justified from everything you could not be justified from by the law of Moses. [40]Take care that what the prophets have said does not happen to you:

[41]"'Look, you scoffers,
wonder and perish,
for I am going to do something in your days
that you would never believe,
even if someone told you.'"

[42]As Paul and Barnabas were leaving the synagogue, the people invited them to speak further about these things on the next Sabbath. [43]When the congregation was dismissed, many of the Jews and devout converts to Judaism followed Paul and Barnabas, who talked with them and urged them to continue in the grace of God.

[44]On the next Sabbath almost the whole city gathered to hear the word of the Lord. [45]When the Jews saw the crowds, they were filled with jealousy and talked abusively against what Paul was saying.

[46]Then Paul and Barnabas answered them boldly: "We had to speak the word of God to you first.

---

[a] *18* Some manuscripts *and cared for them*   [b] *33* Or *have begotten you*   [c] *33* Psalm 2:7   [d] *34* Isaiah 55:3   [e] *35* Psalm 16:10
[f] *41* Hab. 1:5

Since you reject it and do not consider yourselves worthy of eternal life, we now turn to the Gentiles. [47]For this is what the Lord has commanded us:

> " 'I have made you[a] a light for the Gentiles,
> that you[a] may bring salvation to the ends of the earth.'[b]"

[48]When the Gentiles heard this, they were glad and honored the word of the Lord; and all who were appointed for eternal life believed.

[49]The word of the Lord spread through the whole region. [50]But the Jews incited the God-fearing women of high standing and the leading men of the city. They stirred up persecution against Paul and Barnabas, and expelled them from their region. [51]So they shook the dust from their feet in protest against them and went to Iconium. [52]And the disciples were filled with joy and with the Holy Spirit.

IN ICONIUM

14 At Iconium Paul and Barnabas went as usual into the Jewish synagogue. There they spoke so effectively that a great number of Jews and Gentiles believed. [2]But the Jews who refused to believe stirred up the Gentiles and poisoned their minds against the brothers. [3]So Paul and Barnabas spent considerable time there, speaking boldly for the Lord, who confirmed the message of his grace by enabling them to do miraculous signs and wonders. [4]The people of the city were divided; some sided with the Jews, others with the apostles. [5]There was a plot afoot among the Gentiles and Jews, together with their leaders, to mistreat them and stone them. [6]But they found out about it and fled to the Lycaonian cities of Lystra and Derbe and to the surrounding country, [7]where they continued to preach the good news.

IN LYSTRA AND DERBE

[8]In Lystra there sat a man crippled in his feet, who was lame from birth and had never walked. [9]He listened to Paul as he was speaking. Paul looked directly at him, saw that he had faith to be healed [10]and called out, "Stand up on your feet!" At that, the man jumped up and began to walk.

[11]When the crowd saw what Paul had done, they shouted in the Lycaonian language, "The gods have come down to us in human form!" [12]Barnabas they called Zeus, and Paul they called Hermes because he was the chief speaker. [13]The priest of Zeus, whose temple was just outside the city, brought bulls and wreaths to the city gates because he and the crowd wanted to offer sacrifices to them.

[14]But when the apostles Barnabas and Paul heard of this, they tore their clothes and rushed out into the crowd, shouting: [15]"Men, why are you doing this? We too are only men, human like you. We are bringing you good news, telling you to turn from these worthless things to the living God, who made heaven and earth and sea and everything in them. [16]In the past, he let all nations go their own way. [17]Yet he has not left himself without testimony: He has shown kindness by giving you rain from heaven and crops in their seasons; he provides you with plenty of food and fills your hearts with joy." [18]Even with these words, they had difficulty keeping the crowd from sacrificing to them.

[19]Then some Jews came from Antioch and Iconium and won the crowd over. They stoned Paul and dragged him outside the city, thinking he was dead. [20]But after the disciples had gathered around him, he got up and went back into the city. The next day he and Barnabas left for Derbe.

THE RETURN TO ANTIOCH IN SYRIA

[21]They preached the good news in that city and won a large number of disciples. Then they returned to Lystra, Iconium and Antioch, [22]strengthening the disciples and encouraging them to remain true to the faith. "We must go through many hardships to enter the kingdom of God," they said. [23]Paul and Barnabas appointed elders[c] for them in each church and, with prayer and fasting, committed them to the Lord, in whom they had put their trust. [24]After going through Pisidia, they came into Pamphylia, [25]and when they had preached the word in Perga, they went down to Attalia.

[26]From Attalia they sailed back to Antioch, where they had been committed to the grace of God for the work they had now completed. [27]On arriving there, they gathered the church together and reported all that God had done through them and how he had opened the door of faith to the Gentiles. [28]And they stayed there a long time with the disciples.

---

[a] *47* The Greek is singular.   [b] *47* Isaiah 49:6   [c] *23* Or *Barnabas ordained elders*; or *Barnabas had elders elected*

THE COUNCIL AT JERUSALEM

15 Some men came down from Judea to Antioch and were teaching the brothers: "Unless you are circumcised, according to the custom taught by Moses, you cannot be saved." [2]This brought Paul and Barnabas into sharp dispute and debate with them. So Paul and Barnabas were appointed, along with some other believers, to go up to Jerusalem to see the apostles and elders about this question. [3]The church sent them on their way, and as they traveled through Phoenicia and Samaria, they told how the Gentiles had been converted. This news made all the brothers very glad. [4]When they came to Jerusalem, they were welcomed by the church and the apostles and elders, to whom they reported everything God had done through them.

[5]Then some of the believers who belonged to the party of the Pharisees stood up and said, "The Gentiles must be circumcised and required to obey the law of Moses."

[6]The apostles and elders met to consider this question. [7]After much discussion, Peter got up and addressed them: "Brothers, you know that some time ago God made a choice among you that the Gentiles might hear from my lips the message of the gospel and believe. [8]God, who knows the heart, showed that he accepted them by giving the Holy Spirit to them, just as he did to us. [9]He made no distinction between us and them, for he purified their hearts by faith. [10]Now then, why do you try to test God by putting on the necks of the disciples a yoke that neither we nor our fathers have been able to bear? [11]No! We believe it is through the grace of our Lord Jesus that we are saved, just as they are."

[12]The whole assembly became silent as they listened to Barnabas and Paul telling about the miraculous signs and wonders God had done among the Gentiles through them. [13]When they finished, James spoke up: "Brothers, listen to me. [14]Simon[a] has described to us how God at first showed his concern by taking from the Gentiles a people for himself. [15]The words of the prophets are in agreement with this, as it is written:

[16] " 'After this I will return
  and rebuild David's fallen tent.
  Its ruins I will rebuild,
  and I will restore it,
[17]that the remnant of men may seek the Lord,
  and all the Gentiles who bear my name,
  says the Lord, who does these things'[b]
[18] that have been known for ages.[c]

[19]"It is my judgment, therefore, that we should not make it difficult for the Gentiles who are turning to God. [20]Instead we should write to them, telling them to abstain from food polluted by idols, from sexual immorality, from the meat of strangled animals and from blood. [21]For Moses has been preached in every city from the earliest times and is read in the synagogues on every Sabbath."

THE COUNCIL'S LETTER TO GENTILE BELIEVERS

[22]Then the apostles and elders, with the whole church, decided to choose some of their own men and send them to Antioch with Paul and Barnabas. They chose Judas (called Barsabbas) and Silas, two men who were leaders among the brothers. [23]With them they sent the following letter:

The apostles and elders, your brothers,

To the Gentile believers in Antioch, Syria and Cilicia:

Greetings.

[24]We have heard that some went out from us without our authorization and disturbed you, troubling your minds by what they said. [25]So we all agreed to choose some men and send them to you with our dear friends Barnabas and Paul— [26]men who have risked their lives for the name of our Lord Jesus Christ. [27]Therefore we are sending Judas and Silas to confirm by word of mouth what we are writing. [28]It seemed good to the Holy Spirit and to us not to burden you with anything beyond the following requirements: [29]You are to abstain from food sacrificed to

---

[a] 14 Greek *Simeon*, a variant of *Simon*; that is, Peter   [b] 17 Amos 9:11,12   [c] 17,18 Some manuscripts *things'— / [18]known to the Lord for ages is his work*

idols, from blood, from the meat of strangled animals and from sexual immorality. You will do well to avoid these things.

Farewell.

[30] The men were sent off and went down to Antioch, where they gathered the church together and delivered the letter. [31] The people read it and were glad for its encouraging message. [32] Judas and Silas, who themselves were prophets, said much to encourage and strengthen the brothers. [33] After spending some time there, they were sent off by the brothers with the blessing of peace to return to those who had sent them.[a] [35] But Paul and Barnabas remained in Antioch, where they and many others taught and preached the word of the Lord.

NOW OR NEVER
AC 15:36–41

The Bible doesn't tell us who was right and who was wrong in Paul and Barnabas's disagreement. The important thing is that their falling out didn't last forever. Paul's continued love and respect for Barnabas can be seen in more than one of his letters (see 1 Corinthians 9:6; Colossians 4:10).

DISAGREEMENT BETWEEN PAUL AND BARNABAS

[36] Some time later Paul said to Barnabas, "Let us go back and visit the brothers in all the towns where we preached the word of the Lord and see how they are doing." [37] Barnabas wanted to take John, also called Mark, with them, [38] but Paul did not think it wise to take him, because he had deserted them in Pamphylia and had not continued with them in the work. [39] They had such a sharp disagreement that they parted company. Barnabas took Mark and sailed for Cyprus, [40] but Paul chose Silas and left, commended by the brothers to the grace of the Lord. [41] He went through Syria and Cilicia, strengthening the churches.

TIMOTHY JOINS PAUL AND SILAS

16 He came to Derbe and then to Lystra, where a disciple named Timothy lived, whose mother was a Jewess and a believer, but whose father was a Greek. [2] The brothers at Lystra and Iconium spoke well of him. [3] Paul wanted to take him along on the journey, so he circumcised him because of the Jews who lived in that area, for they all knew that his father was a Greek. [4] As they traveled from town to town, they delivered the decisions reached by the apostles and elders in Jerusalem for the people to obey. [5] So the churches were strengthened in the faith and grew daily in numbers.

PAUL'S VISION OF THE MAN OF MACEDONIA

[6] Paul and his companions traveled throughout the region of Phrygia and Galatia, having been kept by the Holy Spirit from preaching the word in the province of Asia. [7] When they came to the border of Mysia, they tried to enter Bithynia, but the Spirit of Jesus would not allow them to. [8] So they passed by Mysia and went down to Troas. [9] During the night Paul had a vision of a man of Macedonia standing and begging him, "Come over to Macedonia and help us." [10] After Paul had seen the vision, we got ready at once to leave for Macedonia, concluding that God had called us to preach the gospel to them.

Overcoming Mistakes

Whatever happened to John Mark, the guy whose desertion split up one of the greatest missionary partnerships in Christian history? We do know that he wrote a book about Jesus' life. You can find it starting on page 1309 of this Bible. It's called the Gospel of Mark. You should also know that by the end of his life, Paul was so impressed with Mark that he asked him to visit him. He even called Mark "helpful" (2 Timothy 4:11). Mark proves that no matter how badly you blow it, God can offer you another chance to serve him.

» live the adventure » Ac 15:36–41

---

[a] 33 Some manuscripts *them,* [34]*but Silas decided to remain there*

LYDIA'S CONVERSION IN PHILIPPI

¹¹From Troas we put out to sea and sailed straight for Samothrace, and the next day on to Neapolis. ¹²From there we traveled to Philippi, a Roman colony and the leading city of that district of Macedonia. And we stayed there several days.

¹³On the Sabbath we went outside the city gate to the river, where we expected to find a place of prayer. We sat down and began to speak to the women who had gathered there. ¹⁴One of those listening was a woman named Lydia, a dealer in purple cloth from the city of Thyatira, who was a worshiper of God. The Lord opened her heart to respond to Paul's message. ¹⁵When she and the members of her household were baptized, she invited us to her home. "If you consider me a believer in the Lord," she said, "come and stay at my house." And she persuaded us.

PAUL AND SILAS IN PRISON

¹⁶Once when we were going to the place of prayer, we were met by a slave girl who had a spirit by which she predicted the future. She earned a great deal of money for her owners by fortune-telling.
¹⁷This girl followed Paul and the rest of us, shouting, "These men are servants of the Most High God, who are telling you the way to be saved." ¹⁸She kept this up for many days. Finally Paul became so troubled that he turned around and said to the spirit, "In the name of Jesus Christ I command you to come out of her!" At that moment the spirit left her.

¹⁹When the owners of the slave girl realized that their hope of making money was gone, they seized Paul and Silas and dragged them into the marketplace to face the authorities. ²⁰They brought them before the magistrates and said, "These men are Jews, and are throwing our city into an uproar ²¹by advocating customs unlawful for us Romans to accept or practice."

²²The crowd joined in the attack against Paul and Silas, and the magistrates ordered them to be stripped and beaten. ²³After they had been severely flogged, they were thrown into prison, and the jailer was commanded to guard them carefully. ²⁴Upon receiving such orders, he put them in the inner cell and fastened their feet in the stocks.

²⁵About midnight Paul and Silas were praying and singing hymns to God, and the other prisoners were listening to them. ²⁶Suddenly there was such a violent earthquake that the foundations of the prison were shaken. At once all the prison doors flew open, and everybody's chains came loose. ²⁷The jailer woke up, and when he saw the prison doors open, he drew his sword and was about to kill himself because he thought the prisoners had escaped. ²⁸But Paul shouted, "Don't harm yourself! We are all here!"

²⁹The jailer called for lights, rushed in and fell trembling before Paul and Silas. ³⁰He then brought them out and asked, "Sirs, what must I do to be saved?"

³¹They replied, "Believe in the Lord Jesus, and you will be saved—you and your household." ³²Then they spoke the word of the Lord to him and to all the others in his house. ³³At that hour of the night the jailer took them and washed their wounds; then immediately he and all his family were baptized. ³⁴The jailer brought them into his house and set a meal before them; he was filled with joy because he had come to believe in God—he and his whole family.

³⁵When it was daylight, the magistrates sent their officers to the jailer with the order: "Release those men." ³⁶The jailer told Paul, "The magistrates have ordered that you and Silas be released. Now you can leave. Go in peace."

³⁷But Paul said to the officers: "They beat us publicly without a trial, even though we are Roman cit-

Answering the Big Question

What is it that we're supposed to believe about Jesus? That he's God's Son? That he lived a sinless life? That he died for us? That he rose from the dead? Yes, yes, yes and yes. But there's more to it than just facts. Believing in Jesus means putting all your eggs in one basket. It means depending on him—and him alone—to save you from the punishment you deserve for your sins.

»» live the adventure »» Ac 16:30-31

izens, and threw us into prison. And now do they want to get rid of us quietly? No! Let them come themselves and escort us out."

[38]The officers reported this to the magistrates, and when they heard that Paul and Silas were Roman citizens, they were alarmed. [39]They came to appease them and escorted them from the prison, requesting them to leave the city. [40]After Paul and Silas came out of the prison, they went to Lydia's house, where they met with the brothers and encouraged them. Then they left.

IN THESSALONICA

17 When they had passed through Amphipolis and Apollonia, they came to Thessalonica, where there was a Jewish synagogue. [2]As his custom was, Paul went into the synagogue, and on three Sabbath days he reasoned with them from the Scriptures, [3]explaining and proving that the Christ[a] had to suffer and rise from the dead. "This Jesus I am proclaiming to you is the Christ,[a]" he said. [4]Some of the Jews were persuaded and joined Paul and Silas, as did a large number of God-fearing Greeks and not a few prominent women.

[5]But the Jews were jealous; so they rounded up some bad characters from the marketplace, formed a mob and started a riot in the city. They rushed to Jason's house in search of Paul and Silas in order to bring them out to the crowd.[b] [6]But when they did not find them, they dragged Jason and some other brothers before the city officials, shouting: "These men who have caused trouble all over the world have now come here, [7]and Jason has welcomed them into his house. They are all defying Caesar's decrees, saying that there is another king, one called Jesus." [8]When they heard this, the crowd and the city officials were thrown into turmoil. [9]Then they made Jason and the others post bond and let them go.

IN BEREA

[10]As soon as it was night, the brothers sent Paul and Silas away to Berea. On arriving there, they went to the Jewish synagogue. [11]Now the Bereans were of more noble character than the Thessalonians, for they received the message with great eagerness and examined the Scriptures every day to see if what Paul said was true. [12]Many of the Jews believed, as did also a number of prominent Greek women and many Greek men.

[13]When the Jews in Thessalonica learned that Paul was preaching the word of God at Berea, they went there too, agitating the crowds and stirring them up. [14]The brothers immediately sent Paul to the coast, but Silas and Timothy stayed at Berea. [15]The men who escorted Paul brought him to Athens and then left with instructions for Silas and Timothy to join him as soon as possible.

IN ATHENS

[16]While Paul was waiting for them in Athens, he was greatly distressed to see that the city was full of idols. [17]So he reasoned in the synagogue with the Jews and the God-fearing Greeks, as well as in the marketplace day by day with those who happened to be there. [18]A group of Epicurean and Stoic philosophers began to dispute with him. Some of them asked, "What is this babbler trying to say?" Others remarked, "He seems to be advocating foreign gods." They said this because Paul was preaching the good news about Jesus and the resurrection. [19]Then they took him and brought him to a meeting of the Areopagus, where they said to him, "May we know what this new teaching is that you are presenting? [20]You are bringing some strange ideas to our ears, and we want to know what they mean." [21](All the Athenians and the foreigners who lived there spent their time doing nothing but talking about and listening to the latest ideas.)

[22]Paul then stood up in the meeting of the Areopagus and said: "Men of Athens! I see that in every way you are very religious. [23]For as I walked around and looked carefully at your objects of worship, I even found an altar with this inscription: TO AN UNKNOWN GOD. Now what you worship as something unknown I am going to proclaim to you.

[24]"The God who made the world and everything in it is the Lord of heaven and earth and does not live in temples built by hands. [25]And he is not served by human hands, as if he needed anything, because he himself gives all men life and breath and everything else. [26]From one man he made every nation of men, that they should inhabit the whole earth; and he determined the times set for them and the exact places where they should live. [27]God did this so that men would seek him and perhaps reach out

---

[a] *3 Or Messiah*   [b] *5 Or the assembly of the people*

jason

the mob

» A Christian convert in Thessalonica
» Showed hospitality to the missionaries Paul and Silas
» Was roughed up by an angry mob

» Led by a group of Jews who rejected Paul and Silas's message
» Accused Paul and Silas of treason against Caesar
» Dragged Jason to the authorities

The Main Event

Pretend you're Jason. You're just a regular guy living in Thessalonica. One day you hear a traveling preacher named Paul speak, and everything he says makes perfect sense. He talks about the death and resurrection of a man named Jesus. He explains how this man is the Christ—the Messiah spoken of by the prophets, the Savior sent by God to deliver the world from sin. According to Paul, this Jesus is the King above all kings, the absolute Lord of the universe.

Paul's words go straight to your heart. His message rings true. You embrace it, and immediately you are ushered into a totally new kind of life. And since you have a decent-sized home, you invite Paul and his entourage to stay with you. All day and night, believers are coming and going. They include Jews, Gentiles and women—people who normally didn't associate with each other before finding a common faith in Jesus. It's nonstop excitement. You're growing in your newfound faith and seeing many other people meet Christ too.

One day everything abruptly changes. Maybe you're in the middle of a Scripture discussion or a prayer time with some of your new friends when you hear a commotion outside. Someone—make that a whole lot of someones—is pounding on your door. The next thing you know, you're being yanked out of your own house (along with the rest of your fellow believers) by an angry mob. They rough you up, spit on you and verbally abuse you as they literally drag you down the street to the nearest police station. Once there, you endure a round of questioning from the city officials. Only after you've posted bond are you free to leave.

What is this about? you wonder. *Why is this mob so angry and violent? Is this kind of treatment going to be a regular part of my new life?*

The Outcome

The apostle Paul (who was absent when the mob came looking for him) would say, "Hey, Jason, you might as well get used to such treatment." In fact, that's precisely what he told another young believer named Timothy: "Everyone who wants to live a godly life in Christ Jesus will be persecuted" (2 Timothy 3:12).

Jason's experience is helpful to us because sooner or later we're all going to face opposition to our faith. The "mob" you face may not be as violent as the one Jason faced. The abuse they toss your way may be more emotional, social and verbal than physical. But if you stand openly with Jesus and his followers, you'd better be prepared to stand against the crowd.

Are you up for that? Do you, like Jason, have a group of Christian brothers and sisters who will stand by you when you go through such trials?

The prospect and promise of trouble isn't fun to ponder, but look at it this way: You'll be part of a small group responsible for turning the world upside down.

Read more about Jason and the mob in Acts 17:1–9 (page 1435).

for him and find him, though he is not far from each one of us. 28'For in him we live and move and have our being.' As some of your own poets have said, 'We are his offspring.'

29"Therefore since we are God's offspring, we should not think that the divine being is like gold or silver or stone—an image made by man's design and skill. 30In the past God overlooked such ignorance, but now he commands all people everywhere to repent. 31For he has set a day when he will judge the world with justice by the man he has appointed. He has given proof of this to all men by raising him from the dead."

32When they heard about the resurrection of the dead, some of them sneered, but others said, "We want to hear you again on this subject." 33At that, Paul left the Council. 34A few men became followers of Paul and believed. Among them was Dionysius, a member of the Areopagus, also a woman named Damaris, and a number of others.

Explaining Difficult Bible Teachings

» live the adventure » Ac 17:20-34

Which of Jesus' teachings do you think seems the strangest to your non-Christian friends? His idea of showing love to your enemies? His idea of turning the other cheek to someone who hurts you? Maybe his idea of losing your life in order to find it? If you're serious about introducing your friends to Jesus, then how are you going to explain your faith to them? Try helping them see the logic in Jesus' teachings . . . help them understand that sometimes "strange" is good.

IN CORINTH

18

After this, Paul left Athens and went to Corinth. 2There he met a Jew named Aquila, a native of Pontus, who had recently come from Italy with his wife Priscilla, because Claudius had ordered all the Jews to leave Rome. Paul went to see them, 3and because he was a tentmaker as they were, he stayed and worked with them. 4Every Sabbath he reasoned in the synagogue, trying to persuade Jews and Greeks.

5When Silas and Timothy came from Macedonia, Paul devoted himself exclusively to preaching, testifying to the Jews that Jesus was the Christ.a 6But when the Jews opposed Paul and became abusive, he shook out his clothes in protest and said to them, "Your blood be on your own heads! I am clear of my responsibility. From now on I will go to the Gentiles."

7Then Paul left the synagogue and went next door to the house of Titius Justus, a worshiper of God. 8Crispus, the synagogue ruler, and his entire household believed in the Lord; and many of the Corinthians who heard him believed and were baptized.

9One night the Lord spoke to Paul in a vision: "Do not be afraid; keep on speaking, do not be silent. 10For I am with you, and no one is going to attack and harm you, because I have many people in this city." 11So Paul stayed for a year and a half, teaching them the word of God.

12While Gallio was proconsul of Achaia, the Jews made a united attack on Paul and brought him into court. 13"This man," they charged, "is persuading the people to worship God in ways contrary to the law."

14Just as Paul was about to speak, Gallio said to the Jews, "If you Jews were making a complaint about some misdemeanor or serious crime, it would be reasonable for me to listen to you. 15But since it involves questions about words and names and your own law—settle the matter yourselves. I will not be a judge of such things." 16So he had them ejected from the court. 17Then they all turned on Sosthenes the synagogue ruler and beat him in front of the court. But Gallio showed no concern whatever.

AC 18:5-6

For everyone who ever asked, "How could a loving God send people to hell?" here's the answer. Those who spend an eternity in hell have no one to blame but themselves for refusing to listen to and believe the truth that Jesus is Lord.

---

a 5 Or *Messiah;* also in verse 28

PRISCILLA, AQUILA AND APOLLOS

18Paul stayed on in Corinth for some time. Then he left the brothers and sailed for Syria, accompanied by Priscilla and Aquila. Before he sailed, he had his hair cut off at Cenchrea because of a vow he had taken. 19They arrived at Ephesus, where Paul left Priscilla and Aquila. He himself went into the synagogue and reasoned with the Jews. 20When they asked him to spend more time with them, he declined. 21But as he left, he promised, "I will come back if it is God's will." Then he set sail from Ephesus. 22When he landed at Caesarea, he went up and greeted the church and then went down to Antioch.

23After spending some time in Antioch, Paul set out from there and traveled from place to place throughout the region of Galatia and Phrygia, strengthening all the disciples.

24Meanwhile a Jew named Apollos, a native of Alexandria, came to Ephesus. He was a learned man, with a thorough knowledge of the Scriptures. 25He had been instructed in the way of the Lord, and he spoke with great fervor[a] and taught about Jesus accurately, though he knew only the baptism of John. 26He began to speak boldly in the synagogue. When Priscilla and Aquila heard him, they invited him to their home and explained to him the way of God more adequately.

27When Apollos wanted to go to Achaia, the brothers encouraged him and wrote to the disciples there to welcome him. On arriving, he was a great help to those who by grace had believed. 28For he vigorously refuted the Jews in public debate, proving from the Scriptures that Jesus was the Christ.

PAUL IN EPHESUS

19 While Apollos was at Corinth, Paul took the road through the interior and arrived at Ephesus. There he found some disciples 2and asked them, "Did you receive the Holy Spirit when[b] you believed?"

They answered, "No, we have not even heard that there is a Holy Spirit."

3So Paul asked, "Then what baptism did you receive?"

"John's baptism," they replied.

4Paul said, "John's baptism was a baptism of repentance. He told the people to believe in the one coming after him, that is, in Jesus." 5On hearing this, they were baptized into[c] the name of the Lord Jesus. 6When Paul placed his hands on them, the Holy Spirit came on them, and they spoke in tongues[d] and prophesied. 7There were about twelve men in all.

8Paul entered the synagogue and spoke boldly there for three months, arguing persuasively about the kingdom of God. 9But some of them became obstinate; they refused to believe and publicly maligned the Way. So Paul left them. He took the disciples with him and had discussions daily in the lecture hall of Tyrannus. 10This went on for two years, so that all the Jews and Greeks who lived in the province of Asia heard the word of the Lord.

11God did extraordinary miracles through Paul, 12so that even handkerchiefs and aprons that had touched him were taken to the sick, and their illnesses were cured and the evil spirits left them.

13Some Jews who went around driving out evil spirits tried to invoke the name of the Lord Jesus over those who were demon-possessed. They would say, "In the name of Jesus, whom Paul preaches, I command you to come out." 14Seven sons of Sceva, a Jewish chief priest, were doing this. 15⌊One day⌋ the evil spirit answered them, "Jesus I know, and I know about Paul, but who are you?" 16Then the man who had the evil spirit jumped on them and overpowered them all. He gave them such a beating that they ran out of the house naked and bleeding.

17When this became known to the Jews and Greeks living in Ephesus, they were all seized with fear, and the name of the Lord Jesus was held in high honor. 18Many of those who believed now came and openly confessed their evil deeds. 19A number who had practiced sorcery brought their scrolls together and burned them publicly. When they calculated the value of the scrolls, the total came to fifty thousand drachmas.[e] 20In this way the word of the Lord spread widely and grew in power.

21After all this had happened, Paul decided to go to Jerusalem, passing through Macedonia and Achaia. "After I have been there," he said, "I must visit Rome also." 22He sent two of his helpers, Timothy and Erastus, to Macedonia, while he stayed in the province of Asia a little longer.

THE RIOT IN EPHESUS

23About that time there arose a great disturbance about the Way. 24A silversmith named Demetrius, who made silver shrines of Artemis, brought in no little business for the craftsmen. 25He called

---

[a] 25 Or with fervor in the Spirit   [b] 2 Or after   [c] 5 Or in   [d] 6 Or other languages   [e] 19 A drachma was a silver coin worth about a day's wages.

demetrius

» A pagan silversmith
» Made lots of money selling silver images of the goddess Artemis
» Became angry at Paul for threatening his livelihood

paul

» An apostle of Jesus Christ
» Unafraid to speak the truth
» Was willing to go into the amphitheater at Ephesus to face an angry mob of violent opponents

The Main Event

The showdown between Demetrius and Paul occurred in Ephesus, a hotbed of pagan religions. Ephesus was not only a center for those immersed in the occult, but it was also home to the great temple of the goddess Artemis, or Diana, as she was also called.

The courageous Paul entered the godless city of Ephesus and began proclaiming the truth about Jesus. God performed incredible miracles through Paul, and people began turning to Christ in droves, which meant they were turning *away* from their old beliefs and practices.

Demetrius was a merchant who made a living selling supplies and religious artifacts to Artemis worshipers. In fact, he did pretty well for himself in the trade. But with Paul preaching that Jesus was the one true God, there were fewer and fewer shoppers . . . which meant Demetrius saw a huge drop in his revenue and profit margin.

Demetrius decided to act. He called an emergency meeting of all the other shop owners in the city. Under the guise of civic pride and religious devotion, he incited a near riot. "Are we going to let this guy come in here, insult our belief system and tarnish the name of Artemis?" the silversmith asked.

"No!" the other craftsmen roared. Then they proceeded to shout at everybody and nobody for two hours straight. Pretty soon they had the whole town in an uproar, and a mob of angry citizens was marching its way to the local amphitheater.

What's really amazing about this story is that Paul was ready to go right into that amphitheater—right into the lion's mouth—to address the fuming crowd. Unconcerned for his own safety, all Paul could see was a group of people who desperately needed to hear the good news about Jesus.

The apostle's friends talked him out of his plan. And eventually the mayor of Ephesus restored order in the city. But the gospel was in Ephesus to stay. And it's a pretty good bet that Demetrius saw his once-great profits continue to shrink.

The Outcome

There are a lot of guys like Demetrius—guys whose number-one priority is cash flow. All they care about is making a good living. Their focus is on the material world. And they are not above using religion to collect a buck or two.

However, God calls his followers to be like the apostle Paul. Paul's twin passions in life were knowing Christ and making him known to others. In any contest between spiritual truth and material desire, the truth always took priority in Paul's life. He saw clearly that souls matter far more than sales.

Perhaps God will lead you to go into business some day. If so, commit yourself to being the rare kind of man who uses his position to further the gospel . . . and not the other way around.

Read more about Demetrius and Paul in Acts 19:23–41 (pages 1438–1440).

them together, along with the workmen in related trades, and said: "Men, you know we receive a good income from this business. 26And you see and hear how this fellow Paul has convinced and led astray large numbers of people here in Ephesus and in practically the whole province of Asia. He says that man-made gods are no gods at all. 27There is danger not only that our trade will lose its good name, but also that the temple of the great goddess Artemis will be discredited, and the goddess herself, who is worshiped throughout the province of Asia and the world, will be robbed of her divine majesty."

28When they heard this, they were furious and began shouting: "Great is Artemis of the Ephesians!" 29Soon the whole city was in an uproar. The people seized Gaius and Aristarchus, Paul's traveling companions from Macedonia, and rushed as one man into the theater. 30Paul wanted to appear before the crowd, but the disciples would not let him. 31Even some of the officials of the province, friends of Paul, sent him a message begging him not to venture into the theater.

32The assembly was in confusion: Some were shouting one thing, some another. Most of the people did not even know why they were there. 33The Jews pushed Alexander to the front, and some of the crowd shouted instructions to him. He motioned for silence in order to make a defense before the people. 34But when they realized he was a Jew, they all shouted in unison for about two hours: "Great is Artemis of the Ephesians!"

35The city clerk quieted the crowd and said: "Men of Ephesus, doesn't all the world know that the city of Ephesus is the guardian of the temple of the great Artemis and of her image, which fell from heaven? 36Therefore, since these facts are undeniable, you ought to be quiet and not do anything rash. 37You have brought these men here, though they have neither robbed temples nor blasphemed our goddess. 38If, then, Demetrius and his fellow craftsmen have a grievance against anybody, the courts are open and there are proconsuls. They can press charges. 39If there is anything further you want to bring up, it must be settled in a legal assembly. 40As it is, we are in danger of being charged with rioting because of today's events. In that case we would not be able to account for this commotion, since there is no reason for it." 41After he had said this, he dismissed the assembly.

THROUGH MACEDONIA AND GREECE

20 When the uproar had ended, Paul sent for the disciples and, after encouraging them, said good-by and set out for Macedonia. 2He traveled through that area, speaking many words of encouragement to the people, and finally arrived in Greece, 3where he stayed three months. Because the Jews made a plot against him just as he was about to sail for Syria, he decided to go back through Macedonia. 4He was accompanied by Sopater son of Pyrrhus from Berea, Aristarchus and Secundus from Thessalonica, Gaius from Derbe, Timothy also, and Tychicus and Trophimus from the province of Asia. 5These men went on ahead and waited for us at Troas. 6But we sailed from Philippi after the Feast of Unleavened Bread, and five days later joined the others at Troas, where we stayed seven days.

EUTYCHUS RAISED FROM THE DEAD AT TROAS

7On the first day of the week we came together to break bread. Paul spoke to the people and, because he intended to leave the next day, kept on talking until midnight. 8There were many lamps in the upstairs room where we were meeting. 9Seated in a window was a young man named Eutychus, who was sinking into a deep sleep as Paul talked on and on. When he was sound asleep, he fell to the ground from the third story and was picked up dead. 10Paul went down, threw himself on the young man and put his arms around him. "Don't be alarmed," he said. "He's alive!" 11Then he went upstairs again and broke bread and ate. After talking until daylight, he left. 12The people took the young man home alive and were greatly comforted.

PAUL'S FAREWELL TO THE EPHESIAN ELDERS

13We went on ahead to the ship and sailed for Assos, where we were going to take Paul aboard. He had made this arrangement because he was going there on foot. 14When he met us at Assos, we took him aboard and went on to Mitylene. 15The next day we set sail from there and arrived off Kios. The day after that we crossed over to Samos, and on the following day arrived at Miletus. 16Paul had decided to sail past Ephesus to avoid spending time in the province of Asia, for he was in a hurry to reach Jerusalem, if possible, by the day of Pentecost.

17From Miletus, Paul sent to Ephesus for the elders of the church. 18When they arrived, he said to them: "You know how I lived the whole time I was with you, from the first day I came into the province of Asia. 19I served the Lord with great humility and with tears, although I was severely tested by the plots of the Jews. 20You know that I have not hesitated to preach anything that would be helpful to you but have taught you publicly and from house to house. 21I have declared to both Jews and Greeks that they must turn to God in repentance and have faith in our Lord Jesus.

22"And now, compelled by the Spirit, I am going to Jerusalem, not knowing what will happen to me there. 23I only know that in every city the Holy Spirit warns me that prison and hardships are facing me. 24However, I consider my life worth nothing to me, if only I may finish the race and complete the task the Lord Jesus has given me—the task of testifying to the gospel of God's grace.

25"Now I know that none of you among whom I have gone about preaching the kingdom will ever see me again. 26Therefore, I declare to you today that I am innocent of the blood of all men. 27For I have not hesitated to proclaim to you the whole will of God. 28Keep watch over yourselves and all the flock of which the Holy Spirit has made you overseers.[a] Be shepherds of the church of God,[b] which he bought with his own blood. 29I know that after I leave, savage wolves will come in among you and will not spare the flock. 30Even from your own number men will arise and distort the truth in order to draw away disciples after them. 31So be on your guard! Remember that for three years I never stopped warning each of you night and day with tears.

32"Now I commit you to God and to the word of his grace, which can build you up and give you an inheritance among all those who are sanctified. 33I have not coveted anyone's silver or gold or clothing. 34You yourselves know that these hands of mine have supplied my own needs and the needs of my companions. 35In everything I did, I showed you that by this kind of hard work we must help the weak, remembering the words the Lord Jesus himself said: 'It is more blessed to give than to receive.' "

36When he had said this, he knelt down with all of them and prayed. 37They all wept as they embraced him and kissed him. 38What grieved them most was his statement that they would never see his face again. Then they accompanied him to the ship.

ON TO JERUSALEM

21

After we had torn ourselves away from them, we put out to sea and sailed straight to Cos. The next day we went to Rhodes and from there to Patara. 2We found a ship crossing over to Phoenicia, went on board and set sail. 3After sighting Cyprus and passing to the south of it, we sailed on to Syria. We landed at Tyre, where our ship was to unload its cargo. 4Finding the disciples there, we stayed with them seven days. Through the Spirit they urged Paul not to go on to Jerusalem. 5But when our time was up, we left and continued on our way. All the disciples and their wives and children accompanied us out of the city, and there on the beach we knelt to pray. 6After saying good-by to each other, we went aboard the ship, and they returned home.

7We continued our voyage from Tyre and landed at Ptolemais, where we greeted the brothers and stayed with them for a day. 8Leaving the next day, we reached Caesarea and stayed at the house of Philip the evangelist, one of the Seven. 9He had four unmarried daughters who prophesied.

10After we had been there a number of days, a prophet named Agabus came down from Judea. 11Coming over to us, he took Paul's belt, tied his own hands and feet with it and said, "The Holy Spirit says, 'In this way the Jews of Jerusalem will bind the owner of this belt and will hand him over to the Gentiles.' "

12When we heard this, we and the people there pleaded with Paul not to go up to Jerusalem. 13Then Paul answered, "Why are you weeping and breaking my heart? I am ready not only to be bound, but also to die in Jerusalem for the name of the Lord Jesus." 14When he would not be dissuaded, we gave up and said, "The Lord's will be done."

15After this, we got ready and went up to Jerusalem. 16Some of the disciples from Caesarea accompanied us and brought us to the home of Mnason, where we were to stay. He was a man from Cyprus and one of the early disciples.

PAUL'S ARRIVAL AT JERUSALEM

17When we arrived at Jerusalem, the brothers received us warmly. 18The next day Paul and the rest

---

a 28 Traditionally bishops   b 28 Many manuscripts of the Lord of us went to see James, and all the elders were present. [19]Paul greeted them and reported in detail what God had done among the Gentiles through his ministry.

[20]When they heard this, they praised God. Then they said to Paul: "You see, brother, how many thousands of Jews have believed, and all of them are zealous for the law. [21]They have been informed that you teach all the Jews who live among the Gentiles to turn away from Moses, telling them not to circumcise their children or live according to our customs. [22]What shall we do? They will certainly hear that you have come, [23]so do what we tell you. There are four men with us who have made a vow. [24]Take these men, join in their purification rites and pay their expenses, so that they can have their heads shaved. Then everybody will know there is no truth in these reports about you, but that you yourself are living in obedience to the law. [25]As for the Gentile believers, we have written to them our decision that they should abstain from food sacrificed to idols, from blood, from the meat of strangled animals and from sexual immorality."

[26]The next day Paul took the men and purified himself along with them. Then he went to the temple to give notice of the date when the days of purification would end and the offering would be made for each of them.

PAUL ARRESTED

[27]When the seven days were nearly over, some Jews from the province of Asia saw Paul at the temple. They stirred up the whole crowd and seized him, [28]shouting, "Men of Israel, help us! This is the man who teaches all men everywhere against our people and our law and this place. And besides, he has brought Greeks into the temple area and defiled this holy place." [29](They had previously seen Trophimus the Ephesian in the city with Paul and assumed that Paul had brought him into the temple area.)

[30]The whole city was aroused, and the people came running from all directions. Seizing Paul, they dragged him from the temple, and immediately the gates were shut. [31]While they were trying to kill him, news reached the commander of the Roman troops that the whole city of Jerusalem was in an uproar. [32]He at once took some officers and soldiers and ran down to the crowd. When the rioters saw the commander and his soldiers, they stopped beating Paul.

[33]The commander came up and arrested him and ordered him to be bound with two chains. Then he asked who he was and what he had done. [34]Some in the crowd shouted one thing and some another, and since the commander could not get at the truth because of the uproar, he ordered that Paul be taken into the barracks. [35]When Paul reached the steps, the violence of the mob was so great he had to be carried by the soldiers. [36]The crowd that followed kept shouting, "Away with him!"

PAUL SPEAKS TO THE CROWD

[37]As the soldiers were about to take Paul into the barracks, he asked the commander, "May I say something to you?"

"Do you speak Greek?" he replied. [38]"Aren't you the Egyptian who started a revolt and led four thousand terrorists out into the desert some time ago?"

[39]Paul answered, "I am a Jew, from Tarsus in Cilicia, a citizen of no ordinary city. Please let me speak to the people."

[40]Having received the commander's permission, Paul stood on the steps and motioned to the crowd.

22 When they were all silent, he said to them in Aramaic[a]: [1]"Brothers and fathers, listen now to my defense."

[2]When they heard him speak to them in Aramaic, they became very quiet.

Then Paul said: [3]"I am a Jew, born in Tarsus of Cilicia, but brought up in this city. Under Gamaliel I was thoroughly trained in the law of our fathers and was just as zealous for God as any of you are today. [4]I persecuted the followers of this Way to their death, arresting both men and women and throwing them into prison, [5]as also the high priest and all the Council can testify. I even obtained letters from them to their brothers in Damascus, and went there to bring these people as prisoners to Jerusalem to be punished.

[6]"About noon as I came near Damascus, suddenly a bright light from heaven flashed around me. [7]I fell to the ground and heard a voice say to me, 'Saul! Saul! Why do you persecute me?'

[8]" 'Who are you, Lord?' I asked.

---

[a] 40 Or possibly *Hebrew*; also in 22:2

" 'I am Jesus of Nazareth, whom you are persecuting,' he replied. [9]My companions saw the light, but they did not understand the voice of him who was speaking to me.

[10]" 'What shall I do, Lord?' I asked.

" 'Get up,' the Lord said, 'and go into Damascus. There you will be told all that you have been assigned to do.' [11]My companions led me by the hand into Damascus, because the brilliance of the light had blinded me.

[12]"A man named Ananias came to see me. He was a devout observer of the law and highly respected by all the Jews living there. [13]He stood beside me and said, 'Brother Saul, receive your sight!' And at that very moment I was able to see him.

[14]"Then he said: 'The God of our fathers has chosen you to know his will and to see the Righteous One and to hear words from his mouth. [15]You will be his witness to all men of what you have seen and heard. [16]And now what are you waiting for? Get up, be baptized and wash your sins away, calling on his name.'

[17]"When I returned to Jerusalem and was praying at the temple, I fell into a trance [18]and saw the Lord speaking. 'Quick!' he said to me. 'Leave Jerusalem immediately, because they will not accept your testimony about me.'

[19]" 'Lord,' I replied, 'these men know that I went from one synagogue to another to imprison and beat those who believe in you. [20]And when the blood of your martyr[a] Stephen was shed, I stood there giving my approval and guarding the clothes of those who were killing him.'

[21]"Then the Lord said to me, 'Go; I will send you far away to the Gentiles.' "

PAUL THE ROMAN CITIZEN

[22]The crowd listened to Paul until he said this. Then they raised their voices and shouted, "Rid the earth of him! He's not fit to live!"

[23]As they were shouting and throwing off their cloaks and flinging dust into the air, [24]the commander ordered Paul to be taken into the barracks. He directed that he be flogged and questioned in order to find out why the people were shouting at him like this. [25]As they stretched him out to flog him, Paul said to the centurion standing there, "Is it legal for you to flog a Roman citizen who hasn't even been found guilty?"

[26]When the centurion heard this, he went to the commander and reported it. "What are you going to do?" he asked. "This man is a Roman citizen."

[27]The commander went to Paul and asked, "Tell me, are you a Roman citizen?"

"Yes, I am," he answered.

[28]Then the commander said, "I had to pay a big price for my citizenship."

"But I was born a citizen," Paul replied.

[29]Those who were about to question him withdrew immediately. The commander himself was alarmed when he realized that he had put Paul, a Roman citizen, in chains.

BEFORE THE SANHEDRIN

[30]The next day, since the commander wanted to find out exactly why Paul was being accused by the Jews, he released him and ordered the chief priests and all the Sanhedrin to assemble. Then he brought Paul and had him stand before them.

23 Paul looked straight at the Sanhedrin and said, "My brothers, I have fulfilled my duty to God in all good conscience to this day." [2]At this the high priest Ananias ordered those standing near Paul to strike him on the mouth. [3]Then Paul said to him, "God will strike you, you whitewashed wall! You sit there to judge me according to the law, yet you yourself violate the law by commanding that I be struck!"

[4]Those who were standing near Paul said, "You dare to insult God's high priest?"

[5]Paul replied, "Brothers, I did not realize that he was the high priest; for it is written: 'Do not speak evil about the ruler of your people.'[b]"

[6]Then Paul, knowing that some of them were Sadducees and the others Pharisees, called out in the Sanhedrin, "My brothers, I am a Pharisee, the son of a Pharisee. I stand on trial because of my hope in the resurrection of the dead." [7]When he said this, a dispute broke out between the Pharisees and the

---

[a] 20 Or *witness*   [b] 5 Exodus 22:28

Sadducees, and the assembly was divided. [8](The Sadducees say that there is no resurrection, and that there are neither angels nor spirits, but the Pharisees acknowledge them all.)

[9]There was a great uproar, and some of the teachers of the law who were Pharisees stood up and argued vigorously. "We find nothing wrong with this man," they said. "What if a spirit or an angel has spoken to him?" [10]The dispute became so violent that the commander was afraid Paul would be torn to pieces by them. He ordered the troops to go down and take him away from them by force and bring him into the barracks.

[11]The following night the Lord stood near Paul and said, "Take courage! As you have testified about me in Jerusalem, so you must also testify in Rome."

THE PLOT TO KILL PAUL

[12]The next morning the Jews formed a conspiracy and bound themselves with an oath not to eat or drink until they had killed Paul. [13]More than forty men were involved in this plot. [14]They went to the chief priests and elders and said, "We have taken a solemn oath not to eat anything until we have killed Paul. [15]Now then, you and the Sanhedrin petition the commander to bring him before you on the pretext of wanting more accurate information about his case. We are ready to kill him before he gets here."

[16]But when the son of Paul's sister heard of this plot, he went into the barracks and told Paul.

[17]Then Paul called one of the centurions and said, "Take this young man to the commander; he has something to tell him." [18]So he took him to the commander.

The centurion said, "Paul, the prisoner, sent for me and asked me to bring this young man to you because he has something to tell you."

[19]The commander took the young man by the hand, drew him aside and asked, "What is it you want to tell me?"

[20]He said: "The Jews have agreed to ask you to bring Paul before the Sanhedrin tomorrow on the pretext of wanting more accurate information about him. [21]Don't give in to them, because more than forty of them are waiting in ambush for him. They have taken an oath not to eat or drink until they have killed him. They are ready now, waiting for your consent to their request."

[22]The commander dismissed the young man and cautioned him, "Don't tell anyone that you have reported this to me."

PAUL TRANSFERRED TO CAESAREA

[23]Then he called two of his centurions and ordered them, "Get ready a detachment of two hundred soldiers, seventy horsemen and two hundred spearmen[a] to go to Caesarea at nine tonight. [24]Provide mounts for Paul so that he may be taken safely to Governor Felix."

[25]He wrote a letter as follows:

[26]Claudius Lysias,

To His Excellency, Governor Felix:

Greetings.

[27]This man was seized by the Jews and they were about to kill him, but I came with my troops and rescued him, for I had learned that he is a Roman citizen. [28]I wanted to know why they were accusing him, so I brought him to their Sanhedrin. [29]I found that the accusation had to do with questions about their law, but there was no charge against him that deserved death or imprisonment. [30]When I was informed of a plot to be carried out against the man, I sent him to you at once. I also ordered his accusers to present to you their case against him.

[31]So the soldiers, carrying out their orders, took Paul with them during the night and brought him as far as Antipatris. [32]The next day they let the cavalry go on with him, while they returned to the barracks. [33]When the cavalry arrived in Caesarea, they delivered the letter to the governor and handed Paul over to him. [34]The governor read the letter and asked what province he was from. Learning that he was from Cilicia, [35]he said, "I will hear your case when your accusers get here." Then he ordered that Paul be kept under guard in Herod's palace.

---

[a] 23 The meaning of the Greek for this word is uncertain.

THE TRIAL BEFORE FELIX

24 Five days later the high priest Ananias went down to Caesarea with some of the elders and a lawyer named Tertullus, and they brought their charges against Paul before the governor. ²When Paul was called in, Tertullus presented his case before Felix: "We have enjoyed a long period of peace under you, and your foresight has brought about reforms in this nation. ³Everywhere and in every way, most excellent Felix, we acknowledge this with profound gratitude. ⁴But in order not to weary you further, I would request that you be kind enough to hear us briefly.

⁵"We have found this man to be a troublemaker, stirring up riots among the Jews all over the world. He is a ringleader of the Nazarene sect ⁶and even tried to desecrate the temple; so we seized him. ⁸By ᵃ examining him yourself you will be able to learn the truth about all these charges we are bringing against him."

⁹The Jews joined in the accusation, asserting that these things were true.

¹⁰When the governor motioned for him to speak, Paul replied: "I know that for a number of years you have been a judge over this nation; so I gladly make my defense. ¹¹You can easily verify that no more than twelve days ago I went up to Jerusalem to worship. ¹²My accusers did not find me arguing with anyone at the temple, or stirring up a crowd in the synagogues or anywhere else in the city. ¹³And they cannot prove to you the charges they are now making against me. ¹⁴However, I admit that I worship the God of our fathers as a follower of the Way, which they call a sect. I believe everything that agrees with the Law and that is written in the Prophets, ¹⁵and I have the same hope in God as these men, that there will be a resurrection of both the righteous and the wicked. ¹⁶So I strive always to keep my conscience clear before God and man.

¹⁷"After an absence of several years, I came to Jerusalem to bring my people gifts for the poor and to present offerings. ¹⁸I was ceremonially clean when they found me in the temple courts doing this. There was no crowd with me, nor was I involved in any disturbance. ¹⁹But there are some Jews from the province of Asia, who ought to be here before you and bring charges if they have anything against me. ²⁰Or these who are here should state what crime they found in me when I stood before the Sanhedrin— ²¹unless it was this one thing I shouted as I stood in their presence: 'It is concerning the resurrection of the dead that I am on trial before you today.' "

²²Then Felix, who was well acquainted with the Way, adjourned the proceedings. "When Lysias the commander comes," he said, "I will decide your case." ²³He ordered the centurion to keep Paul under guard but to give him some freedom and permit his friends to take care of his needs.

²⁴Several days later Felix came with his wife Drusilla, who was a Jewess. He sent for Paul and listened to him as he spoke about faith in Christ Jesus. ²⁵As Paul discoursed on righteousness, self-control and the judgment to come, Felix was afraid and said, "That's enough for now! You may leave. When I find it convenient, I will send for you." ²⁶At the same time he was hoping that Paul would offer him a bribe, so he sent for him frequently and talked with him.

²⁷When two years had passed, Felix was succeeded by Porcius Festus, but because Felix wanted to grant a favor to the Jews, he left Paul in prison.

THE TRIAL BEFORE FESTUS

25 Three days after arriving in the province, Festus went up from Caesarea to Jerusalem, ²where the chief priests and Jewish leaders appeared before him and presented the charges against Paul. ³They urgently requested Festus, as a favor to them, to have Paul transferred to Jerusalem, for they were preparing an ambush to kill him along the way. ⁴Festus answered, "Paul is being held at Caesarea, and I myself am going there soon. ⁵Let some of your leaders come with me and press charges against the man there, if he has done anything wrong."

⁶After spending eight or ten days with them, he went down to Caesarea, and the next day he con-

NOW OR NEVER
AC 24:5-8

If you were ever put on trial for being a follower of Jesus, would there be enough evidence to convict you? What kind of testimony would your friends and family have to give about the true nature of your faith?

ᵃ 6-8 Some manuscripts *him and wanted to judge him according to our law.* ⁷*But the commander, Lysias, came and with the use of much force snatched him from our hands* ⁸*and ordered his accusers to come before you. By* vened the court and ordered that Paul be brought before him. 7When Paul appeared, the Jews who had come down from Jerusalem stood around him, bringing many serious charges against him, which they could not prove.

8Then Paul made his defense: "I have done nothing wrong against the law of the Jews or against the temple or against Caesar."

9Festus, wishing to do the Jews a favor, said to Paul, "Are you willing to go up to Jerusalem and stand trial before me there on these charges?"

10Paul answered: "I am now standing before Caesar's court, where I ought to be tried. I have not done any wrong to the Jews, as you yourself know very well. 11If, however, I am guilty of doing anything deserving death, I do not refuse to die. But if the charges brought against me by these Jews are not true, no one has the right to hand me over to them. I appeal to Caesar!"

12After Festus had conferred with his council, he declared: "You have appealed to Caesar. To Caesar you will go!"

FESTUS CONSULTS KING AGRIPPA

13A few days later King Agrippa and Bernice arrived at Caesarea to pay their respects to Festus. 14Since they were spending many days there, Festus discussed Paul's case with the king. He said: "There is a man here whom Felix left as a prisoner. 15When I went to Jerusalem, the chief priests and elders of the Jews brought charges against him and asked that he be condemned.

16"I told them that it is not the Roman custom to hand over any man before he has faced his accusers and has had an opportunity to defend himself against their charges. 17When they came here with me, I did not delay the case, but convened the court the next day and ordered the man to be brought in. 18When his accusers got up to speak, they did not charge him with any of the crimes I had expected. 19Instead, they had some points of dispute with him about their own religion and about a dead man named Jesus who Paul claimed was alive. 20I was at a loss how to investigate such matters; so I asked if he would be willing to go to Jerusalem and stand trial there on these charges. 21When Paul made his appeal to be held over for the Emperor's decision, I ordered him held until I could send him to Caesar."

22Then Agrippa said to Festus, "I would like to hear this man myself."

He replied, "Tomorrow you will hear him."

PAUL BEFORE AGRIPPA

23The next day Agrippa and Bernice came with great pomp and entered the audience room with the high ranking officers and the leading men of the city. At the command of Festus, Paul was brought in. 24Festus said: "King Agrippa, and all who are present with us, you see this man! The whole Jewish community has petitioned me about him in Jerusalem and here in Caesarea, shouting that he ought not to live any longer. 25I found he had done nothing deserving of death, but because he made his appeal to the Emperor I decided to send him to Rome. 26But I have nothing definite to write to His Majesty about him. Therefore I have brought him before all of you, and especially before you, King Agrippa, so that as a result of this investigation I may have something to write. 27For I think it is unreasonable to send on a prisoner without specifying the charges against him."

26 Then Agrippa said to Paul, "You have permission to speak for yourself."

So Paul motioned with his hand and began his defense: 2"King Agrippa, I consider myself fortunate to stand before you today as I make my defense against all the accusations of the Jews, 3and especially so because you are well acquainted with all the Jewish customs and controversies. Therefore, I beg you to listen to me patiently.

4"The Jews all know the way I have lived ever since I was a child, from the beginning of my life in my own country, and also in Jerusalem. 5They have known me for a long time and can testify, if they are willing, that according to the strictest sect of our religion, I lived as a Pharisee. 6And now it is because of my hope in what God has promised our fathers that I am on trial today. 7This is the promise our twelve tribes are hoping to see fulfilled as they earnestly serve God day and night. O king, it is because of this hope that the Jews are accusing me. 8Why should any of you consider it incredible that God raises the dead?

9"I too was convinced that I ought to do all that was possible to oppose the name of Jesus of Nazareth. 10And that is just what I did in Jerusalem. On the authority of the chief priests I put many of the saints in prison, and when they were put to death, I cast my vote against them. 11Many a time I went from one synagogue to another to have them punished, and I tried to force them to blaspheme. In my obsession against them, I even went to foreign cities to persecute them.

[12]"On one of these journeys I was going to Damascus with the authority and commission of the chief priests. [13]About noon, O king, as I was on the road, I saw a light from heaven, brighter than the sun, blazing around me and my companions. [14]We all fell to the ground, and I heard a voice saying to me in Aramaic,[a] 'Saul, Saul, why do you persecute me? It is hard for you to kick against the goads.'

[15]"Then I asked, 'Who are you, Lord?'

" 'I am Jesus, whom you are persecuting,' the Lord replied. [16]Now get up and stand on your feet. I have appeared to you to appoint you as a servant and as a witness of what you have seen of me and what I will show you. [17]I will rescue you from your own people and from the Gentiles. I am sending you to them [18]to open their eyes and turn them from darkness to light, and from the power of Satan to God, so that they may receive forgiveness of sins and a place among those who are sanctified by faith in me.'

[19]"So then, King Agrippa, I was not disobedient to the vision from heaven. [20]First to those in Damascus, then to those in Jerusalem and in all Judea, and to the Gentiles also, I preached that they should repent and turn to God and prove their repentance by their deeds. [21]That is why the Jews seized me in the temple courts and tried to kill me. [22]But I have had God's help to this very day, and so I stand here and testify to small and great alike. I am saying nothing beyond what the prophets and Moses said would happen— [23]that the Christ[b] would suffer and, as the first to rise from the dead, would proclaim light to his own people and to the Gentiles."

[24]At this point Festus interrupted Paul's defense. "You are out of your mind, Paul!" he shouted. "Your great learning is driving you insane."

[25]"I am not insane, most excellent Festus," Paul replied. "What I am saying is true and reasonable. [26]The king is familiar with these things, and I can speak freely to him. I am convinced that none of this has escaped his notice, because it was not done in a corner. [27]King Agrippa, do you believe the prophets? I know you do."

[28]Then Agrippa said to Paul, "Do you think that in such a short time you can persuade me to be a Christian?"

[29]Paul replied, "Short time or long—I pray God that not only you but all who are listening to me today may become what I am, except for these chains."

NOW OR NEVER
AC 26:28

What if someone threw down that same evasive challenge ("Do you actually think you can persuade me to become a Christian?") to you? How would you respond? What would be your first move?

[30]The king rose, and with him the governor and Bernice and those sitting with them. [31]They left the room, and while talking with one another, they said, "This man is not doing anything that deserves death or imprisonment."

[32]Agrippa said to Festus, "This man could have been set free if he had not appealed to Caesar."

PAUL SAILS FOR ROME

27 When it was decided that we would sail for Italy, Paul and some other prisoners were handed over to a centurion named Julius, who belonged to the Imperial Regiment. [2]We boarded a ship from Adramyttium about to sail for ports along the coast of the province of Asia, and we put out to sea. Aristarchus, a Macedonian from Thessalonica, was with us.

[3]The next day we landed at Sidon; and Julius, in kindness to Paul, allowed him to go to his friends so they might provide for his needs. [4]From there we put out to sea again and passed to the lee of Cyprus because the winds were against us. [5]When we had sailed across the open sea off the coast of Cilicia and Pamphylia, we landed at Myra in Lycia. [6]There the centurion found an Alexandrian ship sailing for Italy and put us on board. [7]We made slow headway for many days and had difficulty arriving off Cnidus. When the wind did not allow us to hold our course, we sailed to the lee of Crete, opposite Salmone. [8]We moved along the coast with difficulty and came to a place called Fair Havens, near the town of Lasea.

[9]Much time had been lost, and sailing had already become dangerous because by now it was after

---

[a] 14 Or *Hebrew*   [b] 23 Or *Messiah*

the Fast.[a] So Paul warned them, [10]"Men, I can see that our voyage is going to be disastrous and bring great loss to ship and cargo, and to our own lives also." [11]But the centurion, instead of listening to what Paul said, followed the advice of the pilot and of the owner of the ship. [12]Since the harbor was unsuitable to winter in, the majority decided that we should sail on, hoping to reach Phoenix and winter there. This was a harbor in Crete, facing both southwest and northwest.

THE STORM

[13]When a gentle south wind began to blow, they thought they had obtained what they wanted; so they weighed anchor and sailed along the shore of Crete. [14]Before very long, a wind of hurricane force, called the "northeaster," swept down from the island. [15]The ship was caught by the storm and could not head into the wind; so we gave way to it and were driven along. [16]As we passed to the lee of a small island called Cauda, we were hardly able to make the lifeboat secure. [17]When the men had hoisted it aboard, they passed ropes under the ship itself to hold it together. Fearing that they would run aground on the sandbars of Syrtis, they lowered the sea anchor and let the ship be driven along. [18]We took such a violent battering from the storm that the next day they began to throw the cargo overboard. [19]On the third day, they threw the ship's tackle overboard with their own hands. [20]When neither sun nor stars appeared for many days and the storm continued raging, we finally gave up all hope of being saved.

[21]After the men had gone a long time without food, Paul stood up before them and said: "Men, you should have taken my advice not to sail from Crete; then you would have spared yourselves this damage and loss. [22]But now I urge you to keep up your courage, because not one of you will be lost; only the ship will be destroyed. [23]Last night an angel of the God whose I am and whom I serve stood beside me [24]and said, 'Do not be afraid, Paul. You must stand trial before Caesar; and God has graciously given you the lives of all who sail with you.' [25]So keep up your courage, men, for I have faith in God that it will happen just as he told me. [26]Nevertheless, we must run aground on some island."

ΠΟШ ΟΡ ΠЄVЄΡ

AC 27:25

Your faith can make a major difference in other people's lives. Seeing you stay calm in the face of difficulty can help them stay calm too. It may also spark their curiosity about why you have peace in the middle of a storm.

THE SHIPWRECK

[27]On the fourteenth night we were still being driven across the Adriatic[b] Sea, when about midnight the sailors sensed they were approaching land. [28]They took soundings and found that the water was a hundred and twenty feet[c] deep. A short time later they took soundings again and found it was ninety feet[d] deep. [29]Fearing that we would be dashed against the rocks, they dropped four anchors from the stern and prayed for daylight. [30]In an attempt to escape from the ship, the sailors let the lifeboat down into the sea, pretending they were going to lower some anchors from the bow. [31]Then Paul said to the centurion and the soldiers, "Unless these men stay with the ship, you cannot be saved." [32]So the soldiers cut the ropes that held the lifeboat and let it fall away.

[33]Just before dawn Paul urged them all to eat. "For the last fourteen days," he said, "you have been in constant suspense and have gone without food—you haven't eaten anything. [34]Now I urge you to take some food. You need it to survive. Not one of you will lose a single hair from his head." [35]After he said this, he took some bread and gave thanks to God in front of them all. Then he broke it and began to eat. [36]They were all encouraged and ate some food themselves. [37]Altogether there were 276 of us on board. [38]When they had eaten as much as they wanted, they lightened the ship by throwing the grain into the sea.

[39]When daylight came, they did not recognize the land, but they saw a bay with a sandy beach, where they decided to run the ship aground if they could. [40]Cutting loose the anchors, they left them in the sea and at the same time untied the ropes that held the rudders. Then they hoisted the foresail to the wind and made for the beach. [41]But the ship struck a sandbar and ran aground. The bow stuck fast and would not move, and the stern was broken to pieces by the pounding of the surf.

[42]The soldiers planned to kill the prisoners to prevent any of them from swimming away and escap-

---

[a] 9 That is, the Day of Atonement (Yom Kippur)   [b] 27 In ancient times the name referred to an area extending well south of Italy.
[c] 28 Greek twenty orguias (about 37 meters)   [d] 28 Greek fifteen orguias (about 27 meters)

ing. ⁴³But the centurion wanted to spare Paul's life and kept them from carrying out their plan. He ordered those who could swim to jump overboard first and get to land. ⁴⁴The rest were to get there on planks or on pieces of the ship. In this way everyone reached land in safety.

Putting Some Adventure in Your Faith

For guys like Paul, Barnabas, Silas and Peter, the Christian life was an adventure. They raced from place to place to spread the Good News, often just one step ahead of those who wanted to kill them. They lived under the constant threat of being arrested and executed. They endured shipwrecks, deadly snake bites, vicious beatings and earthquakes. But they didn't let that stop them. Their attitude was, "As long as we're alive, we're going to talk to people about Jesus—no matter what." What do you think would happen if you started treating your Christian life as the ultimate adventure?

ASHORE ON MALTA

28

Once safely on shore, we found out that the island was called Malta. ²The islanders showed us unusual kindness. They built a fire and welcomed us all because it was raining and cold. ³Paul gathered a pile of brushwood and, as he put it on the fire, a viper, driven out by the heat, fastened itself on his hand. ⁴When the islanders saw the snake hanging from his hand, they said to each other, "This man must be a murderer; for though he escaped from the sea, Justice has not allowed him to live." ⁵But Paul shook the snake off into the fire and suffered no ill effects. ⁶The people expected him to swell up or suddenly fall dead, but after waiting a long time and seeing nothing unusual happen to him, they changed their minds and said he was a god. ⁷There was an estate nearby that belonged to Publius, the chief official of the island. He welcomed us to his home and for three days entertained us hospitably. ⁸His father was sick in bed, suffering from fever and dysentery. Paul went in to see him and, after prayer, placed his hands on him and healed him. ⁹When this had happened, the rest of the sick on the island came and were cured. ¹⁰They honored us in many ways and when we were ready to sail, they furnished us with the supplies we needed.

ARRIVAL AT ROME

¹¹After three months we put out to sea in a ship that had wintered in the island. It was an Alexandrian ship with the figurehead of the twin gods Castor and Pollux. ¹²We put in at Syracuse and stayed there three days. ¹³From there we set sail and arrived at Rhegium. The next day the south wind came up, and on the following day we reached Puteoli. ¹⁴There we found some brothers who invited us to spend a week with them. And so we came to Rome. ¹⁵The brothers there had heard that we were coming, and they traveled as far as the Forum of Appius and the Three Taverns to meet us. At the sight of these men Paul thanked God and was encouraged. ¹⁶When we got to Rome, Paul was allowed to live by himself, with a soldier to guard him.

PAUL PREACHES AT ROME UNDER GUARD

¹⁷Three days later he called together the leaders of the Jews. When they had assembled, Paul said to them: "My brothers, although I have done nothing against our people or against the customs of our ancestors, I was arrested in Jerusalem and handed over to the Romans. ¹⁸They examined me and wanted to release me, because I was not guilty of any crime deserving death. ¹⁹But when the Jews objected, I was compelled to appeal to Caesar—not that I had any charge to bring against my own people. ²⁰For this reason I have asked to see you and talk with you. It is because of the hope of Israel that I am bound with this chain."

²¹They replied, "We have not received any letters from Judea concerning you, and none of the brothers who have come from there has reported or said anything bad about you. ²²But we want to hear what your views are, for we know that people everywhere are talking against this sect."

²³They arranged to meet Paul on a certain day, and came in even larger numbers to the place where he was staying. From morning till evening he explained and declared to them the kingdom of God and tried to convince them about Jesus from the Law of Moses and from the Prophets. ²⁴Some were convinced by what he said, but others would not believe. ²⁵They disagreed among themselves and began

to leave after Paul had made this final statement: "The Holy Spirit spoke the truth to your forefathers when he said through Isaiah the prophet:

> 26 " 'Go to this people and say,
>   "You will be ever hearing but never understanding;
>   you will be ever seeing but never perceiving."
> 27 For this people's heart has become calloused;
>   they hardly hear with their ears,
>   and they have closed their eyes.
> Otherwise they might see with their eyes,
>   hear with their ears,
>   understand with their hearts
> and turn, and I would heal them.'[a]

28"Therefore I want you to know that God's salvation has been sent to the Gentiles, and they will listen!"[b]

30For two whole years Paul stayed there in his own rented house and welcomed all who came to see him. 31Boldly and without hindrance he preached the kingdom of God and taught about the Lord Jesus Christ.

---

a 27 Isaiah 6:9,10   b 28 Some manuscripts listen!" 29After he said this, the Jews left, arguing vigorously among themselves.

« AT A GLANCE

Author
The apostle Paul

Audience
Christians in Rome

Date
About A.D. 57

Setting
Paul, who was in Corinth, was about to visit Rome after making a stop in Jerusalem. Before his visit he wrote to the Christians there to introduce himself and to tell them about God's plan of salvation.

Verse to Remember
I am not ashamed of the gospel, because it is the power of God for the salvation of everyone who believes: first for the Jew, then for the Gentile (1:16).

Theme to Consider
The book of Romans is a handbook on the Christian faith: All of us are sinners; Christ died to forgive sin; we are made right with God through faith; and this faith comes through a relationship with Jesus.

UNCHANGING TRUTH » Who helps you "keep it real"? Who makes sure you never forget who you are at the core of your being? Who keeps you from getting too wrapped up in yourself? Who gives you a reality check when you need one?

For the Christians in Rome, the apostle Paul was that person. In his letter to the Romans, Paul hammered home the truth that the only reason any of us are able to . . .

- call God our heavenly Father
- call Jesus our Savior and Lord
- escape punishment for our sins
- look forward to eternity in heaven

. . . is God's amazing grace.

You aren't a Christian because you did something special to deserve God's love. You didn't earn the right to have your sins forgiven. God gave you a gift and you accepted it. That's why you're a Christian.

If you want to keep your relationship with God real, you'll need to remember that. It's good to be humble and remember that we did nothing to earn our standing before God. Only then can we fully appreciate just how incredible God is and how awesome it is that we can walk with him in this life and for all of eternity.

LIFE LESSONS »

1 Judging others is a dangerous business because no matter what we fault them for, we're guilty of something equally bad in God's sight (2:1).

2 Faith in Jesus is the only thing that can save us from the punishment we deserve for our sin (3:21–24).

3 Making Jesus Lord of your life changes your attitude toward sin forever (8:5).

4 If something you do causes problems for someone else's spiritual growth, your job is to remove the "obstacle" for that person (14:13).

1 Paul, a servant of Christ Jesus, called to be an apostle and set apart for the gospel of God— [2]the gospel he promised beforehand through his prophets in the Holy Scriptures [3]regarding his Son, who as to his human nature was a descendant of David, [4]and who through the Spirit[a] of holiness was declared with power to be the Son of God[b] by his resurrection from the dead: Jesus Christ our Lord. [5]Through him and for his name's sake, we received grace and apostleship to call people from among all the Gentiles to the obedience that comes from faith. [6]And you also are among those who are called to belong to Jesus Christ.

[7]To all in Rome who are loved by God and called to be saints:

Grace and peace to you from God our Father and from the Lord Jesus Christ.

PAUL'S LONGING TO VISIT ROME

[8]First, I thank my God through Jesus Christ for all of you, because your faith is being reported all over the world. [9]God, whom I serve with my whole heart in preaching the gospel of his Son, is my witness how constantly I remember you [10]in my prayers at all times; and I pray that now at last by God's will the way may be opened for me to come to you.

[11]I long to see you so that I may impart to you some spiritual gift to make you strong— [12]that is, that you and I may be mutually encouraged by each other's faith. [13]I do not want you to be unaware, brothers, that I planned many times to come to you (but have been prevented from doing so until now) in order that I might have a harvest among you, just as I have had among the other Gentiles.

[14]I am obligated both to Greeks and non-Greeks, both to the wise and the foolish. [15]That is why I am so eager to preach the gospel also to you who are at Rome.

[16]I am not ashamed of the gospel, because it is the power of God for the salvation of everyone who believes: first for the Jew, then for the Gentile. [17]For in the gospel a righteousness from God is revealed, a righteousness that is by faith from first to last,[c] just as it is written: "The righteous will live by faith."[d]

GOD'S WRATH AGAINST MANKIND

[18]The wrath of God is being revealed from heaven against all the godlessness and wickedness of men who suppress the truth by their wickedness, [19]since what may be known about God is plain to them, because God has made it plain to them. [20]For since the creation of the world God's invisible qualities—his eternal power and divine nature—have been clearly seen, being understood from what has been made, so that men are without excuse.

[21]For although they knew God, they neither glorified him as God nor gave thanks to him, but their thinking became futile and their foolish hearts were darkened. [22]Although they claimed to be wise, they became fools [23]and exchanged the glory of the immortal God for images made to look like mortal man and birds and animals and reptiles.

[24]Therefore God gave them over in the sinful desires of their hearts to sexual impurity for the degrading of their bodies with one another. [25]They exchanged the truth of God for a lie, and worshiped and served created things rather than the Creator—who is forever praised. Amen.

[26]Because of this, God gave them over to shameful lusts. Even their women exchanged natural relations for unnatural ones. [27]In the same way the men also abandoned natural relations with women and were inflamed with lust for one another. Men committed indecent acts with other men, and received in themselves the due penalty for their perversion.

NOW OR NEVER
RO 1:24–25

If you know people who are caught in the trap of living to please themselves, make it a goal to pray for them regularly. Ask God to help them recognize how empty their lives are without Jesus, and ask him to use you in demonstrating to your friends exactly what God has to offer.

[28]Furthermore, since they did not think it worthwhile to retain the knowledge of God, he gave them over to a depraved mind, to do what ought not to be done. [29]They have become filled with every kind of wickedness, evil, greed and depravity. They are full of envy, murder, strife, deceit and malice. They are gossips, [30]slanderers, God-haters, insolent, arrogant and boastful; they invent ways of doing evil;

---

[a] 4 Or *who as to his spirit* [b] 4 Or *was appointed to be the Son of God with power* [c] 17 Or *is from faith to faith* [d] 17 Hab. 2:4

they disobey their parents; [31]they are senseless, faithless, heartless, ruthless. [32]Although they know God's righteous decree that those who do such things deserve death, they not only continue to do these very things but also approve of those who practice them.

GOD'S RIGHTEOUS JUDGMENT

2 You, therefore, have no excuse, you who pass judgment on someone else, for at whatever point you judge the other, you are condemning yourself, because you who pass judgment do the same things. [2]Now we know that God's judgment against those who do such things is based on truth. [3]So when you, a mere man, pass judgment on them and yet do the same things, do you think you will escape God's judgment? [4]Or do you show contempt for the riches of his kindness, tolerance and patience, not realizing that God's kindness leads you toward repentance?

[5]But because of your stubbornness and your unrepentant heart, you are storing up wrath against yourself for the day of God's wrath, when his righteous judgment will be revealed. [6]God "will give to each person according to what he has done." [a] [7]To those who by persistence in doing good seek glory, honor and immortality, he will give eternal life. [8]But for those who are self-seeking and who reject the truth and follow evil, there will be wrath and anger. [9]There will be trouble and distress for every human being who does evil: first for the Jew, then for the Gentile; [10]but glory, honor and peace for everyone who does good: first for the Jew, then for the Gentile. [11]For God does not show favoritism.

[12]All who sin apart from the law will also perish apart from the law, and all who sin under the law will be judged by the law. [13]For it is not those who hear the law who are righteous in God's sight, but it is those who obey the law who will be declared righteous. [14](Indeed, when Gentiles, who do not have the law, do by nature things required by the law, they are a law for themselves, even though they do not have the law, [15]since they show that the requirements of the law are written on their hearts, their consciences also bearing witness, and their thoughts now accusing, now even defending them.) [16]This will take place on the day when God will judge men's secrets through Jesus Christ, as my gospel declares.

THE JEWS AND THE LAW

[17]Now you, if you call yourself a Jew; if you rely on the law and brag about your relationship to God; [18]if you know his will and approve of what is superior because you are instructed by the law; [19]if you are convinced that you are a guide for the blind, a light for those who are in the dark, [20]an instructor of the foolish, a teacher of infants, because you have in the law the embodiment of knowledge and truth— [21]you, then, who teach others, do you not teach yourself? You who preach against stealing, do you steal? [22]You who say that people should not commit adultery, do you commit adultery? You who abhor idols, do you rob temples? [23]You who brag about the law, do you dishonor God by breaking the law? [24]As it is written: "God's name is blasphemed among the Gentiles because of you." [b]

[25]Circumcision has value if you observe the law, but if you break the law, you have become as though you had not been circumcised. [26]If those who are not circumcised keep the law's requirements, will they not be regarded as though they were circumcised? [27]The one who is not circumcised physically and yet obeys the law will condemn you who, even though you have the [c] written code and circumcision, are a lawbreaker.

[28]A man is not a Jew if he is only one outwardly, nor is circumcision merely outward and physical. [29]No, a man is a Jew if he is one inwardly; and circumcision is circumcision of the heart, by the Spirit, not by the written code. Such a man's praise is not from men, but from God.

GOD'S FAITHFULNESS

3 What advantage, then, is there in being a Jew, or what value is there in circumcision? [2]Much in every way! First of all, they have been entrusted with the very words of God.

[3]What if some did not have faith? Will their lack of faith nullify God's faithfulness? [4]Not at all! Let God be true, and every man a liar. As it is written:

> "So that you may be proved right when you speak
> and prevail when you judge." [d]

[5]But if our unrighteousness brings out God's righteousness more clearly, what shall we say? That God is unjust in bringing his wrath on us? (I am using a human argument.) [6]Certainly not! If that were

---

[a] 6 Psalm 62:12; Prov. 24:12   [b] 24 Isaiah 52:5; Ezek. 36:22   [c] 27 Or who, by means of a   [d] 4 Psalm 51:4

so, how could God judge the world? [7]Someone might argue, "If my falsehood enhances God's truthfulness and so increases his glory, why am I still condemned as a sinner?" [8]Why not say—as we are being slanderously reported as saying and as some claim that we say—"Let us do evil that good may result"? Their condemnation is deserved.

NO ONE IS RIGHTEOUS

[9]What shall we conclude then? Are we any better[a]? Not at all! We have already made the charge that Jews and Gentiles alike are all under sin. [10]As it is written:

> "There is no one righteous, not even one;
> [11]   there is no one who understands,
>   no one who seeks God.
> [12]All have turned away,
>   they have together become worthless;
> there is no one who does good,
>   not even one."[b]
> [13]"Their throats are open graves;
>   their tongues practice deceit."[c]
> "The poison of vipers is on their lips."[d]
> [14]   "Their mouths are full of cursing and bitterness."[e]
> [15]"Their feet are swift to shed blood;
> [16]   ruin and misery mark their ways,
> [17]and the way of peace they do not know."[f]
> [18]   "There is no fear of God before their eyes."[g]

NOW OR NEVER

RO 3:12

Do you ever feel like you've arrived—like you're done growing spiritually and you've maxed out the strength of your faith? If you don't feel like that now, you might later in life. And when that feeling comes . . . fight it. It's a lie. No one does good apart from Christ. Life is a race that doesn't end until we die.

---

[19]Now we know that whatever the law says, it says to those who are under the law, so that every mouth may be silenced and the whole world held accountable to God. [20]Therefore no one will be declared righteous in his sight by observing the law; rather, through the law we become conscious of sin.

RIGHTEOUSNESS THROUGH FAITH

[21]But now a righteousness from God, apart from law, has been made known, to which the Law and the Prophets testify. [22]This righteousness from God comes through faith in Jesus Christ to all who believe. There is no difference, [23]for all have sinned and fall short of the glory of God, [24]and are justified freely by his grace through the redemption that came by Christ Jesus. [25]God presented him as a sacrifice of atonement,[h] through faith in his blood. He did this to demonstrate his justice, because in his forbearance he had left the sins committed beforehand unpunished— [26]he did it to demonstrate his justice at the present time, so as to be just and the one who justifies those who have faith in Jesus.

[27]Where, then, is boasting? It is excluded. On what principle? On that of observing the

---

NOW OR NEVER

RO 3:23

Did you ever believe that you could earn your way into heaven by doing good deeds and living a nice, clean life? What made you realize that no human effort could ever meet God's standard? That is, what was it that helped you understand what grace is really all about?

---

law? No, but on that of faith. [28]For we maintain that a man is justified by faith apart from observing the law. [29]Is God the God of Jews only? Is he not the God of Gentiles too? Yes, of Gentiles too, [30]since there is only one God, who will justify the circumcised by faith and the uncircumcised through that same faith. [31]Do we, then, nullify the law by this faith? Not at all! Rather, we uphold the law.

---

[a] 9 Or worse   [b] 12 Psalms 14:1-3; 53:1-3; Eccles. 7:20   [c] 13 Psalm 5:9   [d] 13 Psalm 140:3   [e] 14 Psalm 10:7
[f] 17 Isaiah 59:7,8   [g] 18 Psalm 36:1   [h] 25 Or as the one who would turn aside his wrath, taking away sin

ABRAHAM JUSTIFIED BY FAITH

4 What then shall we say that Abraham, our forefather, discovered in this matter? ²If, in fact, Abraham was justified by works, he had something to boast about—but not before God. ³What does the Scripture say? "Abraham believed God, and it was credited to him as righteousness."[a]

⁴Now when a man works, his wages are not credited to him as a gift, but as an obligation. ⁵However, to the man who does not work but trusts God who justifies the wicked, his faith is credited as righteousness. ⁶David says the same thing when he speaks of the blessedness of the man to whom God credits righteousness apart from works:

⁷ "Blessed are they
   whose transgressions are forgiven,
   whose sins are covered.
⁸Blessed is the man
   whose sin the Lord will never count against him."[b]

⁹Is this blessedness only for the circumcised, or also for the uncircumcised? We have been saying that Abraham's faith was credited to him as righteousness. ¹⁰Under what circumstances was it credited? Was it after he was circumcised, or before? It was not after, but before! ¹¹And he received the sign of circumcision, a seal of the righteousness that he had by faith while he was still uncircumcised. So then, he is the father of all who believe but have not been circumcised, in order that righteousness might be credited to them. ¹²And he is also the father of the circumcised who not only are circumcised but who also walk in the footsteps of the faith that our father Abraham had before he was circumcised.

¹³It was not through law that Abraham and his offspring received the promise that he would be heir of the world, but through the righteousness that comes by faith. ¹⁴For if those who live by law are heirs, faith has no value and the promise is worthless, ¹⁵because law brings wrath. And where there is no law there is no transgression.

¹⁶Therefore, the promise comes by faith, so that it may be by grace and may be guaranteed to all Abraham's offspring—not only to those who are of the law but also to those who are of the faith of Abraham. He is the father of us all. ¹⁷As it is written: "I have made you a father of many nations."[c] He is our father in the sight of God, in whom he believed—the God who gives life to the dead and calls things that are not as though they were.

¹⁸Against all hope, Abraham in hope believed and so became the father of many nations, just as it had been said to him, "So shall your offspring be."[d] ¹⁹Without weakening in his faith, he faced the fact that his body was as good as dead—since he was about a hundred years old—and that Sarah's womb was also dead. ²⁰Yet he did not waver through unbelief regarding the promise of God, but was strengthened in his faith and gave glory to God, ²¹being fully persuaded that God had power to do what he had promised. ²²This is why "it was credited to him as righteousness." ²³The words "it was credited to him" were written not for him alone, ²⁴but also for us, to whom God will credit righteousness—for us who believe in him who raised Jesus our Lord from the dead. ²⁵He was delivered over to death for our sins and was raised to life for our justification.

challengenotes

To: my_son

RO 5:6-8

heavenly_father: the next time someone tries to convince you that I don't love you (or anyone else), remember what it cost me to offer you salvation. if that's not love, what is? I loved you while you were still lost in your sin.

PEACE AND JOY

5 Therefore, since we have been justified through faith, we[e] have peace with God through our Lord Jesus Christ, ²through whom we have gained access by faith into this grace in which we now stand. And we[e] rejoice in the hope of the glory of God. ³Not only so, but we[e] also rejoice in our sufferings, because we know that suffering produces perseverance; ⁴perseverance, character; and character, hope. ⁵And hope does not disappoint us, because God has poured out his love into our hearts by the Holy Spirit, whom he has given us.

⁶You see, at just the right time, when we were still powerless, Christ died for the ungodly. ⁷Very rare-

---

ª *3* Gen. 15:6; also in verse 22   ᵇ *8* Psalm 32:1,2   ᶜ *17* Gen. 17:5   ᵈ *18* Gen. 15:5   ᵉ *1,2,3* Or *let us* ly will anyone die for a righteous man, though for a good man someone might possibly dare to die. 8But God demonstrates his own love for us in this: While we were still sinners, Christ died for us.

9Since we have now been justified by his blood, how much more shall we be saved from God's wrath through him! 10For if, when we were God's enemies, we were reconciled to him through the death of his Son, how much more, having been reconciled, shall we be saved through his life! 11Not only is this so, but we also rejoice in God through our Lord Jesus Christ, through whom we have now received reconciliation.

DEATH THROUGH ADAM, LIFE THROUGH CHRIST

12Therefore, just as sin entered the world through one man, and death through sin, and in this way death came to all men, because all sinned— 13for before the law was given, sin was in the world. But sin is not taken into account when there is no law. 14Nevertheless, death reigned from the time of Adam to the time of Moses, even over those who did not sin by breaking a command, as did Adam, who was a pattern of the one to come.

15But the gift is not like the trespass. For if the many died by the trespass of the one man, how much more did God's grace and the gift that came by the grace of the one man, Jesus Christ, overflow to the many! 16Again, the gift of God is not like the result of the one man's sin: The judgment followed one sin and brought condemnation, but the gift followed many trespasses and brought justification. 17For if, by the trespass of the one man, death reigned through that one man, how much more will those who receive God's abundant provision of grace and of the gift of righteousness reign in life through the one man, Jesus Christ.

18Consequently, just as the result of one trespass was condemnation for all men, so also the result of one act of righteousness was justification that brings life for all men. 19For just as through the disobedience of the one man the many were made sinners, so also through the obedience of the one man the many will be made righteous.

20The law was added so that the trespass might increase. But where sin increased, grace increased all the more, 21so that, just as sin reigned in death, so also grace might reign through righteousness to bring eternal life through Jesus Christ our Lord.

DEAD TO SIN, ALIVE IN CHRIST

6 What shall we say, then? Shall we go on sinning so that grace may increase? 2By no means! We died to sin; how can we live in it any longer? 3Or don't you know that all of us who were baptized into Christ Jesus were baptized into his death? 4We were therefore buried with him through baptism into death in order that, just as Christ was raised from the dead through the glory of the Father, we too may live a new life.

5If we have been united with him like this in his death, we will certainly also be united with him in his resurrection. 6For we know that our old self was crucified with him so that the body of sin might be done away with,a that we should no longer be slaves to sin— 7because anyone who has died has been freed from sin.

8Now if we died with Christ, we believe that we will also live with him. 9For we know that since Christ was raised from the dead, he cannot die again; death no longer has mastery over him. 10The death he died, he died to sin once for all; but the life he lives, he lives to God. 11In the same way, count yourselves dead to sin but alive to God in Christ Jesus. 12Therefore do not

---

a 6 Or be rendered powerless

Rejoicing When Things Get Tough

No one in their right mind loves life during football training camp or preseason conditioning drills. No one high-fives their teammates when their legs are burning after running their tenth straight wind sprint. No one feels like celebrating when their muscles are screaming after their fourth set of bicep curls. Yet deep down all players know that the more they suffer during preseason, the better they'll be when game time arrives. Why not apply that same attitude—that suffering prepares you for what's to come—to your Christian life?

40 THINGS TO TALK ABOUT WITH YOUR PARENTS

Proverbs 1:8–9 says: "Listen, my son, to your father's instruction and do not forsake your mother's teaching. They are a garland to grace your head and a chain to adorn your neck." Proverbs 23:22 adds: "Listen to your father, who gave you life, and do not despise your mother when she is old."

The point? Your parents might seem old and goofy to you—and they probably are, at least a little bit. You might think they have a weird perspective on some things and aren't right about everything—that's also probably true. But even if you think they can't relate to you or understand where you're coming from—well, then this list should be that much more helpful to you. When you come home from a long day of school, instead of flipping on the TV or surfing the Web, here are some things you could talk about with them:

» ⑩ TO REMEMBER

- » 01 Your relationship with your sibling(s)
- » 02 Their childhood
- » 03 Rules
- » 04 Boundaries in your life
- » 05 The transition from boyhood to manhood
- » 06 Dating
- » 07 College
- » 08 What they think your gifts and talents are
- » 09 Career options
- » 10 Marriage

You are going to encounter many opportunities to talk with your parents, so here are a few more ideas to keep the conversation flowing:

- » 11 School/grades
- » 12 God—what it means to know and love and serve him
- » 13 What you appreciate about each other
- » 14 How things are going with your job/team/club
- » 15 Pressure you face from friends

let sin reign in your mortal body so that you obey its evil desires. ¹³Do not offer the parts of your body to sin, as instruments of wickedness, but rather offer yourselves to God, as those who have been brought from death to life; and offer the parts of your body to him as instruments of righteousness. ¹⁴For sin shall not be your master, because you are not under law, but under grace.

SLAVES TO RIGHTEOUSNESS

¹⁵What then? Shall we sin because we are not under law but under grace? By no means! ¹⁶Don't you know that when you offer yourselves to someone to obey him as slaves, you are slaves to the one whom you obey—whether you are slaves to sin, which leads to death, or to obedience, which leads to righteousness? ¹⁷But thanks be to God that, though you used to be slaves to sin, you wholeheartedly obeyed the form of teaching to which you were entrusted. ¹⁸You have been set free from sin and have become slaves to righteousness.

¹⁹I put this in human terms because you are weak in your natural selves. Just as you used to offer the parts of your body in slavery to impurity and to ever-increasing wickedness, so now offer them in slavery to righteousness leading to holiness. ²⁰When you were slaves to sin, you were free from the control of righteousness. ²¹What benefit did you reap at that time from the things you are now ashamed of? Those things result in death! ²²But now that you have been set free from sin and have become slaves to God, the benefit you reap leads to holiness, and the result is eternal life. ²³For the wages of sin is death, but the gift of God is eternal life in[a] Christ Jesus our Lord.

NOW OR NEVER

RO 6:15

Don't fall into the trap of believing that since God forgives sin, you can do anything you want as long as you confess it after the fact. For one thing, that kind of attitude shows that your repentance isn't genuine—and God only responds to genuine repentance.

AN ILLUSTRATION FROM MARRIAGE

7 Do you not know, brothers—for I am speaking to men who know the law—that the law has authority over a man only as long as he lives? ²For example, by law a married woman is bound to her husband as long as he is alive, but if her husband dies, she is released from the law of marriage. ³So then, if she marries another man while her husband is still alive, she is called an adulteress. But if her husband dies, she is released from that law and is not an adulteress, even though she marries another man.

⁴So, my brothers, you also died to the law through the body of Christ, that you might belong to another, to him who was raised from the dead, in order that we might bear fruit to God. ⁵For when we were controlled by the sinful nature,[b] the sinful passions aroused by the law were at work in our bodies, so that we bore fruit for death. ⁶But now, by dying to what once bound us, we have been released from the law so that we serve in the new way of the Spirit, and not in the old way of the written code.

STRUGGLING WITH SIN

⁷What shall we say, then? Is the law sin? Certainly not! Indeed I would not have known what sin was except through the law. For I would not have known what coveting really was if the law had not said, "Do not covet."[c] ⁸But sin, seizing the opportunity afforded by the commandment, produced in me every kind of covetous desire. For apart from law, sin is dead. ⁹Once I was alive apart from law; but when the commandment came, sin sprang to life and I died. ¹⁰I found that the very commandment that was intended to bring life actually brought death. ¹¹For sin, seizing the opportunity afforded by the commandment, deceived me, and through the commandment put me to death. ¹²So then, the law is holy, and the commandment is holy, righteous and good.

¹³Did that which is good, then, become death to me? By no means! But in order that sin might be recognized as sin, it produced death in me through what was good, so that through the commandment sin might become utterly sinful.

¹⁴We know that the law is spiritual; but I am unspiritual, sold as a slave to sin. ¹⁵I do not understand what I do. For what I want to do I do not do, but what I hate I do. ¹⁶And if I do what I do not want to do,

---

ª 23 Or through ᵇ 5 Or the flesh; also in verse 25 ᶜ 7 Exodus 20:17; Deut. 5:21

I agree that the law is good. [17]As it is, it is no longer I myself who do it, but it is sin living in me. [18]I know that nothing good lives in me, that is, in my sinful nature.[a] For I have the desire to do what is good, but I cannot carry it out. [19]For what I do is not the good I want to do; no, the evil I do not want to do—this I keep on doing. [20]Now if I do what I do not want to do, it is no longer I who do it, but it is sin living in me that does it.

[21]So I find this law at work: When I want to do good, evil is right there with me. [22]For in my inner being I delight in God's law; [23]but I see another law at work in the members of my body, waging war against the law of my mind and making me a prisoner of the law of sin at work within my members. [24]What a wretched man I am! Who will rescue me from this body of death? [25]Thanks be to God—through Jesus Christ our Lord!

So then, I myself in my mind am a slave to God's law, but in the sinful nature a slave to the law of sin.

NOW OR NEVER
RO 7:15-20

If there's a particular sin you struggle with, try talking about it with a trusted Christian friend or mentor. Be honest about your struggles, no matter how embarrassing it is for you. Knowing that someone else is praying for you and keeping you accountable might open the door for God to purify your life.

» live the adventure » Ro 7:15-25

Dealing With Problem Sins

Does this passage resonate with you—wanting to live a certain way but always doing something to blow it? Wanting to stop going back to the same old sinful habit, but not having the willpower to break the cycle? If the apostle Paul couldn't live perfectly without ever blowing it, what chance do we have? By ourselves . . . we have no chance whatsoever. But we're not alone. Jesus can rescue us from the power of sin.

LIFE THROUGH THE SPIRIT

8 Therefore, there is now no condemnation for those who are in Christ Jesus,[b] [2]because through Christ Jesus the law of the Spirit of life set me free from the law of sin and death. [3]For what the law was powerless to do in that it was weakened by the sinful nature,[c] God did by sending his own Son in the likeness of sinful man to be a sin offering.[d] And so he condemned sin in sinful man,[e] [4]in order that the righteous requirements of the law might be fully met in us, who do not live according to the sinful nature but according to the Spirit.

[5]Those who live according to the sinful nature have their minds set on what that nature desires; but those who live in accordance with the Spirit have their minds set on what the Spirit desires. [6]The mind of sinful man[f] is death, but the mind controlled by the Spirit is life and peace; [7]the sinful mind[g] is hostile to God. It does not submit to God's law, nor can it do so. [8]Those controlled by the sinful nature cannot please God.

[9]You, however, are controlled not by the sinful nature but by the Spirit, if the Spirit of God lives in you. And if anyone does not have the Spirit of Christ, he does not belong to Christ. [10]But if Christ is in you, your body is dead because of sin, yet your spirit is alive because of righteousness. [11]And if the Spirit of him who raised Jesus from the dead is living in you, he who raised Christ from the dead will also give life to your mortal bodies through his Spirit, who lives in you.

[12]Therefore, brothers, we have an obligation—but it is not to the sinful nature, to live according to it. [13]For if you live according to the sinful nature, you will die; but if by the Spirit you put to death the misdeeds of the body, you will live, [14]because those who are led by the Spirit of God are sons of God. [15]For you did not receive a spirit that makes you a slave again to fear, but you received the Spirit of sonship.[h] And by him we cry, *"Abba,*[i] *Father."* [16]The Spirit himself testifies with our spirit that we are God's children. [17]Now if we are children, then we are

---

[a] *18* Or *my flesh*   [b] *1* Some later manuscripts *Jesus, who do not live according to the sinful nature but according to the Spirit,*
[c] *3* Or *the flesh*; also in verses 4, 5, 8, 9, 12 and 13   [d] *3* Or *man, for sin*   [e] *3* Or *in the flesh*   [f] *6* Or *mind set on the flesh*
[g] *7* Or *the mind set on the flesh*   [h] *15* Or *adoption*   [i] *15* Aramaic for *Father*

heirs—heirs of God and co-heirs with Christ, if indeed we share in his sufferings in order that we may also share in his glory.

FUTURE GLORY

¹⁸I consider that our present sufferings are not worth comparing with the glory that will be revealed in us. ¹⁹The creation waits in eager expectation for the sons of God to be revealed. ²⁰For the creation was subjected to frustration, not by its own choice, but by the will of the one who subjected it, in hope ²¹that[a] the creation itself will be liberated from its bondage to decay and brought into the glorious freedom of the children of God.

²²We know that the whole creation has been groaning as in the pains of childbirth right up to the present time. ²³Not only so, but we ourselves, who have the firstfruits of the Spirit, groan inwardly as we wait eagerly for our adoption as sons, the redemption of our bodies. ²⁴For in this hope we were saved. But hope that is seen is no hope at all. Who hopes for what he already has? ²⁵But if we hope for what we do not yet have, we wait for it patiently.

²⁶In the same way, the Spirit helps us in our weakness. We do not know what we ought to pray for, but the Spirit himself intercedes for us with groans that words cannot express. ²⁷And he who searches our hearts knows the mind of the Spirit, because the Spirit intercedes for the saints in accordance with God's will.

MORE THAN CONQUERORS

²⁸And we know that in all things God works for the good of those who love him,[b] who[c] have been called according to his purpose. ²⁹For those God foreknew he also predestined to be conformed to the likeness of his Son, that he might be the first-born among many brothers. ³⁰And those he predestined, he also called; those he called, he also justified; those he justified, he also glorified.

³¹What, then, shall we say in response to this? If God is for us, who can be against us? ³²He who did not spare his own Son, but gave him up for us all—how will he not also, along with him, graciously give us all things? ³³Who will bring any charge against those whom God has chosen? It is God who justifies. ³⁴Who is he that condemns? Christ Jesus, who died—more than that, who was raised to life—is at the right hand of God and is also interceding for us. ³⁵Who shall separate us from the love of Christ? Shall trouble or hardship or persecution or famine or nakedness or danger or sword? ³⁶As it is written:

> "For your sake we face death all day long;
>   we are considered as sheep to be slaughtered."[d]

³⁷No, in all these things we are more than conquerors through him who loved us. ³⁸For I am convinced that neither death nor life, neither angels nor demons,[e] neither the present nor the future, nor any powers, ³⁹neither height nor depth, nor anything else in all creation, will be able to separate us from the love of God that is in Christ Jesus our Lord.

GOD'S SOVEREIGN CHOICE

9 I speak the truth in Christ—I am not lying, my conscience confirms it in the Holy Spirit— ²I have great sorrow and unceasing anguish in my heart. ³For I could wish that I myself were

» live the adventure » Ro 8:37–39

Being Secure in Your Salvation

Who could possibly be more powerful than God? This isn't a trick question. If you said, "no one," you're right. Remember that the next time Satan tries to convince you that God doesn't care or that you've messed up so badly that he doesn't love you anymore. You see, if you're a Christian, you're not the one holding your relationship with God together; he is. And his grip is unbreakable. You still live in a fallen world where you'll face all kinds of problems, but nothing can separate you from God because his grace is never-ending.

---

[a] 20,21 Or subjected it in hope. ²¹For   [b] 28 Some manuscripts And we know that all things work together for good to those who love God   [c] 28 Or works together with those who love him to bring about what is good—with those who   [d] 36 Psalm 44:22   [e] 38 Or nor heavenly rulers

cursed and cut off from Christ for the sake of my brothers, those of my own race, [4]the people of Israel. Theirs is the adoption as sons; theirs the divine glory, the covenants, the receiving of the law, the temple worship and the promises. [5]Theirs are the patriarchs, and from them is traced the human ancestry of Christ, who is God over all, forever praised![a] Amen.

[6]It is not as though God's word had failed. For not all who are descended from Israel are Israel. [7]Nor because they are his descendants are they all Abraham's children. On the contrary, "It is through Isaac that your offspring will be reckoned."[b] [8]In other words, it is not the natural children who are God's children, but it is the children of the promise who are regarded as Abraham's offspring. [9]For this was how the promise was stated: "At the appointed time I will return, and Sarah will have a son."[c]

[10]Not only that, but Rebekah's children had one and the same father, our father Isaac. [11]Yet, before the twins were born or had done anything good or bad—in order that God's purpose in election might stand: [12]not by works but by him who calls—she was told, "The older will serve the younger."[d] [13]Just as it is written: "Jacob I loved, but Esau I hated."[e]

[14]What then shall we say? Is God unjust? Not at all! [15]For he says to Moses,

> "I will have mercy on whom I have mercy,
>   and I will have compassion on whom I have compassion."[f]

[16]It does not, therefore, depend on man's desire or effort, but on God's mercy. [17]For the Scripture says to Pharaoh: "I raised you up for this very purpose, that I might display my power in you and that my name might be proclaimed in all the earth."[g] [18]Therefore God has mercy on whom he wants to have mercy, and he hardens whom he wants to harden.

[19]One of you will say to me: "Then why does God still blame us? For who resists his will?" [20]But who are you, O man, to talk back to God? "Shall what is formed say to him who formed it, 'Why did you make me like this?' "[h] [21]Does not the potter have the right to make out of the same lump of clay some pottery for noble purposes and some for common use?

[22]What if God, choosing to show his wrath and make his power known, bore with great patience the objects of his wrath—prepared for destruction? [23]What if he did this to make the riches of his glory known to the objects of his mercy, whom he prepared in advance for glory— [24]even us, whom he also called, not only from the Jews but also from the Gentiles? [25]As he says in Hosea:

> "I will call them 'my people' who are not my people;
>   and I will call her 'my loved one' who is not my loved one,"[i]

[26]and,

> "It will happen that in the very place where it was said to them,
>   'You are not my people,'
> they will be called 'sons of the living God.' "[j]

[27]Isaiah cries out concerning Israel:

> "Though the number of the Israelites be like the sand by the sea,
>   only the remnant will be saved.
> [28]For the Lord will carry out
>   his sentence on earth with speed and finality."[k]

[29]It is just as Isaiah said previously:

> "Unless the Lord Almighty
>   had left us descendants,
> we would have become like Sodom,
>   we would have been like Gomorrah."[l]

ISRAEL'S UNBELIEF

[30]What then shall we say? That the Gentiles, who did not pursue righteousness, have obtained it, a righteousness that is by faith; [31]but Israel, who pursued a law of righteousness, has not attained it.

---

[a] 5 Or *Christ, who is over all. God be forever praised!* Or *Christ. God who is over all be forever praised!*   [b] 7 Gen. 21:12
[c] 9 Gen. 18:10,14   [d] 12 Gen. 25:23   [e] 13 Mal. 1:2,3   [f] 15 Exodus 33:19   [g] 17 Exodus 9:16   [h] 20 Isaiah 29:16; 45:9
[i] 25 Hosea 2:23   [j] 26 Hosea 1:10   [k] 28 Isaiah 10:22,23   [l] 29 Isaiah 1:9

battlelines

» Society of Selves (Respect)

Q: What has God been teaching you lately?
A: What has God been teaching me? Wow. I think you're the first person who's ever asked me that question.

Q: Well, it's about time somebody bothered to ask!
A: Hmm . . . give me a second. OK, how about this: God is teaching me that people, including myself, are pretty self-centered. We hardly ever think about what other people are going through.

Q: Give me an example of what you mean.
A: There's this girl at school named Lindsey. She's not real popular. She's not the sort of girl you'd pick out of a crowd. Anyway, she's got all kinds of health problems, but nobody really seems to notice. I've never seen anyone reach out to her.

Q: That's sad.
A: Yeah, it really is. Everybody's just so into themselves. Here's another example. There's this smart kid named Melvin—

Q: Why are guys named Melvin always smart?
A: I have no idea, but you're missing the point. He went to some national history competition or something and came in second place—in the whole nation! That's a pretty big deal, don't you think?

Q: I'd say so.
A: Me too. But other than a little blurb in the school paper, I haven't heard one person around here even mention what he did. I don't know; that just seems flat-out wrong to me.

» Celebrating Others

This passage from the apostle Paul's letter to the Romans is a great, concise statement on how we ought to think about and treat others:

"Be devoted to one another in brotherly love. Honor one another above yourselves . . . Share with God's people who are in need. Practice hospitality. Bless those who persecute you; bless and do not curse. Rejoice with those who rejoice; mourn with those who mourn. Live in harmony with one another. Do not be proud, but be willing to associate with people of low position. Do not be conceited" (Romans 12:10,13–16).

How about it? Are you up for the challenge? Are you ready to treat people in a way that will make a difference in their lives?

Read more about respecting others at www.RevolutionBible.com.

32Why not? Because they pursued it not by faith but as if it were by works. They stumbled over the "stumbling stone." 33As it is written:

"See, I lay in Zion a stone that causes men to stumble
and a rock that makes them fall,
and the one who trusts in him will never be put to shame."a

10 Brothers, my heart's desire and prayer to God for the Israelites is that they may be saved. 2For I can testify about them that they are zealous for God, but their zeal is not based on knowledge. 3Since they did not know the righteousness that comes from God and sought to establish their own, they did not submit to God's righteousness. 4Christ is the end of the law so that there may be righteousness for everyone who believes.

5Moses describes in this way the righteousness that is by the law: "The man who does these things will live by them."b 6But the righteousness that is by faith says: "Do not say in your heart, 'Who will ascend into heaven?'c" (that is, to bring Christ down) 7"or 'Who will descend into the deep?'d" (that is, to bring Christ up from the dead). 8But what does it say? "The word is near you; it is in your mouth and in your heart,"e that is, the word of faith we are proclaiming: 9That if you confess with your mouth, "Jesus is Lord," and believe in your heart that God raised him from the dead, you will be saved. 10For it is with your heart that you believe and are justified, and it is with your mouth that you confess and are saved. 11As the Scripture says, "Anyone who trusts in him will never be put to shame."f 12For there is no difference between Jew and Gentile—the same Lord is Lord of all and richly blesses all who call on him, 13for, "Everyone who calls on the name of the Lord will be saved."g

14How, then, can they call on the one they have not believed in? And how can they believe in the one of whom they have not heard? And how can they hear without someone preaching to them? 15And how can they preach unless they are sent? As it is written, "How beautiful are the feet of those who bring good news!"h

now or never
RO 10:14-15

Everyone needs to hear the truth. Don't leave any of your friends, family members, classmates or neighbors hanging. Tell them what you know about Jesus and make sure that they hear God's truth at least once in their lives. Give them the chance to receive Jesus as their Savior.

16But not all the Israelites accepted the good news. For Isaiah says, "Lord, who has believed our message?"i 17Consequently, faith comes from hearing the message, and the message is heard through the word of Christ. 18But I ask: Did they not hear? Of course they did:

"Their voice has gone out into all the earth,
their words to the ends of the world."j

19Again I ask: Did Israel not understand? First, Moses says,

"I will make you envious by those who are not a nation;
I will make you angry by a nation that has no understanding."k

20And Isaiah boldly says,

"I was found by those who did not seek me;
I revealed myself to those who did not ask for me."l

21But concerning Israel he says,

"All day long I have held out my hands
to a disobedient and obstinate people."m

---

a 33 Isaiah 8:14; 28:16   b 5 Lev. 18:5   c 6 Deut. 30:12   d 7 Deut. 30:13   e 8 Deut. 30:14   f 11 Isaiah 28:16   g 13 Joel 2:32
h 15 Isaiah 52:7   i 16 Isaiah 53:1   j 18 Psalm 19:4   k 19 Deut. 32:21   l 20 Isaiah 65:1   m 21 Isaiah 65:2

THE REMNANT OF ISRAEL

11 I ask then: Did God reject his people? By no means! I am an Israelite myself, a descendant of Abraham, from the tribe of Benjamin. ²God did not reject his people, whom he foreknew. Don't you know what the Scripture says in the passage about Elijah—how he appealed to God against Israel: ³"Lord, they have killed your prophets and torn down your altars; I am the only one left, and they are trying to kill me"ª? ⁴And what was God's answer to him? "I have reserved for myself seven thousand who have not bowed the knee to Baal."ᵇ ⁵So too, at the present time there is a remnant chosen by grace. ⁶And if by grace, then it is no longer by works; if it were, grace would no longer be grace.ᶜ

⁷What then? What Israel sought so earnestly it did not obtain, but the elect did. The others were hardened, ⁸as it is written:

> "God gave them a spirit of stupor,
> eyes so that they could not see
> and ears so that they could not hear,
> to this very day."ᵈ

⁹And David says:

> "May their table become a snare and a trap,
> a stumbling block and a retribution for them.
> ¹⁰May their eyes be darkened so they cannot see,
> and their backs be bent forever."ᵉ

INGRAFTED BRANCHES

¹¹Again I ask: Did they stumble so as to fall beyond recovery? Not at all! Rather, because of their transgression, salvation has come to the Gentiles to make Israel envious. ¹²But if their transgression means riches for the world, and their loss means riches for the Gentiles, how much greater riches will their fullness bring!

¹³I am talking to you Gentiles. Inasmuch as I am the apostle to the Gentiles, I make much of my ministry ¹⁴in the hope that I may somehow arouse my own people to envy and save some of them. ¹⁵For if their rejection is the reconciliation of the world, what will their acceptance be but life from the dead? ¹⁶If the part of the dough offered as firstfruits is holy, then the whole batch is holy; if the root is holy, so are the branches.

¹⁷If some of the branches have been broken off, and you, though a wild olive shoot, have been grafted in among the others and now share in the nourishing sap from the olive root, ¹⁸do not boast over those branches. If you do, consider this: You do not support the root, but the root supports you. ¹⁹You will say then, "Branches were broken off so that I could be grafted in." ²⁰Granted. But they were broken off because of unbelief, and you stand by faith. Do not be arrogant, but be afraid. ²¹For if God did not spare the natural branches, he will not spare you either.

²²Consider therefore the kindness and sternness of God: sternness to those who fell, but kindness to you, provided that you continue in his kindness. Otherwise, you also will be cut off. ²³And if they do not persist in unbelief, they will be grafted in, for God is able to graft them in again. ²⁴After all, if you were cut out of an olive tree that is wild by nature, and contrary to nature were grafted into a cultivated olive tree, how much more readily will these, the natural branches, be grafted into their own olive tree!

ALL ISRAEL WILL BE SAVED

²⁵I do not want you to be ignorant of this mystery, brothers, so that you may not be conceited: Israel has experienced a hardening in part until the full number of the Gentiles has come in. ²⁶And so all Israel will be saved, as it is written:

> "The deliverer will come from Zion;
> he will turn godlessness away from Jacob.
> ²⁷And this isᶠ my covenant with them
> when I take away their sins."ᵍ

ª *3* 1 Kings 19:10,14   ᵇ *4* 1 Kings 19:18   ᶜ *6* Some manuscripts *be grace. But if by works, then it is no longer grace; if it were, work would no longer be work.*   ᵈ *8* Deut. 29:4; Isaiah 29:10   ᵉ *10* Psalm 69:22,23   ᶠ *27* Or *will be*   ᵍ *27* Isaiah 59:20,21; 27:9; Jer. 31:33,34

[28]As far as the gospel is concerned, they are enemies on your account; but as far as election is concerned, they are loved on account of the patriarchs, [29]for God's gifts and his call are irrevocable. [30]Just as you who were at one time disobedient to God have now received mercy as a result of their disobedience, [31]so they too have now become disobedient in order that they too may now[a] receive mercy as a result of God's mercy to you. [32]For God has bound all men over to disobedience so that he may have mercy on them all.

DOXOLOGY

[33]Oh, the depth of the riches of the wisdom and[b] knowledge of God!
How unsearchable his judgments,
and his paths beyond tracing out!
[34]"Who has known the mind of the Lord?
Or who has been his counselor?"[c]
[35]"Who has ever given to God,
that God should repay him?"[d]
[36]For from him and through him and to him are all things.
To him be the glory forever! Amen.

LIVING SACRIFICES

12 Therefore, I urge you, brothers, in view of God's mercy, to offer your bodies as living sacrifices, holy and pleasing to God—this is your spiritual[e] act of worship. [2]Do not conform any longer to the pattern of this world, but be transformed by the renewing of your mind. Then you will be able to test and approve what God's will is—his good, pleasing and perfect will.

[3]For by the grace given me I say to every one of you: Do not think of yourself more highly than you ought, but rather think of yourself with sober judgment, in accordance with the measure of faith God has given you. [4]Just as each of us has one body with many members, and these members do not all have the same function, [5]so in Christ we who are many form one body, and each member belongs to all the others. [6]We have different gifts, according to the grace given us. If a man's gift is prophesying, let him use it in proportion to his[f] faith. [7]If it is serving, let him serve; if it is teaching, let him teach; [8]if it is encouraging, let him encourage; if it is contributing to the needs of others, let him give generously; if it is leadership, let him govern diligently; if it is showing mercy, let him do it cheerfully.

LOVE

[9]Love must be sincere. Hate what is evil; cling to what is good. [10]Be devoted to one another in brotherly love. Honor one another above yourselves. [11]Never be lacking in zeal, but keep your spiritual fervor, serving the Lord. [12]Be joyful in hope, patient in affliction, faithful in prayer. [13]Share with God's people who are in need. Practice hospitality.

[14]Bless those who persecute you; bless and do not curse. [15]Rejoice with those who rejoice; mourn with those who mourn. [16]Live in harmony with one another. Do not be proud, but be willing to associate with people of low position.[g] Do not be conceited.

[17]Do not repay anyone evil for evil. Be careful to do what is right in the eyes of everybody. [18]If it is possible, as far as it depends on you, live at peace with everyone. [19]Do not take revenge, my friends, but leave room for God's wrath, for it is written: "It is mine to avenge; I will repay,"[h] says the Lord. [20]On the contrary:

Dedicating Your Body to God

Remember back in the Old Testament when people offered sacrifices regularly to the Lord? Sometimes they sacrificed bulls and sometimes they sacrificed sheep; whatever the sacrifice was, it had to be a pure and spotless animal—the very best a person had to offer. Nothing less than perfect was acceptable to God. If you're going to make yourself a "living sacrifice" to God, you need to make sure that your offering is as pure and spotless as you can make it. That means allowing yourself to be transformed by God's mercy and avoiding the things that pollute your body and mind and damage your devotion to God.

»» live the adventure »» Ro 12:1-2

---

battlelines

» X-Ray Vision (Lust)

Q: Finish this sentence: "It's springtime, and that means . . ."
A: Cute girls wearing short skirts.

Q: Wow, that was quick. I thought you might say "baseball" or "allergies" or "warm weather."
A: I figured you wanted me to be honest.

Q: Well, OK . . . So, the girls, huh? That's it? That's what you think of?
A: Oh, don't act like you haven't noticed! How could a guy not think of girls this time of year? Almost all of them have been going to tanning booths. Dieting. Exercising. Getting ready for bikini season. Now, here it is—the first bit of warm weather and boom! They're everywhere. Short shorts. Tube tops. Everywhere I look there's a cute girl showing skin!

Q: Yeah, it is kind of hard to look away. And the clothes seem to get skimpier every year.
A: Tell me about it!

Q: Which is why, in my book, it's a good idea to try taming the old imagination, if you get my drift.
A: Yeah, well, that's easier said than done. At least for me.

Q: Are you struggling?
A: (Embarrassed) Well . . . yeah! Doesn't every guy?

Q: I would say it affects all guys some of the time, and some guys all of the time.
A: Yeah, well, I'm in the second category.

» A New View

It's flat-out wrong the way some women dress. And it doesn't help when some Christian girls follow suit. But the fashion industry probably isn't about to change for the better anytime soon. All we can do is try, with God's help, to control our thoughts.

Here are some reminders to help you:

- Appreciating a beautiful girl isn't wrong. God made us to respond to beauty.

- Lust is the problem—undressing women with your mind, viewing them as sexual objects instead of priceless creatures made in the image of God.

- Your mind *can* be disciplined (see Romans 12:2). Tempting thoughts *can* be turned away, certain mental habits *can* be changed, and certain positive images *can* be summoned to replace negative ones. Want to give it a shot? Start by memorizing Job 31:1 or Romans 6.

- Remember, behind that gorgeous female body is a person with fears, dreams, hopes and goals. She's somebody's daughter, somebody's sister and somebody's future bride. That's why it's important to treat her the way you want other men to treat the woman you'll eventually marry. (That gives you a whole new perspective, doesn't it?)

Read more about overcoming lust at www.RevolutionBible.com.

"If your enemy is hungry, feed him;
if he is thirsty, give him something to drink.
In doing this, you will heap burning coals on his head."[a]

[21]Do not be overcome by evil, but overcome evil with good.

SUBMISSION TO THE AUTHORITIES

13 Everyone must submit himself to the governing authorities, for there is no authority except that which God has established. The authorities that exist have been established by God. [2]Consequently, he who rebels against the authority is rebelling against what God has instituted, and those who do so will bring judgment on themselves. [3]For rulers hold no terror for those who do right, but for those who do wrong. Do you want to be free from fear of the one in authority? Then do what is right and he will commend you. [4]For he is God's servant to do you good. But if you do wrong, be afraid, for he does not bear the sword for nothing. He is God's servant, an agent of wrath to bring punishment on the wrongdoer. [5]Therefore, it is necessary to submit to the authorities, not only because of possible punishment but also because of conscience.

[6]This is also why you pay taxes, for the authorities are God's servants, who give their full time to governing. [7]Give everyone what you owe him: If you owe taxes, pay taxes; if revenue, then revenue; if respect, then respect; if honor, then honor.

LOVE, FOR THE DAY IS NEAR

[8]Let no debt remain outstanding, except the continuing debt to love one another, for he who loves his fellowman has fulfilled the law. [9]The commandments, "Do not commit adultery," "Do not murder," "Do not steal," "Do not covet,"[b] and whatever other commandment there may be, are summed up in this one rule: "Love your neighbor as yourself."[c] [10]Love does no harm to its neighbor. Therefore love is the fulfillment of the law.

[11]And do this, understanding the present time. The hour has come for you to wake up from your slumber, because our salvation is nearer now than when we first believed. [12]The night is nearly over; the day is almost here. So let us put aside the deeds of darkness and put on the armor of light. [13]Let us behave decently, as in the daytime, not in orgies and drunkenness, not in sexual immorality and debauchery, not in dissension and jealousy. [14]Rather, clothe yourselves with the Lord Jesus Christ, and do not think about how to gratify the desires of the sinful nature.[d]

THE WEAK AND THE STRONG

14 Accept him whose faith is weak, without passing judgment on disputable matters. [2]One man's faith allows him to eat everything, but another man, whose faith is weak, eats only vegetables. [3]The man who eats everything must not look down on him who does not, and the man who does not eat everything must not condemn the man who does, for God has accepted him. [4]Who are you to judge someone else's servant? To his own master he stands or falls. And he will stand, for the Lord is able to make him stand.

[5]One man considers one day more sacred than another; another man considers every day alike. Each one should be fully convinced in his own mind. [6]He who regards one day as special, does so to the Lord. He who eats meat, eats to the Lord, for he gives thanks to God; and he who abstains, does so to the Lord and gives thanks to God. [7]For none of us lives to himself alone and none of us dies to himself alone. [8]If we live, we live to the Lord; and if we die, we die to the Lord. So, whether we live or die, we belong to the Lord.

[9]For this very reason, Christ died and returned to life so that he might be the Lord of both the dead and the living. [10]You, then, why do you judge your brother? Or why do you look down on your brother? For we will all stand before God's judgment seat. [11]It is written:

" 'As surely as I live,' says the Lord,
'every knee will bow before me;
every tongue will confess to God.' "[e]

[12]So then, each of us will give an account of himself to God.

---

[a] 20 Prov. 25:21,22   [b] 9 Exodus 20:13-15,17; Deut. 5:17-19,21   [c] 9 Lev. 19:18   [d] 14 Or the flesh   [e] 11 Isaiah 45:23

[13]Therefore let us stop passing judgment on one another. Instead, make up your mind not to put any stumbling block or obstacle in your brother's way. [14]As one who is in the Lord Jesus, I am fully convinced that no food[a] is unclean in itself. But if anyone regards something as unclean, then for him it is unclean. [15]If your brother is distressed because of what you eat, you are no longer acting in love. Do not by your eating destroy your brother for whom Christ died. [16]Do not allow what you consider good to be spoken of as evil. [17]For the kingdom of God is not a matter of eating and drinking, but of righteousness, peace and joy in the Holy Spirit, [18]because anyone who serves Christ in this way is pleasing to God and approved by men.

[19]Let us therefore make every effort to do what leads to peace and to mutual edification. [20]Do not destroy the work of God for the sake of food. All food is clean, but it is wrong for a man to eat anything that causes someone else to stumble. [21]It is better not to eat meat or drink wine or to do anything else that will cause your brother to fall.

[22]So whatever you believe about these things keep between yourself and God. Blessed is the man who does not condemn himself by what he approves. [23]But the man who has doubts is condemned if he eats, because his eating is not from faith; and everything that does not come from faith is sin.

15

We who are strong ought to bear with the failings of the weak and not to please ourselves. [2]Each of us should please his neighbor for his good, to build him up. [3]For even Christ did not please himself but, as it is written: "The insults of those who insult you have fallen on me."[b] [4]For everything that was written in the past was written to teach us, so that through endurance and the encouragement of the Scriptures we might have hope.

[5]May the God who gives endurance and encouragement give you a spirit of unity among yourselves as you follow Christ Jesus, [6]so that with one heart and mouth you may glorify the God and Father of our Lord Jesus Christ.

[7]Accept one another, then, just as Christ accepted you, in order to bring praise to God. [8]For I tell you that Christ has become a servant of the Jews[c] on behalf of God's truth, to confirm the promises made to the patriarchs [9]so that the Gentiles may glorify God for his mercy, as it is written:

> "Therefore I will praise you among the Gentiles;
> I will sing hymns to your name."[d]

[10]Again, it says,

> "Rejoice, O Gentiles, with his people."[e]

[11]And again,

> "Praise the Lord, all you Gentiles,
> and sing praises to him, all you peoples."[f]

[12]And again, Isaiah says,

> "The Root of Jesse will spring up,
> one who will arise to rule over the nations;
> the Gentiles will hope in him."[g]

[13]May the God of hope fill you with all joy and peace as you trust in him, so that you may overflow with hope by the power of the Holy Spirit.

---

challenge notes

To: my_son

RO 15:1-3

heavenly_father: remember the people who helped you grow spiritually when you were a young christian—the ones who answered your questions, helped you work through your doubts and warned you when they saw things in your life that didn't belong there? I want you to do the same thing for other new christians.

---

[a] 14 Or that nothing   [b] 3 Psalm 69:9   [c] 8 Greek circumcision   [d] 9 2 Samuel 22:50; Psalm 18:49   [e] 10 Deut. 32:43
[f] 11 Psalm 117:1   [g] 12 Isaiah 11:10

PAUL THE MINISTER TO THE GENTILES

[14] I myself am convinced, my brothers, that you yourselves are full of goodness, complete in knowledge and competent to instruct one another. [15] I have written you quite boldly on some points, as if to remind you of them again, because of the grace God gave me [16] to be a minister of Christ Jesus to the Gentiles with the priestly duty of proclaiming the gospel of God, so that the Gentiles might become an offering acceptable to God, sanctified by the Holy Spirit.

[17] Therefore I glory in Christ Jesus in my service to God. [18] I will not venture to speak of anything except what Christ has accomplished through me in leading the Gentiles to obey God by what I have said and done— [19] by the power of signs and miracles, through the power of the Spirit. So from Jerusalem all the way around to Illyricum, I have fully proclaimed the gospel of Christ. [20] It has always been my ambition to preach the gospel where Christ was not known, so that I would not be building on someone else's foundation. [21] Rather, as it is written:

> "Those who were not told about him will see,
> and those who have not heard will understand." [a]

[22] This is why I have often been hindered from coming to you.

PAUL'S PLAN TO VISIT ROME

[23] But now that there is no more place for me to work in these regions, and since I have been longing for many years to see you, [24] I plan to do so when I go to Spain. I hope to visit you while passing through and to have you assist me on my journey there, after I have enjoyed your company for a while. [25] Now, however, I am on my way to Jerusalem in the service of the saints there. [26] For Macedonia and Achaia were pleased to make a contribution for the poor among the saints in Jerusalem. [27] They were pleased to do it, and indeed they owe it to them. For if the Gentiles have shared in the Jews' spiritual blessings, they owe it to the Jews to share with them their material blessings. [28] So after I have completed this task and have made sure that they have received this fruit, I will go to Spain and visit you on the way. [29] I know that when I come to you, I will come in the full measure of the blessing of Christ.

[30] I urge you, brothers, by our Lord Jesus Christ and by the love of the Spirit, to join me in my struggle by praying to God for me. [31] Pray that I may be rescued from the unbelievers in Judea and that my service in Jerusalem may be acceptable to the saints there, [32] so that by God's will I may come to you with joy and together with you be refreshed. [33] The God of peace be with you all. Amen.

PERSONAL GREETINGS

16 I commend to you our sister Phoebe, a servant[b] of the church in Cenchrea. [2] I ask you to receive her in the Lord in a way worthy of the saints and to give her any help she may need from you, for she has been a great help to many people, including me.

[3] Greet Priscilla[c] and Aquila, my fellow workers in Christ Jesus. [4] They risked their lives for me. Not only I but all the churches of the Gentiles are grateful to them.

[5] Greet also the church that meets at their house.

Greet my dear friend Epenetus, who was the first convert to Christ in the province of Asia.

[6] Greet Mary, who worked very hard for you.

[7] Greet Andronicus and Junias, my relatives who have been in prison with me. They are outstanding among the apostles, and they were in Christ before I was.

[8] Greet Ampliatus, whom I love in the Lord.

[9] Greet Urbanus, our fellow worker in Christ, and my dear friend Stachys.

[10] Greet Apelles, tested and approved in Christ.

Greet those who belong to the household of Aristobulus.

[11] Greet Herodion, my relative.

Greet those in the household of Narcissus who are in the Lord.

[12] Greet Tryphena and Tryphosa, those women who work hard in the Lord.

Greet my dear friend Persis, another woman who has worked very hard in the Lord.

[13] Greet Rufus, chosen in the Lord, and his mother, who has been a mother to me, too.

[14] Greet Asyncritus, Phlegon, Hermes, Patrobas, Hermas and the brothers with them.

---

[a] 21 Isaiah 52:15   [b] 1 Or deaconess   [c] 3 Greek Prisca, a variant of Priscilla

15 Greet Philologus, Julia, Nereus and his sister, and Olympas and all the saints with them.
16 Greet one another with a holy kiss.

All the churches of Christ send greetings.

17 I urge you, brothers, to watch out for those who cause divisions and put obstacles in your way that are contrary to the teaching you have learned. Keep away from them. 18 For such people are not serving our Lord Christ, but their own appetites. By smooth talk and flattery they deceive the minds of naive people. 19 Everyone has heard about your obedience, so I am full of joy over you; but I want you to be wise about what is good, and innocent about what is evil.

20 The God of peace will soon crush Satan under your feet.

The grace of our Lord Jesus be with you.

21 Timothy, my fellow worker, sends his greetings to you, as do Lucius, Jason and Sosipater, my relatives.

22 I, Tertius, who wrote down this letter, greet you in the Lord.

23 Gaius, whose hospitality I and the whole church here enjoy, sends you his greetings.

Erastus, who is the city's director of public works, and our brother Quartus send you their greetings.ᵃ

25 Now to him who is able to establish you by my gospel and the proclamation of Jesus Christ, according to the revelation of the mystery hidden for long ages past, 26 but now revealed and made known through the prophetic writings by the command of the eternal God, so that all nations might believe and obey him— 27 to the only wise God be glory forever through Jesus Christ! Amen.

ᵃ 23 Some manuscripts *their greetings.* 24 *May the grace of our Lord Jesus Christ be with all of you. Amen.*

1 CORINTHIANS

« AT A GLANCE

Author
The apostle Paul

Audience
The church at Corinth

Date
About A.D. 55

Setting
Paul started the church in Corinth, a city in Greece, during his second missionary journey. Corinth was full of sexual immorality and idolatry, and these sins were affecting the church.

Verses to Remember
Do you not know that your body is a temple of the Holy Spirit, who is in you, whom you have received from God? You are not your own; you were bought at a price. Therefore honor God with your body (6:19–20).

Theme to Consider
As Christians, we need to think and act differently than the world. Read 1 Corinthians and discover how to live up to God's standards on such issues as gossip, immorality, sex and divorce. Then determine to honor Jesus.

UNCHANGING TRUTH » When you look around your church on Sunday mornings, who do you see? Do you see your closest friends? Do you see mentors? Do you see people who are an important part of your life? Do you see people who need you?

Do you see people who are gifts from God?

Believe it or not, that's exactly what the people in your church are—gifts from God. Just like you're a gift from God to them.

Let's face it: This world isn't exactly "Christian friendly." Trying to live a life that pleases God can be difficult, frustrating and even lonely—especially if you don't have a lot of Christian friends. That's where the church comes in. What better place is there to go for encouragement, support, advice and friendship than the family of God?

If you have plenty of Christian pals already, maybe you need to become a friend for someone else in your church who really needs one. Maybe you can "adopt" a retired person who could use some company (and some help around the house). Perhaps you can hang out with a younger kid who needs a trustworthy "big brother." In other words, you can start to build the kind of relationships that change lives.

That's what God had in mind when he set up the church 2,000 years ago. In fact, God is so intent on having church members play vital roles in each other's lives that he included specific instructions to the church in Corinth that show us how we should treat each other and handle conflict with one another.

LIFE LESSONS »

1 It's a mistake to put too much importance on any human leader—especially when it detracts from your unity with other believers (1:11–13).

2 Everyone in God's church has at least one spiritual gift—including you. If you're not using your spiritual gift(s), the entire body of Christ suffers (12:7–11).

3 Thanks to Jesus' resurrection, Christians have absolutely no reason to fear death (15:55).

1 Paul, called to be an apostle of Christ Jesus by the will of God, and our brother Sosthenes,

²To the church of God in Corinth, to those sanctified in Christ Jesus and called to be holy, together with all those everywhere who call on the name of our Lord Jesus Christ—their Lord and ours:

³Grace and peace to you from God our Father and the Lord Jesus Christ.

THANKSGIVING

⁴I always thank God for you because of his grace given you in Christ Jesus. ⁵For in him you have been enriched in every way—in all your speaking and in all your knowledge— ⁶because our testimony about Christ was confirmed in you. ⁷Therefore you do not lack any spiritual gift as you eagerly wait for our Lord Jesus Christ to be revealed. ⁸He will keep you strong to the end, so that you will be blameless on the day of our Lord Jesus Christ. ⁹God, who has called you into fellowship with his Son Jesus Christ our Lord, is faithful.

DIVISIONS IN THE CHURCH

¹⁰I appeal to you, brothers, in the name of our Lord Jesus Christ, that all of you agree with one another so that there may be no divisions among you and that you may be perfectly united in mind and thought. ¹¹My brothers, some from Chloe's household have informed me that there are quarrels among you. ¹²What I mean is this: One of you says, "I follow Paul"; another, "I follow Apollos"; another, "I follow Cephas[a]"; still another, "I follow Christ."

¹³Is Christ divided? Was Paul crucified for you? Were you baptized into[b] the name of Paul? ¹⁴I am thankful that I did not baptize any of you except Crispus and Gaius, ¹⁵so no one can say that you were baptized into my name. ¹⁶(Yes, I also baptized the household of Stephanas; beyond that, I don't remember if I baptized anyone else.) ¹⁷For Christ did not send me to baptize, but to preach the gospel—not with words of human wisdom, lest the cross of Christ be emptied of its power.

1CO 1:18-20

heavenly_father: people will try to tell you that my word is a bunch of foolishness—that Jesus isn't the only way to me or that hell is a fictional place. I'm telling you now that to disbelieve my word—that's the very definition of foolishness.

CHRIST THE WISDOM AND POWER OF GOD

¹⁸For the message of the cross is foolishness to those who are perishing, but to us who are being saved it is the power of God. ¹⁹For it is written:

"I will destroy the wisdom of the wise;
  the intelligence of the intelligent I will frustrate."[c]

²⁰Where is the wise man? Where is the scholar? Where is the philosopher of this age? Has not God made foolish the wisdom of the world? ²¹For since in the wisdom of God the world through its wisdom did not know him, God was pleased through the foolishness of what was preached to save those who believe. ²²Jews demand miraculous signs and Greeks look for wisdom, ²³but we preach Christ crucified: a stumbling block to Jews and foolishness to Gentiles, ²⁴but to those whom God has called, both Jews and Greeks, Christ the power of God and the wisdom of God. ²⁵For the foolishness of God is wiser than man's wisdom, and the weakness of God is stronger than man's strength.

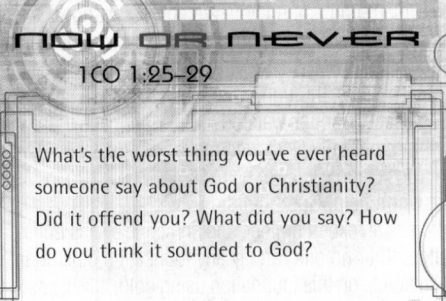

NOW OR NEVER

1CO 1:25-29

What's the worst thing you've ever heard someone say about God or Christianity? Did it offend you? What did you say? How do you think it sounded to God?

---

[a] *12* That is, Peter   [b] *13* Or *in*; also in verse 15   [c] *19* Isaiah 29:14

26Brothers, think of what you were when you were called. Not many of you were wise by human standards; not many were influential; not many were of noble birth. 27But God chose the foolish things of the world to shame the wise; God chose the weak things of the world to shame the strong. 28He chose the lowly things of this world and the despised things—and the things that are not—to nullify the things that are, 29so that no one may boast before him. 30It is because of him that you are in Christ Jesus, who has become for us wisdom from God—that is, our righteousness, holiness and redemption. 31Therefore, as it is written: "Let him who boasts boast in the Lord."[a]

2 When I came to you, brothers, I did not come with eloquence or superior wisdom as I proclaimed to you the testimony about God.[b] 2For I resolved to know nothing while I was with you except Jesus Christ and him crucified. 3I came to you in weakness and fear, and with much trembling. 4My message and my preaching were not with wise and persuasive words, but with a demonstration of the Spirit's power, 5so that your faith might not rest on men's wisdom, but on God's power.

WISDOM FROM THE SPIRIT

6We do, however, speak a message of wisdom among the mature, but not the wisdom of this age or of the rulers of this age, who are coming to nothing. 7No, we speak of God's secret wisdom, a wisdom that has been hidden and that God destined for our glory before time began. 8None of the rulers of this age understood it, for if they had, they would not have crucified the Lord of glory. 9However, as it is written:

> "No eye has seen,
>   no ear has heard,
>   no mind has conceived
>   what God has prepared for those who love him"[c]—

10but God has revealed it to us by his Spirit.

The Spirit searches all things, even the deep things of God. 11For who among men knows the thoughts of a man except the man's spirit within him? In the same way no one knows the thoughts of God except the Spirit of God. 12We have not received the spirit of the world but the Spirit who is from God, that we may understand what God has freely given us. 13This is what we speak, not in words taught us by human wisdom but in words taught by the Spirit, expressing spiritual truths in spiritual words.[d] 14The man without the Spirit does not accept the things that come from the Spirit of God, for they are foolishness to him, and he cannot understand them, because they are spiritually discerned. 15The spiritual man makes judgments about all things, but he himself is not subject to any man's judgment:

> 16 "For who has known the mind of the Lord
>   that he may instruct him?"[e]

But we have the mind of Christ.

ON DIVISIONS IN THE CHURCH

3 Brothers, I could not address you as spiritual but as worldly—mere infants in Christ. 2I gave you milk, not solid food, for you were not yet ready for it. Indeed, you are still not ready. 3You are still worldly. For since there is jealousy and quarreling among you, are you not worldly? Are you not acting like mere men? 4For when one says, "I follow Paul," and another, "I follow Apollos," are you not mere men?

5What, after all, is Apollos? And what is Paul? Only servants, through whom you came to believe—as the Lord has assigned to each his task. 6I planted the seed, Apollos watered it, but God made it grow. 7So neither he who plants nor he who waters is anything, but only God, who makes things grow. 8The man who plants and the man who waters have one purpose, and each will be rewarded according to his own labor. 9For we are God's fellow workers; you are God's field, God's building.

10By the grace God has given me, I laid a foundation as an expert builder, and someone else is building on it. But each one should be careful how he builds. 11For no one can lay any foundation other than the one already laid, which is Jesus Christ. 12If any man builds on this foundation using gold, silver, costly stones, wood, hay or straw, 13his work will be shown for what it is, because the Day will bring it to light. It will be revealed with fire, and the fire will test the quality of each man's work. 14If what he has built

---

a 31 Jer. 9:24   b 1 Some manuscripts as I proclaimed to you God's mystery   c 9 Isaiah 64:4   d 13 Or Spirit, interpreting spiritual truths to spiritual men   e 16 Isaiah 40:13

survives, he will receive his reward. [15]If it is burned up, he will suffer loss; he himself will be saved, but only as one escaping through the flames.

now or never

1CO 3:16–17

When Paul wrote about being God's temple, he was referring to all the believers in the Corinthian church. He was warning them about doing things that hurt the body of Christ. Look around you. What are ways that you can build up (rather than destroy) the "body" of believers around you?

[16]Don't you know that you yourselves are God's temple and that God's Spirit lives in you? [17]If anyone destroys God's temple, God will destroy him; for God's temple is sacred, and you are that temple.

[18]Do not deceive yourselves. If any one of you thinks he is wise by the standards of this age, he should become a "fool" so that he may become wise. [19]For the wisdom of this world is foolishness in God's sight. As it is written: "He catches the wise in their craftiness"[a]; [20]and again, "The Lord knows that the thoughts of the wise are futile."[b] [21]So then, no more boasting about men! All things are yours, [22]whether Paul or Apollos or Cephas[c] or the world or life or death or the present or the future—all are yours, [23]and you are of Christ, and Christ is of God.

APOSTLES OF CHRIST

4 So then, men ought to regard us as servants of Christ and as those entrusted with the secret things of God. [2]Now it is required that those who have been given a trust must prove faithful. [3]I care very little if I am judged by you or by any human court; indeed, I do not even judge myself. [4]My conscience is clear, but that does not make me innocent. It is the Lord who judges me. [5]Therefore judge nothing before the appointed time; wait till the Lord comes. He will bring to light what is hidden in darkness and will expose the motives of men's hearts. At that time each will receive his praise from God.

[6]Now, brothers, I have applied these things to myself and Apollos for your benefit, so that you may learn from us the meaning of the saying, "Do not go beyond what is written." Then you will not take pride in one man over against another. [7]For who makes you different from anyone else? What do you have that you did not receive? And if you did receive it, why do you boast as though you did not?

[8]Already you have all you want! Already you have become rich! You have become kings—and that without us! How I wish that you really had become kings so that we might be kings with you! [9]For it seems to me that God has put us apostles on display at the end of the procession, like men condemned to die in the arena. We have been made a spectacle to the whole universe, to angels as well as to men. [10]We are fools for Christ, but you are so wise in Christ! We are weak, but you are strong! You are honored, we are dishonored! [11]To this very hour we go hungry and thirsty, we are in rags, we are brutally treated, we are homeless. [12]We work hard with our own hands. When we are cursed, we bless; when we are persecuted, we endure it; [13]when we are slandered, we answer kindly. Up to this moment we have become the scum of the earth, the refuse of the world.

[14]I am not writing this to shame you, but to warn you, as my dear children. [15]Even though you have ten thousand guardians in Christ, you do not have many fathers, for in Christ Jesus I became your father through the gospel. [16]Therefore I urge you to imitate me. [17]For this reason I am sending to you Timothy, my son whom I love, who is faithful in the Lord. He will remind you of my way of life in Christ Jesus, which agrees with what I teach everywhere in every church.

[18]Some of you have become arrogant, as if I were not coming to you. [19]But I will come to you very soon, if the Lord is willing, and then I will find out not only how these arrogant people are talking, but what power they have. [20]For the kingdom of God is not a matter of talk but of power. [21]What do you prefer? Shall I come to you with a whip, or in love and with a gentle spirit?

EXPEL THE IMMORAL BROTHER!

5 It is actually reported that there is sexual immorality among you, and of a kind that does not occur even among pagans: A man has his father's wife. [2]And you are proud! Shouldn't you rather have been filled with grief and have put out of your fellowship the man who did this? [3]Even though I am not physically present, I am with you in spirit. And I have already passed judgment on the

[a] *19* Job 5:13   [b] *20* Psalm 94:11   [c] *22* That is, Peter

one who did this, just as if I were present. [4]When you are assembled in the name of our Lord Jesus and I am with you in spirit, and the power of our Lord Jesus is present, [5]hand this man over to Satan, so that the sinful nature[a] may be destroyed and his spirit saved on the day of the Lord.

[6]Your boasting is not good. Don't you know that a little yeast works through the whole batch of dough? [7]Get rid of the old yeast that you may be a new batch without yeast—as you really are. For Christ, our Passover lamb, has been sacrificed. [8]Therefore let us keep the Festival, not with the old yeast, the yeast of malice and wickedness, but with bread without yeast, the bread of sincerity and truth.

[9]I have written you in my letter not to associate with sexually immoral people— [10]not at all meaning the people of this world who are immoral, or the greedy and swindlers, or idolaters. In that case you would have to leave this world. [11]But now I am writing you that you must not associate with anyone who calls himself a brother but is sexually immoral or greedy, an idolater or a slanderer, a drunkard or a swindler. With such a man do not even eat.

[12]What business is it of mine to judge those outside the church? Are you not to judge those inside? [13]God will judge those outside. "Expel the wicked man from among you."[b]

LAWSUITS AMONG BELIEVERS

6 If any of you has a dispute with another, dare he take it before the ungodly for judgment instead of before the saints? [2]Do you not know that the saints will judge the world? And if you are to judge the world, are you not competent to judge trivial cases? [3]Do you not know that we will judge angels? How much more the things of this life! [4]Therefore, if you have disputes about such matters, appoint as judges even men of little account in the church![c] [5]I say this to shame you. Is it possible that there is nobody among you wise enough to judge a dispute between believers? [6]But instead, one brother goes to law against another—and this in front of unbelievers!

[7]The very fact that you have lawsuits among you means you have been completely defeated already. Why not rather be wronged? Why not rather be cheated? [8]Instead, you yourselves cheat and do wrong, and you do this to your brothers.

[9]Do you not know that the wicked will not inherit the kingdom of God? Do not be deceived: Neither the sexually immoral nor idolaters nor adulterers nor male prostitutes nor homosexual offenders [10]nor thieves nor the greedy nor drunkards nor slanderers nor swindlers will inherit the kingdom of God. [11]And that is what some of you were. But you were washed, you were sanctified, you were justified in the name of the Lord Jesus Christ and by the Spirit of our God.

SEXUAL IMMORALITY

[12]"Everything is permissible for me"—but not everything is beneficial. "Everything is permissible for me"—but I will not be mastered by anything. [13]"Food for the stomach and the stomach for food"—but God will destroy them both. The body is not meant for sexual immorality, but for the Lord, and the Lord for the body. [14]By his power God raised the Lord from the dead, and he will raise us also. [15]Do you not know that your bodies are members of Christ himself? Shall I then take the members of Christ and unite them with a prostitute? Never! [16]Do you not know that he who unites himself with a prostitute is one with her in body? For it is said, "The two will become one flesh."[d] [17]But he who unites himself with the Lord is one with him in spirit.

---

[a] 5 Or *that his body*; or *that the flesh*   [b] 13 Deut. 17:7; 19:19; 21:21; 22:21,24; 24:7   [c] 4 Or *matters, do you appoint as judges men of little account in the church?*   [d] 16 Gen. 2:24

[18]Flee from sexual immorality. All other sins a man commits are outside his body, but he who sins sexually sins against his own body. [19]Do you not know that your body is a temple of the Holy Spirit, who is in you, whom you have received from God? You are not your own; [20]you were bought at a price. Therefore honor God with your body.

MARRIAGE

7 Now for the matters you wrote about: It is good for a man not to marry.[a] [2]But since there is so much immorality, each man should have his own wife, and each woman her own husband. [3]The husband should fulfill his marital duty to his wife, and likewise the wife to her husband. [4]The wife's body does not belong to her alone but also to her husband. In the same way, the husband's body does not belong to him alone but also to his wife. [5]Do not deprive each other except by mutual consent and for a time, so that you may devote yourselves to prayer. Then come together again so that Satan will not tempt you because of your lack of self-control. [6]I say this as a concession, not as a command. [7]I wish that all men were as I am. But each man has his own gift from God; one has this gift, another has that.

[8]Now to the unmarried and the widows I say: It is good for them to stay unmarried, as I am. [9]But if they cannot control themselves, they should marry, for it is better to marry than to burn with passion.

[10]To the married I give this command (not I, but the Lord): A wife must not separate from her husband. [11]But if she does, she must remain unmarried or else be reconciled to her husband. And a husband must not divorce his wife.

[12]To the rest I say this (I, not the Lord): If any brother has a wife who is not a believer and she is willing to live with him, he must not divorce her. [13]And if a woman has a husband who is not a believer and he is willing to live with her, she must not divorce him. [14]For the unbelieving husband has been sanctified through his wife, and the unbelieving wife has been sanctified through her believing husband. Otherwise your children would be unclean, but as it is, they are holy.

[15]But if the unbeliever leaves, let him do so. A believing man or woman is not bound in such circumstances; God has called us to live in peace. [16]How do you know, wife, whether you will save your husband? Or, how do you know, husband, whether you will save your wife?

[17]Nevertheless, each one should retain the place in life that the Lord assigned to him and to which God has called him. This is the rule I lay down in all the churches. [18]Was a man already circumcised when he was called? He should not become uncircumcised. Was a man uncircumcised when he was called? He should not be circumcised. [19]Circumcision is nothing and uncircumcision is nothing. Keeping God's commands is what counts. [20]Each one should remain in the situation which he was in when God called him. [21]Were you a slave when you were called? Don't let it trouble you—although if you can gain your freedom, do so. [22]For he who was a slave when he was called by the Lord is the Lord's freedman; similarly, he who was a free man when he was called is Christ's slave. [23]You were bought at a price; do

1CO 6:18-20

---

[a] *1* Or "*It is good for a man not to have sexual relations with a woman.*"

battlelines

» The Lighter Side (Smoking/Tobacco)

Q: Whew! You stink, man! Please tell me you haven't taken up smoking.
A: What? No. I was just hanging out with my friends.

Q: At what? A chain-smoker's convention?
A: No, we were just driving around, looking for something to do.

Q: So your friends smoke?
A: Yeah. We had just gotten in the car, and before I realized it, everyone but me had lit up. Someone offered me a cigarette, but, without thinking, I automatically said, "No, thanks."

Q: I'm glad to hear that.
A: But don't you see? I said no because I've always been taught to say no. But I don't even know why.

Q: Sure you do. Smoking is terrible for you. It causes cancer.
A: Everything causes cancer.

Q: Oh, come on; don't be ridiculous! Smoking is addictive.
A: Not for everybody. Besides, eating is addictive for some people.

Q: OK, it'll make your breath smell like an ashtray.
A: There's always gum.

» Light Your World

You've heard all the reasons not to smoke:

- It causes lung cancer, emphysema and a host of other medical problems. (By the way, lung cancer is one of the leading causes of death in the United States.)

- It's an expensive habit. Even if you limited yourself to, say, one pack a week, you'd be spending a few hundred dollars a year on cigarettes alone. And if you became addicted (like most smokers do) and smoked, say, a pack a day, you'd be spending *thousands* of dollars a year on your new pastime.

- It's a nasty habit that causes bad breath, stained teeth, and smelly hair and clothes.

- Most state laws say you have to be 18 just to purchase tobacco products, and the Bible commands us to obey civil authorities (see Romans 13:1–5).

On top of all these reasons, there are passages like 1 Corinthians 6:12, which reminds us: " 'Everything is permissible for me'—but not everything is beneficial. 'Everything is permissible for me'—but I will not be mastered by anything."

Be honest: Can you think of even one good reason to smoke?

Learn more about smoking at www.RevolutionBible.com.

not become slaves of men. 24Brothers, each man, as responsible to God, should remain in the situation God called him to.

Searching for God's Will

Do you ever wonder why God put you in the situation you're in right now? Why did he give you the family you have? Why did he give you the teachers and coaches you have? Why did he put you in the school you're in right now? Why does he allow you to experience the good and bad things that happen to you? There are definitely reasons— God has a reason for everything. You may never discover what his reasons are for everything, but remembering that God is in control and learning to trust him in any situation will draw you closer to him and give you peace wherever you are.

25Now about virgins: I have no command from the Lord, but I give a judgment as one who by the Lord's mercy is trustworthy. 26Because of the present crisis, I think that it is good for you to remain as you are. 27Are you married? Do not seek a divorce. Are you unmarried? Do not look for a wife. 28But if you do marry, you have not sinned; and if a virgin marries, she has not sinned. But those who marry will face many troubles in this life, and I want to spare you this.

29What I mean, brothers, is that the time is short. From now on those who have wives should live as if they had none; 30those who mourn, as if they did not; those who are happy, as if they were not; those who buy something, as if it were not theirs to keep; 31those who use the things of the world, as if not engrossed in them. For this world in its present form is passing away.

32I would like you to be free from concern. An unmarried man is concerned about the Lord's affairs—how he can please the Lord. 33But a married man is concerned about the affairs of this world—how he can please his wife— 34and his interests are divided. An unmarried woman or virgin is concerned about the Lord's affairs: Her aim is to be devoted to the Lord in both body and spirit. But a married woman is concerned about the affairs of this world—how she can please her husband. 35I am saying this for your own good, not to restrict you, but that you may live in a right way in undivided devotion to the Lord.

36If anyone thinks he is acting improperly toward the virgin he is engaged to, and if she is getting along in years and he feels he ought to marry, he should do as he wants. He is not sinning. They should get married. 37But the man who has settled the matter in his own mind, who is under no compulsion but has control over his own will, and who has made up his mind not to marry the virgin—this man also does the right thing. 38So then, he who marries the virgin does right, but he who does not marry her does even better.[a]

39A woman is bound to her husband as long as he lives. But if her husband dies, she is free to marry anyone she wishes, but he must belong to the Lord. 40In my judgment, she is happier if she stays as she is—and I think that I too have the Spirit of God.

FOOD SACRIFICED TO IDOLS

8 Now about food sacrificed to idols: We know that we all possess knowledge.[b] Knowledge puffs up, but love builds up. 2The man who thinks he knows something does not yet know as he ought to know. 3But the man who loves God is known by God.

4So then, about eating food sacrificed to idols: We know that an idol is nothing at all in the world and that there is no God but one. 5For even if there are so-called gods, whether in heaven or on earth (as indeed there are many "gods" and many "lords"), 6yet for us there is but one God, the Father, from whom all things came and for whom we live; and there is but one Lord, Jesus Christ, through whom all things came and through whom we live.

7But not everyone knows this. Some people are still so accustomed to idols that when they eat such food they think of it as having been sacrificed to an idol, and since their conscience is weak, it is defiled. 8But food does not bring us near to God; we are no worse if we do not eat, and no better if we do.

a. 36-38 Or 36If anyone thinks he is not treating his daughter properly, and if she is getting along in years, and he feels she ought to marry, he should do as he wants. He is not sinning. He should let her get married. 37But the man who has settled the matter in his own mind, who is under no compulsion but has control over his own will, and who has made up his mind to keep the virgin unmarried—this man also does the right thing. 38So then, he who gives his virgin in marriage does right, but he who does not give her in marriage does even better. b. 1 Or "We all possess knowledge," as you say

⁹Be careful, however, that the exercise of your freedom does not become a stumbling block to the weak. ¹⁰For if anyone with a weak conscience sees you who have this knowledge eating in an idol's temple, won't he be emboldened to eat what has been sacrificed to idols? ¹¹So this weak brother, for whom Christ died, is destroyed by your knowledge. ¹²When you sin against your brothers in this way and wound their weak conscience, you sin against Christ. ¹³Therefore, if what I eat causes my brother to fall into sin, I will never eat meat again, so that I will not cause him to fall.

THE RIGHTS OF AN APOSTLE

9 Am I not free? Am I not an apostle? Have I not seen Jesus our Lord? Are you not the result of my work in the Lord? ²Even though I may not be an apostle to others, surely I am to you! For you are the seal of my apostleship in the Lord.

³This is my defense to those who sit in judgment on me. ⁴Don't we have the right to food and drink? ⁵Don't we have the right to take a believing wife along with us, as do the other apostles and the Lord's brothers and Cephas ᵃ? ⁶Or is it only I and Barnabas who must work for a living?

⁷Who serves as a soldier at his own expense? Who plants a vineyard and does not eat of its grapes? Who tends a flock and does not drink of the milk? ⁸Do I say this merely from a human point of view? Doesn't the Law say the same thing? ⁹For it is written in the Law of Moses: "Do not muzzle an ox while it is treading out the grain." ᵇ Is it about oxen that God is concerned? ¹⁰Surely he says this for us, doesn't he? Yes, this was written for us, because when the plowman plows and the thresher threshes, they ought to do so in the hope of sharing in the harvest. ¹¹If we have sown spiritual seed among you, is it too much if we reap a material harvest from you? ¹²If others have this right of support from you, shouldn't we have it all the more?

But we did not use this right. On the contrary, we put up with anything rather than hinder the gospel of Christ. ¹³Don't you know that those who work in the temple get their food from the temple, and those who serve at the altar share in what is offered on the altar? ¹⁴In the same way, the Lord has commanded that those who preach the gospel should receive their living from the gospel.

¹⁵But I have not used any of these rights. And I am not writing this in the hope that you will do such things for me. I would rather die than have anyone deprive me of this boast. ¹⁶Yet when I preach the gospel, I cannot boast, for I am compelled to preach. Woe to me if I do not preach the gospel! ¹⁷If I preach voluntarily, I have a reward; if not voluntarily, I am simply discharging the trust committed to me. ¹⁸What then is my reward? Just this: that in preaching the gospel I may offer it free of charge, and so not make use of my rights in preaching it.

NOW OR NEVER
1 CO 9:20-23

What can you do to fit in at school with certain crowds that you've never really been a part of before? What would it take to share the gospel with them in a way they could relate to?

¹⁹Though I am free and belong to no man, I make myself a slave to everyone, to win as many as possible. ²⁰To the Jews I became like a Jew, to win the Jews. To those under the law I became like one under the law (though I myself am not under the law), so as to win those under the law. ²¹To those not having the law I became like one not having the law (though I am not free from God's law but am under Christ's law), so as to win those not having the law. ²²To the weak I became weak, to win the weak. I have become all things to all men so that by all possible means I might save some. ²³I do all this for the sake of the gospel, that I may share in its blessings.

²⁴Do you not know that in a race all the runners run, but only one gets the prize? Run in such a way as to get the prize. ²⁵Everyone who competes in the games goes into strict training. They do it to get a crown that will not last; but we do it to get a crown that will last forever. ²⁶Therefore I do not run like a man running aimlessly; I do not fight like a man beating the air. ²⁷No, I beat my body and make it my slave so that after I have preached to others, I myself will not be disqualified for the prize.

WARNINGS FROM ISRAEL'S HISTORY

10 For I do not want you to be ignorant of the fact, brothers, that our forefathers were all under the cloud and that they all passed through the sea. ²They were all baptized into Moses in the cloud and in the sea. ³They all ate the same spiritual food ⁴and drank the

---

ᵃ *5 That is, Peter*   ᵇ *9 Deut. 25:4*

battlelines

» Giving In (Sex)

Q: So it's that bad, huh?
A: Yeah, it's that bad. Even if I lived on a deserted island, I'd have a hard time staying sexually pure! As it is, I live in a world where practically every commercial has some awesome-looking babe in it. It doesn't matter what they're selling—it could be lawnmowers—you know they'll show some skin if it'll get people to watch.

Q: You're right.
A: Like just about every other guy my age, I think about sex all the time. And then you've got movies and videos and magazines. Plus the way girls dress. And people talking about sex nonstop at school. With all of that going against me, how am I supposed to wait until marriage?

Q: Try thinking of the risks. What about pregnancy and disease—not to mention the spiritual damage that premarital sex causes?
A: I hear you. And right now I can process that stuff and think clearly. But put me at a party dancing with some tanned, gorgeous girl, and . . . I don't know.

Q: I've got to tell you, I'm shocked.
A: Why? I know giving in would be wrong, but the pressure is nonstop. I might be able to resist 49 times, but what about the 50th?

Q: Aw, man, that's *weak*. You know God can give you all the strength you need. You've stayed pure so far! Besides, what are friends for? I'll tell you what. The next time you think you're about to give in to temptation, call me, text me or email me. I'll come over here and throw you in a cold shower if I have to.
A: (Laughing) I wish I had your commitment.

» Giving Up

You may not feel as though you have much strength or commitment when it comes to waiting for sex, but you do have this rock-solid promise:

"No temptation has seized you except what is common to man. And God is faithful; he will not let you be tempted beyond what you can bear. But when you are tempted, he will also provide a way out so that you can stand up under it" (1 Corinthians 10:13).

God absolutely will *not* allow you to face irresistible temptations. Saying "I couldn't help myself" is a cop-out. "I *wouldn't* stop myself" is closer to the truth. God always provides "a way out," an escape from every tantalizing situation.

Read more about dealing with sexual temptation at www.RevolutionBible.com.

same spiritual drink; for they drank from the spiritual rock that accompanied them, and that rock was Christ. ⁵Nevertheless, God was not pleased with most of them; their bodies were scattered over the desert.

⁶Now these things occurred as examples[a] to keep us from setting our hearts on evil things as they did. ⁷Do not be idolaters, as some of them were; as it is written: "The people sat down to eat and drink and got up to indulge in pagan revelry."[b] ⁸We should not commit sexual immorality, as some of them did—and in one day twenty-three thousand of them died. ⁹We should not test the Lord, as some of them did—and were killed by snakes. ¹⁰And do not grumble, as some of them did—and were killed by the destroying angel.

¹¹These things happened to them as examples and were written down as warnings for us, on whom the fulfillment of the ages has come. ¹²So, if you think you are standing firm, be careful that you don't fall! ¹³No temptation has seized you except what is common to man. And God is faithful; he will not let you be tempted beyond what you can bear. But when you are tempted, he will also provide a way out so that you can stand up under it.

NOW OR NEVER
1CO 10:13

How cool is that? God makes sure that every temptation comes with its own escape plan! That means if you really want to get away from a tempting situation, you'll be able to. In fact, in most cases, all you'll have to do is *run*.

IDOL FEASTS AND THE LORD'S SUPPER

¹⁴Therefore, my dear friends, flee from idolatry. ¹⁵I speak to sensible people; judge for yourselves what I say. ¹⁶Is not the cup of thanksgiving for which we give thanks a participation in the blood of Christ? And is not the bread that we break a participation in the body of Christ? ¹⁷Because there is one loaf, we, who are many, are one body, for we all partake of the one loaf.

¹⁸Consider the people of Israel: Do not those who eat the sacrifices participate in the altar? ¹⁹Do I mean then that a sacrifice offered to an idol is anything, or that an idol is anything? ²⁰No, but the sacrifices of pagans are offered to demons, not to God, and I do not want you to be participants with demons. ²¹You cannot drink the cup of the Lord and the cup of demons too; you cannot have a part in both the Lord's table and the table of demons. ²²Are we trying to arouse the Lord's jealousy? Are we stronger than he?

THE BELIEVER'S FREEDOM

²³"Everything is permissible"—but not everything is beneficial. "Everything is permissible"—but not everything is constructive. ²⁴Nobody should seek his own good, but the good of others.

²⁵Eat anything sold in the meat market without raising questions of conscience, ²⁶for, "The earth is the Lord's, and everything in it."[c]

²⁷If some unbeliever invites you to a meal and you want to go, eat whatever is put before you without raising questions of conscience. ²⁸But if anyone says to you, "This has been offered in sacrifice," then do not eat it, both for the sake of the man who told you and for conscience' sake[d]— ²⁹the other man's conscience, I mean, not yours. For why should my freedom be judged by another's conscience? ³⁰If I take part in the meal with thankfulness, why am I denounced because of something I thank God for?

³¹So whether you eat or drink or whatever you do, do it all for the glory of God. ³²Do not cause anyone to stumble, whether Jews, Greeks or the church of God— ³³even as I try to please everybody in every way. For I am not seeking my own good but the good of many, so that they may be saved.

11 ¹Follow my example, as I follow the example of Christ.

PROPRIETY IN WORSHIP

²I praise you for remembering me in everything and for holding to the teachings,[e] just as I passed them on to you.

---

a *6* Or *types*; also in verse 11   b *7* Exodus 32:6   c *26* Psalm 24:1   d *28* Some manuscripts *conscience' sake, for "the earth is the Lord's and everything in it"*   e *2* Or *traditions*

[3]Now I want you to realize that the head of every man is Christ, and the head of the woman is man, and the head of Christ is God. [4]Every man who prays or prophesies with his head covered dishonors his head. [5]And every woman who prays or prophesies with her head uncovered dishonors her head— it is just as though her head were shaved. [6]If a woman does not cover her head, she should have her hair cut off; and if it is a disgrace for a woman to have her hair cut or shaved off, she should cover her head. [7]A man ought not to cover his head,[a] since he is the image and glory of God; but the woman is the glory of man. [8]For man did not come from woman, but woman from man; [9]neither was man created for woman, but woman for man. [10]For this reason, and because of the angels, the woman ought to have a sign of authority on her head.

[11]In the Lord, however, woman is not independent of man, nor is man independent of woman. [12]For as woman came from man, so also man is born of woman. But everything comes from God. [13]Judge for yourselves: Is it proper for a woman to pray to God with her head uncovered? [14]Does not the very nature of things teach you that if a man has long hair, it is a disgrace to him, [15]but that if a woman has long hair, it is her glory? For long hair is given to her as a covering. [16]If anyone wants to be contentious about this, we have no other practice—nor do the churches of God.

THE LORD'S SUPPER

[17]In the following directives I have no praise for you, for your meetings do more harm than good. [18]In the first place, I hear that when you come together as a church, there are divisions among you, and to some extent I believe it. [19]No doubt there have to be differences among you to show which of you have God's approval. [20]When you come together, it is not the Lord's Supper you eat, [21]for as you eat, each of you goes ahead without waiting for anybody else. One remains hungry, another gets drunk. [22]Don't you have homes to eat and drink in? Or do you despise the church of God and humiliate those who have nothing? What shall I say to you? Shall I praise you for this? Certainly not!

[23]For I received from the Lord what I also passed on to you: The Lord Jesus, on the night he was betrayed, took bread, [24]and when he had given thanks, he broke it and said, "This is my body, which is for you; do this in remembrance of me." [25]In the same way, after supper he took the cup, saying, "This cup is the new covenant in my blood; do this, whenever you drink it, in remembrance of me." [26]For whenever you eat this bread and drink this cup, you proclaim the Lord's death until he comes.

[27]Therefore, whoever eats the bread or drinks the cup of the Lord in an unworthy manner will be guilty of sinning against the body and blood of the Lord. [28]A man ought to examine himself before he eats of the bread and drinks of the cup. [29]For anyone who eats and drinks without recognizing the body of the Lord eats and drinks judgment on himself. [30]That is why many among you are weak and sick, and a number of you have fallen asleep. [31]But if we judged ourselves, we would not come under judgment. [32]When we are judged by the Lord, we are being disciplined so that we will not be condemned with the world.

[33]So then, my brothers, when you come together to eat, wait for each other. [34]If anyone is hungry, he should eat at home, so that when you meet together it may not result in judgment.

And when I come I will give further directions.

SPIRITUAL GIFTS

12

Now about spiritual gifts, brothers, I do not want you to be ignorant. [2]You know that when you were pagans, somehow or other you were influenced and led astray to mute idols. [3]Therefore I tell you that no one who is speaking by the Spirit of God says, "Jesus be cursed," and no one can say, "Jesus is Lord," except by the Holy Spirit.

[4]There are different kinds of gifts, but the same Spirit. [5]There are different kinds of service, but the same Lord. [6]There are different kinds of working, but the same God works all of them in all men.

[7]Now to each one the manifestation of the Spirit is given for the common good. [8]To one there is given through the Spirit the message of wisdom, to another the message of knowledge by means of the same Spirit, [9]to another faith by the same Spirit, to another gifts of healing by that one Spirit, [10]to another miraculous powers, to another prophecy, to another distinguishing between spirits, to another

---

[a] 4-7 Or [4]Every man who prays or prophesies with long hair dishonors his head. [5]And every woman who prays or prophesies with no covering of hair, on her head dishonors her head—she is just like one of the "shorn women." [6]If a woman has no covering, let her be for now with short hair, but since it is a disgrace for a woman to have her hair shorn or shaved, she should grow it again. [7]A man ought not to have long hair

speaking in different kinds of tongues,[a] and to still another the interpretation of tongues.[a] 11All these are the work of one and the same Spirit, and he gives them to each one, just as he determines.

ONE BODY, MANY PARTS

12The body is a unit, though it is made up of many parts; and though all its parts are many, they form one body. So it is with Christ. 13For we were all baptized by[b] one Spirit into one body—whether Jews or Greeks, slave or free—and we were all given the one Spirit to drink.

14Now the body is not made up of one part but of many. 15If the foot should say, "Because I am not a hand, I do not belong to the body," it would not for that reason cease to be part of the body. 16And if the ear should say, "Because I am not an eye, I do not belong to the body," it would not for that reason cease to be part of the body. 17If the whole body were an eye, where would the sense of hearing be? If the whole body were an ear, where would the sense of smell be? 18But in fact God has arranged the parts in the body, every one of them, just as he wanted them to be. 19If they were all one part, where would the body be? 20As it is, there are many parts, but one body.

21The eye cannot say to the hand, "I don't need you!" And the head cannot say to the feet, "I don't need you!" 22On the contrary, those parts of the body that seem to be weaker are indispensable, 23and the parts that we think are less honorable we treat with special honor. And the parts that are unpresentable are treated with special modesty, 24while our presentable parts need no special treatment. But God has combined the members of the body and has given greater honor to the parts that lacked it, 25so that there should be no division in the body, but that its parts should have equal concern for each other. 26If one part suffers, every part suffers with it; if one part is honored, every part rejoices with it.

27Now you are the body of Christ, and each one of you is a part of it. 28And in the church God has appointed first of all apostles, second prophets, third teachers, then workers of miracles, also those having gifts of healing, those able to help others, those with gifts of administration, and those speaking in different kinds of tongues. 29Are all apostles? Are all prophets? Are all teachers? Do all work miracles? 30Do all have gifts of healing? Do all speak in tongues[c]? Do all interpret? 31But eagerly desire[d] the greater gifts.

NOW OR NEVER

1CO 12:7–11

Do you know what your spiritual gifts are? When was the last time you put them into action? How did it go? How else could you use your gifts for the benefit of others in your church?

Pulling Your Weight

The body of Christ isn't some volunteer organization. If you're a Christian, you can't *choose* whether or not you want to participate. You're automatically a part of the body the moment you trust Jesus as Lord and Savior. The question is, are you a productive part of the body or are you dead weight? Are you putting your skills to use in your church, or are you just sitting back and watching other people do all the work?

LOVE

And now I will show you the most excellent way.

13 If I speak in the tongues[e] of men and of angels, but have not love, I am only a resounding gong or a clanging cymbal. 2If I have the gift of prophecy and can fathom all mysteries and all knowledge, and if I have a faith that can move mountains, but have not love, I am nothing. 3If I give all I possess to the poor and surrender my body to the flames,[f] but have not love, I gain nothing.

---

[a] 10 Or *languages*; also in verse 28   [b] 13 Or *with*; or *in*   [c] 30 Or *other languages*   [d] 31 Or *But you are eagerly desiring*
[e] 1 Or *languages*   [f] 3 Some early manuscripts *body that I may boast*

4Love is patient, love is kind. It does not envy, it does not boast, it is not proud. 5It is not rude, it is not self-seeking, it is not easily angered, it keeps no record of wrongs. 6Love does not delight in evil but rejoices with the truth. 7It always protects, always trusts, always hopes, always perseveres.

8Love never fails. But where there are prophecies, they will cease; where there are tongues, they will be stilled; where there is knowledge, it will pass away. 9For we know in part and we prophesy in part, 10but when perfection comes, the imperfect disappears. 11When I was a child, I talked like a child, I thought like a child, I reasoned like a child. When I became a man, I put childish ways behind me. 12Now we see but a poor reflection as in a mirror; then we shall see face to face. Now I know in part; then I shall know fully, even as I am fully known.

13And now these three remain: faith, hope and love. But the greatest of these is love.

NOW OR NEVER
1CO 13:4–8

Which qualities of love come naturally to you? Which ones do you think you could get the hang of with a little more practice? Which ones seem completely impossible for you to embrace?

GIFTS OF PROPHECY AND TONGUES

14 Follow the way of love and eagerly desire spiritual gifts, especially the gift of prophecy. 2For anyone who speaks in a tongue[a] does not speak to men but to God. Indeed, no one understands him; he utters mysteries with his spirit.[b] 3But everyone who prophesies speaks to men for their strengthening, encouragement and comfort. 4He who speaks in a tongue edifies himself, but he who prophesies edifies the church. 5I would like every one of you to speak in tongues,[c] but I would rather have you prophesy. He who prophesies is greater than one who speaks in tongues,[c] unless he interprets, so that the church may be edified.

6Now, brothers, if I come to you and speak in tongues, what good will I be to you, unless I bring you some revelation or knowledge or prophecy or word of instruction? 7Even in the case of lifeless things that make sounds, such as the flute or harp, how will anyone know what tune is being played unless there is a distinction in the notes? 8Again, if the trumpet does not sound a clear call, who will get ready for battle? 9So it is with you. Unless you speak intelligible words with your tongue, how will anyone know what you are saying? You will just be speaking into the air. 10Undoubtedly there are all sorts of languages in the world, yet none of them is without meaning. 11If then I do not grasp the meaning of what someone is saying, I am a foreigner to the speaker, and he is a foreigner to me. 12So it is with you. Since you are eager to have spiritual gifts, try to excel in gifts that build up the church.

13For this reason anyone who speaks in a tongue should pray that he may interpret what he says. 14For if I pray in a tongue, my spirit prays, but my mind is unfruitful. 15So what shall I do? I will pray with my spirit, but I will also pray with my mind; I will sing with my spirit, but I will also sing with my mind. 16If you are praising God with your spirit, how can one who finds himself among those who do not understand[d] say "Amen" to your thanksgiving, since he does not know what you are saying? 17You may be giving thanks well enough, but the other man is not edified.

18I thank God that I speak in tongues more than all of you. 19But in the church I would rather speak five intelligible words to instruct others than ten thousand words in a tongue.

20Brothers, stop thinking like children. In regard to evil be infants, but in your thinking be adults. 21In the Law it is written:

> "Through men of strange tongues
> and through the lips of foreigners
> I will speak to this people,
> but even then they will not listen to me,"[e]
>
> says the Lord.

22Tongues, then, are a sign, not for believers but for unbelievers; prophecy, however, is for believers, not for unbelievers. 23So if the whole church comes together and everyone speaks in tongues, and

---

[a] 2 Or *another language*; also in verses 4, 13, 14, 19, 26 and 27   [b] 2 Or *by the Spirit*   [c] 5 Or *other languages*; also in verses 6, 18, 22, 23 and 39   [d] 16 Or *among the inquirers*   [e] 21 Isaiah 28:11,12

some who do not understand[a] or some unbelievers come in, will they not say that you are out of your mind? 24But if an unbeliever or someone who does not understand[b] comes in while everybody is prophesying, he will be convinced by all that he is a sinner and will be judged by all, 25and the secrets of his heart will be laid bare. So he will fall down and worship God, exclaiming, "God is really among you!"

ORDERLY WORSHIP

26What then shall we say, brothers? When you come together, everyone has a hymn, or a word of instruction, a revelation, a tongue or an interpretation. All of these must be done for the strengthening of the church. 27If anyone speaks in a tongue, two—or at the most three—should speak, one at a time, and someone must interpret. 28If there is no interpreter, the speaker should keep quiet in the church and speak to himself and God.

29Two or three prophets should speak, and the others should weigh carefully what is said. 30And if a revelation comes to someone who is sitting down, the first speaker should stop. 31For you can all prophesy in turn so that everyone may be instructed and encouraged. 32The spirits of prophets are subject to the control of prophets. 33For God is not a God of disorder but of peace.

As in all the congregations of the saints, 34women should remain silent in the churches. They are not allowed to speak, but must be in submission, as the Law says. 35If they want to inquire about something, they should ask their own husbands at home; for it is disgraceful for a woman to speak in the church.

36Did the word of God originate with you? Or are you the only people it has reached? 37If anybody thinks he is a prophet or spiritually gifted, let him acknowledge that what I am writing to you is the Lord's command. 38If he ignores this, he himself will be ignored.[c]

39Therefore, my brothers, be eager to prophesy, and do not forbid speaking in tongues. 40But everything should be done in a fitting and orderly way.

THE RESURRECTION OF CHRIST

15 Now, brothers, I want to remind you of the gospel I preached to you, which you received and on which you have taken your stand. 2By this gospel you are saved, if you hold firmly to the word I preached to you. Otherwise, you have believed in vain.

3For what I received I passed on to you as of first importance[d]: that Christ died for our sins according to the Scriptures, 4that he was buried, that he was raised on the third day according to the Scriptures, 5and that he appeared to Peter,[e] and then to the Twelve. 6After that, he appeared to more than five hundred of the brothers at the same time, most of whom are still living, though some have fallen asleep. 7Then he appeared to James, then to all the apostles, 8and last of all he appeared to me also, as to one abnormally born.

9For I am the least of the apostles and do not even deserve to be called an apostle, because I persecuted the church of God. 10But by the grace of God I am what I am, and his grace to me was not without effect. No, I worked harder than all of them—yet not I, but the grace of God that was with me. 11Whether, then, it was I or they, this is what we preach, and this is what you believed.

THE RESURRECTION OF THE DEAD

12But if it is preached that Christ has been raised from the dead, how can some of you say that there is no resurrection of the dead? 13If there is no resurrection of the dead, then not even Christ has been raised. 14And if Christ has not been raised, our preaching is useless and so is your faith. 15More than that, we are then found to be false witnesses about God, for we have testified about God that he raised Christ from the dead. But he did not raise him if in fact the dead are not raised. 16For if the dead are not raised, then Christ has not been raised either. 17And if Christ has not been raised, your faith is futile; you are still in your sins. 18Then those also who have fallen asleep in Christ are lost. 19If only for this life we have hope in Christ, we are to be pitied more than all men.

20But Christ has indeed been raised from the dead, the firstfruits of those who have fallen asleep. 21For since death came through a man, the resurrection of the dead comes also through a man. 22For as in Adam all die, so in Christ all will be made alive. 23But each in his own turn: Christ, the firstfruits; then, when he comes, those who belong to him. 24Then the end will come, when he hands over the king-

---

[a] 23 Or some inquirers   [b] 24 Or or some inquirer   [c] 38 Some manuscripts If he is ignorant of this, let him be ignorant   [d] 3 Or you at the first   [e] 5 Greek Cephas

dom to God the Father after he has destroyed all dominion, authority and power. ²⁵For he must reign until he has put all his enemies under his feet. ²⁶The last enemy to be destroyed is death. ²⁷For he "has put everything under his feet."ᵃ Now when it says that "everything" has been put under him, it is clear that this does not include God himself, who put everything under him. ²⁸When he has done this, then the Son himself will be made subject to him who put everything under him, so that God may be all in all.

²⁹Now if there is no resurrection, what will those do who are baptized for the dead? If the dead are not raised at all, why are people baptized for them? ³⁰And as for us, why do we endanger ourselves every hour? ³¹I die every day—I mean that, brothers—just as surely as I glory over you in Christ Jesus our Lord. ³²If I fought wild beasts in Ephesus for merely human reasons, what have I gained? If the dead are not raised,

now or never

1CO 15:25-28

When Christ died, it was the ultimate form of humiliation . . . and victory. Because he was killed and rose from the dead three days later, he conquered the power of death. That's real power.

"Let us eat and drink,
for tomorrow we die."ᵇ

³³Do not be misled: "Bad company corrupts good character." ³⁴Come back to your senses as you ought, and stop sinning; for there are some who are ignorant of God—I say this to your shame.

THE RESURRECTION BODY

³⁵But someone may ask, "How are the dead raised? With what kind of body will they come?" ³⁶How foolish! What you sow does not come to life unless it dies. ³⁷When you sow, you do not plant the body that will be, but just a seed, perhaps of wheat or of something else. ³⁸But God gives it a body as he has determined, and to each kind of seed he gives its own body. ³⁹All flesh is not the same: Men have one kind of flesh, animals have another, birds another and fish another. ⁴⁰There are also heavenly bodies and there are earthly bodies; but the splendor of the heavenly bodies is one kind, and the splendor of the earthly bodies is another. ⁴¹The sun has one kind of splendor, the moon another and the stars another; and star differs from star in splendor.

⁴²So will it be with the resurrection of the dead. The body that is sown is perishable, it is raised imperishable; ⁴³it is sown in dishonor, it is raised in glory; it is sown in weakness, it is raised in power; ⁴⁴it is sown a natural body, it is raised a spiritual body.

If there is a natural body, there is also a spiritual body. ⁴⁵So it is written: "The first man Adam became a living being"ᶜ; the last Adam, a life-giving spirit. ⁴⁶The spiritual did not come first, but the natural, and after that the spiritual. ⁴⁷The first man was of the dust of the earth, the second man from heaven. ⁴⁸As was the earthly man, so are those who are of the earth; and as is the man from heaven, so also are those who are of heaven. ⁴⁹And just as we have borne the likeness of the earthly man, so shall weᵈ bear the likeness of the man from heaven.

⁵⁰I declare to you, brothers, that flesh and blood cannot inherit the kingdom of God, nor does the perishable inherit the imperishable. ⁵¹Listen, I tell you a mystery: We will not all sleep, but we will all be changed— ⁵²in a flash, in the twinkling of an eye, at the last trumpet. For the trumpet will sound, the dead will be raised imperishable, and we will be changed. ⁵³For the perishable must clothe itself with the imperishable, and the mortal with immortality. ⁵⁴When the perishable has been clothed with the imperishable, and the mortal with immortality, then the saying that is written will come true: "Death has been swallowed up in victory."ᵉ

⁵⁵ "Where, O death, is your victory?
Where, O death, is your sting?"ᶠ

⁵⁶The sting of death is sin, and the power of sin is the law. ⁵⁷But thanks be to God! He gives us the victory through our Lord Jesus Christ.

ᵃ *27* Psalm 8:6 ᵇ *32* Isaiah 22:13 ᶜ *45* Gen. 2:7 ᵈ *49* Some early manuscripts *so let us* ᵉ *54* Isaiah 25:8 ᶠ *55* Hosea 13:14

[58]Therefore, my dear brothers, stand firm. Let nothing move you. Always give yourselves fully to the work of the Lord, because you know that your labor in the Lord is not in vain.

THE COLLECTION FOR GOD'S PEOPLE

16 Now about the collection for God's people: Do what I told the Galatian churches to do. [2]On the first day of every week, each one of you should set aside a sum of money in keeping with his income, saving it up, so that when I come no collections will have to be made. [3]Then, when I arrive, I will give letters of introduction to the men you approve and send them with your gift to Jerusalem. [4]If it seems advisable for me to go also, they will accompany me.

NOW OR NEVER

1CO 15:58

When was the last time you took a rock-solid stand for God? What made you stand up for the truth? What will you do differently the next time someone challenges your faith?

PERSONAL REQUESTS

[5]After I go through Macedonia, I will come to you—for I will be going through Macedonia. [6]Perhaps I will stay with you awhile, or even spend the winter, so that you can help me on my journey, wherever I go. [7]I do not want to see you now and make only a passing visit; I hope to spend some time with you, if the Lord permits. [8]But I will stay on at Ephesus until Pentecost, [9]because a great door for effective work has opened to me, and there are many who oppose me.

[10]If Timothy comes, see to it that he has nothing to fear while he is with you, for he is carrying on the work of the Lord, just as I am. [11]No one, then, should refuse to accept him. Send him on his way in peace so that he may return to me. I am expecting him along with the brothers.

[12]Now about our brother Apollos: I strongly urged him to go to you with the brothers. He was quite unwilling to go now, but he will go when he has the opportunity.

[13]Be on your guard; stand firm in the faith; be men of courage; be strong. [14]Do everything in love.

[15]You know that the household of Stephanas were the first converts in Achaia, and they have devoted themselves to the service of the saints. I urge you, brothers, [16]to submit to such as these and to everyone who joins in the work, and labors at it. [17]I was glad when Stephanas, Fortunatus and Achaicus arrived, because they have supplied what was lacking from you. [18]For they refreshed my spirit and yours also. Such men deserve recognition.

FINAL GREETINGS

[19]The churches in the province of Asia send you greetings. Aquila and Priscilla[a] greet you warmly in the Lord, and so does the church that meets at their house. [20]All the brothers here send you greetings. Greet one another with a holy kiss.

[21]I, Paul, write this greeting in my own hand.

[22]If anyone does not love the Lord—a curse be on him. Come, O Lord[b]!

[23]The grace of the Lord Jesus be with you.

[24]My love to all of you in Christ Jesus. Amen.[c]

[a] 19 Greek *Prisca*, a variant of *Priscilla*   [b] 22 In Aramaic the expression *Come, O Lord* is *Marana tha.*   [c] 24 Some manuscripts do not have *Amen.*

2 CORINTHIANS

Author
The apostle Paul

Audience
The church at Corinth

Date
About A.D. 55

Setting
False teachers in the church in Corinth were denying Paul's authority over them as an apostle.

Verse to Remember
Therefore, if anyone is in Christ, he is a new creation; the old has gone, the new has come! (5:17).

Theme to Consider
Paul speaks out against false teachers and defends his own character, conduct and calling as an apostle of Jesus Christ. Do you live with that kind of personal integrity?

UNCHANGING TRUTH » Have you ever heard the expression "A man is only as good as his word"? If that's true, how good would your friends and family say you are? When you borrow something from a buddy and promise to give it back, do you return it as soon as you're finished with it? When you tell your little brother that you'll play catch with him, do you always follow through? When you tell a friend that the two of you will hang out on Saturday, do you do it—even if a better offer comes along?

You might ask, "What's the big deal about forgetting some minor promise or changing your plans at the last minute or deciding you really don't want to do something?" The big deal can be summed up in one word: integrity. When you fail to keep your promises, what does that say to God, who was so faithful to his promises that he sent his Son to die on the cross? Besides, how can anyone trust you with big, important stuff if you can't keep "little" promises?

The apostle Paul faced a situation in which false teachers in the church at Corinth were accusing him of not following through on his promises. Instead of blowing off the accusations and saying, "Yeah, whatever," Paul faced them head-on and responded with the truth. His reputation and dependability were important to him, and he went to a lot of trouble to defend them to the Corinthian believers.

Paul understood that if you can't be trusted in minor areas like following through on daily commitments, you can't expect to be trusted in major areas like helping people grow in their relationship with Christ. If Paul were here today, he'd tell you to guard your integrity the way you'd guard your life savings. It's a lot more valuable than you may realize.

LIFE LESSONS »

1   God gives us his peace and comfort so that we can then comfort others (1:3–4).

2   Anyone who has been forgiven for a sin needs to be restored to fellowship with the body of Christ. It's our responsibility to make sure that happens (2:7).

3   The persecution and rejection we experience in this life because of our faith will be far outweighed by the blessings we'll receive in heaven (4:17).

4   God answers all prayers; after all, "no" is an answer too (12:8–10).

1

Paul, an apostle of Christ Jesus by the will of God, and Timothy our brother,

To the church of God in Corinth, together with all the saints throughout Achaia:

²Grace and peace to you from God our Father and the Lord Jesus Christ.

THE GOD OF ALL COMFORT

³Praise be to the God and Father of our Lord Jesus Christ, the Father of compassion and the God of all comfort, ⁴who comforts us in all our troubles, so that we can comfort those in any trouble with the comfort we ourselves have received from God. ⁵For just as the sufferings of Christ flow over into our lives, so also through Christ our comfort overflows. ⁶If we are distressed, it is for your comfort and salvation; if we are comforted, it is for your comfort, which produces in you patient endurance of the same sufferings we suffer. ⁷And our hope for you is firm, because we know that just as you share in our sufferings, so also you share in our comfort.

⁸We do not want you to be uninformed, brothers, about the hardships we suffered in the province of Asia. We were under great pressure, far beyond our ability to endure, so that we despaired even of life. ⁹Indeed, in our hearts we felt the sentence of death. But this happened that we might not rely on ourselves but on God, who raises the dead. ¹⁰He has delivered us from such a deadly peril, and he will deliver us. On him we have set our hope that he will continue to deliver us, ¹¹as you help us by your prayers. Then many will give thanks on our[a] behalf for the gracious favor granted us in answer to the prayers of many.

PAUL'S CHANGE OF PLANS

¹²Now this is our boast: Our conscience testifies that we have conducted ourselves in the world, and especially in our relations with you, in the holiness and sincerity that are from God. We have done so not according to worldly wisdom but according to God's grace. ¹³For we do not write you anything you cannot read or understand. And I hope that, ¹⁴as you have understood us in part, you will come to understand fully that you can boast of us just as we will boast of you in the day of the Lord Jesus.

¹⁵Because I was confident of this, I planned to visit you first so that you might benefit twice. ¹⁶I planned to visit you on my way to Macedonia and to come back to you from Macedonia, and then to have you send me on my way to Judea. ¹⁷When I planned this, did I do it lightly? Or do I make my plans in a worldly manner so that in the same breath I say, "Yes, yes" and "No, no"?

¹⁸But as surely as God is faithful, our message to you is not "Yes" and "No." ¹⁹For the Son of God, Jesus Christ, who was preached among you by me and Silas[b] and Timothy, was not "Yes" and "No," but in him it has always been "Yes." ²⁰For no matter how many promises God has made, they are "Yes" in Christ. And so through him the "Amen" is spoken by us to the glory of God. ²¹Now it is God

---

Learning to Be Sincere

Even though some Corinthians were trying to smear his reputation, Paul said he had a clear conscience. Why? Because he always conducted himself with sincerity. Sincerity—saying what you mean and meaning what you say—is one key to developing and maintaining healthy relationships. Sincerity is what makes you say, "Look, man, I don't want to see you get burned again; I think it'd be a mistake to get back together with her." Sincerity is also what makes you follow through on your commitments. That means if you promise to help a friend study for a big test, you do it—even if your favorite cheerleader invites you to catch a movie with her on the same night.

» live the adventure » 2Co 1:12

NOW OR NEVER
2CO 1:16

When was the last time you backed out of plans you had made with a friend? Did you have a legitimate excuse for canceling, or did you just not feel like doing what you had promised? How did the other person react when you broke your commitment? How do you think that person really felt?

ª 11 Many manuscripts *your*   ᵇ 19 Greek *Silvanus*, a variant of *Silas* who makes both us and you stand firm in Christ. He anointed us, [22]set his seal of ownership on us, and put his Spirit in our hearts as a deposit, guaranteeing what is to come.

[23]I call God as my witness that it was in order to spare you that I did not return to Corinth. [24]Not that we lord it over your faith, but we work with you for your joy, because it is by faith you stand firm.

2 [1]So I made up my mind that I would not make another painful visit to you. [2]For if I grieve you, who is left to make me glad but you whom I have grieved? [3]I wrote as I did so that when I came I should not be distressed by those who ought to make me rejoice. I had confidence in all of you, that you would all share my joy. [4]For I wrote you out of great distress and anguish of heart and with many tears, not to grieve you but to let you know the depth of my love for you.

FORGIVENESS FOR THE SINNER

[5]If anyone has caused grief, he has not so much grieved me as he has grieved all of you, to some extent—not to put it too severely. [6]The punishment inflicted on him by the majority is sufficient for him. [7]Now instead, you ought to forgive and comfort him, so that he will not be overwhelmed by excessive sorrow. [8]I urge you, therefore, to reaffirm your love for him. [9]The reason I wrote you was to see if you would stand the test and be obedient in everything. [10]If you forgive anyone, I also forgive him. And what I have forgiven—if there was anything to forgive—I have forgiven in the sight of Christ for your sake, [11]in order that Satan might not outwit us. For we are not unaware of his schemes.

MINISTERS OF THE NEW COVENANT

[12]Now when I went to Troas to preach the gospel of Christ and found that the Lord had opened a door for me, [13]I still had no peace of mind, because I did not find my brother Titus there. So I said good-by to them and went on to Macedonia.

[14]But thanks be to God, who always leads us in triumphal procession in Christ and through us spreads everywhere the fragrance of the knowledge of him. [15]For we are to God the aroma of Christ among those who are being saved and those who are perishing. [16]To the one we are the smell of death; to the other, the fragrance of life. And who is equal to such a task? [17]Unlike so many, we do not peddle the word of God for profit. On the contrary, in Christ we speak before God with sincerity, like men sent from God.

3 Are we beginning to commend ourselves again? Or do we need, like some people, letters of recommendation to you or from you? [2]You yourselves are our letter, written on our hearts, known and read by everybody. [3]You show that you are a letter from Christ, the result of our ministry, written not with ink but with the Spirit of the living God, not on tablets of stone but on tablets of human hearts.

[4]Such confidence as this is ours through Christ before God. [5]Not that we are competent in ourselves to claim anything for ourselves, but our competence comes from God. [6]He has made us competent as ministers of a new covenant—not of the letter but of the Spirit; for the letter kills, but the Spirit gives life.

THE GLORY OF THE NEW COVENANT

[7]Now if the ministry that brought death, which was engraved in letters on stone, came with glory, so that the Israelites could not look steadily at the face of Moses because of its glory, fading though it was, [8]will not the ministry of the Spirit be even more glorious? [9]If the ministry that condemns men is glorious, how much more glorious is the ministry that brings righteousness! [10]For what was glorious has no glory now in comparison with the surpassing glory. [11]And if what was fading away came with glory, how much greater is the glory of that which lasts!

Spotting "Open Doors"

Have you ever seen God "open a door" in your life? Have you ever had things happen that made it clear to you that God was at work in your life? If you think hard enough, you can probably come up with at least three or four "open doors" that God has provided for you in the past year or so—perhaps a job offer that came out of the blue or a friend's question that led to a discussion about your faith. The thing about open doors is that the more you look for them, the more you will find.

¹²Therefore, since we have such a hope, we are very bold. ¹³We are not like Moses, who would put a veil over his face to keep the Israelites from gazing at it while the radiance was fading away. ¹⁴But their minds were made dull, for to this day the same veil remains when the old covenant is read. It has not been removed, because only in Christ is it taken away. ¹⁵Even to this day when Moses is read, a veil covers their hearts. ¹⁶But whenever anyone turns to the Lord, the veil is taken away. ¹⁷Now the Lord is the Spirit, and where the Spirit of the Lord is, there is freedom. ¹⁸And we, who with unveiled faces all reflect[a] the Lord's glory, are being transformed into his likeness with ever-increasing glory, which comes from the Lord, who is the Spirit.

NOW OR NEVER
2CO 3:6–12

Do you feel competent when it comes to sharing your faith story or talking about Jesus with other people? If not, what would it take to feel more equipped to be a witness for Jesus?

TREASURES IN JARS OF CLAY

4 Therefore, since through God's mercy we have this ministry, we do not lose heart. ²Rather, we have renounced secret and shameful ways; we do not use deception, nor do we distort the word of God. On the contrary, by setting forth the truth plainly we commend ourselves to every man's conscience in the sight of God. ³And even if our gospel is veiled, it is veiled to those who are perishing. ⁴The god of this age has blinded the minds of unbelievers, so that they cannot see the light of the gospel of the glory of Christ, who is the image of God. ⁵For we do not preach ourselves, but Jesus Christ as Lord, and ourselves as your servants for Jesus' sake. ⁶For God, who said, "Let light shine out of darkness,"[b] made his light shine in our hearts to give us the light of the knowledge of the glory of God in the face of Christ.

⁷But we have this treasure in jars of clay to show that this all-surpassing power is from God and not from us. ⁸We are hard pressed on every side, but not crushed; perplexed, but not in despair; ⁹persecuted, but not abandoned; struck down, but not destroyed. ¹⁰We always carry around in our body the death of Jesus, so that the life of Jesus may also be revealed in our body. ¹¹For we who are alive are always being given over to death for Jesus' sake, so that his life may be revealed in our mortal body. ¹²So then, death is at work in us, but life is at work in you.

¹³It is written: "I believed; therefore I have spoken."[c] With that same spirit of faith we also believe and therefore speak, ¹⁴because we know that the one who raised the Lord Jesus from the dead will also raise us with Jesus and present us with you in his presence. ¹⁵All this is for your benefit, so that the grace that is reaching more and more people may cause thanksgiving to overflow to the glory of God.

¹⁶Therefore we do not lose heart. Though outwardly we are wasting away, yet inwardly we are being renewed day by day. ¹⁷For our light and momentary troubles are achieving for us an eternal glory that far outweighs them all. ¹⁸So we fix our eyes not on what is seen, but on what is unseen. For what is seen is temporary, but what is unseen is eternal.

OUR HEAVENLY DWELLING

5 Now we know that if the earthly tent we live in is destroyed, we have a building from God, an eternal house in heaven, not built by human hands. ²Meanwhile we groan, longing to be clothed with our heavenly dwelling, ³because when we are clothed, we will not be found naked. ⁴For while we are in this tent, we groan and are burdened, because we do not wish to be unclothed but to be clothed with our heavenly dwelling, so that what is mortal may be swallowed up by life. ⁵Now it is God who has made us for this very purpose and has given us the Spirit as a deposit, guaranteeing what is to come.

⁶Therefore we are always confident and know that as long as we are at home in the body we are away from the Lord. ⁷We live by faith, not by sight. ⁸We are confident, I say, and would prefer to be away from the body and at home with the Lord. ⁹So we make it our goal to please him, whether we are at home in the body or away from it. ¹⁰For we must all appear before the judgment seat of Christ, that each one may receive what is due him for the things done while in the body, whether good or bad.

---

[a] 18 Or contemplate   [b] 6 Gen. 1:3   [c] 13 Psalm 116:10

THE MINISTRY OF RECONCILIATION

[11]Since, then, we know what it is to fear the Lord, we try to persuade men. What we are is plain to God, and I hope it is also plain to your conscience. [12]We are not trying to commend ourselves to you again, but are giving you an opportunity to take pride in us, so that you can answer those who take pride in what is seen rather than in what is in the heart. [13]If we are out of our mind, it is for the sake of God; if we are in our right mind, it is for you. [14]For Christ's love compels us, because we are convinced that one died for all, and therefore all died. [15]And he died for all, that those who live should no longer live for themselves but for him who died for them and was raised again.

[16]So from now on we regard no one from a worldly point of view. Though we once regarded Christ in this way, we do so no longer. [17]Therefore, if anyone is in Christ, he is a new creation; the old has gone, the new has come! [18]All this is from God, who reconciled us to himself through Christ and gave us the ministry of reconciliation: [19]that God was reconciling the world to himself in Christ, not counting men's sins against them. And he has committed to us the message of reconciliation. [20]We are therefore Christ's ambassadors, as though God were making his appeal through us. We implore you on Christ's behalf: Be reconciled to God. [21]God made him who had no sin to be sin[a] for us, so that in him we might become the righteousness of God.

6 As God's fellow workers we urge you not to receive God's grace in vain. [2]For he says,

"In the time of my favor I heard you,
and in the day of salvation I helped you."[b]

I tell you, now is the time of God's favor, now is the day of salvation.

PAUL'S HARDSHIPS

[3]We put no stumbling block in anyone's path, so that our ministry will not be discredited. [4]Rather, as servants of God we commend ourselves in every way: in great endurance; in troubles, hardships and distresses; [5]in beatings, imprisonments and riots; in hard work, sleepless nights and hunger; [6]in purity, understanding, patience and kindness; in the Holy Spirit and in sincere love; [7]in truthful speech and in the power of God; with weapons of righteousness in the right hand and in the left; [8]through glory and dishonor, bad report and good report; genuine, yet regarded as impostors; [9]known, yet regarded as unknown; dying, and yet we live on; beaten, and yet not killed; [10]sorrowful, yet always rejoicing; poor, yet making many rich; having nothing, and yet possessing everything.

[11]We have spoken freely to you, Corinthians, and opened wide our hearts to you. [12]We are not withholding our affection from you, but you are withholding yours from us. [13]As a fair exchange—I speak as to my children—open wide your hearts also.

DO NOT BE YOKED WITH UNBELIEVERS

[14]Do not be yoked together with unbelievers. For what do righteousness and wickedness have in common? Or what fellowship can light have with darkness? [15]What harmony is there between Christ and Belial[c]? What does a believer have in common with an unbeliever? [16]What agreement is there between the temple of God and idols? For we are the temple of the living God. As God has said: "I will live with them and walk among them, and I will be their God, and they will be my people."[d]

Interacting With Unbelievers

« live the adventure » 2Co 6:14–18

As a Christian, you walk a tightrope. On the one hand, you have a responsibility to share your faith with people who don't know Jesus. To do that, you have to spend time with unbelievers. You have to build relationships with them if you want to be able to show them the love of Christ. On the other hand, you have a responsibility to remain pure—that is, obedient and faithful to God. To do that, you have to avoid being too heavily influenced by the ideas and behaviors of unbelievers. You have to make sure that your friendship with an unbeliever doesn't cause you to compromise your relationship with God.

---

[a] 21 Or be a sin offering   [b] 2 Isaiah 49:8   [c] 15 Greek Beliar, a variant of Belial   [d] 16 Lev. 26:12; Jer. 32:38; Ezek. 37:27

battlelines

» Beauty and the Beast (Girls)

Q: Who was that girl you were just walking with?
A: Amazing, isn't she? That, my friend, is Kacey.

Q: Yeah, well, Kacey's a total hottie. She really seems to like you.
A: You may be right. In fact, I'm pretty sure you're right.

Q: What are you talking about?
A: She just invited me to hang out at her place this Saturday.

Q: Shut up! You? No way. You're pulling my chain.
A: Hey, don't act so surprised.

Q: Dude, how'd you meet her?
A: She's a transfer student. Just started at the beginning of the semester.

Q: Man, you've got to be the luckiest guy in the world. Most transfer students are—hey, wait a minute.
A: What?

Q: What about the junior high retreat this weekend? Didn't you sign up to help with that?
A: Yeah, that's my problem now. I promised John I'd give him a hand. But then Kacey showed up. So now what do I do? I can't just blow off John and leave him hanging. But then there's Kacey.

Q: Well, dude, I'm telling you, she's spectacular. She's flawless. Wish I could hook up with a Christian girl like that.
A: Yeah, well, that's my other problem. I don't know if she's a Christian or not. We never really talked about it, and I'm not sure how to find out . . .

» Missionary Dating

Some Christian guys think it's no big deal to go out with girls who aren't Christians. "It's just one date," they argue. "It's not like we're getting married or anything. Besides, maybe I can help bring her to Christ."

But here's the catch: We marry the people we fall in love with, and we fall in love with the people we spend time with. So it's wise to be super careful about the Kaceys of the world—no matter how nice they look. The apostle Paul put it this way: "Do not be yoked together with unbelievers. For what do righteousness and wickedness have in common? Or what fellowship can light have with darkness? What harmony is there between Christ and Belial? What does a believer have in common with an unbeliever?" (2 Corinthians 6:14–15).

Don't get caught falling for a girl who might be fun to be with yet bad for your faith. Be patient and muster up some self-control. There are plenty of girls worth getting to know who will actually encourage your faith.

Read more about getting along with girls at www.RevolutionBible.com.

> [17] "Therefore come out from them
>   and be separate,
>
>   says the Lord.
>   Touch no unclean thing,
>   and I will receive you."[a]
> [18] "I will be a Father to you,
>   and you will be my sons and daughters,
>
>   says the Lord Almighty."[b]

7 Since we have these promises, dear friends, let us purify ourselves from everything that contaminates body and spirit, perfecting holiness out of reverence for God.

PAUL'S JOY

[2]Make room for us in your hearts. We have wronged no one, we have corrupted no one, we have exploited no one. [3]I do not say this to condemn you; I have said before that you have such a place in our hearts that we would live or die with you. [4]I have great confidence in you; I take great pride in you. I am greatly encouraged; in all our troubles my joy knows no bounds.

[5]For when we came into Macedonia, this body of ours had no rest, but we were harassed at every turn—conflicts on the outside, fears within. [6]But God, who comforts the downcast, comforted us by the coming of Titus, [7]and not only by his coming but also by the comfort you had given him. He told us about your longing for me, your deep sorrow, your ardent concern for me, so that my joy was greater than ever.

[8]Even if I caused you sorrow by my letter, I do not regret it. Though I did regret it—I see that my letter hurt you, but only for a little while— [9]yet now I am happy, not because you were made sorry, but because your sorrow led you to repentance. For you became sorrowful as God intended and so were not harmed in any way by us. [10]Godly sorrow brings repentance that leads to salvation and leaves no regret, but worldly sorrow brings death. [11]See what this godly sorrow has produced in you: what earnestness, what eagerness to clear yourselves, what indignation, what alarm, what longing, what concern, what readiness to see justice done. At every point you have proved yourselves to be innocent in this matter. [12]So even though I wrote to you, it was not on account of the one who did the wrong or of the injured party, but rather that before God you could see for yourselves how devoted to us you are. [13]By all this we are encouraged.

In addition to our own encouragement, we were especially delighted to see how happy Titus was, because his spirit has been refreshed by all of you. [14]I had boasted to him about you, and you have not embarrassed me. But just as everything we said to you was true, so our boasting about you to Titus has proved to be true as well. [15]And his affection for you is all the greater when he remembers that you were all obedient, receiving him with fear and trembling. [16]I am glad I can have complete confidence in you.

GENEROSITY ENCOURAGED

8 And now, brothers, we want you to know about the grace that God has given the Macedonian churches. [2]Out of the most severe trial, their overflowing joy and their extreme poverty welled up in rich generosity. [3]For I testify that they gave as much as they were able, and even beyond their ability. Entirely on their own, [4]they urgently pleaded with us for the privilege of sharing in this service to the saints. [5]And they did not do as we expected, but they gave themselves first to the Lord and then to us in keeping with God's will. [6]So we urged Titus, since he had earlier made a beginning, to bring also to completion this act of grace on your part. [7]But just as you excel in everything—in faith, in speech, in knowledge, in complete earnestness and in your love for us[c]—see that you also excel in this grace of giving.

[8]I am not commanding you, but I want to test the sincerity of your love by comparing it with the earnestness of others. [9]For you know the grace of our Lord Jesus Christ, that though he was rich, yet for your sakes he became poor, so that you through his poverty might become rich.

[10]And here is my advice about what is best for you in this matter: Last year you were the first not only to give but also to have the desire to do so. [11]Now finish the work, so that your eager willingness

---

[a] *17* Isaiah 52:11; Ezek. 20:34,41   [b] *18* 2 Samuel 7:14; 7:8   [c] *7* Some manuscripts *in our love for you*

to do it may be matched by your completion of it, according to your means. ¹²For if the willingness is there, the gift is acceptable according to what one has, not according to what he does not have.

¹³Our desire is not that others might be relieved while you are hard pressed, but that there might be equality. ¹⁴At the present time your plenty will supply what they need, so that in turn their plenty will supply what you need. Then there will be equality, ¹⁵as it is written: "He who gathered much did not have too much, and he who gathered little did not have too little."ᵃ

TITUS SENT TO CORINTH

¹⁶I thank God, who put into the heart of Titus the same concern I have for you. ¹⁷For Titus not only welcomed our appeal, but he is coming to you with much enthusiasm and on his own initiative. ¹⁸And we are sending along with him the brother who is praised by all the churches for his service to the gospel. ¹⁹What is more, he was chosen by the churches to accompany us as we carry the offering, which we administer in order to honor the Lord himself and to show our eagerness to help. ²⁰We want to avoid any criticism of the way we administer this liberal gift. ²¹For we are taking pains to do what is right, not only in the eyes of the Lord but also in the eyes of men.

²²In addition, we are sending with them our brother who has often proved to us in many ways that he is zealous, and now even more so because of his great confidence in you. ²³As for Titus, he is my partner and fellow worker among you; as for our brothers, they are representatives of the churches and an honor to Christ. ²⁴Therefore show these men the proof of your love and the reason for our pride in you, so that the churches can see it.

9 There is no need for me to write to you about this service to the saints. ²For I know your eagerness to help, and I have been boasting about it to the Macedonians, telling them that since last year you in Achaia were ready to give; and your enthusiasm has stirred most of them to action. ³But I am sending the brothers in order that our boasting about you in this matter should not prove hollow, but that you may be ready, as I said you would be. ⁴For if any Macedonians come with me and find you unprepared, we—not to say anything about you—would be ashamed of having been so confident. ⁵So I thought it necessary to urge the brothers to visit you in advance and finish the arrangements for the generous gift you had promised. Then it will be ready as a generous gift, not as one grudgingly given.

SOWING GENEROUSLY

⁶Remember this: Whoever sows sparingly will also reap sparingly, and whoever sows generously will also reap generously. ⁷Each man should give what he has decided in his heart to give, not reluctantly or under compulsion, for God loves a cheerful giver. ⁸And God is able to make all grace abound to you, so that in all things at all times, having all that you need, you will abound in every good work. ⁹As it is written:

"He has scattered abroad his gifts to the
poor;
his righteousness endures forever."ᵇ

¹⁰Now he who supplies seed to the sower and bread for food will also supply and increase your store of seed and will enlarge the harvest of your righteousness. ¹¹You will be made rich in every way so that you can be generous on every occasion, and through us your generosity will result in thanksgiving to God.

ПОШ ОR ПЕVER
2CO 9:7

How much is "enough" when it comes to giving what you have to God? Do you think you have a good spirit of generosity? What could increase your willingness to give back to God what he has given to you?

¹²This service that you perform is not only supplying the needs of God's people but is also overflowing in many expressions of thanks to God. ¹³Because of the service by which you have proved yourselves, men will praise God for the obedience that accompanies your confession of the gospel of Christ, and for your generosity in sharing with them and with everyone else. ¹⁴And in their prayers for you their hearts will go out to you, because of the surpassing grace God has given you. ¹⁵Thanks be to God for his indescribable gift!

ᵃ 15 Exodus 16:18   ᵇ 9 Psalm 112:9

PAUL'S DEFENSE OF HIS MINISTRY

10 By the meekness and gentleness of Christ, I appeal to you—I, Paul, who am "timid" when face to face with you, but "bold" when away! ²I beg you that when I come I may not have to be as bold as I expect to be toward some people who think that we live by the standards of this world. ³For though we live in the world, we do not wage war as the world does. ⁴The weapons we fight with are not the weapons of the world. On the contrary, they have divine power to demolish strongholds. ⁵We demolish arguments and every pretension that sets itself up against the knowledge of God, and we take captive every thought to make it obedient to Christ. ⁶And we will be ready to punish every act of disobedience, once your obedience is complete.

⁷You are looking only on the surface of things.ᵃ If anyone is confident that he belongs to Christ, he should consider again that we belong to Christ just as much as he. ⁸For even if I boast somewhat freely about the authority the Lord gave us for building you up rather than pulling you down, I will not be ashamed of it. ⁹I do not want to seem to be trying to frighten you with my letters. ¹⁰For some say, "His letters are weighty and forceful, but in person he is unimpressive and his speaking amounts to nothing." ¹¹Such people should realize that what we are in our letters when we are absent, we will be in our actions when we are present.

¹²We do not dare to classify or compare ourselves with some who commend themselves. When they measure themselves by themselves and compare themselves with themselves, they are not wise. ¹³We, however, will not boast beyond proper limits, but will confine our boasting to the field God has assigned to us, a field that reaches even to you. ¹⁴We are not going too far in our boasting, as would be the case if we had not come to you, for we did get as far as you with the gospel of Christ. ¹⁵Neither do we go beyond our limits by boasting of work done by others.ᵇ Our hope is that, as your faith continues to grow, our area of activity among you will greatly expand, ¹⁶so that we can preach the gospel in the regions beyond you. For we do not want to boast about work already done in another man's territory. ¹⁷But, "Let him who boasts boast in the Lord."ᶜ ¹⁸For it is not the one who commends himself who is approved, but the one whom the Lord commends.

PAUL AND THE FALSE APOSTLES

11 I hope you will put up with a little of my foolishness; but you are already doing that. ²I am jealous for you with a godly jealousy. I promised you to one husband, to Christ, so that I might present you as a pure virgin to him. ³But I am afraid that just as Eve was deceived by the serpent's cunning, your minds may somehow be led astray from your sincere and pure devotion to Christ. ⁴For if someone comes to you and preaches a Jesus other than the Jesus we preached, or if you receive a different spirit from the one you received, or a different gospel from the one you accepted, you put up with it easily enough. ⁵But I do not think I am in the least inferior to those "super-apostles." ⁶I may not be a trained speaker, but I do have knowledge. We have made this perfectly clear to you in every way.

⁷Was it a sin for me to lower myself in order to elevate you by preaching the gospel of God to you free of charge? ⁸I robbed other churches by receiving support from them so as to serve you. ⁹And when I was with you and needed something, I was not a burden to anyone, for the brothers who came from Macedonia supplied what I needed. I have kept myself from being a burden to you in any way, and will continue to do so. ¹⁰As surely as the truth of Christ is in me, nobody in the regions of Achaia will stop this boasting of mine. ¹¹Why? Because I do not love you? God knows I do! ¹²And I will keep on doing what I am doing in order to cut the ground from under those who want an opportunity to be considered equal with us in the things they boast about.

¹³For such men are false apostles, deceitful workmen, masquerading as apostles of Christ. ¹⁴And no wonder, for Satan himself masquerades as an angel of light. ¹⁵It is not surprising, then, if his servants masquerade as servants of righteousness. Their end will be what their actions deserve.

PAUL BOASTS ABOUT HIS SUFFERINGS

¹⁶I repeat: Let no one take me for a fool. But if you do, then receive me just as you would a fool, so that I may do a little boasting. ¹⁷In this self-confident boasting I am not talking as the Lord would, but

---

ᵃ 7 Or *Look at the obvious facts*   ᵇ 13-15 Or ¹³*We, however, will not boast about things that cannot be measured, but we will boast according to the standard of measurement that the God of measure has assigned us—a measurement that relates even to you.* ¹⁴ . . . ¹⁵*Neither do we boast about things that cannot be measured in regard to the work done by others.*   ᶜ 17 Jer. 9:24

as a fool. [18]Since many are boasting in the way the world does, I too will boast. [19]You gladly put up with fools since you are so wise! [20]In fact, you even put up with anyone who enslaves you or exploits you or takes advantage of you or pushes himself forward or slaps you in the face. [21]To my shame I admit that we were too weak for that!

What anyone else dares to boast about—I am speaking as a fool—I also dare to boast about. [22]Are they Hebrews? So am I. Are they Israelites? So am I. Are they Abraham's descendants? So am I. [23]Are they servants of Christ? (I am out of my mind to talk like this.) I am more. I have worked much harder, been in prison more frequently, been flogged more severely, and have been exposed to death again and again. [24]Five times I received from the Jews the forty lashes minus one. [25]Three times I was beaten with rods, once I was stoned, three times I was shipwrecked, I spent a night and a day in the open sea, [26]I have been constantly on the move. I have been in danger from rivers, in danger from bandits, in danger from my own countrymen, in danger from Gentiles; in danger in the city, in danger in the country, in danger at sea; and in danger from false brothers. [27]I have labored and toiled and have often gone without sleep; I have known hunger and thirst and have often gone without food; I have been cold and naked. [28]Besides everything else, I face daily the pressure of my concern for all the churches. [29]Who is weak, and I do not feel weak? Who is led into sin, and I do not inwardly burn?

[30]If I must boast, I will boast of the things that show my weakness. [31]The God and Father of the Lord Jesus, who is to be praised forever, knows that I am not lying. [32]In Damascus the governor under King Aretas had the city of the Damascenes guarded in order to arrest me. [33]But I was lowered in a basket from a window in the wall and slipped through his hands.

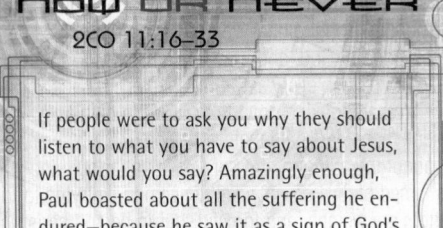

NOW OR NEVER

2CO 11:16–33

If people were to ask you why they should listen to what you have to say about Jesus, what would you say? Amazingly enough, Paul boasted about all the suffering he endured—because he saw it as a sign of God's power and ability to see him through anything. What do you have to boast about?

PAUL'S VISION AND HIS THORN

12 I must go on boasting. Although there is nothing to be gained, I will go on to visions and revelations from the Lord. [2]I know a man in Christ who fourteen years ago was caught up to the third heaven. Whether it was in the body or out of the body I do not know—God knows. [3]And I know that this man—whether in the body or apart from the body I do not know, but God knows— [4]was caught up to paradise. He heard inexpressible things, things that man is not permitted to tell. [5]I will boast about a man like that, but I will not boast about myself, except about my weaknesses. [6]Even if I should choose to boast, I would not be a fool, because I would be speaking the truth. But I refrain, so no one will think more of me than is warranted by what I do or say.

[7]To keep me from becoming conceited because of these surpassingly great revelations, there was given me a thorn in my flesh, a messenger of Satan, to torment me. [8]Three times I pleaded with the Lord to take it away from me. [9]But he said to me, "My grace is sufficient for you, for my power is made perfect in weakness." Therefore I will boast all the more gladly about my weaknesses, so that Christ's power may rest on me. [10]That is why, for Christ's sake, I delight in weaknesses, in insults, in hardships, in persecutions, in difficulties. For when I am weak, then I am strong.

challenge notes

To: my_son

heavenly_father: I want you to come to me in prayer with every request that you have. understand, however, that I may not always give you just the answer you want. but I will give you the strength and endurance you need to accept your situation, grow from it and move forward.

2CO 12:7-10

PAUL'S CONCERN FOR THE CORINTHIANS

[11]I have made a fool of myself, but you drove me to it. I ought to have been commended by you, for I am not in the least inferior to the "super-apostles," even though I am nothing. [12]The things that mark

an apostle—signs, wonders and miracles—were done among you with great perseverance. 13How were you inferior to the other churches, except that I was never a burden to you? Forgive me this wrong!

14Now I am ready to visit you for the third time, and I will not be a burden to you, because what I want is not your possessions but you. After all, children should not have to save up for their parents, but parents for their children. 15So I will very gladly spend for you everything I have and expend myself as well. If I love you more, will you love me less? 16Be that as it may, I have not been a burden to you. Yet, crafty fellow that I am, I caught you by trickery! 17Did I exploit you through any of the men I sent you? 18I urged Titus to go to you and I sent our brother with him. Titus did not exploit you, did he? Did we not act in the same spirit and follow the same course?

19Have you been thinking all along that we have been defending ourselves to you? We have been speaking in the sight of God as those in Christ; and everything we do, dear friends, is for your strengthening. 20For I am afraid that when I come I may not find you as I want you to be, and you may not find me as you want me to be. I fear that there may be quarreling, jealousy, outbursts of anger, factions, slander, gossip, arrogance and disorder. 21I am afraid that when I come again my God will humble me before you, and I will be grieved over many who have sinned earlier and have not repented of the impurity, sexual sin and debauchery in which they have indulged.

FINAL WARNINGS

13 This will be my third visit to you. "Every matter must be established by the testimony of two or three witnesses."a 2I already gave you a warning when I was with you the second time. I now repeat it while absent: On my return I will not spare those who sinned earlier or any of the others, 3since you are demanding proof that Christ is speaking through me. He is not weak in dealing with you, but is powerful among you. 4For to be sure, he was crucified in weakness, yet he lives by God's power. Likewise, we are weak in him, yet by God's power we will live with him to serve you.

5Examine yourselves to see whether you are in the faith; test yourselves. Do you not realize that Christ Jesus is in you—unless, of course, you fail the test? 6And I trust that you will discover that we have not failed the test. 7Now we pray to God that you will not do anything wrong. Not that people will see that we have stood the test but that you will do what is right even though we may seem to have failed. 8For we cannot do anything against the truth, but only for the truth. 9We are glad whenever we are weak but you are strong; and our prayer is for your perfection. 10This is why I write these things when I am absent, that when I come I may not have to be harsh in my use of authority—the authority the Lord gave me for building you up, not for tearing you down.

FINAL GREETINGS

11Finally, brothers, good-by. Aim for perfection, listen to my appeal, be of one mind, live in peace. And the God of love and peace will be with you.

12Greet one another with a holy kiss. 13All the saints send their greetings.

14May the grace of the Lord Jesus Christ, and the love of God, and the fellowship of the Holy Spirit be with you all.

a 1 Deut. 19:15

GALATIANS

GALATIANS GALATIANS

Author
The apostle Paul

Audience
The churches in the Roman province of Galatia, part of the modern nation of Turkey

Date
About A.D. 50

Setting
People called *Judaizers* were teaching that Gentiles had to obey the Jewish laws in order to be saved.

Verses to Remember
I have been crucified with Christ and I no longer live, but Christ lives in me. The life I live in the body, I live by faith in the Son of God, who loved me and gave himself for me. I do not set aside the grace of God, for if righteousness could be gained through the law, Christ died for nothing (2:20–21)!

Theme to Consider
We can never earn God's salvation by what we do or how well we obey the rules. It is by God's grace alone.

UNCHANGING TRUTH » People are naturally suspicious of things that seem too good to be true. If a stranger calls to say you've won a fabulous prize, you know it's a scam . . . or else they're just trying to sell you something dumb like a magazine subscription. If someone you don't know offers you a free slice of pizza at lunch, the first thing you're going to do is check it for spit or some other nasty "hidden topping."

Some people have a hard time accepting God's gift of salvation because it's free. They can't shake the idea that there's got to be some catch; they're convinced that somehow they have to earn the "gift" of eternal life by doing good works, living clean and participating in religious rituals.

The Galatians of Paul's day fit into that category. Judaizers were going around teaching that Gentile (non-Jewish) Christians had to obey Jewish laws and participate in certain rituals and ceremonies in order to be saved. To Paul's amazement, some of the believers in Galatia were actually buying into this messed-up gospel. In response, Paul made it absolutely clear that only one thing ever has, ever does and ever will save people: faith in the Messiah, Jesus Christ.

LIFE LESSONS »

1   The only way to recognize false teaching is to know what God's Word really says (1:6).

2   At some point, we have to choose whether we seek the approval of God or people (1:10).

3   If you know that a close Christian friend is doing something wrong, you have a responsibility to address the sinful behavior (2:11–14).

4   Love, joy, peace, patience, kindness, goodness, faithfulness, gentleness and self-control are "fruits" of the Holy Spirit—signs that he's at work in your life (5:22–23).

1

Paul, an apostle—sent not from men nor by man, but by Jesus Christ and God the Father, who raised him from the dead— [2]and all the brothers with me,

To the churches in Galatia:

[3]Grace and peace to you from God our Father and the Lord Jesus Christ, [4]who gave himself for our sins to rescue us from the present evil age, according to the will of our God and Father, [5]to whom be glory for ever and ever. Amen.

NO OTHER GOSPEL

[6]I am astonished that you are so quickly deserting the one who called you by the grace of Christ and are turning to a different gospel— [7]which is really no gospel at all. Evidently some people are throwing you into confusion and are trying to pervert the gospel of Christ. [8]But even if we or an angel from heaven should preach a gospel other than the one we preached to you, let him be eternally condemned! [9]As we have already said, so now I say again: If anybody is preaching to you a gospel other than what you accepted, let him be eternally condemned!

[10]Am I now trying to win the approval of men, or of God? Or am I trying to please men? If I were still trying to please men, I would not be a servant of Christ.

PAUL CALLED BY GOD

[11]I want you to know, brothers, that the gospel I preached is not something that man made up. [12]I did not receive it from any man, nor was I taught it; rather, I received it by revelation from Jesus Christ.

[13]For you have heard of my previous way of life in Judaism, how intensely I persecuted the church of God and tried to destroy it. [14]I was advancing in Judaism beyond many Jews of my own age and was extremely zealous for the traditions of my fathers. [15]But when God, who set me apart from birth[a] and called me by his grace, was pleased [16]to reveal his Son in me so that I might preach him among the Gentiles, I did not consult any man, [17]nor did I go up to Jerusalem to see those who were apostles before I was, but I went immediately into Arabia and later returned to Damascus.

NOW OR NEVER
GAL 1:23-24

Despite his reputation as a persecutor of Christians, the churches of Judea rejoiced over Paul's conversion. How do you react when someone you think is beyond hope comes to faith in Jesus?

[18]Then after three years, I went up to Jerusalem to get acquainted with Peter[b] and stayed with him fifteen days. [19]I saw none of the other apostles—only James, the Lord's brother. [20]I assure you before God that what I am writing you is no lie. [21]Later I went to Syria and Cilicia. [22]I was personally unknown to the churches of Judea that are in Christ. [23]They only heard the report: "The man who formerly persecuted us is now preaching the faith he once tried to destroy." [24]And they praised God because of me.

PAUL ACCEPTED BY THE APOSTLES

2

Fourteen years later I went up again to Jerusalem, this time with Barnabas. I took Titus along also. [2]I went in response to a revelation and set before them the gospel that I preach among the Gentiles. But I did this privately to those who seemed to be leaders, for fear that I was running or had run my race in vain. [3]Yet not even Titus, who was with me, was compelled to be circumcised, even though he was a Greek. [4]This matter arose because some false brothers had infiltrated our ranks to spy on the freedom we have in Christ Jesus and to make us slaves. [5]We did not give in to them for a moment, so that the truth of the gospel might remain with you.

[6]As for those who seemed to be important—whatever they were makes no difference to me; God does not judge by external appearance—those men added nothing to my message. [7]On the contrary, they saw that I had been entrusted with the task of preaching the gospel to the Gentiles,[c] just as Peter had been to the Jews.[d] [8]For God, who was at work in the ministry of Peter as an apostle to the Jews, was also at work in my ministry as an apostle to the Gentiles. [9]James, Peter[e] and John, those reputed

---

[a] 15 Or from my mother's womb   [b] 18 Greek Cephas   [c] 7 Greek uncircumcised   [d] 7 Greek circumcised; also in verses 8 and 9
[e] 9 Greek Cephas; also in verses 11 and 14

paul

VERSUS

barnabas

» Originally known as Saul
» An apostle who wrote much of the New Testament
» The greatest missionary the church has ever known

» Also known as Joseph from Cyprus
» Given his name because of his great gift for encouraging others
» A respected missionary and generous servant in the early church

The Main Event

Have you ever gotten into an argument with a buddy? Not just a little squabble, but a serious falling out? An all-out, knock-down conflict? A clash in which the two of you were *really* ticked and said some harsh things to each other? One that caused you to avoid each other for a while? Perhaps a long while?

If so, you're in good company. Believe it or not, the apostle Paul and his close missionary side-kick and friend Barnabas once got into a heated debate so fierce they ended up going their separate ways. Here's the skinny on the story.

Paul and Barnabas had been friends from the beginning. In fact, Barnabas was one of the first people to stick up for Paul after his conversion—at a time when many other believers in Jerusalem feared that Paul was just pretending to be a disciple so he could continue persecuting them. On their first missionary journey, Paul and Barnabas agreed to take along Barnabas's young cousin, a recent convert named John Mark. The missionaries hadn't traveled very far when they encountered serious obstacles—including trials, persecution and stress. That's when John Mark bailed. No one knows why he did what he did, but the poor guy may have gotten in way over his head. Missionary life wasn't at all what he had anticipated. He panicked and, almost without warning, split.

It's not until two years later—just before Paul and Barnabas's second missionary journey, in fact—that we see what a huge issue this really was. Barnabas, who was legendary for his warm hearted, encouraging personality, proposed giving Mark another shot. Paul was stunned by the idea. "No way!" he argued. "That kid left us in the lurch once before. I can't embark on another long, hard trip with colleagues who aren't reliable."

Both men had a valid point. And neither would budge. So they went their separate ways.

The Outcome

The dispute between Barnabas and Paul over John Mark is a Biblical snapshot that serves to remind us of some important truths:

1. Even mature Christians can have serious disagreements with one another. Sometimes the best response in such instances is to agree to disagree. Sometimes the issue of "right and wrong" isn't all that black and white.

2. God's global, eternal plan isn't thwarted by our disagreements. The result of Barnabas and Paul's dispute was that instead of one missionary team going out, two went. Barnabas and Mark went one way, and Paul and Silas went another.

3. Our goal should always be to forgive and resolve disputes. It's interesting that in the last letter Paul ever wrote, during the final days of his life, the great apostle told Timothy, "Get [John] Mark and bring him with you, because he is helpful to me in my ministry" (2 Timothy 4:11). Isn't that awesome? Something must have happened between the time of the disagreement and the time that letter was written. Paul and Mark straightened things out and got on the same page—perhaps with the help of their mutual friend Barnabas.

Read more about Paul and Barnabas in Acts 4:36–37 (page 1416); 9:23–31 (page 1425); 11:19–30 (page 1428); 13:1–14:28 (pages 1429–1431); 15:30–41 (page 1433).

to be pillars, gave me and Barnabas the right hand of fellowship when they recognized the grace given to me. They agreed that we should go to the Gentiles, and they to the Jews. [10]All they asked was that we should continue to remember the poor, the very thing I was eager to do.

Not Judging By Appearance

The next time you find yourself in a big crowd of people your age, pay attention to a couple of things: Where do your eyes drift? Who or what catches your attention? What are you thinking about other people as you look at them? What are you thinking about yourself? If you're like most guys, you're a very visual person. Whether you're checking out how a girl looks or how cool another guy is dressed, appearance is everything. But the apostle Paul makes it clear in this passage that appearances of any kind—physical or otherwise—made no difference to him or to the God he served. How about you?

PAUL OPPOSES PETER

[11]When Peter came to Antioch, I opposed him to his face, because he was clearly in the wrong. [12]Before certain men came from James, he used to eat with the Gentiles. But when they arrived, he began to draw back and separate himself from the Gentiles because he was afraid of those who belonged to the circumcision group. [13]The other Jews joined him in his hypocrisy, so that by their hypocrisy even Barnabas was led astray.

[14]When I saw that they were not acting in line with the truth of the gospel, I said to Peter in front of them all, "You are a Jew, yet you live like a Gentile and not like a Jew. How is it, then, that you force Gentiles to follow Jewish customs?

[15]"We who are Jews by birth and not 'Gentile sinners' [16]know that a man is not justified by observing the law, but by faith in Jesus Christ. So we, too, have put our faith in Christ Jesus that we may be justified by faith in Christ and not by observing the law, because by observing the law no one will be justified.

[17]"If, while we seek to be justified in Christ, it becomes evident that we ourselves are sinners, does that mean that Christ promotes sin? Absolutely not! [18]If I rebuild what I destroyed, I prove that I am a lawbreaker. [19]For through the law I died to the law so that I might live for God. [20]I have been crucified with Christ and I no longer live, but Christ lives in me. The life I live in the body, I live by faith in the Son of God, who loved me and gave himself for me. [21]I do not set aside the grace of God, for if righteousness could be gained through the law, Christ died for nothing!" [a]

FAITH OR OBSERVANCE OF THE LAW

3 You foolish Galatians! Who has bewitched you? Before your very eyes Jesus Christ was clearly portrayed as crucified. [2]I would like to learn just one thing from you: Did you receive the Spirit by observing the law, or by believing what you heard? [3]Are you so foolish? After beginning with the Spirit, are you now trying to attain your goal by human effort? [4]Have you suffered so much for nothing—if it really was for nothing? [5]Does God give you his Spirit and work miracles among you because you observe the law, or because you believe what you heard?

[6]Consider Abraham: "He believed God, and it was credited to him as righteousness." [b] [7]Understand, then, that those who believe are children of Abraham. [8]The Scripture foresaw that God would justify the Gentiles by faith, and announced the gospel in advance to Abraham: "All nations will be blessed through you." [c] [9]So those who have faith are blessed along with Abraham, the man of faith.

[10]All who rely on observing the law are under a curse, for it is written: "Cursed is everyone who does

NOW OR NEVER
GAL 3:1

If the apostle Paul were to write a letter to you about your Christian faith, what do you think he would praise you for? What changes do you think he would challenge you to make?

---

[a] *21* Some interpreters end the quotation after verse 14.   [b] *6* Gen. 15:6   [c] *8* Gen. 12:3; 18:18; 22:18

not continue to do everything written in the Book of the Law."[a] 11Clearly no one is justified before God by the law, because, "The righteous will live by faith."[b] 12The law is not based on faith; on the contrary, "The man who does these things will live by them."[c] 13Christ redeemed us from the curse of the law by becoming a curse for us, for it is written: "Cursed is everyone who is hung on a tree."[d] 14He redeemed us in order that the blessing given to Abraham might come to the Gentiles through Christ Jesus, so that by faith we might receive the promise of the Spirit.

THE LAW AND THE PROMISE

15Brothers, let me take an example from everyday life. Just as no one can set aside or add to a human covenant that has been duly established, so it is in this case. 16The promises were spoken to Abraham and to his seed. The Scripture does not say "and to seeds," meaning many people, but "and to your seed,"[e] meaning one person, who is Christ. 17What I mean is this: The law, introduced 430 years later, does not set aside the covenant previously established by God and thus do away with the promise. 18For if the inheritance depends on the law, then it no longer depends on a promise; but God in his grace gave it to Abraham through a promise.

19What, then, was the purpose of the law? It was added because of transgressions until the Seed to whom the promise referred had come. The law was put into effect through angels by a mediator. 20A mediator, however, does not represent just one party; but God is one.

21Is the law, therefore, opposed to the promises of God? Absolutely not! For if a law had been given that could impart life, then righteousness would certainly have come by the law. 22But the Scripture declares that the whole world is a prisoner of sin, so that what was promised, being given through faith in Jesus Christ, might be given to those who believe.

23Before this faith came, we were held prisoners by the law, locked up until faith should be revealed. 24So the law was put in charge to lead us to Christ[f] that we might be justified by faith. 25Now that faith has come, we are no longer under the supervision of the law.

SONS OF GOD

26You are all sons of God through faith in Christ Jesus, 27for all of you who were baptized into Christ have clothed yourselves with Christ. 28There is neither Jew nor Greek, slave nor free, male nor female, for you are all one in Christ Jesus. 29If you belong to Christ, then you are Abraham's seed, and heirs according to the promise.

4 What I am saying is that as long as the heir is a child, he is no different from a slave, although he owns the whole estate. 2He is subject to guardians and trustees until the time set by his father. 3So also, when we were children, we were in slavery under the basic principles of the world. 4But when the time had fully come, God sent his Son, born of a woman, born under law, 5to redeem those under law, that we might receive the full rights of sons. 6Because you are sons, God sent the Spirit of his Son into our hearts, the Spirit who calls out, "Abba,[g] Father." 7So you are no longer a slave, but a son; and since you are a son, God has made you also an heir.

challengenotes

To: my_son

heavenly_father: that word, son, is not just a term of affection. I really do consider you my child. I love you even more than an earthly father can. I want what's best for you. that's why I've made you an heir of my kingdom.

GAL 4:6-7

PAUL'S CONCERN FOR THE GALATIANS

8Formerly, when you did not know God, you were slaves to those who by nature are not gods. 9But now that you know God—or rather are known by God—how is it that you are turning back to those weak and miserable principles? Do you wish to be enslaved by them all over again? 10You are observing special days and months and seasons and years! 11I fear for you, that somehow I have wasted my efforts on you.

12I plead with you, brothers, become like me, for I became like you. You have done me no wrong. 13As you know, it was because of an illness that I first preached the gospel to you. 14Even though my

[a] 10 Deut. 27:26   [b] 11 Hab. 2:4   [c] 12 Lev. 18:5   [d] 13 Deut. 21:23   [e] 16 Gen. 12:7; 13:15; 24:7   [f] 24 Or charge until Christ came   [g] 6 Aramaic for Father

illness was a trial to you, you did not treat me with contempt or scorn. Instead, you welcomed me as if I were an angel of God, as if I were Christ Jesus himself. ¹⁵What has happened to all your joy? I can testify that, if you could have done so, you would have torn out your eyes and given them to me. ¹⁶Have I now become your enemy by telling you the truth?

¹⁷Those people are zealous to win you over, but for no good. What they want is to alienate you ⌐from us⌐, so that you may be zealous for them. ¹⁸It is fine to be zealous, provided the purpose is good, and to be so always and not just when I am with you. ¹⁹My dear children, for whom I am again in the pains of childbirth until Christ is formed in you, ²⁰how I wish I could be with you now and change my tone, because I am perplexed about you!

HAGAR AND SARAH

²¹Tell me, you who want to be under the law, are you not aware of what the law says? ²²For it is written that Abraham had two sons, one by the slave woman and the other by the free woman. ²³His son by the slave woman was born in the ordinary way; but his son by the free woman was born as the result of a promise.

²⁴These things may be taken figuratively, for the women represent two covenants. One covenant is from Mount Sinai and bears children who are to be slaves: This is Hagar. ²⁵Now Hagar stands for Mount Sinai in Arabia and corresponds to the present city of Jerusalem, because she is in slavery with her children. ²⁶But the Jerusalem that is above is free, and she is our mother. ²⁷For it is written:

> "Be glad, O barren woman,
>   who bears no children;
> break forth and cry aloud,
>   you who have no labor pains;
> because more are the children of the desolate woman
>   than of her who has a husband." [a]

²⁸Now you, brothers, like Isaac, are children of promise. ²⁹At that time the son born in the ordinary way persecuted the son born by the power of the Spirit. It is the same now. ³⁰But what does the Scripture say? "Get rid of the slave woman and her son, for the slave woman's son will never share in the inheritance with the free woman's son." [b] ³¹Therefore, brothers, we are not children of the slave woman, but of the free woman.

FREEDOM IN CHRIST

5 It is for freedom that Christ has set us free. Stand firm, then, and do not let yourselves be burdened again by a yoke of slavery.

²Mark my words! I, Paul, tell you that if you let yourselves be circumcised, Christ will be of no value to you at all. ³Again I declare to every man who lets himself be circumcised that he is obligated to obey the whole law. ⁴You who are trying to be justified by law have been alienated from Christ; you have fallen away from grace. ⁵But by faith we eagerly await through the Spirit the righteousness for which we hope. ⁶For in Christ Jesus neither circumcision nor uncircumcision has any value. The only thing that counts is faith expressing itself through love.

⁷You were running a good race. Who cut in on you and kept you from obeying the truth? ⁸That kind of persuasion does not come from the one who calls you. ⁹"A little yeast works through the whole batch of dough." ¹⁰I am confident in the Lord that you will take no other view. The one who is throwing you into confusion will pay the penalty, whoever he may be. ¹¹Brothers, if I am still preaching circumcision, why am I still being persecuted? In that case the offense of the cross has been abolished. ¹²As for those agitators, I wish they would go the whole way and emasculate themselves!

¹³You, my brothers, were called to be free. But do not use your freedom to indulge the sinful nature[c]; rather, serve one another in love. ¹⁴The entire law is summed up in a single command: "Love your neighbor as yourself." [d] ¹⁵If you keep on biting and devouring each other, watch out or you will be destroyed by each other.

LIFE BY THE SPIRIT

¹⁶So I say, live by the Spirit, and you will not gratify the desires of the sinful nature. ¹⁷For the sin-

ᵃ *27* Isaiah 54:1   ᵇ *30* Gen. 21:10   ᶜ *13* Or *the flesh*; also in verses 16, 17, 19 and 24   ᵈ *14* Lev. 19:18

battlelines

» Green With Envy (Jealousy)

Q: Can you believe the weekend Andy had?
A: Yeah, well, I don't see what the big deal is all about.

Q: Dude, you were there! Were you unconscious? The guy dominated! He had the most amazing three runs in a row I've ever seen! I'll bet you anything he qualifies for the X Games. And I'll bet he walks away not only with the $1,000, but with a new girlfriend—Amber.
A: Say whatever you want, but I think Andy's *way* overrated. He's the cockiest dude I've ever seen. You know what? I hope he *does* make the X Games. I'd love to see him get humiliated on national TV. If you ask me, that would be the best thing to ever happen to him. Somebody needs to bring him down to earth.

Q: Know what I think? I think you're just jealous.
A: What? Of Andy? Get out of here! No way.

Q: Yes, you are. It's so obvious. It *kills* you to have to admit that Andy is an unbelievable skater and that the girls are swarming him. Plus, you've had your eye on Amber for two years.
A: Yeah, whatever.

» Getting a Grip

For the sake of argument, let's go ahead and say that Riley *is* a little jealous of Andy. Is that really such a big deal?

Consider what Galatians 5:19–21 says: "The acts of the sinful nature are obvious: sexual immorality, impurity and debauchery; idolatry and witchcraft; hatred, discord, *jealousy*, fits of rage, selfish ambition, dissensions, factions and *envy*; drunkenness, orgies, and the like. I warn you, as I did before, that those who live like this will not inherit the kingdom of God" (emphasis added).

Notice that *envy* is lumped in with idolatry, witchcraft and orgies. Apparently it *is* a big deal.

Envy occurs when we forget that God gives different gifts and abilities to every person. The cure for envy is learning to appreciate what others can do, while working hard to develop your own gifts.

Read more at www.RevolutionBible.com.

ful nature desires what is contrary to the Spirit, and the Spirit what is contrary to the sinful nature. They are in conflict with each other, so that you do not do what you want. [18]But if you are led by the Spirit, you are not under law.

[19]The acts of the sinful nature are obvious: sexual immorality, impurity and debauchery; [20]idolatry and witchcraft; hatred, discord, jealousy, fits of rage, selfish ambition, dissensions, factions [21]and envy; drunkenness, orgies, and the like. I warn you, as I did before, that those who live like this will not inherit the kingdom of God.

[22]But the fruit of the Spirit is love, joy, peace, patience, kindness, goodness, faithfulness, [23]gentleness and self-control. Against such things there is no law. [24]Those who belong to Christ Jesus have crucified the sinful nature with its passions and desires. [25]Since we live by the Spirit, let us keep in step with the Spirit. [26]Let us not become conceited, provoking and envying each other.

now or never
GAL 5:22-23

Of the fruits of the Spirit listed in these verses, which ones are most evident in your life? Which ones are least noticeable in your character?

DOING GOOD TO ALL

6 Brothers, if someone is caught in a sin, you who are spiritual should restore him gently. But watch yourself, or you also may be tempted. [2]Carry each other's burdens, and in this way you will fulfill the law of Christ. [3]If anyone thinks he is something when he is nothing, he deceives himself. [4]Each one should test his own actions. Then he can take pride in himself, without comparing himself to somebody else, [5]for each one should carry his own load.

[6]Anyone who receives instruction in the word must share all good things with his instructor.

[7]Do not be deceived: God cannot be mocked. A man reaps what he sows. [8]The one who sows to please his sinful nature, from that nature[a] will reap destruction; the one who sows to please the Spirit, from the Spirit will reap eternal life. [9]Let us not become weary in doing good, for at the proper time we will reap a harvest if we do not give up. [10]Therefore, as we have opportunity, let us do good to all people, especially to those who belong to the family of believers.

NOT CIRCUMCISION BUT A NEW CREATION

[11]See what large letters I use as I write to you with my own hand!

[12]Those who want to make a good impression outwardly are trying to compel you to be circumcised. The only reason they do this is to avoid being persecuted for the cross of Christ. [13]Not even those who are circumcised obey the law, yet they want you to be circumcised that they may boast about your flesh. [14]May I never boast except in the cross of our Lord Jesus Christ, through which[b] the world has been crucified to me, and I to the world. [15]Neither circumcision nor uncircumcision means anything; what counts is a new creation. [16]Peace and mercy to all who follow this rule, even to the Israel of God.

[17]Finally, let no one cause me trouble, for I bear on my body the marks of Jesus.

[18]The grace of our Lord Jesus Christ be with your spirit, brothers. Amen.

Being a Good Person

Once you get a reputation as a "good guy"—the type who's willing to lend a hand when someone is in trouble or just needs to talk—people are going to seek out your friendship. You may even become overwhelmed by those who want your help. The best way to prevent yourself from burning out is to stay connected to God at all times. Ask him to give you the strength, wisdom and discernment you need to know who to help and how best to help them.

»» live the adventure »» Gal 6:9

---

[a] 8 Or *his flesh, from the flesh*   [b] 14 Or *whom*

EPHESIANS

Author
The apostle Paul

Audience
The church at Ephesus

Date
About A.D. 60

Setting
Paul wrote this letter from Rome while he was in prison. He probably intended this to be a circular letter, to be passed on from the believers in Ephesus to other Christians in the area.

Verses to Remember
There is one body and one Spirit—just as you were called to one hope when you were called—one Lord, one faith, one baptism; one God and Father of all, who is over all and through all and in all (4:4–6).

Theme to Consider
As believers, we are united in Jesus Christ. We should do all we can to live in unity with other believers and get rid of jealousy, backstabbing, anger and bitterness.

UNCHANGING TRUTH » Do you know anyone who's spoiled by their parents? Not just a little spoiled. We're talking about ski trips to Aspen for spring break, a brand new BMW as a 16th birthday present, a closet full of new designer clothes at the beginning of every school year—yeah, that kind of spoiled.

Have you ever wondered what it would be like to have parents like that—a mother and father ready, willing and able to give you anything you need, anytime you ask? Well, wonder no more, because the book of Ephesians makes it clear that we *have* a father like that—God, our heavenly Father.

Instead of being generous with money and material possessions, though, God is generous with spiritual blessings—the kind of wealth that won't disappear the next time an investment goes bad, the market crashes or styles change.

In Ephesians, Paul describes just some of the blessings that are yours as a child of God:
- salvation—the forgiveness and grace that God has "lavished" on you (1:8)
- the Holy Spirit, who is like a deposit guaranteeing your eternal inheritance (1:14)
- wisdom and knowledge to know God better (1:17–18)
- reconciliation with Jesus and with other believers (2:11–22)

Luke 11:9 says simply, "Ask and it will be given to you." God *wants* to bless you. Find out just how deep his spiritual pockets are. Let him spoil you!

LIFE LESSONS »

1. God has equipped us with everything we need to obey him and accomplish his will (2:10).

2. Everyone has a unique and equally important responsibility in the body of Christ (4:11–13).

3. Be prepared to sacrifice your own comfort and preferences for the good of the entire church (5:21).

4. Christians have a God-given responsibility to show respect for the other members of their family (6:1–4).

1

Paul, an apostle of Christ Jesus by the will of God,

To the saints in Ephesus,[a] the faithful[b] in Christ Jesus:

[2]Grace and peace to you from God our Father and the Lord Jesus Christ.

SPIRITUAL BLESSINGS IN CHRIST

[3]Praise be to the God and Father of our Lord Jesus Christ, who has blessed us in the heavenly realms with every spiritual blessing in Christ. [4]For he chose us in him before the creation of the world to be holy and blameless in his sight. In love [5]he[c] predestined us to be adopted as his sons through Jesus Christ, in accordance with his pleasure and will— [6]to the praise of his glorious grace, which he has freely given us in the One he loves. [7]In him we have redemption through his blood, the forgiveness of sins, in accordance with the riches of God's grace [8]that he lavished on us with all wisdom and understanding. [9]And he[d] made known to us the mystery of his will according to his good pleasure, which he purposed in Christ, [10]to be put into effect when the times will have reached their fulfillment—to bring all things in heaven and on earth together under one head, even Christ.

[11]In him we were also chosen,[e] having been predestined according to the plan of him who works out everything in conformity with the purpose of his will, [12]in order that we, who were the first to hope in Christ, might be for the praise of his glory. [13]And you also were included in Christ when you heard the word of truth, the gospel of your salvation. Having believed, you were marked in him with a seal, the promised Holy Spirit, [14]who is a deposit guaranteeing our inheritance until the redemption of those who are God's possession—to the praise of his glory.

THANKSGIVING AND PRAYER

[15]For this reason, ever since I heard about your faith in the Lord Jesus and your love for all the saints, [16]I have not stopped giving thanks for you, remembering you in my prayers. [17]I keep asking that the God of our Lord Jesus Christ, the glorious Father, may give you the Spirit[f] of wisdom and revelation, so that you may know him better. [18]I pray also that the eyes of your heart may be enlightened in order that you may know the hope to which he has called you, the riches of his glorious inheritance in the saints, [19]and his incomparably great power for us who believe. That power is like the working of his mighty strength, [20]which he exerted in Christ when he raised him from the dead and seated him at his right hand in the heavenly realms, [21]far above all rule and authority, power and dominion, and every title that can be given, not only in the present age but also in the one to come. [22]And God placed all things under his feet and appointed him to be head over everything for the church, [23]which is his body, the fullness of him who fills everything in every way.

MADE ALIVE IN CHRIST

2

As for you, you were dead in your transgressions and sins, [2]in which you used to live when you followed the ways of this world and of the ruler of the kingdom of the air, the spirit who is now at work in those who are disobedient. [3]All of us also lived among them at one time, gratifying the cravings of our sinful nature[g] and following its desires and thoughts. Like the rest, we were by nature objects of wrath. [4]But because of his great love for us, God, who is rich in mercy, [5]made us alive with Christ even when we were dead in transgressions—it is by grace you have been saved. [6]And God raised us up with Christ and seated us with him in the heavenly realms in Christ Jesus, [7]in order that in the coming ages he might show the incomparable riches of his grace, expressed in his kindness to us in Christ Jesus. [8]For it is by grace you have been saved, through faith—and this not from yourselves, it is the gift of God— [9]not by works, so that no one can boast. [10]For we are God's workmanship, created in Christ Jesus to do good works, which God prepared in advance for us to do.

ONE IN CHRIST

[11]Therefore, remember that formerly you who are Gentiles by birth and called "uncircumcised" by those who call themselves "the circumcision" (that done in the body by the hands of men)— [12]remember that at that time you were separate from Christ, excluded from citizenship in Israel and foreigners

---

[a] 1 Some early manuscripts do not have in Ephesus.   [b] 1 Or believers who are   [c] 4,5 Or sight in love. [5]He   [d] 8,9 Or us. With all wisdom and understanding, [9]he   [e] 11 Or were made heirs   [f] 17 Or a spirit   [g] 3 Or our flesh

to the covenants of the promise, without hope and without God in the world. ¹³But now in Christ Jesus you who once were far away have been brought near through the blood of Christ.

¹⁴For he himself is our peace, who has made the two one and has destroyed the barrier, the dividing wall of hostility, ¹⁵by abolishing in his flesh the law with its commandments and regulations. His purpose was to create in himself one new man out of the two, thus making peace, ¹⁶and in this one body to reconcile both of them to God through the cross, by which he put to death their hostility. ¹⁷He came and preached peace to you who were far away and peace to those who were near. ¹⁸For through him we both have access to the Father by one Spirit.

¹⁹Consequently, you are no longer foreigners and aliens, but fellow citizens with God's people and members of God's household, ²⁰built on the foundation of the apostles and prophets, with Christ Jesus himself as the chief cornerstone. ²¹In him the whole building is joined together and rises to become a holy temple in the Lord. ²²And in him you too are being built together to become a dwelling in which God lives by his Spirit.

Eliminating Barriers

Eph 2:14 »» live the adventure »»

Do you ever feel as though there are "walls" between you and other people? Some walls are built because of racial issues. Some are built because of differences in backgrounds and upbringing. Some are built because of clashing personalities. One thing these different walls have in common, though, is that none of them can stand against Jesus' power. God is a wall smasher. If you're serious about following him, he will help you eliminate the barriers that separate you from others, and he'll help you find common ground on which to build friendships.

PAUL THE PREACHER TO THE GENTILES

3 For this reason I, Paul, the prisoner of Christ Jesus for the sake of you Gentiles—

²Surely you have heard about the administration of God's grace that was given to me for you, ³that is, the mystery made known to me by revelation, as I have already written briefly. ⁴In reading this, then, you will be able to understand my insight into the mystery of Christ, ⁵which was not made known to men in other generations as it has now been revealed by the Spirit to God's holy apostles and prophets. ⁶This mystery is that through the gospel the Gentiles are heirs together with Israel, members together of one body, and sharers together in the promise in Christ Jesus.

⁷I became a servant of this gospel by the gift of God's grace given me through the working of his power. ⁸Although I am less than the least of all God's people, this grace was given me: to preach to the Gentiles the unsearchable riches of Christ, ⁹and to make plain to everyone the administration of this mystery, which for ages past was kept hidden in God, who created all things. ¹⁰His intent was that now, through the church, the manifold wisdom of God should be made known to the rulers and authorities in the heavenly realms, ¹¹according to his eternal purpose which he accomplished in Christ Jesus our Lord. ¹²In him and through faith in him we may approach God with freedom and confidence. ¹³I ask you, therefore, not to be discouraged because of my sufferings for you, which are your glory.

A PRAYER FOR THE EPHESIANS

¹⁴For this reason I kneel before the Father, ¹⁵from whom his whole family[a] in heaven and on earth derives its name. ¹⁶I pray that out of his glorious riches he may strengthen you with power through his Spirit in your inner being, ¹⁷so that Christ may dwell in your hearts through faith. And I pray that you,

a 15 Or whom all fatherhood

being rooted and established in love, [18]may have power, together with all the saints, to grasp how wide and long and high and deep is the love of Christ, [19]and to know this love that surpasses knowledge— that you may be filled to the measure of all the fullness of God.

[20]Now to him who is able to do immeasurably more than all we ask or imagine, according to his power that is at work within us, [21]to him be glory in the church and in Christ Jesus throughout all generations, for ever and ever! Amen.

UNITY IN THE BODY OF CHRIST

4 As a prisoner for the Lord, then, I urge you to live a life worthy of the calling you have received. [2]Be completely humble and gentle; be patient, bearing with one another in love. [3]Make every effort to keep the unity of the Spirit through the bond of peace. [4]There is one body and one Spirit—just as you were called to one hope when you were called— [5]one Lord, one faith, one baptism; [6]one God and Father of all, who is over all and through all and in all.

[7]But to each one of us grace has been given as Christ apportioned it. [8]This is why it[a] says:

"When he ascended on high,
he led captives in his train
and gave gifts to men."[b]

[9](What does "he ascended" mean except that he also descended to the lower, earthly regions[c]? [10]He who descended is the very one who ascended higher than all the heavens, in order to fill the whole universe.) [11]It was he who gave some to be apostles, some to be prophets, some to be evangelists, and some to be pastors and teachers, [12]to prepare God's people for works of service, so that the body of Christ may be built up [13]until we all reach unity in the faith and in the knowledge of the Son of God and become mature, attaining to the whole measure of the fullness of Christ.

[14]Then we will no longer be infants, tossed back and forth by the waves, and blown here and there by every wind of teaching and by the cunning and craftiness of men in their deceitful scheming. [15]Instead, speaking the truth in love, we will in all things grow up into him who is the Head, that is, Christ. [16]From him the whole body, joined and held together by every supporting ligament, grows and builds itself up in love, as each part does its work.

NOW OR NEVER
EPH 4:11–12

Do you fit in any of the categories Paul mentioned? If you could add a category to describe your role in the church, what would it be? How has God gifted you and how are you using—or not using—those gifts to serve within his church?

LIVING AS CHILDREN OF LIGHT

[17]So I tell you this, and insist on it in the Lord, that you must no longer live as the Gentiles do, in the futility of their thinking. [18]They are darkened in their understanding and separated from the life of God because of the ignorance that is in them due to the hardening of their hearts. [19]Having lost all sensitivity, they have given themselves over to sensuality so as to indulge in every kind of impurity, with a continual lust for more.

[20]You, however, did not come to know Christ that way. [21]Surely you heard of him and were taught in him in accordance with the truth that is in Jesus. [22]You were taught, with regard to your former way of life, to put off your old self, which is being corrupted by its deceitful desires; [23]to be made new in the attitude of your minds; [24]and to put on the new self, created to be like God in true righteousness and holiness.

[25]Therefore each of you must put off falsehood and speak truthfully to his neighbor, for we are all members of one body. [26]"In your anger do not sin"[d]: Do not let the sun go down while you are still angry, [27]and do not give the devil a foothold. [28]He who has been stealing must steal no longer, but must work, doing something useful with his own hands, that he may have something to share with those in need.

[29]Do not let any unwholesome talk come out of your mouths, but only what is helpful for building others up according to their needs, that it may benefit those who listen. [30]And do not grieve the Holy

---

[a] 8 Or God   [b] 8 Psalm 68:18   [c] 9 Or the depths of the earth   [d] 26 Psalm 4:4

Spirit of God, with whom you were sealed for the day of redemption. ³¹Get rid of all bitterness, rage and anger, brawling and slander, along with every form of malice. ³²Be kind and compassionate to one another, forgiving each other, just as in Christ God forgave you.

5 Be imitators of God, therefore, as dearly loved children ²and live a life of love, just as Christ loved us and gave himself up for us as a fragrant offering and sacrifice to God.

³But among you there must not be even a hint of sexual immorality, or of any kind of impurity, or of greed, because these are improper for God's holy people. ⁴Nor should there be obscenity, foolish talk or coarse joking, which are out of place, but rather thanksgiving. ⁵For of this you can be sure: No immoral, impure or greedy person—such a man is an idolater—has any inheritance in the kingdom of Christ and of God.[a] ⁶Let no one deceive you with empty words, for because of such things God's wrath comes on those who are disobedient. ⁷Therefore do not be partners with them.

⁸For you were once darkness, but now you are light in the Lord. Live as children of light ⁹(for the fruit of the light consists in all goodness, righteousness and truth) ¹⁰and find out what pleases the Lord. ¹¹Have nothing to do with the fruitless deeds of darkness, but rather expose them. ¹²For it is shameful even to mention what the disobedient do in secret. ¹³But everything exposed by the light becomes visible, ¹⁴for it is light that makes everything visible. This is why it is said:

> "Wake up, O sleeper,
>   rise from the dead,
> and Christ will shine on you."

¹⁵Be very careful, then, how you live—not as unwise but as wise, ¹⁶making the most of every opportunity, because the days are evil. ¹⁷Therefore do not be foolish, but understand what the Lord's will is. ¹⁸Do not get drunk on wine, which leads to debauchery. Instead, be filled with the Spirit. ¹⁹Speak to one another with psalms, hymns and spiritual songs. Sing and make music in your heart to the Lord, ²⁰always giving thanks to God the Father for everything, in the name of our Lord Jesus Christ.

²¹Submit to one another out of reverence for Christ.

WIVES AND HUSBANDS

²²Wives, submit to your husbands as to the Lord. ²³For the husband is the head of the wife as Christ is the head of the church, his body, of which he is the Savior. ²⁴Now as the church submits to Christ, so also wives should submit to their husbands in everything.

²⁵Husbands, love your wives, just as Christ loved the church and gave himself up for her ²⁶to make her holy, cleansing[b] her by the washing with water through the word, ²⁷and to present her to himself as a radiant church, without stain or wrinkle or any other blemish, but holy and blameless. ²⁸In this same way, husbands ought to love their wives as their own bodies. He who loves his wife loves himself. ²⁹After all, no one ever hated his own body, but he feeds and cares for it, just as Christ does the church— ³⁰for we are members of his body. ³¹"For this reason a man will leave his father and mother and be unit-

---

Avoiding Impurity

As far as God is concerned, there's no "gray area" when it comes to living a holy life. Instead of trying to see how close to the line you can get in the words you use, the jokes you tell and the way you talk about girls, God calls you to demonstrate righteousness by resisting even a hint of evil. If that makes you stand out from the other guys in the locker room . . . well, that's the idea.

NOW OR NEVER
EPH 5:3-4

Name three examples of impurity or sexual immorality that have a foothold in your life. What radical steps do you need to take in order to rid yourself of those sins?

---

[a] 5 Or *kingdom of the Christ and God*   [b] 26 Or *having cleansed*

battlelines

» How Far? (Sexual Purity)

Q: You've been dating Jenna for how long now?
A: Going on two years.

Q: Wow. That's pretty serious.
A: I guess so. We talk about marriage sometimes.

Q: I would guess you face quite a bit of sexual temptation.
A: Well . . . yeah, as a matter of fact, we do. How did you know?

Q: What, you think I've never had a girlfriend?
A: Oh, yeah. I guess it's something everybody struggles with.

Q: So who's winning?
A: Winning?

Q: Yeah—the struggle.
A: Oh. Um . . . I guess temptation wins most of the time. But we haven't gone all the way yet. We're definitely saving that for our wedding night. But we have done a lot of other stuff. Crossed some lines we probably shouldn't have crossed, you know?

Q: So you're up against the old "How far is too far?" question.
A: Yeah, I guess so. I'm not exactly sure what the right answer is. Maybe it's different for every couple. But I know there have been times when, even though we didn't actually have sex, we went *way* too far.

» Boundaries

Every guy who cares about Jesus and who also has red blood pumping through his veins faces the same question: "How far is too far when it comes to physical contact?" Should you stop at handholding, kissing, making out, fondling . . . or some place even further down the road?

But asking this question is really like asking, "How much sin is too much sin?" Maybe the better question is "What do I want to save?" You need to understand that it's not just premarital intercourse that many married Christian guys regret. The church is full of men—cool guys with hearts for God—who desperately wish they hadn't shared so much of themselves with countless girls before they met and married their wives.

Think about this statement from the apostle Paul—and let it be your guide as you seek to answer the question "How far is too far?": "But among you there must not be even a hint of sexual immorality, or of any kind of impurity, or of greed, because these are improper for God's holy people" (Ephesians 5:3).

Read more about dealing with sexual temptation at www.RevolutionBible.com.

ed to his wife, and the two will become one flesh."[a] [32]This is a profound mystery—but I am talking about Christ and the church. [33]However, each one of you also must love his wife as he loves himself, and the wife must respect her husband.

CHILDREN AND PARENTS

6 Children, obey your parents in the Lord, for this is right. [2]"Honor your father and mother"—which is the first commandment with a promise— [3]"that it may go well with you and that you may enjoy long life on the earth."[b]

[4]Fathers, do not exasperate your children; instead, bring them up in the training and instruction of the Lord.

SLAVES AND MASTERS

[5]Slaves, obey your earthly masters with respect and fear, and with sincerity of heart, just as you would obey Christ. [6]Obey them not only to win their favor when their eye is on you, but like slaves of Christ, doing the will of God from your heart. [7]Serve wholeheartedly, as if you were serving the Lord, not men, [8]because you know that the Lord will reward everyone for whatever good he does, whether he is slave or free.

[9]And masters, treat your slaves in the same way. Do not threaten them, since you know that he who is both their Master and yours is in heaven, and there is no favoritism with him.

THE ARMOR OF GOD

[10]Finally, be strong in the Lord and in his mighty power. [11]Put on the full armor of God so that you can take your stand against the devil's schemes. [12]For our struggle is not against flesh and blood, but against the rulers, against the authorities, against the powers of this dark world and against the spiritual forces of evil in the heavenly realms. [13]Therefore put on the full armor of God, so that when the day of evil comes, you may be able to stand your ground, and after you have done everything, to stand. [14]Stand firm then, with the belt of truth buckled around your waist, with the breastplate of righteousness in place, [15]and with your feet fitted with the readiness that comes from the gospel of peace. [16]In addition to all this, take up the shield of faith, with which you can extinguish all the flaming arrows of the evil one. [17]Take the helmet of salvation and the sword of the Spirit, which is the word of God. [18]And pray in the Spirit on all occasions with all kinds of prayers and requests. With this in mind, be alert and always keep on praying for all the saints.

[19]Pray also for me, that whenever I open my mouth, words may be given me so that I will fearlessly make known the mystery of the gospel, [20]for which I am an ambassador in chains. Pray that I may declare it fearlessly, as I should.

FINAL GREETINGS

[21]Tychicus, the dear brother and faithful servant in the Lord, will tell you everything, so that you also may know how I am and what I am doing. [22]I am sending him to you for this very purpose, that you may know how we are, and that he may encourage you.

[23]Peace to the brothers, and love with faith from God the Father and the Lord Jesus Christ. [24]Grace to all who love our Lord Jesus Christ with an undying love.

Honoring Your Parents

The idea of honoring your father and mother goes beyond obeying them and even beyond showing them respect (although these two things are certainly a big part of it). Honoring your parents means treasuring them, being genuinely happy that they are part of your life and telling them how you feel about them. Have you ever thought about being proud of your parents? Beyond that, honoring your parents means caring for them and taking the time to make sure that *their* needs are being met instead of simply worrying about your own.

NOW OR NEVER
EPH 6:13-18

The devil is a beast in spiritual warfare. If you don't protect yourself by getting immersed in God's Word and by praying, Satan will ambush, slash, jab and devour you. Anticipate his attacks, have a steady defense ready and then go on the offensive. It all starts with getting into God's Word.

---

[a] *31* Gen. 2:24   [b] *3* Deut. 5:16

PHILIPPIANS

Author
The apostle Paul

Audience
The church at Philippi

Date
About A.D. 61

Setting
Paul had started the church at Philippi, the first church on the continent of Europe, during his second missionary journey. He wrote this letter from prison in Rome to thank the Philippians for their gifts and to encourage them.

Verse to Remember
Rejoice in the Lord always. I will say it again: Rejoice! (4:4).

Theme to Consider
Joy has nothing to do with our circumstances. According to Paul, if you belong to Christ, then you can have joy in suffering, joy in serving, joy in believing and joy in giving. That's reason to rejoice!

UNCHANGING TRUTH » Do you know how to enjoy life? Dumb question, right? After all, who doesn't know how to have a good time? But what about when things aren't going your way—when the sweet car you paid $2,500 for turns out to be a piece of junk, when your sports injury turns out to be a lot more serious than you first thought, when your favorite uncle dies—do you know how to "enjoy" life then?

That's where the book of Philippians comes in handy. In it, the apostle Paul talks about how to make joy a *permanent* part of your life. The secret is recognizing that circumstances—situations that try to rob us of our joy—are temporary. (Paul was an expert on less-than-joyful circumstances; he was a prisoner in Rome when he wrote this letter.)

The kind of joy that Paul's talking about comes from God. It's the deep pleasure, satisfaction and security that come from knowing that no matter what happens, God loves you and has an incredible future waiting for you. Since God's love is never interrupted, the joy that comes from living in his love is never interrupted either.

That's why you can remain joyful even on the worst days. That's why you can be joyful even when you feel angry or bored or scared or a little depressed. Circumstances can change your mood, but nothing can touch the ultimate source of your joy.

LIFE LESSONS »

1. Salvation is only the first step in God's amazing plan for your life (1:6).

2. Your attitude toward other people—especially toward other believers—should identify you as a Christian (2:1–4,14–15).

3. Learn to be content with what you have (4:12).

4. The fact that God's strength flows through you means you're capable of a lot more than you will ever realize (4:13).

1
Paul and Timothy, servants of Christ Jesus,

To all the saints in Christ Jesus at Philippi, together with the overseers[a] and deacons:

[2] Grace and peace to you from God our Father and the Lord Jesus Christ.

THANKSGIVING AND PRAYER

[3] I thank my God every time I remember you. [4] In all my prayers for all of you, I always pray with joy [5] because of your partnership in the gospel from the first day until now, [6] being confident of this, that he who began a good work in you will carry it on to completion until the day of Christ Jesus.

[7] It is right for me to feel this way about all of you, since I have you in my heart; for whether I am in chains or defending and confirming the gospel, all of you share in God's grace with me. [8] God can testify how I long for all of you with the affection of Christ Jesus.

[9] And this is my prayer: that your love may abound more and more in knowledge and depth of insight, [10] so that you may be able to discern what is best and may be pure and blameless until the day of Christ, [11] filled with the fruit of righteousness that comes through Jesus Christ—to the glory and praise of God.

PAUL'S CHAINS ADVANCE THE GOSPEL

[12] Now I want you to know, brothers, that what has happened to me has really served to advance the gospel. [13] As a result, it has become clear throughout the whole palace guard[b] and to everyone else that I am in chains for Christ. [14] Because of my chains, most of the brothers in the Lord have been encouraged to speak the word of God more courageously and fearlessly.

[15] It is true that some preach Christ out of envy and rivalry, but others out of goodwill. [16] The latter do so in love, knowing that I am put here for the defense of the gospel. [17] The former preach Christ out of selfish ambition, not sincerely, supposing that they can stir up trouble for me while I am in chains.[c] [18] But what does it matter? The important thing is that in every way, whether from false motives or true, Christ is preached. And because of this I rejoice.

Yes, and I will continue to rejoice, [19] for I know that through your prayers and the help given by the Spirit of Jesus Christ, what has happened to me will turn out for my deliverance.[d] [20] I eagerly expect and hope that I will in no way be ashamed, but will have sufficient courage so that now as always Christ will be exalted in my body, whether by life or by death. [21] For to me, to live is Christ and to die is gain. [22] If I am to go on living in the body, this will mean fruitful labor for me. Yet what shall I choose? I do not know! [23] I am torn between the two: I desire to depart and be with Christ, which is better by far; [24] but it is more necessary for you that I remain in the body. [25] Convinced of this, I know that I will remain, and I will continue with all of you for your progress and joy in the faith, [26] so that through my being with you again your joy in Christ Jesus will overflow on account of me.

Encouraging Other People

If you ever want to do a favor for your friends, tell them what you appreciate most about them. Be specific. Talk about their qualities. Maybe it's their sense of humor, the way they make people laugh all the time. Maybe it's their eagerness to serve other people when everyone else is just looking out for themselves. Maybe it's how they've encouraged you in your Christian faith. Whatever it is, let them know how much you appreciate it. Just imagine how you would feel if someone did the same for you.

NOW OR NEVER
PHP 1:9

Can you see yourself growing "more and more in knowledge"? Think of three things you know now about what it means to be a Christian that you didn't know when you were younger.

---

[a] 1 Traditionally *bishops*   [b] 13 Or *whole palace*   [c] 16,17 Some late manuscripts have verses 16 and 17 in reverse order.
[d] 19 Or *salvation*

²⁷Whatever happens, conduct yourselves in a manner worthy of the gospel of Christ. Then, whether I come and see you or only hear about you in my absence, I will know that you stand firm in one spirit, contending as one man for the faith of the gospel ²⁸without being frightened in any way by those who oppose you. This is a sign to them that they will be destroyed, but that you will be saved—and that by God. ²⁹For it has been granted to you on behalf of Christ not only to believe on him, but also to suffer for him, ³⁰since you are going through the same struggle you saw I had, and now hear that I still have.

---

challenge notes

To: my_son

PHP 1:12-13

heavenly_father: never let your life circumstances prevent you from serving me. remember—I have put you where you are for a reason. whether you're living in a mansion or a prison, your job is to obey and stay faithful to me. I'll use your circumstances for good.

IMITATING CHRIST'S HUMILITY

2 If you have any encouragement from being united with Christ, if any comfort from his love, if any fellowship with the Spirit, if any tenderness and compassion, ²then make my joy complete by being like-minded, having the same love, being one in spirit and purpose. ³Do nothing out of selfish ambition or vain conceit, but in humility consider others better than yourselves. ⁴Each of you should look not only to your own interests, but also to the interests of others.

⁵Your attitude should be the same as that of Christ Jesus:

⁶Who, being in very nature[a] God,
did not consider equality with God
something to be grasped,
⁷but made himself nothing,
taking the very nature[b] of a servant,
being made in human likeness.
⁸And being found in appearance as a man,
he humbled himself
and became obedient to death—
even death on a cross!
⁹Therefore God exalted him to the highest place
and gave him the name that is above
every name,
¹⁰that at the name of Jesus every knee
should bow,
in heaven and on earth and under the earth,
¹¹and every tongue confess that Jesus
Christ is Lord,
to the glory of God the Father.

Living With the Right Perspective

« live the adventure » Php 1:21

Paul was in a win-win situation. Because Jesus was the One who brought him joy, Paul would have been happy to go on living for him and telling others about him. On the other hand, death would mean pure joy too, because in death Paul would have been with Jesus in paradise. How do you view death? Does it scare you to think of losing someone you love? Do you get uneasy when you think about the day you will die? Or does it just seem too far off to think much about it? How do you view your years on Earth?

SHINING AS STARS

¹²Therefore, my dear friends, as you have always obeyed—not only in my presence, but now much more in my absence—continue to work out your salvation with fear and trembling, ¹³for it is God who works in you to will and to act according to his good purpose.

¹⁴Do everything without complaining or arguing, ¹⁵so that you may become blameless and pure, children of God without fault in a crooked and depraved generation, in which you shine like stars in the

---

a 6 Or *in the form of*   b 7 Or *the form*

universe ¹⁶as you hold out[a] the word of life—in order that I may boast on the day of Christ that I did not run or labor for nothing. ¹⁷But even if I am being poured out like a drink offering on the sacrifice and service coming from your faith, I am glad and rejoice with all of you. ¹⁸So you too should be glad and rejoice with me.

TIMOTHY AND EPAPHRODITUS

¹⁹I hope in the Lord Jesus to send Timothy to you soon, that I also may be cheered when I receive news about you. ²⁰I have no one else like him, who takes a genuine interest in your welfare. ²¹For everyone looks out for his own interests, not those of Jesus Christ. ²²But you know that Timothy has proved himself, because as a son with his father he has served with me in the work of the gospel. ²³I hope, therefore, to send him as soon as I see how things go with me. ²⁴And I am confident in the Lord that I myself will come soon.

²⁵But I think it is necessary to send back to you Epaphroditus, my brother, fellow worker and fellow soldier, who is also your messenger, whom you sent to take care of my needs. ²⁶For he longs for all of you and is distressed because you heard he was ill. ²⁷Indeed he was ill, and almost died. But God had mercy on him, and not on him only but also on me, to spare me sorrow upon sorrow. ²⁸Therefore I am all the more eager to send him, so that when you see him again you may be glad and I may have less anxiety. ²⁹Welcome him in the Lord with great joy, and honor men like him, ³⁰because he almost died for the work of Christ, risking his life to make up for the help you could not give me.

NO CONFIDENCE IN THE FLESH

3 Finally, my brothers, rejoice in the Lord! It is no trouble for me to write the same things to you again, and it is a safeguard for you.

²Watch out for those dogs, those men who do evil, those mutilators of the flesh. ³For it is we who are the circumcision, we who worship by the Spirit of God, who glory in Christ Jesus, and who put no confidence in the flesh— ⁴though I myself have reasons for such confidence.

If anyone else thinks he has reasons to put confidence in the flesh, I have more: ⁵circumcised on the eighth day, of the people of Israel, of the tribe of Benjamin, a Hebrew of Hebrews; in regard to the law, a Pharisee; ⁶as for zeal, persecuting the church; as for legalistic righteousness, faultless.

⁷But whatever was to my profit I now consider loss for the sake of Christ. ⁸What is more, I consider everything a loss compared to the surpassing greatness of knowing Christ Jesus my Lord, for whose sake I have lost all things. I consider them rubbish, that I may gain Christ ⁹and be found in him, not having a righteousness of my own that comes from the law, but that which is through faith in Christ— the righteousness that comes from God and is by faith. ¹⁰I want to know Christ and the power of his resurrection and the fellowship of sharing in his sufferings, becoming like him in his death, ¹¹and so, somehow, to attain to the resurrection from the dead.

PRESSING ON TOWARD THE GOAL

¹²Not that I have already obtained all this, or have already been made perfect, but I press on to take hold of that for which Christ Jesus took hold of me. ¹³Brothers, I do not consider myself yet to have taken hold of it. But one thing I do: Forgetting what is behind and straining toward what is ahead, ¹⁴I press on toward the goal to win the prize for which God has called me heavenward in Christ Jesus.

¹⁵All of us who are mature should take such a view of things. And if on some point you think differently, that too God will make clear to you. ¹⁶Only let us live up to what we have already attained.

¹⁷Join with others in following my example, brothers, and take note of those who live according to the pattern we gave you. ¹⁸For, as I have often told you before and now say again even with tears, many live as enemies of the cross of Christ. ¹⁹Their destiny is destruction, their god is their stomach, and their glory is in their shame. Their mind is on earthly things. ²⁰But our citizenship is in heaven. And

---

[a] 16 Or hold on to

we eagerly await a Savior from there, the Lord Jesus Christ, [21]who, by the power that enables him to bring everything under his control, will transform our lowly bodies so that they will be like his glorious body.

┌┐□Ш □┌ □┌╪╥╤

PHP 3:12-15

How can you tell if you're becoming a mature Christian? According to Paul, one clear sign is that you'll understand that you haven't arrived yet. The mark of maturity is the realization that you've still got some growing to do.

4 Therefore, my brothers, you whom I love and long for, my joy and crown, that is how you should stand firm in the Lord, dear friends!

EXHORTATIONS

[2]I plead with Euodia and I plead with Syntyche to agree with each other in the Lord. [3]Yes, and I ask you, loyal yokefellow,[a] help these women who have contended at my side in the cause of the gospel, along with Clement and the rest of my fellow workers, whose names are in the book of life.

[4]Rejoice in the Lord always. I will say it again: Rejoice! [5]Let your gentleness be evident to all. The Lord is near. [6]Do not be anxious about anything, but in everything, by prayer and petition, with thanksgiving, present your requests to God. [7]And the peace of God, which transcends all understanding, will guard your hearts and your minds in Christ Jesus.

[8]Finally, brothers, whatever is true, whatever is noble, whatever is right, whatever is pure, whatever is lovely, whatever is admirable—if anything is excellent or praiseworthy—think about such things. [9]Whatever you have learned or received or heard from me, or seen in me—put it into practice. And the God of peace will be with you.

THANKS FOR THEIR GIFTS

[10]I rejoice greatly in the Lord that at last you have renewed your concern for me. Indeed, you have been concerned, but you had no opportunity to show it. [11]I am not saying this because I am in need, for I have learned to be content whatever the circumstances. [12]I know what it is to be in need, and I know what it is to have plenty. I have learned the secret of being content in any and every situation, whether well fed or hungry, whether living in plenty or in want. [13]I can do everything through him who gives me strength.

[14]Yet it was good of you to share in my troubles. [15]Moreover, as you Philippians know, in the early days of your acquaintance with the gospel, when I set out from Macedonia, not one church shared with me in the matter of giving and receiving, except you only; [16]for even when I was in Thessalonica, you sent me aid again and again when I was in need. [17]Not that I am looking for a gift, but I am looking for what may be credited to your account. [18]I have received full payment and even more; I am amply supplied, now that I have received from Epaphroditus the gifts you sent. They are a fragrant offering, an acceptable sacrifice, pleasing to God. [19]And my God will meet all your needs according to his glorious riches in Christ Jesus.

[20]To our God and Father be glory for ever and ever. Amen.

Managing Your Thoughts

>> live the adventure >> Php 4:8

Bad thoughts (whether they involve lust, violence, jealousy or something else) are like an infection in your mind. Unless you do something about them, they begin to spread. The best way to keep bad thoughts from spreading is to fill your mind with good thoughts. If you can't stop thinking about, say, a dirty joke you heard on the radio while driving to school, try thinking about the lyrics to a song with a solid message or your favorite Bible verse. It's difficult to remove evil from your life without replacing it with something good.

[a] 3 Or *loyal Syzygus*

battlelines

» Inertia Boys (Service)

Q: Wow, you seem ticked off. What's the deal?
A: It's my friends—my so-called *Christian* friends. They're such slugs.

Q: What makes you say that?
A: They don't do anything but lie around, watch TV, play video games and occasionally complain that their lives are so boring.

Q: I hate to break it to you, but isn't that what most teenage guys do with their time?
A: Maybe. I don't know. Anyway, the point is, I got a call from this older lady in my neighborhood. She said, "I'm cleaning out my basement, my attic and my storage shed. I'm getting rid of 50 years of stuff, and I need some help. I want to have a big yard sale and give all the profits to my church. And I'm willing to pay you and three of your friends ten dollars an hour to help.

Q: Wow, that sounds like a great deal all the way around.
A: Exactly! We'd be helping an old lady. Her church would benefit. Plus, who knows what kind of cool old stuff we might uncover down in that basement? And to top it off, we'd be making some nice cash.

Q: But your friends won't do it?
A: No. Bunch of selfish lard butts!

» Getting Rolling

Aren't you glad Jesus didn't function the way many of us do? Aren't you glad he didn't moan to the Father, "Become a man? Save the world? That sounds too hard. I'm tired. I need a break"?

Fortunately for us, Jesus was all about other people. He saw his life as one long mission to glorify God by helping others. That's what the apostle Paul had in mind when he encouraged the Philippian believers to be like Jesus:

"Do nothing out of selfish ambition or vain conceit, but in humility consider others better than yourselves. Each of you should look not only to your own interests, but also to the interests of others. Your attitude should be the same as that of Christ Jesus: Who, being in very nature God, did not consider equality with God something to be grasped, but made himself nothing, taking the very nature of a servant" (Philippians 2:3–7).

What are you waiting for?

Discover creative ways to serve others at www.RevolutionBible.com.

euodia

» **A prominent woman in the church at Philippi**

» **Fought with Syntyche**

» **Was instructed by Paul to set aside her differences with Syntyche**

syntyche

» **An influential woman in the Philippian church**

» **Was at odds with Euodia**

» **Was challenged by Paul to settle things with Euodia**

The Main Event

As female leaders in the first-century church, Euodia and Syntyche should have been shining for Christ—working together, serving others, attracting unbelievers to the faith. But instead of projecting a positive image in the greater Philippi area, these Christian women were doing their best impersonation of two female wrestlers in a championship death match.

Nobody knows what started the conflict. And nobody is sure how long the squabble went on. But things must have gotten pretty heated and ugly. By the time the apostle Paul decided to write a short note of encouragement to the church at Philippi, he felt the need to publicly address this nasty, embarrassing split, calling the women by name, and saying, "I plead with Euodia and I plead with Syntyche to agree with each other in the Lord."

That short exhortation was pretty much all Paul said. He didn't go into any gory details. Instead he reminded everyone how much he valued Euodia and Syntyche's ministry and called on other leaders in the church to "help these women." Since the Bible doesn't tell us any more than that, we are left to wonder about the rest of the story. Maybe it's just a hunch or maybe it's pure hope, but don't you get the sneaky feeling that these women figured out a way to resolve their conflict and move on?

The Outcome

Disputes are a sad fact of life. Unfortunately, being a Christian doesn't change that truth. There will always be people—even fellow Christians—with whom you clash and don't see eye to eye.

Do you think Euodia and Syntyche would have been less interested in feuding and quicker to "mend fences" if they had known their dispute was going to be recorded in God's eternal Word for billions of people to read and discuss throughout history?

Our arguments with other believers—if they're not resolved in a quick and healthy manner—can become a cause of public embarrassment to the name of Christ.

Survey the relational landscape in your own life. Are there people you have a hard time looking in the eye? People with whom you have unresolved "issues"? People with whom you need to be reconciled? Pray for wisdom and courage in healing those relationships. Take a page from Paul's book and find a Christian friend or two who can help you and your opponent get right with each other.

Remind yourself that this is no small matter. The world is watching. That's why Jesus told his followers to love one another deeply; that's why he prayed so fervently for our unity (see John 17:20–23).

Read more about Euodia and Syntyche in Philippians 4:2–3 (page 1518).

FINAL GREETINGS

[21]Greet all the saints in Christ Jesus. The brothers who are with me send greetings. [22]All the saints send you greetings, especially those who belong to Caesar's household.

[23]The grace of the Lord Jesus Christ be with your spirit. Amen.[a]

PHP 4:13

challenge notes

To: my_son

heavenly_father: set the bar for your life high. dare to do things that others wouldn't dream of. never let obstacles prevent you from accomplishing your work, and always look to me for your strength. through me, you can do more than you could ever imagine.

---

[a] 23 Some manuscripts do not have *Amen*.

COLOSSIANS

» AT A GLANCE

Author
The apostle Paul

Audience
The church at Colosse

Date
About A.D. 60

Setting
Although Paul had never been to Colosse, a city in Asia Minor (modern-day Turkey), he had heard from prison in Rome that false teachers were convincing the believers to mix pagan philosophy and Jewish legalism with Christian truth.

Verses to Remember
Since, then, you have been raised with Christ, set your hearts on things above, where Christ is seated at the right hand of God. Set your minds on things above, not on earthly things (3:1–2).

Theme to Consider
We have everything we could possibly need in Christ. Jesus alone is our leader, our head and our power source. We need to stay connected to him!

UNCHANGING TRUTH »

Do you think you could spot false teachers if they showed up at your Sunday service or youth group? What would you expect them to say? If they tried to tell you that good works are the way to get to heaven, that would be a pretty good clue. If they tried to tell you that you should follow whatever beliefs seem right to you, that would be another. And if they tried to tell you that Jesus didn't really rise from the dead or that he wasn't the only way to God, that would seal the deal.

Unfortunately, not all false teachers are easy to spot. The believers in the Colossian church found that out the hard way. Paul doesn't spell out exactly what the false teachers were doing in Colosse, but they managed to get inside the heads of some of the believers.

Some false teachers put just enough truth in their teachings to distract you from the dangerous stuff. That's what makes them difficult to identify. The best way to recognize false teachers is to follow the method U.S. Treasury agents use to recognize counterfeit money—study the real thing. If you know what the Bible *really* says, you're not going to be fooled by counterfeit teaching.

LIFE LESSONS »

1. Your ultimate goal should be to please God in everything you do (1:10).

2. Jesus' sacrifice is what makes it possible for us to have a personal relationship with God (1:21–22).

3. Don't listen to anyone who tries to tell you that anything more—or less—than Jesus' sacrifice is required for salvation (2:8).

4. As a result of their new life in Jesus, Christians should live in a way that's noticeably different from the way non-Christians live (3:1–17).

1
¹Paul, an apostle of Christ Jesus by the will of God, and Timothy our brother,

²To the holy and faithful[a] brothers in Christ at Colosse:

Grace and peace to you from God our Father.[b]

THANKSGIVING AND PRAYER

³We always thank God, the Father of our Lord Jesus Christ, when we pray for you, ⁴because we have heard of your faith in Christ Jesus and of the love you have for all the saints— ⁵the faith and love that spring from the hope that is stored up for you in heaven and that you have already heard about in the word of truth, the gospel ⁶that has come to you. All over the world this gospel is bearing fruit and growing, just as it has been doing among you since the day you heard it and understood God's grace in all its truth. ⁷You learned it from Epaphras, our dear fellow servant, who is a faithful minister of Christ on our[c] behalf, ⁸and who also told us of your love in the Spirit.

⁹For this reason, since the day we heard about you, we have not stopped praying for you and asking God to fill you with the knowledge of his will through all spiritual wisdom and understanding. ¹⁰And we pray this in order that you may live a life worthy of the Lord and may please him in every way: bearing fruit in every good work, growing in the knowledge of God, ¹¹being strengthened with all power according to his glorious might so that you may have great endurance and patience, and joyfully ¹²giving thanks to the Father, who has qualified you[d] to share in the inheritance of the saints in the kingdom of light. ¹³For he has rescued us from the dominion of darkness and brought us into the kingdom of the Son he loves, ¹⁴in whom we have redemption,[e] the forgiveness of sins.

COL 1:13

challengenotes

To: my_son

heavenly_father: it's no accident that you're a christian; I chose you to be part of my family. I saw the darkness you were walking in, I knew exactly where you were heading, and I rescued you. listen to my call and trust me to lead you to a better place.

THE SUPREMACY OF CHRIST

¹⁵He is the image of the invisible God, the firstborn over all creation. ¹⁶For by him all things were created: things in heaven and on earth, visible and invisible, whether thrones or powers or rulers or authorities; all things were created by him and for him. ¹⁷He is before all things, and in him all things hold together. ¹⁸And he is the head of the body, the church; he is the beginning and the firstborn from among the dead, so that in everything he might have the supremacy. ¹⁹For God was pleased to have all his fullness dwell in him, ²⁰and through him to reconcile to himself all things, whether things on earth or things in heaven, by making peace through his blood, shed on the cross.

²¹Once you were alienated from God and were enemies in your minds because of[f] your evil behavior. ²²But now he has reconciled you by Christ's physical body through death to present you holy in his sight, without blemish and free from accusation— ²³if you continue in your faith, established and firm, not moved from the hope held out in the gospel. This is the gospel that you heard and that has been proclaimed to every creature under heaven, and of which I, Paul, have become a servant.

NOW OR NEVER

COL 1:23

Who was the first person to tell you the remarkable news that Jesus died for your sins? What led you to believe it? What have you done to spread the same news to others?

---

[a] 2 Or *believing* [b] 2 Some manuscripts *Father and the Lord Jesus Christ* [c] 7 Some manuscripts *your* [d] 12 Some manuscripts *us*
[e] 14 A few late manuscripts *redemption through his blood* [f] 21 Or *minds, as shown by*

PAUL'S LABOR FOR THE CHURCH

[24]Now I rejoice in what was suffered for you, and I fill up in my flesh what is still lacking in regard to Christ's afflictions, for the sake of his body, which is the church. [25]I have become its servant by the commission God gave me to present to you the word of God in its fullness— [26]the mystery that has been kept hidden for ages and generations, but is now disclosed to the saints. [27]To them God has chosen to make known among the Gentiles the glorious riches of this mystery, which is Christ in you, the hope of glory.

[28]We proclaim him, admonishing and teaching everyone with all wisdom, so that we may present everyone perfect in Christ. [29]To this end I labor, struggling with all his energy, which so powerfully works in me.

2 I want you to know how much I am struggling for you and for those at Laodicea, and for all who have not met me personally. [2]My purpose is that they may be encouraged in heart and united in love, so that they may have the full riches of complete understanding, in order that they may know the mystery of God, namely, Christ, [3]in whom are hidden all the treasures of wisdom and knowledge. [4]I tell you this so that no one may deceive you by fine-sounding arguments. [5]For though I am absent from you in body, I am present with you in spirit and delight to see how orderly you are and how firm your faith in Christ is.

FREEDOM FROM HUMAN REGULATIONS THROUGH LIFE WITH CHRIST

[6]So then, just as you received Christ Jesus as Lord, continue to live in him, [7]rooted and built up in him, strengthened in the faith as you were taught, and overflowing with thankfulness.

[8]See to it that no one takes you captive through hollow and deceptive philosophy, which depends on human tradition and the basic principles of this world rather than on Christ.

[9]For in Christ all the fullness of the Deity lives in bodily form, [10]and you have been given fullness in Christ, who is the head over every power and authority. [11]In him you were also circumcised, in the putting off of the sinful nature,[a] not with a circumcision done by the hands of men but with the circumcision done by Christ, [12]having been buried with him in baptism and raised with him through your faith in the power of God, who raised him from the dead.

[13]When you were dead in your sins and in the uncircumcision of your sinful nature,[b] God made you[c] alive with Christ. He forgave us all our sins, [14]having canceled the written code, with its regulations, that was against us and that stood opposed to us; he took it away, nailing it to the cross. [15]And having disarmed the powers and authorities, he made a public spectacle of them, triumphing over them by the cross.[d]

[16]Therefore do not let anyone judge you by what you eat or drink, or with regard to a religious festival, a New Moon celebration or a Sabbath day. [17]These are a shadow of the things that were to come; the reality, however, is found in Christ. [18]Do not let anyone who delights in false humility and the worship of angels disqualify you for the prize. Such a person goes into great detail about what he has seen, and his unspiritual mind puffs him up with idle notions. [19]He has lost connection with the Head, from whom the whole body, supported and held together by its ligaments and sinews, grows as God causes it to grow.

[20]Since you died with Christ to the basic principles of this world, why, as though you still belonged to it, do you submit to its rules: [21]"Do not handle! Do not taste! Do not touch!"? [22]These are all destined to perish with use, because they are based on human commands and teachings. [23]Such regulations indeed have an appearance of wisdom, with their self-imposed worship, their false humility and their harsh treatment of the body, but they lack any value in restraining sensual indulgence.

RULES FOR HOLY LIVING

3 Since, then, you have been raised with Christ, set your hearts on things above, where Christ is seated at the right hand of God. [2]Set your minds on things above, not on earthly things. [3]For you died, and your life is now hidden with Christ in God. [4]When Christ, who is your[e] life, appears, then you also will appear with him in glory.

[5]Put to death, therefore, whatever belongs to your earthly nature: sexual immorality, impurity, lust, evil desires and greed, which is idolatry. [6]Because of these, the wrath of God is coming.[f] [7]You used to

---

[a] 11 Or the flesh   [b] 13 Or your flesh   [c] 13 Some manuscripts us   [d] 15 Or them in him   [e] 4 Some manuscripts our   [f] 6 Some early manuscripts coming on those who are disobedient

battlelines

» Squandering Your Talents? (Laziness)

Q: What is the most aggravating thing in your life right now?
A: My dad.

Q: Wow, it didn't take you any time to come up with that response.
A: You've met him. You know what I'm talking about.

Q: Hey, don't drag me into it.
A: Tell me he's not the most demanding guy in the world. *Nothing* is ever good enough for him.

Q: What do you mean?
A: He's always bugging me. "Be excellent. Why are you so willing to settle for less than your best? God has given you so many talents, and you're *not* using them. How in the world did you get to be so *gifted*, yet so *lazy*?" Yada, yada, yada. It never stops.

Q: I see what you mean. He drives you.
A: Yeah—drives me *crazy*!

Q: But if you look at it objectively, is it possible that he's right . . . maybe a little?
A: Now you're gonna start in on me too?

Q: No, I'm just asking if some of his criticisms might be valid.
A: Look, I'll admit, I'm not always super-motivated like he wants me to be. I mean, why should I kill myself to do a 25-page English paper when I can do a 15-page paper and still get a B-, you know? You've gotta admit, some people take the whole excellence thing to the extreme.

Q: And maybe your dad knows—hint, hint—that you'd rather go to the *other* extreme?
A: OK, OK, you've made your point. Enough already.

» A New Motivation

Imagine how different things might be in your life—and throughout the world—if every person who claims to believe in Jesus would live out these verses:

"Whatever you do, work at it with all your heart, as working for the Lord, not for men, since you know that you will receive an inheritance from the Lord as a reward. It is the Lord Christ you are serving" (Colossians 3:23–24).

How does the attitude described in Colossians 3 differ from the way you approach tasks? What needs to change in your attitudes and actions?

Read more at www.RevolutionBible.com.

walk in these ways, in the life you once lived. ⁸But now you must rid yourselves of all such things as these: anger, rage, malice, slander, and filthy language from your lips. ⁹Do not lie to each other, since you have taken off your old self with its practices ¹⁰and have put on the new self, which is being renewed in knowledge in the image of its Creator. ¹¹Here there is no Greek or Jew, circumcised or uncircumcised, barbarian, Scythian, slave or free, but Christ is all, and is in all.

¹²Therefore, as God's chosen people, holy and dearly loved, clothe yourselves with compassion, kindness, humility, gentleness and patience. ¹³Bear with each other and forgive whatever grievances you may have against one another. Forgive as the Lord forgave you. ¹⁴And over all these virtues put on love, which binds them all together in perfect unity.

¹⁵Let the peace of Christ rule in your hearts, since as members of one body you were called to peace. And be thankful. ¹⁶Let the word of Christ dwell in you richly as you teach and admonish one another with all wisdom, and as you sing psalms, hymns and spiritual songs with gratitude in your hearts to God. ¹⁷And whatever you do, whether in word or deed, do it all in the name of the Lord Jesus, giving thanks to God the Father through him.

RULES FOR CHRISTIAN HOUSEHOLDS

¹⁸Wives, submit to your husbands, as is fitting in the Lord. ¹⁹Husbands, love your wives and do not be harsh with them.

²⁰Children, obey your parents in everything, for this pleases the Lord.

²¹Fathers, do not embitter your children, or they will become discouraged.

²²Slaves, obey your earthly masters in everything; and do it, not only when their eye is on you and to win their favor, but with sincerity of heart and reverence for the Lord. ²³Whatever you do, work at it with all your heart, as working for the Lord, not for men, ²⁴since you know that you will receive an inheritance from the Lord as a reward. It is the Lord Christ you are serving. ²⁵Anyone who does wrong will be repaid for his wrong, and there is no favoritism.

4 Masters, provide your slaves with what is right and fair, because you know that you also have a Master in heaven.

FURTHER INSTRUCTIONS

²Devote yourselves to prayer, being watchful and thankful. ³And pray for us, too, that God may open a door for our message, so that we may proclaim the mystery of Christ, for which I am in chains. ⁴Pray that I may proclaim it clearly, as I should. ⁵Be wise in the way you act toward outsiders; make the most of every opportunity. ⁶Let your conversation be always full of grace, seasoned with salt, so that you may know how to answer everyone.

FINAL GREETINGS

⁷Tychicus will tell you all the news about me. He is a dear brother, a faithful minister and fellow

Letting People See Changes in Your Life

Have your friends or family members noticed any changes in you since you became a Christian? If so, what changes have they specifically mentioned? How does that make you feel? If no one's ever mentioned anything to you . . . perhaps it should bother you a little. God isn't interested in simply saving us; he wants to change our lives from the inside out.

NOW OR NEVER

COL 4:2

Imagine if you were apart from someone close to you like a buddy, a family member or a girlfriend. You'd probably IM, text, email or call each other to keep in touch. Prayer is our lifeline to God. That's why we have to remain devoted to talking with and listening to him.

servant in the Lord. [8]I am sending him to you for the express purpose that you may know about our[a] circumstances and that he may encourage your hearts. [9]He is coming with Onesimus, our faithful and dear brother, who is one of you. They will tell you everything that is happening here.

[10]My fellow prisoner Aristarchus sends you his greetings, as does Mark, the cousin of Barnabas. (You have received instructions about him; if he comes to you, welcome him.) [11]Jesus, who is called Justus, also sends greetings. These are the only Jews among my fellow workers for the kingdom of God, and they have proved a comfort to me. [12]Epaphras, who is one of you and a servant of Christ Jesus, sends greetings. He is always wrestling in prayer for you, that you may stand firm in all the will of God, mature and fully assured. [13]I vouch for him that he is working hard for you and for those at Laodicea and Hierapolis. [14]Our dear friend Luke, the doctor, and Demas send greetings. [15]Give my greetings to the brothers at Laodicea, and to Nympha and the church in her house.

[16]After this letter has been read to you, see that it is also read in the church of the Laodiceans and that you in turn read the letter from Laodicea.

[17]Tell Archippus: "See to it that you complete the work you have received in the Lord."

[18]I, Paul, write this greeting in my own hand. Remember my chains. Grace be with you.

---

[a] 8 Some manuscripts *that he may know about your*

1 THESSALONIANS

Author
The apostle Paul

Audience
The church at Thessalonica

Date
About A.D. 51

Setting
Paul wrote from Corinth to encourage the new Christians at Thessalonica (in modern-day northern Greece) who were being persecuted and to give instructions about the second coming of Christ.

Verses to Remember
May the Lord make your love increase and overflow for each other and for everyone else, just as ours does for you. May he strengthen your hearts so that you will be blameless and holy in the presence of our God and Father when our Lord Jesus comes with all his holy ones (3:12–13).

Theme to Consider
Watch for the practical ways we can live holy lives in the midst of a culture that is hostile to Christian values. Take courage in the knowledge that Christ is with us now and that he *is* coming again.

UNCHANGING TRUTH » The Bible says Christians are supposed to be "lights" in the world—that we're supposed to stand out from unbelievers. The idea is that people should be able to figure out that you follow Jesus by the things they see you do and the things they hear you say.

But how, exactly, do you send that message? What can you do that will make people say, "Oh, he must be a Christian"? That was one of the questions on Paul's mind when he wrote the book of 1 Thessalonians. He offers a couple suggestions for how to live differently from unbelievers.

First, keep lust under control in your life. When other guys are drooling over the latest celebrity sex video circulating around the Internet, keep your distance. When other guys talk crudely about a girl's body—as if a girl's figure is the only thing she has to offer—protect the girl's honor and don't allow that kind of conversation to go on in your presence. When other guys make fun of your morals, ask God for the strength to stand your ground.

Second, demonstrate the love of Christ to everyone around you. Introduce yourself to new people at school and offer to show them the ropes. Help a disabled classmate maneuver through the halls. Include the less likeable types in your circle of friends. Be a friend to someone who's lonely. Above all, show your love to other believers—even if your faith in Jesus is the only thing you have in common.

Standing apart from the crowd can make you feel weird, but God will never let your obedience go to waste. Not only will he reward you for your courage, but he will also use it to change other people's lives.

LIFE LESSONS »

1. If you're not sure how to live in a way that pleases God, try following the example of mature, faithful believers that you know (1:6).

2. As a Christian, you have a responsibility to lovingly challenge other believers to live lives "worthy of God" (2:11–12).

3. You don't have to fear death; it can't keep Jesus from coming back for you (4:13–18).

1

Paul, Silas[a] and Timothy,

To the church of the Thessalonians in God the Father and the Lord Jesus Christ:

Grace and peace to you.[b]

THANKSGIVING FOR THE THESSALONIANS' FAITH

[2]We always thank God for all of you, mentioning you in our prayers. [3]We continually remember before our God and Father your work produced by faith, your labor prompted by love, and your endurance inspired by hope in our Lord Jesus Christ.

[4]For we know, brothers loved by God, that he has chosen you, [5]because our gospel came to you not simply with words, but also with power, with the Holy Spirit and with deep conviction. You know how we lived among you for your sake. [6]You became imitators of us and of the Lord; in spite of severe suffering, you welcomed the message with the joy given by the Holy Spirit. [7]And so you became a model to all the believers in Macedonia and Achaia. [8]The Lord's message rang out from you not only in Macedonia and Achaia—your faith in God has become known everywhere. Therefore we do

NOW OR NEVER
1TH 1:4–5

The good news about Jesus isn't just a bunch of empty words. It's charged with the power of the Holy Spirit. That's why you shouldn't let your concerns about saying the wrong thing keep you from sharing your faith with others. The Holy Spirit can infuse your words with power.

not need to say anything about it, [9]for they themselves report what kind of reception you gave us. They tell how you turned to God from idols to serve the living and true God, [10]and to wait for his Son from heaven, whom he raised from the dead—Jesus, who rescues us from the coming wrath.

PAUL'S MINISTRY IN THESSALONICA

2

You know, brothers, that our visit to you was not a failure. [2]We had previously suffered and been insulted in Philippi, as you know, but with the help of our God we dared to tell you his gospel in spite of strong opposition. [3]For the appeal we make does not spring from error or impure motives, nor are we trying to trick you. [4]On the contrary, we speak as men approved by God to be entrusted with the gospel. We are not trying to please men but God, who tests our hearts. [5]You know we never used flattery, nor did we put on a mask to cover up greed—God is our witness. [6]We were not looking for praise from men, not from you or anyone else.

As apostles of Christ we could have been a burden to you, [7]but we were gentle among you, like a mother caring for her little children. [8]We loved you so much that we were delighted to share with you not only the gospel of God but our lives as well, because you had become so dear to us. [9]Surely you remember, brothers, our toil and hardship; we worked night and day in order not to be a burden to anyone while we preached the gospel of God to you.

[10]You are witnesses, and so is God, of how holy, righteous and blameless we were among you who believed. [11]For you know that we dealt with each of you as a father deals with his own children, [12]encouraging, comforting and urging you to live lives worthy of God, who calls you into his kingdom and glory.

[13]And we also thank God continually because, when you received the word of God, which you heard from us, you accepted it not as the word of men, but as it actually is, the word of God, which is at work in you who believe. [14]For you, brothers, became imitators of God's churches in Judea, which are in Christ Jesus: You suffered from your own countrymen the same things those churches suffered from the Jews, [15]who killed the Lord Jesus and the prophets and also drove us out. They displease God and are hostile to all men [16]in their effort to keep us from speaking to the Gentiles so that they may be saved. In this way they always heap up their sins to the limit. The wrath of God has come upon them at last.[c]

PAUL'S LONGING TO SEE THE THESSALONIANS

[17]But, brothers, when we were torn away from you for a short time (in person, not in thought), out of our intense longing we made every effort to see you. [18]For we wanted to come to you—certainly I,

---

[a] 1 Greek Silvanus, a variant of Silas   [b] 1 Some early manuscripts you from God our Father and the Lord Jesus Christ   [c] 16 Or them fully

Paul, did, again and again—but Satan stopped us. ¹⁹For what is our hope, our joy, or the crown in which we will glory in the presence of our Lord Jesus when he comes? Is it not you? ²⁰Indeed, you are our glory and joy.

3 So when we could stand it no longer, we thought it best to be left by ourselves in Athens. ²We sent Timothy, who is our brother and God's fellow worker[a] in spreading the gospel of Christ, to strengthen and encourage you in your faith, ³so that no one would be unsettled by these trials. You know quite well that we were destined for them. ⁴In fact, when we were with you, we kept telling you that we would be persecuted. And it turned out that way, as you well know. ⁵For this reason, when I could stand it no longer, I sent to find out about your faith. I was afraid that in some way the tempter might have tempted you and our efforts might have been useless.

TIMOTHY'S ENCOURAGING REPORT

⁶But Timothy has just now come to us from you and has brought good news about your faith and love. He has told us that you always have pleasant memories of us and that you long to see us, just as we also long to see you. ⁷Therefore, brothers, in all our distress and persecution we were encouraged about you because of your faith. ⁸For now we really live, since you are standing firm in the Lord. ⁹How can we thank God enough for you in return for all the joy we have in the presence of our God because of you? ¹⁰Night and day we pray most earnestly that we may see you again and supply what is lacking in your faith.

¹¹Now may our God and Father himself and our Lord Jesus clear the way for us to come to you. ¹²May the Lord make your love increase and overflow for each other and for everyone else, just as ours does for you. ¹³May he strengthen your hearts so that you will be blameless and holy in the presence of our God and Father when our Lord Jesus comes with all his holy ones.

LIVING TO PLEASE GOD

4 Finally, brothers, we instructed you how to live in order to please God, as in fact you are living. Now we ask you and urge you in the Lord Jesus to do this more and more. ²For you know what instructions we gave you by the authority of the Lord Jesus.

³It is God's will that you should be sanctified: that you should avoid sexual immorality; ⁴that each of you should learn to control his own body[b] in a way that is holy and honorable, ⁵not in passionate lust like the heathen, who do not know God; ⁶and that in this matter no one should wrong his brother or take advantage of him. The Lord will punish men for all such sins, as we have already told you and warned you. ⁷For God did not call us to be impure, but to live a holy life. ⁸Therefore, he who rejects this instruction does not reject man but God, who gives you his Holy Spirit.

1TH 4:3-6

To: my_son

heavenly_father: want to know how you can be "sanctified"— how you can be more and more the person I want you to be? it's not that complicated. commit yourself to pleasing me instead of yourself by resisting the temptation to misuse my incredible gift of sex.

⁹Now about brotherly love we do not need to write to you, for you yourselves have been taught by God to love each other. ¹⁰And in fact, you do love all the brothers throughout Macedonia. Yet we urge you, brothers, to do so more and more. ¹¹Make it your ambition to lead a quiet life, to mind your own business and to work with your hands, just as we told you, ¹²so that your daily life may win the respect of outsiders and so that you will not be dependent on anybody.

THE COMING OF THE LORD

¹³Brothers, we do not want you to be ignorant about those who fall asleep, or to grieve like the rest of men, who have no hope. ¹⁴We believe that Jesus died and rose again and so we believe that God will bring with Jesus those who have fallen asleep in him. ¹⁵According to the Lord's own word, we tell you

---

a 2 Some manuscripts *brother and fellow worker*; other manuscripts *brother and God's servant*   b 4 Or *learn to live with his own wife*; or *learn to acquire a wife*

battlelines

» Is It Sex? (Sexual Purity)

Q: So you're telling me it's not really sex?
A: Think about it. There's no chance she can get pregnant from it. And she'll still be a virgin. I'm just talking about a safe and fun way to show our feelings for each other.

Q: And she likes the idea?
A: Well . . . it took a couple weeks of convincing, but she's finally warmed up to it.

Q: I'd say you're rationalizing the whole thing—and deep down you know it.
A: No, it's just a matter of where you draw the line. It's no different than kissing or holding hands. It's physical contact that makes you feel good. Period. And it's something we're both ready for.

Q: I can tell you think *you're* ready for it. But it sounds to me like you've been pressuring her to go against her morals.
A: Hey, I'm not forcing her to do anything. It's not like I'm holding a gun to her head.

Q: If you really respect her—
A: Hey, watch it. I *do* respect her—a lot.

Q: So do you really think that pushing her to do this is putting her desires above your own?
A: Show me where the Bible says it's wrong.

Q: You're not answering my question. So try this: If what you're talking about is no big deal, if it isn't really "sex," then tonight when you go over to her house, why don't you do it in the living room, right in front of her parents?
A: What? That's stupid.

Q: You're right. It would be stupid. And you'd never do that in a million years, because deep down you know that what you're talking about *is* a huge deal. It *is* a sexual act.
A: I don't need your preaching. It's my choice—and hers. No one else's. Later.

» Just What Is Sex?

Sex is more than just the act of intercourse. Sex is any physical relationship in which you share your body with someone else in order to experience sexual pleasure. There are no loopholes in God's plan that make certain forms of sex OK before marriage.

Don't misunderstand: There's nothing inherently wrong with sex. God invented it! There's nothing wrong with having sexual desires either. That's the way God wired you.

However, you need to understand that sex is a sacred, special event (see 1 Thessalonians 4:1–8) that bonds two people together in a deep and permanent way (see Hebrews 13:4).

Don't rationalize your way into something like oral sex just to get what you want. And if you're unsure whether or not something you're doing is "crossing the line," ask yourself these questions:

● Am I doing this to give or to get?

● Is this action just making me want to go further physically?

● Would Jesus approve of what I'm doing?

Read more about sex and abstinence at www.RevolutionBible.com

that we who are still alive, who are left till the coming of the Lord, will certainly not precede those who have fallen asleep. ¹⁶For the Lord himself will come down from heaven, with a loud command, with the voice of the archangel and with the trumpet call of God, and the dead in Christ will rise first. ¹⁷After that, we who are still alive and are left will be caught up together with them in the clouds to meet the Lord in the air. And so we will be with the Lord forever. ¹⁸Therefore encourage each other with these words.

5 Now, brothers, about times and dates we do not need to write to you, ²for you know very well that the day of the Lord will come like a thief in the night. ³While people are saying, "Peace and safety," destruction will come on them suddenly, as labor pains on a pregnant woman, and they will not escape.

⁴But you, brothers, are not in darkness so that this day should surprise you like a thief. ⁵You are all sons of the light and sons of the day. We do not belong to the night or to the darkness. ⁶So then, let us not be like others, who are asleep, but let us be alert and self-controlled. ⁷For those who sleep, sleep at night, and those who get drunk, get drunk at night. ⁸But since we belong to the day, let us be self-controlled, putting on faith and love as a breastplate, and the hope of salvation as a helmet. ⁹For God did not appoint us to suffer wrath but to receive salvation through our Lord Jesus Christ. ¹⁰He died for us so that, whether we are awake or asleep, we may live together with him. ¹¹Therefore encourage one another and build each other up, just as in fact you are doing.

FINAL INSTRUCTIONS

¹²Now we ask you, brothers, to respect those who work hard among you, who are over you in the Lord and who admonish you. ¹³Hold them in the highest regard in love because of their work. Live in peace with each other. ¹⁴And we urge you, brothers, warn those who are idle, encourage the timid, help the weak, be patient with everyone. ¹⁵Make sure that nobody pays back wrong for wrong, but always try to be kind to each other and to everyone else.

¹⁶Be joyful always; ¹⁷pray continually; ¹⁸give thanks in all circumstances, for this is God's will for you in Christ Jesus.

¹⁹Do not put out the Spirit's fire; ²⁰do not treat prophecies with contempt. ²¹Test everything. Hold on to the good. ²²Avoid every kind of evil.

²³May God himself, the God of peace, sanctify you through and through. May your whole spirit, soul and body be kept blameless at the coming of our Lord Jesus Christ. ²⁴The one who calls you is faithful and he will do it.

NOW OR NEVER
1TH 4:17–18

How much of what you know about Jesus' return is based on popular fiction books and movies? Make sure you examine what God teaches in his Word to get the real story about Jesus' coming.

²⁵Brothers, pray for us. ²⁶Greet all the brothers with a holy kiss. ²⁷I charge you before the Lord to have this letter read to all the brothers.

²⁸The grace of our Lord Jesus Christ be with you.

2 THESSALONIANS

Author
The apostle Paul

Audience
The church at Thessalonica

Date
About A.D. 51 or 52

Setting
Paul wrote this letter from Corinth to correct the Christians in Thessalonica. They thought the second coming of Christ would happen at any moment. As a result, many became lazy and quit working.

Verse to Remember
Don't let anyone deceive you in any way, for that day will not come until the rebellion occurs and the man of lawlessness is revealed, the man doomed to destruction (2:3).

Theme to Consider
As we wait for Jesus' return, we should heed Paul's advice to the Thessalonians—live purely, use our time well and work for God's kingdom.

UNCHANGING TRUTH » The Lord is coming back; the Bible is very clear about that. But when?

That's the question people have been trying to answer since the day Jesus left for heaven. God gives us some clues in his Word through "warning signs"—events such as the arrival of the antichrist—that signal the beginning of the end. But Bible scholars don't always agree about how to interpret these signs. And even with these clues, God makes it clear that no one will know the hour or day of Jesus' return.

That doesn't stop many people from trying to figure it out, though. Every few years or so, somebody goes public with a new prediction about the date of Jesus' return, armed with obscure timelines and bizarre calculations. If their prediction attracts enough publicity, it usually causes a few overeager (and unwise) believers to sell their possessions, pack their Bibles and head for the hills in preparation for Jesus' return. The result of these predictions is always the same: The target date comes and goes with no sign of Jesus, and the would-be prophets fade into anonymity without so much as admitting their error.

As Paul points out in the book of 2 Thessalonians, the only way to prepare for Jesus' coming is to remain faithfully obedient to God's Word . . . every day. That way you're guaranteed to be doing something pleasing to the Lord when he returns, regardless of the day or the hour.

LIFE LESSONS »

1. Jesus' return is something we should look forward to, not dread (2:1–2).

2. God took the first step in calling you, which says something about how much he loves you (2:14).

3. Don't just sit back and wait for Jesus' return; there's a lot of important work to be done until he comes back (3:6–13).

1

Paul, Silas[a] and Timothy,

To the church of the Thessalonians in God our Father and the Lord Jesus Christ:

[2]Grace and peace to you from God the Father and the Lord Jesus Christ.

challenge notes

To: **my_son**

heavenly_father: accept other believers for who they are. don't allow a personality conflict to sour your attitude toward someone else. the person who annoys and irritates you today may be one of your most important friends sometime in the future.

2TH 1:3

72863 BG C FE

THANKSGIVING AND PRAYER

[3]We ought always to thank God for you, brothers, and rightly so, because your faith is growing more and more, and the love every one of you has for each other is increasing. [4]Therefore, among God's churches we boast about your perseverance and faith in all the persecutions and trials you are enduring.

[5]All this is evidence that God's judgment is right, and as a result you will be counted worthy of the kingdom of God, for which you are suffering. [6]God is just: He will pay back trouble to those who trouble you [7]and give relief to you who are troubled, and to us as well. This will happen when the Lord Jesus is revealed from heaven in blazing fire with his powerful angels. [8]He will punish those who do not know God and do not obey the gospel of our Lord Jesus. [9]They will be punished with everlasting destruction and shut out from the presence of the Lord and from the majesty of his power [10]on the day he comes to be glorified in his holy people and to be marveled at among all those who have believed. This includes you, because you believed our testimony to you.

[11]With this in mind, we constantly pray for you, that our God may count you worthy of his calling, and that by his power he may fulfill every good purpose of yours and every act prompted by your faith. [12]We pray this so that the name of our Lord Jesus may be glorified in you, and you in him, according to the grace of our God and the Lord Jesus Christ.[b]

THE MAN OF LAWLESSNESS

2

Concerning the coming of our Lord Jesus Christ and our being gathered to him, we ask you, brothers, [2]not to become easily unsettled or alarmed by some prophecy, report or letter supposed to have come from us, saying that the day of the Lord has already come. [3]Don't let anyone deceive you in any way, for ⌊that day will not come⌋ until the rebellion occurs and the man of lawlessness[c] is revealed, the man doomed to destruction. [4]He will oppose and will exalt himself over everything that is called God or is worshiped, so that he sets himself up in God's temple, proclaiming himself to be God.

[5]Don't you remember that when I was with you I used to tell you these things? [6]And now you know what is holding him back, so that he may be revealed at the proper time. [7]For the secret power of lawlessness is already at work; but the one who now holds it back will continue to do so till he is taken out of the way. [8]And then the lawless one will be revealed, whom the Lord Jesus will overthrow with the breath of his mouth and destroy by the splendor of his coming. [9]The coming of the lawless one will be in accordance with the work of Satan displayed in all kinds of counterfeit mira-

Holding on to the Truth

Once you learn the truth of God's Word, be prepared to defend it against an onslaught of doubters and critics. You'll find that people will try to chip away at the truth from time to time if you let them. They'll ask things like, "If God is loving, how can he send people to hell?" or "Don't you think it's narrow-minded to believe that Jesus is the *only* way to God?" or "How do you know the Bible is true?" If you're not prepared to face these questions, they can do serious damage to your faith.

» live the adventure » 2Th 2:15

2Th 2:6 »» live the adventure »» 2Th 2:15

SSE 1

[a] *1* Greek *Silvanus*, a variant of *Silas*   [b] *12* Or *God and Lord, Jesus Christ*   [c] *3* Some manuscripts *sin*

cles, signs and wonders, ¹⁰and in every sort of evil that deceives those who are perishing. They perish because they refused to love the truth and so be saved. ¹¹For this reason God sends them a powerful delusion so that they will believe the lie ¹²and so that all will be condemned who have not believed the truth but have delighted in wickedness.

STAND FIRM

¹³But we ought always to thank God for you, brothers loved by the Lord, because from the beginning God chose you[a] to be saved through the sanctifying work of the Spirit and through belief in the truth. ¹⁴He called you to this through our gospel, that you might share in the glory of our Lord Jesus Christ. ¹⁵So then, brothers, stand firm and hold to the teachings[b] we passed on to you, whether by word of mouth or by letter.

¹⁶May our Lord Jesus Christ himself and God our Father, who loved us and by his grace gave us eternal encouragement and good hope, ¹⁷encourage your hearts and strengthen you in every good deed and word.

NOW OR NEVER
2TH 3:1–2

Never be too proud to ask someone to pray for you. Even great leaders like Paul depended on prayer support from other believers. That's what Christian friends are for.

REQUEST FOR PRAYER

3 Finally, brothers, pray for us that the message of the Lord may spread rapidly and be honored, just as it was with you. ²And pray that we may be delivered from wicked and evil men, for not everyone has faith. ³But the Lord is faithful, and he will strengthen and protect you from the evil one. ⁴We have confidence in the Lord that you are doing and will continue to do the things we command. ⁵May the Lord direct your hearts into God's love and Christ's perseverance.

WARNING AGAINST IDLENESS

⁶In the name of the Lord Jesus Christ, we command you, brothers, to keep away from every brother who is idle and does not live according to the teaching[c] you received from us. ⁷For you yourselves know how you ought to follow our example. We were not idle when we were with you, ⁸nor did we eat anyone's food without paying for it. On the contrary, we worked night and day, laboring and toiling so that we would not be a burden to any of you. ⁹We did this, not because we do not have the right to such help, but in order to make ourselves a model for you to follow. ¹⁰For even when we were with you, we gave you this rule: "If a man will not work, he shall not eat."

NOW OR NEVER
2TH 3:10

Everything that we have is a gift from God; none of it is earned. But only a thankful heart can receive the gifts that he's given freely. That's why we should work hard for the food that we eat and the clothes that we wear.

¹¹We hear that some among you are idle. They are not busy; they are busybodies. ¹²Such people we command and urge in the Lord Jesus Christ to settle down and earn the bread they eat. ¹³And as for you, brothers, never tire of doing what is right.

¹⁴If anyone does not obey our instruction in this letter, take special note of him. Do not associate with him, in order that he may feel ashamed. ¹⁵Yet do not regard him as an enemy, but warn him as a brother.

FINAL GREETINGS

¹⁶Now may the Lord of peace himself give you peace at all times and in every way. The Lord be with all of you.

¹⁷I, Paul, write this greeting in my own hand, which is the distinguishing mark in all my letters. This is how I write.

¹⁸The grace of our Lord Jesus Christ be with you all.

ᵃ 13 Some manuscripts *because God chose you as his firstfruits*　ᵇ 15 Or *traditions*　ᶜ 6 Or *tradition*

1 TIMOTHY

« AT A GLANCE

Author
The apostle Paul

Audience
Timothy, Paul's young protégé, and the Ephesian church

Date
About A.D. 64, probably between Paul's first and second imprisonments in Rome

Setting
Paul had previously directed Timothy to lead the church in Ephesus and to fight false teaching there. Paul wrote to give him advice on how to manage the church.

Verse to Remember
Don't let anyone look down on you because you are young, but set an example for the believers in speech, in life, in love, in faith and in purity (4:12).

Theme to Consider
Ever feel you are too young to serve? Then you will want to carefully read Paul's advice to his young friend, Timothy. Put it into practice, and be an example.

UNCHANGING TRUTH » "You're too young; just wait until you get a little older."

How many times have you heard that? It seems as if no matter how old you get, there's always someone ready to tell you that you're still not old enough to buy your own car . . . or go to Florida with your buddies for spring break . . . or plan your own youth group meeting . . . or whatever.

Some things, like getting a driver's license, seeing certain movies and buying certain video games, have age restrictions enforced by an outside source. There's no legal way around them. However, a lot of things that people tell you you're too young to do have more to do with their prejudices than your age.

The truth is that many adults underestimate what young people are capable of. If they knew how much responsibility you could really handle, they'd be blown away. That's why you have to *show* them by taking advantage of the opportunities you do have. When your parents (or a boss or youth leader) give you a responsibility—no matter how small it seems—get it done and do it well. Don't give anyone a single reason to doubt your integrity and maturity. Pretty soon you'll find that they'll begin to trust you with bigger and bigger responsibilities. And that's when you can show them just how much you're *really* capable of!

The apostle Paul accurately understood how much young people can accomplish for God. That's why he left Timothy (a young guy) in charge of the Ephesian church. Paul also understood people's prejudices. That's why he warned Timothy, "Don't let anyone look down on you because you are young" (1 Timothy 4:12).

LIFE LESSONS »

1. No one is ever so far gone that God cannot pour out his grace and mercy on that person (1:12–14).

2. If you want to serve as a spiritual leader, you are going to be held to some pretty high standards (3:13).

3. If acquiring money is your first priority, you're going to lose many more valuable things in the process of getting rich (6:6–10).

1

Paul, an apostle of Christ Jesus by the command of God our Savior and of Christ Jesus our hope,

²To Timothy my true son in the faith:

Grace, mercy and peace from God the Father and Christ Jesus our Lord.

WARNING AGAINST FALSE TEACHERS OF THE LAW

³As I urged you when I went into Macedonia, stay there in Ephesus so that you may command certain men not to teach false doctrines any longer ⁴nor to devote themselves to myths and endless genealogies. These promote controversies rather than God's work—which is by faith. ⁵The goal of this command is love, which comes from a pure heart and a good conscience and a sincere faith. ⁶Some have wandered away from these and turned to meaningless talk. ⁷They want to be teachers of the law, but they do not know what they are talking about or what they so confidently affirm.

⁸We know that the law is good if one uses it properly. ⁹We also know that law[a] is made not for the righteous but for lawbreakers and rebels, the ungodly and sinful, the unholy and irreligious; for those who kill their fathers or mothers, for murderers, ¹⁰for adulterers and perverts, for slave traders and liars and perjurers—and for whatever else is contrary to the sound doctrine ¹¹that conforms to the glorious gospel of the blessed God, which he entrusted to me.

THE LORD'S GRACE TO PAUL

¹²I thank Christ Jesus our Lord, who has given me strength, that he considered me faithful, appointing me to his service. ¹³Even though I was once a blasphemer and a persecutor and a violent man, I was shown mercy because I acted in ignorance and unbelief. ¹⁴The grace of our Lord was poured out on me abundantly, along with the faith and love that are in Christ Jesus.

¹⁵Here is a trustworthy saying that deserves full acceptance: Christ Jesus came into the world to save sinners—of whom I am the worst. ¹⁶But for that very reason I was shown mercy so that in me, the worst of sinners, Christ Jesus might display his unlimited patience as an example for those who would believe on him and receive eternal life. ¹⁷Now to the King eternal, immortal, invisible, the only God, be honor and glory for ever and ever. Amen.

¹⁸Timothy, my son, I give you this instruction in keeping with the prophecies once made about you, so that by following them you may fight the good fight, ¹⁹holding on to faith and a good conscience. Some have rejected these and so have shipwrecked their faith. ²⁰Among them are Hymenaeus and Alexander, whom I have handed over to Satan to be taught not to blaspheme.

» live the adventure » 1Ti 1:13

Understanding Your Value

Saul was a radical Jew who hated Christianity so much that he actually helped kill followers of Jesus. Definitely not the guy to be voted "Most Likely to Change the World Through Christian Teaching and Service." Yet God saw something valuable in Saul that he could use. He saw something that even Saul didn't see. Paul's past (when he was known as Saul) didn't matter to God; his future did. God sees something valuable in you too. And it doesn't matter what your background is or how unqualified for ministry you think you are. God can do incredible things with your life . . . if you give it to him.

INSTRUCTIONS ON WORSHIP

2

I urge, then, first of all, that requests, prayers, intercession and thanksgiving be made for everyone— ²for kings and all those in authority, that we may live peaceful and quiet lives in all godliness and holiness. ³This is good, and pleases God our Savior, ⁴who wants all men to be saved and to come to a knowledge of the truth. ⁵For there is one God and one mediator between God and men, the man Christ Jesus, ⁶who gave himself as a ransom for all men—the testimony given in its proper time. ⁷And for this purpose I was appointed a herald and an apostle—I am telling the truth, I am not lying—and a teacher of the true faith to the Gentiles.

ᵃ 9 Or *that the law*

[8]I want men everywhere to lift up holy hands in prayer, without anger or disputing.

[9]I also want women to dress modestly, with decency and propriety, not with braided hair or gold or pearls or expensive clothes, [10]but with good deeds, appropriate for women who profess to worship God.

[11]A woman should learn in quietness and full submission. [12]I do not permit a woman to teach or to have authority over a man; she must be silent. [13]For Adam was formed first, then Eve. [14]And Adam was not the one deceived; it was the woman who was deceived and became a sinner. [15]But women[a] will be saved[b] through childbearing—if they continue in faith, love and holiness with propriety.

OVERSEERS AND DEACONS

3 Here is a trustworthy saying: If anyone sets his heart on being an overseer,[c] he desires a noble task. [2]Now the overseer must be above reproach, the husband of but one wife, temperate, self-controlled, respectable, hospitable, able to teach, [3]not given to drunkenness, not violent but gentle, not quarrelsome, not a lover of money. [4]He must manage his own family well and see that his children obey him with proper respect. [5](If anyone does not know how to manage his own family, how can he take care of God's church?) [6]He must not be a recent convert, or he may become conceited and fall under the same judgment as the devil. [7]He must also have a good reputation with outsiders, so that he will not fall into disgrace and into the devil's trap.

[8]Deacons, likewise, are to be men worthy of respect, sincere, not indulging in much wine, and not pursuing dishonest gain. [9]They must keep hold of the deep truths of the faith with a clear conscience. [10]They must first be tested; and then if there is nothing against them, let them serve as deacons.

[11]In the same way, their wives[d] are to be women worthy of respect, not malicious talkers but temperate and trustworthy in everything.

[12]A deacon must be the husband of but one wife and must manage his children and his household well. [13]Those who have served well gain an excellent standing and great assurance in their faith in Christ Jesus.

[14]Although I hope to come to you soon, I am writing you these instructions so that, [15]if I am delayed, you will know how people ought to conduct themselves in God's household, which is the church of the living God, the pillar and foundation of the truth. [16]Beyond all question, the mystery of godliness is great:

> He[e] appeared in a body,[f]
>> was vindicated by the Spirit,
> was seen by angels,
> was preached among the nations,
> was believed on in the world,
> was taken up in glory.

INSTRUCTIONS TO TIMOTHY

4 The Spirit clearly says that in later times some will abandon the faith and follow deceiving spirits and things taught by demons. [2]Such teachings come through hypocritical liars, whose consciences have been seared as with a hot iron. [3]They forbid people to marry and order them to abstain from certain foods, which God created to be received with thanksgiving by those who believe and who know the truth. [4]For everything God created is good, and nothing is to be rejected if it is received with thanksgiving, [5]because it is consecrated by the word of God and prayer.

[6]If you point these things out to the brothers, you will be a good minister of Christ Jesus, brought up in the truths of the faith and of the good teaching that you have followed. [7]Have nothing to do with god-

---

NOW OR NEVER

1TI 3:4

At this point in your life, you're probably sick and tired of people telling you that you've got to straighten out your life to be a good son, brother, student, etc. But what if someone told you that you needed to get your act together in order to be a good father, husband or church leader?

---

[a] 15 Greek *she*   [b] 15 Or *restored*   [c] 1 Traditionally *bishop*; also in verse 2   [d] 11 Or *way, deaconesses*   [e] 16 Some manuscripts *God*   [f] 16 Or *in the flesh*

battlelines

» The Narcissus Syndrome (Bodybuilding)

Q: You're *still* working out? Your sister said you left for the gym three hours ago!
A: Yeah, dude. I'm loving it. I'm starting to see big-time results.

Q: You *are* looking bigger. Hey, you're not using steroids, are you?
A: No way! I mean, there's no question, they *do* work. You can turn into an animal in no time. But do I want to shrink myself where it counts, lose my hair, break out all over and start punching lockers? No thanks. I'm just using legal supplements and busting my tail in the gym.

Q: So what's your goal?
A: To get ripped. To be massive. You know, to just look really good. The bigger you are, the more people notice you.

Q: Yeah, but look around you. Here's a bunch of guys spending *hours* a day in front of a mirror. When does trying to look good become an unhealthy obsession?
A: Now you're starting to sound like my sister. She's always saying, "Why don't you spend even ten minutes a day thinking about how you look on the inside?" Hey, look, I know all that stuff. I'm a Christian. Why can't I be a Christian bodybuilder and have an influence on these guys?

Q: You can. No doubt. Let me ask you one last question, and then I'll let you get on with your curls. If something happened and you couldn't be massive, and you had to settle for an average physique, would you feel like you're less of a man? Would you feel inferior?
A: I don't know. Maybe. But I'd rather not think about that right now.

» The Balance

Is it a sin to want to be in good shape? Not at all! But it's not enough to give only our *bodies* a workout. First Timothy 4:7–8 says: "Train yourself to be godly. For physical training is of some value, but godliness has value for all things, holding promise for both the present life and the life to come."

One of the saddest things in the world is the person whose body is strong, but whose character is weak. What happens when the muscles begin to sag? What will you have then?

Read more about working out at www.RevolutionBible.com.

less myths and old wives' tales; rather, train yourself to be godly. ⁸For physical training is of some value, but godliness has value for all things, holding promise for both the present life and the life to come.

Knowing What to Believe

Timothy wasn't the only one who had to worry about "godless myths" and "old wives tales." Here are a few popular ideas you need to recognize as lies: "It doesn't matter what you believe about spiritual things, as long as you believe in something." "Jesus had some good ideas, but he wasn't the Son of God." "It's only a sin if it hurts someone else." "If you give to this ministry, God will make you wealthy." "If you can't accept someone's lifestyle, you're being narrow-minded." "Sex is OK if two people agree to it and really care about each other."

⁹This is a trustworthy saying that deserves full acceptance ¹⁰(and for this we labor and strive), that we have put our hope in the living God, who is the Savior of all men, and especially of those who believe.

¹¹Command and teach these things. ¹²Don't let anyone look down on you because you are young, but set an example for the believers in speech, in life, in love, in faith and in purity. ¹³Until I come, devote yourself to the public reading of Scripture, to preaching and to teaching. ¹⁴Do not neglect your gift, which was given you through a prophetic message when the body of elders laid their hands on you.

¹⁵Be diligent in these matters; give yourself wholly to them, so that everyone may see your progress. ¹⁶Watch your life and doctrine closely. Persevere in them, because if you do, you will save both yourself and your hearers.

ADVICE ABOUT WIDOWS, ELDERS AND SLAVES

5 Do not rebuke an older man harshly, but exhort him as if he were your father. Treat younger men as brothers, ²older women as mothers, and younger women as sisters, with absolute purity.

³Give proper recognition to those widows who are really in need. ⁴But if a widow has children or grandchildren, these should learn first of all to put their religion into practice by caring for their own family and so repaying their parents and grandparents, for this is pleasing to God. ⁵The widow who is really in need and left all alone puts her hope in God and continues night and day to pray and to ask God for help. ⁶But the widow who lives for pleasure is dead even while she lives. ⁷Give the people these instructions, too, so that no one may be open to blame. ⁸If anyone does not provide for his relatives, and especially for his immediate family, he has denied the faith and is worse than an unbeliever.

⁹No widow may be put on the list of widows unless she is over sixty, has been faithful to her husband,ᵃ ¹⁰and is well known for her good deeds, such as bringing up children, showing hospitality, washing the feet of the saints, helping those in trouble and devoting herself to all kinds of good deeds.

¹¹As for younger widows, do not put them on such a list. For when their sensual desires overcome their dedication to Christ, they want to marry. ¹²Thus they bring judgment on themselves, because they have broken their first pledge. ¹³Besides, they get into the habit of being idle and going about from house to house. And not only do they become idlers, but also gossips and busybodies, saying things they ought not to. ¹⁴So I counsel younger widows to marry, to have children, to manage their homes and to give the enemy no opportunity for slander. ¹⁵Some have in fact already turned away to follow Satan.

¹⁶If any woman who is a believer has widows in her family, she should help them and not let the church be burdened with them, so that the church can help those widows who are really in need.

NOW OR NEVER
1Ti 4:7–8

While you're busy pumping up physically, don't let your spiritual muscles go to waste. Try coordinating your physical and spiritual workout schedules. For instance, on the days you work your arms, do your Bible study. On the days you work your chest and abs, do a service project for your church.

ᵃ 9 Or *has had but one husband*

[17]The elders who direct the affairs of the church well are worthy of double honor, especially those whose work is preaching and teaching. [18]For the Scripture says, "Do not muzzle the ox while it is treading out the grain,"[a] and "The worker deserves his wages."[b] [19]Do not entertain an accusation against an elder unless it is brought by two or three witnesses. [20]Those who sin are to be rebuked publicly, so that the others may take warning.

[21]I charge you, in the sight of God and Christ Jesus and the elect angels, to keep these instructions without partiality, and to do nothing out of favoritism.

[22]Do not be hasty in the laying on of hands, and do not share in the sins of others. Keep yourself pure.

[23]Stop drinking only water, and use a little wine because of your stomach and your frequent illnesses.

[24]The sins of some men are obvious, reaching the place of judgment ahead of them; the sins of others trail behind them. [25]In the same way, good deeds are obvious, and even those that are not cannot be hidden.

6 All who are under the yoke of slavery should consider their masters worthy of full respect, so that God's name and our teaching may not be slandered. [2]Those who have believing masters are not to show less respect for them because they are brothers. Instead, they are to serve them even better, because those who benefit from their service are believers, and dear to them. These are the things you are to teach and urge on them.

LOVE OF MONEY

[3]If anyone teaches false doctrines and does not agree to the sound instruction of our Lord Jesus Christ and to godly teaching, [4]he is conceited and understands nothing. He has an unhealthy interest in controversies and quarrels about words that result in envy, strife, malicious talk, evil suspicions [5]and constant friction between men of corrupt mind, who have been robbed of the truth and who think that godliness is a means to financial gain.

[6]But godliness with contentment is great gain. [7]For we brought nothing into the world, and we can take nothing out of it. [8]But if we have food and clothing, we will be content with that. [9]People who want to get rich fall into temptation and a trap and into many foolish and harmful desires that plunge men into ruin and destruction. [10]For the love of money is a root of all kinds of evil. Some people, eager for money, have wandered from the faith and pierced themselves with many griefs.

PAUL'S CHARGE TO TIMOTHY

[11]But you, man of God, flee from all this, and pursue righteousness, godliness, faith, love, endurance and gentleness. [12]Fight the good fight of the faith. Take hold of the eternal life to which you were called when you made your good confession in the presence of many witnesses. [13]In the sight of God, who gives life to everything, and of Christ Jesus, who while testifying before Pontius Pilate made the good confession, I charge you [14]to keep this command without spot or blame until the appearing of our Lord Jesus Christ, [15]which God will bring about in his own time—God, the blessed and only Ruler, the King of kings and Lord of lords, [16]who alone is immortal and who lives in unapproachable light, whom no one has seen or can see. To him be honor and might forever. Amen.

[17]Command those who are rich in this present world not to be arrogant nor to put their hope in wealth, which is so uncertain, but to put their hope in God, who richly provides us with everything for our enjoyment. [18]Command them to do good, to be rich in good deeds, and to be generous and willing to share. [19]In this way they will lay up treasure for themselves as a firm foundation for the coming age, so that they may take hold of the life that is truly life.

[20]Timothy, guard what has been entrusted to your care. Turn away from godless chatter and the opposing ideas of what is falsely called knowledge, [21]which some have professed and in so doing have wandered from the faith.

Grace be with you.

---

[a] *18* Deut. 25:4   [b] *18* Luke 10:7

2 TIMOTHY

Author
The apostle Paul

Audience
Timothy and the Ephesian church

Date
About A.D. 66 or 67

Setting
Paul wrote this, his last letter from a cold dungeon in Rome shortly before he was executed for his faith. He had left Timothy in Ephesus to supervise the church there.

Verses to Remember
Endure hardship with us like a good soldier of Christ Jesus. No one serving as a soldier gets involved in civilian affairs—he wants to please his commanding officer (2:3–4).

Theme to Consider
Like Paul, when we serve Christ, we will likely face persecution and suffering. Like Paul, we will consider it all worthwhile when we achieve our goal of honoring Jesus in all that we do.

UNCHANGING TRUTH » Let's get one thing clear: The good news about Jesus Christ does *not* mean that your life is going to be a breeze. One day we will enter into eternal paradise with Christ—into a life that will make the most luxurious existence on Earth look like a joke. But for those of us who remain on Earth, there is still a race to be run, a battle to be fought and work to be done. For proof, just read the second chapter of 2 Timothy.

The apostle Paul knew that life can be tough. This was a guy who had been beat up, humiliated, arrested, imprisoned and shipwrecked. Why all the harsh treatment? Because he spoke the truth about Jesus.

Nearing the end of his life, Paul wanted to pass on some of the hardest lessons he had learned to a kid whom he had grown to love like a son—a guy named Timothy. Paul's words to Timothy are just as applicable to us now as they were to him nearly 2,000 years ago: Be strong. Run from temptation. Keep your cool under pressure. Speak the truth. Stay away from godless talk. Don't underestimate yourself. This book is filled with exactly the kind of advice that every guy needs to hear.

It's convenient that Paul wrote this letter to Timothy, since he might have been like you in many ways. But you don't have to *imagine* that this letter was written for you. The Holy Spirit inspired Paul's words with you in mind. These words are your road map, your marching orders and your game plan. Read them, believe them and live them.

LIFE LESSONS »

1 Because of all God has done for us, we should not be ashamed or afraid to tell others about him—even if we suffer persecution for doing so (1:8–9).

2 If you're not suffering—at least a little—for being a Christian, it may be a sign that you're not living out your faith as boldly as you ought to (3:12).

3 If your first priority is obtaining the things of this world, your relationship with God (and other believers) will suffer tremendously (4:10).

1

Paul, an apostle of Christ Jesus by the will of God, according to the promise of life that is in Christ Jesus,

2 To Timothy, my dear son:

Grace, mercy and peace from God the Father and Christ Jesus our Lord.

ENCOURAGEMENT TO BE FAITHFUL

3 I thank God, whom I serve, as my forefathers did, with a clear conscience, as night and day I constantly remember you in my prayers. 4 Recalling your tears, I long to see you, so that I may be filled with joy. 5 I have been reminded of your sincere faith, which first lived in your grandmother Lois and in your mother Eunice and, I am persuaded, now lives in you also. 6 For this reason I remind you to fan into flame the gift of God, which is in you through the laying on of my hands. 7 For God did not give us a spirit of timidity, but a spirit of power, of love and of self-discipline.

8 So do not be ashamed to testify about our Lord, or ashamed of me his prisoner. But join with me in suffering for the gospel, by the power of God, 9 who has saved us and called us to a holy life—not because of anything we have done but because of his own purpose and grace. This grace was given us in Christ Jesus before the beginning of time, 10 but it has now been revealed through the appearing of our Savior, Christ Jesus, who has destroyed death and has brought life and immortality to light through the gospel. 11 And of this gospel I was appointed a herald and an apostle and a teacher. 12 That is why I am suffering as I am. Yet I am not ashamed, because I know whom I have believed, and am convinced that he is able to guard what I have entrusted to him for that day.

13 What you heard from me, keep as the pattern of sound teaching, with faith and love in Christ Jesus. 14 Guard the good deposit that was entrusted to you—guard it with the help of the Holy Spirit who lives in us.

15 You know that everyone in the province of Asia has deserted me, including Phygelus and Hermogenes. 16 May the Lord show mercy to the household of Onesiphorus, because he often refreshed me and was not ashamed of my chains. 17 On the contrary, when he was in Rome, he searched hard for me until he found me. 18 May the Lord grant that he will find mercy from the Lord on that day! You know very well in how many ways he helped me in Ephesus.

2

You then, my son, be strong in the grace that is in Christ Jesus. 2 And the things you have heard me say in the presence of many witnesses entrust to reliable men who will also be qualified to teach others. 3 Endure hardship with us like a good soldier of Christ Jesus. 4 No one serving as a soldier gets involved in civilian affairs—he wants to please his commanding officer. 5 Similarly, if anyone competes as an athlete, he does not receive the victor's crown unless he competes according to the rules. 6 The hardworking farmer should be the first to receive a share of the crops. 7 Reflect on what I am saying, for the Lord will give you insight into all this.

8 Remember Jesus Christ, raised from the dead, descended from David. This is my gospel, 9 for which I am suffering even to the point of being chained like a criminal. But God's word is not chained. 10 Therefore I endure everything for the sake of the elect, that they too may obtain the salvation that is in Christ Jesus, with eternal glory. 11 Here is a trustworthy saying:

> If we died with him,
>   we will also live with him;
> 12 if we endure,
>   we will also reign with him.
> If we disown him,
>   he will also disown us;
> 13 if we are faithless,
>   he will remain faithful,
>   for he cannot disown himself.

A WORKMAN APPROVED BY GOD

14 Keep reminding them of these things. Warn them before God against quarreling about words; it is of no value, and only ruins those who listen. 15 Do your best to present yourself to God as one approved,

a workman who does not need to be ashamed and who correctly handles the word of truth. ¹⁶Avoid godless chatter, because those who indulge in it will become more and more ungodly. ¹⁷Their teaching will spread like gangrene. Among them are Hymenaeus and Philetus, ¹⁸who have wandered away from the truth. They say that the resurrection has already taken place, and they destroy the faith of some. ¹⁹Nevertheless, God's solid foundation stands firm, sealed with this inscription: "The Lord knows those who are his,"ᵃ and, "Everyone who confesses the name of the Lord must turn away from wickedness."

²⁰In a large house there are articles not only of gold and silver, but also of wood and clay; some are for noble purposes and some for ignoble. ²¹If a man cleanses himself from the latter, he will be an instrument for noble purposes, made holy, useful to the Master and prepared to do any good work.

²²Flee the evil desires of youth, and pursue righteousness, faith, love and peace, along with those who call on the Lord out of a pure heart. ²³Don't have anything to do with foolish and stupid arguments, because you know they produce quarrels. ²⁴And the Lord's servant must not quarrel; instead, he must be kind to everyone, able to teach, not resentful. ²⁵Those who oppose him he must gently instruct, in the hope that God will grant them repentance leading them to a knowledge of the truth, ²⁶and that they will come to their senses and escape from the trap of the devil, who has taken them captive to do his will.

GODLESSNESS IN THE LAST DAYS

3 But mark this: There will be terrible times in the last days. ²People will be lovers of themselves, lovers of money, boastful, proud, abusive, disobedient to their parents, ungrateful, unholy, ³without love, unforgiving, slanderous, without self-control, brutal, not lovers of the good, ⁴treacherous, rash, conceited, lovers of pleasure rather than lovers of God— ⁵having a form of godliness but denying its power. Have nothing to do with them.

⁶They are the kind who worm their way into homes and gain control over weak-willed women, who are loaded down with sins and are swayed by all kinds of evil desires, ⁷always learning but never able to acknowledge the truth. ⁸Just as Jannes and Jambres opposed Moses, so also these men oppose the truth—men of depraved minds, who, as far as the faith is concerned, are rejected. ⁹But they will not get very far because, as in the case of those men, their folly will be clear to everyone.

PAUL'S CHARGE TO TIMOTHY

¹⁰You, however, know all about my teaching, my way of life, my purpose, faith, patience, love, endurance, ¹¹persecutions, sufferings—what kinds of things happened to me in Antioch, Iconium and Lystra, the persecutions I endured. Yet the Lord rescued me from all of them. ¹²In fact, everyone who wants to live a godly life in Christ Jesus will be persecuted, ¹³while evil men and impostors will go from bad to worse, deceiving and being deceived. ¹⁴But as for you, continue in what you have learned and

Getting Away From Temptation

If you're a normal teenage guy, you don't stand a chance against sexual temptation. Not now, at least. The problem is your hormones—those things you read about in sex ed class. When they get going, lust is never far behind. You can't look at a half-naked girl without getting your hormones fired up, not to mention a few lustful thoughts. That's why the best strategy for keeping both your actions and thoughts pure is to "flee" sexual temptation. Don't give lust a chance to get started. When you see something that you know could spark a hormone stampede, change the channel or turn off the computer.

>> live the adventure >> 2TI 2:22

ᵃ 19 Num. 16:5 (see Septuagint)

battlelines

» Really Quiet Time

Q: How's your quiet time lately?
A: My what?

Q: Your quiet time. You know, your devotional time, the time you spend with God.
A: Oh . . . that. You mean, reading the Bible and praying every day?

Q: Yeah. How's it going?
A: Not so great. I just can't seem to get in the habit. I set my alarm, but then I end up punching the snooze button over and over again. By the time I finally drag myself out of bed, I barely have enough time to get ready for school. So then I tried it at bedtime. But once I get horizontal, I'm out.

Q: Have you tried using any kind of devotional guide?
A: Yeah, a while back I picked up one at church, but after a week, I was already five days behind! How bad is *that*?

Q: What about reading through the Bible in a year?
A: I've tried. I get to the end of Exodus and I'm like, "What the heck is all this stuff?" There's a lot of it I just don't get.

Q: You sound frustrated.
A: Yeah, I am. I know I need to do something to deepen my relationship with God. But, to tell you the truth, it all seems like such a chore. How do you start? How do you stay at it?

» Appointment With God

A "quiet time" is simply a daily appointment with God. The goal is simple: to get alone with God, to be still and to hear what he's saying to you so that you have his perspective and power in your life.

Unfortunately, there's someone who desperately wants to keep you from your daily appointments with God. His name is Satan, and he will do just about anything in his power to interfere with your quiet times. The last thing the devil wants is for you to get tight with his eternal enemy.

So, you see, something *huge* is at stake in your struggle to carve out a quiet time for yourself—something far more important than a few extra minutes of sleep.

The Bible tells us, "All Scripture is God-breathed and is useful for teaching, rebuking, correcting and training in righteousness, so that the man of God may be thoroughly equipped for every good work" (2 Timothy 3:16-17). That's why it has such a powerful effect in people's lives.

God wants to speak to you and equip you for life. Are you willing to make the time to listen?

Learn more about spending daily time with God at www.RevolutionBible.com.

have become convinced of, because you know those from whom you learned it, [15]and how from infancy you have known the holy Scriptures, which are able to make you wise for salvation through faith in Christ Jesus. [16]All Scripture is God-breathed and is useful for teaching, rebuking, correcting and training in righteousness, [17]so that the man of God may be thoroughly equipped for every good work.

4 In the presence of God and of Christ Jesus, who will judge the living and the dead, and in view of his appearing and his kingdom, I give you this charge: [2]Preach the Word; be prepared in season and out of season; correct, rebuke and encourage—with great patience and careful instruction. [3]For the time will come when men will not put up with sound doctrine. Instead, to suit their own desires, they will gather around them a great number of teachers to say what their itching ears want to hear. [4]They will turn their ears away from the truth and turn aside to myths. [5]But you, keep your head in all situations, endure hardship, do the work of an evangelist, discharge all the duties of your ministry.

[6]For I am already being poured out like a drink offering, and the time has come for my departure. [7]I have fought the good fight, I have finished the race, I have kept the faith. [8]Now there is in store for me the crown of righteousness, which the Lord, the righteous Judge, will award to me on that day—and not only to me, but also to all who have longed for his appearing.

PERSONAL REMARKS

[9]Do your best to come to me quickly, [10]for Demas, because he loved this world, has deserted me and has gone to Thessalonica. Crescens has gone to Galatia, and Titus to Dalmatia. [11]Only Luke is with me. Get Mark and bring him with you, because he is helpful to me in my ministry. [12]I sent Tychicus to Ephesus. [13]When you come, bring the cloak that I left with Carpus at Troas, and my scrolls, especially the parchments.

[14]Alexander the metalworker did me a great deal of harm. The Lord will repay him for what he has done. [15]You too should be on your guard against him, because he strongly opposed our message.

[16]At my first defense, no one came to my support, but everyone deserted me. May it not be held against them. [17]But the Lord stood at my side and gave me strength, so that through me the message might be fully proclaimed and all the Gentiles might hear it. And I was delivered from the lion's mouth. [18]The Lord will rescue me from every evil attack and will bring me safely to his heavenly kingdom. To him be glory for ever and ever. Amen.

FINAL GREETINGS

[19]Greet Priscilla[a] and Aquila and the household of Onesiphorus. [20]Erastus stayed in Corinth, and I left Trophimus sick in Miletus. [21]Do your best to get here before winter. Eubulus greets you, and so do Pudens, Linus, Claudia and all the brothers.

[22]The Lord be with your spirit. Grace be with you.

[a] 19 Greek *Prisca*, a variant of *Priscilla*

TITUS

TITUS TITUS

« AT A GLANCE

Author
The apostle Paul

Audience
Titus, a Gentile Christian and Paul's coworker

Date
About A.D. 64

Setting
After visiting the Mediterranean island of Crete, Paul left Titus there to lead the churches. Later Paul wrote this letter to help Titus deal with the false teaching and immoral behavior confronting these churches.

Verse to Remember
This is a trustworthy saying. And I want you to stress these things, so that those who have trusted in God may be careful to devote themselves to doing what is good. These things are excellent and profitable for everyone (3:8).

Theme to Consider
In order to be effective leaders for Christ, we first must be self-disciplined, responsible, living examples of our faith.

UNCHANGING TRUTH »

Don't look now, but someone's watching you. Maybe it's the girl who sits next to you in biology class. Maybe it's your boss at work. Maybe it's your girlfriend's dad. Maybe it's someone you don't even know.

Whoever they may be, people are watching you closely for one reason: They know you're a Christian, and they're not. A part of them wants to see you screw up big-time so they can write off Christians as a bunch of hypocrites. They'd like to hear you tell a dirty joke, take a swing at someone who's bugging you or join the crowd who's making fun of an overweight girl. They want to believe that there's no real difference between you and them.

Another part of them, however, wants to see you live in a way that's completely different from everyone else. They'd like to see you walk away when guys start gossiping. They'd like to see you turn the other cheek when someone gets in your face. They'd like to see you stand up for people who are getting picked on. They'd like to know that there's something special about the way Christians live. They'd like to know that Jesus really can make a difference in someone's life.

Maybe you know exactly who's watching you; maybe you don't. It doesn't really matter. What matters is that you live your life in a way that is genuinely pleasing to God. Then, no matter who's watching and what their motivation is, the only thing they will see is true devotion to God. If you'd like some tips on how to live out such devotion, read Paul's letter to his friend Titus.

LIFE LESSONS »

1. You can't just ignore people who try to bend or stretch God's truth; you have to confront them so that their false teachings don't affect others (1:10–14).

2. Self-control is one of the qualities people look for most in Christians (2:6–8).

3. Because Jesus has done so much good for us, he expects us to do good for other people (3:3–8).

1 Paul, a servant of God and an apostle of Jesus Christ for the faith of God's elect and the knowledge of the truth that leads to godliness— 2a faith and knowledge resting on the hope of eternal life, which God, who does not lie, promised before the beginning of time, 3and at his appointed season he brought his word to light through the preaching entrusted to me by the command of God our Savior,

4To Titus, my true son in our common faith:

Grace and peace from God the Father and Christ Jesus our Savior.

TITUS'S TASK ON CRETE

5The reason I left you in Crete was that you might straighten out what was left unfinished and appointa elders in every town, as I directed you. 6An elder must be blameless, the husband of but one wife, a man whose children believe and are not open to the charge of being wild and disobedient. 7Since an overseerb is entrusted with God's work, he must be blameless—not overbearing, not quick-tempered, not given to drunkenness, not violent, not pursuing dishonest gain. 8Rather he must be hospitable, one who loves what is good, who is self-controlled, upright, holy and disciplined. 9He must hold firmly to the trustworthy message as it has been taught, so that he can encourage others by sound doctrine and refute those who oppose it.

10For there are many rebellious people, mere talkers and deceivers, especially those of the circumcision group. 11They must be silenced, because they are ruining whole households by teaching things they ought not to teach—and that for the sake of dishonest gain. 12Even one of their own prophets has said, "Cretans are always liars, evil brutes, lazy gluttons." 13This testimony is true. Therefore, rebuke them sharply, so that they will be sound in the faith 14and will pay no attention to Jewish myths or to the commands of those who reject the truth. 15To the pure, all things are pure, but to those who are corrupted and do not believe, nothing is pure. In fact, both their minds and consciences are corrupted. 16They claim to know God, but by their actions they deny him. They are detestable, disobedient and unfit for doing anything good.

WHAT MUST BE TAUGHT TO VARIOUS GROUPS

2 You must teach what is in accord with sound doctrine. 2Teach the older men to be temperate, worthy of respect, self-controlled, and sound in faith, in love and in endurance.

3Likewise, teach the older women to be reverent in the way they live, not to be slanderers or addicted to much wine, but to teach what is good. 4Then they can train the younger women to love their husbands and children, 5to be self-controlled and pure, to be busy at home, to be kind, and to be subject to their husbands, so that no one will malign the word of God.

6Similarly, encourage the young men to be self-controlled. 7In everything set them an example by doing what is good. In your teaching show integrity, seriousness 8and soundness of speech that cannot be condemned, so that those who oppose you may be ashamed because they have nothing bad to say about us.

9Teach slaves to be subject to their masters in everything, to try to please them, not to talk back to them, 10and not to steal from them, but to show that they can be fully trusted, so that in every way they will make the teaching about God our Savior attractive.

11For the grace of God that brings salvation has appeared to all men. 12It teaches us to say "No" to ungodliness and worldly passions, and to live self-controlled, upright and godly lives in this present age, 13while we wait for the blessed hope—the glorious appearing of our great God and Savior, Jesus Christ, 14who gave himself for us to redeem us from all wickedness and to purify for himself a people that are his very own, eager to do what is good.

NOW OR NEVER

TIT 2:6–8

In what area of your life do you have the least amount of self-control? Is it what you say or do when you're angry? The way you react when you see something sexually provocative? The way you act when your friends are around? What can you do to develop more self-control in that area?

---

a 5 Or *ordain*   b 7 Traditionally *bishop*

15These, then, are the things you should teach. Encourage and rebuke with all authority. Do not let anyone despise you.

DOING WHAT IS GOOD

3 Remind the people to be subject to rulers and authorities, to be obedient, to be ready to do whatever is good, 2to slander no one, to be peaceable and considerate, and to show true humility toward all men.

3At one time we too were foolish, disobedient, deceived and enslaved by all kinds of passions and pleasures. We lived in malice and envy, being hated and hating one another. 4But when the kindness and love of God our Savior appeared, 5he saved us, not because of righteous things we had done, but because of his mercy. He saved us through the washing of rebirth and renewal by the Holy Spirit, 6whom he poured out on us generously through Jesus Christ our Savior, 7so that, having been justified by his grace, we might become heirs having the hope of eternal life. 8This is a trustworthy saying. And I want you to stress these things, so that those who have trusted in God may be careful to devote themselves to doing what is good. These things are excellent and profitable for everyone.

9But avoid foolish controversies and genealogies and arguments and quarrels about the law, because these are unprofitable and useless. 10Warn a divisive person once, and then warn him a second time. After that, have nothing to do with him. 11You may be sure that such a man is warped and sinful; he is self-condemned.

FINAL REMARKS

12As soon as I send Artemas or Tychicus to you, do your best to come to me at Nicopolis, because I have decided to winter there. 13Do everything you can to help Zenas the lawyer and Apollos on their way and see that they have everything they need. 14Our people must learn to devote themselves to doing what is good, in order that they may provide for daily necessities and not live unproductive lives.

15Everyone with me sends you greetings. Greet those who love us in the faith. Grace be with you all.

Finding Good Things to Do

"Doing what is good" could include *anything* that helps another person or brings glory to God. In ten minutes, you could probably come up with a list of at least a dozen good things you could do this week. Why not give it a shot? To start, write down seven good things you can do in the next seven days to help your family, friends or people you don't even know. Your list might include babysitting a younger sibling so your parents can go out, helping a friend with math homework or raking leaves for the elderly couple down the street.

PHILEMON

PHILEMON PHILEMON

« AT A GLANCE

Author
The apostle Paul

Audience
Philemon, a Christian in Colosse who was a slave owner

Date
About A.D. 60

Setting
A slave named Onesimus had apparently stolen from his master, Philemon, and then run away. Onesimus met Paul in Rome and became a Christian. He was willing to return to his former master to make things right. Paul wrote this letter to Philemon to ask him to forgive and accept Onesimus.

Verses to Remember
Perhaps the reason he was separated from you for a little while was that you might have him back for good—no longer as a slave, but better than a slave, as a dear brother. He is very dear to me but even dearer to you, both as a man and as a brother in the Lord (15–16).

Theme to Consider
What barriers separate you from other believers? Race? Wealth? Where you live? We are called, along with Philemon, to remove those barriers and accept our sisters and brothers in Christ.

UNCHANGING TRUTH » Jesus said, "Blessed are the peacemakers" (Matthew 5:9), the ones who try to unite people on good terms. Peacemakers are the guys who step between two would-be fighters to prevent them from bashing each other's heads in; they don't stand on the sidelines yelling, "Fight! Fight! Fight!" Peacemakers are the guys who won't ruin their friendship with a buddy over a cute girl or macho pride. Peacemakers are the guys who put an end to gossip and rumors by talking instead about people's good qualities.

Paul was a peacemaker. His letter to Philemon was an attempt to fix the relationship between Philemon and a runaway slave named Onesimus. The Bible doesn't tell us what effect Paul's letter had on Philemon, but you know God had to be pleased with the apostle's efforts. After all, he included this brief letter in his Word.

Are you interested in seeing God's blessings take root in your life? Do you have what it takes to be a peacemaker in your family and among your friends?

LIFE LESSONS »

1   One person's Christian love and service can make a serious impact on people's lives (7).

2   The fact that God has forgiven you should make it easy for you to forgive others (17–19).

¹Paul, a prisoner of Christ Jesus, and Timothy our brother,

To Philemon our dear friend and fellow worker, ²to Apphia our sister, to Archippus our fellow soldier and to the church that meets in your home:

³Grace to you and peace from God our Father and the Lord Jesus Christ.

THANKSGIVING AND PRAYER

⁴I always thank my God as I remember you in my prayers, ⁵because I hear about your faith in the Lord Jesus and your love for all the saints. ⁶I pray that you may be active in sharing your faith, so that you will have a full understanding of every good thing we have in Christ. ⁷Your love has given me great joy and encouragement, because you, brother, have refreshed the hearts of the saints.

PAUL'S PLEA FOR ONESIMUS

⁸Therefore, although in Christ I could be bold and order you to do what you ought to do, ⁹yet I appeal to you on the basis of love. I then, as Paul—an old man and now also a prisoner of Christ Jesus— ¹⁰I appeal to you for my son Onesimus,ᵃ who became my son while I was in chains. ¹¹Formerly he was useless to you, but now he has become useful both to you and to me.

¹²I am sending him—who is my very heart—back to you. ¹³I would have liked to keep him with me so that he could take your place in helping me while I am in chains for the gospel. ¹⁴But I did not want to do anything without your consent, so that any favor you do will be spontaneous and not forced. ¹⁵Perhaps the reason he was separated from you for a little while was that you might have him back for good— ¹⁶no longer as a slave, but better than a slave, as a dear brother. He is very dear to me but even dearer to you, both as a man and as a brother in the Lord.

NOW OR NEVER
PHM 19

Are you willing to put yourself on the line for another person, the way Paul did for Onesimus? How far are you willing to go? Are you afraid to speak the truth to certain people because of how cool or intimidating they seem?

¹⁷So if you consider me a partner, welcome him as you would welcome me. ¹⁸If he has done you any wrong or owes you anything, charge it to me. ¹⁹I, Paul, am writing this with my own hand. I will pay it back—not to mention that you owe me your very self. ²⁰I do wish, brother, that I may have some benefit from you in the Lord; refresh my heart in Christ. ²¹Confident of your obedience, I write to you, knowing that you will do even more than I ask.

²²And one thing more: Prepare a guest room for me, because I hope to be restored to you in answer to your prayers.

²³Epaphras, my fellow prisoner in Christ Jesus, sends you greetings. ²⁴And so do Mark, Aristarchus, Demas and Luke, my fellow workers.

²⁵The grace of the Lord Jesus Christ be with your spirit.

ᵃ 10 *Onesimus* means *useful.*

onesimus

VERSUS

philemon

» A runaway slave who belonged to Philemon

» While a fugitive, he was introduced to Christ and discipled by Paul

» Sent back to Philemon by Paul

» A prominent Christian in the Colossian church

» Came to Christ possibly as a result of Paul's ministry

» Onesimus's owner

The Main Event

You're Onesimus. And what a roller coaster you've been on these past few months. Why, it seems like only yesterday that you stole an envelope full of money from your master, Philemon, and made for Rome like a scared rabbit. After you ran out of cash, you met a preacher named Paul, who told you all about Jesus Christ—the Son of God, the Savior of the world. Your heart leaped at this amazing message, but you still have a hard time fathoming all of its claims—like the idea that you're forgiven, that you're a brand-new person inside, and that you have a bright future ahead of you. Even though you don't understand it all, deep down you know you've been changed forever.

You're ready to follow Paul to the ends of the earth to give other people the same message of hope that you received. There's only one problem: You have a past that's just waiting to catch up with you.

When Paul heard your story, he laughed, shook his head and said, "Philemon? From Colosse? He's a friend of mine! You've got to go back to him, Onesimus. It's only right for you to make amends. Besides, he'll show you mercy. He's a follower of Jesus, just like you are!" So now you're heading back to Colosse, uncertain of what awaits you there. You're hoping for the best . . . but fearing the worst.

Now put yourself in Philemon's shoes. Bowing before you on your marble floor is Onesimus. You have half a mind to wring the neck of this thieving, runaway slave. But he's just handed you a postcard from Paul, your spiritual mentor.

In the note, Paul claims that Onesimus is now more than just your servant—he's a servant of Jesus. He's a believer, a disciple. In other words, he's your brother in Christ. What are you going to do about the situation?

The Outcome

In a nutshell that's the wild little story of Onesimus and Philemon. There was a point in time when the two men were at odds. They had a dozen reasons to dislike and distrust each other. One was a slave and the other was free. One was poor and the other was rich. One was stuck at the bottom of society's ladder and the other was doing pretty well. However, once Christ came into the picture, all of their differences melted away and only this remained: their shared need and love for Christ.

Paul was convinced that the bond of Christian faith was greater than the bond of slavery (a pretty radical idea, given that slavery was a commonly accepted practice in the Greco-Roman world). That's because Paul was a reconciler (see 2 Corinthians 5:17–21). That was his business—bringing wandering souls back to God and bringing estranged people back together (see 1 Corinthians 1:10–17; Philippians 4:2–3). Is that description true of you as well? Are you a peacemaker?

Read more about Onesimus and Philemon in Philemon 1–25 (page 1550).

HEBREWS

HEBREWS HEBREWS

≪ AT A GLANCE

Author
Unknown

Audience
Jewish Christians who were being tempted to revert to Judaism

Date
Sometime before the destruction of the temple in Jerusalem in A.D. 70

Setting
These Jewish Christians were being persecuted, probably by both Jews and Romans. They needed reassurance that Jesus was indeed the Messiah.

Verses to Remember
Therefore, since we are surrounded by such a great cloud of witnesses, let us throw off everything that hinders and the sin that so easily entangles, and let us run with perseverance the race marked out for us. Let us fix our eyes on Jesus, the author and perfecter of our faith, who for the joy set before him endured the cross, scorning its shame, and sat down at the right hand of the throne of God (12:1–2).

Theme to Consider
The message of the book of Hebrews is clear: Jesus is better; Christianity is superior; and Christ is sufficient for salvation. Keep your life focused on Jesus—he is all you'll ever need.

UNCHANGING TRUTH ≫

No one is more perfect than God. That's why, when you see a list of people who actually *pleased* God, you pay attention. You'll find a list of exactly those kinds of people in Hebrews 11.

Some of the people on the list lived more than 1,000 years apart. They came from many different backgrounds. Some are men; some are women. They all faced unique challenges and situations. But they all had one thing in common: faith.

We're not talking about the warm, fuzzy feeling that makes you feel good inside. We're talking about believing in God's Word and acting on it, no matter how you feel, because you trust God for a good result. Check out these illustrations of risky faith: Because Noah had faith, he put his life on hold to build an enormous boat—even though the land was dry and dusty. Because Moses had faith, he gave up his royal position in Egypt to be mistreated along with his people. Because Rahab had faith, she hid two Israelite spies—even though it would have meant certain death for her and her family if she'd been caught. Because David had faith, he carried nothing more than a slingshot into battle against a bloodthirsty giant in full battle gear.

It's no wonder people refer to Hebrews 11 as the "Faith Hall of Fame." The question is, do you have what it takes to become a member? How far are you willing to take your faith?

LIFE LESSONS ≫

1 Those who put their trust in Jesus become his brothers and sisters (2:11–12).

2 Because Jesus was fully human (in addition to being fully God), he can relate to any temptation or struggle you face (4:15).

3 If you're serious about your relationship with Jesus, you need to make sure that you're constantly growing in your commitment to him and your understanding of his Word (5:13–14).

4 Christians have a responsibility to challenge and encourage one another to live godly lives (10:24).

THE SON SUPERIOR TO ANGELS

1 In the past God spoke to our forefathers through the prophets at many times and in various ways, ²but in these last days he has spoken to us by his Son, whom he appointed heir of all things, and through whom he made the universe. ³The Son is the radiance of God's glory and the exact representation of his being, sustaining all things by his powerful word. After he had provided purification for sins, he sat down at the right hand of the Majesty in heaven. ⁴So he became as much superior to the angels as the name he has inherited is superior to theirs.

⁵For to which of the angels did God ever say,

> "You are my Son;
> today I have become your Father ᵃ" ᵇ?

Or again,

> "I will be his Father,
> and he will be my Son" ᶜ?

⁶And again, when God brings his firstborn into the world, he says,

> "Let all God's angels worship him." ᵈ

⁷In speaking of the angels he says,

> "He makes his angels winds,
> his servants flames of fire." ᵉ

⁸But about the Son he says,

> "Your throne, O God, will last for ever and ever,
> and righteousness will be the scepter of your kingdom.
> ⁹You have loved righteousness and hated wickedness;
> therefore God, your God, has set you above your companions
> by anointing you with the oil of joy." ᶠ

¹⁰He also says,

> "In the beginning, O Lord, you laid the foundations of the earth,
> and the heavens are the work of your hands.
> ¹¹They will perish, but you remain;
> they will all wear out like a garment.
> ¹²You will roll them up like a robe;
> like a garment they will be changed.
> But you remain the same,
> and your years will never end." ᵍ

¹³To which of the angels did God ever say,

> "Sit at my right hand
> until I make your enemies
> a footstool for your feet" ʰ?

¹⁴Are not all angels ministering spirits sent to serve those who will inherit salvation?

WARNING TO PAY ATTENTION

2 We must pay more careful attention, therefore, to what we have heard, so that we do not drift away. ²For if the message spoken by angels was binding, and every violation and disobedience received its just punishment, ³how shall we escape if we ignore such a great salvation? This salvation, which was first announced by the Lord, was confirmed to us by those who heard him. ⁴God also testified to it by signs, wonders and various miracles, and gifts of the Holy Spirit distributed according to his will.

ᵃ *5 Or have begotten you*   ᵇ *5 Psalm 2:7*   ᶜ *5 2 Samuel 7:14; 1 Chron. 17:13*   ᵈ *6 Deut. 32:43 (see Dead Sea Scrolls and Septuagint)*   ᵉ *7 Psalm 104:4*   ᶠ *9 Psalm 45:6,7*   ᵍ *12 Psalm 102:25-27*   ʰ *13 Psalm 110:1*

JESUS MADE LIKE HIS BROTHERS

[5]It is not to angels that he has subjected the world to come, about which we are speaking. [6]But there is a place where someone has testified:

"What is man that you are mindful of him,
   the son of man that you care for him?
[7]You made him a little[a] lower than the angels;
   you crowned him with glory and honor
[8]   and put everything under his feet."[b]

In putting everything under him, God left nothing that is not subject to him. Yet at present we do not see everything subject to him. [9]But we see Jesus, who was made a little lower than the angels, now crowned with glory and honor because he suffered death, so that by the grace of God he might taste death for everyone.

[10]In bringing many sons to glory, it was fitting that God, for whom and through whom everything exists, should make the author of their salvation perfect through suffering. [11]Both the one who makes men holy and those who are made holy are of the same family. So Jesus is not ashamed to call them brothers. [12]He says,

"I will declare your name to my brothers;
   in the presence of the congregation I will sing your praises."[c]

[13]And again,

"I will put my trust in him."[d]

And again he says,

"Here am I, and the children God has given me."[e]

[14]Since the children have flesh and blood, he too shared in their humanity so that by his death he might destroy him who holds the power of death—that is, the devil— [15]and free those who all their lives were held in slavery by their fear of death. [16]For surely it is not angels he helps, but Abraham's descendants. [17]For this reason he had to be made like his brothers in every way, in order that he might become a merciful and faithful high priest in service to God, and that he might make atonement for[f] the sins of the people. [18]Because he himself suffered when he was tempted, he is able to help those who are being tempted.

JESUS GREATER THAN MOSES

3 Therefore, holy brothers, who share in the heavenly calling, fix your thoughts on Jesus, the apostle and high priest whom we confess. [2]He was faithful to the one who appointed him, just as Moses was faithful in all God's house. [3]Jesus has been found worthy of greater honor than Moses, just as the builder of a house has greater honor than the house itself. [4]For every house is built by someone, but God is the builder of everything. [5]Moses was faithful as a servant in all God's house, testifying to what would be said in the future. [6]But Christ is faithful as a son over God's house. And we are his house, if we hold on to our courage and the hope of which we boast.

WARNING AGAINST UNBELIEF

[7]So, as the Holy Spirit says:

"Today, if you hear his voice,
[8]   do not harden your hearts
   as you did in the rebellion,
   during the time of testing in the desert,
[9]where your fathers tested and tried me
   and for forty years saw what I did.
[10]That is why I was angry with that generation,

---

[a] 7 Or *him for a little while*; also in verse 9   [b] 8 Psalm 8:4-6   [c] 12 Psalm 22:22   [d] 13 Isaiah 8:17   [e] 13 Isaiah 8:18
[f] 17 Or *and that he might turn aside God's wrath, taking away*

and I said, 'Their hearts are always going astray,
and they have not known my ways.'
[11] So I declared on oath in my anger,
'They shall never enter my rest.' "[a]

[12] See to it, brothers, that none of you has a sinful, unbelieving heart that turns away from the living God. [13] But encourage one another daily, as long as it is called Today, so that none of you may be hardened by sin's deceitfulness. [14] We have come to share in Christ if we hold firmly till the end the confidence we had at first. [15] As has just been said:

"Today, if you hear his voice,
do not harden your hearts
as you did in the rebellion."[b]

[16] Who were they who heard and rebelled? Were they not all those Moses led out of Egypt? [17] And with whom was he angry for forty years? Was it not with those who sinned, whose bodies fell in the desert? [18] And to whom did God swear that they would never enter his rest if not to those who disobeyed[c]? [19] So we see that they were not able to enter, because of their unbelief.

A SABBATH-REST FOR THE PEOPLE OF GOD

4 Therefore, since the promise of entering his rest still stands, let us be careful that none of you be found to have fallen short of it. [2] For we also have had the gospel preached to us, just as they did; but the message they heard was of no value to them, because those who heard did not combine it with faith.[d] [3] Now we who have believed enter that rest, just as God has said,

"So I declared on oath in my anger,
'They shall never enter my rest.' "[e]

And yet his work has been finished since the creation of the world. [4] For somewhere he has spoken about the seventh day in these words: "And on the seventh day God rested from all his work."[f] [5] And again in the passage above he says, "They shall never enter my rest."

[6] It still remains that some will enter that rest, and those who formerly had the gospel preached to them did not go in, because of their disobedience. [7] Therefore God again set a certain day, calling it Today, when a long time later he spoke through David, as was said before:

"Today, if you hear his voice,
do not harden your hearts."[b]

[8] For if Joshua had given them rest, God would not have spoken later about another day. [9] There remains, then, a Sabbath-rest for the people of God; [10] for anyone who enters God's rest also rests from his own work, just as God did from his. [11] Let us, therefore, make every effort to enter that rest, so that no one will fall by following their example of disobedience.

[12] For the word of God is living and active. Sharper than any double-edged sword, it penetrates even to dividing soul and spirit, joints and marrow; it judges the thoughts and attitudes of the heart. [13] Nothing in all creation is hidden from God's sight. Everything is uncovered and laid bare before the eyes of him to whom we must give account.

NOW OR NEVER
HEB 4:14–16

How bold are you when you pray? Do you realize that because of Jesus you have direct access to the throne of God? If you know that what you're praying for is consistent with God's character, you should have all the confidence in the world when you talk to him.

JESUS THE GREAT HIGH PRIEST

[14] Therefore, since we have a great high priest who has gone through the heavens,[g] Jesus the Son of God, let us hold firmly to the faith we profess. [15] For we do not have a high priest who is unable to sympathize with our weaknesses, but we have one who has been tempted in every way, just as we are—

---

[a] 11 Psalm 95:7-11   [b] 15,7 Psalm 95:7,8   [c] 18 Or disbelieved   [d] 2 Many manuscripts because they did not share in the faith of those who obeyed   [e] 3 Psalm 95:11; also in verse 5   [f] 4 Gen. 2:2   [g] 14 Or gone into heaven

battlelines

» I Can't Dance (Obedience)

Q: So are you going to the prom?
A: Yeah. I'll be taking Amanda. Woo-hoo.

Q: (Sarcastically) Wow. She must be *quite* a girl.
A: Oh, no. It's not her. She's great. I really like her. It's my parents.

Q: What about them?
A: Oh, man, they're stuck in the 50s. They want the whole world to be just like it was when they were kids!

Q: Meaning?
A: They're telling me I can't go out with everyone afterwards (In a mocking voice) "Why do you need to go to a party after you've just spent three hours at a big party? Besides, it'll already be after midnight." Blah, blah, blah.

Q: So where is it you'd like to go?
A: It's not even like it's a *big* deal. Addison's dad said we could all go up to their lake house. It's got this big fireplace, a huge deck overlooking the water, a big screen TV and everything.

Q: Sounds like a cool place.
A: It is. And you know what? I'm thinking I might just go anyway. Just deal with the consequences later. You know, like they say, "It's easier to get forgiveness than ask permission."

Q: Can I ask you something?
A: Sure.

Q: Why do you think this is such a big deal to you?
A: I don't know. I guess because I'm 18, and in a couple months high school will be over for me. I just want to be with all my friends. It's not like I'm going to go wild or anything. I just want to have some fun.

Q: If you blow your parents off and go anyway, will it be fun *then*—while you're suffering the consequences, I mean?
A: Probably not.

» Breaking Away

There's a terrible tug-of-war in every loving family when children are getting close to leaving the nest. You, as a son, feel adventurous; your parents, on the other hand, likely feel terrified. You want your freedom; they want your safety. You long for your own space; they wish they could literally make time stop so they can hold on to you—because they care about you in ways even they can't understand, much less put into words.

Neither side is wrong. The shame is that we don't look beyond the demands that seem unfair and the behavior that seems rebellious. What's there? A whole ocean full of love.

You may be surprised to know that Jesus once got into a big misunderstanding with his earthly parents for being gone too long (see Luke 2:41–52). But when his parents demanded obedience, Jesus gave it. He could have said, "Hey, I'm God, so deal with it." But instead he quietly toed the line and respected his parents' wishes.

The good news is that Jesus understands the whole parent-child dynamic, and he can give you the patience and willingness you need to be obedient, even when your parents seem to go a little "over the top" (see Hebrews 4:15–16).

Read more about relating to your parents at www.RevolutionBible.com.

yet was without sin. [16]Let us then approach the throne of grace with confidence, so that we may receive mercy and find grace to help us in our time of need.

5 Every high priest is selected from among men and is appointed to represent them in matters related to God, to offer gifts and sacrifices for sins. [2]He is able to deal gently with those who are ignorant and are going astray, since he himself is subject to weakness. [3]This is why he has to offer sacrifices for his own sins, as well as for the sins of the people.

[4]No one takes this honor upon himself; he must be called by God, just as Aaron was. [5]So Christ also did not take upon himself the glory of becoming a high priest. But God said to him,

"You are my Son;
today I have become your Father.[a][b]

[6]And he says in another place,

"You are a priest forever,
in the order of Melchizedek."[c]

[7]During the days of Jesus' life on earth, he offered up prayers and petitions with loud cries and tears to the one who could save him from death, and he was heard because of his reverent submission. [8]Although he was a son, he learned obedience from what he suffered [9]and, once made perfect, he became the source of eternal salvation for all who obey him [10]and was designated by God to be high priest in the order of Melchizedek.

WARNING AGAINST FALLING AWAY

[11]We have much to say about this, but it is hard to explain because you are slow to learn. [12]In fact, though by this time you ought to be teachers, you need someone to teach you the elementary truths of God's word all over again. You need milk, not solid food! [13]Anyone who lives on milk, being still an infant, is not acquainted with the teaching about righteousness. [14]But solid food is for the mature, who by constant use have trained themselves to distinguish good from evil.

6 Therefore let us leave the elementary teachings about Christ and go on to maturity, not laying again the foundation of repentance from acts that lead to death,[d] and of faith in God, [2]instruction about baptisms, the laying on of hands, the resurrection of the dead, and eternal judgment. [3]And God permitting, we will do so.

[4]It is impossible for those who have once been enlightened, who have tasted the heavenly gift, who have shared in the Holy Spirit, [5]who have tasted the goodness of the word of God and the powers of the coming age, [6]if they fall away, to be brought back to repentance, because[e] to their loss they are crucifying the Son of God all over again and subjecting him to public disgrace.

[7]Land that drinks in the rain often falling on it and that produces a crop useful to those for whom it is farmed receives the blessing of God. [8]But land that produces thorns and thistles is worthless and is in danger of being cursed. In the end it will be burned.

[9]Even though we speak like this, dear friends, we are confident of better things in your case—things that accompany salvation. [10]God is not unjust; he will not forget your work and the love you have shown him as you have helped his people and continue to help them. [11]We want each of you to show this same diligence to the very end, in order to make your hope sure. [12]We do not want you to become lazy, but to imitate those who through faith and patience inherit what has been promised.

Relating to Jesus

» live the adventure » Heb 4:15-16

There are two kinds of role models: the ones who say, "Do as I say and not as I do," and the ones who say, "Follow my example." Jesus definitely belongs in the second category. Not only did he talk the talk, but he also walked the walk. He had to deal with the same emotions you struggle with. He faced the same major temptations you face—but he never got beaten by them. He left the earth with the only perfect record against sin. That's great news for you. No matter what you're going through, Jesus can relate to it. Even better, he can give you the strength you need to be victorious over sin.

---

[a] 5 Or *have begotten you*   [b] 5 Psalm 2:7   [c] 6 Psalm 110:4   [d] 1 Or *from useless rituals*   [e] 6 Or *repentance while*

THE CERTAINTY OF GOD'S PROMISE

¹³When God made his promise to Abraham, since there was no one greater for him to swear by, he swore by himself, ¹⁴saying, "I will surely bless you and give you many descendants."[a] ¹⁵And so after waiting patiently, Abraham received what was promised.

¹⁶Men swear by someone greater than themselves, and the oath confirms what is said and puts an end to all argument. ¹⁷Because God wanted to make the unchanging nature of his purpose very clear to the heirs of what was promised, he confirmed it with an oath. ¹⁸God did this so that, by two unchangeable things in which it is impossible for God to lie, we who have fled to take hold of the hope offered to us may be greatly encouraged. ¹⁹We have this hope as an anchor for the soul, firm and secure. It enters the inner sanctuary behind the curtain, ²⁰where Jesus, who went before us, has entered on our behalf. He has become a high priest forever, in the order of Melchizedek.

MELCHIZEDEK THE PRIEST

7 This Melchizedek was king of Salem and priest of God Most High. He met Abraham returning from the defeat of the kings and blessed him, ²and Abraham gave him a tenth of everything. First, his name means "king of righteousness"; then also, "king of Salem" means "king of peace." ³Without father or mother, without genealogy, without beginning of days or end of life, like the Son of God he remains a priest forever.

⁴Just think how great he was: Even the patriarch Abraham gave him a tenth of the plunder! ⁵Now the law requires the descendants of Levi who become priests to collect a tenth from the people—that is, their brothers—even though their brothers are descended from Abraham. ⁶This man, however, did not trace his descent from Levi, yet he collected a tenth from Abraham and blessed him who had the promises. ⁷And without doubt the lesser person is blessed by the greater. ⁸In the one case, the tenth is collected by men who die; but in the other case, by him who is declared to be living. ⁹One might even say that Levi, who collects the tenth, paid the tenth through Abraham, ¹⁰because when Melchizedek met Abraham, Levi was still in the body of his ancestor.

JESUS LIKE MELCHIZEDEK

¹¹If perfection could have been attained through the Levitical priesthood (for on the basis of it the law was given to the people), why was there still need for another priest to come—one in the order of Melchizedek, not in the order of Aaron? ¹²For when there is a change of the priesthood, there must also be a change of the law. ¹³He of whom these things are said belonged to a different tribe, and no one from that tribe has ever served at the altar. ¹⁴For it is clear that our Lord descended from Judah, and in regard to that tribe Moses said nothing about priests. ¹⁵And what we have said is even more clear if another priest like Melchizedek appears, ¹⁶one who has become a priest not on the basis of a regulation as to his ancestry but on the basis of the power of an indestructible life. ¹⁷For it is declared:

Becoming a Mature Christian

In your math classes, what happens after you learn the basics of addition and subtraction? You move on, right? First you go to algebra, then geometry and trig and calculus and all those other GPA-killing classes. How frustrating would it be for a graduating senior to still be reviewing his multiplication tables when he should be studying calculus? The same thing goes for your faith. It's not enough to just keep reviewing the "basics" of salvation over and over again. You've got to move on to higher levels of Christian maturity. That's how you grow as a follower of Jesus, deepening your relationship with God each step of the way.

NOW OR NEVER

HEB 6:18

Everything about God is perfect, including his promises. When he swears an oath to do something, it comes with a forever guarantee. That's why, if you've put your trust in Jesus for salvation, you should hold on to the hope that God will finish what he's started in your life.

ᵃ *14* Gen. 22:17

> "You are a priest forever,
>   in the order of Melchizedek." [a]

[18]The former regulation is set aside because it was weak and useless [19](for the law made nothing perfect), and a better hope is introduced, by which we draw near to God.

[20]And it was not without an oath! Others became priests without any oath, [21]but he became a priest with an oath when God said to him:

> "The Lord has sworn
>   and will not change his mind:
>   'You are a priest forever.' " [a]

[22]Because of this oath, Jesus has become the guarantee of a better covenant.

[23]Now there have been many of those priests, since death prevented them from continuing in office; [24]but because Jesus lives forever, he has a permanent priesthood. [25]Therefore he is able to save completely [b] those who come to God through him, because he always lives to intercede for them.

[26]Such a high priest meets our need—one who is holy, blameless, pure, set apart from sinners, exalted above the heavens. [27]Unlike the other high priests, he does not need to offer sacrifices day after day, first for his own sins, and then for the sins of the people. He sacrificed for their sins once for all when he offered himself. [28]For the law appoints as high priests men who are weak; but the oath, which came after the law, appointed the Son, who has been made perfect forever.

NOW OR NEVER

HEB 7:26

Jesus did what we couldn't do. He lived a perfect, sinless life. He defeated sin on Satan's home court. The fact that Jesus was completely pure made it possible for God to accept his perfect sacrifice on our behalf.

THE HIGH PRIEST OF A NEW COVENANT

8 The point of what we are saying is this: We do have such a high priest, who sat down at the right hand of the throne of the Majesty in heaven, [2]and who serves in the sanctuary, the true tabernacle set up by the Lord, not by man.

[3]Every high priest is appointed to offer both gifts and sacrifices, and so it was necessary for this one also to have something to offer. [4]If he were on earth, he would not be a priest, for there are already men who offer the gifts prescribed by the law. [5]They serve at a sanctuary that is a copy and shadow of what is in heaven. This is why Moses was warned when he was about to build the tabernacle: "See to it that you make everything according to the pattern shown you on the mountain." [c] [6]But the ministry Jesus has received is as superior to theirs as the covenant of which he is mediator is superior to the old one, and it is founded on better promises.

[7]For if there had been nothing wrong with that first covenant, no place would have been sought for another. [8]But God found fault with the people and said [d]:

> "The time is coming, declares the Lord,
>   when I will make a new covenant
>   with the house of Israel
>   and with the house of Judah.
> [9]It will not be like the covenant
>   I made with their forefathers
>   when I took them by the hand
>   to lead them out of Egypt,
>   because they did not remain faithful to my covenant,
>   and I turned away from them,
>
>   declares the Lord.
> [10]This is the covenant I will make with the house of Israel
>   after that time, declares the Lord.
>   I will put my laws in their minds

---

[a] *17,21* Psalm 110:4   [b] *25* Or *forever*   [c] *5* Exodus 25:40   [d] *8* Some manuscripts may be translated *fault and said to the people.*

and write them on their hearts.
I will be their God,
and they will be my people.
[11] No longer will a man teach his neighbor,
or a man his brother, saying, 'Know the Lord,'
because they will all know me,
from the least of them to the greatest.
[12] For I will forgive their wickedness
and will remember their sins no more."[a]

[13] By calling this covenant "new," he has made the first one obsolete; and what is obsolete and aging will soon disappear.

WORSHIP IN THE EARTHLY TABERNACLE

9 Now the first covenant had regulations for worship and also an earthly sanctuary. [2] A tabernacle was set up. In its first room were the lampstand, the table and the consecrated bread; this was called the Holy Place. [3] Behind the second curtain was a room called the Most Holy Place, [4] which had the golden altar of incense and the gold-covered ark of the covenant. This ark contained the gold jar of manna, Aaron's staff that had budded, and the stone tablets of the covenant. [5] Above the ark were the cherubim of the Glory, overshadowing the atonement cover.[b] But we cannot discuss these things in detail now.

[6] When everything had been arranged like this, the priests entered regularly into the outer room to carry on their ministry. [7] But only the high priest entered the inner room, and that only once a year, and never without blood, which he offered for himself and for the sins the people had committed in ignorance. [8] The Holy Spirit was showing by this that the way into the Most Holy Place had not yet been disclosed as long as the first tabernacle was still standing. [9] This is an illustration for the present time, indicating that the gifts and sacrifices being offered were not able to clear the conscience of the worshiper. [10] They are only a matter of food and drink and various ceremonial washings—external regulations applying until the time of the new order.

THE BLOOD OF CHRIST

[11] When Christ came as high priest of the good things that are already here,[c] he went through the greater and more perfect tabernacle that is not man-made, that is to say, not a part of this creation. [12] He did not enter by means of the blood of goats and calves; but he entered the Most Holy Place once for all by his own blood, having obtained eternal redemption. [13] The blood of goats and bulls and the ashes of a heifer sprinkled on those who are ceremonially unclean sanctify them so that they are outwardly clean. [14] How much more, then, will the blood of Christ, who through the eternal Spirit offered himself unblemished to God, cleanse our consciences from acts that lead to death,[d] so that we may serve the living God!

[15] For this reason Christ is the mediator of a new covenant, that those who are called may receive the promised eternal inheritance—now that he has died as a ransom to set them free from the sins committed under the first covenant.

[16] In the case of a will,[e] it is necessary to prove the death of the one who made it, [17] because a will is in force only when somebody has died; it never takes effect while the one who made it is living. [18] This is why even the first covenant was not put into effect without blood. [19] When Moses had proclaimed every commandment of the law to all the people, he took the blood of calves, together with water, scarlet wool and branches of hyssop, and sprinkled the scroll and all the people. [20] He said, "This is the blood of the covenant, which God has commanded you to keep."[f] [21] In the same way, he sprinkled with the blood both the tabernacle and everything used in its ceremonies. [22] In fact, the law requires that nearly everything be cleansed with blood, and without the shedding of blood there is no forgiveness.

[23] It was necessary, then, for the copies of the heavenly things to be purified with these sacrifices, but the heavenly things themselves with better sacrifices than these. [24] For Christ did not enter a man-

---

[a] 12 Jer. 31:31-34   [b] 5 Traditionally *the mercy seat*   [c] 11 Some early manuscripts *are to come*   [d] 14 Or *from useless rituals*
[e] 16 Same Greek word as *covenant*; also in verse 17   [f] 20 Exodus 24:8

made sanctuary that was only a copy of the true one; he entered heaven itself, now to appear for us in God's presence. 25Nor did he enter heaven to offer himself again and again, the way the high priest enters the Most Holy Place every year with blood that is not his own. 26Then Christ would have had to suffer many times since the creation of the world. But now he has appeared once for all at the end of the ages to do away with sin by the sacrifice of himself. 27Just as man is destined to die once, and after that to face judgment, 28so Christ was sacrificed once to take away the sins of many people; and he will appear a second time, not to bear sin, but to bring salvation to those who are waiting for him.

CHRIST'S SACRIFICE ONCE FOR ALL

10 The law is only a shadow of the good things that are coming—not the realities themselves. For this reason it can never, by the same sacrifices repeated endlessly year after year, make perfect those who draw near to worship. 2If it could, would they not have stopped being offered? For the worshipers would have been cleansed once for all, and would no longer have felt guilty for their sins. 3But those sacrifices are an annual reminder of sins, 4because it is impossible for the blood of bulls and goats to take away sins.

5Therefore, when Christ came into the world, he said:

> "Sacrifice and offering you did not desire,
>   but a body you prepared for me;
>   6with burnt offerings and sin offerings
>   you were not pleased.
>   7Then I said, 'Here I am—it is written about me in the scroll—
>   I have come to do your will, O God.' " [a]

8First he said, "Sacrifices and offerings, burnt offerings and sin offerings you did not desire, nor were you pleased with them" (although the law required them to be made). 9Then he said, "Here I am, I have come to do your will." He sets aside the first to establish the second. 10And by that will, we have been made holy through the sacrifice of the body of Jesus Christ once for all.

11Day after day every priest stands and performs his religious duties; again and again he offers the same sacrifices, which can never take away sins. 12But when this priest had offered for all time one sacrifice for sins, he sat down at the right hand of God. 13Since that time he waits for his enemies to be made his footstool, 14because by one sacrifice he has made perfect forever those who are being made holy.

15The Holy Spirit also testifies to us about this. First he says:

> 16"This is the covenant I will make with them
>   after that time, says the Lord.
>   I will put my laws in their hearts,
>   and I will write them on their minds." [b]

17Then he adds:

> "Their sins and lawless acts
>   I will remember no more." [c]

18And where these have been forgiven, there is no longer any sacrifice for sin.

A CALL TO PERSEVERE

19Therefore, brothers, since we have confidence to enter the Most Holy Place by the blood of Jesus, 20by a new and living way opened for us through the curtain, that is, his body, 21and since we have a great priest over the house of God, 22let us draw near to God with a sincere heart in full assurance of faith, having our hearts sprinkled to cleanse us from a guilty conscience and having our bodies washed with pure water. 23Let us hold unswervingly to the hope we profess, for he who promised is faithful. 24And let us consider how we may spur one another on toward love and good deeds. 25Let us not give up meeting together, as some are in the habit of doing, but let us encourage one another—and all the more as you see the Day approaching.

26If we deliberately keep on sinning after we have received the knowledge of the truth, no sacrifice

---

a 7 Psalm 40:6-8 (see Septuagint)   b 16 Jer. 31:33   c 17 Jer. 31:34

for sins is left, 27but only a fearful expectation of judgment and of raging fire that will consume the enemies of God. 28Anyone who rejected the law of Moses died without mercy on the testimony of two or three witnesses. 29How much more severely do you think a man deserves to be punished who has trampled the Son of God under foot, who has treated as an unholy thing the blood of the covenant that sanctified him, and who has insulted the Spirit of grace? 30For we know him who said, "It is mine to avenge; I will repay,"a and again, "The Lord will judge his people."b 31It is a dreadful thing to fall into the hands of the living God.

32Remember those earlier days after you had received the light, when you stood your ground in a great contest in the face of suffering. 33Sometimes you were publicly exposed to insult and persecution; at other times you stood side by side with those who were so treated. 34You sympathized with those in prison and joyfully accepted the confiscation of your property, because you knew that you yourselves had better and lasting possessions.

35So do not throw away your confidence; it will be richly rewarded. 36You need to persevere so that when you have done the will of God, you will receive what he has promised. 37For in just a very little while,

"He who is coming will come and will
    not delay.
38   But my righteous onec will live by
        faith.
    And if he shrinks back,
        I will not be pleased with him."d

39But we are not of those who shrink back and are destroyed, but of those who believe and are saved.

Encouraging Other Christians

What kind of influence do you exert on your Christian friends? Do you ever try to fire them up about an opportunity to help the homeless? Do you ever encourage them to talk about Jesus with their non-Christian friends and family members? Do you ever get together with them just to talk about spiritual things and pray for each other? It's a tremendous privilege and blessing to be a "spur" to your Christian brothers and sisters.

» live the adventure » Heb 10:24-25

BY FAITH

11 Now faith is being sure of what we hope for and certain of what we do not see. 2This is what the ancients were commended for.

3By faith we understand that the universe was formed at God's command, so that what is seen was not made out of what was visible.

4By faith Abel offered God a better sacrifice than Cain did. By faith he was commended as a righteous man, when God spoke well of his offerings. And by faith he still speaks, even though he is dead.

5By faith Enoch was taken from this life, so that he did not experience death; he could not be found, because God had taken him away. For before he was taken, he was commended as one who pleased God. 6And without faith it is impossible to please God, because anyone who comes to him must believe that he exists and that he rewards those who earnestly seek him.

7By faith Noah, when warned about things not yet seen, in holy fear built an ark to save his family. By his faith he condemned the world and became heir of the righteousness that comes by faith.

8By faith Abraham, when called to go to a place he would later receive as his inheritance, obeyed and went, even though he did not know where he was going. 9By faith he made his home in the promised land like a stranger in a foreign country; he lived in tents, as did Isaac and Jacob, who were heirs with him of the same promise. 10For he was looking forward to the city with foundations, whose architect and builder is God.

11By faith Abraham, even though he was past age—and Sarah herself was barren—was enabled to become a father because hee considered him faithful who had made the promise. 12And so from this

---

a 30 Deut. 32:35   b 30 Deut. 32:36; Psalm 135:14   c 38 One early manuscript But the righteous   d 38 Hab. 2:3,4   e 11 Or By faith even Sarah, who was past age, was enabled to bear children because she

barak

VERSUS

jabin

» An Israelite from the tribe of Naphtali

» Became a lieutenant under Deborah, Israel's only female judge

» Defeated the Canaanite forces

» A Canaanite king

» Reigned at Hazor and oppressed Israel for 20 years

» Defeated by Deborah and Barak

The Main Event

King Jabin was a nasty Canaanite king with a fierce army under the command of General Sisera. With a fleet of 900 chariots, his powerful and ruthless Canaanite forces were nothing but trouble to the fledgling nation of Israel. For two decades they made life miserable for the Israelites, constantly attacking with savage cruelty. Why did God allow his people to be oppressed like that? Because they had turned away from him.

Ultimately the Israelites came to their senses. They cried out to God, and God selected a female prophet named Deborah to lead his people out of their mess. Deborah, in turn, selected Barak to lead the armies of Israel into battle.

As you might imagine, this was a big moment for Barak. It was his chance to shine, his opportunity to rise to the occasion, his time to prove that he had what it took to meet the formidable challenge that God laid before him. Unfortunately, Barak let fear and timidity get the best of him. He said he'd go only if Deborah went with him. And so, reluctantly, she agreed. "Fine," she said. "But since you don't have the guts to fully trust God, you won't get the glory when the battle is over. The honor of taking out Sisera will go to a woman."

The battle was a rout. Even with their high-tech iron chariots, the Canaanites were outgunned. Why? Because God was fighting for his people.

King Jabin was never heard from again. Every last one of his troops bit the dust. And just as Deborah predicted, General Sisera died at the hands of a woman—the most disgraceful way imaginable for a man to be killed in the ancient Near Eastern world. The woman, Jael, hammered a tent peg through his head while he slept!

When it was all over, Jael—not Barak—got the major credit for the victory, just as Deborah had predicted.

The Outcome

When we're facing a giant obstacle or a major battle, it's always tempting to look around for help. This tendency isn't wrong—unless God has already promised his presence and power. But if our lack of faith causes us to lean on people more than we lean on the Lord, we'll miss out on a potential blessing. After all, how can people obey God's call to step out in faith if they try to eliminate all the risks of following him?

Barak learned this lesson the hard way. His desperate hunger for human support became a crutch. By relying on Deborah and refusing to trust what she (and, ultimately, God) had promised, he missed out on greater honor—and, more important, on a deeper experience of God's presence and power in his life.

What about you? How do you respond in crisis situations? Do you panic? Do you lean on people—or do you look to God? Trusting God is scary, but it always leads to a maximum reward.

Read more about Barak and Jabin in Judges 4–5 (page 275–279).

one man, and he as good as dead, came descendants as numerous as the stars in the sky and as countless as the sand on the seashore.

¹³All these people were still living by faith when they died. They did not receive the things promised; they only saw them and welcomed them from a distance. And they admitted that they were aliens and strangers on earth. ¹⁴People who say such things show that they are looking for a country of their own. ¹⁵If they had been thinking of the country they had left, they would have had opportunity to return. ¹⁶Instead, they were longing for a better country—a heavenly one. Therefore God is not ashamed to be called their God, for he has prepared a city for them.

¹⁷By faith Abraham, when God tested him, offered Isaac as a sacrifice. He who had received the promises was about to sacrifice his one and only son, ¹⁸even though God had said to him, "It is through Isaac that your offspring[a] will be reckoned."[b] ¹⁹Abraham reasoned that God could raise the dead, and figuratively speaking, he did receive Isaac back from death.

²⁰By faith Isaac blessed Jacob and Esau in regard to their future.

²¹By faith Jacob, when he was dying, blessed each of Joseph's sons, and worshiped as he leaned on the top of his staff.

²²By faith Joseph, when his end was near, spoke about the exodus of the Israelites from Egypt and gave instructions about his bones.

²³By faith Moses' parents hid him for three months after he was born, because they saw he was no ordinary child, and they were not afraid of the king's edict.

²⁴By faith Moses, when he had grown up, refused to be known as the son of Pharaoh's daughter. ²⁵He chose to be mistreated along with the people of God rather than to enjoy the pleasures of sin for a short time. ²⁶He regarded disgrace for the sake of Christ as of greater value than the treasures of Egypt, because he was looking ahead to his reward. ²⁷By faith he left Egypt, not fearing the king's anger; he persevered because he saw him who is invisible. ²⁸By faith he kept the Passover and the sprinkling of blood, so that the destroyer of the firstborn would not touch the firstborn of Israel.

²⁹By faith the people passed through the Red Sea[c] as on dry land; but when the Egyptians tried to do so, they were drowned.

³⁰By faith the walls of Jericho fell, after the people had marched around them for seven days.

³¹By faith the prostitute Rahab, because she welcomed the spies, was not killed with those who were disobedient.[d]

³²And what more shall I say? I do not have time to tell about Gideon, Barak, Samson, Jephthah, David, Samuel and the prophets, ³³who through faith conquered kingdoms, administered justice, and gained what was promised; who shut the mouths of lions, ³⁴quenched the fury of the flames, and escaped the edge of the sword; whose weakness was turned to strength; and who became powerful in battle and routed foreign armies. ³⁵Women received back their dead, raised to life again. Others were tortured and refused to be released, so that they might gain a better resurrection. ³⁶Some faced jeers and flogging, while still others were chained and put in prison. ³⁷They were stoned[e]; they were sawed in two; they were put to death by the sword. They went about in sheepskins and goatskins, destitute, persecuted and mistreated— ³⁸the world was not worthy of them. They wandered in deserts and mountains, and in caves and holes in the ground.

NOW OR NEVER
HEB 11:13

Being a Christian makes you a foreigner in this world. Your real home is with God. Don't get too cozy with worldly lifestyles or too attached to possessions. And if living a God-pleasing life makes you a bit of an outsider, don't get discouraged. God rewards his faithful followers in the end.

challenge notes

To: my_son

heavenly_father: don't assume there was anything super-heroic about the people listed in this chapter. they were all very much like you. none of them knew for sure what their faith would accomplish, but they all believed in me. that's where their strength and courage really came from.

2863   B G C FE

HEB 11:1-40

ᵃ *18* Greek *seed*   ᵇ *18* Gen. 21:12   ᶜ *29* That is, Sea of Reeds   ᵈ *31* Or *unbelieving*   ᵉ *37* Some early manuscripts *stoned; they were put to the test;*

gideon

» A mild-mannered Jewish farmer from the tribe of Manasseh

» Overcame his personal insecurities and became a military warrior

» Used by God to deliver Israel

the midianites

» A desert tribe descended from Abraham's second wife, Keturah

» Formed coalitions with the Moabites and Amalekites

» Used by God to punish Israel

The Main Event

Gideon was a simple farmer trying to scratch out a living and avoid confrontations with Midianite raiders, when an angel of the Lord showed up at his house. To Gideon's great surprise, the heavenly messenger addressed him as a "mighty warrior." An even bigger shock came when the angel said, "Gideon, God is with you and wants to use you to lead a campaign to drive the godless invaders out of Israel."

"Wait a minute! You've got the wrong guy," Gideon protested. "I'm a nobody. Besides, if God cares about us, then where has he been lately? He's been out of the miracle business for a long time now."

It took some prompting and a few tricks with fire and fleece before Gideon would finally trust God. But eventually Gideon found the necessary confidence to tackle the job. He went on a spiritual housecleaning binge first, ridding the land (including his father's property) of idols. Then he gathered an army and set out for a showdown with the Midianites and their allies.

In a bizarre turn of events, God told Gideon that he had too many men and commanded him to pare down his fighting force to a paltry 300 troops. Then God basically said, "Now that the situation is totally impossible for you, just do what I tell you and watch me work."

This was not your ordinary battle. God told the Israelites to use trumpets and jars with torches inside. Then, in the dead of night they launched their surprise attack with trumpets blaring, pottery breaking and lights flashing.

The result was pandemonium. The Midianites panicked and, in the darkness, turned on each other. The few who fled were hunted down, killed and beheaded (presumably with swords, not trumpets).

The Outcome

It's a passage like this that makes you believe the Bible must be true. After all, who in their right mind would make up a religion that includes a wild and crazy story like Gideon's—unless, of course, the events actually happened?

Gideon prevailed against the hated Midianites for a few simple reasons:

1. He chose to believe God's view of himself ("a mighty warrior") instead of his own view of himself ("a nobody from an insignificant family"). It took a long time and a great deal of patience on God's part, but eventually Gideon came to trust God's view of things.

2. When it came right down to it, Gideon stuck his neck out. He took some chances. And with each little success his faith grew a little more.

3. He was willing to obey God even when asked to do things that everyone else must have thought were crazy—including reducing the size of his army and going into battle with band instruments and home furnishings.

Whatever battle you're fighting, you will succeed if you follow Gideon's example.

Read more about Gideon and the Midianites in Judges 6–8 (pages 279–283).

[39]These were all commended for their faith, yet none of them received what had been promised. [40]God had planned something better for us so that only together with us would they be made perfect.

GOD DISCIPLINES HIS SONS

12 Therefore, since we are surrounded by such a great cloud of witnesses, let us throw off everything that hinders and the sin that so easily entangles, and let us run with perseverance the race marked out for us. [2]Let us fix our eyes on Jesus, the author and perfecter of our faith, who for the joy set before him endured the cross, scorning its shame, and sat down at the right hand of the throne of God. [3]Consider him who endured such opposition from sinful men, so that you will not grow weary and lose heart.

[4]In your struggle against sin, you have not yet resisted to the point of shedding your blood. [5]And you have forgotten that word of encouragement that addresses you as sons:

"My son, do not make light of the Lord's
    discipline,
and do not lose heart when he
    rebukes you,
  [6]because the Lord disciplines those he
    loves,
and he punishes everyone he
    accepts as a son." [a]

[7]Endure hardship as discipline; God is treating you as sons. For what son is not disciplined by his father? [8]If you are not disciplined (and everyone undergoes discipline), then you are illegitimate children and not true sons. [9]Moreover, we have all had human fathers who disciplined us and we respected them for it. How much more should we submit to the Father of our spirits and live! [10]Our fathers disciplined us for a little while as they thought best; but God disciplines us for our good, that we may share in his holiness. [11]No discipline seems pleasant at the time, but painful. Later on, however, it produces a harvest of righteousness and peace for those who have been trained by it.

[12]Therefore, strengthen your feeble arms and weak knees. [13]"Make level paths for your feet," [b] so that the lame may not be disabled, but rather healed.

WARNING AGAINST REFUSING GOD

[14]Make every effort to live in peace with all men and to be holy; without holiness no one will see the Lord. [15]See to it that no one misses the grace of God and that no bitter root grows up to cause trouble and defile many. [16]See that no one is sexually immoral, or is godless like Esau, who for a single meal sold his inheritance rights as the oldest son. [17]Afterward, as you know, when he wanted to inherit this blessing, he was rejected. He could bring about no change of mind, though he sought the blessing with tears.

[18]You have not come to a mountain that can be touched and that is burning with fire; to darkness, gloom and storm; [19]to a trumpet blast or to such a voice speaking words that those who heard it begged

Looking Ahead

How far do you think you'd get in a triathlon if you stopped every two miles to complain about how hard the race was? Not very far. The top athletes are the ones who are able to focus not on the race itself but on the finish line. In the same way, successful runners of the Christian "race" are the ones who are able to look past the frustrations and stumbling blocks of life and focus on what God has waiting at the finish line.

NOW OR NEVER
HEB 12:7

God's discipline is kind of like the burn you feel at the end of a tough workout. There's nothing pleasant about it, but when you feel it, you know good things are happening inside.

---

[a] 6 Prov. 3:11,12   [b] 13 Prov. 4:26

that no further word be spoken to them, [20]because they could not bear what was commanded: "If even an animal touches the mountain, it must be stoned."[a] [21]The sight was so terrifying that Moses said, "I am trembling with fear."[b]

[22]But you have come to Mount Zion, to the heavenly Jerusalem, the city of the living God. You have come to thousands upon thousands of angels in joyful assembly, [23]to the church of the firstborn, whose names are written in heaven. You have come to God, the judge of all men, to the spirits of righteous men made perfect, [24]to Jesus the mediator of a new covenant, and to the sprinkled blood that speaks a better word than the blood of Abel.

[25]See to it that you do not refuse him who speaks. If they did not escape when they refused him who warned them on earth, how much less will we, if we turn away from him who warns us from heaven? [26]At that time his voice shook the earth, but now he has promised, "Once more I will shake not only the earth but also the heavens."[c] [27]The words "once more" indicate the removing of what can be shaken—that is, created things—so that what cannot be shaken may remain.

[28]Therefore, since we are receiving a kingdom that cannot be shaken, let us be thankful, and so worship God acceptably with reverence and awe, [29]for our "God is a consuming fire."[d]

CONCLUDING EXHORTATIONS

1 3 Keep on loving each other as brothers. [2]Do not forget to entertain strangers, for by so doing some people have entertained angels without knowing it. [3]Remember those in prison as if you were their fellow prisoners, and those who are mistreated as if you yourselves were suffering.

[4]Marriage should be honored by all, and the marriage bed kept pure, for God will judge the adulterer and all the sexually immoral. [5]Keep your lives free from the love of money and be content with what you have, because God has said,

> "Never will I leave you;
> never will I forsake you."[e]

[6]So we say with confidence,

> "The Lord is my helper; I will not be afraid.
> What can man do to me?"[f]

[7]Remember your leaders, who spoke the word of God to you. Consider the outcome of their way of life and imitate their faith. [8]Jesus Christ is the same yesterday and today and forever.

[9]Do not be carried away by all kinds of strange teachings. It is good for our hearts to be strengthened by grace, not by ceremonial foods, which are of no value to those who eat them. [10]We have an altar from which those who minister at the tabernacle have no right to eat.

NOW OR NEVER
HEB 13:2

[11]The high priest carries the blood of animals into the Most Holy Place as a sin offering, but the bodies are burned outside the camp. [12]And so Jesus also suffered outside the city gate to make the people holy through his own blood. [13]Let us, then, go to him outside the camp, bearing the disgrace he bore. [14]For here we do not have an enduring city, but we are looking for the city that is to come.

The thing about helping strangers is that you never know who the person on the receiving end of your kindness will turn out to be. Good things do happen to guys who aren't afraid to get their hands dirty to help someone else. God makes certain of that.

[15]Through Jesus, therefore, let us continually offer to God a sacrifice of praise—the fruit of lips that confess his name. [16]And do not forget to do good and to share with others, for with such sacrifices God is pleased.

[17]Obey your leaders and submit to their authority. They keep watch over you as men who must give an account. Obey them so that their work will be a joy, not a burden, for that would be of no advantage to you.

---

[a] *20* Exodus 19:12,13   [b] *21* Deut. 9:19   [c] *26* Haggai 2:6   [d] *29* Deut. 4:24   [e] *5* Deut. 31:6   [f] *6* Psalm 118:6,7

¹⁸Pray for us. We are sure that we have a clear conscience and desire to live honorably in every way. ¹⁹I particularly urge you to pray so that I may be restored to you soon.

²⁰May the God of peace, who through the blood of the eternal covenant brought back from the dead our Lord Jesus, that great Shepherd of the sheep, ²¹equip you with everything good for doing his will, and may he work in us what is pleasing to him, through Jesus Christ, to whom be glory for ever and ever. Amen.

²²Brothers, I urge you to bear with my word of exhortation, for I have written you only a short letter. ²³I want you to know that our brother Timothy has been released. If he arrives soon, I will come with him to see you.

²⁴Greet all your leaders and all God's people. Those from Italy send you their greetings. ²⁵Grace be with you all.

JAMES

« AT A GLANCE

Author
James, the brother of Jesus and the leader of the Jerusalem church

Audience
Jewish Christians living in Gentile areas outside of Palestine

Date
Probably about A.D. 49

Setting
James was likely writing to believers who had been part of the early church in Jerusalem and had been scattered to various places because of persecution. He was concerned about issues these Christians were struggling with, such as bitterness, materialism and impatience.

Verses to Remember
Therefore, get rid of all moral filth and the evil that is so prevalent and humbly accept the word planted in you, which can save you. Do not merely listen to the word, and so deceive yourselves. Do what it says (1:21–22).

Theme to Consider
Our faith determines our attitudes and actions. Faith must lead to action because faith without good works is dead.

UNCHANGING TRUTH » Forget about your biceps, abs or quads. The most powerful part of your body (by far) is your tongue. You can hurt someone a lot quicker—and oftentimes, more deeply—with your words than you can with a punch or a kick. Physical scars and bruises heal, but the kind of damage words do can last forever.

Hurting someone's feelings is not the only damage you can do with your tongue though. You can also spread rumors . . . tell lies . . . treat your parents or others with disrespect . . . tell dirty jokes . . . encourage people to do things you know are wrong. The full impact of our words is hard to even imagine.

If you've ever tried to stop yourself from saying something you shouldn't, you know how powerful and difficult it is to tame your tongue. No wonder the New Testament writer James compared it to a spark that starts a raging forest fire. Once your tongue gets going, things can get out of control before you know what's happening.

That's a major problem for Christians. James points out that only a hypocrite would use the same tongue to praise God and cut down other people. If you're serious about your relationship with Jesus, you need to work overtime to control what comes out of your mouth—that's one way to show you possess a genuine faith.

So what do you think? Do you have the strength to fight for control of your tongue?

LIFE LESSONS »

1   God deserves the credit for every good thing in your life (1:17).

2   *Saying* you have faith in God isn't enough; you have to let your faith dictate the way you live (2:14–19).

3   People will judge your character by the words that come out of your mouth (3:10).

4   Never assume that life will play out exactly as you intend it to; always submit your plans to God's will (4:13–15).

1

James, a servant of God and of the Lord Jesus Christ,

To the twelve tribes scattered among the nations:

Greetings.

TRIALS AND TEMPTATIONS

²Consider it pure joy, my brothers, whenever you face trials of many kinds, ³because you know that the testing of your faith develops perseverance. ⁴Perseverance must finish its work so that you may be mature and complete, not lacking anything. ⁵If any of you lacks wisdom, he should ask God, who gives generously to all without finding fault, and it will be given to him. ⁶But when he asks, he must believe and not doubt, because he who doubts is like a wave of the sea, blown and tossed by the wind. ⁷That man should not think he will receive anything from the Lord; ⁸he is a double-minded man, unstable in all he does.

⁹The brother in humble circumstances ought to take pride in his high position. ¹⁰But the one who is rich should take pride in his low position, because he will pass away like a wild flower. ¹¹For the sun rises with scorching heat and withers the plant; its blossom falls and its beauty is destroyed. In the same way, the rich man will fade away even while he goes about his business.

¹²Blessed is the man who perseveres under trial, because when he has stood the test, he will receive the crown of life that God has promised to those who love him.

¹³When tempted, no one should say, "God is tempting me." For God cannot be tempted by evil, nor does he tempt anyone; ¹⁴but each one is tempted when, by his own evil desire, he is dragged away and enticed. ¹⁵Then, after desire has conceived, it gives birth to sin; and sin, when it is full-grown, gives birth to death.

¹⁶Don't be deceived, my dear brothers. ¹⁷Every good and perfect gift is from above, coming down from the Father of the heavenly lights, who does not change like shifting shadows. ¹⁸He chose to give us birth through the word of truth, that we might be a kind of firstfruits of all he created.

LISTENING AND DOING

¹⁹My dear brothers, take note of this: Everyone should be quick to listen, slow to speak and slow to become angry, ²⁰for man's anger does not bring about the righteous life that God desires. ²¹Therefore, get rid of all moral filth and the evil that is so prevalent and humbly accept the word planted in you, which can save you.

²²Do not merely listen to the word, and so deceive yourselves. Do what it says. ²³Anyone who listens to the word but does not do what it says is like a man who looks at his face in a mirror ²⁴and, after looking at himself, goes away and immediately forgets what he looks like. ²⁵But the man who looks intently into the perfect law that gives freedom, and continues to do this, not forgetting what he has heard, but doing it—he will be blessed in what he does.

²⁶If anyone considers himself religious and yet does not keep a tight rein on his tongue, he deceives himself and his religion is worthless. ²⁷Religion that God our Father accepts as pure and faultless is this: to look after orphans and widows in their distress and to keep oneself from being polluted by the world.

NOW OR NEVER
JAS 1:19-20

It's embarrassing to go off about something and find out later that it was all a misunderstanding. The way to avoid humiliating yourself is to listen to others and wait before you react. A moment of reflection can mean the difference between a God-honoring response and one you'll be ashamed of later.

FAVORITISM FORBIDDEN

2

My brothers, as believers in our glorious Lord Jesus Christ, don't show favoritism. ²Suppose a man comes into your meeting wearing a gold ring and fine clothes, and a poor man in shabby clothes also comes in. ³If you show special attention to the man wearing fine clothes and say, "Here's a good seat for you," but say to the poor man, "You stand there" or "Sit on the floor by my feet," ⁴have you not discriminated among yourselves and become judges with evil thoughts?

⁵Listen, my dear brothers: Has not God chosen those who are poor in the eyes of the world to be

battlelines

» The New Guy (Stepparents)

Q: Could you repeat that?
A: I said I wish I had never been born.

Q: Wait a minute. Are you just being dramatic, or do we need to go to the video store and rent *It's a Wonderful Life*?
A: All right, so I'm not ready to jump off a bridge or anything. But what would *you* do? My stepdad and I fight all the time. My mom and I used to be close, but now she's all into him. For seven years it was just me and her. Then, just as I was finally starting to adjust to life without my dad, she brought *him* home.

Q: Is your stepdad weird or something? Does he abuse you?
A: No, it's nothing like that. It's not like I can point to any obvious flaws in his character. He just rubs me the wrong way, you know? We're complete opposites. Whenever we have to be around each other, it's tense. So mostly we try to avoid each other.

Q: How do you two clash?
A: You name it. He likes sports, and I could care less about them. He thinks my interest in music is dumb. We can never find a TV show or movie we both want to watch. We both need the computer at the same time.

Q: The way I see it, one of you has to give.
A: Well, I sure don't think he's going to change.

Q: OK, then, *you* change.
A: What?

Q: Why not? You're a Christian. Just make some little concessions in your life. Give up your resentment and mistrust, and make an effort to get to know the guy.
A: Why do I have to be the one to change?

Q: Because you can. Don't you get it? If you keep doing what you've been doing, you're going to keep getting what you've been getting. This isn't rocket science!

» The New Guise

No one likes to change. But, face it: Stepparents require just that—change. That doesn't mean you have to give up who you are, but it does mean you have to learn to compromise. And that requires understanding, flexibility and forgiveness.

"Blending" a new family is never easy, but it's worth the effort. Communication and patience are the keys. So if you're in a road-blocked relationship, be the bigger person. Move first. Give mercy and acceptance a shot.

Many families seek out Christian counseling if they're struggling in this area. Counseling doesn't mean your family has failed. It's just a sign that you and your family are taking steps to overcome the challenges of life together.

Remember, "Judgment without mercy will be shown to anyone who has not been merciful. Mercy triumphs over judgment!" (James 2:13).

For more, check out the stepparents link on www.RevolutionBible.com.

rich in faith and to inherit the kingdom he promised those who love him? [6]But you have insulted the poor. Is it not the rich who are exploiting you? Are they not the ones who are dragging you into court? [7]Are they not the ones who are slandering the noble name of him to whom you belong?

[8]If you really keep the royal law found in Scripture, "Love your neighbor as yourself,"[a] you are doing right. [9]But if you show favoritism, you sin and are convicted by the law as law-

breakers. [10]For whoever keeps the whole law and yet stumbles at just one point is guilty of breaking all of it. [11]For he who said, "Do not commit adultery,"[b] also said, "Do not murder."[c] If you do not commit adultery but do commit murder, you have become a lawbreaker.

[12]Speak and act as those who are going to be judged by the law that gives freedom, [13]because judgment without mercy will be shown to anyone who has not been merciful. Mercy triumphs over judgment!

Live the Adventure . . . Letting Your Faith Show

» live the adventure » Jas 2:14–18

Putting your faith in the Lord means believing that his plan for your life is the best possible one. If you *really* believe his plan is best, then you'll commit to follow his instructions about how to live. If you follow his instructions, you will, among other things, help people in need, forgive those who hurt you and tell people about Jesus. Those who refuse to do these things should take a closer look at their faith. Something may be missing.

FAITH AND DEEDS

[14]What good is it, my brothers, if a man claims to have faith but has no deeds? Can such faith save him? [15]Suppose a brother or sister is without clothes and daily food. [16]If one of you says to him, "Go, I wish you well; keep warm and well fed," but does nothing about his physical needs, what good is it? [17]In the same way, faith by itself, if it is not accompanied by action, is dead.

[18]But someone will say, "You have faith; I have deeds."

Show me your faith without deeds, and I will show you my faith by what I do. [19]You believe that there is one God. Good! Even the demons believe that—and shudder.

[20]You foolish man, do you want evidence that faith without deeds is useless[d]? [21]Was not our ancestor Abraham considered righteous for what he did when he offered his son Isaac on the altar? [22]You see that his faith and his actions were working together, and his faith was made complete by what he did. [23]And the scripture was fulfilled that says, "Abraham believed God, and it was credited to him as righteousness,"[e] and he was called God's friend. [24]You see that a person is justified by what he does and not by faith alone.

[25]In the same way, was not even Rahab the prostitute considered righteous for what she did when she gave lodging to the spies and sent them off in a different direction? [26]As the body without the spirit is dead, so faith without deeds is dead.

TAMING THE TONGUE

3 Not many of you should presume to be teachers, my brothers, because you know that we who teach will be judged more strictly. [2]We all stumble in many ways. If anyone is never at fault in what he says, he is a perfect man, able to keep his whole body in check.

[3]When we put bits into the mouths of horses to make them obey us, we can turn the whole animal. [4]Or take ships as an example. Although they are so large and are driven by strong winds, they are steered by a very small rudder wherever the pilot wants to go. [5]Likewise the tongue is a small part of the body, but it makes great boasts. Consider what a great forest is set on fire by a small spark. [6]The

---

[a] *8* Lev. 19:18   [b] *11* Exodus 20:14; Deut. 5:18   [c] *11* Exodus 20:13; Deut. 5:17   [d] *20* Some early manuscripts *dead*
[e] *23* Gen. 15:6

tongue also is a fire, a world of evil among the parts of the body. It corrupts the whole person, sets the whole course of his life on fire, and is itself set on fire by hell.

⁷All kinds of animals, birds, reptiles and creatures of the sea are being tamed and have been tamed by man, ⁸but no man can tame the tongue. It is a restless evil, full of deadly poison.

⁹With the tongue we praise our Lord and Father, and with it we curse men, who have been made in God's likeness. ¹⁰Out of the same mouth come praise and cursing. My brothers, this should not be. ¹¹Can both fresh water and salt[a] water flow from the same spring? ¹²My brothers, can a fig tree bear olives, or a grapevine bear figs? Neither can a salt spring produce fresh water.

TWO KINDS OF WISDOM

¹³Who is wise and understanding among you? Let him show it by his good life, by deeds done in the humility that comes from wisdom. ¹⁴But if you harbor bitter envy and selfish ambition in your hearts, do not boast about it or deny the truth. ¹⁵Such "wisdom" does not come down from heaven but is earthly, unspiritual, of the devil. ¹⁶For where you have envy and selfish ambition, there you find disorder and every evil practice.

¹⁷But the wisdom that comes from heaven is first of all pure; then peace-loving, considerate, submissive, full of mercy and good fruit, impartial and sincere. ¹⁸Peacemakers who sow in peace raise a harvest of righteousness.

SUBMIT YOURSELVES TO GOD

4 What causes fights and quarrels among you? Don't they come from your desires that battle within you? ²You want something but don't get it. You kill and covet, but you cannot have what you want. You quarrel and fight. You do not have, because you do not ask God. ³When you ask, you do not receive, because you ask with wrong motives, that you may spend what you get on your pleasures.

⁴You adulterous people, don't you know that friendship with the world is hatred toward God? Anyone who chooses to be a friend of the world becomes an enemy of God. ⁵Or do you think Scripture says without reason that the spirit he caused to live in us envies intensely?[b] ⁶But he gives us more grace. That is why Scripture says:

"God opposes the proud
but gives grace to the humble."[c]

⁷Submit yourselves, then, to God. Resist the devil, and he will flee from you. ⁸Come near to God and he will come near to you. Wash your hands, you sinners, and purify your hearts, you double-minded. ⁹Grieve, mourn and wail. Change your laughter to mourning and your joy to gloom. ¹⁰Humble yourselves before the Lord, and he will lift you up.

¹¹Brothers, do not slander one another. Anyone who speaks against his brother or judges him speaks against the law and judges it. When you judge the law, you are not keeping it, but sitting in judgment on it. ¹²There is only one Lawgiver and Judge, the one who is able to save and destroy. But you—who are you to judge your neighbor?

NOW OR NEVER
JAS 4:1-3

Think of your top prayer request—the one thing you want to see God do more than anything. Why do you want it? If your motive is selfish or if it goes against God's Word, you'd better rethink your priorities. Otherwise, keep praying with passion and persistence. God will answer.

BOASTING ABOUT TOMORROW

¹³Now listen, you who say, "Today or tomorrow we will go to this or that city, spend a year there, carry on business and make money." ¹⁴Why, you do not even know what will happen tomorrow. What is your life? You are a mist that appears for a little while and then vanishes. ¹⁵Instead, you ought to say, "If it is the Lord's will, we will live and do this or that." ¹⁶As it is, you boast and brag. All such boasting is evil. ¹⁷Anyone, then, who knows the good he ought to do and doesn't do it, sins.

ᵃ *11* Greek *bitter* (see also verse 14)   ᵇ *5* Or *that God jealously longs for the spirit that he made to live in us*; or *that the Spirit he caused to live in us longs jealously*   ᶜ *6* Prov. 3:34

WARNING TO RICH OPPRESSORS

5 Now listen, you rich people, weep and wail because of the misery that is coming upon you. ²Your wealth has rotted, and moths have eaten your clothes. ³Your gold and silver are corroded. Their corrosion will testify against you and eat your flesh like fire. You have hoarded wealth in the last days. ⁴Look! The wages you failed to pay the workmen who mowed your fields are crying out against you. The cries of the harvesters have reached the ears of the Lord Almighty. ⁵You have lived on earth in luxury and self-indulgence. You have fattened yourselves in the day of slaughter.[a] ⁶You have condemned and murdered innocent men, who were not opposing you.

PATIENCE IN SUFFERING

⁷Be patient, then, brothers, until the Lord's coming. See how the farmer waits for the land to yield its valuable crop and how patient he is for the autumn and spring rains. ⁸You too, be patient and stand firm, because the Lord's coming is near. ⁹Don't grumble against each other, brothers, or you will be judged. The Judge is standing at the door!

¹⁰Brothers, as an example of patience in the face of suffering, take the prophets who spoke in the name of the Lord. ¹¹As you know, we consider blessed those who have persevered. You have heard of Job's perseverance and have seen what the Lord finally brought about. The Lord is full of compassion and mercy.

¹²Above all, my brothers, do not swear—not by heaven or by earth or by anything else. Let your "Yes" be yes, and your "No," no, or you will be condemned.

THE PRAYER OF FAITH

¹³Is any one of you in trouble? He should pray. Is anyone happy? Let him sing songs of praise. ¹⁴Is any one of you sick? He should call the elders of the church to pray over him and anoint him with oil in the name of the Lord. ¹⁵And the prayer offered in faith will make the sick person well; the Lord will raise him up. If he has sinned, he will be forgiven. ¹⁶Therefore confess your sins to each other and pray for each other so that you may be healed. The prayer of a righteous man is powerful and effective.

¹⁷Elijah was a man just like us. He prayed earnestly that it would not rain, and it did not rain on the land for three and a half years. ¹⁸Again he prayed, and the heavens gave rain, and the earth produced its crops.

¹⁹My brothers, if one of you should wander from the truth and someone should bring him back, ²⁰remember this: Whoever turns a sinner from the error of his way will save him from death and cover over a multitude of sins.

Keeping Your Perspective

Learn to view every day of your life as though it's a gift from God, because each one truly is. No one is guaranteed tomorrow—no matter how young or healthy you are. Instead of just assuming that God will give you a certain amount of time in this world, make a commitment to treat each day as if it's the most important one of your life. Don't put off doing the things that matter—like sharing your faith with loved ones or helping people who need you—until it's more convenient for you. Take advantage of today!

» live the adventure » Jas 4:13–15

---

[a] 5 Or yourselves as in a day of feasting

« AT A GLANCE

Author
The apostle Peter

Audience
Gentile and Jewish Christians in Asia Minor (modern-day Turkey)

Date
About A.D. 62–64, possibly written from Rome

Setting
Christians were being tortured and killed under Emperor Nero, and the church in Jerusalem was being scattered.

Verses to Remember
Dear friends, do not be surprised at the painful trial you are suffering, as though something strange were happening to you. But rejoice that you participate in the sufferings of Christ, so that you may be overjoyed when his glory is revealed (4:12–13).

Theme to Consider
No one likes to go through hard times. But as you read the book of 1 Peter, you'll be reminded that God will use those times to refine and strengthen your faith.

UNCHANGING TRUTH » Why are you a Christian and not a Mormon or a Muslim? How do you know the Bible is really God's Word? What makes you think Jesus rose from the dead? How can you say that only people who believe in him will go to heaven? If God is a loving being, why does he send people to hell?

Have you ever been asked a tough question about your faith? If not, you will be. Sooner or later you're going to run into someone who won't settle for easy answers about God or the Bible. That's why Peter warns, "Always be prepared to give an answer to everyone who asks you to give the reason for the hope that you have. But always do this with gentleness and respect" (1 Peter 3:15).

Put yourself in the place of your unbelieving friends and loved ones. What is it about your faith in Jesus that needs to be explained? What misconceptions might they have?

It's important for you to be prepared to answer their questions. If you need help, talk about it with your youth leader, Sunday school teacher or pastor. Write down the answers they share with you. If you need more help, find a Christian bookstore or church library and ask for books on "apologetics" (defending your faith) for young people.

But remember, having the answers isn't everything. Peter wanted followers of Jesus to share their faith with "gentleness and respect." *How* you react to people's questions about Jesus is just as important as the words you say.

LIFE LESSONS »

1 Live in a way that causes unbelievers to see God's influence in your life so they will desire the same experience in their own lives (2:12).

2 Respectfully obeying authority is a way to stand out when you're under the watchful eyes of unbelievers (2:13–15).

3 If you suffer because of your Christian faith, rejoice; it means you're doing something right (4:14).

1

Peter, an apostle of Jesus Christ,

To God's elect, strangers in the world, scattered throughout Pontus, Galatia, Cappadocia, Asia and Bithynia, [2]who have been chosen according to the foreknowledge of God the Father, through the sanctifying work of the Spirit, for obedience to Jesus Christ and sprinkling by his blood:

Grace and peace be yours in abundance.

PRAISE TO GOD FOR A LIVING HOPE

[3]Praise be to the God and Father of our Lord Jesus Christ! In his great mercy he has given us new birth into a living hope through the resurrection of Jesus Christ from the dead, [4]and into an inheritance that can never perish, spoil or fade—kept in heaven for you, [5]who through faith are shielded by God's power until the coming of the salvation that is ready to be revealed in the last time. [6]In this you greatly rejoice, though now for a little while you may have had to suffer grief in all kinds of trials. [7]These have come so that your faith—of greater worth than gold, which perishes even though refined by fire—may be proved genuine and may result in praise, glory and honor when Jesus Christ is revealed. [8]Though you have not seen him, you love him; and even though you do not see him now, you believe in him and are filled with an inexpressible and glorious joy, [9]for you are receiving the goal of your faith, the salvation of your souls.

[10]Concerning this salvation, the prophets, who spoke of the grace that was to come to you, searched intently and with the greatest care, [11]trying to find out the time and circumstances to which the Spirit of Christ in them was pointing when he predicted the sufferings of Christ and the glories that would follow. [12]It was revealed to them that they were not serving themselves but you, when they spoke of the things that have now been told you by those who have preached the gospel to you by the Holy Spirit sent from heaven. Even angels long to look into these things.

BE HOLY

[13]Therefore, prepare your minds for action; be self-controlled; set your hope fully on the grace to be given you when Jesus Christ is revealed. [14]As obedient children, do not conform to the evil desires you had when you lived in ignorance. [15]But just as he who called you is holy, so be holy in all you do; [16]for it is written: "Be holy, because I am holy." [a]

[17]Since you call on a Father who judges each man's work impartially, live your lives as strangers here in reverent fear. [18]For you know that it was not with perishable things such as silver or gold that you were redeemed from the empty way of life handed down to you from your forefathers, [19]but with the precious blood of Christ, a lamb without blemish or defect. [20]He was chosen before the creation of the world, but was revealed in these last times for your sake. [21]Through him you believe in God, who raised him from the dead and glorified him, and so your faith and hope are in God.

[22]Now that you have purified yourselves by obeying the truth so that you have sincere love for your brothers, love one another deeply, from the heart. [b] [23]For you have been born again, not of perishable seed, but of imperishable, through the living and enduring word of God. [24]For,

"All men are like grass,
   and all their glory is like the flowers of the field;
the grass withers and the flowers fall,
[25]   but the word of the Lord stands forever." [c]

And this is the word that was preached to you.

2

Therefore, rid yourselves of all malice and all deceit, hypocrisy, envy, and slander of every kind. [2]Like newborn babies, crave pure spiritual milk, so that by it you may grow up in your salvation, [3]now that you have tasted that the Lord is good.

THE LIVING STONE AND A CHOSEN PEOPLE

[4]As you come to him, the living Stone—rejected by men but chosen by God and precious to him—[5]you also, like living stones, are being built into a spiritual house to be a holy priesthood, offering spiritual sacrifices acceptable to God through Jesus Christ. [6]For in Scripture it says:

---

[a] *16* Lev. 11:44,45; 19:2   [b] *22* Some early manuscripts *from a pure heart*   [c] *25* Isaiah 40:6-8

> "See, I lay a stone in Zion,
> a chosen and precious cornerstone,
> and the one who trusts in him
> will never be put to shame."[a]

[7]Now to you who believe, this stone is precious. But to those who do not believe,

> "The stone the builders
> rejected
> has become the
> capstone,[b][c]

[8]and,

> "A stone that causes men to
> stumble
> and a rock that makes them
> fall."[d]

They stumble because they disobey the message—which is also what they were destined for.

[9]But you are a chosen people, a royal priesthood, a holy nation, a people belonging to God, that you may declare the praises of him who called you out of darkness into his wonderful light. [10]Once you were not a people, but now you are the people of God; once you had not received mercy, but now you have received mercy.

[11]Dear friends, I urge you, as aliens and strangers in the world, to abstain from sinful desires, which war against your soul. [12]Live such good lives among the pagans that, though they accuse you of doing wrong, they may see your good deeds and glorify God on the day he visits us.

SUBMISSION TO RULERS AND MASTERS

[13]Submit yourselves for the Lord's sake to every authority instituted among men: whether to the king, as the supreme authority, [14]or to governors, who are sent by him to punish those who do wrong and to commend those who do right. [15]For it is God's will that by doing good you should silence the ignorant talk of foolish men. [16]Live as free men, but do not use your freedom as a cover-up for evil; live as servants of God. [17]Show proper respect to everyone: Love the brotherhood of believers, fear God, honor the king.

[18]Slaves, submit yourselves to your masters with all respect, not only to those who are good and considerate, but also to those who are harsh. [19]For it is commendable if a man bears up under the pain of unjust suffering because he is conscious of God. [20]But how is it to your credit if you receive a beating for doing wrong and endure it? But if you suffer for doing good and you endure it, this is commendable before God. [21]To this you were called, because Christ suffered for you, leaving you an example, that you should follow in his steps.

NOW OR NEVER

1PE 2:21

True or false: A Christian life with no suffering is better than one that involves suffering. Explain your answer.

> [22]"He committed no sin,
> and no deceit was found in his mouth."[e]

[23]When they hurled their insults at him, he did not retaliate; when he suffered, he made no threats. Instead, he entrusted himself to him who judges justly. [24]He himself bore our sins in his body on the tree, so that we might die to sins and live for righteousness; by his wounds you have been healed. [25]For you were like sheep going astray, but now you have returned to the Shepherd and Overseer of your souls.

---

[a] *6* Isaiah 28:16   [b] *7* Or *cornerstone*   [c] *7* Psalm 118:22   [d] *8* Isaiah 8:14   [e] *22* Isaiah 53:9

battlelines

» She's Got the Look (Girls)

Q: What is *this*?
A: Some new sports show. It covers the pros, college sports . . . everything.

Q: Looks like it mostly *un*covers cheerleaders.
A: I knew you were going to say something like that. But you're right; they don't miss a chance to flash a little skin. They do that on just about every show—and every commercial too. But that's not why I watch it. I watch it for the game highlights; plus, the commentators are hilarious.

Q: I know. I wasn't pointing the finger at you. I was sort of thinking out loud about how girls are used in the media.
A: No doubt. Good-looking girls mean more viewers. More viewers mean more money. It's all about the money, I guess.

Q: So what do you think goes through the average girl's mind when she sees a show like this with all these gorgeous, overly exposed women?
A: Good question. Do you think she feels jealous or inferior? Or does she watch them and think, *What a bunch of bimbos*? Most of the girls I hang around with would probably never win a beauty contest. Wait—I take that back. Kaitlin and Erin are *really* good-looking. But you know, even with them, once you get past their looks, they're no different than anybody else.

Q: So how exactly do you do that?
A: Do what?

Q: Get past their looks.
A: I don't know. I guess just get to know them. Find out about their lives. Most of my friends like to look *at* them and talk *about* them. I try to talk directly *to* them. When you do that, you find out they're real people.

» Beyond the Make-Up

The world often treats women as objects who exist solely for the benefit of men. Advertisers use their looks to sell everything from shampoo to tires. Pornographers want them to bare their skin so guys can indulge in sexual fantasies. And way too many guys want the women they see to become nothing more than sex toys, providers of sensual pleasure.

In such a twisted culture, it's easy to forget that the gorgeous model in the bathing suit is much more than a collection of incredible body parts. In reality, she's a complex person with hopes, hurts, dreams and fears. She's an immeasurably valuable human being created in the image of God.

Make an effort to see the girls in your life as real people. Though they may like to look good, they also like to be seen and appreciated for who they are on the inside. Take time to go beyond the billboards and behind the make-up (see Proverbs 11:22; 31:10,30).

Read more about getting along with girls at www.RevolutionBible.com.

WIVES AND HUSBANDS

3 Wives, in the same way be submissive to your husbands so that, if any of them do not believe the word, they may be won over without words by the behavior of their wives, ²when they see the purity and reverence of your lives. ³Your beauty should not come from outward adornment, such as braided hair and the wearing of gold jewelry and fine clothes. ⁴Instead, it should be that of your inner self, the unfading beauty of a gentle and quiet spirit, which is of great worth in God's sight. ⁵For this is the way the holy women of the past who put their hope in God used to make themselves beautiful. They were submissive to their own husbands, ⁶like Sarah, who obeyed Abraham and called him her master. You are her daughters if you do what is right and do not give way to fear.

⁷Husbands, in the same way be considerate as you live with your wives, and treat them with respect as the weaker partner and as heirs with you of the gracious gift of life, so that nothing will hinder your prayers.

SUFFERING FOR DOING GOOD

⁸Finally, all of you, live in harmony with one another; be sympathetic, love as brothers, be compassionate and humble. ⁹Do not repay evil with evil or insult with insult, but with blessing, because to this you were called so that you may inherit a blessing. ¹⁰For,

> "Whoever would love life
> and see good days
> must keep his tongue from evil
> and his lips from deceitful speech.
> ¹¹ He must turn from evil and do good;
> he must seek peace and pursue it.
> ¹² For the eyes of the Lord are on the righteous
> and his ears are attentive to their prayer,
> but the face of the Lord is against those who do evil." [a]

¹³Who is going to harm you if you are eager to do good? ¹⁴But even if you should suffer for what is right, you are blessed. "Do not fear what they fear[b]; do not be frightened." [c] ¹⁵But in your hearts set apart Christ as Lord. Always be prepared to give an answer to everyone who asks you to give the reason for the hope that you have. But do this with gentleness and respect, ¹⁶keeping a clear conscience, so that those who speak maliciously against your good behavior in Christ may be ashamed of their slander. ¹⁷It is better, if it is God's will, to suffer for doing good than for doing evil. ¹⁸For Christ died for sins once for all, the righteous for the unrighteous, to bring you to God. He was put to death in the body but made alive by the Spirit, ¹⁹through whom[d] also he went and preached to the spirits in prison ²⁰who disobeyed long ago when God waited patiently in the days of Noah while the ark was being built. In it only a few people, eight in all, were saved through water, ²¹and this water symbolizes baptism that now saves you also—not the removal of dirt from the body but the pledge[e] of a good conscience toward God. It saves you by the resurrection of Jesus Christ, ²²who has gone into heaven and is at God's right hand—with angels, authorities and powers in submission to him.

LIVING FOR GOD

4 Therefore, since Christ suffered in his body, arm yourselves also with the same attitude, because he who has suffered in his body is done with sin. ²As a result, he does not live the rest of his earthly life for evil human desires, but rather for the will of God. ³For you have spent enough time in the past doing what pagans choose to do—living in debauchery, lust, drunkenness, orgies, carousing and detestable idolatry. ⁴They think it strange that you do not

now or never
1PE 4:3–4

Peter's list of what pagans choose to do— "debauchery, lust, drunkenness, orgies"— sounds like a spring break party. So is Peter's description really all that different from the stuff you enjoy watching on TV?

---

[a] 12 Psalm 34:12-16   [b] 14 Or *not fear their threats*   [c] 14 Isaiah 8:12   [d] 18,19 Or *alive in the spirit,* ¹⁹*through which*
[e] 21 Or *response*

plunge with them into the same flood of dissipation, and they heap abuse on you. ⁵But they will have to give account to him who is ready to judge the living and the dead. ⁶For this is the reason the gospel was preached even to those who are now dead, so that they might be judged according to men in regard to the body, but live according to God in regard to the spirit.

⁷The end of all things is near. Therefore be clear minded and self-controlled so that you can pray. ⁸Above all, love each other deeply, because love covers over a multitude of sins. ⁹Offer hospitality to one another without grumbling. ¹⁰Each one should use whatever gift he has received to serve others, faithfully administering God's grace in its various forms. ¹¹If anyone speaks, he should do it as one speaking the very words of God. If anyone serves, he should do it with the strength God provides, so that in all things God may be praised through Jesus Christ. To him be the glory and the power for ever and ever. Amen.

SUFFERING FOR BEING A CHRISTIAN

¹²Dear friends, do not be surprised at the painful trial you are suffering, as though something strange were happening to you. ¹³But rejoice that you participate in the sufferings of Christ, so that you may be overjoyed when his glory is revealed. ¹⁴If you are insulted because of the name of Christ, you are blessed, for the Spirit of glory and of God rests on you. ¹⁵If you suffer, it should not be as a murderer or thief or any other kind of criminal, or even as a meddler. ¹⁶However, if you suffer as a Christian, do not be ashamed, but praise God that you bear that name. ¹⁷For it is time for judgment to begin with the family of God; and if it begins with us, what will the outcome be for those who do not obey the gospel of God? ¹⁸And,

> "If it is hard for the righteous to be saved,
> what will become of the ungodly and the sinner?" [a]

¹⁹So then, those who suffer according to God's will should commit themselves to their faithful Creator and continue to do good.

TO ELDERS AND YOUNG MEN

5 To the elders among you, I appeal as a fellow elder, a witness of Christ's sufferings and one who also will share in the glory to be revealed: ²Be shepherds of God's flock that is under your care, serving as overseers—not because you must, but because you are willing, as God wants you to be; not greedy for money, but eager to serve; ³not lording it over those entrusted to you, but being examples to the flock. ⁴And when the Chief Shepherd appears, you will receive the crown of glory that will never fade away.

⁵Young men, in the same way be submissive to those who are older. All of you, clothe yourselves with humility toward one another, because,

> "God opposes the proud
> but gives grace to the humble." [b]

⁶Humble yourselves, therefore, under God's mighty hand, that he may lift you up in due time. ⁷Cast all your anxiety on him because he cares for you.

⁸Be self-controlled and alert. Your enemy the devil prowls around like a roaring lion looking for

---

> ### Standing Up to Persecution
>
> Don't crawl into your shell when people laugh at you or make fun of you for being a Christian. Instead wear your suffering like a badge of honor, because it means you're doing something right. If people single you out because of your faith, it means they see something different in you. Your response under pressure is the surest test of genuine faith. Don't let anyone drive you underground. Accept other people's negativity as a challenge to become even bolder in doing what's right.

»» live the adventure »» 1Pe 4:16

[a] *18* Prov. 11:31   [b] *5* Prov. 3:34

Guarding Against the Enemy

Where are you most vulnerable to Satan's attacks? What temptations seem hardest for you to resist? It's important to know your weak areas if you're going to be on your guard. If you're vulnerable to sexual temptation, you need to take extra care to avoid porn sites when you're surfing the web. If you struggle with anger, Satan may try to use a couple of really bad days in a row to get you primed for an explosion. At the same time, it's equally important not to drop your guard in areas where you think you're less vulnerable. You may be surprised (unpleasantly) by what can happen.

someone to devour. ⁹Resist him, standing firm in the faith, because you know that your brothers throughout the world are undergoing the same kind of sufferings.

¹⁰And the God of all grace, who called you to his eternal glory in Christ, after you have suffered a little while, will himself restore you and make you strong, firm and steadfast. ¹¹To him be the power for ever and ever. Amen.

FINAL GREETINGS

¹²With the help of Silas,[a] whom I regard as a faithful brother, I have written to you briefly, encouraging you and testifying that this is the true grace of God. Stand fast in it.

¹³She who is in Babylon, chosen together with you, sends you her greetings, and so does my son Mark. ¹⁴Greet one another with a kiss of love.

Peace to all of you who are in Christ.

ᵃ 12 Greek *Silvanus*, a variant of *Silas*

2 PETER

Author
The apostle Peter

Audience
The same people he wrote to in his first letter:
Christians in Asia Minor (modern-day Turkey)

Date
About A.D. 67

Setting
Peter wrote this letter shortly before his death to
warn believers about false teachers.

Verse to Remember
His divine power has given us everything we need
for life and godliness through our knowledge of
him who called us by his own glory and goodness
(1:3).

Theme to Consider
How can we defend against falling prey to wrong
teachings and false teachers? In this book, we learn
that the answer is to continually grow in our relationship with Christ and reject anything that does
not agree with God's Word.

UNCHANGING TRUTH » Not everyone believes the Christian faith is based on truth.
Many doubters are convinced that the disciples simply made up their stories about Jesus—or at least wild-
ly exaggerated the things they saw him do and heard him say.

The problem with that conspiracy theory, however, is that ten of Jesus' original twelve disciples were
put to death because they refused to renounce their belief in the Lord. (The only exceptions were Judas Iscariot, who committed suicide after he betrayed Jesus, and John, who died of natural causes after being
continually persecuted and eventually exiled to an island because of his commitment to Jesus.) If they
made it all up, why didn't they just admit it and save their own hides? Think about it. Who would ever die
for something or someone they knew to be a lie?

The apostle Peter spoke for the other disciples when he wrote, "We did not follow cleverly invented
stories when we told you about the power and coming of our Lord Jesus Christ, but we were eyewitnesses
of his majesty" (2 Peter 1:16).

The stories of Jesus' teachings, miracles and especially his resurrection aren't urban legends; they're
eyewitness testimonies. That's just one of the many reasons you can be sure that you've put your hope in
something trustworthy.

LIFE LESSONS »

I Goodness, knowledge, self-control, perseverance, godliness, kindness and love should be on
the increase as you become more and more mature in your faith (1:5–7).

2 The Bible is completely trustworthy because the Holy Spirit—the spirit of God himself—guided every word that was written (1:21).

3 God works on his own timetable—patiently waiting for people to repent and turn to him. He's
the only One who knows when Jesus will return (3:8).

1

Simon Peter, a servant and apostle of Jesus Christ,

To those who through the righteousness of our God and Savior Jesus Christ have received a faith as precious as ours:

[2] Grace and peace be yours in abundance through the knowledge of God and of Jesus our Lord.

MAKING ONE'S CALLING AND ELECTION SURE

[3] His divine power has given us everything we need for life and godliness through our knowledge of him who called us by his own glory and goodness. [4] Through these he has given us his very great and precious promises, so that through them you may participate in the divine nature and escape the corruption in the world caused by evil desires.

[5] For this very reason, make every effort to add to your faith goodness; and to goodness, knowledge; [6] and to knowledge, self-control; and to self-control, perseverance; and to perseverance, godliness; [7] and to godliness, brotherly kindness; and to brotherly kindness, love. [8] For if you possess these qualities in increasing measure, they will keep you from being ineffective and unproductive in your knowledge of our Lord Jesus Christ. [9] But if anyone does not have them, he is nearsighted and blind, and has forgotten that he has been cleansed from his past sins.

[10] Therefore, my brothers, be all the more eager to make your calling and election sure. For if you do these things, you will never fall, [11] and you will receive a rich welcome into the eternal kingdom of our Lord and Savior Jesus Christ.

PROPHECY OF SCRIPTURE

[12] So I will always remind you of these things, even though you know them and are firmly established in the truth you now have. [13] I think it is right to refresh your memory as long as I live in the tent of this body, [14] because I know that I will soon put it aside, as our Lord Jesus Christ has made clear to me. [15] And I will make every effort to see that after my departure you will always be able to remember these things.

[16] We did not follow cleverly invented stories when we told you about the power and coming of our Lord Jesus Christ, but we were eyewitnesses of his majesty. [17] For he received honor and glory from God the Father when the voice came to him from the Majestic Glory, saying, "This is my Son, whom I love; with him I am well pleased." [a] [18] We ourselves heard this voice that came from heaven when we were with him on the sacred mountain.

[19] And we have the word of the prophets made more certain, and you will do well to pay attention to it, as to a light shining in a dark place, until the day dawns and the morning star rises in your hearts. [20] Above all, you must understand that no prophecy of Scripture came about by the prophet's own interpretation. [21] For prophecy never had its origin in the will of man, but men spoke from God as they were carried along by the Holy Spirit.

FALSE TEACHERS AND THEIR DESTRUCTION

2

But there were also false prophets among the people, just as there will be false teachers among you. They will secretly introduce destructive heresies, even denying the sovereign Lord who bought them—bringing swift destruction on themselves. [2] Many will follow their shameful ways and will bring the way of truth into disrepute. [3] In their greed these teachers will exploit you with stories they have made up. Their condemnation has long been hanging over them, and their destruction has not been sleeping.

[4] For if God did not spare angels when they sinned, but sent them to hell, [b] putting them into gloomy dungeons [c] to be held for judgment; [5] if he did not spare the ancient world when he brought the flood on its ungodly people, but protected Noah, a preacher of righteousness, and seven others; [6] if he condemned the cities of Sodom and Gomorrah by burning them to ashes, and made them an example of what is going to happen to the ungodly; [7] and if he rescued Lot, a righteous man, who was distressed by the filthy lives of lawless men [8] (for that righteous man, living among them day after day, was tormented in his righteous soul by the lawless deeds he saw and heard)— [9] if this is so, then the Lord knows how to rescue godly men from trials and to hold the unrighteous for the day of judgment, while

---

[a] *17* Matt. 17:5; Mark 9:7; Luke 9:35   [b] *4* Greek *Tartarus*   [c] *4* Some manuscripts *into chains of darkness*

battlelines

» Taking Advantage (Cheating)

Q: OK, I'm still not clear on this. The principal called you in for *what*?
A: I made a fake faculty parking permit.

Q: Really? How?
A: It wasn't very hard. I "borrowed" a real permit from a teacher's car, scanned it and then returned it. Then I worked on it until I got it looking just right. You can't tell it's a fake unless you hold it up close.

Q: What do you think will happen to you?
A: Well, they're saying they could kick me out of school. I don't think they will though. I mean, it's my first offense.

Q: Yeah, but what about your scheme last year to get premium cable channels for free? Or that time you emptied the soft drink machine in the teacher's lounge when it was giving out free drinks?
A: Hey, I didn't exactly "empty" the machine. It was like six cans. Maybe eight.

Q: Don't you feel badly about all this? I mean, you say you're a Christian, but you're breaking rules left and right.
A: Look, the parking pass thing—I pay $25 a semester for the right to park, like, a mile from school! And the cable thing—hey, why pay $50 a month for just the regular cable channels? That's a rip-off! And even if I figure out a way to get the premium channels for free, the cable company is still making loads of cash. So why should I feel bad when *they're* the ones who are trying to cheat *us*?

» Doing Right

Two things are true about life in this world:

1. It's dog-eat-dog out there. Life isn't fair, and some people will definitely try to stick it to you.
2. Christians are called to be different, to live lives of integrity.

John's problem is that he's focusing on "them" (the world) instead of "him" (Jesus). If you use the world's standards as your guide, there's not much you won't be able to rationalize. Excuses like, "Everyone does it" or "It's not cheating if you don't get caught" may be common, but they just don't fly with God.

Consider 1 Peter 2:11–12: "Dear friends, I urge you, as aliens and strangers in the world, to abstain from sinful desires, which war against your soul. Live such good lives among the pagans that, though they accuse you of doing wrong, they may see your good deeds and glorify God on the day he visits us."

Read more on the importance of integrity at www.RevolutionBible.com.

50 ESSENTIAL SKILLS AND HABITS FOR THE CHRISTIAN GUY

As followers of Jesus, we are called to live radical, revolutionary lives. Sometimes that means we do spectacular, heroic things. But no one's life is completely filled with nail-biting drama—no matter what Hollywood tries to tell you. Even Jesus, the ultimate revolutionary guy, lived a pretty normal life as a carpenter until his last three years. So for us, living a revolutionary life means doing the right thing—things that guys are supposed to do—day after day. But don't underestimate a life like that. Developing good habits and God-honoring skills will have a huge impact on those around you. Here's a list of 50 essential skills:

01	» Knowing basic car maintenance	GE 46:29
02	» Showing respect to elders	LEV 19:32
03	» Studying the Bible	JOS 1:8
04	» Keeping your promises	JOS 6:22
05	» Listening to and watching for God	1 KI 19:11-14
06	» Blocking out any sensual images, pictures, TV programs, videos, etc. from your life	JOB 31:1
07	» Humbly asking for forgiveness	PS 25:11
08	» Trusting God	PS 31:14
09	» Giving generously	PS 37:21
10	» Saying "I'm sorry"	PS 38:18
11	» Meditating on God	PS 63:6
12	» Asking for discernment and understanding	PS 119:169
13	» Giving to your church	PR 3:9
14	» Seeing spiritual lessons and applications in places you might not expect	PR 6:6
15	» Saving money even though no one else seems to be	PR 6:6-8
16	» Avoiding gossip	PR 11:13
17	» Working hard	PR 12:11
18	» Encouraging a friend	PR 12:25
19	» Planning strategically and setting goals	PR 21:5
20	» Confronting friends	PR 27:5-6

ESSENTIAL SKILLS

continuing their punishment.[a] [10]This is especially true of those who follow the corrupt desire of the sinful nature[b] and despise authority.

Bold and arrogant, these men are not afraid to slander celestial beings; [11]yet even angels, although they are stronger and more powerful, do not bring slanderous accusations against such beings in the presence of the Lord. [12]But these men blaspheme in matters they do not understand. They are like brute beasts, creatures of instinct, born only to be caught and destroyed, and like beasts they too will perish.

[13]They will be paid back with harm for the harm they have done. Their idea of pleasure is to carouse in broad daylight. They are blots and blemishes, reveling in their pleasures while they feast with you.[c] [14]With eyes full of adultery, they never stop sinning; they seduce the unstable; they are experts in greed—an accursed brood! [15]They have left the straight way and wandered off to follow the way of Balaam son of Beor, who loved the wages of wickedness. [16]But he was rebuked for his wrongdoing by a donkey—a beast without speech—who spoke with a man's voice and restrained the prophet's madness.

[17]These men are springs without water and mists driven by a storm. Blackest darkness is reserved for them. [18]For they mouth empty, boastful words and, by appealing to the lustful desires of sinful human nature, they entice people who are just escaping from those who live in error. [19]They promise them freedom, while they themselves are slaves of depravity—for a man is a slave to whatever has mastered him. [20]If they have escaped the corruption of the world by knowing our Lord and Savior Jesus Christ and are again entangled in it and overcome, they are worse off at the end than they were at the beginning. [21]It would have been better for them not to have known the way of righteousness, than to have known it and then to turn their backs on the sacred command that was passed on to them. [22]Of them the proverbs are true: "A dog returns to its vomit,"[d] and, "A sow that is washed goes back to her wallowing in the mud."

NOW OR NEVER

2PE 3:3–4

Don't let anyone raise doubts in your mind about whether or not Jesus will return. The date is decided and the events have been set in motion. What do you think scoffers and doubters will say when that day finally comes?

THE DAY OF THE LORD

3 Dear friends, this is now my second letter to you. I have written both of them as reminders to stimulate you to wholesome thinking. [2]I want you to recall the words spoken in the past by the holy prophets and the command given by our Lord and Savior through your apostles.

[3]First of all, you must understand that in the last days scoffers will come, scoffing and following their own evil desires. [4]They will say, "Where is this 'coming' he promised? Ever since our fathers died, everything goes on as it has since the beginning of creation." [5]But they deliberately forget that long ago by God's word the heavens existed and the earth was formed out of water and by water. [6]By these waters also the world of that time was deluged and destroyed. [7]By the same word the present heavens and earth are reserved for fire, being kept for the day of judgment and destruction of ungodly men.

[8]But do not forget this one thing, dear friends: With the Lord a day is like a thousand years, and a thousand years are like a day. [9]The Lord is not slow in keeping his promise, as some understand slowness. He is patient with you, not wanting anyone to perish, but everyone to come to repentance.

[10]But the day of the Lord will come like a thief. The heavens will disappear with a roar; the elements will be destroyed by fire, and the earth and everything in it will be laid bare.[e]

NOW OR NEVER

2PE 3:15

The fact that Jesus hasn't returned yet is good news for many people who still need to ask God to forgive them for their sins and give their lives to Jesus. What can you do to encourage your unbelieving friends and family members to take that step before it's too late?

---

[a] *9 Or unrighteous for punishment until the day of judgment*   [b] *10 Or the flesh*   [c] *13 Some manuscripts in their love feasts*   [d] *22 Prov. 26:11*   [e] *10 Some manuscripts be burned up*

¹¹Since everything will be destroyed in this way, what kind of people ought you to be? You ought to live holy and godly lives ¹²as you look forward to the day of God and speed its coming.ª That day will bring about the destruction of the heavens by fire, and the elements will melt in the heat. ¹³But in keeping with his promise we are looking forward to a new heaven and a new earth, the home of righteousness.

¹⁴So then, dear friends, since you are looking forward to this, make every effort to be found spotless, blameless and at peace with him. ¹⁵Bear in mind that our Lord's patience means salvation, just as our dear brother Paul also wrote you with the wisdom that God gave him. ¹⁶He writes the same way in all his letters, speaking in them of these matters. His letters contain some things that are hard to understand, which ignorant and unstable people distort, as they do the other Scriptures, to their own destruction.

¹⁷Therefore, dear friends, since you already know this, be on your guard so that you may not be carried away by the error of lawless men and fall from your secure position. ¹⁸But grow in the grace and knowledge of our Lord and Savior Jesus Christ. To him be glory both now and forever! Amen.

Understanding God's Word

When you come across a Bible passage that you have a hard time understanding, don't just gloss over it and move on. Set a personal goal to figure out what the passage means within the next week. If that requires pulling a Bible commentary from your grandpa's old bookshelf or researching the passage in a study Bible, do it. If it means checking out a Bible Q&A page on the Web or talking to your youth leader or church pastor about it, do it. The Bible isn't always easy to understand, but studying it is always well worth the effort.

ª 12 Or *as you wait eagerly for the day of God to come*

« AT A GLANCE

Author
The apostle John

Audience
The churches near Ephesus, in the western part of modern-day Turkey

Date
Between A.D. 85 and 95

Setting
John, who was an eyewitness and close friend of Christ, wrote to encourage Christians to have confidence in God and in their faith.

Verse to Remember
I write these things to you who believe in the name of the Son of God so that you may know that you have eternal life (5:13).

Theme to Consider
When doubts about faith creep in, read the book of 1 John. It will help you understand the reality of God in your life, assure you of your eternal life and encourage you to remain in fellowship with God.

UNCHANGING TRUTH » Is it wrong for a Christian to wear expensive clothes or drive a nice car or own hundreds of video games and DVDs?

Some people think so. They believe that spending money on "things" instead of, say, giving it to needy people or Christian organizations is a sign of mixed-up priorities. Other people argue that God blesses certain Christians with wealth, and if wealthy people are faithful in their tithes and offerings to the Lord, they should be allowed to buy whatever they want with the rest of their money.

The Bible suggests that it all comes down to attitude. The book of 1 John makes it clear that we should not *love* the things of this world. The question is, how do you know when you cross the line between *enjoying* something (whether it's clothes, basketball shoes, video games, computer stuff, DVDs, your iPod or concert tickets) and *loving* it? Here are some clues:

- You're constantly thinking about what you want to buy next.
- You consider shoplifting, cheating or stealing to get what you want.
- You envy people who have what you want.
- You flaunt what you have or try to make other people feel envious of it.
- You start to care more about what you have than who you are.

If any of these descriptions hit a little too close to home, ask God to help you do a self-check in your attitude toward money and material things. Enjoy the blessings that the Lord gives you . . . but always be prepared to walk away from anything that interferes with your relationship with him.

LIFE LESSONS »

1   Your actions say more about who you really are than your words do (1:6).

2   God will forgive any sin that we sincerely confess and for which we seek his forgiveness (1:9).

3   Test everything you hear about God against what the Bible says (4:1).

THE WORD OF LIFE

1 That which was from the beginning, which we have heard, which we have seen with our eyes, which we have looked at and our hands have touched—this we proclaim concerning the Word of life. ²The life appeared; we have seen it and testify to it, and we proclaim to you the eternal life, which was with the Father and has appeared to us. ³We proclaim to you what we have seen and heard, so that you also may have fellowship with us. And our fellowship is with the Father and with his Son, Jesus Christ. ⁴We write this to make our[a] joy complete.

WALKING IN THE LIGHT

⁵This is the message we have heard from him and declare to you: God is light; in him there is no darkness at all. ⁶If we claim to have fellowship with him yet walk in the darkness, we lie and do not live by the truth. ⁷But if we walk in the light, as he is in the light, we have fellowship with one another, and the blood of Jesus, his Son, purifies us from all[b] sin.

⁸If we claim to be without sin, we deceive ourselves and the truth is not in us. ⁹If we confess our sins, he is faithful and just and will forgive us our sins and purify us from all unrighteousness. ¹⁰If we claim we have not sinned, we make him out to be a liar and his word has no place in our lives.

2 My dear children, I write this to you so that you will not sin. But if anybody does sin, we have one who speaks to the Father in our defense—Jesus Christ, the Righteous One. ²He is the atoning sacrifice for our sins, and not only for ours but also for[c] the sins of the whole world.

³We know that we have come to know him if we obey his commands. ⁴The man who says, "I know him," but does not do what he commands is a liar, and the truth is not in him. ⁵But if anyone obeys his word, God's love[d] is truly made complete in him. This is how we know we are in him: ⁶Whoever claims to live in him must walk as Jesus did.

⁷Dear friends, I am not writing you a new command but an old one, which you have had since the beginning. This old command is the message you have heard. ⁸Yet I am writing you a new command; its truth is seen in him and you, because the darkness is passing and the true light is already shining.

⁹Anyone who claims to be in the light but hates his brother is still in the darkness. ¹⁰Whoever loves his brother lives in the light, and there is nothing in him[e] to make him stumble. ¹¹But whoever hates his brother is in the darkness and walks around in the darkness; he does not know where he is going, because the darkness has blinded him.

> ¹²I write to you, dear children,
>> because your sins have been forgiven on account of his name.
> ¹³I write to you, fathers,
>> because you have known him who is from the beginning.
> I write to you, young men,
>> because you have overcome the evil one.
> I write to you, dear children,
>> because you have known the Father.
> ¹⁴I write to you, fathers,
>> because you have known him who is from the beginning.
> I write to you, young men,

Accepting Forgiveness

God doesn't just forgive us; he purifies us. That means he washes away whatever sins we confess, scrubs our hearts clean and forgets about our sin forever. Here's a tip: If God forgets about a sin, you should forget about it too. Don't keep beating yourself up over something you've been forgiven for. Do what you need to do to make things right—apologize to anyone you might have hurt by your actions and seek their forgiveness . . . and then move on.

---

a 4 Some manuscripts *your*   b 7 Or *every*   c 2 Or *He is the one who turns aside God's wrath, taking away our sins, and not only ours but also*   d 5 Or *word, love for God*   e 10 Or *it*

battlelines

» The Lost Boys (Evangelism)

Q: Tell me about those three guys I saw you with at the movies.
A: Those are my friends—Brett, Tyson and Harrison. We've known each other for about four years. We're pretty much inseparable.

Q: You know them from church or what?
A: (Laughing) Or what. They're definitely not church guys. Not that they're against God or anything. They just don't ever mention him or express any kind of interest in church or the Bible.

Q: Do you think they're Christians?
A: Well, I'm not one to judge. I mean, how can I say what they believe deep down inside?

Q: Well, you can look for signs of faith. Do you see any evidence? Do you think any of them have a real relationship with Jesus?
A: If I had to guess, I'd say probably not.

Q: Interesting. Have you ever talked about your own faith with them?
A: Me? You mean, like, witness to them?

Q: Yeah.
A: No. I wouldn't have any idea what to say. I'm 16. What do I know?

» Telling Your Story

Isn't it funny how we can talk so freely about real stuff every day—cars, TV shows, people, personal experiences—but when it comes to Jesus, we suddenly get quiet? Why is that, do you suppose? Isn't Jesus real? Hasn't he made a real difference in your life?

Get over the goofy idea that witnessing means you have to be preachy or insulting or weird or brilliant. That's just not true. Look at the way the apostle John went about it: "That which was from the beginning, which we have heard, which we have seen with our eyes, which we have looked at and our hands have touched—this we proclaim . . . We proclaim to you what we have seen and heard" (1 John 1:1,3).

In other words, just talk about what has happened to you as a result of Christ's work in your life. That's all a witness needs to do.

Learn more about understanding and sharing your faith at www.RevolutionBible.com.

because you are strong,
and the word of God lives in you,
and you have overcome the evil one.

DO NOT LOVE THE WORLD

15Do not love the world or anything in the world. If anyone loves the world, the love of the Father is not in him. 16For everything in the world—the cravings of sinful man, the lust of his eyes and the boasting of what he has and does—comes not from the Father but from the world. 17The world and its desires pass away, but the man who does the will of God lives forever.

WARNING AGAINST ANTICHRISTS

18Dear children, this is the last hour; and as you have heard that the antichrist is coming, even now many antichrists have come. This is how we know it is the last hour. 19They went out from us, but they did not really belong to us. For if they had belonged to us, they would have remained with us; but their going showed that none of them belonged to us. 20But you have an anointing from the Holy One, and all of you know the truth.[a] 21I do not write to you because you do not know the truth, but because you do know it and because no lie comes from the truth. 22Who is the liar? It is the man who denies that Jesus is the Christ. Such a man is the antichrist—he denies the Father and the Son. 23No one who denies the Son has the Father; whoever acknowledges the Son has the Father also.

24See that what you have heard from the beginning remains in you. If it does, you also will remain in the Son and in the Father. 25And this is what he promised us—even eternal life.

26I am writing these things to you about those who are trying to lead you astray. 27As for you, the anointing you received from him remains in you, and you do not need anyone to teach you. But as his anointing teaches you about all things and as that anointing is real, not counterfeit—just as it has taught you, remain in him.

Identifying Your Love for "Things"

If you struggle with a love for the things of this world, look a little deeper to see what's causing it. Are you trying to build a reputation or cultivate an identity for yourself—maybe as one of the best-dressed guys in school or as the one who always has the latest electronic gadget before anyone else does? Are you trying to keep up with your friends? Are you a sucker for cool TV commercials? Once you figure out the root of your problem, you can ask God to help you take care of it and develop a passion for things that really matter.

CHILDREN OF GOD

28And now, dear children, continue in him, so that when he appears we may be confident and unashamed before him at his coming.

29If you know that he is righteous, you know that everyone who does what is right has been born of him.

3 How great is the love the Father has lavished on us, that we should be called children of God! And that is what we are! The reason the world does not know us is that it did not know him. 2Dear friends, now we are children of God, and what we will be has not yet been made known. But we know that when he appears,[b] we shall be like him, for we shall see him as he is. 3Everyone who has this hope in him purifies himself, just as he is pure.

4Everyone who sins breaks the law; in fact, sin is lawlessness. 5But you know that he appeared so

---

NOW OR NEVER

1JN 2:17

Some things "pass away" a lot faster than others. Do you have any CDs in your collection that you'd be embarrassed to listen to now? Any computer software that became obsolete five minutes after you installed it? Why spend your whole life obsessed with stuff that doesn't last?

---

a 20 Some manuscripts *and you know all things*   b 2 Or *when it is made known* that he might take away our sins. And in him is no sin. [6]No one who lives in him keeps on sinning. No one who continues to sin has either seen him or known him.

[7]Dear children, do not let anyone lead you astray. He who does what is right is righteous, just as he is righteous. [8]He who does what is sinful is of the devil, because the devil has been sinning from the beginning. The reason the Son of God appeared was to destroy the devil's work. [9]No one who is born of God will continue to sin, because God's seed remains in him; he cannot go on sinning, because he has been born of God. [10]This is how we know who the children of God are and who the children of the devil are: Anyone who does not do what is right is not a child of God; nor is anyone who does not love his brother.

LOVE ONE ANOTHER

[11]This is the message you heard from the beginning: We should love one another. [12]Do not be like Cain, who belonged to the evil one and murdered his brother. And why did he murder him? Because his own actions were evil and his brother's were righteous. [13]Do not be surprised, my brothers, if the world hates you. [14]We know that we have passed from death to life, because we love our brothers. Anyone who does not love remains in death. [15]Anyone who hates his brother is a murderer, and you know that no murderer has eternal life in him.

[16]This is how we know what love is: Jesus Christ laid down his life for us. And we ought to lay down our lives for our brothers. [17]If anyone has material possessions and sees his brother in need but has no pity on him, how can the love of God be in him? [18]Dear children, let us not love with words or tongue but with actions and in truth. [19]This then is how we know that we belong to the truth, and how we set our hearts at rest in his presence [20]whenever our hearts condemn us. For God is greater than our hearts, and he knows everything.

[21]Dear friends, if our hearts do not condemn us, we have confidence before God [22]and receive from him anything we ask, because we obey his commands and do what pleases him. [23]And this is his command: to believe in the name of his Son, Jesus Christ, and to love one another as he commanded us. [24]Those who obey his commands live in him, and he in them. And this is how we know that he lives in us: We know it by the Spirit he gave us.

NOW OR NEVER

1 JN 3:18

What if someone gathered all of your friends and family members in a room and asked them, "How do you know that [Insert Your Name Here] loves you?" What evidence do you think they would give?

TEST THE SPIRITS

4 Dear friends, do not believe every spirit, but test the spirits to see whether they are from God, because many false prophets have gone out into the world. [2]This is how you can recognize the Spirit of God: Every spirit that acknowledges that Jesus Christ has come in the flesh is from God, [3]but every spirit that does not acknowledge Jesus is not from God. This is the spirit of the antichrist, which you have heard is coming and even now is already in the world.

[4]You, dear children, are from God and have overcome them, because the one who is in you is greater than the one who is in the world. [5]They are from the world and therefore speak from the viewpoint of the world, and the world listens to them. [6]We are from God, and whoever knows God listens to us; but whoever is not from God does not listen to us. This is how we recognize the Spirit[a] of truth and the spirit of falsehood.

GOD'S LOVE AND OURS

[7]Dear friends, let us love one another, for love comes from God. Everyone who loves has been born of God and knows God. [8]Whoever does not love does not know God, because God is love. [9]This is how God showed his love among us: He sent his one and only Son[b] into the world that we might live through him. [10]This is love: not that we loved God, but that he loved us and sent his Son as an atoning sacrifice for[c] our

---

[a] *6 Or spirit*   [b] *9 Or his only begotten Son*   [c] *10 Or as the one who would turn aside his wrath, taking away*

sins. [11]Dear friends, since God so loved us, we also ought to love one another. [12]No one has ever seen God; but if we love one another, God lives in us and his love is made complete in us.

[13]We know that we live in him and he in us, because he has given us of his Spirit. [14]And we have seen and testify that the Father has sent his Son to be the Savior of the world. [15]If anyone acknowledges that Jesus is the Son of God, God lives in him and he in God. [16]And so we know and rely on the love God has for us.

God is love. Whoever lives in love lives in God, and God in him. [17]In this way, love is made complete among us so that we will have confidence on the day of judgment, because in this world we are like him. [18]There is no fear in love. But perfect love drives out fear, because fear has to do with punishment. The one who fears is not made perfect in love.

[19]We love because he first loved us. [20]If anyone says, "I love God," yet hates his brother, he is a liar. For anyone who does not love his brother, whom he has seen, cannot love God, whom he has not seen. [21]And he has given us this command: Whoever loves God must also love his brother.

FAITH IN THE SON OF GOD

5 Everyone who believes that Jesus is the Christ is born of God, and everyone who loves the father loves his child as well. [2]This is how we know that we love the children of God: by loving God and carrying out his commands. [3]This is love for God: to obey his commands. And his commands are not burdensome, [4]for everyone born of God overcomes the world. This is the victory that has overcome the world, even our faith. [5]Who is it that overcomes the world? Only he who believes that Jesus is the Son of God.

[6]This is the one who came by water and blood—Jesus Christ. He did not come by water only, but by water and blood. And it is the Spirit who testifies, because the Spirit is the truth. [7]For there are three that testify: [8]the[a] Spirit, the water and the blood; and the three are in agreement. [9]We accept man's testimony, but God's testimony is greater because it is the testimony of God, which he has given about his Son. [10]Anyone who believes in the Son of God has this testimony in his heart. Anyone who does not believe God has made him out to be a liar, because he has not believed the testimony God has given about his Son. [11]And this is the testimony: God has given us eternal life, and this life is in his Son. [12]He who has the Son has life; he who does not have the Son of God does not have life.

CONCLUDING REMARKS

[13]I write these things to you who believe in the name of the Son of God so that you may know that you have eternal life. [14]This is the confidence we have in approaching God: that if we ask anything according to his will, he hears us. [15]And if we know that he hears us—whatever we ask—we know that we have what we asked of him.

[16]If anyone sees his brother commit a sin that does not lead to death, he should pray and God will give him life. I refer to those whose sin does not lead to death. There is a sin that leads to death. I am not saying that he should pray about that. [17]All wrongdoing is sin, and there is sin that does not lead to death.

[18]We know that anyone born of God does not continue to sin; the one who was born of God keeps him safe, and the evil one cannot harm him. [19]We know that we are children of God, and that the whole world is under the control of the evil one. [20]We know also that the Son of God has come and has given us understanding, so that we may know him who is true. And we are in him who is true—even in his Son Jesus Christ. He is the true God and eternal life.

[21]Dear children, keep yourselves from idols.

---

[a] 7,8 Late manuscripts of the Vulgate *testify in heaven: the Father, the Word and the Holy Spirit, and these three are one. [8]And there are three that testify on earth: the* (not found in any Greek manuscript before the fourteenth century)

battlelines

» The Big Question (Assurance)

Q: Hey, Jake, can I ask you a question?
A: You just did.

Q: Very funny. OK, here goes. If you could ask God any question at all, what would it be?
A: One question?

Q: Just one.
A: I think I'd probably ask him, "Am I really a Christian, and does that mean I'm really going to heaven when I die?"

Q: No kidding?
A: No kidding. I worry about that stuff more than you'd think.

Q: Why?
A: I don't know. Pretty sad, huh? I don't know why I don't know. Maybe it's because I mess up so often. Should I still be sinning so much if I really am a follower of Jesus?

» Beyond a Doubt

If you have doubts similar to Jake's, check out this cool passage from the apostle John:

"And this is the testimony: God has given us eternal life, and this life is in his Son. He who has the Son has life; he who does not have the Son of God does not have life. I write these things to you who believe in the name of the Son of God so that you may know that you have eternal life" (1 John 5:11–13).

Did you get that? God doesn't want us to wonder or wish or hope that we have eternal life. He wants us to *know*. And the way we know is this: If we have put our faith in Jesus, trusting him for salvation and deliverance from sin, then we have him in our lives. And if we have him, according to the passage, we have eternal life—guaranteed! Jesus and eternal life are a package deal.

Salvation is all about grace; there is nothing we can do to earn it. We can never be "good enough" (see Ephesians 2:8–9). The key is to keep trusting in Jesus and asking him to change you (see Philippians 1:6).

Learn more about salvation at www.RevolutionBible.com.

2 JOHN

Author
The apostle John

Audience
John wrote this brief letter to "the chosen lady and her children"

Date
Between A.D. 85 and 95

Setting
"The chosen lady and her children" may have been actual friends of the apostle John, or "the chosen lady" may have been a figure of speech for a church and "her children" were the members.

Verses to Remember
Anyone who runs ahead and does not continue in the teaching of Christ does not have God; whoever continues in the teaching has both the Father and the Son. If anyone comes to you and does not bring this teaching, do not take him into your house or welcome him (9–10).

Theme to Consider
Truth and love go hand-in-hand for believers. This letter is an encouragement to live in the truth, to love God and each other and to watch out for false teachers.

UNCHANGING TRUTH » Everyone deserves your love—the Bible is pretty clear about that. That doesn't mean everyone deserves your companionship, support or encouragement though. The truth is, there are people in this world you need to avoid. Obviously that includes people who pose a threat to your physical safety.

The same goes for people who pose a threat to your spiritual safety. If a stranger approaches you on campus and invites you to something that seems weird and sounds like it might be a cult, politely decline. If you see a non-Christian religious group collecting money for missions work, don't contribute.

If that seems a little harsh, look at the apostle John's words in 2 John 11. The believers John wrote to were apparently very generous. They had opened their homes on several occasions to traveling Christian teachers and had graciously supported their ministries. Unfortunately, some false teachers had helped themselves to the believers' generosity as well. John warned the believers to be careful about whom they were generous to. He wrote, "Anyone who welcomes [a false teacher] shares in his wicked work" (2 John 11).

LIFE LESSONS »

1   Anyone who teaches something about Jesus that disagrees with the Bible should be avoided (7).

2   Anyone who supports (directly or indirectly) the work of false teachers or religions shares in the blame for their wickedness (11).

To the chosen lady and her children, whom I love in the truth—and not I only, but also all who know the truth— 2 because of the truth, which lives in us and will be with us forever:

3 Grace, mercy and peace from God the Father and from Jesus Christ, the Father's Son, will be with us in truth and love.

4 It has given me great joy to find some of your children walking in the truth, just as the Father commanded us. 5 And now, dear lady, I am not writing you a new command but one we have had from the beginning. I ask that we love one another. 6 And this is love: that we walk in obedience to his commands. As you have heard from the beginning, his command is that you walk in love.

7 Many deceivers, who do not acknowledge Jesus Christ as coming in the flesh, have gone out into the world. Any such person is the deceiver and the antichrist. 8 Watch out that you do not lose what you have worked for, but that you may be rewarded fully. 9 Anyone who runs ahead and does not continue in the teaching of Christ does not have God; whoever continues in the teaching has both the Father and the Son. 10 If anyone comes to you and does not bring this teaching, do not take him into your house or welcome him. 11 Anyone who welcomes him shares in his wicked work.

12 I have much to write to you, but I do not want to use paper and ink. Instead, I hope to visit you and talk with you face to face, so that our joy may be complete.

13 The children of your chosen sister send their greetings.

>> live the adventure >> 2 Jn 9

Staying Committed to God

If you've been reading much of this Bible, you've probably read more than one passage in which God promises to be with you, to strengthen you, to protect you, to guide you, etc. These are all good things, right? After all, who doesn't want to be stronger, safer or smarter? Having the Creator of the universe on your side is a pretty good deal. But in this verse, John is giving people a pretty sharp warning. If we walk away from Christ's teachings, we walk away from God. God won't abandon you. The question is: Will *you* ever abandon God?

3 JOHN

Author
The apostle John

Audience
Gaius, a Christian who had welcomed traveling
Christian teachers into his home

Date
Between A.D. 85 and 95

Setting
Church leaders traveled from town to town starting
new churches. They depended on the hospitality of
Christians when they traveled.

Verse to Remember
Dear friend, you are faithful in what you are doing
for the brothers, even though they are strangers to
you (5).

Theme to Consider
One of the most effective ways to demonstrate
God's values and Jesus' love to our sisters and
brothers in Christ is to welcome them into our
homes and lives.

UNCHANGING TRUTH » During the early days of the church, people supported Christian workers by giving them a place to stay when they traveled, by feeding them and by providing them with basic necessities. Have you ever thought about how you can support the Christian workers around you?

Maybe you could arrange with your parents to have visiting missionaries from your church stay at your home, even if it means you have to sleep on the couch for a few days. Maybe you could start a collection among members of your youth group to help someone in your church pay off a medical bill. Maybe you could prepare and deliver a special dinner for an elderly person in your congregation. Maybe you could send your pastor a card, sharing how you've grown as a Christian and expressing your gratitude for his or her leadership.

These may seem like small gestures, but God can use them in incredible ways to help encourage his workers and make them feel appreciated.

LIFE LESSONS »

1 No one is really a stranger to us if he or she is a Christian; they are family (5).

2 Supporting and showing hospitality to other believers is part of the job description for Christians, just like preaching and teaching (8).

¹The elder,

To my dear friend Gaius, whom I love in the truth.

²Dear friend, I pray that you may enjoy good health and that all may go well with you, even as your soul is getting along well. ³It gave me great joy to have some brothers come and tell about your faithfulness to the truth and how you continue to walk in the truth. ⁴I have no greater joy than to hear that my children are walking in the truth.

⁵Dear friend, you are faithful in what you are doing for the brothers, even though they are strangers to you. ⁶They have told the church about your love. You will do well to send them on their way in a manner worthy of God. ⁷It was for the sake of the Name that they went out, receiving no help from the pagans. ⁸We ought therefore to show hospitality to such men so that we may work together for the truth.

⁹I wrote to the church, but Diotrephes, who loves to be first, will have nothing to do with us. ¹⁰So if I come, I will call attention to what he is doing, gossiping maliciously about us. Not satisfied with that, he refuses to welcome the brothers. He also stops those who want to do so and puts them out of the church.

¹¹Dear friend, do not imitate what is evil but what is good. Anyone who does what is good is from God. Anyone who does what is evil has not seen God. ¹²Demetrius is well spoken of by everyone—and even by the truth itself. We also speak well of him, and you know that our testimony is true.

¹³I have much to write you, but I do not want to do so with pen and ink. ¹⁴I hope to see you soon, and we will talk face to face.

Peace to you. The friends here send their greetings. Greet the friends there by name.

NOW OR NEVER

3JN 11

You know the old saying "Actions speak louder than words"? That's especially true for Christians. Whether you know it or not, people are watching you. They want to see if you practice what you preach and whether or not your faith is for real.

diotrephes

VERSUS

gaius

» Had a reputation for being self-absorbed and ambitious

» Known for being a malicious gossip

» Shunned worthy missionaries and harassed those who helped them

» The recipient of John's third letter

» John's friend and child in the faith

» A faithful servant of Jesus who showed love and hospitality to Christian missionaries

The Main Event

Diotrephes was a self-appointed dictator in one of the early churches. If you did things his way, you had no problems. But if you crossed him, challenged him or suggested a different way of doing things, heaven help you. Diotrephes liked calling all the shots, being in charge and getting all the credit. (And you can bet he was quick to blame someone else when things went wrong.) Chances are, he wasn't even a pastor—just someone with lots of money or lots of influence (or both).

One day some good-hearted, Jesus-loving missionaries showed up in town needing a place to stay and maybe a little financial help. They likely had some kind of letter of recommendation from the apostle John. Diotrephes read the letter with disdain and gave the traveling evangelists a look of disgust. "Forget it!" he told them. Then he told the congregation that he would personally deal with anyone who tried to help the missionaries. With that threat, he launched into a tirade against John, making all kinds of bogus accusations against "the disciple whom Jesus loved" (John 13:23).

This was no small insult. Diotrephes' inhospitality was a threat to the missionaries' well-being. There weren't too many hotels in those days, and what few there were generally catered to thieves and other dangerous people. That's why hospitality was so important in that culture—especially for itinerant Christian missionaries.

Still, some of the people in the church did as they were told and ignored the missionaries. But John told Gaius to buck the trend, to welcome the missionaries, to roll out the red carpet for them. John assured Gaius that his hospitality was a sign that God's love was alive and well in his heart . . . and that Diotrephes' inhospitality was a pretty good indicator that God was nowhere to be found in his life.

The Bible doesn't tell us what happened next. Perhaps Diotrephes tried to kick Gaius out of the church for "insubordination." Perhaps other church members shunned him. Whatever the case, it's almost certain there were fireworks of some kind.

Nevertheless John seemed confident that Gaius wouldn't cave in to the pressure. That's why we have the little Bible postcard called 3 John. It's a glowing tribute to a man who stood up to a bully, a guy whose life echoed the words of another believer spoken years earlier: "We must obey God rather than men!" (Acts 5:29).

The Outcome

What kind of man do you want to be? A steamroller like Diotrephes who tries to control others—someone who is feared by everyone but loved and respected by no one? A weak individual (like many of Gaius's peers) who lets others push him around and doesn't stand up to tyrants? Or a humble guy like Gaius—one who pursues God's agenda no matter what?

Gaius is the man's man in this story. The world desperately needs more guys like him. Will you be one?

Read more about Diotrephes and Gaius in 3 John 1–14 (page 1597).

« AT A GLANCE

Author
Jude, the brother of James and Jesus

Audience
Since the address at the beginning of the letter is so general, it may be that Jude intended for his letter to be circulated to several churches.

Date
About A.D. 65

Setting
Jude's original plan was to write about the subject of salvation. But because false teachers were infiltrating the church, Jude shifted the focus of his letter to one of warning.

Verses to Remember
Dear friends, although I was very eager to write to you about the salvation we share, I felt I had to write and urge you to contend for the faith that was once for all entrusted to the saints. For certain men whose condemnation was written about long ago have secretly slipped in among you. They are godless men, who change the grace of our God into a license for immorality and deny Jesus Christ our only Sovereign and Lord (3–4).

Theme to Consider
As believers, we have been given an awesome responsibility—to carry God's truth to others and defend it against false teachers. Nothing is more important!

UNCHANGING TRUTH » Sooner or later, you're going to be tempted to try to play God for a fool. That may sound extreme, but it's true. At some point in your Christian life, you're going to want to take advantage of God's forgiving nature. Maybe you've already been tempted. Maybe you've experienced thoughts that go something like this: *If God will forgive me for anything I do, I might as well run up the bill. After I've had my fun I can ask God for forgiveness and have everything wiped clean.*

That's a dangerous attitude for two reasons. First, it shows a serious disrespect for God. If you try to use his love and forgiveness against him by doing things you know he hates, you're pretty much spitting in his face. Second, it reveals a warped set of priorities on your part. If you've given your life to Jesus, your goal won't be to see how much you can get away with; it will be to honor him in everything you do.

The New Testament writer Jude knew people who were being tempted to take advantage of God's forgiveness. Fortunately for them—and us—God gave Jude some specific instructions for how to deal with this problem. If you want to find out what those instructions are, take a moment to read this brief book.

LIFE LESSONS »

1 Everyone will be judged for the things they do in this life (14–15).

2 No matter what happens around you, keep trusting and obeying God while you look forward to the future he has planned for you (20–21).

¹Jude, a servant of Jesus Christ and a brother of James,

To those who have been called, who are loved by God the Father and kept by[a] Jesus Christ:

²Mercy, peace and love be yours in abundance.

THE SIN AND DOOM OF GODLESS MEN

³Dear friends, although I was very eager to write to you about the salvation we share, I felt I had to write and urge you to contend for the faith that was once for all entrusted to the saints. ⁴For certain men whose condemnation was written about[b] long ago have secretly slipped in among you. They are godless men, who change the grace of our God into a license for immorality and deny Jesus Christ our only Sovereign and Lord.

NOW OR NEVER
JUDE 4

How would you feel if you told your best friend that he was free to use any of your possessions, and then he turned around and stole everything you own? God's eternal grace isn't a license to sin. It's a promise of forgiveness.

⁵Though you already know all this, I want to remind you that the Lord[c] delivered his people out of Egypt, but later destroyed those who did not believe. ⁶And the angels who did not keep their positions of authority but abandoned their own home—these he has kept in darkness, bound with everlasting chains for judgment on the great Day. ⁷In a similar way, Sodom and Gomorrah and the surrounding towns gave themselves up to sexual immorality and perversion. They serve as an example of those who suffer the punishment of eternal fire.

⁸In the very same way, these dreamers pollute their own bodies, reject authority and slander celestial beings. ⁹But even the archangel Michael, when he was disputing with the devil about the body of Moses, did not dare to bring a slanderous accusation against him, but said, "The Lord rebuke you!" ¹⁰Yet these men speak abusively against whatever they do not understand; and what things they do understand by instinct, like unreasoning animals—these are the very things that destroy them.

¹¹Woe to them! They have taken the way of Cain; they have rushed for profit into Balaam's error; they have been destroyed in Korah's rebellion.

¹²These men are blemishes at your love feasts, eating with you without the slightest qualm—shepherds who feed only themselves. They are clouds without rain, blown along by the wind; autumn trees, without fruit and uprooted—twice dead. ¹³They are wild waves of the sea, foaming up their shame; wandering stars, for whom blackest darkness has been reserved forever.

¹⁴Enoch, the seventh from Adam, prophesied about these men: "See, the Lord is coming with thousands upon thousands of his holy ones ¹⁵to judge everyone, and to convict all the ungodly of all the ungodly acts they have done in the ungodly way, and of all the harsh words ungodly sinners have spoken against him." ¹⁶These men are grumblers and faultfinders; they follow their own evil desires; they boast about themselves and flatter others for their own advantage.

A CALL TO PERSEVERE

¹⁷But, dear friends, remember what the apostles of our Lord Jesus Christ foretold. ¹⁸They said to you, "In the last times there

Showing Mercy to Other People

Do you know Christians who struggle with doubts about their faith? Do you know believers who seem particularly vulnerable to false teachings and religious beliefs that aren't compatible with Christianity? There are two ways to deal with people like that. The first option is to cop an attitude and treat them like they're something you scraped off the bottom of your shoe. The second option is to pray for them, encourage them and do whatever you can to support them. Guess which option God wants you to choose? (If you said the first one, go back and read Jude one more time.)

---

michael the archangel

VERSUS the devil

» An angelic "prince" (see Daniel 10:13,21)

» Guarded the Jews from the godless menace of Persia

» Battles Satan on behalf of God

» The rebellious fallen angel formerly known as Lucifer

» The lying, murdering accuser of God's people

» Also called Satan

The Main Event

The wildest wrestling match you've ever seen, the most violent boxing bout ever staged, the fiercest military conflict ever waged on Earth—they're nothing compared to the cosmic fighting going on in the spirit world.

This invisible war began with a revolt in heaven, probably before time and Earth existed. Satan, perhaps the highest of the created beings, became arrogant and sought to overthrow the rule of God and put himself in God's place (see Isaiah 14). He even led other angels in his rebellion (see 2 Peter 2:4; Jude 6). But his coup failed miserably. Why? Because Satan and God are not equals, and they're not opposites. God is the Creator of all. Satan is just a creature. Though the devil has immense power, God has all power and is the giver of everyone else's strength.

Following creation, the battleground shifted to Earth, where the devil turned his wrath on humanity (see Genesis 3; Job 1–2). Here he gained a foothold, becoming known as the "prince of this world" (John 14:30) and "the ruler of the kingdom of the air" (Ephesians 2:2).

When Jesus arrived, Satan pulled out all the stops in a last ditch effort for glory. He unleashed a barrage of temptations in a desperate attempt to defeat God's promised Messiah. He entered Judas's corrupt heart, using one of Jesus' own disciples to betray him to his death. But any hopes for devilish victory were crushed forever when Jesus leaped from the canvas of death and delivered a crippling blow to Satan. Ironic, isn't it? By having Jesus nailed to a tree, Satan was actually handing him the championship belt!

Thanks to Jesus' sacrifice and victory, the outcome of the war is certain; it's no longer in doubt. Currently the big headliners are that loser the devil—who is now more bitter than ever—and Michael the archangel of God. Michael's role apparently is to hold the devil in check. But get this: Even though Satan is already defeated, he's not powerless. That's why, when engaging in some serious combat with the devil, Michael did not accuse Satan directly but left it to God to rebuke him (see Jude 9). Even if you're the greatest angel in heaven, God's power is your only source of victory over evil.

The Outcome

The idea of spiritual warfare is not the product of some religious person's creative imagination. It's a reality spoken of throughout the Bible.

While it's not wise to get to the point where you see the devil behind every tree, it's also unwise to get blasé and forget his presence. The devil is real. He hates believers because we are children of God, and he hates God. He wants to wreck our lives and destroy us (see 1 Peter 5:8–9). He is a master liar (see John 8:44).

So don't get cocky and don't get careless. Put on God's armor and get in the fight. Remember, a desperate and wounded enemy is still a dangerous enemy!

will be scoffers who will follow their own ungodly desires." ¹⁹These are the men who divide you, who follow mere natural instincts and do not have the Spirit.

²⁰But you, dear friends, build yourselves up in your most holy faith and pray in the Holy Spirit. ²¹Keep yourselves in God's love as you wait for the mercy of our Lord Jesus Christ to bring you to eternal life.

²²Be merciful to those who doubt; ²³snatch others from the fire and save them; to others show mercy, mixed with fear—hating even the clothing stained by corrupted flesh.

DOXOLOGY

²⁴To him who is able to keep you from falling and to present you before his glorious presence without fault and with great joy— ²⁵to the only God our Savior be glory, majesty, power and authority, through Jesus Christ our Lord, before all ages, now and forevermore! Amen.

REVELATION

Author
The apostle John

Audience
Seven churches in the Roman province of Asia (in modern-day Turkey)

Date
About A.D. 95

Setting
John wrote the book of Revelation while exiled on the island of Patmos. Christians were being persecuted by the Romans for saying that Jesus is Lord.

Verses to Remember
"Only hold on to what you have until I come. To him who overcomes and does my will to the end, I will give authority over the nations" (2:25–26).

Theme to Consider
Revelation is a book of warning, but it is also a book of hope: God is in control; Christ's return and absolute victory are assured; and all who trust in him will be saved! "Amen. Come, Lord Jesus" (22:20).

UNCHANGING TRUTH »

What would you do if you opened the sports page tomorrow morning and saw the recap and final score of a game that won't be played until next week? Imagine knowing for sure which team was going to win and how the game would turn out. What would you do? Convince your parents to withdraw their life's savings, head to Vegas and bet everything on the winning team?

The book of Revelation is a little like a news report from the future. Thanks to God's revelation to the apostle John, we know how the battle of good versus evil is ultimately going to end. We may not be able to break the bank in Vegas with that knowledge, but we can use it as a great source of encouragement in our lives.

First of all, we can make sure that we're on the right team. Choosing good over evil isn't always an easy decision—especially when it seems as though the people who choose the wrong path often get further ahead, become more popular and enjoy themselves more than the people who choose good. In other words, in the battle between good and evil, evil seems to be winning the early rounds. But since we know how the fight ends, we can stay faithful to God and his plans for us—no matter what other people do.

Second, we've got to get actively involved in the battle. We can take a bold stand for God and for his will. In some cases, this involves making the right personal decision at the right time . . . like choosing not to rent a hotel room on prom night. In other cases, it may mean sharing an unpopular opinion about a controversial topic like evolution or abortion. Or it could mean going against the crowd and choosing not to make fun of a quirky kid at school. Whatever the case, you can expect plenty of opportunities to show the world whose side you're on in the ultimate battle of good versus evil.

LIFE LESSONS »

1 Jesus expects us to be active, not passive, in our faith (3:15–16).

2 Any rebellion against God will end badly for the person doing the rebelling (19:11–21).

3 Just as God punishes evil people for their deeds, he rewards his people for their faithfulness (20:4).

4 Jesus is coming again for his people. In the meantime, our job is simply to remain faithful to him (22:20–21).

PROLOGUE

1 The revelation of Jesus Christ, which God gave him to show his servants what must soon take place. He made it known by sending his angel to his servant John, 2who testifies to everything he saw—that is, the word of God and the testimony of Jesus Christ. 3Blessed is the one who reads the words of this prophecy, and blessed are those who hear it and take to heart what is written in it, because the time is near.

GREETINGS AND DOXOLOGY

4John,

To the seven churches in the province of Asia:

Grace and peace to you from him who is, and who was, and who is to come, and from the seven spirits[a] before his throne, 5and from Jesus Christ, who is the faithful witness, the firstborn from the dead, and the ruler of the kings of the earth.

To him who loves us and has freed us from our sins by his blood, 6and has made us to be a kingdom and priests to serve his God and Father—to him be glory and power for ever and ever! Amen.

> 7Look, he is coming with the clouds,
>   and every eye will see him,
> even those who pierced him;
>   and all the peoples of the earth will mourn because of him.
> So shall it be! Amen.

8"I am the Alpha and the Omega," says the Lord God, "who is, and who was, and who is to come, the Almighty."

ONE LIKE A SON OF MAN

9I, John, your brother and companion in the suffering and kingdom and patient endurance that are ours in Jesus, was on the island of Patmos because of the word of God and the testimony of Jesus. 10On the Lord's Day I was in the Spirit, and I heard behind me a loud voice like a trumpet, 11which said: "Write on a scroll what you see and send it to the seven churches: to Ephesus, Smyrna, Pergamum, Thyatira, Sardis, Philadelphia and Laodicea."

12I turned around to see the voice that was speaking to me. And when I turned I saw seven golden lampstands, 13and among the lampstands was someone "like a son of man,"[b] dressed in a robe reaching down to his feet and with a golden sash around his chest. 14His head and hair were white like wool, as white as snow, and his eyes were like blazing fire. 15His feet were like bronze glowing in a furnace, and his voice was like the sound of rushing waters. 16In his right hand he held seven stars, and out of his mouth came a sharp double-edged sword. His face was like the sun shining in all its brilliance.

17When I saw him, I fell at his feet as though dead. Then he placed his right hand on me and said: "Do not be afraid. I am the First and the Last. 18I am the Living One; I was dead, and behold I am alive for ever and ever! And I hold the keys of death and Hades.

19"Write, therefore, what you have seen, what is now and what will take place later. 20The mystery of the seven stars that you saw in my right hand and of the seven golden lampstands is this: The seven stars are the angels[c] of the seven churches, and the seven lampstands are the seven churches.

TO THE CHURCH IN EPHESUS

2 "To the angel[d] of the church in Ephesus write:

These are the words of him who holds the seven stars in his right hand and walks among the seven golden lampstands: 2I know your deeds, your hard work and your perseverance. I know that you cannot tolerate wicked men, that you have tested those who claim to be apostles but are not, and have found them false. 3You have persevered and have endured hardships for my name, and have not grown weary.

4Yet I hold this against you: You have forsaken your first love. 5Remember the height from

---

a 4 Or *the sevenfold Spirit*   b 13 Daniel 7:13   c 20 Or *messengers*   d 1 Or *messenger*; also in verses 8, 12 and 18 which you have fallen! Repent and do the things you did at first. If you do not repent, I will come to you and remove your lampstand from its place. 6But you have this in your favor: You hate the practices of the Nicolaitans, which I also hate.

7He who has an ear, let him hear what the Spirit says to the churches. To him who overcomes, I will give the right to eat from the tree of life, which is in the paradise of God.

TO THE CHURCH IN SMYRNA

8"To the angel of the church in Smyrna write:

These are the words of him who is the First and the Last, who died and came to life again. 9I know your afflictions and your poverty—yet you are rich! I know the slander of those who say they are Jews and are not, but are a synagogue of Satan. 10Do not be afraid of what you are about to suffer. I tell you, the devil will put some of you in prison to test you, and you will suffer persecution for ten days. Be faithful, even to the point of death, and I will give you the crown of life.

11He who has an ear, let him hear what the Spirit says to the churches. He who overcomes will not be hurt at all by the second death.

TO THE CHURCH IN PERGAMUM

12"To the angel of the church in Pergamum write:

These are the words of him who has the sharp, double-edged sword. 13I know where you live—where Satan has his throne. Yet you remain true to my name. You did not renounce your faith in me, even in the days of Antipas, my faithful witness, who was put to death in your city—where Satan lives.

14Nevertheless, I have a few things against you: You have people there who hold to the teaching of Balaam, who taught Balak to entice the Israelites to sin by eating food sacrificed to idols and by committing sexual immorality. 15Likewise you also have those who hold to the teaching of the Nicolaitans. 16Repent therefore! Otherwise, I will soon come to you and will fight against them with the sword of my mouth.

17He who has an ear, let him hear what the Spirit says to the churches. To him who overcomes, I will give some of the hidden manna. I will also give him a white stone with a new name written on it, known only to him who receives it.

TO THE CHURCH IN THYATIRA

18"To the angel of the church in Thyatira write:

These are the words of the Son of God, whose eyes are like blazing fire and whose feet are like burnished bronze. 19I know your deeds, your love and faith, your service and perseverance, and that you are now doing more than you did at first.

20Nevertheless, I have this against you: You tolerate that woman Jezebel, who calls herself a prophetess. By her teaching she misleads my servants into sexual immorality and the eating of food sacrificed to idols. 21I have given her time to repent of her immorality, but she is unwilling. 22So I will cast her on a bed of suffering, and I will make those who commit adultery with her suffer intensely, unless they repent of her ways. 23I will strike her children dead. Then all the churches will know that I am he who searches hearts and minds, and I will repay each of you according to your deeds. 24Now I say to the rest of you in Thyatira, to you who do not hold to her teaching and have not learned Satan's so-called deep secrets (I will not impose any other burden on you): 25Only hold on to what you have until I come.

Loving Other Believers

If you've ever been a fan of a music group, you've probably heard the term "chemistry." People use it to talk about how well members of a group relate to one another and work together. There's another word for chemistry: *love*. Think of a group that you're a part of—any group. How different would that group be if each person really cared about every other person—that is, if everybody was looking out for each other, serving and sacrificing for one another? That's the kind of living Jesus commands of his people—the first love to which he calls us.

»» live the adventure »» Rev 2:4-5

²⁶To him who overcomes and does my will to the end, I will give authority over the nations—

²⁷'He will rule them with an iron scepter;
he will dash them to pieces like pottery'ᵃ—

just as I have received authority from my Father. ²⁸I will also give him the morning star. ²⁹He who has an ear, let him hear what the Spirit says to the churches.

TO THE CHURCH IN SARDIS

3 "To the angelᵇ of the church in Sardis write:

These are the words of him who holds the seven spiritsᶜ of God and the seven stars. I know your deeds; you have a reputation of being alive, but you are dead. ²Wake up! Strengthen what remains and is about to die, for I have not found your deeds complete in the sight of my God. ³Remember, therefore, what you have received and heard; obey it, and repent. But if you do not wake up, I will come like a thief, and you will not know at what time I will come to you.

REV 3:1-3

challenge notes
To: my_son

heavenly_father: you can fool some of the people some of the time, but you can't fool me any of the time. I know what you do because of your love for me, and I know what you do because you want to impress others. give your heart to me, and let me change your mindset and your passions.

⁴Yet you have a few people in Sardis who have not soiled their clothes. They will walk with me, dressed in white, for they are worthy. ⁵He who overcomes will, like them, be dressed in white. I will never blot out his name from the book of life, but will acknowledge his name before my Father and his angels. ⁶He who has an ear, let him hear what the Spirit says to the churches.

TO THE CHURCH IN PHILADELPHIA

⁷"To the angel of the church in Philadelphia write:

These are the words of him who is holy and true, who holds the key of David. What he opens no one can shut, and what he shuts no one can open. ⁸I know your deeds. See, I have placed before you an open door that no one can shut. I know that you have little strength, yet you have kept my word and have not denied my name. ⁹I will make those who are of the synagogue of Satan, who claim to be Jews though they are not, but are liars—I will make them come and fall down at your feet and acknowledge that I have loved you. ¹⁰Since you have kept my command to endure patiently, I will also keep you from the hour of trial that is going to come upon the whole world to test those who live on the earth.

¹¹I am coming soon. Hold on to what you have, so that no one will take your crown. ¹²Him who overcomes I will make a pillar in the temple of my God. Never again will he leave it. I will write on him the name of my God and the name of the city of my God, the new Jerusalem, which is coming down out of heaven from my God; and I will also write on him my new name. ¹³He who has an ear, let him hear what the Spirit says to the churches.

TO THE CHURCH IN LAODICEA

¹⁴"To the angel of the church in Laodicea write:

These are the words of the Amen, the faithful and true witness, the ruler of God's creation. ¹⁵I know your deeds, that you are neither cold nor hot. I wish you were either one or the other! ¹⁶So, because you are lukewarm—neither hot nor cold—I am about to spit you out of my mouth. ¹⁷You say, 'I am rich; I have acquired wealth and do not need a thing.' But you do not realize that you are wretched, pitiful, poor, blind and naked. ¹⁸I counsel you to buy from me gold

---

ᵃ 27 Psalm 2:9   ᵇ 1 Or messenger; also in verses 7 and 14   ᶜ 1 Or the sevenfold Spirit refined in the fire, so you can become rich; and white clothes to wear, so you can cover your shameful nakedness; and salve to put on your eyes, so you can see.

¹⁹Those whom I love I rebuke and discipline. So be earnest, and repent. ²⁰Here I am! I stand at the door and knock. If anyone hears my voice and opens the door, I will come in and eat with him, and he with me.

²¹To him who overcomes, I will give the right to sit with me on my throne, just as I overcame and sat down with my Father on his throne. ²²He who has an ear, let him hear what the Spirit says to the churches."

THE THRONE IN HEAVEN

4 After this I looked, and there before me was a door standing open in heaven. And the voice I had first heard speaking to me like a trumpet said, "Come up here, and I will show you what must take place after this." ²At once I was in the Spirit, and there before me was a throne in heaven with someone sitting on it. ³And the one who sat there had the appearance of jasper and carnelian. A rainbow, resembling an emerald, encircled the throne. ⁴Surrounding the throne were twenty-four other thrones, and seated on them were twenty-four elders. They were dressed in white and had crowns of gold on their heads. ⁵From the throne came flashes of lightning, rumblings and peals of thunder. Before the throne, seven lamps were blazing. These are the seven spirits[a] of God. ⁶Also before the throne there was what looked like a sea of glass, clear as crystal.

In the center, around the throne, were four living creatures, and they were covered with eyes, in front and in back. ⁷The first living creature was like a lion, the second was like an ox, the third had a face like a man, the fourth was like a flying eagle. ⁸Each of the four living creatures had six wings and was covered with eyes all around, even under his wings. Day and night they never stop saying:

"Holy, holy, holy
is the Lord God Almighty,
who was, and is, and is to come."

⁹Whenever the living creatures give glory, honor and thanks to him who sits on the throne and who lives for ever and ever, ¹⁰the twenty-four elders fall down before him who sits on the throne, and worship him who lives for ever and ever. They lay their crowns before the throne and say:

¹¹ "You are worthy, our Lord and God,
to receive glory and honor and
power,
for you created all things,
and by your will they were created
and have their being."

Developing Extreme Faith

Rev 3:14–22 »» live the adventure »»

Jesus expects us to take our faithfulness and obedience to him to the extreme. "Lukewarm" Christianity disgusts him. He wants us to break out of our comfort zone and get radical in living for him. If your Christian faith isn't making a major difference in your life—and in the lives of the people around you—it's time to shake things up.

NOW OR NEVER

REV 4:1

Horoscopes. Psychic hotlines. Tarot cards. Palm reading. Tea leaves. Magic Eight Ball. Ouija Board. Some people will try anything to figure out what the future holds. As far as God is concerned, he's the only One who can show anyone what's in store down the road.

ᵃ 5 Or the sevenfold Spirit

THE SCROLL AND THE LAMB

5 Then I saw in the right hand of him who sat on the throne a scroll with writing on both sides and sealed with seven seals. ²And I saw a mighty angel proclaiming in a loud voice, "Who is worthy to break the seals and open the scroll?" ³But no one in heaven or on earth or under the earth could open the scroll or even look inside it. ⁴I wept and wept because no one was found who was worthy to open the scroll or look inside. ⁵Then one of the elders said to me, "Do not weep! See, the Lion of the tribe of Judah, the Root of David, has triumphed. He is able to open the scroll and its seven seals."

⁶Then I saw a Lamb, looking as if it had been slain, standing in the center of the throne, encircled by the four living creatures and the elders. He had seven horns and seven eyes, which are the seven spirits ᵃ of God sent out into all the earth. ⁷He came and took the scroll from the right hand of him who sat on the throne. ⁸And when he had taken it, the four living creatures and the twenty-four elders fell down before the Lamb. Each one had a harp and they were holding golden bowls full of incense, which are the prayers of the saints. ⁹And they sang a new song:

NOW OR NEVER

REV 4:6

John's description of heaven is difficult to understand, but it gives us a sense of how awesome a place it really is. The most amazing part of it, though, is the One who sits on the throne, whose brilliance is compared to the light that reflects from precious stones. What could be more incredible?

> "You are worthy to take the scroll
> and to open its seals,
> because you were slain,
> and with your blood you purchased men for God
> from every tribe and language and people and nation.
> ¹⁰You have made them to be a kingdom and priests to serve our God,
> and they will reign on the earth."

¹¹Then I looked and heard the voice of many angels, numbering thousands upon thousands, and ten thousand times ten thousand. They encircled the throne and the living creatures and the elders. ¹²In a loud voice they sang:

> "Worthy is the Lamb, who was slain,
> to receive power and wealth and wisdom and strength
> and honor and glory and praise!"

¹³Then I heard every creature in heaven and on earth and under the earth and on the sea, and all that is in them, singing:

> "To him who sits on the throne and to the Lamb
> be praise and honor and glory and power,
> for ever and ever!"

¹⁴The four living creatures said, "Amen," and the elders fell down and worshiped.

THE SEALS

6 I watched as the Lamb opened the first of the seven seals. Then I heard one of the four living creatures say in a voice like thunder, "Come!" ²I looked, and there before me was a white horse! Its rider held a bow, and he was given a crown, and he rode out as a conqueror bent on conquest.

³When the Lamb opened the second seal, I heard the second living creature say, "Come!" ⁴Then another horse came out, a fiery red one. Its rider was given power to take peace from the earth and to make men slay each other. To him was given a large sword.

⁵When the Lamb opened the third seal, I heard the third living creature say, "Come!" I looked, and there before me was a black horse! Its rider was holding a pair of scales in his hand. ⁶Then I heard what

---

ᵃ 6 Or *the sevenfold Spirit*

sounded like a voice among the four living creatures, saying, "A quart[a] of wheat for a day's wages,[b] and three quarts of barley for a day's wages,[b] and do not damage the oil and the wine!"

[7]When the Lamb opened the fourth seal, I heard the voice of the fourth living creature say, "Come!" [8]I looked, and there before me was a pale horse! Its rider was named Death, and Hades was following close behind him. They were given power over a fourth of the earth to kill by sword, famine and plague, and by the wild beasts of the earth.

[9]When he opened the fifth seal, I saw under the altar the souls of those who had been slain because of the word of God and the testimony they had maintained. [10]They called out in a loud voice, "How long, Sovereign Lord, holy and true, until you judge the inhabitants of the earth and avenge our blood?" [11]Then each of them was given a white robe, and they were told to wait a little longer, until the number of their fellow servants and brothers who were to be killed as they had been was completed.

[12]I watched as he opened the sixth seal. There was a great earthquake. The sun turned black like sackcloth made of goat hair, the whole moon turned blood red, [13]and the stars in the sky fell to earth, as late figs drop from a fig tree when shaken by a strong wind. [14]The sky receded like a scroll, rolling up, and every mountain and island was removed from its place.

[15]Then the kings of the earth, the princes, the generals, the rich, the mighty, and every slave and every free man hid in caves and among the rocks of the mountains. [16]They called to the mountains and the rocks, "Fall on us and hide us from the face of him who sits on the throne and from the wrath of the Lamb! [17]For the great day of their wrath has come, and who can stand?"

NOW OR NEVER

REV 6:16–17

People often ask, "When is God going to do something about all the evil in the world?" The thing about God's judgment, though, is that when it does come, a lot of people are sorry they asked for it. God doesn't mess around when it comes to judgment and his eternal glory!

1 44,000 SEALED

7 After this I saw four angels standing at the four corners of the earth, holding back the four winds of the earth to prevent any wind from blowing on the land or on the sea or on any tree. [2]Then I saw another angel coming up from the east, having the seal of the living God. He called out in a loud voice to the four angels who had been given power to harm the land and the sea: [3]"Do not harm the land or the sea or the trees until we put a seal on the foreheads of the servants of our God." [4]Then I heard the number of those who were sealed: 144,000 from all the tribes of Israel.

[5]From the tribe of Judah 12,000 were sealed,
  from the tribe of Reuben 12,000,
  from the tribe of Gad 12,000,
  [6]from the tribe of Asher 12,000,
  from the tribe of Naphtali 12,000,
  from the tribe of Manasseh 12,000,
  [7]from the tribe of Simeon 12,000,
  from the tribe of Levi 12,000,
  from the tribe of Issachar 12,000,
  [8]from the tribe of Zebulun 12,000,
  from the tribe of Joseph 12,000,
  from the tribe of Benjamin 12,000.

NOW OR NEVER

REV 7:1–4

God never loses track of his people, even in the midst of his judgment. No matter how bad things get in this world, God will always be with us . . . or he'll bring us to himself in heaven. Either way, we have nothing to fear.

THE GREAT MULTITUDE IN WHITE ROBES

[9]After this I looked and there before me was a great multitude that no one could count, from every nation, tribe, people and language, standing before the throne and in front of the Lamb. They were wearing white robes and were holding palm branches in their hands. [10]And they cried out in a loud voice:

---

[a] 6 Greek *a choinix* (probably about a liter) [b] 6 Greek *a denarius*

battlelines

» They're All the Same (Prejudice)

Q: What do you mean they're all the same?
A: Look, I'm not prejudiced. But stereotypes exist for a reason. Most of the Mexican girls at this school have the same three characteristics. They can't speak English, they have no money, and they sleep around. I'll bet you ten bucks this girl is like that.

Q: OK, I'm embarrassed for you. You sound like a Neanderthal. How can you say you're not prejudiced?
A: Because to be prejudiced is to pre-judge. I'm post-judging. I've seen and evaluated Mexican girls. Maria is a Mexican girl. Therefore, I can predict with reasonable certainty what she's like. That's called discernment.

Q: All right, how about this: When you get your driver's license, you'll pay almost twice as much for car insurance as your sister does now.
A: Why?

Q: Because guys get behind the wheel of a car or truck and turn into idiots. We drive faster, and we have more wrecks. That's why we have to pay more for insurance.
A: But that's totally not fair. I'm not reckless! Why should I get lumped in with all the bad drivers?

Q: Bingo! That's the same question Maria would ask you if she were standing here.
A: OK, OK, so maybe I assumed a little. But you can't argue with what I said about the Mexican girls here. Am I right or am I right?

Q: First of all, no—you're not right. I think your stereotypes are shallow and uninformed. Second, why is it your goal to be right about stereotyping other people?
A: I just think if the shoe fits . . . well, you know the rest.

Q: You're hopeless.

» You're Not the Same

The opening chapters of the Bible make it clear that God created people—*all* people—in his image. Each of us has great value because of that fact. We also have immeasurable worth in God's eyes because each person on the planet is unique—a true, one-of-a-kind original. The fact that you're a guy, have black hair or read comic books does not mean you're automatically like everyone else who shares those characteristics. That's why stereotypes can be so dangerous and so . . . wrong.

The final chapters of the Bible make it clear that God loves people—all people. When John was granted a sneak peek into heaven, he reported, "After this I looked and there before me was a great multitude that no one could count, from every nation, tribe, people and language, standing before the throne and in front of the Lamb" (Revelation 7:9).

Memo to Pete and all prejudiced people everywhere: God doesn't share your racist views. He's an equal opportunity Creator and Savior (see Luke 24:47)!

Read more about racism at www.RevolutionBible.com.

> "Salvation belongs to our God,
> who sits on the throne,
> and to the Lamb."

11 All the angels were standing around the throne and around the elders and the four living creatures. They fell down on their faces before the throne and worshiped God, 12 saying:

> "Amen!
> Praise and glory
> and wisdom and thanks and honor
> and power and strength
> be to our God for ever and ever.
> Amen!"

13 Then one of the elders asked me, "These in white robes—who are they, and where did they come from?"

14 I answered, "Sir, you know."

And he said, "These are they who have come out of the great tribulation; they have washed their robes and made them white in the blood of the Lamb. 15 Therefore,

> "they are before the throne of God
> and serve him day and night in his temple;
> and he who sits on the throne will spread his tent over them.
> 16 Never again will they hunger;
> never again will they thirst.
> The sun will not beat upon them,
> nor any scorching heat.
> 17 For the Lamb at the center of the throne will be their shepherd;
> he will lead them to springs of living water.
> And God will wipe away every tear from their eyes."

THE SEVENTH SEAL AND THE GOLDEN CENSER

8 When he opened the seventh seal, there was silence in heaven for about half an hour.

2 And I saw the seven angels who stand before God, and to them were given seven trumpets.

3 Another angel, who had a golden censer, came and stood at the altar. He was given much incense to offer, with the prayers of all the saints, on the golden altar before the throne. 4 The smoke of the incense, together with the prayers of the saints, went up before God from the angel's hand. 5 Then the angel took the censer, filled it with fire from the altar, and hurled it on the earth; and there came peals of thunder, rumblings, flashes of lightning and an earthquake.

THE TRUMPETS

6 Then the seven angels who had the seven trumpets prepared to sound them.

7 The first angel sounded his trumpet, and there came hail and fire mixed with blood, and it was hurled down upon the earth. A third of the earth was burned up, a third of the trees were burned up, and all the green grass was burned up.

8 The second angel sounded his trumpet, and something like a huge mountain, all ablaze, was

---

» live the adventure » Rev 7:9–17

Understanding Worship

If worshiping the Lord doesn't seem like an exciting way to spend eternity, it's because you don't understand what *real* worship can be like. Think of the most exciting sporting event you've ever seen in person. Now think of the most exciting moment in that game—the play that made you jump to your feet and start screaming like a maniac. Think about how exciting it was to experience that moment with hundreds (or thousands) of people who appreciated it as much as you did. That's just a small taste of what worship in heaven will be like. Imagine what your reaction will be when you finally see for yourself just how awesome God really is!

thrown into the sea. A third of the sea turned into blood, ⁹a third of the living creatures in the sea died, and a third of the ships were destroyed.

¹⁰The third angel sounded his trumpet, and a great star, blazing like a torch, fell from the sky on a third of the rivers and on the springs of water— ¹¹the name of the star is Wormwood.ᵃ A third of the waters turned bitter, and many people died from the waters that had become bitter.

¹²The fourth angel sounded his trumpet, and a third of the sun was struck, a third of the moon, and a third of the stars, so that a third of them turned dark. A third of the day was without light, and also a third of the night.

¹³As I watched, I heard an eagle that was flying in midair call out in a loud voice: "Woe! Woe! Woe to the inhabitants of the earth, because of the trumpet blasts about to be sounded by the other three angels!"

9
The fifth angel sounded his trumpet, and I saw a star that had fallen from the sky to the earth. The star was given the key to the shaft of the Abyss. ²When he opened the Abyss, smoke rose from it like the smoke from a gigantic furnace. The sun and sky were darkened by the smoke from the Abyss. ³And out of the smoke locusts came down upon the earth and were given power like that of scorpions of the earth. ⁴They were told not to harm the grass of the earth or any plant or tree, but only those people who did not have the seal of God on their foreheads. ⁵They were not given power to kill them, but only to torture them for five months. And the agony they suffered was like that of the sting of a scorpion when it strikes a man. ⁶During those days men will seek death, but will not find it; they will long to die, but death will elude them.

⁷The locusts looked like horses prepared for battle. On their heads they wore something like crowns of gold, and their faces resembled human faces. ⁸Their hair was like women's hair, and their teeth were like lions' teeth. ⁹They had breastplates like breastplates of iron, and the sound of their wings was like the thundering of many horses and chariots rushing into battle. ¹⁰They had tails and stings like scorpions, and in their tails they had power to torment people for five months. ¹¹They had as king over them the angel of the Abyss, whose name in Hebrew is Abaddon, and in Greek, Apollyon.ᵇ

¹²The first woe is past; two other woes are yet to come.

¹³The sixth angel sounded his trumpet, and I heard a voice coming from the hornsᶜ of the golden altar that is before God. ¹⁴It said to the sixth angel who had the trumpet, "Release the four angels who are bound at the great river Euphrates." ¹⁵And the four angels who had been kept ready for this very hour and day and month and year were released to kill a third of mankind. ¹⁶The number of the mounted troops was two hundred million. I heard their number.

¹⁷The horses and riders I saw in my vision looked like this: Their breastplates were fiery red, dark blue, and yellow as sulfur. The heads of the horses resembled the heads of lions, and out of their mouths came fire, smoke and sulfur. ¹⁸A third of mankind was killed by the three plagues of fire, smoke and sulfur that came out of their mouths. ¹⁹The power of the horses was in their mouths and in their tails; for their tails were like snakes, having heads with which they inflict injury.

²⁰The rest of mankind that were not killed by these plagues still did not repent of the work of their hands; they did not stop worshiping demons, and idols of gold, silver, bronze, stone and wood—idols that cannot see or hear or walk. ²¹Nor did they repent of their murders, their magic arts, their sexual immorality or their thefts.

THE ANGEL AND THE LITTLE SCROLL

10
Then I saw another mighty angel coming down from heaven. He was robed in a cloud, with a rainbow above his head; his face was like the sun, and his legs were like fiery pillars. ²He was holding a little scroll, which lay open in his hand. He planted his right foot on the sea and his left foot on the land, ³and he gave a loud shout like the roar of a lion. When he shouted, the voices of the seven thunders spoke. ⁴And when the seven thunders spoke, I was about to write; but I heard a voice from heaven say, "Seal up what the seven thunders have said and do not write it down."

⁵Then the angel I had seen standing on the sea and on the land raised his right hand to heaven. ⁶And he swore by him who lives for ever and ever, who created the heavens and all that is in them, the earth and all that is in it, and the sea and all that is in it, and said, "There will be no more delay! ⁷But

---

ᵃ *11* That is, Bitterness   ᵇ *11 Abaddon* and *Apollyon* mean *Destroyer.*   ᶜ *13* That is, projections in the days when the seventh angel is about to sound his trumpet, the mystery of God will be accomplished, just as he announced to his servants the prophets."

⁸Then the voice that I had heard from heaven spoke to me once more: "Go, take the scroll that lies open in the hand of the angel who is standing on the sea and on the land."

⁹So I went to the angel and asked him to give me the little scroll. He said to me, "Take it and eat it. It will turn your stomach sour, but in your mouth it will be as sweet as honey." ¹⁰I took the little scroll from the angel's hand and ate it. It tasted as sweet as honey in my mouth, but when I had eaten it, my stomach turned sour. ¹¹Then I was told, "You must prophesy again about many peoples, nations, languages and kings."

THE TWO WITNESSES

11 I was given a reed like a measuring rod and was told, "Go and measure the temple of God and the altar, and count the worshipers there. ²But exclude the outer court; do not measure it, because it has been given to the Gentiles. They will trample on the holy city for 42 months. ³And I will give power to my two witnesses, and they will prophesy for 1,260 days, clothed in sackcloth." ⁴These are the two olive trees and the two lampstands that stand before the Lord of the earth. ⁵If anyone tries to harm them, fire comes from their mouths and devours their enemies. This is how anyone who wants to harm them must die. ⁶These men have power to shut up the sky so that it will not rain during the time they are prophesying; and they have power to turn the waters into blood and to strike the earth with every kind of plague as often as they want.

⁷Now when they have finished their testimony, the beast that comes up from the Abyss will attack them, and overpower and kill them. ⁸Their bodies will lie in the street of the great city, which is figuratively called Sodom and Egypt, where also their Lord was crucified. ⁹For three and a half days men from every people, tribe, language and nation will gaze on their bodies and refuse them burial. ¹⁰The inhabitants of the earth will gloat over them and will celebrate by sending each other gifts, because these two prophets had tormented those who live on the earth.

¹¹But after the three and a half days a breath of life from God entered them, and they stood on their feet, and terror struck those who saw them. ¹²Then they heard a loud voice from heaven saying to them, "Come up here." And they went up to heaven in a cloud, while their enemies looked on.

¹³At that very hour there was a severe earthquake and a tenth of the city collapsed. Seven thousand people were killed in the earthquake, and the survivors were terrified and gave glory to the God of heaven.

¹⁴The second woe has passed; the third woe is coming soon.

THE SEVENTH TRUMPET

¹⁵The seventh angel sounded his trumpet, and there were loud voices in heaven, which said:

"The kingdom of the world has become the kingdom of our Lord and of his
Christ,
and he will reign for ever and ever."

¹⁶And the twenty-four elders, who were seated on their thrones before God, fell on their faces and worshiped God, ¹⁷saying:

"We give thanks to you, Lord God Almighty,
the One who is and who was,
because you have taken your great power
and have begun to reign.
¹⁸The nations were angry;
and your wrath has come.
The time has come for judging the dead,
and for rewarding your servants the prophets
and your saints and those who reverence your name,
both small and great—
and for destroying those who destroy the earth."

[19] Then God's temple in heaven was opened, and within his temple was seen the ark of his covenant. And there came flashes of lightning, rumblings, peals of thunder, an earthquake and a great hailstorm.

THE WOMAN AND THE DRAGON

12 A great and wondrous sign appeared in heaven: a woman clothed with the sun, with the moon under her feet and a crown of twelve stars on her head. [2] She was pregnant and cried out in pain as she was about to give birth. [3] Then another sign appeared in heaven: an enormous red dragon with seven heads and ten horns and seven crowns on his heads. [4] His tail swept a third of the stars out of the sky and flung them to the earth. The dragon stood in front of the woman who was about to give birth, so that he might devour her child the moment it was born. [5] She gave birth to a son, a male child, who will rule all the nations with an iron scepter. And her child was snatched up to God and to his throne. [6] The woman fled into the desert to a place prepared for her by God, where she might be taken care of for 1,260 days.

[7] And there was war in heaven. Michael and his angels fought against the dragon, and the dragon and his angels fought back. [8] But he was not strong enough, and they lost their place in heaven. [9] The great dragon was hurled down—that ancient serpent called the devil, or Satan, who leads the whole world astray. He was hurled to the earth, and his angels with him.

[10] Then I heard a loud voice in heaven say:

"Now have come the salvation and the power and the kingdom of our God,
        and the authority of his Christ.
For the accuser of our brothers,
        who accuses them before our God day and night,
        has been hurled down.
[11] They overcame him
        by the blood of the Lamb
        and by the word of their testimony;
they did not love their lives so much
        as to shrink from death.
[12] Therefore rejoice, you heavens
        and you who dwell in them!
But woe to the earth and the sea,
        because the devil has gone down to you!
He is filled with fury,
        because he knows that his time is short."

[13] When the dragon saw that he had been hurled to the earth, he pursued the woman who had given birth to the male child. [14] The woman was given the two wings of a great eagle, so that she might fly to the place prepared for her in the desert, where she would be taken care of for a time, times and half a time, out of the serpent's reach. [15] Then from his mouth the serpent spewed water like a river, to overtake the woman and sweep her away with the torrent. [16] But the earth helped the woman by opening its mouth and swallowing the river that the dragon had spewed out of his mouth. [17] Then the dragon was enraged at the woman and went off to make war against the rest of her offspring—those who obey God's commandments and hold to the testimony of Jesus. [1] And the dragon[a] stood on the shore of the sea.

13

THE BEAST OUT OF THE SEA

And I saw a beast coming out of the sea. He had ten horns and seven heads, with ten crowns on his horns, and on each head a blasphemous name. [2] The beast I saw resembled a leopard, but had feet like those of a bear and a mouth like that of a lion. The dragon gave the beast his power and his throne and great authority. [3] One of the heads of the beast seemed to have had a fatal wound, but the fatal wound had been healed. The whole world was astonished and followed the beast. [4] Men worshiped the dragon because he had given authority to the beast, and they also worshiped the beast and asked, "Who is like the beast? Who can make war against him?"

[5] The beast was given a mouth to utter proud words and blasphemies and to exercise his authority

---

[a] 1 Some late manuscripts *And I*

for forty-two months. ⁶He opened his mouth to blaspheme God, and to slander his name and his dwelling place and those who live in heaven. ⁷He was given power to make war against the saints and to conquer them. And he was given authority over every tribe, people, language and nation. ⁸All inhabitants of the earth will worship the beast—all whose names have not been written in the book of life belonging to the Lamb that was slain from the creation of the world.[a]

⁹He who has an ear, let him hear.

> ¹⁰If anyone is to go into captivity,
>   into captivity he will go.
> If anyone is to be killed[b] with the sword,
>   with the sword he will be killed.

This calls for patient endurance and faithfulness on the part of the saints.

THE BEAST OUT OF THE EARTH

¹¹Then I saw another beast, coming out of the earth. He had two horns like a lamb, but he spoke like a dragon. ¹²He exercised all the authority of the first beast on his behalf, and made the earth and its inhabitants worship the first beast, whose fatal wound had been healed. ¹³And he performed great and miraculous signs, even causing fire to come down from heaven to earth in full view of men. ¹⁴Because of the signs he was given power to do on behalf of the first beast, he deceived the inhabitants of the earth. He ordered them to set up an image in honor of the beast who was wounded by the sword and yet lived. ¹⁵He was given power to give breath to the image of the first beast, so that it could speak and cause all who refused to worship the image to be killed. ¹⁶He also forced everyone, small and great, rich and poor, free and slave, to receive a mark on his right hand or on his forehead, ¹⁷so that no one could buy or sell unless he had the mark, which is the name of the beast or the number of his name.

¹⁸This calls for wisdom. If anyone has insight, let him calculate the number of the beast, for it is man's number. His number is 666.

THE LAMB AND THE 144,000

14 Then I looked, and there before me was the Lamb, standing on Mount Zion, and with him 144,000 who had his name and his Father's name written on their foreheads. ²And I heard a sound from heaven like the roar of rushing waters and like a loud peal of thunder. The sound I heard was like that of harpists playing their harps. ³And they sang a new song before the throne and before the four living creatures and the elders. No one could learn the song except the 144,000 who had been redeemed from the earth. ⁴These are those who did not defile themselves with women, for they kept themselves pure. They follow the Lamb wherever he goes. They were purchased from among men and offered as firstfruits to God and the Lamb. ⁵No lie was found in their mouths; they are blameless.

THE THREE ANGELS

⁶Then I saw another angel flying in midair, and he had the eternal gospel to proclaim to those who live on the earth—to every nation, tribe, language and people. ⁷He said in a loud voice, "Fear God and give him glory, because the hour of his judgment has come. Worship him who made the heavens, the earth, the sea and the springs of water."

⁸A second angel followed and said, "Fallen! Fallen is Babylon the Great, which made all the nations drink the maddening wine of her adulteries."

⁹A third angel followed them and said in a loud voice: "If anyone worships the beast and his image and receives his mark on the forehead or on the hand, ¹⁰he, too, will drink of the wine of God's fury, which has been poured full strength into the cup of his wrath. He will be tormented with burning sulfur in the presence of the holy angels and of the Lamb. ¹¹And the smoke of their torment rises for ever and ever. There is no rest day or night for those who worship the beast and his image, or for anyone who receives the mark of his name." ¹²This calls for patient endurance on the part of the saints who obey God's commandments and remain faithful to Jesus.

---

^a 8 Or *written from the creation of the world in the book of life belonging to the Lamb that was slain*   ^b 10 Some manuscripts *anyone kills*

[13] Then I heard a voice from heaven say, "Write: Blessed are the dead who die in the Lord from now on."

"Yes," says the Spirit, "they will rest from their labor, for their deeds will follow them."

THE HARVEST OF THE EARTH

[14] I looked, and there before me was a white cloud, and seated on the cloud was one "like a son of man"[a] with a crown of gold on his head and a sharp sickle in his hand. [15] Then another angel came out of the temple and called in a loud voice to him who was sitting on the cloud, "Take your sickle and reap, because the time to reap has come, for the harvest of the earth is ripe." [16] So he who was seated on the cloud swung his sickle over the earth, and the earth was harvested.

[17] Another angel came out of the temple in heaven, and he too had a sharp sickle. [18] Still another angel, who had charge of the fire, came from the altar and called in a loud voice to him who had the sharp sickle, "Take your sharp sickle and gather the clusters of grapes from the earth's vine, because its grapes are ripe." [19] The angel swung his sickle on the earth, gathered its grapes and threw them into the great winepress of God's wrath. [20] They were trampled in the winepress outside the city, and blood flowed out of the press, rising as high as the horses' bridles for a distance of 1,600 stadia.[b]

SEVEN ANGELS WITH SEVEN PLAGUES

15 I saw in heaven another great and marvelous sign: seven angels with the seven last plagues—last, because with them God's wrath is completed. [2] And I saw what looked like a sea of glass mixed with fire and, standing beside the sea, those who had been victorious over the beast and his image and over the number of his name. They held harps given them by God [3] and sang the song of Moses the servant of God and the song of the Lamb:

> "Great and marvelous are your deeds,
>   Lord God Almighty.
> Just and true are your ways,
>   King of the ages.
> [4] Who will not fear you, O Lord,
>   and bring glory to your name?
> For you alone are holy.
> All nations will come
>   and worship before you,
> for your righteous acts have been revealed."

[5] After this I looked and in heaven the temple, that is, the tabernacle of the Testimony, was opened. [6] Out of the temple came the seven angels with the seven plagues. They were dressed in clean, shining linen and wore golden sashes around their chests. [7] Then one of the four living creatures gave to the seven angels seven golden bowls filled with the wrath of God, who lives for ever and ever. [8] And the temple was filled with smoke from the glory of God and from his power, and no one could enter the temple until the seven plagues of the seven angels were completed.

THE SEVEN BOWLS OF GOD'S WRATH

16 Then I heard a loud voice from the temple saying to the seven angels, "Go, pour out the seven bowls of God's wrath on the earth."

[2] The first angel went and poured out his bowl on the land, and ugly and painful sores broke out on the people who had the mark of the beast and worshiped his image.

[3] The second angel poured out his bowl on the sea, and it turned into blood like that of a dead man, and every living thing in the sea died.

[4] The third angel poured out his bowl on the rivers and springs of water, and they became blood. [5] Then I heard the angel in charge of the waters say:

> "You are just in these judgments,
>   you who are and who were, the Holy One,
>   because you have so judged;

---

[a] 14 Daniel 7:13   [b] 20 That is, about 180 miles (about 300 kilometers)

⁶for they have shed the blood of your saints and prophets,
and you have given them blood to drink as they deserve."

⁷And I heard the altar respond:

"Yes, Lord God Almighty,
true and just are your judgments."

⁸The fourth angel poured out his bowl on the sun, and the sun was given power to scorch people with fire. ⁹They were seared by the intense heat and they cursed the name of God, who had control over these plagues, but they refused to repent and glorify him.

¹⁰The fifth angel poured out his bowl on the throne of the beast, and his kingdom was plunged into darkness. Men gnawed their tongues in agony ¹¹and cursed the God of heaven because of their pains and their sores, but they refused to repent of what they had done.

¹²The sixth angel poured out his bowl on the great river Euphrates, and its water was dried up to prepare the way for the kings from the East. ¹³Then I saw three evilᵃ spirits that looked like frogs; they came out of the mouth of the dragon, out of the mouth of the beast and out of the mouth of the false prophet. ¹⁴They are spirits of demons performing miraculous signs, and they go out to the kings of the whole world, to gather them for the battle on the great day of God Almighty.

¹⁵"Behold, I come like a thief! Blessed is he who stays awake and keeps his clothes with him, so that he may not go naked and be shamefully exposed."

¹⁶Then they gathered the kings together to the place that in Hebrew is called Armageddon.

¹⁷The seventh angel poured out his bowl into the air, and out of the temple came a loud voice from the throne, saying, "It is done!" ¹⁸Then there came flashes of lightning, rumblings, peals of thunder and a severe earthquake. No earthquake like it has ever occurred since man has been on earth, so tremendous was the quake. ¹⁹The great city split into three parts, and the cities of the nations collapsed. God remembered Babylon the Great and gave her the cup filled with the wine of the fury of his wrath. ²⁰Every island fled away and the mountains could not be found. ²¹From the sky huge hailstones of about a hundred pounds each fell upon men. And they cursed God on account of the plague of hail, because the plague was so terrible.

THE WOMAN ON THE BEAST

17 One of the seven angels who had the seven en bowls came and said to me, "Come, I will show you the punishment of the great prostitute, who sits on many waters. ²With her the kings of the earth committed adultery and the inhabitants of the earth were intoxicated with the wine of her adulteries."

³Then the angel carried me away in the Spirit into a desert. There I saw a woman sitting on a scarlet beast that was covered with blasphemous names and had seven heads and ten horns. ⁴The woman was dressed in purple and scarlet, and was glittering

NOW OR NEVER
REV 16:21

Add up the damage, destruction and suffering that result from God's seal judgments (see Revelation 6), trumpet judgments (see ch. 8) and bowl judgments (see ch. 16). Think about that the next time someone tries to tell you that sin and disobedience are no big deal.

Leaving Vengeance to God

Throughout the Bible, God warns us not to take revenge on people who do evil things to us. Instead, he instructs us to leave vengeance in his hands. This passage (and others like it in Revelation) shows us why that's a good idea. When God judges evil, he will do so in a way that's so extreme, so intense and so perfect that it will shock the world.

» live the adventure » Rev 16:1-21

ᵃ 13 Greek *unclean*

with gold, precious stones and pearls. She held a golden cup in her hand, filled with abominable things and the filth of her adulteries. ⁵This title was written on her forehead:

MYSTERY
BABYLON THE GREAT
THE MOTHER OF PROSTITUTES
AND OF THE ABOMINATIONS OF THE EARTH.

⁶I saw that the woman was drunk with the blood of the saints, the blood of those who bore testimony to Jesus.

When I saw her, I was greatly astonished. ⁷Then the angel said to me: "Why are you astonished? I will explain to you the mystery of the woman and of the beast she rides, which has the seven heads and ten horns. ⁸The beast, which you saw, once was, now is not, and will come up out of the Abyss and go to his destruction. The inhabitants of the earth whose names have not been written in the book of life from the creation of the world will be astonished when they see the beast, because he once was, now is not, and yet will come.

⁹"This calls for a mind with wisdom. The seven heads are seven hills on which the woman sits. ¹⁰They are also seven kings. Five have fallen, one is, the other has not yet come; but when he does come, he must remain for a little while. ¹¹The beast who once was, and now is not, is an eighth king. He belongs to the seven and is going to his destruction.

¹²"The ten horns you saw are ten kings who have not yet received a kingdom, but who for one hour will receive authority as kings along with the beast. ¹³They have one purpose and will give their power and authority to the beast. ¹⁴They will make war against the Lamb, but the Lamb will overcome them because he is Lord of lords and King of kings—and with him will be his called, chosen and faithful followers."

¹⁵Then the angel said to me, "The waters you saw, where the prostitute sits, are peoples, multitudes, nations and languages. ¹⁶The beast and the ten horns you saw will hate the prostitute. They will bring her to ruin and leave her naked; they will eat her flesh and burn her with fire. ¹⁷For God has put it into their hearts to accomplish his purpose by agreeing to give the beast their power to rule, until God's words are fulfilled. ¹⁸The woman you saw is the great city that rules over the kings of the earth."

THE FALL OF BABYLON

18

After this I saw another angel coming down from heaven. He had great authority, and the earth was illuminated by his splendor. ²With a mighty voice he shouted:

"Fallen! Fallen is Babylon the Great!
She has become a home for demons
and a haunt for every evil[a] spirit,
a haunt for every unclean and detestable bird.
³For all the nations have drunk
the maddening wine of her adulteries.
The kings of the earth committed adultery with her,
and the merchants of the earth grew rich from her excessive luxuries."

⁴Then I heard another voice from heaven say:

"Come out of her, my people,
so that you will not share in her sins,
so that you will not receive any of her plagues;
⁵for her sins are piled up to heaven,
and God has remembered her crimes.
⁶Give back to her as she has given;
pay her back double for what she has done.
Mix her a double portion from her own cup.
⁷Give her as much torture and grief
as the glory and luxury she gave herself.

ᵃ 2 Greek *unclean*

In her heart she boasts,
'I sit as queen; I am not a widow,
and I will never mourn.'
8 Therefore in one day her plagues will overtake her:
death, mourning and famine.
She will be consumed by fire,
for mighty is the Lord God who judges her.

9 "When the kings of the earth who committed adultery with her and shared her luxury see the smoke of her burning, they will weep and mourn over her. 10 Terrified at her torment, they will stand far off and cry:

" 'Woe! Woe, O great city,
O Babylon, city of power!
In one hour your doom has come!'

11 "The merchants of the earth will weep and mourn over her because no one buys their cargoes any more— 12 cargoes of gold, silver, precious stones and pearls; fine linen, purple, silk and scarlet cloth; every sort of citron wood, and articles of every kind made of ivory, costly wood, bronze, iron and marble; 13 cargoes of cinnamon and spice, of incense, myrrh and frankincense, of wine and olive oil, of fine flour and wheat; cattle and sheep; horses and carriages; and bodies and souls of men.

14 "They will say, 'The fruit you longed for is gone from you. All your riches and splendor have vanished, never to be recovered.' 15 The merchants who sold these things and gained their wealth from her will stand far off, terrified at her torment. They will weep and mourn 16 and cry out:

" 'Woe! Woe, O great city,
dressed in fine linen, purple and scarlet,
and glittering with gold, precious stones and pearls!
17 In one hour such great wealth has been brought to ruin!'

"Every sea captain, and all who travel by ship, the sailors, and all who earn their living from the sea, will stand far off. 18 When they see the smoke of her burning, they will exclaim, 'Was there ever a city like this great city?' 19 They will throw dust on their heads, and with weeping and mourning cry out:

" 'Woe! Woe, O great city,
where all who had ships on the sea
became rich through her wealth!
In one hour she has been brought to ruin!
20 Rejoice over her, O heaven!
Rejoice, saints and apostles and prophets!
God has judged her for the way she treated you.' "

21 Then a mighty angel picked up a boulder the size of a large millstone and threw it into the sea, and said:

"With such violence
the great city of Babylon will be thrown down,
never to be found again.
22 The music of harpists and musicians, flute players and trumpeters,
will never be heard in you again.
No workman of any trade
will ever be found in you again.
The sound of a millstone
will never be heard in you again.
23 The light of a lamp
will never shine in you again.
The voice of bridegroom and bride
will never be heard in you again.
Your merchants were the world's great men.

By your magic spell all the nations were led astray.
24 In her was found the blood of prophets and of the saints,
and of all who have been killed on the earth."

HALLELUJAH!

19

After this I heard what sounded like the roar of a great multitude in heaven shouting:

"Hallelujah!
Salvation and glory and power belong to our God,
2   for true and just are his judgments.
He has condemned the great prostitute
who corrupted the earth by her adulteries.
He has avenged on her the blood of his servants."

3 And again they shouted:

"Hallelujah!
The smoke from her goes up for ever
and ever."

4 The twenty-four elders and the four living creatures fell down and worshiped God, who was seated on the throne. And they cried:

"Amen, Hallelujah!"

5 Then a voice came from the throne, saying:

"Praise our God,
all you his servants,
you who fear him,
both small and great!"

6 Then I heard what sounded like a great multitude, like the roar of rushing waters and like loud peals of thunder, shouting:

"Hallelujah!
For our Lord God Almighty reigns.
7 Let us rejoice and be glad
and give him glory!
For the wedding of the Lamb has come,
and his bride has made herself
ready.
8 Fine linen, bright and clean,
was given her to wear."

(Fine linen stands for the righteous acts of the saints.)

9 Then the angel said to me, "Write: 'Blessed are those who are invited to the wedding supper of the Lamb!' " And he added, "These are the true words of God."

10 At this I fell at his feet to worship him. But he said to me, "Do not do it! I am a fellow servant with you and with your brothers who hold to the testimony of Jesus. Worship God! For the testimony of Jesus is the spirit of prophecy."

THE RIDER ON THE WHITE HORSE

11 I saw heaven standing open and there before me was a white horse, whose rider is called Faithful and True. With justice he judges and makes war. 12 His eyes are like blazing fire, and on his head are many crowns. He has a name written on him that no one knows but he himself. 13 He is dressed in a robe dipped in blood, and his name is the Word of God. 14 The armies of heaven were following him,

---

Understanding Jesus' Return

»» live the adventure »» Rev 19:11-21

The first time Jesus came to our planet, it was as a tiny, helpless baby. Next time, it will be as the conquering Warrior and King. When he returns, everyone who rejected him or wrote him off as nothing more than a teacher or philosopher will see him as he really is in all his glory and power. That's when they'll realize what a terrible mistake they've made. If you already know what Jesus is really like, your job is to help others see him for who he really is . . . before it's too late.

riding on white horses and dressed in fine linen, white and clean. ¹⁵Out of his mouth comes a sharp sword with which to strike down the nations. "He will rule them with an iron scepter."ᵃ He treads the winepress of the fury of the wrath of God Almighty. ¹⁶On his robe and on his thigh he has this name written:

KING OF KINGS AND LORD OF LORDS.

¹⁷And I saw an angel standing in the sun, who cried in a loud voice to all the birds flying in midair, "Come, gather together for the great supper of God, ¹⁸so that you may eat the flesh of kings, generals, and mighty men, of horses and their riders, and the flesh of all people, free and slave, small and great." ¹⁹Then I saw the beast and the kings of the earth and their armies gathered together to make war against the rider on the horse and his army. ²⁰But the beast was captured, and with him the false prophet who had performed the miraculous signs on his behalf. With these signs he had deluded those who had received the mark of the beast and worshiped his image. The two of them were thrown alive into the fiery lake of burning sulfur. ²¹The rest of them were killed with the sword that came out of the mouth of the rider on the horse, and all the birds gorged themselves on their flesh.

THE THOUSAND YEARS

20 And I saw an angel coming down out of heaven, having the key to the Abyss and holding in his hand a great chain. ²He seized the dragon, that ancient serpent, who is the devil, or Satan, and bound him for a thousand years. ³He threw him into the Abyss, and locked and sealed it over him, to keep him from deceiving the nations anymore until the thousand years were ended. After that, he must be set free for a short time.

⁴I saw thrones on which were seated those who had been given authority to judge. And I saw the souls of those who had been beheaded because of their testimony for Jesus and because of the word of God. They had not worshiped the beast or his image and had not received his mark on their foreheads or their hands. They came to life and reigned with Christ a thousand years. ⁵(The rest of the dead did not come to life until the thousand years were ended.) This is the first resurrection. ⁶Blessed and holy are those who have part in the first resurrection. The second death has no power over them, but they will be priests of God and of Christ and will reign with him for a thousand years.

SATAN'S DOOM

⁷When the thousand years are over, Satan will be released from his prison ⁸and will go out to deceive the nations in the four corners of the earth—Gog and Magog—to gather them for battle. In number they are like the sand on the seashore. ⁹They marched across the breadth of the earth and surrounded the camp of God's people, the city he loves. But fire came down from heaven and devoured them. ¹⁰And the devil, who deceived them, was thrown into the lake of burning sulfur, where the beast and the false prophet had been thrown. They will be tormented day and night for ever and ever.

NOW OR NEVER
REV 20:11–13

In the end, everyone gets exactly what's coming to them. The Lord keeps track of every ungodly decision, every greedy choice, every sexual sin, every betrayal and every lie. Remember: Your actions—good or bad—reveal where your loyalties truly lie.

THE DEAD ARE JUDGED

¹¹Then I saw a great white throne and him who was seated on it. Earth and sky fled from his presence, and there was no place for them. ¹²And I saw the dead, great and small, standing before the throne, and books were opened. Another book was opened, which is the book of life. The dead were judged according to what they had done as recorded in the books. ¹³The sea gave up the dead that were in it, and death and Hades gave up the dead that were in them, and each person was judged according to what he had done. ¹⁴Then death and Hades were thrown into the lake of fire. The lake of fire is the second death. ¹⁵If anyone's name was not found written in the book of life, he was thrown into the lake of fire.

ᵃ *15* Psalm 2:9

THE NEW JERUSALEM

21

Then I saw a new heaven and a new earth, for the first heaven and the first earth had passed away, and there was no longer any sea. [2]I saw the Holy City, the new Jerusalem, coming down out of heaven from God, prepared as a bride beautifully dressed for her husband. [3]And I heard a loud voice from the throne saying, "Now the dwelling of God is with men, and he will live with them. They will be his people, and God himself will be with them and be their God. [4]He will wipe every tear from their eyes. There will be no more death or mourning or crying or pain, for the old order of things has passed away."

[5]He who was seated on the throne said, "I am making everything new!" Then he said, "Write this down, for these words are trustworthy and true."

[6]He said to me: "It is done. I am the Alpha and the Omega, the Beginning and the End. To him who is thirsty I will give to drink without cost from the spring of the water of life. [7]He who overcomes will inherit all this, and I will be his God and he will be my son. [8]But the cowardly, the unbelieving, the vile, the murderers, the sexually immoral, those who practice magic arts, the idolaters and all liars—their place will be in the fiery lake of burning sulfur. This is the second death."

NOW OR NEVER
REV 21:3-4

All real and lasting happiness, joy and fulfillment come from God. The closer we get to him, the happier, more joyful and more fulfilled we become. Someday, we will be in God's actual presence, which means we'll know what it feels like to be perfectly happy, joyful and fulfilled . . . forever.

[9]One of the seven angels who had the seven bowls full of the seven last plagues came and said to me, "Come, I will show you the bride, the wife of the Lamb." [10]And he carried me away in the Spirit to a mountain great and high, and showed me the Holy City, Jerusalem, coming down out of heaven from God. [11]It shone with the glory of God, and its brilliance was like that of a very precious jewel, like a jasper, clear as crystal. [12]It had a great, high wall with twelve gates, and with twelve angels at the gates. On the gates were written the names of the twelve tribes of Israel. [13]There were three gates on the east, three on the north, three on the south and three on the west. [14]The wall of the city had twelve foundations, and on them were the names of the twelve apostles of the Lamb.

[15]The angel who talked with me had a measuring rod of gold to measure the city, its gates and its walls. [16]The city was laid out like a square, as long as it was wide. He measured the city with the rod and found it to be 12,000 stadia[a] in length, and as wide and high as it is long. [17]He measured its wall and it was 144 cubits[b] thick,[c] by man's measurement, which the angel was using. [18]The wall was made of jasper, and the city of pure gold, as pure as glass. [19]The foundations of the city walls were decorated with every kind of precious stone. The first foundation was jasper, the second sapphire, the third chalcedony, the fourth emerald, [20]the fifth sardonyx, the sixth carnelian, the seventh chrysolite, the eighth beryl, the ninth topaz, the tenth chrysoprase, the eleventh jacinth, and the twelfth amethyst.[d] [21]The twelve gates were twelve pearls, each gate made of a single pearl. The great street of the city was of pure gold, like transparent glass.

[22]I did not see a temple in the city, because the Lord God Almighty and the Lamb are its temple. [23]The city does not need the sun or the moon to shine on it, for the glory of God gives it light, and the Lamb is its lamp. [24]The nations will walk by its light, and the kings of the earth will bring their splendor into it. [25]On no day will its gates ever be shut, for there will be no night there. [26]The glory and honor of the nations will be brought into it. [27]Nothing impure will ever enter it, nor will anyone who does what is shameful or deceitful, but only those whose names are written in the Lamb's book of life.

THE RIVER OF LIFE

22

Then the angel showed me the river of the water of life, as clear as crystal, flowing from the throne of God and of the Lamb [2]down the middle of the great street of the city. On each side of the river stood the tree of life, bearing twelve crops of fruit, yielding its fruit every month. And the leaves of the tree are for the healing of the nations. [3]No longer will there be any curse.

---

[a] *16* That is, about 1,400 miles (about 2,200 kilometers) [b] *17* That is, about 200 feet (about 65 meters) [c] *17* Or *high*
[d] *20* The precise identification of some of these precious stones is uncertain.

The throne of God and of the Lamb will be in the city, and his servants will serve him. ⁴They will see his face, and his name will be on their foreheads. ⁵There will be no more night. They will not need the light of a lamp or the light of the sun, for the Lord God will give them light. And they will reign for ever and ever.

⁶The angel said to me, "These words are trustworthy and true. The Lord, the God of the spirits of the prophets, sent his angel to show his servants the things that must soon take place."

JESUS IS COMING

⁷"Behold, I am coming soon! Blessed is he who keeps the words of the prophecy in this book."

⁸I, John, am the one who heard and saw these things. And when I had heard and seen them, I fell down to worship at the feet of the angel who had been showing them to me. ⁹But he said to me, "Do not do it! I am a fellow servant with you and with your brothers the prophets and of all who keep the words of this book. Worship God!"

¹⁰Then he told me, "Do not seal up the words of the prophecy of this book, because the time is near. ¹¹Let him who does wrong continue to do wrong; let him who is vile continue to be vile; let him who does right continue to do right; and let him who is holy continue to be holy."

¹²"Behold, I am coming soon! My reward is with me, and I will give to everyone according to what he has done. ¹³I am the Alpha and the Omega, the First and the Last, the Beginning and the End.

¹⁴"Blessed are those who wash their robes, that they may have the right to the tree of life and may go through the gates into the city. ¹⁵Outside are the dogs, those who practice magic arts, the sexually immoral, the murderers, the idolaters and everyone who loves and practices falsehood.

¹⁶"I, Jesus, have sent my angel to give you[a] this testimony for the churches. I am the Root and the Offspring of David, and the bright Morning Star."

¹⁷The Spirit and the bride say, "Come!" And let him who hears say, "Come!" Whoever is thirsty, let him come; and whoever wishes, let him take the free gift of the water of life.

challengenotes

To: my_son

heavenly_father: *yes, I am coming soon.* that's a promise you can count on. no matter how insane the world gets and no matter how strong satan's influence may seem, never give up hope. always remember that your Lord is coming to make things right.

REV 22:20-21

¹⁸I warn everyone who hears the words of the prophecy of this book: If anyone adds anything to them, God will add to him the plagues described in this book. ¹⁹And if anyone takes words away from this book of prophecy, God will take away from him his share in the tree of life and in the holy city, which are described in this book.

²⁰He who testifies to these things says, "Yes, I am coming soon."

Amen. Come, Lord Jesus.

²¹The grace of the Lord Jesus be with God's people. Amen.

---

[a] *16* The Greek is plural.

CONTENTS

WEIGHTS AND MEASURES

BIBLICAL UNIT	APPROXIMATE AMERICAN EQUIVALENT	APPROXIMATE METRIC EQUIVALENT
WEIGHTS		
talent (60 minas)	75 pounds	34 kilograms
mina (50 shekels)	$1^1/_4$ pounds	0.6 kilogram
shekel (2 bekas)	$^2/_5$ ounce	11.5 grams
pim ($^2/_3$ shekel)	$^1/_3$ ounce	7.6 grams
beka (10 gerahs)	$^1/_5$ ounce	5.5 grams
gerah	$^1/_{50}$ ounce	0.6 gram
LENGTH		
cubit	18 inches	0.5 meter
span	9 inches	23 centimeters
handbreadth	3 inches	8 centimeters
CAPACITY		
Dry Measure		
cor [homer] (10 ephahs)	6 bushels	220 liters
lethek (5 ephahs)	3 bushels	110 liters
ephah (10 omers)	$^3/_5$ bushel	22 liters
seah ($^1/_3$ ephah)	7 quarts	7.3 liters
omer ($^1/_{10}$ ephah)	2 quarts	2 liters
cab ($^1/_{18}$ ephah)	1 quart	1 liter
Liquid Measure		
bath (1 ephah)	6 gallons	22 liters
hin ($^1/_6$ bath)	4 quarts	4 liters
log ($^1/_{72}$ bath)	$^1/_3$ quart	0.3 liter

The figures of the table are calculated on the basis of a shekel equaling 11.5 grams, a cubit equaling 18 inches and an ephah equaling 22 liters. The quart referred to is either a dry quart (slightly larger than a liter) or a liquid quart (slightly smaller than a liter), whichever is applicable. The ton referred to in the footnotes is the American ton of 2,000 pounds.

This table is based upon the best available information, but it is not intended to be mathematically precise; like the measurement equivalents in the footnotes, it merely gives approximate amounts and distances. Weights and measures differed somewhat at various times and places in the ancient world. There is uncertainty particularly about the ephah and the bath; further discoveries may shed more light on these units of capacity.

SUBJECT INDEX

This subject index will help you find just where you need to look to find information about a particular topic. Look through the list, and you'll probably find something you want to read about.

SUBJECT INDEX

PLAN OF SALVATION

CHRISTIANITY 101

Perhaps the greatest mystery of life is that the Creator of the universe loves you. He spins the galaxies and directs the course of history, yet he also wants to have a personal relationship with you. He wants to be closer to you than your parents, a best friend or even a girlfriend.

FIRST, SOME BAD NEWS.

Not only does God exist, but he's also holy. That means he's perfect. He's never made a mistake or done something he's regretted. He's never been guilty of a crime or broken a law. In short, God is free from any hint of sin. He's so holy and perfect that someone who sins can't even stand in his presence. Even worse news for us is that sin *must* be paid for—and the price is high. God said that the "wages of sin is death" (Romans 6:23) and that "without the shedding of blood there is no forgiveness" (Hebrews 9:22). Sin is serious. The Old Testament describes how the Hebrew people offered sacrifices of lambs and goats to make payment for their sins (see Leviticus 1–7).

SECOND, SOME GOOD NEWS.

After thousands of years of sacrifices, God provided a better way. God sent his Son, Jesus Christ, as the perfect Lamb. Jesus was both fully God and fully human. As God, he was perfect in every way. As a man, he knows what it's like to be us. He experienced the same temptations we experience, and he represents us before God at all times. He died on the cross for us (Matthew 27:32–61). Proving he had power over all sin and death, he didn't stay dead. After three days he was raised to life again (Matthew 28). Because he was without fault and sin, he was the perfect sacrifice—a sacrifice so complete that it's powerful enough to forgive all your sins—past, present and future (Hebrews 10:17–18).

Jesus paid the penalty we deserve for our sins. In exchange, he gives us his righteousness. In other words, when God sees us, he doesn't see our sin any more; he sees Jesus' holiness, which has been given to us (2 Corinthians 5:17–21).

SO, WHAT'S CHRISTIANITY?

Simply put, Christianity is aligning yourself with Christ.
- It's admitting that you have sinned and that your sin is really offensive to God (Psalm 53:3).
- It's recognizing that there's nothing you can do to pay for your sins (Romans 3:23).
- It's confessing your sins to God. Even though he already knows them, he wants us to confess them—to come to grips with them (1 John 1:9).
- It's following him—getting to know him, reading his Word and doing your best to follow him daily (Romans 12:1–2).

SO, WHAT'S NEXT?

If you'd like to become a follower of Christ and enjoy friendship with God, here's a great way to get started.

Pray. Here's a prayer that can help you give your life to Jesus:

"God, I believe in you. I know that I am a sinner. Thank you for sending your Son, Jesus, to die for my sins and make me right with you. Please come into my life. I give it to you. I want to live for you from now on."

Read. Spend some regular time getting to know God better. Start with the 30 Days for New Christians reading plan on page 1641. Read some of God's Word each day. Spend some time thinking about what you read and talking with God. Tell him about your day, the things you're learning, the things that frustrate you and the things that you're excited about. As a true friend, he cares about you and your life.

Don't Go It Alone. The Christian life isn't meant to be lived alone. Spend time with other Christians. Get involved in a church or youth group that loves God and wants you to know him better.

Remember . . . Above all else, remember that God's friendship with you is permanent. Sure, there will be times when you make mistakes. You'll fail, you'll sin and you'll even feel guilty. There will be times when you disappoint yourself and others. In those moments, though, remember that God is your constant companion. He remains your proud friend, loving Father and faithful Savior. He'll never leave you; he'll never forsake you. He promises you that (Romans 8:28–39).

If you've recently become a Christian, we'd love to hear your story. Log on to www.RevolutionBible.com, click on the "Tell Us Your Story" link and tell us when and how you decided to follow Christ.

READING PLANS
30 DAYS FOR NEW CHRISTIANS

Day	Theme	Passage
1	The Fall of Humanity	Genesis 3:1–19
2	A People for God	Genesis 28:10–15; 32:22–28
3	The Ten Commandments	Exodus 20:1–17
4	Sacrifices Required Under Law	Leviticus 5:14–19
5	Punishments for Sin Under Law	Leviticus 20:7–27
6	Obedience From Love	Deuteronomy 11:13–21
7	Cycles of Disobedience	Judges 2:10–19
8	The People Demand a King	1 Samuel 8
9	Saul Fails and Is Rejected	1 Samuel 15:17–23
10	Many Kings Fail	Jeremiah 1–17
11	The Sin of the People	Ezekiel 20:5–26
12	An Eternal King Promised	Jeremiah 23:1–6; Isaiah 9:6–7; Zechariah 9:9–10
13	The Promised King Is Born	Luke 2:1–20
14	The Word Became Flesh	John 1:1–18
15	Signs and Miracles of Authority	Matthew 9:1–8; Luke 13:10–17
16	Jesus Fulfills the Law	Matthew 5:17–20; Romans 8:1–4
17	Jesus Teaches About New Life	John 3
18	Jesus Willingly Taken	John 18:1–11
19	Jesus' Death and Resurrection	Luke 23:44—24:12
20	Christ a Sacrifice for All	Hebrews
21	God's Wrath Explained	Romans 1:18–32
22	God's Judgment Explained	Romans 2:5–11
23	Righteousness by Faith	Romans 3:9–26
24	Life Through Christ	Romans 5:12–21
25	Life by the Spirit	Romans 8:1–17; Galatians 5:16–26
26	Living Sacrifices	Romans 12
27	Walking in the Light	1 John 1–2
28	Living for God	1 Peter 1–11
29	Love for one Another	1 John 3:11–24
30	Promise of Eternity	2 Corinthians 5:1–10; Revelation 21:1–4

READING PLANS
30 DAYS WITH JESUS

READING PLANS
30 DAYS IN THE PSALMS

Day	Theme	Passage
1	Blessing	Psalm 67, 72, 84, 128
2	Calling to God	Psalm 4, 5, 22
3	Confidence	Psalm 27, 36, 71, 125
4	Deeds of God	Psalm 9, 18, 118
5	Doubt	Psalm 42, 73, 77
6	Faithfulness of God	Psalm 105, 119: 137–144, 146
7	Fear	Psalm 37, 49, 91
8	Glory of God	Psalm 19, 24, 29
9	God Is a Helper	Psalm 54, 115, 119:169–176
10	Identity	Psalm 8, 139
11	Justice of God	Psalm 7, 26, 82
12	Meditation	Psalm 119:9–16, 41–48
13	Mercy	Psalm 13, 28, 86
14	Music	Psalm 6, 149, 150
15	Nature	Psalm 50, 104, 147, 148
16	Peace	Psalm 23, 133, 119:161–168
17	Power of God	Psalm 68, 93, 135
18	Praise	Psalm, 65, 98, 138
19	Prayer	Psalm 17, 20, 102
20	Protection	Psalm 59, 62, 124
21	Safety in God	Psalm 11, 16, 142, 46
22	Rejoicing	Psalm 30, 47, 97
23	Righteousness	Psalm 1, 15, 112
24	Salvation	Psalm 3, 14, 121
25	Sin and Repentance	Psalm 25, 32, 38, 51
26	Thanksgiving	Psalm 75, 106, 136
27	Trust	Psalm 31, 40, 56
28	Victory	Psalm 21, 76, 144
29	Wisdom	Psalm 90, 107, 111
30	Worship	Psalm 33, 34, 145

30 DAYS IN PROVERBS

1	Proverbs 1	11	Proverbs 11	21	Proverbs 21
2	Proverbs 2	12	Proverbs 12	22	Proverbs 22
3	Proverbs 3	13	Proverbs 13	23	Proverbs 23
4	Proverbs 4	14	Proverbs 14	24	Proverbs 24
5	Proverbs 5	15	Proverbs 15	25	Proverbs 25
6	Proverbs 6	16	Proverbs 16	26	Proverbs 26
7	Proverbs 7	17	Proverbs 17	27	Proverbs 27
8	Proverbs 8	18	Proverbs 18	28	Proverbs 28
9	Proverbs 9	19	Proverbs 19	29	Proverbs 29
10	Proverbs 10	20	Proverbs 20	30	Proverbs 30–31

READING PLANS
30 DAYS OF MATCH-UPS

Day	Match-Up	Passage
1	Cain vs. Abel	Genesis 4:1–16
2	Lot vs. Abraham	Genesis 13–14
3	Isaac vs. Ishmael	Genesis 16–17
4		Genesis 18–19
5		Genesis 20–21
6		Genesis 22–23
7		Genesis 24–26
8	Esau vs. Jacob	Genesis 25:19–34; 27:1—28:5
9		Genesis 32–33
10	Joseph vs. His Ten Brothers	Genesis 37; 39
11		Genesis 40–41
12		Genesis 42–43
13		Genesis 44–45
14	Aaron vs. Moses	Numbers 12:1–15
15	Caleb vs. The Ten Spies	Numbers 13–14
16		Joshua 1–2
17	David vs. Goliath	1 Samuel 17
18	Ahab vs. Elijah	1 Kings 16:29–34; 17–18
19		1 Kings 19–22
20		2 Kings 1–2
21	Nehemiah vs. Sanballat	Nehemiah 1:11–2
22		Nehemiah 3–4
23		Nehemiah 5:1—6:19
24	Haman vs. Mordecai	Esther 1–2
25		Esther 3–4
26		Esther 5–7
27		Esther 8–10
28	Daniel vs. Government Officers	Daniel 1:1–21; 2:10–49; 6:1–28
29	Jonah vs. the Ninevites	Jonah 1–2
30		Jonah 3–4

READING PLANS
30 DAYS OF LIVING THE ADVENTURE

Here are 30 passages that have a corresponding study note next to them. Read both the verses and the study note each day.

Day	Theme	Passage
1	Adventure	Acts 27:42–43
2	Appearances	Galatians 2:6
3	Boldness	Genesis 6:5–9
4	Courage	Genesis 44:18–34
5	Emotion	Esther 7:8–9
6	Excellence	2 Chronicles 3:1–17
7	Faithfulness	1 Chronicles 10:13
8	Holiness	Nehemiah 10:28–29
9	Hope	Job 42:10–17
10	Humility	Numbers 12:1–3
11	Idolatry	Jeremiah 9:23–24
12	Integrity	1 Chronicles 29:17
13	Kindness	2 Samuel 9:1–8
14	Leadership	1 Chronicles 12:22
15	Love	Revelation 2:4–5
16	Lust	Judges 16:16–20
17	Obedience	1Ch 14:10–16
18	Opportunity	1 Kings 5:1–7
19	Persecution	1 Peter 4:16
20	Purity	Genesis 39:10
21	Revenge	2 Samuel 19:18–23
22	Righteousness	Joshua 24:14–15
23	Spiritual Conflict	Ezra 4:1–4
24	Strength	1 Samuel 9:19-21
25	Temptation	2 Timothy 2:22
26	Thankfulness	Psalm 136:1–26
27	Thankfulness	Ps 136:1–26
28	Thoughts	Philippians 4:8
29	Tragedy	1 Kings 17:19–21
30	Weakness	Judges 3:15

READING PLANS
30 STORIES YOU'VE PROBABLY NEVER HEARD

Day	Theme	Passage
1	Fire and Birds: God Lays Down the Law	Numbers 11
2	Miriam: Leprous as Snow	Numbers 12
3	Korah, Dathan and Abiran: Gulp!	Numbers 16
4	Aaron: A Budding Leader	Numbers 17
5	Moses Strikes Out	Numbers 20:1–13
6	Afraid of Snakes?	Numbers 21:4–9
7	Balaam's . . . er, Donkey	Numbers 22
8		Numbers 23–24
9	Laws for a Special People in a Special Time	Deuteronomy 21
10	Moses: End of an Era	Deuteronomy 31
11		Deuteronomy 32:44–52; 34
12	Solar Stand Still	Joshua 10:1–15
13	Ehud: Left Handed Wonder	Judges 3:12–30
14	Deborah and Jael: Girls Power	Judges 4
15	Jephthah: A Hero's Vow	Judges 11
16	A Levite: The Wickedness of Israel	Judges 19
17	David and Abigail: The Good Guy Wins	1 Samuel 25
18	Mephibosheth: Rags to Riches	2 Samuel 9
19	Elisha: Miracle Man	2 Kings 2:23–25; 4:8–37
20		2 Kings 6:1–23
21	Asa: But if You Forsake Him . . .	2 Chronicles 15
22		2 Chronicles 16
23	Joash: Kindness Forgotten	2 Chronicles 22:10—23:21
24		2 Chronicles 24
25	Josiah: Youthful Ruler	2 Chronicles 34
26		2 Chronicles 35
27	Nehemiah: Homesickness	Nehemiah 1
28		Nehemiah 2
29	Jerusalem Falls: Judgment Arrives	Jeremiah 52
30	The Writing on the Wall	Daniel 5

REVOLUTION

GENERAL EDITOR
Christopher D. Hudson

PROJECT MANAGEMENT AND EDITORIAL
Benjamin D. Irwin

Amy Ballor;
Shari Vanden Berg
2007 revision

EDITORIAL ASSISTANCE
Paul J. Brinkerhoff
Donna Huisjen
Julie Zahm

Natalie Block
2007 revision

THEOLOGICAL REVIEW
Benjamin D. Irwin, M.A., Grand Rapids Baptist Seminary
Andrew Sloan, M.Div., Oral Roberts University

PROFESSIONAL CONSULTING
Jeffrey Gorter, M.S.W., CAC-1 (certified addiction counselor)
Outpatient Therapist, Pine Rest Christian Mental Health Services

PRODUCTION MANAGEMENT
Phil Herich

ART DIRECTION
Rob Monacelli

Ron Huizinga
2007 revision

COVER DESIGN
Rob Monacelli

INTERIOR DESIGN
Kirk Luttrell
The Livingstone Corporation

PROOFREADING
Peachtree Editorial and Proofreading Service, Peachtree, GA

INTERIOR TYPESETTING
Blue Heron Bookcraft, Battle Ground, WA

GUARANTEE

THE REVOLUTION MAN'S CREED AND COVENANT

The story of the Bible is of a cosmic battle between good and evil. The heart of every man is the battlefield, and God has called him to Revolution.

CREED

God is the all powerful creator of the universe who gives life. He is perfect in both who he is and what he does (John 1:1–5).

God created human beings in his own image, giving them freedom and making them rulers, providers, protectors, lovers and worshipers. (Genesis 1:26; 2:24; 4:1–4; Luke 4:8).

When humanity disobeyed and rejected God, sin was introduced into the world, bringing a cursed life filled with pain, frustration and death—ultimately resulting in separation from God (Genesis 2:17–19).

Since the fall of humanity, God has been waging a cosmic battle against the evil one in order to win back the hearts of those who will join the revolution (2 Timothy 1:9). Christ's death and resurrection guarantees the final victory over sin. When we align ourselves with Christ and follow him, we are guaranteed that we will share his victory.

COVENANT

The Revolution Man is an adventurer, created in the image of Christ who lived the ultimate adventure in dying for the sins of every person. The Revolution Man lives in freedom to choose what is right. He is a warrior in the struggle for souls, pursuing righteousness, godliness, faith and honor. He is a defender of the weak and one who is passionate about purity. He is bold in witness and courageous in deed. The Revolution Man is a lover of God and others—family, friend and enemy alike. He loves as Christ loved the church, always protecting, cherishing and defending.

But you, man of God, flee [evil] and pursue righteousness, godliness, faith, love, endurance and gentleness. Fight the good fight of the faith. Take hold of the eternal life to which you were called when you made your good confession in the presence of many witnesses.

(1 Timothy 6:11–12)